BICENTENNIAL EDITION

HISTORICAL STATISTICS
of the United States

COLONIAL TIMES TO 1970

PART 2

U.S. Department of Commerce
Rogers C. B. Morton, Secretary

James L. Pate, Assistant Secretary
for Economic Affairs

BUREAU OF THE CENSUS
Vincent P. Barabba, Director

BUREAU OF THE CENSUS

Vincent P. Barabba, Director
Robert L. Hagan, Deputy Director
James W. Turbitt, Associate Director for Field
Operations and User Services

DATA USER SERVICES DIVISION
Michael G. Garland, Chief

ACKNOWLEDGMENTS

Preparation of this edition was
under the direction of
William Lerner
Chief, Statistical Compendia Staff

The bicentennial edition of *Historical Statistics of the United States* is the third in the series of volumes inaugurated in 1949. In both form and content, the bicentennial edition has drawn heavily from, and built upon, the two prior editions. Both the first volume, *Historical Statistics of the United States, 1789 to 1945,* issued in 1949, and the second volume, *Historical Statistics of the United States, Colonial Times to 1957,* issued in 1960, were prepared by the Bureau of the Census with the cooperation of the Social Science Research Council (SSRC). Although the SSRC did not participate in the preparation of the bicentennial edition, its cooperation in the first two volumes was invaluable in establishing those volumes as the basis for continuing work in the field of historical statistics. Similarly, the many individuals and agencies who made important and distinctive contributions to the first two volumes were instrumental in the preparation of the present one. Immediately following the table of contents, therefore, are reprinted the "official roster and credits" pages from the first two volumes. Also, incorporated within the "Acknowledgments for Chapter Contributions," under the title of each edition, are the credits to contributors as they appeared in the first two volumes.

Analytical review and editing of text tables was primarily the responsibility of **Helen E. Teir,** Assistant Chief, Statistical Compendia Staff, Data User Services Division. During the period January 1972 to June 1973, **Elma D. Beynon** was primarily responsible for obtaining the cooperation and assistance of the many subject consultants and for immediate supervision of compilation operations. **Suzanne L. Worth** assisted Mrs. Beynon and, from July 1973 to November 1974, was responsible for working with consultants and for supervision of the technical and clerical staff. **Alma L. Butler,** assisted by **Kay Swenson,** was responsible for final editing and preparation

of manuscript for the printer. The Census Library, **Dorothy W. Kaufman,** Chief, also lent valuable assistance.

The cooperation of the many contributors to this volume and to the prior editions is gratefully acknowledged. Following the practice established by the prior editions, every data series shown in this volume is, to the extent possible, specifically identified by source as to issuing agency and/or individual author, publication title, publisher, and date of issue. Frequently all five items are shown; frequently additional information is given.

Except for material specified in source citations as "copyright," the tables and text in this volume may be reproduced at will. Appropriate reference to this volume (see citation below) for material reproduced would be appreciated since it may be helpful to users of such material. Permission to reproduce copyrighted material should be obtained directly from the copyright owner.

September 1975

For Library of Congress Cataloging in Publication Data, see p. A-32.

Suggested Citation

U.S. Bureau of the Census

Historical Statistics of the United States, Colonial Times to 1970, Bicentennial Edition, Part 1

Washington, D.C., 1975

For sale by the Superintendent of Documents
U.S. Government Printing Office, Washington, D.C 20402
Price $26 per 2 part set (Sold only in sets)
Stock Number 003–024–00120–9

Contents of Parts 1 and 2

Part 1

Part 2

Part 2—Detailed Contents

DETAILED CONTENTS

Replica of
"Official Roster and
Credits Page" from
**Historical Statistics
of the United States,
Colonial Times to 1957**

Bureau of the Census

ROBERT W. BURGESS, *Director*
A. Ross Eckler, *Deputy Director*
Howard C. Grieves, *Assistant Director*
Conrad Taeuber, *Assistant Director*
Morris H. Hansen, *Assistant Director for Statistical Standards*
Lowell T. Galt, *Assistant Director for Operations*
Walter L. Kehres, *Assistant Director for Administration*
Calvert L. Dedrick, *Chief, International Statistical Programs Office*
A. W. von Struve, *Acting Public Information Officer*

HERMAN P. MILLER, *Historical Statistics Project Director*

This volume stems from a joint interest by the Bureau of the Census and the Social Science Research Council. It was planned, assembled, edited, and published by the Bureau, with the advice and assistance of the Committee on Historical Statistics appointed by the Council. Many other individuals and agencies cooperated and made significant contributions to this project. General acknowledgments for each chapter are presented on p. VII; other acknowledgments frequently appear in the text discussions of the various chapters.

The volume was prepared in the Bureau of the Census under the general direction of Edwin D. Goldfield, Chief, Statistical Reports Division. Herman P. Miller served as the Project Director and was primarily responsible for the planning, organizing, and supervising of all aspects of the compilation of the data. Dr. Miller also served

as executive secretary of the Committee on Historical Statistics, handled liaison matters for the Committee, and participated in its selection of experts to serve as consultants. O. Halbert Goolsby acted as staff assistant.

Morris B. Ullman, who supervised the preparation of the previous volume, *Historical Statistics of the United States, 1789–1945*, was responsible for planning during the early stages of the project.

William Lerner, Assistant Chief, Statistical Reports Division, was primarily responsible for the planning and supervising of the publication aspects of the volume and for the review and editing of the text and tables. Dorothy M. Belzer was responsible for the tabular presentation of the data and preparation of the material for the printer. The Census Library Branch, Louise H. Clickner, Chief, also lent valuable assistance.

Social Science Research Council

The Committee on Historical Statistics appointed by the Social Science Research Council participated actively in the preparation of this volume, in the extension of the subjects to be added, and in planning the general procedures for securing expert assistance on each subject. As the project was developed the Committee, especially the Chairman, was primarily responsible for consideration of prob-

lems of data selection and format, for general appraisal of the quality of the series suggested for inclusion, and for the selection of consultant-specialists for the various subjects. The Committee as a whole, or through specially qualified members, reviewed the plans for inclusion of specific series and discussed areas of study which presented unusual problems.

Committee on Historical Statistics of the Social Science Research Council
(Advisory to the Bureau of the Census)

G. Heberton Evans, Jr., *Chairman*
Chairman of Department of Political Economy
The Johns Hopkins University

Herman P. Miller, *Executive Secretary*
Bureau of the Census

Otis Dudley Duncan
Associate Director of Population
Research and Training Center
The University of Chicago

Maurice I. Gershenson
Department of Industrial Relations
State of California

Willard L. Thorp
Director of Merrill Center for
Economics
Amherst College

Solomon Fabricant
Director of Research
National Bureau of Economic
Research, Inc.

Richard M. Scammon
Director of Elections Research
Governmental Affairs Institute

Harold F. Williamson
Professor of Economics
Northwestern University

Paul Webbink, Vice President, Social Science Research Council, attended Committee meetings and acted as the Council's representative. Stanley Lebergott, Office of Statistical Standards, Bureau of the Budget, also participated in the meetings.

Replica of
"Official Roster and
Credits Page" from
**Historical Statistics
of the United States,
1789-1945.**

BUREAU OF THE CENSUS

J. C. CAPT, *Director*
PHILIP M. HAUSER, *Deputy Director*
A. ROSS ECKLER, *Assistant Director*
HOWARD C. GRIEVES, *Assistant Director*
MORRIS H. HANSEN, *Statistical Assistant to the Director*
ROBERT Y. PHILLIPS, *Executive Assistant to the Director*
CALVERT L. DEDRICK, *Coordinator, International Statistics*
FRANK R. WILSON, *Information Assistant to the Director*

While this volume has been planned, assembled, and edited in the Bureau of the Census, with the advice and assistance of the Social Science Research Council, many other individuals and agencies contributed to its preparation, directly and indirectly. In some instances, individuals devoted themselves full-time for the period necessary to complete their phase of the project. In other instances, contributions were prepared by individuals while they maintained heavy responsibilities in their own offices. A number of private publishers, authors, and research organizations generously granted permission to use their materials. In some cases, they also made additional contributions in time and energy. General acknowledgments for each chapter are given on p. IV; other specific acknowledgments appear within the text in the various sections of the volume.

This volume was prepared in the office of Morris H. Hansen, Statistical Assistant to the Director of the Bureau of the Census, under the supervision of Morris B. Ullman, Chief, Statistical Reports Section, by Bruce L. Jenkinson, A. Benjamin Handler, and William Lerner. Mr. Jenkinson, Chief, Statistical Abstract Unit, was primarily responsible for the planning and preparation of the report; Mr. Handler, Executive Secretary of the Social Science Research Council Committee on the Source Book of Historical Statistics, was primarily responsible for procurement of data and relationships with the agencies and individuals who contributed to the publication; and Mr. Lerner, Statistician, Statistical Abstract Unit, was primarily responsible for the review and editing of the materials as to content, adequacy, and coverage.

Dorothy M. Belzer acted as staff assistant, particularly with respect to tabular presentation, and was responsible for preparation of the materials for the printer. Claire F. Cahill checked all citations by reference to the original published sources and offered many constructive suggestions as to the content of the book.

Social Science Research Council

The Social Science Research Council Committee on the Source Book of Historical Statistics, Advisory to the Bureau of the Census, played an important role in the preparation of this volume. The Chairman of the Committee and its members gave considerable time and thought to the review of plans, to advising on proper courses of action, and contributed in other ways. In particular, J. Frederic Dewhurst, Chairman, was in a large measure responsible for the initiation of the project. The completed volume owes much to his original outline of purpose, coverage, and arrangement. For a detailed statement of the origins of this historical volume, see introductory text.

Through a grant by the Committee on Research in Economic History (Arthur H. Cole, Chairman) of the Social Science Research Council, the full-time services of the Executive Secretary of the Advisory Committee were made available to the Bureau of the Census.

The Social Science Research Council Committee on the Source Book of Historical Statistics
(Advisory to the Bureau of the Census)

J. Frederic Dewhurst (Chairman), The Twentieth Century Fund

Shepard Clough
  Columbia University
Arthur H. Cole
  Harvard University
Morris A. Copeland
  National Bureau of Economic Research
Ernest S. Griffith
  The Library of Congress
Edward P. Hutchinson
  University of Pennsylvania

Stacy May
  International Basic Economy Corp.
Walter Mitchell, Jr.
  Controllers Institute of America
Amos E. Taylor
  Bureau of Foreign and Domestic Commerce
Harold Williamson
  Northwestern University
A. Benjamin Handler (Executive Secretary)
  Social Science Research Council

R. H. Coats, University of Toronto, attended meetings of the Committee as a representative of the Social Science Research Council of Canada

Acknowledgments for Chapter Contributions*

Chapter N.   Construction and Housing

Historical Statistics . . . Colonial Times to 1970

Consultants—Samuel J. Dennis, Bureau of the Census; Lawrence N. Bloomberg, Office of Management and Budget

Major contributors—Leonard J. Norry and David Siskind, Bureau of the Census; Robert E. Lipsey, National Bureau of Economic Research, Inc.

Historical Statistics . . . Colonial Times to 1957

Principal consultant—Leo Grebler, University of California, Los Angeles

Review consultant—Raymond W. Goldsmith, National Bureau of Economic Research, Inc.

Historical Statistics . . . 1789–1945

Basic text and series on construction supplied by Keith W. Johnson, Economic Analyst, Samuel J. Dennis, Chief, Construction Economics Unit, and William H. Shaw, Chief, Construction Statistics Unit, Construction Division, in the Bureau of Foreign and Domestic Commerce, Department of Commerce. Material was also supplied by: H. E. Riley, Chief, Construction and Public Employment Division, Bureau of Labor Statistics, Department of Labor; and Fred E. Schnepfe, Chief, Liaison Division, Public Roads Administration, Federal Works Agency.

Material on housing prepared by Bureau of the Census staff.

Chapter P.   Manufactures

Historical Statistics . . . Colonial Times to 1970

Consultants—Daniel Creamer, The Conference Board, Inc.; Solomon Fabricant, New York University

Major contributors—John W. Kendrick, George Washington University; Vivian E. Spencer, University of Connecticut

Historical Statistics . . . Colonial Times to 1957

Principal consultant—Daniel Creamer, National Industrial Conference Board, Inc.

Review consultant—John W. Kendrick, George Washington University

Other contributor—John A. Waring, Washington, D.C.

Historical Statistics . . . 1789–1945

Material on manufactures prepared by Bureau of the Census staff.

Chapter Q.   Transportation

Historical Statistics . . . Colonial Times to 1970

Consultant—Thor Hultgren, University of Wisconsin

Historical Statistics . . . Colonial Times to 1957

Principal consultant—Thor Hultgren, National Bureau of Economic Research, Inc.

Review consultant—George R. Taylor, Amherst College

Other contributor—Bureau of Public Roads

---

* See also Appendix, p. A–1.

Historical Statistics . . . 1789–1945

List of series on railroads suggested by: Bureau of Transport Economics and Statistics, Interstate Commerce Commission; and Bureau of Railway Economics, Association of American Railroads.

Material on water transportation prepared by staff of Bureau of the Census.

Series on road transportation supplied by Division of Research Reports and Statistics, Public Roads Administration, Federal Works Agency.

List of series on air transport suggested by J. Parker Van Zandt, The Brookings Institution, and by Civil Aeronautics Administration, Department of Commerce. Data supplied by Civil Aeronautics Administration.

Chapter R.   Communications

Historical Statistics . . . Colonial Times to 1970

Consultant—Hyman H. Goldin, Boston University

Historical Statistics . . . Colonial Times to 1957

Principal consultants—Hyman H. Goldin and Robert E. Stromberg, Federal Communications Commission

Review consultant—Melville J. Ulmer, American University

Chapter S.   Energy

Historical Statistics . . . Colonial Times to 1970

Consultants—Joel Darmstadter and Sam H. Schurr, Resources for the Future, Inc.

Major contributors—Charles L. Franklin, Federal Power Commission; Paul J. Rederer, Edison Electric Institute; John W. Eden, American Gas Association

Historical Statistics . . . Colonial Times to 1957

Principal consultant—Lawrence D. Jennings, Federal Power Commission Review consultant—Herbert B. Dorau, New York University

Historical Statistics . . . 1789–1945

Basic text and series on power supplied by Division of Finance and Statistics, Bureau of Accounts, Finance, and Rates, Federal Power Commission.

Chapter T.   Distribution and Services

Historical Statistics . . . Colonial Times to 1970

Consultants—Louis Greenberg, Bureau of the Census, and David Schwartzman, New School for Social Research

Historical Statistics . . . Colonial Times to 1957

Principal consultants—Reavis Cox and Charles S. Goodman, University of Pennsylvania

Review consultant—Harold Barger, Columbia University

Chapter U.   International Transactions and Foreign Commerce

Historical Statistics . . . Colonial Times to 1970

Consultant—Robert E. Baldwin, University of Wisconsin
Major contributor—Frances L. Hall, Bureau of International Commerce

Historical Statistics . . . Colonial Times to 1957

FOREIGN TRADE

Principal consultant—Herbert B. Woolley, New York University
Review consultant—Douglass C. North, University of Washington

BALANCE OF INTERNATIONAL PAYMENTS AND INVESTMENT POSITION

Principal consultant—Nancy F. Culbertson, Office of Business Economics
Review consultant—Walter S. Salant, The Brookings Institution
Other contributors—Douglass C. North, University of Washington; Matthew Simon, Pace College

Historical Statistics . . . 1789–1945

Basic text and series for balance of payments supplied by International Economics Division, Bureau of Foreign and Domestic Commerce, Department of Commerce.
Material on foreign trade prepared by Bureau of the Census staff.

Chapter V.   Business Enterprise

Historical Statistics . . . Colonial Times to 1970

Consultants—Martin Gainsbrugh and Bernard Gelb, The Conference Board, Inc.
Major contributors—Lloyd K. Gilmour, Internal Revenue Service; Ralph L. Nelson, Queens College

Historical Statistics . . . Colonial Times to 1957

BUSINESS POPULATION

Principal consultant—Morris A. Adelman, Massachusetts Institute of Technology
Review consultant—Irwin Friend, University of Pennsylvania

CORPORATE ASSETS, LIABILITIES, AND INCOME

Principal consultant—Sergei P. Dobrovolsky, Rensselaer Polytechnic Institute
Review consultant—Irwin Friend, University of Pennsylvania

Chapter W.   Productivity and Technological Development

Historical Statistics . . . Colonial Times to 1970

PRODUCTIVITY INDEXES

Consultants—Jerome A. Mark, Bureau of Labor Statistics; John W. Kendrick, George Washington University
Major contributors—Charles W. Ardolini, Bureau of Labor Statistics; Daniel Creamer, The Conference Board, Inc.

COPYRIGHTS, PATENTS, AND TRADEMARKS

Consultant—Fritz Machlup, Princeton University

RESEARCH AND DEVELOPMENT

Consultant—Daniel J. Kevles, California Institute of Technology
Major contributor—Thomas J. Mills, National Science Foundation

Historical Statistics . . . Colonial Times to 1957

PRODUCTIVITY INDEXES

Principal consultant—Leon Greenberg, Bureau of Labor Statistics
Review consultant—John W. Kendrick, George Washington University
Other contributors—Robert T. Adams and Julian Frechtman, Bureau of Labor Statistics

COPYRIGHTS, PATENTS, AND TRADEMARKS

Principal consultant—Jacob Schmookler, University of Minnesota
Review consultant—Fritz Machlup, The Johns Hopkins University
Other contributor—P. J. Federico, Patent Office

RESEARCH AND DEVELOPMENT

Principal consultant—Kathryn S. Arnow, National Science Foundation
Review consultant—Irving H. Siegel, Council of Economic Advisers

Chapter X.   Financial Markets and Institutions

Historical Statistics . . . Colonial Times to 1970

FLOW OF FUNDS; NET PUBLIC AND PRIVATE DEBT; MONEY SUPPLY AND GOLD; INTEREST RATES AND SECURITY MARKETS; BANKING; NONBANK FINANCIAL INSTITUTIONS

Consultant—Stephen P. Taylor, Board of Governors of the Federal Reserve System
Major contributor—Anna J. Schwartz, National Bureau of Economic Research, Inc.

INSURANCE

Consultant—C. Arthur Williams, Jr., University of Minnesota

Historical Statistics . . . Colonial Times to 1957

BANKING; MONEY SUPPLY AND GOLD; MONEY RATES AND SECURITY MARKETS; CREDIT AND OTHER FINANCE

Principal consultants—Susan S. Burr and Caroline H. Cagle, Board of Governors of the Federal Reserve System
Review consultant—Milton Friedman, The University of Chicago
Other contributor—Clark Warburton, Federal Deposit Insurance Corporation

PRIVATE INSURANCE

Principal consultant—Albert I. Hermalin, Institute of Life Insurance
Review consultant—James J. O'Leary, Life Insurance Association of America

Historical Statistics . . . 1789–1945

Data reviewed and basic text supplied by Division of Research and Statistics, Board of Governors of the Federal Reserve System.

Chapter Y.   Government

Historical Statistics . . . Colonial Times to 1970

ELECTIONS AND POLITICS

Consultant—Richard M. Scammon, Elections Research Center
Major contributor—Walter Dean Burnham, Massachusetts Institute of Technology

GOVERNMENT EMPLOYMENT AND FINANCES

Consultant—Murray L. Weidenbaum, Washington University
Major contributors—Thomas J. Cuny and Carey P. Modlin, Office of Management and Budget; M. Lynden Mannen, Governments Division, Bureau of the Census

ARMED FORCES AND VETERANS

Consultant—James L. Clayton, University of Utah
Major contributor—Howard J. Sharon, Veterans Administration

Historical Statistics . . . Colonial Times to 1957

ELECTIONS AND POLITICS

Principal consultant—Richard M. Scammon, Governmental Affairs Institute
Review consultant—V. O. Key, Harvard University

ACKNOWLEDGMENTS FOR CHAPTER CONTRIBUTIONS

GOVERNMENT EMPLOYMENT AND FINANCES

Principal consultants—Jacob M. Jaffe, Bureau of the Census; James M. Jarrett, Internal Revenue Service; I. M. Labovitz, Library of Congress; and Flora M. Nicholson, Civil Service Commission

Review consultant—I. M. Labovitz, Library of Congress

Other contributors—Paul B. Trescott, Kenyon College; Paul P. Van Riper, Cornell University

ARMED FORCES AND VETERANS

Principal consultants—Milton C. Forster, Veterans Administration; Michael S. March, Bureau of the Budget

Review consultant—Irving H. Siegel, Council of Economic Advisers

Other contributor—Sydney M. Ratcliffe, Department of the Army

Historical Statistics . . . 1789–1945

Series and basic text on elections and State and local finance and employment were supplied by the Governments Division of the Bureau of the Census.

Data on Federal Government finance were prepared in the Bureau of the Census with the cooperation of the Office of the Technical Staff, Treasury Department.

Series and basic text on copyrights, patents, and trade-marks were supplied by P. J. Federico, Examiner-in-Chief, Patent Office, Department of Commerce.

Chapter Z. Colonial and Pre-Federal Statistics

Historical Statistics . . . Colonial Times to 1970

Consultants—Lawrence A. Harper, University of California; Robert C. Klove, Bureau of the Census

Major contributors—Jacob M. Price, University of Michigan; Stella H. Sutherland, Due West, South Carolina

Historical Statistics . . . Colonial Times to 1957

Principal consultant—Lawrence A. Harper, University of California

Review consultant—Richard B. Morris, Columbia University

Other contributors—Robert E. Gallman, Ohio State University; Jacob M. Price, University of Michigan; Stella H. Sutherland, Oakland City College, Indiana

Introduction

This volume is the third in the *Historical Statistics* series issued by the Bureau of the Census as a supplement to the annual *Statistical Abstract of the United States.*

Statistics are a valuable adjunct to historical analysis. They often clarify and enrich qualitative history and on occasion become important parts of a historical record on their own. However, users of historical data are faced with the paradox of over-abundance and scarcity. A burdensome multiplicity of sources has frequently to be consulted in order to reconstruct one quantitative aspect of a particular subject. Just as often, users are confronted by a discouraging barrenness of data, discoverable only after much costly work and delay.

The objective of the *Historical Statistics* volumes is to provide a convenient reference source which has two functions, *collecting* and *referring*. The *collecting* function consists of assembling, selecting, and arranging data from hundreds of sources and making them available within a single source. The *referring* function consists of text annotations to the data which act as a guide to sources of greater detail. The annotations also define terms used in the tables and include essential qualifying statements.

The first volume in this series, *Historical Statistics of the United States, 1789–1945*, was published in 1949. It provided a wide range of series quantifying various aspects of the development of the Nation. An interim *Continuation to 1952* was issued in 1954 to provide data for 1946 to 1952 for the still-active series shown in the first volume. Limited resources confined the scope of the first volume to data most readily available, usually from governmental agency sources. Nevertheless, some 3,000 statistical time series were presented.

Historical Statistics of the United States, Colonial Times to 1957, issued in 1960, represented a substantial expansion of the data shown in the original volume. It presented more than 8,000 time series, mostly annual, on a greater variety of subjects and for longer time periods. The statistics were also more fully annotated and more precise references to original sources were provided. For a greater number of series, in addition, there were more detailed descriptions of the development and reliability of the data. A *Continuation to 1962 and Revisions* was issued in 1965, presenting revisions of data in the basic volume and extensions to 1962 of the more than 6,000 series still current at that time.

Each of the first two volumes was prepared with the cooperation of the Social Science Research Council, the guidance of a distinguished Advisory Committee, and the assistance of numerous scholars, research analysts, and particular subject specialists. A description tracing the development of the first two editions appears below under "Origin of Historical Statistics of the United States."

During the latter 1960's, the supply of copies of *Historical Statistics . . . to 1957* available for sale from the U.S. Superintendent of Documents was exhausted. The edition had already been through a cycle of five printings and a question was raised concerning the advisability of further printings in the light of a possible new edition. The question was timely. Experience with the first two editions and their *Continuation* supplements had shown that a new edition was desirable at 10 to 12 year intervals. The *Continuation* supplements were at best handy stopgaps for researchers, a serviceable minimum seriously lacking in documentation. As each year lengthened the interval between editions, the "convenience" value of both the *Continuation to 1962* and its parent *Historical Statistics . . . to 1957* diminished. More and more time series were revised in part or entirely replaced. Further, the task for the user of updating the still active, unrevised, series became more burdensome despite the special efforts of the an-

nual *Statistical Abstract* to maintain a direct linkage to as many historical series as possible in its current tables. As a result, a decision was made in 1969 to begin preparation of a new edition.

The plans for the new edition immediately encountered the problem of funding and resources. It was clearly impractical at that time, given the available resources, to consider undertaking a full-fledged new edition of *Historical Statistics*. The determination to make a start, however, was very strong and more modest objectives were adopted. In effect, the early plans for the present edition proposed that it comprise little more than: (1) An extension to 1970 of those series for which current data were available; (2) revisions of data which had occurred since issuance of the *Continuation to 1962*; and (3) a reprinting of those series in *Historical Statistics . . . to 1957* which had not been affected by either updating or revisions. No time span was specifically set down to complete the work because there was a clear understanding that it was a part-time staff project.

Two other aspects of this plan differed considerably from the procedures followed for the last edition. For that edition, a large number of consultants were enlisted for their expertise in assembling and developing new time series, reviewing and adjusting old time series, and providing explanatory and bibliographic notes for both. Although most of these consultants, especially those in Federal agencies, contributed their own and their agencies services without compensation, many were compensated from funds provided by the Ford Foundation (by arrangement through the Social Science Research Council). For the new edition, given the limited resources, consultants' contributions were recruited on a public service basis entirely. Partly for the same reason, it was decided not to revive the collaboration of the Census Bureau with the Social Science Research Council which had proved so highly effective for the first two *Historical Statistics* editions. Even more convincing for the Bureau decision to undertake the project alone was the solidity of the base which those editions now provided for the next edition. Seeking such collaboration again seemed unwarranted in the light of the modest objectives outlined above.

As the work slowly progressed and as the many consultants and contributors gave generously of their knowledge and talent, it became clear that our objectives were too restrictive; that our contemplated mere updating would, if adhered to, have to ignore a large accumulation of new time series which were either ineligible for the last edition (at that time they covered a period of less than 20 years) or had not been discovered or properly developed prior to that edition. The gradual accretion of new material plus the additions to old material substantially changed the planned scope of the present edition. What follows are some measures of the changes in content introduced in the present edition.

All of the broad subject fields shown as separate chapters in the last edition are included in this edition and follow the same sequence. Within some of the chapters, however, chapter segments have been regrouped into new subchapters (as in chapters K and X) and in others, the sequence of the subchapters has been changed (as in chapters H, Q, and U) to achieve minor improvements in the juxtaposition of subjects.

In two chapters, two entirely new subchapters have been added: "Input-Output Structure of the U.S. Economy" to chapter F and "Flow of Funds" to chapter X.

The present edition presents more than 12,500 time series, a 50-percent increase over the last edition. Every chapter has undergone some expansion with respect to new time series. Chapter F, national income and wealth, and chapter H, social statistics, doubled in number of series; the former from 345 to 723 and the latter from 543 to 1,170. The increase in chapter F was largely due to newly-added data for economic growth rates, greater detail than was previously shown for national and personal income, and data showing valuation of capital stocks. Unsurprisingly, the largest increase in series occurred in chapter H where the data for social insurance and welfare, education, and crime and correction reflect the great public attention given to these subjects in recent decades. Almost equally large increases took place for chapter K, agriculture, and chapter X, financial markets and institutions (formerly banking and finance); chapter K from 328 series to 623; chapter X from 480 to 962. Partly to accommodate the increase in series, chapter K has been subdivided into 4 parts. Most of the new series in chapter K relate to farm population and farm-operator characteristics, farm marketings, government payments and price supports, and a number of new measures of farm productivity. For chapter X, the bulk of the increase in series is in the new flow-of-funds subchapter.

Several chapters now include for the first time a number of data series below the national level. In all, there are 13 new tables (comprising 484 series) in this category, 9 of which present data for the individual States and 4 for either regions (e.g. the South or the West) or the smaller geographic divisions (e.g. New England, South Atlantic). Perhaps of special interest among these tables are the series on population characteristics and land area for each State (A 195–263), those on selected items for farms and farm population by State (K 17–81), those on voter participation in presidential elections by State (Y 27–78), and those on population censuses taken in the colonies and States during the colonial and pre-Federal period (Z 24–132).

In addition, each of 4 chapters (D, G, Q, and Z) includes at least 200 or more new series and each of 10 chapters (A, B, L, N, P, S, T, U, V, and Y) includes 100 or more. A summary of selected new series included in each chapter is shown on p. XV.

One other important change is the reinstatement of a time period index (see p. A–4) which first appeared in *Historical Statistics . . . , 1789 to 1945*. The index enables users to identify quickly which time series (or statistics for particular subjects) begin in the specified 10- or 20-year time segment (e.g. 1800–1819, 1820–1839).

As a result of the complete review and updating of the contents of the last edition of *Historical Statistics*, many changes, apart from the entirely new series, have occurred in both the tables, the descriptive text, and the bibliographic notes. Most of the changes are due to revisions and corrections made during the interval between the last and present editions by the sources of the data affected. Where users of both editions become aware of discrepancies in what purport to be identical sets of data, it is safe to assume that the figures, descriptive text, and notes in the present edition supersede those in the last edition.

With rare exception, all of the series shown in the last edition are also included here. 76 series were omitted. They were primarily discontinued series replaced on recommendations of consultants by other series of a similar kind or were considered of marginal importance or relatively weak in other respects. In one or two instances, space was also a factor.

Origin of *Historical Statistics of the United States*

The first edition, *Historical Statistics of the United States, 1789–1945*, was formally initiated by a recommendation in 1945 by the Social Science Research Council that the Secretary of Commerce consider compilation and publication by the Bureau of the Census of a source book of economic statistics.

Earlier the same year, J. Frederic Dewhurst urged the development of an historical source book in a proposal to the American Statistical Association and the American Economic Association. A joint committee was named by these associations, joined by the Economic History Association, to explore the practical problems of preparing such a volume. Dr. Dewhurst's proposal coincided closely with

Bureau of the Census plans to prepare an historical supplement to the *Statistical Abstract of the United States*. The formal decision in 1945 by the Bureau of the Census to compile and publish such a volume led to the reconstitution of the joint committee, which then became the Social Science Research Council Committee on the Source Book of Historical Statistics, Advisory to the Bureau of the Census.

After the first edition was issued in June 1949, the Economic History Association, in response to a request from the Bureau of the Census, appointed an advisory committee in September 1950 to evaluate the volume and to make specific recommendations affecting the question of its revision. This committee, formally designated as the Committee of the Economic History Association on the Revision of *Historical Statistics of the United States, 1789–1945*, was under the chairmanship of G. Heberton Evans, Jr., The Johns Hopkins University, and included the following as members: Arthur H. Cole, Harvard University; Shepard Clough, Columbia University; T. C. Cochran, University of Pennsylvania, and Solomon Fabricant, National Bureau of Economic Research, Inc. In April 1952 the committee submitted a report to the Bureau of the Census entitled "On the Revision of *Historical Statistics of the United States, 1789–1945*." The conclusions and comments presented in this report were subsequently influential in getting underway the project for a revised volume.

For the second edition, *Historical Statistics of the United States, Colonial Times to 1957*, the Bureau designated a project director who also acted as secretary of the Committee on Historical Statistics appointed by the Social Science Research Council to serve as an advisory group similar to the committee which participated in the preparation of the first edition. The Census Bureau again assumed the responsibility for publishing the volume as a part of its *Statistical Abstract* program. The Social Science Research Council, in turn, obtained a grant from the Ford Foundation which provided funds for the procurement of services of experts in each field. More than 125 such specialists were engaged to serve as consultants. The Council also made arrangements with some of the consultants for the preparation of bibliographic essays on statistics in selected fields, five of which were subsequently published in the *Journal of the American Statistical Association*.

The Problem of Historical Statistics

The scattered sources of historical statistics of the United States include the annual reports of the executive heads of the agencies of the Federal Government, reports of special Federal commissions, the U.S. census volumes, printed debates of the Congress, published reports of committees of the Congress and transcripts of hearings on important legislative measures, published reports and documents of the State governments, statistical publications of private research organizations and of the universities and colleges of the Nation, together with the great mass of statistical volumes printed by other private organizations and individuals.

It has been noted that on occasion compilers, desiring to save the time and effort required to obtain data directly from the original sources, make use of successive issues of the annual *Statistical Abstract of the United States* to construct long-term time series. The results of such a procedure are not always sound, since the space available in the *Statistical Abstract* for describing major revisions in time series may not permit adequate clarification. Of the many revised figures appearing in each issue, most revisions apply to the immediate preceding years, but revisions of much earlier years are not uncommon. Moreover, the revisions shown have followed no systematic pattern and may be scattered irregularly over many issues.

Impediments to the use of historical statistics, then, include the initial difficulty of determining whether the data in fact exist, of identifying the document in which the data may be found, of constructing time series where the data may not be arranged in suitable form, and of identifying and interpreting changes in concept and coverage. Definitions employed in published historical tables, moreover, may have to be sought in separate publications if, indeed, they have been published at all.

Technical Notes and Explanations

Arrangement of the data. Data are arranged for broad subjects in lettered chapters and for more specific and detailed subjects in numbered series within each chapter. To facilitate reference, subject groups are organized in summary form under chapter and subchapter titles in the table of contents (p. IV). In addition, there is a detailed alphabetical subject index (p. A–10). The data are presented in conventional tabular form, each table comprising a group of subject-related series. Each series or tabular column is assigned a unique letter and number. The letter prefix identifies the chapter and the number represents the order of the series in the chapter. Thus the 44th series in the chapter on agriculture is designated K 44 to distinguish it from the 44th series in the chapter on transportation, Q 44. Because of possible confusion with numerals, the capital letters I and O have been omitted in identifying chapters. Source citations and descriptive text material (see below) are linked to the data series by use of the assigned series numbers.

All series begin with the most recent year for which data have been obtained and run backward in time. This arrangement was selected because it lent itself to more compact, less space-consuming presentation than the alternative of beginning with the earliest year. Insofar as possible, there are uniformly placed spaces above every year ending in 0 or 5. No data are shown for years subsequent to 1970. Figures for later years for most of the current series are presented in the *Statistical Abstract of the United States* beginning with the 1973 edition.

Basic guidelines. The guidelines adopted for this edition to aid Census Bureau staff members, subject matter consultants, and other participants with respect to selection and presentation of the data are quite similar to those of the last edition. As was the case then, however, the guidelines were not followed with complete rigidity. At times, the scope, variety, and complexity of the data involved made it necessary to modify the rules for the sake of clarity or internal consistency. The guidelines applied and the elements subject to application are discussed below.

Area coverage. Except as otherwise specified, data generally represent conterminous United States or the 48 States (including the District of Columbia) prior to the admission of Alaska and Hawaii to statehood and the 50 States thereafter. Asterisks on individual tables or series indicate the first year for which the figures include Alaska and Hawaii to the extent that their inclusion could be ascertained. For some series, especially in chapter K, the notes specifying inclusion or exclusion of Alaska and Hawaii appear in the text. In some instances, the sources used for data failed to specify the area covered. Where practicable, the data were examined and the appropriate qualifications were added.

Because of limitations of space, data are not generally shown for regions, States, or localities. Some exceptions were permitted, however, as noted above with respect to data for regions and States. Other exceptions were of a more specialized nature as in the following instances: Where regional statistics are helpful for correct interpretation of data, such as presentation of merchant marine statistics separately for each coast and for inland waters; where data in the subject field cannot (by definition) be summarized effectively for the United States, such as internal migration data; where summary data for a given subarea or market are indicative of general trend or level, such as prices on the New York Stock Exchange or in specified cities; where data for a given area effectively represent the national picture because of concentration of production, etc., as Pennsylvania anthracite; where data are available for only a given area as in the case of many series concerned with early American history and limited to the Atlantic seaboard.

Time coverage. In general, only annual or census-period data which cover at least 20 years are presented. A major exception was made for series covering the colonial or pre-Federal period. Other exceptions were permitted where newly developed series of recent origin were the only data available to represent an important subject field or where a short series was an important extension of other longer series.

The general requirements as to time coverage were specifically designed to permit inclusion of "lapsed" series, particularly those falling within the nineteenth century or extending into the early twentieth century. The lapsed series, which begin and terminate in the past, represent major fields of interest during various phases of American historical development; frequently they must be sought in out-of-print documents which are available in few libraries.

The identification of time-periods was complicated by failure of some sources to state whether the data were prepared on a calendar-year or on a fiscal-year basis; by shifts in time coverage from calendar to fiscal year during the period of the series, and, in some instances, by the lack of identification of the beginning or ending date of the fiscal year. In all such cases, particularly where time shifts seemed likely to have occurred, an effort was made to identify the correct basis.

Frequency of data. Annual data are given preference but certain series are presented only for years in which a national census was conducted, and, in some instances (for example, telephone and telegraph rates), only for the scattered dates for which the data are available. Where both annual figures and decennial or quinquennial benchmark or census data exist, both series are frequently shown.

Series linkage. No formal attempt was made to extend a single series back through time by linking it to another series which terminated at or near the date on which the first began. In a number of instances, however, such series are presented in adjoining columns, with an overlap for a period of years, when available.

Selection of data. The criteria of selection varied broadly, depending on a number of factors applicable to the subject matter involved. Generally, summary measures or one-dimensional aggregates at gross levels and immediately below were given highest priority for inclusion. Below such levels, selection was governed by the interplay of: The amount of space already devoted to a particular subject; the attempt to achieve a relatively balanced presentation among subject fields; the "uniqueness" (in the sense that other data did or did not fairly cover a particular subject) of the data; the quantity of data available; the quality of the data available; and the extent to which data might be related to and enhance the value of other data.

Among less discretionary factors, both area detail (see above under area coverage) and subject detail, such as cross-classifications or data for specific commodities, were held to a minimum because of space limitations. Inevitably, there were exceptions where synthesis or summarization did serious damage to the value of a series or where it was clearly more meaningful to show series for specific commodities than a group aggregate.

Presentation of absolute rather than derived data. Primary emphasis was placed on the presentation of absolute figures rather than on derived data since the absolute figures offer somewhat greater flexibility to the user. The major exception was the presentation of index numbers. In general, percentage distributions of absolute data already shown are not presented. Other percentage data, and averages, medians, ratios, and rates were used only where they resulted in a significant economy in space or where they significantly facilitated interpretation. No attempt was made to convert various series of index numbers to a base year or period other than that shown in the source. Large numbers (8 digits or more, for example) shown in the source documents have been rounded to thousands, millions, or billions for ease of use and reference only as staff resources allowed.

Omissions of data, "blank" cells. The significance of dashes in tabular cells varies from series to series. In general, the presence of cell "leaders" or "dashes" indicates merely that no information was provided. Dash entries may mean that no information exists for the given year; the entry, if shown, would be zero; the information was not available; or the information is believed to exist in published form but it was not practicable to do the research necessary to locate the appropriate source. The user will have to judge from the context which meaning is appropriate in each particular instance.

The practices of the various sources of information differ as to the meaning of dashes in cells, the extent to which they label data as "not available," the meaning of the term "not available," the use of the zero entry, etc. In general, the policy adopted in preparing this volume was to retain "not available" notations where they appeared for intermediate years in the series; to change them to dashes where they appeared at the beginning or end of the series. Where cells were left blank in the sources, they were filled with dashes unless there was evidence that "not available" was a more appropriate entry.

Since series of varying length taken from different sources are frequently found in adjoining columns in a table, the stub listings for years necessarily encompass the earliest and latest date for which any of the series in the table are shown. In itself, this tends to create many additional blank cells since missing entries have been replaced by dashes in order to make it easier for the user's eye to trace the entries for a given year across the entire table.

Source citations and text. For every series shown, the text notes present the source or sources of the data. In most cases, precise publication dates and page or table numbers are given. However, where numerous issues of a certain publication were used, the source citations are usually limited to "annual issues," "various monthly issues," or similar notations. The term "unpublished data" means that the data were not in published form at the time they were obtained for use in this edition. In many cases, such data were scheduled for inclusion in forthcoming publications.

Where possible the descriptive text includes definitions of concepts and terms used, and sufficient methodological and historical information to permit intelligent use of the data. For many series the text also includes reference to where more detail can be found. Unusual values in a series are explained and major changes which affect comparability are noted. Methods used for adjusted or derived figures are described, often with reference to a more complete description.

Copyright material. Copyright restrictions, where applicable, are noted in source citations. Permission to quote or reprint copyright material should be obtained directly from the copyright owner.

Statistical Reliability and Responsibility

The contents of this volume were obtained from a large number of sources. All data from either censuses and surveys or based on estimates or administrative records are subject to error arising from a number of sources: Sampling variability (for statistics based on samples), reporting errors in the data for individual units, incomplete coverage, nonresponse, imputation, and processing error. The Bureau of the Census cannot accept responsibility for the accuracy or the limitations of data presented here, other than for those which it collects. Every attempt has been made, within the limits of time and available personnel, to verify and correctly identify the material. Final responsibility for selection of the material, and for its accurate and proper presentation, rests with the Bureau of the Census, even though carried out with the cooperation of many individuals and agencies who devoted much time and energy in providing data and descriptions of series for this publication.

The information presented in this volume supersedes all similar information presented in *Historical Statistics of the United States, Colonial Times to 1957*, and in *Historical Statistics of the United States, Colonial Times to 1957: Continuation to 1962 and Revisions.*

FOR ADDITIONAL INFORMATION ON DATA PRESENTED

please consult the source publications available in local libraries or write to the agency indicated in the source note in the descriptive text for the given statistical series. Write to the Bureau of the Census only if it is indicated as the source.

SUGGESTIONS AND COMMENTS

should be sent to:

The Director
Bureau of the Census
Washington, D.C. 20233

Summary of Selected New Series in This Edition

Chapter and title	Number of new series	Summary of selected new series	Chapter and title	Number of new series	Summary of selected new series
A. Population	198	Urban population characteristics (A 82–90); foreign born, by sex and race (A 105–118); population characteristics and land area, by States (A 195–263); households, by number of persons (A 335–349); inmates of institutions (A 359–371)	**L. Forestry and Fisheries**	153	Forest products production, imports, exports, and consumption (L 56–71, L 87–97, L 138–165, L 178–198); fishery imports and exports (L 224–235); value of landed fish catches (L 244–253); prices received by fishermen (L 321–337)
B. Vital Statistics and Health and Medical Care	180	Fertility and birth rates, by age of mother (B 11–19); illegitimate births and rates (B 28–35); health expenditures (B 221–261); hospital use rates, expenses, personnel, and insurance coverage (B 381–422)	**M. Minerals**	26	Employment and man-hours in mineral industries (M 287–306)
C. Migration	36	Aliens naturalized (C 162–167); passenger arrivals and departures (C 296–331)	**N. Construction and Housing**	120	Wholesale price indexes for construction materials (N 140–155); new publicly-owned housing starts (N 171–179); value and mean age of stocks of residential structures (N 200–231); housing vacancy rates (N 246–258)
D. Labor	227	Working women (D 49–74); unemployment rates (D 87–115); employee output (D 683–704); employee earnings (D 705–786); union membership and work stoppages (D 927–939, D 986–1021)	**P. Manufactures**	132	General statistics (P 58–67); horsepower of power equipment (P 68–73); shipments, inventories, and orders (P 74–92); corporation sales, profits, and equity (P 93–106); shares of largest companies (P 177–204); consumption of selected commodities (P 216–230)
E. Prices	22	GNP implicit price deflators (E 1–22)	**Q. Transportation**	240	Intercity passenger traffic (Q 1–11); revenues and employment, by type of transport (Q 23–46); intercity motor carriers (Q 69–81); long-term public highway debt (Q 136–147); motor vehicle insurance, ownership, and financing (Q 163–186); motor vehicle speed, miles of travel, and accidents (Q 187–232); merchant vessels built, repaired, launched, and active (Q 438–480, Q 487–502)
F. National Income and Wealth	362	GNP growth rates and per capita (F 10–31); GNP summary and by type of industry (F 32–46), F 130–162); national and personal income (F 163–209, F 250–348); national tangible assets (F 349–376); value and age of capital stocks (F 470–534)			
G. Consumer Income and Expenditures	292	Distribution of families and persons, by money income levels (G 1–268); nutritive value of city diets (G 857–865); food used at home (G 866–880)	**R. Communications**	53	Cable TV (R 98–101); radio and TV finances (R 113–120, R 130–137); new books published (R 195–217); newsprint consumption (R 218–223)
H. Social Statistics	675	Employee benefit plans (H 70–114); OASDHI (social security) coverage, benefits, and trust fund (H 186–259); Civil Service retirement (H 260–270); private philanthropy (H 398–411); schools and school enrollment (H 418–432, H 442–522); school retention rates (H 587–597); income, by years of school completed (H 648–663); illiteracy (H 669–688); doctorates, by field (H 766–787); foreign travel, passports issued, and foreign visitors to U.S. (H 894–951); crimes and crime rates (H 952–961); homicides and suicides (H 971–986); criminal justice expenditures (H 1012–1027); lawyers (H 1028–1062); courts (H 1063–1124)	**S. Energy**	124	Consumption of raw materials and fuel resources (S 15–31); privately-owned electric utility generating plants and balance sheet and income items (S 58–73, S 133–146); REA summary of operations (S 147–159); waterpower (S 160–175); natural gas consumption and gas utility industry (S 178–218)
			T. Distribution and Services	100	Annual earnings of full-time employees (T 29–42); legal form of organization of industries (T 43–57); merchant wholesalers sales and stocks (T 375–383); index of national advertising expenditures (T 472–484)
			U. International Transactions and Foreign Commerce	155	Value of direct foreign investment in U.S. (U 47–74); U.S. Government foreign grants and credits (U 75–186); exports and imports, by broad end-use class (U 249–263)
J. Land, Water, and Climate	15	Indian lands (J 16–19); tornadoes, floods, and cyclones (J 268–278)			
K. Agriculture	315	Farm population, land in farms, farm property, farm products sold (K 1–81); farm operator characteristics (K 82–108); balance sheet of farming and value of gross farm product (K 204–239); farm income and farm marketings (K 256–343); farm productivity (K 407–495)	**V. Business Enterprise**	115	Number of firms, by type of ownership (V 1–12); income of unincorporated firms (V 66–77); manufacturing and trade sales and inventories (V 78–107); gross product and unit costs of nonfinancial corporations

INTRODUCTION

Summary of Selected New Series in This Edition—Con.

Chapter and title	Number of new series	Summary of selected new series	Chapter and title	Number of new series	Summary of selected new series
		(V 141–166); business expenditures for new plant and equipment (V 306–332)	Y. Government	158	Voter participation in presidential elections (Y 28–78); costs of presidential elections (Y 187–188); congressional bills vetoed (Y 199–203); Federal Government full-time civilian employment (Y 318–331); Federal grants to State and local governments (Y 638–651); selective service registrants (Y 917–926); defendants charged with violation of selective service acts (Y 927–942)
W. Productivity and Technological Development	60	Indexes of output per man-hour and per employed person (W 22–29); funds for research and development (W 109–125, W 161–167); employment of natural scientists and engineers (W 168–180)			
X. Financial Markets and Institutions	517	Flow of funds (X 1–392); sales of stocks and bonds on registered exchanges (X 517–530); savings and other time deposits, by institution (X 687–697); assets and liabilities of mutual savings banks and savings and loan associations (X 821–844); selected items of property-liability insurance (X 918–932); stock and mutual insurance companies (X 933–956)	Z. Colonial and Pre-Federal Statistics	200	Population censuses taken in the colonies and States (Z 24–132); components of private wealth for the thirteen colonies (Z 169–191); exports to and imports from Scotland, by colonies and States (Z 227–244); commodity imports and exports, shipping earnings, and value of slaves imported (Z 286–290); vessels built in colonies and West Florida (Z 510–529)

XVI

Part 2
Chapter N—Chapter Z

For Chapter A—Chapter M,
see Part 1

Construction and Housing

Construction (Series N 1-155)

N 1-60. General note.

On July 1, 1959, full responsibility for compiling and publishing value-in-place estimates for new construction was placed in the U.S. Department of Commerce. Prior to that date, the U.S. Department of Labor was responsible for the estimates of value of private housekeeping residential construction and of all public construction, and the U.S. Department of Commerce was responsible for the estimates of all other new construction, of maintenance and repair expenditures, and of expenditures in constant prices for all types of construction.

Specific definitions of the terms used here and discussion of sources and methodology are given in the source publications. New construction includes the complete, original erection of structures and essential service facilities, as well as major additions and alterations. It does not include mobile structures, special purpose equipment (e.g. steam tables in restaurants, printing presses, refrigerators and dishwashers, church pews, etc.), demolition of structures if not part of a construction contract, oil and gas well drilling, digging and shoring of mines, and farming operations such as plowing, terracing, or digging of drainage ditches.

The value of construction put in place is a measure of the value of construction installed or erected at the site during a given period. For an individual project, this includes the cost of material installed or erected, the cost of labor performed (both by the contractors and by force account employees) and a proportionate share of the cost of construction equipment used, the contractor's profit, the project owner's overhead costs, the cost of architectural and engineering work, and miscellaneous costs chargeable to the project on the owner's books.

The total value in place for a given period is the sum of the value put in place on all projects underway during this period, regardless of when work on each individual project was started or when payment was made to the contractors.

The estimates do not always conform completely to the value-in-place concept. For some categories, the published estimates represent payments made during a period rather than the value of work actually done during that period. For other categories, the estimates are derived by distributing the total construction cost of the project in accordance with fixed construction progress patterns.

Estimates of the value of new construction by States are available only for 1939-1952 in Department of Commerce, *Construction and Building Materials, Statistical Supplement*, "New Construction by Regions and States, 1939-1952."

Significant revisions in basic data were made for all or part of the period beginning in 1960 in four categories: New private housing units, private nonresidential buildings, farm construction, and privately owned public utilities. These revisions are noted in the text for those series.

The estimates for other series have only small revisions made necessary by the incorporation of newly available basic data.

Except as indicated in footnotes, all these series are essentially comparable back to 1946, as the result of revisions made in 1964 to establish historical comparability. For series N 1-29, two sets of data are given for 1946 in order to show comparability also between 1946 and earlier years. For a description of the revisions beginning with 1946, see Bureau of the Census, *Construction Reports*, series C 30-61 Supplement, October 1964.

N 1-29. Value of new private and public construction put in place, 1915-1970.

Source: 1915-1957 (except as indicated in footnote 9), U.S. Business and Defense Services Administration, *Construction Statistics, 1915-1964*, a supplement to *Construction Review*, January 1966, pp. 2-7. 1958-1970, U.S. Bureau of the Census, *Construction Reports*, series C 30-74-5, pp. 8 and 9, and unpublished data.

N 1-3, total new, total new private, and total new private residential construction. Series N 1 is the sum of series N 2 and N 19; series N 2 is the sum of series N 3, N 7, N 11, N 12, and N 18; series N 3 is the sum of series N 4-6.

N 4, new housing units. This series covers all new houses and apartments, including housing at all levels of value and quality, such as prefabricated units, shell houses, basement (or capped) houses, and houses built of used materials. The estimates for 1941-1970 are based on monthly reports of the value of new housing units authorized by local building permits and on monthly field surveys in a sample of areas not issuing building permits. Values in building permit reports are adjusted to reflect the construction cost of housing units in all permit-issuing places, reporting and nonreporting, to compensate for the typical understatement of costs in permits, and to allow for lapses of permits. The permit and nonpermit segments are then combined and further adjustments are made to cover architect and engineering fees and site development costs not covered elsewhere. An expenditure pattern is developed for these adjusted estimates of total costs to estimate the amount of work put in place in the months following start of construction. Beginning 1960, this series was revised to incorporate the results of new procedures and to include farm housing, which was previously included in the farm series. In this volume, series N 4 includes, and series N 11 excludes, farm housing (shown separately in the first source cited) for all years except 1958 and 1959.

For 1921-1940, the data are based mainly on the value of permits issued during each year, with rough adjustments for nonreporting permit areas and nonpermit areas and for the other items mentioned above. Only slight adjustment is made for year-to-year differences in the amount of carryover of expenditures for units started near the end of the year. The estimates for 1915-1920 are projected back from the 1921-1922 average by using link relatives indicated by year-to-year changes in the value of residential building contracts awarded as reported by the F. W. Dodge Corporation.

Residential construction expenditures for new 1 unit- and 2 or more unit-structures are presented in *Construction Reports*, series C 30, beginning with data for 1960. For a rough segregation of residential construction expenditures into 1- to 4-family housing and multifamily housing, see Raymond W. Goldsmith, *A Study of Saving in the United States*, vol. I, Princeton University Press, 1955, table R-28.

Series N 4 excludes group quarters, transient accommodations, residential units in buildings which are primarily nonresidential, new units provided by conversion of residential or nonresidential space to additional housing units, mobile homes, house trailers, and houseboats.

N 5, residential additions and alterations. This series includes all remodeling of or additions to housing units subsequent to their original completion, the construction of additional housing units in existing residential structures, the finishing of basements or attics, and the modernization of kitchens, bathrooms, etc. Work representing normal maintenance and repair is not included.

Private residential construction is the only type of construction activity for which the source publishes estimates of additions and alterations separately, and the data cover housekeeping structures only. For a discussion of the problems of estimating dependable data on residential additions and alterations, particularly prior to 1960, see Marvin Wilkerson, "Revised Estimates of Residential Additions and Alterations, 1945–56," *Construction Review*, June 1957.

N 6, nonhousekeeping residential buildings. These include fixed structures providing residential facilities other than housekeeping units, such as hotels (other than apartment hotels), motels, dormitories, nurses' homes, etc. The sources and estimating procedures are the same as those for private nonresidential building. Revised data were introduced for 1968 through 1970. They were obtained from the Bureau of the Census' newly introduced Progress Reporting Survey for the 13 Western States, and 37 Eastern States which accounts for an average of about 23 percent of this series.

See also text for series N 7–10 and series N 78–100.

N 7–10, new private nonresidential buildings. Estimates are based on monthly records of the value of contract awards in the District of Columbia and the 37 States east of the Rocky Mountains, as compiled by the F. W. Dodge Division of the McGraw-Hill Information Systems Company (see text for series N 78–100). These were adjusted for undercoverage, cancellations, and duplication of construction reported by public utilities. Prior to 1968, data for the 13 Western States were derived by applying an adjustment factor to the data for the Eastern States. Beginning 1968, the series are based not only on the previously used survey data for the 37 Eastern States but also on the results of the new survey covering the 13 Western States (see text for series N 6). The net effect of the new procedure was to lower the estimates for total new private nonresidential building construction for 1968 by 3.4 percent in comparison to the old method. In order to maintain a continuous series, the estimates for total private nonresidential building were adjusted. The previously published totals were reduced starting in 1965 and continuing through 1967, i.e., 0.1 percent decrease in March 1965, 0.2 percent in April, etc. down to the 3.4 percent decrease in December 1967. A corresponding adjustment could not be made by type of construction for those years.

Also beginning 1968, the classification system for new projects was revised from a building basis, i.e., the classification of the building itself, to an establishment basis, i.e., classification based upon the classification of the establishment at which the construction is taking place or classification of the entire project of which the individual building or subproject is part. For example, under the new classification, a cafeteria building at a hospital is classified under hospital and institutional; under the previous classification, following an adjustment in the data, it would have been classified as commercial.

Through June 1962, the adjusted value of monthly contract awards is converted to monthly estimates of expenditures on the assumption that all projects are started in the month following the contract award and on the basis of an expenditure pattern over subsequent months. Beginning July 1962 (January 1968 in the 13 Western States), monthly estimates of expenditures are derived from a monthly survey of construction progress.

N 11, farm construction, nonresidential. This series includes buildings and structures such as barns, storage houses, smoke houses, wells, fences, etc., which are constructed on places classified as farms. Annual estimates of total expenditures on farm buildings are prepared by the Economic Research Service of the U.S. Department of Agriculture. They are based chiefly on data from sample surveys of construction expenditures of farm operators for 1934–1937, 1939, 1946, 1949, 1955, and 1971. Estimates for other years are made by interpolation and extrapolation, based in part on inferences from relevant data reported in Bureau of the Census, *Current Industrial Reports*, and in part on regression analyses of selected series of farm income and construction expenditures for past benchmark years.

N 12, total, privately owned public utilities. This series is the sum of series N 13–17. Recent revisions for public utilities result from the incorporation of late basic data for the years 1967 through 1969 and from revision of estimating procedures in 1970.

N 13, railroad. Railroad estimates are based on an annual summary of construction expenditures prepared by the Interstate Commerce Commission from reports by all Class I railroads which account for over 95 percent of all railroad expenditures. These data are adjusted to include estimates for Class II railroads based on ICC data on railroad investment in roads and equipment. Prior to 1955, local transit estimates of capital and maintenance expenditures were included from the annual *Transit Fact Book* of the American Transit Association. Outlays by municipally owned transit companies were deducted from these expenditures. The estimates for 1955–1958 are projections based on an assumed gradual decline in expenditure from the 1954 level to zero in 1959. For both railroads and local transit, the estimates for 1915–1921 are extrapolations based on miles of track added or rebuilt.

N 14, petroleum pipeline. Capital expenditures on pipelines for 1919–1970 were obtained from reports filed with the Interstate Commerce Commission. Adjustment was made for the purchase of existing lines and for expenditures by companies not required to file information with the Commission on the basis of data on gross capital investment compiled by the Chase Manhattan Bank. Only rough estimates by the Bureau of Foreign and Domestic Commerce are available for 1915–1918.

N 15, electric light and power. Annual estimates are based on reports to the Federal Power Commission by privately owned electric companies and on data reported to the Rural Electrification Administration by REA cooperative companies. For 1937–1970, annual additions to electric plants reported to the Federal Power Commission were adjusted to include small companies not reporting and to allow for work in progress and existing property purchased. For 1921–1936, data from the Edison Electric Institute were used. For 1915–1920, the data are based on an estimated year-by-year distribution of the 5-year increments in plant and equipment derived from data reported in the Census of Electrical Industries for 1912, 1917, and 1922.

N 16, gas. Annual estimates are based on reports to the Federal Power Commission and data compiled by the American Gas Association. For 1929–1970, annual data published by the American Gas Association were adjusted to eliminate equipment expenditures. For 1915–1928, estimates were obtained by extrapolation on the basis of year-to-year changes in the fixed capital accounts of 50 large gas companies.

N 17, telephone and telegraph. Estimated construction expenditures of the telephone industry for 1915–1970 were obtained from the American Telephone and Telegraph Co.; they include expenditures for Bell System companies and estimates for independent companies. Construction expenditures of the telegraph industry were derived from capital expenditures reported by the Western Union Telegraph Co. for 1927–1970 and by the Postal Telegraph and Cable Co. for 1919–1943. Extrapolation back to 1915 was made on the basis of annual increments in the value of plant and equipment.

N 18, all other private construction. This series includes unclassified items such as private dams and reservoirs not constructed by public utility companies, sewer and water installations, roads, bridges, parks and playgrounds, and airfields.

N 19, total new public construction. This series is the sum of series N 20–21 and N 25–29. The distinction between private and public construction is made on the basis of ownership rather than source of funds. Some types of private institutional construction involve Federal, State, or local aids to projects built by nonprofit organizations. To this extent, the public construction estimates do not account for all public expenditures for new construction.

N 20, public residential construction. The estimates are based on reports of the Public Housing Administration, the New York City

Housing Authority, and other State and local agencies. They include direct Federal construction during World War I, the depression of the 1930's, and the defense and World War II periods (1940's); the Federal low-rent public housing program initiated in 1937 and executed by State and local agencies with Federal loans and grants; similar programs executed by State and local agencies without Federal aid; and the Veterans Temporary Re-Use Housing Program of the Federal Government initiated in 1945 and terminated in 1950. For the number of housing units under the major programs, see series N 180–191.

Most of the estimates for federally owned construction are based on monthly reports from Federal bureaus and agencies administering residential construction programs. In a few instances, they are based on information presented in the Federal budget documents.

For State and local residential construction prior to 1963, the estimates are based on contract award data compiled from various sources, such as the F. W. Dodge Corporation, the Public Housing Administration, regional offices of the Housing and Home Finance Agency, and State and local agencies responsible for construction of public housing. For 1963–1968, the estimates are based on quarterly expenditures data obtained by the Census Bureau in its quarterly survey of construction expenditures of State and local governments. Beginning 1968, they are based on monthly data on new construction expenditures of State and local governments collected by the Census Bureau in a monthly survey inaugurated with reports for October 1968.

N 21–24, public nonresidential buildings. Series N 21 is the sum of series N 22–24. For Federal construction and State and local projects under Federal-aid programs, the estimates are based on reports of Federal agencies since 1941. For prior years, and for public construction other than Federal or Federal-aid projects prior to 1963, they were derived from the compilations of contract awards by the F. W. Dodge Corporation, adjusted as explained in the text for series N 7–10. For years beginning 1963, see text for series N 20.

N 25, military facilities. This series covers certain construction owned by the Department of Defense, such as troop housing, administration and training buildings, warehouses, mess halls, recreation centers, educational facilities, airfields and airport buildings, missile sites, etc. It also covers construction of Coast Guard facilities.

Estimates for 1940–1970 are based on monthly reports by the Department of Defense. Navy Department construction expenditures for 1915–1936 were derived from special tabulations of the Bureau of Supplies and Accounts. Expenditures of the Navy for 1937–1939 and the War Department for 1915–1939 are based upon expenditures shown in various issues of Bureau of the Budget, *Budget of the United States Government*.

N 26, highways, roads, and streets. This series includes streets, bridges, vehicular tunnels, viaducts, and forest and park roads owned by Federal agencies other than the Department of Defense. It also includes the following items if built in connection with a Federal road: Culverts, right-of-way drainage, erosion control, lighting, guard rails, and earthwork protective structures.

For 1921–1962, estimates for State-administered highways are based on annual reports of the Bureau of Public Roads adjusted to include expenditures by county, municipal, and other local bodies. The adjustments are based upon ratios developed from the analysis of total highway construction and State highway construction. For years beginning 1963, see text for series N 20. Estimates for 1915–1919 were derived from the 1920 *Yearbook of Agriculture*. The 1920 estimates were obtained by straight line interpolation.

N 27, sewer and water systems. For 1915–1942, estimates are based upon data published annually in Bureau of the Census, *Financial Statistics of Cities*. Using the expenditure patterns of the city-size groups reporting, expenditure ratios were derived for the smaller municipalities and rural incorporated areas. For 1943–1962, estimates are based upon contracts awarded as reported by the F. W. Dodge Corporation with adjustments for undercoverage. For years beginning 1963, see text for series N 20.

N 28, conservation and development. For 1915–1942, expenditures for reclamation, improvement of rivers and harbors, and flood control work were derived from annual reports of the Corps of Engineers and the Bureau of Reclamation. The fiscal-year basis of the reports was converted to calendar year by taking one-half of the figure for each fiscal year included within that calendar year. For 1943–1970, estimates are based upon project reports furnished by the same two agencies. Tennessee Valley Authority expenditures are available in its annual reports. For Bureau of Indian Affairs, Forest Service, National Park Service, Soil Conservation Service, Bonneville Power Administration, Office of Saline Water, Southwestern Power Administration, International Boundary and Water Commission, and St. Lawrence Seaway Development Corporation, expenditures were derived from special tabulations prepared by those agencies and from the Office of Management and Budget, *Budget of the United States Government*.

The estimates, with minor exceptions for earlier years, refer only to expenditures by the Federal Government. State and local government expenditures for this type of construction are included in "All other public," series N 29.

N 29, all other public construction. This series combines "miscellaneous public service enterprises" and "all other public construction" shown separately in the source. Construction expenditures by Federal agencies not included in other series are, for the most part, based on monthly or quarterly reports of the agencies or, in cases of minor or occasional construction work, derived from fiscal-year data in the Office of Management and Budget, *Budget of the United States Government*. Outlays for municipal public service enterprises prior to 1963 were obtained directly from the municipalities or estimated from information reported in Bureau of the Census, *Financial Statistics of Cities*. Miscellaneous public construction estimates prior to 1963, other than those of the Federal Government, were derived primarily from reports of contracts awarded, compiled by the F. W. Dodge Corporation, from the *Engineering News-Record*, and from other publications reporting contract awards. For years beginning 1963, see text for series N 20.

N 30–60. Value of new private and public construction put in place, 1957–59 dollars, 1915–1970.

Source: 1915–1959, see first source for series N 1–29, pp. 8–12. 1960–1970, U.S. Bureau of the Census, *Construction Reports*, series C 30, various issues.

Measurement of construction expenditures in constant prices is an indirect way of approximating changes in the physical volume of construction. These estimates are based on a deflation of each type of construction by an appropriate construction cost index. For a description of the cost indexes used for each type of construction, see the source publication.

These series, revised back to 1947 on a 1967 constant dollar base, are scheduled for issuance in 1975.

Beginning 1946, data are not entirely comparable with those for earlier years; see text for series N 1–29.

N 61. Construction expenditures for maintenance and repair, 1915–1963.

Source: See first source for series N 1–29.

The estimates are, in general, much less reliable than those for new construction and, to judge from past revisions and occasional partial surveys, probably understate actual expenditures.

Estimates of nonfarm residential building for 1947–1963 are based on the annual *Survey of Consumer Finances* of the Board of Governors of the Federal Reserve System, the consumer expenditure survey for 1950 by the Bureau of Labor Statistics, and a 1950 survey of outlays of owners of tenant-occupied dwelling units by the Office of the Housing Expediter (conducted for purposes of rent control). Data for earlier years are based on estimates of the value of all residential properties and on ratios of maintenance and repair expenditures to value. These ratios were derived from various studies, such as surveys of consumer purchases by the Department of Agriculture and the Department of Labor, and wartime surveys made for purposes of rent control.

Estimates for nonresidential building are based on corporate income tax returns covering manufacturing activities; cost analyses for office buildings in the National Association of Building Owners and Managers, *Experience Exchange Reports;* and reports by State school agencies to the Office of Education.

Other maintenance expenditures were estimated from the same sources used for the new construction figures. See text for series N 11–18 and N 21–29.

The source also presents maintenance and repair expenditures for major classes of construction. Beginning 1964, maintenance and repair expenditures are available for residential construction only; see Bureau of the Census *Residential Alterations and Repairs*, series C 50.

N 62–65. Expenditures for private nonfarm residential building, 1889–1921.

Source: Robert E. Lipsey and Doris Preston, *Source Book of Statistics Relating to Construction*, National Bureau of Economic Research (NBER), New York, 1966, pp. 35–38 (copyright).

New housekeeping units data, series N 62–63, are from David M. Blank, *The Volume of Residential Construction, 1889–1950*, Technical Paper 9, NBER, 1954, table 18. Blank's estimates were intended primarily to extend the official current dollar series (see series N 4), which begins in 1915, to earlier years. Blank presented his data for 1915–1920 as an improvement over the official series, and accepted the official series beginning 1921. Although Blank's estimating procedure was, in general, the same as that used for series N 4, more comprehensive source material and more refined techniques were used for the Blank estimates.

Blank estimated the permit value of new construction from Bureau of Labor Statistics-Works Progress Administration permit data by the same methods used in the Bureau of the Census *Construction Reports* (C 20), except that the calculation for all nonfarm housing units had to take account of the fact that rural nonfarm units had lower average values than urban nonfarm units. The permit valuations were then increased to allow for undervaluation of construction costs and to cover architects' and engineers' fees, land development costs, and builders' profit margins on construction operations. They were then converted to a construction-put-in-place basis, by extending the carryover of construction from one year to the next.

The constant dollar series was derived by deflating the current dollar data by a construction cost index developed by Blank. The index for 1910–1921 is based on the Boeckh index of residential construction. Earlier years are extrapolated by indexes of building-trade wage rates and building materials prices.

Data for additions and alterations to housekeeping units, series N 64–65, are from Leo Grebler, David M. Blank, and Louis Winnick, *Capital Formation in Residential Real Estate: Trends and Prospects*, NBER, 1956, pp. 40–52, 336, and 362. Additions and alterations are defined as in the Commerce series (see series N 61). Official Commerce estimates were carried back from 1921 by a crude graphic extrapolation using the movement of housekeeping construction expenditures but reducing the amplitude of fluctuation.

N 66–69. Value of new public construction put in place, by ownership and source of funds, 1915–1970.

Source: 1915–1946 (comparable with earlier years), U.S. Departments of Labor and Commerce, "Construction Volume and Costs, 1915–1946," statistical supplement to *Construction Review*, 1958, p. 10; 1946 (comparable with later years), U.S. Business and Defense Services Administration, "Construction Statistics, 1915–1964," supplement to *Construction Review*, January 1966, p. 14, and unpublished data; 1963–1970, U.S. Bureau of the Census, *Construction Reports*, series C 30, and unpublished data.

The sources also present detailed data by types of public construction. For bases of estimates, see text for series N 20–29.

N 70–77. Expenditures for new construction, private residential and nonresidential and public, in current and constant (1929) dollars, 1869–1955.

Source: Robert E. Lipsey and Doris Preston, *Source Book of Statistics Relating to Construction*, National Bureau of Economic Research (NBER), New York, 1966, pp. 29–32, 35–36, and 39–40 (copyright).

These series are a selection from the large number of annual estimates, partly unpublished, which underlie the five-year moving averages published with explanatory notes in Simon Kuznets, *Capital in the American Economy: Its Formation and Financing*, Princeton University Press for NBER, 1961.

N 70–71, total new construction. Kuznets' current price figures for 1952–1955 are U.S. Department of Commerce estimates of "Total New Construction Activity" plus "Petroleum and Natural Gas Well Drilling" from the *Survey of Current Business*, July 1956, table 31, p. 22. The constant (1929) price estimates for 1953–1955 were calculated, for private construction, from the current price estimates and an implicit price index derived from current and constant dollar figures in the *Economic Report of the President*, January 1956, pp. 165 and 168, and for public construction, by extrapolating the 1952 estimate by the constant price series in *Construction Review*, October 1956, p. 18.

For earlier years, Kuznets calculated total gross construction as the sum of (1) cost of oil and gas wells drilled and (2) all other construction.

The cost of oil and gas wells drilled in current prices was obtained as follows: For 1889–1928, the Kuznets' data were calculated by multiplying the series in 1929 prices by the price index for petroleum pipe lines. For 1915–1928, this price index was calculated from Business and Defense Services Administration (BDSA), *Construction and Building Materials, Statistical Supplement*, May 1954, pp. 33 and 82; it was extrapolated back from 1915 by the total construction cost index described in Kuznets, *National Product Since 1869*, NBER, 1946, table IV-4. For 1929–1938, this index was calculated from Office of Business Economics (OBE), *National Income*, 1954 edition, p. 209; 1939–1945, from BDSA, *Construction and Building Materials . . .*, p. 56; and 1946–1955, from OBE, *U.S. Income and Output*, 1958. The Commerce Department (BDSA and OBE) estimates represent all costs of drilling, including the cost of casings. The cost of installed production equipment, such as flowing and pumping equipment, is excluded. The figures are based on the cost of drilling oil and gas wells, as reported in the Census of Mineral Industries, 1939 and 1958, interpolated and extrapolated by annual data on the number of wells completed and on average cost per well.

The calculations for "all other construction" in current prices were as follows: 1889–1918: Calculated by multiplying the series in 1929 prices by the underlying price index. The latter was computed for 1915 and later years from *Construction and Building Materials . . .*, pp. 33 and 82, and was extrapolated from 1915 by the total construction cost index described in Kuznets, *National Product . . .*, table IV-4, notes to line 1. 1919–1951: Sum of (a) new private nonfarm residential construction including additions and alterations and excluding nonhousekeeping, from Grebler, Blank, and Winnick, *Capital Formation . . .* (cited in text for series N 62–65), appendix B, table B-6, and (b) all other new construction, from *Construction and Building Materials . . .*, tables 2 and 3.

The cost, in 1929 dollars, of oil and gas wells drilled was calculated as follows: Kuznets' data for 1889–1918 were extrapolated from the 1919 figure by the number of wells drilled each year (see pp. 526–527 of Kuznets, *Capital in the American Economy . . .*, for derivation). For 1919–1928, data were extrapolated from the 1929 figure by the series described in Kuznets, *National Income and Its Composition, 1919–1938*, NBER, 1941, p. 645. This series is based on individual State data for number of wells drilled and 1935 costs. For 1929–1945, Kuznets used the Commerce series in current prices divided by the price index for petroleum pipelines, calculated from *Construction and Building Materials* . . . , pp. 33 and 82, and adjusted to a 1929 base. For 1946–1955, the sources used were the same as for the current price series.

The value of "all other construction" in 1929 dollars was calculated as follows: 1889–1914: Output of construction materials for domestic consumption, multiplied by 1.54056, the ratio of new construction to cost of construction materials consumed in 1919–1933. The method of estimation is described in Kuznets, *Capital in the American Economy*, table R–30, notes to column 10, and Kuznets, *National Product* . . . , table II–5, notes to column 7. For data on output of construction materials, see William H. Shaw, *Value of Commodity Output Since 1869*, NBER, 1947 (series D 7). 1915–1920: Sum of (1) new private nonfarm residential construction including additions and alterations, in Grebler, Blank, and Winnick, *Capital Formation* . . . , appendix B, table B–6, and (2) other new construction from *Construction and Building Materials* . . . , tables 15 and 16, adjusted to 1929 prices. 1921–1952: Given in *Construction and Building Materials* . . . , tables 15 and 16, adjusted to 1929 prices.

N 72–73, private nonfarm residential building. Gross private nonfarm residential construction is composed of housekeeping residential construction plus additions and alterations.

Current dollar figures were taken from the following sources: 1889–1920: New construction, from David M. Blank, *The Volume of Residential Construction 1889–1950*, table 18, plus a rough estimate of additions and alterations from Leo Grebler, David M. Blank, and Louis Winnick, *Capital Formation* . . . , table D–2, p. 363. The new construction series was built up originally from the BLS–WPA building permit surveys (see Blank, *The Volume of Residential Construction*, p. 33). Blank estimated the permit value of construction started and the total cost of construction started. He then converted construction started to construction put in place, by using an estimate of the average carryover into the following year of construction started in a given year (*ibid.*, pp. 52–56). 1921–1952: BLS–Commerce estimates published in *Construction and Building Materials* . . . , p. 6, and *Survey of Current Business*, July 1956, table 31.

The constant (1929) dollar figures were calculated as follows: The series in current prices was deflated by residential construction cost indexes. For 1889–1952, the index in Grebler, Blank, and Winnick, *Capital Formation* . . . , table B–10, column 1, was used. This is the Boeckh residential construction cost index extrapolated back from 1910 by building-trade wage rates and building material prices. The index for 1953–55 was the index implicit in the series for all private residential nonfarm building (including nonhousekeeping) in 1947–49 prices, *Construction Review*, September 1956.

N 74–75, private nonresidential construction. These series were calculated as a residual by subtracting from Kuznets' *Capital in the American Economy* total new construction series, C 1 and C 2 (here identified as series N 70–71), his series on gross private nonfarm residential building, C 3 and C 4 (series N 72–73), gross nonmilitary public construction, C 7 and C 8 (series N 76–77), and gross military construction (an earlier version of BLS–Commerce series C 55 and C 56); see source.

N 76–77, public construction. Current dollar figures were taken from the following sources: 1889–1914: Sum of separate estimates for Federal, State, and local governments. The Federal Government series are derived mainly from those published in U.S. Bureau of the Census, *Historical Statistics of the United States, 1789–1945*, 1949, and the State and local government series are derived mainly from the Census Bureau's publications on government finances. A detailed description is given in Kuznets, *Capital* . . . , notes to table R–30, pp. 580–584. 1915–1955: BLS–Commerce estimates published in *Construction and Building Materials* . . . , table 3 ("total public construction" minus "military facilities"), and *Survey of Current Business*, July 1956, table 31.

The constant (1929) dollar figures were taken from the following sources: 1889–1914: The components of the current price series were

converted to 1929 prices by separate price indexes, each derived by extrapolating that implicit in the estimate for 1915 by the cost of construction index described in *National Product* . . . , table IV–4, notes to line 1. (See Kuznets, *Capital* . . . , table R–30 notes for further detail.) 1915–1955: BLS–Commerce estimates, from *Construction and Building Materials* . . . , table 16, adjusted to a 1929 price base, and extrapolated from 1952 to 1955 by the series in 1947–49 prices given in *Construction Review*, September 1956, table 4, p. 11.

N 78–100. Construction contracts awarded (Dodge)—value, and floor space of buildings, by class of construction, 1901–1970.

Source: 1901–1924, Robert E. Lipsey and Doris Preston, *Source Book of Statistics Relating to Construction*, National Bureau of Economic Research, New York, 1966, pp. 15–21 (copyright); 1925–1970, F. W. Dodge Division, McGraw-Hill Information Systems Company, New York (propriety data provided by special permission).

These series, except the part of residential buildings comprising privately owned one- and two-family houses, are based upon daily reports by the F. W. Dodge field staff. This field staff contacts owners, architects, engineers, contractors, financial institutions, real estate brokers, and others able to supply reliable information on construction projects. The series include new construction, additions, and major alterations within 60 days of work start. They exclude maintenance and repair work, farm building, ship building, and a part of force-account work done by firms and public agencies.

Geographic coverage has been increased in several steps since the series began. The earliest data beginning 1901 cover total construction in the New England States. Data covering 27 northeastern States and the District of Columbia are available from 1910; the addition of nine southern States between 1920 to 1923 brought the total to 36. Texas was added in 1924. The 37 States covered then excluded Montana, Idaho, Wyoming, Colorado, New Mexico, Arizona, Utah, Nevada, Washington, Oregon, and California. For the remaining 11 western States, information gathered from permit places, publications, and a sample of areas was used. From 1956 to 1969, the 48 conterminous States were covered; beginning 1970, all 50 States.

Valuation represents, as nearly as possible, actual construction costs, including subcontracts for such items as plumbing, heating, electrical work, roofing, and normal connecting utilities, and excluding land and architects' fees. Cost of industrial equipment not an integral part of the structure is excluded, except for special purpose equipment in petroleum refineries; outdoor chemical plants; electrical generating, power, and heating plants; and water and sewage treatment plants.

Floor space figures represent footage under roof, exclusive of basement. Where building permit data are the basis of the statistics, floor area is estimated from construction costs, with local building cost differentials applied to nationally established cost-per-square-foot rates.

N 101–110. Construction bidding volume (Engineering News-Record), by type, 1913–1970.

Source: *Engineering News-Record*, McGraw-Hill Inc., New York, various issues (copyright).

Data are based on daily reports by a field staff in 50 States and the District of Columbia. For 1963 to 1970, they consist of low bids for public construction and contract awards for private construction. Excluded are homebuilding, design-and-construct contracts (under which the contractor is responsible for design as well as the construction) and projects of investment builders or owner-builders serving as their own general contractors. They thus exclude a large proportion of chemical process and powerplant (design-and-construct) contracts and substantial volumes of commercial and apartment projects handled by owner-builders. Beginning 1963, data cover only projects reported by *Engineering News-Record* as new plans and which have advanced to the low bid or contract award stage. Although data prior to 1963, which are contract awards, are not strictly comparable with later data, the earlier and later figures are adequately comparable in coverage to describe long-term trends consistently for the separate series. In the aggregate they represent over 65 percent of the annual volume reported by series N 78–89. The following types of construction are included: Water supply, sewers and waste disposal, bridges, streets and roads, earthwork and waterways, public buildings, multiunit residential structures, commercial building, industrial plants, and an unclassified category. Only larger projects are included, and the minimum cost of projects covered by the reports has varied over time. For 1963 to 1970, the minimum cost of projects covered was: $100,000 for public works other than buildings, industrial and unclassified; $500,000 for buildings other than industrial. Because of the emphasis on heavy engineering works and the difference in geographic coverage, as well as other reasons, the data are not comparable to series N 78–89.

N 111–117.   General note.

While comprehensive estimates of construction expenditures by types of construction, such as presented in series N 1–29, are generally preferred for most purposes, building permit data are available for a considerably longer period. Permit values are based on estimates by builders of the costs of building for which permits are granted or plans filed. Permit data generally cover private, rather than public, construction; building, rather than nonbuilding, types of construction; and are generally limited to construction within the corporate limits of the cities covered. On the average, the cost of the projects covered is underestimated; small projects are generally not covered at all. Permit data are less frequently available for smaller cities and for earlier years. It follows that building permit data in unadjusted form are unsatisfactory as measures of the total absolute volume of new construction. Permit data are often more satisfactory when used in the form of relatives or indexes of permit values, as in the case of series N 111–114.

Although the absolute amount of construction activity is not adequately indicated by early permit data, the data clearly indicate the presence and approximate timing of cycles in private building. However, the relatively few cities upon which permit indexes are based during the earlier years suggests caution in the drawing of quantitative conclusions, particularly as to the amplitude of building cycles. Nonbuilding construction of various types and public building construction have fluctuated somewhat differently from building permit indexes, so that the data available for the analysis of cycles in total new construction over an extended period of years are particularly inadequate. The mere comparison of the various series on building permits purporting to measure roughly the same type of activity should warn the user against placing too much confidence in the data.

N 111.   Index of new building permit values (Long), 1868–1939.

Source: Clarence D. Long, Jr., *Building Cycles and the Theory of Investment*, Princeton University Press, 1940, pp. 213–223 (copyright).

This index was obtained by averaging the monthly indexes given in the source. The number of cities covered by the index has ranged from 1 to 37 (or 33 if all the boroughs of New York City are combined). For a list of cities and years covered, see source. The aggregate permit volume each year was divided by the aggregate volume for the same cities in 1930. For additional explanation, see general note for series N 111–117.

N 112–113.   Index of new building permit values (Newman), 1875–1933.

Source: William H. Newman, "The Building Industry and Business Cycles," *The Journal of Business of the University of Chicago*, vol. VIII, No. 3, pp. 63–71, copyright, University of Chicago.

These are annual indexes and annual averages of monthly indexes. Series N 112 is based on Bradstreet's building permit values, 120 identical cities, 1911–1933; Babson's monthly values of building permits in 20 cities, 1903–1910; Ayres' permits in 50 cities, 1900–1902; and permit data from 13 cities, 1875–1900. Series N 113 is obtained from series N 112 by the use of the following building cost indexes: The American Appraisal Co.'s building construction cost index, 1913–1933; an arithmetic average of the American Appraisal Co.'s cost indexes for frame, brick, and reinforced concrete buildings, 1900–1913; and an average of the frame- and the brick-building cost indexes, 1875–1900. For additional explanation, see general note for series N 111–117.

N 114.   Index of new building permit values (Riggleman-Isard), 1830–1933.

Source: Miles L. Colean and Robinson Newcomb, *Stabilizing Construction: The Record and Potential*, McGraw-Hill, Inc., New York, 1952, appendix N, table 2 (copyright).

This index is based on the per capita value of building permits as estimated in an unpublished doctoral dissertation by John R. Riggleman, *Variations in Building Activity in United States Cities*, Johns Hopkins University, 1934. The data cover Manhattan, Boston, and Washington, D.C., from 1830 through 1848. The coverage then increases gradually to a total of 10 cities in 1868, which were augmented to cover 70 cities in 1900 and subsequent years (counting the 5 boroughs of New York City separately). For the cities covered, see the source, appendix N, table 4, footnote c, p. 240. By eliminating the population adjustment and weighting the data on the basis of the relative volume of activity from 1920 to 1929 in the areas covered, Isard developed a series more comparable to that of Long (series N 111) in general movement (see Walter Isard, *The Economic Dynamics of Transport Technology*, unpublished doctoral dissertation, Yale University, 1947). The data back to 1830 have decreasing credibility.

N 115.   Index of dollar volume of new construction (Newcomb), 1868–1914.

Source: See source for series N 114, appendix N, table 3.

This index is based on a 3-year moving average of the figures for series N 114 for 1868–1878, and on a 3-year moving average of the figures for series N 111 for 1879–1914, adjusted by (1) weighting residential building at one-third instead of approximately one-half used by Long, series N 111, and (2) changing the base to 1920–29 = 100. The purpose of these adjustments by Robinson Newcomb of the original series is to make their year-to-year movement more closely comparable to that of construction expenditures which fluctuate less than building permits, and to reduce the weight of residential construction for early years to that found in the official estimates of construction expenditures beginning in 1915, series N 1–29. Newcomb notes that the index figures for 1868–1914 are suggestive only, since the raw data are not sufficient for a reliable index. The source extends the index to 1951 by using the official estimates of construction expenditures, series N 1–29.

N 116–117.   Index of urban dwelling units (Blank), 1870–1929.

Source: David M. Blank, *The Volume of Residential Construction, 1889–1950*, National Bureau of Economic Research, New York, Technical Paper 9, 1954, table 11 (copyright).

This index is based on building permit data covering Manhattan for 1870–1874 and gradually augmented to cover 67 cities in 1900 and 314 in 1929. For list of cities and years covered, see source, table 23. This is a chain index computed by first deriving relatives of the aggregate number of dwelling units authorized and the aggregate permit valuation of such units in identical cities in the sample between pairs of successive years. The data are unadjusted for lapses of building permits (with certain exceptions for New York City) and for understatement of valuations in building permits. The valuations are not converted to a work-put-in-place basis to reflect construction expenditures.

N 118–137. Construction cost indexes, 1913–1970.

Source: U.S. Bureau of the Census. 1915–1968, unpublished data. The indexes for **series N 132,** 1915–1968, **series N 133–134,** 1946–1968, **series N 135,** 1962–1968, and **series N 136,** 1967 and 1968, were provided on a 1967 base by the source agencies; all other indexes, except series N 137, represent conversions of those given on a 1957–59 base in U.S. Business and Defense Services Administration, *Construction Statistics, 1915–1964,* pp. 58 and 59, and in Bureau of the Census, *Construction Reports,* series C 30, various issues. 1969 and 1970, *Construction Reports,* series C 30-74-7, p. 8. **Series N 137,** see source for series N 114, appendix Q.

Construction cost indexes are useful in the conversion of construction expenditure data from current prices to constant prices and in the study of cost trends. However, no single cost index is satisfactory for all types of construction since the movements of cost differ for different types of construction. Series N 118, however, is a composite index weighted by the relative importance of the major classes of construction.

Construction cost indexes generally are not fully adequate for the making of cost comparisons over an extended period of time. Changes in the productivity and the proportions used of the various productive factors cannot be allowed for easily in the assignment of weights to labor, materials, and other cost items. An aggregative index proportional to the total construction cost of a standardized project, or a component part thereof, is not easily computed for most types of construction and suffers from the disadvantage of the probable eventual obsoleteness of any adequately specified standard project. For further discussion, see chapter IV of source cited above for series N 137; Lowell J. Chawner, "Construction Cost Indexes as Influenced by Technological Changes and Other Factors," *Journal of the American Statistical Association,* 1935, vol. 30, pp. 561–576; and Leo Grebler, David M. Blank, and Louis Winnick, *Capital Formation in Residential Real Estate,* Princeton University Press, 1956, appendix C.

N 118, Department of Commerce composite cost index. This index is a combination of various indexes weighted by the relative importance of the major classes of construction. It is an implicit index computed by dividing the total estimate of new construction activity in current prices by the total expressed in 1967 prices. Since the total in 1967 prices is obtained by adding the estimates for the separately deflated classes of construction, the composite cost index is the equivalent of a variably weighted index, reflecting changes not only in the component indexes, but also in the relative importance of the major classes of construction which are used as weights. For 1945–1970, the index is an average of the 12 monthly indexes.

N 119, American Appraisal Company index. This index is compiled on the basis of a detailed bill of quantities of material and labor required for four representative types of buildings—frame, brick, concrete, and steel—with allowances for contractor's overhead and profit, in various cities throughout the United States. Workmen's compensation and liability insurance, unemployment insurance, and old-age pension factors are included. The index covers the structural portion of the buildings, but does not include the fixtures such as plumbing, heating, lighting, sprinkler systems, and elevators. The material and labor costs are recomputed monthly in accordance with average prices and wages supplemented by personal investigation of appraisers and information from clients and others as to actual costs. These computations automatically result in weighted averages for the individual buildings. Arithmetic averages are computed for the individual buildings and cities to obtain the city and national averages. The latter covers 24 cities prior to 1925 and 30 cities since that time. The index reflects changes in average price levels but does not reflect costs resulting from overtime wages and bonuses during

boom periods or sacrifice prices and omissions of overhead costs and profits during depression periods.

N 120, Associated General Contractors index. This index is a combination of indexes of wages and materials weighted in the proportion of 40 percent for wages and 60 percent for materials. Wages used in computing this index are for hod carriers and common laborers, and the material prices are those for sand, gravel, crushed stone, portland cement, common brick, lumber (each with a weight of one), hollow tile (weighted $\frac{1}{2}$), and structural and reinforcing steel (each with a weight of $\frac{1}{4}$). Wages and prices are reported by the 12 district offices of the Association as of the 15th of each month.

N 121–123, E. H. Boeckh and Associates indexes. These indexes are based on separate computations for 10 types of buildings in 20 cities (comparable indexes are available from the compilers for a total of more than 40 cities). The basic list of items covered includes current local prices for common brick, common lumber, portland cement, structural steel, common labor, brickmasons, carpenters, structural ironworkers, plasterers, and miscellaneous which includes many specialized items such as heating and plumbing equipment, paint, glass, and hardware. Wage rates are adjusted to reflect efficiency of local labor. State and local sales taxes and Social Security payroll taxes are included. The weights assigned to the different items vary among the 10 types of buildings. An unweighted arithmetic average of the individual indexes for the 20 cities for each of the 10 types of buildings has been computed and these have been further consolidated into the 3 series shown here. The residential index is an unweighted average of the indexes for frame residences and for brick residences; the apartment, hotel, and office building index is an unweighted average of the indexes for brick and wood, brick and concrete, and brick and steel apartment, hotel, and office buildings; the commercial and factory buildings index is an unweighted average of the indexes for wood, steel, brick and wood, brick and steel, and brick and concrete commercial and factory buildings.

N 124–125, Engineering News-Record indexes. The index of construction costs is comprised of (1) steel, which until 1938 was the base price of structural steel shapes at Pittsburgh and, beginning in 1938, is a weighted average of steel prices at Pittsburgh, Gary, and Birmingham; (2) cement, which until 1948 was the consumers' net price, f.o.b. Chicago, and, beginning in 1948, is the ENR 20-city average of bulk cement prices; (3) lumber, which until 1936 was 12 x 12 long leaf yellow pine, wholesale, at New York, and beginning in 1936 is a composite 20-city price average of 2 x 4 Douglas fir and southern or local pine in carload lots; and (4) common labor rate paid in the steel industry for 1913–1920 and since 1920 the average common labor rate in construction (ENR 20-city average of wage rates in force). The 4 components are weighted according to their relative importance in the national economy in 1910, 1913, 1916, and 1919. The index of building costs is identical to the index of construction costs for all components except wage rates, where the trend of skilled labor wage rates is substituted for common labor wage rates. For a detailed description of these two indexes, see U.S. Office of Business Economics, *Business Statistics,* 1971 edition, p. 53.

N 126–127, Economic Research Service farm construction cost indexes for farm housing and other farm construction. This is a weighted index of farm wage rates and prices paid for materials. In compiling the index of farm housing construction costs, prices paid by farmers for building materials are given a weight of 73 percent, farm wage rates a weight of 27 percent. For other farm building construction, the corresponding weights are 78 and 22 percent. The wages paid by farmers for labor for building construction and repairs are higher than the wages paid for ordinary agricultural labor, but they probably fluctuate more comparably to farm labor wage rates than to urban union wage rates.

N 128, George A. Fuller Company index. This is a composite index of 36 major cost elements, in 3 commercial type buildings, including structural elements, elevators, wiring, heating, plumbing, ventilating, and employee benefit costs. The index is adjusted for changes in productivity from job-cost reports showing the number of man-hours of skilled and unskilled labor required. The indexes are simple averages of the quarterly indexes from the job-cost reports made by the compiler.

N 129–131, Handy-Whitman public utility construction cost indexes (compiled by Whitman, Requardt and Associates, Baltimore). These indexes measure changes in construction costs of utility buildings, gas plants, and electric plants. Cost trends of reinforced concrete utility building construction and brick utility building construction are reported semiannually by geographic regions. A single index is computed by averaging the figures for the first, middle, and end of each year for each region and then combining the regions for a United States average. Cost trends of gas plant construction and of steam-operated electric plant construction are also reported semiannually by geographic regions. A single index for each is computed in the same manner as for utility buildings.

N 132, Interstate Commerce Commission railroad construction cost index. The index is the weighted average for the entire United States of 31 separate indexes for individual operations important in railroad construction. Separate indexes covering items such as grading, tunnel excavation, bridges, ballast haul, and tracklaying and surfacing, were developed largely from analysis of major construction contracts covering a period of more than 30 years. The indexes for materials accounts—such as ties, rails, other track material, ballast, and fences—were based on studies of carriers' returns, joint studies made with the various railroad committees, well-known engineering and trade publications, contracts covering major construction projects over a period of 30 years, and other information furnished by individual carriers.

N 133–134, Bell System Telephone plant indexes. The American Telephone and Telegraph Company compiles separate annual cost indexes for construction of telephone company "buildings" and "outside plant," e.g. poles, cable, aerial wire, and underground conduits. These indexes represent changes in the total installed cost of telephone buildings or plant. The "outside plant" index reflects the effect of price changes in the cost of telephone apparatus and the cost of associated installation and engineering.

N 135, Federal Highway Administration index. This index is based upon a record of quarterly variations in contract unit bid prices maintained by the Federal Highway Administration and its predecessor, Public Roads Administration, since 1922. Cost indexes are based on average annual construction on State and Federal aid highway systems during 1925–1929. Average costs for these years are taken as 100 percent. For this period, the total quantity and contract cost of each of the principal cost-controlling contract items were summarized and divided by the total mileage of construction. This operation provided average quantities of each type of work involved per average gross or composite mile of construction. Since unit prices and construction volumes vary not only from State to State but also from year to year, the percentage of each item contributed during this 5-year period by each State was adopted as the contributing State base. The index thus indicates the relative costs at which the average quantities placed per mile in 1925–1929, with the same State distribution, could be replaced at current contract bid prices. Figures for 1915–1922 were extrapolated by the Department of Commerce by means of a weighted average of the Interstate Commerce Commission indexes for grading; tunnel and subway excavation; bridges, culverts, and trestles; and ballast. This index is a composite derived from average unit bid prices for fixed amounts of the following items put in place: Common excavation, surfacing,

and structures. The base quantities involved in measuring this index are: 3,641,885,000 cubic yards of roadway excavation; 154,953,000 square yards of portland cement concrete surfacing with average thickness of 9.1 inches; 111,516,000 tons of bituminous concrete surfacing; 2,206,879,000 pounds of reinforcing steel for structures; 2,581,462,000 pounds of structural steel; and 14,583,000 cubic yards of structural concrete.

N 136, Turner Construction Company index. This index is based on the building cost experience of the Turner Construction Company in eastern cities applied to these factors: Labor rates, material prices, productivity of labor, efficiency of plant and management, and competitive conditions. The series also reflects the payment of sales taxes and employee benefit costs.

N 137, average of contractor indexes of construction cost. This is an average of 4 contractor indexes shown separately in the source. In contrast to the common indexes of construction costs, which usually represent a combination of wages and materials prices according to a fixed relationship and may not take adequate account of changes in efficiency, the contractor indexes are based on estimates of the actual cost for erecting comparable structures. The comparison of these indexes with the common indexes may suggest changes in cost that result from changes in efficiency. For a fuller discussion, see the source, pp. 69–74, and Grebler-Blank-Winnick, appendix C.

N 138. Building cost index (Riggleman), 1868–1933.

Source: See source for series N 114, appendix N, table 4.

The index is from an unpublished doctoral dissertation by John R. Riggleman, *Variations in Building Activity in United States Cities*, Johns Hopkins University, 1934, appendix I. The index was constructed on the basis of several sources, including the American Appraisal Company's cost of industrial buildings in eastern cities to 1903 and the *Engineering News-Record* construction cost index for 1904–1933. The figures for earlier years are less reliable than those for later years, and should be used with caution. The source also presents the index back to 1830.

N 139. Residential construction cost index (Blank), 1889–1933.

Source: David M. Blank, *The Volume of Residential Construction, 1889–1950*, National Bureau of Economic Research, New York, Technical Paper 9, 1954, table 21 (copyright).

For 1889–1914, the index is based on weighted averages of building trade wages and building materials prices, more fully described in the source. For 1915–1933, the index is the Boeckh residential construction cost index shown as series N 121, converted to the 1929 base. The figures for earlier years are less reliable than those for later years and should be used with caution.

N 140–155. Indexes of wholesale prices for construction materials, 1926–1970.

Source: U.S. Bureau of Labor Statistics, *Handbook of Labor Statistics, 1973*, pp. 315–318, and *Wholesale Prices and Price Indexes*, monthly and annual issues.

Data cover materials incorporated as integral part of a building or normally installed during construction and not readily removable. Excluded are consumer durables, such as kitchen ranges, refrigerators, etc.

For compilation and description of wholesale indexes, see series E 23–122.

Series N 1–29.   Value of New Private and Public Construction Put in Place: 1915 to 1970

[In millions of dollars]

Year	Total new construction	Private												
		Total[1]	Residential buildings (including farm)				Nonresidential buildings (excluding farm)[4]				Farm nonresidential[2]	Public utilities		
			Total[2]	New housing units[2]	Additions and alterations[3]	Non-housekeeping	Total[2]	Industrial	Commercial[2]	Other		Total[2][5]	Railroad[2][5]	Petroleum pipeline
	1	2	3	4	5	6	7	8	9	10	11	12	13	14
1970	94,855	66,759	31,864	24,272	6,234	1,358	21,417	6,538	9,754	5,125	1,512	11,020	306	285
1969	93,917	65,953	33,200	25,941	5,882	1,377	21,155	6,783	9,401	4,971	1,322	9,535	453	231
1968	87,093	59,488	30,565	24,030	5,297	1,238	18,164	6,021	7,761	4,382	1,217	8,969	413	357
1967	78,082	52,546	25,568	18,985	5,317	1,266	17,589	(NA)	(NA)	(NA)	1,332	7,603	327	312
1966	76,414	52,407	25,715	19,352	4,941	1,422	18,279	(NA)	(NA)	(NA)	1,126	6,803	378	142
1965	73,747	51,685	27,934	21,712	4,736	1,486	16,509	(NA)	(NA)	(NA)	1,038	5,788	310	122
1964	67,675	47,292	28,010	21,786	(NA)	1,457	12,955	3,565	5,396	3,994	958	5,031	267	166
1963	64,812	45,455	27,874	21,735	4,798	1,341	11,646	2,906	4,995	3,745	958	4,667	253	272
1962	60,205	42,336	25,150	19,443	4,484	1,223	11,617	2,842	5,144	3,631	962	4,330	201	203
1961	56,445	39,297	23,107	17,074	4,973	1,060	10,734	2,780	4,674	3,280	871	4,335	213	109
1960*	54,738	38,875	22,975	17,279	4,831	865	10,149	2,851	4,180	3,118	849	4,621	270	132
1959*	55,392	39,322	[6] 24,251	[6] 19,233	4,253	765	8,859	2,106	3,930	2,823	[7] 1,484	4,521	218	131
1958	50,047	34,590	[6] 19,789	[6] 15,445	3,711	633	8,675	2,382	3,589	2,704	[7] 1,249	4,688	272	156
1957	49,139	35,080	19,543	15,273	3,769	501	9,556	3,557	3,564	2,435	874	4,908	397	159
1956	47,601	34,869	20,707	16,672	3,588	447	8,818	3,084	3,631	2,103	863	4,361	421	123
1955	46,519	34,804	22,409	18,774	3,296	339	7,611	2,399	3,218	1,994	853	3,770	341	130
1954	41,380	29,668	18,759	15,503	2,960	296	6,250	2,030	2,212	2,008	853	3,685	366	224
1953	39,136	27,894	17,213	14,030	2,916	267	5,680	2,229	1,791	1,660	908	3,973	405	330
1952	36,828	26,049	16,468	13,516	2,767	185	5,014	2,320	1,137	1,557	949	3,533	449	267
1951	35,435	26,180	16,546	13,872	2,484	190	5,279	2,117	1,498	1,664	934	3,357	372	173
1950	33,575	26,709	18,768	16,193	2,400	175	3,904	1,062	1,415	1,427	880	3,045	309	197
1949	26,722	20,453	13,111	10,726	2,200	185	3,383	972	1,182	1,229	887	2,994	354	157
1948	26,078	21,374	13,830	11,208	2,467	155	3,765	1,397	1,397	971	938	2,776	398	150
1947	20,041	16,722	10,404	8,319	1,960	125	3,243	1,702	957	584	880	2,126	340	121
1946 [8]	14,308	12,077	6,656	5,204	1,307	145	3,362	1,689	1,153	520	752	1,255	265	63
1946 [9]	12,737	10,375	4,752	3,300	1,307	145	3,341	1,689	1,132	520	447	1,374	293	63
1945	5,809	3,411	1,376	820	516	40	1,020	642	203	175	167	827	282	42
1944	5,259	2,186	923	678	220	25	351	208	56	87	175	725	262	71
1943	8,301	1,979	1,006	831	160	15	233	156	33	44	163	570	225	77
1942	14,075	3,415	1,850	1,575	225	50	635	346	155	134	125	786	209	80
1941	11,957	6,206	3,692	3,222	375	95	1,482	801	409	272	128	872	217	60
1940	8,682	5,054	3,130	2,705	335	90	1,025	442	348	235	95	771	217	30
1939	8,198	4,389	2,786	2,376	320	90	786	254	292	240	106	683	191	35
1938	6,980	3,560	2,069	1,699	295	75	764	232	285	247	92	605	160	21
1937	6,999	3,903	1,975	1,575	320	80	1,085	492	387	206	107	705	238	67
1936	6,497	2,981	1,641	1,286	295	60	713	266	290	157	85	518	194	41
1935	4,232	1,999	1,071	771	250	50	472	158	211	103	65	363	156	20
1934	3,720	1,509	661	416	200	45	456	191	173	92	30	326	158	12
1933	2,879	1,231	499	319	145	35	406	176	130	100	20	261	115	7
1932	3,538	1,676	654	509	105	40	502	74	223	205	13	467	168	37
1931	6,427	3,768	1,624	1,379	175	70	1,099	221	454	424	38	946	361	77
1930	8,741	5,883	2,182	1,677	305	200	2,003	532	893	578	86	1,527	606	30
1929	10,793	8,307	3,772	3,187	340	245	2,694	949	1,135	610	160	1,578	592	97
1928	11,641	9,156	4,926	4,355	315	260	2,573	802	1,121	650	175	1,372	523	53
1927	12,034	9,625	5,320	4,700	290	330	2,534	696	1,145	693	195	1,450	539	80
1926	12,082	9,938	5,737	5,057	270	410	2,513	727	1,107	679	160	1,415	542	36
1925	11,439	9,301	5,656	5,051	250	355	2,060	513	940	607	170	1,302	445	55
1924	10,407	8,506	5,193	4,708	230	255	1,675	460	740	475	165	1,356	421	70
1923	9,332	7,710	4,542	4,102	210	230	1,697	549	716	432	175	1,191	435	53
1922	7,647	5,963	3,479	3,074	200	205	1,457	467	613	377	150	787	261	41
1921	6,004	4,440	2,203	1,893	185	125	1,434	574	570	290	125	604	243	30
1920	6,749	5,397	2,281	1,976	175	130	1,964	1,099	625	240	300	771	266	41
1919	6,296	4,320	2,123	1,918	130	75	1,082	621	--------	--------	380	673	329	56
1918	5,118	2,880	1,118	963	110	45	731	449	--------	--------	275	697	472	24
1917	4,569	3,290	1,389	1,199	125	65	800	364	--------	--------	250	788	515	20
1916	3,849	3,141	1,529	1,324	145	60	716	262	--------	--------	170	658	390	20
1915	3,262	2,543	1,329	1,149	140	40	478	197	--------	--------	120	549	353	20

See footnotes at end of table.

Series N 1–29. Value of New Private and Public Construction Put in Place: 1915 to 1970—Con.

[In millions of dollars]

Year	Private—Con.				Public										
	Public utilities—Con.			All other private [11]	Total [1]	Residential	Nonresidential buildings				Military facilities	High-ways, roads, and streets	Sewer and water systems	Conservation and development	All other public [12]
	Electric light and power [2][10]	Gas [2]	Telephone and telegraph				Total	Industrial	Educational	Other					
	15	16	17	18	19	20	21	22	23	24	25	26	27	28	29
1970	5,808	1,653	2,968	946	28,096	1,107	9,550	499	5,619	3,432	718	9,981	2,638	1,908	2,194
1969	4,764	1,884	2,203	741	27,964	1,047	10,183	518	5,868	3,797	879	9,250	2,680	1,783	2,142
1968	4,452	2,043	1,704	573	27,605	746	9,693	519	6,061	3,113	808	9,321	3,065	1,973	1,999
1967	3,777	1,549	1,638	454	25,536	709	9,272	408	5,988	2,876	695	8,591	2,328	2,124	1,816
1966	3,060	1,614	1,609	484	24,007	655	8,265	369	5,333	2,563	727	8,405	2,366	2,194	1,395
1965	2,589	1,304	1,463	416	22,062	603	7,290	368	4,284	2,638	830	7,550	2,461	2,019	1,309
1964	2,211	1,073	1,314	338	20,383	567	6,610	403	3,790	2,417	910	7,133	2,281	1,750	1,132
1963	2,066	948	1,128	310	19,357	531	6,003	440	3,477	2,086	1,179	7,084	1,829	1,694	1,037
1962	1,899	1,031	996	277	17,869	938	5,154	422	2,984	1,748	1,266	6,365	1,754	1,523	869
1961	1,886	1,147	980	250	17,148	842	5,169	472	3,052	1,645	1,371	5,854	1,581	1,384	947
1960	2,026	1,105	1,088	281	15,863	716	4,795	407	2,818	1,570	1,366	5,437	1,487	1,175	887
1959*	2,007	1,214	951	207	16,070	962	4,514	368	2,656	1,490	1,465	5,761	1,467	1,121	780
1958	2,291	1,065	904	189	15,457	846	4,653	408	2,875	1,370	1,402	5,545	1,387	1,019	605
1957	2,168	1,116	1,068	199	14,059	506	4,507	473	2,825	1,209	1,287	4,934	1,344	971	510
1956	1,720	1,031	1,066	120	12,732	292	4,076	453	2,556	1,067	1,360	4,415	1,275	826	488
1955	1,572	922	805	161	11,715	266	4,196	721	2,442	1,033	1,287	3,852	1,085	701	328
1954	1,717	723	655	121	11,712	336	4,609	1,506	2,134	969	1,003	3,714	982	773	295
1953	1,805	818	615	120	11,242	556	4,350	1,771	1,714	865	1,290	3,021	883	892	250
1952	1,537	710	570	85	10,779	654	4,158	1,684	1,619	855	1,387	2,677	790	900	213
1951	1,315	1,010	487	64	9,255	595	3,496	974	1,513	1,009	887	2,355	775	912	235
1950	1,240	859	440	112	6,866	345	2,387	224	1,133	1,030	177	2,134	659	942	222
1949	1,313	637	533	78	6,269	359	2,049	177	934	938	137	2,015	619	852	238
1948	1,016	499	713	65	4,704	156	1,291	196	618	477	158	1,661	535	670	233
1947	761	394	510	69	3,319	200	591	96	287	208	204	1,344	351	424	205
1946 [8]	425	197	305	52	2,231	374	354	113	101	140	188	764	194	260	97
1946 [9]	443	270	305	52	2,362	374	354	113	101	140	188	895	194	260	97
1945	245	141	117	21	2,398	80	937	755	59	123	690	398	97	130	66
1944	163	146	83	12	3,073	211	1,361	1,230	41	90	837	362	79	163	60
1943	144	63	61	7	6,322	739	2,010	1,870	63	77	2,550	446	107	285	185
1942	255	87	155	19	10,660	545	3,685	3,437	128	120	5,016	734	169	357	154
1941	305	111	179	32	5,751	430	1,646	1,280	158	208	1,620	1,066	252	500	237
1940	311	91	122	33	3,628	200	615	164	156	295	385	1,302	338	528	260
1939	303	61	93	28	3,809	65	970	23	468	479	125	1,381	371	570	327
1938	267	65	92	30	3,420	35	672	12	311	349	62	1,421	355	551	324
1937	218	80	102	31	3,096	93	550	2	253	295	37	1,226	311	605	274
1936	139	77	67	24	3,516	61	701	4	366	331	29	1,362	342	658	363
1935	87	48	52	28	2,233	9	328	2	153	173	37	845	175	700	139
1934	66	43	47	36	2,211	1	363	11	148	204	47	1,000	173	518	109
1933	59	35	45	45	1,648	--------	230	2	52	176	36	847	95	359	81
1932	109	66	87	40	1,862	--------	415	(1)	130	285	34	958	156	150	149
1931	225	117	166	61	2,659	--------	612	(1)	285	327	40	1,355	270	156	226
1930	377	181	333	85	2,858	--------	660	(1)	364	296	29	1,516	343	137	173
1929	350	185	354	103	2,486	--------	659	(1)	389	270	19	1,266	253	115	174
1928	338	212	246	110	2,485	--------	638	(1)	378	260	15	1,289	300	72	171
1927	362	257	212	126	2,409	--------	596	(1)	367	229	12	1,222	312	63	204
1926	362	248	227	113	2,144	--------	603	(1)	399	204	11	1,067	285	61	117
1925	421	171	210	113	2,138	--------	573	(1)	400	173	8	1,082	278	73	124
1924	463	206	196	117	1,901	--------	494	(1)	353	141	9	987	263	79	69
1923	412	133	158	105	1,622	--------	481	(1)	346	135	16	805	203	65	52
1922	229	139	117	90	1,684	--------	481	(1)	342	139	25	876	201	48	53
1921	163	66	102	74	1,564	--------	387	(1)	274	113	49	853	178	52	45
1920	262	78	124	81	1,352	--------	283	(1)	190	93	161	656	153	55	44
1919	156	56	76	62	1,976	14	246	(1)	--------	--------	1,089	429	124	39	35
1918	102	26	73	59	2,238	28	199	(1)	--------	--------	1,555	296	94	29	37
1917	123	45	85	63	1,279	--------	192	(1)	--------	--------	608	320	91	27	41
1916	117	70	61	68	708	--------	207	(1)	--------	--------	21	314	95	28	43
1915	92	41	43	67	719	--------	217	(1)	--------	--------	17	302	106	36	41

* Denotes first year for which figures include Alaska and Hawaii, except that the nonfarm component of series N 4 should be interpreted as including estimates for Alaska and Hawaii beginning 1946.

NA   Not available.

[1] Public industrial and commercial building not segregable from private construction, 1915–1932; amount believed negligible.

[2] Beginning 1946, figures not entirely comparable with those for earlier years.

[3] Prior to 1960, excludes farm housing.

[4] Excludes building by privately owned public utilities. Beginning 1968, figures not comparable with earlier years because of revision in survey.

[5] Prior to 1959, includes local transit; thereafter, local transit included in "All other private."

[6] Excludes farm.

[7] Includes farm housing units.

[8] Comparable with later years.

[9] Comparable with earlier years. Source: U.S. Department of Commerce and U.S. Department of Labor, *Construction Volume and Costs, 1915–1956*, a statistical supplement to *Construction Review*, pp. 2–9.

[10] Includes construction with Rural Electrification Administration funds.

[11] Includes sewer and water systems, roads, bridges, and miscellaneous nonstructural items such as parks and playgrounds. Beginning 1959, includes local transit.

[12] Includes publicly owned parks and playgrounds, memorials, etc.

Series N 30–60.   Value of New Private and Public Construction Put in Place, 1957–59 Dollars: 1915 to 1970

[In millions of dollars.   Beginning 1960, figures for these series are essentially comparable with figures for series N 1–29, *except* series N 33 with N 4, new private residential units; series N 36–39 with N 7–10, new private nonresidential buildings; series N 40 with N 11, new farm nonresidential; and series N 41–46 with N 12–17, new privately-owned public utilities.   See text for series N 1–29 and general note for series N 1–60]

Year	Total new construction	Private construction											
		Total [1]	Residential buildings (including farm)				Nonresidential buildings (excluding farm) [3]				Farm, nonresidential	Public utilities	
			Total	New housing units	Additions and alterations [2]	Non-housekeeping	Total	Industrial	Commercial	Other		Total	Railroad [4]
	30	31	32	33	34	35	36	37	38	39	40	41	42
1970	60,170	42,317	[2]20,509	[2]15,345	4,167	[2]997	13,749	3,895	6,332	3,522	----------	----------	----------
1969	64,169	44,911	[2]22,364	[2]17,311	(NA)	[2]1,068	14,874	4,590	6,692	3,592	----------	----------	----------
1968	64,432	43,775	[2]22,369	[2]17,399	(NA)	[2]1,076	13,837	4,427	5,981	3,429	----------	----------	----------
1967	61,144	40,967	[2]19,413	[2]14,623	(NA)	[2]1,036	14,197	5,131	5,312	3,754	----------	----------	----------
1966	62,941	43,208	[2]20,561	[2]15,412	(NA)	[2]1,219	15,131	5,749	5,416	3,966	----------	6,024	----------
1965	62,896	43,780	23,496	[2]17,882	3,893	[2]1,307	13,959	4,541	5,491	3,927	702	5,294	302
1964	59,172	40,861	23,942	[2]18,223	(NA)	[2]1,305	11,185	3,263	4,520	3,402	737	4,719	262
1963	58,102	40,309	24,542	[2]18,756	(NA)	[2]1,236	10,292	2,728	4,291	3,273	750	4,459	243
1962	55,948	39,056	23,286	[2]17,508	(NA)	[2]1,150	10,558	2,732	4,555	3,271	776	4,190	193
1961	53,087	36,428	21,194	[2]15,474	(NA)	[2]1,014	10,004	2,712	4,275	3,017	779	4,226	211
1960*	52,171	36,518	21,304	[2]15,747	(NA)	[2]828	9,690	2,803	3,943	2,944	790	4,474	261
1959*	54,222	38,218	[2]23,641	[2]18,751	4,144	746	8,614	2,080	3,799	2,735	[5]1,359	4,407	215
1958	50,270	34,868	[2]19,930	[2]15,552	3,739	639	8,679	2,392	3,584	2,703	[5]1,384	4,686	271
1957	49,878	35,753	19,862	15,522	3,830	510	9,774	3,582	3,684	2,508	891	5,020	405
1956	50,034	36,651	21,437	17,264	3,712	461	9,501	3,316	3,923	2,262	908	4,673	448
1955	51,717	38,394	24,222	20,295	3,562	365	8,668	2,807	3,623	2,238	938	4,384	390
1954	47,164	33,721	20,883	17,258	3,295	330	7,287	2,400	2,569	2,318	960	4,449	428
1953	44,747	31,818	19,023	15,506	3,223	294	6,694	2,587	2,142	1,965	1,006	4,948	479
1952	42,882	30,334	18,508	15,189	3,110	209	6,071	2,736	1,415	1,920	1,067	4,577	548
1951	42,596	31,387	19,084	15,996	2,868	220	6,641	2,568	1,936	2,137	1,070	4,505	473
1950	43,576	34,309	23,232	20,042	2,975	215	5,321	1,447	1,930	1,944	1,124	4,470	419
1949	36,605	27,779	17,234	14,093	2,898	243	4,718	1,363	1,640	1,715	1,151	4,556	494
1948	34,681	28,385	17,602	14,255	3,149	198	5,210	1,917	1,941	1,352	1,202	4,267	553
1947	29,573	24,682	14,762	11,784	2,797	181	4,994	2,595	1,474	925	1,221	3,584	523
1946	25,668	21,787	11,447	8,928	2,269	250	6,498	3,050	2,348	1,100	1,271	2,465	466
1945	12,251	7,181	2,608	1,551	982	75	2,353	1,426	489	438	309	1,868	542
1944	11,525	4,803	1,878	1,375	452	51	861	491	143	227	342	1,687	525
1943	17,866	4,474	2,223	1,837	354	32	563	351	92	120	351	1,314	452
1942	31,777	8,234	4,343	3,687	531	125	1,628	829	418	381	302	1,911	454
1941	30,144	16,049	9,112	7,958	921	233	4,228	2,160	1,214	854	350	2,274	540
1940	23,217	14,105	8,366	7,236	890	240	3,200	1,310	1,106	784	289	2,149	585
1939	22,379	12,600	7,676	6,549	879	248	2,567	806	944	817	324	1,946	534
1938	18,775	10,361	5,800	4,767	824	209	2,477	714	914	849	278	1,719	437
1937	19,051	11,504	5,690	4,539	921	230	3,443	1,481	1,251	711	318	1,963	633
1936	18,938	9,771	5,268	4,128	947	193	2,609	910	1,069	630	266	1,552	549
1935	12,780	6,764	3,555	2,558	831	166	1,809	564	810	435	206	1,102	449
1934	10,815	5,089	2,145	1,350	649	146	1,738	691	657	390	95	993	455
1933	9,232	4,570	1,763	1,128	512	123	1,725	728	543	454	71	847	342
1932	12,350	6,111	2,309	1,798	370	141	2,078	314	861	903	46	1,531	485
1931	19,559	11,998	4,856	4,124	523	209	4,001	880	1,495	1,626	119	2,826	951
1930	24,511	17,200	5,999	4,609	839	551	6,437	1,865	2,600	1,972	233	4,273	1,506
1929	29,213	23,157	10,096	8,528	911	657	8,144	2,970	3,256	1,918	417	4,194	1,398
1928	32,113	26,127	13,752	12,142	882	728	7,812	2,440	3,327	2,045	459	3,774	1,223
1927	33,238	27,528	14,908	13,166	815	927	7,712	2,118	3,415	2,179	505	4,025	1,239
1926	33,113	28,038	15,856	13,973	748	1,135	7,569	2,156	3,277	2,136	413	3,860	1,232
1925	31,323	26,366	15,793	14,101	699	993	6,246	1,523	2,814	1,909	435	3,552	1,013
1924	28,022	23,796	14,360	13,016	638	706	5,004	1,370	2,172	1,462	430	3,659	930
1923	25,011	21,415	12,386	11,185	574	627	5,040	1,618	2,106	1,316	459	3,222	961
1922	22,524	18,420	10,611	9,372	612	627	4,813	1,543	1,984	1,286	409	2,284	630
1921	16,167	12,745	6,208	5,336	520	352	4,441	1,812	1,713	916	346	1,525	523
1920	14,753	12,333	5,101	4,413	395	293	4,657	2,536	1,540	581	609	1,770	468
1919	----------	----------	6,002	5,405	379	218	----------	1,831	----------	----------	852	1,688	699
1918	----------	----------	3,655	3,129	373	153	----------	1,563	----------	----------	716	1,780	1,118
1917	----------	----------	5,469	4,703	505	261	----------	1,431	----------	----------	780	2,364	1,452
1916	----------	----------	7,108	6,140	685	283	----------	1,263	----------	----------	630	2,508	1,337
1915	----------	----------	6,613	5,710	702	201	----------	1,107	----------	----------	510	2,357	1,316

Year	Private construction—Con.				All other private	Public construction							Military facilities	Highways, roads, and streets
	Public utilities—Con.					Total	Residential	Nonresidential buildings						
	Petroleum pipeline	Electric light and power	Gas	Telephone and telegraph				Total	Industrial	Educational	Hospital and institutional	Other		
	43	44	45	46	47	48	49	50	51	52	53	54	55	56
1970	----------	----------	----------	2,038	539	17,853	776	5,744	325	3,351	504	1,564	501	6,736
1969	----------	----------	----------	1,579	464	19,258	768	6,640	369	3,799	522	1,950	663	6,886
1968	----------	----------	----------	1,367	393	20,657	581	6,881	410	4,272	489	1,710	623	7,565
1967	----------	----------	----------	1,341	331	20,177	581	7,007	340	4,504	477	1,686	573	7,269
1966	----------	----------	----------	1,425	371	19,733	560	6,542	317	4,199	405	1,621	636	7,365
1965	114	2,408	1,117	1,353	329	19,116	527	6,054	324	3,554	434	1,742	733	7,108
1964	156	2,117	943	1,241	278	18,311	507	5,648	367	3,224	398	1,659	835	7,003
1963	256	2,022	853	1,085	265	17,793	486	5,267	413	3,035	370	1,449	1,084	6,998
1962	193	1,884	947	973	246	16,892	882	4,670	408	2,688	357	1,217	1,182	6,447

See footnotes at end of table.

Series N 30-60. Value of New Private and Public Construction Put in Place, 1957-59 Dollars: 1915 to 1970—Con.

[In millions of dollars]

Year	Private construction—Con.					Public construction								
	Public utilities—Con.				All other private	Total [1]	Residential	Nonresidential buildings					Military facilities	Highways, roads, and streets
	Petroleum pipeline	Electric light and power	Gas	Telephone and telegraph				Total	Industrial	Educational	Hospital and institutional	Other		
	43	44	45	46	47	48	49	50	51	52	53	54	55	56
1961	107	1,876	1,071	961	225	16,659	803	4,790	461	2,813	342	1,174	1,320	6,152
1960	127	1,980	1,047	1,059	260	15,653	686	4,551	402	2,664	380	1,105	1,336	5,758
1959*	125	1,963	1,171	933	197	16,004	941	4,387	363	2,579	418	1,027	1,449	5,993
1958	156	2,286	1,060	913	189	15,402	852	4,656	411	2,879	390	976	1,398	5,489
1957	162	2,219	1,154	1,080	206	14,125	515	4,631	478	2,908	365	880	1,297	4,753
1956	134	1,870	1,137	1,084	132	13,383	304	4,381	487	2,748	323	823	1,442	4,443
1955	153	1,866	1,110	865	182	13,323	288	4,751	848	2,742	338	823	1,467	4,396
1954	275	2,101	909	736	142	13,443	374	5,366	1,780	2,466	385	735	1,158	4,109
1953	417	2,276	1,081	695	147	12,929	614	5,107	2,055	2,029	438	585	1,483	3,209
1952	351	2,037	981	660	111	12,548	737	5,034	1,983	1,997	612	442	1,612	2,681
1951	235	1,788	1,429	580	87	11,209	687	4,421	1,180	1,943	678	620	1,060	2,430
1950	290	1,879	1,308	574	162	9,267	430	3,252	304	1,543	682	723	234	2,722
1949	242	2,122	1,015	683	120	8,826	474	2,861	249	1,302	638	672	182	2,684
1948	239	1,717	832	926	104	6,296	199	1,787	267	859	294	367	207	1,831
1947	214	1,413	740	694	121	4,891	300	923	145	449	121	208	293	1,652
1946	129	925	439	506	106	3,881	634	717	209	213	182	113	329	1,067
1945	99	618	366	243	43	5,070	154	2,190	1,730	147	215	98	1,434	611
1944	171	416	388	187	35	6,722	436	3,249	2,904	109	155	81	1,758	535
1943	191	368	169	134	23	13,392	1,647	4,580	4,195	171	121	93	5,144	599
1942	204	657	234	362	50	23,543	1,260	8,749	8,048	366	102	233	10,796	1,081
1941	155	812	316	451	85	14,095	1,056	4,488	3,406	464	134	484	4,144	2,019
1940	88	873	275	328	101	9,112	529	1,913	481	484	182	766	1,055	2,797
1939	103	861	188	260	87	9,779	174	3,220	76	1,555	434	1,155	354	2,877
1938	62	766	197	257	87	8,414	98	2,228	37	1,037	323	831	177	2,893
1937	196	620	243	271	90	7,547	268	1,843	6	853	246	738	104	2,396
1936	129	434	256	184	76	9,167	196	2,743	14	1,441	289	999	88	2,497
1935	64	277	166	146	92	6,016	29	1,342	7	628	155	552	115	1,681
1934	39	213	150	136	118	5,726	3	1,451	40	584	208	619	145	1,899
1933	24	208	137	136	164	4,662	--------	1,028	9	228	218	573	122	1,819
1932	130	398	258	260	147	6,239	--------	1,827	(1)	572	366	889	123	2,623
1931	253	769	420	433	196	7,561	--------	2,346	(1)	1,093	421	832	124	2,951
1930	93	1,255	620	799	258	7,311	--------	2,250	(1)	1,241	402	607	81	2,958
1929	289	1,105	631	771	306	6,056	--------	2,072	(1)	1,223	318	531	50	2,296
1928	160	1,119	735	537	330	5,986	--------	2,007	(1)	1,189	340	478	39	2,260
1927	238	1,220	860	468	378	5,710	--------	1,874	(1)	1,154	251	469	30	2,004
1926	106	1,191	810	521	340	5,075	--------	1,896	(1)	1,255	214	427	27	1,725
1925	160	1,365	550	464	340	4,957	--------	1,801	(1)	1,258	192	351	20	1,681
1924	199	1,497	639	394	343	4,226	--------	1,522	(1)	1,087	185	250	22	1,459
1923	157	1,358	443	303	308	3,596	--------	1,464	(1)	1,053	167	244	38	1,141
1922	129	757	508	260	303	4,104	--------	1,641	(1)	1,167	205	269	66	1,384
1921	90	520	200	192	225	3,422	--------	1,223	(1)	866	126	231	122	1,228
1920	103	752	215	232	196	2,420	--------	685	(1)	459	80	146	321	783
1919	153	503	167	166	190	--------	40	--------	(1)	--------	--------	--------	2,755	665
1918	73	339	84	166	198	--------	95	--------	(1)	--------	--------	--------	4,515	507
1917	69	468	167	208	232	--------	--------	--------	(1)	--------	--------	--------	2,027	663
1916	86	554	355	176	336	--------	--------	--------	(1)	--------	--------	--------	81	749
1915	101	537	253	150	417	--------	--------	--------	(1)	--------	--------	--------	73	763

Year	Public construction—Con.			
	Sewer and water systems	Conservation and development	Public service enterprises	All other public
	57	58	59	60
1970	1,535	1,102	1,459	
1969	1,695	1,134	1,472	
1968	2,108	1,406	1,493	
1967	1,709	1,611	1,427	
1966	1,807	1,676	1,147	
1965	1,956	1,605	1,133	
1964	1,878	1,429	1,011	
1963	1,565	1,445	948	
1962	1,549	1,345	817	
1961	1,431	1,255	908	
1960	1,380	1,089	853	
1959*	1,403	1,073	538	220
1958	1,385	1,017	451	154
1957	1,399	1,007	403	120
1956	1,387	896	416	114
1955	1,238	799	277	107
1954	1,164	917	230	125
1953	1,095	1,109	209	103
1952	1,030	1,175	222	57

Year	Public construction—Con.			
	Sewer and water systems	Conservation and development	Public service enterprises	All other public
	57	58	59	60
1951	1,054	1,238	250	69
1950	947	1,351	241	90
1949	945	1,298	298	84
1948	838	1,048	278	108
1947	613	737	262	111
1946	397	529	182	26
1945	225	299	138	19
1944	190	390	124	40
1943	264	702	124	332
1942	400	913	188	156
1941	609	1,230	320	229
1940	855	1,336	337	290
1939	946	1,441	353	414
1938	879	1,397	349	393
1937	798	1,513	330	295
1936	943	1,794	465	441
1935	540	1,932	213	164
1934	511	1,422	165	130
1933	330	1,101	225	37

Year	Public construction—Con.			
	Sewer and water systems	Conservation and development	Public service enterprises	All other public
	57	58	59	60
1932	573	551	490	52
1931	869	502	714	55
1930	1,038	415	521	48
1929	751	341	478	68
1928	902	216	520	42
1927	935	188	644	35
1926	858	184	367	18
1925	836	219	389	11
1924	770	232	210	11
1923	594	190	148	21
1922	676	161	155	21
1921	544	159	133	13
1920	372	134	112	13
1919	380	119	108	3
1918	314	97	120	3
1917	335	100	153	3
1916	470	138	200	5
1915	659	224	232	6

* Denotes first year for which figures include Alaska and Hawaii, except that the nonfarm component of series N 33 should be interpreted as including estimates for Alaska and Hawaii beginning 1946.

[1] Public industrial and commercial building not segregable from private construction, 1915-1932; amount believed negligible.

[2] Excludes farm housing.
[3] Excludes building by privately owned public utilities.
[4] Includes local transit.
[5] Includes farm housing.

Series N 61. Construction Expenditures for Maintenance and Repair: 1915 to 1963

[In millions of dollars. Includes work relief expenditures, 1933–1943. Beginning 1950, figures not entirely comparable with those for earlier years]

Year	Maintenance and repair 61	Year	Maintenance and repair 61	Year	Maintenance and repair 61	Year	Maintenance and repair 61	Year	Maintenance and repair 61	Year	Maintenance and repair 61
1963	20,540	1954	14,708	1945	6,096	1936	3,795	1927	3,926	1920	2,982
1962	20,305	1953	14,413	1944	5,316	1935	3,145	1926	3,751	1919	2,561
1961	19,777	1952	14,140	1943	4,998	1934	2,942	1925	3,533	1918	2,247
1960	19,237	1951	13,316	1942	4,601	1933	2,478	1924	3,380		
				1941	4,485					1917	1,927
1959*	18,957	1950	12,055			1932	2,576	1923	3,209	1916	1,808
1958	17,558	1949	11,966	1940	4,119	1931	3,232	1922	2,960	1915	1,711
1957	17,920	1948	11,801	1939	3,978	1930	3,874	1921	2,863		
1956	16,978	1947	10,374	1938	3,884	1929	4,201				
1955	15,858	1946	8,062	1937	3,895	1928	3,977				

* Denotes first year for which figures include Alaska and Hawaii.

Series N 62–65. Expenditures for Private Nonfarm Residential Building: 1889 to 1921

[In millions of dollars]

Year	New housekeeping units Current dollars 62	Constant 1929 dollars 63	Additions and alterations to housekeeping units Current dollars 64	Constant 1929 dollars 65	Year	62	63	64	65	Year	62	63	64	65
1921	1,795	1,882	185	194	1910	1,028	1,932	112	211	1899	608	1,579	71	184
1920	1,072	903	140	118	1909	1,272	2,475	118	230	1898	574	1,599	72	201
1919	1,258	1,366	140	152	1908	1,034	2,089	114	230	1897	643	1,869	76	221
1918	391	494	90	114	1907	1,037	2,029	111	217	1896	606	1,726	77	219
1917	769	1,155	110	165	1906	1,170	2,393	111	227	1895	679	1,946	77	221
1916	1,255	2,202	116	204	1905	1,154	2,593	110	247	1894	594	1,678	78	220
1915	1,192	2,228	108	202	1904	690	1,624	98	231	1893	583	1,589	79	215
1914	1,081	2,071	106	203	1903	607	1,412	84	195	1892	763	2,073	80	217
1913	1,108	2,135	106	204	1902	572	1,378	76	183	1891	612	1,615	82	216
1912	1,113	2,069	108	201	1901	610	1,521	73	182	1890	790	2,015	85	217
1911	1,000	1,905	109	208	1900	433	1,067	70	172	1889	806	2,067	85	217

Series N 66–69. Value of New Public Construction Put in Place, by Ownership and Source of Funds: 1915 to 1970

[In millions of dollars]

Year	All public construction 66	Federal ownership 67	State and local ownership Total 68	Federal grants-in-aid [1] 69	Year	66	67	68	69	Year	66	67	68	69
1970	28,096	3,290	24,806		1950	6,866	1,624	5,242	454	1931	2,659	271	2,388	235
1969	27,963	3,313	24,651		1949	6,269	1,488	4,781	461					
1968	27,605	3,367	24,238		1948	4,704	1,177	3,527	417	1930	2,858	209	2,649	104
1967	25,536	3,475	22,061		1947	3,319	840	2,479	409	1929	2,486	155	2,331	80
1966	24,007	3,964	20,043		1946 [2]	2,231	865	1,366	244	1928	2,485	122	2,363	85
										1927	2,409	98	2,311	81
1965	22,062	4,014	18,048		1946 [3]	2,362	870	1,492	244	1926	2,144	92	2,052	82
1964	20,383	3,898	16,485	3,489	1945	2,398	1,737	661	99					
1963	19,357	4,001	15,356	3,150	1944	3,073	2,505	568	126	1925	2,138	100	2,038	89
1962	17,869	3,913	13,956	2,556	1943	6,322	5,609	713	268	1924	1,901	111	1,790	100
1961	17,148	3,879	13,269	2,426	1942	10,660	9,313	1,347	475	1923	1,622	108	1,514	77
1960	15,863	3,622	12,241	2,267	1941	5,751	3,751	2,000	697	1922	1,684	100	1,584	78
1959*	16,070	3,724	12,346	2,711	1940	3,628	1,182	2,446	946	1921	1,564	122	1,442	78
1958	15,457	3,387	12,070	2,106	1939	3,809	759	3,050	1,377	1920	1,352	232	1,120	95
1957	14,059	2,974	11,085	1,269	1938	3,420	717	2,703	1,320	1919	1,976	1,162	814	65
1956	12,732	2,726	10,006	857	1937	3,096	776	2,320	1,117	1918	2,238	1,634	604	10
					1936	3,516	797	2,719	1,566	1917	1,279	654	625	5
1955	11,715	2,769	8,946	739	1935	2,233	814	1,419	567	1916	708	66	642	
1954	11,712	3,428	8,284	675	1934	2,211	626	1,585	721	1915	719	71	648	
1953	11,242	4,139	7,103	700	1933	1,648	516	1,132	286					
1952	10,779	4,186	6,594	550	1932	1,862	333	1,529	111					
1951	9,255	2,982	6,274	464										

* Denotes first year for which figures include Alaska and Hawaii.
[1] Construction programs receiving Federal grant-in-aid funds cover highways, schools, hospitals, airports, and miscellaneous community facilities.
[2] Comparable with later years.
[3] Comparable with earlier years.

Series **N 70–77.** Expenditures for New Construction, Private Residential and Nonresidential and Public, in Current and Constant (1929) Dollars: 1869 to 1955

[In millions of dollars]

Year	Total new construction [1]		Private nonfarm residential building [2]		Private nonresidential construction [1]		Public construction [3]	
	Current dollars	Constant 1929 dollars	Current dollars	Constant 1929 dollars	Current dollars	Constant 1929 dollars	Current dollars	Constant 1929 dollars
	70	**71**	**72**	**73**	**74**	**75**	**76**	**77**
1955	45,153	18,585	16,256	6,557	16,478	6,534	11,122	4,946
1954	39,792	16,852	13,200	5,489	14,663	5,990	10,899	4,926
1953	37,172	15,694	11,663	4,813	14,115	5,825	10,087	4,489
1952	34,624	15,032	10,915	4,582	12,808	5,535	9,513	4,301
1951	32,750	14,680	10,783	4,648	12,549	5,584	8,531	4,043
1950	29,733	14,406	12,425	5,763	10,308	4,964	6,823	3,591
1949	23,858	12,031	8,082	3,956	9,371	4,672	6,268	3,334
1948	22,729	11,309	8,425	4,002	9,479	4,754	4,667	2,475
1947	17,462	9,667	6,185	3,270	7,844	4,321	3,229	1,965
1946	12,653	8,492	3,870	2,479	6,421	4,357	2,174	1,530
1945	6,231	4,836	1,060	752	2,773	2,209	1,708	1,328
1944	5,785	4,653	790	598	1,922	1,636	2,236	1,750
1943	8,648	6,926	870	718	1,456	1,339	3,772	2,900
1942	14,381	12,115	1,665	1,438	2,056	2,091	5,644	4,447
1941	12,380	11,642	3,415	3,116	3,214	3,187	4,131	3,749
1940	9,080	9,065	2,895	2,846	2,557	2,520	3,243	3,293
1939	8,566	8,683	2,590	2,643	2,167	2,175	3,684	3,729
1938	7,380	7,385	1,915	1,988	2,045	1,979	3,358	3,351
1937	7,499	7,540	1,795	1,916	2,608	2,594	3,059	2,990
1936	6,797	7,295	1,505	1,787	1,776	1,933	3,487	3,542
1935	4,532	5,026	960	1,193	1,339	1,468	2,196	2,321
1934	3,920	4,214	580	699	1,129	1,203	2,164	2,257
1933	3,079	3,673	435	571	996	1,160	1,612	1,896
1932	3,738	4,845	590	775	1,286	1,444	1,828	2,579
1931	6,627	7,457	1,495	1,663	2,473	2,668	2,619	3,079
1930	9,041	9,352	1,875	1,923	4,308	4,380	2,829	3,018
1929	11,193	11,193	3,380	3,380	5,327	5,327	2,467	2,467
1928	11,988	12,268	4,510	4,703	4,993	5,113	2,470	2,437
1927	12,439	12,699	4,830	5,052	5,200	5,343	2,397	2,293
1926	12,584	12,773	5,190	5,356	5,250	5,382	2,133	2,025
1925	11,891	12,066	5,160	5,364	4,593	4,712	2,130	1,982
1924	10,792	10,752	4,805	4,958	4,086	4,092	1,892	1,694
1923	9,732	9,653	4,170	4,242	3,940	3,985	1,606	1,412
1922	8,016	8,768	3,155	3,597	3,177	3,524	1,659	1,622
1921	6,359	6,341	1,980	2,076	2,815	2,870	1,515	1,349
1920	6,727	5,414	1,212	1,021	4,163	3,414	1,191	857
1919	6,396	6,300	1,398	1,518	3,022	2,919	887	817
1918	5,126	5,676	481	608	2,407	2,617	683	737
1917	4,641	6,090	879	1,320	2,483	3,148	671	853
1916	4,162	6,783	1,371	2,406	2,083	3,275	687	1,071
1915	3,509	6,363	1,300	2,430	1,490	2,646	702	1,259
1914	3,659	6,701	1,187	2,274	1,808	3,210	645	1,186
1913	4,988	8,879	1,214	2,339	3,183	5,481	591	1,059
1912	4,546	8,280	1,221	2,270	2,765	4,982	560	1,028
1911	4,144	7,678	1,109	2,113	2,459	4,496	576	1,069
1910	4,425	8,234	1,140	2,143	2,764	5,118	521	973
1909	4,467	8,471	1,390	2,705	2,589	4,832	488	934
1908	3,891	7,496	1,148	2,319	2,245	4,210	498	967
1907	4,342	8,049	1,148	2,246	2,750	4,980	444	823
1906	3,951	7,615	1,281	2,620	2,307	4,288	363	707
1905	3,327	6,968	1,264	2,840	1,721	3,414	342	714
1904	3,023	6,625	788	1,855	1,903	4,047	332	723
1903	3,063	6,632	691	1,607	2,085	4,420	287	605
1902	3,107	6,964	648	1,561	2,228	4,897	231	506
1901	2,705	6,241	683	1,703	1,809	4,058	213	480
1900	2,471	5,562	503	1,239	1,761	3,866	207	457
1899	2,069	4,866	679	1,763	1,205	2,678	185	425
1898	1,982	5,118	646	1,800	1,174	2,908	162	410
1897	2,088	5,493	719	2,090	1,219	3,014	150	389
1896	1,875	4,744	683	1,945	1,046	2,435	146	364
1895	2,192	5,598	756	2,167	1,295	3,073	141	358
1894	2,093	5,300	672	1,898	1,282	3,051	139	351
1893	2,190	5,338	662	1,804	1,390	3,199	138	335
1892	2,718	6,570	843	2,290	1,743	3,962	132	318
1891	2,141	5,033	694	1,831	1,320	2,904	127	298
1890	2,393	5,451	875	2,232	1,394	2,937	124	282
1889	1,645	3,735	891	2,284	635	1,181	119	270
1884–1893 [4]	1,894	4,358	---------	---------	---------	---------	---------	---------
1879–1888 [4]	1,330	2,985	---------	---------	---------	---------	---------	---------
1874–1883 [4]	966	2,154	---------	---------	---------	---------	---------	---------
1869–1878 [4]	802	1,671	---------	---------	---------	---------	---------	---------

[1] Includes oil and gas well drilling.
[2] Total housekeeping, including additions and alterations.
[3] Excludes military.
[4] Annual averages per year for overlapping decades.

Series N 78–89. Value of Construction Contracts Awarded (Dodge), by Class of Construction: 1901 to 1970

[In millions of dollars. Includes new structures and alterations to existing structures. Figures for 1901–1909 are for New England States only; 1910–1922, for 27 States except as noted; 1923–1924, for 36 States; 1925–1955, for 37 States; 1956–1969, for 48 States; thereafter, for 50 States. See text]

Year	Total	Nonresidential buildings									Residential buildings	Non-building construction
		Total	Commercial	Industrial	Educational and science	Hospital	Public buildings	Religious	Social and recreational	Miscellaneous		
	78	79	80	81	82	83	84	85	86	87	88	89
1970	68,294	24,455	9,056	3,664	5,253	2,811	1,007	575	1,137	952	24,837	19,001
1969	68,294	25,949	9,786	3,915	5,543	2,817	1,154	674	1,116	944	25,633	16,710
1968	61,732	22,513	7,645	3,768	5,347	2,114	1,112	778	954	795	24,838	14,382
1967	54,514	20,139	6,080	3,701	5,216	1,873	959	793	834	683	21,155	13,220
1966	50,150	19,393	5,835	3,623	4,939	1,721	939	825	855	656	17,827	12,930
1965	49,272	17,219	5,457	3,064	4,164	1,515	842	783	800	596	21,248	10,805
1964	47,330	15,522	4,572	2,970	3,554	1,625	789	814	599	598	20,565	11,244
1963	45,546	14,377	4,445	2,274	3,314	1,485	964	755	648	493	20,502	10,667
1962	41,303	13,010	4,216	2,086	3,060	1,079	677	811	704	377	18,039	10,255
1961	37,135	12,115	3,797	1,814	3,015	985	671	805	623	403	16,123	8,897
1960	36,318	12,240	3,725	2,114	3,005	832	679	789	631	464	15,105	8,973
1959	36,269	11,387	3,496	1,880	2,666	865	605	799	601	474	17,150	7,732
1958	35,090	10,948	3,197	1,400	2,907	879	655	746	500	664	14,696	9,446
1957	32,173	11,293	3,267	2,168	2,936	870	470	699	429	455	13,039	7,841
1956	31,612	11,208	3,140	2,381	2,883	678	428	681	422	595	12,862	7,542
1955	24,632	8,497	2,359	1,878	2,134	475	301	551	270	530	11,072	5,063
1954	20,596	7,110	1,816	1,274	2,063	519	249	486	252	452	9,344	4,142
1953	18,804	6,956	1,489	2,051	1,720	434	203	385	222	452	7,840	4,008
1952	18,070	6,695	979	2,558	1,472	444	233	318	153	538	7,963	3,412
1951	17,151	6,823	915	2,883	1,335	581	158	299	136	515	7,605	2,723
1950	16,592	5,182	1,209	1,142	1,180	655	124	336	261	274	8,832	2,578
1949	11,826	3,644	885	559	824	555	119	276	222	204	5,706	2,476
1948	11,121	3,666	975	840	725	405	84	245	232	161	5,299	2,155
1947	9,175	2,716	785	941	392	192	73	118	122	92	4,569	1,890
1946	7,490	2,716	773	1,317	221	131	25	68	93	88	3,142	1,631
1945	3,299	1,850	346	1,027	100	113	16	35	60	153	563	885
1944	1,994	899	81	473	69	59	12	12	33	161	348	746
1943	3,274	1,424	121	766	62	111	25	7	58	274	868	982
1942	8,255	3,897	302	2,228	148	185	102	24	101	808	1,818	2,541
1941	6,007	2,316	471	1,182	141	89	89	53	78	214	1,954	1,738
1940	4,004	1,295	318	442	147	94	80	46	63	104	1,597	1,112
1939	3,551	966	247	175	201	83	110	38	82	29	1,334	1,251
1938	3,197	1,072	216	121	334	116	114	36	108	28	986	1,139
1937	2,913	1,156	297	314	223	82	105	37	84	15	905	852
1936	2,675	960	249	198	219	74	102	28	75	14	802	914
1935	1,845	681	165	109	168	47	98	24	55	16	479	685
1934	1,543	551	151	116	112	37	56	18	46	15	249	743
1933	1,256	417	99	128	39	37	51	18	27	19	249	589
1932	1,351	488	123	44	81	48	118	27	34	13	280	583
1931	3,093	1,141	311	116	223	121	181	53	99	36	811	1,141
1930	4,523	1,822	616	257	366	163	140	93	117	71	1,101	1,599
1929	5,751	2,425	929	546	370	152	121	106	147	55	1,916	1,410
1928	6,628	2,438	885	509	390	165	76	128	219	67	2,788	1,402
1927	6,303	2,439	933	376	369	163	80	157	261	102	2,573	1,291
1926	6,381	2,418	921	471	373	133	67	149	252	52	2,671	1,292
1925	6,006	2,202	872	327	419	111	55	153	253	12	2,748	1,057

Year	Total	Nonresidential buildings			Residential buildings	Non-building construction	Year	Total	Year	Total
		Total¹	Commercial	Industrial	Public and institutional					
	78	79	80	81	83–87	88	89		78		78
1924	4,479	1,583	591	233	721	2,052	844	1914	775	1907	129
1923	3,992	1,456	518	313	601	1,736	801	1913	917	1906	125
1922	3,344	1,395	496	278	599	1,340	609	1912	923	1905	107
1921	2,355	998	332	153	461	879	479	1911	828	1904	97
1920²	2,564	1,394	444	555	345	570	600	1910	859	1903	104
1919²	2,580	1,213	406	498	266	849	517	1909	166	1902	119
1918	1,767					305		1908	112	1901	120
1917	1,691					355					
1916	1,413					483					
1915	978					418					

¹ Includes theaters, not shown separately.
² 25 States only. Totals for 27 States are: 1919, 2,699; 1920, 2,635.

Series N 90–100. Floor Space of Buildings for Which Construction Contracts Awarded (Dodge), by Class of Construction: 1919 to 1970

[In millions of square feet. Includes new structures and alterations to existing structures. Figures for 1919–1922 are for 27 States; 1923–1924, for 36 States; 1925–1955, for 37 States; 1956–1969, for 48 States; thereafter, for 50 States. See text]

Year	Total [1]	Nonresidential buildings									Residential buildings
		Total	Commercial	Industrial	Educational and science	Hospital	Public buildings	Religious	Social and recreational	Miscel-laneous	
	90	91	92	93	94	95	96	97	98	99	100
1970	2,938	1,157	530	212	195	75	29	27	47	42	1,781
1969	3,249	1,374	573	317	221	87	36	33	53	54	1,874
1968	3,129	1,254	496	284	234	69	39	39	46	47	1,876
1967	2,820	1,165	424	270	242	66	37	41	42	43	1,654
1966	2,643	1,227	442	312	245	60	37	45	47	40	1,416
1965	2,843	1,132	415	265	225	60	36	45	47	38	1,711
1964	2,738	1,024	360	239	202	67	34	50	36	36	1,714
1963	2,711	958	347	187	197	65	43	48	38	32	1,753
1962	2,414	894	326	174	191	49	34	53	40	27	1,520
1961	2,203	838	293	150	194	44	33	53	41	29	1,364
1960	2,154	854	283	178	196	36	33	53	44	31	1,300
1959	2,337	824	281	158	181	38	34	54	43	35	1,512
1958	2,101	768	243	113	201	38	37	51	37	47	1,333
1957	2,003	809	245	176	207	40	27	50	31	33	1,195
1956	2,017	823	244	192	200	33	27	48	30	48	1,194
1955	1,695	604	173	125	155	23	18	37	20	53	1,089
1954	1,486	532	138	100	154	28	16	34	19	44	953
1953	1,306	490	123	112	124	23	13	28	17	50	814
1952	1,288	441	82	115	107	26	15	22	12	62	845
1951	1,279	470	77	148	110	38	11	25	11	50	805
1950	1,475	483	122	115	111	45	10	29	24	28	989
1949	1,038	344	86	61	79	42	8	25	21	22	694
1948	1,060	385	101	110	72	35	6	21	22	18	673
1947	1,060	349	100	143	41	20	6	12	14	12	707
1946	946	432	119	235	26	15	2	8	11	15	516
1945	397	285	63	158	13	11	2	5	8	26	111
1944	229	156	12	84	10	8	2	1	5	33	74
1943	448	245	22	106	12	20	5	1	13	66	201
1942	1,296	848	74	446	31	34	20	3	23	216	449
1941	941	440	106	188	24	15	14	9	15	69	503
1940	690	268	67	95	25	14	12	7	12	37	421
1939	513	179	49	44	34	12	15	6	12	6	333
1938	429	186	42	25	57	17	16	5	18	6	241
1937	446	204	62	61	36	11	12	6	14	1	236
1936	410	183	57	40	42	10	14	4	13	1	223
1935	252	114	35	21	26	6	14	4	8	1	135
1934	152	86	28	18	17	4	9	3	7	1	64
1933	147	73	23	19	6	6	10	3	6	2	73
1932	156	80	24	9	14	7	16	4	6	1	74
1931	366	171	50	20	37	17	24	6	14	3	190
1930	510	272	97	48	57	19	17	11	16	7	230
1929	791	398	161	106	59	20	13	13	22	6	388
1928	967	394	159	93	61	20	11	15	28	6	568
1927	851	351	142	68	54	19	10	17	34	7	495
1926	884	356	152	76	54	15	8	16	30	4	521
1925	936	362	160	67	61	14	8	19	32	1	559

Year	Total	Nonresidential buildings				Resi-dential buildings	Year	Total	Nonresidential buildings				Resi-dential buildings
		Total [2]	Commer-cial	Industrial	Public and institu-tional				Total [2]	Commer-cial	Industrial	Public and institu-tional	
	90	91	92	93	96–99	100		90	91	92	93	96–99	100
1924	695	274	112	48	109	422	1921	385	180	65	35	74	205
1923	674	281	110	68	99	393	1920	402	264	84	125	49	138
1922	570	259	95	62	98	312	1919	557	315	110	152	47	242

[1] For early years, includes a small amount of floor space reported for public works and utilities.

[2] Includes theaters, not shown separately.

Series N 101–110. Construction Bidding Volume (Engineering News-Record), by Type: 1913 to 1970

[In millions of dollars]

Year	Total volume	Public works — Water-works	Sewerage	Bridges	Earth-work, irrigation, drainage	Streets, roads	Buildings	Private buildings — Industrial	Commercial, multi-unit residential	Un-classified
	101	102	103	104	105	106	107	108	109	110
1970	31,128	902	1,653	1,027	1,596	6,689	7,391	3,254	6,228	2,388
1969	28,982	712	1,289	1,337	648	5,993	7,649	3,505	5,268	2,581
1968	28,760	591	1,247	696	774	4,813	6,313	4,457	7,779	2,090
1967	29,451	723	911	822	1,039	5,142	5,582	5,135	8,366	1,731
1966	24,828	431	730	485	1,067	4,181	4,816	4,635	7,187	1,296
1965	24,025	401	685	347	1,407	4,096	4,197	3,632	7,888	1,372
1964	21,895	470	790	540	1,138	4,259	3,176	3,708	6,405	1,409
1963	21,370	460	950	640	1,055	4,070	2,810	2,750	7,165	1,470
1962	22,123	391	777	601	1,075	4,037	[1]3,490	2,544	7,376	1,832
1961	21,981	431	819	651	804	3,712	[1]3,427	2,817	7,636	1,685
1960	22,654	455	619	794	780	3,401	[1]3,300	2,792	8,051	2,462
1959[*]	20,423	376	655	570	915	2,899	[1]3,195	2,993	6,861	1,958
1958	19,165	306	618	713	1,045	3,729	[1]3,664	1,756	5,534	1,799
1957	17,986	369	556	781	969	2,965	[1]2,995	3,081	4,795	1,475
1956	21,712	356	579	622	730	2,475	[1]2,417	5,335	7,358	1,841
1955	18,722	314	402	546	546	2,137	[1]1,987	2,951	7,794	2,046
1954	14,412	245	388	510	339	1,919	[1]2,017	1,876	5,653	1,465
1953	15,171	247	431	752	374	1,793	[1]2,112	3,178	4,621	1,663
1952	15,689	231	304	413	496	1,397	[1,2]4,899	2,722	3,845	1,382
1951	13,605	209	335	316	505	1,167	[1]2,701	4,124	2,632	1,617
1950	13,342	215	287	369	417	1,268	[1]3,754	1,683	4,092	1,256
1949	8,157	207	277	357	524	897	[1]1,736	950	2,406	803
1948	7,219	209	228	303	519	996	1,161	1,096	1,888	820
1947	5,659	139	175	196	327	794	615	862	1,898	652
1946	5,176	109	114	129	328	769	414	1,113	1,846	354
1945	2,289	61	35	53	57	227	463	635	387	371
1944	1,730	33	32	17	64	196	658	174	140	416
1943	[3]3,062	46	41	26	47	227	1,419	167	231	858
1942	[4]9,306	151	118	50	251	531	5,678	200	292	2,034
1941	5,869	77	89	112	245	583	2,786	496	486	996
1940	3,987	70	91	120	234	678	1,196	594	400	603
1939	3,003	163	160	151	233	644	593	283	388	390
1938	2,792	131	136	135	268	638	503	152	550	279
1937	2,437	104	95	133	110	415	333	477	460	309
1936	2,387	92	121	188	182	483	436	309	275	300
1935	1,590	81	100	98	259	325	298	172	109	148
1934	1,361	92	61	99	266	345	204	105	81	106
1933	1,068	67	22	98	137	288	121	152	106	77
1932	1,219	35	25	84	101	380	241	93	166	95
1931	2,432	57	73	116	143	545	384	166	561	387
1930	3,173	49	83	131	77	585	356	331	1,034	528

Year	Total volume (101)	Private industrial buildings (108)
1929	3,950	547
1928	3,551	353
1927	3,254	321
1926	2,854	312
1925	2,559	228
1924	1,999	205
1923	1,904	282
1922	1,557	198
1921	1,194	118
1920	1,523	453
1919	1,176	381
1918	993	261
1917	739	175
1916	933	260
1915	585	91
1914	583	38
1913	601	41

[*] Denotes first year for which figures include Alaska and Hawaii.
[1] Includes contracts awarded for atomic energy plants as follows (in millions): 1949, $247; 1950, $2,020; 1951, $123; 1952, $2,829; 1953, $72; 1954, $19; 1955, $131; 1956, $86; 1957, $64; 1958, $84; 1959, $241; 1960, $59; 1961, $82; 1962, $106.
[2] Deduct $400 million for cost savings on Portsmouth, Ohio, atomic energy plant originally estimated to cost $1.2 billion.
[3] Add $1,357 million for atomic bomb plants.
[4] $1,800 million canceled by War Production Board.

Series N 111–117. Indexes of Building Activity: 1830 to 1939

Year	New building permits, value — Long (1930=100)	Newman — In current prices (1920-30=100)	Newman — In 1913 prices (1913=100)	Riggleman-Isard (1920-29=100)	Dollar volume of new construction, Newcomb (1920-29=100)	Urban dwelling units, Blank (1929=100) — Number of units started	Permit valuation
	111	112	113	114	115	116	117
1939	78.8						
1938	70.6						
1937	67.0						
1936	59.4						
1935	39.8						
1934	21.4						
1933	19.0	10.8	22	12.63			
1932	28.0	14.0	28	15.77			
1931	78.8	40.5	71	41.55			
1930	100.0	56.5	86	54.49			
1929	187.3	100.3	149	97.55		100.0	100.0
1928	199.1	114.3	170	109.16		155.5	153.9
1927	214.4	118.5	176	113.36		172.8	173.3
1926	239.6	130.9	194	128.49		192.3	190.1
1925	252.3	137.7	204	135.95		208.1	207.0
1924	213.3	119.9	173	115.50		193.9	187.1
1923	212.7	116.4	167	113.20		193.7	178.5
1922	167.6	94.3	151	92.49		155.5	140.3
1921	107.6	61.1	90	60.81		94.2	83.3

Series N 111–117. Indexes of Building Activity: 1830 to 1939—Con.

Year	New building permits, value Long (1930 = 100)	Newman In current prices (1920–30 = 100)	Newman In 1913 prices (1913 = 100)	Riggleman-Isard (1920–29 = 100)	Dollar volume of new construction, Newcomb (1920–29 = 100)	Urban dwelling units, Blank (1929 = 100) Number of units started	Urban dwelling units, Blank (1929 = 100) Permit valuation	Year	New building permits, value Long (1930 = 100)	Newman In current prices (1920–30 = 100)	Newman In 1913 prices (1913 = 100)	Riggleman-Isard (1920–29 = 100)	Dollar volume of new construction, Newcomb (1920–29 = 100)	Urban dwelling units, Blank (1929 = 100) Number of units started	Urban dwelling units, Blank (1929 = 100) Permit valuation
	111	112	113	114	115	116	117		111	112	113	114	115	116	117
1920	87.6	50.9	58	48.93	--------	47.2	43.6	1893	24.3	12.6	55	12.87	16.0	55.1	20.5
1919	81.9	47.9	70	44.84	--------	68.6	55.3	1892	34.2	19.3	84	17.02	16.0	77.8	29.3
1918	24.1	14.5	27	14.74	--------	24.6	13.5	1891	31.3	17.6	76	15.75	17.0	67.9	24.7
1917	49.7	26.2	59	24.10	--------	48.3	26.9								
1916	74.2	37.2	100	37.56	--------	101.3	54.2	1890	29.5	17.5	75	18.11	17.0	84.5	31.7
								1889	29.0	15.4	63	17.06	16.0	88.3	33.3
1915	62.8	31.2	94	30.26	--------	101.0	50.4	1888	21.0	11.2	46	13.83	15.0	74.7	25.2
1914	56.1	29.9	92	28.81	30.0	93.2	44.4	1887	25.1	11.8	47	14.40	14.0	91.1	32.8
1913	62.3	33.1	100	32.12	33.0	96.2	47.2	1886	22.5	12.9	51	13.24	13.0	82.1	29.1
1912	69.2	35.6	108	35.37	36.0	105.9	52.7								
1911	65.5	33.2	104	32.79	37.0	106.4	50.9	1885	19.5	11.2	47	11.60	11.0	71.8	25.6
								1884	17.3	10.5	44	9.97	10.0	63.5	20.2
1910	64.9	34.5	109	33.97	35.0	106.7	53.3	1883	17.1	10.4	39	10.13	11.0	52.9	19.6
1909	65.6	38.8	125	35.68	31.0	118.5	60.4	1882	16.5	8.9	33	8.99	11.0	38.2	18.6
1908	57.6	27.3	89	26.43	29.0	92.0	43.5	1881	15.3	6.7	27	7.33	10.0	36.4	16.9
1907	50.4	31.4	98	29.63	28.0	102.9	45.6								
1906	57.9	34.6	109	31.92	31.0	121.3	52.7	1880	11.5	5.4	22	5.64	7.0	32.1	12.4
								1879	8.9	4.1	19	4.53	5.0	21.4	10.8
1905	56.1	31.9	106	29.66	30.0	134.0	53.2	1878	6.1	4.0	17	3.90	4.3	16.3	7.3
1904	41.6	22.9	80	22.09	25.0	83.6	32.6	1877	5.5	4.5	19	4.55	4.5	17.5	6.6
1903	36.9	19.8	71	18.29	22.0	59.9	24.1	1876	6.5	4.6	18	5.12	5.3	21.0	7.1
1902	36.0	18.4	69	17.99	21.0	49.5	21.7								
1901	35.3	17.0	66	17.72	19.0	75.1	30.3	1875	7.5	5.4	20	6.22	5.9	24.9	8.5
								1874	8.4	--------		6.42	8.2	24.5	8.0
1900	22.5	11.6	46	11.69	18.0	49.3	20.8	1873	12.6			11.97	10.2	25.8	8.9
1899	30.0	16.7	70	14.89	15.0	84.9	33.6	1872	14.1			12.30	13.2	27.3	13.0
1898	23.0	12.7	58	11.93	17.0	65.3	25.0	1871	21.5			15.41	13.8	39.3	20.2
1897	25.3	14.5	67	13.57	16.0	75.4	28.0								
1896	23.4	13.3	60	12.64	18.0	58.7	23.3	1870	17.5			13.79	14.7	27.8	16.0
								1869	20.3			14.88	14.0	--------	--------
1895	28.0	16.5	73	15.26	17.0	73.6	27.7	1868	17.4			13.25	12.9	--------	--------
1894	21.0	12.2	55	11.56	16.0	54.4	20.9								

Year	Value of new building permits, Riggleman-Isard (1920–29 = 100) 114	Year	Value of new building permits, Riggleman-Isard (1920–29 = 100) 114	Year	Value of new building permits, Riggleman-Isard (1920–29 = 100) 114	Year	Value of new building permits, Riggleman-Isard (1920–29 = 100) 114	Year	Value of new building permits, Riggleman-Isard (1920–29 = 100) 114
1867	10.55	1859	4.61	1850	4.04	1841	1.35	1833	1.97
1866	8.92	1858	3.95	1849	3.01			1832	1.63
		1857	6.70	1848	2.71	1840	1.28	1831	1.02
1865	6.10	1856	6.46	1847	2.96	1839	1.70		
1864	3.91			1846	2.08	1838	1.82	1830	.71
1863	5.34	1855	5.94			1837	2.27		
1862	3.34	1854	6.07	1845	1.41	1836	4.45		
1861	3.68	1853	5.96	1844	.99				
		1852	5.28	1843	.80	1835	2.61		
1860	5.29	1851	4.35	1842	1.01	1834	2.10		

Series N 118–137. Construction Cost Indexes: 1913 to 1970

[1967 = 100, except series N 137. Excludes Alaska and Hawaii for all years]

Year	Department of Commerce composite	American Appraisal Company	Associated General Contractors	E. H. Boeckh and Associates Residences	E. H. Boeckh and Associates Apartments, hotels, and office buildings	E. H. Boeckh and Associates Commercial and factory buildings	Engineering News-Record Building	Engineering News-Record Construction	Dept. of Agriculture, Economic Research Service Farm housing	Dept. of Agriculture, Economic Research Service Other farm construction	George A. Fuller Co., commercial buildings	Handy-Whitman public utility Buildings	Handy-Whitman public utility Gas plant	Handy-Whitman public utility Electric light and power plants
	118	119	120	121	122	123	124	125	126	127	128	129	130	131
1970	122	124	126	122.4	124.4	123.1	124.4	128.9	---------	118	127	121	117	119
1969	114	116	114	116.2	116.1	114.5	117.7	118.7	---------	115	116	113	110	110
1968	106	107	105	107.3	107.0	106.8	107.4	107.9	108	106	105	105	104	104
1967	100	100	100	100.0	100.0	100.0	100.0	100.0	100	100	100	100	100	100
1966	96	95	96	94.3	94.3	93.9	96.9	95.2	96	96	98	97	97	96
1965	93	91	93	90.4	90.7	90.0	93.3	90.8	92	93	96	93	94	94
1964	90	88	90	87.6	87.7	87.1	91.1	87.4	90	91	94	92	92	90
1963	88	86	86	85.2	85.2	84.6	88.5	84.2	90	92	91	90	90	89
1962	86	83	84	83.4	83.2	82.8	86.3	81.5	89	91	89	88	88	89
1961	84	81	83	82.1	81.3	81.1	84.6	79.2	88	91	85	87	86	88

Series N 118–137. Construction Cost Indexes: 1913 to 1970—Con.

[1967 = 100]

Year	Department of Commerce composite	American Appraisal Company	Associated General Contractors	E. H. Boeckh and Associates Residences	E. H. Boeckh and Associates Apartments, hotels, and office buildings	E. H. Boeckh and Associates Commercial and factory buildings	Engineering News-Record Building	Engineering News-Record Construction	Dept. of Agriculture, Economic Research Service Farm housing	Dept. of Agriculture, Economic Research Service Other farm construction	George A. Fuller Co., commercial buildings	Handy-Whitman public utility Buildings	Handy-Whitman public utility Gas plant	Handy-Whitman public utility Electric light and power plants
	118	119	120	121	122	123	124	125	126	127	128	129	130	131
1960	83	80	81	81.8	80.3	80.4	83.3	76.9	88	91	82	87	85	89
1959	82	77	78	80.5	78.7	79.1	81.6	74.5	86	90	81	87	84	89
1958	81	75	76	77.9	76.1	76.4	78.2	71.0	84	87	78	84	81	88
1957	80	73	73	77.2	74.8	74.9	75.7	67.6	84	86	74	82	77	86
1956	77	70	70	75.7	72.5	72.3	73.1	64.7	82	83	71	76	73	81
1955	73	67	67	72.5	69.2	68.7	69.9	61.6	79	80	68	70	67	74
1954	71	65	64	70.4	67.2	66.5	66.4	58.7	77	78	66	67	64	72
1953	71	64	62	71.0	66.6	65.7	64.1	56.0	78	79	64	65	60	69
1952	69	61	59	69.7	64.6	63.5	61.9	53.2	77	78	61	61	58	67
1951	68	59	58	68.0	62.5	61.4	59.7	50.7	76	76	60	61	57	65
1950	62	55	55	63.0	58.0	56.8	55.9	47.7	69	69	56	56	52	58
1949	60	54	52	59.8	55.5	54.6	52.4	44.5	64	72	57	54	50	54
1948	60	54	51	61.4	54.8	54.0	51.3	43.0	67	73	56	51	48	51
1947	54	47	45	54.6	48.6	47.8	46.6	38.6	62	67	52	45	43	46
1946	45	35	39	45.1	41.3	40.7	39.1	32.3	49	54	43	38	36	40
1945	39	30	35	41.1	37.8	37.3	35.6	28.8	45	50	36	33	31	35
1944	37	29	34	38.3	35.5	35.2	35.0	27.9	42	47	36	32	31	34
1943	38	28	33	35.2	33.3	32.9	34.1	27.1	38	43	35	31	30	34
1942	35	26	32	33.8	32.0	31.6	33.1	25.9	33	39	34	31	30	34
1941	31	24	30	31.9	30.4	30.2	31.5	24.1	29	33	30	29	28	33
1940	29	23	29	29.6	29.0	28.7	30.2	22.6	26	31	29	26	27	32
1939	28	23	29	28.6	28.5	28.3	29.4	22.0	25	30	29	26	27	31
1938	30	22	29	28.1	28.2	28.0	29.3	22.0	25	31	29	26	27	31
1937	30	22	29	27.3	27.1	27.0	29.2	21.9	27	31	27	27	27	31
1936	28	19	27	24.4	24.3	24.2	25.7	19.2	25	30	25	24	24	28
1935	27	18	27	23.6	23.6	23.5	24.7	18.3	25	30	25	24	23	28
1934	28	17	27	24.2	23.9	23.9	24.8	18.5	25	30	26	24	23	27
1933	25	17	24	22.2	21.7	21.9	22.0	15.9	22	26	23	21	21	25
1932	23	17	26	22.2	21.2	21.4	21.0	14.7	22	26	23	21	21	25
1931	27	20	30	26.3	24.9	24.8	25.3	17.0	25	30	26	23	23	26
1930	29	23	30	28.5	26.9	26.8	27.6	19.0	30	34	29	25	23	26
1929	30	24	31	29.3	27.4	27.2	28.4	19.4	31	36	29	26	23	28
1928	30	24	30	28.0	26.8	26.4	28.0	19.3	31	35	29	26	23	26
1927	30	24	30	27.9	26.6	26.4	27.7	19.2	31	36	29	26	24	26
1926	30	24	30	28.3	27.0	26.7	27.6	19.5	31	36	29	27	24	26
1925	30	24	30	28.0	26.8	26.5	27.2	19.3	31	37	29	27	25	27
1924	30	24	31	28.3	26.5	26.7	27.6	20.1	31	36	29	29	26	27
1923	30	25	30	28.7	27.1	26.8	27.7	20.0	31	35	28	26	24	26
1922	27	23	28	25.7	24.5	24.0	23.1	16.3	29	33	26	23	22	27
1921	30	24	34	27.9	26.1	25.9	24.7	18.8	28	33	28	26	27	27
1920	37	31	37	34.7	32.4	31.6	30.8	23.5	39	46	31	34	29	30
1919	30	26	30	26.9	25.4	25.4	23.6	18.5	36	41	25	29	27	27
1918	27	20	27	23.2	22.3	23.1	23.7	17.7	29	36	23	29	25	26
1917	23	16	23	19.5	19.7	21.0	24.9	16.9	24	30	23	28	21	22
1916	18	13	17	16.6	16.4	17.2	19.5	12.1	20	25	21	19	15	18
1915	16	11	15	15.6	14.6	14.8	14.2	8.7	18	22	19	17	13	15

Year	ICC, railroad construction	Bell System Telephone plant, telephone and telegraph Buildings	Bell System Telephone plant, telephone and telegraph Outside plant	Federal Highway Administration	Turner Construction Company	Average of contractor indexes (1913 = 100)
	132	133	134	135	136	137
1970	------------	125.0	124.0	125.6	129	
1969	------------	114.7	111.2	111.8	117	
1968	------------	105.5	104.5	103.4	106	
1967	100	100.0	100.0	100.0	100	
1966	98	95.7	96.5	96.1	97	
1965	96	91.9	91.1	90.3	94	
1964	95	88.9	89.8	86.9	91	
1963	95	86.5	89.3	86.4	89	
1962	95	84.4	87.2	84.3	87	
1961	95	83.6	87.1	80.7	86	
1960	96	83.5	88.9	80.0	85	
1959	95	82.6	86.4	82.0	84	
1958	93	81.0	84.4	85.5	83	
1957	91	78.9	85.9	87.7	83	
1956	87	76.6	86.0	84.0	78	
1955	81	72.8	81.5	74.2	71	------------
1954	79	70.7	78.5	76.4	71	------------
1953	79	68.8	77.7	81.0	72	------------
1952	76	66.7	76.4	84.1	71	------------
1951	73	64.9	74.3	81.7	68	413
1950	68	61.2	67.7	66.6	61	379
1949	67	60.2	68.6	73.7	59	371
1948	67	58.2	67.8	76.4	61	375
1947	60	53.0	65.0	68.3	55	346
1946	53	46.1	53.0	60.1	46	292
1945	49	35.7	46.1	55.1	38	246
1944	46	31.0	44.3	57.1	35	237
1943	46	30.2	42.6	63.1	37	236
1942	43	30.2	40.9	55.0	35	229
1941	37	27.9	38.3	41.1	31	210

Series N 118–137. Construction Cost Indexes: 1913 to 1970—Con.

[1967 = 100]

Year	ICC, railroad construction	Bell System Telephone plant, telephone and telegraph Buildings	Outside plant	Federal Highway Administration	Turner Construction Company	Average of contractor indexes (1913 = 100)
	132	133	134	135	136	137
1940	35	27.1	37.4	36.1	28	191
1939	34	26.4	37.4	36.6	26	184
1938	34	26.4	37.4	36.8	27	187
1937	35	25.6	37.4	40.1	28	189
1936	33	23.3	34.8	41.9	24	169
1935	32	22.5	34.8	40.7	23	163
1934	32	21.7	35.7	42.4	23	163
1933	31	20.2	34.8	38.8	20	148
1932	32	20.9	34.8	30.9	20	147
1931	35	23.3	35.7	38.8	21	163
1930	38	26.4	35.7	43.3	24	182
1929	40	----------	----------	46.6	27	192
1928	40	----------	----------	48.1	28	193
1927	40	----------	----------	51.5	28	195
1926	41	----------	----------	52.2	28	200

Year	ICC, railroad construction	Federal Highway Administration	Turner Construction Company	Average of contractor indexes (1913 = 100)
	132	135	136	137
1925	41	54.3	28	199
1924	42	57.1	28	198
1923	42	59.6	28	196
1922	39	53.5	25	174
1921	43	58.7	26	187
1920	53	70.8	36	232
1919	44	54.5	28	184
1918	39	49.2	24	176
1917	33	40.7	21	151
1916	27	35.5	18	128
1915	25	33.5	14	113
1914	----------	----------	----------	102
1913	----------	----------	----------	100

Series N 138–139. Construction Cost Indexes: 1868 to 1933

Year	Building cost, Riggleman (1913 = 100)	Residential construction cost, Blank (1929 = 100)	Year	Building cost, Riggleman (1913 = 100)	Residential construction cost, Blank (1929 = 100)	Year	Building cost, Riggleman (1913 = 100)	Residential construction cost, Blank (1929 = 100)	Year	Building cost, Riggleman (1913 = 100)
	138	139		138	139		138	139		138
1933	170.0	76.2	1916	115.6	57.0	1899	74.4	38.5	1883	81.9
1932	157.0	76.1				1898	67.5	35.9	1882	81.5
1931	181.4	89.9	1915	100.9	53.5	1897	66.5	34.4	1881	77.6
			1914	98.3	52.2	1896	68.3	35.1		
1930	202.9	97.5	1913	100.0	51.9				1880	73.2
1929	207.0	100.0	1912	90.7	53.8	1895	69.8	34.9	1879	67.3
1928	206.8	95.9	1911	93.4	52.5	1894	69.2	35.4	1878	69.7
1927	206.2	95.6				1893	71.1	36.7	1877	73.6
1926	208.0	96.9	1910	96.3	53.2	1892	70.9	36.8	1876	79.0
			1909	90.9	51.4	1891	70.9	37.9		
1925	206.7	96.2	1908	97.2	49.5				1875	82.0
1924	215.4	96.9	1907	100.6	51.1	1890	73.3	39.2	1874	90.2
1923	214.0	98.3	1906	95.1	48.9	1889	75.3	39.0	1873	97.0
1922	174.5	87.7				1888	75.2	----------	1872	99.2
1921	201.8	95.4	1905	90.6	44.5	1887	77.8	----------	1871	99.4
			1904	87.4	42.5	1886	78.1	----------		
1920	251.3	118.7	1903	84.0	43.0				1870	95.3
1919	212.8	92.1	1902	83.8	41.5	1885	73.1	----------	1869	105.4
1918	170.9	79.2	1901	83.6	40.1	1884	73.3	----------	1868	104.3
1917	142.9	66.6	1900	79.9	40.6					

Series N 140–155. Indexes of Wholesale Prices for Construction Materials: 1926 to 1970

[1967 = 100]

Year	All construction materials	Softwood lumber Douglas fir	Southern pine	Millwork	Plywood	Building paper and board	Finished steel products Structural shapes	Reinforcing bars	Nonferrous metal products	Plumbing fixtures [1]	Heating equipment	Concrete Ingredients	Products	Structural clay products [2]	Gypsum products	Asphalt roofing
	140	141	142	143	144	145	146	147	148	149	150	151	152	153	154	155
1970	112.5	108.7	114.7	116.0	108.5	101.2	115.3	110.3	125.0	112.5	110.6	114.6	112.2	109.8	100.0	102.9
1969	111.6	131.7	126.0	117.8	122.5	105.5	108.1	100.3	113.5	107.3	105.4	106.7	106.5	106.2	103.6	102.8
1968	105.6	120.3	113.7	105.8	115.7	100.9	101.8	99.3	103.5	103.3	102.7	103.2	102.6	102.6	103.6	103.1
1967	100.0	100.0	100.0	100.0	100.0	100.0	100.0	100.0	100.0	100.0	100.0	100.0	100.0	100.0	100.0	100.0
1966	98.8	96.8	100.2	98.0	104.0	100.8	99.9	100.8	100.0	98.1	99.8	98.1	97.7	98.2	99.6	102.1
1965*	95.8	92.3	91.2	96.0	103.5	100.9	96.2	99.7	95.3	93.3	98.9	97.5	96.3	96.6	101.2	98.7
1964	94.7	93.1	89.6	96.7	103.5	102.3	96.2	91.5	87.6	91.3	99.2	97.1	95.7	95.8	105.3	94.5
1963	93.6	91.5	89.5	92.7	104.8	104.4	94.1	90.3	82.0	90.5	100.2	97.3	96.5	95.5	102.5	95.7
1962	93.4	88.1	89.8	90.7	103.6	105.8	93.4	99.7	82.1	90.6	100.5	97.5	97.3	95.0	102.1	100.9
1961	93.7	85.6	89.9	90.8	107.3	109.7	93.4	104.8	83.0	93.4	101.8	97.1	97.2	94.2	101.0	104.9

See footnotes at end of table.

Series N 140–155. Indexes of Wholesale Prices for Construction Materials: 1926 to 1970—Con.

[1967 = 100]

Year	All construction materials	Softwood lumber — Douglas fir	Softwood lumber — Southern pine	Millwork	Plywood	Building paper and board	Finished steel products — Structural shapes	Finished steel products — Reinforcing bars	Nonferrous metal products	Plumbing fixtures ¹	Heating equipment	Concrete — Ingredients	Concrete — Products	Structural clay products²	Gypsum products	Asphalt roofing
	140	141	142	143	144	145	146	147	148	149	150	151	152	153	154	155
1960	95.5	89.3	93.9	93.1	109.6	110.3	93.4	107.3	85.9	93.3	105.8	97.0	97.2	93.7	99.1	97.4
1959	97.1	97.7	95.4	92.6	115.5	110.8	93.4	107.8	84.2	91.9	107.9	95.7	96.1	92.2	99.0	105.7
1958	94.0	85.7	92.3	87.3	110.9	108.5	91.4	105.4	79.0	87.5	107.4	94.8	94.9	90.1	98.2	102.4
1957	94.1	87.3	93.7	87.4	110.0	107.2	87.7	101.7	85.0	92.0	108.4	92.7	93.6	89.4	94.6	111.1
1956	94.1	97.0	97.5	88.0	116.0	103.7	76.2	93.8	96.5	94.7	105.9	89.0	91.1	88.1	94.6	101.4
1955	90.4	97.5	94.2	87.7	120.4	99.1	71.0	87.8	88.3	88.7	102.5	85.2	88.0	83.8	90.9	96.3
1954	86.6	89.2	90.5	88.9	117.7	96.7	67.3	84.9	76.8	83.7	101.8	82.5	87.1	80.5	94.5	94.5
1953	86.4	87.6	94.7	89.6	124.8	91.9	64.7	77.9	77.3	82.0	102.3	80.1	85.5	79.2	90.1	97.4
1952	85.2	95.1	95.6	86.5	119.8	87.4	61.3	70.0	76.3	83.1	101.3	77.1	83.4	77.8	87.5	93.4
1951	86.2	96.1	94.7	88.7	131.4	85.9	60.0	68.1	76.8	86.6	102.0	77.1	83.3	78.0	87.4	95.2
1950	78.9	87.8	88.3	78.2	121.5	81.5	56.6	64.0	64.4	76.5	93.5	72.8	78.2	72.1	77.8	92.0
1949	73.5	71.2	78.7	73.4	108.6	78.9	52.8	61.9	61.0	72.6	92.2	71.8	76.4	69.0	76.1	93.4
1948	75.0	81.5	87.1	71.7	124.3	77.9	48.1	55.6	65.4	72.6	90.1	69.5	74.7	67.1	76.8	93.6
1947	67.7	71.4	79.5	59.4	109.4	70.4	39.5	48.3	59.1	67.0	84.9	63.5	71.3	62.3	70.3	85.4
1946	49.6	-------	-------	46.3	-------	-------	-------	-------	43.0	56.0	-------	58.1	62.7	-------	-------	74.9
1945	44.2	-------	-------	41.0	-------	-------	-------	-------	37.3	52.5	-------	55.7	59.2	-------	-------	71.6
1944	43.3	-------	-------	40.7	-------	-------	-------	-------	37.3	52.9	-------	54.3	59.2	-------	-------	70.3
1943	41.8	-------	-------	39.5	-------	-------	-------	-------	37.4	55.0	-------	53.5	59.2	-------	-------	69.6
1942	41.3	-------	-------	39.2	-------	-------	-------	-------	37.2	56.6	-------	53.5	59.2	-------	-------	69.7
1941	38.7	-------	-------	35.8	-------	-------	-------	-------	36.6	51.0	-------	52.0	57.3	-------	-------	71.5
1940	35.5	-------	-------	31.4	-------	-------	-------	-------	35.2	50.0	-------	51.5	49.3	-------	-------	69.3
1939	33.9	-------	-------	28.8	-------	-------	-------	-------	34.0	47.1	-------	51.7	55.4	-------	-------	63.5
1938	33.8	-------	-------	29.3	-------	-------	-------	-------	31.7	47.1	-------	51.8	55.6	-------	-------	61.4
1937	35.7	-------	-------	32.6	-------	-------	-------	-------	38.9	47.7	-------	51.5	60.6	-------	-------	76.0
1936	32.5	-------	-------	27.2	-------	-------	-------	-------	31.1	46.7	-------	51.7	60.3	-------	-------	69.5
1935	32.0	-------	-------	25.3	-------	-------	-------	-------	29.8	40.9	-------	51.6	56.7	-------	-------	70.5
1934	32.4	-------	-------	25.6	-------	-------	-------	-------	29.4	46.8	-------	51.3	62.1	-------	-------	67.2
1933	28.9	-------	-------	24.6	-------	-------	-------	-------	25.9	44.8	-------	48.4	62.1	-------	-------	62.4
1932	26.9	-------	-------	23.4	-------	-------	-------	-------	21.7	45.7	-------	44.5	61.2	-------	-------	61.0
1931	29.8	-------	-------	23.8	-------	-------	-------	-------	26.9	56.1	-------	46.8	66.3	-------	-------	66.6
1930	33.7	-------	-------	28.4	-------	-------	-------	-------	35.9	59.5	-------	51.3	70.4	-------	-------	64.3
1929	35.8	-------	-------	30.1	-------	-------	-------	-------	46.2	62.8	-------	51.0	69.4	-------	-------	62.8
1928	35.3	-------	-------	29.9	-------	-------	-------	-------	40.9	66.4	-------	50.7	70.5	-------	-------	71.2
1927	35.6	-------	-------	30.0	-------	-------	-------	-------	40.4	65.3	-------	45.0	70.5	-------	-------	79.5
1926	37.5	-------	-------	30.0	-------	-------	-------	-------	43.4	72.9	-------	46.3	70.5	-------	-------	84.3

* Denotes first year for which figures include Alaska and Hawaii.
¹ Includes brass fittings.
² Excludes refractories.

Housing (Series N 156-307)

N 156–169. New housing units started, by ownership, type of structure, location, and construction cost, 1889–1970.

Source: U.S. Bureau of the Census, 1889–1962, *Housing Construction Statistics, 1889 to 1964*, tables A-1 and A-5; 1963–1970, *Construction Reports*, Housing Starts, series C 20-73-7, July 1973.

The data for 1889–1919 are from David M. Blank, *The Volume of Residential Construction, 1889–1950*, Technical Paper No. 9, National Bureau of Economic Research, 1954; data for 1920–1929 are from David L. Wickens and Ray R. Foster, *Nonfarm Residential Construction, 1920–1936*, National Bureau of Economic Research, Bulletin No. 65, 1937. The data for 1930–1944 are from U.S. Department of Labor, *Construction, 1948 in Review*, Bulletin No. 983, 1950; data for 1930–1936 represent a revision by the Bureau of Labor Statistics of the Wickens-Foster data. Data for 1945–1970 are Census Bureau estimates derived from its monthly estimates based on building permits and supplemented by sample surveys of housing starts in non-permit-issuing areas. Data for 1945–1958 are revisions of data from the Bureau of Labor Statistics; detail data, such as number of units by type of structure, are not available for these years.

For methods used by Blank and Wickens-Foster, see the sources. Blank's data are based on a comprehensive tabulation of historical building permit data collected by the Works Progress Administration and made available by the Bureau of Labor Statistics (BLS). For methods used by BLS, see BLS Bulletin No. 1168, *Techniques of Preparing Major BLS Statistical Series*, December 1954, chapter 2.

Basically, compilation of the housing starts series depends on four steps. First, an estimate is made of the number of housing units for which building permits have been issued in all permit-issuing places each month. For the country as a whole, about 85 percent of the private housing units were constructed in permit-issuing places in recent years. Since 1967, the series have pertained to approximately 13,000 places identified in 1967 as having local building permit systems. Coverage from 1963 to 1967 was based on a permit-issuing universe of 12,000 places, identified as permit-issuing in 1962. Back to 1959, the series relate to the 10,000 places identified as permit-issuing in 1959. Prior to 1959, 6,600 places was the universe. Second, a survey is made each month in a sample of permit places. In each place, a sample of building permits is selected each month and an inquiry is made of the owner or the builder to find out whether and when the units covered by the permits have been started. From this sample of permits, ratios are calculated, by type of structure, of the number of units started to the number of units covered by permits. These ratios are then applied to the total number of units authorized by permits in the corresponding months to provide estimates of the total number of units started each month with permit authorization. Third, the estimates of the number of one-family units started in each month with permit authorization are adjusted upward by 3.3 percent to take care of the units started within permit-issuing areas but without permit authorization. The fourth step in estimating total housing starts is to estimate the number of units started in areas where building permit systems do not exist. In a sample of 100 areas, visits are made to a select group of persons who are presumed most likely to know about local housing activities. A list is obtained from them of all residential buildings they know to have been started within the nonpermit portions of these areas during the preceding month. Within those portions of the sample area, a sub-sample of areas is canvassed for all units started since the previous month, identifying those not reported by the sources as well as those reported by them. This canvass provides a basis for estimating the number of units not reported by the local sources. The number of units not reported is then added to the number of units reported, to provide an estimate of total housing starts in areas not covered by building permit systems.

The housing units covered in these series are permanent housekeeping units in new residential structures. Excluded are temporary units; accommodations without housekeeping facilities such as transient hotels, dormitories, and clubhouses; mobile homes, trailers, houseboats, sheds, and shacks used for housing purposes; units provided by conversion of existing structures; and housing units in nonresidential structures such as factories, warehouses, or public buildings.

For regional estimates of the number of new private nonfarm housing units started, 1920–1950, see Leo Grebler, David M. Blank, and Louis Winnick, *Capital Formation in Residential Real Estate: Trends and Prospects*, Princeton University Press, 1956, table H-1. Regional estimates for later years appear in Bureau of the Census, *Construction Reports*, series C 20.

N 157–158, new housing units started, by ownership. For bases of estimates for privately financed housing units, see text for series N 156–169. Publicly owned housing includes housing units in buildings for which construction contracts were awarded by Federal, State, or local governments. Information on public housing is obtained, for the most part, from the agencies involved, e.g., Department of Housing and Urban Development, Department of Defense, New York City Housing Authority, and others. The criterion for classifying housing units as public is ownership of the facilities rather than the source of funds. Thus, low-rent housing projects owned by local housing authorities are classified as public even though they may be financed by local bonds issued to private investors, and military housing units owned by the Department of Defense are also classified as public even though they may be financed by mortgages held by private lending institutions. Figures exclude temporary dwellings built during the defense period and World War II (1940's), veterans temporary re-use housing (see text for series N 186–191), and temporary structures on military posts and similar installations. Units in structures built by private developers for sale upon completion to local public housing authorities under the Department of Housing and Urban Development "Turnkey" program are classified as private housing.

N 162–163, new housing units started, by location. The distribution of housing starts between units inside and outside standard metropolitan statistical areas (SMSA's) is based on the definitions published by the Office of Management and Budget in *Standard Metropolitan Statistical Areas*. Data for 1959–1960 are based on 1959 definitions; for 1961–1963 on 1961 definitions; for January 1964–March 1968 on 1964 definitions; and for April 1968–1970 on 1967 definitions. The term, "urban" was applied to all incorporated places with a population of 2,500 or more and to a relatively small number of areas urban under special rule. "Rural-nonfarm" housing included all housing (except farm housing) in unincorporated areas and in incorporated places of less than 2,500 inhabitants. This classification for 1920–1929 was based on the 1930 Census of Population and for 1930–1944 on the 1940 census. This classification system was abandoned in 1954 because of the difficulties of resolving differences between the geographic areas used for building permit systems and the urban areas as newly defined in the 1950 census. Beginning in 1950, housing starts have been classified by those inside and outside the standard metropolitan statistical areas.

N 164–169, construction cost. The construction cost data for the privately owned units are not reported directly but are based on permit valuations adjusted for understatement of construction cost and relationship between costs in permit places and nonpermit areas. They cover the cost of labor, material, and subcontracted work, and that part of the builder's overhead and profit chargeable directly to the building of the housing units started. Included is the cost of equipment which becomes an integral part of the housing unit and is essential to its general use. Excluded are the costs of land, site improvement, architectural fees, and sales profit.

The data for the publicly owned units are based on contract award values or estimated construction costs for individual projects, as reported by the several agencies administering the various public housing programs.

The source, *Housing Construction Statistics, 1889 to 1964*, was designed as an historical supplement to the current data issued by the Bureau of the Census in three publication series of its Construction Reports program—*Housing Starts*, series C 20; *Building Permits, Housing Authorized in Individual Permit-Issuing Places*, series C 40; and *Building Permits, Housing Authorized in Permit-Issuing Places, Summary Statistics*, series C 42.

N 170. Mobile home shipments, 1947–1970.

Source: U.S. Department of Housing and Urban Development, *HUD Statistical Yearbook*, annual issues.

Statistics on manufacturers' shipments of mobile homes are provided by the Mobile Home Manufacturers' Association, and include estimates for firms not associated with the MHMA. Mass production of 10-foot wide homes began in 1955; 12-foot wide homes in 1962.

Manufacturers' shipments of mobile homes are included in this volume because an addition to the housing supply is made by mobile homes as well as by the construction of new housing units. Some of the mobile homes, however, are used as seasonal homes and second homes and do not add to the supply of housing units occupied as usual places of residence. Furthermore, some are used for nonresidential purposes. The number of mobile homes used in these ways is not now known.

N 171–179. New publicly owned housing starts, by ownership and program, 1949–1970.

Source: U.S. Bureau of Domestic Commerce, *Construction Review*, monthly issues.

These series, which are compiled by the U.S. Bureau of the Census, represent an actual count of publicly owned housing starts as reported by the Public Housing Administration (PHA), the Defense Department, the New York City Housing Authority, and other State and local housing authorities. Publicly owned housing units were not reported separately until 1935. It is considered that the volume of permanent publicly owned housing units prior to 1935 is insignificant. Housing provided under the Federal emergency programs, including those of World War II, consisted largely of units in temporary or converted structures and, therefore, are not included in the permanent units shown. Type of program data, i.e., Federal, State, or local, are not available for publicly owned housing prior to 1949.

N 180–185. Privately owned housing units in major Federal programs, 1935–1970.

Source: All series except N 181 and N 185, U.S. Housing and Home Finance Agency, 1935–1956, *Annual Report, 1956*, tables A-6, A-37, A-42, and A-54; 1957, *Annual Report, 1957*, tables A-7, A-48, A-53, and A-68; 1958–1963, *Annual Report, 1964*, table III-3; 1964–1970, U.S. Department of Housing and Urban Development, *1970 HUD Statistical Yearbook*, tables 146, 160, 162, and 164. **Series N 181 and N 185**, U.S. Veterans Administration, Loan Guaranty Service, unpublished data.

Figures are based on reports of the agencies administering the programs. The Federal Housing Administration (FHA) and the Veterans Administration (VA) are agencies which insure or guarantee loans made by private lenders.

N 180–181, new privately owned units started under FHA and VA. Data are based on monthly reports of these agencies. These reports are based on the first of several inspections of newly started units required by the agencies, the timing of which coincides roughly with the definition of housing starts by the Bureau of Labor Statistics and the Bureau of the Census.

The figures may be used roughly to derive the units started under FHA and VA as a percentage of all private housing starts. However, an unknown number of units started under FHA or VA inspection is sold later for cash or with conventional (uninsured or unguaranteed) mortgage loans. On the other hand, the number of units started under the FHA program understates the role of FHA inasmuch as previously unoccupied (new) houses, for which the builder did not apply for FHA insurance before construction, are classified by FHA as "existing construction" when the houses are sold later with FHA-insured loans. In 1956, about one-fifth of the FHA units classified as "existing construction" were previously unoccupied (new). However, by 1970, such previously unoccupied (new) units amounted to less than 3 percent of those classified under "existing construction." For problems of coverage and comparability, see Department of Commerce and Department of Labor, *Construction Review*, "FHA and VA Housing Statistics and the Housing Market," June 1957.

N 182–185, new and existing privately owned units covered by loans under FHA and VA. Data are based on monthly reports of these agencies and refer to loans on both new and existing construction at the time such loans were closed or actually insured. FHA "homes" include 1- to 4-family dwellings; FHA "rental projects" include structures having 5 or more dwelling units. Practically all VA loans are on single-family dwellings. The VA program was authorized in 1944 and the small 1944 activity is included in 1945.

N 186–191. Low-rent public housing units, by progress stage, and war and defense housing and veterans housing units available for occupancy, 1941–1970.

Source: U.S. Department of Housing and Urban Development, Housing and Mortgage Credit-FHA, *HUD Statistical Yearbook*, various issues.

These data comprise low-rent, publicly financed housing units occupied or available for occupancy, units to be constructed, and units that were to go directly under management since they needed no rehabilitation. The data are not comparable with series N 156–159 which relate to new construction starts and include all publicly financed units (Federal, State, and local).

N 192–195. Nonfarm dwelling units standing and selected components of change, 1890–1950.

Source: Leo Grebler, David M. Blank, and Louis Winnick, *Capital Formation in Residential Real Estate: Trends and Prospects*, Princeton University Press, 1956, tables 15 and A-1 (copyright, National Bureau of Economic Research, New York).

Estimates do not represent all components of change in the nonfarm housing inventory; that is, the units added through new construction or conversion minus the units destroyed through demolition or disaster losses during a certain period do not equal the net change in the inventory during the same period. This difference is due mainly to the following factors: (1) The net change in the nonfarm housing inventory reflects the reclassification of farm dwellings, as farmland is absorbed in suburban and urban development; (2) the inventory includes temporary dwelling units, shacks, trailers, and dwellings in nonresidential buildings such as factories or warehouses, which are not included in the estimates of housing starts; (3) the periods of the inventory estimates are not fully reconcilable with the calendar-year estimates of new or converted units and of demolitions; (4) minor changes in census definitions; and (5) deficiencies of estimates, particularly for conversions and demolitions. For a reconciliation of the net change in inventory and the various components of change for 1930–1939, see Bureau of Labor Statistics, Serial No. R. 1421, "Housing and the Increase in Population," 1942. For a similar reconciliation for 1940–1949, see Grebler-Blank-Winnick (cited above), appendix A and appendix D, especially table D 4.

N 192, dwelling units standing. Estimates for 1890–1920 are based on David L. Wickens, *Residential Real Estate*, National Bureau of Economic Research, 1941, p. 55. The 1890 and 1900 estimates apply to June 1, the 1910 estimate to April 15, and the 1920 estimate to January 1. The data were derived by dividing Wickens' estimates of nonfarm private families (now termed households) by the occupancy ratios implicit in Wickens' vacancy estimates. The estimate for 1930 applies to April and is based on figures in the Bureau of Labor Statistics Bulletin cited above, p. 12. The 1940 and 1950 figures apply to April 1 and are from the *Sixteenth Census of the United States: 1940, Housing*, vol. II, part 1, p. 10, and *U.S. Census of Housing: 1950*, vol. I, p. 3.

N 193–194, units added during period. For certain periods, the number of "new units" shown for series N 193 varies from the estimated number of permanent dwelling units started as shown for series N 156. Only for 1890–1919 is there exact agreement as both series for this period are based on the same sources using the same concepts and definitions. A slight difference for 1920–1929 is due to varying estimates for the year 1920. The differences for later periods reflect mainly the factors outlined above under (2) and (5).

N 195, units demolished or destroyed during period. The 1940–1949 estimate is designated in the source as a "preliminary estimate by an interdepartmental committee of Federal agencies," but no revision of it was made thereafter.

N 196–199. Nonfarm residential wealth, 1889–1953.

Source: See Grebler-Blank-Winnick source for series N 192–195, table D-1, columns 1, 2, 4, and 5.

Estimates are for housekeeping dwellings, i.e., do not cover transient hotels, clubs, motels, dormitories, and similar facilities. For an alternative estimate of nonfarm residential wealth, see series F 422–469.

N 197–198, structures. The value of structures in 1929 dollars was obtained by adding to an estimate for the end of 1889 annual estimates of net capital formation in constant dollars (shown in table B-8 of the source). The initial estimate for the end of 1889 is based on the average value of owner-occupied nonfarm mortgaged homes reported in the 1890 Census Report, *Real Estate Mortgages* (see pp. 364–365 of the source). The value of structures in current dollars was obtained by adjusting the value in constant dollars by use of the construction cost index given in series N 121 and N 139.

N 199, land. Estimates are based on ratios of land value to total property value, i.e., land and structures, which are estimated to have declined from 40 percent in 1890 to 16.9 percent in 1953, with the move to the suburbs accounting for most of this trend. According to the source (appendix D, p. 364), the ratios are "based on Federal Housing Administration appraisal data and tax assessment data from a number of cities which permit the separation of residential from other real estate. These data do not extend back of the thirties but, together with the bench-mark estimate for the twenties and one for 1907, are sufficient to approximate both the level of the ratio and the direction of the trend." The estimates are fully explained in Louis Winnick, *Wealth Estimates for Residential Real Estate, 1890–1950*, unpublished doctoral dissertation, Columbia University, 1953.

N 200–215. Value of gross and net stocks of residential structures in current and constant (1958) dollars, 1925–1970.

Source: U.S. Bureau of Economic Analysis, *Survey of Current Business*, November 1971, pp. 24–25.

Constant-cost (or "real" or "physical-volume") capital stock

measures are derived by valuing all assets at the prices of a specific period (1958 prices in these series) regardless of their actual prices in the years of original purchase. To calculate constant-cost stocks, the gross investment flows must be expressed in constant prices. This is done by applying appropriate price indexes to the current-dollar investment flows. The constant-cost stock measures the physical volume of residential capital.

Beginning with 1963, the current-dollar residential investment series which are components of the gross national product (GNP) are deflated by the Census Bureau's price index for new 1-family houses. Data for years prior to 1963 are deflated by a privately compiled residential construction cost index.

Estimates of gross stocks were derived by using the perpetual inventory method. This method cumulates past flows of residential investment and deducts the investment discarded from the stock. To illustrate, assume a constant rate of investment of $10 million per year in a new type of residential structure with a life of 40 years. Abstracting from price changes, the gross stock of this type of structure, calculated as the difference between cumulated past investment and cumulated discards, would equal $10 million at the end of year 1, $20 million at the end of year 2, and so on, reaching $400 million at the end of year 40. In succeeding years, the stock would stay at $400 million as annual investment was offset by annual discards. Under this "gross" concept, an asset enters the stock with a specific value and carries that value as long as it is in the stock. In other words, assets in the gross stock are not adjusted for any physical wear and tear or obsolescence which may occur during their lives.

Net stock measures, on the other hand, represent the depreciated value of the capital stock. There is no general agreement as to the correct method of computing economic depreciation, the value of productive services of an asset used up each year. One widely accepted accounting method uses the "straight line" pattern, which assumes equal dollar depreciation each year over the life of the asset. Another important method uses the "declining balance" pattern, which assumes equal percentage depreciation each year over the life of the asset. The annual declining balance depreciation charge for an asset will equal a certain fixed percentage of the net (depreciated) value of the asset at the beginning of the year.

The depreciation method used here to compute the net stock estimates was of the declining balance type. A rate of 2 percent per year was applied to the net value of 1–4 unit structures and 2.4 percent per year to the net value of housekeeping structures with 5 or more units. These rates are consistent with the evidence provided in several studies conducted in the 1930's which shows that depreciation of residential housekeeping structures tended to follow a declining balance formula with the annual rate of depreciation in the neighborhood of 2 percent of the net value.

The depreciation rates used for nonhousekeeping residential structures and mobile homes are higher, because of the shorter service lives involved. For all types of residential capital, the declining balance depreciation rates used in this study are equivalent to roughly $1\frac{1}{2}$ times the first year percentage depreciation under straight line method.

The current-dollar value of the total stock of residential structures increased from $80 billion in 1925 to $800 billion in 1970. About five-sixths of this increase was due to price increases, while about one-sixth represented growth of the real net stock.

Several fairly distinct periods of price change can be identified. In the late 1920's, prices changed little and the increase in the current-dollar net stock was due almost entirely to an increase in the real stock. On the other hand, virtually all of the 25 percent drop in the current-dollar stock from 1929 to 1934 was due to a decrease in the price level, and price increases accounted for virtually all of the doubling in value of the stock between 1934 and 1945.

About three-fourths of the increase in the current-dollar net stock since 1945 has been due to inflation. Price increases were particularly significant in the growth of the stock in the immediate postwar period and in the 1960's, but during the 1950's the growth of the real net stock accounted for 60 percent of the increase in the current-dollar stock.

The Nation's stock of housing has been and continues to be composed predominantly of 1–4 unit structures, most of which are single-family houses. At the end of 1970, private nonfarm 1–4 unit structures accounted for 81 percent of the value of the constant-dollar gross stock of residential structures. Privately owned apartment buildings (structures with 5 or more units) formed the next largest component, accounting for 9 percent of the stock. Farm housing accounted for 4 percent of the stock, while public housing, mobile homes, and private nonhousekeeping residential structures each accounted for about 2 percent.

The annual investment flows used in implementing the perpetual inventory method were those which enter the estimates of the GNP beginning 1929 and are taken from the following sources: *The National Income and Product Accounts of the United States, 1929–65, Statistical Tables,* and July issues of the *Survey of Current Business.*

See also text for series F 470–534.

N 216–231. Mean age of stocks of residential structures, 1925–1970.

Source: See source for series N 200–215.

Information on the age structure of capital stocks is useful in analyzing the condition of the housing stock. Three measures of age structure are presented in the source: The ratio of net to gross stocks, the age distribution of the gross stock, and the average age of gross and net stocks, which is presented here. The net/gross ratios show the extent to which the services available in new residential capital remain intact, while the average age provides information on the absolute ages of gross and net stocks. These two measures can be used interchangeably for many purposes, but each of them also provides specific information. The age distribution of the gross stock shows the proportion of the stock that is of a given age.

The data on the age structure of the gross stock show the effect of the curtailment of residential investment in the depression and World War II years and of the boom in the postwar years. The average age of the gross stock of residential structures increased from 27 years in 1925 to 34 years in 1945. The average age has since declined until in recent years it has approached the level of the late 1920's. The average age of the gross stock of private apartment structures (5 or more units) increased from 15 years in the late 1920's to 26 years by the end of World War II. This trend continued until 1958, when the average age was almost 30 years. As a result of the boom in apartment construction in the 1960's, the average age had declined to 20 years by 1970. In 1970, over half of the gross stock of private apartments had been built in the past ten years. Farm housing, the oldest component of the stock, has steadily increased in age. More than half of the gross stock in 1970 was over 50 years of age.

See also text for series F 470–534 and N 200–215.

N 232–237. Comparison of residential wealth estimates, 1890–1950.

Source: See Grebler-Blank-Winnick source for series N 192–195, table D–3.

There are basically two procedures for estimating residential wealth (as well as other wealth components). One procedure uses a benchmark estimate of wealth in an initial year and adds to it the yearly net capital increments. This procedure yields cumulated wealth estimates, series N 232–234. The other procedure is based on census or similar estimates of wealth at different dates, benchmark wealth estimates, series N 235–237. For a description of the conceptual and estimating problems involved in these two procedures and for the sources of the estimates, see appendix D of the source.

The juxtaposition of wealth estimates derived by various methods indicates clearly the fairly large variations that may result from the employment of these methods, and should caution the user against placing excessive confidence in any particular wealth figures.

N 238–245. Occupied housing units and tenure of homes, 1890–1970.

Source: U.S. Bureau of the Census, 1890–1950, except 1910 and 1945, *U.S. Census of Housing: 1950,* vol. I, part 1, tables J and L; 1945, *Special Census Reports on Housing,* "Characteristics of Occupied Dwelling Units for the United States: November 1945," series H 46, No. 1; 1956, *National Housing Inventory, Components of Change: 1950–1956;* 1960 and 1970, *U.S. Census of Housing: 1960,* vol. I, part 1 and *1970,* vol. I, part 1. The 1910 figure for farm population, series N 239, is an estimate which appears in Leon E. Truesdell, *Farm Population of the United States, 1920,* Census Monographs VI, Washington, D.C., 1926, p. 45. The 1910 figure for nonfarm population was derived by subtracting the estimated farm population from the total population.

The first nationwide census of housing was taken in 1940. In 1940, 1950, 1956, 1960, and 1970, a housing (dwelling) unit was defined in general as the living quarters occupied or intended for occupancy by one household. Figures for 1890 to 1930 rest on the fairly close correspondence between the concept of occupied housing unit used in the housing censuses since 1940 and concepts used in previous censuses of population. Perfect comparability of all the figures in the series is not possible because of various relatively minor changes in definition. The figures for 1890, 1910, and 1920 include the small number of institutions, hotels, military installations, dormitories, etc., which were not included in the counts for any of the other years. For 1940, 1960, and 1970, the count of occupied housing units includes living quarters with five lodgers or more whereas for 1950 and 1956 such living quarters were not included.

For all years, the figures for population per occupied housing unit were obtained by dividing the total population by the number of occupied housing units. The figures for 1950–1970 shown here are not identical with the population per occupied housing unit as shown in the census volumes because the latter figures were derived by dividing the total population living in occupied housing units by the number of occupied units.

The number of occupied housing units is closely comparable to the number of households as shown in series A 288. Since 1950, the number of occupied housing units has been identical by definition to the number of households. The small difference between the number of households and the number of occupied housing units is due to occasional errors in the separate tabulation processes of the census of population and the census of housing. In 1940, small differences existed by definition between the number of occupied housing units and the number of households. The usual occupants of a housing unit who were temporarily away and were enumerated elsewhere were included in the count of households but their housing unit was not considered to be occupied. In addition, a small number of lodginghouses in 1940 (those with 11 or more lodgers) were counted as occupied units, but the heads of these units were not counted as household heads. The figures shown for occupied dwelling units for 1890–1930 are identical to those shown for heads of households in series A 288.

With reference to the farm-nonfarm classification, enumeration of the 1960 and 1970 censuses was conducted primarily through self-enumeration; however, enumerators in the National Housing Inventory of 1956 and the 1950 census were specifically instructed to base the classification of a dwelling unit on the respondent's answer to the question, "Is this house on a farm?" Farm residence was, therefore, determined without regard to the occupation of the members of the household. Housing units located on farmland for which cash rent was paid for the house and yard only, and housing units on institutional grounds and in summer camps and tourist courts, were classed as nonfarm, regardless of the answer to the foregoing question.

For 1960 and 1970, occupied housing units were classified as farm units if they were located on places of 10 or more acres from which sales of farm products amounted to $50 or more in 1959 and 1969, respectively; or on places of less than 10 acres from which sales of farm products amounted to $250 or more in 1959 and 1969, respectively.

For 1930–1950, "farm" consists of rural-farm units only. The classification "rural farm" used in 1950 differs slightly from that used in 1940. As a result, there was, in 1950, an expansion in the urban fringe of cities, tending to reduce the number of farms. On the other hand, in 1940 some areas were classified as urban which were not so classified in 1950. Thus, the differences partly offset each other. In addition, the number of farms was reduced in 1950 by the exclusion of renter-occupied units on farms paying rent for the use of house and yard only.

A housing unit is classified as owner occupied if it is owned wholly or in part by the head of the household or by some related member of his family living in the housing unit. A cooperative or condominium unit is owner occupied only if the owner or co-owner lives in it. All other occupied units are renter occupied whether or not cash rent is actually paid.

N 246–258. Housing units vacancy rates, by region, 1940–1970.

Source: U.S. Bureau of the Census, 1940, *U.S. Census of Housing*, vol. II, part 1, table 28; 1950, *U.S. Census of Housing*, vol. I, part 1, table 17; 1956–1970, Current Housing Reports, *Housing Vacancies*, series H 111, No. 43, tables F and 1 and series H 111-73-5, tables 1 and 4.

A housing unit is vacant if no one is living in it at the time of enumeration, unless its occupants are only temporarily absent. In addition, a vacant unit may be one which is entirely occupied by persons who have a usual residence elsewhere. New units not yet occupied are classified as vacant housing units if construction has reached a point where all exterior windows and doors are installed and final usable floors are in place. Vacant units are excluded if unfit for human habitation, that is, roof, walls, windows or doors no longer protect the interior from the elements, or if there is positive evidence (such as a sign on the house or in the block) that the unit is to be demolished or is condemned. Also excluded are quarters being used entirely for nonresidential purposes, such as a store or an office, or quarters used for storage of business supplies or inventory, machinery, or agricultural products. Vacant sleeping rooms in lodging houses, transient accommodations, barracks, and other quarters not defined as housing units are not included in these series.

Homeowner vacancy rate. The percentage relationship between the vacant units for sale and the total homeowner inventory is termed the homeowner vacancy rate. It is computed by dividing the number of vacant units for sale by the total homeowner units. The total homeowner units comprise owner-occupied units, vacant units sold and awaiting occupancy, and the vacant units for sale. Vacant units that are seasonal or held off the market are excluded. Vacant units for sale that were rated as dilapidated are also excluded.

Rental vacancy rate. The percentage relationship of the vacant units for rent to the total rental inventory is termed the rental vacancy rate. It is computed by dividing the number of vacant units for rent by the total rental units. Total rental units comprise renter-occupied units, vacant units rented but not yet occupied at the time of enumeration, and the vacant units for rent. Excluded are seasonal vacant units, units held off the market, and vacant units rated as dilapidated.

Year-round vacant units are those intended for occupancy at any time of the year, even though they may not be in use the year round. In resort areas, a housing unit which is usually occupied on a year-round basis was considered a year-round unit. On the other hand, a housing unit located in the closely built-up area of a nonresort city was considered a "year-round" unit even though it may be occupied only part of the year.

Seasonal housing units are those intended for occupancy during only a season of the year and are found primarily in resort areas. In farm areas, housing units used for only a portion of the year to house migratory workers employed during the crop season are classified as seasonal.

The enumeration of vacant units in the 1950 Census of Housing was not entirely comparable with the procedures used in 1940 nor with those used in the Current Population Survey to obtain the data for 1956–1970. In 1950, all vacant units, whether or not dilapidated, were included if they were intended for occupancy as living quarters. Where there was little or no demand for housing, many houses were not enumerated because they were used for storage or were abandoned and no longer intended for occupancy as living quarters.

N 259–261. General note.

The development of price indexes for any kind of urban real estate is unusually difficult because of the great heterogeneity of the product and the local nature of real estate markets. The problem of heterogeneity is somewhat less serious in the case of 1-family houses. For a discussion of the conceptual difficulties of using construction cost indexes for measuring price changes for homes and of distinguishing between prices for new and old homes, see Grebler-Blank-Winnick (cited as source for series N 192–195), appendix C. Only a few attempts have been made to measure price changes of urban real estate. For additional data of this type, see Herman Wyngarden, "An Index of Local Real Estate Prices," *Michigan Business Studies*, vol. 1, No. 2, University of Michigan, Bureau of Business Research, 1927; William M. Hoad, *Real Estate Prices, a Study of Residential Real Estate Transfers in Lucas County, Ohio*, unpublished doctoral dissertation, University of Michigan, 1942; and data for Cleveland and Seattle given in Grebler-Blank-Winnick, table C-2. See also Ernest M. Fisher, *Urban Real Estate Markets: Characteristics and Financing*, National Bureau of Economic Research, 1951, pp. 51–56. Beginning 1963, the Bureau of the Census has developed a price index for new 1-family houses sold, including value of lot on a 1967 = 100 base. See U.S. Bureau of Domestic Commerce, *Construction Review*, May 1974, p. 58.

N 259–260. Price indexes for 1-family owner-occupied houses, 1890–1934.

Source: See Grebler-Blank-Winnick source for series N 192–195, tables C-1 and C-3.

Unadjusted figures were derived from detailed information for a sample of residential properties in 22 cities in Department of Commerce, *Financial Survey of Urban Housing, 1937*. This survey, among other things, ascertained the value of the property in 1934, the year of acquisition by the then-present owner, and original cost to the owner at time of acquisition, regardless of whether the house was new or old at that time. From these data, a relative for each year was calculated for each city, based on the ratio of the total acquisition cost of the single-family owner-occupied houses acquired in each given year in a given city to their value in 1934. The unadjusted figures are median relatives derived from the data for all of the 22 cities and are subject to a downward bias due to the changing age structure of properties included in each year's sample, and to an upward bias due to value increments in the form of structural additions and alterations. The adjusted figures are corrected for the resulting net downward bias, by allowing 1⅜ percent compound annual depreciation. See the source, appendix C, for details of correction.

N 261. Median asking price for existing 1-family houses, Washington, D.C., 1918–1947.

Source: Ernest M. Fisher, *Urban Real Estate Markets: Characteristics and Financing*, National Bureau of Economic Research, New York, 1951, table 6 (copyright).

This series represents the results of an experimental study by the National Housing Agency (a predecessor of the U.S. Department of Housing and Urban Development) of a sample of newspaper advertisements. Similar experimental indexes, but for shorter periods, were developed for 100 metropolitan areas. The principal limitations of the study, fully recognized by the originating source, are as follows:

(1) Because of the changing composition of the sample, the type of houses included may vary from period to period. Consequently, fluctuations in median prices may be due either to change in asking prices or to change in the type of houses advertised; (2) because of the omission of houses advertised without listing price and of houses sold without newspaper advertisement, a sizable segment of total sales is not considered in the series; and (3) there may be cyclical differences in the spread between asking prices and selling prices.

N 262–272. Residential nonfarm mortgage debt outstanding, by type of holder, 1890–1970.

Source: 1890–1952, see Grebler-Blank-Winnick source for series N 192–195, tables N-1 and N-2; 1952–1956, Saul B. Klaman, *The Volume of Mortgage Debt in the Postwar Decade: Appraisal and Development of Statistics*, Technical Paper 13, National Bureau of Economic Research, New York, 1958 (copyright); 1956–1970, Board of Governors of the Federal Reserve System, *Federal Reserve Bulletin*, various monthly issues.

The Grebler-Blank-Winnick estimates are based largely on Raymond W. Goldsmith, *A Study of Saving in the United States*, vol. I, Princeton University Press, 1955. Because of the paucity of reliable data, particularly for earlier years, and the consequent employment of ratios found for benchmark years and interpolations or extrapolations, the estimates must be used with caution. The Grebler-Blank-Winnick figures were slightly modified to take account of later revisions by the Federal Home Loan Bank Board (FHLBB) of its estimates of debt on 1- to 4-family houses for 1938–1952; see Federal Home Loan Bank Board, *Estimated Home Mortgage Debt and Financing Activity, 1955* (release, March 1956).

The study by Klaman contains alternative estimates for 1945–1952 which are not entirely comparable with the figures shown here. Because of new information and improved estimating techniques, these data are superior to those in Grebler-Blank-Winnick for overlapping years. The differences reflect mainly lower estimates by Klaman for the mortgage debt on multifamily residences and are fully explained in Klaman's paper. The Klaman paper presents also a comprehensive methodology and a more detailed classification of mortgage debt estimates. See also J. E. Morton, *Urban Mortgage Lending: Comparative Markets and Experience*, Princeton University Press, 1956.

Federal Reserve Board figures are based on data from the Federal Deposit Insurance Corporation, Departments of Agriculture and Commerce, Federal National Mortgage Association, Government National Mortgage Association, Federal Housing Administration, Public Housing Administration, Veterans Administration, Federal Home Loan Mortgage Corporation, Comptroller of the Currency, Federal Home Loan Bank Board, and the Institute of Life Insurance.

N 262, total debt, including real estate bonds. For 1910–1949, the underlying estimates for real estate bonds outstanding on residential property are those of Goldsmith, table R-43. For 1950–1952, figures are estimates based on extrapolation of Goldsmith's data for 1946–1949 for total bonds and assume that 40 percent of these were secured by residential property. This is the ratio applied by Goldsmith for 1910–1949. For the 1890–1909 figures, it was assumed that there were no residential real estate bonds outstanding.

N 263, total debt, excluding real estate bonds. For 1890–1920, figures are based on Goldsmith's estimates of the residential mortgage debt (table R-40) for 1890 and 1920 modified as explained in appendix L of Grebler-Blank-Winnick. The annual estimates between 1890 and 1920 are derived, following Goldsmith's procedures, by interpolating the ratios of nonfarm residential to total nonfarm mortgage debt between the ratios for the two benchmark years. For 1921–1924, figures are those of Goldsmith, derived by interpolation between the 1920 estimate and the 1925 estimate, except that revised FHLBB data for the 1925 debt on 1- to 4-family houses were used. For basis of 1925–1952 figures, see text for series N 273–275 and N 276–277.

N 264–265, noninstitutional and institutional debt. Noninstitu-

tional figures represent the difference between series N 263 and N 265. Institutional figures are the sum of series N 266–272. The estimates for noninstitutional debt are probably the weakest component from the viewpoint of reliability. They represent largely a residual derived from the independent estimates of total debt and those of institutional holdings. Data for 1956–1970 include estimates for insurance companies other than life, mortgage companies, pension funds, credit unions, and installment investment companies.

N 266, debt held by commercial banks. For 1896–1924, figures are based on estimates of total nonfarm mortgages of operating and closed commercial banks shown in Grebler-Blank-Winnick, tables N-10 and N-12, with the 1925 ratio of residential to total nonfarm mortgages for operating banks applied to the entire period. For 1925–1952, figures represent the sum of (1) FHLBB estimates of the holdings of mortgages on 1- to 4-family housing by operating commercial banks, plus those of closed banks (given in Grebler-Blank-Winnick, table N-12), and (2) FHLBB estimates for 1925–1934 and of the Federal Reserve Board for 1935–1952. For 1953–1956, figures are from Klaman, table 4.

N 267, debt held by mutual savings banks. For 1896–1924, figures are based on estimates of total nonfarm mortgages held by mutual savings banks shown in Grebler-Blank-Winnick, table N-8, and on the application of the 1925 ratio of residential to total nonfarm mortgages. For 1925–1938, figures are the sum of (1) FHLBB estimates for mortgages on 1- to 4-family housing and (2) estimates of multifamily residential mortgages based on recent ratios of such mortgages to total nonfarm mortgages other than those on 1- to 4-family housing. For 1939–1952, figures are from *Federal Reserve Bulletin*, March 1954, p. 289 and for 1953–1956, are from Klaman, table 4.

N 268, debt held by savings and loan associations. For 1896–1924, figures are from Goldsmith, table M-4. For most of the period, these estimates are derived by applying to aggregate assets of savings and loan associations the ratio of mortgage loans obtained from a sample of States accounting for nearly two-thirds of aggregate savings and loan assets. For 1925–1950, figures are FHLBB estimates plus the holdings of closed savings and loan associations as given in Grebler-Blank-Winnick, table N-12. For 1951 and 1952, figures are FHLBB estimates.

N 269, debt held by life insurance companies. For 1896–1924, figures are based on estimates of total nonfarm mortgages held by life insurance companies, given in Grebler-Blank-Winnick, table N-9, and application of the 1925 ratio of residential to total holdings. For 1925–1952, figures are the sum of (1) FHLBB estimates of holdings of mortgages on 1- to 4-family houses and (2) estimates of mortgages on multifamily residential property. The latter are from Goldsmith, table M-10, for 1925–1937; from a FHLBB release, *Mortgage Investments of Life Insurance Companies*, 1951, for 1938–1951; and from the Institute of Life Insurance for 1952. For 1953–1956, figures are from Klaman, table 4.

N 270, debt held by the Home Owners' Loan Corporation (HOLC). Figures are from reports of HOLC and include outstandings on both original HOLC loans and on loans originating from the sale of property acquired by HOLC through foreclosure or similar proceedings.

N 271, debt held by the Federal National Mortgage Association (FNMA). Figures are from reports of FNMA and cover all programs of that agency. Under law, only mortgage loans insured by the Federal Housing Administration or guaranteed by the Veterans Administration are eligible for purchase by FNMA. Beginning 1968, "old" FNMA was split between FNMA and the Government National Mortgage Association.

N 272, debt held by other institutions. Figures for 1896–1952 combine data given separately in the source for insurance companies other than life, mortgage companies, and installment investment companies. Figures for 1956–1970, provided by the Federal Reserve Board, include only data for other Federal agencies (Veterans Administration, Federal Housing Administration, Federal National

Mortgage Association, Federal Home Loan Mortgage Corporation, and Government National Mortgage Association (guaranteed pools)).

N 273–275. Residential nonfarm mortgage debt outstanding on 1- to 4-family homes, 1925–1970.

Source: 1925–1955, U.S. Housing and Home Finance Agency, *Annual Report, 1956*, table A-24; 1956–1970, Board of Governors of the Federal Reserve System, *Federal Reserve Bulletin*, various monthly issues.

The total debt on 1- to 4-family structures is estimated by the Federal Home Loan Bank Board (FHLBB) in its annual releases, "Estimated Home Mortgage Debt and Financing Activity." Mainly because such property may be owner occupied, tenant occupied, or vacant, the data are not comparable to census figures on mortgage debt of owner-occupied housing. The estimates are based on reports to FHLBB of savings and loan associations, mortgage investment data reported by life insurance companies, information on mutual savings banks' holdings from call reports and other data collated by FHLBB, similar information collated by the Board of Governors of the Federal Reserve System for commercial banks, financial statements of the Home Owners' Loan Corporation, the Federal National Mortgage Association, and the Government National Mortgage Association, and less reliable information for holdings of individuals and others. The latter group includes mortgages held by trusts and trust departments of commercial banks, pension funds, philanthropic and educational institutions, casualty and fire insurance companies, real estate and mortgage companies, RFC Mortgage Company, Federal Housing Administration (FHA) and Veterans Administration (VA), and individuals. The estimates for holdings of individuals and others are based on residential finance surveys of the Bureau of the Census, trends in nonfarm mortgage recordings, FHA and VA records, and other information. See source for data by type of mortgagee.

The data for government-underwritten mortgages are the outstanding balances of loans insured by FHA and guaranteed by the VA, as estimated by these agencies from their records.

For rough estimates of mortgage debt on 1- to 4-family structures for 1890–1924, see Goldsmith's *A Study of Saving* . . . (cited in text for series N 262–272), vol. I, table R-34.

N 276–277. Residential nonfarm mortgage debt outstanding on 5- or-more unit structures, 1925–1970.

Source: See sources for series N 273–275.

The estimates for total of 5 or more units represent revisions of those in Grebler-Blank-Winnick (see source for series N 192–195), table L-4, which were undertaken by the Board of Governors, Federal Reserve System. Because of these revisions, the sum of series N 273 and N 276 does not equal the totals shown in series N 263.

The data for FHA-insured mortgages are estimates of the Federal Housing Administration based on unpublished data.

N 278–290. General note.

While the annual changes in the amount of residential mortgage debt outstanding, series N 262–277, indicate the net flow of funds, measures of the gross flow of funds are useful for many purposes. However, these measures are far from adequate. For estimates of the gross flow of funds into *new* residential construction for 1911–1955, see Grebler-Blank-Winnick series N 192–195, appendix M and table 80.

N 278–284. Mortgage loans on 1- to 4-family houses, by type of lender, 1925–1950.

Source: See Grebler-Blank-Winnick source for series N 192–195, table N-13. (Figures are from Federal Home Loan Bank Board, *Estimated Home Mortgage Debt and Lending Activity, 1950.*)

These series represent only rough approximations except for the

Home Owners' Loan Corporation and for savings and loan associations since the late thirties. The estimates were based on scattered reports of national and State supervisory authorities, special reports to the Home Loan Bank Board by life insurance companies, and, for 1939–1950, on mortgage recordings figures, series N 285–290. Estimates for the earlier years, and for "individuals and others" throughout, are highly tentative.

N 285–290. Mortgage recordings of $20,000 or less, by type of lender, 1939–1964.

Source: Federal Home Loan Bank Board, *Savings and Home Financing Source Book*, annual issues.

Estimates are computed on the basis of monthly reports of co-operating institutions. These reports cover approximately 500 areas containing about 54 percent of the total nonfarm 1-family housing units. Activity in the remaining areas is estimated usually by reference to the closest reporting area. To relate the series as closely as possible to home-financing operations, it is limited to mortgages of $20,000 or less, but it includes small mortgages secured by non-residential real estate and omits large mortgages secured by residences.

The *Savings and Home Financing Source Book, 1966*, contains the following: "Since almost every mortgage is recorded, the series provides an adequate means of determining trends in real estate financing activity, as well as the role being played by various types of lenders. Summaries are made on the basis of the originating mortgagees, and, for this reason, assignments of mortgages are not reflected in the series. To the extent that certain lenders (e.g., insurance companies) purchase mortgages originated and recorded by other lenders (e.g., mortgage companies), the recording statistics may overstate or understate the importance of a particular type of lender as the ultimate source of mortgage credit. It should also be pointed out that mortgage recording data are not directly comparable with estimates on home mortgage lending; the periods covered are not necessarily the same, because lending statistics are reported as of the date of loan commitment, while recording figures reflect the actual date of mortgage registration. Furthermore, alterations in the terms of an existing contract may necessitate a new registration. In the case of refinancing an institution's own mortgage, for example, the face amount of the instrument would appear in the recording totals, whereas only that portion which represented an increase of funds loaned would be included in the lending figures."

N 291–300. Major Federal housing finance programs, 1934–1970.

Source: **Series N 291–297** and **N 300**, 1934–1970 (except N 297, 1950–1970), see source for series N 273–275, Real Estate Credit section. **Series N 297**, 1950–1964, Housing and Home Finance Agency, *Annual Report, 1964*, table B-72; 1965–1970, U.S. Veterans Administration, unpublished data. **Series N 298–299**, Federal National Mortgage Association, unpublished data.

The figures are based on records of the Federal Housing Administration (FHA), Veterans Administration (VA), Federal National Mortgage Association (FNMA), Federal Home Loan Bank Board (FHLBB), and Government National Mortgage Association (GNMA).

N 291–296, loans made with FHA insurance. Figures are from FHA. Homes include 1- to 4-family houses. Projects include multifamily housing. Under law, only new multifamily projects are eligible for FHA-insured mortgage loans, although such projects are later eligible for refinancing loans. For the FHA classification of new and existing houses, see text for series N 180–181.

N 297, loans made with VA guaranty. Figures are from VA and show the total principal amount of loans, not the guaranteed portion which is smaller. In addition to the loans made by private lenders under its guaranty program, the VA has made direct loans for home purchase to veterans in certain areas since fiscal year 1951. The cumulative amount of direct loans disbursed through December 31, 1970, was $3 billion.

N 298–299, FNMA purchases and sales. Figures are from FNMA and include all its programs. Beginning 1954, FNMA established three independent portfolios of FNMA-owned mortgages with separate accountability. The three portfolios resulted from separate operations predicated on different purposes and objectives: (1) Secondary market operations, basically a privately financed activity; (2) special assistance functions, operated for the account of the government; and (3) management and liquidating functions, under which the FNMA managed and operated for the government the portfolio of mortgages acquired since 1938 under the FHA. Beginning 1968, FNMA separated into two organizations, the Government National Mortgage Association, which maintains the special assistance functions and the management and liquidating functions portfolios; and the "new" FNMA which maintains the secondary market operation portfolio.

N 300, advances outstanding of the Federal Home Loan Banks. Figures are from FHLBB and represent advances to member institutions of the Federal Home Loan Bank System, mainly savings and loan associations.

N 301. Real estate foreclosures of nonfarm properties, 1926–1970.

Source: Federal Home Loan Bank Board, *Savings and Home Financing Source Book*, annual issues.

Estimates for the old series are based on reports for approximately 1,700 counties, cities, townships, or other governmental divisions in 1968. The reporting areas include approximately three-fifths of all nonfarm single-family housing units. Foreclosures in the remaining areas are estimated usually by reference to the closest reporting area. Figures represent the number of nonfarm properties, residential and nonresidential, acquired by mortgage lenders through foreclosure proceedings; they do not include voluntary transfers to such lenders in lieu of foreclosure, or defaults on real estate contracts.

Foreclosure estimates consist of completed foreclosures—those that result in a sale or final action.

N 302–307. Mortgage status of nonfarm owner-occupied housing units, 1890–1970.

Source: **Series N 302–306,** U.S. Bureau of the Census, 1890–1950, *U.S. Census of Housing: 1950*, vol. I, part 1; 1956, *National Housing Inventory, 1956*, vol. II; and 1960 and 1970, *U.S. Census of Housing: 1960*, vol. V, and *1970*, vol. V, respectively. **Series N 307,** 1890–1950, see Grebler-Blank-Winnick source for series N 192–195, table 59 (based on census data for value and debt); 1956, 1960, and 1970, same as for series N 302–306.

For 1940, 1950, 1956, 1960, and 1970, the mortgage statistics are for owner-occupied housing units in 1- to 4-family housing unit structures without business. For 1890–1920, they are for owner-occupied units in all types of structures. These differences are not large enough to invalidate comparisons.

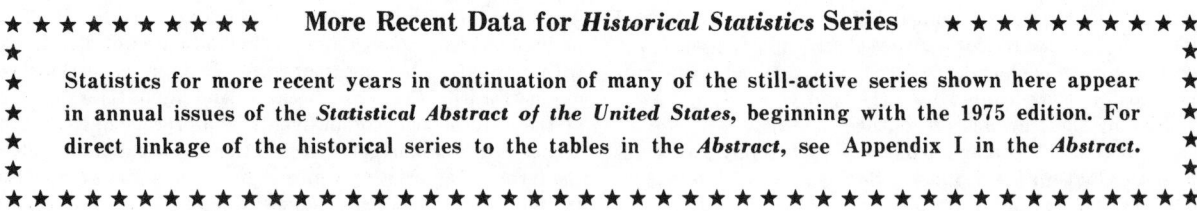

★ ★ ★ ★ ★ ★ ★ ★ ★   **More Recent Data for *Historical Statistics* Series**   ★ ★ ★ ★ ★ ★ ★ ★ ★
★   ★
★   Statistics for more recent years in continuation of many of the still-active series shown here appear   ★
★   in annual issues of the *Statistical Abstract of the United States*, beginning with the 1975 edition. For   ★
★   direct linkage of the historical series to the tables in the *Abstract*, see Appendix I in the *Abstract*.   ★
★   ★
★ ★

Series N 156–169. New Housing Units Started, by Ownership, Type of Structure, Location, and Construction Cost: 1889 to 1970

Year	New housing units started (1,000)								Construction cost (mil. dol.)			Construction cost, average per unit (dol.)		
	Total	Ownership		In structures with—			Inside SMSA's [1]	Outside SMSA's [1]	Total	Privately owned	Publicly owned	Total	Privately owned	Publicly owned
		Private	Public	1 unit	2 units	3 units or more								
	156	157	158	159	160	161	162	163	164	165	166	167	168	169
INCLUDES FARM HOUSING														
1970	1,469	1,434	35	815	48	606	1,035	435	22,655	22,148	507	15,450	15,450	15,200
1969	1,500	1,467	33	811	48	640	1,097	403	23,292	22,807	485	15,525	15,550	14,700
1968	1,545	1,508	38	900	54	591	1,116	429	23,153	22,622	531	14,975	15,000	14,050
1967	1,322	1,292	30	845	48	429	920	402	19,072	18,674	397	14,425	14,450	13,100
1966	1,196	1,165	31	780	41	376	809	387	16,969	16,575	394	14,175	14,225	12,625
1965	1,510	1,473	37	965	58	486	1,035	475	20,528	20,061	466	13,600	13,625	12,625
1964	1,561	1,529	32	972	62	527	1,098	463	20,375	19,975	400	13,050	13,075	12,450
1963	1,635	1,603	32	1,013	61	561	1,147	487	20,756	20,378	378	12,650	12,650	11,925
1962	1,492	1,463	30	996	56	440	1,054	439	18,720	18,373	347	12,550	12,550	11,700
1961	1,365	1,313	52	989	50	326	948	417	17,085	16,476	609	12,525	12,550	11,725
1960	1,296	1,252	44	1,009	51	237	889	407	16,357	15,831	528	12,625	12,650	12,025
1959	1,554	1,517	37	1,251	59	244	1,077	477	19,214	18,782	432	12,400	12,400	11,775
EXCLUDES FARM HOUSING														
1962	1,469	1,439	30	973	56	440	1,053	416	18,400	18,053	347	12,525	12,550	11,700
1961	1,337	1,285	52	961	50	326	946	391	16,740	16,132	609	12,525	12,550	11,725
1960	1,274	1,230	44	987	51	237	888	386	16,124	15,596	528	12,650	12,675	12,025
1959	1,531	1,495	37	1,229	59	244	1,076	455	18,981	18,549	432	12,400	12,400	11,775
(columns 162/163 headed:)							Urban areas	Rural nonfarm areas						
1958	1,382	1,314	68	-----	-----	-----	-----	-----	16,565	15,744	821	12,000	11,975	12,075
1957	1,224	1,175	49	-----	-----	-----	-----	-----	14,913	14,346	567	12,175	12,225	11,550
1956	1,349	1,325	24	-----	-----	-----	-----	-----	15,781	15,519	262	11,700	11,725	10,825
1955	1,646	1,627	19	-----	-----	-----	-----	-----	18,017	17,818	199	10,950	10,950	10,225
1954	1,551	1,532	19	-----	-----	-----	-----	-----	15,863	15,694	169	10,225	10,250	9,050
1953	1,438	1,402	36	-----	-----	-----	-----	-----	13,665	13,358	307	9,500	9,525	8,650
1952	1,504	1,446	58	-----	-----	-----	-----	-----	13,636	13,133	503	9,050	9,075	8,600
1951	1,491	1,420	71	-----	-----	-----	-----	-----	13,402	12,787	615	8,975	9,000	8,625
1950	1,952	1,908	44	-----	-----	-----	-----	-----	16,481	16,111	370	8,450	8,450	8,450
1949	1,466	1,430	36	-----	-----	-----	-----	-----	10,992	10,663	329	7,525	7,450	9,050
1948	1,362	1,344	18	-----	-----	-----	-----	-----	10,514	10,340	174	7,725	7,700	9,625
1947	1,268	1,265	3	-----	-----	-----	-----	-----	8,430	8,404	26	6,650	6,650	7,650
1946	1,023	1,015	8	-----	-----	-----	-----	-----	5,746	5,690	56	5,625	5,600	7,000
1945	326	325	1	-----	-----	-----	-----	-----	1,504	1,498	6	4,625	4,625	5,350
1944	142	139	3	118	11	14	96	46	496	483	13	3,500	3,475	4,125
1943	191	184	7	144	18	30	124	67	689	660	29	3,600	3,600	3,925
1942	356	301	55	293	20	43	227	129	1,344	1,134	210	3,775	3,775	3,825
1941	706	620	87	604	34	68	434	272	2,826	2,531	295	4,000	4,075	3,400
1940	603	530	73	486	37	80	397	206	2,299	2,072	227	3,825	3,925	3,125
1939	515	458	57	399	29	87	359	156	1,948	1,764	184	3,775	3,850	3,250
1938	406	399	7	317	18	71	262	144	1,584	1,562	22	3,900	3,900	3,325
1937	336	332	4	267	16	53	218	118	1,382	1,366	17	4,125	4,100	4,600
1936	319	304	15	244	14	61	211	108	1,271	1,194	77	3,975	3,925	5,225
1935	221	216	5	183	8	30	117	104	757	732	25	3,425	3,400	4,700

[1] SMSA = Standard Metropolitan Statistical Area.

Series N 156–169.   New Housing Units Started, by Ownership, Type of Structure, Location, and Construction Cost: 1889 to 1970—Con.

Year	New housing units started (1,000)						Construction cost	
	Total	In structures with—			Urban areas	Rural nonfarm areas	Total (mil. dol.)	Average per unit (dol.)
		1 unit	2 units	3 units or more				
	156	159	160	161	162	163	164	167
EXCLUDES FARM HOUSING—Con.								
1934	126	109	5	12	49	77	368	2,925
1933	93	76	5	12	45	48	285	3,075
1932	134	118	7	9	64	70	407	3,050
1931	254	187	22	45	174	80	1,105	4,350
1930	330	227	29	74	236	94	1,494	4,525
1929	509	316	51	142	400	109	2,453	4,825
1928	753	436	78	239	594	159	3,613	4,800
1927	810	454	99	257	643	167	3,910	4,825
1926	849	491	117	241	681	168	4,112	4,850
1925	937	573	157	208	752	185	4,475	4,775
1924	893	534	173	186	716	177	4,065	4,550
1923	871	513	175	183	698	173	3,775	4,325
1922	716	437	146	133	574	142	2,957	4,125
1921	449	316	70	63	359	90	1,771	3,950
1920	247	202	24	21	196	51	1,068	4,325
1919	315	239	36	40	230	85	1,258	4,000
1918	118	91	13	14	86	32	391	3,325
1917	240	166	31	43	175	65	769	3,200
1916	437	267	69	101	319	118	1,255	2,875
1915	433	262	73	98	316	117	1,192	2,750
1914	421	263	72	86	308	113	1,081	2,575
1913	421	264	72	85	307	114	1,108	2,625
1912	426	258	71	97	311	115	1,113	2,625
1911	395	249	62	84	288	107	1,000	2,525
1910	387	251	57	79	283	104	1,028	2,650
1909	492	328	73	91	322	170	1,272	2,575
1908	416	286	65	65	272	144	1,034	2,475
1907	432	291	59	82	283	149	1,037	2,400
1906	487	316	69	102	319	168	1,170	2,400
1905	507	336	64	107	332	175	1,154	2,275
1904	315	207	45	63	206	109	690	2,200
1903	253	175	30	48	166	87	607	2,400
1902	240	171	32	37	157	83	572	2,375
1901	275	177	32	66	180	95	610	2,225
1900	189	123	31	35	124	65	433	2,300
1899	282	--------	--------	--------	159	123	608	2,150
1898	262	--------	--------	--------	148	114	574	2,200
1897	292	--------	--------	--------	165	127	643	2,200
1896	257	--------	--------	--------	145	112	606	2,350
1895	309	--------	--------	--------	175	134	679	2,200
1894	265	--------	--------	--------	150	115	594	2,250
1893	267	--------	--------	--------	151	116	583	2,175
1892	381	--------	--------	--------	215	166	763	2,000
1891	298	--------	--------	--------	169	129	612	2,050
1890	328	--------	--------	--------	185	143	790	2,400
1889	342	--------	--------	--------	193	149	806	2,350

Series N 170.   Mobile Home Shipments: 1947 to 1970

Year	Mobile home shipments	Year	Mobile home shipments	Year	Mobile home shipments	Year	Mobile home shipments	Year	Mobile home shipments
	170		170		170		170		170
1970	401,190	1965	216,470	1960	103,700	1955	111,900	1950	63,100
1969	412,690	1964	191,320	1959	120,500	1954	76,000	1949	46,200
1968	317,950	1963	150,840	1958	102,000	1953	76,900	1948	85,500
1967	240,360	1962	118,000	1957	119,300	1952	83,000	1947	60,000
1966	217,300	1961	90,200	1956	124,330	1951	67,300		

Series N 171–179.   New Publicly-Owned Housing Starts, by Ownership and Program: 1949 to 1970

[In units]

Year	All public programs	Federally owned			State and locally owned				
		Total	Military	All other	Total	Federally aided (PHA)		New York City Housing Authority (excluding federally aided)	All other
						Total	New York City Housing Authority		
	171	172	173	174	175	176	177	178	179
1970	35,363	2,873	2,814	59	32,490	28,848	2,309	–	3,642
1969	32,779	4,010	3,977	33	28,769	26,958	1,486	–	1,811
1968	37,802	4,690	4,597	93	33,112	31,020	1,298	225	1,867
1967	30,329	3,470	3,199	271	26,859	25,303	2,005	1,333	223
1966	30,942	289	31	258	30,653	28,721	1,290	440	1,492
1965	36,907	4,686	4,432	254	32,221	30,077	3,061	96	2,048
1964	33,264	4,580	–	4,580	28,684	22,712	1,033	1,335	4,637
1963	31,758	3,181	–	3,181	28,577	23,970	4,328	874	3,733
1962	29,653	4,363	2,532	1,831	25,290	19,781	3,581	2,562	2,947
1961	52,001	14,047	13,153	894	37,954	28,190	4,522	5,263	4,501
1960	43,897	13,801	13,182	619	30,096	26,533	4,203	771	2,792
1959 *	36,690	14,999	14,590	409	21,691	13,860	2,003	3,966	3,865
1958	67,907	36,312	34,667	1,645	31,595	19,970	1,102	6,319	5,306
1957	49,103	25,518	23,642	1,876	23,585	17,473	2,856	2,762	3,350
1956	24,236	8,752	3,783	4,969	15,484	4,794	981	5,189	5,501
1955	19,596	5,012	----	5,012	14,584	8,572	3,916	3,870	2,142
1954	18,638	246	----	246	18,392	14,155	2,289	3,656	581
1953	35,483	104	----	104	35,379	31,314	2,246	2,955	1,110
1952	58,520	622	----	622	57,898	52,747	5,862	1,731	3,420
1951	71,207	1,060	----	1,060	70,147	65,201	2,641	1,436	3,510
1950	43,648	1,055	----	1,055	42,593	26,875	5,259	4,399	11,319
1949	36,321	3,963	----	3,963	32,358	781	----	19,660	11,917

* Denotes first year for which figures include Alaska and Hawaii.   – Represents zero.

Series N 180–185.   Privately Owned Housing Units in Major Federal Programs: 1935 to 1970

[In thousands.   FHA = Federal Housing Administration; VA = Veterans Administration]

Year	New privately owned units started under [1]—		New and existing privately owned units covered by loans			
	FHA inspection	VA inspection	FHA (mortgages insured)			VA (mortgages guaranteed)
			Total	Homes	Rental projects	
	180	181	182	183	184	185
1970	432.8	61.0	716	515	201	168
1969	240.5	51.2	576	495	81	214
1968	227.1	56.1	529	453	76	211
1967	179.7	52.5	453	412	41	201
1966	158.4	36.8	469	436	33	157
1965	196.6	49.4	591	554	37	163
1964	204.6	59.2	557	503	54	186
1963	221.0	71.0	476	423	53	211
1962	259.5	77.8	469	405	64	188
1961	243.6	83.3	435	376	59	134
1960	260.9	74.6	422	373	49	145
1959	332.5	109.3	549	505	44	213
1958	295.4	102.1	454	389	65	146
1957	168.4	128.3	245	202	43	307
1956	2 189.3	270.7	264	253	11	508
1955	276.7	392.9	328	318	9	650
1954	276.3	307.0	251	223	28	411
1953	252.0	156.5	303	272	31	322
1952	279.9	141.3	286	246	40	307
1951	263.5	148.6	335	261	74	447
1950	486.7	191.2	506	352	155	498
1949	363.8	90.8	453	320	133	277
1948	294.1	71.1	400	321	79	350
1947	229.0	160.3	197	150	47	542
1946	69.0	91.8	88	86	2	412
1945	41.2	8.8	107	103	4	3 43

Year	New privately owned units started under FHA inspection [1]	New and existing privately owned units covered by FHA loans (mortgages insured)		
		Total	Homes	Rental projects
	180	182	183	184
1944	93.3	170	157	12
1943	146.2	210	190	20
1942	165.7	242	236	6
1941	220.4	220	216	4
1940	180.1	187	183	4
1939	158.1	185	171	13
1938	118.7	134	122	12
1937	60.0	114	111	3
1936	49.4	85	84	1
1935	14.0	26	25	1

[1] Based on first compliance inspection.   Includes homes and housing units in multi-family projects; excludes mobile homes and non-housing unit activity.
[2] Excludes 2,567 Capehart units.
[3] Estimated.

Series N 186–191.　Low-Rent Public Housing Units, by Progress Stage, and War and Defense Housing and Veterans Housing Units Available for Occupancy: 1941 to 1970

[Low-rent public housing units cover those units subsidized by U.S. Department of Housing and Urban Development under annual contributions contracts, including new, conventional, and turnkey units and existing housing either acquired or leased.　Includes Puerto Rico and Virgin Islands]

Year	Low-rent public housing (1,000)[1]				Year	Low-rent public housing (1,000)[1]				War and defense housing available for occupancy[4]	Veterans re-use housing available for occupancy[4]
	Total	Under management[2]	Under construction	Not under construction[3]		Total	Under management[2]	Under construction	Not under construction[3]		
	186	187	188	189		186	187	188	189	190	191
1970	1,155.3	893.5	126.8	135.0	1955[5]	489.7	413.6	21.1	55.1	109	---
1969	1,034.7	822.6	84.8	127.4	1954	455.7	390.1	33.4	32.2	3,441	---
1968	923.7	744.5	73.5	105.7	1953	455.2	343.8	61.5	50.0	6,559	---
1967	850.2	673.2	48.8	128.2	1952	436.8	271.3	87.6	77.9	5,577	---
1966	778.2	635.9	45.6	96.7	1951	404.8	211.3	90.6	102.9	---	---
1965	735.7	604.9	42.4	88.4	1950[5]	302.1	201.7	31.5	68.9	---	381
1964	714.3	576.7	38.5	99.0	1949	204.9	191.6	1.7	11.5	---	695
1963	682.3	553.4	37.4	91.5	1948	193.8	190.9	1.5	1.4	1,550	27,168
1962	646.6	527.2	41.1	78.4	1947	192.0	189.7	.1	2.1	---	106,631
1961	624.1	499.0	47.4	77.7	1946	---	---	---	---	4,051	128,871
1960	593.3	478.2	36.4	78.8	1945	---	---	---	---	40,171	1,906
1959	585.2	465.2	23.9	96.1	1944	---	---	---	---	150,327	---
1958	557.2	444.2	30.0	83.0	1943	---	---	---	---	347,404	---
1957	534.6	429.5	24.0	81.1	1942	---	---	---	---	120,729	---
1956	533.6	423.9	14.0	95.7	1941	---	---	---	---	59,786	---

[1] As of December 31.
[2] Occupied or available for occupancy.
[3] Comprises units to be constructed and units that will go directly into "under management" category because they need no rehabilitation.
[4] Refers to period between completion of construction and actual occupancy.
[5] Excludes units which have been sold to mutual housing associations, limited dividend corporations (PWA), and homestead associations on which HUD has mortgages for collection.

Series N 192–195.　Nonfarm Dwelling Units Standing and Selected Components of Change: 1890 to 1950

[In thousands]

Year	Dwelling units standing	Year	Dwelling units standing	Period	Units added		Units demolished or destroyed	Period	Units added		Units demolished or destroyed
					New units started	Converted units			New units started	Converted units	
	192		192		193	194	195		193	194	195
1950	39,625	1910	14,281	1940–1949	5,393	2,000	1,000	1910–1919	3,593	103	414
1940	29,683	1900	10,589	1930–1939	2,646	1,070	397	1900–1909	3,606	81	297
1930	25,692	1890	8,319	1920–1929	7,004	125	580	1890–1899	2,941	62	208
1920	17,733										

Series N 196–199.　Nonfarm Residential Wealth: 1889 to 1953

[In millions of dollars]

Year	Total, current dollars	Structures		Land, current dollars	Year	Total, current dollars	Structures		Land, current dollars	Year	Total, current dollars	Structures		Land, current dollars
		1929 dollars	Current dollars				1929 dollars	Current dollars				1929 dollars	Current dollars	
	196	197	198	199		196	197	198	199		196	197	198	199
1953	282,751	96,933	234,966	47,785	1931	96,761	80,724	72,571	24,190	1910	38,337	48,499	25,801	12,536
1952	270,918	94,173	224,320	46,598						1909	36,369	47,406	24,367	12,002
1951	257,833	91,575	212,454	45,379	1930	105,430	80,775	78,756	26,674	1908	33,977	45,715	22,629	11,348
					1929	108,429	80,563	80,563	27,866	1907	34,255	44,378	22,677	11,578
1950	233,623	88,855	191,571	42,052	1928	102,438	78,938	75,702	26,736	1906	31,971	43,085	21,069	10,902
1949	212,430	84,951	173,555	38,875	1927	98,639	75,939	72,598	26,041					
1948	214,358	82,790	174,273	40,085	1926	95,999	72,519	70,271	25,728	1905	28,118	41,385	18,416	9,702
1947	188,396	80,556	152,412	35,984						1904	25,739	39,425	16,756	8,983
1946	153,140	78,974	123,278	29,862	1925	90,802	68,715	66,104	24,698	1903	25,494	38,418	16,520	8,974
					1924	86,633	64,818	62,809	23,824	1902	24,256	37,640	15,621	8,635
1945	137,348	78,178	110,153	27,195	1923	83,501	61,245	60,204	23,297	1901	23,116	36,892	14,794	8,322
1944	130,960	79,111	104,506	26,454	1922	71,329	58,316	51,143	20,186					
1943	122,450	80,219	97,225	25,225	1921	74,791	55,976	53,401	21,390	1900	22,936	35,984	14,610	8,326
1942	118,922	81,230	94,064	24,858						1899	21,607	35,525	13,677	7,930
1941	113,548	81,535	89,362	24,186	1920	92,155	55,122	65,430	26,715	1898	19,703	34,522	12,393	7,310
					1919	72,163	55,317	50,947	21,216	1897	18,387	33,459	11,510	6,877
1940	104,102	80,149	81,512	22,590	1918	61,972	55,008	43,566	18,406	1896	18,103	32,080	11,260	6,843
1939	99,264	79,006	77,426	21,838	1917	52,987	55,613	37,038	15,949					
1938	96,831	78,028	75,140	21,690	1916	45,527	55,510	31,641	13,886	1895	17,403	30,816	10,755	6,648
1937	94,297	77,692	72,797	21,500						1894	16,867	29,301	10,373	6,494
1936	84,770	77,420	65,188	19,582	1915	41,986	54,306	29,054	12,932	1893	16,833	28,024	10,285	6,548
					1914	40,251	53,051	27,693	12,558	1892	16,257	26,814	9,868	6,389
1935	81,314	77,273	62,205	19,109	1913	39,401	51,927	26,950	12,451	1891	15,742	25,087	9,508	6,234
1934	84,669	77,724	64,433	20,236	1912	40,063	50,711	27,283	12,780	1890[1]	15,540	23,786	9,324	6,216
1933	79,100	78,685	59,958	19,142	1911	38,417	49,539	26,008	12,409	1889	14,333	22,050	8,600	5,733
1932	80,537	79,796	60,725	19,812										

[1] As of June 1.

Series N 200–215. Value of Gross and Net Stocks of Residential Structures in Current and Constant (1958) Dollars: 1925 to 1970

[In billions of dollars]

Year	Gross stocks of residential structures								Net stocks of residential structures							
	Total, all types	Private nonfarm		Public		Farm	Private non-house-keeping	Mobile homes	Total, all types	Private nonfarm		Public		Farm	Private non-house-keeping	Mobile homes
		1–4 unit	5 or more unit	Federal	State and local					1–4 unit	5 or more unit	Federal	State and local			
	200	201	202	203	204	205	206	207	208	209	210	211	212	213	214	215
CURRENT DOLLARS																
1970	1,284.7	1,050.2	111.1	8.5	20.5	50.5	27.9	16.0	804.2	661.6	72.2	5.3	14.9	24.7	15.9	9.6
1969	1,197.3	983.4	100.3	8.0	18.9	47.7	25.6	13.4	749.5	620.0	65.1	5.0	13.8	23.0	14.6	8.0
1968	1,094.4	903.3	88.4	7.4	16.7	44.3	23.4	10.9	682.6	567.9	56.4	4.7	12.3	21.6	13.4	6.3
1967	1,010.6	836.5	79.0	6.9	15.3	42.6	21.2	9.1	633.3	529.5	49.6	4.5	11.3	21.2	12.1	5.1
1966	941.8	782.1	72.5	6.5	13.9	39.5	19.4	7.9	593.0	497.1	45.2	4.3	10.4	20.5	11.1	4.4
1965	888.9	739.8	67.0	6.2	12.8	39.5	16.7	6.9	559.7	470.2	41.4	4.2	9.7	20.3	10.0	3.9
1964	848.0	707.2	62.2	5.9	12.1	38.4	16.3	5.9	533.1	450.1	37.7	4.1	9.3	19.7	8.9	3.3
1963	807.5	675.1	57.2	5.8	11.2	38.3	14.9	5.0	505.1	428.5	33.7	4.0	8.7	19.6	7.9	2.7
1962	765.7	641.3	52.2	5.6	10.6	38.0	13.6	4.4	477.6	407.0	29.8	3.9	8.4	19.3	6.9	2.3
1961	731.6	614.1	48.2	5.3	9.6	37.9	12.6	3.9	453.4	389.2	26.7	3.7	7.7	18.1	6.0	2.0
1960	713.5	600.8	45.6	4.9	9.0	37.7	11.9	3.6	440.9	380.4	24.6	3.5	7.1	18.1	5.3	1.9
1959	689.0	579.8	43.9	4.6	8.5	37.6	11.4	3.2	424.4	366.8	23.4	3.3	6.9	18.0	4.7	1.8
1958	645.1	540.9	41.6	4.0	7.9	37.2	10.8	2.7	395.4	340.6	21.9	2.8	6.5	17.9	4.2	1.5
1957	618.4	517.7	40.1	3.6	7.2	37.0	10.5	2.3	376.7	324.3	21.0	2.5	6.0	17.8	3.8	1.3
1956	593.7	496.0	39.0	3.4	6.8	36.4	10.2	1.9	359.4	308.6	20.4	2.3	5.8	17.7	3.6	1.0
1955	556.7	463.4	37.4	3.2	6.4	35.0	9.8	1.5	335.5	286.5	19.7	2.3	5.4	17.6	3.3	.7
1954	517.1	427.7	35.7	3.1	5.8	34.0	9.5	1.3	308.3	261.1	18.9	2.3	5.2	17.1	3.1	.6
1953	498.8	410.5	35.1	3.1	5.4	34.0	9.5	1.2	293.9	247.5	18.8	2.3	4.8	17.0	3.0	.5
1952	486.8	398.1	35.0	3.1	5.9	34.0	9.7	1.0	283.7	237.9	18.8	2.3	4.5	16.7	3.0	.5
1951	465.0	378.6	34.0	3.0	5.2	33.8	9.6	.8	268.0	223.5	18.5	2.4	3.8	16.4	3.0	.4
1950	428.4	347.8	32.1	2.9	3.4	32.2	9.3	.7	244.5	202.8	17.6	2.3	3.1	15.4	2.9	.4
1949	386.2	312.0	29.6	2.7	3.0	29.4	8.9	.6	216.4	177.8	16.2	2.2	2.6	14.5	2.8	.3
1948	369.3	297.8	28.5	2.7	2.5	28.5	8.8	.5	205.2	167.7	15.5	2.2	2.3	14.4	2.8	.3
1947	342.6	274.4	26.8	2.6	2.4	27.5	8.6	.3	187.9	152.1	14.6	2.2	2.2	13.9	2.7	.2
1946	286.7	228.8	22.9	2.4	1.7	23.3	7.5	.1	155.9	125.3	12.6	2.1	1.5	11.9	2.4	.1
1945	243.4	194.8	19.9	2.3	1.0	18.9	6.5	(Z)	132.3	105.9	11.1	2.1	.9	10.2	2.1	(Z)
1944	226.2	181.3	18.5	2.0	1.0	17.2	6.2	--------	124.9	99.7	10.6	1.9	.9	9.7	2.1	--------
1943	211.5	168.2	17.2	1.7	1.8	16.8	5.8	--------	117.3	93.9	10.0	1.6	.8	8.9	2.1	--------
1942	195.1	155.4	15.8	.9	1.7	15.8	5.5	--------	108.9	88.0	9.4	.8	.8	7.9	2.0	--------
1941	179.3	144.3	14.7	.5	.5	14.2	5.1	--------	101.2	82.4	8.9	.4	.6	6.9	2.0	--------
1940	162.9	131.3	13.5	.2	.3	12.9	4.7	--------	91.7	74.9	8.3	.2	.3	6.1	1.9	--------
1939	151.4	121.7	12.6	.2	.1	12.3	4.5	--------	85.0	69.4	7.8	.2	.1	5.7	1.8	--------
1938	146.4	117.5	12.1	.2	(Z)	12.3	4.3	--------	82.4	67.2	7.6	.2	(Z)	5.6	1.8	--------
1937	142.3	114.0	11.8	.2	--------	12.1	4.2	--------	80.9	65.6	7.5	.2	--------	5.8	1.8	--------
1936	132.2	105.9	10.9	.1	--------	11.3	4.0	--------	76.0	61.4	7.0	.1	--------	5.8	1.7	--------
1935	121.8	97.5	10.0	(Z)	--------	10.6	3.7	--------	70.9	57.0	6.6	(Z)	--------	5.6	1.7	--------
1934	119.3	95.4	9.8	(Z)	--------	10.5	3.6	--------	70.2	56.4	6.6	(Z)	--------	5.5	1.7	--------
1933	114.2	91.2	9.4	--------	--------	10.2	3.4	--------	68.0	54.7	6.4	--------	--------	5.2	1.7	--------
1932	109.1	86.9	9.0	--------	--------	9.9	3.3	--------	65.9	53.0	6.3	--------	--------	4.9	1.7	--------
1931	122.2	97.1	10.1	--------	--------	11.3	3.7	--------	75.1	60.1	7.2	--------	--------	5.6	2.2	--------
1930	140.5	111.6	11.5	--------	--------	13.2	4.2	--------	87.3	69.7	8.4	--------	--------	6.8	2.4	--------
1929	147.4	117.1	12.0	--------	--------	14.0	4.3	--------	92.8	73.8	8.9	--------	--------	7.6	2.5	--------
1928	143.6	113.8	11.3	--------	--------	14.4	4.1	--------	90.7	72.1	8.4	--------	--------	7.8	2.4	--------
1927	136.3	108.1	10.1	--------	--------	14.4	3.7	--------	86.0	68.5	7.5	--------	--------	7.8	2.2	--------
1926	131.6	105.3	8.2	--------	--------	14.6	3.5	--------	83.2	66.6	6.6	--------	--------	7.9	2.1	--------
1925	127.8	101.7	8.2	--------	--------	14.8	3.1	--------	79.5	64.0	5.8	--------	--------	7.9	1.8	--------
CONSTANT (1958) DOLLARS																
1970	870.3	707.2	74.8	5.8	13.7	34.0	18.8	16.0	544.6	445.5	48.6	3.6	10.0	16.6	10.7	9.6
1969	843.3	688.7	70.1	5.7	13.0	34.2	18.2	13.4	526.9	433.3	45.5	3.6	9.4	16.7	10.4	8.0
1968	823.2	676.5	66.1	5.6	12.3	34.3	17.5	10.9	514.5	426.6	42.2	3.6	9.0	16.8	10.0	6.3
1967	802.2	662.0	62.5	5.6	11.7	34.5	16.8	9.1	502.2	419.0	39.2	3.6	8.8	16.9	9.6	5.1
1966	786.4	650.7	60.3	5.6	11.1	34.7	16.1	7.9	492.3	412.1	37.6	3.7	8.4	16.9	9.2	4.4
1965	769.6	638.5	57.8	5.5	10.7	34.9	15.3	6.9	482.2	405.1	35.7	3.7	8.2	17.0	8.6	3.9
1964	749.5	623.5	54.9	5.4	10.3	35.1	14.4	5.9	469.2	396.1	33.3	3.7	7.9	17.0	7.9	3.3
1963	729.7	609.1	51.6	5.3	9.9	35.3	13.5	5.0	455.7	387.0	30.5	3.7	7.7	17.0	7.1	2.7
1962	709.5	594.2	48.4	5.2	9.6	35.5	12.6	4.0	441.5	376.8	27.7	3.6	7.7	17.0	6.4	2.3
1961	690.5	579.6	45.5	5.0	8.9	35.7	11.9	3.9	427.5	367.0	25.2	3.5	7.2	17.0	5.6	2.0
1960	679.5	572.0	43.6	4.7	8.4	35.8	11.4	3.6	419.6	362.0	23.5	3.3	6.8	17.1	5.0	1.9
1959	663.8	559.0	42.3	4.4	8.0	35.9	11.0	3.2	408.1	352.3	22.5	3.2	6.5	17.2	4.6	1.8
1958	634.7	532.8	41.0	3.9	7.6	36.0	10.7	2.7	388.0	334.5	21.6	2.8	6.2	17.3	4.1	1.5
1957	618.0	518.2	40.2	3.6	7.1	36.0	10.5	2.4	375.1	323.2	21.0	2.5	5.9	17.4	3.8	1.3
1956	601.2	502.9	39.6	3.4	6.8	36.1	10.4	2.0	363.9	312.9	20.7	2.4	5.7	17.5	3.6	1.1
1955	583.9	486.5	39.3	3.4	6.5	36.2	10.4	1.6	350.8	300.3	20.7	2.4	5.6	17.6	3.4	.8
1954	564.8	468.2	38.9	3.4	6.2	36.3	10.4	1.4	333.8	283.5	20.7	2.5	5.4	17.7	3.4	.6
1953	546.1	450.1	38.6	3.4	5.8	36.4	10.5	1.3	320.8	270.8	20.6	2.5	5.2	17.8	3.3	.6
1952	530.0	435.0	38.2	3.4	5.2	36.5	10.6	1.1	309.0	259.5	20.6	2.6	4.7	17.8	3.3	.5
1951	515.3	421.3	38.0	3.4	4.5	36.5	10.7	.9	298.2	249.1	20.6	2.6	4.2	17.9	3.4	.4

Z Less than $0.05 billion.

Series N 200–215. Value of Gross and Net Stocks of Residential Structures in Current and Constant (1958) Dollars: 1925 to 1970—Con.

[In billions of dollars]

Year	Gross stocks of residential structures								Net stocks of residential structures							
	Total, all types	Private nonfarm		Public		Farm	Private non-house-keeping	Mobile homes	Total, all types	Private nonfarm		Public		Farm	Private non-house-keeping	Mobile homes
		1–4 unit	5 or more unit	Federal	State and local					1–4 unit	5 or more unit	Federal	State and local			
	200	201	202	203	204	205	206	207	208	209	210	211	212	213	214	215
	CONSTANT (1958) DOLLARS—Con.															
1950	500.1	406.8	37.6	3.4	4.0	36.6	10.9	0.8	285.6	237.4	20.6	2.7	3.6	17.5	3.4	0.4
1949	480.2	388.1	36.8	3.4	3.7	36.5	11.0	.7	268.5	221.5	20.1	2.8	3.2	17.0	3.5	.4
1948	466.2	375.3	35.9	3.4	3.5	36.4	11.1	.6	256.9	211.1	19.5	2.8	3.1	16.5	3.5	.4
1947	451.6	361.6	35.3	3.4	3.3	36.3	11.3	.4	247.4	201.8	19.3	2.9	3.0	16.5	3.6	.3
1946	439.4	350.1	35.0	3.7	2.7	36.3	11.4	.2	237.9	192.4	19.3	3.3	2.4	16.6	3.7	.2
1945	434.5	346.0	34.9	4.0	1.8	36.3	11.4	.1	231.7	186.0	19.5	3.7	1.6	17.0	3.8	.1
1944	434.2	345.3	35.0	3.9	1.8	36.5	11.7	--------	235.1	188.7	20.0	3.6	1.6	17.2	4.0	--------
1943	433.9	345.0	35.1	3.5	1.8	36.6	11.9	--------	239.0	191.9	20.5	3.3	1.6	17.5	4.2	--------
1942	432.3	344.7	35.1	2.0	1.7	36.7	12.1	--------	241.2	194.8	20.8	1.9	1.6	17.6	4.5	--------
1941	429.9	343.3	35.0	1.1	1.2	37.1	12.2	--------	241.8	195.9	21.2	1.1	1.2	17.7	4.7	--------
1940	422.9	337.3	34.7	.6	.7	37.4	12.2	--------	237.8	192.7	21.3	.6	.7	17.7	4.8	--------
1939	417.0	332.4	34.4	.6	.2	37.2	12.2	--------	234.5	189.9	21.3	.6	.2	17.6	4.9	--------
1938	411.6	327.9	33.9	.6	(Z)	37.1	12.1	--------	232.3	187.8	21.2	.6	(Z)	17.7	5.0	--------
1937	408.2	324.9	33.6	.5	--------	37.1	12.1	--------	232.2	187.3	21.4	.5	--------	17.8	5.2	--------
1936	404.6	322.0	33.2	.2	--------	37.1	12.1	--------	231.8	187.0	21.4	.2	--------	17.9	5.3	--------
1935	401.6	319.5	32.9	(Z)	--------	37.2	12.0	--------	232.2	187.0	21.6	(Z)	--------	18.1	5.5	--------
1934	400.5	318.3	32.9	(Z)	--------	37.3	12.0	--------	234.3	188.3	22.0	(Z)	--------	18.3	5.7	--------
1933	400.7	318.3	32.9	--------	--------	37.5	12.0	--------	237.9	190.9	22.5	--------	--------	18.6	5.9	--------
1932	400.8	318.3	32.9	--------	--------	37.6	12.0	--------	242.1	193.9	23.0	--------	--------	19.0	6.2	--------
1931	400.6	317.9	32.9	--------	--------	37.8	12.0	--------	245.6	196.3	23.5	--------	--------	19.3	6.5	--------
1930	397.4	315.1	32.5	--------	--------	37.9	11.9	--------	246.8	196.9	23.6	--------	--------	19.6	6.7	--------
1929	392.9	311.5	32.0	--------	--------	37.9	11.5	--------	247.0	197.0	23.6	--------	--------	19.7	6.7	--------
1928	384.8	305.8	30.4	--------	--------	37.7	10.9	--------	242.9	194.2	22.5	--------	--------	19.8	6.4	--------
1927	373.0	297.3	27.9	--------	--------	37.5	10.3	--------	235.1	188.7	20.5	--------	--------	19.8	6.1	--------
1926	360.1	288.2	25.1	--------	--------	37.3	9.5	--------	226.1	182.6	18.1	--------	--------	19.8	5.6	--------
1925	346.3	278.2	22.5	--------	--------	37.2	8.4	--------	215.5	174.8	15.9	--------	--------	19.9	4.9	--------

Z Less than $0.05 billion.

Series N 216–231. Mean Age of Stocks of Residential Structures: 1925 to 1970

[In years]

Year	Gross stocks of residential structures								Net stocks of residential structures							
	Total, all types	Private nonfarm		Public		Farm	Private non-house-keeping	Mobile homes	Total, all types	Private nonfarm		Public		Farm	Private non-house-keeping	Mobile homes
		1–4 unit	5 or more unit	Federal	State and local					1–4 unit	5 or more unit	Federal	State and local			
	216	217	218	219	220	221	222	223	224	225	226	227	228	229	230	231
1970	27.6	27.7	19.7	21.1	13.9	49.0	11.5	4.2	18.7	19.1	12.2	18.5	11.9	35.1	7.1	2.8
1969	27.6	27.5	20.4	20.4	13.7	49.1	11.5	4.2	18.6	18.9	12.6	17.8	11.8	35.3	6.8	2.7
1968	27.6	27.4	21.3	19.7	13.4	49.1	11.6	4.3	18.6	18.7	13.3	17.3	11.7	35.4	6.6	2.8
1967	27.7	27.4	22.0	18.9	13.0	49.0	11.9	4.4	18.6	18.6	13.8	16.5	11.4	35.5	6.4	2.9
1966	27.7	27.3	22.4	18.0	12.7	49.0	12.2	4.3	18.5	18.4	14.0	15.6	11.2	35.6	6.2	2.9
1965	27.7	27.2	23.1	17.2	12.3	48.8	12.8	4.2	18.4	18.3	14.6	14.9	10.9	35.6	6.2	2.8
1964	27.9	27.3	24.0	16.6	11.7	48.7	13.6	4.1	18.5	18.2	15.4	14.5	10.4	35.5	6.3	2.8
1963	28.1	27.4	25.3	15.9	11.2	48.5	14.6	4.1	18.6	18.2	16.7	13.8	10.0	35.4	6.6	2.8
1962	28.3	27.5	26.8	15.3	10.7	48.3	15.9	4.1	18.7	18.2	18.5	13.3	9.5	35.4	7.1	2.8
1961	28.5	27.6	27.9	14.9	10.5	48.2	16.9	3.9	18.9	18.3	20.0	13.0	9.4	35.4	7.7	2.7
1960	28.7	27.7	28.8	14.7	10.2	48.0	18.0	3.6	19.0	18.3	21.2	13.0	9.2	35.4	8.4	2.5
1959	28.9	27.8	29.2	14.6	9.7	47.8	19.0	3.4	19.1	18.3	22.0	13.2	8.8	35.2	9.2	2.3
1958	29.2	28.2	29.5	15.3	9.3	47.5	19.9	3.4	19.4	18.6	22.7	14.4	8.5	35.0	10.1	2.2
1957	29.4	28.4	29.5	15.8	8.9	47.0	20.7	3.4	19.6	18.8	23.0	15.4	8.2	34.9	11.1	2.0
1956	29.6	28.6	29.3	15.5	8.4	47.0	21.2	3.5	19.8	18.9	23.1	15.4	7.7	34.7	11.9	2.0
1955	30.0	29.0	29.0	14.5	7.8	46.8	21.6	3.8	20.1	19.3	22.8	14.5	7.2	34.7	12.9	2.2
1954	30.5	29.6	28.6	13.6	7.1	46.6	21.8	4.0	20.7	19.7	22.6	13.5	6.5	34.5	13.6	2.5
1953	30.9	30.1	28.2	12.5	6.6	46.4	21.9	3.8	21.1	20.5	22.4	12.5	6.0	34.6	14.2	2.5
1952	31.3	30.6	27.8	11.6	6.3	46.3	21.8	3.6	21.6	20.9	22.1	11.6	5.8	34.7	14.7	2.4
1951	31.6	31.0	27.4	10.6	6.3	46.2	21.6	3.3	22.0	21.5	21.8	10.6	5.8	34.9	14.9	2.5
1950	32.1	31.5	27.0	9.6	6.4	46.2	21.3	2.8	22.7	22.1	21.5	9.6	6.0	35.2	15.1	2.3
1949	32.8	32.4	27.0	8.6	6.0	46.2	21.1	2.3	23.7	23.3	21.8	8.6	5.7	35.6	15.2	1.9
1948	33.2	32.9	27.0	7.7	5.6	46.0	20.8	1.6	24.4	24.1	22.2	7.7	5.4	36.2	15.4	1.4
1947	33.7	33.5	26.9	6.5	4.7	46.5	20.4	1.2	25.2	25.0	22.4	6.5	4.5	36.9	15.5	1.1
1946	34.1	33.9	26.6	5.1	4.3	46.5	20.0	.8	25.9	25.9	22.3	5.0	4.2	37.4	15.3	.7
1945	34.2	34.1	26.1	3.8	4.6	46.4	19.7	.5	26.4	26.4	21.9	3.6	4.6	37.7	15.5	.5
1944	33.6	33.5	25.3	2.9	3.6	45.6	19.1	--------	25.7	25.8	21.1	2.8	3.6	36.7	14.9	--------
1943	33.0	32.9	24.5	2.1	2.7	44.8	18.4	--------	25.1	25.2	20.3	2.0	2.6	35.8	14.2	--------
1942	32.5	32.2	23.7	2.4	1.8	44.1	17.7	--------	24.6	24.5	19.5	2.3	1.8	34.9	13.4	--------
1941	32.1	31.8	23.0	2.8	1.2	43.5	17.2	--------	24.3	24.1	18.8	2.6	1.2	34.2	12.9	--------

Series N 216–231. Mean Age of Stocks of Residential Structures: 1925 to 1970—Con.

[In years]

Year	Gross stocks of residential structures							Net stocks of residential structures						
	Total, all types	Private nonfarm		Public		Farm	Private non-house-keeping	Total, all types	Private nonfarm		Public		Farm	Private non-house-keeping
		1–4 unit	5 or more unit	Federal	State and local				1–4 unit	5 or more unit	Federal	State and local		
	216	217	218	219	220	221	222	224	225	226	227	228	229	230
1940	32.0	31.7	22.4	3.7	0.8	43.0	16.7	24.4	24.3	18.3	3.7	0.8	33.8	12.6
1939	31.9	31.6	21.9	2.8	.6	42.4	16.3	24.4	24.3	17.8	2.7	.6	33.2	12.3
1938	31.6	31.4	21.4	1.8	.5	42.0	15.8	24.3	24.3	17.4	1.8	.5	33.0	12.0
1937	31.3	31.0	20.8	1.0	-------	41.6	15.4	24.0	24.0	16.8	1.0	-------	32.6	11.6
1936	30.9	30.6	20.2	.7	-------	41.2	14.9	23.7	23.7	16.2	.7	-------	32.3	11.2
1935	30.4	30.2	19.5	.6	-------	40.8	14.3	23.4	23.3	15.5	.6	-------	31.8	10.7
1934	29.9	29.6	18.7	.5	-------	40.3	13.7	22.8	22.8	14.7	.5	-------	31.4	10.1
1933	29.2	28.9	17.9	-------	-------	39.7	13.0	22.1	22.1	13.8	-------	-------	30.7	9.4
1932	28.5	28.2	17.0	-------	-------	39.0	12.4	21.4	21.4	12.9	-------	-------	30.0	8.7
1931	27.8	27.5	16.1	-------	-------	38.4	11.7	20.6	20.7	12.0	-------	-------	29.3	7.9
1930	27.3	27.0	15.4	-------	-------	37.8	11.0	20.1	20.2	11.3	-------	-------	28.7	7.2
1929	26.8	26.5	14.8	-------	-------	37.4	10.7	19.6	19.7	10.6	-------	-------	28.2	6.8
1928	26.6	26.2	14.7	-------	-------	37.0	10.4	19.5	19.5	10.4	-------	-------	27.9	6.5
1927	26.6	26.2	15.0	-------	-------	36.6	10.3	19.6	19.6	10.7	-------	-------	27.6	6.3
1926	26.8	26.3	15.8	-------	-------	36.3	10.4	19.9	19.8	11.4	-------	-------	27.4	6.3
1925	27.0	26.4	16.7	-------	-------	35.9	10.8	20.2	20.1	12.3	-------	-------	27.0	6.7

Series N 232–237. Comparison of Residential Wealth Estimates: 1890 to 1950

[In billions of current dollars. June and April figures are for the first day of the month; December figures, last day of the month; where month is not specified, the specific date was not available. These estimates were compiled from the various sources shown in the footnotes]

Date	Cumulated wealth estimates			Date	Benchmark wealth estimates		
	Total	Structures	Land		Total	Structures	Land
	232	233	234		235	236	237
1949 December	212.5	173.6	38.9	1950 April [1]	260.0	(NA)	(NA)
1939 December	99.2	77.4	21.8	1940 April [2]	87.4	(NA)	(NA)
1938 December	96.8	75.1	21.7	1938 [3]	92.0	44.0	48.0
1929 December	108.5	80.6	27.9	1930 [3]	107.7	51.6	56.1
				1930 April [4]	99.0	46.8	52.2
1922 December	71.3	51.1	20.2	1930 April [5]	122.6	98.1	24.5
1912 December	40.1	27.3	12.8	1922 [3]	65.0	30.0	34.9
1900 December	22.9	14.6	8.3	1912 June [6]	39.2	20.7	18.5
1890 June	15.0	9.0	6.0	1900 June [6]	20.0	9.5	10.5
				1890 June [6]	14.4	6.7	7.7

NA   Not available.
[1] Derived from Census of Housing, 1950, Preliminary Reports, series HC–5, No. 1.
[2] Housing—Special Reports, Bureau of the Census, series H–1943, No. 1.
[3] Robert R. Doane, *The Anatomy of Wealth*, Harper, 1940.

[4] E. A. Keller, *A Study of the Physical Assets, Sometimes Called Wealth of the United States, 1922–1933*, University of Notre Dame Press, 1939.
[5] David L. Wickens, *Residential Real Estate*, NBER, 1941.
[6] Simon Kuznets, *National Product since 1869*, NBER, 1946.

Series N 238–245. Occupied Housing Units and Tenure of Homes: 1890 to 1970

Year [1]	Total occupied housing units (1,000)	Total population		Occupied units reporting tenure (1,000)	Tenure of homes			
		Number of persons (1,000)	Per occupied housing unit		Owner occupied		Renter occupied	
					Number (1,000)	Percent	Number (1,000)	Percent
	238	239	240	241	242	243	244	245
TOTAL								
1970[2]	63,450	203,211	3.2	63,450	39,885	62.9	23,565	37.1
1960*	53,024	179,326	3.4	53,024	32,796	61.9	20,227	38.1
1956[3]	49,874	(NA)	(NA)	49,874	30,121	60.4	19,753	39.6
1950	42,826	150,697	3.5	42,826	23,560	55.0	19,266	45.0
1945[3]	37,600	140,186	3.7	37,600	20,009	53.2	17,591	46.8
1940	34,855	131,669	3.8	34,855	15,196	43.6	19,659	56.4
1930	29,905	122,775	4.1	29,322	14,002	47.8	15,320	52.2
1920	24,353	105,711	4.3	23,811	10,867	45.6	12,944	54.4
1910	20,256	91,972	4.5	19,782	9,084	45.9	10,698	54.1
1900	15,964	75,995	4.8	15,429	7,205	46.7	8,224	53.3
1890	12,690	62,948	5.0	12,690	6,066	47.8	6,624	52.2
NONFARM								
1970[2]	60,351	192,624	3.2	60,351	37,393	62.0	22,957	38.0
1960*	49,458	165,851	3.4	49,458	30,164	61.0	19,294	39.0
1950	37,105	127,649	3.4	37,105	19,802	53.4	17,304	46.6
1945[3]	31,281	(NA)	(NA)	31,281	15,878	50.8	15,403	49.2
1940	27,748	101,453	3.7	27,748	11,413	41.1	16,335	58.9
1930	23,300	92,618	4.0	22,917	10,550	46.0	12,367	54.0
1920	17,600	74,096	4.2	17,229	7,041	40.9	10,188	59.1
1910	14,132	[4]59,895	[4]4.2	13,672	5,245	38.4	8,427	61.6
1900	10,274	------	------	9,780	3,567	36.5	6,213	63.5
1890	7,923	------	------	7,923	2,924	36.9	4,999	63.1
FARM								
1970[2]	3,095	10,589	3.4	3,095	2,492	80.5	603	19.5
1960*	3,566	13,475	3.8	3,566	2,633	73.8	933	26.2
1950	5,721	23,049	4.0	5,721	3,758	65.7	1,963	34.3
1945[3]	6,319	(NA)	(NA)	6,319	4,131	65.4	2,188	34.6
1940	7,107	30,216	4.3	7,107	3,783	53.2	3,324	46.8
1930	6,605	30,158	4.6	6,405	3,452	53.9	2,953	46.1
1920	6,751	31,614	4.7	6,581	3,826	58.1	2,755	41.9
1910	6,124	[4]32,077	[4]5.2	6,110	3,838	62.8	2,271	37.2
1900	5,690	------	------	5,649	3,638	64.4	2,011	35.6
1890	4,767	------	------	4,767	3,143	65.9	1,624	34.1

* Denotes first year for which figures include Alaska and Hawaii.
NA   Not available.
[1] Figures for 1956 are for December 31; figures for 1945 are for November 1; figures for decennial years, 1890 to 1970, are for census dates.

[2] Farm-nonfarm breakdown will not add to total; "Total" figures were revised as a result of errors found after the tabulations were completed.
[3] These figures are not comparable with other years; based on sample surveys.
[4] Estimated; see text.

Series N 246–258. Housing Units Vacancy Rates, by Region: 1940 to 1970

[In percent. Annual averages, except as noted. For composition of regions, see text for series A 172–194]

Year	All housing units vacancy rate			Homeowner vacancy rate					Rental vacancy rate				
	Total	Year-round vacancy	Seasonal vacancy	United States	Northeast	North Central	South	West	United States	Northeast	North Central	South	West
	246	247	248	249	250	251	252	253	254	255	256	257	258
1970	8.8	6.3	2.5	1.0	0.8	1.0	1.2	1.1	5.3	2.7	5.8	7.2	5.6
1969	9.1	6.5	2.6	1.0	.8	.9	1.2	1.2	5.5	3.0	5.7	7.2	6.1
1968	9.3	6.7	2.6	1.1	.8	1.0	1.4	1.3	5.9	3.7	5.4	7.5	7.1
1967	9.9	7.2	2.7	1.3	.7	1.0	1.7	2.0	6.8	4.8	5.7	8.0	8.9
1966	10.3	7.5	2.8	1.4	.9	1.0	1.8	2.1	7.7	5.3	6.5	8.5	10.9
1965	10.5	7.6	2.9	1.5	1.0	1.2	2.0	1.9	8.3	5.6	7.2	9.0	11.9
1964	10.3	7.3	3.0	1.5	1.1	1.3	1.9	1.8	8.3	5.2	7.9	9.1	11.0
1963	10.3	7.2	3.1	1.5	1.0	1.4	1.9	1.9	8.3	5.1	8.7	9.2	10.2
1962	10.1	7.4	2.7	1.4	1.1	1.2	1.7	1.6	8.1	4.7	9.0	9.9	9.5
1961	10.2	7.6	2.6	1.4	1.1	1.2	1.7	1.3	8.7	4.9	9.3	10.4	10.7
1960*	10.1	7.4	2.7	1.3	1.0	1.2	1.6	1.4	8.1	4.9	8.3	9.5	11.0
1959	10.0	7.0	3.0	1.2	1.0	1.1	1.2	1.4	7.0	3.9	7.1	9.4	8.5
1958	9.9	6.7	3.2	1.2	1.0	1.4	1.0	1.2	6.5	3.8	7.3	7.9	7.5
1957	9.1	6.2	2.9	1.0	.7	.9	.9	1.3	5.6	3.4	5.4	6.7	7.4
1956	8.8	6.2	2.6	1.0	.9	.8	1.0	1.4	6.1	3.1	5.6	8.1	8.7
1950[1]	6.9	4.4	2.5	.9									
1940[1]	6.6	4.5	2.0										

* Denotes first year for which figures include Alaska and Hawaii.   [1] As of April.

Series N 259-261. Price Indexes for 1-Family Houses: 1890 to 1947

Year	Owner-occupied houses, 22 cities (1929 = 100)		Median asking price for existing houses, Washington, D.C.	Year	Owner-occupied houses, 22 cities (1929 = 100)		Median asking price for existing houses, Washington, D.C.	Year	Owner-occupied houses, 22 cities (1929 = 100)		Year	Owner-occupied houses, 22 cities (1929 = 100)	
	Unadjusted	Adjusted for depreciation			Unadjusted	Adjusted for depreciation			Unadjusted	Adjusted for depreciation		Unadjusted	Adjusted for depreciation
	259	260	261		259	260	261		259	260		259	260
1947			$12,309	1932	78.7	82.0	$6,515	1917	80.1	68.0	1903	64.9	45.5
1946			12,638	1931	87.9	90.4	6,796	1916	78.5	65.8	1902	63.9	42.4
											1901	54.2	37.0
1945			10,131	1930	95.7	97.1	7,146	1915	71.7	59.2			
1944			8,649	1929	100.0	100.0	7,246	1914	78.1	63.7	1900	64.6	43.5
1943			8,011	1928	102.1	100.7	7,333	1913	75.3	60.5	1899	56.5	37.5
1942			7,573	1927	100.6	97.9	7,682	1912	75.3	59.7	1898	59.1	38.7
1941			6,954	1926	104.5	100.4	7,748	1911	72.5	56.7	1897	55.5	35.9
											1896	53.8	34.3
1940			6,558	1925	108.9	103.1	7,809	1910	74.2	57.3			
1939			6,416	1924	103.5	96.7	7,720	1909	68.7	52.3	1895	62.1	39.0
1938			6,420	1923	103.3	95.2	7,400	1908	70.3	52.8	1894	68.4	42.4
1937			6,622	1922	101.8	92.5	7,197	1907	77.9	37.7	1893	58.7	35.9
1936			6,145	1921	100.4	90.0	7,019	1906	70.6	51.6	1892	56.3	34.0
											1891	55.3	32.9
1935			6,296	1920	102.7	90.8	6,296	1905	59.5	42.9			
1934	77.9	78.3	5,972	1919	93.7	81.7	5,626	1904	67.9	48.3	1890	61.3	36.0
1933	75.7	80.0	5,759	1918	85.2	73.3	4,821						

Series N 262-272. Residential Nonfarm Mortgage Debt Outstanding, by Type of Holder: 1890 to 1970

[In millions of dollars]

Year	Total debt, including real estate bonds	Debt, excluding real estate bonds									
		Total	Non-institutional	Institutional							
				Total	Commercial banks	Mutual savings banks	Savings and loan associations	Life insurance companies	Home Owners' Loan Corp.	Federal National Mortgage Assn. [1]	Other
	262	263	264	265	266	267	268	269	270	271	272
1970		338,198	35,733	302,465	45,640	49,936	138,800	42,737		20,708	4,644
1969		318,984	34,361	284,623	44,573	48,682	129,658	42,083		15,797	3,830
1968		298,587	32,688	265,899	41,433	46,748	120,839	41,784		11,420	3,675
1967		279,970	31,119	248,851	37,642	44,641	112,804	41,480		8,912	3,372
1966		263,952	30,062	233,890	34,876	42,242	106,028	40,522		7,109	3,113
1965		250,120	29,445	220,675	32,387	40,096	102,347	38,400		4,769	2,676
1964		231,142	28,673	202,469	28,933	36,487	94,236	35,761		4,464	2,588
1963		211,229	27,244	183,985	26,476	32,718	84,882	32,674		4,729	2,506
1962		192,295	25,898	166,397	23,482	29,181	74,103	31,122		6,032	2,477
1961		175,895	24,564	151,331	21,225	26,341	65,447	29,899		6,216	2,203
1960		161,636	22,493	139,143	20,362	24,306	57,569	28,744		6,297	1,865
1959		149,522	21,120	128,402	20,320	22,486	51,187	27,249		5,581	1,579
1958		134,535	19,701	114,834	18,591	20,935	44,122	25,921		3,937	1,328
1957		122,947	17,757	105,190	17,147	19,010	38,885	24,992		4,011	1,145
1956 [2]		113,880	16,707	97,173	17,004	17,703	34,761	23,745		3,085	875
1956 [3]	112,051	(NA)	(NA)	(NA)	17,004	17,703	35,014	23,745		3,047	(NA)
1955	100,670	(NA)	(NA)	(NA)	15,888	15,568	30,832	21,213		2,615	(NA)
1954	87,280	(NA)	(NA)	(NA)	14,152	13,211	25,670	18,557		2,436	(NA)
1953	77,117	(NA)	(NA)	(NA)	12,925	11,334	21,523	16,558		2,463	(NA)
1952 [3]	68,878	(NA)	(NA)	(NA)	12,188	9,883	18,028	15,045		2,242	(NA)
1952 [4]	69,561	69,121	10,990	58,131	12,188	9,883	17,590	15,112		2,210	1,198
1951	62,506	62,026	10,604	51,422	11,270	8,595	14,801	13,865		1,818	1,073
1950	54,882	54,362	10,422	43,938	10,431	7,054	13,104	11,035	10	1,328	978
1949	46,456	45,896	10,461	35,435	8,676	5,569	11,117	8,232	231	806	804
1948	41,461	40,861	10,189	30,672	8,066	4,758	9,841	6,754	369	198	686
1947	35,701	[5] 35,071	9,689	25,382	6,933	3,937	8,475	5,005	486	4	542
1946	30,139	29,459	8,809	20,650	5,146	3,588	6,843	4,021	636	6	410
1945	25,383	24,643	7,874	16,769	3,395	3,387	5,162	3,632	852	7	334
1944	24,820	24,000	7,348	16,652	3,218	3,476	4,638	3,819	1,091	50	360
1943	24,956	24,056	7,181	16,875	3,256	3,558	4,422	3,835	1,338	60	406
1942	25,647	24,667	7,316	17,351	3,335	3,725	4,449	3,625	1,567	206	444
1941	25,915	24,875	7,462	17,413	3,308	3,884	4,481	3,235	1,777	203	525
1940	24,930	23,810	7,278	16,532	2,997	3,914	4,073	2,887	1,956	178	527
1939	23,940	22,740	7,156	15,584	2,719	3,875	3,748	2,557	2,038	144	503
1938	23,326	22,046	7,105	14,941	2,535	3,830	3,523	2,226	2,169	80	578
1937	23,284	21,924	7,089	14,835	2,415	3,851	3,414	2,163	2,398		594
1936	23,435	21,915	6,967	14,948	2,285	3,897	3,257	2,142	2,763		604
1935	23,891	22,211	6,984	15,227	2,225	3,984	3,301	2,200	2,897		620
1934	24,811	22,811	7,377	15,434	2,183	4,109	3,749	2,370	2,379		644
1933	25,464	23,083	8,356	14,727	2,528	4,293	4,473	2,626	132		675
1932	27,438	24,918	9,208	15,710	2,561	4,554	5,020	2,854			721
1931	29,293	26,673	9,940	16,733	2,769	4,568	5,704	2,948			744

See footnotes at end of table.

647

Series N 262–272. Residential Nonfarm Mortgage Debt Outstanding, by Type of Holder: 1890 to 1970—Con.

[In millions of dollars]

Year	Total debt, including real estate bonds	Debt, excluding real estate bonds							
		Total	Non-institutional	Institutional					
				Total	Commercial banks	Mutual savings banks	Savings and loan associations	Life insurance companies	Other
	262	263	264	265	266	267	268	269	272
1930	30,176	27,649	10,629	17,020	2,844	4,388	6,149	2,878	761
1929	29,440	27,001	10,350	16,651	2,896	4,135	6,182	2,704	734
1928	27,238	24,958	9,301	15,657	2,805	4,016	5,757	2,406	673
1927	24,358	22,491	8,379	14,112	2,508	3,700	5,214	2,088	602
1926	21,500	19,956	7,409	12,547	2,319	3,349	4,570	1,775	534
1925	18,393	17,231	6,469	10,762	1,858	3,037	3,994	1,408	465
1924	15,514	14,794	5,360	9,434	1,621	2,756	3,519	1,132	406
1923	13,446	12,924	4,940	7,984	1,323	2,437	2,917	946	361
1922	11,441	11,080	4,283	6,797	1,055	2,167	2,468	788	319
1921	10,273	10,017	4,041	5,976	860	1,945	2,179	698	294
1920	9,354	9,120	3,846	5,274	800	1,782	1,860	558	274
1919	7,998	7,809	3,129	4,680	733	1,613	1,552	549	233
1918	7,555	7,407	3,031	4,376	651	1,535	1,387	578	225
1917	7,210	7,082	2,836	4,246	621	1,554	1,293	563	215
1916	6,495	6,387	2,391	3,996	580	1,501	1,175	541	199
1915	6,104	6,012	2,222	3,790	566	1,416	1,098	522	188
1914	5,800	5,724	2,118	3,606	520	1,362	1,013	531	180
1913	5,389	5,329	1,907	3,422	493	1,331	930	499	169
1912	4,933	4,881	1,659	3,222	485	1,264	847	469	157
1911	4,690	4,644	1,643	3,001	461	1,184	768	439	149
1910	4,466	4,426	1,634	2,792	445	1,111	690	403	143
1909	4,168	4,168	1,598	2,570	408	1,042	628	361	131
1908	3,948	3,948	1,586	2,362	357	974	575	334	122
1907	3,795	3,795	1,565	2,230	337	925	538	316	114
1906	3,676	3,676	1,584	2,092	328	885	487	287	105
1905	3,520	3,520	1,600	1,920	293	822	448	254	103
1904	3,341	3,341	1,567	1,774	251	768	423	238	94
1903	3,194	3,194	1,539	1,655	221	727	394	223	90
1902	3,102	3,102	1,543	1,559	195	694	378	207	85
1901	3,011	3,011	1,535	1,476	173	658	367	194	84
1900	2,917	2,917	1,493	1,424	158	632	371	183	80
1899	2,835	2,835	1,466	1,369	148	595	376	172	78
1898	2,783	2,783	1,430	1,353	144	570	396	169	74
1897	2,746	2,746	1,411	1,335	140	550	403	169	73
1896	2,711	2,711	1,369	1,342	141	532	429	166	74
1890	2,292	2,292							

NA   Not available.
[1] Includes debt also held by Government National Mortgage Association.
[2] Federal Reserve Board estimates.
[3] Klaman estimates.
[4] Grebler-Blank-Winnick estimates.
[5] Estimate shown in source is 35,061.   Change was made so that components would add to total.

Series N 273–277. Residential Nonfarm Mortgage Debt Outstanding, by Type of Property, and Government-Underwritten Debt: 1925 to 1970

[In billions of dollars.   As of December 31.   FHA = Federal Housing Administration; VA = Veterans Administration]

Year	1- to 4-family structures			5-or-more unit structures		Year	1- to 4-family structures			5-or-more unit structures	
	Total	Government-underwritten		Total	FHA insured		Total	Government-underwritten		Total	FHA insured
		FHA insured	VA guaranteed					FHA insured	VA guaranteed		
	273	274	275	276	277		273	274	275	276	277
1970	280.2	59.9	37.3	58.0	12.0	1960	141.3	26.7	29.7	20.3	5.9
1969	266.8	54.5	35.7	52.2	10.0	1959	130.9	23.8	30.0	18.7	5.4
1968	251.2	50.6	33.8	47.3	9.0	1958	117.7	19.7	30.4	16.8	5.0
1967	236.1	47.4	32.5	43.9	8.3	1957	107.6	16.5	30.7	15.3	4.4
1966	223.6	44.8	31.3	40.3	8.0	1956	99.0	15.5	28.4	14.9	3.9
1965	212.9	42.0	31.1	37.2	8.0	1955	88.2	14.3	24.6	14.3	4.0
1964	197.6	38.3	30.9	33.6	7.9	1954	75.7	12.8	19.3	13.5	4.1
1963	182.2	35.0	30.9	29.0	7.5	1953	66.1	12.0	16.1	12.9	4.0
1962	166.5	32.3	29.9	25.8	7.2	1952	58.5	10.8	14.6	12.3	3.9
1961	153.1	29.5	29.6	23.0	6.4	1951	51.7	9.7	13.2	11.5	3.7

Series N 273–277. Residential Nonfarm Mortgage Debt Outstanding, by Type of Property, and Government-Underwritten Debt: 1925 to 1970—Con.

[In billions of dollars]

Year	1- to 4-family structures Total	Government-underwritten FHA insured	Government-underwritten VA guaranteed	5-or-more unit structures Total	FHA insured	Year	1- to 4-family structures Total	Government-underwritten, FHA insured	5-or-more unit structures Total	FHA insured
	273	274	275	276	277		273	274	276	277
1950	45.2	8.6	10.3	10.1	3.2	1937	15.5	0.6	4.5	(Z)
1949	37.6	6.9	8.1	8.6	2.1	1936	15.4	.2	4.6	(Z)
1948	33.3	5.3	7.2	7.5	1.1	1935	15.4	(Z)	4.8	(Z)
1947	28.2	3.8	5.5	6.6	.5	1934	15.6	----	5.1	----
1946	23.0	3.7	2.4	6.1	.2	1933	15.4	----	5.7	----
1945	18.6	4.1	.2	5.7	.2	1932	16.7	----	6.0	----
1944	17.9	4.2	----	5.6	.2	1931	18.1	----	6.2	----
1943	17.8	4.1	----	5.8	.2					
1942	18.2	3.7	----	5.8	.1	1930	18.9	----	6.5	----
1941	18.4	3.0	----	5.9	.1	1929	18.9	----	6.0	----
						1928	17.9	----	5.4	----
1940	17.4	2.3	----	5.7	.1	1927	16.4	----	5.0	----
1939	16.3	1.8	----	5.6	.1	1926	14.8	----	4.6	----
1938	15.8	1.0	----	4.4	(Z)	1925	13.0	----	4.2	----

Z Less than $50 million.

Series N 278–284. Mortgage Loans on 1- to 4-Family Houses, by Type of Lender: 1925 to 1950

[In millions of dollars. Excludes Alaska and Hawaii]

Year	Total	Commercial banks	Mutual savings banks	Savings and loan associations	Life insurance companies	Home Owners' Loan Corporation	Individuals and others	Year	Total	Commercial banks	Mutual savings banks	Savings and loan associations	Life insurance companies	Home Owners' Loan Corporation	Individuals and others
	278	279	280	281	282	283	284		278	279	280	281	282	283	284
1950	16,008	3,429	1,400	5,237	1,742	--------	4,200	1937	2,588	513	196	897	232	27	723
1949	11,069	2,236	990	3,636	1,093	2	3,112	1936	2,302	472	202	755	140	128	605
1948	11,357	2,636	980	3,607	1,132	2	3,000								
1947	11,207	2,986	658	3,811	906	2	2,844	1935	2,259	474	118	564	77	583	443
1946	10,011	2,677	556	3,584	492	2	2,700	1934	3,170	195	95	451	16	2,263	150
								1933	1,093	233	104	414	10	132	200
1945	4,867	923	267	1,913	209	4	1,551	1932	1,408	257	254	543	54		300
1944	4,004	726	189	1,454	300	31	1,304	1931	2,232	368	353	892	169	--------	450
1943	3,362	654	160	1,184	272	54	1,038								
1942	3,319	721	179	1,051	374	40	954	1930	3,189	455	352	1,262	400		720
1941	3,931	847	243	1,379	371	63	1,028	1929	4,442	538	468	1,791	525	--------	1,120
								1928	4,947	696	544	1,932	525		1,250
1940	3,510	838	204	1,200	324	143	801	1927	4,857	585	517	1,895	500	--------	1,360
1939	2,912	604	157	986	274	151	740	1926	4,863	819	475	1,824	465	--------	1,280
1938	2,437	470	177	798	242	81	669	1925	4,240	650	450	1,620	400	--------	1,120

Series N 285–290. Mortgage Recordings of $20,000 or Less, by Type of Lender: 1939 to 1964

[In millions of dollars. Excludes Alaska and Hawaii]

Year	Total	Commercial banks	Mutual savings banks	Savings and loan associations	Life insurance companies	All others	Year	Total	Commercial banks	Mutual savings banks	Savings and loan associations	Life insurance companies	All others
	285	286	287	288	289	290		285	286	287	288	289	290
1964	36,921	6,656	2,182	15,759	1,408	10,916	1951	16,405	3,370	1,013	5,295	1,615	5,112
1963	36,925	6,354	2,061	16,716	1,339	10,455	1950	16,179	3,365	1,064	5,060	1,618	5,073
1962	34,187	5,851	1,958	15,144	1,212	10,022	1949	11,828	2,446	750	3,646	1,046	3,940
1961	31,157	4,997	1,741	13,662	1,160	9,597	1948	11,882	2,664	745	3,629	1,016	3,829
							1947	11,729	3,004	596	3,650	847	3,631
1960	29,341	4,520	1,557	12,158	1,318	9,788	1946	10,589	2,712	548	3,483	503	3,343
1959	32,235	5,832	1,780	13,094	1,523	10,006							
1958	27,388	5,204	1,640	10,516	1,460	8,568	1945	5,650	1,097	217	2,017	250	2,069
1957	24,244	4,264	1,429	9,217	1,472	7,862	1944	4,606	878	165	1,560	257	1,746
1956	27,088	5,458	1,824	9,532	1,799	8,475	1943	3,861	753	152	1,238	280	1,439
							1942	3,943	886	166	1,171	362	1,359
1955	28,484	5,617	1,857	10,452	1,932	8,626	1941	4,732	1,166	218	1,490	404	1,454
1954	22,974	4,239	1,501	8,312	1,768	7,154							
1953	19,747	3,680	1,327	7,365	1,480	5,895	1940	4,031	1,006	170	1,284	334	1,238
1952	18,018	3,600	1,137	6,452	1,420	5,409	1939	3,507	891	143	1,058	287	1,128

Series N 291–300. Major Federal Housing Finance Programs: 1934 to 1970

[In millions of dollars. Includes Alaska and Hawaii for all years]

Year	Loans made with Federal Housing Administration insurance						Loans made with Veterans Administration guaranty	Federal National Mortgage Association [1]		Advances outstanding of the Federal Home Loan Banks [3][4]
	Property improvement loans, net proceeds	Mortgage loans						Purchases [2]	Sales [2] (gross)	
		Total	Homes			Projects				
			Total	New	Existing					
	291	292	293	294	295	296	297	298	299	300
1970	617	11,364	8,114	2,667	5,447	3,250	3,442	5,712	154	10,615
1969	693	8,437	7,121	1,551	5,570	1,316	4,072	5,119	61	9,289
1968	656	7,619	6,496	1,572	4,924	1,123	3,774	4,534	21	5,259
1967	623	6,527	5,885	1,369	4,516	642	3,405	1,400	12	4,386
1966	641	6,678	6,095	1,729	4,366	583	2,600	2,081	----------	6,935
1965	634	8,056	7,465	1,705	5,760	591	2,652	757	47	5,997
1964	663	7,468	6,573	1,608	4,965	895	[5] 2,851	198	78	5,325
1963	804	6,412	5,569	1,664	3,905	843	[5] 3,042	181	780	4,784
1962	834	6,349	5,270	1,849	3,421	1,079	2,650	547	391	3,479
1961	855	5,691	4,765	1,783	2,982	926	1,836	624	522	2,662
1960	982	5,311	4,600	2,197	2,403	711	1,984	980	42	1,981
1959	997	6,698	6,069	2,563	3,507	628	2,788	735	3	2,134
1958	868	5,480	4,551	1,666	2,885	929	1,864	260	466	1,298
1957	869	2,846	2,251	880	1,371	595	3,758	1,021	3	1,265
1956	692	2,769	2,638	1,133	1,505	130	5,866	575	5	1,228
1955	646	3,161	3,085	1,269	1,816	76	7,154	86	–	1,417
1954	891	2,174	1,942	1,035	907	232	4,256	–	–	868
1953	1,334	2,548	2,289	1,259	1,030	259	2,464	----------	----------	952
1952	848	2,264	1,942	969	974	322	2,678	----------	----------	864
1951	707	2,512	1,928	1,216	713	584	4,252	----------	----------	806
1950	694	3,649	2,492	1,637	856	1,157	3,073	----------	----------	816
1949	594	3,231	2,210	1,317	892	1,021	1,424	----------	----------	433
1948	614	2,725	2,116	1,432	684	609	1,877	----------	----------	515
1947	534	1,255	895	477	418	360	3,283	----------	----------	436
1946	321	435	422	120	302	13	2,302	----------	----------	294
1945	171	494	474	257	217	20	[6] 192	----------	----------	195
1944	114	763	707	484	224	56	----------	----------	----------	131
1943	86	848	763	553	210	85	----------	----------	----------	110
1942	126	994	973	766	208	21	----------	----------	----------	129
1941	228	924	911	728	183	14	----------	----------	----------	219
1940	216	775	762	587	175	13	----------	----------	----------	202
1939	179	747	695	486	208	52	----------	----------	----------	181
1938	138	533	486	240	246	48	----------	----------	----------	199
1937	54	435	424	169	256	10	----------	----------	----------	200
1936	222	311	309	95	214	2	----------	----------	----------	145
1935	201	96	94	22	72	2	----------	----------	----------	103
1934	27	(7)	(7)	(7)	(7)	(7)	----------	----------	----------	87

– Represents zero.
[1] Includes Alaska, Hawaii, Puerto Rico, Guam, and Virgin Islands for all years. Beginning 1968, includes purchases and sales of Government National Mortgage Association; see text.
[2] Purchases and sales during the year.

[3] Includes Alaska, Hawaii, Puerto Rico, and Guam for all years.
[4] Loans outstanding at the end of the year.
[5] Includes direct loans sold with a guaranty.
[6] Includes 1944 activity.
[7] Included in 1935 figures.

Series N 301. Real Estate Foreclosures of Nonfarm Properties: 1926 to 1970

[New series is based on a new, 1967, benchmark and includes Alaska and Hawaii and farm foreclosures; the old series excludes them]

Year	Number 301	Year	Number 301	Year	Number 301	Year	Number 301	Year	Number 301	Year	Number 301
NEW SERIES		**OLD SERIES—Con.**		**OLD SERIES—Con.**		**OLD SERIES—Con.**		**OLD SERIES—Con.**			
1970	101,070	1964	108,620	1954	26,211	1944	17,153	1934	230,350		
1969	95,856	1963	98,195	1953	21,473	1943	25,281	1933	252,400		
1968	110,404	1962	86,444	1952	18,135	1942	41,997	1932	248,700		
1967	134,203	1961	73,074	1951	18,141	1941	58,559	1931	193,800		
OLD SERIES		1960	51,353	1950	21,537	1940	75,556	1930	150,000		
		1959	44,075	1949	17,635	1939	100,410	1929	134,900		
1968	90,941	1958	42,367	1948	13,052	1938	118,357	1928	116,000		
1967	110,541	1957	34,204	1947	10,559	1937	151,366	1927	91,000		
1966	117,473	1956	30,963	1946	10,453	1936	185,439	1926	68,100		
1965	116,664	1955	28,529	1945	12,706	1935	228,713				

Series N 302–307. Mortgage Status of Nonfarm Owner-Occupied Housing Units: 1890 to 1970

[In thousands, except as indicated]

Year	Total owner-occupied housing units	Reporting mortgage status	Mortgaged Number	Mortgaged Percent	Not mortgaged	Median debt-to-value ratio of mortgaged units (percent)
	302	303	304	305	306	307
1970[1]	33,206	33,206	20,110	60.6	13,096	52.0
1960*	27,862	27,862	15,816	56.8	12,046	53.3
1956	25,637	25,637	14,203	55.4	11,434	(NA)
1950	19,802	17,796	7,825	44.0	9,971	42.0
1940	11,413	10,611	4,805	45.3	5,806	52.4
1930	10,550	(NA)	(NA)	(NA)	(NA)	
1920	7,041	6,868	2,736	39.8	4,132	42.6
1910	5,245	5,110	1,701	33.3	3,409	
1900	3,567	3,395	1,087	32.0	2,308	
1890	2,924	2,924	810	27.7	2,114	39.8

* Denotes first year for which figures include Alaska and Hawaii.
NA Not available.

[1] Data as of 1971.

Chapter P

Manufactures

P 1-374. General note.

Manufacturing is the mechanical or chemical transformation of inorganic or organic substances into new products. The assembly of component parts of products is also considered to be manufacturing if the resulting product is neither a structure nor other fixed improvement. These activities are usually carried on in plants, factories, or mills, which characteristically use power-driven machines and materials-handling equipment.

Manufacturing production is usually carried on for the wholesale market, for transfer to other plants of the same company, or to the order of industrial users rather than for direct sale to the household consumer. However, some manufacturers (e.g., baking, milk bottling, etc.) sell chiefly at retail to household consumers through the mail, house-to-house routes, or salesmen. Some activities of a service nature (enameling, binding, platemaking, etc.) are included in manufacturing when they are performed primarily for the trade; but they are considered nonmanufacturing when they are performed primarily to the order of the household consumer. On the other hand, some manufacturing industries include business firms which do not undertake physical production but perform only the entrepreneurial functions of buying the materials, designing, and marketing the product, and have the actual production done on contract (e.g., apparel jobbers).

In addition to the production of goods and manufacturing services, manufacturing plants engage in related and diverse supporting activities. These activities encompass the acquisition of materials to be processed, their movement into the manufacturing facility, their storage at the manufacturing site, the operation and maintenance of plant and equipment, the design of flow of work through the production process, and necessary arrangements for shipment of output to customers. Also included are a host of subsidiary activities associated with the conduct of the establishment as a manufacturing entity; e.g., management and policy formation, product and market orientation, engineering and quality control, record keeping and accounting, physical security of plant and equipment, and the like. Such subsidiary activities may be performed by personnel located at the manufacturing facility or at an auxiliary unit serving one or more manufacturing locations of the same company. Where these activities are carried on at a different physical location or are performed for more than one plant, they are excluded from the figures for operating manufacturing establishments and are included in the data shown for central administrative offices and auxiliaries in the source reports.

The *Standard Industrial Classification* (SIC) *Manual*, published by the Office of Management and Budget, is a classification structure for the entire national economy. It was first issued in 1939. For the manufacturing industries, a revised manual was issued in 1945 which, with minor modifications, was used in the 1947 Census of Manufactures. For the 1954 census, the classification structure used in 1947 was again employed, again with minor modifications. In 1957, the SIC system was extensively revised for manufacturing industries and historical comparability of some data was seriously affected. This revision and its effects on census series are described in the introduction and appendixes to the 1958 Census of Manufactures volumes. A minor revision of the SIC occurred between 1958 and 1963. Another extensive revision of the SIC was issued in 1972.

In the manufacturing sector, the SIC *Manual* built upon the Bureau of the Census manufacturing industry classifications developed over the years. The SIC system was developed for use in classifying establishments by type of activity in which they are engaged in order to facilitate the collection, tabulation, and publication of data relating to establishments and to promote uniformity and comparability in the presentation of statistical data by government agencies, trade associations, research organizations, and others. The SIC system divides all activities into broad industrial divisions (manufacturing, mining, retail trade, agriculture, etc.). It further subdivides each division into major industry groups, then into industry groups, and finally into detailed industries.

Except as noted, Alaska and Hawaii are included in census of manufactures data and in annual survey of manufactures data beginning 1958.

P 1-12. Manufactures summary, 1849-1970.

Source: U.S. Bureau of the Census, *Annual Survey of Manufactures, 1970-1971*, p. 10.

The basic source of comprehensive data on manufactures has been the census of manufactures conducted by the Bureau of the Census. The first census of manufactures covered 1809. A census was taken at 10-year intervals thereafter to 1899 (with the exception of 1829), at 5-year intervals for 1904-1919, and biennially for 1921-1939. The census was suspended during World War II, but was resumed for 1947. Legislation enacted in 1948 provided for a census of manufactures every 5 years, with annual sample surveys authorized for interim years. The 1954 census was the first to be taken as a result of this legislation. Subsequently, the census intervals were revised and censuses were taken in 1958, 1963, and 1967. Annual surveys of manufactures were conducted every year beginning 1949, except during census years. The data from the annual surveys represent estimates derived from a sample of manufacturing establishments canvassed. These estimates may differ from the results that would have been obtained from a complete canvass of all manufacturing establishments. The relative standard errors (measures of the potential differences) associated with these estimates are published in the annual survey volumes.

There have been changes in scope from one census of manufactures to another. For "factories and hand and neighborhood industries," data for 1849-1899 are for all establishments with products valued at $500 or more. For "factories, excluding hand and neighborhood industries," data for 1899-1919 are for establishments reporting value of shipments of $500 or more; for 1921-1939, for establishments reporting value of shipments of $5,000 or more, while data beginning 1947 are for establishments employing one or more persons at any time during the census year. These changes in the minimum size limit have not appreciably affected the historical comparability of the census figures except for data on number of establishments.

There have also been a number of changes in the definition of manufacturing industries. Among the more important were changes in the treatment of "railroad repair shops" and "manufactured gas." These industries are included in the figures for 1899-1933, but excluded for 1935-1970. When the change results in the omission of an entire industry for which separate tabulations are available during each census, the adjustments are usually carried back through the previous censuses. Beginning 1954, the figures cover the logging camps and contractors industry, which was not included within the scope of the 1947 census; and establishments engaged in the processing and distribution of fluid milk, which were not included in the figures for earlier census years. Beginning 1958, the figures cover establishments classified in the ready-mixed concrete industry, and establishments classified in the miscellaneous machinery industry that were engaged exclusively or almost exclusively in machine shop repair work. Data for such establishments are excluded for 1939 to 1957 but included for 1929 and earlier years.

For a discussion of changes between 1929 and 1958, see U.S. Bureau of the Census, *Census Working Paper*, No. 9, 1959, by Harold T. Goldstein. There have been no major changes since 1958.

P 1–2, number of establishments. The reporting units in each census have been establishments rather than legal entities or companies. Conceptually, an establishment is a geographically isolated manufacturing unit maintaining independent bookkeeping records, regardless of its managerial or financial affiliations. An establishment may be a single plant, a group of closely located plants operated as a unit, or a group of closely located plants operated by a single company without separate records for each. The establishment is also the basic unit of industrial classification, being assigned to an industry on the basis of its reported product of chief total value. Establishments owned and operated by the Federal Government are excluded from census coverage.

P 3–5, persons engaged in manufacturing. The figures for 1939–1970 exclude personnel reported by manufacturing establishments as in distribution and in construction work (the 1939 and subsequent censuses required separate reporting for such employees). Therefore, the employee figures for earlier years probably are not strictly comparable with those for 1939–1970. It is not known how many of the wage earners and the salaried employees reported in previous censuses were engaged in distribution and construction, and how many were engaged in manufacturing. The figures for nonproduction employees are derived by subtracting the figures for production workers from those for all employees shown in the source. For nonproduction employees, series P 4, the figures for 1939 and earlier years refer to one payroll period, usually in October; for 1947, to an average of 12 monthly figures; for 1949 to 1954, to an average for the payroll period ended nearest the 12th of March, May, August, and November; and for 1955 to 1970, to the payroll period ended nearest the 12th of March. For production workers, series P 5, the figures for 1947 and earlier years represent the average of 12 monthly figures; for 1949 to 1970, they are based on employment for the payroll period ended nearest the 12th of March, May, August, and November.

Employees comprise all full-time and part-time employees on the payrolls of operating establishments who worked or received pay for any part of the pay period specified on the report form. Officers of corporations are included as employees; proprietors and partners of unincorporated firms are, however, excluded from the total. In recent censuses, employment at separate administrative offices and auxiliary units is excluded from this category.

There has not been a consistent treatment of employees in central administrative offices. The latter are defined as offices which operate one or more manufacturing plants located in a city or cities other than that in which the administrative office is located. For the censuses of 1909–1923, data on employees in such offices were collected on a separate "administrative schedule" and were tabulated and included with those for salaried employees (and, therefore, with all employees) of the manufacturing plants. Thereafter, these data were collected and tabulated for the censuses of 1925, 1929, and 1937. Beginning 1954, separate data on employment in administrative offices and auxiliary establishments were compiled in census years and are shown in census of manufactures publications. The figures for nonproduction employees for 1925 and 1929 include employees in central administrative offices. To make the 1937 figure for nonproduction employees more comparable to the figures for 1929 and earlier years (except 1927), 130,854 employees in central administrative offices should be added to the 1937 figure (*1937 Census of Manufactures*, p. 1652), and to make the 1954 figure more comparable to the figures for 1929 and earlier years (except 1927), 474,256 employees in administrative and auxiliary units should be added to the 1954 figure (*U.S. Census of Manufactures: 1954*, vol. II, part 1, p. 2).

Collection of data on proprietors and partners was discontinued after the 1963 census.

Production workers are defined as workers (up through the working foreman level) engaged in fabricating, processing, assembling, inspection, receiving, storage, handling, packing, warehousing, shipping (but not delivering), maintenance, repair, janitorial, watchman services, product development, auxiliary production for plants' own use (e.g., power plant), recordkeeping, and other services closely associated with these production operations at the establishment covered by the report. Supervisory employees above the working foreman level are excluded from this category.

Decennial estimates of wage earners (production and related workers) excluding hand and neighborhood industries have been prepared for 1869–1899 by John W. Kendrick and Maude Pech for the National Bureau of Economic Research. The following is the estimated number of wage earners for each of these years: 1869, 1,803,000; 1879, 2,454,000; 1889, 3,562,000; 1899, 4,496,000. This estimate for 1899 differs from the official Census Bureau estimate (series P 5) by only one-tenth of one percent. For details of estimating procedure, see John W. Kendrick, *Productivity Trends in the United States*, National Bureau of Economic Research, New York, 1961, appendix D.

P 6, man-hours, production workers. This series covers all plant man-hours of production and related workers. It represents all man-hours worked or paid for except hours paid for vacations, holidays, or sick leave and includes actual overtime hours. Where employees elected to work during vacation periods, only the actual hours they worked were reported. The man-hour figures issued by the Census Bureau differ from those published by the Bureau of Labor Statistics which cover all hours paid for, whether or not worked.

P 7–9, payroll. These figures include gross earnings paid in the calendar year to all employees on the payroll of operating manufacturing establishments. They include all forms of compensation such as salaries, wages, commissions, dismissal pay, all bonuses, vacation and sick leave pay, and compensation in kind, prior to such deductions as employees' Social Security contributions, withholding taxes, group insurance, union dues, and savings bonds. Salaries of officers of these establishments are included for corporations; payments to proprietors and partners are excluded for unincorporated concerns. Also excluded are payments to members of Armed Forces and pensioners carried on the active payrolls of manufacturing establishments. Employers' Social Security contributions or other nonlabor costs such as pension plans, group insurance, and workmen's compensation are also excluded.

P 10, value added by manufacture. The standard formula for calculating value added by manufacture since 1958 differs from the one used for 1954 and earlier years. Prior to 1958, the value added of an establishment was calculated by subtracting the cost of materials, supplies, containers, fuels, purchased electric energy, and contract work from the value of shipments for products manufactured plus miscellaneous receipts for services rendered. This is known as unadjusted value added. Beginning 1958, the measure of value added has been adjusted for each establishment in two respects. Value added now includes: (1) Value added by merchandising, i.e., the difference between the sales value and cost of merchandise sold without further manufacture, processing or assembly; and (2) an adjustment for the net change in finished goods and work-in-process inventories between the beginning and end of the year. The resulting figure is the adjusted value added. This procedure avoids the duplication in the "value of shipments" figures which results from the use of products of some establishments as materials by others. The "value added by manufacture" concept should not be confused with "national income originating in manufacturing," as presented in the national income estimates (see chapter F). The latter is obtained by subtracting from the value of shipments not only the cost of materials, but also such other costs as depreciation charges, State and local taxes (other than corporate income taxes), allowance for bad debts, and purchases of services from nonmanufacturing enterprises such as services of engineering and management consultants, advertising, telephone and telegraph expense, insurance, royalties, patent fees, etc. It is, therefore, a more "net" concept of value added than that used in the census of manufactures. Value added by manufacture in 1967, for example, exceeded national income originating in manufacturing, as estimated by the U.S. Office of Business Economics, by 34 percent.

Robert E. Gallman prepared estimates of value added for the census years 1839 to 1879 by adjusting manufacturing totals to exclude nonmanufacturing industries and by correcting for industries omitted from or poorly covered by the various censuses. These estimates are extrapolations based on data prepared by Richard A. Easterlin and published in "Estimates of Manufacturing Activity," *Population Redistribution and Economic Growth, United States, 1870–1950*, vol. I, by Everett S. Lee, Ann Ratner, Carol P. Brainerd, and Richard A. Easterlin, American Philosophical Society, Philadelphia, 1957, pp. 635–681. The following are Gallman's estimates:

Table I. Value Added by Manufacture

[In millions of dollars]

Year	Current prices	Prices of 1879
1899	5,044	6,252
1889	3,727	4,156
1879	1,962	1,962
1869	1,631	1,078
1859	815	859
1849	447	488
1839	240	190

Source: Robert E. Gallman, "Commodity Output in the United States, 1839–1899," *Studies in Income and Wealth*, National Bureau of Economic Research, New York, 1961, vol. 24, table A 13.

P 11, capital expenditures, new. Manufacturers were asked to report expenditures made during the year for permanent additions and major alterations to their plants, as well as for new machinery and equipment purchases that were chargeable to fixed-asset accounts of manufacturing establishments and were of a type for which depreciation accounts are ordinarily maintained. Excluded are costs of maintenance and repairs charged as current operating expense, new facilities and equipment leased from other companies, new facilities owned by the Federal Government but operated under contract by private companies, and plant and equipment furnished to manufacturers by communities and organizations. Beginning 1951, the figures include expenditures for plants under construction and not yet in operation. (In the series by major groups, P 58–67, however, such expenditures are included beginning only in 1958.)

P 12, end-of-year inventories. Respondents were asked to report their inventories at approximate current costs if feasible; otherwise at book values. See also text for series P 74–92.

P 13. FRB index of manufacturing production, 1919–1970.

Source: Board of Governors of the Federal Reserve System, *Industrial Production, 1971 Edition*, S-45.

In the 1971 revision of the FRB industrial production index detailed adjustments were made to independently compiled Census-Federal Reserve benchmark and annual production levels for this series. All of the revisions have been carried back in detail to 1954 and in more limited fashion to 1939. The index comparison base has been updated to the single year 1967. Conversion to the new base has been carried back to the beginning of the index in 1919.

In this revision the manufacturing series was adjusted in detail to changes in the comprehensive Census-Federal Reserve production benchmarks for the years 1954 to 1958 and 1958 to 1963; the index had previously been adjusted to such benchmark changes for manufacturing from 1939 to 1947 and from 1947 to 1954. Where adequate product data were not available for the intervening years

1955–62 and for years 1964 through 1970, annual levels were adjusted to the detailed results of a new annual production index program for all 4-digit manufacturing industries based largely on deflated data from the Census Bureau's *Annual Survey of Manufactures*. Revised production levels for 1940 through 1946 are based on a combination of several types of independent annual data adjusted to the Census-Federal Reserve benchmark indexes from 1939 to 1947.

The year 1967 was selected for use as the weight base for the most recent period, beginning 1967. The year 1963 is used for the 1963–66 period, 1958 for the 1958–62 period, and 1954 for the 1954–57 period. The year 1947 continues to be used as the weight base for the 1947–52 period and 1939 weights have been introduced for the 1939–46 period.

For a more detailed description of the revised production series, see the source report of the *Federal Reserve Bulletin* for July 1971.

P 14. NBER index of manufacturing production, 1929–1966.

Source: John W. Kendrick, *Postwar Productivity Trends in the United States, 1948–1969*, National Bureau of Economic Research, New York, 1973, table A 32 (copyright).

The manufacturing output index is based on the Census-Federal Reserve Board (FRB) benchmark production indexes for 1947, 1954, 1958, and 1963, interpolated and extrapolated to 1966 by the FRB indexes of manufacturing production.

See also John W. Kendrick, *Productivity Trends in the United States*, National Bureau of Economic Research, 1961.

P 15–16. NBER index of manufacturing production, 1899–1919.

Source: U.S. Bureau of the Census, unpublished data.

These data were prepared by extending and shifting the production indexes originally prepared from census of manufactures data by Solomon Fabricant, National Bureau of Economic Research. The original data were first presented in Solomon Fabricant, *The Output of Manufacturing Industries, 1899–1937*, National Bureau of Economic Research, New York, 1940. These indexes cover only those years for which a census of manufactures was taken. Because of the inadequacy of data for most groups, no attempt was made to interpolate between intercensal years. For details of method of construction, see Fabricant's book, chapter 2 and appendix A.

P 17. Frickey index of manufacturing production, 1860–1914.

Source: Edwin Frickey, *Production in the United States, 1860–1914*, Harvard Economic Studies, Harvard University Press, 1947, p. 54.

In the derivation of these indexes, Frickey employed the weighted arithmetic mean of quantity relatives. With respect to weighting, he took the value-added principle as his standard and conformed to this standard as nearly as possible with existing data. For details on constituent series, see the source, appendixes A and B.

Making use of the figures for series P 13–17 and other data, John W. Kendrick has constructed an index of manufacturing, with 1929 as the base, for benchmark years 1869, 1879, and 1889, and annually thereafter through 1953. See appendix table D-II for figures and appendix D for description of this index in Kendrick's *Productivity Trends in the United States*, National Bureau of Economic Research, New York, 1961.

P 18–39. Indexes of manufacturing production (FRB), by industry group, 1947–1970.

Source: Board of Governors of the Federal Reserve System, *Federal Reserve Bulletin*, July 1971 and later issues, and unpublished data.

See text for series P 13. For description of industry groups, see text for series P 58–67.

P 40–57. Indexes of manufacturing production, by industry group, 1899–1954.

Source: U.S. Bureau of the Census, unpublished data.

See text for series P 15 and 16.

For a listing of changes in industry classifications as of 1947, see *Census of Manufactures, 1947, Indexes of Production*, footnote to table 1, p. 1. For an annual index of durable and nondurable production (1899 = 100) for 1860–1914, see text for series P 17.

P 58–67. General statistics for manufacturing industries, by major groups, 1899–1970.

Source: U.S. Bureau of the Census. For all series except P 67, earliest year shown to 1967, *Census of Manufactures, 1967*, vol. II, parts 1, 2, and 3, table 1 for each major group; 1968–1970, *Annual Survey of Manufactures*, 1971. **Series P 67**, earliest year shown to 1929, *Fifteenth Census of the United States: 1939*, vol. II, Manufactures, 1929; 1939, *Census of Manufactures: 1954*, vol. II, parts 1 and 2; 1954 and 1962, *Census of Manufactures: 1963*, vol. I, pp. 6–10.

See general note for series P 1–374 and text for series P 1–12.

Food and kindred products. This group includes establishments manufacturing foods and beverages for human consumption and certain related products, such as manufactured ice, chewing gum, vegetable and animal fats and oils, and prepared feeds for animals and fowls. Also included are establishments primarily engaged in processing and distributing fluid milk and cream and those primarily engaged in extracting animal and vegetable oils.

Figures are not shown prior to 1921 because they are not sufficiently comparable with those for later years owing to numerous changes in classification.

Tobacco manufactures. This group includes establishments manufacturing cigarettes, cigars, smoking and chewing tobacco, and snuff, and stemming and redrying tobacco.

Textile mill products. This group includes establishments: (1) Manufacturing yarn, thread, cordage, and twine; (2) manufacturing woven fabric, carpets and rugs, braids, laces, knit fabric, knit garments, and other products from yarn; (3) dyeing and finishing fibers, yarn, and fabrics; and (4) coating, waterproofing, and otherwise treating fabric. Also included are establishments weaving or knitting fabrics and also manufacturing finished apparel or other fabricated textile products in the same establishment.

Apparel and other textile products. This group includes establishments producing clothing and fabricated products by cutting and sewing purchased woven or knit textile fabrics and related materials such as leather, rubberized fabrics, plastics and furs. Excluded from this group are knitting mills primarily engaged in manufacturing apparel from yarns knitted in the same establishment and weaving mills that further process the fabric at the same establishment into such end products as sheets, towels, and pillowcases, both of which are classified in textile mill products. Custom tailors and dressmakers, who manufacture and sell apparel in the same retail establishment, are classified as nonmanufacturing.

Three types of establishments are included in this group: (1) The regular factories or "manufacturers," (2) the apparel "jobbers," and (3) the contract factories or "contractors." The manufacturers purchase fabric, employ production workers in their own plants to cut and sew the materials into apparel, and sell the final product. The jobbers primarily perform entrepreneurial functions such as buying raw materials, designing and preparing samples, arranging for the manufacture of the garments from their materials, and selling of the finished apparel. The actual processing (cutting, sewing, etc.) is performed on contract by the apparel contractors, although many jobbers perform the cutting operation in their own establishments. Apparel jobbers are included in manufacturing. However, jobbers of miscellaneous fabricated textile products, such as curtains, draperies, etc., are classified in wholesale trade.

Lumber and wood products. This group includes logging camps cutting timber and pulpwood, merchant sawmills, lath mills, shingle mills, cooperage-stock mills, planing mills, and plywood mills and veneer mills producing lumber and wood basic materials; and establishments manufacturing finished articles made entirely or mainly of wood or wood substitutes. See also furniture and fixtures and miscellaneous manufacturing.

Woodworking in connection with construction, in the nature of reconditioning and repair, or performed to individual order, is classified in nonmanufacturing.

Furniture and fixtures. This group includes establishments manufacturing household, office, public building, and restaurant furniture; and office and store fixtures. Establishments primarily engaged in woodworking to individual order or in reconditioning and repair are classified in nonmanufacturing.

Paper and allied products. This group includes the manufacture of pulps primarily from wood, and from rags and other cellulose fibers; the conversion of these pulps into paper or board; and the manufacture of paper and paperboard into converted products such as coated paper, paper bags, paperboard boxes, and envelopes. Certain types of converted paper products—such as abrasive paper, carbon paper, and photo-sensitized and blueprint paper—are classified in other groups.

Printing and publishing. This group includes establishments engaged in printing, such as letterpress, lithography, gravure, or screen; establishments which perform printing services such as bookbinding, typesetting, engraving, photoengraving, and electrotyping and establishments publishing newspapers, books, and periodicals, regardless of whether or not they do their own printing. News syndicates are classified in service industries, and textile printing and finishing in textile mill products. Prior to 1935, data reported by religious, social, charitable, educational, and other nonprofit organizations are not included; thereafter, data are included only for such nonprofit organizations whose employees are covered by the Social Security system.

Chemicals and allied products. This group includes establishments producing basic chemicals, and establishments manufacturing products by predominantly chemical processes. Establishments classified in this group manufacture three general classes of products: (1) Basic chemicals such as acids, alkalies, salts, and organic chemicals; (2) chemical products to be used in further manufacture such as synthetic fibers, plastics materials, dry colors, and pigments; and (3) finished chemical products to be used for ultimate consumption, such as drugs, cosmetics, and soaps, or to be used as materials or supplies in other industries, such as paints, fertilizers, and explosives. Establishments primarily packaging, repacking, and bottling purchased chemicals and allied products are classified in trade industries.

Petroleum and coal products. This group includes establishments primarily engaged in petroleum refining, manufacturing paving and roofing materials, and compounding lubricating oils and greases from purchased materials. Establishments manufacturing and distributing gas to consumers are classified in public utilities industries, and those primarily engaged in producing coke and byproducts in primary metal industries. Establishments primarily engaged in producing crude petroleum, natural gas, natural gasoline, and cycle condensation are classified in mining industries.

Rubber and plastics products, not elsewhere classified. This group includes establishments manufacturing from natural, synthetic, or reclaimed rubber, gutta percha, balata, or gutta siak, rubber products such as tires, rubber footwear, mechanical rubber goods; heels and soles, flooring, and rubber sundries. It also includes establishments manufacturing or rebuilding retreaded tires, but automobile tire repair shops engaged in recapping and retreading automobile tires are classified in services. This group also includes establishments molding primary plastics for the trade and manufacturing miscellaneous finished plastics products. Elastic webbing, products made of elastic webbing and garments made from rubberized fabrics, synthetic rubber, and plastics materials in the form of sheets, rods, tubes, granules, powders, and liquids are classified elsewhere.

Leather and leather products. This group includes establishments tanning, currying, and finishing hides and skins; establishments manufacturing finished leather and artificial leather products and some similar products made of other materials; and leather converters.

Stone, clay, and glass products. This group includes establishments manufacturing flat glass and other glass products, cement, structural clay products, pottery, concrete, and gypsum products, cut-stone products, abrasive and asbestos products, etc., from materials taken principally from the earth in the form of stone, clay, and sand. When separate reports are available for mines and quarries operated by these establishments, the mining activities are classified in mining industries; otherwise, the mining activities are classified here.

Primary metal industries. This group includes establishments smelting and refining ferrous and nonferrous metals from ore, pig, or scrap; rolling, drawing, and alloying of ferrous and nonferrous metals; manufacturing castings, forgings, and other basic products of ferrous and nonferrous metals; and manufacturing nails, spikes, and insulated wire and cable. It also includes the production of coke.

Figures are not shown prior to 1937 because of large elements of noncomparability in the earlier statistics of a number of the industries included.

Fabricated metal products. This group includes establishments primarily manufacturing a wide variety of fabricated metal products. Other important segments of the metal fabricating industries are classified in machinery, transportation equipment, instruments and related products, furniture and fixtures, and miscellaneous manufacturing industries.

The industries included here encompass a varied group of finished products (cutlery, hardware, oil burners, plumbing fixtures, metal doors, safes, etc.), materials or components for incorporation into other products (sheet metal work, steel springs, bolts and nuts, etc.), containers (metal cans, metal shipping barrels and drums, and collapsible tubes), and service operations performed on a job or order basis for the trade (for example, galvanizing, coating, and engraving).

Figures are not shown prior to 1937 because they are not sufficiently comparable with those for later years principally owing to the inclusion in earlier years of establishments primarily manufacturing valves and fittings, except plumbers', and the exclusion of establishments primarily manufacturing stamped, pressed, and spun aluminum ware.

Machinery, except electrical. This group includes establishments primarily producing a wide variety of machinery and equipment items. The industries included encompass the whole range of industrial machinery, other than electrical. To a considerable extent, the products fall into the producers' heavy equipment category, are frequently of a complex character, and are produced both to individual order and as standard items. Industries in some of the subgroups are defined in terms of end products, and the parts, attachments, and accessories for these items are included in the industry of the end product unless specifically classified elsewhere in the Standard Industrial Classification. The volume of shipments of machinery parts and accessories in some industries constitutes a significant portion of total shipments. These parts producers are generally smaller establishments but there are a large number of them. The machine shops subgroup includes plants producing a broad variety of miscellaneous parts made by job machine shops.

Plants primarily rebuilding machinery or equipment on a factory basis were formerly included in this group. However, such rebuilding activities are now classified according to the original industry classification of the product being rebuilt. Plants primarily rebuilding automotive parts are included in the transportation equipment group. Plants primarily rebuilding machine tools, metalworking machinery, and office and store machines are included in the industry of the plants producing the original equipment.

Figures are not shown prior to 1937 because they are not sufficiently comparable with those for later years, owing principally to their inclusion of establishments primarily engaged in manufacture of aircraft engines and in machine shop repairs.

Electrical equipment and supplies. This group covers establishments primarily manufacturing machinery, apparatus and supplies for the generation, storage, transmission, transformation, and utilization of electrical energy. Products included consist of equipment and apparatus for industrial or commercial use as well as goods for household consumption—for example, electric lamps, lighting fixtures, wiring devices and supplies, ranges, ovens, water heaters, fans and small electric appliances, household refrigerators and freezers, household laundry equipment, sewing machines, and vacuum cleaners.

A number of products which are sometimes considered "as belonging" in electrical equipment are classified in other groups in the 1957 edition of the *SIC Manual* in use for 1963. For example, machinery or equipment powered by built-in or detachable electric motors, such as machine tools and other metalworking equipment, commercial laundry and dry cleaning equipment, industrial vacuum cleaners, and office and store machines are classified as machinery, except electrical. Establishments primarily producing glass insulators, glass blanks for bulbs, and porcelain electrical supplies are classified in the stone, clay, glass, and concrete products group.

Industries included here are typically defined in terms of products and may include both electrical and electronic equipment. Electronic components are frequently produced and consumed at the same location by establishments classified in this group. Thus, there are (1) plants solely engaged in producing electronic components, (2) plants producing electronic components and assembling them into finished products, and (3) plants which assemble components produced elsewhere either in other plants of the same company or by other companies. Other types of components and equipment such as motors, generators, and motor-generator sets are not uncommonly produced for incorporation into other products made in the same plant.

Transportation equipment. This group covers establishments primarily manufacturing equipment for transportation of passengers and cargo by land, air, and water. Important products include motor vehicles, aircraft, ships, boats, railroad equipment, and miscellaneous transportation equipment such as motorcycles, bicycles, etc. It also includes, since 1967, guided missile components, not elsewhere classified; and receipts from research and development on aircraft parts, guided missile components, not elsewhere classified, and airplane and missile engines.

Certain products sometimes associated with or considered a part of transportation equipment are classified in other groups in the SIC. For example, wheeltype tractors, tracklaying tractors, mining cars, and industrial trucks, tractors, trailers, and stackers are classified as machinery, except electrical; and ignition systems and storage batteries as electrical equipment and supplies.

Railroad shops are not classified as manufacturing by the SIC and, therefore, such activities are not included in employment and other establishment totals for this group.

Figures are not shown prior to 1937 because they are not sufficiently comparable with later years owing to their exclusion of establishments primarily engaged in manufacture of aircraft engines and of a number of large establishments classified prior to 1937 in other industry groups.

Instruments and related products. This group covers establishments primarily manufacturing mechanical measuring, engineering, laboratory, and scientific research instruments; optical instruments and lenses; surgical, medical, and dental instruments, equipment, and supplies; ophthalmic goods; photographic equipment and supplies; and watches and clocks. Establishments primarily manufacturing instruments for indicating, measuring, and recording electrical quantities and characteristics are classified in electrical equipment and supplies.

During 1958 to 1963, reports received from some large establishments indicated a change from the manufacture primarily of such individual instruments as those used for indicating air speed, rate-of-climb, angle-of-yaw and similar flight characteristics, and gyroscopes which are sold separately, to the manufacture primarily of complete instrumentation systems for navigation, guidance, check-out etc. The major impact of this change has been on the classification of products and, consequently, the SIC coding of these large establishments.

As a result, the annual data for 1958–1962 were revised. Because of the shift in recent years from instruments classified in this group to complete systems classified in the electrical equipment and supplies group, the year-to-year changes are of dubious validity for the industries considered separately. The two industries taken in combination however, would yield significant measures of activity in the general area.

Miscellaneous manufacturing industries. This group covers establishments primarily manufacturing products not classified in any other group. Industries in this group fall into the following categories: Jewelry, and silverware and plated ware; musical instruments; toys, and sporting and athletic goods; pens, pencils, and other office and artists' materials; buttons, costume novelties, and miscellaneous notions; brooms and brushes; morticians' goods; and other miscellaneous manufacturing industries.

For 1953 and earlier years, data for ordnance and accessories are included with this group. For 1954 and subsequent years data for the ordnance and accessories group are published separately in the source volumes.

Figures are not shown prior to 1947 because they are not sufficiently comparable with those for later years owing to their exclusion of establishments primarily manufacturing rubber dolls, carousels and other amusement park rides, electric vibrators, exercisers and reducers, blasting and detonating caps, safety fuses, and pressed and molded pulp goods; and inclusion of establishments primarily manufacturing cellophane bags, aluminum tags, and hair clippers for human use.

P 68–73. Horsepower of power equipment in manufacturing industries, 1869–1962.

Source: U.S. Bureau of the Census, *Census of Manufactures, 1963*, vol. I, p. 6–9.

The first census of power equipment available in manufacturing establishments was made by the Bureau of the Census in 1870 covering the year 1869. Because certain industries included in earlier censuses were not covered by the 1939 census, the power equipment statistics from 1899 through 1929 were adjusted in 1939 to provide a comparable series for the 70-year period. The comparability of the 1954 and 1962 statistics with those for 1939 is affected by (a) the exclusion from the 1954 and 1962 inquiry of fractional horsepower motors included in the 1939 totals, and (b) the omission of data for selected industry groups in 1954 included in the 1939 and 1962 totals.

The aggregate horsepower figure, series P 68, represents the unduplicated rating for total installed equipment and thus provides a measure of the mechanical power available in manufacturing establishments. The figure is derived by summing the horsepower rating of prime movers, series P 69, and that for electric motors driven by purchased electricity, series P 71. To secure the latter figure the total horsepower for electric motors was distributed, by establishment, into two categories: Motors driven by purchased electricity and motors driven by energy generated at the establishment. For the relatively small number of establishments which both generate and purchase electricity, the total horsepower for electric motors was prorated on the basis of the ratio of the net quantity purchased to the net total for electricity consumed.

The horsepower ratings for prime movers include information for such types of power equipment as internal combustion engines, steam and hydraulic turbines, and reciprocating steam engines. The totals for prime movers are further separated between those driving electric generators and those used for other purposes. The statistics for prime movers not driving generators exclude data for automobiles, trucks, and other highway equipment.

Respondents were requested to report horsepower of standby equipment as well as equipment in operation at the end of the year, including all prime movers and motors in mobile (except automobiles, trucks, and other highway equipment) as well as in stationary equipment. Information for fractional horsepower motors, however, was not reported for either 1954 or 1962.

Data on aggregate horsepower per 100 (factory) production workers, series P 73, are comparable for all years, except for 1954 and for years prior to 1899. The figures for 1954 exclude data for all establishments in the printing trade services industry, and those in the apparel and other fabricated textile products industry except for miscellaneous ap- parel. The number of wage earners as published in the census reports prior to 1899 includes those in factory as well as in hand trades and neighborhood industries (carpentry, millinery, painting, etc.) and custom grist milling, custom saw milling, and cotton ginning. Changes in the minimum size limit set for establishments included in the several censuses, or the number of manufacturing establishments requested to report power equipment data are believed to have an insignificant effect on the totals.

P 74–92. Value of manufacturers' shipments, inventories, and orders, 1947–1970.

Source: U.S. Bureau of the Census, *Manufacturers' Shipments, Inventories, and Orders: 1947–1963 Revised, 1961–1968,* and *1966–1972 Revised*, series M 3–1.

Shipments, as used here, represents manufacturers' receipts, billings, or the value of products shipped, less discounts, returns, and allowances, and exclude freight charges and excise taxes. Shipments for export as well as for domestic use are included. Shipments by foreign subsidiaries are excluded, but shipments to a foreign subsidiary by a domestic firm are included. The shipments figures from the Annual Survey of Manufactures to which this series is benchmarked include interplant transfers as well as commercial sales.

Inventory data are book values of stocks on hand at the end of the period, and include materials and supplies, goods in process, and finished goods. Inventories associated with nonmanufacturing activities are excluded from the benchmark. In general, inventories are as valued by the manufacturer.

New orders are net of cancellations received during the period. Unfilled orders at the end of a reporting period are orders that have not passed through the sales account and are equal to unfilled orders at the beginning of the period plus net new orders received during the period less net sales.

The manufacturers' shipments, inventories, and orders survey provides monthly figures that are comparable to the annual totals published each year in the annual survey of manufactures. The sample panel is defined as a probability sample drawn as a subsample of the companies with 100 or more employees in the annual survey of manufactures. The monthly reporting panel consists of approximately 5,000 reporting units and includes virtually all companies with 1,000 or more employees and a sample of the smaller ones.

P 77–86, inventories. Respondents are asked to report inventories of individual establishments at approximate current cost if feasible; otherwise, "at book values." Since different methods of inventory valuation are used, the definition of the aggregate inventories for establishments in an industry is not precise. The figures on the change in inventories from one period to the next are of greater significance than the actual aggregates.

Inventories are reported by stage of fabrication: (a) Finished goods; (b) work in process; and (c) materials, supplies, fuel, and other inventories. In using inventories by stage of fabrication at the all manufacturing level, as well as for the durable and nondurable goods sectors, it should be noted that a finished product of one industry may be a raw material for another industry at the next stage of fabrication.

P 87–92, new orders and unfilled orders. Orders are net of cancellations. They include orders received during the period and also filled during the period as well as orders received for future delivery. They also include the net sales value of contract change documents which increase or decrease the sales value of the unfilled orders to which they relate. Orders include only those supported by binding legal documents such as signed contracts, letters of award, or letters of intent. In case of letters of intent, the full amount of the sales value is included if the parties are in substantial agreement on the amount; otherwise, only the funds specifically authorized to be expended are included.

Unfilled orders include orders as defined above that have not yet passed through the sales account. Generally, unfilled orders at the end of the reporting period are equal to unfilled orders at the beginning of the period plus net new orders received less net sales.

While both new orders and unfilled orders are used in reviewing individual company reports for consistency, only unfilled orders are estimated directly in the tabulated totals. New orders are derived from the shipments plus net change in unfilled orders for each industry category.

P 93–106. Manufacturing corporations—sales, profits, and stockholders' equity, 1947–1970.

Source: U.S. Council of Economic Advisers, *Economic Report of the President*, January 1972, table B–74.

Data are from the U.S. Federal Trade Commission and U.S. Securities and Exchange Commission. The annual figures presented here appear originally in the Federal Trade Commission's *Quarterly Financial Report for Manufacturing Corporations* for the fourth quarter of the year.

These data are based on uniform, confidential financial statements collected from a probability sample of all enterprises which are required to file Form 1120, U.S. Corporation Income Tax Return, and are classified as manufacturers. Included are domestic corporations organized within the United States, resident foreign corporations incorporated abroad but engaged in trade or business in the United States, associations and joint-stock companies which are taxed as corporations, and small business corporations electing to be taxed through their shareholders. Excluded are inactive corporations with no income or deductions, tax-exempt farmers' cooperatives, tax-exempt nonprofit organizations, and corporations not classified in their tax returns as manufacturers.

The first sample was drawn from Form 1120 for the taxable year 1943. A second sample was drawn for the taxable year 1949. The third sample was drawn for the taxable year 1954 and each taxable year thereafter. Each sample has been supplemented by a quarterly sample of applications for a Federal Social Security Employer's Identification Number filed with the the Social Security Administration.

The first sample was used to provide estimates for each of the quarters in calendar years 1947 to 1951, inclusive; the second sample, from third quarter 1951 to second quarter 1956, inclusive; the third sample, from second quarter 1956 to 1970. To splice the estimates based upon the first and second samples, an overlap was provided for third and fourth quarters 1951; the second and third samples, an overlap was provided for second quarter 1956. Within the third sample, an overlap was provided for each quarter in calendar year 1958 to splice the estimates based upon the 1945 and 1957 editions of the *Standard Industrial Classification Manual* (SIC).

The classification of a corporation has been determined, in general, on the basis of the consolidated operations of the reporting company (as opposed to the establishment). In the reports for 1947 through 1958, classification was based on the 1945 edition of the SIC manual. Beginning 1959, estimates were based on the classification of corporations within the framework of the 1957 edition. In 1963, the *Enterprise Standard Industrial Classification* (ESIC) was used in the classification of companies. The structure of the 1968 revision of the ESIC follows closely that of the 1967 edition of the SIC.

For further description concerning compilation of these series, see Federal Trade Commission, *Quarterly Financial Report for Manufacturing Corporations*. Specific information concerning significant changes and revisions is contained in the following issues of the *Report*: Third quarter 1953, third quarter 1956, first quarter 1959, and first quarter 1965.

P 107–112. Purchases of structures and equipment, in manufacturing industries, 1863–1970.

Source: U.S. Bureau of Economic Analysis, *Fixed Nonresidential Business Capital in the United States, 1925–1973*, National Technical

Information Service, Springfield, Va., January 1974, pp. 425–427 and 437–439; and unpublished data.

Private purchases of structures and equipment for manufacturing establishments were derived from the estimates of gross private domestic investment in new industrial buildings and producers' durable equipment that are included in the gross national product estimates of the Department of Commerce. The outlays on structures and equipment were adjusted to benchmarks based on expenditures for new plant and equipment in the census of manufactures for 1939, 1947, 1954, 1958, 1963, and 1967, and the annual survey of manufactures for other years beginning with 1950 and ending with 1966. The census controls were extended through 1970 by data from plant and equipment expenditure surveys conducted jointly by the Bureau of Economic Analysis (formerly Office of Business Economics) and the Securities and Exchange Commission.

The purchases of structures and of equipment were converted to constant (1958) cost by the indexes used to deflate the corresponding individual series in the gross national product.

For a more detailed discussion and for tabulations derived from these and related series, see source.

P 113–118. Depreciation (straight-line) on manufacturing structures and equipment, 1925–1970.

Source: See source for series P 107–112, pp. 7–9 and 50.

Information on the service lives of capital assets is deficient. Not enough is known either about the average service lives of the producers' durable equipment and structures that make up the stock of fixed capital, or about how the service lives of individual items depart from average. Differences in the basic physical characteristics of capital assets, variations among the practices of their owners with respect to use and retirement, technological changes and changes in demand, all make for a large dispersion of service lives and help to explain the dearth of information about them. The useful life information was drawn largely from *Income Tax, Depreciation and Obsolescence, Estimated Useful Lives, and Depreciation Rates*, Bulletin F, Internal Revenue Service. The actual service lives used were 85 percent of Bulletin F for equipment, and 68 percent of Bulletin F for structures. (See pages T-4 and T-5 of source for reasons behind the use of shorter service lives.)

Average service lives were estimated for each of the 20 types of equipment and 10 types of structures which are detailed in the GNP gross investment series with which the calculation starts. Average life for each type of nonfarm equipment was derived by assigning service lives as shown in Bulletin F to each of the equipment items of that type and deriving an average for the type for each year based on weights reflecting shipments of each item as shown in the censuses and annual surveys of manufactures. Altogether, Bulletin F service lives for about 180 items of equipment were used in obtaining averages for the 20 types. Average lives for farm equipment were derived from several unpublished Department of Agriculture studies.

Depreciation at constant cost has been estimated by applying information on the length of useful lives to the constant dollar purchases of structures and equipment.

Underlying the average service life of a given type of asset is a distribution of discards. For example, trucks have an average service life of 10 years, but some trucks are wrecked after a few months and others are used for 15 or 20 years. To take into account that similar assets are discarded at different ages, a pattern labeled the Winfrey S-3 distribution was introduced. It is a minor modification of the original Winfrey S-3 curve. (See Robley Winfrey, *Statistical Analysis of Industrial Property Retirement*, Iowa Engineering Experiment Station Bulletin 125, Dec. 11, 1935.) The new pattern is a bell-shaped distribution whose mean is the average service life of the asset in question, with discards starting at 45 percent of the average life and continuing until 155 percent of the average life has been attained. In the absence of sufficient information to support any alternative course, that service life distribution was applied uniformly to all the gross investment series to derive the gross capital stocks and related estimates.

P 119–122. Real net value of assets in manufacturing industries, in 1958 dollars, 1925–1970.

Source: See source for series P 107–112, pp. T–25, 286, 287, and 397.

Estimates are for privately owned structures and equipment assets in manufacturing establishments (in contrast to the firm), and represent the undepreciated value remaining in past acquisitions including the purchases of Government surplus assets at original acquisition prices. The latter were derived from the estimates of gross private domestic investment in newly constructed nonresidential structures and producers' durable equipment that are included in the gross national product estimates of the Department of Commerce. The outlays on structures were adjusted to benchmarks, based mainly on expenditures for new plant construction by establishments included in the census of manufactures. Data on gross investment by manufacturing establishments from censuses and annual surveys of manufactures were used as industry totals. The asset detail was developed on the basis of unpublished Internal Revenue Service studies on lives of depreciable assets and several specialized industry studies which provided detailed information on the composition of assets in manufacturing. Purchases of equipment were converted to constant (1958) cost by the indexes used to deflate the corresponding component of the gross national product. Purchases of structures were deflated by constant cost 2, which is a closer approximation to a price index than is constant cost 1. For the composition of these costs, see table 4, pp. T–17 to T–19 of source.

Depreciation was allocated over the useful life by the double-declining balance method, under which twice the straight-line rate of depreciation is charged in the first year, and the same percentage rate is applied in successive years to the remaining value of the asset. (See page T–12 of source.)

For a discussion of the data and methodology of estimation of Government-owned, privately operated assets for each of the four major owning agencies—Department of Defense, Atomic Energy Commission, Maritime Administration, and National Aeronautics and Space Administration—see pages T–22 and T–23 of source.

P 123–176. Capital in manufacturing industries, in book value and in 1929 dollars (Creamer), 1879–1957.

Source: 1879–1937, Daniel Creamer, Sergei Dobrovolsky, and Israel Borenstein, *Capital in Manufacturing and Mining: Its Formation and Financing*, Princeton University Press, 1960, Appendix A, tables 8 and 9; 1948–1957, Daniel Creamer, *Capital Expansion and Capacity in Postwar Manufacturing*, National Industrial Conference Board, Inc., New York, *Studies in Business Economics*, No. Seventy-Two, 1961, Appendix G, tables G–1 and G–2. (Copyright.)

Estimates for 1879–1919 are based on data in various reports of the census of manufactures. For 1929–1957, the estimates are based on balance sheet data of corporations (raised to the level of all firms) published by the Internal Revenue Service (formerly Bureau of Internal Revenue) in *Statistics of Income*. Fixed capital includes land, buildings, and equipment (all net of depreciation). Working capital includes all other assets, other than investments in securities (chiefly cash, accounts and notes receivable, and inventories). Structures and equipment owned by the Federal Government but operated by private firms are excluded in all years. For a detailed description of data, adjustments and limitations, see Appendix A, section A, of the first source.

Figures in 1929 dollars were derived by dividing the estimates of capital in book values, by price indexes of book values expressed in 1929 prices. The latter are the implicit indexes derived by dividing the sum of the reported book values of the 15 major industry groups

comprising all manufactures by the sum of the book values expressed in 1929 prices of the 15 major groups.

The general procedure for deflating capital is to derive a composite index of prices underlying book values of buildings, machinery and equipment, and working capital for each of the 15 major industrial groups shown here. A construction cost index weighted by volume of construction depreciated over 50 years is used to represent the changes in the book value of land and buildings. This component of the composite index is identical for all 15 groups. For machinery and equipment, a price index of general machinery and equipment is used for all 15 groups, but in each group the index is weighted by volume of machinery and equipment produced, depreciated according to length of life typical for a given industry as reported by the Internal Revenue Service in *Income Tax, Depreciation and Obsolescence, Estimated Useful Lives, and Depreciation Rates*, Bulletin F. Because of these changing industry weights, a different deflator for machinery and equipment is obtained for each major group. The wholesale price index of the output of a given major industry is used to deflate working capital.

For derivation of the deflators for each of the 15 major groups, see Appendix A, section B, of the first source.

P 177–196. Share of total value added by manufacture accounted for by the 200 largest manufacturing companies, and by the 50 and 100 largest identical manufacturing companies, 1947–1970.

Source: U.S. Bureau of the Census. 1947–1967, *1967 Census of Manufactures*, vol. I, p. 9–6; 1970, Annual Survey of Manufactures, *Value of Shipment Concentration Ratios*, M70 (AS)–9.

Data for 1962 and 1966 are based on the annual survey of manufactures; other years on the census of manufactures.

These data reflect the activity of the largest companies in the industrial sector as a whole. A company is defined as the total of its industrial establishments, including not only its manufacturing plants but also auxiliary establishments such as warehouses and central administrative offices. Value added for all manufacturing establishments of a given company was aggregated irrespective of the industry classification of the individual establishments. The companies were then arrayed by magnitude of value added in each specified year and totals were computed for the 50, 100, 150, and 200 largest companies.

The rankings in 1947 and 1954 were based on unadjusted value added; those for later years on adjusted value added. See text for series P 10.

For series P 177–180, companies were classified in size groups in each particular year based on their size in that year. The largest companies are those which were the largest in each of the specified years. Thus, a size group, such as the top four, does not necessarily include the same companies from year to year.

For series P 181–196, the 100 largest companies in each year specified in the stub of the table were selected and their proportion of total value added by manufacture in each of the years shown in the column headings was computed. These data thus measure the changes in concentration ratios for a fixed group of companies from one year to another. In case of mergers, the larger of the two at the time of merger was considered to be the predecessor company.

P 197–204. Concentration in manufacturing, by industry group, 1901, 1947, and 1954.

Source: **Series P 197**, G. Warren Nutter, *The Extent of Enterprise Monopoly in the United States*, tables 10 and 39, copyright 1951 by The University of Chicago. **Series P 198**, M. A. Adelman, "The Measurement of Industrial Concentration," *Review of Economics and Statistics*, vol. 33, November 1951, table 14 (copyright, Harvard College; based on *Hearings Before the Subcommittee on Study of Monopoly Power*, House of Representatives, 81st Congress, 1st session, Serial No. 14, part 2–B, pp. 1436–1456). **Series P 199–200** are tabulations prepared by the Bureau of the Census from data reported in the census of manufactures. **Series P 201–204**, Irving Rottenberg, "New Statistics on Companies and on Concentration in Manufacturing From the 1954 Census," *Proceedings of the American Statistical Association*, 1957, table 5 (copyright).

The basic source of most of the data in all columns is the census of manufactures. The concentration ratio is defined as the percent of total industry sales (or, occasionally, value added) made by the four largest sellers.

The entries for series P 197–198 represent the value added by manufacture in 4-digit SIC industries (see general note for series P 1–374) with concentration ratios of 50 or higher, as a percentage of value added by all 4-digit industries included in each 2-digit industry group (e.g., "food and kindred products" is a 2-digit group containing "meat-packing plants" and 2 other 4-digit meat industries, "creamery butter" and 5 other 4-digit dairy industries, etc.).

The figures for series P 199–204 are average concentration ratios for each 2-digit industry group, i.e., the concentration ratio of each 4-digit industry is weighted in proportion to its employment or value added, as indicated, as a proportion of total employment or total value added by the whole 2-digit group.

Series P 199–200 include all industries for the given year—452 in 1947, and 434 in 1954. Because of changes in 4-digit industry definitions, concentration ratios are not fully comparable. Series P 201–204 are based on 375 comparable industries accounting for 85 percent of all value added by manufacture in 1947, and for 82 percent in 1954.

The first total line is a set of weighted averages based on value-added weights derived from the basic data for the respective years shown. Figures on the second total line (for series P 201–204) are averages of the concentration ratios shown for the 20 industry groups.

Where the change in concentration, 1947–1954, as shown in series P 199–200, is substantially different from that shown in series P 201–204, the difference is due to industry redefinition and to inclusion or exclusion of industries from the census of manufactures. A striking example is in group 39, "miscellaneous manufactures" from which major group 19, "ordnance and accessories," was omitted for national security reasons.

P 205–211. Selected statistics for operating manufacturing establishments, by legal form of organization, 1939–1967.

Source: U.S. Bureau of the Census, 1939, *Sixteenth Census of the United States: 1940, Census of Manufactures, 1939*, vol. I, p. 230; 1947–1967, *1967 Census of Manufactures*, vol. I, p. 3–4.

Each establishment included in the censuses of manufactures was classified into one of the following legal forms of organization:

Corporate—an establishment (other than a cooperative) owned by an organization or company legally incorporated under State laws.

Noncorporate—individual proprietorships, partnerships, cooperatives, establishments operated by estate administrators, trusteeships, receiverships, public and quasi-public organizations, and, in addition, misassignments of small establishments that were not corrected because they were not statistically significant.

Individual proprietorship—an establishment owned by one person, who may or may not actively participate in the operation of the business.

Partnership—an establishment owned by two or more persons, each of whom has a financial interest in and responsibility for the business. A partner may or may not actively participate in the operation of the business.

See also text for series P 1–12.

P 212–215. Percent distribution of production workers and of value added in manufacturing establishments, by legal form of ownership, 1899–1967.

Source: U.S. Bureau of the Census. 1899, *Census of Manufactures: 1905*, part I, p. liv; 1904 and 1909, *Thirteenth Census of the United*

States, 1910, Manufactures: 1909, vol. VIII, p. 135; 1914 and 1919, *Fourteenth Census of the United States, 1920, Manufactures: 1919*, vol. VIII, p. 108; 1929, *Fifteenth Census of the United States, 1930, Manufactures: 1929*, vol. I, p. 95; 1939, *Sixteenth Census of the United States, 1940, Manufactures: 1939*, vol. I, p. 229; 1947–1967, *U.S. Census of Manufactures, 1967*, vol. I.

Percentages were computed from figures published in the various Bureau of the Census reports cited as sources.

See also data and text for series P 205–211.

P 216–226. Consumption of energy materials, 1899–1967.

Source: U.S. Bureau of the Census. *Thirteenth Census of the United States: 1910*, vol. X, p. 662; *Census of Manufactures: 1963*, vol. I, pp. 7–90 and 7–91; and *Census of Manufactures: 1967*, Special Report MC67(S)-4, *Fuels and Electric Energy Consumed*, pp. 8–9.

Data for fuels consumed for heat and power were converted to kilowatt-hour equivalents, the international unit of energy, and then added to the quantity of purchased electric energy. The conversion factors used for each fuel are shown in the source reports. For fuels, quantities include both fuels purchased for use as fuel and fuels made and used in the same establishment.

P 227. Coffee imported, 1860–1970.

Source: 1860–1914, see source for series P 17, pp. 8–9 and 143–144; 1915–1929, see Arthur F. Burns, pp. 292–293, cited as source for series P 231; 1930–1947, U.S. Bureau of the Census, *Foreign Commerce and Navigation of the United States*; 1948–1962, same agency, *Quarterly Summary of Foreign Commerce of the United States*, for those years; 1963–1970, same agency, *U.S. Imports of Merchandise for Consumption*, Reports FT 110, FT 125, and FT 135, calendar year issues.

The data for 1860–1933 are described as net imports (general imports) minus foreign exports; for 1934–1970, they are described as imports for consumption minus foreign exports. However, on duty-free commodities, like coffee, general imports equal imports for consumption. Data cover U.S. customs area, which includes Alaska, Hawaii, and Puerto Rico.

P 228. Raw cotton used in textiles, 1860–1970.

Source: U.S. Bureau of the Census. 1860–1909, *Bulletin 160, Cotton Production and Distribution, 1926*, p. 49; 1910–1945, *Bulletin 183, Cotton Production and Distribution, 1946*, pp. 26–31; 1946–1962, *Cotton Production and Distribution*, annual reports; 1963–1970, Current Industrial Reports, series M22P, *Cotton, Man-Made Fiber Staple, and Linters, Summary for Cotton Season*, various annual issues.

Data are for years ending August 31 through 1910, July 31 thereafter. Figures are in running bales, except that for 1860–1870, they are in equivalent 500-pound bales. Data exclude linters for 1860–1908 and include them thereafter.

P 229. Wool used in textiles, 1918–1970.

Source: U.S. Bureau of the Census. 1922–1957, *Facts for Industry, Wool Consumption and Stocks*, monthly issues. (Title may vary for this report.) 1958–1970, Current Industrial Reports, series M 220, *Consumption on the Woolen and Worsted Systems*, monthly issues.

Figures relate to scoured wool plus greasy wool reduced to a scoured basis, assuming average yields varying with class, origin, grade, and whether shorn or pulled. For 1946–1970, they include raw wool consumed in woolen and worsted systems only.

For a series on apparent consumption of all wool, 1870–1929, see Arthur F. Burns, pp. 296–297, cited as source for series P 231.

P 230. Unmanufactured silk imports for consumption, 1883–1970.

Source: 1883–1929, see Arthur F. Burns, pp. 294–295, cited as source for series P 231; 1930–1931, U.S. Bureau of Foreign and Domestic Commerce, *Foreign Commerce and Navigation of the U.S.*, vol. I, for respective years; 1932, U.S. Bureau of the Census, *Statistical Abstract of the United States, 1940*, p. 732; 1933–1949, *Statistical Abstract, 1950*, p. 638; 1950–1955, Textile Economics Bureau, Inc., New York, *Textile Organon*, vol. XXXVII, No. 3, March 1966; 1955–1970, *Textile Organon*, March 1971.

Figures are derived by subtracting foreign exports from general imports of all types of unmanufactured silk. Spun silk is not included.

For a series on raw silk imports (excluding silk from cocoons and waste) for 1860–1914, see source for series P 17, pp. 8–9 and 153–155; and for 1870–1929, see Arthur F. Burns, cited above.

P 231.   Wheat flour produced, 1860–1970.

Source: 1860–1914, see source for series P 17, pp. 8–9 and 135–139; 1915–1929, Arthur F. Burns, *Production Trends in the United States Since 1870*, National Bureau of Economic Research, New York, 1934, pp. 299 and 339 (copyright); 1931 and 1933, Solomon Fabricant, *The Output of Manufacturing Industries, 1899–1937*, National Bureau of Economic Research, New York, 1940, p. 395 (copyright; data from census of manufactures); 1935–1970, U.S. Dept. of Agriculture, Economic Research Service, Agricultural Economic Report No. 138, *Food Consumption, Prices, and Expenditures*, and Supplement for 1970.

Reported data in hundredweights were converted to barrels containing 196 pounds of flour. These estimates are based on commercial production of wheat flour reported by the Bureau of the Census. They include flour milled in bond from foreign wheat plus the estimated flour equivalent of farm wheat ground for flour or exchanged for flour for farm household use.

P 232.   Refined sugar produced, 1860–1970.

Source: 1860–1914, see source for series P 17, pp. 8–9 and 139–143; 1919–1933, see Solomon Fabricant, pp. 382 and 387, cited as source for series P 231; 1934–1945, U.S. Department of Agriculture, *Agricultural Statistics, 1952*, p. 111; 1946–1960, *Agricultural Statistics, 1967*, p. 83; 1961–1970, *Agricultural Statistics, 1971*, p. 88.

Figures represent production in cane-sugar refineries and in beet-sugar factories.

P 233.   Canned corn produced, 1885–1970.

Source: 1885–1908, see Arthur F. Burns, pp. 300–301 and 341, cited as source for series P 231; 1909–1970, National Canners Association, *Canned Food Pack Statistics, 1971–72*.

A case consists of 24 No. 2 cans.

P 234.   Canned tomatoes produced, 1885–1970.

Source: 1885–1898, 1900–1903, and 1905–1907, see Arthur F. Burns, pp. 300–301 and 341, cited as source for series P 231. National Canners Association, 1899 and 1904, *Canned Food Pack Statistics, 1969–70*; 1908–1970, *Canned Food Pack Statistics, 1971–72*.

A case consists of 24 No. 2 cans. The figures for 1885–1907 were published in the unit case of 24 No. 3 cans. They have been converted to a unit case of 24 No. 2 cans by multiplying by 1.707. The conversion factor is taken from National Canners Association, Washington, D.C., *Canned Food Pack Statistics: 1940, part 1—Vegetables*, March 1941, p. 19.

Except for some of the early historical data which came from reports of the Bureau of the Census, the data have been compiled by the National Canners Association with the cooperation of State, regional, and commodity associations.

P 235.   Beer produced, 1870–1970.

Source: 1870–1929, see Arthur F. Burns, pp. 292–293, cited as source for series P 231. U.S. Internal Revenue Service (formerly

Bureau of Internal Revenue), 1930–1932, unpublished data; 1933, *Annual Report of the Commissioner of Internal Revenue, 1936*; 1934–1970, U.S. Bureau of Alcohol, Tobacco and Firearms, *Alcohol, Tobacco and Firearms, Summary Statistics*, 1973, p. 41.

The unit "barrel" contains 31 wine gallons. For 1921–1933, only cereal beverages were permitted to be produced.

P 236–236a.   Distilled spirits produced, 1870–1970.

Source: 1870–1929, see Arthur F. Burns, pp. 292–293, cited as source for series P 231. U.S. Internal Revenue Service (formerly Bureau of Internal Revenue), 1930–1933, *Annual Report of the Commissioner of Internal Revenue*, annual issues. 1934–1970, see source for series P 235, p. 20.

The computation of taxable gallons excludes all fractional parts of a proof gallon less than one-tenth. Figures are for years ending June 30 and include data for Hawaii; beginning 1928, they also include data for Puerto Rico. Series P 236 includes industrial alcohol for all years. Series P 236a was derived by subtracting figures for industrial alcohol (i.e., tax-free withdrawals) from total distilled spirits production.

P 237–238.   Fats and oils produced, 1922–1970.

Source: U.S. Bureau of the Census. 1922–1940, *Animal and Vegetable Fats and Oils*, annual issues; 1941–1970, Current Industrial Reports, series M20J and M20K, *Fats and Oils*, 1970 and earlier years, summary issues (prior to 1958, series M 17-1, M 17-2, and M 28).

P 239.   Manufactured tobacco and snuff products, 1870–1970.

Source: 1870–1879, see source for series P 17, pp. 14–15 and 192–193; 1880–1929, see Arthur F. Burns, pp. 296–297, cited as source for series P 231; 1930–1970, U.S. Department of Agriculture, *Agricultural Statistics, 1952, 1957, 1962, 1967*, and *1971* editions.

Primary source of the figures is the *Annual Report of the Commissioner of Internal Revenue*.

P 240.   Cigars, 1870–1970.

Source: 1870–1879, see source for series P 17, pp. 14–15 and 189–191; 1880–1929, see Arthur F. Burns, pp. 298–299, cited as source for series P 231. U.S. Internal Revenue Service (formerly Bureau of Internal Revenue), 1930–1939 and 1941–1949, *Annual Report of the Commissioner of Internal Revenue*, various issues; 1940 and 1950–1970, *Alcohol and Tobacco Summary Statistics*, annual issues.

For 1870–1949, figures exclude cigars weighing not more than 3 pounds per 1,000.

P 241.   Cigarettes, 1870–1970.

Source: 1870–1879, see source for series P 17, pp. 14–15 and 192; 1880–1929, see Arthur F. Burns, pp. 298–299, cited as source for series P 231; 1930–1970, see source for series P 240.

Figures represent large and small cigarettes and small cigars for 1870–1949, excluding those manufactured in bonded manufacturing warehouses. For 1954–1970, small cigars are excluded.

P 242–243.   Apparel products, 1927–1970.

Source: U.S. Bureau of the Census, Current Industrial Reports, series MA23A, *Annual Apparel Survey*, 1970 and earlier years, summary issues.

Men's and boys' suits and separate coats represent (1) men's suits, excluding ski, slack, snow, and uniform, (2) men's tailored dress and sport coats and jackets, excluding uniform, (3) boys' tailored dress and sport coats, and (4) boys' suits, including students', cadets', and junior boys'.

Women's, misses', and juniors' dresses include both dresses sold at a unit price and those sold at a dozen-price.

P 244.   Rayon and acetate yarns available, 1911–1970.

Source: 1911–1939, Textile Economics Bureau, Inc., New York, *Textile Organon—Base Book of Textile Statistics*, vol. XXXIII, No. 1, January 1962; 1940–1955, *Textile Organon*, January–February, 1971; 1956–1970, *Textile Organon*, March 1971.   (Copyright.)

Figures represent producers' domestic shipments plus imports of yarn and exclude staple, tow, waste, and other rayon and acetate products.   Data for rayon relate to manmade fibers produced by the viscose, cuprammonium, and nitrocellulosic (discontinued after 1934) processes.   Rayon horsehair and straw are included in the filament yarn figures for 1952–1970 (for 1940–51, production of these items averaged just under 1 million pounds per year).   Acetate means manmade fibers composed of cellulose acetate and triacetate.

For 1941–1970, figures for rayon and acetate are as actually reported by the entire industry; earlier data are estimated totals based on reports obtained from 86 percent or more of the industry, with adjustments for complete coverage in accordance with information from the census of manufactures.

P 245.   Non-cellulosic yarn available, 1940–1970.

Source: See source for series P 244, 1940–1970.

Data include producers' domestic shipments plus imports of yarn and exclude staple and tow.

P 246.   Finished knit cloth shipped, 1933–1970.

Source: U.S. Bureau of the Census, Current Industrial Reports. 1933–1946, series M67C, *Underwear and Allied Products: Underwear, Knit Cloth, and Knit Fabric Gloves; and Underwear and Knit Cloth for Sale;* 1947–1965, series M22K, *Knit Cloth for Sale;* 1966–1970, series MQ22K, *Shipments of Knit Cloth*, summary issues.

P 247.   Carpets and rugs shipped, 1899–1970.

Source: U.S. Bureau of the Census.   1899–1947, *Census of Manufactures* reports; 1954–1970, Current Industrial Reports, series M22L and MQ22K, *Carpets and Rugs*, summary issues.

P 248–250.   Sodium hydroxide and ammonia produced, 1899–1970.

Source: U.S. Bureau of the Census. 1899–1939, *Census of Manufactures* reports; thereafter, Current Industrial Reports, series M28A, *Inorganic Chemicals*, summary issues.

P 251.   Sulfuric acid produced, 1899–1970.

Source: U.S. Bureau of the Census. 1899–1927, unpublished data; 1929–1970, Current Industrial Reports, series M28A, *Inorganic Chemicals*, summary issues.

Figures are combined totals for sulfuric acid produced by the contact and chamber processes, including spent acid fortified in the contact plants with the simultaneous production of new acid. Production of Government-owned plants, which was large during the war period, is not included for that period; for the most part, this production was available only for military use.   However, for 1954–1970, appreciable amounts of sulfuric acid produced in Government-owned privately operated plants are included.   Figures for 1946–1950 include estimates based on annual totals of byproduct operations of a few smelters reporting to the Bureau of Mines; the estimated data included vary from 4 percent in 1946 to 2 percent in 1950.   For 1899–1939, figures are based on reports of the Census of Manufactures; they are shown in those reports on a 50° Baume basis but are here converted to 100 percent H_2SO_4. Beginning January 1948, figures are not strictly comparable with earlier data because of the inclusion of additional plants; however, the addition of these plants increased the production of the specified chemical by less than 3.5 percent.

P 252.   Paints, varnishes, and lacquers produced, 1899–1970.

Source: U.S. Bureau of the Census. 1899–1947, *Census of Manufactures*, reports for various census years; 1953–1970, Current Industrial Reports, series M28F, *Paint, Varnish, and Lacquer*, summary issues.

P 253.   Superphosphates produced, 1860–1970.

Source: 1860–1954, U.S. Department of Agriculture, *Statistics on Fertilizers and Liming Materials in the United States*, Statistical Bulletin No. 191, p. 43, April 1957; 1955–1957, U.S. Bureau of the Census, *Facts for Industry*, series M19D-06 and M19D-08; 1958–1970, Current Industrial Reports, series M28B, *Inorganic Fertilizer Materials and Related Acids*, summary issues.

P 254.   Light products of distillation, 1918–1970.

Source: U.S. Bureau of Mines, *Mineral Industry Surveys*, "Petroleum Statements," annual issues.

These figures relate essentially to the production of gasoline and naphtha.   Figures for 1918–1927, 1929–1956, and 1962–1963 are not strictly comparable.   The figure for 1929 on a basis comparable with preceding years is 438 million barrels.   For 1953–1970, figures for jet fuel are excluded.

P 255.   Illuminating oils (kerosene) produced, 1916–1970.

Source: U.S. Bureau of Mines, *Mineral Industry Surveys*, "Petroleum Statements," annual issues.

Figures for 1916–1927, 1929–1956, and 1962–1963 are not strictly comparable.   The figure for 1929 comparable with the preceding years is 55.7 million barrels.   For 1953–1959, figures exclude jet fuel. Beginning 1960, data include jet fuel used in commercial aircraft; beginning 1965, they include kerosene–type jet fuels.

P 256.   Fuel oils produced, 1916–1970.

Source: See source for series P 255.

Figures for 1916–1927, 1929–1956, and 1962–1963 are not strictly comparable.   The figure for 1929 comparable with the preceding years is 390 million barrels.   For 1953–1970, jet fuels are excluded.

P 257.   Lubricating oils produced, 1916–1970.

Source: See source for series P 255.

Figures for 1916–1927 and 1929–1956 are not strictly comparable. The figure for 1929 comparable with preceding years is 37 million barrels.

P 258.   Paraffin wax produced, 1916–1970.

Source: See source for series P 255.

For 1929–1956, figures are labeled petroleum wax.   The basic source of these data is the Bureau of Mines, *Minerals Yearbook*.

P 259.   Pneumatic motor vehicle tires produced, 1914–1967.

Source: U.S. Bureau of the Census, *Census of Manufactures*, reports for various census years.

P 260–261.   Men's and women's shoes produced, 1899–1970.

Source: 1899–1919, see Solomon Fabricant, cited as source for series P 231; U.S. Bureau of the Census, 1921–1946, *Statistical Abstract of the United States*, various editions, *1929–1947;* 1947–1954, unpublished data; 1955–1970, Current Industrial Reports, series M31A, *Shoes and Slippers*, summary issues.

Figures represent pairs of leather uppers for men's and women's shoes.   They do not include youths' and boys', misses', children's, infants', athletic, part leather, or nonleather shoes. For 1930–1970, figures for men's shoes are not strictly comparable with earlier years because large quantities of heavy footwear included with men's shoes for later years were included with athletic shoes for earlier years.

P 262. Rails produced, 1860–1970.

Source: 1860–1872, see source for series P 17; 1873–1970, American Iron and Steel Institute, *Annual Statistical Report*, various issues, 1965–1970 (copyright); and unpublished data.

Figures include both iron and steel rails, rerolled rails, and girder and high T rails. Rails are a component of "hot rolled iron and steel," series P 270. For 1860–1867, figures include production of iron rails only.

P 263. Structural iron and steel shapes produced, 1879–1970.

Source: 1879–1889, see source for series P 17; 1892–1970, American Iron and Steel Institute, *Annual Statistical Report*, various issues (copyright), and unpublished data.

Structural shapes are a component of "hot rolled iron and steel," series P 270.

P 264. Common and face brick produced, 1869–1970.

Source: 1869–1899 (decennially), 1904, 1909, 1914, 1919–1939 (biennially), 1947, 1954, 1958, 1963, and 1967, U.S. Bureau of the Census, *Census of Manufactures*, reports for various years; 1895–1912, U.S. Geological Survey, *Mineral Resources of the United States*, various issues; 1913–1959, U.S. Bureau of the Census, Facts for Industry, *Clay Construction Products*, summary issues; 1960–1970, Current Industrial Reports, series M320, *Clay Construction Products*, summary issues.

The figures for 1869 and 1879 are for common brick only. For 1889, 1899, and 1904, the production of "fancy or ornamental brick" has been added to the production of "face brick," the reason being that "the best grade of 'face' or 'front' brick appears to have been classified as 'fancy or ornamental' brick" in these years. Beginning 1943, common and face brick are classified as "unglazed" brick.

P 265–269. Raw steel produced, 1860–1970.

Source: American Iron and Steel Institute, *Annual Statistical Report*, various issues (copyright).

For 1934–1970, figures include only that part of steel castings made in foundries producing steel ingots.

P 270. Hot rolled iron and steel produced, 1864–1970.

Source: American Iron and Steel Institute, *Annual Statistical Report*, various issues, 1965–1970 (copyright), and unpublished data.

Figures include rails, plates and sheets, merchant bar and skelp production, wire rods, and structural shapes.

P 271. Copper and copper base alloy, rolled, drawn, and extruded products shipped, 1925–1970.

Source: U.S. Bureau of the Census. 1925–1947, see source for series P 259; 1952–1970, Current Industrial Reports, series BDSAF-84, *Shipments of Copper-Base Mill and Foundry Products*, summary issues.

P 272–274. Fabricated metal products, 1941–1970.

Source: U.S. Bureau of the Census, Current Industrial Reports, series M34D, *Metal Cans*, and series M34N, *Heating and Cooking Equipment (Except Electric)*, summary issues.

Warm air-furnaces, P 273, include oil- and gas-fired furnaces sold as component parts of "year-round air–conditioning units."

P 275–276. Gasoline and diesel engines produced, 1947–1970.

Source: U.S. Bureau of the Census, Current Industrial Reports, series MA35L, *Internal Combustion Engines*, summary issues.

Production data exclude engines for outboard, automotive, and aircraft purposes.

P 277. Wheel tractors, complete, produced, 1922–1970.

Source: U.S. Bureau of the Census, Current Industrial Reports, series M35S, *Tractors (Except Garden Tractors)*, summary issues.

P 278. Metal cutting machines shipped, 1947–1970.

Source: U.S. Bureau of the Census, Current Industrial Reports, series M35W, *Metalworking Machinery*, summary issues.

P 279. Typewriters shipped, 1900–1970.

Source: U.S. Bureau of the Census, Current Industrial Reports, series M35C, *Typewriters*, summary issues.

Except as indicated in footnotes, standard electric and manual and portable models are included.

P 280. Room air-conditioners shipped, 1945–1970.

Source: U.S. Bureau of the Census, Current Industrial Reports, series M35M, *Air-Conditioning and Refrigeration Equipment*, summary issues.

P 281–282. Fractional horsepower motors and integral horsepower motors and generators shipped, 1914–1970.

Source: U.S. Bureau of the Census. 1914–1958, see source for series P 259; thereafter, Current Industrial Reports, series M36H, *Motors and Generators*, summary issues.

P 283–285. Domestic ranges, electric, shipped; household refrigerators produced; and household washing machines, mechanical, shipped, 1921–1967.

Source: Series P 284, 1921–1937, see Solomon Fabricant, p. 585, cited as source for series P 231; all other data, see source for series P 259.

P 286–287. Electric lamps produced, 1899–1970.

Source: U.S. Bureau of the Census. 1899–1939, see source for series P 259; thereafter, Current Industrial Reports, series M36B and M36D, *Electric Lamps*.

P 288–290. Home-type radio receivers, home-type radio-phonograph combinations, and phonographs shipped, 1899–1970.

Source: U.S. Bureau of the Census. 1899–1939, see source for series P 259; thereafter, Current Industrial Reports, series MA36M, *Home-Type Radio Receivers and Television Sets, Automobile Radios, Phonographs, and Record Player Attachments*.

Home-type radio receivers and radio-phonograph combinations for 1923–1939 include automobile sets.

P 291. Trailer coaches, housing type, shipped, 1937–1967.

Source: See source for series P 259.

P 292. Truck trailers shipped, 1935–1970.

Source: U.S. Bureau of the Census. 1935–1939, see source for series P 259; thereafter, Current Industrial Reports, series M37L, *Truck Trailers*, summary issues.

P 293.   Locomotives produced, 1880–1967.

Source: 1880–1929, see Arthur F. Burns, pp. 300–301, cited as source for series P 231; 1930–1945, American Railway Car Institute, *Railway Age, Annual Statistical and Outlook Number*, January 6, 1945, p. 91, and *Annual Statistical and Outlook Number*, January 5, 1946, p. 88 (copyright); 1947–1967, see source for series P 259.

For 1905–1945, Canadian output is included although the U.S. output is shown separately beginning with 1929 (see, for example, *Railway Age, Annual Statistical Number*, January 4, 1947). For 1880–1911, locomotives built in railroad repair shops are excluded. For 1942–1944, figures exclude locomotives built for U.S. Government and for lend-lease program.

This series was discontinued when the new traction power was supplied almost exclusively by diesel units. A locomotive may be composed of one or more diesel units.

Data for 1947–1967, which are from the census of manufactures, represent shipments.

P 294.   Railroad passenger cars produced, 1871–1967.

Source: 1871–1914, see source for series P 17, pp. 14–15 and 196–197; 1915–1957, see source for series P 295; 1958–1967, see source for series P 259.

For 1871–1919, figures represent domestic production of passenger cars, exclusive of that in railroad repair shops; thereafter, figures include production in railroad repair shops. For 1920–1957, figures represent "passenger train cars delivered."

Data for 1958–1967, which are from the census of manufactures, represent shipments.

P 295.   Railroad freight cars produced, 1871–1967.

Source: 1871–1914, see source for series P 17, pp. 14–15 and 193–196; 1915–1919, American Railway Car Institute, *Railway Age, Annual Statistical and Outlook Number*, January 7, 1939, p. 83; 1920–1957, *Railway Age, Annual Statistical and Outlook Number* (most recently entitled *Review and Outlook*), various issues, 1950–1958 (copyright); 1958–1967, see source for series P 259.

For 1871–1919, figures represent domestic production of freight cars, exclusive of that in railroad repair shops; thereafter, figures include production in railroad repair shops. For 1920–1957, figures represent "freight cars delivered."

Data for 1958–1967, which are from the census of manufactures, represent shipments.

P 296–297.   Horse-drawn vehicles produced, 1899–1967.

Source: 1899–1937, see Solomon Fabricant, p. 585, cited as source for series P 231; 1939–1967, see source for series P 259.

For 1899–1914, figures for farm wagons, trucks, and business vehicles include patrol wagons, ambulances, handcarts, and push-carts; for 1919–1925, they exclude mail carrier wagons and public conveyances and relate to products made within the industry (as classified by the Bureau of the Census); for 1927–1967, figures relate to all products made regardless of the industry classification of the establishment.

For 1899–1925, figures for carriages, buggies, and sulkies exclude sulkies; for 1933, include two-wheeled carts.

P 298.   Bicycles produced, 1899–1967.

Source: 1899–1937, see Solomon Fabricant, p. 590, cited as source for series P 231; 1939–1967, see source for series P 259.

For 1899–1921, figures relate to products made within the industry (as classified by the Bureau of the Census); for 1923–1967, figures relate to all products made regardless of the industry classification of the establishment.

P 299–300.   Pianos and organs produced, 1899–1967.

Source: 1899–1937, see Solomon Fabricant, pp. 597 and 598, cited as source for series P 231; 1939–1967, see source for series P 259.

For organs, series P 300, the data represent reed organs for 1899–1935, electronic organs thereafter.

P 301–317.   General note.

Capacity is rarely calculated on the basis of full-time operation of an industry (i.e., 365 days a year, 24 hours a day), but at varying criteria short of that. Capacity as of January 1 is generally used as the basis of computation. Exceptions to these general rules are noted in the text for each series, where applicable.

P 301.   Blast furnaces (pig iron), 1898–1960.

Source: American Iron and Steel Institute, *Annual Directory* and *Annual Statistical Report*, New York, various issues (copyright).

Figures include a 6.1 percent deduction from full-time operation to allow for rebuilding, relining, and repairing the equipment. Capacity is based on April 1 for 1898; November 1, 1901 and 1907; June 1, 1904; and the average of January 1 and July 1 for 1941–1944 and 1950.

None or negligible capacity in Alaska and Hawaii.

P 302.   Steel ingots and steel for castings, 1887–1960.

Source: See source for series P 301.

Figures include a 9.1 percent deduction from full-time operation to allow for rebuilding, relining, and repairing equipment, and for holiday shutdowns. Capacity is based on an average of January 1 and July 1 for 1941–1944.

None or negligible capacity in Alaska and Hawaii.

P 303.   Copper refining, 1907–1970.

Source: 1907–1930, Edwin G. Nourse, *America's Capacity to Produce*, The Brookings Institution, Washington, D.C., 1934, p. 557; 1931–1970, American Bureau of Metal Statistics, *Year Book*, New York, various issues. (Copyright.)

None or negligible capacity in Alaska and Hawaii.

P 304–305.   Lead refining, 1921–1970.

Source: American Bureau of Metal Statistics, *Year Book*, New York, various issues (copyright).

None or negligible capacity in Alaska and Hawaii.

P 306.   Zinc refining, 1921–1970.

Source: See source for series P 304–305.

Figures are not comparable throughout because of changes in components. For 1921–1925, figures represent distillation zinc; 1926–1940, distillation and electrolytic zinc; 1941–1970, slab zinc. As an alternative source for data, see U.S. Bureau of Mines, *Minerals Yearbook*, various issues.

None or negligible capacity in Alaska and Hawaii.

P 307.   Aluminum ingots, 1889–1970.

Source: 1889–1895, J. D. Edwards, et al., *The Aluminum Industry*, McGraw-Hill Publishing Co., New York, 1930 (copyright); 1910–1919, U.S. Business and Defense Services Administration (now Bureau of Domestic Commerce), *Materials Survey, Aluminum*, 1956; 1927–1938, U.S. Surplus Property Board, *Aluminum Plants and Facilities Report*, 1945; 1939–1970, American Bureau of Metal Statistics, *Year Book*, New York, various issues (copyright).

The general practice in this industry is to rate potline capacity on full-time operation. As an alternative source for data, see U.S. Bureau of Mines, *Minerals Yearbook*, various issues.

None or negligible capacity in Alaska and Hawaii.

P 308. Portland cement, 1910–1970.

Source: U.S. Geological Survey, 1910–1923, *Mineral Resources of the United States*, annual volumes; U.S. Bureau of Mines, 1924–1931, *Mineral Resources of the United States*, annual volumes; 1932–1970, *Minerals Yearbook*, annual volumes.

A deduction from full-time operation is taken for estimated average number of days required for repair or other unavoidable shutdowns. Favorable labor, fuel, and transportation conditions are assumed.

No capacity in Alaska; figures include Hawaii beginning 1960.

P 309. Crude petroleum refining, 1918–1970.

Source: U.S. Bureau of Mines, 1918–1961, *Petroleum Refineries, Including Cracking Plants in the United States, January 1, 1961* (also shown in *Minerals Yearbook*); 1962–1970, *Mineral Industry Survey*, Petroleum Refineries in the United States and Puerto Rico, January 1, annual issues.

Capacity is defined as the maximum daily average throughput (converted to an annual basis) of the plant in complete operation, with allowance for necessary shutdown time for routine maintenance, repairs, etc. It approximates the maximum daily average crude runs to stills that can be maintained for an extended period. Capacity is based on November 1 for 1924.

Includes Alaska for all years, Hawaii beginning 1960.

P 310–311. Coke, 1909–1961.

Source: 1909–1920, see first source cited for series P 303; 1921–1961, see sources cited for series P 308.

None or negligible capacity in Alaska and Hawaii.

P 312. Carbon black, 1928–1970.

Source: See source for series P 308.

None or negligible capacity in Alaska and Hawaii.

P 313. Sulfuric acid, 1945–1970.

Source: 1945, reprinted with permission from *Chemical and Engineering News*, Washington, D.C., July 10, 1945 (copyright by American Chemical Society); 1950–1970, U.S. Bureau of Domestic Commerce (formerly Business and Defense Services Administration), *Chemical Industry Report*, various issues.

Capacity is based on 350 days a year.

None or negligible capacity in Alaska and Hawaii.

P 314. Phosphatic fertilizers, 1900–1970.

Source: 1900–1951, U.S. Agricultural Research Service, *Statistics on Fertilizers and Liming Materials in the United States*, Statistical Bulletin No. 191, April 1957; 1952–1957, National Plant Food Institute, *Plant Food Review*, vol. 4, Nos. 2 and 3, 1958; 1958–1970, U.S. Bureau of Domestic Commerce (formerly Business and Defense Services Administration), unpublished data.

These data are the total of normal superphosphate, concentrated superphosphate, and miscellaneous phosphatic materials. Capacity of normal superphosphate is based on 300 two-shift days a year. Capacity of concentrated superphosphate and other phosphatic materials is based on 350 days a year, continuous operations.

None or negligible capacity in Alaska and Hawaii.

P 315. Total combined nitrogen, 1924–1970.

Source: 1924–1950, see source for series P 314; 1951–1955, U.S. Business and Defense Services Administration, *Summary Information on Anhydrous Ammonia*, Bulletin No. 142, February 1956; 1956–1970, U.S. Bureau of Domestic Commerce (formerly Business and Defense Services Administration), unpublished data.

This series was entitled "synthetic nitrogen" from 1924–1955. Capacity is based on 350 days a year, continuous operations.

None or negligible capacity in Alaska and Hawaii.

P 316. Rayon and acetate yarn, staple and tow, 1911–1970.

Source: 1911, *New York Times*, Special Chemistry Section, September 2, 1951; 1931–1970, Textile Economics Bureau, *Textile Organon* (prior to 1952, *Rayon Organon*), New York, various issues. (Copyright.)

Data for 1931–1938 are for yarn only; staple and tow data are not available for those years.

Capacity is as of November for all years except 1933 (July) and 1944 (April). Allowance was made for periodic shutdowns of machines for repair, overhaul, or cleaning on a set time schedule.

None or negligible capacity in Alaska and Hawaii.

P 317. Paper and paperboard, 1900–1970.

Source: American Paper Institute, *The Statistics of Paper, 1957*, and subsequent annual issues, New York (copyright).

Historic capacity, used until 1955, is based on 310 days a year, 24 hours a day, for paper and building paper and 313 days for paperboard. From 1956 to 1969, practical maximum capacity was used, based on 340 days a year for paper, 339 days for paperboard, and 326 days for construction paper and board and wet machine board. In 1970, practical maximum capacity was based on 346 days for all grades, 348 days for paper, 346 days for paperboard, and 334 days for construction paper and board and wet machine board.

Includes Alaska and Hawaii beginning 1960.

P 318–374. Value of output of finished commodities and construction materials destined for domestic consumption at current producers' prices, and implicit price indexes for major commodity groups (Shaw), 1869–1939.

Source: William H. Shaw, *Value of Commodity Output Since 1869*, National Bureau of Economic Research, New York, 1947, pp. 30, 66, and 290 (copyright).

These estimates are derived from census of manufactures data, supplemented by less complete data for nonmanufactured finished commodities and construction materials and for intercensal year interpolations. The estimates before 1919 are based necessarily on less adequate information.

The estimates of finished commodities measure the value of commodities that have reached the form in which they are used by ultimate recipients—largely households in the case of consumers' goods, chiefly business and public enterprises in the case of producers' goods. The amount "destined for domestic consumption" is derived as the sum of domestic production, minus exports, plus imports. In most years and for most commodities, the differences between domestic production of finished commodities and finished commodities destined for domestic consumption were modest. Changes in the latter, therefore, can be used as an approximate measure of changes in domestic manufacturing output. For figures on domestic output of finished commodities at producers' prices for 1919–1933, see Simon Kuznets, *Commodity Flow and Capital Formation*, vol. 1, National Bureau of Economic Research, New York, 1938, pp. 136–138 and 348.

The estimates presented here exclude transportation and distribution costs incurred after the production stage, and hence are not in terms of prices to final users. Nor do they measure domestic consumption for they make no allowance for inventory changes.

Perishable commodities include those usually lasting less than 6 months; semidurable, those usually lasting from 6 months to 3 years; and durable, those usually lasting more than 3 years. For a detailed discussion of sources and procedures, see the source, part II for estimates of the value of output, part III for exports and imports, and part IV for price indexes.

Series P 1-12. Manufactures Summary: 1849 to 1970

Year	Establishments		Persons engaged in manufacturing (1,000)			Man-hours, production workers (mil.)	Payroll (mil. dol.)			Value added by manufacture [2] (mil. dol.)	Capital expenditures, new (mil. dol.)	End-of-year inventories (mil. dol.)
	Total	With 20 or more employees	Proprietors and partners	Non-production employees	Production workers [1]		Total	Salaries	Wages			
	1	2	3	4	5	6	7	8	9	10	11	12
FACTORIES, EXCLUDING HAND AND NEIGHBORHOOD INDUSTRIES												
1970				4,462	13,528	26,669	141,886	50,277	91,609	300,228	22,164	101,285
1969				4,798	14,358	28,600	142,645	49,186	93,460	304,441	22,291	98,206
1968				4,640	14,041	28,157	132,568	45,088	87,480	285,059	20,613	90,505
1967	305,680	107,138		4,537	13,955	27,838	123,481	42,087	81,394	261,984	21,503	84,406
1966				4,374	13,827	28,103	117,157	38,901	78,256	250,880	20,236	77,721
1965				4,174	13,076	26,568	106,643	35,281	71,362	226,940	16,615	68,009
1964				4,082	12,403	25,246	98,685	32,846	65,839	206,194	13,294	63,211
1963	306,617	99,352	169	4,000	12,232	24,509	93,283	31,190	62,094	192,083	11,370	59,913
1962				4,028	12,127	24,270	89,819	30,685	59,134	179,071	10,436	58,067
1961				3,951	11,779	23,289	83,677	28,912	54,765	164,281	9,780	54,744
1960				3,940	12,210	24,174	83,673	28,117	55,556	163,999	10,098	53,560
1959				3,790	12,273	24,444	81,204	26,489	54,714	161,536	9,140	52,552
1958	299,017	95,278	186	3,742	11,681	22,679	73,875	24,270	49,605	141,541	9,544	49,947
1957				3,782	12,839	25,208	76,315	23,745	52,569	147,838	12,144	
1956				3,563	13,131	26,089	74,015	21,974	52,041	144,909	11,233	
1955				3,381	12,954	25,898	69,097	19,878	49,218	135,023	8,233	
1954	286,814	90,470	198	3,273	12,372	24,334	62,963	18,372	44,591	117,032	8,201	40,341
1953	285,000			3,192	13,501	27,066	66,493	17,513	48,979	121,659	8,048	
1952	267,000			3,026	12,706	25,618	59,598	15,834	43,764	109,162	7,883	
1951	262,000			2,800	12,509	25,264	54,742	14,087	40,655	102,086	7,782	
1950	260,000			2,688	11,779	23,717	46,643	12,043	34,600	89,750	5,041	
1949				2,550	11,016	21,770	41,482	11,228	30,254	75,367	5,067	
1947	240,807		189	2,376	11,918	24,317	39,696	9,452	30,244	74,291	5,998	26,129
1939 [3]	173,802		[4] 124	[5] 1,719	7,808		[5] 12,706	[5] 3,708	[5] 8,998	24,487		9,632
1937	166,794		99	1,217	8,569		12,830	2,717	10,113	25,174		9,863
1935	167,916		82	1,058	7,204		9,565	2,253	7,311	18,553		
1933	139,325		72	[6] 770	5,788		[6] 6,238	[6] 1,298	4,940	14,008		
1931	171,450				6,163				6,689	18,601		
1929	206,663		133	1,290	8,370		14,284	3,399	10,885	30,591		
1927	187,629		132	1,224	7,848		13,123	3,023	10,100	26,325		
1925	183,877		133	1,271	7,871		12,958	2,978	9,980	25,668		
1923	192,096		148	1,280	8,194		12,997	2,848	10,149	24,570		
1921	192,059		172	1,081	6,476		9,870	2,419	7,451	17,253		
1919	270,231		250	1,371	8,465		12,427	2,763	9,664	23,842		
1914	268,436		259	911	6,602		5,016	1,234	3,782	9,386		
1909	264,810		272	759	6,262		4,106	900	3,205	8,160		
1904	213,444		225	493	5,182		2,991	550	2,441	6,019		
1899	204,754			348	4,502		2,259	366	1,893	4,647		
FACTORIES AND HAND AND NEIGHBORHOOD INDUSTRIES												
1899	509,490			380	5,098		2,596	389	2,207	5,475		
1889	353,864			457	4,129		2,209	388	1,821	4,102		
1879	253,852				2,733				948	1,973		
1869	252,148				2,054				621	1,395		
1859	140,433				1,311				379	854		
1849	123,025				957				237	464		

[1] The Bureau of Labor Statistics annual averages for employment in manufacturing indicates 1943 as the year of maximum employment, with 15,147,000 production workers. See series D 145.

[2] For 1849–1933, cost of contract work was not subtracted from value of products in calculating value added by manufacture. For 1935–1953, value added by manufacture represents unadjusted value added; beginning 1954, it represents adjusted value.

[3] Except as noted, figures have been revised by retabulation of returns to exclude data for establishments classified as manufacturing in 1939 but as nonmanufacturing beginning 1947. Value added by manufacture in 1939, prior to revision and on a basis comparable with prior years, was $24.7 billion.

[4] Includes establishments classified as manufacturing in 1939 and prior years but as nonmanufacturing thereafter.

[5] Figures revised on basis of estimates rather than by retabulation of 1939 reports. Estimates made as follows: For nonproduction employees, by multiplying the retabulated figure for number of production workers by the ratio of all employees to production workers computed from unrevised 1939 data; for salaries and wages, by multiplying the retabulated wage figure by the ratio for salaries and wages also derived from the unrevised 1939 data.

[6] Excludes data for salaried officers of corporations and their salaries; therefore, not strictly comparable with figures for other years.

Series P 13–17. Indexes of Manufacturing Production: 1860 to 1970

Year	FRB [1] (1967 = 100) 13	NBER [2] (1958 = 100) 14	Year	FRB [1] (1967 = 100) 13	NBER [2] (1958 = 100) 14	Year	NBER [2] (1947 = 100) 15	NBER [2] (1939 = 100) 16	Frickey [3] (1899 = 100) 17	Year	Frickey [3] (1899 = 100) 17
1970	105	----	1945	43	82	1919	34			1890	71
1969	111	----	1944	51	86	1914	29		192	1889	66
1968	106	----	1943	47	87	1913			203	1888	62
1967	100	----	1942	38	83	1912			194	1887	60
1966	98	131	1941	32	80	1911			162	1886	57
1965	89	129	1940	25	74	1910			172	1885	47
1964	81	125	1939	22	69	1909	24		166	1884	47
1963	76	121	1938	18	60	1908			127	1883	50
1962	71	117	1937	23	66	1907			156	1882	49
1961	66	113	1936	22	66	1906			152	1881	46
1960	65	109	1935	18	63	1905			140	1880	42
1959	64	107	1934	15	57	1904		19	121	1879	36
1958	57	100	1933	14	53	1903			126	1878	32
1957	61	100	1932	12	46	1902			127	1877	30
1956	61	99	1931	15	52	1901			111	1876	28
1955	58	98	1930	19	54	1900			100	1875	28
1954	52	91	1929	23	56	1899		15	100	1874	29
1953	55	90	1928	21	----	1898			91	1873	30
1952	51	86	1927	20	----	1897			80	1872	31
1951	49	86	1926	20	----	1896			74	1871	26
1950	45	87	1925	19	----	1895			81	1870	25
1949	39	79	1924	17	----	1894			68	1869	25
1948	41	78	1923	18	----	1893			70	1868	23
1947	39	76	1922	15	----	1892			79	1867	22
1946	35	73	1921	12	----	1891			73	1866	21
			1920	15	----					1865	17
			1919	15	----					1864	18
										1863	17
										1862	15
										1861	16
										1860	16

[1] Federal Reserve Board index of manufacturing production.
[2] National Bureau of Economic Research index of physical volume, all manufacturing industries.
[3] Edwin Frickey's indexes of manufacturing production.

Series P 18–39. Indexes of Manufacturing Production (FRB), by Industry Group: 1947 to 1970

[1967 = 100]

Year	Total manufacturing 18	Durable manufactures									
		Total 19	Primary metals 20	Fabricated metal products 21	Machinery 22	Transportation equipment 23	Instruments and related products 24	Stone, clay, and glass products 25	Lumber and products 26	Furniture and fixtures 27	Miscellaneous manufactures 28
1970	105	102	107	109	100	90	111	106	106	99	117
1969	111	110	114	114	107	108	116	113	109	107	116
1968	106	106	103	106	102	110	107	106	105	105	107
1967	100	100	100	100	100	100	100	100	100	100	100
1966	98	99	109	101	99	101	95	105	98	101	100
1965	89	89	104	93	84	91	83	101	95	93	94
1964	81	79	96	83	74	80	71	96	91	86	84
1963	76	74	84	78	68	76	66	91	86	81	78
1962	71	69	78	76	65	69	60	86	82	78	75
1961	66	62	73	70	57	60	57	81	78	71	70
1960	65	63	74	72	56	64	58	81	74	72	68
1959	64	62	75	72	54	62	55	84	79	73	65
1958	57	54	64	64	45	54	48	73	70	65	60
1957	61	62	80	71	52	69	51	76	68	69	66
1956	61	62	84	69	52	64	49	77	75	69	69
1955	58	60	85	68	47	66	44	72	76	66	65
1954	52	52	65	60	42	58	40	62	68	57	51
1953	55	59	80	67	----	66	39	63	68	53	55
1952	51	52	71	59	----	53	36	62	64	51	49
1951	49	49	78	60	----	45	30	64	65	49	48
1950	45	44	71	57	----	41	26	58	65	52	49
1949	39	36	57	46	----	34	23	48	54	43	44
1948	41	40	67	51	----	34	25	52	61	46	47
1947	39	38	65	50	----	31	25	48	59	45	44

Series P 18–39.   Indexes of Manufacturing Production (FRB), by Industry Group: 1947 to 1970—Con.

[1967 = 100]

Year		Nondurable manufactures									
	Total	Textile mill products	Apparel products	Leather and products	Paper and products	Printing and publishing	Chemicals and products	Petroleum and products	Rubber and plastics products	Food	Tobacco products
	29	30	31	32	33	34	35	36	37	38	39
1970	111	106	98	91	113	104	120	113	116	112	100
1969	111	113	103	96	114	106	120	108	120	108	97
1968	106	109	102	106	106	103	110	105	113	104	100
1967	100	100	100	100	100	100	100	100	100	100	100
1966	97	102	101	105	100	98	93	97	97	97	100
1965	90	95	98	104	92	90	82	93	84	92	100
1964	84	87	94	101	86	84	74	91	74	90	101
1963	79	81	89	99	81	77	67	88	69	86	97
1962	75	78	86	101	76	73	62	84	64	83	94
1961	71	73	82	98	72	71	55	80	57	81	93
1960	69	71	82	99	68	70	53	77	54	78	90
1959	67	72	80	104	67	68	51	74	54	76	88
1958	61	64	73	97	59	63	44	70	45	73	85
1957	61	65	75	99	59	65	42	70	46	71	79
1956	60	68	75	100	60	63	40	70	43	70	75
1955	57	66	74	99	57	59	37	66	43	66	74
1954	51	58	67	90	51	54	32	60	35	63	72
1953	51	62	67	92	51	52	32	58	34	61	74
1952	49	60	67	92	47	49	29	55	32	60	75
1951	48	61	63	86	49	49	28	54	31	59	73
1950	46	61	64	92	46	49	25	48	31	58	69
1949	42	54	60	85	38	46	20	44	24	56	68
1948	42	58	60	89	40	45	20	45	25	55	68
1947	41	55	58	94	39	43	18	42	25	56	67

Series P 40–57.   Indexes of Manufacturing Production, by Industry Group: 1899 to 1954

[1947 = 100]

Year	All manufacturing industries	Durable manufactures							
		Primary metals	Fabricated metal products	Machinery, except electrical	Electrical machinery	Transportation equipment	Stone, clay, and glass products	Lumber and furniture	Instruments and miscellaneous [1]
	40	41	42	43	44	45	46	47	48
1954	128	103	114	116	165	189	124	116	178
1947	100	100	100	100	100	100	100	100	100
1939	57	52	50	38	35	49	87	72	52
1937	58	58	51			60	88	69	
1935	46	39				48	61	54	
1933	35	27				22	42	42	
1931	40	32				30	60	57	
1929	56	65				66	89	91	
1927	49	52				45	88	90	
1925	46	53				50	81	93	
1923	43	52				50		82	
1921	30	26				25		76	
1919	34	40				40		71	
1914	29	29				13		75	
1909	24	28				7		75	
1904	19	18				5		69	
1899	15	14				5		74	

Year	Nondurable manufactures								
	Textiles and apparel	Rubber products	Leather	Paper	Printing and publishing	Chemicals	Petroleum and coal products	Food	Tobacco
	49	50	51	52	53	54	55	56	57
1954	109	114	90	131	126	164	131	109	108
1947	100	100	100	100	100	100	100	100	100
1939	80	55	87	68	69	46	65	65	66
1937	72	51	86	63	73	43	61	61	65
1935	67	45	79	53	62	35	49	52	56
1933	57	39	68	44	52	29	42	37	48
1931	58	39	142	45	60	30	45	41	51
1929	67	57	79	52	72	35	54	46	55
1927	63	52	76	46	65	29	45	42	50
1925	58	48	67	40	59	24	40	40	45
1923	56	41	75	36	52	22	34	38	41
1921	43	24	60	26	37	15	30	31	36
1919	45	30	142	27	39	18	21	32	38
1914	48		64	24	34	15	12	34	29
1909	41		65	19	25	11	9	28	24
1904	32		58	14	19	8	6	24	21
1899	26		50	10	12	6	5	19	16

[1] Includes ordnance and accessories.

Series P 58–67. General Statistics for Manufacturing Industries, by Major Groups: 1899 to 1970

[Represents operating manufacturing establishments only]

Industry group and year	Establishments		All employees [1]		Production workers [1]			Value added by manufacture	Capital expenditures, new	Aggregate horsepower rating of power equipment
	Total	With 20 employees or more	Number	Payroll	Number	Man-hours	Wages			
	58	59	60	61	62	63	64	65	66	67
	Number	Number	1,000	Mil. dol.	1,000	Millions	Mil. dol.	Mil. dol.	Mil. dol.	1,000
FOOD AND KINDRED PRODUCTS										
1970			1,619	11,698	1,105	2,216	7,095	32,289	2,144	
1969			1,653	11,135	1,132	2,265	6,782	29,997	1,917	
1968			1,632	10,497	1,114	2,234	6,390	28,202	1,740	
1967	32,518	13,514	1,650	10,077	1,122	2,259	6,063	26,621	1,730	
1966			1,643	9,542	1,098	2,240	5,676	24,896	1,692	
1965			1,641	9,162	1,095	2,233	5,446	23,538	1,476	
1964			1,646	9,028	1,095	2,270	5,367	25,053	1,413	
1963	37,521	14,113	1,643	8,637	1,098	2,228	5,159	21,826	1,249	
1962			1,683	8,593	1,119	2,287	5,060	20,870	1,235	11,884
1961			1,702	8,363	1,138	2,317	4,934	20,124	1,044	
1960			1,719	8,210	1,155	2,348	4,857	19,753	1,034	
1959			1,718	7,910	1,155	2,345	4,702	18,646	1,078	
1958	41,970	14,890	1,718	7,622	1,153	2,310	4,549	17,701	1,021	
1957			1,688	7,141	1,133	2,304	4,244	16,347	923	
1956			1,706	6,964	1,167	2,378	4,202	15,939	887	
1955			1,674	6,544	1,154	2,344	3,940	14,790	798	
1954 [2]	42,373	13,648	1,647	6,200	1,138	2,316	3,758	13,767	788	8,311
1953			1,455	5,267	1,059	2,160	3,436	11,938	545	
1952	36,829		1,480	5,098	1,075	2,216	3,313	11,340	527	
1951	38,237		1,474	4,819	1,079	2,218	3,143	10,579	687	
1950	38,466		1,493	4,415	1,075	2,218	2,858	10,104	649	
1949			1,463	4,199	1,077	2,222	2,707	9,426	723	
1947	42,802		1,461	3,833	1,112	2,368	2,617	9,116	821	
1939	43,667				802		888	3,485		5,642
1937	48,763				891		981	3,371		
1935	48,982		932	1,068	800		804	2,804		
1933 [3]	40,325		768	777	669		624	2,413		
1931	48,729				647		740	2,745		
1929	55,325		872	1,203	741		896	3,340		4,608
1927 [4]	48,947		796	1,104	668		817	2,840		4,135
1925	48,151		793	1,062	667		799	2,718		3,882
1923	51,173		818	1,084	676		792	2,506		3,723
1921	51,502		760	1,016	621		742	2,120		
TOBACCO MANUFACTURES										
1970			71	448	63	119	362	2,489	56	
1969			72	411	63	117	329	2,221	61	
1968			74	396	65	121	323	2,141	50	
1967	329	195	75	377	66	126	304	2,032	53	
1966			72	356	64	122	289	1,872	58	
1965			75	349	66	125	285	1,766	59	
1964			79	353	70	138	291	1,772	59	
1963	394	231	77	331	69	132	272	1,681	54	
1962			76	328	67	134	265	1,642	49	295
1961			78	317	69	135	258	1,590	49	
1960			81	313	73	142	258	1,546	47	
1959			83	304	75	145	255	1,480	53	
1958	504	380	85	295	76	147	248	1,414	48	
1957			88	284	81	151	240	1,246	42	
1956			93	279	85	156	237	1,173	47	
1955			96	271	88	166	230	1,083	27	
1954	627	391	95	260	87	163	220	1,004	28	256
1953			95	253	87	166	213	987	29	
1952			93	241	86	163	202	868	22	
1951			94	230	86	162	192	856	18	
1950			93	213	85	160	177	806	18	
1949			101	208	93	174	174	779	22	
1947	1,086		112	206	103	198	175	641	36	

[1] Beginning 1947, for food and kindred products, excludes driver-salesmen in bakery products industry. Number of driver-salesmen for 1939 was at least 120,000.

[2] Beginning 1954, includes milk bottling plants. Value added for this industry in 1954 was $1,476 million.

[3] Beginning 1933, excludes establishments primarily engaged in manufacture of ethyl alcohol.

[4] Beginning 1927, includes establishments primarily engaged in manufacture of vegetable cooking oils.

Series P 58–67. General Statistics for Manufacturing Industries, by Major Groups: 1899 to 1970—Con.

Industry group and year	Establishments		All employees		Production workers			Value added by manufacture	Capital expenditures, new	Aggregate horsepower rating of power equipment
	Total	With 20 employees or more	Number	Payroll	Number	Man-hours	Wages			
	58	59	60	61	62	63	64	65	66	67
	Number	*Number*	*1,000*	*Mil. dol.*	*1,000*	*Millions*	*Mil. dol.*	*Mil. dol.*	*Mil. dol.*	*1,000*
TOBACCO MANUFACTURES — Con.										
1939	765		96	87	88		69	350		100
1937	852		98	82	92		70	325		
1935	890		96	71	91		59	284		
1933	804		91	59	87		51	250		
1931	1,228				100		69	370		
1929	1,888		126	118	116		95			65
1927	2,156		141	129	129		105			52
1925	2,623		143	134	132		111			42
1923	3,672		162	151	146		121			44
1921	4,312		165	148	150		121			
1919	10,291		173	153	157		124			43
1914	13,951		196	100	179		78			35
1909	15,822		180	86	167		69			28
1904	16,827		170	71	159		63			24
1899	14,959		140	57	133		48			22
TEXTILE MILL PRODUCTS										
1970			925	5,082	813	1,629	4,036	9,334	811	
1969			968	5,132	859	1,748	4,129	9,605	849	
1968			959	4,850	854	1,758	3,945	9,184	691	
1967	7,080	4,453	929	4,391	828	1,690	3,557	8,153	733	
1966			927	4,244	828	1,728	3,446	8,028	887	
1965			894	3,912	798	1,671	3,189	7,469	618	
1964			876	3,647	782	1,626	2,963	6,672	504	
1963	7,104	4,368	863	3,385	775	1,568	2,768	6,123	382	
1962			880	3,358	787	1,590	2,723	6,055	376	5,043
1961			876	3,183	782	1,552	2,575	5,609	322	
1960			901	3,214	809	1,602	2,626	5,591	326	
1959			930	3,252	835	1,689	2,681	5,692	300	
1958 [1]	7,680	4,621	903	2,943	812	1,571	2,412	4,870	215	
1957			989	3,183	893	1,736	2,632	5,197	289	
1956			1,044	3,298	949	1,874	2,750	5,456	297	
1955			1,059	3,241	966	1,921	2,708	5,312	262	
1954	8,070	4,862	1,037	3,033	948	1,821	2,527	4,709	226	4,463
1953			1,158	3,455	1,060	2,086	2,910	5,412	256	
1952	7,584		1,135	3,343	1,037	2,039	2,823	5,257	323	
1951	7,758		1,195	3,438	1,097	2,155	2,925	5,421	406	
1950	8,434		1,245	3,364	1,142	2,301	2,861	5,642	420	
1949			1,170	2,973	1,066	2,071	2,510	4,741	419	
1947	8,157		1,232	2,833	1,146	2,307	2,448	5,323	368	
1939 [2]	6,388				1,082		907	1,818		3,670
1937 [2]	6,096				1,138		974	1,786		
1935	6,433		1,130	986	1,070		847	1,461		
1933	5,957				972		664	1,342		
1931	6,490				904		762	1,525		
1929	7,415		1,190	1,293	1,120		1,082	2,321		4,146
1927	7,633		1,208	1,314	1,143		1,128	2,273		4,173
1925	7,892		1,201	1,272	1,135		1,093	2,212		3,987
1923	8,249		1,263	1,345	1,190		1,152	2,413		3,783
1921	7,695		1,072	1,071	1,012		916	1,824		
1919	7,869		1,139	1,108	1,076		932	2,300		3,248
1914	6,756		1,013	476	976		417	781		2,717
1909	6,490				932		362	752		
1904	5,798		813	307	786		271	515		
1899	5,930		716	250	698		224	441		

[1] Beginning 1958, excludes establishments primarily producing hats, except cloth and millinery, and those primarily producing hard-surface floor covering except asbestos, plastic, or rubber; therefore, data are not entirely comparable with those for earlier years. The 1957 employment was 12,428 for the hats except millinery industries and 8,736 for the hard-surface floor covering industry. Also, prior to 1958, excludes establishments primarily engaged in shrinking and sponging of cloth; such establishments had 1,723 employees in 1958.

[2] For 1937 and 1939, includes establishments that cut and stitch products from knit cloth made in separate mills of integrated companies.

Series **P 58–67.**   General Statistics for Manufacturing Industries, by Major Groups: 1899 to 1970—Con.

Industry group and year	Establishments		All employees		Production workers			Value added by manufacture	Capital expenditures, new	Aggregate horsepower rating of power equipment
	Total	With 20 employees or more	Number	Payroll	Number	Man-hours	Wages			
	58	59	60	61	62	63	64	65	66	67
	Number	*Number*	*1,000*	*Mil. dol.*	*1,000*	*Millions*	*Mil. dol.*	*Mil. dol.*	*Mil. dol.*	*1,000*
APPAREL AND OTHER TEXTILE PRODUCTS										
1970			1,341	6,267	1,171	2,119	4,806	11,598	300	
1969			1,381	6,402	1,210	2,203	4,944	11,571	311	
1968			1,356	6,012	1,194	2,177	4,681	10,881	267	
1967	26,393	12,705	1,357	5,582	1,200	2,179	4,341	10,064	208	
1966			1,360	5,207	1,202	2,213	4,038	9,181	206	
1965			1,335	4,955	1,183	2,179	3,878	8,684	168	
1964			1,303	4,684	1,147	2,107	3,640	8,163	123	
1963	28,457	13,011	1,280	4,423	1,133	2,053	3,482	7,861	129	
1962			1,235	4,162	1,085	1,952	3,224	7,135	98	250
1961			1,214	3,877	1,066	1,891	3,000	6,707	80	
1960			1,238	3,865	1,089	1,932	3,012	6,587	84	
1959			1,237	3,827	1,090	1,990	3,001	6,495	88	
1958 [1]	29,363	13,034	1,181	3,587	1,042	1,837	2,771	6,001	91	
1957			1,264	3,664	1,123	1,989	2,867	6,067	107	
1956			1,271	3,612	1,134	2,031	2,842	5,973	88	
1955			1,248	3,408	1,117	2,000	2,684	5,650	86	
1954	31,472	13,380	1,190	3,202	1,070	1,899	2,521	5,166	77	
1953			1,227	3,358	1,106	1,995	2,652	5,415	60	
1952	29,079		1,143	3,079	1,018	1,876	2,404	4,849	55	
1951	28,931		1,123	2,955	1,002	1,819	2,295	4,699	69	
1950	26,145		1,151	2,765	1,005	1,815	2,170	4,176	63	
1949			1,161	2,717	1,009	1,813	2,094	4,245	54	
1947	30,063		1,082	2,525	973	1,811	2,015	4,440	84	
1939 [2]	20,375				753		656	1,386		[3] 24
1937 [2]	16,389				693		600	1,245		
1935	18,952				631		545	1,123		
1933	14,801				513		366	826		
1931	19,750				531		503	1,370		
1929	22,470		681	901	606		687	1,927		40
1927	22,077		648	859	571		673	1,878		34
1925	18,609				515		602	1,685		33
1923	20,333		635	816	545		627	1,748		40
1921	20,049		586	733	515		584	1,408		
1919	22,501		640	769	554		578	1,618		
1914	18,015		618	356	548		270	682		
1909	16,747				537		247	614		
1904	12,416		428	194	391		159	414		
1899	12,619		364	150	338		123	309		
LUMBER AND WOOD PRODUCTS										
1970			542	3,241	475	925	2,591	5,869	535	
1969			566	3,246	502	986	2,630	6,331	590	
1968			552	3,019	491	973	2,471	5,916	484	
1967	36,795	5,803	554	2,799	496	977	2,291	4,973	426	
1966			572	2,693	506	1,015	2,214	4,791	485	
1965			572	2,586	507	1,009	2,124	4,474	482	
1964			559	2,436	490	985	2,048	4,365	362	
1963	36,150	5,765	563	2,339	497	979	1,943	4,021	395	
1962			553	2,170	493	972	1,780	3,644	300	7,710
1961			556	2,084	494	961	1,714	3,413	242	
1960			594	2,169	529	1,028	1,779	3,495	334	
1959			617	2,230	552	1,071	1,850	3,806	301	
1958 [4]	37,882	5,904	585	2,008	509	967	1,642	3,213	297	
1957			646	2,111	579	1,072	1,723	3,285	204	
1956			698	2,276	631	1,187	1,887	3,817	293	
1955			693	2,187	628	1,202	1,820	3,744	302	
1954	41,484	6,387	645	1,934	582	1,107	1,605	3,242	217	5,151
1953			720	2,087	658	1,236	1,803	3,501	183	
1952			743	2,072	687	1,270	1,786	3,449	178	
1951			771	2,015	714	1,308	1,738	3,523	240	
1950 [5]	41,506		751	1,748	692	1,272	1,510	3,166	192	
1949 [5]			649	1,422	601	1,083	1,210	2,284	147	
1947 [6]	26,312		642	1,352	601	1,255	1,191	2,520	172	

[1] Prior to 1958, excludes establishments producing hats, except cloth and millinery. In 1954, these establishments had 12,988 employees and $61,886 thousand value added by manufacture. Also prior to 1958, includes establishments primarily engaged in shrinking and sponging of cloth. In 1958, such establishments had 1,723 employees and $10,709 thousand value added by manufacture.

[2] For 1937 and 1939, excludes establishments that cut and stitch products from knit cloth made in separate mills of integrated companies.

[3] Horsepower of prime movers only.

[4] Prior to 1958, excludes establishments primarily engaged in manufacture of hard pressed wood fiberboard and those primarily engaged in manufacturing fabricated hardboard products.

[5] In 1949 and 1950, there was a significant undercoverage in the sample for this major group, especially in the logging camps and logging contractors industry.

[6] For 1937–1947, excludes logging contractors and independent logging camps not operating sawmills as well as establishments primarily engaged in manufacture of venetian blinds.

Series P 58–67. General Statistics for Manufacturing Industries, by Major Groups: 1899 to 1970—Con.

Industry group and year	Establishments		All employees		Production workers			Value added by manufacture	Capital expenditures, new	Aggregate horsepower rating of power equipment
	Total	With 20 employees or more	Number	Payroll	Number	Man-hours	Wages			
	58	59	60	61	62	63	64	65	66	67
	Number	*Number*	*1,000*	*Mil. dol.*	*1,000*	*Millions*	*Mil. dol.*	*Mil. dol.*	*Mil. dol.*	*1,000*
LUMBER AND WOOD PRODUCTS—Con.										
1939 [1]	13,208				423		355	731		2,998
1937 [1]	11,747				438		369	714		
1935	11,280		415	340	384		283	542		
1933	8,456		314	211	294		182	379		
1931	11,141				327		277	524		
1929 [2]	20,928		651	759	603		632	1,322		3,674
1927	14,949		649	748	602		632	1,179		3,332
1925	16,878		726	815	674		693	1,333		3,473
1923 [3]	16,471		746	820	693		701	1,399		3,336
1921	16,548		566	581	521		483	853		
1919	35,872		715	774	663		668	1,299		3,410
1914 [4]	37,949		718	410	672		349	647		3,176
1909	44,822				758		347	708		
1904	29,308				596		272	578		
1899 [2][3]	32,456				563		209	437		
FURNITURE AND FIXTURES										
1970			437	2,691	361	715	1,938	4,876	231	
1969			456	2,693	381	761	1,968	5,031	190	
1968			433	2,453	364	733	1,793	4,562	178	
1967	10,008	3,449	425	2,258	358	716	1,654	4,170	198	
1966			429	2,188	361	735	1,621	3,990	186	
1965			407	2,013	342	699	1,487	3,612	151	
1964			388	1,845	324	663	1,375	3,227	108	
1963	10,478	3,313	377	1,727	315	640	1,290	3,068	110	
1962			368	1,638	307	632	1,205	2,841	96	1,265
1961			351	1,503	293	590	1,097	2,558	77	
1960			364	1,531	304	615	1,124	2,619	76	
1959			368	1,522	309	628	1,131	2,614	84	
1958	10,329	3,265	354	1,414	292	575	1,039	2,396	83	
1957			375	1,432	311	618	1,049	2,514	84	
1956			376	1,417	315	638	1,057	2,510	92	
1955			366	1,329	309	627	996	2,306	79	
1954	10,373	3,012	341	1,197	287	571	893	1,998	62	949
1953			361	1,259	310	629	973	2,047	59	
1952	8,778		332	1,123	285	589	853	1,904	55	
1951	8,369		336	1,077	290	590	818	1,804	55	
1950			346	1,013	296	617	774	1,667	58	
1949			310	862	270	549	653	1,412	41	
1947	7,551		316	807	278	584	642	1,346	77	
1939 [5]	5,178				189		187	418		566
1937 [6]	4,469				199		202	424		
1935	4,319		171	171	151		133	274		
1933	3,491		137	111	123		91	193		
1931	4,554				147		147	322		
1929	5,491		248	359	219		276	615		504
1927	4,666		237	338	210		266	569		456
1925 [7]	4,776		232	321	204		254	562		403
1923	4,532		217	293	192		232	510		345
1921	4,326		162	214	142		165	347		
1919	4,821		183	214	160		162	366		265
1914	4,844		169	110	149		84	174		240
1909 [8]	4,337				142		73	151		
1904	3,497		137	69	127		58	116		163
1899 [7][8]	2,614				98		40	82		112

[1] For 1937–1947, excludes logging contractors and independent logging camps not operating sawmills as well as establishments primarily engaged in manufacture of venetian blinds.

[2] For 1899–1929, excludes establishments primarily engaged in manufacture of wood and vehicle stock. For 1931, value added by manufacture on a basis comparable with 1929 is $523.8 million; 1931, on new basis, $524.4 million.

[3] For 1899–1923, includes establishments engaged in manufacture of rules made of metal and other materials as well as wood; figures for later years include establishments making wooden rules only.

[4] Beginning 1914, excludes establishments primarily engaged in manufacture of windows and door screens. For 1914, excludes establishments engaged in manufacture of laths and shingles; value added by manufacture on a basis comparable with prior years was $652 million.

[5] Beginning 1939, includes establishments primarily engaged in manufacture of metal partitions. For 1939, value added by manufacture on a basis comparable with prior years was $411 million.

[6] Beginning 1937, includes establishments primarily engaged in manufacture of venetian blinds. For 1937, value added by manufacture on a basis comparable with prior years was $418 million.

[7] For 1899–1925, excludes establishments primarily engaged in manufacture of sewing machine cases, cabinets, and tables.

[8] For 1899–1909, excludes establishments primarily engaged in manufacture of window and door screens. For 1914, value added by manufacture on a basis comparable with prior years was $169 million.

Series P 58–67. General Statistics for Manufacturing Industries, by Major Groups: 1899 to 1970—Con.

Industry group and year	Establishments		All employees		Production workers			Value added by manufacture	Capital expenditures, new	Aggregate horsepower rating of power equipment
	Total	With 20 employees or more	Number	Payroll	Number	Man-hours	Wages			
	58	59	60	61	62	63	64	65	66	67
	Number	Number	1,000	Mil. dol.	1,000	Millions	Mil. dol.	Mil. dol.	Mil. dol.	1,000
PAPER AND ALLIED PRODUCTS										
1970			659	5,374	520	1,076	3,850	11,590	1,397	
1969			670	5,200	531	1,128	3,757	11,426	1,421	
1968			643	4,750	510	1,086	3,436	10,466	1,238	
1967	5,890	3,812	639	4,436	508	1,071	3,206	9,756	1,585	
1966			634	4,236	503	1,076	3,071	9,417	1,422	
1965			610	3,896	485	1,029	2,829	8,464	1,186	
1964			593	3,686	471	1,007	2,678	7,806	902	
1963	5,713	3,552	588	3,508	468	989	2,551	7,396	709	
1962			576	3,336	460	971	2,424	6,997	742	12,477
1961			570	3,179	456	958	2,315	6,660	685	
1960			575	3,089	461	964	2,235	6,509	659	
1959			569	2,998	459	977	2,201	6,393	686	
1958 [1]	5,259	3,214	551	2,759	445	927	2,022	5,669	634	
1957			563	2,721	458	956	2,010	5,724	767	
1956			563	2,616	461	982	1,952	5,610	750	
1955			546	2,419	451	968	1,818	5,141	556	
1954	5,004	3,277	528	2,205	436	920	1,657	4,630	533	8,256
1953			533	2,180	442	950	1,647	4,463	397	
1952	4,334		482	1,878	402	868	1,425	3,883	371	
1951	4,406		495	1,823	415	898	1,389	4,180	389	
1950	4,849		478	1,607	401	874	1,240	3,438	299	
1949			447	1,420	377	801	1,083	2,777	315	
1947 [2]	4,100		454	1,295	392	857	1,018	2,913	407	
1939 [3]	3,328				270		315	888		4,131
1937 [4]	3,084				267		310	863		
1935	2,945		267	313	236		236	636		
1933	2,697		221	220	196		173	518		
1931 [5]	2,917				197		217	606		
1929	2,973		258	373	229		282	782		3,167
1927	2,851		246	344	218		264	686		2,814
1925	2,614		242	327	216		256	612		2,575
1923	2,582		241	317	214		244	564		2,314
1921	2,511		202	256	181		198	392		
1919	2,558		227	268	203		208	517		1,967
1914	2,344		182	114	164		87	201		1,697
1909	2,316		155	85	142		67	168		
1904	2,031		129	62	120		51	122		
1899	1,895		100	44	94		35	90		
PRINTING AND PUBLISHING										
1970			1,077	8,682	653	1,265	4,903	17,232	873	
1969			1,091	8,338	667	1,262	4,702	16,793	853	
1968			1,040	7,627	636	1,204	4,280	15,329	757	
1967	37,989	8,035	1,031	7,152	632	1,196	4,011	14,355	788	
1966			1,018	6,751	619	1,209	3,832	13,265	709	
1965			982	6,269	597	1,156	3,575	12,099	543	
1964			935	5,848	570	1,124	3,350	11,192	465	
1963	38,090	7,215	913	5,515	560	1,083	3,191	10,476	464	
1962			922	5,411	566	1,084	3,101	9,998	436	1,746
1961			913	5,201	559	1,075	2,983	9,551	414	
1960			907	5,065	560	1,082	2,935	9,342	420	
1959			885	4,812	553	1,054	2,799	8,788	403	
1958	35,457	6,859	865	4,489	531	998	2,596	7,973	422	
1957			867	4,295	533	1,019	2,466	7,913	327	
1956			854	4,118	527	1,017	2,386	7,547	289	
1955			823	3,837	507	985	2,225	6,938	254	
1954	32,530	6,054	804	3,620	499	961	2,112	6,403	237	975
1953			760	3,387	474	924	2,014	5,916	195	
1952	30,147		773	3,267	471	999	1,909	5,660	189	
1951	29,704		765	3,068	474	991	1,791	5,289	244	
1950	29,427		763	2,909	472	1,019	1,702	4,907	244	
1949			756	2,744	462	994	1,569	4,659	254	
1947 [6]	29,078		715	2,276	438	888	1,318	4,249	226	

[1] Beginning 1958, excludes hard pressed wood fiberboard mills.
[2] Beginning 1947, includes establishments primarily engaged in the manufacture of tags.
[3] Beginning 1939, includes establishments primarily engaged in the manufacture of printed paper patterns and laminated enamel hard pressed insulating wallboards of vegetable fiber. In 1939, value added by manufacture on a basis comparable with prior years was $870 million.
[4] Beginning 1937, includes establishments primarily engaged in the manufacture of fiber products, fiber conduits, and molded pulp products. In 1937, value added by manufacture on a basis comparable with prior years was $853 million.
[5] Beginning 1931, includes establishments primarily engaged in manufacture of papeteries. In 1931, value added by manufacture on a basis comparable with prior years was $600 million.
[6] Prior to 1947, includes establishments primarily engaged in the manufacture of tags.

Series P 58–67.   General Statistics for Manufacturing Industries, by Major Groups: 1899 to 1970—Con.

Industry group and year	Establishments		All employees		Production workers			Value added by manufacture [1]	Capital expenditures, new	Aggregate horsepower rating of power equipment
	Total	With 20 employees or more	Number	Payroll	Number	Man-hours	Wages			
	58	59	60	61	62	63	64	65	66	67
	Number	*Number*	*1,000*	*Mil. dol.*	*1,000*	*Millions*	*Mil. dol.*	*Mil. dol.*	*Mil. dol.*	*1,000*
PRINTING AND PUBLISHING—Con.										
1939 [2]	24,878	----------	552	978	324	----------	493	1,765	----------	771
1937	22,674	----------	555	951	351	----------	530	1,785	----------	----------
1935	22,505	----------	473	792	303	----------	444	1,547	----------	----------
1933 [3]	19,216	----------	398	579	262	----------	353	1,245	----------	----------
1931	24,664	----------	----------	----------	315	----------	535	1,768	----------	----------
1929	27,364	----------	566	1,139	358	----------	636	2,233	----------	649
1927	25,375	----------	524	1,027	331	----------	589	1,936	----------	570
1925	23,646	----------	497	924	317	----------	544	1,757	----------	486
1923	22,897	----------	481	838	310	----------	494	1,527	----------	430
1921	22,559	----------	428	718	284	----------	436	1,306	----------	----------
1919	33,262	----------	448	594	304	----------	352	1,091	----------	379
1914	34,241	----------	406	340	286	----------	207	627	----------	342
1909	32,137	----------	374	281	270	----------	174	519	----------	----------
1904	28,369	----------	299	203	228	----------	133	424	----------	----------
1899	24,363	----------	244	144	202	----------	104	300	----------	----------
CHEMICALS AND ALLIED PRODUCTS										
1970	----------	----------	881	8,004	556	1,121	4,327	27,930	3,111	----------
1969	----------	----------	883	7,603	566	1,151	4,181	27,319	2,843	----------
1968	----------	----------	856	6,939	551	1,116	3,845	25,810	2,789	----------
1967	11,799	4,348	841	6,443	541	1,086	3,555	23,550	2,936	----------
1966	----------	----------	822	6,129	529	1,077	3,400	22,656	2,899	----------
1965	----------	----------	780	5,594	502	1,023	3,105	20,956	2,482	----------
1964	----------	----------	749	5,244	480	986	2,928	19,166	1,862	----------
1963	11,996	3,985	737	4,970	474	963	2,780	17,586	1,546	----------
1962	----------	----------	727	4,755	470	953	2,647	16,009	1,382	20,553
1961	----------	----------	713	4,524	460	932	2,521	14,805	1,500	----------
1960	----------	----------	726	4,422	470	944	2,473	14,415	1,285	----------
1959	----------	----------	718	4,233	471	949	2,410	14,336	1,103	----------
1958	11,372	3,753	698	3,941	453	908	2,242	12,308	1,244	----------
1957	----------	----------	757	4,036	506	1,018	2,322	12,373	1,264	----------
1956	----------	----------	755	3,852	515	1,040	2,266	11,894	1,082	----------
1955	----------	----------	741	3,566	508	1,027	2,117	11,108	761	----------
1954	11,074	3,959	734	3,377	499	1,011	1,994	9,547	927	13,521
1953	----------	----------	768	3,400	536	1,094	2,103	9,320	944	----------
1952	11,007	----------	739	3,117	513	1,063	1,904	8,539	1,019	----------
1951	10,909	----------	703	2,784	498	1,029	1,733	8,165	981	----------
1950	10,339	----------	643	2,342	457	955	1,471	7,237	603	----------
1949 [4]	----------	----------	612	2,092	440	922	1,320	5,848	598	----------
1947	10,019	----------	626	1,899	464	975	1,236	5,317	805	----------
1939 [5]	8,839	----------	----------	----------	276	----------	342	1,819	----------	3,763
1937 [6]	8,337	----------	----------	----------	303	----------	366	1,732	----------	----------
1935	8,225	----------	----------	----------	294	----------	282	1,363	----------	----------
1933 [7]	7,297	----------	302	306	254	----------	217	1,121	----------	----------
1931	8,324	----------	----------	----------	248	----------	259	1,359	----------	----------
1929 [8]	9,327	----------	382	550	307	----------	352	1,737	----------	2,312
1927 [9]	8,594	----------	348	492	278	----------	319	1,474	----------	1,848
1925 [10]	8,160	----------	----------	----------	261	----------	297	1,320	----------	1,748
1923	8,253	----------	340	459	264	----------	286	1,185	----------	1,654
1921	8,208	----------	279	369	212	----------	218	834	----------	----------
1919	10,688	----------	388	497	294	----------	306	1,198	----------	1,721
1914	10,698	----------	269	192	208	----------	106	457	----------	1,459
1909	10,380	----------	235	144	185	----------	82	401	----------	----------
1904	8,370	----------	191	103	158	----------	56	286	----------	----------
1899 [11]	7,669	----------	170	80	144	----------	51	212	----------	----------

[1] Printing and publishing—for 1909–1933, cost of contract work was subtracted from value of products in calculating value added by manufacture only for the industries in which it was significant. For 1899 and 1904, cost of contract work was not subtracted from value of products for any industries.   In 1909, value added by manufacture on a basis comparable with prior years was $556 million.

[2] Prior to 1939, includes establishments primarily engaged in the manufacture of paper patterns.

[3] For 1933, excludes establishments engaged solely in music publishing.

[4] Beginning 1949, includes Government-owned plants operated by private firms for the account of the Federal Government.

[5] Beginning 1939, excludes establishments primarily engaged in manufacture of electrometallurgical products.   In 1939, value added by manufacture on a basis comparable with prior years was $1,838 million.

[6] Beginning 1937, excludes establishments primarily engaged in mining of rock salt or in smelting and refining of aluminium; in 1937, value added by manufacture on a basis comparable with prior years was $1,759 million.   Also beginning 1937, excludes woods employees of the gum naval stores industry; in 1937, production workers numbered 30,880 with wages of $8.6 million.

[7] Beginning 1933, includes establishments primarily engaged in manufacture of ethyl alcohol.

[8] Beginning 1929, excludes establishments other than petroleum refineries engaged in manufacture of lubricating oils.

[9] Beginning 1927, excludes establishments primarily engaged in manufacture of vegetable cooking oils.

[10] Beginning 1925, excludes certain establishments primarily engaged in manufacture of rubber cement.   In 1925, value added by manufacture on a basis comparable with prior years was $1,321 million.

[11] For 1899, includes establishments primarily engaged in manufacture of candles. In 1904, value added by manufacture on a basis comparable with 1899 was $287 million.

Series P 58–67. General Statistics for Manufacturing Industries, by Major Groups: 1899 to 1970—Con.

Industry group and year	Establishments		All employees		Production workers			Value added by manufacture	Capital expenditures, new	Aggregate horsepower rating of power equipment
	Total	With 20 employees or more	Number	Payroll	Number	Man-hours	Wages			
	58	59	60	61	62	63	64	65	66	67
	Number	*Number*	*1,000*	*Mil. dol.*	*1,000*	*Millions*	*Mil. dol.*	*Mil. dol.*	*Mil. dol.*	*1,000*
PETROLEUM AND COAL PRODUCTS										
1970			144	1,487	100	205	942	5,478	1,218	
1969			142	1,369	98	197	857	5,703	1,072	
1968			141	1,284	98	201	825	5,567	1,065	
1967	1,880	704	142	1,216	99	202	786	5,426	999	
1966			140	1,128	99	198	742	4,754	669	
1965			142	1,107	102	204	733	4,131	604	
1964			148	1,127	105	214	743	3,780	413	
1963	1,839	689	154	1,134	109	217	745	3,713	414	
1962			154	1,097	110	222	724	3,439	479	9,916
1961			160	1,118	114	229	745	3,382	495	
1960			171	1,145	124	250	773	3,308	485	
1959			171	1,128	124	247	761	2,894	431	
1958	1,708	821	179	1,117	131	255	758	2,518	682	
1957			186	1,150	135	268	771	3,249	900	
1956			184	1,083	136	271	744	3,318	701	
1955			183	1,001	136	271	692	2,793	545	
1954 [1]	1,262	659	183	953	136	269	659	2,241	674	6,506
1953			229	1,140	176	351	821	2,795	833	
1952	1,024		220	1,036	170	338	751	2,619	612	
1951	889		218	970	170	347	712	2,687	332	
1950	1,142		208	850	162	330	624	2,139	332	
1949			208	820	167	336	614	1,744	474	
1947 [2]	1,411		208	726	165	354	543	1,991	400	
1939 [3]	1,227				108		177	697		2,410
1937	934				116		189	638		
1935 [4]	928		124	187	105		143	471		
1933	835		103	141	90		113	395		
1931	859				91		140	432		
1929 [5]	922				112		180	829		1,755
1927	645		116	202	100		159	543		1,513
1925	750		113	193	97		154	635		1,242
1923	781		125	210	103		163	562		1,093
1921	692		103	176	87		136	430		
1919	787		118	182	97		143	511		710
1914	591		60	49	51		36	112		465
1909	590		51	34	46		27	76		
1904 [6]	376		39	23	36		19	57		
1899 [6]	308		31	16	29		14	37		
RUBBER AND PLASTICS PRODUCTS, N.E.C.										
1970			546	3,999	427	849	2,759	8,503	828	
1969			567	4,026	451	916	2,846	8,431	857	
1968			542	3,705	430	875	2,624	7,730	760	
1967	6,456	3,122	517	3,287	410	816	2,313	6,800	677	
1966			492	3,072	391	800	2,174	6,277	600	
1965			465	2,814	369	747	1,985	5,681	516	
1964			430	2,457	341	696	1,799	4,991	399	
1963	5,728	2,449	415	2,364	329	659	1,672	4,654	344	
1962			398	2,250	314	637	1,585	4,316	354	3,549
1961			371	2,019	288	577	1,402	3,916	283	
1960			378	1,998	296	590	1,400	3,773	299	
1959			379	1,968	300	600	1,406	3,793	214	
1958 [7]	4,562	1,827	348	1,723	271	531	1,211	3,277	197	
1957			260	1,310	205	403	954	2,462	149	
1956			265	1,260	211	415	931	2,418	152	
1955			265	1,257	213	437	947	2,377	127	
1954	1,406	753	247	1,059	196	377	776	1,954	128	2,211
1953			270	1,140	219	432	866	2,021	127	
1952	730		255	1,042	206	409	786	1,744	127	
1951	743		253	963	207	415	735	1,729	114	
1950	838		239	837	196	392	644	1,620	80	
1949			222	713	180	342	533	1,195	63	
1947	872		258	781	214	424	613	1,300	110	

[1] Beginning 1954, excludes beehive and byproduct coke ovens.
[2] For 1947, excludes byproduct coke plants operated in conjunction with public utilities manufacturing and distributing gas, and includes establishments primarily engaged in shipping lubricants and greases made from animal and vegetable oils.
[3] Prior to 1939, excludes byproduct coke ovens owned by city gas companies. In 1939, such ovens represented less than 2 percent of the total value of products for this commodity group.
[4] For 1935, excludes a few establishments primarily engaged in blending and compounding lubricating oils.

[5] Beginning 1929, excludes lubricants not elsewhere classified and paving mixtures and blocks. In 1929, these industries represented 4 percent of the production workers and 5 percent of the value added by manufacture for this commodity group.
[6] For 1899 and 1904, excludes fuel briquets and roofing felts and coatings. In 1909 these industries represented 6 percent of the production workers and 9 percent of the value added by manufacture for this commodity group.
[7] Beginning 1958, includes establishments engaged in molding plastics products for the trade and fabricating miscellaneous finished plastics products.

Series P 58–67. General Statistics for Manufacturing Industries, by Major Groups: 1899 to 1970—Con.

Industry group and year	Establishments		All employees		Production workers			Value added by manufacture	Capital expenditures, new	Aggregate horsepower rating of power equipment [1]
	Total	With 20 employees or more	Number	Payroll	Number	Man-hours	Wages			
	58	59	60	61	62	63	64	65	66	67
	Number	Number	1,000	Mil. dol.	1,000	Millions	Mil. dol.	Mil. dol.	Mil. dol.	1,000
RUBBER AND PLASTICS PRODUCTS, N.E.C.—Con.										
1939	695		150	227	121		161	406		989
1937	578		150	216	130		171	369		
1935	566		132	169	115		134	309		
1933	408		121	125	106		99	261		
1931	553				99		113	361		
1929	525		172	263	149		207	539		821
1927	516		169	259	142		198	565		791
1925 [2]	530				142		191	539		660
1923	529		160	231	138		182	457		606
1921	596		125	171	103		124	327		
1919	577		206	279	159		194	544		429
1914	342		89	60	74		44	138		199
1909	367		56	33	49		25	75		125
1904	365		48	25	44		20	68		86
1899	301		39	19	37		15	40		71
LEATHER AND LEATHER PRODUCTS										
1970			296	1,526	261	480	1,184	2,820	63	
1969			327	1,593	291	538	1,252	2,898	64	
1968			334	1,582	298	561	1,253	2,912	79	
1967	3,685	1,967	329	1,459	293	549	1,147	2,627	62	
1966			341	1,426	303	574	1,125	2,481	62	
1965			336	1,348	299	563	1,065	2,322	47	
1964			327	1,286	292	553	1,022	2,265	38	
1963	4,047	2,073	328	1,228	292	543	982	2,079	35	
1962			346	1,256	308	569	1,000	2,102	36	587
1961			351	1,225	312	568	970	2,041	35	
1960			358	1,227	317	582	972	2,044	35	
1959			363	1,246	324	601	993	2,121	34	
1958	4,549	2,227	349	1,146	310	566	912	1,898	32	
1957			362	1,157	323	590	939	1,892	32	
1956			367	1,149	329	607	939	1,882	37	
1955			366	1,102	330	613	896	1,778	37	
1954	4,845	2,267	357	1,027	321	587	834	1,641	28	505
1953			375	1,099	338	630	987	1,711	25	
1952	5,012		361	1,016	324	605	834	1,597	19	
1951	4,883		354	945	318	576	768	1,475	22	
1950	4,903		385	949	342	629	773	1,499	26	
1949			375	892	338	610	722	1,387	30	
1947	5,308		383	874	349	677	725	1,533	31	
1939	3,505				327		294	583		461
1937	3,249				329		308	584		
1935	3,506		336	333	311		280	530		
1933	3,265		302	254	282		223	452		
1931	3,702				273		262	524		
1929	4,285		351	444	319		360	774		436
1927	4,372		350	444	316		365	781		420
1925	4,352				314		355	751		413
1923	4,981				346		390	797		413
1921	4,827		314	385	280		315	610		
1919	6,423		394	469	350		364	898		383
1914	6,798		341	214	308		170	353		311
1909	5,785		340	191	311		156	325		
1904	5,476		284	141	266		121	246		
1899	5,785		265	117	250		102	187		

[1] Prior to 1939, for rubber and plastics products, excludes plastics products.
[2] Beginning 1925, includes establishments primarily engaged in manufacture of rubber cement and rubber toy balloons. In 1925, value added by manufacture on a basis comparable with prior years was $537 million.

Series P 58–67. General Statistics for Manufacturing Industries, by Major Groups: 1899 to 1970—Con.

Industry group and year	Establishments		All employees		Production workers			Value added by manufacture	Capital expenditures, new	Aggregate horsepower rating of power equipment
	Total	With 20 employees or more	Number	Payroll	Number	Man-hours	Wages			
	58	59	60	61	62	63	64	65	66	67
	Number	Number	1,000	Mil. dol.	1,000	Millions	Mil. dol.	Mil. dol.	Mil. dol.	1,000
STONE, CLAY, AND GLASS PRODUCTS										
1970			591	4,531	470	951	3,321	9,786	920	
1969			608	4,440	484	987	3,257	9,851	908	
1968			590	4,065	469	951	2,971	9,212	734	
1967	15,580	4,911	590	3,826	469	948	2,784	8,333	821	
1966			616	3,838	488	999	2,812	8,495	940	
1965			605	3,602	480	981	2,640	7,996	773	
1964			581	3,369	459	949	2,447	7,493	627	
1963 [1]	15,838	4,655	574	3,213	456	929	2,350	7,044	608	
1962			573	3,103	463	939	2,280	6,589	549	8,716
1961			567	2,938	457	923	2,153	6,288	554	
1960			581	2,950	474	960	2,187	6,370	541	
1959			596	2,939	488	981	2,199	6,504	557	
1958 [1]	15,047	4,484	553	2,586	446	884	1,935	5,333	489	
1957			526	2,355	437	869	1,803	4,980	656	
1956			536	2,345	450	911	1,815	5,036	725	
1955			525	2,178	442	899	1,703	4,637	461	
1954 [1]	11,162		492	1,938	412	827	1,496	3,866	301	4,811
1953			506	1,949	431	873	1,539	3,753	282	
1952	10,435		510	1,842	436	895	1,457	3,531	251	
1951	10,700		529	1,828	455	946	1,459	3,561	323	
1950	9,707		491	1,530	418	863	1,220	3,138	222	
1949			453	1,323	388	778	1,044	2,451	191	
1947 [1]	11,643		461	1,207	405	838	992	2,299	285	
1939 [1]	6,778		314	410	267		307	856		3,026
1937 [1]	6,114		331	420	297		346	860		
1935	5,846		265	293	235		228	600		
1933	4,757				175		144	404		
1931	6,549				234		250	616		
1929	8,788		372	548	331		436	1,054		2,854
1927	8,574		390	575	348		463	1,023		2,709
1925	8,491		392	565	351		466	1,043		2,348
1923	8,209		389	544	349		451	990		1,936
1921	8,227		282	377	251		305	605		
1919	12,326		331	397	295		324	680		1,585
1914	14,793		405	249	335		206	379		1,494
1909	16,207		372	224	344		190	352		
1904	10,744		305	171	286		149	271		
1899	11,571		243	116	230		102	185		
PRIMARY METAL INDUSTRIES										
1970			1,261	11,252	1,014	2,009	8,410	21,445	2,737	
1969			1,311	11,447	1,064	2,172	8,688	22,729	2,816	
1968			1,275	10,479	1,033	2,090	7,922	20,974	3,102	
1967	6,837	4,082	1,281	9,851	1,042	2,089	7,457	19,978	3,134	
1966			1,296	9,911	1,066	2,191	7,649	20,899	2,765	
1965			1,250	9,238	1,026	2,105	7,176	18,924	2,257	
1964			1,181	8,488	973	1,994	6,578	16,692	1,886	
1963	6,513	3,583	1,127	7,734	922	1,839	5,934	15,261	1,446	
1962			1,128	7,482	917	1,796	5,658	13,678	1,159	33,304
1961			1,100	7,060	891	1,723	5,271	12,759	1,222	
1960			1,175	7,215	957	1,837	5,424	13,283	1,615	
1959			1,144	7,057	947	1,830	5,354	13,578	1,076	
1958	6,447	3,412	1,092	6,281	883	1,670	4,696	11,542	1,544	
1957			1,272	7,019	1,053	2,057	5,440	13,320	2,150	
1956			1,319	6,893	1,110	2,195	5,444	13,848	1,651	
1955			1,274	6,418	1,076	2,192	5,117	12,963	977	
1954 [2]			1,152	5,260	967	1,866	4,105	9,772	910	25,546
1953			1,288	6,002	1,103	2,253	4,867	11,004	1,212	
1952	5,500		1,240	5,215	1,066	2,071	4,204	9,051	1,603	
1951	5,490		1,244	5,137	1,079	2,256	4,219	9,761	1,127	
1950	5,322		1,129	4,158	978	2,009	3,400	7,951	548	
1949			1,016	3,465	868	1,702	2,770	5,710	568	
1947	5,465		1,158	3,602	1,012	2,054	2,983	5,733	592	
1939	3,512				672		978	2,169		12,670
1937 [3]	3,245				792		1,205	2,520		

[1] For 1939, 1947, and 1954, excludes establishments primarily engaged in producing ready-mixed concrete. In 1958, the value added in such establishments represented 12 percent of the total value added for this commodity group and, in 1937, less than 1 percent. The value added at quarries operated in conjunction with manufacturing establishments (including value added in producing mineral products consumed in the same establishment) was $194 million in 1954, $361 million in 1958, and $321 million in 1963.

[2] Beginning 1954, includes beehive and byproduct coke ovens.

[3] For 1937, includes establishments primarily engaged in producing certain nonferrous bearings and aluminum products (ship bunks, ornamental metal work, stampings, novelties, valves and fittings, machined castings and tags) and excludes establishments primarily engaged in making electrometallurgical products, nonferrous die castings and forgings, cast aluminum cooking ware, and in the heat treatment of steel. In 1939, value added by manufacture on a basis comparable with 1937 was $2,131 million.

Series P 58–67. General Statistics for Manufacturing Industries, by Major Groups: 1899 to 1970—Con.

Industry group and year	Establishments		All employees		Production workers			Value added by manufacture	Capital expenditures, new	Aggregate horsepower rating of power equipment
	Total	With 20 employees or more	Number	Payroll	Number	Man-hours	Wages			
	58	59	60	61	62	63	64	65	66	67
	Number	*Number*	*1,000*	*Mil. dol.*	*1,000*	*Millions*	*Mil. dol.*	*Mil. dol.*	*Mil. dol.*	*1,000*
FABRICATED METAL PRODUCTS										
1970			1,334	10,780	1,025	2,080	7,430	20,888	1,140	
1969			1,399	10,773	1,097	2,228	7,551	20,740	1,287	
1968			1,358	10,038	1,068	2,193	7,062	19,505	1,041	
1967	27,418	10,741	1,342	9,320	1,057	2,161	6,542	18,043	1,118	
1966			1,252	8,245	984	2,038	5,762	15,792	953	
1965			1,173	7,414	915	1,901	5,182	14,171	806	
1964			1,116	6,853	870	1,795	4,803	12,693	727	
1963	27,075	9,210	1,082	6,388	844	1,721	4,484	11,791	570	
1962			1,084	6,234	834	1,717	4,283	11,128	530	6,974
1961			1,050	5,810	803	1,629	3,953	10,291	416	
1960			1,086	5,889	836	1,699	4,038	10,331	484	
1959			1,089	5,805	843	1,714	4,004	10,488	505	
1958	24,783	8,323	1,061	5,425	815	1,609	3,734	9,440	464	
1957			1,114	5,383	880	1,751	3,803	9,544	528	
1956			1,102	5,127	881	1,774	3,669	9,244	498	
1955			1,094	4,863	885	1,787	3,533	8,775	459	
1954	22,516	7,348	1,019	4,397	821	1,652	3,174	7,653	433	5,127
1953			1,118	4,765	916	1,885	3,555	8,144	446	
1952	17,953		1,008	4,124	820	1,692	3,037	7,168	328	
1951	17,552		1,035	3,988	853	1,765	2,970	7,139	354	
1950	17,975		989	3,404	807	1,658	2,524	6,211	317	
1949			872	2,884	710	1,429	2,088	4,834	231	
1947	16,877		973	2,834	823	1,695	2,189	4,920	305	
1939	9,532				451		547	1,401		1,740
1937[1]	8,688				493		605	1,389		
MACHINERY, EXCEPT ELECTRICAL										
1970			1,891	16,638	1,306	2,624	10,222	31,814	1,855	
1969			1,944	16,442	1,377	2,830	10,402	32,009	1,866	
1968			1,849	14,755	1,320	2,701	9,428	28,778	1,743	
1967	37,892	10,627	1,865	14,226	1,349	2,785	9,236	27,836	1,868	
1966			1,804	13,470	1,310	2,796	8,843	27,035	1,658	
1965			1,653	11,742	1,196	2,515	7,660	22,762	1,228	
1964			1,539	10,607	1,109	2,327	6,892	20,302	939	
1963	33,703	8,426	1,459	9,571	1,045	2,151	6,209	17,311	783	
1962			1,451	9,202	1,035	2,101	5,825	16,106	718	8,643
1961			1,382	8,405	984	1,961	5,248	14,240	658	
1960			1,426	8,482	1,014	2,045	5,398	14,410	701	
1959			1,414	8,203	1,022	2,062	5,310	14,582	607	
1958	29,868	7,363	1,350	7,314	956	1,856	4,654	12,414	670	
1957			1,707	9,050	1,266	2,573	6,061	15,978	1,038	
1956			1,717	8,897	1,308	2,717	6,156	16,176	888	
1955			1,064	7,812	1,222	2,513	5,438	13,753	653	
1954	25,600	7,521	1,541	7,186	1,171	2,368	4,977	12,333	714	[2]9,497
1953			1,691	7,876	1,307	2,744	5,686	13,381	755	
1952			1,651	7,380	1,284	2,733	5,352	12,807		
1951	18,734		1,604	6,729	1,260	2,693	4,914	11,219	631	
1950	17,909		1,368	5,063	1,064	2,183	3,609	8,765	337	
1949			1,295	4,559	1,005	2,013	3,175	7,689	351	
1947	17,910		1,552	4,830	1,249	2,591	3,610	7,834	518	
1939	8,860				536		770	2,037		2,613
1937[3]	7,327				654		970	2,366		

[1] For 1937, excludes establishments primarily engaged in producing lawn sprinklers, spun ware, nonferrous metal novelties, tackle blocks, aluminum ornamental work, aluminum stampings, and machine knives (except metalworking) and includes establishments primarily engaged in making caulking guns, toilet seats, brooders, cast aluminum cooking ware, and hair clippers. In 1939, value added by manufacture on a basis comparable with 1937 was $1,340 million.
[2] Includes electrical machinery.

[3] For 1937, includes establishments primarily engaged in manufacture of thermostats and gauges, heat treating of steel, machine knives, and tackle blocks, and excludes establishments primarily engaged in manufacture of vacuum cleaners, turbo-generators and water-wheel generator sets, hair clippers for animal use, brooders, nonferrous bearings, certain industrial furnaces and ovens, time-stamps and time-recording machines, dictating machines, certain valves and fittings (except plumbers'), and caulking guns. In 1939, value added by manufacture on a basis comparable with 1937 was $1,990 million.

Series P 58–67. General Statistics for Manufacturing Industries, by Major Groups: 1899 to 1970—Con.

Industry group and year	Establishments		All employees		Production workers			Value added by manufacture	Capital expenditures, new	Aggregate horsepower rating of power equipment
	Total	With 20 employees or more	Number	Payroll	Number	Man-hours	Wages			
	58	59	60	61	62	63	64	65	66	67
	Number	*Number*	*1,000*	*Mil. dol.*	*1,000*	*Millions*	*Mil. dol.*	*Mil. dol.*	*Mil. dol.*	*1,000*
ELECTRICAL EQUIPMENT AND SUPPLIES										
1970			1,832	14,827	1,237	2,417	8,321	27,774	1,520	
1969			1,918	14,830	1,324	2,619	8,446	28,211	1,641	
1968			1,883	13,808	1,304	2,597	7,986	26,425	1,478	
1967	10,706	5,572	1,875	12,968	1,324	2,611	7,607	24,487	1,537	
1966			1,811	11,988	1,319	2,642	7,259	23,482	1,388	
1965			1,605	10,450	1,139	2,313	6,232	20,162	1,046	
1964			1,484	9,407	1,030	2,070	5,569	17,765	761	
1963	9,948	4,722	1,512	9,284	1,049	2,091	5,406	17,011	702	
1962			1,523	9,083	1,046	2,121	5,318	16,416	653	4,813
1961			1,432	8,207	970	1,951	4,681	14,433	639	
1960			1,377	7,515	962	1,932	4,466	13,484	637	
1959			1,274	6,752	927	1,855	4,196	12,826	554	
1958 [1]	8,086	3,797	1,141	5,755	817	1,606	3,558	10,624	468	
1957			1,084	5,133	795	1,565	3,292	9,620	524	
1956			1,080	4,903	817	1,618	3,261	9,112	475	
1955			1,001	4,314	759	1,521	2,896	8,002	335	
1954	5,758	2,837	959	3,951	722	1,422	2,646	7,300	341	(2)
1953			1,096	4,425	851	1,703	3,078	7,876	406	
1952	4,421		957	3,750	741	1,521	2,629	6,873		
1951	4,294		877	3,193	692	1,396	2,278	5,753	296	
1950	4,019		766	2,533	610	1,221	1,800	4,815	195	
1949			663	2,145	506	1,026	1,460	3,902	187	
1947 [3]	3,970		796	2,258	635	1,278	1,637	3,860	225	
1939 [4]	1,979				248		323	941		1,019
1937	1,597		374	559	306		408	1,102		
1935 [5]	1,589		275	348	224		241	686		
1933	1,365		202	212	164		145	404		
1931	1,596				217		240	763		
1929	1,861		421	650	343		474	1,389		894
1927 [6]	1,837		322	509	256		356	1,049		661
1925	1,807		309	463	251		338	940		589
1923	1,782		332	474	255		330	806		480
1921	1,487		240	339	179		216	547		
1919	1,570		305	379	241		272	672		438
1914	1,048		156	118	128		80	201		226
1909 [7]	1,027		111	73	93		52	121		158
1904	798		75	45	64		34	80		102
1899	592		49	26	43		21	44		41
TRANSPORTATION EQUIPMENT										
1970			1,689	16,073	1,201	2,393	10,230	29,990	1,612	
1969			1,920	17,651	1,398	2,823	11,455	34,053	1,943	
1968			1,888	16,811	1,377	2,893	11,135	32,866	1,599	
1967	7,483	3,354	1,834	15,174	1,337	2,746	9,918	28,174	1,822	
1966			1,830	14,852	1,355	2,844	9,858	28,277	1,880	
1965			1,684	13,273	1,241	2,640	8,813	26,331	1,506	
1964			1,563	11,887	1,120	2,370	7,772	22,734	1,177	
1963	7,180	2,852	1,551	11,406	1,108	2,356	7,389	21,854	981	
1962			1,601	11,334	1,129	2,367	7,169	20,872	856	10,699
1961			1,506	10,113	1,056	2,157	6,313	17,433	720	
1960			1,593	10,360	1,161	2,393	6,842	18,369	731	
1959			1,615	10,254	1,172	2,454	6,696	18,084	723	
1958 [8]	6,634	2,674	1,562	9,186	1,139	2,275	6,037	15,315	630	
1957			1,901	10,491	1,402	2,845	7,178	18,492	723	
1956			1,793	9,707	1,358	2,793	6,743	16,633	1,142	
1955			1,813	9,407	1,418	2,959	6,843	17,071	1,437	
1954	5,349	2,318	1,706	8,300	1,328	2,711	6,006	13,428	925	9,041
1953			1,912	8,987	1,530	3,155	6,731	14,534	710	
1952	3,393		1,650	7,423	1,317	2,750	5,585	12,042		
1951			1,469	6,067	1,200	2,448	4,672	9,789	600	
1950	2,780		1,218	4,680	1,006	2,060	3,657	8,547	343	
1949			1,140	4,098	936	1,873	3,163	7,054	264	
1947	3,703		1,175	3,695	981	1,961	2,921	5,842	353	
1939	2,012				545		867	1,773		2,926
1937 [9]	1,958				662		1,029	1,987		

[1] Beginning 1958, includes establishments primarily engaged in manufacture of household refrigerators and home and farm freezers; household laundry equipment and sewing machines; water heaters, except electric; and other household appliances. Excludes those primarily engaged in manufacture of hearing aids; high frequency, induction, and dielectric heating apparatus; commercial food warming equipment; industrial electric heating units and devices; and insulated wire and cable made from purchased wire.   [2] Included with machinery, except electrical.
[3] Beginning 1947, includes establishments primarily engaged in manufacture of electric (dry) shavers.
[4] Beginning 1939, excludes establishments primarily engaged in manufacture of vacuum cleaners, turbo-generators and water-wheel generator sets, dictating machines and electric industrial furnaces and ovens. In 1939, value added by manufacture on a basis comparable with prior years was $1,000 million.

[5] Beginning 1935, excludes establishments primarily engaged in manufacture of certain types of beauty and barber shop equipment.
[6] Beginning 1927, excludes establishments primarily engaged in manufacture of certain types of mechanical refrigerators.
[7] Beginning 1909, excludes establishments primarily engaged in manufacture of signs and advertising novelties.
[8] Beginning 1958, includes establishments primarily engaged in manufacture of truck and bus bearings, convertible tops for automobiles, rebuilt automotive parts, and aircraft and related engine and power take-off gears and excludes those primarily engaged in manufacture of parachutes.
[9] For 1937, includes railroad repair shops. In 1939, value added by manufacture on a basis comparable with 1937 was $1,794 million.

Series P 58–67.   General Statistics for Manufacturing Industries, by Major Groups: 1899 to 1970—Con.

Industry group and year	Establishments		All employees		Production workers			Value added by manufacture	Capital expenditures, new	Aggregate horsepower rating of power equipment
	Total	With 20 employees or more	Number	Payroll	Number	Man-hours	Wages			
	58	59	60	61	62	63	64	65	66	67
	Number	*Number*	*1,000*	*Mil. dol.*	*1,000*	*Millions*	*Mil. dol.*	*Mil. dol.*	*Mil. dol.*	*1,000*
INSTRUMENTS AND RELATED PRODUCTS										
1970			405	3,358	262	502	1,746	7,905	436	
1969			413	3,272	271	535	1,757	7,676	388	
1968			400	3,002	266	525	1,625	7,174	397	
1967	4,453	1,614	394	2,822	266	530	1,569	6,418	392	
1966			362	2,509	249	494	1,426	5,833	307	
1965			329	2,228	226	452	1,275	5,002	232	
1964			308	2,014	209	421	1,149	4,314	192	
1963	3,949	1,343	306	1,913	208	417	1,101	3,992	192	
1962			308	1,871	206	416	1,051	3,690	178	
1961			316	1,908	208	415	1,037	3,574	179	860
1960			326	1,908	217	437	1,067	3,641	162	
1959			311	1,783	214	432	1,033	3,410	145	
1958 [1]	3,518	1,189	286	1,510	197	390	898	2,781	115	
1957			307	1,571	211	428	947	2,872	146	
1956			297	1,458	211	426	897	2,690	145	
1955			283	1,295	202	406	814	2,367	106	
1954 [2]	3,141	984	273	1,200	196	391	760	2,131	94	667
1953			286	1,233	212	434	824	2,169	90	
1952			279	1,179	205	420	779	1,995		
1951	2,686		253	1,001	190	390	671	1,608	85	
1950	2,697		226	813	169	342	532	1,389	64	
1949			205	683	156	306	447	1,123	58	
1947 [2]	2,605		245	706	194	390	502	1,141	56	
1939 [3]	1,292				85		108	333		165
1937 [4]	1,026				84		113	298		
1935 [5]	1,000		84	108	68		74	200		
1933	830				50		46	142		
1931	1,029				60		66	201		
1929 [6]	1,109		98	149	82		108	301		
1927 [7]	1,108				79		103	274		
1925 [8]	1,286		88	124	73		91	263		
1923	1,593		93	127	77		92	245		
1921	1,592		83	109	67		78	189		
1919	2,037		109	125	91		93	236		
1914 [9]	1,572		71	50	60		36	98		
1909	1,239				51		28	73		
1904	1,027		46	26	42		21	46		
1899	1,101		35	18	32		15	32		
MISCELLANEOUS MANUFACTURING INDUSTRIES										
1970			429	2,685	337	643	1,752	5,433	253	
1969			449	2,665	363	690	1,796	5,296	240	
1968			431	2,461	349	669	1,667	4,951	209	
1967	14,072	3,845	423	2,291	344	662	1,553	4,599	214	
1966			418	2,150	340	666	1,463	4,338	181	
1965			416	2,042	340	661	1,393	4,092	166	
1964			394	1,924	315	631	1,314	3,763	137	
1963	14,723	3,618	391	1,812	315	613	1,254	3,562	131	
1962			378	1,705	305	597	1,163	3,330	130	[10] 2,215
1961			375	1,608	303	585	1,097	3,082	113	
1960			374	1,655	301	588	1,091	3,003	111	
1959			376	1,556	305	591	1,084	2,888	124	
1958 [11]	13,797	3,336	365	1,467	291	559	1,034	2,678	111	
1957			495	1,886	403	776	1,313	3,327	122	
1956			506	1,861	417	814	1,324	3,305	158	
1955 [12]			489	1,734	404	783	1,225	3,042	117	
1954	16,517	4,289	467	1,625	385	748	1,149	2,746	115	2,036
1953			844	3,232	686	1,368	2,366	5,272	205	
1952	14,572		682	2,375	564	1,102	1,731	3,984	155	
1951	15,057		519	1,711	432	862	1,233	2,842		
1950			488	1,452	404	800	1,055	2,534	98	
1949			447	1,263	370	728	917	2,109	77	
1947	14,148		463	1,205	396	811	918	2,066	107	

[1] Beginning 1958, includes establishments primarily engaged in manufacture of laboratory precision balances, laboratory furniture, revolution counters, operating room and other hospital furniture, surgical corsets, and hearing aids and excludes those primarily engaged in manufacture of sanitary napkins and tampons.

[2] For 1947 and 1954–1970, includes establishments primarily engaged in manufacture of automatic temperature controls.

[3] Beginning 1939, includes establishments primarily engaged in manufacture of thermostats and gauges and excludes those primarily engaged in manufacture of time-recording stamps and machines. In 1939, value added on a basis comparable with prior years was $314 million.

[4] Beginning 1937, includes establishments primarily engaged in manufacture of certain mechanical measuring instruments. In 1937, value added by manufacture on a basis comparable with prior years was $295 million.

[5] Beginning 1935, includes establishments primarily engaged in manufacture of certain dental equipment and supplies (chairs, cabinets, and electrical devices).

[6] Beginning 1929, excludes establishments primarily engaged in manufacture of gas machines. In 1929, value added by manufacture on a basis comparable with prior years was $306 million. [7] Beginning 1927, excludes dental laboratories operating on a custom basis. In 1927, value added by manufacture on a basis comparable with prior years was $280 million.

[8] Beginning 1925, excludes establishments primarily engaged in grinding lenses for spectacles and eyeglasses to individual prescription.

[9] Beginning 1914, includes establishments primarily engaged in manufacture of motion-picture machines. In 1914, value added by manufacture on a basis comparable with prior years was $96 million. [10] Includes ordnance.

[11] Beginning 1958, excludes establishments primarily engaged in manufacture of plastics products not elsewhere classified, cork products, soda-fountain and bar equipment, and jewelry, instrument, and musical instrument cases and includes those primarily engaged in manufacture of linoleum and other hard surface floor covering, n.e.c.

[12] Prior to 1955, includes ordnance and accessories.

Series P 68–73. Horsepower of Power Equipment in Manufacturing Industries: 1869 to 1962

[In thousands]

Year	Aggregate	Prime movers	Electric motors			Aggregate per 100 production workers	Year	Aggregate	Prime movers	Electric motors			Aggregate per 100 production workers
			Total	Driven by purchased energy	Driven by energy generated at establishment					Total	Driven by purchased energy	Driven by energy generated at establishment	
	68	69	70	71	72	73		68	69	70	71	72	73
1962	151,498	45,770	126,783	105,728	21,054	¹1,249	1909	18,062	16,393	4,582	1,669	2,913	288
1954*	108,100	35,763	91,505	72,337	19,168	958	1904	13,033	12,605	1,517	428	1,089	252
1939	49,893	21,077	44,827	28,816	16,011	652	1899	9,811	9,633	475	178	297	218
1929	41,122	19,328	33,844	21,794	12,050	491							
1927	37,126	18,902	29,153	18,224	10,929	473	1899²	10,988	10,805	494	183	311	207
1925	34,359	19,243	25,092	15,116	9,976	437	1889²	--------	5,939	15	--------	--------	140
1919	28,397	19,432	15,612	8,965	6,647	333	1879²	--------	3,410	--------	--------	--------	125
1914	21,565	17,858	8,392	3,707	4,684	326	1869²	--------	2,346	--------	--------	--------	114

* Denotes first year for which figures include Alaska and Hawaii.
¹ Figure comparable with 1954, based on 1954 industry coverage (see text), is 1,365.
Figures for earlier censuses are comparable with 1962, except as noted in text.

² Includes hand trades and neighborhood industries.

Series P 74–92. Value of Manufacturers' Shipments, Inventories, and Orders: 1947 to 1970

[In billions of dollars, except ratios. As of December 31, except shipments are for calendar year]

Year	Shipments			Inventories			Ratios of inventories to sales¹			Inventories by stages of fabrication				New orders			Unfilled orders		
	Total	Durable goods industries	Non-durable goods industries	Total	Durable goods industries	Non-durable goods industries	Total	Durable goods	Non-durable goods	All manufacturing				Total	Durable goods industries	Non-durable goods industries	Total	Durable goods industries	Non-durable goods industries
										Total	Materials and supplies	Work in process	Finished goods						
	74	75	76	77	78	79	80	81	82	83	84	85	86	87	88	89	90	91	92
1970	630.7	336.7	294.0	101.4	66.4	34.9	1.90	2.33	1.40	101.4	32.7	35.2	33.6	620.0	325.9	294.0	73.8	70.8	2.9
1969	642.7	353.5	289.2	96.6	62.9	33.8	1.76	2.08	1.36	96.6	31.8	33.9	30.9	643.7	354.6	289.2	84.5	81.6	2.9
1968	603.4	332.3	271.1	90.5	58.7	31.8	1.76	2.11	1.34	90.5	30.0	32.0	28.4	606.1	335.0	271.0	85.4	82.4	2.9
1967	557.4	302.5	254.8	84.4	54.6	29.8	1.77	2.10	1.37	84.4	28.5	29.1	26.8	561.2	306.3	254.9	83.9	80.9	3.0
1966	538.4	295.6	242.8	77.7	49.5	28.2	1.73	2.01	1.39	77.7	27.0	25.9	24.8	550.9	308.3	242.7	79.8	76.7	3.0
1965	492.0	267.0	225.5	68.0	42.0	26.0	1.66	1.89	1.39	68.0	24.1	22.0	22.3	502.0	276.0	226.0	67.2	64.0	3.1
1964	448.0	236.0	212.4	63.0	38.0	25.0	1.69	1.94	1.42	63.0	22.4	19.5	21.3	455.4	243.1	212.3	58.0	55.0	3.0
1963	420.4	219.0	201.4	60.0	36.0	24.3	1.71	1.95	1.45	60.0	21.3	18.1	20.4	424.0	222.3	202.0	50.2	47.3	3.0
1962	397.4	205.2	192.1	58.0	34.3	24.0	1.75	1.97	1.46	58.0	21.0	17.1	20.0	396.1	204.3	191.8	47.0	44.0	3.0
1961	371.0	187.0	184.2	55.0	32.2	23.0	1.77	2.08	1.47	55.0	20.1	16.0	19.0	373.0	188.4	184.4	48.0	45.0	3.0
1960*	370.0	190.0	180.0	54.0	32.0	22.0	1.74	2.02	1.44	54.0	20.0	15.5	18.3	361.4	183.0	179.0	46.0	43.2	3.0
1959	363.0	187.0	176.1	52.5	31.5	21.0	1.74	2.02	1.43	52.5	20.0	16.0	17.0	368.1	191.4	177.0	54.1	50.4	4.0
1958	327.4	163.0	164.5	50.0	30.0	20.1	1.83	2.20	1.47	50.0	19.0	15.0	16.1	323.0	158.0	165.0	49.0	46.0	3.1
1957	345.0	183.0	162.0	52.0	32.0	20.3	1.81	2.07	1.50	52.0	20.0	16.0	17.0	330.2	169.0	161.3	53.3	50.5	2.8
1956	333.0	177.0	156.3	51.0	30.4	20.3	1.83	2.07	1.56	51.0	20.0	15.0	16.0	341.0	185.0	156.0	67.5	64.1	3.4
1955	318.0	169.0	149.0	45.2	26.4	19.0	1.71	1.88	1.51	45.2	18.2	13.2	14.0	329.1	179.4	150.0	60.0	56.4	4.0
1954	280.2	142.0	138.3	42.0	24.0	18.0	1.80	2.01	1.57	42.0	16.5	13.3	13.3	267.8	129.0	139.0	48.2	45.2	3.0
1953	298.0	160.0	138.0	44.2	26.0	18.2	1.79	1.95	1.59	44.2	17.8	13.1	13.4	282.4	145.3	137.1	60.3	58.0	2.5
1952	271.0	136.1	135.0	42.0	24.0	18.0	1.84	2.11	1.57	42.0	17.0	12.3	12.6	278.4	145.0	134.0	75.5	72.3	3.2
1951	260.4	126.0	135.0	39.2	21.1	18.0	1.80	2.01	1.60	39.2	16.0	11.0	12.4	287.0	154.1	133.0	67.0	63.1	4.0
1950	223.4	106.0	117.4	32.0	16.0	16.0	1.70	1.77	1.62	32.0	13.1	9.0	10.0	241.3	122.0	119.3	41.2	35.2	6.0
1949	193.1	86.0	107.1	26.5	13.1	13.4	1.65	1.83	1.50	26.5	10.3	6.8	9.4	187.4	80.0	108.0	24.0	20.0	4.4
1948	217.3	100.0	117.2	29.0	15.0	14.1	1.59	1.77	1.44	29.0	--------	--------	--------	212.3	98.0	115.0	31.0	26.5	4.1
1947	186.0	80.2	106.0	26.1	13.1	13.0	1.69	1.96	1.47	26.1	--------	--------	--------	183.1	77.0	106.4	34.3	28.4	6.0

* Denotes first year for which figures include Alaska and Hawaii.

¹ Ratios of average inventories to average monthly sales.

Series P 93–106. Manufacturing Corporations—Sales, Profits, and Stockholders' Equity: 1947 to 1970

[In billions of dollars]

Year	All manufacturing corporations						Durable goods industries				Nondurable goods industries			
	Sales (net)	Net profits		Stockholders' equity [1]	Cash dividends	Retained earnings	Sales (net)	Net profits		Stockholders' equity [1]	Sales (net)	Net profits		Stockholders' equity [1]
		Before Federal income taxes	After Federal income taxes					Before Federal income taxes	After Federal income taxes			Before Federal income taxes	After Federal income taxes	
	93	94	95	96	97	98	99	100	101	102	103	104	105	106
1970	708.8	48.1	28.6	306.8	15.1	13.5	363.1	23.0	12.9	155.1	345.7	25.2	15.7	151.7
1969 [2]	694.6	58.1	33.2	289.9	15.1	18.2	366.5	31.5	16.9	147.6	328.1	26.6	16.4	142.3
1968	631.9	55.4	32.1	265.9	14.2	17.9	335.5	30.6	16.5	135.6	296.4	24.8	15.5	130.3
1967	575.4	47.8	29.0	247.6	13.3	15.7	300.6	25.7	14.6	125.0	274.8	22.0	14.4	122.6
1966	554.2	51.8	30.9	230.3	13.0	18.0	291.7	29.2	16.4	115.2	262.4	22.6	14.6	115.1
1965	492.2	46.5	27.5	211.7	12.0	15.5	257.0	26.2	14.5	105.4	235.2	20.3	13.0	106.3
1964	443.1	39.6	23.2	199.8	10.8	12.4	226.3	21.2	11.6	98.5	216.8	18.3	11.6	101.3
1963	412.7	34.9	19.5	189.7	9.9	9.6	209.0	18.5	9.5	93.3	203.6	16.4	10.0	96.3
1962	389.9	31.9	17.7	181.4	9.3	8.4	195.5	16.7	8.6	89.1	194.4	15.1	9.2	92.3
1961	356.4	27.5	15.3	172.6	8.6	6.8	175.2	13.6	6.9	84.9	181.2	13.9	8.5	87.7
1960	345.7	27.5	15.2	165.4	8.3	6.9	173.9	14.0	7.0	82.3	171.8	13.5	8.2	83.1
1959	338.0	29.7	16.3	157.1	7.9	8.4	169.4	15.8	8.1	77.9	168.5	13.9	8.3	79.2
1958	305.3	22.7	12.7	147.4	7.4	5.3	148.6	11.4	5.8	72.8	156.7	11.3	6.9	74.6
1957	320.0	28.2	15.4	141.1	7.6	7.9	166.0	15.8	7.9	70.5	154.1	12.4	7.5	70.6
1956	307.3	29.8	16.2	131.6	7.4	8.8	159.5	16.5	8.3	65.2	147.8	13.2	7.8	66.4
1955	278.4	28.6	15.1	120.1	6.8	8.3	142.1	16.5	8.1	58.8	136.3	12.1	7.0	61.3
1954	248.5	20.9	11.2	113.1	5.9	5.3	122.8	11.4	5.6	54.9	125.7	9.6	5.6	58.2
1953	265.9	24.4	11.3	108.2	5.6	5.7	137.9	14.0	5.8	52.4	128.0	10.4	5.5	55.7
1952	250.2	22.9	10.7	103.7	5.5	5.2	122.0	12.9	5.5	49.8	128.0	10.0	5.2	53.9
1951	245.0	27.4	11.9	98.3	5.5	6.3	116.8	15.4	6.1	47.2	128.1	12.1	5.7	51.1
1950	181.9	23.2	12.9	83.3	5.7	7.2	86.8	12.9	6.7	39.9	95.1	10.3	6.1	43.5
1949	154.9	14.4	9.0	77.6	4.5	4.5	70.3	7.5	4.5	37.0	84.6	7.0	4.6	40.6
1948	165.6	18.4	11.5	72.2	4.3	7.2	75.3	8.9	5.4	34.1	90.4	9.5	6.2	38.1
1947	150.7	16.6	10.1	65.1	3.7	6.4	66.6	7.6	4.5	31.1	84.1	9.0	5.6	34.0

[1] Annual data are average equity for the year (using four end-of-quarter figures).   [2] Beginning 1969, includes newspapers.

Series P 107–122. Capital in Manufacturing Industries: 1863 to 1970

[In billions of dollars]

Year	Purchases of structures and equipment						Depreciation on structures and equipment						Real net value of assets in 1958 dollars			
	In current dollars			In 1958 dollars			In current dollars			In 1958 dollars			Structures and equipment	Structures	Equipment	Government owned, privately operated [1]
	Total	Structures	Equipment	Total	Structures	Equipment	Total	Structures	Equipment	Total	Structures	Equipment				
	107	108	109	110	111	112	113	114	115	116	117	118	119	120	121	122
1970	22.4	5.7	16.6	17.0	3.8	13.3	18.2	4.8	13.3	13.7	3.1	10.6	101.5	38.8	62.7	5.2
1969	22.5	5.8	16.7	18.1	4.2	14.0	16.4	4.3	12.1	13.1	3.1	10.0	99.2	38.2	61.0	5.8
1968	20.9	5.3	15.6	17.5	4.2	13.4	14.9	3.8	11.0	12.4	3.0	9.4	95.2	37.1	58.1	6.2
1967	21.7	5.7	16.0	18.7	4.7	14.0	13.6	3.6	10.1	11.7	2.9	8.8	91.3	36.0	55.3	6.4
1966	20.4	5.2	15.2	18.2	4.4	13.7	12.4	3.3	9.0	11.0	2.8	8.2	85.4	34.3	51.1	6.4
1965	16.7	4.2	12.6	15.4	3.7	11.7	11.3	3.1	8.2	10.3	2.7	7.6	79.0	32.7	46.2	6.3
1964	13.4	3.2	10.2	12.6	3.0	9.7	10.6	3.0	7.7	9.9	2.7	7.3	74.5	31.8	42.7	6.4
1963	11.5	3.0	8.5	11.0	2.8	8.2	10.2	2.8	7.3	9.6	2.6	7.0	72.2	31.6	40.7	6.5
1962	10.6	2.7	7.9	10.2	2.6	7.6	9.9	2.7	7.2	9.4	2.6	6.8	71.2	31.4	39.8	6.8
1961	9.9	2.7	7.2	9.6	2.7	7.0	9.6	2.7	7.0	9.3	2.6	6.7	70.7	31.5	39.3	7.1
1960*	10.3	2.8	7.4	10.0	2.8	7.2	9.4	2.6	6.8	9.1	2.5	6.6	70.6	31.3	39.3	7.4
1959	9.0	2.5	6.6	8.8	2.4	6.4	9.1	2.6	6.6	8.9	2.5	6.4	70.1	31.2	39.0	8.0
1958	9.7	3.3	6.5	9.7	3.3	6.5	8.8	2.5	6.3	8.8	2.5	6.3	70.9	31.4	39.5	8.7
1957	12.3	3.9	8.4	12.5	3.9	8.6	8.3	2.4	5.9	8.5	2.4	6.1	70.8	30.9	39.9	9.4
1956	11.4	3.5	7.9	12.3	3.7	8.6	7.4	2.2	5.2	8.1	2.4	5.7	67.8	29.7	38.1	10.0
1955	8.6	2.4	6.2	10.0	2.8	7.1	6.5	2.0	4.6	7.7	2.3	5.4	64.5	28.7	35.8	10.3
1954	8.5	2.5	6.0	10.1	2.9	7.2	6.1	1.9	4.2	7.4	2.3	5.1	62.8	28.1	34.7	10.1
1953	8.4	2.6	5.8	10.0	3.0	7.1	5.8	1.9	3.9	7.0	2.2	4.8	61.0	27.8	33.2	9.3
1952	8.0	2.6	5.5	9.8	3.0	6.8	5.4	1.9	3.5	6.7	2.2	4.5	58.9	27.3	31.6	8.7
1951	8.0	2.6	5.4	9.9	3.1	6.8	5.0	1.8	3.2	6.3	2.2	4.1	56.8	26.8	30.0	8.7
1950	5.6	1.5	4.0	7.5	2.1	5.5	4.3	1.6	2.7	6.0	2.2	3.8	53.9	26.0	27.9	8.8
1949	5.6	1.7	3.9	7.8	2.4	5.4	3.9	1.6	2.4	5.7	2.2	3.5	52.8	25.9	26.9	9.7
1948	6.8	2.2	4.6	9.9	3.0	6.8	3.6	1.6	2.0	5.3	2.1	3.2	50.9	25.2	25.8	11.4
1947	6.7	2.4	4.3	10.6	3.6	6.9	3.0	1.4	1.6	4.8	2.1	2.8	45.9	23.2	22.6	14.3
1946	5.2	2.4	2.8	9.5	4.4	5.1	2.4	1.1	1.3	4.4	2.0	2.4	38.7	20.6	18.1	18.0

See footnotes at end of table.

Series P 107–122. Capital in Manufacturing Industries: 1863 to 1970—Con.

[In billions of dollars]

Year	Purchases of structures and equipment						Depreciation on structures and equipment						Real net value of assets in 1958 dollars			
	In current dollars			In 1958 dollars			In current dollars			In 1958 dollars			Structures and equipment	Structures	Equipment	Government owned, privately operated [1]
	Total	Structures	Equipment	Total	Structures	Equipment	Total	Structures	Equipment	Total	Structures	Equipment				
	107	108	109	110	111	112	113	114	115	116	117	118	119	120	121	122
1945	2.9	0.8	2.1	5.5	1.7	3.7	2.0	.9	1.1	4.1	1.9	2.2	31.7	16.6	15.1	22.8
1944	1.7	.3	1.5	3.2	.6	2.6	1.9	.9	1.1	4.1	2.0	2.1	29.9	16.3	13.6	23.5
1943	1.4	.2	1.2	2.5	.4	2.1	1.9	.9	1.0	4.1	2.1	2.1	30.5	17.4	13.1	22.2
1942	1.7	.5	1.2	3.3	1.1	2.2	1.9	.9	1.0	4.2	2.1	2.1	31.9	18.8	13.2	16.0
1941	2.6	1.1	1.6	6.0	2.9	3.1	1.7	.8	1.0	4.2	2.1	2.0	32.7	19.5	13.2	5.0
1940	1.9	.7	1.3	4.7	2.0	2.8	1.6	.7	.9	4.1	2.1	2.0	30.7	18.5	12.2	1.0
1939	1.3	.4	.9	3.5	1.4	2.1	1.5	.7	.8	4.1	2.1	2.0	29.8	18.3	11.5	–
1938	1.1	.4	.8	2.9	1.1	1.8	1.6	.7	.9	4.2	2.2	2.0	30.1	18.7	11.4	–
1937	1.8	.7	1.1	4.7	2.1	2.6	1.5	.7	.8	4.2	2.2	2.0	31.0	19.4	11.6	–
1936	1.3	.4	.9	3.7	1.4	2.3	1.4	.6	.8	4.2	2.2	2.0	30.1	19.2	10.9	–
1935	.9	.2	.6	2.6	.9	1.7	1.4	.6	.7	4.2	2.3	1.9	30.2	19.7	10.5	–
1934	.8	.3	.5	2.3	1.1	1.2	1.4	.6	.8	4.3	2.3	2.0	31.4	20.7	10.7	–
1933	.6	.3	.3	2.2	1.1	1.0	1.3	.6	.7	4.4	2.3	2.1	33.0	21.7	11.3	–
1932	.4	.1	.3	1.4	.5	.9	1.3	.6	.8	4.5	2.4	2.1	34.9	22.7	12.2	–
1931	.9	.3	.6	2.8	1.3	1.6	1.5	.7	.8	4.6	2.4	2.2	37.8	24.4	13.4	–
1930	1.7	.8	.9	4.8	2.7	2.1	1.6	.8	.9	4.7	2.4	2.2	39.6	25.5	14.1	–
1929	2.7	1.5	1.2	7.3	4.4	2.8	1.7	.8	.9	4.6	2.4	2.2	39.6	25.3	14.3	–
1928	2.3	1.2	1.1	6.3	3.7	2.6	1.7	.8	.9	4.4	2.3	2.1	37.2	23.3	13.9	–
1927	2.1	1.1	1.0	5.7	3.2	2.4	1.6	.7	.9	4.3	2.2	2.1	35.5	22.0	13.5	–
1926	2.2	1.1	1.1	6.0	3.3	2.7	1.6	.7	.8	4.2	2.2	2.0	34.4	21.1	13.3	–
1925	1.8	.8	1.0	4.8	2.3	2.5	1.5	.7	.8	4.0	2.1	1.9	32.7	20.0	12.8	–

Year	Purchases of structures and equipment					
	In current dollars			In 1958 dollars		
	Total	Structures	Equipment	Total	Structures	Equipment
	107	108	109	110	111	112
1924	1.6	0.7	0.9	4.2	2.1	2.1
1923	1.8	.9	1.0	4.9	2.5	2.4
1922	1.4	.7	.7	4.2	2.4	1.8
1921	1.4	.8	.6	3.9	2.5	1.4
1920	2.4	1.4	1.1	5.4	3.1	2.3
1919	1.6	.7	.9	3.9	2.0	1.9
1918	1.4	.5	.9	3.6	1.6	2.1
1917	1.3	.5	.7	4.1	1.8	2.3
1916	1.0	.4	.6	4.0	2.0	2.0
1915	.6	.3	.3	3.1	1.7	1.3
1914	.6	.3	.3	3.4	2.1	1.3
1913	.9	.5	.4	4.6	2.9	1.7
1912	.9	.5	.3	4.6	3.1	1.5
1911	.7	.4	.3	3.9	2.6	1.3
1910	.7	.4	.3	4.1	2.5	1.5
1909	.7	.4	.3	3.7	2.4	1.3
1908	.5	.3	.2	3.2	2.0	1.1
1907	.7	.3	.3	3.7	2.0	1.7
1906	.7	.3	.3	3.6	1.9	1.7
1905	.5	.3	.3	3.0	1.6	1.4
1904	.5	.2	.2	2.7	1.6	1.1
1903	.6	.3	.3	3.7	2.2	1.5
1902	.6	.3	.2	3.5	2.3	1.2
1901	.4	.2	.2	2.6	1.5	1.1
1900	.4	.2	.2	2.3	1.3	1.1
1899	.3	.2	.2	2.2	1.3	.8
1898	.3	.2	.1	2.1	1.4	.7
1897	.3	.2	.1	2.7	2.1	.7
1896	.4	.2	.1	3.1	2.1	1.0
1895	.3	.2	.1	2.5	1.6	.8
1894	.3	.2	.1	2.0	1.4	.6

Year	Purchases of structures and equipment					
	In current dollars			In 1958 dollars		
	Total	Structures	Equipment	Total	Structures	Equipment
	107	108	109	110	111	112
1893	0.3	0.2	0.1	2.2	1.5	0.7
1892	.3	.2	.1	2.2	1.5	.8
1891	.3	.2	.1	2.2	1.4	.7
1890	.3	.2	.1	2.0	1.3	.6
1889	.2	.1	.1	1.6	1.0	.6
1888	.2	.1	.1	1.1	.6	.6
1887	.2	.1	.1	1.0	.5	.4
1886	.1	.1	.1	.7	.5	.3
1885	.1	.1	(Z)	.7	.5	.2
1884	.1	.1	.1	.9	.6	.3
1883	.1	.1	.1	.8	.5	.3
1882	.2	.1	.1	.9	.5	.4
1881	.2	.1	.1	.8	.5	.4
1880	.1	(Z)	(Z)	.4	.2	.2
1879	.1	(Z)	(Z)	.4	.2	.2
1878	.1	(Z)	(Z)	.4	.2	.2
1877	.1	(Z)	(Z)	.3	.2	.1
1876	.1	(Z)	(Z)	.3	.2	.1
1875	(Z)	(Z)	(Z)	.2	.2	(Z)
1874	.1	(Z)	(Z)	.4	.3	.1
1873	.1	1.1	(Z)	.4	.4	.1
1872	.1	(Z)	(Z)	.4	.3	.1
1871	.1	(Z)	(Z)	.4	.3	.1
1870	.1	.1	(Z)	.4	.4	.1
1869	.1	(Z)	(Z)	.3	.3	(Z)
1868	(Z)	(Z)	(Z)	.2	.2	(Z)
1867	(Z)	(Z)	(Z)	.2	.2	(Z)
1866	(Z)	(Z)	(Z)	.1	.1	(Z)
1865	(Z)	(Z)	(Z)	.1	.1	(Z)
1864	(Z)	–	(Z)	(Z)	–	(Z)
1863	(Z)	–	(Z)	(Z)	–	(Z)

* Denotes first year for which figures include Alaska and Hawaii.
– Represents zero.   Z Less than $50 million.

[1] Includes both structures and equipment, all agencies.

Series P 123–176. Capital in Manufacturing Industries, in Book Value and in 1929 Dollars (Creamer): 1879 to 1957

[In millions of dollars]

Series No.	Industry	1957[1][2][3]	1953[1][2][3]	1948[1][2]	1937[1]	1929[1]	1919[4]	1914[4]	1909[4]	1904[4]	1899[4]	1899[5]	1889[5]	1879[5]
	BOOK VALUE													
123	**Total manufacturing capital**	214,613	166,224	113,617	50,166	59,072	40,289	20,784	16,937	11,588	8,168	8,663	5,697	2,718
124	Fixed capital	97,210	70,605	45,891	23,282	27,410	(NA)	(NA)	(NA)	5,596	(NA)	4,223	2,646	-------
125	Working capital	117,403	95,619	67,726	26,884	31,662	(NA)	(NA)	(NA)	5,992	(NA)	4,440	3,051	-------
126	**Food and kindred products**	22,495	19,921	16,071	8,069	8,881	6,272	3,668	2,935	2,230	1,576	1,647	925	498
127	Bakery and confectionery	-------	-------	1,757	1,131	1,568	911	426	295	173	114	123	72	28
128	Canned products	-------	-------	1,681	820	853	378	172	119	90	59	59	25	9
129	Mill products	-------	-------	1,060	496	471	802	380	349	265	189	219	208	177
130	Packinghouse products	-------	-------	1,975	1,114	1,385	1,185	537	378	238	189	189	117	49
131	Sugar	-------	-------	780	599	1,053	473	316	283	221	204	204	24	28
132	Liquor and beverages	4,282	3,900	3,158	1,371	692	782	1,016	873	660	516	534	310	135
133	Tobacco products	3,044	2,826	2,330	961	1,150	605	304	246	324	112	124	96	40
134	Other food products	-------	-------	3,302	1,577	1,709	1,136	517	392	259	193	193	195	32
135	**Textiles and textile products**	12,417	12,077	10,397	4,770	7,687	6,205	2,881	2,550	1,783	1,366	1,494	1,119	602
136	Cotton goods	-------	-------	3,693	866	1,603	2,145	1,039	936	702	528	528	392	246
137	Silk and rayon goods	-------	-------	-------	441	869	533	210	152	110	81	81	51	19
138	Woolen and worsted goods	-------	-------	-------	415	601	868	403	429	313	264	264	203	117
139	Carpets, floorcovering, tapestries, etc	-------	-------	483	199	262	179	112	97	69	53	53	43	25
140	Knit goods	-------	-------	929	433	709	516	216	164	107	82	82	51	16
141	Clothing	4,049	3,924	3,018	1,036	1,758	1,447	633	568	345	257	350	292	114
142	Textiles, n.e.c.[6]	-------	-------	2,253	1,380	1,887	517	268	204	137	101	136	87	65
143	**Leather products**	1,542	1,394	1,303	751	1,167	1,523	743	659	452	335	369	274	157
144	Boots and shoes	-------	-------	710	410	625	581	255	197	123	100	102	95	43
145	Other leather products	-------	-------	592	341	542	942	488	462	329	235	267	179	114
146	**Rubber products**	3,369	2,614	1,791	795	1,088	960	268	162	99	78	78	37	9
147	Tires and tubes	-------	-------	1,383	586	918	635	130	-------	-------	-------	-------	-------	-------
148	Other rubber products	-------	-------	361	209	170	325	138	-------	-------	-------	-------	-------	-------
149	**Forest products**	8,225	6,347	4,820	2,405	3,842	2,726	1,932	1,767	1,174	872	1,110	825	361
150	Sawmill and planing mill products	-------	-------	3,000	1,562	2,660	1,730	1,193	1,122	694	520	731	518	219
151	Other wood products	-------	-------	1,805	843	1,182	996	739	645	480	352	379	307	142
152	**Paper, pulp, and products**	8,161	5,499	3,692	1,942	2,060	1,195	689	523	354	218	219	115	58
153	**Printing, publishing, and allied industries**	6,632	5,202	3,984	2,320	2,622	1,189	745	611	450	342	342	234	80
154	**Chemicals and allied substances**	19,138	14,450	9,109	3,537	3,942	2,594	1,280	911	634	457	458	288	137
155	Fertilizers	-------	-------	334	198	335	312	217	122	69	61	61	41	18
156	Chemicals proper, acids, etc	-------	-------	2,580	1,125	973	941	390	273	194	144	145	96	49
157	Allied chemical substances, drugs, oils, etc	-------	-------	5,917	2,214	2,634	1,341	673	516	371	252	252	151	70
158	**Petroleum refining**	30,174	19,960	15,363	5,814	5,745	1,170	326	182	136	95	95	77	27
159	**Stone, clay, and glass products**	6,681	4,482	2,934	1,825	2,351	1,267	990	860	554	336	351	217	83
160	**Iron and steel and products**	26,572	20,212	13,609	6,383	6,226	5,671	2,836	2,411	1,544	870	860	646	318
161	Iron and steel	-------	-------	9,521	4,394	4,155	4,456	2,147	1,845	1,185	657	657	469	258
162	Metal building materials and supplies	-------	-------	2,309	805	756	665	417	340	202	97	87	73	10
163	Hardware, tools, etc	-------	-------	1,177	1,184	1,315	549	273	225	156	116	117	104	49
164	**Nonferrous metals and products**	6,516	4,288	2,655	2,090	2,194	1,484	827	705	455	360	381	187	86
165	Precious metals, products and processes	-------	-------	515	247	352	315	196	181	126	97	97	70	29
166	Other metals, products and processes	-------	-------	2,663	1,843	1,842	1,169	631	524	329	263	284	117	57
167	**Machinery, excluding transportation equipment**	29,735	24,104	14,674	4,979	5,833	4,700	2,331	1,860	1,309	924	924	557	242
168	Electrical machinery and equipment; radios	10,014	8,936	4,874	1,120	1,514	963	390	282	183	87	86	19	2
169	Agricultural machinery	-------	-------	1,745	749	730	367	339	256	197	158	158	145	62
170	Office equipment, etc	-------	-------	815	413	430	167	95	72	41	24	24	8	6
171	Factory, household, and miscellaneous machinery	-------	-------	6,962	2,697	3,159	3,203	1,507	1,250	888	655	656	385	172
172	**Transportation equipment**	23,117	17,885	8,944	3,294	3,264	2,326	685	390	169	173	167	73	9
173	Motor vehicles	12,680	9,982	6,006	2,504	2,575	1,816	426	184	29	36	30	2	-------
174	Locomotive and railroad equipment	-------	-------	927	610	578	491	259	206	139	137	137	71	9
175	Airplanes	-------	-------	1,114	180	111	18	-------	-------	-------	-------	-------	-------	-------
176	**Miscellaneous manufacturing**	9,839	7,789	4,271	1,192	2,168	1,007	583	411	245	166	168	123	51

See footnotes at end of table.

Series **P 123–176.** Capital in Manufacturing Industries, in Book Value and in 1929 Dollars (Creamer): 1879 to 1957—Con.

[In millions of dollars]

Series No.	Industry	1957 [123]	1953 [123]	1948 [12]	1937 [1]	1929 [1]	1919 [4]	1914 [4]	1909 [4]	1904 [4]	1899 [4]	1899 [5]	1889 [5]	1879 [5]
	1929 DOLLARS													
123	**Total manufacturing capital**	110,455	97,843	78,067	55,319	63,022	46,094	36,737	31,563	23,295	17,452	18,626	11,157	4,821
124	Fixed capital	51,061	43,862	36,639	25,851	30,853	(NA)	(NA)	(NA)	12,316	(NA)	9,651	5,553	-------
125	Working capital	59,394	53,981	41,428	29,468	32,169	(NA)	(NA)	(NA)	10,979	(NA)	8,975	6,336	-------
126	**Food and kindred products**	13,361	12,878	10,488	9,180	9,591	7,593	6,515	5,517	4,656	3,598	3,760	1,839	897
127	Bakery and confectionery			1,146	1,287	1,693	1,103	757	555	361	256	281	143	50
128	Canned products			1,097	933	921	458	306	224	188	135	135	50	16
129	Mill products			691	564	509	971	675	656	553	432	500	414	319
130	Packinghouse products			1,288	1,267	1,496	1,435	954	711	497	432	432	233	88
131	Sugar			509	681	1,137	573	561	532	461	466	466	48	50
132	Liquor and beverages	3,092	3,233	2,061	1,560	747	947	1,805	1,641	1,378	1,178	1,219	616	243
133	Tobacco products	1,948	1,907	1,520	1,093	1,242	732	540	462	676	256	283	191	72
134	Other food products			2,154	1,794	1,846	1,375	918	737	541	441	445	145	58
135	**Textiles and textile products**	7,758	7,846	6,892	5,638	8,195	6,752	5,163	4,636	3,482	2,876	3,145	2,024	998
136	Cotton goods			2,447	1,024	1,709	2,334	1,862	1,702	1,371	1,112	1,112	709	408
137	Silk and rayon goods				521	926	580	376	276	215	171	171	92	32
138	Woolen and worsted goods				491	641	945	722	780	611	556	556	367	194
139	Carpets, floorcovering, tapestries, etc			320	235	279	195	201	176	135	112	112	78	41
140	Knit goods			616	512	756	561	387	298	209	173	173	92	27
141	Clothing	2,657	2,638	2,001	1,225	1,874	1,575	1,134	1,033	674	541	737	528	189
142	Textiles, n.e.c.[6]			1,493	1,631	2,012	563	480	371	268	213	286	157	108
143	**Leather products**	940	821	817	808	1,213	1,411	1,351	1,359	1,066	809	891	640	328
144	Boots and shoes			445	441	650	538	464	406	290	242	246	222	90
145	Other leather products			371	367	563	873	887	953	776	568	645	418	238
146	**Rubber products**	1,842	1,660	1,422	816	1,131	704	265	139	93	74	74	36	10
147	Tires and tubes			1,098	602	954	466	129	-------	-------	-------	-------	-------	-------
148	Other rubber products			287	215	177	238	136	-------	-------	-------	-------	-------	-------
149	**Forest products**	3,634	3,252	2,934	2,548	4,083	3,155	3,475	3,591	2,662	2,253	2,868	1,950	847
150	Sawmill and planing mill products			1,826	1,655	2,827	2,002	2,146	2,280	1,574	1,344	1,889	1,225	514
151	Other wood products			1,099	893	1,256	1,153	1,329	1,311	1,088	910	979	726	333
152	**Paper, pulp, and products**	4,039	3,086	2,476	2,062	2,239	1,524	1,246	1,002	670	453	455	200	90
153	**Printing, publishing, and allied industries**	2,832	2,622	2,571	2,505	2,737	1,556	1,444	1,265	939	801	801	466	144
154	**Chemicals and allied substances**	10,564	8,845	6,487	3,965	4,221	2,777	2,078	1,531	1,134	869	871	478	206
155	Fertilizers			237	222	359	334	352	205	123	116	116	68	27
156	Chemicals proper, acids, etc			1,830	1,261	1,042	1,007	633	459	347	274	276	159	74
157	Allied chemical substances, drugs, oils, etc			4,196	2,482	2,820	1,436	1,093	867	664	479	479	251	105
158	**Petroleum refining**	16,134	12,455	11,188	6,503	6,092	1,380	552	327	254	195	195	151	37
159	**Stone, clay, and glass products**	3,375	2,631	2,128	1,975	2,592	1,676	1,937	1,755	1,138	709	741	408	156
160	**Iron and steel and products**	13,090	11,701	9,649	6,719	6,666	6,735	5,166	4,305	2,886	1,599	1,581	1,143	472
161	Iron and steel			6,598	4,625	4,449	5,292	3,911	3,295	2,215	1,208	1,208	830	383
162	Metal building materials and supplies			1,600	847	809	790	760	607	378	178	160	129	15
163	Hardware, tools, etc			816	1,246	1,408	652	497	402	292	213	215	184	73
164	**Nonferrous metals and products**	3,229	2,508	1,837	2,338	2,364	1,808	1,365	1,203	804	610	646	276	116
165	Precious metals, products and processes			379	276	379	384	323	309	223	164	164	103	39
166	Other metals, products and processes			1,960	2,062	1,985	1,424	1,041	894	581	446	481	173	77
167	**Machinery, excluding transportation equipment**	14,388	13,773	10,352	5,286	6,166	5,595	4,293	3,654	2,710	1,917	1,917	1,160	414
168	Electrical machinery and equipment; radios	5,099	5,517	3,438	1,189	1,600	1,146	718	554	379	180	178	40	3
169	Agricultural machinery			1,226	795	772	437	624	503	408	328	328	302	106
170	Office equipment, etc			573	438	455	199	175	141	85	50	50	17	10
171	Factory, household, and miscellaneous machinery			4,892	2,863	3,339	3,813	2,775	2,456	1,839	1,359	1,361	802	295
172	**Transportation equipment**	10,450	9,387	6,017	3,672	3,476	2,480	991	567	333	349	337	156	17
173	Motor vehicles	6,150	5,425	4,016	2,792	2,742	1,936	616	267	57	73	60	4	-------
174	Locomotive and railroad equipment			618	680	616	523	375	299	274	276	276	152	17
175	Airplanes			743	201	118	19	-------	-------	-------	-------	-------	-------	-------
176	**Miscellaneous manufacturing**	4,819	4,378	2,809	1,304	2,256	948	896	712	468	340	344	230	89

NA Not available.
[1] Covers factories having annual production of $5,000 or more.
[2] Some minor groups are not adjusted for investment in emergency facilities after "normal" depreciation or intangible assets. Therefore, sum of detail does not equal totals.
[3] Includes firms engaged in shipbuilding which were excluded in other years.
[4] Covers factories having annual production of $500 or more.
[5] Includes custom and neighborhood shops.
[6] N.e.c. means not elsewhere classified.

Series **P 177-180.** Share of Total Value Added by Manufacture Accounted for by the 200 Largest Manufacturing Companies: 1947 to 1970

Series No.	Company rank group	Percent of total value added by manufacture							
		1970	1967	1966	1963	1962	1958	1954	1947
177	Largest 50 companies_____	24	25	25	25	24	23	23	17
178	Largest 100 companies_____	33	33	33	33	32	30	30	23
179	Largest 150 companies_____	38	38	38	37	36	35	34	27
180	Largest 200 companies_____	43	42	42	41	40	38	37	30

Series **P 181-196.** Share of Total Value Added by Manufacture Accounted For by the 50 and 100 Largest Identical Manufacturing Companies: 1947 to 1970

Series No.	Specified year and company rank group	Percent of value added by manufacture in each year accounted for by the largest companies in the specified year shown in stub							
		1970	1967	1966	1963	1962	1958	1954	1947
	1970								
181	Largest 50 companies_____	24	23	24	23	22	20	19	12
182	Largest 100 companies_____	33	31	31	29	29	26	25	18
	1967								
183	Largest 50 companies_____	24	25	25	24	24	22	21	15
184	Largest 100 companies_____	32	33	33	32	31	29	28	20
	1966								
185	Largest 50 companies_____	23	24	25	24	24	22	21	14
186	Largest 100 companies_____	31	32	33	32	31	29	28	21
	1963								
187	Largest 50 companies_____	23	24	24	25	24	23	22	15
188	Largest 100 companies_____	31	32	33	33	32	30	29	22
	1962								
189	Largest 50 companies_____	23	24	25	25	24	23	22	15
190	Largest 100 companies_____	31	33	33	32	32	30	29	21
	1958								
191	Largest 50 companies_____	22	23	24	24	24	23	23	16
192	Largest 100 companies_____	29	31	31	32	31	30	29	22
	1954								
193	Largest 50 companies_____	21	23	23	24	23	23	23	16
194	Largest 100 companies_____	28	31	31	31	30	30	30	21
	1947								
195	Largest 50 companies_____	19	20	21	21	21	20	21	17
196	Largest 100 companies_____	26	27	27	28	27	27	27	23

Series P 197–204. Concentration in Manufacturing, by Industry Group: 1901, 1947, and 1954

[Concentration ratio is defined as the percent of total "4-digit" SIC industry sales (or value added) made by 4 largest sellers. See text]

SIC code No.	Industry group (1947 and 1954 census classification)	Value added by 4-digit industries with concentration ratio over 50 as percent of value added by all industries in a 2-digit industry group		Average concentration ratios					
				1947 value-added weights	1954 value-added weights	1947 employment weights		1954 employment weights	
		1901 [1]	1947 [2]	1947	1954 [3]	1947	1954	1947	1954
		197	198	199	200	201	202	203	204
	Total, all industries, value-added weights	32.9	24.0	35.3	36.9	36.3	37.0	37.7	39.0
	Total, all industries, employment weights	---	---	---	---	34.6	35.9	34.7	35.3
20	Food and kindred products	39.1	18.8	34.9	33.8	32.4	33.2	31.3	32.4
21	Tobacco manufactures	49.9	77.7	76.2	73.4	66.0	62.9	67.4	64.1
22	Textile mill products	20.3	9.0	24.3	26.5	27.6	28.8	26.5	27.8
23	Apparel and related products		2.2	12.6	13.0	14.0	14.7	13.6	14.3
24	Lumber and wood products	.5	2.0	11.2	10.8	12.3	11.3	10.8	10.7
25	Furniture and fixtures		8.1	21.9	20.3	16.5	18.7	17.4	16.7
26	Pulp, paper, and products	71.0	1.6	21.2	24.8	24.2	24.3	24.5	24.4
27	Printing and publishing	1.0	-	19.7	17.7	18.8	17.2	18.6	16.9
28	Chemicals and products	24.3	33.7	51.0	48.6	25.8	29.7	29.7	32.5
29	Petroleum and coal products	46.8	13.6	39.5	36.6	39.5	37.0	39.4	36.7
30	Rubber products	100.0	59.9	58.6	54.1	57.0	56.0	52.1	51.0
31	Leather and leather products	26.3	-	26.2	26.4	26.1	26.6	25.9	26.6
32	Stone, clay, and glass products	13.3	43.9	43.4	46.4	80.6	78.8	79.0	77.7
33	Primary metal products	[4] 45.7	21.0	43.8	49.5	40.6	45.3	41.4	46.7
34	Fabricated metal products		8.4	25.3	26.1	26.7	26.0	26.6	25.4
35	Machinery, except electrical	[5] 41.4	18.5	38.0	33.2	38.2	38.9	37.6	37.8
36	Electrical machinery		53.2	54.1	48.2	53.4	50.5	50.8	47.9
37	Transportation equipment	57.3	84.2	54.4	58.7	54.0	63.3	53.7	56.6
38	Instruments and related products		45.0	45.3	47.4	52.8	52.5	54.0	53.5
39	Miscellaneous manufactures	2.7	21.2	34.9	16.1	31.5	30.1	29.0	28.6

- Represents zero.
[1] 319 (4-digit) industries. Various years 1895–1904; central date was approximately 1901 but weighting factors used were as of 1899.
[2] 452 (4-digit) industries.
[3] 434 (4-digit) industries.
[4] Excludes steel works and rolling mills for which the concentration ratio is 78.8.
[5] Includes electrical machinery.

Series P 205–211. Selected Statistics for Operating Manufacturing Establishments, by Legal Form of Organization: 1939 to 1967

Item	Establishments	All employees		Production workers		Value added by manufacture	Capital expenditures, new
		Total	Payroll	Total	Wages		
	205	206	207	208	209	210	211
		1,000	*Mil. dol.*	*1,000*	*Mil. dol.*	*Mil. dol.*	*Mil. dol.*
ALL ESTABLISHMENTS							
1967 [1]	305,681	18,498	123,550	13,955	81,394	261,984	21,503
1963	306,617	16,235	93,289	12,232	62,394	192,103	11,371
1958	298,182	15,381	73,773	11,367	48,471	143,159	9,531
1954	286,814	15,645	62,963	12,372	44,591	117,032	8,201
1947	240,807	14,294	39,696	11,918	30,244	74,290	5,998
1939	184,230	---	---	[2]7,887	---	24,683	---
CORPORATE							
1967	153,892	17,697	119,530	13,260	78,429	253,261	20,988
1963	176,190	15,245	89,356	11,426	59,064	184,100	10,791
1958	162,749	14,215	69,885	10,398	45,455	135,644	8,926
1954	148,461	14,273	59,051	11,206	41,480	109,669	7,752
1947	118,102	12,856	36,580	10,649	27,637	68,294	---
1939	95,187	---	---	[2]7,051	---	22,790	---
NONCORPORATE							
1967	33,165	530	2,709	433	2,008	5,636	370
1963	130,427	990	3,932	806	3,030	8,002	580
1958	135,433	1,165	3,787	969	3,016	7,515	605
1954	138,353	1,372	3,912	1,166	3,111	7,363	449
1947	122,705	1,438	3,115	1,269	2,607	5,996	---
1939	89,043	---	---	[2]836	---	1,893	---

See footnotes at end of table.

Series P 205–211. Selected Statistics for Operating Manufacturing Establishments, by Legal Form of Organization: 1939 to 1967—Con.

Item	Establishments	All employees		Production workers		Value added by manufacture	Capital expenditures, new
		Total	Payroll	Total	Wages		
	205	206	207	208	209	210	211
		1,000	*Mil. dol.*	*1,000*	*Mil. dol.*	*Mil. dol.*	*Mil. dol.*
NONCORPORATE—Con.							
Individual proprietorship:							
1967	24,897	243	1,187	210	933	2,361	141
1963	99,174	536	2,033	440	1,595	3,916	315
1958	91,276	542	1,637	461	1,349	3,115	317
1954	88,224	593	1,527	507	1,237	2,735	176
1947	69,498	586	1,184	522	1,001	2,162	
1939	58,834			[2] 443		957	
Partnership:							
1967	6,731	193	971	157	730	1,895	114
1963	27,677	334	1,034	277	1,062	2,726	141
1958	41,958	543	1,836	452	1,458	3,663	223
1954	47,885	703	2,108	602	1,684	4,054	216
1947	50,771	757	1,687	673	1,432	3,347	
1939	27,651			[2] 368		863	

[1] Includes establishments for which legal form of organization was not available.   [2] Average for year.

Series P 212–215. Percent Distribution of Production Workers and of Value Added in Manufacturing Establishments, by Legal Form of Ownership: 1899 to 1967

Year	Production workers, percent in establishments owned by—		Value added, percent in establishments owned by—		Year	Production workers, percent in establishments owned by—		Value added, percent in establishments owned by—	
	Corporations	Other [1]	Corporations	Other [1]		Corporations	Other [1]	Corporations	Other [1]
	212	213	214	215		212	213	214	215
1967	95.0	5.0	96.7	3.3	1929	89.9	10.1	91.5	8.5
1963	93.4	6.6	95.8	4.2	1919	86.6	13.4	87.7	12.3
1958	91.7	8.3	94.7	5.3	1914	80.3	19.7	83.2	16.8
1954	90.6	9.4	93.7	6.3	1909	75.6	24.4	77.2	22.8
1947	89.4	10.6	91.9	8.1	1904	70.6	29.4	71.9	28.1
1939	89.4	10.6	92.3	7.7	1899			[2] 65.0	[2] 35.0

[1] Includes individual proprietorships, partnerships, and other forms of ownership, mostly cooperative societies.   [2] Based on value of product. Establishments covered include 66,143 establishments not covered by census of manufactures. These establishments produced value of products of $290 million in a total value of product of all manufactures of $11,701 million.

Series P 216–230. Physical Consumption of Selected Commodities in Manufacturing Industries: 1860 to 1970

Year	Energy materials										
	Used for heat and power						Used as raw material				
	Total	Coal	Coke	Fuel oil	Gas	Purchased electric energy	Coal	Coke	Crude petroleum	Fuel oil	Natural gas
	216	217	218	219	220	221	222	223	224	225	226
	Bil. kwh	*1,000 short tons*	*1,000 short tons*	*Mil. bbl.*	*Bil. cu. ft.*	*Bil. kwh*	*1,000 short tons*	*1,000 short tons*	*Mil. bbl.*	*Mil. bbl.*	*Bil. cu. ft.*
1967	5,348	75,100	61,105	262.3	11,638	427	92,940	1,390	3,621	11.1	607
1963	4,632	89,438	55,941	271.0	9,341	314	71,470	1,122	3,198	8.3	300
1958	4,184	81,784	49,806	226.9	8,628	253	77,817	1,265	2,850	6.0	365
1954	4,359	91,458	54,372	246.6	8,977	187	85,441	1,860	2,499	4.0	338
1947	3,195	110,869	66,171	215.6	4,866	103	108,053	2,551	1,884		485
1939	1,595	80,161	35,001	97.4	1,840	45	63,189	1,744	1,250	36.0	968
1937	[1] 2,588	[2] 169,523	[2] 42,194	[2] 136.3	[2] 2,489	46	(2)	(2)		(2)	(2)
1929	[1] 2,510	[2] 206,232	[2] 51,406	[2] 132.2	[2] 1,174	36	(2)	(2)	1,040	(2)	(2)
1927	[3] 1,533	[2] 199,705					(2)				
1923	[3] 1,711	[2] 222,848					(2)				
1919	[1] 2,097	[2] 202,576	[2] 41,785	[2] 69.6	[2] 566		(2)	(2)	365	(2)	(2)
1914	[1] 1,626	[2] 168,892	[2] 31,370	[2] 32.7	[2] 280		(2)	(2)	191	(2)	(2)
1909	[1] 1,630	[2] 165,593	[2] 38,530	[2] 19.7	[2] 309		(2)	(2)	121	(2)	(2)
1904									67		
1899									52		

See footnotes at end of table.

Series P 216–230. Physical Consumption of Selected Commodities in Manufacturing Industries: 1860 to 1970—Con.

Year	Coffee imported 227 (Mil. lb.)	Raw cotton used in textiles 228 (1,000 bales)	Wool used in textiles 229 (Mil. lb.)	Unmanufactured silk imports for consumption 230 (Mil. lb.)	Year	Coffee imported 227 (Mil. lb.)	Raw cotton used in textiles 228 (1,000 bales)	Wool used in textiles 229 (Mil. lb.)	Unmanufactured silk imports for consumption 230 (Mil. lb.)	Year	Coffee imported 227 (Mil. lb.)	Raw cotton used in textiles 228 (1,000 bales)
1970	2,609	9,119	240.3	1.8	1925	1,269	6,852	349.9	63.1	1882	484	1,849
1969	2,676	9,367	312.8	3.3	1924	1,395	6,217	342.2	50.5	1881	426	1,866
1968	3,357	10,072	329.7	4.0	1923	1,388	7,312	422.4	49.1			
1967	2,819	10,650	315.5	2.8	1922	1,220	6,549	406.5	50.1	1880	396	1,501
1966	2,918	10,950	307.2	4.6	1921	1,304	5,409	343.4	44.9	1879	438	1,457
										1878	325	1,459
1965	2,844	10,557	387.0	5.8	1920	1,248	6,762	314.2	29.3	1877	349	1,314
1964	3,054	9,967	356.7	6.7	1919	1,256	6,224	329.1	44.3	1876	267	1,256
1963	3,185	9,747	411.7	6.4	1918	1,014	7,685	399.3	32.3			
1962	4 3,238	10,292	429.1	6.5	1917	1,218	7,658	---------	36.0	1875	360	1,098
1961	4 2,954	9,560	412.1	6.7	1916	1,132	7,279	---------	32.0	1874	283	1,213
										1873	292	1,116
1960	4 2,917	10,471	411.0	6.9	1915	1,137	6,009	---------	30.8	1872	289	1,147
1959	4 3,066	9,913	435.3	8.0	1914	975	5,885	---------	25.5	1871	308	1,027
1958	4 2,667	9,101	331.1	5.3	1913	845	5,786	---------	27.8			
1957	4 2,713	10,166	368.8	8.3	1912	938	5,368	---------	24.7	1870	272	797
1956	4 2,776	10,930	440.7	12.7	1911	796	4,705	---------	20.7	1869	235	860
										1868	235	844
1955	2,569	10,315	413.8	11.0	1910	797	4,799	---------	21.5	1867	220	715
1954	2,234	9,900	380.8	8.5	1909	1,126	5,241	---------	22.1	1866	175	615
1953	2,767	10,783	494.0	7.8	1908	926	4,493	---------	18.6			
1952	2,665	10,426	466.4	12.6	1907	930	4,974	---------	15.6	1865	126	344
1951	2,678	12,050	484.1	7.2	1906	844	4,877	---------	16.7	1864	105	220
										1863	101	287
1950	2,429	10,467	634.8	10.5	1905	859	4,523	---------	15.4	1862	94	369
1949	2,913	9,201	500.4	4.0	1904	1,074	3,981	---------	16.4	1861	146	842
1948	2,752	10,510	693.1	7.4	1903	740	4,187	---------	11.5	1860	180	845
1947	2,458	11,009	698.3	3.2	1902	901	4,080	---------	13.6			
1946	2,664	10,218	737.5	13.5	1901	1,028	3,604	---------	12.2			
1945	2,705	11,049	645.1	1.0	1900	741	3,687	---------	8.1			
1944	2,604	11,308	622.8	---------	1899	852	3,672	---------	11.7			
1943	2,194	12,401	636.2	---------	1898	781	3,472	---------	8.4			
1942	1,712	12,658	603.6	.2	1897	787	2,841	---------	10.0			
1941	2,250	11,081	648.0	25.6	1896	621	2,500	---------	4.9			
1940	2,044	8,845	407.9	47.6	1895	634	2,984	---------	9.1			
1939	2,001	7,709	396.5	55.3	1894	601	2,300	---------	7.8			
1938	1,981	6,463	284.5	57.1	1893	535	2,416	---------	4.4			
1937	1,689	8,769	380.8	64.2	1892	601	2,847	---------	7.8			
1936	1,732	7,085	406.1	67.5	1891	574	2,604	---------	7.1			
1935	1,745	6,080	417.5	72.4	1890	481	2,518	---------	4.6			
1934	1,514	6,467	229.6	60.4	1889	534	2,309	---------	5.8			
1933	1,574	6,898	317.1	73.0	1888	507	2,205	---------	5.4			
1932	1,484	5,503	230.1	77.6	1887	423	2,050	---------	4.8			
1931	1,730	5,977	311.0	87.6	1886	521	2,095	---------	4.8			
1930	1,585	6,911	263.2	80.6	1885	534	1,687	---------	3.9			
1929	1,475	7,970	368.1	85.9	1884	494	1,814	---------	3.4			
1928	1,447	7,614	333.2	74.4	1883	488	2,038	---------	3.3			
1927	1,419	7,996	354.1	72.7								
1926	1,482	7,260	342.7	65.6								

1 Includes energy equivalents for fuel used as raw material.
2 Use as raw material is included with use for heat and power.
3 Energy equivalent for coal only, including that used as raw material.
4 Imports for consumption of raw or green coffee.

Series P 231–300. Physical Output of Selected Manufactured Commodities: 1860 to 1970

Year	Foods produced — Wheat flour 1 231 (Mil. bbl.)	Refined sugar 232 (Mil. lb.)	Canned corn 233 (1,000 cases)	Canned tomatoes 234 (1,000 cases)	Beverages produced 2 — Beer 235 (1,000 bbl.)	Distilled spirits Total, including industrial alcohol 236 (1,000 tax gal.)	Beverage alcohol 236a (1,000 tax gal.)	Fats and oils produced — Soybean oil, crude 237 (Mil. lb.)	Shortening and salad and cooking oils 3 238 (Mil. lb.)	Tobacco products produced — Manufactured tobacco and snuff 239 (Mil. lb.)	Cigars 240 (Millions)	Cigarettes 241 (Millions)	Apparel products — Mens' and boys' suits and separate coats 242 (1,000)	Womens', misses', and juniors' dresses 243 (1,000)
1970	129.1	20,848	38,536	31,994	134,654	917,457	355,240	8,086	6,977	165	4 7,979	4 562,154	5 43,642	251,540
1969	129.7	19,816	40,497	26,270	122,657	985,641	336,456	6,805	6,624	161	4 7,499	4 573,002	5 49,310	266,856
1968	129.7	20,098	48,608	39,706	117,524	905,459	331,306	6,150	6,308	159	4 7,696	4 570,748	5 50,320	277,971
1967	125.2	18,838	40,400	32,084	116,564	873,010	301,949	6,150	6,148	158	4 7,303	4 572,790	5 47,987	282,192
1966	129.2	18,664	37,331	26,783	109,736	889,352	306,813	5,811	6,136	162	4 7,992	562,667	6 44,641	273,080
1965	127.9	18,426	32,075	29,532	108,015	865,240	275,616	5,236	5,566	167	4 8,883	4 562,368	6 44,039	282,071
1964	133.6	18,596	30,792	29,873	103,018	838,978	273,750	4,944	5,510	180	4 8,648	534,973	40,815	271,718
1963	132.8	17,746	36,205	27,094	97,961	800,830	266,648	5,053	4,945	168	4 6,657	543,688	41,348	259,979
1962	133.9	17,874	37,510	29,144	96,418	809,518	292,767	4,889	5,221	169	4 6,843	529,883	41,937	251,734
1961	133.0	16,840	37,857	27,908	93,496	801,799	248,439	4,442	4,580	173	4 6,648	518,031	37,810	252,155

See footnotes at end of table.

Series P 231–300. Physical Output of Selected Manufactured Commodities: 1860 to 1970—Con.

Year	Foods produced				Beverages produced[2]			Fats and oils produced		Tobacco products produced			Apparel products	
						Distilled spirits							Mens' and boys' suits and separate coats	Womens', misses', and juniors' dresses
	Wheat flour[1]	Refined sugar	Canned corn	Canned tomatoes	Beer	Total, including industrial alcohol	Beverage alcohol	Soybean oil, crude	Shortening and salad and cooking oils[3]	Manufactured tobacco and snuff	Cigars	Cigarettes		
	231	232	233	234	235	236	236a	237	238	239	240	241	242	243
	Mil. bbl.	Mil. lb.	1,000 cases	1,000 cases	1,000 bbl.	1,000 tax gal.	1,000 tax gal.	Mil. lb.	Mil. lb.	Mil. lb.	Millions	Millions	1,000	1,000
1960	130.4	*16,710	*28,926	*25,413	94,548	803,751	273,258	4,392	4,228	173	[4]6,937	[4]506,127	40,622	253,606
1959	128.1	16,082	33,810	24,126	90,974	754,539	271,797	4,344	4,061	176	[4]7,298	[4]489,865	39,283	257,677
1958	126.8	15,790	27,075	30,465	89,011	718,848	244,316	3,943	2,006	180	[4]6,395	[4]470,068	33,053	243,273
1957	122.2	15,150	31,533	21,686	89,882	650,366	207,946	3,475	1,809	179	[4]5,952	[4]442,328	34,968	255,605
1956	117.6	15,532	35,668	29,883	90,698	720,754	217,814	3,200	1,842	185	[4]5,830	[4]424,247	35,640	257,336
1955	115.6	14,760	24,075	24,727	89,791	593,982	194,888	2,827	1,975	199	[4]5,834	[4]412,309	34,091	260,389
1954	113.5	15,066	30,619	21,827	92,561	563,496	167,319	2,378	1,961	204	[4]5,882	[4]401,849	29,421	248,169
1953	113.9	13,900	30,982	22,334	90,434	619,456	135,240	2,515	1,675	209	[4]5,973	[4]423,070	34,659	259,312
1952	117.0	13,820	32,329	27,981	89,601	689,256	69,294	2,478	1,611	220	[4]5,892	[4]435,549	33,057	258,263
1951	117.6	13,276	25,576	31,770	88,976	846,388	342,768	2,473	1,403	227	[4]5,664	[4]418,803	30,471	240,964
1950	115.4	14,665	18,241	21,108	88,807	521,770	194,025	2,075	1,710	235	[4]5,468	[4]391,956	36,000	248,195
1949	120.3	13,235	29,795	21,537	89,736	617,558	291,722	1,859	1,487	239	5,453	385,046	29,737	266,674
1948	143.2	12,202	31,483	24,393	91,291	576,409	270,587	1,604	1,441	245	5,645	386,916	32,005	227,279
1947	156.7	13,753	26,089	27,709	87,857	563,956	219,656	1,543	1,375	242	5,488	369,763	34,168	203,247
1946	143.2	10,224	30,951	23,857	84,978	634,454	225,077	1,454	1,451	253	5,618	350,132	35,086	213,073
1945	141.1	11,204	28,237	16,758	86,604	1,174,391	87,515	1,392	1,441	331	5,275	332,345		
1944	125.4	12,160	25,089	26,099	81,726	1,011,763	–	1,246	1,364	307	5,199	323,734	20,729	204,878
1943	122.8	10,635	28,755	29,269	71,018	772,267	246,262	1,234	1,438	327	5,363	296,305	19,425	223,995
1942	114.6	9,637	32,118	41,252	63,717	675,959	254,815	762	1,300	330	5,841	257,657		
1941	112.7	13,437	26,109	31,759	55,214	474,054	192,416	586	1,409	342	5,610	218,083		
1940	110.9	12,098	15,524	29,533	54,892	387,183	159,707	533	1,190	344	[4]5,370	[4]189,373		
1939	114.1	11,749	14,567	24,465	53,871	346,344	166,763	458	1,404	343	5,198	180,828	[7]27,354	194,383
1938	111.8	11,908	20,470	23,131	56,340	351,190	183,288	323	1,514	345	5,015	171,842		
1937	109.4	11,684	23,541	26,235	58,748	482,138	299,207	194	1,595	341	5,303	170,171	[7]23,743	178,300
1936	111.0	11,181	14,621	24,414	51,812	449,994	274,108	225	1,587	348	5,172	159,076		
1935	106.4	10,891	21,471	26,985	45,229	349,772	183,668	105	1,547	343	4,685	140,147	24,287	[8]172,247
1934		10,256	11,268	22,376	[9]37,678	241,610	101,612	35	1,204	346	4,526	130,287		
1933	97.2	11,132	10,193	20,461	[10]9,798	123,405		27	953	342	4,300	115,087	19,300	145,238
1932			9,358	20,367	2,766	150,391		39	945	347	4,383	106,915		
1931	115.0	11,172	19,415	16,341	3,137	170,394		39	1,172	371	5,348	117,402	21,624	167,192
1930			15,692	29,015	3,681	197,221		14	1,211	372	5,894	124,193		
1929	123.6	12,376	17,487	24,146	3,900	203,300		11	1,220	381	6,519	122,822	30,342	162,837
1928	120.6		14,497	14,575	4,200	170,500		5	1,143	386	6,373	109,131		
1927	122.0	12,046	10,347	22,425	4,400	185,500		3	1,179	396	6,519	100,260	31,846	109,080
1926	116.2		19,069	16,140	4,900	203,800		3	1,141	411	6,499	92,523		
1925	117.5	12,972	24,320	33,747	5,100	167,500		3	1,153	414	6,463	82,712		
1924	118.7		12,131	21,370	4,900	137,500		1	830	414	6,598	73,256		
1923	114.7	10,358	14,106	25,045	5,300	124,600		1	751	413	6,950	67,239		
1922	113.8		11,419	19,695	6,300	82,200		1	784	420	6,722	56,413		
1921	97.2	9,586	8,843	6,857	9,200	87,900				387	6,726	52,770		
1920	130.4		15,040	19,405	9,200	101,300				413	8,097	48,091		
1919	122.5	9,478	13,550	18,452	27,700	100,800				424	7,072	53,865		
1918	115.4		11,722	27,111	50,300	178,800				497	7,054	47,528		
1917	115.8		10,803	25,735	60,800	286,100				483	7,560	36,323		
1916	118.7		9,130	22,433	58,600	253,300				466	7,042	26,203		
1915	119.2		10,124	14,457	59,800	140,700				442	6,599	18,945		
1914	115.0	8,617	9,789	25,984	66,200	181,900				441	7,174	17,944		
1913	113.6	8,274	7,283	24,250	65,300	193,600				444	7,572	16,530		
1912	110.8	7,904	13,109	23,936	62,200	187,600				435	7,044	14,239		
1911	110.8	7,350	14,301	16,642	63,300	183,400				424	7,049	11,700		
1910	107.2	7,317	10,063	15,764	59,500	163,900				447	6,810	9,782		
1909	107.5	6,986	5,787	18,750	56,300	139,900				431	6,668	7,880		
1908	109.8	6,479	6,779	19,595	58,800	133,900				408	6,489	6,833		
1907	111.5	6,451	6,654	22,051	58,600	174,700				388	7,302	6,345		
1906	109.5	6,433	9,137	14,733	54,700	150,100				391	7,148	5,502		
1905	105.4	5,699	13,019	9,517	49,500	153,300				368	6,748	4,477		
1904	104.7	5,963	11,163	16,065	48,300	139,500				354	6,640	4,170		
1903	111.8	5,467	4,861	17,335	46,700	148,200				351	6,806	3,959		
1902	109.1	5,725	4,191	15,810	44,600	132,800				348	6,232	3,647		
1901	108.4	5,156	5,028	7,227	40,600	128,600				314	6,139	3,503		
1900	105.8	4,858	6,486	9,385	39,500	109,200				301	5,566	3,870		
1899	104.0	4,578	6,366	14,852	36,700	100,200				295	4,910	4,367		
1898	100.3	4,107	4,315	9,651	37,500	83,700				275	4,459	4,843		
1897	95.7	4,241	2,787	6,767	34,500	64,300				297	4,136	4,927		
1896	96.5	3,957	2,539	5,845	35,900	90,000				261	4,048	4,967		
1895	93.6	3,961	2,992	6,888	33,600	81,900				274	4,099	4,238		
1894	93.7	4,281	3,278	10,971	33,400	92,200				269	4,164	3,621		
1893	92.5	4,050	4,184	7,337	34,600	131,000				251	4,341	3,661		
1892	92.1	3,896	3,417	5,502	31,900	118,400				274	4,675	3,282		
1891	86.3	4,069	2,837	5,660	30,500	117,800				271	4,422	3,137		

See footnotes at end of table.

Series **P 231–300.**   Physical Output of Selected Manufactured Commodities: 1860 to 1970—Con.

Year	Foods produced—Con.				Beverages produced—Con.		Tobacco products produced—Con.		
	Wheat flour [1]	Refined sugar	Canned corn	Canned tomatoes	Fermented malt liquor [2]	Distilled spirits [2]	Manufactured tobacco and snuff	Cigars	Cigarettes
	231	232	233	234	235	236	239	240	241
	Mil. bbl.	Mil. lb.	1,000 cases	1,000 cases	1,000 bbl.	1,000 tax gal.	Mil. lb.	Millions	Millions
1890	83.3	3,233	1,523	5,280	27,600	111,100	253	4,229	2,505
1889	80.8	3,170	1,726	5,022	25,100	91,100	246	3,787	2,413
1888	79.5	3,048	3,437	5,580	24,700	71,700	209	3,668	2,212
1887	79.5	3,014	2,276	4,720	23,100	79,400	226	3,662	1,865
1886	75.7	2,949	1,675	3,921	20,700	81,800	210	3,462	1,607
1885	74.0	2,912	1,062	2,362	19,200	76,400	207	3,294	1,080
1884	72.5	2,732			19,000	76,500	172	3,373	920
1883	70.8	2,466			17,800	75,300	194	3,232	844
1882	67.8	2,368			17,000	107,300	159	3,118	599
1881	65.6	1,940			14,300	119,500	172	2,806	595
1880	64.3	1,988			13,300	91,400	146	2,510	533
1879	61.9	1,709			11,100	72,900	136	2,217	371
1878	59.8	1,778			10,200	57,300	125	1,923	210
1877	56.5	1,698			9,800	61,400	123	1,816	157
1876	56.1	1,583			9,900	58,600	124	1,776	113
1875	54.4	1,642			9,500	62,700	124	1,828	59
1874	53.6	1,638			9,600	69,600	124	1,835	35
1873	51.3	1,526			9,600	71,200	118	1,755	28
1872	49.2	1,454			8,700	69,400	112	1,578	24
1871	49.0	1,413			7,700	57,000	107	1,353	20
1870	47.9	1,196			6,600	72,600	102	1,183	16
1869	46.8	1,254							
1868	44.9	1,149							
1867	44.3	841							
1866	42.8	886							
1865	42.5	733							
1864	42.4	565							
1863	42.5	607							
1862	42.4	590							
1861	41.6	978							
1860	39.8	788							

Year	Textile mill products				Chemicals and allied products						Refined petroleum products				
						Inorganic chemicals									
	Rayon and acetate yarns available	Noncellulosic yarn available	Finished knit cloth shipped[11]	Carpets and rugs shipped	Sodium hydroxide (caustic soda)	Ammonia anhydrous	Ammonia aqua (100% NH₃)	Sulfuric acid (100% H₂SO₄)	Paints, varnishes, and lacquers	Superphosphates (100% P₂O₅)	Light products of distillation	Illuminating oils (kerosene)[12]	Fuel oils	Lubricating oils	Paraffin wax
	244	245	246	247	248	249	250	251	252	253	254	255	256	257	258
	Mil. lb.	Mil. lb.	1,000 lb.	1,000 sq. yd.	1,000 short tons	1,000 short tons	1,000 short tons	1,000 short tons	Mil. gal.	1,000 short tons	Mil. bbl.	Mil. bbl.	Mil. bbl.	Mil. bbl.	1,000 bbl.
1970	699.6	1,803.8	782,279	633,662	10,064	13,570	33	29,577	827	4,596	2,136	314	1,155	66	6,294
1969	743.5	1,649.0	744,003	597,885	9,917	12,769	39	29,537	881	4,289	2,057	320	1,114	65	6,049
1968	794.5	1,555.7	698,124	546,840	8,868	12,120	42	28,544	843	4,149	1,968	295	1,116	66	6,049
1967	739.8	1,184.7	603,951	467,909	8,398	12,194	65	28,815	782	4,695	1,873	264	1,081	65	5,719
1966	780.8	1,081.9	558,617	445,527	7,596	10,605	73	28,385	837	4,450	1,822	228	1,050	65	5,772
1965	782.5	927.7	450,128	411,220	6,842	8,869	81	24,851	775	3,834	1,733	202	1,034	63	5,456
1964	768.6	797.4	416,642	357,653	6,399	7,634	63	22,924	725	3,482	1,687	168	1,009	64	5,352
1963	687.4	655.2	345,607	305,470	5,814	6,693	60	20,936	678	3,231	1,625	165	1,041	63	5,126
1962	668.9	570.7	314,597	268,235	5,486	5,810	64	19,701	643	2,823	1,583	156	1,015	63	5,353
1961	627.8	477.3	276,048	[13]178,625	4,914	5,207	56	17,848	623	2,744	1,533	141	1,012	59	5,781
1960	624.9	400.8	247,671	[13]151,984	4,972	4,818	45	17,883	663	2,672	*1,522	*136	*999	*59	5,896
1959	722.2	378.9	243,042	[13]132,523	4,748	4,520	56	17,609	650	2,610	1,489	111	1,027	56	5,630
1958	643.5	311.3	210,635	166,737	3,993	3,879	51	15,950	595	2,381	1,440	110	995	51	5,252
1957	685.8	314.8	193,518	[13]99,651	4,336	3,733	41	16,460	[14]518	2,455	1,438	109	1,084	56	5,461
1956	727.0	273.1	186,458	[13]83,177	4,227	3,378	37	16,495	[14]503	2,439	1,429	123	1,092	59	5,367
1955	857.7	258.2	181,884	[13]77,822	3,915	3,252	39	16,255	[14]515	2,272	1,374	117	1,023	56	5,293
1954	721.2	214.1	165,030	128,023	3,410	2,737	54	14,376	[14]416	2,215	1,261	122	959	53	5,290
1953	865.6	186.4	164,193		3,263	2,288	34	14,003	[14]421	2,147	1,266	123	978	53	4,978
1952	845.2	160.8	170,518		3,031	2,052	34	13,310		2,165	1,193	132	974	56	4,331
1951	865.5	134.4	148,747		3,106	1,777	35	13,372		2,045	1,140	136	945	61	4,814
1950	955.6	97.6	162,803		2,949	1,566	28	13,029		1,994	1,024	119	824	52	4,462
1949	782.8	75.6	147,853		[15]2,650	1,294		11,432		1,891	961	102	766	45	3,208
1948	846.7	59.3			[15]2,938	1,090		11,456		1,900	920	122	859	51	3,515
1947	729.3	43.7	153,778	91,160	[15]2,909	1,114	24	10,780	520	1,857	842	110	760	52	3,624
1946	666.5	33.6	146,666		[15]2,292	726		9,203		1,566	776	104	719	46	3,003
1945	602.4	29.4	129,958		[15]2,322	549		9,522		1,447	793	81	719	42	2,921
1944	539.1	24.9	107,908		[15]2,328	544		9,242		1,340	741	78	701	41	2,883

See footnotes at end of table.

MANUFACTURES

Series P 231–300. Physical Output of Selected Manufactured Commodities: 1860 to 1970—Con.

Year	Rayon and acetate yarns available	Non-cellulosic yarn available	Finished knit cloth shipped[11]	Carpets and rugs shipped	Sodium hydroxide (caustic soda)	Ammonia anhydrous (100% NH₃)	Ammonia aqua (100% NH₃)	Sulfuric acid (100% H₂SO₄)	Paints, varnishes, and lacquers	Superphosphates (100% P₂O₅)	Light products of distillation	Illuminating oils (kerosene)	Fuel oils	Lubricating oils	Paraffin wax
	244	245	246	247	248	249	250	251	252	253	254	255	256	257	258
	Mil. lb.	Mil. lb.	1,000 lb.	1,000 sq. yd.	1,000 short tons	1,000 short tons	1,000 short tons	1,000 short tons	Mil. gal.	1,000 short tons	Mil. bbl.	Mil. bbl.	Mil. bbl.	Mil. bbl.	1,000 bbl.
1943	494.2	17.7	112,560		[15] 2,249	543		8,442		1,273	609	72	629	39	2,697
1942	468.8	12.2			[15] 1,574	543		7,754		1,071	610	67	556	39	2,502
1941	452.5	7.5			[15] 1,429	501		6,770		955	704	73	532	40	2,393
1940	388.8	2.7								876	616	74	500	37	1,833
1939	359.9		79,756	63,676	[15] 1,045	311	[16] 16	4,795	265	758	611	69	468	35	1,659
1938	274.1									685	568	65	447	31	1,555
1937	267.2		76,377	64,799	969	[16] 108	[16] 13	6,029	280	805	571	65	459	35	1,863
1936	297.6									627	516	56	414	31	1,689
1935	252.8		49,587	59,152	759	[16] 69	[16] 12	4,890	219	532	470	56	360	28	1,608
1934	194.8									509	424	54	335	26	1,674
1933	211.9		41,484	41,876	687	[16] 75	[16] 6		(NA)	463	411	49	316	24	1,677
1932	152.1				659	[16] 64	[16] 9	4,627	171	307	403	44	295	22	1,639
1931	157.8			44,181						478	442	42	337	27	1,705
1930	118.4									794	444	49	372	34	1,956
1929	131.8		73,411		762	[16] 87	[16] 15	6,456	239		445	56	449	34	2,261
1928	100.3										388	59	427	35	2,257
1927	100.1		67,193		573	[16] 23	25	5,577	201		340	56	393	32	2,089
1926	60.9										307	62	365	32	2,310
1925	58.4		72,100		497	[16] 16	51	5,325	176		269	60	365	31	2,135
1924	42.4										225	60	320	27	1,845
1923	32.8		83,242		437	12	34	4,984	152		196	56	287	26	1,665
1922	25.0										158	55	255	23	1,651
1921	19.8		52,906		239	15	39	3,323	94	863	132	46	230	21	1,553
1920	8.7										124	55	211	25	1,933
1919	9.3		52,182		313	14	23	4,222	109		101	56	182	20	1,668
1918	6.0										91	43	174	20	1,805
1917	6.8											41	155	18	1,719
1916	6.6											35	111	15	1,379
1915	6.6														
1914	5.1			66,340	[16] 292	[16] 8	[16] 18	3,096	77						
1913	4.0														
1912	2.9														
1911	2.1														
1909				81,219	[16] 132	6	[16] 11	2,254	70						
1904				82,671	[16] 87	[16] 3		1,421	46						
1899				76,410	[16] 167	[16] 1		1,177	40						
1890											84				
1880											35				
1870											12				
1860											1				

Year	Pneumatic motor vehicle tires produced	Men's	Women's	Rails produced[17]	Structural iron and steel shapes produced[17]	Common and face brick produced	Total[18]	Bessemer[17]	Open hearth[17]	Crucible[17]	Electric and all other[17]	Hot rolled iron and steel produced[17]	Copper and copper base alloy, rolled, drawn, and extruded products shipped[11]
	259	260	261	262	263	264	265	266	267	268	269	270	271
	Millions	Mil. pairs	Mil. pairs	1,000 short tons	1,000 short tons	Billions	1,000 short tons	1,000 short tons	1,000 short tons	1,000 short tons	1,000 short tons	1,000 short tons	1,000 short tons
1970		119.7	230.2	900	[19] 5,566	6.73	131,514	-	48,022		20,162	[20] 90,798	2,821
1969		117.6	237.6	830	[19] 5,766	7.81	141,262	-	60,894		20,132	[20] 93,877	3,274
1968		125.6	283.7	847	7,098	7.91	131,462	(21)	[21] 65,835		16,814	99,115	2,912
1967	186	123.7	258.0	763	6,986	7.57	127,213	(21)	[21] 70,690		15,089	93,084	2,987
1966		126.9	284.2	878	7,687	8.26	134,101	278	85,025		14,870	99,205	3,447
1965		118.2	280.0	766	7,641	8.21	131,462	586	94,193		13,804	99,304	3,144
1964	158	117.7	278.0	701	6,809	7.87	127,076	858	98,097		12,678	93,635	2,950
1963		110.7	275.2	531	5,856	7.41	109,261	963	88,834		10,920	81,851	2,592
1962		112.7	288.2	544	5,278	6.89	98,328	805	82,957		9,013	74,998	2,478
1961		103.3	273.4	472	5,517	6.68	98,014	881	84,502		8,664	73,412	2,255

See footnotes at end of table.

Series P 231-300. Physical Output of Selected Manufactured Commodities: 1860 to 1970—Con.

Year	Pneumatic motor vehicle tires produced	Shoes produced (except athletic) Men's	Women's	Construction materials Rails produced[17]	Structural iron and steel shapes produced[17]	Common and face brick produced	Primary and fabricated metals — Raw steel produced Total[18]	Bessemer[17]	Open hearth[17]	Crucible[17]	Electric and all other[17]	Hot rolled iron and steel produced[17]	Copper and copper base alloy, rolled, drawn, and extruded products shipped[11]
	259	260	261	262	263	264	265	266	267	268	269	270	271
	Millions	Mil. pairs	Mil. pairs	1,000 short tons	1,000 short tons	Billions	1,000 short tons	1,000 short tons	1,000 short tons	1,000 short tons	1,000 short tons	1 000 short tons	1,000 short tons
1960		100.6	279.8	711	6,125	6.94	99,282	1,189	86,368		8,379	76,446	2,149
1959		110.1	292.4	631	5,259	7.34	93,446	1,380	81,669		8,533	71,856	2,407
1958	112	101.4	270.7	587	5,220	6.32	85,255	1,396	75,879		6,656	65,105	2,021
1957		104.3	274.2	1,308	8,595	6.66	112,715	2,475	101,658		7,971	85,887	2,214
1956		106.9	273.4	1,301	7,167	8.09	115,216	3,228	102,841		8,641	89,284	2,435
1955		103.7	270.9	1,227	6,336	7.90	117,036	3,320	105,359		8,050	90,658	2,564
1954	102	91.1	202.0	1,171	5,706	6.72	88,312	2,548	80,327		5,436	68,465	2,114
1953		98.8	186.9	1,982	6,538	5.87	111,610	3,856	100,474		7,280	85,944	2,525
1952		100.7	183.9	1,472	5,355	5.89	93,168	3,524	82,846		6,798	71,349	2,465
1951		104.5	169.4	1,854	6,348	6.63	105,200	4,891	93,167		7,142	81,911	
1950		102.5	195.2	1,850	5,442	6.33	96,836	4,535	86,263		6,039	75,191	---------
1949		97.4	178.0	1,901	4,672	5.52	77,978	3,947	70,249		3,783	60,882	---------
1948		104.4	176.5	2,208	5,456	5.84	88,640	4,243	79,340		5,057	69,192	---------
1947	112	106.2	191.6	2,441	5,607	5.14	84,894	4,233	76,874		3,788	66,202	2,438
1946		106.0	181.4	1,966	4,388	4.87	66,603	3,328	60,712		2,563	50,937	---------
1945		107.7	120.2	2,418	4,467	2.29	79,702	4,305	71,940	(Z)	3,457	59,812	---------
1944		108.5	118.1	2,491	4,676	1.88	89,642	5,040	80,364	(Z)	4,238	65,804	---------
1943		129.3	154.7	2,127	4,576	1.92	88,837	5,625	78,622	(Z)	4,589	63,293	---------
1942		143.0	181.7	2,096	5,816	(NA)	86,032	5,553	76,502	2	3,975	62,446	---------
1941		135.8	184.9	1,928	5,724	(NA)	82,839	5,578	74,390	2	2,869	62,324	---------
1940		102.4	151.9	1,679	4,232	4.10	66,983	3,709	61,573	1	1,700	48,660	---------
1939	[22]64	103.8	167.7	1,313	3,359	4.73	52,799	3,359	48,410	1	1,029	39,068	1,224
1938		96.7	147.8	698	2,083	3.53	31,752	2,106	29,080	(Z)	566	23,569	---------
1937	[22]59	102.9	149.7	1,619	3,670	4.19	56,637	3,864	51,825	1	947	41,178	1,060
1936	[22]53	103.8	161.9	1,366	3,245	3.82	53,500	3,873	48,760	1	865	37,858	---------
1935		99.5	145.2	797	1,960	2.28	38,184	3,175	34,401	1	606	26,840	634
1934		91.4	133.0	1,131	1,596	1.40	29,182	2,422	26,355	1	405	21,246	---------
1933	[22]45	88.8	130.7	466	1,243	1.29	25,725	2,717	22,653	(Z)	354	18,743	495
1932		74.5	113.9	451	1,050	1.40	15,123	1,712	13,243	(Z)	168	11,705	---------
1931	[22]52	77.4	112.6	1,297	2,310	3.22	28,607	3,373	24,953	1	280	21,477	625
1930		77.1	112.6	2,098	3,934	5.11	44,591	5,623	38,587	2	379	33,055	---------
1929	[22]70	94.8	131.3	3,049	5,351	7.64	61,742	7,945	53,152	6	638	45,998	1,245
1928		91.0	123.8	2,965	4,588	8.83	56,623	7,385	48,689	7	542	42,182	---------
1927	[22]67	95.3	116.3	3,143	4,192	9.47	49,273	6,894	41,921	9	449	36,825	[24]558
1926		86.6	110.4	3,604	4,381	9.96	52,902	7,721	44,764	16	401	39,755	---------
1925	[22]61	86.5	104.8	3,119	4,037	10.04	49,705	7,474	41,804	20	406	37,393	[24]545
1924		84.7	104.1	2,725	3,678	9.19	41,446	6,551	34,597	24	274	31,457	---------
1923	[22]50	100.3	109.7	3,253	3,814	9.21	49,017	9,431	39,200	48	338	37,270	---------
1922		90.0	105.4	2,432	3,045	7.32	38,945	6,578	32,106	31	230	29,626	---------
1921	[22]29	69.5	101.5	2,440	1,425	5.32	21,639	4,461	17,065	8	104	16,547	---------
1920				2,917	3,704	5.64	46,183	9,841	35,846	79	417	36,230	---------
1919	[22]38	95.0	104.8	2,468	2,928	5.54	38,099	8,038	29,665	69	327	28,114	---------
1918				2,846	3,192	3.91	49,010	10,335	38,065	128	482	34,894	---------
1917				3,297	3,483	6.62	49,787	11,572	37,783	138	294	37,036	---------
1916				3,197	3,394	8.40	46,793	12,234	34,278	135	146	36,266	---------
1915				2,469	2,729	7.71	35,180	9,178	25,838	108	55	27,320	---------
1914	12	98.0	80.9	2,179	2,275	7.96	25,606	6,895	18,603	88	20	20,575	---------
1913				3,923	3,366	8.92	34,087	10,604	23,340	117	26	27,766	---------
1912				3,727	3,188	9.37	34,079	11,492	22,457	114	17	27,616	---------
1911				3,162	2,142	9.20	25,937	8,841	16,970	94	32	21,324	---------
1910				4,072	2,539	9.92	28,330	10,478	17,672	122	58	24,216	---------
1909		98.0	86.6	3,387	2,549	10.61	26,218	10,414	15,682	107	16	22,002	---------
1908				2,152	1,213	8.40	15,383	6,828	8,492	63	---------	13,248	---------
1907				4,070	2,173	10.38	25,375	13,031	12,206	138	---------	22,249	---------
1906				4,455	2,373	10.64	25,443	13,712	11,594	137	---------	21,939	---------
1905				3,781	1,860	10.36	21,880	12,231	9,537	112	---------	18,861	---------
1904		83.4	69.5	2,559	1,063	9.10	15,205	8,787	6,325	93	---------	13,455	---------
1903				3,352	1,227	8.90	15,865	9,605	6,146	114	---------	14,793	---------
1902				3,302	1,456	8.93	16,402	10,222	6,054	126	---------	15,617	---------
1901				3,220	1,135	8.45	14,784	9,752	4,924	108	---------	13,831	---------
1900				2,672	913	7.49	11,227	7,481	3,638	109	---------	10,626	---------
1899		67.7	65.0	2,545	952	8.13	11,739	8,494	3,135	111	---------	11,530	---------
1898				2,219	786	6.16	9,888	7,401	2,388	99	---------	9,535	---------
1897				1,846	654	5.60	7,940	6,131	1,731	77	---------	7,842	---------
1896				1,257	555	5.97	5,849	4,388	1,396	65	---------	6,178	---------
1895				1,463	580	6.36	6,785	5,494	1,219	72	---------	6,932	---------
1894				1,144	404	---------	4,899	3,995	845	58	---------	5,199	---------
1893				1,273	434	---------	4,471	3,596	805	69	---------	5,573	---------
1892				1,738	508	---------	5,492	4,663	732	96	---------	6,906	---------
1891				1,464	---------	---------	4,349	3,635	631	82	---------	6,038	---------

See footnotes at end of table.

Series P 231–300. Physical Output of Selected Manufactured Commodities: 1860 to 1970—Con.

Year	Construction materials			Primary and fabricated metals					
	Rails produced	Structural iron and steel shapes produced	Common and face brick produced	Raw steel produced					Hot rolled iron and steel produced
				Total	Bessemer	Open hearth	Crucible		
	262	263	264	265	266	267	268		270
	1,000 short tons	*1,000 short tons*	*Billions*	*1,000 short tons*	*1,000 short tons*	*1,000 short tons*	*1,000 short tons*		*1,000 short tons*
1890	2,112			4,779	4,131	566	82		6,746
1889	1,705	276	8.05	3,784	3,282	413	89		5,865
1888	1,572			3,238	2,813	345	80		5,171
1887	2,396			3,733	3,288	356	89		5,864
1886	1,793			2,870	2,541	245	83		4,853
1885	1,094			1,917	1,702	149	66		2,975
1884	1,145			1,737	1,541	132	65		3,077
1883	1,361			1,874	1,655	134	86		3,645
1882	1,689			1,945	1,696	161	88		3,955
1881	1,844			1,779	1,539	147	93		3,999
1880	1,462			1,397	1,203	113	81		3,301
1879	1,113	87	3.82	1,048	929	56	62		2,741
1878	883			820	732	36	51		2,115
1877	765			638	561	25	52		1,909
1876	880			597	526	21	50		1,922

Year	Construction materials—Con.		Primary and fabricated metals—Con.					Year	Construction materials—Con.	Primary and fabricated metals—Con.			
	Rails produced	Common and face brick produced	Raw steel produced—Con.				Hot rolled iron and steel produced		Rails produced	Raw steel produced—Con.			Hot rolled iron and steel produced
			Total	Bessemer	Open hearth	Crucible				Total	Bessemer	Crucible	
	262	264	265	266	267	268	270		262	265	266	268	270
	1,000 short tons	*Billions*	*1,000 short tons*	*1,000 short tons*	*1,000 short tons*	*1,000 short tons*	*1,000 short tons*		*1,000 short tons*	*1,000 short tons*	*1,000 short tons*	*1,000 short tons*	*1,000 short tons*
1875	793		437	376	9	52	1,890	1867	463	22	3	19	1,042
1874	729		242	192	7	43	1,840	1866	431	19		19	1,026
1873	890		223	171	4	49	1,966	1865	356	15		15	856
1872	1,000		160	120	3	37	1,942	1864	335	10		10	872
1871	776		82	45	2	35	1,486	1863	276	9		9	
1870	620		77	42	2	34	1,325	1862	214				
1869	594	2.80	35	12	1	22	1,236	1861	190				
1868	506		30	9		22	1,105	1860	205	13		13	

Year	Fabricated metal products			Machinery, except electrical						Electrical machinery			
	Metal cans shipped[25]	Warm air-furnaces shipped	Non-electric cooking stoves and ranges shipped	Gasoline engines produced	Diesel engines produced	Wheel tractors, complete, produced	Metal cutting machines shipped	Type-writers shipped	Room air-conditioners shipped	Fractional horse-power motors (excluding hermetics) shipped[11]	Integral horse-power motors and generators shipped[11]	Domestic ranges, electric, shipped[11]	House-hold refrigerators produced
	272	273	274	275	276	277	278	279	280	281	282	283	284
	1,000 base boxes	*1,000*	*1,000*	*1,000*	*1,000*	*1,000*	*1,000*	*1,000*	*1,000*	*1,000*	*1,000*	*1,000*	*1,000*
1970	159,299	1,783	2,114	9,558	226	172	188	[26] 1,371	5,438	135,134	2,836		
1969	152,617	1,865	2,291	10,528	254	196	230	1,626	5,115	150,463	2,776		
1968	145,862	1,741	2,326	9,822	252	213	226	1,842	3,887	142,696	2,726		
1967	133,980	1,449	2,097	9,102	252	242	236	1,928	3,941	122,419	2,834	2,273	4,578
1966	129,389	1,528	2,132	8,900	254	271	243	1,889	3,269	136,820	2,595		
1965	121,050	1,583	2,187	7,908	247	244	184	1,486	2,868	131,572	2,139		
1964	116,213	1,535	2,068	6,734	238	213	154	1,438	2,592	106,587	1,923		
1963	110,949	1,363	2,016	6,862	179	203	140	1,307	1,990	98,926	1,433	2,205	4,221
1962	114,506	1,238	1,878	7,126	155	188	139	1,306	1,628	81,373	1,724		
1961	[27] 109,358	1,175	1,773	5,968	150	171	124	1,130	1,562	74,552	1,428		
1960	4,862	1,253	1,822	6,022	139	152	134	1,191	1,523	76,027	1,409		
1959	4,949	1,435	2,037	7,181	180	260	143	1,283	1,773				
1958	4,761	1,235	1,825	5,756	132	241	110	1,224	1,675	58,877	1,639	[28] 789	3,038
1957	4,595	1,131	1,956	4,924	127	229		1,645	1,586				
1956	4,786	1,355	2,274	5,883	141	215		1,501	1,828				

See footnotes at end of table.

Series P 231–300. Physical Output of Selected Manufactured Commodities: 1860 to 1970—Con.

Year	Fabricated metal products			Machinery, except electrical						Electrical machinery			
	Metal cans shipped [25]	Warm air-furnaces shipped	Non-electric cooking stoves and ranges shipped	Gasoline engines produced	Diesel engines produced	Wheel tractors, complete, produced	Metal cutting machines shipped	Typewriters shipped	Room air-conditioners shipped	Fractional horsepower motors (excluding hermetics) shipped [11]	Integral horsepower motors and generators shipped [11]	Domestic ranges, electric, shipped [11]	Household refrigerators produced
	272	273	274	275	276	277	278	279	280	281	282	283	284
	1,000 base boxes	1,000	1,000	1,000	1,000	1,000	1,000	1,000	1,000	1,000	1,000	1,000	1,000
1955	4,484	1,406	2,509	4,932	139	330		1,258	1,283				
1954	4,143	1,152	2,203	3,670	105	246	121	[29] 1,111	1,353	57,643	1,744	1,209	3,387
1953	4,082	997	2,386	2,989	118	390		1,295	[30] 1,018				
1952	3,842	928	2,424	2,945	121	415		1,383	[30] 372				
1951	3,805	872	2,624	3,104	129	564		1,533	[30] 229				
1950	3,893	1,100	3,388	2,458	99	499		[29] 1,408	194				
1949	3,277	770	2,475			556		[29] 1,074	89				
1948	3,245	777	3,532			530		[29] 1,173	74				
1947	2,956	885	3,519	2,141	100	433	191	[29] 1,493	43	43,375	1,904	1,210	3,975
1946	2,760	699	[31] 2,811			258			30				
1945	2,442	373	[31] 1,889			244			1				
1944	2,072	281	[31] 1,424			249							
1943	1,684	[32] 173	[31] 1,055			105							
1942		[32] 256				172							
1941		[32] 518				313							
1940						249							
1939						186		930		11,256	456	275	1,773
1938						172							
1937						238		1,116		20,666	520	[33] 341	[34] 2,824
1936						194							
1935						138		824		7,782	327	[33] 195	[34] 1,882
1934													
1933								416		3,818	189	[33] 51	[34] 1,160
1932													
1931						62		529		3,845	309	[33] 110	[34] 1,050
1930						176							
1929						196		962		4,832	713	[33] 225	[34] 890
1928						152							
1927						185		862		3,046	524	[33] 113	[34] 390
1926						170							
1925						158		742		2,288	446	[33] 85	[34] 75
1924						112							
1923						127		698		1,995	413	[35] 49	[34] 18
1922						95							
1921								489		993	250	27	[34] 5
1919										198	1,153		
1914										64	283		
1900								145					

Year	Household washing machines, mechanical, shipped [11]	Electric lamps produced		Home-type radio receivers shipped [11]	Home-type radio-phonograph combinations shipped [11]	Phonographs shipped	Transportation equipment					Horse-drawn vehicles produced		Bicycles produced
		Large incandescent	Fluorescent, hot cathode				Trailer coaches, housing type, shipped [11]	Truck trailers shipped	Loco-motives produced	Railroad passenger cars produced	Railroad freight cars produced	Carriages, buggies, and sulkies	Farm wagons, trucks, and business vehicles	
	285	286	287	288	289	290	291	292	293	294	295	296	297	298
	1,000	Mil.	Mil.	1,000	1,000	1,000	1,000	1,000			1,000	1,000	1,000	Mil.
1970		1,582	267	4,359	1,660	3,051		106						
1969		1,476	261	5,941	1,842	3,941		138						
1968		1,467	258	7,455	1,982	3,705		114						
1967	4,596	1,391	224	9,362	1,730	3,828	226	97	[36] 1,418	[37] 72	[37] 63		92	[37] 4.87
1966		1,394	256	13,536	1,702	4,323		113						
1965		1,320	225	12,744	1,662	4,057		104						
1964		1,264	198	9,404	1,454	3,242		87						
1963	4,227	1,254	179	9,313	1,244	3,699	151	78	686	[37] 266	[37] 33		94	[37] 3.81
1962		1,238	164	10,112	1,243	3,668		68						
1961		1,155	142	10,350	853	3,343		51						

See footnotes at end of table.

Series P 231–300. Physical Output of Selected Manufactured Commodities: 1860 to 1970—Con.

Year	Household washing machines, mechanical, shipped [11]	Electric lamps produced		Home-type radio receivers shipped [11]	Home-type radio-phonograph combinations shipped [11]	Phonographs shipped	Trailer coaches, housing type, shipped [11]	Truck trailers shipped	Locomotives produced	Railroad passenger cars produced	Railroad freight cars produced	Horse-drawn vehicles produced		Bicycles produced
		Large incandescent	Fluorescent, hot cathode									Carriages, buggies, and sulkies	Farm wagons, trucks, and business vehicles	
	285	286	287	288	289	290	291	292	293	294	295	296	297	298
	1,000	*Mil.*	*Mil.*	*1,000*	*1,000*	*1,000*	*1,000*	*1,000*			*1,000*	*1,000*	*1,000*	*Mil.*
1960	--------	1,142	140	9,763	654	3,242	--------	58	--------	--------	--------	--------	--------	----
1959		1,212	131	9,568	771	3,481		68						
1958	3,974	1,052	113	8,012	787	3,750	135	49	1,140	[37] 116	[37] 32		107	[37] 2.05
1957		1,112	119	8,604	735	3,943		58		705	97			
1956		1,132	126	8,974	602	3,949		64		396	67			
1955		1,057	104	7,929	507	3,919		74		886	38			
1954	3,697	960	93	6,448	377	2,659	72	52	1,409	315	36		108	1.75
1953		1,028	92	7,260	524	1,494		93		386	84			
1952		864	65	6,556	566	830		55		117	79			
1951		1,070	111					65		179	96			
1950		1,200	98					66		964	44			
1949		975	71					34		933	95			
1948		1,030	94					47		891	115			
1947	4,148	999	89	14,067	3,415	760	76	53	1,718	861	96		218	2.88
1946		774	52					73		1,337	60			
1945		787	37					[38] 33	3,213	931	55			
1944								209	1,438	1,003	82			
1943								197	1,164	685	75			
1942								80	1,018	418	71			
1941								[38] 42	1,107	349	83			
1940								[38] 27	560	257	64			
1939		1,393	517	9,839	475		12	24	355	276	26	1	52	1.25
1938									346	434	17			
1937		1,493	501	7,728	58		18	22	615	629	79	1	106	1.13
1936									202	191	47			
1935		1,208	388	5,669	23		19		205	205	9	1	98	.66
1934									110	195	25			
1933		1,017	306	3,648	30				63	7	2	1	53	.32
1932									123	71	3			
1931		818	320	3,743	74				222	290	14	1	27	.26
1930									1,134	1,481	77			
1929		956	352	4,980	152	[39] 603			1,161	2,202	85	4	106	.31
1928									747	1,462	48			
1927		760	335	1,980	59	[39] 988			1,176	1,975	64	8	112	.26
1926									1,770	2,800	91			
1925			267	2,350	([39])	[39] 642			1,285	2,383	109	22	196	.30
1924									2,036	2,491	115			
1923			233	190	([39])	[39] 997			3,785	1,963	178	40	193	.49
1922									1,534	1,096	68			
1921			155		([39])	[39] 596			1,823	1,159	46	34	67	.22
1920									3,672	903	76			
1919			[40] 225		([39])	[39] 2,230			3,272	391	157	216	342	.47
1918									6,475	1,572	108			
1917									5,446	1,955	140			
1916									4,075	1,802	129			
1915									2,085	1,866	70			
1914			[40] 89			514			2,235	3,366	98	538	534	.30
1913									5,332	2,779	186			
1912									4,915	2,818	126			
1911									3,530	3,466	62			
1910									4,755	4,288	171			
1909			[40] 67			345			2,887	2,749	87	828	588	.17
1908									2,342	1,637	68			
1907									7,362	5,353	275			
1906									6,952	3,084	233			
1905			[40] 113						5,491	2,500	163	937	644	.23
1904									3,441	2,144	61			
1903									5,152	2,007	153			
1902									4,070	1,948	163			
1901									3,384	2,055	137			
1900									3,153	1,636	116			
1899			[40] 25			151			2,475	1,305	120	905	570	1.11

See footnotes at end of table.

Series P 231–300. Physical Output of Selected Manufactured Commodities: 1860 to 1970—Con.

Year	Locomotives produced	Railroad passenger cars produced	Railroad freight cars produced	Year	Locomotives produced	Railroad passenger cars produced	Railroad freight cars produced	Year	Locomotives produced	Railroad passenger cars produced	Railroad freight cars produced	Year	Railroad passenger cars produced	Railroad freight cars produced
	293	294	295		293	294	295		293	294	295		294	295
		1,000				*1,000*				*1,000*				*1,000*
1898	1,875	699	100	1890	2,300	1,654	104	1882	2,282	1,711	68	1875	185	9
1897	1,251	494	44	1889	1,860	1,580	71	1881	1,977	1,188	74	1874	256	5
1896	1,175	474	51	1888	2,180	1,452	72	1880	1,405	685	46	1873	280	6
1895	1,101	430	38	1887	2,044	1,277	78	1879		524	26	1872	387	9
1894	695	516	17	1886	1,436	953	42	1878		211	9	1871	185	2
1893	2,011	1,986	57	1885	800	813	13	1877		708	7			
1892	2,012	2,195	98	1884	1,149	1,063	25	1876		836	8			
1891	2,165	1,640	96	1883	2,067	2,135	45							

Year	Miscellaneous — Pianos produced	Miscellaneous — Organs produced	Year	Miscellaneous — Pianos produced	Miscellaneous — Organs produced	Year	Miscellaneous — Pianos produced	Miscellaneous — Organs produced	Year	Miscellaneous — Pianos produced	Miscellaneous — Organs produced
	299	300		299	300		299	300		299	300
	1,000	*1,000*		*1,000*	*1,000*		*1,000*	*1,000*		*1,000*	*1,000*
1967	199		1939	111		1927	212	3.1	1914	323	40.5
1963	214	[41]141.9	1937	103		1925	303	4.4	1909	364	64.1
1958	159	88.6	1935	61	1.7	1923	344	7.8	1904	261	113
1954	152		1931	51	1.3	1921	218	7.9	1899	172	107
1947	148		1929	121	2.7	1919	338	26.4			

* Denotes first year for which figures include Alaska and Hawaii.
– Represents zero. NA Not available. Z Less than 500 short tons.
[1] Figures for 1915–1929 are for crop years ending June; all others are for calendar years. The 1914 crop year figure is 114.2 million barrels. The 1929 calendar year figure is 120.0 million barrels.
[2] Figures are for years ending June 30.
[3] Prior to 1959, shortening only; figures for salad and cooking oils not collected.
[4] Includes large and small sizes.
[5] Data for 53 weeks.
[6] Includes boys' uniform clothing.
[7] Excludes separate coats.
[8] Includes children's and infants'.
[9] Alcoholic content limited to 3.2 percent by weight from Apr. 7–Dec. 5, 1933.
[10] Includes 1,589 thousand barrels produced prior to Apr. 7 (effective date of the Act of Mar. 22, 1933).
[11] From beginning of series through 1939, represents amount produced.
[12] Beginning 1964, includes kerosene type jet fuel.
[13] Tufted only.
[14] Represents only reported quantities produced; not adjusted to include estimated production for establishments not reporting.
[15] For 1939–1949, excludes flakes and powders; for 1939–1942, also excludes solids.
[16] Amount for sale.
[17] Beginning 1959, includes Hawaii.
[18] Beginning 1953, includes production by basic oxygen process, not shown separately here.
[19] Represents shipments of heavy steel structural shapes; comparable figure for 1968 is 5,557 thousand.
[20] Represents shipments of steel products; comparable figure for 1968 is 91,856 thousand.

[21] Bessemer included with open hearth.
[22] Includes bicycle tires.
[23] Excludes motorcycle tires.
[24] Excludes amount produced and consumed in same works.
[25] Prior to 1961, represents thousands of short tons of metal consumed in manufacture of cans. Comparable figure for 1961 is 5,039 thousand.
[26] For October–December, excludes standard portable typewriters and specialized typewriters (i.e., specialized composing typewriters, coded media typewriters, and input/output typewriters).
[27] Represents tinplate cans shipped.
[28] Excludes other than free-standing ranges.
[29] Excludes specialized typewriters.
[30] Listed as self-contained window sill type.
[31] Amount produced.
[32] Represents orders booked rather than shipments; comparable figure for 1944 is 226 thousand.
[33] 2½ kw. and over.
[34] Represents sales.
[35] Includes disk stoves and hotplates.
[36] Includes rebuilt locomotives.
[37] Represents shipments. For bicycles, 1963 and 1967, excludes children's 2-wheel sidewalk cycles with semipneumatic tires.
[38] Civilian only.
[39] For phonographs, amount produced, 1921–1929. Radio-phonograph combinations included with phonographs, 1919–1925.
[40] Not strictly comparable with later years because of changes in classification.
[41] Represents electronic organs shipped.

Series P 301–317. Total Production Capacity of Selected Manufacturing Industries: 1887 to 1970

[In thousands of short tons unless otherwise stated. Capacity is usually rated as of January 1. See text for exception]

Year	Blast furnaces (pig iron)	Steel ingots and steel for castings [1]	Copper refining [2]	Lead refining — Silver-lead refineries	Lead refining — Smelters and refiners of Missouri lead	Zinc refining [3]	Aluminum ingots	Portland cement	Crude petroleum refining (mil. 42-gal. bbl.)	Coke — By-product (slot type)	Coke — Beehive	Carbon black	Sulfuric acid	Phosphatic fertilizers [4]	Total combined nitrogen	Rayon and acetate yarn, staple and tow	Paper and paperboard
	301	302	303	304	305	306	307	308	309	310	311	312	313	314	315	316	317
1970			2,676	350	435	1,253	4,121	93,349	4,407			1,877	29,676	4,496	13,135	857	58,372
1969			2,676	422	415	1,288	3,863	93,682	4,285			1,832	29,537	4,290	12,713	865	56,241
1968			2,643	422	390	1,310	3,668	93,521	4,221			1,668	28,544	4,149	12,120	858	53,978
1967			2,522	500	300	1,294	3,319	91,588	3,927			1,551	28,815	4,695	12,194	843	51,410
1966			2,431	402	120	1,264	2,968	89,194	3,830			1,464	28,385	4,450	10,605	860	48,073
1965			2,421	488	120	1,278	2,795	88,664	3,933			1,467	24,857	3,834	8,869	855	46,250
1964			2,365	488	120	1,267	2,553	88,451	3,801			1,327	22,924	3,482	7,634	818	44,671
1963			2,335	488	120	1,252	2,509	86,757	3,693			1,282	20,936	3,231	6,693	747	43,423
1962			2,335	488	120	1,203	2,489	81,878	3,682			1,287	19,701	2,823	5,810	727	42,800
1961			2,342	488	120	1,199	2,484	80,265	3,654	78,877	4,616	1,264	17,848	2,743	5,207	711	41,334

See footnotes at end of table.

Series P 301–317. Total Production Capacity of Selected Manufacturing Industries: 1887 to 1970—Con.

[In thousands of short tons unless otherwise stated]

Year	Blast furnaces (pig iron)	Steel ingots and steel for castings [1]	Copper refining [2]	Lead refining — Silver-lead refineries	Lead refining — Smelters and refiners of Missouri lead	Zinc refining [3]	Aluminum ingots	Portland cement	Crude petroleum refining (mil. 42-gal. bbl.)	Coke — By-product (slot type)	Coke — Beehive	Carbon black	Sulfuric acid	Phosphatic fertilizers [4]	Total combined nitrogen	Rayon and acetate yarn, staple and tow	Paper and paperboard
	301	302	303	304	305	306	307	308	309	310	311	312	313	314	315	316	317
1960	96,521	148,571	2,332	488	248	1,191	2,464	[5]77,906	[6]3,624	81,448	4,369	1,174	17,883	2,672	4,818	734	*40,232
1959	94,635	147,634	2,309	488	248	1,176	2,403	74,596	3,584	82,498	5,020	1,051	17,609	2,641	4,520	732	38,641
1958	91,000	140,743	2,109	560	248	1,173	2,230	70,385	3,434	80,299	5,503	1,028	15,950	2,423	3,879	709	37,351
1957	86,818	133,459	2,064	560	258	1,159	1,776	64,699	3,330	79,965	5,766	1,085	19,500	4,550	3,711	768	35,021
1956	85,485	128,363	2,064	628	258	1,161	1,589	58,562	3,159	79,676	6,285	1,016	18,600	4,590	3,631	750	33,169
1955	83,971	125,828	1,862	628	258	1,110	1,388	55,324	3,074	78,596	8,078	990	17,440	4,642	3,194	785	30,025
1954	82,001	124,330	1,896	628	258	1,094	1,311	54,050	2,923	78,258	10,073	966	15,970	4,329	2,474	826	29,089
1953	79,380	117,547	1,647	628	242	1,014	1,142	52,624	2,788	76,428	12,005	975	14,560	3,720	2,002	805	27,854
1952	73,782	108,588	1,599	628	238	995	846	52,156	2,684	74,228	13,859	1,030	14,220	3,432	1,955	745	26,789
1951	72,472	104,230	1,599	628	238	966	750	49,712	2,542	72,488	11,572	942	13,410	3,349	1,593	708	26,059
1950	71,560	99,983	1,557	628	238	986	633	48,000	2,444	73,710	8,672	744	13,000	2,896	1,565	641	25,048
1949	70,542	96,121	1,547	628	238	974	679	47,326	2,350	74,500	9,076	758			1,389	587	23,389
1948	67,439	94,233	1,557	653	238	1,000	676	46,362	2,209	72,549	8,844	736		2,834	1,389	586	22,025
1947	65,709	91,241	1,585	653	238	1,000	762	45,086	2,033	71,113	8,427	743		2,604	1,394	511	20,420
1946	67,341	91,891	1,720	737	238	1,100	785	45,108	1,940	71,399	8,095	668			1,384	446	20,282
1945	67,314	95,505	1,720	767	246	1,084	704	44,915	1,935	72,330	10,438	663	10,500	2,291	1,327		19,260
1944	67,921	93,854	1,595	767	279	1,097	1,164	45,319	1,864	71,378	11,230	472			1,191	370	18,830
1943	64,188	90,589	1,563	767	(Z)	1,069	771	46,669	1,789	64,555	10,409	395			797		18,755
1942	60,607	88,887	1,561	767	361	950	391	46,416	1,809	62,562	11,210	330			455		18,492
1941	57,775	85,158	1,549	845	313	787	245	47,707	1,722	62,220	(Z)	313			390	300	16,891
1940	55,724	81,619	1,572	851	317	1,313	188	48,142	1,694	62,955	(Z)	317		1,692	380	253	16,557
1939	56,326	81,829	1,642	851	317	1,346	131	48,071	1,646	61,272	(Z)	313			375	220	16,191
1938	56,782	80,186	1,642	863	317	1,413	144	47,982	1,588	62,727	(Z)	317			370	183	15,573
1937	55,557	78,148	1,642	809	317	1,368	133	48,035	1,568	62,076	(Z)	317			359	163	14,458
1936	55,854	78,164	1,613	785	333	1,379	130	49,240	1,507	62,403	(Z)	261			342	147	13,986
1935	57,098	78,452	1,624	799	333	1,489	130	49,389	1,481	62,757	(Z)	265			341		13,888
1934	57,243	78,128	1,624	895	417	1,489	132	50,645	1,430	63,050	(Z)	240			341		13,728
1933	56,511	76,767	1,612	823	417	1,458	134	51,006	1,420	62,645	(Z)	231			347	105	13,728
1932	57,949	76,898	1,612	781	417	1,424	132	51,108	1,469	63,491	(Z)	227			357		13,972
1931	58,979	75,328	1,630	775	417	1,447	125	50,768	1,439	61,468	(Z)	249			261	81	13,643
1930	57,855	71,042	1,528	771	407	1,491	113	48,676	1,374	60,167	(Z)	270		1,644	236		13,704
1929	57,382	69,584	1,520	711	407	1,575	100	45,816	1,281	60,357	(Z)	263			212		12,933
1928	56,596	66,960	1,520	711	437	1,697	83	42,691	1,190	57,852	(Z)	228			116		12,536
1927	58,701	65,344	1,490		437	1,692	82	40,476	1,117	52,666	(Z)				66		12,000
1926	57,288	62,925	1,375		437	1,625	(NA)	36,389	1,041	48,184	(Z)				65		11,623
1925	59,847	65,962	1,335		427	1,478	(NA)	32,919	1,032	46,809	(Z)				55		10,500
1924	59,006	64,137	1,318		372	1,485	(NA)	30,429	1,027	45,058	(Z)				54		9,725
1923	59,009	63,383	1,348		372	1,409	(NA)	27,486		43,763	(Z)						8,970
1922	58,786	63,135	1,348		348	1,439	(NA)	26,693	770	43,854							8,614
1921	57,950	61,928	1,348		342	1,439	(NA)	27,523	689	42,821							8,540
1920	56,249	60,220	1,384				(NA)	25,209	559	38,200	49,300			1,447			7,671
1919	55,182	59,174	1,408				63	25,869	473	33,700	51,000						7,500
1918	53,701	57,083	1,408				(NA)	25,709	434	25,900	53,000						7,000
1917	51,368	53,914	1,244				(NA)	25,132		21,600	55,000						
1916	50,438	49,266	946				(NA)	24,402		18,400	55,000						
1915	49,734	44,454	889				45	21,620		16,600	56,300						6,440
1914	49,723	42,678	884				(NA)	21,620		15,000	57,200						
1913	48,448		824				(NA)	20,680		12,800	57,900						
1912			747				(NA)	21,150		10,200	58,900						
1911			724				(NA)	18,362		8,600	59,100					1	
1910			644				17	17,578		(Z)	58,200			943			5,293
1909			587							(Z)	57,100						
1908		36,545	581														
1907	34,074		568														
1905																	3,858
1904	27,262	26,919															
1901	23,961	23,276															
1900														336			2,782
1898	18,124	15,639															
1896		13,236															
1895						(Z)											
1894		10,780				(Z)											
1892		8,332															
1891						(Z)											
1889		7,195				(Z)											
1887		5,852															

* Denotes first year for which figures include Alaska and Hawaii.
NA Not available.   Z Less than 500 tons.
[1] From open hearth, Bessemer, crucible, and electric furnaces.
[2] 1944–1970 includes electrolytic refining capacity plus Lake Superior and fire-refined; 1907–1943, electrolytic capacity only.
[3] 1941–1970, slab zinc; 1926–1940, distillation and electrolytic zinc; 1921–1925, distillation zinc.
[4] Available phosphoric oxide (P_2O_3).
[5] Beginning 1960, includes Hawaii.
[6] Beginning 1960, includes Hawaii; includes Alaska for all years.

Series **P 318–374.** Value of Output of Finished Commodities and Construction Materials Destined for Domestic Consumption at Current Producers' Prices, and Implicit Price Indexes for Major Commodity Groups (Shaw): 1869 to 1939

[In millions of dollars]

Year	Total, all finished commodities	Perishable								Semidurable				
		Total	Food and kindred products		Cigars, cigarettes, and tobacco	Drug, toilet, and household preparations	Magazines, newspapers, misc. paper supplies, etc.	Fuel and lighting products		Total	Dry goods and notions	Clothing and personal furnishings	Shoes and other footwear	House-furnishings
			Manufactured	Non-manufactured				Manufactured	Non-manufactured					
	318	319	320	321	322	323	324	325	326	327	328	329	330	331
1939	31,277.7	16,073.5								5,490.6				
1938	28,156.7	15,721.6								4,852.7				
1937	33,667.8	17,295.3	9,402.3	3,683.0	1,274.1	818.4	601.9	1,335.0	180.6	5,591.3	712.9	3,258.6	828.3	340.1
1936	30,258.1	16,239.0								4,775.8				
1935	26,744.7	14,571.7	7,884.9	3,183.6	1,096.4	727.7	527.2	952.2	199.7	4,937.6	576.0	3,039.1	693.4	273.7
1934	23,166.7	12,987.2								4,501.6				
1933	18,454.1	10,872.9	5,509.5	2,451.1	910.7	626.0	470.1	707.2	198.3	3,772.8	390.4	2,274.6	597.3	218.2
1932	17,727.8	10,754.9	5,183.0	2,408.1	1,006.6	624.4	492.6	830.6	209.5	3,526.1	317.5	2,183.4	546.3	187.5
1931	24,243.3	13,431.7	6,730.2	3,133.4	1,154.9	809.0	573.5	740.2	290.5	4,931.4	1 459.4	3,087.9	705.1	256.6
1930	31,260.7	16,590.5	8,497.5	3,996.8	1,141.8	891.0	644.8	1,052.2	366.3	6,069.4	574.4	3,767.8	860.3	347.8
1929	37,782.6	18,384.0	9,463.9	4,358.3	1,243.6	984.2	683.9	1,237.8	412.3	7,458.3	791.0	4,516.4	1,081.9	416.5
1928	35,892.9	17,911.1	9,111.7	4,466.9	1,168.7	932.3	661.6	1,153.3	416.4	7,383.2	769.1	4,385.6	1,074.9	401.5
1927	34,410.2	17,263.6	8,827.3	4,360.2	1,164.5	851.9	648.4	958.9	452.5	7,390.7	798.6	4,360.2	1,077.6	396.9
1926	35,856.6	17,784.6	9,039.8	4,467.4	1,127.2	783.3	632.8	1,220.7	513.4	7,295.6	803.5	4,186.6	1,073.9	438.1
1925	34,046.3	16,870.5	8,684.0	4,335.8	1,094.4	767.0	615.7	990.1	383.5	7,134.0	816.0	4,149.2	1,044.8	404.8
1924	30,957.7	15,573.6	7,981.3	3,948.0	1,073.2	718.6	563.0	781.3	508.2	6,401.4	700.7	3,743.9	1,061.7	358.4
1923	32,168.5	15,176.0	7,554.6	4,012.9	1,050.3	698.5	550.7	746.4	562.7	7,230.3	861.9	4,347.4	1,128.2	377.3
1922	27,393.8	14,059.4	6,837.6	3,843.0	1,002.1	624.6	499.9	888.4	363.9	6,313.9	681.5	3,865.4	993.0	307.1
1921	25,864.0	14,022.9	6,548.7	4,182.4	1,053.0	562.2	474.5	714.9	487.3	5,631.7	607.4	3,345.3	953.5	277.9
1920	37,285.2	19,236.2	10,301.4	4,696.3	1,195.5	765.6	675.9	1,044.8	556.8	7,872.8	903.6	4,382.8	1,368.2	390.5
1919 2	34,032.4	17,392.4	9,468.2	4,720.2	1,008.4	667.8	439.8	668.4	419.5	7,019.9	806.5	3,932.9	1,254.2	324.0
1919 2	33,265.3	17,215.5	9,312.4	4,709.0	1,000.0	660.1	458.7	630.7	444.5	6,770.2	890.9	3,817.9	1,187.6	212.0
1918	29,979.8	15,807.2	8,583.6	4,280.8	864.0	636.1	445.5	580.7	416.5	6,076.1	854.8	3,361.1	1,043.2	199.9
1917	24,545.5	13,174.1	6,925.7	3,907.2	629.5	511.5	407.5	425.7	366.9	4,790.6	620.3	2,622.7	863.4	156.7
1916	18,389.4	9,893.2	5,380.1	2,693.6	522.4	420.7	352.2	262.5	261.7	3,573.7	461.6	2,025.3	705.5	112.2
1915	13,986.1	8,079.8	4,342.1	2,310.3	478.6	331.0	255.6	141.7	220.5	2,635.7	317.0	1,533.9	520.6	85.8
1914	14,054.0	8,296.5	4,484.8	2,380.1	500.9	289.0	254.4	160.4	226.9	2,709.5	337.8	1,598.1	523.8	90.0
1913	14,632.8	8,230.2	4,441.9	2,315.9	506.8	294.9	243.9	191.3	235.3	2,900.2	348.6	1,721.6	583.8	95.5
1912	14,028.0	8,100.8	4,342.3	2,410.5	468.9	289.4	233.6	142.0	214.0	2,754.4	363.2	1,656.7	531.4	85.5
1911	12,749.4	7,491.3	3,980.1	2,235.7	460.4	278.8	211.3	119.1	205.9	2,571.4	326.3	1,560.0	500.8	80.0
1910	3 12,659.2	7,386.0	3,823.5	2,306.1	464.0	266.8	209.9	121.0	194.8	2,417.3	349.5	1,408.3	486.0	83.0
1909	11,825.3	6,922.1	3,617.7	2,112.5	430.5	250.3	210.6	124.7	175.8	2,447.0	368.0	1,459.7	467.9	75.0
1908	10,191.1	5,988.1	2,974.7	1,915.7	399.8	234.1	156.8	125.8	181.3	2,155.5	295.5	1,287.0	452.1	60.1
1907	11,524.3	6,452.7	3,389.7	1,886.9	405.2	249.3	196.7	128.5	196.5	2,310.1	375.5	1,335.4	454.4	68.2
1906	10,752.5	5,912.7	3,121.0	1,719.6	398.1	225.4	184.3	102.9	161.3	2,244.2	348.2	1,314.7	448.9	69.5
1905	9,451.0	5,403.6	2,856.7	1,540.0	357.2	215.8	172.5	94.4	167.0	1,925.3	318.3	1,099.7	395.9	55.7
1904	8,734.3	5,167.7	2,601.5	1,614.9	339.2	182.3	159.7	109.2	160.8	1,746.5	285.1	992.6	368.9	52.9
1903	8,702.1	5,012.7	2,516.7	1,518.9	346.0	183.1	154.7	111.5	182.3	1,734.7	302.1	981.8	352.5	53.9
1902	8,227.5	4,764.7	2,403.1	1,519.3	325.1	174.0	151.3	89.7	102.2	1,613.8	298.7	892.8	325.9	53.2
1901	7,782.2	4,620.5	2,365.0	1,420.9	327.9	155.2	134.9	84.7	132.0	1,528.5	271.1	837.9	327.4	49.4
1900	7,120.8	4,100.8	2,083.9	1,249.1	304.0	136.2	122.3	100.3	105.0	1,465.7	271.9	817.4	289.8	49.8
1899	6,586.2	3,820.9	1,955.5	1,160.9	267.4	134.6	113.0	87.7	101.8	1,374.4	255.8	743.7	292.9	42.5
1898	5,708.0	3,431.7	1,707.9	1,121.4	226.9	122.4	103.2	63.9	86.0	1,175.8	227.4	608.2	261.9	35.9
1897	5,376.1	3,222.6	1,633.7	1,032.1	197.3	115.6	92.6	62.4	89.0	1,154.0	232.3	596.8	246.3	35.7
1896	5,003.4	2,944.0	1,436.2	927.5	193.0	112.7	90.0	92.8	91.9	1,064.6	215.5	549.5	228.9	35.5
1895	5,227.2	3,119.1	1,443.7	1,079.0	202.4	111.3	94.1	95.8	92.9	1,114.7	265.7	542.2	236.0	36.4
1894	4,752.3	2,916.3	1,337.9	1,012.3	218.1	102.9	92.9	61.9	90.3	970.9	209.9	478.1	228.0	32.4
1893	5,500.4	3,314.4	1,555.3	1,182.7	218.5	104.9	98.3	54.0	100.7	1,124.2	259.4	566.9	233.6	35.9
1892	5,331.3	2,908.8	1,251.4	1,062.3	230.5	104.7	109.3	52.1	98.5	1,255.8	297.2	632.8	263.8	37.0
1891	5,284.3	2,964.9	1,308.5	1,079.2	226.6	97.9	101.2	62.7	88.9	1,196.9	289.3	603.3	244.2	35.3
1890	5,002.2	2,705.3	1,155.5	991.4	215.4	90.1	97.3	75.4	80.2	1,196.0	299.6	588.8	249.8	34.5
1889	5,080.4	2,905.7	1,434.3	956.6	202.5	81.6	93.9	59.5	77.2	1,132.9	281.7	560.8	236.1	32.1
1879	3,441.7	1,996.1	962.9	716.5	119.7	40.4	61.5	39.7	55.5	828.2	263.1	358.2	173.7	16.2
1869	2,813.3	1,594.2	673.1	699.1	74.7	37.7	30.6	29.4	49.7	665.4	224.5	229.8	185.3	12.8

See footnotes at end of table.

MANUFACTURES

Series P 318–374. Value of Output of Finished Commodities and Construction Materials Destined for Domestic Consumption at Current Producers' Prices, and Implicit Price Indexes for Major Commodity Groups (Shaw): 1869 to 1939—Con.

[In millions of dollars]

Year	Toys, games, and sporting goods	Tires and tubes	Total	Household furniture	Heating and cooking apparatus, etc.	Electrical household appliances and supplies	Radios	Housefurnishings	China and household utensils	Musical instruments	Jewelry, silverware, clocks, and watches	Printing and publishing books	Luggage	Passenger vehicles, motor
	332	333	334	335	336	337	338	339	340	341	342	343	344	345
1939			4,973.1											
1938			3,747.3											
1937	190.2	261.2	5,742.1	478.7	341.0	332.6	218.0	640.9	241.6	52.0	272.6	161.6	42.5	2,212.9
1936			5,158.0											
1935	140.3	215.1	4,256.8	323.7	237.5	217.8	167.4	468.3	204.8	31.5	189.5	131.1	31.0	1,688.3
1934			3,307.2											
1933	95.8	196.7	2,321.3	226.9	147.1	110.3	98.0	311.6	150.4	24.1	116.0	92.1	19.1	725.3
1932	96.9	194.5	2,047.4	205.4	123.0	82.2	94.2	252.0	138.9	35.0	108.5	102.9	18.4	603.2
1931	149.1	273.4	3,251.9	333.2	206.2	144.4	154.7	373.6	185.9	48.7	178.8	141.5	29.4	1,074.1
1930	182.2	336.9	4,272.6	441.4	254.2	160.0	230.6	402.7	196.4	103.4	263.8	174.3	44.5	1,538.0
1929	214.6	437.8	6,312.0	600.4	347.3	176.7	366.0	643.3	274.0	111.9	402.7	192.3	70.3	2,567.0
1928	200.9	551.0	5,936.1	629.3	314.2	152.7	298.7	627.5	275.7	148.6	396.3	179.7	67.9	2,294.9
1927	182.5	574.9	5,435.8	625.5	339.4	146.3	181.5	584.7	229.3	176.2	387.6	172.1	65.9	1,967.8
1926	177.2	616.3	6,109.0	638.2	364.3	137.5	206.7	591.6	271.6	189.3	398.9	155.4	66.4	2,504.3
1925	164.2	555.1	5,785.7	622.9	346.1	106.3	168.2	604.0	240.1	173.6	384.3	149.8	66.4	2,340.2
1924	154.6	382.0	5,034.3	614.0	322.2	83.4	139.3	547.1	181.5	178.5	363.9	145.0	57.8	1,922.5
1923	167.1	348.3	5,366.7	578.9	322.0	76.3	50.3	600.0	239.0	215.1	388.1	130.7	69.2	2,188.8
1922	131.1	335.8	4,056.5	501.1	239.2	58.6	26.9	470.0	167.7	187.7	327.0	124.9	52.6	1,546.1
1921	124.1	323.5	3,270.3	466.6	186.5	63.2	12.2	374.6	166.8	166.4	263.1	122.0	51.0	1,115.5
1920	148.8	678.9	4,899.3	620.5	345.6	82.8	17.0	574.8	265.7	264.2	383.2	140.0	78.2	1,628.3
1919 [2]	155.8	546.6	4,075.6	509.0	242.5	65.1	14.3	430.2	201.7	242.0	427.8	128.2	70.4	1,292.6
1919 [2]	146.4	515.4	3,921.2	494.7	263.5	84.5	--------	375.2	230.1	248.3	409.7	127.4	64.2	1,286.9
1918	125.8	491.3	2,646.9	329.0	216.8	67.5	--------	320.1	197.6	144.2	194.9	99.2	52.2	762.7
1917	198.5	329.1	2,799.0	300.6	194.2	58.8	--------	288.6	221.7	134.7	219.2	89.8	36.7	996.7
1916	113.0	156.1	2,396.1	271.7	142.5	41.2	--------	234.9	160.9	116.2	221.7	76.7	39.6	873.7
1915	73.5	104.9	1,700.2	212.3	119.4	23.7	--------	181.4	126.1	90.2	144.1	73.3	25.9	537.8
1914	67.1	92.7	1,570.4	222.5	110.5	18.8	--------	190.7	125.9	91.6	154.6	68.1	26.5	399.6
1913	64.0	86.6	1,675.1	236.7	124.9	22.2	--------	209.3	130.2	104.4	196.0	77.8	34.0	372.8
1912	59.3	58.3	1,538.4	220.5	131.5	19.7	--------	199.1	122.4	95.2	190.9	66.3	33.9	311.3
1911	58.7	45.5	1,339.2	204.1	104.1	15.7	--------	187.5	116.7	81.3	186.1	59.1	36.1	209.2
1910	54.4	36.0	1,331.6	202.4	97.3	16.3	--------	195.7	114.1	77.6	186.1	60.3	32.8	203.8
1909	52.9	23.4	1,212.8	192.0	93.8	11.8	--------	184.2	102.9	76.8	175.9	62.9	28.5	154.3
1908	43.3	17.5	1,011.0	152.6	84.2	7.7	--------	147.1	93.6	63.0	128.6	53.8	23.6	132.2
1907	60.9	15.6	1,178.1	185.1	101.2	10.2	--------	182.8	120.7	87.8	180.9	56.8	27.7	89.6
1906	50.4	12.5	1,129.5	190.3	103.4	8.0	--------	185.8	122.6	81.2	174.0	55.9	23.9	62.7
1905	46.3	9.3	954.8	160.8	85.8	4.7	--------	156.7	108.7	71.1	144.1	56.7	20.1	35.6
1904	41.3	5.7	826.9	142.4	73.6	3.3	--------	146.2	91.7	57.7	120.9	53.6	18.9	21.4
1903	40.1	4.3	825.7	139.2	78.8	3.8	--------	152.5	90.8	65.1	120.5	51.5	15.8	11.3
1902	37.8	5.5	786.3	129.4	78.6	3.2	--------	146.8	78.5	57.2	117.0	49.2	14.9	9.3
1901	36.5	6.2	718.9	118.7	70.7	2.6	--------	128.8	73.5	48.8	103.6	47.4	13.1	7.8
1900	29.0	7.8	658.7	106.9	61.9	2.4	--------	126.8	69.5	42.4	100.0	44.3	12.0	6.0
1899	27.0	12.7	634.3	104.1	59.2	1.9	--------	115.6	60.9	34.2	97.1	45.0	12.6	4.2
1898	23.4	19.0	528.9	89.4	46.3	--------	--------	95.4	52.0	27.8	74.0	40.8	8.8	--------
1897	24.8	18.1	506.5	88.4	50.7	--------	--------	96.0	51.0	24.5	63.6	33.7	8.8	--------
1896	25.4	9.8	475.2	90.2	45.6	--------	--------	90.6	51.0	22.8	58.5	34.6	9.2	--------
1895	26.4	7.9	497.7	94.0	35.5	--------	--------	102.6	45.9	27.9	69.2	35.6	8.9	--------
1894	22.4	--------	429.3	82.4	31.0	--------	--------	88.9	39.3	19.9	58.3	28.4	11.1	--------
1893	28.4	--------	496.3	100.2	35.3	--------	--------	100.1	43.5	23.2	71.7	34.3	12.9	--------
1892	25.0	--------	579.3	115.0	38.9	--------	--------	112.6	52.9	34.6	90.3	34.9	15.6	--------
1891	24.8	--------	556.8	100.5	39.1	--------	--------	114.9	51.7	33.0	86.7	33.4	13.9	--------
1890	23.3	--------	538.7	95.3	37.9	--------	--------	103.9	49.3	32.9	90.2	33.9	13.4	--------
1889	22.3	--------	499.2	93.4	38.9	--------	--------	97.6	46.4	28.2	74.5	34.7	10.7	--------
1879	17.0	--------	304.3	65.2	23.0	--------	--------	56.7	31.2	14.3	43.3	19.1	7.1	--------
1869	13.0	--------	262.7	58.5	26.4	--------	--------	40.1	26.0	10.8	41.6	8.4	7.7	--------

See footnotes at end of table.

Series **P 318–374.** Value of Output of Finished Commodities and Construction Materials Destined for Domestic Consumption at Current Producers' Prices, and Implicit Price Indexes for Major Commodity Groups (Shaw): 1869 to 1939—Con.

[In millions of dollars]

Year	Consumer durable—Con.						Producer durable							
	Motor vehicle accessories	Passenger vehicles (horse drawn) and accessories	Motorcycles and bicycles	Pleasure craft	Ophthalmic products and artificial limbs	Monuments and tombstones	Total	Industrial machinery and equipment	Tractors	Electrical equipment, industrial and commercial	Farm equipment	Office and store machinery and equipment	Office and store furniture and fixtures	Locomotive and railroad cars
	346	347	348	349	350	351	352	353	354	355	356	357	358	359
1939							4,740.5							
1938							3,835.1							
1937	594.6		30.8	25.4	70.9	26.0	5,039.1	1,883.7	223.7	673.8	668.5	204.9	176.8	119.1
1936							4,085.3							
1935	463.6		16.8	14.1	50.1	21.3	2,978.6	1,126.0	133.3	361.2	345.3	140.6	111.1	33.0
1934							2,370.7							
1933	228.2		7.5	4.8	39.1	20.8	1,487.1	577.1	12.6	200.9	78.8	78.8	70.3	13.6
1932	211.9		4.6	9.3	32.0	25.7	1,399.4	525.8	15.8	215.5	70.9	78.5	74.9	37.0
1931	273.1		7.7	16.8	40.3	43.6	2,628.3	938.2	19.6	499.5	163.4	116.5	151.7	78.0
1930	326.1		9.2	24.6	48.3	54.9	4,328.2	1,457.8	95.4	722.2	338.5	165.3	203.5	352.7
1929	407.6		10.6	26.2	52.1	63.6	5,628.4	2,017.2	121.8	1,000.1	386.5	217.8	288.7	347.6
1928	411.7		12.0	17.4	48.7	61.0	4,662.5	1,644.1	104.1	895.0	356.5	213.6	245.8	245.1
1927	419.8		10.1	17.8	49.7	61.9	4,320.2	1,476.0	91.3	741.2	340.4	201.2	249.0	318.5
1926	440.2		11.9	22.4	46.6	63.8	4,667.5	1,606.8	87.4	776.4	355.4	200.1	242.3	399.3
1925	444.3		11.3	15.0	46.6	66.8	4,256.0	1,486.4	70.3	666.2	306.5	196.4	236.1	353.1
1924	337.2		13.0	14.0	48.6	66.4	3,948.5	1,303.8	52.1	655.0	265.9	179.2	229.5	481.1
1923	355.8		16.3	12.1	58.5	65.6	4,395.5	1,510.9	63.5	598.1	315.5	182.0	201.3	635.5
1922	243.4		8.9	6.2	48.6	47.6	2,964.0	1,085.2	43.4	415.8	160.7	132.4	136.8	265.6
1921	169.5		10.2	9.4	46.6	46.9	2,939.1	922.8	49.6	406.6	248.1	114.0	115.5	313.6
1920	313.4		20.8	14.7	67.8	82.3	5,277.0	1,635.8	197.4	557.9	270.6	160.6	135.1	563.3
1919 [2]	282.6		24.0	13.9	58.2	73.4	5,544.5	1,434.3	171.6	460.8	394.6	156.4	100.3	560.7
1919 [2]	168.0	26.4	19.0	5.1	45.0	73.4	5,358.4	1,440.5	152.6	365.7	343.8	125.4	86.4	460.9
1918	85.8	35.3	18.9	1.5	71.1	50.0	5,449.7	1,575.8	136.6	339.9	301.8	157.8	65.7	734.0
1917	120.5	38.8	16.7	3.3	36.5	42.3	3,781.8	1,358.1	50.7	325.2	250.0	140.5	61.3	610.6
1916	104.0	31.0	16.3	4.0	23.9	37.9	2,526.3	906.0	25.8	253.9	237.1	98.8	51.6	363.4
1915	61.0	30.5	13.3	3.4	20.2	37.5	1,570.4	536.8	22.7	160.2	205.1	63.0	43.3	142.2
1914	49.9	35.6	16.2	3.6	15.5	41.0	1,477.6	460.2	16.7	147.0	187.8	50.9	50.8	203.2
1913	46.1	40.1	21.9	4.1	12.3	42.1	1,827.3	543.4	4.4	177.1	202.4	55.4	54.3	422.5
1912	39.3	41.6	12.0	3.9	10.6	40.3	1,634.5	517.1	8.1	162.1	187.3	50.2	54.3	303.4
1911	26.3	45.9	9.4	4.3	10.9	42.4	1,347.6	476.6		133.5	168.2	43.8	48.7	161.7
1910	26.9	53.3	7.3	4.4	10.7	42.6	[3]1,524.2	512.4		144.4	170.6	48.4	50.1	203.3
1909	21.1	49.8	5.6	4.3	10.5	38.4	1,243.4	446.9		111.2	166.5	40.1	48.6	127.0
1908	17.3	48.8	4.9	3.4	9.3	40.9	1,036.5	331.2		83.2	137.7	27.9	40.4	137.1
1907	11.3	63.8	6.5	6.1	9.4	38.3	1,583.5	510.9		127.5	161.6	42.7	49.1	351.2
1906	7.8	62.4	4.9	4.3	7.9	34.5	1,466.1	504.6		119.9	160.5	38.8	50.7	299.4
1905	4.3	61.2	5.4	3.8	7.1	28.7	1,167.3	404.7		84.9	130.2	28.0	43.1	214.3
1904	2.5	57.8	2.5	3.1	5.6	25.7	993.2	327.1		75.9	125.2	20.3	38.2	162.7

Year	Consumer durable—Con.					Producer durable—Con.						
	Passenger vehicles (horse drawn) and accessories	Motorcycles and bicycles	Pleasure craft	Ophthalmic products and artificial limbs	Monuments and tombstones	Total	Industrial machinery and equipment	Electrical equipment, industrial and commercial	Farm equipment	Office and store machinery and equipment	Office and store furniture and fixtures	Locomotive and railroad cars
	347	348	349	350	351	352	353	355	356	357	358	359
1903	56.7	4.2	3.6	5.8	25.9	1,129.0	405.9	91.9	120.2	23.9	37.8	194.6
1902	58.8	6.4	3.5	5.7	27.9	1,062.7	371.3	80.6	152.9	21.9	33.6	157.8
1901	64.1	7.7	3.7	5.2	23.2	914.3	330.3	68.5	110.4	18.9	30.2	127.4
1900	50.1	10.5	2.7	4.7	18.4	895.6	347.6	68.2	100.6	19.7	27.2	130.0
1899	53.5	18.9	2.1	4.8	20.3	756.6	267.5	56.1	99.4	14.3	24.2	114.1
1898	43.5	27.8	1.4	4.3	17.5	571.6	194.9	34.3	85.6	10.6	21.4	82.1
1897	40.9	27.0	1.2	4.0	16.6	492.9	182.3	24.4	58.4	9.7	21.8	67.7
1896	39.3	14.9	1.2	3.8	13.4	519.6	209.8	20.5	46.6	11.6	22.5	75.2
1895	45.2	14.1	1.3	3.7	13.8	495.7	193.1	20.0	59.3	10.7	23.7	53.7
1894	50.9		1.0	3.3	14.9	435.7	157.7	15.8	58.7	8.6	21.2	47.4
1893	58.5		1.4	3.3	11.9	565.5	184.9	16.6	71.2	9.5	26.1	104.1
1892	63.3		1.5	3.2	16.6	587.4	196.5	22.7	75.4	9.8	30.1	90.9
1891	62.4		1.6	2.9	16.7	565.7	185.5	23.7	75.3	9.0	26.8	87.6
1890	60.4		1.5	2.6	17.3	562.2	185.6	21.8	89.0	8.7	25.8	81.5
1889	54.0	1.9	1.5	2.3	15.2	542.6	184.5	13.1	83.9	8.2	25.6	87.3
1879	35.1		.9	.8	7.5	313.1	98.6	1.9	67.3	3.6	15.9	36.3
1869	35.7		.6	.4	6.6	291.0	110.4		50.0	3.1	13.6	40.8

See footnotes at end of table.

Series **P 318–374.** Value of Output of Finished Commodities and Construction Materials Destined for Domestic Consumption at Current Producers' Prices, and Implicit Price Indexes for Major Commodity Groups (Shaw): 1869 to 1939—Con.

[In millions of dollars]

Year	Producer durable—Con.							Construction materials			Implicit price index (1913 = 100)				
	Ships and boats	Business vehicles, motor	Business vehicles, horse-drawn	Aircraft	Professional and scientific equipment	Carpenters' and mechanics' tools	Misc. subsidiary durable equipment	Total	Manufactured	Non-manufactured	Perishable	Semidurable	Consumer durable	Producer durable	Construction materials
	360	361	362	363	364	365	366	367	368	369	370	371	372	373	374
1939	------	------	------	------	------	------	------	3,701.6	------	------	[4]110.6	[4]123.1	[4]92.1	[5]110.4	159.0
1938	------	------	------	------	------	------	------	3,159.0	------	------	[4]114.6	[4]122.7	[4]92.8	[4]112.8	159.0
1937	128.6	496.6	------	48.4	49.8	95.3	269.9	3,945.8	------	------	126.4	132.6	91.9	112.1	167.3
1936	------	------	------	------	------	------	------	3,331.5	------	------	[4]122.6	[4]120.6	[4]90.8	[4]102.0	152.2
1935	48.2	359.3	------	19.1	36.4	66.3	198.8	2,375.0	------	------	122.4	119.2	93.6	99.6	149.8
1934	------	------	------	------	------	------	------	1,909.9	------	------	[4]107.8	[4]120.6	[4]98.5	[4]107.6	151.4
1933	30.4	159.0	------	16.5	32.0	49.1	168.1	1,536.1	------	------	95.0	105.0	96.8	104.6	136.0
1932	49.7	125.5	------	14.1	31.7	31.0	129.0	1,362.7	------	------	96.7	93.6	98.0	112.9	126.8
1931	82.0	247.0	------	30.0	48.6	53.9	199.9	2,552.1	------	------	114.1	109.2	99.8	117.2	140.2
1930	94.9	373.0	------	28.8	91.6	99.8	304.7	3,779.8	------	------	135.1	122.0	104.3	125.6	158.4
1929	78.2	510.8	------	56.0	109.6	124.6	369.7	5,007.5	------	------	147.4	130.7	106.4	131.1	167.8
1928	60.4	318.3	------	51.1	92.1	131.6	304.9	4,793.8	------	------	150.0	131.7	105.4	136.5	165.6
1927	70.8	302.3	------	19.4	87.7	104.2	318.4	4,845.2	------	------	146.9	137.4	104.0	138.5	166.6
1926	86.5	377.2	------	17.6	86.5	110.2	321.9	5,111.5	------	------	154.3	150.4	98.8	138.4	175.6
1925	55.7	389.6	------	10.5	74.9	109.8	300.4	4,950.4	------	------	154.3	160.0	103.3	135.0	178.5
1924	67.4	323.4	------	10.9	66.0	106.4	208.0	4,465.3	------	------	143.5	164.9	108.5	134.8	179.5
1923	73.1	321.8	------	11.5	64.7	115.4	302.1	4,647.3	------	------	147.7	177.6	108.2	138.7	190.4
1922	93.6	237.2	------	8.8	51.7	87.8	245.1	3,568.9	------	------	141.2	163.2	113.4	135.2	170.7
1921	272.7	170.4	------	6.1	48.8	62.1	208.6	2,956.7	------	------	146.5	173.8	139.8	164.5	172.2
1920	808.1	332.9	------	8.7	74.8	128.7	403.0	4,777.1	------	------	213.4	265.6	157.8	181.0	262.0
1919 [2]	1,381.3	344.3	------	10.0	62.0	120.6	347.6	3,508.1	------	------	196.5	219.0	134.5	184.1	202.7
1919 [2]	1,389.5	344.0	42.5	8.4	74.5	174.8	349.3	3,703.2	3,224.5	478.7	199.9	212.4	136.4	185.0	202.7
1918	805.3	417.0	50.6	174.7	119.2	210.6	360.7	3,217.5	2,824.6	392.8	182.8	206.2	121.9	175.7	174.5
1917	243.8	189.1	51.1	21.3	57.0	131.7	291.6	3,058.6	2,702.9	355.7	161.1	161.0	100.8	145.5	154.9
1916	103.7	111.6	37.4	1.4	32.5	97.5	205.6	2,627.8	2,309.5	318.2	120.6	117.6	90.4	120.5	119.0
1915	66.8	68.6	34.0	.6	29.4	57.0	140.6	2,010.7	1,732.9	277.8	103.7	96.5	90.3	106.4	94.6
1914	43.5	36.2	36.9	.2	23.7	49.6	171.0	2,043.8	1,758.7	285.2	101.4	96.5	94.4	100.3	93.1
1913	47.6	47.1	39.9	.2	17.7	53.6	161.7	2,384.4	2,083.2	301.2	100.0	100.0	100.0	100.0	100.0
1912	44.4	49.9	41.9	.3	14.2	48.5	152.8	2,154.1	1,854.9	299.2	102.8	98.6	66.2	97.6	97.9
1911	42.7	25.9	44.2	------	13.4	41.9	147.1	1,942.8	1,655.4	287.4	96.2	97.4	95.8	99.1	97.0
1910	40.8	12.5	48.3	------	12.6	49.1	151.6	2,049.7	1,728.0	321.7	100.0	100.9	93.5	95.3	97.6
1909	38.2	7.3	43.0	------	12.4	47.7	154.6	1,992.5	1,686.7	305.8	96.9	99.3	90.4	94.3	94.8
1908	34.4	3.5	40.2	------	8.0	35.7	157.4	1,820.1	1,513.9	306.3	92.3	96.0	96.6	89.3	93.3
1907	66.3	2.3	49.5	------	11.8	52.7	157.9	2,111.5	1,770.1	341.4	89.7	102.6	97.7	93.6	101.0
1906	54.8	1.8	46.2	------	10.7	43.4	135.2	1,911.1	1,622.8	288.3	84.9	98.2	89.1	90.6	96.6
1905	55.6	1.5	43.1	------	8.2	37.9	115.6	1,578.1	1,334.0	244.1	86.9	90.5	85.3	89.7	87.0
1904	53.6	1.4	38.9	------	6.4	34.7	108.7	1,394.3	1,167.3	227.0	85.5	86.0	83.5	88.8	81.7
1903	61.3	------	37.6	------	7.8	37.7	110.4	1,447.4	1,218.9	228.4	83.3	86.0	82.7	86.2	84.5
1902	60.8	------	37.9	------	7.5	35.7	102.8	1,493.6	1,270.6	223.0	84.1	83.5	79.9	89.7	82.5
1901	64.7	------	40.2	------	5.0	29.2	89.5	1,306.3	1,119.2	187.1	79.6	81.9	77.5	88.9	80.7
1900	46.9	------	31.4	------	5.3	26.9	91.8	1,222.7	1,046.8	175.8	80.2	86.7	77.0	90.0	85.8
1899	36.1	------	32.5	------	4.0	24.5	83.9	1,006.3	855.7	150.6	75.4	81.0	70.0	88.1	80.7
1898	24.4	------	25.9	------	3.2	19.8	69.4	937.8	795.8	141.9	74.9	77.3	67.5	82.5	69.9
1897	20.7	------	24.2	------	2.7	16.8	64.2	963.4	821.0	142.4	72.0	75.5	63.0	75.9	67.1
1896	20.8	------	23.0	------	3.2	18.6	67.9	880.3	751.4	128.9	70.9	75.5	63.8	66.1	71.8
1895	22.7	------	25.7	------	3.0	19.1	64.8	1,033.2	881.2	152.0	75.0	77.1	67.4	72.2	70.7
1894	17.8	------	28.4	------	2.5	16.6	61.0	1,004.1	867.0	137.1	76.3	80.5	72.3	78.2	71.6
1893	23.9	------	32.1	------	3.0	22.5	71.7	1,074.3	933.1	141.3	84.7	90.5	74.8	78.4	75.4
1892	24.9	------	34.1	------	3.5	24.6	74.9	1,335.3	1,164.8	170.7	79.8	92.6	79.2	80.0	75.9
1891	26.9	------	33.5	------	3.2	24.7	69.5	1,076.0	940.0	136.0	84.8	92.6	82.1	81.1	80.2
1890	24.6	------	32.0	------	3.2	23.6	66.5	1,216.5	1,070.5	146.1	86.1	94.9	82.3	87.7	84.3
1889	24.7	------	28.4	------	2.9	20.8	63.3	838.9	712.2	126.7	88.3	95.6	81.9	88.2	85.0
1879	19.4	------	18.0	------	1.6	13.4	37.1	444.2	365.9	78.3	86.6	102.2	83.2	95.4	81.4
1869	11.5	------	18.1	------	1.6	10.5	31.4	377.4	324.8	52.6	141.2	158.5	119.4	163.8	107.4

[1] Does not agree with source, which is in error.
[2] Shaw's estimates for 1869–1919; Kuznets' estimates adjusted by Shaw for 1919–1939. See source, p. 104, for explanation.
[3] Agrees with source; however, figures for components do not add to total shown.
[4] Indexes derived by weighting the individual group indexes by the average current price estimates for 1933, 1935, and 1937. The composite indexes thus calculated were used to interpolate and extrapolate the implicit indexes for 1933, 1935, and 1937.
[5] Based on the movement of the NBER price index for processed capital equipment goods.

Transportation

Highway Transportation (Series Q 1-263)

Q 1–263. General note.

In 1894, the Federal Government created an Office of Road Inquiry to initiate experiments and conduct inquiries concerning the best methods of road building. It was succeeded by the Office of Public Roads and Rural Engineering in 1916 and by the Bureau of Public Roads in 1918 (the latter was called the Public Roads Administration during 1939–1949). The bureau was transferred to the Department of Transportation in 1966 and its functions assigned to the Federal Highway Administration. Surveys of highway mileage, revenues, and expenditures were made in 1904, 1909, and 1914.

In 1916, Congress passed the first of the many Federal-aid highway acts, under which the Federal Government has contributed to the cost of constructing highways designated as parts of the Federal-aid system. The Federal Highway Administration administers Federal legislation providing for the improvement, in cooperation with the States, of roads on the Federal-aid primary, secondary, and interstate highway systems. As the principal road-building agency of the Federal Government, it also cooperates with the Forest Service, the National Park Service, and other Federal agencies in the construction of roads in national forests, parks, and other areas.

The principal sources (1973) of data on public roads and on ownership and operation of motor vehicles is the Federal Highway Administration's annual *Highway Statistics* and its *Highway Statistics, Summary to 1965*. Another major source of data is the Interstate Commerce Commission. Among its publications are the monthly *Transport Economics* and the *Annual Report*, containing data on all types of domestic transport and the annual *Transport Statistics in the United States*.

Various censuses conducted by the U.S. Bureau of the Census also provide data relating to transportation. Reports of the census of manufactures and the census of business and the *Annual Survey of Manufactures* present statistics on the motor vehicle and equipment industry and on retail, wholesale, and services aspects of this industry.

Q 1–11. Volume of domestic intercity passenger traffic, by type of transport, 1950–1970.

Source: U.S. Interstate Commerce Commission, *Annual Report* and *Transport Economics*, various issues.

Q 12–22. Volume of domestic intercity freight traffic, by type of transport, 1939–1970.

Source: U.S. Interstate Commerce Commission, 1939–1959, *Intercity Ton-Miles, 1939–1959*, Statement No. 6103; 1960–1970, *Annual Report* and *Transport Economics*, various issues.

This study is intended to show, on as nearly comparable a base as possible, the intercity ton-miles by the various means of transport. Information sufficient in quantity and accuracy is not available to cover all modes of transport on a comparable basis before 1939. Estimates of intercity ton-miles for a period from sometime before 1939 through part of World War II are contained in the Bureau of Transport Economics and Statistics release, *Postwar Traffic Levels*, Statement No. 4440, issued in 1944. These estimates, however, are not on bases comparable with those in the 1939–1959 series.

A ton, as used here, is 2,000 pounds; and a mile is 5,280 feet. A ton-mile is a ton of freight carried one mile. These definitions apply to all means of transport covered. To this extent, all figures presented here are comparable. Further, as far as possible, local switching, local delivery, lighterage, and rural to rural movements have been eliminated to confine operations to intercity only.

Q 23–35. Operating revenues, by type of transport, 1936–1970.

Source: Except for series Q 28, U.S. Interstate Commerce Commission, 1936–1956, *Statistics of Class I, II, and III Motor Carriers, 1939–1956*, Statement No. 589; 1957–1970, *Annual Report* and *Transport Economics*, various issues, and unpublished data. **Series Q 28**, U.S. Federal Aviation Administration, *FAA Statistical Handbook of Aviation*, various editions.

Q 36–46. Employment in selected types of transportation, 1947–1970.

Source: U.S. Bureau of Labor Statistics, *Employment and Earnings, United States, 1909–72*, Bulletin 1312–9, pp. 526–532.

Q 36, total. Represents about 80 percent of all employment in transportation. Data for types of transportation other than those shown here are available in the source only for shorter and current periods.

Q 47–49. Indexes of transportation output, 1889–1966.

Source: 1889–1946, National Bureau of Economic Research, New York, Harold Barger, *The Transportation Industries, 1889 to 1946* (copyright); 1947–1966, estimates by John W. Kendrick, George Washington University.

Sources of figures and methods of computation are described in Barger's book. The components of passenger traffic, series Q 48, are airlines, intercity buslines, waterways, and steam railroads. For freight traffic, series Q 49, the components are motor trucking, pipelines, waterways, and steam railroads.

Q 50–55. Mileage of rural roads and municipal streets, 1904–1970.

Source: U.S. Bureau of Public Roads, 1904–1920, *Highway Statistics, Summary to 1955*. U.S. Federal Highway Administration, 1921–1965, *Highway Statistics, Summary to 1965*; 1966–1970, *Highway Statistics*, annual issues.

Rural roads are defined roughly as those roads located outside of incorporated communities or delimited places generally having more than 1,000 inhabitants. Estimates for earlier years for total mileage of rural roads are (in thousands of miles): 1904, 2,151; 1909, 2,200; 1914, 2,446.

Municipal and other mileage figures for 1934 and 1935 represent only mileage on municipal extensions of State systems, which are State administered. Mileage not on State or county systems was initially included in 1936 (67,000 miles). Mileage on local city streets was first included in 1941 (274,000 miles for that year). Municipal extensions are continuations of State System roads through communities with more than 1,000 inhabitants. Although mileage in places having more than 2,500 inhabitants was not originally included in Federal-aid programs, those places have been eligible for such aid in more recent years.

Q 56–58. Surfaced mileage, 1904–1970.

Source: 1904–1940, see first source for series Q 50–55; 1941–1970, see other sources for series Q 50–55.

High-type surfaced roads include bituminous penetration, sheet asphalt, bituminous concrete, portland cement concrete, vitrified brick, and block pavements of asphalt, wood, and stone. For some years, they also include dual-type surfaces and a small amount of unclassified mileage. Low-type surfaced roads include sand, clay, selected soil, untreated gravel, bituminous surface-treated, mixed bituminous and treated gravel, chert, shale, waterbound macadam.

Q 59–63. Mileage built by State highway departments, 1923–1970.

Source: 1920–1933, see first source for series Q 50–55; 1934–1970, see other sources for series Q 50–55.

Mileage built is mileage on which construction work creates a newly located road or is regarded as significantly improving the condition of an existing road. It does not include work designed to maintain or restore the condition of an existing road without material betterment. Mileage resurfaced or rebuilt to higher standards is the bulk of mileage built. Construction of earth roads consists of aligning, grading, and draining. See also text for series Q 56–58.

Q 64–68. Mileage and cost of Federal-aid highway systems, 1917–1970.

Source: **Series Q 64**, U.S. Federal Highway Administration, 1923–1965, *Highway Statistics, Summary to 1965;* 1966–1970, *Highway Statistics*, annual issues. **Series Q 65–68**, U.S. Bureau of Public Roads, 1917–1955, *Highway Statistics, Summary to 1955;* 1956–1965, *Highway Statistics*, annual issues; 1966–1970, see source for series Q 64.

In 1912, the Congress authorized $500,000 for an experimental program of rural post-road construction. However, it was not until the Federal-Aid Road Act of 1916 that the present cooperative Federal-State highway program was established on a continuing basis. In order to accelerate the improvement of the main traveled roads, Congress in 1921 authorized designation of a system of principal interstate and intercounty roads, limited to 7 percent of the total rural mileage then existing. The use of Federal aid was restricted to this system, and to rural mileage only.

Urban highway improvement first came in for its share of the Federal-State program when the Federal-Aid Highway Act of 1944 specifically authorized the use of funds for Federal-aid highways in urban areas. In addition, the Act provided for the designation of a Federal-aid secondary system and a National System of Interstate Highways. The Federal-Aid Highway Act of 1956 provided substantially increased sums for the Federal-aid primary and secondary systems for a 3-year period, and established a long-range plan for financing accelerated completion of the 41,000-mile interstate system.

Federal funds are available for expenditure only on the designated Federal-aid systems and, in general, must be matched by an equal amount of State funds. However, under the Federal-aid Act of 1954 the Federal share for the Interstate System was raised to 60 percent, and under the 1956 Act the proportion was increased to 90 percent. Federal aid may not be expended for maintenance. The cost of most Federal-aid projects is paid initially out of State highway funds, or in some cases by counties or other local governments. The Federal share is paid as reimbursement to the States as work progresses, with final payment made after completion.

Federal authorizations have usually been made on a biennial basis and apportioned among the States for use within a 3-year period. Figures for State funds shown here are based on legal matching ratios determined by applicable Federal-aid acts. In States having public lands in excess of 5 percent of their total area, the Federal share is proportionally increased.

Q 69–81. Class I intercity motor carriers of passengers and property, 1939–1970.

Source: U.S. Interstate Commerce Commission, *Transport Statistics in the United States*, part 7, annual issues.

Prior to 1950, class I for-hire motor carriers were classified by the Interstate Commerce Commission as those with $100,000 or more of gross annual operating revenue; for 1950–1958, those having gross operating revenue of $200,000 for a 3-year period; and, beginning 1969, those having gross operating revenue of $1,000,000 for a 3-year period.

Q 82–96. State highway finances, 1890–1970.

Source: 1890–1920, see first source for series Q 50–55; 1921–1970, see other sources for series Q 50–55.

A State highway-user tax is defined as a special tax or fee (except tolls) levied upon motor-vehicle users because of their use of the highways. Highway-user taxes include motor-fuel taxes, motor-vehicle registration and associated fees, and special taxes applicable only to motor carriers; these taxes are separable and apart from property, excise, business, or other taxes paid by the general public.

In many States, specific portions of the revenue from each type of highway-user tax are allocated to particular highway purposes. A number of States, however, place all highway-user revenue in a highway fund, and a few have a general State fund into which go all types of revenue.   For the latter group of States, each particular appropriation or expenditure for highway purposes is considered to have been made from motor-fuel taxes, motor-vehicle registration fees, and motor-carrier taxes in proportion to the relative amount of revenue received from each of these three sources.

The largest share of receipts from State highway-user taxes is expended on State highways, but a portion is also allocated for local roads and streets, and a small amount used for nonhighway purposes.

Q 97–112. Receipts and disbursements of highway funds by counties and townships, 1921–1970.

Source: U.S. Federal Highway Administration, 1921–1964, *Highway Statistics, Summary to 1965*, tables LF-201 and LF-202; 1965–1970, *Highway Statistics*, annual issues, tables LF-1 and LF-2.

Q 113–128. Receipts and disbursements of highway funds by municipalities, 1921–1970.

Source: U.S. Federal Highway Administration, 1921–1964, *Highway Statistics, Summary to 1965*, tables UF-201 and UF-202; 1965–1970, *Highway Statistics*, annual issues, tables UF-1 and UF-2.

Q 129–135. Highway construction—contracts awarded, 1947–1970.

Source: U.S. Bureau of Domestic Commerce (formerly Business and Defense Services Administration), *Construction Review*, various issues.

Highways include streets, roads, alleys, bridges, vehicular tunnels, viaducts, sidewalks, curbs, and gutters, except when installed by private builders as a part of land development; forest and park roads; new culverts and extension of old culverts; right-of-way drainage, erosion control, lighting, and guard rails; and earth-work protective structures in connection with road improvements.

The data for State and locally owned highways were compiled by the Bureau of Domestic Commerce (formerly the Business and Defense Services Administration), Department of Commerce, from: (1) Information published by a number of private construction news services; (2) information received from selected State and local government agencies; and (3) data compiled by the Bureau of Public Roads (now the Federal Highway Administration) and the Bureau of Labor Statistics.

Data on contracts awarded for federally owned construction were compiled by BLS from reports submitted by the various Federal agencies having construction operations.

Q 136–147. Public highway debt—long–term highway obligations of State and local governments, 1945–1970.

Source: U.S. Federal Highway Administration (formerly Bureau of Public Roads), releases.

Q 148–151. Motor-vehicle factory sales, 1900–1970.

Source: Automobile Manufacturers Association, *Automobile Facts and Figures*, various issues.

Production of passenger cars was discontinued in February 1942 to economize resources for World War II purposes, but some vehicles remaining in factory stocks were sold under rationing orders in subsequent war years. The War Production Board authorized resumption of production as of July 1, 1945, but no new cars were actually produced until 1946.

Q 152–155. Motor-vehicle registrations, 1900–1970.

Source: U.S. Federal Highway Administration, 1900–1965, *Highway Statistics, Summary to 1965*; 1966–1970, *Summary of Motor Vehicle Registrations by Years*, table MV-200, and unpublished data.

Figures are based on reports and unpublished data of State motor-vehicle registration departments. They include both privately and publicly owned vehicles.

Motor-vehicle data for the early years of the century are incomplete, largely because few States required their registration, and hence had no records of the number of vehicles using roads and streets. As production of vehicles increased, shortly before the first World War, so did the number of registration laws. By 1921, all States had adopted some form of motor-vehicle registration.

Accompanying the growth in motor-vehicle registrations has been a corresponding diversity in the registration practices among the States. In general, motor vehicles are classified as private passenger cars, passenger carriers for hire, trucks, trailers, motorcycles, and property carriers for hire. Several States, however, still register buses with either trucks or passenger cars. These differences have made it necessary for the data-compiling agency to supplement the data submitted by the States with information obtained from special studies and from other sources.

Q 156–162. Motor-fuel usage, 1919–1970.

Source: U.S. Federal Highway Administration, 1919–1965, *Highway Statistics, Summary to 1965*; 1966–1970, *Analysis of Motor Fuel Consumption*, table G221, and unpublished data.

Fuel consumption figures for which reports from State authorities were not available have been estimated by the Federal Highway Administration (formerly Bureau of Public Roads). Motor fuel includes all gasoline used for any purpose (private and public), except military, plus any diesel or other fuels used solely for the propulsion of motor vehicles on public highways. Exports from the United States are excluded, and there is no duplication because of interstate shipment. Tractor fuels are not included. Nonhighway consumption includes all use off the highway, such as aviation, agriculture, marine, industrial, etc., and usually falls under the exemption or refund provisions of the motor-fuel tax law.

Q 163–174. Automobile insurance, 1946–1970.

Source: The Spectator, Philadelphia, 1946–1954, *Insurance Yearbook*; 1955–1965, *Insurance by States*; 1966–1969, *Property Liability Insurance Review*, annual. 1970, The National Underwriter Co., Cincinnati, *Argus F.C. & S. Chart*, annual (copyright).

Q 175–186. Percent distribution of automobile ownership, and financing, 1947–1970.

Source: The University of Michigan, Survey Research Center, Ann Arbor, *Survey of Consumer Finances* (copyright).

Q 187–198. Speed of motor vehicles on highways, 1945–1970.

Source: U.S. Federal Highway Administration, *Traffic Speed Trends*, and unpublished data.

Comparatively few speed studies were conducted on main rural highways until immediately prior to World War II. At that time, the average speeds of trucks, passenger cars, and buses were 41, 48, and 51 miles/hour, respectively. The low average speeds during World War II resulted from wartime restrictions on travel speeds and from gasoline rationing.

Speeds of passenger cars did not return to their prewar level until 1947. Trucks reached their prewar level in 1946, and buses in 1948. From 1948 through 1950 there was little change in vehicle speeds. Since then speeds consistently increased until 1970.

Q 199–205. Miles of travel by motor vehicles, 1921–1970.

Source: 1921–1935, U.S. Federal Works Agency, unpublished data, and U.S. Public Roads Administration, unpublished data; 1936–1965, see U.S. Federal Highway Administration sources for series Q 50–55.

Traffic volume information is obtained from automatic traffic recorders operating continuously at selected locations on the roads and streets of each State. The recorders are generally supplemented by periodic manual classification counts to determine the proportion of vehicles of each type, and each highway category, and by portable machine counts on the many road and street sections.

Q 206–207. Average miles of travel per vehicle, 1936–1970.

Source: See U.S. Federal Highway Administration sources for series Q 50–55.

Q 208–223. Motor-vehicle deaths and death rates, by age, 1913–1970.

Source: National Safety Council, Chicago, *Accident Facts, 1969*, p. 60; and *1974*, p. 60 (copyright).

Data for 1913 to 1932 were calculated from U.S. National Center for Health Statistics data for registration States. Data for 1933 to 1963, 1965 to 1967, 1969, and 1970 are national totals; those for 1964 and 1968 are National Safety Council estimates.

Q 224–232. Motor-vehicle accidents—number and deaths, by type of accident, 1913–1970.

Source: National Safety Council, Chicago, *Accident Facts, 1974*, and various annual issues (copyright).

Q 233–234. State and Federal gasoline tax rates, 1930–1970.

Source: See U.S. Federal Highway Administration sources for series Q 50–55.

State average tax is weighted by net gallons taxed at the various rates in the several States. No data are shown before 1930 because it was the first year in which all States had motor fuel taxes in effect for the whole year.

The precise dates of the changes in the Federal tax are as follows: June 21, 1932, 1 cent; June 17, 1933, 1.5 cents; January 1, 1934, 1 cent; July 1, 1940, 1.5 cents; November 1, 1951, 2 cents; July 1, 1956, 3 cents; October 1, 1959, 4 cents.

Q 235–250. Public transit mileage, equipment, passengers, and passenger revenue, 1917–1970.

Source: American Transit Association, *Transit Fact Book*, various annual issues (copyright); *The Transit Industry in the United States, Basic Data and Trends*, 1943 (copyright); mimeographed release on number of passengers, January 3, 1938.

Figures are estimates based on reports for more than 85 percent of the industry, which includes local motorbuses, electric street railways, elevated and subway lines, interurban electric railways, and transit coach lines.

Mileage estimates for trolley coaches, series Q 236, are miles of negative overhead wire. Mileage estimates for motorbuses, series Q 237, are miles of route, round trip. Equipment owned, railway cars, series Q 238, includes surface, subway, and elevated cars. The estimates for 1933 and 1934 for motorbuses owned, series Q 240, are probably understated. Revenue and nonrevenue passenger figures, series Q 241–244, exceed revenue passenger figures, series Q 245, chiefly because of free transfers.

Q 251–263. Oil pipelines operated and oil originated, 1921–1970.

Source: U.S. Interstate Commerce Commission, 1921–1953, *Sta-*

tistics of Railways in the United States, various annual issues; 1954–1970, *Transport Statistics in the United States*, part 6, *Oil Pipe Lines*.

Figures refer to pipelines operating in interstate commerce and regulated by ICC. Crude oil originated, series Q 252, includes both gathering and trunk lines.

For a discussion of statistics of oil pipelines, see ICC, *A Review of Statistics of Oil Pipe Lines, 1921–1941*, Statement 4280, mimeographed, 1942. The figure for mileage in 1938, which appears to have been revised, is from this Statement.

Figures for barrels of oil carried are as follows, in millions: 1925, 831; 1926, 836; 1927, 989; 1928, 1,053; 1929, 1,156; 1930, 1,172; 1931, 987. In these figures, a barrel handled by two or more pipelines in succession is counted each time it is handled. In the figures for barrels originated, this duplication is avoided.

★ ★ ★ ★ ★ ★ ★ ★ ★   **More Recent Data for *Historical Statistics* Series**   ★ ★ ★ ★ ★ ★ ★ ★ ★
★   ★
★   Statistics for more recent years in continuation of many of the still-active series shown here appear   ★
★   in annual issues of the *Statistical Abstract of the United States*, beginning with the 1975 edition. For   ★
★   direct linkage of the historical series to the tables in the *Abstract*, see Appendix I in the *Abstract*.   ★
★   ★
★ ★

Series **Q 1–11.** Volume of Domestic Intercity Passenger Traffic, by Type of Transport: 1950 to 1970

[**In billions of passenger-miles, except percent.** Airways, prior to 1959, and other types of transportation, prior to 1960, exclude Alaska and Hawaii. A passenger-mile is the movement of 1 passenger for the distance of 1 mile. Comprises public and private traffic, both revenue and nonrevenue]

Year	Total traffic, volume	Private automobiles		Airways [1]		Buses [2]		Railroads [3]		Inland waterways [4]	
		Volume	Percent of total	Volume	Percent of total	Volume	Percent of total	Volume	Percent of total	Volume	Percent of total
	1	2	3	4	5	6	7	8	9	10	11
1970	1,185	1,026	86.6	119	10.0	25	2.1	11	0.9	4.0	0.3
1969	1,138	977	85.9	120	10.5	25	2.2	12	1.1	3.8	.3
1968	1,079	936	86.8	101	9.4	25	2.3	13	1.2	3.4	.3
1967	1,021	890	87.2	87	8.6	25	2.4	15	1.5	3.4	.3
1966	971	856	88.2	69	7.1	25	2.5	17	1.8	3.4	.4
1965	920	818	88.7	58	6.3	24	2.6	18	1.9	3.1	.3
1964	896	802	89.5	49	5.5	23	2.6	18	2.1	2.8	.3
1963	853	766	89.8	43	5.0	23	2.6	19	2.2	2.8	.3
1962	818	736	90.0	37	4.6	22	2.7	20	2.5	2.7	.3
1961	791	714	90.2	35	4.4	20	2.6	21	2.6	2.3	.3
1960	784	706	90.1	34	4.3	19	2.5	22	2.8	2.7	.3
1959	765	687	89.9	33	4.3	20	2.7	22	2.9	2.0	.3
1958	760	685	90.1	29	3.8	21	2.7	24	3.1	2.1	.3
1957	748	670	89.6	28	3.8	21	2.9	26	3.5	1.9	.3
1956	751	670	89.2	26	3.4	25	3.4	29	3.8	1.9	.3
1955	716	637	89.0	23	3.2	25	3.6	29	4.0	1.7	.2
1954	673	597	88.7	20	2.9	26	3.8	29	4.4	1.7	.3
1953	655	576	87.9	17	2.7	28	4.3	32	4.9	1.5	.2
1952	575	496	86.1	15	2.6	29	5.0	35	6.0	1.4	.2
1951	535	458	85.6	13	2.4	27	5.1	35	6.6	1.3	.3
1950	508	438	86.2	10	2.0	26	5.2	32	6.4	1.2	.2

[1] Includes domestic commercial revenue service and private pleasure and business flying.
[2] Excludes schoolbuses.
[3] Includes electric railways.
[4] Includes Great Lakes.

Series **Q 12–22.** Volume of Domestic Intercity Freight Traffic, by Type of Transport: 1939 to 1970

[**In billions of ton-miles, except percent.** Motor vehicles and airways, prior to 1959, and other types of transportation, prior to 1960, exclude Alaska and Hawaii, except as noted. A ton-mile is the movement of 1 ton (2,000 pounds) of freight for the distance of 1 mile. Comprises public and private traffic, both revenue and nonrevenue]

Year	Total traffic, volume	Railroads [1]		Motor vehicles		Inland waterways [2]		Oil pipelines		Airways [3]	
		Volume	Percent of total	Volume	Percent of total	Volume	Percent of total	Volume	Percent of total	Volume	Percent of total
	12	13	14	15	16	17	18	19	20	21	22
1970	1,936	771	39.8	412	21.3	319	16.5	431	22.3	3.3	0.2
1969	1,895	774	40.8	404	21.3	303	16.0	411	21.7	3.2	.2
1968	1,839	757	41.2	396	21.6	291	15.9	391	21.3	2.9	.2
1967	1,776	742	41.8	389	21.9	281	15.9	361	20.3	2.6	.1
1966	1,759	762	43.3	381	21.7	281	16.0	333	18.9	2.3	.1
1965	1,651	721	43.7	359	21.8	262	15.9	306	18.6	1.9	.1
1964	1,556	679	43.7	356	22.9	250	16.1	269	17.3	1.5	.1
1963	1,469	644	43.8	336	22.9	234	15.9	253	17.3	1.3	.1
1962	1,387	616	44.4	309	22.3	223	16.1	238	17.1	1.3	.1
1961	1,326	586	44.2	296	22.4	210	15.8	233	17.6	.9	.1
1960	1,330	595	44.7	285	21.5	220	16.6	229	17.2	.8	.1
1959	1,303	599	46.0	279	21.4	197	15.1	227	17.4	.7	.1
1958	1,231	575	46.7	256	20.8	189	15.4	211	17.2	.6	(Z)
1957	1,354	645	47.6	254	18.8	232	17.1	223	16.5	.6	(Z)
1956	1,376	677	49.2	249	18.1	220	16.0	230	16.7	.6	(Z)
1955	1,298	655	50.4	223	17.2	217	16.7	203	15.7	.6	(Z)
1954	1,144	578	50.5	213	18.6	174	15.2	179	15.7	.4	(Z)
1953	1,232	643	52.1	217	17.6	4 202	16.4	170	13.8	.4	(Z)
1952	1,172	651	55.6	195	16.6	168	14.4	158	13.4	.4	(Z)
1951	1,209	686	56.8	188	15.6	4 182	15.1	152	12.6	.4	(Z)
1950	1,094	628	57.4	173	15.8	163	14.9	129	11.8	.3	(Z)
1949	947	567	59.9	125	13.2	139	14.7	115	12.1	.2	(Z)
1948	1,086	689	63.4	115	10.6	4 162	14.9	120	11.0	.2	(Z)
1947	1,060	707	66.6	102	9.6	147	13.8	105	9.9	.2	(Z)
1946	944	643	68.1	82	8.7	124	13.1	96	10.1	.1	(Z)
1945	1,072	736	68.6	67	6.2	143	13.3	127	11.8	.1	(Z)
1944	1,136	795	70.0	58	5.1	150	13.2	133	11.7	.1	(Z)
1943	1,076	780	72.5	57	5.3	142	13.2	98	9.1	.1	(Z)
1942	973	689	70.9	60	6.2	149	15.3	75	7.7	(Z)	(Z)
1941	811	521	64.2	81	10.0	140	17.3	68	8.4	(Z)	(Z)
1940	651	412	63.2	62	9.5	118	18.1	59	9.1	(Z)	(Z)
1939	575	370	64.4	53	9.2	96	16.7	56	9.7	(Z)	(Z)

Z Less than 50 million ton-miles, or less than 0.05 percent.
[1] Includes electric railways, express, and mail.
[2] Includes Great Lakes. Includes Alaska for all years and Hawaii beginning 1959.
[3] Domestic revenue service only. Includes express, mail, and excess baggage.
[4] Part of this increase resulted from coverage of waterways previously existing but not covered.

Series Q 23-35. Operating Revenues, by Type of Transport: 1936 to 1970

[Excludes Alaska and Hawaii, except as noted]

Year	Revenues (mil. dol.)								Index (1967 = 100)				
	Electric railways [1]	Railway express [2]	Railroads [3]	Waterlines [4]	Pipelines (oil)	Domestic scheduled air carriers [5][6]	Motor carriers of property	Motor carriers of passengers	Railroads [2]	Pipelines (oil)	Domestic scheduled air carriers [5][6]	Motor carriers of property	Motor carriers of passengers
	23	24	25	26	27	28	29	30	31	32	33	34	35
1970	11	313	12,511	502	1,188	7,131	14,585	882	115	119	146	129	93
1969	13	270	11,951	450	1,103	6,857	13,958	1,007	110	111	140	123	107
1968	12	299	11,357	435	1,023	5,607	12,400	991	104	103	115	110	105
1967	12	323	10,875	426	995	4,887	11,308	945	100	100	100	100	100
1966	14	324	11,163	460	941	4,070	10,862	901	103	95	83	96	95
1965	13	316	10,738	426	904	3,609	10,068	885	99	91	74	89	94
1964	13	298	10,252	405	865	3,095	9,155	802	94	87	63	81	85
1963	14	275	9,921	395	840	2,723	8,548	759	91	84	56	76	80
1962	22	271	9,792	394	811	2,498	8,131	729	90	82	51	72	77
1961	22	257	9,540	389	787	2,245	7,463	690	88	79	46	66	73
1960	23	*248	*9,955	427	[7]770	2,129	*7,214	667	*92	[7]77	44	*64	71
1959	25	247	10,207	430	765	1,955	7,145	631	94	77	40	63	67
1958	30	258	9,924	415	721	1,624	6,131	599	91	72	33	54	63
1957	45	248	10,920	450	730	1,515	6,166	599	100	73	31	55	63
1956	49	257	10,963	476	737	1,342	5,829	565	101	74	27	52	60
1955	60	241	10,495	452	678	1,215	5,535	560	97	68	25	49	59
1954	56	235	9,708	399	617	1,043	4,737	561	89	62	21	42	59
1953	78	242	11,063	391	591	937	4,926	614	102	59	19	44	65
1952	82	248	10,966	340	562	818	4,417	602	101	56	17	39	64
1951	81	223	10,773	336	524	702	4,169	578	99	53	14	37	61
1950	79	223	9,820	330	442	558	3,737	539	90	44	11	33	57
1949	70	251	8,885	275	376	486	2,911	554	82	38	10	26	59
1948	77	295	10,002	237	377	434	2,698	565	92	39	9	24	60
1947	80	313	8,973	225	325	365	2,214	534	83	33	7	20	57
1946	79	326	7,852	148	294	316	1,699	554	72	30	6	15	59
1945	87	284	9,136	173	304	215	1,840	652	84	31	4	16	69
1944	100	255	9,676	188	310	161	1,756	624	89	31	3	16	66
1943	99	208	9,288	196	277	123	1,347	544	85	28	3	12	58
1942	68	155	7,691	123	245	108	1,189	398	71	25	2	11	42
1941	59	135	5,541	258	252	97	1,095	237	51	25	2	10	25
1940	53	120	4,559	212	226	77	922	182	42	23	2	8	19
1939	50	112	4,140	111	212	56	796	168	38	21	1	7	18
1938	49	110	3,687	104	228	43	700	151	34	23	1	6	16
1937	51	110	4,321	108	249	----	----	----	40	25	----	----	----
1936	52	103	4,197	104	219	----	----	----	39	22	----	----	----

* Denotes first year for which figures include Alaska and Hawaii.
[1] The electric railway decrease is overstated through the years because of non-comparability of reporting.
[2] Through 1969, excludes payments to others for express privileges.
[3] Includes pullman (prior to 1965), line-haul, and switching and terminal companies.
[4] Includes only revenues from domestic traffic of carriers under jurisdiction of Interstate Commerce Commission.
[5] Revenues for scheduled passenger cargo operations.
[6] Includes Hawaii for all years and Alaska beginning 1955.
[7] Beginning 1960, includes operations in Alaska.

Series Q 36–46.   Employment in Selected Types of Transportation: 1947 to 1970

[In thousands, except percent. Annual averages]

Year	Total	Trucking and warehousing [1]		Railroad [2]		Air [3]		Local and suburban [4]		Intercity highway [5]	
		Number	Percent of total	Number	Percent of total	Number	Percent of total	Number	Percent of total	Number	Percent of total
	36	37	38	39	40	41	42	43	44	45	46
1970	2,149	1,083	50.4	627	29.2	319	14.8	77	3.6	43	2.0
1969	2,166	1,083	50.0	642	29.6	320	14.8	78	3.6	43	2.0
1968	2,128	1,045	49.1	661	31.1	298	14.0	81	3.8	43	2.0
1967	2,106	1,019	48.4	691	32.8	269	12.8	83	3.9	44	2.1
1966	2,070	1,005	48.6	718	34.7	223	10.8	82	4.0	42	2.0
1965	2,030	964	47.5	735	36.2	206	10.1	83	4.1	42	2.1
1964	1,991	919	46.2	756	38.0	191	9.6	83	4.2	42	2.1
1963	1,986	904	45.5	772	38.9	181	9.1	88	4.4	41	2.1
1962	1,989	885	44.5	796	40.0	176	8.8	91	4.6	41	2.1
1961	1,977	845	42.7	817	41.3	175	8.9	99	5.0	41	2.1
1960	2,055	856	41.7	885	43.1	172	8.4	101	4.9	41	2.0
1959*	2,074	844	40.7	925	44.6	161	7.8	103	5.0	41	2.0
1958	2,032	778	38.3	957	47.1	149	7.3	105	5.2	43	2.1
1957	2,230	804	36.1	1,121	50.3	148	6.6	112	5.0	45	2.0
1956	2,287	803	35.1	1,190	52.0	131	5.7	120	5.2	43	1.9
1955	2,254	765	33.9	1,205	53.5	114	5.1	127	5.6	43	1.9
1954	2,221	719	32.4	1,215	54.7	105	4.7	138	6.2	44	2.0
1953	2,403	731	30.4	1,377	57.3	105	4.4	141	5.9	49	2.0
1952	2,389	699	29.3	1,400	58.6	97	4.1	145	6.1	48	2.0
1951	2,409	676	28.1	1,449	60.1	86	3.6	151	6.3	47	2.0
1950	2,290	619	27.0	1,391	60.7	76	3.3	157	6.9	47	2.1
1949	2,232	567	25.4	1,367	61.2	77	3.4	169	7.8	52	2.3
1948	2,399	573	23.9	1,517	63.2	78	3.3	176	7.3	55	2.3
1947	2,443	551	22.6	1,557	63.7	82	3.4	199	8.1	54	2.2

* Denotes first year for which figures include Alaska and Hawaii.
[1] Covers establishments furnishing local or long-distance trucking, transfer, and draying services, or engaged in storage of farm products, furniture and other household goods, or commercial goods. Includes terminal facilities for handling freight.
[2] Includes companies furnishing transportation by line-haul railroad and certain allied services, such as sleeping and dining car services, railway express, and switching and terminal companies.

[3] Covers certificated and noncertificated air carriers engaged in passenger and cargo or freight transportation. Excludes employment in related facilities and services.
[4] Covers companies or systems primarily engaged in furnishing passenger transportation confined principally to a municipality, contiguous municipalities, or a municipality and its suburban areas, including transportation by railway but excluding taxicab, schoolbus, and charter service.
[5] Covers intercity, interurban, and interstate bus lines, and includes intercity motor vehicle passenger transportation not operated on regular schedules.

Series Q 47–49.   Indexes of Transportation Output: 1889 to 1966

Year	All traffic [1]	Year	All traffic [1]	Passenger	Freight	Year	All traffic [1]	Passenger	Freight
	47		47	48	49		47	48	49
	1958 = 100		1939 = 100				1939 = 100—Con.		
1966	152.7	1953	220			1935	79	87	77
1965	139.4	1952	219			1934	76	84	74
1964	128.0	1951	226			1933	70	76	68
1963	119.9					1932	66	79	62
1962	114.0	1950	206			1931	82	94	79
1961	107.7	1949	182						
		1948	205			1930	97	108	95
1960	108.1	1947	203			1929	110	118	108
1959	106.4	1946	192	248	176	1928	106	117	103
1958	100.0					1927	106	119	102
1957	103.4	1945	213	(NA)	(NA)	1926	108	121	104
1956	108.5	1944	222	(NA)	(NA)				
		1943	216	(NA)	(NA)	1925	102	120	97
1955	103.2	1942	183	(NA)	(NA)	1924	98	121	91
1954	93.9	1941	137	(NA)		1923	102	122	96
1953	98.4					1922	88	116	81
1952	98.0	1940	110	108	114	1921	81	115	72
1951	100.1	1939	100	100	100	1920	103	127	96
		1938	89	97	87				
1950	89.6	1937	101	103	101	1889	18.5	25.5	16.5
1949	86.5	1936	93	99	92				
1948	92.1								

NA   Not available.

[1] In combining passenger and freight traffic, passenger-miles were weighted by revenue per passenger-mile and ton-miles by revenue per ton-mile.

TRANSPORTATION

Series Q 50–63. Mileage of Rural Roads and Municipal Streets: 1904 to 1970

Year	Total mileage	Rural roads					Surfaced mileage	Under State control[4]		Mileage built by State highway departments	Roads under State control			
	Total	Total	State administered Primary	Secondary and county roads	County roads under local control[1]	Municipal and other mileage[2]	Total[3]	High-type roads	Low-type roads	Total[5]	Total	Earth roads	High-type surface	Low-type surface
	50	51	52	53	54	55	56	57	58	59	60	61	62	63
	1,000 miles	1,000 miles	1,000 miles	1,000 miles	1,000 miles	1,000 miles	1,000 miles	1,000 miles	1,000 miles	Miles	Miles	Miles	Miles	Miles
1970	3,730	3,169	408	273	2,488	561	2,946	410	322	40,438	33,834	68	24,637	9,129
1969	3,710	3,162	406	273	2,483	548	2,914	403	324	37,123	30,034	212	20,394	9,428
1968	3,684	3,152	425	252	2,475	532	2,870	392	330	47,425	37,279	403	23,617	13,259
1967	3,705	3,184	424	250	2,510	521	2,827	386	331	46,257	36,763	209	24,915	11,639
1966	3,698	3,188	418	252	2,518	510	2,800	376	333	50,872	38,968	249	27,152	11,567
1965	3,690	3,009	414	249	2,346	681	2,776	367	333	47,573	36,442	278	24,194	11,970
1964	3,644	3,003	411	248	2,344	641	2,730	359	334	45,452	36,203	275	22,664	13,264
1963	3,620	3,002	409	247	2,346	618	2,693	350	335	49,974	36,980	210	23,623	13,147
1962	3,600	3,005	407	247	2,351	595	2,647	341	337	52,560	41,052	433	26,305	14,314
1961	3,573	2,995	406	243	2,346	578	2,588	331	338	44,279	33,449	372	20,554	12,523
1960*	3,546	2,989	403	241	2,345	557	2,557	322	338	49,428	36,944	328	22,013	14,603
1959*	3,511	2,974	403	237	2,334	537	2,503	314	338	50,232	36,282	185	21,892	14,205
1958	3,479	2,959	395	234	2,330	520	2,448	301	338	54,753	39,824	313	23,644	15,867
1957	3,453	2,952	391	232	2,329	501	2,371	290	338	53,235	39,675	374	19,476	19,825
1956	3,430	2,945	389	226	2,330	485	2,323	281	335	57,454	44,016	486	20,726	22,804
1955	3,418	2,954	387	222	2,345	464	2,273	270	340	53,559	41,210	694	17,672	22,754
1954	3,395	2,941	379	218	2,344	454	2,228	262	333	55,488	42,053	866	19,730	21,457
1953	3,366	2,925	377	214	2,334	441	2,160	252	332	52,886	41,744	1,264	17,807	22,673
1952	3,343	2,925	371	219	2,335	418	2,070	245	328	57,847	46,354	1,238	17,811	27,305
1951	3,326	2,925	367	217	2,341	401	1,998	236	323	51,471	41,864	1,603	15,122	25,139
1950	3,313	2,922	363	210	2,349	391	1,939	227	316	55,487	44,265	1,784	13,379	29,102
1949	3,322	2,934	358	206	2,370	388	1,865	174	350	45,171	35,236	1,517	7,482	26,237
1948	3,323	2,929	350	206	2,373	394	1,815	172	338	41,968	35,085	1,403	7,753	25,929
1947	3,326	2,933	337	212	2,384	393	1,780	170	332	32,865	29,574	1,013	6,219	22,342
1946	3,316	2,934	342	205	2,387	382	1,730	170	317	21,711	20,856	417	4,898	15,541
1945	3,319	2,939	339	202	2,398	380	1,721	168	312	15,278	14,827	250	3,971	10,606
1944	3,311	2,932	335	200	2,397	379	1,655	167	309	15,080	13,924	289	3,925	9,710
1943	3,311	2,930	333	200	2,397	381	1,646	166	306	15,971	14,692	458	4,446	9,788
1942	3,309	2,925	334	199	2,392	384	1,630	165	302	19,670	18,078	1,038	4,167	12,873
1941	3,309	2,926	332	196	2,398	383	1,608	163	297	32,629	30,549	1,343	6,299	22,907
1940	3,287	2,920	329	195	2,396	367	1,367	153	296	32,588	29,689	1,423	5,217	23,049
1939	3,274	2,913	328	194	2,391	361	1,318	151	286	32,990	30,665	1,720	5,015	23,930
1938	3,257	2,898	327	194	2,377	359	1,276	149	277	36,322	34,598	1,187	5,751	27,660
1937	3,245	2,894	327	189	2,378	351	1,232	144	265	35,627	28,945	1,828	6,532	20,585
1936	3,267	2,920	340	177	2,403	347	1,175	131	262	32,274	32,274	3,361	4,706	24,207
1935	3,310	3,032	332	173	2,527	278	1,080	128	246	26,814	26,814	3,284	3,806	19,724
1934	3,309	3,034	325	170	2,539	275	992	124	237	41,730	41,730	5,917	6,386	29,427
1933	3,286	3,029	346	135	2,548	257	914	116	195	--------	33,471	6,258	7,412	19,801
1932	3,296	3,040	358	84	2,598	256	879	110	156	--------	35,971	6,394	10,009	19,568
1931	3,291	3,036	329	45	2,662	255	830	96	146	--------	44,634	10,095	12,513	22,026
1930	3,259	3,009	324	--------	2,685	250	694	84	142	--------	35,277	7,813	10,787	16,677
1929	3,272	3,024	314	--------	2,710	248	662	75	133	--------	32,522	7,451	8,847	16,224
1928	3,262	3,016	306	--------	2,710	246	626	68	125	--------	29,252	8,675	8,748	11,829
1927	3,257	3,013	293	--------	2,720	244	589	60	117	--------	26,723	7,151	6,733	12,839
1926	3,242	3,000	288	--------	2,712	242	550	54	109	--------	26,552	7,060	6,132	13,360
1925	3,246	3,006	275	--------	2,731	240	521	48	97	--------	23,152	5,316	6,686	11,150
1924	3,243	3,004	261	--------	2,743	239	472	41	90	--------	23,164	5,957	6,697	10,510
1923	3,233	2,996	252	--------	2,744	237	439	34	78	--------	20,311	5,814	5,628	8,869
1922	3,196	2,960	227	--------	2,733	236	412	--------	--------	--------	--------	--------	--------	--------
1921	3,160	2,925	203	--------	2,722	235	387	--------	--------	--------	--------	--------	--------	--------

Year	Surfaced mileage, total (56)
	1,000 miles
1920	369
1919	350
1918	332
1917	313
1916	295
1915	276
1914	257
1913	244
1912	231
1911	217
1910	204
1909	190
1908	183
1907	176
1906	168
1905	161
1904	154

* Denotes first year for which figures include Alaska and Hawaii.
NA   Not available.
[1] Includes municipal extensions of county, town, and township roads prior to 1962, and mileage in National and State parks, forests, reservations, etc. prior to 1936 that were not parts of State or local systems.
[2] Includes mileage in National and State parks, forests, reservations, etc. that did not form parts of State or local road system.   Prior to 1936 these roads were included with county, town, and township roads.
[3] Includes all surfaced mileage whether under State or local control.
[4] Includes State highway extensions within cities.
[5] Excludes mileage of local roads and streets on Federal-aid secondary system which were built by State highway departments or by local authorities when financed partially or entirely by Federal funds.

Series Q 64–68. Mileage and Cost of Federal-Aid Highway Systems: 1917 to 1970

Year	Miles of highway		Cost (mil. dol.) [3]			Year or period	Miles of highway		Cost (mil. dol.) [3]		
	Total designated as part of Federal systems [1]	Completed during year [2]	Total	Federal funds	State funds		Total designated as part of Federal systems [1]	Completed during year [2]	Total	Federal funds	State funds
	64	65	66	67	68		64	65	66	67	68
1970	895,208	10,745	4,625	3,515	1,110	1945	308,741	3,035	101	76	25
1969	890,094	10,569	4,826	3,706	1,120	1944	367,690	4,473	135	109	26
1968	886,181	11,871	4,132	3,167	965	1943	338,705	7,753	273	219	54
1967	887,465	14,150	5,178	4,039	1,139	1942	330,051	6,898	226	143	83
1966	885,050	16,281	5,362	4,151	1,211	1941	316,432	9,734	274	148	126
1965	908,722	17,433	4,569	3,430	1,139	1940	235,482	11,549	269	150	119
1964	901,120	19,487	4,560	3,385	1,175	1939	232,834	11,776	306	176	130
1963	891,927	19,561	3,790	2,767	1,023	1938	229,905	11,766	309	183	125
1962	886,678	21,051	3,423	2,437	986	1937	226,829	21,330	521	348	173
1961	879,539	21,313	3,265	2,339	925	1936	224,450	12,258	238	225	13
1960	866,841	20,969	3,264	2,273	992	1935	219,869	12,811	242	218	24
1959*	854,294	32,633	3,709	2,518	1,191	1934	212,496	21,203	358	311	47
1958	830,569	28,137	2,744	1,669	1,075	1933	207,194	18,219	264	223	41
1957	810,466	22,424	1,714	969	746	1932	205,025	10,855	205	95	110
1956	777,514	23,609	1,444	757	687	1931	198,967	15,902	325	228	97
1955	749,166	22,571	1,287	666	621	1930	193,652	10,339	237	100	137
1954	725,963	20,548	1,146	591	555	1929	189,853	8,581	197	80	117
1953	704,150	21,136	1,078	559	519	1928	188,017	9,756	196	83	113
1952	675,121	22,147	978	505	472	1927	187,035	10,220	189	84	105
1951	664,464	17,060	772	390	382	1926	184,162	10,723	215	93	122
1950	643,939	19,876	753	390	364	1925	179,501	11,001	221	100	121
1949	632,037	19,876	829	425	404	1924	174,507	10,946	205	93	112
1948	611,332	21,725	763	397	366	1923	169,007	7,494	130	57	73
1947	599,338	15,473	422	224	198	1922	----------	11,188	186	80	106
1946	556,787	5,057	147	86	61	1917–1921	----------	12,919	222	95	127

* Denotes first year for which figures include Alaska and Hawaii.
[1] Includes estimates on Federal-aid primary system throughout, Federal-aid secondary systems beginning in 1942, and national system of interstate and defense highways beginning in 1951. Estimates as of end of calendar year.
[2] Comprises new and rebuilt mileage.
[3] Represents actual expenditures of funds on calendar-year basis. Beginning 1935, includes money spent on public works and defense highways. Beginning 1940, includes secondary highways.

Series Q 69–81. Class I Intercity Motor Carriers of Passengers and Property: 1939 to 1970

[Carriers subject to ICC regulations]

Year	Carriers of passengers							Carriers of property					
	Carriers reporting [1]	Operating revenue	Expenses	Net income after income taxes	Vehicles in service [2]	Vehicle-miles, passenger [3]	Average fare per passenger, per carrier (intercity)	Carriers reporting	Operating revenue	Expenses	Net income after income taxes	Owned revenue vehicles	Intercity vehicle-miles
	69	70	71	72	73	74	75	76	77	78	79	80	81
		Mil. dol.	Mil. dol.	Mil. dol.		Millions	Dollars		Mil. dol.	Mil. dol.	Mil. dol.	1,000	Millions
1970	71	722	639	52	13,282	871	3.81	1,376	11,137	10,763	150	483	11,498
1969	70	677	594	56	12,992	869	3.55	1,311	10,770	10,337	200	466	11,699
1968	173	695	613	61	15,398	977	2.91	1,252	9,593	9,129	235	428	10,902
1967	177	670	591	52	15,406	997	2.79	1,198	8,091	7,796	144	394	9,815
1966	166	644	550	54	14,298	988	2.71	1,159	7,897	7,505	217	384	9,814
1965	156	607	514	52	13,287	947	2.73	1,114	7,131	6,760	209	355	9,154
1964	161	655	570	52	16,157	1,056	2.43	1,025	6,199	5,918	152	318	8,209
1963	148	610	529	48	[4] 13,608	1,009	2.38	1,004	5,756	5,520	122	309	7,882
1962	151	589	511	43	[4] 13,873	998	2.30	1,004	5,428	5,204	112	298	7,567
1961	144	485	423	31	[4] 11,036	865	2.20	972	4,908	4,718	84	285	7,023
1960*	143	463	405	28	12,680	843	2.12	935	4,763	4,645	37	279	7,203
1959	143	439	380	29	[4] 10,763	810	2.00	890	4,590	4,392	92	265	7,085
1958	136	410	366	20	[4] 10,791	816	1.91	866	3,851	3,723	54	243	6,101
1957	144	407	371	20	[4] 11,301	867	1.70	837	3,836	3,702	62	238	6,399
1956	145	377	343	17	[4] 11,062	859	1.51	2,293	4,290	4,141	77	304	7,529
1955	146	362	331	16	13,127	859	1.37	2,244	4,030	3,870	82	289	7,559
1954	155	363	331	15	[4] 12,314	887	1.29	2,110	3,431	3,323	54	260	6,538
1953	161	395	354	18	[4] 12,940	972	1.24	2,027	3,493	3,360	60	251	6,802
1952	160	395	348	22	[4] 13,106	975	1.20	1,868	3,059	2,924	67	229	6,137
1951	166	393	345	25	[4] 13,431	1,011	1.12	1,737	2,728	2,603	58	213	5,848
1950	172	351	315	19	14,566	959	1.01	1,621	2,380	2,215	93	191	5,532
1949	262	380	346	20	[4] 14,863	1,066	.91	2,012	1,895	1,794	64	169	4,338
1948	260	401	351	31	[4] 15,290	1,130	.85	1,825	1,663	1,553	72	151	3,810
1947	253	367	313	33	[4] 14,149	1,056	.80	1,603	1,233	1,174	37	128	3,059
1946	254	381	299	50	[4] 13,168	1,043	.80	1,516	884	852	21	112	2,407
1945	231	378	265	32	[4] 12,865	931	.79	1,445	746	745	-2	100	2,165
1944	194	375	245	36	[4] 12,019	905	.80	1,337	711	696	8	98	2,132
1943	157	344	214	37	[4] 11,000	832	.81	1,165	646	626	9	89	2,006
1942	136	251	164	24	[4] 9,677	702	.80	1,083	588	556	17	84	2,040
1941	132	149	120	20	[4] 7,891	556	.83	1,076	560	533	18	84	2,121
1940	135	115	98	15	[4] 6,678	482	.84	991	431	412	13	69	1,761
1939	149	113	95	20	[4] 6,408	466	.88	957	378	360	15	62	1,343

* Denotes first year for which figures include Alaska and Hawaii.
[1] Excludes carriers subject to ICC jurisdiction engaged preponderantly in local or suburban service and carriers engaged in transportation of both property and passengers.
[2] Regular route intercity and local.
[3] Vehicles owned, leased, and operated under "purchased transportation" arrangements, operated in all revenue service.
[4] Excludes intercity service.

Series Q 82–96. State Highway Finances: 1890 to 1970

[In millions of dollars]

Year	Revenues								Disbursements						
	Total	Receipts from current State imposts				Federal funds [2]	Receipts from issue of bonds, notes, etc. [3]	All other [4]	Total [5]	For State-administered highways			For county and local roads and streets	All other [7]	State highway debt outstanding
		Highway-user revenue			Other [1]					Capital outlay for roads and bridges	Maintenance	Other [6]			
		Total	Motor-fuel taxes	Motor vehicle and carrier taxes											
	82	83	84	85	86	87	88	89	90	91	92	93	94	95	96
1970	16,501	8,843.1	6,090.9	2,752.1	1,175.0	4,737.1	1,301.5	444.5	16,534	8,866.0	1,928.8	2,774.9	2,965.1	--------	14,020.0
1969	15,293	8,238.5	5,687.1	2,551.3	1,009.2	4,190.2	1,421.1	434.6	14,919	7,876.1	1,723.1	2,644.7	2,675.1	--------	13,514.3
1968	14,563	7,426.5	5,122.8	2,303.6	921.6	4,431.0	1,374.7	409.7	14,253	7,866.3	1,593.6	2,283.6	2,510.0	--------	12,903.3
1967	13,161	6,886.9	4,758.1	2,128.7	813.2	4,001.3	1,011.3	449.0	13,315	7,339.8	1,513.5	2,108.0	2,354.2	--------	12,177.4
1966	13,217	6,577.4	4,494.1	2,083.3	755.2	4,229.7	1,295.3	359.7	12,553	7,056.3	1,402.2	1,871.8	2,223.1	--------	11,813.9
1965	12,532	7,012.7	4,505.7	2,507.0	771.1	3,862.4	591.1	295.3	12,437	6,458.2	1,309.7	1,662.6	2,037.0	--------	11,058.7
1964	12,363	6,582.8	4,217.5	2,365.3	712.4	4,000.6	783.7	283.4	12,017	6,562.3	1,210.3	1,564.9	1,943.9	969.5	10,930.6
1963	11,091	6,116.8	3,929.0	2,187.8	630.7	3,499.5	611.1	233.0	11,248	6,047.7	1,133.9	1,491.5	1,787.8	936.3	10,596.3
1962	10,697	5,831.9	3,764.1	2,067.8	622.7	2,933.0	1,077.9	231.9	10,451	5,608.4	1,093.2	1,352.8	1,689.1	707.5	10,472.1
1961	9,758	5,511.3	3,542.7	1,968.5	590.0	2,729.4	709.6	217.7	9,626	5,105.0	1,019.8	1,192.3	1,650.4	659.2	9,783.5
1960	9,276	5,313.0	3,399.6	1,913.4	527.5	2,521.4	707.2	207.0	8,956	4,669.3	985.6	1,147.8	1,556.6	597.3	9,382.9
1959*	9,542	5,075.7	3,256.3	1,819.3	481.7	3,058.9	722.9	202.6	9,276	5,075.8	903.0	1,115.9	1,517.3	664.5	9,008.2
1958	8,451	4,688.1	2,976.1	1,711.9	404.2	2,246.7	916.0	196.4	8,478	4,713.6	867.1	955.8	1,431.2	510.8	8,605.0
1957	7,067	4,544.5	2,894.7	1,649.8	357.3	1,256.0	727.1	182.4	7,702	4,139.3	812.4	903.5	1,347.6	499.4	7,945.2
1956	6,789	4,394.9	2,788.2	1,606.8	392.6	775.6	1,064.6	160.9	6,896	3,661.9	756.4	748.4	1,236.1	493.4	7,495.9
1955	5,794	4,014.4	2,533.1	1,481.3	295.1	670.2	658.1	156.6	6,053	3,412.9	675.6	686.7	1,130.4	438.0	6,618.5
1954	6,913	3,648.5	2,301.7	1,346.8	221.0	587.8	2,338.0	118.0	5,720	2,962.5	647.7	653.3	1,044.1	412.6	6,164.0
1953	5,401	3,420.5	2,167.9	1,252.6	213.2	540.8	1,101.5	125.3	4,884	2,271.4	620.4	566.3	994.0	432.4	4,015.4
1952	4,651	3,094.0	1,958.1	1,135.8	184.7	485.2	798.6	88.6	4,247	1,941.8	602.5	472.4	905.4	325.4	3,116.1
1951	4,051	2,863.2	1,809.3	1,053.9	158.1	415.6	536.9	77.2	3,980	1,739.5	562.2	484.0	808.8	385.7	2,475.8
1950	3,613	2,587.0	1,652.2	934.7	125.0	425.5	410.1	65.5	3,561	1,533.8	501.4	447.5	752.4	326.1	2,141.0
1949	3,278	2,337.0	1,473.3	863.7	153.0	429.1	303.1	56.5	3,201	1,361.9	488.0	355.8	735.3	259.8	1,928.3
1948	2,950	2,081.0	1,348.1	732.9	144.1	364.8	312.7	47.4	2,873	1,138.6	465.6	343.4	652.8	273.2	1,735.3
1947	2,345	1,838.7	1,196.4	642.2	91.5	288.3	89.3	37.0	2,383	882.3	374.5	344.0	537.3	244.8	1,536.9
1946	2,107	1,602.8	1,046.3	556.4	176.4	147.2	150.0	31.3	1,788	502.3	327.3	404.9	400.4	153.0	1,571.5
1945	1,449	1,235.7	773.8	461.9	87.2	59.9	47.6	18.5	1,301	210.4	287.7	344.0	309.8	149.7	1,637.9
1944	1,361	1,136.9	684.9	451.9	44.3	91.9	72.1	15.6	1,243	210.3	258.9	290.0	297.8	186.6	1,794.5
1943	1,425	1,117.3	663.6	453.7	56.4	152.1	83.8	15.2	1,309	268.6	224.8	303.1	315.5	197.1	1,869.5
1942	1,572	1,321.3	855.2	466.1	44.5	154.9	33.0	18.3	1,489	401.6	216.7	263.7	359.3	247.9	1,962.1
1941	1,899	1,452.0	948.0	503.9	45.7	168.8	204.8	27.6	1,888	525.2	234.8	505.8	359.0	263.9	2,069.6
1940	1,780	1,321.0	866.2	454.8	38.1	196.1	202.2	22.7	1,678	563.0	218.7	318.1	333.1	244.8	2,159.0
1939	1,611	1,226.9	816.6	410.2	34.1	203.8	120.2	26.0	1,606	500.1	211.9	337.0	333.5	224.0	2,177.8
1938	1,578	1,175.7	769.8	405.8	33.4	197.6	145.9	25.4	1,619	558.3	232.6	329.9	296.8	201.2	2,250.1
1937	1,634	1,195.6	767.4	428.1	30.2	264.0	111.5	33.2	1,601	589.2	223.7	270.6	312.8	205.2	2,243.6
1936	1,590	1,057.9	683.0	374.9	25.3	349.7	134.2	23.6	1,578	631.7	222.0	256.3	257.3	211.0	2,210.3
1935	1,330	940.4	615.5	324.8	24.8	219.3	117.1	28.7	1,257	438.3	187.1	219.8	233.2	179.2	2,169.2
1934	1,388	883.7	565.1	318.5	27.5	354.8	103.0	19.4	1,325	580.3	181.5	191.1	216.3	155.7	2,114.8
1933	1,187	820.9	519.4	301.5	43.7	223.5	79.8	19.1	1,221	529.2	179.3	189.0	196.8	126.6	2,108.8
1932	1,168	838.1	514.0	324.0	48.4	138.8	104.6	38.8	1,243	571.0	178.1	190.1	196.3	108.2	2,038.5
1931	1,389	881.7	537.4	344.3	47.6	218.3	174.7	67.4	1,391	796.9	162.9	167.2	217.5	47.1	1,879.7
1930	1,296	850.7	494.6	356.0	55.1	94.1	222.2	74.5	1,330	728.8	193.9	167.1	200.5	40.0	1,572.4
1929	1,209	778.9	431.3	347.5	75.8	77.9	191.2	85.5	1,089	575.4	173.6	136.9	171.0	32.4	1,438.9
1928	998	626.8	304.3	322.4	57.6	81.2	133.4	98.8	985	558.4	160.2	96.3	141.1	27.6	1,187.8
1927	879	559.6	258.7	300.9	52.0	80.1	90.9	96.4	847	418.8	139.1	129.3	136.4	23.9	1,085.8
1926	825	475.8	187.6	288.2	49.2	79.1	137.8	83.1	747	366.0	125.7	116.6	115.6	22.9	933.0
1925	783	405.6	145.4	260.2	56.1	93.3	141.4	86.5	759	403.8	119.3	115.9	101.4	18.8	789.3
1924	634	302.0	78.7	223.2	39.4	92.9	101.6	98.6	688	397.6	104.8	89.8	75.6	20.1	678.3
1923	521	216.5	30.8	185.7	62.4	73.3	88.1	80.6	501	279.9	75.3	74.4	57.8	14.0	565.4
1922	545	153.5	10.8	142.7	65.8	79.7	143.0	102.9	494	287.4	75.3	54.3	68.0	9.6	473.2
1921	432	130.3	5.3	125.0	69.7	77.7	114.8	40.1	443	300.6	64.8	41.8	29.7	6.8	372.9
1920	358	102.9	1.3	101.5	97.5	61.9	38.2	57.4	358	240.3	58.4	25.4	29.6	4.2	225.4
1919	221	65.7	1.0	64.6	27.7	11.7	34.3	81.7	221	124.9	53.0	19.2	19.0	4.9	191.4
1918	139	51.4	--------	51.4	30.2	2.1	7.0	48.8	139	71.9	34.9	13.5	14.7	4.5	159.5
1917	116	37.5	--------	37.5	6.3	--------	21.6	50.8	116	61.6	27.6	10.2	14.1	2.8	154.0
1916	87	25.8	--------	25.8	23.0	--------	4.8	33.5	87	49.8	18.4	6.7	10.2	1.9	134.4
1915	90	18.2	--------	18.2	20.1	--------	25.3	27.0	90	55.9	19.2	5.8	7.5	2.0	130.2
1914	75	12.3	--------	12.3	26.1	--------	11.6	25.1	75	53.8	14.5	5.2	1.8	--------	105.4

Year	State highway debt outstanding	Year	State highway debt outstanding	Year	State highway debt outstanding	Year	State highway debt outstanding
	96		96		96		96
1913	94.2	1907	18.4	1901	13.1	1895	2.6
1912	65.6	1906	16.4	1900	12.7	1894	1.3
1911	52.4	1905	15.4	1899	12.2	1893	.5
1910	38.3	1904	15.0	1898	10.0	1892	(Z)
1909	31.6	1903	14.5	1897	8.2	1891	(Z)
1908	24.4	1902	14.0	1896	6.7	1890	(Z)

* Denotes first year for which figures include Alaska and Hawaii.
Z   Less than 50,000.
[1] Includes road, bridge, and ferry tolls; property taxes; appropriations from general funds; and other State imposts.
[2] Includes funds of Federal Highway Administration and other agencies paid as reimbursement to the States. Does not include direct Federal expenditures for highways.
[3] Includes refunding issues and toll revenue bonds.

[4] Includes funds transferred from local governments and miscellaneous receipts.
[5] Beginning 1966, excludes amounts allocated for collection and nonhighway purposes, and bonds redeemed by refunding.
[6] Includes administration, engineering, and equipment; State highway police; interest on obligations for State highways; and retirement of obligations for State highways.
[7] Includes expenditures and funds transferred for nonhighway purposes and expense of collecting and administering highway-user revenue.

Series Q 97–112. Receipts and Disbursements of Highway Funds by Counties and Townships: 1921 to 1970

[In millions of dollars]

| Year | Total receipts | Local receipts | | | | | Transfers from other governments | | | Total disbursements [5] | Capital outlays [3] | Maintenance and operation | Administration and other | Interest [6] | Debt retirement [6] | Transfers to other governments |
| | | Total | Local highway user imposts | Tolls | Borrowing [1] | Property tax, general fund, misc. | Total [2] | Federal [3] | State | | | | | | | |
	97	98	99	100	101	102	103	104	105	106	107	108	109	110	111	112
1970	3,075	1,511	50	24	222	1,216	1,565	72	1,485	3,028	915	1,463	269	65	193	124
1969	2,913	1,478	42	21	236	1,179	1,435	53	1,376	2,818	846	1,392	218	62	191	109
1968	2,693	1,372	18	21	272	1,061	1,321	44	1,255	2,639	806	1,272	201	55	167	138
1967	2,609	1,321	20	20	272	1,009	1,288	41	1,202	2,577	761	1,205	163	53	220	175
1966	2,410	1,216	18	20	201	977	1,194	45	1,146	2,345	714	1,138	146	46	162	139
1965	2,247	1,114	12	19	216	867	1,133	43	1,087	2,203	681	1,080	133	48	166	95
1964	2,135	1,053	11	18	203	821	1,082	33	1,044	2,068	649	1,008	123	45	148	95
1963	2,012	1,015	10	17	159	829	997	30	964	1,996	618	959	108	45	158	108
1962	1,990	1,035	9	16	220	790	955	30	922	1,934	605	939	99	41	144	106
1961	1,926	979	8	16	186	769	947	29	916	1,896	579	922	99	40	149	107
1960	1,753	878	9	19	115	735	875	28	845	1,737	500	923	95	33	108	78
1959	1,762	926	9	20	184	713	836	21	812	1,745	521	874	92	32	126	99
1958	1,695	891	4	19	167	701	804	26	776	1,704	549	847	81	32	116	77
1957	1,619	810	4	16	141	649	809	28	779	1,603	518	784	76	32	112	72
1956	1,518	768	3	15	128	622	750	21	728	1,509	425	764	65	31	109	58
1955	1,531	835	4	15	229	587	696	17	678	1,429	450	701	64	29	109	62
1954	1,371	697	4	14	113	566	674	18	655	1,369	436	677	59	29	107	48
1953	1,329	691	3	13	126	549	638	18	619	1,297	401	649	55	28	102	51
1952	1,253	650	3	13	121	513	603	17	584	1,200	355	618	51	27	97	42
1951	1,128	582	2	12	98	470	546	9	536	1,106	285	596	47	29	101	35
1950	1,067	565	2	12	104	447	502	6	495	1,043	266	557	44	29	100	38
1949	1,010	538	2	11	120	405	472	5	466	990	279	498	39	31	96	39
1948	936	489	1	10	98	380	447	4	442	929	255	478	33	32	91	37
1947	856	485	1	8	127	349	371	2	369	826	208	432	27	33	96	27
1946	702	375	1	7	64	303	327	3	323	685	147	373	24	35	85	17
1945	575	310	1	5	39	265	265	4	261	556	74	308	20	38	103	9
1944	519	276	1	5	28	242	243	2	241	506	58	271	19	41	105	8
1943	516	266	1	5	18	242	250	2	248	470	52	237	18	45	107	7
1942	669	320	1	5	57	257	349	79	270	643	173	246	18	49	142	8
1941	847	364	1	4	94	265	483	191	292	836	311	254	22	55	175	13
1940	931	348	–	3	68	277	583	299	283	925	432	249	19	58	149	12
1939	987	354	–	3	69	282	633	362	271	989	495	240	19	63	152	14
1938	1,023	370	–	3	86	281	653	394	259	1,031	533	239	18	68	150	17
1937	869	389	–	1	108	280	480	223	257	876	353	234	19	72	168	26
1936	901	326	1	–	56	269	575	341	234	909	449	222	24	73	116	23
1935	624	314	1	–	50	263	310	95	215	629	194	202	23	80	120	9
1934	660	282	1	–	31	250	378	154	224	662	238	187	26	81	116	10
1933	567	320	1	–	24	295	247	25	222	576	130	191	27	81	124	12
1932	664	456	1	–	67	388	208	–	208	686	168	235	28	87	133	24
1931	812	602	1	–	109	492	210	1	209	847	248	262	38	91	165	41
1930	818	622	–	–	95	527	196	–	196	852	297	284	36	83	113	39
1929	790	636	–	–	111	525	154	–	154	808	257	260	50	78	106	57
1928	835	700	–	–	150	550	135	–	135	832	282	260	37	80	103	70
1927	841	716	–	–	181	535	125	–	125	829	289	238	41	75	105	81
1926	775	667	–	–	169	498	108	–	108	752	266	213	42	67	91	73
1925	683	581	–	–	144	437	102	–	102	689	265	197	29	52	74	72
1924	690	646	–	–	158	488	44	–	44	688	256	195	27	55	67	88
1923	638	598	–	–	129	469	40	–	40	645	242	184	46	50	56	67
1922	731	645	–	–	150	495	86	–	86	733	330	185	40	35	48	95
1921	657	635	–	–	202	433	22	–	22	670	337	186	40	34	40	33

– Represents zero.
[1] Includes long and short-term notes. The latter are for two years or less.
[2] Beginning 1940, includes small amount from municipalities, not shown separately.
[3] Includes Federal work-relief funds (mainly Works Progress Administration) for 1933–42 respectively, as follows (in millions of dollars): 25, 150, 91, 339, 221, 389, 352, 295, 189, and 78.

[4] Includes expenditures by local rural agencies for highways. The major share of the expenditures were for the local highway system. However, in some instances, outlays for State-administered highways and local city streets are included.
[5] For 1931–1959, includes small amount for nonhighway purposes, not shown separately.
[6] Includes debt service for long and short-term notes. The latter are for two years or less.

Series Q 113–128.   Receipts and Disbursements of Highway Funds by Municipalities: 1921 to 1970

[In millions of dollars]

Year	Total receipts	Local receipts					Transfers from other governments			Total disbursements [4]	Capital outlays	Maintenance and operation	Administration and other	Interest [5]	Debt retirement [3]	Transfers to other governments
		Total	Local highway user imposts	Tolls	Borrowing [1]	Property tax, general fund, misc.	Total [2]	Federal	State							
	113	114	115	116	117	118	119	120	121	122	123	124	125	126	127	128
1970	3,580	2,578	96	93	525	1,864	1,002	20	895	3,570	1,074	1,240	668	138	397	52
1969	3,269	2,430	91	89	447	1,803	839	10	764	3,273	1,017	1,136	525	131	384	80
1968	3,046	2,288	87	85	458	1,658	758	5	686	2,982	935	1,066	445	118	339	79
1967	2,826	2,116	74	82	499	1,461	710	6	664	2,786	894	970	381	111	354	76
1966	2,632	1,994	74	81	444	1,395	638	5	602	2,530	808	893	332	102	333	62
1965	2,362	1,748	71	77	394	1,206	614	11	574	2,305	722	854	234	101	345	49
1964	2,228	1,652	67	65	371	1,149	576	22	523	2,199	731	801	214	97	303	53
1963	2,170	1,680	61	60	475	1,084	490	5	435	2,117	694	789	189	94	309	42
1962	1,968	1,523	67	58	377	1,021	445	1	395	2,046	679	758	165	91	302	51
1961	2,003	1,592	67	53	450	1,022	411	2	365	1,949	645	738	163	83	275	45
1960	1,987	1,572	67	54	507	944	415	3	389	1,954	666	685	152	80	323	48
1959	1,892	1,491	66	54	503	868	401	–	364	1,815	631	659	133	75	263	54
1958	1,702	1,313	62	53	347	851	389	–	351	1,773	656	614	155	63	241	40
1957	1,725	1,390	68	52	436	834	335	1	305	1,682	615	567	123	57	264	38
1956	1,550	1,266	57	49	365	795	284	–	264	1,523	563	542	105	47	220	16
1955	1,485	1,224	56	46	385	737	261	–	243	1,347	507	479	82	52	180	25
1954	1,314	1,068	49	43	290	686	246	1	232	1,269	464	456	71	50	194	16
1953	1,186	971	49	42	236	644	215	1	204	1,153	415	442	70	43	151	15
1952	1,302	1,113	35	41	443	594	189	1	178	1,256	379	409	70	44	329	14
1951	962	792	25	37	205	525	171	–	162	959	336	377	56	42	133	10
1950	918	753	23	31	187	512	165	–	154	901	329	346	51	42	115	13
1949	1,014	860	23	26	300	511	154	–	145	971	320	347	50	43	200	8
1948	776	662	20	24	136	482	114	–	106	756	253	324	43	40	86	7
1947	671	565	17	21	132	395	106	–	101	635	212	265	34	39	78	4
1946	485	407	16	10	53	328	78	–	76	463	100	220	24	37	75	4
1945	399	350	15	8	31	296	49	–	48	389	55	191	18	38	84	1
1944	310	261	14	11	19	217	49	–	43	381	53	193	13	39	79	2
1943	297	248	12	10	22	204	49	–	43	322	41	176	14	41	43	2
1942	407	358	7	11	66	274	49	–	46	372	81	168	21	48	49	2
1941	495	437	8	9	79	341	58	1	52	494	112	170	26	59	122	2
1940	504	429	10	9	86	324	75	6	63	509	171	133	24	60	114	2
1939	471	404	20	7	80	297	67	9	54	479	172	153	33	62	54	1
1938	448	393	17	5	74	297	55	5	47	433	140	144	31	62	53	1
1937	489	432	11	5	39	377	57	2	50	488	130	134	29	63	128	1
1936	396	367	–	–	19	348	29	–	25	430	125	154	26	60	65	–
1935	373	352	–	–	17	335	21	–	17	408	107	145	24	68	64	–
1934	392	366	–	–	29	337	26	–	21	376	110	148	25	75	18	–
1933	407	386	–	–	13	373	21	–	17	501	135	147	24	82	113	–
1932	536	516	–	–	42	474	20	–	15	630	208	166	27	87	142	–
1931	737	716	–	–	73	643	21	–	16	790	344	193	32	88	133	–
1930	910	899	–	–	112	787	11	–	11	946	473	197	33	91	152	–
1929	860	847	–	–	122	725	13	–	13	779	427	196	32	82	42	–
1928	841	833	–	–	115	718	8	–	8	745	441	180	30	74	20	–
1927	848	845	–	–	115	730	3	–	3	747	451	182	30	69	15	–
1926	729	724	–	–	100	624	5	–	5	644	372	167	28	62	15	–
1925	694	691	–	–	113	578	3	–	3	591	356	147	24	54	10	–
1924	573	573	–	–	91	482	–	–	–	492	285	130	22	45	10	–
1923	403	403	–	–	–	403	–	–	–	403	226	120	20	37	–	–
1922	376	376	–	–	–	376	–	–	–	376	213	115	19	29	–	–
1921	337	337	–	–	–	337	–	–	–	337	191	108	18	20	–	–

– Represents zero.

[1] Includes long and short-term notes.   The latter are for two years or less.

[2] Beginning 1931, includes small amount from county and townships, not shown separately.

[3] Represents expenditures for highways and streets by local municipal governments. The major share of the expenditures were for the local highway system However, in some instances, outlays for State-administered highways and local county-level streets are included.

[4] For 1937–1958, includes small amount for nonhighway purposes, not shown separately.

[5] Includes debt service for long and short-term notes.   The latter are for two years or less.

Series Q 129–135. Highway Construction—Contracts Awarded: 1947 to 1970

[In millions of dollars. Covers federally and State owned highways only; includes force-account construction authorized to start]

Year	Highways			Federally aided projects		Independent State projects		Year	Highways			Federally aided projects		Independent State projects	
	Total	Federally owned	State owned	Total value	Federal funds	Total value	Total facilities		Total	Federally owned	State owned	Total value	Federal funds	Total value	Total facilities
	129	130	131	132	133	134	135		129	130	131	132	133	134	135
1970	6,520	52	6,468	4,877	3,619	1,591	49	1958	[1] 4,585	96	3,996	3,489	2,504	507	44
1969	6,625	38	6,587	5,048	3,784	1,539	78	1957	[1] 3,917	92	3,311	2,390	1,614	921	343
1968	5,305	84	5,220	3,711	2,766	1,510	63	1956	[1] 3,303	92	2,718	1,737	963	981	337
1967	5,522	78	5,444	4,112	3,077	1,332	213								
1966	5,459	127	5,332	4,173	3,131	1,159	99	1955	2,619	59	2,560	1,256	667	1,304	695
								1954	[1] 2,746	62	2,300	1,218	630	1,082	459
1965	4,935	135	4,800	3,896	2,976	904	49	1953	[1] 2,713	53	2,287	998	519	1,289	800
1964	4,868	123	4,745	4,055	3,084	690	82	1952	[1] 2,088	90	1,654	912	476	743	146
1963	4,418	142	4,275	3,730	2,770	546	27	1951	[1] 1,743	71	1,362	780	409	582	68
1962	4,336	95	4,241	3,253	2,506	988	326								
1961	[1] 4,482	92	3,803	3,168	2,289	634	92	1950	1,528	36	1,492	798	415	694	228
								1949	[1] 1,448	47	1,150	643	332	507	120
1960*	4,030	129	3,901	3,097	2,218	804	165	1948	[1] 1,436	28	1,145	740	386	405	46
1959	[1] 3,805	86	3,213	2,638	1,877	575	59	1947	917	25	892	635	329	257	(NA)

* Denotes first year for which figures include Alaska and Hawaii.
NA Not available.

[1] Includes locally owned; therefore, details do not add to total.

Series Q 136–147. Public Highway Debt—Long-Term Highway Obligations of State and Local Governments: 1945 to 1970

[In millions of dollars. State data are for calendar years; local data are for varying fiscal years. Excludes duplicated and interunit obligations, except as noted. Municipal obligations include data for all municipalities and other political subdivisions urban in character]

Year	Debt issued				Debt redeemed				Debt outstanding			
	Total [1]	State	County and local rural	Municipal	Total [2]	State	County and local rural	Municipal	Total	State	County and local rural	Municipal
	136	137	138	139	140	141	142	143	144	145	146	147
1970	1,886	1,305	174	407	1,252	782	152	318	19,107	13,903	1,685	3,519
1969	2,022	1,351	241	430	1,122	705	137	280	18,572	13,380	1,658	3,534
1968	1,991	1,377	241	373	1,071	657	136	278	17,672	12,734	1,554	3,384
1967	1,633	1,012	194	427	965	540	136	289	16,749	12,014	1,450	3,285
1966	1,680	1,156	158	366	915	519	126	270	16,080	11,542	1,394	3,144
1965	1,070	586	169	315	855	459	123	273	15,316	10,905	1,363	3,048
1964	1,097	634	156	307	752	381	116	255	15,114	10,778	1,317	3,019
1963	981	458	114	409	732	382	114	236	14,773	10,525	1,281	2,967
1962	1,535	1,017	184	334	679	340	110	229	14,537	10,449	1,285	2,803
1961	1,272	718	153	401	665	330	117	218	13,718	9,772	1,252	2,694
1960	1,206	680	190	336	616	300	96	220	13,166	9,384	1,280	2,502
1959*	1,158	669	153	336	610	308	92	210	12,576	9,004	1,186	2,386
1958	1,352	913	140	299	543	252	94	197	12,278	8,641	1,130	2,507
1957	1,200	702	123	375	535	253	92	190	11,422	7,945	1,084	2,393
1956	1,439	1,067	105	267	438	190	97	151	10,659	7,496	1,035	2,128
1955	1,174	646	205	323	421	191	89	141	9,658	6,619	1,027	2,012
1954	2,684	2,317	94	273	433	168	109	156	8,905	6,164	911	1,830
1953	1,353	1,038	119	196	344	139	86	119	6,654	4,015	926	1,713
1952	1,102	797	100	205	339	157	78	104	5,645	3,116	893	1,636
1951	790	535	79	176	349	156	82	111	4,883	2,476	868	1,539
1950	652	400	90	162	322	143	83	96	4,436	2,096	872	1,468
1949	533	254	98	181	[3] 261	106	81	84	[3] 4,077	1,838	888	1,402
1948	476	270	83	123	[3] 266	117	79	78	[3] 3,797	1,690	870	1,298
1947	308	80	107	122	[3] 258	115	78	75	[3] 3,589	1,537	866	1,254
1946	[3] 161	55	49	62	[3] 261	124	78	72	[3] 3,538	1,571	837	1,207
1945	[3] 49	11	22	20	[3] 258	115	87	78	[3] 3,640	1,638	869	1,218

* Denotes first year for which figures include Alaska and Hawaii.
[1] Excludes refunding issues.
[2] Excludes redemptions by refunding.
[3] Duplicated and interunit obligations have been excluded from totals only.

Series Q 148–162.   Motor-Vehicle Factory Sales and Registrations, and Motor-Fuel Usage: 1900 to 1970

[Number sold includes sales of military vehicles. Value of sales does not include Federal excise taxes.   Beginning 1937, standard equipment is included in the value estimate]

Year	Motor-vehicle factory sales				Motor-vehicle registrations				Motor-fuel usage						
	Passenger cars		Motor trucks and buses [1]		Total	Auto-mobiles	Buses	Trucks	Total	Highway	Non-highway	Passenger vehicles	Trucks and combinations	Consumption per vehicle	Average mileage per gallon, per vehicle
	Number	Wholesale value	Number	Wholesale value											
	148	149	150	151	152	153	154	155	156	157	158	159	160	161	162
	1,000	Mil. dol.	1,000	Mil. dol.	1,000	1,000	1,000	1,000	Mil. gal.	Mil. gal.	Mil. gal.	Mil. gal.	Mil. gal.	Gallons	
1970	6,546.8	14,500	1,692.4	4,500	108,407.3	89,279.8	379.0	18,748.4	96,331	92,328	4,002	66,728	25,600	830	12.1
1969	8,223.7	18,751	1,923.1	4,936	105,096.6	86,861.3	364.2	17,870.9	92,240	88,135	4,105	63,395	24,727	821	12.2
1968	8,822.1	19,352	1,896.0	4,670	100,884.7	83,591.6	351.7	16,941.2	87,154	82,948	4,206	59,456	23,482	804	12.3
1967	7,436.7	15,653	1,539.4	3,592	96,930.9	80,414.1	337.9	16,178.8	81,911	77,730	4,180	56,020	21,673	786	12.4
1966	8,598.3	17,554	1,731.0	3,953	93,962.0	78,122.9	322.1	15,516.8	78,979	74,664	4,314	54,208	20,415	778	12.5
1965	9,305.5	18,380	1,751.8	3,733	90,357.6	75,257.5	314.2	14,785.7	75,312	71,104	4,208	51,169	19,935	775	12.5
1964	7,751.8	14,836	1,540.4	3,225	86,301.2	71,982.7	305.3	14,013.1	72,097	67,901	4,196	48,431	19,470	778	12.5
1963	7,637.7	14,427	1,462.7	3,090	82,713.7	69,055.4	297.8	13,360.4	68,760	64,516	4,244	46,084	18,432	773	12.5
1962	6,933.2	13,071	1,240.1	2,581	79,173.3	66,108.2	285.2	12,779.8	66,101	61,697	4,404	44,608	17,089	774	12.4
1961	5,542.7	10,285	1,133.8	2,155	75,958.2	63,417.3	279.6	12,261.1	64,534	59,306	5,228	42,863	16,443	776	12.4
1960	6,674.7	12,164	1,194.4	2,350	73,868.6	61,682.3	272.1	11,914.2	63,210	57,877	5,332	41,996	15,882	777	12.4
1959*	5,591.2	10,543	1,137.3	2,338	71,354.4	59,453.9	265.1	11,635.3	61,715	56,331	5,383	40,879	15,453	782	12.4
1958	4,257.8	8,010	877.2	1,730	68,296.5	56,890.5	270.1	11,135.8	58,589	53,418	5,171	38,904	14,514	776	12.4
1957	6,113.3	11,198	1,107.1	2,082	67,124.9	55,917.8	264.0	10,942.9	56,954	51,864	5,089	37,594	14,271	767	12.5
1956	5,816.1	9,754	1,104.4	2,077	65,148.2	54,210.9	258.7	10,678.6	55,149	50,214	4,935	36,128	13,978	768	12.5
1955	7,920.1	12,452	1,249.1	2,020	62,688.7	52,144.7	255.2	10,288.8	52,565	47,730	4,834	34,319	13,308	759	12.7
1954	5,558.8	8,218	1,042.1	1,660	58,505.3	48,468.4	248.3	9,788.5	49,118	44,365	4,753	31,670	12,541	757	12.7
1953	6,116.9	9,002	1,206.2	2,089	56,217.4	46,429.2	244.2	9,543.9	47,381	42,731	4,649	30,384	12,245	757	12.8
1952	4,320.7	6,455	1,218.1	2,319	53,262.4	43,823.0	240.4	9,198.8	45,037	40,584	4,452	28,735	11,849	766	12.7
1951	5,338.4	7,241	1,426.8	2,323	51,912.7	42,688.3	230.4	8,993.9	42,473	38,128	4,345	26,910	11,171	730	12.9
1950	6,665.8	8,468	1,337.1	1,707	49,161.6	40,339.0	223.6	8,598.9	39,830	35,652	4,177	25,037	10,566	728	12.9
1949	5,119.4	6,650	1,134.1	1,394	44,690.2	36,457.9	208.9	8,023.4	36,440	32,431	4,009	23,645	8,666	727	13.1
1948	3,909.2	4,870	1,376.2	1,880	41,085.5	33,355.2	196.7	7,533.5	34,329	30,460	3,868	22,149	8,189	741	13.1
1947	3,558.1	3,936	1,239.4	1,731	37,841.4	30,849.3	187.4	6,804.6	31,680	28,215	3,464	20,864	7,243	746	13.2
1946	2,148.6	1,979	940.9	1,043	34,373.0	28,217.0	173.5	5,982.3	28,876	25,648	3,227	19,502	6,068	747	13.3
1945	69.5	57	655.6	1,181	31,035.4	25,796.9	162.1	5,076.3	22,046	19,148	2,897	14,023	5,055	617	13.1
1944	.6	(Z)	737.5	1,700	30,479.3	25,566.4	152.5	4,760.2	19,292	16,429	2,862	11,805	4,576	540	13.0
1943	.1	(Z)	699.6	1,451	30,888.1	36,009.0	152.3	4,726.7	18,642	16,004	2,638	11,424	4,534	519	13.1
1942	222.8	163	818.6	1,427	33,003.6	27,972.8	135.9	4,894.8	22,438	19,939	2,499	[2] 14,974	4,889	604	13.5
1941	3,779.6	2,567	1,060.8	1,069	34,894.1	29,624.2	119.7	5,150.1	26,429	24,192	2,237	18,502	5,754	694	13.8
1940	3,717.3	2,370	754.9	567	32,453.2	27,465.8	101.1	4,886.2	24,038	22,001	2,037	16,759	5,156	678	13.8
1939	2,888.5	1,770	700.3	489	31,009.9	26,226.3	92.2	4,691.2	22,571	20,714	1,857	15,826	4,807	668	13.8
1938	2,019.5	1,241	488.8	329	29,813.7	25,250.4	87.6	4,475.5	21,311	19,611	1,700	15,069	4,465	658	13.9
1937	3,929.2	2,240	891.0	537	30,058.8	25,467.2	83.1	4,508.5	21,115	19,455	1,659	15,018	4,365	648	13.9
1936	3,679.2	2,014	782.2	463	28,506.8	24,182.6	62.6	4,261.6	19,561	18,099	1,462	14,026	4,003	635	14.0
1935	3,273.8	1,707	697.3	380	26,546.1	22,567.8	58.9	3,919.3	17,637	16,344	1,292	--------	--------	--------
1934	2,160.8	1,140	576.2	326	25,261.7	21,544.7	51.5	3,665.4	16,557	15,414	1,143	--------	--------	--------
1933	1,560.5	773	329.2	175	24,159.2	20,657.2	44.9	3,457.0	15,367	14,348	1,019	--------	--------	--------
1932	1,103.5	616	228.3	137	24,391.0	20,901.4	43.4	3,446.1	15,427	14,339	1,088	--------	--------	--------
1931	1,948.1	1,108	432.2	265	26,093.9	22,396.2	41.8	3,655.8	16,621	15,456	1,164	--------	--------	--------
1930	2,787.4	1,644	575.3	390	26,749.8	23,034.7	40.5	3,674.5	15,777	14,753	1,023	--------	--------	--------
1929	4,455.1	2,790	881.9	622	26,704.8	23,120.8	33.9	3,549.9	15,051	14,139	911	--------	--------	--------
1928	3,775.4	2,572	583.3	460	24,688.6	21,362.2	31.9	3,294.4	13,090	12,361	728	--------	--------	--------
1927	2,936.5	2,164	464.7	420	23,303.4	20,193.3	27.6	3,082.4	11,936	11,331	605	--------	--------	--------
1926	3,692.3	2,607	608.6	484	22,200.1	19,267.9	24.3	2,907.8	10,552	10,063	488	--------	--------	--------
1925	3,735.1	2,458	530.6	458	20,068.5	17,481.0	17.8	2,569.7	9,143	8,749	394	--------	--------	--------
1924	3,185.8	1,970	416.6	318	17,612.9	15,436.1	--------	2,176.8	7,809	7,497	312	--------	--------	--------
1923	3,624.7	2,196	409.2	308	15,102.1	13,253.0	--------	1,849.0	6,313	6,078	235	--------	--------	--------
1922	2,274.1	1,494	269.9	226	12,273.5	10,704.0	--------	1,569.5	5,014	4,841	173	--------	--------	--------
1921	1,468.0	1,038	148.0	166	10,493.6	9,212.1	--------	1,281.5	4,064	3,935	129	--------	--------	--------
1920	1,905.5	1,809	321.7	423	9,239.1	8,131.5	--------	1,107.6	3,448	3,346	102	--------	--------	--------
1919	1,651.6	1,365	224.7	371	7,576.8	6,679.1	--------	897.7	2,747	2,672	75	--------	--------	--------
1918	943.4	801	227.2	434	6,160.4	5,554.9	--------	605.4	--------	--------	--------	--------	--------	--------
1917	1,745.7	1,053	128.1	220	5,118.5	4,727.4	--------	391.0	--------	--------	--------	--------	--------	--------
1916	1,525.5	921	92.1	161	3,617.9	3,367.8	--------	250.0	--------	--------	--------	--------	--------	--------
1915	895.9	575	74.0	125	2,490.9	2,332.4	--------	158.5	--------	--------	--------	--------	--------	--------
1914	548.1	420	24.9	44	1,763.0	1,664.0	--------	99.0	--------	--------	--------	--------	--------	--------
1913	461.5	399	23.5	44	1,258.0	1,190.3	--------	67.6	--------	--------	--------	--------	--------	--------
1912	356.0	335	22.0	43	944.0	901.5	--------	42.4	--------	--------	--------	--------	--------	--------
1911	199.3	225	10.6	21	639.8	618.7	--------	20.7	--------	--------	--------	--------	--------	--------
1910	181.0	215	6.0	9	468.5	458.3	--------	10.1	--------	--------	--------	--------	--------	--------
1909	123.9	159	3.2	5	312.0	305.9	--------	6.0	--------	--------	--------	--------	--------	--------
1908	63.5	135	1.5	2	198.4	194.4	--------	4.0	--------	--------	--------	--------	--------	--------
1907	43.0	91	1.0	1	143.2	140.3	--------	2.9	--------	--------	--------	--------	--------	--------
1906	33.2	61	.8	1	108.1	105.9	--------	2.2	--------	--------	--------	--------	--------	--------
1905	24.2	38	.7	1	78.8	77.4	--------	1.4	--------	--------	--------	--------	--------	--------
1904	22.1	23	.7	1	55.2	54.5	--------	.7	--------	--------	--------	--------	--------	--------
1903	11.2	13	--------	--------	32.9	32.9	--------	--------	--------	--------	--------	--------	--------	--------
1902	9.0	10	--------	--------	23.0	23.0	--------	--------	--------	--------	--------	--------	--------	--------
1901	7.0	8	--------	--------	14.8	14.8	--------	--------	--------	--------	--------	--------	--------	--------
1900	4.1	4	--------	--------	8.0	8.0	--------	--------	--------	--------	--------	--------	--------	--------

* Denotes first year for which figures include Alaska and Hawaii.
Z   Less than $500,000.
[1] A substantial portion of the number of trucks and buses (series Q 150) consists of chassis only, without bodies; hence the value of bodies for these chassis (series Q 151) is not included.
[2] Beginning 1942, includes travel by military vehicles.

Series Q 163–174. Automobile Insurance: 1946 to 1970

[Money figures in millions of dollars.   1950, net basis; 1955, direct writing basis; 1960 and 1965, direct premiums earned and direct losses incurred; 1969, premiums written basis; 1970, premiums earned basis]

Year	Total insurance			Automobile liability						Physical damage [3]		
		Losses paid [1]		Bodily injury			Property damage [2]				Losses paid [1]	
	Premiums written	Total	Percent of premiums written	Premiums written	Losses paid [1]		Premiums written	Losses paid [1]		Premiums written	Total	Percent of premiums written
					Total	Percent of premiums written		Total	Percent of premiums written			
	163	164	165	166	167	168	169	170	171	172	173	174
1970	14,612	11,198	76.6	6,723	5,256	78.2	2,836	2,291	80.8	5,053	3,651	72.3
1969	12,906	7,715	59.8	5,892	3,093	52.5	2,544	1,693	66.5	4,470	2,929	65.5
1968	11,693	6,642	56.8	5,383	2,802	52.1	2,280	1,416	62.1	4,030	2,424	60.1
1967	10,800	5,814	53.8	4,991	2,580	51.7	2,091	1,224	58.5	3,718	2,011	54.1
1966	10,008	5,235	52.3	4,610	2,351	51.0	1,894	1,090	59.6	3,504	1,794	51.2
1965	8,358	5,221	62.5	3,948	2,459	62.3	1,567	1,025	65.4	2,843	1,737	61.1
1964	7,582	4,787	63.1	3,612	2,266	62.7	1,418	940	66.3	2,552	1,581	62.0
1963	7,341	4,459	60.7	3,333	2,017	60.5	1,328	826	62.2	2,680	1,616	60.3
1962	6,922	4,034	58.3	3,144	1,849	58.8	1,276	748	58.6	2,502	1,437	57.4
1961	6,668	3,723	55.8	2,977	1,744	58.6	1,285	705	54.9	2,406	1,274	53.0
1960*	6,448	3,645	56.5	2,841	1,697	59.7	1,219	675	55.4	2,388	1,273	53.3
1959	6,060	3,445	56.8	2,596	1,615	62.2	1,185	655	55.3	2,279	1,175	51.6
1958	5,404	2,846	52.7	2,432	1,280	52.6	1,087	572	52.6	1,885	994	52.7
1957	5,037	2,714	53.9	2,180	1,141	52.3	989	541	54.7	1,868	1,032	55.2
1956	4,541	2,363	52.0	1,899	923	48.6	925	488	52.8	1,717	952	55.4
1955	4,644	2,122	45.7	1,735	820	47.3	896	415	46.3	2,013	887	43.6
1954	4,175	1,869	44.8	1,642	746	45.4	877	387	44.1	1,656	736	44.4
1953	4,165	1,810	43.5	1,562	661	42.3	833	374	44.9	1,770	775	43.8
1952	3,608	1,646	45.6	1,332	569	42.7	715	369	51.5	1,561	708	45.4
1951	2,995	1,406	47.0	1,126	493	43.8	575	313	54.5	1,294	600	46.3
1950	2,625	1,069	40.7	931	396	42.5	482	231	47.9	1,212	442	36.5
1949	2,332	901	38.7	879	343	39.0	453	205	45.3	999	353	41.0
1948	2,019	802	39.7	744	286	38.4	366	171	46.9	910	345	37.9
1947	1,657	673	40.6	636	235	36.9	289	138	37.9	732	300	41.0
1946	1,250	582	46.6	500	189	37.7	193	107	55.1	557	287	51.5

* Denotes first year for which figures include Alaska and Hawaii.
[1] For 1970, includes adjusting expenses.
[2] Covers real property against damage by autos.
[3] Covers auto fire, theft, collision, and comprehensive.

Series Q 175–186. Percent Distribution of Automobile Ownership, and Financing: 1947 to 1970

[In percent.   Excludes Alaska and Hawaii]

Years	Families owning automobiles			Method of financing purchases								
	Total	Owning 1 automobile	Owning 2 or more automobiles	All passenger cars [1]			New passenger cars [1]			Used passenger cars [1]		
				Total	Full cash [2]	Installment credit and other borrowing	Total	Full cash [2]	Installment credit and other borrowing	Total	Full cash [2]	Installment credit and other borrowing
	175	176	177	178	179	180	181	182	183	184	185	186
1970	82	54	28	100	47	53	100	34	66	100	52	48
1969	79	52	27	100	47	53	100	34	66	100	51	49
1968	79	53	26	100	42	58	100	31	69	100	50	50
1967	78	53	25	100	48	52	100	38	62	100	53	47
1966	79	54	25	100	48	52	100	37	63	100	52	48
1965	79	55	24	100	48	52	100	40	60	100	53	47
1964	78	55	22	100	47	53	100	40	60	100	51	49
1963	80	58	22	100	45	55	100	38	62	100	49	51
1962	74	57	17	100	44	56	100	38	62	100	48	50
1961	76	58	18	100	48	52	100	39	61	100	52	48
1960	77	62	15	100	38	62	100	33	67	100	41	59
1959	74	59	15	100	38	61	100	33	66	100	41	57
1958	70	60	10	100	43	56	100	36	63	100	45	54
1957	75	62	13	100	38	60	100	36	63	100	39	58
1956	72	61	9	100	36	61	100	34	63	100	38	60
1955	70	60	10	100	38	60	100	39	60	100	37	60
1954	66	58	8	100	37	61	100	38	61	100	36	61
1953	61	55	5	100	38	61	100	40	59	100	37	62
1952	60	56	4	100	35	63	100	41	57	100	33	65
1951	60	56	4	100	44	55	100	52	47	100	39	60
1950	59	52	7	100	47	52	100	54	46	100	41	57
1949	56	³48	³3	100	50	49	100	56	43	100	47	52
1948	54	----------	----------	100	59	39	100	66	33	100	55	42
1947	----------	----------	----------	100	65	35	100	71	29	100	63	37

[1] Refers to purchases during preceding year.   Includes cars received as gifts, whether cash or credit purchased.   Detail in purchases excludes buyers for whom method of financing was not ascertained.
[2] Includes trade-in allowance.
[3] Based on spending units (persons living in the same dwelling and related by blood, marriage, or adoption) who pooled their income for major items of expense.

Series Q 187–198.　Speed of Motor Vehicles on Highways: 1945 to 1970

[Excludes Alaska and Hawaii.　Based on actual speed of each vehicle recorded on tangent sections of main rural highways during off-peak hours]

Year	Vehicles recorded (1,000)	Average speed (m.p.h.)				Percent of vehicles exceeding—						
		All vehicles	Passenger cars	Trucks	Buses	40 m.p.h.	45 m.p.h.	50 m.p.h.	55 m.p.h.	60 m.p.h.	65 m.p.h.	70 m.p.h.
	187	188	189	190	191	192	193	194	195	196	197	198
1970	488	59.2	60.6	54.7	58.8	97	93	83	68	47	27	12
1969	388	60.0	61.3	54.9	59.4	98	93	82	67	46	27	13
1968	480	59.0	60.4	54.0	60.5	97	92	81	66	45	26	12
1967	478	58.0	59.5	53.1	59.4	96	91	79	64	44	24	12
1966	519	57.3	58.8	52.6	58.8	96	89	76	59	40		
1965	552	56.4	57.8	51.8	57.4	95	88	73	56	34		
1964	569	55.9	57.2	51.0	57.8	95	87	71	53	32		
1963	539	55.8	57.1	51.3	58.1	95	88	72	52	29		
1962	602	53.8	55.1	49.4	56.0	93	84	64	43	21		
1961	574	52.6	53.7	48.2	55.3	92	80	60	38	18		
1960	459	52.6	53.8	48.2	55.5	92	80	58	37	16		
1959	396	52.0	53.3	47.3	53.5	90	77	56	36	16		
1958	515	51.7	52.8	47.3	53.6	90	77	55	33	15		
1957	344	51.4	52.6	47.0	52.6	89	75	52	33	15		
1956	381	50.5	51.8	46.2	52.3	87	72	49	30	14		
1955	395	50.5	52.0	45.6	52.3	87	72	50	29	14		
1954	236	49.7	51.1	45.2	51.8	86	69	46	26	12		
1953	241	49.7	51.1	44.9	51.5	85	69	47	27	13		
1952	341	49.5	50.8	45.0	52.1	84	68	45	26	12		
1951	273	48.9	50.1	44.4	51.2	82	63	42	24	11		
1950	280	47.6	48.7	43.0	49.8	77	58	37	20	8		
1949	223	47.6	48.7	43.5	50.3	78	60	38	21	9		
1948	164	47.7	48.8	43.1	50.0	77	59	36	20	9		
1947	132	46.9	48.1	42.5	48.4	75	56	34	18	8		
1946	158	45.2	46.1	40.2	47.8	68	48	29	15	7		
1945 [1]	96	44.0	45.0	39.8	45.5	64	42	24	11	5		

[1] August 15 to December 31.

Series Q 199–207.　Miles of Travel by Motor Vehicles: 1921 to 1970

[In million vehicle-miles]

Year	All motor vehicles			Passenger vehicles [1]		Trucks and combinations		Average miles per vehicle		Year	All motor vehicles		
	Total travel	Urban travel	Rural travel	Urban travel	Rural travel	Urban travel	Rural travel	Passenger vehicles [1]	Trucks and combinations		Total travel	Urban travel	Rural travel
	199	200	201	202	203	204	205	206	207		199	200	201
1970	1,120,705	577,373	543,332	496,767	409,268	80,606	134,064	9,798	11,450	1935	228,568	118,327	110,241
1969	1,070,575	544,547	526,028	468,275	395,620	76,272	130,408	9,650	11,565	1934	215,563	112,513	103,050
1968	1,015,649	513,289	502,360	440,936	378,062	72,353	124,298	9,507	11,571	1933	200,642	105,578	95,064
1967	961,553	485,493	476,060	417,209	361,888	68,284	114,172	9,420	11,268	1932	200,517	106,366	94,151
1966	930,497	469,777	460,720	402,573	354,019	67,204	106,701	9,407	11,207	1931	216,151	115,580	100,571
1965	887,640	423,853	463,787	358,796	355,188	65,057	108,599	9,278	11,737	1930	206,320	111,202	95,118
1964	846,500	405,086	441,414	342,755	339,474	62,331	101,940	9,311	11,723	1929	197,720	107,409	90,311
1963	805,423	385,422	420,001	327,079	322,775	58,343	97,226	9,265	11,644	1928	172,856		
1962	766,852	368,089	398,763	318,937	314,626	49,152	84,137	9,467	10,406	1927	158,453		
1961	737,535	339,633	397,902	294,191	314,762	45,442	83,140	9,492	10,461	1926	140,735		
1960	718,845	331,585	387,260	286,898	305,538	44,687	81,722	9,474	10,583	1925	122,346		
1959*	700,478	323,790	376,688	279,931	297,393	43,859	79,295	9,559	10,552	1924	104,838		
1958	664,653	307,069	357,584	265,729	283,454	41,340	74,130	9,524	10,348	1923	84,995		
1957	647,004	296,699	350,305	256,563	277,235	40,136	73,070	9,425	10,328	1922	67,697		
1956	631,161	287,200	343,961	246,961	271,955	40,239	72,006	9,389	10,813	1921	55,027		
1955	605,646	275,105	330,541	235,384	261,445	39,721	69,096	9,400	10,697				
1954	561,963	247,551	314,412	210,671	246,733	36,880	67,679	9,354	10,883				
1953	544,433	236,058	308,375	199,754	240,046	36,304	68,329	9,417	10,927				
1952	513,581	224,118	289,463	189,987	224,534	34,131	64,929	9,442	10,940				
1951	491,093	222,671	268,422	188,670	207,579	34,001	60,843	9,208	10,790				
1950	458,246	218,248	239,998	184,476	183,218	33,772	56,780	9,078	10,776				
1949	424,461	205,364	219,097	175,686	171,044	29,678	48,053	9,468	9,915				
1948	397,957	199,082	198,875	170,331	153,617	28,751	45,258	9,648	10,030				
1947	370,894	184,088	186,806	158,770	145,921	25,318	40,885	9,814	9,955				
1946	340,880	170,049	170,831	148,497	136,153	21,552	34,678	10,033	9,630				
1945	250,173	130,161	120,012	111,401	92,831	18,760	27,181	7,870	9,270				
1944	212,713	110,750	101,963	93,679	77,264	17,071	24,699	6,647	8,998				
1943	208,192	108,990	99,202	91,942	74,592	17,048	24,610	6,366	9,034				
1942	268,224	138,235	129,989	119,653	102,780	18,582	27,209	7,910	9,616				
1941	333,612	163,591	170,021	143,101	135,558	20,490	34,463	9,663	10,750				
1940	302,188	149,993	152,195	130,269	121,988	19,724	30,207	9,129	10,626				
1939	285,402	142,253	143,149	122,805	115,378	19,448	27,771	9,025	10,504				
1938	271,177	136,264	134,913	117,537	109,145	18,727	25,768	8,923	10,383				
1937	270,110	138,072	132,038	118,216	107,743	19,856	24,295	8,819	10,264				
1936	252,128	129,450	122,678	110,419	100,602	19,031	22,076	8,675	10,098				

* Denotes first year for which figures include Alaska and Hawaii.　　　　[1] Passenger cars, buses, and taxicabs.

Series Q 208–223. Motor Vehicle Deaths and Death Rates, by Age: 1913 to 1970

[Rates are deaths per 100,000 population]

Year or period	All ages Number 208	Rate [1] 209	Under 5 years Number 210	Rate 211	5–14 years Number 212	Rate 213	15–24 years Number 214	Rate 215	25–44 years Number 216	Rate 217	45–64 years Number 218	Rate 219	65–74 years Number 220	Rate 221	75 years and over [2] Number 222	Rate 223
1970	54,633	25.3	1,915	11.2	4,159	10.2	16,720	46.7	13,446	27.9	11,099	26.5	4,084	32.7	3,210	42.2
1969	55,791	27.6	2,077	11.6	4,045	9.8	17,443	49.8	13,868	28.9	11,012	26.6	4,210	35.2	3,136	41.5
1968	55,200	28.8	2,100	11.0	4,200	10.2	16,600	51.6	13,600	28.5	11,300	27.8	4,100	34.5	3,300	46.7
1967	52,924	27.8	2,067	10.7	3,845	9.4	15,646	49.2	12,987	27.6	10,902	26.9	4,285	36.5	3,192	45.7
1966	53,041	28.3	2,182	11.0	3,869	9.6	15,298	48.8	13,282	28.6	11,051	27 9	4,217	36.4	3,142	45.6
1965	49,163	26.5	2,059	10.1	3,526	8.9	13,395	44.2	12,595	27.1	10,509	27.0	4,077	35.5	3,002	45.0
1964	47,700	26.1	2,120	10.2	3,430	8.8	12,400	42.7	12,500	26.8	10,200	26.6	4,150	36.4	2,900	44.9
1963	43,564	24.3	1,991	9.6	3,063	8.0	11,123	40.1	11,356	24.4	9,506	25.1	3,786	33.4	2,739	43 9
1962	40,804	23.1	1,903	9.2	3,028	8.1	10,157	38.4	10,701	22.9	8,812	23.6	3,696	32.8	2,507	41.5
1961	38,091	22.0	1,891	9.2	2,802	7.6	9,088	36.5	10,212	21.8	8,267	22.5	3,467	31.0	2,364	40.5
1960	38,137	22.4	1,953	9.6	2,814	7.9	9,117	37.7	10,189	21.8	8,294	22.9	3,457	31.3	2,313	41.1
1959	37,910	22.7	1,842	9.2	2,719	7.9	8,969	38.2	10,358	22.2	8,263	23.2	3,487	32.3	2,272	41.8
1958	36,981	22.5	1,791	9.1	2,710	8.1	8,388	37.0	10,414	22.2	7,922	22.6	3,535	33.5	2,221	42.3
1957	38,702	24.1	1,785	9.2	2,604	8.0	8,667	39.7	11,230	23.9	8,545	24.8	3,560	34.4	2,311	45.5
1956	39,628	25.1	1,770	9.4	2,640	8.4	9,169	42.9	11,551	24.6	8,573	25.3	3,657	36.2	2,268	46.4
1955	38,426	24.6	1,875	10.2	2,406	8.0	8,656	40.9	11,448	24.5	8,372	25.2	3,455	35.1	2,214	47.1
1954	35,586	23.0	1,864	10.4	2,332	8.1	7,571	36.2	10,502	22.6	7,848	24.0	3,247	33.9	2,203	49.0
1953	37,955	24.9	2,019	11.5	2,368	8.5	8,169	39.1	11,302	24.5	8,318	25.8	3,508	37.7	2,271	52.6
1952	37,794	25.0	1,951	11.3	2,295	8.7	8,115	38.6	11,380	24.7	8,463	26.7	3,472	38.5	2,118	50.8
1951	36,996	24.6	1,875	10.9	2,300	9.2	7,713	36.0	11,253	24.7	8,276	26.5	3,444	39.5	2,135	53.0
1950	34,763	23.3	1,767	10.8	2,152	8.8	7,600	34.5	10,214	22.5	7,728	25.1	3,264	38.8	2,038	52.4
1949	31,701	21.5	1,667	10.7	2,158	9.0	6,772	30.7	8,892	19.9	7,073	23.4	3,116	37.8	2,023	53.9
1948	32,259	22.3	1,635	11.0	2,337	9.8	7,218	32.5	8,702	19.8	7,190	24.3	3,173	39.6	2,001	55.4
1947	32,697	23.0	1,502	10.5	2,275	9.7	7,251	32.8	8,775	20.3	7,468	25.7	--------	--------	5,426	48.2
1946	33,411	24.0	1,568	11.9	2,508	10.8	7,445	34.4	8,955	21.1	7,532	26.4	--------	--------	5,403	49.6
1945	28,076	21.4	1,290	10.0	2,386	10.3	5,358	27.8	7,578	19.7	6,794	24.2	--------	--------	4,670	44.1
1944	24,282	18.3	1,203	9.6	2,093	9.1	4,561	22.6	6,514	16.7	5,982	21.6	--------	--------	3,929	38.2
1943	23,823	17.7	1,132	9.4	1,959	8.6	4,522	20.6	6,454	16.1	5,996	22.0	--------	--------	3,760	37.6
1938–1942 avg	33,549	25.5	1,187	11.1	2,453	10.8	6,705	28.5	9,173	23.1	8,594	32.8	--------	--------	5,437	59.8
1933–1937 avg	36,313	29.3	1,273	12.4	3,054	12.7	6,790	29.3	10,224	26.9	9,521	39.8	--------	--------	5,451	69.8
1928–1932 avg	30,900	26.4	1,500	12.8	3,600	14.5	5,600	25.1	8,200	22.6	7,500	35.0	--------	--------	4,500	67.5
1923–1927 avg	21,700	19.6	1,300	11.1	3,800	15.8	3,500	16.8	5,400	15.9	4,800	24.7	--------	--------	2,900	48.6
1918–1922 avg	12,500	12.3	950	8.3	3,100	14.1	1,650	8.8	2,900	9.4	2,500	14.5	--------	--------	1,400	27.9
1913–1917 avg	6,700	7.0	450	3.8	1,600	7.7	950	5.1	1,700	5.9	1,400	8.9	--------	--------	600	13.4

[1] Based on populations standardized for age (base 1940) to remove influence of changes in age distribution that occurred between 1913 and 1969.

[2] Includes "age unknown." In 1967, those deaths numbered about 23.

Series Q 224–232. Motor-Vehicle Accidents—Number and Deaths, by Type of Accident: 1913 to 1970

Year	Total motor-vehicle accidents (1,000) 224	Traffic deaths [1] Total 225	Non-collision accidents 226	Collision accidents With other motor vehicles 227	With pedestrians 228	With fixed objects 229	Traffic death rates Per 100,000 population 230	Per 10,000 motor vehicles 231	Per 100 million vehicle miles 232
1970	16,000	54,633	[2] 15,400	23,200	9,900	[2] 3,800	26.8	4.9	4.9
1969	15,500	55,791	15,700	23,700	10,100	3,900	27.7	5.2	5.2
1968	14,600	54,862	17,400	22,400	9,900	2,700	27.5	5.3	5.4
1967	13,700	52,924	16,700	22,000	9,400	2,350	26.8	5.4	5.5
1966	13,600	53,041	16,300	22,200	9,400	2,500	27.1	5.5	5.7
1965	13,200	49,163	14,900	20,800	8,900	2,200	25.4	5.4	5.5
1964	12,300	47,700	14,600	19,600	9,000	2,100	25.0	5.5	5.6
1963	11,500	43,564	13,800	17,600	8,200	1,900	23.1	5.2	5.4
1962	11,000	40,804	12,900	16,400	7,900	1,750	22.0	5.1	5.3
1961	10,400	38,091	12,200	14,700	7,650	1,700	20.8	5.0	5.2
1960	10,400	38,137	11,900	14,800	7,850	1,700	21.2	5.1	5.3
1959	10,200	37,910	11,800	14,900	7,850	1,600	21.5	5.3	5.4
1958	10,000	36,981	11,600	14,200	7,650	1,650	21.3	5.4	5.6
1957	10,200	38,702	11,800	15,400	7,850	1,700	22.7	5.7	6.0
1956	10,300	39,628	13,000	15,200	7,900	1,600	23.7	6.1	6.3
1955	9,900	38,426	12,100	14,500	8,200	1,600	23.4	6.1	6.3
1954	9,550	35,586	11,500	12,800	8,000	1,500	22.1	6.1	6.3
1953	9,900	37,955	12,200	13,400	8,750	1,500	24.0	6.7	7.0
1952	9,500	37,794	11,900	13,500	8,900	1,450	24.3	7.1	7.4
1951	9,400	36,996	11,200	13,100	9,150	1,400	24.1	7.1	7.5

See footnotes at end of table.

Series Q 224-232. Motor-Vehicle Accidents—Number and Deaths, by Type of Accident: 1913 to 1970—Con.

Year	Total motor-vehicle accidents (1,000)	Traffic deaths [1]					Traffic death rates		
		Total	Non-collision accidents	Collision accidents			Per 100,000 population	Per 10,000 motor vehicles	Per 100 million vehicle miles
				With other motor vehicles	With pedestrians	With fixed objects [2]			
	224	225	226	227	228	229	230	231	232
1950	8,300	34,763	10,600	11,650	9,000	1,300	23.0	7.1	7.6
1949	7,600	31,701	9,100	10,500	8,800	1,100	21.3	7.1	7.5
1948	8,200	32,259	8,950	10,200	9,950	1,000	22.1	7.9	8.1
1947	8,400	32,697	8,800	9,900	10,450	1,000	22.8	8.6	8.8
1946	6,150	33,411	8,900	9,400	11,600	950	23.9	9.7	9.8
1945	5,500	28,076	6,600	7,150	11,000	800	21.2	9.1	11.2
1944	4,800	24,282	5,600	5,700	9,900	700	18.3	8.0	11.4
1943	4,400	23,823	5,690	5,300	9,900	700	17.8	7.7	11.4
1942	5,200	28,309	6,740	7,300	10,650	850	21.1	8.6	10.6
1941	7,000	39,969	9,450	12,500	13,550	1,350	30.0	11.5	12.0
1940	6,100	34,501	7,800	10,100	12,700	1,100	26.1	10.6	11.4
1939	5,700	32,386	7,900	8,700	12,400	1,000	24.7	10.4	11.4
1938	5,800	32,582	7,350	8,900	12,850	940	25.1	10.9	12.0
1937	7,000	39,643	9,690	10,320	15,500	1,160	30.8	13.2	14.7
1936		38,089	9,410	9,500	15,250	1,060	29.7	13.4	15.1
1935		36,369	9,720	8,750	14,350	1,010	28.6	13.7	15.9
1934		36,101	9,820	8,110	14,480	1,040	28.6	14.3	16.8
1933		31,363	8,680	6,470	12,840	900	25.0	13.0	15.6
1932		29,500	7,000	6,070	11,490	800	23.6	12.2	16.1
1931		33,700	7,850	6,820	13,370	870	27.2	13.0	17.0
1930		32,900	8,730	5,880	12,900	720	26.7	12.4	17.4
1929		31,200	8,430	5,400	12,250	620	25.7	11.8	17.3
1928		28,000	7,360	4,310	11,420	540	23.4	11.4	17.4
1927		25,800	7,280	3,430	10,820	500	21.8	11.2	17.7
1926		23,400					20.1	10.6	18.0
1925		21,900					19.1	11.0	17.9
1924		19,400					17.1	11.0	
1923		18,400					16.5	12.2	
1922		15,300							
1921		13,900							
1920		12,500							
1919		11,200							
1918		10,700							
1917		10,200							
1916		8,200							
1915		6,600							
1914		4,700							
1913		4,200							

[1] Totals may not quite equal sums of various types because totals for most types are estimated, and these have been rounded. [2] Data based on improved reporting procedure; therefore, not entirely comparable with other years.

Series Q 233-234. State and Federal Gasoline Tax Rates: 1930 to 1970

[In cents per gallon. When 2 figures appear in a cell, the first is tax in effect at beginning of year, the other is tax at end of year]

Year	State average	Federal tax [1]	Year	State average	Federal tax [1]	Year	State average	Federal tax [1]
	233	234		233	234		233	234
1970	7.01	4	1955	5.35	2	1940	3.96	1–1.5
1969	6.84	4	1954	5.19	2	1939	3.96	1
1968	6.62	4	1953	5.10	2	1938	3.96	1
1967	6.45	4	1952	4.83	2	1937	3.91	1
1966	6.42	4	1951	4.74	1.5–2	1936	3.85	1
1965	6.41	4	1950	4.65	1.5	1935	3.80	1
1964	6.31	4	1949	4.52	1.5	1934	3.66	1
1963	6.22	4	1948	4.35	1.5	1933	3.65	1–1.5
1962	6.18	4	1947	4.25	1.5	1932	3.60	0–1
1961	6.09	4	1946	4.16	1.5	1931	3.48	
1960	5.94	4	1945	4.10	1.5	1930	3.35	
1959*	5.86	3–4	1944	4.06	1.5			
1958	5.65	3	1943	4.05	1.5			
1957	5.58	3	1942	3.99	1.5			
1956	5.54	2–3	1941	3.99	1.5			

* Denotes first year for which figures include Alaska and Hawaii.
[1] The 4-cent gasoline tax applies to all gallonage imported or produced. Effective July 1, 1955, the entire tax became refundable for fuel used for farming; thereafter, the additional two cents (one cent levied July 1, 1956, and one cent levied Oct. 1, 1959) became refundable for nonhighway uses, and for use by local transit systems.

Series Q 235–250. Public Transit Mileage, Equipment, Passengers, and Passenger Revenue: 1917 to 1970

Year	Mileage (Dec. 31)			Equipment owned (Dec. 31)			Revenue and nonrevenue passengers (millions)				Revenue passengers (mil.)	Passenger revenue (mil. dol.)	Employees (1,000)	Employee payroll (mil. dol.)	Passengers carried, railway (millions)	
	Railway track	Trolley coach	Motor bus	Railway cars	Trolley coaches	Motor buses	Total	Railway	Trolley coach	Motor bus					Surface	Subway and elevated
	235	236	237	238	239	240	241	242	243	244	245	246	247	248	249	250
1970	2,081	563	112,700	10,600	1,050	49,700	7,332	2,116	182	5,034	5,932	1,639.1	138	1,274	235	1,881
1969	2,081	563	117,300	10,665	1,082	49,600	7,803	2,229	199	5,375	6,310	1,554.7	141	1,184	249	1,980
1968	2,045	616	121,000	10,745	1,185	50,000	8,019	2,181	228	5,610	6,491	1,470.2	144	1,110	253	1,928
1967	2,049	616	123,600	10,645	1,244	50,180	8,172	2,201	248	5,723	6,616	1,457.4	146	1,055	263	1,938
1966	2,153	676	122,100	10,680	1,326	50,130	8,083	2,035	284	5,764	6,671	1,385.4	144	995	282	1,753
1965	2,173	766	120,900	10,664	1,453	49,600	8,253	2,134	305	5,814	6,798	1,340.1	145	964	276	1,858
1964	2,173	986	118,300	10,614	1,865	49,200	8,328	2,166	349	5,813	6,854	1,326.0	145	917	289	1,877
1963	2,236	1,119	117,000	10,634	2,155	49,400	8,400	2,165	413	5,822	6,915	1,316.3	147	892	329	1,836
1962	2,557	1,849	114,300	11,084	3,161	48,800	8,695	2,283	547	5,865	7,122	1,330.2	149	878	284	1,704
1961	2,601	2,017	111,500	11,419	3,593	49,000	8,883	2,289	601	5,993	7,242	1,320.9	152	856	434	1,855
1960	3,143	2,196	108,700	11,866	3,826	49,600	9,395	2,313	657	6,425	7,521	1,334.9	156	857	463	1,850
1959*	3,445	2,491	106,300	11,983	4,297	49,500	9,557	2,349	749	6,459	7,650	1,308.0	159	832	521	1,828
1958	3,844	2,723	104,500	12,201	4,848	50,100	9,732	2,387	843	6,502	7,778	1,282.2	165	831	572	1,815
1957	5,019	3,007	102,400	12,759	5,412	50,800	10,389	2,522	993	6,874	8,338	1,319.8	177	840	679	1,843
1956	5,746	3,293	100,700	13,225	5,748	51,400	10,941	2,756	1,142	7,043	8,756	1,351.1	186	852	876	1,880
1955	6,197	3,428	99,800	14,532	6,157	52,400	11,529	3,077	1,202	7,250	9,189	1,358.9	198	864	1,207	1,870
1954	6,765	3,630	99,000	15,600	6,598	54,000	12,392	3,401	1,367	7,624	9,858	1,410.0	211	895	1,489	1,912
1953	7,352	3,663	100,000	17,234	6,941	54,700	13,902	4,076	1,566	8,260	11,036	1,448.6	220	913	2,036	2,040
1952	8,532	3,736	99,600	19,176	7,180	55,980	15,119	4,601	1,640	8,878	12,022	1,438.1	227	903	2,477	2,124
1951	9,457	3,678	99,700	20,604	7,071	57,660	16,125	5,290	1,633	9,202	12,281	1,411.6	232	872	3,101	2,189
1950	10,813	3,513	98,000	22,986	6,504	56,820	17,246	6,168	1,658	9,420	13,845	1,386.8	240	835	3,904	2,264
1949	11,931	3,337	96,400	24,728	6,366	57,035	19,008	7,185	1,661	10,162	15,251	1,419.7	253	841	4,839	2,346
1948	12,964	2,905	96,500	26,280	5,687	58,540	21,368	9,112	1,528	10,728	17,312	1,416.8	261	829	6,506	2,606
1947	14,976	2,699	95,300	30,158	4,707	56,917	22,540	10,852	1,356	10,332	18,287	1,324.2	266	790	8,096	2,756
1946	16,716	2,354	91,100	33,479	3,916	52,450	23,372	11,862	1,311	10,199	19,119	1,331.5	261	713	9,027	2,835
1945	17,702	2,313	90,400	36,377	3,711	49,670	23,254	12,124	1,244	9,886	18,982	1,313.7	242	632	9,426	2,698
1944	18,082	2,245	87,700	37,199	3,561	48,400	23,017	12,137	1,234	9,646	18,735	1,296.9	242	599	9,516	2,621
1943	18,181	2,248	87,000	37,505	3,501	47,100	22,000	11,806	1,175	9,019	17,918	1,235.6	2.9	554	9,150	2,656
1942	18,171	2,273	85,500	37,508	3,385	46,000	18,000	9,856	899	7,245	14,501	979.1	219	462	7,290	2,566
1941	18,342	2,041	82,100	37,670	3,029	39,300	14,085	8,502	652	4,931	11,302	758.8	205	386	6,074	2,421
1940	19,602	1,925	78,000	37,662	2,802	35,000	13,098	8,325	534	4,239	10,504	701.5	203	360	5,943	2,382
1939	20,600	1,543	74,300	40,372	2,184	32,600	12,837	8,539	445	3,853	10,252	681.5	202	352	6,171	2,368
1938	21,800	1,398	70,400	42,605	2,032	28,500	12,645	8,781	389	3,475	9,985	662.9	202	344	6,545	2,236
1937	23,770	1,166	67,000	45,312	1,655	27,500	13,246	9,468	289	3,489	10,436	689.7	209	348	7,161	2,307
1936	25,300	859	62,200	48,103	1,136	23,900	13,146	9,824	143	3,179	10,512	685.5	206	328	7,501	2,323
1935	26,700	548	58,100	50,466	578	23,800	12,226	9,512	96	2,618	9,782	642.3	204	311	7,276	2,236
1934	28,500	423	54,700	54,118	441	18,700	12,038	9,600	68	2,370	--------	--------	204	303	7,394	2,206
1933	--------	--------	--------	58,124	310	17,200	11,327	9,207	45	2,075	--------	--------	201	287	7,074	2,133
1932							12,025	9,852	37	2,136						
1931							13,924	11,583	28	2,313						
1930							15,567	13,072	16	2,479						
1929							16,985	14,358	5	2,622						
1928							16,989	14,518	3	2,468						
1927							17,201	14,901	--------	2,300						
1926							17,234	15,225	--------	2,009						
1925							16,651	15,167	--------	1,484						
1924							16,301	15,312	--------	989						
1923							16,311	15,650	--------	661						
1922							15,735	15,331	--------	404						
1921							--------	14,574	--------	--------						
1920								15,541								
1919								14,916								
1918								14,243								
1917								14,507								

* Denotes first year for which figures include Alaska and Hawaii.

Series Q 251–263. Oil Pipelines Operated and Oil Originated: 1921 to 1970

Year	Miles of line operated	Oil originated		Oil delivered out of system			Companies reporting	Investment in carrier property	Current assets	Current liabilities	Retained income	Capital- ization	Net income
		Crude	Refined	Total	To con- necting carriers	Terminated							
	251	252	253	254	255	256	257	258	259	260	261	262	263
		Mil. bbl.	*Mil. bbl.*	*Mil. bbl.*	*Mil. bbl.*	*Mil. bbl.*	*Number*	*Mil. dol.*	*Mil. dol.*	*Mil. dol.*	*Mil. dol.*	*Mil. dol.*	*Mil. dol.*
1970	175,735	3,568	2,449	8,147	2,320	5,827	101	5,786	628	480	1,124	2,518	312
1969	170,824	3,405	2,316	7,745	2,243	5,499	99	5,379	644	441	1,037	2,267	273
1968	169,307	3,203	2,203	7,269	2,048	5,221	97	5,139	562	431	950	2,130	262
1967	165,478	3,017	2,035	6,800	1,890	4,910	90	4,745	519	354	873	1,943	[1] 261
1966	163,155	2,826	1,774	6,238	1,770	4,468	87	4,433	572	333	858	1,790	236
1965	161,412	2,618	1,629	5,864	1,757	4,107	89	4,178	555	301	835	1,635	218
1964	159,583	2,567	1,381	5,565	1,684	3,881	90	4,040	530	293	812	1,620	210
1963	156,812	2,467	1,182	5,322	1,648	3,673	94	3,915	535	254	843	1,685	201
1962	155,053	2,379	1,078	5,109	1,624	3,485	92	3,518	432	184	798	1,383	204
1961	153,737	2,336	966	4,923	1,646	3,277	89	3,407	432	190	769	1,397	181
1960*	151,968	2,239	909	4,783	1,639	3,144	87	3,300	393	187	701	1,439	169
1959	149,159	2,182	849	4,659	1,624	3,035	85	3,197	384	175	673	1,385	183
1958	144,354	2,018	757	4,317	1,509	2,807	82	2,949	347	154	633	1,383	162
1957	145,236	2,183	668	4,472	1,590	2,883	82	2,843	364	161	600	1,357	159
1956	142,686	2,195	663	4,458	1,613	2,845	83	2,716	368	217	467	1,304	178
1955	140,374	2,038	586	4,039	1,444	2,595	84	2,586	353	185	432	1,282	153
1954	138,962	1,829	502	3,705	1,355	2,349	81	2,501	316	155	403	1,266	124
1953	133,900	1,861	435	3,627	1,279	2,349	78	2,312	301	173	372	1,177	109
1952	132,715	1,810	385	3,359	1,198	2,161	75	2,064	323	182	328	1,024	97
1951	131,457	1,774	345	3,201	1,126	2,075	76	1,822	233	166	279	759	82
1950	128,589	1,525	297	2,740	937	1,803	76	1,656	192	126	219	660	81
1949	124,984	1,415	241	2,448	792	1,656	73	1,498	175	97	202	549	58
1948	124,092	1,586	227	2,697	880	1,817	73	1,381	168	110	180	439	57
1947	119,298	1,431	187	2,474	851	1,623	71	1,225	127	105	148	339	53
1946	116,544	1,319	154	2,260	766	1,494	70	1,106	104	83	129	298	56
1945	113,351	1,292	150	2,365	964	1,401	74	1,043	115	78	120	301	66
1944	111,615	1,277	147	2,389	1,043	1,347	75	1,001	104	91	93	283	66
1943	108,783	1,123	144	2,077	866	1,211	74	965	108	82	71	297	61
1942	106,485	981	92	1,764	692	1,072	69	919	81	75	62	301	57
1941	105,435	971	82	1,642	563	1,079	71	885	56	91	30	293	79
1940	100,156	886	72	1,407	451	956	66	842	47	52	51	295	80
1939	98,681	803	70	---------	---------	907	63	830	32	48	40	310	81
1938	95,938	793	65	---------	---------	868	59	808	35	45	40	295	93
1937	96,612	885	63	---------	---------	910	58	803	44	51	42	323	103
1936	93,926	755	52	---------	---------	788	52	774	42	43	38	309	92
1935	92,037	723	44	---------	---------	709	53	763	47	40	59	346	78
1934	93,070	557	35	---------	---------	---------	51	758	72	11	101	348	84
1933	93,724	538	29	---------	---------	---------	48	766	66	20	92	360	106
1932	92,782	508	25	---------	---------	---------	46	764	77	21	89	368	112
1931	93,090	489	16	---------	---------	---------	49	845	132	37	171	474	121
1930	88,728	---------	---------	---------	---------	---------	40	773	133	36	167	458	124
1929	85,796	---------	---------	---------	---------	---------	37	741	129	25	186	428	142
1928	81,676	---------	---------	---------	---------	---------	33	659	130	30	186	388	117
1927	76,070	---------	---------	---------	---------	---------	32	609	125	27	150	388	93
1926	72,846	---------	---------	---------	---------	---------	33	539	93	22	130	342	80
1925	70,009	---------	---------	---------	---------	---------	35	511	88	13	102	346	88
1924	68,185	---------	---------	---------	---------	---------	36	496	159	54	107	496	72
1923	64,760	---------	---------	---------	---------	---------	34	432	144	77	78	497	63
1922	57,349	---------	---------	---------	---------	---------	36	382	130	36	152	472	59
1921	55,260	---------	---------	---------	---------	---------	33	365	127	61	148	337	34

* Denotes first year for which figures include Alaska and Hawaii.
[1] After extraordinary and prior period items.

Chapter Q

Rail Transportation (Series Q 264-412)

Q 264–412. General note.

The principal sources of these series are various issues of two annual publications of the Interstate Commerce Commission: For 1954–1970, *Transport Statistics in the United States*, part 1; and for all years prior to 1954, *Statistics of Railways in the United States*.

No attempt has been made to adjust the figures for the effect of changes in methods of accounting and reporting; hence, the data for the various years are often only approximately comparable.

Although railroads regulated by the ICC are still described legally as "steam railways," most train and switching operations, since 1957, are performed by diesel locomotives, and some divisions of the railways included are electrified. The Commission has also regulated a small and diminishing number of railways of the interurban electric type which are not included in the figures shown here.

Railway *operating* companies are those whose officers direct the actual transportation service and whose books contain operating as well as financial accounts. *Lessor* companies maintain a separate legal existence, but their properties are operated by the lessees. *Proprietary* companies are also nonoperating companies. Their outstanding capitalization is owned by other railway companies. The term "circular" refers to roads (operating or nonoperating) for which brief circulars showing date of incorporation, mileage, and a few other facts were filed with the Interstate Commerce Commission. They include intrastate roads and roads under construction. The term "unofficial" is used to indicate roads for which official returns were not received by the ICC—the figures having been taken from the returns by roads in prior years, and items contained in railway and engineering periodicals and newspapers, corrected in accordance with the best information available.

Switching and terminal companies are those operating separately for joint account or for revenue. Services such as those of switching and terminal companies are mostly performed directly by the line-haul carriers as an ordinary part of their business. Line haul denotes train movements between terminals and stations on main and branch lines of the road, exclusive of switching.

Beginning in 1911, the ICC classified operating companies on the basis of operating revenues. Those of class I had annual revenues above $1,000,000; class II, above $100,000; and class III, below $100,000. Beginning in 1956, the minimum for class I was raised to $3,000,000 and the other two classes were consolidated. Effective January 1965, the classification was changed to the following: Class I, $5,000,000 or more; and class II, under $5,000,000. If the revenues of a company fall below the limit, the company is not reclassified until the decline appears to be permanent. The relative importance of class I railroads has increased since 1911 because of the growth of traffic and the absorption of small roads in larger systems. The ratio of operating revenues of class I line-haul companies to the total revenues of classes I, II, and III was 96.48 percent in 1911, 97.45 in 1916, 98.07 in 1926, 98.76 in 1941, 99.06 in 1945, and 98.21 in 1969.

A collection of definitions of words or phrases frequently used in discussions of railway statistics has been issued by the ICC, entitled *Railway Statistical Terms*, Statement No. 4119, June 1941. For financial terms, see ICC, *Uniform System of Accounts for Steam Railroads*.

Statistics of mileage in existence and stocks of equipment, and balance sheet items, pertain to the end of the year indicated.

There are no class I railroads in Alaska or Hawaii.

Q 264–273. Electric railways—summary, 1890–1937.

Source: U.S. Bureau of the Census, *Census of Electrical Industries, Report on Street Railways and Trolley-Bus and Motorbus Operations*.

The census of street railways, which was first taken in 1890, and which was taken at quinquennial intervals from 1902 through 1937, covers all street railways, without regard to kind of motive power, and all interurban railways using other than steam as motive power. The nonelectric railroads included are those operated principally by cable and gasoline engines. Operations of electrified divisions of steam-railway companies are not included. Figures in these series do not include data for motorbus and trolley-bus operations of electric street railways. For motorbus and trolley-bus statistics from census reports, see source.

Q 274–282. Railroad passenger and freight service, 1865–1890.

Source: U.S. Interstate Commerce Commission, *Railway Statistics Before 1890*, Statement No. 32151 (mimeographed), 1932.

Before 1890, the principal source of continuous information on railroads is the annual *Poor's Manual of Railroads*. The figures in the *Manual* were revised in successive issues. The Interstate Commerce Commission consulted the issues from 1869 to 1900 and evidently took account of the revisions. Earnings and traffic figures are understatements of actual level; mileage covered is shown in the table below. Similar but not identical figures, with the degree of coverage similarly indicated in terms of mileage, appear in Bureau of the Census, *Report on Transportation Business in the United States at the Eleventh Census*, 1890, part I.

Table I. Miles of Road Operated by Railroads

Year	Roads reporting earnings [1]	Roads reporting earnings and traffic statistics	Year	Roads reporting earnings [1]
1890	158,037	157,976	1879	79,009
1889	153,945	153,689	1878	78,960
1888	145,387	145,341	1877	74,112
1887	137,028	136,986	1876	73,508
1886	125,185	125,146		
			1875	71,759
1885	123,320	122,110	1874	69,273
1884	115,704	113,172	1873	66,237
1883	110,414	106,938	1872	57,323
1882	104,971	95,752	1871	44,614
1881	92,971			
1880	82,146		1851	8,836

[1] Includes elevated railways.

All figures are based on reports of individual railroads for fiscal years ending in the calendar year indicated. The period of time covered is, therefore, not the same for all carriers included. Balance sheet data pertain to the ends of such fiscal years.

Data for 1890 shown in these series do not agree with 1890 data shown for series Q 284–312 because of different sources.

Q 283. Freight service, ton-miles carried, 13 railroads, 1865–1885.

Source: H. V. and H. W. Poor, *Manual of Railroads*, New York City, 1888, p. XXVIII (reprinted with permission, Standard & Poor Corporation).

The roads represented are 7 eastern roads (Pennsylvania; Pittsburgh, Fort Wayne, and Chicago; New York Central; Lake Shore; Michigan Central; Boston and Albany; New York, Lake Erie and Western) and 6 western roads (Illinois Central; Chicago and Alton; Chicago and Rock Island; Chicago, Burlington and Quincy; Chicago and Northwestern; Chicago, Milwaukee, and St. Paul).

Q 284–312. Railroad mileage, equipment, and passenger traffic and revenue, 1890–1970.

Source: All series, except series Q 293–294, see general note for series Q 264–412. **Series Q 293**, 1913–1970, and **series Q 294**, 1911–1956, American Railway Car Institute, New York, *Railroad Car Facts*, annual issues (copyright); **series Q 294**, 1957–1970, U.S. Interstate Commerce Commission, *Transport Statistics in the United States*, part 1, annual issues.

Q 285, mileage constructed. Miles on which operations were begun during the year. Figures exclude relocated road or road constructed to shorten distance without serving new territory.

Q 286, mileage abandoned. Miles on which operation was permanently abandoned during the year, the cost of which was written out of the investment accounts or was scheduled to be written out at the end of the year.

Q 289, track operated, first main track. Equivalent to miles of road operated. Figures exceed those for series Q 287, road owned, in most years because of two or more roads operating on same line under trackage agreements.

Q 300, average tractive effort. Figures represent the force in pounds exerted by locomotives, measured at the rim of the driving wheels.

Q 301–303, passenger-train cars. Includes coaches and parlor, sleeping, dining, club, lounge, observation, postal, baggage, express, and other cars, as well as cars serving a combination of purposes.

Q 311, passenger revenue. Excludes revenue from services such as handling of excess baggage or mail; sleeping and parlor or chair car reservations; dining and buffet service on trains; station, train, and boat privileges; parcel rooms; storage of baggage; or other miscellaneous services and facilities connected with the transportation of passengers. Passenger revenue depends upon the established tariffs (the published schedules of rates and fares) and includes extra fares on limited trains, additional railway fares for the exclusive use of space, mileage and scrip coupons honored, or revenue from the transportation of corpses.

Q 312, revenue per passenger mile. Represents figures for series Q 311 divided by those for series Q 307.

Q 313–314. Railroad revenue passenger-miles per car-mile and per train-mile, 1890–1970.

Source: U.S. Interstate Commerce Commission, 1890–1965, *Revenue Traffic Statistics*, December issues; 1966–1970, *Transport Economics*, June 1970, and unpublished data.

Figures for revenue passenger-miles per car-mile for 1908–1919, and for passenger-miles per train-mile for 1890–1932, were computed by the National Bureau of Economic Research from figures for passenger-miles, car-miles, and train-miles presented in *Statistics of Railways in the United States*.

Q 315. Passenger train-miles per train-hour, 1936–1970.

Source: U.S. Interstate Commerce Commission, 1936–1957, *Passenger Train Performance*, December issues; 1958–1968, *Annual Report*, 1968 and 1969; 1969 and 1970, *Transport Economics*, June 1970, and unpublished data.

The train-hour figures upon which these figures are based are reckoned from the time a train leaves its original terminal to the time it arrives at its final terminal. Time spent in stopping to take on and discharge traffic and other delays on the road is included.

Q 316–318. Railroad freight revenue ton-miles per loaded car-mile, train-mile, and mile of road, 1890–1970.

Source: See general note for series Q 264–412.

Q 319. Freight train-miles per train-hour, 1920–1970.

Source: U.S. Interstate Commerce Commission, 1920–1955, *Freight Train Performance*, December issues; 1956–1965, *Annual Report*, 1967 and 1969; 1966–1970, *Transport Economics*, June 1970, and unpublished data.

For explanation of train-hour figures, see text for series Q 315.

Q 320. Freight car-miles per car-day, 1921–1970.

Source: U.S. Interstate Commerce Commission. See general note for series Q 264–412; 1956–1962, *Annual Report*, various issues; 1963–1965, *Transport Statistics in the United States*, 1967; 1966–1970, *Transport Economics*, June 1970, and unpublished data.

Q 321–328. Railroad mileage and equipment, 1830–1890.

Source: See source for series Q 274–282.

Equipment data pertain to the ends of fiscal years. See also text for series Q 274–282.

Q 329. Miles of railroad built, 1830–1925.

Source: 1830–1879, U.S. Bureau of the Census, Tenth Census Reports, vol. IV, *Report on the Agencies of Transportation in the United States*, p. 289. 1893–1925, *Railway Age*, vol. 104, No. 1, Simmons-Boardman Publishing Corp., New York, January 1, 1938, p. 66 (copyright).

For a more detailed discussion of the problems of estimating miles of railroad built, see E. R. Wicker, "Railroad Investment Before the Civil War," and the "Comment" by George R. Taylor and by Charles J. Kennedy, in *Studies in Income and Wealth*, vol. 24, National Bureau of Economic Research, New York.

The Tenth Census report (pp. 289–293, 300–375) contains materials on history of construction which includes figures on mileage built and existent, by groups of States, for individual companies, annually from 1830 to 1880. Somewhat similar data appear in Bureau of the Census, *Report on Transportation Business in the United States at the Eleventh Census: 1890*, part 1, pp. 3–5, 54–107.

According to the Bureau of the Census, information was received from every railroad known to exist in 1880. The letter of instructions from the Superintendent of the Census to the railroads said: "In cases . . . in which the records have been lost, the officers of such companies and roads are requested to obtain . . . this information in the best form possible. The recollection of officers and employees long in the service of a road may be used . . . if more reliable data be not accessible."

The *Railway Age* obtained its figures at annual intervals from individual railroads and from State railroad commissions.

It is not clear just when a mile of road would be reported as built. Construction of some lines extended over several years. Each annual segment may have been reported when finished, or nothing may have been reported until the whole line was completed. The year of physical completion may have differed from the year in which traffic was first carried. In such cases, the mileage may have been assigned to either year.

The Census Bureau figures pertain only to miles in operation in the census year. The figures for any year are, therefore, understatements to the extent that mileage constructed in that year may have been abandoned by June 1, 1880 (the date of the 1880 Census).

The change from year to year in miles operated, series Q 321, or miles owned, series Q 322, is sometimes used as a measure of miles constructed. The annual change in miles operated, however, is also affected by acquisitions of trackage rights, as a result of which the same line may be counted in the operation of two or more railroads. The changes in miles operated and in miles owned are affected by abandonments during the year (regardless of when constructed).

Q 330. Miles of railroad operated by receivers or trustees, 1894–1970.

Source: See general note for series Q 264–412.

Q 331–345. Railroad freight traffic and revenue, 1890–1970.

Source: See general note for series Q 264–412 except series Q 331, 332, and 338, 1964–1970, from U.S. Interstate Commerce Commission, *Freight Commodity Statistics of Class I Railroads in the United States,* annual issues.

Revenue-tons and ton-miles exclude the movement of a railroad company's materials and supplies on its own lines. A carload is a shipment of 10,000 pounds or more of one commodity from one shipper to one consignee.

Tons originated are tons identified as not having had previous line-haul transportation by other rail carriers; such shipments include import traffic and traffic from outlying possessions of the United States received from water carriers at the port of entry, and finished products from transit points. Ton-miles are computed by multiplying the weight of each shipment by the distance it moves and summing the products.

For definitions of class I, II, and III roads, see general note for series Q 264–412.

Q 333, products of agriculture. Includes not only raw farm products but simple manufactures such as flour, corn meal, cottonseed meal, cake, and linters. On the other hand, such products as vegetable oils, sugar and molasses, canned fruits and vegetables, and manufactured tobacco are included in series Q 337, manufactures and miscellaneous.

Q 335, products of mines. Includes coke as well as coal and other raw minerals.

Q 336, products of forests. Includes not only raw forest products but lumber, shingles, lath; box, crate, and cooperage materials; veneer and built-up wood.

Q 343, freight revenue. Includes revenue from the transportation of freight and from transit, stop, diversion, and reconsignment arrangements upon the basis of tariffs. Excludes revenue from such activities as switching of freight-train cars; water transfers of freight, vehicles, and livestock; movement of freight trains at a rate per train-mile or for a lump sum; storage of freight; demurrage; grain elevators; stockyards; or other miscellaneous services and facilities connected with the transportation of freight.

Q 346–355. Railroad property investment, capital, income, and expenses, 1850–1890.

Source: See source for series Q 274–282.

See also text for same series.

Q 356–363. Railroad property investment and capital, 1890–1970.

Source: See general note for series Q 264–412.

Q 356, investment, book value. Figures represent recorded value, in the accounts of carriers, of land, fixed improvements such as roadbed and track, rolling stock, maintenance machinery, etc., owned by them. Figures include property held under contract for purchase.

Q 357, depreciation reserve. Figures represent the accumulated accounting allowance for loss in service value not restored by current maintenance. The loss in value is incurred in connection with the consumption or prospective retirement of physical property in the course of service from causes against which carriers are not protected by insurance, which are known to be in current operation, and the effect of which can be forecast with a reasonable approach to accuracy.

Q 361, funded debt unmatured. Funded debt is debt maturing more than one year from date of issue.

Q 362, net capitalization. Figures represent railway capital outstanding, series Q 358, minus stocks and debt of railroad companies held by other railroad companies.

Q 364–366. Railroad capital expenditures for additions and betterments, 1921–1970.

Source: Association of American Railroads, 1921–1950, *Railroad Transportation*; 1951–1970, *Yearbook of Railroad Facts, 1971.*

Additions comprise: Additional facilities such as equipment (rolling stock), tracks, buildings and other structures; additions to such facilities, such as extensions to tracks, buildings and other structures; additional ties laid in existing tracks; and additional devices applied to facilities such as airbrakes applied to cars not previously thus equipped.

Betterments comprise improvements of existing facilities through the substitution of superior parts for inferior parts retired, such as the substitution of steel-tired wheels for cast wheels under equipment, the application of heavier rail in tracks, the strengthening of bridges by the substitution of heavier members, and the application of superior floors or roofs in buildings.

Q 367–377. Railroad income and expenses, and interest and dividends, 1890–1970.

Source: See general note for series Q 264–412.

Q 367, operating revenue. Includes revenue from freight, passenger, and other transportation and incidental services.

Q 368–370, operating expenses. Includes current depreciation.

Q 371, tax accruals. Taxes imposed by any form of government whether based on an assessed value of the property, on amounts of stocks and bonds, on earnings, income, dividends declared, payroll, number of passengers, quantity of freight, length of road, rolling stock, or other basis. Tax accruals do not include special assessments for street and other improvements, nor special benefit taxes such as water assessments.

Q 372, operating income. Figures represent net revenue from railway operations, series Q 367 minus series Q 368, less tax accruals, series Q 371.

Q 373, net operating income. Figures represent operating income, series Q 372, minus net payable balance of equipment and joint facility rents. The equipment rents deducted at this point are those for equipment leased for less than one year, or interchanged. They are usually on a per day or per mile basis.

Q 374, net income. Figures represent net operating income, series Q 373, plus other income, minus miscellaneous deductions and fixed and contingent charges. Fixed charges are mainly rent for leased roads and equipment (i.e., equipment leased for one year or more), and interest (except contingent interest).

Q 377, interest accrued on funded debt. Figures include interest not paid during year on debt in default of interest; they exclude interest on debt owed by the issuing company, or on debt incurred for new lines, extensions, additions or betterments, accrued before such property is completed or comes into service.

Q 378–384. Railroad tax accruals, 1921–1970.

Source: See general note for series Q 264–412.

Other taxes, series Q 384, are largely property taxes levied by State or local governments.

Q 385–387. Railroad highway grade crossings, 1925–1970.

Source: See general note for series Q 264–412.

Specially protected highway grade crossings, series Q 386, include crossings with operated gates, watchmen, or both, during at least part of the day, and those with audible signals, visible signals, or both; they exclude those with fixed signs only.

Q 388–397. Fuel received, ties and rails laid, and purchases by railroads, 1917–1970.

Source: **Series Q 388–393,** see general note for series Q 264–412. **Series Q 394–397,** Association of American Railroads, 1923–1964,

Railroad Transportation; 1965–1969, *Yearbook of Railroad Facts*, annual issues.

Q 388–390, fuel received. Figures include not only fuel for operation of trains but fuel for station, shop, or other use, except that figures for 1964–1970 include only the operation of locomotives and motorcars.

Q 391, new rails laid. Figures include both rails laid in replacement and rails laid in additional tracks, new lines, and extensions, except that figures for 1917–1926 include only rails laid in replacement.

Q 392–393, cross-ties laid. Figures for 1917–1926 include only ties laid in replacement. Of the total ties laid in 1927, 78,340,000 were in replacement. Treated ties are those which have been subjected to some preservative process, e.g., creosoting, before being placed in the track.

Q 398–399. Railroad employees and compensation, 1890–1970.

Source: See general note for series Q 264–412.

An employee is defined as a person in the service of a railroad, subject to its continuing authority to supervise and direct the manner of rendition of his service. Persons such as lawyers engaged to render only specifically defined service for specific cases and not under general or continuing retainer are not classed as employees. For 1890–1914, the number of employees represents the number on the payroll June 30. Thereafter, the nature of the figures included for the smaller (class II and III) roads is not clear in the source. For class I roads they appear to be averages of 4 quarterly counts, 1915–1920; and of 2 quarterly and 6 monthly counts, 1921; beginning 1922, they are averages of 12 monthly counts.

Q 400–409. Railroad accidents and fatalities, 1890–1970.

Source: U.S. Federal Railroad Administration, *Accident Bulletin*,

annual issues (formerly issued by U.S. Interstate Commerce Commission), and related monthly reports.

Reportable railroad accidents are divided into three groups: (1) Train accidents, (2) train-service accidents, and (3) nontrain accidents. Train accidents are those arising from the operation or movement of trains, locomotives, or cars which result in a reportable death or injury and more than $750 damage to equipment, track, or roadbed; or a collision, derailment, or other train accident, with more than $750 damage to equipment, track, or roadbed. Train-service accidents are those arising from the operation or movement of trains, locomotives, or cars which result in a reportable death or injury but not more than $750 damage to equipment, track, or roadbed. Nontrain accidents are those which do not result from the operation or movement of trains, locomotives, or cars.

Q 410–412. Pullman company operations, 1915–1968.

Source: U.S. Interstate Commerce Commission, *Statistics of Railways in the United States* and *Transport Statistics in the United States*, part 2, and, beginning 1963, part 1, *The Pullman Company (Sleeping Car Companies)*, various annual issues; except series Q 411, 1915–1921, U.S. Office of Business Economics, *Survey of Current Business*, January 1939, p. 18.

Figures for series Q 411 exceed those in series Q 310, parlor and sleeping car passenger-miles, mainly because travel of railroad employees etc. (for which railroad companies receive no revenue) is not included in series Q 310; but if Pullman accommodations are paid for, the travel is included in series Q 411.

The number of Pullman employees, series Q 412, is the number on the payroll at the end of the year. The Pullman Company ceased operation in 1969.

★ ★ ★ ★ ★ ★ ★ ★ **More Recent Data for *Historical Statistics* Series** ★ ★ ★ ★ ★ ★ ★ ★ ★

★   ★
★   Statistics for more recent years in continuation of many of the still-active series shown here appear   ★
★   in annual issues of the *Statistical Abstract of the United States*, beginning with the 1975 edition. For   ★
★   direct linkage of the historical series to the tables in the *Abstract*, see Appendix I in the *Abstract*.   ★
★   ★

★ ★

Series Q 264–273. Electric Railways—Summary: 1890 to 1937

Series No.	Item	1937 [1]	1932	1927	1922	1917	1912	1907	1902	1890
264	Number of companies	[2] 478	[2] 706	[2] 963	[2] 1,200	[2] 1,307	1,260	1,236	987	789
265	Miles of line operated [3]	14,214	20,110	27,948	31,264	32,548	30,438	25,547	16,645	5,783
266	Miles of all track operated [3]	23,770	31,548	40,722	43,932	44,835	41,065	34,382	22,577	8,123
267	Value of road and equipment__$1,000_	4,399,768	4,143,381	(NA)	5,058,762	5,136,442	4,596,563	3,637,669	2,167,634	389,357
268	Number of employees [4]	152,476	[5] 182,165	264,575	300,119	294,826	282,461	221,429	140,769	70,764
269	Number of passenger cars	44,864	59,692	70,309	77,301	79,914	76,162	70,016	60,290	32,505
270	Revenue passengers, including pay-transfer___1,000_	7,485,290	[6] 7,955,981	12,174,592	12,666,558	11,304,660	9,545,555	7,441,115	4,774,212	2,023,010
271	Operating revenues [7]___$1,000_	513,129	566,290	927,774	1,016,719	709,825	567,512	418,188	247,554	90,617
272	Operating expenses [7]___$1,000_	406,119	442,607	694,460	727,795	452,796	332,896	251,309	142,313	62,011
273	Operating ratio___percent_	79.1	78.2	74.9	71.6	63.8	58.7	60.1	57.5	68.4

NA Not available.
[1] Excludes data for 22 companies, operating on a part-year basis.
[2] Includes certain companies in Pennsylvania which maintained separate organizations, though controlled through stock ownership by other companies. For 1912, these companies were treated as merged and not included in the number reported.
[3] Includes small mileage of track lying outside United States.
[4] Number reported as of June 30 for 1890, 1922, 1927, and 1932; for 1902, average for the year; for 1912, as of Sept. 16. Figures for 1937 represent an average of numbers reported on June 30 and Dec. 31.
[5] Includes 334 trolley-bus operators.
[6] Includes 29,721,000 trolley-bus passengers.
[7] Includes auxiliary operating revenues of $91,242,000 for 1922 and $8,905,000 for 1927; auxiliary expenses, $49,232,000 for 1922 and $7,822,000 for 1927. Data for operating revenues and operating expenses of auxiliary operations excluded so far as possible for earlier years.

Series Q 274–283. Railroad Passenger and Freight Service: 1865 to 1890

Year	Passenger service				Freight service						Year	Passenger revenue service	Freight service		Year	Freight service	
	Passenger revenue	Passengers carried	Passenger miles	Revenue per passenger-mile	Freight revenue	Total revenue-tons carried [1]	Ton-miles carried, all roads	Revenue per ton-mile	Revenue ton-miles per train-mile	Ton-miles carried, 13 railroads			Freight revenue	Ton-miles carried, 13 railroads		Freight revenue	Ton-miles carried, 13 railroads
	274	275	276	277	278	279	280	281	282	283		274	278	283		278	283
	Mil. dol.	Mil.	Mil.	Cents	Mil. dol.	Mil.	Mil.	Cents		Bil.		Mil. dol.	Mil. dol.	Bil.		Mil. dol.	Bil.
1890	272	520	12,522	2.174	734	691	79,193	0.927	163.99	--------	1880	147	467	14.48	1870	(NA)	4.92
1889	259	494	11,965	2.169	665	619	68,677	.970	159.91	--------	1879	142	386	13.07	1869	300	4.22
1888	251	451	11,191	2.246	639	590	65,423	.977	159.36	--------	1878	124	365	10.68	1868	--------	3.44
1887	240	428	10,570	2.276	636	552	61,561	1.034	156.16	--------	1877	125	347	8.75	1867	--------	3.03
1886	211	382	9,660	2.194	550	482	52,802	1.042	150.99	--------	1876	136	361	8.74	1866	--------	2.62
															1865	--------	2.16
1885	200	351	9,134	2.199	509	437	49,152	1.057	143.59	17.83	1875	139	363	7.84			
1884	206	334	8,779	2.356	502	399	44,725	1.124	133.58	16.81	1874	140	379	7.73			
1883	206	312	8,541	2.422	539	400	44,065	1.224	125.86	17.09	1873	137	389	7.48			
1882	188	289	7,688	2.447	485	360	39,302	1.236	128.81	16.23	1872	132	340	6.42			
1881	173	--------	--------	--------	551	--------	--------	--------	--------	16.06	1871	108	294	5.57			

NA Not available.   [1] 72.5 million revenue tons were carried in 1870; 55.1 million in 1861.

Series Q 284–312. Railroad Mileage, Equipment, and Passenger Traffic and Revenue: 1890 to 1970

[Includes intercorporate duplications. Unless otherwise noted, covers class I, II, and III railroads, except that prior to 1908 includes returns for switching and terminal companies where applicable]

Year ending—	Number of operating railroads [1]	Mileage								New cars delivered for domestic use		Equipment [5]					
		Con-structed	Aban-doned	Road owned [2]	Track operated				Road operated, passenger service [4]			Locomotives in service					
					Total [3]	First main track	Other main tracks	Yard tracks and sidings		Freight train	Passenger train [4]	Total [6]	Steam	Electric [7]	Diesel	Other	Average tractive effort [8] (lb.)
	284	285	286	287	288	289	290	291	292	293	294	295	296	297	298	299	300
DEC. 31																	
1970	351	80	1,283	205,782	360,330	220,107	28,682	111,541	49,533	66,185	302	29,122	(9)	270	28,773	79	--------
1969	361	49	1,166	207,005	364,915	222,164	29,564	113,187	56,484	69,028	240	29,090	(9)	278	28,711	101	--------
1968	360	63	747	208,111	366,238	222,924	30,002	113,312	59,259	56,232	65	29,448	(9)	307	29,031	110	--------
1967	370	169	1,039	209,292	368,030	222,039	30,387	113,604	67,827	83,095	146	29,874	67	324	29,428	55	65,267
1966	375	89	786	210,573	370,104	225,528	30,906	113,670	73,173	90,104	113	30,124	76	347	29,644	57	70,900
1965	372	59	963	211,384	370,636	226,015	31,113	113,508	76,993	77,822	666	30,061	89	365	29,552	55	63,096
1964	380	24	882	212,059	372,300	226,753	31,535	114,012	81,795	69,330	399	30,296	93	402	29,745	56	62,311
1963	395	23	777	214,387	374,522	227,282	32,153	115,087	84,928	44,960	156	30,506	112	438	29,898	58	61,533
1962	395	41	1,353	215,090	376,290	227,851	32,719	115,720	86,302	36,554	304	30,701	136	441	30,057	67	61,415
1961	397	34	930	216,445	379,415	229,369	33,853	116,193	88,854	31,720	214	30,889	210	484	30,123	72	61,969
1960	*407	*21	*693	*217,552	*381,745	*230,169	*34,800	*116,776	93,816	57,047	251	*31,178	*374	*498	*30,240	*66	*61,314
1959	411	14	1,034	217,565	383,912	230,930	35,746	117,236	100,243	37,819	66	31,539	871	517	30,097	54	61,408
1958	412	50	941	218,399	385,264	231,494	36,448	117,322	107,131	42,760	143	31,616	1,488	562	29,515	51	61,312
1957	415	49	1,194	219,067	386,978	232,177	37,123	117,678	112,724	99,590	232	32,391	2,608	597	29,137	49	61,515
1956	422	74	613	220,221	389,668	233,509	37,908	118,251	115,951	67,080	396	32,593	3,918	616	28,001	58	68,745

See footnotes at end of table.

Series Q 284–312. Railroad Mileage, Equipment, and Passenger Traffic and Revenue: 1890 to 1970—Con.

Year ending—	Number of operating railroads [1]	Mileage			Track operated				Road operated, passenger service [4]	Equipment [5]							
		Constructed	Abandoned	Road owned [2]	Total [3]	First main track	Other main tracks	Yard tracks and sidings		New cars delivered for domestic use		Locomotives in service					Average tractive effort [8] (lb.)
										Freight train	Passenger train [4]	Total [6]	Steam	Electric [7]	Diesel	Other	
	284	285	286	287	288	289	290	291	292	293	294	295	296	297	298	299	300
DEC. 31 —Con.																	
1955	441	105	502	220,670	390,965	233,955	38,825	118,185	119,745	37,545	886	33,533	6,266	639	26,563	65	65,005
1954	443	49	694	221,098	392,580	234,342	39,520	118,718	124,572	35,696	349	35,033	9,041	669	25,256	67	63,152
1953	448	50	666	221,758	393,736	234,959	39,794	118,983	128,943	81,021	386	37,251	12,274	713	24,209	55	61,339
1952	454	76	965	222,508	394,631	235,545	39,977	119,109	132,903	77,833	117	39,697	16,737	790	22,118	52	59,966
1951	462	71	456	223,427	395,831	236,476	40,157	119,198	139,178	95,993	179	42,473	22,590	817	19,014	52	58,476
1950	471	33	755	223,779	396,380	236,857	40,456	119,067	146,468	43,991	964	42,951	26,680	827	15,396	48	57,075
1949	481	100	620	224,511	397,232	237,564	40,639	119,029	156,821	92,562	933	43,272	30,344	856	12,025	47	56,333
1948	485	71	529	225,149	397,203	237,756	40,845	118,602	160,140	112,640	891	44,474	34,581	867	8,981	45	55,170
1947	502	79	709	225,806	397,355	238,209	40,954	118,192	161,115	68,522	861	44,344	36,942	864	6,495	43	54,506
1946	513	20	381	226,438	398,037	239,069	41,015	117,953	161,407	41,955	1,337	45,511	39,592	867	5,008	44	53,735
1945	517	40	551	226,696	398,054	239,438	41,106	117,510	161,701	43,864	931	46,253	41,018	885	4,301	49	53,217
1944	524	46	705	227,335	398,437	240,215	41,178	117,044	162,290	43,003	1,003	46,305	41,921	902	3,432	50	52,822
1943	534	34	1,149	227,999	398,730	240,745	41,093	116,892	162,429	31,836	685	45,406	41,983	907	2,476	40	52,451
1942	543	38	2,886	229,174	399,627	241,737	41,137	116,753	163,658	62,873	418	44,671	41,755	892	1,978	46	51,811
1941	559	22	1,695	231,971	403,625	244,263	41,166	118,196	167,951	80,623	349	44,375	41,911	895	1,517	52	51,217
1940	574	19	1,284	233,670	405,975	245,740	41,373	118,862	170,429	62,341	257	44,333	42,410	900	967	56	50,905
1939	600	1	1,697	235,064	408,350	246,922	41,445	119,983	172,031	25,132	276	45,172	43,604	879	639	50	50,395
1938	611	35	1,621	236,842	411,324	248,474	41,589	121,261	173,616	16,470	434	46,544	45,210	882	403	49	49,803
1937	631	149	1,642	238,539	414,572	250,582	41,579	122,411	175,543	77,498	629	47,555	46,342	872	293	48	49,412
1936	641	38	1,577	240,104	416,381	251,542	41,731	123,108	178,491	46,612	191	48,009	46,923	858	175	53	48,972
1935	661	25	1,974	241,822	419,228	252,930	41,916	124,382	--------	7,515	205	49,541	48,477	884	130	50	48,367
1934	678	33	1,784	243,857	422,401	254,882	42,109	125,410	--------	25,176	275	51,423	50,465	805	104	49	47,712
1933	700	122	2,016	245,703	425,664	256,741	42,397	126,526	--------	2,163	9	54,228	53,302	789	85	52	46,916
1932	709	321	1,370	247,595	428,402	258,869	42,556	126,977	--------	3,252	77	56,732	55,831	764	80	57	46,299
1931	749	502	779	248,829	429,823	259,999	42,780	127,044	--------	13,203	323	58,652	57,820	709	80	43	45,764
1930	775	460	954	249,052	429,883	260,440	42,742	126,701	--------	74,920	1,534	60,189	59,406	663	77	43	45,225
1929	809	671	782	249,433	429,054	260,570	42,711	125,773	--------	81,590	2,455	61,257	60,572	621	25	39	44,801
1928	849	946	710	249,309	427,750	260,546	42,432	124,772	--------	46,060	1,571	63,311	62,642	617	(9)	52	43,838
1927	880	819	797	249,131	424,737	259,639	42,071	123,027	--------	63,370	2,087	65,348	64,843	467	(9)	38	42,798
1926	929	881	892	249,138	421,341	258,815	41,686	120,840	--------	88,862	2,814	66,847	66,381	435	11	20	41,886
1925	947	595	753	249,398	417,954	258,631	40,962	118,361	--------	105,735	2,428	68,098	67,713	379	1	5	40,666
1924	995	635	617	250,156	415,028	258,238	39,916	116,874	--------	113,711	2,517	69,486	69,114	372	--------	--------	39,891
1923	1,023	441	537	250,222	412,993	258,084	38,697	116,212	--------	175,748	2,034	69,414	69,005	409	--------	--------	39,177
1922	1,041	318	1,188	250,413	409,359	257,425	37,888	114,046	--------	66,289	977	68,518	68,121	397	--------	--------	37,441
1921	1,058	331	687	251,176	407,531	258,362	37,614	111,555	--------	40,292	1,161	69,122	68,733	389	--------	--------	36,935
1920	1,085	--------	--------	252,845	406,580	259,941	36,894	109,744	--------	50,955	831	68,942	68,554	388	--------	--------	36,365
1919	1,111	--------	--------	253,152	403,891	258,525	36,730	108,637	--------	94,981	126	68,977	68,592	385	--------	--------	35,789
1918	1,131	--------	--------	253,529	402,343	258,507	36,228	107,608	--------	67,063	750	67,936	67,563	373	--------	--------	34,995
1917	1,168	--------	--------	253,626	400,353	259,705	35,066	105,582	--------	115,705	1,684	66,070	65,699	371	--------	--------	33,932
1916	1,216	--------	--------	254,037	397,014	259,705	34,325	102,984	--------	111,516	1,344	65,595	65,253	342	--------	--------	32,840
JUNE 30																	
1916	1,243	--------	--------	254,251	394,944	259,211	33,864	101,869	--------	[10] 58,226	[10] 1,513	65,314	65,021	293	--------	--------	32,380
1915	1,260	--------	--------	253,789	391,142	257,569	33,662	99,910	--------			66,502	66,229	273	--------	--------	31,501
1914	1,297	--------	--------	252,105	387,208	256,547	32,376	98,285	--------	[10] 97,626	[10] 3,589	67,012			--------	--------	31,006
1913	1,296	--------	--------	249,777	379,508	253,470	30,827	95,211	--------	[10] 176,049	[10] 2,654	65,597			--------	--------	30,258
1912	1,298	--------	--------	246,777	371,238	249,852	29,367	92,019	--------		[10] 2,509	63,463			--------	--------	29,049
1911	1,312	--------	--------	243,979	362,824	246,238	27,613	88,974	--------		[10] 3,362	62,463			--------	--------	28,291
1910	1,306	--------	--------	240,293	351,767	240,831	25,354	85,582	--------			60,019					27,282
1909	1,316	--------	--------	236,834	342,351	235,402	24,573	82,377	--------			58,219					26,601
1908	1,323	--------	--------	233,468	333,646	230,494	23,699	79,453	--------			57,698					26,356
1907	1,564	--------	--------	229,951	327,975	227,455	22,771	77,749	--------			55,388					25,781
1906	1,491	--------	--------	224,363	317,083	222,340	20,982	73,761	--------			51,672					24,741
1905	1,380	--------	--------	218,101	306,797	216,974	19,881	69,942	--------			48,357					23,666
1904	1,314	--------	--------	213,904	297,073	212,243	18,338	66,492	--------			46,743					22,804
1903	1,281	--------	--------	207,977	283,822	205,314	16,948	61,560	--------			43,871					21,781
1902	1,219	--------	--------	202,472	274,196	200,155	15,820	58,221	--------			41,225					--------
1901	1,213	--------	--------	197,237	265,352	195,562	14,876	54,915	--------			39,584					--------
1900	1,224	--------	--------	193,346	258,784	192,556	14,075	52,153	--------			37,663					--------
1899	1,206	--------	--------	189,295	250,143	187,535	13,384	49,224	--------			36,703					
1898	1,192	--------	--------	186,396	245,334	184,648	13,096	47,589	--------			36,234					
1897	1,158	--------	--------	184,428	242,013	183,284	12,795	45,934	--------			35,986					
1896	1,111	--------	--------	182,777	239,140	181,983	12,440	44,718	--------			35,950					
1895	1,104	--------	--------	180,657	233,276	177,746	12,348	43,181	--------			35,699					
1894	1,043	--------	--------	178,709	229,796	175,691	12,163	41,941	--------			35,492					
1893	1,034	--------	--------	176,461	221,864	169,780	11,633	40,451	--------			34,788					
1892	1,002	--------	--------	171,564	211,051	162,397	10,846	37,808	--------			33,136					
1891	991	--------	--------	168,403	207,446	161,275	10,428	35,742	--------			32,139					
1890	1,013	--------	--------	163,597	199,876	156,404	9,760	33,711	--------			30,140					

See footnotes at end of table.

Series Q 284–312. Railroad Mileage, Equipment, and Passenger Traffic and Revenue: 1890 to 1970—Con.

Year ending—	Equipment [5]—Con.					Passenger traffic and revenue						
	Passenger-train cars in service			Freight-train cars in service [12]			Passenger-miles				Revenue	
	Railroad only	Class I railroads and Pullman Co. [11]		Number	Average capacity [8]	Passengers	Total	Commutation [4]	Coach [4]	Parlor and sleeping car [4]	Total	Per passenger-mile
		Total	Air conditioned									
	301	302	303	304	305	306	307	308	309	310	311	312
					Tons	1,000	Mil.	Mil.	Mil.	Mil.	$1,000	Cents
DEC. 31												
1970	11,378	11,177	----------	1,453,708	67.1	289,469	10,786	4,592	5,414	765	423,191	3.924
1969	12,630	14,619	----------	1,464,194	65.8	301,673	12,214	4,546	6,601	1,021	441,503	3.615
1968	14,816	15,384	----------	1,484,571	64.3	301,372	13,164	4,383	7,559	1,178	446,704	3.393
1967	17,822	18,610	7,159	1,510,963	63.4	304,028	15,264	4,281	9,329	1,592	488,549	3.201
1966	18,974	20,016	7,589	1,523,741	61.4	307,530	17,162	4,193	10,799	2,104	547,139	3.188
1965	20,022	21,327	8,079	1,515,169	59.8	305,822	17,454	4,128	11,069	2,191	555,986	3.185
1964	21,510	23,057	8,980	1,517,564	58.2	314,386	18,271	4,199	11,632	2,416	579,287	3.170
1963	22,616	23,568	9,950	1,542,456	56.8	310,999	18,519	4,101	11,785	2,611	589,521	3.183
1962	23,430	24,634	10,423	1,581,213	56.3	313,084	19,926	4,046	12,757	3,102	620,290	3.113
1961	24,433	25,899	11,259	1,635,342	55.7	318,359	20,308	4,132	12,893	3,262	625,874	3.082
1960	*25,746	*27,414	*11,787	*1,690,396	*55.4	*327,172	*21,284	4,197	13,422	3,643	*641,496	*3.014
1959	27,419	29,160	12,993	1,708,116	55.0	353,647	22,075	4,549	13,704	3,798	652,316	2.955
1958	28,999	(NA)	13,675	1,755,775	54.8	381,623	23,295	4,776	14,225	4,249	676,316	2.903
1957	29,564	32,231	14,323	1,777,557	54.5	412,625	25,914	4,901	15,803	5,185	736,408	2.842
1956	30,817	(NA)	14,551	1,738,631	54.0	429,994	28,216	4,841	17,074	6,275	757,625	2.685
1955	32,118	35,455	14,784	1,723,747	53.7	433,308	28,548	4,776	17,314	6,441	743,688	2.605
1954	33,035	37,768	15,733	1,761,386	53.7	440,770	29,310	4,753	17,687	6,850	767,987	2.620
1953	34,106	39,532	16,231	1,801,874	53.5	458,252	31,679	4,757	18,955	7,950	842,663	2.660
1952	34,942	41,011	16,320	1,783,352	53.2	470,979	34,033	4,755	19,758	9,504	906,838	2.665
1951	36,326	42,406	16,502	1,777,878	52.9	485,468	34,640	4,866	19,524	10,226	901,019	2.601
1950	37,359	43,372	16,747	1,745,778	52.6	488,019	31,790	4,990	17,443	9,338	814,741	2.563
1949	38,006	43,578	16,008	1,778,811	52.4	556,741	35,133	5,478	20,273	9,349	862,139	2.454
1948	39,406	44,447	15,249	1,785,067	51.9	645,535	41,224	5,855	24,315	11,015	965,630	2.342
1947	39,057	44,841	14,628	1,759,758	51.5	706,551	45,972	6,011	27,660	12,261	965,005	2.099
1946	38,697	45,637	13,967	1,768,400	51.3	794,824	64,754	5,857	39,039	19,801	1,261,416	1.948
1945	38,633	46,863	12,685	1,787,073	51.1	897,384	91,826	5,418	59,415	26,912	1,719,316	1.872
1944	38,217	46,588	13,175	1,797,012	50.8	915,817	95,663	5,344	63,288	26,944	1,793,322	1.875
1943	38,331	45,764	13,165	1,784,472	50.7	887,674	87,925	5,261	57,909	24,675	1,655,814	1.883
1942	38,446	----------	----------	1,773,735	50.5	672,420	53,747	4,761	30,910	17,853	1,030,486	1.917
1941	38,334	----------	----------	1,732,673	50.3	488,668	29,406	4,088	16,106	9,166	515,851	1.754
1940	38,308	----------	----------	1,684,171	50.0	456,088	23,816	3,997	12,485	7,288	417,955	1.755
1939	38,977	----------	----------	1,680,519	49.7	454,032	22,713	4,012	11,118	7,527	417,716	1.839
1938	39,931	----------	----------	1,731,096	49.4	454,508	21,657	4,032	10,247	7,354	406,406	1.877
1937	40,949	----------	----------	1,776,428	49.2	499,688	24,695	4,116	12,417	8,126	443,532	1.796
1936	41,390	----------	----------	1,790,043	48.8	492,493	22,460	4,188	----------	----------	413,189	1.840
1935	42,426	----------	----------	1,867,381	48.3	448,059	18,509	4,118	----------	----------	358,423	1.936
1934	44,884	----------	----------	1,973,247	48.0	452,176	18,069	4,163	----------	----------	346,870	1.920
1933	47,677	----------	----------	2,072,632	47.5	434,848	16,368	4,308	----------	----------	329,816	2.015
1932	50,598	----------	----------	2,184,690	47.0	480,718	16,997	4,986	----------	----------	377,511	2.221
1931	52,096	----------	----------	2,245,904	47.0	599,227	21,933	6,018	----------	----------	551,726	2.515
1930	53,584	----------	----------	2,322,267	46.9	707,987	26,876	6,669	----------	----------	730,766	2.719
1929	53,838	----------	----------	2,323,683	46.3	786,432	31,165	6,898	----------	----------	875,929	2.811
1928	54,800	----------	----------	2,346,751	45.8	798,476	31,718	6,626	----------	----------	905,271	2.854
1927	55,729	----------	----------	2,378,800	45.5	840,030	33,798	6,650	----------	----------	980,528	2.901
1926	56,855	----------	----------	2,403,967	45.1	874,589	35,673	6,605	----------	----------	1,049,210	2.941
1925	56,814	----------	----------	2,414,083	44.8	901,963	36,167	6,592	----------	----------	1,064,806	2.944
1924	57,451	----------	----------	2,411,627	44.3	950,459	36,368	6,407	----------	----------	1,085,672	2.985
1923	57,159	----------	----------	2,379,131	43.8	1,008,538	38,294	6,401	----------	----------	1,158,925	3.026
1922	56,827	----------	----------	2,352,483	43.1	989,509	35,811	6,132	----------	----------	1,087,516	3.037
1921	56,950	----------	----------	2,378,510	42 5	1,061,131	37,706	----------	----------	----------	1,166,252	3.093
1920	56,102	----------	----------	2,388,424	42.4	1,269,913	47,370	----------	----------	----------	1,304,815	2.755
1919	56,290	----------	----------	2,426,889	41.9	1,211,022	46,838	----------	----------	----------	1,193,431	2.548
1918	56,611	----------	----------	2,397,943	41.6	1,122,963	43,212	----------	----------	----------	1,046,166	2.421
1917	55,939	----------	----------	2,379,472	41.5	1,109,943	40,100	----------	----------	----------	840,910	2.097
1916	55,193	----------	----------	2,329,475	40.9	1,048,987	35,220	----------	----------	----------	722,359	2.051

See footnotes at end of table.

Series Q 284–312. Railroad Mileage, Equipment, and Passenger Traffic and Revenue: 1890 to 1970—Con.

Year ending—	Passenger-train cars in service, railroads only	Freight-train cars in service [12] Number	Average capacity [8]	Passengers	Total passenger-miles	Revenue Total	Revenue Per passenger-mile	Year ending—	Passenger-train cars in service, railroads only	Freight-train cars in service [12]	Passengers	Total passenger-miles	Revenue Total	Revenue Per passenger-mile
	301	304	305	306	307	311	312		301	304	306	307	311	312
			Tons	1,000	Mil.	$1,000	Cents				1,000	Mil.	$1,000	Cents
JUNE 30								JUNE 30 —Con.						
1916	54,774	2,343,378	40.5	1,015,338	34,309	689,627	2.010	1902	36,987	1,546,101	649,879	19,690	392,963	1.986
1915	55,810	2,341,567	39.7	985,676	32,475	646,475	1.991	1901	35,969	1,464,328	607,278	17,354	351,356	2.013
1914	54,492	2,349,734	39.1	1,063,249	35,357	703,484	1.990							
1913	52,717	2,298,478	38.3	1,043,603	34,673	[13] 695,988	[13] 2.008	1900	34,713	1,365,531	576,831	16,038	323,716	2.003
1912	51,583	2,229,163	37.4	1,004,081	33,132	660,373	1.987	1899	33,850	1,295,510	523,177	14,591	291,113	1.978
1911	49,906	2,208,997	36.9	997,410	33,202	657,638	1.974	1898	33,595	1,248,826	501,067	13,380	266,970	1.973
1910	47,179	2,148,478	35.9	971,683	32,338	628,992	1.938	1897	33,626	1,221,730	489,445	12,257	251,136	2.022
1909	45,664	2,086,835	35.3	891,472	29,109	563,609	1.928	1896	33,003	1,221,887	511,773	13,049	266,563	2.019
1908	45,292	2,100,784	34.9	890,010	29,083	566,833	1.937							
1907	43,973	1,991,557	33.8	873,905	27,719	564,606	2.014	1895	33,112	1,196,119	507,421	12,188	252,246	2.040
1906	42,262	1,837,914	32.2	797,946	25,167	510,033	2.003	1894	33,018	1,205,169	540,688	14,289	285,350	1.986
								1893	31,384	1,013,307	593,561	14,229	301,492	2.108
1905	40,713	1,731,409	30.8	738,835	23,800	472,695	1.962	1892	28,876	966,998	560,958	13,363	286,806	2.126
1904	39,752	1,692,194	30.1	715,420	21,923	444,327	2.006	1891	27,949	947,300	531,184	12,844	281,179	2.142
1903	38,140	1,653,782	29.4	694,892	20,916	421,705	2.006	1890	26,820	918,491	492,431	11,848	260,786	2.167

* Denotes first year for which figures include Alaska and Hawaii.
[1] Includes circular and unofficial.
[2] First track. Includes lessors, proprietary, unofficial and, through 1963, circular companies.
[3] For railroads reporting track by class. Excludes circular and unofficial, figures for which cover road, first track only.
[4] Class I railroads.
[5] Includes switching and terminal companies.
[6] For 1890–1927, number of locomotives; for 1928–1970, number of units, except for steam locomotives. (A unit is the least number of wheel bases together with super-structure capable of independent propulsion, but not necessarily equipped with an independent control.)
[7] For 1915–1922, identified as "other than steam," but all or almost all of the locomotives must be electric.
[8] For 1916–1956, represents steam locomotives and freight cars of class I railroads excluding switching and terminal companies; for 1957–1967, includes all class I locomotives excluding switching and terminal companies.
[9] Included with "Other."   [10] Calendar-year data.
[11] Beginning 1969, excludes Pullman Co.
[12] Excludes caboose cars.   [13] Class I and II railroads.

Series Q 313–320. Railroad Passenger and Freight Operations: 1890 to 1970

[Tons are of 2,000 pounds. Class I, II, and III railroads except as follows: Series Q 313, class I beginning 1911; series Q 314, class I beginning 1933; and series Q 315, Q 319, Q 320, class I for all years]

Year ending—	Passenger service Revenue passenger-miles per— Car-mile	Train-mile	Train-miles per train-hour	Freight service Revenue ton-miles per— Loaded car-mile [1]	Train-mile	Mile of road	Train-miles per train-hour	Car-miles per car-day	Year ending—	Passenger service Revenue passenger-miles per— Car-mile	Train-mile	Train-miles per train-hour	Freight service Revenue ton-miles per— Loaded car-mile [1]	Train-mile	Mile of road	Train-miles per train-hour	Car-miles per car-day
	313	314	315	316	317	318	319	320		313	314	315	316	317	318	319	320
DEC. 31									DEC. 31 —Con.								
1970	25.8	116.2	40.1	44.32	1,774.14	3,468,168	20.1	51.8									
1969	24.7	113.6	41.0	42.75	1,754.54	3,456,667	20.1	52.6	1940	14.0	60.3	35.8	25.40	764.30	1,525,579	16.7	35.6
1968	22.4	107.0	41.0	41.77	1,714.88	3,385,901	20.4	51.3	1939	13.5	57.6	35.4	24.59	727.45	1,355,052	16.7	32.3
1967	20.7	101.5	41.7	41.24	1,693.38	3,237,648	20.3	49.1	1938	13.1	54.5	34.7	23.80	676.57	1,171,637	16.6	28.5
1966	20.2	104.1	41.3	40.34	1,669.77	3,312,186	20.3	50.6	1937	14.0	59.0	34.5	24.68	708.35	1,446,921	16.1	32.9
									1936	13.6	55.4	34.0	24.32	687.49	1,353,406	15.8	30.7
1965	19.5	100.9	41.3	39.02	1,638.44	3,120,778	20.1	49.0									
1964	20.3	99.4	41.4	37.63	1,572.60	2,917,502	20.2	47.2	1935	11.2	47.5		23.49	646.17	1,119,290	16.0	25.8
1963	19.6	97.3	40.9	36.27	1,537.72	2,750,078	20.1	44.6	1934	10.9	46.7		23.19	623.62	1,058,609	15.9	24.2
1962	20.0	102.6	40.9	34.87	1,490.70	2,612,129	20.0	42.8	1933	10.2	42.5		23.26	619.13	972,262	15.7	21.3
1961	19.8	101.5	40.9	33.80	1,441.87	2,460,997	19.9	40.6	1932	9.8	39.9		22.56	585.49	908,296	15.5	19.8
									1931	10.5	44.7		23.44	652.87	1,196,960	14.8	24.5
1960	19.3	100.9	40.7	*33.11	*1,399.31	*2,496,638	19.5	40.9									
1959	18.9	97.6	40.3	32.32	1,374.99	2,505,800	19.5	41.2	1930	11.3	48.9		24.28	699.27	1,481,199	13.8	28.7
1958	18.6	94.0	40.2	32.10	1,362.05	2,394,040	19.2	39.6	1929	12.5	54.4		24.52	713.03	1,727,786	13.2	32.3
1957	18.1	93.9	40.2	32.42	1,369.56	2,676,573	18.8	43.7	1928	12.9	55.1		24.31	705.86	1,677,089	12.9	31.2
1956	18.1	96.9	40.0	31.98	1,347.21	2,789,340	18.6	45.0	1927	13.5	57.9		24.60	689.68	1,668,800	12.3	30.3
									1926	14.2	60.4		24.96	688.56	1,732,295	11.9	30.4
1955	17.8	95.2	39.8	30.94	1,296.86	2,679,482	18.6	45.7									
1954	17.4	92.0	39.5	30.27	1,216.54	2,356,646	18.7	41.2	1925	14.8	61.5		24.55	662.53	1,613,862	11.8	28.5
1953	17.7	94.8	39.1	30.66	1,219.03	2,592,188	18.2	44.3	1924	15.3	62.1		24.47	634.43	1,518,556	11.5	26.8
1952	18.1	98.4	38.3	31.02	1,210.90	2,622,463	17.6	44.0	1923	16.3	65.9		25.18	632.32	1,615,741	10.9	27.8
1951	18.1	97.2	37.7	31.38	1,211.06	2,748,700	17.0	45.0	1922	15.9	64.6		24.31	599.12	1,330,460	11.1	23.5
									1921	16.4	66.4		24.60	566.74	1,199,328	11.5	22.4
1950	17.0	88.5	37.4	29.97	1,131.47	2,496,927	16.8	43.6									
1949	18.0	92.0	37.0	29.48	1,044.83	2,229,430	16.9	40.3	1920	19.8	82.4		26.71	639.03	1,597,133	10.3	---
1948	19.4	100.8	36.7	30.90	1,080.30	2,695,708	16.2	45.1	1919	20.5	84.7		25.44	622.51	1,423,390	---	---
1947	21.1	110.2	36.1	30.61	1,052.43	2,752,915	16.0	46.9	1918	19.9	79.4		26.96	620.68	1,582,796	---	---
1946	24.7	143.7	35.1	29.25	992.95	2,488,499	16.0	43.5	1917	17.2	67.6		24.75	588.29	1,538,211	---	---
									1916	15.5	59.2		22.83	552.26	1,409,957	---	---
1945	30.4	189.7	34.7	30.18	1,034.49	2,852,615	15.7	47.7									
1944	32.2	199.8	34.8	30.62	1,045.67	3,084,195	15.7	50.6									
1943	31.7	188.6	34.7	31.36	1,027.64	3,032,199	15.4	49.7									
1942	23.7	124.9	35.7	29.76	947.87	2,638,067	15.8	47.4									
1941	16.0	72.7	36.1	26.28	827.48	1,950,166	16.5	41.6									

See footnotes at end of table.

Series Q 313–320. Railroad Passenger and Freight Operations: 1890 to 1970—Con.

[Tons are of 2,000 pounds]

Year ending—	Passenger service, revenue passenger-miles per—		Freight service, revenue ton-miles per—			Year ending—	Passenger service, revenue passenger-miles per train-mile	Freight service, revenue ton-miles per—	
	Car-mile	Train-mile	Loaded car-mile [1]	Train-mile	Mile of road			Train-mile	Mile of road
	313	314	316	317	318		314	317	318
JUNE 30						JUNE 30 —Con.			
1916_____	15.3	58.2	22.39	536.67	1,325,089				
1915_____	15.0	56.0	21.14	476.13	1,075,962	1900_____	44.2	270.86	735,352
1914_____	15.4	58.4	21.09	446.96	1,125,084	1899_____	41.2	243.52	659,565
1913_____	15.4	58.5	[2] 21.12	[2] 445.43	1,190,397	1898_____	39.1	226.45	617,810
1912_____	15.1	56.5	20.18	406.76	1,078,580	1897_____	36.6	204.62	519,079
1911_____	15.6	57.9	19.74	383.10	1,053,566	1896_____	39.2	198.81	523,832
1910_____	15.7	58.9	19.84	380.38	1,071,086	1895_____	38.3	189.69	479,490
1909_____	15.4	57.5	19.26	362.57	953,986	1894_____	43.7	179.80	457,252
1908_____	15.5	57.5	19.62	351.80	974,654	1893_____	42.4	183.97	551,232
1907_____		54.5	19.68	357.35	1,052,119	1892_____	42.0	181.89	543,365
1906_____		52.5	18.92	344.39	982,401	1891_____	41.7	181.67	502,705
1905_____		51.7	18.14	322.26	861,396	1890_____	41.4	175.12	487,245
1904_____		49.8	17.72	307.76	829,476				
1903_____		49.2	17.60	310.54	855,442				
1902_____		48.5	16.92	296.47	793,351				
1901_____		45.1	16.55	281.26	760,414				

* Denotes first year for which figures include Alaska and Hawaii.
[1]This average was obtained by dividing the revenue ton-miles by the total loaded car-miles, the latter item including some cars loaded with nonrevenue freight. The method is necessary to preserve comparability with figures for the earlier years; they differ slightly from the average "net tons per loaded car" shown in the regular monthly statements, *Freight and Passenger Service Operating Statistics*, based on revenue and nonrevenue ton-miles and car-miles.
[2] Class I and II railroads.

Series Q 321–328. Railroad Mileage and Equipment: 1830 to 1890

Year	Mileage			Equipment [2]					Year	Miles of road operated (Dec. 31)	Year	Miles of road operated (Dec. 31)
	Road operated (Dec. 31)	Road owned [1]	All track (Dec. 31)	Loco-motives	Revenue cars							
					Total	Passenger	Freight	Baggage, mail, express				
	321	322	323	324	325	326	327	328		321		321
				1,000	*1,000*	*1,000*	*1,000*	*1,000*				
1890_____	166,703	163,359	208,152	31.8	1,091	21.7	1,062	7.3	1870_____	52,922	1850_____	9,021
1889_____	161,276	159,934	202,088	30.6	1,081	21.5	1,051	7.1	1869_____	46,844	1849_____	7,365
1888_____	156,114	154,222	191,376	29.1	1,032	20.2	1,005	6.8	1868_____	42,229	1848_____	5,996
1887_____	149,214	147,953	184,935	27.3	977	19.3	951	6.6	1867_____	39,050	1847_____	5,598
1886_____	136,338	133,565	167,952	26.1	871	18.4	846	6.3	1866_____	36,801	1846_____	4,930
1885_____	128,320	127,689	160,506	25.7	828	16.5	806	6.0	1865_____	35,085	1845_____	4,633
1884_____	125,345	125,119	156,414	24.4	821	16.6	798	5.9	1864_____	33,908	1844_____	4,377
1883_____	121,422	120,519	149,101	23.4	801	16.2	779	5.8	1863_____	33,170	1843_____	4,185
1882_____	114,677	114,428	140,878	21.9	751	14.9	730	5.6	1862_____	32,120	1842_____	4,026
1881_____	103,108	103,530	130,455	19.9	667	13.9	648	5.0	1861_____	31,286	1841_____	3,535
1880_____	93,262	92,147	115,647	17.9	557	12.8	539	4.8	1860_____	30,626	1840_____	2,818
1879_____	86,556	84,393	104,756	17.1	497	12.0	480	4.5	1859_____	28,789	1839_____	2,302
1878_____	81,747	80,832	103,649	16.4	439	11.7	423	4.4	1858_____	26,968	1838_____	1,913
1877_____	79,082	79,208	97,308	15.9	408	12.1	392	3.9	1857_____	24,503	1837_____	1,497
1876_____	76,808	76,305	94,665	15.6	340	[3] 14.6	385	_____	1856_____	22,076	1836_____	1,273
1875_____	74,096	74,096	_____	_____	_____	_____	_____	_____	1855_____	18,374	1835_____	1,098
1874_____	72,385	72,623	_____	_____	_____	_____	_____	_____	1854_____	16,720	1834_____	633
1873_____	70,268	70,651	_____	_____	_____	_____	_____	_____	1853_____	15,360	1833_____	380
1872_____	66,171	57,323	_____	_____	_____	_____	_____	_____	1852_____	12,908	1832_____	229
1871_____	60,301	51,455	_____	_____	_____	_____	_____	_____	1851_____	10,982	1831_____	95
											1830_____	23

[1] Prior to 1882, includes elevated railways.
[2] Prior to 1881, includes elevated railways.
[3] Includes baggage, mail, and express.

Series Q 329. Miles of Railroad Built: 1830 to 1925

Year	Miles 329	Year	Miles 329	Year	Miles 329	Year	Miles 329	Year	Miles 329	Year	Miles 329	Year	Miles 329	Year	Miles 329
1925	644	1915	933	1905	4,388	1894	1,760	1871	6,660	1860	1,500	1850	1,261	1840	491
1924	579	1914	1,532	1904	3,832	1893	3,024	1870	5,658	1859	1,707	1849	1,048	1839	386
1923	427	1913	3,071	1903	5,652			1869	4,103	1858	1,966	1848	1,056	1838	453
1922	324	1912	2,997	1902	6,026	1879	5,006	1868	2,468	1857	2,077	1847	263	1837	348
1921	475	1911	3,066	1901	5,368	1878	2,428	1867	2,541	1856	1,471	1846	333	1836	280
						1877	2,280	1866	1,404						
1920	314	1910	4,122	1900	4,894	1876	2,575			1855	2,453	1845	277	1835	138
1919	686	1909	3,748	1899	4,569			1865	819	1854	3,442	1844	180	1834	214
1918	721	1908	3,214	1898	3,265	1875	1,606	1864	947	1853	2,170	1843	288	1833	116
1917	979	1907	5,212	1897	2,109	1874	2,584	1863	574	1852	2,288	1842	505	1832	191
1916	1,098	1906	5,623	1896	1,692	1873	5,217	1862	720	1851	1,274	1841	606	1831	99
				1895	1,420	1872	7,439	1861	1,016					1830	40

Series Q 330. Miles of Railroad Operated by Receivers or Trustees: 1894 to 1970

[As of end of year. Class I, II, and III railroads]

Year ending—	Miles 330	Year ending—	Miles 330	Year ending—	Miles 330	Year ending—	Miles 330	Year ending—	Miles 330	Year ending—	Miles 330	Year ending—	Miles 330
DEC. 31		DEC. 31— Con.		DEC. 31— Con.		DEC. 31— Con.		JUNE 30				JUNE 30— Con.	
1970	23,190	1955	11,685	1940	75,270	1927	16,752	1916	37,353			1905	796
1969	649	1954	11,608	1939	77,013	1926	17,632	1915	30,223			1904	1,323
1968	650	1953	12,054	1938	76,938	1925	18,687	1914	18,608			1903	1,185
1967	2,476	1952	11,942	1937	70,884	1924	8,105	1913	16,286			1902	1,475
1966	1,612	1951	12,212	1936	69,712	1923	12,623	1912	9,786			1901	2,497
						1922	15,259	1911	4,593				
1965	1,690	1950	12,223	1935	68,345	1921	13,512					1900	4,178
1964	1,732	1949	12,679	1934	42,168			1910	5,257			1899	9,853
1963	1,748	1948	13,283	1933	41,698	1920	16,290	1909	10,530			1898	12,745
1962	2,113	1947	22,750	1932	22,545	1919	16,590	1908	9,529			1897	18,862
1961	2,365	1946	34,389	1931	12,970	1918	19,208	1907	3,926			1896	30,475
						1917	17,376	1906	3,971				
1960*	1,259	1945	39,714	1930	9,486	1916	34,804					1895	37,856
1959	1,097	1944	50,497	1929	5,703							1894	40,819
1958	1,040	1943	64,758	1928	5,256								
1957	1,022	1942	66,904										
1956	1,594	1941	69,859										

* Denotes first year for which figures include Alaska and Hawaii.

Series Q 331–345. Railroad Freight Traffic and Revenue: 1890 to 1970

[In tons of 2,000 pounds]

Year ending—	Revenue freight originated (class I railroads)								Freight and revenue (class I, II, and III railroads)						
	All tonnage	In carloads						Less than carload	Revenue tons originated	Ton-miles	Haul per ton [2]	Deprecia-tion and retirements	Revenue		
		Total	Products of agriculture	Animals and products	Products of mines	Products of forests	Manufactures and misc. [1]						Total	Per ton [2]	Per ton-mile
	331	332	333	334	335	336	337	338	339	340	341	342	343	344	345
	1,000	1,000	1,000	1,000	1,000	1,000	1,000	1,000	Mil.	Mil.	Miles	$1,000	Mil. dol.	Dol.	Cents
DEC. 31															
1970	1,484,919	1,484,110						809	1,572	771,012	490.41	812,684	11,124	7.08	1.443
1969	1,473,457	1,472,620						837	1,558	773,830	496.82	788,837	10,538	6.77	1.362
1968	1,431,308	1,430,441						867	1,515	750,468	495.37	775,356	9,942	6.56	1.325
1967	1,407,628	1,406,668						960	1,498	727,075	485.21	765,768	9,329	6.23	1.283
1966	1,448,901	1,447,852						1,049	1,544	746,699	483.70	744,800	9,487	6.15	1.271
1965	1,387,423	1,386,090						1,333	1,479	705,705	477.15	714,052	9,037	6.11	1.281
1964	1,354,612	1,373,117						1,496	1,420	662,089	466.17	685,785	8,575	6.04	1.295
1963	1,285,061	1,283,382	160,589	9,378	662,461	78,319	372,635	1,679	1,347	625,170	463.97	676,584	8,271	6.14	1.323
1962	1,233,597	1,231,415	155,301	9,452	634,747	78,105	353,809	2,183	1,294	595,774	460.57	660,586	8,115	6.27	1.362
1961	1,193,740	1,191,154	153,819	9,341	615,646	74,924	337,424	2,586	1,253	566,295	452.00	652,271	7,859	6.27	1.388
1960	1,240,789	1,237,575	150,350	9,463	649,228	79,211	349,323	3,213	*1,301	*575,360	*442.14	634,778	*8,152	*6.26	*1.417
1959	1,232,201	1,228,277	145,531	9,994	632,870	80,397	359,485	3,923	1,293	578,637	447.66	625,888	8,442	6.53	1.459
1958	1,190,353	1,185,951	146,746	9,895	628,911	73,287	327,112	4,402	1,247	554,534	444.55	618,062	8,193	6.57	1.477
1957	1,380,327	1,374,884	137,618	11,074	769,675	77,497	379,020	5,443	1,449	621,907	429.20	596,355	9,064	6.26	1.457
1956	1,447,422	1,440,937	138,093	13,198	796,480	87,799	405,367	6,485	1,521	651,188	428.08	569,605	9,089	5.97	1.396
1955	1,396,339	1,389,346	133,789	13,161	761,993	82,584	397,819	6,993	1,459	626,893	429.75	554,597	8,665	5.94	1.382
1954	1,223,969	1,217,005	131,733	13,128	650,074	75,650	346,420	6,964	1,279	552,197	431.65	547,267	7,915	6.19	1.433
1953	1,384,301	1,376,046	131,137	13,768	754,292	82,107	394,742	8,255	1,448	608,954	420.66	534,457	9,078	6.27	1.491
1952	1,382,604	1,373,294	138,415	14,601	752,699	83,480	384,097	9,310	1,447	617,942	426.93	513,059	8,915	6.16	1.443
1951	1,477,402	1,467,023	140,811	14,362	819,373	86,522	405,955	10,379	1,547	649,831	419.99	485,160	8,758	5.66	1.348

See footnotes at end of table.

Series Q 331–345. Railroad Freight Traffic and Revenue: 1890 to 1970—Con.

[In tons of 2,000 pounds]

Year ending—	All tonnage	Revenue freight originated (class I railroads)								Freight and revenue (class I, II, and III railroads)						
		In carloads						Less than carload	Revenue-tons orig- inated	Ton- miles	Haul per ton[2]	Deprecia- tion and retire- ments	Revenue		
		Total	Products of agri- culture	Animals and products	Prod- ucts of mines	Prod- ucts of forests	Manu- factures and misc.[1]						Total	Per ton[2]	Per ton- mile
	331	332	333	334	335	336	337	338	339	340	341	342	343	344	345
	1,000	1,000	1,000	1,000	1,000	1,000	1,000	1,000	Mil.	Mil.	Miles	$1,000	Mil. dol.	Dol.	Cents
DEC. 31— Con.															
1950	1,354,196	1,343,308	129,175	14,321	746,808	78,860	374,144	10,888	1,421	591,550	416.32	466,589	7,934	5.58	1.341
1949	1,226,503	1,213,911	140,383	15,284	653,759	69,257	335,228	12,592	1,284	529,111	412.02	441,658	7,151	5.57	1.352
1948	1,506,878	1,488,612	145,176	16,865	845,640	86,104	394,827	18,266	1,580	641,104	405.64	409,310	8,090	5.12	1.262
1947	1,537,546	1,514,985	158,168	19,716	847,807	87,027	402,267	22,561	1,613	657,878	407.82	385,763	7,141	4.43	1.085
1946	1,366,617	1,342,230	149,941	21,587	717,806	84,817	368,079	24,387	1,432	594,943	415.48	365,902	5,866	4.10	.986
1945	1,424,913	1,404,080	159,571	23,748	732,942	75,604	412,215	20,833	1,493	684,148	458.14	1,186,844	6,617	4.43	.967
1944	1,491,491	1,471,366	145,685	25,413	785,265	83,731	431,272	20,125	1,565	740,586	473.28	540,461	7,087	4.53	.957
1943	1,481,225	1,462,314	148,971	22,936	797,163	80,899	412,345	18,911	1,557	730,132	469.07	465,525	6,866	4.41	.940
1942	1,421,187	1,403,612	117,318	20,620	804,577	84,570	376,527	17,575	1,498	640,992	427.76	338,181	6,026	4.02	.940
1941	1,227,650	1,209,559	100,173	16,810	684,433	71,540	336,603	18,091	1,296	477,576	368.54	233,340	4,510	3.48	.944
1940	1,009,421	994,728	88,821	15,456	570,220	58,221	262,010	14,693	1,069	375,369	351.13	205,860	3,584	3.35	.955
1939	901,669	886,794	91,564	15,049	496,939	50,156	233,086	14,875	955	335,375	351.21	201,852	3,297	3.45	.983
1938	771,862	757,470	95,390	14,760	408,835	43,973	194,512	14,392	820	291,866	356.05	201,825	2,901	3.54	.994
1937	1,015,586	998,398	89,460	15,233	569,745	58,658	265,302	17,188	1,075	362,815	337.43	197,035	3,428	3.19	.945
1936	958,830	942,538	86,648	16,209	541,488	53,156	245,037	16,292	1,012	341,182	337.29	193,502	3,357	3.32	.984
1935	789,627	775,588	76,338	15,125	445,136	42,483	196,506	14,039	832	283,637	341.05	194,625	2,831	3.40	.998
1934	765,296	750,951	79,305	20,363	436,380	35,650	179,253	14,345	802	270,292	336.91	192,387	2,672	3.33	.989
1933	698,943	684,592	81,702	17,651	395,065	33,165	157,009	14,351	733	250,651	341.77	199,917	2,529	3.45	1.009
1932	646,223	630,989	80,917	18,055	362,226	26,109	143,682	15,234	679	235,309	346.63	209,111	2,485	3.66	1.056
1931	894,186	871,412	97,487	21,632	501,903	43,024	207,366	22,774	945	311,073	329.23	221,611	3,302	3.50	1.062
1930	1,153,197	1,123,530	110,728	23,129	642,537	69,371	277,765	29,667	1,220	385,815	316.21	243,253	4,145	3.40	1.074
1929	1,339,091	1,303,048	115,343	24,907	737,879	94,855	330,064	36,043	1,419	450,189	317.17	259,375	4,899	3.45	1.088
1928	1,285,943	1,248,989	118,022	25,634	696,583	96,737	312,013	36,954	1,371	436,087	318.00	241,719	4,772	3.48	1.094
1927	1,281,611	1,243,171	113,342	26,003	713,402	99,351	291,073	38,440	1,373	432,014	314.75	239,184	4,729	3.45	1.095
1926	1,336,142	1,296,651	111,787	26,244	757,703	104,851	296,066	39,491	1,440	447,444	310.81	231,497	4,906	3.41	1.096
1925	1,247,242	1,206,655	109,313	26,324	678,336	107,391	285,291	40,587	1,351	417,418	308.93	223,925	4,648	3.44	1.114
1924	1,187,296	1,146,747	116,587	27,747	637,582	108,094	256,737	40,549	1,287	391,945	304.44	208,064	4,437	3.45	1.132
1923	1,279,030	1,234,692	109,318	28,254	713,735	115,618	257,767	44,338	1,388	416,256	299.94	205,070	4,712	3.40	1.132
1922	1,023,745	980,516	111,787	26,230	532,998	89,059	220,442	43,229	1,112	342,188	307.77	169,808	4,086	3.67	1.194
1921	940,183	898,191	114,069	24,263	511,271	76,419	172,169	41,992	1,018	309,533	304.11	155,968	4,004	3.93	1.294
1920	[3] 1,255,421	[3] 1,202,219	110,840	26,595	712,155	100,765	251,864	53,202	1,363	413,699	303.52	------	4,421	3.24	1.069
1919	[3] 1,096,449	[3] 1,045,148	115,033	35,494	589,951	94,076	210,256	51,301	1,190	367,161	308.60	------	3,625	3.05	.987
1918	1,263,344	1,209,957	116,051	35,777	734,796	97,256	226,077	53,387	1,377	408,778	296.89	------	3,522	2.56	.862
1917	1,264,016	1,210,247	104,629	31,858	732,653	100,838	240,269	53,769	1,382	398,263	288.18	------	2,897	2.10	.728
1916	[3] 1,203,367	[3] 1,150,456	113,635	30,473	680,123	93,819	231,039	52,911	1,317	366,173	277.98	------	2,631	2.00	.719
JUNE 30															
1916									1,263	343,477	271.98	------	2,469	1.96	.719
1915	[3] 925,697	[3] 878,761	109,483	26,001	507,250	76,674	157,085	46,936	1,024	277,135	270.69	------	2,038	1.99	.735
1914	[3] 1,023,131	[3] 982,892	98,825	26,352	574,000	91,094	177,950	40,239	1,130	288,637	255.43	------	2,127	1.88	.737
1913	[3] 1,067,978	[3] 1,026,817	102,658	25,669	592,164	93,762	196,947	41,161	1,183	301,730	255.15	------	[4] 2,199	[4] 1.92	[4] .729
1912	926,990	[3] 889,999	86,433	24,064	506,306	74,796	166,134	36,991	1,031	264,081	256.87	------	1,969	1.91	.744
1911	[3] 901,573	[3] 866,398	81,780	22,833	483,861	79,345	163,380	35,175	1,003	253,784	254.10	------	1,926	1.92	.757
1910									1,026	255,017	249.68		1,926	1.88	.753
1909									881	218,803	251.10		1,678	1.90	.763
1908									870	218,382	253.94		1,655	1.90	.754
1907									977	236,601	242.05		1,824	1.87	.759
1906									896	215,878	240.89		1,640	1.83	.748
1905									785	186,463	237.56		1,451	1.85	.766
1904									714	174,522	244.30		1,379	1.93	.780
1903									715	173,221	242.35		1,338	1.87	.763
1902									658	157,289	239.10		1,207	1.84	.757
1901									584	147,077	251.98		1,119	1.92	.750
1900									583	141,597	242.73		1,049	1.80	.729
1899									502	123,667	246.58		914	1.82	.724
1898										114,078			877	------	.753
1897										95,139			773	------	.798
1896										95,328			787	------	.806
1895										85,228			730	------	.839
1894										80,335			699	------	.860
1893										93,588			829	------	.878
1892										88,241			799	------	.898
1891										81,074			737	------	.895
1890										76,207			714	------	.941

* Denotes first year for which figures include Alaska and Hawaii.
[1] Includes forwarder traffic beginning 1939.
[2] United States as a system, i.e., ton-miles or revenue of connecting roads is included in the numerator, but only tonnage originated in the denominator.

[3] Includes the following amounts of unassigned carload tonnage (thousands): 1911, 35,199; 1912, 32,266; 1913, 15,617; 1914, 14,671; 1915, 2,268; 1916, 1,367; and 1919, 338.
[4] Class I and II railroads.

Series Q 346–355. Railroad Property Investment, Capital, Income, and Expenses: 1850 to 1890

[In millions of dollars]

Year	Investment in railroad and equipment	Stock, mortgage bonds, equipment, obligations, etc.			Stock paying dividends	Total traffic earnings	Operating expenses	Net earnings	Dividends paid	Interest paid on funded debt
		Total	Capital stock	Bonded debt						
	346	347	348	349	350	351	352	353	354	355
EXCLUDING ELEVATED RAILWAYS										
1890		10,020	4,590	5,055		1,086		342	83	224
1889		9,576	4,447	4,784		991		317	79	216
1888		9,281	4,392	4,585		950		297	78	205
1887		8,595	4,146	4,155		931		331	90	202
1886		8,089	3,956	3,853		822	524	297	80	182
1885		7,775	3,778	3,740		765	498	266	77	179
1884		7,617	3,726	3,647		763		266	93	167
1883		7,423	3,675	3,479		807		291	101	[1] 171
1882		6,960	3,478	3,214						
INCLUDING ELEVATED RAILWAYS										
1890	8,789	10,122	4,640	5,105	1,721	1,097		346	85	226
1889	8,598	9,680	4,495	4,828	1,790	1,002		322	81	218
1888	8,344	9,369	4,438	4,624	1,769	960		301	80	207
1887	7,799	8,673	4,191	4,186	1,805	940		334	91	203
1886	7,254	8,163	3,999	3,882	1,675	829		300	81	189
1885	7,037	7,842	3,817	3,765	1,304	772		269	77	187
1884	6,924	7,676	3,762	3,669	1,658	777		270	94	178
1883	6,684	7,477	3,708	3,500	1,713	823		298	102	173
1882	6,035	7,016	3,511	3,235	1,673	770		280	102	150
1881	5,577	6,278	3,177	2,878	(NA)	701		272	93	128
1880	4,653	5,402	2,708	2,530	(NA)	613		255	77	107
1879	4,416	4,872	2,395	2,319	(NA)	525		216	61	112
1878	4,166	4,772	2,292	2,297	(NA)	490	302	187	53	103
1877	4,180	4,806	2,313	2,255	(NA)	472	301	170	58	98
1876	4,086	[2] 4,468	2,248	2,165	937	497	310	186	68	93
1875		4,658	2,198	[3] 2,459		503	(NA)	185	74	
1874		4,221	1,990	[3] 2,230		520	330	189	67	
1873		3,784	1,947	[3] 1,836		526	342	183	67	
1872		3,159	1,647	[3] 1,511		465	(NA)	165	64	
1871		2,664	1,481	(NA)		403	(NA)	141	56	
1870		2,476	(NA)	(NA)		(NA)	(NA)	(NA)	(NA)	
1869		2,041	(NA)	(NA)		(NA)	(NA)	(NA)	(NA)	
1868		1,869	(NA)	(NA)		(NA)	(NA)	(NA)	(NA)	
1867		1,172	756	416		334	228	105		32
1863	(NA)	(NA)	(NA)	(NA)		190	(NA)			
1861		(NA)	(NA)	(NA)		130	(NA)			
1860		1,149	(NA)	(NA)		(NA)	(NA)			
1855		763	424	299		84	42			
1851		(NA)				39				
1850		318								

NA Not available.
[1] Includes other interest.
[2] Sum of capital stock, bonded debt, and $55 million Pacific R.R., U.S. subsidiary bonds.
[3] Includes other debt.

Series Q 356–366. Railroad Property Investment, Capital, and Capital Expenditures: 1890 to 1970

[In millions of dollars. Includes intercorporate duplications. Figures subject to general exception that, prior to 1908, the returns for switching and terminal companies were included where applicable. Capital expenditure represents total money outlay without deductions for property retired]

Year ending—	Property investment and capital (class I, II, III railroads and their lessors)								Capital expenditures for additions and betterments (class I railroads)		
	Road and equipment		Railroad capital outstanding [3]				Net capitalization	Stock paying dividends	Total	Equipment	Roadway and structures
	Investment, book value [1]	Depreciation reserve [2]	Total	Common stock	Preferred stock	Funded debt unmatured					
	356	357	358	359	360	361	362	363	364	365	366
DECEMBER 31											
1970	37,918	9,929	14,339	5,605	718	8,016		3,594	1,350	993	357
1969	37,383	9,688	14,701	5,758	814	8,129		4,347	1,509	1,088	420
1968	36,720	9,450	14,577	5,754	821	8,002		4,629	1,186	818	368
1967	37,250	9,664	14,690	5,828	889	7,973		4,727	1,522	1,148	374
1966	36,618	9,479	14,800	5,639	1,091	8,070		4,709	1,952	1,554	398
1965	35,489	9,341	14,857	5,580	1,116	8,161		4,845	1,630	1,303	327
1964	34,868	9,265	14,876	5,537	1,164	8,175		4,926	1,417	1,139	277
1963	34,519	9,143	15,011	5,592	1,189	8,230	12,840	4,462	1,043	784	258
1962	34,361	8,982	15,013	5,537	1,201	8,275	12,968	4,285	832	593	239
1961	35,541	8,792	15,179	5,526	1,212	8,441	13,184	4,361	646	427	219

See footnotes at end of table.

Series Q 356–366. Railroad Property Investment, Capital, and Capital Expenditures: 1890 to 1970—Con.

[In millions of dollars]

Year ending—	Property investment and capital (class I, II, III railroads and their lessors)								Capital expenditures for additions and betterments (class I railroads)		
	Road and equipment		Railroad capital outstanding [3]				Net capitalization	Stock paying dividends	Total	Equipment	Roadway and structures
	Investment, book value [1]	Depreciation reserve [2]	Total	Common stock	Preferred stock	Funded debt unmatured					
	356	357	358	359	360	361	362	363	364	365	366
DEC. 31—Con.											
1960*	35,513	8,532	16,134	6,185	1,218	8,731	14,150	5,617	919	633	285
1959	35,157	8,295	16,365	6,233	1,246	8,886	14,287	5,750	818	567	250
1958	34,934	8,043	16,603	6,243	1,266	9,094	14,529	5,290	738	479	258
1957	34,614	7,800	16,775	6,291	1,369	9,115	14,682	6,465	1,394	1,007	386
1956	33,714	7,542	17,399	6,911	1,395	9,093	15,285	6,785	1,227	821	406
1955	33,034	7,313	17,422	7,341	1,310	8,771	15,171	7,300	909	568	341
1954	32,708	7,175	17,590	7,316	1,530	8,744	15,336	6,618	820	498	321
1953	32,416	7,009	17,658	7,023	1,868	8,767	15,365	7,252	1,259	857	401
1952	31,822	6,926	18,067	7,243	1,954	8,870	15,487	6,734	1,340	935	405
1951	31,077	6,837	18,220	7,235	1,977	9,008	15,489	6,700	1,413	1,050	363
1950	30,174	6,629	18,274	7,207	1,977	9,090	15,618	6,768	1,065	779	286
1949	29,519	6,438	18,343	7,234	1,988	9,121	15,609	5,924	1,312	981	330
1948	28,664	6,279	18,249	7,250	1,992	9,007	15,467	6,446	1,273	917	356
1947	27,686	6,037	18,050	7,250	1,975	8,825	15,301	5,184	864	565	298
1946	27,277	5,800	18,449	7,448	1,961	9,040	15,309	5,221	561	319	242
1945	26,967	5,549	18,681	7,442	1,981	9,258	15,667	5,383	562	314	248
1944	26,631	4,382	19,403	7,464	1,984	9,955	16,276	5,523	560	328	231
1943	26,145	3,939	19,914	7,517	1,912	10,485	16,755	5,466	454	255	198
1942	25,838	3,561	20,471	7,565	1,935	10,971	17,315	5,355	534	349	185
1941	25,668	3,240	20,708	7,546	1,953	11,209	17,568	3,861	543	367	175
1940	25,646	3,095	21,047	7,734	2,036	11,277	17,630	3,741	429	271	157
1939	25,538	3,102	23,609	8,025	2,050	13,534	17,698	3,190	262	133	128
1938	25,595	3,044	23,855	8,040	2,049	13,766	17,988	3,139	226	115	111
1937	25,636	2,950	24,123	8,064	2,050	14,009	18,319	3,890	509	322	186
1936	25,432	2,809	24,003	7,993	2,036	13,974	18,336	3,594	298	159	139
1935	25,500	2,771	22,080	7,907	2,018	12,155	18,342	3,412	188	79	108
1934	25,681	2,764	24,570	7,994	2,044	14,532	18,653	3,411	212	92	120
1933	25,901	2,707	24,723	8,057	2,042	14,624	18,831	3,119	103	15	88
1932	26,086	2,632	24,837	8,067	2,047	14,723	18,894	3,298	167	36	130
1931	26,094	2,520	24,344	8,031	2,049	14,264	18,941	7,325	361	73	288
1930	26,051	2,360	22,783	7,953	2,059	12,771	19,066	7,702	872	328	544
1929	25,465	2,169	23,983	7,853	2,065	14,065	18,680	7,506	853	321	532
1928	24,875	2,043	23,747	7,809	2,034	13,904	18,511	7,159	676	224	452
1927	24,453	1,946	23,614	7,683	1,980	13,951	18,137	6,701	771	288	482
1926	23,800	1,811	23,677	7,560	1,925	14,192	18,234	6,473	885	371	513
1925	23,217	1,681	21,734	7,492	1,921	12,321	18,191	6,278	748	338	410
1924	22,182	1,549	23,636	7,539	1,935	14,162	18,202	6,042	874	493	381
1923	21,372	1,408	22,839	7,398	1,852	13,589	17,810	5,646	1,059	681	377
1922	20,580	1,335	22,290	7,307	1,834	13,149	17,280	5,321	429	245	183
1921	20,329	1,237	22,292	7,275	1,801	13,216	17,083	5,059	557	319	237
1920	19,849	1,081	20,098	6,958	1,885	11,255	16,994	5,075	----------	----------	----------
1919	19,300	1,009	20,950	7,193	1,898	11,859	16,550	5,298	----------	----------	----------
1918	18,984	936	20,785	7,249	1,806	11,730	16,454	5,138	----------	----------	----------
1917	18,574	796	21,249	7,454	1,848	11,947	16,402	5,610	----------	----------	----------
1916	17,842	628	21,049	7,594	1,455	12,000	16,333	5,430	----------	----------	----------
JUNE 30											
1916	17,689	571	21,092	7,603	1,456	12,033	16,336	5,279	----------	----------	----------
1915	17,441	511	19,720	7,287	1,348	11,085	16,308	5,219	----------	----------	----------
1914	17,153	435	[4] 20,247	[4] 7,304	[4] 1,376	[4] 11,567	[4] 15,759	5,667	----------	----------	----------
1913	16,588	[5] 327	[4] 19,796	[4] 7,232	[4] 1,379	[4] 11,185	[4] 15,366	5,780	----------	----------	----------
1912	16,004	[5] 259	19,753	7,249	1,374	11,130	15,126	5,581	----------	----------	----------
1911	15,612	[5] 210	19,209	7,075	1,396	10,738	15,044	5,730	----------	----------	----------
1910	[6] 14,557	----------	18,417	6,710	1,403	10,304	14,376	5,412	----------	----------	----------
1909	13,609	----------	17,488	6,218	1,468	9,802	13,914	4,920	----------	----------	----------
1908	13,213	----------	16,768	5,911	1,463	9,394	12,834	4,843	----------	----------	----------
1907	13,030	----------	16,082	5,933	1,424	8,725	(NA)	4,948	----------	----------	----------
1906	12,420	----------	14,570	5,403	1,401	7,766	11,672	4,526	----------	----------	----------
1905	11,951	----------	13,805	5,181	1,373	7,251	11,167	4,119	----------	----------	----------
1904	11,511	----------	13,213	5,051	1,289	6,873	10,712	3,643	----------	----------	----------
1903	10,973	----------	12,600	4,877	1,279	6,444	10,282	3,450	----------	----------	----------
1902	10,658	----------	12,134	4,722	1,302	6,110	9,926	3,337	----------	----------	----------
1901	10,405	----------	11,688	4,475	1,331	5,882	9,483	2,977	----------	----------	----------
1900	10,263	----------	11,491	4,522	1,323	5,646	9,548	2,668	----------	----------	----------
1899	9,961	----------	11,034	4,323	1,192	5,519	9,432	2,239	----------	----------	----------
1898	9,760	----------	10,819	4,269	1,119	5,431	9,297	1,818	----------	----------	----------
1897	9,709	----------	10,635	4,367	998	5,270	9,168	1,603	----------	----------	----------
1896	9,500	----------	10,567	4,257	970	5,340	9,066	1,559	----------	----------	----------
1895	9,203	----------	10,347	4,202	760	5,385	8,900	1,485	----------	----------	----------
1894	9,073	----------	10,191	4,104	730	5,357	8,647	1,767	----------	----------	----------
1893	8,937	----------	9,895	3,982	687	5,226	8,332	1,809	----------	----------	----------
1892	[7] 8,690	----------	9,686	3,979	654	5,053	8,295	1,825	----------	----------	----------
1891	[7] 8,444	----------	9,291	3,796	655	4,840	8,008	1,796	----------	----------	----------
1890	[7] 8,133	----------	8,984	3,803	606	4,575	7,577	1,598	----------	----------	----------

* Denotes first year for which figures include Alaska and Hawaii.
NA Not available.
[1] Increase in investment over a period of years cannot be obtained accurately by subtraction of 1 year's investment from that of another owing to reorganization, sale or abandonment, reclassification, etc. For 1921–1924, includes investment of lessor companies; and for 1925–1970, investment of lessor and proprietary companies.
[2] Includes depreciation on "Miscellaneous physical property" prior to 1920 and amortization of defense projects accrued in 1941–1950.

[3] Prior to 1958, includes securities nominally issued and nominally outstanding as well as those outstanding. Funded debt unmatured (series Q 361) does not include equipment obligations subsequent to 1942 but they are included here to preserve comparability of figures.
[4] Class I and II railroads and their lessor subsidiaries.
[5] Class I railroads.
[6] Includes $170 million estimated reserve for accrued depreciation to place figure on comparable basis with other years.
[7] Represents 1893 investments less increases each year on account of change in classification in 1893.

Series Q 367–377. Railroad Income and Expenses, and Interest and Dividends: 1890 to 1970

[In thousands of dollars, except as indicated. Includes intercorporate duplications. Unless otherwise noted, covers class I, II, and III railroads, subject to general exception that, prior to 1908, the returns for switching and terminal companies were included where applicable]

Year ending—	Income and expenses									Interest and dividends [1]	
	Operating revenue	Operating expenses			Tax accruals	Operating income	Net operating income	Net income [1]	Ratio of operating expenses to operating revenues (percent)	Dividends declared	Interest accrued on funded debt
		Total	Maintenance of way and structures	Maintenance of equipment							
	367	368	369	370	371	372	373	374	375	376	377
DECEMBER 31											
1970	12,209,237	9,805,555	1,650,302	2,188,863	1,103,988	1,299,694	505,669	[2] 126,429	80.31	486,132	553,763
1969	11,658,525	9,209,137	1,540,481	2,025,511	1,065,134	1,384,254	667,157	[2] 517,066	78.99	534,849	501,856
1968	11,061,902	8,723,664	1,441,112	1,938,988	979,700	1,358,538	694,143	[2] 623,440	78.86	560,048	473,213
1967	10,581,560	8,359,369	1,326,630	1,895,376	941,272	1,280,919	689,548	[2] 367,689	79.00	582,088	455,059
1966	10,880,467	8,277,294	1,342,632	1,872,661	1,001,510	1,601,663	1,065,232	957,359	76.07	547,567	423,486
1965	10,425,052	8,002,685	1,273,099	1,802,103	949,215	1,473,152	980,066	865,899	76.76	532,649	402,889
1964	9,985,187	7,830,168	1,250,697	1,779,807	891,248	1,263,771	828,433	733,220	78.42	492,443	384,413
1963	9,684,636	7,542,306	1,207,801	1,747,395	906,456	1,235,874	815,952	681,325	77.88	412,815	377,556
1962	9,562,991	7,507,757	1,179,466	1,758,967	925,572	1,129,663	735,266	600,593	78.51	394,116	376,149
1961	9,309,696	7,361,751	1,141,223	1,698,617	1,011,814	956,131	547,045	410,140	79.08	385,017	383,313
1960*	9,641,593	7,657,329	1,217,241	1,775,528	1,020,471	963,793	594,618	473,175	79.42	411,650	386,774
1959	9,954,828	7,796,855	1,262,683	1,813,550	1,070,093	1,087,900	760,140	607,924	78.32	[3] 431,860	390,467
1958	9,686,289	7,631,341	1,248,596	1,735,067	977,277	1,077,671	772,898	630,033	78.78	444,982	393,159
1957	10,625,452	8,321,577	1,458,888	1,928,912	1,090,818	1,213,057	934,645	765,227	78.32	466,415	382,175
1956	10,686,492	8,199,792	1,433,037	1,907,606	1,144,446	1,342,254	1,083,708	908,416	76.73	476,083	373,207
1955	10,229,600	7,724,496	1,412,877	1,798,579	1,100,920	1,404,185	1,144,347	958,849	75.51	476,207	373,502
1954	9,484,015	7,460,507	1,376,478	1,704,985	877,304	1,146,203	887,817	712,252	78.66	405,403	376,020
1953	10,787,891	8,218,223	1,612,390	1,993,602	1,205,366	1,364,302	1,122,512	939,887	76.18	445,145	378,218
1952	10,702,877	8,154,811	1,546,613	1,965,327	1,282,144	1,285,922	1,091,657	900,472	76.01	394,042	376,907
1951	10,511,612	8,122,521	1,505,488	1,956,438	1,223,644	1,165,447	956,699	757,934	77.27	373,574	367,244
1950	9,587,000	7,135,055	1,311,775	1,718,660	1,212,084	1,239,861	1,055,309	854,951	74.42	348,811	367,218
1949	8,680,791	6,968,296	1,309,857	1,617,800	845,089	867,406	693,957	496,103	80.27	306,995	365,393
1948	9,784,332	7,552,630	1,374,058	1,713,967	1,043,056	1,188,666	1,014,815	767,949	77.19	335,313	361,879
1947	8,784,214	6,869,806	1,234,978	1,568,124	949,273	965,136	790,534	537,405	78.21	280,397	374,150
1946	7,709,171	6,422,494	1,169,887	1,478,302	506,480	780,197	624,868	334,966	83.31	283,171	406,147
1945	8,986,954	7,115,391	1,431,221	2,157,678	835,434	1,036,130	858,864	502,250	79.17	295,294	449,917
1944	9,524,628	6,345,035	1,283,208	1,597,155	1,961,652	1,317,941	1,113,153	733,461	66.62	292,248	488,877
1943	9,138,419	5,714,804	1,125,873	1,449,356	1,862,940	1,560,675	1,370,568	946,150	62.54	263,919	515,617
1942	7,547,826	4,653,705	811,206	1,219,460	1,211,775	1,682,347	1,499,364	992,843	61.66	254,088	564,114
1941	5,413,972	3,709,921	615,533	1,000,375	555,970	1,148,081	1,009,592	557,672	68.52	239,438	543,954
1940	4,354,712	3,131,598	508,328	826,242	402,953	820,161	690,554	243,148	71.91	216,522	547,333
1939	4,050,047	2,959,438	477,697	773,080	361,617	728,992	595,961	141,134	73.07	179,412	512,283
1938	3,616,072	2,762,681	431,021	683,529	346,236	507,155	376,865	−87,468	76.40	136,270	521,758
1937	4,226,325	3,165,154	508,319	834,820	351,013	730,158	597,841	146,351	74.89	227,596	532,237
1936	4,108,658	2,973,566	466,284	790,240	324,858	810,434	675,600	221,591	72.37	231,733	548,452
1935	3,499,126	2,630,177	404,105	688,678	240,760	626,973	505,415	52,177	75.17	202,568	559,187
1934	3,316,861	2,479,997	375,410	644,989	243,646	592,034	465,896	23,282	74.77	211,767	569,760
1933	3,138,186	2,285,218	331,653	605,409	253,522	598,222	477,326	26,543	72.82	158,790	590,230
1932	3,168,537	2,441,814	361,337	625,606	279,263	446,417	325,332	−121,630	77.06	150,774	591,340
1931	4,246,385	3,273,906	544,300	825,923	308,492	663,084	528,204	169,287	77.10	401,463	592,866
1930	5,356,484	3,993,621	723,525	1,030,482	353,881	1,007,907	874,154	577,923	74.56	603,150	588,742
1929	6,373,004	4,579,162	877,067	1,216,045	402,698	1,389,955	1,262,656	977,230	71.85	560,902	580,770
1928	6,212,464	4,508,606	861,846	1,181,251	395,631	1,306,620	1,182,467	855,018	72.57	510,018	578,831
1927	6,245,716	4,662,521	895,063	1,234,655	383,112	1,198,547	1,077,842	741,924	74.65	[4] 567,281	583,452
1926	6,508,679	4,766,235	894,886	1,300,680	396,538	1,344,010	1,229,020	883,422	73.23	473,683	581,709
1925	6,246,884	4,633,497	844,186	1,278,227	365,790	1,245,622	1,136,728	771,053	74.17	409,645	583,875
1924	6,045,252	4,608,807	821,793	1,279,680	347,437	1,086,578	984,463	623,399	76.24	385,130	588,301
1923	6,419,210	4,999,383	843,224	1,485,555	339,577	1,078,226	974,918	632,118	77.88	411,882	551,705
1922	5,674,483	4,509,991	755,030	1,269,971	308,145	854,779	769,411	434,459	79.48	338,806	538,594
1921	5,632,665	4,668,998	787,537	1,271,921	283,163	678,551	601,139	350,540	82.89	456,482	529,398
1920	6,310,151	5,954,394	1,069,436	1,613,950	289,272	75,402	12,101	481,951	94.36	331,103	500,354
1919	5,250,420	4,498,817	800,912	1,245,264	239,136	511,546	454,132	496,609	85.68	335,242	476,075
1918	4,985,290	4,071,522	673,084	1,120,611	229,533	684,004	646,223	442,336	81.67	339,186	468,286
1917	4,115,413	2,906,283	460,447	700,073	218,632	988,776	950,557	658,225	70.62	381,852	474,123
1916	3,691,065	2,426,251	439,195	609,105	161,825	1,102,171	1,058,506	735,341	65.73	366,561	481,426

See footnotes at end of table.

Series Q 367–377. Railroad Income and Expenses, and Interest and Dividends: 1890 to 1970—Con.

[In thousands of dollars, except as indicated]

Year ending—	Income and expenses										Interest and dividends [1]	
	Operating revenue	Operating expenses			Tax accruals	Operating income	Net operating income	Net income [1]	Ratio of operating expenses to operating revenues (percent)		Dividends declared	Interest accrued on funded debt
		Total	Maintenance of way and structures	Maintenance of equipment								
	367	368	369	370	371	372	373	374	375		376	377
JUNE 30												
1916	3,472,642	2,277,202	421,501	570,326	150,015	1,044,603	1,002,935	671,398	65.58		342,109	474,535
1915	2,956,193	2,088,683	381,532	509,819	137,775	729,069	694,276	354,787	70.65		328,478	464,186
1914	3,127,730	2,280,416	[5] 419,278	[5] 532,139	140,470	706,844	674,190	395,492	72.91		451,653	442,595
1913	[5] 3,193,118	[5] 2,235,923	[5] 421,232	[5] 511,561	[5] 122,005	[5] 835,190	[5] 805,266	[6] 546,761	[5] 70.02		369,078	[6] 434,753
1912	2,906,416	2,035,058	367,448	450,373	113,819	757,540	727,458	453,281	70.02		400,315	429,027
1911	2,852,855	1,976,332	366,025	428,367	102,657	773,866	744,669	547,281	69.28		460,195	410,327
1910	2,812,142	1,881,879	368,507	413,110	98,035	832,228	805,097	583,191	66.92		405,771	399,582
1909	2,473,205	1,650,034	308,450	363,913	85,140	738,032	710,474	441,063	66.72		321,072	382,675
1908	2,440,659	1,710,402	329,373	368,354	78,674	651,562	634,794	443,987	70.08		390,695	368,296
1907	2,589,106	1,748,516	343,545	368,062	73,743	----------	766,846	488,014	67.53		308,089	344,243
1906	2,325,765	1,536,877	311,721	328,555	69,064	----------	719,824	434,229	66.08		272,796	322,556
1905	2,082,482	1,390,602	275,046	288,441	58,712	----------	633,168	364,811	66.78		237,964	310,632
1904	1,975,174	1,338,896	261,280	267,185	56,802	----------	579,476	317,308	67.79		221,941	297,675
1903	1,900,847	1,257,539	266,422	240,430	53,522	----------	590,056	338,324	66.16		196,728	283,953
1902	1,726,380	1,116,249	248,382	213,381	50,054	----------	560,077	314,989	64.66		185,392	274,422
1901	1,588,526	1,030,397	231,057	190,300	46,708	----------	511,421	273,450	64.86		156,736	262,095
1900	1,487,045	961,429	211,221	181,174	44,445	----------	481,171	252,760	64.65		139,598	252,950
1899	1,313,610	856,969	180,411	150,919	44,397	----------	412,244	177,225	65.24		111,010	251,158
1898	1,247,326	817,973	173,315	142,625	41,929	----------	387,424	147,167	65.58		96,153	246,127
1897	1,122,090	752,525	159,434	122,762	41,119	----------	328,446	85,802	67.06		87,111	247,880
1896	1,150,169	772,989	160,345	133,382	37,962	----------	339,219	94,794	67.20		87,603	249,624
1895	1,075,371	725,720	143,976	113,789	38,146	----------	311,505	60,133	67.48		85,288	252,513
1894	1,073,362	731,414	143,669	112,895	36,556	----------	305,391	60,174	68.14		95,515	252,780
1893	1,220,752	827,921	169,258	136,876	35,071	----------	357,760	114,015	67.82		100,930	250,177
1892	1,171,407	780,998	164,189	128,712	32,751	----------	357,658	120,091	66.67		97,615	240,075
1891	1,096,761	731,888	153,672	117,048	32,052	----------	332,822	114,965	66.73		91,118	219,521
1890	1,051,878	692,094	152,719	114,039	29,806	----------	329,978	106,270	65.80		87,072	221,500

* Denotes first year for which figures include Alaska and Hawaii.
[1] Includes lessors.
[2] After extraordinary and prior period items.
[3] Includes $10,000 dividend declared from "capital surplus."

[4] Includes unusual items, amounting to $76,300,000, not representing cash.
[5] Class I and II railroads.
[6] Class I and II railroads and their lessor subsidiaries.

Series Q 378–384. Railroad Tax Accruals: 1921 to 1970

[In millions of dollars. Class I railroads]

Year	Total	U.S. Government taxes					Other taxes	Year	Total	U.S. Government taxes					Other taxes
		Total	Old-age retirement	Un-employment insurance	Income and excess profits	All other				Total	Old-age retirement	Un-employment insurance	Income and excess profits	All other	
	378	379	380	381	382	383	384		378	379	380	381	382	383	384
1970	1,068.5	665.3	468.3	107.6	88.4	1.0	403.2	1945	823.5	548.0	119.8	110.8	305.7	11.9	275.5
1969	1,029.1	640.0	422.3	110.6	106.2	.9	389.1	1944	1,846.0	1,560.4	120.2	110.8	1,304.4	25.0	285.6
1968	946.6	579.6	398.9	113.8	66.1	.8	366.7	1943	1,849.2	1,578.5	110.0	101.6	1,335.1	31.8	270.7
1967	910.2	544.3	359.3	117.5	66.3	.9	365.8	1942	1,198.8	950.6	85.5	85.5	755.1	24.5	248.2
1966	968.4	626.4	318.1	121.0	186.3	1.0	342.0	1941	547.2	323.3	69.1	69.0	173.8	11.4	223.9
1965	916.5	560.4	271.2	124.0	163.7	1.5	356.1	1940	396.4	181.5	58.2	58.2	59.9	5.2	214.9
1964	870.6	524.0	256.3	128.3	137.9	1.6	346.6	1939	355.7	118.7	50.3	28.7	32.8	6.9	237.0
1963	886.4	539.5	242.3	131.6	164.1	1.5	346.9	1938	340.8	75.4	47.1	5.9	18.9	3.5	265.4
1962	905.0	540.0	246.0	135.8	156.8	1.5	365.0	1937	325.7	66.7	25.1	4.5	32.0	5.1	259.0
1961	991.1	608.2	233.8	130.1	242.5	1.9	382.9	1936	319.8	91.8	47.3	8.8	30.7	5.0	228.0
1960	998.8	598.6	253.2	141.0	202.9	1.6	400.2	1935	236.9	24.7	--------	--------	18.9	5.8	212.2
1959	1,047.4	643.4	244.7	129.2	267.6	1.9	404.2	1934	239.6	19.8	--------	--------	14.3	5.5	219.8
1958	957.2	559.0	225.5	90.3	240.9	2.2	398.2	1933	249.6	19.3	--------	--------	12.7	6.6	230.3
1957	1,068.4	664.2	258.7	82.9	320.3	2.4	404.2	1932	275.1	11.9	--------	--------	--------		263.2
1956	1,121.3	728.5	269.3	64.9	392.0	2.3	392.8	1931	303.5	10.2	--------	--------	--------		293.3
1955	1,080.4	700.9	262.5	21.3	414.3	2.7	379.5	1930	348.6	39.9	--------	--------	--------		308.6
1954	861.3	499.6	250.6	20.0	226.4	2.6	361.7	1929	396.7	89.4	--------	--------	--------		307.2
1953	1,185.0	822.4	266.8	21.2	533.1	1.3	362.6	1928	389.4	88.0	--------	--------	--------		301.4
1952	1,261.8	906.4	269.8	21.6	612.6	2.4	355.4	1927	376.1	84.6	--------	--------	--------		291.5
1951	1,203.3	855.8	264.1	22.0	567.1	2.6	347.5	1926	388.9	108.3	--------	--------	--------		280.6
1950	1,194.6	866.5	242.1	20.2	601.2	3.0	328.1	1925	358.5	86.5	--------	--------	--------		272.0
1949	832.5	517.8	233.8	19.4	261.6	3.0	314.7	1924	340.3	73.4	--------	--------	--------		266.9
1948	1,028.5	721.2	243.9	21.1	448.4	7.9	307.3	1923	331.9	77.1	--------	--------	--------		254.8
1947	936.4	654.0	232.2	121.2	297.6	3.0	282.4	1922	301.0	51.9	--------	--------	--------		249.1
1946	498.1	242.1	136.9	117.4	-15.7	3.4	256.0	1921	275.9	37.3	--------	--------	--------		238.6

Series Q 385–387. Railroad Highway Grade Crossings: 1925 to 1970

[Class I railroads. Includes switching and terminal companies]

Year	Total	Specially protected	Eliminated durng year by separation of grades	Year	Total	Specially protected	Eliminated durng year by separation of grades
	385	386	387		385	386	387
1970	210,954	46,674	95	1945	226,153	33,321	7
1969	211,740	45,961	49	1944	226,357	33,211	14
1968	211,993	45,502	207	1943	226,938	33,124	37
1967	213,723	45,213	132	1942	227,496	33,075	149
1966	214,417	44,432	173	1941	229,722	32,859	182
1965	215,961	44,333	59	1940	230,285	32,421	209
1964	218,723	43,990	159	1939	231,104	31,775	204
1963	220,165	43,484	72	1938	231,400	31,448	235
1962	221,653	43,127	132	1937	232,322	31,119	400
1961	223,735	42,256	100	1936	232,902	30,466	521
1960	224,513	42,267	102	1935	234,231	30,200	164
1959	225,394	41,720	130	1934	234,820	30,226	231
1958	225,938	41,155	78	1933	235,827	30,628	221
1957	223,381	39,884	113	1932	237,035	30,809	189
1956	224,519	39,324	72	1931	238,017	31,052	361
1955	226,318	39,060	84	1930	240,673	30,287	403
1954	226,522	38,528	80	1929	242,809	30,190	275
1953	227,110	37,990	53	1928	240,089	29,215	270
1952	227,291	37,242	95	1927	236,283	28,724	245
1951	227,415	36,682	50	1926	235,158	27,927	195
1950	227,364	35,968	61	1925	233,633	27,241	----------
1949	226,791	35,243	53				
1948	226,844	34,507	26				
1947	226,501	33,789	24				
1946	226,143	33,320	23				

Series Q 388–397. Fuel Received, Ties and Rails Laid, and Purchases by Railroads: 1917 to 1970

[Class I line-haul railroads]

Year	Fuel received [1]			New rails laid	Cross-ties laid		Purchases			
	Bituminous coal	Fuel oil	Diesel oil		Total	Treated	Total, incl. miscellaneous	Fuel	Forest products	Iron and steel products
	388	389	390	391	392	393	394	395	396	397
	1,000 short tons	Mil. gal.	Mil. gal.	1,000 short tons	1,000	1,000	Mil. dol.	Mil. dol.	Mil. dol.	Mil. dol.
1970	1	–	3,812	549	19,611	19,473	----------	----------	----------	----------
1969	1	33	3,924	575	20,088	19,895	1,654	446	123	454
1968	2	42	3,922	547	19,006	18,811	1,534	439	104	425
1967	2	47	3,889	474	17,458	17,319	1,591	415	126	462
1966	3	65	3,925	605	17,699	17,399	1,605	401	125	483
1965	4	77	3,742	446	16,982	16,731	1,498	374	104	447
1964	7	85	3,630	383	16,546	16,488	1,476	365	97	437
1963	1,566	221	3,636	370	15,120	15,027	1,401	376	85	396
1962	1,834	229	3,578	312	15,206	15,138	1,311	364	81	374
1961	1,870	224	3,507	293	13,427	13,357	1,262	366	70	334
1960	2,229	233	3,560	382	16,417	16,290	1,463	365	97	446
1959	2,717	237	3,620	481	18,267	18,077	1,430	392	93	419
1958	3,658	239	3,453	413	17,722	17,426	1,231	376	76	320
1957	8,160	279	3,633	782	25,123	24,497	1,816	460	128	609
1956	12,280	443	3,639	883	27,323	26,848	1,884	477	155	613
1955	15,188	613	3,453	963	27,173	26,490	1,637	454	119	510
1954	15,964	656	3,160	993	25,728	24,531	1,425	433	114	406
1953	28,005	1,153	3,067	1,302	33,462	32,144	1,920	510	176	613
1952	37,829	1,668	2,759	1,086	34,231	32,910	1,818	539	177	513
1951	54,226	2,335	2,323	1,282	32,457	30,804	2,176	621	188	704
1950	63,906	2,519	1,923	1,368	33,091	31,553	1,740	609	121	510
1949	64,671	2,638	1,486	1,448	32,926	31,198	1,641	564	142	454
1948	98,826	3,759	1,170	1,548	40,472	38,281	2,183	833	166	590
1947	109,884	4,052	785	1,639	40,206	37,920	1,909	692	172	504
1946	108,148	4,144	544	1,388	40,150	37,671	1,571	553	149	416
1945	123,007	4,706	441	1,823	46,624	43,657	1,572	555	137	418
1944	135,579	4,744	316	1,773	51,259	47,695	1,611	586	159	432
1943	129,738	4,802	219	1,448	49,344	44,822	1,394	527	150	340
1942	120,910	4,135	174	1,353	53,241	47,932	1,260	426	115	354
1941	104,100	3,368	114	1,355	50,077	43,872	1,161	350	104	380

See footnotes at end of table.

Series Q 388–397. Fuel Received, Ties and Rails Laid, and Purchases by Railroads: 1917 to 1970—Con.

Year	Fuel received [1]			New rails laid	Cross-ties laid		Purchases			
	Bituminous coal	Fuel oil	Diesel oil		Total	Treated	Total, incl. miscellaneous	Fuel	Forest products	Iron and steel products
	388	389	390	391	392	393	394	395	396	397
	1,000 short tons	*Mil. gal.*	*Mil. gal.*	*1,000 short tons*	*1,000*	*1,000*	*Mil. dol.*	*Mil. dol.*	*Mil. dol.*	*Mil. dol.*
1940	88,595	2,752	73	1,134	45,326	38,698	854	274	82	264
1939	81,813	2,573	44	992	46,410	39,654	769	257	70	236
1938	74,784	2,426	----------	679	42,508	34,589	583	244	57	127
1937	91,718	2,875	----------	1,163	49,738	39,674	966	294	105	311
1936	91,707	2,569	----------	1,043	49,117	38,206	803	272	77	239
1935	81,286	2,282	----------	658	45,260	33,939	593	233	57	135
1934	79,494	2,108	----------	715	44,131	32,367	600	217	64	151
1933	75,487	1,943	----------	457	38,007	26,818	466	181	42	104
1932	74,670	1,984	----------	456	40,137	30,107	445	178	52	95
1931	91,136	2,380	----------	1,154	54,449	41,851	695	245	76	189
1930	108,651	2,870	----------	1,783	69,325	54,529	1,039	307	135	305
1929	124,152	3,208	----------	2,281	81,964	64,724	1,330	364	158	407
1928	119,820	2,847	----------	2,404	84,585	64,331	1,271	385	161	375
1927	130,606	2,921	----------	2,477	86,243	62,963	1,396	439	176	407
1926	139,602	3,173	----------	2,475	[2] 80,746	[2] 55,558	1,559	473	186	507
1925	131,452	3,114	----------	2,184	82,717	50,090	1,392	459	170	419
1924	126,340	3,095	----------	2,006	83,073	44,490	1,343	472	181	366
1923	157,900	3,017	----------	1,937	84,435	41,656	1,739	618	233	465
1922	120,654	----------	----------	1,557	86,642	40,630	----------	----------	----------	----------
1921	127,630	----------	----------	1,640	86,522	36,072	----------	----------	----------	----------
1920	----------	----------	----------	1,581	86,829	37,792	----------	----------	----------	----------
1919	----------	----------	----------	2,615	80,903	----------	----------	----------	----------	----------
1918	----------	----------	----------	2,109	76,139	----------	----------	----------	----------	----------
1917	----------	----------	----------	2,293	79,070	----------	----------	----------	----------	----------

– Represents zero.
[1] Beginning 1964, represents fuel consumed by locomotives and rail motor cars.
[2] Figures for this and earlier years less inclusive than for later years.

Series Q 398–409. Railroad Employment and Wages, and Accidents and Fatalities: 1890 to 1970

[Statistics on accidents and fatalities not strictly comparable because of changing definition of a reportable accident]

Year ending—	Employees [1]		Railroad accidents and fatalities (all steam railroads)									
	Number	Compensation	Total		Passengers [2][3]		Employees [4]		Other persons [3]		Trespassers [3][5]	
			Killed	Injured	Killed	Injured	Killed	Injured	Killed	Injured	Killed	Injured
	398	399	400	401	402	403	404	405	406	407	408	409
	1,000	*Mil. dol.*										
DECEMBER 31												
1970	577	5,646	2,225	21,327	8	489	172	16,285	1,452	3,907	593	646
1969	590	5,451	2,299	23,356	6	862	190	17,255	1,476	4,565	627	674
1968	602	5,197	2,359	24,608	11	1,329	150	18,116	1,570	4,500	628	663
1967	624	5,026	2,483	24,523	12	1,054	176	18,055	1,649	4,718	646	696
1966	645	4,975	2,684	25,552	23	1,244	168	18,651	1,815	4,955	678	702
1965	655	4,887	2,399	25,789	11	1,189	184	19,133	1,570	4,799	634	668
1964	675	4,758	2,423	27,614	8	1,489	188	20,499	1,608	4,915	619	711
1963	691	4,690	2,141	27,456	13	2,135	173	19,992	1,384	4,671	571	658
1962	711	4,722	2,106	26,880	27	2,109	190	19,733	1,272	4,360	617	678
1961	727	4,684	2,127	27,118	17	1,887	145	20,194	1,341	4,359	624	678
1960*	793	4,957	2,248	19,577	32	1,463	198	13,710	1,401	3,840	617	564
1959	828	5,049	2,094	19,909	10	1,352	178	14,198	1,265	3,740	641	619
1958	853	4,991	2,311	19,343	61	1,628	187	13,305	1,352	3,750	711	660
1957	999	5,422	2,393	18,688	15	1,566	195	12,246	1,441	4,259	742	617
1956	1,058	5,388	2,578	28,676	57	2,756	288	19,608	1,415	5,588	818	724
1955	1,071	5,045	2,761	27,840	24	2,253	282	19,011	1,588	5,896	867	680
1954	1,078	4,907	2,575	25,547	30	2,247	235	17,219	1,440	5,354	870	727
1953	1,221	5,381	3,039	29,214	49	2,503	343	20,170	1,603	5,745	1,044	796
1952	1,242	5,382	3,011	30,001	24	2,049	386	21,339	1,558	5,806	1,043	807
1951	1,292	5,328	3,459	34,454	150	3,184	432	24,266	1,735	6,178	1,142	826
1950	1,237	4,645	3,486	33,267	180	3,419	392	22,586	1,699	6,320	1,215	942
1949	1,209	4,469	3,426	32,123	37	2,545	450	22,993	1,652	5,664	1,287	921
1948	1,345	4,821	3,883	43,107	59	3,607	622	31,961	1,757	6,575	1,445	964
1947	1,371	4,399	4,285	48,819	79	4,246	791	36,880	1,935	6,675	1,480	1,018
1946	1,378	4,214	4,508	52,026	128	4,714	738	39,472	2,007	6,853	1,635	987
1945	1,439	3,901	4,812	61,515	156	4,840	972	48,632	2,092	7,031	1,592	1,012
1944	1,434	3,898	4,908	61,251	267	4,854	1,087	48,613	2,004	6,820	1,550	964
1943	1,375	3,556	5,051	60,348	278	5,166	1,072	46,971	1,946	7,076	1,755	1,135
1942	1,291	2,966	5,337	48,123	122	3,501	1,005	36,032	2,197	7,237	2,013	1,353
1941	1,159	2,360	5,191	37,829	48	3,009	807	25,866	2,141	7,378	2,195	1,576

See footnotes at end of table.

Series Q 398–409. Railroad Employment and Wages, and Accidents and Fatalities: 1890 to 1970—Con.

Year ending—	Employees [1]		Railroad accidents and fatalities (all steam railroads)									
	Number	Compensation	Total		Passengers [2][3]		Employees [4]		Other persons [3]		Trespassers [3][5]	
			Killed	Injured	Killed	Injured	Killed	Injured	Killed	Injured	Killed	Injured
	398	399	400	401	402	403	404	405	406	407	408	409
	1,000	*Mil. dol.*										
DECEMBER 31—Con.												
1940	1,046	1,991	4,740	29,606	83	2,597	583	18,350	1,979	6,886	2,095	1,773
1939	1,007	1,889	4,492	28,144	40	2,580	536	17,383	1,564	6,225	2,352	1,956
1938	958	1,771	4,649	27,275	81	2,345	513	16,569	1,695	6,253	2,360	2,108
1937	1,137	2,014	5,502	36,713	34	2,594	712	24,114	2,102	7,703	2,654	2,302
1936	1,086	1,874	5,550	34,723	41	2,548	720	22,409	1,988	7,348	2,801	2,418
1935	1,014	1,666	5,258	28,108	30	1,949	600	16,742	1,842	6,711	2,786	2,706
1934	1,027	1,541	5,020	28,641	38	1,945	556	17,338	1,729	6,573	2,697	2,785
1933	991	1,424	5,180	27,516	51	2,067	533	15,932	1,704	5,915	2,892	3,602
1932	1,052	1,535	4,905	29,232	27	1,912	579	17,742	1,722	6,214	2,577	3,364
1931	1,283	2,125	5,271	35,671	46	2,104	677	23,358	2,059	7,232	2,489	2,977
1930	1,517	2,589	5,665	49,443	61	2,666	977	35,872	2,218	8,230	2,409	2,675
1929	1,694	2,940	6,690	77,013	114	3,846	1,428	60,739	2,724	10,082	2,424	2,346
1928	1,692	2,874	6,680	86,205	91	3,468	1,329	70,873	2,773	9,497	2,487	2,367
1927	1,776	2,963	6,992	104,817	88	3,893	1,570	88,223	2,608	9,976	2,726	2,725
1926	1,822	3,002	7,090	130,235	152	4,461	1,672	111,903	2,705	11,326	2,561	2,545
1925	1,786	2,916	6,766	137,435	171	4,952	1,599	119,224	2,412	10,571	2,584	2,688
1924	1,795	2,883	6,617	143,739	149	5,354	1,543	125,319	2,369	10,213	2,556	2,853
1923	1,902	3,062	7,385	171,712	138	5,847	2,026	152,678	2,442	10,140	2,779	3,047
1922	1,670	2,693	6,325	134,871	200	6,153	1,657	117,197	2,038	8,677	2,430	2,844
1921	1,705	2,824	5,996	120,685	205	5,584	1,446	104,530	4,345	10,571	--------	--------
1920	2,076	3,754	6,958	168,309	229	7,591	2,578	149,414	4,151	11,304	--------	--------
1919	1,960	2,898	6,978	149,053	273	7,456	2,138	131,018	4,567	10,579	--------	--------
1918	1,892	2,665	9,286	174,575	471	7,316	3,419	156,013	5,396	11,246	--------	--------
1917	1,786	1,783	10,087	194,805	301	7,582	3,199	174,247	6,587	12,976	--------	--------
1916	1,701	1,507	10,001	196,722	246	7,152	2,941	176,923	6,814	12,647	--------	--------
JUNE 30												
1916	1,654	1,404	9,364	180,375	239	7,488	2,687	160,663	6,438	12,224	--------	--------
1915	1,548	1,278	8,621	162,040	199	10,914	2,152	138,092	6,270	13,034	--------	--------
1914	1,710	1,381	10,302	192,662	232	13,887	3,259	165,212	6,811	13,563	--------	--------
1913	[6]1,815	[6]1,374	10,964	200,308	350	15,130	3,715	171,417	6,899	13,761	--------	--------
1912	1,716	1,252	10,585	169,538	283	14,938	3,635	142,442	6,667	12,158	--------	--------
1911	1,670	1,208	10,396	150,159	299	12,042	3,602	126,039	6,495	12,078	--------	--------
1910	1,699	1,144	9,682	119,507	324	12,451	3,382	95,671	5,976	11,385	--------	--------
1909	1,503	988	8,722	95,626	253	10,311	2,610	75,006	5,859	10,309	--------	--------
1908	1,436	1,035	10,188	104,230	381	11,556	3,405	82,487	6,402	10,187	--------	--------
1907	1,672	1,072	11,839	111,016	610	13,041	4,534	87,644	6,695	10,331	--------	--------
1906	1,521	901	10,618	97,706	359	10,764	3,929	76,701	6,330	10,241	--------	--------
1905	1,382	840	9,703	86,008	537	10,457	3,361	66,833	5,805	8,718	--------	--------
1904	1,296	818	10,046	84,155	441	9,111	3,632	67,067	5,973	7,977	--------	--------
1903	1,313	757	9,840	76,553	355	8,231	3,606	60,481	5,879	7,841	--------	--------
1902	1,189	676	8,588	64,662	345	6,683	2,969	50,524	5,274	7,455	--------	--------
1901	1,071	611	8,455	53,339	282	4,988	2,675	41,142	5,498	7,209	--------	--------
1900	1,018	577	7,865	50,320	249	4,128	2,550	39,643	5,066	6,549	--------	--------
1899	929	523	7,123	44,620	239	3,442	2,210	34,923	4,674	6,255	--------	--------
1898	875	495	6,859	40,882	221	2,945	1,958	31,761	4,680	6,176	--------	--------
1897	823	466	6,437	36,731	222	2,795	1,693	27,667	4,522	6,269	--------	--------
1896	827	469	6,448	38,687	181	2,873	1,861	29,969	4,406	5,845	--------	--------
1895	785	446	6,136	33,748	170	2,375	1,811	25,696	4,155	5,677	--------	--------
1894	780	----------	6,447	31,889	324	3,034	1,823	23,422	4,300	5,433	--------	--------
1893	874	----------	7,346	40,393	299	3,229	2,727	31,729	4,320	5,435	--------	--------
1892	821	----------	7,147	36,652	376	3,227	2,554	28,267	4,217	5,158	--------	--------
1891	784	----------	7,029	33,881	293	2,972	2,660	26,140	4,076	4,769	--------	--------
1890	749	----------	6,335	29,027	286	2,425	2,451	22,396	3,598	4,206	--------	--------

* Denotes first year for which figures include Alaska and Hawaii.
[1] See headnote for series Q 367–377.
[2] Passengers on trains and travelers not on trains.
[3] Casualties sustained in nontrain accidents included with "Other persons." *Nontrain accidents* are those not caused directly by operation or movement of trains, locomotives, or cars, but attributable to shop machinery or use of tools and apparatus that result in reportable casualties.

[4] Prior to 1921 casualties sustained by employees not on duty in nontrain accidents included with "Other persons."
[5] Trespassers included with "Other persons" prior to 1922.
[6] Class I and II railroads.

Series Q 410–412.   Pullman Company Operations: 1915 to 1968

Year	Average miles of road over which operations conducted	Revenue passenger-miles [1] (millions)	Employees	Year	Average miles of road over which operations conducted	Revenue passenger-miles [1] (millions)	Employees
	410	411	412		410	411	412
1968	33,464	1,002	2,945	1940	109,595	8,214	20,877
1967	42,713	1,434	4,179	1939	109,886	8,485	21,335
1966	45,807	1,969	4,905	1938	110,728	8,270	20,750
				1937	111,507	9,170	23,406
1965	51,057	2,014	5,347	1936	111,522	8,355	21,711
1964	52,994	2,218	5,544				
1963	59,798	2,516	5,902	1935	112,117	7,146	20,436
1962	61,278	2,905	6,392	1934	112,420	6,891	19,066
1961	63,035	3,046	6,688	1933	112,298	6,142	15,887
				1932	118,061	6,757	17,132
1960	67,467	3,358	7,320	1931	125,703	9,891	22,546
1959	71,448	3,462	8,020				
1958	79,555	4,300	10,234	1930	129,578	12,516	26,165
1957	85,068	5,388	14,890	1929	130,019	14,059	29,250
1956	87,472	6,630	16,793	1928	128,753	13,938	26,815
				1927	123,334	14,099	27,359
1955	89,124	6,882	18,061	1926	126,907	14,409	26,185
1954	91,920	7,271	19,866				
1953	94,518	8,200	21,529	1925	126,840	14,016	26,919
1952	96,390	9,336	22,588	1924	124,795	13,082	25,091
1951	99,592	9,893	23,862	1923	124,794	12,982	23,579
				1922	123,547	11,759	19,066
1950	102,722	10,558	22,820	1921	----------	11,295	----------
1949	104,287	10,544	22,286				
1948	104,940	12,172	23,724	1920	----------	14,334	----------
1947	105,950	13,516	29,046	1919	----------	13,720	----------
1946	100,653	20,672	36,982	1918	----------	10,679	----------
				1917	----------	11,072	----------
1945	95,765	27,276	41,601	1916	----------	9,285	----------
1944	103,766	28,267	39,703				
1943	104,128	25,891	33,182	1915	----------	8,925	----------
1942	106,408	19,072	26,591				
1941	108,034	10,070	22,704				

[1] 1939–1967 includes Pullman operations on Canadian and Mexican railroads; excludes chartered car operations.

Water Transportation (Series Q 413-564)

Q 413–564. General note.

Basic governmental sources of historical merchant-marine and water-traffic statistics include *American State Papers: Class IV, Commerce and Navigation*, vols. 1 and 2, for 1789–1823; the various annual issues of *Foreign Commerce and Navigation of the United States*, for 1821–1946, originally issued by the Register of the Treasury and then by the Treasury Department, later by the Department of Commerce and Labor, and finally by the Department of Commerce; the *Annual Report of the Commissioner of Navigation*, 1884–1923, the issuance of which followed a similar succession beginning with the Treasury Department; annual issues of *Merchant Marine Statistics*, 1924–1965, originally prepared by the Department of Commerce as successor to the statistical section of the *Annual Report of the Commissioner of Navigation*, and issued annually by the Bureau of Customs until 1965, supplemented by records of the U.S. Coast Guard, and the various annual issues of the *Annual Report of the Office of the Chief of Engineers*, Corps of Engineers. The *Statistical Abstract of the United States*, a secondary source, also contains historical merchant-marine and water-traffic statistics. The *Statistical Abstract* has been issued by the following agencies: 1878–1902, Bureau of Statistics, Treasury Department; 1903–1911, Bureau of Statistics, Department of Commerce and Labor; 1912, Bureau of Foreign and Domestic Commerce, Department of Commerce and Labor; 1913–1937, Bureau of Foreign and Domestic Commerce, Department of Commerce; 1938 and thereafter, Bureau of the Census, Department of Commerce.

Congressional documents also contain historical series on the merchant marine, foreign commerce, and related fields. For 1789–1882, a particularly valuable collection of documents was found in the library of the Department of Commerce, bound together under the title *Decadence of American Shipping and Compulsory Pilotage*. The documents included are as follows: *Foreign Commerce and Decadence of American Shipping*, H. R. Ex. Doc. No. 111, 41st Congress, 2d session; *Causes of the Reduction of American Tonnage and the Decline of Navigation Interest . . .*, H. R. Report No. 28, 41st Congress, 2d session; *Foreign Commerce and the Practical Workings of Maritime Reciprocity*, H. R. Ex. Doc. No. 76, 41st Congress, 3d session; *Causes of the Decadence of Our Merchant Marine; Means for Its Restoration and the Extension of Our Foreign Commerce*, H. R. Report No. 342, 46th Congress, 3d session; *American Shipping*, H. R. Report No. 1827, 47th Congress, 2d session; *American Merchant Marine*, H. R. Report No. 363, 48th Congress, 1st session; *Ship-Building and Ship-Owning Interests*, H. R. Report No. 750, 48th Congress, 1st session; and reports of lesser interest, H. R. Misc. Doc. No. 37 and Report No. 1848, both of the 48th Congress, 1st session.

Since 1921, publications of the Maritime Commission and its predecessor agencies should also be consulted, particularly the reports entitled, *Ocean-Going Merchant Fleets of Principal Maritime Nations, Iron and Steel, Steam and Motor, Vessels of 2,000 Gross Tons and Over*, issued quarterly or semiannually, 1921–1941, and *Employment of American Flag Steam and Motor Merchant Vessels of 1,000 Gross Tons and Over*, issued quarterly, 1923–1941. Finally, the Bureau of the Census (and its predecessor Census Office) published the results of five censuses of water transportation, for the years 1880, 1889, 1906, 1916, and 1926 (see general note for series Q 414–505, below).

Q 413. Persons entering the United States by ship, 1933–1970.

Source: U.S. Department of the Treasury, *Annual Report of the Secretary of the Treasury on the State of the Finances*, various issues.

Data include persons entering by documented vessels, excluding ferryboats.

Q 414–505. General note.

Statistics on documented merchant vessels and shipbuilding are from *Merchant Marine Statistics*, various annual issues, supplemented by records of the U.S. Coast Guard. Many are from the 1936 issue. Some of the estimates from the 1936 report have been modified, however, as explained below in table II. The text statements, and the correction of errors found in the published tables are based on reference to the primary sources, as follows: For 1789–1823, see *American State Papers: Class IV, Commerce and Navigation*, vols. 1 and 2 (published in 1834); for 1821–1892, see annual issues of *Commerce and Navigation of the United States*; for 1884–1923, see issues of *Annual Report of the Commissioner of Navigation*; for 1924–1945, see annual issues of *Merchant Marine Statistics*.

Of the Maritime Commission reports cited in the general note for series Q 413–564, above, the first, *Ocean-Going Merchant Fleets. . .*, provides data for each leading maritime nation on ocean-going merchant vessels of 2,000 gross tons and over, showing number and tonnage of such fleets classified by age, speed, size, boilers, engines, draft, etc., by major vessel type. The second, *Employment of American Flag Steam and Motor Merchant Vessels . . .*, shows for seagoing merchant vessels of 1,000 gross tons and over the number and tonnage of such vessels employed in U.S. foreign and domestic trade, arranged by major vessel type, ownership (government and private), and area of operation.

Census statistics on water transportation are not presented here. For reports of these censuses, see *Tenth Census Reports*, vol. IV, *Report on Agencies of Transportation*, 1880; *Eleventh Census Reports*, *Report on Transportation Business*, part 1, "Transportation by Water"; *Transportation by Water, 1906*; *Water Transportation, 1916*; and *Water Transportation, 1926*.

The first census, for 1880, was limited to steam vessels. The report of this census includes a detailed history of steam navigation in the United States with separate discussion and single-year construction statistics by geographic region, from the beginning to 1880. (See T. C. Purdy, "Report on Steam Navigation in the United States," *Tenth Census Reports*, 1880, vol. IV.) The report of the shipbuilding census, also taken the same year, includes a detailed technical history of shipbuilding in all aspects, with particular reference to sailing craft. Single-year figures are shown for New England shipbuilding, 1674–1714, classified by type of vessel and place where built. (See Henry Hall, "Report on the Ship-Building Industry of the United States," *Tenth Census Reports*, 1880, vol. VIII.)

The censuses of 1889 and 1906 included all classes of vessels. However, the 1889 census included fishing vessels for the Pacific Division only and the 1906 census excluded fishing vessels. The censuses of 1916 and 1926 provided data for all U.S. vessels and craft of 5 tons net register and over, documented and undocumented, whether propelled by machinery or sails, or unrigged, except that certain specified types of vessels were excluded. (See Bureau of the Census, *Water Transportation, 1926*, p. 5.) While the census reports of 1850 and 1860 contain some statistics relating to water transportation, these statistics apparently were collected by other agencies.

Data shown here are for documented merchant vessels only, exclusive of yachts. The following definitions are those currently applicable:

Documented vessels include all vessels granted registers, enrollments and licenses, or licenses, as "vessels of the United States," and as such have certain benefits and privileges. Vessels of 5 net tons and over owned by citizens of the United States and otherwise complying with the requirements for documentation may be documented to engage in the foreign or coasting trades or the fisheries.

Registers are ordinarily issued to vessels engaged in the foreign trade or the whale fisheries. Historically, this group has included the major portion of the whaling fleet.

Enrollments and licenses are issued to vessels of 20 net tons and over engaged in the coasting trade or fisheries.

Licenses may be issued to vessels of less than 20 net tons engaged in the coasting trade or fisheries.

Undocumented craft are those not registered, enrolled, or licensed· Barges, scows, lighters, and canal boats, without any propelling power of their own, operated exclusively in a harbor, on the canals or other internal waters of a State, or on the rivers or lakes of the United States, not in any case carrying passengers, and vessels under 5 net tons are exempt from the requirements of the laws governing documentation.

Gross tonnage refers to *space* measurement, 100 cubic feet equaling 1 ton; it is not a measure of weight. Gross tonnage is the capacity of the entire space within the frames and the ceiling of the hull, together with those closed-in spaces above deck available for cargo, stores, passengers, or crew, with certain minor exemptions. Before 1865, 95 cubic feet equaled 1 ton, and the admeasurement method differed in other respects.

Changes in maritime law: Admeasurement method. "Admeasurement" refers to the method of calculating gross tonnage of ships or vessels. The first law of the United States on the subject appears to have been enacted September 1, 1789 (1 Stat. 55). The enactment then made was reenacted with certain minor amendments in the Acts of August 4, 1790 (1 Stat. 169), and of March 2, 1799 (1 Stat. 675), and as so enacted was in force until January 1, 1865.

A basic change in admeasurement method was provided in the act of May 6, 1864, effective January 1, 1865 (13 Stat. 70–72, R. S. 4153, 46 U. S. C. 77). The method described in the act of May 6, 1864, appears to have been substantially the same as that in force in 1945.

For the transition period, 1865–1868, the total tonnage figures for the fleet are "mixed." During those years, the total fleet tonnage was obtained by combining the "old admeasurement" tonnage of vessels not yet readmeasured and the "new admeasurement" tonnage of vessels which had been readmeasured or newly built. For a recapitulation of the "old" and "new" *components* of the fleet tonnage (not the same vessels) for each year, 1865–1868, see *Commerce and Navigation, 1870,* p. 798.

No table has been located comparing the tonnage of a substantial number of vessels under "new" and "old" admeasurement; hence, neither the magnitude nor the direction of the change can be stated here. Apparently it varied for different types of vessels. "Brigs, schooners, and sloops measure less under the 'new' admeasurement ... while ships, barks, steamboats, and vessels having closed-in spaces above their hulls have their tonnage largely increased." Further, the difference between "old" and "new" was not believed to affect a comparison of New England shipbuilding for the years 1855 and 1868. (See *Treasury Annual Report,* 1868, p. 496.)

Another type of change in maritime law affecting the statistics is illustrated by the act of April 18, 1874 (18 Stat. 31), which exempted the greater amount of canalboat and other unrigged tonnage from documentation. (See U.S. Code, title 46, sec. 336.) For 1874–1876,

the "balance sheets of tonnage," published annually in the source volumes, record the removal of 879,000 tons of vessels for this reason alone. However, *Merchant Marine Statistics, 1936,* lists 843,000 tons exempted in 1876, whereas the 1876 balance sheet of tonnage specified 601,000 tons exempted. The reason for this discrepancy is not clear. The tonnage exempted annually, 1874–1936, is shown on pp. 54–55 of *Merchant Marine Statistics, 1936.*

At irregular intervals, steps were taken to remove from the tonnage accounts those vessels lost, abandoned, captured, sold to aliens, etc., which had not been officially reported for removal purposes. From the outset, the failure to remove such vessels annually resulted in a cumulative error which inflated the statistics of tonnage. When general clearances of this cumulative error were made, the effect was concentrated in a single year or a small group of years.

For a basic statement on this subject, see *American State Papers,* cited above, vol. 1, p. 494, where Albert Gallatin, Secretary of the Treasury, outlines the problem and discusses the first attempt (1800) to deal with it. Recurrently, in the annual tonnage reports found in the source volumes, the problem is discussed, the announcement is made that the rolls have been finally cleared, and assurance is given that the problem has been solved for the future. However, as late as 1867, in spite of repeated clearances in earlier years, the "First Annual Report of the Director of the Bureau of Statistics" stated, "The tonnage returns were swelled with thousands of ghostly ships— ships that had gone to the bottom years ago." (See *Annual Report of the Secretary of Treasury, 1867,* p. 244.)

In 1869, the Register of the Treasury attributed the entire decline of tonnage reported for 1869 to this factor. (See *Treasury Report, 1869,* p. 300.) In the same year, Francis A. Walker, Deputy Special Commissioner of Revenue in Charge of the Bureau of Statistics, stated that the process of assigning a number to each vessel and the institution of an annual list of vessels, as required by the Act of July 28, 1866, "has succeeded in clearing from the lists of vessels ... a vast amount of purely fictitious tonnage, which have been carried forward from year to year although thousands of vessels which this tonnage originally represented had been meanwhile lost at sea, broken up, or sold abroad." (See *Treasury Report, 1869,* p. 342.)

In the "balance sheets of tonnage" published annually in the source volumes, clearances of cumulative error are generally identified as "not heretofore credited" to distinguish them from listings of removals of the various types routinely reported as having occurred during the given year.

Some of the more important clearances of this cumulative error, and the tons of shipping thereby removed, were: 1800–1901, 197,000; 1811, amount not stated but the effect is evident in series Q 418; 1818, 182,000; 1829–1830, 604,000; 1837, 96,000; 1841–1842, 267,000; and 1855–1858, 945,000.

In later years, the terms "obsolete," "obsolete, not heretofore reported," and "correction of balance" found in annual balance sheets of tonnage, frequently reflect removal of cumulative errors. Examples are (in tons): 1864, 188,000; 1866, 1,063,000; 1867, 260,000; 1868, 128,000; 1869, 338,000; 1870, 58,000; 1871, 103,000; 1881, 157,000.

Other factors which require that early merchant-vessel statistics should be used with some caution are the following: (1) In some instances, systematic differences in identically described statistical series appear in the source volumes (see text for series Q 433–437) which reflect conflicting series of figures, possibly originating from different primary sources of data (see table II below); (2) transcription and typographical errors have crept into historical tables in the source volumes in the process of repeated recopying and retypesetting; (3) statistically significant footnotes which appeared in early reports frequently were dropped in later years; and (4) caution is suggested in referring back to the earlier volumes in the search for explanations of discrepancies or major changes, since the earlier data may reflect the same or similar errors.

In this volume (see table II below), a number of the copying and typesetting errors have been corrected where the exact nature of the discrepancy could be determined beyond reasonable doubt; several broad differences in figures have been pointed out; and a few detailed tabular notes have been added based on information in various annual issues selected largely at random.

Table II. Merchant Marine Tonnage—Changes in Figures From Those Shown in Source

[Source is *Merchant Marine Statistics, 1936*]

Series No.	Year	In source volume	In this volume
Q 417	1868	[1] 28,118	[1] 28,167
Q 418	1886	[2] 4,131,116	[3] 4,131,136
	1868	4,318,309	4,351,758
	1817	[4] 1,339,912	[5] 1,399,912
	1815	1,368,182	1,368,128
Q 419	1928	14,343,679	14,346,679
	1913	5,335,541	5,333,247
	1851	582,607	583,607
Q 425	1868	2,475,067	2,508,516
	1863	4,357,537	4,579,537
	1824	1,367,453	1,367,553
	1817	1,330,986	1,390,986
Q 426	1921	1,232,728	1,242,728
	1913	1,043,347	1,045,641
Q 427	1928	14,064,199	14,064,119
Q 429	1858	2,301,408	2,301,148
	1818	589,944	589,954
Q 430	1927	9,432,869	9,532,869
	1856	2,447,663	2,247,663
Q 431	1833	101,666	101,636
Q 432	1879	79,855	79,885
	1878	86,447	86,547
	1841	77,783	77,873
	1831	170,189	107,189
Q 435	1893	134,308	134,368
Q 436	1894	37,824	37,827
Q 437	1901	83,743	83,783
	1895	6,978	6,948
Q 459	1895	87,127	67,127
	1894	90,099	80,099
	1885	12,010	121,010
Q 460	1917	52,536	52,526
	1881	54,888	54,488
Q 461	1881	59,801	59,861
Q 463	1914	64,523	64,550
	1910	184,239	174,239
	1892	60,710	60,770
Q 481	1936	12,511,777	12,511,523
	1868	3,141,540	3,174,935
Q 482	1876	1,447,844	1,147,844
	1873	1,051,991	1,055,019
	1868	1,012,749	1,046,198
Q 483	1873	2,242,890	2,242,862
	1868	1,962,279	1,962,225
Q 485	1932	1,856,563	1,856,553
	1887	683,721	783,721
Q 486	1868	481,271	481,218

[1] Number of vessels.   [2] As shown in table 10, p. 16, of source.
[3] As shown in table 16, p. 30, of source.   [4] As shown in table 10, p. 14, of source.
[5] As shown in table 16, p. 28, of source.

Q 414–416. Employment on U.S. flag merchant vessels—basic wage scale for able-bodied seamen, 1929–1970.

Source: U.S. Maritime Administration, *Seafaring Wage Rates*, and unpublished data.

Seamen on both coasts receive extra pay for Saturdays and Sundays at sea. Beginning November 1955, West Coast incorporated this extra pay into base wages but East Coast did not. Monthly wage rate represents basic wage, over and above subsistence (board and room), paid to seamen having qualifying experience and employed on U.S. flag merchant vessels.

See also general note for series Q 414–505.

Q 417–432. Documented merchant vessels, by major classes, material of which built, and trade, 1789–1970.

Source: U.S. Bureau of Marine Inspection and Navigation, *Merchant Marine Statistics, 1936* and *1965* (annual report now published

by the U.S. Coast Guard), and U.S. Bureau of Customs, unpublished data. (Series Q 427–428, 1884, U.S. Department of the Treasury, *Annual Report of Commission of Navigation, 1884*, p. 161.)

See also general notes for series Q 413–564 and Q 414–505.

For 1789–1793, tonnage figures are the "duty tonnage," i.e., the tonnage of vessels on which duties were collected during the year. (See *American State Papers*, cited above in general note for series Q 414–505, vol. 1, p. 895.) The "duty tonnage" appears to have been the tonnage on which duties were collected on registered vessels, including "the repeated voyages of the same vessel," plus tonnage of the enrolled and licensed vessels which paid tonnage duties once each year. (See *American State Papers*, vol. 1, pp. 494, 498, 528.) Beginning in 1794, "district tonnage returns" were used, derived from reports of District Collectors of Customs, which gave the tonnage of vessels in each district based on registers, enrollments, and licenses outstanding, as of December 31.

For 1794–1801, figures are district tonnage returns, with no attempt to correct for the cumulative error caused by failure to remove vessels lost, abandoned, sold to aliens, etc. (See *American State Papers*, vol. 1, pp. 494, 499.) The figures for 1800–1801 ignore the first clearing of tonnage accounts which took place during these years. (See *American State Papers*, vol. 1, pp. 494–499, 527–531.) The correction for the cumulative error for *registered vessels only* would reduce the 1800 total to 819,571 tons and the 1801 total to 903,235 tons. The sharp drop attributable to the clearing of tonnage accounts would thereby be shifted back to 1800 instead of appearing in 1802.

For 1802–1818, the figures in series Q 418 consist of the "corrected registered" tonnage plus the uncorrected enrolled or licensed tonnage (see 1813 tonnage report in *American State Papers*, vol. 1, p. 1017). The figures for 1811 and 1818 reflect two additional attempts to clear out the cumulative error of registered vessels improperly retained on the registers. (See *American State Papers*, vol. 1, pp. 876, 958, and vol. 2, p. 406.)

The figures shown below in table III are those which were derived by a method authorized by Secretary of the Treasury Gallatin. They were reported to Congress in the annual tonnage reports in *American State Papers* as being the "actual" or "more nearly correct" tonnage.

Table III. "Actual Tonnage" of Documented Vessels: 1800 to 1818

[In thousands of gross tons]

Year	Tons	Year	Tons
1818	1,150	1808	1,173
1817	1,341	1807	1,208
1816	1,264	1806	1,166
1815	1,262	1805	1,085
1814	1,029	1804	983
1813	1,032	1803	917
1812	1,127	1802	865
1811	1,131	1801	850
1810	1,329	1800	768
1809	1,266		

These were obtained by taking the "corrected registered tonnage" and adding to it the "duty tonnage" for enrolled and licensed vessels. Since duties were paid only once each year on enrolled and licensed vessels, and owners were not likely to pay duties on nonexistent vessels, it was reasoned that the lower "duty tonnage" figure more accurately reflected the true total for the enrolled or licensed craft than did the district returns of tonnage based on outstanding marine documents. This correction for enrolled and licensed craft was dropped after 1818, probably because, beginning 1819, the "duty tonnage" for this group exceeded the district tonnage returns for the group.

In *American State Papers*, vol. 1, p. 499, the tonnage described as "actual tonnage" in the comparative table for 1794–1799 is, in fact, the district returns of tonnage without correction of any kind. Elsewhere in the tonnage report for 1800 (pp. 494–499), and in tonnage reports for later years, the term "actual tonnage" normally means the district returns based on outstanding marine documents (registers, enrollments, and licenses) corrected for cumulative error. In table III, the term "actual tonnage" is used in the latter sense; the figures are from annual tonnage reports, 1800–1818, in *American State Papers*, vols. 1 and 2.

Q 427–428, vessels, by material of which built. The source publication also classifies tonnage of each material by type of propulsion (steam, motor, sail, canalboat, and barge).

Q 429–432, vessels, by trade in which engaged. The source publication also presents the number of vessels engaged in each type of trade as well as tonnage. The statutes do not recognize for documenting purposes any fisheries except the cod, mackerel, and whale. Vessels engaged in catching any other fish, such as salmon or menhaden, are documented for the mackerel fishery.

Figures in early reports identified as "registered," or as "registered in foreign trade," commonly include the registered vessels engaged in the whale fishery. Accordingly, figures on "whale fishery" found in early reports should be examined carefully to determine whether they represent the entire whaling fleet or only the "enrolled or licensed" portion. The term "fisheries" as used in early volumes refers to cod and, later, to cod and mackerel fisheries. It rarely includes the whale fishery.

In terms of documentation as "registered," "enrolled," "licensed," series Q 429–432 are composed broadly as follows:

Series Q 429 (foreign trade) represents the total "registered" minus "registered whale fishery." The "registered" whaling tonnage is, however, included for 1794–1798.

Series Q 430 (coastwise and internal) represents the portion of the enrolled or licensed group engaged in this trade. The rest of the enrolled or licensed group is in series Q 432 (cod and mackerel fisheries).

Series Q 431 (whale fishery) is the "registered whale fishery" portion of the registered fleet plus the "whale fishery" portion of the enrolled or licensed fleet. For 1794–1798, however, the registered whaling tonnage is not included here, but in series Q 429.

Series Q 432 (cod and mackerel fishery) is the cod and mackerel fishery portion of the enrolled or licensed fleet. The rest of the enrolled or licensed group is in series Q 430 (coastwise and internal).

Q 433–437. Merchant vessels built and documented, by type, 1797–1964.

Source: See source for series Q 417–432.

The source publication also presents statistics separately for steam, motor, and sailing vessels, canalboats, and barges. Statistics for motor vessels begin in 1893.

Beginning 1938, figures are not comparable with those for earlier years and are probably understated. They represent those vessels built during the 12-month period which were still existent and documented as part of the merchant fleet at the end of the period. Hence, they exclude vessels completed during the period which were lost, sold to U.S. Government, sold to aliens, or otherwise removed from merchant vessel documentation before the end of the period.

See also general notes for series Q 413–564 and Q 414–505.

Q 438–448. Merchant vessels completed by U.S. shipyards, 1914–1970.

Source: 1914–1960, American Bureau of Shipping, New York, *The Bulletin*, annual issues. 1961–1970, U.S. Maritime Administration, *New Ship Construction*, annual issues.

See general notes for series Q 413–564 and Q 414–505.

Q 449–458. Shipbuilding in private shipyards—summary, 1949–1970.

Source: Shipbuilders Council of America, Washington, D.C., *Annual Report*, various issues.

Q 459–463. Gross tonnage of merchant vessels built and documented, by region, 1840–1936.

Source: U.S. Bureau of Marine Inspection and Navigation, *Merchant Marine Statistics, 1936*, pp. 46–48, and table 2.

See general notes for series Q 413–564 and Q 414–505.

Q 464–466. Gross tonnage of merchant vessels built and documented, by region, 1817–1850.

Source: U.S. Department of the Treasury, fold-in table on the history of shipbuilding (1817–1868) at back of the *Annual Report of the Secretary of the Treasury*, 1868.

Source also presents figures separately for "The United States," "The Lakes," and "Western Rivers." For a discussion of these data see the *Annual Report*. The source table, with a more detailed discussion appears as Plate XXII in H.R., Ex. Doc. No. 111, 41st Congress, 2d session, where the period covered is extended to 1869, and as Plate X (extended to 1870) in H.R. Ex. Doc. No. 76, 41st Congress, 3d session. These three series do not add to series Q 434.

See also general notes for series Q 413–564 and Q 414–505.

Q 467–472. Vessels repaired or converted in private shipbuilding and ship repair yards, 1943–1970.

Source: See source for series Q 449–458.

Q 473–480. Merchant vessels launched and owned—world and United States, 1895–1970.

Source: Lloyd's Register of Shipping, London, England, *Statistical Tables*, annual issues; and *Annual Summary of Merchant Ships Launched in the World*, various issues. (copyright.)

Q 481–486. Documented merchant vessels, by geographic region, 1816–1965.

Source: See source for series Q 417–432.

See general notes for series Q 413–564 and Q 414–505.

Q 486a. Documented merchant vessels, western rivers (Haites), 1811–1868.

Source E. F. Haites, J. Mak, and G. M. Walton, *Western River Transportation During the Era of Early Internal Improvements, 1810–1860*, Johns Hopkins University Press, 1975, Appendix B (copyright).

This series was calculated by the authors from W. M. Lytle, *Merchant Steam Vessels of the United States 1807–1868*, Mystic, Conn., The Steamship Historical Society of America, 1952, and *Supplements* 2 (1954) and 3 (1958), edited by F. R. Holdcamper.

The Lytle List is an alphabetical listing of steamboats based on the original records for documented merchant vessels constructed in the United States between 1807 and 1868. The entry for each steamboat includes its gross measured tonnage (by the pre-1865 calculation), year of construction, port of construction, and year of termination of service. Steamboats operating on the western rivers during this era were of a special design. Steamboats not built on the western rivers were not well suited to operate there; steamboats built to operate there generally did not leave the river system. The western river steamboats were, therefore, isolated on the basis of their port of construction. The number and tonnage of the western river steamboats starting and terminating service each year was then calculated and these series were combined to give the tonnage in operation at the end of the calendar year.

Series Q 486a differs from series Q 486 primarily in the treatment of the steamboats that ceased operation. Figures for series Q 486a exclude steamboats in the year during which they ceased to operate. Figures for series Q 486 exclude such steamboats only at irregular intervals.

See also general notes for series Q 413–564 and Q 414–505.

Q 487–502. U.S. flag merchant vessels, steam and motor, 1934–1970.

Source: U.S. Maritime Administration, *Employment Report of United States Flag Merchant Fleet Oceangoing Vessels 1,000 Gross Tons and Over*, annual issues.

See general notes for series Q 413–564 and Q 414–505.

Q 503–505. Documented merchant vessels, by type of service, 1934–1970.

Source: See source for series Q 417–432.

Series Q 505 includes cable, cod, dredging, elevator, ferry, fireboat, fishing, ice breaker, lightering, oil exploitation, oystering, passenger, pile driving, pilot boat, police boat, patrol boat, refrigerator, towing, waterboat, whaling, welding, wrecking, and miscellaneous. The source presents details for each of these in recent years.

See also general notes for series Q 413–564 and Q 414–505.

Q 506–517. General note.

Net tonnage capacity, as used here, refers to net or registered tonnage of the vessel, not weight of cargo. The net tonnage is what remains after deducting from the gross tonnage (defined in general note for series Q 414–505) the spaces occupied by the propelling machinery, fuel, crew quarters, master's cabin, and navigation spaces. It represents, substantially, space available for cargo and passengers. It is the usual basis for tonnage taxes and port charges. The net tonnage capacity of a ship recorded as "entered with cargo" may bear little relation to actual weight of cargo. Gross tonnage and net tonnage are both measures of cubic capacity, not of weight, 100 cubic feet equaling 1 ton. These terms should not be confused with the cargo ton of 2,000 pounds. Tonnage figures shown in series Q 507 and Q 513 for U.S. vessels entered and cleared, respectively, in foreign trade are greater than the total tonnage of U.S. vessels documented for the foreign trade because the "entered" and "cleared" series include tonnage for each vessel as often as it "enters" or "clears" each year. The documented tonnage, series Q 418, includes the tonnage of each vessel once for each year.

These figures include the tonnage of all types of watercraft engaged in the foreign trade, whether entering or clearing with cargo or in ballast, which are required to make formal entrance and clearance under U.S. customs regulations. Vessels engaged in trade on the Great Lakes with Canada as well as in trade with Mexico are also included. Vessels touching at a U.S. port in distress or for other temporary causes without discharging cargo, and Army and Navy vessels carrying no commercial cargo, are not required by customs regulations to enter or clear and thus are not included in the figures.

Vessels are reported as entered at the first port in the United States at which entry is made, regardless of whether any cargo is unladen at that port; arrivals at subsequent ports are not counted. Vessels are reported as cleared from the last port in the United States where loading of outward cargo is completed or where the vessel cleared in ballast; departures from prior ports are not counted.

Q 506–508. Vessels entered, all ports, 1789–1970.

Source: 1789–1820, Fred J. Guetter and Albert E. McKinley, *Statistical Tables Relating to the Economic Growth of the United States*, McKinley Publishing Co., Philadelphia, 1924, p. 39 (copyright). 1821–1879, U.S. Bureau of Marine Inspection and Navigation, *Merchant Marine Statistics, 1936*, p. 93. 1880–1940, *Statistical Abstract of the United States*, 1880–1888, *1908* edition, p. 286; 1889–1916, *1916* edition, p. 338; 1917–1930, *1931* edition, p. 474; 1931–1940, *1947* edition, p. 558. (See general note for series Q 413–564 for the various agencies which have issued the *Statistical Abstract*.) 1941–1946, U.S. Bureau of the Census, *Foreign Commerce and Navigation of the United States*, various issues; 1947–1970, same agency, *Vessel Entrances and Clearances*, Summary Report FT 975, various issues, and unpublished data.

Q 509. Total vessels entered at seaports, 1840–1970.

Source: *Statistical Abstract of the United States*. 1840, *1946* edition, p. 546; 1844–1855, *1878* edition, p. 134; 1856–1879, *1880* edition, p. 138. 1880–1970, see source for series Q 506–508.

Q 510–511. U.S. and foreign vessels entered at seaports, 1856–1970.

Source: 1856–1879, see source for series Q 509; 1880–1970, see source for series Q 506–508.

Q 512–514. Vessels cleared, all ports, 1821–1970.

Source: See sources cited for specific periods for series Q 506–508. The following page numbers apply, respectively, to the sources cited for 1821–1940: 93, 287, 475, 558, and 592.

Q 515. Total vessels cleared at seaports, 1840–1970.

Source: *Statistical Abstract of the United States*. 1840 and 1850, *1946* edition, p. 546; 1853–1879, *1881* edition, p. 138. 1880–1970, see source for series Q 506–508.

Q 516–517. U.S. and foreign vessels cleared at seaports, 1857–1970.

Source: 1857–1879, *Statistical Abstract of the United States, 1881*, p. 136; 1880–1970, see source for series Q 506–508.

Q 518–523. Value of waterborne imports and exports (including re-exports) of merchandise, 1790–1970.

Source: 1790–1820, see source for series Q 506–508; 1821–1858, U.S. Bureau of Marine Inspection and Navigation, *Merchant Marine Statistics, 1936*, p. 91; 1859–1935, *Statistical Abstract of the United States*, 1859–1866, *1895* edition, pp. 399–400; 1867–1912, *1913* edition, pp. 318–319; 1913–1923, *1924* edition, p. 417; 1924–1935, *1946* edition, p. 552. (See general note for series Q 413–564 for the various agencies which have issued the *Statistical Abstract*.) U.S. Bureau of the Census, 1943–1946, *Foreign Commerce and Navigation of the United States*, annual issues, 1947–1950, *Waterborne Trade by United States Port*, FT 972, annual issues, 1951–1970, *Waterborne Foreign Trade Statistics*, FT 985, annual issues (title changed to *U.S. Waterborne Foreign Trade* in July 1965).

The primary source of figures for 1790–1820 is J. R. Soley, "The Maritime Industries of America," *The United States of America* (N. S. Shaler, Editor), vol. II, 1894, pp. 522–527, 534, 536, 538. The report gives the percent of imports and exports in U.S. vessels. Guetter and McKinley (cited above for series Q 506–508) have derived absolute figures by applying these percentages to total imports and exports of merchandise and specie. The primary source of figures for 1821–1935 is *Foreign Commerce and Navigation of the United States*, annual issues. Starting with 1943, import or export statistics by method of transportation, showing shipping weight as well as dollar value, have been compiled by the Bureau of the Census.

See also general note for series U 187–352.

Q 524–529. Tonnage of waterborne imports and exports, by flag of carrier vessel, 1921–1970.

Source: U.S. Bureau of the Census, 1921–1945, *Foreign Commerce and Navigation of the United States*, annual issues; 1946–1957, releases and unpublished data; 1958–1970, *Statistical Abstract of the United States*, various issues.

Excludes cargoes (small in the aggregate) carried by ships of less than 100 tons gross capacity prior to 1946. Beginning 1946, excludes Army and Navy cargo, and includes Alaska, Hawaii, and Puerto Rico. Beginning July 1950, excludes commodities classified for security reasons as "special category." From July 1953 to December 1955 and July 1956 through December 1962, exports exclude shipments under $500 in value regardless of shipping weight; for January–

June 1956, exports exclude shipments under $1,000. For 1963 and later years, exports exclude shipments to Canada individually valued under $2,000 and to other countries under $500. Under $100 shipments are excluded for all years. Beginning 1954, imports exclude shipments under 2,000 pounds shipping weight regardless of value, as well as shipments valued at less than $100 regardless of shipping weight. For January 1960 through June 1965, imports exclude formal entry shipments valued at less than $100 and informal entry shipments valued under $251. For July–December 1965 and later years, imports exclude all shipments under $251.

Q 530–541. Waterborne cargo tonnage, foreign and domestic, 1924–1970.

Source: U.S. Corps of Engineers, 1924–1946, *Annual Report of the Chief of Engineers*, part 2; 1947–1970, *Waterborne Commerce of the United States*, 1971, part 5, *National Summaries*, pp. 5 and 6.

In 1954, part 2 of the *Annual Report* was superseded by a separate publication entitled *Waterborne Commerce of the United States* (published in several regional parts). Part 5 of this report, *National Summaries*, presents separate figures for series Q 534–535 for "Canadian" and "overseas."

Cargo tonnage refers to the weight of cargo and should not be confused with gross tonnage shown in series Q 417–505 or the net or registered tonnage capacity shown in series Q 506–517, which are measures of cubic capacity, not of weight. See also text for those series.

Domestic commerce includes all commercial movements between points in the United States, Puerto Rico, and the U.S. Virgin Islands. Traffic with the Canal Zone is treated as foreign commerce.

Foreign commerce includes all movements between the United States and foreign countries, and between Puerto Rico and the U.S. Virgin Islands (considered a single unit) and foreign countries. Trade between U.S. outlying areas (Guam, Wake, American Samoa, etc.) and foreign countries is excluded.

"Coastwise" commerce, series Q 537, refers to domestic traffic receiving a carriage over the ocean, or the Gulf of Mexico; and to traffic between Great Lakes ports and seacoast ports, when having a carriage over the ocean.

"Lakewise" commerce, series Q 538, refers to traffic between U.S. ports on the Great Lakes System.

"Local and intraport" commerce, series Q 539, refers to movements of freight within the confines of a port whether the port has only one or several arms or channels, except car-ferry and general ferry. The term is also applied to marine products, sand, and gravel taken directly from the Great Lakes.

"Internal" commerce, series Q 540, covers traffic between ports or landings where the entire movement takes place on inland waterways; movements involving carriage on both inland waterways and waters of the Great Lakes; inland movements that cross short stretches of open waters which link inland systems; marine products, sand, and gravel taken directly from beds of the oceans, the Gulf of Mexico, and important arms thereof; and movements between offshore installations and inland waterways.

"Intraterritory" commerce, series Q 541, refers to traffic between ports in Puerto Rico and the U.S. Virgin Islands, which are considered as a single unit.

Q 542–547. Waterborne bulk freight traffic on the Great Lakes, 1900–1970.

Source: Lake Carriers' Association, *Annual Report, 1970*, pp. 51–52 and 76–77 (copyright).

Includes tonnage moving to or from Canadian or U.S. lake ports, in Canadian or U.S. bulk carriers.

Q 548–552. Freight traffic on the Sault Ste. Marie canals, 1855–1900.

Source: U.S. Corps of Engineers, *Statistical Report of Lake Commerce Passing Through Canals at Sault Ste. Marie*, 1931.

These series include traffic moving through the American and Canadian canals. Figures for later years may be obtained from various issues of Corps of Engineers, *Annual Report*, part 2, *Commercial Statistics*. They are not shown here because they pertain only to traffic between Lake Superior and the other lakes; series Q 542–547, therefore, provide more comprehensive totals of Great Lakes traffic.

Q 553–555. Commercial ocean traffic on the Panama Canal, 1915–1970.

Source: 1915–1924, Governor of the Panama Canal, *Annual Report, 1948*, p. 10; 1925–1970, Panama Canal Company, *Annual Report*, various issues (copyright).

Does not include U.S. Government traffic.

Q 556–557. Tonnage moved on New York State canals, 1837–1970.

Source: State of New York, Department of Public Works, *Annual Report of the Superintendent*, annual issues, and unpublished data.

Q 558. Federal expenditures for rivers and harbors, 1822–1970.

Source: 1822–1882, *Statement of Appropriations and Expenditures for Public Buildings, Rivers and Harbors, Forts, Arsenals, Armories, and Other Public Works from March 4, 1789 to June 30, 1882*, U.S. Senate Ex. Doc., vol. 7, No. 196, 47th Congress, 1st session (Treasury Department Doc. No. 373), pp. 521–522; 1883–1919, Federal Works Agency, records (compiled from Treasury Department accounts); 1920–1970, U.S. Corps of Engineers, *Annual Report of the Chief of Engineers on Civil Works Activities*, vol. I, annual issues.

Figures include expenditures for rivers, harbors, and flood control prior to 1928. In 1928, expenditures for flood control amounted to less than $13,500,000. Figures for 1929–1970 exclude expenditures for flood control. The figures include amounts expended from emergency relief and Public Works Administration funds, 1933–1937, but exclude $5,500,000 for purchase of Cape Cod Canal, 1928, expended by and accounted for by the Treasury Department.

Q 559–564. Investment in canals, by region and agency of enterprise, 1815–1860.

Source: H. Jerome Cranmer, "Canal Investment, 1815–1860," *Studies in Income and Wealth*, vol. 24, National Bureau of Economic Research, New York, 1960, pp. 555 and 556. (Copyright, Princeton University Press.)

The development of data on annual canal investment was based on an averaging process applied to the experience of a sample of 24 canals for which annual expenditure figures were available. For a list of those canals and description of the estimating operations, see source.

Adjusted estimates of annual expenditures were made for every canal or canal system undertaken between 1815 and 1860. Expenditures for river and harbor improvements were not included, nor for slack water navigation except when the expenditures were part of a canal project. The estimates were then aggregated by region and by agency of enterprise within each region. The regional estimates were then aggregated to provide estimates of annual investment in canals for the entire United States, together with estimates for State and private enterprise.

The Northeast consists of the New England and Middle Atlantic States, including Maryland and the District of Columbia. The South encompasses the area south of the Potomac and Ohio Rivers; and the West, the region north of the Ohio River, except that the Louisville and Portland canal which, though actually located in Kentucky, south of the Ohio River, is included in the West region.

Series **Q 413.** Persons Entering the United States by Ship: 1933 to 1970

[**In thousands.** For years ending June 30. Covers persons disembarking, as reported on U.S. Customs Service forms, and differs from series C 315]

Year	Persons entering 413	Year	Persons entering 413	Year	Persons entering 413	Year	Persons entering 413
1970	723	1960	773	1950	762	1940	733
1969	728	1959*	762	1949	676	1939	1,019
1968	715	1958	781	1948	641	1938	1,072
1967	719	1957	848	1947	548	1937	1,011
1966	767	1956	842	1946	1,660	1936	898
1965	782	1955	843	1945	1,286	1935	812
1964	1 847	1954	845	1944	676	1934	754
1963	743	1953	865	1943	389	1933	795
1962	677	1952	900	1942	305		
1961	805	1951	723	1941	443		

* Denotes first year for which figures include Alaska and Hawaii.   1 Includes Puerto Rico.

Series **Q 414–416.** Employment on U.S. Flag Merchant Vessels—Basic Wage Scale for Able-Bodied Seamen: 1929 to 1970

[Except as indicated, employment data as of June 30 and wage rate data as of June 16]

Date	Employment 1 (1,000) 414	Date	Employment 1 (1,000) 414	Date	East coast monthly wage rate 4 415	Date	West coast monthly wage rate 4 416
1970	37.6	1949	67.2	1970—Jan	$470	1970—Jan	$652
1969	47.5	1948	82.1	1969—Jan	444	1969—Jan	600
1968	54.2	1947—Dec. 20	110.8	1968	444	1968	600
1967	54.6	1946—June 20	120.1	1967	423	1967	578
1966	51.9			1966	393	1966	558
		1945—June 20	158.9				
1965	2 39.1	1944—June 20	125.3	1965	393	1965	539
1964	48.0	1943—June 20	75.0	1964	393	1964	522
1963	48.0	1942	47.4	1963	393	1963	522
1962	47.3	1941	51.3	1962	393	1962	522
1961	2 30.9			1961	384	1961—Oct	522
		1940	49.8				
1960	49.2	1939	52.0	1960—Jan	369	1960—Oct	512
1959	50.2	1938	49.8	1959	353	1959	478
1958	51.5	1937	59.2	1958	353	1958—Oct	478
1957	61.1	1936	57.2	1957	353	1957—Oct	478
1956	57.2			1956	333	1956—Oct	453
		1935	56.2				
1955	57.5	1934	3 56.3	1955	314	1955—Nov	432
1954	55.8	1933	3 54.6	1954	314	1954—Oct	302
1953	69.1	1932	3 52.6	1953	314	1953	314
1952	70.7	1931	3 57.2	1952	302	1952	302
1951	69.5	1930	3 62.4	1951	257	1951	249
1950	56.6	1929	3 63.8	1950—Oct. 15	248	1950—Oct. 15	249

1 Estimates of personnel employed on U.S. merchant ships, 1,000 gross tons and over. Excludes vessels on inland waterways, Great Lakes, and those owned by, or operated for, the U.S. Army and Navy, and special types such as cable ships, tugs, etc.   2 Decrease due to seafaring strike.   3 Average monthly employment.   4 Seamen on both coasts receive extra pay for Saturdays and Sundays at sea. Beginning 1955, West Coast incorporated this extra pay into base wages but East Coast did not.

Series **Q 417–432.** Documented Merchant Vessels, by Major Classes, Material of Which Built, and Trade: 1789 to 1970

[Gross tonnage of documented vessels of 5 tons or more. As of December 31, 1789–1834; September 30, 1835–1842; June 30, 1843–1940; January 1 thereafter]

Year	Number of vessels	Gross tonnage (1,000) Total	Major classes Steam and motor, total	Steam Total 1	Steam Coal burning 1	Steam Oil burning 1	Motor Total 2	Motor Diesel and semi-Diesel engines 1	Sailing 3	Canal-boats and barges	Material of which built Metal 4	Material of which built Wood	Trade in which engaged For-eign	Trade in which engaged Coast-wise and internal	Trade in which engaged Whale fish-eries	Trade in which engaged Cod and mackerel fisheries 5
	417	418	419	420	421	422	423	424	425	426	427	428	429	430	431	432
1970	49,993	28,613	19,074	16,447			2,627		6	9,533						
1969	49,991	28,455	19,433	16,868			2,565		6	9,016						
1968	49,545	27,932	19,396	16,871			2,525		6	8,530						
1967	48,700	27,251	(NA)	(NA)			(NA)		(NA)	(NA)						
1966	47,223	26,522	(NA)	(NA)			(NA)		(NA)	(NA)						
1965	45,579	26,516	19,730	17,560	1,497	16,063	2,170	2,040	8	6,778	25,318	1,198	12,628	13,839	1	1
1964	44,669	26,160	20,018	17,896	1,664	16,232	2,122	1,988	17	6,125	24,900	1,260	12,580	13,276	1	1
1963	44,077	25,691	20,079	17,987	1,760	16,226	2,092	1,952	18	5,595	24,377	1,314	12,289	13,089	1	1
1962	43,566	25,456	20,076	17,990	1,903	16,088	2,085	1,942	18	5,362	24,107	1,349	12,393	12,775	1	1
1961	43,367	26,403	21,175	19,125	2,049	17,076	2,050	1,902	18	5,210	25,028	1,375	13,126	13,260	1	1

See footnotes at end of table.

Series Q 417–432. Documented Merchant Vessels, by Major Classes, Material of Which Built, and Trade: 1789 to 1970—Con.

Year	Number of vessels	Total	Steam and motor, total	Steam Total[1]	Steam Coal burning[1]	Steam Oil burning[1]	Motor Total[2]	Motor Diesel and semi-Diesel engines[1]	Sailing[3]	Canal-boats and barges	Metal[4]	Wood	Foreign	Coastwise and internal	Whale fisheries	Cod and mackerel fisheries[5]
	417	418	419	420	421	422	423	424	425	426	427	428	429	430	431	432
1960	43,088	28,581	23,553	21,526	2,125	19,401	2,027	1,876	23	5,005	27,184	1,397	14,737	13,833	1	1
1959	42,409	28,895	24,333	22,306	2,176	20,131	2,027	1,871	23	4,539	27,470	1,425	15,600	13,284	1	1
1958	41,276	28,586	24,599	22,596	2,171	20,426	2,002	1,844	23	3,965	27,118	1,469	16,206	12,376	1	1
1957	40,191	29,421	25,785	23,788	2,190	21,597	1,998	1,836	24	3,612	27,935	1,486	17,265	12,154	1	1
1956	39,499	29,610	26,251	24,210	2,204	22,005	2,041	1,886	34	3,326	28,073	1,537	17,765	11,843	1	1
1955	39,242	29,958	26,792	24,706	2,252	22,454	2,086	1,907	40	3,125	28,336	1,622	18,143	11,812	1	1
1954	39,008	30,764	27,631	25,489	2,321	23,168	2,142	1,960	46	3,087	28,982	1,782	18,974	11,787	1	2
1953	38,072	30,546	27,507	25,377	2,387	22,990	2,130	1,951	55	2,984	28,761	1,785	19,007	11,537	1	2
1952	37,389	30,416	27,459	25,356	2,405	22,951	2,103	1,923	66	2,891	28,559	1,857	19,280	11,134	1	2
1951	36,745	30,341	27,424	25,390	2,441	22,948	2,033	1,865	71	2,846	28,417	1,924	18,876	11,462	1	2
1950	36,083	31,215	28,327	26,273	2,507	23,765	2,055	1,885	82	2,806	29,263	1,952	19,154	12,048	[6]11	2
1949	35,264	32,182	29,323	27,225	2,543	24,682	2,099	1,932	87	2,771	30,212	1,969	20,654	11,525	1	3
1948	33,843	33,167	30,469	28,401	2,606	25,796	2,067	1,902	87	2,611	31,211	1,956	22,021	11,143	1	3
1947	32,760	37,832	35,149	32,941	2,699	30,242	2,208	2,058	95	2,588	35,897	1,936	26,535	11,294	1	3
1946	31,386	38,501	35,928	33,779	2,884	30,895	2,149	2,002	98	2,475	36,571	1,929	29,705	8,791	1	3
1945	29,797	32,813	30,247	28,669	2,931	25,737	1,578	1,433	115	2,452	30,898	1,915	26,043	6,766	1	3
1944	28,690	25,795	23,217	21,674	3,014	18,660	1,543	1,392	129	2,449	23,837	1,959	18,685	7,105	1	4
1943	27,612	16,762	14,052	12,547	3,048	9,499	1,505	1,361	142	2,568	14,647	2,115	9,285	7,471	2	5
1942	27,325	13,860	11,072	9,704	2,965	6,739	1,369	1,213	166	2,621	11,641	2,218	4,109	9,744	2	6
1941	27,075	13,722	11,047	9,814	3,058	6,756	1,233	1,075	182	2,493	11,393	2,329	3,047	10,654	14	7
1940	27,212	14,018	11,353	10,102	3,159	6,943	1,251	1,090	200	2,466	(NA)	(NA)	3,638	10,352	20	8
1939	27,470	14,632	11,952	10,760	3,250	7,510	1,192	1,028	221	2,459	12,159	2,473	3,312	11,288	21	11
1938	27,155	14,651	12,007	10,835	3,325	7,510	1,172	1,005	261	2,384	12,130	2,521	3,551	11,064	21	16
1937	26,588	14,676	12,170	11,055	3,322	7,559	1,115	878	312	2,194	12,233	2,443	3,833	10,798	20	25
1936	25,392	14,497	12,267	11,161	3,371	7,617	1,105	867	379	1,851	12,263	2,234	4,159	10,300	9	28
1935	24,919	14,654	12,535	11,433	3,496	7,748	1,102	841	441	1,677	12,469	2,185	4,560	10,049	9	35
1934	24,904	14,862	12,687	11,599	3,539	7,860	1,087	824	500	1,675	12,601	2,261	4,598	10,220	9	35
1933	24,868	15,060	12,862	11,788	3,615	7,971	1,075	812	563	1,635	12,736	2,324	4,701	10,313	9	37
1932	25,156	15,839	13,568	12,499	3,991	8,308	1,069	810	625	1,646	13,421	2,417	5,071	10,728	2	38
1931	25,471	15,908	13,528	12,475	4,103	8,202	1,053	792	673	1,707	13,344	2,565	5,576	10,286	7	40
1930	25,214	16,068	13,757	12,775	4,209	8,429	982	715	757	1,554	13,514	2,554	6,296	9,723	7	42
1929	25,326	16,477	14,162	13,301	4,462	8,751	861	609	825	1,490	13,910	2,567	6,906	9,526	7	39
1928	25,385	16,680	14,344	13,614	4,557	9,002	730	494	915	1,421	14,064	2,619	6,934	9,706	7	36
1927	25,778	16,888	14,507	13,874	4,919	8,907	633	397	989	1,392	14,160	2,728	7,309	9,533	8	38
1926	26,343	17,311	14,848	14,318	5,370	8,895	530	293	1,092	1,371	14,473	2,838	7,719	9,552	3	38
1925	26,367	17,406	14,976	14,495	5,512	8,931	481	254	1,125	1,304	14,499	2,907	8,151	9,216	4	35
1924	26,575	17,741	15,315	14,870	5,921	8,947	445	128	1,185	1,240	14,627	3,114	8,794	8,911	3	32
1923	27,017	18,285	15,821	15,426	6,556	8,870	397	17	1,254	1,209	14,775	3,510	9,069	9,177	4	35
1922	27,358	18,463	15,982	15,607	6,908	8,699	375	16	1,288	1,193	14,805	3,658	10,720	7,703	4	36
1921	28,012	18,282	15,745	15,371	7,069	8,302	374	15	1,294	1,243	14,426	3,856	11,077	7,163	4	37
1920	28,183	16,324	13,823	13,466	7,551	5,915	357	24	1,272	1,228	12,448	3,876	9,925	6,358	4	38
1919	27,513	12,907	10,416	------	------	------	------	------	1,200	1,292	9,236	3,671	6,665	6,201	4	36
1918	26,711	9,925	7,471	------	------	------	------	------	1,210	1,244	6,814	3,110	3,599	6,282	4	38
1917	26,397	8,871	6,433	------	------	------	------	------	1,278	1,159	5,856	3,015	2,441	6,393	6	32
1916	26,444	8,470	6,070	------	------	------	------	------	1,311	1,089	5,476	2,994	2,185	6,245	7	33
1915	26,701	8,389	5,944	------	------	------	------	------	1,384	1,061	5,305	3,085	1,863	6,486	9	32
1914	26,943	7,929	5,428	------	------	------	------	------	1,433	1,069	4,733	3,196	1,066	6,818	10	34
1913	27,070	7,887	5,333	------	------	------	------	------	1,508	1,046	4,608	3,278	1,019	6,817	9	42
1912	26,528	7,714	5,180	------	------	------	------	------	1,539	995	4,433	3,282	923	6,737	9	45
1911	25,991	7,639	5,074	------	------	------	------	------	1,598	967	4,299	3,340	863	6,720	9	46
1910	25,740	7,508	4,900	------	------	------	------	------	1,655	952	4,117	3,391	783	6,669	9	47
1909	25,868	7,389	4,749	------	------	------	------	------	1,711	928	3,925	3,464	879	6,451	9	50
1908	25,425	7,365	4,711	------	------	------	------	------	1,761	893	3,860	3,505	930	6,372	10	54
1907	24,911	6,939	4,279	------	------	------	------	------	1,814	845	3,438	3,501	861	6,011	10	57
1906	25,006	6,675	3,975	------	------	------	------	------	1,899	801	3,115	3,560	928	5,674	11	61
1905	24,681	6,457	3,741	------	------	------	------	------	1,962	753	2,850	3,607	944	5,442	11	60
1904	24,558	6,292	3,595	------	------	------	------	------	1,945	751	2,669	3,623	889	5,335	10	58
1903	24,425	6,087	3,408	------	------	------	------	------	1,966	713	2,440	3,647	879	5,141	10	58
1902	24,273	5,798	3,177	------	------	------	------	------	1,942	679	2,180	3,618	873	4,859	9	57
1901	24,057	5,524	2,921	------	------	------	------	------	1,933	670	1,901	3,623	880	4,583	10	52
1900	23,333	5,165	2,658	------	------	------	------	------	1,885	622	1,593	3,572	817	4,287	10	52
1899	22,728	4,864	2,476	------	------	------	------	------	1,825	563	1,376	3,489	837	3,965	11	51
1898	22,705	4,750	2,372	------	------	------	------	------	1,836	542	1,224	3,526	726	3,960	11	52
1897	22,633	4,769	2,359	------	------	------	------	------	1,904	506	1,207	3,562	793	3,897	13	67
1896	22,908	4,704	2,307	------	------	------	------	------	1,928	468	1,090	3,614	830	3,790	15	69
1895	23,240	4,636	2,213	------	------	------	------	------	1,965	458	970	3,666	822	3,729	16	69
1894	23,586	4,684	2,189	------	------	------	------	------	2,023	472	930	3,754	900	3,696	16	72
1893	24,512	4,825	2,183	------	------	------	------	------	2,118	524	896	3,930	883	3,855	17	71
1892	24,383	4,765	2,074	------	------	------	------	------	2,178	512	786	3,979	978	3,701	17	69
1891	23,899	4,685	2,016	------	------	------	------	------	2,172	497	742	3,943	989	3,610	17	69
1890	23,467	4,424	1,859	------	------	------	------	------	2,109	456	627	3,798	928	3,409	19	68
1889	23,623	4,307	1,766	------	------	------	------	------	2,099	443	554	3,753	1,000	3,211	22	74
1888	23,281	4,192	1,648	------	------	------	------	------	2,124	419	494	3,698	919	3,172	24	76
1887	23,063	4,106	1,543	------	------	------	------	------	2,170	393	475	3,631	989	3,011	26	80
1886	23,534	4,131	1,523	------	------	------	------	------	2,210	398	444	3,687	1,088	2,939	23	81

See footnotes at end of table.

Series Q 417–432. Documented Merchant Vessels, by Major Classes, Material of Which Built, and Trade: 1789 to 1970—Con.

Year	Number of vessels	Gross tonnage (1,000)									
		Total	Major classes			Material of which built		Trade in which engaged			
			Steam and motor	Sailing [3]	Canal-boats and barges	Metal [4]	Wood	Foreign	Coastwise and internal	Whale fisheries	Cod and mackerel fisheries
	417	418	419	425	426	427	428	429	430	431	432
1885	23,963	4,266	1,495	2,374	397	430	3,836	1,263	2,895	25	83
1884	24,082	4,271	1,466	2,414	391	387	3,885	1,277	2,884	27	83
1883	24,217	4,235	1,413	2,387	436	----------	----------	1,270	2,838	32	95
1882	24,368	4,166	1,356	2,361	449	----------	----------	1,259	2,796	33	78
1881	24,065	4,058	1,265	2,350	442	----------	----------	1,297	2,646	39	76
1880	24,712	4,068	1,212	2,366	490			1,314	2,638	38	78
1879	25,211	4,170	1,176	2,423	571			1,452	2,598	40	80
1878	25,264	4,213	1,168	2,521	524			1,589	2,497	40	87
1877	25,386	4,243	1,171	2,580	491			1,571	2,540	41	91
1876	25,934	4,279	1,172	2,609	498			1,554	2,599	39	88
1875	32,285	4,854	1,169	2,585	1,100			1,516	3,220	38	80
1874	32,486	4,801	1,186	2,474	1,141			1,390	3,293	39	78
1873	32,672	4,696	1,156	2,383	1,156			1,379	3,163	45	110
1872	31,114	4,438	1,112	2,325	1,001			1,359	2,930	52	98
1871	29,651	4,283	1,088	2,286	909			1,364	2,765	61	93
1870	28,998	4,247	1,075	2,363	808			1,449	2,638	68	91
1869	27,487	4,145	1,104	2,400	641			1,496	2,516	70	63
1868	28,167	4,352	1,199	2,509	644			1,487	2,702	78	84
1867	------------	4,304	1,192	3,113	----------			1,516	2,660	52	76
1866	------------	4,311	1,084	3,227	----------			1,388	2,720	105	98

Year	Gross tonnage (1,000)						
	Total	Major classes		Trade in which engaged			
		Steam and motor	Sailing	Foreign	Coastwise and internal	Whale fisheries	Cod and mackerel fisheries
	418	419	425	429	430	431	432
1865	5,097	1,067	4,030	1,518	3,382	84	113
1864	4,986	978	4,008	1,487	3,245	95	159
1863	5,155	576	4,580	1,927	2,961	99	168
1862	5,112	710	4,402	2,174	2,617	118	204
1861	5,540	877	4,663	2,497	2,705	146	193
1860	5,354	868	4,486	2,379	2,645	167	163
1859	5,145	769	4,376	2,322	2,481	186	157
1858	5,050	729	4,320	2,301	2,401	199	149
1857	4,941	706	4,235	2,268	2,337	196	140
1856	4,872	673	4,199	2,302	2,248	189	132
1855	5,212	770	4,442	2,348	2,543	187	134
1854	4,803	677	4,126	2,152	2,322	182	147
1853	4,407	605	3,802	1,910	2,134	193	169
1852	4,138	643	3,495	1,706	2,056	194	183
1851	3,772	584	3,189	1,545	1,900	182	146
1850	3,535	526	3,010	1,440	1,798	146	152
1849	3,334	462	2,872	1,259	1,770	180	125
1848	3,154	428	2,726	1,169	1,659	193	133
1847	2,839	405	2,434	1,047	1,489	194	109
1846	2,562	348	2,214	943	1,316	187	116
1845	2,417	326	2,091	904	1,223	191	98
1844	2,280	272	2,008	900	1,110	169	101
1843	2,159	237	1,922	857	1,076	153	73
1842	2,092	230	1,863	824	1,046	152	71
1841	2,131	175	1,956	788	1,107	157	78
1840	2,181	202	1,978	763	1,177	137	104
1839	2,096	195	1,901	702	1,154	132	108
1838	1,996	193	1,802	703	1,041	125	127
1837	1,897	155	1,742	683	957	129	127
1836	1,882	146	1,737	753	873	146	110
1835	1,825	123	1,702	788	797	98	142
1834	1,759	123	1,636	749	784	108	117
1833	1,606	102	1,504	649	744	102	111
1832	1,439	91	1,349	614	650	73	102
1831	1,268	69	1,198	538	540	83	107
1830	1,192	64	1,127	538	517	40	98
1829	1,261	54	1,207	593	509	57	102
1828	1,741	39	1,702	758	843	55	86
1827	1,621	40	1,580	702	789	46	84
1826	1,534	34	1,500	696	722	42	74

Year	Gross tonnage (1,000)						
	Total	Major classes		Trade in which engaged			
		Steam and motor	Sailing	Foreign	Coastwise and internal	Whale fisheries	Cod and mackerel fisheries
	418	419	425	429	430	431	432
1825	1,423	23	1,400	665	641	35	81
1824	1,389	22	1,368	637	642	33	77
1823	1,337	25	1,312	600	618	41	78
1822	1,325	23	1,304	583	624	49	69
1821	1,299	23	1,276	594	615	28	62
1820	1,280	22	1,258	584	588	36	72
1819	1,261	17	1,243	581	571	32	76
1818	1,225	13	1,213	590	549	17	69
1817	1,400	9	1,391	805	525	5	65
1816	1,372	6	1,366	801	522	1	48
1815	1,368	3	1,365	854	476	1	37
1814	1,159	3	1,156	675	466	1	18
1813	1,167	3	1,164	673	471	3	20
1812	1,270	2	1,268	759	478	3	30
1811	1,233	1	1,231	764	420	5	43
1810	1,425	1	1,424	981	405	4	35
1809	1,350	1	1,350	907	405	4	34
1808	1,243	(Z)	1,242	765	421	5	52
1807	1,269	(Z)	1,268	840	349	9	70
1806	1,209	----------	1,209	799	341	11	59
1805	1,140	----------	1,140	744	333	6	57
1804	1,042	----------	1,042	661	318	12	52
1803	949	----------	949	586	299	12	52
1802	892	----------	892	558	290	3	42
1801	948	----------	948	631	275	3	39
1800	972	----------	972	667	272	3	29
1799	939	----------	939	657	247	6	30
1798	898	----------	898	603	251	1	43
1797	877	----------	877	598	237	1	41
1796	832	----------	832	577	218	2	35
1795	748	----------	748	529	184	3	31
1794	629	----------	629	439	163	4	23
1793	521	----------	521	368	122	---------	31
1792 [7]	564	----------	564	411	121	---------	32
1791 [7]	502	----------	502	363	106	---------	33
1790 [7]	478	----------	478	346	104	---------	28
1789 [7]	202	----------	202	124	69	---------	9

NA   Not available.
Z   Less than 500 tons.
[1] For 1920–1937, tonnage for vessels with electric screw included in total (series Q 420 or Q 423) but excluded from series Q 421, Q 422, and Q 424. Maximum such tonnage included in series Q 420 is 201,246 in 1933 and maximum in series Q 423 is 91,470 in 1934.
[2] Includes gasoline engines, not shown separately.

[3] Includes canalboats and barges prior to 1868.
[4] Includes iron, steel, composite, concrete, bronze, and aluminum.
[5] Beginning 1937, excludes mackerel.
[6] Increase due to documentation of 1 large vessel on Atlantic Coast.
[7] Figures for 1789 are for ships paying tonnage duties during the last 5 months of the year. Figures for 1790–1792 are for ships paying duties at some time during the year.

Series Q 433–437. Merchant Vessels Built and Documented, by Type: 1797 to 1964

[Gross tonnage of documented vessels of 5 tons or more.   As of December 31, 1797–1834; September 30, 1835–1842; June 30, 1843–1940; January 1 thereafter.   Includes Alaska, Hawaii, Puerto Rico, Guam, and the Virgin Islands]

Year	All vessels		Gross tonnage		
	Number of vessels	Gross tons	Steam and motor	Sailing [1]	Canalboats and barges
	433	434	435	436	437
1964	1,551	867.910	265,850	99	601,961
1963	1,365	942,809	460,442	6	482,361
1962	1,175	821,431	419,586	94	401,751
1961	877	620,287	388,927	–	231,360
1960	949	629,295	352,271	–	277,024
1959	1,180	791,640	385,874	–	405,766
1958	1,390	836,799	406,272	–	430,527
1957	1,582	585,048	248,801	–	336,247
1956	1,385	445,617	152,359	8	293,250
1955	1,116	400,076	117,011	24	283,041
1954	1,186	589,317	369,016	10	220,291
1953	1,190	633,966	477,421	28	156,517
1952	990	437,378	313,296	–	124,082
1951	992	308,825	165,064	–	143,761
1950	861	194,370	103,358	7	91,005
1949	978	195,190	85,288	39	109,863
1948	1,118	200,290	108,206	–	92,084
1947	1,259	267,331	186,109	16	81,206
1946	1,275	548,262	509,538	7	38,717
1945	1,744	6,313,977	6,258,608	–	55,369
1944	1,723	8,032,009	8,009,277	129	22,603
1943	1,901	10,431,734	10,339,670	23	92,041
1942	1,108	4,543,946	4,504,398	14	39,534
1941	703	647,097	586,443	–	60,654
1940 [2]	705	446,894	385,894	87	61,126
1940 [3]	319	193,229	172,433	17	20,779
1939	673	339,899	269,188	22	70,689
1938	753	237,374	(NA)	(NA)	(NA)
1937	1,939	471,364	113,661	71	357,632
1936	1,207	224,084	59,020	79	164,985
1935	748	62,919	30,341	50	32,528
1934	724	66,649	26,916	33	39,700
1933	642	190,803	168,488	46	22,269
1932	722	212,892	164,620	18	48,254
1931	1,302	386,906	212,996	52	173,858
1930	1,020	254,296	172,969	210	81,117
1929	808	128,976	75,725	797	52,454
1928	969	257,180	172,901	230	84,049
1927	917	245,144	181,504	326	63,314
1926	924	224,673	140,586	263	83,824
1925	967	199,846	141,053	2,869	55,924
1924	1,049	223,968	145,493	914	77,561
1923	770	335,791	241,802	17,442	76,547
1922	845	661,232	597,137	25,459	38,636
1921	1,361	2,265,115	2,071,221	91,743	102,151
1920	2,067	3,880,639	3,660,023	132,184	88,432
1919	1,953	3,326,621	3,157,091	79,234	90,296
1918	1,528	1,300,868	1,090,996	83,629	126,243
1917	1,297	664,479	513,243	43,185	108,051
1916	937	325,413	250,125	14,765	60,523
1915	1,157	225,122	154,990	8,021	62,111
1914	1,151	316,250	224,225	13,749	78,276
1913	1,475	346,155	243,408	28,610	74,137
1912	1,505	232,669	153,493	21,221	57,955
1911	1,422	291,162	227,231	10,092	53,839
1910	1,361	342,068	257,993	19,358	64,717
1909	1,247	238,090	148,208	28,950	60,932
1908	1,457	614,216	481,624	31,981	100,611
1907	1,157	471,332	365,405	24,907	81,020
1906	1,221	418,745	315,707	35,209	67,829
1905	1,012	330,316	197,702	79,418	53,196
1904	1,184	378,542	255,744	64,908	57,890
1903	1,311	436,152	271,781	89,979	74,392
1902	1,491	468,831	308,178	97,698	62,955
1901	1,580	483,489	273,591	126,165	83,733
1900	1,447	393,790	202,528	116,460	74,802
1899	1,273	300,038	151,058	98,073	50,907
1898	952	180,458	105,838	34,416	40,204
1897	891	232,233	106,154	64,308	61,771
1896	723	227,097	138,029	65,236	23,832
1895	694	111,602	69,754	34,900	6,948
1894	838	131,195	83,720	37,827	9,648
1893	956	211,639	134,368	49,348	27,923
1892	1,395	199,633	92,531	83,217	23,885
1891	1,384	369,302	185,037	144,290	39,975
1890	1,051	294,123	159,046	102,873	32,204
1889	1,077	231,134	159,318	50,570	21,246
1888	1,014	218,087	142,007	48,590	27,490
1887	844	150,450	100,074	34,633	15,743
1886	715	95,453	44,468	41,238	9,747
1885	920	159,056	84,333	65,362	9,361
1884	1,190	225,514	91,328	120,621	13,565
1883	1,268	265,430	107,229	137,046	21,155
1882	1,371	282,270	121,843	118,798	41,629
1881	1,108	280,459	118,070	81,209	81,180

Year	All vessels		Gross tonnage		
	Number of vessels	Gross tons	Steam and motor	Sailing [1]	Canalboats and barges
	433	434	435	436	437
1880	902	157,410	78,854	59,057	19,499
1879	1,132	193,031	86,361	66,867	39,803
1878	1,258	235,504	81,860	106,066	47,578
1877	1,029	176,592	47,514	106,331	22,747
1876	1,112	203,586	69,251	118,672	15,663
1875	1,301	297,639	62,460	206,884	28,295
1874	2,147	432,725	101,930	216,316	114,479
1873	2,261	359,246	88,011	144,629	126,606
1872	1,643	209,052	62,210	76,291	70,551
1871	1,755	273,227	87,842	97,179	88,206
1870	1,618	276,953	70,621	146,340	59,992
1869	1,726	275,230	65,066	149,029	61,135
1868	1,802	285,304	63,940	142,742	78,622
1867	1,518	305,594	72,010	233,584	----------
1866	1,898	336,146	125,183	210,963	----------
1865	1,789	394,523	146,433	248,090	----------
1864	2,388	415,740	147,499	268,241	----------
1863	1,816	311,045	94,233	216,812	----------
1862	864	175,076	55,449	119,627	----------
1861	1,146	233,194	60,986	172,208	----------
1860	1,071	214,798	69,370	145,428	----------
1859	875	156,602	35,305	121,297	----------
1858	1,241	244,712	65,374	179,338	----------
1857	1,443	378,804	74,459	304,345	----------
1856	1,703	469,393	74,865	394,528	----------
1855	2,024	583,450	78,127	505,323	----------
1854	1,774	535,616	91,037	444,579	----------
1853	1,710	425,572	109,402	316,170	----------
1852	1,444	351,493	98,624	252,869	----------
1851	1,357	298,203	78,197	220,006	----------
1850	1,360	272,218	56,911	215,307	----------
1849	1,547	256,577	61,241	195,336	----------
1848	1,851	318,075	66,652	251,423	----------
1847	1,598	243,732	53,979	189,753	----------
1846	1,420	188,203	51,778	136,425	----------
1845	1,038	146,018	40,926	105,092	----------
1844	766	103,537	30,976	72,561	----------
1843 [4]	482	63,617	17,624	45,992	----------
1842	1,021	129,083	29,158	99,925	----------
1841	761	118,893	27,941	90,950	----------
1840	871	118,309	19,811	98,498	----------
1839	899	125,260	34,219	91,041	----------
1838	913	115,905	23,607	92,298	----------
1837	972	125,913	33,811	92,102	----------
1836	911	116,230	26,630	89,600	----------
1835 [4]	725	75,107	12,347	62,760	----------
1834	957	118,389	13,905	104,484	----------
1833	1,187	161,492	12,620	148,872	----------
1832	1,065	144,544	17,386	127,158	----------
1831	712	85,556	11,437	74,119	----------
1830	648	58,560	8,269	50,291	----------
1829	796	79,408	10,281	69,127	----------
1828	886	98,964	5,881	93,083	----------
1827	951	106,456	11,010	95,446	----------
1826	1,033	130,373	12,818	117,555	----------
1825	1,000	116,464	9,171	107,293	----------
1824	793	92,798	5,216	87,582	----------
1823	630	75,857	3,766	72,091	----------
1822	639	77,569	1,861	75,708	----------
1821	519	57,275	3,017	54,258	----------
1820	557	51,394	5,572	45,822	----------
1819	876	86,670	5,824	80,846	----------
1818	923	87,346	3,695	83,651	----------
1817	1,087	87,626	2,543	85,083	----------
1816	1,431	135,186	2,926	132,260	----------
1815	1,329	155,579	546	155,033	----------
1814	490	29,751	593	29,158	----------
1813	371	32,583	1,140	31,443	----------
1812	(NA)	85,148	118	85,030	----------
1811	(NA)	146,691	1,145	145,546	----------
1810	(NA)	127,575	–	127,575	----------
1809	(NA)	91,397	458	90,939	----------
1808 [5]	(NA)	31,755	182	31,673	----------
1807	(NA)	99,783	78	99,705	----------
1806	(NA)	126,093	----------	126,093	----------
1805	(NA)	128,507	----------	128,507	----------
1804	(NA)	103,753	----------	103,753	----------
1803	(NA)	88,448	----------	88,448	----------
1802	(NA)	(NA)	----------	(NA)	----------
1801	(NA)	124,755	----------	124,755	----------
1800	995	106,261	----------	106,261	----------
1799	767	77,921	----------	77,921	----------
1798	635	49,435	----------	49,435	----------
1797	----------	56,679	----------	56,679	----------

– Represents zero.   NA Not available.
[1] Includes canalboats and barges prior to 1868.
[2] Jan. 1–Dec. 31.
[3] July 1, 1939–June 30, 1940.
[4] 9-month period.
[5] Figures by class of vessel do not add to the total for this year.

Series **Q 438–448.** Merchant Vessels Completed by U.S. Shipyards: 1914 to 1970

[**Tons in thousands.** Represents self-propelled steel vessels of 2,000 gross tons and over for domestic use. Excludes Alaska and Hawaii]

Year	Merchant vessels		Passenger-cargo/transport			Cargo			Tanker		
	Number	Gross tons	Number	Gross tons	Deadweight tons	Number	Gross tons	Deadweight tons	Number	Gross tons	Deadweight tons
	438	439	440	441	442	443	444	445	446	447	448
1970	13	342	–	–	–	6	120	134	7	222	427
1969	22	418	–	–	–	14	217	247	8	201	381
1968	21	319	–	–	–	18	256	291	3	63	113
1967	12	143	–	–	–	12	143	150	–	–	–
1966	13	146	–	–	–	12	125	161	1	21	36
1965	13	173	–	–	–	11	121	154	2	52	92
1964	15	213	1	14	9	10	104	123	4	95	166
1963	35	418	6	51	31	23	250	289	6	117	200
1962	27	392	1	14	10	23	265	303	3	113	186
1961	25	369	–	–	–	18	190	224	7	179	298
1960	26	410	–	–	–	15	134	163	11	276	456
1959	30	714	1	5	1	3	40	73	26	668	1,095
1958	30	572	4	61	35	5	48	67	21	463	759
1957	19	297	–	–	–	3	8	6	16	289	457
1956	8	113	–	–	–	2	7	15	6	106	169
1955	9	119	–	–	–	7	84	95	2	35	55
1954	39	585	1	4	6	11	106	159	27	475	764
1953	45	570	1	4	4	22	212	324	22	354	555
1952	31	399	6	101	57	17	170	289	8	127	202
1951	10	148	2	47	24	4	29	43	4	71	116
1950	26	405	–	–	–	3	27	44	23	378	609
1949	33	541	–	–	–	–	–	–	33	541	863
1948	24	159	1	15	11	17	92	159	6	52	88
1947	39	247	8	74	68	28	154	224	3	19	36
1946	83	646	9	77	85	66	487	729	8	82	121
1945	1,041	7,615	46	509	311	807	5,336	7,206	188	1,770	2,787
1944	1,463	11,403	48	461	330	1,175	8,455	11,858	240	2,486	3,955
1943	1,661	12,486	20	220	180	1,410	10,103	14,921	231	2,163	3,420
1942	724	5,393	11	102	81	652	4,679	6,843	61	612	982
1941	95	749	6	58	57	61	423	598	28	268	434
1940	53	445	6	69	61	31	227	335	16	149	238
1939	28	241	3	30	20	14	92	128	11	119	193
1938	24	181	–	–	–	6	39	56	18	142	228
1937	15	122	–	–	–	–	–	–	15	122	192
1936	8	63	–	–	–	–	–	–	8	63	105
1935	2	19	–	–	–	–	–	–	2	19	30
1934	2	10	–	–	–	2	10	15	–	–	–
1933	4	50	4	50	32	–	–	–	–	–	–
1932	15	145	13	129	83	2	16	22	–	–	–
1931	14	151	9	109	85	–	–	–	5	42	70
1930	18	164	5	50	39	2	16	24	11	97	161
1929	8	65	2	24	20	5	33	49	1	9	15
1928	7	72	3	44	37	–	–	–	4	28	44
1927	19	155	7	51	27	9	73	104	3	30	50
1926	8	54	5	29	16	2	16	26	1	9	15
1925	12	84	3	19	11	9	65	92	–	–	–
1924	12	84	7	44	20	4	34	48	1	7	11
1923	18	117	7	34	26	9	68	110	2	16	23
1922	19	168	3	41	34	10	78	156	6	48	71
1921	183	1,359	22	256	243	57	317	485	104	786	1,158
1920	467	2,396	12	100	111	375	1,758	2,696	80	538	778
1919	723	3,370	2	10	11	679	3,086	4,680	42	273	395
1918	414	1,770	5	30	24	375	1,508	2,283	34	232	339
1917	125	642	1	10	10	92	414	627	32	218	314
1916	74	370	1	6	7	49	201	300	24	163	247
1915	24	128	3	20	13	17	88	131	4	20	30
1914	26	135	1	3	1	17	88	130	8	45	67

– Represents zero.

Series **Q 449–458.** Shipbuilding in Private Shipyards—Summary: 1949 to 1970

[**Tons in thousands; gross tons for commercial vessels, light displacement tons for naval vessels.** Covers steel self-propelled vessels of 1,000 tons or over]

Year	Commercial vessels					Naval vessels				
	Under construction		Contracted for	Launched	Delivered	Under construction		Contracted for	Launched	Delivered
	Jan. 1	Dec. 31				Jan. 1	Dec. 31			
	449	450	451	452	453	454	455	456	457	458
1970: Number	49	49	13	11	13	108	82	6	23	32
Tons	1,388	¹ 1,609	580	322	370	621	588	132	117	166
1969: Number	63	49	8	13	22	133	108	6	28	31
Tons	1,495	1,388	309	271	416	701	621	80	142	159
1968: Number	64	63	23	27	24	134	133	15	26	16
Tons	1,211	1,495	613	454	329	686	701	153	138	138
1967: Number	48	64	29	15	13	147	134	8	15	21
Tons	596	¹ 1,211	740	182	162	745	686	50	137	109
1966: Number	45	48	16	11	13	106	147	54	25	13
Tons	513	596	244	134	161	573	745	246	129	74

See footnotes at end of table.

Series Q 449–458. Shipbuilding in Private Shipyards—Summary: 1949 to 1970—Con.

[Tons in thousands; gross tons for commercial vessels, light displacement tons for naval vessels]

Year	Commercial vessels					Naval vessels				
	Under construction		Contracted for	Launched	Delivered	Under construction		Contracted for	Launched	Delivered
	Jan. 1	Dec. 31				Jan. 1	Dec. 31			
	449	450	451	452	453	454	455	456	457	458
1965: Number	47	45	16	17	18	101	106	23	15	18
Tons	550	513	166	221	203	537	573	158	102	122
1964: Number	45	47	18	20	16	83	101	39	22	21
Tons	517	550	244	239	223	450	537	195	133	108
1963: Number	54	45	25	18	34	71	83	29	23	17
Tons	648	517	291	261	422	² 383	450	148	125	81
1962: Number	66	54	15	37	27	67	71	19	18	15
Tons	859	648	174	429	385	362	385	99	79	76
1961: Number	57	66	34	20	25	59	67	24	13	16
Tons	789	² 859	² 438	320	369	² 403	362	132	69	173
1960: Number	60	58	23	31	25	52	59	19	16	12
Tons	979	844	270	471	404	334	410	115	170	39
1959: Number	75	60	19	28	32	55	52	13	15	16
Tons	1,514	954	196	587	717	335	334	63	66	64
1958: Number	93	75	22	32	31	46	55	17	15	8
Tons	2,156	1,543	176	719	573	281	335	78	56	24
1957: Number	84	93	35	26	23	55	46	14	15	23
Tons	1,855	2,172	751	389	320	286	273	100	39	114
1956: Number	25	84	68	12	9	42	55	22	17	9
Tons	312	1,902	1,715	156	126	247	284	87	110	49
1955: Number	15	25	18	3	8	44	43	13	13	14
Tons	225	315	196	48	105	307	253	93	73	146
1954: Number	48	15	7	31	38	31	44	26	14	13
Tons	672	210	122	473	564	212	303	138	132	48
1953: Number	92	48	4	41	45	45	31	2	16	16
Tons	1,298	680	19	516	570	254	219	16	41	51
1952: Number	96	92	27	37	31	31	45	18	8	6
Tons	1,222	1,303	478	428	397	158	254	107	33	14
1951: Number	29	96	77	10	10	11	32	22	7	1
Tons	411	1,251	987	146	148	45	214	170	30	765
1950: Number	39	29	16	26	26	11	11	–	–	–
Tons	636	401	181	422	415	42	42	–	–	–
1949: Number	71	40	5	39	34	21	11	–	–	7
Tons	1,130	661	72	631	539	194	42	–	–	58

– Represents zero.
¹ Adjusted to account for major changes made during construction.
² Tonnages revised.

Series Q 459–466. Gross Tonnage of Merchant Vessels Built and Documented, by Region: 1817 to 1936

[Documented vessels of 5 tons or more.   As of December 31, 1817–1834; September 30, 1835–1842; June 30 thereafter]

Year	Seaboard			Northern lakes and western rivers	Year	Seaboard			Northern lakes and western rivers
	Total	New England coast	Mid-Atlantic and Gulf coasts	Pacific coast		Total	New England coast	Mid-Atlantic and Gulf coasts	Pacific coast	
	459	460	461	462	463		459	460	461	462	463
1936	175,398	711	166,671	8,016	48,686	1910	167,829	23,442	127,517	16,870	174,239
						1909	131,748	27,237	81,752	22,759	106,342
1935	49,054	1,910	38,452	8,692	13,865	1908	266,937	70,903	138,984	57,050	347,279
1934	49,946	862	37,390	11,694	16,703	1907	219,753	44,428	140,134	35,191	251,579
1933	181,593	25,851	151,823	3,919	9,210	1906	146,883	32,311	94,311	20,261	271,862
1932	195,529	52,163	133,625	9,741	17,363						
1931	355,771	26,639	287,884	41,248	31,135	1905	230,716	119,377	91,224	20,115	99,600
						1904	208,288	51,417	135,263	21,608	170,254
1930	193,116	18,601	143,656	30,859	61,180	1903	288,196	66,973	177,887	43,336	147,956
1929	104,769	12,766	71,750	20,253	24,207	1902	290,122	75,852	161,211	53,059	178,709
1928	181,681	11,434	146,532	23,715	75,499	1901	291,516	82,971	153,977	54,568	191,973
1927	176,207	6,574	124,068	45,565	68,937						
1926	159,658	4,995	131,994	22,669	65,015	1900	249,006	72,179	135,473	41,354	144,784
						1899	196,120	68,761	85,825	41,534	103,918
1925	123,933	5,615	76,784	41,534	75,913	1898	112,879	23,944	39,146	49,789	67,579
1924	145,837	3,174	106,414	36,249	78,131	1897	103,504	21,942	74,067	7,495	128,729
1923	262,769	13,057	199,026	50,686	73,022	1896	102,544	39,582	52,143	10,819	124,553
1922	637,708	56,973	448,197	132,538	23,524						
1921	2,147,555	150,745	1,383,185	613,625	117,560	1895	67,127	26,783	33,200	7,144	44,475
						1894	80,099	28,665	46,042	5,392	51,096
1920	3,475,872	208,023	1,931,514	1,336,335	404,767	1893	102,830	37,091	52,018	13,721	108,809
1919	2,815,733	177,758	1,274,472	1,363,503	510,888	1892	138,863	60,624	57,469	20,770	60,770
1918	1,080,437	88,302	473,698	518,437	220,431	1891	237,462	105,491	112,901	19,070	131,840
1917	518,958	52,526	298,958	167,474	145,521						
1916	275,749	37,568	188,550	49,631	49,664	1890	169,091	78,577	78,179	12,335	125,032
						1889	111,852	39,983	53,930	17,939	119,282
1915	203,156	18,551	152,906	31,699	21,966	1888	105,125	33,813	49,356	21,956	112,962
1914	251,700	14,985	200,220	36,495	64,550	1887	83,061	24,035	49,886	9,140	67,389
1913	247,318	27,131	175,523	44,664	98,837	1886	64,458	30,624	27,920	5,914	30,995
1912	136,485	23,052	81,329	32,104	96,184						
1911	190,612	23,653	139,725	27,234	100,550						

See footnotes at end of table.

Series Q 459–466.   Gross Tonnage of Merchant Vessels Built and Documented, by Region: 1817 to 1936—Con.

Year	Seaboard Total	New England coast	Mid-Atlantic and Gulf coasts	Pacific coast	Northern lakes and western rivers	Year	Seaboard Total	New England coast	Mid-Atlantic and Gulf coasts	Northern lakes and western rivers
	459	460	461	462	463		459	460	461	463
1885	121,010	48,128	61,844	11,038	38,046	1842	109,100	64,237	44,863	19,983
1884	178,419	84,046	83,753	10,620	47,095	1841	104,268	63,771	40,497	14,625
1883	210,349	110,226	83,385	16,738	55,081	1840	110,683	65,189	45,494	7,626
1882	188,084	93,965	78,342	15,777	94,186					
1881	125,766	54,488	59,861	11,417	154,693					

ALTERNATIVE SERIES

Year	The Coast [3]	Western lakes and rivers	New England States [3]
	464	465	466

Year	Seaboard Total 459	New England coast 460	Mid-Atlantic and Gulf coasts 461	Pacific coast 462	Northern lakes and western rivers 463	Year	The Coast [3] 464	Western lakes and rivers 465	New England States [3] 466
1880	101,720	46,374	46,403	8,943	55,690				
1879	115,683	55,874	48,602	11,207	77,348				
1878	155,138	90,386	53,419	11,333	80,366				
1877	132,996	90,992	29,286	12,718	43,596				
1876	163,826	95,288	51,716	16,822	39,760				
1875	244,474	151,497	79,549	13,428	53,165	1850	247,847	24,372	142,367
1874	277,093	136,251	129,953	10,859	155,632	1849	217,264	39,313	120,234
1873	218,139	76,406	136,258	5,475	141,107	1848	262,581	55,495	146,111
1872	128,097	46,269	79,552	2,276	80,955	1847	185,493	58,240	104,682
1871	156,249	64,366	86,559	5,324	116,978	1846	149,332	38,872	82,347
						1845	116,156	29,862	63,835
1870	182,836	110,584	59,532	12,720	94,117	1844	71,732	31,805	36,268
1869	191,194	103,604	72,058	15,532	84,036	1843	90,017	26,293	46,251
1868	173,722	98,915	67,956	6,851	111,582	1842	108,302	20,782	56,234
1867 [1]	229,583	135,189	90,070	4,324	73,945	1841	103,576	15,318	63,770
1866	232,788	121,335	105,329	6,124	103,358				
1865 [1]	280,899	135,253	141,830	3,816	102,910	1840	109,706	8,603	65,189
1864	328,710	112,615	211,242	4,853	87,030	1839	107,232	13,757	59,204
1863 [1]	215,410	79,578	133,161	2,671	95,474	1838	100,074	13,061	53,054
1862	112,486	45,597	64,365	2,524	62,589	1837	98,997	23,990	51,981
1861	181,586	104,678	72,192	4,716	51,608	1836	98,130	15,497	58,330
1860	169,836	134,289	33,524	2,023	44,962	1835	101,906	14,072	60,054
1859 [1]	134,499	79,316	53,127	2,056	23,103	1834	105,683	12,647	61,779
1858 [1]	177,799	103,864	71,811	2,124	64,487	1833	153,455	8,171	95,143
1857	285,681	183,686	100,810	1,185	93,123	1832	130,064	14,475	100,585
1856	369,679	252,974	116,343	362	99,714	1831	80,541	5,222	49,793
1855	505,450	326,431	176,901	2,118	78,000				
1854	454,933	289,599	164,311	1,023	80,683	1830	52,686	5,398	24,169
1853	357,233	222,791	134,291	151	68,339	1829	71,055	6,044	38,117
1852	301,274	179,804	121,470	----------	50,218	1828	95,349	3,027	54,282
1851	265,378	133,351	131,957	70	32,825	1827	99,343	5,000	57,156
1850	248,865	142,369	106,374	122	23,353	1826	121,908	4,530	72,668
1849	209,189	120,237	88,952	----------	47,388	1825	112,616	2,381	65,616
1848	264,268	146,113	118,155	----------	53,807	1824	89,166	1,773	52,445
1847	185,618	104,745	80,873	----------	58,114	1823	73,942	1,066	42,725
1846	149,571	82,347	67,224	----------	38,632	1822	75,242	105	44,206
						1821	55,607	249	36,651
1845	116,443	63,837	52,606	----------	29,575				
1844	71,832	36,268	35,564	----------	31,705	1820	47,696	88	29,353
1843 [2]	53,220	26,512	26,708	----------	10,397	1819	79,551	267	50,614
						1818	82,232	189	48,823
						1817	85,144	1,250	46,605

[1] Figures for these years do not add to series Q 434.
[2] 9-month period.

[3] Figures for New England States included in series Q 464 "The Coast."

Series Q 467–472.   Vessels Repaired or Converted in Private Shipbuilding and Ship Repair Yards: 1943 to 1970

Year	All vessels Number	All vessels Yards reporting [1]	Vessels under 1,000 gross tons Number	Vessels under 1,000 gross tons Yards reporting	Vessels over 1,000 gross tons Number	Vessels over 1,000 gross tons Yards reporting	Year	All vessels Number	All vessels Yards reporting [1]	Vessels under 1,000 gross tons Number	Vessels under 1,000 gross tons Yards reporting	Vessels over 1,000 gross tons Number	Vessels over 1,000 gross tons Yards reporting
	467	468	469	470	471	472		467	468	469	470	471	472
1970	39,200	122	26,800	110	12,400	75	1955	35,413	144	21,122	130	14,291	89
1969	36,000	126	22,120	116	13,880	78	1954	39,870	154	24,458	136	15,412	99
1968	37,200	128	24,300	114	12,900	81	1953	44,663	163	27,006	142	17,657	106
1967	37,400	130	24,500	112	12,900	85	1952	42,774	131	20,878	113	21,896	82
1966	33,100	135	19,600	110	13,500	75	1951	38,513	138	20,307	123	18,106	59
1965	35,600	136	22,900	117	12,700	93	1950	33,287	118	17,993	111	15,294	80
1964	37,500	146	26,777	132	10,723	93	1949	27,441	114	15,135	103	12,306	69
1963	39,990	139	27,804	129	12,186	102	1948	30,937	105	14,651	97	16,286	70
1962	42,686	151	29,912	137	12,774	95	1947	30,888	102	12,866	84	18,022	67
1961	36,816	122	26,027	106	10,789	73	1946	38,091	126	19,462	107	18,629	87
1960	37,774	159	24,991	132	12,783	93	1945	23,558	----------	----------	----------	23,558	----------
1959	37,501	149	24,837	130	12,664	87	1944	22,014	----------	----------	----------	22,014	----------
1958	42,809	154	28,331	134	14,478	88	1943	22,957	----------	----------	----------	22,957	----------
1957	40,827	152	26,106	139	14,721	82							
1956	45,555	165	29,401	144	16,154	93							

[1] Not additive.

Series Q 473–480. Merchant Vessels Launched and Owned—World and United States: 1895 to 1970

[Vessels of 100 gross tons and over. Excludes sailing ships, nonpropelled craft, and all ships built of wood. Figures for 1895 to 1935 represent annual average 5-year span beginning with the year shown; for example, the figure shown for 1895 is the annual average for 1895 to 1899, that for 1900, the annual average for 1900 to 1904, etc]

	World				United States			
	Launched		Owned		Launched		Owned	
Year	Number	Gross tons (1,000)	Number	Gross tons (1,000)	Number	Gross tons (1,000)	Number	Gross tons (1,000)
	473	474	475	476	477	478	479	480
1970	2,700	21,690	50,472	227,138	150	338	2,822	18,423
1969	2,819	19,315	48,246	211,294	174	400	2,972	19,507
1968	2,798	16,908	45,343	193,770	199	441	3,049	19,623
1967	2,778	15,780	42,234	181,709	231	242	3,115	20,286
1966	2,561	14,307	40,822	170,730	191	167	3,140	20,750
1965	2,280	12,216	39,628	159,979	130	270	3,224	21,478
1964	2,147	10,264	38,602	152,584	80	276	3,344	22,380
1963	2,001	8,539	37,310	145,438	78	294	3,506	23,082
1962	1,901	8,375	36,364	139,549	90	449	3,542	23,220
1961	1,990	7,940	35,465	135,477	56	343	3,728	24,184
1960	2,020	8,356	34,056	129,339	60	485	3,845	24,781
1959	1,808	8,746	33,924	124,494	47	597	3,964	25,227
1958	1,936	9,270	32,857	117,578	64	732	4,054	25,526
1957	1,950	8,501	31,421	109,778	54	359	4,116	25,843
1956	1,815	6,670	30,620	104,720	50	169	4,157	26,074
1955	1,437	5,315	29,967	100,069	26	73	4,225	26,343
1954	1,223	5,251	29,766	96,899	46	477	4,404	27,252
1953	1,134	5,095	29,174	92,826	68	528	4,431	27,144
1952	1,065	4,394	28,751	89,636	64	468	4,458	27,139
1951	1,002	3,639	28,374	86,678	58	164	4,484	27,226
1950	990	3,489	27,922	83,996	51	437	4,531	27,404
1949	899	3,126	27,194	81,954	66	633	4,605	27,707
1948	840	2,303	26,479	79,714	49	126	4,807	29,060
1947	741	2,093	(NA)	(NA)	61	163	(NA)	(NA)
1946	655	2,108	(NA)	(NA)	95	501	(NA)	(NA)
1945	1,311	7,189	(NA)	(NA)	880	5,968	(NA)	(NA)
1944	1,690	11,157	(NA)	(NA)	1,237	9,332	(NA)	(NA)
1943	2,067	13,881	(NA)	(NA)	1,620	11,577	(NA)	(NA)
1942	1,285	7,812	(NA)	(NA)	861	5,671	(NA)	(NA)
1941	489	2,487	(NA)	(NA)	184	1,035	(NA)	(NA)
1940	495	1,754	(NA)	(NA)	167	579	(NA)	(NA)
1939	}1,040	2,595{	31,186	69,440	}117	244{	3,270	11,874
1935			30,979	64,886			3,585	12,773
1930	484	1,020	32,713	69,608	25	83	4,105	13,947
1925	873	2,469	32,905	65,638	74	159	4,790	15,314
1920	942	2,582	31,484	57,281	99	315	5,381	15,997
1915	1,637	4,616	30,643	49,246	605	2,217	3,180	5,846
1910	1,426	2,588	29,943	41,884	140	222	3,180	5,018
1905	1,474	2,218	29,574	35,949	206	352	3,457	3,996
1900	1,611	2,354	27,840	28,957	242	347	3,135	2,750
1895	1,205	1,844	30,288	25,086	155	200	3,200	2,165

NA Not available.

Series Q 481–486a. Documented Merchant Vessels, by Geographic Region: 1816 to 1965

[In thousands of tons. Gross tonnage of documented vessels of 5 net tons or more. As of December 31, 1789–1834; September 30, 1835–1842; June 30, 1843–1940; January 1 thereafter]

| Year | Total seaboard | New England coast | Mid-Atlantic and Gulf coasts [1] | Pacific coast [2] | Northern lakes | Western rivers |
	481	482	483	484	485	486
1965	21,430	17,074		4,356	1,878	3,208
1964	21,482	17,077		4,405	1,858	2,820
1963	21,083	16,547		4,537	1,932	2,676
1962	21,010	555	15,922	4,533	2,056	2,389
1961	22,064	692	16,059	5,313	2,121	2,218
1960	24,708	814	18,112	5,782	1,728	2,145
1959	25,577	827	18,439	6,312	1,627	1,691
1958	25,520	898	17,955	6,667	1,638	1,429
1957	26,605	1,007	18,634	6,964	1,569	1,247
1956	26,952	1,091	18,732	7,129	1,558	1,100
1955	27,405	1,191	19,211	7,004	1,590	962
1954	28,299	1,239	19,908	7,152	1,616	849
1953	28,184	1,204	19,886	7,094	1,624	738
1952	28,136	1,335	19,604	7,196	1,556	725
1951	28,040	1,559	18,409	8,072	1,565	736
1950	28,866	1,505	18,915	8,446	1,628	721
1949	29,407	1,679	18,639	9,089	2,076	699
1948	30,484	1,719	18,397	10,368	2,079	604
1947	35,238	1,834	20,340	13,064	2,091	504
1946	35,829	1,644	19,927	14,258	2,183	489
1945	30,306	1,472	17,186	11,648	2,061	446
1944	23,569	972	13,596	9,001	1,793	434
1943	14,714	440	10,051	4,224	1,620	428
1942	11,856	544	9,372	1,939	1,624	379
1941	11,776	494	9,318	1,964	1,641	305
1940	12,064	453	9,563	2,047	1,669	285
1939	12,668	418	9,779	2,471	1,712	252
1938	12,666	454	9,730	2,483	1,739	246
1937	12,733	515	9,630	2,588	1,713	230
1936	12,512	517	9,254	2,741	1,767	218
1935	12,700	589	9,248	2,863	1,773	181
1934	12,883	620	9,312	2,951	1,802	177
1933	13,077	641	9,465	2,970	1,814	170
1932	13,793	708	9,970	3,115	1,857	189
1931	12,958	712	9,157	3,089	2,767	184
1930	13,131	798	9,106	3,227	2,758	178
1929	13,527	815	9,447	3,264	2,771	179
1928	13,728	878	9,494	3,355	2,773	182
1927	13,914	918	9,747	3,249	2,805	168
1926	14,306	936	10,079	3,290	2,844	161
1925	14,390	953	10,155	3,282	2,853	162
1924	14,785	1,014	10,344	3,428	2,791	164
1923	15,388	1,113	10,780	3,496	2,758	138
1922	15,604	984	11,147	3,474	2,724	135
1921	15,320	920	10,932	3,468	2,840	122
1920	13,065	872	8,867	3,326	3,139	120
1919	9,762	616	6,329	2,816	3,024	122
1918	7,004	600	4,757	1,647	2,798	123
1917	5,959	604	4,146	1,210	2,779	133
1916	5,574	616	3,827	1,131	2,761	135
1915	5,433	658	3,652	1,123	2,818	139
1914	4,904	767	3,036	1,101	2,883	141
1913	4,800	766	2,986	1,049	2,940	146
1912	4,618	765	2,868	985	2,950	146
1911	4,544	775	2,795	974	2,944	168
1910	4,459	800	2,723	937	2,895	154
1909	4,444	828	2,681	934	2,782	163
1908	4,469	822	2,685	962	2,729	167
1907	4,328	784	2,656	887	2,440	172
1906	4,273	781	2,651	840	2,234	168
1905	4,220	813	2,586	822	2,062	174
1904	4,059	795	2,458	807	2,019	213
1903	3,970	772	2,386	812	1,903	215
1902	3,759	758	2,227	774	1,817	222
1901	3,568	750	2,104	714	1,706	249
1900	3,341	771	1,957	613	1,566	258
1899	3,155	742	1,873	540	1,446	263
1898	3,051	775	1,779	497	1,438	262
1897	3,087	818	1,830	439	1,410	272
1896	3,105	857	1,810	438	1,324	275

See footnotes at end of table.

Series **Q 481–486a.** Documented Merchant Vessels, by Geographic Region: 1816 to 1965—Con.

[In thousands of tons]

Year	Total seaboard	New England coast	Mid-Atlantic and Gulf coasts [1]	Pacific coast [2]	Northern lakes	Western rivers Official	Western rivers Haites	Year	Total seaboard	New England coast	Mid-Atlantic and Gulf coasts [1]	Pacific coast [2]	Northern lakes	Western rivers Official	Western rivers Haites
	481	482	483	484	485	486	486a		481	482	483	484	485	486	486a
1895	3,113	846	1,834	434	1,241	281	--------	1855	4,877	2,004	2,779	93	206	129	173
1894	3,169	879	1,834	456	1,227	287	--------	1854	4,531	1,806	2,623	102	161	111	169
1893	3,265	907	1,901	457	1,261	299	--------	1853	3,872	1,679	2,088	105	254	282	169
1892	3,271	932	1,874	465	1,184	311	--------	1852	3,566	1,557	1,906	103	217	355	153
1891	3,222	944	1,836	441	1,155	308	--------	1851	3,259	1,414	1,785	59	196	318	143
1890	3,067	947	1,691	428	1,063	294	--------	1850	3,051	1,368	1,665	19	181	303	135
1889	3,036	957	1,643	436	972	299	--------	1849	2,874	1,289	1,584	1	174	286	130
1888	3,013	1,009	1,603	400	874	305	--------	1848	2,729	1,258	1,470	--------	148	277	133
1887	2,995	998	1,640	356	784	327	--------	1847	2,464	1,125	1,339	--------	134	241	122
1886	3,034	1,055	1,631	348	763	335	--------	1846	2,257	1,071	1,186	--------	91	215	106
1885	3,170	1,090	1,720	361	750	346	--------	1845	2,143	1,010	1,133	--------	86	188	96
1884	3,182	1,142	1,705	335	733	356	--------	1844	2,033	963	1,071	--------	72	174	90
1883	3,151	1,121	1,702	328	724	361	--------	1843	1,940	923	1,017	--------	66	152	80
1882	3,062	1,095	1,664	302	711	393	--------	1842	1,888	915	973	--------	61	143	76
1881	3,000	1,045	1,669	286	663	394	--------	1841	1,936	984	951	--------	58	137	85
1880	2,989	1,073	1,644	272	605	474	--------	1840	2,014	1,012	1,002	--------	49	118	83
1879	3,070	1,095	1,705	270	597	502	--------	1839	(3)	(3)	(3)	--------	(3)	(3)	78
1878	3,150	1,140	1,757	253	605	458	--------	1838	1,837	901	936	--------	50	109	65
1877	3,196	1,146	1,799	252	610	436	--------	1837	1,771	889	882	--------	35	91	64
1876	3,266	1,148	1,864	253	613	401	--------	1836	1,773	877	896	--------	30	79	57
1875	3,597	1,143	2,225	229	838	419	--------	1835	1,735	896	840	--------	17	73	50
1874	3,521	1,077	2,232	212	842	438	--------	1834	(3)	(3)	(3)	--------	(3)	(3)	41
1873	3,489	1,055	2,243	191	788	418	--------	1833	1,530	811	718	--------	17	60	37
1872	3,265	1,053	2,031	180	724	448	--------	1832	1,367	700	667	--------	16	56	35
1871	3,164	1,050	1,947	167	712	407	--------	1831	1,215	576	639	--------	9	44	29
1870	3,164	1,057	1,917	190	685	398	--------	1830	1,146	581	565	--------	13	33	25
1869	3,090	1,066	1,839	185	661	393	--------	1829	(3)	(3)	(3)	--------	(3)	(3)	22
1868	3,175	1,046	1,962	167	696	481	212	1828	1,692	787	905	--------	10	39	19
1867	3,340	1,008	2,171	161	613	352	232	1827	1,590	714	876	--------	9	22	20
1866	3,515	1,126	2,209	180	572	224	238	1826	1,501	706	795	--------	9	24	17
1865	4,180	1,269	2,756	154	671	246	229	1825	1,397	641	756	--------	7	19	13
1864	4,100	1,341	2,654	105	698	189	193	1824	1,362	613	748	--------	9	18	10
1863	4,382	1,646	2,618	118	631	142	160	1823	1,312	600	711	--------	7	18	12
1862	4,425	1,805	2,516	104	561	127	157	1822	1,298	601	697	--------	7	20	13
1861	4,888	1,839	2,959	90	479	173	165	1821	1,265	580	684	--------	7	27	14
1860	3,723	1,828	2,810	85	463	168	195	1820	1,245	565	681	--------	7	27	14
1859	4,675	1,833	2,754	88	329	142	193	1819	1,228	551	678	--------	7	25	13
1858	4,648	1,739	2,824	85	261	141	196	1818	1,194	528	667	--------	6	25	6
1857	4,562	1,777	2,701	85	238	140	200	1817	1,320	562	758	--------	7	13	3
1856	4,525	1,863	2,579	84	222	124	188	1816	1,357	569	788	--------	5	10	[4]2

[1] Includes Puerto Rico and Virgin Islands.
[2] Includes Alaska, Hawaii, and Guam.
[3] No returns reported.   [4] First 5 years of the series are as follows (in thousands of tons): 1811, 0.4; 1812, 0.4; 1813, 0.4; 1814, 0.7; and 1815, 1.5.

Series **Q 487–502.** United States Flag Merchant Vessels, Steam and Motor: 1934 to 1970

[Dead-weight tonnage in thousands. As of June 30, except as indicated. Covers oceangoing vessels of 1,000 gross tons and over engaged in foreign and domestic trade, and inactive vessels. Excludes special types and vessels employed on Great Lakes]

Year and type of vessel	All vessels		Active vessels												Inactive vessels	
			Total		Foreign trade		Domestic trade						Special service			
							Total		Coastwise		Intercoastal and noncontiguous					
	Number	Tons	Number	Tons	Number	Tons	Number	Tons	Number	Tons	Number	Tons	Number	Tons	Number	Tons
	487	488	489	490	491	492	493	494	495	496	497	498	499	500	501	502
1970	1,780	23,280	819	14,073	386	5,775	245	5,368	142	3,599	103	1,769	188	2,930	961	9,208
Combination	177	1,147	13	117	10	94	2	13	-	-	2	13	1	10	164	1,031
Cargo	1,302	14,298	557	7,173	344	4,605	68	837	10	116	58	721	145	1,731	745	7,125
Tanker	301	7,835	249	6,783	32	1,076	175	4,518	132	3,483	43	1,035	42	1,189	52	1,052
1969	2,013	25,079	1,013	15,180	447	6,021	199	4,062	105	2,619	94	1,445	367	5,097	1,000	9,898
Combination	187	1,214	22	198	20	187	2	11	-	-	2	11	-	-	165	1,015
Cargo	1,521	16,462	780	9,412	398	5,100	69	823	8	111	61	713	313	3,489	741	7,050
Tanker	305	7,403	211	5,570	29	734	128	3,228	97	2,508	31	721	54	1,608	94	1,833
1968	2,101	25,699	1,104	16,416	481	6,332	242	4,934	134	3,105	108	1,829	381	5,150	997	9,284
Combination	205	1,343	26	227	22	200	1	4	-	-	1	4	3	23	179	1,116
Cargo	1,581	16,993	811	9,569	421	5,180	65	797	9	123	56	674	325	3,592	770	7,425
Tanker	315	7,363	267	6,620	38	952	176	4,133	125	2,982	51	1,151	53	1,535	48	743
1967	2,209	26,560	1,107	16,273	460	6,037	233	4,654	142	3,333	91	1,323	414	5,582	1,102	10,286
Combination	222	1,454	27	231	24	214	1	4	-	-	1	4	2	13	195	1,223
Cargo	1,670	17,843	818	9,547	400	4,963	66	810	9	120	57	691	352	3,774	852	8,296
Tanker	317	7,263	262	6,495	36	860	166	3,840	133	3,213	33	628	60	1,795	55	767

- Represents zero.

Series Q 487–502. United States Flag Merchant Vessels, Steam and Motor: 1934 to 1970—Con.

[Dead-weight tonnage in thousands]

Year and type of vessel	All vessels		Active vessels												Inactive vessels	
			Total		Foreign trade		Domestic trade						Special service			
							Total		Coastwise		Intercoastal and noncontiguous					
	Number	Tons	Number	Tons	Number	Tons	Number	Tons	Number	Tons	Number	Tons	Number	Tons	Number	Tons
	487	488	489	490	491	492	493	494	495	496	497	498	499	500	501	502
1966	2,292	27,393	1,043	15,388	494	6,576	248	4,825	139	3,202	109	1,623	301	3,987	1,249	12,004
Combination	225	1,476	29	250	26	233	1	4	-	-	1	4	2	13	196	1,225
Cargo	1,739	18,565	760	8,913	420	5,093	83	1,050	11	160	72	890	257	2,770	979	9,652
Tanker	328	7,352	254	6,225	48	1,250	164	3,771	128	3,042	36	729	42	1,204	74	1,127
1965	2,425	28,755	779	11,821	512	6,877	217	3,953	118	2,667	99	1,286	50	993	1,646	16,934
Combination	236	1,558	19	158	18	153	1	4	-	-	1	4	-	-	217	1,402
Cargo	1,840	19,561	561	6,679	440	5,249	92	1,056	13	142	79	914	29	375	1,279	12,883
Tanker	349	7,636	199	4,985	54	1,475	124	2,892	105	2,525	19	368	21	618	150	2,651
1964	2,598	30,084	940	13,868	584	7,271	295	5,504	184	3,964	111	1,540	61	1,093	1,658	16,219
Combination	271	1,787	35	307	32	290	1	4	-	-	1	4	2	13	236	1,480
Cargo	1,959	20,612	642	7,493	509	5,971	100	1,137	19	220	81	918	33	385	1,317	13,121
Tanker	368	7,685	263	6,067	43	1,010	194	4,362	165	3,744	29	618	26	695	105	1,618
1963	2,691	30,753	946	13,812	587	7,344	299	5,479	207	4,349	92	1,130	60	989	1,745	16,940
Combination	290	1,924	33	288	30	271	1	4	-	-	1	4	2	13	257	1,636
Cargo	2,013	21,047	649	7,498	512	5,979	103	1,157	26	290	77	867	34	362	1,364	13,549
Tanker	388	7,784	264	6,027	45	1,095	195	4,318	181	4,059	14	259	24	614	124	1,756
1962	2,716	30,954	940	13,473	543	6,616	340	5,951	231	4,640	109	1,311	57	906	1,776	17,481
Combination	289	1,925	34	294	29	260	2	14	-	-	2	14	3	20	255	1,630
Cargo	2,018	21,024	628	7,083	482	5,554	115	1,233	32	362	83	872	31	296	1,390	13,941
Tanker	409	8,006	278	6,096	32	803	223	4,703	199	4,278	24	425	23	590	131	1,911
1961	2,810	31,525	644	8,837	415	5,066	182	3,107	115	2,325	67	783	47	664	2,166	22,690
Combination	300	2,012	20	172	17	152	-	-	-	-	-	-	3	20	280	1,840
Cargo	2,086	21,575	456	5,025	365	4,135	64	642	17	173	47	469	27	248	1,630	16,549
Tanker	424	7,941	168	3,641	33	781	118	2,465	98	2,152	20	313	17	395	256	4,301
1960	2,934	32,601	951	12,922	558	6,541	372	5,926	237	4,284	135	1,642	21	455	1,983	19,679
Combination	305	2,038	36	320	34	305	2	14	-	-	2	14	-	-	269	1,717
Cargo	2,204	22,813	633	6,907	479	5,265	148	1,589	35	375	113	1,215	6	53	1,571	15,906
Tanker	425	7,750	282	5,695	45	972	222	4,323	202	3,910	20	413	15	402	143	2,055
1959	3,047	33,565	963	12,636	533	5,935	375	5,912	229	4,054	146	1,858	55	789	2,084	20,930
Combination	288	1,950	39	343	36	323	2	14	-	-	2	14	1	6	249	1,607
Cargo	2,347	24,333	646	6,986	473	5,189	142	1,512	35	336	107	1,176	31	285	1,701	17,348
Tanker	412	7,283	278	5,306	24	422	231	4,386	194	3,718	37	668	23	498	134	1,977
1958	3,047	33,316	970	12,358	551	6,208	356	5,369	229	3,811	127	1,558	63	781	2,077	20,958
Combination	238	1,638	44	413	36	344	3	30	-	-	3	30	5	39	194	1,225
Cargo	2,425	25,125	657	7,051	487	5,348	133	1,366	37	345	96	1,021	37	337	1,768	18,076
Tanker	384	6,553	269	4,895	28	516	220	3,973	192	3,466	28	507	21	406	115	1,658
1957	3,032	32,900	1,199	14,874	721	8,406	399	5,595	262	4,082	137	1,513	79	873	1,833	18,027
Combination	230	1,594	50	467	38	363	3	30	-	-	3	30	9	74	180	1,127
Cargo	2,450	25,412	822	8,779	611	6,649	161	1,675	41	398	120	1,277	50	455	1,628	16,634
Tanker	352	5,894	327	5,628	72	1,393	235	3,891	221	3,684	14	207	20	344	25	266
1956	3,150	34,052	1,127	13,988	644	7,538	402	5,639	281	4,269	121	1,370	81	811	2,023	20,065
Combination	247	1,683	48	443	38	359	1	10	-	-	1	10	9	74	199	1,240
Cargo	2,511	26,007	738	7,864	524	5,688	149	1,569	42	411	107	1,158	65	607	1,773	18,140
Tanker	392	6,363	341	5,680	82	1,489	252	4,061	239	3,858	13	202	7	130	51	685
1955	3,235	35,017	1,163	14,232	601	6,992	425	5,880	271	3,999	154	1,881	137	1,360	2,072	20,786
Combination	249	1,687	50	453	39	361	1	10	-	-	1	10	10	82	199	1,234
Cargo	2,560	26,539	772	8,182	492	5,383	160	1,650	43	385	117	1,265	120	1,149	1,788	18,358
Tanker	426	6,790	341	5,597	70	1,248	264	4,220	228	3,614	36	606	7	129	85	1,193
1954	3,333	35,860	1,123	13,645	623	7,299	398	5,324	265	3,854	133	1,470	102	1,022	2,210	22,216
Combination	252	1,695	54	466	39	361	5	23	-	-	5	23	10	82	198	1,230
Cargo	2,636	26,435	730	6,876	489	5,226	154	1,581	44	396	110	1,185	87	69	1,906	19,559
Tanker	445	7,730	339	6,303	95	1,713	239	3,719	221	3,458	18	261	5	871	106	1,427
1953	3,349	36,255	1,415	16,738	629	7,390	437	5,725	303	4,275	134	1,450	349	3,623	1,934	19,517
Combination	257	2,039	55	479	40	378	5	23	-	-	5	23	10	78	202	1,560
Cargo	2,630	27,228	964	10,060	461	4,890	167	1,638	59	517	108	1,121	336	3,532	1,666	17,168
Tanker	462	6,988	396	6,199	128	2,122	265	4,064	244	3,758	21	306	3	13	66	790
1952	3,350	36,081	1,447	16,976	782	9,052	395	5,190	291	4,033	104	1,158	270	2,734	1,903	19,106
Combination	260	2,044	62	552	44	393	1	4	-	-	1	4	17	155	198	1,491
Cargo	2,629	27,210	967	10,047	582	6,177	135	1,302	58	517	77	786	250	2,567	1,662	17,164
Tanker	461	6,827	418	6,378	156	2,481	259	3,884	233	3,516	26	368	3	13	43	451
1951	3,386	36,336	1,654	19,284	988	11,425	426	5,333	287	3,924	139	1,408	240	2,523	1,732	17,053
Combination	266	2,067	63	537	46	404	5	24	-	-	5	24	12	109	203	1,530
Cargo	2,650	27,376	1,144	12,015	743	7,892	176	1,721	55	484	121	1,236	225	2,401	1,506	15,361
Tanker	470	6,893	447	6,731	199	3,129	245	3,587	232	3,440	13	146	3	13	23	162
1950	3,408	36,526	1,145	13,828	711	8,353	434	5,474	279	3,716	155	1,757	--------	--------	2,263	22,698
Combination	83	639	51	417	45	389	6	28	-	-	6	28	--------	--------	32	222
Cargo	2,846	28,927	682	7,075	505	5,367	177	1,708	66	559	111	1,149	--------	--------	2,164	21,851
Tanker	479	6,959	412	6,335	161	2,597	251	3,737	213	3,157	38	580	--------	--------	67	624

- Represents zero.

Series Q 487–502. United States Flag Merchant Vessels, Steam and Motor: 1934 to 1970—Con.

[Dead-weight tonnage in thousands]

Year and type of vessel	All vessels		Active vessels												Inactive vessels	
			Total		Foreign trade		Domestic trade						Special service			
							Total		Coastwise		Intercoastal and noncontiguous					
	Number	Tons	Number	Tons	Number	Tons	Number	Tons	Number	Tons	Number	Tons	Number	Tons	Number	Tons
	487	488	489	490	491	492	493	494	495	496	497	498	499	500	501	502
1949	3,379	36,228	1,386	16,044	1,004	11,416	382	4,628	262	3,437	120	1,191	--------	--------	1,993	20,184
Combination	79	609	47	388	43	375	4	13	–	–	4	13	--------	--------	32	221
Cargo	2,799	28,442	969	10,063	813	8,626	156	1,437	53	416	103	1,021	--------	--------	1,830	18,379
Tanker	501	7,177	370	5,593	148	2,415	222	3,178	209	3,021	13	157	--------	--------	131	1,584
1948	3,490	36,774	1,723	19,552	1,246	13,767	477	5,785	327	4,329	150	1,456	--------	--------	1,767	17,222
Combination	77	601	48	385	41	357	7	28	–	–	7	28	--------	--------	29	216
Cargo	2,887	28,674	1,221	12,424	1,023	10,592	198	1,832	68	569	130	1,263	--------	--------	1,666	16,250
Tanker	526	7,499	454	6,743	182	2,818	272	3,925	259	3,760	13	165	--------	--------	72	756
1947 [1]	3,696	38,882	2,114	23,651	1,603	17,238	511	6,413	381	5,104	130	1,309	--------	--------	1,582	15,231
Combination	95	742	38	284	32	259	6	25	–	–	6	25	--------	--------	57	458
Cargo	2,977	29,206	1,628	16,561	1,434	14,779	194	1,782	82	659	112	1,123	--------	--------	1,349	12,645
Tanker	624	8,934	448	6,806	137	2,200	311	4,606	299	4,445	12	161	--------	--------	176	2,128
1946 [2]	4,852	50,263	2,762	29,127	1,890	20,592	442	4,807	297	3,483	145	1,324	430	3,728	2,090	21,136
Combination	117	800	56	412	15	127	10	38	–	–	10	38	31	247	61	388
Cargo	3,829	36,675	2,220	21,408	1,607	16,200	226	1,910	101	730	125	1,180	387	3,298	1,609	15,267
Tanker	906	12,785	486	7,305	268	4,264	206	2,858	196	2,753	10	106	12	183	420	5,480
1941	1,168	10,096	1,137	9,919	471	4,052	663	5,836	488	4,261	175	1,575	3	31	31	177
Combination	94	541	88	526	43	348	44	165	34	118	10	47	1	13	6	15
Cargo	716	5,472	693	5,324	358	2,966	333	2,340	179	937	154	1,402	2	18	23	148
Tanker	358	4,083	356	4,070	70	739	286	3,331	275	3,205	11	125	–	–	2	13
1940	1,300	11,019	1,119	9,653	425	3,749	693	5,893	500	4,172	193	1,721	1	10	181	1,367
Combination	140	873	112	696	66	514	46	182	36	129	10	53	–	–	28	176
Cargo	790	6,020	642	4,892	291	2,443	350	2,438	188	988	162	1,450	1	10	148	1,129
Tanker	370	4,126	365	4,065	68	791	297	3,273	276	3,054	21	218	–	–	5	62
1939	1,398	11,699	1,092	9,308	319	2,804	772	6,499	543	4,359	229	2,141	1	5	306	2,391
Combination	163	1,079	131	856	78	621	53	235	37	139	16	96	–	–	32	224
Cargo	851	6,364	609	4,545	193	1,619	415	2,921	229	1,197	186	1,724	1	5	242	1,819
Tanker	384	4,256	352	3,908	48	565	304	3,343	277	3,022	27	320	–	–	32	348
1938	1,422	11,814	1,060	9,019	366	3,301	694	5,718	494	3,946	200	1,772	–	–	362	2,795
Combination	167	1,108	125	764	76	562	49	202	38	145	11	57	–	–	42	344
Cargo	882	6,557	592	4,436	213	1,808	379	2,629	205	1,073	174	1,556	–	–	290	2,121
Tanker	373	4,149	343	3,819	77	931	266	2,888	251	2,728	15	159	–	–	30	330
1937	1,517	12,335	1,231	10,251	426	3,643	805	6,608	563	4,467	242	2,141	–	–	286	2,085
Combination	185	1,204	159	1,051	99	753	60	298	40	147	20	151	–	–	26	153
Cargo	975	7,231	721	5,344	275	2,286	446	3,058	241	1,253	205	1,806	–	–	254	1,887
Tanker	357	3,900	351	3,856	52	604	299	3,252	282	3,067	17	184	–	–	6	44
1936	1,563	12,323	1,208	9,697	430	3,714	776	5,958	537	3,878	239	2,079	2	25	355	2,626
Combination	201	1,281	171	1,083	104	770	67	313	46	170	21	143	–	–	30	198
Cargo	1,007	7,405	694	5,072	250	2,087	442	2,961	243	1,227	199	1,734	2	25	313	2,333
Tanker	355	3,637	343	3,541	76	857	267	2,684	248	2,482	19	202	–	–	12	95
1935	1,637	12,809	1,145	9,194	434	3,748	709	5,425	488	3,479	221	1,946	2	21	492	3,615
Combination	217	1,347	176	1,099	108	802	68	296	47	149	21	147	–	–	41	248
Cargo	1,065	7,847	645	4,741	253	2,096	390	2,624	215	1,085	175	1,539	2	21	420	3,106
Tanker	355	3,615	324	3,354	73	850	251	2,504	226	2,245	25	260	–	–	31	261
1934	1,673	12,986	1,097	8,767	438	3,753	657	4,993	440	3,005	217	1,987	2	21	576	4,219
Combination	233	1,389	184	1,123	111	823	73	300	50	143	23	157	–	–	49	266
Cargo	1,079	7,946	596	4,382	258	2,168	336	2,194	200	1,025	136	1,169	2	21	483	3,564
Tanker	361	3,652	317	3,262	69	763	248	2,499	190	1,838	58	661	–	–	44	390

– Represents zero.
[1] Data as of December 31.
[2] Data as of September 30.

Series Q 503–505. Gross Tonnage of Documented Merchant Vessels, by Type of Service: 1934 to 1970

[In thousands of tons. Documented vessels of 5 tons or more. As of June 30, 1934–1940; January 1, thereafter. Includes Puerto Rico and Guam]

Year	Freight (dry cargo)	Tanker	All other	Year	Freight (dry cargo)	Tanker	All other	Year	Freight (dry cargo)	Tanker	All other
	503	504	505		503	504	505		503	504	505
1970	18,896	6,412	3,305	1955	22,298	5,279	2,381	1945	23,931	6,835	2,047
1969	19,183	6,139	3,134	1954	22,818	5,520	2,427	1944	18,878	4,802	2,115
1968	18,823	5,976	3,134	1953	22,605	5,478	2,463	1943	11,365	3,128	2,268
				1952	22,556	5,451	2,409	1942	8,226	3,261	2,373
1965	18,045	5,673	2,798	1951	22,598	5,354	2,389	1941	8,115	3,053	2,553
1964	17,731	5,645	2,784								
1963	17,393	5,599	2,699	1950	23,209	5,554	2,452	1940	8,267	3,028	2,723
1962	17,236	5,535	2,685	1949	23,766	6,001	2,414	1939	8,615	3,089	2,929
1961	18,320	5,404	2,679	1948	24,047	4,171	4,949	1938	8,702	2,989	2,960
				1947	27,407	8,196	2,230	1937	8,671	2,881	3,123
1960	20,637	5,261	2,683	1946	28,087	8,336	2,077	1936	8,702	2,686	3,109
1959	21,342	4,908	2,645								
1958	21,420	4,632	2,534					1935	8,748	2,668	3,238
1957	22,024	4,934	2,464					1934	8,887	2,674	3,301
1956	22,280	4,945	2,386								

Series Q 506–517.   Net Tonnage Capacity of Vessels Entered and Cleared: 1789 to 1970

[In thousands of net tons.   For years ending September 20, 1789–1842; June 30, 1843–1918; December 31 thereafter.   Excludes domestic trade.   Includes Alaska, Hawaii, Puerto Rico, and, beginning 1935, the Virgin Islands]

Year	Vessels entered						Vessels cleared					
	All ports			Seaports [1]			All ports			Seaports [1]		
	Total	U.S. vessels	Foreign vessels	Total	U.S. vessels	Foreign vessels	Total	U.S. vessels	Foreign vessels	Total	U.S. vessels	Foreign vessels
	506	507	508	509	510	511	512	513	514	515	516	517
1970	254,154	26,239	227,915	226,666	24,234	202,431	253,136	26,953	226,183	225,925	24,898	201,027
1969	238,085	26,662	211,423	213,008	25,264	187,741	237,986	27,235	210,758	212,746	25,738	187,013
1968	229,850	30,389	199,465	203,664	27,456	176,210	230,324	31,198	199,126	204,086	28,244	175,839
1967	220,681	30,830	189,848	195,871	26,990	168,878	220,231	30,827	189,404	195,845	27,089	168,756
1966	217,894	31,487	186,407	191,684	28,621	163,063	219,437	32,738	186,699	193,433	29,925	163,507
1965	209,000	34,041	174,960	183,724	30,919	152,806	208,736	34,016	174,721	183,540	31,048	152,492
1964	199,330	34,956	164,373	174,625	30,909	143,715	202,262	35,337	166,924	177,636	31,409	146,225
1963	186,700	33,300	153,400	165,124	29,677	135,447	187,539	34,106	153,433	166,103	30,440	135,663
1962	178,334	33,774	144,560	158,606	29,963	128,644	178,953	34,165	144,788	159,330	30,337	128,993
1961	166,548	31,144	135,404	148,955	28,266	120,688	168,878	31,941	136,936	151,295	29,062	122,233
1960	162,765	30,189	132,575	145,828	26,708	119,119	166,715	31,280	135,434	149,778	27,649	122,127
1959	154,213	26,417	127,796	137,845	21,897	115,947	155,505	26,623	128,883	139,262	22,042	117,221
1958	149,097	26,842	122,255	136,291	23,642	112,648	148,816	26,449	122,366	136,102	23,324	112,778
1957	162,925	35,898	127,027	146,144	31,189	114,956	162,578	35,118	127,460	145,954	30,569	115,385
1956	147,844	36,247	111,598	130,767	31,254	99,514	148,269	36,317	111,952	131,391	31,510	99,881
1955	128,405	34,321	94,084	113,807	30,407	83,400	129,368	34,407	94,961	114,806	30,615	84,192
1954	109,524	33,860	75,664	97,198	30,133	67,065	109,899	33,579	76,321	97,674	29,969	67,706
1953	112,559	39,319	73,240	97,344	34,969	62,375	112,935	39,188	73,747	97,627	34,775	62,852
1952	116,375	45,223	71,152	101,263	40,732	60,532	114,797	43,726	71,071	99,703	39,273	60,429
1951	108,081	44,571	63,515	93,674	40,482	53,192	110,236	46,763	63,472	96,257	43,024	53,233
1950	86,629	35,376	51,251	73,451	31,757	41,693	87,829	36,043	51,778	74,785	32,510	42,269
1949	85,700	41,251	44,451	74,701	37,626	37,076	84,286	39,681	44,604	73,063	36,136	36,927
1948	90,927	47,726	43,199	76,910	43,270	33,640	89,449	45,775	43,667	75,714	41,348	34,358
1947	93,796	53,627	40,170	80,889	49,044	31,844	97,160	54,088	43,072	84,508	49,558	34,949
1946	80,258	53,045	27,213	69,520	49,143	20,378	77,225	49,124	28,101	66,376	45,113	21,263
1945	94,021	61,375	32,646	81,182	56,499	24,682	94,559	61,460	33,099	81,452	56,332	25,120
1944	81,860	48,071	33,789	66,305	42,196	24,109	87,385	53,050	34,335	71,717	46,919	24,798
1943	61,084	29,292	31,792	44,739	24,508	20,231	66,716	33,682	33,034	50,232	28,826	21,406
1942	43,942	13,611	30,331	28,258	10,326	17,932	47,706	16,354	31,352	31,976	13,149	18,827
1941	59,061	20,940	38,121	42,616	16,767	25,849	62,596	21,869	40,726	46,142	17,701	28,441
1940	58,544	19,220	39,324	45,393	15,740	29,652	62,171	20,248	41,923	48,996	16,766	32,230
1939	68,992	17,769	51,223	57,973	14,553	43,421	70,306	18,156	52,150	59,218	14,903	44,316
1938	70,516	19,020	51,496	59,223	15,899	43,324	71,286	18,829	52,456	60,064	15,742	44,322
1937	71,560	19,527	52,033	59,980	16,747	43,233	72,880	19,938	52,942	61,177	17,134	44,043
1936	65,972	20,682	45,290	55,038	17,510	37,528	66,066	20,069	45,997	55,381	16,967	38,414
1935	64,612	22,372	42,240	54,289	18,893	35,395	64,887	22,126	42,761	54,722	18,651	36,071
1934	63,787	23,192	40,594	53,132	19,186	33,946	63,702	22,799	40,903	53,162	18,901	34,261
1933	60,936	22,488	38,448	51,564	19,051	32,513	61,287	22,434	38,853	52,083	19,093	32,990
1932	64,837	24,278	40,559	55,229	20,643	34,587	64,446	23,865	40,582	54,900	20,204	34,695
1931	72,782	26,907	45,875	60,427	21,499	38,929	73,501	26,854	46,647	61,204	21,417	39,787
1930	81,253	31,866	49,387	66,499	24,620	41,879	81,307	31,560	49,747	66,500	24,154	42,346
1929	82,602	32,241	50,361	66,853	25,208	41,645	82,343	31,927	50,416	67,030	25,045	41,985
1928	80,211	31,285	48,926	62,809	22,991	39,818	80,667	31,734	48,933	63,331	23,180	40,151
1927	74,310	29,289	45,021	58,921	22,001	36,920	75,440	29,793	45,647	59,759	22,078	37,681
1926	76,933	26,890	50,043	63,759	21,091	42,668	79,041	28,532	50,509	65,583	22,234	43,349
1925	69,378	27,947	41,431	55,636	21,148	34,487	70,229	27,808	42,421	57,160	21,394	35,766
1924	68,292	29,628	38,664	54,726	22,462	32,264	68,910	30,092	38,818	55,294	22,896	32,397
1923	66,319	27,725	38,594	52,775	20,984	31,791	66,624	27,932	38,692	53,215	21,305	31,910
1922	65,191	31,738	33,453	51,701	23,633	28,068	64,839	31,759	33,080	51,799	23,755	28,044
1921	62,285	31,185	31,100	49,958	24,402	25,556	62,665	30,181	32,484	50,423	23,432	26,991
1920	64,104	32,119	31,985	51,531	26,225	25,306	67,817	34,053	33,764	54,980	27,875	27,106
1919	46,702	21,933	24,769	36,381	16,224	20,157	51,257	24,992	26,265	40,751	19,133	21,617
1918 [2]	45,456	19,284	26,173	31,101	11,256	19,845	46,014	19,206	26,808	31,869	11,280	20,589
1917	50,472	18,725	31,747	36,521	10,898	25,623	52,077	19,146	32,931	38,094	11,339	26,755
1916	51,550	17,928	33,622	37,744	9,446	28,298	52,423	17,902	34,521	38,946	9,763	29,182
1915	46,710	13,275	33,435	35,032	6,830	28,202	46,885	13,418	33,467	35,458	7,110	28,347
1914	53,389	13,730	39,659	40,052	5,436	34,616	53,183	13,740	39,443	39,743	5,185	34,558
1913	50,639	13,073	37,567	37,973	5,241	32,732	51,152	13,946	37,206	37,566	5,289	32,277
1912	46,158	11,257	34,901	34,659	4,572	30,087	46,417	11,703	34,713	34,706	4,794	29,912
1911	42,675	9,693	32,982	32,457	4,302	28,155	42,437	9,753	32,684	32,299	4,427	27,871
1910	40,236	8,888	31,347	30,917	4,214	26,703	39,706	8,809	30,897	30,510	4,196	26,314
1909	39,058	8,771	30,287	30,243	4,403	25,840	38,196	8,492	29,705	29,604	4,215	25,389
1908	38,539	8,473	30,066	30,444	4,314	26,130	38,282	8,435	29,846	30,198	4,288	25,910
1907	36,622	8,116	28,507	29,248	3,924	25,324	35,990	8,093	27,898	28,499	3,797	24,702
1906	34,155	7,613	26,543	27,401	4,023	23,379	33,784	7,581	26,204	26,970	3,923	23,047
1905	30,983	7,081	23,903	24,793	4,120	20,673	31,158	7,203	23,955	25,020	4,259	20,760
1904	29,952	6,679	23,273	24,111	3,806	20,305	30,016	6,641	23,374	24,192	3,836	20,356
1903	31,094	6,907	24,187	24,698	3,881	20,817	31,316	6,975	24,341	24,823	3,931	20,892
1902	30,654	6,961	23,693	24,361	4,020	20,342	30,444	6,822	23,623	24,242	3,956	20,287
1901	29,768	6,381	23,387	24,791	3,980	20,811	29,820	6,417	23,403	24,889	4,020	20,870
1900	28,163	6,136	22,027	23,534	3,974	19,559	28,281	6,209	22,072	23,618	4,006	19,612
1899	26,111	5,341	20,770	21,963	3,333	18,631	26,266	5,472	20,794	22,177	3,463	18,714
1898	25,579	5,240	20,339	21,700	3,362	18,338	25,748	5,111	20,637	21,892	3,231	18,661
1897	23,760	5,525	18,235	20,003	3,611	16,391	23,709	5,618	18,091	19,878	3,637	16,241
1896	20,989	5,196	15,793	17,453	3,673	13,779	21,415	5,330	16,085	17,819	3,741	14,078
1895	19,295	4,473	14,822	16,725	3,677	13,049	19,751	4,504	15,246	17,024	3,616	13,408
1894	19,990	4,655	15,335	17,025	3,649	13,376	20,272	4,740	15,532	17,306	3,747	13,560
1893	19,582	4,359	15,223	16,679	3,493	13,186	19,761	4,403	15,357	16,825	3,537	13,288
1892	21,013	4,470	16,543	18,180	3,747	14,434	21,161	4,536	16,625	18,258	3,751	14,507
1891	18,204	4,381	13,823	15,394	3,670	11,724	18,261	4,455	13,805	15,411	3,716	11,695

See footnotes at end of table.

Series Q 506–517. Net Tonnage Capacity of Vessels Entered and Cleared: 1789 to 1970—Con.

[In thousands of net tons]

Year	Vessels entered — All ports			Vessels entered — Seaports [1]			Vessels cleared — All ports			Vessels cleared — Seaports [1]		
	Total	U.S. vessels	Foreign vessels	Total	U.S. vessels	Foreign vessels	Total	U.S. vessels	Foreign vessels	Total	U.S. vessels	Foreign vessels
	506	507	508	509	510	511	512	513	514	515	516	517
1890	18,107	4,083	14,024	15,366	3,405	11,961	18,149	4,067	14,082	15,429	3,390	12,039
1889	15,952	3,724	12,228	13,312	3,128	10,184	16,343	3,988	12,355	13,672	3,342	10,329
1888	15,393	3,367	12,026	12,956	2,914	10,042	15,669	3,415	12,254	13,252	2,944	10,308
1887	15,816	3,366	12,451	13,532	2,871	10,661	15,753	3,259	12,494	13,511	2,771	10,740
1886	15,136	3,232	11,904	12,230	2,762	9,468	15,328	3,303	12,024	12,413	2,806	9,607
1885	15,305	3,132	12,173	12,287	2,709	9,578	15,515	3,232	12,283	12,496	2,809	9,688
1884	15,069	3,202	11,867	12,085	2,821	9,264	15,205	3,237	11,968	12,206	2,845	9,361
1883	16,382	3,256	13,126	13,361	2,835	10,526	16,541	3,307	13,234	13,565	2,895	10,670
1882	17,601	3,341	14,260	14,656	2,968	11,688	17,757	3,318	14,439	14,846	2,936	11,911
1881	18,319	3,254	15,066	15,631	2,919	12,711	18,470	3,376	15,094	15,794	3,040	12,754
1880	18,011	3,437	14,574	15,251	3,140	12,111	18,043	3,397	14,646	15,296	3,078	12,218
1879	16,193	3,415	12,778	13,768	3,050	10,718	16,075	3,464	12,611	13,617	3,071	10,545
1878	14,464	3,642	10,821	11,531	3,009	8,521	14,808	3,872	10,935	11,844	3,196	8,647
1877	13,455	3,663	9,791	10,406	2,958	7,449	13,442	3,765	9,677	10,389	3,043	7,345
1876	12,511	3,611	8,899	9,716	2,928	6,788	12,655	3,732	8,923	9,839	3,037	6,802
1875	11,693	3,574	8,119	9,143	2,887	6,256	11,897	3,737	8,160	9,341	3,061	6,279
1874	13,092	3,894	9,198	10,010	2,915	7,095	13,189	3,982	9,207	10,058	2,961	7,097
1873	11,696	3,613	8,083	8,395	2,443	5,951	11,822	3,757	8,065	8,515	2,574	5,941
1872	10,806	3,712	7,095	7,770	2,585	5,185	10,734	3,682	7,051	7,739	2,598	5,141
1871	10,009	3,743	6,266	6,994	2,604	4,391	9,898	3,747	6,152	6,918	2,635	4,283
1870	9,156	3,486	5,670	6,270	2,452	3,818	9,169	3,507	5,662	6,362	2,530	3,832
1869	8,750	3,403	5,348	6,032	2,459	3,573	7,754	3,381	4,373	6,114	2,502	3,612
1868	8,046	3,551	4,495	5,572	2,466	3,106	8,279	3,718	4,561	5,811	2,625	3,186
1867	7,774	3,455	4,319	5,266	2,146	3,121	7,885	3,420	4,465	5,501	2,270	3,230
1866	7,782	3,372	4,410	5,008	1,891	3,117	7,822	3,383	4,438	5,161	2,030	3,131
1865	6,161	2,944	3,217	3,827	1,615	2,212	6,620	3,025	3,595	4,161	1,710	2,450
1864	6,538	3,066	3,471	4,167	1,655	2,512	6,832	3,091	3,741	4,279	1,662	2,617
1863	7,255	4,615	2,640	4,205	2,308	1,898	7,511	4,447	3,064	4,343	2,266	2,077
1862	7,363	5,118	2,245	4,191	2,629	1,562	7,339	4,962	2,377	4,205	2,568	1,637
1861	7,241	5,024	2,218	4,559	3,025	1,534	7,151	4,889	2,262	4,410	2,874	1,536
1860	8,275	5,921	2,354	5,000	3,302	1,698	8,790	6,166	2,624	5,257	3,501	1,756
1859	7,806	5,266	2,540	4,913	3,328	1,585	7,916	5,297	2,618	4,867	3,315	1,552
1858	6,605	4,396	2,209	4,338	3,051	1,287	7,803	4,490	3,313	4,436	3,128	1,309
1857	7,186	4,721	2,465	4,843	3,482	1,361	7,071	4,581	2,490	4,882	3,483	1,398
1856	6,872	4,385	2,487	4,464	3,194	1,270	7,000	4,538	2,462	4,695	--------	--------

Year	Vessels entered — All ports			Vessels entered — Seaports [1]	Vessels cleared — All ports			Vessels cleared — Seaports [1]	Year	Vessels entered, all ports		
	Total	U.S. vessels	Foreign vessels		Total	U.S. vessels	Foreign vessels			Total	U.S. vessels	Foreign vessels
	506	507	508	509	512	513	514	515		506	507	508
1855	5,945	3,861	2,084	4,178	6,179	4,069	2,110	4,435	1820	880	801	79
1854	5,884	3,752	2,132	4,343	6,019	3,911	2,108	4,524	1819	869	784	86
1853	6,282	4,004	2,278	4,157	6,066	3,767	2,299	4,289	1818	917	755	161
1852	5,293	3,236	2,057	3,926	5,278	3,231	2,048	(NA)	1817	992	780	212
1851	4,993	3,054	1,939	3,466	5,130	3,201	1,930	(NA)	1816	1,136	877	259
1850	3,749	2,573	1,176	3,013	4,361	2,633	1,728	3,167	1815	918	701	217
1849	4,369	2,658	1,711	2,890	4,429	2,754	1,676	(NA)	1814	108	60	48
1848	3,799	2,393	1,405	2,503	3,865	2,461	1,404	(NA)	1813	351	238	114
1847	3,322	2,101	1,220	2,429	3,379	2,202	1,177	(NA)	1812	715	668	47
1846	3,111	2,151	960	2,022	3,189	2,221	968	(NA)	1811	981	948	33
1845	2,946	2,035	911	2,011	2,984	2,054	930	(NA)	1810	989	909	80
1844	2,894	1,977	917	1,897	2,918	2,011	907	(NA)	1809	705	605	99
1843	1,678	1,144	535	(NA)	1,792	1,268	524	(NA)	1808	586	539	48
1842	2,243	1,510	733	(NA)	2,277	1,536	740	(NA)	1807	1,203	1,116	87
1841	2,368	1,632	736	(NA)	2,371	1,634	737	(NA)	1806	1,135	1,044	91
1840	2,289	1,577	712	1,788	2,353	1,647	706	1,861	1805	1,010	922	88
1839	2,116	1,491	625	--------	2,090	1,478	612	--------	1804	944	822	122
1838	1,895	1,303	592	--------	2,013	1,409	604	--------	1803	951	787	164
1837	2,065	1,300	766	--------	2,023	1,267	756	--------	1802	944	799	146
1836	1,936	1,255	680	--------	1,990	1,316	674	--------	1801	1,007	849	157
1835	1,994	1,353	641	--------	2,031	1,401	631	--------	1800	804	683	121
1834	1,643	1,075	568	--------	1,712	1,134	578	--------	1799	732	625	108
1833	1,608	1,111	497	--------	1,639	1,142	497	--------	1798	610	522	88
1832	1,343	950	393	--------	1,362	975	388	--------	1797	681	608	73
1831	1,405	923	482	--------	1,244	973	272	--------	1796	722	675	47
1830	1,099	967	132	--------	1,105	972	133	--------	1795	637	580	57
1829	1,004	873	131	--------	1,078	945	133	--------	1794	609	526	83
1828	1,019	868	150	--------	1,048	897	151	--------	1793	611	448	164
1827	1,056	918	138	--------	1,112	981	131	--------	1792	659	415	244
1826	1,048	942	106	--------	1,052	953	99	--------	1791	604	364	241
1825	974	881	93	--------	1,055	960	95	--------	1790	606	355	251
1824	952	850	102	--------	1,022	919	103	--------	1789	234	127	107
1823	895	775	119	--------	931	811	120	--------				
1822	889	788	101	--------	911	814	97	--------				
1821	847	765	82	--------	888	805	83	--------				

NA Not available.
[1] Comprises all ports except northern border ports.
[2] As of June 30; figures (in thousands of tons) for July-Dec. are as follows:

Series Q 506, 25,029; series Q 507, 11,006; series Q 508, 14,023; series Q 509, 16,113; series Q 510, 5,747; series Q 511, 10,366; series Q 512, 25,472; series Q 513, 11,223; series Q 514, 14,249; series Q 515, 16,112; series Q 516, 5,614; and series Q 517, 10,498.

Series Q 518–523. Value of Waterborne Imports and Exports (Including Reexports) of Merchandise: 1790 to 1970

[In millions of dollars. For years ending September 30, 1790–1842; June 30, 1843–1915; December 31 thereafter. Includes gold and silver coin and bullion to 1879, imports and exports by land prior to 1871; and all waterborne foreign commerce of ports on the Great Lakes]

Year	Imports Total	Imports U.S. vessels	Imports Foreign vessels	Exports Total	Exports U.S. vessels	Exports Foreign vessels
	518	519	520	521	522	523
1970	24,728			24,394		
1969	21,570			19,915		
1968	21,139			19,359		
1967	17,434			18,636		
1966	17,319			18,520		
1965	14,943			16,926		
1964	13,441			17,089		
1963	12,382			14,793		
1962	11,805			13,705		
1961	10,644			13,635		
1960	11,140			13,164		
1959	11,633			10,618		
1958	9,700			10,664		
1957	9,244			12,948		
1956	8,899			11,045		
1955	8,073			9,227		
1954	7,334			8,286		
1953	8,292			7,852		
1952	8,118			9,031		
1951	8,441			10,109		
1950	6,754			7,097		
1949	4,965			8,475		
1948	5,197			8,877		
1947	4,368			11,026		
1946	3,691	2,239	1,452	7,705	4,692	3,013
1945	(NA)	(NA)	(NA)	7,860	4,052	3,808
1944	(NA)	(NA)	(NA)	11,382	5,582	5,800
1943	(NA)	(NA)	(NA)	10,275	4,828	5,447
1935	1,813	649	1,164	1,973	705	1,268
1934	1,446	528	917	1,837	658	1,179
1933	1,287	461	826	1,471	515	956
1932	1,164	431	734	1,385	476	909
1931	1,829	619	1,210	2,043	732	1,311
1930	2,635	898	1,737	3,168	1,117	2,051
1929	3,807	1,205	2,602	4,322	1,487	2,835
1928	3,550	1,133	2,418	4,277	1,472	2,804
1927	3,662	1,215	2,447	4,097	1,434	2,663
1926	3,891	1,195	2,696	4,050	1,401	2,649
1925	3,716	1,151	2,565	4,224	1,473	2,751
1924	3,145	1,012	2,133	4,010	1,532	2,478
1923	3,312	1,040	2,272	3,539	1,358	2,181
1922	2,704	921	1,783	3,281	1,261	2,020
1921	2,187	765	1,422	3,888	1,402	2,486
1920	4,731	1,988	2,743	7,252	3,165	4,087
1919	3,414	1,228	2,186	7,090	2,596	4,494
1918	2,577	717	1,860	5,226	986	4,240
1917	2,590	733	1,857	5,403	946	4,457
1916	2,157	532	1,625	4,820	665	4,155
1915 [1]	1,526	281	1,245	2,466	291	2,176
1914	1,738	199	1,539	2,048	170	1,878
1913	1,698	193	1,505	2,075	188	1,887
1912	1,551	171	1,380	1,880	152	1,729
1911	1,436	147	1,290	1,774	134	1,641
1910	1,467	147	1,319	1,516	114	1,403
1909	1,241	151	1,090	1,481	108	1,373
1908	1,123	152	971	1,670	121	1,550
1907	1,340	177	1,164	1,662	142	1,521
1906	1,140	168	971	1,550	154	1,396
1905	1,039	161	878	1,355	130	1,225
1904	923	132	791	1,308	97	1,211
1903	960	124	836	1,281	91	1,190
1902	847	102	745	1,258	84	1,174
1901	776	93	683	1,376	84	1,292
1900	806	104	701	1,284	91	1,193
1899	664	82	582	1,143	79	1,065
1898	586	94	492	1,158	68	1,090
1897	729	109	620	986	80	906
1896	744	117	627	821	70	751
1895	699	108	591	758	62	695
1894	625	122	504	843	74	769
1893	822	127	695	804	71	733
1892	788	139	649	997	81	916
1891	804	127	677	853	79	774
1890	749	125	624	825	78	747
1889	707	121	586	714	83	631
1888	692	124	568	674	67	606
1887	665	121	543	695	73	622
1886	611	119	492	660	78	582
1885	556	113	444	718	82	636
1884	648	135	513	714	99	615
1883	700	136	564	799	104	694
1882	702	130	572	738	97	641
1881	625	134	492	894	117	777
1880	653	149	503	830	109	721
1879	454	144	310	729	128	601
1878	454	146	307	736	167	570
1877	481	152	330	695	165	530
1876	465	143	321	660	168	492
1875	541	158	383	658	156	502
1874	581	176	405	708	174	534
1873	647	175	472	666	172	495
1872	623	177	445	562	168	394
1871	526	163	363	583	190	393
1870	462	153	309	530	200	330
1869	437	137	301	439	153	286
1868	372	123	249	477	175	302
1867	418	117	301	461	181	281
1866	446	112	333	565	214	352
1865	249	74	174	356	93	263
1864	330	81	248	340	103	237
1863	253	110	143	332	132	200
1862	206	92	113	230	125	105
1861	336	202	134	249	180	69
1860	362	228	134	400	279	121
1859	339	216	123	357	250	107
1858	283	204	79	325	243	81
1857	361	259	102	363	251	112
1856	315	250	65	327	232	95
1855	261	202	59	275	203	72
1854	301	215	86	276	191	84
1853	268	192	76	231	155	76
1852	208	155	53	210	139	70
1851	216	164	53	218	152	66
1850	178	140	38	152	100	52
1849	148	120	27	146	101	45
1848	155	129	26	154	110	44
1847	147	113	33	154	100	54
1846	122	106	16	113	87	27
1845	117	102	15	115	87	28
1844	108	94	14	111	78	33
1843	65	50	15	84	65	19
1842	100	89	11	105	80	25
1841	128	113	15	122	95	27
1840	107	93	14	132	106	26
1839	162	144	18	121	95	26
1838	115	104	11	108	89	19
1837	141	122	19	117	91	26
1836	189	171	18	129	97	32
1835	150	135	15	122	94	28
1834	127	114	13	104	78	27
1833	108	98	10	90	68	22
1832	101	90	11	87	66	21
1831	103	94	9	81	66	16
1830	71	66	4	74	64	10
1829	74	69	5	72	62	10
1828	89	82	7	72	61	11
1827	79	75	5	82	72	10
1826	85	81	4	78	70	8
1825	96	92	4	100	89	11
1824	81	75	5	76	67	9
1823	78	72	6	75	65	9
1822	83	77	6	72	61	11
1821	63	58	5	65	55	10
1820	74	67	7	70	62	8
1819	87	67	20	70	58	13
1818	122	103	18	93	75	19
1817	99	78	21	88	65	23
1816	147	107	40	82	56	26
1815	113	87	26	53	37	15
1814	13	8	5	7	4	3
1813	22	16	6	28	18	10
1812	77	65	12	39	31	8
1811	53	48	5	61	53	9
1810	85	79	6	67	60	7
1809	59	52	7	52	44	8
1808	57	53	4	22	20	3
1807	139	130	8	108	98	11
1806	129	120	9	102	90	11
1805	121	112	8	96	85	11
1804	85	77	8	78	67	11
1803	65	56	9	56	46	9
1802	76	67	9	72	61	11
1801	111	101	10	93	81	12
1800	91	83	8	71	62	9
1799	79	71	8	79	68	10
1798	69	62	6	61	53	8
1797	75	69	6	51	45	6
1796	81	77	5	59	53	6
1795	70	64	6	48	42	6
1794	35	31	3	33	28	5
1793	31	26	6	26	20	6
1792	32	21	10	21	13	8
1791	29	17	12	19	10	9
1790	23	9	14	20	8	12

[1] Figures (in millions of dollars) for July-Dec. are as follows: Series Q 518, 817; Q 519, 179; Q 520, 638; Q 521, 1,625; Q 522, 200; Q 523, 1,425.

Series Q 524–529. Tonnage of Waterborne Imports and Exports, by Flag of Carrier Vessel: 1921 to 1970

[In thousands of short tons]

Year	Imports Total	Imports U.S. vessels	Imports Foreign vessels	Exports Total	Exports U.S. vessels	Exports Foreign vessels	Year	Imports Total	Imports U.S. vessels	Imports Foreign vessels	Exports Total	Exports U.S. vessels	Exports Foreign vessels
	524	525	526	527	528	529		524	525	526	527	528	529
1970	299,159	15,438	283,721	239,774	14,940	224,834	1945 [1]	39,426	31,415	8,011	61,603	37,729	23,874
1969	288,620	10,985	277,635	199,286	13,060	186,226	1944 [1]	33,320	26,209	7,111	55,215	34,002	21,213
1968	282,751	16,321	266,430	194,483	15,599	178,884	1943 [1]	30,988	24,740	6,248	47,765	25,302	22,463
1967	256,806	13,526	243,280	187,427	15,365	172,062	1942 [1]	27,393	17,399	9,994	41,670	16,227	25,443
1966	266,075	15,598	250,477	185,978	17,358	168,620							
							1940	44,667	17,322	27,345	60,929	12,939	47,990
1965	255,596	15,573	240,023	171,811	19,048	152,762	1939	42,054	12,459	29,595	61,697	10,557	51,140
1964	233,774	16,278	217,496	171,431	23,937	147,494	1938	36,756	13,527	23,230	62,286	11,602	50,684
1963	212,542	15,682	196,860	156,122	20,885	135,237	1937	47,110	14,967	32,143	61,105	12,189	48,916
1962	210,631	18,373	192,257	134,001	19,535	114,466	1936	43,003	14,780	28,223	44,480	9,650	34,830
1961	187,887	15,155	172,732	127,519	18,411	109,108							
							1935	38,042	15,820	22,221	42,723	9,789	32,935
1960	198,830	19,627	179,203	123,887	20,133	103,754	1934	33,392	14,299	19,092	42,360	10,567	31,792
1959	200,481	19,219	181,262	108,281	17,724	90,557	1933	29,755	12,340	17,415	36,272	9,357	26,914
1958	175,605	20,628	154,977	114,748	18,686	96,062	1932	32,156	14,923	17,232	35,666	9,125	26,541
1957	172,030	34,558	137,472	165,796	29,092	136,704	1931	40,168	19,168	21,000	44,855	12,396	32,459
1956	159,472	39,394	120,078	144,755	27,304	117,451							
							1930	53,270	27,801	25,469	55,699	16,703	38,995
1955	141,123	37,409	103,715	112,796	22,144	90,652	1929	57,103	28,260	28,844	64,372	20,071	44,301
1954	120,685	36,291	84,395	78,178	18,378	59,800	1928	53,083	27,089	25,993	65,889	21,602	44,287
1953	119,003	38,468	80,535	80,549	19,448	61,101	1927	47,245	24,033	23,212	63,768	20,939	42,829
1952	107,421	41,683	65,738	103,048	30,417	72,630	1926	50,049	23,638	26,411	76,316	19,177	57,140
1951	100,603	42,836	57,767	115,690	43,232	72,458							
							1925	48,311	23,760	24,551	55,626	17,603	38,024
1950	96,703	42,268	54,435	62,685	20,379	42,306	1924	45,807	24,968	20,839	58,533	20,515	38,018
1949	77,371	41,364	36,007	71,865	26,136	45,729	1923	48,491	25,518	22,973	54,970	18,131	36,838
1948	67,416	40,528	26,888	88,312	34,501	53,810	1922	50,044	31,286	18,758	47,602	18,871	28,731
1947	59,203	37,682	21,521	124,317	61,062	63,254	1921	37,167	26,269	10,898	54,477	20,784	33,692
1946	49,184	32,340	16,844	87,043	49,799	37,244							

[1] Excludes U.S. Army and Navy cargo and Great Lakes.

Series Q 530–541. Waterborne Cargo Tonnage, Foreign and Domestic: 1924 to 1970

[In thousands of short tons of 2,000 pounds. For definition of cargo tonnage, see text. Net totals are derived by deducting two types of duplications from unadjusted totals: (1) Traffic between seaports and river points, and (2) "Other duplications," comprising principally coastwise and lake traffic passing through canals and connecting channels other than the St. Marys Falls Canal and the Detroit River]

Year	Foreign and domestic commerce	Foreign commerce Total	Through seaports Imports	Through seaports Exports	Great Lakes ports Imports	Great Lakes ports Exports	Net total [1]	Between ports Coastwise	Between ports Lakewise	Local and intraport [2]	Internal	Intraterritory [3]
	530	531	532	533	534	535	536	537	538	539	540	541
1970	1,531,697	580,969	312,934	205,698	26,406	35,932	950,727	238,440	157,059	81,475	472,123	1,630
1969	1,448,712	521,312	295,648	168,944	24,645	32,075	927,399	216,708	160,844	87,536	460,945	1,366
1968	1,395,839	507,950	278,827	166,580	32,110	30,434	887,889	214,251	151,116	90,730	430,174	1,618
1967	1,336,606	465,972	248,245	162,443	27,720	27,564	870,634	214,647	153,597	102,320	398,593	1,478
1966	1,334,116	471,391	257,173	155,759	26,674	31,785	862,725	208,375	164,037	99,215	389,852	1,247
1965	1,272,896	443,727	244,874	142,121	24,961	31,771	829,169	201,508	153,695	102,865	369,615	1,486
1964	1,238,094	421,925	224,433	142,874	24,152	30,465	816,168	205,688	151,405	99,579	357,916	1,580
1963	1,173,767	385,659	209,370	129,782	18,006	28,502	788,108	213,853	141,741	98,981	331,902	1,630
1962	1,129,404	358,599	207,041	110,492	15,649	25,417	770,805	215,461	135,744	102,277	316,062	1,262
1961	1,062,155	329,330	188,179	105,959	11,986	23,205	732,825	206,899	136,841	93,929	294,052	1,104
1960	1,099,850	339,277	198,466	104,810	12,851	23,151	760,573	209,197	155,109	104,193	291,057	1,017
1959	1,052,402	325,670	198,608	91,629	14,878	20,555	726,732	205,509	131,220	106,747	282,269	987
1958	1,004,516	308,851	181,480	101,555	8,004	17,811	695,665	194,050	132,289	105,425	261,069	2,832
1957	1,131,401	358,540	176,236	146,890	10,116	25,298	772,862	196,419	182,150	110,824	281,066	2,403
1956	1,092,913	326,690	163,349	126,448	10,865	26,027	766,223	205,910	173,991	114,364	269,734	2,225
1955	1,016,136	271,103	144,276	95,404	8,681	22,742	745,033	195,718	184,809	112,863	249,693	1,951
1954	867,640	213,844	123,503	65,244	5,921	19,176	653,796	187,240	145,364	102,719	217,061	1,411
1953	923,548	217,396	120,595	63,780	7,387	25,635	706,151	188,758	148,621	102,562	224,957	1,253
1952	887,722	227,326	108,674	85,072	7,287	26,293	660,396	184,207	154,112	103,972	216,644	1,460
1951	924,128	232,056	101,813	97,603	6,935	25,705	692,073	186,759	178,463	112,029	213,405	1,417
1950	820,584	169,225	96,299	43,640	5,683	23,603	651,359	182,544	169,881	106,906	190,789	1,239
1949	740,721	165,358	77,153	65,740	4,839	17,626	575,363	161,431	145,592	102,637	165,703	----------
1948	793,200	162,971	68,078	65,404	4,219	25,270	630,229	174,081	172,491	113,959	169,698	----------
1947	766,817	188,256	57,366	101,996	4,796	24,098	578,561	153,098	163,180	112,668	149,615	----------
1946	617,032	148,877	47,948	76,589	4,163	20,177	468,155	137,609	138,617	91,225	81,668	----------
1945	618,906	172,094	44,526	100,333	6,511	20,724	446,812	90,705	157,900	97,822	87,073	----------
1944	605,928	153,736	39,441	82,613	8,055	23,627	452,192	70,806	164,971	106,194	95,821	----------
1943	580,581	127,284	33,077	63,086	7,120	24,001	453,297	60,009	159,458	106,278	93,689	----------
1942	589,900	99,221	25,974	46,023	4,488	22,736	490,679	74,016	172,606	104,189	92,748	----------
1941	653,600	120,652	54,616	40,605	4,628	20,802	532,948	155,927	163,161	98,728	85,368	----------

See footnotes at end of table.

Series Q 530–541. Waterborne Cargo Tonnage, Foreign and Domestic: 1924 to 1970—Con.

[In thousands of short tons of 2,000 pounds]

Year	Foreign and domestic commerce	Foreign commerce						Domestic commerce				
		Total	Through seaports		Great Lakes ports		Net total [1]	Between ports		Local and intraport [2]	Internal
			Imports	Exports	Imports	Exports		Coast-wise	Lake-wise		
	530	531	532	533	534	535	536	537	538	539	540
1940	607,900	111,255	40,740	49,568	4,118	16,829	496,645	157,027	141,103	97,632	70,217
1939	569,400	112,667	37,854	57,711	4,941	12,161	456,733	150,983	113,309	87,710	62,014
1938	466,900	105,182	33,886	55,476	5,110	10,710	361,718	138,545	72,846	76,216	56,034
1937	583,100	114,413	43,764	52,910	4,102	13,637	468,687	149,740	135,075	91,059	55,295
1936	525,842	90,247	37,507	37,154	5,423	10,163	435,595	132,515	115,250	88,024	44,337
1935	453,331	81,639	33,942	33,922	4,716	9,059	371,692	115,561	83,628	76,583	35,720
1934	414,308	77,898	30,553	33,570	4,287	9,488	336,410	113,349	71,685	60,998	34,894
1933	394,104	69,466	27,670	31,197	3,034	7,565	324,638	110,675	68,911	55,207	26,030
1932	342,489	70,429	29,843	30,039	3,072	7,475	272,060	94,434	39,544	54,845	27,242
1931	445,648	89,525	37,375	38,841	4,016	9,293	356,123	113,949	71,788	67,530	37,327
1930	520,280	114,110	46,448	48,148	7,590	11,924	406,170	117,821	109,791	79,414	37,591
1929	583,800	127,510	51,591	55,761	6,385	13,773	456,290	124,999	135,838	89,528	41,995
1928	539,200	126,768	46,690	56,151	8,548	15,379	412,432	119,254	119,301	75,728	39,870
1927	532,500	120,523	43,388	56,550	8,098	12,487	411,977	121,036	112,805	78,020	40,559
1926	540,500	131,293	44,834	69,859	6,424	10,176	409,207	108,023	115,791	88,270	36,798
1925	483,400	108,548	42,793	49,251	7,317	9,187	374,852	105,090	110,626	59,981	49,787
1924	453,700	101,562	36,425	49,008	4,962	11,167	352,138	88,554	92,563	77,270	34,101

[1] Figures for 1924–1945 are approximations; there are some minor duplications in figures for foreign traffic. Domestic commerce, for 1924–1946, includes "rivers, canals, and connecting channels," not shown separately.

[2] Includes figures for harbor traffic of New York, Philadelphia, and San Francisco; local traffic of other seaports, and local traffic of lake ports.

[3] Beginning 1959, excludes traffic in Alaska and Hawaii; such traffic included in other domestic traffic categories.

Series Q 542–547. Waterborne Bulk Freight Traffic on the Great Lakes: 1900 to 1970

[In thousands of short tons]

Year	Dry bulk					Bulk trade in petroleum products	Year	Dry bulk				
	Total	Iron ore	Coal	Grain	Stone			Total	Iron ore	Coal	Grain	Stone
	542	543	544	545	546	547		542	543	544	545	546
1970	209,531	97,550	49,684	23,820	38,477	13,873	1935	82,887	31,766	35,289	6,750	9,082
1969	196,267	96,664	46,924	16,595	36,083	13,149	1934	75,739	24,919	35,477	7,951	7,392
1968	191,947	93,667	48,862	16,325	33,093	12,834	1933	71,373	24,218	31,777	8,713	6,665
1967	192,503	90,279	52,891	17,617	31,717	12,110	1932	41,673	3,997	24,857	8,890	3,929
1966	210,128	95,506	55,585	25,014	34,022	12,980	1931	74,149	26,284	31,176	9,480	7,209
1965	195,332	88,063	54,574	21,875	30,819	11,168	1930	112,529	52,173	38,072	9,851	12,433
1964	192,041	87,489	52,143	21,637	30,771	10,790	1929	138,574	73,028	39,255	10,021	16,270
1963	174,341	75,374	51,643	18,777	28,547	12,417	1928	127,331	60,458	34,823	16,372	15,678
1962	157,490	70,656	46,184	15,919	24,731	13,893	1927	120,760	57,240	34,794	14,693	14,033
1961	154,201	68,205	43,970	16,608	25,418	14,874	1926	121,289	65,563	31,011	12,087	12,628
1960	169,857	81,842	46,701	14,135	27,179	14,295	1925	113,292	60,571	28,049	13,320	11,352
1959	144,622	57,625	47,228	13,609	26,160	14,410	1924	98,047	47,737	25,861	15,223	9,226
1958	141,434	61,362	44,950	12,626	22,496	14,025	1923	121,029	66,122	33,137	11,850	9,920
1957	196,206	97,752	56,780	11,235	30,439	16,628	1922	89,455	47,727	19,869	14,267	7,592
1956	192,267	89,819	57,375	14,320	30,753	16,137	1921	68,034	24,977	26,661	12,470	3,926
1955	193,759	99,871	53,378	10,788	29,722	15,532	1920	106,519	65,551	26,410	6,736	7,822
1954	151,298	68,090	46,367	11,866	24,975	14,901	1919	91,762	52,839	26,424	6,092	6,407
1953	199,697	107,346	51,035	14,317	26,999	16,810	1918	114,614	68,495	32,102	6,549	7,448
1952	168,677	83,900	46,284	15,215	23,278	17,448	1917	115,102	69,998	31,193	7,162	6,749
1951	189,750	99,783	50,946	13,150	25,871	16,297	1916	117,053	72,503	28,440	10,556	5,554
1950	177,953	87,591	57,640	9,327	23,395	13,331	1915	93,050	51,877	26,220	11,099	3,854
1949	151,697	77,902	40,930	12,543	20,322	12,607	1914	72,940	35,864	27,282	9,794	
1948	185,612	92,890	60,564	9,877	22,282	10,956	1913	100,018	54,959	33,362	11,697	
1947	177,606	87,246	58,060	11,409	20,891	10,145	1912	87,174	53,129	24,673	9,372	
1946	147,955	66,478	53,727	10,198	17,552	10,217	1911	68,646	35,987	25,700	6,959	
1945	175,083	84,801	55,246	18,718	16,318	9,364	1910	80,015	47,733	26,478	5,804	
1944	184,159	90,911	60,163	16,229	16,856	10,196	1909	71,954	46,686	18,617	6,651	
1943	175,653	94,534	51,969	11,810	17,340	9,450	1908	53,791	28,479	19,288	6,024	
1942	182,731	103,125	52,534	8,502	18,570	8,940	1907	74,743	46,245	21,487	7,011	
1941	172,287	89,732	53,535	11,387	17,633	9,387	1906	66,152	42,015	17,274	6,863	
1940	145,216	71,358	49,320	9,645	14,893		1905	58,008	37,494	14,401	6,113	
1939	114,230	50,482	40,368	11,172	12,208		1904	40,331	23,774	12,370	4,187	
1938	75,118	21,575	34,623	10,679	8,241		1903	45,571	26,488	13,351	5,732	
1937	134,688	70,111	44,319	5,829	14,429		1902	44,374	30,284	9,196	4,894	
1936	114,415	50,201	44,699	7,434	12,081		1901	37,064	22,576	9,820	4,668	
							1900	35,298	20,799	8,908	5,591	

Series Q 548–552. Freight Traffic on the Sault Ste. Marie Canals: 1855 to 1900

[In thousands of short tons, except grain in thousands of bushels]

Year	Total traffic	Iron ore	Coal	Grain	Stone	Year	Total traffic	Iron ore	Coal	Grain	Stone
	548	549	550	551	552		548	549	550	551	552
1900	25,643	16,444	4,487	56,664	49	1875	833	493	101	1,486	3
1899	25,256	15,328	3,941	88,398	39	1874	655	428	61	1,270	(Z)
1898	21,235	11,707	3,776	88,418	5	1873	888	504	97	2,430	2
1897	18,983	10,634	3,039	80,814	6	1872	746	383	81	1,013	5
1896	16,239	7,909	3,023	90,705	18	1871	586	327	47	1,686	6
1895	15,063	8,062	2,574	54,547	24	1870	540	410	16	354	5
1894	13,196	6,549	2,797	36,414	21	1869	368	239	28	324	----------
1893	10,797	4,015	3,008	45,887	19	1868	299	192	26	285	----------
1892	11,214	4,901	2,904	42,661	40	1867	325	223	23	249	----------
1891	8,889	3,560	2,508	39,849	44	1866	239	152	20	230	----------
1890	9,041	4,775	2,177	18,262	48	1865	182	147	----------	----------	----------
1889	7,516	4,096	1,629	18,325	34	1864	284	214	11	144	----------
1888	6,411	2,571	2,105	20,619	34	1863	237	182	8	78	----------
1887	5,495	2,498	1,353	23,872	13	1862	162	113	11	59	----------
1886	4,528	2,088	1,010	19,707	9	1861	88	45	12	77	----------
1885	3,257	1,235	895	15,697	8	1860	154	120	----------	133	----------
1884	2,875	1,136	706	12,503	6	1859	122	66	9	72	----------
1883	2,267	792	714	6,677	2	1858	57	31	4	21	----------
1882	2,030	987	430	4,202	5	1857	52	26	5	41	----------
1881	1,568	748	296	3,825	1	1856	34	12	4	82	----------
1880	1,322	677	171	4,659	2	1855	15	1	1	----------	----------
1879	1,051	540	111	3,578	2						
1878	937	556	92	2,138	3						
1877	913	568	92	1,728	3						
1876	1,074	610	125	2,396	2						

Z Less than 500 short tons.

Series Q 553–555. Commercial Ocean Traffic on the Panama Canal: 1915 to 1970

[For years ending June 30. Includes oceangoing tolls-paying vessels and foreign naval vessels of 300 net tons and over (Panama Canal measurement) for vessels rated on net tonnage, or 500 tons displacement and over for vessels rated on displacement tonnage]

Year	Number of transits	Tolls ($1,000)	Cargo (1,000 long tons)	Year	Number of transits	Tolls ($1,000)	Cargo (1,000 long tons)	Year	Number of transits	Tolls ($1,000)	Cargo (1,000 long tons)
	553	554	555		553	554	555		553	554	555
1970	13,658	94,620	114,257	1950	5,448	24,430	28,872	1930	6,027	27,060	30,018
1969	13,146	87,423	101,373	1949	4,793	20,541	25,305	1929	6,289	27,111	30,648
1968	13,199	83,907	96,550	1948	4,678	19,957	24,118	1928	6,253	26,922	29,616
1967	12,412	76,769	86,193	1947	4,260	17,597	21,671	1927	5,293	24,212	27,734
1966	11,925	69,095	81,704	1946	3,747	14,774	14,978	1926	5,087	22,920	26,030
1965	11,834	65,443	76,573	1945	1,939	7,244	8,604	1925	4,592	21,394	23,957
1964	11,808	61,098	70,550	1944	1,562	5,456	7,003	1924	5,158	24,285	26,993
1963	11,017	56,368	62,247	1943	1,822	7,357	10,600	1923	3,908	17,504	19,566
1962	11,149	57,290	67,525	1942	2,688	9,752	13,607	1922	2,665	11,192	10,883
1961	10,866	54,128	63,670	1941	4,727	18,158	24,951	1921	2,791	11,269	11,596
1960	10,795	50,939	59,258	1940	5,370	21,145	27,299	1920	2,393	8,508	9,372
1959	9,718	45,529	51,153	1939	5,903	23,661	27,867	1919	1,948	6,164	6,910
1958	9,187	41,796	48,125	1938	5,524	23,170	27,387	1918	1,989	6,429	7,526
1957	8,579	38,444	49,702	1937	5,387	23,102	28,108	1917	1,738	5,621	7,055
1956	8,209	36,154	45,119	1936	5,382	23,479	26,506	1916 [1]	724	2,403	3,093
1955	7,997	33,849	40,646	1935	5,180	23,307	25,310	1915 [2]	1,058	4,367	4,888
1954	7,784	33,248	39,095	1934	5,234	24,047	24,704				
1953	7,410	31,918	36,095	1933	4,162	19,602	18,161				
1952	6,524	26,923	33,611	1932	4,362	20,695	19,799				
1951	5,593	23,906	30,073	1931	5,370	24,625	25,065				

[1] Canal closed about 7 months by slides.

[2] Canal opened Aug. 15, 1914.

Series Q 556–557.   Tonnage Moved on New York State Canals: 1837 to 1970

[In short tons of 2,000 pounds]

Year	All canals 556	Erie division, freight originating 557	Year	All canals 556	Erie division, freight originating 557	Year	All canals 556	Erie division, freight originating 557	Year	All canals 556	Erie division, freight originating 557
1970	2,734,963	983,986	1935	4,489,172	3,898,506	1900	3,345,941	2,145,876	1865	4,729,654	2,523,490
1969	3,248,440	1,492,071	1934	4,142,728	3,645,125	1899	3,686,051	2,419,084	1864	4,852,941	2,535,792
1968	3,249,035	1,409,769	1933	4,074,002	3,574,951	1898	3,360,063	2,338,020	1863	5,557,692	2,955,302
1967	3,219,994	1,332,853	1932	3,643,433	3,186,094	1897	3,617,804	2,584,906	1862	5,598,785	3,204,277
1966	3,147,129	1,314,250	1931	3,722,012	3,277,936	1896	3,714,894	2,742,438	1861	4,507,635	2,500,782
1965	3,270,796	1,508,546	1930	3,605,457	3,044,271	1895	3,500,314	2,356,084	1860	4,650,214	2,253,533
1964	3,194,696	1,500,946	1929	2,876,160	2,422,204	1894	3,882,560	3,144,144	1859	3,781,684	1,753,954
1963	3,225,526	1,541,251	1928	3,089,998	2,535,684	1893	4,331,963	3,235,726	1858	3,665,192	1,767,004
1962	3,279,944	1,610,959	1927	2,581,892	2,047,774	1892	4,281,995	2,978,832	1857	3,344,061	1,566,624
1961	3,223,558	1,583,098	1926	2,369,367	1,935,278	1891	4,563,472	3,097,853	1856	4,116,082	2,107,678
1960	3,415,095	1,772,789	1925	2,344,013	1,945,466	1890	5,246,102	3,303,929	1855	4,022,617	2,202,463
1959	3,719,919	1,976,739	1924	2,032,317	1,691,766	1889	5,370,369	3,673,554	1854	4,165,862	2,224,008
1958	4,000,580	2,056,733	1923	2,006,284	1,626,062	1888	4,942,948	3,321,516	1853	4,247,853	2,196,308
1957	4,468,539	2,675,853	1922	1,873,434	1,485,109	1887	5,553,805	3,840,513	1852	3,863,441	2,129,334
1956	4,858,044	3,053,219	1921	1,270,407	993,639	1886	5,293,982	3,808,642	1851	3,582,733	1,955,265
1955	4,616,399	2,779,491	1920	1,421,434	891,221	1885	4,731,784	3,208,207	1850	3,076,617	1,635,089
1954	3,859,335	2,395,291	1919	1,238,844	842,164	1884	5,009,488	3,389,555	1849	2,894,732	1,622,444
1953	4,497,231	3,211,932	1918	1,159,270	667,374	1883	5,664,056	3,587,102	1848	2,796,230	1,599,965
1952	4,487,858	3,112,480	1917	1,297,225	675,083	1882	5,467,423	3,694,364	1847	2,869,810	1,661,575
1951	5,211,472	3,673,104	1916	1,625,050	917,689	1881	5,179,192	3,598,721	1846	2,268,662	1,264,408
1950	4,615,613	3,620,346	1915	1,858,114	1,155,235	1880	6,457,656	4,608,651	1845	1,977,565	1,038,700
1949	3,949,739	2,685,635	1914	2,080,850	1,361,764	1879	5,362,372	3,820,027	1844	1,816,586	945,944
1948	4,513,817	3,121,411	1913	2,602,035	1,788,453	1878	5,171,320	3,608,684	1843	1,513,439	819,216
1947	3,790,050	2,514,643	1912	2,606,116	1,795,069	1877	4,955,963	3,254,367	1842	1,236,931	712,310
1946	2,820,541	1,685,516	1911	3,097,068	2,031,735	1876	4,172,129	2,418,422	1841	1,521,661	906,442
1945	2,968,682	1,665,447	1910	3,073,412	2,023,185	1875	4,859,958	2,787,226	1840	1,416,046	829,960
1944	2,506,840	1,729,448	1909	3,116,536	2,031,307	1874	5,804,588	3,097,122	1839	1,435,713	845,007
1943	2,824,160	2,166,393	1908	3,051,877	2,177,443	1873	6,364,782	3,602,535	1838	1,333,011	744,848
1942	3,539,101	2,760,596	1907	3,407,914	2,415,548	1872	6,673,370	3,562,560	1837	1,171,296	667,151
1941	4,505,059	3,512,829	1906	3,540,907	2,385,491	1871	6,467,888	3,580,922			
1940	4,768,160	3,587,086	1905	3,226,896	1,999,824	1870	6,173,769	3,083,132			
1939	4,689,037	3,643,782	1904	3,138,547	1,945,708	1869	5,859,080	2,845,072			
1938	4,709,488	3,349,250	1903	3,615,385	2,414,018	1868	6,442,225	3,346,986			
1937	5,010,464	4,173,700	1902	3,274,610	2,105,876	1867	5,688,325	2,920,578			
1936	5,014,206	4,220,397	1901	3,420,613	2,257,035	1866	5,775,220	2,896,027			

Series Q 558.   Federal Expenditures for Rivers and Harbors: 1822 to 1970

[In thousands of dollars.   For years ending June 30]

Year	Total 558	Year	Total 558	Year	Total 558	Year	Total 558	Year	Total 558
1970	1,050,803	1940	107,082	1910	29,273	1880	8,080	1850	42
1969	1,124,790	1939	115,987	1909	34,579	1879	8,267	1849	26
1968	1,170,845	1938	135,921	1908	30,361	1878	3,791	1848	24
1967	1,182,958	1937	178,825	1907	23,310	1877	4,655	1847	44
1966	1,208,301	1936	106,239	1906	25,955	1876	5,736	1846	219
1965	1,092,588	1935	162,375	1905	22,814	1875	6,434	1845	529
1964	993,916	1934	104,873	1904	22,546	1874	5,704	1844	313
1963	1,004,022	1933	76,788	1903	19,590	1873	6,312	1843	111
1962	889,936	1932	84,260	1902	14,948	1872	4,962	1842	82
1961	863,600	1931	80,903	1901	19,544	1871	4,421	1841	79
1960	800,948	1930	73,970	1900	18,736	1870	3,528	1840	145
1959	721,767	1929	57,299	1899	16,094	1869	3,545	1839	780
1958	624,558	1928	70,197	1898	20,792	1868	3,457	1838	1,054
1957	545,032	1927	60,620	1897	13,686	1867	1,217	1837	1,362
1956	489,118	1926	63,464	1896	18,119	1866	295	1836	869
1955	455,612	1925	69,882	1895	19,944	1865	305	1835	569
1954	475,418	1924	62,025	1894	19,888	1864	102	1834	598
1953	272,130	1923	47,478	1893	14,804	1863	65	1833	704
1952	214,957	1922	43,393	1892	13,024	1862	37	1832	538
1951	204,699	1921	57,166	1891	12,253	1861	172	1831	652
1950	190,456	1920	47,188	1890	11,740	1860	228	1830	574
1949	160,431	1919	33,078	1889	11,234	1859	290	1829	524
1948	115,728	1918	29,594	1888	7,007	1858	427	1828	188
1947	89,170	1917	30,487	1887	7,786	1857	268	1827	136
1946	79,542	1916	32,450	1886	4,197	1856	161	1826	87
1945	57,146	1915	46,834	1885	10,558	1855	791	1825	40
1944	64,366	1914	50,762	1884	8,237	1854	937	1824	26
1943	84,368	1913	42,275	1883	13,839	1853	489	1823	---
1942	88,664	1912	35,861	1882	11,624	1852	40	1822	1
1941	86,530	1911	33,968	1881	9,072	1851	70		

Series Q 559-564. Investment in Canals, by Region and Agency of Enterprise: 1815 to 1860

[In millions of dollars]

Year	United States			Northeast	South	West	Year	United States			Northeast	South	West
	Total	State	Private					Total	State	Private			
	559	560	561	562	563	564		559	560	561	562	563	564
1860	1.2	1.0	0.1	1.1	0.1	----------	1837	8.2	3.9	4.3	4.4	1.2	2.7
1859	1.9	1.4	.5	1.7	.2	----------	1836	4.4	1.8	2.6	2.9	.3	1.2
1858	2.8	1.6	1.1	2.3	.4	0.1	1835	3.5	2.0	1.5	2.9	.1	.5
1857	3.5	2.9	.7	3.0	.5	.1	1834	4.4	2.8	1.6	3.9	.1	.4
1856	4.2	3.2	1.0	3.6	.4	.2	1833	5.3	2.7	2.6	4.9	.2	.2
1855	5.3	4.2	1.1	4.6	.3	.4	1832	4.6	2.9	1.7	4.2	.1	.4
1854	4.7	3.8	.9	4.0	.3	.5	1831	3.7	2.2	1.5	3.0	.1	.7
1853	3.8	2.4	1.4	3.3	.2	.3	1830	7.5	5.1	2.4	6.1	.5	1.0
1852	3.4	1.9	1.5	2.8	.5	.1	1829	7.0	3.7	3.2	5.2	.8	.9
1851	4.7	2.0	2.8	3.8	.8	.1	1828	7.8	4.0	3.7	6.0	.7	1.0
1850	4.9	2.3	2.5	4.2	.7	-	1827	5.6	2.3	3.3	4.3	.4	.9
1849	3.4	1.9	1.6	2.9	.4	.1	1826	4.0	1.5	2.5	3.0	.3	.8
1848	4.5	1.5	3.0	3.9	.3	-.3	1825	2.7	1.5	1.2	2.2	.4	.1
1847	4.7	1.1	3.6	3.5	.6	.6	1824	2.5	1.8	.7	1.9	.6	----------
1846	1.8	.8	1.0	.5	.7	.7	1823	2.8	2.2	.7	2.4	.4	----------
1845	2.0	1.1	.9	.7	.3	1.0	1822	2.7	2.3	.3	2.2	.4	----------
1844	1.0	.7	.3	.2	-	.8	1821	1.6	1.3	.2	1.3	.3	----------
1843	1.0	.7	.3	.3	.1	.6	1820	1.1	.8	.2	.8	.3	----------
1842	3.1	2.6	.6	1.8	.3	1.1	1819	.8	.6	.2	.7	.1	----------
1841	11.7	9.8	1.9	8.8	.5	2.4	1818	.7	.6	.1	.6	----------	----------
1840	14.3	11.3	3.0	8.4	1.2	4.7	1817	.2	.1	----------	.2	----------	----------
1839	13.6	9.5	4.1	7.3	1.9	4.4	1816	(Z)	----------	----------	----------	----------	----------
1838	12.3	7.2	5.1	6.0	1.9	4.4	1815	(Z)	----------	----------	----------	----------	----------

- Represents zero.   Z Less than $50,000.

Chapter Q

Air Transportation (Series Q 565-637)

Q 565–637. General note.

Only scattered data on air transportation are available for years before 1926. Regular collection of national statistics began with the establishment in that year of an Aeronautics Branch in the Department of Commerce. In 1934 a Bureau of Air Commerce was organized in that department. The Civil Aeronautics Act of 1938 created the Civil Aeronautics Authority, an independent regulatory agency, which was reorganized in 1940 into 2 separate entities, the Civil Aeronautics Board and the Civil Aeronautics Administration. In 1958, the latter's functions were transferred to the Federal Aviation Agency, which in turn was made a part of the Department of Transportation in 1966 and renamed the Federal Aviation Administration (FAA). The FAA's annual *Statistical Handbook of Civil Aviation* is the source for the statistics presented here.

Federal promotion and regulation of civil aviation are carried out by the Civil Aeronautics Board and the Federal Aviation Administration. The Board issues certificates permitting persons to engage in air transportation as a business, fixes air mail rates which they may charge, and may establish maximum and minimum rates for transportation of passengers and goods. The responsibility for investigation of aviation accidents, formerly held by the Civil Aeronautics Board, now (1975) resides with the National Transportation Safety Board of the Department of Transportation.

The principal activities of the Federal Aviation Administration are: Controlling the use of navigable airspace; prescribing regulations dealing with the competence of airmen, airworthiness of aircraft, and aircraft control; operation of air route traffic control centers, airport traffic control towers, and flight service stations; the design, construction, maintenance, and inspection of navigation, traffic control, and communications equipment for the airways; and promotion of air safety.

These agencies publish annual operational data on the use of airway facilities; data related to the location of airmen, aircraft, and airports; the activity volume in the field of non-air carrier (general aviation) flying; and aircraft production and registration.

Statistics of domestic scheduled airline operations cover trunk airlines, local service airlines, helicopter carriers, and territorial airlines except those operating in Alaska. Scheduled intrastate airlines are not included anywhere, nor are those operating locally in Alaska. Statistics of international scheduled airline operations include not only operations to and from foreign countries but overseas operations to American possessions. They also include the service of Northwest Airlines and Pan American World Airways between the United States and Alaska. Some companies operate in both the domestic and the international fields, but the statistics are segregated.

Operations of scheduled carriers of cargo only are generally not included.

Q 565–576. Aircraft production and exports, 1913–1970.

Source: U.S. Federal Aviation Administration, *FAA Statistical Handbook of Aviation*, various annual issues (including, in some cases, subsequent revisions).

There is no aircraft production in Alaska or Hawaii.

Q 577–590. Scheduled air transportation, domestic and international, 1926–1970.

Source: See source for series Q 565–576.

The term *certificated route air carrier* refers to air carriers holding certificates of public convenience and necessity, issued by the Civil Aeronautics Board, authorizing the performance of scheduled air transportation over specified routes and a limited amount of non-scheduled operations. Certificated route air carriers are often referred to as "scheduled airlines," although they also perform non-scheduled service. *Nonscheduled service* comprises revenue flights that are not operated in regular scheduled service, such as charter flights, and all nonrevenue flights incident to such flights. *Scheduled service* is transport service operated over an air carrier's certificated routes, based on published flight schedules, including extra sections and related nonrevenue flights.

For series Q 579, the figures are for "route mileage operated" from the beginning of the series through 1961. Thereafter, they represent the total route miles for passenger/cargo and all-cargo carriers, reported separately in the source.

Series Q 589, average available seats, was derived by dividing passenger seat-miles by revenue miles flown in passenger service.

Q 591–603. Scheduled airline revenues and expenses, 1938–1970.

Source: See source for series Q 565–576.

Q 604–623. Airports, aircraft, pilots, and miles flown, 1926–1970.

Source: See source for series Q 565–576.

Figures for airports and landing fields, series Q 604–605, include civil, military, and FAA (formerly CAA) fields but exclude seaplane facilities prior to 1953. Growth of airports after 1940 was stimulated by Federal defense expenditures during World War II and by the Federal-aid airport program thereafter.

Estimates of the number of certificated pilots, series Q 607–610, refer to persons certificated by FAA in the various classifications. Some may not have been actively engaged in the classification for which they were certificated. The count of certificated pilots after 1941 is not directly comparable with the previous years as the Civil Aeronautics Regulations were amended to permit pilot certificates currently effective on April 1, 1942, to continue in effect indefinitely. This amendment expired on July 1, 1947. The number of commercial pilots, series Q 609, rose sharply after 1944 because the CAA awarded many veterans commercial certificates on the basis of their military flying experience. The number of private pilots, series Q 610, increased sharply after 1939 because of the federally subsidized civilian pilot training program which was initiated in 1939. It gave preliminary training to hundreds of thousands of men who went into the military service. Miles flown, series Q 614–618, includes business flying (by corporate executives or employees or by individuals, including farmers, on personal business), commercial flying (contract, charter, crop-dusting, photographic, etc.), instructional flying, pleasure flying, and other flying (testing, experimental, ferrying, Civil Air Patrol, etc.). Separate data on these five categories are given in the source.

Q 624–637. Air transportation accidents, 1927–1970.

Source: 1927–1962, see source for series Q 565–576; 1963–1970, U.S. Civil Aeronautics Board, *Handbook of Airline Statistics, 1971*.

An aircraft accident is considered to be any occurrence, while the aircraft is operating as such, which results in fatal or serious injury to persons or appreciable damage to the aircraft. The aircraft is considered to be "operating as such" from the time the engine is started for purposes of flight until the flight is completed; in the case of gliders, while they are under tow or gliding.

Propeller accidents to persons are included. A collision between two or more aircraft is counted as one accident.

Data include military contract operations for 1956–1970 but not for earlier years. Scheduled cargo carriers are included for 1949–1970, but not for earlier years.

Series Q 565–576. Aircraft Production and Exports: 1913 to 1970

Year	Number of aircraft produced									Exports [2]		
	Total	For U.S. Military	Civil						Value of all products [1] ($1,000)	Aircraft exported [3]		Value of all exports [4] ($1,000)
			Total	Transports	General aviation			Rotor-craft		Number	Value ($1,000)	
					Total	Single-engine	Multi-engine					
	565	566	567	568	569	570	571	572	573	574	575	576
1970			8,190	313	7,381	6,029	1,352	496	13,466,000	2,383	1,316,041	2,769,345
1969			13,600	509	12,581	10,193	2,388	510	12,764,000	3,322	1,235,336	2,848,745
1968			14,969	702	13,749	11,479	2,270	518	13,850,000	3,682	1,403,930	2,817,654
1967			14,479	500	13,536	11,530	2,006	443	11,894,000	3,881	787,682	1,924,976
1966			16,397	322	15,723	13,226	2,497	352	8,725,000	3,611	553,908	1,393,422
1965			12,646	221	12,053	10,023	2,030	372	7,057,000	3,129	482,236	1,802,098
1964			10,067	158	9,459	7,812	1,647	450	6,431,000	2,577	287,345	1,212,442
1963			8,121	80	7,628	6,317	1,311	413	5,617,000	2,251	244,101	1,241,132
1962			7,249	146	6,797	5,765	1,032	306	5,900,000	2,131	323,340	1,435,477
1961	9,053	1,639	7,414	180	6,943	5,980	963	291	5,842,000	2,459	334,790	1,233,863
1960	10,324	2,143	8,181	238	7,726	6,438	1,288	217	6,429,000	2,336	537,133	1,329,494
1959	11,227	2,985	8,242	262	7,802	6,785	1,017	178	7,134,000	1,628	152,984	769,130
1958	11,117	4,235	6,882	218	6,478	5,609	869	186	(5)	1,689	204,051	971,541
1957	12,419	5,614	6,805	322	6,173	5,250	923	310	(5)	2,025	248,943	1,028,729
1956	13,307	6,102	7,205	205	6,765	5,715	1,050	235	(5)	1,711	171,097	1,064,888
1955	12,852	8,032	4,820	113	4,563	3,755	808	144	(5)	1,714	129,924	727,549
1954	12,129	8,740	3,389	191	3,072	2,717	355	126	(5)	1,053	102,736	(NA)
1953	14,760	10,626	4,134	213	3,811	3,681	130	110	(5)	1,377	91,003	(NA)
1952	12,811	9,302	3,509	194	3,247	3,137	110	68	(5)	1,180	26,620	(NA)
1951	7,923	5,446	2,477	74	2,386	2,337	49	17	(5)	894	18,606	(NA)
1950	6,293	2,773	3,520	129	3,391	-----	-----	-----	(5)	756	44,287	(NA)
1949	6,137	2,592	3,545	166	3,379	-----	-----	-----	(5)	881	27,165	(NA)
1948	9,838	2,536	7,302	263	7,039	-----	-----	-----	(5)	2,259	66,354	153,629
1947	17,739	2,122	15,617	278	15,339	-----	-----	-----	(5)	3,125	74,477	172,190
1946	36,418	1,417	35,001	433	34,568	-----	-----	-----	(5)	2,302	65,258	115,320
1945	48,912	46,865	2,047	-----	-----	-----	-----	-----	[6]8,279,000	7,599	663,129	1,148,852
1944	95,272	95,272	–	-----	-----	-----	-----	-----	[6]16,047,000	16,544	1,589,801	2,825,927
1943	85,433	85,433	–	-----	-----	-----	-----	-----	[6]12,514,000	13,865	1,215,848	2,142,611
1942	47,675	47,675	–	-----	-----	-----	-----	-----	[6]5,817,000	10,448	879,995	1,357,345
1941	26,289	19,445	[7]6,844	-----	-----	-----	-----	-----	[6]1,804,000	6,001	422,764	626,929
1940	12,813	6,028	[7]6,785	-----	-----	-----	-----	-----	[6]370,000	3,522	196,261	311,871
1939	5,856	2,195	3,661						247,905	1,220	67,113	117,807
1938	3,623	1,800	1,823						198,293	875	37,977	68,228
1937	3,773	949	2,824						114,093	628	21,076	39,404
1936	3,010	1,141	1,869						78,149	527	11,601	23,143
1935	1,710	459	1,251						42,506	333	6,599	14,291
1934	1,615	437	1,178						43,892	490	8,195	17,663
1933	1,324	466	858						33,357	406	5,391	9,180
1932	1,396	593	803						34,861	280	4,359	7,947
1931	2,800	812	1,988						48,540	140	1,813	4,868
1930	3,437	747	2,690						60,846	321	4,820	8,818
1929	6,193	677	5,516						91,051	348	5,485	9,125
1928	4,346	1,219	3,127						64,662	162	1,760	3,665
1927	1,995	621	1,374						30,897	63	849	1,904
1926	1,186	532	654						17,695	50	303	1,027
1925	789	447	342						12,775	80	511	784
1924	377	317	60						(NA)	59	413	798
1923	743	687	56						13,142	48	309	434
1922	263	226	37						(NA)	37	157	495
1921	437	389	48						7,431	48	315	473
1920	328	256	72						(NA)	65	598	1,153
1919	780	682	98						14,373	85	778	13,167
1918	14,020	13,991	29						(NA)	20	206	9,084
1917	2,148	2,013	135						(NA)	135	1,002	4,135
1916	411	142	269						(NA)	269	2,158	7,002
1915	178	26	152						(NA)	152	958	1,541
1914	49	15	34						790	34	189	226
1913	43	14	29						-----	29	82	108

– Represents zero.   NA Not available.

[1] Value of aircraft, engines, parts, parachutes, etc. For 1959–1970, represents net sales value of "complete aircraft and parts" plus "aircraft engines and parts."
[2] 1913–1918, fiscal years; 1919–1957, calendar years. Data for the second half of 1918 are included with calendar year 1919.
[3] Exclusive of gliders and barrage balloons. 1949–1954, civil aircraft only.
[4] Total value of aircraft, engines, parts, etc. Prior to 1922, engine values were not reported separately but were probably included with either "other" internal combustion engines or with "parts" of aircraft. Values for parachutes and their parts have been included only since 1932.

[5] Comparable data not available.
[6] Values are for military aircraft produced in the United States only. These data were computed by the War Production Board in terms of August 1943 unit cost. The values are not meant to measure output at current prices or expenditures. The 1940 figure is only for the second half of that year; the 1945 figure covers only the first 8 months.
[7] Represents domestic civil only; data on new aircraft produced for export not available.

Series Q 577–590. Scheduled Air Transportation, Domestic and International: 1926 to 1970

[As of December 31 or for years ending December 31. All data reflect scheduled operations exclusively. Domestic data include intra-Alaska carriers beginning 1941 for series Q 586 and Q 587; 1948 for series Q 580 and Q 585; 1949 for series Q 582; and 1961 for series Q 581]

Year	Number of operators	Aircraft in service [1]	Route mileage in operation	Average passenger-revenue per passenger-mile	Persons employed	Revenue miles flown (1,000)	Revenue passengers carried Duplicated [2] (1,000)	Revenue passengers carried Unduplicated [3] (1,000)	Revenue passenger-miles flown (millions)	Ton-miles flown Express and freight (1,000)	Ton-miles flown Mail (1,000)	Fuel consumed, gasoline (mil. gal.)	Average available seats	Average speed (m.p.h.)
	577	578	579	580	581	582	583	584	585	586	587	588	589	590
DOMESTIC														
1970	33	2,437	171,615	$0.0587	242,206	2,013,484	--------	153,408	104,156	1,966,009	705,711	--------	110.4	350
1969	33	2,423	150,431	.0590	255,386	2,000,269	--------	158,405	102,717	1,916,472	801,416	27	109.8	394
1968	38	2,317	125,581	.0561	244,742	1,715,857	--------	145,774	87,508	1,578,992	564,084	113	100.8	373
1967	39	2,194	119,768	.0564	223,380	1,462,240	--------	128,479	75,487	1,314,409	405,352	223	94.4	354
1966	40	2,027	111,488	.0583	196,298	1,178,458	--------	105,789	60,591	1,108,691	291,277	332	91.2	320
1965	40	1,896	114,110	.0606	169,952	1,088,112	--------	92,073	51,887	943,128	225,992	448	89.2	314
1964	40	1,863	115,147	.0612	153,243	957,575	--------	79,139	44,141	743,963	189,782	507	86.1	297
1963	40	1,832	114,089	.0617	143,112	888,793	--------	69,366	38,457	603,725	174,439	554	83.4	287
1962	40	1,831	112,944	.0644	138,673	827,694	--------	60,738	33,623	554,599	166,801	696	79.4	274
1961	41	1,867	102,309	.0628	136,987	795,165	--------	56,900	31,062	454,142	150,452	743	72.9	253
1960	42	1,594	101,414	.0609	133,717	820,756	--------	56,352	30,567	386,933	135,923	922	65.5	235
1959	39	1,596	95,063	.0588	132,042	841,925	--------	54,955	29,308	344,728	120,308	1,142	58.7	223
1958	39	1,546	89,569	.0564	119,746	784,200	--------	48,297	25,375	294,018	107,018	1,188	55.8	220
1957	40	1,494	88,325	.0531	119,333	791,265	--------	48,761	25,379	268,791	100,218	1,165	53.7	215
1956	40	1,347	84,189	.0533	103,489	694,050	--------	41,738	22,399	247,255	94,523	1,005	52.4	213
1955	42	1,212	78,992	.0536	95,548	627,336	--------	38,025	19,852	229,966	88,751	912	51.2	208
1954	43	1,175	78,294	.0541	84,765	556,880	--------	32,343	16,802	189,765	82,768	776	50.1	206
1953	44	1,139	78,384	.0546	84,651	525,374	--------	28,721	14,794	179,063	74,106	692	46.1	198
1952	46	1,078	77,894	.0557	79,687	465,477	--------	25,010	12,559	162,047	70,443	588	42.7	191
1951	49	981	78,913	.0561	72,898	411,878	--------	22,652	10,590	144,790	64,734	(NA)	39.6	185
1950	52	960	77,440	.0554	61,903	369,826	--------	17,345	8,007	152,223	47,740	418	37.5	180
1949	51	913	72,667	.0576	59,886	355,501	--------	15,081	6,752	123,603	41,889	375	35.0	179
1948	39	878	68,702	.0574	60,416	338,217	--------	13,168	5,976	102,360	38,198	332	32.4	172
1947	27	810	62,215	.0505	58,998	325,054	--------	12,890	6,105	64,637	33,086	294	30.0	168
1946	23	674	53,981	.0463	69,182	309,889	--------	12,213	5,945	38,590	32,969	236	25.3	160
1945	19	421	48,516	.0495	50,313	208,969	--------	6,576	3,360	22,175	65,103	135	19.7	155
1944	18	288	47,384	.0534	31,198	138,732	--------	4,046	2,177	16,974	51,146	90	19.1	156
1943	18	204	42,537	.0535	29,654	105,355	--------	3,020	1,632	15,618	36,067	65	18.3	--------
1942	19	186	41,596	.0527	26,910	111,341	--------	3,137	1,418	11,896	21,167	69	17.9	--------
1941	19	370	45,163	.0504	19,223	134,406	3,849	[4] 3,464	1,385	5,257	13,108	82	17.5	--------
1940	19	369	42,757	.0507	15,984	110,101	2,803	[4] 2,523	1,052	3,476	10,118	66	16.5	--------
1939	[5] 18	[5] 276	[5] 36,654	.0510	[5] 10,639	82,925	1,735	[4] 1,561	683	2,713	8,611	47	14.7	--------
1938	[6] 16	[6] 260	[6] 34,879	.0518	[6] 9,008	68,610	1,197	[4] 1,077	480	2,182	7,449	38	13.9	--------
1937	22	291	32,006	.056	7,586	66,791	985	[4] 887	412	2,162	6,698	34	12.5	--------
1936	24	280	29,797	.057	7,079	64,307	932	--------	[7] 439	1,866	5,741	31	10.7	--------
1935	26	363	29,190	.057	5,945	55,918	679	--------	[7] 316	1,098	4,133	27	10.3	--------
1934	24	423	28,609	.059	4,201	41,526	[8] 475	--------	[7] 190	[9] 597	[10] 2,237	19	8.9	--------
1933	25	418	28,283	.061	4,369	49,256	[8] 502	--------	[7] 175	[9] 423	[11] 2,568	22	7.6	--------
1932	32	456	28,956	.061	4,020	45,894	[8] 476	--------	[7] 127	[9] 290	[11] 2,701	20	6.6	--------
1931	39	490	30,857	.067	4,314	43,109	[8] 472	--------	[7] 107	[9] 221	[11] 3,140	16	--------	--------
1930	43	497	30,293	.083	2,778	32,645	[8] 385	--------		[7] 85	[9] 101	--------	12	--------	--------
1929	38	442	--------	.12	1,958	22,729	[8] 162	--------	--------	[9] 70	--------	6	--------	--------
1928	34	268	--------	.11	[12] 1,496	10,528	[8] 48	--------	--------	[9] 59	--------	2	--------	--------
1927	18	--------	--------	.106	--------	5,856	[8] 9	--------	--------	[9] 13	--------	1	--------	--------
1926	13	--------	--------	.12	--------	4,318	[8] 6	--------	--------	[9] 1	--------	1	--------	--------
INTERNATIONAL														
1970	3	--------	205,666	.0500	48,520	369,870	--------	16,260	27,563	942,008	548,845	--------	154.9	482
1969	3	--------	193,554	.0495	53,954	359,446	--------	13,493	22,703	936,554	463,099	92	121.9	477
1968	9	--------	163,534	.0495	50,283	408,136	--------	16,407	26,451	927,250	679,357	9	135.6	476
1967	10	--------	158,823	.0501	46,510	350,719	--------	14,020	23,259	796,964	560,402	18	132.2	482
1966	10	--------	156,745	.0516	42,398	285,711	--------	12,272	19,298	721,609	452,635	31	129.3	468
1965	10	--------	152,293	.0529	36,882	247,766	--------	10,847	16,789	597,324	254,093	41	129.1	451
1964	10	--------	154,096	.0545	34,695	214,375	--------	9,381	14,352	394,681	180,991	46	127.2	441
1963	10	--------	153,294	.0582	32,327	192,140	--------	8,037	11,905	296,404	181,257	61	124.8	423
1962	10	--------	153,219	.0587	30,400	171,500	--------	7,079	10,138	264,729	172,017	91	118.7	394
1961	11	--------	138,668	.0608	29,506	161,297	--------	6,112	8,769	217,164	144,804	128	108.7	357
1960	13	174	148,303	.0635	29,054	162,634	--------	5,904	8,306	191,585	103,335	205	89.9	307
1959	13	173	139,820	.0629	28,648	172,143	--------	5,341	7,064	159,349	81,997	333	67.5	263
1958	12	185	140,105	.0646	27,404	172,713	--------	4,773	6,124	133,958	75,635	330	64.4	258
1957	10	170	133,884	.0655	27,857	161,571	--------	4,552	5,882	128,239	66,894	325	61.4	253
1956	11	196	113,694	.0668	28,014	151,806	--------	3,949	5,226	115,172	64,355	275	59.0	249
1955	9	147	117,282	.0666	26,655	135,441	--------	3,416	4,499	96,378	61,233	258	56.4	244
1954	9	161	112,488	.0676	24,776	120,322	--------	2,875	3,810	86,840	43,554	205	56.7	242
1953	8	161	111,826	.0684	24,741	114,153	--------	2,699	3,451	79,579	31,630	189	52.3	230
1952	7	149	110,465	.0701	24,385	106,158	--------	2,365	3,065	75,706	28,201	182	49.1	227
1951	6	140	108,763	.0710	22,855	98,703	--------	2,042	2,614	71,665	27,089	(NA)	46.4	224

See footnotes at end of table.

Series Q 577–590. Scheduled Air Transportation, Domestic and International: 1926 to 1970—Con.

Year	Number of operators	Aircraft in service [1]	Route mileage	Average passenger-revenue per passenger-mile	Persons employed	Revenue miles flown (1,000)	Revenue passengers carried, unduplicated [3] (1,000)	Revenue passenger-miles flown (millions)	Ton-miles flown Express and freight (1,000)	Ton-miles flown Mail (1,000)	Fuel consumed, gasoline (mil. gal.)	Average available seats	Average speed (m.p.h.)
	577	578	579	580	581	582	584	585	586	587	588	589	590
INTERNATIONAL—Con.													
1950	6	160	106,401	.0728	20,883	94,626	1,675	2,214	60,588	26,228	154	41.0	218
1949	5	177	109,011	.0772	21,108	105,119	1,520	2,060	56,190	24,410	143	36.6	207
1948	5	175	105,853	.0801	24,192	98,053	1,373	1,894	45,603	20,664	123	35.1	199
1947	5	154	95,503	.0777	26,154	86,481	1,360	1,814	32,904	15,503	103	35.2	191
1946	5	147	66,419	.0831	27,372	59,376	1,041	1,104	15,096	8,165	60	27.2	166
1945	5	97	38,885	.0868	17,968	32,609	476	450	8,728	4,772	25	18.9	151
1944	4	70	29,708	.0783	11,409	22,273	341	312	6,215	2,630	16	18.5	149
1943	4	70	27,211	.0794	9,625	18,458	279	246	5,096	2,763	14	17.5	--------
1942	4	68	(NA)	.0886	12,803	18,681	269	237	--------	--------	17	17.7	--------
1941	3	83	(NA)	.0861	7,235	14,410	229	163	--------	--------	11	18.0	--------
1940	3	68	52,322	.0883	6,067	9,652	163	100	--------	--------	9	18.3	--------
1939	2	84	43,455	.0857	5,275	7,607	129	72	--------	--------	9	17.7	--------
1938	2	73	34,968	.0833	4,266	7,043	109	53	--------	--------	8	16.9	--------
1937	2	92	31,979	--------	4,000	7,909	[8] 112	[7] 54	--------	--------	7	--------	--------
1936	2	94	31,990	--------	2,916	6,904	[8] 88	[7] 42	--------	--------	7	--------	--------
1935	2	101	31,261	--------	2,407	7,950	[8] 111	[7] 46	--------	--------	6	--------	--------
1934	2	99	22,192	--------	2,276	7,539	[8] 97	[7] 37	--------	--------	6	--------	--------
1933	3	86	19,404	--------	1,926	5,857	[8] 74	[7] 25	--------	--------	4	--------	--------
1932	3	108	19,574	--------	1,590	5,278	[8] 72	[7] 21	--------	--------	4	--------	--------
1931	3	100	19,543	--------	1,353	4,537	[8] 59	[7] 14	--------	--------	3	--------	--------
1930	3	103	19,256	--------	697	4,301	[8] 33	[7] 19	--------	--------	2	--------	--------
1929	4	83	--------	--------	387	2,413	[8] 11	--------	--------	--------	1	--------	--------
1928	1	57	--------	--------	[13]	146	[8] 1	--------	--------	--------	--------	--------	--------
1927	1	--------	--------	--------	--------	14	--------	--------	--------	--------	--------	--------	--------
1926	--------	--------	--------	--------	--------	--------	--------	--------	--------	--------	--------	--------	--------

NA Not available.
[1] Figures for 1961–1970 for domestic airlines are for total aircraft in service, domestic and international.
[2] Duplication exists where (a) the same passengers were carried on more than 1 route of an air carrier; and (b) where the same passengers were carried by more than 1 air carrier.
[3] Duplication has been eliminated where the same passengers were carried on more than 1 route of an air carrier, but still exists where the same passengers were carried by more than 1 air carrier.
[4] Computed by CAA from reports of duplicated revenue passengers.

[5] Excludes Marine Airlines.
[6] Excludes Colonial and Marine Airlines.
[7] Includes nonrevenue passenger-miles flown.
[8] Includes nonrevenue passengers.
[9] Excludes Colonial Airlines, Inc., and Hawaiian Airlines, Ltd.
[10] Excludes 224,236 ton-miles flown by U.S. Army.
[11] Excludes Colonial Airlines, Inc.
[12] Includes employees of Pan American Airways.
[13] Included with domestic air transportation.

Series Q 591–603. Scheduled Airline Revenues and Expenses: 1938 to 1970

[In thousands of dollars]

Year	Operating revenues Total	Passenger	Mail (including subsidy)	Express and freight	Excess baggage	Other	Operating expenses Total	Aircraft Total	Flying	Direct maintenance flight equipment	Depreciation flight equipment	Ground and indirect expense	Net operating income or loss [1]
	591	592	593	594	595	596	597	598	599	600	601	602	603
DOMESTIC													
1970	7,180,121	6,246,416	206,679	498,322	12,134	216,570	7,180,938	4,005,322	2,119,362	1,135,808	750,152	3,175,616	−817
1969	6,935,606	5,943,446	224,120	462,139	11,699	294,202	6,613,425	3,702,356	1,947,738	1,057,917	696,701	2,911,069	322,181
1968	5,607,054	4,911,881	185,654	343,392	8,943	157,184	5,297,594	2,948,964	1,505,477	911,297	532,190	2,348,630	309,460
1967	4,886,572	4,260,000	170,180	287,254	7,236	161,902	4,475,594	2,501,951	1,229,479	831,715	440,757	1,973,643	411,152
1966 [2]	4,070,323	3,534,335	161,796	251,344	5,954	116,894	3,589,659	2,007,928	974,179	680,413	353,336	1,581,731	480,664
1965	3,608,506	3,142,048	157,525	219,612	12,041	77,280	3,165,073	1,810,851	854,650	639,942	316,259	1,354,222	443,433
1964 [2]	3,094,628	2,701,111	149,122	181,396	16,674	46,325	2,777,925	1,614,993	755,846	580,092	279,055	1,162,932	316,703
1963 [2]	2,722,464	2,374,392	142,775	152,414	17,473	35,410	2,579,821	1,539,303	698,696	523,111	317,496	1,040,518	142,643
1962 [2]	2,497,900	2,167,476	139,451	135,947	19,661	35,366	2,407,935	1,448,288	659,136	496,408	292,744	959,646	89,965
1961 [2]	2,245,495	1,951,491	129,589	114,500	20,399	29,514	2,244,237	1,362,055	633,187	445,859	283,009	882,183	1,257
1960	2,129,311	1,860,369	113,123	102,766	21,365	31,688	2,091,423	1,043,016	600,840	257,788	184,388	1,048,407	37,888
1959	1,955,116	1,722,491	94,998	91,235	21,362	25,030	1,848,332	932,907	551,399	230,404	151,104	915,425	106,784
1958	1,636,231	1,432,207	81,814	77,622	19,490	25,098	1,538,700	786,406	474,654	186,690	125,062	752,294	97,531
1957	1,530,228	1,347,530	74,734	68,591	18,644	20,729	1,488,973	780,401	469,587	176,099	134,715	708,572	41,255
1956 [3]*	1,359,480	1,193,370	66,558	64,004	15,175	20,373	1,258,423	637,082	371,623	168,490	96,969	621,341	101,057
1955	[4]1,201,266	1,060,590	55,536	61,102	12,168	11,856	1,077,122	551,626	323,220	135,487	92,919	525,493	124,142
1954	[4]1,042,793	905,840	65,726	49,901	10,631	10,680	[4]941,582	487,376	279,971	110,299	97,106	454,200	101,211
1953	[4]937,482	803,869	64,484	47,791	8,704	12,622	[4]850,448	438,088	253,091	102,401	82,596	412,356	87,032
1952	[4]817,680	695,456	58,887	42,828	7,348	13,152	[4]723,409	361,464	208,665	92,696	60,103	361,939	94,271
1951	[4]702,365	591,187	57,422	36,914	6,069	10,733	[4]595,363	287,942	173,023	71,687	43,232	307,421	107,001

See footnotes at end of table.

Series Q 591–603. Scheduled Airline Revenues and Expenses: 1938 to 1970—Con.

[In thousands of dollars]

Year	Operating revenues						Operating expenses						Net operating income or loss [1]
								Aircraft				Ground and indirect expense	
	Total	Passenger	Mail (including subsidy)	Express and freight	Excess baggage	Other	Total	Total	Flying	Direct maintenance flight equipment	Depreciation flight equipment		
	591	592	593	594	595	596	597	598	599	600	601	602	603
DOMESTIC—Con.													
1950	557,803	444,506	63,788	35,122	5,077	9,310	494,645	241,060	141,816	57,841	41,403	253,585	63,158
1949	486,034	388,931	59,333	27,987	4,452	5,331	461,733	223,193	127,398	54,028	41,767	238,540	24,301
1948	434,295	343,290	59,309	24,372	3,953	3,371	431,634	199,991	109,636	49,035	41,320	231,643	2,661
1947	364,840	308,576	29,445	19,378	3,572	3,869	386,199	169,165	88,840	42,903	37,422	217,034	−21,360
1946	316,233	275,594	20,982	13,620	2,993	3,044	322,219	129,250	70,410	33,273	25,567	192,969	−5,986
1945	214,743	166,520	33,694	10,835	2,298	1,397	180,626	69,223	43,421	16,393	9,409	111,403	34,117
1944	160,928	116,441	33,317	8,306	2,031	833	124,522	45,150	28,238	11,893	5,019	79,372	36,406
1943	123,105	87,481	24,213	8,382	1,720	1,309	95,563	34,613	20,739	9,132	4,742	60,950	27,542
1942	108,249	74,819	23,470	6,978	1,260	1,722	84,366	36,392	21,866	8,664	5,862	47,974	23,882
1941	97,311	69,791	22,696	2,919	766	1,139	89,919	44,932	27,392	9,789	7,751	44,987	7,392
1940	76,864	53,308	20,090	2,078	551	837	[5] 70,897	35,179	22,093	7,496	5,590	35,028	5,967
1939	55,948	34,844	18,482	1,619	346	657	[5] 51,392	26,294	15,809	5,651	4,834	24,692	4,556
1938	42,845	24,861	15,798	1,278	283	625	[6] 43,865	24,987	14,737	5,345	4,905	18,878	−1,020
INTERNATIONAL													
1970	1,913,592	1,380,388	110,197	197,031	15,109	210,867	1,894,391	944,148	515,182	241,077	187,889	950,243	19,201
1969	1,689,387	1,176,349	99,041	185,502	14,232	214,263	1,638,275	832,503	456,431	219,053	157,019	805,772	51,112
1968	1,958,327	1,309,173	135,904	185,856	15,823	311,571	1,746,831	920,029	495,035	244,024	180,970	826,802	211,496
1967 [2]	1,769,682	1,165,862	145,051	163,558	13,419	281,792	1,496,540	792,026	424,135	211,874	156,017	704,514	273,142
1966 [2]	1,474,480	995,185	131,804	149,529	14,092	183,865	1,220,894	634,423	329,427	181,475	123,521	586,471	253,586
1965 [2]	1,199,403	887,335	82,158	131,119	13,481	85,310	1,001,362	508,710	262,597	146,043	100,070	492,651	198,041
1964 [2]	1,027,916	781,649	71,321	100,296	11,149	63,501	896,187	471,764	238,427	145,186	88,151	424,423	131,729
1963 [2]	920,303	692,801	73,989	80,378	11,665	61,470	799,462	430,073	216,834	117,729	95,510	369,389	120,841
1962 [2]	810,446	595,221	70,368	71,252	10,334	63,269	723,853	398,381	193,422	113,602	91,357	325,472	86,593
1961 [2]	722,390	533,159	59,527	63,265	9,570	56,869	698,685	400,537	186,561	109,493	104,483	298,148	23,706
1960	684,672	527,568	47,544	58,802	10,136	40,622	639,477	303,953	179,712	58,392	65,849	335,524	45,195
1959	592,226	444,618	40,469	51,877	8,845	46,417	573,653	281,988	170,391	57,522	54,075	291,665	18,573
1958	530,881	395,604	37,962	45,420	8,963	42,932	519,604	259,825	163,516	47,859	48,450	259,779	11,277
1957	508,827	385,183	32,895	42,879	9,228	38,642	480,495	241,820	150,763	44,828	46,229	238,675	28,332
1956 [3]	471,160	349,019	39,320	38,292	8,271	36,258	436,257	211,783	132,529	47,634	31,620	224,474	34,903
1955	385,157	295,442	27,221	32,013	7,385	23,093	366,562	171,427	108,954	34,867	27,606	195,135	18,597
1954 [7]	359,491	254,653	49,191	29,784	6,997	18,866	333,337	157,728	99,044	30,856	27,828	175,610	26,155
1953	[4] 337,711	232,867	53,746	27,385	5,248	18,454	318,489	151,308	91,751	32,827	26,730	167,178	19,221
1952	[4] 315,141	212,581	51,532	26,910	4,822	19,290	304,423	146,965	87,442	33,043	26,480	157,456	10,718
1951	287,936	184,692	53,213	25,245	3,809	20,977	269,865	129,221	75,102	29,856	24,263	140,644	18,071
1950	260,131	160,672	55,689	21,664	3,244	18,862	248,323	122,776	70,980	26,158	25,638	125,547	11,808
1949	274,155	158,480	75,197	22,127	4,178	14,173	252,863	122,334	72,347	26,311	23,676	130,529	21,291
1948	249,234	151,338	57,331	20,809	4,135	15,621	235,287	110,993	67,163	24,241	19,589	124,294	13,947
1947	209,009	140,652	32,300	17,526	4,388	14,143	209,294	93,766	53,189	21,997	18,580	115,528	−284
1946	146,754	91,417	25,061	11,413	3,296	15,567	139,843	52,045	32,027	11,064	8,954	87,798	6,911
1945	69,111	38,859	12,246	7,315	1,571	9,120	61,765	22,918	15,297	5,199	2,422	38,847	7,346
1944	38,882	24,287	2,889	5,405	1,066	5,235	39,227	13,353	8,471	3,030	1,852	25,874	−344
1943	32,839	19,334	3,624	4,401	803	4,677	32,079	11,992	8,074	2,174	1,744	20,087	760
1942	40,870	20,971	9,039	4,319	936	5,605	35,223	----	----	----	----	----	5,647
1941	37,990	14,021	15,473	1,475	382	6,639	35,309	----	----	----	----	----	2,681
1940	26,922	8,812	13,439	893	306	3,472	25,666	----	----	----	----	----	1,256
1939	19,653	6,156	11,066	613	237	1,581	18,201	----	----	----	----	----	1,452
1938	15,153	4,435	8,599	562	219	1,338	14,303	----	----	----	----	----	850

* Denotes first year for which figures include Intra-Alaskan and Intra-Hawaiian carriers.

[1] Minus sign denotes loss.

[2] Items of aircraft operating expense are not comparable with prior years and include items of ground and indirect expenses as follows: (a) direct maintenance flight equipment (series Q600) also includes direct maintenance ground equipment, and indirect maintenance; (b) depreciation flight equipment (series Q 601) also includes other depreciation and amortization expenses; (c) ground and indirect expense (series Q 602) includes only those expenses chargeable to general services and administration.

[3] Operating expenses for 1956 are not directly comparable with those for subsequent years because of the revision in the *Uniform System of Accounts and Reports* put into effect on January 1, 1957. The time period covered and the number of air carriers involved precluded a full conversion to the new reporting system, and only limited adjustments in data for 1956 were made by CAB.

[4] Sum of the items does not agree with total due to rounding procedure.

[5] Includes total operating expenses for Colonial Airlines, Inc., for which distribution by type of expense was not available.

[6] Excludes Colonial Airlines, Inc.

[7] Excludes Midet Aviation Corporation due to inadequacies in reporting.

Series Q 604–623.   Airports, Aircraft, Pilots, and Miles Flown: 1926 to 1970

[As of December 31 or for years ending December 31, except as noted.   Includes Alaska, Hawaii, and outlying areas for all years]

Year	Airports and landing fields [1]		Total civil aircraft [2]	Certificated airplane pilots [3]				Federal aid to airports, cumulative since 1947 (mil. dol.)		
	Total	Lighted		Total	Airline transport	Commercial	Private	Total funds	Federal funds	Sponsor funds
	604	605	606	607	608	609	610	611	612	613
1970	11,261	3,554	154,450	732,729	34,430	186,821	303,779	2,453	1,199	1,254
1969	11,050	3,430	190,749	720,028	31,442	176,585	299,491	2,447	1,198	1,249
1968	10,470	3,312	179,285	691,695	28,607	164,458	281,728	2,362	1,165	1,197
1967	10,126	3,149	166,598	617,931	25,817	150,135	253,312	2,193	1,090	1,103
1966	9,673	2,988	155,132	548,757	23,917	131,539	222,427	2,052	1,018	1,034
1965	9,566	2,878	142,078	479,770	22,440	116,665	196,393	1,887	935	952
1964	9,490	2,773	137,189	431,041	21,572	108,428	175,574	1,754	866	888
1963	8,814	2,672	129,975	378,700	20,269	96,341	152,209	1,624	799	825
1962	8,084	2,481	124,273	830,220	23,220	275,495	531,505	1,198	578	620
1961	7,715	2,299	117,904	804,707	22,042	268,707	513,958	1,183	571	613
1960	6,881	2,133	111,580	783,232	20,985	262,437	499,810	1,184	573	611
1959	6,426	1,943	105,309	758,368	19,364	255,377	483,627	1,047	509	538
1958	6,018	1,809	98,893	731,078	18,303	245,541	467,234	882	431	451
1957	6,412	1,713	93,189	702,519	16,900	237,149	448,470	782	385	397
1956	7,028	1,399	87,531	669,079	15,295	221,096	432,688	660	326	334
1955	6,839	1,247	85,320	643,201	13,700	211,142	418,359	460	224	236
1954	6,977	1,108	92,067	613,695	13,341	201,441	398,913	382	185	197
1953	[4] 6,760	[4] 1,050	91,102	585,974	12,757	195,363	377,854	388	193	195
1952	6,042	1,858	89,313	581,218	11,357	193,575	376,286	388	194	194
1951	6,237	(NA)	88,545	580,574	10,813	197,900	371,861	368	182	186
1950	6,403	1,670	92,809	(NA)	(NA)	(NA)	(NA)	342	165	177
1949	6,484	1,480	92,622	525,174	9,025	187,769	328,380	277	133	144
1948	6,414	1,521	95,997	[5] 491,306	[5] 7,762	[5] 176,845	[5] 306,699	216	103	112
1947	5,759	1,447	94,821	[6] 433,241	[6] 7,059	[6] 181,912	[6] 244,270	142	68	74
1946	4,490	1,019	81,002	400,061	7,654	203,251	189,156			
1945	4,026	1,007	37,789	296,895	5,815	162,873	128,207			
1944	3,427	964	27,919	183,383	3,046	68,449	111,888			
1943	2,769	859	27,180	173,206	2,315	63,940	106,951			
1942	2,809	700	27,170	166,626	2,177	55,760	108,689			
1941	2,484	662	26,013	129,947	1,587	34,578	93,782			
1940	2,331	776	17,928	69,829	1,431	18,791	49,607			
1939	2,280	735	13,772	33,706	1,197	11,677	20,832			
1938	2,374	719	11,159	22,983	1,159	7,839	13,985			
1937	2,299	720	10,836	17,681	1,064	6,411	10,206			
1936	2,342	705	9,229	15,952	842	7,288	7,822			
1935	2,368	698	9,072	14,805	736	7,362	6,707			
1934	2,297	664	8,322	13,949	676	7,484	5,789			
1933	2,188	626	9,284	13,960	554	7,635	5,771			
1932	2,117	701	10,324	18,594	[7] 330	7,967	10,297			
1931	2,093	680	10,780	17,739		8,513	9,226			
1930	1,782	640	9,818	15,280		7,847	7,433			
1929	1,550		9,922	10,430		6,165	4,265			
1928	1,364		5,104	4,887						
1927	1,036		2,740	1,572						
1926										

See footnotes at end of table.

Series Q 604–623. Airports, Aircraft, Pilots, and Miles Flown: 1926 to 1970—Con.

Year	Estimated miles flown in civil flying other than scheduled air carrier (millions)					Fuel consumed (general aviation) (mil. gal.)	Domestic air cargo, revenue ton-miles flown [10] (millions)			
	Total	Business [8]	Commercial [9]	Instructional	Personal and other		Total	Scheduled carriers	Nonscheduled carriers [11]	Supplemental carriers [12]
	614	615	616	617	618	619	620	621	622	623
1970	3,207	1,134	791	450	832	759	2,581	2,216	80	285
1969	3,926	1,426	723	910	867	690	2,769	2,126	365	278
1968	[13] 3,701	[13] 1,406	[13] 666	[13] 814	[13] 814	610	2,327	1,775	248	305
1967	[13] 3,440	[13] 1,431	[13] 569	[13] 713	[13] 727	541	2,168	1,498	406	264
1966	[13] 3,336	[13] 1,536	[13] 516	[13] 646	[13] 638	486	1,944	1,301	389	254
1965	[13] 2,562	[13] 1,204	[13] 461	[13] 359	[13] 538	378	1,661	1,112	330	220
1964	[13] 2,181	[13] 1,047	[13] 393	[13] 284	[13] 458	307	1,288	894	209	185
1963	[14] 2,049	[14] 983	[14] 369	[14] 266	[14] 430	[14] 285	1,095	715	210	171
1962	[15] 1,965	[15] 935	[15] 367	[15] 256	[15] 407	[15] 264	1,102	637	351	115
1961	[14] 1,858	[14] 888	[14] 333	[14] 203	[14] 434	[14] 257	829	533	182	114
1960	[14] 1,769	[14] 881	[14] 299	[14] 194	[14] 395	[14] 246	724	476	135	112
1959	[14] 1,716	[14] 858	[14] 292	[14] 223	[14] 343	[14] 221	651	450	138	63
1958	[14] 1,660	[14] 847	[14] 299	[14] 232	[14] 282	[14] 209	567	387	119	61
1957	1,426	721	249	202	254	213	554	396	111	47
1956	[14] 1,315	[14] 672	[14] 247	[14] 158	[14] 238	[14] 201	457	351	47	59
1955	[14] 1,216	[14] 628	[14] 246	[14] 121	[14] 222	[14] 193	379	319	20	41
1954	1,119	553	226	124	216	180	277	248	6	24
1953	1,045	499	210	121	216	172	281	254	10	18
1952	972	420	218	144	190	141	259	244	5	10
1951	975	380	190	190	190	215	261	217	26	18
1950	[14] 1,062	[14] 340	[14] 181	[14] 287	[14] 255	[14] 134	239	211	16	13
1949	1,129	309	166	379	275	135	153	134	5	13
1948	1,470	299	143	755	273	183	109	102	7	----------
1947	1,502	228	150	849	275	160	69	65	4	----------
1946	875	122	108	479	166	101	----------	----------	----------	----------
1942	294	30	47	188	29	26	----------	----------	----------	----------
1941	346	27	51	197	71	30	----------	----------	----------	----------
1940	264	26	32	126	80	23	----------	----------	----------	----------
1939	178	25	34	66	52	17	----------	----------	----------	----------
1938	129	19	25	46	39	10	----------	----------	----------	----------
1937	103	16	23	35	30	11	----------	----------	----------	----------
1936	93	12	25	30	27	11	----------	----------	----------	----------
1935	85	13	23	23	26	11	----------	----------	----------	----------
1934	76	12	21	17	26	10	----------	----------	----------	----------
1933	71	12	20	16	23	9	----------	----------	----------	----------
1932	78	12	22	18	26	11	----------	----------	----------	----------
1931	94	13	26	25	29	12	----------	----------	----------	----------
1930	108	----------	----------	----------	----------	14	----------	----------	----------	----------
1929	110	----------	----------	----------	----------	14	----------	----------	----------	----------
1928	60	----------	----------	----------	----------	8	----------	----------	----------	----------
1927	30	----------	----------	----------	----------	4	----------	----------	----------	----------
1926	19	----------	----------	----------	----------	2	----------	----------	----------	----------

NA Not available.
[1] Includes seaplane bases, heliports, and, beginning 1954, military fields having joint civil-military use. Prior to 1954, all military fields are included.
[2] 1946–1962 includes gliders. Beginning 1950, active and inactive aircraft.
[3] Beginning 1963, data are for active certified airplane pilots only. Also beginning 1963, total includes student, helicopter, glider, and other pilots, not shown separately.
[4] As of Mar. 1, 1954.
[5] As of May 1, 1949.
[6] As of Apr. 1, 1948.
[7] Airline transport rating became effective May 5, 1932.
[8] Corporation and individual business transportation, not for hire.

[9] Passenger and cargo transportation for hire, aerial application (crop dusting, spraying, seeding, etc.), patrol, survey, and other miscellaneous work use.
[10] Comprises express and freight ton-miles.
[11] Includes some military ton-miles and may include a small amount of international traffic.
[12] Civil and military.
[13] Estimated from information received on Aircraft Use and Inspection Reports.
[14] No survey was conducted. Data for 1958–61 have been revised using a correction factor based on the 1962 survey of aircraft use in general aviation. Data for 1963 are based on hours and use reported on aircraft inspection reports adjusted by the same correction factor.
[15] The 1962 general aviation survey excluded gliders, dirigibles, and balloons. These data have been adjusted to include them.

Series Q 624–637. Air Transportation Accidents: 1927 to 1970

Year	Domestic scheduled air carriers [1]					International scheduled air carriers [1]					Non-air-carrier flying operations			
	Total accidents	Number of fatal accidents	Total passenger-fatalities	Plane-miles flown per fatal accident (1,000)	Passenger-fatalities per 100 million passenger-miles flown [2]	Total accidents	Number of fatal accidents	Total passenger fatalities	Plane-miles flown per fatal accident (1,000)	Passenger-fatalities per 100 million passenger-miles flown	Total accidents	Fatal accidents	Fatalities	Miles flown per fatal accident (1,000)
	624	625	626	627	628	629	630	631	632	633	634	635	636	637
1970	31	1	—	[3]2,024,703	—	8	1	2	[3]390,630	(Z)	4,640	622	1,254	5,155
1969	37	7	132	[3]287,246	.1	11	—	—	(X)	(X)	4,767	647	1,495	6,068
1968	44	11	258	[3]157,037	(Z)	10	2	47	[3]209,282	.2	4,968	692	1,399	5,348
1967	43	8	226	[3]184,176	.3	8	—	—	(X)	(X)	6,115	603	1,228	5,972
1966	50	4	59	[3]297,369	.1	3	—	—	(X)	(X)	5,712	573	1,151	5,822
1965	55	6	205	[3]183,152	.4	8	1	21	[3]254,587	.1	5,196	538	1,029	4,762
1964	45	6	106	[3]161,371	.1	8	3	94	[3]73,635	.6	5,070	504	1,056	4,327
1963	39	4	48	[3]224,180	.1	10	1	73	[3]198,337	.6	4,690	482	893	4,250
1962	35	5	158	[3]166,660	.3	8	—	—	(X)	(X)	4,840	430	857	4,568
1961	56	5	124	[3]160,476	.4	[4]2	—	—	(X)	(X)	4,625	426	761	4,361
1960	62	[5]10	326	[3]82,948	.9	5	2	10	[3]84,246	.1	4,793	429	787	4,122
1959	61	9	209	[3]94,619	.7	6	1	59	[3]178,667	.8	4,576	450	823	3,813
1958	42	4	114	[3]198,553	.4	12	2	10	[3]89,387	.2	4,584	384	717	4,323
1957	44	4	32	208,014	.1	7	1	36	179,624	.6	4,200	438	800	3,256
1956	55	4	143	178,957	.6	3	—	—	(X)		3,474	356	669	3,693
1955	[6]45	8	156	80,042	.8	5	1	2	144,921	.04	3,343	384	619	3,166
1954	[7]49	4	16	141,123	.1	5	—	—	(X)	(X)	3,381	393	684	2,848
1953	37	5	86	107,331	.6	6	2	2	59,250	.1	3,232	387	635	2,701
1952	44	6	46	79,600	.4	11	3	94	36,275	3.0	3,657	401	691	2,424
1951	45	11	142	39,051	1.3	10	1	31	102,534	1.1	3,824	441	750	2,211
1950	39	4	96	96,123	1.1	6	2	48	47,956	2.1	4,505	499	871	2,127
1949	35	8	96	44,622	1.3	9	—	—	(X)	(X)	5,459	562	896	2,008
1948	56	5	83	67,889	1.3	12	2	44	50,144	1.0	7,850	850	1,384	1,728
1947	44	8	199	40,832	3.2	9	3	20	29,392	1.1	9,253	882	1,352	1,703
1946	33	9	75	34,633	1.2	14	3	40	30,355	3.5	7,618	690	1,009	1,267
1945	40	8	76	26,171	2.2	5	2	17	16,304	3.7	4,652	322	508	(NA)
1944	30	5	48	27,768	2.2	7	1	17	22,272	5.3	3,343	169	257	(NA)
1943	23	2	22	52,716	1.3	2	1	10	18,457	3.9	3,871	167	257	(NA)
1942	23	5	55	22,354	3.7	2	—	—	(X)	(X)	3,324	143	220	2,053
1941	27	4	35	33,729	2.3	5	1	2	14,410	1.2	4,252	217	312	1,595
1940	30	3	35	36,837	3.0	6	—	—	(X)	(X)	3,471	232	359	1,137
1939	28	2	9	41,616	1.2	6	1	10	7,042	12.8	2,222	203	315	876
1938	23	5	25	13,818	4.5	9	3	7	2,347	13.0	1,861	176	274	734
1937	42	5	40	13,358	8.3	8	1	11	7,909	13.9	1,900	184	280	560
1936	65	8	44	8,038	10.0	5	2	2	3,452	4.8	1,674	155	261	602
1935	58	8	15	6,989	4.7	4	—	—	(X)	(X)	1,503	161	253	526
1934	71	8	17	5,190	9.0	2	2	4	3,769	10.9	1,491	184	323	410
1933	100	9	8	5,472	4.6	1	—	—	(X)	(X)	1,589	177	299	402
1932	108	16	19	2,868	14.9	7	1	6	5,278	28.9	1,936	207	318	377
1931	118	13	25	3,316	23.4	8	1	1	4,537	7.1	2,197	251	398	375
1930	88	9	24	3,627	28.2	3	—	—	(X)	(X)	2,029	300	504	360
1929	124	21	14	1,082	-------						1,586	287	457	-------
1928	85	11	14	957	-------						1,036	215	362	-------
1927	25	4	1	1,464	-------						253	95	146	-------

− Represents zero.   X Not applicable.   Z Less than 1/10 of a person.
[1] Includes scheduled revenue operators only.
[2] Rates computed on basis of total passengers carried and passenger-miles flown, revenue and nonrevenue. Applies to passenger-carrying service only. Excludes passenger deaths occurring in dynamite/sabotage accidents; July 25, 1957, 1 passenger; Jan. 6, 1960, 29 passengers; May 22, 1962, 37 passengers; May 7, 1964, 41 passengers.
[3] Represents aircraft revenue-miles per fatal accident.
[4] Midair collision, nonfatal to air-carrier occupants.
[5] Includes 2 midair collisions nonfatal to air-carrier occupants.
[6] Excludes sabotage disaster at Longmont, Colo., on Nov. 1, 1955 in which 5 crew members and 39 passengers were fatally injured.
[7] Includes 1 ground collision between 2 air-carrier aircraft, 1 in scheduled passenger service and 1 in other revenue operations.

Chapter R

Communications

Telephone and Telegraph Systems (Series R 1-92)

R 1-92. General note.

Among the primary sources of governmental historical statistics relating to the telephone and telegraph industries are the following:

1. U.S. Bureau of the Census. *Compendium of the Seventh Census of the United States, 1850; Compendium of the Tenth Census of the United States, 1880; Statistics of Manufactures, 1890,* Census Bulletin No. 196, June 1892.

2. U.S. Bureau of the Census. Quinquennial censuses of the telephone and telegraph industry, 1902-1937: Bulletin No. 17, *Special Reports: Telephones and Telegraphs, 1902; Special Reports: Telephones, 1907;* Bulletin No. 102, *Telegraph Systems: 1907; Telephones and Telegraphs and Municipal Electric Fire-Alarm and Police-Patrol Signaling Systems, 1912; Census of Electrical Industries: 1917, Telegraphs and Municipal Electric Fire-Alarm and Police-Patrol Signaling Systems; Census of Electrical Industries: Telephones—1917, 1922, and 1927; Census of Electrical Industries: Telegraphs—1917, 1922, and 1927; Census of Electrical Industries: Telephones and Telegraphs, 1932 and 1937.* (Multiple year titles represent different volumes for each year.)

3. U.S. Interstate Commerce Commission. Reports of telephone and telegraph carriers, 1914-1933:

  a. *Memorandum Concerning Telephone Companies and Telegraph Companies Reporting to the Interstate Commerce Commission for the Years 1916 and 1917* (processed).

  b. *Annual Report on Telephone Companies, 1920-1927, 1928-1932,* and *1933* (processed); *Annual Report on Telegraph Companies, 1926-1927, 1928-1932,* and *1933* (processed).

4. U.S. Congress. *Report on Communication Companies* (Splawn Report), issued as House Report No. 1273, 73d Cong., 2d sess. (1934) in connection with the consideration of the Communications Act of 1934. This report contains detailed data from the carrier reports filed with the Interstate Commerce Commission and also the results of a questionnaire to the telephone, telegraph, and radio industries for 1922-1932.

5. U.S. Federal Communications Commission. Reports of telephone and telegraph companies filed monthly and annually with that agency, 1934-1970. Selected data from these reports have been issued either monthly or quarterly, and annually (in processed form), in the Commission's annual reports to Congress and beginning 1939, in the FCC's annual *Statistics of the Communications Industry in the United States.*

6. U.S. Federal Communications Commission, *Investigation of the Telephone Industry in the United States,* House Document No. 340, 76th Cong., 1st sess. (1939). This report includes the results of the Commission's investigation of the American Telephone and Telegraph Company (AT&T). Page 609 of the report refers to a number of staff reports, or exhibits, containing more detailed statistical and other material prepared in connection with the investigation and issued in processed form. These staff exhibits and reports are listed under the title, *Special Investigation Docket No. 1.*

7. Statistics for 1926-1934 obtained by the Federal Communications Commission from telephone and telegraph companies and designed to afford the FCC a basis for determining whether carrier rates were just and reasonable and in enforcement of other statutory responsibilities. (The text of the tele-

phone inquiry appears in "Telephone Division Order No. 9," FCC, *Reports,* vol. 1, p. 49; the text of the telegraph inquiry is in "Telegraph Division Order No. 12," FCC, *Reports,* vol. 1, p. 88. Responses are available to the public at the Commission.)

Other major sources of telephone and telegraph statistics are the annual reports to stockholders by AT&T (Bell), the Western Union Telegraph Company, and statistics of independent (i.e., non-Bell) telephone companies compiled and published by the United States Independent Telephone Association.

A major factor affecting the statistics of the telephone and telegraph carriers has been the prescription of uniform systems of accounts for these companies by the Interstate Commerce Commission and by the Federal Communications Commission after its formation in 1934. The ICC prescribed a uniform system of accounts for telephone companies having annual operating revenues exceeding $50,000, effective January 1, 1913, and for telegraph carriers, effective January 1, 1914. The ICC issued more detailed accounting systems, effective January 1, 1933, for Class A companies, and condensed classifications for Class B companies, effective January 1, 1934. The FCC adopted a revised uniform system of accounts for Class A and Class B telephone companies, effective January 1, 1937. The outstanding change was a requirement that telephone plant be recorded in the accounts at original cost, i.e., cost at time of first dedication to public use. The FCC adopted a revised uniform system of accounts for Class C telephone companies, effective January 1, 1939 (the earlier ICC system had been established, effective January 1, 1915). The FCC differentiates among Class A, B, and C companies on the basis of operating revenues, which have had varying limits over the years.

The reporting authority of the FCC relates only to telephone and telegraph carriers engaged in interstate and foreign communication which cross State or national boundary lines over their own facilities or through connection with facilities of an affiliated carrier having such facilities. Thus, carriers filing reports with the FCC (with the exception of a small number of companies filing voluntarily) exclude a large number of small, and a few large, telephone companies.

R 1-45. General note.

The Bell System provides the great bulk of local exchange and interexchange or toll telephone facilities and service in the United States. It includes the parent company of the Bell operating telephone companies, consolidated with "associated holding and operating companies in the United States, not including connected independent or sublicensee companies." The figures as presented are "statements of the Bell Telephone business as a whole, eliminating all duplications and showing the figures and results as 'if operated by a single company.'" The parent company has been American Telephone and Telegraph Company since January 1, 1900; prior to that date it was the American Bell Telephone Company. The number of companies included within the Bell group has varied from time to time. In 1914, approximately 35 companies were included and in 1915-1916 the number increased to 39. Subsequent consolidations reduced the number to 29 in 1920 and to 25, including Cincinnati Bell, Inc., and Southern New England Telephone Company in 1970. Since 1936, however, AT&T in its consolidated financial statements has excluded these 2 large noncontrolled companies. For comparability with previous years, however, the figures have been adjusted to include these 2 companies using reports filed by them with the FCC. "Bell companies" and "Bell System" are at times used interchangeably herein. Unless otherwise specified, the reference is to "Bell System."

Included in the Bell organization in 1970 were the following:

1. AT&T, which is the parent company.

2. 21 regional subsidiaries owned and controlled by AT&T, plus a subsidiary of one of these regional companies. These 22 Bell System principal telephone subsidiaries furnish exchange and intrastate toll service, as well as interstate toll telephone service; they constitute, with the parent, the Bell System of 1970.

3. Two other major companies, Cincinnati Bell, Inc. and Southern New England Telephone Company, in which AT&T has substantial minority interests. These 2 companies, together with the 22 above, are referred to as the Associated Companies.

4. Bell Telephone Laboratories, Inc., a scientific research and development organization, and Western Electric Company, Inc., which is the Bell manufacturing and supply organization.

In addition, a number of Bell Company affiliates have varying degrees of stock interest in various other telephone companies. Data for series R 1–30 relating to the Bell companies exclude operations of Bell Telephone Laboratories and of Western Electric, except as their operations affect operating expenses and miscellaneous income of the Bell companies. Bell Telephone Laboratories operates on a nonprofit basis and the profits of Western Electric on sales to the Bell companies are not eliminated in the consolidated statements.

The historical growth of the Western Electric Company is described in the FCC *Report . . . on the Investigation of the Telephone Industry . . .* , pp. 56–64. More recent data appear in the "Report on Preliminary Survey and Investigation of Western Electric Company, Inc.," prepared by a committee of National Association of Railroad and Utilities Commissioners and FCC representatives (July 15, 1948, processed), and in annual supplements since 1948. In 1970, AT&T's annual share of the net income of Western Electric was over $253 million.

Independent companies are referred to as non-Bell companies, although AT&T or Bell companies have financial interests in some of them. The independents participate with Bell in providing toll service, and have contractual arrangements with AT&T and the Bell Associated companies.

R 1 and R 3–8. Total telephones, Bell System telephones, and telephones of independent companies, 1876–1970.

Source: U.S. Federal Communications Commission, unpublished data; American Telephone and Telegraph Company, unpublished data; and the following U.S. Bureau of the Census reports: *Telephones and Telegraphs, 1902*, table 2, for total telephones in 1880, 1890; table 4, for total telephones in 1902; table 6, for Bell System telephones in 1902; *Telephones, 1907*, table 51, for total telephones in 1907; table 54, for Bell System telephones; *Telephones and Telegraphs . . . , 1912*, table 1, for total telephones and Bell System telephones in 1912; p. 37 for telephones connecting with the Bell System; *Telephones and Telegraphs, 1932*, table A for total telephones in 1917, 1922, 1927, and 1932; table 12, for Bell System telephones in 1922, 1927, and 1932; *Telephones and Telegraphs, 1937*, table 1, for total telephones and Bell System telephones in 1937.

The data for 1876–1934 (except census data) were taken from FCC records consisting of *Special Investigation Docket No. 1*, "Report on Control of Telephone Communications," vol. III, Exhibit 2096-D, p. 11 (June 15, 1937, processed), and "Report on American Telephone and Telegraph Company Corporate and Financial History," vol. I, Exhibit 1360-A, pp. 115 and 150. The data for 1935–1956 were supplied to FCC by AT&T; substantially the same data are also available in the AT&T annual reports to stockholders. The data for 1957–1970 were supplied by AT&T, compiled from annual reports and unpublished data.

The number of telephones comprises the total number of instruments and extensions in the system. Telephones also include tele-

graph and teletypewriter stations through 1930 and private line telephones through 1934, but not thereafter. Lines, basically for internal use, on which outside calls to public phones cannot be placed constitute private line telephones.

The households with telephones are based on census figures, utilized by AT&T in conjunction with the number of telephones in residences.

R 2. Telephones per 1,000 population, 1876–1970.

Source: 1876–1956, U.S. Federal Communications Commission, unpublished data (except for census data). For census data and 1957–1970, see source for series R 1 and R 3–8.

Annual figures are based on data supplied to FCC by AT&T.

R 9–12. Average daily conversations, 1880–1970.

Source: U.S. Federal Communications Commission, unpublished data. Figures are based on data supplied to FCC by AT&T.

Generally, exchange service is telephone service within an exchange area. A local call is defined as a call originating in and completed within the same public exchange area; a toll call is one which originates in one exchange destined to another exchange area, whether located nearby or across the continent. In instances in which there is a high community of interest between exchanges, accompanied by considerable calling on a message toll basis, "extended area service" has been established under which adjacent and nearby exchanges are included in the subscriber's local service area. The growth of this type of service each year has significantly affected the number of calls classified as local, which otherwise would have been classified and charged as toll. Moreover, elimination of toll charges through the establishment of extended area service has tended to stimulate telephone usage within the service area.

Conversations are those completed calls originating from company and service telephones, excluding private line telephones. Local calls include both completed and uncompleted calls. Bell System toll messages consist of interstate and intrastate completed calls originated or terminated at Bell System Associated Company telephones, and toll messages originated or terminated at connecting (i.e., independent) company telephones, provided their transmission utilized toll line facilities of a Bell operating company. Toll messages handled wholly over facilities of connecting or nonconnecting independent companies are shown under Independent Companies. Toll message figures include ship-to-shore messages and international messages. Since a toll ticket is made for each toll call, the count can be relatively exact. In very large exchanges, some counts of local calls are automatically accumulated in message registers but in small exchanges the counts are estimates based upon samples.

R 13–16. Telephone toll rates between New York City and selected cities, 1902–1970.

Source: 1902, U.S. Bureau of the Census, *Special Reports: Telephones and Telegraphs, 1902*, p. 77; 1911–1970, U.S. Federal Communications Commission, unpublished data.

Data for 1911–1917 are based on records of AT&T, newspapers, and other published reports. Data for 1919–1937 are based on information in FCC, Telephone Rate and Research Department, "The Classified Toll Rate Structure and Basic Rate Practices for Message Toll Telephone Service," pp. 40–47 (Jan. 15, 1938, processed). Data for 1940–1970 are based on unpublished data and tariffs of the FCC. Considerable historical toll rate data also appear in the report of a committee of National Association of Railroad and Utilities Commissioners (NARUC) and FCC representatives, *Message Toll Telephone Rates and Disparities*, annual October issues.

The three major classes of toll telephone messages are dial station-to-station, operator station-to-station, and person-to-person. Dial station-to-station service denotes that service where the person originating the call from other than a coin telephone station dials the telephone number desired and the call is completed without the assistance of a telephone company operator.

In interstate toll service, operator station rates are over 10 percent higher than dial station rates, and person-to-person rates are over twice the amount of the rates for dial station service. On station calls, the starting point is computed at the time communication is established between the calling and called stations; on person-to-person calls, the chargeable period begins when the person called is reached. There was generally no rate differentiation between station and person service until January 21, 1919.

A paucity of historical data exists with respect to local exchange rates. Such data can only be laboriously constructed from the records of the Bell System companies and other telephone companies or from the tariffs filed with each State which has regulatory authority over the intrastate telephone rates. One source of data pertaining to exchange rates is the Bureau of Census report, *Telephones and Telegraphs and Municipal Electric Fire-Alarm and Police-Patrol Signaling Systems, 1912*, pp. 49–156, which presents telephone rates of selected cities in 38 States and the District of Columbia. Another source of exchange rate data is provided by the responses of telephone companies to FCC, "Telephone Division Order No. 9," which called for rates in effect in selected size exchanges between 1907 and 1933. These responses are on file at the FCC.

R 17–18. Telephone plant, book value and depreciation reserves, 1880–1970.

Source: 1885–1935, U.S. Federal Communications Commission, unpublished data consisting of *Special Investigation, Docket No. 1* "Report on American Telephone and Telegraph Company Corporate and Financial History," vol. I, Exhibit No. 1360-A (Jan. 16, 1937, processed), pp. 73, 102; vol. II, Exhibit No. 1360-B, Schedule 2 (appendix); "Report on Associated Bell Telephone Companies Financial and Operating Data," Exhibit No. 1364 (Jan. 23, 1937), Schedule A-15; 1936–1956, American Telephone and Telegraph Company, annual reports, and FCC, unpublished data; 1957–1970, AT&T, annual reports and unpublished data.

Census data are from the following U.S. Bureau of the Census volumes: *Compendium of the Tenth Census, 1880*, p. 1332; *Telephones and Telegraphs, 1902*, table 6, p. 7; *Telephones and Telegraphs . . . , 1912*, table 29; *Telephones, 1917*, table 33; *Telephones, 1922*, table 34; *Telephones and Telegraphs, 1932*, table 17, and *1937*, table 1 (see general note for series R 1–92 for complete list of census sources).

The FCC's uniform system of accounts, which became effective January 1, 1937, requires establishment of telephone plant accounts on the basis of original cost (cost at time of first dedication to the public use). This applies to all plants ordinarily having a service life of more than one year as well as franchises, patents, rights of way, leaseholds, and other interests in land.

The depreciation policies of the Bell System have undergone various changes from a simple maintenance reserve set up for the purpose of equalizing maintenance charges over a period of years and providing for deferred maintenance expenses, to depreciation rates prescribed by the FCC. Prescription of depreciation rates for Bell companies began in 1949 and initial prescriptions were completed in 1953. For a discussion of Bell System depreciation policies, see *Report of the Federal Communications Commission on the Investigation of the Telephone Industry in the United States*, pp. 325–349.

R 19. Miles of wire, 1880–1970.

Source: 1880–1884, American Telephone and Telegraph Company, unpublished financial report; 1885–1935, U.S. Federal Communications Commission, unpublished data consisting of *Special Investigation Docket No. 1*, Exhibit No. 1360-A, pp. 76, 115; 1936–1956, AT&T, annual reports, and FCC, unpublished data; 1957–1970, see source for series R 17–18.

Census data are from the following U.S. Bureau of the Census volumes: *Compendium of the Tenth Census, 1880*, p. 1327; *Telephones*

and Telegraphs, 1902, table 2; *Telephones, 1922*, table 21; *Telephones and Telegraphs, 1937*, table 14.

Miles of wire are not an adequate index of the growth in telephone capacity for a variety of reasons: The shift from single open wire lines to complex cable systems including coaxial tubes; use of carrier systems to increase significantly the number of communication channels over a band of frequencies transmitted over an electrical circuit; and use of microwave radio systems not included in the statistics of wire lines.

R 20–22 and R 27–28. Operating revenues, net income, and dividends, 1880–1970.

Source: 1881–1914, U.S. Federal Communications Commission, unpublished data consisting of *Special Investigation Docket No. 1*, Exhibit No. 1360-A, pp. 39, 54, 73, 81, 89, 109 (for operating revenues and division between local and toll revenues, 1900–1914, Schedule B-2 of *Special Investigation Docket No. 1*, Exhibit No. 1364 combined with Long Lines revenues from p. 395 of Exhibit 1360-B); 1915–1956, American Telephone and Telegraph Company, annual reports, and FCC, unpublished data; 1957–1970, see source for series R 17–18.

Census data are from the following U.S. Bureau of the Census reports (see general note for series R 1–92 for detailed listing of sources): *Compendium of the Tenth Census, 1880*, p. 1329; *Statistics of Manufactures, 1890*, pp. 1, 5; *Telephones, 1907*, table 36; *Telephones and Telegraphs . . . , 1912*, table 29; *Telephones, 1917*, tables 21, 30, and 31; *Telephones, 1922*, tables 2, 31, 32; *Telephones, 1927*, table 1; *Telephones and Telegraphs, 1932*, table 1, and *1937*, table 1.

Figures for series R 20–22 for 1900–1914 have been adjusted by the FCC by subtracting uncollectible operating revenues so that they are comparable with figures for 1915–1970.

Operating revenues include monthly service charges; amounts charged for connection, restoration and termination of service, and for moves, instrument changes, and similar service requirements; initial nonrecurring charges for plant or equipment, except initial charges based on the cost of specially assembled private branch exchanges; and amounts of service charges for supplemental or auxiliary equipment as extension stations and auxiliary receivers. Operating revenues include the telegraph services of the Bell System, including revenues derived from teletypewriter exchange service (TWX), and private line service; international radiotelephone service; directory advertising and sales; and rent revenues.

Net income is net operating income and other income, including dividend income and interest income, including interest charged to construction; minus miscellaneous deductions from income and fixed charges (as interest deductions). All of the Bell System operations are included; however, as noted below (see text for series R 25), prior to 1933 only the dividends from controlled companies not consolidated were included.

Dividends declared refer to the entire Bell System operations, excluding dividends paid by one system company to another.

R 23. Operating expenses, 1880–1970.

Source: 1885–1907, U.S. Federal Communications Commission, unpublished data consisting of *Special Investigation Docket No. 1*, Exhibit 1360-A, pp. 54, 73, 109 (figures for operating expenses derived by subtracting net earnings from revenues); 1908–1935, American Telephone and Telegraph Company, annual reports; 1936–1956, AT&T, annual reports, and FCC, unpublished data; 1957–1970, see source for series R 17–18. For census data, see source for series R 20–22 and R 27–28.

For 1885–1907, FCC's figures include all taxes (including Federal income taxes) and interest expense and miscellaneous income. For 1908–1913, figures also include Federal income taxes. For 1914–1920, figures were adjusted to exclude estimated amounts of Federal income taxes by use of annual reports of the individual Bell Telephone companies to the Interstate Commerce Commission. For 1921–1935, the Federal income tax adjustment was obtained from AT&T unpublished data.

Figures include that portion of the expenses of Bell Telephone Laboratories absorbed by AT&T.

R 24. Federal income taxes, 1914–1970.

Source: 1914–1920, U.S. Federal Communications Commission, unpublished data (approximations derived from annual reports of individual Bell System companies to the ICC); 1921–1935, American Telephone and Telegraph Company, unpublished data; 1936–1956, AT&T, annual reports, and FCC, unpublished data; 1957–1970, see source for series R 17–18.

R 25. Other income, net, 1882–1970.

Source: 1882–1956, American Telephone and Telegraph Company, annual reports, and U.S. Federal Communications Commission, unpublished data; 1957–1970, see source for series R 17–18.

Since 1933, instead of including under this item only the dividends from controlled companies not consolidated, the AT&T has included its proportionate interest in the total earnings or deficits of such companies.

R 26. Interest expenses, 1885–1970.

Source: 1885–1956, American Telephone and Telegraph Company, annual reports, and U.S. Federal Communications Commission, unpublished data; 1957–1970, see source for series R 17–18. Census data are from the following U.S. Bureau of the Census reports: *Special Reports, Telephones, 1907*, table 57; *Census of Electrical Industries: 1917, Telephones*, table 30; *Census of Electrical Industries: Telephones, 1922*, table 31.

Interest expense includes interest on all classes of debt owing to the public but excludes intercompany interest payment.

R 29–30. Employees and wages, 1880–1970.

Source: **Series R 29**, 1885–1899 and 1907–1935, U.S. Federal Communications Commission, unpublished data consisting of *Special Investigation Docket No. 1*, Exhibit No. 1360-A, pp. 76, 136, 147; **series R 29–30**, 1900–1906, and **series R 30**, 1913–1935, American Telephone and Telegraph Company, unpublished data; **series R 29–30**, 1936–1956, AT&T, annual reports to stockholders, and FCC, unpublished data; 1957–1970, see source for series R 17–18.

Census data are from the following U.S. Bureau of the Census reports (see general note for series R 1–92 for detailed description of sources): *Compendium of the Tenth Census, 1880*, p. 1327; *Statistics of Manufactures, 1890*, p. 1; *Telephones and Telegraphs, 1902*, tables 2, 6; *Telephones and Telegraphs . . . , 1912*, tables 3, 29; *Telephones, 1917*, table 1; *Telephones, 1922*, table 1; *Telephones 1927*, table 1; *Telephones and Telegraphs, 1932*, table 1; *Telephones and Telegraphs, 1937*, table 1.

Employee figures for 1885–1935 exclude Western Electric Company.

Figures for 1939–1956 also appear in the FCC annual issues of *Statistics of the Communications Industry in the United States*. These issues also contain detailed reports of the occupational classifications and wage rates of Bell System employees.

R 31–45. Independent telephone companies—property, revenues, expenses, interest, net income, dividends, employees, and wages, 1916–1970.

Source: U.S. Federal Communications Commission, 1916–1934, unpublished data. United States Independent Telephone Association (USITA), 1935–1962, *Annual Statistical Volume of the United States Independent Telephone Association*, various issues (copyright); 1963–1970, *Independent Telephone Statistics*, annual issues (copyright).

Census data are from the following U.S. Bureau of the Census reports (see general note for series R 1–92 for detailed description of sources): *Telephones, 1917*, tables 1, 30, 31, 33; *Telephones, 1922*, tables 1, 22, 32; *Census of Electrical Industries: Telephones, 1927*, tables 1, 34; *Telephones and Telegraphs, 1932*, table 1, and *1937*, table 1.

The large discrepancy between the census figures and the Federal Communications Commission and USITA figures is due to the major differences in coverage. The following excerpt from Bureau of the Census, *Telephones, 1922*, refers to census coverage:

> Unit of enumeration ("system" or "line").—So far as practicable, a report was secured for each system or line operated under separate ownership. The terms "system" and "line" are sometimes used synonymously but, in general, the former is employed with reference to the aggregations of lines operated by the larger companies while the latter is more commonly used to denote the small farmer or rural lines. A farmer or rural line may be merely an individual line connected with an exchange under different ownership, or may be a party line without an exchange or connected with an exchange owned jointly with other lines or under independent ownership.

Figures for 1916–1933 were based on ICC annual summaries (which did not differentiate between the Bell System and the independent telephone companies) and were derived by subtraction from the ICC figures of those amounts for each company included on a consolidated basis in the data shown for series R 17–30.

Figures for 1935–1970 were obtained by USITA from reports of independent telephone companies to the USITA. For recent years, the publications provide detailed data on companies reporting to the USITA, and limited data in respect to companies not reporting to the USITA. Certain totals for combined reporting and nonreporting independent companies are shown for 1961–1970 in the USITA *1971 Annual Statistical Volume*.

A discussion of the relations between the Bell System and the Independents is presented in the FCC *Report . . . on the Investigation of the Telephone Industry . . .*, pp. 123–146; and a Report of Committee of National Association of Railroad and Utilities Commissioners and FCC representatives, *Message Toll Telephone Rates and Disparities*.

R 46–74. General note.

Since the 1850's, the Western Union Telegraph Company has been the dominant carrier in the domestic telegraph industry. Established in 1851 as the New York & Mississippi Valley Printing Telegraph Company, this company succeeded by 1866 in acquiring or merging dozens of competing telegraph companies and emerging as the sole telegraph company in the United States. (See Robert Luther Thompson, *Wiring a Continent; the History of the Telegraph Industry in the United States, 1832–1866*, Princeton University Press, 1947.) In succeeding decades, smaller telegraph companies were formed, serving a region or major cities, often with the intent of forcing Western Union to acquire them. Western Union developed close contractual ties with the railways. Telegraph pole lines were constructed along railroad rights-of-way. The lines were used jointly for general telegraph and railroad telegraph communication and signaling; and railroad stations and personnel were used for the pick-up and delivery of telegraph messages.

Western Union's most serious telegraph rival, Postal Telegraph, was acquired by the Mackay interests in the 1880's as the domestic pick-up and delivery agent for Mackay's Commercial Cable Company (later the International Telephone and Telegraph Company). Until the 1920's, Postal Telegraph competed with Western Union for the larger and more profitable routes. Beginning in the 1920's, Postal Telegraph attempted to provide a nationwide service in full competition with Western Union. Postal Telegraph expanded its own facilities and also made arrangements with the telephone companies, gasoline stations, and others for the pick-up and delivery of telegrams.

The expansion of Postal Telegraph coincided roughly with the emergence of more effective competition from other sources. Predominantly, such competition came from the growth and development of toll telephone service, the expansion of domestic airmail, the introduction of the Bell System's teletypewriter exchange service (TWX), which was sold to Western Union in 1971, and the provision of domestic radiotelegraph service by the international radiotelegraph carriers, RCA Global Communications and the Mackay Companies. (In 1942, as a war measure, domestic radiotelegraph service was discontinued and was not subsequently resumed.) Postal Telegraph's share of domestic telegraph revenues was less than 25 percent. In 1943, Postal Telegraph merged with Western Union. (See U.S. Federal Communications Commission, *Reports*, vol. 10, pp. 148–198, September 27, 1943, for Commission approval of the specific terms of the merger.)

R 46–55. Western Union Telegraph Company—summary of facilities, traffic, and finances, 1866–1915.

Source: **Series R 46–49** (except 1913), The Western Union Telegraph Company, annual reports; 1913, Moody's Investors Service, *Moody's Public Utilities Reports*, 1919, New York (copyright). **Series R 50–55** (except R 52, 1914–1915), U.S. Interstate Commerce Commission, Bureau of Valuation, *Accounting Reports, The Western Union Telegraph Company* (December 31, 1915 and June 30, 1919); **series R 52**, 1914 and 1915, U.S. Federal Communications Commission, unpublished data. Census data are from the following U.S. Bureau of the Census reports: 1880, *Compendium of the Tenth Census, 1880*, pp. 1310–1325; *Special Reports: Telephones and Telegraphs, 1902*, tables 39, 41; *Telegraph Systems: 1907*, tables 1–8; *Telephones and Telegraphs . . . , 1912*, tables 2, 3.

The data for series R 52, 1914 and 1915, are based on ICC Bureau of Valuation report cited above, Exhibit V, sheets 2 and 3.

According to the *Compendium of the Seventh Census, 1854*, p. 189, there were 89 telegraph lines having 23,261 miles of wire in 1853. In 1854, the miles of wire were estimated at over 30,000.

The 1880 census data include many companies in addition to Western Union, and the later census data include Postal Telegraph as well as reports from some 15 to 20 small companies. Included in the Postal Telegraph data were the telephone operations of that company. The 1902 census data include the several domestic ocean-cable systems, while the 1880, 1907, and 1912 census figures exclude ocean-cable systems other than the Western Union Cable Division.

Other statistics appear in 60th Cong., 2d sess., *Investigation of Western Union and Postal Telegraph-Cable Companies*, U.S. Senate Document No. 725 (1909); State of New York, *Proceedings of Joint Committee Investigation of Telephone and Telegraph Companies* (1910); and *Submarine and Land Telegraph Systems of the World*, an excerpt from the Treasury Department, *Monthly Summary of Commerce and Finance*, January 1899.

R 56–70. Domestic telegraph industry—messages, property, revenues, expenses, net income, dividends, employees, and wages, 1916–1970.

Source: 1916–1928, U.S. Interstate Commerce Commission and U.S. Federal Communications Commission, unpublished data (annual reports of Western Union Telegraph Company and Postal Telegraph-Cable Company to the ICC); 1929–1955, FCC, *Statistics of the Communications Industry in the United States*, 1955, pp. 110–115; 1956–1970, FCC, *Statistics of Communications Common Carriers*, annual issues, and unpublished data (data are from the annual reports of Western Union Telegraph Company to the FCC). Census data are from the following U.S. Bureau of the Census reports (see general note for series R 1–92 for detailed identification of sources): *Census of Electrical Industries: 1917, Telegraphs . . . ,* tables 1, 2, 4, 5; *Tele-*

graphs, 1922, tables 2, 3, 5, 6; *Telegraphs, 1927*, tables 2, 3, 5, 6; *Telegraphs, 1932*, tables 2, 3, 4; *Telephones and Telegraphs, 1937*, tables 2, 3, 4.

For 1916–1928, the Western Union reported landline (domestic) and cable operations on a merged basis; therefore, supplementary material was obtained from Western Union relating to the landline operations. Necessarily, these involve estimates and allocations, the precise bases of which were not specified. For 1929–1955, figures were obtained from annual reports of the telegraph carriers to the ICC and to the FCC, supplemented by correspondence and reference to the reports of the telegraph companies.

Each census report, 1917–1937, included Western Union Cable Division with Western Union telegraph plant. Similarly, the census reports of 1917, 1922, and 1927, in reporting Western Union operating revenues, operating expenses, net income, and dividends declared, include Western Union cables. Apparently, in each census report, number of employees and wages and salaries were for Western Union landline system only.

The census data refer to approximately 15 to 20 minor domestic telegraph companies, in addition to Western Union and Postal Telegraph. In 1943, Western Union acquired Postal Telegraph, and the telegraph company data, beginning in 1944, relate to the single merged carrier.

R 56, messages handled. Prior to 1935, the annual count of revenue messages handled was based on a count of messages during the month of January and was partly estimated. For 1935–1950, most of the Western Union message data were based on an actual count for 2 days in each month at some 400 of the largest offices which together accounted for about 80 percent of total message revenues. The Postal Telegraph data continued to be based on counts and estimates for the month of January projected to annual totals. For 1950–1970, Western Union used a scientifically constructed random message sample, the results of which provide generally reliable monthly and annual message data by service classes and rate zones.

Data include telegraph traffic with Canada and Mexico. Such traffic forms only a small portion of the message data.

R 57, private-line telegraph service revenues of telegraph companies. For 1916–1935, data were furnished to FCC by Western Union and added to annual report figures for Postal Telegraph; for 1936–1943, figures are from annual reports of Western Union and Postal Telegraph.

Private line, or leased circuit, revenues are derived from the lease of wires, cables, channels, circuits, and similar wire-telegraph facilities to banks, airlines, governmental agencies, and other large organizations for the exclusive use of these customers. The charge for such service is based on contractual rent agreements providing for definite periodic terms without regard to the extent of the service obtained by the users of such facilities.

R 58, private-line telegraph service revenues of telephone companies. Data for 1916–1938 apply to the Bell System telephone companies only. Data for 1916–1926 and 1935–1938 were obtained from unpublished data of the Bell System. Data for 1927–1934 were obtained from the Bell System response to the FCC, "Telegraph Division Order No. 12," and appear in "Some Aspects of Competition Affecting the Land Wire Telegraph Industry" (1937), an unpublished FCC staff study. For 1939–1970, data include all telephone companies reporting on an annual basis to the FCC (roughly varying between 60 and 125).

R 59–60, telegraph plant. Effective January 1, 1914, the ICC prescribed a Uniform System of Accounts for telegraph and cable companies and required the carriers to keep their accounts in conformity with this system. All charges made to plant and equipment or other property accounts with respect to any property acquired on or after January 1, 1914, were to be the actual money costs of the property. The ICC did not attempt to prescribe the depreciation rates of the carriers.

In 1940, the FCC adopted a revised uniform system of accounts for wire telegraph and ocean cable carriers, to go into effect January 1, 1942. The effective date was later postponed to January 1, 1943. The new system was designed to supplant the previous system in use since 1914. The FCC prescribed depreciation rates for the telegraph carrier, effective January 1, 1948. After the merger of Western Union and Postal Telegraph, the Commission required that the merged carrier reclassify its plant as of January 1, 1943.

Telegraph plant book costs for 1946–1970 were affected by two conflicting factors: Accelerated retirement of old plant, and addition of new plant as part of the general modernization program of the Western Union Telegraph Company begun in 1946. As part of its modernization program the Western Union Telegraph Company leased substantial plant, in the form of voice channels, from the Bell System.

Census figures on book cost of plant include Western Union cables in all years.

R 61, miles of wire. Wire figures are not a satisfactory measure of the capacity of the domestic telegraph industry for various reasons, including the shift from less efficient open wire to more efficient cable; the introduction of multiplex terminal equipment, which has permitted a significant subdivision of each telegraph channel and the simultaneous transmission of messages on each such subdivision; the leasing from the Bell System telephone companies of voice-frequency channels and the subdivision of these channels into a substantially greater number of telegraph channels; operation by Western Union of its microwave radio system for the transmission of messages; and use of modernized routing and switching systems.

R 62–68, finances, employees, and wages and salaries. Operating revenues are derived, in the bulk, from various transmission and non-transmission telegraph services. However, a small proportion has been derived from incidental services, such as errand service, time service, and code registration. The operations of the former Postal Telegraph toll telephone system were included until February 1, 1952, when Western Union disposed of this service. Also included in operating revenues are revenues derived by the domestic telegraph carrers in handling the domestic haul of insular, mobile, and foreign cable and radiotelegraph communications. Such domestic haul is between the "gateway" cities and the interior of the nation.

To obtain data on total operating expenses, the domestic telegraph carriers (Western Union and Postal Telegraph) were required to subdivide their expense accounts as between domestic and international operations in respect to compensation, overhead, materials and supplies, and other charges. Such allocations are subject to some arbitrariness.

Census data for 1917, 1922, and 1927 with respect to operating revenues, expenses, and net income differ from the other data as a result of the inclusion of Western Union cable operations and the inclusion of minor companies, in addition to Western Union and Postal Telegraph.

No adjustments were made in the annual reported income statements. Thus, the net loss shown for 1945 resulted from a substantial retroactive wage award made by the War Labor Board. This was shown in the 1945 statement of the Western Union Telegraph Company as an extraordinary charge (less recoverable income taxes).

Income taxes (through 1963, when the cables were sold) are total Western Union income taxes minus those assigned by the company itself to its cable operations. The amounts assigned to Western Union cables were obtained by the FCC from Western Union on an informal basis. Income taxes for 1924 and prior years are not available separately and are included in total operating expenses.

Dividends declared (through 1963, when the international operations were sold), include the entire operations of Western Union, domestic and international. No basis exists for allocating them.

Number of employees was reported as of different periods: 1929–1934, at the end of June; 1935–1945, at the end of December; and 1946–1970, at the end of October. However, wages and salaries are uniformly reported for the calendar year ending December 31.

R 69–70, Bell Teletypewriter Exchange (TWX) Service. For 1931–1934, data are from responses to FCC, "Telegraph Division Order No. 12"; for 1935–1938, from the FCC *Annual Report*.

Teletypewriter exchange service (TWX) was initiated November 21, 1931. The revenues from this service, as well as the private line telegraph revenues of telephone companies, are not included in total operating revenues, which is limited to the revenues of domestic telegraph carriers. The TWX service of the telephone industry was purchased by Western Union in 1971.

R 71–74. Domestic telegraph message rates and TWX rates between New York City and selected cities, 1850–1970.

Source: U.S. Federal Communications Commission, unpublished data.

The 1850 rates are cited in William Holmes, *History of Telegraph Rates, 1860 to 1913* (an unpublished study obtained by the FCC from the Western Union Telegraph Company), p. 2. The same source states, p. 8, that the New York-Chicago rate from 1866 to October 1, 1869, was $1.85, although James D. Reid, *The Telegraph in America* (1886), p. 746, states that the Chicago rate was $2.05 between 1866 and 1869, and U.S. Senate, 60th Cong., 2d sess., *Investigation of Western Union and Postal Telegraph Cable Companies*, Document No. 725 (1909), p. 24, claims that in 1866 this rate was $2.20. Holmes, p. 8, is the source for the 1866 and 1869 New York-Philadelphia rates. Reid, p. 746, quotes the New York-San Francisco rates for 1866 and 1869. The *Investigation of Western Union . . .*, p. 24, is also the source for the New York-Denver rate as of 1866. The 1870 rates are mentioned in 51st Cong., 1st sess., *Hearings before the House Committee on the Post-Office and Post-Roads on Postal Telegraph Facilities*, p. 131. In addition, Holmes, p. 9, states that in 1870 the maximum rate from States north of Washington, D.C., to San Francisco was reduced from $7.45 in currency (or $6.75 if paid in gold) to $5.00 in currency (or $4.00 in gold). The 1873 rates are shown in *Investigation of Western Union . . .*, p. 24. Holmes, p. 10, states that the $2.50 San Francisco rate became effective February 1, 1873, and a reason given was that $2.50 was the denomination of a coin in common use on the Pacific Coast. The same source, p. 12, describes the New York-Chicago rate in 1875 as having been 25 cents and in 1877 as being successively increased to 40 cents, 50 cents, and 60 cents. Holmes also states, p. 11, that the New York-Denver rate became $2.00 in March 1876 and that the San Francisco rate was reduced to $2.00 in August 1876. However, Reid mentions, p. 747, March 1877 as the date $2.00 was fixed as the maximum rate between New York City and points east of the Rocky Mountains. The 1883 rates are also from *Investigation of Western Union . . .*, p. 24. Holmes, p. 17, states that the $1.00 San Francisco rate became effective in March 1884 as part of a general reduction which established $1.00 as the maximum rate for a 10-word full rate telegram between any two points in the Western Union system. Holmes also reports, p. 17, that in June 1884 the rate between New York and Chicago charged by Western Union was 50 cents, by Postal Telegraph, 25 cents, and by the Baltimore and Ohio Telegraph Company, 40 cents. The 1888 rates are based on State of New York, *Report of the Joint Committee of the Senate and Assembly of the State of New York Appointed to Investigate Telephone and Telegraph Companies* (transmitted to the Legislature March 21, 1910), p. 687, and the annual report of Western Union to stockholders for 1888, p. 5. The 1890 rates are from *Hearings Before the House Committee on the Post-Office and Post-Roads on Postal Telegraph Facilities*, p. 68. The rates in effect as of 1908 are from *Investigation of Western Union . . .*, p. 24, although there is evidence from other sources that some of these rates were put into effect in 1907. The 1919 rates were the result of a 20 percent increase in domestic telegraph rates as set forth in the 1919 Western Union annual report to stockholders, p. 8.

The 1931 TWX rates are from testimony on behalf of AT&T by Mr. Carroll O. Bickelhaupt in the hearings pursuant to FCC, "Telegraph Division Order No. 12."

All rates beginning with the 1946 increase are derived from official tariffs filed with the FCC.

The census report, *Special Reports: Telephones and Telegraphs, 1902*, states (p. 14) that the first telegraph rate was applicable in 1845 between Baltimore and Washington and was one cent for each group of four characters. The rates shown here are mainly those of the Western Union Telegraph Company. During some of the early years, lower rates were sometimes published by competing companies. The frequent changes in the New York-Chicago rate illustrate particularly the effects of competition. New companies appeared offering lower rates on this basic route and Western Union was forced to meet the competition until such time as it succeeded in acquiring the competing company. Moreover, it is not certain that the published rates were adhered to uniformly, particularly in the early years of telegraph development and in periods of depression. Under the stress of competition, rebates were sometimes allowed.

The rate for the full-rate telegram is the keystone of the telegraph rate structure. Rates for most other public message telegraph services (day letters, night letters, etc.) are a percentage of the rates for the full-time telegram. Between 1908 and 1946, there was no change in the level of the full-rate telegram, except for the increase effected in 1919. However, while maintaining the rate level on its full-rate telegrams, Western Union introduced various new classifications (including the fixed text social message and serials) which in effect provided discounts to the message customer.

TWX is provided only by the Bell Telephone System but this service was sold to Western Union in 1971. As contrasted with message telegraph service, which is a 1-way communication service, TWX provides 2-way, instantaneous communication service between TWX subscribers. The maximum number of words which can be transmitted in the 3-minute rate period depends on the speed of the transmitting operator (provided by the subscriber) and the maximum rated speed of the TWX equipment. In addition to the charges for specific use (measured in time units and distance) of the facilities, TWX subscribers beginning July 1, 1953, were billed a monthly service charge of $10. This was increased to $40 on September 1, 1966, and to $45 on February 1, 1970, for 60-speed service.

R 75–88. General note.

The first successful cable linking North America with Europe was laid in 1866. Radio was not a significant factor in overseas telegraphy until 1920 when the newly formed Radio Corporation of America (RCA) entered the field as successor to Marconi Company of America. The record of hearings held in 1929 before the Committee on Interstate Commerce, United States Senate, 71st Cong., 1st sess., on S. 6, a "Bill to Provide for the Regulation of the Transmission of Intelligence by Wire or Wireless," contains (pp. 960-972) a list of submarine cables of the world, and the year in which each was laid. Few of these cables are now in use, having been replaced by circuits in telephone ocean cables laid since the mid-1950's and, since 1965, also by circuits in microwave radio relayed by satellite. Information on the beginnings of international radiotelegraphy appears in the *Report of the Federal Trade Commission on the Radio Industry* (1924).

The first overseas radio telephone service was opened in 1927 between New York and London by American Telephone and Telegraph Company. The only overseas telephone service available during 1921-1926 was to and from Cuba by means of cable.

The census data are derived from the special quinquennial census reports of the telephone and telegraph industries (see general note for series R 1-92). With respect to international telegraph, these reports suffer from two major shortcomings. First, the Bureau of the Census was unable to obtain from the Western Union Telegraph Company a division between its landline system and its cable operations with respect to plant and financial operations. Prior to the 1932 census, Western Union provided separate data for its cable operations only in the categories of messages and cable mileage.

In the censuses of 1932 and 1937, Western Union also supplied operating revenue information for its cable system. The absence of Western Union's Cable Division from the census data on the ocean-cable companies largely accounts for the significant differences between the census data and the annual series with respect to telegraph plant book cost and depreciation reserves, operating revenues, operating expenses, and net income.

A second shortcoming of the census data is the lack of adequate coverage of the radiotelegraph industry. The financial information included in the 1922 and 1937 census compilations is seriously distorted because of the failure to exclude various activities of the Radio Corporation of America not related to its telegraph communications business. In the 1932 census, no information on radiotelegraph appeared, while in the 1937 census the published statistics relate only to messages and operating revenue. Consequently, the only census data shown with respect to radiotelegraph are the message statistics, and $9,515,000 in operating revenues included within the 1937 cable-radiotelegraph total.

R 75–77, R 79–81, R 83–88. Telegraph messages, plant, nautical miles of ocean-telegraph cable, operating revenues and expenses, Federal income taxes, net income, employees, and wages, 1907–1970.

Source: U.S. Federal Communications Commission, 1916–1928, unpublished data; 1929–1956, *Statistics of the Communications Industry in the United States*, 1955 and 1956 issues, table 19; 1957–1970, *Statistics of Communications, Common Carriers*, annual issues. Census data beginning 1907 are from the following U.S. Bureau of the Census reports (see general note for series R 1–92 for detailed description of sources): *Telegraph Systems: 1907*, pp. 10, 19; *Telephones and Telegraphs . . ., 1912*, pp. 165, 167; *Telegraphs, 1927*, pp. 19, 25; *Telephones and Telegraphs, 1937*, pp. 49, 52.

Annual data prior to 1929 were derived in part from annual reports of the carriers filed with the Interstate Commerce Commission. In large part, these data were obtained through field examinations by the staff of the FCC and from data supplied by the carriers upon specific request.

Figures include Hawaii and Puerto Rico for all years. There is no international telegraph industry in Alaska; however, international telegrams originating or terminating there are included in series R 75–77.

Cable and radiotelegraph messages (series R 75–77) include communications sent from, received in, and transiting the United States and its outlying areas. In addition, radiotelegraph messages include ship-shore messages, and domestic telegraph messages handled over radiotelegraph circuits prior to the closure of such circuits on June 30, 1942.

Plant and depreciation figures (series R 79–80) are on the basis of the currently effective systems of accounts. The radiotelegraph accounts became effective January 1, 1940, and the ocean-cable uniform system accounts January 1, 1943 (replacing an earlier cable accounts system promulgated by the ICC, effective January 1, 1914).

The miles of ocean cable (series R 81) as published have been adjusted in view of the fact that some of the cables were reported and tabulated in statute miles rather than nautical miles.

Federal income taxes prior to 1929 are included in operating expenses (series R 84) in amounts which are not ascertainable. The substantial decline in net income in 1912 compared with 1907 may have been accounted for in large measure by the introduction of depreciation charges which were absent from the 1907 accounts.

Included in employees and compensation (series R 87–88) are the foreign employees of the carriers. The reporting dates for number of employees have varied: For 1929–1934, as of the end of June; for 1935–1945, as of the end of December; for 1946–1970, as of the end of October.

R 78. Overseas telephone calls, 1921–1970.

Source: 73d Cong., 2d sess., *Report on Communication Companies*, House Report No. 1273, pt. III, No. 2, p. 1459 (1935); and American Telephone and Telegraph Company, unpublished data.

Figures include calls to and from ships on the high seas and most international points. Additional data on radiotelephone service are contained in the *Statistics of the Communications Industry in the United States.* See also *Census of Electrical Industries: Telephones and Telegraphs, 1937*, table 9.

R 82. Overseas countries served by direct radiotelegraph circuits, 1912–1970.

Source: U.S. Federal Communications Commission, unpublished data (supplemented and confirmed in *Report of the Federal Trade Commission on the Radio Industry* and *Report on Communication Companies*, House Report No. 1273, pt. III, No. 1, pp. 990, 998; pt. III, No. 4, pp. 3934, 3948, and 4188).

R 89–92. International cable and radiotelegraph rates and international telephone rates between New York City and selected cities, 1866–1970.

Source: 1866–1928, scattered sources as indicated below; 1929–1970, U.S. Federal Communications Commission, unpublished data.

New York to London. The first successful transatlantic cable was laid in 1866. James D. Reid, *The Telegraph in America* (1886), p. 748, indicates that the first telegraph rate on the cable (presumably New York to London) was $100 for 10 words. Three months later, the same source states, the rate was reduced to $50 and subsequently to $25. By 1868, the rate for 10 words had declined to $15.75, and in 1885 it stood at 40 cents per word. A staff document of American Cable & Radio, Inc., prepared in connection with FCC Docket No. 8777 (1948) indicates that the Western Union Telegraph Company had a 50 cents per word rate in 1884, and that on December 24 of that year the Commercial Cable Company entered the field with a rate of 40 cents per word. The same source indicates that the cable companies other than Commercial Cable reduced their rates to 12 cents per word on May 6, 1886, and Commercial Cable in turn lowered its per word rate from 40 cents to 25 cents. On September 16, 1887, Commercial Cable further reduced its rate to the 12 cent level. Then on September 1, 1888, all the cable companies raised their rate between New York and London to 25 cents per word.

Exhibit No. 190, introduced by RCA Communications, Inc., in the same hearing (Docket No. 8777) shows the same rates, but with somewhat different effective dates; while William Holmes, *History of Telegraph Rates, 1860 to 1913*, p. 23, cites rates which differ in part from those shown here.

In 1916, it became possible to send messages from New York to London through Canada via Marconi Wireless for 17 cents per full rate word. According to the Federal Trade Commission *Report on the Radio Industry*, p. 36, RCA, on March 1, 1920, began transmitting radiotelegraph messages to Great Britain. The rate initially was 17 cents per word, with an increase to 18 cents on January 1, 1921, and to 20 cents on April 15, 1923. At this point the international cable companies reduced their rate to 20 cents to meet the radio competition. Since then, the rates for cable and radio have been identical.

The rate reductions effective May 1, 1945, provided for a uniform 20 cents per word basic rate from the United States "gateway" cities to a large part of the world (see FCC, *Eleventh Annual Report for Fiscal Year Ended June 30, 1945*, p. 45). Effective May 1,

1946, all international cable and radiotelephone rates were established on a country-to-country basis at 20 cents and 30 cents per word, respectively.

The reductions in rates, effective July 1, 1950, are the result of "unification" of the full rate and the code rate on all cable and radiotelegraph service. The rates were unified at 75 percent of the existing rate per full-rate word. This had the effect of lowering the charge for full-rate messages but increasing the charge for code messages which at that time formed a substantial portion of international telegraph traffic.

New York to Cairo. Telegraphic communication between New York and Cairo began, probably, in 1870 or shortly thereafter. A Commercial Cable Company tariff book, dated January 1903, indicates a rate of 61 cents per word as of that time. A July 1905 tariff book of the Western Union Telegraph Company shows a New York-Cairo rate of 56 cents per word; 25 cents was the rate for the New York-London haul and 31 cents for the rate beyond London. No record has been found of rates in effect between 1905 and 1925. Data since 1925 are from the FCC based on filed tariffs and correspondence with companies.

New York to Tokyo. No specific record has been found dating the beginning of telegraphic communication with Tokyo. In the hearings before the Senate Committee on Foreign Relations, 54th Cong., 1st sess., Senate Document No. 194 (1896), conflicting testimony was presented with respect to the early rates. The Commercial Cable Company tariff book of January 1903 stated that the rate at that time was $1.76 per word. Shortly thereafter Commercial Pacific Cable Company opened its trans-Pacific cable and the rate fell to $1.53 per word. This rate included 12 cents per word for the domestic landline haul from New York to San Francisco, and $1.41 for the San Francisco-Tokyo leg. *Report on Communication Companies*, 73d Cong., 2d sess., House Report No. 1273, pt. III, No. 4, p. 3926, is the source of the New York-Tokyo rates between 1903 and 1929. FCC is the source of rates since 1929. For data on radiotelegraph rates lower than cable rates prior to 1925, see FTC, *Report on the Radio Industry*, p. 35, and testimony before the House Committee on the Merchant Marine and Fisheries, pursuant to H.R. 7357, 68th Cong., 1st sess., p. 170.

New York to Buenos Aires. The 1880 rate is stated in the *1956 Annual Report of the American Cable and Radio Corporation to Stockholders*, p. 16. Rates between 1882 and 1927 are derived from testimony before the Senate Committee on Interstate and Foreign Commerce, 71st Cong., 2d sess., on S. 6 (1929–1930) beginning p. 2201, and *A Half Century of Cable Service to the Three Americas* (1928) published by All America Cables, Inc. When radio service was opened in 1924 the rate was fixed at the same level as the existing cable rate. FCC is the source for rates since 1929.

New York international radiotelephone rates to selected cities. The first overseas radiotelephone service was opened on January 7, 1927, between New York and London. Service to Buenos Aires began April 3, 1930, and to Tokyo, December 8, 1934. The circuit to Cairo, opened August 8, 1932, operated via London until January 7, 1946, when a direct circuit to Cairo was placed in operation. As in telegraph, the Tokyo radiotelephone rate included a landline haul charge until 1946 for the New York–San Francisco haul. Initially $9.00, the landline charge was reduced to $6.75 on July 1, 1937, and to $4.50 on August 1, 1940. All radiotelephone rates presented are for 3 minute weekday person-to-person daytime calls. In addition, there are lower night and Sunday rates on some routes, and on three of the routes station-to-station service is available at either a 25-percent or a 33⅓-percent discount from the person-to-person rates.

Series R 1-12. Telephones and Average Daily Conversations (Bell and Independent Companies): 1876 to 1970

[In thousands, except series R 2 and R 3.   Census figures in *italics*]

Year	Telephones [1] Total					Bell System [2]	Independent companies Connecting with Bell System	Independent companies Not connecting with Bell System	Average daily conversations Bell System [2] Local exchange	Bell System [2] Toll	Independent companies Local exchange	Independent companies Toll
	Number	Per 1,000 population	Households with (percent)	Residence	Business							
	1	2	3	4	5	6	7	8	9	10	11	12
1970	120,218	583.4	90.5	87,137	33,081	99,903	20,315	–	356,400	22,500	102,000	4,300
1969	115,222	565.2	89.8	83,210	32,012	95,943	19,279	–	337,900	20,700	97,500	4,100
1968	109,256	541.5	88.5	79,029	30,227	91,122	18,134	–	311,800	18,400	92,800	3,900
1967	103,752	519.3	87.1	74,963	28,789	86,776	16,976	–	298,600	16,700	87,100	3,600
1966	98,787	499.6	86.3	71,481	27,308	82,813	15,976	–	288,000	15,400	82,800	3,300
1965	93,656	479.0	84.6	67,729	25,927	78,632	15,024	–	273,400	14,000	77,400	3,000
1964	88,793	459.5	82.8	64,124	24,669	74,659	14,134	–	256,500	12,800	73,200	2,700
1963	84,453	442.9	81.4	60,876	23,577	71,152	13,301	–	246,282	11,784	68,400	2,400
1962	80,969	430.7	80.2	58,289	22,680	68,393	12,576	–	237,942	11,164	65,158	2,242
1961	77,422	418.0	78.9	55,737	21,685	65,507	11,915	–	222,320	10,539	62,177	2,074
1960	74,342	407.8	78.3	53,537	20,805	62,989	11,353	(Z)	215,317	10,068	58,005	1,996
1959	*70,820	*394.8	78.0	(NA)	(NA)	60,110	10,710	*(Z)	204,491	9,549	*53,525	*1,785
1958	66,645	379.3	76.4	47,831	18,814	56,759	9,886	(Z)	193,627	8,834	48,192	1,645
1957	63,624	368.2	75.5	45,433	18,191	54,241	9,380	3	185,304	8,490	44,174	1,602
1956	60,190	354.5	73.8	42,832	17,358	51,344	8,843	3	175,848	8,015	41,863	1,518
1955	56,243	337.2	71.5	39,854	16,389	48,028	8,212	3	166,438	7,420	37,722	1,430
1954	52,806	322.1	69.6	37,272	15,534	45,039	7,764	3	157,423	6,799	35,946	1,380
1953	50,373	312.7	68.0	35,411	14,962	43,010	7,359	4	151,667	6,552	34,645	1,365
1952	48,056	303.3	66.0	33,667	14,389	41,014	7,038	4	147,400	6,358	27,292	73
1951	45,636	292.9	64.0	31,939	13,697	38,943	6,685	8	143,235	6,230	26,384	74
1950	43,004	280.9	61.8	30,077	12,927	36,795	6,200	9	138,881	6,118	25,539	85
1949	40,709	270.4	60.2	28,327	12,382	34,175	6,524	10	130,403	6,125	23,961	102
1948	38,205	258.1	58.2	26,314	11,891	32,698	5,495	12	123,481	6,065	22,520	90
1947	34,867	239.7	54.9	23,708	11,159	29,773	5,081	13	113,075	5,908	20,353	86
1946	31,611	221.3	51.4	21,239	10,372	26,900	4,697	14	103,827	5,544	18,645	82
1945	27,867	198.1	46.2	18,409	9,458	23,547	4,306	14	89,362	4,852	17,667	99
1944	26,859	192.9	45.1	17,791	9,068	22,653	4,190	16	84,618	4,377	17,227	107
1943	26,381	191.6	45.0	17,706	8,675	22,301	4,014	66	85,000	4,046	17,138	93
1942	24,919	183.4	42.2	16,619	8,300	21,000	3,853	66	86,314	3,544	17,141	68
1941	23,521	175.3	39.3	15,453	8,068	19,742	3,709	70	84,360	3,222	16,659	69
1940	21,928	165.1	36.9	14,271	7,657	18,311	3,550	67	79,515	2,852	16,110	306
1939	20,831	158.3	35.6	13,446	7,385	17,329	3,435	67	74,020	2,705	15,292	294
1938	19,953	153.0	34.6	12,727	7,226	16,536	3,349	68	70,070	2,596	14,739	283
1937	*19,453*	*150.0*				*15,332*						
1937	19,453	150.4	34.3	12,341	7,112	16,097	3,288	68	68,833	2,682	14,678	287
1936	18,433	143.5	33.1	11,654	6,779	15,192	3,170	71	64,960	2,589	14,124	281
1935	17,424	136.4	31.8	11,003	6,421	14,280	3,073	71	58,809	2,276	14,631	284
1934	16,869	133.0	31.4	10,683	6,186	13,805	2,992	72	56,648	2,142	14,332	278
1933	16,628	132.0	31.3	10,475	6,153	13,501	3,051	76	55,199	2,047	14,481	273
1932	*17,424*	*139.0*				*13,793*						
1932	17,341	138.5	33.5	11,054	6,287	14,011	3,246	84	58,813	2,251	15,637	299
1931	19,602	157.5	39.2	12,754	6,848	15,692	3,816	94	62,205	2,700	17,245	350
1930	20,103	162.6	40.9	13,153	6,950	15,983	4,017	103	62,365	2,933	17,860	362
1929	19,970	163.1	41.6	13,135	6,835	15,838	4,022	110	61,034	3,139	18,107	370
1928	19,256	158.9	40.8	12,645	6,611	14,955	4,157	144	56,196	2,839	17,895	370
1927	*18,523*	*155.0*				*13,726*						
1927	18,446	153.9	39.7	12,086	6,360	14,155	4,133	158	52,581	2,615	18,100	369
1926	17,680	149.5	39.2	11,689	5,991	13,402	4,106	172	49,980	2,375	18,453	372
1925	16,875	144.6	38.7	11,270	5,605	12,622	4,037	216	46,702	2,098	18,148	352
1924	16,015	139.2	37.8	10,773	5,242	11,857	3,908	250	43,981	1,835	18,260	324
1923	15,316	135.4	37.3	10,345	4,971	10,857	4,090	369	41,109	1,683	18,516	322
1922	*14,347*	*130.0*				*9,515*						
1922	14,294	128.7	35.6	9,642	4,652	9,950	3,912	432	36,831	1,523	18,329	317
1921	13,817	126.4	35.3	9,342	4,475	9,328	3,994	495	33,671	1,356	18,447	281
1920	13,273	123.4	35.0	9,021	4,252	8,736	3,810	727	31,836	1,327	18,371	280
1919	12,669	119.7				7,739	4,057	873	29,286	1,167	18,158	276
1918	12,078	115.2				7,202	3,864	1,012	30,001	1,067	18,753	285
1917	*11,717*	*112.0*				*7,327*	*3,165*					
1917	11,717	112.7				7,032	3,458	1,226	30,845	1,009	19,785	302
1916	11,241	109.5				6,545	3,348	1,348	28,530	890	19,856	302
1915	10,524	103.9				5,968	3,204	1,351	25,184	819	18,535	282
1914	10,046	100.6				5,585	3,074	1,388	22,775	799	17,198	262
1913	9,543	97.2				5,255	2,878	1,409	22,255	806	17,640	272
1912	*8,730*	*92.0*				*5,087*	*2,369*					
1912	8,730	90.7				4,804	2,496	1,430	21,532	738	18,064	275
1911	8,349	88.3				4,352	2,281	1,716	19,773	645	17,466	266
1910	7,635	82.0				3,933	1,950	1,753	18,256	602	17,043	260
1909	6,996	76.5				3,522	1,621	1,853	16,777	517	16,213	247
1908	6,484	72.4				3,176	1,188	2,119	15,576	463	15,717	239
1907	*6,119*	*70.0*				*3,132*						
1907	6,119	69.6				3,013	826	2,280	15,266	494	13,814	210
1906	4,933	57.2				2,774	297	1,862	13,875	461	11,430	175
1905	4,127	48.8				2,285	246	1,596	11,404	368	9,756	148
1904	3,353	40.4				1,838	167	1,348	9,388	301	7,884	120
1903	2,809	34.5				1,564	121	1,124	8,316	258	6,903	105
1902	*2,371*	*30.0*				*1,317*						
1902	2,371	29.7				1,317	84	970	7,850	240	6,146	94
1901	1,801	23.0				1,061	48	692	6,342	187	4,468	68
1900	1,356	17.6				836	20	500	4,773	149	2,916	44
1899	1,005	13.3				667	10	328	5,174	133		

See footnotes at end of table.

Series R 1–12. Telephones and Average Daily Conversations (Bell and Independent Companies): 1876 to 1970—Con.

[In thousands, except series R 2 and R 3. Census figures in *italics*]

Year	Telephones [1]				Average daily conversations			
	Total		Bell System [2]	Independent companies not connecting with Bell System	Bell System [2]		Independent companies	
	Number	Per 1,000 population			Local exchange	Toll	Local exchange	Toll
	1	2	6	8	9	10	11	12
1898	681	9.2	496	185	3,823	95		
1897	515	7.1	415	100	3,099	75		
1896	404	5.7	354	50	2,630	63		
1895	340	4.8	310	30	2,351	51	170	3
1894	285	4.1	270	15	2,088	38		
1893	266	3.9	266		1,872	34		
1892	261	3.9	261		1,868	41		
1891	239	3.7	239		1,585	34		
1890	*234*	*3.7*						
1890	228	3.6	228		1,438	10		
1889	212	3.4	212		1,240	8		
1888	195	3.2	195		1,052	7		
1887	181	3.0	181		1,012	7		
1886	167	2.9	167		856	7		
1885	156	2.7	156		747	7		
1884	148	2.6	148		698	8		
1883	124	2.3	124		590	5		
1882	98	1.8	98					
1881	71	1.4	71					
1880	*54*	*1.1*						
1880	48	.9	48		237	2		
1879	31	.6	31					
1878	26	.6	26					
1877	9	.2	9					
1876	3	.1	3					

* Denotes first year for which figures include Alaska and Hawaii.
– Represents zero. NA Not available.
Z Less than 500.

[1] Beginning 1920, excludes private line telephones and "Bell" figures derived through totaling data for the Bell Systems, the Southern New England Telephone Company, the Cincinnati Bell Inc., and Bell service telephones.
[2] Bell System has no operations in Alaska and Hawaii.

Series R 13–16. Telephone Toll Rates Between New York City and Selected Cities: 1902 to 1970

[Rate for station-to-station, daytime, 3-minute call]

Effective date	Between New York City and—				Effective date	Between New York City and—			
	Philadelphia	Chicago	Denver	San Francisco		Philadelphia	Chicago	Denver	San Francisco
	13	14	15	16		13	14	15	16
1970, Feb	$0.50	$1.05	$1.25	$1.35	1936, Sept	$0.50	$2.50	$5.25	$7.50
1968, Aug	.50	1.30	1.55	1.70	1930, Jan	.50	3.00	6.00	9.00
1967, Dec	.50	1.40	1.60	1.75					
					1929, Feb	.60	3.00	6.00	9.00
1965, Dec	.50	1.40	1.70	2.00	1927, Dec	.60	3.25	6.00	9.00
1960, Feb	.50	1.45	1.80	2.25	1926, Oct	.60	3.40	7.25	11.30
1959, Sept	.50	1.45	1.95	2.25					
					1919, Jan	.55	4.65	10.40	16.50
1952, Mar	.50	1.50	2.20	2.50	1917, June	[1] .75	[1] 5.00	11.25	18.50
1946, Feb	.45	1.55	2.20	2.50	1917, Mar	(NA)	(NA)	11.25	19.80
1945, July	.45	1.75	2.35	2.50					
					1915, Jan	(NA)	(NA)	11.25	20.70
1941, July	.45	1.75	3.25	4.00	1911	(NA)	(NA)	11.25	
1940, May	.45	1.90	3.25	4.00	1902 [2]	.55	5.45		
1937, Jan	.45	2.20	4.50	6.50					

NA Not available.
[1] Rates in effect immediately prior to Jan. 21, 1919, according to an item in the New York Times for Jan. 23, 1919.

[2] Toll rates were $0.006 per mile for all mileages.

Series R 17–30. Bell Telephone Companies—Property, Revenues, Expenses, Interest, Net Income, Dividends, Employees, and Wages: 1880 to 1970

[In thousands, except series R 29. Census figures in *italics*. Bell companies have no operations in Alaska and Hawaii]

Year	Telephone plant Book value	Telephone plant Depreciation reserves	Miles of wire [1]	Operating revenues Total [2]	Operating revenues Local	Operating revenues Toll	Operating expenses [3]	Federal income taxes	Other income, net [4]	Interest expenses	Net income	Dividends declared [5]	Employees Number [6]	Employees Wages and salaries
	17	18	19	20	21	22	23	24	25	26	27	28	29	30
1970	$56,171,376	$12,609,552	601,912	$17,368,544	$8,685,479	$8,042,160	$12,867,499	$1,608,526	$438,275	$1,028,356	$2,303,227	$1,508,445	793,196	$6,640,908
1969	50,479,993	11,553,823	553,868	16,057,755	7,979,015	7,450,709	11,401,821	2,018,380	390,178	720,435	2,307,298	1,424,155	755,065	5,911,857
1968	46,091,402	10,511,655	512,250	14,428,866	1,366,128	6,472,036	10,025,833	1,990,741	313,821	573,848	2,152,630	1,389,124	696,749	5,136,622
1967	42,508,397	9,445,322	480,308	13,310,606	6,910,073	5,852,380	9,245,691	1,695,744	275,199	493,757	2,150,612	1,290,838	673,316	4,791,543
1966	39,316,832	8,551,263	453,521	12,419,140	6,517,473	5,378,439	8,577,644	1,633,247	281,048	412,992	2,076,305	1,250,184	666,982	4,517,006
1965	36,228,981	7,793,812	422,623	11,320,328	6,114,439	4,705,856	7,857,118	1,466,287	261,214	371,193	1,886,943	1,144,416	627,278	4,169,473
1964	33,384,997	7,158,004	394,360	10,549,386	5,778,936	4,291,054	7,233,111	1,476,741	260,748	356,707	1,743,574	1,085,182	604,577	3,890,458
1963	30,854,403	6,583,840	368,594	9,796,302	5,527,789	3,814,370	6,647,813	1,455,070	207,412	343,700	1,557,130	934,275	585,941	3,659,869
1962	28,656,559	6,126,180	346,697	9,192,520	5,219,431	3,543,591	6,271,299	1,360,144	214,568	314,414	1,456,158	915,846	578,403	3,512,691
1961	26,586,552	5,749,767	327,319	8,614,337	4,921,320	3,284,038	5,903,602	1,244,867	172,368	288,158	1,350,079	871,249	581,245	3,369,059
1960	24,721,830	5,402,334	307,876	8,108,793	4,665,116	3,058,181	5,584,190	1,172,131	184,052	262,422	1,274,101	769,701	594,860	3,282,991
1959	22,818,918	5,084,804	282,287	7,569,869	4,362,374	2,843,466	5,233,097	1,080,302	140,874	226,773	1,170,571	730,682	597,107	3,137,533
1958	21,225,314	4,760,297	260,464	6,936,364	4,049,465	2,543,114	4,910,866	939,687	132,005	216,108	1,001,709	649,497	606,340	3,029,099
1957	19,654,439	4,487,207	243,730	6,466,160	3,743,800	2,406,830	4,788,708	773,481	140,702	176,186	868,486	607,655	656,100	3,042,598
1956	17,555,690	4,228,966	220,154	5,964,876	3,457,640	2,220,488	4,437,810	714,260	127,604	147,778	792,632	546,924	653,074	2,883,990
1955	15,773,373	4,007,118	201,235	5,424,246	3,168,480	1,999,553	4,039,159	644,404	90,084	133,910	696,857	483,619	629,773	2,631,154
1954	14,525,346	3,766,530	185,809	4,901,162	2,914,754	1,755,241	3,746,294	524,995	79,777	132,347	577,303	439,327	591,364	2,443,560
1953	13,419,650	3,555,901	173,375	4,523,707	2,713,501	1,603,608	3,500,599	472,994	69,359	117,668	501,805	389,057	600,363	2,327,884
1952	12,301,975	3,352,297	162,120	4,135,537	2,460,438	1,500,063	3,240,896	403,031	54,622	118,773	427,459	339,186	591,783	2,151,286
1951	11,250,819	3,125,706	152,112	3,727,632	2,205,117	1,369,682	2,929,122	350,134	54,244	118,857	383,763	296,541	563,416	1,927,900
1950	10,375,100	2,904,820	144,264	3,341,308	1,995,659	1,207,509	2,652,421	248,328	41,455	114,637	367,377	262,901	534,751	1,741,907
1949	9,688,160	2,724,745	135,400	2,965,852	1,746,771	1,092,395	2,530,899	125,878	52,224	113,469	247,830	227,929	528,015	1,704,105
1948	8,848,572	2,597,371	126,424	2,693,027	1,551,742	1,030,474	2,324,762	105,154	63,649	91,497	235,264	214,061	559,408	1,621,347
1947	7,552,159	2,447,046	114,850	2,282,446	1,311,401	880,227	2,013,725	77,024	40,613	63,420	168,890	198,469	536,602	1,395,042
1946	6,474,011	2,286,952	107,343	2,146,894	1,198,802	874,497	1,789,686	104,121	9,829	42,950	219,966	193,802	508,391	1,273,137
1945	5,865,065	2,108,385	101,813	1,978,418	1,072,731	845,008	1,454,174	259,213	[7] 30,198	47,177	187,656	187,961	396,567	910,929
1944	5,670,879	1,934,419	100,271	1,814,113	1,017,244	746,694	1,308,926	283,062	7,037	48,998	180,163	181,281	345,703	784,178
1943	5,543,094	1,763,868	99,400	1,690,720	981,094	666,238	1,214,015	243,605	5,989	52,525	188,061	177,865	350,912	731,276
1942	5,450,471	1,601,916	99,709	1,507,336	923,765	544,234	1,089,074	195,906	4,023	52,147	174,232	178,000	334,957	651,904
1941	5,196,319	1,482,590	97,206	1,333,064	872,089	424,521	986,412	110,375	17,118	49,886	203,509	179,341	321,108	586,207
1940	4,887,900	1,397,339	91,273	1,205,435	811,400	360,792	913,023	64,419	39,297	43,349	223,941	180,298	282,224	522,095
1939	4,727,050	1,339,563	87,411	1,136,412	766,956	338,391	870,762	41,387	23,222	43,597	203,888	180,360	266,707	497,276
1938	4,621,914	1,286,582	85,295	1,080,591	734,687	317,290	849,079	35,015	14,655	43,256	167,896	180,847	264,275	488,888
1937	*4,389,549*			*1,051,379*	*703,444*	*321,503*								*463,642*
1937	4,516,998	1,231,712	83,391	1,079,004	724,658	327,229	833,789	31,740	27,302	43,320	197,457	183,400	275,634	476,164
1936	4,380,881	1,156,227	--------	1,020,698	685,110	311,489	766,287	28,807	27,287	51,267	201,624	184,209	262,888	421,447
1935	4,196,671	1,061,650	80,458	934,371	640,993	273,483	726,510	20,843	12,894	52,373	147,539	183,145	244,599	387,264
1934	4,177,950	968,214	80,118	884,532	607,676	258,691	685,951	19,586	3,918	57,561	125,352	183,181	248,996	371,727
1933	4,169,370	891,883	80,281	872,406	617,253	243,906	684,424	17,109	[7] 1,942	54,351	114,580	183,240	248,563	356,287
1932	*4,269,268*		*80,586*	*956,355*	*670,737*	*263,148*							*281,350*	*414,342*
1932	4,188,749	820,195	80,491	943,540	670,737	263,148	747,713	19,073	17,717	55,135	139,336	185,032	266,288	414,342
1931	4,195,064	788,586	79,239	1,066,895	723,920	326,269	824,115	21,249	36,568	64,720	193,379	180,904	294,689	483,614
1930	4,043,422	740,006	76,248	1,094,883	728,709	348,541	852,703	21,931	47,626	66,229	201,646	156,625	324,343	534,468
1929	3,671,100	699,035	69,519	1,063,633	691,359	354,286	807,988	22,924	43,966	59,582	217,105	132,224	344,402	526,684
1928	3,275,687	650,621	62,193	969,237	644,209	309,334	728,544	25,591	27,621	51,635	191,088	119,349	333,794	466,362
1927	*3,085,613*		*56,819*	*894,699*	*604,266*	*271,174*							*308,865*	*429,877*
1927	3,013,985	600,664	56,823	888,987	604,266	271,174	670,397	23,908	21,888	50,511	166,059	112,401	309,005	429,877
1926	2,783,023	576,216	50,861	817,928	557,490	248,087	611,675	22,712	21,329	49,809	155,061	100,614	300,557	408,418
1925	2,524,906	530,071	45,474	736,648	506,026	219,913	557,295	16,829	19,920	45,941	136,503	93,243	293,095	381,857
1924	2,266,923	485,661	39,894	653,459	454,326	190,318	511,905	13,091	20,314	41,531	107,246	82,603	278,838	365,071
1923	1,978,948	443,130	34,524	598,153	412,009	178,427	470,556	11,748	21,526	37,751	99,624	72,429	271,979	333,786
1922	*1,758,079*	*395,297*	*30,614*	*546,820*	*374,719*	*163,098*	*438,592*		*15,186*	*36,790*	*86,623*	*60,305*	*242,710*	*299,350*
1922	1,729,220	395,297	30,617	543,747	374,719	163,098	426,302	10,162	17,209	37,869	86,623	60,305	243,045	297,301
1921	1,543,866	350,642	27,766	495,244	343,133	146,459	397,226	7,471	13,652	36,774	67,425	47,848	224,277	274,990
1920	1,363,826	309,556	25,377	448,233	301,283	141,883	376,171	4,246	11,693	31,724	47,785	40,000	231,316	263,729
1919	1,215,944	276,304	24,163	387,659	--------	--------	--------	6,635	--------	27,693	48,621	39,840	209,860	199,183
1918	1,142,498	235,395	23,349	326,524	--------	--------	--------	5,893	--------	23,111	46,383	39,735	187,458	156,451
1917	1,140,640	206,863	23,134	303,864	214,119	86,814	237,002	--------	5,539	21,266	51,135	37,021	198,700	144,915
1917	1,064,893	201,090	22,610	293,666	207,472	84,560	224,766	4,342	7,976	21,820	50,714	36,863	192,364	137,861
1916	946,293	168,044	19,850	263,095	188,888	72,972	197,772	1,103	7,080	18,379	52,921	35,160	179,032	116,549
1915	880,069	142,307	18,506	232,721	169,156	62,930	171,888	674	6,023	18,096	48,086	32,897	156,294	99,454
1914	847,205	122,338	17,476	224,500	160,311	58,466	166,102	603	1,452	18,940	40,307	30,304	142,527	99,048
1913	797,159	105,720	16,111	214,126	151,260	57,009	156,883	--------	1,447	16,653	42,037	30,302	156,928	95,209
1912	*780,018*		*15,133*	*206,131*			*163,024*				*43,107*	*29,710*	*141,903*	*76,901*
1912	742,288	92,458	14,611	197,798	139,630	53,037	142,285	--------	1,374	14,205	42,681	29,460	141,340	--------
1911	666,661	73,832	12,933	178,267	126,238	47,413	127,892	--------	1,211	13,611	37,975	25,967	129,724	--------
1910	611,000	54,051	11,642	164,245	114,896	45,004	114,618	--------	1,368	11,557	39,438	25,161	121,310	--------
1909	557,417	38,980	10,480	148,951	103,502	40,095	101,547	--------	964	10,222	38,146	23,911	104,956	--------
1908	528,717	17,819	9,831	137,363	93,964	35,800	93,377	--------	781	10,874	33,894	20,719	98,533	--------
1907	*526,079*		*8,947*	*138,804*			*99,830*				*7,527*	*31,447*	*20,202*	*95,811*	*50,576*
1907	502,988	12,246	8,611	127,859	88,682	34,411	87,395	--------	721	--------	30,676	18,152	100,789	--------
1906	450,061	--------	7,469	111,080	77,243	30,192	77,967	--------	685	--------	25,582	16,990	104,646	--------

See footnotes at end of table.

Series R 17–30.　Bell Telephone Companies—Property, Revenues, Expenses, Interest, Net Income, Dividends, Employees, and Wages: 1880 to 1970—Con.

[In thousands, except series R 29.　Census figures in *italics*]

Year	Telephone plant, book value	Miles of wire [1]	Operating revenues			Operating expenses [3]	Other income, net [4]	Interest expenses	Net income	Dividends declared [5]	Employees	
			Total [2]	Local	Toll						Number [6]	Wages and salaries
	17	19	20	21	22	23	25	26	27	28	29	30
1905	$368,065	5,780	$96,923	$67,620	$26,412	$66,189	$577	$5,836	$25,474	$15,818	89,661	----------
1904	316,521	4,671	85,296	59,841	22,638	58,152	577	----------	22,487	15,436	67,756	----------
1903	284,568	9,359	75,089	52,710	19,879	50,946	553	----------	20,321	14,096	61,476	----------
1902		*3,388*						*1,745*		*13,714*	*56,405*	*$28,875*
1902	250,013	3,282	64,176	44,845	16,906	44,338	457	----------	16,129	10,608	55,403	----------
1901	211,780	2,445	54,177	37,971	14,329	35,824	373	----------	15,464	9,884	45,990	----------
1900	180,700	1,962	46,086	32,414	12,098	30,632	300	2,390	13,364	7,894	37,067	----------
1899	145,511	1,519	----------	----------	----------		198	----------	12,095	6,647	29,818	----------
1898	118,124	1,159	----------	----------	----------		168	----------	10,577	6,294	22,955	----------
1897	104,488	951	----------	----------	----------		144	----------	9,735	6,127	19,603	----------
1896	95,242	806	----------	----------	----------		144	----------	8,833	5,481	16,558	----------
1895	87,859	675	24,059	----------	----------	15,488	138	656	8,053	5,067	14,699	----------
1894	77,731	577	----------	----------	----------		117	----------	7,708	4,662	12,553	----------
1893	73,136	508	----------	----------	----------		105	----------	8,630	4,967	11,862	----------
1892	67,636	441	----------	----------	----------		84	----------	8,114	4,631	11,602	----------
1891	62,190	382	----------	----------	----------		83	----------	6,741	4,398	9,713	----------
1890		*240*	*16,405*			*11,144*				*3,168*	*8,645*	
1890	58,512	332	16,153	----------	----------	9,068	59	279	6,866	4,101	8,740	----------
1889	51,572	280	----------	----------	----------		60	----------	6,202	3,802	7,550	----------
1888	44,436	244	----------	----------	----------		75	----------	5,747	3,658	7,445	----------
1887	40,799	203	----------	----------	----------		42	----------	5,506	3,444	6,683	----------
1886	38,325	172	----------	----------	----------		32	----------	5,160	3,246	6,162	----------
1885	38,619	156	10,002	----------	----------	5,124	32	28	4,882	3,107	5,766	----------
1884		137	----------	----------	----------			----------	----------	----------	5,769	----------
1883		115	----------	----------	----------			----------	----------	----------		----------
1882		83	----------	----------	----------		8	----------	----------	----------		----------
1881		52	----------	----------	----------			----------	----------	----------		----------
1880	*15,702*	*34*	*3,098*			*2,374*				*303*	*3,338*	
1880	----------	30	----------	----------	----------			----------	----------	----------		----------

[1] Beginning 1957, excludes drop and block wire.
[2] Includes miscellaneous revenues not shown elsewhere.
[3] Excludes Federal income taxes.
[4] Nonoperating income including Western Electric income less non-operating deductions from income.
[5] Excludes intercompany payments.
[6] As of Dec. 31.
[7] Represents net loss.

Series R 31–45.　Independent Telephone Companies—Property, Revenues, Expenses, Interest, Net Income, Dividends, Employees, and Wages: 1916 to 1970

[In thousands, except series R 31 and R 44.　Census figures, in *italics*, represent "systems and lines"; see text.　Includes Alaska and Hawaii for all years]

Year	Companies included	Telephone plant		Miles of wire	Operating revenues			Operating expenses [2]	Federal income taxes	Miscellaneous income items (net)	Interest expenses	Net income	Dividends declared	Employees	
		Book value	Depreciation reserves		Total [1]	Local	Toll							Number	Wages and salaries
	31	32	33	34	35	36	37	38	39	40	41	42	43	44	45
1970	684	$11,175,403	$2,203,425	------	$2,791,304	$1,453,662	$1,232,084	$1,952,904	$224,326	$47,146	$304,859	$356,094	$243,387	142,000	$1,001,008
1969	688	9,917,622	1,934,273	------	2,461,750	1,313,635	1,054,210	1,695,175	230,715	41,347	246,246	325,927	233,338	133,000	871,301
1968	654	8,714,127	1,705,577	------	2,152,316	1,178,891	891,800	1,477,393	214,630	32,366	196,501	293,484	202,747	123,000	781,627
1967	670	7,620,505	1,487,127	------	1,872,943	1,072,533	729,944	1,299,707	172,198	23,963	159,677	263,881	186,501	114,000	670,777
1966	666	6,877,526	1,333,240	------	1,734,341	1,000,283	668,752	1,183,853	174,322	16,877	133,991	257,241	159,156	110,000	612,105
1965	669	6,055,508	1,167,922	------	1,529,709	916,736	560,551	1,040,236	161,993	11,487	112,041	224,873	137,550	101,000	537,412
1964	663	5,452,292	1,039,244	------	1,386,143	849,035	491,720	934,421	161,036	10,154	97,494	201,013	125,829	95,000	485,065
1963	613	4,847,391	911,183	------	1,247,652	778,371	428,596	835,445	153,868	7,319	85,602	177,432	113,030	90,000	440,233
1962	601	4,334,646	792,986	35,017	1,119,531	710,073	372,005	754,569	137,506	7,597	75,889	157,003	103,427	86,000	404,428
1961	554	3,819,984	689,526	31,586	993,827	640,202	320,193	681,357	122,138	8,609	64,661	133,241	93,136	84,000	380,469
1960	550	3,395,865	600,405	28,594	905,744	585,004	289,400	630,187	107,092	6,974	57,249	116,998	80,880	85,000	359,341
1959	533	2,968,027	522,174	25,188	801,289	519,394	254,147	560,257	94,248	6,168	48,379	103,215	72,432	82,000	330,726
1958	504	2,609,007	460,755	22,667	703,792	459,906	217,470	502,806	76,461	5,638	42,634	86,409	63,968	81,000	310,270
1957	477	2,271,141	409,560	20,502	633,815	411,704	198,618	453,644	69,181	5,239	35,314	80,002	57,979	81,000	292,681
1956	437	1,926,743	364,616	17,478	570,929	370,587	178,728	402,318	67,472	2,035	25,749	76,686	51,584	78,000	261,218
1955	406	1,655,903	326,327	15,201	503,153	329,355	155,431	354,386	61,129	1,608	21,669	66,846	42,840	72,000	224,122
1954	392	1,444,320	293,008	13,587	449,464	295,965	137,820	327,318	48,841	1,767	19,271	55,136	37,209	70,000	214,073
1953	372	1,279,632	264,581	13,037	407,738	268,435	125,962	297,702	44,201	1,099	17,326	49,112	35,063	70,000	197,693
1952	372	1,124,094	239,885	11,337	347,307	226,436	109,943	265,597	31,140	984	15,038	36,368	24,598	68,000	163,349
1951	369	981,071	216,863	10,277	303,060	195,352	98,343	234,478	26,366	917	13,244	29,202	--------	65,000	156,007
1950	379	878,167	203,265	9,176	270,347	170,536	91,512	211,493	18,762	1,217	11,974	28,765		63,000	147,317
1949	305	791,486	186,789		233,064	145,007	80,829	199,288						60,000	134,033
1948	291	667,762	174,735	7,128	203,578	124,219	72,898	161,499	12,843	874	8,015	21,621	4,877	54,000	112,565
1947	281	574,100	162,380	6,566	176,358	107,235	63,784	140,500	11,213	124	5,176	17,939	11,117	50,000	93,900
1946	265	498,567	151,959	6,609	154,757	93,857	56,754	117,195	12,522	1,188	5,067	18,781	11,108	44,000	73,211

See footnotes at end of table.

Series R 31–45. Independent Telephone Companies—Property, Revenues, Expenses, Interest, Net Income, Dividends, Employees, and Wages: 1916 to 1970—Con.

[In thousands, except series R 31 and R 44. Census figures, in *italics*, represent "systems and lines"; see text. Includes Alaska and Hawaii for all years]

| Year | Companies included | Telephone plant | | Miles of wire | Operating revenues | | | Operating expenses² | Federal income taxes | Miscellaneous income items (net) | Interest expenses | Net income | Dividends declared | Employees | |
| | | Book value | Depreciation reserves | | Total¹ | Local | Toll | | | | | | | Number | Wages and salaries |
	31	32	33	34	35	36	37	38	39	40	41	42	43	44	45
1945	227	$449,739	$138,333	5,637	$135,494	$84,155	$48,019	$94,889	$19,697	$382	$5,285	$14,414	$4,466	36,000	$54,478
1944	229	438,962	126,970	5,521	126,081	80,752	42,519	86,482	18,704	327	5,289	14,329	4,538	31,409	46,177
1943	231	432,734	114,347	5,573	117,011	77,015	37,488	78,602	17,862	837	5,143	14,106	5,880	30,309	41,386
1942	210	412,440	98,980	5,829	97,071	68,786	25,801	66,459	11,875	283	5,323	12,725	6,695	32,196	40,473
1941	210	400,836	92,055		88,519	64,276	21,878	68,712		173	5,346	13,705			
1940	210	383,315	85,453		80,846	59,993	18,676	61,478		181	5,541	11,768			
1939	201	369,809	81,047		75,768	56,539	17,172	55,992		338	5,809	12,444			
1938	201	357,472	76,290		71,508	53,678	15,923	53,366		338	5,823	10,573			
1937	200	351,350	73,127		69,957	51,956	16,145	51,634		338	5,771	10,823			
1937	*50,534*	*612,254*		*9,253*	*128,649*	*96,058*	*29,258*							*57,461*	*52,998*
1936	201	346,061	70,889		65,500	49,041	14,803	47,481		346	6,148	10,259			
1935	202	341,949	67,001		61,170	46,273	13,029	43,974		396	6,347	8,830			
1934	211	374,654	71,263	4,803	63,934			48,466	1,283			6,229	6,977	27,048	25,010
1933	261	429,087	74,832	5,027	68,533			51,940	1,073			6,727	8,179	28,836	23,861
1932	271	428,189	67,967	5,141	77,067			55,725	1,147			9,616	11,786	29,462	
1932	*55,353*	*522,634*		*7,092*	*105,176*	*70,351*	*17,900*							*52,735*	*43,775*
1931	287	431,749	64,909	5,154	87,867			61,538	1,293			15,355	12,437	33,660	
1930	314	418,456	59,758	4,880	90,884			63,860	1,454			16,628	12,940	35,715	
1929	323	410,294	60,701	5,023	90,926			63,549	1,661			17,612	12,075	35,434	
1928	316	376,955	56,284	4,756	83,866			59,446	1,740			14,966	10,834	35,310	
1927	312	334,944	51,725	4,476	76,411			55,550	1,878			12,555	10,288	31,505	
1927	*60,123*	*463,262*		*7,017*	*128,874*	*76,955*	*23,451*							*66,407*	*56,720*
1926	293	327,450	50,623	4,728	78,240			57,376	1,661			12,476	9,988	33,848	
1925	268	289,157	49,051	4,045	73,122			54,339				11,714	8,809		
1924	274	271,607	43,508	4,169	69,236			52,163				9,936	7,361		
1923	268	270,076	48,686	3,770	67,486			51,078				9,231	6,816		
1922	1,134	339,963		4,837	85,130			67,945				11,036	8,726		
1922	*57,227*	*422,104*	*64,302*	*6,652*	*119,854*	*72,348*	*16,972*	*66,812*				*10,041*	*5,730*	*69,305*	*53,576*
1921	1,083	339,733		4,565	79,704			66,781				7,809	6,284		
1920	1,034	349,795		4,735	80,561			67,548				7,559	8,204		
1917	702	245,787		3,890	50,485	40,967	9,152	37,260				8,507	7,397	37,381	
1917	*53,089*	*351,689*	*27,515*	*5,693*	*79,582*	*48,579*	*10,436*	*46,411*		*310*	*5,603*	*8,264*	*5,246*	*63,929*	*30,755*
1916	694	258,417		3,871	48,591			34,521				9,268	6,843	38,952	

¹ Includes miscellaneous revenues not shown elsewhere.

² Excludes Federal income taxes.

Series R 46–55. Western Union Telegraph Company—Summary of Facilities, Traffic, and Finances: 1866 to 1915

[In thousands, except series R 46. Census figures in *italics*. Covers landline (domestic) and cable (international) operations]

| As of, or for, year ending— | Telegraph offices | Miles of wire | Messages handled | Total book capitalization | Revenues | Expenses¹ | Miscellaneous income items (net) | Interest expenses | Net income | Dividends declared |
	46	47	48	49	50	51	52	53	54	55
1915, Dec. 31	25,142	1,584		$167,338	$51,100	$40,797	$1,213	$1,348	$10,168	$4,986
1914, Dec. 31	25,784	1,582		162,678	45,880	40,138	972	1,343	5,371	3,989
1913, Dec. 31	25,060	1,561		158,855	45,784	42,327	1,116	1,338	3,235	2,992
1913, June 30	26,300	1,543		158,692	43,978	40,432	927	1,338	3,135	2,991
1912, Dec. 31	*30,864*	*1,814*	*109,378*	*226,387*	*62,822*	*55,610*	*1,941*	*2,769*	*6,384*	*6,180*
1912, June 30	25,392	1,517		159,394	39,438	34,846	1,107	1,697	4,002	2,991
1911, June 30	24,926	1,487		166,762	33,598	27,825	1,424	1,826	5,371	2,990
1910, June 30	24,825	1,429	75,135	164,382	30,741	24,544	1,133	1,951	5,379	2,987
1909, June 30	24,321	1,383	68,053	159,246	27,600	21,364	1,333	1,956	5,614	2,739
1908, June 30	23,853	1,359	62,371	156,371	25,890	23,553	1,063	1,731	1,670	1,715
1907, Dec. 31	*29,110*	*1,578*	*103,794*	*220,294*	*49,685*	*39,227*	*1,899*	*2,653*	*9,704*	*7,477*
1907, June 30	24,760	1,321	74,805	153,585	29,939	24,674	1,058	1,420	4,903	4,867
1906, June 30	24,323	1,256	71,487	146,349	27,828	21,838	1,093	1,335	5,749	4,867
1905, June 30	23,814	1,185	67,477	145,993	26,347	20,227	1,066	1,227	5,959	4,867
1904, June 30	23,458	1,155	67,904	141,271	26,571	19,783	1,116	1,175	6,729	4,867
1903, June 30	23,120	1,089	69,791	138,409	26,525	19,262	2,353	1,166	8,450	4,867
1902, Dec. 31	*27,377*	*1,318*	*91,655*	*162,947*	*39,486*	*28,999*	*1,444*	*1,950*	*9,982*	*6,257*
1902, June 30	23,567	1,030	69,375	133,150	25,602	18,941	670	1,008	6,323	4,867
1901, June 30	23,238	973	65,657	129,715	23,865	17,979	1,773	956	6,703	4,867
1900, June 30	22,900	933	63,168	128,856	22,811	16,934	405	991	5,292	4,867
1899, June 30	22,285	905	61,398	123,818	22,048	16,463	422	1,027	4,980	4,866
1898, June 30	22,210	874	62,174	123,718	21,683	16,231	671	992	5,130	4,866
1897, June 30	21,769	841	58,152	123,484	20,630	15,515	629	896	4,849	4,791
1896, June 30	21,725	827	58,760	121,436	20,820	15,406	474	909	4,980	4,766

See footnotes at end of table.

Series R 46–55. Western Union Telegraph Company—Summary of Facilities, Traffic, and Finances: 1866 to 1915—Con.

[In thousands, except series R 46. Census figures in *italics*]

As of, or for, year ending—	Telegraph offices	Miles of wire	Messages handled	Total book capital- ization	Revenues	Expenses [1]	Miscel- laneous income items (net)	Interest expenses	Net income	Dividends declared
	46	47	48	49	50	51	52	53	54	55
1895, June 30	21,360	803	58,307	$121,278	$20,421	$14,756	$477	$898	$5,244	$4,766
1894, June 30	21,166	791	58,682	120,285	20,059	14,763	513	904	4,906	4,739
1893, June 30	21,078	769	66,592	120,364	22,983	16,057	575	899	6,602	4,632
1892, June 30	20,700	739	62,387	118,423	21,769	14,926	599	932	6,511	4,308
1891, June 30	20,098	716	59,148	116,255	21,135	15,012	499	903	5,719	4,308
1890, June 30	19,382	679	55,879	115,273	20,055	13,701	637	898	6,093	4,955
1889, June 30	18,470	648	54,108	108,430	19,075	13,328	725	820	5,651	4,308
1888, June 30	17,241	616	51,464	101,968	17,584	13,493	535	494	4,132	4,041
1887, June 30	15,658	525	47,395	96,481	15,683	12,021	504	608	3,557	812
1886, June 30	15,142	490	43,290	93,794	14,871	11,384	511	580	3,418	3,400
1885, June 30	14,184	462	42,097	92,616	15,298	11,029	509	505	4,274	5,198
1884, June 30	13,761	451	42,076	92,459	16,693	12,012	565	503	4,744	5,597
1883, June 30	12,917	433	41,181	90,961	16,596	10,490	459	433	6,132	4,999
1882, June 30	12,068	374	38,842	88,971	14,819	9,035	579	430	5,933	4,798
1881, June 30	10,737	327	32,500	87,123	11,552	7,630	2,228	437	5,713	3,733
1880, June 30	9,077	234	29,216	64,080	10,581	5,863	437	435	4,720	3,280
1880, June 1	*12,510*	*291*	*31,703*	*96,031*	*16,697*	*10,218*	--------	*564*	*5,970*	*4,137*
1879, June 30	8,534	212	25,070	62,699	9,118	5,239	395	438	3,836	2,295
1878, June 30	8,014	206	23,919	58,287	8,637	5,656	179	462	2,698	2,085
1877, June 30	7,500	194	21,159	56,318	9,089	6,096	194	443	2,694	1,521
1876, June 30	7,072	184	18,730	55,844	9,143	6,061	314	535	2,862	2,532
1875, June 30	6,565	179	17,154	54,673	[2] 4,330	[2] 2,832	[2] 33	[2] 228	[2] 1,304	1,351
1874, Dec. 31 [3]	6,188	176	16,329	54,773	8,872	5,935	148	333	2,752	151
1873, Dec. 31 [3]	5,740	154	14,457	53,331	8,612	6,506	155	266	1,995	269
1872, Dec. 31 [3]	5,237	137	12,444	----------	8,471	5,558	97	370	2,640	259
1871, Dec. 31 [3]	4,606	121	10,646	----------	7,384	4,916	74	318	2,224	222
1870, Dec. 31 [3]	3,972	112	9,158	----------	6,731	4,539	116	327	1,982	1,035
1869, Dec. 31 [3]	3,607	105	7,935	48,402	6,672	4,346	225	325	2,226	1,810
1868, Dec. 31 [3]	3,219	98	6,405	47,677	6,636	3,873	139	346	2,557	832
1867, Dec. 31 [3]	2,565	85	5,879	47,426	5,964	3,693	182	371	2,082	1,608
1866, Dec. 31 [3]	2,250	76	----------	24,205	4,619	2,686	185	162	1,956	1,051

[1] Including facility rentals and taxes.
[2] Income data are for 6 months ending June 30.
[3] Telegraph offices, miles of wire, messages handled, and total book capitalization are as of June 30.

Series R 56–70. Domestic Telegraph Industry—Messages, Property, Revenues, Expenses, Net Income, Dividends, Employees, and Wages: 1916 to 1970

[In thousands, except series R 67 and R 69. Census figures in *italics*]

Year	Messages handled	Private-line telegraph service revenues		Telegraph plant		Miles of wire	Operat- ing revenues	Operat- ing ex- penses [2]	Federal income taxes [3]	Net income	Divi- dends declared	Employees		Bell Teletypewriter Exchange (TWX) Service	
		Tele- graph com- panies	Tele- phone com- panies [1]	Book value	Depre- ciation reserves							Number	Wages and salaries	Number of teletype- writers	Rev- enues
	56	57	58	59	60	61	62	63	64	65	66	67	68	69	70
1970	69,679	$125,188	$130,050	$1,029,149	$331,360	621	$402,456	$368,446	–	$26,074	$19,681	24,293	$209,294	40,766	$75,214
1969	77,059	122,294	138,091	968,401	307,518	683	391,338	358,445	–	22,724	18,076	25,164	203,836	42,605	71,051
1968	85,645	111,815	128,328	916,712	284,677	753	358,202	328,622	–	21,569	16,776	26,502	196,621	46,411	71,118
1967	89,078	104,950	121,461	871,425	279,647	829	334,983	310,791	–	22,062	15,917	26,524	190,085	47,200	72,367
1966	92,682	94,074	118,425	778,810	262,843	891	319,329	294,435	–	20,712	13,935	27,198	180,172	48,663	77,207
1965	94,302	93,319	118,508	688,757	242,974	964	305,615	281,835	–	17,833	11,085	26,179	164,793	56,675	72,902
1964	97,448	91,922	112,190	634,636	221,783	984	299,410	278,324	($1,200)	16,974	10,501	26,607	161,129	59,843	72,470
1963	104,220	84,687	115,953	596,587	198,930	1,010	286,822	266,660	1,000	[4] 24,931	10,490	28,015	160,650	57,598	70,321
1962	112,487	61,981	118,746	541,419	183,099	1,043	264,119	257,139	(3,730)	10,405	10,484	30,021	168,278	56,693	69,338
1961	117,263	58,968	123,661	434,933	177,850	1,044	265,727	253,374	3,295	11,833	9,704	31,425	165,856	57,920	67,859

See footnotes at end of table.

Series R 56–70. Domestic Telegraph Industry—Messages, Property, Revenues, Expenses, Net Income, Dividends, Employees, and Wages: 1916 to 1970—Con.

[In thousands, except series R 67 and R 69. Census figures in *italics*]

| Year | Messages handled | Private-line telegraph service revenues | | Telegraph plant | | Miles of wire | Operating revenues | Operating expenses [2] | Federal income taxes | Net income | Dividends declared | Employees | | Bell Teletypewriter Exchange (TWX) Service | |
| | | Telegraph companies | Telephone companies [1] | Book value | Depreciation reserves | | | | | | | Number | Wages and salaries | Number of teletypewriters | Revenues |
	56	57	58	59	60	61	62	63	64	65	66	67	68	69	70
1960	124,319	$54,841	$118,384	$398,023	$168,605	1,063	$262,365	$246,768	$4,350	$10,205	$8,9⁻0	32,655	$164,524	54,744	$62,539
1959	130,993	49,763	108,943	380,216	157,382	1,058	260,849	235,762	11,000	14,755	7,941	33,151	159,842	51,631	58,111
1958	131,867	39,186	85,850	364,498	149,693	1,075	240,729	225,146	4,975	11,062	7,505	33,620	154,032	47,491	51,284
1957	143,947	34,414	77,735	350,860	147,334	1,078	245,549	228,219	5,993	12,911	7,165	36,467	159,157	44,923	47,944
1956	151,600	29,859	66,074	332,727	141,490	1,088	238,362	219,231	6,665	12,060	6,226	37,754	153,625	41,628	44,872
1955	153,910	24,458	55,309	310,968	135,826	1,100	228,816	206,024	9,613	10,331	5,695	37,785	143,289	38,946	41,758
1954	152,582	20,163	48,732	300,126	130,183	1,129	209,635	194,657	6,208	4,480	3,730	37,009	137,521	36,672	38,349
1953	162,188	17,458	44,619	289,448	128,776	1,151	208,578	193,863	5,743	13,242	3,690	38,957	139,489	35,272	33,174
1952	151,712	15,031	40,828	286,372	126,580	1,194	184,336	183,395	199	[5] 724	3,689	39,853	126,974	33,338	26,503
1951	180,151	12,669	36,265	284,293	123,825	1,225	192,089	182,023	4,007	4,711	3,381	40,319	127,818	30,815	23,344
1950	178,904	9,139	31,747	294,451	128,227	1,298	177,994	167,280	2,050	7,353	2,459	40,482	116,937	28,393	20,445
1949	175,323	7,528	28,017	306,316	133,979	1,438	171,393	173,505		[5] 3,468		41,660	125,871	25,526	17,940
1948	191,013	5,696	25,225	310,295	136,267	1,632	183,429	185,362		1,265	1,228	48,967	140,901	23,423	16,302
1947	213,780	4,320	21,829	314,275	142,664	1,743	191,654	185,314	2,176	906		53,572	138,976	20,208	13,743
1946	212,072	3,681	20,732	361,618	161,826	2,044	175,536	183,366		[5] 10,030		57,644	137,293	14,838	12,946
1945	236,169	3,572	23,627	357,784	157,243	2,247	182,048	174,848		[5] 7,834	2,433	63,446	126,662	13,031	16,798
1944	225,462	3,655	20,727	358,882	152,795	2,272	173,207	160,169	2,267	5,117	2,167	61,481	112,553	15,979	20,613
1943	231,692	3,688	17,590	366,347	153,730	2,303	166,953	159,020	3,236	[5] 746	2,090	61,037	111,8 2	16,013	23,456
1942	223,148	3,889	19,318	384,352	120,863	2,294	145,789	134,031	4,448	3,836	2,090	64,674	92,450	16,607	16,233
1941	210,928	3,079	14,830	380,501	114,174	2,281	130,519	121,841	1,450	4,016	2,090	65,363	84,267	16,130	10,169
1940	191,645	2,170	14,621	375,021	97,746	2,269	114,587	110,856		372	1,045	59,670	74,736	14,855	8,436
1939	189,055	2,185	15,744	388,837	87,569	2,277	109,899	106,995		[5] 3,152		57,513	71,287	14,266	7,782
1938	185,639	2,056	16,834	387,897	83,827	2,279	106,813	105,996		[5] 5,248		57,190	70,124		6,803
1937	200,711	1,981	19,098	387,749	80,678	2,275	117,228	111,614		[5] 523	1,568	64,084	77,745	12,499	6,775
1937	*206,937*			*418,231*		[6] *2,302*	*117,032*				*1,604*	*64,254*	*77,928*		
1936	193,566	1,897	18,538	384,946	42,398	2,270	115,772	103,991	116	5,129	784	67,862	71,155	10,646	5,722
1935	176,250	1,782	17,007	383,216	42,574	2,245	106,262	96,076		3,213	2,090	62,257	65,030	7,894	3,864
1934	155,215	1,749	19,131	383,165	42,940	2,247	102,557	96,069		[5] 387		62,839	65,810	5,776	2,300
1933	143,553	1,856	20,023	383,886	43,947	2,245	96,613	90,669		330		58,368	60,401	3,578	995
1932	143,075	1,830	21,284	383,960	44,191	2,239	97,902	96,339		[5] 5,099	1,045	60,997	65,760	2,524	514
1932	*147,941*			*415,694*		[6] *2,260*	*97,729*					*60,933*	*66,988*		
1931	183,373	1,787	25,245	382,737		2,250	126,697	120,166		537	7,838	72,916	90,084	1,479	7
1930	211,971	1,881	27,034	379,869	53,095	2,269	148,223	139,141	486	3,942	8,188	84,962	108,557		
1929	234,050	1,947	25,197	357,343	53,710	2,251	163,358	146,867	1,307	12,796	8,188	87,435	113,928		
1928	211,559	1,754	21,057	307,113	50,791	2,202	153,329	135,081	1,798	13,889	8,085	77,644	94,415		
1927	203,365	1,853	18,016	292,817	46,991	2,095	147,845	128,940	2,126	14,105	7,981	76,183	91,493		
1927	*215,595*			*338,143*		[6] *2,138*	*159,682*	*142,213*		*16,090*	*8,191*	*74,903*	*89,984*		
1926	203,035	1,899	16,548	281,503	43,432	1,977	149,721	131,473	2,070	13,841	7,981	79,755	101,003		
1925	185,187	1,601	15,153	266,571	40,675	1,944	141,680	122,613	2,062	15,153	7,232	73,262	90,911		
1924	162,700	1,510	13,207	252,678	38,146	1,884	125,490	111,853		12,152	6,983	68,561	80,692		
1923	158,468	1,502	13,106	238,923	35,326	1,836	124,172	109,197		13,094	6,983	69,045	79,341		
1922	149,219	1,689	12,145	230,644	32,100	1,807	116,659	100,352		14,311	6,983	62,576	70,497		
1922	*181,519*			*254,030*		*1,845*	*128,639*	*111,724*		*15,675*	*7,143*	*62,299*	*68,737*		
1921	139,544	1,873	11,270	224,876	23,293	1,787	111,707	101,817		7,932	6,983	64,395	71,942		
1920	155,884	1,489	10,541	214,986	19,289	1,711	124,379	113,253		9,199	6,983	74,448	86,037		
1919	139,435	1,318	7,969	203,010	16,967	1,686	105,409	93,165		9,595	6,983	65,181	66,351		
1918	134,031	1,121	5,811	190,712	12,965	1,620	90,369	80,511		8,103	6,983	69,528	58,376		
1917	129,273	1,300	5,202	184,351	10,792	1,863	81,623	67,084		12,336	6,983	60,122	46,953		
1917	*151,725*			*183,488*		*1,889*	*91,313*	*79,409*		*12,125*	*7,166*	*60,376*	*40,512*		
1916		1,365	4,162			1,877	66,471	54,335		11,764	5,985				

− Represents zero.
[1] Includes minor amounts for Hawaiian Telephone Co.
[2] Excludes Federal income taxes.
[3] Figures in parentheses represent reversal of income taxes charged in previous years. The Western Union Telegraph Company has numerous items deductible from taxable income, but not recorded in the accounts as income deductions; this accounts for the fact that it reported net income in the late sixties with no concurrent liability for income taxes.

[4] This figure is affected by the $18,126,223 loss on the sale of the Western Union cables system recorded as a cables loss and the $8,250,000 tax reduction therefore recorded as a domestic telegraph gain.
[5] Figures represent net loss.
[6] Excludes wire owned and operated wholly by Class I railroads and landwire of ocean-cable companies.

Series R 71–74. Domestic Telegraph Message Rates and Teletypewriter Exchange Service (TWX) Rates Between New York City and Selected Cities: 1850 to 1970

Year	Between New York City and—				Year	Between New York City and—			
	Philadelphia	Chicago	Denver	San Francisco		Philadelphia	Chicago	Denver	San Francisco
	71	72	73	74		71	72	73	74
TELEGRAPH RATES [1]					**TELEGRAPH RATES** [1]—Con.				
In effect Jan. 1, 1970	$2.25	$2.25	$2.25	$2.25	In effect in—Con.				
					1876	(NA)	$0.50	$2.00	$2.00
Made effective:					1875	(NA)	.25	(NA)	(NA)
1968, Nov. 1	2.25	2.25	2.25	2.25	1873	$0.30	1.00	2.50	2.50
1966, Jan. 1	1.27	1.70	2.23	2.23	1870	.25	1.00	(NA)	5.00
1963, July 10	1.20	1.60	2.10	2.10	1869	.45	2.05	(NA)	7.45
1960, Oct. 17	1.10	1.45	1.90	1.90	1866	.25	1.85	7.00	7.45
1958, Aug. 1	1.05	1.40	1.85	1.85	1850	.25	1.55		
1956, Aug. 26	.95	1.30	1.75	1.75					
					TELETYPEWRITER EXCHANGE SERVICE RATES [2]				
1954, July 15	.85	1.25	1.70	1.70					
1952, July 6	.65	1.10	1.55	1.70	In effect Jan. 1, 1970	.25	.45	.55	.60
1951, Sept. 1	.60	1.00	1.45	1.60					
1950, Feb. 1	.40	.75	1.25	1.45	Made effective:				
1946, Dec. 29	.36	.72	1.08	1.44	1966, Sept. 1	.25	.45	.55	.60
1946, June 12	.33	.66	.99	1.32	1960, Feb. 7	.45	1.15	1.65	1.75
1919, Apr. 1	.30	.60	.90	1.20	1953, July 1	.45	1.20	1.65	1.75
					1946, Feb. 1	.35	1.05	1.55	1.75
In effect in—					1931, Nov. 21 [3]	.35	1.10	1.80	2.40
1908	.25	.50	.75	1.00					
1890	.20	.40	.75	1.00					
1888	.25	.50	.75	1.00					
1884	(NA)	.50	(NA)	1.00					
1883	.15	.50	1.25	1.50					
1877	(NA)	.60	(NA)	(NA)					

NA Not available.
[1] Beginning Sept. 1, 1951, minimum charge for 15 text words or less; prior to that, for 10 text words or less.

[2] Prior to September 1966, telephone company rates for 3 minutes or less, 2-way; thereafter, for each minute or fraction thereof. Since 1959, the telegraph company has offered similar service called "Telex" with a different rate structure.
[3] Beginning of service.

Series R 75–88. International Telegraph Industry—Messages, Property, Ocean-Cable Mileage, Countries Served by Radiotelegraph, Revenues, Expenses, Net Income, Employees, and Wages: 1907 to 1970

[In thousands, except series R 82 and R 87.   Census figures in *italics*.   Includes Hawaii and Puerto Rico]

Year	Telegraph messages [1]			Overseas telephone calls [2]	Telegraph plant		Nautical miles of ocean-telegraph cable	Overseas countries served by direct radio-telegraph circuits [3]	Operating revenues	Operating expenses [4]	Federal income taxes	Net income	Employees [5]	
	Total	Cable	Radio		Book value	Depreciation reserves							Number	Wages and salaries
	75	76	77	78	79	80	81	82	83	84	85	86	87	88
1970	32,241	6,548	25,693	25,813	$351,674	$93,355	—	60	$193,808	$155,708	$11,887	$42,346	7,599	$71,709
1969	32,235	6,832	25,403	20,660	320,629	81,351	8	62	179,993	142,413	12,421	37,253	7,938	65,463
1968	30,705	6,560	24,145	15,166	282,412	79,225	8	64	153,547	123,997	8,527	21,212	7,727	59,873
1967	29,953	6,577	23,376	12,332	250,722	70,561	8	66	132,427	107,565	6,784	19,324	7,541	55,437
1966	29,925	6,663	23,262	9,932	213,359	62,623	8	68	121,516	96,133	6,550	14,779	7,437	52,217
1965	28,830	6,467	22,363	8,108	189,242	56,584	8	69	106,696	87,374	5,448	13,110	7,581	50,531
1964	30,102	9,365	20,737	6,382	191,412	71,452	38	70	107,560	91,109	5,439	9,158	9,041	53,131
1963	29,390	11,260	18,130	5,290	153,445	66,939	42	71	97,822	85,102	3,611	[6] 8,638	9,968	51,905
1962	28,568	11,318	17,250	4,914	163,360	72,394	55	72	92,372	82,104	4,083	8,118	10,522	50,651
1961	28,345	11,323	17,022	4,365	172,050	85,210	71	74	90,049	78,379	4,926	8,467	10,734	48,876
1960	28,278	11,186	17,092	3,713	163,798	82,610	71	77	86,976	76,885	4,511	7,991	11,011	47,636
1959	28,133	10,807	17,326	3,039	157,557	83,679	75	83	84,377	71,726	5,815	8,328	11,239	44,531
1958	26,876	10,420	16,456	2,688	154,439	82,018	76	86	77,281	67,044	4,868	6,605	11,182	42,855
1957	27,838	10,647	17,191	2,421	149,449	80,069	76	84	76,845	66,258	5,386	5,921	11,502	41,994
1956	27,348	11,012	16,336	2,024	139,818	77,629	76	85	73,472	60,862	5,783	6,186	11,306	41,288
1955	25,642	10,671	14,971	1,742	135,178	76,432	76	85	68,050	58,366	6,328	5,020	11,844	40,548
1954	24,357	10,619	13,738	1,529	133,667	75,987	78	85	63,811	54,654	4,854	5,333	11,814	39,241
1953	23,725	10,085	13,640	1,440	131,168	75,348	78	85	59,727	53,217	4,308	3,390	11,686	37,507
1952	23,880	9,756	14,124	1,364	127,101	72,923	78	85	57,606	51,557	2,434	4,393	11,540	36,055
1951	24,043	10,059	13,984	1,263	127,310	73,929	78	85	56,949	49,087	3,504	4,526	11,081	33,120
1950	22,578	9,969	12,609	1,000	136,168	82,757	88	83	50,333	45,226	1,304	4,538	10,759	30,240
1949	20,891	10,390	10,501	853	134,332	82,897	88	83	46,595	45,959	525	619	11,150	31,269
1948	22,136	11,022	11,114	798	135,626	82,087	90	81	46,348	47,435	519	[7] 778	11,755	31,717
1947	23,960	11,835	12,125	664	132,534	79,426	91	76	45,579	49,358	263	[7] 2,715	12,404	33,678
1946	22,272	11,069	11,203	632	129,147	76,769	91	75	45,199	44,999	230	836	11,557	30,497
1945	21,047	10,531	10,516	360	137,623	86,197	91	72	49,879	37,905	7,190	7,907	9,579	25,153
1944	17,266	10,386	6,880	173	136,329	84,550	91	69	46,981	34,340	6,983	7,454	7,898	20,002
1943	15,991	10,159	5,832	154	138,436	83,909	95	68	40,254	29,450	6,424	6,508	7,591	16,533
1942	13,020	8,012	5,008	135	139,360	83,807	95	65	35,812	28,423	4,600	4,525	7,232	14,553
1941	16,511	7,434	9,077	117	141,292	82,723	95	61	36,022	28,425	3,201	3,814	8,206	13,723
1940	16,619	7,667	8,952	73	142,015	81,240	95	60	32,087	27,035	1,359	3,598	8,083	12,809
1939	18,725	9,300	9,425	76	146,236	81,860	95	55	30,612	26,518	524	2,074	8,176	12,663
1938	18,306	9,612	8,694	75	147,747	81,263	95	53	26,895	25,577	219	[7] 27	8,229	12,383
1937	*16,331*	*11,129*	*5,202*		*88,533*		*104*		*28,275*				*5,403*	*7,408*
1937	19,768	10,376	9,392	75	148,082	79,517	95	52	29,648	25,511	530	2,936	8,428	12,302
1936	17,641	9,819	7,822	48	147,723	78,082	95	52	27,173	24,042	306	2,004	8,182	11,538
1935	15,669	9,050	6,619	28	147,708	76,613	95	50	25,360	23,693	186	693	8,134	11,033
1934	14,464	9,287	5,177	27	147,662	75,473	97	49	25,449	23,177	259	1,395	7,851	10,754
1933	15,365	10,456	4,909	30	146,602	74,528	97	48	24,649	21,532	227	3,467	7,337	9,615
1932	*10,437*	*10,437*			*90,751*		*96*		*16,927*				*5,790*	*6,961*
1932	14,940	10,443	4,497	28	145,913	73,066	98	46	23,442	21,707	169	2,368	7,553	10,009
1931	17,414	12,551	4,863	33	148,847	62,050	98	43	28,584	23,919	201	5,610	8,114	11,178

See footnotes at end of table.

Series **R 75–88.** International Telegraph Industry—Messages, Property, Ocean-Cable Mileage, Countries Served by Radiotelegraph, Revenues, Expenses, Net Income, Employees, and Wages: 1907 to 1970—Con.

[**In thousands, except series R 82 and R 87.** Census figures in *italics*. Includes Hawaii and Puerto Rico]

Year	Telegraph messages [1]			Overseas telephone calls [2]	Telegraph plant		Nautical miles of ocean-tele-graph cable	Overseas countries served by direct radio-tele-graph circuits [3]	Operat-ing revenues	Operat-ing expenses [4]	Federal income taxes	Net income	Employees [5]	
	Total	Cable	Radio		Book value	Depre-ciation reserves							Number	Wages and salaries
	75	76	77	78	79	80	81	82	83	84	85	86	87	88
1930	20,409	15,258	5,151	33	$147,236	$64,994	98	42	$35,360	$27,010	$366	$9,775	8,999	$13,604
1929	21,565	16,473	5,092	30	135,797	72,671	97	34	39,656	27,559	798	13,705	8,579	13,129
1928	17,562	14,812	2,750	23	126,770	69,124	93	30	34,264	21,643	--------	11,368	2,299	3,392
1927	*17,765*	*13,987*	*3,778*	--------	*88,556*		*99*	--------	*20,137*	*11,549*	--------	*7,755*	*6,595*	*9,536*
1927	16,093	13,793	2,300	12	122,635	67,668	91	26	32,083	21,340	--------	9,814	2,332	3,395
1926	15,493	13,298	2,195	9	116,179	60,904	88	20	32,672	22,293	--------	11,159	2,309	3,469
1925	7,580	5,520	2,060	10	110,106	59,370	83	16	34,811	22,726	--------	11,526	2,352	3,659
1924	7,088	5,198	1,890	12	107,357	54,834	83	14	33,636	21,360	--------	10,962	2,340	3,463
1923	6,165	4,465	1,700	11	101,011	52,011	79	12	32,173	21,725	--------	9,768	2,349	3,459
1922	*11,968*	*9,603*	*2,365*	--------	*72,632*		*77*	--------	*21,319*	*12,450*	--------	*8,193*	*6,333*	*7,425*
1922	5,437	3,992	1,445	10	92,073	49,142	73	10	34,191	22,539	--------	11,058	2,603	3,902
1921	4,947	3,987	960	5	90,139	46,467	76	9	35,976	22,570	--------	10,399	3,111	4,283
1920	4,387	4,037	350		83,799	42,059	75	8	40,507	24,287	--------	11,463	3,062	4,882
1919		581			74,090	37,145	69	4	22,584	12,267	--------	5,357	2,688	3,938
1918		418	--------		64,058	31,481	69	4	17,299	10,425	--------	2,965		
1917	*6,573*	*6,451*	*122*		*59,871*		*71*	--------	*16,749*	*9,281*	--------	*5,707*	*4,347*	*3,252*
1917		485			63,116	26,763	69	4	15,274	7,838	--------	3,434		
1916		378			63,256	21,349	68	4	10,878	4,706	--------	3,318		
1912	*6,121*	*5,841*	*280*	--------	*58,136*	*7,600*	*68*	*1*	*8,469*	*4,008*	--------	*2,953*	*[8] 1,656*	*1,167*
1907	*6,024*	*5,869*	*155*	--------	*57,438*	--------	*46*	--------	*7,672*	*2,205*	--------	*4,029*	*1,207*	*915*

– Represents zero.

[1] Numbers of cable and radio telegraph messages depend on whether they were reported by what were formerly known as cable or radio carriers. Since 1956, radio carriers have been using circuits in cables in addition to radio for transmission of messages; since 1965, cable carriers have been using radio circuits via satellite relay in addition to cables.

[2] Overseas telephone calls inserted for information purposes only; not handled by International Telegraph Industry. Beginning 1956, includes Alaska, Guam, and Virgin Islands. Excludes calls over landwire to Canada and Mexico.

[3] Number of overseas countries served by direct radiotelegraph circuits decreased during the sixties as they were displaced by submarine cable and satellite circuits; even some of the remaining circuits are for fallback use only.

[4] Excludes Federal income taxes.

[5] Prior to 1929, employment and compensation figures represent incomplete reportings to FCC by all carriers.

[6] Figure represents net loss resulting from the sale, charged against income, of a cable system.

[7] Figures represent net loss.

[8] As of September 16.

Series **R 89–92.** International Cable and Radiotelegraph Rates and International Telephone Rates Between New York City and Selected Cities: 1866 to 1970

[Prior to 1924, rate changes are for messages by cable only (except as noted for radiotelegraph messages). Since 1924, rate changes are for both cable and radiotelegraph messages]

Effective date	New York City to—				Effective date	New York City to—			
	London	Cairo	Tokyo	Buenos Aires		London	Cairo	Tokyo	Buenos Aires
	89	90	91	92		89	90	91	92
INTERNATIONAL CABLE AND RADIOTELEGRAPH RATES [1]					**INTERNATIONAL CABLE AND RADIOTELEGRAPH RATES** [1]—Con.				
1970, Jan. 1	$0.23	$0.34	$0.34	$0.31	1892, May 1	$0.25	----------	$2.21	$1.50
1969, Jan. 1	.23	.34	.34	.31	1892, Jan. 26	.25		2.21	1.70
1966, Apr. 12	.23	.34	.34	.31	1890	.25			1.82
1958, Aug. 1	.21	.34	.34	.31	1888	.25			3.98
1950, July 1	.19	.30	.30	.27	1886	.12			3.98
1949, Feb. 2	.25	.40	.40	.35	1884	.40			3.98
1948, Apr. 28	.25	.30	.30	.28	1882	.50			3.98
1947, Aug. 5	.25	.30	.30	.22	1882	.50			4.60
1946, May 1	.20	.30	.20	.20	1880	.50			7.50
1945, May 1	.20	.42	.24	.20	1868	1.58			
1943, Aug. 16	.20	.42	.72	.26	1866	10.00			
1940	.20	.42	.72	.42	**INTERNATIONAL TELEPHONE RATES** [3]				
1937	.20	.42	.72	.42	1970, Mar. 1	9.60	$12.00	12.00	12.00
1931	.20	.39	.80	.42	1969	12.00	12.00	12.00	12.00
1928	.20	.39	.80	.42	1946	12.00	12.00	12.00	12.00
1927	.20	.45	.80	.42	1945	12.00	30.00	19.50	12.00
1925	.20	.42	.85	.42	1944	21.00	30.00	19.50	12.00
1924	.20	(NA)	.109	.50	1940	21.00	30.00	19.50	15.00
1924	.20	(NA)	.85	.50	1939	21.00	30.00	30.75	15.00
1923 [2]	.20	(NA)	.109	.50	1937	21.00	30.00	30.75	21.00
1921 [2]	.18	(NA)	.85	.50	1936	21.00	30.00	33.00	21.00
1919	.25	(NA)	1.09	.50	1934	30.00	36.00	39.00	30.00
1917	.25	(NA)	1.33	.50	1932	30.00	36.00		30.00
1916 [2]	.17	(NA)	.92	.65	1930	30.00			30.00
1912	.25	(NA)	1.33	.65	1930	30.00			36.00
1910	.25	(NA)	1.33	.85	1928	45.00			
1905	.25	.56	1.33	1.00	1927	75.00			
1903	.25	(NA)	1.53	1.00					
1903, Jan	.25	.61	1.76	1.00					
1901	.25	----------	1.76	1.00					

NA Not available.

[1] Per plain language telegraph-word, including address and signature.

[2] Change in radiotelegraph messages.

[3] For 3-minute person-to-person telephone conversations.

Chapter R

Radio and Television (Series R 93-162)

R 93-162. General note.

Federal regulation of radio communication has been continuous since 1912 when the Department of Commerce was given authority to license radio equipment and radio operators, and broadcast stations, which began operation in 1921. On February 23, 1927, Congress established the Federal Radio Commission with broad authority for the regulation of radio. In 1934, the powers of the Federal Radio Commission were transferred to the Federal Communications Commission.

Principal governmental sources of statistics in respect to broadcast and nonbroadcast radio services include the following:

    1. U.S. Bureau of the Census, *Census of Business, 1935: Radio Broadcasting*; Fifteenth Census Reports, *Population*, vol. VI, *Families*, 1930; Sixteenth Census Reports, *Housing*, vol. II, part 1, 1940; *U.S. Census of Housing: 1950, 1960*, and *1970*, vol. I, part 1.

    2. U.S. Department of Commerce, *Annual Report of the Secretary of Commerce*, 1913-1926.

    3. Federal Radio Commission, *Annual Report of the Federal Radio Commission*, 1927-1933; *Commercial Radio Advertising*, 1931.

    4. U.S. Federal Communications Commission, *Annual Report of the Federal Communications Commission*, 1938-1970; *Report on Chain Broadcasting*, 1941; *The Public Service Responsibilities of Broadcast Stations*, 1946; "An Economic Study of Standard Broadcasting," October 1947 (processed); House Report No. 1297, 85th Cong., 2d sess., *Network Broadcasting*, 1958.

    5. House Report No. 1273, 73d Cong., 2d sess., *Report on Communication Companies*, 1934.

Since 1937, the FCC has obtained annual financial reports from networks and broadcast stations. Statistical tabulations of the data so reported have been made available by the FCC in its annual reports; in its annual *Statistics of the Communications Industry in the United States;* and in annual processed reports. Unlike the telephone and telegraph industries, radio broadcasting is not classified as a common carrier and is not subject to rate or earnings regulation. The FCC, therefore, does not prescribe a uniform system of accounts for the radio industry. However, the Commission's Annual Report Form No. 324, and the accompanying instructions, ensures general uniformity in the reported data. The individual financial reports of networks and stations filed with the FCC are not available for public inspection. However, some individual network and station data have been published from time to time, as for example, in a Committee Print, 84th Cong., 2d sess. (Senator John W. Bricker), *The Network Monopoly: Report Prepared for Use of the Committee on Interstate and Foreign Commerce*, 1956; *Monopoly Problems in Regulated Industries; Hearings before the Antitrust Subcommittee of the Committee on the Judiciary*, 84th Cong., 2d sess., 4 vols., part 2, 1956.

R 93-97. General note.

Statistics of broadcast stations are commonly presented in terms of "authorized" and of "licensed" stations. A broadcast station is authorized when it receives a construction permit from the U.S. Federal Communications Commission (or predecessor licensing agencies). Normally, a station is expected to complete construction and begin regular operation within 8 months thereafter. However, not all authorized stations complete this process and be-

come operating stations. This has occurred mainly in the broadcast services of frequency modulation (FM) and television (TV).

Similarly, statistics of "licensed" stations can be misleading. A station permittee who has completed construction in accordance with the specifications of the construction permit or a modification thereof, usually receives a regular license, prior to start of regular on-the-air program service. However, for a variety of reasons, the FCC has permitted stations to undertake regular broadcast service under a Special Temporary Authorization. Many stations have operated under such authority for a number of years. Here, again, this statement applies particularly to FM and TV stations.

Figures for these series are for the most part presented in terms of operating stations. Stations are recorded in FCC records as operating when they have received permission to conduct program tests. In some instances, considerable time may elapse before such stations are in regular, daily operation. Adjustments for this factor have been made by the FCC on the basis of trade sources, and such adjustments are incorporated here. In sum, the data on operating stations are not precise, but are believed to be reasonably accurate.

R 93. Standard broadcast (AM) stations operating, 1921-1970.

Source: 1921, U.S. Federal Communications Commission, unpublished data; 1922-1926, *Annual Report of the Secretary of Commerce*, various issues; 1927-1932, *Seventh Annual Report of the Federal Radio Commission for Fiscal Year 1933*, p. 18; 1933-1970, FCC, *Annual Report*, various issues.

Prior to 1948, data pertain to licensed stations which, in the AM service, generally approximated operating stations.

Figures are not available annually on the number of noncommercial AM stations because there is no separate noncommercial service. Usually, such stations are supported by educational or public bodies. In the early growth of radio prior to 1927, educational institutions were prominent in radio (see S. E. Frost, *Education's Own Stations; the History of Broadcast Licenses Issued to Educational Institutions*, University of Chicago Press, 1937). From 1945-1970, the number of noncommercial AM stations declined from about 35 to 25. In addition, a small number of educational institutions operate commercial stations.

The decline in the number of AM stations between 1927 and 1929 followed the transfer of the licensing function from the Secretary of Commerce to the Federal Radio Commission. The latter body tightened the licensing requirements, resulting in the withdrawal or deletion of a number of operating stations.

R 94-95. Frequency modulation (FM) stations operating, 1940-1970.

Source: U.S. Federal Communications Commission, *Annual Report*, various issues.

FM was authorized as a regular service in 1940, effective January 1, 1941, and the first commercial station was licensed in 1941. Noncommercial FM is a separate service with a specific spectrum allocation. The stations are licensed to nonprofit educational organizations.

R 96-97. Television (TV) stations operating, 1941-1970.

Source: See source for series R 94-95.

Television was authorized on a regular commercial basis, effective July 1, 1941, and 2 stations in New York began operating as of that date. Figures include very high frequency (VHF) stations, first authorized in 1941, and ultra high frequency stations (UHF), first authorized in 1952. Some stations (almost entirely UHF stations) began operation and subsequently ceased operation, but retained their FCC authorization. Such stations are not included in the years of nonoperation.

R 98-101. Cable television, 1952-1970.

Source: John Blair & Company, New York, N.Y., *Statistical Trends in Broadcasting*, annual issues (copyright).

Cable television (CATV) is a system whereby program signals are sent through a cable attached to a television set, as opposed to commercial television and on-the-air transmission of signals.

R 102-103. Sets produced, 1922-1970.

Source: Electronic Industries Association, 1922-1934, *Electronics Industry Fact Book*, 1957, pp. 4, 5; 1935-1970, *Electronic Market Data Book*, 1971. (Copyright.)

Figures are based on reports of members of the Electronic Industries Association (formerly Radio-Electronic-Television Manufacturers Association) adjusted for estimated production of nonmembers. The figures also include sets produced for export. Radio set figures include home sets for all years; auto sets, 1930-1970; portable sets, 1939-1970; and clock sets, 1951-1970. As of 1970, automobile sets constituted over 40.3 percent of total radio-set production. As of 1970, year end, Electronic Industries Association estimated that there were 336 million radio sets in working order in the United States, including 85 million in automobiles.

R 104. Households with radio sets, 1922-1970.

Source: Annual figures, National Broadcasting Company (NBC), unpublished estimates. U.S. Bureau of the Census data, as follows: 1930, Fifteenth Census Reports, *Population*, vol. VI, *Families*, table 39; 1940, Sixteenth Census Reports, *Housing*, vol. II, part 1, table 10; 1950, 1960, and 1970, *U.S. Census of Housing: 1950*, vol. I, part 1, table 13; *1960*, vol. I, part 1, table 7; *1970*, vol. I, part 1, table 34.

NBC accredits data on radio ownership prior to 1950 to the National Association of Broadcasters (NAB), which is the national trade association of broadcasters, and to Broadcast Measurement Bureau, a private survey group, which conducted a detailed nationwide survey of radio listening. A survey conducted by the Columbia Broadcasting System (CBS), the results of which were published as "Lost and Found," purported to show 2,450,000 households with radios not enumerated in the 1930 Census of Population. Accordingly, the NAB adjusted the 1930 census figure to 14,499,000. Similarly, 964,026 occupied dwelling units did not report concerning radio ownership in the 1940 Census of Population. The NAB estimated that 786,043 of these should be added to the 1940 census figure of 28,048,219 occupied units with radio.

The figures include radio sets which may not be in working order. Sets temporarily out of order or being repaired at the time of enumeration were included in the census data. The figures exclude radio sets in places of business, institutions, and hotels.

R 105. Households with television sets, 1946-1970.

Source: National Broadcasting Company, unpublished estimates. U.S. Bureau of the Census data as follows: 1950, 1960, and 1970, *U.S. Census of Housing: 1950*, vol. I, part 1, table 13; *1960*, vol. I, part 1, table 7; *1970*, vol. I, part 1, table 34.

An indication of the accuracy of the estimates is provided by several surveys of TV ownership in the Nation's households conducted by the Bureau of the Census for the Advertising Research Foundation. These studies have yielded the following estimates:

	June 1955	March 1956	August 1956	January 1969
Total sets in TV homes	33,269,000	37,277,000	39,568,000	79,660,000
TV homes	32,106,000	35,495,000	37,410,000	58,250,000
Second sets in TV homes	1,163,000	1,782,000	2,158,000	21,410,000
TV homes as percent of total homes	67.2	72.8	76.1	95.0

All figures exclude sets in places of business, institutions, and hotels, but include households with television sets which may not be in current working order.

R 106-109 and R 123-126. Radio and television advertising expenditures, 1935-1970.

Source: 1935-1956 and 1958-1968, *Printers' Ink Advertisers' Guide to Marketing*, various issues; 1957, *Printers' Ink*, Feb. 6, 1959, p. 9; 1969 and 1970, *Marketing Communications*, July 1971.

Historical-time series on advertising expenditures were first developed by L. D. H. Weld of the McCann-Erickson Advertising Agency, New York, in 1938. After Dr. Weld's death in 1946, McCann-Erickson continued to prepare the estimates under the supervision of Dr. Hans Zeisel and, since 1950, Robert J. Coen.

Total advertising expenditures in radio and television are total time sales of networks and stations including commissions of advertising agencies and station representatives, as reported by the Federal Communications Commission, multiplied by estimated "adjustment" factors. For a description of the method used in developing the annual adjustment factors, see the source. Total advertising expenditures are larger than total broadcast revenues as reported by the FCC in two respects: The inclusion of commissions paid to advertising agencies and station representatives; and the inclusion of sums paid by advertisers for talent, program, and production to organizations which do not operate networks or broadcast stations (included in the "adjustment" figures).

The networks included in radio are the four national networks—American Broadcasting Company (ABC), Columbia Broadcasting System (CBS), National Broadcasting Company (NBC), and the Mutual Broadcasting System (MBS). The three large regional networks included for most years are the Don Lee Network, the Yankee Network, and the Texas State Network. The networks included in television are ABC, CBS, NBC (each of which operates a network in both radio and television) and, until September 1955, the DuMont Network. At that time DuMont withdrew from the network field.

For a detailed discussion of the network system, see the FCC and other reports listed in the general note for series R 93-162; and 84th Cong., 2d sess., Robert F. Jones, *Investigation of Television Networks and the UHF-VHF Problems; Progress Report Prepared for the Committee on Interstate and Foreign Commerce*, 1955.

R 107 and **R 124**, network expenditures. Figures are total expenditures of network advertisers in radio or television for time (i.e., access to the individual stations broadcasting the program); for the program, including talent and production; and for the production of the commercial announcements. Such sums include commissions to advertising agencies but exclude discounts and allowances received by the advertiser. The figures are before disbursements by the networks to their affiliated and owned stations, and exclude the nonnetwork time sales of the stations owned by the networks.

R 108 and **R 125**, national spot expenditures. This type of advertising is commonly confused with commercial, or "spot," announcements. The term "spot" in this context refers to the purchase of time by national advertisers on individual stations "spotted" or selected in various communities. Predominantly, the advertiser expenditures are for commercial announcements adjacent to network or other programs carried by the individual stations. In addition, national spot advertisers sponsor programs or purchase "participations" in station-supplied programs. Thus, national spot advertiser expenditures include total time sales (after discounts but including commissions to advertising agencies and station representatives) multiplied by an estimated "adjustment" factor for program and production.

R 109 and R 126, local advertising expenditures. These include total time sales (after trade discounts but including commissions to advertising agencies) multiplied by an estimated "adjustment" factor for program and production. Local advertiser expenditures are made both in connection with the broadcast of commercial announcements and the supply of a program service. The main distinction between national spot and local advertising is as follows: National spot advertisers are connected with firms or companies which produce or distribute goods or services on a national or regional basis, and which usually place their advertising message on a number of selected stations. Local advertisers are usually local retailers and other organizations whose goods or services are primarily for local distribution. As such, a local advertiser will place his advertising message only on the stations in his community or marketing area. However, in practice, the "national" and "local" categories are not completely differentiated.

R 110–122 and R 127–139.   Networks and stations reporting, broadcast revenues, expenses, income, gross investment, and employees, 1935–1970.

Source: U.S. Bureau of the Census, 1935, *Census of Business, 1935, Radio Broadcasting,* pp. 15, 25; U.S. Federal Communications Commission, 1937–1947, *Annual Report,* various issues; 1948–1970, *AM-FM Broadcast Financial Data* and *TV Broadcast Financial Data,* various issues.

The basic sources of figures shown in the *Annual Report* are *Statistics of the Communications Industry in the United States,* annual issues, and processed releases of the FCC.

FCC began the regular annual collection of financial and operating data from networks and stations in 1937. The respondents each year usually include over 90 percent of commercial stations in operation, accounting for well over 95 percent of total industry revenues, expenses, and income. Statistics based on these reports, particularly prior to 1952, have included considerable detail. These statistics have been made available to the public in the *Annual Report* of the FCC, 1938–1970; *Statistics of the Communications Industry in the United States,* annual issues; and in processed releases.

R 110–111 and R 127–128, reporting networks and stations. Prior to 1949 the radio data are limited to commercial standard broadcasting (AM) stations and networks operating in the United States, Puerto Rico, and outlying areas. Since 1949, the radio data also include reports of joint AM-FM stations, and reports of FM-only stations. The television data include stations operating in the United States, Puerto Rico, and outlying areas.

R 112–114 and R 129–131, broadcasting revenues. Figures include the amounts received by networks and stations from the sale of time (net of all trade and cash discounts and commissions to advertising agencies and station representatives) and from other broadcast activities as follows: Gross amount received for services of talent under contract to and in the pay of networks or stations; net commissions, fees, and profits for services in obtaining, or for placing with others, talent not under contract to and in the pay of respondent; amounts received for furnishing manuscripts, transcriptions, productions, or other program materials or services; and amounts received for incidental broadcast activities such as charges for studio facilities and special charges in connection with remote broadcasts, fees or other charges for conducting studio tours, and fees or profits received for the right to operate concessions.

R 115–117 and R 132–134, broadcasting expenses. The broad expense categories reported include technical, program, selling, and general and administrative expenses. Among the expenses required to be included are the following: Salaries and wages; talent expenses;

film and transcription expense; commissions to staff salesmen; insurance; depreciation and amortization of broadcast investments; rents paid for use of broadcast property; taxes (other than Federal taxes on income); and losses on notes, accounts, and other amounts receivable.

R 118–120 and R 135–137, broadcasting income. Figures represent net operating revenues (before Federal income tax), excluding income derived by the networks and stations from sources and operations other than broadcasting.

R 121 and R 138, gross investment. Figures represent investment in tangible broadcast property, before depreciation. The FCC report form requires that the costs be reported on an original-cost basis, and not on the basis of cost readjustments resulting from the sales or transfers of stations. Tangible broadcast property includes land and buildings, if owned, and transmitter and studio property; it excludes financial assets and good will. In the case of stations which have been sold, it represents that portion of the price assigned by the licensee to the property. Tangible broadcast property is, therefore, not a measure of total investment in broadcasting.

R 122 and R 139, employees. Figures include all employees, staff and nonstaff, full and part time, not excluding general officers and other managerial officials, but excluding "uncompensated" employees. Figures for 1935 are employees reported as of the 15th of each month, summed and divided by 12; 1938, week beginning Dec. 11; 1939–1943, middle week in October; 1944–1946, as of Dec. 31; 1946–1948, middle week in October; 1955–1970, as of Dec. 31.

R 140–148.   Safety and special radio stations authorized, by class, 1913–1970.

Source: 1913–1926, U.S. Department of Commerce, *Annual Report of the Secretary of Commerce,* various issues; 1927–1934, Federal Radio Commission, *Annual Report,* various issues; 1935–1970, U.S. Federal Communications Commission, *Annual Report,* various issues.

Prior to 1948, the only data available to measure the use of radio in various nonbroadcast safety and special radio services were the number of authorized stations. The term "station," however, has not had a uniform significance among these services or within the same service over time. Primarily, the term reflects licensing procedures. A station is a single authorization issued by the FCC (or its predecessor licensing agencies) authorizing the use of one or more transmitters on assigned frequencies. A station may include one of the following: One or more transmitters at a fixed (land or fixed stations) location; one or more mobile transmitters; a system including a transmitter at a fixed location and one or more mobile transmitters or one of these in a combination with more than one frequency. Within most of the services, station authorizations have been changed from one to another form in an effort to simplify licensing procedures. As a result, year-to-year changes in the number of stations must be interpreted with caution, particularly if a decrease is shown.

Most of the nonbroadcast radio services are grouped together as the safety and special radio services, which constitute the greatest number of radio stations licensed by the FCC. Utilization of these services by individuals, industry, commerce, and State and local governments cover broad fields of operations in connection with protection of life and property, industrial and agricultural production, transportation, disaster, and civil defense.

R 149–162.   Authorized land stations and mobile transmitters in the safety and special radio services, 1948–1970.

Source: See source for series R 140–148.

The distinctive characteristics of a land station are that it is located at a fixed site, has a fixed antenna and a panel control, and is used for communication in the mobile services (aviation, land transportation, etc.). In the land mobile radio services, a land station is referred to as a base station. Thus, in the taxicab radio service, the base station is used to send and receive communications to and from the associated mobile transmitter-receivers located in the taxicabs. In the marine radio services, coastal stations are examples of land stations, and in the aviation radio services, aeronautical stations are the land stations.

Fixed stations are similar to land stations but are employed in the nonmobile radio services to communicate, or transmit messages, to other land points.

Mobile transmitters, as the name implies, are installed in moving vehicles, or are hand carried or are used as pack set units. They have relatively simple antenna and switching equipment and, in conjunction with a receiver, are used for transmitting and/or receiving information. Such transmitters usually tie in with a land station, the latter serving as a central control point for communicating with the various mobile units.

One major shortcoming of the transmitter data, however, is that they measure authorized rather than operating transmitters. This divergence is not too great in the case of the land or fixed transmitters. It is estimated that over 90 percent of the authorized transmitters are in operation. However, an entirely different situation prevails with respect to mobile transmitters. The number of mobile transmitters is an approximation of the number of transmitters in actual operation. Approximately 50 percent of the authorized mobile transmitters are included in these figures. Licensees, in applying for authorizations, have wide latitude in estimating the number of mobile units they expect to have in operation within the license period.

See also text for series R 140–148.

★ ★ ★ ★ ★ ★ ★ ★ ★   **More Recent Data for *Historical Statistics* Series**   ★ ★ ★ ★ ★ ★ ★ ★ ★

Statistics for more recent years in continuation of many of the still-active series shown here appear in annual issues of the *Statistical Abstract of the United States*, beginning with the 1975 edition. For direct linkage of the historical series to the tables in the *Abstract*, see Appendix I in the *Abstract*.

Series **R 93–105.** Radio and Television Stations, Sets Produced, and Households With Sets: 1921 to 1970

[Figures as of June 30, except for census figures in *italics* which are as of Apr. 1]

Year	Operating broadcast stations [1]					Cable television				Sets produced [2]		Households with—	
	Standard broadcast (AM)	Frequency modulation (FM)		Television (TV)		Systems	Subscribers (households)			Radio (1,000)	Television (1,000)	Radio sets (1,000)	Television sets (1,000)
		Commercial	Noncommercial	Commercial	Noncommercial		Total (1,000)	Percent of U.S.	Average per system				
	93	94	95	96	97	98	99	100	101	102	103	104	105
1970	4,288	2,126	416	691	190	2,490	4,500	7.6	1,807	16,406	4,852	62,000	59,550
1970												[3] *46,108*	*60,594*
1969	4,254	2,018	375	680	177	2,260	3,600	6.1	1,593	20,549	5,309	60,600	58,250
1968	4,203	1,850	348	655	156	2,000	2,800	4.4	1,400	22,566	5,813	58,500	56,670
1967	4,135	1,708	318	626	127	1,770	2,100	3.8	1,186	21,698	5,104	57,500	55,130
1966	4,075	1,515	291	613	108	1,570	1,575	2.9	1,003	23,595	7,285	57,000	53,850
1965	4,025	1,343	262	589	92	1,325	1,275	2.4	962	24,119	8,382	55,200	52,700
1964	3,976	1,181	243	582	79	1,200	1,085	2.1	904	19,176	8,107	54,000	51,600
1963	3,860	1,120	221	581	70	1,000	950	1.9	950	18,282	7,130	52,300	50,300
1962	3,745	1,012	201	571	59	800	850	1.7	1,063	19,162	6,471	51,305	48,855
1961	3,602	889	186	553	54	700	725	1.5	1,036	17,374	6,178	50,695	47,200
1960	3,483	741	165	579	47	640	650	1.4	1,016	17,127	5,708	50,193	45,750
1960												*48,504*	*46,312*
1959	3,377	622	154	566	43	560	550	1.3	982	15,622	6,349	*49,450	*43,950
1958	3,253	548	147	556	32	525	450	1.1	857	11,747	4,920	48,500	41,924
1957	3,079	530	135	519	26	500	350	.9	700	14,505	6,399	47,600	38,900
1956	2,896	530	126	496	20	450	300	.9	667	13,518	7,387	46,800	34,900
1955	2,732	540	124	458	11	400	150	.5	375	14,133	7,757	45,900	30,700
1954	2,583	553	117	402	6	300	65	(Z)	217	10,028	7,347	45,100	26,000
1953	2,458	580	106	198	1	150	30	(Z)	200	12,852	7,216	44,800	20,400
1952	2,355	629	92	108	–	70	14	(Z)	200	10,431	6,096	42,800	15,300
1951	2,281	649	83	107						11,928	5,385	41,900	10,320
1950	2,144	691	62	104						13,468	7,464	40,700	3,875
1950												*40,411*	*5,030*
1949	2,006	737	34	69						11,400	3,000	39,300	940
1948	2,034	1,020	46	108						16,500	975	37,623	172
1947	1,795	918	38	66						20,000	179	35,900	14
1946	1,215	511	24	30						15,955	6	33,998	8
1945	955	53	12	9						(4)		33,100	
1944	924	52	8	9						(4)		32,500	
1943	912	48	7	8						(4)		30,800	
1942 [4]	925	42	8	10						4,307		30,600	
1941	897	49	7	2						13,642		29,300	
1940	847	–	3							11,831		28,500	
1940												*28,048*	

Year	Operating standard broadcast stations (AM)	Radio sets produced (1,000)	Households with radio sets (1,000)	Year	Operating standard broadcast stations (AM)	Radio sets produced (1,000)	Households with radio sets (1,000)	Year	Operating standard broadcast stations (AM)	Radio sets produced (1,000)	Households with radio sets (1,000)
	93	102	104		93	102	104		93	102	104
1939	778	10,763	27,500	1932	604	2,446	18,450	1926	528	1,750	4,500
1938	743	7,142	26,667	1931	612	3,594	16,700	1925	571	2,000	2,750
1937	704	8,083	24,500	1930	618	3,789	13,750	1924	530	1,500	1,250
1936	656	8,249	22,869	*1930*			*12,049*	1923	556	500	400
1935	623	6,030	21,456	1929	606	4,428	10,250	1922	30	100	60
1934	593	4,479	20,400	1928	677	3,250	8,000	1921	[5] 1		
1933	598	4,157	19,250	1927	681	2,350	6,750				

* Denotes first year for which figures include Alaska and Hawaii.
– Represents zero.
Z Less than 0.05 percent.
[1] Includes Alaska, Hawaii, Puerto Rico, Guam, and Virgin Islands for all years. Prior to 1948, the FCC did not keep records on the number of stations on the air. Therefore, data for 1933–1948 are for authorized stations and may include a number that were not actually on the air.

[2] No production in Alaska and Hawaii.
[3] In 1970 Census of Housing, only battery-operated radios were enumerated.
[4] Authorization of new radio stations and production of radio receivers for commercial use halted from April 1942 until Oct. 1945.
[5] First station to receive regular license as of Sept. 15; other stations in operation experimentally.

Series R 106–122. Radio Advertising Expenditures, Finances, and Employment: 1935 to 1970

Year	Advertising expenditures (mil. dol.)				Networks reporting [1]	Number of stations reporting	Broadcast revenues, net (mil. dol.)		
	Total	Network	National spot	Local			Total	Network [1]	Other stations
	106	107	108	109	110	111	112	113	114
1970	1,308	56	371	881	7	4 898	1,137	88	1,049
1969	1,264	59	368	837	7	4,815	1,086	86	1,000
1968	1,190	63	360	767	7	4,594	1,023	81	942
1967	1,031	64	310	657	4	4,481	907	77	830
1966	1,010	64	308	638	4	4,400	872	79	793
1965	917	60	275	582	4	4,279	793	74	719
1964	846	59	256	531	4	4,202	719	71	648
1963	789	56	243	490	4	4,126	670	69	601
1962	736	46	233	457	4	3,977	627	64	563
1961	683	43	221	420	4	3,859	584	62	522
1960	692	43	222	428	4	3,688	598	63	535
1959	656	44	206	406	4	3,528	556	60	495
1958	619	58	190	372	7	3,290	521	69	451
1957	618	64	187	368	7	3,164	515	74	442
1956	567	61	161	346	7	2,967	479	70	409
1955	545	84	134	326	7	2,742	452	78	374
1954	559	114	135	309	7	2,598	449	89	360
1953	611	141	146	324	7	2,479	475	97	377
1952	624	162	142	321	7	2,380	469	101	368
1951	606	180	138	289	7	2,266	449	104	345
1950	605	196	136	273	7	2,229	443	111	333
1949	571	203	123	245	7	2,125	414	108	306
1948	562	211	121	230	7	1,927	407	109	298
1947	506	201	106	199	7	1,516	364	104	260
1946	454	200	98	157	8	1,033	323	102	221
1945	424	198	92	134	10	906	299	101	198
1944	394	192	87	114	9	879	275	95	180
1943	314	157	71	86	9	846	215	76	139
1942	260	129	59	73	10	856	179	63	116
1941	247	125	52	70	8	817	169	62	107
1940	216	113	42	60	8	765	147	53	94
1939	184	99	35	50	3	705	124	49	75
1938	167	89	34	44	3	660	111	45	66
1937	165	89	28	48	3	629	114	41	73
1936	122	76	23	24	(NA)	(NA)	(NA)	(NA)	(NA)
1935	113	63	15	35	8	561	86	30	56

Year	Broadcast expenses (mil. dol.)			Broadcast income [2] (mil. dol.)			Gross investment (mil. dol.)	Employees (1,000)
	Total	Network [1]	Other stations	Total	Network [1]	Other stations		
	115	116	117	118	119	120	121	122
1970	1,044	90	955	93	−1	94	823	71.0
1969	985	88	897	101	−2	103	780	70.0
1968	910	86	824	113	−5	118	723	70.6
1967	826	79	747	81	−2	83	671	67.2
1966	775	76	699	97	4	93	623	64.8
1965	715	71	644	78	3	75	567	62.2
1964	645	67	579	73	4	69	521	60.2
1963	612	63	549	58	6	52	493	58.0
1962	580	62	518	47	2	45	466	56.1
1961	552	61	490	32	(Z)	32	426	54.3
1960	552	66	486	46	−3	49	423	53.0
1959	512	65	447	44	−5	49	373	50.4
1958	483	73	410	38	−4	42	333	48.8
1957	461	74	387	54	(NA)	54	328	48.9
1956	430	70	360	50	(Z)	49	298	47.6
1955	406	72	334	46	6	40	287	45.3
1954	406	80	326	43	8	34	279	(NA)
1953	419	87	332	56	10	45	276	(NA)
1952	408	89	318	61	11	50	267	(NA)
1951	390	94	296	59	10	49	255	(NA)
1950	372	92	281	71	19	52	244	(NA)
1949	363	87	267	56	17	39	231	52.0
1948	343	91	252	64	18	46	202	48.3
1947	292	92	200	72	20	52	150	(NA)
1946	246	73	173	76	19	57	108	40.0
1945	216	78	138	84	23	60	88	37.8
1944	185	68	116	90	26	64	83	34.3
1943	149	53	96	66	23	43	81	31.8
1942	134	47	87	45	17	28	81	29.6
1941	124	44	80	45	17	27	78	27.6
1940	114	39	75	33	13	20	71	25.7
1939	100	37	62	24	11	13	64	23.9
1938	93	36	57	19	8	11	61	22.5
1937	92	33	59	19	6	13	55	28.8
1936	---	---	---	---	---	---	---	(NA)
1935	---	---	---	---	---	---	---	14.6

NA Not available.
Z Less than $500,000.

[1] Includes network owned and operated stations.
[2] Before Federal income tax.

Series R 123–139. Television Advertising Expenditures, Finances, and Employment: 1945 to 1970

Year	Advertising expenditures (mil. dol.)				Networks reporting [1]	Number of stations reporting	Broadcast revenues, net (mil. dol.)		
	Total	Network	National spot	Local			Total	Network [1]	Other stations
	123	124	125	126	127	128	129	130	131
1970	3,596	1,658	1,234	704	3	686	2,808	1,457	1,351
1969	3,585	1,678	1,253	654	3	673	2,796	1,467	1,329
1968	3,231	1,523	1,131	577	3	658	2,521	1,308	1,213
1967	2,909	1,455	988	466	3	637	2,275	1,217	1,059
1966	2,823	1,393	988	442	3	608	2,203	1,166	1,037
1965	2,515	1,237	892	386	3	588	1,965	1,024	941
1964	2,289	1,132	806	351	3	575	1,793	929	865
1963	2,032	1,025	698	309	3	565	1,597	820	777
1962	1,897	976	629	292	3	554	1,486	754	732
1961	1,691	887	548	256	3	540	1,318	675	643
1960	1,627	820	527	281	3	530	1,269	641	628
1959	1,529	776	486	267	3	519	1,164	576	588
1958	1,387	742	397	248	3	514	1,030	517	513
1957	1,286	690	352	244	3	501	943	468	475
1956	1,225	643	329	253	3	474	897	442	455
1955	1,035	550	260	225	4	437	745	374	371
1954	809	422	207	180	4	410	593	307	286
1953	606	320	146	141	4	334	433	232	201
1952	454	256	94	104	4	122	324	180	144
1951	332	181	70	82	4	108	236	128	107
1950	171	85	31	55	4	107	106	56	50
1949	58	29	9	19	4	98	34	19	15
1948						47	9	5	4
1947						15	2		
1946						10	1		
1945						6	(Z)		

Year	Broadcast expenses (mil. dol.)			Broadcast income [2] (mil. dol.)			Gross investment (mil. dol.)	Employees (1,000)
	Total	Network [1]	Other stations	Total	Network [1]	Other stations		
	132	133	134	135	136	137	138	139
1970	2,354	1,290	1,065	454	167	286	1,497	58.4
1969	2,243	1,241	1,001	554	226	328	1,445	57.8
1968	2,026	1,129	897	495	179	316	[3] 1,307	55.2
1967	1,861	1,057	804	415	160	255	1,185	51.7
1966	1,710	980	731	493	187	306	1,014	50.3
1965	1,517	862	655	448	162	286	860	47.8
1964	1,378	772	606	416	157	259	781	45.7
1963	1,254	684	570	343	136	207	(NA)	43.6
1962	1,175	643	532	312	111	200	673	41.8
1961	1,081	588	493	237	87	150	631	40.1
1960	1,025	546	479	244	95	149	593	40.6
1959	942	488	453	222	88	134	563	40.3
1958	858	440	418	172	77	95	523	39.4
1957	783	397	386	160	71	89	478	37.8
1956	707	357	350	190	85	104	430	35.7
1955	595	306	289	150	68	82	365	32.3
1954	503	270	232	90	37	54	315	29.4
1953	361	214	147	71	18	53	233	18.2
1952	269	170	98	56	10	46	124	14.1
1951	194	117	77	42	11	31	93	
1950	115	66	50	[3] 9	[3] 10	1	70	
1949	60	31	28	[3] 25	[3] 12	[3] 13	56	
1948	24	11	12	[3] 15	6	9		

NA Not available.
Z Less than $500,000.
[1] Includes network owned and operated stations.
[2] Before Federal income tax.
[3] Loss.

Series **R 140–148.** Safety and Special Radio Stations Authorized, by Class: 1913 to 1970

[As of June 30. Includes Alaska, Hawaii, Puerto Rico, and outlying areas. See text for definition of stations]

Year	Amateur and disaster services	Aviation services	Citizens services	Industrial services	Land transportation services	Marine services	Public safety services	Experimental services [1]	Radio operators (1,000)
	140	141	142	143	144	145	146	147	148
1970	283,461	150,955	886,951	222,500	22,262	206,251	72,215	1,049	3,688
1969	285,175	143,997	860,624	204,266	21,291	186,295	67,730	1,019	3,545
1968	282,525	140,799	867,552	185,046	20,016	164,000	63,160	966	3,405
1967	279,093	122,568	848,237	169,417	18,613	143,612	58,831	898	3,240
1966	285,600	105,133	865,414	152,315	16,914	137,469	54,839	928	3,088
1965	280,343	109,897	744,713	141,360	15,635	114,075	50,888	812	2,971
1964	280,818	107,557	682,307	124,347	14,815	161,593	47,389	698	2,870
1963	270,838	106,202	446,590	107,796	14,089	143,227	43,168	730	3,186
1962	251,659	106,923	305,138	93,073	13,278	127,633	38,676	757	2,789
1961	234,681	92,779	206,106	77,773	12,075	110,433	36,658	757	2,499
1960	228,206	91,180	126,034	64,804	11,452	97,411	32,906	728	2,154
1959	205,588	77,682	49,269	49,679	10,625	84,947	29,363	891	1,897
1958	187,362	62,684	38,611	39,978	10,190	72,514	26,512	834	1,682
1957	165,908	49,699	27,931	35,711	9,592	63,844	23,270	788	1,469
1956	154,337	48,745	18,602	30,597	8,990	56,915	20,718	716	1,259
1955	142,387	43,855	12,334	24,854	7,668	50,714	18,415	625	1,123
1954	124,324	40,154	7,054	21,598	6,891	46,299	15,697	586	963
1953	111,579	39,315	3,829	17,378	5,922	40,357	13,631	444	839
1952	113,163	32,603	1,401	13,680	5,027	35,500	11,143	369	790
1951	90,587	34,061	560	9,551	4,253	29,544	9,129	404	701
1950	87,967	23,794	335	6,099	3,495	24,921	7,607	466	624
1949	81,675	27,227	----------	4,266	3,588	20,004	5,700	501	[2] 564
1948	78,434	20,858	----------	2,855	3,122	15,024	4,903	652	[2] 506
1947	75,000	15,943	----------	1,787	1,692	11,955	4,620	532	442
1946	70,000	6,205	----------	702	156	8,676	4,760	1,374	----------
1945	60,000	3,793	----------	576	----------	----------	4,446	487	----------
1944	60,000	3,445	----------	468	----------	6,817	4,144	572	----------
1943	60,000	3,553	----------	386	----------	6,609	3,772	453	----------
1942	60,000	4,713	----------	356	----------	----------	3,455	497	----------
1941	60,000	3,000	----------	306	----------	5,822	2,967	450	----------
1940	56,295	2,099	----------	340	----------	4,945	2,334	295	----------
1939	53,558	1,824	----------	307	----------	4,036	1,536	372	----------
1938	49,911	1,460	----------	232	----------	3,516	662	2,842	----------
1937	47,444	1,212	----------	221	----------	2,422	535	1,971	----------
1936	46,850	812	----------	195	----------	2,219	403	1,576	----------
1935	45,561	678	----------	146	----------	2,157	298	975	----------

Year	Amateur and disaster services	Aviation services	Industrial services	Marine services	Public safety services	Experimental services [1]	Year	Amateur and disaster services	Marine services	Public safety services
	140	141	143	145	146	147		140	145	146
1934	46,390	671	129	2,195	220	681	1923	16,570	----------	3
1933	41,555	646	121	2,192	152	255	1922		----------	----------
1932	30,374	579	134	2,225	123	168	1921			
1931	22,739	463	130	2,392	91	160	1920	5,719	----------	1
1930	18,994	281	----------	2,173	20	----------	1919			
1929	16,829	131	----------	----------	12	----------	1918			
1928	16,928	----------	----------	----------	----------	----------	1917			
1927	16,926	----------	----------	----------	----------	----------	1916			1
1926	14,902	----------	----------	1,954	----------	----------	1915			
1925	15,000	----------	----------	1,901	4	----------	1914			
1924	15,540	----------	----------	2,741	3	----------	1913	1,312	701	----------

[1] The Experimental Radio Service is the means by which the Federal Communications Commission encourages and promotes basic radio research and development of new radio techniques and systems.

[2] Estimated.

Series R 149–162. Authorized Land Stations and Mobile Transmitters in the Safety and Special Radio Services: 1948 to 1970

[Includes Alaska, Hawaii, Puerto Rico, and outlying areas. See text for series R 140–148 for definition of stations]

Year	Aviation		Citizens [1]		Land transportation [1]		Marine		Public safety	
	Land or fixed stations	Portable or mobile units	Land or fixed stations	Portable or mobile units	Land or fixed stations	Portable or mobile units	Land or fixed stations	Portable or mobile units	Land or fixed stations	Portable or mobile units
	149	150	151	152	153	154	155	156	157	158
1970, June 30	21,352	220,813	4,663	3,987,075	25,802	548,020	8,610	242,026	68,972	709,497
1969, June 30	20,958	210,035	4,402	2,838,243	24,766	526,801	7,147	219,036	64,743	667,350
1968, June 30	20,105	205,771	5,115	2,753,996	23,440	498,941	6,530	192,708	60,441	624,015
1967, June 30	19,527	177,196	4,934	2,776,167	21,961	467,874	5,565	168,889	56,246	583,309
1966, June 30	17,330	151,704	4,440	2,714,065	20,215	425,999	4,951	144,678	52,474	544,814
1965, June 30	17,449	159,109	----------	2,545,606	19,056	397,331	4,760	134,028	48,730	496,002
1964, June 30	17,696	154,967	----------	2,383,082	18,203	378,008	4,402	191,268	45,372	464,428
1963, June 30	16,036	153,786	----------	2,183,302	18,340	369,943	4,553	160,934	60,017	430,860
1962, June 30	15,294	154,401	----------	1,429,088	17,270	351,989	4,122	143,245	51,975	388,464
1961, June 30	14,400	132,350	----------	963,688	15,785	325,150	4,015	123,757	45,582	369,890
1960, June 30	13,502	130,752	----------	650,000	11,913	246,935	3,878	103,007	39,047	332,940
1959, June 30	11,524	111,547	----------	431,000	17,100	425,371	3,642	90,007	37,077	292,131
1958, Jan. 1	11,884	69,451	----------	----------	10,145	331,608	3,619	75,000	31,184	273,216
1957, Jan. 1	8,996	53,616	----------	----------	9,371	297,322	3,094	62,000	23,565	220,022
1956, Jan. 1	7,978	40,735	----------	----------	8,069	243,457	2,106	56,265	18,526	207,195
1955, Jan. 1	5,373	36,595	----------	----------	6,616	154,358	1,385	49,742	13,731	187,670
1954, Jan. 1	4,657	37,467	----------	----------	6,041	132,944	1,250	42,573	11,742	152,811
1953, Mar. 1	6,145	37,951	----------	----------	5,277	110,514	1,174	37,629	10,306	131,549
1952, Jan. 1	2,716	39,307	----------	----------	4,302	92,000	1,102	34,187	7,732	104,559
1951, Jan. 1	3,181	32,575	----------	----------	3,721	74,966	1,273	28,085	6,579	80,433
1949, June 15	1,987	28,037	----------	----------	2,759	51,774	443	19,170	4,301	59,122
1949, Jan. 1	----------	24,695	----------	----------	----------	[2] 49,650	----------	17,414	----------	53,783
1948, Jan. 1	----------	20,517	----------	----------	----------	[3] 31,852	----------	13,180	----------	38,929

Year	Industrial		Amateur and disaster		Year	Industrial		Amateur and disaster	
	Land or fixed stations	Portable or mobile units	Land or fixed stations	Portable or mobile units		Land or fixed stations	Portable or mobile units	Land or fixed stations	Portable or mobile units
	159	160	161	162		159	160	161	162
1970, June 30	177,598	1,840,649	283,461		1958, Jan. 1	35,170	381,421	184,566	
1969, June 30	164,456	1,693,936	290,298		1957, Jan. 1	28,073	297,147	160,931	
1968, June 30	150,219	1,538,525	287,164		1956, Jan. 1	22,987	252,265	148,509	8,408
1967, June 30	139,033	1,412,377	283,412						
1966, June 30	126,558	1,273,673	292,194		1955, Jan. 1	16,009	164,262	129,029	3,123
					1954, Jan. 1	13,515	132,425	116,286	1,173
1965, June 30	119,328	1,196,170	286,325		1953, Mar. 1	12,074	115,024	116,902	252
1964, June 30	106,921	1,054,584	289,338		1952, Jan. 1	8,676	81,418	113,159	335
1963, June 30	97,008	926,631	279,978		1951, Jan. 1	6,458	64,172	90,601	61
1962, June 30	88,328	804,234	233,038						
1961, June 30	76,065	680,880	218,101		1949, June 15	2,765	33,608	81,675	----------
					1949, Jan. 1	----------	[4] 27,842	----------	----------
1960, June 30	66,795	573,395	221,362		1948, Jan. 1	----------	10,924	----------	----------
1959, June 30	54,779	480,174	205,595						

[1] Data for "Citizens" are included with "Land transportation" before 1960.
[2] Includes Class 2 experimental stations as follows: 46,085 taxicab units and 668 trucks and buses.
[3] Includes 30,000 Class 2 experimental taxicab units.
[4] Includes 68 Class 2 experimental industrial units.

Chapter R

Postal Service, Newspapers, and Books (Series R 163-257)

R 163. Post offices, 1789-1970.

Source: U.S. Post Office Department, *Annual Report of the Post-master General, 1970.*

The source also presents a classification of the number of post offices into first, second, third, and fourth class for 1946-1970.

R 164-165. Revenues and expenditures, 1789-1970.

Source: See source for series R 163.

For 1789-1953, revenues and expenses are stated on a cash basis and therefore include payments and receipts in one year applicable to the expenses and revenues of prior years. For 1954-1962, revenues and expenses are stated on an accrual basis, with expenses reported in the year which gave rise to the earnings, whether collected or accrued. For 1963-1970, revenues and expenses are stated on an accrued cost basis.

Comparability of figures from year-to-year are affected by various factors. For example, the Post Office discontinued payment of subsidies to airlines in 1954; the Department also began receiving reimbursement for penalty and franked mail in 1954, costs which the Post Office had previously absorbed.

Expenses include expenditures for plant and equipment of a capital nature and for inventories and supplies, but no provision for depreciation is made. Expenses also include certain public service costs paid by the Post Office Department, but which the Department considered to be unrelated to the determination of the proper operating costs of the Postal Service. These include unreimbursed services for other Government agencies; specific rate subsidies for mailings of second- and third-class mail by certain nonprofit organizations, free-in-county second-class mail, classroom publications, and mail for the blind; excess rates paid to foreign air carriers; and custodial services for other Government departments and agencies. These costs were estimated to have been approximately $740 million for 1970.

Expenses of the Post Office Department do not include costs applicable to postal operations which are paid by other Government departments and agencies for retirement pay accrual, workmen's compensation and unemployment compensation for postal employees, and certain custodial and maintenance expenses. These expenses amounted to $424 million in 1970.

R 166-167. Ordinary postage stamps and stamped envelopes and wrappers issued, 1848-1970.

Source: See source for series R 163.

R 168. Postal cards issued, 1873-1970.

Source: See source for series R 163.

The Government postal card was authorized in 1872. The post card, or private mailing card, was introduced in 1898. The rate for this service has been practically identical with that of the postal cards. Business reply cards and letters as a postal service was initiated in 1928.

R 169. Pieces of matter of all kinds handled, 1886-1970.

Source: See source for series R 163.

With the establishment of the cost ascertainment system in 1926, data on the volume of mail have been obtained from sample counts conducted quarterly for one week at representative post offices, ranging in number from 255 to over 500. These sample data were then projected to include all originating mail at all post offices in the United States. The methods of estimating the number of pieces of matter handled prior to 1926 could not be ascertained. See also general note for series R 172-186.

R 170. Surplus or deficit, 1926-1970.

Source: See source for series R 163.

The Post Office Department operated with a deficit in fiscal year 1970 as it had in all but a few years of its history. The last period in which there was a surplus was during the three World War II years, 1943 through 1945.

The accounts of the Department are maintained in such a way as to reflect the deficit in three ways—the cash deficit, the operating deficit, and the postal fund deficit. The "cash deficit" represents the excess of disbursements over receipts. The "operating deficit," which is utilized in the series, represents the excess of expense over income. The "postal fund deficit" represents the excess of obligations incurred over postal revenues.

R 171. Sales of postage stamps and other stamped paper, 1937-1970.

Source: See source for series R 163.

R 172-186. General note.

The bulk of postal revenues and postal expenses cannot be allocated directly to the various classes of mail handled or to special services performed.

Postal revenues (except for about 10 percent which can be directly allocated or computed) are derived from postage acquired in the form of stamps and stamped paper and from payments under permits, which may be used by the purchaser generally on any class of mail. The result is a large common pool of revenues from numerous sources. Similarly, the several classes of mail and the special services are to a considerable extent handled by the same employees using the same buildings, equipment, operating facilities, house services, and supplies.

Pursuant to a Congressional Act of February 28, 1925 (39 U.S.C. 826), a regular, continuing cost ascertainment system was established in 1926 to collect and develop data on the revenue received (including volume and weight of mail) and cost incurred by the Post Office Department. This system was succeeded by the revenue-cost analysis system which incorporated incremental costs concepts into the system for the first time. The latter system represents the culmination of many changes and improvements for the Revenue and Cost Analysis Report (formerly the Cost Ascertainment Report).

The statistics of expenses as published annually are subject to later readjustments as a result of increases in the charges of railroad, air, or other transportation services, or increases in the salaries of Post Office Department employees, if such increases are made retroactive to an earlier fiscal year.

R 172-174. First-class mail, 1926-1970.

Source: U.S. Post Office Department, 1926-1946, *Budget Digest,* 1949, chapter IV, tables 5-11; 1947-1968, *Cost Ascertainment Report,* 1956, 1958, and 1968 issues; 1969-1970, *Revenue and Cost Analysis,* 1970.

Figures cover letters, matter wholly or partially in writing or typewriting, and packages (including local delivery letters), single or double postal and post cards, bills and statements of account, and matter closed against postal inspection. Each piece may not weigh more than 70 pounds or measure more than 100 inches in length and girth combined. Postage may be paid by adhesive stamps, stamped cards or envelopes, meter stamps, or permit imprint. For 1926–1929, domestic airmail could not be segregated and is included with first-class mail. Mail fees are included for 1950–1970. Box rent revenues, previously reported as unassignable are allocated to classes of mail, 1951–1955, and classified with special services for 1956–1970. For 1951–1970, the expense of free mail from members of the Armed Forces is included in first-class mail expenditures.

See also text for series R 188–189.

R 175–177. Second-class mail, 1926–1970.

Source: See source for series R 172–174.

Newspapers and periodical publications, both domestic and foreign, which meet all of the requirements set forth in part 132, Postal Service Manual, may be mailed at the second-class rates of postage. Revenues include postage payments (stamps or money order permit) and, since 1932, payment of fees for use of the second-class privilege; transient second-class matter (mailings of second-class publications by other than the publisher or news agents); publishers' second-class matter forwarded or returned, 1950–1970; mailing fees, 1951–1970; and box rent revenue allocation, 1951–1970.

Expenses include cost of publishers' second-class matter forwarded or returned, 1950–1970, and, for 1953–1970, also includes the expense of sending notices to publishers regarding undelivered mail.

R 178–180. Third-class mail, 1926–1970.

Source: See source for series R 172–174.

Third-class mail embraces all matter less than 16 ounces in weight and not qualifying as first or second class. A significant proportion of the matter mailed under third class is advertising material. Also included are keys, identification cards and tags, or similar identification devices that are without cover and bear, contain, or have securely attached the name and complete post office address of a person, organization, or concern with instructions to return to such address and a statement guaranteeing the payment of the postage due on delivery. In 1928, a special "bulk rate" was made applicable to separately addressed identical pieces of third-class matter mailed at one time. The present law requires such matter be mailed in quantities of at least 50 pounds or at least 200 pieces. Also, there is a single piece third-class rate. Revenues include postage revenues and fees for permits; domestic mail fees, 1951–1970; and box rent revenue allocation, 1951–1970.

Prior to 1953, the revenues and expenses applicable to controlled circulation publications (publications consisting primarily of advertising and distributed free or mainly free) were included with third-class and fourth-class services. For 1953–1970, controlled circulation publications are shown separately.

R 181–183. Fourth-class mail, 1926–1970.

Source: See source for series R 172–174.

This class includes mailable matter 16 ounces or more in weight, not qualifying as first or second class. The major development in this class of mail was the establishment of the parcel post system effective January 1, 1913. Books, special fourth-class and library rate items, catalogs, and matter for the blind, included in fourth class, carry special rates. Mailers of fourth-class articles may use any method of paying postage. Revenues include domestic mail fees for 1951–1970; box rent revenue allocations, 1951–1970; and special handling fees.

R 184–186. Domestic airmail, 1929–1970.

Source: See source for series R 172–174.

Since September 1948, domestic airmail includes a parcel post service and since January 1949 airmail postal and post card service. Paid airmail to and from the Armed Forces overseas and the outlying areas of the United States, formerly in international airmail, is included with domestic airmail, 1947–1970. For 1951–1970, airmail expenses include the cost of free mail from members of the Armed Forces.

Airmail expenditures include subsequent payments, as of June 30, 1950, to airlines for retroactive rate increases where effective. The decline in airmail expenses between 1953 and 1954 resulted from the transfer of subsidy payments to airlines from the Post Office Department to the Civil Aeronautics Board effective October 1, 1953. The *Cost Ascertainment Report* for 1953 and prior years shows division of service costs and subsidy payments.

For 1954–1970, the Post Office Department experimented with the transporting of all mail by air between a number of major cities. Such mail, carrying first-class postage, is counted within first-class service.

R 187. Post Office employees, 1926–1970.

Source: U.S. Post Office Department, *Annual Report of the Postmaster General, 1970.*

Included are regular or full-time employees and substitute, hourly rate, and part-time employees. Part-time employees are a substantial part of the Post Office labor force.

Prior to October 1933, the operating force for public buildings housing post offices and other Government agencies was on the rolls of the Treasury Department. On that date, the personnel were transferred to the Post Office Department. This increased the regular labor force of the Post Office Department by 8,000 employees.

R 188–190. Postal rates for first-class mail, letters and postal cards, 1792–1970.

Source: 1792–1956, U.S. Post Office Department, *United States Domestic Postage Rates, 1789–1956,* table I; 1958–1970, Public Law 85–426 (Postal Policy Act of 1958), Public Law 87–793 (Postal Service and Employee Salary Act of 1962), and Public Law 90–206 (Postal Service and Employee Salary Act of 1967).

The postage rates in effect in 1789 were those fixed by the Continental Congress in the Ordinance of 1782. These rates were continued until 1792. It was not until 1863 that mail was divided into "classes." In the early days of the postal service the recipient rather than the sender ordinarily paid the postage. In 1847 postage stamps were introduced, and in 1885 compulsory prepayment for all domestic letter mail was established.

The rates shown are for regular service. During the earlier years of the westward expansion, special local rates were often improvised. Thus, the first letter rate on the "pony express," which operated between Missouri and California from 1860 to 1861, was $5 for a half ounce, reduced in May 1861 to $2 for a half ounce, and in July 1861 to $1 for a half ounce because of a Government subsidy.

A considerable part of the domestic mail service between 1792 and 1863 was carried by ship, and was subject to shipletter rates. These rates are detailed in the source, table II, p. 24. In 1863, a ship and steamboat rate, double the regular rate, was made applicable to domestic mail conveyed by ships not regularly employed in carrying mail. This classification is omitted after 1879 because of its diminishing importance but the double rate is still in effect although little or no matter is mailed under these rates.

In 1863, first-class mail was defined to include letters and matter wholly or partly in writing, except book manuscripts and corrected proof sheets. In 1872, first-class mail was described as including letters and all correspondence, wholly or partly in writing, except book manuscripts and corrected proof sheets passing between authors and publishers. In 1879, it was redefined to include letters, postal cards, and all matter wholly or partly in writing, except such writing as is authorized to be placed on mail of other classes. See Jane Kennedy, "Development of Postal Rates: 1845–1955," *Land Economics*, May 1957 issue, pp. 93–112, for additional materials on postal rates, particularly rates for second-, third-, and fourth-class mail.

R 191. Postal rates for domestic airmail, 1918–1970.

Source: See source for series R 188–189, table III, p. 25.

Until 1948, domestic airmail rates applied not only to letters but also to other mailable matter, including sealed parcels up to specified maxima (prescribed according to weight or according to length and girth). Effective September 1, 1948, an Air Parcel Post Service was established. Matter carried by air weighing 8 ounces or less was classified as "airmail" and over 8 ounces "air parcel post." In 1968, air parcel post and first class mail weighing more than 13 ounces were combined and classified "priority mail."

R 192–217. New books and new editions published, by subject, 1880–1970.

Source: **Series R 192 and R 193**, 1890, *Bookman Literary Yearbook*, 1898, Dodd, Mead Co. All other series reprinted from various issues of *Publishers Weekly*, published by R. R. Bowker Co., a Xerox Education Co., copyright © by Xerox Corporation.

Figures represent the number of titles published, not the number of books which were printed. Beginning 1967, books are counted by title rather than by volume. Beginning 1959, United Nations Educational, Scientific, and Cultural Organization definition of a "book" (a volume over 49 pages) was adopted. Previously, all hardbound books and all paperbacks that were specialized (workbooks, laboratory manuals, etc.), over 65 pages, or had mass market distribution, were counted. Years prior to 1959, therefore, are not strictly comparable with subsequent years. The data are compiled from information and actual books submitted to R. R. Bowker Company by the various book publishing firms. The source also contains the number of publications for some foreign nations.

R 218–223. Newsprint consumption and newspaper pages, 1940–1970.

Source: U.S. Domestic and International Business Administration, unpublished data.

R 224–231. Newspapers—number and circulation of daily and Sunday newspapers, 1920–1970.

Source: Editor and Publisher, New York, N.Y., *International Year Book Number*, various issues (copyright).

The term "daily" refers to papers that are published either morning or evening. About 90 percent of the circulation figures are credited by the Audit Bureau of Circulations. The remaining 10 percent is based on publishers' statements to the U.S. Post Office Department. The compilation is checked annually with a questionnaire to every daily newspaper in the country. The source also presents data for individual States.

R 232–243. Newspapers and periodicals, 1935–1970.

Source: N. W. Ayer and Son, Inc., Philadelphia, Pa., *Ayer Directory of Newspapers, Magazines and Trade Publications*, annual issues (copyright).

R 244–257. Number and circulation of newspapers and periodicals, 1850–1967.

Source: 1850–1899, Twelfth Census Reports, *Manufactures*, vol. IX, part III; 1904–1909, Thirteenth Census Reports, *Manufactures*, vol. X; 1914–1927, census of manufactures for each census year; 1929–1947, census of manufactures; 1947, *Product Supplement*, pp. 67 and 68; 1954, *U.S. Census of Manufactures: 1954*, vol. II, part I, p. 27A–16; 1958, *U.S. Census of Manufactures: 1958*, vol. II, part I, p. 27A–28; 1963, *U.S. Census of Manufactures: 1963*, vol. II, part I, p. 27A–35; 1967, *U.S. Census of Manufactures: 1967*, vol. II, part I, p. 27A–23.

For data prior to 1850, which is not comparable to the data since that time, see Tenth Census Reports, S. N. D. North, *History and Present Conditions of the Newspaper and Periodical Press of the United States*, p. 47; and W. S. Rossiter, *A Century of Population Growth in the United States*, Government Printing Office, 1909, p. 32.

★ ★ ★ ★ ★ ★ ★ ★ ★   **More Recent Data for *Historical Statistics* Series**   ★ ★ ★ ★ ★ ★ ★ ★ ★

Statistics for more recent years in continuation of many of the still-active series shown here appear in annual issues of the *Statistical Abstract of the United States*, beginning with the 1975 edition. For direct linkage of the historical series to the tables in the *Abstract*, see Appendix I in the *Abstract*.

Series **R 163–171.** Postal Service—Post Offices, Revenues and Expenditures, Postage Stamps, Stamped Envelopes and Postal Cards Issued, and Pieces of Mail Handled: 1789 to 1970

[In thousands, except number of post offices. For years ending June 30. Includes Alaska, Hawaii, Puerto Rico, and all outlying areas except the Canal Zone]

Year	Post offices [1]	Revenues [2]	Expenditures [2]	Ordinary postage stamps issued [3]	Stamped envelopes and wrappers issued [4]	Postal cards issued [5]	Pieces of matter of all kinds handled	Surplus or deficit	Sales of postage stamps and other stamped paper
	163	164	165	166	167	168	169	170	171
1970	32,002	$7,701,695	$7,867,269	26,182,562	1,368,098	830,650	84,881,833	$−165,574	$1,936,147
1969	32,064	7,025,898	7,168,489	27,383,827	1,374,121	846,695	82,004,501	−142,591	1,936,578
1968	32,260	6,423,515	6,543,920	34,667,494	1,853,427	1,431,311	79,516,731	−120,405	1,799,492
1967	32,626	5,101,982	6,249,027	26,320,986	1,512,996	1,011,675	78,366,572	−1,147,044	1,636,057
1966	33,121	4,784,186	5,726,523	23,503,959	1,627,789	1,289,000	75,607,302	−942,336	1,579,338
1965	33,624	4,483,390	5,275,840	22,691,106	1,670,726	1,092,380	71,873,166	−792,450	1,528,289
1964	34,040	4,276,123	4,927,825	24,692,326	1,928,982	1,563,165	69,676,477	−651,702	1,504,180
1963	34,498	3,879,128	4,698,528	31,669,175	2,344,717	2,487,038	67,852,738	−819,400	1,381,749
1962	34,797	3,557,041	4,331,617	25,405,929	1,789,415	1,463,665	66,493,190	−837,277	1,262,316
1961	34,955	3,423,059	4,249,414	23,001,808	2,021,032	1,653,595	64,932,859	−875,355	1,252,681
1960	35,238	3,276,588	3,873,953	23,773,570	2,005,442	1,773,090	63,674,604	−634,534	1,244,909
1959	35,750	3,035,232	3,640,368	27,980,885	2,228,813	2,969,055	61,247,220	−605,117	1,245,231
1958	36,308	2,550,221	3,440,810	22,879,828	2,040,211	2,375,065	60,129,911	−890,577	1,016,930
1957	37,012	2,496,614	3 044,438	24,257,860	1,966,336	2,046,515	59,077,633	−547,824	1,015,237
1956	37,515	2,419,354	2,883,305	23,722,489	2,571,416	2,911,276	56,441,216	−463,951	1,010,523
1955	38,316	2,349,477	2,712,150	23,105,454	2,189,521	2,515,392	55,233,564	−362,673	999,985
1954	39,405	2,268,517	2,667,664	22,219,068	2,265,309	2,360,534	52,213,170	−399,147	998,965
1953	40,609	2,091,714	2,742,126	22,960,962	2,338,622	2,330,921	50,948,156	−650,412	985,172
1952	40,919	1,947,316	2,666,860	22,067,083	2,274,660	2,984,124	49,905,875	−719,544	948,430
1951	41,193	1,776,816	2,341,399	21,521,807	2,004,569	4,183,748	46,908,410	−564,583	883,357
1950	41,464	1,677,487	2,222,949	20,647,165	2,052,156	3,872,301	45,063,737	−545,462	862,313
1949	41,607	1,571,851	2,149,322	21,047,376	2,219,744	3,468,719	43,555,108	−551,130	856,266
1948	41,695	1,410,971	1,687,805	20,432,059	2,117,573	3,656,591	40,280,374	−308,972	820,904
1947	41,760	1,299,141	1,504,799	19,542,257	1,996,450	2,951,300	37,427,706	−263,368	801,437
1946	41,751	1,224,572	1,353,654	19,180,427	1,815,916	2,477,854	36,318,158	−148,083	843,417
1945	41,792	1,314,240	1,145,002	20,239,986	2,064,773	2,282,280	37,912,067	+162,642	953,770
1944	42,161	1,112,877	1,068,987	19,106,171	1,902,313	1,912,990	34,930,685	+37,789	787,836
1943	42,654	966,227	952,529	19,123,977	1,797,400	2,316,990	32,818,262	+1,335	658,054
1942	43,358	859,817	873,950	19,492,121	1,676,573	2,370,062	30,117,633	−11,825	571,651
1941	43,739	812,828	836,859	16,381,321	1,645,255	2,400,188	29,235,791	−26,964	543,584
1940	44,024	766,949	807,629	16,381,427	1,649,549	2,256,520	27,749,467	−42,225	521,753
1939	44,327	745,955	784,550	15,073,796	1,605,076	2,170,572	26,444,846	−40,827	514,869
1938	44,586	728,634	772,308	14,912,093	1,643,815	2,186,721	26,041,979	−44,697	515,118
1937	44,877	726,201	772,743	15,108,639	1,663,818	2,226,153	25,801,279	−44,704	521,675
1936	45,230	665,343	753,616	13,835,400	1,647,891	1,917,793	23,571,315	−90,975	-----------
1935	45,686	630,795	696,503	13,610,497	1,617,677	1,754,030	22,331,752	−69,802	-----------
1934	46,506	586,733	630,733	12,525,717	1,580,820	1,590,257	20,625,827	−46,667	-----------
1933	47,641	587,631	699,887	11,917,442	1,644,993	1,389,524	19,868,456	−110,007	-----------
1932	48,159	588,172	793,684	14,650,970	2,384,793	1,334,753	24,306,744	−206,886	-----------
1931	48,733	656,463	802,485	15,559,164	2,847,439	1,531,246	26,544,352	−146,545	-----------
1930	49,063	705,484	803,667	16,268,856	3,164,127	1,643,212	27,887,823	−98,449	-----------
1929	49,482	696,948	782,344	16,917,275	3,228,587	1,783,897	27,951,548	−86,310	-----------
1928	49,944	693,634	725,700	16,676,493	3,201,459	1,872,040	26,837,005	−33,363	-----------
1927	50,266	683,122	714,577	15,999,701	3,145,946	1,834,456	26,686,556	−28,915	-----------
1926	50,601	659,820	679,704	16,333,410	3,001,858	1,668,241	25,483,529	−37,906	-----------
1925	50,957	599,591	639,282	17,386,556	2,997,177	1,497,367	-----------	-----------	-----------
1924	51,266	572,949	587,377	15,954,475	2,964,464	1,293,185	-----------	-----------	-----------
1923	51,613	532,828	556,851	15,478,095	2,721,475	1,253,196	23,054,832	-----------	-----------
1922	51,950	484,854	545,644	14,261,949	2,364,373	1,111,124	-----------	-----------	-----------
1921	52,168	463,491	620,994	13,869,935	2,738,934	1,081,207	-----------	-----------	-----------
1920	52,641	437,150	454,323	13,212,790	2,350,073	986,156	-----------	-----------	-----------
1919	53,084	[6] 436,239	362,498	15,020,470	1,844,885	456,924	-----------	-----------	-----------
1918	54,347	[6] 388,976	324,834	13,065,785	1,819,307	707,111	-----------	-----------	-----------
1917	55,414	329,726	319,839	12,451,522	2,161,108	1,112,338	-----------	-----------	-----------
1916	55,935	312,058	306,204	11,671,842	1,853,791	1,047,895	-----------	-----------	-----------
1915	56,380	287,248	298,546	11,226,386	1,793,764	975,542	-----------	-----------	-----------
1914	56,810	287,935	283,544	11,112,254	1,864,714	962,072	-----------	-----------	-----------
1913	58,020	266,620	262,068	10,812,508	1,724,730	946,862	18,567,445	-----------	-----------
1912	58,729	246,744	248,525	9,929,174	1,684,624	909,411	17,588,659	-----------	-----------
1911	59,237	237,880	237,649	10,046,069	1,690,775	975,139	16,900,552	-----------	-----------
1910	59,580	224,129	229,977	9,067,165	1,506,862	726,441	14,850,102	-----------	-----------
1909	60,144	203,562	221,004	8,731,875	1,509,626	926,479	14,004,577	-----------	-----------
1908	60,704	191,479	208,352	7,651,400	1,266,003	809,427	13,364,069	-----------	-----------
1907	62,658	183,585	190,238	7,061,037	1,418,840	805,569	12,255,666	-----------	-----------
1906	65,600	167,933	178,450	6,284,450	1,230,288	798,918	11,361,091	-----------	-----------
1905	68,131	152,827	167,399	5,751,018	1,074,918	728,285	10,187,506	-----------	-----------
1904	71,131	143,582	152,362	5,330 887	1,020,255	702,907	9,502,450	-----------	-----------
1903	74,169	134,224	138,784	5,270,549	948,654	770,658	8,887,467	-----------	-----------
1902	75,924	121,848	124,786	4,621,286	853,128	547,204	8,085,447	-----------	-----------
1901	76,945	111,631	115,555	4,239,274	772,839	659,615	7,424,390	-----------	-----------

See footnotes at end of table.

Series R 163–171. Postal Service—Post Offices, Revenues and Expenditures, Postage Stamps, Stamped Envelopes and Postal Cards Issued, and Pieces of Mail Handled: 1789 to 1970—Con.

[In thousands, except number of post offices]

Year	Post offices [1]	Revenues [2]	Expenditures [2]	Ordinary postage stamps issued [3]	Stamped envelopes and wrappers issued [4]	Postal cards issued [5]	Pieces of matter of all kinds handled
	163	164	165	166	167	168	169
1900	76,688	$102,354	$107,740	3,998,545	707,555	587,815	7,129,990
1899	75,000	95,021	101,632	3,692,776	628,456	573,634	6,576,310
1898	73,570	89,013	98,054	3,418,458	606,447	556,381	6,214,447
1897	71,022	82,665	94,077	3,063,634	585,032	523,608	5,781,002
1896	70,360	82,499	90,933	3,025,481	616,040	524,820	5,693,719
1895	70,064	76,983	87,180	2,795,425	598,849	492,306	5,134,281
1894	69,805	75,080	84,994	2,602,278	571,475	468,500	4,919,090
1893	68,403	75,897	81,582	2,750,293	636,279	530,506	5,021,841
1892	67,119	70,930	76,981	2,543,270	593,685	511,434	4,776,575
1891	64,329	65,932	73,060	2,397,503	556,226	424,217	4,369,900
1890	62,401	60,882	66,260	2,219,737	513,833	429,515	4,005,408
1889	58,999	56,176	62,317	1,961,981	451,864	386,809	3,860,200
1888	57,376	52,695	56,458	1,867,173	433,636	381,798	3,576,100
1887	55,157	48,838	53,006	1,746,986	381,611	356,939	3,495,100
1886	53,614	43,948	51,005	1,620,784	354,008	355,648	3,747,000
1885	51,252	42,561	50,046	1,465,123	322,751	339,417	----------
1884	48,434	43,326	47,225	1,459,768	322,232	362,877	----------
1883	46,820	45,509	43,283	1,202,744	259,266	379,517	----------
1882	46,231	41,876	40,482	1,114,560	256,565	351,498	----------
1881	44,512	36,785	39,593	954,128	227,067	308,537	----------
1880	42,989	33,315	36,543	875,682	207,137	272,550	----------
1879	40,588	30,042	33,450	774,359	177,562	221,797	----------
1878	38,253	29,278	34,165	742,462	183,500	200,630	----------
1877	37,345	27,532	33,486	689,581	170,651	170,015	----------
1876	36,383	28,644	33,263	698,799	165,520	150,815	----------
1875	35,547	26,791	33,611	682,342	149,766	107,616	----------
1874	34,294	26,471	32,126	632,733	136,419	91,079	----------
1873	33,244	22,997	29,085	601,932	131,173	31,094	----------

Year	Post offices [1]	Revenues [2]	Expenditures [2]	Ordinary postage stamps issued [3]	Stamped envelopes and wrappers issued [4]
	163	164	165	166	167
1872	31,863	$21,915	$26,658	541,445	113,926
1871	30,045	20,037	24,390	498,126	104,675
1870	28,492	18,880	23,999	468,118	86,290
1869	27,106	17,314	23,698	421,047	81,675
1868	26,481	16,292	22,731	383,471	73,365
1867	25,163	15,237	19,235	371,600	63,087
1866	29,389	14,387	15,352	347,734	39,095
1865	28,882	14,556	13,695	387,419	[7] 26,206
1864	28,878	12,438	12,645	334,055	28,219
1863	29,047	11,164	11,314	338,340	25,549
1862	28,875	8,300	11,125	251,307	27,234
1861	28,586	8,349	13,607	211,789	[8] 26,027
1860	28,498	8,518	14,875	216,371	29,280
1859	28,539	7,968	15,754	192,202	30,280
1858	27,977	7,487	12,722	176,761	30,971
1857	26,586	7,354	11,508	154,729	33,033
1856	25,565	6,921	10,405	126,045	33,764
1855	24,410	6,642	9,968	72,977	23,452
1854	23,548	6,256	8,577	56,330	21,384
1853	22,320	5,241	7,983	56,344	5,000
1852	20,901	5,185	7,108	54,136	----------
1851	19,796	6,411	6,278	1,247	----------
1850	18,417	5,500	5,213	1,541	----------
1849	16,749	4,705	4,479	956	----------
1848	16,159	4,555	4,327	860	----------

Year	Post offices [1]	Revenues [2]	Expenditures [2]	Year	Post offices [1]	Revenues [2]	Expenditures [2]	Year	Post offices [1]	Revenues [2]	Expenditures [2]
	163	164	165		163	164	165		163	164	165
1847	15,146	$3,880	$3,980	1827	7,300	$1,525	$1,470	1807	1,848	$479	$454
1846	14,601	3,487	4,076	1826	6,150	1,448	1,367	1806	1,710	446	417
1845	14,183	4,290	4,321	1825	5,677	1,307	1,229	1805	1,558	421	377
1844	14,103	4,237	4,299	1824	5,182	1,198	1,188	1804	1,405	389	338
1843	13,814	4,296	4,375	1823	4,043	1,130	1,157	1803	1,258	352	322
1842	13,733	4,547	4,628	1822	4,709	1,117	1,168	1802	1,114	327	282
1841	13,778	4,408	4,500	1821	4,650	1,059	1,165	1801	1,025	320	255
1840	13,468	4,544	4,718	1820	4,500	1,112	1,161	1800	903	281	214
1839	12,780	4,485	4,637	1819	4,000	1,205	1,118	1799	677	265	188
1838	12,519	4,239	4,431	1818	3,618	1,130	1,036	1798	639	233	179
1837	11,767	4,102	3,288	1817	3,459	1,003	917	1797	554	214	150
1836	11,091	3,408	2,842	1816	3,260	962	804	1796	468	195	132
1835	10,770	2,994	2,757	1815	3,000	1,043	748	1795	453	161	118
1834	10,693	2,824	2,911	1814	2,670	730	727	1794	450	129	90
1833	10,127	2,617	2,930	1813	2,708	703	631	1793	209	105	72
1832	9,205	2,259	2,266	1812	2,610	649	540	1792	195	67	55
1831	8,686	1,998	1,936	1811	2,403	587	499	1791	89	46	37
1830	8,450	1,851	1,933	1810	2,300	552	496	1790	75	38	32
1829	8,004	1,707	1,782	1809	2,012	507	498	1789	75	[9] 8	[9] 8
1828	7,530	1,660	1,690	1808	1,944	461	463				

[1] Excludes branches and stations.
[2] Accounting basis changed from cash to accrual basis in 1954; from accrual basis to accrued cost basis in 1963.
[3] First issued under act of Mar. 3, 1847, and placed on sale at New York, July 1, 1847.
[4] Stamped envelopes first issued June 1853, under act of Aug. 31, 1852.
[5] First issued May 1, 1873, under act of June 8, 1872.
[6] For 1918 and 1919, includes $44,500,000 and $71,392,000, respectively, war-tax revenue accruing from increased postage.
[7] Special-request envelopes first issued in this year.
[8] Newspaper wrappers first issued under act of Feb. 27, 1861; they were not made after Oct. 9, 1934.
[9] For 3 months only.

Series R 172–187. Postal Service—Revenues, Expenses, and Volume of Mail, by Classes of Mail, and Employees: 1926 to 1970

[In millions, except employees in thousands. Includes Alaska, Hawaii, Puerto Rico, and all outlying areas except the Canal Zone]

Year	First-class mail [1]			Second-class mail			Third-class mail			Fourth-class mail			Airmail, domestic [1][3]			Post Office employees
	Revenues [2]	Expenses	Pieces	Revenues [2]	Expenses	Pieces	Revenues [2]	Expenses	Pieces	Revenues [2]	Expenses	Pieces	Revenues [2]	Expenses	Pieces	
	172	173	174	175	176	177	178	179	180	181	182	183	184	185	186	187
1970	$3,290	$1,985	48,640	$155	$292	9,351	$827	$531	19,974	$778	$554	977	$484	$188	1,718	741
1969 [4]	3,135	1,692	46,411	147	350	9,206	782	460	19,622	831	542	1,031	485	165	1,836	739
1968	2,722	2,660	43,183	134	569	8,907	743	1,144	20,665	767	939	1,039	425	304	2,065	731
1967	2,442	2,407	41,998	129	551	8,711	704	1,116	20,985	742	933	1,070	329	271	2,111	717
1966	2,334	2,176	40,422	126	524	8,634	682	1,041	20,305	712	896	1,066	277	221	1,828	675
1965	2,193	1,965	38,068	119	499	8,600	650	999	19,454	702	846	1,045	243	198	1,629	596
1964	2,109	1,814	36,943	108	481	8,559	612	899	18,599	659	815	1,066	216	181	1,505	585
1963	1,824	1,691	35,833	98	454	8,227	563	874	18,407	645	806	1,076	200	172	1,545	587
1962	1,615	1,605	35,333	94	455	8,090	510	787	17,837	634	787	1,024	185	163	1,545	588
1961	1,558	1,547	34,289	89	442	7,966	498	787	17,569	626	774	978	171	151	1,453	582
1960	1,510	1,395	33,235	81	412	7,535	441	711	17,910	607	736	1,016	157	137	1,356	563
1959	1,439	1,303	32,274	69	373	7,099	391	678	16,978	576	709	1,038	153	131	1,368	550
1958	1,092	1,229	32,218	66	351	7,148	288	611	15,849	584	699	1,170	137	127	1,435	538
1957	1,066	1,040	31,561	66	327	6,888	281	528	15,702	586	641	1,184	140	119	1,483	521
1956	1,014	978	30,078	66	318	6,915	266	472	14,676	593	608	1,173	137	114	1,487	509
1955	968	906	28,713	66	299	6,740	270	442	15,050	595	593	1,136	130	109	1,467	512
1954	908	845	27,085	62	293	6,483	252	399	13,866	587	609	1,195	127	119	1,470	507
1953	909	822	27,257	58	298	6,762	218	374	12,004	491	623	1,245	121	157	1,430	507
1952	843	787	26,502	51	288	6,956	171	361	11,630	485	619	1,257	121	148	1,391	524
1951	785	678	25,578	49	245	6,520	158	286	10,534	431	537	1,235	95	116	1,094	498
1950	741	665	24,500	45	242	6,265	154	292	10,343	404	506	1,179	74	109	853	501
1949	706	629	23,206	44	234	6,987	136	267	9,389	356	485	1,209	65	104	856	518
1948	668	518	21,948	41	210	6,344	112	201	8,188	272	368	1,143	54	83	796	503
1947	627	500	20,665	39	201	6,124	96	171	6,803	235	298	1,067	54	68	772	503
1946	598	454	20,059	33	181	5,832	83	135	6,055	209	250	994	68	50	716	487
1945	615	374	21,009	29	145	5,522	76	99	5,446	233	232	1,028	81	50	876	436
1944	540	370	20,510	29	138	4,635	63	88	4,409	202	217	961	79	49	1,092	390
1943	(NA)	(NA)	(NA)	(NA)	(NA)	(NA)	(NA)	(NA)	(NA)	(NA)	(NA)	(NA)	(NA)	(NA)	(NA)	374
1942	459	293	16,972	27	113	4,571	74	98	5,435	151	169	779	33	37	463	360
1941	432	278	15,989	26	109	4,607	83	105	6,075	142	161	738	24	31	323	361
1940	413	267	15,224	25	110	4,577	75	101	5,556	134	156	712	19	28	259	353
1939	400	263	14,657	24	111	4,310	70	94	5,181	133	151	693	16	25	221	349
1938	389	259	14,226	24	114	4,377	71	95	5,272	129	146	670	15	22	210	345
1937	384	254	13,882	24	113	4,529	72	92	5,356	132	146	685	12	19	168	345
1936	355	247	12,731	22	113	4,353	63	86	4,674	122	140	618	10	17	134	332
1935	344	229	12,498	20	107	4,138	55	76	4,030	112	133	573	7	13	89	309
1934	325	206	11,557	21	99	3,956	50	67	3,612	102	121	531	6	15	57	314
1933	332	227	10,878	20	108	3,869	51	79	3,753	100	132	530	6	23	60	322
1932	310	277	14,598	23	125	4,552	51	80	3,641	114	146	617	6	24	89	333
1931	336	278	15,824	27	124	4,857	58	82	4,100	138	158	766	6	18	88	339
1930	359	279	16,901	31	120	4,968	61	83	4,325	152	167	837	5	15	69	340
1929	361	276	17,170	30	124	4,834	62	81	4,341	143	163	770	4	11	56	340
1928	356	268	16,706	35	120	4,678	66	72	3,838	144	151	752	-------	-------	-------	337
1927	345	262	16,284	35	119	4,753	69	73	4,062	141	146	743	-------	-------	-------	332
1926	321	247	15,266	34	118	4,658	69	71	3,962	145	148	770	-------	-------	-------	329

NA Not available.

[1] For 1926–1929, domestic airmail included with first-class mail.

[2] For 1951–1955, box rent revenue, previously classified as unassignable, allocated to classes of mail; thereafter, classified as "Special services."

[3] Beginning 1947, includes airmail to and from Armed Forces overseas, previously included with foreign mail. Beginning 1954, excludes reimbursement for airmail transportation.

[4] In fiscal year 1969 the department changed from a fully distributed cost system to an attributable cost system.

Series R 188–190. Postal Rates for First-Class Mail, Letters and Postal Cards: 1792 to 1970

[First-class mail as a mail category not officially established until 1863. Ship and steamboat letters, 1792–1863, carried special rates]

Year of rate change	Letters, nonlocal	Postal cards (cents)	Year of rate change and distance	Single letters [5] (cents)	Year of rate change and distance	Single letters [5] (cents)
	188	189		190		190
1968–1970	6¢ per oz.	5	**1855:**		1815, over 500 miles	50% increase
1963	5¢ per oz.	4	Not over 3,000 miles	3	**1799:**	
1958, Aug. 1	4¢ per oz.	3	Over 3,000 miles, all prepaid	10	Not over 40 miles	8
1952	3¢ per oz.	2	**1851:**		41–90 miles	10
1940	(1)	(1)	Not over 3,000 miles, prepaid	3	91–150 miles	12½
1932	3¢ per oz.	1	Not over 3,000 miles, not prepaid	5	151–300 miles	17
			Over 3,000 miles, prepaid	6	301–500 miles	20
1919	2¢ per oz.	1	Over 3,000 miles, not prepaid	10	Over 500 miles	25
1917	3¢ per oz.	2	**1847**	(6)	1794, over 500 miles	[8] 25
1885	2¢ per oz.	1	**1845:**		**1792:**	
1883	2¢ per ½ oz.	1	Not over 300 miles	5	Not over 30 miles	6
1872	3¢ per ½ oz.	[2] 1	Over 300 miles	10	31–60 miles	8
1863 [3]	3¢ per ½ oz.		**1816:**		61–100 miles	10
1861 [4]	----[4] do----		Not over 30 miles	6	101–150 miles	12½
			31–80 miles	10	151–200 miles	15
			81–150 miles	12½	201–250 miles	17
			151–400 miles	[7] 18½	251–350 miles	20
			Over 400 miles	25	351–450 miles	22
			Over 500 miles	increase repealed	Over 450 miles	25

[1] The 1940 rate change provided that the 3¢ letter rate was not to apply to first-class matter for local delivery or for delivery within a county with a population of over 1 million if county was entirely within a corporate city.

[2] Government postal cards first authorized in 1872.

[3] A uniform rate regardless of distance, a free city delivery service, and a letter unit of ½ ounce instead of the former "single letter" were inaugurated.

[4] Rate between any point in the U.S. east of the Rocky Mountains and any State or Territory on the Pacific. For other rates, see those for 1855.

[5] A communication of 1 sheet. Proportionately higher rates charged for letters of 2, 3, and 4 or more sheets (packet).

[6] Various acts between 1847 and 1850 established special rates for the western and southwestern U.S.

[7] In 1825, rates for single letters, 151 to 400 miles, increased to 18¾ cents.

[8] Between 1794 and 1863, extra fees were charged for city delivery service. The proceeds went to the letter carrier.

Series R 191. Postal Rates for Domestic Airmail: 1918 to 1970

[Includes Alaska, Hawaii, Puerto Rico, and all outlying areas except the Canal Zone]

Effective date	Rate (191)	Effective date	Rate (191)	Effective date	Rate (191)
1968, Jan. 7 to 1970	10¢ per oz., 8¢ each for airmail postal and post cards	1932, July 6	8¢ first oz.; 13¢ each additional oz.	1926, Feb. 15	Government routes: Daytime zone rate, 8¢ per oz. New York to Chicago (overnight), 10¢ per oz.
		1928, Aug. 1	5¢ first oz.; 10¢ each additional oz.		
1963, Jan. 7	8¢ per oz., 6¢ each for airmail postal and post cards	1927, Feb. 1	10¢ per ½ oz., regardless of distance (both contract and Government-operated air routes)	1925, July 1	10¢ per oz. for Government-operated overnight service New York to Chicago; 8¢ per oz. daytime zone rate
1958, Aug. 1	7¢ per oz., 5¢ each for airmail postal and post cards	1926, Feb. 15	Contract air routes: Under 1,000 miles, 10¢ per oz. — 1,000–1,500 miles, 15¢ per oz. — Over 1,500 miles, 20¢ per oz. } plus 5¢ for each airmail zone		
1949, Jan. 1	6¢ per oz., 4¢ each for airmail postal and post cards [1]			1924, July 1	8¢ per oz., per zone [3]
				1919, July 18	2¢ per oz. [4]
1948, Sept. 1	(2)			1918, Dec. 15	6¢ per oz.
1946, Oct. 1	5¢ per oz.			1918, July 15	16¢ per oz. and 6¢ each additional oz., of which 10¢ was for special delivery
1944, Mar. 26	8¢ per oz.				
1934, July 1	6¢ per oz.			1918, May 15	24¢ per oz., of which 10¢ was for special delivery

[1] Airmail postal and post card service started Jan. 1, 1949.

[2] Prior to 1948, weight and size limits for airmail were the same as for first-class mail; beginning Sept. 1, 1948, matter carried by air weighing 8 oz. or less was classified as "airmail," and over 8 oz. as "air-parcel post."

[3] Zones were (1) New York-Chicago, (2) Chicago-Cheyenne, (3) Cheyenne-San Francisco.

[4] Not strictly an "airmail rate." Between July 18, 1919, and July 1, 1924, there was no airmail rate and no offer of airmail service. Some mail, however, was carried by planes at the regular first-class rate of 2¢ per oz.

Series R 192–217. New Books and New Editions Published, by Subject: 1880 to 1970

Year	Books published[1]			New books									
	Total	New books	New editions	Agriculture	Art	Biography	Business	Education	Fiction	General works	History	Home economics	Juvenile
	192	193	194	195	196	197	198	199	200	201	202	203	204
1970	36,071	24,288	11,783	200	852	735	658	842	1,998	568	1,010	235	2,472
1969	29,579	21,787	7,792	216	856	718	566	721	1,816	508	1,191	267	1,321
1968	30,387	23,321	7,066	191	930	786	644	917	1,822	521	1,048	245	2,318
1967	[2] 28,762	21,877	6,885	218	844	783	509	781	1,981	426	1,015	203	2,390
1966	30,050	21,819	8,231	212	779	819	478	886	1,699	410	959	219	2,375
1965	28,595	20,234	8,361	214	763	455	437	789	1,615	384	909	241	2,473
1964	28,451	20,542	7,909	209	776	697	411	934	1,703	361	834	188	2,533
1963	25,784	19,057	6,727	219	664	680	396	777	1,859	346	847	205	2,605
1962	21,904	16,448	5,456	215	590	667	308	559	1,787	279	812	156	2,328
1961	18,060	14,238	3,822	194	539	622	286	461	1,645	231	796	143	1,513
1960	15,012	12,069	2,943	121	422	746	240	308	1,642	233	695	155	1,628
1959	[3] 14,876	12,017	2,859	101	354	671	327	368	1,675	326	750	141	1,540
1958	13,462	11,012	2,450	122	409	608	283	276	1,592	213	750	142	1,424
1957	13,142	10,561	2,581	120	304	699	266	254	1,433	360	773	115	1,420
1956	12,538	10,007	2,531	106	283	676	222	229	1,500	305	521	159	1,384
1955	12,589	10,226	2,363	125	305	735	228	231	1,459	315	572	205	1,372
1954	11,901	9,690	2,211	111	285	687	196	223	1,512	339	529	192	1,193
1953	12,050	9,724	2,326	126	265	710	225	201	1,495	360	495	197	1,264
1952	11,840	9,399	2,441	114	267	650	180	238	1,354	336	454	237	1,094
1951	11,255	8,765	2,490	105	272	586	180	229	1,329	329	435	186	982
1950	11,022	8,634	2,388	111	317	538	190	209	1,211	262	456	150	907

New books—Continued

Year	Language	Law	Literature	Medicine	Music	Philosophy, psychology	Poetry, drama	Religion	Science	Sociology, economics	Sports, recreation	Technology	Travel
	205	206	207	208	209	210	211	212	213	214	215	216	217
1970	339	355	1,349	1,144	217	843	973	1,315	1,955	3,867	583	930	848
1969	355	363	1,348	928	227	678	944	1,278	1,999	3,216	585	884	802
1968	387	432	1,301	1,022	210	669	791	1,511	2,011	3,107	501	1,072	885
1967	382	392	1,172	935	165	633	739	1,502	1,835	2,761	391	1,051	885
1966	459	316	1,185	1,007	207	629	728	1,477	2,079	2,632	441	1,091	769
1965	385	291	1,166	871	183	582	775	1,428	1,850	2,372	474	942	732
1964	414	256	1,038	876	156	528	681	1,441	1,923	2,445	452	939	635
1963	334	269	861	752	139	505	578	1,459	1,648	1,932	427	960	747
1962	226	219	771	688	137	436	505	1,174	1,309	1,603	367	780	595
1961	248	203	617	595	114	433	517	1,098	1,193	1,289	381	665	455
1960	--------	303	560	388	82	496	404	983	833	651	233	[4] 574	372
1959	--------	245	630	445	93	505	395	984	814	566	204	585	298
1958	--------	245	495	393	89	467	373	941	781	494	201	443	271
1957	--------	252	477	359	73	480	378	883	697	416	195	316	291
1956	--------	221	570	334	88	425	337	810	531	448	160	404	294
1955	--------	240	529	407	85	362	423	747	623	443	175	355	290
1954	--------	226	493	345	69	386	389	774	522	463	201	325	230
1953	--------	196	485	328	58	425	412	725	522	467	194	294	280
1952	--------	236	518	350	71	427	424	715	513	478	168	311	264
1951	--------	223	445	336	80	393	400	636	521	430	151	287	230
1950	--------	228	510	312	88	380	453	626	499	447	153	366	221

Year	Books published[1]		
	Total	New books	New editions
	192	193	194
1949	10,892	8,460	2,432
1948	9,897	7,807	2,090
1947	9,182	7,243	1,939
1946	7,735	6,170	1,565
1945	6,548	5,386	1,162
1944	6,970	5,807	1,163
1943	8,325	6,764	1,561
1942	9,525	7,786	1,739
1941	11,112	9,337	1,775
1940	11,328	9,515	1,813
1939	10,640	9,015	1,625
1938	11,067	9,464	1,603
1937	10,912	9,273	1,639
1936	10,436	8,584	1,852
1935	8,766	6,914	1,852
1934	8,198	6,788	1,410
1933	8,092	6,813	1,279
1932	9,035	7,556	1,479
1931	10,307	8,506	1,801
1930	10,027	8,134	1,893
1929	10,187	8,342	1,845
1928	10,354	7,614	1,562
1927	10,153	7,450	1,449
1926	9,925	6,832	1,527
1925	9,574	6,680	1,493
1924	9,012	6,380	1,158
1923	8,863	6,257	921
1922	8,638	5,998	865
1921	8,329	5,438	1,008
1920	8,422	5,101	1,086
1919	8,594	7,625	969
1918	9,237	8,085	1,152
1917	10,060	8,849	1,211
1916	10,445	9,160	1,285
1915	9,734	8,349	1,385
1914	12,010	10,175	1,835
1913	12,230	10,607	1,623
1912	10,903	10,135	768
1911	[5] 11,123	10,440	783
1910	13,470	11,671	1,799
1909	10,901	10,193	708
1908	9,254	8,745	509
1907	9,620	8,925	695
1906	7,139	6,724	415
1905	8,112	7,514	598
1904	8,291	6,971	1,320
1903	7,865	5,793	2,072
1902	7,833	5,485	2,348
1901	8,141	5,496	2,645
1900	6,356	4,490	1,866
1899	5,321	4,749	572
1898	4,886	4,332	554
1897	4,928	4,171	757
1896	5,703	5,189	514
1895	5,469	5,101	368
1894	4,484	3,837	647
1893	5,134	4,281	853
1892	4,862	4,074	788
1891	4,665	(NA)	(NA)
1890	4,559	4,113	446
1889	4,014	--------	--------
1888	4,631	--------	--------
1887	4,437	--------	--------
1886	4,676	--------	--------
1885	4,030	--------	--------
1884	4,088	--------	--------
1883	3,481	--------	--------
1882	3,472	--------	--------
1881	2,991	--------	--------
1880	2,076	--------	--------

NA Not available.

[1] 1880–1919, includes pamphlets; 1920–1928, pamphlets included in total only; thereafter, pamphlets excluded entirely.

[2] Beginning 1967, counting methods were revised; prior years not strictly comparable with subsequent years. See text.

[3] Beginning 1959, data not strictly comparable with previous years because of change in definition of "book." See text.

[4] Prior to 1961, includes military.

[5] Agrees with source; however, figures for components do not add to total shown.

Series R 218–223. Newsprint Consumption and Newspaper Pages: 1940 to 1970

[Consumption figures in 1,000 short tons]

Year	Total	Newspapers Total	Advertising	Other content	Daily	Sunday
	218	219	220	221	222	223
1970	9,754	9,071	5,579	3,492	47	145
1969	9,820	9,133	5,662	3,471	56	191
1968	9,162	8,521	5,274	3,247	55	186
1967	9,159	8,518	5,213	3,305	53	178
1966	9,099	8,462	5,221	3,241	53	180
1965	8,442	7,851	4,750	3,101	50	167
1964	8,092	7,482	4,616	2,866	47	154
1963	7,577	7,047	4,313	2,734	46	148
1962	7,412	6,893	4,205	2,688	45	145
1961	7,358	6,843	4,126	2,717	43	139
1960	7,312	6,800	4,148	2,652	43	142
1959*	7,073	6,578	4,026	2,552	42	141
1958	6,515	6,059	3,635	2,424	39	135
1957	6,768	6,300	3,843	2,457	40	138
1956	6,807	6,320	3,925	2,395	41	135
1955	6,484	6,173	3,827	2,346	40	132
1954	6,103	5,732	3,376	2,356	36	122
1953	6,109	5,713	3,394	2,319	37	121
1952	5,915	5,569	3,286	2,283	36	117
1951	5,872	5,557	3,295	2,262	36	113
1950	5,863	5,521	3,279	2,242	36	112
1949	5,532	5,142	2,977	2,165	34	107
1948	5,136	4,781	2,811	1,970	32	102
1947	4,658	4,420	2,550	1,870	29	94
1946	4,192	3,995	2,177	1,818	27	84
1945	3,451	3,237	1,667	1,570	22	70
1944	3,218	3,048	1,530	1,518	23	68
1943	3,559	3,409	1,568	1,841	26	78
1942	3,721	3,587	1,442	2,145	26	82
1941	3,922	3,694	1,481	2,213	27	88
1940	3,739	3,507	1,403	2,104	27	86

* Denotes first year for which figures include Alaska and Hawaii.
[1] Apparent consumption; equals production plus imports minus exports adjusted for year-end changes in newspaper publishers, inventories, and domestic mill stocks.

[2] Based on information of Media Records, Inc. Through 1968, newspaper pages per issue based on average in 39 cities; thereafter, on average in 110 cities.

Series R 224–231. Newspapers—Number and Circulation of Daily and Sunday Newspapers: 1920 to 1970

[Circulation in thousands. Figures as of October 1 of each year]

Year	Daily Total Number	Daily Total Circulation	Morning Number	Morning Circulation	Evening Number	Evening Circulation	Sunday Number	Sunday Circulation
	224	225	226	227	228	229	230	231
1970	[1] 1,748	62,108	334	25,934	1,429	36,174	586	49,217
1969	[1] 1,758	62,060	333	25,812	1,443	36,248	585	49,675
1968	[1] 1,752	62,535	328	25,838	1,443	36,697	578	49,693
1967	[1] 1,749	61,561	327	25,282	1,438	36,279	573	49,224
1966	[1] 1,754	61,397	324	24,806	1,444	36,592	578	49,282
1965	[1] 1,751	60,358	320	24,107	1,444	36,251	562	48,600
1964	[1] 1,763	60,412	323	24,365	1,452	36,048	561	48,383
1963	[1] 1,754	58,905	311	23,459	1,453	35,446	550	46,830
1962	[1] 1,760	59,849	318	24,563	1,451	35,286	558	48,888
1961	[1] 1,761	59,261	312	24,094	1,458	35,167	558	48,216
1960	[1] 1,763	58,882	312	24,029	1,459	34,853	563	47,699
1959	[1] 1,755	58,300	306	23,547	1,455	34,753	564	47,848
1958	[1] 1,755	57,418	307	23,161	1,456	34,258	556	46,955
1957	[1] 1,755	57,805	309	23,171	1,453	34,635	544	47,044
1956	[1] 1,761	57,102	314	22,492	1,454	34,610	546	47,162
1955	[1] 1,760	56,147	316	22,183	1,454	33,964	541	46,448
1954	[1] 1,765	55,072	317	21,705	1,448	33,367	544	46,176
1953	1,785	54,472	327	21,412	1,458	33,060	544	45,949
1952	1,786	53,951	327	21,160	1,459	32,791	545	46,210
1951	1,773	54,018	319	21,223	1,454	32,795	543	46,279
1950	1,772	53,829	322	21,266	1,450	32,563	549	46,582
1949	1,780	52,846	329	21,005	1,451	31,841	546	46,399
1948	1,781	52,285	328	21,082	1,453	31,203	530	46,308
1947	1,769	51,673	328	20,762	1,441	30,911	511	45,151
1946	1,763	50,928	334	20,546	1,429	30,382	497	43,665
1945	1,749	48,384	330	19,240	1,419	29,144	485	39,680
1944	1,744	45,955	338	18,059	1,406	27,896	481	37,946
1943	1,754	44,393	333	17,078	1,421	27,315	467	37,292
1942	1,787	43,375	345	17,111	1,442	26,264	474	35,294
1941	1,857	42,080	377	16,519	1,480	25,561	510	33,436
1940	1,878	41,132	380	16,114	1,498	25,018	525	32,371
1939	1,888	39,671	383	--------	1,505	--------	524	31,519
1938	1,936	39,572	398	--------	1,538	--------	523	30,481
1937	1,983	41,419	406	--------	1,577	--------	539	30,957
1936	1,989	40,292	405	--------	1,584	--------	520	29,962
1935	1,950	38,156	390	--------	1,560	--------	518	28,147
1934	1,929	36,709	385	--------	1,544	--------	505	26,545
1933	1,911	35,175	378	--------	1,533	--------	506	24,041
1932	1,913	36,408	380	--------	1,533	--------	518	24,860
1931	1,923	38,761	384	--------	1,539	--------	513	25,702
1930	1,942	39,589	388	--------	1,554	--------	521	26,413
1929	1,944	39,426	381	--------	1,563	--------	528	26,880
1928	1,939	37,973	397	--------	1,542	--------	522	25,772
1927	1,949	37,967	411	--------	1,538	--------	526	25,469
1926	2,001	36,002	425	--------	1,576	--------	545	24,435
1925	2,008	33,739	427	--------	1,581	--------	548	23,355
1924	2,014	32,999	429	--------	1,585	--------	539	22,220
1923	2,036	31,454	426	--------	1,610	--------	547	21,463
1922	2,033	29,780	426	--------	1,607	--------	546	19,713
1921	2,028	28,424	427	--------	1,601	--------	545	19,041
1920	2,042	27,791	437	--------	1,605	--------	522	17,084

[1] Total is adjusted to account for "all-day" papers listed in both morning and evening figures. Circulations are divided between morning and evening totals.

Series R 232–243. Newspapers and Periodicals: 1935 to 1970

[Data refer to year of complication of the Directory, i.e., generally to year preceding year shown]

Year	Newspapers					Periodicals						
	Total	Semi-weekly	Weekly	Daily	Other	Total	Weekly	Semi-monthly	Monthly	Bi-monthly	Quarterly	Other
	232	233	234	235	236	237	238	239	240	241	242	243
1970	11,383	423	8,903	1,838	219	9,573	1,856	589	4,314	957	1,108	749
1969	11,336	413	8,855	1,833	235	9,434	1,787	587	4,353	899	1,084	724
1968	11,293	387	8,858	1,833	215	9,400	1,796	606	4,331	899	1,078	690
1967	11,307	366	8,915	2,026		9,238	1,808	573	[1] 4,296	859	1,051	651
1966	12,365	382	9,785	1,972	226	10,002	1,884	335	4,796	912	1,119	956
1965	11,383	357	8,989	1,843	194	8,990	1,716	550	[1] 4,195	876	1,030	623
1964	12,332	390	9,761	1,963	218	9,798	1,724	334	4,847	910	1,065	918
1963	12,295	391	9,739	1,974	191	9,643	1,792	313	4,744	858	1,025	911
1962	12,293	376	9,774	1,970	173	9,483	1,740	305	4,705	826	1,030	877
1961	12,285	361	9,783	1,968	173	9,275	1,656	301	4,634	801	998	885
1960 *	11,315	324	8,979	1,854	158	8,422	1,580	527	[1] 4,113	743	895	564
1959	12,294	359	9,812	1,977	146	9,004	1,592	302	4,577	712	950	871
1958	12,207	332	9,768	1,969	138	8,927	1,705	292	4,490	676	914	850
1957	12,299	354	9,854	1,946	145	8,722	1,681	288	4,457	639	842	815
1956	12,256	338	9,813	1,963	142	8,718	1,748	283	4,450	614	831	792
1955	11,415	324	9,126	1,860	105	7,648	1,602	503	[1] 3,782	608	674	479
1954	12,398	328	9,960	1,999	111	8,092	1,584	260	4,218	604	695	731
1953	12,645	346	10,173	2,009	117	7,792	1,494	242	4,115	598	673	670
1952	12,833	341	10,381	1,998	113	7,711	1,485	246	4,118	558	665	639
1951	13,009	362	10,514	2,018	115	7,635	1,491	239	4,132	517	633	623
1950	12,115	337	9,794	1,894	90	6,960	1,443	416	[1] 3,694	436	604	367
1949	12,814	326	10,386	2,014	88	7,570	1,537	244	4,073	458	635	623
1948	12,900	301	10,511	2,001	87	7,346	1,498	262	3,970	412	576	628
1947	12,877	284	10,523	2,003	67	7,083	1,394	272	3,805	401	609	602
1946	12,804	286	10,424	2,020	74	6,693	1,331	253	3,595	345	595	574
1945	12,791	283	10,430	2,004	74	6,569	1,359	246	3,503	309	578	574
1944	12,889	308	10,504	2,006	71	6,672	1,456	226	3,500	285	588	617
1943	13,456	356	10,967	2,043	90	7,040	1,489	215	3,826	274	586	650
1942	14,100	408	11,474	2,131	87	7,374	1,609	248	3,983	288	601	645
1941	14,284	397	11,617	2,153	117	7,141	1,449	222	3,966	277	595	632
1940	13,314	368	10,860	2,086		6,432	1,399	427	[1] 3,466	241	538	361
1939	14,213	380	11,516	2,216	101	6,846	1,408	213	3,821	250	563	591
1938	14,112	383	11,421	2,242	66	6,412	1,220	202	3,663	219	530	578
1937	14,336	401	11,592	2,272	71	6,320	1,251	253	3,512	203	530	571
1936	13,928	368	11,288	2,189	83	6,670	1,546	216	3,622	197	497	592
1935	14,091	369	11,438	2,197	87	6,546	1,484	203	3,608	196	493	562

* Denotes first year for which figures include Alaska and Hawaii.   [1] Includes fortnightly.

Series R 244–257. Newspapers and Periodicals—Number and Circulation: 1850 to 1967

[Circulation in thousands. Data for 1947 and 1954 are for establishments having 1 or more regularly paid employees for whom a social security account was maintained at the Bureau of Old-Age and Survivors Insurance. Data for 1921–1939 are for establishments reporting annual receipts of $5,000 or more. For prior years the corresponding limit was $500. Circulation figures are the totals of average circulation per issue]

Year	Newspapers										Periodicals			
	Total		Daily		Sunday		Weekly		Other		Total		Weekly	
	Number	Circulation	Number	Circulation	Number	Circulation	Number	Circulation	Number	Circulation	Number	Circulation	Number	Circulation
	244	245	246	247	248	249	250	251	252	253	254	255	256	257
1967	(NA)	(NA)	(NA)	66,527	(NA)	52,129	(NA)	5,377	(NA)	(NA)	(NA)	427,915	(NA)	(NA)
1963	7,703	136,600	1,766	63,831	560	51,669	5,377	[1] 17,500	(NA)	[1] 3,600	(NA)	(NA)	(NA)	(NA)
1958	8,645	136,803	1,778	58,713	552	48,262	6,315	26,177	(NA)	3,651	4,455	408,364	478	105,147
1954	9,022	136,353	1,820	56,410	510	46,350	6,249	30,336	443	3,257	3,427	449,285	487	82,066
1947	10,282	119,568	1,854	53,287	416	42,736	7,705	21,408	307	2,137	4,610	384,628	892	69,393
1939	9,173	96,477	2,040	42,966	542	33,007	6,212	18,295	379	2,209	4,985	239,693	1,109	55,825
1937	8,826	95,296	2,065	43,345	528	32,713	5,839	17,287	394	1,951	4,202	224,275	954	56,115
1935	8,266	87,096	2,037	40,871	523	29,196	5,337	15,185	369	1,844	4,019	178,621	966	42,648
1933	6,884	76,298	1,903	37,630	489	25,444	4,218	12,048	274	1,166	3,459	174,759	878	39,365
1931	9,299	86,457	2,044	41,294	555	27,453	6,313	16,173	387	1,537	4,887	183,527	1,066	30,782
1929	10,176	91,778	2,086	42,015	578	29,012	7,075	18,884	437	1,867	5,157	202,022	1,158	34,495
1927	9,693	87,617	2,091	41,368	511	27,696	6,661	16,879	430	1,674	4,659	191,000	1,099	39,107
1925	9,569	80,705	2,116	37,407	597	25,630	6,435	15,990	421	1,678	4,496	179,281	1,133	34,826
1923	9,248	[2] 76,408	2,271	35,471	602	24,512	5,903	16,425	472		3,829		984	31,436
1921	9,419	[2] 75,411	2,334	33,742	538	20,853	6,059	20,816	488		3,747		995	23,090
1919	15,697	[2] 73,139	2,441	33,029	604	19,369	12,145	20,741	507		4,796		1,230	31,162
1914	[3] 16,944	[2] 67,108	2,580	28,777	571	16,480	13,793	21,851					1,379	28,486
1909	[3] 17,023	[2] 58,505	2,600	24,212	520	13,347	13,903	20,946					1,194	19,877
1904	[3] 16,459	[2] 50,464	2,452	19,633	494	12,022	13,513	18,809					1,493	17,418
1900			[4] 2,226	[4] 15,102										
1890			[4] 1,610	[4] 8,387										
1880			[4] 971	[4] 3,566										
1870			[4] 574	[4] 2,602										
1860			[4] 387	[4] 1,478										
1850			[4] 254	[4] 758										

NA Not available.
[1] Data are estimates based on the yearly subscription rate of reporting newspapers, as many small newspapers did not report circulation.

[2] Does not include circulation of "Other" newspapers (series R 253), not available prior to 1925. [3] Does not include a number of "Other" newspapers (series R 252), not available prior to 1919.
[4] Includes a small number of periodicals.

Energy

S 1–218. General note.

Energy to meet the expanding power needs of our economy has been secured from various animate and inanimate sources. Among those of historical significance, whose use is generally within the control of mankind, are human and animal power; waterpower; windpower; wood and other vegetable matter used as fuel; coal; oil; and natural gas; and, since 1957, atomic energy. Currently, efforts are being made to develop and control solar energy, internal heat of the earth, and, through chemical processing, certain additional natural resources such as shale and sea water. For those interested in developing a comprehensive understanding of power problems the following books are suggested: Eugene Ayers and Charles A. Scarlott, *Energy Sources—The Wealth of the World*, McGraw-Hill Publishing Company, Inc., New York, 1952; P. C. Putnam, *Energy in the Future*, D. Van Nostrand Company, Inc., New York, 1953; Fred Cottrell, *Energy and Society*, McGraw-Hill Publishing Company, Inc., New York, 1955; J. F. Dewhurst and Associates, *America's Needs and Resources, A New Survey*, The Twentieth Century Fund, New York, 1955; Ali Bulet Cambel, editor, *Energy R&D and National Progress*, Government Printing Office, 1964; Hans H. Landsberg and Sam H. Schurr, *Energy in the United States, Sources, Uses, and Policy Issues*, Random House, New York, 1968; Warren E. Morrison and Charles L. Readling, *Energy Model for the United States, Energy Balances for the Years 1947–1965, and Projections and Forecasts*, U.S. Bureau of Mines Information Circular 8384, 1968; N. B. Guyol, *The World Electric Power Industry*, University of California Press, Berkeley and Los Angeles, 1969; M. King Hubbert, "Energy Resources," in *Resources and Man*, W. H. Freeman and Co., San Francisco, 1969; U.S. Congress, Joint Committee on Atomic Energy, *Environmental Effects of Producing Electric Power*, selected materials and hearings issued in 4 vols., 1969 and 1970; U.S. Senate, Committee on the Judiciary, hearings of the Subcommittee on Anti-Trust & Monopoly, *Competitive Aspects of the Energy Industry*, parts 1 and 2, 1970; U.S. Bureau of the Census, *1967 Census of Manufactures—Fuels and Electric Energy Consumed*, Report MC 67(S)4, Government Printing Office, 1971; Joel Darmstadter with Perry D. Teitelbaum and J. G. Polach, for Resources for the Future, Inc., *Energy in the World Economy: A Statistical Review of Trends in Output, Trade, and Consumption Since 1925*, Johns Hopkins University Press, Baltimore, 1971; National Petroleum Council, *U.S. Energy Outlook—An Initial Appraisal (1971–1985)*, Washington, D.C., 1971; Resources for the Future, Inc., in cooperation with M.I.T. Environmental Laboratory, *Energy Research Needs*, a report to the National Science Foundation, document No. PB 207–516, National Technical Information Service, Springfield, Va., 1971; U.S. Federal Power Commission, *The 1970 National Power Survey*, issued in 4 parts, 1971 and 1972; Walter G. Dupree, Jr., and James A. West, *United States Energy Through the Year 2000*, U.S. Dept. of the Interior, 1972; Edison Electric Institute, *Statistical Yearbook of the Electric Utility Industry*, New York, annual; U.S. Federal Power Commission, *World Power Data*, annual; U.S. Bureau of Mines, *Minerals Yearbook*, vols. I–II combined, *Metals, Minerals, and Fuels*, annual; United Nations Statistical Office, *World Energy Supplies*, Statistical Papers, Series J, New York, annual; U.S. Senate Committee on Interior and Insular Affairs, *A National Fuels and Energy Policy Study*, Pursuant to Senate Resolution 45, 1972–1974; Federal Power Commission, *Natural Gas Survey*, forthcoming.

Preparation of historical tables showing energy from various sources and total energy input on a per capita or other basis is complicated. The amounts shown will differ greatly depending on the basis and point of measurement used. End-use data, for example, will show far larger increases in total per capita over the last 100 years than will data presenting physical measures such as tons, gallons, cubic feet, or B.t.u.'s because of increased efficiency in conversion and utilization.

Data on energy available from mineral fuels, waterpower for electric energy, and fuel wood are shown in series M 76–92. For total waterpower, net imports from waterpower sources in Canada and the energy equivalent of waterpower not converted to electric energy (direct drive from water wheels) must also be considered. Statistics available for power sources not included here are presented in some of the sources cited above. Data on the development and use of energy for power and related purposes are compiled or summarized and published by: Federal agencies such as the Bureau of Mines, Bureau of the Census, Rural Electrification Administration, Bureau of Labor Statistics, Federal Power Commission, Federal Reserve Board, Interstate Commerce Commission; the various trade associations such as the Edison Electric Institute, American Gas Association, Bituminous Coal Institute, American Petroleum Institute; and various technical journals, particularly in their statistical issues.

S 1–14. Total horsepower of all prime movers, 1849–1970.

Source: 1849–1952, J. F. Dewhurst and Associates, *America's Needs and Resources, A New Survey*, © 1955 by The Twentieth Century Fund, New York, p. 1117; 1955, estimates prepared by John A. Waring for *Transactions of Canadian Sectional Meeting, World Power Conference, 1958*; 1960–1970, unpublished estimates from John A. Waring.

Data for 1849–1952 for series S 4 (work animals), S 10 (sailing vessels), and S 12 (windmills), as shown on p. 1117 of *America's Needs and Resources*, are based on data presented in appendix 25-3 of that volume. All other data for 1849–1919 are from C. R. Daugherty, A. H. Horton, and R. W. Davenport, *Power Capacity and Production in the United States*, Water Supply Paper No. 579, U.S. Geological Survey, 1928. The original data from Daugherty *et al.* were for 1849 and subsequent 10-year intervals through 1919. Estimates for 1850 and subsequent 10-year intervals through 1940 are based on straight-line interpolation of original data.

All data for 1929, 1939, 1950, and 1952 shown in Dewhurst were prepared by John A. Waring. According to Waring, estimates for 1952 as shown in Dewhurst are too low for mines and farms, and too high for railroad locomotives.

A technical and statistical bibliography of early data pertaining to the development of horsepower equipment in the United States appears on pp. 43 and 44 of Daugherty *et al.* This source also contains a section on the sources and accuracy of the data. The following appraisal of the data appears on p. 21: "In general the accuracy of the statistics presented . . . increases with each successive decade. The data for the early years are almost wholly estimated, but it is believed that the estimates are supported by bases accurate enough to lend a degree of authenticity to them."

In addition to the classifications shown in series S 1–14, the installed mechanical horsepower in a number of special industries was also calculated for 1960 by Waring, as follows (in thousands): Municipal waterworks pumping engines, 2,188; gas utility stations, 1,775; natural gas pipeline pumping stations, 6,110; underground gas storage pool compressor engines, 470; petroleum pipeline pumping stations, 4,560; standby communications generator sets, 632; isolated nonindustrial generator sets, 5,204; construction and contractors' building equipment, 89,182; inboard powered motor boats and yachts, 29,870; outboard powered motor boats, 60,500; portable chain saws, 2,020; and power lawn mowers, 36,800. These total 239,311 thousand horsepower, which, when added to the 1960 total of 11,007,889 thousand shown in series S 1, result in an aggregate of 11,247,200 thousand horsepower.

S 15–24. Consumption of raw materials in constant 1967 dollars, by broad use classes, 1900–1969.

Source: U.S. Bureau of the Census and U.S. Bureau of Mines, *Raw Materials in the United States Economy: 1900–1969* (Working Paper No. 35), table A5.

The raw-materials series presented in the source are regrouped in these series in terms of the major purposes for which the materials are used. This classification represents materials used in the entire U.S. economy, including the raw-materials industries.

Minerals usually used for energy purposes are increasingly being absorbed for nonfuel uses. Some such uses are for synthetic rubber, carbon black, and other chemical raw materials; for lubricants, asphalt, road oil, waxes; and as carbon in iron and electrodes. The approximate significance of such uses is indicated by the following figures:

Period	Mineral fuels used for nonfuel purposes as a percent of total mineral fuels use
1960–1969	6.7
1950–1959	5.0
1940–1949	4.2
1930–1939	3.3
1920–1929	2.6
1910–1919	1.4
1900–1909	1.2

The figures in series S 15–24 exclude such uses from the figures presented for "energy materials" and include them in "physical-structure materials."

It should be noted that the relative importance of the foods, energy materials, and physical-structure materials segments of the consumption pattern is somewhat influenced by the consumption of raw materials within the raw-materials industries. The value of purchased feed for farm animals and seed are excluded here. However, the mineral fuels consumed in producing raw materials are included, as well as the indirect consumption of raw materials represented by the capital-goods requirements of the raw-materials industries. Available staff facilities did not permit extensive analysis of the magnitude of consumption of raw materials within the raw-materials industries. It appears, however, that 4 to 7 percent of all energy has been used in mineral-fuel production.

See also series K 392–406, L 56–71, and M 38–53 for raw material consumption by agricultural materials, forest products, and minerals, respectively.

S 25–31. Consumption of fuel resources, by major consumer group, 1947–1970.

Source: U.S. Bureau of Mines, *Minerals Yearbook* and *Mineral Industry Surveys*, annual issues.

Most of the uses in the residential and commercial classification have the common characteristic of contributing personal comfort: Lighting, heating, and cooling in homes, schools, theaters, offices, and stores; and the operation of dozens of other appliances from kitchen stoves to office equipment. The line between the two is particularly thin in the case of large apartment houses, which, for the purpose of most energy statistics, are classified as commercial. Industry comprises manufacturing and mining. The transportation category takes in both private vehicles operated by their owners and public transportation—long distance as well as short haul, passenger as well as freight, and water and air as well as land.

Miscellaneous is a "catch-all" category embracing such diverse uses and users as street lighting, the defense establishment, construc-

tion activities, transportation activities other than those identifiable in published statistics, and agriculture, which includes all uses of energy in farming, etc.

S 32–175. General note.

Some data on the production and use of electric energy are available since the beginning of commercial production in 1882. Data for 1882–1920, however, are difficult to evaluate because of changing bases of measurement and variations in coverage of the various censuses or other surveys made during the period. The Bureau of the Census published the results of censuses of the electric light and power industries made at 5-year intervals for 1902–1937, and the reports of the census of manufactures and of mineral industries contain important data on industrial use and production of electric energy. The Geological Survey, the *Electrical World* (McGraw-Hill Publishing Company, Inc., New York), and the National Electric Light Association also published considerable data applicable to the industry during this early period.

The chief gaps in the data for these years are in the production of electric energy by industrial establishments for their own use, and in the measurement of the sales by electric railroads and railways for public distribution. Early data on capacity must be converted from horsepower (hp.) to kilowatts (kw.) to be comparable; and capacity data in kilovolt-amperes (kv.-a.) were often tabulated as kw. without adjustment for the power factor. Data on generation were also often reported without allowance for the kilowatt-hours (kw.-hr.) used in production and, in many instances, where the prime mover was used both for direct drive and for electric generation, the kw.-hr. equivalent of power used directly was reported as generation. End uses were reported by appliances, as number of lamps, arc lights, or motors, rather than as kw.-hr. These variations in units of measurements, in classification, and in coverage often resulted in differences in estimated totals of as much as 20 to 25 percent. In presenting historical data on electric energy since 1902, efforts have been made to resolve such differences and place the data on a comparable basis.

Referring to various historical sources, one will note that data published in later years will frequently show material revisions to reflect changes in classification and coverage. In the utility series prior to 1945, for example, when a large generating plant was purchased from an industrial concern, the utility series would be adjusted to include the capacity and generation of this plant in prior years. Where such revisions have been made, the revised data are shown.

Since 1920, comprehensive statistics on capacity and generation of electric utilities for public use have been compiled and published by the Geological Survey for 1920–1936, and by the Federal Power Commission since 1936. Data on capacity and generation by non-utility establishments since 1939 have been compiled and published by the FPC. The Commission also published financial, operating, sales, and rate statistics for the electric utility industry. Data on customers, revenues, sales, and related matters since 1926 are published by the Edison Electric Institute and the McGraw-Hill Publishing Co., Inc., *Electrical World*.

During the years there has been a marked growth in the application of power from various fuels through electric energy produced not only in generating plants but by generators in mobile equipment of many types. Among these are power plants in ships, railroad locomotives, trailers, barges, trucks, tractors, buses, and in machines used in mining and heavy construction which produce electric energy for driving and operating the mobile unit and for other services related thereto, or to supplement generating plants for temporary periods. Also of interest are the electric generators for auxiliary purposes operated directly or indirectly by the prime movers in automobiles, airplanes, and other mobile engines or by independent power units in refrigerator cars and trailers and many other installations to furnish electric energy directly or to maintain the electric charge in batteries for use as required. The importance of these small generators is indicated by the fact that the 108 million motor vehicles registered in the United States in 1970 alone have a total generator capacity in excess of that of all the federally owned electric utilities. Except where large units in the general classification of mobile plants are connected to utility systems for power for extended periods, neither capacity nor generation are included in the data indicating production and use of electric energy in the United States. In some cases, however, industries will report the horsepower of such equipment as driving generators, but, in general, do not indicate power output in kw.-hr.

S 32–35. Net production of electric energy, by electric utility and industrial generating plants, by type of plant, 1902–1970.

Source: Summation of series S 36–43.

S 36–39. Net production of electric energy, by electric utility generating plants, by type of plant, 1902–1970.

Source: 1902–1917, U.S. Bureau of the Census, *Census of Electrical Industries: Central Electric Light and Power Stations;* 1920–1970, U.S. Federal Power Commission, *Production of Energy and Capacity of Plants,* monthly and annual reports.

Census data for 1902–1917 were adjusted in some instances for classification and coverage by the late L. D. Jennings of the Federal Power Commission. The figures for electric energy produced by waterpower for 1912 and 1917, for example, differ from those published in *Central Electric Light and Power Stations: 1917,* table 26, because they have been adjusted to exclude electricity produced by steam and internal combustion engines at plants which also produced energy by waterpower, and energy produced in plants subsequently included in series S 40–43.

For 1920–1970, data are based on monthly reports by electric utilities to the FPC. Coverage is substantially 100 percent. Included are plants of the privately owned electric utilities, the cooperatively owned systems, and the publicly owned electric utilities. The latter group is composed of the following classes: Municipal electric utilities, Federal projects, public utility power districts, and State power projects.

S 40–43. Net production of electric energy, by industrial generating plants, by type of plant, 1902–1970.

Source: U.S. Federal Power Commission, 1902–1941, unpublished data; 1942–1970, *Production of Energy and Capacity of Plants,* monthly and annual reports.

Data include the generation of electric energy by manufacturing and extracting industries and by electric railroads and railways, but exclude electric energy generated by the following sources: Nonutility generating plants of less than 100 kw. capacity; plants operated by hotels, apartment houses, office buildings, or other commercial, transport, or service establishments; and plants in military installations. The total generating plant generation excluded is estimated at about 1½ percent of the annual total shown for both utility and industrial plants. This percentage has declined in recent years with the development of mobile type generators.

S 44–52. Net production of electric energy, by class of ownership, 1902–1970.

Source: **Series S 44–51,** see source for series S 36–39; **series S 52,** see source for series S 40–43.

The Federal Power Commission reports cited above show data for "noncentral stations" within the publicly owned group for 1920–1951. This category included plants supplying electric power primarily for such functions as public street lighting, water pumping, and sewage disposal. Such plants were included in municipal or other named classifications effective 1952. A similar adjustment using records available was made for 1920–1951.

Data for cooperatively owned utilities (series S 47) are shown in the source combined with power districts and State projects. The

separate data for series S 47 were obtained from the detailed records of the FPC. These amounts are slightly below those reported by the Rural Electrification Administration, *Annual Statistical Report— Rural Electrification Borrowers,* because a few plants financed by the REA are included in other classifications or are not, for various reasons, included in the FPC totals.

S 53–57. Number of electric utility generating plants, and production per kilowatt of installed generating capacity, 1902–1970.

Source: See source for series S 36–39.

Figures for series S 57 are based on beginning- and end-of-year average installed generating capacity, except for 1902–1920 when capacity as of the end of the year was used.

In counting the number of generating plants, each prime mover type in combination plants was included separately. Generating capacity represents the manufacturer's maximum nameplate rating of generators.

S 58–73. Privately owned electric utility generating plants, by type of plant and plant size, 1920–1970.

Source: U.S. Federal Power Commission, *Statistics of Privately Owned Electric Utilities in the U.S.,* annual issues.

See text for series S 36–39.

S 74–85. General note.

Gas turbine (plant type) generating capacity is included with steam. Separate data for gas turbines are available from the Federal Power Commission beginning with 1969. Amounts for 1969 and 1970 are as follows (in thousands of kilowatts):

	Electric utilities	*Industrial establishments*
1970	15,460	441
1969	10,094	424

S 74–77. Installed generating capacity in electric utility and industrial generating plants, by type of plant, 1902–1970.

Source: Summation of series S 78–85.

See also text for series S 36–39 and S 40–43.

S 78–81. Installed generating capacity in electric utility generating plants, by type of plant, 1902–1970.

Source: See source for series S 36–39.

See also text for series S 36–39.

S 82–85. Installed generating capacity in industrial generating plants, by type of plant, 1902–1970.

Source: See source for series S 40–43.

See also text for series S 40–43.

S 86–94. Installed generating capacity, by class of ownership, 1902–1970.

Source: **Series S 86–93,** see source for series S 36–39; **series S 94,** see source for series S 40–43.

See also text for series S 44–52.

S 95–106. Consumption of fuels by electric utilities, 1920–1970.

Source: U.S. Federal Power Commission, *Fuel Consumption of Electric Power Plants,* monthly and annual reports, and unpublished data.

For series S 105–106, data for years prior to 1940 are from the records of the Federal Power Commission or may be computed from the data shown for fuel used and electric energy generated. For 1920–1938, the distribution of energy generated for plants using two or more kinds of fuel was estimated.

The data are based on individual generating plant reports submitted monthly by all electric utilities to the FPC. Both the privately owned and publicly owned operations are included. The coal figures include anthracite, bituminous, and lignite coal—processed separately for the detailed report—and small amounts of coke; those for oil include crude oil, fuel oil, distillate pitch, sludge, and small quantities of other liquid fuels. The consumption of gas includes both natural gas and byproduct manufactured gas. In general, the minor fuels are reported in units equivalent to those for the major class of fuel with which they are combined. The quantities of each fuel include the consumption of generating plants operating on a standby or other intermittent basis.

Data on fuels used in industrial electric generating plants are not solicited as many establishments do not keep such records separate from fuels used for other purposes.

Kilowatt-hour production represents the summation of net station output after deduction for energy used in the operation of auxiliary equipment and facilities within the generating plants. Where two or more kinds of fuel are used at a particular plant during the same month, allocation of the kilowatt-hour production to each fuel is reported. Where such allocations are not made by the reporting utility, they are estimated on the basis of the latest available annual average B.t.u. content of each fuel used at that plant and the average B.t.u. per kw.-hr. generated reported for each kind of fuel.

S 107. Overall heat rate, 1925–1970.

Source: Edison Electric Institute, *Statistical Year Book of the Electric Utility Industry*, annual issues.

These data are estimates computed by the Edison Electric Institute by the application of an appropriate calorific factor for each fuel in series S 104–106.

S 108. Annual use of electric energy per residential customer, 1912–1970.

Source: 1912, U.S. Bureau of the Census, *Census of Electrical Industries, 1912;* 1917–1925, National Electric Light Association, *Statistical Supplement to the Electric Light and Power Industry in the United States,* Publication 1106, New York, 1931, p. 27; 1926–1970, Edison Electric Institute, *Edison Electric Institute Statistical Bulletin,* New York, 1952 and 1970 issues.

Averages are based on data for customers and on use reported by the electric utilities. Data for appliances used and related matters are published annually in the statistical issue of *Electrical Merchandising* (McGraw-Hill Publishing Company, Inc., New York).

S 109–111. Percentage of dwelling units with electric service, 1907–1956.

Source: For census years, U.S. Bureau of the Census, census of housing (decennial) and census of agriculture (quinquennial); for intercensal years, various annual issues of the following: National Electric Light Association, *Statistical Supplement to the Electric Light and Power Industry in the United States,* New York; McGraw-Hill Publishing Company, Inc., *Electrical World,* New York (copyright); and Edison Electric Institute, *Edison Electric Institute Statistical Bulletin,* New York.

Some adjustments for comparability and coverage have been made in the source data by the late L. D. Jennings of the Federal Power Commission.

In the annual *Statistical Bulletin* of the Edison Electric Institute and in the statistical reports of their predecessor organization, the National Electric Light Association (cited above), data on the electrification of farms (series S 110) are presented. The information shown in these publications includes Bureau of the Census data and data compiled by the Rural Electrification Administration as well as material collected by the Institute or the Association. In the annual statistical numbers of the *Electrical World* (cited above), data are presented showing the percent of the population living in wired homes (series S 109). These percentages are generally based on the relation between the number of residential electric customers and population

in census years. Percentages presented by the different sources indicated may vary from one to the other for intercensal years, depending on the statistical procedures used to determine the number of farms and dwelling units and related concepts applied. Among the items causing variations in the percentages of farms electrified, for example, are the inclusion or exclusion of farms without permanent dwelling units, farms with their own electric power plants, farms without service where distribution lines are within ¼ mile of the dwelling unit, or interpolation for the number of farms in intervening years between the various censuses of agriculture. The percentages shown are those considered reasonable and comparable to those for census years.

S 112–115, and S 117. Average price of electricity by class of service, 1907–1970.

Source: 1907–1924, based on a study by W. G. Vincent, Pacific Gas and Electric Company, *Edison Electric Institute Bulletin,* June 1936, p. 224 (adjusted by the late L. D. Jennings for comparability with the Federal Power Commission series); Federal Power Commission, 1925–1934, annual report, *Typical Electric Bills: Cities of 50,000 Population and More* (except that average prices have been adjusted from as of October 1, as originally published, to as of January 1 for comparability with the series subsequent to 1934); 1935–1970, *Typical Electric Bills, 1964,* p. VI and *1970,* p. IX.

Prior to 1935 for series S 113–115 and for all years for S 112, the average bills for specified consumption are based on typical bills for residential and industrial service in cities with 50,000 or more inhabitants. These cities include about one-third of the total U.S. population. Beginning 1935 for series S 113–115, typical bills are based on residential service in communities with 2,500 or more population. These communities include about two-thirds of the U.S. population. Commercial and industrial service is still based on service in cities of 50,000 or more inhabitants. Since populations in adjacent areas are frequently served under the rate schedules effective in these cities, the bills reported indicate rate levels applicable to more than 70 percent of the total population.

Specifications for the computation of typical net monthly bills are prepared by the Federal Power Commission. Special rates for refrigeration, cooking, or water heating, where generally applicable, are used in computing the bill. Fuel adjustments, commodity adjustments, and tax adjustments where the tax is imposed upon the utility and not upon the customer, and other similar adjustments, have been included in the computations where applicable. Sales taxes computed separately and added to the bill computed under the rate schedules are not included in the bills reported.

Average bills are determined by multiplying the bill as of January 1 for each city by its population and dividing the sum of these products by the sum of the populations. Where two or more utilities serve a community with different bills, the population for each bill is determined by the proportion of customers served by class of service. For service where bills are presented under more than one rate schedule, the lowest bill generally applicable is used.

S 116, S 118, and S 119. Average price of electricity for all users, by class of user, 1902–1970.

Source: 1902–1925, U.S. Bureau of the Census, *Census of Electrical Industries,* 1917 and 1922 reports; 1926–1970, Edison Electric Institute, *Edison Electric Institute Statistical Bulletin,* New York, 1952 and 1970 issues.

These averages indicate the average revenue from electric service and will vary with average use and rate levels.

S 120. Electric energy, total use, 1902–1970.

Source: Prior to 1955, summation of series S 121–132; thereafter, summation of series S 121–131.

Total amount is equal to (a) utility sales of electric energy by class of service, plus (b) industrial generation minus sales to utilities, plus

(c) use by utilities except in connection with the operation of generating plants, plus (d) energy furnished others without charge, plus (e) reported losses and unaccounted for, plus (f) estimated production for nonutility generating plants not included in industrial generation, series S 40, minus sales to utilities as shown by utility reports on purchased energy. This total by years was compared with total net generation of utility and industrial plants, series S 32, plus net imports, series S 132, plus estimates of energy produced by generating plants not included in series S 32. Differences of significance were analyzed, sources checked, explanations of the differences considered and adjustments made as necessary to account for all production or use. For 1939–1970, an appreciable portion of the energy estimated for plants not included in series S 32 and related series are variously reported to the Federal Power Commission or available from related material. For prior years, the amount estimated is based on relationships in benchmark years for which census or comparable type data on capacity, production, or use were available.

Beginning 1955, series is more refined, reflecting ultimate use rather than being based on rate classifications. Included is self-generation at Atomic Energy Commission installations; excluded is self-generation at shopping centers, apartment buildings, and offices.

Imports are classified according to ultimate use; "net imports" as a category is not included.

S 121–122. Electric energy, residential and commercial use, 1912–1970.

Source: 1912–1925, based on McGraw-Hill Publishing Company, Inc., *Electrical World*, annual statistical numbers, New York (copyright), and U.S. Bureau of the Census, *Census of Electrical Industries*, 1902–1927, reports at 5-year intervals; 1926–1944, Edison Electric Institute, *Electric Light and Power Industry in the United States*, New York; 1945–1970, U.S. Federal Power Commission, *Sales of Electric Energy by Class of Service*, monthly reports.

For 1912–1945, some combinations and adjustments were necessary for comparability with data for later years. These adjustments were made by the late L. D. Jennings of the Federal Power Commission.

Series S 121 includes residential use on farms and in rural areas but does not include (a) residential service charged in the rent of dwelling units, (b) service where energy is submetered by large apartment houses or operators of housing projects, (c) residential service secured in connection with commercial or other enterprises purchasing energy usually under commercial service classifications, or (d) irrigation sometimes included in the sales classification "Rural (district rural rates)." The FPC data include some residential service rendered by industrial and certain classes of publicly owned plants excluded from the Edison Electric Institute series.

Series S 122 includes purchases under commercial rate schedules for residential services by operators of apartment houses or housing projects where electric service is included in the rent of the facilities, and submetered service to small industrial establishments. Generally excluded are sales to very large commercial enterprises included in series S 130.

S 123. Electric energy, total industrial use, 1912–1970.

Source: Prior to 1963, summation of series S 124 and S 129; thereafter, see source for series S 121–122.

S 124. Use of electric energy for manufacturing industries, 1912–1962.

Source: 1912–1938, based on data in units of horsepower or kilowatt-hours presented in U.S. Bureau of the Census reports of the census of manufactures; 1939–1962, based on reports of the census of manufactures and U.S. Federal Power Commission report, *Industrial Electric Power, 1939–1946*, and unpublished data.

Estimates or reported data were checked with information on industrial or large light and power sales of electric energy plus data available or developed for industrial generation with allowances for

data applicable to series S 129, and, to a limited extent, series S 130. Adjustments that appeared reasonable in view of all information available, including that for later years, were made by the late L. D. Jennings of the Federal Power Commission for changes or variations in classification and coverage.

S 125. Use of electric energy for manufacture of nuclear fuels and related products, 1943–1970.

Source: 1943, U.S. Atomic Energy Commission, unpublished data; 1944–1970, U.S. Federal Power Commission, unpublished data.

Data for 1955–1970 were reported by suppliers of major installations of the Atomic Energy Commission and by the Commission itself.

S 126. Use of electric energy for paper and chemical industries, 1912–1954.

Source: See source for series S 124.

The figures combine data for two major industry groups—paper and chemicals; they exclude major nuclear energy projects where included in the chemical industry group.

S 127. Use of electric energy for primary metals, 1912–1962.

Source: See source for series S 124.

Figures include ferrous and nonferrous metals.

S 128. Use of electric energy for other manufacturing industries, 1912–1962.

Source: See source for series S 124.

S 129. Use of electric energy for extracting industries, 1912–1962.

Source: U.S. Bureau of the Census, 1912–1939, based on *Census of Mineral Industries*, reports for 1919, 1929, and 1939; U.S. Federal Power Commission, 1940–1946, *Industrial Electric Power, 1939–1946*; 1947–1962, unpublished data.

Data for 1947–1962 are based on generation reported by industrial plants in this classification. Data from trade associations and from technical publications on total output and on electric energy per unit computed for intercensal years for representative establishments were used to check data estimated for these years by other methods.

S 130. Use of electric energy for miscellaneous light and power, 1912–1970.

Source: See source for series S 121–122.

Figures include uses variously classified as other, industrial or large light and power (but not included in manufacturing or mineral industries), street and highway lighting, other sales to public authorities where service is not rendered under commercial or industrial rate schedules or purchased for resale by publicly owned systems, railroads and railways, interdepartmental or company use or furnished without charge by electric power systems, rural or other sales for irrigation, and generation in generating plants and used by enterprises of various kinds not included in the use classifications shown separately. The figures include energy for certain classes of residential and commercial uses, series S 121–122, as noted for those series, and may also include some manufacturing and extracting plants for which data were not included in these series, S 124–129, for reasons indicated in text for series S 120.

S 131. Electric energy losses and use unaccounted for, 1912–1970.

Source: 1912–1936, Edison Electric Institute, *Edison Electric Institute Statistical Bulletin*, New York, monthly and annual issues, and *Electric Light and Power Industry in the United States*, annual; McGraw-Hill Publishing Company, Inc., *Electrical World*, annual, New York (copyright); and U.S. Bureau of the Census, *Census of Electrical Industries*, 1912–1932, reports at 5-year intervals. 1937–1970, U.S. Federal Power Commission, unpublished data.

Relation to total energy used varies from year to year with changes in the proportion of energy metered on the low or on the high side of transformers at the point of delivery or at the generating plant, as well as for changes in technological efficiency in the transmission and distribution of electric energy and its relation to the quantities handled.

S 132. Electric energy, net imports, 1912–1970.

Source: U.S. Federal Power Commission, unpublished data.

Data for 1940–1970 are based on annual surveys for staff use. For prior years, data are based on FPC S-15, *Movement of Electric Energy Across State Lines and International Boundaries, 1940,* and on historical records and files to include exports and imports for industrial as well as utility purposes. Monthly and annual *Electric Power Statistics* published by the Dominion Bureau of Statistics, Ottawa, Canada, were also considered. Coverage in reports for the earlier years varied as did the treatment of energy delivered or received on long-term exchange agreements.

Beginning 1955, data classified in ultimate use; "net imports" as a category is not included in total.

S 133–146. Electric utilities—selected balance sheet and income account items of privately owned companies, 1937–1970.

Source: U.S. Federal Power Commission, *Statistics of Privately Owned Electric Utilities in the United States, 1971,* tables 10 and 13.

S 147–159. Rural Electrification Administration—electric program, summary of operations, 1935–1970.

Source: U.S. Rural Electrification Administration, *Annual Statistical Report—Rural Electrification Borrowers,* various issues.

The Rural Electrification Administration was established in May 1935, to initiate, formulate, administer, and supervise a program of approved projects with respect to the generation, transmission, and distribution of electric energy in rural areas. Later, the Rural Electrification Administration (REA) was authorized to make loans for a maximum of 35 years with interest at 2 percent per annum for the construction or improvement of rural electric systems.

The following definitions are used by REA:

Borrowers. Organizations, mainly cooperatives, to which loans for extending central station electric service in rural areas are made.
Systems. Rural electric distribution, generation, and transmission systems in operation by REA borrowers.
Miles energized. Pole miles of electric distribution and transmission lines in service.
Consumers served. The number of individual customers receiving service by borrowers as of the end of the calendar year.
Energy generated. The kilowatt-hours of energy produced during the calendar year by electric generating plants owned by the borrowers of REA loan funds.
Energy purchased. The kilowatt-hours of energy purchased during the calendar year by REA borrowers from all suppliers.
Revenue. Gross revenue received by REA borrowers mainly from the sale of electric energy.

S 160–175. Developed and undeveloped water power, by geographic division, 1920–1970.

Source: U.S. Federal Power Commission, *Electric Power Statistics,* annual summaries and related monthly reports.

The data for developed water power are based on monthly reports submitted to the Federal Power Commission by the electric utilities. FPC practice is to record generating unit capacity as that given by the manufacturer on the nameplate which is placed on each generator. Included are plants of the privately owned electric utilities, municipal utilities, Federal projects, public utility power districts and State power projects. For 1946–1970, the data also include hydroelectric plants of industrial establishments based on their monthly reports to the FPC.

The data for undeveloped water power resources are based on river basin studies of the years shown. The discovery of new sites, changing criteria, and re-evaluation of needs, as well as the development of sites and a host of other reasons may cause the listed amounts of undeveloped water resources to increase or decrease from year to year. Therefore, the yearly changes in the figures for undeveloped resources cannot be directly related to the amounts of developed water power resources.

S 176–189. Natural gas—consumption and value, 1922–1970.

Source: U.S. Bureau of Mines, *Minerals Yearbook,* annual volumes.

Data on natural-gas consumption and value are collected by annual surveys of oil and gas producers, natural gas processing plants, gas pipeline companies, and gas utility companies with separate reports obtained for each State in which they operate.

Volumes are reported at the pressure base selected by the reporting company; however, prior to 1967, if the reported pressure base deviated more than 5 percent from 14.65 pounds per square in absolute (p.s.i.a.) at 60° F, it was corrected to this base. Beginning 1967, gas volumes are reported or converted to a pressure base of 14.73 (p.s.i.a.).

S 190–204. Gas utility industry—customers, sales, and revenues, by type of service, 1932–1970.

Source: American Gas Association, Arlington, Va., 1932–1959, *Historical Statistics of the Gas Industry,* 1965, pp. 163, 213, and 263; 1960–1970, *Gas Facts,* 1971, pp. 58, 78, and 98. (Copyright.)

American Gas Association (A.G.A.) statistics are based on data provided by individual gas companies to A.G.A.'s department of statistics on the Uniform Statistical Report, a detailed questionnaire distributed annually to the industry. This questionnaire, periodically reviewed by the financial community to insure the inclusion of all items important to security analysis and insurance companies, is also utilized by many gas companies in reporting their operations to the financial community.

Data relating to customers, sales, and revenues are based upon responses submitted to A.G.A. on this questionnaire by gas companies representing 96 percent of the industry. For the small remaining portion of the industry, data have been obtained from reports filed with regulatory commissions, supplemented by investigation of financial publications and other secondary sources.

Revised monthly sales and quarterly customers, sales, and revenues, as well as interim income statements, are based on information previously published in the *Monthly Bulletin of Utility Gas Sales,* and the *Quarterly Report of Gas Industry Operations.*

The three rate classifications are:

1. *Residential service.*

   a. *Without space heating.*

   Service to customers supplied for residential purposes (cooking, water heating, kitchen heating, where another fuel is principal heat for premises, etc.) by individual meter in a single family dwelling or building, or in an individual flat or apartment, or to not over four households served by a single meter (one customer) in a multiple family dwelling, or portion thereof. Service for residential purposes supplied to five or more households served as a *single customer* (one meter) under one rate classification contract is considered as commercial and is counted as only one customer.

   Residential premises also used regularly for professional or business purposes (such as a doctor's office in a home, or where a small store is integral with the living space) are considered as residential where the residential use is half or more of the total gas volume; otherwise, these are commercial.

Dormitories, hotels, religious and eleemosynary institutions (such as orphan homes), boarding and rooming houses, motor courts, camps, etc., are considered as commercial customers for statistical purposes even though they are supplied by the company on a residential rate contract.

b. *With space heating.*

Service to customers using gas to supply the principal space heating requirements of a dwelling; other residential uses are included if supplied under the same rate classification.

c. *Air conditioning service.*

Service to customers using gas to supply the principal air cooling requirements of a dwelling; other residential uses (cooking, water heating, etc.) are included if supplied under the same rate classification.

2. *Commercial service.*

Service to customers primarily engaged in wholesale or retail trade, agriculture, forestry, fisheries, transportation, communication, sanitary services, finance, insurance, real estate, personal services (clubs, hotels, rooming houses, five or more households served as a single customer, auto repair, etc.), government, and to service that does not directly come in one of the other classifications. The size of the customer or volume of use is not a criterion for determining commercial service. The nature of the customer's primary business or economic activity at the location served determines the customer classification. If a particular load to a manufacturing or processing plant represents the cafeteria of the plant, or a heating load, with or without any processing load, whether or not separately metered, the account is classified as industrial service. Gas supplied to commercial customers for air conditioning or space heating is included under com-

mercial service, whether or not supplied under a separate rate contract.

3. *Industrial service.*

Service to customers engaged primarily in a process which creates or changes raw or unfinished materials into another form or product. This includes establishments in mining and manufacturing. The size of the customer or volume of use is not a criterion for determining industrial service. The nature of the company's primary business or economic activity at the location served determines the classification used. If a manufacturing corporation has only a sales office, *no plant*, at a particular location, the classification commercial service is used on the basis of primary activity. If, however, the sales office is part of a manufacturing plant, the classification is industrial service. Gas supplied to these customers for air conditioning or for space heating is included under industrial service, whether or not supplied under a separate rate contract.

Other services comprise service to municipalities or divisions (agencies) of State or Federal Governments under special contracts or agreements or service classifications, which are applicable only to public authorities using gas for general or institutional purposes. They exclude sales properly included under commercial or industrial service such as manufacturing arsenals or publicly owned power systems.

S 205–218. Gas utility and pipeline industry—balance sheet and income account, 1937–1970.

Source: American Gas Association, Arlington, Va., 1937–1959, *Historical Statistics of the Gas Industry*, 1965, pp. 391 and 397; 1960–1970, *Gas Facts*, various issues. (Copyright.)

See text for series S 190–204.

★ ★ ★ ★ ★ ★ ★ ★ **More Recent Data for *Historical Statistics* Series** ★ ★ ★ ★ ★ ★ ★ ★

★   ★

★   Statistics for more recent years in continuation of many of the still-active series shown here appear   ★

★   in annual issues of the ***Statistical Abstract of the United States***, beginning with the 1975 edition. For   ★

★   direct linkage of the historical series to the tables in the ***Abstract***, see Appendix I in the ***Abstract***.   ★

★   ★

★ ★

Series S 1–14. Total Horsepower of All Prime Movers: 1849 to 1970

[In thousands]

Year	Total	Automotive [1]	Nonautomotive Total	Work animals	Inanimate Total	Factories [2]	Mines	Railroads [3]	Merchant ships, powered	Sailing vessels	Farms [4]	Windmills	Electric generating plants	Aircraft [3][5]
	1	2	3	4	5	6	7	8	9	10	11	12	13	14
1970	20,408,000	19,325,000	1,083,000	1,500	1,081,500	54,000	45,000	54,000	22,000	1	[6] 288,500	[6]	435,000	183,000
1969	19,115,000	18,075,000	1,040,250	1,250	1,039,000	53,000	44,000	53,000	19,000	1	[6] 302,000	[6]	404,000	165,000
1968	17,912,144	16,937,725	974,419	1,460	972,959	52,000	43,400	57,607	20,413	1	290,600	24	371,756	137,158
1967	17,050,693	16,152,371	898,322	1,620	896,702	51,000	42,500	49,067	21,493	1	273,606	24	342,918	116,093
1966	15,959,175	15,101,836	857,339	1,800	855,539	49,700	41,200	47,098	22,622	1	274,227	27	323,800	96,864
1965	15,096,332	14,306,300	790,032	2,000	788,032	48,400	40,300	43,838	24,015	2	269,822	30	307,025	54,600
1964	14,272,244	13,512,653	759,591	2,250	757,341	47,000	39,327	46,548	23,715	2	258,451	33	287,111	55,154
1963	13,413,072	12,713,712	699,360	2,500	696,860	45,770	37,000	46,390	23,890	2	217,928	37	273,085	52,758
1962	12,586,417	11,930,000	656,417	2,600	653,817	44,600	[2] 36,300	46,694	22,867	2	204,740	39	249,059	49,516
1961*	11,611,311	10,972,210	639,101	2,700	636,401	43,250	[2] 35,400	47,453	23,046	2	205,463	41	235,746	46,000
1960*	11,007,889	10,366,880	641,009	2,790	638,219	42,000	34,700	46,856	23,890	2	237,020	44	217,173	36,534
1955	7,158,229	6,632,121	526,108	4,141	521,967	35,579	[7] 30,768	60,304	[8] 24,155	[8] 5	[7] 207,742	59	137,576	[8] 25,779
1952	5,736,886	5,361,386	375,500	5,980	369,520	35,045	9,523	101,690	23,207	9	73,590	62	103,453	22,941
1950	4,754,038	4,403,617	350,421	7,040	343,381	32,921	8,500	110,969	23,890	[8] 11	57,533	59	87,965	[8] 22,000
1940	2,773,316	2,511,312	262,004	12,510	249,494	21,768	7,332	92,361	[8] 9,408	[8] 26	57,472	130	53,542	[8] 7,455
1939	--------	2,400,000	--------	--------	--------	21,239	7,149	90,500	10,000	--------	40,750	--------	52,115	6,000
1930	1,663,944	1,426,568	237,376	17,660	219,716	19,519	5,620	109,743	9,115	100	28,610	200	43,427	3,382
1929	--------	1,424,980	--------	--------	--------	19,328	5,450	111,881	9,017	--------	27,261	--------	40,014	3,091
1920	453,450	280,900	172,550	22,430	150,120	19,422	5,146	80,182	6,508	169	21,443	200	17,050	--------
1919	--------	230,432	--------	--------	--------	19,432	5,112	76,660	6,229	--------	20,796	--------	15,250	--------
1910	138,810	24,686	114,124	21,460	92,664	16,697	4,473	51,308	3,098	220	10,460	180	6,228	--------
1909	--------	7,714	--------	--------	--------	16,393	4,401	48,491	2,750	--------	9,311	--------	5,225	--------
1900	63,952	100	63,852	18,730	45,122	10,309	2,919	24,501	1,663	251	4,009	120	1,350	--------
1899	--------	32	--------	--------	--------	9,633	2,754	21,835	1,542	--------	3,420	--------	1,200	--------
1890	44,086	--------	44,086	15,970	28,116	6,308	1,445	16,980	1,124	280	1,452	80	447	--------
1889	--------	--------	--------	--------	--------	5,939	1,300	16,440	1,078	--------	1,233	--------	120	--------
1880	26,314	--------	26,314	11,580	14,734	3,664	715	8,592	741	314	668	40	--------	--------
1879	--------	--------	--------	--------	--------	3,411	650	7,720	703	--------	605	--------	--------	--------
1870	16,931	--------	16,931	8,660	8,271	2,453	380	4,462	632	314	--------	30	--------	--------
1869	--------	--------	--------	--------	--------	2,346	350	4,100	624	--------	--------	--------	--------	--------
1860	13,763	--------	13,765	8,630	5,133	1,675	170	2,156	515	597	--------	20	--------	--------
1859	--------	--------	--------	--------	--------	1,600	150	1,940	503	--------	--------	--------	--------	--------
1850	8,495	--------	8,495	5,960	2,535	1,150	60	586	325	400	--------	14	--------	--------
1849	--------	--------	--------	--------	--------	1,100	50	435	305	--------	--------	--------	--------	--------

* Denotes first year for which figures include Alaska and Hawaii.
[1] Includes passenger cars, trucks, buses, and motorcycles.
[2] Excludes electric motors.
[3] Beginning 1965, not strictly comparable with earlier years.
[4] Excludes horses and other work animals, which are included in series S 4.
[5] Includes private planes and commercial airliners.
[6] Windmills included in series S 11.
[7] Beginning 1955, not strictly comparable with earlier years.
[8] Includes Alaska and Hawaii.

Series S 15–24. Consumption of Raw Materials in Constant 1967 Dollars, by Broad Use Classes: 1900 to 1969

[In millions of dollars]

Year	Raw materials, total	Food	Energy materials Total	Coal	Oil and gas	Fuel wood	Physical-structure materials Total	Agricultural and fishery nonfoods and wildlife products	Forest products	Minerals
	15	16	17	18	19	20	21	22	23	24
1969	68,590	32,275	19,170	2,467	16,527	176	17,145	4,031	3,401	9,713
1968	67,095	31,735	18,202	2,430	15,590	182	17,158	4,193	3,400	9,565
1967	64,417	30,844	17,123	2,341	14,594	188	16,450	4,093	3,217	9,140
1966	63,547	29,938	16,513	2,370	13,935	208	17,096	4,357	3,386	9,353
1965	61,463	29,322	15,737	2,253	13,257	227	16,404	4,221	3,362	8,821
1964	59,880	29,183	15,158	2,154	12,757	247	15,539	4,068	3,254	8,217
1963	57,890	28,534	14,704	2,046	12,392	266	14,652	3,952	3,082	7,618
1962	56,514	27,702	14,212	1,923	12,003	286	14,600	4,132	2,949	7,519
1961	54,487	27,279	13,648	1,862	11,477	309	13,560	3,842	2,805	6,913
1960	53,644	26,636	13,532	1,925	11,280	327	13,476	3,814	2,831	6,831
1959	53,737	26,411	13,295	1,904	11,034	357	14,031	3,983	3,004	7,044
1958	51,192	25,579	12,820	1,857	10,605	358	12,793	3,644	2,724	6,425
1957	51,523	25,710	12,724	2,094	10,259	371	13,089	3,750	2,727	6,612
1956*	52,232	25,891	12,701	2,161	10,136	404	13,640	4,017	3,064	6,559
1955	50,594	25,076	12,269	2,130	9,721	418	13,249	3,925	2,952	6,372
1954	47,630	24,182	11,319	1,955	8,940	424	12,129	3,673	2,804	5,652
1953	48,067	23,922	11,400	2,182	8,779	439	12,745	3,948	2,822	5,975
1952	46,718	23,340	11,101	2,242	8,397	462	12,277	3,952	2,807	5,518
1951	46,334	22,881	11,059	2,506	8,065	488	12,394	4,184	2,820	5,390
1950	45,532	22,672	10,384	2,479	7,409	496	12,476	4,367	2,811	5,298
1949	41,903	22,045	9,482	2,355	6,564	563	10,376	3,635	2,378	4,363
1948	43,181	21,885	9,950	2,904	6,494	552	11,346	4,150	2,705	4,491
1947	42,996	22,583	9,627	2,993	6,083	551	10,786	4,078	2,536	4,172
1946	41,976	22,586	8,740	2,717	5,477	546	10,650	4,389	2,428	3,833

Series S 15–24. Consumption of Raw Materials in Constant 1967 Dollars, by Broad Use Classes: 1900 to 1969—Con.

[In millions of dollars]

Year	Raw materials, total	Food	Energy materials				Physical-structure materials			
			Total	Coal	Oil and gas	Fuel wood	Total	Agricultural and fishery nonfoods and wildlife products	Forest products	Minerals
	15	16	17	18	19	20	21	22	23	24
1945	41,931	22,710	9,085	3,046	5,463	576	10,136	4,063	2,086	3,987
1944	42,271	22,784	8,998	3,252	5,165	581	10,489	4,143	2,289	4,057
1943	40,448	21,140	8,507	3,249	4,693	565	10,801	4,207	2,322	4,272
1942	39,351	20,261	7,954	2,974	4,394	586	11,136	4,197	2,528	4,411
1941	38,615	19,557	7,864	2,679	4,482	703	11,194	4,356	2,498	4,340
1940	34,901	18,985	7,261	2,453	4,074	734	8,655	3,580	2,140	2,935
1939	33,063	18,514	6,729	2,184	3,774	771	7,820	3,353	1,982	2,485
1938	30,098	17,541	6,198	1,978	3,438	782	6,359	2,838	1,756	1,765
1937	32,171	17,439	6,751	2,407	3,589	755	7,981	3,359	2,012	2,610
1936	31,675	17,543	6,542	2,412	3,350	780	7,590	3,372	1,876	2,342
1935	28,810	16,766	5,941	2,109	3,029	803	6,103	2,909	1,576	1,618
1934	28,753	17,606	5,726	2,069	2,815	842	5,421	2,781	1,342	1,298
1933	27,753	17,003	5,428	1,912	2,651	865	5,322	2,783	1,262	1,277
1932	26,258	16,644	5,225	1,850	2,526	849	4,389	2,358	1,060	971
1931	28,529	16,927	5,732	2,208	2,749	775	5,870	2,675	1,408	1,787
1930	29,890	16,830	6,071	2,670	2,690	711	6,989	2,744	1,928	2,317
1929	31,979	16,834	6,508	3,005	2,857	646	8,637	3,197	2,411	3,029
1928	30,545	16,430	6,157	2,927	2,583	647	7,958	2,952	2,279	2,727
1927	30,304	16,307	5,980	2,943	2,392	645	8,017	3,034	2,342	2,641
1926	30,518	16,390	6,092	3,128	2,333	631	8,036	2,843	2,459	2,734
1925	29,652	16,007	5,732	2,853	2,219	660	7,913	2,811	2,487	2,615
1924	28,840	15,953	5,656	2,924	2,051	681	7,231	2,495	2,412	2,324
1923	29,190	15,954	5,804	3,125	1,993	686	7,432	2,394	2,538	2,500
1922	26,312	15,217	4,822	2,463	1,631	728	6,273	2,042	2,253	1,978
1921	22,832	13,475	4,723	2,497	1,436	790	4,634	1,400	1,914	1,320
1920	26,706	14,406	5,285	3,071	1,435	779	7,015	2,628	2,274	2,113
1919	25,376	14,130	4,834	2,909	1,144	781	6,412	2,267	2,207	1,938
1918	25,984	13,913	5,019	3,230	982	807	7,052	2,779	2,110	2,163
1917	25,868	13,809	5,036	3,228	1,025	783	7,023	2,564	2,306	2,153
1916	24,427	12,879	4,642	3,006	851	785	6,906	2,112	2,485	2,309
1915	23,605	13,388	4,232	2,699	753	780	5,985	1,834	2,312	1,839
1914	24,643	13,819	4,047	2,593	662	792	6,777	2,767	2,438	1,572
1913	24,028	13,298	4,276	2,843	659	774	6,454	2,033	2,548	1,873
1912	24,027	13,757	4,085	2,685	624	776	6,185	1,769	2,608	1,808
1911	23,397	13,229	3,890	2,529	547	814	6,278	2,090	2,503	1,685
1910	23,075	12,952	3,867	2,558	507	802	6,256	1,850	2,601	1,805
1909	22,395	12,899	3,357	2,170	398	789	6,139	1,798	2,604	1,737
1908	21,498	12,593	3,350	2,163	384	803	5,555	1,737	2,462	1,356
1907	21,676	12,166	3,619	2,467	358	794	5,891	1,634	2,652	1,605
1906	21,797	12,426	3,258	2,125	331	802	6,113	1,892	2,573	1,648
1905	20,748	12,005	3,223	2,052	350	821	5,520	1,629	2,415	1,476
1904	20,351	12,140	2,972	1,850	281	841	5,239	1,677	2,353	1,209
1903	19,385	11,476	3,013	1,894	261	858	4,896	1,311	2,274	1,311
1902	18,679	11,056	2,628	1,532	221	875	4,995	1,407	2,210	1,378
1901	17,594	10,504	2,608	1,564	151	893	4,482	1,198	2,107	1,177
1900	17,358	10,448	2,447	1,418	120	909	4,463	1,317	2,030	1,116

Series S 25–31. Consumption of Fuel Resources, by Major Consumer Group: 1947 to 1970

[In trillions of British thermal units]

Year	Total	House-hold and com-mercial	Industrial	Transpor-tation [1]	Electrical genera-tion, utilities [2]	Miscella-neous	Utility electricity pur-chased [3]	Year	Total	House-hold and com-mercial	Industrial	Transpor-tation [1]	Electrical genera-tion, utilities [2]	Miscella-neous	Utility electricity pur-chased [3]
	25	26	27	28	29	30	31		25	26	27	28	29	30	31
1970	67,444	13,988	20,339	16,472	16,430	215	5,226	1958	41,696	9,467	13,507	10,275	7,317	1,130	2,213
1969	64,979	13,606	20,107	15,784	15,254	228	4,924	1957	41,706	8,685	14,503	10,229	7,330	959	2,167
1968	61,763	13,109	19,363	15,156	13,892	243	4,529	1956	41,700	8,963	14,588	10,132	7,082	935	2,065
1967	58,265	13,014	18,230	14,015	12,728	278	4,142								
1966	56,412	12,388	18,028	13,345	12,054	597	3,905	1955	39,703	8,595	13,991	9,826	6,595	696	1,881
								1954	36,263	7,968	12,515	9,113	5,940	727	1,617
1965	53,343	11,830	17,176	12,714	11,075	548	3,600	1953	37,586	7,757	13,752	9,205	5,891	981	1,518
1964	51,240	11,143	16,698	12,261	10,375	763	3,356	1952	36,458	7,979	13,098	9,168	5,518	695	1,370
1963	49,308	11,016	15,908	11,962	9,683	739	3,128	1951	36,775	7,857	13,698	9,206	5,281	733	1,294
1962	47,422	10,948	15,249	11,415	9,093	717	2,910								
1961	45,319	10,373	14,631	10,986	8,537	792	2,710	1950	33,992	7,593	12,325	8,616	4,981	477	1,129
								1949	31,488	6,884	11,369	8,075	4,616	544	998
1960	44,569	10,174	14,642	10,818	8,263	672	2,586	1948	33,880	7,039	12,322	8,781	4,724	1,014	969
1959	43,140	9,711	14,040	10,387	7,873	1,129	2,435	1947	33,035	6,775	12,795	8,791	4,264	410	879

[1] Includes bunkers and military transportation.
[2] Represents fossil fuels burned in steam-electric plants with hydropower and nuclear power converted to national average heat rates for fossil-fueled steam-electric plants as reported by Federal Power Commission. [3] Electricity generated and imported.

Series S 32–43. Net Production of Electric Energy, by Electric Utility and Industrial Generating Plants, by Type of Plant: 1902 to 1970

[In millions of kilowatt-hours]

Year	Total utility and industrial				Electric utilities				Industrial establishments			
	Total	Hydro	Steam	Internal combustion	Total	Hydro	Steam	Internal combustion	Total	Hydro	Steam	Internal combustion
	32	33	34	35	36	37	38	39	40	41	42	43
1970	1,639,771	250,699	1,375,252	13,820	1,531,609	247,456	1,278,091	6,062	108,162	3,243	97,161	7,758
1969	1,552,757	253,468	1,285,448	13,841	1,442,182	250,192	1,186,410	5,580	110,575	3,276	99,038	8,261
1968	1,436,029	225,874	1,196,587	13,568	1,329,443	222,491	1,101,767	5,185	106,586	3,383	94,820	8,383
1967	1,317,301	224,948	1,079,508	12,844	1,214,365	221,518	987,991	4,856	102,935	3,430	91,517	7,988
1966	1,249,444	197,938	1,038,645	12,861	1,144,350	194,756	944,430	5,164	105,094	3,182	94,215	7,697
1965	1,157,583	196,984	947,890	12,709	1,055,252	193,851	856,312	5,089	102,331	3,133	91,578	7,620
1964	1,083,741	180,301	890,887	12,553	983,990	177,073	801,907	5,010	99,751	3,228	88,980	7,543
1963	1,011,417	168,990	830,285	12,142	916,793	165,755	745,992	5,046	94,624	3,235	84,293	7,096
1962	946,526	172,086	763,313	11,127	854,796	168,579	681,340	4,878	91,730	3,507	81,973	6,249
1961	881,495	155,630	716,161	9,705	794,273	152,158	637,436	4,680	87,223	3,472	78,725	5,026
1960	844,188	149,515	683,941	10,733	755,374	145,796	605,031	4,547	88,814	3,719	78,910	6,186
1959*	797,567	141,500	645,164	10,903	711,822	138,028	569,355	4,438	85,745	3,471	75,808	6,465
1958	724,752	143,614	571,037	10,101	645,098	140,262	500,764	4,072	79,654	3,352	70,273	6,029
1957	716,356	133,358	571,405	11,593	631,507	130,232	497,212	4,062	84,849	3,125	74,193	7,531
1956	684,804	125,237	548,306	11,261	600,668	122,029	474,552	4,087	84,136	3,208	73,754	7,174
1955	629,010	116,236	502,388	10,386	547,038	112,975	430,119	3,944	81,972	3,261	72,269	6,442
1954	544,645	111,640	423,151	9,854	471,686	107,069	360,834	3,783	72,959	4,571	62,317	6,071
1953	514,169	109,617	394,726	9,826	442,664	105,233	333,541	3,890	71,505	4,384	61,185	5,936
1952	463,055	109,708	344,695	8,652	399,224	105,102	290,385	3,737	63,831	4,606	54,310	4,915
1951	433,358	104,376	321,705	7,277	370,673	99,750	267,252	3,671	62,685	4,626	54,453	3,606
1950	388,674	100,884	281,000	6,790	329,141	95,938	229,543	3,660	59,533	4,946	51,457	3,130
1949	345,066	94,773	244,429	5,864	291,099	89,748	197,878	3,473	53,967	5,025	46,551	2,391
1948	336,808	86,992	243,730	6,086	282,698	82,470	196,928	3,300	54,110	4,522	46,802	2,786
1947	307,400	83,066	218,985	5,349	255,739	78,426	174,500	2,813	51,661	4,640	44,485	2,536
1946	269,609	83,150	181,825	4,634	223,178	78,406	142,412	2,360	46,431	4,744	39,413	2,274
1945	271,255	84,747	181,708	4,800	222,486	79,970	140,435	2,081	48,769	4,777	41,273	2,719
1944	279,525	78,905	195,664	4,956	228,189	73,945	152,328	1,916	51,336	4,960	43,336	3,040
1943	267,540	79,077	183,952	4,511	217,759	73,632	142,381	1,746	49,781	5,445	41,571	2,765
1942	233,146	69,133	159,725	4,288	185,979	63,871	120,479	1,629	47,167	5,262	39,246	2,659
1941	208,306	55,357	149,157	3,792	164,788	50,863	112,319	1,606	43,518	4,494	36,838	2,186
1940	179,907	51,659	124,941	3,307	141,837	47,321	93,002	1,514	38,070	4,338	31,939	1,793
1939	161,308	47,691	110,635	2,982	127,642	43,564	82,783	1,295	33,666	4,127	27,852	1,687
1938	141,955	48,394	93,561		113,812	44,279	68,423	1,110	28,143	4,115	24,028	
1937	146,476	48,272	98,204		118,913	44,013	73,891	1,009	27,563	4,259	23,304	
1936	136,006	42,750	93,256		109,316	39,058	69,359	899	26,690	3,692	22,998	
1935	118,935	42,253	76,682		95,287	38,372	56,144	771	23,648	3,881	19,767	
1934	110,404	35,922	74,482		87,258	32,684	53,939	635	23,146	3,238	19,908	
1933	102,655	36,730	65,925		81,740	33,457	47,709	574	20,915	3,273	17,642	
1932	99,359	35,998	63,361		79,393	32,878	45,922	593	19,966	3,120	16,846	
1931	109,373	32,106	77,267		87,350	29,028	57,685	637	22,023	3,078	18,945	
1930	114,637	34,874	79,763		91,112	31,190	59,293	629	23,525	3,684	19,841	
1929	116,747	37,038	79,709		92,180	32,648	58,965	567	24,567	4,390	20,177	
1928	108,069	37,297	70,772		82,794	32,874	49,370	550	25,275	4,423	20,852	
1927	101,390	32,924	68,466		75,418	28,474	46,615	329	25,972	4,450	21,522	
1926	94,222	30,355	63,867		69,353	25,603	43,422	328	24,869	4,752	20,117	
1925	84,666	26,112	58,554		61,451	21,798	39,367	286	23,215	4,314	18,901	
1924	75,892	24,138	51,754		54,662	19,489	34,955	218	21,230	4,649	16,581	
1923	71,399	23,421	47,978		51,229	18,940	32,093	196	20,170	4,481	15,689	
1922	61,204	21,262	39,942		43,632	16,875	26,579	178	17,572	4,387	13,185	
1921	53,125	18,732	34,393		37,180	14,703	22,311	166	15,945	4,029	11,916	
1920	56,559	20,311	36,248		39,405	15,760	23,489	156	17,154	4,551	12,603	
1917	43,429	13,948	29,481		25,438	10,100	15,338		17,991	3,848	14,143	
1912	24,752	7,387	17,365		11,569	4,500	7,069		13,183	2,887	10,296	
1907	14,121	4,003	10,118		5,862	----------	----------------		8,259	----------	----------------	
1902	5,969	2,166	3,803		2,507	----------	----------------		3,462	----------	----------------	

* Denotes first year for which figures include Alaska and Hawaii.

Series S 44–52. Net Production of Electric Energy, by Class of Ownership: 1902 to 1970

[In millions of kilowatt-hours]

Year	Total utility and industrial	Electric utilities							Industrial establishments
		Total	Privately owned	Cooperatively owned [1]	Publicly owned				
					Total	Municipal	Federal	Other [1]	
	44	45	46	47	48	49	50	51	52
1970	1,639,771	1,531,609	1,183,190	23,459	324,960	71,394	185,753	67,813	108,162
1969	1,552,757	1,442,182	1,102,162	17,513	322,507	69,614	183,245	69,648	110,575
1968	1,436,029	1,329,443	1,019,312	14,141	295,990	63,804	170,834	61,352	106,586
1967	1,317,301	1,214,365	928,439	12,389	273,538	57,789	162,399	53,350	102,935
1966	1,249,444	1,144,350	880,837	11,175	252,338	52,627	153,067	46,644	105,094
1965	1,157,583	1,055,252	809,474	8,571	237,207	49,940	145,231	42,036	102,331
1964	1,083,741	983,990	756,183	7,934	219,873	50,263	129,936	39,674	99,751
1963	1,011,417	916,793	701,253	6,949	208,591	46,293	124,340	37,958	94,624
1962	946,526	854,796	653,076	6,180	195,540	41,840	115,926	37,773	91,730
1961	881,495	794,273	606,737	5,294	182,242	38,872	112,375	30,995	87,223
1960	844,188	755,374	580,286	5,006	170,082	37,029	112,509	20,545	88,814
1959*	797,567	711,822	545,741	4,441	161,639	34,721	109,217	17,702	85,745
1958	724,752	645,098	490,402	3,422	151,274	28,329	110,437	12,508	79,654
1957	716,356	631,507	480,943	3,029	147,535	27,850	109,176	10,509	84,849
1956	684,804	600,668	459,015	3,413	138,240	28,005	100,711	9,524	84,136
1955	629,010	547,038	420,869	3,034	123,135	25,852	89,064	8,219	81,972
1954	544,645	471,686	370,970	2,476	98,240	23,505	67,804	6,931	72,959
1953	514,169	442,664	354,271	1,897	86,496	21,625	58,064	6,807	71,505
1952	463,055	399,224	322,126	1,526	75,572	17,490	52,492	5,590	63,831
1951	433,358	370,673	301,845	1,264	67,564	17,617	44,120	5,827	62,685
1950	388,674	329,141	266,860	1,010	61,271	15,244	40,388	5,639	59,533
1949	345,066	291,099	233,112	847	57,140	13,410	38,102	5,628	53,967
1948	336,808	282,698	228,231	673	53,794	13,122	35,373	5,299	54,110
1947	307,400	255,739	208,105	406	47,228	12,415	29,877	4,936	51,661
1946	269,609	223,178	181,020	300	41,858	10,801	26,960	4,097	46,431
1945	271,255	222,486	180,926	242	41,318	9,624	28,000	3,694	48,769
1944	279,525	228,189	185,850	200	42,139	9,637	28,867	3,635	51,336
1943	267,540	217,759	180,247	187	37,325	9,223	24,485	3,617	49,781
1942	233,146	185,979	158,052	123	27,804	7,610	16,893	3,301	47,167
1941	208,306	164,788	144,290	78	20,420	7,023	10,793	2,604	43,518
1940	179,907	141,837	125,411	37	16,389	6,188	8,584	1,617	38,070
1939	161,308	127,642	115,078	------------	12,564	5,688	5,476	1,400	33,666
1938	141,955	113,812	104,090	------------	9,722	5,237	3,029	1,456	28,143
1937	146,476	118,913	110,464	------------	8,449	5,270	1,843	1,336	27,563
1936	136,006	109,316	102,293	------------	7,023	4,705	1,072	1,246	26,690
1935	118,935	95,287	89,330	------------	5,957	4,228	555	1,174	23,648
1934	110,404	87,258	82,079	------------	5,179	3,834	357	988	23,146
1933	102,655	81,740	76,668	------------	5,072	3,583	458	1,031	20,915
1932	99,359	79,393	74,488	------------	4,905	3,517	445	943	19,966
1931	109,373	87,350	82,597	------------	4,753	3,435	497	821	22,023
1930	114,637	91,112	86,109	------------	5,003	3,604	465	934	23,525
1929	116,747	92,180	87,514	------------	4,666	3,497	300	869	24,567
1928	108,069	82,794	78,207	------------	4,587	3,245	356	986	25,275
1927	101,390	75,418	70,920	------------	4,498	3,051	668	779	25,972
1926	94,222	69,353	65,480	------------	3,873	2,832	518	523	24,869
1925	84,666	61,451	58,685	------------	2,766	2,302	103	361	23,215
1924	75,892	54,662	52,315	------------	2,347	1,940	58	349	21,230
1923	71,399	51,229	49,044	------------	2,185	1,852	63	270	20,170
1922	61,204	43,632	41,660	------------	1,972	1,637	55	280	17,572
1921	53,125	37,180	35,456	------------	1,724	1,422	52	250	15,945
1920	56,559	39,405	37,716	------------	1,689	1,373	59	257	17,154
1917	43,429	25,438	24,399	------------	1,039	1,039	------------	------------	17,991
1912	24,752	11,569	11,032	------------	537	537	------------	------------	13,183
1907	14,121	5,862	5,573	------------	289	289	------------	------------	8,259
1902	5,969	2,507	2,311	------------	196	196	------------	------------	3,462

* Denotes first year for which figures include Alaska and Hawaii.

[1] Prior to 1940, "cooperatively owned" included in "other publicly owned."

Series S 53–57. Number of Electric Utility Generating Plants, and Production Per Kilowatt of Installed Generating Capacity: 1902 to 1970

Year	Number of plants				Production per kilowatt of capacity (kw.-hr.)	Year	Number of plants				Production per kilowatt of capacity (kw.-hr.)
	Total	Hydro	Steam	Internal combustion			Total	Hydro	Steam	Internal combustion	
	53	54	55	56	57		53	54	55	56	57
1970	3,519	1,183	1,330	1,006	4,490	1940	3,918	1,474	1,153	1,291	3,601
1969	3,472	1,188	1,272	1,012	4,602	1939	3,938	1,487	1,195	1,256	3,346
1968	3,429	1,207	1,206	1,016	4,568	1938	3,903	1,479	1,252	1,172	3,110
1967	3,378	1,211	1,149	1,018	4,510	1937	3,918	1,473	1,283	1,162	3,364
1966	3,290	1,217	1,085	988	4,617	1936	3,896	1,471	1,337	1,088	3,145
1965	3,290	1,231	1,068	991	4,469	1935	4,023	1,476	1,424	1,123	2,777
1964	3,377	1,274	1,072	1,031	4,427	1934	3,999	1,471	1,454	1,074	2,540
1963	3,402	1,284	1,074	1,044	4,354	1933	4,012	1,482	1,514	1,016	2,374
1962	3,435	1,301	1,068	1,066	4,583	1932	4,027	1,460	1,553	1,014	2,337
1961	3,476	1,333	1,062	1,081	4,540	1931	4,037	1,461	1,577	999	2,646
1960	3,497	1,343	1,072	1,082	4,635	1930	4,043	1,446	1,626	971	2,926
1959*	3,518	1,366	1,061	1,091	(NA)	1929	3,838	1,389	1,693	756	3,197
1958	3,481	1,359	1,051	1,071	4,748	1928	3,830	1,370	1,717	743	3,127
1957	3,517	1,360	1,043	1,114	5,056	1927	3,707	1,299	1,869	539	3,111
1956	3,534	1,365	1,037	1,132	5,108	1926	3,742	1,287	1,964	491	3,094
1955	3,587	1,381	1,045	1,161	5,037	1925	3,738	1,250	2,004	484	3,138
1954	3,627	1,387	1,045	1,195	4,862	1924	3,783	1,221	2,169	393	3,276
1953	3,686	1,406	1,041	1,239	5,098	1923	3,768	1,191	2,224	353	3,434
1952	3,698	1,412	1,030	1,256	5,051	1922	3,722	1,142	2,276	304	3,145
1951	3,806	1,428	1,048	1,330	5,124	1921	3,726	1,120	2,324	282	2,839
1950	3,867	1,458	1,051	1,358	4,984	1920	3,831	1,125	2,422	284	3,101
1949	3,888	1,465	1,054	1,369	4,862	1917	4,364	---------	---------	---------	2,828
1948	3,879	1,467	1,045	1,367	5,191	1912	3,520	---------	---------	---------	2,240
1947	3,865	1,479	1,045	1,341	4,984	1907	3,200	---------	---------	---------	2,164
1946	3,854	1,488	1,046	1,320	4,441	1902	2,250	---------	---------	---------	2,068
1945	3,886	1,505	1,057	1,324	4,487						
1944	3,933	1,510	1,082	1,341	4,699						
1943	3,959	1,507	1,101	1,351	4,687						
1942	3,899	1,489	1,100	1,310	4,257						
1941	3,882	1,473	1,116	1,293	4,003						

* Denotes first year for which figures include Alaska and Hawaii.　　　　NA Not available.

Series S 58–73. Privately Owned Electric Utility Generating Plants, by Type of Plant and Plant Size: 1920 to 1970

[Plant size interval in kilowatts]

Year	Total plants	Steam plants						Nuclear plants	Hydro plants					Internal combustion		
		Total	Under 100,000	100,001–200,000	200,001–500,000	500,001–1,000,000	Over 1,000,000		Total	Under 5,000	5,001–25,000	25,001–100,000	Over 100,000	Total [1]	Under 5,000	Over 5,000
	58	59	60	61	62	63	64	65	66	67	68	69	70	71	72	73
								NUMBER OF PLANTS								
1970	1,923	661	219	109	178	108	47	13	702	336	203	117	46	547	223	89
1969	1,893	656	224	116	176	97	43	10	719	354	202	117	46	508	229	80
1968	1,843	657	231	114	185	91	36	8	734	369	202	118	45	444	229	68
1967	1,794	657	239	114	192	86	26	8	739	373	204	117	45	390	231	58
1966	1,726	651	243	117	196	76	19	8	749	386	207	115	41	318	226	41
1965	1,724	653	255	115	194	72	17	7	754	393	205	116	40	310	234	36
1964	1,755	664	280	117	184	69	14	7	786	432	204	113	37	298	237	61
1963	1,798	674	299	117	186	60	12	7	812	462	204	111	35	305	251	54
1962	1,818	686	317	121	181	57	10	7	821	476	206	107	32	304	262	42
1961	1,858	696	339	122	176	50	9	5	839	498	205	105	31	318	282	36
1960	1,896	707	362	121	177	42	5	4	866	523	209	105	29	319	291	28
1959*	1,905	694	371	116	168	35	4	3	888	543	211	107	27	320	295	25
1958	1,911	689	388	118	152	27	4	3	897	553	212	106	26	322	299	23
1957	1,929	690	421	125	119	23	2	3	900	569	211	101	19	336	314	22
1956	1,934	684	427	122	117	17	1	--------	903	578	210	97	18	347	325	22
1955	1,965	691	451	116	108	16	--------	--------	924	602	207	96	19	350	328	22
1954	2,003	703	483	112	97	11	--------	--------	934	618	204	94	18	366	342	24
1953	2,038	695	499	108	80	8	--------	--------	959	646	202	93	18	384	363	21
1952	2,038	684	513	94	70	7	--------	--------	964	660	195	93	16	390	371	19
1951	2,088	688	526	94	62	6	--------	--------	973	679	190	89	15	427	410	17
1950	2,116	684	543		141			--------	990	702	186	87	15	442	428	14
1949	2,133	685	559		126			--------	993	710	187	83	13	455	443	12
1948	2,123	670	564		106			--------	991	709	187	83	12	462	452	10
1947	2,060	653	553		100			--------	984	707	183	83	11	423	419	4
1946	2,045	650	556		94			--------	986	709	184	82	11	409	405	4
1945	2,039	655	561		94			--------	988	715	181	82	10	396	392	4

See footnotes at end of table.

Series S 58–73. Privately Owned Electric Utility Generating Plants, by Type of Plant and Plant Size: 1920 to 1970—Con.

[Plant size interval in kilowatts]

Year	Total plants	Steam plants						Nuclear plants	Hydro plants					Internal combustion		
		Total	Under 100,000	100,001–200,000	200,001–500,000	500,001–1,000,000	Over 1,000,000		Total	Under 5,000	5,001–25,000	25,001–100,000	Over 100,000	Total [1]	Under 5,000	Over 5,000
	58	59	60	61	62	63	64	65	66	67	68	69	70	71	72	73
						CAPACITY (1,000 kilowatts)										
1970	259,662	220,536	8,375	15,676	58,619	75,314	62,552	5,622	18,638	654	2,415	5,802	9,767	14,866	437	1,987
1969	241,230	209,950	8,637	16,943	58,561	67,524	58,285	3,110	18,252	685	2,356	5,867	9,344	9,918	452	1,721
1968	223,121	196,787	8,837	16,639	61,477	61,836	47,998	1,940	18,166	703	2,376	5,867	9,220	6,228	441	1,507
1967	203,838	180,726	8,854	16,634	63,620	58,200	33,418	1,415	17,876	690	2,392	5,847	8,947	3,821	447	576
1966	186,325	167,105	8,977	17,217	64,876	51,271	24,764	931	16,149	695	2,439	5,672	7,343	2,140	413	347
1965	177,478	159,141	9,273	16,900	63,509	48,412	21,047	856	15,840	701	2,418	5,749	6,972	1,641	424	308
1964	167,426	150,379	10,059	17,260	60,556	45,742	16,762	836	15,043	747	2,410	5,573	6,313	1,168	432	736
1963	158,576	142,309	10,601	17,332	60,556	39,432	14,388	836	14,400	767	2,426	5,492	5,715	1,031	429	602
1962	150,992	135,959	10,634	17,826	57,955	37,481	12,063	803	13,369	767	2,443	5,293	4,866	861	427	434
1961	142,158	127,719	11,011	18,025	56,405	31,730	10,548	473	13,165	792	2,434	5,232	4,707	801	439	362
1960	133,839	119,820	11,588	17,702	57,695	27,158	5,677	321	13,010	812	2,498	5,259	4,441	688	447	241
1959*	123,991	110,375	11,909	17,154	54,520	22,175	4,617	112	12,854	826	2,512	5,373	4,143	650	436	214
1958	112,687	99,554	12,026	17,187	46,701	17,023	4,617	112	12,398	831	2,494	5,272	3,801	623	425	198
1957	97,439	85,581	12,825	18,738	37,094	14,534	2,390	112	11,127	858	2,518	5,037	2,714	619	435	184
1956	90,826	79,462	12,625	18,199	36,299	11,259	1,080	--------	10,738	854	2,497	4,811	2,576	626	442	184
1955	87,009	75,301	13,596	17,312	33,296	11,097	--------	--------	11,084	877	2,459	4,837	2,911	624	446	178
1954	79,408	67,957	14,183	16,647	30,052	7,075	--------	--------	10,806	891	2,417	4,694	2,804	645	449	196
1953	71,345	60,013	14,159	15,810	24,930	5,114	--------	--------	10,692	923	2,383	4,639	2,747	640	468	172
1952	64,354	53,488	14,017	13,774	21,200	4,497	--------	--------	10,251	923	2,275	4,658	2,395	615	464	151
1951	60,237	49,797	13,160	13,945	18,785	3,907	--------	--------	9,841	935	2,243	4,423	2,240	599	477	122
1950	54,833	44,633	13,355		31,278		--------	--------	9,626	950	2,202	4,248	2,226	574	469	105
1949	50,376	40,643	12,952		27,691		--------	--------	9,181	945	2,179	4,075	1,982	552	459	93
1948	44,983	35,474	12,367		23,107		--------	--------	9,002	950	2,174	4,018	1,860	507	433	74
1947	41,863	32,594	11,392		21,202		--------	--------	8,885	905	2,136	4,070	1,774	384	352	32
1946	40,123	30,954	11,028		19,926		--------	--------	8,863	912	2,148	4,029	1,774	306	276	30
1945	39,978	30,972	10,948		20,024		--------	--------	8,717	923	2,129	4,033	1,632	289	259	30

Year	Capacity (1,000 kilowatts)				Year	Capacity (1,000 kilowatts)			
	Total plants	Steam plants	Hydro plants	Internal combustion		Total plants	Steam plants	Hydro plants	Internal combustion
	58	59	66	71		58	59	66	71
1944	39,733	30,626	8,747	360	1930	30,285	22,322	7,697	267
1943	39,128	30,114	8,647	367	1929	27,953	20,722	7,023	208
1942	37,442	28,454	8,613	375	1928	25,990	18,848	6,943	200
1941	36,041	27,170	8,492	379	1927	23,418	17,241	6,048	129
					1926	21,819	16,000	5,700	120
1940	34,399	25,551	8,469	379					
1939	33,908	24,999	8,537	372	1925	20,045	14,618	5,316	111
1938	33,246	24,302	8,584	360	1924	16,740	11,945	4,711	84
1937	31,958	23,088	8,520	351	1923	14,787	10,449	4,264	75
1936	31,787	23,000	8,494	293	1922	13,419	9,441	3,908	69
					1921	12,797	9,028	3,703	66
1935	31,820	23,091	8,437	292					
1934	31,547	22,888	8,365	294	1920	12,022	8,443	3,511	68
1933	32,163	23,499	8,368	296					
1932	32,033	23,414	8,314	306					
1931	31,498	23,041	8,172	286					

* Denotes first year for which figures include Alaska and Hawaii.

[1] Beginning 1965, includes gas turbine plants.

ENERGY

Series S 74–85. Installed Generating Capacity in Electric Utility and Industrial Generating Plants, by Type of Plant: 1902 to 1970

[In thousands of kilowatts. As of December 31]

Year	Total utility and industrial				Electric utilities				Industrial establishments			
	Total	Hydro	Steam	Internal combustion	Total	Hydro	Steam	Internal combustion	Total	Hydro	Steam	Internal combustion
	74	75	76	77	78	79	80	81	82	83	84	85
1970	360,327	55,751	298,803	5,773	341,090	55,056	281,684	4,350	19,237	696	17.119	1,422
1969	332,606	53,447	273,534	5,625	313,349	52,753	256,391	4,205	19,257	694	17,143	1,420
1968	310,181	51,874	252,975	5,331	291,058	51,168	235,912	3,978	19,123	706	17,063	1,353
1967	288,185	48,832	234,195	5,158	269,252	48,112	217,322	3,818	18,933	720	16,873	1,340
1966	266,816	45,691	216,309	4,816	247,843	44,977	199,357	3,509	18,973	714	16,952	1,307
1965	254,519	44,490	205,423	4,606	236,126	43,782	188,979	3,365	18,393	708	16,444	1,241
1964	240,471	42,899	193,026	4,546	222,285	42,188	176,777	3,320	18,186	711	16,249	1,226
1963	228,757	40,928	183,348	4,480	210,549	40,214	167,090	3,245	18,208	714	16,259	1,235
1962	209,576	38,162	167,015	4,398	191,747	37,418	151,197	3,132	17,829	744	15,819	1,267
1961	199,216	36,301	158,588	4,326	181,312	35,557	142,746	3,009	17,904	745	15,841	1,318
1960	186,534	33,180	149,161	4,193	168,569	32,423	133,282	2,865	17,965	757	15,880	1,328
1959*	175,000	31,884	139,073	4,043	157,347	31,132	123,490	2,725	17,653	752	15,583	1,318
1958	160,651	30,089	126,625	3,936	142,597	29,359	110,633	2,604	18,054	730	15,992	1,332
1957	146,221	27,761	114,660	3,800	129,123	27,036	99,542	2,545	17,098	725	15,119	1,254
1956	137,342	26,386	107,251	3,705	120,697	25,654	92,591	2,452	16,645	732	14,660	1,253
1955	130,895	25,742	101,698	3,455	114,472	25,005	87,112	2,355	16,423	737	14,586	1,100
1954	118,878	24,238	91,250	3,390	102,592	23,211	77,102	2,279	16,286	1,027	14,148	1,111
1953	107,354	23,054	80,960	3,340	91,502	22,045	67,235	2,222	15,852	1,009	13,725	1,118
1952	97,312	21,416	72,620	3,276	82,227	20,419	59,679	2,129	15,085	997	12,941	1,147
1951	90,127	19,870	67,372	2,885	75,775	18,868	54,865	2,042	14,352	1,002	12,507	843
1950	82,850	18,674	61,495	2,681	68,919	17,675	49,333	1,911	13,931	999	12,162	770
1949	76,570	17,662	56,472	2,436	63,100	16,654	44,640	1,806	13,470	1,008	11,832	630
1948	69,615	16,635	50,751	2,229	56,560	15,652	39,304	1,604	13,055	983	11,447	625
1947	65,151	15,956	47,242	1,953	52,322	14,971	36,034	1,317	12,829	985	11,208	636
1946	63,066	15,828	45,442	1,796	50,317	14,848	34,313	1,156	12,749	980	11,129	640
1945	62,868	15,892	45,248	1,728	50,111	14,912	34,112	1,087	12,757	980	11,136	641
1944	62,066	15,696	44,637	1,733	49,189	14,586	33,541	1,062	12,877	1,110	11,096	671
1943	60,539	14,991	43,840	1,708	47,951	13,884	33,015	1,052	12,588	1,107	10,825	656
1942	57,237	13,947	41,593	1,697	45,053	12,842	31,169	1,042	12,184	1,105	10,424	655
1941	53,995	12,912	39,474	1,609	42,405	11,817	29,599	989	11,590	1,095	9,875	620
1940	50,962	12.304	37,138	1,520	39,927	11,224	27,775	928	11,035	1,080	9,363	592
1939	49,438	12,075	35,932	1,431	38,863	11,004	27,009	850	10,575	1,071	8,923	581
1938	46,873	11,682	35,191		37,492	10,657	26,066	769	9,381	1,025	8,356	
1937	44,370	11,186	33,184		35,620	10,176	24,763	681	8,750	1,010	7,740	
1936	43,582	11,037	32,545		35,082	10,037	24,441	604	8,500	1,000	7,500	
1935	42,828	10,399	32,429		34,436	9,399	24,471	566	8,392	1,000	7,392	
1934	42,545	10,345	32,200		34,119	9,345	24,253	521	8,426	1,000	7,426	
1933	43,037	10,330	32,707		34,587	9,334	24,759	494	8,450	996	7,454	
1932	42,849	10,258	32,591		34,387	9,258	24,646	483	8,462	1,000	7,462	
1931	42,287	10,190	32,097		33,698	9,090	24,162	446	8,589	1,100	7,489	
1930	41,153	9,650	31,503		32,384	8,585	23,385	414	8,769	1,065	7,704	
1929	38,708	8,925	29,783		29,839	7,813	21.704	322	8,869	1,112	7,757	
1928	36,782	8,800	27,982		27,805	7,702	19,790	313	8,977	1,098	7,879	
1927	34,574	7,927	26,647		25,079	6,802	18,078	199	9,495	1,125	8,370	
1926	32,936	7,650	25,286		23,386	6,405	16,792	189	9,550	1,245	8,305	
1925	30,087	7,150	22,937		21,472	5,922	15,368	182	8,615	1,228	7,387	
1924	25,923	6,224	19,699		17,681	5,024	12,535	122	8,242	1,200	7,042	
1923	23,235	5,682	17,553		15,643	4,507	11,026	110	7,592	1,175	6,417	
1922	21,317	5,229	16,088		14,192	4,129	9,965	98	7,125	1,100	6,025	
1921	20,605	5,002	15,603		13,519	3,902	9,527	90	7,086	1,100	5,986	
1920	19,439	4,804	14,635		12,714	3,704	8,920	90	6,725	1,100	5,625	
1917	15,494	3,886	11,608		8,994	2,786	6,128	80	6,500	1,100	5,400	
1912	10,980	2,794	8,186		5,165	1,694	3,395	76	5,815	1,100	4,715	
1907	6,809	1,906	4,903		2,709	906	1,765	38	4,100	1,000	3,100	
1902	2,987	1,140	1,847		1,212	230	914	8	1,775	850	925	

* Denotes first year for which figures include Alaska and Hawaii.

Series S 86–94. Installed Generating Capacity, by Class of Ownership: 1902 to 1970

[In thousands of kilowatts. As of December 31]

Year	Total utility and industrial	Electric utilities							Industrial estab-lishments
		Total	Privately owned	Cooperatively owned [1]	Publicly owned				
					Total	Municipal	Federal	Other [1]	
	86	87	88	89	90	91	92	93	94
1970	360,327	341,090	262,675	5,161	73,253	20,941	38,718	13,594	19,237
1969	332,606	313,349	240,078	4,319	68,953	20,035	36,130	12,788	19,257
1968	310,181	291,058	220,766	3,434	66,858	19,429	34,956	12,473	19,123
1967	288,185	269,252	203,580	3,019	62,652	18,049	33,640	10,964	18,933
1966	266,816	247,843	185,670	2,758	59,415	16,548	32,608	10,258	18,973
1965	254,519	236,126	177,570	2,309	56,248	15,407	31,690	9,151	18,393
1964	240,471	222,285	167,704	2,017	52,564	15,199	28,342	9,022	18,186
1963	228,757	210,549	158,448	1,873	50,228	14,222	27,315	8,691	18,208
1962	209,576	191,747	145,111	1,591	45,046	12,991	24,345	7,710	17,829
1961	199,216	181,312	137,270	1,491	42,552	12,250	23,287	7,015	17,904
1960	186,534	168,569	128,912	1,423	38,233	11,539	22,380	4,314	17,965
1959*	175,000	157,347	119,403	1,168	36,775	10,953	21,906	3,917	17,653
1958	160,651	142,597	108,202	977	33,418	9,817	20,436	3,165	18,054
1957	146,221	129,123	97,376	924	30,823	8,640	19,649	2,534	17,098
1956	137,342	120,697	91,146	792	28,759	8,325	18,336	2,096	16,645
1955	130,895	114,472	86,887	776	26,809	7,795	16,962	2,052	16,423
1954	118,878	102,592	79,127	750	22,715	7,225	13,567	1,923	16,286
1953	107,354	91,502	71,201	619	19,682	6,570	11,358	1,754	15,852
1952	97,312	82,227	64,349	522	17,356	6,019	9,678	1,659	15,085
1951	90,127	75,775	60,192	482	15,101	5,293	8,099	1,709	14,352
1950	82,850	68,919	55,176	375	13,368	4,970	6,921	1,477	13,931
1949	76,570	63,100	50,484	283	12,333	4,727	6,210	1,396	13,470
1948	69,615	56,560	45,381	230	10,949	4,105	5,525	1,319	13,055
1947	65,151	52,322	41,986	168	10,168	3,825	5,027	1,316	12,829
1946	63,066	50,317	40,335	105	9,877	3,708	4,919	1,250	12,749
1945	62,868	50,111	40,307	87	9,717	3,586	5,081	1,050	12,757
1944	62,066	49,189	39,733	70	9,386	3,447	4,886	1,053	12,877
1943	60,539	47,951	39,128	66	8,757	3,419	4,322	1,016	12,588
1942	57,237	45,053	37,442	45	7,566	3,331	3,216	1,019	12,184
1941	53,995	42,405	36,041	30	6,334	3,158	2,371	805	11,590
1940	50,962	39,927	34,399	13	5,515	2,977	1,944	594	11,035
1939	49,438	38,863	33,908	----------	4,955	2,807	1,650	498	10,575
1938	46,873	37,492	33,246	----------	4,246	2,631	1,156	459	9,381
1937	44,370	35,620	31,958	----------	3,662	2,476	833	353	8,750
1936	43,582	35,082	31,787	----------	3,295	2,164	804	327	8,500
1935	42,828	34,436	31,820	----------	2,616	2,002	300	314	8,392
1934	42,545	34,119	31,547	----------	2,572	1,963	288	321	8,426
1933	43,037	34,587	32,163	----------	2,424	1,879	232	313	8,450
1932	42,849	34,387	32,033	----------	2,354	1,828	232	294	8,462
1931	42,287	33,698	31,498	----------	2,200	1,696	231	273	8,589
1930	41,153	32,384	30,285	----------	2,099	1,601	226	272	8,769
1929	38,708	29,839	27,952	----------	1,887	1,424	214	249	8,869
1928	36,782	27,805	25,991	----------	1,814	1,347	213	254	8,977
1927	34,574	25,079	23,418	----------	1,661	1,210	209	242	9,495
1926	32,936	23,386	21,819	----------	1,567	1,204	205	158	9,550
1925	30,087	21,472	20,045	----------	1,427	1,125	198	104	8,615
1924	25,923	17,681	16,740	----------	941	824	14	103	8,242
1923	23,235	15,643	14,787	----------	856	752	14	90	7,592
1922	21,317	14,192	13,419	----------	773	685	10	78	7,125
1921	20,605	13,519	12,797	----------	722	634	10	78	7,086
1920	19,439	12,714	12,023	----------	691	601	10	80	6,725
1917	15,494	8,994	8,412	----------	582	582	----------	----------	6,500
1912	10,980	5,165	4,769	----------	396	396	----------	----------	5,815
1907	6,809	2,709	2,500	----------	209	209	----------	----------	4,100
1902	2,987	1,212	1,099	----------	113	113	----------	----------	1,775

* Denotes first year for which figures include Alaska and Hawaii.

[1] Prior to 1940, "cooperatively owned" included in "other publicly owned."

Series S 95–107. Consumption of Fuels by Electric Utilities: 1920 to 1970

Year	Net generation, by fuel					Fuel consumed				Per kilowatt-hour			Overall heat rate
	Total [1]	Coal	Fuel oil	Gas	Nuclear	Total coal equivalent	Coal	Oil	Gas	Coal	Oil	Gas	
	95	96	97	98	99	100	101	102	103	104	105	106	107
	Mil. kw.-hr.	Mil. kw.-hr.	Mil. kw.-hr.	Mil. kw.-hr.	Mil. kw.-hr.	1,000 short tons	1,000 short tons	1,000 42-gal. bbl.	Mil. cu. ft.	Lb.	Gal.	Cu. ft.	B.t.u. per kw.-hr.
1970	1,284,153	706,102	182,488	372,884	21,797	583,456	320,818	335,504	3,931,996	0.91	0.077	10.5	10,508
1969	1,191,989	706,001	137,847	333,279	13,928	524,476	310,641	251,027	3,487,642	.88	.076	10.5	10,457
1968	1,106,952	684,905	104,276	304,433	12,528	481,275	297,779	188,642	3,147,909	.87	.076	10.3	10,371
1967	992,847	630,483	89,271	264,806	7,655	431,769	274,185	161,278	2,746,352	.87	.076	10.4	10,396
1966	949,594	613,475	78,926	251,151	5,520	412,478	266,477	140,949	2,609,949	.87	.075	10.4	10,399
1965	861,401	570,926	64,801	221,559	3,657	369,331	244,788	115,203	2,321,101	.86	.075	10.5	10,384
1964	806,917	526,230	56,954	220,038	3,343	345,666	225,425	101,141	2,322,896	.86	.075	10.6	10,407
1963*	751,038	493,927	52,001	201,602	3,212	321,341	211,332	93,314	2,144,473	.86	.075	10.6	10,438
1962	684,031	450,249	46,983	184,301	2,270	293,573	193,238	85,768	1,965,974	.86	.077	10.7	10,493
1961	640,189	421,871	47,120	169,286	1,692	276,369	182,121	85,736	1,825,117	.86	.076	10.8	10,552
1960	607,660	403,067	46,105	157,970	518	266,064	176,634	85,340	1,724,762	.88	.078	10.9	10,701
1959	572,071	378,424	46,840	146,619	188	254,525	168,423	88,263	1,628,509	.89	.079	11.1	10,879
1958	504,662	344,366	40,372	119,759	165	228,136	155,724	77,668	1,372,853	.90	.081	11.5	11,090
1957	501,108	346,386	40,500	114,212	10	232,576	160,769	79,693	1,336,141	.93	.083	11.7	11,365
1956	478,487	338,503	35,947	104,037	--------	223,733	158,279	72,711	1,239,311	.94	.085	11.9	11,456
1955	433,786	301,363	37,138	95,285	--------	206,929	148,759	75,274	1,153,280	.95	.085	12.1	11,699
1954	364,354	239,146	31,520	93,688	--------	180,367	118,385	66,745	1,165,498	.99	.089	12.4	12,180
1953	337,042	218,846	38,404	79,791	--------	178,491	115,897	82,238	1,034,272	1.06	.090	13.0	12,889
1952	293,640	195,437	29,750	68,453	--------	160,872	107,071	67,218	910,117	1.10	.095	13.3	13,361
1951	270,531	185,204	28,712	56,616	--------	154,498	105,768	63,945	763,898	1.14	.094	13.5	13,641
1950	232,813					138,421	91,871	75,420	628,919	1.19	.094	14.1	14,030
1949	200,965					124,574	83,963	66,301	550,121	1.24	.098	14.9	15,033
1948	199,796					130,122	99,586	42,645	478,097	1.30	.107	15.9	15,738
1947	176,983					115,672	89,531	45,309	373,054	1.31	.112	16.2	15,600
1946	144,555					93,471	72,197	36,316	306,942	1.29	.108	16.3	15,700
1945	142,331					92,642	74,725	20,228	326,212	1.30	.109	16.5	15,800
1944	153,868					99,251	80,084	20,862	358,784	1.29	.109	16.6	15,850
1943	143,785					93,275	77,301	17,986	301,937	1.30	.111	17.0	16,000
1942	121,585					79,075	66,257	15,236	235,208	1.30	.115	16.7	16,100
1941	113,272					75,700	62,668	20,077	201,763	1.34	.112	16.9	16,550
1940	93,963					62,942	51,474	16,325	180,096	1.34	.112	16.5	16,400
1939	83,628					57,958	44,539	17,139	188,878	1.38	.100	16.4	16,700
1938	69,255					48,560	38,394	12,942	165,504	1.40	.113	17.1	17,450
1937	74,502					53,560	42,929	13,829	169,127	1.44	.119	17.1	17,850
1936	69,823					50,144	40,085	14,079	154,084	1.44	.118	17.1	17,800
1935	56,688					40,797	32,715	11,257	124,118	1.44	.118	17.0	17,850
1934	54,418					39,367	34,414	10,258	127,071	1.45	.120	17.2	17,950
1933	48,170					35,274	28,543	9,606	101,985	1.46	.122	17.3	18,150
1932	46,422					34,489	28,056	7,583	107,103	1.49	.122	17.6	18,450
1931	58,014					43,954	36,115	7,922	138,458	1.52	.128	18.0	18,800
1930	59,588					47,544	40,278	8,805	119,553	1.60	.132	19.0	19,800
1929	59,154					49,039	41,827	9,783	112,353	1.66	.137	19.7	20,550
1928	49,622					43,020	38,042	6,818	77,155	1.73	.143	20.9	21,550
1927	46,660					42,492	38,199	6,552	62,485	1.82	.153	21.5	22,600
1926	43,472					41,342	36,842	8,999	52,647	1.90	.157	22.9	23,600
1925	39,443					40,014	35,615	9,794	45,472	2.03	.165	23.9	25,175
1924	34,963					38,855	32,790	16,060	47,301	2.22	.182	26.3	---------
1923	32,088					38,404	33,636	13,925	29,340	2.39	.195	29.3	---------
1922	26,561					33,402	29,193	12,443	24,996	2.52	.209	31.2	---------
1921	22,343					30,436	26,604	11,505	21,701	2.72	.220	31.0	---------
1920	23,495					35,791	31,640	12,690	22,136	3.05	.254	36.9	---------

* Denotes first year for which figures include Alaska and Hawaii.
[1] Excludes generation by wood and waste fuels. Beginning 1961, includes limited output by use of wood, waste, and geothermal power, as follows, in million kw.-hr: 220 in 1961, 228 in 1962, 296 in 1963, 352 in 1964, 458 in 1965, 522 in 1966, 632 in 1967, 811 in 1968, 935 in 1969, and 882 in 1970.

Series S 108–119. Growth of Residential Service, and Average Prices for Electric Energy: 1902 to 1970

Year	Annual use per customer [1] (kw.-hr.)	Percentage of dwelling units with electric service			Average price (cents per kw.-hr.) monthly use of—				All consumption [1] (cents per kw.-hr.)	Large light and power, average price		Average prices, all services [1] (cents per kw.-hr.)
		All dwellings	Farm	Urban and rural nonfarm	25 kw.-hr.	100 kw.-hr. [2]	250 kw.-hr. [2]	500 kw.-hr. [2]		Monthly use, 200,000 kw.-hr. [3]	All customers [1] (cents per kw.-hr.)	
	108	109	110	111	112	113	114	115	116	117	118	119
1970	7,066					4.09	3.00	2.10	2.10	1.75	0.95	1.59
1969	6,571					4.05	2.96	2.06	2.09	1.72	.91	1.54
1968	6,057					4.03	2.95	2.07	2.12	1.71	.90	1.55
1967	5,577					4.03	2.95	2.07	2.17	1.71	.90	1.56
1966	5,265					4.00	2.94	2.07	2.20	1.70	.89	1.56
1965	4,933					4.02	2.95	2.08	2.25	1.71	.90	1.59
1964	4,703					4.03	2.97	2.12	2.31	1.71	.91	1.62
1963	4,442					4.06	2.99	2.13	2.37	1.72	.93	1.65
1962	4,259					4.06	2.99	2.13	2.41	1.68	.96	1.68
1961	4,019					4.05	2.98	2.13	2.45	1.67	.97	1.69
1960	*3,854					4.04	2.98	2.12	*2.47	1.65	*.97	*1.69
1959	3,618					3.98	2.94	2.10	2.51	1.64	.96	1.69
1958	3,389					3.93	2.92	2.09	2.54	1.64	.97	1.71
1957	3,198				*5.28	*3.89	*2.89	*2.08	2.56	*1.62	.94	1.67
1956	2,989	98.8	95.9	99.2	5.28	3.88	2.88	2.07	2.61	1.60	.92	1.64
1955	2,773	98.4	94.4	98.8	5.20	3.86	2.87	2.06	2.65	1.58	.94	1.67
1954	2,573	97.9	93.0		5.16	3.82	2.84	2.05	2.70	1.58	.99	1.77
1953	2,369	97.2	91.4		5.12	3.81	2.83	2.04	2.74	1.58	1.00	1.77
1952	2,186	96.1	86.9		4.96	3.76	2.79	2.02	2.77	1.52	1.01	1.79
1951	2,021	95.2	82.2		4.96	3.74	2.78	2.00	2.81	1.51	1.00	1.78
1950	1,845	94.0	77.7	96.6	4.96	3.76	2.79	2.02	2.88	1.51	1.02	1.81
1949	1,684	93.0	72.9		5.00	3.78	2.80	2.04	2.95	1.55	1.05	1.86
1948	1,563	89.6	66.8		4.96	3.74	2.77	2.02	3.01	1.50	1.01	1.79
1947	1,438	86.2	60.2		4.92	3.75	2.77	2.01	3.09	1.45	.97	1.77
1946	1,329	85.5	53.3		5.12	3.85	2.82	2.03	3.22	1.44	.98	1.81
1945	1,229	85.0	48.0	93.0	5.28	3.89	2.84	2.04	3.41	1.43	.93	1.73
1944	1,151	84.0	42.2		5.32	3.92	2.86	2.05	3.51	1.44	.91	1.65
1943	1,070	81.3	40.0		5.32	3.94	2.88	2.05	3.60	1.43	.90	1.66
1942	1,022	81.2	37.8		5.36	3.96	2.90	2.07	3.67	1.41	.94	1.79
1941	986	80.0	35.0		5.36	3.98	2.92	2.08	3.73	1.41	1.00	1.90
1940	952	78.7	32.6	90.8	5.44	4.06	2.95	2.11	3.84	1.41	1.06	2.06
1939	897	77.3	27.4		5.60	4.12	2.98	2.17	4.00	1.43	1.12	2.16
1938	853	74.9	23.9		5.72	4.20	3.09	2.21	4.14	1.43	1.20	2.30
1937	805	73.1	18.3		5.80	4.25	3.13	2.30	4.30	1.48	1.14	2.17
1936	735	70.3	14.5		6.12	4.39	3.28	2.47	4.67	(NA)	1.19	2.27
1935	677	68.0	12.6	83.9	6.40	4.67	3.56	2.77	5.01	1.54	1.30	2.46
1934	629	67.1	12.1		6.52	4.49	3.60		5.33		1.35	2.58
1933	600	66.7	11.8		6.68	4.55	3.65		5.52		1.38	2.66
1932	601	67.0	11.2		6.76	4.61	3.69		5.60		1.53	2.85
1931	583	67.4	10.7		6.80	4.86	4.00		5.78		1.47	2.75
1930	547	68.2	10.4	84.8	6.92	5.00	4.12		6.03		1.41	2.66
1929	502	67.9	9.2		7.04	5.21	4.33		6.33		1.38	2.57
1928	463	65.0	7.3		7.24	5.44	4.62		6.63		1.40	2.66
1927	446	63.1	5.9		7.54	5.70	4.87		6.82		1.46	2.71
1926	430	57.9	4.8		7.52	5.85	5.09		7.00		1.49	2.71
1925	396	53.2	3.9	69.4	7.68	6.03	5.14		7.30		(NA)	(NA)
1924	378	48.6	3.5		7.8	6.3	5.4		7.20		(NA)	(NA)
1923	368	44.2	3.0		7.9	6.4	5.6		7.20		(NA)	(NA)
1922	359	40.0	2.5		8.0	6.7	5.9		7.38		1.8	2.83
1921	347	37.8	2.0		8.2	6.7	5.9		7.39		(NA)	(NA)
1920	339	34.7	1.6	47.4	8.4	6.9	6.0		7.45		(NA)	(NA)
1917	268	24.3			7.9	6.6	5.9		7.52		1.2	2.1
1912	264	15.9			9.5	8.6	8.0		9.10		(NA)	
1907		8.0			10.9	10.3	9.5		10.5			2.7
1902									16.2			

* Denotes first year for which figures include Alaska and Hawaii.
NA Not available.
[1] Beginning 1950, figures revised to allocate rural service to other appropriate classes of service; not comparable with previous years.
[2] Composite series using population weights and uniform bills for cities having population of 2,500 or more, beginning 1935; prior years, 50,000 or more.
[3] Peak demand of 1,000 kilowatts.

Series S 120–132. Use of Electric Energy: 1902 to 1970

[In millions of kilowatt-hours]

Year	Total [1]	Residential	Commercial	Industrial Total industrial	Manufacturing Total	Nuclear energy	Paper and chemicals	Primary metals	Other	Extracting	Miscellaneous light and power	Losses and use unaccounted for	Net imports [2]
	120	121	122	123	124	125	126	127	128	129	130	131	132
1970	1,641,731	453,015	295,057	685,693		19,672					78,743	129,223	1,960
1969	1,553,829	413,599	272,248	672,345		21,020					73,508	122,129	1,072
1968	1,435,398	370,033	248,670	628,657		24,901					71,486	116,552	−631
1967	1,317,001	331,118	225,710	588,560		29,828					65,670	105,943	−299
1966	1,250,536	308,162	208,819	571,613		34,107					61,092	100,850	1,092
1965	1,157,442	282,255	190,916	534,297		38,707					57,969	92,005	−141
1964	1,085,696	263,441	171,436	508,991		46,464					55,257	86,571	1,955
1963	1,011,515	243,486	156,924	477,325		51,167					50,786	82,994	98
1962	947,018	226,430	145,276	449,270	388,222	51,501	(3)	93,721	3 243,000	61,048	47,920	78,122	536
1961	883,749	208,172	129,961	424,235	366,858	55,326	(3)	86,753	3 224,779	57,377	47,432	73,949	2,254
1960*	848,723	196,296	121,437	415,699	361,965	56,873	(3)	87,704	3 217,388	53,734	44,421	70,870	4,535
1959	798,858	181,889	112,955	394,770	350,592	56,998	(3)	84,216	3 209,271	44,178	40,931	68,313	3,607
1958	728,070	159,930	101,969	358,099	319,258	56,950	(3)	73,096	3 189,212	38,841	44,208	63,864	3,318
1957	719,957	147,969	94,994	372,476	325,445	58,938	(3)	77,766	3 188,741	47,031	42,909	61,609	3,601
1956	689,352	135,620	87,499	364,779	323,334	60,655	(3)	78,702	3 183,977	41,445	41,327	60,127	4,548
1955	633,078	121,526	80,031	334,088	299,261	50,105	(3)	75,960	3 173,196	34,827	39,623	57,810	4,068
1954	553,727	116,228	72,141	263,527	247,666	26,559	58,146	66,781	96,180	15,861	45,687	53,804	2,340
1953	522,419	104,146	66,533	254,260	238,480	14,727	57,725	68,897	97,131	15,780	44,818	50,654	2,008
1952	472,071	93,545	63,935	224,487	209,507	8,473	51,049	54,493	95,492	14,980	39,949	47,886	2,269
1951	442,046	83,093	58,643	214,522	200,322	5,533	49,494	54,497	90,798	14,200	38,798	44,803	2,187
1950	396,346	72,200	52,091	194,835	181,335	3,794	45,123	50,111	82,307	13,500	34,166	41,268	1,786
1949	351,831	63,369	44,830	169,274	156,524	3,614	38,227	44,344	70,339	12,750	34,720	38,050	1,588
1948	343,410	57,421	41,698	172,658	159,358	3,477	38,970	45,206	71,705	13,300	33,096	36,992	1,545
1947	313,926	49,417	37,152	157,197	144,247	3,233	34,996	40,645	65,373	12,950	34,788	33,457	1,915
1946	276,044	42,919	32,060	137,308	125,598	3,548	32,104	34,895	55,051	11,710	32,584	28,782	2,391
1945	275,028	37,749	28,091	146,261	134,955	3,099	36,780	37,371	57,705	11,306	33,364	27,001	2,562
1944	283,718	34,636	29,837	156,365	145,015	1,164	40,285	43,158	60,408	11,350	31,965	28,400	2,515
1943	270,215	31,271	28,192	155,671	143,995	31	39,670	44,973	59,321	11,676	26,017	26,567	2,497
1942	235,477	29,187	27,233	133,899	122,762		33,463	36,257	53,042	11,137	19,958	22,782	2,418
1941	210,389	26,574	24,628	113,931	104,037		27,830	29,630	46,577	9,894	22,574	20,351	2,331
1940	181,706	24,068	22,373	92,390	83,276		22,776	22,782	37,718	9,114	23,173	17,588	2,114
1939	162,921	21,433	20,722	78,603	70,518		19,040	17,632	33,846	8,085	24,378	15,891	1,894
1938	143,375	19,371	19,137	65,850	58,452		15,829	14,504	28,119	7,398	22,982	14,227	1,808
1937	147,941	17,691	18,075	73,300	64,757		17,536	16,068	31,153	8,543	22,124	14,924	1,827
1936	137,366	15,659	15,612	70,500	62,949		17,046	15,620	30,283	7,551	20,266	13,773	1,556
1935	120,124	13,978	13,588	63,265	56,706		15,356	14,070	27,280	6,559	15,902	12,054	1,337
1934	111,508	12,658	12,278	56,695	50,593		13,700	12,554	24,339	6,102	17,561	11,082	1,234
1933	103,682	11,747	11,589	52,358	46,561		12,609	11,553	22,399	5,797	16,599	10,422	967
1932	100,353	11,875	12,106	48,614	43,504		11,781	10,795	20,928	5,110	16,952	10,162	644
1931	110,467	11,738	13,544	56,512	50,410		13,651	12,508	24,251	6,102	16,240	11,224	1,209
1930	115,783	11,018	13,944	61,023	53,930		14,604	13,382	25,944	7,093	16,453	11,753	1,592
1929	117,914	9,773	13,106	63,279	55,122		14,983	13,543	26,596	8,157	18,396	11,937	1,423
1928	109,150	8,619	11,692	59,750	52,699		14,271	13,076	25,352	7,051	16,753	10,763	1,573
1927	102,404	7,676	10,766	57,383	51,012		13,814	12,658	24,540	6,371	15,118	9,842	1,619
1926	95,164	6,827	9,485	52,750	46,350		12,551	11,501	22,298	6,400	15,524	9,085	1,493
1925	85,513	6,020	9,345	45,500	39,725		10,757	9,857	19,111	5,775	15,294	8,081	1,273
1924	76,651	5,080	8,634	40,300	34,967		9,468	8,677	16,822	5,333	14,132	7,215	1,290
1923	72,113	4,580	8,027	38,250	32,585		8,824	8,085	15,676	5,665	13,137	6,788	1,331
1922	61,816	3,916	7,180	32,200	27,364		7,410	6,790	13,164	4,836	11,752	5,803	965
1921	53,656	3,532	6,125	28,000	23,993		6,497	5,953	11,543	4,007	10,026	4,964	1,009
1920	57,125	3,190	6,150	31,500	26,913		7,288	6,678	12,947	4,587	10,065	5,280	940
1917	43,863	1,731	5,213	23,750	20,750		5,619	5,149	9,982	3,000	8,532	3,421	1,216
1912	25,000	910	4,076	11,250	9,250		2,505	2,295	4,450	2,000	6,671	1,562	531
1907	14,262												
1902	6,029												

* Denotes first year for which figures include Alaska and Hawaii.
[1] Beginning 1955, represents a more refined series reflecting ultimate use rather than being based on rate classifications. Includes self-generation at Atomic Energy Commission installations; excludes self-generation at shopping centers, apartment buildings, and offices.
[2] Beginning 1955, classified in ultimate use; "net imports" not included in total.
[3] Paper and chemicals included in other.

Series S 133–146. Electric Utilities—Selected Balance Sheet and Income Account Items of Privately Owned Companies: 1937 to 1970

[In millions of dollars]

Year	Total assets, liabilities	Assets and debits			Liabilities and credits				Income accounts		Gross income			Net income
		Net utility plant	Current assets	Other	Capital stock	Long-term debt	Retained earnings	Other liabilities and credits	Operating revenues	Net operating revenues	Total	Operating	Other	
	133	134	135	136	137	138	139	140	141	142	143	144	145	146
1970	87,417	79,928	5,321	2,168	20,782	41,938	9,363	15,335	23,128	4,885	5,658	4,885	773	3,408
1969	78,317	71,449	4,810	2,057	18,584	37,072	8,608	14,053	21,085	4,490	4,628	4,493	136	3,196
1968	71,099	64,901	4,439	1,760	17,746	33,519	7,742	12,092	19,405	4,106	4,233	4,109	124	2,996
1967	65,197	59,421	4,156	1,619	17,080	30,358	6,997	10,761	17,935	3,896	4,005	3,899	106	2,908
1966	60,359	54,791	4,020	1,549	16,212	27,728	6,407	10,012	16,959	3,639	3,743	3,642	101	2,749
1965	56,395	51,267	3,639	1,489	15,668	25,502	5,712	9,512	15,820	3,405	3,506	3,409	97	2,581
1964	53,753	48,644	3,634	1,475	15,621	24,589	5,142	8,401	14,991	3,154	3,277	3,156	121	2,393
1963	51,389	46,566	3,411	1,412	15,074	23,632	4,640	8,043	14,180	3,020	3,108	3,023	85	2,178
1962	49,191	44,486	3,320	1,386	14,325	22,912	4,481	7,474	13,468	2,833	2,908	2,835	73	2,053
1961	47,009	42,549	3,152	1,309	13,801	22,028	4,011	7,168	12,604	2,560	2,630	2,563	67	1,875
1960	44,742	40,456	3,066	1,220	13,322	21,035	3,736	6,649	11,920	2,395	2,476	2,398	79	1,783
1959	42,106	37,889	2,943	1,273	12,636	19,818	3,356	6,296	11,129	2,220	2,286	2,222	64	1,656
1958	39,278	35,293	2,773	1,212	12,074	18,558	3,042	5,604	10,195	2,074	2,074	2,016	58	1,519
1957	36,401	32,436	2,799	1,166	11,434	17,037	2,718	5,212	9,670	1,849	1,916	1,852	64	1,413
1956	33,242	29,500	2,618	1,124	10,934	15,211	2,414	4,683	9,054	1,745	1,808	1,748	61	1,332
1955	30,992	27,318	2,567	1,107	10,404	14,316	2,191	4,081	8,360	1,617	1,683	1,620	63	1,244
1954	28,975	25,359	2,437	1,179	9,924	13,313	2,051	3,687	7,588	1,456	1,526	1,459	67	1,134
1953	26,615	23,165	2,377	1,073	9,314	12,030	1,868	3,403	7,136	1,318	1,369	1,321	49	1,080
1952	24,502	20,636	2,443	1,423	8,764	10,797	1,645	3,298	6,549	1,192	1,266	1,195	70	947
1951	22,365	18,654	2,307	1,404	8,146	9,983	1,444	2,792	6,508	1,056	1,122	1,060	62	814
1950	20,523	17,075	2,058	1,389	7,621	9,179	1,346	2,377	5,528	1,028	1,101	1,033	68	822
1949	18,906	15,581	1,899	1,427	7,016	8,532	1,197	2,161	5,069	951	1,022	956	66	757
1948	17,266	13,929	1,985	1,352	6,404	7,693	1,036	2,132	4,830	825	896	830	66	657
1947	15,573	12,487	1,763	1,323	6,071	6,581	888	2,033	4,291	811	883	815	67	643
1946	14,649	11,647	1,704	1,298	5,804	6,129	833	1,882	3,815	824	891	829	62	638
1945	14,452	11,446	1,672	1,333	5,950	6,117	766	1,619	3,682	828	887	833	54	534
1944	15,181	11,951	1,655	1,576	6,271	6,371	866	1,673	3,615	781	842	786	56	507
1943	15,525	12,286	1,583	1,655	6,353	6,587	845	1,739	3,464	752	817	759	58	502
1942	15,612	12,542	1,365	1,705	6,487	6,754	863	1,508	3,216	737	802	744	59	490
1941	15,600	12,640	1,217	1,742	6,504	6,822	868	1,406	3,029	762	836	770	67	527
1940	15,477	12,494	1,123	1,860	6,471	6,895	860	1,251	2,797	797	873	805	68	548
1939	15,318	12,352	1,042	1,924	6,387	6,971	811	1,148	2,647	786	864	794	70	535
1938	15,469	12,419	1,084	1,966	6,376	7,060	788	1,245	2,549	746	821	754	67	487
1937	15,272	12,356	959	1,957	6,432	6,850	802	1,188	2,532	761	840	769	71	509

Series S 147–159. Rural Electrification Administration—Electric Program, Summary of Operations: 1935 to 1970

Year	Net loans approved [1]		Systems in operation [2]			Borrowers' operations during year [3]				Average monthly consumption per consumer		Total utility plant	Employees
	Borrowers	Amount	Systems	Miles energized	Consumers served	Energy generated	Energy purchased	Energy sold	Revenue	All consumers	Residential consumers [4]		
	147	148	149	150	151	152	153	154	155	156	157	158	159
		Mil. dol.		1,000	1,000	Mil. kw.-hr.	Mil. kw.-hr.	Mil. kw.-hr.	Mil. dol.	Kw.-hr.	Kw.-hr.	Mil. dol.	
1970	1,096	7,496	1,050	1,676	6,442	23,814	60,478	76,009	1,309	948	687	7,175	37,013
1969	1,098	7,151	1,049	1,650	6,197	18,073	56,031	66,421	1,168	876	643	6,593	35,771
1968	1,101	6,822	1,052	1,627	5,986	14,509	50,917	58,304	1,060	812	593	6,167	34,563
1967	1,101	6,403	1,052	1,606	5,806	13,710	45,400	52,880	977	751	543	5,776	33,457
1966	1,101	6,145	1,051	1,587	5,653	11,547	42,825	48,439	912	708	515	5,353	32,597
1965	1,103	5,793	1,052	1,567	5,541	8,834	39,104	42,668	847	654	479	4,979	31,702
1964	1,105	5,477	1,051	1,547	5,386	8,039	36,907	39,837	802	616	456	4,696	30,799
1963	1,101	5,073	1,046	1,527	5,238	7,002	33,005	35,357	746	565	425	4,406	29,816
1962	1,096	4,786	1,042	1,504	5,095	6,043	30,134	31,880	697	526	401	4,104	29,046
1961	1,091	4,509	1,038	1,483	4,956	5,118	27,754	28,967	651	487	375	3,897	28,084
1960	1,087	4,256	1,038	1,465	4,826	4,922	26,057	27,269	615	466	357	3,697	---------
1959	1,085	4,011	1,032	1,446	4,722	4,464	24,033	25,071	575	432	334	3,486	---------
1958	1,081	3,847	1,030	1,424	4,596	3,482	21,500	21,902	525	393	311	3,244	---------
1957	1,079	3,634	1,030	1,405	4,466	3,291	19,266	19,677	490	364	283	3,059	---------
1956	1,077	3,343	1,026	1,383	4,362	3,612	17,266	18,197	460	345	263	2,879	---------
1955	1,077	3,125	1,026	1,362	4,251	3,255	14,996	15,739	420	312	242	2,706	---------
1954	1,075	2,946	1,024	1,333	7,174	2,721	13,450	13,829	383	285	223	2,542	---------
1953	1,078	2,778	1,022	1,297	4,025	2,103	11,786	11,804	343	254	201	2,351	---------
1952	1,081	2,669	1,020	1,245	3,858	1,640	10,351	10,128	306	230	182	2,143	---------
1951	1,076	2,484	1,016	1,179	3,666	1,413	8,828	8,567	270	206	166	---------	---------

See footnotes at end of table.

Series S 147–159. Rural Electrification Administration—Electric Program, Summary of Operations: 1935 to 1970—Con.

Year	Net loans approved [1]		Systems in operation [2]			Borrowers' operations during year [3]				Average monthly consumption per consumer	
	Borrowers	Amount	Systems	Miles energized	Consumers served	Energy generated	Energy purchased	Energy sold	Revenue	All consumers	Residential consumers [4]
	147	148	149	150	151	152	153	154	155	156	157
		Mil. dol.		1,000	1,000	Mil. kw.-hr.	Mil. kw.-hr.	Mil. kw.-hr.	Mil. dol.	Kw.-hr.	Kw.-hr.
1950	1,076	2,312	1,007	1,089	3,413	1,077	7,270	6,884	229	180	147
1949	1,066	1,999	995	943	3,040	903	5,879	5,564	188	166	134
1948	1,044	1,575	952	759	2,518	718	4,514	4,252	145	153	121
1947	1,029	1,191	911	603	2,046	443	3,379	3,056	111		
1946	1,009	958	869	507	1,684	320	2,497	2,244	87		
1945	961	667	848	450	1,409	258	2,159	1,951	71		
1944	904	518	826	410	1,217	213	1,974	1,795	63		
1943	873	474	811	390	1,088	199	1,721	1,572	54		
1942	868	460	803	378	1,012	131	1,305	1,151	47		
1941	869	434	773	348	902	83	854	724	35		
1940	791	351	685	268	674	34	402	311	17		
1939	688	268	548	181	436						
1938		181	350	67	176						
1937		82	126	17	44						
1936		44	29	3	8						
1935		7	2	–	–						

– Represents zero.
[1] Excludes loans rescinded. Cumulative as of Dec. 31. Prior to 1948, includes amounts not yet under loan contract.
[2] As of Dec. 31. Includes data at time of repayment of loan for borrowers whose loans have been repaid in full.
[3] Excludes energy sales and revenues of power sold by one REA borrower to another, except for 1940–1942, for which such sales and revenues are included.
[4] Includes rural-nonfarm and farm consumers.

Series S 160–175. Developed and Undeveloped Water Power, by Geographic Division: 1920 to 1970

[In thousands of kilowatts. As of December 31. For composition of divisions, see text for series A 172–194]

Year	Developed water power [1]								Undeveloped water power							
	United States	New England	Middle Atlantic	North Central	South Atlantic	South Central	Mountain	Pacific	United States	New England	Middle Atlantic	North Central	South Atlantic	South Central	Mountain	Pacific
	160	161	162	163	164	165	166	167	168	169	170	171	172	173	174	175
1970	51,952	1,473	4,264	3,664	5,265	7,170	6,202	23,914	127,990	3,330	4,455	5,966	9,556	7,089	26,655	70,939
1969	50,248	1,495	4,231	3,718	5,271	6,951	6,097	22,481	128,900	3,300	4,545	5,892	9,708	7,054	26,923	71,478
1968	48,741	1,487	4,243	3,665	5,255	6,874	6,095	21,122	129,709	3,302	4,545	5,892	9,716	7,063	26,923	72,268
1967	45,826	1,491	4,247	3,703	5,349	6,530	6,083	18,425	130,444	3,304	4,514	5,619	9,468	7,008	26,891	73,640
1966	44,288	1,487	4,246	3,625	5,184	6,298	6,022	17,426	130,640	3,312	4,332	5,312	9,812	7,031	26,822	74,019
1965	42,948	1,488	4,237	3,460	4,700	6,088	5,551	17,424	124,087	3,240	4,986	5,497	9,977	7,343	26,530	66,514
1964	41,827	1,491	4,237	3,302	4,635	5,851	5,218	17,093	117,793	3,125	4,950	5,691	10,017	7,549	27,253	59,208
1963	40,230	1,497	4,218	3,197	4,600	5,419	4,845	16,454	115,734	3,128	5,179	5,866	9,903	8,023	26,652	56,983
1962	37,835	1,508	4,239	2,942	4,099	5,164	4,773	15,110	116,100	3,100	5,200	6,800	11,000	8,200	26,900	54,900
1961	36,193	1,518	3,852	2,618	3,795	4,897	4,821	14,694	112,700	2,800	5,700	9,000	8,900	8,100	24,100	54,100
1960	33,180	1,520	2,472	2,522	3,773	4,695	4,621	13,578	114,200	2,900	7,600	9,400	8,400	8,500	23,600	53,800
1959	*31,794	1,513	2,475	2,369	3,788	4,697	4,511	*12,439	*114,287	2,858	7,465	9,591	8,388	8,499	23,243	*54,243
1958	30,089	1,521	2,113	2,276	3,732	4,697	4,157	11,592	93,783	2,708	7,869	9,323	8,393	7,854	23,141	34,495
1957	27,761	1,528	1,600	2,277	3,732	4,674	3,785	10,165	90,242	2,728	8,382	8,967	7,645	7,480	21,245	33,795
1956	26,386	1,388	1,479	2,243	3,611	4,524	3,701	9,440	90,102	2,728	8,012	9,000	7,586	7,721	21,333	33,722
1955	25,742	1,385	1,789	1,905	3,536	4,524	3,706	8,898	86,895	2,586	8,023	9,335	7,943	7,213	20,668	31,127
1954	24,238	1,335	1,750	1,783	3,423	4,418	3,629	7,901	82,804	2,990	6,395	9,211	8,058	7,035	20,105	29,010
1953	23,055	1,282	1,704	1,620	3,212	4,374	3,438	7,425	85,562	3,122	6,449	9,412	8,281	7,464	21,618	29,216
1952	21,416	1,262	1,707	1,564	2,834	4,054	3,181	6,814	87,992	3,233	6,415	9,480	8,677	7,784	21,895	30,508
1951	19,871	1,254	1,677	1,559	2,785	3,547	2,627	6,421	86,174	3,239	6,598	8,117	8,255	8,168	22,089	29,708
1950	18,675	1,239	1,678	1,530	2,767	3,195	2,286	5,980	87,604	3,250	6,572	8,119	8,151	8,304	23,440	29,768
1949	17,662	1,202	1,687	1,469	2,687	2,993	2,202	5,423	88,070	3,249	6,503	8,192	8,184	8,374	23,426	30,142
1948	16,635	1,192	1,668	1,437	2,662	2,731	2,056	4,888	(NA)	(NA)	(NA)	(NA)	(NA)	(NA)	(NA)	(NA)
1947	15,956	1,165	1,662	1,435	2,662	2,618	2,026	4,387	77,130	3,348	5,175	7,309	7,462	7,446	17,755	28,635
1946	15,828	1,167	1,669	1,434	2,663	2,618	2,008	4,269								
1945	14,912	895	1,591	1,300	2,222	2,592	2,002	4,309								
1944	14,586	894	1,593	1,303	2,086	2,393	2,003	4,314								
1943	13,884	893	1,587	1,314	2,085	2,151	1,924	3,929								
1942	12,842	891	1,596	1,294	2,084	1,936	1,784	3,256								
1941	11,817	855	1,589	1,280	1,912	1,588	1,692	2,902								

See footnotes at end of table.

Series S 160–175. Developed and Undeveloped Water Power, by Geographic Division: 1920 to 1970—Con.

[In thousands of kilowatts]

Year	Developed water power [1]							Year	Developed water power [1]						
	United States	New England	Middle Atlantic	North Central	South Atlantic	South Central	Mountain	Pacific		United States	New England	Middle Atlantic	North Central	South Atlantic	South Central	Mountain	Pacific
	160	161	162	163	164	165	166	167		160	161	162	163	164	165	166	167
1940	11,224	858	1,588	1,219	1,882	1,397	1,612	2,668	1930	8,585	753	1,290	881	1,603	882	784	2,391
1939	11,004	833	1,563	1,204	1,803	1,279	1,581	2,741	1929	7,831	554	1,218	879	1,351	841	680	2,308
1938	10,657	824	1,561	1,204	1,728	1,223	1,381	2,736	1928	7,702	557	1,205	862	1,346	840	679	2,213
1937	10,176	832	1,550	1,147	1,710	1,114	1,160	2,662	1927	6,802	496	1,151	842	963	700	673	1,977
1936	10,037	832	1,533	1,111	1,709	1,079	1,152	2,622	1926	6,405	474	1,115	835	945	618	592	1,826
1935	9,399	804	1,517	1,071	1,678	924	792	2,613	1925	5,922	415	1,027	813	878	482	570	1,738
1934	9,345	767	1,489	1,071	1,680	924	782	2,631	1924	5,024	381	905	741	760	280	544	1,413
1933	9,334	768	1,489	1,065	1,680	916	791	2,624	1923	4,507	350	766	705	659	248	520	1,259
1932	9,258	768	1,457	1,058	1,634	954	788	2,599	1922	4,128	337	757	664	534	195	509	1,132
1931	9,091	762	1,338	1,056	1,635	945	788	2,566	1921	3,902	314	741	632	536	187	494	998
									1920	3,704	291	662	629	589	174	487	872

* Denotes first year for which figures include Alaska and Hawaii.
NA Not available.

[1] Nameplate capacity of existing installations only. Includes capacity at electric utility and industrial plants, but excludes pumped storage capacity. Prior to 1946, includes capacity at electric utility plants only.

Series S 176–189.   Natural Gas—Consumption and Value: 1922 to 1970

Year	Total consumption [1] (bil. cu. ft.)				Value of gas consumed								Consumers (1,000)	
	Total	Residential	Commercial	Industrial	Total (mil. dol.)	Residential (mil. dol.)	Commercial (mil. dol.)	Industrial (mil. dol.)	Average per 1,000 cu. ft. [1] (cents)				Residential	Commercial
									Total	Residential	Commercial	Industrial		
	176	177	178	179	180	181	182	183	184	185	186	187	188	189
1970	22,046	4,837	2,057	15,152	11,825	5,272	1,682	4,871	53.6	109.0	81.8	32.1	38,604	3,253
1969	20,923	4,728	1,955	14,240	10,769	4,954	1,526	4,289	51.5	104.7	78.1	30.1	38,096	3,222
1968	19,460	4,450	1,801	13,209	9,800	4,635	1,398	3,767	50.3	104.1	77.6	28.5	37,259	3,121
1967	18,173	4,313	1,717	12,143	9,442	4,501	1,338	3,603	51.9	104.3	77.9	29.7	36,434	3,077
1966	17,192	4,138	1,623	11,431	8,996	4,318	1,238	3,440	52.3	104.3	76.3	30.1	36,084	3,120
1965	16,033	3,903	1,443	10,687	8,368	4,091	1,115	3,162	52.2	104.8	77.3	29.6	35,302	2,991
1964	15,536	3,787	1,375	10,374	8,020	3,990	1,059	2,971	51.9	105.9	77.5	28.8	34,575	2,884
1963	14,640	3,589	1,268	9,783	7,497	3,750	996	2,751	51.2	104.5	78.6	28.1	33,451	2,788
1962	13,890	3,479	1,207	9,204	7,145	3,629	940	2,576	51.4	104.3	77.9	28.0	32,655	2,712
1961	13,082	3,249	1,077	8,756	6,667	3,475	838	2,354	51.0	107.0	77.8	26.9	32,052	2,641
1960 [2]	12,509	3,103	1,020	8,386	6,270	3,209	791	2,270	50.1	103.4	77.5	27.1	31,148	2,584
1959	11,820	2,913	975	7,932	5,642	2,946	703	1,993	47.7	101.1	72.1	25.1	30,692	2,608
1958	10,761	2,714	872	7,175	4,968	2,665	606	1,697	46.2	98.2	69.5	23.6	29,282	2,405
1957	10,280	2,500	776	7,004	4,435	2,325	534	1,576	43.1	93.0	68.9	22.5	28,792	2,344
1956	9,707	2,328	717	6,662	4,025	2,126	465	1,434	41.5	91.3	64.9	21.5	27,887	2,255
1955	9,070	2,124	629	6,317	3,626	1,885	395	1,346	40.0	88.7	62.7	19.6	26,084	2,140
1954	8,403	1,894	585	5,924	3,205	1,692	378	1,135	38.1	89.3	64.7	19.2	25,227	2,076
1953	7,979	1,686	531	5,762	2,829	1,458	323	1,048	35.5	86.5	61.0	18.2	24,186	2,042
1952	7,613	1,622	516	5,475	2,527	1,347	294	886	33.2	83.1	57.0	16.2	22,569	1,855
1951	7,103	1,475	464	5,164	2,119	1,121	246	752	29.8	76.0	52.9	14.6	21,444	1,614
1950	6,026	1,198	388	4,440	1,604	826	184	594	26.6	69.0	47.6	13.4	16,906	1,347
1949	5,195	993	348	3,854	1,321	666	158	497	25.4	67.1	45.5	12.9	14,690	1,231
1948	4,945	896	323	3,726	1,194	585	142	467	24.1	65.3	44.0	12.5	13,508	1,145
1947	4,427	802	285	3,340	1,028	526	126	376	23.2	65.6	44.1	11.3	12,204	1,039
1946	4,013	661	242	3,110	883	447	103	333	22.0	67.6	42.4	10.7	11,472	965
1945	3,900	607	230	3,063	834	415	98	321	21.4	68.3	42.4	10.5	10,959	889
1944	3,696	562	221	2,913	794	388	92	314	21.5	69.1	41.7	10.8	10,669	845
1943	3,403	529	205	2,669	759	371	88	300	22.3	70.0	42.3	11.3	10,354	811
1942	3,045	499	184	2,362	691	353	80	258	22.7	70.7	43.7	10.9	10,135	779
1941	2,805	442	145	2,218	620	318	68	234	22.1	72.0	47.2	10.5	9,730	767
1940	2,655	444	135	2,076	577	316	64	197	21.7	71.1	47.8	9.5	9,245	741
1939	2,474	391	118	1,965	534	288	58	188	21.6	73.5	49.4	9.6	8,888	715
1938	2,294	368	114	1,812	501	273	56	172	21.8	74.2	49.2	9.4	8,570	695
1937	2,403	372	117	1,914	528	274	57	197	22.0	73.6	48.7	10.3	8,348	680
1936	2,161	343	112	1,706	476	252	54	170	22.0	73.3	48.1	10.0	8,017	657
1935	1,910	313	100	1,497	428	234	49	145	22.4	74.6	49.3	9.7	7,391	613
1934	1,765	288	91	1,386	394	215	45	134	22.3	74.6	49.6	9.7	6,984	582
1933	1,553	283	86	1,184	368	210	43	115	23.7	74.0	49.8	9.8	6,691	541
1932	1,554	298	87	1,169	384	223	44	117	24.7	74.8	50.4	10.0	6,506	531
1931	1,684	294	86	1,304	392	208	41	143	23.3	70.7	47.8	10.9	6,443	518
1930	1,942	296	81	1,565	416	201	39	176	21.4	67.8	47.8	11.3	5,035	413
1929	1,917	360		1,557	413	223		190	21.5	62.0	12.2		5,098	
1928	1,568	321		1,247	364	199		165	23.2	62.0	13.2		4,344	
1927	1,445	296		1,149	318	180		138	22.0	60.8	12.0		3,984	
1926	1,313	289		1,024	300	169		131	22.9	58.4	12.8		3,731	
1925	1,188	272		916	265	152		113	22.3	56.0	12.3		3,508	
1924	1,141	285		856	254	154		100	22.2	54.0	11.6		3,443	
1923	1,007	277		730	240	142		98	23.8	51.4	13.4		3,234	
1922	763	254		509	222	127		95	29.1	49.9	18.6		3,015	

[1] Beginning 1967, data volumes are converted to a pressure base of 14.73 p.s.i.a.;   [2] Beginning 1960, includes Alaska.
prior years are converted to a pressure base of 14.65 p.s.i.a.

Series S 190–204. Gas Utility Industry—Customers, Sales, and Revenues, by Type of Service: 1932 to 1970

Year	Customers [1] (1,000)					Sales [2] (mil. therms [3])					Revenues [2] (mil. dol.)				
	Total	Residential	Commercial	Industrial	Other	Total	Residential	Commercial	Industrial	Other	Total	Residential	Commercial	Industrial	Other
	190	191	192	193	194	195	196	197	198	199	200	201	202	203	204
1970	41,482	38,097	3,131	199	55	160,435	49,237	20,066	84,392	6,740	10,283	5,207	1,620	3,181	274
1969	40,854	37,538	3,074	193	49	153,916	48,204	18,781	81,358	5,573	9,480	4,883	1,459	2,919	219
1968	39,930	36,691	3,004	188	47	144,724	45,527	17,049	75,951	6,197	8,781	4,567	1,315	2,675	223
1967	39,077	35,915	2,934	181	47	134,883	43,653	15,776	70,143	5,311	8,261	4,383	1,224	2,461	193
1966	38,228	35,142	2,868	174	45	128,591	41,754	14,628	66,533	5,676	7,870	4,195	1,135	2,335	205
1965	37,338	34,341	2,790	166	41	119,803	39,990	13,448	61,465	4,900	7,407	4,030	1,054	2,148	176
1964	36,463	33,551	2,712	159	41	115,912	38,697	12,735	59,120	5,360	7,133	3,895	998	2,049	191
1963	35,551	32,711	2,640	162	39	107,663	36,680	11,366	54,381	5,236	6,727	3,728	910	1,906	183
1962	34,683	31,893	2,598	156	37	102,348	35,369	10,929	51,001	5,049	6,445	3,603	874	1,796	171
1961	33,831	31,118	2,529	147	37	95,890	33,210	9,881	47,856	4,943	5,993	3,377	789	1,658	169
1960*	33,054	30,418	2,458	141	37	92,877	31,881	9,198	47,094	4,704	5,617	3,177	723	1,563	153
1959 [4]	32,066	29,530	2,364	136	36	87,917	29,739	8,275	45,631	4,273	5,065	2,870	633	1,431	131
1958	31,242	28,786	2,287	134	35	80,285	28,125	7,649	40,764	3,748	4,568	2,658	571	1,229	111
1957	30,476	28,101	2,211	132	32	77,034	25,985	6,989	40,476	3,585	4,134	2,379	506	1,150	99
1956	29,536	27,241	2,141	125	29	72,541	24,643	6,558	38,687	2,654	3,850	2,237	471	1,066	77
1955	28,479	26,283	2,048	121	27	66,586	22,387	6,029	35,351	2,819	3,450	2,007	424	938	81
1954	27,528	25,398	1,990	112	28	61,026	20,031	5,405	33,096	2,494	3,049	1,783	378	821	68
1953	26,705	24,647	1,926	107	25	56,073	18,033	4,980	30,373	2,687	2,716	1,574	339	739	63
1952	25,850	23,852	1,869	104	25	52,392	17,348	4,929	27,990	2,125	2,466	1,457	321	639	48
1951	24,953	23,042	1,787	101	23	48,222	16,205	4,559	25,522	1,936	2,228	1,335	294	557	42
1950	24,001	22,146	1,739	100	16	42,090	13,839	4,104	22,887	1,261	1,948	1,177	266	480	26
1949	23,035	21,264	1,657	97	17	35,790	11,827	3,724	18,979	1,260	1,689	1,031	238	396	24
1948	22,245	20,562	1,571	94	18	33,885	11,153	3,535	17,981	1,216	1,579	958	221	377	23
1947	21,416	19,835	1,474	91	16	29,882	10,087	3,107	15,792	897	1,396	862	191	326	18
1946	20,636	19,157	1,377	87	15	26,379	8,482	2,630	14,602	665	1,213	754	161	284	13
1945	19,977	18,607	1,278	80	12	25,868	7,749	2,497	14,523	1,098	1,153	705	149	281	18
1944	19,585	18,320	1,177	82	6	25,120	7,313	2,208	14,635	964	1,108	667	133	293	15
1943	19,064	17,838	1,141	77	8	23,415	7,001	2,083	13,582	748	1,064	648	128	277	11
1942	18,734	17,511	1,137	78	8	20,849	6,679	1,990	11,723	457	994	623	127	238	7
1941	18,126	16,904	1,137	78	7	19,009	5,862	1,650	11,206	292	914	575	114	220	5
1940	17,600	16,381	1,138	73	8	17,235	5,823	1,598	9,544	271	872	573	112	182	5
1939	17,128	15,926	1,121	73	8	15,927	5,289	1,469	8,768	401	814	538	105	165	6
1938	16,876	15,697	1,094	75	10	14,682	4,956	1,380	7,941	405	777	523	101	145	9
1937	16,605	15,466	1,056	74	9	15,773	4,987	1,382	9,041	364	802	528	100	167	7
1936	16,170	15,026	1,058	77	9	14,693	4,784	1,369	8,280	260	770	516	97	151	5
1935	15,819	14,725	1,014	72	8	12,924	4,445	1,211	7,221	47	727	503	91	130	2
1934	15,512	14,440	990	74	8	12,063	4,202	1,102	6,699	62	703	494	87	119	3
1933	15,195	14,141	978	68	8	10,531	4,237	1,150	5,114	29	680	495	88	95	2
1932	15,532	14,452	999	73	8	10,441	4,672	1,193	4,534	42	723	537	93	91	3

* Denotes first year for which figures include Alaska and Hawaii.
[1] Yearly averages.
[2] Excludes sales for resale.

[3] A therm is equivalent to 100,000 British thermal units. A B.t.u. is the quantity of heat required to raise the temperature of 1 pound of water 1° F. at or near its point of maximum density.
[4] Includes Hawaii.

Series S 205–218. Gas Utility and Pipeline Industry—Balance Sheet and Income Account: 1937 to 1970

[In millions of dollars]

Year	Total assets, liabilities	Assets and other debits			Liabilities and other credits					Operating revenues	Net operating revenues	Utility operating income	Gross income	Net income
		Utility plant and adjustments	Current and accrued assets	Other [1]	Capital stock and surplus	Long-term debt	Reserve for depreciation, retirements, etc.	Current and accrued liabilities	Other [2]					
	205	206	207	208	209	210	211	212	213	214	215	216	217	218
1970	45,625	38,541	3,674	3,410	8,735	15,681	10,696	4,832	5,681	16,380	2,074	2,086	2,384	1,427
1969	[3] 42,952	36,593	3,328	3,031	8,101	14,423	10,010	4,902	5,388	14,896	1,958	1,966	2,264	1,459
1968	40,245	34,400	3,120	2,725	8,115	13,610	9,310	4,325	4,885	13,770	1,702	1,710	2,000	1,312
1967	37,620	32,030	2,965	2,625	7,885	12,770	8,535	3,890	4,540	12,850	1,654	1,662	1,925	1,300
1966	35,175	30,175	2,765	2,235	7,475	12,055	7,855	3,620	4,170	12,219	1,536	1,543	1,740	1,179
1965	32,845	28,205	2,545	2,095	7,290	11,515	7,205	3,035	3,800	11,525	1,462	1,469	1,626	1,107
1964	31,000	26,410	2,605	1,985	7,085	11,070	6,615	2,850	3,380	11,074	1,373	1,380	1,559	1,063
1963	29,535	25,055	2,610	1,870	6,885	10,605	6,045	2,940	3,060	10,435	1,299	1,305	1,409	890
1962	28,500	23,940	2,650	1,910	6,745	10,450	5,615	2,890	2,800	10,019	1,274	1,280	1,416	907
1961	26,555	22,385	2,340	1,830	6,455	10,080	5,025	2,460	2,535	9,282	1,158	1,164	1,254	818
1960	24,570	20,835	2,185	1,550	5,930	9,130	4,570	2,420	2,520	8,696	1,109	1,112	1,222	830
1959	22,845	19,200	2,150	1,495	5,650	8,740	4,065	2,195	2,195	7,690	994	997	1,075	732
1958	20,730	17,465	1,905	1,360	5,185	8,005	3,690	1,960	1,890	6,856	890	892	976	668
1957	19,150	16,155	1,790	1,205	4,820	7,465	3,280	1,885	1,700	6,194	814	816	895	627
1956	16,885	14,490	1,605	790	4,370	6,390	3,055	1,630	1,440	5,661	764	766	821	600
1955	15,435	13,305	1,465	665	4,105	5,900	2,775	1,390	1,265	5,063	665	667	715	509
1954	14,230	12,195	1,375	660	3,780	5,615	2,525	1,160	1,150	4,454	582	584	630	435
1953	13,240	11,315	1,225	700	3,445	5,260	2,270	1,120	1,145	4,074	534	537	566	389
1952	11,770	10,095	1,145	530	3,145	4,540	2,045	1,030	1,010	3,462	455	457	489	352
1951	10,515	9,005	1,060	450	2,770	3,945	1,885	995	920	2,999	421	423	451	336
1950	9,010	7,620	970	420	2,540	3,145	1,740	735	850	2,553	371	372	405	317
1949	7,890	6,730	780	380	2,290	2,615	1,655	550	780	2,129	302	302	330	251
1948	7,165	5,945	805	415	2,090	2,370	1,475	535	695	1,954	263	263	290	222
1947	6,620	5,600	690	330	2,015	1,970	1,505	450	680	1,700	238	238	271	213
1946	5,940	5,065	615	260	1,915	1,580	1,495	365	585	1,465	233	232	255	195
1945	5,610	4,770	590	250	1,825	1,495	1,400	350	540	1,363	211	211	226	152
1944	5,550	4,735	570	245	1,750	1,515	1,335	360	590	1,308	219	215	217	145
1943	5,435	4,635	510	290	1,715	1,520	1,250	320	630	1,264	203	199	203	133
1942	5,155	4,445	440	270	1,680	1,525	1,070	310	570	1,188	194	190	195	124
1941	4,970	4,295	405	270	1,690	1,460	960	275	585	1,108	202	198	205	132
1940	4,980	4,330	360	290	1,740	1,575	870	245	550	1,054	215	214	223	145
1939	4,865	4,240	325	300	1,720	1,580	830	235	500	1,000	200	199	211	129
1938	4,815	4,195	330	290	1,665	1,650	740	235	525	964	191	185	195	105
1937	4,815	4,200	300	315	1,665	1,695	750	235	470	995	205	201	213	121

[1] Includes investment and fund accounts, capital stock discount and expense, and reacquired securities.

[2] Includes deferred credits, reserve for deferred income taxes, other reserves, contributions in aid of construction, and retained income.

[3] Liability breakdown will not add to total because of error in reporting units.

Chapter T

Distribution and Services

T 1–491. General note.

Users of these statistics are cautioned to keep in mind that data relate to establishments or firms classified under the Standard Industrial Classification (SIC) System (U.S. Office of Management and Budget, *Standard Industrial Classification Manual*, various issues, Washington, D.C.) as being engaged in wholesale trade, retail trade, or in performing services. As defined in the SIC, services does not include finance, insurance and real estate. Data for such establishments are included in Chapter X.

Where two or more activities are carried on at a single location under a single ownership, all activities are generally grouped together and the entire establishment classified in its major activity. The activities of leased departments are generally combined with the parent establishment in which they are located. Data as presented for the various censuses and annual data do not include the activities engaged in at administrative offices or in auxiliary establishments. Neither do they include the operations of chain store warehouses.

T 1–14. National income originating in distribution and selected service industries, 1869–1970.

Source: 1869–1929, Harold Barger, "Income Originating in Trade, 1869–1929," *Studies in Income and Wealth*, vol. 24, Conference on Research in Income and Wealth, National Bureau of Economic Research, Princeton. U.S. Bureau of Economic Analysis (formerly Office of Business Economics), 1929–1963, *National Income and Product Accounts of the United States, 1929–1965*, table 1.12; 1964–1967, *U.S. National Income and Product Accounts, 1964–67*, table 1.12; 1968–1970, *Survey of Current Business*, July 1972, table 1.12.

Data for 1929–1948 are based on the 1942 Standard Industrial Classification System (SIC); data for 1948–1970 are based on the 1957 SIC System. For all series, data for 1948 are shown according to both systems. See reference in general note for series T 1–491.

T 15–28. Persons engaged in distribution and selected service industries, 1869–1970.

Source: 1869–1919, see source for series T 1–14; 1929–1970, see sources for series T 1–14, table 6.6.

These figures are in terms of full-time equivalent employment, which measures man-years of full-time employment and its equivalent work performed by part-time workers. Full-time employment is defined simply in terms of the number of hours which is customary at a particular time and place. For a full explanation of the concept, see U.S. Office of Business Economics, *Survey of Current Business*, June 1945, pp. 17 and 18.

Unpaid family workers are excluded due to unresolved difficulties in their definition and measurement.

For explanation of the two series presented for 1948, see the text for series T 1–14.

T 29–42. Average annual earnings per full-time employee in distribution and selected service industries, 1929–1970.

Source: U.S. Bureau of Economic Analysis (formerly Office of Business Economics), 1929–1963, *The National Income and Product Accounts of the United States, 1929–1965*, table 6.5; 1964–1967, *U.S. National Income and Product Accounts, 1964–67*, table 6.5; 1968–1970, *Survey of Current Business*, July 1972, table 6.5.

For definition of full-time employment, see text for series T 15–28.

Average annual earnings per full-time employee measures wage-and-salary income per man-year of full-time work. Wages and salaries comprise all payments accruing to persons in an employee status as compensation for their work. They include commissions, tips, and bonuses, as well as cash payments commonly referred to as wages and salaries, together with the value of those payments in kind that clearly represent an addition to the recipient's income. Income in kind is valued, so far as possible, at its cost to the employer. Service industries in which it is a perceptible portion of wages and salaries include hotels and other lodging places and educational services.

Series T 29–42 do not include dismissal pay, directors' fees, employer contributions to social insurance funds and private pension plans, nor accident compensation payments.

For further details, see *Survey of Current Business*, June 1945, pp. 17 and 18.

T 43–57. Distribution and selected services, legal form of organization, 1935–1967.

Source: U.S. Bureau of the Census. 1935, *U.S. Census of Business: 1935, Wholesale Distribution*, vol. 1, p. 119. 1939, *Sixteenth Census of the U.S.: 1940, Census of Business: 1939*, vol. I, p. 71; vol. II, p. 200; and vol. III, p. 104. 1948, *U.S. Census of Business: 1948*, vol. I, p. 6.05; vol. IV, p. 5.02; and vol. VI, p. 5.02. 1954, *U.S. Census of Business: 1954*, vol. I, p. 5–2; vol. III, p. 7–2; and vol. V, p. 5–2. 1958, *U.S. Census of Business: 1958*, vol. I, p. 5–2; vol. III, p. 5–2; and vol. V, p. 5–2. 1963, *1963 Census of Business*, vol. I, p. 5–1; vol. IV, p. 7–1; and vol. VI, p. 5–1. 1967, *1967 Census of Business*, BC67–RS5, p. 5–103; BC67–WS8, p. 8–126; and BC67–SS8, p. 8–57.

Each establishment included in the censuses of business was classified into one of the following legal forms of organization: (1) *Individual proprietorship*—an establishment owned by one person, who may or may not actively participate in the operation of the business. (2) *Partnership*—an establishment owned by two or more persons each of whom has a financial interest in and responsibility for the business. Any partner may or may not actively participate in the operation of the business. (3) *Corporation*—an establishment (other than a cooperative) owned by an organization or company legally incorporated under State laws. In the 1939 and 1948 censuses of business, cooperative associations incorporated under either regular corporation laws or under the special cooperative association laws of the States were classified as corporations. Beginning with the 1954 Census of Business, a separate legal form was established for cooperatives. (4) *Cooperative*—an establishment owned by an association of customers of the establishment whether or not they are incorporated. In general, the distinguishing features of a cooperative are patronage dividends based on the volume of expenditures by the member, and a limitation of one vote per member regardless of the amount of stock owned. The establishments are open to the public as a rule, but generally are patronized primarily by members of the association operating the business. In the 1939 and 1948 censuses of business, cooperatives were defined as either "corporations," if the cooperative was incorporated, or as "other legal forms." (5) *Other legal forms*—These are establishments whose legal form of organization is not one of those defined above. Included in this legal form are liquor stores owned or operated by State, county, or municipal governments, and other miscellaneous ownership types such as estates, receiverships, some nonprofit organizations, and joint ventures. In the 1939 and 1948 censuses of business, cooperatives not incorporated were also included in this category.

T 58–78. Book value of inventories at end of year, 1929–1970.

Source: U.S. Bureau of Economic Analysis (formerly Office of Business Economics). **Series T 58–66**: 1938, unpublished data; 1939–1946, *1969 Business Statistics*, p. 63; 1947–1967, *1971 Business Statistics*, p. 63; 1968–1970, *Survey of Current Business*, December 1971, p. 55. **Series T 67–69**: 1938–1945, *1953 Business Statistics*, p. 16; 1946–1947, unpublished data; 1948–1970, *1971 Business Statistics*, p. 24. **Series T 70–78**: 1929–1952, *1957 Business Statistics*, pp. 17–20 except for series T 70, T 71, and T 75 for 1947–1952, which are revised figures from unpublished data; 1953–1970, *1971 Business Statistics*, pp. 30–33.

In these series, trade inventories are valued at the cost of merchandise on hand; manufacturers' inventories at cost or market price, whichever is lower. About 15 percent of manufacturers' inventories are valued on a last-in-first-out basis; this basis is much less prevalent in trade, although it is used extensively by department stores. Changes in book values reflect changes in unit costs as well as changes in physical quantities.

Retail store inventories, series T 58–66, for 1938–45 were linked to the census of business for 1939 and 1948, the Internal Revenue Service's *Statistics of Income*, and Federal Reserve Board data on department store inventories. Data for 1946–1970 are based on sample information which is used to extrapolate year-end estimates from the 1952–1970 *Annual Retail Trade Reports* of the Bureau of the Census. Adjustments have been made to the data from 1961 forward to make them directly comparable to retail sales estimates derived from a new sample introduced in 1968.

Inventories of merchant wholesalers, series T 67–69, include wholesalers of farm products and raw materials. Figures for 1938–1946 include some types of nonmerchant wholesalers and are not comparable with data for later years. Figures for 1947–1958 are adjusted to the levels of the 1958 Census of Business sample from data based on samples selected from the 1948 and 1954 censuses of business. Figures for 1959 and later years are based on a sample designed to conform to the 1963 Census of Business. Inventories are valued at the cost of merchandise on hand; changes thus reflect changes in unit prices as well as changes in physical quantities.

Manufacturers' inventories for 1929–1946, series T 70, 71, and 75, and inventories by stage of fabrication for 1938–1952, series T 72–74 and T 76–78, are based on a sample of manufacturing companies. The data were collected by the Office of Business Economics and benchmarked to Internal Revenue Service's *Statistics of Income* reports. These data are not directly comparable to the series for later years because of differences in the conceptual basis of the two series, particularly in figures for inventories by stage of fabrication. Total manufacturers' inventories for 1947–1970 and inventories by stage of fabrication for 1953–1970 are based on sample reports collected from manufacturers by the Bureau of the Census and benchmarked to establishment data from its *Annual Survey of Manufactures*, which is benchmarked to the *Census of Manufactures*.

T 79–196. Retail establishments, sales, and persons engaged, by kind of business, 1929–1967.

Source: U.S. Bureau of the Census. 1929, *Fifteenth Census of the United States, 1930, Distribution*, vol. I, *Retail Distribution*, part 1. 1933, *Census of American Business: 1933*, United States Summaries; 1935, *Census of Business: 1935, Retail Distribution*, part 1, vol. I, *U.S. Summary*; 1939, *Sixteenth Census of the United States, 1940, Census of Business*, vol. I, *Retail Trade: 1939*, part 1; 1948, *Census of Business: 1948*, vol. I, *Retail Trade, General Statistics*, part 1; 1954, *Census of Business: 1954*, vol. I, *Retail Trade—Summary Statistics*; 1958, *Census of Business: 1958*, vol. I, *Retail Trade—Summary Statistics*; 1963, *Census of Business: 1963*, vol. I, *Retail Trade—Summary Statistics*, part 1; 1967, *Census of Business: 1967*, vol. I, *Retail Trade—Subject Reports*.

Stores are classified according to their principal kind of business. Where a number of lines are carried, changes in relative importance may serve to shift a particular establishment from one category to another between censuses. Sales figures shown are for kinds of establishments, *not* kinds of products.

Certain of these series have been adjusted or combined for some years prior to 1958, by Professors Charles S. Goodman and Reavis Cox (presently and formerly, respectively) of the Wharton School of Finance and Commerce, University of Pennsylvania, in order to provide historical series that are as comparable as possible. Figures for 1933, in particular, have been adjusted for comparability. The reports of the census of business provide considerably more detail as to kinds of business.

Sales and excise taxes are included in sales figures for 1954 and later years and excluded for 1948 and 1939.

Figures for persons engaged represent the total of the reported number of active proprietors and employees for the week including March 12 for 1967, of active proprietors and employees for the payroll period ended nearest November 15 for 1939–1963, and of active proprietors plus the average annual number of full-time and part-time employees for 1939 and earlier years. Unpaid family workers are excluded from figures for persons engaged.

Establishments without paid employment and with less than $2,500 sales were excluded in 1954 and 1958. The 1948 figures exclude stores which operated the entire year but had sales of less than $500. The corresponding cutoff point for 1939 was $100. Nonemployer establishments which did not operate the entire year were included in 1963 and 1967 if their receipts during the period they operated were at a rate which would have reached an annual total of $2,500 or more had they operated the entire year.

There have been many changes in enumeration methods, in accuracy, and in classifications over the years. The principal ones are noted here; others are described in the various census volumes. Users of the data are cautioned to consult original sources for more complete discussion of factors affecting the comparability of data. The 1954 and subsequent censuses were conducted by mail canvasses of all firms included in the active records of the Internal Revenue Service as subject to the payment of Federal Insurance Contributions Act (FICA) taxes and which were in appropriate kind-of-business classifications. Such data cover only firms with paid employees. The nonemployer segment was derived from a 50-percent sample of 1954, 1958, and 1963 tax returns. This procedure was modified for the 1967 census by the use of tax records instead of census returns for small employers, and the use of tax records for all nonemployers rather than for a 50-percent sample. The 1948 and earlier censuses were conducted by field enumeration. The differences in enumeration affect particularly the coverage of establishments without easily recognized places of business (e.g., nonstore retailers) and those leaving business prior to the end of the year. The data for the 1954 and subsequent censuses thus have better coverage in these areas. The 1933 and 1935 censuses were not taken under mandatory reporting requirements and may be subject to some underenumeration.

Dairies which processed milk and cream were included as retailers in 1948 and earlier years if the major portion of their sales was by route delivery to the homes of consumers. They were excluded in 1954 and later years.

Nonstore retailers are treated as a separate kind of business for 1954 and later years. For earlier years, such retailers (to the extent enumerated) were classified in their appropriate kind of business. For 1954, each leased department is treated as a separate establishment; for all other years, data for such departments were consolidated with the establishments in which they were located.

Two sets of data are shown for 1948. The data for 1948 (comparable with later years) represent retabulations of 1948 data to make them comparable with later years as to treatment of dairies, nonstore retailers, and cutoff points for tabulation. Similarly, two sets of data are shown for the number of persons engaged in retail establishments in 1939. The data for 1939 (comparable with later years) represent the sum of active proprietors and paid employees for the payroll period ended nearest November 15 and are comparable with data for 1948 and later years. The figures for 1939 (comparable with earlier years) represent the number of active proprietors and the average number of employees for the year, and are comparable with data for 1935 and earlier years.

T 197–219. Retail sales of stores of multiunit retail firms, by kind of business, 1929–1970.

Source: U.S. Bureau of Economic Analysis (formerly Office of Business Economics), 1929–1938, unpublished data; 1939–1970, *1971 Business Statistics*, p. 64, and unpublished data, except 1970 (new basis) and 1960 (old basis) from U.S. Bureau of the Census, *Monthly Retail Trade Report*, January 1961 and December 1971 issues.

For 1929–1951, these series were originally designated as "Retail Sales of Chain Stores and Mail-Order Houses" and represent sales of firms with 4 or more retail stores. Data from the census of business for 1929, 1933, 1935, 1939, and 1948 were used as benchmarks. The intercensal estimates were based on sample groups of organizations with 4 or more stores.

For 1951–1970, the series are based on a sample of firms which operated 11 or more retail units in the most recently available census. Adjustments reflecting changes in industry classification, and in the firms to be included in the sample, were made for 1956 based on 1954 census results; for 1960 based on the 1958 census; for 1964 based on the 1963 census; and for 1970 based on the 1967 census.

Since no adjustments were made for entries and exits from the "11 or more" category between censuses, the data shown cannot be subtracted from total retail sales to obtain sales by organizations operating 10 or fewer stores.

T 220–224. Chains and chain stores, 1872–1928.

Source: U.S. Federal Trade Commission, *Chain Stores: Growth and Development of Chain Stores* (72d Congress, 1st session, Senate Document No. 100), p. 80.

Figures include chains of two or more stores reporting to the Federal Trade Commission or known to that agency. Grocery and meat chains have been combined with grocery chains. Ready-to-wear chains include men's ready-to-wear chains, women's ready-to-wear chains, and men's and women's ready-to-wear chains but not chains specializing in furnishings, accessories, millinery, and the like, nor dry goods chains whether carrying apparel or not. Data for each of the 26 lines of business shown in the total column are found in the source. The source publication also contains estimates of the number of chain outlets in different years but such data embody substantial estimating difficulties.

T 225–244. Retail trade margins, by kind of store, 1869–1947.

Source: Harold Barger, *Distribution's Place in the American Economy Since 1869*, National Bureau of Economic Research, Princeton University Press, 1955, pp. 57, 60, and 81 (copyright).

The retail margin estimates are shown as a percent of retail value of sales, and include both net profit and expenses of doing business. With regard to the reliability of the data, the source volume notes that "because of the extremely heterogeneous nature of the source material, it is not possible to offer any measures of dispersion within categories for the data." The source concludes, however, that we may "have some confidence that at least the larger differences reported . . . have a real existence."

T 245–271. Retail store sales, by kind of business, 1929–1970.

Source: U.S. Bureau of Economic Analysis (formerly Office of Business Economics), 1929–1938, unpublished data; 1939–1946, *1969 Business Statistics*, pp. 58–59; 1947–1967, *1971 Business Statistics*, pp. 58–59; 1968–1970, *Survey of Current Business*, December issues.

Sales figures include multiunit stores. The classification of durable goods stores and nondurable goods stores is based on the durability of the commodities accounting for a major portion of the sales of each kind-of-business group. Data from censuses of retail trade were used as benchmarks for annual 1929–1946 data. Estimates for intercensal years in this period were developed from sales tax collection data, special Internal Revenue Service compilations, business population trends, the Federal Reserve Board index of department store sales, and data from the Bureau of Public Roads and the American Petroleum Institute. Methods of compilation are described in *1969 Business Statistics*, p. 58.

Data for 1946–1961 were based on a new method of estimating retail sales and are not comparable with those shown for prior years. Estimates of retail sales were developed from a sample representing all sizes of stores, firms, or organizations, and all kinds of retail business. These data were not linked to a census of retail trade as were the old, a factor that accounts for most of the difference between the levels of retail sales indicated by the old and new series for 1946. In 1957 the data were revised back to January 1951 to exclude milk dealers engaged in processing on the premises. (This change conforms with the treatment of such establishments as manufacturing plants in the 1954 Census of Business.) Data for 1961–1970 reflect a new sample design and classification changes resulting from the 1963 census. In addition, data by kind-of-business group were revised by shifting all "nonstore" establishments into the general merchandise group. Nonstore establishments (mail order, house-to-house, and vending machine businesses) were previously shown in such kind-of-business groups as food, eating and drinking places, and furniture and appliance. The sampling procedure for the new series is described in *1971 Business Statistics*.

T 272–273. Index of department store sales and stocks, 1919–1970.

Source: Board of Governors of the Federal Reserve System, unpublished data.

The index for sales is based on the average per trading day. The stocks index is the annual average of monthly data of end-of-month stocks.

T 274–371. Wholesale establishments, sales, operating expenses, and persons engaged, by kind of business, 1929–1967.

Source: U.S. Bureau of the Census. 1929, *Fifteenth Census of the United States, 1930, Distribution*, vol. II, *Wholesale Distribution*; 1933, *Census of American Business: 1933*, United States Summaries; 1935, *Census of Business: 1935, Wholesale Distribution*, part 1, vol. I, *U.S Summary*; 1939, *Sixteenth Census of the United States, 1940, Census of Business*, vol. II, *Wholesale Trade: 1939*; 1948, *Census of Business: 1948*, vol. IV, *Wholesale Trade—General Statistics* and *Commodity Line Sales Statistics*; 1954, *Census of Business: 1954*, vol. III, *Wholesale Trade—Summary Statistics*; 1958, *Census of Business: 1958*, vol. III, *Wholesale Trade—Summary Statistics*; 1963, *Census of Business: 1963*, vol. IV, *Wholesale Trade—Summary Statistics*, part 1; 1967, *Census of Business: 1967*, vol. III, *Wholesale Trade—Subject Reports*.

Data shown are for wholesale establishments, other than chain store warehouses. Adjustments have been made in the data prior to 1958 for certain years by Professors Charles S. Goodman and Reavis Cox (presently and formerly, respectively) of the Wharton School of Finance and Commerce, University of Pennsylvania, in order to attain maximum comparability.

Data for persons engaged represent the total of the reported number of active proprietors and employees for the week including March 12, for 1967; of active proprietors and employees for the payroll period nearest November 15, for 1948–1963; and of active proprietors plus the average annual number of full-time and part-time employees for 1939 and earlier years.

There have been numerous changes over the years in the definitions of kinds of business, scope of the census (especially size minimums for enumeration), enumeration methods, and completeness of data. The statistics shown have been adjusted where possible to maintain maximum comparability over time. Significant changes are noted below. For treatment of lesser differences, see source publications.

The 1954 and later censuses were conducted by mail canvass. Report forms were mailed to all firms included in the active records of the Internal Revenue Service as subject to the payment of Federal Insurance Contributions Act (FICA) taxes and which were classified in appropriate kinds of business or were unclassified at the time the forms were mailed. Data for such censuses, therefore, omit all wholesalers who had no employees subject to FICA taxes. The 1948 and earlier censuses were conducted by field canvasses and were restricted to firms which operated from recognizable places of business, whether or not they had any employees subject to FICA taxes. The 1933 and 1935 censuses were not taken under mandatory reporting requirements and may therefore be subject to some underenumeration.

Data for 1954 and later years are for establishments with paid employees. The original 1948 tabulations include all establishments with sales of $5,000 or more irrespective of employment. For 1939, the corresponding cutoff point was $500. No mention of cutoff point is made in sources of data for years prior to 1939.

The figures for 1948 (comparable with later years) have been revised to reflect 1954 coverage and to incorporate certain changes in classification.

The figures for 1963 (comparable with later years) have been revised to reflect the scope of the 1967 Census of Business. Significant changes are (1) kinds of business data for 1967 are in accordance with the 1967 edition of the U.S. Office of Management and Budget (formerly Bureau of the Budget) *Standard Industrial Classification Manual*, whereas the 1963 data are in conformity with the 1957 edition and its supplements; (2) the number of paid employees in 1967 was obtained from administrative records of the Internal Revenue Service while, in 1963, all census information was obtained directly from the companies; and (3) the number of active proprietors for 1967 is based on crediting sole proprietorships with one proprietor and partnerships with two proprietors for firms with first quarter 1967 payroll; for 1963, on crediting proprietors similarly but for all sole proprietorships and partnerships operated at any time during 1963.

T 372–374. Sales of wholesale establishments, 1939–1962.

Source: U.S. Bureau of Economic Analysis (formerly Office of Business Economics), 1939–1946, *Survey of Current Business*, October 1951, p. 24; 1946–1962, unpublished data (monthly averages published in *1963 Business Statistics*, p. 22).

These estimates exclude sales of corporate manufacturers, sales branches and offices, and the marketing stations of petroleum refiners which are included in the manufacturing series of the former Office of Business Economics. Sales of agents and brokers are included here on the basis of actual receipts of the agents and brokers rather than on the total value of goods sold. For 1939–1946, data are based on 1948 Census of Business definitions and classifications. The 1939 census data have been recast to conform to the 1948 census. Data for 1946–1962 are based on definitions and classifications in the 1954 Census of Business, with the 1948 census data adjusted to the scope of the 1954 census.

T 375–383. Sales, stocks, and stock-sales ratios of merchant wholesalers, 1948–1970.

Source: U.S. Bureau of Economic Analysis (formerly Office of Business Economics), *1971 Business Statistics*, p. 23.

The estimates are confined to merchant wholesalers since information on other types of wholesalers is not available except for years when the census of wholesale trade was taken. The 1963 Census of Business (to which the merchant wholesale data conform for the period since 1959) indicated that merchant wholesalers accounted for 44 percent of the sales and 74 percent of the inventories of all wholesale establishments.

The data exclude manufacturers' sales branches and sales offices, petroleum bulk stations and terminals, agents and brokers, and assemblers of farm products.

Sales include sales of merchandise and receipts from repairs or other services to customers, after deduction of returns, allowances, and discounts; and sales of merchandise for others on a commission basis. Local and State sales taxes and Federal excise taxes are included. Inventories represent stocks, at cost, of merchandise on hand for sale at the end of the month; they do not include goods held on a consignment basis or such items as fixtures, equipment, and supplies not held for sale.

The stock-sales ratios for a given year are derived by dividing the weighted average of seasonally adjusted end-of-month inventories (using the 13 observations including the yearend figures for the given and previous year) by the monthly average sales for that year. No adjustments have been made to bring inventory book values, which are typically valued at the lower of cost or market, up to the level of selling prices.

Figures for 1948–1958 are based on samples selected from the 1948 and 1954 censuses of business, and were adjusted by the former Office of Business Economics to the level of the sample selected from the 1958 Census of Business and Social Security Administration lists of wholesalers since 1958. These estimates are extrapolations based on data collected by the Census Bureau in the past, compiled with different samples.

In February 1966 a revised sample was introduced which included over 17,000 firms drawn from 1963 Census of Business lists representing all wholesalers (with paid employees) in business in 1963, and Social Security Administration lists of wholesalers (with paid employees) entering business (or requesting new Employer Identification numbers) since 1963. The Office of Business Economics in cooperation with the Bureau of the Census applied ratios calculated from the overlapping data to the previous estimates for 1959 through 1965 to make them comparable with the 1966 figures.

T 384–390. Wholesale trade margins of independent wholesalers, 1869–1947.

Source: See source for series T 225–244, p. 84.

See text for series T 225–244 for definition of "margin" and statement regarding reliability of the data.

Independent or regular wholesalers are types of wholesalers handling finished goods or construction materials for eventual distribution through some kind of retail outlet. This category excludes other kinds of wholesalers, such as brokers, commission merchants, manufacturers' sale branches, and chain-store warehouses.

T 391–443. Selected service establishments and receipts, 1929–1967.

Source: U.S. Bureau of the Census. 1929, unpublished data; 1933, *Census of American Business: 1933*, United States Summaries; 1935, *Census of Business: 1935*, Service Establishments, vol. I, *U.S. Summary* and *Census of Business: 1935*, Miscellaneous; 1939, *Census of Business: 1939*, vol. III, *Service Establishments*; 1948, *Census of Business: 1948*, vol. VI, *Service Trade—General Statistics*; 1954, *Census of Business: 1954*, vol. V, *Selected Service Trades—Summary Statistics*; 1958, *Census of Business: 1958*, vol. V, *Selected Services— Summary Statistics*; 1963, *Census of Business: 1963*, vol. VI, *Selected Services—Summary Statistics*; 1967, *Census of Business: 1967*, vol. V, *Selected Services—Area Statistics*, part 1.

Certain series have been combined for some years in order to provide as comparable historical series as possible. For some of the series, as noted below, data for some years were collected in other census programs. The series presented here cover that very limited segment of the services sector which bears greatest similarity to retail trade, specifically, personal, repair, and automotive services; hotels; and motels.

There have been numerous changes in enumeration methods, in accuracy, and in classifications over the years. The principal ones are noted here; others can be noted by reference to the various census volumes. The 1954 and later censuses were conducted by mail canvasses of firms included in the active records of the Internal Revenue Service as subject to the payment of Federal Insurance Contributions Act (FICA) taxes and which were in appropriate kind-of-business classifications. Such data cover only firms with paid employees. The nonemployer segment was derived from a 50-percent sample of 1954, 1958, and 1963 tax returns. In the 1967 census, data for all nonemployers were compiled from tax records. The 1948 and earlier censuses were conducted by field enumeration. The differences in enumeration methods affect particularly the coverage of establishments without easily recognizable places of business and those leaving business prior to the end of the year. The 1954–1967 data are thus more complete in those areas. The 1933 and 1935 censuses were not taken under mandatory reporting requirements and may therefore be subject to some underenumeration. There are important gaps in enumerators' reports for 1933 so that substantial underenumeration, particularly of the smaller establishments, exists for 1933. Underenumerations have more effect on the number of establishments than on receipts.

In the 1963 and 1967 censuses, nonemployer establishments which did not operate the entire year have been included if, during the period they operated, their receipts were at a rate which would have reached an annual total of $1,000 or more had they operated the entire year. Establishments without paid employment and with less than $1,000 receipts were excluded in 1954 and 1958 tabulations. The data for 1948 (comparable with later years) show 1948 figures adjusted to this cutoff point. The data for 1948 (comparable with earlier years) exclude establishments which operated the entire year but had receipts less than $500. For 1939 and earlier years establishments having receipts of $100 or more are included (except as noted). Where two estimates are shown for 1939, the figures for 1939 (comparable with later years) represent a revision to conform to 1948 kind-of-business definitions.

Receipts for 1954 and later years include sales and excise taxes; receipts for 1948 and 1939 exclude them.

Establishments are classified according to their principal kinds of business. Changes in relative importance may thus serve to shift particular establishments among service categories or between service and retailing classifications from one census to another. Many service establishments derive some receipts from sales of merchandise; conversely, many establishments primarily engaged in the sale of goods, and hence included in retail trade, obtain some income from services. Receipts reported in each case *represent total receipts of establishments comprising the classification*, not receipts for the particular service indicated.

T 402–403, total personal services. Data for 1933 and 1935 represent groupings that correspond most closely to the 1939 scope.

T 410–411, photographic studios. Since the 1954–1967 data were obtained by mail canvass, they are believed to be substantially more complete than data for earlier years. For this industry, nonrecognizable establishments are likely to result in substantial underenumeration in a field canvass.

T 412–417, laundry, cleaning, and garment services. Included in series T 412 are power laundries, cleaning plants, press shops, linen supply, diaper service, industrial launderers, garment repair, and hand laundries. For 1933 and 1935, power laundries and dry cleaning plants with receipts of less than $5,000 were omitted. While series T 414 does not include the count of outlets owned and operated by dry cleaning plants, series T 415 does include the receipts of such outlets.

T 426–427, automobile repair shops. Data for 1935 include specialized shops as enumerated in the census of service establishments, and general repair garages as enumerated in the *1935 Census of Business, Retail Distribution*, table 1A. Data for 1933 cover only general repair garages, as enumerated in the *1933 Census of American Business, Retail Distribution*, table 1A, and the following types of

specialized shops as reported in *1933 Census of American Business, Service Industries*: Paint shops, radiator shops, top and body repair shops, tire repair shops, and brake repair shops.

T 434–437, miscellaneous repair services. Separate data are available for some or all of the indicated years for several of the repair services in this group including shops engaged in armature rewinding, bicycle repair, blacksmithing, harness and leather goods repair, musical instrument repair, saw and tool repair, typewriter repair, upholstering and furniture repair, watch, clock, and jewelry repair, etc. Since the 1954–1967 data were obtained by mail canvass, they are believed to be substantially more complete than data for earlier years. In these industries, nonrecognizable establishments are likely to result in substantial underenumeration in a field canvass.

T 438–439, hotels, tourist courts, motels, trailer parks, and camps. Data for 1954–1967 are for establishments with payrolls only.

T 444–471. Volume of advertising, by medium, 1867–1970.

Source: Printers' Ink Publications, New York, N.Y., 1867–1934, *Printers' Ink Advertisers' Annual*, 1955 edition; 1935–1968, *Printers' Ink Advertisers' Guide to Marketing*, annual issues; 1969 and 1970, *Marketing/Communications*, July 1971.

The data were prepared by Robert J. Coen of McCann–Erickson, Inc., from information furnished by the American Newspaper Publishers Association, A. C. Nielsen Company, Publishers' Information Bureau, Farm Publication Reports, Inc., the Direct Mail Advertising Association, A. R. Venezian, Outdoor Advertising, Inc., and the Federal Communications Commission.

The data include the cost of preparation, and the cost of talent in the case of radio and television as well as the charges for space and time.

T 472–484. Indexes of national advertising expenditures, by medium, 1935–1970.

Source: Compiled by Robert J. Coen of McCann–Erickson, Inc., from annual dollar figures prepared and published in *Advertising Age*, Crain Communications, Inc., Chicago.

The general index, series T 472, is designed to reflect the changes in advertising dollar expenditures by national advertisers in major media. The national advertiser is usually a manufacturer of a product or service who does business in many markets across the country. National advertisers usually place their advertising through the facilities of an advertising agency and national media sales representative.

The index numbers for all media are based on estimates of the total expenditures made by advertisers to cover space and time charges as well as charges for programming, art and mechanical production expenses, and all commercial production items.

Estimates for the individual media are developed according to several general sources. Broadcast media estimates are derived from the financial reports of the Federal Communications Commission (FCC). The FCC provides comprehensive data on time sales revenue and also program revenue for network television, network radio, spot television, and spot radio. Adjustments are made to these figures to include additional allowances for commercial production expenses and some programming and talent charges not channeled through the stations or networks.

Magazine estimates are primarily based on the reports of the Publishers Information Bureau. Newspaper estimates are primarily based on the reports provided by the Bureau of Advertising of the American Newspaper Publishers Association. Business publications estimates are developed from data collected by the American Business Press. Outdoor estimates are developed from data provided by the Institute of Outdoor Advertising.

The above sources relate to the figures for the most recent years.

In some cases older historical data were derived from sources that are no longer in existence. All data are adjusted and linked in order to make the historical series comparable from year to year.

Data for all media include Alaska and Hawaii as well as expenditures for media in outlying areas of the United States.

T 485–491. Newspaper advertising—linage for 52 cities, 1928–1970.

Source: U.S. Bureau of Economic Analysis (formerly Office of Business Economics). 1928–1938, unpublished data; 1939–1946, *1969 Business Statistics*, p. 57; 1947–1970, *1971 Business Statistics*, p. 57.

Data represent newspaper linage in all newspapers, daily and Sunday, in the following 52 cities: Akron, Albany, Albuquerque, Atlanta, Baltimore, Birmingham, Boston, Buffalo, Chicago, Cincinnati, Cleveland, Columbus, Dallas, Dayton, Denver, Detroit, El Paso, Fort Worth, Hartford, Houston, Indianapolis, Jacksonville, Knoxville, Los Angeles, Memphis, Milwaukee, Minneapolis, Nashville, New Orleans, Oakland, Oklahoma City, Omaha, Pittsburgh, Portland (Oreg.), Reading, Richmond, Rochester, Salt Lake City, San Antonio, San Diego, San Francisco, Seattle, South Bend, Spokane, St. Louis, Syracuse, Tacoma, Toledo, Tulsa, Washington, Worcester, and Youngstown.

Series T 1–14. National Income Originating in Distribution and Selected Service Industries: 1869 to 1970

[**In millions of dollars.** Data represent net value added at factor costs]

Year	Whole-sale trade	Retail trade [1]	Hotels and other lodging places	Personal services	Miscellaneous business services	Automobile repair, services, and garages [1]	Miscellaneous repair services	Motion pictures	Amusement and recreation, except motion pictures	Medical and other health services	Legal services	Educational services	Miscellaneous professional services	Nonprofit membership organizations
	1	2	3	4	5	6	7	8	9	10	11	12	13	14
1970	44,715	76,473	4,204	7,417	13,888	3,621	2,121	1,551	3,239	29,775	6,426	7,292	9,886	8,411
1969	41,872	72,939	4,051	7,384	12,980	3,449	2,092	1,465	2,863	26,604	5,631	6,648	9,092	7,762
1968	38,394	67,675	3,744	7,265	11,490	3,106	1,866	1,535	2,783	23,250	5,114	5,975	8,009	6,955
1967	35,238	62,280	3,435	6,955	10,600	2,879	1,735	1,350	2,512	20,640	4,820	5,394	7,397	6,346
1966	33,380	58,012	3,192	6,570	9,547	2,637	1,689	1,343	2,419	18,075	4,522	4,719	6,552	5,785
1965	30,341	53,961	2,788	5,993	8,413	2,450	1,501	1,205	2,221	16,256	4,069	4,191	5,719	5,306
1964	28,656	50,663	2,577	5,691	7,490	2,368	1,378	1,053	2,120	14,865	3,724	3,768	5,231	4,907
1963	26,768	46,646	2,423	5,282	6,614	2,174	1,315	910	1,970	13,519	3,424	3,374	4,743	4,562
1962	25,505	44,823	2,270	5,036	6,122	2,017	1,227	890	1,849	12,609	3,162	3,010	4,385	4,298
1961	24,243	42,006	2,134	4,795	5,541	1,824	1,181	933	1,789	11,482	2,982	2,713	4,011	4,041
1960 *	23,126	41,270	2,111	4,608	5,093	1,762	1,105	894	1,661	10,731	2,636	2,449	3,761	3,870
1959	22,710	40,622	2,048	4,462	4,735	1,616	1,072	908	1,492	9,974	2,488	2,208	3,593	3,620
1958	20,754	37,492	1,885	4,236	4,088	1,445	993	828	1,369	9,046	2,231	2,040	3,339	3,378
1957	20,314	36,929	1,905	4,195	3,843	1,322	1,037	899	1,235	8,275	2,131	1,887	3,287	3,120
1956	19,326	35,480	1,812	3,916	3,493	1,336	973	949	1,196	7,530	1,979	1,723	2,850	2,873
1955	17,841	34,429	1,717	3,661	3,011	1,172	873	979	1,121	7,097	1,926	1,524	2,324	2,675
1954	15,825	32,426	1,623	3,500	2,672	1,034	822	953	1,039	5,874	1,758	1,405	2,026	2,486
1953	15,777	31,487	1,592	3,416	2,484	1,012	833	849	984	5,801	1,606	1,300	1,934	2,310
1952	15,593	31,087	1,557	3,277	2,204	958	812	869	880	5,273	1,515	1,222	1,776	2,096
1951	15,376	29,715	1,464	3,164	1,945	932	750	877	820	4,827	1,455	1,170	1,504	1,971
1950	13,307	27,636	1,388	3,021	1,684	864	665	866	788	4,412	1,344	1,109	1,252	1,803
1949	12,187	26,848	1,362	2,908	1,474	841	648	885	803	4,045	1,257	1,040	1,164	1,686
1948 [2]	12,857	27,004	1,341	2,840	1,439	908	701	902	830	3,925	1,176	972	1,140	1,492
1948 [3]	13,083	28,591	1,341	2,840	1,859	---------	934	902	830	4,020	1,176	865	782	1,492
1947	11,679	25,872	1,289	2,640	1,641	---------	934	1,045	796	3,542	1,036	810	589	1,308
1946	10,448	24,156	1,320	2,561	1,483	---------	837	1,128	815	3,025	957	658	480	1,193
1945	8,244	19,766	1,087	2,121	1,182	---------	703	929	613	2,459	930	569	335	983
1944	7,647	18,121	990	2,015	1,056	---------	701	882	507	2,341	874	532	320	916
1943	6,923	16,959	878	1,899	916	---------	610	830	436	1,988	814	503	344	819
1942	6,223	14,200	675	1,552	829	---------	419	652	388	1,806	793	461	385	716
1941	5,276	12,135	585	1,292	781	---------	350	513	368	1,575	763	439	264	640
1940	4,500	9,960	532	1,154	668	---------	261	448	310	1,463	719	424	193	599
1939	3,876	8,728	485	1,053	642	---------	261	434	288	1,381	692	415	181	556
1938	3,845	8,251	460	1,028	601	---------	259	426	266	1,330	666	409	164	556
1937	3,971	8,383	473	1,113	610	---------	247	437	305	1,323	680	394	156	547
1936	3,287	7,481	418	962	578	---------	230	391	253	1,253	647	376	144	546
1935	2,972	6,436	383	865	483	---------	218	329	211	1,115	624	365	121	528
1934	2,545	5,765	361	790	432	---------	203	283	197	1,036	600	361	113	532
1933	1,810	3,815	291	707	338	---------	191	210	154	948	561	363	98	527
1932	2,201	4,331	335	814	363	---------	228	194	177	1,037	591	393	102	569
1931	3,221	6,690	465	1,040	450	---------	276	361	268	1,306	701	412	152	626
1930	4,085	8,272	577	1,218	568	---------	306	438	336	1,476	683	413	184	649
1929 [2]	4,261	9,250	623	1,287	568	---------	315	440	379	1,536	689	402	206	640
1929 [3][4]	4,120	8,960	---------	---------	---------	---------	---------	---------	---------	---------	---------	---------	---------	---------
1919 [4]	3,130	5,920	---------	---------	---------	---------	---------	---------	---------	---------	---------	---------	---------	---------
1909 [4]	1,300	2,320	---------	---------	---------	---------	---------	---------	---------	---------	---------	---------	---------	---------
1899 [4]	810	1,340	---------	---------	---------	---------	---------	---------	---------	---------	---------	---------	---------	---------
1889 [4]	360	1,020	---------	---------	---------	---------	---------	---------	---------	---------	---------	---------	---------	---------
1879 [4]	220	560	---------	---------	---------	---------	---------	---------	---------	---------	---------	---------	---------	---------
1869 [4]	210	500	---------	---------	---------	---------	---------	---------	---------	---------	---------	---------	---------	---------

* Denotes first year for which figures include Alaska and Hawaii.
[1] For 1948 and prior years, "Automobile repair, services, and garages" included with "Retail trade."
[2] Comparable with later years.
[3] Comparable with earlier years.
[4] Excludes inventory valuation adjustment.

Series T 15–28.   Persons Engaged in Distribution and Selected Service Industries: 1869 to 1970

[In thousands.   Data represent man-years of full-time equivalent employment by persons working for wages or salaries and by active proprietors of unincorporated businesses devoting the major portion of their time to the business]

Year	Whole-sale trade	Retail trade [1]	Hotels and other lodging places	Personal services	Miscellaneous business services	Automobile repair, services, and garages [1]	Miscellaneous repair services	Motion pictures	Amusement and recreation, except motion pictures	Medical and other health services	Legal services	Educational services	Miscellaneous professional services	Nonprofit membership organizations
	15	16	17	18	19	20	21	22	23	24	25	26	27	28
1970	3,838	11,386	799	1,452	1,627	512	324	191	523	3,359	405	1,271	850	1,387
1969	3,767	11,157	793	1,468	1,573	500	312	193	505	3,176	383	1,247	814	1,358
1968	3,647	10,730	760	1,485	1,442	492	306	186	488	2,996	371	1,210	745	1,318
1967	3,561	10,374	732	1,488	1,353	483	295	185	469	2,813	368	1,162	698	1,273
1966	3,487	10,118	722	1,482	1,255	465	304	179	448	2,654	363	1,093	662	1,218
1965	3,358	9,813	704	1,424	1,144	456	300	173	433	2,479	346	1,036	617	1,175
1964	3,252	9,483	683	1,394	1,056	446	294	169	426	2,350	338	989	590	1,128
1963	3,180	9,179	662	1,360	982	426	287	168	414	2,239	327	947	565	1,103
1962	3,141	9,132	652	1,333	928	407	279	170	401	2,128	327	902	545	1,082
1961	3,100	9,077	641	1,311	860	394	279	177	384	2,041	314	861	518	1,042
1960 *	3,090	9,209	639	1,289	810	388	265	179	370	1,968	310	823	503	1,028
1959	3,018	9,041	624	1,250	754	359	259	185	348	1,895	298	779	489	983
1958	2,966	8,902	612	1,258	678	350	265	188	331	1,807	277	743	468	948
1957	2,976	9,002	625	1,280	654	333	268	203	320	1,719	266	703	482	911
1956	2,953	8,955	621	1,248	609	322	259	213	316	1,642	262	658	456	885
1955	2,842	8,750	618	1,223	549	310	249	216	307	1,558	257	625	404	843
1954	2,795	8,541	641	1,218	500	302	240	218	296	1,484	254	588	383	801
1953	2,820	8,660	656	1,223	486	305	255	221	297	1,417	251	564	378	780
1952	2,793	8,605	638	1,230	455	308	264	228	291	1,355	246	543	354	750
1951	2,740	8,505	625	1,232	425	306	254	233	294	1,307	243	530	314	738
1950	2,605	8,178	605	1,217	395	310	232	234	296	1,239	235	519	273	713
1949	2,591	8,071	611	1,218	382	325	235	235	296	1,170	228	502	271	697
1948 [2]	2,664	8,087	636	1,241	385	340	253	234	298	1,132	217	482	275	649
1948 [3]	2,712	8,597	640	1,241	486	---------	504	234	299	1,131	217	421	160	554
1947	2,625	8,376	636	1,243	455	---------	535	237	284	1,071	212	387	144	599
1946	2,419	7,973	632	1,210	418	---------	504	236	275	983	210	364	131	572
1945	2,052	6,862	584	1,073	343	---------	399	222	232	892	195	346	112	493
1944	1,936	6,598	584	1,053	320	---------	394	221	232	895	200	344	104	479
1943	1,912	6,648	573	1,090	305	---------	378	211	234	894	211	340	110	455
1942	2,041	6,916	561	1,115	310	---------	328	200	255	878	228	335	129	448
1941	2,136	7,126	557	1,095	314	---------	320	191	256	861	245	329	103	427
1940	2,015	6,768	538	1,050	296	---------	293	181	240	841	244	324	91	390
1939	1,942	6,440	526	996	290	---------	300	179	223	813	242	318	86	328
1938	1,857	6,218	522	1,008	276	---------	314	178	212	807	236	312	82	331
1937	1,857	6,305	520	1,034	269	---------	311	184	230	785	230	304	80	332
1936	1,690	5,949	494	994	265	---------	311	171	212	750	225	297	78	342
1935	1,572	5,608	469	950	233	---------	311	155	197	711	223	293	74	338
1934	1,530	5,431	453	910	231	---------	309	141	193	695	216	287	72	339
1933	1,393	5,038	403	860	204	---------	312	124	180	679	217	286	69	335
1932	1,395	5,058	417	886	198	---------	315	128	200	691	214	289	69	341
1931	1,533	5,507	465	941	192	---------	299	147	248	725	212	292	77	354
1930	1,685	5,839	504	996	207	---------	281	153	277	749	202	291	85	358
1929	1,744	6,077	518	1,008	209	---------	264	153	295	750	194	287	83	351
1919	1,233	3,977	---------	---------	---------	---------	---------	---------	---------	---------	---------	---------	---------	---------
1909	1,034	3,177	---------	---------	---------	---------	---------	---------	---------	---------	---------	---------	---------	---------
1899	783	2,218	---------	---------	---------	---------	---------	---------	---------	---------	---------	---------	---------	---------
1889	397	1,775	---------	---------	---------	---------	---------	---------	---------	---------	---------	---------	---------	---------
1879	250	1,087	---------	---------	---------	---------	---------	---------	---------	---------	---------	---------	---------	---------
1869	169	716	---------	---------	---------	---------	---------	---------	---------	---------	---------	---------	---------	---------

* Denotes first year for which figures include Alaska and Hawaii.
[1] For 1948 and prior years, "Automobile repair, services, and garages" included with "Retail trade."

[2] Comparable with later years.
[3] Comparable with earlier years.

Series T 29–42.   Average Annual Earnings Per Full-Time Employee in Distribution and Selected Service Industries: 1929 to 1970

[In dollars]

Year	Whole-sale trade	Retail trade [1]	Hotels and other lodging places	Personal services	Miscellaneous business services	Automobile repair, services, and garages [1]	Miscellaneous repair services	Motion pictures	Amusement and recreation, except motion pictures	Medical and other health services	Legal services	Educational services	Miscellaneous professional services	Nonprofit membership organizations
	29	30	31	32	33	34	35	36	37	38	39	40	41	42
1970	9,458	5,913	4,756	5,424	7,652	6,723	8,815	7,157	6,289	5,641	7,549	5,511	9,902	5,494
1969	8,921	5,627	4,513	5,177	7,273	6,333	8,350	7,100	5,937	5,046	6,777	5,063	9,353	5,180
1968	8,391	5,358	4,244	4,919	6,921	5,865	7,784	6,814	5,642	4,579	6,140	4,718	8,752	4,794
1967	7,935	5,057	4,026	4,653	6,626	5,442	7,380	6,433	5,368	4,197	5,624	4,410	8,377	4,537
1966	7,588	4,865	3,822	4,422	6,383	5,141	6,947	6,265	5,112	3,884	5,401	4,132	7,958	4,346
1965	7,238	4,721	3,691	4,253	6,214	4,946	6,535	6,044	4,893	3,736	5,126	3,887	7,489	4,171
1964	6,983	4,574	3,610	4,120	6,072	4,808	6,350	5,538	4,763	3,641	4,994	3,684	7,205	4,035
1963	6,687	4,418	3,490	3,935	5,809	4,643	6,077	5,200	4,592	3,452	4,791	3,465	6,878	3,843
1962	6,445	4,264	3,393	3,805	5,718	4,482	5,862	5,038	4,484	3,317	4,576	3,257	6,629	3,724
1961	6,215	4,108	3,313	3,664	5,545	4,320	5,684	4,970	4,348	3,184	4,399	3,078	6,362	3,640

See footnotes at end of table.

Series T 29-42. Average Annual Earnings Per Full-Time Employee in Distribution and Selected Service Industries: 1929 to 1970—Con.

[In dollars]

Year	Whole-sale trade	Retail trade 1	Hotels and other lodging places	Personal services	Miscel-laneous business services	Automobile repair, services, and garages 1	Miscel-laneous repair services	Motion pictures	Amusement and recreation, except motion pictures	Medical and other health services	Legal services	Educational services	Miscel-laneous profes-sional services	Nonprofit member-ship organiza-tions
	29	30	31	32	33	34	35	36	37	38	39	40	41	42
1960 *	6,047	4,015	3,242	3,550	5,343	4,169	5,504	4,651	4,240	3,061	4,185	2,913	6,142	3,538
1959	5,849	3,876	3,120	3,414	5,159	4,022	5,250	4,506	4,077	2,907	4,077	2,802	5,913	3,475
1958	5,574	3,709	2,992	3,240	5,043	3,845	4,911	4,233	3,915	2,787	3,919	2,677	5,711	3,371
1957	5,403	3,592	2,904	3,122	4,904	3,772	4,741	4,073	3,631	2,660	3,794	2,599	5,501	3,239
1956	5,169	3,447	2,746	2,975	4,754	3,560	4,519	3,901	3,397	2,523	3,597	2,507	5,318	3,073
1955	4,844	3,329	2,652	2,827	4,514	3,405	4,141	3,757	3,263	2,497	3,320	2,380	4,892	3,004
1954	4,626	3,189	2,551	2,717	4,379	3,306	3,927	3,476	3,125	2,405	3,120	2,326	4,686	2,935
1953	4,465	3,079	2,454	2,609	4,193	3,235	3,924	3,265	2,950	2,338	2,951	2,265	4,574	2,801
1952	4,247	2,925	2,362	2,469	4,021	3,032	3,721	3,197	2,809	2,230	2,771	2,210	4,409	2,644
1951	4,103	2,815	2,250	2,336	3,816	2,883	3,491	3,049	2,632	2,099	2,534	2,169	4,042	2,524
1950	3,839	2,734	2,156	2,223	3,583	2,674	3,202	2,938	2,500	1,998	2,391	2,099	3,728	2,412
1949	3,623	2,612	2,107	2,158	3,369	2,553	3,180	2,933	2,473	1,912	2,286	2,056	3,577	2,319
1948	3,574	2,520	2,026	2,084	3,239	2,520	3,150	2,911	2,415	1,824	2,196	2,002	3,443	2,220
1947	3,322	2,368	1,902	1,978	3,023	---------	2,974	3,031	2,345	1,821	1,971	2,113	3,495	2,077
1946	3,021	2,141	1,745	1,854	2,861	---------	2,766	2,978	2,185	1,605	1,757	1,802	3,280	1,984
1945	2,751	1,879	1,612	1,709	2,739	---------	2,810	2,567	1,888	1,401	1,856	1,641	3,258	1,876
1944	2,600	1,709	1,455	1,570	2,584	---------	2,901	2,379	1,663	1,262	1,653	1,562	3,237	1,795
1943	2,416	1,555	1,269	1,384	2,332	---------	2,641	2,250	1,461	1,127	1,423	1,469	3,063	1,679
1942	2,177	1,395	1,097	1,196	2,072	---------	2,152	2,124	1,328	1,036	1,324	1,344	2,654	1,482
1941	1,943	1,299	1,025	1,075	1,967	---------	1,891	2,016	1,292	955	1,265	1,264	2,245	1,379
1940	1,754	1,236	997	1,042	1,889	---------	1,579	1,948	1,280	927	1,224	1,240	1,902	1,408
1939	1,698	1,224	958	1,034	1,886	---------	1,603	1,971	1,277	908	1,198	1,234	1,973	1,546
1938	1,686	1,217	946	992	1,899	---------	1,552	1,942	1,270	899	1,205	1,228	1,909	1,529
1937	1,693	1,218	941	978	1,966	---------	1,544	1,972	1,269	876	1,231	1,211	1,774	1,497
1936	1,652	1,159	897	940	1,915	---------	1,456	1,896	1,232	851	1,200	1,180	1,759	1,465
1935	1,640	1,139	878	915	1,884	---------	1,429	1,892	1,193	829	1,163	1,162	1,600	1,435
1934	1,550	1,102	863	905	1,709	---------	1,339	1,844	1,190	801	1,160	1,175	1,609	1,440
1933	1,477	1,066	816	889	1,653	---------	1,286	1,891	1,185	810	1,168	1,189	1,619	1,442
1932	1,672	1,173	908	996	1,844	---------	1,464	1,959	1,218	865	1,260	1,279	1,714	1,545
1931	1,934	1,324	1,030	1,136	2,255	---------	1,684	2,179	1,244	919	1,333	1,323	1,897	1,653
1930	2,039	1,384	1,097	1,200	2,412	---------	1,793	2,175	1,268	933	1,394	1,329	2,027	1,698
1929	2,072	1,409	1,098	1,219	2,274	---------	1,814	2,169	1,273	925	1,378	1,312	2,314	1,712

* Denotes first year for which figures include Alaska and Hawaii.

1 Prior to 1948, "Automobile repair, services, and garages" included with "Retail trade."

Series T 43-57. Distribution and Selected Services, Legal Form of Organization: 1935 to 1967

Year	Total					Corporations					All other legal forms				
	Establish-ments	Sales	Payroll, entire year	Payroll, workweek ended nearest Nov. 15	Paid em-ployees, workweek ended nearest Nov. 15	Establish-ments	Sales	Payroll, entire year	Payroll, workweek ended nearest Nov. 15	Paid em-ployees, workweek ended nearest Nov. 15	Establish-ments	Sales	Payroll, entire year	Payroll, workweek ended nearest Nov. 15	Paid em-ployees, workweek ended nearest Nov. 15
	43	44	45	46	47	48	49	50	51	52	53	54	55	56	57
	1,000	Mil. dol.	Mil. dol.	Mil. dol.	1,000	1,000	Mil. dol.	Mil. dol.	Mil. dol.	1,000	1,000	Mil. dol.	Mil. dol.	Mil. dol.	1,000
RETAIL TRADE															
1967	1,763	310,214	36,175	--------	1 9,381	451	209,153	27,068	--------	1 6,377	1,312	101,062	9,107	--------	1 3,004
1963 *	1,708	244,202	27,632	553	8,410	359	151,093	19,293	383	5,329	1,349	93,109	8,339	171	3,081
1958	1,788	199,646	21,589	413	7,911	278	106,099	13,659	258	4,438	1,511	93,547	7,930	155	3,473
1954	1,722	169,968	18,199	354	7,124	230	82,229	10,999	210	3,848	1,491	87,739	7,200	144	3,276
1948	1,770	130,521	13,568	--------	6,918	211	61,203	8,154	--------	3,617	1,559	69,317	5,414	--------	3,301
1939	1,770	42,042	4,529	--------	2 4,600	211	19,810	2,824	--------	2 2,454	1,560	22,231	1,705	--------	2 2,146
WHOLESALE TRADE															
1967	311	459,476	23,922	--------	1 3,519	200	393,997	21,098	--------	1 2,950	111	65,479	2,824	--------	1 569
1963 *	308	358,386	18,101	349	3,089	197	298,662	15,743	303	2,536	111	59,724	2,358	47	553
1958	286	284,971	13,199	269	2,797	162	225,124	10,997	222	2,180	124	59,846	2,202	47	618
1954	252	234,974	11,021	--------	2,590	128	167,647	8,477	--------	1,830	125	67,327	2,544	--------	761
1948	243	188,689	7,991	153	2,383	121	142,862	6,659	127	1,849	122	45,827	1,332	27	534
1939	201	55,266	2,624	--------	2 1,562	3 98	41,013	2,186	--------	2 1,181	103	14,253	438	--------	2 381
1935	177	42,803	2,022	--------	2 1,261	88	32,987	1,736	--------	2 1,001	88	9,816	286	--------	2 260
SELECTED SERVICES															
1967	1,188	60,542	17,524	--------	1 3,841	157	37,607	12,000	--------		1,030	22,935	5,524	--------	
1963 *	1,062	44,586	12,192	241	3,262	138	28,342	8,653	170	2,057	923	16,245	3,539	71	1,205
1958	975	32,376	9,006	167	2,889	91	17,945	5,637	103	1,581	885	14,431	3,369	64	1,308
1954 4	786	23,487	6,526	126	2,361	66	12,429	4,017	76	1,271	719	11,058	2,509	50	1,089
1948	665	13,296	4,164	81	2,100	46	6,026	2,333	44	1,042	619	7,270	1,831	37	1,057
1939	646	3,420	1,070	--------	2 1,102	28	1,283	601	--------	2 505	618	2,137	468	--------	2 597

* Denotes first year for which figures include Alaska and Hawaii.
1 Paid employees for week including March 12.
2 Average annual number of full-time and part-time employees.

3 Includes 17,530 petroleum bulk stations operated on a commission basis by operators having a proprietary interest in the business.
4 For 1954, legal form of organization data were withheld for some establishments to avoid disclosure.

Series T 58–78. Book Value of Inventories at End of Year: 1929 to 1970

[In millions of dollars. All data except series T 70–78 for 1929–1939 adjusted for seasonal variations]

Year	Retail stores									Merchant wholesale trade [2]		
	Total inventories	Durable goods stores, total [1]	Automotive group	Furniture and appliance group	Lumber, building, hardware group	Nondurable goods stores, total [1]	Apparel group	Food group	General merchandise group	Total inventories	Durable goods establishments	Nondurable goods establishments
	58	59	60	61	62	63	64	65	66	67	68	69
1970	46,555	20,490	9,021	3,451	2,809	26,065	4,467	5,188	10,163	26,604	15,565	11,039
1969	45,376	20,647	9,866	3,315	2,719	24,729	4,518	4,849	9,567	24,363	14,579	9,784
1968	41,973	19,167	8,926	3,117	2,751	22,806	4,177	4,449	8,753	22,528	13,454	9,074
1967	38,952	17,277	7,395	2,903	2,663	21,675	4,084	4,239	8,022	21,557	12,543	9,014
1966	38,073	17,258	8,041	2,813	2,635	20,815	4,009	4,057	7,673	20,691	12,112	8,579
1965	34,405	15,253	7,316	2,392	2,529	19,152	3,751	3,856	6,827	18,274	10,575	7,699
1964	31,094	13,318	5,784	2,227	2,609	17,776	3,385	3,628	6,276	16,977	9,809	7,168
1963	29,386	12,572	5,623	2,080	2,403	16,814	3,288	3,435	5,709	16,048	9,119	6,929
1962	27,941	11,798	5,013	1,935	2,359	16,143	3,326	3,281	5,395	14,936	8,631	6,305
1961 *	26,221	11,062	4,487	1,802	2,381	15,159	3,044	3,132	4,917	14,488	8,315	6,173
1960	26,813	11,923	5,015	1,987	2,408	14,890	3,323	3,171	4,278	14,120	8,121	5,999
1959	25,305	11,029	4,105	1,983	2,435	14,276	3,194	2,984	4,198	13,879	7,861	6,018
1958	24,113	10,526	3,966	1,879	2,406	13,587	2,967	2,943	3,865	12,739	7,150	5,589
1957	24,451	11,283	4,520	1,922	2,394	13,168	3,024	2,852	3,843	12,730	7,115	5,615
1956	23,402	10,495	3,727	1,957	2,388	12,907	2,912	2,719	3,834	13,260	7,074	6,186
1955	22,769	10,532	4,012	1,878	2,355	12,237	2,682	2,560	3,706	11,678	6,261	5,417
1954	20,926	9,270	3,013	1,785	2,281	11,656	2,601	2,469	3,401	10,637	5,477	5,160
1953	21,488	9,781	3,283	1,895	2,340	11,707	2,620	2,287	3,686	10,686	5,547	5,139
1952	21,031	9,491	3,033	1,905	2,400	11,540	2,489	2,196	3,736	10,210	5,312	4,898
1951	21,050	9,628	3,130	1,951	2,380	11,422	2,491	2,181	3,587	9,886	5,207	4,679
1950	19,460	8,290	2,455	1,881	2,098	11,170	2,488	2,171	3,508	9,284	4,691	4,593
1949	15,470	6,261	1,881	1,266	1,530	9,209	2,113	1,725	2,867	7,706	3,818	3,888
1948	16,007	6,572	1,992	1,483	1,532	9,435	2,126	1,780	2,855	³7,957	³3,999	³3,958
1947	14,241	5,346	1,526	1,238	1,279	8,895	1,896	1,683	2,819	7,123	3,069	4,054
1946 ³	12,062	3,851	1,000	950	888	8,211	1,615	1,573	2,621	6,203	2,521	3,682
1946 ⁴	11,852	3,949	977	938	1,056	7,903	1,567	1,596	2,603	6,583	2,595	3,988
1945	7,948	2,431	517	480	683	5,517	1,116	1,034	1,686	4,555	1,497	3,058
1944	7,640	2,243	491	422	690	5,397	1,244	969	1,596	3,912	1,148	2,764
1943	7,561	2,209	562	446	593	5,352	1,207	1,080	1,679	3,684	1,073	2,611
1942	8,023	2,752	813	570	676	5,271	1,148	1,119	1,665	3,781	1,101	2,680
1941	7,776	3,175	951	599	881	4,601	948	961	1,590	4,044	1,388	2,656
1940	6,119	2,469	772	430	709	3,650	761	687	1,340	3,238	1,110	2,128
1939	5,534	2,088	575	395	640	3,446	748	656	1,269	3,052	1,008	2,044
1938	5,276	1,977	545	377	623	3,299	717	612	1,202	2,894	940	1,954

Year	Manufacturers' total inventories	Manufacturers' durable goods industries				Manufacturers' nondurable goods industries			
		Total	Purchased materials	Goods-in-process	Finished goods	Total	Purchased materials	Goods-in-process	Finished goods
	70	71	72	73	74	75	76	77	78
1970	100,476	65,152	19,056	29,233	16,863	35,324	13,026	5,055	17,243
1969	96,673	63,160	18,678	28,963	15,519	33,513	12,583	5,135	15,795
1968	90,737	58,969	17,393	27,503	14,073	31,768	12,103	4,829	14,836
1967	84,563	54,888	16,432	24,992	13,464	29,675	11,729	4,412	13,534
1966	77,950	49,793	15,430	21,995	12,368	28,157	11,210	4,245	12,702
1965	68,221	42,227	13,299	18,152	10,776	25,994	10,488	3,823	11,683
1964	63,386	38,436	11,927	16,253	10,256	24,950	10,185	3,519	11,246
1963	60,043	35,813	11,001	14,997	9,815	24,230	10,003	3,410	10,817
1962	58,213	34,605	10,798	14,205	9,602	23,608	9,841	3,304	10,463
1961 *	54,939	32,509	10,242	13,211	9,056	22,430	9,464	3,193	9,773
1960	53,814	32,360	10,286	12,780	9,190	21,454	9,113	2,935	9,353
1959	52,707	31,839	10,585	12,952	8,143	20,868	9,089	2,928	8,857
1958	50,070	30,095	9,847	12,294	7,749	19,975	8,671	2,800	8,498
1957	51,871	31,728	10,608	12,837	8,125	20,143	8,775	2,864	8,624
1956	50,642	30,447	10,417	12,317	7,565	20,195	8,971	2,721	8,622
1955	45,069	26,405	9,194	10,756	6,348	18,664	8,556	2,571	7,666
1954	41,612	23,710	7,894	9,721	6,040	17,902	8,167	2,440	7,415
1953	43,948	25,878	8,966	10,720	6,206	18,070	8,317	2,472	7,409
1952	41,136	23,731	7,300	10,200	6,900	17,405	8,600	2,700	8,100
1951	39,306	20,991	7,400	8,600	6,800	18,315	9,100	2,700	8,200
1950	31,078	15,539	6,100	6,000	4,700	15,539	8,400	2,500	6,600
1949	26,321	13,060	4,600	4,700	4,700	13,261	6,500	2,100	6,300
1948	28,543	14,662	5,600	5,400	4,700	13,881	7,300	2,200	6,500
1947	25,897	13,061	5,100	5,200	4,000	12,836	7,200	2,200	5,200
1946	24,457	11,997	4,500	4,600	2,900	12,460	6,500	1,800	4,200
1945	18,390	8,767	3,200	3,500	2,100	9,623	4,900	1,500	3,200
1944	19,507	10,433	3,300	5,000	2,100	9,074	4,700	1,400	3,000
1943	20,098	11,175	3,900	5,200	2,100	8,923	4,500	1,400	3,000
1942	19,287	10,441	3,700	4,600	2,200	8,846	4,300	1,200	3,300
1941	16,960	8,601	3,100	3,200	2,300	8,359	4,000	1,200	3,200
1940	12,819	6,304	2,100	2,000	2,200	6,515	2,600	900	3,000
1939	11,465	5,334	1,800	1,500	2,100	6,131	2,400	800	2,900
1938 ³	10,750	5,019	---	---	---	5,731	---	---	---
1938 ⁴	10,803	5,017	---	---	---	5,786	---	---	---
1937	12,071	5,693	---	---	---	6,378	---	---	---
1936	10,731	4,813	---	---	---	5,918	---	---	---
1935	9,145	4,052	---	---	---	5,093	---	---	---
1934	8,764	3,741	---	---	---	5,023	---	---	---
1933	8,189	3,533	---	---	---	4,656	---	---	---
1932	7,369	3,375	---	---	---	3,994	---	---	---
1931	9,151	4,241	---	---	---	4,910	---	---	---
1930	11,321	5,300	---	---	---	6,021	---	---	---
1929	12,839	5,919	---	---	---	6,920	---	---	---

* Denotes first year for which figures include Alaska and Hawaii.
[1] Includes kinds of business, not shown separately.
[2] Data prior to 1947 include estimates for nonmerchant wholesalers and are not comparable with data for later years.
[3] Comparable with later years; see text. 1948 data comparable with earlier years are (in millions of dollars): Series 67, 7,879; series 68, 3,683; series 69, 4,186.
[4] Comparable with earlier years; see text.

Series T 79–196. Retail Establishments, Sales, and Persons Engaged, by Kind of Business: 1929 to 1967

	All establishments			Establishments with payroll						Establishments of multiunit firms			Active proprietors of unincorporated businesses
		Sales				Payroll			Paid employees, workweek ended nearest Nov. 15		Sales		
Year	Number	Amount (mil. dol.)	Per capita	Number	Sales	Entire year		Workweek ended nearest Nov. 15 (mil. dol.)		Number	Amount (mil. dol.)	Percent of total retail	
						Amount (mil. dol.)	Percent of sales						
	79	80	81	82	83	84	85	86	87	88	89	90	91
1967	1,763,324	310,214	1,557	1,191,546	295,170	36,175	12.3	------	¹9,380,616	220,142	123,505	39.8	1,624,451
1963 *	1,707,931	244,202	1,294	1,206,087	233,085	27,632	11.9	553	8,410,199	219,783	89,455	36.6	1,545,999
1958	1,788,325	199,646	1,152	1,180,641	187,090	21,589	11.5	413	7,911,081	182,735	67,209	33.7	1,818,666
1954	1,721,650	169,968	1,054	1,124,040	157,933	18,199	11.5	354	7,124,331	167,027	51,187	30.1	1,765,752
1948 ²	1,688,479	128,849	882	1,118,692	118,352	(NA)	(NA)	------	(NA)	(NA)	(NA)	(NA)	
1948 ³	1,769,540	130,521	866	1,100,223	119,379	13,568	11.4	------	6,918,061	162,655	38,691	29.6	1,742,046
1939	1,770,355	42,042	321	1,017,062	38,190	4,529	11.9	------	4,821,806	123,195	9,106	21.7	1,613,673
1935	1,587,196	32,791	258	------	------	3,568		------	⁴3,898,258	131,430	7,653	23.3	1,440,108
1933	1,526,119	25,037	199	------	------	2,910		------	⁴2,703,325	(NA)	(NA)	(NA)	1,574,341
1929	1,476,365	48,330	396	------	------	5,044		------	⁴4,286,516	151,712	9,965	20.3	1,434,704

	Food group											
	Total ⁵			Grocery stores			Meat markets			Fruit stores, vegetable markets		
Year	Number	Sales (mil. dol.)	Persons engaged	Number	Sales (mil. dol.)	Persons engaged	Number	Sales (mil. dol.)	Persons engaged	Number	Sales (mil. dol.)	Persons engaged
	92	93	94	95	96	97	98	99	100	101	102	103
ALL ESTABLISHMENTS												
1967	294,243	70,251	1,723,306	218,130	65,074	1,446,094	⁶17,943	⁶1,831	⁶59,645	8,890	448	19,088
1963 *	319,433	57,079	1,579,759	244,838	52,566	1,315,615	16,457	1,530	50,274	8,874	412	19,347
1958	355,508	49,022	1,563,691	259,796	43,696	1,251,229	23,844	2,327	83,820	12,689	505	27,385
1954	384,616	39,762	1,439,397	287,572	34,901	1,132,789	22,896	1,944	71,836	13,136	484	27,691
1948 ²	460,913	29,207	1,515,618	350,754	24,730	1,066,748	23,920	1,641	66,427	13,482	394	32,273
1948 ³	504,439	30,965	1,515,618	377,939	24,770	1,066,748	24,242	1,641	66,427	15,763	399	32,273
1939 ²	560,549	10,165	1,331,722	387,337	7,722	905,015	35,630	700	85,485	27,666	222	48,564
1939 ³	560,549	10,165	1,315,438	387,337	7,722	891,983	35,630	700	83,684	27,666	222	48,357
1935	532,010	8,362	1,235,069	354,971	6,352	844,483	32,555	565	77,236	32,632	216	56,463
1933	470,149	6,776	1,170,291	303,910	5,004	624,337	(NA)	(NA)	(NA)	21,897	170	43,419
1929	481,891	10,837	1,174,665	307,425	7,353	719,765	43,788	1,253	113,407	22,904	308	46,277
ESTABLISHMENTS WITH PAYROLL												
1967	171,700	66,041	------	128,675	61,771	------	9,243	1,383	------	3,222	324	------
1963 *	178,170	53,028	------	132,129	49,187	------	10,483	1,314	------	3,638	304	------
1958	190,074	44,978	------	138,176	40,425	------	16,810	2,097	------	4,323	350	------
1954	200,468	35,233	------	148,028	31,280	------	14,984	1,697	------	4,648	331	------
1948	232,532	24,375	------	168,131	20,699	------	------	------	------	------	------	------

	Food group—Con.						Eating places			Drinking places		
	Candy, nut, confectionery stores			Bakery products stores			Number	Sales (mil. dol.)	Persons engaged	Number	Sales (mil. dol.)	Persons engaged
Year	Number	Sales (mil. dol.)	Persons engaged	Number	Sales (mil. dol.)	Persons engaged						
	104	105	106	107	108	109	110	111	112	113	114	115
ALL ESTABLISHMENTS												
1967	13,981	541	34,252	19,598	1,340	116,377	236,563	18,879	1,969,462	111,327	4,964	410,048
1963 *	14,979	499	34,233	18,631	1,080	110,882	223,876	13,919	1,705,797	110,605	4,493	381,954
1958	17,593	528	41,380	19,235	905	104,017	229,815	11,038	1,570,189	114,925	4,164	388,334
1954	20,507	568	46,892	19,034	862	104,929	195,128	8,731	1,280,398	123,887	4,360	438,559
1948 ²	27,165	586	75,021	19,500	722	103,415	179,185	6,440	1,175,331	146,604	4,204	533,899
1948 ³	32,876	649	75,021	20,152	725	103,415	194,123	6,468	1,175,331	152,433	4,215	533,899
1939 ²	48,015	295	77,170	16,985	168	43,217	169,792	2,135	777,884	135,594	1,385	358,398
1939 ³	48,015	295	76,353	16,985	168	41,225	169,792	2,135	764,650	135,594	1,385	348,452
1935	55,197	314	91,164	14,150	99	28,939	153,468	1,666	652,334	98,005	724	252,167
1933	54,243	271	91,237	19,380	188	63,563	170,434	1,324	606,600	29,901	105	54,798
1929	63,265	571	127,311	12,013	201	41,907	134,293	2,124	615,385	------	------	------
ESTABLISHMENTS WITH PAYROLL												
1967	6,284	369	------	15,711	1,249	------	189,418	17,955	------	81,764	4,263	------
1963 *	7,121	337	------	15,877	1,030	------	180,874	13,329	------	83,067	4,001	------
1958	6,147	316	------	14,483	826	------	172,701	10,220	------	82,223	3,577	------
1954	7,777	351	------	15,102	802	------	149,996	8,142	------	94,413	3,878	------
1948	------	------	------	------	------	------	141,163	5,982	------	104,316	3,626	------

See footnotes at end of table.

Series T 79–196. Retail Establishments, Sales, and Persons Engaged, by Kind of Business: 1929 to 1967—Con.

Year	General merchandise group stores			Department stores			Variety stores			Apparel group — Total [5]			Shoe stores		
	Number	Sales (mil. dol.)	Persons engaged	Number	Sales (mil. dol.)	Persons engaged	Number	Sales (mil. dol.)	Persons engaged	Number	Sales (mil. dol.)	Persons engaged	Number	Sales (mil. dol.)	Persons engaged
	116	117	118	119	120	121	122	123	124	125	126	127	128	129	130
ALL ESTABLISHMENTS															
1967	67,307	43,537	1,696,237	5,792	32,344	1,175,402	21,046	5,407	297,346	110,164	16,672	741,706	(NA)	(NA)	(NA)
1963 *	62,063	30,003	1,513,314	4,251	20,537	970,956	22,378	4,538	325,265	116,223	14,040	718,771	24,568	2,390	105,945
1958	86,644	21,879	1,406,092	3,157	13,359	807,898	21,017	3,621	340,422	118,759	12,525	749,614	24,437	2,130	111,153
1954	76,198	17,872	1,342,824	2,761	10,558	735,138	20,917	3,066	347,997	119,743	11,078	707,702	23,847	1,895	101,843
1948 [2]	70,807	15,796	1,391,319	2,558	9,432	843,740	18,917	2,504	345,812	110,944	9,716	685,156	19,201	1,460	87,203
1948 [3]	52,544	15,975	1,391,319	2,580	10,645	843,740	20,210	2,506	345,812	115,246	9,803	685,156	19,551	1,467	87,203
1939 [2]	50,267	5,665	1,002,246	4,074	3,975	637,749	16,946	976	239,341	106,959	3,258	499,725	20,487	617	78,262
1939 [3]	50,267	5,665	903,369	4,074	3,975	566,612	16,946	976	221,658	106,959	3,258	471,066	20,487	617	76,151
1935	44,651	4,620	761,355	4,201	3,311	492,846	11,741	780	177,221	95,968	2,656	401,043	18,967	511	68,799
1933	49,712	3,891	570,157	3,544	2,545	365,936	12,046	678	163,002	86,548	1,923	341,202	18,836	424	63,193
1929	54,636	6,444	862,758	4,221	4,350	543,836	12,110	904	167,058	114,296	4,240	494,524	24,259	806	83,355
ESTABLISHMENTS WITH PAYROLL															
1967	51,770	43,127	----------	5,792	32,344	----------	19,028	5,348	----------	91,430	16,223	----------	21,110	2,917	----------
1963 *	51,417	29,786	----------	4,251	20,537	----------	20,176	4,501	----------	96,015	13,650	----------	21,450	2,319	----------
1958	49,698	21,085	----------	3,157	13,359	----------	18,139	3,565	----------	97,664	12,168	----------	20,143	2,042	----------
1954	50,554	17,327	----------	2,761	10,558	----------	17,639	3,014	----------	97,829	10,701	----------	19,723	1,817	----------
1948	48,758	15,418	----------			----------			----------	85,163	9,306	----------	15,248	1,390	----------

Year	Apparel group—Con. — Women's ready-to-wear			Furniture, homefurnishings, appliance group — Total [5]			Furniture stores			Household appliance, radio, TV		
	Number	Sales (mil. dol.)	Persons engaged	Number	Sales (mil. dol.)	Persons engaged	Number	Sales (mil. dol.)	Persons engaged	Number	Sales (mil. dol.)	Persons engaged
	131	132	133	134	135	136	137	138	139	140	141	142
ALL ESTABLISHMENTS												
1967	31,883	5,380	261,224	98,826	14,542	487,372	33,274	6,564	205,610	[7] 43,619	[7] 6,017	[7] 191,150
1963 *	29,696	4,428	249,278	93,649	10,926	428,883	37,216	5,317	199,510	30,685	3,385	126,693
1958	(NA)	(NA)	(NA)	103,417	10,074	489,654	36,096	4,783	217,214	40,985	3,499	169,810
1954	(NA)	(NA)	(NA)	91,797	8,619	440,362	(NA)	(NA)	(NA)	40,542	3,237	163,186
1948 [2]	29,788	3,277	255,426	80,423	6,592	456,186	28,465	3,413	190,551	35,331	2,410	165,307
1948 [3]	30,677	3,305	255,426	85,585	6,914	456,186	29,031	3,427	190,551	36,931	2,543	165,307
1939 [2]	25,820	1,009	164,696	52,827	1,733	263,441	[8] 19,902	[8] 973	[8] 125,607	20,913	533	89,651
1939 [3]	25,820	1,009	154,297	52,827	1,733	256,126	[8] 19,902	[8] 973	[8] 121,512	20,913	533	88,342
1935	21,975	795	124,537	45,215	1,289	209,795	[8] 17,043	[8] 694	[8] 92,760	18,396	438	84,006
1933	17,759	568	99,702	42,976	958	197,663	[8] 17,418	[8] 553	[8] 93,419	17,922	312	79,446
1929	18,253	1,087	131,116	58,941	2,754	319,212	25,854	1,578	159,624	25,366	950	129,877
ESTABLISHMENTS WITH PAYROLL												
1967	27,792	5,288	----------	71,264	13,824	----------	27,375	6,355	----------	25,384	4,796	----------
1963 *	26,066	4,364	----------	69,393	10,474	----------	26,982	5,125	----------	24,793	3,267	----------
1958	26,559	4,009	----------	72,929	9,544	----------	28,342	4,634	----------	28,189	3,276	----------
1954	26,893	3,577	----------	65,773	8,151	----------	25,475	4,170	----------	27,774	3,003	----------
1948			----------	60,275	6,212	----------			----------			----------

Year	Total, automotive group [5]			Passenger car dealers, franchised			Passenger car dealers, nonfranchised			Tire, battery, accessory dealers			Gasoline service stations		
	Number	Sales (mil. dol.)	Persons engaged	Number	Sales (mil. dol.)	Persons engaged	Number	Sales (mil. dol.)	Persons engaged	Number	Sales (mil. dol.)	Persons engaged	Number	Sales (mil. dol.)	Persons engaged
	143	144	145	146	147	148	149	150	151	152	153	154	155	156	157
ALL ESTABLISHMENTS															
1967	105,500	55,631	992,368	[9] 62,023	[9] 48,636	[9] 785,868	(9)	(9)	(9)	29,189	4,236	158,799	216,059	22,709	800,331
1963 *	98,514	45,376	871,525	33,349	37,375	630,817	27,984	3,087	72,857	25,899	3,336	131,141	211,473	17,760	732,542
1958	93,656	31,808	803,872	38,555	25,326	593,996	25,331	2,983	72,332	20,912	2,425	108,701	206,302	14,178	699,472
1954	85,953	29,915	788,246	41,407	25,108	623,740	20,140	2,423	56,552	18,845	1,814	91,292	181,747	10,743	558,449
1948 [2]	85,285	20,100	711,200	43,960	15,951	556,668	16,634	2,440	49,841	20,224	1,358	90,384	179,647	6,470	482,486
1948 [3]	86,162	20,104	711,200	43,999	15,952	556,668	16,874	2,441	49,841	20,628	1,359	90,384	188,253	6,483	482,486
1939 [2]	60,132	5,548	451,404	33,609	4,810	353,757	6,980	193	20,552	18,525	523	74,224	241,858	2,822	478,075
1939 [3]	60,132	5,548	440,536	33,609	4,810	345,771	6,980	193	19,789	18,525	523	72,025	241,858	2,822	467,002
1935	50,459	4,236	356,374	30,294	3,725	282,638	4,751	122	14,603	14,343	373	56,135	197,568	1,967	383,623
1933	48,545	2,367	285,817	[9] 30,646	[9] 2,127	[9] 237,185	(9)	(9)	(9)	16,027	226	44,510	170,404	1,531	328,263
1929	69,379	7,043	477,510	42,204	6,266	386,356	3,097	140	10,867	22,313	599	75,147	121,513	1,787	245,278
ESTABLISHMENTS WITH PAYROLL															
1967	76,887	54,597	----------	32,898	45,480	----------	11,502	2,433	----------	22,521	4,044	----------	165,190	20,589	----------
1963 *	75,538	44,686	----------	33,145	37,362	----------	13,401	2,622	----------	21,896	3,245	----------	165,863	16,354	----------
1958	71,464	31,213	----------	36,869	25,277	----------	13,199	2,633	----------	15,992	2,323	----------	149,004	12,640	----------
1954	68,573	29,351	----------	39,465	25,007	----------	11,362	2,115	----------	14,451	1,723	----------	120,855	9,292	----------
1948	72,655	19,565	----------			----------			----------			----------	112,372	5,310	----------

See footnotes at end of table.

Series T 79–196. Retail Establishments, Sales, and Persons Engaged, by Kind of Business: 1929 to 1967—Con.

Lumber, building, hardware group

Year	Total[5] Number	Sales (mil. dol.)	Persons engaged	Lumber, building materials dealers Number	Sales (mil. dol.)	Persons engaged	Hardware stores Number	Sales (mil. dol.)	Persons engaged	Farm equipment dealers Number	Sales (mil. dol.)	Persons engaged
	158	159	160	161	162	163	164	165	166	167	168	169
ALL ESTABLISHMENTS												
1967	86,373	17,200	476,186	(NA)	(NA)	(NA)	27,162	2,813	108,028	16,739	4,832	103,869
1963 *	92,703	14,606	473,759	28,979	7,023	205,927	29,595	2,560	114,058	16,362	3,626	92,437
1958	108,248	14,309	544,677	34,867	7,123	237,717	34,670	2,717	136,249	19,008	3,186	100,864
1954	100,519	13,123	540,326	30,177	6,502	232,329	34,858	2,694	143,323	18,689	2,804	99,825
1948 [2]	97,342	11,143	566,626	25,978	5,126	227,722	34,009	2,491	149,182	17,509	2,386	94,182
1948 [3]	98,938	11,151	566,626	26,110	5,127	227,722	34,674	2,493	149,182	17,615	2,386	94,182
1939 [2]	79,313	2,734	323,396	25,067	1,478	152,959	29,147	629	86,707	10,499	344	35,831
1939 [3]	79,313	2,734	318,051	25,067	1,478	149,275	29,147	629	85,471	10,499	344	36,646
1935	73,186	1,864	253,829	21,149	866	101,677	26,996	467	72,130	9,637	291	31,879
1933	76,098	1,342	261,249	21,015	603	97,488	22,844	311	60,886	9,958	177	28,953
1929	90,386	3,845	405,836	26,377	1,981	164,571	25,330	706	81,277	12,242	518	43,443
ESTABLISHMENTS WITH PAYROLL												
1967	69,015	16,644	---------	24,296	7,864	---------	19,339	2,556	---------	13,342	4,708	---------
1963 *	74,803	14,183	---------	25,655	6,942	---------	22,189	2,377	---------	13,974	3,563	---------
1958	80,644	13,736	---------	27,539	6,980	---------	24,522	2,482	---------	16,028	3,115	---------
1954	78,507	12,642	---------	25,429	6,395	---------	25,266	2,478	---------	16,399	2,744	---------
1948	79,899	10,767	---------							15,944	2,332	---------

Year	Drug and proprietary stores Number	Sales (mil. dol.)	Persons engaged	Liquor stores Number	Sales (mil. dol.)	Persons engaged	Fuel, ice dealers Number	Sales (mil. dol.)	Persons engaged	Hay, grain, feed stores Number	Sales (mil. dol.)	Persons engaged
	170	171	172	173	174	175	176	177	178	179	180	181
ALL ESTABLISHMENTS												
1967	53,722	10,930	450,367	39,719	6,663	136,509	22,258	3,598	117,578	(NA)	(NA)	(NA)
1963 *	54,732	8,487	405,798	40,188	5,189	129,256	24,956	3,401	120,891	13,926	3,340	65,550
1958	56,232	6,779	400,754	37,068	4,202	115,659	28,559	3,473	135,003	16,782	3,117	71,669
1954	56,009	5,251	354,261	31,240	3,180	85,244	27,070	2,842	121,292	16,530	3,455	75,725
1948 [2]	55,282	4,011	334,716	32,949	2,578	82,041	21,473	2,425	127,215	17,970	2,796	75,374
1948 [3]	55,796	4,013	334,716	33,422	2,579	82,041	22,670	2,424	127,215	18,213	2,790	75,374
1939 [2]	57,903	1,562	241,969	19,136	586	40,735	41,172	1,013	149,094	16,772	624	50,321
1939 [3]	57,903	1,562	239,076	19,136	586	39,346	41,172	1,013	142,694	16,772	624	49,304
1935	56,697	1,232	207,493	12,105	328	25,234	35,293	859	123,199	11,132	346	28,376
1933	58,407	1,066	205,300	3,767	16	5,806	[10] 23,875	[10] 623	[10] 104,858	(NA)	(NA)	(NA)
1929	58,258	1,690	233,210	---------	---------	---------	[10] 19,113	[10] 1,013	[10] 109,191	21,394	990	66,072
ESTABLISHMENTS WITH PAYROLL												
1967	49,079	10,713	---------	31,039	6,209	---------	16,596	3,447	---------	11,625	3,845	---------
1963 *	50,952	8,381	---------	31,860	4,837	---------	17,816	3,252	---------	11,264	3,259	---------
1958	50,792	6,641	---------	28,040	3,888	---------	18,557	3,273	---------	13,512	3,030	---------
1954	49,489	5,103	---------	21,926	2,853	---------	16,986	2,668	---------	13,196	3,345	---------
1948	47,628	3,832	---------	21,282	2,201	---------	17,855	2,350	---------			

Year	Jewelry stores Number	Sales (mil. dol.)	Persons engaged	Cigar stores and stands Number	Sales (mil. dol.)	Persons engaged	Florists Number	Sales (mil. dol.)	Persons engaged	Gift, novelty, souvenir stores Number	Sales (mil. dol.)	Persons engaged	Secondhand stores Number	Sales (mil. dol.)	Persons engaged
	182	183	184	185	186	187	188	189	190	191	192	193	194	195	196
ALL ESTABLISHMENTS															
1967	23,689	2,207	88,186	5,560	352	13,869	22,451	1,102	80,705	(NA)	(NA)	(NA)	(NA)	(NA)	(NA)
1963 *	20,935	1,560	79,275	4,899	275	12,551	19,801	780	63,865	12,606	397	31,860	19,862	782	56,688
1958	23,751	1,495	91,405	5,336	233	12,801	19,176	638	60,601	13,987	389	34,115	16,737	551	47,041
1954	24,266	1,407	90,908	6,068	233	14,255	16,279	495	50,111	12,149	283	27,538	14,364	424	41,041
1948 [2]	20,550	1,209	89,322	12,791	385	30,658	13,565	375	46,459	10,266	185	26,938	13,387	298	37,917
1948 [3]	21,269	1,224	89,322	14,526	535	30,658	14,749	377	46,459	12,516	195	26,938	16,969	304	37,917
1939 [2]	14,559	361	50,686	18,504	207	31,197	16,055	148	38,635	7,429	53	13,665	23,962	138	48,146
1939 [3]	14,559	361	48,326	18,504	207	31,173	16,055	148	39,202	7,429	53	13,544	23,962	138	46,814
1935	12,447	234	36,805	15,350	183	28,828	11,242	98	28,296	5,512	31	9,655	22,550	113	43,543
1933	14,313	175	38,197	20,175	189	39,417	7,728	66	21,297	(NA)	(NA)	(NA)	20,869	105	45,305
1929	19,998	536	62,853	33,248	410	67,377	9,328	176	37,889	5,186	61	13,771	15,065	148	33,516
ESTABLISHMENTS WITH PAYROLL															
1967	14,626	2,018	--------	2,852	282	--------	14,587	972	--------	7,501	487	--------	10,162	676	--------
1963 *	14,265	1,452	--------	2,953	225	--------	13,265	692	--------	6,798	328	--------	11,882	691	--------
1958	15,223	1,367	--------	2,680	175	--------	11,662	534	--------	7,179	306	--------	9,667	473	--------
1954	15,548	1,287	--------	3,270	181	--------	10,247	421	--------	6,063	216	--------	7,956	359	--------
1948	14,583	1,128	--------												

* Denotes first year for which figures include Alaska and Hawaii.
NA Not available.   [1] For 1967, paid employees for week including March 12.
[2] Comparable with later years.   [3] Comparable with earlier years.
[4] Average annual number of full-time and part-time employees for year; comparable figure for 1939 is 4,600,217.

[5] Totals include subclasses not shown separately.
[6] Figures include fish (sea food) markets. Separate figures not available.
[7] Includes music stores.   [8] Excludes interior decorators.
[9] Nonfranchised dealers combined with franchised dealers.
[10] Excludes fuel oil dealers.

Series T 197–219. Retail Sales of Stores of Multiunit Retail Firms, by Kind of Business: 1929 to 1970

[In millions of dollars]

Year	All stores	Total sales [1]	Automotive group		Furniture, appliance group		Lumber, building, hardware group		Total sales [1]	Apparel group					Drug and proprietary stores	Eating and drinking places
			Motor vehicle, other automotive dealers	Tire, battery, accessory dealers	Furniture, home-furnishings stores	Household appliance, radio stores	Total	Lumber, building materials dealers		Total [1]	Men's and boys' wear stores [2]	Women's apparel, accessory stores [3]	Family and other apparel stores	Shoe stores		
	197	198	199	200	201	202	203	204	205	206	207	208	209	210	211	212
FIRMS WITH 11 OR MORE STORES																
1970[4]	117,245	8,617	--------	1,827	1,508		--------	--------	108,628	5,475	819	1,875	--------	1,473	4,358	2,859
1970[5]	110,848	5,750	--------	1,747	1,281		--------	--------	105,098	6,191	852	2,250	--------	1,712	4,307	2,683
1969	103,070	5,892	--------	1,816	1,354		--------	--------	97,178	5,921	905	2,090	--------	1,598	3,777	2,487
1968[6]	94,194	5,415	--------	1,736	1,303		--------	--------	88,779	5,186	767	1,837	--------	1,335	3,373	2,122
1967	85,203	6,184	--------	1,529	1,362		--------	--------	79,019	5,069	612	1,855	--------	1,367	3,120	2,554
1966	80,323	5,979	--------	1,472	1,276		--------	--------	74,344	4,770	573	1,779	--------	1,269	2,663	2,222
1965	73,356	5,506	--------	1,312	1,193		--------	--------	67,850	4,445	557	1,656	--------	1,168	2,300	1,891
1964[7]	68,306	5,320	--------	1,242	1,126		--------	--------	62,986	4,287	531	1,622	--------	1,155	2,029	1,677
1964[8]	63,191	5,032	--------	1,196	1,246		--------	--------	58,159	4,145	387	1,757	--------	1,142	1,896	1,446
1963	58,280	4,469	--------	1,098	1,115		--------	--------	53,811	3,796	355	1,607	--------	1,054	1,728	1,253
1962	55,576	4,271	--------	1,087	1,070		--------	--------	51,305	3,683	351	1,490	--------	1,082	1,640	1,202
1961	52,531	4,013	--------	1,001	1,050		--------	--------	48,518	3,567	357	1,442	--------	1,030	1,526	1,141
1960[9]*	50,681	3,985	--------	990	999		--------	--------	46,696	3,515	348	1,414	--------	1,025	1,452	1,115
1960[10]*	48,603	3,960	--------	980	970		(11)	(11)	44,643	3,144	228	1,337	(11)	992	1,309	999
1959	46,673	3,365	--------	973	965		1,192	825	43,308	3,046	231	1,302	578	935	1,223	950
1958	43,853	3,146	--------	867	957		1,098	765	40,707	2,805	223	1,198	532	852	1,118	871
1957	41,900	3,031	--------	815	924		1,053	723	38,868	2,696	232	1,141	523	800	1,032	868
1956[12]	39,754	3,097	--------	763	953		1,131	810	36,657	2,616	219	1,093	534	770	943	821
1956[13]	36,291	2,836	--------	732	784		1,316	818	33,455	2,249	175	863	433	788	836	756
1955	33,918	2,790	--------	700	347	366	1,300	838	31,128	2,166	186	852	404	724	785	707
1954	31,690	2,582	--------	609	346	378	1,178	750	29,108	2,041	187	794	385	675	760	662
1953	30,929	2,580	--------	636	321	390	1,155	728	28,349	2,079	205	821	402	651	759	671
1952	30,120	2,605	--------	611	317	383	1,224	785	27,515	2,068	214	834	378	642	737	622
1951	28,536	2,521	(11)	568	287	392	1,208	798	26,015	2,009	215	786	356	652	722	590
FIRMS WITH 4 OR MORE STORES																
1951	34,000	3,825	389	575	569	572	1,582	1,147	30,175	2,763	342	1,137	539	745	905	779
1950	31,232	3,863	408	551	592	622	1,561	1,147	27,369	2,588	338	1,042	512	696	852	724
1949	29,041	3,240	331	448	519	482	1,336	957	25,801	2,588	342	1,049	517	680	847	721
1948	29,737	3,407	287	454	562	465	1,505	1,107	26,330	2,729	366	1,117	548	698	869	742
1947	26,958	3,100	262	437	533	417	1,315	962	23,858	2,566	385	1,012	483	686	864	714
1946	22,514	2,510	191	467	436	281	998	715	20,004	2,434	355	1,013	425	641	830	676
1945	17,280	1,627	96	295	277	112	739	565	15,653	2,090	272	968	329	521	704	593
1944	16,234	1,416	91	270	240	81	636	500	14,818	1,957	264	923	286	484	681	558
1943	14,926	1,316	82	254	224	71	589	478	13,610	1,791	241	843	232	475	654	518
1942	14,376	1,291	79	236	211	101	588	486	13,085	1,594	237	668	182	507	571	439
1941	12,635	1,465	200	293	226	134	552	480	11,170	1,280	229	504	135	412	479	374
1940	10,500	1,157	165	241	175	104	427	385	9,343	1,062	182	428	97	355	425	330
1939	9,570	1,024	136	236	151	88	375	350	8,546	992	173	394	80	345	400	304
1938	8,872	931	115	221	126	77	362	339	7,941	913	156	349	76	332	377	288
1937	9,426	1,065	182	225	150	93	381	357	8,361	989	177	371	90	351	378	290
1936	8,960	986	190	208	127	81	351	330	7,974	913	174	326	90	323	352	270
1935	8,040	813	168	187	97	65	274	256	7,227	758	141	260	78	279	317	248
1933	6,618	528	115	76	86	60	180	162	6,090	589	112	214	41	222	267	182
1929	10,412	1,683	624	122	235	157	509	488	8,729	1,197	271	413	144	369	312	299

See footnotes at end of table.

Series T 197–219. Retail Sales of Stores of Multiunit Retail Firms, by Kind of Business: 1929 to 1970—Con.

[In millions of dollars]

FIRMS WITH 11 OR MORE STORES

Year	Food group Total	Grocery stores	Gasoline service stations	General merchandise group Total [1]	Department stores, excl. mail order	Mail order (catalog sales)	Variety stores
	213	214	215	216	217	218	219
1970 [4]	44,072	43,183	--------	46,102	31,893	--------	5,417
1970 [5]	40,965	40,557	--------	45,302	31,105	--------	5,627
1969	37,619	37,163	--------	41,997	28,934	--------	5,232
1968 [6]	34,707	34,295	--------	38,395	26,184	--------	4,821
1967	32,241	31,150	--------	30,953	20,984	--------	5,029
1966	30,940	29,906	--------	28,988	19,653	--------	4,593
1965	28,598	27,627	--------	26,112	17,593	--------	4,096
1964 [7]	27,081	26,198	--------	23,645	15,807	--------	3,770
1964 [8]	25,634	24,903	--------	21,375	13,361	--------	3,928
1963	24,357	23,692	--------	19,018	11,817	--------	3,542
1962	23,695	23,046	--------	17,568	10,751	--------	3,404
1961	22,774	22,119	--------	16,249	9,875	--------	3,147
1960 [9]*	22,076	21,424	--------	15,478	9,374	--------	3,018
1960 [10]*	21,472	20,602	--------	14,991	8,839	--------	3,053
1959	20,368	19,502	--------	14,521	8,607	--------	2,977
1958	19,461	18,590	--------	13,414	7,939	--------	2,779
1957	18,221	17,377	([11])	13,092	7,790	--------	2,668
1956 [12]	16,636	15,895	732	12,805	7,630	([11])	2,619
1956 [13]	16,546	15,454	625	10,341	4,918	1,306	2,613
1955	15,250	14,223	561	9,726	4,575	1,233	2,508
1954	14,345	13,359	538	8,862	4,092	1,130	2,357
1953	13,392	12,404	498	8,962	4,058	1,233	2,350
1952	12,552	11,606	474	8,916	4,002	1,254	2,322
1951	11,705	10,718	478	8,575	3,820	1,220	2,233

FIRMS WITH 4 OR MORE STORES

Year	Food group Total	Grocery stores	Gasoline service stations	General merchandise group Total [1]	Department stores, excl. mail order	Mail order (catalog sales)	Variety stores
	213	214	215	216	217	218	219
1951	12,921	11,569	609	9,950	6,149	1,284	2,326
1950	11,344	10,140	548	9,300	5,743	1,235	2,143
1949	10,636	9,468	505	8,560	5,159	1,156	2,077
1948	10,493	9,319	470	8,930	5,373	1,301	2,077
1947	9,418	8,284	416	7,916	4,636	1,171	1,937
1946	7,259	6,192	357	6,713	3,788	959	1,812
1945	5,614	4,705	271	4,925	2,630	608	1,559
1944	5,499	4,657	241	4,621	2,380	609	1,510
1943	5,111	4,318	234	4,222	2,125	581	1,406
1942	5,211	4,520	285	4,094	2,050	628	1,325
1941	4,328	3,729	331	3,666	1,828	621	1,147
1940	3,635	3,106	294	2,978	1,421	491	1,008
1939	3,340	2,833	288	2,693	1,226	464	952
1938	3,110	2,618	316	2,448	1,075	424	900
1937	3,170	2,643	375	2,590	1,155	467	917
1936	3,083	2,608	403	2,428	1,060	445	878
1935	2,916	2,468	423	2,124	898	386	801
1933	2,594	2,209	544	1,589	673	220	696
1929	3,475	2,833	605	2,275	1,013	447	815

* Denotes first year for which figures include Alaska and Hawaii.
[1] Includes data for kinds of business not shown separately.
[2] Includes men's and boys' clothing and furnishings stores, and custom tailors.
[3] Includes women's ready-to-wear; other apparel, accessory, specialty shops; and furriers.
[4] New basis; adjusted to reflect the classification, definition, and distribution of firms by size according to the 1967 Census of Business.
[5] Old basis; based on the 1963 Census of Business.
[6] Data for series T 198–219 not comparable with previous years because of industry classification changes, and the shift of "nonstore" operations into the general merchandise group.
[7] New basis; adjusted to reflect the classification, definition, and distribution of firms by size according to the 1963 Census of Business.
[8] Old basis; based on the 1958 Census of Business.
[9] New basis; adjusted to reflect the classification, definition, and distribution of firms by size according to the 1958 Census of Business.
[10] Old basis; based on the 1954 Census of Business.
[11] No longer available separately; included in total for group
[12] New basis; adjusted to reflect the classification, definition, and distribution of firms by size according to the 1954 Census of Business.
[13] Old basis; based on the 1948 Census of Business.

Series T 220–224. Chains and Chain Stores: 1872 to 1928

Year	26 lines of merchandise	Grocery	Drug	Shoes	Ready-to-wear
	220	221	222	223	224
1928	1,718	315	179	220	294
1927	1,689	335	175	206	281
1926	1,565	310	166	182	258
1925	1,440	301	162	167	231
1924	1,267	270	150	146	201
1923	1,164	249	145	128	184
1922	1,056	232	131	114	165
1921	905	198	117	95	137
1920	808	180	107	79	125
1919	733	168	101	63	110
1918	645	148	89	46	104
1917	607	135	86	44	96
1916	557	125	80	40	87
1915	505	112	81	38	73
1914	450	103	70	36	61
1913	376	85	52	27	52
1912	324	78	45	21	44

Year	26 lines of merchandise	Grocery	Drug	Shoes	Ready-to-wear
	220	221	222	223	224
1911	292	69	39	17	39
1910	257	62	36	13	34
1909	231	59	30	12	31
1908	212	53	26	12	29
1907	193	49	25	10	28
1906	173	45	24	9	23
1905	154	44	19	9	21
1904	132	41	16	8	15
1903	107	36	13	7	10
1902	87	29	12	6	9
1901	66	23	9	4	7
1900	58	21	7	3	5
1899	42	17	3	2	5
1898	38	15	3	1	5
1897	35	14	2	1	4
1896	25	11	1	1	3
1895	21	11	1	1	1

Year or period	26 lines of merchandise	Grocery	Drug
	220	221	222
1894	19	11	1
1893	17	10	1
1892	14	9	1
1891	12	7	1
1890	10	6	1
1889	9	5	1
1888	8	4	1
1887	6	3	1
1886	5	3	-------
1885	4	2	-------
1875–1884	3	1	-------
1874	2	1	-------
1873	2	1	-------
1872	1	1	-------

Series T 225–244. Retail Trade Margins, by Kind of Store: 1869 to 1947

[Percent of retail value of sales]

Year	Grocery Independent	Grocery Chain	Meat	Country general	Department	Mail order	Dry goods	Variety	Apparel
	225	226	227	228	229	230	231	232	233
1947	18.0	17.5	20.3	17.9	35.6	28.0	28.0	36.0	37.7
1939	19.0	18.2	23.6	17.9	36.4	27.4	28.0	34.6	36.0
1929	19.5	18.5	24.7	18.4	33.4	26.8	28.0	34.7	34.1
1919	19.5	18.0	25.8	19.0	32.8	26.2	29.0	34.7	31.8
1909	19.5	17.0	26.8	18.7	29.3	25.6	27.0	33.3	29.6
1899	19.5	----------	28.0	18.1	25.6	25.0	21.4	31.0	27.5
1889	19.0	----------	29.0	17.8	22.2	24.4	19.2	----------	25.4
1879	18.5	----------	----------	17.5	----------	----------	18.7	----------	23.2
1869	18.0	----------	----------	----------	----------	----------	----------	----------	21.1

Year	Shoes Independent	Shoes Chain	Furniture, independent	Automobile accessories	Filling stations	Coal and lumber	Hardware	Farm implements	Restaurants	Drugs	Weighted mean [1]
	234	235	236	237	238	239	240	241	242	243	244
1947	34.5	27.6	40.0	32.6	19.5	25.8	29.0	23.0	58.0	33.0	[2] 29.7
1939	32.9	28.9	41.2	32.6	19.0	25.0	27.8	21.9	56.3	33.0	29.7
1929	31.2	30.5	41.2	29.1	16.5	24.0	26.4	20.6	54.3	34.6	28.6
1919	29.5	32.0	39.0	26.5	14.0	22.5	25.0	19.2	52.4	34.6	28.0
1909	28.0	33.5	31.2	26.5	22.0	20.5	23.6	18.0	52.0	33.6	27.6
1899	26.3	----------	31.2	----------	----------	19.5	22.2	18.0	----------	31.8	26.2
1889	24.7	----------	30.6	----------	----------	19.0	23.7	19.6	----------	30.2	25.1
1879	23.1	----------	30.0	----------	----------	18.5	25.2	21.4	----------	28.4	24.1
1869	21.4	----------	----------	----------	----------	18.0	----------	23.0	----------	----------	23.2

[1] Includes classes not shown.   [2] 1948 data.

Series T 245–271. Retail Store Sales, by Kind of Business: 1929 to 1970

[In millions of dollars. Includes nonstores; see text]

Year	All stores	Total sales [1]	Durable goods stores Automotive group Passenger car, other automotive dealers	Tire, battery, accessory dealers	Furniture and appliance group Total [2]	Furniture, home-furnishings stores	Household appliance, T.V., radio stores	Lumber, building, hardware group Lumber, building materials dealers [3]	Hardware stores	Jewelry stores	Nondurable goods stores Total sales [1]	Apparel group Total	Men's and boys' wear stores	Women's apparel, accessory stores
	245	246	247	248	249	250	251	252	253	254	255	256	257	258
1970	375,527	114,288	59,388	5,578	17,778	10,483	6,073	11,995	3,351	----------	261,239	19,810	4,630	7,582
1969	362,935	115,517	63,091	5,126	17,291	10,523	5,693	11,630	3,367	----------	247,418	19,866	4,753	7,499
1968	339,324	110,245	60,660	4,601	16,540	10,227	5,235	10,984	(NA)	----------	229,079	19,265	4,516	7,429
1967	313,809	100,173	53,966	4,307	15,267	(NA)	(NA)	9,781	2,894	----------	213,636	18,123	(NA)	(NA)
1966	303,956	98,301	54,144	3,945	14,558	(NA)	(NA)	9,769	2,804	----------	205,655	17,291	(NA)	(NA)
1965	284,128	94,186	53,484	3,400	13,352	(NA)	(NA)	9,731	2,657	----------	189,942	15,765	(NA)	(NA)
1964	261,870	84,593	46,029	3,268	12,724	(NA)	(NA)	9,089	2,505	----------	177,277	15,295	(NA)	(NA)
1963	246,666	79,927	43,609	3,127	11,267	(NA)	(NA)	9,169	2,399	----------	166,739	14,233	(NA)	(NA)
1962	235,563	74,894	40,472	3,010	10,497	(NA)	(NA)	9,017	2,401	----------	160,669	14,164	(NA)	(NA)
1961 [4]	218,992	67,302	34,695	2,777	10,078	(NA)	(NA)	8,697	2,358	----------	151,690	13,614	(NA)	(NA)
1961 [5]	218,811	66,968	34,523	2,492	10,370	(NA)	(NA)	8,316	2,495	----------	151,343	13,601	(NA)	(NA)
1960*	219,529	70,560	37,038	2,541	10,591	(NA)	(NA)	8,567	2,655	----------	148,969	13,631	2,644	5,295
1959	215,413	71,608	36,901	2,560	11,042	(NA)	(NA)	9,086	2,737	----------	143,805	13,239	2,544	5,271
1958	200,353	63,409	31,577	2,282	10,324	6,636	3,688	8,154	2,653	----------	136,944	12,559	2,349	4,994
1957	200,002	68,352	36,298	2,292	10,584	6,601	3,983	7,950	2,737	----------	131,650	12,277	2,487	4,914
1956	189,729	65,810	34,050	2,072	10,667	6,568	4,099	8,312	2,893	----------	123,919	11,610	2,469	4,541
1955	183,851	66,978	36,267	1,959	10,055	6,116	3,939	8,242	2,788	----------	116,873	10,791	2,294	4,207
1954	169,135	58,173	29,962	1,703	9,079	5,291	3,788	7,433	2,702	----------	110,962	10,147	2,239	4,009
1953	169,094	60,371	31,498	1,822	9,125	5,136	3,989	7,715	2,706	[6]	108,723	10,256	2,249	4,089
1952	162,353	55,270	26,393	1,944	8,926	5,255	3,671	7,572	2,628	1,452	107,083	10,633	2,497	4,233
1951	156,548	54,479	26,282	1,874	8,604	5,095	3,509	7,470	2,738	1,351	102,069	10,209	2,461	4,049
1950	147,213	54,275	27,405	1,766	8,795	4,997	3,798	7,155	2,526	1,256	92,938	9,485	2,306	3,722
1949	133,783	44,983	22,211	1,417	7,240	4,284	2,956	5,648	2,248	1,174	88,800	9,493	2,317	3,817
1948	133,619	42,888	19,212	1,514	7,356	4,503	2,853	6,007	2,398	1,136	90,731	9,971	2,450	4,086
1947	122,406	37,542	16,198	1,423	6,760	4,167	2,593	5,204	2,171	1,225	84,864	9,467	2,451	3,753
1946 [4]	104,802	28,231	10,912	1,420	5,132	3,366	1,766	3,935	1,836	1,247	76,571	9,054	2,331	3,706
1946 [5]	102,488	27,570	10,647	1,275	4,839	3,264	1,575	4,106	1,911	1,260	74,918	8,880	2,195	3,591

See footnotes at end of table.

Series T 245–271.   Retail Store Sales, by Kind of Business: 1929 to 1970—Con.

[In millions of dollars]

Durable goods stores: Total sales (246); Automotive group (247–248); Furniture and appliance group (249–251); Lumber, building, hardware group (252–253); Jewelry stores (254). Nondurable goods stores: Total sales (255); Apparel group (256–258).

Year	All stores	Total sales[1]	Passenger car, other automotive dealers	Tire, battery, accessory dealers	Total[2]	Furniture, home-furnishings stores	Household appliance, T.V., radio stores	Lumber, building materials dealers[3]	Hardware stores	Jewelry stores	Total sales[1]	Total	Men's and boys' wear stores	Women's apparel, accessory stores
	245	246	247	248	249	250	251	252	253	254	255	256	257	258
1945	78,034	16,026	5,000	855	2,740	2,101	639	2,502	1,237	997	62,008	7,689	1,769	3,338
1944	70,208	13,942	4,420	739	2,310	1,848	462	2,102	1,030	909	56,266	6,704	1,524	2,964
1943	63,235	12,221	3,768	670	2,107	1,692	415	2,024	903	894	51,014	6,158	1,405	2,670
1942	57,212	12,320	3,404	623	2,370	1,776	594	2,332	973	710	44,892	5,089	1,268	2,042
1941	55,274	17,213	8,185	704	2,576	1,780	796	2,442	905	566	38,061	4,137	1,076	1,635
1940	46,375	13,576	6,429	560	2,011	1,386	625	2,023	712	422	32,799	3,451	886	1,388
1939	42,042	11,312	5,025	524	1,733	1,200	533	1,761	629	362	30,730	3,259	840	1,323
1938	38,053	9,475	3,909	457	1,490	1,014	476	1,530	563	299	28,578	2,998	765	1,211
1937	42,150	12,048	5,568	499	1,846	1,254	592	1,739	651	347	30,102	3,323	878	1,325
1936	38,339	10,751	5,102	457	1,615	1,082	533	1,463	576	297	27,588	3,102	855	1,205
1935	32,791	8,321	3,863	374	1,290	852	438	1,105	467	235	24,470	2,656	727	1,026
1933	24,517	5,384	2,142	226	959	646	313	854	311	175	19,133	1,930	542	754
1929	48,459	15,610	6,432	599	2,755	1,813	942	2,621	706	536	32,849	4,241	1,358	1,408

Nondurable goods stores—Con.: Apparel group—Con. (259–260); Drug and proprietary stores (261); Eating and drinking places (262); Food group (263–264); Gasoline service stations (265); General merchandise group (266–270); Liquor stores (271).

Year	Family and other apparel stores	Shoe stores	Drug and proprietary stores	Eating and drinking places	Total	Grocery stores	Gasoline service stations	Total[1][7]	Department stores, excl. mail order	Mail order (catalog sales)[8]	Variety stores	Other general merchandise	Liquor stores
	259	260	261	262	263	264	265	266	267	268	269	270	271
1970		3,501	13,366	29,689	86,114	79,756	27,994	61,320	37,295	3,853	6,959		7,980
1969		3,618	12,224	26,970	83,362	77,942	25,909	57,606	35,659	3,538	6,426		7,384
1968		3,196	11,458	25,285	72,881	67,925	24,526	54,493	33,323	3,256	6,152		6,969
1967		(NA)	10,721	23,473	69,113	(NA)	22,739	49,820	29,589	(NA)	(NA)		6,409
1966		(NA)	9,988	22,098	68,137	(NA)	21,792	46,961	27,868	(NA)	(NA)		6,081
1965		(NA)	9,186	20,201	64,016	(NA)	20,611	42,299	25,014	(NA)	(NA)		5,674
1964		(NA)	8,476	18,462	60,224	(NA)	19,196	38,289	22,224	(NA)	(NA)		5,410
1963		(NA)	8,068	17,194	57,254	(NA)	18,319	34,232	(NA)	(NA)	(NA)		5,138
1962		(NA)	7,917	16,434	55,643	(NA)	17,644	32,537	(NA)	(NA)	(NA)		4,892
1961[4]		(NA)	7,629	15,549	53,398	(NA)	17,007	29,874	(NA)	(NA)	(NA)		4,433
1961[5]		(NA)	7,752	16,488	55,739	50,369	17,959	25,059	(NA)	(NA)	(NA)		4,927
1960 *		2,437	7,538	16,146	54,023	48,610	17,588	24,085	(NA)	(NA)	(NA)	[6]	4,893
1959		2,330	7,150	15,618	51,739	46,132	16,793	23,420	(NA)	(NA)	(NA)		4,743
1958		2,222	6,600	14,792	50,263	44,547	15,757	21,667	12,563	1,536	3,609	3,943	4,439
1957		2,091	6,325	14,787	47,786	42,444	15,070	21,157	(NA)	1,477	3,523	4,254	4,212
1956		2,068	5,775	14,317	44,223	39,180	13,738	20,762	11,327	1,407	3,423	4,605	3,944
1955		2,009	5,232	13,662	42,010	36,919	12,411	20,100	10,882	1,331	3,295	4,592	3,546
1954		1,809	4,940	13,127	40,106	34,993	11,443	18,857	10,272	1,222	3,027	4,336	3,415
1953		1,736	4,790	13,003	39,130	33,623	10,556	19,006	10,370	1,327	3,095	4,214	3,325
1952		1,693	4,717	12,688	38,039	32,238	9,976	18,694	10,277	1,339	2,996	4,082	3,165
1951		1,684	4,547	12,207	35,951	30,346	9,151	18,202	10,095	1,309	2,859	3,939	2,975
1950		1,556	4,205	11,158	31,889	26,886	8,240	17,275	9,649	1,258	2,632	3,736	2,669
1949		1,498	4,074	10,994	30,101	25,248	7,590	16,339	9,083	1,178	2,555	3,523	2,598
1948		1,510	4,050	11,218	30,093	25,215	7,077	17,170	9,579	1,328	2,556	3,707	2,711
1947		1,487	3,904	11,183	27,577	22,907	5,979	16,088	9,108	1,194	2,363	3,423	2,782
1946[4]		1,417	3,759	11,152	23,315	18,980	4,922	14,755	8,431	976	2,197	3,151	2,823
1946[5]	[6]	1,377	3,723	10,619	24,155	18,640	4,511	14,724	9,183		2,158	3,383	2,688
1945	1,442	1,140	3,155	9,575	19,233	14,593	3,284	11,802	7,092		1,845	2,865	2,288
1944	1,215	1,001	2,924	8,305	17,918	13,665	2,812	11,076	6,488		1,774	2,814	1,926
1943	1,114	969	2,628	7,216	16,447	12,481	2,628	10,162	5,889		1,642	2,631	1,557
1942	865	914	2,213	5,699	14,788	11,368	3,089	9,204	5,389		1,536	2,279	1,212
1941	700	726	1,847	4,570	12,244	9,312	3,466	7,973	4,862		1,320	1,791	854
1940	545	632	1,636	3,787	10,732	8,169	2,970	6,859	4,128		1,153	1,578	681
1939	479	617	1,563	3,529	10,156	7,722	2,822	6,475	3,872		1,080	1,523	586
1938	431	591	1,474	3,188	9,505	7,187	2,696	6,145	(NA)	(NA)	1,015	1,536	539
1937	484	636	1,527	3,293	9,699	7,266	2,641	6,673	(NA)	(NA)	1,025	1,755	558
1936	456	586	1,409	2,748	9,008	6,850	2,318	6,366	(NA)	(NA)	967	1,731	475
1935	392	511	1,233	2,395	8,358	6,352	1,968	5,730	2,833	386	873	1,638	328
1933	209	425	1,066	1,434	6,772	5,004	1,532	4,982	(NA)	(NA)	756	1,766	17
1929	596	807	1,690	2,132	10,960	7,353	[9] 1,787	9,015	3,903	447	904	3,761	

* Denotes first year for which figures include Alaska and Hawaii.
NA   Not available.
[1] Totals include subclasses not shown separately.
[2] Beginning 1959, includes music stores, not shown separately.
[3] Includes lumber yards; building materials dealers; and paint, plumbing, and electrical stores.
[4] Comparable with later years; see text.
[5] Comparable with earlier years; see text.
[6] No longer available separately; included in total for group.
[7] Includes nonstores, i.e., establishments selling merchandise primarily through coin-operated vending machines, house-to-house canvass, and mail orders.
[8] Includes sales made by mail order catalog desks located within department stores of mail order firms.
[9] Excludes garages primarily selling gasoline and oil.

Series T 272–273. Index of Department Store Sales and Stocks: 1919 to 1970

[1957–59 = 100]

Year	Sales index 272	Stocks index 273	Year	Sales index 272	Stocks index 273	Year	Sales index 272	Stocks index 273	Year	Sales index 272	Stocks index 273	Year	Sales index 272	Stocks index 273
1970	239	279	1960	106	109	1950	72	69	1940	25	24	1930	24	28
1969	230	250	1959	105	103	1949	67	62	1939	23	22	1929	25	30
1968	212	231	1958	98	97	1948	70	67	1938	21	22	1928	25	30
1967	190	213	1957	96	99	1947	66	59	1937	23	24	1927	25	30
1966	179	192	1956	94	95	1946	60	48	1936	20	21	1926	24	30
												1925	24	30
1965	160	166	1955	87	85	1945	46	37	1935	19	20	1924	23	30
1964	142	150	1954	80	80	1944	41	36	1934	18	20	1923	23	29
1963	127	135	1953	80	82	1943	37	34	1933	16	18	1922	20	26
1962	118	121	1952	77	76	1942	33	40	1932	16	20	1921	20	26
1961	109	110	1951	76	82	1941	29	29	1931	21	24	1920	22	30
												1919	18	23

Series T 274–371. Wholesale Establishments, Sales, Operating Expenses, and Persons Engaged, by Kind of Business: 1929 to 1967

[Sales, inventories, and payroll in millions of dollars; paid employees and active proprietors in thousands]

Year	All wholesale establishments [1]						Merchant wholesalers [2]							
					Persons engaged						Payroll, entire year		Persons engaged	
	Number	Sales	Inventories, end of year	Payroll, entire year	Paid employees workweek ended nearest Nov. 15	Active proprietors of unincorporated businesses	Number	Sales	Operating expenses (percent)	Inventories, end of year	Amount	Ratio to sales	Paid employees workweek ended nearest Nov. 15	Active proprietors of unincorporated businesses
	274	275	276	277	278	279	280	281	282	283	284	285	286	287
1967	311,464	459,476	28,117	23,922	[3]3,519	122	212,993	206,055	13.5	21,463	15,368	13.4	[3]2,417	98
1963 [4]*	308,177	358,386	20,150	18,101	3,089	138	208,997	157,392	13.5	14,992	11,545	13.6	2,064	104
1963 [5]*	308,177	358,386	20,150	18,101	3,089	138	208,997	157,392	13.5	14,992	11,545	13.6	2,064	108
1958	285,996	284,977	14,943	13,199	2,791	1	190,492	122,060	13.4	11,253	8,278	14.8	1,843	120
1954	250,322	233,976	13,046	10,868	2,555	150	163,157	100,103	13.0	9,492	6,865	15.8	1,651	104
1948 [4]	216,099	180,577	9,965	7,734	2,305	131	129,117	76,533	11.5	7,056	4,849	15.8	1,441	85
1948 [5]	243,366	188,689	10,167	7,991	2,383	163	146,518	79,767	11.6	7,207	5,064	15.8	1,508	107
1939 [6]	190,379	53,766	3,822	2,511	[7]1,553	126	100,961	22,538	13.1	2,621	1,498	15.0	949	72
1935	176,756	42,803	3,107	2,022	[7]1,261	97	88,931	17,662	7.6	2,068	1,162	15.2	760	62
1933 [6]	163,583	30,010	(NA)	1,659	[7]1,188	(NA)	82,844	12,960	15.0	1,971	925	14.0	636	---------
1929 [6]	163,830	65,378	5,195	2,922	[7]1,550	87	79,840	29,556	11.7	3,383	1,713	17.3	912	---------

Year	Merchant wholesalers [2]—Con.											
	Groceries, confectionery, meat				Farm products [8] (edible)				Beer, wine, and distilled spirits			
	Number	Sales	Operating expenses (percent)	Persons engaged	Number	Sales	Operating expenses (percent)	Persons engaged	Number	Sales	Operating expenses (percent)	Persons engaged
	288	289	290	291	292	293	294	295	296	297	298	299
1967	18,960	32,720.5	8.7	267,391	10,091	8,830.3	12.5	113,124	6,862	10,444.1	11.9	95,435
1963 [4]*	19,814	25,332.9	8.7	243,445	10,065	6,794.7	11.8	92,905	7,164	8,194.7	12.0	87,614
1963 [5]*	19,225	24,059.2	8.9	239,945	10,065	6,794.7	11.8	93,282	7,164	8,194.7	12.0	87,769
1958	18,582	18,712.1	8.6	213,231	11,440	6,488.8	12.0	100,599	7,325	6,510.2	11.9	82,659
1954	18,334	15,980.6	9.0	216,928	11,461	6,077.2	11.8	110,422	7,309	5,686.9	12.0	78,340
1948 [4]	15,707	11,213.1	8.8	195,072	10,966	5,858.6	9.0	106,809	6,701	4,049.8	10.9	68,305
1948 [5]	17,345	11,356.7	8.8	196,636	13,539	7,500.9	11.6	169,393	7,195	4,069.7	10.9	69,059
1939	15,681	3,940.8	11.3	165,550	10,945	2,110.8	13.0	104,508	6,232	1,249.2	12.9	50,718
1935	15,989	3,636.7	10.5	164,486	11,188	1,941.1	11.0	89,043	5,496	698.5	13.1	37,266
1933	18,088	3,121.2	12.8	---------	10,386	1,589.9	14.8	---------	2,880	129.0	17.0	---------
1929	15,224	5,386.9	10.2	---------	8,972	3,061.2	---------	---------	---------	---------	---------	---------

See footnotes at end of table.

Series **T 274–371.** Wholesale Establishments, Sales, Operating Expenses, and Persons Engaged, by Kind of Business: 1929 to 1967—Con.

[Sales in millions of dollars]

	Merchant wholesalers [2]—Con.											
Year	Tobacco distributors				Drugs, chemicals, and allied products				Dry goods, apparel [9]			
	Numbers	Sales	Operating expenses (percent)	Persons engaged	Number	Sales	Operating expenses (percent)	Persons engaged	Number	Sales	Operating expenses (percent)	Persons engaged
	300	301	302	303	304	305	306	307	308	309	310	311
1967	2,515	5,315.4	5.9	35,370	7,701	7,807.9	15.5	107,182	8,846	8,861.4	14.2	95,887
1963 [4] *	2,753	4,682.1	5.6	33,536	7,792	5,996.1	15.9	91,483	9,227	7,026.8	13.5	79,992
1963 [5] *	2,753	4,682.1	5.6	33,570	7,792	5,996.1	15.9	91,590	9,227	7,026.8	13.5	80,161
1958	2,759	3,668.3	5.6	30,994	7,097	4,640.8	15.1	82,481	9,199	5,900.9	13.5	80,852
1954	2,858	3,208.9	5.9	30,848	5,837	3,369.9	15.9	71,366	9,389	5,689.7	13.3	83,811
1948 [4]	2,701	2,487.1	5.2	28,406	4,124	2,243.3	15.9	57,775	9,604	5,529.5	11.9	84,977
1948 [5]	3,019	2,529.6	5.2	28,886	4,671	2,282.2	15.8	58,679	11,733	5,727.7	11.8	88,745
1939	2,717	1,106.2	4.9	21,122	3,298	801.8	17.3	41,824	8,275	1,889.0	13.1	75,385
1935	2,253	783.4	5.5	16,862	2,989	722.9	15.6	35,926	7,567	1,634.3	12.8	69,624
1933	1,738	523.7	6.4	----------	2,543	575.7	11.0	----------	6,392	1,262.2	14.5	----------
1929	1,721	858.3	7.4	----------	[10] 2,376	[10] 948.0	[10] 15.9	----------	7,543	2,849.3	13.4	----------

	Merchant wholesalers [2]—Con.											
Year	Furniture, homefurnishings [11]				Paper and allied products				Farm products (raw materials)			
	Number	Sales	Operating expenses (percent)	Persons engaged	Number	Sales	Operating expenses (percent)	Persons engaged	Number	Sales	Operating expenses (percent)	Persons engaged
	312	313	314	315	316	317	318	319	320	321	322	323
1967	6,047	4,328.6	19.1	70,164	7,663	6,421.7	17.4	105,672	4,044	16,176.3	3.4	39,217
1963 [4] *	6,265	3,400.1	19.4	61,956	7,046	4,714.6	17.2	85,851	3,565	13,689.9	3.3	36,790
1963 [5] *	6,265	3,400.1	19.4	62,054	7,046	4,714.6	17.2	85,951	3,565	13,689.9	3.3	36,968
1958	5,359	2,510.1	19.2	54,162	5,182	3,564.1	15.3	67,424	4,195	9,593.8	4.5	41,768
1954	5,324	2,274.6	18.6	52,793	5,057	2,961.0	15.9	61,123	3,853	9,231.9	4.0	41,317
1948 [4]	3,189	1,249.2	17.3	34,402	3,630	1,880.0	15.5	50,553	2,059	6,771.0	3.6	24,326
1948 [5]	3,813	1,314.9	16.6	34,929	4,044	1,901.7	15.5	51,468	2,594	6,904.0	3.6	26,592
1939	2,214	373.5	17.2	20,265	2,898	575.0	17.2	33,605	2,086	1,628.7	6.9	29,281
1935	1,959	243.5	17.8	15,871	2,549	408.9	18.3	27,543	2,199	1,562.5	6.7	23,712
1933	1,788	175.0	22.5	----------	2,221	333.4	20.7	----------	2,433	1,224.7	6.9	----------
1929	1,750	494.8	18.9	----------	2,297	704.4	16.4	----------	3,240	3,665.9	4.5	----------

	Merchant wholesalers [2]—Con.											
Year	Automotive wholesalers				Electrical, electronics appliance distributors				Hardware, plumbing and heating			
	Number	Sales	Operating expenses (percent)	Persons engaged	Number	Sales	Operating expenses (percent)	Persons engaged	Number	Sales	Operating expenses (percent)	Persons engaged
	324	325	326	327	328	329	330	331	332	333	334	335
1967	28,513	14,093.4	18.5	274,698	11,376	13,622.1	14.5	157,041	8,830	7,425.8	18.6	127,421
1963 [4] *	26,946	10,444.7	19.5	240,711	10,978	9,910.6	14.7	133,170	8,404	6,012.9	18.0	110,661
1963 [5] *	26,500	10,303.9	19.5	237,749	10,978	9,910.6	14.7	133,350	8,404	6,012.9	18.0	110,769
1958	20,823	7,098.4	20.0	191,875	9,488	7,928.2	14.4	128,346	7,526	5,307.4	17.8	112,029
1954	15,540	3,977.5	22.6	144,532	7,123	6,337.7	14.0	111,299	6,183	4,397.7	17.2	103,860
1948 [4]	13,563	3,917.6	18.1	145,023	5,041	4,309.3	12.8	91,772	5,189	3,680.2	15.2	100,721
1948 [5]	14,693	4,091.6	17.8	146,459	5,443	4,424.6	12.7	93,325	5,576	3,730.5	15.2	101,913
1939	7,818	1,055.4	17.5	72,616	3,072	788.0	16.6	40,147	3,568	972.0	18.4	64,358
1935	5,672	780.4	16.8	53,820	2,438	576.5	17.3	31,698	2,872	671.4	18.8	49,821
1933	5,237	438.0	23.0	----------	2,125	275.8	22.3	----------	2,614	484.9	22.5	----------
1929	3,451	1,383.1	15.0	----------	2,182	846.7	16.9	----------	2,953	1,212.7	19.3	----------

See footnotes at end of table.

Series **T 274–371.** Wholesale Establishments, Sales, Operating Expenses, and Persons Engaged, by Kind of Business: 1929 to 1967—Con.

[Sales in millions of dollars]

	Merchant wholesalers [2]—Con.											
	Lumber, construction materials wholesalers [1]				Machinery, equipment supplies distributors [12]				Metals, metalwork (except scrap) distributors			
Year	Number	Sales	Operating expenses (percent)	Persons engaged	Number	Sales	Operating expenses (percent)	Persons engaged	Number	Sales	Operating expenses (percent)	Persons engaged
	336	337	338	339	340	341	342	343	344	345	346	347
1967	10,877	9,073.7	15.6	123,603	40,999	25,279.4	20.4	456,048	5,395	11,862.7	11.9	103,459
1963 [4] *	11,643	8,712.6	15.2	129,483	38,419	17,471.3	21.1	363,964	5,547	7,934.5	12.4	83,174
1963 [5] *	11,643	8,712.6	15.2	129,693	38,865	17,612.1	21.1	368,905	5,547	7,934.5	12.4	83,261
1958	9,463	6,271.5	13.4	102,748	32,593	13,259.1	20.5	299,285	4,792	5,540.9	13.6	74,689
1954	10,314	6,586.2	16.1	132,724	27,150	10,039.9	20.2	254,060	[13] 3,235	[13] 3,362.6	[13] 14.5	[13] 53,641
1948 [4]	5,576	3,890.0	14.1	89,427	19,573	6,723.1	18.2	203,642	1,706	1,951.1	12.9	33,844
1948 [5]	5,890	3,934.7	14.0	90,036	21,755	6,827.8	18.1	207,062	1,803	2,056.7	12.1	34,395
1939	3,303	804.4	15.2	38,918	11,270	1,440.4	20.0	96,311	1,017	516.0	12.0	17,705
1935	2,817	491.9	16.7	29,110	[14] 7,583	[14] 863.5	[14] 21.1	[14] 67,379	810	282.0	13.2	11,343
1933	2,636	278.7	22.7		[14] 6,226	[14] 505.6	[14] 25.4		748	160.5	15.8	
1929	3,774	1,283.9	15.8		6,988	1,268.8	19.1		856	672.6	8.1	

	Merchant wholesalers [2]—Con.				Manufacturers' sales branches (with stocks)				Manufacturers' sales offices (without stocks)			
	Scrap, waste materials dealers											
Year	Number	Sales	Operating expenses (percent)	Persons engaged	Number	Sales	Operating expenses (percent)	Persons engaged	Number	Sales	Operating expenses (percent)	Persons engaged
	348	349	350	351	352	353	354	355	356	357	358	359
1967	7,814	4,423.0	17.3	84,536	16,709	67,174.6	11.3	491,613	13,970	89,921.9	4.1	193,425
1963 [4] *	8,174	3,484.3	17.8	78,105	16,408	54,857.4	10.6	435,573	12,476	61,585.9	4.2	164,855
1963 [5] *	8,174	3,484.3	17.8	78,391	16,408	54,857.4	10.6	435,575	12,476	61,585.9	4.2	164,885
1958	9,491	2,898.3	18.7	81,528	15,088	41,797.7	10.8	419,415	10,093	45,959.8	4.8	140,954
1954	8,189	2,405.6	17.8	75,499	[13] 14,759	[13] 36,811.2	[13] 10.5	[13] 404,098	[15] 7,831	[15] 32,722.5	[15] 4.5	[15] 111,888
1948 [4]	6,440	2,663.6	11.8	65,582	15,687	28,609.3	10.0	410,199	8,019	22,191.1	4.0	89,992
1948 [5]	7,717	2,699.3	11.9	67,227	15,716	29,229.7	10.0	412,252	8,052	23,508.9	4.3	90,144
1939	6,059	656.0	14.7	52,379	12,844	9,610.3	12.5	267,774	5,082	4,643.3	6.9	47,699
1935	4,793	399.7	14.5	34,830	11,541	7,403.6	11.8	[16] 212,452	4,065	3,535.1	6.4	[16] 39,607
1933	3,360	272.2	10.8		12,444	5,144.7	14.9		4,429	2,412.7	7.4	
1929	3,919	474.5	12.3		[17] 16,863	[17] 16,174.0			([17])	([17])		

	Petroleum bulk stations, terminals				Agents and brokers				Assemblers (mainly farm products)			
Year	Number	Sales	Operating expenses (percent)	Persons engaged	Number	Sales	Commissions earned (percent)	Persons engaged	Number	Sales	Operating expenses (percent)	Persons engaged
	360	361	362	363	364	365	366	367	368	369	370	371
1967	30,229	24,821.8	0.3	156,708	26,462	61,347.0	4.0	195,838	11,101	10,155.5	8.6	88,564
1963 [4] *	30,873	21,485.4	(NA)	151,541	25,313	53,245.0	3.6	184,459	14,110	9,820.5	9.0	117,849
1963 [5] *	30,873	21,485.4	(NA)	151,613	25,313	53,245.0	3.6	184,678	14,110	9,820.2	9.0	117,986
1958	30,424	20,130.8	11.9	147,351	26,567	46,422.6	3.3	169,597	14,096	8,998.6	9.0	123,314
1954	29,189	16,038.4	10.0	154,760	22,131	39,250.5	3.1	148,595	[18] 13,255	[18] 9,050.8	[18] 8.1	[18] 130,337
1948 [4]	28,351	10,483.1	9.0	134,897	18,138	32,839.7	2.5	116,148	16,787	9,920.3	6.1	158,956
1948 [5]	29,451	10,615.7	9.0	136,418	24,361	34,610.1	2.6	123,470	19,268	10,957.9	6.1	169,182
1939	30,825	3,807.9	11.0	123,017	21,083	11,779.5	[19] 2.8	111,125	28,931	2,509.6	9.3	168,673
1935	27,333	2,704.0	14.5	[16] 105,118	18,147	8,908.1	[19] 2.9	88,064	26,515	2,463.0	6.7	115,381
1933	[20] 26,176	[20] 1,884.6	[20] 19.8		13,818	6,502.4	[19] 3.2		23,962	1,774.1	9.8	
1929	19,587	2,101.1	16.0		18,467	14,517.2	[19] 3.2		34,143	4,452.1		

* Denotes first year for which figures include Alaska and Hawaii.
NA Not available.
[1] Beginning 1954, excludes ready-mixed concrete distributors, no longer part of wholesale trade but included in selected service trade.
[2] Includes subclasses not shown separately.
[3] For workweek ended nearest March 12.
[4] Comparable with later years.
[5] Comparable with earlier years.
[6] Data for series T 274–279 for 1939, 1933, and 1929 are revised; revised data for other series for these years not available.
[7] Average annual number of full-time and part-time employees.
[8] Fresh fruit and vegetable wholesalers and poultry and dairy products distributors. Milk bottling plants are included in the 1948 (unrevised) and earlier data.
[9] Includes dressed furs.
[10] Includes 42 distilled spirits wholesalers with sales of 13 million dollars and operating expenses of 24.7 percent.
[11] Beginning 1954, includes musical instruments and sheet music wholesalers.
[12] Beginning 1948, includes air conditioning and ventilating equipment distributors. Such distributors were classified in the plumbing and heating category in earlier years but were of negligible importance.

[13] For 1954, 142 sales branches (with stocks) of steel works and rolling mill companies are included in metal distributors rather than manufacturers' sales branches. They had sales of 172 million dollars.
[14] Excludes wholesalers of shoe finding and cut stock; in 1929, 555 such establishments had sales of 56 million dollars. Persons engaged in optical goods segment partially estimated.
[15] Includes a moderate amount of underenumeration because, in the mail canvass, the activities of some branches and offices were reported as those of the manufacturing plant or an auxiliary establishment.
[16] Partly estimated.
[17] Figures not available separately for "manufacturers' sales branches (with stocks)" and "manufacturers' sales offices (without stocks);" figure shown is for both.
[18] Beginning 1954, excludes fish and seafood assemblers, which are included in the grocery, confectionery, meat group. In 1948 (adjusted) there were 544 such establishments with sales of 117 million dollars, and operating expenses of 23.5 percent.
[19] Operating expenses.
[20] Includes district and general sales offices.

Series T 372–374. Sales of Wholesale Establishments: 1939 to 1962

[In billions of dollars]

Year	Total	Durable goods establishments	Non-durable goods establishments	Year	Total	Durable goods establishments	Non-durable goods establishments	Year	Total	Durable goods establishments	Non-durable goods establishments	Year	Total	Durable goods establishments	Non-durable goods establishments
	372	373	374		372	373	374		372	373	374		372	373	374
1962	156.7	54.2	102.5	1955	127.4	48.2	79.2	1948	90.6	29.2	61.4	1942	41.1	9.6	31.5
1961 *	150.7	51.4	99.3	1954	116.8	40.0	76.8	1947	82.9	26.0	57.0	1941	36.4	10.2	26.2
				1953	117.7	41.4	76.3	1946 ¹	67.9	18.7	49.2				
1960	148.0	53.3	94.7	1952	114.8	39.3	75.4	1946 ²	71.9	17.6	54.3	1940	28.9	7.5	21.4
1959	147.5	55.4	92.1	1951	112.4	39.6	72.8	1945	53.7	10.9	42.8	1939	26.2	6.3	20.0
1958	133.1	47.3	85.8												
1957	135.2	50.5	84.8	1950	101.0	35.4	65.7	1944	49.8	10.1	39.7				
1956	135.3	52.8	82.5	1949	86.6	27.2	59.3	1943	46.0	9.4	36.5				

* Denotes first year for which figures include Alaska and Hawaii.
¹ Beginning 1946, excludes wholesale establishments with no paid employment.
² Comparable with earlier data.

Series T 375–383. Sales, Stocks, and Stock-Sales Ratios of Merchant Wholesalers: 1948 to 1970

Year	All establishments			Durable goods establishments			Nondurable goods establishments		
	Sales	Stocks, end of year	Stock-sales ratio	Sales	Stocks, end of year	Stock-sales ratio	Sales	Stocks, end of year	Stock-sales ratio
	375	376	377	378	379	380	381	382	383
1970	246,643	26,604	1.23	111,778	15,565	1.61	134,865	11,039	0.92
1969	236,708	24,363	1.19	109,578	14,579	1.53	127,130	9,784	.89
1968	219,943	22,528	1.20	100,012	13,454	1.54	119,930	9,074	.91
1967	205,188	21,557	1.21	90.447	12,543	1.61	114,741	9,014	.90
1966	203,751	20,691	1.14	91,026	12,112	1.49	112,724	8,579	.85
1965	187,141	18,274	1.14	82,691	10,575	1.49	104,450	7,699	.87
1964	174,329	16,977	1.13	75,722	9,809	1.49	98,607	7,168	.86
1963	160,578	16,048	1.15	68,696	9,119	1.54	91,882	6,929	.85
1962	152,082	14,936	1.16	64,541	8,631	1.57	87,541	6,305	.86
1961	143,850	14,488	1.20	59,836	8,315	1.63	84,014	6,173	.89
1960	139,866	14,120	1.22	58,581	8,121	1.69	81,285	5,999	.89
1959	137,893	13,879	1.15	59,349	7,861	1.53	78,544	6,018	.87
1958	123,083	12,739	1.24	50,437	7,150	1.66	72,646	5,589	.94
1957	125,705	12,730	1.23	53,760	7,115	1.53	71,945	5,615	.96
1956	126,153	13,260	1.19	56,308	7,074	1.43	69,845	6,186	1.00
1955	118,713	11,678	1.13	51,412	6,261	1.36	67,301	5,417	.95
1954	107,920	10,637	1.18	42,639	5,477	1.54	65,281	5,160	.95
1953	108,624	10,686	1.17	44,079	5,547	1.52	64,545	5,139	.93
1952	105,379	10,210	1.12	41,905	5,312	1.47	63,474	4,898	.89
1951	103,163	9,886	1.16	42,229	5,207	1.47	60,934	4,679	.95
1950	92,336	9,284	1.07	37,695	4,691	1.29	54,641	4,593	.91
1949	78,163	7,706	1.19	29,014	3,818	1.61	49,149	3,888	.95
1948	81,699	7,957	1.13	31,101	3,999	1.42	50,598	3,958	.95

Series T 384–390. Wholesale Trade Margins of Independent Wholesalers: 1869 to 1947

[Percent of wholesale value of sales]

Year	Dry goods	Furniture	Automobile accessories	Gasoline and oil	Lumber	Hardware	Drug (general line)	Year	Dry goods	Furniture	Lumber	Hardware	Drug (general line)
	384	385	386	387	388	389	390		384	385	388	389	390
1947	18	22.0	23.0	16.5	17.0	24.0	15.6	1899	17	14.0	10.0	19.0	13.6
1939	18	22.0	24.0	17.5	16.0	24.0	15.2	1889	16	14.0	10.0	19.0	12.2
1929	18	18.0	25.5	17.8	14.2	23.0	16.0	1879	15	14.0	10.0	19.0	11.0
1919	18	16.2	25.0	16.0	13.0	22.0	16.6	1869	14	14.0	10.0	19.0	10.0
1909	18	15.0	25.0	18.0	11.5	20.0	15.2						

Series T 391–443.   Selected Service Establishments and Receipts: 1929 to 1967

[Receipts and payroll in millions of dollars; paid employees and active proprietors in thousands]

Year	Establishments		Receipts					Payroll		Paid employees, workweek ended nearest Nov. 15	Active proprietors of unincorporated businesses
	Number	With payroll	All establishments	Establishments with payroll		Establishments without payroll		Entire year	Workweek ended nearest Nov. 15		
				Total	Average per establishment (dollars)	Total	Average per establishment (dollars)				
	391	392	393	394	395	396	397	398	399	400	401
1967	1,187,814	521,410	60,542	55,527	106,494	5,015	7,526	17,524	----------	[1] 3,841	1,082
1963 *	1,061,673	504,356	44,586	41,023	81,338	3,563	6,393	12,192	241	3,262	1,017
1958 *	975,250	442,584	32,376	29,001	65,526	3,375	6,336	9,006	167	2,889	992
1954	785,589	375,149	23,508	21,263	56,680	2,245	5,469	6,534	126	2,362	782
1948 [2]	617,002	----------	13,230	(NA)	(NA)	(NA)	(NA)	(NA)	(NA)	(NA)	(NA)
1948 [3]	665,475	----------	13,296	12,164	32,879	1,132	3,830	4,164	81	2,100	667
1939 [2]	656,482	----------	4,872	----------	----------	----------	----------	1,384	----------	1,497	651
1939 [3]	646,028	----------	3,420	----------	----------	----------	----------	1,070	----------	[4] 1,102	652
1935	631,309	----------	3,001	----------	----------	----------	----------	(NA)	----------	(NA)	(NA)
1933	502,416	----------	2,761	----------	----------	----------	----------	702	----------	[4] 657	546

Year	Personal services															
	Total [5]		Barber, beauty shops		Funeral services, crematories		Shoe repair shops, shoeshine parlors, hat cleaning shops		Photographic studios (incl. commercial photography)		Laundry, cleaning, and garment services					
											Total [5]		Dry cleaning plants		Coin-operated laundry and dry cleaning	
	Number	Receipts	Number	Receipts	Number	Receipts	Number	Receipts	Number	Receipts	Number	Receipts	Number	Receipts	Number	Receipts
	402	403	404	405	406	407	408	409	410	411	412	413	414	415	416	417
1967	498,935	11,750	291,706	3,375	20,191	[6] 1,517	16,270	207	26,558	745	111,926	5,432	[7] 31,519	[7] 2,004	29,551	557
1963 *	447,080	9,163	257,236	2,525	20,529	1,299	21,486	208	19,544	495	109,740	4,357	33,580	1,511	26,153	373
1958	413,180	7,422	215,451	1,811	20,767	1,016	27,775	232	20,028	423	107,204	3,708	34,311	1,357	(NA)	(NA)
1954	348,843	5,773	169,684	1,206	18,387	744	29,385	202	17,293	334	106,520	3,180	29,200	1,138	(NA)	(NA)
1948 [2]	325,246	4,421	153,764	834	18,480	572	39,275	215	13,788	211	96,106	2,530	25,313	844	7,844	65
1948 [3]	351,985	4,440	169,081	845	18,675	572	44,151	219	14,712	212	101,127	2,533	25,534	844	8,523	65
1939	[2] 389,726	[2] 1,822	205,268	481	18,196	262	59,371	119	10,957	64	90,048	874	12,616	193	----------	----------
1935	369,081	1,517	186,810	402	17,144	230	61,046	110	10,402	48	90,335	713	6,910	141	----------	----------
1933	320,863	1,223	159,905	321	12,655	172	57,452	97	8,330	32	79,907	587	3,864	98	----------	----------

Year	Personal services—Con.		Miscellaneous business services				Automobile repair, garage, other services									
	Power laundries [8]		Total		Advertising		Total [5]		Automobile repair shops		Automobile, truck rentals (without drivers)		Automobile storage, parking		Automobile laundries	
	Number	Receipts	Number	Receipts	Number	Receipts	Number	Receipts	Number	Receipts	Number	Receipts	Number	Receipts	Number	Receipts
	418	419	420	421	422	423	424	425	426	427	428	429	430	431	432	433
1967	[7] 6,350	[7] 942	211,835	22,595	20,124	8,342	139,243	7,028	109,946	4,086	[7] 5,832	[7] 2,060	10,606	484	[7] 3,918	[7] 236
1963 *	[7] 10,050	[7] 1,040	147,668	15,193	12,896	6,384	139,611	5,444	114,459	3,588	[7] 4,323	[7] 1,187	11,269	416	[7] 2,338	[7] 139
1958	[7] 11,262	[7] 1,022	114,450	9,919	12,180	4,926	125,691	3,869	103,724	2,759	4,714	616	10,998	366	2,660	90
1954	[7] 9,612	[7] 914	88,661	6,317	8,239	3,498	94,342	2,223	79,709	1,589	2,872	278	8,572	292	1,657	44
1948 [2]	6,770	913	27,251	1,030	5,910	652	90,762	1,558	80,705	1,269	994	84	8,033	190	717	10
1948 [3]	6,783	913	32,007	1,630	5,986	652	95,444	1,561	84,875	1,272	1,011	84	8,533	190	792	10
1939	6,773	454	26,188	487	[9] 1,628	[9] 97	78,881	441	66,178	316	648	20	11,095	102	960	3
1935	6,470	370	29,859	510	[9] 1,212	[9] 71	92,471	538	79,553	433	765	16	11,246	87	907	3
1933	5,122	296	36,442	469	1,479	190	100,149	585	[10] 93,760	[10] 550	381	5	5,275	27	733	2

See footnotes at end of table.

Series T 391-443.   Selected Service Establishments and Receipts: 1929 to 1967—Con.

[Receipts and payroll in millions of dollars; paid employees and active proprietors in thousands]

Year	Miscellaneous repair services				Hotels, tourist courts, motels, trailer parks, and camps		Motion pictures		Amusement recreation services, except motion pictures	
	Total		Electrical repair shops							
	Number	Receipts	Number	Receipts	Number	Receipts	Number	Receipts	Number	Receipts
	434	435	436	437	438	439	440	441	442	443
1967	138,014	3,827	47,886	1,329	87,006	7,039	16,752	3,476	96,029	4,827
1963 *	146,116	3,022	61,186	1,116	84,706	5,049	16,381	2,583	79,451	3,990
1958	145,163	2,270	51,269	763	85,890	3,924	19,657	2,431	75,164	2,673
1954	113,429	1,796	32,195	502	66,962	3,027	20,843	2,352	52,509	2,021
1948 [2]	71,338	941	17,076	213	52,518	2,366	18,532	1,353	30,630	1,058
1948 [3]	80,023	947	19,440	215	55,569	2,368	18,631	1,614	31,716	735
1939 [2]	75,262	224	15,644	48	41,508	900	---	---	---	---
1939 [3]	72,130	195	15,644	48	41,508	900	15,115	673	29,802	325
1935	[11] 71,426	[11] 148	10,131	23	38,670	744	12,024	508	25,653	191
1933	53,010	91	[12] 6,892	[12] 17	[13] 29,462	[13] 516	10,265	415	19,472	105
1929	---	---	---	---	[14] 3,328	[14] 963	---	---	---	---

* Denotes first year for which figures include Alaska and Hawaii.
NA Not available.
[1] Paid employees for week including March 12.
[2] Comparable with later years. 1939 data comparable with earlier years are: Series 402, 388,918; series 403, 1,820 mil. dol.
[3] Comparable with earlier years.
[4] Average annual number of full-time and part-time employees.
[5] Includes subclasses not shown separately.
[6] About 7 percent represents repayment of cash advances which are not part of the cost of the complete funeral service. Receipts in prior censuses did not include such advances.
[7] Establishments with payroll only.

[8] Data prior to 1933 are as follows:

Year	Number of establishments	Receipts (mil. dol.)
1931	6,400	466.0
1929	6,776	541.2
1927	6,013	454.0
1925	4,859	362.3
1919 [2]	4,881	233.8
1919 [3]	5,678	236.1
1914	6,097	142.5

[9] For advertising agencies only.
[10] Covers only general repair garages, paint shops, radiator shops, top and body repair shops, tire repair shops, and brake repair shops.
[11] Includes boat repair shops not included in other years.
[12] Excludes refrigerator repair and washing machine repair establishments.
[13] Hotels only.
[14] Limited to hotels with 25 or more guest rooms.

Series T 444-471.   Volume of Advertising, by Medium: 1867 to 1970

[In millions of dollars]

Year	Total	National	Local	Newspapers			Magazines					Television			
				Total	National	Local	Total	Weeklies	Women's	Monthlies	Farm, national	Total	Network	Spot	Local
	444	445	446	447	448	449	450	451	452	453	454	455	456	457	458
1970	19,600	11,485	8,115	5,745	1,014	4,731	1,323	617	301	374	31	3,665	1,712	1,247	706
1969	19,482	11,518	7,964	5,753	1,059	4,694	1,376	662	308	374	32	3,585	1,678	1,253	654
1968	18,127	10,883	7,244	5,265	990	4,275	1,318	657	284	342	35	3,231	1,523	1,131	577
1967	16,866	10,250	6,616	4,942	936	4,006	1,280	651	282	312	35	2,889	1,455	968	466
1966	16,670	10,213	6,457	4,896	975	3,920	1,291	658	280	316	37	2,823	1,393	988	442
1965	15,255	9,398	5,857	4,457	869	3,587	1,199	610	269	282	37	2,515	1,237	892	386
1964	14,155	8,745	5,410	4,148	848	3,300	1,108	583	231	260	34	2,289	1,132	806	351
1963	13,107	8,148	4,959	3,804	765	3,039	1,034	540	218	244	32	2,032	1,025	698	309
1962	12,381	7,683	4,698	3,681	782	2,900	973	519	200	223	31	1,897	976	629	292
1961	11,845	7,270	4,575	3,623	802	2,821	924	508	187	200	29	1,691	887	548	256
1960	11,932	7,296	4,636	3,703	836	2,867	941	525	184	200	32	1,590	783	527	281
1959	11,255	6,835	4,420	3,546	826	2,720	866	478	168	185	35	1,494	740	486	267
1958	10,302	6,331	3,971	3,193	769	2,424	767	425	151	158	33	1,354	709	397	248
1957	10,311	6,253	4,057	3,283	810	2,474	814	451	164	161	38	1,265	670	352	244
1956	9,905	5,926	3,979	3,236	789	2,447	795	440	166	153	37	1,207	625	329	253
1955	9,194	5,407	3,788	3,088	743	2,345	729	396	161	133	39	1,025	540	260	225
1954	8,164	4,812	3,352	2,695	635	2,060	668	363	152	114	39	809	422	207	180
1953	7,755	4,521	3,235	2,645	643	2,002	667	351	158	118	41	606	320	146	141
1952	7,156	4,096	3,060	2,473	562	1,910	616	325	149	101	41	454	256	94	104
1951	6,426	3,701	2,725	2,258	549	1,709	574	297	144	95	38	332	181	70	82

Series T 444–471. Volume of Advertising, by Medium: 1867 to 1970—Con.

[In millions of dollars]

Year	Total	National	Local	Newspapers			Magazines					Television			
				Total	National	Local	Total	Weeklies	Women's	Monthlies	Farm, national	Total	Network	Spot	Local
	444	445	446	447	448	449	450	451	452	453	454	455	456	457	458
1950	5,710	3,257	2,453	2,076	533	1,542	515	261	129	88	37	171	85	31	55
1949	5,202	2,965	2,237	1,916	476	1,440	493	245	129	84	35	58	29	9	19
1948	4,864	2,776	2,088	1,750	394	1,356	513	258	133	87	35	------	------	------	------
1947	4,260	2,487	1,772	1,475	336	1,139	493	246	133	85	29	------	------	------	------
1946	3,364	1,963	1,401	1,158	248	911	427	202	127	76	22	------	------	------	------
1945	2,875	1,775	1,099	921	211	710	365	188	97	59	20	------	------	------	------
1944	2,724	1,669	1,054	888	197	691	324	173	82	51	18	------	------	------	------
1943	2,496	1,452	1,045	900	182	718	275	154	65	39	16	------	------	------	------
1942	2,156	1,212	944	798	144	654	199	107	51	28	12	------	------	------	------
1941	2,236	1,259	977	844	165	680	214	117	52	32	12	------	------	------	------
1940	2,088	1,163	925	815	163	652	198	104	49	34	12	------	------	------	------
1939	1,980	1,086	895	793	153	640	180	88	48	32	11	------	------	------	------
1938	1,904	1,031	873	782	150	632	169	75	52	31	11	------	------	------	------
1937	2,072	1,103	969	873	173	700	193	83	60	38	12	------	------	------	------
1936	1,902	1,003	899	844	171	673	162	67	57	30	8	------	------	------	------
1935	1,690	859	831	762	152	610	136	54	52	25	6	------	------	------	------

Year	Radio				Farm papers	Direct mail	Business papers	Outdoor			Miscellaneous			Year	Total
	Total	Network	Spot	Local				Total	National	Local	Total	National	Local		
	459	460	461	462	463	464	465	466	467	468	469	470	471		444
1970	1,278	58	355	865	31	2,734	740	234	154	80	3,850	2,148	1,702	1934	1,627
1969	1,264	59	368	837	32	2,670	752	213	138	75	3,837	2,165	1,672	1933	1,302
1968	1,190	63	360	767	33	2,612	714	208	137	71	3,556	2,035	1,521	1932	1,627
1967	1,031	64	310	658	33	2,488	707	191	126	65	3,306	1,917	1,389	1931	2,282
1966	1,010	64	308	639	34	2,461	712	178	118	60	3,267	1,904	1,363		
1965	917	60	275	582	34	2,324	671	180	120	60	2,959	1,751	1,209	1930	2,607
1964	846	59	256	531	33	2,184	623	175	117	58	2,750	1,614	1,138	1929	3,426
1963	789	56	243	490	34	2,078	615	171	115	56	2,551	1,519	1,032	1928	3,262
1962	736	46	233	457	34	1,933	597	171	115	56	2,359	1,400	959	1927	3,262
1961	683	43	221	420	33	1,850	578	180	122	59	2,283	1,296	987	1926	3,262
1960	692	43	222	428	35	1,830	609	203	137	66	2,328	1,368	960	1925	3,099
1959	656	44	206	406	36	1,688	569	193	130	63	2,206	1,278	928	1924	2,935
1958	619	58	190	372	34	1,589	525	192	129	62	2,030	1,199	830	1923	2,935
1957	618	64	187	368	34	1,471	568	199	134	65	2,059	1,184	874	1922	2,607
1956	567	61	161	346	36	1,419	496	201	136	65	1,948	1,115	833	1921	2,282
1955	545	84	134	326	34	1,299	446	192	130	63	1,836	1,040	796	1920	2,935
1954	559	114	135	309	32	1,202	408	187	126	61	1,604	895	710	1919	2,282
1953	611	141	146	324	31	1,099	395	176	119	57	1,525	845	679	1918	1,468
1952	624	162	142	321	29	1,024	365	162	109	53	1,409	766	643	1917	1,627
1951	606	180	138	289	26	924	292	149	101	49	1,265	693	572	1916	1,468
1950	605	196	136	273	21	803	251	143	96	46	1,125	610	515	1915	1,302
1949	571	203	123	245	21	756	248	131	88	43	1,010	540	470	1914	1,302
1948	562	211	121	230	20	689	251	132	89	43	947	509	438	1909	1,142
1947	506	201	106	199	20	580	233	121	79	43	833	461	372	1904	821
1946	454	200	98	157	14	334	211	86	60	26	680	385	294	1900	542
1945	424	198	92	134	12	290	204	72	50	22	587	366	221	1890	360
1944	394	192	87	114	11	326	177	56	39	17	549	328	221	1880	200
1943	314	157	71	86	9	322	142	42	30	13	493	274	219	1867	50
1942	260	129	59	73	6	329	98	44	31	13	422	224	198		
1941	247	125	52	70	7	353	89	53	37	16	430	224	205		
1940	216	113	42	60	7	334	76	45	34	11	398	204	194		
1939	184	99	35	50	6	333	69	44	33	11	372	184	188		
1938	167	89	34	44	3	324	61	43	32	11	356	172	183		
1937	165	89	28	48	7	333	70	44	33	11	388	185	204		
1936	122	76	23	24	4	319	61	38	29	10	353	164	189		
1935	113	63	15	35	4	282	51	31	23	8	312	137	175		

Series T 472–484.   Indexes of National Advertising Expenditures, by Medium: 1935 to 1970

[1967 = 100]

| Year | General index | Magazines | | | | | Network radio | Spot radio | Network television | Spot television | News-papers | Business papers | Outdoor advertising |
| | | Total | Weekly | Women's | General | Farm | | | | | | | |
	472	473	474	475	476	477	478	479	480	481	482	483	484
1970	112	103	95	107	120	89	88	118	114	125	108	105	122
1969	114	108	102	109	120	91	92	117	115	127	113	106	110
1968	106	103	101	101	110	100	98	115	105	114	106	101	109
1967	100	100	100	100	100	100	100	100	100	100	100	100	100
1966	100	101	101	99	101	106	100	98	96	100	104	101	94
1965	91	94	94	95	90	106	94	88	85	90	93	95	95
1964	84	87	90	82	83	97	92	82	78	82	91	88	93
1963	78	81	83	77	78	91	88	77	70	71	82	87	91
1962	74	76	80	71	71	89	72	74	67	64	84	84	91
1961	70	72	78	66	64	83	67	70	61	55	86	82	97
1960	70	74	81	65	64	91	67	71	54	53	89	86	109
1959	66	68	73	60	59	100	69	66	51	49	88	80	103
1958	60	60	65	53	51	94	91	61	49	40	82	74	102
1957	61	64	69	58	52	109	100	60	46	36	87	80	106
1956	58	62	68	59	49	106	95	51	43	33	84	70	108
1955	52	57	61	57	43	111	131	43	37	26	79	63	103
1954	46	52	56	54	37	111	178	43	29	21	68	58	100
1953	44	52	54	56	38	117	220	46	22	15	69	56	94
1952	39	48	50	53	32	117	253	45	18	10	60	52	87
1951	36	45	46	51	30	109	281	44	12	7	59	41	80
1950	31	40	40	46	28	106	306	43	6	3	57	36	76
1949	28	39	38	46	27	100	317	39	2	1	51	35	70
1948	27	40	40	47	28	100	330	39	--------	--------	42	36	71
1947	25	39	38	47	27	83	314	34	--------	--------	36	33	63
1946	21	33	31	45	24	63	313	31	--------	--------	26	30	48
1945	19	29	29	34	19	57	309	29	--------	--------	23	29	40
1944	17	25	27	29	16	51	300	28	--------	--------	21	25	31
1943	15	21	24	23	12	46	245	23	--------	--------	19	20	24
1942	11	16	16	18	9	34	202	19	--------	--------	15	14	25
1941	12	17	18	18	10	34	195	17	--------	--------	18	13	29
1940	11	15	16	17	11	34	177	13	--------	--------	17	11	27
1939	10	14	14	17	10	31	154	11	--------	--------	16	10	26
1938	9	13	12	18	10	31	139	11	--------	--------	16	9	25
1937	10	15	13	21	12	34	139	9	--------	--------	18	10	26
1936	9	13	10	20	10	23	119	7	--------	--------	18	9	23
1935	7	11	8	18	8	17	98	5	--------	--------	16	7	18

Series T 485–491.   Newspaper Advertising—Linage for 52 Cities: 1928 to 1970

[In thousands of lines]

| Year | Total | Classified | Display | | | | | Year | Total | Classified | Display | | | | |
| | | | Total | Auto-motive | Financial | General [1] | Retail | | | | Total | Auto-motive | Financial | General [1] | Retail |
	485	486	487	488	489	490	491		485	486	487	488	489	490	491
1970	3,443,755	917,262	2,526,512	161,570	74,907	275,156	2,014,880	1948	2,263,446	522,446	1,741,000	82,737	25,791	338,641	1,293,831
1969	3,575,126	1,017,084	2,558,042	173,263	81,677	300,080	2,003,022	1947	2,008,536	473,600	1,534,936	68,672	24,417	314,605	1,127,242
1968	3,381,058	923,725	2,457,334	170,958	72,839	296,134	1,917,404	1946	1,729,713	423,662	1,306,051	42,106	26,376	266,285	971,284
1967	3,297,750	878,114	2,419,636	158,506	66,943	297,106	1,897,081								
1966	3,354,253	924,255	2,429,998	182,894	73,184	310,287	1,863,632	1945	1,391,629	320,156	1,071,474	34,656	22,090	246,052	768,676
								1944	1,361,244	308,891	1,052,353	31,479	18,365	250,926	751,584
1965	3,164,577	865,631	2,298,946	170,366	63,350	288,528	1,776,702	1943	1,396,418	335,042	1,061,377	32,358	17,758	247,424	763,837
1964	2,973,466	787,135	2,186,331	159,729	60,867	292,549	1,673,186	1942	1,241,672	257,312	984,360	26,823	17,623	196,653	743,261
1963	2,856,483	749,734	2,106,749	150,555	58,841	285,778	1,611,576	1941	1,313,233	272,568	1,040,666	56,445	20,478	194,053	769,690
1962	2,798,250	725,507	2,072,743	149,307	58,017	301,495	1,563,923								
1961	2,776,958	697,740	2,079,217	147,598	59,175	323,043	1,549,401	1940	1,268,632	262,811	1,005,821	62,006	19,424	188,629	735,761
								1939	1,243,550	252,725	990,825	52,678	20,308	191,859	725,980
1960	2,888,617	735,212	2,153,405	165,208	54,234	345,694	1,588,269	1938	1,225,166	255,012	970,154	47,255	19,170	191,948	711,781
1959	2,865,238	727,574	2,137,664	155,080	54,704	363,580	1,564,299	1937	1,409,666	283,416	1,126,250	67,802	22,480	247,155	788,813
1958	2,685,618	628,748	2,056,869	141,761	46,400	360,844	1,507,864	1936	1,380,121	265,475	1,114,646	72,822	25,025	251,510	765,289
1957	2,829,132	685,470	2,143,662	181,400	47,515	377,714	1,537,033								
1956	2,910,781	724,610	2,186,170	170,021	45,274	408,645	1,562,231	1935	1,246,942	228,972	1,017,969	72,929	21,309	216,976	706,755
								1934	1,178,880	205,322	973,559	73,306	19,128	211,384	669,741
1955	2,843,395	704,461	2,138,934	191,034	40,593	376,201	1,531,107	1933	1,065,515	197,262	868,253	62,642	20,179	188,045	597,386
1954	2,581,175	602,772	1,978,403	143,015	36,347	358,040	1,441,002	1932	1,164,770	220,361	944,409	63,790	23,680	201,830	655,109
1953	2,610,670	648,841	1,961,829	140,145	33,424	368,049	1,420,212	1931	1,464,868	265,270	1,199,598	80,613	40,984	261,817	816,183
1952	2,505,393	617,512	1,887,881	107,424	32,284	349,131	1,399,041								
1951	2,478,463	582,014	1,896,449	109,996	30,164	366,661	1,389,629	1930	1,654,246	298,950	1,355,296	107,186	59,255	303,051	885,804
								1929	1,897,213	345,441	1,551,772	150,473	74,177	338,875	988,248
1950	2,440,150	510,633	1,929,517	120,592	28,274	389,564	1,391,086	1928	1,802,482	345,835	1,456,647	142,325	66,005	289,779	958,538
1949	2,301,968	484,024	1,817,944	105,485	25,345	354,781	1,332,333								

[1] Advertising of specific products on general sale, as distinguished from the advertising of retail stores, and automotive or financial advertising.

Chapter U

International Transactions and Foreign Commerce

International Transactions and Foreign Aid (Series U 1-186)

U 1–74. General note.

This section presents statistics on the balance of international payments and the international investment position of the United States. Separate tables show the value of U.S. direct investments in foreign countries and of foreign direct investments in the United States, both by area and industry groups. The balance of international payments shows the economic transactions between residents of the United States and those of all other areas of the world during a stated time period. The international investment position indicates the value of U.S. investments abroad and of foreign investments in the United States at specified points of time. The change in the international investment position of the United States results partly from the movement of foreign and U.S. capital, as presented in the balance of international payments, and partly from other factors, such as changes in the valuation of assets or liabilities, including changes in the market value of securities, defaults, expropriations, writeoffs, and reinvested earnings of subsidiaries operating abroad and of foreign subsidiaries operating in the United States. U.S. direct investments in foreign countries include all foreign enterprises whose voting stock is owned to the extent of at least 25 percent by U.S. organizations or individuals, or in the management of which Americans have an important voice. In addition, they include unincorporated foreign branches or other direct foreign operations of U.S. interests, including mining claims, oil concessions, and other property held for business purposes such as real estate. Similarly, foreign direct investments in the United States cover U.S. business enterprises, including real estate investments, in which there was a foreign interest or ownership of 25 percent or more.

In all the series of this section, international organizations, such as the International Monetary Fund, the International Bank for Reconstruction and Development, and the United Nations, though located within the United States, are considered extra-territorial. Consequently, transactions between the United States and these organizations are considered international transactions of the United States, while transactions between them and foreign countries do not enter the balance of payments of the United States. U.S. holdings of their obligations and U.S. liabilities to them are part of the U.S. investment position.

U 1–25. Balance of international payments, 1790–1970.

Source: U.S. Office of Business Economics, 1790–1918 (except series U 24, 1874–1900), unpublished data; series U 24, 1874–1900, U.S. Department of the Treasury, *Annual Report, Director of the Mint*, 1921, p. 130. U.S. Bureau of Economic Analysis (formerly Office of Business Economics), 1919–1945, *Balance of Payments Statistical Supplement*, 1958, pp. 10–13; 1946–1970, *Survey of Current Business*, June 1970, p. 34; October 1972, pp. 26–27; June 1972, pp. 26 and 30.

Basically the figures for 1790–1918 are from publications by private authors; therefore, they are unofficial figures. However, the figures, as shown by these authors, have been rearranged and adjusted, and in some cases supplemented, for this volume by the former U.S. Office of Business Economics (OBE). The reclassified figures fit into the concepts and framework currently used in the official balance of payments statements prepared by OBE.

The original figures are from the following private publications:

1790–1860, Douglass C. North, "The United States Balance of Payments, 1790–1860," *Studies in Income and Wealth*, Princeton University Press, vol. 24, 1960; 1861–1900, Matthew Simon, "The United States Balance of Payments, 1861–1900," *Studies in Income and Wealth*, Princeton University Press, vol. 24, 1960; and 1901–1918 (with the exception of exports and imports of merchandise trade and silver), Paul D. Dickens, "The Transitional Period of American International Financing, 1897–1914" (unpublished doctoral dissertation, George Washington University, 1933), and C. J. Bullock, John H. Williams, and Rufus S. Tucker, "The Balance of Trade of the United States," *Review of Economic Statistics*, July 1919. Data on merchandise trade and silver for 1901–1918 were taken from Department of Commerce, *Monthly Summary of Foreign Commerce*, various issues.

The estimates for 1901–1918 were revised primarily to make them consistent with, and to link them to, data prepared for subsequent years. The revised estimates were published by Raymond W. Goldsmith in *Study of Savings in the United States*, Princeton University Press, 1956, vol. 1, pp. 1078, 1080, 1081, 1084, and 1086.

The Department of Commerce began its series in 1922, later extending the data backward to cover 1919–1921. Data for quarterly U.S. international transactions, total and with individual regions of the rest of the world, are available currently in the March, June, September, and December issues of the *Survey of Current Business*.

The balance of payments statement reflects all the exchanges of goods, services, gold, and capital claims between residents of the United States and residents of all other areas of the world. Since 1919, residents of the United States comprise residents of conterminous United States, Alaska, Hawaii, Puerto Rico, American Samoa, and Virgin Islands. Beginning 1940, residents of the Panama Canal Zone are also included. As noted above, international organizations are not regarded as residents of the United States.

Transactions entering into the balance of payments are divided into four categories—goods and services, unilateral transfers, capital movements, and transactions in U.S. official reserve assets. The balance of payments statement is built on a double entry system, whereby, in principle, every transaction is recorded both as a debit and a credit. Debits represent increases in assets or decreases in liabilities, and credits represent decreases in assets or increases in liabilities. Thus, an export of merchandise in return for a check drawn on a foreign account in a bank in this country results in a credit for the export (a reduction in an asset) and a debit for the reduction in foreign-held bank deposits (a reduction in a liability). Unilateral transfers to foreign countries (payments) are debits (as are expense items in accounting), and unilateral transfers from foreign countries (receipts) are credits (as are income items in accounting). While all transactions have a debit and credit phase which are necessarily equal, both sides are not estimated simultaneously nor from the same sources; hence, the possibility of error. The resulting discrepancy, referred to as "errors and omissions," series U 25, is given a plus or minus sign, depending upon which is necessary to make the accounts balance.

The procedure generally followed by North and Simon in their studies was to estimate receipts and payments on account of merchandise trade, transportation, travel, interest, dividends, and remittances. The authors then assumed that the balance indicated net flows of U.S. and foreign capital. For 1790–1900, series U 18–23 represents this balance which, of course, includes any errors and omissions in the estimates.

Data on exports and imports of merchandise used in the study by North are reported to include gold and silver prior to 1821 (see *Statistical Abstract of the United States, 1957*, p. 890). A separate estimate, however, was made by North for net movements of gold, because he concluded on the basis of his research that specie movements were in fact not included in the merchandise trade figures prior to 1821. (See "The United States Balance of Payments, 1790–1860," pp. 24–25.) This estimate is included in series U 2 and U 9. Although the annual amounts are small, varying from net exports of $1 million to $2.5 million to net imports of $1 million to $4 million, the residual item, or net movement of capital, may be in error by the same amount.

North indicates that the reliability of the data on exports prior to 1820 is doubtful and that data on imports are incomplete. The paucity of information also made the estimates for other transactions for this period considerably less satisfactory than for subsequent years. Consequently, North suggests that 5-year averages may be more reliable than the annual data. Such averages are included in his study.

For the classification and contents of series U 1–25, 1900–1918, see Raymond W. Goldsmith, cited above. Three transactions have been entered which did not appear in this study. See text below for series U 17 and U 18.

For methods of estimating later data, see *Balance of Payments of the United States, 1949–1951*, a supplement to the *Survey of Current Business*, Office of Business Economics. Continued changes and improvements in the methods of collecting data have been made and the figures have become progressively more reliable over time. For an evaluation of data for recent years, see Report of the Review Committee for Balance of Payments Statistics to the Bureau of the Budget, *The Balance of Payments Statistics of the United States: A Review and Appraisal*, April 1965.

U 2 and **U 9**, merchandise. The estimates for ship sales for 1790–1900 are included in exports, series U 2. For 1790–1819, the net export or import of specie is included in series U 2 or U 9, respectively. The gross movements of specie were not available. For 1820–1860, exports of specie are included in series U 2 and imports in series U 9. Exports and imports of gold for 1861–1873, of nonmonetary gold for 1874–1900, and of silver for 1861–1900 are included in series U 2 and U 9, respectively.

The data for 1901–1918 include merchandise trade proper, silver, and nonmonetary gold. The basic data on merchandise trade for 1919–1970 are the official trade statistics published until 1965 in *Foreign Commerce and Navigation* and since then in the foreign trade reports of the Bureau of the Census. For 1919–1970, adjustments in both exports and imports have been made to correct for known overvaluation or undervaluation, to exclude noncommercial items, to include an estimate for unrecorded trade, and to adjust for certain differences in territorial coverage, e.g., to exclude the trade with the Panama Canal Zone, beginning with 1940. For World War II and early postwar years, data on Government purchases were substituted for certain import data. For Government-financed transfers of merchandise, the figures based on fiscal records were used instead of the figures appearing in the recorded export statistics. For the years after World War I and World War II, sales and other transfers of surplus property located abroad were added to recorded export statistics. Prior to 1946, series U 2 also includes the transfers with or without compensation to allied countries of military equipment, including that purchased abroad under the Mutual Defense Assistance Program. A small amount of services connected with these transfers was also included. Series U 2 and U 9 include nonmonetary movements of gold. For the treatment of gold, see series U 24 below.

U 3 and **U 10**, transportation. For 1790–1819, series U 3 represents gross earnings on freight carried in U.S. ships. Some adjustment was made to eliminate earnings from ships carrying U.S. imports.

For 1820–1860, series U 3 includes earnings by U.S. ships from carrying U.S. exports and from carrying freight between foreign ports. It also includes American port charges paid by foreign ships. Transportation payments, series U 10, consist of freight payments to foreign ships for carrying U.S. imports, and expenditures of American ships in foreign ports. Port expenditures and receipts are estimated as a percentage of freight earnings by American and foreign ships, respectively. (Fare payments to American ships by immigrants are included in the estimate for immigrant funds. See discussion of series U 16, private unilateral transactions. For fare payments of tourists, see discussion of travel, series U 4 and U 11.) For 1861–1900, series U 3 includes ocean freight earnings from carrying U.S. exports and from carrying freight between foreign ports, and port expenditures in the United States of the foreign merchant marine and of passenger steamships. The estimates for the years 1871–1900 also include earnings from carrying overland freight. Payments for transportation, series U 10, includes ocean freight payments on U.S. imports, and expenditures in foreign ports by the U.S. merchant marine. Passenger fares are included in the travel account (series U 4 and U 11). The data for 1900–1918 include receipts and payments on account of ocean freight, and port charges. For 1916–1918, payments for charter hire were added.

For 1919–1970, the transportation category includes international freight, fares and shipboard expenses of travelers, revenues and expenditures resulting from the charter of vessels and the rental of freight cars, and the expenses of U.S. transportation companies abroad and foreign transportation companies in the United States. The data cover air and surface transportation.

U 4 and **U 11**, travel. For 1790–1819, no estimate was made for international travel expenditures. For 1820–1860, series U 4 includes tourist expenditures in the United States and their fare payments to American ships; series U 11 represents American tourist expenditures abroad. North assumed that American tourists going abroad and, for the most part, foreigners coming to the United States traveled on American ships during this period. The method employed in the source study for estimating tourism precludes the transfer of fare payments to the transportation account. For 1861–1900, series U 4 includes outlays of foreign travelers in the United States. It was assumed that alien travelers came to the United States on foreign lines and, therefore, no estimate was made for receipt of fares. Series U 11 includes payments abroad by American tourists for maintenance and for ocean fares. Simon assumed that the bulk of the travel during 1861–1900 was on foreign ships. The outlays for procurement of sundry items and luxury consumption goods were not included in his estimate for expenditures abroad by American tourists.

The data for 1900–1918 include fares paid to U.S. ships by foreign tourists and to foreign ships by U.S. tourists.

For 1919–1970, all expenditures made in the United States by foreign residents, except those of diplomats and other official personnel stationed here, are included in the travel receipts. Expenditures made in foreign countries by U.S. travelers for food, lodging, amusements, gifts, and other personal purchases constitute travel payments. Expenditures for transportation within or between foreign countries when purchased abroad are, in general, included as travel expenditures. However, passenger fares for overseas transportation to the ultimate destination (even if the ticket permits stopovers enroute) when paid to foreign carriers by U.S. residents, and when paid to U.S. carriers by foreign residents, are included in the transportation account.

U 5, **U 6**, and **U 13**, income on investments. For 1790–1900, series U 13 represents net payments of income on investments by the United States. The income was computed by applying an assumed yield rate to the net indebtedness of the United States.

For 1900–1918, separate estimates were made for receipts and payments. Series U 5 for 1915–1918 includes income on private and Government war loans. See Goldsmith, cited above, p. 1078.

For 1919–1970, income includes all interest, dividends, and branch profits effectively paid or credited during the period, after payment of all taxes in the country in which the payer of income resides.

Private income, series U 5, for 1919–1970 includes interest, dividends, and branch profits from direct investments, and interest and dividends received from holdings of foreign bonds by residents in the United States, from stocks issued by foreign corporations which are not U.S. direct investments, from loans by banks and other financial or commercial organizations, from miscellaneous assets such as commercial real estate, insurance policies, commercial claims of various kinds, trusts and estates, and mortgages. Reinvested earnings, or the parent company's equity in the undistributed earnings on common stock of foreign subsidiary companies, are not included except for 1919–1929. Reinvested earnings are, however, regularly tabulated and used for computing changes in the international investment position of the United States.

Government income, series U 6, for 1919–1970 includes interest received by the U.S. Government on long- and short-term loans and other investments.

Income payments, series U 13, for 1919–1970 include payments of interest, dividends, and branch profits by foreign direct investment companies in the United States, interest and dividend payments to foreign holders of other American bonds and stocks (including U.S. Government securities), and payments of income on various miscellaneous assets such as estates and trusts.

U 7 and U 14, other transactions. Marine insurance and brokers' commissions constitute series U 14 for 1790–1819. No estimate was made for these transactions between 1820 and 1860. For 1861–1900, series U 7 consists of receipts on marine insurance; series U 14 comprises payments for marine insurance and net payments for brokers' commissions.

For 1900–1918, no estimates were made.

For 1919–1970, the coverage of miscellaneous service items has expanded and now includes receipts and payments from insurance transactions, communications, management services, motion picture and other royalties; receipts from fees of American engineering, construction, and consulting firms, from foreign contracts, from foreign governments in the United States, and expenditures of U.S. Government agencies abroad, except expenditures by the Department of Defense. The latter is included in series U 12, while receipts from abroad by the military agencies are included in series U 2.

U 12, military expenditures. This item includes direct outlays by the military agencies in dollars and in foreign currencies, as well as expenditures in the foreign economies by troops, civilian personnel of the military agencies, and post exchanges. It does not include expenditures of deutsche marks received from the Federal Republic of Germany or of yen received from Japan for the support of Allied and U.S. Forces stationed in the respective countries. Offshore procurement under military assistance programs and the purchase of goods and services to be transferred to other foreign countries under aid programs are included in the expenditures by military agencies.

U 16–17, unilateral transfers, net. No estimate was made prior to 1820 for series U 16. For 1820–1860, series U 16 represents the excess of funds brought into the United States by immigrants and their fare payments to American shipping companies over the amounts remitted abroad after their arrival in this country. For 1861–1916, series U 16 consists of the immigrant remittances and funds carried by immigrants into the country (+) and out (−). The estimate for immigrant remittances includes remittances through banks and an estimate for outlays by U.S. residents for prepayment of passage for friends and relatives planning to emigrate to the United States. For 1917 and subsequent years, remittances in cash and kind by religious, educational, and charitable institutions are also included. For series U 17, the entries of $0.6 million for 1794–1796 represent annual payments to the Barbary pirates. The payment of $11.2 million in 1803 was to France for the purchase of Louisiana Territory. The United States acquired sovereignty over this territory in 1803 and issued bonds for the amount of the purchase. These

bonds carried an interest rate of 6 percent per year and were redeemed between 1812–1823. The interest during this period amounted to $8.2 million, $5.6 million of which was paid in the first 10 years. (See E. M. Douglas, *Boundaries, Areas, Geographic Centers and Altitudes of the United States and the Several States*, Washington, D.C., 1930.) Presumably the interest is included in the estimate for income payments, series U 13. The entries of $5.5 million for 1836–1838 represent receipts by the U.S. Government from France on behalf of American citizens in satisfaction of claims for indemnities arising from the Napoleonic wars. (See J. T. Adams, ed., *Dictionary of American History*, Scribner's, New York, 1940, vol. II, p. 348.) Interest of $0.5 million ($0.3, $0.1, and $0.1 million for 1836–1838, respectively) is included. In 1848, at the end of the Mexican War, the United States and Mexico signed the treaty of Guadelupe-Hidalgo which gave to the United States the present States of Arizona, New Mexico, California, Nevada, Utah, and Colorado west of the Rockies. The payment by the United States of $15 million for this territory, plus interest of $1.4 million, is represented by the entries for 1849–1852. These entries were referred to in the study, "United States Balance of Payments, 1790–1860," as indemnity payments and entered in the capital account. The entries for 1854–1856, aggregating $10 million, represent the Gadsden purchase. Russia, in March 1867, agreed to sell Alaska to the United States for $7.2 million in gold. The United States took possession in fiscal year 1868, but payment was not made until fiscal year 1869. During the Civil War, Great Britain had sold to the Confederate States ships which were used as privateers to sink the Union ships. An international tribunal in 1873 held Great Britain liable to the extent of $15.5 million. Payment was made to the United States in 1873, as indemnity on behalf of its citizens. The treaty of peace with Spain in 1898, as a result of which the Philippines, Guam, and Puerto Rico were ceded to the United States, stipulated a payment to Spain of $20 million.

The figures for series U 17 include two transactions which are not included in Goldsmith's *Study of Saving . . .*, mentioned earlier for the 1900–1918 period. In 1904, the U.S. Government paid $10 million to the Republic of Panama for lease of the Panama Canal, and in 1917, the United States bought the Virgin Islands from Denmark for $25 million. These transactions appear in series U 17.

For 1919–1970, series U 17 consists of Government transfers of goods, services, or cash, in both dollars and foreign currencies, for which payment by the foreign country has not been made, is not expected, or has not been specified, less reverse lend-lease, counterpart funds on certain foreign-aid programs, and other receipts. Series U 17 also includes Government payments of pensions, receipts or payments for idemnities, intangible rights, or other considerations.

U 18–23, U.S. capital flows, net, and foreign capital flows, net. For 1790–1900, the data for series U 18 and U 23 represent the net flow of U.S. and foreign capital, and were estimated as residuals, to balance the other items in the balance of payments. Consequently, they reflect errors and omissions in the estimates of the other items. For some of these years, particularly 1861–1900, the data shown here differ from those in the source studies because of adjustments in some of the other series. For 1900–1918, see Goldsmith, cited above, pp. 1080–1081.

In 1904, the figure for series U 18 includes the payment by the U.S. Government of $40 million for the original Panama Canal Company. This transaction was not included in Goldsmith's *Study of Saving.*

For 1919–1970, the data for series U 18–21 represent changes in assets or in investments of the United States abroad. The long-term transactions represent shifts in capital claims of indefinite maturity or of a stated original maturity of more than one year from the date of issuance. Short-term transactions represent changes in claims on foreigners with a maturity of one year or less. For 1919–1970, series U 18 (long-term) includes disbursements of foreign loans, net of repayments, by all U.S. Government agencies, whether made in dollars or in foreign currencies. Also included are movements of capital related to the operation by the U.S. Government of productive facilities abroad, and U.S. capital contributions to international organizations such as the International Monetary Fund, the International Bank for Reconstruction and Development, and the International Finance Corporation. Loan operations between these organizations and foreign countries are not included since such organizations are regarded as foreign entities in the U.S. balance of payments. Loans made by private banks and guaranteed by the Export-Import Bank are included in series U 20. Real property purchased by the Government for administrative purposes is included in series U 14, other transactions, while all expenditures of religious, educational, and charitable institutions are included in series U 16, unilateral transfers, even if they involve the purchase of fixed assets. For 1919–1970, series U 18 (short-term) includes changes in the U.S. Government short-term claims arising from holdings of foreign currencies (received as a counterpart to foreign grants or through sales of agricultural and other surplus products), deposits abroad, and various advances.

For 1919–1970, the shifts in capital claims in series U 19 and U 20 refer not only to securities (stocks, bonds, mortgages, etc.) but also to real property (farms, branch factories, and real estate). Series U 19 consists of net purchases of stocks in, and of changes in, net claims by U.S. parent companies against foreign incorporated companies in the management of which U.S. companies have an important voice, and net changes in the equity in foreign branches of U.S. companies. Series U 20, other private long-term capital movements, consists of U.S. purchases of newly issued foreign securities, amortizations of foreign bonds, net transactions in outstanding foreign securities, and net changes in long-term claims reported by U.S. banks (including loans made by private banks and guaranteed by the Export-Import Bank) and other commercial enterprises.

Series U 21 includes changes in bank deposits, brokerage and commercial balances, and uncollected bills.

For 1919–1970, the data for series U 22–23 represent changes in liabilities of the United States to residents of foreign countries, or changes in assets held in the United States by residents of foreign countries. Series U 22 represents shifts in foreign claims on the United States with an original maturity of more than one year, including changes in the investments of foreign corporations in their branches and subsidiaries in the United States, and transactions by foreigners in the U.S. public debt obligations. Series U 23 represents shifts in the liabilities of the U.S. Government and of private individuals and institutions with an original maturity of one year or less. Foreign short-term claims on the U.S. Government include deposits with the Treasury and other Government agencies and changes in foreign holdings of U.S. Government short-term obligations. Foreign short-term claims on private Americans include foreign deposits in U.S. banks, changes in holdings of privately issued short-term securities, and other commercial liabilities. The data also include an estimate of movements of U.S. currency and coins.

U 24, transactions in U.S. official reserve assets, net. This entry measures net changes in the official reserve assets of the United States, which consist of U.S. holdings of monetary gold, special drawing rights (SDR), convertible foreign currencies, and gold tranche position in the International Monetary Fund (IMF).

Monetary gold includes the U.S. gold stock held by the U.S. Treasury and the Exchange Stabilization Fund. (On December 9, 1974, Treasury acquired all gold held by the Exchange Stabilization Fund.) The transactions also included gold sold to the United States by the IMF with the right to repurchase, and gold deposited by the IMF to mitigate the impact on the U.S. gold stock of foreign purchases for gold subscription to the IMF under quota increases. Special drawing rights are international reserve assets created through amendments to the Articles of Agreement of the IMF to provide orderly and adequate growth in international liquidity. Thus far (1974) there have been three annual allocations to the United States and other participating nations made on January 1, of 1970, 1971, and 1972. U.S. holdings of special drawing rights in the Special

Drawing Account in the IMF include allocations and acquisitions, net of use. Convertible foreign currencies represent Treasury and Federal Reserve System holdings of convertible foreign currencies in U.S. dollar equivalents. The U.S. gold tranche position in the IMF represents the amount that the United States could purchase in foreign currencies automatically if needed; it is equivalent to the U.S. quota in the IMF minus the Fund's holdings of U.S. dollars.

U 25, errors and omissions. As indicated above, this is the residual item which has been given the sign (+ or −) necessary to make the statement balance. It compensates for missing data, possible errors in the estimates, as well as for seasonal and other leads and lags in the reporting of the debt and credit phases of transactions which are compensating over a period of time.

U 26–39. International investment position of the United States, 1843–1970.

Source: 1843–1914, Cleona Lewis, *America's Stake in International Investments*, The Brookings Institution, Washington, D.C., 1938 (copyright). 1919–1945, U.S. Office of Business Economics, various publications. 1946–1970, U.S. Bureau of Economic Analysis (formerly Office of Business Economics), *Balance of Payments Statistical Supplement, Revised Edition;* and *Survey of Current Business,* August 1963 and 1964, September 1965 and 1966, and October 1968–1972.

The estimates for 1919–1945 are based on the following publications: (1) *The United States in the World Economy,* Office of Business Economics, Economic Series No. 23, Washington, D.C., 1943, p. 123; (2) *The Balance of International Payments of the United States in 1931,* Bureau of Foreign and Domestic Commerce, Trade Information Bulletin No. 803, Washington, D.C., 1932, pp. 44, 48, and 62; (3) *Foreign Investments in the United States,* Bureau of Foreign and Domestic Commerce, Washington, D.C., 1937, p. 5; (4) Cleona Lewis (see source above for 1843–1914); (5) *International Transactions of the United States During the War 1940–45* (as revised), Office of Business Economics, Economic Series No. 65, 1948, p. 110.

In *America's Stake in International Investments,* direct investments are based on book value wherever possible; portfolio investments are calculated at par value for bonds and preferred stocks, and at market value for common stocks. Similar practices were followed in the estimates of the Department of Commerce for 1930, 1931, and 1935; miscellaneous portfolio investments for the same years were calculated at market values wherever possible. For 1940, 1945, and 1946–1970, the values of bonds and preferred stocks as well as of common stocks were calculated at market prices wherever possible.

The estimates for these series prior to 1919 were prepared by compilers who used different valuation methods and whose data varied in completeness. While the estimates are therefore not homogeneous, they do present rough indications of the magnitudes involved.

U 40. International investment position of the United States (net liabilities), 1789–1900.

Source: 1789–1860, Douglass C. North, "The United States Balance of Payments, 1789–1860," cited in text for series U 1–25; and 1861–1900, Matthew Simon, "The United States Balance of Payments, 1861–1900," also cited in text for series U 1–25. (Copyright.)

In the source studies, a net liability of $60 million was estimated for 1789. For the following years, the changes were computed by adding the annual net international flow of capital which is the balancing item, series U 18–23, for exports and imports of goods, services, and unilateral transactions. For certain years, adjustments were made for defaults. Differences between the accumulating "net indebtedness" in the source studies and the data in series U 40 are due to adjustments incorporated in series U 1–25 as explained in the text for those series.

U 41–46. Value of direct investment in foreign countries, by area and industry groups, 1929–1970.

Source: See source for series U 26–39.

See also general note for series U 1–74, and text for series U 18–23.

U 47–74. Value of foreign direct investment in the United States, by area and industry, 1937–1970.

Source: U.S. Office of Business Economics, 1937–1961, *Foreign Business Investments in the United States*, 1962; 1962–1970, *Survey of Current Business*, various issues (usually September or October).

The basic data for these series were derived from reports filed with the Department of Commerce by enterprises in the United States in which there was a foreign interest of 25 percent or more. Reports were required by law under section 8 of the Bretton Woods Agreements Act (59 Stat. 515, 22 U.S.C. 286f). Forms and instructions were mailed directly to lists of companies developed from tax records, news reports, previous census studies, and records of the Office of Business Economics.

In general, a report was required for every U.S. business enterprise, including real estate investments, in which a foreign person or organization owned 25 percent or more of the voting stock, and for similar interests in noncorporate enterprises. A report was required both when the 25 percent foreign interest was direct in a U.S. primary organization or was indirect in a subsidiary, called a secondary organization.

There were certain exemptions from filing a report, as follows: (a) If the value of total assets was less than $50,000, a report was required only for information identifying the reporter; (b) reports were not required from religious bodies, charitable organizations, or other nonprofit organizations in the United States; (c) reports were not required in connection with real or personal property acquired for personal use or occupancy.

The coverage is believed to be quite complete for substantial industrial investments. However, there are probably many small trading organizations and holdings of real estate not covered. The extent of these investments is not believed to be significant.

It should be noted that this survey does not cover portfolio foreign holdings of U.S. corporate securities, or other miscellaneous investments here.

Direct foreign investments in the United States included the following U.S. business enterprises for which reports were required: (1) A U.S. corporation in which 25 percent or more of the voting stock was owned directly or indirectly by a foreign person or organization; (2) branches of foreign corporations resident in the United States; (3) partnerships and proprietorships resident in the United States in which 25 percent or more ownership was held by a foreign person or organization; (4) U.S. enterprises held as part of an estate or trust created under the laws of the United States in which foreign beneficial owners held an interest of 25 percent or more; (5) real estate and other real property, including leaseholds, acquired for commercial purposes, in which an interest of 25 percent or more was held by a foreign person or organization.

These series cover the 50 States, the District of Columbia, the Commonwealth of Puerto Rico, the Panama Canal Zone, and outlying areas of the United States.

Each reporter or foreign-owned U.S. company was classified by the country of the foreign parent organization. Secondary reporters or subsidiaries of the primary organization were given the same country classification as the primary.

The major areas for classification were Canada, United Kingdom, other Western Europe, Latin American Republics, Asia, Africa, and Australia. The investment was generally quite small for countries in Asia, Africa, or Latin America.

The Standard Industrial Classification (SIC) issued by the then Bureau of the Budget was the basic guide used for classifying reporters by industry. However, certain departures were made in

connection with grouping certain industries into major divisions. This change in grouping consisted, for the most part, in shifting certain industries to major divisions on the basis of their relationship or integration of operations. For example, reporters engaged in petroleum production and others engaged in petroleum refining were classified under petroleum as a major industrial division. The SIC had no such classification and production is included under mining (not shown separately here) and refining under manufacturing. Similarly, other integrated operations of oil companies were included under petroleum.

Frequently a reporter was engaged in more than one business activity, especially in those cases where the report furnished was a consolidation of several companies in different lines of business. Such a report was classified according to the basic activity involved.

Reporters who were primarily holding companies of U.S. operating companies were classified according to the industry of the operating companies.

U 75–186. U.S. Government foreign grants and credits, by country, 1945–1970.

Source: U.S. Bureau of Economic Analysis, unpublished summary of data published in more detail in "Foreign Aid by the United States Government, 1940–1951," a 1952 supplement to the *Survey of Current Business*, and in the periodic report, *Foreign Grants and Credits by the United States Government*.

The following text was excerpted from *Annual Report of the Bretton Woods Agreement Act* (Communication from the Chairman, National Advisory Council on International Monetary and Financial Policies), 93d Congress, 1st session, House Doc. No. 93–34, pp. 120–122.

These series were compiled by the Bureau of Economic Analysis from information made available by agencies operating the grant, credit, and other assistance programs, and include some estimates for transactions not yet recorded on the operating agencies' books. Items based on estimates have been adjusted or qualified on the basis of information received to the date of preparation of these series, but in some instances are subject to future adjustments.

The data on credits are comparable, with minor exceptions, to those appearing in *Foreign Credits by the United States Government*, a semiannual publication of the Department of the Treasury, in which a detailed enumeration of every active foreign credit of the U.S. Government, showing its current status, is presented.

The data are divided into three categories—grants, credits, and other assistance through net accumulation of foreign currency claims under programs for the sale of agricultural commodities. The Government's capital investments in, or contributions to, the international financial institutions constitute an additional measure taken by this Government to promote foreign economic recovery and development. Payments to these institutions do not result in immediate equivalent aid to foreign countries. Use of available dollar funds is largely determined by the managements of the institutions, in some instances subject to certain controls which can be exercised by the U.S. Government. Changes in the procedures for disbursing the U.S. Government contributions, initiated in 1965, have retarded such actual Government payments to agree more closely with the actual disbursement of assistance by the international institution to the foreign country.

Grants are transfers for which no payment is expected, or which at most involve an obligation on the part of the receiver to extend aid to the United States or other countries to achieve a common objective. *Credits* are loan disbursements or transfers under other agreements which give rise to specific obligations to repay, over a period of years, usually with interest. *Other assistance* represents the transfer of U.S. farm products in exchange for foreign currencies (*plus*—since the enactment of Public Law 87–128—principal and interest collections in foreign currencies for credits extended under the farm products sales program) *less* the Government's disbursements of the currencies as grants, credits, or for purchases. The net acquisition of currencies represents net transfers of resources to foreign countries under the agricultural programs, in addition to those classified as grants or credits.

Occasionally, assistance has been given under indeterminate conditions, subject to future settlement. Indeterminate aid on this basis is included with grants, in the period rendered. When settlement for such indeterminate aid is agreed upon, the terms may call for a cash settlement or may establish a long-term credit. Cash settlements are included in returned grants. Amounts of the newly established credits are added to outstanding indebtedness.

The U.S. Government receives some returns on its gross grants and credits. The returns which are deducted from gross grants and credits to arrive at net grants and credits include (1) reverse lend-lease; (2) the dollar value of the portion of grant counterpart funds paid to the United States for its use; (3) returned lend-lease and civilian supply ships; (4) returns of military equipment "loaned"; (5) cash received in war-account settlements for lend-lease and other aid; and (6) principal repaid on credits, but not interest. The Government's disbursements of currencies are deducted from the accumulation of currency claims in calculating net other assistance.

The measure of foreign grants and credits generally is in terms of (1) dollars disbursed by the U.S. Government to or for the account of a foreign government or other foreign entity or individual, and (2) dollar equivalents of goods delivered or shipped, services rendered, or foreign currencies disbursed to or for such foreign account. Correspondingly, returns are measured in terms of the dollars received by the U.S. Government, or the dollar equivalents of goods, services, and foreign currencies received. Dollar equivalents are, of necessity, frequently estimated.

Assistance is shown by country, or general area, where possible. In certain instances (particularly in the earlier postwar period), data for parent countries include those for their dependent area; for example, although goods have been shipped to a then dependent area, Tunisia, such aid was reported as rendered to the parent country, France.

Transactions shown for a country are *not* necessarily with the government of such country, but are often with individuals, relief organizations, international organizations, or other private entities located in the designated country and considered to be within its economy.

★ ★ ★ ★ ★ ★ ★ ★ ★   **More Recent Data for *Historical Statistics* Series**   ★ ★ ★ ★ ★ ★ ★ ★ ★

★   ★

★   Statistics for more recent years in continuation of many of the still-active series shown here appear   ★

★   in annual issues of the *Statistical Abstract of the United States,* beginning with the 1975 edition. For   ★

★   direct linkage of the historical series to the tables in the *Abstract,* see Appendix I in the *Abstract.*   ★

★   ★

★ ★

Series U 1–25. Balance of International Payments: 1790 to 1970

[In millions of dollars. For fiscal years, 1790–1900; thereafter, calendar years]

Year	Exports of goods and services [1]							Imports of goods and services						
	Total	Merchandise, adjusted [2]	Transportation	Travel	Income on investments abroad		Other transactions [5]	Total	Merchandise, adjusted	Transportation	Travel	Direct military expenditures	Income on foreign investments in U.S. [6]	Other transactions [5]
					Private [3][4]	Government								
	1	2	3	4	5	6	7	8	9	10	11	12	13	14
1970	62,870	41,963	3,627	2,319	10,517	909	3,536	59,307	39,799	4,034	3,973	4,852	5,167	1,484
1969	55,502	36,417	3,112	2,058	9,607	932	3,376	53,591	35,796	3,547	3,407	4,856	4,564	1,422
1968	50,603	33,576	2,948	1,775	8,468	765	3,071	48,178	32,964	3,258	3,030	4,535	3,013	1,377
1967	46,177	30,638	2,792	1,646	7,672	638	2,791	41,041	26,821	2,994	3,207	4,378	2,423	1,217
1966	43,277	29,287	2,609	1,590	6,988	593	2,210	38,108	25,463	2,922	2,657	3,764	2,206	1,095
1965	39,408	26,438	2,415	1,380	6,583	509	2,083	32,310	21,496	2,675	2,438	2,952	1,797	952
1964	37,281	25,478	2,317	1,207	5,943	456	1,880	28,715	18,647	2,462	2,211	2,880	1,524	991
1963	32,603	22,252	2,103	1,015	5,041	498	1,695	26,646	17,011	2,316	2,114	2,961	1,386	860
1962	30,507	20,779	1,955	957	4,748	471	1,598	25,382	16,218	2,128	1,939	3,105	1,167	827
1961	28,772	20,107	1,803	947	4,223	381	1,310	23,173	14,519	1,943	1,785	2,998	1,050	878
1960	27,490	19,650	1,782	919	3,591	348	1,201	23,383	14,744	1,915	1,750	3,087	1,098	789
1959	23,652	16,458	1,646	902	3,237	349	1,060	23,342	15,310	1,759	1,610	3,107	860	696
1958	23,217	16,414	1,638	825	2,980	307	1,053	20,861	12,952	1,636	1,460	3,435	703	675
1957	26,653	19,562	1,967	785	3,058	205	1,076	20,752	13,291	1,569	1,372	3,216	675	629
1956	23,772	17,556	1,617	705	2,906	194	794	19,627	12,803	1,408	1,275	2,949	606	586
1955	19,948	14,424	1,406	654	2,543	274	647	17,795	11,527	1,204	1,153	2,901	520	490
1954	17,889	12,929	1,171	595	2,283	272	639	15,904	10,353	1,026	1,009	2,642	443	457
1953	17,078	12,412	1,198	574	1,963	252	679	16,546	10,975	1,081	929	2,615	483	463
1952	18,122	13,449	1,488	550	1,916	204	515	15,766	10,838	1,115	840	2,054	445	474
1951	18,864	14,243	1,556	473	1,956	198	438	15,047	11,176	974	757	1,270	434	436
1950	13,893	10,203	1,033	419	1,730	109	399	12,001	9,081	818	754	576	379	393
1949	15,834	12,213	1,238	392	1,517	98	376	9,616	6,874	700	700	621	342	379
1948	16,861	13,265	1,317	334	1,451	102	392	10,343	7,557	646	631	799	291	419
1947	19,819	16,097	1,738	364	1,237	66	317	8,202	5,973	583	573	455	256	362
1946	14,792	11,764	1,383	271	957	21	396	6,985	5,067	459	462	493	222	282
1945	16,273	12,473	1,308	162	572	17	1,741	10,232	5,245	420	309	2,434	231	1,593
1944	21,438	16,969	1,306	117	556	17	2,473	8,986	5,043	399	225	1,982	161	1,176
1943	19,134	15,115	1,110	84	497	12	2,316	8,096	4,599	343	173	1,763	155	1,063
1942	11,769	9,187	689	82	496	18	1,297	5,356	3,499	263	155	953	158	328
1941	6,896	5,343	562	70	535	9	377	4,486	3,416	343	212	162	187	166
1940	5,355	4,124	402	95	561	3	170	3,636	2,698	334	190	61	210	143
1939	4,432	3,347	303	135	539	2	106	3,366	2,409	367	290	46	230	24
1938	4,336	3,243	267	130	583	2	111	3,045	2,173	303	303	41	200	25
1937	4,553	3,451	236	135	576	1	154	4,256	3,181	366	348	41	295	25
1936	3,539	2,590	158	117	567	2	105	3,424	2,546	247	297	38	270	26
1935	3,265	2,404	139	101	521	--------	100	3,137	2,462	206	245	41	155	28
1934	2,975	2,238	133	81	437	--------	86	2,374	1,763	196	218	34	135	28
1933	2,402	1,736	108	66	417	20	55	2,044	1,510	154	199	41	115	25
1932	2,474	1,667	171	65	460	67	44	2,067	1,343	255	259	47	135	28
1931	3,641	2,494	247	94	674	92	40	3,125	2,120	366	341	48	220	30
1930	5,448	3,929	325	129	876	164	25	4,416	3,104	477	463	49	295	28
1929	7,034	5,347	390	139	982	157	19	5,886	4,463	509	483	50	330	51
1928	6,842	5,249	372	121	922	158	20	5,465	4,159	460	448	44	275	79
1927	6,456	4,982	360	114	821	160	19	5,383	4,240	417	400	38	240	48
1926	6,381	4,922	370	110	793	160	26	5,555	4,500	415	372	43	200	25
1925	6,348	5,011	318	83	752	160	24	5,261	4,291	391	347	39	170	23
1924	5,911	4,741	315	77	602	160	16	4,560	3,684	361	303	36	140	36
1923	5,494	4,266	302	71	676	164	15	4,652	3,866	332	260	33	130	31
1922	4,954	3,929	286	61	544	126	8	3,957	3,184	341	243	42	105	42
1921	5,505	4,586	394	76	405	40	4	3,383	2,572	334	200	65	105	107
1920	10,264	8,481	1,119	67	588	8	1	6,741	5,384	848	190	123	120	76
1919	10,776	8,891	1,109	56	544	175	1	5,908	3,995	818	123	757	130	85
1918	7,272	6,432	346	44	450	--------	--------	4,814	3,103	510	83	1,018	100	--------
1917	7,072	6,398	290	34	350	--------	--------	3,597	3,006	391	100	--------	100	--------
1916	6,029	5,560	197	22	250	--------	--------	2,927	2,423	263	123	--------	118	--------
1915	3,948	3,686	38	24	200	--------	--------	2,200	1,813	91	160	--------	136	--------
1914	2,445	2,230	31	39	145	--------	--------	2,389	1,815	102	272	--------	200	--------
1913	2,816	2,600	29	50	137	--------	--------	2,442	1,829	92	311	--------	210	--------
1912	2,738	2,532	34	49	123	--------	--------	2,481	1,866	112	306	--------	197	--------
1911	2,405	2,228	22	41	114	--------	--------	2,131	1,576	76	289	--------	190	--------
1910	2,160	1,995	19	38	108	--------	--------	2,114	1,609	68	265	--------	172	--------
1909	2,013	1,857	15	41	100	--------	--------	1,987	1,522	50	251	--------	164	--------
1908	2,022	1,880	14	39	89	--------	--------	1,595	1,159	44	232	--------	160	--------
1907	2,192	2,051	19	35	87	--------	--------	1,896	1,469	60	214	--------	153	--------
1906	2,052	1,921	18	27	86	--------	--------	1,756	1,365	52	191	--------	148	--------
1905	1,859	1,751	14	18	76	--------	--------	1,561	1,215	41	160	--------	145	--------
1904	1,657	1,563	11	13	70	--------	--------	1,378	1,062	35	140	--------	141	--------
1903	1,663	1,575	12	9	67	--------	--------	1,323	1,019	38	127	--------	139	--------
1902	1,550	1,473	11	9	57	--------	--------	1,292	996	35	124	--------	137	--------
1901	1,651	1,585	11	8	47	--------	--------	1,213	912	36	130	--------	135	--------
1900 [7]	1,686	1,623	17	8	38	--------	--------	1,179	869	53	120	--------	137	--------
1900 [8]	1,578	1,534	23	19	--------	--------	1	1,149	894	30	98	--------	114	13
1899	1,400	1,363	19	17	--------	--------	1	973	735	26	77	--------	124	11
1898	1,340	1,304	19	16	--------	--------	1	896	653	25	76	--------	133	10
1897	1,173	1,136	21	15	--------	--------	1	1,041	803	30	69	--------	127	12
1896	1,082	1,048	18	15	--------	--------	1	1,048	816	26	71	--------	122	13

See footnotes at end of table.

Series U 1–25. Balance of International Payments: 1790 to 1970—Con.

[In millions of dollars]

Year	Exports of goods and services[1]					Imports of goods and services					
	Total	Merchandise, adjusted[2]	Transportation	Travel	Other transactions	Total	Merchandise, adjusted	Transportation	Travel	Income on foreign investments in U.S.[6]	Other transactions
	1	2	3	4	7	8	9	10	11	13	14
1895	888	855	18	14	1	1,015	774	28	75	126	12
1894	981	943	17	20	1	883	692	22	45	113	10
1893	1,021	974	20	26	1	1,140	898	26	62	139	15
1892	1,122	1,084	23	14	1	1,142	888	28	69	143	14
1891	1,035	997	24	13	1	1,124	875	31	69	134	15
1890	960	921	23	15	1	1,109	866	36	68	125	15
1889	880	841	23	14	1	1,046	817	35	62	118	14
1888	786	750	22	14	1	1,013	791	34	67	107	14
1887	810	774	21	14	1	967	759	31	65	98	14
1886	817	781	20	15	1	894	698	30	60	93	13
1885	830	792	20	17	2	818	635	28	58	86	12
1884	862	822	23	15	2	921	730	31	56	90	14
1883	915	875	25	13	2	927	748	31	45	89	14
1882	859	824	26	7	2	915	747	30	39	84	14
1881	971	936	26	6	2	834	672	27	34	88	12
1880	963	929	25	7	2	848	694	28	35	79	13
1879	813	784	22	5	2	612	469	20	36	78	8
1878	813	780	26	4	3	595	462	20	29	76	8
1877	716	687	24	3	3	614	475	21	23	86	9
1876	654	620	26	4	3	634	478	23	29	96	9
1875	623	590	26	3	3	722	556	26	30	99	11
1874	707	669	31	3	4	767	593	31	30	102	12
1873	675	631	39	2	4	856	683	36	25	99	13
1872	578	539	31	4	4	824	662	30	32	86	13
1871	603	564	29	6	4	704	557	24	28	84	11
1870	507	473	27	3	4	608	475	22	22	80	9
1869	395	365	24	2	3	567	450	23	17	69	9
1868	428	395	28	2	4	505	382	22	26	67	8
1867	401	369	27	1	4	550	430	29	25	58	9
1866	481	446	29	1	5	572	459	27	25	51	10
1865	279	261	16	----------	2	343	256	15	22	45	5
1864	304	288	14	----------	2	418	339	21	17	34	7
1863	313	287	19	1	7	328	260	13	15	31	9
1862	272	248	20	1	4	272	211	11	14	30	5
1861	303	261	36	1	5	406	344	17	15	24	6
1860	438	401	35	2	----------	438	376	17	20	25	----------
1859	384	358	25	1	----------	416	352	14	26	23	----------
1858	350	326	23	2	----------	334	293	8	17	15	----------
1857	385	366	18	2	----------	416	375	10	16	15	----------
1856	359	329	27	2	----------	378	327	9	19	23	----------
1855	303	279	22	2	----------	325	272	8	23	22	----------
1854	314	281	28	4	----------	377	316	15	25	20	----------
1853	258	231	23	4	----------	333	279	13	25	16	----------
1852	232	211	17	4	----------	265	221	9	20	15	----------
1851	251	219	28	4	----------	271	225	10	23	13	----------
1850	166	153	9	4	----------	210	185	5	8	12	----------
1849	166	146	16	3	----------	173	154	6	2	12	----------
1848	174	155	17	2	----------	188	161	6	2	12	[9] 8
1847	181	160	19	2	----------	178	151	7	4	9	[9] 8
1846	133	114	17	2	----------	143	126	5	3	9	----------
1845	135	115	19	1	----------	138	120	5	4	9	----------
1844	126	112	14	1	----------	126	111	4	5	7	----------
1843	101	85	15	1	----------	81	66	6	3	7	----------
1842	119	105	13	1	----------	119	102	4	5	8	----------
1841	136	122	13	1	----------	148	130	4	6	8	----------
1840	160	133	27	1	----------	134	109	7	6	12	----------
1839	135	121	12	1	----------	188	165	4	5	14	----------
1838	128	109	19	1	----------	135	116	5	5	10	----------
1837	133	118	13	2	----------	161	144	4	4	9	----------
1836	141	129	11	2	----------	209	194	4	4	9	----------
1835	132	122	9	1	----------	166	153	3	3	7	----------
1834	116	105	10	1	----------	140	129	3	2	6	----------
1833	101	90	9	1	----------	119	110	3	1	5	----------
1832	101	88	12	1	----------	112	103	4	1	5	----------
1831	97	82	14	1	----------	112	103	4	1	4	----------
1830	86	74	11	1	----------	79	71	3	1	5	----------
1829	83	73	10	----------	----------	83	75	3	2	5	----------
1828	84	73	10	1	----------	97	89	3	2	4	----------
1827	98	83	14	----------	----------	90	80	3	2	5	----------
1826	91	78	13	----------	----------	95	85	3	2	5	----------
1825	112	100	12	----------	----------	106	96	3	2	5	----------
1824	90	77	14	----------	----------	90	81	3	1	5	----------
1823	89	75	14	----------	----------	87	78	3	1	5	----------
1822	83	73	10	----------	----------	92	83	3	1	5	----------
1821	76	66	11	----------	----------	72	63	3	2	5	----------
1820	84	70	14	----------	----------	84	75	3	2	5	----------

See footnotes at end of table.

Series U 1–25. Balance of International Payments: 1790 to 1970—Con.

[In millions of dollars]

Year	Exports of goods and services [1]			Imports of goods and services					Year	Exports of goods and services [1]			Imports of goods and services				
	Total	Merchandise, adjusted [2]	Transportation	Total	Merchandise, adjusted	Transportation	Income on foreign investments in U.S. [6]	Other transactions		Total	Merchandise, adjusted [2]	Transportation	Total	Merchandise, adjusted	Transportation	Income on foreign investments in U.S. [6]	Other transactions
	1	2	3	8	9	10	13	14		1	2	3	8	9	10	13	14
1819	91	72	19	105	94	4	6	2	1804	114	81	34	102	87	7	5	4
1818	116	95	20	141	128	4	6	3	1803	88	59	30	80	67	6	4	3
1817	103	89	14	113	102	3	7	2	1802	98	75	23	91	78	5	5	3
1816	105	84	21	163	151	4	5	3	1801	134	95	39	132	114	8	5	5
1815	81	55	26	96	85	5	4	2	1800	107	74	33	108	93	7	5	4
1814	11	8	3	20	16	1	3	------	1799	111	80	30	96	81	6	6	3
1813	45	32	13	30	22	3	4	------	1798	83	62	21	84	72	4	6	3
1812	75	39	36	96	83	7	3	3	1797	79	57	21	90	77	4	5	3
1811	114	63	51	78	61	10	5	2	1796	94	67	27	97	84	5	5	3
1810	117	68	49	110	91	10	6	4	1795	72	48	24	85	73	5	4	3
1809	88	55	33	76	61	7	6	2	1794	55	36	19	46	36	4	5	1
1808	55	26	29	71	58	6	5	2	1793	43	28	15	42	33	3	5	1
1807	162	109	53	167	146	11	5	6	1792	32	23	9	40	33	2	4	1
1806	148	105	43	155	137	9	4	6	1791	29	21	8	37	31	2	4	1
1805	134	97	37	144	128	7	4	5	1790	29	21	7	30	24	2	4	1

Year	Balance on goods and services	Unilateral transfers, net [to foreign countries (−)]		U.S. capital flows, net [outflow of funds (−)]				Foreign capital flows, net [outflow of funds (−)]		Transactions in U.S. official reserve assets, net [increase(−)]	Errors and omissions, net
		Private	Government [1]	Government, long- and short-term	Private			Long-term	Short-term		
					Direct long-term [3]	Other long-term	Short-term				
	15	16	17	18	19	20	21	22	23	24	25
1970	3,563	−1,012	−2,196	−1,584	−4,400	−1,353	−1,132	3,545	2,401	2,477	−1,174
1969	1,911	−895	−2,050	−2,193	−3,254	−1,601	−569	3,969	8,341	−1,187	−2,470
1968	2,425	−796	−2,113	−2,268	−3,209	−1,088	−1,087	6,029	3,383	−880	−399
1967	5,136	−837	−2,243	−2,421	−3,137	−1,292	−1,228	2,411	4,441	52	−881
1966	5,170	−613	−2,277	−1,534	−3,661	−257	−414	2,156	1,165	568	−302
1965	7,098	−659	−2,177	−1,598	−3,468	−1,079	754	−68	451	1,222	−477
1964	8,568	−587	−2,167	−1,676	−2,328	−2,103	−2,147	110	3,209	171	−1,048
1963	5,957	−563	−2,179	−1,661	−1,976	−1,698	−786	326	2,656	377	−455
1962	5,126	−467	−2,164	−1,094	−1,654	−1,227	−546	274	1,423	1,533	−1,206
1961	5,599	−424	−2,088	−926	−1,598	−1,025	−1,556	442	2,026	606	−1,054
1960	4,107	−414	−1,878	−1,104	−1,674	−856	−1,349	430	1,690	2,145	−1,098
1959	310	−599	−1,849	−353	−1,372	−926	−77	709	2,862	1,035	+260
1958	2,356	−563	−1,798	−971	−1,181	−1,444	−311	73	1,186	2,292	+361
1957	5,901	−570	−1,775	−958	−2,442	−859	−276	399	733	−1,165	+1,012
1956	4,145	−555	−1,868	−629	−1,951	−603	−517	593	1,864	−869	+390
1955	2,153	−456	−2,042	−310	−823	−241	−191	390	967	182	+371
1954	1,959	−504	−1,776	93	−667	−320	−635	274	1,036	480	+60
1953	532	−503	−1,978	−218	−735	185	167	228	846	1,256	+220
1952	2,356	−443	−2,088	−420	−852	−214	−94	166	1,507	−415	+497
1951	3,817	−409	−3,106	−156	−508	−437	−103	205	376	−33	+354
1950	1,892	−454	−3,563	−156	−621	−495	−149	68	1,844	1,758	−124
1949	6,218	−532	−5,106	−652	−660	−80	187	119	55	−266	+717
1948	6,518	−697	−3,828	−1,024	−721	−69	−116	−172	730	−1,736	+1,115
1947	11,617	−682	−1,943	−4,224	−749	−49	−189	−98	−1,229	−3,315	+861
1946	7,807	−673	−2,249	−3,019	−230	127	−310	−347	−638	−623	+155
1945	6,041	−473	−6,640	−1,019	−100	−354	−96	−104	2,189	548	+8
1944	12,452	−357	−13,785	−231	71	−62	−85	175	509	1,350	−37
1943	11,038	−249	−12,658	−109	98	−58	−12	−63	1,222	757	+34
1942	6,413	−123	−6,213	−221	19	−84	96	−84	182	23	−8
1941	2,410	−179	−957	−391	47	19	21	−327	−400	−719	+476

See footnotes at end of table.

Series U 1–25. Balance of International Payments: 1790 to 1970—Con.

[In millions of dollars]

Year	Balance on goods and services	Unilateral transfers, net [to foreign countries (−)]		U.S. capital flows, net [outflow of funds (−)]				Foreign capital flows, net [outflow of funds (−)]		Transactions in U.S. official reserve assets, net [increase(−)]	Errors and omissions, net
		Private	Government [1]	Government, long- and short-term	Private			Long-term	Short-term		
					Direct long-term [3]	Other long-term	Short-term				
	15	16	17	18	19	20	21	22	23	24	25
1940	1,719	−178	−32	−51	32	36	177	−90	1,353	−4,243	+1,277
1939	1,066	−151	−27	−14	9	104	226	−86	1,259	−3,174	+788
1938	1,291	−153	−29	−9	16	24	36	57	317	−1,799	+249
1937	297	−175	−60	2	35	241	43	245	311	−1,364	+425
1936	115	−176	−32	3	−12	189	52	600	376	−1,272	+157
1935	128	−162	−20	1	34	82	427	320	648	−1,822	+364
1934	601	−162	−10	−5	−17	202	104	[10] 15	126	−1,266	+412
1933	358	−191	−17	−7	32	−80	42	[10] 125	−454	131	+61
1932	407	−217	−21	26	−16	267	227	−26	−673	−53	+79
1931	516	−279	−40	14	−222	350	628	66	−1,265	133	+99
1930	1,032	−306	−36	77	−294	−70	−191	66	−288	−310	+320
1929	1,148	−343	−34	38	−602	−34	−200	358	196	−143	−384
1928	1,377	−346	−19	49	−558	−752	−231	463	−117	238	−104
1927	1,073	−355	−2	46	−351	−636	−349	−50	934	113	−423
1926	826	−361	−20	30	−351	−470	−36	95	455	−93	−75
1925	1,087	−373	−30	27	−268	−603	−46	[11] 301	−60	100	−135
1924	1,351	−339	−25	28	−182	−703	−109	[11] 185	228	−256	−178
1923	842	−328	−37	91	−148	−235	−82	[11] 338	49	−315	−175
1922	997	−314	−38	31	−153	−669	----------	7	----------	−269	+408
1921	2,122	−450	−59	30	−111	−477	----------	−4	----------	−735	−316
1920	3,523	−634	−45	−175	−154	−400	----------	−278	----------	68	−1,905
1919	4,868	−832	−212	−2,328	−94	−75	----------	−215	----------	166	−1,278
1918	2,458	−268	----------	−4,028	----------	−396	----------	----------	422	−5	+1,817
1917	3,475	−180	−25	−3,656	----------	−594	----------	−36	400	−312	+928
1916	3,102	−150	----------	----------	----------	−1,064	----------	−391	−900	−531	−66
1915	1,748	−150	----------	----------	----------	−790	----------	−789	450	−499	+30
1914	56	−170	----------	----------	−76	−14	----------	−432	450	100	+86
1913	374	−207	----------	----------	−138	−27	----------	252	----------	−25	−229
1912	257	−212	----------	----------	−139	−70	----------	232	----------	−81	+13
1911	274	−224	----------	----------	−95	−28	----------	171	----------	−90	−8
1910	46	−204	----------	----------	−124	34	----------	345	----------	−71	−26
1909	26	−187	----------	----------	−88	−24	----------	171	----------	18	+84
1908	427	−192	----------	----------	−48	−87	----------	89	----------	−44	−145
1907	296	−177	----------	----------	−89	24	----------	136	----------	−154	−36
1906	296	−147	----------	----------	−92	46	----------	114	----------	−171	−46
1905	298	−133	----------	----------	−46	−93	----------	56	----------	−71	−11
1904	279	−127	−10	−40	−80	11	----------	59	----------	−25	−67
1903	340	−115	----------	----------	−81	40	----------	20	----------	−71	−133
1902	258	−105	----------	----------	−65	−40	----------	−30	----------	−71	+53
1901	438	−104	----------	----------	−89	−123	----------	−33	----------	−61	−28
1900 [7]	507	−95	----------	----------	−56	−87	----------	−75	----------	−91	−103
1900 [8]	429	−54				−296				−78	
1899	427	−48	−20			−229				−130	
1898	444	−44				−279				−121	
1897	132	−41				−23				−68	
1896	34	−49				40				−25	
1895	−127	−55				137				44	
1894	98	−54				−66				22	
1893	−119	−44				146				17	
1892	−20	−54				41				33	
1891	−90	−50				136				4	
1890	−150	−45				194				1	([12])
1889	−166	−44				202				8	
1888	−226	−30				287				−30	
1887	−157	−28				231				−46	
1886	−77	−28				137				−32	
1885	12	−27				34				−19	
1884	−59	−24				105				−23	
1883	−12	−22				51				−17	
1882	−55	−13				110				−42	
1881	137	−5				−41				−91	

See footnotes at end of table.

Series U 1–25. Balance of International Payments: 1790 to 1970—Con.

[In millions of dollars]

Year	Balance on goods and services (15)	Unilateral transfers, net [to foreign countries (−)] Private (16)	Government [1] (17)	U.S. and foreign capital flows, net [outflow of funds (−)] (18–23)	Transactions in U.S. official reserve assets, net [increase (−)] (24)
1880	114	−4		30	−140
1879	202	−8		−160	−34
1878	218	−11		−162	−44
1877	102	−13		−57	−33
1876	20	−11		2	−10
1875	−99	−14		87	27
1874	−61	−11		82	−11
1873	−181	−2	16	167	
1872	−246	4		242	
1871	−101			101	
1870	−101	1		100	
1869	−172	4	−7	176	
1868	−77	4		73	
1867	−149	4		145	
1866	−91	−4		95	
1865	−64	5		59	
1864	−114	3		111	
1863	−15	3		13	
1862					
1861	−103	−1		103	
1860	−1	8		−7	
1859	−32	6		26	
1858	17	7		−23	
1857	−30	14		17	
1856	−20	9	−1	12	
1855	−22	10	−2	15	
1854	−63	28	−7	42	
1853	−75	19		56	
1852	−33	20	−3	16	
1851	−20	18	−3	6	

Year	Balance on goods and services (15)	Unilateral transfers, net [to foreign countries (−)] Private (16)	Government [1] (17)	U.S. and foreign capital flows, net [outflow of funds (−)] (18–23)
1850	−44	20	−4	29
1849	−8	16	−6	−3
1848	−15	13		2
1847	3	16		−19
1846	−10	11		−1
1845	−2	6		−4
1844		4		−4
1843	20	2		−22
1842	1	6		−6
1841	−12	4		8
1840	26	4		−31
1839	−53	4		49
1838	−7	2	1	3
1837	−28	6	1	22
1836	−68	6	4	59
1835	−33	3		30
1834	−24	6		19
1833	−19	5		14
1832	−12	5		7
1831	−15	1		14
1830	6	2		−8
1829		2		−2
1828	−14	2		11
1827	8	2		−10
1826	−4	1		3
1825	6	1		−7
1824		1		−1
1823	2			−2
1822	−9			8
1821	4	1		−5
1820	1	1		−1

Year	Balance on goods and services (15)	Unilateral transfers, net [to foreign countries (−)], government [1] (17)	U.S. and foreign capital flows, net [outflow of funds (−)] (18–23)
1819	−15		15
1818	−25		25
1817	−11		11
1816	−58		58
1815	−15		15
1814	−9		9
1813	15		−15
1812	−21		21
1811	35		−35
1810	7		−7
1809	12		−12
1808	−17		17
1807	−5		5
1806	−7		7
1805	−10		10
1804	12		−12
1803	8	−11	3
1802	7		−7
1801	2		−2
1800	−2		2
1799	15		−15
1798	−2		2
1797	−11		11
1796	−3	−1	4
1795	−12	−1	13
1794	10	−1	−9
1793	2		−2
1792	−8		8
1791	−8		8
1790	−1		1

[1] Prior to 1946, includes transfers of goods and services under U.S. military grant programs.
[2] Includes receipts from military cash and credit transactions, the major portion of which is merchandise.
[3] 1919–1929, includes reinvested earnings of subsidiaries.
[4] Beginning 1946, income on investments includes direct investment fees and royalties.
[5] 1919–1939, includes certain adjustments to merchandise transactions.
[6] Net for 1790–1900.
[7] Comparable with later years.
[8] Comparable with earlier years.
[9] Military expenditures in Mexico.
[10] 1933, includes a net outflow of $40 million and, 1934, a net inflow of $30 million of funds through arbitrage operation in securities which cannot be divided between domestic and foreign securities.
[11] Includes transactions in securities which cannot be separated between domestic and foreign.
[12] Included in figures for series 18–23.

Series U 26–39. International Investment Position of the United States: 1843 to 1970

[In billions of dollars]

Year	U.S. investments abroad Total [1] (26)	Private Total private (27)	Private Long-term Total long-term (28)	Private Long-term Direct [2] (29)	Private Long-term Other (30)	Private Short-term (31)	U.S. Government [1] (32)	Foreign investments in the U.S. Total (33)	Long-term Total long-term (34)	Long-term Direct (35)	Long-term Other (36)	Short-term Total short-term (37)	Short-term Private obligations (38)	Short-term U.S. Govt. obligations [3] (39)
1970	166.9	120.2	105.0	78.2	26.8	15.2	46.7	97.7	48.7	13.3	35.4	49.0	28.1	20.9
1969	158.1	110.4	96.3	71.0	25.3	14.1	47.7	90.8	41.1	11.8	29.3	49.7	37.9	11.9
1968	146.8	102.5	89.5	65.0	24.5	13.0	44.3	81.2	40.4	10.8	29.5	40.9	22.6	18.3
1967	134.7	93.6	81.7	59.5	22.2	11.9	41.1	69.7	32.0	9.9	22.1	37.7	23.0	14.8
1966	125.2	86.4	75.8	54.8	21.0	10.6	38.8	60.4	27.0	9.1	18.0	33.4	20.8	12.6
1965	120.4	81.5	71.4	49.5	21.9	10.2	38.8	58.8	26.4	8.8	17.6	32.4	18.2	14.2
1964	114.7	75.9	65.0	44.5	20.5	10.9	38.8	56.9	25.0	8.4	16.6	31.9	17.5	14.4
1963	103.9	66.6	58.4	40.7	17.6	8.2	37.4	51.5	22.8	7.9	14.8	28.7	14.9	13.8
1962	96.5	60.1	52.8	37.3	15.5	7.3	36.4	46.3	20.2	7.6	12.6	26.1	13.3	12.7
1961	92.0	55.6	49.1	34.7	14.3	6.5	36.4	46.0	21.4	7.4	14.1	24.5	13.4	11.2

See footnotes at end of table.

Series U 26–39. International Investment Position of the United States: 1843 to 1970—Con.

[In billions of dollars]

Year	U.S. investments abroad							Foreign investments in the U.S.						
	Total [1]	Private					U.S. Government [1]	Total	Long-term			Short-term		
		Total private	Long-term			Short-term			Total long-term	Direct	Other	Total short-term	Private obligations	U.S. Govt. obligations [3]
			Total long-term	Direct [2]	Other									
	26	27	28	29	30	31	32	33	34	35	36	37	38	39
1960	85.6	49.3	44.5	31.9	12.6	4.8	36.3	40.9	18.4	6.9	11.5	22.4	11.7	10.8
1959	82.2	44.8	41.2	29.8	11.4	3.6	37.4	39.1	18.0	6.6	11.4	21.1	10.8	10.2
1958	79.2	41.1	37.6	27.4	10.2	3.5	38.1	34.4	16.4	6.1	10.3	18.0	10.9	7.1
1957	76.4	36.9	33.7	25.4	8.4	3.2	39.5	30.7	13.8	5.7	8.1	17.0	9.9	7.1
1956	70.8	33.4	30.4	22.5	7.9	2.9	37.4	30.5	14.3	5.5	8.8	16.3	9.4	6.8
1955	65.1	29.1	26.7	19.4	7.4	2.4	35.9	27.8	13.4	5.1	8.3	14.4	8.4	6.0
1954	62.4	26.6	24.4	17.6	6.7	2.2	35.8	25.0	11.6	4.6	7.0	13.5	8.5	5.0
1953	60.2	23.8	22.2	16.3	5.9	1.6	36.4	21.9	9.6	4.3	5.4	12.2	7.6	4.6
1952	59.1	22.7	21.0	14.7	6.3	1.7	36.4	20.8	9.4	3.9	5.4	11.5	7.2	4.2
1951	56.4	20.8	19.2	13.0	6.2	1.7	35.6	18.7	8.8	3.7	5.1	10.0	6.6	3.3
1950	54.4	19.0	17.5	11.8	5.7	1.5	35.4	17.6	8.0	3.4	4.6	9.6	6.6	3.1
1949	53.9	16.9	15.6	10.7	4.9	1.3	37.0	14.8	7.1	2.9	4.2	7.7	5.7	2.0
1948	52.5	16.3	14.7	9.6	5.1	1.6	36.2	14.4	6.8	2.8	4.0	7.7	5.5	2.1
1947	48.3	14.9	13.4	8.4	5.1	1.5	33.4	13.8	6.8	2.6	4.2	7.0	5.0	2.0
1946	39.4	13.5	12.3	[4] 7.2	5.0	1.3	25.9	15.2	7.0	2.5	4.5	8.3	5.3	3.0
1945	36.9	14.7	13.7	8.4	5.3	1.0	22.2	17.0	8.0	2.5	5.5	9.0	5.3	3.7
1940	34.3	12.2	11.3	7.3	4.0	.9	22.1	13.5	8.1	2.9	5.2	5.4	5.1	.3
1935	23.6	13.5	12.6	7.8	4.8	.9	10.1	6.4	5.1	1.6	3.5	1.2	1.2	--------
1931	20.1	15.9	14.6	8.1	6.5	1.3	4.2	3.8	2.3	--------	--------	1.5		
1930	21.5	17.2	15.2	8.0	7.2	2.0	4.3	8.4	[5] 5.7	[5] 1.4	[5] 4.3	2.7	2.7	--------
1927	17.9	13.8	12.5	6.6	5.9	1.3	4.1	6.6	3.7	--------	--------	2.9		
1924	15.1	10.9	10.0	5.4	4.6	.8	4.2	3.9	2.9	1.0	1.9	1.0	1.0	--------
1919	9.7	7.0	6.5	3.9	2.6	.5	2.7	3.3	2.5	.9	1.6	.8	.8	--------
1914 (June 30)	5.0	3.5	3.5	2.7	.8	--------	1.5	7.2	6.7	1.3	5.4	.5	.5	--------
1908	2.5	2.5	2.5	1.6	.9			6.4	6.4					
1897	.7	.7	.7	.6	.1			3.4	3.1			.3		
1869	.1	.1	--------	--------	--------			1.5	1.4			.2		
1843	(Z)	--------	--------	--------	--------		.2							

Z   Less than 50 million.
[1] Beginning 1914, includes U.S. monetary gold stock.
[2] Beginning 1960, excludes Cuba.
[3] Includes long-term and short-term.

[4] New series for direct investments, based on *Investments of the United States*, Government Printing Office, 1953; not comparable with earlier years.
[5] For 1929.

Series U 40. International Investment Position of the United States (Net Liabilities): 1789 to 1900

[In millions of dollars]

Year	Amount [40]	Year	Amount [40]	Year	Amount [40]	Year	Amount [40]	Year	Amount [40]	Year	Amount [40]	Year	Amount [40]	Year	Amount [40]
1900	2,501	1886	1,980	1872	1,595	1858	358	1844	213	1830	75	1816	[1] 118	1802	74
1899	2,797			1871	1,353	1857	381	1843	217	1829	83			1801	81
1898	3,026	1885	1,843			1856	364	1842	[1] 239	1828	85	1815	80		
1897	3,305	1884	1,809	1870	1,252			1841	[1] 257	1827	74	1814	65	1800	83
1896	3,328	1883	1,704	1869	1,152	1855	352			1826	84	1813	56	1799	81
		1882	1,653	1868	976	1854	337	1840	261			1812	71	1798	96
1895	3,288	1881	1,543	1867	903	1853	295	1839	292	1825	81	1811	50	1797	94
1894	3,151			1866	758	1852	239	1838	243	1824	88			1796	83
1893	3,217	1880	1,584			1851	223	1837	240	1823	89	1810	85		
1892	3,071	1879	1,554	1865	663			1836	218	1822	91	1809	92	1795	79
1891	3,030	1878	1,714	1864	604	1850	217			1821	83	1808	104	1794	66
		1877	1,876	1863	493	1849	188	1835	159			1807	87	1793	75
1890	2,894	1876	1,933	1862	480	1848	191	1834	129	1820	88	1806	82	1792	77
1889	2,700			1861	480	1847	189	1833	110	1819	[1] 89			1791	69
1888	2,498	1875	1,931			1846	208	1832	96	1818	[1] 104	1805	75		
1887	2,211	1874	1,844	1860	377			1831	89	1817	[1] 109	1804	65	1790	61
		1873	1,762	1859	384	1845	209					1803	77	1789	60

[1] Includes defaults of $20 million in 1816 and 1817; $30 million in 1818 and 1819; and $12 million in 1841 and 1842.

Series U 41–46. Value of Direct Investment in Foreign Countries, by Area and Industry Groups: 1929 to 1970

[In millions of dollars]

Year and industry group	Total, all areas	Canada	Latin American Republics	Western Europe [1]	Western Hemisphere dependencies	Other countries [2]
	41	42	43	44	45	46
TOTAL						
1970	78,178	22,790	12,252	24,516	2,508	16,113
1969	71,016	21,127	11,694	21,650	2,147	14,398
1968	64,983	19,535	11,033	19,407	2,068	12,941
1967	59,491	18,102	10,270	17,926	1,779	11,414
1966	54,799	17,017	9,876	16,234	1,622	10,051
1965	49,474	15,318	9,441	13,985	1,445	9,285
1964	44,480	13,855	8,942	12,129	1,312	8,242
1963	40,736	13,044	8,712	10,340	1,229	7,411
1962	37,276	12,133	8,474	8,930	1,050	6,689
1961	34,717	11,602	8,286	7,742	954	6,134
1960	31,865	11,179	7,481	6,691	884	5,630
1959	29,827	10,310	8,120	5,323	768	5,306
1958	27,409	9,470	7,773	4,573	696	4,897
1957	25,394	8,769	7,434	4,151	618	4,422
1956	22,505	7,795	6,844	3,561	454	3,851
1955	19,395	6,761	6,031	3,002	211	3,390
1954	17,631	6,043	5,741	2,643	189	3,015
1953	16,253	5,349	5,589	2,375	185	2,755
1952	14,721	4,641	5,355	2,153	159	2,413
1951	12,979	3,969	4,818	1,989	131	2,072
1950	11,788	3,579	4,445	1,733	131	1,900
1940	7,000	2,103	2,771	1,420	(3)	706
1936	6,691	1,952	2,847	1,245	(3)	[4] 647
1929	7,528	2,010	3,519	1,353	(3)	646
AGRICULTURE [5]						
1940	435	13	359	--------	(3)	63
1936	482	10	400	--------	(3)	71
1929	880	21	817	--------	(3)	43
MINING AND SMELTING						
1970	6,168	2,989	1,391	75	679	1,035
1969	5,658	2,769	1,363	72	577	878
1968	5,435	2,638	1,410	61	519	806
1967	4,876	2,342	1,277	61	431	765
1966	4,365	2,089	1,198	54	367	658
1965	3,931	1,851	1,164	54	310	552
1964	3,665	1,713	1,154	56	250	492
1963	3,419	1,549	1,143	55	210	462
1962	3,244	1,489	1,145	50	176	384
1961	3,094	1,367	1,153	48	179	347
1960	2,997	1,325	1,143	49	176	304
1959	2,848	1,089	1,254	50	158	297
1958	2,558	938	1,180	52	137	251
1957	2,361	856	1,112	55	120	218
1956	2,419	1,002	1,039	51	106	221
1955	2,197	904	961	45	86	201
1954	2,066	822	954	40	78	172
1953	1,920	698	968	36	69	149
1952	1,622	564	845	34	55	124
1951	1,292	406	719	32	32	103
1950	1,129	334	628	31	38	98
1940	782	187	512	53	(3)	30
1936	1,032	239	708	43	(3)	42
1929	1,185	400	732	(3)	(3)	53
MANUFACTURING						
1970	32,261	10,059	4,336	13,706	285	3,876
1969	29,527	9,406	4,078	12,280	270	3,493
1968	26,414	8,568	3,711	10,796	293	3,045
1967	24,172	8,095	3,310	9,798	276	2,694
1966	22,078	7,692	3,081	8,879	236	2,190
1965	19,339	6,872	2,745	7,606	200	1,916
1964	16,935	6,198	2,341	6,587	166	1,643
1963	14,937	5,761	2,102	5,634	111	1,329
1962	13,250	5,312	1,898	4,883	46	1,111
1961	11,997	5,076	1,684	4,255	23	959
MANUFACTURING—Con.						
1960	11,051	4,827	1,500	3,804	21	899
1959	9,707	4,565	1,396	2,947	21	778
1958	8,673	4,164	1,316	2,475	18	700
1957	8,009	3,924	1,270	2,195	10	610
1956	7,561	3,526	1,521	1,952	10	552
1955	6,623	3,093	1,351	1,685	3	491
1954	5,899	2,777	1,221	1,478	2	421
1953	5,340	2,540	1,133	1,310	1	356
1952	4,967	2,303	1,152	1,194	1	317
1951	4,348	2,009	981	1,074	1	283
1950	3,831	1,897	780	932	1	221
1940	1,926	943	210	639	(3)	133
1936	1,710	799	192	611	(3)	108
1929	1,813	820	231	629	(3)	134
TRANSPORTATION, COMMUNICATION, AND PUBLIC UTILITIES						
1970 [6]	--------	--------	--------	--------	--------	--------
1969	2,719	629	627	84	74	1,305
1968	2,672	599	628	94	58	1,294
1967	2,393	506	621	78	51	1,138
1966	2,284	495	624	67	48	1,050
1965	2,136	486	596	60	45	949
1964	2,020	471	568	53	47	880
1963	2,061	457	715	44	47	798
1962	1,989	473	692	50	47	727
1961	1,988	471	681	47	49	739
1960	2,215	626	820	45	49	676
1959	2,445	633	1,103	44	49	616
1958	2,270	601	1,049	41	48	531
1957	2,145	581	1,001	38	48	477
1956	1,778	353	1,033	41	31	320
1955	1,647	329	987	32	26	273
1954	1,566	304	977	31	16	238
1953	1,516	303	962	30	14	207
1952	1,477	290	953	29	14	191
1951	1,432	287	926	28	15	176
1950	1,425	284	927	27	15	172
1940	1,514	407	962	74	(3)	71
1936	1,640	520	937	91	(3)	92
1929	1,610	542	887	145	(3)	36
TRADE						
1970 [6]	--------	--------	--------	--------	--------	--------
1969	5,855	1,225	1,309	2,432	98	791
1968	5,280	1,123	1,251	2,129	94	683
1967	5,015	1,043	1,207	2,060	94	612
1966	4,716	996	1,159	1,933	87	540
1965	4,219	882	1,041	1,730	91	476
1964	3,688	805	947	1,446	89	401
1963	3,307	747	882	1,237	82	359
1962	2,985	699	813	1,084	76	312
1961	2,670	646	775	893	80	276
1960	2,353	630	674	736	64	248
1959	2,039	564	636	586	47	206
1958	1,786	524	567	480	37	178
1957	1,668	499	545	433	26	165
1956	1,483	464	510	326	2	181
1955	1,296	411	432	297	2	154
1954	1,170	377	401	256	2	134
1953	1,047	342	351	234	1	119
1952	963	289	340	218	1	115
1951	876	262	300	207	1	106
1950	762	240	242	186	3	91
1940	523	112	82	245	(3)	84
1936	391	79	100	144	(3)	68
1929	368	38	119	139	(3)	72

See footnotes at end of table.

Series U 41–46. Value of Direct Investment in Foreign Countries, by Area and Industry Groups: 1929 to 1970—Con.

[In millions of dollars]

Year and industry group	Total, all areas	Canada	Latin American Republics	Western Europe [1]	Western Hemisphere dependencies	Other countries [2]	Year and industry group	Total, all areas	Canada	Latin American Republics	Western Europe [1]	Western Hemisphere dependencies	Other countries [2]
	41	42	43	44	45	46		41	42	43	44	45	46
PETROLEUM							**OTHER [7]**						
1970	21,714	4,807	3,173	5,466	765	7,503	1970	18,035	4,935	3,353	5,269	778	3,701
1969	19,882	4,361	3,079	4,818	644	6,980	1969	7,374	2,737	1,238	1,964	484	950
1968	18,887	4,094	3,014	4,636	667	6,477	1968	6,295	2,513	1,019	1,691	436	636
1967	17,399	3,819	2,903	4,423	569	5,684	1967	5,636	2,298	952	1,507	358	520
1966	16,222	3,608	2,897	4,003	578	5,136	1966	5,134	2,137	917	1,297	306	477
1965	15,298	3,356	3,034	3,427	512	4,969	1965	4,550	1,871	861	1,107	287	424
1964	14,328	3,196	3,100	3,122	489	4,421	1964	3,844	1,473	832	864	271	403
1963	13,652	3,134	3,095	2,776	541	4,106	1963	3,359	1,396	775	594	238	357
1962	12,725	2,875	3,162	2,385	480	3,823	1962	3,083	1,285	763	477	226	332
1961	12,190	2,828	3,254	2,152	420	3,536	1961	2,778	1,215	738	347	203	275
1960	10,810	2,664	2,739	1,763	382	3,261	1960	2,438	1,107	606	293	192	240
1959	10,324	2,467	2,862	1,452	346	3,197	1959	2,463	993	868	244	148	210
1958	9,822	2,293	2,830	1,320	322	3,057	1958	2,300	950	832	205	134	179
1957	9,055	2,016	2,702	1,253	296	2,788	1957	2,157	894	805	177	119	162
1956	7,355	1,759	1,940	990	258	2,408	1956	1,908	692	801	201	48	166
1955	5,899	1,381	1,550	762	72	2,134	1955	1,733	643	751	180	23	136
1954	5,297	1,165	1,466	668	73	1,925	1954	1,632	598	723	169	19	123
1953	4,914	941	1,471	609	84	1,809	1953	1,515	526	705	157	16	111
1952	4,273	719	1,376	532	79	1,567	1952	1,419	476	690	146	8	99
1951	3,687	563	1,218	512	76	1,318	1951	1,344	443	674	137	7	83
1950	3,390	418	1,233	426	70	1,243	1950	1,251	406	635	130	4	76
1940	1,278	120	572	306	(3)	280	1940	544	320	74	104	(3)	46
1936	1,074	108	453	275	(3)	238	1936	362	197	57	80	(3)	28
1929	1,117	55	617	231	(3)	214	1929	555	136	116	209	(3)	94

[1] Includes Eastern Europe in 1929, 1936, and 1940, amounting to $89 million, $93 million, and $259 million, respectively. Excludes Turkey for 1936 and 1940.
[2] Includes Turkey for 1936 and 1940, and Western European dependencies for 1929, 1936, and 1940.
[3] Combined with "Other countries."
[4] Includes $26 million reported as "International."
[5] Beginning 1950, included in "Other."
[6] For 1970, "Transportation, communication, and public utilities" and "Trade" included in "Other."
[7] Excludes insurance in 1929; includes "Agriculture" beginning 1950; includes "Transportation, communication, and public utilities" and "Trade" in 1970.

Series U 47–74. Value of Foreign Direct Investment in the United States, by Area and Industry: 1937 to 1970

[In millions of dollars. Book value at yearend. Covers U. S. business enterprises, including real estate investments, in which there was a foreign interest or ownership of 25 percent or more]

Year	All areas Total [1]	Petroleum	Manufacturing	Finance and insurance	Canada Total [1]	Petroleum	Manufacturing	Finance and insurance	Europe Total [1]	Petroleum	Manufacturing	Finance and insurance	United Kingdom Total [1]	Petroleum
	47	48	49	50	51	52	53	54	55	56	57	58	59	60
1970	13,270	2,992	6,140	2,256	3,117	190	1,836	324	9,554	2,777	4,091	1,805	4,127	1,220
1969	11,818	2,493	5,344	2,189	2,834	132	1,644	325	8,510	2,322	3,530	1,766	3,496	829
1968	10,815	2,261	4,475	2,305	2,659	100	1,413	376	7,750	2,146	2,941	1,855	3,409	749
1967	9,923	1,885	4,181	2,193	2,575	99	1,397	354	7,005	1,772	2,669	1,758	3,156	612
1966	9,054	1,740	3,789	2,072	2,439	98	1,342	386	6,273	1,620	2,335	1,611	2,864	558
1965	8,797	1,710	3,478	2,169	2,388	208	1,219	370	6,076	1,481	2,167	1,724	2,852	511
1964	8,363	1,612	3,213	2,181	2,284	205	1,129	382	5,819	1,404	2,005	1,723	2,796	498
1963	7,944	1,513	3,018	2,045	2,183	213	1,063	337	5,491	1,306	1,881	1,640	2,665	480
1962	7,612	1,419	2,885	1,943	2,064	212	1,015	269	5,245	1,203	1,797	1,611	2,474	416
1961	7,392	1,325	2,754	2,025	1,989	194	975	274	5,129	1,125	1,708	1,690	2,484	381
1960	6,910	1,238	2,611	1,810	1,934	203	932	246	4,707	1,028	1,611	1,504	2,248	339
1959	6,604	1,184	2,471	1,734	1,896	207	907	227	4,452	972	1,501	1,451	2,167	316
1958	6,115	1,099	2,232	1,660	1,835	214	863	222	4,070	885	1,332	1,384	2,024	283
1957	5,710	1,043	2,083	1,496	1,773	211	816	208	3,753	832	1,248	1,238	1,881	271
1956	5,459	937	1,940	1,534	1,690	200	775	196	3,598	737	1,155	1,289	1,833	227
1955	5,076	853	1,759	1,499	1,542	196	711	179	3,369	657	1,040	1,272	1,749	204
1954	4,633	776	1,582	1,371	1,427	192	651	168	3,049	584	925	1,158	1,590	180
1953	4,251	706	1,451	1,219	1,350	168	611	162	2,751	538	836	1,014	1,422	163
1952	3,945	552	1,377	1,170	1,218	90	592	149	2,575	462	782	977	1,345	137
1951	3,658	466	1,274	1,105	1,119	62	525	150	2,410	404	747	912	1,273	118
1950	3,391	405	1,138	1,065	1,029	56	468	153	2,228	349	669	870	1,168	95
1941	2,312	222	714	521	530	--------	--------	--------	1,569	--------	--------	--------	712	--------
1937	1,882	283	729	412	463	--------	--------	--------	1,337	--------	--------	--------	833	--------

See footnotes at end of table.

Series U 47–74. Value of Foreign Direct Investment in the United States, by Area and Industry: 1937 to 1970—Con.

[In millions of dollars]

Year	United Kingdom—Con.		Netherlands				Switzerland			Other Europe				Other areas [2]
	Manufacturing	Finance and insurance	Total [1]	Petroleum	Manufacturing	Finance and insurance	Total [1]	Manufacturing	Finance and insurance	Total [1]	Petroleum	Manufacturing	Finance and insurance	
	61	62	63	64	65	66	67	68	69	70	71	72	73	74
1970	1,391	1,141	2,151	1,311	652	58	1,545	1,147	351	1,731	246	901	256	599
1969	1,176	1,143	1,966	1,275	535	55	1,395	1,026	323	1,653	218	793	245	474
1968	1,076	1,239	1,750	1,215	426	54	1,238	863	331	1,353	182	576	231	406
1967	1,009	1,189	1,508	1,021	388	41	1,096	744	309	1,245	139	529	219	343
1966	906	1,075	1,402	953	356	39	949	615	287	1,059	109	458	210	341
1965	839	1,176	1,304	887	328	36	940	590	303	980	83	410	209	332
1964	812	1,154	1,231	842	296	39	896	530	321	897	64	367	209	259
1963	779	1,085	1,134	772	275	36	825	477	307	867	54	350	212	269
1962	762	1,023	1,082	736	248	43	836	454	339	855	51	333	207	302
1961	750	1,091	1,023	693	231	43	830	433	345	791	51	294	211	274
1960	722	953	947	639	213	42	773	427	300	739	50	249	209	269
1959	698	927	892	607	197	42	716	395	280	677	49	210	201	256
1958	640	889	816	553	176	41	636	344	261	594	49	172	193	210
1957	611	794	747	512	155	39	576	324	223	549	49	158	182	184
1956	566	841	681	461	142	38	557	304	230	527	49	143	180	171
1955	510	836	613	411	127	37	522	282	223	485	42	121	176	165
1954	460	751	533	364	98	36	466	257	201	460	40	110	170	157
1953	419	647	480	333	80	35	415	237	176	434	42	100	156	150
1952	395	626	423	289	68	34	390	224	165	417	36	95	152	152
1951	388	583	376	257	54	34	369	215	155	392	29	90	140	139
1950	337	554	334	226	44	34	348	204	147	377	28	84	135	134
1941			336				138							213
1937			179				74							82

[1] Includes industries not shown separately: Mining and smelting, transportation and utilities, trade, and miscellaneous.
[2] Includes balance of North America, and South America, Africa, Asia, and Oceania.

Series U 75–186. U. S. Government Foreign Grants and Credits, by Country: 1945 to 1970

[In millions of dollars. Negative figures (−) occur when the total of grant returns, principal repayments, and/or foreign currencies disbursed by the Government exceeds new credits utilized and/or acquisitions of foreign currencies through new sales of farm products]

Series No.	Program and country	Total, 1945–1970	1970	1969	1968	1967	1966	1965	1964	1963	1962	1961	1960
75	Total, net [1]	133,777	5,695	6,697	6,787	6,673	5,505	5,052	4,923	5,055	4,528	4,236	4,590
76	Investment in 5 international financial agencies [2]	1,928	234	184	127	194	−101	−	112	62	122	172	153
77	Under assistance programs, net	131,848	5,462	6,513	6,660	6,479	5,606	5,052	4,811	4,993	4,406	4,064	4,437
78	Net new military grants	48,640	2,548	2,954	2,923	2,506	2,112	1,673	1,394	1,628	1,622	1,515	1,812
79	Gross new grants	49,137	2,551	2,958	2,927	2,511	2,118	1,682	1,403	1,637	1,758	1,523	1,822
80	Less: Reverse grants and returns	495	3	4	4	4	5	9	8	9	136	8	11
81	Western Europe (excluding Greece and Turkey)	16,681	66	62	133	148	137	243	289	447	363	412	623
82	Near East (incl. Greece, Turkey, and U.A.R.) and South Asia	7,283	200	266	283	345	255	330	309	383	337	241	332
83	Africa (excluding U.A.R.)	314	19	26	34	29	34	24	25	30	30	18	12
84	Far East and Pacific	22,740	2,235	2,561	2,405	1,915	1,609	1,014	687	685	789	689	743
85	Western Hemisphere	1,207	25	36	64	64	72	59	59	56	74	133	77
86	Unspecified areas	417	4	4	4	5	5	3	26	27	28	22	24
87	Net new economic and technical aid grants [3]	55,353	1,734	1,649	1,709	1,805	1,910	1,808	1,888	1,917	1,916	1,855	1,671
88	Developed countries [4]	21,171	10	6	19	10	12	21	21	28	40	44	50
89	Developing countries [4]	34,182	1,724	1,643	1,690	1,795	1,898	1,787	1,867	1,889	1,877	1,812	1,622
90	Gross new grants	57,036	1,735	1,651	1,712	1,808	1,914	1,814	1,901	1,937	1,934	1,882	1,705
91	Less: Reverse grants and returns	1,683	1	2	3	3	4	6	14	19	17	27	34
92	Net new credits [3][5]	25,066	1,280	2,111	2,208	2,445	1,388	1,598	1,559	1,162	727	489	430
93	Developed countries [4]	3,604	−284	206	121	367	−283	−255	−3	−401	−802	−818	−168
94	Developing countries [4]	21,462	1,564	1,905	2,087	2,078	1,671	1,853	1,562	1,563	1,529	1,306	597
95	New credits	43,320	2,993	3,300	3,587	3,443	2,613	2,463	2,270	2,142	2,006	1,757	1,039
96	Less: Principal collections	18,254	1,713	1,190	1,378	998	1,225	865	711	980	1,279	1,268	609
97	Other assistance (through net accumulation of foreign currency claims) [6]	2,780	−101	−201	−179	−278	195	−27	−30	285	141	206	524
98	Developed countries [4]	436	−20	−17	−17	−15	−14	−29	17	35	9	31	85
99	Developing countries [4]	2,344	−80	−184	−162	−263	210	2	−46	250	132	175	439
100	Currency claims acquired	15,752	451	486	700	851	953	1,079	1,394	1,284	1,140	1,147	1,186
101	Less: Currencies disbursed	12,972	552	687	879	1,128	757	1,106	1,424	999	998	941	662

See footnotes at end of table.

Series U 75–186. U. S. Government Foreign Grants and Credits, by Country: 1945 to 1970—Con.

[In millions of dollars]

Series No.	Program and country	Total, 1945–1970	1970	1969	1968	1967	1966	1965	1964	1963	1962	1961	1960
102	Other grants, credits, and other assistance (through net accumulation of foreign currency claims)	83,201	2,914	3,559	3,738	3,972	3,493	3,379	3,417	3,365	2,785	2,550	2,625
103	Developed countries [4]	25,213	−295	194	123	363	−285	−263	34	−337	−753	−743	−32
104	Developing countries [4]	57,988	3,208	3,364	3,614	3,610	3,779	3,642	3,383	3,702	3,537	3,293	2,657
105	Western Europe	23,865	−278	142	152	284	−243	−100	126	−249	−690	−594	−16
106	Austria	1,079	−6	−12	(Z)	−1	−2	4	8	5	−12	4	9
107	Belgium and Luxembourg	651	5	−8	−8	12	−6	−8	−8	−6	−18	−8	4
108	Denmark	260	−1	−1	−1	−1	−2	−2	−2	−2	−2	−2	−2
109	France	4,123	−27	−3	12	−2	−96	−205	−38	−244	−541	−68	−48
110	Germany, Federal Republic of	2,849	−16	−4	8	13	−207	(Z)	−5	−14	−3	−587	−28
111	Ireland	146	23	4	−6	−2	−3	−3	−2	−2	−2	−2	−1
112	Italy	3,028	−8	224	−22	41	−122	32	78	5	−176	−27	12
113	Netherlands	761	(Z)	(Z)	−66	(Z)	(Z)	−2	−1	−72	−12	−52	−11
114	Norway	229	−2	−2	−2	−1	−3	−4	−5	−4	−4	−6	−7
115	Portugal	131	−34	−2	6	−4	5	12	30	17	20	1	2
116	Spain	1,040	1	15	45	69	31	19	−10	1	12	110	90
117	Sweden	99	2	3	2	6	–	(Z)	−1	(Z)	−16	−1	(Z)
118	United Kingdom	6,570	−143	−42	185	126	57	−20	−14	−75	−77	−83	−89
119	Yugoslavia	1,939	−36	−28	(Z)	7	94	72	87	131	143	123	49
120	Eastern Europe	1,584	5	−29	2	−13	−13	−12	46	43	54	53	123
121	Czechoslovakia	191	–	–	–	–	–	–	–	–	–	–	–
122	Poland	945	−19	−19	10	−3	−5	−5	52	48	61	57	127
123	U.S.S.R.	358	−10	−9	−8	−9	−7	−5	−5	−5	−6	−4	−4
124	Near East and South Asia	21,668	991	1,107	1,202	1,462	1,461	1,673	1,789	1,741	1,499	1,238	1,227
125	Afghanistan	337	2	13	15	24	28	34	37	33	13	30	13
126	Ceylon	159	11	21	18	14	6	4	4	5	9	10	8
127	Egypt	1,126	(Z)	4	7	5	60	97	194	184	185	110	108
128	Greece	1,673	(Z)	6	−2	11	5	27	35	30	21	31	28
129	India	8,237	434	466	576	841	761	854	864	740	534	373	523
130	Iran	971	58	107	70	18	31	8	−6	20	46	129	33
131	Iraq	46	−2	−1	−1	2	4	7	12	5	1	1	1
132	Israel	1,184	84	105	35	26	61	61	34	49	58	41	42
133	Jordan	597	14	13	13	19	58	38	45	55	53	61	62
134	Lebanon	103	7	4	4	1	1	(Z)	−2	3	4	8	10
135	Nepal	140	11	9	8	11	12	16	17	14	9	10	8
136	Pakistan	3,878	242	209	282	331	221	349	377	380	323	218	229
137	Saudi Arabia	99	−16	27	8	3	54	1	3	−2	−26	−7	2
138	Turkey	2,280	88	84	94	104	125	140	132	175	203	153	101
139	UNRWA [7]	550	32	32	28	27	27	28	32	35	31	34	22
140	Africa	3,817	275	279	276	337	412	376	288	308	365	296	180
141	Algeria	178	1	3	(Z)	11	27	8	39	40	42	2	1
142	Ethiopia	185	9	14	15	11	19	11	8	18	24	14	7
143	Ghana	223	2	34	26	35	62	33	8	13	3	2	2
144	Liberia	240	(Z)	7	13	37	23	25	12	11	35	19	8
145	Libya	206	(Z)	1	3	−6	(Z)	3	6	16	20	23	34
146	Morocco	690	64	38	53	34	50	51	39	56	50	98	61
147	Nigeria	251	36	33	30	35	31	26	25	15	11	6	3
148	South Africa	−92	−2	−2	−2	−2	−4	−13	−11	−16	−13	−13	−13
149	Tunisia	623	49	49	44	49	39	55	44	38	54	77	55
150	Zaire	365	11	12	21	35	38	51	40	43	73	30	11
151	Far East and Pacific	19,677	985	1,144	1,033	1,001	974	648	573	776	775	748	786
152	Australia	355	−17	26	159	153	33	12	3	−14	−6	18	−3
153	Burma	108	1	5	1	1	2	3	5	10	3	4	13
154	Cambodia [8]	257	(Z)	(Z)	(Z)	(Z)	(Z)	2	7	20	20	24	25
155	China (Taiwan)	2,245	14	12	32	38	30	49	45	76	82	119	109
156	Indonesia	1,229	189	153	125	52	27	−3	32	78	89	54	45
157	Japan	2,422	−54	22	−124	−9	47	−57	−49	32	57	26	18
158	Korea, Republic of	4,885	198	260	191	193	168	167	158	240	238	230	261
159	Laos [8]	697	53	51	44	58	56	58	39	32	30	51	33
160	Philippines	1,310	63	29	34	33	22	46	49	11	26	12	24
161	Ryukyu Islands	384	14	19	13	16	12	19	22	8	11	5	10
162	Thailand	544	34	38	50	39	20	25	18	29	31	29	42
163	Trust Territory of the Pacific Islands	280	48	46	30	20	18	18	13	18	8	6	5
164	Vietnam, South [8]	4,536	418	446	437	401	503	301	221	212	157	151	186
165	Western Hemisphere	8,966	541	605	806	655	739	644	448	576	587	711	194
166	Argentina	368	20	5	−14	−20	−3	−3	5	11	66	41	47
167	Bolivia	488	24	28	38	24	21	30	34	45	29	24	13
168	Brazil	2,440	93	99	199	143	236	153	213	139	159	270	42
169	Chile	1,187	56	106	151	50	88	102	97	111	88	122	10
170	Colombia	888	118	101	108	86	59	35	38	69	45	53	−7
171	Costa Rica	151	8	13	11	12	10	14	10	7	9	7	4
172	Dominican Republic	400	33	37	46	60	54	79	22	48	22	(Z)	(Z)
173	Ecuador	205	8	11	15	27	21	17	17	14	12	11	7
174	El Salvador	109	10	7	7	11	17	11	10	11	6	8	1
175	Guatemala	219	10	10	17	15	8	11	9	10	9	14	16
176	Haiti	114	4	3	4	3	3	5	4	3	10	14	5
177	Honduras	96	10	9	7	6	7	10	4	5	4	8	4
178	Jamaica	51	8	3	6	10	6	4	3	3	2	1	1
179	Mexico	575	−1	16	53	50	54	38	−55	−18	3	83	21
180	Nicaragua	135	21	17	10	9	11	7	7	7	7	9	8
181	Panama	187	15	12	10	17	22	21	10	19	11	9	12
182	Paraguay	97	6	9	8	3	4	5	7	9	4	10	6
183	Peru	356	13	10	24	24	30	33	17	4	5	−20	−16
184	Uruguay	115	9	16	23	4	4	2	(Z)	8	4	3	20
185	Venezuela	323	16	33	33	48	41	40	−40	43	64	32	6
186	Other international organizations and unspecified areas	3,623	396	311	266	247	163	149	148	170	194	98	131

See footnotes at end of table.

Series U 75–186. U. S. Government Foreign Grants and Credits, by Country: 1945 to 1970—Con.

[In millions of dollars]

Series No.	Program and country	1959	1958	1957	1956	1955	1954	1953	1952	1951	1950	1949	1948	1947	1946	1945
75	**Total, net**	**3,924**	**4,926**	**5,070**	**4,986**	**4,909**	**5,095**	**6,352**	**5,043**	**4,621**	**4,180**	**5,673**	**5,480**	**6,080**	**5,710**	**1,987**
76	Investment in 5 international financial agencies [2]	(Z)	–	–	35	–	–	–	–	–	–	–	–	318	317	(Z)
77	Under assistance programs, net	3,923	4,926	5,070	4,951	4,909	5,095	6,352	5,043	4,621	4,180	5,673	5,480	5,763	5,392	1,987
78	Net new military grants	2,031	2,368	2,483	2,634	2,672	3,431	4,266	2,656	1,440	519	213	473	97	69	610
79	Gross new grants	2,052	2,379	2,496	2,649	2,681	3,439	4,329	2,722	1,456	523	213	540	97	69	610
80	Less: Reverse grants and returns	21	11	12	16	9	8	63	66	16	4	–	67	------	------	------
81	Western Europe (excluding Greece and Turkey)	823	726	1,059	1,570	1,423	1,984	3,102	1,888	859	324	–	–	–	–	–
82	Near East (incl. Greece, Turkey, and U.A.R.) and South Asia	445	648	511	337	335	342	329	289	185	118	171	250	43	–	–
83	Africa (excluding U.A.R.)	7	9	9	2	3	2	2	–	–	–	–	–	–	–	–
84	Far East and Pacific	669	885	814	643	862	1,037	769	382	292	63	42	224	54	69	610
85	Western Hemisphere	59	71	66	56	30	47	31	60	67	–	–	–	–	–	–
86	Unspecified areas	28	28	25	25	19	20	33	36	37	15	–	–	–	–	–
87	Net new economic and technical aid grants [3]	1,633	1,643	1,603	1,741	1,933	1,661	1,845	1,980	3,040	3,506	4,984	3,864	1,887	2,830	1,340
88	Developed countries [4]	67	107	149	286	601	848	919	1,189	2,320	2,909	4,327	3,127	1,241	1,956	867
89	Developing countries [4]	1,565	1,535	1,454	1,455	1,331	813	925	791	721	597	657	736	646	874	473
90	Gross new grants	1,667	1,682	1,676	1,796	1,974	1,726	1,947	2,065	3,164	3,658	5,227	3,928	2,126	2,954	1,453
91	Less: Reverse grants and returns	34	39	72	55	42	65	103	85	123	153	243	65	239	124	113
92	Net new credits [3][5]	5	646	363	18	−26	−201	233	408	141	155	476	1,143	3,779	2,494	37
93	Developed countries [4]	−609	−137	187	−161	−135	−236	−138	147	−167	−53	382	1,058	3,572	2,192	19
94	Developing countries [4]	614	783	177	179	109	36	371	261	308	208	94	85	208	301	17
95	New credits	1,030	1,180	1,001	484	384	290	710	828	446	443	669	1,561	4,061	2,562	81
96	Less: Principal collections	1,025	534	638	466	410	491	477	420	305	288	193	418	282	69	44
97	Other assistance (through net accumulation of foreign currency claims) [6]	254	270	620	558	330	203	8								
98	Developed countries [4]	1	31	46	104	80	102	8								
99	Developing countries [4]	254	239	573	454	250	101									
100	Currency claims acquired	934	1,023	1,233	1,079	556	248	8								
101	Less: Currencies disbursed	679	753	614	520	226	46									
102	Other grants, credits, and other assistance (through net accumulation of foreign currency claims)	1,892	2,559	2,587	2,318	2,237	1,664	2,086	2,388	3,182	3,661	5,460	5,006	5,666	5,323	1,377
103	Developed countries [4]	−541	1	382	229	546	714	789	1,336	2,153	2,856	4,709	4,185	4,813	4,148	886
104	Developing countries [4]	2,433	2,558	2,205	2,089	1,691	950	1,297	1,051	1,029	805	751	821	853	1,175	491
105	Western Europe	−438	157	503	351	692	810	867	1,378	2,064	2,676	4,202	3,799	4,291	3,275	713
106	Austria	3	17	25	24	9	15	36	82	147	101	194	197	146	73	18
107	Belgium and Luxembourg	−11	−2	−7	−6	−6	−4	−2	13	42	176	240	80	−2	153	36
108	Denmark	−2	−3	−2	−1	2	−1	7	8	75	52	102	39	1	(Z)	–
109	France	−76	−16	−49	46	286	268	263	343	416	460	765	781	588	1,158	149
110	Germany, Federal Republic of	−205	−23	−11	25	37	83	35	103	361	467	948	1,130	417	300	26
111	Ireland	−1	−1	−1	−1	–	–	(Z)	(Z)	24	55	67	–	–	(Z)	–
112	Italy	−4	30	100	71	57	101	109	175	268	269	445	422	313	500	136
113	Netherlands	−14	−19	−15	−25	−19	2	10	44	102	224	286	123	85	133	63
114	Norway	−9	−11	−12	−9	−1	12	15	26	41	61	64	61	24	8	(Z)
115	Portugal	2	1	(Z)	9	3	12	5	8	20	18	–	(Z)	(Z)	–	–
116	Spain	88	131	88	157	89	44	21	24	17	(Z)	–	–	–	–	–
117	Sweden	−1	−1	−1	−1	(Z)	(Z)	−1	−4	27	43	39	3	–	(Z)	1
118	United Kingdom	−323	−52	242	−43	58	102	229	398	118	624	1,009	937	2,662	750	34
119	Yugoslavia	111	100	133	94	130	97	98	80	120	36	–	–	34	150	115
120	Eastern Europe	61	98	63	−3	−1	7	4	−4	−15	−9	−13	13	178	663	274
121	Czechoslovakia	–	–	–	–	2	1	–	(Z)	(Z)	(Z)	−6	3	31	106	54
122	Poland	66	99	56	−6	−5	−4	−4	−3	−1	(Z)	1	19	96	251	75
123	U.S.S.R.	−4	–	–	–	(Z)	(Z)	–	–	−13	−9	−8	−8	45	285	133
124	Near East and South Asia	983	800	642	687	551	302	362	442	468	221	183	157	150	182	148
125	Afghanistan	19	19	13	13	6	4	4	6	11	(Z)	(Z)	–	–	–	–
126	Ceylon	19	20	8	2	(Z)	–	(Z)	(Z)	(Z)	(Z)	(Z)	–	–	–	–
127	Egypt	75	2	7	47	27	3	2	(Z)	1	(Z)	4	−5	(Z)	9	(Z)
128	Greece	37	23	31	69	74	47	66	123	189	108	108	164	156	168	121
129	India	320	243	187	119	118	29	37	94	108	1	(Z)	−4	−3	−9	29
130	Iran	91	50	47	61	64	65	52	11	4	4	15	−3	−3	3	1
131	Iraq	2	4	3	3	3	2	2	(Z)	(Z)	(Z)	–	−1	(Z)	1	–
132	Israel	56	51	35	57	46	62	49	109	66	50	7	–	–	–	–
133	Jordan	60	57	20	5	14	7	4	1	1	–	–	–	–	–	–
134	Lebanon	10	28	4	5	7	4	3	1	(Z)	(Z)	(Z)	−1	(Z)	2	–
135	Nepal	3	6	2	2	2	1	(Z)	(Z)	(Z)	–	–	–	–	–	–
136	Pakistan	142	145	100	154	67	12	91	8	(Z)	(Z)	(Z)	(Z)	–	–	–
137	Saudi Arabia	1	12	21	−1	−1	(Z)	(Z)	(Z)	2	(Z)	−1	−3	5	10	1
138	Turkey	111	122	141	123	97	47	40	59	52	39	34	10	9	−1	–
139	UNRWA [7]	27	16	23	27	23	18	9	22	24	20	15	–	–	–	–

See footnotes at end of table.

Series U 75–186. U. S. Government Foreign Grants and Credits, by Country: 1945 to 1970—Con.

[In millions of dollars]

Series No.	Program and country	1959	1958	1957	1956	1955	1954	1953	1952	1951	1950	1949	1948	1947	1946	1945
	Other grants, credits, and other assistance (through net accumulation of foreign currency claims) —Con.															
140	Africa	125	69	44	45	59	46	40	56	8	9	4	2	−87	4	1
141	Algeria	1	(Z)	1	(Z)	(Z)	(Z)	1	−	−	−	−	−	(Z)	(Z)	(Z)
142	Ethiopia	10	6	7	3	4	1	1	1	−1	1	(Z)	(Z)	1	(Z)	−
143	Ghana	1	1	(Z)	(Z)	(Z)	−	(Z)	−	−	(Z)	−	−	−	−	−
144	Liberia	9	8	5	3	2	2	−2	3	2	4	4	2	3	4	1
145	Libya	33	18	17	13	17	4	1	2	(Z)	(Z)	−	−	−	−	−
146	Morocco	45	26	18	−1	−2	−4	−3	9	3	4	1	−	−	−	−
147	Nigeria	1	(Z)	(Z)	(Z)	(Z)	(Z)	(Z)	−	−	−	−	−	−	−	−
148	South Africa	−13	−14	−5	11	21	31	35	26	(Z)	−1	−	(Z)	−91	−	−
149	Tunisia	33	26	6	3	1	(Z)	(Z)	(Z)	(Z)	(Z)	(Z)	−	−	−	−
150	Zaire	(Z)	(Z)	(Z)	(Z)	(Z)	(Z)	−1	(Z)	1	(Z)					
151	Far East and Pacific	716	785	977	1,004	784	390	397	383	506	608	902	857	914	832	178
152	Australia	2	−2	−2	−8	−1	4	1	(Z)	(Z)	−1	−1	1	(Z)	−11	10
153	Burma	14	3	18	3	(Z)	1	5	7	5	−1	(Z)	(Z)	5	−	−
154	Cambodia [8]	21	37	32	41	28	(Z)	−	−	−	−	−	−	−	−	−
155	China (Taiwan)	86	84	98	112	109	89	90	80	65	18	33	151	187	315	121
156	Indonesia	17	24	51	51	9	23	17	34	(Z)	36	41	20	−	62	4
157	Japan	48	−6	47	123	65	7	−3	36	241	226	521	372	469	367	2
158	Korea, Republic of	232	311	373	307	279	169	206	155	118	102	77	134	84	33	1
159	Laos [8]	35	30	38	52	37	(Z)	−	−	−	−	−	−	−	−	−
160	Philippines	24	42	39	28	21	9	24	10	13	200	203	131	150	42	29
161	Ryukyu Islands	3	5	5	2	2	3	9	29	38	26	29	46	19	13	7
162	Thailand	48	30	33	39	16	4	5	4	5	(Z)	(Z)	1	(Z)	5	−
163	Trust Territory of the Pacific Islands	5	6	5	5	5	6	5	5	3	1	1	1	1	2	3
164	Vietnam, South [8]	177	218	236	229	203	41	(Z)	−	−	−	−	−	−	−	−
165	Western Hemisphere	338	568	253	151	102	68	375	91	114	64	73	58	111	84	10
166	Argentina	73	48	−6	12	−5	−9	3	5	92	(Z)	(Z)	(Z)	(Z)	(Z)	(Z)
167	Bolivia	22	22	25	31	21	17	3	5	7	3	3	2	9	6	(Z)
168	Brazil	35	145	16	28	37	24	328	4	4	(Z)	5	9	30	28	2
169	Chile	33	47	32	10	−1	−3	(Z)	(Z)	−2	33	28	18	6	5	2
170	Colombia	32	92	19	10	2	2	−5	10	4	6	3	4	2	1	1
171	Costa Rica	8	10	9	3	5	2	2	2	1	(Z)	(Z)	(Z)	(Z)	2	1
172	Dominican Republic	(Z)	(Z)	(Z)	(Z)	1	(Z)	(Z)	(Z)	(Z)	(Z)	(Z)	−1	(Z)	(Z)	(Z)
173	Ecuador	2	3	4	8	6	4	1	4	2	2	2	3	1	1	2
174	El Salvador	1	1	1	1	1	1	1	(Z)	(Z)	(Z)	(Z)	(Z)	(Z)	(Z)	1
175	Guatemala	9	12	23	20	11	(Z)	(Z)	1	(Z)	1	2	2	1	2	(Z)
176	Haiti	13	5	4	9	14	10	3	1	(Z)	(Z)	−1	(Z)	(Z)	(Z)	(Z)
177	Honduras	6	5	3	2	2	1	1	1	(Z)	(Z)	(Z)	(Z)	1	(Z)	(Z)
178	Jamaica	−3	−8	−1	(Z)	(Z)	−3	−1	5	11	4	−	−	−	(Z)	−
179	Mexico	14	78	23	−8	−10	27	18	29	−5	19	33	20	58	35	2
180	Nicaragua	4	5	3	2	2	1	1	1	1	(Z)	(Z)	1	(Z)	2	1
181	Panama	6	7	5	3	3	−1	1	3	1	1	(Z)	(Z)	(Z)	1	(Z)
182	Paraguay	7	4	8	5	1	1	1	1	−1	(Z)	(Z)	(Z)	(Z)	1	(Z)
183	Peru	52	60	53	24	13	2	11	7	1	1	(Z)	(Z)	5	1	(Z)
184	Uruguay	13	−1	4	(Z)	2	(Z)	(Z)	2	(Z)	(Z)	(Z)	2	(Z)	1	(Z)
185	Venezuela	−3	7	−1	−3	(Z)	−3	(Z)	4	1	(Z)	1	2	1	(Z)	(Z)
186	Other international organizations and unspecified areas	108	80	105	82	51	41	40	42	37	93	108	119	108	283	53

− Represents zero.

Z Less than $500,000 or net minus (−) of less than $500,000.

[1] Beginning 1964, Department of Defense transactions estimated.

[2] Asian Development Bank, Inter-American Development Bank, International Bank for Reconstruction and Development, International Development Association, and International Finance Corporation.

[3] Net new grants not adjusted for settlements for postwar relief and other grants under agreements, and net new credits exclude prior grants converted into credits, which were as follows: July 1945–December 1955, $2,198 million; 1956–66, $491 million. Repayments on these settlements included in net new credits.

[4] Developed countries include Australia, Canada, Japan, New Zealand, Republic of South Africa, and countries of Eastern and Western Europe except Spain, Yugoslavia, and Malta. Developing countries include all other countries.

[5] Outstanding credits on Dec. 31, 1970, totaled $27,568 million representing net credits extended since organization of Export-Import Bank, Feb. 12, 1934, less charge-offs, and net adjustments due to exchange rates ($989 million), and excluding World War I debts. The amount repayable in dollars at U.S. Government option was $20,131 million; the remainder was repayable in foreign currencies, commodities, or services, at the option of the borrowers.

[6] Equivalent value of currencies still available to be used, including some funds advanced from foreign governments and after loss by exchange rate fluctuations ($1,334 billion), was $1,446 billion on December 31, 1970.

[7] United Nations Relief and Works Agency for Palestine refugees.

[8] Separate data became available during 1954. For earlier periods, data shown as Indochina.

Foreign Commerce (Series U 187-352)

U 187-352. General note.

Statistics on foreign trade of the United States are among the most useful, revealing, and, in spite of their deficiencies, reliable series relating to the growth of the American economy. This situation is especially true for the first 100 years of the Republic. The United States was more heavily dependent upon foreign markets and sources at that time than it has been in the 20th century. For a fuller discussion of the usefulness of such data, see G. G. Huebner's review of foreign trade of the United States in Emory Johnson, *History of Domestic and Foreign Commerce of the United States*, Carnegie Institution, Washington, D.C., 1915. This study has an excellent bibliography of material on foreign trade available at that time.

Since the first appearance of the *Statistical Abstract of the United States* in 1878, official time series on foreign trade have been presented in that publication and it is, therefore, cited here as a primary source for certain of the foreign trade data shown.

Foreign trade data are subject to a variety of special statistical problems relating to compilation, publication, coverage, valuation, and classification as to composition and direction. The record of gold movements, in particular, has been found to be subject to considerable error owing to its peculiar qualities which make it both a useful form of money and a likely candidate for smuggling (see R. G. D. Allen and J. Edward Ely, *International Trade Statistics*, John Wiley and Sons, New York, 1953; and Oskar Morgenstern, *Validity of International Gold Movement Statistics*, Special Paper in International Economics No. 2, International Finance Section, Princeton University Press, November 1955).

The first Congress of the United States provided for the compilation of statistics on foreign trade, and the Treasury Department, through its customhouses, began keeping a record of foreign trade beginning August 1, 1789. According to the Treasury Department, government records of the total values of our imports for 1790 to 1820 are fairly complete but do not show, except for a few years, the articles imported. They show, however, domestic exports by articles, but do not distinguish the values of merchandise from coin and bullion imported and exported, nor the value of the commerce with each country (see *Statistical Tables Exhibiting the Commerce of the United States With European Countries From 1790–1890*, Washington, D.C., 1893, p. vii).

Compared with currently compiled statistics, these earliest records left a great deal to be desired. J. Edward Ely, writing on the historical development of foreign trade statistics, observes that:

> The United States may be said to have had an adequate set of import and export statistics only since about 1821. Prior to that time no information was compiled on the amount of imports of articles which were free of duty upon importation into the United States. No value figures were compiled on imports subject to specific rates of duty and the dollar value for imports subject to ad valorem rates of duty, although apparently accurate, was compiled only as a total with no information on how much of each commodity was imported. Existing figures on the total dollar value of imports during the years 1795 to 1801 were apparently estimated at the time by the Secretary of the Treasury, and the figures for 1790–1794 and from 1802–1820 were apparently estimated many years later. (Allen and Ely, cited above, p. 269.)

Douglass North observes that the 1789–1820 figures were "officially overhauled and published in the Report of the Secretary of the Treasury on Finances for 1835" (see North's "United States

Balance of Payments, 1790–1860," *Studies in Income and Wealth*, vol. 24, National Bureau of Economic Research, 1960). In employing the early records, North found a number of deficiencies, and users of figures for 1790–1820 should note his revised figures and consider the criticisms in the appendix to his paper. The adequacy of the early records, of course, depends upon the use made of them. Some of the earliest records were not published officially and scholars have had to depend on information from *A View of the United States of America*, published by Tench Coxe in 1794, giving official documents for 1790, 1791, and 1792; *A Statistical Manual for the United States of America*, by Samuel Blodget, Jr.; *A Statistical View of Commerce of the United States of America*, by Timothy Pitkin, New Haven, 1835 (reprinted by Johnson Reprint Corporation in 1967), presenting many tables obtained directly from the Treasury books; and *Statistical Annals* by Dr. Adam Seybert, covering the period 1789–1818, and giving statistics of population, commerce, public land, etc. Such data as were published annually for 1790–1820 were brought together later in U.S. Congress, *American State Papers*, Class 4, "Commerce and Navigation," two volumes, Gales and Seaton, Washington, D.C., 1832 (vol. I) and 1834 (vol. II).

In 1820, Congress passed a law to provide for obtaining accurate statements of the foreign commerce of the United States and, at the same time, established the Division of Commerce and Navigation in the office of the Register of the Treasury. It required collectors of customs to compile and transmit annual reports to that office showing the detailed trade with foreign countries and the navigation employed therein. Beginning with 1821, these reports were consolidated and published annually in *Commerce and Navigation of the United States*.

Foreign trade statistics published by the Federal Government after 1820 are regarded as superior to those for the earlier period but still subject to some deficiencies, notably with respect to valuation of imports. They also suffered in respect to coverage of overland exports (see North, cited above, app. II, and Allen and Ely, cited above, pp. 270–271).

The Civil War introduced two special difficulties. For the last three quarters of fiscal year ending June 30, 1861, certain ports of the Southern States failed to make reports, and it was necessary for the Treasury Department to introduce estimates of the exports of cotton by the Southern States during the war based on records of the main recipient countries in Europe (see Treasury Department, *Statistics of the Foreign and Domestic Commerce of the United States*, Washington, D.C., 1864, p. 39).

The second difficulty was introduced in 1862 when the United States abandoned the specie backing for its money. The dollar fluctuated against foreign currencies and gold with each reverse or success of the northern forces. While imports and reexports continued to be valued in specie (dollars of a fixed parity to gold), since these goods were initially expressed in foreign currencies, domestic exports were recorded in "mixed values"—partly gold dollars and partly dollars of a fluctuating value—from 1862 until the resumption of specie payment in 1879. These deficiencies were recognized at the time both officially by the Director of the Bureau of Statistics (established in the Treasury Department in 1866) and by private observers (see, for example, Louis Blodgett's criticism and evaluation of U.S. foreign trade statistics in the early 1860's in *The Commercial and Financial Strength of the United States as Shown in the Balances of Foreign Trade and the Increased Production of Staple Articles*, King and Baird, Philadelphia, 1864). Treasury statisticians sought to adjust mixed currency values to specie values of total imports and exports and some other broad aggregates. The adjustments, however, were not carried through completely to country and commodity detail, and only a limited number of domestic export series are available for 1862–1879 in terms of "specie values" while the domestic export figures for countries and individual commodities are only available in mixed currency values.

When Congress established the Bureau of Statistics in 1866, it also specified that the kinds, quantities, and values of all articles exported and imported should be distinctly set forth in the statistical accounts, by countries of destination or of shipment, and that the exports of articles produced or manufactured in the United States should be shown separately from the reexports of foreign articles imported into the United States. Prior to 1866, only annual statistics of the foreign commerce of the United States were published; since then, monthly statistics have also been published.

The first report of the Director of the Bureau of Statistics in 1867 contains several pointed criticisms of the previous statistics, and the subsequent annual reports of *Foreign Commerce and Navigation* emphasized the shortcomings of the figures presented, especially the difficulty which became important in the post-Civil War period of reporting on trade with Canada in the absence of any mandatory reporting requirement on the railroads (see, for example, the *Annual Report of the Chief of the Bureau of Statistics on the Commerce and Navigation of the United States for the Fiscal Year Ended June 30, 1877*, 1878, pp. xii–xiii, table showing ". . . the imports into Ontario, Quebec, and Manitoba, from the United States in excess of the domestic exports from the United States to Canada, as returned to the Bureau of Statistics by U.S. collectors of customs during the fiscal year ended June 30, 1877."). An act of March 3, 1893, provided for obtaining information on exports by rail and apparently eliminated this deficiency in the subsequent figures, but prior to that time trade totals and figures on trade with Canada suffer lack of coverage in varying degrees.

For additional comments on foreign trade data for 1861–1900, see Matthew Simon, "Statistical Estimates of the Balance of International Payments and the International Capital Movements of the United States, 1861–1900," *Studies in Income and Wealth*, vol. 24, National Bureau of Economic Research, 1960.

In 1923, the function of compiling foreign trade statistics was transferred to the Department of Commerce; however, the release and publication of the annual figures had been done by that Department since 1903. In 1941, the function was transferred from the Bureau of Foreign and Domestic Commerce to the Bureau of the Census.

A problem affecting comparability of value statistics arose between January 31, 1934, and March 10, 1953, when the foreign exchange value of the dollar was permitted to depreciate as a result of the restriction placed on gold shipments to foreign countries. For this period, unless otherwise noted, values stated are in U.S. dollars without reference to changes in the gold content of the dollar.

World War II and the special foreign aid programs following it introduced new complications into the handling of U.S. foreign trade statistics. Lend-lease during the war, surplus property disposal immediately after the war, War Department shipments to relieve disease and unrest, economic and military aid, and security shipments have all complicated the presentation as will be noted below.

Import data compiled by the Department of Commerce are from import entries (various Customs forms) which importers are required to file with customs officials for each shipment arriving. Import values are, in general, based on market or selling price and are f.o.b. the exporting country. Values do not include import duties. The country of origin is defined as the country in which the merchandise was grown, mined, or manufactured. If the importer cannot obtain the information as to the country of origin, the merchandise is credited (for statistical purposes) to the country of shipment.

Imports are classified either as general imports or imports for consumption. General imports represent total arrivals of imported goods (except for intransit shipments), that is, merchandise released from Customs custody immediately upon arrival plus merchandise entered into a customs-bonded storage, manufacturing, or refining warehouse immediately upon arrival. Imports for consumption comprise merchandise entered into the U.S. consumption channels, that is, merchandise released from Customs custody immediately upon arrival, merchandise entered into a customs-bonded manufacturing warehouse (other than smelting or refining warehouse), merchandise withdrawn from a customs-bonded storage warehouse for release into domestic consumption channels, and imported ores and crude metals which have been processed in a customs-bonded smelting warehouse and then withdrawn for consumption and export.

During past periods, data for some low-valued imports have been fully compiled while data for others have been estimated. The following changes have occurred in the methods of compiling data on low-valued imports: Effective January 1954–1957, imports valued at $250 or less, reported on formal consumption and informal entries, were estimated from a 5-percent sample. From January 1958–June 1965, formal entries valued under $100 and informal entries valued $250 or less, were estimated from a 1-percent sample. Effective July 1965, all formal and informal entries valued $250 and under have been estimated from a 1-percent sample except a 5-percent sample, in effect every 3 years, was used to estimate data for 1967 and 1970. The estimated import values are excluded from detailed commodity statistics but are included in the over-all totals and are distributed in the appropriate country, district, and economic class totals, and in the totals for groupings of commodity classifications (i.e., commodity group or subgroup). The total value so excluded generally amounts to about 1 percent of the annual import total. Some indication of the undercounting in the detailed commodity statistics for imports is presented in the appendixes to the annual issues, from 1954–1965, of Bureau of the Census, Report FT 110, *United States Imports of Merchandise for Consumption*, and beginning 1967, Bureau of the Census, Report FT 135, *Imports, Commodity by Country*. Explanations of the sampling procedures are given in Report FT 110 for 1956; monthly issues of Report FT 135, *Foreign Commerce and Navigation of the United States, 1965*; and annual issues of *Guide to Foreign Trade Statistics*.

Export data are from Shippers' Export Declarations which exporters are required to file with customs officials for each shipment leaving the United States. Export data include shipments made after World War II under the Department of the Army Civilian Supply Program only for 1948 and subsequent years. In addition, export data include United States exports under the Lend-Lease, United Nations Relief and Rehabilitation Administration, Economic Cooperation Administration, Mutual Defense Assistance, and other mutual security programs. Shipments to U.S. Armed Forces for their own use are not included in export statistics for any period.

Export value figures are based on the selling price (or on the cost, if not sold) of the commodity shipped and include inland freight, insurance, and other charges to the U.S. place of export. Transportation and other costs beyond the United States port of exportation are excluded. The country of destination is defined as the country of ultimate destination or country where the merchandise is to be consumed, further processed, or manufactured. In the event the exporter does not have definite information as to the country of ultimate destination for a shipment, it is credited (for statistical purposes) to the country to which it is consigned.

Certain export commodity classifications were grouped for security reasons into special categories beginning with May 1949, with periodic amendments to include additional commodities. With the adoption of new security regulations, effective July 1950, the publication of the country of destination and customs district detail for the special category commodities and groups was discontinued. Effective January 1965, some changes were made in the security restrictions primarily because of revisions in export commodity classifications. Permission was granted to release data on exports of some commodities which were previously classified as special category commodities with the result that security restrictions were applied to considerably fewer commodities than before. In addition, permission was granted to release some commodity data for 1964 and prior years, which was withheld when statistics for those years were initially released. Data for special category commodities are included, however, in all total export statistics, series U 187, U 190, U 191, U 213, U 225, U 226, and U 317; in the category of finished manufactures, series U 218, U 235, and U 236; and in the commodity categories of series U 274–294 (except automobiles and parts, series U 287, from which machinery and vehicles manufactured to military specifications have been excluded beginning in July 1949).

Shipments individually valued, prior to October 1969, at less than $100 and, thereafter, at $250 and under, are not classified by commodity, but are reported in a single separate category. Effective with the statistics for July 1953 and continuing through December 1955, data for export shipments individually valued from $100 to $499 (about 4 to 6 percent of the total export value) were estimated on the basis of a 10-percent sample. From January through June 1956, the 10-percent sample was applied to shipments individually valued from $100 to $999 but, subsequently, the level was reduced to the previous level of $499. From July 1956–December 1959, shipments valued $100–$499 were based on a 10-percent sample; from January 1960–December 1962, on a 10-percent sample for Canada and a 50-percent sample for other countries. From January 1963–September 1969, shipments to Canada valued $100–$1,999 were based on a 10-percent sample; shipments to other countries valued $100–$499 were based on a 50-percent sample. From October 1969–December 1969, shipments to Canada valued $251–$1,999 were based on a 10-percent sample; shipments to other countries valued $251–$499, on a 50-percent sample; from January 1970–August 1970, shipments to other countries valued $251–$499 were fully compiled. For Canadian shipments valued $251–$1,999, sampling procedures were applied. Effective September 1970, shipments to Canada valued $251–$1,999 were based on a 10-percent sample; shipments to other countries valued $251–$499 on a 50-percent sample. Value data for shipments less than $100, prior to October 1969, and less than $251 thereafter, were estimated each month from factors established by observation of the percentage relationship of the under-$251 (under $100 prior to October 1969) shipments to the individual country totals in past periods. Details concerning sampling error and procedures are given in the Bureau of the Census, *Quarterly Summary of Foreign Commerce of the United States*, January-December 1956; *Foreign Commerce and Navigation of the United States, 1965*; monthly issues of Report FT 410, *Exports, Schedule B Commodity by Country*; and annual issues of *Guide to Foreign Trade Statistics*.

The geographic area covered by these statistics, except as noted, is the United States customs area, which includes Alaska, Hawaii, and Puerto Rico, and for 1935–1939, the Virgin Islands.

U 187–189. Total merchandise, gold, and silver exports and imports, 1821–1970.

Source: 1821–1880, except as noted, U.S. Bureau of Foreign and Domestic Commerce, *Foreign Commerce and Navigation of the United States*, 1912, pp. 43–44 (1821, series U 187 and U 189, revised estimates prepared by the U.S. Bureau of the Census); U.S. Bureau of the Census, 1881–1903, *Statistical Abstract of the United States*, *1924* edition, pp. 420, 421; 1904–1941, *1948* edition, p. 903; 1942–1949 (except series U 187 for 1948 and 1949), *1951* edition, p. 828; 1950–1957, *1958* edition, p. 880; 1958–1967, various editions; and 1968–1970, unpublished data. **Series U 187**, 1948 and 1949, *1953* edition, p. 899.

U 190–196. Merchandise exports and imports, 1790–1970.

Source: **Series U 190–192** and **U 196**, U.S. Bureau of Foreign and Domestic Commerce, 1790, *Foreign Commerce and Navigation of the*

United States, 1912, p. 43. U.S. Department of the Treasury, Bureau of Statistics, 1791–1880, *Monthly Summary of Imports and Exports of the United States for the Fiscal Year, 1896*, pp. 622–623 (except 1821, series U 190, U 192, and U 196, revised estimates prepared by Bureau of the Census). U.S. Bureau of the Census, *Statistical Abstract of the United States, 1924* edition, pp. 420, 421, and 424; 1904–1941, *1948* edition, pp. 902–903; 1942–1946, *Summary of Foreign Commerce of the United States*, various annual issues; 1947–1965, *Foreign Commerce and Navigation of the United States, 1964* and *1965*; 1966–1970, *Highlights of Exports and Imports*, FT 990, December 1972, pp. 37 and 79. **Series U 193–195**, U.S. Bureau of Foreign and Domestic Commerce, 1821–1880, *Foreign Commerce and Navigation of the United States, 1912*, p. 50; 1881–1915, *Foreign Commerce and Navigation of the United States, 1924*, p. lxvii. U.S. Bureau of the Census, 1916–1941, *Statistical Abstract of the United States, 1948* edition, p. 939; 1942–1946, *1951* edition, p. 854; 1947–1965, *Foreign Commerce and Navigation of the United States, 1964* and *1965*; 1966–1970, *Statistical Abstract, 1972* edition, p. 788.

Merchandise export statistics include data on all shipments of commodities and merchandise leaving the United States customs area except: (*1*) Gold and silver (prior to 1968) and evidences of debt; (*2*) intransit merchandise; (*3*) bunker fuel, stores, supplies, and equipment for vessels and planes; (*4*) temporary exports; (*5*) merchandise having small value or no commercial value; (*6*) shipments of military and naval supplies and equipment to the U.S. Armed Forces; and (*7*) shipments of office equipment and related items to U.S. Government agencies or establishments.

Exports of U.S. merchandise, series U 191, consist of commodities grown, produced, or manufactured in the United States, and commodities of foreign origin which have been changed in the United States from the form in which they were imported, or which have been enhanced in value by further manufacture in the United States.

Reexports, series U 192, comprise withdrawals from customs-bonded storage warehouses for exportation and exports of foreign merchandise (principally duty-free articles) which have previously been formally entered through customs. Exports of foreign merchandise consist of commodities of foreign origin which have entered the United States as imports and which, at the time of exportation, are in the same condition as when imported.

Merchandise import statistics include data on all commodities and merchandise reaching the United States except: (*1*) Merchandise not entering the U.S. customs area, such as articles excluded from the United States by law; (*2*) bunker fuel, and ships' stores; (*3*) intransit merchandise; (*4*) certain domestic merchandise returned from foreign countries; (*5*) gold and silver (prior to 1968) and evidences of debt; (*6*) merchandise having small value or no commercial value; and (*7*) commodities entered under special provisions, such as articles consigned to diplomatic officers. General imports, series U 193, consist of entries for immediate consumption and entries into bonded warehouses, and therefore comprise the total arrivals of merchandise, whether they enter consumption channels immediately or are entered into warehouses under customs custody to be subsequently withdrawn for consumption or withdrawn for exportation. Imports for consumption are the total of the entries for immediate consumption and the withdrawals from warehouse for consumption. The terms "entered for immediate consumption" and "withdrawn from warehouse for consumption" are taken from the language used in handling the transactions through customs, and are sometimes misleading in their implication that the merchandise is immediately assimilated by being processed, merchandised, or consumed. Although all customs barriers to such assimilation have been removed, merchandise for "immediate consumption" may, in fact, be warehoused by the importer outside of customs custody. In the case of withdrawal for "consumption," although duties have been paid and the goods released from customs control, they may remain in storage for a further period of time. Any of this "for consumption" merchandise could conceivably be exported subsequent to its release from customs custody and thus never enter actual U.S. consumption channels.

U 197–200. Gold and silver exports and imports, 1821–1970.

Source: U.S. Bureau of Foreign and Domestic Commerce, 1821–1864, *Foreign Commerce and Navigation of the United States, 1912,* p. 43. U.S. Department of the Treasury, 1865–1880, *Statistical Abstract, 1887,* pp. 41, 42. U.S. Bureau of the Census, 1881–1941, see source for series U 187–189 above; 1942–1946, *Summary of Foreign Commerce of the United States,* various annual issues; 1947–1965, *Foreign Commerce and Navigation of the United States, 1964* and *1965;* 1966–1970, *U.S. Foreign Trade, Gold Movements,* FT 2402, December issues.

Prior to 1895, figures for gold and silver relate to coin and bullion only; subsequently, they include ore also. Domestic exports of gold and silver cannot be separately stated prior to 1864, but it is probable that the greater portion of the exports was gold. In the series shown here, the data on exports of gold prior to 1864 include domestic exports of silver. The exports of silver for years prior to 1864, therefore, consist of only foreign exports or reexports.

U 201–206. Foreign trade related to various measures of production, 1869–1970.

Source: **Series U 201–202,** 1869–1939, computed as the ratios respectively of series U 190 and U 193 to gross national product (using series F 1 for all years except 1909–1918; for these years, the estimates of gross national product are from U.S. Senate, 79th Congress, 1st session, "Report to the Committee on Banking and Currency," *Basic Facts on Employment and Production,* Senate Committee Print No. 4); 1940–1957, U.S. Bureau of Foreign Commerce, *Exports in Relation to United States Production, 1957,* p. 2; 1958–1962, U.S. Bureau of International Commerce, *Exports in Relation to U.S. Production, 1962,* Overseas Business Reports No. 63–118, p. 2; 1963–1970, ratios computed from foreign trade data, as published by BIC in *U.S. Foreign Trade Annual, 1966–1972,* Overseas Business Reports No. 73–12, p. 2, and gross national product data as published by U.S. Bureau of Economic Analysis in *Survey of Current Business,* July 1973, p. 52. **Series U 203–204,** 1919–1927, 1931, and 1935, U.S. Bureau of Foreign Commerce, *World Trade Information Service Statistical Reports,* part 3, No. 58–22; 1929, 1933, and 1937–1962, see source for series U 201–202, 1940–1957 and 1958–1962; 1963–1970, value of production corresponds to aggregate for agricultural production (U.S. Department of Agriculture, *Farm Income Situation,* No. 222, July 1973, table 29, and U.S. Bureau of Economic Analysis, *Survey of Current Business,* July 1973, p. 24), manufacturing (U.S. Bureau of the Census, *Annual Survey of Manufactures, 1971,* No. M71 (AS), p. 3), mineral production (U.S. Department of the Interior, *Statistical Summary—Minerals Yearbook,* 1972), and freight receipts (U.S. Interstate Commerce Commission, *Annual Report on Transport Statistics of the United States*). **Series U 205,** 1910–1950, U.S. Foreign Agricultural Service, *United States Farm Products in Foreign Trade,* Statistical Bulletin No. 112, p. 10; 1951–1955, *The Problem of Maintaining High Level Agricultural Exports,* November 1957, p. 13; 1956–1970, U.S. Bureau of Economic Analysis, *1971 Business Statistics,* biennial supplement to *Survey of Current Business,* p. 111, and U.S. Department of Agriculture, Economic Research Service, *Agricultural Statistics, 1972,* p. 562. **Series U 206,** Don D. Humphrey, *American Imports,* © 1955 by the Twentieth Century Fund, New York, pp. 527–528.

For additional data on the relation of foreign trade to the domestic economy, see the following: Bureau of International Commerce, *Overseas Business Reports: Contribution of Imports to United States Raw Material Supplies,* No. 63–8; and *Contribution of Imports to U.S. Food Supplies,* No. 63–51. Also see Bureau of the Census, *U.S. Commodity Exports and Imports as Related to Output, 1970 and 1969.*

U 207–212. Value of merchandise imports and duties, 1821–1970.

Source: See source for series U 193–195.

Imports are "imports for consumption" consisting of entries for immediate consumption and withdrawals from warehouses for consumption. The term "entry for consumption" is the technical name of the import entry made at the customhouse, and implies that the goods have been delivered into the custody of the importer and that the duties have been paid on the dutiable portion. Some of them may be exported afterwards.

For 1821–1866, the figures for import values, series U 207–209, represent net general imports (total imports less reexports), the amount of duty collected (calculated) being the annual amounts collected on merchandise only. For 1867–1970, the figures of import values represent imports entered for consumption.

U 210, duties calculated. The series described here as "duties calculated" is the series identified in annual volumes of *Foreign Commerce and Navigation . . .,* through the 1925 issue, as "duties collected"; subsequent issues describe it as "duties calculated." In spite of its description, it was a computed figure at least back to 1876. The evidence indicates that the earlier years, at least in part, were on a "duties collected" basis. This series should not be confused with the modern series called "duties collected" (not shown here) which represents the total amount of duties actually collected (on individual shipments) as reported to the Treasury Department by customs officials, subject in certain cases to subsequent refund as well as drawback. In contrast, "duties calculated" is a statistical measure derived by applying the appropriate rates to totals for all imports of the given commodity received at all ports of entry; it does not reflect drawbacks or refunds and is subject to some time lag in reporting.

U 211–212, ratio of duties to total. The calculated ratio of duties to total is simply the relationship of series U 210 to series U 207 and series U 209, respectively, expressed in percentage form. Series U 211–212 are similar to, but not identical with, the series described as "ratios of duties to total" shown in annual issues of *Foreign Commerce and Navigation . . .,* 1925 to 1946, and as *"average ad valorem rates"* in earlier issues. These series have been computed as shown here because of conflicts in source volumes with respect to early years.

U 213–224. Value of merchandise exports and imports, by economic class, 1820–1970.

Source: U.S. Bureau of the Census. 1820–1918, *Statistical Abstract of the United States, 1820–1881, 1907* edition, pp. 698–701; 1882–1903, *1926* edition, pp. 448, 449; 1904–1918, *1947* edition, pp. 896, 897. 1919–1970, *Indexes of U.S. Exports and Imports by Economic Class: 1919 to 1971,* tables 1 and 5.

For definition of terms, see text for series U 190–196, U 207–212, and U 225–248.

The economic classes shown here are broad categories based on groupings of more than 2,000 individual commodities listed in *Schedule B: Statistical Classification of Domestic and Foreign Commodities Exported From the United States,* issued and kept current by the Bureau of the Census. Following are some of the important and typical commodities included in each of the economic classes:

Class	Exports	Imports
Crude materials	Crude petroleum	Crude rubber
	Coal	Raw silk
	Raw cotton	Hides and skins
Crude foodstuffs	Grains	Coffee
	Fruits	Tea
	Vegetables	Fruits
Manufactured foodstuffs	Meat	Sugar
	Lard	Meat
	Prepared fruits	Wheat flour
Semimanufactures	Iron and steel plates	Wood pulp
	Lumber	Copper in bars, etc.
	Refined copper	Tin in bars, etc.
Finished manufactures	Aircraft	Wool manufactures
	Cigarettes	Newsprint
	Radios and television sets	Automobiles and parts

In a report on *Exports of Manufactures From the United States and Their Distribution by Articles and Countries, 1800–1906* (1907), the Department of Commerce and Labor presented trade figures by economic classes annually back to 1850 and for selected years back to

1820. This study provided a different grouping of commodities than the Bureau of Statistics of the Treasury Department had previously employed for exports. In "Exports of Domestic Manufactures and Their Distribution" (*Monthly Summary of Commerce and Finance of the United States*, April 1903, p. 3239 ff.) the Treasury tabulated domestic exports for 1800–1850 by decade years and for 1851–1902 annually according to economic sector ("sources of production") as follows (p. 3249): Agriculture, manufactures, mining, forest, fisheries, and miscellaneous. But it tabulated imports "according to degree of manufacture and uses" for 1821, 1830, 1840, 1850, and 1851–1902 as follows (p. 3279–3280): Food and live animals, crude articles for domestic industries, articles manufactured wholly or partially for use as material in the mechanic arts, articles manufactured ready for consumption, and articles of voluntary use, luxuries, etc. This report noted that values for exports were in fluctuating currency for 1862–1879 and for those years gave specie values both for total exports and for exports of manufactures (p. 3315).

Trade in agricultural and forest products have been of special concern to the Department of Agriculture. Bulletin No. 51 of the Bureau of Statistics of the Department of Agriculture (1909) provides the "only compilation . . . ever to be completed (to that time)" of the "Foreign Trade of the United States in Forest Products, 1851–1908." Bulletins No. 74 and 75 in the same series, published in 1910, reviewed the "Imports of Farm Products Into the United States, 1851–1908" and "Exports of Farm Products From the United States, 1851–1908," respectively.

U 225–248. Indexes of quantity and unit value of exports and imports, by economic class, 1879–1970.

Source: 1879–1921 (1913 = 100 base), Robert E. Lipsey, *Price and Quantity Trends in the Foreign Trade of the United States*, Princeton University Press for the National Bureau of Economic Research, 1963 (copyright); U.S. Bureau of International Commerce, 1913 (1967 = 100 base), unpublished data; 1919–1970 (1967 = 100 base), *Indexes of U.S. Exports and Imports by Economic Class: 1919–1971*.

The Bureau of International Commerce indexes are computed by the Fisher formula, chained annually so that weights are taken from the given and preceding years. Commodities not directly entering into the calculations are taken into account in the weighting within the economic classes on the basis of certain assumptions regarding similarity of their price movements to price changes of commodities specifically covered.

The National Bureau of Economic Research indexes for the years 1879–1921 also used the Fisher formula linked from four time segments, within each of which weights are taken from the given year and the latest year of the segment. The National Bureau supplemented the U.S. foreign trade data with price information from other sources. Descriptions of methods used for the two sets of indexes are available in the sources.

All commodities in U.S. export and import trade have been grouped into one of five economic classes as follows: (1) Crude foods—products for edible use (by man or animals) which have not been substantially processed after sale by the farmer, fisherman, rancher, or other primary producer; (2) manufactured foods—processed forms of crude foods, edible and refined oils, and oilcake and meal; (3) crude materials—products of farms, forests, fisheries, and mines which are for nonfood use and which are unprocessed by manufacturing; (4) semimanufactures—manufactured materials in the early stages of processing; and (5) finished manufactures—highly processed bulk materials and products manufactured from semimanufactures or other finished products.

U 249–263. Value of exports and imports, by broad end-use class, 1923–1970.

Source: 1923–1967 (excluding World War II years), U.S. Office of Business Economics, *U.S. Exports and Imports Classified by OBE End-Use Commodity Categories, 1923–1968*, tables 1 and 2; 1968–1970, U.S. Bureau of Economic Analysis (formerly Office of Business Economics), *Survey of Current Business*, March issues.

The Bureau of Economic Analysis (BEA), (formerly Office of Business Economics (OBE)) end-use series presented in series U 249–263 are constructed from basic data provided by the Bureau of the Census, which has primary responsibility for compiling the official statistics of U.S. merchandise exports and imports. The Census Bureau currently collects foreign trade data on the basis of some 14,000 individual commodity numbers which are contained in its commodity classification schedules: almost 4,000 in Schedule B, for exports; over 10,000 in the Tariff Schedules of the United States Annotated (TSUSA), for imports.

BEA's-OBE's end-use categories are constructed by assigning each of these 14,000 basic "building blocks" to one of 228 basic end-use commodity groupings—116 for exports and 112 for imports—each of which is identified by a 4-digit code number. These 4-digit commodity groupings aggregate into broader intermediate groupings, identified by 3-digit and 2-digit codes. The intermediate groupings, in turn, combine at the broadest level into the principal 1-digit end-use categories—7 for exports, 6 for imports, as shown in series U 249–263.

BEA's-OBE's classification scheme was designed to fill a gap in the presentation of foreign trade statistics by regrouping commodity exports and imports as compiled by the Bureau of the Census into new, broad commodity categories based on a concept of end-use demand. The data have customarily been classified in terms of the physical nature of commodities and their stage of processing, or in terms of the principal industries *producing* the commodities. The end-use classification is associated with the principal sectors of the economy *using or consuming* the commodities.

It should be noted that inasmuch as the BEA-OBE end-use categories are constructed from the Census Bureau's Schedule B (export) and TSUSA (import) classifications, the validity of the assignments of individual commodities to end-use categories is subject to the limitations of the census classifications systems. The 14,000 basic "individual" commodities classified in Schedule B and TSUSA very frequently represent not a single commodity but rather a number of different items not separately classified. These items are related by their material content or general function, but not necessarily by their end-use. This is especially true of "basket" classifications. For example, "rubber products, n.e.s." may include erasers and soap dishes for consumer use, as well as rubber flanges, rings, and valves for industrial use. In cases of this kind, the products deemed to comprise most of the value of the "basket" commodity—based on advice of foreign trade commodity specialists—determine the end-use assignment it will receive. In another case, the commodity "ball bearings" is a machinery part that has been assigned to the export end-use category "Capital goods, except automotive" even though it includes ball bearings for autos and trucks which would be assigned, if they were separately identifiable, to the end-use category "Automotive vehicles, parts, and engines."

U 250 and U 258, foods, feeds, and beverages. This category is comprised of food for human consumption and animal feeds, and includes edible animals. It excludes work animals and animals for breeding, which are included in "Materials associated with nondurable goods and farm output," a grouping within the industrial supplies and materials category. Tobacco is not included in the foods category: cigarettes, etc., are in the consumer goods (nonfood) category, while unmanufactured tobacco is considered to be an industrial material (used in the manufacture of cigarettes and other tobacco products). A distinction is made in the foods category between *agricultural* and *nonagricultural* commodities in exports, but not in imports. This category, unlike the other principal end-use categories, does not distinguish between *manufactured* and *unmanufactured* commodity classes in either exports or imports.

U 251 and U 259, industrial supplies and materials. This category encompasses crude and processed materials and supplies primarily associated with, or used in, the producing sectors of the economy—

manufacturing, farming, and construction. Both the export and import sides are set up so as to separate *manufactured* from *unmanufactured* goods. *Agricultural* and *nonagricultural* aggregates can be obtained for exports but not for imports.

The industrial supplies and materials end-use category is subdivided on the import side into five major intermediate groupings as follows: (1) Fuels and lubricants; (2) paper and paper base stocks; (3) materials associated with nondurable goods and farm output; (4) selected building materials, except metals; (5) materials associated with durable goods output. These aggregates were established in order to facilitate analysis of the relationships between domestic economic conditions and imports of industrial supplies and materials. For example, shifts in imports of materials associated with durable goods output can be examined for their relationship to changes in the Federal Reserve Board's production index of durable manufactures, and imports of selected building materials can be related to domestic construction and housing indicators.

On the export side, the industrial supplies and materials category is broken down between agricultural and nonagricultural goods; intermediate groupings similar to (3), (4), and (5), listed above, are not constructed.

(1) *Fuels and lubricants*—comprised of coal, oil, and gas. This grouping excludes petrochemicals, which are included with chemicals in another grouping within the industrial supplies and materials category. Although fuels and lubricants are partly associated with consumer goods as well as industrial supplies, it was not considered feasible to try to distinguish between fuel for home heating, for example, and fuel for industrial heating and energy.

Fuels and lubricants have been established as an independent major subcomponent of the industrial supplies and materials category on both the export and import sides because of their magnitude in our international trade, and because of the difficulty of associating them with the output of nondurable as distinguished from durable goods.

(2) *Paper and paper base stocks*—consists of pulpwood, woodpulp, and scrap materials for making paper; also paper products, mainly newsprint, but including also kraft paper, paperboard, and similar products. Excluded are such paper products as stationery, which are allocated to the consumer goods end-use category. The predominance of newsprint imports in the paper grouping, and the unique nature of this product, led to the establishment of paper, like the fuels and lubricants grouping, as a separate major subcomponent of industrial supplies and materials for both exports and imports.

(3) *Materials associated with nondurable goods and farm output*—consists of supplies and materials related to the manufacture of products considered to be *nondurables*. It includes such goods as crude and processed textiles, but not those manufactured into final products such as apparel and house-furnishings. The latter are in the consumer goods category. Also included are unmanufactured tobacco, chemicals (except medicinals), hides and skins, undressed furs, soap and perfumery ingredients, etc. Seeds, fertilizers, farm work animals and breeding animals, and eggs for hatching are included as materials associated with farm output. This grouping is constructed only for imports.

(4) *Selected building materials, except metals*—consists of such major (nonmetal) building materials as lumber, plywood and veneers, stone, sand, cement, lime, glass (except automotive), asbestos, gypsum, millwork, molding, prefabricated structures, etc. Excludes metals used in building (steel beams, copper tubing, wire, pipe, latches and locks, etc.). This grouping is constructed only for imports.

(5) *Materials associated with durable goods output*—consists of supplies and materials related to the manufacture of products defined to be *durables*. Includes primary metals and metal shapes, and fabricated metal manufactures for further assembly or incorporation in other goods (door hinges, latches, locks, and parts

and components not included elsewhere). This grouping is constructed only for imports.

It should be noted that the allocation of individual commodities to the various subcomponents outlined above is based on end-use demand and not on the nature of the commodities from a production (supply) viewpoint. To illustrate—imports of primary rubber, a "nondurable" commodity, is classified under "Materials associated with durable goods output" because its major end-use—as a tire-making material—is associated with the production of such durable goods as motor vehicles (including tractors), and aircraft.

U 252 and **U 260**, capital goods, except automotive. This end-use category is designed to include all (nonmilitary) machinery, equipment, apparatus, and instruments—and their parts, components, accessories, and attachments. These products are associated with investment outlays for industrial and agricultural plant and equipment; for commercial, scientific, professional, and service-industry capital goods; and for natural resource development (petroleum and mining), and construction. Also included is transport equipment such as civilian aircraft and parts, railway rolling stock, and, for exports only, commercial cargo and passenger-carrying vessels. Automotive products are *excluded* from the capital goods end-use category as are other transportation items classifiable as consumer goods (yachts and other pleasure craft, motorcycles, etc.).

U 253 and **U 261**, automotive vehicles, parts, and engines. This category contains commodities that might have qualified for assignment to two other end-use categories; passenger cars and parts to consumer goods (nonfood), and trucks and buses and parts to capital goods. However, because it has not been possible to distinguish parts for passenger cars from parts for trucks and buses, and because of the overall magnitude and importance of U.S. automotive trade, a separate automotive category was established. There are groupings within the category for passenger cars, trucks and buses, and automotive parts and engines (including engine parts).

U 254 and **U 262**, consumer goods (nonfood), except automotive. Designed to cover products used by the final consumer, this category has been subdivided into *durables* and *nondurables*, as well as *manufactured* and *unmanufactured*. The overall category encompasses a broad variety of products including consumer-type transportation equipment other than automotive—pleasure craft, motorcycles, etc.—and furniture, rugs, appliances, radios and TV, clocks and watches, precious stones, and other *durables;* and apparel and household softgoods, leather, rubber and plastic articles, notions and toiletries, medicinal preparations, and other *nondurables*. In general, consumer goods have been classified as *durables* or *nondurables* on the basis of whether they are, respectively, *hardgoods* or *softgoods*. Rugs are an exception, being classified as durable goods because of their long life and relatively high cost, and because they can be characterized as consumer "capital goods" along with furniture and appliances. The consumer goods category consists predominantly of manufactured products, but also includes such unmanufactured items as gem stones, Christmas trees, nursery stock, and pet birds.

U 255, special category, domestic (military-type goods). This is an export category only. It includes military aircraft, engines, turbines, missiles and rockets, military trucks, warships, ordnance, and other military material classified confidential by the Department of Defense as to country of destination. (Prior to 1965, DOD classified many military items confidential as to their identity as well as their destination.) A few other military items currently of minor value, not classified as special category—military cars and buses—are included in the category "Exports not elsewhere classified."

Parts for aircraft (exports) are not separately identifiable from 1958 on as between military and civilian aircraft, and all aircraft parts have thus been included, with civilian aircraft, in the capital goods category.

Imports of military aircraft and parts are included in the category "Imports not elsewhere shown." Other military imports are either minimal in value or are unidentifiable, and are included, as appropriate, in other end-use categories.

U 256 and **U 263**, exports, n.e.c., and imports, n.e.s. This category includes transactions and commodities not elsewhere classified or shown. "Exports, n.e.c." includes reexports (exports of foreign merchandise imported into the United States and then reexported with no significant change in form or content), low-value shipments (commodity detail unavailable), a few military items not classified as special category, and special transactions such as goods imported for repair and exported. "Imports, n.e.s." includes low-value shipments, U.S. goods returned (after having been exported), U.S. Government purchases of uranium ores and oxides, and of military aircraft and parts; also includes movies, exhibits, and laboratory, zoo, and show animals, etc. (Exports of uranium, and non-Government imports of uranium, are included in the industrial supplies and materials category.)

U 264–273. Value of merchandise exports and imports, by groups of customs districts, 1860–1970.

Source: U.S. Bureau of the Census, 1860–1880, *Statistical Abstract of the United States, 1923* edition, pp. 824–825; 1881–1903, *1924* edition, p. 441; 1904–1944, *1947* edition, p. 921; 1945–1970, unpublished data. Data are published for individual customs districts in Bureau of the Census, *Foreign Commerce and Navigation of the United States* and *Highlights of Exports and Imports*, FT 990.

The customs district in which merchandise is entered or withdrawn for consumption is the district shown in the "imports for consumption" statistics. The customs district shown in the "general imports" statistics is the district through which merchandise enters the United States either as an entry for immediate consumption or as an entry into a customs-bonded warehouse. Except for shipments by mail, vessels under their own power or afloat, and certain low-valued shipments, the customs district through which a shipment clears when it leaves the country is the district to which the export is credited statistically. Shipments are not credited on the basis of the district in which export shipments originate or to which import shipments are destined. For definition of terms, see text for series U 190–196 and U 207–212. Export figures for 1865 and 1870–1878 represent mixed gold and currency values and hence do not agree with the specie values given for total exports elsewhere.

U 274–316. General note.

The totals of the selected imports and exports, series U 274 and U 295, are shown to provide a means of judging the extent to which the selected items account for the total trade of this country. They include only the values of the items shown for each year and are, therefore, a total with a variable composition. Additional information on the composition of the foreign trade of the United States may be found in M. B. Hammond, *The Cotton Industry*, American Economic Association Series 2, No. 1, New York, 1897, and in reports by the U.S. Department of Treasury, Bureau of Statistics, on the grain, provision, cotton, coal, iron and steel, and lumber trades of the United States which appeared in the *Monthly Summary of Commerce and Finance* (hereafter abbreviated as *MSCF*) for 1899–1900, 1900–1901, and 1902–1903.

Export commodity information is compiled in accordance with the classifications in Schedule B, Statistical Classification of Domestic and Foreign Commodities Exported From the United States. For earlier years Schedule B, Statistical Classification of Domestic Commodities Exported From the United States, and Schedule F, Statistical Classification of Foreign Commodities Exported From the United States, were used. Export commodity information has been compiled in accordance with the Schedule B classifications in effect during those years. Commodities were classified according to physical characteristics or use. These groupings were made on the basis of the materials of which articles were made, the use for which they were intended, and the extent of their refinement or manufacture. In 1965, a revised edition of Schedule B based on the Standard International Trade Classification, Revised (SITC), was put in effect. The 1965 edition was developed with the primary

objective of instituting a classification system providing for those detailed characteristics which permit comparison of the U.S. export statistics with foreign trade statistics of other countries reporting in terms of SITC, as well as data on domestic production. The statistics shown for 1960–1964, which were initially compiled in accordance with the Schedule B classifications in effect during those years, have been recompiled in terms of SITC classifications. It should be noted that some difficulties were encountered in relating the Schedule B classifications to the SITC and, because of differences between these two classification systems, it was necessary to assign some Schedule B numbers to SITC groups on the basis of judgment. Therefore, comparisons of 1960–1970 data for SITC groups with corresponding data for prior periods should be made with caution.

For periods prior to 1963, import commodity information was compiled in terms of the commodity classifications contained in Schedule A, Statistical Classifications of Commodities Imported Into the United States. Effective with the statistics for 1963, import data are compiled in accordance with the classifications in the Tariff Schedules of the United States Annotated (TSUSA), an official publication of the U.S. Tariff Commission embracing the legal text of the Tariff Schedules of the United States (enacted into law by the Tariff Classification Act of 1962) together with statistical annotations.

Effective with the statistics for 1964, a revised Schedule A classification system was established, based on the Standard International Trade Classification, Revised (SITC). This edition of Schedule A was constructed (1) to provide for the summarization of data for the approximately 10,000 TSUSA classifications into about 2,300 commodity groupings that are meaningful in terms of commodities important in the U.S. import trade and (2) to provide data in terms of the SITC outline that are comparable, insofar as comparison is possible, to the foreign trade statistics compiled by other trading nations.

As with export commodity statistics, difficulties were encountered in relating Schedule A classifications to TSUSA and SITC classifications; therefore, comparisons between 1963–1970 data and prior periods should be made with caution.

U 274. Exports, total selected commodities, value, 1802–1970.

Source: See general note for series U 274–316.

U 275–276. Cotton, unmanufactured, exports, quantity and value, 1791–1970.

Source: 1791–1889, U.S. Department of the Treasury, Bureau of Statistics, *MSCF*, 1895–6, p. 290; 1890–1897, *MSCF*, March 1900, p. 2561; 1898–1940, following editions of the *Statistical Abstract of the United States:*

Period	Edition	Page
1898–1905	1907	417–477
1906–1915	1916	392–438
1916–1919	1920	435–511
1920–1922	1924	448–536
1923–1925	1928	480–552
1926–1929	1931	528–609
1930–1932	1934	440–521
1933–1935	1937	467–554
1936–1940	1942	575–669

1941–1962, U.S. Bureau of the Census, *Summary of Foreign Commerce*, various issues. 1960–1970 (SITC), U.S. Bureau of the Census, *U.S. Foreign Trade—Highlights of Exports and Imports*, FT 990, December issues; and unpublished data.

U 277–278. Leaf tobacco, unmanufactured, exports, quantity and value, 1790–1970.

Source: 1790–1894, U.S. Department of the Treasury, Bureau of Statistics, *MSCF*, June 1895, pp. 1418–1421; 1898–1970, see source for series U 275–276.

U 279–280. Wheat exports, quantity and value, 1790–1970.

Source: 1790–1897, see source for series U 277–278; 1898–1970, see source for series U 275–276.

U 281–294. Value of exports of selected U.S. merchandise, 1810–1970.

Source: 1810–1961, the following editions of the *Statistical Abstract of the United States* except as noted below for series U 287 and U 294:

Period	Edition	Page
1810–1881	1924	446–447
1882–1904 (1882–1907 for imports)	1926	470–473
1905–1945 (1908–1945 for imports)	1948	916–919
1946–1949	1954	910–911
1950–1954	1958	885–886
1955–1961	1962	877

Series U 287, 1860–1900, *Statistical Abstract, 1924*, p. 447. **Series U 294**, 1903–1907, *Statistical Abstract, 1947*, p. 905; 1962, unpublished data. 1960–1970 (SITC), see source for series U 275–276.

U 295. Imports, total selected commodities, value, 1821–1962.

Source: See general note for series U 274–316.

U 296–297. Coffee imports, quantity and value, 1790–1970.

Source: 1790–1896, U.S. Department of the Treasury, Bureau of Statistics, *MSCF*, October 1896, pp. 670–672 and 679–681; 1898–1970, see source for series U 275–276.

U 298–299. Tea imports, quantity and value, 1790–1970.

Source: 1790–1896, see source for series U 296–297, pp. 684–685 and 688–689; 1898–1970, see source for series U 275–276.

U 300–301. Sugar imports, quantity and value, 1790–1970.

Source: 1790–1897, U.S. Department of the Treasury, Bureau of Statistics, *MSCF*, November 1902, pp. 1366 and 1375; 1898–1970, see source for series U 275–276.

U 302–305. Crude rubber and raw silk imports, quantity and value, 1855–1970.

Source: 1855–1897, U.S. Department of Commerce, *Statistical Abstract of the United States, 1924*, p. 445; 1898–1970, see source for series U 275–276.

U 306–316. Value of imports of selected products, 1820–1970.

Source: See source for series U 281–294.

U 317–352. General note.

Imports are shown according to country of origin and exports according to ultimate destination. When the final destination is not known the shipment is credited statistically to the country to which it is consigned. Accurate information on country of origin is difficult to obtain. Consequently, the directional breakdown of foreign trade is at best approximate.

Trade with Canada and the United Kingdom, particularly, is difficult to measure. Considerable U.S. merchandise normally moves to foreign destinations via Canada and some moves across Canada to destinations in the United States, notably from ports in Michigan to ports in New York. At times such movements have been counted as trade with Canada. Also, considerable Canadian trade with other countries moves through the United States. A good deal of United States merchandise has been consigned to the United Kingdom and reexported to other markets by the United Kingdom, as can be observed by the difference between general imports and retained imports in the United Kingdom's record of trade with the United States.

Special studies of U.S.-Canadian trade have been made from time to time. In this connection, see the headnote to the table, p. 295 of *Commerce Yearbook*, vol. II, for 1931; and see *MSCF*, June and July 1898, pp. 2084–2089, where it is also noted (p. 2075) that "exports to Canada are incomplete prior to April 1, 1893, the date on which the law requiring exporters to clear their goods exported by railways went into effect." For an effort at adjusting the U.S. trade record for this deficiency and the similar lack of coverage in the report of trade with Mexico, see tables 2 and 3 of Matthew Simon's "The United States Balance of Payments, 1861–1900" published by the National Bureau of Economic Research in *Studies in Income and Wealth*, vol. 24, 1960. For a discussion of shortcomings in the U.S. record of trade with the United Kingdom in the early years of the Civil War, see the Treasury's report in 1864 to Congress, *Statistics of the Foreign and Domestic Commerce of the United States*, p. 37 ff.

For certain periods, like the Civil War and the greenback era, partners' records of trade with the United States are more reliable than the U.S. record and in some ways more revealing of certain aspects of the trade.

For 1862–1879, exports of domestic merchandise are mixed gold and currency values. Imports and reexports, however, are specie values. The extent of the adjustment can be observed by comparing figures from series U 317 with those in series U 190.

Prior to 1873, trade figures for Canada are actually trade figures for all of British North America, a somewhat larger area than the Dominion of Canada. Asia includes the Philippines in all years and Turkey in Europe for 1926–1951. Oceania includes Hawaii prior to 1901. Europe includes the Soviet Republic in Asia since 1923 and Iceland in all years (Iceland was included with northern North America in *Historical Statistics of the United States, 1789–1945*).

The source for these series for 1821–1881 is the Treasury Department, Bureau of Statistics, *Monthly Summary of Commerce and Finance*, hereafter abbreviated as *MSCF*.

U 317–334. Value of exports (including reexports) of U.S. merchandise, by country of destination, 1790–1970.

Source: 1790–1820, **series U 317**, see source for series U 190. 1790–1820, **series U 318–334**, U.S. Department of the Treasury, Bureau of Statistics, *Statistical Tables Exhibiting the Commerce of the U.S. With European Countries 1790–1890*, 1893, pp. xiii, xiv, xviii, and xix. 1821–1881, **series U 317**, *MSCF*, April 1898, p. 1632; **series U 319**, 1821–1872, *MSCF*, June 1898, p. 2091; 1873–1881, U.S. Department of Commerce and Labor, *Statistical Abstract of the United States, 1907*, p. 317; **series U 320–322**, *MSCF*, August 1901, pp. 618, 626–627, and 632–633; **series U 324–328**, *MSCF*, October 1896, pp. 718, 730–732, and 745–746; **series U 329–332**, *MSCF*, April 1898, pp. 1632, 1637, and 1638 (except for China, 1865–1881, *Statistical Abstract, 1907*, p. 350); **series U 333–334**, 1821–1864, *MSCF*, June 1896, pp. 1612, 1621, and 1622; 1865–1881, *Statistical Abstract, 1907*, pp. 366, 376 (data for total America and "other" series were obtained as residuals for 1821–1881); 1882–1946 and 1966–1970, the following editions of the *Statistical Abstract:*

Period	Edition	Page
1882–1889	1907	284, 288–369
1890–1906	1910	328–376
1907–1915	1916	347–381
1916–1920	1920	398–425
1921–1923	1926	452, 458–463
1924–1928	1930	482, 492–497
1929–1932	1934	418, 424–429
1933–1936	1938	456, 460–464
1937–1940	1943	530, 534–538
1941–1945	1948	922, 926–930
1946	1952	856, 858–860
1966–1968	1969	808–811
1969–1970	1972	778–781

1947–1964, U.S. Bureau of the Census, *Foreign Commerce and Navigation of the United States, 1964 and 1965*.

U 335–352. Value of general imports, by country of origin, 1790–1970.

Source: See source for series U 317–334.

See also general note for series U 317–352.

Series U 187-200. Value of Exports and Imports: 1790 to 1970

[In millions of dollars. For years ending September 30, 1790-1842; June 30, 1843-1915; thereafter, calendar years]

Year	Total merchandise, gold, and silver			Merchandise [1]							Gold		Silver [3]	
			Excess of exports (+) or imports (−)	Exports and reexports			General imports			Excess of exports (+) or imports (−)				
	Exports	Imports		Total	Exports of U.S. merchandise	Re-exports	Total	For immediate consumption	For warehouse		Exports [2]	Imports	Exports [2]	Imports
	187	188	189	190	191	192	193	194	195	196	197	198	199	200
1970	43,265	40,189	+3,076	43,224	42,590	634	39,952	38,064	1,888	+3,272	41	237	--------	--------
1969	38,018	36,279	+1,739	38,006	37,462	544	36,043	34,238	1,805	+1,964	12	237	--------	--------
1968	35,475	33,452	+2,023	34,636	34,199	437	33,226	31,439	1,787	+1,410	839	226	--------	--------
1967	32,632	26,925	+5,708	31,526	31,142	384	26,812	25,330	1,483	+4,714	1,005	33	101	80
1966	30,891	25,663	+5,229	30,320	29,884	436	25,542	23,870	1,673	+4,777	457	42	114	78
1965	28,809	21,533	+7,276	27,470	27,127	343	21,364	19,661	1,705	+6,105	1,285	102	54	65
1964	27,075	18,791	+8,284	26,508	26,156	352	18,684	17,087	1,597	+7,824	423	41	144	66
1963	23,593	17,253	+6,339	23,347	23,062	285	17,138	15,644	1,493	+6,209	204	44	42	71
1962	22,096	16,606	+5,491	21,700	21,431	269	16,380	14,928	1,451	+5,320	381	151	15	75
1961	21,812	14,815	+6,997	20,999	20,755	245	14,714	13,361	1,353	+6,286	775	56	38	45
1960	20,603	15,046	+5,557	20,575	20,375	200	14,654	13,282	1,372	+5,922	2	335	26	57
1959	17,646	15,574	+2,072	17,634	17,451	183	15,207	13,908	1,299	+2,427	2	304	10	63
1958	17,945	13,215	+4,730	17,910	17,745	165	12,792	11,780	1,012	+5,118	31	291	4	132
1957	21,029	13,413	+7,617	20,850	20,671	180	12,982	11,894	1,088	+7,868	168	273	11	158
1956	19,124	12,877	+6,247	19,090	18,940	150	12,615	11,591	1,024	+6,475	27	133	7	129
1955	15,563	11,562	+4,001	15,547	15,419	128	11,384	10,467	917	+4,163	7	105	8	73
1954	15,136	10,333	+4,803	15,110	14,981	129	10,215	9,442	773	+4,894	22	38	5	80
1953	15,827	11,015	+4,812	15,774	15,652	122	10,873	9,972	902	+4,900	45	47	9	95
1952	15,262	11,525	+3,737	15,201	15,049	152	10,717	9,768	949	+4,483	56	740	5	67
1951	15,672	11,152	+4,520	15,032	14,879	153	10,967	9,600	1,367	+4,065	631	81	9	103
1950	10,816	9,125	+1,691	10,275	10,142	133	8,852	7,815	1,037	+1,423	534	163	7	110
1949	12,160	7,467	+4,693	12,051	11,936	115	6,622	5,942	680	+5,429	85	771	24	74
1948	12,967	9,176	+3,791	12,653	12,532	121	7,124	6,361	763	+5,529	301	1,981	13	71
1947	14,674	7,904	+6,770	[4] 14,430	14,252	177	5,756	5,074	682	+8,673	213	2,080	31	68
1946	9,996	5,533	+4,464	[4] 9,738	9,500	238	4,942	4,285	657	+4,796	221	533	36	58
1945	10,097	4,280	+5,816	9,806	9,585	221	[5] 4,159	3,689	458	+5,646	200	94	91	27
1944	15,345	4,066	+11,279	[4] 14,259	14,162	97	[5] 3,929	3,515	404	+10,330	959	114	127	23
1943	13,028	3,511	+9,517	12,965	12,842	123	3,381	3,034	347	+9,583	33	102	31	28
1942	8,081	3,113	+4,968	8,079	8,003	76	[5] 2,756	2,286	459	+5,323	(Z)	316	2	41
1941	5,153	4,375	+778	5,147	5,020	127	3,345	2,716	629	+1,802	(Z)	982	6	47
1940	4,030	7,433	−3,403	4,021	3,934	87	2,625	2,170	455	+1,396	5	4,749	4	58
1939	3,192	5,978	−2,786	3,177	3,123	54	2,318	1,918	400	+859	1	3,575	15	85
1938	3,107	4,170	−1,063	3,094	3,057	37	1,960	1,666	294	+1,134	6	1,979	7	231
1937	3,407	4,807	−1,400	3,349	3,299	50	3,084	2,614	470	+265	46	1,632	12	92
1936	2,495	3,750	−1,254	2,456	2,419	37	2,423	2,095	328	+33	28	1,144	12	183
1935	2,304	4,143	−1,839	2,283	2,243	40	2,047	1,762	285	+235	2	1,741	19	355
1934	2,202	2,944	−742	2,133	2,100	33	1,655	1,388	267	+478	53	1,187	17	103
1933	2,061	1,703	+358	1,675	1,647	28	1,450	1,254	196	+225	367	193	19	60
1932	2,434	1,706	+729	1,611	1,576	35	1,323	1,198	125	+288	810	363	14	20
1931	2,918	2,731	+186	2,424	2,378	46	2,091	1,881	210	+334	467	612	26	29
1930	4,013	3,500	+514	3,843	3,781	62	3,061	2,765	296	+782	116	396	54	43
1929	5,441	4,755	+686	5,241	5,157	84	4,399	3,925	474	+842	117	292	83	64
1928	5,776	4,328	+1,448	5,128	5,030	98	4,091	3,655	436	+1,037	561	169	87	68
1927	5,142	4,447	+695	4,865	4,759	107	4,185	3,720	465	+681	201	208	76	55
1926	5,017	4,714	+303	4,809	4,712	97	4,431	3,949	482	+378	116	214	92	70
1925	5,272	4,419	+852	4,910	4,819	91	4,227	3,702	524	+683	263	128	99	65
1924	4,763	4,004	+759	4,591	4,498	93	3,610	3,153	457	+981	62	320	110	74
1923	4,269	4,189	+79	4,167	4,091	77	3,792	3,341	451	+375	29	323	72	74
1922	3,931	3,459	+473	3,832	3,765	67	3,113	2,776	337	+719	37	275	63	71
1921	4,560	3,264	+1,297	4,485	4,379	106	2,509	2,280	230	+1,976	24	691	52	63
1920	8,664	5,784	+2,880	8,228	8,080	148	5,278	4,789	490	+2,950	322	417	114	88
1919	8,528	4,070	+4,457	7,920	7,750	171	3,904	3,828	76	+4,016	368	77	239	89
1918	6,443	3,165	+3,278	6,149	6,048	101	3,031	2,865	166	+3,118	41	62	253	71
1917	6,690	3,558	+3,131	6,234	6,170	64	2,952	2,667	285	+3,281	372	552	84	53
1916	5,709	3,110	+2,599	5,483	5,423	60	2,392	2,179	213	+3,091	156	686	71	32
1915 [6]	2,966	1,875	+1,091	2,769	2,716	52	1,674	1,648	26	+1,094	146	172	51	29
1914	2,532	1,991	+541	2,365	2,330	35	1,894	1,906	−12	+471	112	67	55	30
1913	2,615	1,923	+692	2,466	2,429	37	1,813	1,767	46	+653	78	69	72	41
1912	2,327	1,749	+577	2,204	2,170	34	1,653	1,641	13	+551	57	49	65	47
1911	2,137	1,647	+490	2,049	2,014	36	1,527	1,528	−1	+522	23	74	65	46

See footnotes at end of table.

Series U 187–200. Value of Exports and Imports: 1790 to 1970—Con.

[In millions of dollars]

Year	Total merchandise, gold, and silver			Merchandise [1]							Gold		Silver	
				Exports and reexports			General imports							
	Exports	Imports	Excess of exports (+) or imports (−)	Total	Exports of U.S. merchandise	Reexports	Total	For immediate consumption	For warehouse	Excess of exports (+) or imports (−)	Exports [2]	Imports	Exports [2]	Imports
	187	188	189	190	191	192	193	194	195	196	197	198	199	200
1910	1,919	1,646	+273	1,745	1,710	35	1,557	1,547	10	+188	119	43	55	45
1909	1,810	1,400	+410	1,663	1,638	25	1,312	1,282	30	+351	92	44	56	44
1908	1,991	1,387	+604	1,861	1,835	26	1,194	1,183	11	+666	72	148	58	45
1907	1,989	1,592	+397	1,881	1,854	27	1,434	1,415	19	+446	51	115	57	43
1906	1,848	1,367	+481	1,744	1,718	26	1,227	1,213	13	+517	39	96	66	44
1905	1,660	1,199	+461	1,519	1,492	27	1,118	1,087	30	+401	93	54	49	27
1904	1,592	1,118	+474	1,461	1,435	26	991	982	9	+470	81	99	49	28
1903	1,511	1,095	+417	1,420	1,392	28	1,026	1,008	18	+394	47	45	44	24
1902	1,480	984	+496	1,382	1,355	26	903	900	4	+478	49	52	50	28
1901	1,605	926	+680	1,488	1,460	27	823	808	15	+665	53	66	64	36
1900	1,499	930	+570	1,394	1,371	24	850	831	19	+545	48	45	57	35
1899	1,321	817	+504	1,227	1,204	23	697	685	12	+530	38	89	56	31
1898	1,302	767	+535	1,231	1,210	21	616	587	29	+615	15	120	55	31
1897	1,153	880	+273	1,051	1,032	19	765	789	−25	+286	40	85	62	31
1896	1,056	842	+214	883	863	19	780	760	20	+103	112	34	61	29
1895	921	789	+133	808	793	14	732	731	1	+76	66	36	47	20
1894	1,020	741	+279	892	869	23	655	630	25	+237	77	72	50	13
1893	997	911	+86	848	831	17	866	833	34	−19	109	21	41	23
1892	1,113	897	+216	1,030	1,016	15	827	804	23	+203	50	50	33	20
1891	993	881	+112	884	872	12	845	845	1	+40	86	18	23	18
1890	910	823	+87	858	845	13	789	766	24	+69	17	13	35	21
1889	839	774	+65	742	730	12	745	735	10	−3	60	10	37	19
1888	742	783	−41	696	684	12	724	707	17	−28	18	44	28	15
1887	752	752	(Z)	716	703	13	692	680	13	+24	10	43	26	17
1886	752	674	+78	680	666	14	635	624	11	+44	43	21	30	18
1885	784	621	+164	742	727	16	578	579	−2	+165	8	27	34	17
1884	808	705	+103	741	725	16	668	668	(Z)	+73	41	23	26	15
1883	856	752	+104	824	804	20	723	701	22	+101	12	18	20	11
1882	800	767	+33	751	733	17	725	717	8	+26	33	34	17	8
1881	922	753	+169	902	884	18	643	651	−8	+260	3	100	17	11
1880	853	761	+92	836	824	12	668	628	40	+168	4	81	14	12
1879	735	466	+269	710	698	12	446	440	6	+265	5	6	20	15
1878	729	467	+262	695	681	14	437	439	−2	+258	9	13	25	16
1877	659	492	+167	602	590	13	451	440	11	+151	27	26	30	15
1876	597	477	+120	540	526	15	461	465	−4	+80	31	8	25	8
1875	606	554	+52	513	499	14	533	526	7	−20	67	14	25	7
1874	653	596	+57	586	569	17	567	568	(Z)	+19	34	20	33	9
1873	607	664	−57	522	505	17	642	663	−21	−120	45	9	40	13
1872	524	640	−116	444	428	16	627	560	67	−182	50	9	30	5
1871	541	541	(Z)	443	428	14	520	500	20	−77	67	7	32	14
1870	451	462	−11	393	377	16	436	426	10	−43	34	12	25	14
1869	343	437	−94	286	275	11	418	394	23	−131	36	14	21	6
1868	376	372	+4	282	269	13	357	345	13	−75	72	9	21	5
1867	355	418	−62	295	280	15	396	378	18	−101	39	17	22	5
1866	435	446	−11	349	338	11	435	423	11	−86	71	8	15	3
1865	234	249	−15	166	137	29	239	210	29	−73	58	6	9	3
1864	264	330	−65	159	144	15	316	301	15	−158	101	11	5	2
1863	268	253	+15	204	186	18	243	225	18	−39	62	6	2	4
1862	228	206	+22	191	180	11	189	178	11	+1	35	14	1	3
1861	249	336	−86	220	205	15	289	275	15	−70	27	42	2	4
1860	400	362	+38	334	316	17	354	336	17	−20	58	3	8	6
1859	357	339	+18	293	278	15	331	317	15	−38	61	2	3	5
1858	325	283	+42	272	251	21	263	243	21	+9	50	12	3	8
1857	363	361	+2	294	279	15	348	334	15	−55	65	7	4	6
1856	327	315	+12	281	266	15	310	296	15	−29	45	1	1	3
1855	275	261	+14	219	193	26	258	232	26	−39	55	1	1	3
1854	278	305	−26	237	215	22	298	276	22	−61	40	3	1	4
1853	231	268	−37	203	190	14	264	250	14	−60	25	2	2	2
1852	210	213	−3	167	155	12	207	195	12	−40	40	4	3	2
1851	218	216	+2	189	179	10	211	200	10	−22	23	4	7	2

See footnotes at end of table.

INTERNATIONAL TRANSACTIONS AND FOREIGN COMMERCE

Series U 187–200.   Value of Exports and Imports: 1790 to 1970—Con.

[In millions of dollars]

Year	Total merchandise, gold, and silver			Merchandise [1]							Gold		Silver	
				Exports and reexports			General imports				Exports [2]	Imports	Exports [2]	Imports
	Exports	Imports	Excess of exports (+) or imports (−)	Total	Exports of U.S. merchandise	Re-exports	Total	For immediate consumption	For warehouse	Excess of exports (+) or imports (−)				
	187	188	189	190	191	192	193	194	195	196	197	198	199	200
1850	152	178	−26	144	135	9	174	164	9	−29	5	2	3	3
1849	146	148	−2	140	132	9	141	133	9	−1	2	4	3	3
1848	154	155	−1	138	130	8	149	141	8	−10	11	3	5	3
1847	159	147	+12	157	151	6	122	116	6	+34	1	22	1	3
1846	113	122	−8	110	102	8	118	110	8	−8	2	1	2	3
1845	115	117	−3	106	98	8	113	106	8	−7	3	1	6	3
1844	111	108	+3	106	100	6	103	96	6	+3	1	2	4	4
1843 [7]	84	65	+20	83	78	5	42	37	5	+40	(Z)	17	1	5
1842	105	100	+5	100	92	8	96	88	8	+4	2	1	3	3
1841	122	128	−6	112	104	8	123	115	8	−11	4	1	6	4
1840	132	107	+25	124	112	12	98	86	12	+25	4	3	5	6
1839	121	162	−41	112	102	11	156	146	11	−44	5	1	4	4
1838	108	114	−5	105	96	9	96	87	9	+9	1	12	2	6
1837	117	141	−24	111	94	17	130	113	17	−19	3	2	3	8
1836	129	190	−61	124	107	18	177	159	18	−52	1	7	4	6
1835	122	150	−28	115	100	15	137	122	15	−22	1	2	5	11
1834	104	127	−22	102	81	22	109	87	22	−6	1	4	1	14
1833	90	108	−18	88	70	18	101	83	18	−14	1	1	2	6
1832	87	101	−14	82	62	20	95	75	20	−14	2	1	4	5
1831	81	103	−22	72	59	13	96	83	13	−24	3	1	6	6
1830	74	71	+3	72	59	13	63	50	13	+9	1	1	1	7
1829	72	74	−2	67	55	12	67	55	12	(Z)	2	1	3	7
1828	72	89	−16	64	50	14	81	67	14	−17	2	1	7	7
1827	82	79	+3	74	58	16	71	55	16	+3	2	1	6	7
1826	78	85	−7	73	52	20	78	58	20	−5	1	1	4	6
1825	100	96	+3	91	67	24	90	66	24	+1	(Z)	1	8	6
1824	76	81	−5	69	51	18	72	54	18	−3	(8)	(8)	8 7	8 8
1823	75	78	−3	68	47	21	72	51	21	−4	(8)	(8)	8 6	8 5
1822	72	83	−11	61	50	11	80	68	11	−19	(8)	(8)	8 11	8 3
1821	65	63	+2	55	41	11	55	44	11	(Z)	(8)	(8)	8 10	8 8

Year	Merchandise [1]					Year	Merchandise [1]					Year	Merchandise [1]				
	Exports and reexports			General imports	Excess of exports(+) or imports(−)		Exports and reexports			General imports	Excess of exports(+) or imports(−)		Exports and reexports			General imports	Excess of exports(+) or imports(−)
	Total	Exports of U.S. merchandise	Re-exports				Total	Exports of U.S. merchandise	Re-exports				Total	Exports of U.S. merchandise	Re-exports		
	190	191	192	193	196		190	191	192	193	196		190	191	192	193	196
1820	70	52	18	74	−5	1810	67	42	24	85	−19	1800	71	32	39	91	−20
1819	70	51	19	87	−17	1809	52	31	21	59	−7	1799	79	33	46	79	(Z)
1818	93	74	19	122	−28	1808	22	9	13	57	−35	1798	61	28	33	69	−7
1817	88	68	19	99	−12	1807	108	49	60	139	−30	1797	51	24	27	75	−24
1816	82	65	17	147	−65	1806	102	41	60	129	−28	1796	59	32	26	81	−23
1815	53	46	7	113	−60	1805	96	42	53	121	−25	1795	48	40	8	70	−22
1814	7	7	(Z)	13	−6	1804	78	41	36	85	−7	1794	33	27	7	35	−2
1813	28	25	3	22	+6	1803	56	42	14	65	−9	1793	26	24	2	31	−5
1812	39	30	8	77	−39	1802	72	36	36	76	−4	1792	21	19	2	32	−11
1811	61	45	16	53	+8	1801	93	46	47	111	−18	1791	19	19	1	29	−10
												1790	20	--------	--------	23	−3

NA   Not available.   Z   Less than $500,000 or less than −$500,000.
[1] Includes gold and silver prior to 1821.   Beginning 1961, includes exports and imports of uranium, thorium, and related products; beginning 1968, includes silver ore and bullion.
[2] Prior to 1864, domestic exports of silver included with gold.
[3] Beginning 1968, silver ore and bullion included in merchandise exports and imports.
[4] Figures which include estimates of civilian supplies shipped to occupied areas through U.S. Armed Forces and other relief agencies are as follows (in millions of dollars): 1944, 14,414; 1945, 10,530; 1946, 10,184; 1947, 15,338.

[5] Does not add due to revisions not carried to detail.
[6] Figures for 6-month period July 1, 1915–Dec. 31, 1915, are as follows (in millions of dollars): Series U 187, 1,905; series U 188, 1,239; series U 189, +667; series U 190, 1,853; series U 191, 1,820; series U 192, 33; series U 193, 913; series U 196, +940; series U 197, 24; series U 198, 307; series U 199, 29; and series U 200, 19.
[7] Period beginning Oct. 1, 1842, and ending June 30, 1843.
[8] Data shown under silver are for gold and silver.

Series U 201–206. Foreign Trade Related to Various Measures of Production: 1869 to 1970

Year	Percent of gross national product [1]		Percent of production of movable goods [1]		Farm exports as percent of farm income [2]	Index of finished goods imports as percent of output of finished goods (1919 = 100)
	Exports	General imports	Exports	General imports		
	201	202	203	204	205	206
1970	4.4	4.1	10.5	9.9	14.3	----------
1969	4.0	3.9	9.2	8.9	12.4	----------
1968	4.0	3.8	9.1	8.8	14.2	----------
1967	3.9	3.4	8.9	7.7	15.1	----------
1966	4.0	3.4	8.9	7.6	16.0	----------
1965	4.0	3.1	8.8	7.0	16.0	
1964	4.2	3.0	9.3	6.7	17.2	
1963	3.9	2.9	8.6	6.4	15.1	
1962	3.8	2.9	8.5	6.5	14.0	
1961	4.0	2.8	8.9	6.3	14.4	
1960	4.1	3.0	8.8	6.5	14.3	
1959	3.6	3.2	7.6	6.9	11.8	
1958	4.0	3.0	8.5	6.4	11.5	
1957	4.7	3.0	9.7	6.2	15.1	
1956	4.6	3.0	9.1	6.1	13.6	
1955	3.9	2.9	7.8	5.9	10.8	
1954	4.2	2.8	8.5	5.8	10.2	
1953	4.3	3.0	8.6	5.9	9.0	
1952	4.4	3.1	8.8	6.2	10.5	
1951	4.6	3.3	9.0	6.6	12.3	
1950	3.6	3.1	7.0	6.1	10.0	
1949	4.7	2.6	9.5	5.3	12.8	
1948	4.9	2.7	9.0	5.1	11.5	
1947	6.5	2.5	12.2	4.7	13.4	
1946	[3]4.8	2.3	9.8	4.9	12.7	
1945	[3]4.9	1.9	10.2	4.1	10.4	
1944	[3]6.8	1.9	13.6	3.7	10.2	
1943	6.7	1.8	12.9	3.4	10.6	
1942	5.1	1.7	9.0	3.1	7.7	
1941	4.1	2.7	7.8	5.2	6.0	
1940	4.0	2.6	8.3	5.5	6.2	
1939	3.5	2.5	7.5	5.6	8.4	66
1938	3.6	2.3	----------	----------	10.7	
1937	3.7	3.4	7.4	6.9	9.0	84
1936	3.0	2.9	----------	----------	8.5	
1935	3.1	2.8	6.6	6.0	10.6	70
1934	3.3	2.5	----------	----------	11.6	
1933	3.0	2.6	6.5	5.7	13.1	70
1932	2.8	2.3	----------	----------	14.0	67
1931	3.2	2.7	7.2	6.4	12.9	77
1930	4.2	3.4	----------	----------	13.3	87
1929	5.0	4.2	9.6	8.2	15.0	103
1928	5.2	4.2	----------	----------	17.0	100
1927	5.1	4.3	9.9	8.7	17.6	108
1926	4.9	4.5	----------	----------	17.2	110
1925	5.4	4.6	10.0	8.7	19.4	110
1924	5.2	4.1	----------	----------	20.7	103
1923	4.8	4.4	9.1	8.5	19.1	105
1922	5.2	4.2	----------	----------	21.9	99
1921	6.1	3.4	13.1	7.5	26.2	86
1920	9.3	5.9	----------	----------	27.3	124
1919	10.0	4.9	16.4	8.3	28.1	100
1918	9.3	4.6	----------	----------	20.4	88
1917	10.5	5.0	----------	----------	18.4	105
1916	11.5	5.0	----------	----------	22.7	113

Year or period	Percent of gross national product [1]		Farm exports as percent of farm income [2]	Index of finished goods imports as percent of output of finished goods (1919 = 100)
	Exports	General imports		
	201	202	205	206
1915	6.6	4.0	25.1	111
1914	6.1	4.9	16.5	115
1913	6.2	4.5	18.3	111
1912	5.7	4.3	18.8	117
1911	5.6	4.1	17.8	109
1910	4.8	4.2	15.9	113
1909	4.9	3.9	----------	114
1908				99
1907				112
1906				111
1905				113
1904				107
1903				104
1902				106
1901				101
1900				104
1899				109
1898				99
1897				125
1896				124
1895				140
1894				128
1893				129
1892				145
1891				142
1890				151
1889				138
1879				136
1869				147
1917–1921	8.7	4.7	----------	----------
1912–1916	7.6	4.7	----------	----------
1907–1911	5.8	4.4	----------	----------
1902–1906	6.2	4.4	----------	----------
1897–1901	7.4	4.3	----------	----------
1892–1896	6.6	5.7	----------	----------
1889–1893	6.5	6.0	----------	----------
Kuznets concept: [4]				
1889–1893	6.7	6.2	----------	----------
1887–1891	6.3	6.2	----------	----------
1882–1886	6.6	5.9	----------	----------
1877–1881	8.2	5.8	----------	----------
1872–1876	6.9	7.5	----------	----------
1869–1873	6.2	7.9	----------	----------

[1] Trade data cover U.S. customs area, which includes Alaska, Hawaii, and Puerto Rico for all years; gross national product data include Alaska and Hawaii beginning 1959; measures of production used for estimates of movable goods exclude Alaska and Hawaii except output of minerals are included beginning 1953 and value added in manufacturing beginning 1958.

[2] Excludes Alaska and Hawaii for all years.

[3] Includes an estimate for civilian supplies shipped to occupied areas through U.S. Armed Forces, which were not tabulated with the foreign trade statistics prior to 1947.

[4] For an explanation of this concept, see text for series F 1–5 and F 71–97.

Series U 207–212. Value of Merchandise Imports and Duties: 1821 to 1970

[Merchandise imports entered for consumption. For years ending September 30, 1821–1842; June 30, 1843–1915; thereafter, calendar years]

Year	Value of imports for consumption[1]			Duties calculated	Ratio of duties calculated to total imports		Year	Value of imports for consumption			Duties calculated	Ratio of duties calculated to total imports	
	Total	Free	Dutiable		Free and dutiable	Dutiable		Total	Free	Dutiable		Free and dutiable	Dutiable
	207	208	209	210	211	212		207	208	209	210	211	212
	Mil. dol.	Mil. dol.	Mil. dol.	Mil. dol.	Percent	Percent		Mil. dol.	Mil. dol.	Mil. dol.	Mil. dol.	Percent	Percent
1970	39,756	13,870	25,886	2,584	6.50	9.98	1895	731	377	354	149	20.44	42.19
1969	35,863	13,057	22,805	2,551	7.11	11.19	1894	630	372	258	130	20.56	50.29
1968	33,066	12,342	20,724	2,341	7.08	11.30	1893	833	432	400	199	23.91	49.75
1967	26,733	10,215	16,518	2,016	7.54	12.20	1892	804	449	356	174	21.65	48.98
1966	25,360	9,344	16,016	1,920	7.57	11.99	1891	845	379	466	217	25.65	46.50
1965	21,282	7,434	13,848	1,643	7.72	11.86							
1964	18,601	7,029	11,572	1,340	7.20	11.58	1890	766	258	508	227	29.59	44.63
1963	17,001	6,258	10,743	1,240	7.29	11.54	1889	735	250	485	221	30.02	45.49
1962	16,242	6,216	10,026	1,220	7.50	12.17	1888	707	239	468	216	30.55	46.15
1961	14,658	5,923	8,735	1,057	7.21	12.10	1887	680	229	450	214	31.52	47.57
							1886	624	210	414	189	30.35	45.78
1960	14,650	5,780	8,870	1,084	7.40	12.22	1885	579	192	387	178	30.75	46.05
1959	14,994	5,823	9,170	1,052	7.02	11.53	1884	668	211	457	190	28.50	41.67
1958	12,739	5,342	7,398	821	6.44	11.09	1883	701	207	494	211	30.04	42.61
1957	12,951	6,036	6,914	746	5.76	10.79	1882	717	211	506	216	30.16	42.71
1956	12,516	6,235	6,281	710	5.67	11.30	1881	651	202	448	194	29.79	43.23
1955	11,337	6,037	5,300	633	5.59	11.95							
1954	10,240	5,668	4,572	529	5.17	11.58	1880	628	208	420	183	29.12	43.54
1953	10,779	5,920	4,859	584	5.42	12.02	1879	440	143	297	133	30.33	44.90
1952	10,747	6,257	4,491	570	5.30	12.69	1878	439	141	297	127	29.00	42.77
1951	10,817	5,993	4,824	591	5.47	12.26	1877	440	140	299	128	29.20	42.91
							1876	465	140	324	145	31.25	44.76
1950	8,743	4,767	3,976	522	5.97	13.14	1875	526	146	380	155	29.36	40.66
1949	6,592	3,883	2,708	365	5.53	13.46	1874	568	151	416	161	28.29	38.58
1948	7,092	4,175	2,918	405	5.71	13.87	1873	663	178	485	185	27.90	38.12
1947	5,666	3,455	2,212	428	7.55	19.34	1872	560	47	513	213	37.99	41.46
1946	4,825	2,935	1,890	478	9.90	25.28	1871	500	40	460	202	40.51	44.04
1945	4,098	2,749	1,349	381	9.29	28.24							
1944	3,887	2,718	1,170	367	9.45	31.41	1870	426	20	406	192	44.89	47.13
1943	3,390	2,193	1,197	393	11.57	32.79	1869	394	22	373	177	44.76	47.37
1942	2,780	1,779	1,002	320	11.51	31.96	1868	345	15	330	161	46.56	48.70
1941	3,222	2,031	1,191	438	13.59	36.75	1867	378	17	361	169	44.56	46.66
							1866	423	57	366	177	41.81	48.33
1940	2,541	1,649	892	318	12.51	35.63	1865	210	40	170	81	38.46	47.56
1939	2,276	1,397	879	328	14.41	37.33	1864	301	38	263	96	32.04	36.69
1938	1,950	1,183	767	301	15.46	39.30	1863	225	30	195	64	28.28	32.62
1937	3,010	1,765	1,245	471	15.63	37.80	1862	178	50	128	47	26.08	36.20
1936	2,424	1,385	1,039	408	16.84	39.28	1861	275	67	207	39	14.21	18.84
1935	2,039	1,206	833	357	17.52	42.88							
1934	1,636	991	645	301	18.41	46.70	1860	336	68	268	53	15.67	19.67
1933	1,433	904	529	284	19.80	53.58	1859	317	67	250	49	15.43	19.56
1932	1,325	886	440	260	19.59	59.06	1858	243	55	187	42	17.33	22.44
1931	2,088	1,392	697	371	17.75	53.21	1857	334	50	284	64	19.09	22.45
							1856	296	50	246	64	21.68	26.05
1930	3,114	2,081	1,033	462	14.83	44.71	1855	232	30	202	54	23.36	26.83
1929	4,339	2,880	1,458	585	13.48	40.10	1854	276	23	254	65	23.52	25.61
1928	4,078	2,679	1,399	542	13.30	38.76	1853	250	25	225	58	23.37	25.94
1927	4,163	2,680	1,483	575	13.81	38.76	1852	195	22	174	48	24.35	27.38
1926	4,408	2,908	1,500	590	13.39	39.34	1851	200	18	183	49	24.26	26.63
1925	4,176	2,709	1,467	552	13.21	37.61							
1924	3,575	2,118	1,457	532	14.89	36.53	1850	164	16	148	40	24.50	27.14
1923	3,732	2,165	1,567	567	15.18	36.17	1849	133	14	119	31	23.41	26.11
1922	3,074	1,888	1,186	451	14.68	38.07	1848	141	15	126	33	23.49	26.28
1921	2,557	1,564	993	292	11.44	29.46	1847	116	16	100	28	24.20	28.02
							1846	110	19	91	30	27.70	33.35
1920	5,102	3,116	1,986	326	6.38	16.40	1845	106	16	90	31	29.34	34.45
1919	3,828	2,711	1,116	237	6.20	21.27	1844	96	17	80	29	30.50	36.88
1918	2,952	2,229	723	171	5.79	23.65	1843[5]	37	12	26	8	20.13	29.19
1917	2,919	2,141	778	205	7.01	26.28	1842	88	23	65	17	18.96	25.81
1916	2,359	1,615	744	214	9.08	28.80	1841	115	57	58	20	17.37	34.56
1915[2]	1,648	1,033	616	206	12.49	33.46							
1914	1,906	1,152	754	284	14.88	37.63	1840	86	42	44	15	17.60	34.39
1913	1,767	987	780	313	17.69	40.08	1839	146	65	81	26	17.57	31.77
1912	1,641	882	759	305	18.58	40.16	1838	87	38	48	20	23.11	41.33
1911	1,528	777	751	310	20.29	41.27	1837	113	51	62	18	16.05	29.19
							1836	159	70	89	31	19.51	34.94
1910	1,547	761	786	327	21.11	41.56	1835	122	58	64	26	21.25	40.38
1909	[3]1,282	509	682	295	22.99	43.19	1834	87	40	47	19	21.83	40.19
1908	1,183	526	657	283	23.88	42.98	1833	83	20	63	24	28.99	38.25
1907	1,415	642	773	329	23.28	42.60	1832	75	7	68	29	38.97	42.96
1906	1,213	549	665	294	24.22	44.22	1831	83	6	77	37	44.23	47.38
1905	1,087	517	570	258	23.77	45.33							
1904	982	454	528	258	26.29	48.92	1830	50	4	46	28	57.32	61.69
1903	1,008	437	571	281	27.85	49.20	1829	55	3	51	28	50.73	54.17
1902	900	397	503	251	27.95	49.97	1828	67	4	63	30	44.74	47.59
1901[4]	808	339	469	234	28.91	49.83	1827	55	3	52	28	50.93	53.76
							1826	58	5	53	26	45.28	49.26
1900[4]	831	367	464	229	27.62	49.46	1825	66	4	63	32	47.72	50.54
1899	685	300	386	202	29.48	52.38	1824	54	3	51	26	47.39	50.26
1898	587	292	296	145	24.77	49.20	1823	51	3	49	22	43.69	46.04
1897	789	382	407	173	21.89	42.41	1822	68	4	65	24	35.23	37.16
1896	760	369	391	157	20.67	40.18	1821	44	2	42	19	43.21	45.00

[1] Beginning 1961, includes uranium, thorium, and related products; beginning 1968, includes silver ore and bullion.

[2] Figures for 6-month period July 1, 1915–Dec. 31, 1915, are as follows (in millions of dollars): Series U 207, 935; series U 208, 631; series U 209, 303; series U 210, 96; series U 211, 10.26 percent; and series U 212, 31.61 percent.

[3] Agrees with source; however, figures for components do not add to total shown.

[4] During the period May 1, 1900–July 25, 1901, merchandise brought from Puerto Rico was dutiable at 15 percent of regular rates. The duties collected thereon were as follows: May 1, 1900–June 30, 1900, $134,593.88; July 1, 1900–July 25, 1901, $448,193.91.

[5] Period beginning Oct. 1, 1842, and ending June 30, 1843.

Series U 213–224. Value of Merchandise Exports and Imports, by Economic Class: 1820 to 1970

[In millions of dollars. General imports through 1933; thereafter, imports for consumption. For years ending September 30, 1821–1840; June 30, 1850–1915; thereafter, calendar years. Excludes trade in silver prior to 1947 and military grant-aid beginning 1950]

Year	U.S. domestic exports						U.S. general imports					
	Total	Crude materials	Crude food	Manufactured food [1]	Semimanufactures [2]	Finished manufactures [2]	Total	Crude materials	Crude food	Manufactured food [1]	Semimanufactures	Finished manufactures
	213	214	215	216	217	218	219	220	221	222	223	224
1970	42,029	4,492	2,748	1,921	6,866	26,001	39,963	4,129	2,580	3,523	7,268	22,463
1969	36,788	3,475	2,085	1,782	5,774	23,671	36,043	4,124	2,141	3,043	6,768	19,967
1968	33,626	3,467	2,334	1,671	5,117	21,036	33,226	4,012	2,294	2,882	7,141	16,897
1967	30,646	3,293	2,595	1,596	4,489	18,673	26,889	3,707	1,981	2,518	5,592	13,091
1966	29,054	3,143	3,198	1,582	4,368	16,763	25,618	3,851	2,117	2,309	5,631	11,710
1965	26,399	2,888	2,587	1,590	4,114	15,220	21,427	3,653	2,008	1,877	5,013	8,876
1964	25,479	2,896	2,540	1,687	4,090	14,265	18,749	3,474	2,034	1,819	4,045	7,377
1963	22,183	2,577	2,273	1,496	3,348	12,488	17,068	3,141	1,725	1,998	3,810	6,393
1962	20,717	2,234	2,010	1,366	3,042	12,065	16,326	3,086	1,776	1,792	3,677	5,995
1961	19,981	2,545	1,898	1,151	3,287	11,102	14,703	2,875	1,717	1,602	3,415	5,094
1960	19,459	2,588	1,645	1,117	3,535	10,574	15,068	3,012	1,720	1,566	3,493	5,276
1959	16,243	1,913	1,448	1,078	2,478	9,327	15,476	3,097	1,824	1,599	3,763	5,194
1958	16,211	2,139	1,280	1,102	2,285	9,405	13,344	2,749	1,942	1,517	3,191	3,946
1957	19,337	3,110	1,332	1,163	3,255	10,476	13,387	3,211	2,020	1,272	3,277	3,607
1956	17,193	2,515	1,333	1,264	2,782	9,300	12,805	3,087	2,036	1,167	3,219	3,296
1955	14,172	1,907	930	1,012	2,311	8,011	11,519	2,845	1,998	1,118	2,933	2,624
1954	12,728	1,899	741	832	1,820	7,437	10,396	2,413	2,200	1,117	2,433	2,232
1953	12,142	1,626	962	759	1,424	7,371	10,889	2,613	2,185	1,108	2,752	2,232
1952	13,053	1,982	1,369	736	1,622	7,344	10,847	2,937	2,068	1,083	2,627	2,132
1951	13,820	2,471	1,401	881	1,668	7,399	10,919	3,365	2,077	1,022	2,514	1,942
1950	9,864	1,886	760	634	1,121	5,463	8,845	2,466	1,750	898	2,172	1,558
1949	11,938	1,780	1,342	908	1,356	6,553	6,679	1,857	1,333	741	1,457	1,292
1948	12,533	1,488	1,266	1,367	1,371	7,042	7,178	2,150	1,272	731	1,679	1,346
1947	14,274	1,579	849	1,528	1,734	8,583	5,743	1,770	1,017	656	1,279	1,022
1946	9,500	1,416	648	1,522	895	5,019	4,825	1,729	814	504	931	847
1945	9,585	871	432	1,246	780	6,257	4,098	1,183	693	462	928	832
1944	14,162	554	134	1,633	1,097	10,744	3,887	1,078	841	521	706	741
1943	12,842	662	109	1,551	1,089	9,431	3,390	1,037	584	421	678	670
1942	8,003	418	68	926	920	5,672	2,780	1,061	349	275	640	457
1941	5,020	362	84	418	771	3,385	3,222	1,376	376	322	724	423
1940	3,934	464	74	167	900	2,330	2,541	1,011	285	277	559	409
1939	3,123	545	111	202	599	1,667	2,276	745	291	313	487	440
1938	3,057	607	249	184	494	1,523	1,950	576	260	311	385	418
1937	3,299	731	105	178	669	1,617	3,010	971	413	440	634	551
1936	2,419	670	58	144	393	1,154	2,424	733	349	386	490	466
1935	2,243	683	59	157	350	994	2,039	582	322	319	410	406
1934	2,100	653	59	168	342	879	1,636	461	254	264	307	350
1933 [3]	1,647	591	48	155	237	617	1,450	418	216	201	292	322
1932	1,576	514	89	152	197	624	1,323	358	233	174	217	341
1931	2,378	567	127	247	318	1,120	2,091	642	305	222	372	549
1930	3,781	829	179	363	513	1,898	3,061	1,002	400	293	608	757
1929	5,157	1,142	270	484	729	2,532	4,399	1,559	539	424	885	994
1928	5,030	1,293	295	466	716	2,260	4,091	1,467	550	406	763	906
1927	4,759	1,193	421	463	700	1,982	4,185	1,601	505	451	750	879
1926	4,712	1,261	335	503	656	1,957	4,431	1,792	540	418	804	877
1925	4,819	1,422	318	574	662	1,843	4,227	1,748	495	433	755	796
1924	4,498	1,333	393	573	611	1,588	3,610	1,258	425	522	656	749
1923	4,091	1,208	257	583	564	1,478	3,792	1,407	363	530	721	771
1922	3,765	988	459	588	438	1,292	3,113	1,180	330	387	553	663
1921	4,379	984	673	685	410	1,627	2,509	859	300	368	362	620
1920	8,080	1,883	918	1,117	958	3,205	5,278	1,784	578	1,238	802	877
1919	7,750	1,623	678	1,963	922	2,564	3,904	1,701	545	556	609	493
1918	6,048	972	547	1,406	1,053	2,069	3,031	1,234	346	397	650	405
1917	6,170	833	509	807	1,315	2,706	2,952	1,286	386	352	537	392
1916	5,423	816	421	648	912	2,625	2,392	1,029	260	339	419	346
1915 [4]	2,716	591	507	455	356	807	1,674	591	224	286	237	336
1914	2,330	800	137	293	374	725	1,894	650	248	228	319	449
1913	2,429	740	182	321	409	776	1,813	649	212	194	349	408
1912	2,170	731	100	319	348	672	1,653	573	230	196	294	360
1911	2,014	721	103	282	309	598	1,527	525	181	172	288	361
1910	1,710	574	110	259	268	499	1,557	578	145	182	285	368
1909	1,638	529	136	303	231	440	1,312	461	164	166	222	299
1908	1,835	563	189	332	261	489	1,194	374	146	147	196	332
1907	1,854	601	167	346	259	481	1,434	488	150	159	274	364
1906	1,718	507	177	347	226	460	1,227	424	134	140	220	308
1905	1,492	479	118	283	210	402	1,118	396	146	145	178	252
1904	1,435	467	136	309	175	349	991	328	132	118	160	253
1903	1,392	416	185	323	141	327	1,026	336	119	117	196	258
1902	1,355	388	185	329	132	322	903	309	120	95	148	231
1901	1,460	411	246	337	148	318	823	254	110	126	128	206

See footnotes at end of table.

Series U 213–224. Value of Merchandise Exports and Imports, by Economic Class: 1820 to 1970—Con.

[In millions of dollars]

Year	U.S. domestic exports						U.S. general imports					
	Total	Crude materials	Crude food	Manufactured food [1]	Semimanufactures	Finished manufactures	Total	Crude materials	Crude food	Manufactured food [1]	Semimanufactures	Finished manufactures
	213	214	215	216	217	218	219	220	221	222	223	224
1900	1,371	340	226	320	153	332	850	282	98	133	134	203
1899	1,204	286	233	305	118	263	697	213	99	123	92	170
1898	1,210	296	305	285	102	223	616	194	104	86	79	153
1897	1,032	304	181	235	98	213	765	201	128	129	88	218
1896	863	257	129	219	76	182	780	203	130	119	101	227
1895	793	269	99	219	62	144	732	188	141	107	96	200
1894	869	283	133	250	67	136	655	135	133	155	83	149
1893	831	252	153	247	49	130	866	217	132	154	136	229
1892	1,016	320	262	250	50	133	827	195	176	140	113	205
1891	872	351	106	226	48	140	845	193	151	148	136	218
1890	845	309	132	225	46	133	789	180	128	133	117	231
1889	730	291	99	175	43	123	745	172	123	122	115	212
1888	684	274	86	170	40	114	724	164	116	111	122	211
1887	703	253	125	176	37	112	692	151	106	112	120	203
1886	666	257	101	163	34	112	635	145	92	113	92	195
1885	727	251	123	202	39	111	578	120	93	103	78	183
1884	725	244	130	195	38	118	668	131	103	131	95	208
1883	804	294	163	186	38	122	723	146	93	142	99	243
1882	733	238	155	178	37	125	725	143	105	139	99	239
1881	884	281	242	226	33	102	643	125	102	123	88	204
1880	824	243	266	193	29	93	668	142	100	118	111	197
1879	698	202	189	174	30	103	446	81	82	103	50	130
1878	681	216	155	170	29	110	437	79	84	102	47	125
1877	590	205	91	150	32	113	451	76	86	115	49	126
1876	526	204	94	122	31	74	461	78	94	92	51	146
1875	499	208	79	110	27	75	533	89	90	113	63	178
1874	569	229	119	114	26	81	567	89	94	120	72	192
1873	505	233	70	101	25	76	642	108	83	122	97	232
1872	428	198	59	84	21	65	627	103	77	122	88	238
1871	428	224	49	67	14	76	520	78	64	103	72	203
1870	377	214	42	51	14	56	436	57	54	96	56	174
1869	275	145	25	44	14	47	418	50	53	95	63	157
1868	269	133	35	42	17	43	357	41	52	78	53	133
1867	280	167	21	34	15	44	396	43	51	65	56	181
1866	338	228	17	41	12	39	435	48	61	72	56	198
1865	137	34	14	48	11	30	239	30	35	48	30	96
1864	144	29	25	55	10	25	316	40	44	52	52	128
1863	186	30	45	66	11	33	243	48	30	35	35	95
1862	180	18	56	70	8	27	189	33	32	35	24	66
1861	205	58	49	54	8	36	289	31	40	54	33	132
1860	316	217	12	39	13	36	354	40	46	60	35	172
1859	278	190	10	32	11	35	331	39	44	57	40	151
1858	251	155	18	39	10	30	263	34	36	46	31	116
1857	279	158	31	49	11	30	348	34	41	72	39	163
1856	266	145	29	53	8	31	310	27	39	46	41	157
1855	193	109	11	33	11	29	258	27	33	34	35	129
1854	5 214	108	22	47	11	27	298	23	25	33	45	173
1853	190	124	8	27	6	24	264	18	26	33	42	144
1852	155	101	7	20	6	21	207	14	24	29	21	120
1851	179	125	5	20	6	23	211	17	20	29	27	118
1850	135	84	8	20	6	17	174	13	18	21	26	95
1840	112	76	5	16	5	11	98	12	15	15	11	44
1830	59	37	3	10	4	5	63	5	7	10	5	36
1821	---	---	---	---	---	---	55	3	6	11	4	31
1820	52	31	2	10	5	3	---	---	---	---	---	---

[1] Includes beverages.

[2] Beginning 1950, for security reasons, a small amount of semimanufactures included with finished manufactures.

[3] Imports for consumption are as follows (in millions of dollars): Series U 219, 1,433; series U 220, 420; series U 221, 215; series U 222, 191; series U 223, 290; and series U 224, 317.

[4] Figures for 6-month period July 1, 1915–Dec. 31, 1915, are as follows (in millions of dollars): Series U 213, 1,820; series U 214, 303; series U 215, 158; series U 216, 293; series U 217, 268; series U 218, 799; series, U 219, 913; series U 220, 378; series U 221, 130; series U 222, 113; series U 223, 144; and series U 224, 147.

[5] Excludes exports from San Francisco valued at $1,343,064.

Series U 225–248. Indexes of Quantity and Unit Value of Exports and Imports, by Economic Class: 1879 to 1970

Year	U.S. domestic exports [1]											
	Total		Crude materials		Crude foods		Manufactured foods		Semimanufactures		Finished manufactures	
	Quantity	Unit value	Quantity	Unit value	Quantity	Unit value	Quantity	Unit value	Quantity	Unit value	Quantity	Unit value
	225	226	227	228	229	230	231	232	233	234	235	236
	1967 = 100											
1970	123.9	110.7	127.1	107.3	106.9	99.0	114.2	105.4	150.8	101.4	120.5	115.6
1969	114.7	104.7	105.9	99.6	83.2	96.6	109.9	101.6	133.7	96.2	116.1	109.2
1968	108.2	101.4	107.5	97.9	94.0	95.7	104.0	100.7	119.2	95.6	108.0	104.3
1967	100.0	100.0	100.0	100.0	100.0	100.0	100.0	100.0	100.0	100.0	100.0	100.0
1966	96.6	98.1	92.8	102.8	124.6	98.9	98.0	101.2	94.5	103.0	93.3	96.2
1965	90.5	95.2	88.7	98.9	103.8	96.0	104.9	95.0	90.3	101.5	87.3	93.4
1964	90.2	92.2	93.1	95.2	98.5	99.4	117.3	90.1	94.9	96.0	84.8	90.1
1963	79.3	91.3	82.2	95.2	88.6	98.9	106.5	88.0	78.2	95.4	75.1	89.1
1962	73.9	91.5	70.9	95.7	80.3	96.5	98.2	87.2	69.0	98.2	72.4	89.3
1961	70.8	92.1	81.1	95.3	77.5	94.4	81.3	88.7	70.9	103.2	66.6	89.3
1960	70.2	90.4	86.5	90.8	69.1	91.8	80.3	87.2	75.1	104.8	64.8	87.4
1959	59.1	89.7	63.3	91.7	60.5	92.2	76.0	88.8	52.8	104.6	58.2	85.8
1958	59.1	89.5	68.2	95.2	53.1	92.9	71.6	96.5	49.9	102.0	59.9	84.1
1957	69.7	90.5	97.5	96.9	54.4	94.3	76.5	95.2	63.7	113.8	67.8	82.8
1956	64.0	87.6	79.4	96.2	54.0	95.1	86.4	91.7	53.4	116.1	63.8	78.0
1955	54.7	84.5	59.8	96.9	38.0	94.4	67.8	93.6	49.2	104.7	57.3	74.9
1954	49.7	83.6	59.3	97.1	29.2	97.6	50.8	102.7	41.2	98.3	54.0	73.8
1953	46.8	84.7	51.7	95.5	33.9	109.3	45.3	102.7	32.0	99.0	52.8	74.8
1952	49.8	85.6	59.4	101.3	45.3	116.4	46.3	99.7	35.5	101.7	53.1	74.1
1951	52.4	86.0	69.6	107.8	50.3	107.3	52.0	106.1	36.0	103.2	53.8	73.7
1950	42.9	75.0	63.0	90.9	30.4	96.2	46.9	84.7	29.7	84.0	44.1	66.4
1949	50.6	77.0	61.6	87.7	46.2	111.9	57.2	99.5	35.1	86.1	51.6	68.0
1948	49.4	82.8	48.9	92.5	38.4	127.0	68.4	125.2	33.6	90.8	52.8	71.4
1947	59.8	77.9	59.5	80.6	26.5	123.5	78.2	122.5	46.2	83.7	68.1	67.5
1946	47.5	65.3	62.1	69.2	23.3	107.1	98.5	99.0	31.5	64.7	46.3	57.7
1945	45.3	69.0	43.1	61.3	17.0	97.9	83.9	96.0	28.2	62.8	50.4	66.0
1944	66.8	69.2	27.6	60.9	5.8	89.6	107.3	97.5	39.0	64.0	86.5	66.3
1943	69.4	60.4	34.4	58.5	5.3	79.5	114.1	86.3	40.1	61.8	88.7	56.8
1942	47.6	54.8	24.1	52.7	4.1	63.0	72.2	80.8	35.0	59.8	59.6	50.9
1941	36.2	45.2	24.1	45.6	6.1	52.5	45.4	58.7	31.8	55.2	43.7	41.4
1940	30.6	42.0	35.7	39.4	6.3	45.1	21.3	49.2	40.8	50.2	31.3	39.9
1939	26.0	39.2	44.6	37.1	11.0	38.9	26.3	48.3	28.7	47.4	24.2	36.9
1938	24.9	40.1	48.7	37.8	20.8	46.2	22.3	51.8	23.7	47.5	21.9	37.2
1937	24.8	43.3	51.3	42.7	7.1	56.5	18.5	60.3	28.7	53.8	22.8	37.9
1936	19.4	40.7	46.5	43.6	4.3	52.7	16.0	56.4	20.2	44.4	17.1	36.2
1935	18.4	39.8	48.6	42.7	4.6	48.9	17.9	55.0	19.1	41.6	14.8	35.9
1934	17.5	39.1	47.2	42.0	4.7	48.2	22.2	47.3	18.5	41.9	13.4	35.2
1933	16.2	33.2	56.4	31.8	4.5	41.5	23.3	41.5	14.6	36.8	10.1	32.8
1932	16.1	31.9	57.4	27.2	8.3	41.6	23.8	40.0	12.6	35.6	9.8	34.2
1931	21.0	36.9	53.7	32.1	10.0	49.0	29.6	52.3	16.8	43.1	16.0	37.6
1930	25.8	47.9	52.9	47.6	9.7	70.7	34.0	66.9	22.2	52.6	21.8	46.6
1929	31.3	53.7	56.6	61.3	13.2	78.7	41.5	73.2	27.3	60.7	27.8	48.7
1928	30.3	54.1	62.0	63.3	13.8	82.3	40.8	73.0	28.4	57.4	24.4	49.5
1927	29.2	53.2	65.3	55.5	18.5	87.6	38.6	75.2	27.6	57.6	21.2	50.1
1926	27.2	56.6	67.2	57.0	14.7	88.0	38.5	81.9	24.4	61.2	19.0	55.3
1925	25.4	61.8	58.5	73.8	12.0	101.9	42.1	85.5	24.2	62.1	17.9	55.1
1924	24.1	61.0	49.5	81.7	17.1	88.4	50.2	71.6	23.5	59.0	15.6	54.5
1923	21.5	66.2	42.0	87.3	13.1	75.4	51.2	71.4	20.8	61.6	14.3	55.2
1922	21.2	58.0	43.7	68.6	23.5	75.3	52.6	70.1	17.5	56.8	12.0	57.8
1921	22.9	62.5	54.0	55.3	29.1	89.1	54.3	79.1	14.5	64.1	12.3	70.8
1920	27.5	95.9	53.2	107.4	23.0	153.9	54.3	129.0	23.6	92.5	19.2	89.5
1919	28.5	88.6	52.1	94.6	18.8	138.6	87.5	140.6	24.2	86.4	17.5	78.4
1913	18.3	40.3	61.6	38.3	11.4	57.3	35.0	58.1	20.4	43.5	9.2	40.1

[1] Data on 1967 base exclude trade in silver prior to 1947 and exclude military grant-aid beginning 1950.

Series U 225–248.   Indexes of Quantity and Unit Value of Exports and Imports, by Economic Class: 1879 to 1970—Con.

Year	U.S. domestic exports											
	Total		Crude materials		Crude foods		Manufactured foods		Semimanufactures		Finished manufactures	
	Quantity	Unit value	Quantity	Unit value	Quantity	Unit value	Quantity	Unit value	Quantity	Unit value	Quantity	Unit value
	225	226	227	228	229	230	231	232	233	234	235	236
	1913 = 100											
1921	113.4	157.5	81.3	156.4	252.8	155.7	153.9	136.2	72.2	143.5	125.6	163.9
1920	141.8	232.5	84.8	285.3	192.2	268.2	161.2	217.2	120.8	210.5	202.2	197.7
1919	146.6	215.7	86.7	241.3	156.3	241.7	257.6	237.4	126.4	199.5	179.9	174.4
1918	119.7	206.1	57.0	219.0	132.8	234.6	203.9	214.2	129.5	202.8	153.4	169.7
1917	142.2	177.0	64.4	166.8	134.4	214.8	147.0	170.5	168.5	198.4	225.0	150.4
1916	163.3	135.5	90.9	115.5	168.6	144.2	164.8	118.4	155.8	156.5	252.0	130.6
1915	135.7	105.1	103.1	86.0	200.6	133.8	160.5	106.5	111.7	113.2	163.6	100.9
1914	86.6	97.7	74.9	87.9	140.0	114.5	93.0	103.3	87.4	97.6	86.0	94.3
1913	100.0	100.0	100.0	100.0	100.0	100.0	100.0	100.0	100.0	100.0	100.0	100.0
1912	101.1	95.5	115.3	89.3	79.4	104.2	97.8	97.0	97.9	100.3	95.5	97.2
1911	90.0	93.5	96.2	90.9	68.5	97.9	103.2	93.3	89.7	93.2	84.0	95.5
1910	73.1	102.1	79.4	108.4	55.1	98.7	73.6	107.3	77.0	93.4	69.0	98.7
1909	73.7	94.3	83.5	91.4	65.1	104.2	94.3	93.7	69.8	91.0	60.7	97.4
1908	78.4	90.1	91.3	79.8	98.3	99.8	114.6	87.9	64.5	92.4	56.4	100.5
1907	81.3	95.2	89.3	87.4	118.2	95.0	121.8	86.5	62.6	109.9	62.5	102.2
1906	80.5	89.9	84.2	83.8	126.1	81.7	131.8	80.7	60.0	105.9	61.8	97.5
1905	78.0	83.7	84.7	75.6	108.8	82.4	129.8	75.7	58.4	93.6	58.5	94.5
1904	67.0	86.9	73.1	84.3	73.2	80.3	113.4	77.8	60.2	85.9	48.4	98.8
1903	68.8	86.6	77.2	81.0	123.1	81.4	123.1	81.8	46.0	87.3	43.2	98.9
1902	66.9	81.4	73.8	69.1	112.1	82.0	120.6	83.8	44.4	83.5	43.6	94.0
1901	74.0	79.4	77.0	67.9	182.7	77.4	143.4	76.0	40.0	86.0	42.9	94.2
1900	72.8	81.0	75.7	72.2	168.4	74.4	142.9	71.3	48.6	89.5	42.2	98.9
1899	70.3	72.3	66.8	55.1	183.9	73.2	148.2	66.9	41.8	84.9	41.4	90.3
1898	73.2	68.4	82.0	48.9	197.1	76.9	139.8	68.0	41.8	70.4	36.3	82.6
1897	63.4	69.1	67.2	54.3	178.6	71.5	121.8	64.8	39.6	69.6	30.6	88.1
1896	56.4	71.0	65.6	61.0	141.4	63.6	114.3	63.5	34.5	70.1	25.6	96.8
1895	45.7	71.8	59.0	56.7	83.1	69.5	100.5	69.5	25.5	71.7	22.2	91.4
1894	46.5	70.5	62.8	55.3	87.7	67.8	100.8	74.2	25.6	67.7	20.7	82.0
1893	43.3	80.2	54.7	66.4	97.3	77.9	89.6	85.6	23.1	71.8	19.7	87.0
1892	45.8	81.9	53.8	67.8	127.1	86.8	108.6	77.7	17.2	78.7	17.5	91.8
1891	44.2	87.9	60.1	74.1	107.6	100.3	94.5	76.7	18.3	81.7	17.1	100.3
1890	40.4	85.0	52.3	78.5	87.2	76.8	97.1	73.6	16.1	82.5	16.3	104.4
1889	38.4	86.0	55.4	77.5	77.6	75.5	82.9	76.7	15.8	81.9	15.6	106.7
1888	30.7	89.7	46.7	78.1	51.2	86.2	63.6	81.3	13.7	84.7	13.0	110.9
1887	33.4	85.5	46.6	74.5	77.0	81.8	72.4	76.3	12.8	82.2	13.1	106.1
1886	33.1	85.7	46.6	74.9	80.4	80.6	70.6	76.3	12.0	80.5	12.8	109.0
1885	30.0	91.0	39.0	80.2	64.0	85.6	73.8	80.9	12.1	83.7	12.1	115.5
1884	30.5	97.6	43.4	83.3	69.7	91.6	64.8	92.2	12.3	86.4	11.8	122.3
1883	31.1	101.4	43.7	82.1	74.7	104.2	64.1	99.7	12.1	90.8	12.6	121.8
1882	28.4	107.0	40.4	88.3	73.5	109.2	51.7	106.8	11.7	93.0	12.1	123.3
1881	31.8	103.8	39.8	86.8	106.3	102.9	67.2	97.6	10.4	92.1	11.6	124.8
1880	35.0	101.5	41.1	89.4	146.5	96.3	80.1	86.6	9.5	87.5	8.7	132.4
1879	33.1	92.5	37.0	80.1	134.1	93.6	74.4	76.7	10.1	79.3	9.7	119.3

Series U 225–248. Indexes of Quantity and Unit Value of Exports and Imports, by Economic Class: 1879 to 1970—Con.

Year	U.S. general imports [1]											
	Total		Crude materials		Crude foods		Manufactured foods		Semimanufactures		Finished manufactures	
	Quantity	Unit value	Quantity	Unit value	Quantity	Unit value	Quantity	Unit value	Quantity	Unit value	Quantity	Unit value
	237	238	239	240	241	242	243	244	245	246	247	248
	1967 = 100											
1970	133.2	111.6	105.8	105.3	106.4	122.4	124.4	112.5	118.0	110.1	152.9	112.2
1969	128.6	104.2	106.1	104.9	103.0	104.9	113.3	106.6	116.3	104.1	147.1	103.7
1968	122.3	101.0	107.9	100.3	114.5	101.1	113.0	101.3	124.1	102.9	128.7	100.3
1967	100.0	100.0	100.0	100.0	100.0	100.0	100.0	100.0	100.0	100.0	100.0	100.0
1966	96.0	99.2	100.6	103.3	103.7	103.1	93.8	97.8	102.0	98.7	91.6	97.7
1965	82.6	96.5	98.2	100.4	101.4	100.0	81.4	91.6	91.4	98.1	71.2	95.2
1964	73.0	95.5	93.4	100.3	102.2	100.5	78.9	91.5	76.8	94.2	59.4	94.9
1963	68.1	93.2	84.7	100.0	104.8	83.1	84.9	93.4	74.6	91.3	51.4	95.0
1962	65.7	92.4	83.8	99.4	107.9	83.1	82.8	85.9	71.4	92.1	48.3	94.9
1961	57.8	94.6	76.6	101.3	102.1	84.9	73.7	86.3	63.3	96.5	40.2	96.8
1960	58.4	96.0	77.0	105.5	97.7	88.9	72.4	85.9	63.6	98.2	41.9	96.1
1959	60.9	94.5	81.5	102.5	101.8	90.4	72.7	87.4	69.9	96.2	42.1	94.2
1958	51.6	96.2	72.8	101.8	96.2	101.9	68.7	87.6	59.4	96.1	32.0	94.3
1957	49.2	101.2	79.4	109.1	94.5	107.9	56.9	88.7	55.8	105.0	28.7	95.9
1956	48.0	99.3	79.1	105.3	93.4	110.1	54.7	84.7	53.9	106.9	26.7	94.3
1955	43.6	98.3	74.4	103.2	88.5	114.0	52.6	84.3	52.2	100.5	21.7	92.5
1954	39.2	98.5	66.8	97.5	83.4	133.2	51.9	85.5	46.8	92.9	18.1	94.0
1953	42.0	96.5	70.1	100.5	99.2	111.2	50.9	86.5	51.4	95.7	18.1	94.1
1952	40.1	100.6	71.1	111.5	94.6	110.4	49.4	87.0	46.5	101.0	17.0	95.8
1951	38.2	106.2	67.1	135.2	95.6	109.6	46.8	86.6	45.2	99.4	15.3	96.9
1950	38.8	84.7	71.8	92.6	90.9	97.2	45.0	79.3	49.3	78.8	14.4	82.7
1949	31.8	78.0	59.4	84.3	95.2	70.7	37.1	79.2	32.3	80.6	11.7	84.7
1948	32.6	81.9	66.0	87.9	87.3	73.5	35.1	82.8	33.9	88.5	11.7	87.5
1947	28.8	74.1	61.2	78.1	77.2	66.5	32.0	81.4	29.3	77.9	9.7	80.4
1946	30.3	60.2	66.9	70.4	86.9	47.3	30.3	66.0	28.3	61.4	10.4	64.2
1945	28.2	54.2	46.1	69.8	93.3	37.5	31.8	57.7	30.6	54.8	11.4	55.5
1944	27.6	52.6	43.5	67.5	117.0	36.3	37.8	54.8	23.6	54.2	10.5	53.8
1943	25.7	49.2	44.5	63.4	89.9	32.8	31.2	53.6	23.2	52.7	10.5	48.6
1942	22.9	45.3	50.6	57.1	58.1	30.3	21.9	49.7	22.9	50.6	7.9	44.0
1941	30.8	39.0	73.9	50.7	83.7	22.7	34.7	36.9	28.4	46.0	8.1	39.9
1940	26.0	36.4	56.5	48.7	78.2	18.4	32.6	33.8	23.0	43.7	8.3	37.7
1939	24.9	34.1	45.6	44.5	76.0	19.3	35.4	35.1	22.3	39.4	9.8	34.3
1938	21.6	33.6	38.6	40.7	67.0	19.6	34.2	36.1	17.5	39.7	9.2	34.5
1937	29.9	37.6	54.5	48.5	85.8	24.3	42.4	41.2	26.2	43.6	13.0	32.3
1936	26.9	33.6	48.8	40.9	86.3	20.4	38.2	40.2	22.7	39.0	11.4	31.2
1935	24.3	31.3	46.1	34.4	83.4	19.5	33.9	37.3	19.4	38.0	9.7	31.9
1934	19.9	30.7	38.3	32.7	61.4	20.9	30.9	33.8	14.4	38.4	8.3	32.4
1933	20.1	26.9	41.5	27.4	59.5	18.3	26.6	30.1	16.2	32.5	8.1	30.5
1932	18.3	26.9	36.9	26.4	58.8	20.0	23.9	28.9	12.8	30.6	8.0	32.6
1931	22.6	34.5	46.7	37.4	65.2	23.6	25.2	35.1	17.5	38.3	10.5	40.0
1930	25.8	44.2	49.7	54.9	66.8	30.3	29.8	39.1	22.7	48.3	12.3	46.9
1929	30.4	53.9	61.1	69.4	66.3	41.0	35.5	47.4	28.3	56.3	14.5	52.5
1928	26.6	57.4	53.5	74.6	63.9	43.4	29.2	55.2	25.1	54.7	12.1	57.4
1927	26.3	59.4	53.3	81.7	62.6	40.2	28.8	62.2	23.5	57.6	12.2	55.1
1926	25.9	63.7	50.1	97.3	63.4	43.0	31.5	52.6	25.0	58.0	11.7	57.4
1925	24.1	65.3	48.2	98.7	57.4	43.5	30.5	56.3	23.5	57.8	10.1	60.4
1924	22.4	60.1	42.8	80.1	60.6	35.4	25.6	81.0	21.2	55.8	10.3	55.5
1923	23.0	61.4	46.4	82.6	61.3	29.9	23.3	90.3	22.4	58.1	10.2	57.5
1922	22.1	52.4	46.2	69.5	55.9	29.8	28.6	53.8	19.0	52.4	9.2	55.3
1921	17.1	54.6	37.0	63.2	56.3	26.9	19.2	76.2	11.3	57.5	7.7	61.7
1920	20.4	96.7	42.8	113.4	64.8	45.0	22.3	220.5	17.0	85.0	8.3	80.7
1919	18.8	77.6	45.0	102.8	62.9	43.8	20.8	106.0	14.8	74.1	5.3	70.5
1913	15.4	43.7	24.0	63.0	39.6	28.0	18.8	41.2	16.1	42.9	8.5	37.0

[1] 1934–1963, based on imports for consumption. Data on 1967 base exclude trade in silver prior to 1947.

Series U 225–248. Indexes of Quantity and Unit Value of Exports and Imports, by Economic Class: 1879 to 1970—Con.

Year	U.S. general imports											
	Total		Crude materials		Crude foods		Manufactured foods		Semimanufactures		Finished manufactures	
	Quantity	Unit value	Quantity	Unit value	Quantity	Unit value	Quantity	Unit value	Quantity	Unit value	Quantity	Unit value
	237	238	239	240	241	242	243	244	245	246	247	248
	1913 = 100											
1921	111.8	125.2	140.3	99.8	135.8	101.1	100.7	179.0	75.8	135.0	86.6	164.6
1920	134.4	219.1	159.9	179.1	155.7	166.4	133.3	472.4	112.7	204.2	89.9	223.5
1919	120.4	181.0	171.7	161.6	150.6	159.4	112.4	255.7	86.5	183.1	63.0	195.2
1918	104.9	161.3	137.2	147.3	132.4	110.5	92.9	216.5	92.3	180.4	63.4	180.1
1917	113.4	145.3	149.1	139.8	154.9	106.7	89.5	196.9	96.1	160.4	69.7	136.1
1916	111.0	120.2	144.9	113.1	117.0	98.7	98.1	172.3	96.8	128.1	75.2	112.2
1915	102.1	97.2	126.6	89.7	120.6	89.9	96.6	142.9	77.3	99.8	79.3	90.3
1914	106.5	93.7	106.0	92.8	117.5	91.1	117.1	110.7	87.1	93.3	110.2	90.7
1913	100.0	100.0	100.0	100.0	100.0	100.0	100.0	100.0	100.0	100.0	100.0	100.0
1912	100.4	101.0	104.6	100.4	103.2	104.0	87.8	119.0	97.0	96.9	103.0	95.4
1911	89.0	96.1	83.2	99.9	90.8	94.5	83.5	109.7	95.8	90.4	92.7	90.2
1910	92.2	94.6	85.1	104.8	85.6	80.9	86.0	113.8	102.4	85.7	99.7	86.5
1909	93.5	88.0	90.4	95.3	106.4	71.1	82.7	104.3	94.6	81.2	96.9	86.3
1908	70.7	88.0	65.6	89.7	87.0	72.8	74.8	105.8	64.2	83.9	74.5	90.4
1907	80.0	99.2	70.7	106.2	86.7	78.2	78.7	101.8	77.0	103.1	96.1	97.1
1906	77.8	94.7	71.0	100.7	79.6	75.9	75.0	97.1	78.8	97.4	90.2	93.2
1905	72.6	90.6	70.0	93.5	81.6	74.2	70.9	113.2	70.5	85.4	76.9	90.1
1904	67.3	85.8	62.4	89.2	89.9	73.0	73.6	93.7	60.3	83.4	68.3	87.7
1903	66.1	84.0	58.6	88.5	78.8	67.3	63.1	88.2	66.6	82.9	73.7	87.6
1902	67.0	80.8	61.8	83.0	79.0	67.9	67.6	80.5	66.2	80.0	71.5	86.0
1901	59.4	82.6	56.6	82.0	77.5	66.1	64.0	96.0	52.0	82.4	60.8	88.6
1900	53.2	86.7	47.7	87.7	64.2	72.9	58.8	101.4	48.8	82.7	58.8	87.4
1899	54.1	81.5	48.6	83.2	67.5	66.4	61.4	99.1	50.6	73.4	56.0	82.8
1898	46.3	75.7	40.7	76.2	59.3	68.4	49.3	92.6	43.6	60.8	50.9	79.4
1897	54.0	75.9	51.9	71.4	64.9	81.8	56.4	84.7	44.1	63.4	62.3	79.4
1896	46.6	80.7	35.7	71.0	53.2	99.5	56.6	94.3	40.7	64.9	60.4	81.2
1895	55.7	79.5	50.6	70.0	55.8	111.6	53.2	80.7	50.8	63.4	75.8	80.3
1894	44.4	83.5	37.6	68.5	52.5	114.8	58.2	101.7	40.9	65.2	48.2	80.4
1893	44.7	92.0	37.1	75.6	48.2	123.9	54.6	122.4	45.4	73.7	59.5	84.6
1892	50.4	88.4	42.9	74.9	52.1	113.7	54.4	112.7	50.3	72.4	64.0	84.8
1891	47.7	92.0	38.6	77.6	49.9	122.8	63.7	116.1	50.7	74.3	58.8	86.1
1890	46.9	93.2	36.4	82.2	49.0	123.7	49.6	113.3	49.7	75.3	71.6	86.4
1889	43.6	93.9	35.2	83.0	48.4	112.4	43.1	131.6	47.3	72.5	64.7	87.6
1888	43.4	88.8	32.2	81.3	49.4	108.4	45.8	110.1	47.6	69.5	64.8	85.1
1887	41.4	90.9	29.7	85.8	43.9	118.9	44.8	97.6	50.5	71.8	61.7	87.5
1886	40.3	87.5	29.7	84.5	48.2	87.3	45.7	107.4	43.7	73.1	57.9	87.4
1885	35.6	87.7	25.3	84.6	46.9	88.3	43.8	105.0	37.0	71.8	48.0	90.7
1884	35.1	95.4	23.4	91.9	46.1	95.5	42.4	116.6	36.0	80.1	51.5	96.1
1883	35.9	101.8	23.1	96.9	45.0	94.6	38.9	145.8	41.0	80.8	54.0	101.6
1882	37.0	108.3	23.0	104.5	46.1	105.2	37.7	159.6	43.8	84.9	59.1	103.6
1881	33.1	107.7	21.5	99.3	42.9	112.4	32.4	157.6	38.4	83.8	51.3	103.2
1880	32.8	113.1	22.9	104.2	36.8	123.3	31.5	158.7	41.4	91.1	52.8	105.4
1879	26.7	102.4	17.9	95.0	38.8	114.3	28.4	132.4	28.9	78.0	37.4	102.8

Series U 249–263. Value of Exports and Imports, by Broad End-Use Class: 1923 to 1970

[In millions of dollars]

Year	Exports								Imports						
	Total [1]	Foods, feeds, and beverages	Industrial supplies and materials	Capital goods, except automotive	Automotive vehicles, parts, and engines	Consumer goods (nonfood), except automotive	Special category, domestic (military-type goods)	Exports, n.e.c., and reexports	Total [1][2]	Foods, feeds, and beverages	Industrial supplies and materials [1]	Capital goods, except automotive	Automotive vehicles, parts, and engines	Consumer goods (nonfood), except automotive	Imports, n.e.c. [2][3]
	249	250	251	252	253	254	255	256	257	258	259	260	261	262	263
1970	43,224	5,839	13,782	14,371	3,652	2,718	1,359	1,503	39,952	6,154	15,106	3,783	5,956	7,553	1,399
1969	37,988	4,687	11,758	12,322	3,888	2,596	1,650	1,089	36,052	5,239	14,163	3,331	5,346	6,503	1,469
1968	34,636	4,813	11,006	11,072	3,453	2,334	1,110	849	33,226	5,271	14,159	2,825	4,295	5,330	1,347
1967	31,622	4,998	9,971	9,913	2,784	2,111	1,103	743	26,889	4,586	11,856	2,382	2,634	4,213	1,219
1966	30,430	5,489	9,613	8,892	2,354	2,035	1,249	798	25,618	4,499	12,162	2,136	1,910	3,912	1,000
1965	27,521	4,928	8,917	8,039	1,929	1,799	1,229	680	21,520	3,946	11,024	1,458	939	3,305	849
1964	26,650	4,849	9,185	7,463	1,729	1,751	951	723	18,749	3,915	9,563	1,039	767	2,694	771
1963	23,387	4,282	7,822	6,604	1,468	1,558	1,025	629	17,205	3,753	8,874	823	586	2,389	781
1962	21,714	3,829	7,132	6,443	1,301	1,455	971	583	16,453	3,573	8,573	758	521	2,276	752
1961	21,037	3,418	7,705	5,910	1,188	1,441	826	549	14,759	3,331	7,714	693	383	1,889	749
1960	20,600	3,170	7,924	5,511	1,266	1,396	840	493	15,072	3,286	7,887	562	633	1,901	802
1959	17,642	2,871	6,146	4,617	1,187	1,371	967	484	15,688	3,445	8,343	591	844	1,632	834
1958	17,912	2,590	6,436	4,752	1,123	1,314	1,149	548	13,419	3,472	6,944	460	555	1,195	793
1957	20,859	2,781	8,669	4,487	1,349	1,336	1,861	377	13,412	3,306	7,595	400	339	1,210	562
1956	19,096	2,807	7,383	3,834	1,395	1,246	2,074	357	12,902	3,190	7,674	364	145	1,133	396
1955	15,553	2,119	6,065	3,071	1,276	1,134	1,592	297	11,562	3,108	6,843	254	85	991	280
1954	15,112	1,713	5,479	2,919	1,072	1,097	2,549	282	10,369	3,317	5,764	220	53	787	228
1953	15,775	1,838	4,826	2,929	998	1,086	3,801	299	10,983	3,282	6,456	224	53	757	211
1952	15,203	2,201	5,553	2,812	1,024	1,015	2,274	323	10,817	3,156	6,537	227	56	663	178
1951	15,038	2,433	6,190	2,526	1,218	1,111	1,269	291	11,068	3,087	6,952	170	38	666	156
1950	10,277	1,482	4,358	2,144	746	850	445	253	8,954	2,642	5,493	111	23	540	145
1949	12,053	2,335	4,877	2,562	772	923	311	274	6,706	2,068	4,011	106	13	404	104
1948	12,654	2,659	4,865	2,626	939	1,033	254	278	7,207	1,986	4,508	103	35	434	141
1947	15,359	3,178	5,997	3,199	1,153	1,333	175	324	5,829	1,673	3,626	55	6	375	94
1946	[4] 9,770	2,206	3,864	1,660	556	1,084	99	301	5,003	1,328	3,065	32	5	492	82
1940	4,021	246	2,045	954	259	234	169	114	2,625	556	1,778	9	1	166	115
1939	3,177	321	1,670	583	260	219	54	70	2,318	600	1,431	13	1	198	75
1938	3,094	433	1,560	528	277	202	37	58	1,960	566	1,150	16	2	186	40
1937	3,349	283	1,899	509	354	217	22	66	3,084	844	1,856	23	1	255	105
1936	2,456	203	1,424	342	246	182	14	45	2,423	728	1,443	17	1	215	19
1935	2,283	216	1,372	265	232	145	10	44	2,047	635	1,183	14	(Z)	182	33
1934	2,133	224	1,308	218	192	127	12	53	1,655	514	933	11	(Z)	155	42
1933	1,674	204	1,105	134	92	96	6	38	1,450	403	861	7	(Z)	141	38
1932	1,611	243	996	131	78	102	5	55	1,333	404	742	8	(Z)	142	37
1931	2,424	374	1,321	326	152	176	5	71	2,091	523	1,268	14	1	239	46
1930	3,843	542	2,111	547	284	255	7	96	3,061	684	1,943	29	2	347	56
1929	5,240	753	2,827	657	547	343	8	104	4,399	955	2,837	39	3	516	49
1928	5,128	762	2,879	543	509	308	6	122	4,091	951	2,618	27	3	446	46
1927	4,865	883	2,685	478	397	287	5	130	4,185	950	2,727	24	2	439	43
1926	4,809	835	2,784	445	328	289	6	122	4,431	953	2,979	23	2	433	41
1925	4,910	890	2,854	415	324	287	5	135	4,227	918	2,855	16	1	394	43
1924	--------	--------	--------	--------	--------	--------	--------	--------	3,610	942	2,245	14	1	369	39
1923	--------	--------	--------	--------	--------	--------	--------	--------	3,792	891	2,468	17	1	364	51

Z Less than $500,000.

[1] Beginning 1946, includes exports and imports of silver ore and bullion.

[2] To achieve time series comparability, adjustments have been made to the census data for 1946–1959 to include U.S. Government imports of uranium ores, concentrates, and oxides which are excluded from Census data for these years.

[3] For 1933–1940, includes differences between total imports, which are on a "general imports" basis, and the sum total of the commodity categories, which are on an "imports for consumption" basis.

[4] For 1946, excludes an estimated $499 million of civilian supplies, mainly foodstuffs, shipped to occupied areas. Beginning 1947, similar civilian supply shipments are included.

Series U 264–273.   Value of Merchandise Exports and Imports, by Groups of Customs Districts: 1860 to 1970

[In millions of dollars.   Exports include reexports; general imports through 1933; thereafter, imports for consumption.   For years ending June 30, 1860–1915; thereafter, calendar years]

Year	Atlantic coast		Gulf coast		Mexican border		Pacific coast		Northern border	
	Exports [1]	Imports	Exports [1]	Imports	Exports [1]	Imports	Exports [1]	Imports	Exports [1]	Imports
	264	265	266	267	268	269	270	271	272	273
1970	16,144	17,335	7,107	3,497	1,287	711	7,119	6,301	9,237	11,579
1969	13,384	15,576	5,525	3,021	1,110	579	6,231	5,518	9,400	10,855
1968	12,798	15,400	5,928	3,055	1,061	493	5,124	4,423	8,074	9,365
1967	11,721	12,941	5,687	2,423	939	382	4,386	3,453	7,223	7,243
1966	11,346	12,961	5,632	2,341	907	403	3,801	3,195	6,883	6,194
1965	10,002	10,954	5,495	2,182	869	304	3,476	2,766	5,958	4,836
1964	10,281	9,754	5,697	1,993	821	278	3,103	2,435	5,206	3,958
1963	9,218	9,093	4,552	1,773	639	281	3,036	2,152	4,503	3,525
1962	8,127	4,057	4,127	1,576	571	256	2,322	2,045	4,063	3,274
1961	7,897	3,727	2,778	1,413	603	227	2,356	1,764	3,740	2,961
1960	7,594	8,249	4,084	1,559	595	194	2,472	1,799	3,735	2,612
1959	6,292	8,390	3,262	1,643	545	203	1,630	1,822	3,707	2,707
1958	6,679	7,171	3,257	1,403	654	216	1,900	1,460	3,228	2,294
1957	7,759	7,389	3,980	1,336	671	189	2,052	1,446	3,646	2,469
1956	6,949	7,239	3,165	1,340	629	143	1,789	1,275	3,675	2,423
1955	6,089	6,604	2,343	1,196	509	138	1,417	1,076	2,964	2,228
1954	5,233	5,917	2,265	1,157	480	111	1,299	926	2,544	2,033
1953	4,870	6,297	2,014	1,190	485	138	1,132	915	2,732	2,141
1952	5,260	6,324	2,588	1,217	478	190	1,314	854	2,529	2,059
1951	6,105	6,525	2,799	1,219	544	109	1,271	903	2,397	1,953
1950	(NA)	5,310	(NA)	882	356	122	(NA)	723	1,844	1,622
1949	(NA)	3,826	(NA)	765	360	113	(NA)	549	1,779	1,279
1948	(NA)	4,319	(NA)	725	391	114	(NA)	523	1,752	1,328
1947	7,874	3,570	2,235	570	483	102	1,071	426	1,918	953
1946	5,413	3,220	1,691	407	405	103	689	267	1,347	787
1945	5,733	2,268	1,150	453	256	117	1,302	233	[2] 1,212	[2] 942
1944	9,255	1,903	1,079	475	240	117	1,819	267	1,615	1,026
1943	7,744	1,692	1,068	395	185	120	2,377	250	1,538	889
1942	4,999	1,464	708	360	131	64	785	243	1,431	600
1941	3,246	2,161	364	227	91	31	376	308	1,032	459
1940	2,374	1,738	522	163	51	13	363	252	694	346
1939	1,640	1,601	576	157	86	13	390	179	470	301
1938	1,532	1,371	627	160	80	10	387	151	453	237
1937	1,680	2,116	662	214	102	11	404	232	483	404
1936	1,202	1,681	546	163	56	8	275	192	360	350
1935	1,105	1,408	534	153	57	11	280	170	308	273
1934	1,018	1,158	510	113	48	6	259	123	298	217
1933	720	1,038	502	101	42	4	198	121	210	177
1932	665	914	467	94	33	8	203	130	234	168
1931	1,168	1,461	502	139	48	14	303	195	389	265
1930	1,801	2,041	822	198	102	26	449	343	648	427
1929	2,424	2,931	1,140	284	116	40	595	524	939	585
1928	2,290	2,677	1,228	285	95	30	561	505	925	564
1927	2,297	2,775	1,101	285	77	28	506	511	856	555
1926	2,309	2,953	1,121	326	73	26	519	546	759	543
1925	2,404	2,839	1,295	300	76	24	427	527	681	507
1924	2,246	2,358	1,164	282	73	20	447	477	639	442
1923	2,070	2,534	992	238	60	20	372	481	674	487
1922	1,938	2,024	914	188	57	11	312	430	610	440
1921	2,379	1,726	1,077	158	104	10	312	190	615	408
1920	4,905	3,802	1,683	340	84	38	511	391	1,044	666
1919	5,211	2,630	1,235	220	58	35	599	463	817	529
1918	3,759	1,830	776	156	48	52	539	569	1,027	403
1917	4,288	1,798	663	144	48	46	390	539	844	404
1916	3,826	1,654	624	114	24	43	338	295	670	269
1915 [3]	1,739	1,213	508	102	15	21	174	159	332	165
1914	1,304	1,375	566	120	17	33	136	138	341	205
1913	1,349	1,376	543	104	25	27	147	129	402	154
1912	1,263	1,268	464	92	27	23	128	111	322	138
1911	1,166	1,164	488	82	30	20	94	103	270	138
1910	1,018	1,227	399	69	29	23	73	89	225	129
1909	977	1,019	410	60	27	16	70	86	179	113
1908	1,156	907	397	59	33	11	94	82	181	15
1907	1,080	1,133	469	63	41	18	92	91	199	109
1906	1,062	975	369	54	35	17	102	66	177	98
1905	917	888	320	48	26	15	103	62	152	90
1904	897	779	335	44	29	12	66	57	134	84
1903	904	821	285	38	26	13	79	56	126	82
1902	895	724	263	31	24	14	88	54	111	68
1901	1,003	671	285	27	21	10	70	48	108	57

See footnotes at end of table.

Series U 264–273. Value of Merchandise Exports and Imports, by Groups of Customs Districts: 1860 to 1970—Con.

[In millions of dollars]

Year	Atlantic coast		Gulf coast		Mexican border		Pacific coast		Northern border	
	Exports	Imports	Exports	Imports	Exports	Imports	Exports	Imports	Exports	Imports
	264	265	266	267	268	269	270	271	272	273
1900	964	693	234	24	22	5	70	59	104	60
1899	871	576	194	17	16	5	56	46	89	46
1898	862	502	202	13	12	5	74	50	81	39
1897	733	639	181	20	14	4	59	44	64	50
1896	636	645	131	18	11	4	44	49	60	56
1895	590	614	122	17	9	2	36	40	50	51
1894	670	538	127	21	7	8	35	41	53	42
1893	624	717	126	25	12	14	42	48	43	53
1892	753	689	175	22	7	13	56	50	40	46
1891	637	698	152	23	8	11	53	54	35	50
1890	629	654	141	18	6	9	45	51	37	50
1889	548	610	108	17	4	8	49	51	34	51
1888	523	596	105	14	3	6	36	49	29	51
1887	539	578	104	12	3	5	41	42	29	47
1886	505	534	105	10	2	4	40	39	27	44
1885	564	482	98	11	3	2	48	36	30	42
1884	543	583	110	13	5	2	46	37	37	32
1883	597	625	131	12	5	2	53	47	36	37
1882	557	620	94	16	5	2	65	42	30	43
1881	687	553	141	17	4	3	41	39	31	32
1880	651	590	118	13	4	2	39	36	24	28
1879	560	385	90	9	3	2	37	30	22	21
1878	540	374	110	14	3	2	29	27	27	21
1877	479	388	101	12	3	1	35	30	28	20
1876	437	391	118	15	3	2	28	29	24	25
1875	421	468	100	15	3	2	27	25	23	23
1874	463	493	126	17	2	1	28	27	30	29
1873	404	551	137	24	3	1	27	33	22	32
1872	344	544	119	22	2	1	11	28	16	31
1871	323	454	131	22	3	1	14	16	20	27
1870	293	371	146	17	2	1	15	16	15	32
1865	257	194	4	1	--------	--------	11	16	16	28
1860	160	305	154	22	1	1	5	7	14	19

NA Not available.
[1] For security reasons, effective July 1950, data for certain commodities and Department of Defense controlled cargo are excluded from export figures for individual customs districts, but are included in total export statistics.

[2] Includes Omaha beginning April 1, 1945.
[3] Figures for 6-month period July 1, 1915–Dec. 31, 1915, are as follows (in millions of dollars): Series U 264, 1,304; series U 265, 638; series U 266, 224; series U 367, 44; series U 268, 10; series U 269, 13; series U 270, 97; series U 271, 105; series U 272, 218; and series U 273, 105.

Series U 274–294. Exports of Selected U. S. Merchandise: 1790 to 1970

[In millions of dollars and units. For years ending September 30, 1790–1842; June 30, 1843–1915; thereafter, calendar years]

Year	Total selected commodities, value [1]	Cotton, unmanufactured		Leaf tobacco, unmanufactured [2]		Wheat		Wheat and wheat flour, value	Cotton manufactures, value [3]	Animal fats and oils, value [4]	Fruits and nuts, value [5]	Meat products, value [6]	Naval stores, gums, and resins, value	Automobiles, incl. engines and parts, value [7]	Sawmill products, value [8]	Other wood manufactures, value [8]	Coal and related fuels, value [9]	Petroleum and products, value	Iron and steel mill products, value	Machinery, value	Copper and manufactures, value
		Quantity (lb.)	Value	Quantity (lb.)	Value	Quantity (60-lb. bu.)	Value														
	274	275	276	277	278	279	280	281	282	283	284	285	286	287	288	289	290	291	292	293	294
	SCHEDULE B—SITC CLASSIFICATIONS																				
1970	------	1,491	372	452	481	641	1,012	1,112	------	493	406	175	------	3,245	193	------	962	488	1,188	11,685	358
1969	------	1,199	280	523	529	444	726	831	------	308	370	199	------	3,514	175	------	594	433	941	10,137	282
1968	------	1,935	459	537	511	592	993	1,101	------	274	303	162	------	3,123	151	------	503	454	583	8,844	282
1967	------	1,987	464	527	487	642	1,120	1,207	------	338	338	151	------	2,503	135	------	483	539	539	8,280	209
1966	------	1,799	432	516	472	826	1,396	1,536	------	357	340	159	------	2,154	132	------	468	434	537	7,678	307
1965	------	1,898	486	447	378	640	1,064	1,184	------	472	339	162	------	1,744	119	------	477	418	607	6,935	293
1964	------	2,621	682	495	409	756	1,362	1,532	------	414	307	177	------	1,749	120	------	463	461	664	6,525	228
1963	------	2,170	577	489	401	642	1,148	1,331	------	303	295	144	------	1,518	108	------	474	479	505	5,702	208
1962	------	1,925	528	459	372	548	1,058	1,136	------	301	300	138	------	1,365	91	------	376	430	454	5,447	222
1961	------	3,196	875	494	390	659	1,227	1,300	------	272	280	133	------	1,188	87	------	340	432	454	4,968	271
1960	------	3,766	980	488	379	535	967	1,029	------	295	265	115	------	1,270	104	------	354	468	635	4,476	291

See footnotes at end of table.

Series U 274–294.   Exports of Selected U. S. Merchandise: 1790 to 1970—Con.

[In millions of dollars and units]

Year	Total selected commodities, value [1]	Cotton, unmanufactured Quantity (lb.)	Cotton, unmanufactured Value	Leaf tobacco, unmanufactured [2] Quantity (lb.)	Leaf tobacco, unmanufactured [2] Value	Wheat Quantity (60-lb. bu.)	Wheat Value	Wheat and wheat flour, value	Cotton manufactures, value [3]	Animal fats and oils, value [4]	Fruits and nuts, value [5]	Meat products, value [6]	Naval stores, gums, and resins value	Automobiles, incl. engines and parts, value [7]	Sawmill products, value [8]	Other wood manufactures, value [8]	Coal and related, value [9]	Petroleum products, value	Iron and steel mill products, value	Machinery, value	Copper and manufactures, value
	274	275	276	277	278	279	280	281	282	283	284	285	286	287	288	289	290	291	292	293	294
1962	10,704	2,050	537	459	371	517	934	1,060	262	148	259	152	48	1,362	91	53	385	443	438	4,851	244
1961	10,798	3,376	884	494	390	629	1,114	1,227	272	181	238	148	53	1,201	87	56	349	445	429	4,497	341
1960	10,614	3,909	988	495	370	504	852	971	284	176	229	125	68	1,298	104	51	362	479	610	4,121	378
1959	8,800	2,013	452	459	346	357	613	719	274	176	210	106	45	1,258	90	53	388	480	372	3,706	125
1958	9,223	2,368	661	381	279	330	570	686	280	151	367	83	36	1,087	78	44	534	462	563	3,682	230
1957	12,285	3,648	1,059	492	359	415	732	848	314	198	214	113	42	1,309	89	46	846	994	1,377	4,178	299
1956	10,880	2,511	729	506	333	409	694	798	293	207	230	99	39	1,357	88	42	745	766	[10]1,075	3,813	266
1955	8,667	1,415	477	535	355	222	386	483	293	190	161	70	39	1,238	89	33	495	646	[10]818	3,057	218
1954	7,982	2,231	788	450	303	192	350	427	317	181	171	61	38	1,036	70	30	312	658	[10]516	2,875	199
1953	7,845	1,497	521	513	339	236	506	590	329	130	129	60	27	963	65	29	346	692	[10]495	3,013	117
1952	8,825	2,141	874	391	245	369	841	942	370	147	125	52	25	987	77	33	510	793	[10]621	2,868	156
1951	9,415	2,618	1,146	518	325	423	887	997	478	214	108	60	48	1,191	96	37	605	783	611	2,615	101
1950	6,491	2,963	1,024	471	250	206	405	489	263	112	100	43	42	723	48	25	278	499	472	2,035	88
1949	7,750	2,708	874	493	252	340	835	1,002	366	135	140	51	32	753	60	31	308	562	732	2,355	97
1948	8,188	1,474	511	415	214	328	909	1,393	499	89	194	57	30	930	64	36	492	657	649	2,259	114
1947	8,789	1,380	423	493	270	167	429	868	852	111	199	129	48	1,149	121	68	632	641	824	2,352	102
1946	5,747	1,999	536	642	350	187	391	610	375	95	171	341	27	549	50	36	316	436	447	1,369	39
1945	4,949	1,282	279	470	239	129	240	330	236	103	128	290	13	588	34	55	198	753	457	1,191	55
1944	5,398	531	115	280	146	10	16	76	232	163	126	535	14	643	31	43	182	960	551	1,478	103
1943	4,407	842	184	393	170	12	16	56	192	144	80	617	14	279	26	38	172	517	615	1,194	109
1942	3,266	539	99	237	68	7	7	28	131	95	51	358	13	433	27	24	152	350	592	763	82
1941	2,608	625	83	263	65	13	11	35	135	41	52	99	15	339	30	21	119	285	501	740	48
1940	2,456	2,046	213	217	44	14	11	33	76	14	36	22	12	254	37	21	87	310	516	671	110
1939	2,198	2,562	243	327	77	63	37	61	68	23	83	32	15	254	41	14	67	385	236	502	97
1938	2,226	2,442	229	473	155	87	78	101	57	20	99	28	12	270	38	14	56	390	184	486	87
1937	2,513	3,223	369	418	134	35	39	64	60	18	82	25	22	347	56	18	67	378	300	479	94
1936	1,821	2,974	361	407	137	2	2	19	44	16	81	25	19	240	45	14	57	265	112	335	51
1935	1,719	3,234	391	381	134	(NA)	(NA)	15	39	15	93	28	17	227	42	13	52	251	88	265	49
1934	1,612	3,149	373	419	125	17	10	27	43	31	74	35	15	190	44	13	57	228	89	218	50
1933	1,268	4,523	398	420	82	8	5	19	39	40	70	26	15	91	33	11	40	201	46	132	25
1932	1,200	4,803	345	388	65	55	33	51	46	38	77	19	12	76	27	9	45	209	29	131	21
1931	1,782	3,667	326	504	110	80	50	84	60	60	109	36	15	148	47	17	65	271	63	316	55
1930	2,905	3,492	497	561	145	88	88	157	89	88	111	66	23	279	82	26	90	495	139	513	105
1929	3,963	3,982	771	555	146	90	112	192	135	124	137	79	31	541	115	37	106	562	200	604	183
1928	3,861	4,579	920	575	154	96	120	194	135	119	129	68	26	502	113	33	100	527	180	491	170
1927	3,641	4,897	826	506	139	168	240	325	133	116	122	71	34	389	111	34	110	487	161	433	150
1926	3,683	4,692	814	479	137	138	202	285	129	135	112	107	37	320	102	33	204	555	174	398	141
1925	3,707	4,384	1,060	468	153	87	149	234	146	148	102	127	32	318	103	32	107	474	144	366	161
1924	3,496	3,483	951	547	163	166	237	328	131	158	98	121	25	210	106	28	116	444	150	310	157
1923	3,124	2,743	807	475	152	99	116	205	136	158	69	154	25	171	107	30	166	367	167	281	129
1922	2,711	3,153	673	431	146	165	206	292	137	116	76	140	19	103	70	23	96	346	136	234	104
1921	3,263	3,339	534	515	205	280	433	551	116	140	70	157	11	84	55	26	171	401	236	408	98
1920	5,848	3,179	1,136	468	245	218	597	821	398	192	84	279	35	303	114	60	360	593	498	588	142
1919	5,229	3,368	1,137	766	260	148	357	650	270	326	126	698	31	156	80	49	126	377	450	362	131
1918	4,155	2,118	674	404	123	111	261	505	179	181	32	668	10	101	57	25	120	371	632	270	207
1917	3,534	2,476	575	251	46	106	246	384	157	100	35	274	14	124	42	25	119	275	645	356	363
1916	2,746	3,645	545	477	63	154	227	313	127	85	37	198	16	123	35	19	73	221	376	278	237
1915	1,804	4,404	376	348	44	260	334	428	70	79	35	132	11	70	31	15	58	148	85	120	102
1914	1,822	4,761	610	447	54	92	88	142	49	81	32	68	20	35	71	25	63	162	91	168	151
1913	1,831	4,562	547	414	49	92	89	142	52	89	37	68	26	33	78	30	68	150	124	195	143
1912	1,633	5,535	566	375	43	30	28	79	51	86	31	72	27	26	68	25	56	123	102	161	117
1911	1,528	4,034	585	352	39	24	22	71	41	86	24	66	25	16	64	23	48	105	79	151	105
1910	1,290	3,207	450	353	38	47	48	95	33	72	19	62	19	11	54	20	44	107	60	117	89
1909	1,255	4,448	417	283	31	67	68	119	32	87	17	82	15	6	45	19	40	112	47	99	87
1908	1,413	3,817	438	323	34	100	100	164	25	92	14	102	22	5	55	22	42	113	58	121	106
1907	1,404	4,518	481	332	33	77	60	122	32	94	18	108	22	6	59	20	38	94	55	125	97
1906	1,247	3,634	401	302	29	35	29	88	53	92	15	115	20	3	45	20	31	93	51	108	83
1905	1,102	4,305	380	328	30	4	4	44	50	70	16	99	16	2	37	17	31	88	45	89	88
1904	1,089	3,063	371	305	29	44	36	105	22	71	21	101	16	2	42	18	30	88	31	84	58
1903	1,044	3,543	316	357	35	114	88	162	32	72	18	104	13	1	34	19	23	77	21	76	41
1902	1,030	3,501	291	291	27	155	113	179	32	73	9	121	12	1	28	16	22	81	26	68	44
1901	1,058	3,331	314	307	27	132	97	166	32	68	11	121	13	11	32	15	24	78	40	73	45
1900	973	3,101	242	335	29	102	73	141	24	62	12	114	12	10	29	17	21	84	39	78	59
1899	875	3,773	210	272	25	139	104	177	24	61	8	109	10	10	24	14	14	63	29	61	36
1898	874	3,850	230	252	22	148	146	215	17	55	9	104	9	10	20	13	12	62	19	44	33
1897	725	3,104	231	(NA)	(NA)	80	60	116	21	43	8	88	9	10	22	14	12	68	11	38	34
1896	610	2,335	190	(NA)	(NA)	61	40	92	17	47	6	81	9	5	17	12	11	67	5	29	22
1895	586	3,517	205	(NA)	(NA)	76	44	95	14	48	5	81	7	2	15	10	11	50	3	24	16
1894	655	2,683	211	269	23	88	59	129	14	57	2	80	7	3	14	11	12	45	3	22	22
1893	651	2,212	189	248	22	117	94	169	12	51	4	79	7	3	15	9	10	47	3	22	9
1892	797	2,935	258	241	20	157	161	237	13	49	7	83	8	3	15	9	9	49	3	21	13
1891	703	2,907	291	237	21	55	51	106	14	51	2	81	8	5	15	9	8	56	3	21	12
1890	645	2,472	251	244	21	54	45	102	10	48	4	78	7	5	17	10	7	54	3	20	8
1889	576	2,385	238	212	19	46	42	87	10	36	5	59	6	3	16	10	7	52	2	16	10
1888	564	2,264	223	249	22	66	56	111	13	32	4	52	6	2	13	8	6	49	2	12	9
1887	575	2,169	206	294	26	102	91	143	15	32	3	53	6	2	11	8	5	49	1	11	4
1886	518	2,058	205	282	27	58	50	89	14	27	4	54	5	2	11	8	4	52	1	10	6
1885	565	1,892	202	219	22	85	73	125	12	32	4	63	5	2	11	8	5	52	1	11	10
1884	564	1,863	197	207	18	70	75	126	12	36	2	64	7	3	12	10	5	48	2	16	6
1883	659	2,288	247	236	19	106	120	175	13	35	3	61	8	4	13	11	4	46	1	17	7
1882	593	1,740	200	224	19	95	113	149	13	37	2	69	7	3	12	10	4	52	1	14	1
1881	654	2,191	248	227	19	151	168	213	14	------	------	134	5	2	18	------	------	------	------	------	1

SCHEDULE B CLASSIFICATION

See footnotes at end of table.

Series U 274–294. Exports of Selected U. S. Merchandise: 1790 to 1970—Con.

[In millions of dollars and units]

SCHEDULE B CLASSIFICATION—Con. (Left half)

Year	Total selected commodities, value [1]	Cotton, unmanufactured		Leaf tobacco, unmanufactured [2]		Wheat	
		Quantity (lb.)	Value	Quantity (lb.)	Value	Quantity (60-lb. bu.)	Value
	274	275	276	277	278	279	280
1880	600	1,822	212	216	16	153	191
1879	483	1,628	162	322	25	122	131
1878	471	1,608	180	284	25	72	97
1877	409	1,445	171	282	29	40	47
1876	421	1,491	193	218	23	55	68
1875	395	1,260	191	224	25	53	60
1874	475	1,359	211	318	30	71	101
1873	421	1,200	227	214	23	39	51
1872	341	934	181	235	24	26	39
1871	358	1,463	218	216	20	34	45
1870	359	959	227	186	21	37	47
1869	208	644	163	182	21	18	24
1868	206	785	153	206	23	16	30
1867	229	661	201	185	20	6	8
1866	318	651	281	191	29	6	8
1865	154	9 [11]	7 [11]	149	42	10	19
1864	64	12 [11]	10 [11]	110	23	24	31
1863	74	11 [11]	7 [11]	112	20	36	47
1862	56	5 [11]	1 [11]	107	12	37	43
1861	86	308	34	161	14	31	38
1860	270	1,768	192	167	16	4	4
1859	185	1,386	161	199	21	3	3
1858	157	1,119	131	128	17	9	9
1857	174	1,048	132	157	20	15	22
1856	155	1,351	128	117	12	8	15
1855	151	1,008	88	150	15	1	1
1854	116	988	94	126	10	8	12
1853	124	1,112	109	160	11	4	4
1852	101	1,093	88	137	10	3	3
1851	122	927	112	96	9	1	1
1850	101	635	72	146	10	1	1
1849	74	1,027	66	102	6	2	2
1848	73	814	62	131	8	2	3
1847	66	527	53	136	7	4	6
1846	53	548	43	150	8	2	2
1845	59	873	52	147	7	(Z)	(Z)
1844	63	664	54	163	8	1	1
1843 [12]	54	792	49	94	5	(Z)	(Z)
1842	59	585	48	159	10	1	1
1841	68	530	54	148	13	1	1
1840	94	744	64	119	10	2	2
1839	71	414	61	79	10	(Z)	(Z)
1838	69	596	62	111	7	(Z)	(Z)
1837	69	444	63	100	6	(Z)	(Z)
1836	81	424	71	109	10	(Z)	(Z)

SCHEDULE B CLASSIFICATION—Con. (Right half)

Year	Total selected commodities, value [1]	Cotton, unmanufactured		Leaf tobacco, unmanufactured [2]		Wheat	
		Quantity (lb.)	Value	Quantity (lb.)	Value	Quantity (60-lb. bu.)	Value
	274	275	276	277	278	279	280
1835	73	387	65	94	8	(Z)	(Z)
1834	56	385	49	88	7	(Z)	(Z)
1833	42	325	36	83	6	(Z)	(Z)
1832	38	322	32	107	6	(Z)	(Z)
1831	31	277	25	87	5	(Z)	(Z)
1830	45	298	30	84	6	(Z)	(Z)
1829	32	265	27	77	5	(Z)	(Z)
1828	27	211	22	96	5	(Z)	(Z)
1827	36	294	29	100	7	(Z)	(Z)
1826	30	205	25	64	5	(Z)	(Z)
1825	43	176	37	76	6	(Z)	(Z)
1824	27	142	22	78	5	(Z)	(Z)
1823	26	174	20	99	6	(Z)	(Z)
1822	30	145	24	83	6	(Z)	(Z)
1821	26	125	20	67	6	(Z)	(Z)
1820	39	128	22	84	8	(Z)	(Z)
1819	29	88	21	69	8	(Z)	(Z)
1818	41	94	31	84	10	(Z)	(Z)
1817	32	86	23	62	9	(Z)	(Z)
1816	37	82	24	69	13	(Z)	--------
1815	26	83	18	85	8	(Z)	--------
1814	3	18	3	3	(Z)	(Z)	--------
1813	2	19	2	5	2	(Z)	--------
1812	5	29	3	26	2	(Z)	--------
1811	12	62	10	36	2	(Z)	--------
1810	27	93	15	84	5	(Z)	--------
1809	13	51	9	54	4	(Z)	--------
1808	3	11	2	10	1	(Z)	--------
1807	19	64	14	62	5	1	--------
1806	15	36	8	83	7	(Z)	--------
1805	15	38	9	71	6	(Z)	--------
1804	14	38	8	83	6	(Z)	--------
1803	14	41	8	86	6	1	--------
1802	11	28	5	78	6	(Z)	--------
1801	--------	21	--------	104	--------	(Z)	--------
1800	--------	18	--------	79	--------	(Z)	--------
1799	--------	10	--------	96	--------	1	--------
1798	--------	9	--------	69	--------	(Z)	--------
1797	--------	4	--------	58	--------	1	--------
1796	--------	6	--------	69	--------	(Z)	--------
1795	--------	6	--------	61	--------	(Z)	--------
1794	--------	2	--------	77	--------	1	--------
1793	--------	(Z)	--------	60	--------	1	--------
1792	--------	(Z)	--------	112	--------	1	--------
1791	--------	(Z)	--------	101	3	1	1
1790	--------	--------	--------	118	4	1	1

SCHEDULE B CLASSIFICATION—Con. (Left half, lower)

Year	Wheat and wheat flour, value	Cotton manufactures, value [3]	Meat products, value [6]	Naval stores, value	Automobiles, incl. engines and parts, value [7]	Other wood manufactures, value [8]	Copper and manufactures, value
	281	282	285	286	287	289	294
1880	226	10	114	5	1	15	1
1879	160	11	102	4	1	15	3
1878	122	11	107	5	2	17	2
1877	69	10	101	5	1	20	3
1876	93	8	79	4	1	17	3
1875	83	4	68	5	1	17	1
1874	131	3	71	6	2	21	(Z)
1873	71	3	71	6	2	18	(Z)
1872	57	2	55	6	1	15	(Z)
1871	69	4	30	3	1	13	(Z)

SCHEDULE B CLASSIFICATION—Con. (Right half, lower)

Year	Wheat and wheat flour, value	Cotton manufactures, value [3]	Meat products, value [6]	Naval stores, value	Automobiles, incl. engines and parts, value [7]	Other wood manufactures, value [8]	Copper and manufactures, value
	281	282	285	286	287	289	294
1870	68	4	21	3	1	13	1
1865	47	3	35	(Z)	1	18	1
1860	20	11	14	4	1	10	2
1855	12	6	16	3	(Z)	10	1
1850	8	5	--------	1	(Z)	5	(Z)
1840	12	4	--------	1	(Z)	3	(Z)
1830	6	1	--------	(Z)	(Z)	2	(Z)
1820	5	--------	--------	1	(Z)	4	(Z)
1810	7	--------	--------	--------	(Z)	--------	(Z)

NA Not available. Z Less than one-half the unit indicated.

[1] Where both are available, total includes "Wheat and wheat flour, value" but not "Wheat."

[2] Prior to 1865, quantity in hogsheads. Includes some leaf tobacco which has been partly processed.

[3] Includes semimanufactures.

[4] Includes margarine of vegetable origin since 1948. Excludes inedible fish oils. Excludes lard compounds since 1921; now classified as vegetable cooking fats.

[5] Includes fruit and nut preparations since 1946.

[6] 1855–1881, "Meats and meat products"; 1882–1904, "Meats."

[7] "Cars, carriages, automobiles, etc.," prior to 1902. Excludes machinery and vehicles manufactured to military specifications beginning July 1949.

[8] Includes box, crate, and package shooks (except fruit and vegetables) beginning 1949; classified as "Sawmill products" in prior years. Prior to 1881, "Sawmill products" combined with "Other wood manufactures."

[9] "Coal and coke" prior to 1946.

[10] Includes a small amount of nonferrous metal articles.

[11] No record of cotton exports for southern ports.

[12] For 9 months.

INTERNATIONAL TRANSACTIONS AND FOREIGN COMMERCE

Series U 295–316. Imports of Selected Products: 1790 to 1970

[In millions of dollars and units. For years ending September 30, 1790–1842; June 30, 1843–1915; thereafter, calendar years. Last 6 months of 1915 omitted]

Year	Total selected commodities, value	Coffee		Tea		Sugar		Rubber, crude		Raw silk		Wool and mohair, value	Wool manufactures (including rags, noil, waste), value	Iron and steel manufactures, value	Tin, including ore, value	Cotton manufactures, value [1]	Copper and manufactures, value [2]	Hides and skins, value	Furs and manufactures, value [3]	Fruits and nuts, value	Forest products, value [4]	Petroleum and products, value
		Quantity (lb.)	Value	Quantity (lb.)	Value	Quantity (lb.)	Value	Quantity (lb.)	Value	Quantity (lb.)	Value											
	295	296	297	298	299	300	301	302	303	304	305	306	307	308	309	310	311	312	313	314	315	316
									TSUSA–SITC CLASSIFICATIONS													
1970		2,609	1,160	137	53	10,490	729	1,246	236	---	---	116	---	1,952	190	---	532	51	59	---	---	2,770
1969		2,676	894	140	53	9,528	638	1,321	279	---	---	155	---	1,724	189	---	486	62	94	---	---	2,560
1968		3,357	1,140	156	61	9,944	640	1,223	192	---	---	199	---	1,962	184	---	855	78	103	---	---	2,343
1967		2,819	963	143	58	9,430	588	1,026	174	---	---	168	---	1,289	167	---	656	61	92	---	---	2,086
1966		2,919	1,067	133	57	8,453	501	974	181	---	---	277	---	1,183	154	---	611	89	126	---	---	2,127
1965		2,816	1,058	130	57	7,703	442	1,015	188	---	---	282	---	1,140	167	---	425	80	113	---	---	2,092
1964		3,019	1,197	134	60	7,182	458	1,004	206	---	---	263	---	715	104	---	400	82	102	---	---	1,907
1963		3,152	955	126	58	(NA)	611	(NA)	197	---	---	280	---	598	109	---	331	65	114	---	---	1,814
									SCHEDULE A CLASSIFICATION													
1962	7,099	3,248	989	130	60	9,143	505	943	228	5	27	209	308	149	117	303	273	66	117	220	1,763	1,765
1961	6,570	2,962	964	109	54	8,447	458	876	216	6	27	198	251	122	120	217	279	64	101	220	1,636	1,643
1960	6,886	2,917	1,003	115	56	9,367	507	920	322	6	27	197	266	125	119	265	401	71	109	230	1,644	1,544
1959	6,880	3,076	1,097	110	52	9,082	496	1,285	383	7	25	224	234	111	127	209	298	87	108	218	1,676	1,535
1958	6,311	2,668	1,171	103	48	9,464	520	1,063	248	4	16	164	175	77	102	155	246	54	88	195	1,427	1,625
1957	6,431	2,761	1,376	102	51	8,273	459	1,243	349	6	25	211	191	(NA)	130	143	384	49	87	194	1,234	1,548
1956	6,619	2,810	1,439	101	51	8,287	437	1,297	398	8	32	242	196	(NA)	178	161	502	66	86	192	1,354	1,286
1955	6,142	2,602	1,357	104	64	7,806	414	1,423	442	8	34	260	168	(NA)	179	132	455	57	88	201	1,266	1,026
1954	5,503	2,260	1,486	115	62	7,485	409	284	262	7	31	223	128	(NA)	184	83	363	53	72	177	1,141	829
1953	5,747	2,786	1,468	108	48	7,613	426	1,450	331	5	26	296	140	(NA)	271	80	433	74	73	188	1,131	762
1952	5,895	2,681	1,376	93	39	7,667	415	1,804	619	8	34	382	165	(NA)	298	67	411	60	79	164	1,094	692
1951	6,143	2,693	1,361	87	41	7,278	387	1,642	807	5	19	714	152	(NA)	159	81	280	133	114	169	1,125	601
1950	5,040	2,442	1,092	113	53	7,349	381	1,800	458	8	21	428	114	(NA)	202	81	243	119	109	169	978	592
1949	3,796	2,924	796	95	46	7,457	372	1,480	240	3	7	222	72	(NA)	212	50	224	73	109	147	748	478
1948	3,911	2,774	698	91	45	6,397	313	1,646	309	6	15	308	79	(NA)	176	53	203	108	165	161	862	416
1947	3,233	2,501	600	68	28	8,330	411	1,587	317	2	16	209	40	(NA)	86	31	176	86	126	136	721	250
1946	2,673	2,738	472	94	34	5,284	196	840	228	13	128	289	41	(NA)	69	45	86	77	238	143	468	159
1945	2,005	2,717	346	84	29	6,574	202	312	99	(NA)	1	241	25	(NA)	42	38	195	50	144	110	331	152
1944	1,722	2,608	326	90	30	7,728	212	239	76	(NA)	(NA)	186	17	(NA)	47	12	166	61	126	68	282	113
1943	1,577	2,200	273	89	29	6,684	184	117	33	(NA)	(NA)	296	16	(NA)	38	12	157	66	91	41	256	85
1942	1,499	1,715	205	50	18	3,968	107	620	118	(NA)	(NA)	311	27	(NA)	51	10	165	78	69	35	268	37
1941	1,974	2,255	177	107	29	5,807	117	2,294	418	23	62	205	28	(AN)	177	23	142	83	109	62	260	82
1940	1,529	2,055	127	99	23	5,829	113	1,825	318	45	125	85	25	(NA)	131	31	73	50	80	61	217	70
1939	1,243	2,014	140	98	21	5,807	125	1,114	178	52	121	50	26	(NA)	71	40	44	47	55	58	223	44
1938	1,034	1,987	138	81	18	5,949	130	917	130	55	89	23	18	(NA)	45	35	38	30	46	55	200	39
1937	1,560	1,697	151	95	21	6,395	166	1,339	248	58	107	96	32	(NA)	104	57	53	71	86	67	256	45
1936	1,255	1,739	134	82	18	5,939	158	1,091	159	60	102	53	30	(NA)	76	49	30	55	82	58	210	41
1935	1,063	1,756	137	86	17	5,910	133	1,045	119	68	96	30	20	(NA)	70	41	33	46	53	55	175	38
1934	894	1,524	133	76	16	5,994	118	1,036	102	56	72	17	15	(NA)	45	32	28	35	41	46	157	37
1933 [5]	820	1,586	124	97	14	5,669	105	938	46	67	103	21	16	(NA)	51	32	18	46	38	37	143	26
1932		1,501	137	95	12	5,943	97	929	33	74	114	6	13	(NA)	16	28	24	22	28	44	149	61
1931	1,207	1,742	175	87	19	6,353	113	1,124	74	84	191	22	23	(NA)	37	41	49	50	56	60	204	93
1930	1,695	1,599	209	85	23	6,990	130	1,090	141	74	263	37	40	(NA)	60	46	105	92	69	75	259	146
1929	2,477	1,482	302	89	26	9,777	209	1,263	241	87	427	87	79	(NA)	92	69	154	137	126	87	296	145
1928	2,346	1,457	310	90	27	7,737	207	978	245	75	368	80	78	(NA)	87	69	98	151	122	90	280	134
1927	2,430	1,433	264	89	28	8,431	258	955	340	74	390	83	79	(NA)	101	66	85	113	138	85	285	115
1926	2,653	1,493	323	96	31	9,420	233	926	506	66	393	107	71	(NA)	105	67	100	97	120	88	286	126

See footnotes at end of table.

Series U 295–316. Imports of Selected Products: 1790 to 1970—Con.

[In millions of dollars and units]

SCHEDULE A CLASSIFICATION—Con.

Year	Total selected commodities, value	Coffee Quantity (lb.)	Coffee Value	Tea Quantity (lb.)	Tea Value	Sugar Quantity (lb.)	Sugar Value	Rubber, crude Quantity (lb.)	Rubber, crude Value	Raw silk Quantity (lb.)	Raw silk Value	Wool and mohair, value	Wool manufactures (including rags, noil, waste), value	Iron and steel manufactures, value	Tin, including ores, value	Cotton manufactures, value [1]	Copper and manufactures, value	Hides and skins, value	Furs and manufactures, value [3]	Fruits and nuts, value	Forest products, value [4]	Petroleum and products, value
	295	296	297	298	299	300	301	302	303	304	305	306	307	308	309	310	311	312	313	314	315	316
1925	2,534	1,284	286	101	31	8,920	246	888	430	64	396	142	74	(NA)	95	79	84	97	117	89	259	109
1924	2,190	1,421	249	93	27	8,272	364	735	174	51	328	93	69	44	69	91	96	75	88	72	248	103
1923	2,302	1,410	190	105	30	7,709	380	692	185	49	392	130	69	54	63	100	96	119	89	70	255	80
1922	1,831	1,246	161	97	24	9,722	252	674	102	51	366	87	59	48	46	87	67	107	69	72	195	89
1921	1,429	1,341	143	76	14	5,967	235	415	74	45	259	60	51	29	22	75	46	68	41	74	159	79
1920	3,212	1,297	252	90	24	8,065	1,115	567	243	30	285	127	58	50	93	138	90	244	92	102	231	68
1919	2,309	1,334	261	81	20	7,020	393	536	216	45	329	217	19	27	63	53	86	307	76	79	130	33
1918	1,608	1,052	99	134	30	5,167	241	326	146	33	180	252	23	25	105	41	134	108	34	49	114	27
1917	1,692	1,287	123	127	26	4,941	222	406	233	37	184	172	23	28	68	56	138	210	29	45	113	22
1916	1,373	1,167	119	105	19	5,530	227	270	160	32	145	126	16	24	56	55	95	173	21	45	77	15
1915	908	1,119	107	97	18	5,093	166	172	83	26	81	68	30	23	31	46	32	104	10	41	57	11
1914	934	1,002	111	91	17	4,948	99	132	71	29	98	53	34	32	39	71	55	120	14	51	54	15
1913	913	863	119	95	17	4,533	99	113	90	26	82	36	16	34	53	66	60	117	24	41	48	11
1912	844	885	118	101	18	3,663	104	110	93	22	67	33	15	27	46	65	45	102	25	43	38	5
1911	749	876	91	103	18	3,703	90	72	76	22	73	23	19	36	38	67	40	71	24	40	40	3
1910	823	871	69	86	14	3,913	102	101	101	20	65	51	24	40	31	68	40	112	27	37	40	2
1909	711	1,050	79	115	19	4,184	96	88	62	23	79	45	18	22	26	63	38	78	21	30	34	1
1908	603	891	68	94	16	3,365	80	62	37	15	64	24	19	28	25	69	32	55	16	37	32	1
1907	755	985	78	86	14	4,384	93	77	59	17	70	42	22	41	38	75	48	83	22	36	34	------
1906	654	852	73	94	15	3,970	85	58	45	15	53	39	23	29	31	64	33	84	22	29	29	------
1905	626	1,048	85	103	16	3,658	97	67	50	18	60	46	18	24	23	50	25	65	18	26	23	------
1904	516	995	70	113	18	3,684	71	59	40	13	44	25	18	27	21	50	22	52	15	24	19	------
1903	535	915	59	109	16	4,163	71	55	30	14	49	22	20	52	24	53	21	58	15	24	21	------
1902	463	1,091	71	76	9	2,941	53	50	25	13	42	18	17	27	19	45	25	58	16	21	17	------
1901	438	855	63	90	11	3,865	88	55	28	9	29	13	15	18	20	40	21	48	11	20	13	------
1900	475	788	52	85	11	4,007	100	49	31	11	45	20	16	20	19	42	15	58	12	19	15	------
1899	387	832	55	74	9	3,917	93	51	32	10	32	9	14	12	12	32	7	42	11	18	9	------
1898	343	871	65	72	10	2,589	58	46	25	10	31	17	15	13	9	27	4	37	8	15	9	------
1897	355	(NA)	(NA)	(NA)	(NA)	4,720	94	------	17	------	18	53	49	16	7	35	2	28	6	17	13	------
1896	449	581	85	94	13	3,709	84	------	17	------	26	32	53	25	7	33	2	31	9	19	13	------
1895	416	646	95	97	13	3,516	75	------	18	------	22	26	39	23	7	33	1	26	10	17	11	------
1894	386	532	87	94	14	4,286	125	------	15	------	16	6	19	21	3	22	1	17	8	19	13	------
1893	475	541	77	89	14	3,733	115	------	18	------	29	21	38	35	12	34	1	28	11	24	18	------
1892	485	633	127	90	14	3,542	104	------	20	------	24	20	36	29	9	28	1	27	10	21	15	------
1891	483	520	96	83	14	3,479	106	------	18	------	18	18	41	54	8	30	1	28	10	26	15	------
1890	440	499	78	84	12	2,934	96	------	15	------	23	15	57	42	7	30	(Z)	22	8	21	13	------
1889	418	578	75	80	13	2,762	89	------	12	------	19	18	53	42	7	27	(Z)	25	7	19	12	------
1888	397	424	61	85	13	2,700	74	------	16	------	19	16	48	49	9	29	(Z)	24	7	21	11	------
1887	392	526	56	90	17	3,136	78	------	14	------	19	16	45	49	7	29		24	7	21	10	------
1886	362	565	43	82	16	2,690	81	------	12	------	17	17	41	38	6	30	1	27	7	17	9	------
1885	317	573	47	72	14	2,718	73	------	9	------	12	9	36	34	4	27	(Z)	21	5	17	9	------
1884	376	535	50	68	14	2,756	98	------	14	------	12	12	41	40	5	29	1	22	8	20	10	------
1883	403	516	42	73	17	2,138	92	------	16	------	14	11	44	58	6	37	(Z)	28	8	20	10	------
1882	403	460	46	79	19	1,990	90	------	14	------	13	11	37	68	5	34	1	28	8	19	10	------
1881	320	455	57	82	21	1,947	87	------	11	------	11	10	31	61	------	31		------	------	------	------	------

See footnotes at end of table.

INTERNATIONAL TRANSACTIONS AND FOREIGN COMMERCE

Series U 295–316. Imports of Selected Products: 1790 to 1970—Con.

[In millions of dollars and units]

Year	Total selected commodities, value	Coffee Quantity (lb.)	Coffee Value	Tea Quantity (lb.)	Tea Value	Sugar Quantity (lb.)	Sugar Value
	295	296	297	298	299	300	301
			SCHEDULE A CLASSIFICATION—Con.				
1880	341	447	60	72	20	1,830	80
1879	217	378	47	60	15	1,834	72
1878	222	310	52	65	16	1,538	73
1877	239	332	54	58	16	1,654	85
1876	231	340	57	63	20	1,494	58
1875	272	318	51	65	23	1,797	73
1874	298	285	55	56	21	1,701	82
1873	344	293	44	65	24	1,568	83
1872	334	299	38	64	23	1,509	81
1871	260	318	31	51	17	1,276	65
1870	205	235	24	47	14	1,197	57
1869	99	254	25	44	14	1,247	60
1868	85	249	25	38	11	1,121	49
1867	69	187	21	40	12	849	36
1866	73	181	21	43	11	998	41
1865	101	106	11	20	5	651	27
1864	57	132	16	37	11	632	30
1863	37	80	10	30	8	517	19
1862	41	123	14	25	7	557	20
1861	59	184	21	26	7	809	31
1860	170	202	22	32	9	694	31
1859	63	264	25	29	7	656	31
1858	48	189	18	33	7	519	23
1857	71	241	22	20	6	776	43
1856	53	236	22	23	7	544	24
1855	118	191	17	25	7	474	15
1854	36	162	15	24	7	455	14
1853	39	199	16	23	8	464	15
1852	36	194	14	29	7	457	15
1851	31	153	13	17	5	368	13
1850	87	145	11	30	5	218	8
1849	21	165	9	16	4	259	8
1848	23	151	8	24	6	255	9
1847	23	157	9	17	4	236	10
1846	18	133	8	20	5	128	5
1845	17	108	6	20	6	114	5
1844	21	161	10	16	4	185	7
1843 [6]	12	93	6	14	4	71	2
1842	20	113	9	16	5	172	6
1841	22	115	10	12	3	184	9
1840	47	95	9	20	5	121	6
1839	22	107	10	9	2	195	10
1838	19	88	8	14	3	154	8
1837	22	88	9	17	6	136	7
1836	28	94	10	16	5	191	13
1835	23	103	11	14	5	126	7
1834	21	80	9	16	6	115	6
1833	21	100	11	15	5	98	5
1832	15	92	9	10	3	66	3
1831	12	82	6	5	1	109	5
1830	29	51	4	9	2	86	5
1829	11	51	5	7	2	63	4
1828	11	55	5	8	2	57	4
1827	11	50	4	6	2	77	5
1826	13	37	4	10	4	85	5
1825	13	45	5	10	4	72	4
1824	13	39	5	9	3	94	5
1823	12	37	7	8	2	61	3
1822	13	26	6	7	2	88	5
1821	9	21	4	5	1	60	4
1819		23		7		74	
1818		29		6		68	
1817		31		7		93	
1816		26		3		55	
1815		20		2		45	
1814		8		(Z)		30	
1813		12		1		33	
1812		28		3		83	
1811		30		3		77	
1810		31		8		55	
1809		36		1		77	
1808		37		5		104	
1807		59		8		221	
1806		56		7		199	
1805		56		5		187	
1804		53		3		128	
1803		17		6		74	
1802		41		4		99	
1801		57		4		137	
1800		47		5		113	
1799		30		5		104	
1798		58		2		88	
1797		49		2		73	
1796		61		2		60	
1795		54		3		64	
1794		37		3		49	
1793		34		3		48	
1792		9		3		24	
1791		4		1		25	
1790		4		3		18	

Year	Rubber, crude, value	Raw silk, value	Wool and mohair, value	Wool manufactures, value	Iron and steel manufactures, value	Cotton manufactures, value [1]
	303	305	306	307	308	310
			SCHEDULE A CLASSIFICATION—Con.			
1880	10	12	24	34	71	30
1879	6	8	5	24	20	20
1878	5	5	8	25	19	19
1877	6	7	7	26	19	19
1876	4	5	8	33	23	23
1875	5	5	11	45	31	28
1874	6	4	8	47	47	28
1873	7	6	20	51	74	35
1872	5	6	26	52	68	35
1871	4	6	10	44	53	30
1870	3	3	7	34	40	23
1865	1	1	8	22	17	9
1860	1		5	43	26	33
1855	2		2	28	29	18
1850			2	20	20	21
1840			1	11	8	7
1830				6	6	6
1820				6		8

NA Not available. Z Less than one-half the unit of measure indicated.
[1] Includes semimanufactures.
[2] Copper including ore and manufactures since 1946.
[3] Includes fur hats beginning 1921; formerly classified as miscellaneous textile products.
[4] Includes sawmill products, wood pulp, and paper and manufactures.

[5] Value in millions of dollars for imports for consumption as follows: Series U 302, 19; series U 303, 16; series U 307, 51; series U 308, 31; series U 309, 15; series U 310, 45; series U 313, 37; series U 314, 37; series U 315, 144; series U 316, 26.
[6] For 9 months.

Series U 317–334. Value of Exports (Including Reexports) of U.S. Merchandise, by Country of Destination: 1790 to 1970

[In millions of dollars. Figures shown here are mixed values for 1862–1879. For years ending September 30, 1790–1842; June 30, 1843–1915; thereafter, calendar years. Beginning 1961, includes uranium, thorium, and related products. Beginning 1869, includes silver ores, base bullion, and refined bullion]

Year	Total value [1]	America						Europe					Asia				Australia and Oceania	Africa
		Total	Canada [2]	Cuba	Mexico	Brazil	Other	Total	United Kingdom	France	Germany [3]	Other	Total	Mainland China [4]	Japan [5]	Other		
	317	318	319	320	321	322	323	324	325	326	327	328	329	330	331	332	333	334
1970	43,224	15,612	9,079	(Z)	1,704	840	3,989	14,817	2,536	1,483	2,741	8,057	10,027	-----	4,652	5,375	1,189	1,580
1969	38,006	14,713	9,137	(Z)	1,450	672	3,454	12,641	2,335	1,195	2,142	6,969	8,261	-----	3,490	4,771	998	1,392
1968	34,636	13,411	8,072	(Z)	1,378	705	3,257	11,347	2,289	1,095	1,709	6,254	7,582	(Z)	2,954	4,628	1,026	1,269
1967	31,526	11,883	7,165	(Z)	1,222	547	2,949	10,297	1,960	1,025	1,706	5,606	7,146	(Z)	2,695	4,451	1,017	1,182
1966	30,320	11,429	6,661	(Z)	1,180	575	3,013	10,003	1,737	1,007	1,674	5,585	6,733	(Z)	2,364	4,369	805	1,349
1965	27,470	9,908	5,642	(Z)	1,104	341	2,821	9,364	1,615	971	1,649	5,129	6,012	(Z)	2,080	3,932	956	1,229
1964	26,508	9,207	4,915	(Z)	1,107	402	2,783	9,436	1,532	990	1,606	5,308	5,802	3	2,009	3,790	803	1,259
1963	23,347	7,944	4,251	36	873	405	2,379	8,338	1,213	813	1,582	4,730	5,448	4	1,844	3,600	565	1,054
1962	21,700	7,724	4,045	13	821	449	2,396	7,758	1,128	735	1,581	4,314	4,676	23	1,574	3,079	519	1,023
1961	20,999	7,673	3,826	14	828	545	2,460	7,370	1,206	704	1,343	4,117	4,652	7	1,837	2,808	445	859
1960	20,575	7,684	3,810	225	831	464	2,354	7,398	1,487	699	1,272	3,940	4,186	–	1,447	2,739	514	793
1959	17,634	7,692	3,825	442	755	435	2,235	5,554	1,097	483	878	3,096	3,284	3	1,079	2,202	376	728
1958	17,910	7,999	3,539	553	904	567	2,436	5,566	905	570	887	3,204	3,411	5	987	2,419	282	652
1957	20,850	9,001	4,041	628	917	512	2,903	6,838	1,162	708	1,330	3,638	3,961	9	1,319	2,633	295	755
1956	19,090	8,243	4,149	528	860	326	2,380	6,434	982	829	943	3,680	3,417	–	998	2,419	265	731
1955	15,547	6,903	3,404	463	719	273	2,044	5,126	1,006	536	607	2,977	2,581	3	683	1,895	295	642
1954	15,110	6,520	2,966	439	649	507	1,959	5,118	808	783	505	3,022	2,577	6	693	1,878	264	630
1953	15,774	6,514	3,197	436	663	379	1,839	5,711	826	1,236	363	3,286	2,783	–	686	2,097	203	563
1952	15,201	6,682	3,003	525	683	597	1,874	5,089	787	1,013	450	2,839	2,541	–	633	1,908	267	621
1951	15,032	6,607	2,693	548	730	739	1,897	5,121	1,000	843	523	2,755	2,410	(Z)	601	1,809	270	624
1950	10,275	4,902	2,039	464	526	365	1,508	3,306	548	475	441	1,842	1,539	37	418	1,084	151	376
1949	12,051	4,861	1,959	380	468	383	1,671	4,239	700	497	822	2,220	2,135	83	468	1,584	195	622
1948	12,653	5,307	1,944	441	522	497	1,903	4,380	644	591	863	2,282	2,029	273	325	1,431	153	785
1947	14,430	6,183	2,114	492	630	643	2,304	5,269	1,103	817	128	3,221	1,835	353	60	1,422	320	821
1946	9,738	3,684	1,442	272	505	356	1,109	4,122	855	709	83	2,475	1,327	465	102	760	117	489
1945	9,806	2,564	1,178	196	307	219	664	5,515	2,193	472	2	2,848	849	108	1	740	354	524
1944	14,259	2,627	1,441	167	264	218	537	9,364	5,243	18	(Z)	4,103	996	52	-----	944	410	861
1943	12,965	2,418	1,444	134	187	156	497	7,633	4,505	-----	-----	3,128	838	53	2	783	569	1,507
1942	8,079	2,205	1,334	133	148	105	485	4,009	2,529	1	-----	1,479	688	80	-----	608	361	816
1941	5,147	2,047	994	126	159	148	620	1,847	1,637	2	(Z)	208	625	95	60	470	123	504
1940	4,021	1,501	713	85	97	111	495	1,645	1,011	252	(Z)	382	619	78	227	314	94	161
1939	3,177	1,131	489	82	83	80	397	1,290	505	182	46	557	562	56	232	274	80	115
1938	3,094	1,040	468	76	62	62	372	1,326	521	134	107	564	517	35	240	242	94	118
1937	3,349	1,158	509	92	109	69	379	1,360	536	165	126	533	580	47	289	241	99	152
1936	2,456	821	384	67	76	49	245	1,043	440	129	102	372	399	47	204	148	79	114
1935	2,283	706	323	60	66	44	213	1,029	433	117	92	387	378	38	203	137	74	96
1934	2,133	648	302	45	55	40	206	950	383	116	109	342	401	69	210	122	57	77
1933	1,675	455	211	25	38	30	151	850	312	122	140	276	292	52	143	97	35	43
1932	1,611	462	241	29	32	29	131	784	288	112	134	250	292	56	135	101	37	36
1931	2,424	750	396	47	52	29	226	1,187	456	122	166	443	386	98	156	132	42	60
1930	3,843	1,357	659	94	116	54	434	1,838	678	224	278	658	448	90	165	193	108	92
1929	5,241	1,934	948	129	134	109	614	2,341	848	266	410	817	643	124	259	260	192	131
1928	5,128	1,802	915	128	116	100	543	2,375	847	241	467	820	655	138	288	229	180	117
1927	4,865	1,691	837	155	109	89	501	2,314	840	229	482	763	560	83	258	219	194	107
1926	4,809	1,620	739	160	135	95	491	2,310	973	264	364	709	565	110	261	194	213	101
1925	4,910	1,541	649	199	145	87	461	2,604	1,034	280	470	820	487	94	230	163	189	89
1924	4,591	1,404	624	200	135	65	380	2,445	983	282	440	740	515	109	253	153	157	70
1923	4,167	1,355	652	192	120	46	345	2,093	882	272	317	622	511	109	267	135	146	61
1922	3,832	1,142	577	128	110	43	284	2,083	856	267	316	644	449	100	222	127	102	56
1921	4,485	1,403	594	188	222	58	341	2,364	942	225	372	825	533	108	238	187	113	73
1920	8,228	2,553	972	515	208	157	701	4,466	1,825	676	311	1,654	872	146	378	348	172	166
1919	7,920	1,738	734	278	131	115	480	5,188	2,279	893	93	1,923	772	106	366	300	126	98
1918	6,149	1,628	887	227	98	57	359	3,859	2,061	931	-----	867	498	53	274	171	105	59
1917	6,234	1,573	829	196	111	66	371	4,062	2,009	941	(Z)	1,112	469	40	186	243	77	51
1916	5,483	1,145	605	165	54	48	273	3,813	1,887	861	2	1,063	388	32	109	247	83	54
1915	2,769	576	301	76	34	26	139	1,971	912	369	29	661	139	16	41	82	53	29
1914	2,365	654	345	69	39	30	171	1,486	594	160	345	387	141	25	51	65	56	28
1913	2,466	763	415	71	54	43	180	1,479	597	146	332	404	140	21	58	61	54	29
1912	2,204	648	329	62	53	35	169	1,342	564	135	307	336	141	24	53	64	48	24
1911	2,049	566	270	61	61	27	147	1,308	577	135	287	309	105	19	37	49	46	24
1910	1,745	479	216	53	58	23	129	1,136	506	118	250	262	78	16	22	40	34	19
1909	1,663	387	163	44	50	18	112	1,147	515	109	235	288	83	19	27	37	30	17
1908	1,861	409	167	47	56	19	120	1,284	581	116	277	310	113	22	41	50	35	20
1907	1,881	432	183	49	66	19	115	1,298	608	114	257	319	101	26	39	36	33	17
1906	1,744	383	157	48	58	15	105	1,200	583	98	235	284	111	44	38	29	30	20
1905	1,519	318	141	38	46	11	82	1,021	523	76	194	228	135	53	52	30	27	19
1904	1,461	286	131	27	46	11	71	1,058	537	84	215	222	65	13	25	27	28	24
1903	1,420	256	123	22	42	11	58	1,029	524	77	194	234	62	19	21	22	33	38
1902	1,382	242	110	27	40	10	55	1,008	549	72	173	214	69	25	21	23	29	33
1901	1,488	241	106	26	36	12	61	1,137	631	79	192	235	53	10	19	24	31	26
1900	1,394	227	95	26	35	12	59	1,040	534	83	187	236	68	15	29	24	41	19
1899	1,227	194	88	19	25	12	50	937	512	61	156	208	49	14	17	18	29	19
1898	1,231	174	84	10	21	13	46	974	541	95	155	183	45	10	20	15	22	18
1897	1,051	159	65	8	23	12	51	813	483	58	125	147	39	12	13	14	23	17
1896	883	153	60	8	19	14	52	673	406	47	98	122	26	7	8	11	17	14

See footnotes at end of table.

INTERNATIONAL TRANSACTIONS AND FOREIGN COMMERCE

Series U 317–334.   Value of Exports (Including Reexports) of U.S. Merchandise, by Country of Destination: 1790 to 1970—Con.

[In millions of dollars]

Year	Total value [1]	America						Europe					Asia				Australia and Oceania	Africa
		Total	Canada [2]	Cuba	Mexico	Brazil	Other	Total	United Kingdom	France	Germany [3]	Other	Total	Mainland China [4]	Japan [5]	Other		
	317	318	319	320	321	322	323	324	325	326	327	328	329	330	331	332	333	334
1895	808	143	53	13	15	15	47	628	387	45	92	104	18	4	5	9	13	6
1894	892	153	57	20	13	14	49	701	431	55	92	123	22	6	4	12	12	5
1893	848	152	47	24	20	12	49	662	421	47	84	110	17	4	3	10	12	5
1892	1,030	139	43	18	14	14	50	851	499	99	106	147	20	7	3	10	11	5
1891	884	131	38	12	15	14	52	705	445	61	93	106	26	9	5	12	16	5
1890	858	133	40	13	13	12	55	684	448	50	86	100	20	3	5	12	16	5
1889	742	125	41	12	11	9	52	579	383	46	68	82	19	6	5	8	16	4
1888	696	110	36	10	10	7	47	549	362	39	56	92	20	5	4	11	15	3
1887	716	104	35	11	8	8	42	575	366	57	59	93	20	6	3	11	14	3
1886	680	98	33	10	8	7	40	541	348	42	62	89	23	8	3	12	15	3
1885	742	104	38	9	8	7	42	599	398	47	62	92	21	6	3	12	14	4
1884	741	123	44	11	13	9	46	584	386	51	61	86	17	5	3	9	13	3
1883	824	129	44	15	17	9	44	660	425	59	66	110	17	4	3	10	14	4
1882	751	113	37	12	15	9	40	600	408	50	54	88	19	6	3	10	13	4
1881	902	108	38	11	11	9	39	766	481	94	70	121	13	5	1	7	10	6
1880	836	93	29	11	8	9	36	719	454	100	57	108	12	1	3	8	7	5
1879	712	91	30	13	7	8	33	594	349	90	57	98	12	3	3	6	10	5
1878	710	100	37	12	7	9	35	584	387	55	55	87	12	4	2	6	9	4
1877	645	99	37	13	6	8	35	525	346	45	58	76	10	2	1	7	8	3
1876	610	96	33	13	6	7	37	497	336	40	51	70	8	1	1	6	5	4
1875	574	100	35	15	6	8	36	459	317	34	50	58	7	1	2	4	5	3
1874	651	110	42	17	6	8	37	528	345	43	63	77	5	1	1	3	5	3
1873	594	102	33	16	6	7	40	479	317	34	62	66	5	1	1	3	5	3
1872	492	89	29	14	6	6	34	393	265	31	41	56	4	3	1	—	4	3
1871	493	89	32	15	8	6	28	394	273	27	35	59	3	2	1	1	4	3
1870	471	79	25	14	6	6	28	381	248	46	42	45	4	3	1	—	5	2
1869	382	74	23	12	5	6	28	291	185	33	38	35	7	5	1	1	6	3
1868	383	81	24	15	6	6	30	287	198	26	31	32	6	4	1	1	6	3
1867	398	77	21	14	5	5	32	307	225	34	22	26	5	4	1	—	6	3
1866	479	80	24	15	5	6	30	386	288	51	22	25	5	3	1	2	7	2
1865	281	110	29	[6]19	16	6	40	158	103	11	20	24	4	3	(Z)	1	7	2
1864	235	92	27	[6]13	9	5	40	138	97	13	13	15	4	9	(Z)	(Z)	1	
1863	268	83	28	[6]14	9	5	27	173	128	14	14	17	5	6	(Z)	(Z)	7	
1862	193	57	21	[6]9	2	4	21	127	86	20	10	11	3	5	(Z)	(Z)	7	
1861	220	61	23	10	2	5	21	147	108	15	11	13	6	7	(Z)	(Z)	6	
1860	334	69	23	12	5	6	23	249	169	39	15	26	8	9	(Z)	(Z)	8	
1859	293	70	28	12	3	6	21	210	133	30	15	32	6	7	(Z)	(Z)	7	
1858	272	62	24	11	3	5	19	199	129	28	12	30	5	6	(Z)	(Z)	6	
1857	294	64	24	9	4	5	22	218	135	32	15	36	4	4	(Z)	(Z)	8	
1856	281	66	29	7	4	5	21	204	128	35	13	28	3	3	—	(Z)	8	
1855	219	62	28	8	3	4	19	148	92	29	9	18	3	2	(Z)	—	—	6
1854	237	60	24	8	3	4	21	170	117	25	9	19	2	1	(Z)	—	—	5
1853	203	43	12	6	4	4	17	151	103	22	7	19	4	4	—	—	—	5
1852	167	34	10	6	2	3	13	124	81	19	6	18	3	3	—	—	—	6
1851	189	39	12	5	2	3	17	146	101	21	6	18	2	2	—	—	—	2
1850	144	30	10	5	2	3	10	109	71	18	5	15	3	2	—	—	—	2
1849	140	29	8	5	2	3	11	107	78	13	3	13	3	2	—	—	—	1
1848	138	35	8	7	4	3	13	99	67	15	4	13	3	2	—	—	—	1
1847	157	31	7	6	1	3	14	123	87	19	5	12	2	2	—	—	—	1
1846	110	31	7	5	2	3	14	76	46	14	5	11	2	2	—	—	—	1
1845	106	29	6	6	1	3	13	73	45	12	6	10	3	2	—	—	—	1
1844	106	28	6	5	2	3	12	76	49	13	4	10	2	2	—	—	—	1
1843 [7]	83	16	3	3	1	2	7	63	41	12	4	6	3	2	—	—	—	1
1842	100	27	6	5	2	3	11	72	40	17	5	10	2	1	—	—	—	
1841	112	30	6	6	2	3	13	80	47	18	5	10	2	1	—	—	—	1
1840	124	30	6	6	3	2	13	92	55	20	4	13	1	1	—	—	—	1
1839	112	24	4	6	3	2	9	86	57	18	3	8	1	2	—	—	—	1
1838	105	23	2	6	2	2	11	80	52	15	3	10	1	2	—	—	—	1
1837	111	24	3	6	4	2	9	86	52	19	3	11	1	2	—	—	—	
1836	124	26	3	6	6	2	9	96	58	21	4	13	2	1	—	—	—	1
1835	115	30	3	5	9	2	11	83	52	19	4	8	1	1	—	—	—	1
1834	102	27	3	5	5	2	12	74	44	15	5	10	1	2	—	—	—	
1833	88	29	4	5	5	3	12	57	32	14	3	8	2	1	—	—	—	
1832	82	26	3	5	3	2	13	55	29	12	4	10	1	1	—	—	—	
1831	72	26	3	5	6	2	10	45	31	6	3	5	1	1	—	—	—	
1830	72	23	3	5	5	2	8	48	26	11	2	9	1	1	—	—	—	
1829	67	21	2	5	2	2	10	45	24	10	3	8	1	1	—	—	—	
1828	64	23	2	6	3	2	10	39	20	9	3	7	2	1	—	—	—	
1827	74	21	2	6	4	2	7	49	26	11	3	9	2	4	—	—	—	
1826	73	30	2	6	6	2	14	42	21	11	3	8	1	3	—	—	—	
1825	91	30	3	5	6	2	14	59	37	10	3	9	2	6	—	—	—	
1824	69	28	2	6	—	2	18	40	21	10	2	7	2	6	—	—	—	
1823	68	22	2	5	—	1	14	44	22	9	3	10	2	5	—	—	—	
1822	61	20	2	3	—	1	14	40	24	6	3	7	2	6	—	—	—	
1821	55	15	2	4	—	1	8	36	19	6	2	9	2	4	—	—	—	

See footnotes at end of table.

Series U 317–334. Value of Exports (Including Reexports) of U.S. Merchandise, by Country of Destination: 1790 to 1970—Con.

[In millions of dollars]

Year	Total value	Europe					Year	Total value	Europe					Year	Total value	Europe				
		Total	United Kingdom	France	Germany[3]	Other			Total	United Kingdom	France	Germany[3]	Other			Total	United Kingdom	France	Germany[3]	Other
	317	324	325	326	327	328		317	324	325	326	327	328		317	324	325	326	327	328
1820	70	48	24	8	3	13	1810	67	47	12	(Z)	2	33	1800	71	41	19	(Z)	8	14
1819	70	47	24	9	4	10	1809	52	34	6	-	2	26	1799	79	45	19	-	18	8
1818	93	68	38	12	3	15	1808	22	7	3	3	(Z)	1	1798	61	39	12	1	15	11
1817	88	58	33	9	3	13	1807	108	71	23	13	3	32	1797	51	29	6	4	10	9
1816	82	59	30	10	4	15	1806	102	65	16	11	6	32	1796	59	39	17	3	10	9
1815	53	38	18	7	2	11	1805	96	61	15	13	4	29	1795	48	31	6	8	10	7
1814	7	1	-	(Z)	-	1	1804	78	51	13	9	6	23	1794	33	21	6	1	5	9
1813	28	22	-	4	(Z)	18	1803	56	37	18	4	4	11	1793	26	15	6	2	2	5
1812	39	27	6	3	(Z)	18	1802	72	44	16	8	6	14	1792	21	12	5	2	1	4
1811	61	40	14	2	(Z)	24	1801	93	59	31	4	11	13	1791	19	10	6	1	(Z)	3
														1790	20	13	7	1	(Z)	5

- Represents zero.   Z Less than $500,000.

[1] For security reasons, exports of special category commodities are excluded from totals for certain countries. Beginning 1950, exports reflect declassification of special category data authorized July 28, 1965 and January 5, 1968, and relaxation of security restrictions as authorized July 17, 1969.

[2] Prior to 1873, data are for trade with British North American Provinces which is a somewhat larger area than the Dominion of Canada. In the year ending June 30, 1873, the U.S. traded with British North American Provinces the following amounts: Exports, $34.6 million and imports, $37.6 million. Beginning 1950, includes Newfoundland and Labrador.

[3] Prior to January 1952, East and West Germany; thereafter, only West Germany.

[4] Figures in italics include gold and silver.

[5] Beginning 1954, excludes Ryukyu Islands. No records available prior to 1855.

[6] Includes Puerto Rico.

[7] For 9 months.

Series U 335–352. Value of General Imports, by Country of Origin: 1790 to 1970

[In millions of dollars. Totals shown here in mixed values. For years ending September 30, 1790–1842; June 30, 1843–1915; thereafter, calendar years. Beginning 1961, includes uranium, thorium, and related products]

Year	Total value[1]	America						Europe					Asia				Australia and Oceania	Africa
		Total	Canada[2]	Cuba	Mexico	Brazil	Other	Total	United Kingdom	France	Germany[3]	Other	Total	Mainland China[4]	Japan[5]	Other		
	335	336	337	338	339	340	341	342	343	344	345	346	347	348	349	350	351	352
1970	39,952	16,928	11,092	(Z)	1,219	670	3,947	11,395	2,194	942	3,127	5,132	9,621	(Z)	5,875	3,746	871	1,113
1969	36,043	15,547	10,384	(Z)	1,029	617	3,517	10,334	2,120	842	2,603	4,769	8,274	(Z)	4,888	3,386	828	1,046
1968	33,226	14,148	9,005	(Z)	910	670	3,563	10,337	2,058	842	2,721	4,716	6,911	(Z)	4,054	2,857	696	1,122
1967	26,812	11,741	7,107	(Z)	749	559	3,326	8,227	1,710	690	1,955	3,872	5,348	(Z)	2,999	2,349	581	906
1966	25,542	10,829	6,125	(Z)	750	600	3,354	7,857	1,786	698	1,796	3,577	5,276	(Z)	2,963	2,313	593	979
1965	21,364	9,203	4,833	(Z)	638	512	3,220	6,292	1,405	615	1,341	2,931	4,528	(Z)	2,414	2,114	453	878
1964	18,684	8,390	4,239	(Z)	643	535	2,973	5,307	1,143	495	1,171	2,498	3,620	(Z)	1,768	1,852	440	917
1963	17,138	7,850	3,829	(Z)	594	562	2,865	4,811	1,079	431	1,003	2,298	3,192	(Z)	1,498	1,694	502	777
1962	16,380	7,591	3,660	7	578	541	2,805	4,621	1,005	428	962	2,226	2,960	(Z)	1,358	1,602	440	754
1961	14,714	6,995	3,270	35	538	562	2,590	4,141	898	435	856	1,952	2,583	(Z)	1,055	1,528	320	672
1960	14,654	6,864	2,901	357	443	570	2,593	4,268	993	396	897	1,982	2,721	(Z)	1,149	1,572	266	534
1959	15,207	7,071	3,042	475	435	628	2,491	4,607	1,137	462	920	2,088	2,603	(Z)	1,029	1,574	338	589
1958	12,792	6,703	2,674	524	454	565	2,486	3,340	864	308	629	1,539	1,983	(Z)	666	1,317	208	557
1957	12,982	7,048	2,907	482	430	700	2,529	3,147	766	256	607	1,518	1,985	(Z)	601	1,384	216	587
1956	12,615	6,856	2,894	457	401	745	2,359	2,963	726	236	494	1,507	1,996	(Z)	558	1,438	203	597
1955	11,384	6,262	2,653	422	397	633	2,157	2,453	616	202	366	1,269	1,876	(Z)	432	1,444	174	619
1954	10,215	5,896	2,377	401	328	682	2,108	2,083	501	157	278	1,147	1,467	(Z)	279	1,188	165	605
1953	10,873	6,117	2,462	431	355	768	2,101	2,335	546	186	277	1,326	1,626	1	262	1,363	201	593
1952	10,717	6,025	2,386	440	410	808	1,981	2,029	485	167	212	1,165	1,813	28	229	1,556	243	607
1951	10,967	5,826	2,275	418	326	911	1,896	2,119	466	263	233	1,157	1,983	45	205	1,733	451	589
1950	8,852	5,063	1,960	406	315	715	1,667	1,449	335	132	104	878	1,638	146	182	1,310	208	494
1949	6,622	3,995	1,551	388	243	552	1,261	981	228	61	45	647	1,184	106	82	996	125	338
1948	7,124	4,099	1,593	375	246	514	1,371	1,171	290	73	32	776	1,296	120	63	1,113	164	394
1947	5,756	3,398	1,127	510	247	446	1,068	877	205	47	6	619	998	117	35	846	156	327
1946	4,942	2,762	883	324	232	408	915	804	158	63	3	580	887	93	81	713	183	306
1945	4,159	2,874	1,125	337	231	311	870	409	90	13	1	305	407	6	(Z)	401	171	297
1944	3,929	2,965	1,260	387	204	293	821	289	84	(Z)	(Z)	205	322	11	(Z)	311	130	222
1943	3,381	2,458	1,024	292	192	228	722	240	105	(Z)	(Z)	135	235	12	(Z)	223	245	204
1942	2,756	1,762	717	161	124	165	595	220	134	1	(Z)	85	340	16	(Z)	324	231	204
1941	3,345	1,657	554	181	98	184	640	281	136	5	3	137	1,088	87	78	923	159	161
1940	2,625	1,089	424	105	76	105	379	390	155	37	5	193	981	93	158	730	35	131
1939	2,318	898	340	105	56	107	290	617	149	62	52	354	700	62	161	477	27	77
1938	1,960	753	260	106	49	98	240	567	118	54	65	330	570	47	127	396	16	55
1937	3,084	1,113	398	148	60	121	386	843	203	76	92	472	967	104	204	659	68	92
1936	2,423	910	376	127	49	102	256	718	200	65	80	373	708	74	172	462	36	51

See footnotes at end of table.

Series U 335–352.   Value of General Imports, by Country of Origin: 1790 to 1970—Con.

[In millions of dollars]

Year	Total value	America						Europe					Asia				Australia and Oceania	Africa
		Total	Canada[2]	Cuba	Mexico	Brazil	Other	Total	United Kingdom	France	Germany[3]	Other	Total	Mainland China[4]	Japan[5]	Other		
	335	336	337	338	339	340	341	342	343	344	345	346	347	348	349	350	351	352
1935	2,047	776	286	104	42	100	244	599	155	58	78	308	605	64	153	388	26	42
1934	1,655	628	232	79	36	91	190	490	115	61	69	245	489	44	119	326	15	33
1933	1,450	520	185	58	31	83	163	463	111	50	78	224	425	38	128	259	13	28
1932	1,323	539	174	58	37	82	188	390	75	45	74	196	362	26	134	202	8	24
1931	2,091	824	266	90	48	110	310	641	135	79	127	300	574	67	206	301	19	33
1930	3,061	1,195	402	122	80	131	460	911	210	114	177	410	854	101	279	474	33	68
1929	4,399	1,621	503	207	118	208	585	1,334	330	171	255	578	1,279	166	432	681	57	109
1928	4,091	1,530	489	203	125	221	492	1,249	349	159	222	519	1,169	140	384	645	53	90
1927	4,185	1,504	475	257	138	203	431	1,265	358	168	201	538	1,268	152	402	714	55	93
1926	4,431	1,580	476	251	169	235	449	1,278	383	152	198	545	1,409	143	401	865	68	96
1925	4,227	1,499	454	262	179	222	382	1,239	413	157	164	505	1,319	169	384	766	78	92
1924	3,610	1,461	399	362	167	179	354	1,096	366	148	139	443	931	118	340	473	49	73
1923	3,792	1,469	416	376	140	143	394	1,157	404	150	161	442	1,020	188	347	485	59	87
1922	3,113	1,181	364	268	132	120	297	991	357	143	117	374	827	135	354	338	49	65
1921	2,509	1,051	335	230	119	96	271	765	239	142	80	304	618	101	251	266	35	40
1920	5,278	2,424	612	722	179	228	683	1,228	514	166	89	459	1,397	193	415	789	80	150
1919	3,904	1,844	495	419	149	234	547	751	309	124	11	307	1,108	154	410	544	89	112
1918	3,031	1,585	452	279	159	98	597	318	149	60	(Z)	109	939	111	302	526	103	86
1917	2,952	1,471	414	249	130	145	533	551	280	99	(Z)	172	821	125	254	442	37	73
1916	2,392	1,086	237	244	105	132	368	633	305	109	6	213	551	80	182	289	60	62
1915	1,674	734	160	186	78	99	211	614	256	77	91	190	272	40	99	133	29	25
1914	1,894	650	161	131	93	101	164	896	294	141	190	271	305	39	107	159	24	19
1913	1,813	580	121	126	78	120	135	893	296	137	189	271	298	39	92	167	17	26
1912	1,653	549	109	120	66	124	130	820	273	125	171	251	249	30	81	138	13	23
1911	1,527	488	101	110	57	101	119	768	261	115	163	229	231	34	79	118	13	27
1910	1,557	503	95	123	59	108	118	806	271	132	169	234	210	30	66	114	20	17
1909	1,312	418	79	97	48	98	96	654	209	108	144	193	207	29	70	108	18	15
1908	1,194	364	75	83	47	75	84	608	190	102	143	173	191	26	68	97	15	16
1907	1,434	424	73	97	57	98	99	747	246	128	162	211	224	33	69	122	18	21
1906	1,227	375	68	85	51	80	91	633	210	108	135	180	192	29	53	110	12	13
1905	1,118	378	62	86	46	100	84	541	176	90	118	157	175	28	52	95	13	11
1904	991	319	52	77	44	76	70	499	166	81	109	143	156	29	47	80	8	9
1903	1,026	297	55	63	41	67	71	547	190	90	120	147	159	27	44	88	10	13
1902	903	271	48	35	40	79	69	475	166	83	102	124	136	21	38	77	8	13
1901	823	255	42	43	29	71	70	430	143	75	100	112	122	18	29	75	7	9
1900	850	224	39	31	29	58	67	441	160	73	97	111	146	27	33	86	29	11
1899	697	199	31	25	23	58	62	354	118	62	84	90	112	19	27	66	23	10
1898	616	183	32	15	19	62	55	306	109	53	70	74	96	20	25	51	23	7
1897	765	213	40	18	19	69	67	430	168	68	111	83	92	20	24	48	20	10
1896	780	236	41	40	17	71	67	419	170	66	94	89	95	22	26	47	20	11
1895	732	246	37	53	16	79	61	384	159	62	81	82	84	21	24	39	13	6
1894	655	267	31	76	29	79	52	295	107	48	69	71	75	17	19	39	14	3
1893	866	286	38	79	34	76	59	458	183	76	96	103	99	21	27	51	17	6
1892	827	325	35	78	28	119	65	392	156	69	83	84	89	20	24	45	17	5
1891	845	282	39	62	27	83	71	459	195	77	97	90	79	19	19	41	20	4
1890	789	238	39	54	23	59	63	450	186	78	99	87	81	16	21	44	17	3
1889	745	243	43	52	21	60	67	403	178	70	82	73	76	17	17	42	19	4
1888	724	224	43	49	17	54	61	407	178	71	78	80	73	17	19	37	16	3
1887	692	211	38	50	15	53	55	391	165	68	81	77	72	19	17	36	15	4
1886	635	191	37	51	11	42	50	358	154	63	69	72	69	19	15	35	14	3
1885	578	183	37	42	9	45	50	319	137	57	63	62	61	16	12	33	12	3
1884	668	212	38	57	9	50	58	371	163	71	65	72	68	16	11	41	13	4
1883	723	222	44	66	8	44	60	410	189	98	57	66	73	20	15	38	13	5
1882	725	238	51	70	8	49	60	398	196	89	56	57	73	20	14	39	12	5
1881	643	215	38	63	8	53	53	341	174	70	53	44	74	22	14	38	8	5
1880	668	212	33	65	7	52	55	371	211	69	52	39	74	22	15	37	7	4
1879	446	172	26	64	5	39	38	216	109	51	36	20	52	16	10	26	4	2
1878	437	176	25	60	5	43	43	204	107	43	35	19	51	16	7	28	4	2
1877	451	182	24	66	5	43	44	214	114	48	33	19	49	11	14	24	4	2
1876	461	170	29	56	5	45	35	232	123	51	35	23	53	12	15	26	3	2
1875	533	191	28	65	5	42	51	281	155	60	40	26	52	13	8	31	5	3
1874	567	209	34	85	4	44	42	302	180	52	44	26	50	18	6	26	3	3
1873	642	204	37	77	4	39	47	361	237	34	61	29	66	26	8	33	5	5
1872	627	191	36	67	4	30	54	365	249	43	46	27	60	27	7	26	5	6
1871	520	170	33	58	3	31	45	297	221	28	25	23	48	20	5	23	1	4

See footnotes at end of table.

Series U 335–352. Value of General Imports, by Country of Origin: 1790 to 1970—Con.

[In millions of dollars]

Year	Total value	America						Europe					Asia				Australia and Oceania	Africa
		Total	Canada²	Cuba	Mexico	Brazil	Other	Total	United Kingdom	France	Germany³	Other	Total	Mainland China⁴	Japan⁵	Other		
	335	336	337	338	339	340	341	342	343	344	345	346	347	348	349	350	351	352
1870	436	153	36	54	3	25	35	241	152	43	27	19	37	15	3	19	2	3
1869	418	147	29	57	2	25	34	235	159	30	25	21	31	13	3	15	2	3
1868	357	130	26	50	2	24	28	196	132	25	22	17	28	11	2	15	1	2
1867	396	111	25	38	1	19	28	245	172	29	27	17	30	12	3	15	7	3
1866	⁶435	132	49	38	2	17	26	266	202	23	26	15	23	10	2	11	4	3
1865	⁶239	100	33	30	6	10	21	109	85	7	10	7	13	5	(Z)	8	1	3
1864	316	112	30	33	6	14	29	179	142	11	14	12	19	10	(Z)	9	6	
1863	243	71	17	21	3	11	19	148	113	11	13	11	20	11	(Z)	9	4	
1862	189	69	19	21	1	13	15	105	75	8	14	8	13	7	(Z)	6	2	
1861	289	94	23	31	1	18	21	166	105	32	15	14	26	11	(Z)	15	3	
1860	354	104	24	32	2	21	25	217	138	43	19	17	29	14	(Z)	15	4	
1859	331	102	19	33	1	22	27	201	126	41	18	16	25	11	(Z)	14	3	
1858	263	79	16	23	1	17	22	153	89	33	14	17	28	11	(Z)	17	3	
1857	348	116	22	45	1	21	27	205	127	46	15	17	25	8	(Z)	17	2	
1856	310	86	21	24	1	19	21	199	122	49	15	13	23	10	(Z)	13	2	
1855	258	70	15	18	1	15	21	165	106	32	13	14	21	11	(Z)	-------	2	
1854	298	72	9	17	1	14	31	204	146	36	17	5	20	11	-------	-------	2	
1853	264	55	7	19	1	15	13	190	130	33	14	13	17	11	-------	-------	2	
1852	207	54	5	18	1	12	18	134	89	25	8	12	18	11	-------	-------	1	
1851	211	49	5	17	1	12	14	148	93	31	10	14	12	7	-------	-------	2	
1850	174	38	5	10	1	9	13	124	75	27	9	13	11	7	-------	-------	1	
1849	141	31	2	10	1	8	10	100	58	24	8	10	9	6	-------	-------	1	
1848	149	33	3	12	1	8	9	103	60	28	6	9	12	8	-------	-------	1	
1847	122	30	1	12	(Z)	7	10	83	48	24	4	7	8	6	-------	-------	1	
1846	118	27	1	8	1	7	10	80	45	24	3	8	10	7	-------	-------	1	
1845	113	25	1	6	1	6	11	78	45	21	3	9	10	7	-------	-------	(Z)	
1844	103	28	1	10	1	7	9	67	41	17	2	7	8	5	-------	-------	(Z)	
1843⁷	42	16	(Z)	4	1	4	7	20	12	5	1	2	6	4	-------	-------	1	
1842	96	26	1	7	1	6	11	61	34	17	2	8	9	5	-------	-------	(Z)	
1841	123	33	1	11	1	6	14	83	46	24	2	11	7	4	-------	-------	(Z)	
1840	98	25	1	9	1	5	9	62	33	16	3	10	10	7	-------	-------	1	
1839	156	35	2	12	1	5	15	114	65	32	5	12	6	4	-------	-------	1	
1838	96	26	1	11	1	3	10	62	36	16	3	7	7	5	-------	-------	1	
1837	130	28	2	11	1	5	9	86	45	21	6	14	14	9	-------	-------	2	
1836	177	35	2	13	1	7	12	128	76	32	5	15	13	7	-------	-------	1	
1835	137	28	1	11	1	6	9	99	60	22	4	13	9	6	-------	-------	1	
1834	109	26	1	8	1	5	11	71	41	15	3	12	11	8	-------	-------	1	
1833	101	27	1	10	1	5	10	63	38	13	2	10	11	8	-------	-------	(Z)	
1832	95	22	1	7	1	4	9	63	37	12	3	11	9	5	-------	-------	1	
1831	96	22	1	8	1	2	10	68	44	14	4	6	5	3	-------	-------	1	
1830	63	17	(Z)	5	1	2	9	40	24	8	2	6	5	4	-------	-------	1	
1829	67	17	(Z)	5	1	2	9	44	25	9	2	8	6	5	-------	-------	(Z)	
1828	81	20	(Z)	6	1	3	10	54	33	9	3	9	7	5	-------	-------	(Z)	
1827	71	19	(Z)	7	1	2	9	48	30	8	2	8	4	4	-------	-------	(Z)	
1826	78	20	(Z)	7	1	2	10	46	26	8	3	9	11	7	-------	-------	1	
1825	90	21	(Z)	7	1	2	11	59	37	11	3	8	10	8	-------	-------	(Z)	
1824	72	22	(Z)	7	-------	2	13	44	28	7	2	7	6	6	-------	-------	(Z)	
1823	72	18	(Z)	7	-------	1	10	43	28	6	2	7	11	7	-------	-------	(Z)	
1822	80	19	(Z)	7	-------	1	11	51	35	6	2	8	9	5	-------	-------	1	
1821	55	15	(Z)	5	-------	1	9	35	24	4	1	6	5	3	-------	-------	(Z)	

Year	Total, value 335	Year	Total, value 335	Year	Total, value 335	Year	Total, value 335	Year	Total, value 335	Year	Total, value 335
1820	74	1815	113	1810	85	1805	121	1800	91	1795	70
1819	87	1814	13	1809	59	1804	85	1799	79	1794	35
1818	122	1813	22	1808	57	1803	65	1798	69	1793	31
1817	99	1812	77	1807	139	1802	76	1797	75	1792	32
1816	147	1811	53	1806	129	1801	111	1796	81	1791	29
										1790	23

Z   Less than $500,000.
¹ Beginning 1962, includes data on imports from countries which could not be identified because of illegible reporting on import entries for low valued shipments not included in the detail figures.
² Prior to 1873, data are for trade with British North American Provinces which is a somewhat larger area than the Dominion of Canada. In the year ending June 30, 1873, the U.S. traded with British North American Provinces the following amounts: Exports, $34.6 million and imports, $37.6 million. Beginning 1947, includes Newfoundland and Labrador.
³ Prior to January 1952, East and West Germany; thereafter, only West Germany.
⁴ Figures in italics include gold and silver.
⁵ Beginning 1954, excludes Ryukyu Islands. No records available prior to 1855.
⁶ Agrees with source; however, figures for components do not add to total shown.
⁷ For 9 months.

Business Enterprise

Business Population (Series V 1-107)

V 1-107. General note.

Statistics on the total number and the size distribution of business firms must be used with caution. No governmental process records all firms, and an entirely satisfactory definition of a firm seems impossible. The boundary between self-employment and conduct of a business firm is hazy at best. In addition, there are problems of inactive or partly (e.g., seasonally) inactive firms, joint ventures, partial interests, ownership of multiple firms by individuals and families, etc. Moreover, the characteristic which causes an enterprise to be counted as, for example, a corporation, an employer subject to social security, or an operator of an establishment requiring a sanitary or safety license, varies with laws creating these categories and with degree of thoroughness of administration of these laws.

These difficulties are compounded when an attempt is made to group firms into industrial categories, because industry boundaries must be arbitrary, and the assignment of a firm on one side of the boundary or another may be based on a 50-percent rule or on some convention lacking analytic justification. Or the activity may not fit well into any recognized category.

The statistical importance of these problems is great because of the unusual size distribution of the business population, which contains a large number of very small firms, and a minute proportion of larger firms accounting for a substantial or even predominant fraction of total activity. Many small firms are on the boundary line between recognition and nonrecognition (enumeration or nonenumeration), so that a slight difference in method or source, particularly one of which the statistician is unaware, may generate considerable but spurious change or absence of change in the total number of firms. If, however, the object of estimation is not number of firms but total activity, the radically unequal size distribution becomes a great advantage because it permits more efficient sample design at lower cost.

The number and percentage of business firms, therefore, must be used with a realization that the meaning of a business firm is not always certain and that the figures are subject to considerable error. The most meaningful statistics of the business population are those which are based on some consistent criterion or definition over a period of years. The business population studies of the U.S. Bureau of Economic Analysis may be said to have inaugurated the publication of such satisfactory statistics.

The record of one particular year's activity is in effect a single observation out of the infinite number which might be generated by the structural condition which is the object of measurement. Strikes, accidents, and cyclical fluctuations, with highly unequal impact upon various branches of industry, cause a divergence of the actual year's activity from the theoretically true or representative (average) year. Furthermore, if the incidence of mergers (series V 38–39) is substantial, a given year may be the peak or trough of a short-run change in concentration. Moreover, concentration measures may be strongly affected by the arbitrary nature of industry subdivisions, changes in industry classification between census years, and turnover of companies among those designated as the largest.

V 1-12. Proprietorships, partnerships, and corporations—Number, receipts, and profit, 1939–1970.

Source: U.S. Internal Revenue Service. *Statistics of Income, Business Income Tax Returns,* 1965 and 1968 issues; *Statistics of Income, Individual Income Tax Returns* and *Statistics of Income, Corporation Income Tax Returns,* various issues; and unpublished data.

Proprietorships, partnerships, and corporations encompass virtually all American businesses except those reported to the Internal Revenue Service by fiduciary agents of estates and trusts and the business activities of "exempt" organizations.

"Proprietor" applies to anyone with income from a single-owner business who had specified minimums of self-employment income or gross income during the year. (For historical details, see *Statistics of Income, Individual Income Tax Returns,* 1965, p. 206.) Thus, the proprietorship data cover the farmers, businessmen, and professionals who are in business for themselves on a full-time or part-time basis. Generally, a proprietor corresponds to a "self-employed" person, other than partners. However, some types of persons defined as self-employed in the Internal Revenue Code are not considered as businessmen in the tax returns report. The most important of these are clergymen and public officials, such as sheriffs, notaries public, etc. Often, classification of a person as a proprietor depended entirely on how he reported his income.

"Partnership" applies to any group of two or more persons conducting a business for profit unless it is specifically classified as a corporation for tax purposes.

"Corporation" includes most businesses incorporated under State law and, in addition, many unincorporated associations, such as mutual insurance societies, savings and loan associations, and real estate investment trusts.

V 1, V 4, V 7, and **V 10,** number of business organizations. Represents the number of active businesses operated as proprietorships by individuals, the number of active partnerships, and, for corporations, the number of active corporation tax returns filed, including those for small business corporations. The total number of corporations is slightly understated to the extent that subsidiary corporations are included in a consolidated return filed by a parent corporation.

V 5-6, business receipts and net profit (less loss) for proprietorships. In general, series V 5 represents gross receipts from sales and operations reduced by the cost of returned goods and allowances. Receipts include incidental income from such things as sale of scrap or cash rebates. Dividends, interest, rents, royalties, and other investment-type income are generally excluded, although rents or interest that represent income from business operations are sometimes included (e.g. rents received by real estate operators and interest received by small loan companies). Series V 6 represents the difference between business receipts and the sum of cost of goods sold and other business deductions. It does not reflect investment income; and salaries to owners and contributions or gifts are not allowed as deductions from proprietorship business receipts.

V 8-9, total receipts and net profit (less loss) for partnerships. Series V 8 represents the sum of business receipts (the income from the partnership's principal business activity), investment income such as interest, rents, royalties, nonqualifying dividends, net gain from sale or exchange of noncapital assets, income from farms and other partnerships, and other income. Total receipts do not reflect net losses from the foregoing sources.

Series V 9 represents the difference between total receipts and the sum of cost of sales and operations and other business deductions. The deductions for partnerships exclude both contributions or gifts and additional first-year depreciation.

The term "net profit" is used for both proprietorships and partnerships although it is not strictly comparable for the two forms of business organization. Three differences are (1) investment income is reflected in the partnership, but not in the proprietorship, net profit, (2) salaries paid to the owner(s) are a business deduction for partnerships but not for proprietorships, and (3) additional first-year depreciation is a deduction in the computation of proprietorship, but not partnership, net profit.

V 11–12, total receipts and net profit (less loss) for corporations. Series V 11 includes the gross taxable receipts (i.e., business receipts, taxable investment, income, and certain foreign income) before deduction of cost of sales and operations and net losses from sales of noncapital assets. It also includes nontaxable interest, but excludes all other nontaxable income recognized by the corporation.

The source refers to series V 12 as "net income (or deficit)." It is defined as the difference between gross taxable receipts and the sum of cost of sales and operations and other business deductions allowable for tax purposes. The concept of net income for corporations is not strictly comparable with the concept of net profit for proprietorships and partnerships.

V 13–19. Number of firms in operation, by major industry group, 1929–1963.

Source: U.S. Bureau of Economic Analysis (formerly Office of Business Economics). 1929–1939, *Survey of Current Business*, January 1954, p. 12; 1940–1950, unpublished data; 1951–1958, *Survey of Current Business*, May 1959, p. 18; 1959–1963, *Survey of Current Business*, June 1963, p. 2.

These estimates are based primarily on data from the Bureau of Old-Age and Survivors Insurance and the Internal Revenue Service, and are revised from time to time by the Bureau of Economic Analysis (BEA), formerly the Office of Business Economics. The last substantial revision was made in January 1963 and revealed errors in the earlier estimates for absolute number and rate of growth; these errors were due partly to the cumulative effect of imperfect estimates for discontinued businesses. BEA defines a firm as a business organization under one management; it may include one or more plants or outlets. A self-employed person is considered a firm only if he has either one or more employees or has an established place of business. Concerns owned or controlled by the same interests are not combined. Agriculture and professional services are excluded. A firm conducting more than one kind of business is classified by industry according to the major activity of the firm as a whole. Revisions of the Standard Industrial Classification (see Bureau of the Budget, *Standard Industrial Classification Manual*, 1963) have, therefore, affected the industrial distribution of firms.

V 20–30. Business formation and business failures, 1857–1970.

Source: Series **V 20** and **V 23–30,** Dun & Bradstreet, Inc., 1857–1919, *Dun & Bradstreet Reference Book and Failure Statistics* (a printed mail folder distributed by Dun & Bradstreet); 1920–1970, *The Failure Record Through 1971*, and unpublished data. Series **V 21–22,** U.S. Bureau of Economic Analysis. Series **V 21,** *1971 Business Statistics*, p. 37; series **V 22,** *Business Conditions Digest*, June 1971, series B 12.

V 20, total concerns in business. This series represents the number of business enterprises listed in the *Reference Book*. The figures are for conterminous United States (i.e., excluding Alaska and Hawaii) and represent listings in the books published nearest to July 1 of each year. The listings include types of business which are seekers of commercial credit in the accepted sense of the term; namely, manufacturers, wholesalers, retailers, building contractors, and certain types of commercial service, including public utilities, water carriers, motor carriers, and airlines. Specific types of business not covered are finance, insurance, and real estate companies; railroads; terminals; amusements; and many small one-man services. Neither professions nor farmers are included.

V 21, new business incorporations. This series represents the total number of stock corporations issued charters under the general business corporation laws of the various States and the District of Columbia. The statistics include completely new businesses that have incorporated, existing businesses changed from the noncorporate to the corporate form of organization, existing corporations given certificates of authority to operate also in another State, and existing corporations transferred to a new State. Data for incorporations in the District of Columbia are included beginning January 1963.

V 22, index of net business formation. This series is compiled from monthly national data on number of new business incorporations, number of business failures, and confidential data on telephones installed. These components are adjusted for seasonal variation and number of trading days before being combined into the index.

V 23–26, business failure rate and business failures. The failure rate is obtained by dividing total failures by the total number of industrial and commercial enterprises listed in the Dun & Bradstreet *Reference Book*. Failures are defined as concerns involved in court procedures or voluntary actions, probably ending in loss to creditors. These include, but are not limited to, discontinuances following assignment or attachment of goods, bankruptcy petitions, foreclosure, etc.; voluntary withdrawals with known loss to creditors; enterprises involved in court action such as receivership; businesses making voluntary arrangements with creditors out of court; and since June 1934 (enactment of the Bankruptcy Act), reorganization which may or may not lead to discontinuance.

V 27–30, liabilities. Average liability per failure is obtained by dividing total liabilities by total concerns. Liabilities represent primarily current indebtedness, including accounts and notes payable on secured or unsecured obligations held by banks, officers, affiliates, suppliers, or government at all levels. Beginning in 1933, certain types of enterprises characterized by heavy deferred obligations were eliminated from the data, thus conferring a slight downward bias in average liability figures as compared with earlier years. These series have undergone two revisions. In 1933, they were revised to exclude real estate and finance companies. This revision brought the failure record more nearly in accordance with type of concerns covered by series V 20. In 1939, the series were revised to include voluntary discontinuances with loss to creditors, and small concerns forced out of business with insufficient assets to cover all claims.

V 31–37. Number of new, discontinued, and transferred businesses, by major industry group, 1940–1962.

Source: See source for series V 13–19.

New businesses include only firms which have been newly established. Discontinued businesses include closures of all kinds without reference to the reason for going out of business. A firm which is maintained as a business entity but undergoes a change of ownership is counted as a transferred business, not as a discontinuance. Partnerships in which a member is added or dropped, corporations that are reorganized or reincorporated, and businesses sold or otherwise acquired by new owners or changed in legal form of organization (such as partnership to corporation) are considered transfers. Note should be taken of the large differences between figures for failures in series V 24 and those for discontinued businesses in series V 31.

V 38–40. Recorded mergers in manufacturing and mining, 1895–1970.

Source: 1895–1918, Ralph L. Nelson, *Merger Movements in American Industry*, table 14, p. 37, Princeton University Press, 1959 (copyright, National Bureau of Economic Research, New York); 1919–1930, Carl Eis, *The 1919–1930 Merger Movement in American Industry*, table 1 (reprinted from *The Journal of Law and Economics*, vol. XII (2), October 1969, The University of Chicago (copyright)); U.S. Federal Trade Commission, 1919–1955, *Report on Corporate Mergers and Acquisitions*, 1955; 1956–1970, *Current Trends in Merger Activity, 1970*.

Methods of estimation of the Nelson figures are explained in chapters II and III of his book; the basic source of the figures is chiefly the *Commercial and Financial Chronicle*. The Eis figures are an extension of the same series, using essentially the same source material.

Federal Trade Commission (FTC) estimates include mergers reported by Moody's Investors Service, Inc., and Standard and Poor's Corporation. For 1919–1939, the estimates were first made by Willard L. Thorp in various publications, and then continued by the FTC. For complete sources and related data, see the FTC reports cited above.

The annual totals of reported mergers are only a small fraction of all "transferred businesses," as shown in series V 31–37. Series V 38–39 are essentially a count of all mergers and acquisitions involving corporations with widely held or publicly traded securities outstanding. There are two offsetting biases of uncertain amount: Mergers may be announced but not actually consummated; small acquisitions by registered manufacturing companies may be consummated without announcement in the sources used.

The FTC series and the Nelson-Eis series use different sources, each of which changes in degree of coverage over time, and are not comparable. The FTC estimates include a more complete recording of smaller mergers, so that average capitalization or assets per merger would on this account tend to decrease, and total assets to increase. However, value data are not available for this series because the FTC does not collect such data for concerns with assets of less than $10 million. Such concerns represented 93 percent of the 1,351 concerns acquired in 1970.

V 41–53. Number of corporations, by industrial division, 1916–1970.

Source: 1916–1933, U.S. Bureau of Internal Revenue, *Statistics of Income*, various annual issues; 1934–1970, U.S. Internal Revenue Service, *Statistics of Income, Corporation Income Tax Returns*, various annual issues.

After 1925, trade is divided into wholesale trade, retail trade, and trade not allocable. The latter, series V 48, varies widely owing to changes in inclusion. The joint figure of wholesale and retail trade for 1916 is not comparable with figures for subsequent years because the "merchandising companies" group was not as inclusive as the "wholesale trade" and "retail trade" groups. This is reflected in the very large figure for all other active corporations. The same is true of "finance, insurance, and real estate" (series V 50) for 1916, then labeled "banks and insurance companies."

V 54–65. Percent of total corporate net income reported by small and large corporations (with net income only), 1918–1939.

Source: U.S. Office of Business Economics, *Survey of Current Business*, March 1944, p. 11.

The data are based on a special tabulation of corporate income tax records by the then Bureau of Internal Revenue. See general note for series V 1–107.

V 66–77. Income of unincorporated enterprises, by industry, 1929–1970.

Source: U.S. Bureau of Economic Analysis (formerly Office of Business Economics). 1929–1963, *The National Income and Product Accounts of the United States, 1929–1965*; 1964–1967, *U.S. National Income and Product Accounts, 1964–67*; 1968–1970, *Survey of Current Business*, July 1972. Table 6.8.

These series measure the earnings of unincorporated business—sole proprietorships, partnerships, and producers' cooperatives—from their current business operations, other than the supplementary income of individuals derived from renting property. Capital gains and losses are excluded, and no deduction is made for depletion.

Estimation in this field has generally required laborious piecing together and adjustment of various types of data from numerous sources. The estimates rely heavily on tax-return tabulations of the incomes of sole proprietorships and partnerships prepared by the Internal Revenue Service.

For a general summary of estimation sources and methods, see Office of Business Economics, *National Income*, 1954 edition, p. 76 ff.

V 78–107. Manufacturing and trade—sales and inventories, 1948–1970.

Source: U.S. Bureau of Economic Analysis (formerly Office of Business Economics), *1971 Business Statistics*, pp. 23–25.

V 78–87, sales. These are estimated aggregate dollar values for the year. "Sales" means essentially billings or shipments for manufacturing and sales or shipments for retail and wholesale trade. In wholesale trade, however, some respondents probably report orders (bookings) as sales.

V 79–81, sales, manufacturing. As used here, "sales" represents manufacturers' receipts, billings, or the value of products shipped, less discounts, returns, and allowances, and exclude freight charges and excise taxes. Shipments for export as well as for domestic use are included. Shipments by foreign subsidiaries are excluded, but those to a foreign subsidiary by a domestic firm are included. The shipments figures from the Bureau of the Census, *Annual Survey of Manufactures*, to which these series are benchmarked, include interplant transfers as well as commercial sales. The figures include adjustments for trading-day and calendar-month variations.

V 82–84, sales, retail trade. The definition of sales of retail stores is in accordance with the 1963 Census of Business. Sales are total receipts from customers after deductions of refunds and allowances for merchandise returned by customers, and include receipts from repairs and from other services to customers, sales for resale, and sales and excise taxes. The data represent total sales and receipts of all establishments engaged primarily in retail trade; they do not include sales at retail by manufacturers, wholesalers, service establishments, or other businesses whose primary activity is not retail trade. The breakdown into durable goods stores and nondurable goods stores is based on the durability of the commodities accounting for the major portion of the sales of each kind-of-business group.

Retail sales estimates are developed as direct measures from a sample representing all sizes of stores, firms, or organizations, and all kinds of retail business throughout the country. Because the estimates obtained are based on a sample, the results are not expected to be in exact agreement with those that would be obtained from a complete census of retail stores in which the same enumeration procedure would be used. For details concerning the sample, see *1971 Business Statistics*, blue pp. 58–59.

V 85–87, sales, merchant wholesalers. See text for series T 375–383.

V 89–91, inventories, manufacturing. Inventory data are book values of stocks on hand at the end of the period, and include materials and supplies, goods in process, and finished goods. Inventories associated with the nonmanufacturing activities of the company are excluded. Manufacturers' inventories are generally valued at the lower of cost or market price while retail and wholesale inventories are valued at cost of merchandise on hand. About one-fifth of manufacturers' inventories are valued on a last-in-first-out basis (see general note for series V 108–305) which is much less prevalent in trade although it is used extensively by department stores. Changes in the book value of inventories reflect movements of replacement costs as well as changes in physical volume.

V 92–94, inventories, retail trade. These data represent estimated book values of nationwide retailers' inventories, valued at the cost of merchandise on hand. Data for Alaska and Hawaii are included beginning 1946.

The breakdown into durable and nondurable inventories is based on the durability of the commodities accounting for the major portion of the retailers' sales. Thus, nondurable items carried by the retailers dealing primarily in durable goods would be reported in durable goods inventories.

V 95–97, inventories, merchant wholesalers. See the text for series T 375–383.

V 98–107, inventory-sales ratios. See the text for stock-sales ratios, series T 375–383.

Series **V 1–12.** Proprietorships, Partnerships, and Corporations—Number, Receipts, and Profit: 1939 to 1970

[Number in thousands; money figures in billions of dollars. Based on sample of unaudited tax returns filed for accounting periods ending between July 1 of year shown and June 30 of following year]

Year	Total business enterprises			Proprietorships			Partnerships			Corporations		
	Number	Receipts	Net profit (less loss)	Number	Business receipts	Net profit (less loss)	Number	Total receipts	Net profit (less loss)	Number	Total receipts	Net profit (less loss)
	1	2	3	4	5	6	7	8	9	10	11	12
1970	12,000	2,082	109	9,399	238	33	936	93	10	1,665	1,751	66
1969	12,008	2,001	124	9,429	234	34	920	87	10	1,659	1,680	80
1968	11,672	1,813	129	9,212	222	32	918	83	11	1,542	1,508	86
1967	11,566	1,666	119	9,126	211	30	906	80	11	1,534	1,375	78
1966	11,479	1,594	121	9,087	207	30	923	80	10	1,469	1,307	81
1965	11,417	1,469	112	9,078	199	28	914	75	10	1,424	1,195	74
1964	11,489	1,351	97	9,193	189	26	922	75	9	1,374	1,087	62
1963	11,383	1,264	87	9,136	182	24	924	73	9	1,323	1,009	54
1962	11,383	1,201	83	9,183	178	24	932	74	9	1,268	949	50
1961	11,371	1,119	78	9,242	171	23	939	75	9	1,190	873	46
1960	11,171	1,094	73	9,090	171	21	941	74	8	1,141	849	44
1959	11,166	1,071	78	9,142	176	22	949	78	9	1,074	817	47
1958	10,744	(NA)	69	8,800	163	21	954	78	9	990	735	39
1957	10,648	(NA)	73	8,738	163	20	971	82	9	940	720	44
1956	(NA)	(NA)	(NA)	8,973	(NA)	21	(NA)	(NA)	(NA)	886	680	47
1955	(NA)	(NA)	(NA)	8,239	139	18	(NA)	(NA)	(NA)	807	642	47
1954	(NA)	(NA)	(NA)	7,786	(NA)	17	(NA)	(NA)	(NA)	723	555	36
1953	9,371	783	64	7,715	144	17	959	79	8	698	558	39
1952	(NA)	(NA)	(NA)	6,873	(NA)	16	(NA)	(NA)	(NA)	672	531	38
1951	(NA)	(NA)	(NA)	7,340	132	17	(NA)	(NA)	(NA)	652	517	44
1950	(NA)	(NA)	(NA)	6,865	(NA)	15	(NA)	(NA)	(NA)	629	458	43
1949	(NA)	(NA)	(NA)	6,901	110	14	(NA)	(NA)	(NA)	615	393	28
1948	(NA)	(NA)	(NA)	7,208	(NA)	17	(NA)	(NA)	(NA)	594	411	34
1947	8,065	530	54	6,624	101	15	889	60	8	552	368	31
1946	(NA)	(NA)	(NA)	6,944	(NA)	15	(NA)	(NA)	(NA)	491	289	25
1945	6,738	382	40	5,689	79	12	627	47	7	421	255	21
1944	(NA)	(NA)	(NA)	6,134	66	12	(NA)	(NA)	(NA)	412	262	26
1943	(NA)	(NA)	(NA)	5,121	58	11	(NA)	(NA)	(NA)	421	250	28
1942	(NA)	(NA)	(NA)	(NA)	(NA)	9	(NA)	(NA)	(NA)	443	218	23
1941	(NA)	(NA)	(NA)	3,169	38	6	(NA)	(NA)	(NA)	469	190	16
1940	(NA)	(NA)	(NA)	2,018	31	4	(NA)	(NA)	(NA)	473	148	9
1939	1,793	172	12	1,052	24	3	271	13	2	470	133	7

NA Not available.

Series **V 13–19.** Number of Firms in Operation, by Major Industry Group: 1929 to 1963

[**In thousands.** Annual averages, 1929–1939; thereafter, as of January 1]

Year	All industries	Contract construction	Manufacturing	Wholesale trade	Retail trade	Service industries	All other [1]
	13	14	15	16	17	18	19
1963	4,797	470	313	332	2,032	942	708
1962	4,755	473	317	327	2,022	918	698
1961	4,713	477	322	322	2,011	895	686
1960	4,658	476	323	317	1,997	872	674
1959	4,583	464	323	312	1,977	848	658
1958	4,533	466	329	309	1,955	828	647
1957	4,471	465	332	304	1,926	810	634
1956	4,381	452	327	297	1,903	790	612
1955	4,287	430	326	292	1,874	773	592
1954	4,240	417	331	288	1,861	760	582
1953	4,188	405	331	283	1,846	750	573
1952	4,118	387	328	276	1,831	740	557
1951	4,067	377	323	269	1,821	733	545
1950	4,009	353	318	263	1,802	736	536
1949	3,984	339	322	260	1,783	739	541
1948	3,873	310	316	254	1,730	728	535
1947	3,651	268	302	243	1,627	686	523
1946	3,242	199	264	209	1,458	614	498
1945	2,995	160	253	186	1,356	567	472
1944	2,839	147	246	170	1,291	536	449
1943	3,030	164	243	182	1,401	579	461
1942	3,295	187	241	201	1,561	620	485
1941	3,276	194	230	190	1,561	615	486
1940	3,319	202	222	184	1,580	639	492
1939	3,222	199	221	176	1,535	615	476
1938	3,074	193	202	167	1,452	605	455
1937	3,136	199	214	171	1,469	631	452
1936	3,070	192	211	165	1,430	629	443
1935	2,992	180	205	157	1,387	616	447
1934	2,884	180	188	152	1,337	592	435
1933	2,782	185	167	142	1,291	575	422
1932	2,828	202	166	142	1,302	588	428
1931	2,916	219	195	144	1,317	592	449
1930	2,994	230	228	147	1,326	599	464
1929	3,029	234	257	148	1,327	591	472

[1] Mining and quarrying; transportation, communication, and other public utilities; and finance, insurance, and real estate.

Series V 20–30. Business Formation and Business Failures: 1857 to 1970

Year	Total concerns in business (1,000)	New business incorporations (number)	Index of net business formation (1967=100)	Business failure rate [2]	Number of failures — Total	Number of failures — Under $100,000	Number of failures — $100,000 and over	Current liabilities Total (mil. dol.)	Current liabilities Under $100,000	Current liabilities $100,000 and over	Average liability per failure ($1,000)
	20	21	22	23	24	25	26	27	28	29	30
1970	2,442	264,209	108.1	44	10,748	8,019	2,729	1,888	269	1,618	175.6
1969	2,444	274,267	116.2	37	9,154	7,192	1,962	1,142	231	911	124.8
1968	2,481	233,635	109.8	39	9,636	7,829	1,807	941	241	700	97.7
1967	2,519	206,569	100.1	49	12,364	10,144	2,220	1,265	298	967	102.3
1966	2,520	200,010	98.2	52	13,061	10,833	2,228	1,386	322	1,064	106.1
1965	2,527	203,897	98.5	53	13,514	11,340	2,174	1,322	322	1,000	97.8
1964	2,524	197,724	97.2	53	13,501	11,346	2,155	1,329	314	1,016	98.5
1963	2,544	186,404	93.3	56	14,374	12,192	2,182	1,353	321	1,032	94.1
1962	2,589	182,057	90.7	61	15,782	13,772	2,010	1,214	347	867	76.9
1961	2,641	181,535	88.4	64	17,075	15,006	2,069	1,090	370	720	63.8
1960	2,708	182,713	92.4	57	15,445	13,650	1,795	939	327	611	60.8
1959	2,708	193,067	96.7	52	14,053	12,707	1,346	693	279	414	49.3
1958	2,675	150,781	89.4	56	14,964	13,499	1,465	728	298	431	48.7
1957	2,652	137,112	90.3	52	13,739	12,547	1,192	615	267	348	44.8
1956	2,629	141,163	95.0	48	12,686	11,615	1,071	563	240	323	44.4
1955	2,633	139,915	98.9	42	10,969	10,113	856	449	206	243	41.0
1954	2,632	117,411	91.3	42	11,086	10,226	860	463	211	251	41.7
1953	2,667	102,706	94.4	33	8,862	8,075	787	394	168	227	44.5
1952	2,637	92,946	98.1	29	7,611	7,081	530	283	132	151	37.2
1951	2,608	83,778	98.2	31	8,058	7,626	432	260	132	128	32.2
1950	2,687	93,092	93.1	34	9,162	8,746	416	248	151	97	27.1
1949	2,679	85,640	87.9	34	9,246	8,708	538	308	161	147	33.3
1948	2,550	96,346	112.5	20	5,250	4,853	397	235	94	141	44.7
1947	2,405	112,897	--------	14	3,474	3,103	371	205	64	141	58.9
1946	2,142	132,916	--------	5	1,129	1,003	126	67	16	52	59.7
1945	1,909	--------	--------	4	809	759	50	30	11	19	37.4
1944	1,855	--------	--------	7	1,222	1,176	46	32	15	17	25.9
1943	2,023	--------	--------	16	3,221	3,155	66	45	30	15	14.1
1942	2,152	--------	--------	45	9,405	9,282	123	101	80	21	10.7
1941	2,171	--------	--------	55	11,848	11,685	163	136	101	35	11.5
1940	2,156	--------	--------	63	13,619	13,400	219	167	120	47	12.2
1939 [3]	2,116	--------	--------	70	14,768	14,541	227	183	133	50	12.4
1938	2,102	--------	--------	61	12,836	12,553	283	247	140	106	19.2
1937	2,057	--------	--------	46	9,490	9,203	287	183	102	81	19.3
1936	2,010	--------	--------	48	9,607	9,285	322	203	(NA)	(NA)	21.1
1935	1,983	--------	--------	62	12,244	11,691	553	311	(NA)	(NA)	25.4
1934	1,974	--------	--------	61	12,091	11,421	670	334	(NA)	(NA)	27.6
1933 [3]	1,961	--------	--------	100	19,859	18,880	979	458	216	242	23.0
1932	2,077	--------	--------	154	31,822	(NA)	(NA)	928	(NA)	(NA)	29.2
1931	2,125	--------	--------	133	28,285	(NA)	(NA)	736	(NA)	(NA)	26.0
1930	2,183	--------	--------	122	26,355	(NA)	(NA)	668	(NA)	(NA)	25.4
1929	2,213	--------	--------	104	22,909	22,165	744	483	262	222	21.1
1928	2,199	--------	--------	109	23,842	--------	--------	490	--------	--------	20.5
1927	2,172	--------	--------	106	23,146	--------	--------	520	--------	--------	22.5
1926	2,158	--------	--------	101	21,773	--------	--------	409	--------	--------	18.8
1925	2,113	--------	--------	100	21,214	--------	--------	444	--------	--------	20.9
1924	2,047	--------	--------	100	20,615	--------	--------	543	--------	--------	26.4
1923	1,996	--------	--------	93	18,718	--------	--------	539	--------	--------	28.8
1922	1,983	--------	--------	120	23,676	--------	--------	624	--------	--------	26.4
1921	1,927	--------	--------	102	19,652	--------	--------	627	--------	--------	31.9

Year	Total concerns in business (1,000)	Business failure rate [2]	Number of failures	Current liabilities Total (mil. dol.)	Current liabilities Average liability per failure ($1,000)	Year	Total concerns in business (1,000)	Business failure rate [2]	Number of failures	Current liabilities Total (mil. dol.)	Current liabilities Average liability per failure ($1,000)
	20	23	24	27	30		20	23	24	27	30
1920	1,821	48	8,881	295	33.2	1900	1,174	92	10,774	138	12.9
1919	1,711	37	6,451	113	17.6	1899	1,148	82	9,337	91	9.7
1918	1,708	59	9,982	163	16.3	1898	1,106	111	12,186	131	10.7
1917	1,733	80	13,855	182	13.2	1897	1,059	125	13,351	154	11.6
1916	1,708	100	16,993	196	11.5	1896	1,152	133	15,088	226	15.0
1915	1,675	133	22,156	302	13.6	1895	1,209	112	13,197	173	13.1
1914	1,655	118	18,280	358	19.6	1894	1,114	123	13,885	173	12.5
1913	1,617	98	16,037	273	17.0	1893	1,193	130	15,242	347	22.8
1912	1,564	100	15,452	203	13.1	1892	1,173	89	10,344	114	11.0
1911	1,525	88	13,441	191	14.2	1891	1,143	107	12,273	190	15.5
1910	1,515	84	12,652	202	15.9	1890	1,111	99	10,907	190	17.4
1909	1,486	87	12,924	154	11.9	1889	1,051	103	10,882	149	13.7
1908	1,448	108	15,690	222	14.2	1888	1,047	103	10,679	124	11.6
1907	1,418	83	11,725	197	16.8	1887	994	97	9,634	168	17.4
1906	1,393	77	10,682	119	11.2	1886	970	101	9,834	115	11.7
1905	1,357	85	11,520	103	8.9	1885	920	116	10,637	134	11.7
1904	1,320	92	12,199	144	11.8	1884	905	121	10,968	226	20.6
1903	1,281	94	12,069	155	12.9	1883	864	106	9,184	173	18.8
1902	1,253	93	11,615	117	10.1	1882	822	82	6,738	102	15.1
1901	1,219	90	11,002	113	10.3	1881	782	71	5,582	81	14.5

See footnotes at end of table.

Series V 20–30. Business Formation and Business Failures: 1857 to 1970—Con.

Year	Total concerns in business (1,000)	Business failures [1]				Year	Total concerns in business (1,000)	Business failures [1]			
		Business failure rate [2]	Number of failures	Current liabilities				Business failure rate [2]	Number of failures	Current liabilities	
				Total (mil. dol.)	Average liability per failure ($1,000)					Total (mil. dol.)	Average liability per failure ($1,000)
	20	23	24	27	30		20	23	24	27	30
1880	747	63	4,735	66	13.9	1868	(NA)	(NA)	2,608	64	24.4
1879	702	95	6,658	98	14.7	1867	(NA)	(NA)	2,780	97	34.8
1878	661	158	10,478	234	22.4	1866	(NA)	(NA)	1,505	54	35.7
1877	637	139	8,872	191	21.5	1865	(NA)	(NA)	530	18	33.3
1876	639	142	9,092	191	21.0	1864	(NA)	(NA)	520	9	16.5
1875	603	128	7,740	201	26.0	1863	(NA)	(NA)	495	8	16.0
1874	559	104	5,830	155	26.6	1862	(NA)	(NA)	1,652	23	14.0
1873	494	105	5,183	229	44.1	1861	(NA)	(NA)	6,993	207	29.6
1872	500	81	4,069	121	29.8	1860	(NA)	(NA)	3,676	80	21.7
1871	457	64	2,915	85	29.2	1859		230	170	3,913	64	16.5
1870	427	83	3,546	88	24.9	1858	(NA)	(NA)	4,225	96	22.7
1869	(NA)	(NA)	2,799	75	26.8	1857	204		242	4,932	292	59.2

NA Not available.
[1] Commercial and industrial failures only. Excludes failures of banks and railroads and, beginning 1933, of real estate, insurance, holding, and financial companies, steamship lines, travel agencies, etc.
[2] Failure rate per 10,000 listed enterprises.
[3] Series revised; not strictly comparable with earlier data.

Series V 31–37. Number of New, Discontinued, and Transferred Businesses, by Major Industry Group: 1940 to 1962

[In thousands. As of January 1]

Year	All industries	Contract construction	Manufacturing	Wholesale trade	Retail trade	Service industries	All other [1]	Year	All industries	Contract construction	Manufacturing	Wholesale trade	Retail trade	Service industries	All other [1]
	31	32	33	34	35	36	37		31	32	33	34	35	36	37
NEW BUSINESSES								DISCONTINUED BUSINESSES—Con.							
1962	430	60	25	25	168	91	61	1950	290	39	25	16	115	58	37
1961	431	62	25	25	170	89	61	1949	306	41	31	18	116	61	41
1960	438	66	27	24	170	89	62	1948	282	36	27	19	98	62	38
1959	422	67	27	23	161	82	62	1947	239	32	27	18	76	49	38
1958	397	58	24	22	160	76	56	1946	209	26	24	11	66	44	38
1957	398	57	25	23	166	71	56	1945	176	17	26	7	59	38	28
1956	431	68	31	24	170	73	64	1944	175	15	20	8	63	40	28
1955	408	69	29	22	161	67	59	1943	337	26	22	20	160	71	38
1954	366	62	25	21	147	61	50	1942	386	30	21	24	199	70	43
1953	352	60	28	21	140	56	47	1941	271	27	21	12	117	56	38
1952	346	61	28	21	130	54	50	1940	318	30	22	14	138	74	41
1951	327	54	28	21	123	53	48	TRANSFERRED BUSINESSES							
1950	348	64	30	22	133	56	44	1958	371	12	14	11	248	59	27
1949	331	54	26	21	136	58	37	1957	376	13	15	12	252	56	28
1948	393	65	35	24	151	73	45	1956	393	14	17	13	261	58	30
1947	461	74	40	30	180	90	48	1955	384	13	17	13	259	55	28
1946	617	95	63	45	234	117	64	1954	371	13	15	12	250	53	27
1945	423	56	37	30	161	84	54	1953	378	14	17	13	253	55	26
1944	331	28	27	24	128	71	52	1952	370	12	17	13	248	54	27
1943	146	9	25	8	50	28	26	1951	358	11	16	11	241	53	25
1942	121	8	23	5	39	29	18	1950	419	15	21	14	278	63	29
1941	290	20	31	23	117	62	38	1949	435	16	22	16	286	66	29
1940	275	22	29	20	118	49	37	1948	501	17	29	17	327	79	33
DISCONTINUED BUSINESSES								1947	572	18	31	20	375	94	34
								1946	627	18	37	26	399	107	39
1962	387	63	29	20	158	67	50	1945	473	10	21	16	308	83	36
1961	389	65	30	21	159	65	50	1944	359	7	17	11	227	65	33
1960	384	64	29	19	157	65	49	1943	250	4	17	7	122	60	39
1959	346	56	27	18	140	59	46	1942	292	7	17	7	104	121	36
1958	347	59	30	19	138	56	45	1941	320	10	23	9	74	158	48
1957	335	57	29	17	137	53	43	1940	241	7	18	6	60	105	44
1956	342	54	26	17	148	53	43								
1955	314	47	28	17	133	50	38								
1954	319	48	30	18	134	48	40								
1953	299	48	28	16	124	46	37								
1952	276	43	25	14	115	44	34								
1951	276	44	23	13	113	47	37								

[1] Mining and quarrying; transportation, communications, and other public utilities; and finance, insurance, and real estate.

Series V 38–40. Recorded Mergers in Manufacturing and Mining: 1895 to 1970

[Merger values in millions of dollars]

Year	Recorded mergers (FTC) 38	Year	Recorded mergers (FTC) 38	Year	Recorded mergers (FTC) 38	Year	Recorded mergers (FTC) 38	Recorded mergers (Eis) Number 39	Recorded mergers (Eis) Merger values 40	Year	Recorded mergers (Nelson) Number 39	Recorded mergers (Nelson) Merger values 40	Year	Recorded mergers (Nelson) Number 39	Recorded mergers (Nelson) Merger values 40
1970	1,351	1957	585	1944	324	1931	464	—	—	1918	71	254	1905	226	243
1969	2,307	1956	673	1943	213	1930	799	281	1,757	1917	195	679	1904	79	110
1968	2,407			1942	118	1929	1,245	587	1,993	1916	117	470	1903	142	298
1967	1,496			1941	111	1928	1,058	507	1,653				1902	379	911
1966	995	1955	683			1927	870	306	727	1915	71	158	1901	423	2,053
		1954	387	1940	140	1926	856	265	1,135	1914	39	160			
		1953	295	1939	87					1913	85	176	1900	340	442
1965	1,008	1952	288	1938	110	1925	554	257	721	1912	82	322	1899	1,208	2,263
1964	854	1951	235	1937	124	1924	368	149	466	1911	103	210	1898	303	651
1963	861			1936	126	1923	311	143	1,171				1897	69	120
1962	853	1950	219			1922	309	122	502	1910	142	257	1896	26	25
1961	954	1949	126	1935	130	1921	487	70	430	1909	49	89			
		1948	223	1934	101					1908	50	188	1895	43	41
1960	844	1947	404	1933	120	1920	760	163	809	1907	87	185			
1959	835	1946	419	1932	203	1919	438	159	777	1906	128	378			
1958	589	1945	333												

Series V 41–53. Number of Corporations, by Industrial Division: 1916 to 1970

[In thousands]

Year	Total corporations 41	Active corporations — Total 42	Agriculture, forestry, and fisheries 43	Mining 44	Manufacturing 45	Wholesale trade 46	Retail trade 47	Trade not allocable 48	Services 49	Finance, insurance, and real estate 50	Public utilities 51	Contract construction 52	All other 53
1970	1,747.6	1,665.5	37.2	14.5	197.8	165.6	350.8	1.7	281.2	406.2	67.4	138.9	4.1
1969	1,737.9	1,658.8	32.0	14.0	202.1	172.1	351.8	0.6	261.6	429.0	66.9	127.7	0.9
1968	1,614.7	1,541.7	31.2	12.8	191.9	153.1	314.0	4.3	228.9	407.2	65.6	126.6	6.1
1967	1,609.9	1,534.4	32.4	14.4	197.0	142.5	315.6	7.7	220.6	399.1	66.0	123.2	15.7
1966	1,537.9	1,468.7	27.9	14.8	187.6	151.2	298.4	3.6	202.1	402.7	59.9	112.4	8.0
1965	1,490.1	1,424.0	27.5	13.3	185.9	146.6	287.6	6.2	188.2	388.4	59.7	113.3	7.4
1964	1,437.2	1,373.5	25.9	14.5	185.0	142.6	272.2	6.8	176.9	383.7	56.3	104.1	5.5
1963	1,381.7	1,323.2	23.3	14.9	181.8	137.6	257.4	8.4	163.8	375.4	56.3	96.5	7.9
1962	1,318.8	1,268.0	22.1	13.5	183.1	132.3	245.1	11.3	150.1	359.2	52.7	90.6	7.8
1961	1,240.8	1,190.3	19.0	13.7	173.6	123.4	230.2	11.3	138.0	340.2	49.0	83.8	8.1
1960	1,187.6	1,140.6	17.1	13.0	165.9	117.4	217.3	20.9	121.0	334.4	43.9	72.3	17.3
1959	1,119.8	1,074.1	15.6	12.9	156.3	109.6	199.6	25.4	110.0	318.6	43.2	66.3	16.5
1958	1,032.6	990.4	13.9	12.1	150.7	102.3	186.4	22.7	97.2	293.9	37.9	59.8	13.3
1957	984.5	940.1	11.8	12.7	138.6	103.5	178.5	23.2	90.6	276.9	37.8	53.6	13.1
1956	925.0	885.7	11.0	11.7	132.8	95.0	168.3	23.0	81.6	265.0	36.2	48.3	12.8
1955	842.1	807.3	10.3	10.7	129.8	86.3	154.9	23.8	72.9	234.0	33.0	41.6	10.0
1954	754.0	722.8	8.8	9.6	120.9	77.1	140.0	21.5	64.8	205.3	29.1	36.1	9.6
1953	731.0	698.0	9.4	9.1	121.1	74.1	134.6	19.6	63.5	195.2	29.9	34.9	6.5
1952	705.5	672.1	8.9	9.1	119.4	72.1	131.5	17.7	61.6	185.9	28.5	31.8	5.6
1951	687.3	652.4	8.7	9.0	120.2	71.6	129.2	15.5	58.3	177.8	26.8	29.6	5.7
1950	666.0	629.3	8.3	9.1	115.9	68.9	125.5	15.0	55.2	171.8	26.3	27.7	5.6
1949	650.0	614.8	8.0	9.2	117.3	67.9	118.8	17.3	54.0	166.3	25.9	25.7	4.4
1948	630.7	594.2	7.7	9.1	116.7	64.8	110.8	21.1	50.5	160.6	25.2	23.5	4.2
1947	587.7	551.8	7.3	8.3	112.2	56.0	99.0	22.2	46.0	151.0	23.7	20.3	5.7
1946	526.4	491.2	6.7	7.7	98.1	47.7	84.8	19.1	39.6	144.4	21.8	15.8	5.5
1945	454.5	421.1	6.2	7.3	79.1	35.7	71.2	14.1	35.1	135.6	19.7	11.8	5.3
1944	446.8	412.5	6.4	7.6	76.6	33.6	69.1	14.6	34.7	133.9	19.2	11.5	5.0
1943	455.9	420.5	6.9	8.1	78.7	34.4	72.6	13.8	35.6	133.7	19.3	12.1	5.3
1942	479.7	442.7	7.3	8.9	82.2	36.3	78.3	14.4	38.4	136.9	20.2	13.7	6.1
1941	509.1	468.9	7.9	9.7	84.4	37.6	84.5	16.5	40.5	143.5	21.9	15.0	7.3
1940	516.8	473.0	8.4	10.4	85.6	37.5	85.8	16.5	41.4	142.6	22.1	15.7	7.0
1939	516.0	469.6	8.6	10.8	86.2	36.0	86.3	15.9	41.0	142.3	22.1	16.1	4.3
1938	520.5	471.0	9.0	10.9	88.1	37.0	86.7	15.5	41.0	140.4	22.0	16.3	4.1
1937	529.1	477.8	8.7	13.6	92.0	34.5	78.5	30.1	60.2	117.1	24.7	16.9	1.5
1936	530.8	478.9	8.9	13.8	92.0	35.2	83.0	27.3	59.7	115.7	24.9	16.6	1.8
1935	533.6	477.1	9.1	13.7	91.7	34.2	83.6	27.1	49.6	124.9	25.4	16.1	1.7
1934	528.9	469.8	9.3	13.5	91.3	33.2	79.7	27.9	45.9	126.1	25.4	15.9	1.6
1933	504.1	446.8	9.3	11.8	88.6	30.7	81.2	20.9	43.0	121.7	21.8	16.3	1.5
1932	508.6	451.9	9.8	12.0	87.9	29.9	77.9	24.6	43.3	125.1	21.7	17.3	2.4
1931	516.4	459.7	9.9	12.1	89.1	30.0	80.0	22.9	38.2	134.6	21.6	18.1	3.4
1930	518.7	463.0	9.9	12.2	91.5	30.2	79.2	22.1	38.2	136.6	21.6	18.5	2.9
1929	509.4	456.0	9.4	12.5	92.2	29.1	77.9	22.1	36.0	133.9	21.6	18.4	2.9
1928	495.9	443.6	9.2	12.9	91.6	28.5	73.0	24.9	33.5	129.1	21.3	17.3	2.3
1927	475.0	425.7	8.9	13.0	89.8	29.6	65.9	24.2	31.1	122.7	20.8	16.4	3.3
1926	455.3	[1]455.3	10.7	19.3	93.2	39.5	47.5	25.7	32.3	130.4	25.1	16.8	[1]14.8
1925	430.1	[1]430.1	9.9	19.1	88.7		109.6		29.0	115.9	23.6	15.3	[1]19.0
1924	417.4	[1]417.4	9.8	18.4	86.8		105.3		26.3	104.8	22.4	13.2	[1]30.4
1923	398.9	[1]398.9	9.4	18.5	85.2		100.6		25.1	96.8	21.1	12.6	[1]29.6
1922	382.9	[1]382.9	9.1	17.1	82.5		95.7		23.1	91.1	20.5	11.4	[1]32.4
1921	356.4	[1]356.4	8.7	17.7	79.7		88.2		19.1	82.8	19.1	10.4	[1]30.7
1920	345.6	[1]345.6	9.2	17.5	78.2		78.9		17.5	78.9	20.6	10.0	[1]34.8
1919	320.2	[1]320.2	8.3	18.5	67.8		70.2		15.7	72.8	20.5	8.2	[1]38.2
1918	317.6	[1]317.6	7.9	10.7	67.3		70.1		14.9	68.1	18.2	7.7	[1]52.7
1917	351.4	[1]351.4	9.6	12.9	79.6		91.1		18.6	68.4	26.4	10.7	[1]34.1
1916	341.3	[1]341.3	7.3	12.0	80.2		30.6		[2]	30.0	22.9	[2]	[1]158.3

[1] Includes inactive corporations.   [2] Included in "All other."

Series V 54–65. Percent of Total Corporate Net Income Reported by Small and Large Corporations (With Net Income Only): 1918 to 1939

[Size measured by net income]

Year	All industries				All industries except finance				Manufacturing			
	Total	Smallest 75%	Next 20%	Largest 5%	Total	Smallest 75%	Next 20%	Largest 5%	Total	Smallest 75%	Next 20%	Largest 5%
	54	55	56	57	58	59	60	61	62	63	64	65
1939	100.00	3.40	12.11	84.49	------	------	------	------	------	------	------	------
1938	100.00	3.52	12.05	84.43	------	------	------	------	------	------	------	------
1937	100.00	3.07	11.58	85.35	------	------	------	------	------	------	------	------
1936	100.00	3.32	12.85	83.83	------	------	------	------	------	------	------	------
1935	100.00	3.90	14.73	81.37	------	------	------	------	------	------	------	------
1934	100.00	3.70	14.77	81.53	------	------	------	------	------	------	------	------
1933	100.00	3.08	13.10	83.82	------	------	------	------	------	------	------	------
1932	100.00	2.71	10.70	86.59	------	------	------	------	------	------	------	------
1931	100.00	4.46	10.78	84.76	------	------	------	------	------	------	------	------
1930	100.00	4.09	10.63	85.28	100.00	3.50	9.84	86.66	100.00	3.42	11.82	84.76
1929	100.00	3.97	11.69	84.34	100.00	3.62	11.14	85.24	100.00	4.49	13.42	82.09
1928	100.00	4.43	13.03	82.54	100.00	4.03	12.45	83.52	100.00	4.94	14.69	80.37
1927	100.00	4.66	14.63	80.71	100.00	4.17	13.90	81.93	100.00	5.54	16.56	77.90
1926	100.00	4.52	14.35	81.13	100.00	3.94	13.29	82.77	100.00	5.28	15.12	79.60
1925	100.00	4.97	15.44	79.59	100.00	4.91	14.04	81.05	100.00	5.98	16.29	77.73
1924	100.00	5.52	16.06	78.42	100.00	4.96	15.23	79.81	100.00	6.16	16.92	76.92
1923	100.00	5.28	16.44	78.28	100.00	5.53	15.53	78.94	100.00	6.40	18.07	75.53
1922	100.00	5.62	16.71	77.67	100.00	5.51	16.21	78.28	100.00	6.72	19.19	74.09
1921	100.00	6.34	16.06	77.60	100.00	5.36	15.85	78.79	100.00	7.28	19.18	73.54
1920	100.00	5.77	15.31	78.92	100.00	5.77	16.16	78.07	100.00	6.42	17.92	75.66
1919	100.00	7.01	16.26	76.73	(NA)	(NA)	(NA)	(NA)	(NA)	(NA)	(NA)	(NA)
1918	100.00	6.03	14.37	79.60	100.00	6.56	14.51	78.93	100.00	6.33	17.58	76.09

NA Not available.

Series V 66–77. Income of Unincorporated Enterprises, by Industry: 1929 to 1970

[In millions of dollars]

Year	Total, all industries	Agriculture, forestry, and fisheries	Mining	Contract construction	Manufacturing	Transportation	Communication	Electric, gas, and sanitary services	Wholesale trade	Retail trade	Finance, insurance, and real estate	Services
	66	67	68	69	70	71	72	73	74	75	76	77
1970	67,538	17,596	103	4,962	1,652	1,237	39	99	3,359	10,673	3,172	24,646
1969	67,969	17,522	37	5,157	1,849	1,219	15	104	3,355	10,746	4,055	23,910
1968	64,948	15,342	335	4,766	1,873	1,243	64	101	3,303	10,724	4,636	22,561
1967	62,435	15,471	355	4,533	1,880	1,118	26	99	2,975	10,430	4,272	21,276
1966	61,688	16,698	209	4,517	2,109	1,204	21	89	3,019	10,148	4,054	19,620
1965	57,633	15,440	239	4,332	1,979	1,194	23	80	2,866	9,682	3,965	17,833
1964	52,394	12,712	250	3,921	1,885	1,008	25	85	3,032	9,338	3,420	16,718
1963	51,047	13,580	268	3,698	1,815	987	19	67	3,113	8,800	3,257	15,443
1962	50,094	13,525	273	3,597	1,877	933	16	56	3,003	9,013	3,091	14,710
1961	48,401	13,285	284	3,558	1,818	848	17	58	2,966	8,637	3,155	13,775
1960	46,228	12,394	276	3,357	1,841	794	16	55	2,822	8,681	3,163	12,829
1959	46,690	11,846	277	3,551	1,907	808	16	56	2,871	9,407	3,405	12,546
1958	46,663	13,861	370	3,284	1,867	796	17	66	2,793	8,796	3,312	11,501
1957	44,363	11,714	413	3,475	2,003	787	17	51	2,862	8,928	3,173	10,940
1956	43,237	11,843	404	3,290	2,095	767	18	38	2,770	8,795	2,983	10,234
1955	41,899	11,868	339	3,167	2,035	754	18	43	2,430	8,713	2,915	9,617
1954	40,037	12,878	291	2,929	1,906	764	21	43	1,899	8,715	2,395	8,196
1953	40,680	13,468	298	3,208	2,103	754	18	38	2,203	8,404	2,160	8,026
1952	41,910	15,401	277	3,272	2,082	730	18	33	2,050	8,556	2,019	7,472
1951	42,290	16,222	306	3,123	2,168	693	14	27	2,216	8,617	1,860	7,044
1950	38,569	13,860	295	3,088	2,047	655	11	23	2,052	8,024	1,831	6,683
1949	34,822	13,005	288	2,653	1,581	601	8	17	1,409	7,685	1,353	6,222
1948	40,628	17,832	401	2,654	1,825	601	8	18	1,592	8,370	1,172	6,155
1947	36,959	15,395	270	2,124	1,658	556	8	18	1,808	8,651	966	5,505
1946	38,229	15,099	164	1,723	2,302	487	7	17	2,323	9,755	1,036	5,316
1945	31,528	12,371	129	1,094	2,365	432	8	15	1,740	7,943	899	4,532
1944	29,890	11,742	163	992	2,203	465	7	12	1,635	7,577	718	4,376
1943	28,788	11,770	166	1,119	1,882	479	6	9	1,462	7,305	640	3,950
1942	24,198	9,879	126	1,248	1,439	417	5	7	1,176	5,956	526	3,419
1941	18,122	6,514	98	968	993	360	4	6	892	4,835	485	2,967
1940	13,090	4,529	69	697	523	286	3	4	594	3,310	433	2,642
1939	12,011	4,471	70	654	409	250	3	4	487	2,758	405	2,500
1938	11,076	4,430	59	616	276	230	3	4	429	2,273	370	2,386
1937	13,232	6,067	85	591	374	233	3	4	432	2,517	408	2,518
1936	11,075	4,342	61	628	411	218	2	2	405	2,274	398	2,334
1935	10,808	5,321	39	392	307	197	1	2	299	1,814	343	2,093
1934	7,729	2,995	31	324	253	174	1	2	235	1,503	285	1,926
1933	6,440	2,627	4	206	210	158	–	1	156	1,030	348	1,700
1932	5,359	2,143	9	248	29	163	1	2	80	530	263	1,891
1931	8,554	3,471	−16	618	130	187	2	5	181	1,158	342	2,476
1930	11,129	4,367	35	875	300	214	3	6	274	1,729	508	2,818
1929	14,966	6,215	64	1,139	572	222	3	6	390	2,533	827	2,995

– Represents zero.

Series V 78–107. Manufacturing and Trade—Sales and Inventories: 1948 to 1970

[Money figures in billions of dollars]

Year	Total	Manufacturing			Retail trade			Merchant wholesalers		
		Total	Durable goods	Nondurable goods	Total	Durable goods	Nondurable goods	Total	Durable goods	Nondurable goods
	SALES									
	78	79	80	81	82	83	84	85	86	87
1970	1,264	653	352	301	365	110	255	247	112	135
1969	1,232	644	354	289	352	113	239	237	110	127
1968	1,163	603	332	271	339	110	229	220	100	120
1967	1,076	557	303	255	314	100	214	205	90	115
1966	1,046	538	296	243	304	98	206	204	91	113
1965	963	492	267	225	284	94	190	187	83	104
1964	884	448	236	212	262	85	177	174	76	99
1963	828	420	219	201	247	80	167	161	69	92
1962	785	397	205	192	236	75	161	152	65	88
1961	734	371	187	184	219	67	152	144	60	84
1960 *	729	370	190	180	220	71	149	140	59	81
1959	716	363	187	176	215	72	144	138	59	79
1958	651	327	163	165	200	63	137	123	50	73
1957	671	345	183	162	200	68	132	126	54	72
1956	649	333	177	156	190	66	124	126	56	70
1955	620	318	169	149	184	67	117	119	51	67
1954	557	280	142	138	169	58	111	108	43	65
1953	576	298	160	138	169	60	109	109	44	65
1952	538	270	136	135	162	55	107	105	42	63
1951	520	261	126	135	157	54	102	103	42	61
1950	463	224	106	117	147	54	93	92	38	55
1949	405	194	86	107	134	45	89	78	29	49
1948	423	208	91	117	134	43	91	82	31	51
	INVENTORIES, BOOK VALUE									
	88	89	90	91	92	93	94	95	96	97
1970	170	100	65	35	45	19	26	27	16	11
1969	164	97	63	34	45	20	25	24	15	10
1968	154	91	59	32	42	19	23	23	13	9
1967	144	85	55	30	39	17	22	22	13	9
1966	135	78	50	28	38	17	21	21	12	9
1965	120	68	42	26	34	15	19	18	11	8
1964	110	63	38	25	31	13	18	17	10	7
1963	104	60	36	24	29	13	17	16	9	7
1962	100	58	35	24	28	12	16	15	9	6
1961	95	55	33	22	26	11	15	14	8	6
1960 *	94	54	32	21	27	12	15	14	8	6
1959	91	53	32	21	25	11	14	14	8	6
1958	86	50	30	20	24	11	14	13	7	6
1957	88	52	32	20	24	11	13	13	7	6
1956	86	51	30	20	23	10	13	13	7	6
1955	78	45	26	19	23	11	12	12	6	5
1954	72	42	24	18	21	9	12	11	5	5
1953	75	44	26	18	21	10	12	11	6	5
1952	71	41	24	17	21	9	12	10	5	5
1951	69	39	21	18	21	10	11	10	5	5
1950	59	31	16	16	19	8	11	9	5	5
1949	49	26	13	13	15	6	9	8	4	4
1948	52	29	15	14	16	7	9	8	4	4
	INVENTORY—SALES RATIO [1]									
	98	99	100	101	102	103	104	105	106	107
1970	1.60	1.82	2.20	1.37	1.47	2.13	1.18	1.23	1.61	0.92
1969	1.56	1.75	2.07	1.36	1.47	2.05	1.19	1.19	1.53	.89
1968	1.55	1.74	2.05	1.36	1.43	1.97	1.17	1.20	1.54	.91
1967	1.57	1.76	2.09	1.37	1.46	2.03	1.19	1.21	1.61	.90
1966	1.47	1.62	1.85	1.34	1.44	2.00	1.17	1.14	1.49	.85
1965	1.45	1.60	1.81	1.34	1.39	1.86	1.16	1.14	1.49	.87
1964	1.47	1.64	1.87	1.38	1.40	1.86	1.18	1.13	1.49	.86
1963	1.49	1.69	1.94	1.42	1.39	1.79	1.20	1.15	1.54	.85
1962	1.51	1.72	1.98	1.44	1.38	1.82	1.17	1.16	1.57	.86
1961	1.54	1.74	2.05	1.43	1.43	2.00	1.18	1.20	1.63	.89
1960 *	1.56	1.76	2.07	1.42	1.45	2.02	1.18	1.22	1.69	.89
1959	1.50	1.70	2.00	1.39	1.40	1.86	1.16	1.15	1.53	.87
1958	1.60	1.84	2.23	1.45	1.43	2.01	1.17	1.24	1.66	.94
1957	1.59	1.80	2.07	1.51	1.44	1.91	1.19	1.23	1.58	.96
1956	1.55	1.73	1.94	1.49	1.47	1.92	1.22	1.19	1.43	1.00
1955	1.47	1.62	1.75	1.47	1.43	1.79	1.22	1.13	1.36	.95
1954	1.60	1.81	2.06	1.56	1.51	1.96	1.27	1.18	1.54	.95
1953	1.58	1.76	1.91	1.58	1.53	1.96	1.29	1.17	1.52	.93
1952	1.58	1.78	2.00	1.58	1.52	2.00	1.28	1.12	1.47	.89
1951	1.55	1.66	1.77	1.55	1.64	2.00	1.40	1.16	1.47	.95
1950	1.36	1.48	1.55	1.41	1.38	1.52	1.29	1.07	1.29	.91
1949	1.53	1.75	2.04	1.51	1.41	1.77	1.23	1.19	1.61	.95
1948	1.42	1.57	1.83	1.36	1.39	1.71	1.23	1.13	1.42	.95

* Denotes first year for which figures include Alaska and Hawaii, except 1961 for merchant wholesalers, and 1946 for retail trade inventories.

[1] Average inventories to average monthly sales. Average inventories based on weighted averages of end-of-month figures.

Chapter V

Corporate Assets, Liabilities, and Income (Series V 108-332)

V 108–305. General note.

Aggregate balance sheet and income data for all U.S. corporations combined and for corporations classified by major industry have been published annually since 1926 by the Internal Revenue Service (and its predecessor, Bureau of Internal Revenue) in *Statistics of Income*, part 2.   Data classified by asset-size class are also available since 1931. Series V 108–140 and V 167–196 are based on the materials assembled in *Statistics of Income*. Other sources provide balance sheet and income data for public utilities, railroads, and commercial banks over considerably longer periods. Data for public utility corporations are presented, in condensed form, in series V 197–212. Data for railroads are presented in chapter Q, Transportation, and for commercial banks in chapter X, Financial Markets and Institutions.

Most of the series shown here include aggregates based on the values reported by corporations in their accounting statements. These book values are seldom, if ever, equal to current market values, nor do they correspond to theoretical values computed by economic analysts (e.g., values arrived at on the basis of the expected revenue streams). When the general price level remains stable, individual differences between the book value and the market value (or between the book value and the theoretical economic value) may largely cancel out in the process of aggregation. In times of a persistent inflation, however, book values show a general tendency to fall below current market valuations, while in times of persistent deflation the reverse is generally true. Some specific valuation problems, arising in connection with different types of business assets, are briefly discussed below.

Physical assets. Physical assets owned by business firms include inventories (both finished goods and goods in process) and fixed assets (land, plant, and equipment).

Inventories are usually shown on the balance sheet at "cost or market, whichever is lower." Consequently, in periods of rising prices, book values tend to be below current market values. In periods of falling prices, however, conservative accounting practices require an adjustment in the book value so as to bring it down to the level of the current market value.

Book charges for inventories used up in production were formerly based almost universally on the "fifo" (first in, first out) method of valuation, but a substantial number of firms have switched to the "lifo" (last in, first out) method. These two valuation methods yield different results with respect to reported costs and profits and also with respect to the book value of the year-end inventory. Under "lifo" procedure, the most recent prices are used for the computation of costs. Consequently, reported profits (and, therefore, income tax liability) are reduced in periods of rising prices, but are increased in periods of falling prices, as compared with the amount that would be reported under "fifo."

On the other hand, the year-end inventories are valued at less recent prices on a "lifo" than on a "fifo" basis. Consequently, in periods of price instability the use of "lifo" tends to widen the gap between the book value and the current market value of the year-end inventories.

Except in special cases, a comparison of year-end inventory values does not provide an adequate indication of changes in the physical volume of inventories. When "lifo" is used, a change in the book value of inventory will correctly indicate the change in the physical volume valued at current prices, as long as the volume is increasing. If the physical volume is decreasing, however, a valuation adjustment is required in order to arrive at the current value of the physical

decrement. When "fifo" is used, a valuation adjustment must be made whether the physical volume is increasing or decreasing.

Since the aggregate inventory values represent a combination of "fifo" and "lifo" inventories (the former being the predominant component), an inventory valuation adjustment is clearly required before any inferences regarding changes in the physical stock are to be drawn from these figures.

Fixed assets include durable capital goods, which are generally entered at cost and are written off gradually over a period of years by means of annual depreciation charges. A detailed balance sheet usually includes (*a*) the gross amount before depreciation, (*b*) the depreciation reserve accumulated to date, and (*c*) the net amount after depreciation, which is equal to (*a*) minus (*b*).

If the prices of capital goods remained constant, the gross amount of plant and equipment would equal their replacement cost (the cost of replacing the existing items, which vary in age from almost new to being close to the time of retirement, with brand new items of the same type). During periods of continual price increases, however, the gross amount falls considerably short of the replacement cost; while during periods of continual price declines, the opposite is true.

The net amount of plant and equipment would approach the current market value only if the annual depreciation allowances corresponded to the actual loss of value through wear and tear as well as obsolescence (and, furthermore, if the prices of new capital goods remained constant). This, however, hardly ever happens in actual practice. Most corporations have been using the "straight line" method of depreciation, under which durable equipment has been written off by equal amounts every year during its entire lifetime, irrespective of the actual degree of wear and tear or obsolescence. During and after World War II accelerated writeoffs were allowed in industries working for defense, whereby plant and equipment could be written off over an arbitrary 5-year period. This procedure, coupled with the fact that prices generally rose at a relatively fast rate during the war and the postwar period, has served to further widen the gap between the net book values and the actual market values of fixed assets.

Neither the gross nor the net amount of plant and equipment may be taken to reflect accurately changes in the physical stock of durable capital goods. If prices remained constant, changes in the gross amount would indicate changes in quantity, though not in quality, of capital goods. For example, if a firm owned 100 units of machinery and added 10 new units next year, the gross amount would show a 10-percent rise (assuming no retirements during the year); but the gross amount could not show the decline in quality of the original 100 units through the process of aging. The net amount does reflect the aging of durable equipment but, as stated above, the prevailing depreciation methods do not—and are not intended to—align the book values with changes in the actual market value over time.

Financial assets. Financial assets of corporations represent their claims on other business units, individuals, and government. Current (short-term) financial assets include cash, bank deposit accounts, notes receivable and marketable securities (mostly U.S. Government but frequently including marketable corporate stock as well). Noncurrent (long-term) financial assets consist of bonds, other long-term debt instruments, and nonmarketable securities which are largely permanent holdings of corporate stock. The problem of market valuation does not, of course, arise in connection with cash and bank deposits. If receivables are salable, their market value does not ordinarily deviate from the book amount by more than a moderate discount. But in the case of securities, especially common stocks, the current market value may differ widely from the original cost to the owner. Bonds tend to rise in price when the current interest rate declines relative to the coupon rate. Stocks tend to rise when the expected rate of profit and/or dividends earned by the issuer increases. Conservative accounting practice requires that securities be valued at "cost or market, whichever is lower." Thus, while the book values are not expected to exceed the market values for any considerable length of time the reverse relationship may continue indefinitely.

While the market value of stocks tends to rise with—though not necessarily in proportion to—the general level of prices, the market value of bonds is not directly affected by this factor. In fact, in times of inflation or deflation, the fixed amount debt instruments become especially variable in terms of real purchasing power represented by them.

A special problem arises in connection with financial assets when aggregate balance sheets are compiled. In a closed economic system all financial claims and liabilities would cancel out. A consolidated balance sheet for the entire system would show only physical property on the asset side and net claims to this property by individuals on the liability side.

Since the corporate sector of our economy is not a closed system, a consolidated balance sheet for all corporations combined would not eliminate all financial assets and liabilities, although it would eliminate a substantial part representing intercompany claims.

The aggregate balance sheets presented in this section are essentially unconsolidated data. Some large corporations submitted consolidated balance sheets comprising the parent company and its subsidiaries. (Consolidated returns were permitted prior to 1934 and then again after 1942. See text for series V 108–140 and V 167–196.) But, in the main, the total amounts were obtained by mere aggregation rather than consolidation of individual companies' statements.

As a result, the total amounts of both receivables and payables include a certain (undetermined) amount owed by corporations to other corporations. The total amount of investments includes a certain (undetermined) amount of corporate securities owned by corporations. When claims of the creditor corporations on the debtor corporations are included in total assets of the sector as a whole, the total is inflated by the double-counting involved.

Liabilities. The valuation problems encountered in connection with corporate liabilities are generally similar to those discussed above in connection with financial assets. When the price level rises, the amount of debt shrinks in terms of real purchasing power. When the market value of assets increases, the dollar amount of debt remains unchanged, but its magnitude in relation to net worth (valued at market prices) declines. When unconsolidated data are aggregated, the total amount of debt is inflated because no adjustment is made for intercompany liabilities.

The item designated as "other liabilities" (series V 123) includes accrued income tax and other accrued liabilities. Tax accruals were a relatively minor item during the 1920's and 1930's, but assumed major proportions during and after World War II, when the income tax rates were sharply raised and the excess profits tax was imposed (during 1940–1945 and again during 1950–1953). Tax accruals rose substantially also in the years of World War I, but a sharp decline occurred after the war. These movements are reflected in the sample data for large manufacturing corporations, extending over the 1914–1943 period (see text for series V 285–305).

The amount of accrued taxes has not been reported as a separate balance sheet item in *Statistics of Income*. Until recently, the year-end amount of tax accruals usually was fairly close to the current year's total tax liability (series V 137, V 180, and V 195), but the acceleration program enacted in 1954 placed large corporate taxpayers on a pay-as-you-go basis, which tended to reduce their tax reserves.

The rise in the income tax accruals on the liability side of corporate balance sheets was accompanied by an increase in government security holding on the asset side. Thus, in a completely consolidated statement for the corporate sector, the debt owed by corporations to the government would be largely offset by the debt owed by the government to corporations, and the net balance of such claims would be relatively small.

Net worth. Net worth (or equity) is the stockholders' share in the total assets of a corporation. It is not measured by the capital stock account alone, but is equal to the sum of capital stock, capital reserves, paid-in surplus, and earned surplus; or, alternatively, it represents the difference between total assets on the one hand and the sum of all short-term and long-term liabilities on the other. Since the dollar amount of liabilities is fixed at any one time, a revaluation of assets results in a corresponding change in net worth.

In a newly established firm, net worth is equal to the amount of capital paid in by its first stockholders. This amount may be registered in the capital stock account alone, or partly (usually up to the par value per share) in the capital stock account and partly in the paid-in surplus (or capital surplus) account. A going concern, on the other hand, can increase its net worth from two sources—by selling additional shares of stock and by retaining profits. The latter method (known as internal financing) has generally been a very important source of funds for American corporations.

Net profit retained in a given year is reflected in the year-end balance sheet as an increase in the earned surplus account. However, the amount of earned surplus shown on the balance sheet may not generally be taken to represent the sum of all profit retentions over the company's entire lifetime. Many companies declare stock dividends from time to time, and this involves transfers from the earned surplus to the capital stock account. Other companies make occasional transfers from earned surplus to various reserve or special fund accounts. In some cases, earned surplus and paid-in surplus are combined into one account, which makes it impossible to separate paid-in equity from retained funds. Thus, generally speaking, while the balance sheet data for any one year indicate the total amount of net worth, they contain no accurate information as to what portion of net worth has been built up by stock sales and what portion has been accumulated through profit retentions.

Sales, income, and dividends. The sales, income, and dividend figures also represent unconsolidated aggregates, with no adjustment for intercompany transactions. Goods and services sold by corporations to other corporations are included in the total amount of sales two or more times. For example, the value of steel sold by steel producers to automobile manufacturers is included in the sales of the steel industry and also in the sales of the automobile industry (as part of the total value of the automobiles sold). In other words, total reported sales of all industries would exceed by a large margin the net value of corporate production (the sum of all net values added by individual companies) in any given period.

The net income and dividend totals also contain some duplication, since no adjustment has been made for intercompany dividends. When dividends are paid by one company to another, this is obviously a transfer payment which does not increase the actual total income of the corporate sector as a whole. Yet, since such payments are included in net income of the receiving companies without being deducted from net income of the paying companies, the aggregate amount of net income of all corporations is correspondingly inflated.

Problems of asset valuation and income computation have been extensively discussed in the accounting and economic literature. Useful basic discussions may be found in the following books: J. C. Bonbright, *The Valuation of Property*, McGraw-Hill, New York, 1937; N. S. Buchanan, *The Economics of Corporate Enterprise*, Henry Holt & Co., New York, 1940; B. Graham and D. L. Dodd, *Security Analysis*, McGraw-Hill, New York, 4th ed. 1962; J. P. Powelson, *Economic Accounting*, McGraw-Hill, New York, 1955.

The problems encountered in compiling the national income data from the balance sheets submitted by business firms are discussed in Office of Business Economics, *National Income*, 1954 edition, and *U.S. Income and Output*, 1958.

V 108–140 and V 167–196.   General note.

Aggregate balance sheet data for all corporations submitting such data with their income tax returns have been published in *Statistics of Income* since 1926.   Aggregate income data for all corporations submitting income tax returns have been available since 1916, but income data for corporations submitting balance sheets have been compiled only since 1931.

Companies which did not submit balance sheet data for 1926–1955 represented only a small fraction of the total corporate population in terms of total income and assets.   Thus, companies not submitting balance sheets accounted for only 3 percent of the total compiled receipts in 1931 and 1 percent in 1953.   The data presented here may, therefore, be taken as a fairly close approximation of the entire corporate population.

For 1926–1950, annual tabulations have been derived from all corporation returns filed.   For 1951–1955, the aggregate data for small corporations were estimated on the basis of 10- and 20-percent samples, in order to reduce the cost and delay involved in tabulating all returns.   In 1951, sampling procedures were confined to corporations with total assets under $250,000.   The sample amounted to 10 percent of this population.   In 1952, the companies with total assets under $250,000 were represented by a 10-percent sample.   Furthermore, the companies with total assets between $250,000 and $500,000 were represented by a 20-percent sample.   All returns with total assets of $500,000 and over together with all consolidated returns, life and mutual insurance companies, personal holding companies, and taxable returns with total income (total gross receipts less cost of sales or operations) of $200,000 and over, regardless of size of total assets, were tabulated.

For 1953–1957, sampling rates were based on gross receipts instead of total assets.   For 1953–1955, companies with gross receipts below $100,000 were sampled at a 10-percent rate; 20-percent of the companies with gross receipts between $100,000 and $500,000 were sampled and all companies with gross receipts over $500,000 were included.   In 1956–1957, the 20-percent sample was expanded to include companies with gross receipts between $100,000 and $1,000,000.   For 1956–1957, all companies with gross receipts over $1,000,000 were tabulated.

In 1958, total assets and net income (deficit) were included with gross receipts as a basis for sample selection.   In addition, strata were introduced to cover Small Business Corporation returns (Form 1120S).   These were filed for the first time under the Technical Amendments Act of 1958.

Beginning 1959, total assets and net income (deficit) only are the basis for sample selection.   In addition, separate sampling plans were developed for "special" returns such as life and mutual insurance companies, etc.   As a result, there were eighteen sampling classes and eleven sampling rates in 1968 as compared with seven classes and three rates in 1958.

Although small companies account for a very large share of the total corporate universe in terms of the number of returns, they represent a relatively small share of the total in terms of assets and receipts.   Thus, in 1952 the total assets of small companies accounted for only 7 percent of the aggregate figure for all corporations combined.

The data in each volume of *Statistics of Income* are from returns for the calendar year indicated, for fiscal years ending within the period from July of one year through June of the succeeding year, and for partial years with the greater number of months of the accounting period falling within the calendar year.   The information is compiled from the returns as filed, prior to revisions that may be made as a result of audit by the Internal Revenue Service.   Also, the data do not reflect loss carrybacks, renegotiation of war contracts, or recomputation of amortization of emergency facilities.

The returns included in each report are those filed for comparable periods of time.   There are factors, however, which interfere with the precise comparability of the data over a period of years.   While their influence has not been so strong as to obscure major historical trends, they must, of course, be borne in mind, especially when close comparisons are attempted.   Some of the more important interfering factors are indicated below.

In general, the items for 1926–1933 are not precisely comparable with those for 1934–1941, because of the discontinuance, under the Revenue Act of 1934, of the privilege of filing consolidated income tax returns (except by railroad corporations and their related holding and leasing companies and, for 1940 and 1941, Pan-American trade corporations), and the consequent appearance, in the separate returns filed by corporations formerly included in an affiliated group, of items which, owing to "intercompany eliminations," did not appear on the consolidated return.

The discontinuance of consolidated returns also resulted in changes in industrial classification.   A corporation is classified industrially according to the business reported on the return.   When diversified activities are reported, the classification is determined by the industry which accounts for the largest percentage of receipts.   Therefore, industrial groups may contain data for activities other than those on which the classification is based.   Prior to 1934, a consolidated return was classified on the predominant activity of the group of affiliated concerns, whereas, for 1934 and subsequent years, the separate return filed by each concern which was formerly a part of an affiliated group is classified on its predominant industry.   Beginning 1942, the consolidated return privilege was again extended, in general, to all corporations.

On the basis of the data contained in the 1934 issue of *Statistics of Income*, two sets of figures are given for 1934 in series V 167–181.   In 1934 (comparable with later years), corporations which submitted consolidated returns in 1933 are classified according to the business reported on the deconsolidated returns for 1934.   In 1934 (comparable with earlier years, insofar as industrial classification is concerned), corporations which submitted consolidated returns in 1933 are classified according to the business reported on consolidated returns in 1933.   The latter data for 1934, however, are still not fully consistent with those for 1933 because they include items which are eliminated in consolidated returns but are present in deconsolidated statements.

There have been other changes in the content of various items, which have affected historical comparability.   For example, notes payable with maturity of one year or more were included with bonds and mortgages for 1929–1936, but not for succeeding years.   Surplus reserves were included with "surplus and undivided profits" for 1926–1937, whereas they have been shown as a separate item since 1938.

The changes in the Standard Industrial Classification System from time to time do not substantially affect the comparability of these data.   The figures have been revised historically to reflect these changes which are indicated in the annual volumes of *Statistics of Income*.

V 108–140.   Corporate asset, liability, income, deduction, tax, and profit items, and dividends paid, for all industries, 1926–1970.

Source: U.S. Internal Revenue Service (and predecessor Bureau of Internal Revenue), *Statistics of Income, Corporation Income Tax Returns*, various issues.

Prior to 1959, the statistics represent only the amounts reported by corporations which supplied balance sheet information; thereafter the statistics also include estimated amounts for corporations which owned assets but did not furnish balance sheet information, as well as selected items (other than assets and liabilities) for returns with zero assets.

V 108, number of corporate returns.   Except for 1926, excludes returns of inactive corporations.

V 110, cash.   Includes bank deposits.

V 111, notes and accounts receivable.   For 1958 and prior years, includes loans to stockholders.

V 113, investments in government obligations.   Consists of obligations of all governmental units within the United States and its outlying areas. Where investments are not segregated between "government" and "other," the entire amount is included in "other investments."

V 115, capital assets. Includes depreciable tangible assets such as buildings, fixed mechanical equipment, manufacturing and transportation facilities, furniture and fixtures; depletable tangible assets— natural resources; land; and, for 1939–1970, intangible assets such as patents, franchises, formulas, copyrights, leaseholds, goodwill, and trademarks. Prior to 1939, intangible assets were included in "other assets."

V 116, other assets. Consists of noncurrent assets which were not allocable to a specific account and certain accounts for which no distinction could be made between current and noncurrent status. Includes such items as deferred charges reported as noncurrent by the corporation, interest discounts, guaranty deposits, and intangible assets not subject to amortization. Beginning 1959, includes loans to stockholders and "other current assets" such as nontrade receivables, coupons and dividends receivable, claims and judgments, and short term marketable securities. Prior to 1959, loans to stockholders are included in notes and accounts receivable; and other current assets are included in other assets, other investments, or notes and accounts receivable, except for 1956–1958 data, which represent prepaid expenses and supplies only. Prior to 1956, prepaid expenses are included in other assets. For banks, other assets include property held in trust if included in the banks' assets while, for life insurance companies, they include market value of real estate and that portion of stock and bond holdings in excess of book value.

V 118, notes and accounts payable. Consists of accounts payable and mortgages, notes, and bonds payable with maturity less than one year.

V 119, bonded debt and mortgages. Includes bonds and mortgages payable, regardless of length of time of original maturity, and notes payable with original maturity of one year or more.

V 120, accounts payable. For 1958 and prior years, includes loans from stockholders.

V 123, other liabilities. Consists of obligations which were not allocable to a specific account and were either noncurrent accounts, in general not due within one year, or accounts which could not be identified as either current or long-term. Includes deferred or unearned income not reported as part of a current account, provisions for future taxes based on the effects of either accelerated depreciation or possible income tax adjustments such as for the investment credit, and principal amounts of employee and similar funds. Beginning 1959, includes loans from stockholders; and "other current liabilities" such as accrued expenses, taxes accrued or payable, accrued employee accounts such as payrolls and contributions to benefit plans, dividends payable, overdrafts, accrued interest or rent, and deposits and withdrawable shares of banking and savings institutions. Prior to 1959, loans from stockholders are included in accounts payable; and other current liabilities are included in accounts payable or in other liabilities, except 1957 and 1958 data, which represent accrued expenses only.

V 126, retained earnings, appropriated. Included with surplus and retained earnings, unappropriated, for 1926–1937.

V 127, surplus and retained earnings, unappropriated. Consists of paid-in or capital surplus, and, for 1926–1937, retained earnings, appropriated.

V 130, gross sales and receipts from operations. Gross sales consist of amounts received for goods, less returns and allowances, in transactions where inventories are an income-determining factor. Cost of goods sold is shown as a deduction. Gross receipts from operations consist of amounts received from transactions in which inventories are not an income-determining factor. Cost of operations is shown as a deduction. Gross receipts from operations and cost of operations are not available prior to 1932. The figure shown for 1931 represents gross profit from operations.

V 139, dividends paid in cash and assets other than own stock. Excludes liquidating dividends.

V 141–166. Nonfinancial corporations, gross product and unit costs, 1948–1970.

Source: U.S. Bureau of Economic Analysis, *Survey of Current Business*, March 1972, p. 22.

The data presented here consist of annual estimates of the output of nonfinancial corporations, capital stocks and inputs, labor inputs consistent with the Bureau of Economic Analysis (BEA) compensation and employment series, combined labor and capital inputs (total factor input), and profits. The output, profit, and stock estimates are based on the assumption of consistent depreciation practices. Total factor productivity is estimated, as well as the partial productivity of labor and capital separately. Also, rates of return to capital stock are calculated, relating property income to the capital stock valued at current replacement cost.

In interpreting these results it should be kept in mind that the capital input measure is based upon the constant dollar stock of capital owned by nonfinancial corporations, and is thus not adjusted for changes in the degree of utilization of the capital stock. Also, labor input is measured by total man-hours worked instead of the more sophisticated techniques underlying other studies of factor input and productivity, for instance, Edward F. Denison's 1962 study, *The Sources of Economic Growth in the United States and the Alternatives Before Us.*

The output measure most appropriate for comparison with total factor inputs is output valued at factor cost in constant (1958) dollars, because it excludes capital consumption allowances and indirect business taxes which are not returns to factors of production. This measure is derived by deducting from BEA's measure of constant dollar gross product originating in nonfinancial corporations the sum of constant dollar capital consumption allowances, indirect business taxes (net of subsidies received) and business transfer payments.

The gross product of nonfinancial corporations in current dollars, series V 141, is estimated from the income side of the national income and product accounts. The estimates of compensation of employees, series V 147, are largely based upon data collected from establishments reporting under the unemployment insurance system, with legal form allocations based on data from the economic censuses. The estimates of capital consumption allowances, series V 143, business transfer payments, included in series V 145, net interest, series V 150, and profits, series V 152–156, are based upon statistical tabulations of income tax returns. Indirect business taxes and subsidies are obtained from government accounting records, with allocations of indirect business taxes by legal form of organization made on the basis of the value of output produced.

The constant dollar measure of gross corporate product, series V 158, is derived from BEA's estimates of gross product by industry by multiplying each industry's real gross product by the percentage of that industry's output attributable to corporations and summing to a total for nonfinancial corporations. Capital consumption allowances and indirect business taxes (net of subsidies) and business transfer payments are estimated in constant (1958) dollars and deducted from gross corporate product in order to provide output valued at factor cost in constant (1958) dollars.

The capital consumption allowances shown in BEA's regular presentation of data on nonfinancial corporations are valued at historical cost and are affected by changes in depreciation practices permitted under Federal tax laws and regulations. To obtain constant dollar output at factor cost, this measure is replaced with an estimate of capital consumption allowances in constant (1958) dollars that is based on the assumption of straight-line depreciation with service lives averaging 85 percent of those shown in Bulletin F of the Internal Revenue Service.

In order to obtain profits based on consistent depreciation practices and current cost valuation, this new measure of capital consumption was also valued at current prices and then deducted from the sum of profits and capital consumption allowances as shown in the regular presentation. In series V 141–166, the difference between the regularly shown capital consumption allowances at historical cost and the newly computed measure in current prices is shown as the "depreciation adjustment," series V 144. The method for deriving capital consumption allowances in current and constant dollars is discussed in the section on capital stock in the source publication. For the source study, a constant dollar measure of indirect business taxes was derived, and this measure was used to extrapolate the $½ billion 1958 value of business transfer payments less subsidies. Constant dollar indirect business taxes were obtained by extrapolating the value of indirect taxes in 1958 by the output of the taxes commodities and services. Taxes on heavily taxed products or products whose output fluctuated more than average were estimated separately. The value of the automobile excise tax in 1958 was extrapolated by constant dollar auto product; liquor taxes by constant dollar personal consumption expenditures for alcoholic beverages; tobacco taxes by constant dollar personal consumption expenditures for tobacco products; gasoline taxes by the number of gallons consumed; and property taxes on residential structures by the constant dollar net stock of these structures owned by nonfinancial corporations. All other taxes, accounting for 65 percent of the 1958 total, were extrapolated by an estimate of constant dollar net corporate product at market prices excluding corporate product associated with the separately extrapolated items.

V 167–181. Selected corporate asset, liability, income, and tax items, and dividends paid, by industrial division, 1926–1970.

Source: See source for series V 108–140.

Includes Alaska and Hawaii for all years.

V 172, investments. Consists of investments in government obligations, other investments, and mortgage and real estate loans.

V 174, accounts payable and short-term debt. Consists of accounts payable and mortgages, notes, and bonds payable in less than one year.

V 175, long-term debt. Consists of mortgages, notes, and bonds payable in one year or more.

V 177, surplus and retained earnings. Consists of paid-in or capital surplus and retained earnings, appropriated and unappropriated.

V 182–196. Selected corporate asset, liability, income, and tax items, and dividends paid, by size of total assets, 1931–1970.

Source: See source for series V 108–140.

Includes Alaska and Hawaii for all years.

V 187, investments. Consists of investments in government obligations, other investments, and mortgage and real estate loans.

V 189, accounts payable and short-term debt. Consists of accounts payable and mortgages, notes, and bonds payable in less than one year.

V 190, long-term debt. Consists of mortgages, notes, and bonds payable in one year or more.

V 192, surplus and retained earnings. Consists of paid-in or capital surplus and retained earnings, appropriated and unappropriated.

V 197–212. Assets, liabilities, and selected income items for privately owned Class A and B electric companies, 1937–1970.

Source: U.S. Federal Power Commission, all series except V 200–202 for 1937–1956, *Statistics of Electrical Utilities in the United States,* various annual issues; **series V 200–202,** 1937–1956, unpublished data.

These data cover reports of all Class A and B companies: Class A companies having annual electric operating revenue of $2,500,000 or more; Class B companies having annual electric operating revenue of more than $1,000,000 but less than $2,500,000. In recent years, these concerns have represented approximately 98 percent of the total privately owned electric utility industry.

V 197, total assets or liabilities. For total assets, series V 197 is the sum of series V 198, V 199, V 202, and V 203. For total liabilities, series V 197 is the sum of series V 204–209.

V 198, current assets. Includes cash, special deposits, working funds, temporary cash investments, receivables (less reserve for uncollectible accounts), materials and supplies, prepayments, other current and accrued assets.

V 199, investments. Includes investments in associated companies (less reserve), other investments (less reserve), physical property other than utility plant (less reserve), sinking funds, miscellaneous special funds.

V 200–202, plant and equipment in service. Prior to 1932, firms in the electric utility industry included in their electric utility plant and equipment accounts an increasing amount of "phantom assets" which were created by "writing up" assets above their original cost. Changes in economic conditions and government regulation forced a "write-down" of these "assets" at intervals over subsequent years. Until such "write-downs" were made, however, the figures as published in the annual reports of the Federal Power Commission included decreasing amounts of "phantom assets." However, the figures shown here for series V 197–202 represent revised estimates of the Federal Power Commission and exclude "phantom assets."

V 203, other assets. Includes the "phantom assets" deducted from electric plant and equipment (see text for series V 200–202); electric plant not in service such as plant under construction, leased to others, or held for future use; net utility plant and equipment other than electric; deferred debits; capital stock discount and expenses; and reacquired securities. Although there was some decline in deferred debits, capital stock discount and expense, and reacquired securities, the major portion of the decline in this series between 1937 and 1945 is attributable to the writeoff of "phantom assets." The distribution of these assets for significant years was as follows (in millions):

Item	1937	1948	1956
Total other assets	$4,833.9	$3,657.3	$5,207.1
"Phantom assets"	2,100.0		
Electric plant not in service	450.0	1,472.1	1,945.0
Net utility plant other than electric	1,683.6	1,876.6	2,959.4
Other asset items	600.3	308.6	302.7

If the "phantom assets" were to be completely excluded from the asset side, a corresponding adjustment would have to be made in the companies' net worth. This has not been done, because it has been deemed advisable to present the capital and surplus figures as reported by the electric companies.

V 204, current liabilities. Includes notes and accounts payable, dividends declared, customers' deposits, accrued taxes and interest, miscellaneous current and accrued liabilities.

V 205, long-term debt. Includes bonds, receivers' certificates, advances from associated companies, miscellaneous long-term debt. Bonds held in treasury were deducted from the total amount of long-term debt outstanding.

V 206, other liabilities. Includes deferred credits, insurance, and other reserves.

V 207, capital stock. Includes common and preferred stock.

V 208, other paid-in capital. Includes premium on capital stock, capital stock discount and expenses, other capital stock items, and reacquired capital stock.

V 209, net surplus. Includes capital and earned surplus.

V 210, total revenue. Includes operating revenues and other income, gross of operating expenses, and all other deductions.

V 211, net income. Equals total revenue less all operating and nonoperating income deductions (including depreciation, interest, and taxes).

V 212, dividends. Includes dividends on preferred and common shares. Excludes stock dividends.

V 213–227.   Assets, liabilities, and selected income items for central electric light and power stations, commercial, 1902–1937.

Source: U. S. Bureau of the Census. 1902–1912, *Electrical Industries*, special reports and bulletins for 1902, 1907, and 1912; 1917–1937, *Census of Electrical Industries*, reports for 1917, 1922, 1927, 1932, and 1937.

See also text for series V 197–212.

Central electric stations are defined as plants owned or operated by individuals, companies, corporations, or municipalities, and furnishing current for public or commercial uses.

Although central electric stations, as defined by the Bureau of the Census, do not represent a group completely identical with Class A and B electric companies, as defined by the Federal Power Commission, the coverage is nearly the same in terms of assets, liabilities, and revenues, as the figures for 1937 show. Consequently, the data in series V 197–212 and V 213–227 may be taken to indicate, with a high degree of approximation, financial trends in the electric utility industry over the entire 1902–1937 period.

Unfortunately, complete balance sheet data for series V 213–227 are available only for 1927, 1932, and 1937. The data for 1912, 1917, and 1922 do not include reserve for depreciation. Consequently, total assets for these years include the gross rather than net value of plant and equipment. The only balance sheet item available for 1902 and 1907 is the gross amount of plant and equipment. The gross revenue, net income, and dividend figures, however, are available for the entire 1902–1937 period.

The accounting nomenclature in series V 213–227 and also in series V 228–272 is similar to that described above for series V 197–212. However, financial statements were much less detailed in the early years and accounting procedures did not remain fully consistent over the entire 1902–1937 period.

V 228–242.   Assets, liabilities, and selected income items for street and electric railways, 1902–1937.

Source: See source for series V 213–227.

See also text for series V 197–212.

These data relate to all electric railways in the United States irrespective of their length or location and all street railways irrespective of their motive power.

Data for 1902–1922 include companies which operated street and electric railways and were also engaged in other activities, while the data for 1922–1937 include only companies which were exclusively engaged in the operation of street and electric railways. The double set of figures given for 1922 should enable users to make an adjustment required for comparing the figures for 1927–1937 with those for 1902–1917. For 1917–1937, the total assets include net value of plant and equipment. For 1902–1912, they include gross value of plant and equipment because of the lack of data on depreciation.

V 243–270.   Assets, liabilities, and selected income items for telephone and telegraph companies, 1902–1937.

Source: See source for series V 213–227.

See also text for series V 197–212.

The data available for the telephone and telegraph companies for 1902–1937 are even more incomplete than those for the electric utilities. After 1922, the only data collected by the Bureau of the Census were value of plant and equipment, gross income, and dividends paid. During the entire 1902–1937 period, reserves for depreciation were included with other reserves on the liability side and could not, therefore, be used to obtain net value of plant and equipment. Treasury stocks and bonds were reported as a single item (Treasury securities) and could not, therefore, be subtracted from long-term debt and capital stock respectively, as was done for the other electrical industries.

Despite these serious deficiencies, the data throw some light on the rapid development of the telephone and telegraph industries in the early decades of the 20th century and should, therefore, be useful to those interested in financial trends of these two industries.

V 271–284.   Net value of plant and equipment in regulated industries, 1870–1951.

Source: Melville J. Ulmer, *Capital in Transportation, Communications, and Public Utilities*, National Bureau of Economic Research, Princeton University Press, 1959 (copyright).

All values in these series are net of depreciation and relate to reproducible fixed assets: Road, plant, and equipment. Investment in land and land rights has not been included. The coverage is confined to privately owned enterprises.

In general, the series have been obtained by cumulative addition (or subtraction) of the annual figures on net capital formation to a base value in some selected year. The series in 1929 dollars reflect changes in net physical stock of reproducible fixed assets. The series in current dollars indicate changes in the replacement value of such assets, less depreciation.

More specifically, the derivation of the series in 1929 dollars involved the following steps:

a. Finding a base-year figure. For steam railroads, the base-year value was derived from an ICC estimate for January 1, 1937. For electric light and power companies, the value of plant and equipment was assumed to be zero as of January 1, 1881. For telephones, the value for 1880 was derived from estimates of gross capital expenditures in 1878 and 1879. For street and electric railways, the value for 1870 was obtained from the reports submitted to State railroad commissions. For local buslines, it was assumed that net value for 1910 was less than $100,000.

b. Converting the base-year figure into 1929 dollars.

c. Deriving the series on net capital expenditures in 1929 prices. This series was obtained by deducting the estimated annual amounts of "true" depreciation from the figures on gross capital expenditures for the corresponding years.

d. Applying the series on net capital expenditures to the base-year value.

The series in current dollars for each class of utilities was obtained by multiplying the values in 1929 dollars by the construction cost index applicable to that class.

V 285–305.   Assets, liabilities, and selected income items for two samples of large manufacturing corporations, 1914–1943.

Source: National Bureau of Economic Research, unpublished data.

These series represent financial data for two samples of large corporations (companies with total assets over $10 million each). The data for 1914–1922 are based on a sample of 81 corporations, and the data for 1922–1943 are based on a sample of 84 corporations. These sample materials make it possible to examine financial developments in manufacturing during World War I and the early part of the interwar period, for which time no aggregate data are available.

For both samples, companies were selected from among the largest and most important concerns in 11 major manufacturing industries. A few of the very large corporations (e.g., Ford Motor Company) had to be omitted because of lack of published financial statements, but the number of such omissions was small. Consequently, both samples, though small in terms of the number of firms included, represent substantial portions of the entire manufacturing universe in terms of total assets and total volume of operations. For example, in 1933 the sample represented 29 percent of the total assets of all manufacturing corporations and as much as 45 percent of the total assets of all large manufacturing corporations (with total assets over $10 million). (See A. R. Koch, *The Financing of Large Corporations*, National Bureau of Economic Research, New York, 1943, p. 13.)

In the sample for 1914–1922, data were not available for 8 companies in 1914, 3 companies in 1915, 1 company in 1916, and 1 company in 1917. In the sample for 1922–1943, 3 companies had to be omitted in 1922, 1 in 1923, 1 in 1924, and 1 in 1925. Since the excluded firms were among the smallest in the samples, however, their omission had a relatively minor effect on the composite balance sheets and income statements.

The amounts of total assets, income, and dividends for the sample for 1922–1943 are considerably greater than those for the sample for earlier years. This is due to the fact that in a number of cases larger companies were substituted in the sample for 1922–1943 for smaller concerns included in the sample for 1914–1922. These differences should be borne in mind when trends over the entire period are examined.

For a more detailed description of these samples, see the unpublished manuscript, *Corporate Financial Data for Studies in Business Finance*, May 1945, available at the National Bureau of Economic Research.

The accounting terms used in these series are defined as follows:

Total assets: Sum of all asset items less depreciation and revaluation reserves.

Cash: Cash on hand and bank deposits.

Marketable securities: Government securities; call and time loans.

Receivables: Notes and accounts receivable less bad debt reserve.

Inventory: Raw materials; goods and work in process; finished goods; supplies—less reserves for inventory.

Investments and advances: Investment in, or advances to, subsidiaries or affiliated; other stocks and bonds.

Fixed assets (net): Land; plant; machinery; equipment; nonoperating property—less reserves for depreciation, depletion, and obsolescence.

Other assets: Prepaid expenses; deferred charges; intangibles; due from officers, directors, and stockholders; cash set aside for specific purposes or not available for immediate use.

Notes payable: All notes or bills to banks, trade, and others.

Accounts payable: Accounts payable to trade.

Other current liabilities: Accruals and current reserves.

Long-term debt: All funded debt or mortgages, whether current or not, less sinking fund when listed on asset side; purchase obligations.

Other liabilities: Minority interest; deferred liabilities; amounts appropriated from surplus for specific purposes; due to officers, employees, and affiliates.

Preferred stock: Preferred and debenture stock less treasury preferred stock when listed on asset side.

Common stock: Common stock (A and B) or capital stock less common treasury stock when listed on asset side.

Capital reserves: Special appropriations from income or surplus for contingencies.

Surplus: Capital and earned surplus less profit and undivided surplus when carried on asset side.

Net income: Net amount after all expenses, interest, and taxes.

Dividends: Cash dividends on preferred and common shares. Stock dividends are not included.

V 306–332. Business expenditures for new plant and equipment 1947–1970.

Source: U.S. Office of Business Economics (OBE), 1947–1969, *Survey of Current Business*, January 1970, p. 25–39; 1970, *Survey of Current Business*, March 1971, p. 20. Series prepared jointly with U.S. Securities and Exchange Commission (SEC).

These series measure estimated expenditures for new structures and additions to existing plants (including major alterations), as well as expenditures for new machinery and equipment that are chargeable to fixed asset accounts. They include expenditures for replacement purposes and for additions and modernization and exclude expenditures for land, costs of maintenance and repairs, items charged off as current operating expense, new facilities owned by the Federal Government and operated under contract by private companies, and plant and equipment furnished a company by communities and organizations.

Coverage is extended to all private nonagricultural business except real estate operators; medical, legal, educational, and cultural services; and nonprofit membership organizations. The data generally reflect company expenditures, aggregated on a fully consolidated basis, rather than individual establishment data. Each company is assigned an industry classification on the basis of its primary activity, utilizing the Standard Industrial Classification system. Thus, the total capital expenditures of a company for both its primary and secondary activity are included under the assigned industry category. The possible effect of the aggregation of company data in this manner is that the expenditures of one industry could be included in a different industry's total.

Data on plant and equipment expenditures appearing prior to 1947 in a similar OBE-SEC series are not entirely comparable to the series for 1947 to 1970, due to revisions that have occurred. The effect of the revisions, which are benchmarked to data from the 1958 and 1963 censuses, was to increase the rate of growth of capital expenditures over the period for both manufacturing and nonmanufacturing industries.

The gross national product (GNP) series on fixed nonresidential investment (F 54–56) differs from these series in definition and industry coverage. The GNP investment accounts cover capital expenditures of farm enterprises, professional persons, real estate operators, and nonprofit institutions and include oil well drilling costs charged to current expense, automobile costs used for business purposes, net purchases of used capital goods from government, and dealers' margins on used capital purchases, all of which are not covered or included by these series. The national accounts investment data are derived in a largely indirect manner from a variety of sources, with the equipment component resulting from the utilization, basically, of the commodity flow technique that provides commodity detail. The structures component is obtained in an equally indirect manner from Census Bureau construction data and other sources. In contrast, the OBE-SEC series is based primarily on sample survey results and provides expenditure estimates by purchasing industry.

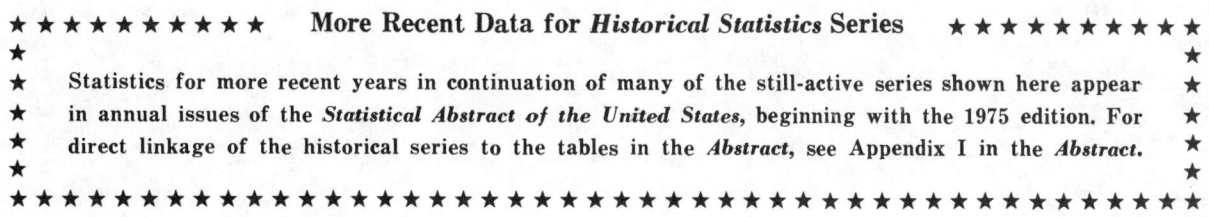

★ ★ ★ ★ ★ ★ ★ ★ ★ ★   **More Recent Data for *Historical Statistics* Series**   ★ ★ ★ ★ ★ ★ ★ ★ ★ ★

★ Statistics for more recent years in continuation of many of the still-active series shown here appear in annual issues of the *Statistical Abstract of the United States*, beginning with the 1975 edition. For direct linkage of the historical series to the tables in the *Abstract*, see Appendix I in the *Abstract*.

Series V 108–140. Corporate Asset, Liability, Income, Deduction, Tax, and Profit Items, and Dividends Paid, for All Industries: 1926 to 1970

[In millions of dollars, except number of tax returns]

Series No.	Item	1970	1969	1968	1967	1966	1965	1964	1963	1962
108	Number of corporate tax returns	1,665,477	1,658,820	1,541,670	1,534,360	1,468,725	1,423,980	1,373,517	1,323,187	1,268,042
109	Total assets	2,634,707	2,445,628	2,215,625	2,010,443	1,844,775	1,723,524	1,585,619	1,481,236	1,388,127
110	Cash	176,925	162,615	150,295	139,984	126,255	117,060	113,742	108,775	(NA)
111	Notes and accounts receivable less allowance	594,637	562,102	499,397	449,222	414,384	392,252	345,322	330,953	(NA)
112	Inventories	190,402	184,583	164,433	151,581	141,019	126,341	112,960	106,340	100,327
113	Investments in government obligations	196,625	178,235	185,394	173,181	157,573	156,916	155,335	150,553	(NA)
114	Other investments	728,982	670,558	607,045	538,902	497,410	463,378	428,611	383,014	(NA)
115	Capital assets less reserves	599,465	561,306	504,865	467,446	432,034	395,297	365,551	342,026	(NA)
116	Other assets	147,671	126,230	104,195	90,129	76,101	72,282	64,097	59,577	(NA)
117	Total liabilities	2,634,707	2,445,628	2,215,625	2,010,443	1,844,775	1,723,524	1,585,619	1,481,236	1,388,127
120	Accounts payable	148,813	144,177	124,111	110,780	99,226	89,612	82,582	95,303	(NA)
	Bonds, notes, and mortgages payable:									
121	Maturity less than 1 year [1]	170,884	157,349	125,490	104,564	98,167	84,667	72,420	68,775	(NA)
122	Maturity 1 year or more [1]	362,700	326,039	285,612	252,423	232,506	210,274	192,878	180,952	(NA)
123	Other liabilities	1,199,898	1,090,505	1,013,801	929,631	847,794	802,974	734,334	659,650	(NA)
124	Capital stock, preferred	} 201,214	195,548	181,314	176,709	167,778	161,357	158,120	154,602	(NA)
125	Capital stock, common									
126	Retained earnings, appropriated	16,657	15,598	18,845	18,873	17,800	18,619	18,689	20,596	(NA)
127	Surplus and retained earnings, unappropriated [2]	534,540	516,413	466,451	417,462	381,503	356,022	326,596	301,357	(NA)
129	Total receipts	1,750,728	1,680,482	1,507,786	1,374,599	1,306,518	1,194,601	1,086,739	1,008,743	949,305
130	Gross sales and receipts from operations	1,620,887	1,560,830	1,403,500	1,285,000	1,224,370	1,120,382	1,018,889	949,549	895,120
131	Other receipts	129,842	119,652	104,286	89,599	82,148	74,219	67,850	59,194	54,185
132	Total compiled deductions	1,682,779	1,598,348	1,420,309	1,295,348	1,225,225	1,119,860	1,023,680	953,006	898,463
133	Cost of goods sold and of operations	1,146,263	1,104,572	989,550	908,598	866,425	792,953	722,477	672,972	638,036
134	Depreciation, depletion, and amortization	59,310	55,483	50,710	46,567	42,803	39,189	36,486	34,129	32,007
135	Other deductions	477,206	438,293	380,049	340,183	315,997	287,718	264,717	245,905	228,420
136	Total receipts less total deductions	67,949	82,135	87,477	79,250	81,293	74,742	63,059	55,737	50,842
137	Income and excess profits taxes	33,293	39,374	39,694	33,301	34,449	31,662	27,857	26,298	23,930
138	Compiled net profit after taxes	34,656	42,761	47,783	45,949	46,844	43,079	35,202	29,438	26,912
	Dividends paid:									
139	Cash and assets other than own stock	32,013	32,951	31,563	28,239	27,033	25,997	23,305	21,105	19,565
140	Corporation's own stock	1,923	2,715	3,304	3,233	2,677	2,240	3,092	2,118	2,149

Series No.	Item	1961	1960	1959	1958	1957	1956	1955	1954	1953
108	Number of corporate tax returns	1,190,286	1,140,574	1,074,120	990,381	940,147	827,916	746,962	667,856	640,073
109	Total assets	1,289,516	1,206,662	1,136,668	1,064,481	996,400	948,951	888,621	805,300	761,877
110	Cash	101,965	97,162	91,856	93,248	89,222	89,780	87,375	81,723	80,171
111	Notes and accounts receivable less allowance	259,541	242,416	227,994	210,141	198,226	210,392	191,779	158,738	148,282
112	Inventories	94,818	91,334	88,304	80,047	80,560	78,744	70,920	62,914	65,519
113	Investments in government obligations	144,760	135,180	134,293	132,947	121,621	122,071	131,898	131,409	123,599
114	Other investments	332,882	308,293	284,440	260,419	236,356	198,829	179,558	160,553	147,188
115	Capital assets less reserves	310,266	293,215	275,772	259,613	244,463	225,862	206,388	191,437	180,612
116	Other assets	45,285	39,061	34,008	28,065	25,952	23,273	20,703	18,527	16,506
117	Total liabilities	1,289,516	1,206,662	1,136,668	1,064,481	996,400	948,951	888,621	805,300	[3]761,877
120	Accounts payable	70,873	62,933	62,755	59,792	54,842	50,886	45,590	38,153	35,554
	Bonds, notes and mortgages payable:									
121	Maturity less than 1 year [1]	50,183	49,381	43,171	36,697	35,893	34,230	30,458	23,239	21,394
122	Maturity 1 year or more [1]	165,521	153,566	142,913	132,082	122,515	108,928	98,399	90,797	86,607
123	Other liabilities	568,745	531,815	498,826	466,753	438,799	427,240	408,727	373,343	353,141
124	Capital stock, preferred	17,702	16,952	16,522	16,302	16,419	15,627	15,796	15,632	15,815
125	Capital stock, common	128,669	123,396	118,573	112,104	107,941	103,977	96,832	90,730	88,121
126	Retained earnings, appropriated	19,417	17,085	16,757	18,855	16,033	15,289	14,265	14,197	13,294
127	Surplus and retained earnings, unappropriated [2]	268,405	251,533	237,152	221,896	203,957	192,775	178,555	159,210	155,606
129	Total receipts	873,178	849,132	816,800	735,338	720,414	673,493	634,508	547,001	551,984
130	Gross sales and receipts from operations	823,943	802,791	772,915	696,594	684,883	640,679	605,408	521,478	528,638
131	Other receipts	49,235	46,341	43,885	38,744	35,530	32,814	29,100	25,523	23,344
132	Total compiled deductions	826,144	804,633	769,145	696,114	675,340	626,309	586,907	510,515	512,402
133	Cost of goods sold and of operations	586,557	577,039	557,062	505,252	499,972	468,813	443,172	384,226	388,214
134	Depreciation, depletion, and amortization	28,246	26,899	25,299	23,825	22,777	20,466	18,592	15,729	14,178
135	Other deductions	211,341	200,695	186,784	167,038	152,589	137,030	125,143	110,561	110,009
136	Total receipts less total deductions	47,034	44,499	47,655	39,224	45,073	47,184	47,601	36,486	39,582
137	Income and excess profits taxes	22,188	21,866	22,525	18,814	20,582	21,222	21,536	16,682	19,693
138	Compiled net profit after taxes	24,846	22,633	25,130	20,410	24,491	25,962	26,065	19,804	19,889
	Dividends paid:									
139	Cash and assets other than own stock	18,038	17,193	16,242	14,952	14,914	14,359	13,468	11,832	11,533
140	Corporation's own stock	2,177	1,966	2,174	1,604	1,778	2,717	1,980	1,344	1,106

Series No.	Item	1952	1951	1950	1949	1948	1947	1946	1945	1944
108	Number of corporate tax returns	615,698	596,385	569,961	554,573	536,833	496,821	440,750	374,950	363,056
109	Total assets	721,864	647,524	598,369	543,562	525,136	494,615	454,705	441,461	418,324
110	Cash	79,597	76,853	71,018	63,864	65,737	64,369	58,502	57,717	52,783
111	Notes and accounts receivable less allowance	140,902	119,314	108,639	85,526	84,597	75,959	61,371	51,630	47,894
112	Inventories	64,520	63,776	54,496	44,726	48,293	44,009	36,965	26,067	26,476
113	Investments in government obligations	120,303	108,939	109,822	110,969	104,819	108,774	109,910	129,935	111,219
114	Other investments	132,512	104,883	96,760	91,152	84,202	78,363	77,089	74,026	74,392
115	Capital assets less reserves	169,546	159,325	144,691	135,617	125,650	112,194	100,329	92,057	95,128
116	Other assets	14,485	14,434	12,944	11,709	11,838	10,946	10,541	10,029	10,431

See footnotes at end of table.

Series V 108–140. Corporate Asset, Liability, Income, Deduction, Tax, and Profit Items, and Dividends Paid, for All Industries: 1926 to 1970—Con.

[In millions of dollars, except number of tax returns]

Series No.	Item	1952	1951	1950	1949	1948	1947	1946	1945	1944
117	Total liabilities	721,864	647,524	598,369	543,562	525,136	494,615	454,705	441,461	418,324
120	Accounts payable	35,827	33,352	31,298	24,896	26,302	25,537	21,336	17,455	17,805
	Bonds, notes, and mortgages payable:									
121	Maturity less than 1 year [1]	20,996	19,240	15,845	11,801	12,225	11,289	9,504	7,208	7,056
122	Maturity 1 year or more [1]	80,628	72,835	65,719	61,851	57,326	50,108	44,968	40,987	42,454
123	Other liabilities	330,406	283,058	261,899	236,716	232,064	227,114	214,283	221,286	200,550
124	Capital stock, preferred	15,831	15,595	14,906	15,365	14,957	15,007	14,857	14,764	15,112
125	Capital stock, common	85,365	82,804	79,310	78,944	76,774	72,463	68,334	64,747	64,785
126	Retained earnings, appropriated	13,472	12,739	12,410	11,178	11,345	11,303	11,004	11,057	12,200
127	Surplus and retained earnings, unappropriated [2]	146,464	135,310	124,951	111,078	102,262	90,101	78,836	72,528	67,557
128	Less: Deficit [4]	7,125	7,411	7,968	8,269	8,118	8,307	8,416	8,571	9,195
129	Total receipts	525,011	511,849	452,523	387,636	405,430	361,521	283,917	252,636	258,880
130	Gross sales and receipts from operations	503,365	492,373	434,666	372,005	390,382	347,946	270,984	241,456	249,129
131	Other receipts	21,647	19,476	17,856	15,629	15,049	13,575	12,933	11,180	9,750
132	Total compiled deductions	486,504	468,354	409,988	359,505	371,182	330,314	258,893	231,417	232,426
133	Cost of goods sold and of operations	371,597	363,046	317,373	275,585	290,405	258,146	199,552	178,187	183,179
134	Depreciation, depletion, and amortization	12,433	11,090	9,489	8,521	7,939	6,383	4,972	6,531	5,563
135	Other deductions	102,474	94,218	83,128	75,400	72,838	65,782	54,370	46,698	43,686
136	Total receipts less total deductions	38,507	43,495	42,535	28,130	34,248	31,207	25,025	21,220	26,454
137	Income and excess profits taxes	19,002	21,902	17,168	9,688	11,771	10,787	8,710	10,702	14,769
138	Compiled net profit after taxes	19,504	21,593	25,368	18,442	22,477	20,420	16,314	10,518	11,685
	Dividends paid:									
139	Cash and assets other than own stock	11,196	11,219	11,471	9,464	9,305	8,285	7,378	6,009	5,957
140	Corporation's own stock	1,360	1,425	1,289	678	1,022	696	523	332	235

Series No.	Item	1943	1942	1941	1940	1939	1938	1937	1936	1935
108	Number of corporate tax returns	366,870	383,534	407,053	413,716	412,759	411,941	416,902	415,654	415,205
109	Total assets	389,524	360,018	340,452	320,478	306,801	300,022	303,357	303,180	303,150
110	Cash	50,271	46,464	41,629	41,423	34,054	27,973	24,346	26,102	23,664
111	Notes and accounts receivable less allowance	45,728	46,155	49,255	42,864	39,451	37,763	40,329	40,219	38,690
112	Inventories	27,187	26,832	25,058	19,463	17,718	16,582	18,515	16,584	14,788
113	Investments in government obligations	86,655	61,191	36,548	29,570	27,353	25,527	23,988	24,313	21,863
114	Other investments	72,064	70,899	80,354	80,429	81,155	82,701	85,065	86,208	90,163
115	Capital assets less reserves	97,728	99,772	100,698	100,214	100,226	99,299	100,320	97,873	100,480
116	Other assets	9,889	8,706	6,911	6,514	6,846	10,176	10,794	11,882	13,501
117	Total liabilities	389,524	360,018	340,452	320,478	306,801	300,022	303,357	303,180	303,150
118	Notes and accounts payable	-------	-------	-------	-------	-------	-------	-------	25,580	25,332
119	Bonded debt and mortgages	-------	-------	-------	-------	-------	-------	-------	47,023	49,822
120	Accounts payable	17,495	17,055	16,350	14,696	14,506	13,747	14,748	-------	-------
	Bonds, notes, and mortgages payable:									
121	Maturity less than 1 year [1]	6,770	7,205	9,242	7,987	8,027	8,104	10,373	-------	-------
122	Maturity 1 year or more [1]	43,735	45,040	49,542	49,199	49,388	50,278	49,326	-------	-------
123	Other liabilities	175,859	151,088	122,728	110,210	98,016	90,455	87,276	97,109	89,066
124	Capital stock, preferred	15,067	15,473	16,214	17,138	17,213	18,108	18,364	18,591	19,533
125	Capital stock, common	64,481	65,828	71,577	72,292	73,482	74,792	77,339	78,072	82,733
126	Retained earnings, appropriated	12,409	10,581	10,065	8,358	7,889	7,301	}	58,524	48,043	48,828
127	Surplus and retained earnings, unappropriated [2]	63,427	58,201	56,593	53,275	51,302	50,367	}			
128	Less: Deficit [4]	9,720	10,454	11,858	12,676	13,022	13,131	12,594	11,237	12,163
129	Total receipts	245,796	213,777	186,137	145,427	130,365	117,596	138,907	126,269	112,098
130	Gross sales and receipts from operations	236,610	204,981	176,717	136,535	121,601	109,210	130,004	117,375	102,884
131	Other receipts	9,186	8,795	9,420	8,891	8,763	8,384	8,903	8,895	9,214
132	Total compiled deductions	217,863	190,497	169,546	135,955	123,129	113,452	131,130	118,651	106,599
133	Cost of goods sold and of operations	171,698	146,596	125,737	97,240	86,828	78,271	94,149	84,447	73,926
134	Depreciation, depletion, and amortization	5,169	4,800	4,280	3,931	3,805	3,711	3,756	3,551	3,611
135	Other deductions	40,994	39,102	39,528	34,784	32,497	31,470	33,224	30,653	29,061
136	Total receipts less total deductions	27,933	23,280	16,592	9,472	7,236	4,144	7,777	7,618	5,500
137	Income and excess profits taxes	15,752	12,138	7,064	2,525	1,217	844	1,246	1,145	722
138	Compiled net profit after taxes	12,181	11,141	9,528	6,947	6,019	3,300	6,531	6,473	4,778
	Dividends paid:									
139	Cash and assets other than own stock	5,628	5,512	6,556	6,019	5,639	4,834	7,281	7,163	5,896
140	Corporation's own stock	212	69	166	136	86	73	183	343	135

Series No.	Item	1934	1933	1932	1931	1930	1929	1928	1927	1926
108	Number of corporate tax returns	410,626	388,564	392,021	381,088	403,173	398,815	384,548	379,156	359,449
109	Total assets	301,307	268,206	280,083	296,497	334,002	335,778	307,218	287,542	262,179
110	Cash	19,961	15,236	15,917	15,880	21,012	22,371	21,952	16,851	16,802
111	Notes and accounts receivable less allowance (except 1926)	40,529	35,835	39,564	48,667	59,675	66,810	62,804	50,959	23,552
112	Inventories	14,311	13,597	12,372	15,140	18,771	21,911	20,751	21,005	20,939
113	Investments in government obligations	19,084	13,571	11,917	10,667	10,228	10,338	10,116	9,781	8,694
114	Other investments	90,573	70,474	75,630	75,305	83,809	[5] 55,844	(5)	(5)	(5)
115	Capital assets less reserves	102,751	104,958	108,553	114,303	120,994	116,446	109,931	104,945	97,523
116	Other assets	14,097	14,535	16,129	16,534	19,511	[5] 42,057	[5] 81,663	[5] 84,001	[5] 94,669

See footnotes at end of table.

Series V 108–140. Corporate Assets, Liability, Income, Deduction, Tax, and Profit Items, and Dividends Paid, for All Industries: 1926 to 1970—Con.

[In millions of dollars, except number of tax returns]

Series No.	Item	1934	1933	1932	1931	1930	1929	1928	1927	1926
117	Total liabilities	301,307	268,206	280,083	296,497	334,002	335,778	307,218	287,542	262,179
118	Notes and accounts payable	27,021	19,362	20,562	23,251	26,870	29,453	27,437	24,126	24,042
119	Bonded debt and mortgages	48,604	45,883	47,222	48,101	50,282	46,643	42,943	37,740	31,801
123	Other liabilities	84,096	75,384	78,730	81,782	95,568	99,314	93,950	93,274	87,076
124	Capital stock, preferred	19,976	18,394	19,076	19,217	19,117	19,738	18,475	17,800	17,146
125	Capital stock, common	84,970	74,088	78,413	79,794	87,067	85,520	77,256	74,081	67,517
126	Retained earnings, appropriated	}								
127	Surplus and retained earnings, unappropriated [2]	48,986	44,792	45,664	51,976	61,832	60,699	52,069	45,415	39,154
128	Less: Deficit [4]	12,347	9,696	9,584	7,624	6,734	5,588	4,913	4,893	4,557
129	Total receipts	99,095	82,148	79,701	105,238					
130	Gross sales and receipts from operations	90,738	74,952	71,226	[6] 94,989					
131	Other receipts	8,357	7,196	8,475	10,249					
132	Total compiled deductions	96,058	82,787	83,211	105,725					
133	Cost of goods sold and of operations	64,656	51,969	50,261	[6] 57,374					
134	Depreciation, depletion, and amortization	3,593	3,666	3,866	4,194					
135	Other deductions	27,808	27,151	29,084	44,158	} (7)	(7)	(7)	(7)	(7)
136	Total receipts less total deductions	3,037	[8] 639	[8] 3,511	[8] 487					
137	Income and excess profits taxes	586	417	282	393					
138	Compiled net profit after taxes	2,451	[8] 1,056	[8] 3,792	[8] 880					
	Dividends paid:									
139	Cash and assets other than own stock	4,788	3,091	3,854	6,092					
140	Corporation's own stock	212	90	142	162	}				

NA Not available.
[1] Prior to 1954, based on original maturity date; beginning 1954, based on date of balance sheet.
[2] Net amount beginning in 1954. For 1937–1953, this is the sum of all positive amounts reported; for 1926–1936, the sum of positive net surplus and undivided profits.
[3] Includes deficit of $7,655 million.
[4] For 1937–1953, this is the sum of all deficits reported (1953 deficit, $7,655 million); for 1926–1936, sum of net deficits.
[5] "Other investments" were included in "Other assets" for all corporations, 1926–1928, and for life insurance companies, 1929.
[6] For 1931, gross profit was reported in lieu of gross receipts and cost of operations.
[7] Not available separately for returns with balance sheets.
[8] Loss.

Series V 141–166. Nonfinancial Corporations, Gross Product and Unit Costs: 1948 to 1970

Series No.	Item	1970	1969	1968	1967	1966	1965	1964	1963	1962	1961	1960	1959
		BILLIONS OF DOLLARS											
141	Gross product in current dollars	516.2	502.0	469.9	430.8	413.0	377.6	346.0	320.0	302.8	278.4	273.1	263.7
142	Capital consumption allowances less depreciation adjustment	55.6	50.0	44.4	40.5	36.7	33.5	31.2	29.5	28.2	27.0	26.0	25.0
143	Capital consumption allowances	54.1	49.5	45.4	41.7	38.4	35.4	32.9	31.0	29.3	25.6	24.3	23.0
144	Depreciation adjustment [1]	−1.5	−.4	.9	1.2	1.7	1.9	1.7	1.5	1.2	−1.4	−1.7	−2.0
145	Indirect business taxes plus transfer payments less subsidies	49.9	47.1	43.7	39.2	36.8	35.7	33.8	31.5	29.7	27.7	26.4	24.6
146	Income originating in nonfinancial corporations	410.7	405.0	381.8	351.0	339.5	308.4	281.0	259.0	245.0	223.6	220.6	214.0
147	Compensation of employees	344.2	330.5	301.5	275.8	261.0	236.3	218.9	204.4	194.7	181.3	179.0	170.6
148	Wages and salaries	305.2	293.7	268.6	246.6	233.3	212.7	197.5	184.5	176.2	165.0	163.3	156.4
149	Supplements	39.0	36.9	33.0	29.2	27.7	23.6	21.4	19.9	18.5	16.3	15.7	14.3
150	Net interest	14.8	12.9	10.3	9.0	7.3	6.0	5.1	4.5	4.1	3.5	3.0	2.7
151	Corporate profits and inventory valuation and depreciation adjustments	51.8	61.6	70.0	66.3	71.2	66.0	57.0	50.1	46.1	38.8	38.6	40.7
152	Profits before tax	57.8	67.6	72.4	66.2	71.2	65.8	55.8	49.1	44.7	40.3	40.1	43.2
153	Profits tax liability	27.1	33.4	34.0	28.4	30.1	27.6	24.3	22.9	20.9	19.8	19.5	20.8
154	Profits after tax	30.7	34.2	38.3	37.8	41.2	38.2	31.4	26.2	23.9	20.5	20.6	22.5
155	Dividends	21.1	20.9	20.9	18.9	18.2	16.9	15.0	14.3	12.8	11.6	11.6	10.9
156	Undistributed profits	9.6	13.3	17.5	19.0	23.0	21.3	16.5	11.9	11.1	8.9	9.0	11.6
157	Inventory valuation adjustment	−4.5	−5.5	−3.3	−1.1	−1.8	−1.7	−.5	−.5	.3	−.1	.2	−.5
		BILLIONS OF 1958 DOLLARS											
158	Gross product in 1958 dollars	425.0	430.5	415.0	390.2	385.0	357.8	329.7	308.0	292.9	270.6	267.1	260.8
		DOLLARS											
159	Current dollar cost per unit of 1958 dollar gross product	1.215	1.166	1.132	1.104	1.073	1.055	1.050	1.039	1.034	1.029	1.022	1.011
160	Capital consumption allowances less depreciation adjustment	.131	.116	.107	.104	.095	.094	.095	.096	.096	.100	.097	.096
161	Indirect business taxes plus transfer payments less subsidies	.117	.109	.105	.100	.096	.100	.103	.102	.101	.103	.099	.094
162	Compensation of employees	.810	.768	.727	.707	.678	.660	.664	.664	.665	.670	.670	.654
163	Net interest	.035	.030	.025	.023	.019	.017	.015	.015	.014	.013	.011	.010
164	Corporate profits and inventory valuation and depreciation adjustments	.122	.143	.169	.170	.185	.185	.173	.163	.158	.144	.144	.156
165	Profits tax liability	.064	.078	.082	.073	.078	.077	.074	.074	.071	.073	.073	.080
166	Profit after tax plus inventory valuation and depreciation adjustments	.058	.066	.087	.097	.107	.107	.099	.088	.086	.070	.071	.077

See footnotes at end of table.

Series V 141–166. Nonfinancial Corporations, Gross Product and Unit Costs: 1948 to 1970—Con.

Series No.	Item	1958	1957	1956	1955	1954	1953	1952	1951	1950	1949	1948
		BILLIONS OF DOLLARS										
141	Gross product in current dollars_____	236.0	241.9	231.2	216.3	191.6	194.7	182.0	174.3	151.7	133.3	137.0
142	Capital consumption allowances less depreciation adjustment_____	23.9	22.8	20.7	18.5	17.3	16.6	15.9	14.7	12.6	11.3	10.3
143	Capital consumption allowances_____	21.5	20.4	18.5	17.1	14.7	12.9	11.3	10.1	8.6	7.8	6.9
144	Depreciation adjustment [1]_____	−2.4	−2.4	−2.2	−1.5	−2.6	−3.7	−4.6	−4.6	−4.0	−3.5	−3.4
145	Indirect business taxes plus transfer payments less subsidies__	22.8	22.4	20.8	19.2	17.4	18.2	16.8	15.2	14.0	12.6	12.1
146	Income originating in nonfinancial corporations_____	189.3	196.7	189.7	178.6	156.9	159.9	149.3	144.5	125.0	109.4	114.6
147	Compensation of employees_____	155.6	158.7	151.0	138.2	126.2	128.4	118.0	110.0	94.6	85.1	87.6
148	Wages and salaries_____	143.5	146.7	140.3	128.7	117.9	120.6	110.8	103.2	89.1	80.9	83.6
149	Supplements_____	12.1	12.0	10.8	9.4	8.2	7.8	7.2	6.8	5.5	4.2	4.0
150	Net interest_____	2.7	2.2	1.7	1.6	1.6	1.3	1.2	1.1	.9	1.0	.9
151	Corporate profits and inventory valuation and depreciation adjustments_____	31.1	35.9	36.9	38.8	29.1	30.2	30.1	33.3	29.5	23.3	26.2
152	Profits before tax_____	33.7	39.8	41.8	42.0	32.1	34.9	33.8	39.1	38.5	24.9	31.8
153	Profits tax liability_____	16.3	18.9	19.8	19.8	15.7	18.5	17.8	21.0	16.7	9.5	11.9
154	Profits after tax_____	17.5	20.9	22.1	22.2	16.3	16.4	16.0	18.1	21.7	15.4	19.9
155	Dividends_____	10.2	10.4	10.1	9.4	8.2	8.0	7.8	7.8	7.9	6.5	6.5
156	Undistributed profits_____	7.3	10.5	11.9	12.8	8.1	8.4	8.1	10.3	13.8	8.9	13.4
157	Inventory valuation adjustment_____	−.3	−1.5	−2.7	−1.7	−.3	−1.0	1.0	−1.2	−5.0	1.9	−2.2
		BILLIONS OF 1958 DOLLARS										
158	Gross product in 1958 dollars_____	236.0	247.2	244.0	237.2	213.4	219.8	207.1	203.5	186.4	165.6	172.9
		DOLLARS										
159	Current dollar cost per unit of 1958 dollars gross product_____	1.000	0.979	0.948	0.912	0.898	0.886	0.879	0.857	0.814	0.805	0.793
160	Capital consumption allowances less depreciation adjustment_____	.101	.092	.085	.078	.081	.076	.077	.072	.068	.068	.060
161	Indirect business taxes plus transfer payments less subsidies__	.097	.090	.085	.081	.081	.083	.081	.075	.075	.076	.070
162	Compensation of employees_____	.659	.642	.619	.582	.591	.584	.570	.541	.507	.514	.507
163	Net interest_____	.011	.009	.007	.007	.007	.006	.006	.005	.005	.006	.005
164	Corporate profits and inventory valuation and depreciation adjustments_____	.132	.145	.151	.164	.137	.137	.145	.164	.158	.141	.151
165	Profits tax liability_____	.069	.076	.081	.084	.074	.084	.086	.103	.090	.057	.069
166	Profits after tax plus inventory valuation and depreciation adjustments_____	.063	.069	.070	.080	.063	.053	.060	.061	.069	.083	.083

[1] This is the difference between depreciation claimed on Federal tax returns, and depreciation valued at current (i.e., replacement) cost and computed on the straight-line pattern with service lives 15 percent shorter than those shown in the Internal Revenue Service's Bulletin F.

Series V 167–181. Selected Corporate Asset, Liability, Income, and Tax Items, and Dividends Paid, by Industrial Division: 1926 to 1970

[In millions of dollars, except number of returns. Excludes returns not allocable to any industrial division]

Industrial division and tax year	Number of returns	Total assets or liabilities	Cash	Notes and accounts receivable less allowance	Inventories	Investments	Capital assets less reserves	Accounts payable and short-term debt	Long-term debt	Capital stock	Surplus and retained earnings	Total receipts	Total receipts less total deductions	Income tax	Dividends paid in cash and assets other than own stock
	167	168	169	170	171	172	173	174	175	176	177	178	179	180	181
Mining:															
1970_____	14,465	23,973	1,252	3,348	1,289	4,519	11,744	3,332	4,158	2,686	11,013	17,748	1,820	1,052	1,178
1969_____	14,028	22,773	1,185	3,517	1,253	4,091	11,307	3,264	3,920	2,386	10,187	16,233	1,545	931	1,274
1968_____	12,813	19,813	1,318	2,725	1,064	3,423	9,956	2,630	3,214	2,316	9,066	14,550	1,602	898	1,181
1967_____	14,441	18,176	1,166	2,547	984	3,040	9,258	2,376	2,768	2,515	8,259	13,680	1,461	738	1,039
1966_____	14,831	17,605	1,182	2,683	890	3,000	8,879	2,498	2,666	2,604	7,910	14,609	1,725	832	1,088
1965_____	13,285	16,546	1,120	2,495	850	2,870	8,223	2,179	2,346	2,277	7,839	12,602	1,389	658	909
1964_____	14,487	17,724	1,232	2,673	939	2,951	8,901	2,177	2,921	2,681	7,996	13,314	1,230	620	934
1963_____	14,878	17,341	1,150	2,602	948	2,922	8,676	2,124	2,752	2,867	7,936	13,055	1,213	660	1,067
1962_____	13,539	17,942	(NA)	(NA)	1,004	(NA)	(NA)	(NA)	(NA)	(NA)	(NA)	12,529	797	534	946
1961_____	13,731	17,944	1,217	2,409	1,000	3,229	9,437	2,061	2,977	3,150	8,035	12,258	865	534	898
1960_____	13,017	16,949	1,074	2,259	921	3,159	8,938	1,850	2,854	3,068	7,609	10,926	741	505	814
1959_____	12,920	16,039	1,034	1,991	883	2,979	8,618	1,877	3,009	2,954	7,114	10,355	649	473	719
1958_____	10,971	15,062	1,142	1,977	828	2,846	7,829	2,049	2,353	2,919	6,820	9,992	855	483	758
1957_____	11,532	14,572	1,041	1,811	923	2,763	7,643	1,876	2,122	2,941	6,595	11,193	957	553	692
1956_____	10,861	14,015	1,071	1,827	757	2,707	7,236	1,847	2,069	2,668	6,334	10,732	1,157	640	837

See footnotes at end of table.

Series V 167–181. Selected Corporate Asset, Liability, Income, and Tax Items, and Dividends Paid, by Industrial Division: 1926 to 1970—Con.

[In millions of dollars, except number of returns]

Industrial division and tax year	Number of returns	Total assets or liabilities	Selected assets					Selected liabilities				Total receipts	Total receipts less total deductions	Income tax	Dividends paid in cash and assets other than own stock
			Cash	Notes and accounts receivable less allowance	Inventories	Investments	Capital assets less reserves	Accounts payable and short-term debt	Long-term debt	Capital stock	Surplus and retained earnings				
	167	168	169	170	171	172	173	174	175	176	177	178	179	180	181
Mining—Con.:															
1955	9,683	13,265	1,119	1,706	631	2,483	6,959	1,580	2,067	2,667	5,819	9,631	1,085	603	780
1954	8,704	11,891	1,059	1,496	640	2,221	6,111	1,245	1,713	2,563	5,407	8,181	736	425	736
1953	8,164	11,967	917	1,426	761	2,721	5,866	1,277	1,677	2,515	5,545	9,230	951	509	648
1952	7,998	12,034	970	1,423	803	2,349	6,208	1,321	1,833	2,577	5,354	9,475	973	504	613
1951	8,136	11,659	1,032	1,415	755	2,273	5,878	1,258	1,610	2,755	5,030	9,562	1,114	553	593
1950	8,045	10,844	1,031	1,312	643	2,187	5,395	1,139	1,629	2,682	4,584	8,493	1,086	443	549
1949	8,094	9,261	871	889	569	2,000	4,636	933	1,278	2,493	3,901	6,730	698	265	417
1948	8,025	9,042	971	991	551	2,023	4,271	916	1,176	2,526	3,653	7,782	1,143	408	463
1947	7,280	7,186	785	789	410	1,506	3,516	825	830	2,266	2,755	5,881	788	286	315
1946	6,759	5,949	641	601	341	1,152	3,050	639	719	2,055	2,162	4,240	332	131	207
1945	6,394	5,563	556	492	306	1,140	2,906	602	550	2,093	1,987	3,903	246	117	156
1944	6,581	5,480	527	480	273	1,106	2,919	569	561	2,135	1,831	3,969	318	156	187
1943	7,036	5,434	516	476	281	1,013	2,980	547	578	2,277	1,614	3,680	342	168	197
1942	7,619	6,221	527	485	343	1,039	3,625	618	619	2,778	1,753	3,945	392	195	264
1941	8,227	7,065	482	568	339	1,354	4,128	712	941	3,009	2,014	3,754	370	138	311
1940	8,885	7,362	488	556	309	1,355	4,432	753	1,056	3,285	1,937	3,219	212	67	280
1939	9,287	7,331	408	550	321	1,372	4,450	804	1,000	3,374	1,858	2,843	138	37	216
1938	9,468	7,545	314	502	342	1,406	4,688	838	999	3,547	1,846	2,489	52	28	200
1937	11,467	9,146	333	677	340	1,737	5,748	1,004	1,125	4,458	2,165	3,273	297	58	361
1936	11,531	9,199	315	678	278	1,671	5,850	1,041	1,046	4,590	1,853	2,756	168	36	274
1935	11,491	9,519	295	597	317	1,840	5,914	1,172	1,047	4,807	1,750	2,418	70	22	255
1934 [1]	11,362	10,228	265	738	374	2,139	6,116	1,299	1,039	5,366	1,775	2,361	67	22	265
1934 [2]	11,488	10,030	281	774	401	2,569	5,464	1,027	973	5,597	1,531	2,388	89	22	188
1933	9,950	9,007	255	504	411	1,213	6,053	730	928	5,046	1,460	1,936	[3] 149	10	91
1932	10,020	9,485	236	515	392	1,366	6,415	768	957	5,460	1,528	1,653	[3] 186	7	102
1931	9,576	10,050	242	603	474	1,455	6,633	849	996	5,564	1,776	2,191	[3] 202	7	170
1930	10,025	11,395	331	730	444	1,734	7,259	1,028	941	5,785	2,166				
1929	10,219	11,832	421	837	694	1,611	7,264	975	1,037	6,252	2,566				
1928	10,366	10,799	413	745	516	264	6,647	854	976	5,793	2,004				
1927	11,298	11,565	360	703	681	262	7,495	918	912	6,240	1,863				
1926	11,641	12,172	409	763	636	299	7,967	902	1,008	6,714	1,638				
Manufacturing:															
1970	197,807	612,913	21,173	132,068	112,824	94,854	204,009	115,429	110,030	65,112	248,572	722,911	30,456	16,981	14,616
1969	202,102	572,127	21,026	125,403	108,635	89,330	191,253	106,172	95,725	64,673	239,523	710,084	40,386	21,621	16,029
1968	191,915	500,564	21,271	105,122	98,231	75,725	170,505	85,609	81,132	60,177	216,589	648,965	43,560	22,427	14,461
1967	197,023	448,026	20,432	92,521	91,955	63,185	155,823	73,556	69,703	59,848	198,661	590,822	39,486	18,589	13,215
1966	187,642	405,967	18,993	84,669	85,829	56,624	140,711	65,561	59,844	56,996	180,233	571,009	43,490	20,143	12,879
1965	185,924	311,524	18,673	76,544	75,994	57,902	125,493	56,159	50,997	56,096	165,482	514,719	39,509	18,415	12,205
1964	184,961	335,190	17,817	67,449	68,108	53,486	113,693	48,849	43,969	55,230	150,132	464,820	32,552	15,488	11,509
1963	181,800	310,207	17,463	55,906	64,664	53,781	104,782	43,692	38,673	54,029	139,432	429,507	28,825	14,323	10,330
1962	183,149	292,640	(NA)	(NA)	60,941	(NA)	(NA)	(NA)	(NA)	(NA)	(NA)	407,865	25,386	12,643	9,508
1961	173,558	275,964	16,064	48,810	57,523	45,900	96,917	37,893	35,133	52,429	124,087	377,580	22,538	11,403	8,409
1960	165,862	262,308	15,373	43,378	55,763	44,190	94,201	34,870	33,177	51,047	118,022	371,093	22,200	11,362	8,028
1959	156,297	252,134	15,239	42,245	54,799	42,559	89,997	33,444	32,132	49,498	112,392	363,157	25,026	12,435	7,666
1958	145,581	235,836	16,231	39,609	49,643	36,414	87,733	30,226	31,274	47,778	107,072	326,940	18,424	9,877	7,239
1957	133,558	224,910	15,165	36,083	50,358	33,574	83,801	28,434	29,032	46,194	100,081	330,749	22,677	11,481	7,366
1956	128,457	216,363	15,514	36,276	49,788	32,274	77,330	29,338	26,121	44,923	94,065	316,679	24,504	12,209	7,121
1955	124,199	201,360	15,999	32,380	44,422	34,095	69,892	25,853	22,426	42,986	88,007	303,211	25,816	12,891	6,770
1954	115,820	181,891	15,745	27,767	39,872	28,730	65,364	22,257	21,547	40,519	79,384	264,966	18,194	9,385	5,818
1953	115,254	176,805	14,847	26,368	42,992	27,267	61,657	22,258	20,392	39,265	74,549	278,495	21,290	12,054	5,848
1952	113,711	170,282	14,748	26,907	41,801	25,922	57,723	22,783	19,372	38,730	70,767	258,969	20,228	11,348	5,665
1951	114,142	160,876	14,542	24,011	40,774	26,014	52,643	20,823	15,797	37,676	67,049	252,956	24,697	14,060	5,715
1950	109,537	141,600	13,370	21,753	33,008	24,528	46,377	17,559	12,269	35,502	61,539	218,272	23,608	10,575	6,037
1949	110,269	123,755	12,610	16,067	27,780	20,789	44,118	13,286	12,262	34,780	54,105	185,285	14,158	5,446	4,838
1948	110,078	121,708	11,778	17,090	30,355	18,685	41,227	15,253	11,757	33,347	50,506	198,260	17,985	6,760	4,617
1947	105,390	111,356	11,884	16,138	27,634	17,774	35,380	14,750	9,906	32,577	44,097	178,173	16,477	6,241	4,143
1946	92,771	96,300	11,042	13,517	23,282	16,561	29,414	12,647	7,879	30,015	37,574	137,087	11,508	4,543	3,378
1945	75,215	91,030	11,270	13,569	17,256	21,076	25,145	11,056	6,385	28,445	35,701	140,155	10,179	6,064	2,801
1944	72,170	95,999	11,918	14,552	18,421	21,836	25,921	12,501	6,332	28,335	34,735	152,673	14,754	9,318	2,828
1943	73,149	94,768	11,752	15,010	19,155	18,501	27,037	12,540	6,573	27,378	33,310	144,560	16,428	10,430	2,596
1942	76,334	85,092	9,075	13,809	18,433	14,537	26,607	11,133	6,219	27,113	27,958	117,895	13,554	8,158	2,486
1941	78,645	70,071	6,149	10,858	16,178	10,781	24,727	9,151	5,702	25,476	22,922	91,606	10,310	4,881	2,800
1940	80,198	60,547	5,744	8,412	12,334	9,349	23,605	7,311	5,418	25,429	18,734	66,246	5,313	1,544	2,390
1939	80,860	56,739	4,570	7,427	10,993	9,507	23,060	6,996	5,255	25,640	16,756	57,603	3,571	629	2,170
1938	82,155	54,792	4,003	6,761	10,192	9,444	21,544	6,456	5,274	25,847	15,413	50,489	1,615	372	1,634
1937	85,474	55,723	3,283	7,004	11,454	9,525	21,537	7,271	4,904	25,951	15,288	61,560	3,686	641	2,899
1936	85,350	54,262	3,522	7,368	10,029	9,524	20,690	7,096	4,256	25,622	12,845	55,378	3,636	587	2,867
1935	85,817	52,682	3,389	7,376	8,705	9,688	20,231	6,745	4,387	25,882	11,729	47,473	2,494	355	2,184
1934 [1]	85,499	52,531	3,006	7,483	8,319	9,663	20,451	6,768	4,025	26,930	11,201	40,581	1,387	263	1,578
1934 [2]	88,371	66,626	3,371	10,178	8,612	17,130	22,889	9,653	5,122	33,347	13,981	44,754	1,959	289	2,071
1933	82,836	57,753	3,084	6,765	8,084	11,481	24,384	5,722	5,021	30,398	12,943	34,943	502	206	1,159
1932	82,083	59,023	3,343	6,541	7,310	11,651	25,622	5,507	5,226	31,186	12,790	31,850	[3] 1,468	100	1,324
1931	80,106	63,801	3,458	7,819	9,003	10,120	27,286	6,017	5,581	32,329	15,310	43,534	[3] 308	164	2,276
1930	85,520	69,245	3,960	8,730	11,157	11,062	28,987	6,852	5,879	33,855	18,267				
1929	86,112	70,282	3,847	9,572	12,614	9,154	28,235	7,418	5,450	33,228	19,466				
1928	84,925	67,060	3,895	9,502	12,011	2,183	27,025	7,449	5,446	32,491	17,526				
1927	84,776	65,582	3,525	8,946	11,884	2,036	26,007	7,349	4,806	31,553	16,496				
1926	84,251	64,727	3,528	8,567	12,284	1,822	26,619	7,216	4,340	31,412	14,862				

See footnotes at end of table.

Series V 167–181. Selected Corporate Asset, Liability, Income, and Tax Items, and Dividends Paid, by Industrial Division: 1926 to 1970—Con.

[In millions of dollars, except number of returns]

Industrial division and tax year	Number of returns	Total assets or liabilities	Selected assets					Selected liabilities				Total receipts	Total receipts less total deductions	Income tax	Dividends paid in cash and assets other than own stock
			Cash	Notes and accounts receivable less allowance	Inventories	Investments	Capital assets less reserves	Accounts payable and short-term debt	Long-term debt	Capital stock	Surplus and retained earnings				
	167	168	169	170	171	172	173	174	175	176	177	178	179	180	181
Public utilities:															
1970	67,398	287,740	5,335	15,039	6,999	26,392	219,812	21,642	114,438	51,166	70,504	135,492	7,561	4,372	5,838
1969	66,945	262,357	4,917	14,543	6,035	21,142	203,320	19,905	101,598	47,672	66,184	125,262	10,068	5,573	5,678
1968	65,554	238,568	4,986	12,012	5,189	17,173	188,705	16,205	93,636	45,890	60,673	112,587	10,526	5,639	5,439
1967	66,045	221,144	4,647	10,892	4,947	15,889	175,641	13,123	85,760	44,594	57,458	102,398	10,617	5,029	5,146
1966	59,925	204,061	4,674	9,999	4,243	14,848	161,985	11,561	77,090	42,742	53,444	97,098	11,628	5,383	4,953
1965	59,676	186,854	4,257	8,357	3,812	13,150	150,025	9,832	69,454	40,746	49,092	88,957	10,711	4,951	4,590
1964	56,338	174,913	4,023	7,384	3,471	12,962	140,084	8,258	65,027	40,496	44,458	81,726	9,760	4,741	4,214
1963	56,291	167,379	4,120	6,951	3,310	12,499	133,984	8,340	62,211	39,650	41,133	77,870	8,947	4,570	3,801
1962	52,701	161,025	(NA)	(NA)	3,112	(NA)	(NA)	(NA)	(NA)	(NA)	(NA)	73,156	8,026	4,180	3,579
1961	49,048	155,535	3,893	6,140	3,126	12,322	124,624	7,241	60,955	38,779	35,941	68,154	7,496	3,916	3,440
1960	43,852	144,774	3,632	5,747	3,093	10,296	117,081	7,606	55,791	36,287	33,877	65,922	6,602	3,695	3,199
1959	43,195	137,319	3,559	5,439	3,007	10,437	110,216	6,961	52,321	35,414	32,421	62,309	6,798	3,528	3,040
1958	35,161	128,678	3,672	5,019	2,710	9,736	103,747	6,379	49,166	34,151	30,637	55,788	5,719	2,994	2,803
1957	34,492	121,316	3,666	4,834	3,004	9,200	97,083	6,315	45,905	32,350	28,623	55,834	5,753	2,953	2,682
1956	32,895	113,838	3,641	4,603	3,050	9,155	89,978	6,123	41,317	32,150	25,726	52,070	5,953	3,017	2,535
1955	29,704	106,378	3,634	3,904	2,623	9,436	83,444	5,164	38,727	30,183	24,157	47,983	5,763	2,895	2,380
1954	26,067	98,637	3,658	3,495	2,468	8,567	77,608	4,260	36,556	28,811	21,641	42,038	4,424	2,296	2,057
1953	26,314	95,220	3,281	3,732	2,381	10,429	72,862	4,213	35,053	28,517	20,303	40,570	5,018	2,537	2,012
1952	25,139	90,041	3,503	3,703	2,352	10,537	67,517	4,111	33,062	27,159	18,824	38,348	4,900	2,472	1,909
1951	23,641	84,707	3,170	3,553	2,360	10,258	62,955	3,902	31,275	26,084	16,747	36,007	4,676	2,299	1,782
1950	22,973	79,209	3,178	3,296	1,909	10,259	57,444	3,633	28,912	25,034	15,714	31,857	4,312	1,752	1,640
1949	22,496	71,620	2,853	2,621	1,756	8,295	53,986	3,411	25,534	24,349	13,624	28,410	2,835	1,041	1,303
1948	21,749	73,705	2,876	2,565	2,059	13,993	50,001	3,573	26,125	23,033	13,033	29,272	3,413	1,189	1,432
1947	20,376	68,037	2,921	2,476	1,811	12,512	46,092	3,349	23,425	24,182	11,947	25,957	2,662	979	1,292
1946	18,561	63,812	2,858	2,276	1,427	12,256	42,756	2,669	21,463	23,964	10,685	22,738	2,336	891	1,338
1945	16,656	63,217	2,754	2,203	1,115	12,962	41,955	2,287	20,902	23,619	10,701	22,485	2,928	1,538	1,238
1944	16,183	64,958	2,703	2,275	1,096	12,945	43,635	2,221	21,854	23,804	9,967	22,328	4,188	2,382	1,221
1943	16,227	64,910	3,130	2,391	991	12,171	44,117	2,233	22,863	23,593	9,149	21,186	4,500	2,402	1,171
1942	16,873	63,581	2,476	2,059	1,027	11,336	44,647	2,090	23,652	23,765	8,267	18,450	3,624	1,567	1,118
1941	18,405	58,472	2,024	1,628	1,013	6,179	45,966	2,059	23,709	21,926	6,183	15,739	1,918	695	1,068
1940	18,680	56,748	1,851	1,440	745	5,243	45,977	2,118	23,331	21,661	5,955	13,574	1,320	359	1,067
1939	18,744	60,230	1,582	1,394	715	8,031	46,694	2,801	23,994	23,602	6,250	12,945	1,179	215	1,196
1938	18,595	60,843	1,444	1,422	692	8,159	47,064	2,830	24,418	23,815	6,468	12,037	687	166	1,114
1937	20,775	64,648	1,181	1,592	818	8,825	49,629	2,925	25,803	25,420	7,172	13,235	1,084	192	1,334
1936	20,667	62,715	1,499	1,602	651	8,377	47,673	2,987	24,619	24,786	5,263	11,938	980	166	1,285
1935	21,149	66,478	1,233	1,869	617	10,050	49,581	3,189	26,391	26,116	6,243	11,353	638	126	1,281
1934 [1]	21,265	68,461	1,306	2,660	629	10,535	50,472	3,908	25,654	27,131	6,785	10,997	631	126	1,213
1934 [2]	21,329	83,990	1,510	4,027	729	23,505	50,501	5,178	29,726	34,352	8,291	11,556	669	118	1,299
1933	17,706	69,049	1,290	2,210	741	11,323	50,141	2,798	26,959	26,191	8,000	10,110	249	92	994
1932	17,547	72,149	1,299	2,539	713	12,956	50,058	3,382	27,006	27,793	8,036	10,735	341	97	1,300
1931	16,457	72,337	1,333	2,826	889	11,616	52,214	3,494	27,024	26,642	10,332	13,297	958	104	1,789
1930	17,248	80,479	1,693	3,670	973	14,505	55,060	4,146	28,739	28,345	12,431				
1929	17,258	77,792	1,634	3,974	1,119	9,614	52,205	4,449	26,619	28,131	10,955				
1928	16,770	71,380	1,571	3,628	1,000	475	48,887	3,585	25,696	25,741	9,837				
1927	16,858	66,559	1,549	2,115	1,024	272	46,487	2,604	23,542	25,296	7,594				
1926	18,297	57,245	1,358	1,528	942	285	40,699	2,337	19,932	20,466	6,045				
Trade:															
1970	518,062	192,181	13,533	51,998	58,747	16,748	39,084	66,173	24,835	23,304	55,708	522,546	9,636	4,485	2,069
1969	524,586	184,644	12,666	51,349	58,695	15,034	35,488	63,934	22,115	23,464	53,376	508,265	10,728	4,889	2,470
1968	471,987	162,115	11,878	46,232	51,054	13,501	30,538	54,626	19,110	21,232	48,774	451,898	10,317	4,570	2,138
1967	465,841	144,129	11,163	41,023	45,794	11,597	27,212	47,802	15,950	20,638	43,739	410,370	8,834	3,641	1,885
1966	453,174	135,943	10,011	39,834	43,300	11,009	25,307	45,994	14,979	19,969	40,226	389,155	8,215	3,361	1,780
1965	440,304	125,487	9,708	37,696	39,410	10,353	22,693	41,329	13,563	19,049	36,744	365,166	7,623	3,193	1,653
1964	421,553	113,939	9,343	34,055	34,892	9,428	20,434	35,361	12,475	18,769	33,803	335,319	6,641	2,843	1,462
1963	403,435	105,722	8,723	30,665	32,523	9,812	18,761	31,531	11,949	18,447	51,543	309,590	5,366	2,593	1,250
1962	388,852	101,563	(NA)	(NA)	30,715	(NA)	(NA)	(NA)	(NA)	(NA)	(NA)	298,336	5,179	2,508	1,314
1961	364,947	94,591	8,262	27,566	28,783	9,429	16,257	27,947	10,390	17,479	29,278	270,847	4,573	2,272	1,239
1960	355,623	92,219	8,423	26,386	28,434	9,296	15,891	27,247	9,894	17,401	29,057	269,581	4,535	2,359	1,232
1959	334,717	87,557	7,651	26,113	26,704	9,122	14,998	25,252	9,624	16,508	28,253	256,648	5,573	2,640	1,131
1958	311,477	79,346	7,484	23,654	24,230	7,635	14,001	22,559	8,350	15,656	26,355	225,939	4,411	2,228	982
1957	305,117	76,830	7,046	21,767	24,021	7,582	13,843	21,888	7,335	15,534	25,568	229,816	4,725	2,392	1,036
1956	270,951	73,468	6,917	21,134	23,124	6,856	13,280	21,134	6,478	15,017	24,496	215,914	5,239	2,532	1,060
1955	248,071	69,113	6,808	20,287	21,578	6,533	12,037	19,460	5,795	14,366	23,500	204,924	5,099	2,435	993
1954	222,801	59,132	6,317	16,594	18,138	5,651	10,695	15,402	4,973	12,856	21,066	170,589	3,629	1,867	909
1953	212,931	56,370	6,185	15,193	17,828	5,445	10,263	13,902	4,968	12,608	20,197	167,705	3,922	2,050	926
1952	205,848	55,792	6,023	15,365	17,802	5,169	10,145	14,043	4,572	12,468	20,058	166,063	4,388	2,226	989
1951	201,594	55,102	5,992	14,682	18,089	5,272	9,831	13,536	4,401	12,282	19,856	166,422	5,473	2,754	1,076
1950	193,496	51,759	5,547	14,068	17,394	4,558	9,028	13,115	3,951	11,518	18,585	152,895	6,273	2,593	1,135
1949	187,520	42,985	5,348	10,778	13,446	4,257	8,081	9,528	3,286	10,946	15,853	129,965	3,810	1,469	965
1948	181,353	42,270	5,322	10,354	14,016	4,120	7,417	9,770	3,088	10,505	15,025	135,092	5,681	2,094	1,063
1947	163,300	38,122	5,049	9,169	12,758	4,044	6,158	9,279	2,621	9,516	12,876	120,960	5,969	2,174	980
1946	139,816	31,958	4,300	7,130	10,746	4,213	4,732	7,803	2,017	8,434	10,459	94,936	5,487	1,992	915

See footnotes at end of table.

Series V 167–181. Selected Corporate Asset, Liability, Income, and Tax Items, and Dividends Paid, by Industrial Division: 1926 to 1970—Con.

[In millions of dollars, except number of returns]

Industrial division and tax year	Number of returns	Total assets or liabilities	Cash	Notes and accounts receivable less allowance	Inventories	Investments	Capital assets less reserves	Accounts payable and short-term debt	Long-term debt	Capital stock	Surplus and retained earnings	Total receipts	Total receipts less total deductions	Income tax	Dividends paid in cash and assets other than own stock
	167	168	169	170	171	172	173	174	175	176	177	178	179	180	181
Trade—Con.:															
1945	110,587	24,041	3,946	4,636	6,582	4,675	3,532	5,034	1,366	7,182	8,045	65,654	3,337	1,886	547
1944	106,193	22,674	3,505	4,678	5,941	4,289	3,543	4,673	1,305	6,999	7,320	60,660	3,228	1,895	543
1943	107,667	21,489	3,152	4,494	6,032	3,495	3,661	4,426	1,311	7,026	6,615	57,193	3,057	1,760	530
1942	114,165	21,063	2,687	5,021	6,313	2,564	3,870	4,977	1,467	7,063	5,795	54,642	2,548	1,385	487
1941	123,439	22,134	1,920	6,454	6,841	2,325	4,068	6,356	1,718	7,500	5,099	56,512	2,071	853	576
1940	125,474	19,514	1,684	5,626	5,522	2,203	4,003	5,366	1,537	7,494	4,172	46,060	1,089	292	504
1939	124,627	19,030	1,501	5,224	5,157	2,714	3,961	5,071	1,544	7,822	3,824	41,849	830	165	497
1938	124,765	18,346	1,452	4,990	4,808	2,660	3,655	4,781	1,461	7,900	3,456	37,974	435	113	432
1937	128,200	18,853	1,287	5,180	5,328	2,561	3,671	5,382	1,279	7,902	3,348	44,199	845	166	702
1936	130,073	18,224	1,314	5,224	5,054	2,160	3,615	5,381	998	7,648	2,788	40,532	915	167	736
1935	130,317	17,486	1,270	4,832	4,568	2,168	3,662	5,030	1,029	7,725	2,560	36,669	558	107	505
1934 [1]	127,457	17,434	1,251	4,787	4,374	2,267	3,698	4,951	892	8,054	2,445	32,170	415	93	392
1934 [2]	126,086	16,651	1,134	4,258	3,970	2,651	3,672	3,947	1,112	8,003	2,528	28,571	392	84	351
1933	120,064	15,654	990	3,944	3,809	2,032	3,810	3,625	1,126	7,732	2,155	23,653	36	62	213
1932	119,346	15,759	1,041	4,006	3,368	2,068	4,158	3,443	1,204	8,237	1,936	22,609	[3] 705	30	249
1931	113,886	17,900	1,033	4,688	3,986	2,120	4,729	4,074	1,315	8,520	2,925	29,540	[3] 453	45	430
1930	119,792	20,115	1,269	5,652	5,046	2,032	4,889	5,029	1,331	9,174	3,619	--------	--------	--------	--------
1929	117,583	21,842	1,283	6,305	5,862	1,764	4,967	5,730	1,252	9,317	4,204	--------	--------	--------	--------
1928	114,068	21,481	1,293	6,297	5,908	325	4,910	5,646	1,044	9,252	4,359	--------	--------	--------	--------
1927	110,280	20,083	1,198	5,614	5,631	403	4,309	5,046	846	8,858	3,832	--------	--------	--------	--------
1926	100,395	19,140	1,164	5,632	5,569	357	4,079	4,997	584	8,558	3,502	--------	--------	--------	--------
Service:															
1970	281,218	61,875	4,655	9,900	2,557	8,893	29,000	13,374	17,989	7,136	13,154	69,571	1,187	1,063	558
1969	261,640	55,398	4,204	9,296	2,414	7,702	26,328	12,248	16,286	6,549	11,928	60,037	1,654	1,115	656
1968	228,904	47,234	4,052	7,921	2,345	6,756	22,160	10,370	13,420	5,735	10,567	51,046	2,016	1,032	565
1967	220,561	39,984	3,584	6,737	1,883	4,742	19,558	9,034	11,865	5,186	8,255	47,441	1,976	864	521
1966	202,065	36,858	3,092	6,481	1,800	4,349	19,171	8,530	10,832	4,991	7,271	43,083	1,820	797	423
1965	188,177	33,481	2,773	5,864	1,585	4,329	16,507	7,684	9,536	4,628	6,378	38,377	1,582	699	377
1964	176,902	29,951	2,545	5,017	1,546	3,751	14,840	6,713	8,806	4,489	5,438	34,101	1,154	587	297
1963	163,766	27,526	2,345	4,661	1,319	3,466	13,624	6,025	7,851	4,327	5,181	31,615	908	558	285
1962	150,082	25,219	(NA)	(NA)	1,113	(NA)	(NA)	(NA)	(NA)	(NA)	(NA)	28,095	837	524	221
1961	137,955	22,829	2,072	4,001	1,095	3,249	10,762	5,040	6,353	3,723	4,811	25,920	893	525	233
1960	121,024	19,853	1,787	3,449	856	2,799	9,538	4,418	5,444	3,272	4,401	23,347	853	486	277
1959	110,005	18,355	1,736	3,160	807	2,720	8,737	4,003	4,790	3,056	4,448	22,227	970	491	215
1958	89,494	15,870	1,613	2,902	837	2,129	7,558	3,605	3,963	2,581	3,173	18,295	749	412	181
1957	82,429	14,858	1,506	2,481	772	2,159	7,111	3,244	3,734	2,593	3,705	17,779	784	423	187
1956	74,372	13,090	1,430	2,220	718	1,881	6,190	2,823	2,904	2,317	3,661	16,273	840	409	189
1955	66,011	11,264	1,296	1,808	630	1,666	5,334	2,244	2,413	2,169	3,283	14,103	699	361	173
1954	58,117	10,017	1,228	1,420	574	1,588	4,756	1,813	2,241	1,902	3,028	12,267	585	319	159
1953	56,473	9,471	1,110	1,309	551	1,469	4,652	1,543	2,133	1,962	2,897	11,815	607	318	157
1952	54,690	8,916	1,043	1,260	602	1,304	4,398	1,410	1,925	1,858	2,807	11,168	620	324	174
1951	51,357	8,667	973	1,144	633	1,328	4,284	1,321	1,903	1,855	2,711	10,432	637	325	179
1950	47,834	8,053	913	996	570	1,271	4,004	1,252	1,717	1,834	2,461	9,350	568	236	170
1949	46,588	7,063	854	810	467	911	3,726	1,059	1,531	1,750	2,059	8,850	534	212	154
1948	43,882	6,950	827	779	546	990	3,516	1,035	1,493	1,689	2,061	8,766	623	241	172
1947	39,896	6,517	814	724	618	919	3,135	1,003	1,389	1,595	1,867	8,285	720	260	184
1946	34,229	5,869	755	631	537	991	2,692	816	1,273	1,517	1,631	7,143	785	284	203
1945	30,043	5,017	660	502	419	994	2,240	640	1,193	1,354	1,283	5,801	596	312	130
1944	29,389	4,739	556	481	391	901	2,198	567	1,147	1,344	1,143	5,481	575	317	114
1943	29,799	4,584	530	427	351	756	2,331	573	1,122	1,370	1,000	4,964	537	303	104
1942	31,692	4,475	411	423	301	672	2,458	610	1,197	1,417	813	4,457	357	179	86
1941	33,296	4,366	313	420	264	611	2,605	656	1,307	1,465	614	4,029	189	74	97
1940	34,094	4,273	303	386	213	640	2,586	675	1,269	1,485	573	3,702	117	38	90
1939	34,177	4,255	261	388	218	626	2,610	686	1,289	1,579	422	3,512	85	26	85
1938	33,816	4,294	241	406	205	625	2,496	714	1,311	1,564	400	3,409	59	23	83
1937	49,751	10,835	356	558	175	970	8,271	1,384	5,128	3,101	529	4,605	36	33	148
1936	48,590	10,853	365	602	167	1,077	8,085	1,408	5,002	3,185	175	4,345	13	31	156
1935	40,093	8,427	285	526	157	826	6,033	1,231	3,560	2,734	[3] 18	3,528	[3] 97	18	71
1934 [1]	37,171	7,771	246	597	166	677	5,447	1,166	3,004	2,705	54	3,231	[3] 144	15	63
1934 [2]	36,999	7,903	248	819	168	983	5,088	1,149	2,856	2,858	155	3,177	[3] 151	14	58
1933	34,546	7,429	204	625	139	744	5,070	954	2,724	2,761	179	2,662	[3] 255	9	42
1932	34,552	8,480	231	637	145	1,228	5,611	983	3,008	3,078	712	2,953	[3] 371	9	71
1931	28,545	6,555	211	636	198	1,189	3,719	878	1,636	2,427	1,045	3,486	[3] 67	11	115
1930	30,312	7,518	292	686	241	1,705	3,880	963	1,719	2,573	1,716	--------	--------	--------	--------
1929	28,710	7,820	440	833	191	1,876	3,814	954	1,563	2,519	1,982	--------	--------	--------	--------
1928	26,505	5,857	249	548	178	43	3,521	928	1,291	2,386	697	--------	--------	--------	--------
1927	25,388	5,618	240	459	177	37	3,340	869	1,163	2,189	736	--------	--------	--------	--------
1926	23,264	4,873	300	384	184	42	2,783	821	842	1,963	596	--------	--------	--------	--------

See footnotes at end of table.

Series V 167–181. Selected Corporate Asset, Liability, Income, and Tax Items, and Dividends Paid, by Industrial Division: 1926 to 1970—Con.

[In millions of dollars, except number of returns]

Industrial division and tax year	Number of returns	Total assets or liabilities	Cash	Notes and accounts receivable less allowance	Inventories	Investments	Capital assets less reserves	Accounts payable and short-term debt	Long-term debt	Capital stock	Surplus and retained earnings	Total receipts	Total receipts less total deductions	Income tax	Dividends paid in cash and assets other than own stock
	167	168	169	170	171	172	173	174	175	176	177	178	179	180	181
Finance, insurance, real estate, and lessors of real property:															
1970	406,235	1,401,154	126,317	366,858	1,289	769,284	80,364	82,205	82,872	45,609	153,328	161,630	15,690	4,443	7,387
1969	428,972	1,298,161	114,512	343,461	1,237	706,846	79,405	79,632	78,835	45,386	151,108	164,291	15,832	4,292	9,068
1968	407,199	1,202,918	102,771	312,700	873	671,818	70,462	66,007	68,355	40,507	139,396	146,905	17,477	4,226	7,395
1967	399,115	1,097,348	95,224	283,550	622	610,292	67,978	55,977	60,422	38,506	119,461	131,983	15,146	3,640	6,062
1966	402,740	1,007,717	84,934	259,895	293	562,048	66,665	50,818	61,848	35,621	109,579	119,815	12,731	3,202	5,612
1965	388,428	955,902	77,347	251,348	357	528,586	63,158	45,370	59,770	33,673	103,027	110,466	12,429	3,115	5,924
1964	383,727	883,959	76,053	220,127	355	497,949	59,643	43,745	55,546	31,942	97,983	101,297	10,640	3,059	4,627
1963	375,375	825,415	72,434	222,048	216	448,210	54,814	63,195	53,556	30,848	91,753	93,343	9,739	3,119	4,080
1962	359,229	764,797	(NA)	(NA)	231	(NA)	(NA)	(NA)	(NA)	(NA)	(NA)	81,859	9,847	3,092	3,778
1961	340,210	699,888	68,380	163,801	176	401,151	46,495	33,339	46,795	26,885	81,099	75,584	10,051	3,138	3,618
1960	334,388	650,591	64,935	154,916	141	371,608	42,512	29,633	44,017	25,678	71,525	70,842	9,161	3,101	3,466
1959	318,592	606,825	60,780	142,887	96	348,808	38,583	28,406	38,912	24,285	65,408	65,912	7,949	2,559	3,283
1958	272,305	572,513	61,134	130,276	81	332,652	34,542	26,868	34,985	22,139	61,800	59,335	8,085	2,724	2,780
1957	255,976	528,509	59,159	124,872	94	301,072	31,201	24,754	32,763	21,920	51,746	39,019	9,154	2,214	2,688
1956	244,755	504,571	59,773	138,584	59	266,632	28,590	19,911	28,824	19,881	50,639	35,718	8,676	2,015	2,491
1955	213,680	474,858	57,210	126,800	47	255,680	25,581	18,176	25,697	17,825	45,124	32,320	8,543	2,030	2,238
1954	187,172	432,477	52,413	103,697	48	243,959	24,129	13,502	22,724	17,484	39,979	29,406	8,308	2,068	2,027
1953	175,653	401,976	52,637	96,456	31	222,418	22,609	11,364	21,378	16,911	35,153	25,829	7,167	1,879	1,817
1952	166,749	374,891	52,174	88,544	27	206,476	20,970	10,818	18,779	16,424	32,351	23,343	6,662	1,745	1,712
1951	158,335	317,026	50,129	70,912	23	167,642	21,309	9,331	16,850	15,769	26,788	20,017	6,088	1,515	1,700
1950	151,540	298,624	46,104	64,529	20	162,872	20,111	8,406	16,508	15,750	24,318	18,233	5,849	1,228	1,748
1949	146,120	281,983	40,447	52,065	6	165,077	19,053	7,061	17,397	18,236	22,504	16,768	5,411	992	1,656
1948	140,872	265,124	43,254	50,699	11	148,524	17,380	6,628	13,143	15,928	19,550	15,132	4,612	792	1,428
1947	131,825	257,833	42,318	44,933	46	149,696	16,282	6,353	11,448	15,828	18,167	13,581	3,982	628	1,265
1946	124,564	246,364	38,404	35,984	69	151,177	16,363	5,294	11,232	15,822	17,878	12,097	4,146	713	1,261
1945	116,186	249,119	38,105	29,407	46	162,424	15,221	4,352	10,286	15,562	16,457	10,612	3,680	654	1,076
1944	113,221	221,043	33,152	24,624	35	143,870	15,836	3,675	10,937	16,000	14,818	9,614	3,123	544	1,004
1943	112,892	194,564	30,714	22,026	51	122,082	16,384	3,241	10,916	13,654	13,459	9,001	2,686	455	965
1942	114,866	175,483	30,837	23,185	68	101,264	17,255	3,937	11,507	17,631	13,079	8,749	2,385	387	1,004
1941	120,647	174,403	30,434	28,333	107	94,928	17,740	5,684	15,734	26,732	17,515	10,199	1,499	315	1,631
1940	120,725	168,414	31,103	25,616	61	90,565	18,131	5,609	16,159	28,264	17,394	9,455	1,369	192	1,622
1939	120,945	155,975	25,518	23,777	42	85,668	18,099	5,410	15,944	27,136	16,711	8,768	1,386	127	1,421
1938	118,631	150,926	20,314	23,040	53	85,377	18,439	5,504	16,451	28,582	16,688	8,548	1,273	127	1,326
1937	98,438	140,402	17,685	24,611	47	84,835	19,785	6,349	10,674	27,156	16,966	8,927	1,757	134	1,736
1936	96,869	144,109	18,872	24,028	65	87,108	10,238	6,814	10,707	29,046	13,606	8,692	1,834	136	1,738
1935	104,146	144,747	16,986	22,886	109	86,809	13,320	7,147	13,037	33,100	14,143	8,662	1,817	81	1,535
1934 [1]	105,535	140,840	13,702	23,640	134	83,626	14,689	8,031	13,611	32,739	14,074	8,022	721	59	1,226
1934 [2]	103,294	112,073	13,231	19,841	130	61,971	13,370	5,250	8,387	18,768	9,798	6,904	142	50	800
1933	100,989	105,475	9,252	21,235	141	56,518	13,712	4,825	8,652	18,482	9,965	7,422	[3] 936	34	560
1932	104,141	110,753	9,581	24,647	151	57,397	14,634	5,625	9,395	19,635	10,619	8,155	[3] 954	35	753
1931	107,892	121,043	9,385	31,202	249	57,611	17,638	6,962	11,000	21,583	12,167	10,565	[3] 328	53	1,222
1930	114,275	140,035	13,207	39,158	462	62,136	18,792	7,640	11,079	24,356	16,177	—	—	—	—
1929	113,463	140,724	14,471	44,129	921	41,401	17,819	8,654	10,135	23,682	15,108	—	—	—	—
1928	108,123	125,692	14,278	41,029	675	6,690	16,969	7,724	8,103	18,056	11,995	—	—	—	—
1927	106,016	112,917	9,721	32,131	1,068	6,652	15,251	6,179	6,047	15,725	9,394	—	—	—	—
1926	98,417	99,452	9,778	5,790	923	5,823	13,429	6,682	4,740	13,733	7,436	—	—	—	—
Construction:															
1970	138,905	42,720	4,049	14,105	5,345	3,550	9,265	14,597	5,186	3,599	8,637	90,611	1,541	781	299
1969	127,670	39,643	3,616	13,505	5,059	3,065	8,704	13,866	4,815	3,367	7,964	83,913	1,660	814	398
1968	125,999	35,896	3,512	11,673	4,570	3,329	7,946	12,063	4,801	3,471	7,409	72,263	1,713	768	281
1967	123,180	32,538	3,210	10,793	4,434	2,411	7,139	11,145	4,026	3,141	6,622	68,022	1,549	699	282
1966	112,373	28,809	2,909	9,880	3,674	2,204	6,240	10,600	3,567	2,957	5,744	63,030	1,392	612	200
1965	113,284	26,725	2,673	9,098	3,532	2,223	5,525	10,126	3,051	2,939	4,917	56,695	1,258	519	240
1964	104,134	23,309	2,356	7,744	2,942	2,103	4,788	8,410	2,734	2,721	4,257	49,741	946	424	187
1963	96,466	21,395	2,153	7,295	2,635	2,089	4,234	7,741	2,637	2,674	3,928	45,649	650	369	143
1962	90,604	19,467	(NA)	(NA)	2,559	(NA)	(NA)	(NA)	(NA)	(NA)	(NA)	41,065	621	367	134
1961	83,791	17,745	1,781	6,130	2,535	1,753	3,279	6,438	1,962	2,383	3,575	37,413	512	329	140
1960	72,332	15,367	1,625	5,584	1,643	1,453	2,905	5,669	1,549	2,115	3,208	32,893	382	297	116
1959	66,260	14,222	1,559	5,589	1,562	1,424	2,639	5,096	1,344	1,971	3,068	32,140	581	332	91
1958	56,181	13,204	1,659	6,132	1,303	1,314	2,321	3,943	1,308	1,856	3,067	28,234	670	356	89
1957	50,425	11,935	1,401	5,894	1,040	1,057	2,117	3,520	1,034	1,692	2,838	26,744	745	383	95
1956	45,223	10,386	1,184	5,167	929	882	1,835	3,243	731	1,500	2,452	23,257	680	326	80
1955	38,653	9,319	1,052	4,530	693	1,042	1,664	2,864	784	1,347	2,354	19,722	479	251	85
1954	33,700	8,254	1,074	3,694	886	789	1,438	2,302	631	1,216	2,189	17,215	483	252	75
1953	32,158	7,414	974	3,474	664	680	1,346	1,976	628	1,115	1,959	15,914	512	271	74
1952	29,433	7,307	918	3,372	793	673	1,336	1,904	713	1,035	1,946	15,047	596	304	75
1951	27,315	6,698	788	3,149	773	596	1,199	1,859	629	972	1,783	13,946	554	287	72
1950	25,344	5,661	661	2,670	614	502	1,025	1,496	434	911	1,568	11,262	545	238	81
1949	23,402	4,637	693	2,052	428	429	889	1,043	291	832	1,388	9,691	511	196	71
1948	21,293	4,203	523	1,881	475	364	810	1,020	297	749	1,168	9,198	569	207	67
1947	18,398	3,419	409	1,457	460	328	651	897	252	633	866	6,899	386	137	42
1946	14,406	2,497	319	993	332	287	459	645	181	517	636	4,234	231	83	38

See footnotes at end of table.

Series **V 167–181.** Selected Corporate Asset, Liability, Income, and Tax Items, and Dividends Paid, by Industrial Division: 1926 to 1970—Con.

[In millions of dollars, except number of returns]

Industrial division and tax year	Number of returns	Total assets or liabilities	Selected assets					Selected liabilities				Total receipts	Total receipts less total deductions	Income tax	Dividends paid in cash and assets other than own stock
			Cash	Notes and accounts receivable less allowance	Inventories	Investments	Capital assets less reserves	Accounts payable and short-term debt	Long-term debt	Capital stock	Surplus and retained earnings				
	167	168	169	170	171	172	173	174	175	176	177	178	179	180	181
Construction—Con.:															
1945	10,726	1,619	257	559	159	275	291	364	102	405	482	2,903	113	62	29
1944	10,326	1,629	263	555	147	308	274	345	101	401	492	3,106	138	89	25
1943	10,707	1,826	315	678	147	291	308	410	115	415	506	4,177	255	165	30
1942	11,729	2,082	315	934	177	262	309	568	107	430	500	4,661	337	204	32
1941	12,894	1,714	195	768	140	205	325	532	107	444	358	3,406	178	81	32
1940	13,795	1,445	157	608	117	182	321	434	93	458	260	2,439	70	23	30
1939	14,162	1,370	146	529	121	159	326	395	95	482	213	2,159	35	11	28
1938	14,308	1,364	134	460	116	188	385	341	98	515	225	1,882	28	10	23
1937	14,807	1,702	140	543	170	240	494	415	152	604	287	2,355	47	14	49
1936	14,574	1,689	126	544	159	244	493	436	135	608	188	1,927	38	11	49
1935	14,117	1,613	123	426	125	288	485	372	140	668	158	1,425	5	7	29
1934 [1]	14,082	1,700	110	418	125	325	546	392	131	707	198	1,220	[3] 23	4	23
1934 [2]	14,059	1,624	106	403	113	365	469	366	162	690	199	1,147	[3] 17	4	23
1933	14,398	1,833	100	390	125	479	555	376	235	734	263	1,035	[3] 51	3	28
1932	15,382	2,141	132	479	138	517	674	448	274	791	332	1,384	[3] 84	3	40
1931	15,350	2,475	155	643	180	545	704	580	297	809	450	2,131	[3] 4	7	63
1930	16,496	3,012	215	800	248	554	896	773	350	932	524	--------	--------	--------	
1929	16,355	3,095	208	876	305	476	857	846	350	884	510	--------	--------	--------	
1928	15,289	2,690	197	816	263	84	756	818	220	808	442	--------	--------	--------	
1927	14,955	2,739	191	743	306	78	743	691	237	738	426	--------	--------	--------	
1926	13,981	2,358	213	668	273	48	654	645	233	639	317	--------	--------	--------	
Agriculture, forestry, and fisheries:															
1970	37,238	11,909	579	1,233	1,328	1,347	6,127	2,854	3,174	2,526	1,622	14,278	68	114	66
1969	31,979	10,407	480	982	1,232	1,066	5,474	2,453	2,730	2,035	2,028	12,127	258	138	92
1968	31,248	8,343	491	951	1,089	693	4,563	2,036	1,917	1,935	1,630	9,451	269	132	95
1967	32,448	8,411	491	967	878	836	4,651	2,108	1,797	1,980	1,805	9,296	184	99	86
1966	27,945	7,557	433	875	970	876	3,993	1,758	1,607	1,788	1,636	8,605	286	118	91
1965	27,530	6,845	411	811	794	861	3,619	1,560	1,527	1,855	1,186	7,524	238	111	97
1964	25,933	6,453	359	829	697	882	3,384	1,429	1,376	1,688	1,249	6,329	138	93	73
1963	23,270	5,946	358	741	711	736	3,074	1,348	1,280	1,618	1,065	7,986	99	90	147
1962	22,130	5,176	(NA)	(NA)	632	(NA)	(NA)	(NA)	(NA)	(NA)	(NA)	6,289	162	81	61
1961	18,981	4,691	272	599	568	534	2,432	1,026	899	1,406	968	5,340	111	71	52
1960	17,139	4,063	255	545	472	515	2,048	881	746	1,270	878	4,402	38	58	50
1959	15,603	3,587	214	429	434	494	1,837	703	676	1,168	792	3,838	106	62	32
1958	12,618	3,523	246	477	395	512	1,766	722	610	1,147	827	3,523	145	77	53
1957	10,676	2,885	190	355	318	382	1,529	588	524	953	651	2,953	114	62	48
1956	9,892	2,678	199	383	304	367	1,335	550	385	900	683	2,700	133	68	44
1955	9,023	2,600	207	269	284	338	1,380	499	379	881	697	2,508	122	67	46
1954	7,790	2,620	191	452	278	376	1,251	508	334	870	696	2,226	122	65	49
1953	8,259	2,392	190	256	299	304	1,264	354	356	855	689	2,333	119	72	49
1952	7,738	2,355	191	257	332	318	1,186	384	332	827	683	2,500	139	77	58
1951	7,618	2,462	186	369	360	349	1,138	499	323	827	671	2,404	254	105	99
1950	7,094	2,260	177	211	322	321	1,174	435	246	799	640	2,052	287	99	106
1949	6,820	1,934	164	183	254	295	990	286	232	762	554	1,833	172	64	59
1948	6,539	1,855	160	176	266	256	934	278	205	754	510	1,812	217	78	62
1947	6,153	1,757	145	172	250	264	873	273	173	665	535	1,599	206	74	58
1946	5,554	1,583	139	149	207	270	764	232	152	648	437	1,239	181	66	33
1945	5,114	1,477	120	183	168	305	662	242	135	615	397	965	133	63	26
1944	5,224	1,436	117	174	160	262	684	215	141	631	357	896	119	62	31
1943	5,557	1,422	118	125	160	250	730	189	159	662	323	828	112	61	29
1942	5,893	1,409	85	109	152	232	793	195	159	675	284	771	81	39	25
1941	6,312	1,502	69	103	146	306	844	281	192	716	243	717	64	22	32
1940	6,816	1,516	62	107	141	259	900	233	224	762	216	617	19	9	25
1939	7,048	1,502	50	100	138	306	867	292	216	767	168	585	15	6	23
1938	7,304	1,523	57	107	145	290	872	299	212	828	122	575	[3] 1	4	19
1937	7,046	1,987	77	141	179	346	1,174	362	254	1,055	214	746	26	8	48
1936	7,126	2,064	82	151	177	352	1,214	372	244	1,100	170	697	36	9	56
1935	7,143	2,107	76	151	187	340	1,229	392	217	1,135	186	566	18	6	35
1934 [1]	7,445	2,243	68	169	187	409	1,303	447	219	1,227	175	513	[3] 11	4	26
1934 [2]	7,375	2,218	70	186	182	436	1,234	405	247	1,214	190	556	[3] 36	4	26
1933	7,295	1,913	58	144	147	211	1,217	311	231	1,047	159	380	[3] 84	2	5
1932	7,716	2,143	51	168	150	307	1,340	370	234	1,152	187	354	[3] 77	1	14
1931	7,567	2,136	57	203	155	246	1,334	362	240	975	373	467	[3] 70	1	25
1930	7,862	2,031	41	219	196	262	1,188	393	229	1,001	264	--------	--------	--------	
1929	7,443	2,140	60	218	198	230	1,231	376	222	1,051	341	--------	--------	--------	
1928	7,130	2,054	51	210	189	41	1,177	399	161	1,059	297	--------	--------	--------	
1927	7,195	2,177	57	197	217	32	1,230	387	178	1,082	202	--------	--------	--------	
1926	7,681	2,050	47	192	118	16	1,242	407	114	1,071	210	--------	--------	--------	

NA Not available.
[1] Comparable with later years.
[2] Comparable with earlier years. Adjusted for comparability with industry classification in 1933 when consolidated returns were permitted to be filed.
[3] Deficit or loss.

Series V 182–196. Selected Corporate Asset, Liability, Income, and Tax Items, and Dividends Paid, by Size of Total Assets: 1931 to 1970

[In millions of dollars, except number of returns. Figures for 1962 not available, except for asset classes of $50 million or more]

Size of total assets and tax year	Number of returns	Total assets or liabilities	Cash	Notes and accounts receivable less allowance	Inventories	Investments	Capital assets less reserves	Accounts payable and short-term debt	Long-term debt	Capital stock	Surplus and retained earnings [1]	Total receipts	Total receipts less total deductions [1]	Income tax	Dividends paid in cash and assets other than own stock
	182	183	184	185	186	187	188	189	190	191	192	193	194	195	196
Less than $50,000:															
1970	[2]	[2]	[2]	[2]	[2]	[2]	[2]	[2]	[2]	[2]	[2]	[2]	[2]	[2]	[2]
1969	673,173	12,296	1,843	2,222	1,664	577	4,441	3,636	1,897	4,518	907	49,047	164	383	634
1968	635,659	11,693	1,780	2,189	1,539	523	4,225	3,594	1,784	4,177	667	55,214	824	608	1,055
1967	646,277	11,842	1,721	2,272	1,616	477	4,338	3,466	1,784	4,735	872	47,141	460	367	752
1966	619,597	11,344	1,606	2,249	1,614	489	4,084	3,532	1,828	4,297	906	42,486	702	478	514
1965	608,259	11,146	1,595	2,242	1,621	470	3,939	3,420	1,813	4,203	927	40,520	441	321	507
1964	592,184	10,859	1,516	2,245	1,548	565	3,860	3,403	1,746	4,274	964	37,772	48	236	504
1963	573,319	10,613	1,428	2,216	1,557	548	3,729	3,306	1,785	4,176	1,081	34,782	153	230	680
1961	506,738	9,607	1,289	2,050	1,434	527	3,384	3,210	1,649	3,888	817	32,754	151	285	431
1960	494,298	9,116	1,204	1,957	1,388	556	3,246	3,194	1,606	3,833	905	30,447	319	217	333
1959	468,453	8,469	1,151	1,816	1,290	573	3,012	2,955	1,525	3,416	543	32,334	48	303	244
1958	370,757	7,749	1,077	1,749	1,184	507	2,775	2,740	1,395	3,221	441	20,225	123	108	66
1957	357,046	7,516	993	1,629	1,150	491	2,689	2,597	1,293	3,102	412	20,022	105	115	86
1956	332,685	6,921	966	1,507	1,087	431	2,503	2,380	1,072	2,953	349	18,038	11	115	82
1955	299,564	6,280	878	1,354	983	367	2,342	2,126	976	2,790	451	16,271	37	101	63
1954	273,045	5,750	802	1,229	962	322	2,108	1,825	933	2,597	292	14,623	87	86	66
1953	261,920	5,624	783	1,152	974	328	2,101	1,651	971	2,628	246	14,550	14	92	46
1952	253,029	5,429	752	1,089	971	333	2,055	1,560	936	2,462	139	13,905	46	97	57
1951	245,803	5,299	723	1,067	955	280	2,073	1,581	890	2,474	160	13,870	86	103	66
1950	236,854	5,081	658	1,016	939	262	1,987	1,519	835	2,453	274	12,381	59	78	74
1949	242,765	5,159	714	997	914	277	2,021	1,454	853	2,556	175	12,936	81	64	70
1948	234,590	5,007	719	946	920	261	1,913	1,347	797	2,463	114	13,215	54	84	80
1947	218,623	4,661	732	884	858	248	1,716	1,223	730	2,273	108	12,062	178	98	80
1946	199,076	4,196	749	778	740	243	1,496	1,064	652	2,095	97	10,902	363	119	86
1945	177,788	3,648	722	668	540	242	1,308	904	599	1,965	250	9,031	268	108	61
1944	176,212	3,528	624	652	558	229	1,313	967	614	2,034	441	9,004	257	106	66
1943	181,961	3,559	578	671	572	206	1,381	1,027	610	2,133	586	9,188	225	111	62
1942	196,642	3,753	477	753	663	175	1,521	1,198	668	2,328	799	9,461	132	82	50
1941	213,086	4,013	372	884	763	183	1,666	1,467	767	2,468	1,009	10,010	44	49	59
1940	225,000	4,136	354	958	738	206	1,740	1,610	731	2,722	1,260	9,617	96	24	56
1939	226,877	4,141	337	969	744	199	1,739	1,615	735	2,803	1,330	9,697	120	18	49
1938	227,491	4,140	324	977	748	193	1,604	1,563	673	2,875	1,313	9,347	204	15	53
1937	228,721	4,180	320	976	795	182	1,585	1,616	543	2,857	1,255	10,923	131	20	95
1936	227,343	4,151	339	998	778	168	1,528	1,602	459	2,875	1,244	10,325	101	22	90
1935	227,545	4,131	327	976	764	171	1,499	1,563	425	2,987	1,308	9,364	183	17	56
1934	223,073	4,038	302	961	730	173	1,495	1,498	419	3,023	1,315	8,588	250	15	62
1933	211,586	3,876	255	925	669	175	1,458	1,324	365	2,962	1,136	6,810	377	9	38
1932	206,477	3,870	237	934	636	177	1,503	1,323	340	2,994	1,136	6,340	609	5	40
1931	182,447	3,703	231	924	640	166	1,390	1,248	283	2,632	722	6,952	412	3	65
$50,000 to $99,999:															
1970 [2]	961,021	32,154	4,261	5,963	4,785	1,638	11,893	8,990	5,259	9,285	1,945	100,270	601	594	836
1969	273,193	19,686	2,381	3,818	3,139	1,105	7,338	5,204	3,479	4,617	3,448	43,065	829	285	263
1968	254,517	18,339	2,248	3,708	2,907	963	6,702	4,654	3,172	4,302	3,376	39,448	863	277	259
1967	260,181	18,815	2,230	3,859	3,083	915	7,057	4,945	3,257	4,611	3,243	39,841	894	253	244
1966	244,880	17,575	2,031	3,603	2,918	919	6,499	4,548	2,980	4,532	2,974	37,013	817	241	218
1965	237,903	17,071	1,971	3,732	2,829	877	6,278	4,561	2,961	4,500	2,378	35,915	790	229	248
1964	231,457	16,614	1,860	3,645	2,714	1,069	6,078	4,377	2,990	4,392	2,401	34,433	687	226	181
1963	221,887	15,937	1,756	3,508	2,628	1,027	5,844	4,181	2,849	4,316	2,205	32,205	517	230	172
1961	206,039	14,756	1,562	3,342	2,475	987	5,321	4,054	2,683	4,092	2,093	30,337	397	206	155
1960	190,316	13,694	1,437	3,093	2,294	1,020	5,014	3,849	2,456	3,833	2,015	28,367	380	192	114
1959	177,542	12,774	1,405	2,895	2,155	993	4,621	3,726	2,332	3,587	1,847	26,227	493	208	87
1958	166,581	12,050	1,325	2,802	2,018	966	4,414	3,485	2,117	3,535	1,877	24,372	338	187	74
1957	158,511	11,344	1,201	2,617	1,930	903	4,126	3,199	1,976	3,325	1,800	23,587	337	188	68
1956	150,165	10,734	1,172	2,490	1,860	819	3,918	3,096	1,701	3,234	1,679	22,473	416	197	84
1955	131,510	9,481	1,089	2,150	1,634	744	3,468	2,658	1,474	2,858	1,598	19,811	353	171	68
1954	117,001	8,430	981	1,858	1,494	585	3,153	2,160	1,334	2,631	1,491	17,606	260	144	61
1953	115,719	8,339	942	1,818	1,540	593	3,118	1,958	1,426	2,661	1,556	17,696	298	152	63
1952	109,780	7,939	941	1,689	1,518	599	2,952	1,846	1,347	2,541	1,555	16,711	390	166	68
1951	106,268	7,725	861	1,595	1,557	484	3,004	1,792	1,368	2,511	1,424	16,593	424	168	78
1950	101,645	7,317	785	1,527	1,475	422	2,865	1,727	1,243	2,452	1,331	15,257	438	138	89
1949	99,878	7,177	861	1,434	1,340	435	2,860	1,561	1,212	2,557	1,310	15,282	288	114	85
1848	96,747	6,948	844	1,352	1,366	414	2,710	1,512	1,137	2,462	1,245	15,544	471	152	92
1947	89,002	6,376	844	1,224	1,244	395	2,426	1,404	1,031	2,216	1,132	14,161	590	178	93
1946	76,821	5,491	801	1,034	985	387	2,075	1,133	904	1,972	953	11,904	649	185	92
1945	61,431	4,379	707	778	622	384	1,719	819	778	1,731	658	8,651	377	147	60
1944	56,831	4,050	584	704	589	364	1,661	750	746	1,683	524	7,929	351	148	64
1943	56,579	4,036	542	716	606	307	1,719	793	762	1,743	390	7,887	339	165	62
1942	58,338	4,164	442	797	685	249	1,843	935	809	1,844	245	7,772	270	123	51
1941	61,525	4,385	324	941	780	242	1,966	1,150	919	1,964	54	8,211	200	72	58
1940	61,053	4,342	297	942	693	269	2,015	1,152	886	2,083	58	7,358	57	30	65
1939	60,256	4,292	277	933	661	271	2,011	1,124	853	2,086	30	6,900	41	21	54
1938	59,582	4,238	261	912	642	266	1,878	1,095	784	2,151	86	6,412	21	16	48
1937	60,238	4,282	250	912	701	267	1,857	1,202	659	2,207	141	7,608	38	21	96
1936	59,528	4,233	263	936	664	259	1,790	1,171	609	2,205	150	7,156	56	23	103

See footnotes at end of table.

Series V 182–196. Selected Corporate Asset, Liability, Income, and Tax Items, and Dividends Paid, by Size of Total Assets: 1931 to 1970—Con.

[In millions of dollars, except number of returns]

Size of total assets and tax year	Number of returns	Total assets or liabilities	Cash	Notes and accounts receivable less allowance	Inventories	Investments	Capital assets less reserves	Accounts payable and short-term debt	Long-term debt	Capital stock	Surplus and retained earnings [1]	Total receipts	Total receipts less total deductions [1]	Income tax	Dividends paid in cash and assets other than own stock
	182	183	184	185	186	187	188	189	190	191	192	193	194	195	196
$50,000 to $99,999—Con.:															
1935	58,434	4,161	258	900	623	268	1,767	1,103	575	2,354	194	6,089	10	17	57
1934	57,840	4,120	243	893	582	278	1,777	1,062	547	2,326	197	5,402	47	14	44
1933	56,205	4,007	209	873	542	271	1,725	953	526	2,283	131	4,317	113	9	33
1932	58,320	4,153	204	924	534	286	1,827	1,067	543	2,415	149	4,101	312	9	38
1931	61,144	4,367	219	1,031	616	283	1,829	1,133	514	2,363	40	5,398	214	5	61
$100,000 to $249,999:															
1970	335,741	53,758	5,656	11,185	9,145	3,732	19,453	14,239	9,426	10,180	12,447	108,518	2,065	756	490
1969	333,802	53,497	5,368	11,597	8,906	3,884	19,259	13,807	9,421	10,352	12,957	103,980	2,684	899	566
1968	310,238	49,570	5,421	10,830	8,203	3,204	18,024	12,611	8,943	9,740	12,125	94,623	2,618	820	609
1967	302,373	48,226	5,167	10,910	8,034	2,835	17,481	12,399	8,598	9,726	11,445	93,142	2,576	737	567
1966	291,520	46,675	4,800	10,704	7,711	2,797	17,195	12,088	8,531	9,496	10,828	90,755	2,462	714	501
1965	280,271	44,698	4,502	10,447	7,210	2,879	16,388	11,636	8,246	9,332	9,577	85,735	2,437	670	499
1964	269,744	42,988	4,345	10,083	6,930	3,458	15,460	11,213	7,895	9,188	9,153	82,073	2,005	606	385
1963	260,714	41,428	4,049	9,701	6,821	3,253	15,103	10,725	7,867	9,192	8,432	78,234	1,659	628	406
1961	239,057	38,023	3,591	8,984	6,330	3,134	13,809	10,042	7,142	8,614	7,995	71,057	1,370	588	317
1960	229,142	36,392	3,303	8,725	6,168	3,162	13,024	9,862	6,756	8,346	7,622	69,952	1,218	546	285
1959	212,573	33,842	3,134	8,182	5,623	3,205	12,099	9,243	7,094	7,817	6,422	64,464	1,446	575	194
1958	195,025	31,090	3,095	7,781	5,161	2,855	11,015	8,414	5,661	7,347	7,005	58,619	1,122	502	201
1957	179,341	28,200	2,670	6,813	4,861	2,550	10,137	7,498	5,152	6,809	6,205	55,300	1,072	493	182
1956	171,122	27,157	2,651	6,573	4,733	2,490	9,668	7,373	4,476	6,809	6,025	53,507	1,283	527	190
1955	150,350	23,923	2,431	5,822	4,259	2,216	8,339	6,394	3,830	5,994	5,445	48,805	1,179	478	186
1954	134,229	21,379	2,263	5,025	3,772	1,847	7,681	5,247	3,488	5,635	5,121	42,249	834	391	160
1953	127,949	20,306	2,086	4,523	3,757	1,788	7,472	4,382	3,744	5,352	5,086	40,521	891	405	165
1952	122,123	19,362	2,070	4,375	3,698	1,714	6,984	4,175	3,534	5,213	4,796	39,489	1,101	451	175
1951	118,366	18,714	1,916	4,003	3,892	1,280	7,147	3,941	3,494	5,053	4,741	38,984	1,243	500	200
1950	111,503	17,687	1,760	3,844	3,605	1,246	6,713	3,817	3,195	4,924	4,342	35,585	1,371	448	224
1949	104,262	16,436	1,838	3,336	2,998	1,224	6,513	3,230	3,008	4,923	4,004	32,953	938	340	210
1948	100,341	15,832	1,767	3,119	3,086	1,152	6,161	3,166	2,829	4,731	3,689	33,606	1,388	480	236
1947	90,709	14,306	1,741	2,814	2,741	1,117	5,390	2,909	2,480	4,345	3,167	30,072	1,575	541	228
1946	76,592	12,094	1,563	2,267	2,152	1,123	4,557	2,361	2,181	3,820	2,509	23,988	1,495	509	217
1945	60,308	9,526	1,317	1,600	1,309	1,132	3,817	1,588	1,851	3,308	1,906	16,660	838	396	141
1944	56,782	8,964	1,150	1,487	1,220	1,085	3,694	1,461	1,774	3,256	1,632	15,587	848	433	145
1943	56,105	8,855	1,090	1,508	1,260	918	3,771	1,484	1,803	3,343	1,373	15,291	851	463	152
1942	57,365	9,067	935	1,686	1,420	735	3,992	1,731	1,864	3,493	1,150	14,808	729	367	130
1941	60,386	9,547	722	2,043	1,589	714	4,212	2,087	2,035	3,730	868	15,071	561	215	155
1940	59,059	9,316	653	2,015	1,331	781	4,279	1,986	1,981	3,924	633	12,742	275	83	154
1939	58,119	9,188	622	1,922	1,246	837	4,287	1,953	1,937	4,041	486	11,561	193	51	138
1938	57,733	9,112	577	1,853	1,195	841	4,096	1,902	1,789	4,112	391	10,535	50	37	120
1937	58,817	9,283	564	1,888	1,294	879	4,089	2,122	1,588	4,232	319	12,308	178	52	234
1936	58,442	9,229	600	1,930	1,212	872	3,980	2,097	1,511	4,337	160	11,394	225	53	258
1935	58,208	9,204	620	1,865	1,125	894	4,018	1,933	1,422	4,444	215	9,688	72	39	142
1934	58,186	9,231	566	1,835	1,065	963	4,080	1,898	1,399	4,616	138	8,466	28	32	113
1933	56,745	8,992	481	1,848	995	937	3,948	1,727	1,368	4,506	216	6,780	188	20	63
1932	59,500	9,414	457	1,994	945	1,000	4,249	1,779	1,427	4,751	247	6,561	484	11	83
1931	63,428	10,072	491	2,308	1,135	993	4,335	2,038	1,382	4,816	578	8,803	340	13	141
$250,000 to $499,999:															
1970	169,847	59,586	5,266	13,685	10,554	4,741	20,898	16,458	11,184	9,398	15,068	113,023	2,306	999	434
1969	172,995	60,345	5,192	14,626	10,529	4,657	20,847	16,675	11,069	9,439	15,712	112,730	2,832	1,093	698
1968	155,647	54,528	4,812	13,411	9,366	4,011	19,244	15,041	10,224	8,709	13,894	101,100	2,928	1,040	566
1967	151,626	53,214	4,696	13,385	9,247	3,551	18,656	14,525	10,182	8,892	13,150	98,333	2,727	924	526
1966	144,699	50,616	4,263	12,966	8,619	3,634	17,845	13,774	9,861	8,431	12,389	92,528	2,673	863	493
1965	137,481	48,007	4,080	12,262	8,239	3,515	16,803	13,244	9,406	8,162	11,171	86,867	2,383	806	419
1964	131,188	45,826	3,980	11,820	7,374	4,172	15,985	12,193	8,858	8,360	10,542	84,221	2,080	761	378
1963	124,958	43,528	3,589	11,036	7,130	4,138	15,141	11,600	8,712	8,037	9,870	76,686	1,644	696	289
1961	111,593	38,925	3,204	10,070	6,336	3,951	13,222	10,455	7,618	7,531	9,017	67,513	1,360	624	278
1960	105,174	36,622	2,897	9,368	6,001	3,854	12,641	9,860	7,297	7,174	8,425	64,340	1,226	580	252
1959	99,583	34,739	2,964	9,068	5,730	3,799	11,619	9,205	6,605	6,917	8,518	63,631	1,547	662	212
1958	88,311	30,827	2,741	8,072	5,052	3,313	10,609	8,157	5,760	6,185	7,950	54,947	1,221	537	188
1957	82,274	28,213	2,490	7,212	4,841	2,986	9,636	7,338	5,080	5,848	7,201	53,495	1,212	563	193
1956	76,929	26,753	2,424	6,831	4,522	3,136	8,930	7,076	4,505	5,552	6,854	50,181	1,363	596	197
1955	70,483	24,560	2,290	6,356	4,391	2,708	7,997	6,425	3,970	5,202	6,441	48,144	1,291	562	191
1954	60,356	21,046	2,143	5,193	3,686	2,235	7,044	5,088	3,416	4,622	5,835	39,745	966	447	176
1953	55,447	19,387	1,953	4,539	3,541	2,116	6,562	4,059	3,476	4,487	5,427	37,348	994	478	206
1952	52,976	18,571	1,884	4,343	3,488	2,072	6,303	3,927	3,292	4,239	5,197	36,678	1,143	545	202
1951	52,395	18,330	1,842	4,119	3,655	1,750	6,492	3,738	3,227	4,349	5,171	36,981	1,412	661	229
1950	49,735	17,365	1,721	3,954	3,503	1,576	6,112	3,618	2,934	4,250	4,859	33,737	1,605	621	259
1949	44,634	15,567	1,762	3,229	2,746	1,567	5,770	2,827	2,664	4,159	4,428	29,310	1,106	434	234
1948	43,366	15,145	1,681	3,039	2,924	1,521	5,489	2,872	2,510	4,042	4,121	30,510	1,577	603	262
1947	39,571	13,842	1,625	2,727	2,699	1,475	4,843	2,669	2,217	3,787	3,583	27,387	1,701	647	246
1946	34,264	11,997	1,464	2,254	2,228	1,493	4,135	2,217	1,945	3,469	2,951	22,270	1,584	603	253

See footnotes at end of table.

Series V 182–196. Selected Corporate Asset, Liability, Income, and Tax Items, and Dividends Paid, by Size of Total Assets: 1931 to 1970—Con.

[In millions of dollars, except number of returns]

Size of total assets and tax year	Number of returns	Total assets or liabilities	Cash	Notes and accounts receivable less allowance	Inventories	Investments	Capital assets less reserves	Accounts payable and short-term debt	Long-term debt	Capital stock	Surplus and retained earnings [1]	Total receipts	Total receipts less total deductions [1]	Income tax	Dividends paid in cash and assets other than own stock
	182	183	184	185	186	187	188	189	190	191	192	193	194	195	196
$250,000 to $499,999—Con.:															
1945	27,583	9,667	1,256	1,567	1,398	1,561	3,523	1,527	1,663	3,063	2,255	15,829	914	511	154
1944	26,496	9,322	1,199	1,518	1,262	1,646	3,368	1,338	1,627	3,036	2,024	14,778	995	588	161
1943	26,757	9,418	1,236	1,585	1,294	1,474	3,538	1,348	1,655	3,096	1,858	14,646	1,015	606	171
1942	27,300	9,611	1,158	1,831	1,381	1,259	3,721	1,487	1,694	3,268	1,623	13,647	893	500	158
1941	28,751	10,122	975	2,270	1,493	1,152	3,986	1,830	1,860	3,455	1,407	13,053	691	289	189
1940	27,832	9,787	867	2,191	1,204	1,226	4,056	1,664	1,836	3,669	1,145	10,286	345	102	187
1939	27,447	9,649	812	2,064	1,130	1,302	4,092	1,590	1,819	3,796	1,013	9,335	248	59	175
1938	27,371	9,629	747	1,991	1,050	1,415	4,005	1,545	1,749	3,896	955	8,495	106	41	152
1937	27,992	9,868	720	2,007	1,159	1,523	4,052	1,745	1,706	3,990	915	9,794	242	59	256
1936	28,342	9,995	808	2,040	1,104	1,519	4,059	1,798	1,596	4,123	761	9,185	283	60	281
1935	28,605	10,076	775	1,933	1,016	1,483	4,160	1,687	1,486	4,363	633	7,888	132	41	162
1934	28,673	10,096	693	1,886	973	1,550	4,261	1,697	1,495	4,500	571	6,885	21	33	134
1933	26,773	9,421	535	1,823	891	1,420	3,976	1,419	1,419	4,222	733	5,505	*129*	22	69
1932	28,422	9,988	491	2,023	846	1,533	4,322	1,486	1,500	4,521	790	5,297	*379*	12	96
1931	31,052	10,930	555	2,436	1,036	1,557	4,544	1,747	1,547	4,685	1,071	7,210	*251*	17	159
$500,000 to $999,999:															
1970	93,468	64,947	4,860	15,680	11,532	5,523	22,457	19,086	12,998	8,727	16,119	117,785	2,317	1,189	469
1969	96,206	66,565	4,666	17,037	12,304	5,532	22,180	20,014	12,985	8,961	16,523	119,916	2,925	1,436	464
1968	87,050	60,245	4,727	15,882	10,589	5,177	19,591	17,531	11,344	8,171	15,661	109,065	3,344	1,461	588
1967	81,440	56,359	4,436	14,098	9,611	4,613	19,730	16,042	11,312	8,160	13,999	100,742	2,756	1,164	506
1966	78,652	54,538	4,078	14,619	9,300	4,641	18,298	15,830	10,808	7,869	13,221	95,350	2,890	1,174	475
1965	72,936	50,384	3,905	12,972	8,440	4,604	17,195	14,159	10,072	7,383	11,959	86,655	2,710	1,051	432
1964	67,268	46,305	3,613	11,920	7,317	5,529	15,466	12,477	9,402	7,274	10,849	77,426	1,972	868	385
1963	64,950	44,955	3,565	11,882	7,165	5,047	14,880	12,018	9,190	7,162	10,743	75,553	1,871	902	287
1961	58,065	40,247	3,309	10,507	6,311	4,908	13,043	10,355	7,861	6,852	10,036	65,796	1,612	797	343
1960	54,991	38,203	3,112	9,869	6,209	4,966	11,961	10,030	7,245	6,642	9,590	62,682	1,390	760	319
1959	52,048	36,138	2,939	9,391	5,949	4,945	11,327	9,124	7,012	6,233	9,281	61,857	1,626	783	261
1958	46,346	32,053	2,898	8,535	5,264	4,264	10,028	8,074	6,025	5,834	8,502	53,077	1,346	672	236
1957	43,634	29,740	2,678	7,572	4,854	4,063	9,491	7,183	5,333	5,527	8,030	51,352	1,386	697	248
1956	41,336	28,775	2,666	7,328	4,735	4,224	8,866	6,877	4,672	5,148	7,958	48,810	1,596	749	249
1955	39,301	27,382	2,659	6,934	4,643	3,998	8,254	6,389	4,251	5,050	7,689	48,675	1,638	757	242
1954	33,617	23,491	2,475	5,728	3,788	3,357	7,409	4,976	3,617	4,628	6,982	38,904	1,214	594	232
1953	31,845	22,239	2,323	5,140	3,800	3,434	6,892	4,142	3,842	4,476	6,312	38,192	1,255	657	245
1952	31,290	21,847	2,375	5,162	3,847	3,230	6,697	4,077	3,418	4,562	6,474	37,896	1,462	762	258
1951	30,355	21,208	2,329	4,793	4,087	2,672	6,808	3,935	3,379	4,506	6,154	37,891	1,797	917	302
1950	29,093	20,338	2,181	4,610	3,824	2,779	6,402	3,805	3,055	4,437	5,929	34,453	1,991	830	352
1949	25,651	17,903	2,142	3,786	2,878	2,843	5,847	2,908	2,629	4,241	5,367	28,963	1,296	528	311
1948	24,803	17,362	2,048	3,593	3,119	2,718	5,497	2,898	2,410	4,133	5,040	30,900	1,861	721	346
1947	23,258	16,293	2,032	3,271	2,982	2,695	4,936	2,842	2,127	4,020	4,474	28,718	2,029	781	331
1946	20,803	14,585	1,878	2,692	2,544	2,739	4,324	2,435	1,909	3,772	3,744	23,611	1,840	718	305
1945	17,669	12,437	1,805	1,934	1,643	2,919	3,764	1,658	1,692	3,454	3,001	17,398	1,196	718	204
1944	17,625	12,391	1,804	1,959	1,508	2,974	3,746	1,513	1,627	3,463	2,782	16,545	1,304	817	215
1943	17,893	12,606	1,922	2,116	1,517	2,761	3,924	1,494	1,682	3,553	2,572	15,938	1,351	842	218
1942	18,109	12,715	1,906	2,475	1,601	2,295	4,119	1,615	1,717	3,699	2,301	14,785	1,185	702	208
1941	18,424	12,915	1,598	2,956	1,697	1,907	4,470	1,908	1,925	4,009	1,995	13,538	892	401	251
1940	17,505	12,227	1,338	2,687	1,322	1,987	4,607	1,714	1,977	4,174	1,683	10,419	427	135	220
1939	17,232	12,056	1,228	2,485	1,240	2,114	4,699	1,659	2,012	4,338	1,540	9,391	316	72	219
1938	17,079	11,966	1,087	2,370	1,144	2,275	4,597	1,627	1,953	4,415	1,481	8,406	162	51	190
1937	17,587	12,325	1,038	2,388	1,259	2,432	4,705	1,846	1,919	4,605	1,436	9,830	317	73	314
1936	17,941	12,560	1,142	2,394	1,192	2,467	4,807	1,909	1,836	4,766	1,243	9,214	364	77	333
1935	18,102	12,705	1,041	2,279	1,133	2,467	4,936	1,907	1,760	5,096	1,093	8,014	178	49	242
1934	18,339	12,856	923	2,248	1,076	2,571	5,175	1,923	1,764	5,310	1,062	7,115	55	39	209
1933	16,592	11,577	691	2,101	966	2,259	4,665	1,428	1,645	4,894	1,193	5,476	*101*	27	98
1932	17,590	12,289	655	2,394	891	2,450	5,018	1,499	1,730	5,219	1,229	5,088	*395*	15	125
1931	19,335	13,531	722	2,892	1,092	2,543	5,289	1,765	1,794	5,463	1,570	7,079	*252*	19	198
$1,000,000 to $4,999,999:															
1970	74,420	150,895	10,259	37,212	22,809	23,222	46,004	39,259	28,174	15,716	37,391	214,232	5,161	3,159	956
1969	78,657	158,074	10,581	40,676	25,008	24,461	46,343	41,322	27,914	17,395	39,094	226,259	7,056	3,854	1,405
1968	71,904	146,176	11,093	37,432	22,619	24,157	41,298	36,118	25,298	15,858	36,589	202,510	7,403	3,853	1,105
1967	65,999	135,538	10,450	35,152	20,125	22,794	38,702	31,995	23,360	15,257	34,172	184,887	6,830	3,232	1,053
1966	63,988	132,529	10,123	34,952	19,513	23,606	37,005	30,705	22,769	15,086	31,990	180,236	6,853	3,202	1,063
1965	62,601	130,154	10,586	35,056	17,870	24,660	34,796	28,734	21,242	15,000	30,854	166,533	6,495	2,987	1,043
1964	58,905	122,868	10,320	32,718	15,789	25,413	32,804	26,684	20,243	14,901	28,747	149,074	5,314	2,607	952
1963	55,771	116,988	10,012	31,317	15,171	24,558	30,142	25,244	19,145	14,776	27,425	140,502	4,560	2,426	852
1961	49,262	103,911	9,679	27,476	13,143	23,525	25,352	20,971	15,596	13,664	25,691	117,735	3,918	2,075	826
1960	47,983	100,945	9,416	26,472	12,628	23,749	24,418	19,326	14,827	13,456	25,049	116,550	3,789	2,021	894
1959	46,104	97,228	9,227	25,450	12,320	23,899	22,738	18,632	13,635	13,045	24,120	114,483	4,525	2,253	837
1958	43,321	91,202	9,441	23,759	11,274	22,667	21,582	16,762	12,386	12,396	23,697	102,156	3,749	1,938	756
1957	41,780	87,461	9,161	22,749	10,647	22,144	20,226	15,357	11,853	12,552	21,655	101,667	4,137	2,090	857
1956	39,861	85,884	9,380	21,479	10,961	22,619	19,272	13,909	9,984	11,497	21,849	97,748	4,738	2,302	843

See footnotes at end of table.

Series V 182–196. Selected Corporate Asset, Liability, Income, and Tax Items, and Dividends Paid, by Size of Total Assets: 1931 to 1970—Con.

[In millions of dollars, except number of returns]

Size of total assets and tax year	Number of returns	Total assets or liabilities	Selected assets					Selected liabilities				Total receipts	Total receipts less total deductions [1]	Income tax	Dividends paid in cash and assets other than own stock
			Cash	Notes and accounts receivable less allowance	Inventories	Investments	Capital assets less reserves	Accounts payable and short-term debt	Long-term debt	Capital stock	Surplus and retained earnings [1]				
	182	183	184	185	186	187	188	189	190	191	192	193	194	195	196
$1,000,000 to $4,999,999— Con.:															
1955	40,853	87,950	10,225	22,331	10,799	23,468	19,038	13,421	9,857	11,996	22,255	97,583	4,820	2,338	881
1954	35,770	76,940	9,604	18,349	9,186	20,812	17,071	10,580	9,194	11,292	19,028	82,325	3,650	1,857	774
1953	33,805	72,960	9,284	17,089	9,255	19,759	15,960	8,984	8,467	10,373	18,980	81,805	3,996	2,115	880
1952	33,579	72,539	9,286	17,131	9,493	19,250	16,058	9,276	8,164	10,684	18,761	81,150	4,411	2,351	861
1951	32,041	68,596	9,437	15,645	9,872	16,287	16,069	8,790	7,644	10,665	18,100	81,724	5,297	2,804	970
1950	30,643	65,455	8,809	15,421	8,974	16,341	14,748	8,436	6,590	10,444	17,320	73,903	5,576	2,390	1,111
1949	27,793	59,298	8,453	12,846	6,900	16,400	13,670	6,154	5,728	10,281	15,398	61,613	3,663	1,401	973
1948	27,414	58,797	8,353	12,304	7,540	16,732	12,833	6,325	5,261	10,072	14,545	65,995	4,978	1,860	1,054
1947	26,447	57,167	8,458	10,937	7,272	17,774	11,696	6,307	4,747	10,009	13,282	61,785	5,336	1,995	1,014
1946	24,618	53,375	8,219	8,936	6,412	18,183	10,548	5,566	4,330	9,634	11,651	50,624	4,627	1,781	937
1945	22,057	47,907	8,199	6,572	4,477	18,114	9,486	4,241	3,906	9,359	9,676	42,251	3,450	2,047	680
1944	21,590	46,107	7,777	6,526	4,252	16,677	9,712	3,945	3,965	9,355	9,328	41,476	4,019	2,511	684
1943	20,737	43,611	7,291	6,664	4,245	14,255	10,060	3,804	3,930	9,488	8,817	39,471	4,139	2,567	681
1942	19,582	40,790	6,622	7,399	4,262	10,905	10,659	3,868	4,261	9,774	8,015	35,138	3,590	2,121	675
1941	18,832	39,214	5,313	8,155	4,324	8,694	11,927	4,399	5,032	10,898	7,149	31,307	2,655	1,214	838
1940	17,627	36,756	4,703	7,356	3,363	8,479	12,088	3,839	5,134	11,339	6,308	23,456	1,401	424	749
1939	17,337	36,150	4,144	6,770	3,140	8,887	12,404	3,782	5,232	11,573	6,031	21,091	1,104	211	740
1938	17,187	35,789	3,465	6,338	2,850	9,482	12,218	3,587	5,381	11,903	5,913	18,544	561	137	597
1937	17,897	37,278	3,266	6,541	3,246	10,115	12,701	4,262	5,338	12,455	6,024	21,930	1,108	220	974
1936	18,277	37,955	3,486	6,566	2,968	10,326	12,930	4,455	5,122	12,986	5,126	20,545	1,167	218	968
1935	18,407	38,298	3,067	6,273	2,691	10,533	13,542	4,699	5,288	13,986	4,785	18,446	674	132	817
1934	18,499	38,603	2,666	6,235	2,571	10,677	14,094	4,937	5,084	14,571	4,732	16,101	285	102	650
1933	15,840	32,723	1,928	5,549	2,220	8,829	11,835	3,095	4,299	12,781	4,424	11,448	*258*	67	315
1932	16,705	34,432	1,927	6,321	1,972	9,359	12,658	3,138	4,512	13,573	4,730	10,744	*834*	35	378
1931	18,345	37,955	2,067	7,666	2,438	9,843	13,440	3,710	4,649	14,118	5,625	14,595	*539*	52	591
$5,000,000 to $9,999,999:															
1970	12,559	88,837	6,375	24,755	9,064	24,660	18,271	15,233	11,675	6,777	18,731	77,755	2,313	1,383	522
1969	13,211	92,535	6,625	27,190	9,617	26,894	17,652	15,900	11,364	6,946	18,730	80,572	3,061	1,674	661
1968	9,898	69,427	5,595	19,520	7,384	20,765	12,745	11,072	7,994	5,301	14,582	59,153	2,788	1,410	455
1967	11,329	80,261	6,386	23,662	7,608	24,219	14,530	12,484	8,971	6,205	16,318	60,533	2,962	1,384	537
1966	11,048	78,025	6,410	22,310	7,369	24,589	14,133	11,609	8,649	6,359	15,518	62,638	3,235	1,486	557
1965	10,874	76,074	6,610	21,557	7,645	25,138	12,880	10,572	7,882	6,046	15,059	57,551	3,004	1,360	605
1964	9,714	68,149	6,117	18,976	5,704	23,043	11,643	8,952	7,177	5,778	13,548	49,149	2,337	1,134	484
1963	9,289	65,102	5,986	18,782	5,246	21,679	10,933	9,876	6,692	5,643	13,382	45,542	2,038	1,018	436
1961	8,564	59,865	6,053	15,897	4,890	20,875	10,231	7,269	6,245	5,590	12,948	41,906	1,974	970	441
1960	8,280	57,818	5,801	14,712	4,961	20,718	9,990	6,722	5,879	5,265	12,882	41,660	1,917	979	485
1959	8,022	55,994	5,709	13,945	4,798	20,730	9,378	6,383	5,315	5,172	12,574	40,877	2,280	1,085	471
1958	7,870	54,797	6,137	14,566	4,489	19,587	8,952	7,296	4,617	5,181	12,299	38,335	1,907	961	462
1957	7,667	53,392	6,159	13,720	4,498	19,247	8,799	6,391	4,877	4,969	11,670	38,682	2,056	1,052	479
1956	7,295	51,200	5,963	12,364	4,627	19,109	8,270	5,128	3,995	4,833	11,513	38,049	2,343	1,151	491
1955	6,794	47,606	5,761	11,618	4,247	17,527	7,675	4,576	3,627	4,809	11,053	35,489	2,295	1,090	485
1954	6,324	44,205	5,713	9,718	3,916	16,765	7,323	3,707	3,433	4,493	10,536	32,269	1,870	926	470
1953	6,181	43,046	5,620	9,005	4,036	16,479	7,217	3,489	3,494	4,463	9,993	32,684	2,092	1,104	471
1952	6,139	42,817	5,635	9,280	4,195	15,757	7,298	3,619	3,257	4,698	9,955	32,718	2,205	1,188	501
1951	5,303	37,018	5,395	8,291	4,339	11,447	6,916	3,430	2,745	4,603	9,263	32,393	2,524	1,350	528
1950	4,987	34,767	4,882	7,778	3,857	11,266	6,430	3,046	2,406	4,574	8,833	28,430	2,631	1,117	598
1949	4,650	32,383	4,715	6,615	3,088	11,218	6,182	2,309	2,259	4,668	8,073	24,261	1,772	661	540
1948	4,733	33,061	4,869	6,524	3,641	11,339	6,154	2,635	2,222	4,728	8,026	28,292	2,545	927	604
1947	4,576	31,950	4,830	5,853	3,340	11,737	5,649	2,517	2,057	4,527	7,379	25,355	2,525	929	598
1946	4,241	29,627	4,409	4,669	2,922	11,860	5,179	2,063	1,901	4,565	6,591	20,234	2,133	809	548
1945	3,948	27,591	4,491	3,381	2,057	12,317	4,743	1,662	1,699	4,444	5,725	17,749	1,719	989	411
1944	3,646	25,285	4,055	3,170	2,066	10,357	5,015	1,687	1,891	4,504	5,346	18,684	2,073	1,292	388
1943	3,232	22,397	3,539	3,049	2,022	8,169	5,039	1,627	1,760	4,445	5,003	16,754	2,152	1,322	373
1942	2,905	20,258	3,153	3,168	2,014	6,141	5,181	1,617	1,895	4,566	4,479	14,552	1,766	1,072	356
1941	2,812	19,571	2,695	3,578	1,901	5,136	5,815	1,821	2,275	5,016	4,316	12,605	1,369	651	457
1940	2,603	18,142	2,404	3,105	1,434	4,912	5,894	1,550	2,376	5,221	3,863	9,186	687	212	390
1939	2,537	17,613	2,031	2,773	1,244	5,164	5,992	1,445	2,645	5,373	3,423	8,026	541	96	373
1938	2,542	17,584	1,745	2,639	1,158	5,428	5,961	1,470	2,718	5,631	3,198	7,192	302	63	312
1937	2,620	18,187	1,612	2,712	1,314	5,685	6,169	1,736	2,770	5,867	3,211	8,452	542	96	466
1936	2,719	18,967	1,711	2,806	1,265	5,920	6,459	1,861	2,776	6,180	2,998	8,352	605	101	498
1935	2,769	19,342	1,512	2,771	1,145	6,152	6,895	1,955	3,015	6,709	3,005	7,434	343	58	414
1934	2,844	19,789	1,323	2,931	1,108	6,337	7,151	2,215	2,994	7,000	2,903	6,589	172	50	332
1933	2,344	16,224	1,015	2,395	930	5,147	5,873	1,252	2,394	5,978	2,491	4,811	*110*	33	191
1932	2,442	16,857	1,005	2,698	801	5,187	6,241	1,248	2,528	6,257	2,630	4,627	*335*	21	228
1931	2,588	17,965	1,055	3,311	942	5,385	6,241	1,393	2,432	6,185	3,091	5,588	*138*	28	345
$10,000,000 to $49,999,999:															
1970	13,706	287,787	20,024	75,559	18,231	117,532	41,561	32,472	28,662	15,130	50,573	158,598	6,160	3,180	1,806
1969	13,235	277,024	18,353	73,659	18,189	114,093	39,885	30,955	26,966	14,986	50,063	154,116	7,423	3,755	2,273
1968	12,597	261,852	18,457	67,055	17,157	110,425	37,569	27,833	24,375	14,858	47,466	142,390	8,272	3,938	1,883
1967	11,314	235,595	16,741	59,771	15,956	98,638	34,720	25,797	22,213	14,128	43,944	131,545	7,495	3,308	1,829
1966	10,746	223,779	15,840	53,954	16,128	95,213	34,076	22,979	21,645	13,773	42,089	132,041	8,134	3,569	1,973

See footnotes at end of table.

Series V 182–196. Selected Corporate Asset, Liability, Income, and Tax Items, and Dividends Paid, by Size of Total Assets: 1931 to 1970—Con.

[In millions of dollars, except number of returns]

| Size of total assets and tax year | Number of returns | Total assets or liabilities | Selected assets | | | | | Selected liabilities | | | | Total receipts | Total receipts less total deductions ¹ | Income tax | Dividends paid in cash and assets other than own stock |
| | | | Cash | Notes and accounts receivable less allowance | Inventories | Investments | Capital assets less reserves | Accounts payable and short-term debt | Long-term debt | Capital stock | Surplus and retained earnings ¹ | | | | |
	182	183	184	185	186	187	188	189	190	191	192	193	194	195	196
$10,000,000 to $49,999,999— Con.:															
1965	10,254	214,023	15,855	50,714	14,609	92,934	32,173	20,414	20,186	13,494	40,058	119,550	7,618	3,335	2,678
1964	9,846	204,211	15,644	46,271	13,542	91,299	30,777	18,623	19,239	13,392	39,507	112,874	6,526	3,066	1,845
1963	9,264	192,004	15,111	49,247	12,971	78,090	29,399	22,300	18,150	13,173	39,727	106,882	5,914	2,881	1,634
1961	8,336	171,786	14,807	37,118	11,977	76,440	26,361	14,456	15,530	12,476	37,700	92,923	5,572	2,593	1,574
1960	7,912	162,350	14,173	34,760	11,805	71,784	25,537	13,278	14,228	12,479	35,972	93,603	5,391	2,639	1,650
1959	7,476	154,136	13,465	32,521	11,630	68,522	24,237	12,081	12,970	12,166	34,950	89,434	6,169	2,903	1,710
1958	7,220	146,166	14,177	31,223	10,590	64,032	23,198	11,148	12,216	11,421	33,567	81,649	5,233	2,518	1,580
1957	6,769	138,249	13,776	29,794	11,129	58,326	22,366	10,826	11,425	11,782	32,039	82,826	6,000	2,848	1,677
1956	6,547	134,887	14,254	30,746	11,495	53,423	22,491	10,312	11,557	11,738	31,527	83,432	6,685	3,167	1,769
1955	6,246	126,472	13,607	27,557	10,153	52,241	20,622	8,796	9,665	11,257	29,799	77,254	6,530	3,039	1,723
1954	5,718	116,343	13,300	24,148	9,440	47,158	20,080	7,270	9,263	11,202	27,969	70,567	5,272	2,512	1,566
1953	5,550	112,999	13,163	22,922	9,928	44,569	20,407	7,116	9,344	11,928	26,537	73,302	5,966	3,130	1,631
1952	5,220	104,753	13,040	21,129	9,825	39,083	19,590	7,481	9,054	11,862	24,984	71,725	5,953	3,122	1,660
1951	4,481	90,506	12,394	18,330	10,143	29,064	18,637	7,326	8,063	11,647	23,378	71,510	7,195	3,803	1,805
1950	4,217	84,676	11,233	16,944	8,707	28,415	17,652	6,671	7,375	11,668	22,176	64,717	6,910	2,878	1,887
1949	3,761	75,812	10,051	13,006	7,015	27,606	16,505	4,603	6,862	11,334	19,448	53,752	4,486	1,589	1,529
1948	3,709	75,045	10,390	12,794	7,666	26,735	15,904	4,904	6,688	11,456	18,215	56,134	5,653	2,002	1,624
1947	3,565	71,789	10,063	11,646	7,208	26,977	14,325	5,040	5,708	11,613	16,511	51,621	5,188	1,878	1,487
1946	3,341	67,896	9,486	9,505	6,201	28,115	13,062	4,239	5,310	11,585	14,799	40,362	4,114	1,507	1,341
1945	3,197	65,335	9,724	7,523	4,591	30,143	11,852	3,798	4,817	11,134	13,513	39,917	3,900	2,163	1,072
1944	2,942	60,260	8,741	6,961	4,664	25,969	12,212	3,980	4,827	11,094	12,923	40,606	4,764	2,855	1,041
1943	2,719	55,215	7,966	6,757	4,670	21,737	12,487	3,763	5,003	11,063	12,047	37,959	5,093	3,120	1,016
1942	2,467	50,148	7,230	6,880	4,748	16,934	13,005	3,733	5,132	11,064	11,099	32,681	4,472	2,581	975
1941	2,411	49,186	6,615	7,685	4,249	14,964	14,576	3,646	6,288	12,671	10,877	29,132	3,071	1,440	1,252
1940	2,266	46,494	6,443	6,590	3,236	14,456	14,722	2,926	6,665	13,117	9,979	21,850	1,849	506	1,139
1939	2,217	45,767	5,485	6,186	3,009	15,156	14,887	2,838	6,972	13,651	9,465	19,199	1,565	246	1,154
1938	2,213	45,225	4,616	5,727	2,770	15,446	14,813	2,758	7,210	14,070	8,978	16,641	958	165	926
1937	2,281	46,642	4,263	6,086	3,040	16,063	15,228	3,495	7,100	14,536	9,325	19,522	1,640	252	1,372
1936	2,311	47,405	4,264	5,986	2,715	16,923	15,346	3,743	6,939	15,174	7,821	17,174	1,528	224	1,370
1935	2,393	49,080	3,926	6,122	2,428	17,935	16,313	4,244	8,050	16,268	8,099	16,386	1,202	152	1,308
1934	2,411	49,405	3,323	6,601	2,325	17,648	16,975	4,643	7,869	16,898	8,051	14,408	748	118	1,105
1933	1,885	38,592	2,365	4,932	2,029	13,314	13,657	2,391	6,194	16,270	6,270	10,430	68	78	589
1932	1,947	39,839	2,494	5,628	1,752	13,369	14,122	2,485	6,271	14,319	6,054	9,905	*495*	48	595
1931	2,117	43,167	2,482	7,051	2,141	13,859	14,857	2,980	6,282	14,890	7,154	13,365	*36*	68	880
$50,000,000 to $99,999,999:															
1970	2,080	144,514	8,402	29,147	9,132	67,998	21,815	13,527	15,307	7,776	29,160	73,354	2,929	1,500	1,265
1969	1,875	130,753	7,134	27,030	8,671	60,794	20,947	12,832	14,294	7,473	27,305	68,451	3,580	1,721	1,476
1968	1,839	127,956	7,652	27,048	8,025	59,913	19,636	11,741	13,617	7,105	26,162	62,739	3,919	1,785	1,323
1967	1,664	115,830	6,832	22,776	7,982	54,975	18,584	9,395	12,313	6,638	24,088	58,487	3,854	1,643	1,189
1966	1,576	109,554	6,391	20,688	7,821	52,157	18,476	9,298	11,894	6,665	23,216	58,148	4,281	1,827	1,291
1965	1,500	104,339	6,469	19,894	7,139	49,589	17,490	8,177	10,557	6,526	21,962	54,857	3,928	1,709	1,226
1964	1,453	100,494	6,661	18,591	6,354	47,805	17,293	7,568	10,407	6,928	21,463	52,052	3,572	1,587	1,219
1963	1,376	95,606	6,356	20,972	6,138	40,726	17,078	8,546	10,213	7,253	21,875	50,685	3,463	1,520	1,267
1962	1,289	89,559	(NA)	(NA)	5,727	(NA)	(NA)	(NA)	(NA)	(NA)	(NA)	46,680	3,018	1,414	1,089
1961	1,204	84,155	6,179	15,715	5,761	37,653	16,391	5,239	9,527	7,066	20,278	45,206	3,204	1,452	1,267
1960	1,145	79,745	5,930	14,744	5,692	35,418	15,848	5,568	8,442	6,934	19,449	43,748	3,166	1,471	1,211
1959	1,043	73,108	5,464	13,282	5,390	32,433	14,411	5,135	7,424	6,399	18,478	43,459	3,432	1,549	1,132
1958	1,001	69,915	5,759	12,790	5,042	30,659	14,084	4,813	7,384	6,050	18,642	40,610	2,789	1,283	1,152
1957	955	66,769	5,765	11,741	5,229	28,896	13,697	4,684	6,581	6,241	17,016	42,301	3,131	1,435	1,155
1956	896	62,304	5,930	13,503	4,785	23,829	12,929	4,141	6,146	6,101	16,169	36,598	3,432	1,519	1,178
1955	834	57,696	5,615	12,040	4,260	22,480	12,019	3,696	5,655	6,240	14,110	32,560	3,136	1,413	1,064
1954	794	55,544	5,801	10,288	4,234	21,808	12,026	3,204	5,431	6,297	13,580	31,400	2,667	1,223	972
1953	742	51,984	5,493	9,892	4,435	19,120	11,801	3,284	5,531	6,169	12,385	32,349	2,764	1,384	877
1952	708	49,986	5,551	8,995	4,224	18,463	11,542	3,230	5,442	6,012	11,748	30,361	2,755	1,382	926
1951	626	44,109	5,431	7,278	4,158	14,812	11,385	2,916	4,932	6,302	10,978	28,710	3,280	1,721	934
1950	596	41,555	4,989	7,113	3,659	14,191	10,555	2,594	5,145	6,335	9,798	27,249	3,205	1,297	959
1949	556	38,957	4,698	5,730	3,285	13,330	10,330	2,217	5,097	6,668	8,927	24,692	2,229	780	896
1948	529	37,169	4,760	5,358	3,443	13,415	9,146	2,142	4,442	6,263	7,909	23,985	2,507	866	849
1947	509	35,740	4,934	4,704	3,262	13,180	8,674	2,037	4,192	6,492	6,578	21,619	2,147	757	744
1946	463	32,457	4,125	3,660	2,645	12,918	8,235	1,712	3,808	6,463	6,125	15,675	1,587	559	651
1945	427	29,834	3,960	3,117	1,755	13,136	7,068	1,362	3,396	5,797	5,452	15,626	1,522	768	593
1944	415	28,953	3,927	2,950	2,112	11,740	7,274	1,555	3,623	5,820	5,023	17,351	1,986	1,169	506
1943	396	27,308	3,767	2,945	2,129	9,770	7,545	1,528	3,965	5,767	4,771	16,665	2,186	1,282	497
1942	371	25,623	3,545	2,975	2,072	8,546	7,567	1,422	3,895	5,833	4,141	13,665	1,760	952	477
1941	400	27,879	3,432	3,328	2,169	8,691	9,444	1,496	5,345	7,391	4,908	11,683	1,577	697	689
1940	368	25,565	3,200	2,822	1,624	7,861	9,383	1,152	5,209	7,265	4,523	8,488	939	245	643
1939	342	23,741	2,438	2,529	1,344	7,438	9,248	1,266	5,252	7,023	4,223	7,637	649	106	548
1938	349	24,220	2,134	2,613	1,260	7,927	9,334	1,400	5,348	7,357	4,383	7,210	474	84	527
1937	355	24,647	1,894	2,752	1,516	8,186	9,353	1,632	5,307	7,578	4,534	9,283	752	105	748
1936	355	24,295	2,000	2,646	1,223	8,610	8,848	1,614	4,977	7,703	3,667	7,201	775	92	729
1935 ³	742	156,153	12,138	15,571	3,864	72,123	47,351	6,241	27,803	46,059	20,335	28,790	3,093	217	2,697
1934 ³	761	153,168	9,922	16,939	3,882	69,461	47,743	7,149	27,033	46,701	20,695	25,542	2,080	183	2,140
1933 ³	594	142,796	7,759	15,390	4,356	51,692	57,820	5,773	27,671	41,414	21,037	26,571	706	150	1,693
1932 ³	618	149,241	8,448	16,648	3,993	54,185	58,614	6,538	28,371	43,440	21,684	27,037	332	132	2,270
1931 ³	632	154,807	8,059	21,049	5,100	51,343	62,378	7,236	29,218	43,858	25,946	36,247	1,694	187	3,654

See footnotes at end of table.

Series V 182–196. Selected Corporate Asset, Liability, Income, and Tax Items, and Dividends Paid, by Size of Total Assets: 1931 to 1970—Con.

[In millions of dollars, except number of returns]

Size of total assets and tax year	Number of returns	Total assets or liabilities	Cash	Notes and accounts receivable less allowance	Inventories	Investments	Capital assets less reserves	Accounts payable and short-term debt	Long-term debt	Capital stock	Surplus and retained earnings [1]	Total receipts	Total receipts less total deductions [1]	Income tax	Dividends paid in cash and assets other than own stock
	182	183	184	185	186	187	188	189	190	191	192	193	194	195	196
$100,000,000 or more:															
1970	2,635	1,752,228	111,821	381,451	95,149	676,562	397,113	160,433	240,016	118,225	381,093	787,192	44,098	20,533	25,234
1969	2,473	1,574,853	100,471	344,247	86,557	606,798	362,414	141,180	206,650	110,859	359,341	722,347	51,581	24,274	27,227
1968	2,321	1,415,840	88,511	302,322	76,644	563,300	325,832	109,406	178,862	103,093	324,909	641,545	54,517	24,502	23,721
1967	2,157	1,254,764	81,326	263,337	68,321	499,065	293,666	84,296	150,433	98,357	284,684	559,946	48,695	20,290	21,035
1966	2,019	1,120,139	70,711	238,337	60,026	446,939	264,421	73,032	133,541	91,271	254,700	515,304	49,246	20,895	19,948
1965	1,901	1,027,629	61,486	223,374	51,740	415,627	237,354	59,361	117,910	86,709	232,551	460,418	44,936	19,193	18,339
1964	1,758	927,303	59,687	189,052	45,689	381,593	216,185	49,513	104,920	83,632	210,041	407,665	38,538	16,766	16,972
1963	1,659	855,075	56,924	172,292	41,513	354,500	199,776	56,283	96,348	80,876	189,375	367,671	34,182	15,752	15,081
1962	1,543	788,388	(NA)	(NA)	38,527	(NA)	(NA)	(NA)	(NA)	(NA)	(NA)	335,359	30,231	13,806	13,936
1961	1,428	728,241	52,292	128,385	36,161	305,643	183,150	35,005	91,669	76,599	162,881	307,951	27,584	12,598	12,405
1960	1,333	671,778	49,889	118,715	34,187	278,246	171,536	30,627	84,832	72,287	148,518	297,782	26,286	12,461	11,649
1959	1,276	630,239	46,397	111,445	33,419	259,635	162,329	29,442	79,000	70,344	138,262	280,035	25,952	12,205	11,032
1958	1,203	588,633	46,598	98,866	29,973	244,515	152,961	25,601	74,224	67,268	127,652	254,257	21,481	9,953	10,171
1957	1,129	545,515	44,329	94,379	31,421	218,371	143,296	25,659	68,946	64,205	114,847	245,047	25,686	10,985	9,858
1956	1,080	514,338	44,374	107,572	29,938	190,821	129,015	24,823	60,820	61,739	104,838	224,658	25,316	10,898	9,274
1955	1,027	477,272	42,818	95,618	25,551	185,706	116,634	21,567	55,092	56,431	94,882	209,917	26,395	11,587	8,566
1954	932	432,171	38,641	77,202	22,435	177,072	107,541	17,334	50,689	52,965	83,157	177,314	19,840	8,502	7,355
1953	915	404,992	38,523	72,202	24,254	162,600	99,083	17,884	46,312	51,399	75,217	183,538	21,340	10,175	6,949
1952	854	378,622	38,062	67,708	23,261	152,314	90,066	17,632	42,183	48,925	69,478	164,378	19,040	8,938	6,490
1951	747	336,020	36,525	54,193	21,116	135,746	80,793	15,143	37,093	46,289	61,590	153,193	20,238	9,875	6,107
1950	688	304,127	33,999	46,701	15,954	130,085	71,224	11,908	32,941	42,678	55,080	126,812	18,751	7,370	5,916
1949	623	274,870	28,631	34,547	13,562	126,649	65,918	9,434	31,539	42,921	47,206	103,853	12,434	3,778	4,617
1948	601	260,770	30,306	35,569	14,590	114,736	59,843	10,726	29,029	41,379	42,811	107,250	13,214	4,077	4,159
1947	561	242,492	29,110	31,899	12,402	111,540	52,540	9,878	24,819	38,187	37,099	88,741	9,832	2,982	3,464
1946	531	222,988	25,806	25,575	10,136	109,938	46,716	8,051	22,029	35,816	32,199	64,349	6,632	1,920	2,947
1945	542	231,137	25,537	24,491	7,676	124,013	44,778	7,104	20,587	35,255	33,078	69,525	7,035	2,855	2,687
1944	517	219,462	22,922	21,966	8,244	114,571	47,135	7,665	21,759	35,654	31,419	76,920	9,858	4,852	2,687
1943	491	202,520	22,340	19,718	8,871	98,922	48,227	7,397	22,564	34,916	29,872	71,997	10,584	5,273	2,396
1942	455	183,889	20,997	18,191	7,986	84,851	48,042	6,654	23,105	35,433	26,074	57,268	8,482	3,621	2,431
1941	426	163,621	19,583	17,414	6,092	75,221	42,637	5,788	23,096	36,187	24,235	41,527	5,534	2,036	2,608
1940	403	153,712	21,165	14,199	4,519	69,823	41,431	5,091	22,404	35,917	22,139	32,026	3,587	764	2,417
1939	395	144,205	16,679	12,819	3,961	67,140	40,866	5,260	21,929	36,010	21,068	27,526	2,700	336	2,188
1938	394	138,119	13,016	12,343	3,764	64,956	40,792	4,906	22,673	36,490	20,637	24,815	1,755	236	1,911
1937	394	136,664	10,419	14,067	4,191	63,721	40,581	5,466	22,398	37,375	21,563	29,257	2,716	347	2,725
1936 [3]	396	134,389	11,489	13,918	3,463	63,457	38,126	5,331	21,198	36,315	16,423	25,723	2,716	274	2,533

NA   Not available.
[1] Figures in *italics* represent deficit or loss.
[2] For 1970, "Less than $50,000" asset-size classification included with "$50,000 to $99,999."
[3] For 1931–1935, data for returns with assets of $100,000,000 or more are included under the asset-size classification "$50,000,000 to $99,999,999."

Series V 197–270. Assets, Liabilities, and Selected Income Items for Selected Utility Industries: 1902 to 1970

[In millions of dollars]

Year	Total assets or liabilities [1]	Current assets	Investments	Electric plant and equipment in service — Gross	Reserve for depreciation	Net	Other assets	Current liabilities	Long-term debt	Other liabilities	Capital stock	Other paid-in capital	Net surplus	Total revenue	Net income	Dividends
	197	198	199	200	201	202	203	204	205	206	207	208	209	210	211	212
							CLASS A AND B ELECTRIC COMPANIES, PRIVATELY OWNED									
1970	87,417.3	5,321.1	1,742.2	82,653.7	20,253.2	62,400.5	17,953.5	7,308.6	41,937.5	3,626.9	20,781.7	4,400.0	9,362.7	23,901.4	3,407.5	2,521.2
1969	78,316.5	4,810.1	1,680.2	75,665.3	18,674.9	56,990.3	14,835.9	6,948.4	37,071.8	3,418.3	18,583.8	3,686.1	8,608.2	21,221.0	3,196.0	2,311.6
1968	71,099.5	4,439.0	1,464.4	69,863.6	17,245.7	52,617.9	12,578.2	5,646.2	33,519.4	3,186.2	17,745.6	3,259.9	7,742.2	19,529.3	2,995.5	2,198.5
1967	65,196.7	4,156.5	1,353.2	64,953.1	16,011.3	48,941.7	10,745.2	4,943.2	30,358.5	2,991.7	17,079.5	2,826.5	6,997.2	18,040.9	2,908.3	2,066.3
1966	60,359.4	4,019.5	1,294.9	60,256.6	14,791.9	45,464.7	9,580.3	4,495.1	27,728.5	2,810.6	16,211.9	2,706.6	6,406.7	17,059.9	2,749.1	1,938.3
1965	56,395.1	3,639.1	1,247.2	57,025.2	13,630.6	43,394.6	8,114.1	4,221.7	25,502.5	2,667.8	[2]15,668.5	2,622.3	5,712.4	15,917.3	2,580.7	1,864.4
1964	53,753.4	3,634.1	1,210.9	53,954.7	12,574.5	41,380.1	7,528.2	3,736.2	24,589.0	2,517.5	15,620.9	2,147.7	5,142.1	15,111.5	2,393.4	1,681.7
1963	51,388.9	3,410.9	1,148.4	51,321.0	11,510.7	39,810.3	7,019.1	3,618.6	23,631.8	2,434.4	15,074.2	1,989.7	4,640.1	14,265.0	2,178.4	1,576.5
1962	49,191.3	3,319.6	1,125.4	48,640.2	10,550.1	38,090.1	6,656.4	3,284.8	22,912.2	2,198.6	14,324.8	1,990.5	4,480.5	13,541.1	2,053.5	1,461.9
1961	47,010.7	3,151.9	1,083.2	45,820.3	9,674.4	36,145.9	6,629.7	3,286.1	22,028.4	1,979.4	13,801.1	1,903.3	4,012.4	12,674.6	1,874.9	1,376.1
1960	44,742.3	3,065.7	1,004.5	43,197.0	8,889.0	34,308.1	6,364.0	3,112.2	21,034.9	1,789.7	13,322.3	1,747.2	3,736.0	11,998.2	1,783.1	1,307.6
1959*	42,105.8	2,943.5	1,057.8	39,938.0	8,064.3	31,873.6	6,230.9	2,965.7	19,818.0	1,601.5	12,635.7	1,728.7	3,356.3	11,192.6	1,655.8	1,217.8
1958	39,276.7	2,772.5	1,008.1	36,632.2	7,358.7	29,273.5	6,222.6	2,781.2	18,558.3	1,339.0	12,073.6	1,483.1	3,041.5	10,254.6	1,518.8	1,133.9
1957	36,401.3	2,799.1	979.2	33,317.7	6,771.4	26,546.3	6,076.7	2,803.6	17,036.8	1,086.0	11,434.3	1,322.2	2,718.4	9,734.6	1,412.5	1,069.1
1956	33,241.8	2,617.6	937.2	30,817.4	6,222.0	24,595.4	5,091.6	2,627.4	15,210.8	862.0	10,934.3	1,193.4	2,414.0	9,114.4	1,332.2	1,021.8

See footnotes at end of table.

Series V 197–270. Assets, Liabilities, and Selected Income Items for Selected Utility Industries: 1902 to 1970—Con.

[In millions of dollars]

Year	Total assets or liabilities [1]	Assets						Liabilities						Total revenue	Net income	Dividends
		Current assets	Invest-ments	Electric plant and equipment in service			Other assets	Current liabil-ities	Long-term debt	Other liabil-ities	Capital stock	Other paid-in capital	Net surplus			
				Gross	Reserve for depre-ciation	Net										

CLASS A AND B ELECTRIC COMPANIES, PRIVATELY OWNED—Con.

	197	198	199	200	201	202	203	204	205	206	207	208	209	210	211	212
1955__	30,992.4	2,567.3	932.9	28,681.1	5,712.5	22,968.6	4,523.6	2,381.0	14,315.9	617.2	10,404.0	1,083.1	2,191.2	8,423.5	1,244.1	942.2
1954__	28,974.5	2,436.9	1,009.1	26,011.4	5,251.4	20,760.0	4,768.5	2,254.3	13,312.9	465.6	9,924.5	966.6	2,050.7	7,654.8	1,134.1	868.0
1953__	26,615.5	2,377.1	912.0	23,369.1	4,845.7	18,523.4	4,803.0	2,227.8	12,030.2	311.7	9 314.2	863.8	1,867.8	7,185.3	1,030.2	780.4
1952__	24,502.4	2,442.6	1,255.2	20,996.3	4,512.3	16,484.0	4,320.6	2,090.4	10,796.5	284.7	8,763.6	922.5	1,644.7	6,619.4	947.1	724.8
1951__	22,365.0	2,307.5	1,234.5	19,191.1	4,161.0	15,030.1	3,792.9	1,857.2	9,983.0	277.5	8,145.8	657.1	1,444.4	6,121.0	814.2	651.4
1950__	20,522.7	2,058.1	1,234.9	17,275.6	3,851.6	13,424.0	3,805.7	1,527.2	9,178.8	260.5	7,621.0	589.2	1,346.0	5,595.7	821.9	619.1
1949__	18,906.0	1,898.7	1,272.4	15,583.2	3,567.3	12,015.9	3,719.0	1,358.5	8,532.1	262.6	7,015.8	539.9	1,197.1	5,134.4	757.3	559.8
1948__	17,265.8	1,985.2	1,154.6	13,838.8	3,369.1	10,469.7	3,656.3	1,359.7	7,693.4	267.6	6,404.3	505.1	1,035.7	4,895.9	656.8	493.1
1947__	15,573.3	1,763.4	1,096.0	12,472.0	2,915.5	9,556.5	3,157.4	1,203.5	6,581.0	342.2	6,071.1	487.4	888.1	4,358.4	642.7	494.1
1946__	14,648.6	1,703.9	1,066.8	11,827.5	2,715.8	9,111.7	2,828.1	1,003.4	6,129.3	378.6	5,804.0	499.9	833.4	3,877.2	637.6	458.1
1945__	14,451.9	1,672.4	1,089.4	11,495.6	2,502.2	8,993.4	2,766.5	964.8	6,117.4	371.5	5,950.4	282.3	765.5	3,735.9	534.5	407.0
1944__	15,181.3	1,654.7	1,297.4	11,279.2	2,272.3	9,006.9	3,292.2	959.8	6,370.8	434.0	6,271.0	279.2	866.5	3,670.7	506.8	397.6
1943__	15,524.7	1,582.9	1,289.8	11,098.1	2,055.9	9,042.2	3,664.6	986.6	6,587.5	445.9	6,353.1	306.4	845.2	3,522.4	501.5	410.1
1942__	15,611.8	1,364.7	1,320.0	10,825.6	1,860.4	8,965.2	4,053.9	908.0	6,753.6	384.5	6,487.3	215.4	863.0	3,275.0	489.9	407.5
1941__	15,599.8	1,217.2	1,321.0	10,501.1	1,710.2	8,790.9	4,369.0	807.7	6,821.7	333.5	6,503.7	265.0	868.2	3,096.1	526.6	437.2
1940__	15,477.2	1,122.9	1,380.4	10,165.0	1,593.8	8,571.2	4,504.7	692.0	6,895.5	303.6	6,470.8	254.9	860.4	2,864.8	547.7	447.4
1939__	15,317.6	1,041.7	1,420.8	9,924.3	1,501.8	8,422.5	4,532.3	655.2	6,971.4	276.7	6,387.1	216.1	811.1	2,717.4	534.8	444.1
1938__	15,469.0	1,083.7	1,468.4	9,710.3	1,413.9	8,296.4	4,742.9	750.4	7,060.3	270.4	6,375.9	224.2	787.8	2,615.5	487.2	417.6
1937__	15,272.1	959.1	1,462.4	9,469.1	1,346.4	8,122.7	4,833.9	692.4	6,850.2	280.9	6,431.8	214.5	802.3	2,603.1	509.5	431.8

CENTRAL ELECTRIC LIGHT AND POWER STATIONS, COMMERCIAL

	213	214	215	216	217	218	219	220	221	222	223		224	225	226	227
1937__	15,553.6	972.5	1,308.1	14,048.7	1,346.4	12,702.3	570.6	707.5	6,837.6	467.1	6,540.5		1,000.9	2,603.3	514.2	434.0
1932__	15,871.6	943.0	957.0	14,370.4	1,141.1	13,229.3	742.2	641.3	6,678.8	627.2	6,935.8		988.6	2,266.1	538.6	493.7
1927__	12,239.6	982.2	622.4	10,586.8	700.2	9,886.6	748.3	671.6	5,309.0	450.7	5,095.1		712.3	1,841.2	505.8	338.2
1922__	5,333.3	424.3	421.2	4,290.3			197.5	390.9	2,125.2	446.9	2,110.4		259.9	986.7	258.5	129.2
1917__	3,555.1	178.9	238.9	2,964.2			173.1	348.6	1,262.7	234.6	1,543.5		165.8	486.6	91.5	64.6
1912__	2,434.1	140.1	164.4	2,098.6			30.9	200.9	876.0	103.4	1,138.2		115.7	279.1	61.6	34.6
1907__				1,054.0										161.6	37.8	19.3
1902__				482.7										78.7	15.9	6.2

STREET AND ELECTRIC RAILWAYS

	228	229	230	231	232	233	234	235	236	237	238		239	240	241	242
1937__	6,454.6	289.1	397.4	5,867.2	666.5	5,200.7	567.4	556.2	3,022.3	854.3	2,073.1		−51.2	513.1	46.1	59.8
1932__	3,967.6	137.0	693.6	3,314.0	308.4	3,005.6	131.4	363.6	1,914.1	446.3	1,294.8		−51.3	527.3	−20.2	19.0
1927__	4,160.0	170.4	472.0	3,487.7	218.7	3,268.9	248.7	359.5	2,052.8	316.5	1,447.8		−16.6	813.3	40.7	32.8
1922 [3]_	4,113.8	164.1	439.4	3,417.1	130.7	3,286.4	224.0	409.3	2,041.2	227.6	1,506.2		−70.4	784.9	35.7	22.7
1922 [4]_	6,110.8	230.3	633.8	5,147.9	181.1	4,966.8	279.9	570.9	2,969.3	289.7	2,307.6		−26.7	1,049.8	74.2	53.7
1917__	6,042.1	143.4	556.2	5,216.0	73.9	5,142.1	200.3	357.5	2,997.7	152.1	2,456.6		78.1	730.6	81.8	73.3
1912__	5,317.4	178.9	399.9	4,596.6			142.1	441.1	2,273.1	159.5	2,348.5		95.3	586.4	81.4	71.0
1907__	4,236.3	173.8	347.1	3,637.7			77.7	399.4	1,658.6	85.0	2,022.9		70.4	430.2	68.8	54.5
1902__	2,533.8	61.1	152.5	2,167.6			152.6	118.7	974.1	133.4	1,266.9		40.7	250.5	47.4	33.0

TELEPHONES

	243	244	245	246	247	248	249	250	251	252	253		254	255	256	257
1937__				4,941.3										1,167.4		
1932__				4,734.7										1,046.4		
1927__				3,475.2										996.9		
1922__	2,135.8	187.6	193.4	2,129.8	459.6	1,670.2	84.6	75.9	737.2	91.3	1,005.1		226.3	637.5	96.7	73.9
1917__	1,424.5	108.5	75.2	1,435.9	234.4	1,201.5	39.3	46.4	497.3	60.9	670.9		149.0	363.8	59.4	45.3
1912__	1,295.6	96.6	104.5	1,081.4			13.1	88.0	405.8	151.0	590.1		60.8	255.1	51.3	34.1
1907__	940.3	83.0	60.7	794.1			2.6	85.0	302.5	45.2	459.4		48.2	176.7	41.2	23.4
1902__	466.4	52.6	24.2	389.3			.3	44.5	[5] 102.5	38.3	[5] 269.7		21.3	86.8	21.7	15.0

TELEGRAPHS

	258	259	260	261			262	263	264	265	266		267	268	269	270
1937__				506.8										135.8		3.1
1932__				506.4										114.7		(NA)
1927__				426.7										177.6		14.2
1922__	459.5	50.0	78.9	326.7			3.9	34.3	71.4	106.0	177.2		70.5	146.8	23.9	10.7
1917__	363.1	59.4	56.0	243.4			4.3	31.9	61.8	67.3	167.3		34.8	107.0	17.8	9.8
1912__	298.3	42.3	33.9	222.0				35.2	62.7	20.8	163.6		15.8	60.4	6.4	6.2
1907__	261.8	15.3	36.5	210.0				12.9	65.2	8.3	155.1		20.3	45.3	9.7	7.5
1902__	195.5	7.3	30.7	156.9			.6	6.6	45.9	7.9	117.1		18.1	35.3	10.0	6.3

* Denotes first year for which figures include Alaska and Hawaii.
NA Not available.
[1] Includes net value of plant and equipment when a reserve for depreciation is shown; otherwise, gross value.

[2] Reflects assignment of par value to stock previously without par value and transfer to premium on capital stock of difference between par value and stated value.
[3] Comparable with later years. [4] Comparable with earlier years.
[5] Intercompany holdings of independent companies not deducted.

Series V 271–284. Net Value of Plant and Equipment in Regulated Industries: 1870 to 1951

[In millions of dollars. As of January 1]

Year	All regulated industries		Steam railroads		Electric light and power		Telephones		Street and electric railways		Local bus lines		All other	
	Current dollars	1929 dollars	Current dollars	1929 dollars	Current dollars	1929 dollars	Current dollars	1929 dollars	Current dollars	1929 dollars	Current dollars	1929 dollars	Current dollars	1929 dollars
	271	272	273	274	275	276	277	278	279	280	281	282	283	284
1951	87,254	48,394	39,213	22,601	19,145	9,335	8,377	5,056	1,299	749	628	351	18,592	10,303
1950	81,881	46,950	38,243	22,509	17,265	8,822	7,520	4,784	1,314	773	680	380	16,860	9,682
1949	77,416	45,299	37,695	22,265	15,069	8,145	6,650	4,341	1,375	812	696	405	15,932	9,331
1948	68,020	43,187	34,099	22,028	12,630	7,523	5,479	3,591	1,311	847	621	395	13,880	8,803
1947	58,495	41,752	30,769	22,009	10,326	7,136	3,978	3,007	1,356	970	449	333	11,617	8,295
1946	51,423	41,171	27,868	22,135	8,867	7,037	3,064	2,683	1,278	1,015	356	309	9,991	7,992
1945	49,842	41,260	26,905	22,217	8,726	7,089	3,001	2,668	1,301	1,074	349	308	9,559	7,904
1944	50,008	41,569	26,829	22,265	8,966	7,254	3,021	2,731	1,376	1,142	355	315	9,461	7,862
1943	48,430	42,150	25,369	22,391	9,052	7,383	3,057	2,810	1,376	1,215	380	340	9,195	8,011
1942	43,794	42,029	22,180	22,314	8,724	7,343	2,877	2,693	1,289	1,297	330	321	8,394	8,061
1941	40,475	41,555	20,533	22,270	8,171	7,174	2,478	2,487	1,251	1,357	264	274	7,777	7,993
1940	39,686	41,600	20,018	22,292	7,946	7,094	2,446	2,387	1,548	1,724	228	243	7,500	7,860
1939	39,855	41,909	20,220	22,517	7,899	7,110	2,398	2,355	1,590	1,771	212	223	7,535	7,933
1938	40,864	42,259	20,960	22,733	7,895	7,068	2,309	2,334	1,695	1,838	198	220	7,807	8,066
1937	38,021	42,012	19,491	22,638	7,166	6,985	2,308	2,284	1,640	1,904	169	201	7,247	8,000
1936	37,809	42,245	19,467	22,769	6,996	7,024	2,371	2,324	1,683	1,974	136	162	7,151	7,992
1935	37,898	42,920	19,453	23,076	7,010	7,161	2,446	2,418	1,740	2,064	115	133	7,133	8,068
1934	36,246	43,722	18,716	23,366	6,582	7,345	2,339	2,533	1,745	2,179	101	123	6,763	8,176
1933	37,560	44,714	19,434	23,729	6,629	7,533	2,466	2,656	1,900	2,320	103	120	7,029	8,357
1932	41,424	45,371	21,579	24,030	7,090	7,599	2,699	2,690	2,204	2,454	107	120	7,745	8,478
1931	43,584	45,212	23,273	24,142	7,090	7,424	2,568	2,576	2,466	2,558	109	115	8,078	8,397
1930	43,857	43,857	23,774	23,774	6,934	6,934	2,242	2,242	2,648	2,648	110	110	8,149	8,149
1929	41,728	42,407	23,120	23,401	6,215	6,535	1,968	1,899	2,711	2,744	98	100	7,616	7,728
1928	41,667	41,377	23,571	23,154	5,746	6,139	1,871	1,718	2,897	2,846	83	85	7,500	7,435
1927	40,516	40,234	23,132	22,858	5,427	5,683	1,773	1,596	2,990	2,955	75	74	7,119	7,069
1926	39,449	39,020	22,752	22,482	5,100	5,241	1,649	1,457	3,118	3,081	61	58	6,769	6,701
1925	39,503	37,947	23,270	22,204	4,606	4,729	1,526	1,332	3,355	3,201	47	44	6,699	6,437
1924	38,568	36,627	23,223	21,785	3,963	4,145	1,355	1,201	3,534	3,316	33	31	6,460	6,149
1923	33,937	35,388	20,367	21,260	3,317	3,633	1,246	1,112	3,254	3,397	14	12	5,739	5,974
1922	37,302	35,025	22,629	21,228	3,416	3,416	1,325	1,066	3,710	3,480	4	3	6,218	5,832
1921	46,384	35,060	28,841	21,191	3,591	3,343	1,291	1,064	4,920	3,615	4	3	7,737	5,845
1920	39,785	35,053	24,679	21,220	3,205	3,264	1,033	1,076	4,354	3,743	4	3	6,510	5,747
1919	36,123	35,276	22,309	21,410	3,085	3,310	992	1,112	3,980	3,819	3	2	5,755	5,623
1918	29,951	35,361	18,343	21,454	2,682	3,382	940	1,140	3,274	3,829	1	1	4,711	5,555
1917	23,992	34,822	14,776	21,322	2,110	3,216	762	1,109	2,656	3,833	1	1	3,687	5,341
1916	20,706	34,684	12,832	21,315	1,687	3,177	730	1,101	2,326	3,864	1	1	3,130	5,226
1915	20,318	34,614	12,687	21,358	1,595	3,133	738	1,143	2,286	3,849	1	1	3,011	5,131
1914	20,517	34,025	12,877	21,075	1,560	3,029	747	1,150	2,357	3,839	1	1	2,975	4,932
1913	19,464	32,989	12,184	20,443	1,535	2,925	709	1,145	2,288	3,825	(Z)	(Z)	2,748	4,652
1912	18,411	31,743	11,630	19,847	1,315	2,605	689	1,096	2,254	3,847	(Z)	(Z)	2,523	4,348
1911	17,638	30,463	11,265	19,190	1,109	2,311	650	1,079	2,255	3,816	(Z)	(Z)	2,359	4,068
1910	16,326	29,049	10,459	18,413	964	2,042	621	1,055	2,152	3,750	(Z)	(Z)	2,130	3,789
1909	15,219	27,925	9,790	17,735	792	1,795	590	1,067	2,086	3,745	--------	--------	1,961	3,583
1908	14,789	26,792	9,527	17,105	728	1,568	611	1,077	2,046	3,647	--------	--------	1,877	3,396
1907	13,584	25,533	8,848	16,477	629	1,413	545	1,000	1,855	3,422	--------	--------	1,707	3,221
1906	12,072	24,387	7,940	15,976	543	1,268	448	856	1,613	3,200	--------	--------	1,528	3,087
1905	11,197	23,524	7,483	15,688	474	1,130	385	752	1,444	2,970	--------	--------	1,411	2,984
1904	10,925	22,855	7,455	15,531	407	1,000	337	676	1,338	2,746	--------	--------	1,388	2,902
1903	10,356	22,271	7,179	15,439	361	875	292	585	1,205	2,542	--------	--------	1,319	2,830
1902	9,788	21,750	6,898	15,362	306	746	254	516	1,085	2,365	--------	--------	1,245	2,761
1901	9,681	21,276	6,944	15,295	267	638	226	456	1,012	2,190	--------	--------	1,232	2,697
1900	9,021	20,785	6,560	15,185	234	569	186	384	892	2,019	--------	--------	1,149	2,628
1899	8,091	20,328	6,000	15,113	185	490	144	321	749	1,839	--------	--------	1,013	2,566
1898	7,757	20,095	5,867	15,239	146	408	119	276	647	1,642	--------	--------	979	2,530
1897	7,869	19,973	6,100	15,444	108	347	90	235	580	1,440	--------	--------	991	2,508
1896	7,754	19,881	6,104	15,652	102	311	72	182	497	1,248	--------	--------	979	2,488
1895	7,736	19,735	6,194	15,801	96	264	59	137	430	1,072	--------	--------	957	2,461
1894	7,845	19,274	6,363	15,635	82	230	42	98	381	915	--------	--------	977	2,396
1893	7,462	18,200	6,098	14,873	69	193	40	92	328	783	--------	--------	927	2,259
1892	7,212	17,212	5,936	14,168	56	152	37	86	287	670	--------	--------	896	2,136
1891	7,184	16,747	5,955	13,882	48	123	38	84	252	576	--------	--------	891	2,083
1890	6,982	16,313	5,827	13,614	34	87	34	75	220	502	--------	--------	867	2,035
1889	6,872	15,907	5,766	13,348	23	60	29	64	195	441	--------	--------	859	1,995
1888	6,683	15,470	5,626	13,022	15	39	28	61	173	392	--------	--------	841	1,956
1887	6,509	14,964	5,494	12,631	9	23	27	60	150	337	--------	--------	829	1,913
1886	6,342	14,681	5,354	12,394	5	13	30	65	139	313	--------	--------	815	1,896
1885	6,378	14,529	5,390	12,278	3	8	26	56	133	294	--------	--------	827	1,893
1884	6,502	14,259	5,482	12,048	2	5	23	47	134	284	--------	--------	861	1,876
1883	6,412	13,789	5,401	11,641	1	2	20	38	131	272	--------	--------	859	1,836
1882	5,850	13,028	4,922	10,986	(Z)	1	14	29	119	254	--------	--------	795	1,759
1881	5,357	12,121	4,494	10,191	(Z)	(Z)	9	18	116	248	--------	--------	738	1,664
1880	4,594	11,573	3,852	9,728	--------	--------	4	9	98	235	--------	--------	640	1,602
1879	4,576	11,384	3,853	9,584	--------	--------			93	219	--------	--------	630	1,580
1878	4,828	11,229	4,061	9,467	--------	--------			93	203	--------	--------	674	1,559
1877	5,199	11,086	4,380	9,360	--------	--------			94	188	--------	--------	725	1,538
1876	5,486	10,994	4,630	9,298	--------	--------			93	175	--------	--------	763	1,521
1875	5,729	10,912	4,844	9,244	--------	--------			91	162	--------	--------	794	1,506
1874	5,993	10,740	5,076	9,114	--------	--------			90	150	--------	--------	827	1,476
1873	5,656	10,340	4,799	8,789	--------	--------			81	138	--------	--------	776	1,413
1872	4,899	9,662	4,172	8,229	--------	--------			68	126	--------	--------	659	1,307
1871	4,484	8,810	3,829	7,523	--------	--------			61	112	--------	--------	594	1,175
1870	4,437	8,053	3,787	6,886	--------	--------			65	108	--------	--------	585	1,059

Z Less than $500,000.

Series V 285–305.   Assets, Liabilities, and Selected Income Items for Two Samples of Large Manufacturing Corporations: 1914 to 1943

[In millions of dollars]

Year	Total assets or liabilities	Current assets					Investments and advances	Fixed assets (net)	Other assets
		Total [1]	Cash	Marketable securities	Receivables	Inventory			
	285	286	287	288	289	290	291	292	293
1943	24,632.3	13,259.6	2,610.4	2,666.1	3,241.6	4,741.5	1,775.5	8,727.0	870.2
1942	23,074.1	11,664.6	2,120.6	1,751.2	3,168.2	4,624.6	1,833.5	8,853.4	722.6
1941	21,071.8	9,643.3	2,059.2	1,280.6	2,097.8	4,205.7	1,902.8	8,911.1	614.6
1940	19,048.2	7,858.0	2,184.0	602.5	1,511.0	3,560.5	1,985.9	8,715.6	488.7
1939	18,212.5	7,033.9	1,772.1	576.0	1,297.9	3,387.9	1,850.8	8,807.4	520.4
1938	17,769.2	6,641.1	1,593.9	451.9	1,223.8	3,371.5	1,650.2	8,937.8	540.1
1937	18,034.0	6,663.3	1,105.4	493.9	1,282.2	3,781.8	1,637.9	9,156.9	575.9
1936	16,985.4	6,280.8	1,270.1	522.6	1,266.7	3,221.4	1,594.0	8,592.7	517.9
1935	16,338.9	5,933.0	1,299.1	613.8	1,093.2	2,926.9	1,547.6	8,356.4	501.9
1934	16,257.0	5,553.1	1,109.1	705.8	947.8	2,790.4	1,604.7	8,600.2	499.0
1933	16,588.0	5,448.2	1,041.3	899.2	962.5	2,545.2	1,673.7	8,757.5	708.6
1932	16,799.4	5,360.4	1,219.5	782.2	987.3	2,371.4	1,466.2	9,391.6	581.2
1931	18,035.6	6,031.3	1,080.4	1,030.3	1,180.8	2,739.8	1,362.1	10,021.3	620.9
1930	18,689.2	6,855.1	1,219.1	910.0	1,453.9	3,272.1	1,434.7	9,735.3	664.1
1929	18,684.2	7,394.1	1,124.3	1,059.1	1,675.7	3,535.0	1,643.8	8,972.7	673.6
1928	17,292.3	6,999.5	1,187.2	1,079.6	1,529.9	3,202.8	1,221.7	8,459.8	611.3
1927	16,360.7	6,467.1	1,026.7	928.5	1,403.3	3,108.6	1,089.7	8,255.1	548.8
1926	16,048.3	6,651.5	937.1	877.9	1,658.2	3,178.3	1,035.9	7,847.6	513.3
1925	15,029.9	6,218.9	911.9	694.4	1,595.0	3,017.6	1,029.5	7,302.9	478.6
1924	14,030.1	5,728.9	818.6	665.0	1,472.8	2,772.5	1,025.7	6,752.3	523.8
1923	13,761.3	5,555.9	735.9	620.0	1,437.3	2,762.7	1,104.7	6,571.7	529.0
1922 [2]	12,701.1	5,102.3	650.7	583.9	1,379.6	2,488.1	1,032.6	6,005.8	560.4
1922 [3]	9,911.5	3,753.2	547.7	430.8	943.7	1,826.7	785.3	4,882.3	490.7
1921	9,915.1	3,786.5	526.6	432.2	985.4	1,837.1	775.4	4,874.8	478.4
1920	10,463.5	4,646.3	520.0	369.6	1,209.8	2,464.5	651.2	4,652.4	513.6
1919	9,693.5	4,500.6	573.8	534.7	1,065.5	2,242.2	563.2	4,136.1	493.6
1918	9,340.7	4,512.5	581.6	621.0	1,071.2	2,158.0	455.8	3,866.3	506.1
1917	8,197.0	3,662.7	552.9	461.2	863.0	1,717.6	407.8	3,667.6	458.9
1916	6,754.0	2,579.3	448.3	190.6	674.8	1,216.4	310.4	3,434.7	429.6
1915	5,919.1	1,920.5	316.4	99.8	581.8	886.4	306.1	3,277.1	415.4
1914	5,254.1	1,532.4	236.8	42.0	465.6	780.5	253.6	3,116.6	351.5

Year	Current liabilities				Long-term debt	Other liabilities	Capital				Net income	Dividends
	Total [1]	Notes payable	Accounts payable	Other			Preferred stock	Common stock	Capital reserves	Surplus		
	294	295	296	297	298	299	300	301	302	303	304	305
1943	5,870.8	202.7	1,466.3	4,201.8	1,984.3	495.7	1,831.1	6,843.0	1,408.8	6,198.6	1,247.7	770.7
1942	4,928.9	321.7	1,159.6	3,447.6	1,993.5	461.4	1,898.2	6,830.2	1,208.8	5,753.1	1,154.6	750.2
1941	3,547.7	263.9	925.1	2,358.7	2,014.3	444.5	1,907.4	6,821.4	960.5	5,376.0	1,501.6	949.8
1940	2,081.6	120.4	729.0	1,232.2	2,013.5	421.1	1,946.6	6,805.5	813.3	4,966.6	1,317.6	868.8
1939	1,440.4	88.2	626.2	726.0	2,089.9	423.2	1,963.1	6,856.5	639.2	4,800.2	1,048.4	750.7
1938	1,279.9	145.4	532.2	602.3	2,048.4	454.1	1,956.5	6,840.8	596.3	4,593.2	651.6	562.2
1937	1,597.1	289.2	557.0	750.9	1,717.0	469.5	1,956.0	7,110.4	634.0	4,550.0	1,427.4	1,019.2
1936	1,480.0	197.5	613.0	669.5	1,551.4	374.6	1,871.2	7,015.2	567.3	4,125.7	1,269.3	922.5
1935	1,201.0	193.6	504.0	503.4	1,592.0	440.8	1,882.4	6,805.0	519.9	3,897.8	791.7	514.6
1934	957.1	129.5	448.1	379.5	1,662.3	476.0	1,938.4	6,782.2	492.2	3,948.8	467.2	440.1
1933	787.2	65.0	465.7	256.5	1,768.9	413.0	1,945.2	7,243.3	461.2	3,969.2	314.3	384.0
1932	649.1	34.8	385.2	229.1	1,933.4	406.2	1,955.0	7,307.3	459.3	4,089.1	.5	497.1
1931	757.3	44.7	425.4	287.2	1,972.1	459.6	1,979.6	7,684.6	550.2	4,632.2	289.7	809.8
1930	1,059.6	72.4	588.9	398.3	2,001.2	299.4	1,995.1	7,521.9	544.9	5,267.1	964.1	971.7
1929	1,364.5	161.8	708.2	494.5	1,850.7	329.4	1,964.0	7,421.7	544.8	5,209.1	1,721.1	1,011.6
1928	1,344.7	171.7	685.5	487.5	2,162.2	279.9	1,918.9	6,582.8	456.4	4,547.4	1,485.3	905.3
1927	1,178.1	152.5	575.8	449.8	2,114.3	242.1	1,907.0	6,283.2	460.0	4,176.0	1,098.7	839.5
1926	1,385.0	166.6	760.2	458.2	1,887.0	67.4	2,041.1	5,974.0	429.1	4,264.7	1,311.0	764.8
1925	1,344.2	162.4	790.0	391.8	1,756.8	66.4	1,983.5	5,551.1	447.5	3,880.4	1,214.7	613.9
1924	1,225.9	232.7	689.5	303.7	1,745.2	55.4	1,935.2	5,384.8	423.8	3,260.4	889.7	527.2
1923	1,297.5	319.2	685.1	293.2	1,780.4	59.5	1,913.8	5,251.0	405.7	3,053.4	868.1	499.1
1922 [2]	1,111.0	273.0	604.1	233.9	1,648.6	59.7	1,877.2	4,864.2	435.4	2,705.0	645.2	410.5
1922 [3]	799.1	220.0	289.9	204.5	1,460.3	40.4	1,547.3	3,592.9	505.4	1,966.1	511.1	535.9
1921	948.2	436.9	230.9	198.8	1,470.6	60.0	1,450.1	3,028.0	552.5	2,405.7	139.2	297.2
1920	1,556.1	670.8	370.1	285.1	1,286.2	47.2	1,453.5	2,959.6	474.2	2,686.7	587.8	311.3
1919	1,459.9	511.3	385.0	323.7	1,204.0	88.4	1,404.1	2,610.7	440.7	2,485.7	610.7	297.1
1918	1,737.1	447.2	435.4	700.0	1,221.0	79.8	1,298.4	2,472.9	370.6	2,160.9	627.4	331.9
1917	1,331.3	345.4	332.8	471.1	1,114.2	82.4	1,236.4	2,337.9	237.7	1,857.1	875.1	357.4
1916	658.9	204.4	227.0	122.7	1,067.3	68.3	1,173.3	2,108.0	150.0	1,528.2	914.0	305.6
1915	527.8	177.4	220.0	67.5	1,030.0	122.5	1,149.6	1,955.9	126.8	1,006.5	381.5	172.1
1914	385.0	181.1	111.3	53.4	1,027.9	22.4	1,064.7	1,865.6	77.0	811.5	190.5	154.1

[1] For 1914–1922, exceeds sum of components by amount of unsegregable items.   [3] Comparable with earlier years.
[2] Comparable with later years.

Series V 306–332.   Business Expenditures for New Plant and Equipment: 1947 to 1970

[In billions of dollars]

Year	Total all indus-tries	Manufacturing	Durable goods				Transportation equipment			Stone, glass, and clay	Other durables [2]	Nondurable goods		
		Total	Total	Primary metal	Electrical machinery and equip-ment	Ma-chinery, except electrical	Total	Motor vehicles	Aircraft and other [1]			Total	Food and beverages	Textile
	306	307	308	309	310	311	312	313	314	315	316	317	318	319
1970	79.71	31.95	15.80	3.24	2.27	3.47	2.43	1.59	0.84	0.99	3.41	16.15	2.84	0.56
1969	75.56	31.68	15.96	3.23	2.03	3.44	2.76	1.65	1.11	1.07	3.44	15.72	2.59	.63
1968	67.76	28.37	14.12	3.36	1.78	2.84	2.48	1.36	1.11	.86	2.82	14.25	2.21	.53
1967	65.47	28.51	14.06	3.24	1.70	2.94	2.72	1.54	1.17	.96	2.50	14.45	2.08	.58
1966	63.51	28.20	14.06	2.97	1.62	2.87	2.95	1.80	1.16	1.16	2.48	14.14	2.10	.82
1965	54.42	23.44	11.50	2.54	1.12	2.31	2.54	1.89	.64	.92	2.07	11.94	1.83	.66
1964	46.97	19.34	9.28	2.16	.86	1.79	1.98	1.39	.60	.74	1.74	10.07	1.72	.52
1963	40.77	16.22	7.53	1.51	.79	1.39	1.58	1.00	.59	.68	1.58	8.70	1.53	.43
1962	38.39	15.06	6.79	1.27	.80	1.31	1.33	.78	.55	.70	1.38	8.26	1.51	.38
1961	35.91	14.33	6.31	1.30	.88	1.20	1.10	.69	.41	.70	1.12	8.02	1.52	.33
1960	36.75	15.09	7.23	1.82	.90	1.25	1.25	.79	.46	.75	1.26	7.85	1.34	.37
1959	33.55	12.77	5.81	1.26	.66	1.02	.96	.56	.39	.69	1.23	6.95	1.22	.30
1958	31.89	12.38	5.61	1.56	.60	.92	.85	.48	.37	.55	1.12	6.77	1.10	.22
1957	37.94	16.51	7.84	2.45	.77	1.25	1.46	.90	.55	.76	1.15	8.68	1.16	.32
1956	35.73	15.40	7.45	1.61	.77	1.05	1.89	1.44	.45	.89	1.25	7.95	1.05	.38
1955	29.53	11.89	5.41	1.02	.54	.80	1.26	.97	.28	.64	1.16	6.48	.90	.31
1954	27.19	11.24	4.91	.96	.54	.68	1.32	1.12	.19	.44	.98	6.33	.93	.30
1953	28.20	11.86	5.31	1.55	.57	.78	1.06	.87	.19	.41	.93	6.56	.95	.34
1952	26.43	11.45	5.21	1.94	.45	.69	.98	.77	.22	.38	.76	6.24	.86	.40
1951	25.46	10.71	4.82	1.44	.42	.68	1.00	.77	.22	.45	.83	5.89	.94	.48
1950	20.21	7.39	2.94	.72	.25	.41	.57	.49	.09	.30	.70	4.45	.78	.43
1949	18.98	7.12	2.45	.74	.21	.38	.45	.36	.09	.16	.51	4.68	.92	.46
1948	21.30	9.01	3.30	.94	.29	.53	.58	.47	.10	.26	.70	5.71	1.12	.58
1947	19.33	8.44	3.25	.81	.30	.52	.60	.50	.10	.33	.69	5.19	.95	.51

Year	Manufacturing—Con. Nondurable goods—Con.					Mining	Transportation		Public utilities			Commu-nication	Commer-cial and other [4]
	Paper	Chemical	Petroleum	Rubber	Other non-durables [3]		Railroad	Air and other	Total	Electric	Gas and other		
	320	321	322	323	324	325	326	327	328	329	330	331	332
1970	1.65	3.44	5.62	0.94	1.11	1.89	1.78	4.26	13.14	10.65	2.49	10.10	16.59
1969	1.58	3.10	5.63	1.09	1.10	1.86	1.86	4.19	11.61	8.94	2.67	8.30	16.05
1968	1.32	2.83	5.25	.98	1.13	1.63	1.45	4.15	10.20	7.66	2.54	6.83	15.14
1967	1.56	3.06	5.08	.67	1.31	1.65	1.86	3.77	8.74	6.75	2.00	6.34	14.59
1966	1.43	3.26	4.70	.64	1.18	1.62	2.37	3.38	7.43	5.38	2.05	6.02	14.48
1965	1.22	2.73	4.03	.56	.92	1.46	1.99	2.90	6.13	4.43	1.70	5.30	13.19
1964	.97	2.08	3.59	.44	.75	1.34	1.66	2.52	5.49	3.97	1.51	4.61	12.02
1963	.72	1.73	3.15	.37	.78	1.27	1.26	1.98	4.98	3.67	1.31	4.06	10.99
1962	.66	1.56	3.12	.33	.69	1.40	1.02	2.17	4.90	3.53	1.38	3.85	9.99
1961	.64	1.58	3.00	.31	.63	1.29	.82	1.96	5.00	3.55	1.45	3.39	9.13
1960	.77	1.55	2.89	.31	.62	1.30	1.16	1.96	5.24	3.62	1.62	3.24	8.75
1959	.62	1.17	2.76	.26	.62	1.36	1.02	2.11	5.14	3.60	1.54	2.72	8.44
1958	.57	1.33	2.72	.22	.62	1.43	.86	1.43	5.52	3.99	1.53	2.79	7.48
1957	.80	1.73	3.84	.26	.56	1.69	1.58	1.71	5.67	3.98	1.68	3.19	7.60
1956	.79	1.46	3.47	.27	.52	1.64	1.37	1.66	4.52	3.13	1.39	2.82	8.32
1955	.51	1.02	3.08	.20	.46	1.31	1.02	1.56	4.03	2.87	1.15	2.11	7.63
1954	.45	1.13	2.93	.18	.41	1.28	.93	1.46	3.99	3.04	.95	1.82	6.45
1953	.41	1.43	2.89	.20	.33	1.25	1.42	1.53	4.34	3.18	1.17	1.78	6.02
1952	.36	1.39	2.72	.19	.31	1.21	1.50	1.47	3.74	2.72	1.02	1.61	5.45
1951	.42	1.25	2.22	.19	.38	1.11	1.58	1.47	3.56	2.25	1.31	1.37	5.67
1950	.33	.77	1.63	.14	.37	.84	1.18	1.19	3.24	2.07	1.18	1.14	5.22
1949	.30	.67	1.83	.11	.39	.88	1.42	.88	3.10	2.17	.93	1.34	4.24
1948	.38	.94	2.16	.13	.39	.93	1.37	1.27	2.54	1.90	.64	1.74	4.42
1947	.37	1.06	1.74	.17	.40	.69	.91	1.30	1.54	1.03	.51	1.40	5.05

[1] Includes guided missiles and space vehicles.
[2] Includes fabricated metal, lumber, furniture, instrument, ordnance, and miscellaneous except guided missiles and space vehicles.
[3] Includes apparel, tobacco, leather, printing, and publishing.
[4] Includes trade, service, construction, finance, and insurance.

Productivity and Technological Development
Productivity Indexes (Series W 1-81)

W 1-81. General note.

Work in the field of productivity has been carried on by many individuals and organizations, especially the U.S. Bureau of Labor Statistics (BLS) and the National Bureau of Economic Research (NBER). Extensive work is being done by BLS, which measures productivity for the economy and for selected major sectors and industries.

Productivity can be defined generally as the ratio relating output (goods and services) to one or more of the inputs (labor, land, capital, energy, etc.) associated with that output. A variety of productivity measures can be developed, the particular form depending on the purpose to be served. Output per labor input is useful in understanding changes in employment or labor cost. A more comprehensive measure would be output per unit of labor and capital combined which is useful in studying how the economy has used these resources. The latter measures, which have been developed by John W. Kendrick for NBER, are covered in series W 5-8. Their construction is described in the NBER volume, *Productivity Trends in the United States*, 1961, General Series 71, and in *Postwar Productivity Trends in the United States*, 1973, General Series 98.

Historically, the measure of productivity which is most commonly used has been output per unit of labor input—frequently called "labor productivity." Such a measure reflects not only labor's effort but also other factors, including state of technology, capital per worker, availability of materials, the efficiency of management, rate of operations, and changes in the composition of the work force. Measures of this type have been developed by the BLS.

The output part of a labor productivity ratio may also be defined in several ways. The simplest one, conceptually, is what is called physical output, where the components are physical units such as pounds, bushels, number, etc. To arrive at total measures for an industry or an industry group, the units are weighted by man-hours or the closest equivalent (such as labor cost or value added). This type of measure is a weighted arithmetic average of the productivity change of its components. The BLS industry estimates are of this type. For a more detailed description of the concepts and procedures used, see chapter 26, *BLS Handbook of Methods for Surveys and Studies*, Bulletin 1711, 1971.

Estimates for broad aggregates, such as manufacturing or the total private economy, are constructed in terms of another output concept called value added or net output where purchased "intermediate" products consumed in the production process are excluded. This type of measure in relation to man-hours reflects not only the average of the individual industry productivity changes, but also shifts in the relative importance of low- or high-productivity industries.

Man-hours in labor productivity data can refer to either hours worked or hours paid for. The latter include not only hours worked but also paid leave time such as vacations, sick leave, and holidays.

The specific year chosen for the weight base may affect the trend of the productivity series. For example, output valued in 1954 prices would undoubtedly show a different trend from net output valued in 1958 prices. In general, a current year-weighted productivity index gives a lower trend than a base year-weighted index, since items which increase most in volume of output tend to be those with price declines or lower price increases.

Productivity series suffer from statistical limitations which are common to most production estimates. Quality change cannot be adequately accounted for in measuring changes in output; price indexes often do not cover a sufficiently broad industrial area; and man-hour weights for constructing physical output series are frequently not available. Productivity statistics also have additional limitations arising out of the noncomparability of output and man-hour series.

W 1-11. Indexes of national productivity, 1889-1970.

Source: **Series W 1-8**, John W. Kendrick, 1889-1966, *Productivity Trends in the United States*, National Bureau of Economic Research, Princeton University Press, 1961, (copyright) and *Postwar Productivity Trends in the United States*, National Bureau of Economic Research, 1973 (copyright); 1967-1970, computations supplied by John W. Kendrick. **Series W 9-11**, U.S. Bureau of Labor Statistics, *Productivity, Wages, Prices, and Employment*, press release issued quarterly, tables 1 and 2.

These indexes are measures of aggregate productivity for the total private economy and the major segments thereof. The NBER series (W 1-8) show the change in real gross product per unit of factor input after adjustments to exclude general government and real net factor income from abroad. The BLS series (W 9-11) exclude only general government and retain real net factor income from abroad. Since the latter amount as a percent of total product is extremely small, the difference between the two series in this regard is relatively small. For both series, the numerator is derived from the Department of Commerce gross national product series (with some adjustments), carried back from 1929 in the case of the NBER series, chiefly by the national product estimates of Simon Kuznets, supplemented by estimates of government purchases by John W. Kendrick.

Although the numerator of the indexes is adjusted gross national product, the indexes are actually measures of the net productivity of the economy. This arises as the result of "netting" out all intermediate purchases of goods and services, thus eliminating duplication and measuring only the "end product" of the system. Indexes of net productivity may therefore move differently from gross productivity indexes according to changes in the efficiency of materials utilization which are not reflected in gross output indexes of productivity.

The indexes are "real" in the sense that price fluctuations have been eliminated by various means. In the NBER series, the net goods and services produced were combined in six segments or "comparison periods" by a Marshall-Edgeworth formula using as weights the average prices in the terminal years of each period. The final production index is thus a chain index with shifting weights between links, but fixed weights within links. Over the long period, therefore, the productivity index reflects the overall shifts in the industry composition of the aggregates. The comparison bases are 1929 for 1889 to 1933 and 1958 for 1929 to 1970.

The output measure in the BLS index is derived from constant dollar aggregates of gross national product published by the Department of Commerce. These aggregates represent the deflation of current dollar values by weighted price indexes. The resultant indexes of net output approximate production indexes with 1958 representing the price base and 1967 the comparison base.

W 1-3, real gross private domestic product per man-hour. This series shows changes in over-all productive efficiency in terms of man-hours as the physical unit of labor input. In general, the estimates of man-hours were obtained by multiplying employment by average hours worked per year in the various industrial groupings. The industry hours were combined to the desired level of aggregation without explicit weights. The exception to the general rule for derivation of total hours occurred in the farm sector where the Agricultural Marketing Service estimates of farm labor requirements in terms of "average adult man-hour equivalents" were used. The AMS estimates were adjusted upwards by 10 percent in all years to attain a level comparable to that of the other sectors.

For the private nonfarm sector, employment data are based upon establishment reports or represent extrapolations of establishment-type estimates. The estimates since 1929 are by the U.S. Bureau of Economic Analysis (formerly Office of Business Economics). Prior to 1929, they are extrapolations of various benchmark estimates and are largely those used in previous NBER studies of output and employment.

W 4, product per unit of labor input. This series measures net output per weighted man-hour. Man-hours for industry groups or segments were combined by average hourly earnings, using the Marshall-Edgeworth cross-weighting formula. The comparison periods conforming to those in the output index were used. Aside from making possible a comparative study of the movements of output per weighted and per unweighted man-hour, the construction of this index makes possible the combination of the capital and labor inputs and the derivation of indexes of net output per unit of total factor input.

W 5, product per unit of capital input. This series expresses the change in total productivity in terms of real capital assets. The capital input of the private domestic economy was defined to include land and replaceable assets, such as residential and nonresidential structures, equipment, and inventories. The estimates are based primarily on those by Raymond Goldsmith in *A Study of Saving in the United States*, vol. 3, Princeton University Press, 1956. Index numbers of real capital stocks for separate industry groups were combined by use of the Marshall-Edgeworth formula, using unit capital compensation as weights. The system parallels that used in the index of labor input.

W 6-8, product per unit of total factor input. These series are conceptually more inclusive measures than those shown in series W 1-5 since they relate the quantity of net output to the real quantity of total factor input required to produce it. The index of total factor input is the weighted average of the index of labor input and the index of capital input previously described. The weights are units of factor compensation and the combination was made by applying the Marshall-Edgeworth formula.

W 9-11, real gross private product per man-hour. The output measures used in these productivity estimates—gross product originating developed by the U.S. Bureau of Economic Analysis—are based on a value added concept and represent an unduplicated count of the goods and services produced in an industrial sector. In current dollars, the output data reflect both changes in prices and the physical volume of production. For productivity measurement, only changes in the volume of production are relevant so that output is adjusted for price change and expressed in constant dollars of a base year, which is 1958 for these indexes.

Man-hours refer to hours paid rather than hours worked. They are derived primarily from the BLS establishment data on employment and average weekly hours, supplemented by employment and hours from national income data and the BLS labor force series. The latter is the source of man-hours in the farm sector. Man-hours for the private and nonfarm sectors are the simple aggregate of man-hours computed for each industrial sector. Employment and man-hours data are published in *Employment and Earnings*. A complete description of the methods and procedures used to develop these output per man-hour measures appears in chapter 25 of the *BLS Handbook of Methods*, Bulletin 1711.

W 12. Productivity—index of output per man-hour for production workers, total mining (1929 = 100), 1890-1960.

Source: John W. Kendrick, *Productivity Trends in the United States*, National Bureau of Economic Research, Princeton University Press, 1961 (copyright).

An earlier index appearing in Harold Barger and Sam H. Schurr, *The Mining Industries, 1899-1939: A Study of Output, Employment, and Productivity*, NBER, New York, 1944, provided the basis for this series. The earlier index has been extended back by Kendrick to cover years omitted by Barger and Schurr and to include the later period, 1939-1960. Since Kendrick's study of the mining industry was part of a study of national productivity, the need for consistency between the several sectors caused some modification of the Barger and Schurr index.

The mining industry covers all extraction of minerals including stone quarrying and the pumping of crude petroleum. The output index is a price-weighted aggregate of the Marshall-Edgeworth type and is of "modified chain" construction. Separate indexes were computed for each of several comparison periods using the mean of the commodity prices for the terminal years of each period. The indexes of the comparison periods were then linked to obtain an index covering the entire period.

The general weighting scheme of the original study was followed in the Kendrick revisions, except that he applied national income per unit of output as the weighting factor for combining the broad industry groups into the sector aggregate. These broad groups are metal mining, nonmetallic mining and quarrying, oil and gas wells, bituminous coal, and anthracite. For years prior to 1919, the 1919-1929 weights were used.

Basic sources of quantity and value data for the original production index were *Mineral Resources of the United States*, published annually for 1882-1931; and *Minerals Yearbook*, published annually since 1932-33. These volumes were prepared and issued by the U.S. Geological Survey from 1882 to 1923 and by the U.S. Bureau of Mines since 1924.

Labor input data for 1902 are from the U.S. Bureau of the Census, whereas later data are from accident statistics collected by the Bureau of Mines. The data are man-days used in actual mine operation; in most cases, the average number of employees times the number of days the mine operated during the year. BLS reports on employment and average hours have been used since 1939. The estimates of man-hours are the products of man-days times the "nominal" hours worked per day. Nominal hours are implicitly defined as the number of hours customarily worked on one shift in a regular workday by all persons "engaged in production."

W 13. Productivity—index of output per man-hour for production workers, total mining (1947 = 100), 1880-1950.

Source: U.S. Bureau of Labor Statistics computations, 1880-1935, based on WPA National Research Project, *Production, Employment, and Productivity in the Mineral Extractive Industries, 1880-1938*; 1935-1950, based on BLS, *Productivity Trends in Selected Industries, Indexes Through 1950*, Bulletin No. 1046.

For 1935-1945, the index for mining represents 6 individual mining industries, for 5 of which the BLS published separate series—bituminous coal, anthracite, iron, copper, and lead and zinc. The production index from which the combined index is derived is an average of the 5 separately published series plus a series for crude petroleum and natural gas weighted with current man-hours; the man-hours index is based on totals for the 6 industries. The productivity index for the years before 1935 is based on the WPA National Research Project study.

The individual mining series (W 14-21) are published annually in a BLS release, *Indexes of Output Per Man-Hour: Selected Industries*. The production data for these series are from the U.S. Bureau of Mines. Employment and average weekly hours series are those of BLS for 1939-1970. For 1935-1939, BLS series were used for the coal industry and Bureau of Mines data for metal mining. The employment definition adopted (average number of wage earners employed during the 12 months of each year, including months of no activity) is the concept used by the Bureau of the Census.

W 14–21. Productivity—indexes of output per man-hour for production workers, selected mining industries, 1935–1970.

Source: U.S. Bureau of Labor Statistics, 1939 and 1947–1970, *Indexes of Output Per Man-Hour: Selected Industries, 1973 Edition*, Bulletin No. 1780; all other years, BLS computations.

Production data on which the indexes are based come from the U.S. Bureau of Mines, *Minerals Yearbook*, and the U.S. Bureau of the Census, censuses of mineral industries. The man-hours components of the indexes are derived from the regularly published BLS series on employment and average weekly hours adjusted by data obtained from the censuses of mineral industries. Exceptions to this are the indexes of man-hours for copper mining and iron mining for 1935–1939, which were derived from accident analysis statistics of the Bureau of Mines; and the lead and zinc mining man-hours for 1935–1939, which were derived from special WPA National Research Project tabulations of Bureau of Mines data for 1935–1939. The man-hours cover only production and related workers, and exclude salaried officers, superintendents, other supervisory employees, and professional and technical employees. They include all hours worked or paid for.

W 22–29. Indexes of output per man-hour and output per employed person, 1947–1970.

Source: U.S. Bureau of Labor Statistics, *Handbook of Labor Statistics 1972*, table 85.

The measures of output per man-hour in the private economy refer to the ratio between constant-dollar gross national product (GNP) originating in the private sector of the economy or individual sectors, and the corresponding hours of all persons employed.

Two series of output per man-hour estimates have been developed. One series is based on labor force data from surveys of households, conducted by the U.S. Bureau of the Census for the Bureau of Labor Statistics. The other series, shown here, is based primarily on BLS surveys of establishments.

The output measure (GNP) used in preparing both series represents the market value (in 1958 dollars) of final goods and services produced in the economy. It includes the purchases of goods and services by consumers, business establishments, foreign investors, and the various government agencies. The GNP data are prepared by the U.S. Bureau of Economic Analysis. The establishment series is based on an hours paid concept and includes the hours of all persons on establishment payrolls in the private economy. In the development of the establishment man-hour series, data from the labor force reports and national income series were used to supplement the BLS payroll series data.

These indexes relate output to man-hours and to employment. They do not reflect the specific contributions of labor, capital, or any other factors of production. Rather, they measure the combined effect of a number of interrelated influences, such as skills of workers, managerial skills, changes in technology, capital investment per worker, utilization of capital, layout and flow of materials, and labor-management relations.

For a discussion of the BLS indexes and those prepared by the Department of Agriculture's Economic Research Service, see the text for series W 67–81.

The indexes of output per man-hour in manufacturing (series W 25) measure changes in the real value added per man-hour of all wage and salary workers, proprietors, and unpaid family workers. Annual output data used to prepare these indexes are the gross product originating in manufacturing, in 1958 dollars, developed by the U.S. Bureau of Economic Analysis. Gross product originating excludes the cost of materials and other intermediate products consumed in the production process.

Man-hours data are developed by BLS on the basis of establishment data on employment and average weekly hours and refer to hours paid.

For a complete description of the methods used, see chapter 25 of *BLS Handbook of Methods*, Bulletin 1711.

W 30. Index of output per man-hour for production workers, total manufacturing industries, 1909–1950.

Source: U.S. Bureau of Labor Statistics, 1909, 1914, and 1919–1939 computations based on *Handbook of Labor Statistics, 1947*; 1939, 1947, and 1949–1950, *Trends in Output Per Man-Hour and Man-Hours Per Unit of Output-Manufacturing, 1939–53*, Report No. 100, 1955.

The production index used to derive the index of output per man-hour in manufacturing for 1909, 1914, and the odd-numbered years 1919–1939, is from Solomon Fabricant, *Employment in Manufacturing, 1899–1939*, NBER, New York, 1942. The production index for even-numbered years to 1939 was computed by use of the Federal Reserve Index for Manufactures. The man-hours index was derived from an employment index based on U.S. Bureau of the Census and BLS data and BLS series for average weekly hours for 1909, 1919, and 1923–1939, supplemented with estimates of the WPA National Research Project for 1920–1922. For 1939, 1947, and 1949–1950, the production index was computed by BLS.

For the period before 1936, indexes of productivity are shown in *Production, Employment, and Productivity in 59 Manufacturing Industries, 1919–1936*, a 3-volume report prepared by WPA National Research Project on Reemployment Opportunities and Recent Changes in National Techniques. BLS made some revisions in these indexes and extended most of them to 1940. These measures, together with indexes of payrolls and unit labor cost, appear in the BLS report, *Productivity and Unit Labor Cost in Selected Manufacturing Industries, 1910–1940*, and were later revised. The revised output-per-man-hour series was published in the 1947 *Handbook of Labor Statistics*.

The production pattern changed radically when the United States began its World War II program. Statistics were inadequate for measuring overall changes in manufacturing efficiency during the period of transition from peace to war. Consequently, there is a gap in the measurements between 1939 and 1947.

The index of output per man-hour in manufacturing attempts to compare the labor time required in the current year to manufacture the current year's output of goods with the time required in the base year to produce the same quantity and mixture of goods. That is, it measures the change in output per man-hour, assuming that the proportion of goods produced by each industry and within each industry in each year under consideration was also produced in the base year. It is the ratio of a production index (consisting of an aggregate of quantities produced weighted by the labor time required to produce a single unit) to a man-hours index (based upon the time of production workers). The concept of physical output holds constant the relative importance of industries. Indexes developed under this concept reflect primarily the average change in productivity of plants and industries in manufacturing.

W 31–54. Indexes of output per man-hour for production workers, selected industries, 1919–1970.

Source: U.S. Bureau of Labor Statistics. For data on 1947 base, selected years, *Indexes of Output Per Man-Hour for Selected Industries: 1919–1958*, April 1959; all other years, computations (1919–1936, based on WPA National Research Project, *Production, Employment, and Productivity in 59 Manufacturing Industries*, May 1939; 1936–1939, based on BLS, *Productivity and Unit Labor Cost in Selected Manufacturing Industries, 1919–1940*, 1942; 1939–1950, based on BLS, *Productivity Trends in Selected Industries, Indexes Through 1950*, Bulletin No. 1046); for data on 1967 base, *Indexes of Output Per Man-Hour: Selected Industries, 1973 Edition*, Bulletin No. 1780.

The indexes on the 1939 base were published in 1939 by the National Research Project on Reemployment Opportunities and Recent Changes in Industrial Techniques, a unit of the Works Progress Administration. They were based on data obtained from the U.S. Bureau of the Census, BLS, and other official and private agencies. BLS made some revisions in these series, and extended most of them through 1945. These extended and revised indexes were published, together with indexes of unit labor cost, in a series of BLS publications, *Productivity and Unit Labor Cost in Selected Manufacturing Industries, 1919–1940,* and several supplements to this report. All measures in these series refer to output per production worker and are based on an aggregate of production worker man-hours.

Relative to the data on the 1967 base, the source warns that the industries covered are not necessarily a representative cross section of U.S. industry, and their output per man-hour indexes should not be combined to obtain an overall measure for the entire economy or any sector. Each index represents only the change in output per man-hour for the designated industry or combination of industries.

Output per man-hour indexes are obtained by dividing an output index by an index of aggregate man-hours. Although the measures relate output to one input—labor time—they do not measure the specific contribution of labor or any other factor of production. Rather, they reflect the joint effect of a number of interrelated influences, such as changes in technology, capital investment per worker, and capacity utilization. Industry output per man-hour measures are limited to the extent that they do not account for quality change, and often do not reflect adequately changes in the degree of plant integration and specialization. In addition, there is not always strict comparability between output and labor input estimates. Finally, year-to-year changes in output per man-hour are irregular, and therefore not necessarily indicative of basic changes in long-term trends. Conversely, long-term trends are not necessarily applicable to any one year or period in the future.

W 55–59. Indexes of output per worker in transportation, 1869–1966.

Source: John W. Kendrick, *Productivity Trends in the United States,* National Bureau of Economic Research, Princeton University Press, 1961; and *Postwar Productivity Trends in the United States,* National Bureau of Economic Research, 1973. (Copyright.)

These series represent revisions and extensions of data by Harold Barger, *The Transportation Industries, 1889–1946: A Study of Output, Employment and Productivity,* NBER, New York, 1951. In addition to extending Barger's index, Kendrick also created an index for the trucking industry which was not separately presented in the earlier study. For details concerning underlying data and computations for these series, see the sources cited.

W 55, output per worker in all transportation industries. This index measures the change in the movement of persons and property for hire per worker employed and includes the industry groupings of the national income accounts which follow closely the U.S. Office of Management and Budget, *Standard Industrial Classification Manual.*

The production index used as the numerator is based upon revenue passenger-miles and unweighted ton-miles wherever possible. Where these items were not available, less refined units were substituted, as indicated for individual industries below. Output figures were not available for industries which, in 1929, amounted to some 20 percent of the total. For these industries, output was derived from employment on the assumption that the productivity of the uncovered portion was the same as in the covered portion. The aggregate production index of the industry was derived by weighting together the group indexes using changing national income weights and applying a Marshall-Edgeworth formula.

The employment index is based upon the U.S. Bureau of Economic Analysis (BEA, formerly Office of Business Economics), employment series since 1929. For 1870–1930, the series was extrapolated by estimates of the distribution of gainfully employed workers in census years, adjusted to exclude the unemployed.

Although only output per worker is presented here, the Kendrick series afford measures of output per man-hour for total transportation and for most individual industries.

W 56, output per worker in railroads. The output of this industry includes the freight and passenger activities of Class I, II, and III line-haul roads, switching and terminal companies, the Pullman Company, and the Railway Express Agency and its predecessors.

The production index is a weighted average of simple ton-miles and revenue passenger-miles with different weights for the different classes of passenger service.

W 57, output per worker for pipelines. This index covers companies primarily engaged in the pipeline transportation of crude petroleum and refined petroleum products. Transmission of natural gas is not included. It includes trunkline mileage in interstate as well as intrastate transmission. Gathering lines are excluded.

W 58, output per worker in waterways. The productivity estimates of waterways measure the output per person employed on U.S. flag vessels in coastwise, intercoastal, Great Lakes (domestic), inland, noncontiguous, and international water transportation. The exception is that Great Lakes passenger traffic is not included.

W 59, output per worker in airlines. The productivity estimates for this industry relate to scheduled airlines and unscheduled carriers and companies primarily engaged in operating fixed facilities or providing services to airlines.

W 60–61. Indexes of output per person and per man-hour in distribution, 1869–1969.

Source: See source for series W 55–59.

These indexes represent revisions and extensions of an earlier index prepared by Harold Barger, *Distribution's Place in the American Economy Since 1869,* Princeton University Press, 1955. The original estimates by Barger represented real margin earned per man-hour on those goods reaching the public through retail stores only. The quantities sold through retail stores were weighted by average 1869 and 1929 distributive margins to derive the production aggregate. The index is thus a "net" concept, although it is more inclusive than the usual net productivity index since packaging and other supply materials customarily considered a part of margin are not eliminated.

W 62–63. Indexes of output per employee and per man-hour, 1948–1970.

Source: U.S. Bureau of Labor Statistics, *Indexes of Output Per Man-Hour: Selected Industries, 1973 Edition,* Bulletin No. 1780.

W 62, index of output per employee in air transportation, 1947–70. Output is measured by passenger-miles and freight ton-miles for all of the certificated air carriers. Unit revenue weights are used to combine the different output services. The index series refers to output per employee (production and nonproduction workers); man-hour data are not available. Employment data are from the Civil Aeronautics Board.

W 63, index of output per employee in petroleum pipelines, 1947–69. The output measure is computed from the annual barrel-mile total of crude oil and products. All basic output data are published by the Interstate Commerce Commission. The index series refers to output per employee (production and nonproduction workers). Prior to 1958 man-hour data are not available. However, from 1958 forward, output per man-hour measures are available and are published in the source cited. All employment measures are computed by BLS.

W 64. Index of output per man-hour in railroad transportation, 1916–1970.

Source: U.S. Bureau of Labor Statistics, 1939, 1947–1970, *Indexes of Output Per Man-Hour: Selected Industries, 1973 Edition,* Bulletin No. 1780; all other years, BLS computations (1916–1935, based on Witt Bowden, "Productivity, Hours, and Compensation of Railroad Labor, 1933–1936," *Monthly Labor Review*, July 1937; 1935–1947, based on BLS, *Trends in Output Per Man-Hour, 1935–1955, Selected Nonmanufacturing Industries*, Report No. 105, June 1956).

The index of output per man-hour for railroad transportation refers to Class I railroads and Class I switching and terminal companies. For 1935–1970, the production measure represents aggregate passenger-miles and freight ton-miles, each category being weighted by fixed period average unit revenue weights. The man-hours index represents straight time worked and overtime paid for all employees (production and nonproduction workers) and also includes constructive allowance hours of train and engine employees. Constructive allowance time includes vacations, standby time, held-over time, court time, etc. All basic data are published by the Interstate Commerce Commission.

The indexes for 1916–1934 are based on a somewhat different index prepared by BLS. The components of the production index are combined with 1926 weights; and for 1916 through July 1921, the man-hours represent time worked rather than paid.

W 65. Index of output per man-hour in the gas and electric utilities industry, 1939–70.

Source: U.S. Bureau of Labor Statistics, *Indexes of Output Per Man-Hour: Selected Industries, 1973 Edition*, Bulletin No. 1780.

Output is measured in terms of energy sold (kw.-hr. of electricity and therms of gas) by privately owned gas utilities, privately owned classes A and B electric utilities, and REA borrowers. Unit revenue weights are used to combine the different output series. The index series refers to output per man-hour for all employees (both production and nonproduction workers). Employment and man-hour data are from BLS.

W 66. Indexes of output per man-hour for nonfinancial corporations, 1948–1970.

Source: U.S. Bureau of Labor Statistics, *Productivity, Wages, Prices, and Employment*, press release issued quarterly, table 4.

The nonfinancial corporate sector includes all corporations operating in the United States except banks, commodity and stock brokers, credit agencies, and insurance carriers. Output data used to prepare these indexes are the gross product originating in 1958 dollars. These data and compensation (wages, salaries, and supplements) were developed by the Bureau of Economic Analysis. A description of the methods and procedures used to derive these statistics appears in the May 1967 issue of *Survey of Current Business*.

Man-hours refer to hours paid and are based mainly on BLS establishment data on employment and average weekly hours. Census data by legal form of organization for 2-digit SIC industries are used to adjust man-hours to the nonfinancial corporate levels.

W 67–81. Index of farm production per man-hour, 1910–1970.

Source: U.S. Department of Agriculture, Economic Research Service, *Changes in Farm Production and Efficiency*, Statistical Bulletin No. 233.

For a description of the index of farm production, see the text for series K 414–429. The index of farm production per man-hour is the ratio of farm production to labor input. The index numbers are developed by relating the indexes of farm output and production of individual or groups of farm products to the appropriate index of labor input expressed in man-hours (see text for series K 410–413).

Indexes of farm labor productivity reflect the net effect of all factors that affect either farm production or the labor input. Since labor is one of the more important inputs in agricultural production, changes in the ratio of production to labor provide a useful measure of changes in efficiency of farm production.

These series are published annually in the source cited and in *Agricultural Statistics*.

Caution should be exercised when comparing the ERS series with those of the Bureau of Labor Statistics (BLS) because of differences between "gross" and "net" farm production, and between hours "worked" and hours "required."

BLS computes indexes of production per man-hour for the total private economy, for nonagriculture, and for agriculture. Like the ERS series, the BLS series calculates indexes of farm production in which production data are weighted by constant prices. However, the ERS farm output index is a "gross" index while the production index of BLS follows the GNP approach, which is a "net" index excluding intermediate products.

The BLS series uses both BLS and census labor force data based on hours "worked" and covers men, women, and children over 14 years of age. Thus, the labor input differs from the ERS series which reports hours "required" for agricultural production in terms of man-equivalent hours.

The BLS series is applicable for all agriculture only, while the ERS series permits comparisons.

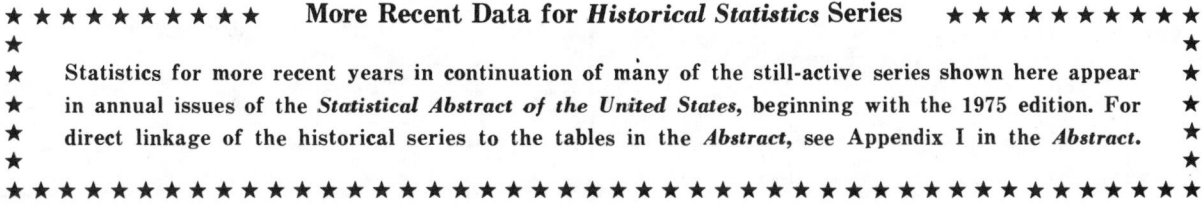

★ ★ ★ ★ ★ ★ ★ ★ ★   **More Recent Data for *Historical Statistics* Series**   ★ ★ ★ ★ ★ ★ ★ ★ ★

Statistics for more recent years in continuation of many of the still-active series shown here appear in annual issues of the ***Statistical Abstract of the United States***, beginning with the 1975 edition. For direct linkage of the historical series to the tables in the ***Abstract***, see Appendix I in the ***Abstract***.

Series W 1–11. Indexes of National Productivity: 1889 to 1970

Year	Real gross private domestic product (NBER)								Real gross private product per man-hour (BLS)		
	Per man-hour			Per unit of labor input	Per unit of capital input	Per unit of total factor input			Total economy	Farm	Non-farm
	Total economy	Farm	Non-farm			Total economy	Farm	Non-farm			
	1	2	3	4	5	6	7	8	9	10	11
	1958 = 100								1967 = 100		
1970	¹137.2			¹132.6	¹107.5	¹126.4			103.8	115.6	103.5
1969	135.6	¹177.5		130.9	112.1	126.5			103.0	110.7	102.7
1968	135.2	164.6		131.0	113.5	126.8			102.5	100.2	102.9
1967	131.5	163.5		127.7	112.8	124.2			100.0	100.0	100.0
1966	129.5	149.4	127.1	125.4	115.3	123.2	126.6	123.7	98.8	90.5	98.4
1965	125.7	144.2	123.8	122.9	114.5	121.0	128.3	121.3	95.8	86.9	95.1
1964	121.6	131.7	120.3	119.4	111.9	117.7	118.9	118.3	93.0	79.5	92.4
1963	117.4	128.7	116.3	115.6	109.4	114.2	118.5	114.5	89.8	78.1	89.1
1962	113.5	118.2	113.0	112.4	108.0	111.4	112.1	111.8	87.1	71.7	86.4
1961	108.5	115.8	107.8	107.7	103.5	106.8	111.2	107.0	88.6	70.0	82.7
1960	104.9	106.5	104.7	104.5	104.1	104.4	105.4	104.6	81.4	64.9	80.3
1959	103.5	101.1	103.5	103.0	104.5	103.3	100.9	103.5	80.1	61.5	79.3
1958	100.0	100.0	100.0	100.0	100.0	100.0	100.0	100.0	77.6	60.4	76.7
1957	97.2	89.8	97.6	96.4	103.4	97.8	92.7	98.0	75.6	54.7	74.8
1956	94.6	84.6	95.6	94.4	105.6	96.6	90.4	96.9	73.8	51.6	73.2
1955	94.2	81.0	95.9	94.4	108.4	97.0	88.1	97.7	73.7	49.5	73.6
1954	89.9	80.1	91.2	90.3	103.2	92.8	86.7	93.2	70.7	49.1	70.5
1953	87.4	76.6	88.8	87.1	108.0	90.8	84.1	91.3	69.3	46.7	68.9
1952	83.5	68.0	85.6	83.8	106.7	87.9	77.1	88.7	66.8	41.2	66.9
1951	82.0	62.3	85.1	82.9	109.5	87.8	72.4	89.1	65.7	37.9	66.3
1950	80.1	61.9	83.8	82.3	109.1	87.1	74.1	88.3	64.3	37.7	65.0
1949	74.0	54.3	78.4	76.8	102.4	81.5	67.3	82.6	59.9	33.1	61.1
1948	71.4	56.2	74.8	73.5	106.7	79.5	70.0	81.0	58.3	34.0	58.8
1947	68.7	49.6	72.8	71.0	105.6	77.2	63.0	79.3	56.0	29.2	57.1
1946	68.7	51.4	73.3	71.7	109.4	78.4	66.7	80.5			
1945	70.7	47.9	76.8	74.0	115.6	81.3	63.0	84.4			
1944	67.2	47.6	72.7	70.1	115.7	77.8	64.3	80.3			
1943	63.0	47.9	67.4	65.8	108.6	73.1	64.7	74.5			
1942	62.0	49.9	66.7	65.7	102.9	72.3	67.9	73.2			
1941	61.8	47.7	67.2	66.3	98.2	72.0	64.2	73.5			
1940	58.5	42.7	66.1	64.9	89.3	69.3	58.3	71.5			
1939	56.9	44.2	63.6	63.5	83.9	67.1	60.5	68.3			
1938	54.7	43.3	61.4	61.5	76.4	64.1	59.1	65.0			
1937	53.1	40.3	59.7	59.3	81.6	63.2	56.5	64.7			
1936	53.2	37.0	60.2	59.2	78.6	62.7	50.1	64.7			
1935	50.6	39.2	57.7	57.8	69.8	59.8	53.9	60.6			
1934	49.0	36.2	55.9	56.2	62.1	56.7	48.7	57.6			
1933	44.5	38.9	50.4	52.1	56.8	52.3	54.6	51.3			
1932	45.4	39.8	51.6	53.2	56.2	53.0	55.8	51.9			
1931	47.2	39.5	53.3	54.0	63.1	55.3	56.1	55.0			
1930	46.8	35.6	52.5	52.3	68.1	55.1	50.1	55.6			
1929	48.6	37.3	54.1	53.5	77.5	57.8	52.6	58.8			

Year	Real gross private domestic product (NBER)								Year	Real gross private domestic product (NBER)							
	Per man-hour			Per unit of labor input	Per unit of capital input	Per unit of total factor input				Per man-hour			Per unit of labor input	Per unit of capital input	Per unit of total factor input		
	Total economy	Farm	Non-farm			Total economy	Farm	Non-farm		Total economy	Farm	Non-farm			Total economy	Farm	Non-farm
	1	2	3	4	5	6	7	8		1	2	3	4	5	6	7	8
	1929 = 100									1929 = 100							
1933	93.5	105.2		99.3	72.5	91.3	104.5		1910	64.4	90.0		67.7	82.4	71.6	92.5	
1932	95.0	102.2		100.8	71.9	91.9	100.9		1909	65.6	88.1	64.7	69.6	84.3	73.4	90.9	71.5
1931	98.4	103.0		102.1	82.3	96.4	103.4		1908	61.1	90.5		65.6	76.2	68.2	93.7	
1930	97.5	94.0		98.8	89.0	96.3	93.9		1907	64.2	89.3		68.0	86.2	72.7	92.5	
1929	100.0	100.0	100.0	100.0	100.0	100.0	100.0	100.0	1906	64.4	94.0		68.5	88.1	73.5	93.1	
1928	95.7	96.1		95.9	96.1	96.0	96.7										
1927	95.7	100.1		95.6	97.5	96.1	100.3		1905	59.9	89.8		64.2	81.7	68.8	93.5	
1926	94.1	93.4		94.4	99.2	95.7	95.3		1904	58.4	89.4		63.5	78.0	67.2	93.3	
									1903	58.5	87.6		62.9	81.7	67.7	91.6	
1925	91.6	94.6		92.5	96.4	93.6	96.6		1902	57.2	85.6		61.9	80.7	66.7	90.0	
1924	91.7	90.0		92.9	95.3	93.6	91.2		1901	59.4	86.8		65.2	83.2	69.8	93.1	
1923	87.8	95.9		88.2	95.9	90.2	96.5		1900	55.6	87.9		61.7	77.0	65.7	92.8	
1922	83.0	90.4		84.9	85.7	85.1	90.2		1899	54.7	87.9	52.8	61.0	77.9	65.4	93.1	61.3
1921	83.8	97.0		86.8	81.1	85.1	85.7		1898	53.7			60.9	73.3	64.1	94.2	
1920	78.3	85.8		79.6	85.4	81.2	86.4		1897	52.9			60.0	74.3	63.7	91.5	
1919	79.0	88.4	79.7	80.4	86.8	82.1	88.4	81.7	1896	49.5			56.3	69.2	59.5	86.3	
1918	74.1	86.2		75.0	86.1	78.0	87.3										
1917	68.6	96.2		69.5	82.6	73.0	97.3		1895	50.7			57.7	73.5	61.7	81.3	
1916	72.3	89.6		73.7	87.5	77.4	89.9		1894	47.7			55.3	67.6	58.5	77.4	
									1893	47.4			54.1	71.9	58.7	75.5	
1915	67.2	101.3		70.2	77.0	72.0	102.1		1892	49.4			56.0	79.6	61.8	78.3	
1914	64.7	92.7		67.9	76.6	70.3	95.3		1891	46.6			53.2	77.1	59.1	83.6	
1913	69.2	85.6		71.8	86.0	75.6	87.2		1890	45.7			52.4	77.8	58.6	81.3	
1912	66.9	97.2		69.7	85.1	73.7	99.8		1889	43.6	77.0	41.1	50.0	74.8	56.0	83.9	51.6
1911	65.7	83.3		69.0	83.0	72.7	85.4										

¹ Preliminary.

Series **W 12–21.** Productivity—Indexes of Output Per Man-Hour for Production Workers in Mining: 1880 to 1970

Year	Total mining (NBER)	Total mining	Total coal mining	Bituminous coal	Copper Recoverable metal	Copper Crude ore mined	Iron Usable ore	Iron Crude ore mined	Lead and zinc Recoverable metal	Lead and zinc Crude ore mined	Year	Total mining (NBER)	Total mining (BLS)
	12	13	14	15	16	17	18	19	20	21		12	13
	1929 = 100	1947 = 100				1967 = 100				1947 = 100		1929 = 100	1947 = 100
1970			102.7	103.2	112.8	126.9	108.7	118.0			1934	119.0	73.3
1969			105.3	105.4	106.9	116.2	109.6	117.8			1933	116.0	70.9
1968			105.4	105.1	103.4	109.6	105.1	110.0			1932	112.9	69.8
1967			100.0	100.0	100.0	100.0	100.0	100.0			1931	108.9	69.5
1966			97.6	97.9	105.0	103.0	102.5	96.1			1930	102.9	65.6
1965			92.4	92.7	102.5	98.5	99.7	95.1			1929	100.0	62.9
1964			86.7	86.6	103.9	96.9	101.4	98.6			1928	98.0	61.2
1963			81.6	80.8	95.4	86.0	91.8	91.1			1927	91.0	58.8
1962			78.7	77.9	95.0	86.5	86.6	82.4			1926	85.9	57.1
1961			74.1	73.6	87.5	79.4	83.9	76.7			1925	84.9	56.3
1960	247.1		67.3	66.7	84.0	77.6	79.7	66.3			1924	79.4	54.6
1959	233.8		63.6	62.8	81.8	75.8	72.0	58.7			1923	78.8	53.1
1958	224.4		62.3	61.6	86.3	74.3	73.1	56.8			1922	75.9	51.8
1957	215.8		56.1	55.6	76.5	67.3	80.9	58.2	123.0	104.3	1921	69.5	48.8
1956	210.5		55.3	54.3	70.1	61.4	81.2	57.6	117.1	107.8	1920	68.2	46.6
1955	206.3		52.8	52.6	73.0	60.5	84.7	55.3	116.6	111.1	1919	65.9	44.6
1954	197.0		49.3	48.8	65.0	53.7	65.1	42.9	114.6	108.1	1918	66.8	44.5
1953	186.5		42.2	42.0	64.6	51.8	75.7	47.3	116.0	102.8	1917	65.2	43.7
1952	176.8		39.2	38.8	68.8	54.8	72.9	45.2	111.1	103.0	1916	64.6	43.3
1951	175.5		37.3	36.7	68.6	52.2	77.4	48.0	116.4	104.4	1915	63.6	43.7
1950	164.0	105.7	37.1	36.9	68.4	52.5	71.2	43.7	127.0	103.2	1902	47.9	30.1
1949	151.9	97.7	34.4	33.7	58.8	43.9	66.7	39.5	114.7	94.1	1890	37.3	23.0
1948	149.9	99.8	32.8	32.0	57.7	42.8	68.7	41.4	108.3	88.8	1880		17.8
1947	144.2	100.0	32.8	32.1	58.9	44.5	68.7	40.8	100.0	100.0			
1946	141.0	96.5	32.5	31.5	52.6	39.3	67.9	39.4	92.0	120.1			
1945	144.1	95.5	31.1	30.3	60.2	44.0	71.0	41.8	103.4	129.5			
1944	136.2	94.2	30.3	29.3	59.0	40.4	63.8	37.0	102.3	124.5			
1943	135.3	91.4	29.0	28.1	53.5	35.0	61.8	36.1	98.5	109.1			
1942	133.2	93.6	30.3	29.4	52.6	32.6	68.6	40.9	119.0	117.7			
1941	138.3	93.5	30.8	29.7	51.5	30.6	74.2	42.9	129.1	124.0			
1940	145.6	91.9	30.4	29.4	53.1	30.4	73.8	41.6	127.6	114.4			
1939	144.9	90.0	29.2	28.2	51.2	28.2	62.8	34.9	132.3	114.7			
1938	138.8	81.1	28.2	27.2	47.6	23.4	44.1	24.6	129.4	107.0			
1937	130.9	79.2	26.9	25.8	48.2	25.4	66.4	37.3	120.2	110.6			
1936	138.6	77.9	26.2	25.2	52.1	23.7	62.0	34.9	123.5	109.0			
1935	127.6	76.4	24.4	24.1	50.1	18.4	55.0	31.9	131.0	101.9			

Series **W 22–29.** Indexes of Output Per Man-Hour and Output Per Employed Person: 1947 to 1970

[1967 = 100. Man-hour estimates based primarily on establishment data]

Year	Output per man-hour in the private economy Total private	Farm	Nonfarm	Manufacturing	Output per employed person in the private economy Total private	Farm	Nonfarm	Manufacturing
	22	23	24	25	26	27	28	29
1970	104.4	119.8	103.4	108.0	102.2	116.9	101.4	106.4
1969	103.3	110.2	102.7	107.4	102.5	108.5	102.1	107.4
1968	102.9	100.2	102.9	104.7	102.4	99.0	102.5	104.9
1967	100.0	100.0	100.0	100.0	100.0	100.0	100.0	100.0
1966	98.0	90.5	98.4	99.9	99.3	91.3	99.7	101.3
1965	94.2	86.9	95.1	98.4	96.2	88.2	96.9	99.6
1964	91.1	79.5	92.4	94.5	92.8	79.7	94.0	94.8
1963	87.7	78.1	89.1	90.1	89.5	78.1	90.8	90.1
1962	84.7	71.7	86.4	86.6	86.6	72.3	88.1	86.4
1961	80.9	70.0	82.7	81.9	82.5	69.7	84.1	81.0
1960	78.2	64.9	80.3	79.9	80.4	65.6	82.2	79.0
1959	76.9	61.5	79.3	78.6	79.5	61.7	81.7	78.6
1958	74.3	60.4	76.7	74.4	76.3	60.6	78.4	73.0
1957	72.0	54.7	74.8	74.4	74.8	55.4	77.2	73.8
1956	70.0	51.6	73.2	72.9	73.6	53.6	76.4	73.2
1955	69.9	49.5	73.6	73.7	74.1	52.5	77.2	74.4
1954	66.9	49.1	70.5	69.5	70.7	52.8	73.5	68.8
1953	65.3	46.7	68.9	68.4	69.7	51.1	72.5	68.8
1952	62.7	41.2	66.9	66.2	67.3	44.6	70.9	66.9
1951	61.5	37.9	66.3	65.9	66.2	41.4	70.3	66.5
1950	59.7	37.7	65.0	64.4	64.4	40.8	68.9	64.9
1949	55.3	33.1	61.1	60.1	59.5	36.4	64.4	58.9
1948	53.6	34.0	58.8	58.0	58.5	38.0	62.7	57.9
1947	51.3	29.2	57.1	54.9	56.5	32.9	61.4	55.2

Series W 30–54. Indexes of Output Per Man-Hour for Production Workers, Selected Industries: 1909 to 1970

Year	Total manufacturing	Canning and preserving	Flour and grain mill products	Bakery products	Sugar	Candy and other confectionery products	Malt liquors	Tobacco products	Cigarettes, chewing and smoking tobacco, and snuff	Cigars	Hosiery	Paper, paperboard, and pulp mills	Petroleum refining	Tires and inner tubes	Footwear
	30	31	32	32a	33	34	35	36	37	38	39	40	41	42	43
								1967 = 100							
1970	--------	105.9	111.2	105.5	111.1	103.0	120.3	103.4	98.8	114.7	126.2	115.8	108.6	105.4	105.3
1969	--------	102.8	105.8	103.1	101.9	101.1	113.3	102.0	98.9	109.3	106.4	110.2	110.6	100.3	97.4
1968	--------	107.2	106.1	101.5	103.7	103.0	105.7	103.2	103.0	103.8	93.1	106.2	103.7	105.0	103.6
1967	--------	100.0	100.0	100.0	100.0	100.0	100.0	100.0	100.0	100.0	100.0	100.0	100.0	100.0	100.0
1966	--------	98.5	100.8	95.6	99.9	97.9	93.9	99.2	98.6	100.8	88.4	101.2	97.1	98.3	102.6
1965	--------	100.8	95.3	95.1	94.4	93.7	88.7	99.5	98.1	102.8	80.1	96.4	89.9	96.7	101.2
1964	--------	96.0	90.5	91.8	90.8	90.8	83.9	94.8	93.5	97.9	80.2	91.3	83.0	94.4	101.7
1963	--------	91.6	84.5	89.3	85.9	89.1	77.9	93.5	95.0	90.5	75.2	86.9	78.5	86.7	102.3
1962	--------	91.1	75.2	84.1	84.4	82.5	71.1	89.1	91.5	84.6	66.9	82.0	73.5	79.8	99.0
1961	--------	91.0	73.9	81.0	77.3	80.9	68.2	85.9	90.4	78.9	64.5	79.0	67.1	74.4	98.3
1960	--------	85.0	72.2	79.8	71.9	81.5	64.9	82.4	88.0	73.7	58.6	73.9	62.1	70.9	98.0
1959	--------	80.4	68.3	79.5	68.2	77.8	62.9	77.0	84.2	66.7	57.2	70.9	59.1	68.2	98.6
1958	--------	77.2	71.8	79.0	64.9	75.7	60.8	72.8	81.3	61.2	57.9	66.7	52.5	62.9	94.4
1957	--------	77.4	69.2	77.3	61.8	74.3	55.4	67.1	79.6	52.3	48.7	64.9	49.9	59.6	92.0
1956	--------	74.9	63.6	73.1	62.8	68.6	53.3	64.1	77.3	48.9	46.3	64.3	49.1	56.3	90.0
1955	--------	70.4	60.6	71.0	60.0	66.8	51.9	60.1	75.3	44.2	45.4	61.0	47.1	54.8	88.1
1954	--------	67.6	57.7	70.0	58.2	63.1	50.5	60.3	76.3	43.8	45.9	57.4	43.1	53.2	84.3
1953	--------	62.6	50.4	67.9	52.0	62.5	48.1	60.4	79.7	42.0	44.2	54.9	40.9	51.9	(NA)
1952	--------	61.8	47.5	65.4	50.0	60.8	48.1	61.8	83.6	42.0	45.9	54.9	39.9	49.3	84.6
1951	--------	61.5	48.2	62.7	46.0	60.6	46.5	60.3	83.1	40.4	42.4	55.6	38.4	50.9	82.9
1950	--------	59.7	48.7	62.0	48.8	54.5	46.4	58.1	78.6	39.4	39.7	53.0	36.6	52.6	80.2
1949	--------	54.1	47.2	61.3	45.1	53.2	45.3	53.6	75.2	35.2	38.0	47.4	31.7	47.9	74.1
1948	--------	49.8	(NA)	(NA)	(NA)	(NA)	(NA)	52.2	73.4	34.3	(NA)	(NA)	(NA)	(NA)	(NA)
1947	--------	48.5	49.8	59.6	41.0	53.3	38.6	48.2	68.5	31.4	35.8	44.4	28.6	43.1	69.6
1939	--------	43.7	44.5	(NA)	(NA)	47.6	33.0	38.6	47.7	28.7	(NA)	48.5	29.9	(NA)	(NA)
								1947 = 100							
1950	114.3	118.3	-----	-----	-----	-----	-----	119.3	115.6	122.5	115.4	118.9	-----	-----	-----
1949	107.2	111.5	-----	-----	-----	-----	-----	113.2	111.8	114.3	110.3	106.7	-----	-----	-----
1948	--------	103.2	-----	-----	-----	-----	-----	106.7	107.9	105.6	-----	-----	-----	-----	-----
1947	100.0	100.0	-----	-----	-----	-----	-----	100.0	100.0	100.0	100.0	100.0	-----	-----	100.0
1946	--------	106.0	-----	-----	-----	-----	-----	98.1	93.5	102.4	108.5	98.0	-----	-----	109.1
1945	--------	102.5	-----	-----	-----	-----	-----	96.5	86.3	106.9	114.4	95.6	-----	-----	104.4
1944	--------	100.5	-----	-----	-----	-----	-----	89.3	81.8	96.6	109.7	95.0	-----	-----	99.5
1943	--------	92.3	-----	-----	-----	-----	-----	84.9	80.0	89.3	106.1	98.1	-----	-----	101.6
1942	--------	93.2	-----	-----	-----	-----	-----	85.3	80.5	89.8	99.6	109.1	-----	-----	100.4
1941	--------	97.8	-----	-----	-----	-----	-----	84.1	78.7	89.3	95.6	115.9	-----	-----	101.8
1940	--------	99.2	-----	-----	-----	-----	-----	80.8	71.5	90.5	94.9	115.0	-----	-----	97.7
1939	93.2	90.0	-----	-----	-----	-----	-----	80.0	69.6	91.3	87.0	109.2	-----	-----	93.8
1938	85.1	85.8	-----	-----	-----	-----	-----	76.1	67.8	84.5	--------	103.2	-----	-----	92.9
1937	83.6	79.8	-----	-----	-----	-----	-----	73.1	66.6	79.5	--------	101.1	-----	-----	89.8
1936	84.5	74.5	-----	-----	-----	-----	-----	75.0	71.3	78.4	--------	99.9	-----	-----	97.3
1935	84.3	90.4	-----	-----	-----	-----	-----	69.4	62.8	75.8	--------	95.5	-----	-----	91.0
1934	79.8	84.3	-----	-----	-----	-----	-----	60.3	56.7	63.6	--------	90.0	-----	-----	84.0
1933	76.0	88.1	-----	-----	-----	-----	-----	61.3	67.1	57.1	--------	94.9	-----	-----	82.5
1932	72.2	76.5	-----	-----	-----	-----	-----	56.1	60.7	52.9	--------	92.7	-----	-----	74.5
1931	77.5	77.5	-----	-----	-----	-----	-----	58.5	59.0	58.1	--------	93.1	-----	-----	68.9
1930	74.3	68.9	-----	-----	-----	-----	-----	52.7	56.9	49.6	--------	81.3	-----	-----	71.0
1929	72.5	61.6	-----	-----	-----	-----	-----	52.5	55.4	50.4	--------	80.8	-----	-----	72.9
1928	69.7	65.2	-----	-----	-----	-----	-----	45.2	44.1	46.2	--------	80.2	-----	-----	72.8
1927	66.2	60.7	-----	-----	-----	-----	-----	44.5	44.2	44.8	--------	76.1	-----	-----	69.3
1926	64.5	64.1	-----	-----	-----	-----	-----	45.8	45.6	45.9	--------	71.8	-----	-----	64.2
1925	62.8	61.9	-----	-----	-----	-----	-----	41.6	39.6	43.4	--------	70.2	-----	-----	58.9
1924	58.9	65.0	-----	-----	-----	-----	-----	39.3	35.3	43.3	--------	66.5	-----	-----	60.0
1923	55.2	59.1	-----	-----	-----	-----	-----	36.7	32.3	41.4	--------	64.2	-----	-----	59.0
1922	56.2	--------	-----	-----	-----	-----	-----	33.0	26.7	40.8	--------	60.5	-----	-----	63.0
1921	51.3	47.4	-----	-----	-----	-----	-----	30.5	23.6	40.0	--------	51.5	-----	-----	59.3
1920	44.6	--------	-----	-----	-----	-----	-----	27.2	18.2	45.8	--------	51.3	-----	-----	62.5
1919	42.1	48.3	-----	-----	-----	-----	-----	27.4	19.5	41.0	--------	49.0	-----	-----	60.3
1914	42.2	--------	-----	-----	-----	-----	-----	--------	--------	--------	--------	--------	-----	-----	--------
1909	36.6	--------	-----	-----	-----	-----	-----	--------	--------	--------	--------	--------	-----	-----	--------

NA Not available.

Series **W 30–54.** Indexes of Output Per Man-Hour for Production Workers, Selected Industries: 1909 to 1970—Con.

Year	Glass containers	Cement, hydraulic	Concrete products	Steel	Primary copper, lead, and zinc	Primary aluminum	Metal cans	Year	Steel	Chemicals	Lumber and timber	Motor vehicles	News- papers and periodicals	Blast furnaces
	44	45	46	47	48	49	49a		47	50	51	52	53	54
			1967 = 100					1947 = 100			1939 = 100			
1970	105.0	109.3	109.0	102.8	111.4	109.8	106.7	1950	111.9					
1969	109.1	111.9	110.3	104.8	113.8	104.8	107.7	1949	102.8					
1968	106.5	110.2	109.7	104.6	112.8	95.6	104.6	1948	100.4					
1967	100.0	100.0	100.0	100.0	100.0	100.0	100.0	1947	100.0					
1966	97.4	99.4	100.2	101.3	111.6	100.7	96.7	1946						
1965	97.7	94.4	93.5	98.7	113.1	97.0	95.6	1945					88.7	
1964	91.9	91.4	91.0	94.8	110.2	94.4	92.2	1944			96.0		87.5	
1963	89.3	86.8	85.9	92.1	106.4	93.2	89.9	1943			95.1		101.4	
1962	86.5	80.9	75.8	89.6	104.8	90.4	90.3	1942			98.1		105.7	
1961	83.1	76.0	74.5	85.4	99.0	87.5	93.8	1941	87.2		105.5		106.2	
1960	81.8	68.2	72.7	82.3	94.4	83.0	88.8	1940	82.3	95.9	111.7	101.3	103.8	113.9
1959	83.8	68.2	76.0	87.7	86.7	78.6	86.7	1939	79.3	100.0	100.0	100.0	100.0	100.0
1958	79.2	64.2	77.4	78.4	91.4	68.2	84.3	1938	67.2	89.6	87.6	99.7	92.8	68.2
1957	81.4	61.2	77.8	81.6	90.7	59.7	80.0	1937	65.9	91.3	82.4	100.4	93.0	98.7
1956	81.5	62.5	78.6	82.3	89.1	58.8	81.0	1936	64.7	88.5	84.9	102.1	93.7	101.2
1955	81.2	59.5	71.9	82.4	88.6	56.3	77.9	1935	62.9	84.1	90.8	99.5	92.1	86.4
1954	78.5	56.7	68.4	74.1	80.7	50.5	73.7	1934	58.6	76.0	89.5	85.2	85.4	68.7
1953	79.1	50.7	64.0	76.0	78.6	44.6	71.5	1933	59.5	86.7	86.1	83.8	75.3	67.8
1952	74.0	45.9	62.1	75.0	79.5	45.6	69.2	1932	55.4	85.7	79.6	69.4	74.4	51.2
1951	74.6	45.3	58.3	72.8	78.0	46.0	69.4	1931	53.0	81.3	90.6	79.6	75.4	83.3
1950	77.4	43.6	55.5	72.5	75.8	47.5	70.2	1930	54.7	72.6	78.5	89.1	74.3	98.8
1949	69.9	43.3	48.0	66.8	69.3	43.0	63.8	1929	57.8	72.1	82.4	84.2	77.3	105.5
1948	(NA)	(NA)	(NA)	65.1	(NA)	(NA)	(NA)	1928	57.5	65.9	78.2	70.6	78.6	92.5
1947	77.4	37.8	39.6	64.7	63.4	42.4	60.1	1927	50.9	64.2	79.4	66.8	75.7	80.4
1939	59.7	39.8	(NA)	(NA)	61.6	(NA)	(NA)	1926	50.3	61.1	76.4	66.1	77.5	82.0
								1925	48.9	51.2	76.5	62.5	69.0	77.5
								1924	43.1	45.9	72.7	59.6	65.0	62.0
								1923	42.4	46.9	71.4	58.8	63.2	67.7
								1922	43.8	43.5	67.5	51.5	59.4	64.7
								1921	34.3	43.5	84.4	47.8	51.8	55.1
								1920	37.7	49.6	75.6	39.1	51.9	59.7
								1919	29.5	29.9	79.0	35.9	43.8	43.5

NA Not available.

Series **W 55–66.** Indexes of Output Per Worker and Output Per Man-Hour in Transportation, Distribution, Gas and Electric Utilities, and Nonfinancial Corporations: 1869 to 1970

Year	Transportation (NBER), output per worker					Distribution (NBER)		Indexes of output (BLS)				
	Transpor- tation	Railroads	Pipelines, etc.	Waterways	Airlines	Output per person	Output per man-hour	Air trans- portation, output per employee	Petroleum pipelines, output per employee	Railroad transpor- tation, output per man-hour	Gas and electric utilities, output per man-hour	Nonfinancial corpora- tions, output per man-hour
	55	56	57	58	59	60	61	62	63	64	65	66
			1958 = 100							1967 = 100		
1970								109.7	120.7	110.1	117.3	106.7
1969							[1] 142.1	107.2	113.5	109.2	113.8	105.5
1968							141.0	104.3	105.4	104.3	107.0	104.3
1967							135.5	100.0	100.0	100.0	100.0	100.0
1966	151.5	170.1	208.9	107.5	188.2	129.8	133.3	93.9	88.1	97.5	95.7	99.0
1965	142.5	158.9	193.1	111.5	170.6	126.1	127.7	83.7	78.6	90.8	89.2	96.5
1964	132.5	147.0	159.7	112.1	150.3	123.1	123.8	75.0	66.2	82.1	85.5	93.0
1963	125.0	136.9	146.0	112.1	136.3	119.1	118.8	68.2	60.3	77.1	79.5	88.8
1962	118.3	127.9	132.1	110.3	124.0	114.7	114.6	61.6	54.6	72.6	74.9	85.7
1961	111.5	119.2	124.8	102.9	110.8	108.4	108.3	55.4	51.9	68.2	69.4	81.1
1960	107.9	111.6	116.7	103.9	106.4	105.8	105.3	52.3	48.7	63.6	65.5	79.2
1959	106.0	107.4	111.8	100.1	109.6	106.0	105.4	51.9	45.7	61.2	61.5	78.1
1958	100.0	100.0	100.0	100.0	100.0	100.0	100.0	48.2	39.7	57.6	56.4	74.8
1957	94.9	96.1	98.5	105.5	98.4	99.0	99.3	46.6	39.0	54.8	53.7	73.8
1956	98.2	95.1	96.7	109.1	96.6	98.1	97.7	45.0	39.6	54.0	51.1	72.0
1955	94.6	89.5	86.6	107.6	96.3	97.9	96.9	43.9	34.8	51.6	47.2	71.5
1954	87.0	79.2	77.8	102.3	87.5	91.8	91.0	38.9	31.2	46.6	42.4	67.8
1953	84.5	77.2	71.5	96.6	78.8	89.9	89.3	35.2	28.4	44.8	39.6	65.6
1952	83.9	77.2	64.2	97.2	72.5	87.7	86.2	32.4	25.9	44.6	37.0	63.6
1951	85.0	78.5	62.9	102.1	71.0	86.8	84.8	31.1	25.0	44.4	34.7	63.3
1950	80.1	75.8	54.4	96.9	61.5	88.9	86.8	27.1	21.7	42.0	31.3	61.5
1949	78.3	71.9	44.1	89.4	51.8	82.3	80.8	23.4	18.0	36.7	28.1	57.2
1948	77.9	77.7	43.7	88.8	45.2	80.2	79.1	20.5	17.5	37.6	27.5	56.1
1947								18.2	16.5	38.3	26.2	
1939										27.9	15.8	

[1] Preliminary.

Series **W 55–66.** Indexes of Output Per Worker and Output Per Man-Hour in Transportation, Distribution, Gas and Electric Utilities, and Nonfinancial Corporations: 1869 to 1970—Con.

Year	Transportation (NBER), output per worker					Distribution (NBER)		Railroad transportation, output per man-hour (BLS)
	Transportation	Railroads	Pipelines, etc.	Waterways	Airlines	Output per person	Output per man-hour	
	55	56	57	58	59	60	61	64
	1929 = 100				1947 = 100	1929 = 100		1947 = 100
1953	255.4	178.6	379.5	206.8	172.5	124.5	157.3	118.0
1952	253.3	179.3	345.0	206.7	160.7			117.3
1951	258.8	181.7	334.5	222.6	157.9			116.7
1950	247.1	172.8	290.7	207.0	142.9			110.5
1949	224.3	160.6	239.6	178.4	123.2			96.9
1948	231.6	174.0	233.5	170.7	108.4	117.1	144.2	98.5
1947	223.8	176.1	221.2	178.1	100.0			100.0
1946	207.3	169.0	211.5		88.2			95.8
1945	225.7	195.5	233.2		95.3			103.6
1944	242.2	211.2	241.6		75.3			110.1
1943	250.7	215.8	216.5		57.2			112.1
1942	231.3	191.0	186.4		60.2			103.7
1941	187.4	151.6	176.8		69.6			85.7
1940	163.7	132.0	159.6	115.7	66.4			78.2
1939	154.2	123.8	157.1	102.0	60.2			74.4
1938	141.0	114.6	148.2	97.5	53.3			70.4
1937	140.5	119.3	141.1	105.9	54.6	99.8	113.5	71.0
1936	132.2	116.7		99.2	57.3			70.0
1935	117.4	103.8		85.8	51.7			66.2
1934	111.5	98.2		84.6	36.4			63.2
1933	104.4	93.5		85.5	33.3			62.7
1932	94.5	83.7		77.2	26.5			55.7
1931	96.8	90.8		85.6	27.3			57.1
1930	97.7	95.3		93.9	37.1			56.7
1929	100.0	100.0	100.0	100.0	22.6	100.0	100.0	56.7
1928	96.1	98.4						55.7
1927	91.4	94.3						53.1
1926	90.6	95.6						53.2
1925	86.2	92.6						51.5
1924	81.1	87.6						48.8
1923	80.3	88.1						47.5
1922	76.0	84.2						46.0
1921	69.3	76.7						44.2
1920	76.2	83.9						43.5
1919	73.6	81.0	40.5	73.8		92.6	89.6	42.9
1918	80.2	88.8						40.4
1917	81.8	91.4						40.9
1916	78.2	87.3		69.7				39.0
1915	72.2	80.6						
1914	65.3	71.2						
1913	65.5	71.2						
1912	64.3	70.2						
1911	61.7	67.2						
1910	62.5	68.2						
1909	62.3	68.2				95.3	85.8	
1908	59.3	64.5						
1907	59.6	64.4						
1906	60.4	65.6		62.9				
1905	59.1	64.1						
1904	56.5	61.2						
1903	56.0	60.5						
1902	56.6	61.4						
1901	56.4	61.7						
1900	56.5	62.2						
1899	55.8	61.5		46.7		90.5	73.7	
1889	42.3	47.5		30.8		82.1	66.0	
1879				18.9		93.0	75.0	
1869				18.1		59.4	47.8	

Series **W 67–81.** Index of Farm Production Per Man-Hour: 1910 to 1970

[**1967 = 100.** Index of farm output (production) divided by index of man-hours used]

Year	All farm work	Livestock and livestock products	Meat animals	Milk cows	Poultry	All crops	Feed grains	Hay and forage	Food grains	Vege-tables	Fruits and nuts	Sugar crops	Cotton	Tobacco	Oil crops
	67	**68**	**69**	**70**	**71**	**72**	**73**	**74**	**75**	**76**	**77**	**78**	**79**	**80**	**81**
1970	113	119	116	123	120	110	101	148	117	106	107	121	125	104	115
1969	112	112	110	115	112	112	109	145	113	106	109	115	117	98	114
1968	106	105	105	106	105	106	102	102	108	101	98	113	130	98	110
1967	100	100	100	100	100	100	100	100	100	100	100	100	100	100	100
1966	94	93	95	93	95	95	93	99	102	99	99	99	92	101	96	101
1965	91	87	90	87	87	92	92	96	101	99	95	88	101	95	100
1964	83	83	89	81	82	85	78	93	97	96	91	90	87	99	89
1963	80	77	83	74	73	82	77	92	90	97	87	97	78	97	94
1962	73	71	78	70	66	77	70	89	89	92	87	82	71	93	92
1961	70	67	74	65	61	73	64	89	86	93	78	82	61	88	90
1960	67	62	70	60	55	71	58	84	93	89	74	79	56	87	84
1959	62	59	68	57	50	66	52	81	77	88	74	75	52	81	82
1958	59	55	65	53	45	65	47	77	85	82	73	67	48	81	81
1957	53	51	63	49	39	56	40	71	62	80	69	67	44	77	69
1956	50	48	62	46	37	52	35	65	54	76	75	59	41	80	67
1955	47	46	62	43	32	48	31	63	50	70	75	53	39	75	60
1954	43	43	59	40	30	45	29	58	46	67	74	51	35	71	54
1953	41	41	58	39	27	43	27	63	43	64	70	49	33	67	51
1952	39	40	56	37	24	42	26	60	46	63	67	43	30	67	50
1951	36	39	56	36	23	38	23	58	38	59	65	39	28	67	46
1950	35	37	55	35	21	39	23	55	40	57	64	38	25	66	47
1940	21	27	50	25	15	22	10	30	21	40	51	27	17	56	18
1930	17	26	48	25	14	17	8	23	17	34	38	22	12	50	13
1920	15	24	45	22	13	17	8	24	11	32	38	18	12	52	10
1910	14	24	44	21	13	15	7	24	10	30	27	18	11	54	9

Chapter W

Copyrights, Patents, and Trademarks (Series W 82-108)

W 82-95. Copyright registrations, by type, 1870-1970.

Source: **Series W 82-91, W 93-95**, U.S. Library of Congress, *Annual Report of the Librarian of Congress* and *Annual Report of the Register of Copyrights*, various issues. **Series W 92**, U.S. Patent Office, 1874-1896, *Annual Report of the Commissioner of Patents*; 1897-1940, unpublished data; 1941-1970, U.S. Library of Congress, *Annual Report of the Librarian of Congress*, various issues.

Additional detail for some series is shown in the source volumes.

Figures are on a calendar-year basis for 1870-1896, and on a fiscal-year basis thereafter. Prior to 1870, copyright claims were entered at Federal District Courts. For additional information on this period, see Martin A. Roberts, *Records in the Copyright Office Deposited by the United States District Courts Covering the Period 1790-1870*, Washington, D.C., 1939.

The term "copyright" may be defined as the right to prevent copying. It has come to mean that body of exclusive rights granted by Federal statute to authors for the protection of their writings. It includes the exclusive right to print, reprint, publish, copy, and vend the copyrighted work; to make other versions of the work; and, with certain limitations, to make recordings of the work and to perform the work in public. The Copyright Office is primarily an office of record, and registers claims if the provisions of the law and the regulations have been complied with. A certificate is issued to the applicant upon completion of each registration.

The first law, 1790, applied only to maps, charts, and books. Subsequent amendments provided for prints (1802); musical compositions (1831); dramatic compositions with the right of public performance (1856); photographs (1865); paintings, drawings, sculpture, and models or designs for works of the fine arts (1870); performance rights in music (1897); motion pictures and photoplays (1912); and performance rights in nondramatic literary works (1952). The original term of copyright was 14 years, with the privilege of renewal for 14 years. In 1831, the first term was increased to 28 years, and in 1909, the renewal term was also increased to 28 years. Before 1891, only citizens or residents of the United States could obtain copyrights. The Act of 1891 extended the privilege to citizens of countries with which the United States had reciprocal copyright agreements. Claims in works by citizens of States adhering to international copyright conventions to which the United States is a party (Mexico City, 1902; Buenos Aires, 1910; and Universal Copyright Convention, 1952) may also be registered, as well as works first published in States adhering to the Universal Copyright Convention.

Detailed information on the various classes of works may be obtained by writing to the Register of Copyrights, Library of Congress, Washington, D.C. 20540.

W 82, total registrations. For 1870-1940, the figures shown in this series exclude commercial prints and labels; see text for series W 92, below.

W 83-85, books, pamphlets, and periodicals. Serial publications issued at regular intervals of less than a year are considered periodicals; otherwise, they are considered books.

W 87, dramatic or dramatico-musical compositions. For 1909 and earlier years, this series pertains only to dramatic compositions.

W 92, commercial prints and labels. Registration of commercial prints and labels in the Patent Office was first authorized by the Act of June 18, 1874. Jurisdiction was transferred to the Register of Copyrights by Public Law 244, 53 Stat. 1142, effective June 30, 1940.

W 94, miscellaneous. Includes lectures, sermons, addresses; reproductions of works of art; drawings or plastic works of a scientific or technical character; and photographs.

W 96-106. General note.

A patent is a grant by the Government to the inventor, his heirs or assigns, of the right to exclude others from making, using, or selling the invention patented. Patents can be obtained for any new and useful machine, manufacture, composition of matter or process, or any new and useful improvement thereof, subject to the requirements and conditions of the law, United States Code, Title 35, Patents. An invention is "useful" if it has lawful purpose and is operative. Since 1946, inventions useful solely in the utilization of fissionable material or atomic energy for atomic weapons have been unpatentable. If the subject matter patented can be used without infringement of the prior rights of others or violation of any applicable statute, the patent, in effect, gives its owner the exclusive right to make, use, or sell the subject of the patent. The subject matter covered by a patent must be sufficiently new as to be not obvious to one skilled in the art to which it relates.

Patents on inventions have been issued by the Federal Government since April 10, 1790. Both the fees charged and the term of patents have been changed occasionally by law. A total fee of $30 was charged on application in 1793; now (1973) a base fee of $65 is charged. Whereas no charge was made prior to 1861 when a patent was granted, modern-day applicants pay an additional minimum fee of $110 at that time. Other smaller fees incidental to the processing of applications may also be charged by the Patent Office.

For 1790-1861, the term of a patent was 14 years. From 1836 until the patents granted in 1861 expired, patents could be extended for an additional 7 years upon application by the patentee and approval of a special board or the Commissioner. About 5 percent of the patents issued during the latter part of this period were extended in this manner. Since 1861, the term of patents on inventions has been fixed at 17 years with extensions possible only by special act of Congress. The number of such extensions has been negligible.

From February 21, 1793, to July 4, 1836, patents were granted on demand of the applicant, upon compliance with the formal requirements, without examination as to novelty and other requirements. Consequently, statistics of patents on inventions issued during this period are more comparable to subsequent statistics of *applications* for patents on inventions (series W 96) than to subsequent statistics of *patents* on inventions. Different sources for patent statistics during this period show minor discrepancies.

Since July 4, 1836, the Patent Office has examined applications for novelty and for compliance with the requirements of the statute and not all applications which are filed become patents. See Department of Commerce, *The Story of the United States Patent Office*, for a brief account of the development of the patent laws; and *General Information Concerning Patents* (revised periodically), for an outline of the patent law.

Other kinds of patents issued are design patents, botanical plant patents, and reissued patents. Reissued patents are patents which are issued to replace another patent to correct some error, and hence have no significance in most uses of patent statistics. They are not shown in this compilation, although reissue applications are included in series W 96 for some years for which they could not be separated. Reissued patents were numbered separately from 1838; the number of the first such patent issued in 1972 is 27,264.

Statistics on various phases of patents on invention are available in various sources. Analyses of aggregate patent statistics appear in Barkev S. Sanders, "The Course of Invention," *Journal of the Patent Office Society*, October 1936; Joseph Rossman and Barkev Sanders, "The Patent Utilization Study," *The Patent, Trademark, and Copyright Journal*, June 1957; Alfred B. Stafford, *Trends of Inven-*

tion in Material Culture, Ph.D. thesis, University of Chicago, 1950; Alfred B. Stafford, "Is the Rate of Invention Declining?" *American Journal of Sociology*, May 1952; Jacob Schmookler, *Invention and Economic Growth*, Harvard University Press, 1966. Statistics of patents issued by industry or by field of technology appear in Simon Kuznets, *Secular Movements in Production and Prices*, Boston, 1930; R. K. Merton, "Fluctuations in the Rate of Industrial Invention," *Quarterly Journal of Economics*, May 1935; *Trends of Invention in Material Culture*, cited above; and *Invention and Economic Growth*, cited above. The basic data used in this work, two volumes bound in one, are on file in the Library of the U.S. Patent Office under the title "Statistics of Patents Classified by Industry, United States, 1837–1957".

Statistics of patents issued by State and country of residence of the inventor appear in the Patent Office, *Annual Report of the Commissioner of Patents*, and in the Bureau of the Census, *Statistical Abstract of the United States*. Since 1966, the annual reports have also included applications filed by country of residence, beginning with calendar year 1961.

International patent statistics are given in P. J. Federico, "Historical Patent Statistics, 1791–1961," *Journal of the Patent Office Society*, vol. 46, Feb. 1964, pages 89–171, which also contains a description of the sources of the statistics for various countries, including the United States. *The English Language International Periodical Industrial Property* (World Intellectual Property Organization, Geneva), published since 1960, has an annual statistical supplement in each December issue, which gives data for a large number of countries including, for many, applications filed by and patents granted to residents of other countries, and additional statistics for the United States.

W 96–98. Patent applications filed on inventions, designs, and botanical plants, 1836–1970.

Source: U.S. Patent Office, 1836–1839, *The Story of the United States Patent Office, 1790–1956*; 1840–1925, *Annual Report of the Commissioner of Patents*; 1926–1970, unpublished data.

Series W 96 involves a slight element of double counting prior to 1940. Before a change in the law on August 5, 1939, made it impossible, an applicant could permit his initial application to lapse and then file a new application covering the same invention. Possibly 2 to 4 percent of the applications filed before 1940 were of this character. For years prior to 1880, series W 96 includes design applications, and for years prior to 1877, also includes reissue applications.

W 99. Total patents issued on inventions, 1790–1970.

Source: 1790–1925, U.S. Patent Office, *Annual Report of the Commissioner of Patents*; 1926–1970, unpublished data.

Patents for inventions are numbered serially, the number of the first patent issued in 1972 being 3,631,539. This numbering system, although instituted later, began with the first patent issued after the Patent Act of July 4, 1836. Most sources of patent statistics give, as the annual number of patents issued, the numbers derived by subtracting the serial numbers of the first patent in each year. However, some serial numbers were not used and are blank; that is, there may not be any patent corresponding to a particular number. This may arise when an application scheduled to be patented, with the patent number assigned, is withdrawn for some reason at a time when it is too late to assign that number to some other case. The blank numbers averaged 26 per year for 1939–1955, but only 7.5 per year for 1961–1970. Beginning with the 1970 edition, the Annual Patent Index includes a listing of the blank numbers, for the period 1920–1970. Through 1971 there were 2,998 blank numbers. In the present series the number of blank numbers has been deducted in each year for which it could be ascertained. Therefore, the statistics of patents on inventions issued since 1836 may run a fraction of a percent below those appearing in some issues of the *Annual Report of the Commissioner of Patents* and in *Historical Statistics of the United*

States, 1789–1945. Reissued patents are not shown in this compilation.

Patents granted in a given year cannot be compared with applications filed in the same year since there is a variable lag between the time of applying and the time of issuing a patent. During the last 10 years this lag varied between 2 years and 6 months and 3 years and 3 months as the average time for issuing patents. In addition, variations in the number of patents issued in a given year may be due to administrative problems such as the loss or addition of examining personnel, or rearrangement of printing schedules.

W 100–103. Patents on inventions issued to individuals, to U.S. and foreign corporations, and to the U.S. Government, 1901–1970.

Source: 1901–1935, U.S. Patent Office, unpublished data; 1936–1955, P. J. Federico, *Distribution of Patents Issued to Corporations, 1939–1955*, Washington, D.C., 1957, Study No. 3, table 6 (a report prepared for the Senate Subcommittee on Patents, Trademarks, and Copyrights); 1956–1970, U.S. Patent Office, unpublished data.

Statistics on patents issued to U.S. and foreign corporations are actual counts for 1931–1937, 1955, and 1961–1970; for the other years they are estimates based on samples. Statistics of patents issued to the U.S. Government are based on actual count. This figure does not include patents issued to the Alien Property Custodian during and after World War II. Patents assigned after grant are not included. The patents issued to individuals are obtained by subtraction from the total.

W 104. Patents issued on designs, 1842–1970.

Source: U.S. Patent Office, *Annual Report of the Commissioner of Patents*, and unpublished data.

Designs became patentable in 1842 and relate to the appearance, not to the structure or use, of articles of manufacture. The term for design patents was initially set at 7 years. Since 1861, the term has been 3½, 7, or 14 years, at the discretion of the applicant. Fees payable vary with the term. Design patents are numbered separately. The number of the first design patent issued in 1972 is 222,801.

W 105. Patents issued on botanical plants, 1931–1970.

Source: U.S. Patent Office, unpublished data.

Botanical plants became subject to patents for the first time in 1930. Patentable plants are those which are asexually reproduced—distinct and new varieties of plants other than tuber-propagated plants. The term and fees for plant patents are the same as for patents on inventions. Plant patents are numbered separately from the other patents. The number of the first plant patent issued in 1972 is 3,063.

W 106. Patents issued to residents of foreign countries, 1836–1970.

Source: U.S. Patent Office, *Annual Report of the Commissioner of Patents*, and unpublished data.

The volume of patents issued to citizens of foreign countries was influenced in the early years of the patent system by discriminatory legislation. For 1800–1836, only aliens who had resided in the United States for 2 years and who had declared their intention of becoming citizens could apply for U.S. patents. For 1836–1861, aliens paid higher fees than citizens on a theory of reciprocity. Discrimination based on nationality was eliminated in 1861.

This series is based on residence and not on citizenship. It includes patents on inventions, designs, and botanical plants. Separate statistics on components are not available except for recent years. For the 7 years 1951–1957, foreign residents received 12.6 percent of invention patents, 3.3 percent of design patents, and 12.5 percent of the plant patents. For the period 1964–1970, foreign residents received 22.4 percent of invention patents, 7.0 percent of design patents, and 13.5 percent of the plant patents.

W 107–108. Trademarks registered and renewed, 1870–1970.

Source: U.S. Patent Office, *Annual Report of the Commissioner of Patents*, and unpublished data.

A trademark is a symbol—a picture, word, or phrase—applied by a manufacturer or merchant to distinguish his goods from those of others. Trademark rights are acquired by adoption of a mark and use of it on the goods in trade. The Federal law provides for the registration in the Patent Office of such marks which are used in interstate and foreign commerce. Applications for registration are examined and registration may be refused if the mark is of a character-prohibited registration (national emblems, deceptive marks, purely descriptive marks, etc.) or if it conflicts with a prior registered mark. Federal registration does not create ownership, but only gives additional advantages to the owner. See Department of Commerce, *General Information Concerning Trademarks*, (revised periodically), for an outline of the requirements for registering a trademark.

The first Federal trademark law, that of 1870, was based on the patent and copyright clause of the Constitution instead of the interstate and foreign commerce clause, and was held unconstitutional in 1879. The Trademark Act of 1881 was limited to marks used in foreign commerce. The Act of 1905 included marks used in interstate commerce as well. An Act of 1920 permitted registration of a secondary class of marks not previously registrable. A completely new Act of 1946, effective 1947, provides for a Principal Register on which marks of the type registrable under the Acts of 1881 and 1905 could be registered, and a Supplemental Register on which marks of the type registrable under the Act of 1920 could be registered. Registrations under the Act of 1946 are for a term of 20 years, with renewal possible for successive 20-year terms. Registrations issued under the Acts of 1881 and 1905 remain in force for their unexpired terms and may be renewed in the same manner as registrations under the Act of 1946. Registrations under the Act of 1920 cannot be renewed unless renewal is required to support a Foreign Registration and in such case may be renewed on the Supplemental Register in the same manner as registrations under the Act of 1946.

Series W 82–95.   Copyright Registrations, by Type: 1870 to 1970

Year	Total copyright registrations [1]	Books and pamphlets		Periodicals	Contributions to periodicals [2]	Dramatic or dramatico-musical compositions	Musical compositions	Maps	Works of art, models, or designs	Prints and pictorial illustrations	Commercial prints and labels [1]	Motion pictures	Miscellaneous	Renewals, all classes [3]
		Total [2]	Printed abroad in foreign language											
	82	83	84	85	86	87	88	89	90	91	92	93	94	95
1970	316,466	88,432	----------	83,862	1,943	3,352	88,949	1,921	6,807	3,373	5,255	2,545	6,711	23,316
1969	301,258	83,603	----------	80,706	1,676	3,213	83,608	2,024	5,630	2,837	4,798	2,364	5,132	25,667
1968	303,451	85,189	----------	81,773	2,026	3,214	80,479	2,560	5,236	3,109	5,972	2,922	5,197	25,774
1967	294,406	80,910	----------	81,647	1,696	3,371	79,291	2,840	4,855	2,740	5,862	2,696	4,999	23,499
1966	286,866	77,300	----------	77,963	1,717	3,215	76,805	1,933	5,164	3,081	6,285	2,889	5,050	25,464
1965	293,617	76,098	----------	78,307	2,095	3,343	80,881	3,262	5,735	2,927	7,509	3,752	6,188	23,520
1964	278,987	71,618	----------	74,611	2,529	3,039	75,256	1,955	5,915	3,325	7,013	4,107	7,045	22,574
1963	264,845	68,445	----------	69,682	2,535	2,730	72,583	2,002	6,262	2,594	7,318	4,216	6,314	20,164
1962	254,776	66,571	----------	67,523	2,993	2,813	67,612	2,073	6,043	2,889	7,167	3,641	6,177	19,274
1961	247,014	62,415	----------	66,251	3,398	2,762	65,500	2,010	5,557	2,955	7,564	4,654	5,754	18,194
1960	243,926	60,034	----------	64,204	3,306	2,445	65,558	1,812	5,271	3,343	8,142	3,457	4,961	21,393
1959	241,735	55,967	----------	62,246	3,042	2,669	70,707	1,865	4,593	3,186	8,786	3,724	3,417	21,533
1958	238,935	57,242	----------	60,691	3,355	2,754	66,515	1,614	5,019	3,413	8,924	3,199	3,616	22,593
1957	225,807	53,503	2,915	59,724	3,214	2,764	59,614	2,084	4,557	3,409	8,687	3,198	3,580	21,473
1956	224,908	53,942	3,115	58,576	3,490	3,329	58,330	2,242	4,168	3,306	9,491	3,012	4,096	20,926
1955	224,732	54,414	3,694	59,448	3,746	3,493	57,527	2,013	3,456	3,793	10,505	2,650	4,168	19,519
1954	222,665	51,763	3,697	60,667	3,294	3,527	58,213	2,390	3,170	4,103	10,784	2,556	3,690	18,558
1953	218,506	49,059	3,875	59,371	3,288	3,884	59,302	2,541	3,029	3,126	12,025	2,175	3,605	17,101
1952	203,705	46,083	3,382	56,509	3,320	3,766	51,538	2,422	3,305	2,891	11,770	2,079	3,332	16,690
1951	200,354	47,125	3,536	55,129	3,408	3,992	48,319	1,992	3,428	3,590	11,981	2,149	2,869	16,372
1950	210,564	50,456	3,710	55,436	4,438	4,427	52,309	1,638	4,013	4,309	13,320	1,895	3,792	14,531
1949	201,190	47,422	2,644	54,163	4,140	5,159	48,210	2,314	3,281	4,358	13,233	1,763	3,472	13,675
1948	238,121	48,811	2,545	59,699	5,963	6,128	72,339	1,456	3,938	6,686	10,619	1,631	5,035	15,816
1947	230,215	49,525	3,970	58,340	4,400	6,456	68,709	1,779	4,044	6,506	9,674	2,084	5,497	13,201
1946	202,144	42,356	3,513	48,289	5,504	5,356	63,367	1,304	3,094	5,384	7,975	2,024	4,975	12,516
1945	178,848	35,688	111	45,763	4,856	4,714	57,835	857	1,821	2,634	7,403	1,735	4,175	11,367
1944	169,269	35,952	82	44,364	4,730	4,875	52,087	494	1,743	2,426	5,953	1,872	4,526	10,247
1943	160,795	36,889	156	42,995	3,568	3,687	48,348	737	1,649	2,317	5,385	1,767	3,803	9,650
1942	182,232	45,157	651	45,145	5,119	4,803	50,023	1,217	2,110	2,917	7,162	2,219	4,872	11,488
1941	180,647	46,040	1,553	42,207	5,845	5,010	49,135	1,398	2,187	3,058	7,152	1,798	6,475	10,342
1940	176,997	50,125	2,504	40,173	13,926	6,450	37,975	1,622	3,081	4,699	2,470	1,611	7,128	10,207
1939	173,135	49,901	4,086	38,307	9,843	6,800	40,961	1,566	3,419	3,126	2,315	1,757	7,278	10,177
1938	166,248	49,156	3,646	39,249	8,195	7,369	35,334	1,200	3,330	3,010	2,415	1,889	7,576	9,940
1937	154,424	45,504	3,841	38,053	7,551	7,176	31,821	1,198	3,002	3,875	2,506	1,751	5,904	8,589
1936	156,962	47,667	3,853	38,418	7,082	6,569	33,250	1,444	2,977	4,117	2,306	1,708	5,550	8,180
1935	142,031	43,134	3,283	36,351	7,875	6,501	27,459	1,343	3,082	3,120	2,408	1,695	4,810	6,661
1934	139,047	40,658	3,593	35,819	7,740	5,945	27,001	1,250	5,447	2,834	2,170	1,513	3,851	6,989
1933	137,424	40,694	4,232	35,464	9,290	6,359	26,846	1,178	2,667	3,143	1,937	1,607	3,765	6,411
1932	151,735	46,576	4,784	39,177	10,489	6,296	29,264	1,774	2,590	3,354	1,975	1,539	4,788	5,888
1931	164,642	46,855	4,339	42,415	12,698	5,784	31,488	2,940	2,551	5,813	2,465	1,926	6,174	5,998
1930	172,792	47,248	4,664	43,939	14,587	5,734	32,129	2,554	2,734	9,170	2,333	2,195	6,565	5,937
1929	161,959	44,040	3,868	44,161	13,574	4,594	27,023	2,232	2,486	9,873	2,707	2,319	6,709	4,948
1928	193,914	50,095	4,405	47,364	26,986	4,473	26,897	2,862	3,152	14,272	2,801	2,304	10,062	5,447
1927	184,000	47,801	3,777	41,475	29,335	4,475	25,282	2,677	2,575	14,833	2,856	1,915	8,946	4,686
1926	177,635	73,455	3,430	41,169	----------	4,130	25,484	2,647	3,173	13,382	2,544	1,623	8,543	4,029
1925	165,848	65,670	3,266	40,880	----------	4,015	25,548	2,222	2,950	10,827	2,015	1,765	8,662	3,309
1924	162,694	61,982	2,306	39,806	----------	3,409	26,734	2,265	2,873	11,110	2,016	1,473	9,549	3,433
1923	148,946	55,561	2,886	37,104	----------	3,778	24,900	2,042	2,790	10,400	2,141	1,277	8,405	2,689
1922	138,633	46,307	1,309	35,471	----------	3,418	27,381	1,930	2,954	9,139	2,101	1,487	7,820	2,726
1921	135,280	41,245	1,134	34,074	----------	3,217	31,054	1,647	2,762	9,362	1,485	1,721	7,992	2,206

See footnotes at end of table.

Series W 82–95. Copyright Registrations, by Type: 1870 to 1970—Con.

Year	Total copy-right regis-trations[1]	Books and pamphlets Total[2]	Printed abroad in foreign language	Periodicals	Contributions to periodicals[2]	Dramatic or dramatico-musical compositions	Musical compositions	Maps	Works of art, models, or designs	Prints and pictorial illustrations	Commercial prints and labels[1]	Motion pictures	Miscellaneous	Renewals, all classes[3]
	82	83	84	85	86	87	88	89	90	91	92	93	94	95
1920	126,562	39,090	939	28,935	--------	2,906	29,151	1,498	2,115	10,945	780	1,714	8,096	2,112
1919	113,003	37,710	855	25,083	--------	2,293	26,209	1,207	1,901	9,997	768	1,429	5,268	1,906
1918	106,728	33,617	636	25,822	--------	2,711	21,849	1,269	1,858	9,161	708	1,838	6,746	1,857
1917	111,438	33,552	914	26,467	--------	3,067	20,115	1,529	2,247	11,514	1,123	2,720	8,235	1,992
1916	115,967	32,897	1,276	26,553	--------	3,223	20,644	1,612	2,220	12,722	1,235	3,240	11,228	1,628
1915	115,193	31,926	1,843	24,938	--------	3,797	21,406	1,772	2,965	12,935	1,083	2,950	11,178	1,326
1914	123,154	31,891	2,860	24,134	--------	3,957	28,493	1,950	3,021	15,438	1,059	2,148	10,891	1,231
1913	119,495	29,572	2,369	23,002	--------	3,700	26,292	2,011	2,871	16,591	918	953	13,438	1,065
1912	120,931	29,286	2,294	22,580	--------	3,767	26,777	2,158	3,224	17,639	893	--------	14,151	1,349
1911	115,198	26,970	1,707	23,393	--------	3,415	25,525	2,318	3,355	14,269	757	--------	15,025	928
1910	109,074	24,740	1,351	21,608	--------	3,911	24,345	2,622	4,383	11,925	235	--------	14,533	1,007
1909	120,131	32,533	--------	21,195	--------	2,937	26,306	--------	--------	--------	1,010	--------	--------	--------
1908	119,742	30,191	--------	22,409	--------	2,382	28,427	--------	--------	--------	915	--------	--------	--------
1907	123,829	30,879	--------	23,078	--------	2,114	31,401	--------	--------	--------	985	--------	--------	--------
1906	117,704	29,261	--------	23,163	--------	1,879	26,435	--------	--------	--------	1,095	--------	--------	--------
1905	113,374	29,860	--------	22,591	--------	1,645	24,595	--------	--------	--------	1,373	--------	--------	--------
1904	103,130	27,824	--------	21,496	--------	1,571	23,110	--------	--------	--------	1,301	--------	--------	--------
1903	97,979	27,466	--------	22,625	--------	1,608	21,161	--------	--------	--------	1,143	--------	--------	--------
1902	92,978	24,272	--------	21,071	--------	1,448	19,706	--------	--------	--------	913	--------	--------	--------
1901	92,351			(NA)	--------	(NA)	(NA)	--------	--------	--------	948	--------	--------	--------

Year	Total copyright regis-trations[1]	Periodicals	Dramatic or dramatico-musical compositions	Musical compositions	Maps	Commercial prints and labels[1]	Year	Total copyright regis-trations[1]	Periodicals	Dramatic or dramatico-musical compositions	Musical compositions	Commercial prints and labels[1]
	82	85	87	88	89	92		82	85	87	88	92
1900	94,798	(NA)	(NA)	(NA)	--------	775	1885	28,411	6,060	625	6,808	391
1899	80,968	(NA)	(NA)	(NA)	--------	448	1884	26,893	5,570	587	6,241	513
1898	75,545	(NA)	(NA)	(NA)	--------	89	1883	25,274	5,489	498	6,280	906
1897	75,000	(NA)	(NA)	(NA)	--------	35	1882	22,918	4,612	458	6,143	304
1896	72,470	12,892	907	20,951	1,198	33	1881	21,075	4,339	415	5,578	202
1895	67,572	12,155	827	18,563	1,432	3	1880	20,686	4,369	496	5,628	203
1894	62,762	12,149	465	18,460	1,922	4	1879	18,125	3,608	414	4,688	355
1893	58,956	11,094	580	16,273	1,814	2	1878	15,798	3,424	372	3,772	492
1892	54,735	10,327	813	14,649	(NA)	6	1877	15,758	--------	--------	--------	392
1891	48,908	9,477	746	11,688	1,912	137	1876	14,882	--------	--------	--------	472
1890	42,794	8,164	715	9,132	--------	304	1875	15,927	--------	--------	--------	232
1889	40,985	7,646	620	8,958	--------	319	1874	16,283	--------	--------	--------	232
1888	38,225	7,086	589	8,066	--------	327	1873	15,352	--------	--------	--------	--------
1887	35,083	6,708	536	7,744	--------	380	1872	14,164	--------	--------	--------	--------
1886	31,241	6,089	672	7,514	--------	378	1871	12,688	--------	--------	--------	--------
							1870[4]	5,600	--------	--------	--------	--------

NA Not available.
[1] Prior to 1941, commercial prints and labels not included in total; jurisdiction moved to copyright office in 1940.
[2] Prior to 1927, contributions to periodicals included with books and pamphlets.
[3] Prior to 1941, excludes renewals of commercial prints and labels.
[4] July–December.

Series W 96–106. Patent Applications Filed and Patents Issued, by Type and by Patentee: 1790 to 1970

Year	Patent applications filed Inventions	Designs	Botanical plants	Patents issued — Inventions Total[1]	Individuals	Corporations U.S.	Corporations Foreign	U.S. Government[2]	Designs	Botanical plants	To residents of foreign countries
	96	97	98	99	100	101	102	103	104	105	106
1970	102,868	5,996	188	64,427	13,511	36,896	12,294	1,726	3,214	52	17,872
1969	98,386	5,496	111	67,557	14,772	38,847	12,188	1,750	3,335	103	17,573
1968	93,136	5,171	95	59,102	13,555	34,886	9,172	1,489	3,352	72	13,722
1967	87,872	4,744	103	65,652	15,647	38,353	9,895	1,757	3,165	85	14,711
1966	88,293	4,853	104	68,406	16,018	41,634	9,222	1,532	3,188	114	14,008
1965	94,632	5,413	105	62,857	16,063	37,158	8,096	1,540	3,424	120	12,782
1964	87,597	5,259	120	47,376	12,504	27,836	5,854	1,182	2,686	128	9,168
1963	85,724	4,968	145	45,679	12,525	26,632	5,501	1,021	2,965	129	8,736
1962	85,029	4,897	151	55,691	15,470	32,560	6,380	1,281	2,300	91	10,255
1961	83,100	4,714	107	48,368	13,383	28,351	5,161	1,473	2,487	108	8,384
1960	79,590	4,525	131	47,170	13,069	28,187	4,670	1,244	2,543	116	7,850
1959	78,594	4,879	114	52,408	16,017	29,888	5,081	1,422	2,768	101	8,340
1958	77,495	4,923	134	48,330	15,706	27,116	4,230	1,278	2,374	120	7,395
1957	74,197	4,714	101	42,744	15,154	23,255	3,372	963	2,362	129	6,282
1956	74,906	4,824	104	46,817	16,643	25,502	3,690	982	2,977	101	6,646

See footnotes at end of table.

Series **W 96-106.**   Patent Applications Filed and Patents Issued, by Type and by Patentee: 1790 to 1970—Con.

	Patent applications filed			Patents issued							
	Inventions	Designs	Botanical plants	Inventions					Designs	Botanical plants	To residents of foreign countries
Year				Total [1]	Individuals	Corporations		U. S. Government [2]			
						U. S.	Foreign				
	96	97	98	99	100	101	102	103	104	105	106
1955	77,188	5,764	118	30,432	11,914	16,084	1,744	689	2,713	103	4,065
1954	77,185	5,465	95	33,809	12,531	18,319	2,301	658	2,536	101	4,433
1953	72,284	5,450	99	40,468	16,284	21,230	2,294	658	2,713	78	4,331
1952	64,554	4,993	84	43,616	18,538	22,340	2,035	695	2,959	101	5,635
1951	60,438	4,279	71	44,326	19,192	22,305	2,163	659	4,163	58	4,888
1950	67,264	6,739	105	43,040	18,960	21,782	1,660	622	4,718	89	4,408
1949	67,592	6,998	70	35,131	14,957	18,536	1,127	485	4,450	93	3,105
1948	68,740	7,048	59	23,963	9,812	13,124	628	352	3,968	44	1,984
1947	75,443	7,644	92	20,139	7,784	11,448	669	155	2,102	52	1,617
1946	81,056	10,698	72	21,803	7,444	13,486	585	147	2,778	56	1,656
1945	67,846	8,066	52	25,695	8,981	15,665	580	87	3,524	17	2,112
1944	54,190	5,063	42	28,053	9,636	16,769	645	106	2,914	38	2,564
1943	45,493	2,986	41	31,054	11,654	18,022	524	48	2,228	47	2,625
1942	45,549	4,218	60	38,449	14,534	22,019	1,286	62	3,728	65	3,943
1941	52,339	7,203	67	41,109	16,322	22,632	2,112	43	6,486	62	5,311
1940	60,863	8,530	91	42,238	17,627	22,165	2,406	40	6,145	85	6,148
1939	64,093	7,137	76	43,073	18,583	21,800	2,640	50	5,592	45	6,338
1938	66,874	8,084	48	38,061	16,304	19,635	2,063	59	5,026	41	5,776
1937	65,324	7,207	45	37,683	15,995	19,831	1,824	33	5,136	55	5,638
1936	62,599	6,478	66	39,782	16,639	21,207	1,903	33	4,556	49	5,734
1935	58,117	5,728	72	40,618	17,757	20,821	2,018	22	3,864	45	5,980
1934	56,643	4,399	28	44,420	19,731	22,529	2,131	29	2,919	32	6,489
1933	56,558	3,600	27	48,774	22,713	23,667	2,343	51	2,411	33	7,170
1932	67,006	4,345	46	53,458	26,274	24,822	2,325	37	2,942	46	7,376
1931	79,740	4,190	37	51,756	26,618	23,149	1,961	28	2,935	5	6,897
1930	89,554	4,182	16	45,226	23,726	19,700	1,800	----------	2,710	----------	6,085
1929	89,752	4,520	----------	45,267	25,367	18,500	1,400	----------	2,905	----------	5,921
1928	87,603	4,761	----------	42,357	23,357	17,800	1,200	----------	3,182	----------	5,218
1927	87,219	4,473	----------	41,717	25,417	15,100	1,200	----------	2,387	----------	4,918
1926	81,365	4,343	----------	44,733	28,633	15,200	900	----------	2,597	----------	5,103
1925	80,208	4,082	----------	46,432	30,332	14,800	1,300	----------	2,819	----------	5,347
1924	87,987	3,635	----------	42,574	29,174	12,400	1,000	----------	2,670	----------	4,723
1923	76,783	3,550	----------	38,616	27,016	10,800	800	----------	1,927	----------	4,133
1922	83,962	4,763	----------	38,369	27,369	10,300	700	----------	1,609	----------	4,455
1921	87,467	5,596	----------	37,798	27,098	9,860	840	----------	3,265	----------	3,963
1920	81,915	4,660	----------	37,060	----------	----------	----------	----------	2,481	----------	3,762
1919	76,710	3,627	----------	36,797	----------	----------	----------	----------	1,521	----------	3,687
1918	57,347	2,234	----------	38,452	----------	----------	----------	----------	1,206	----------	2,883
1917	67,590	2,545	----------	40,935	----------	----------	----------	----------	1,505	----------	3,209
1916	68,075	2,684	----------	43,892	31,742	11,540	610	----------	1,745	----------	3,767
1915	67,138	2,734	----------	43,118	----------	----------	----------	----------	1,538	----------	4,334
1914	67,774	2,454	----------	39,892	----------	----------	----------	----------	1,711	----------	4,595
1913	68,117	2,060	----------	33,917	----------	----------	----------	----------	1,677	----------	4,212
1912	68,968	1,850	----------	36,198	----------	----------	----------	----------	1,341	----------	4,489
1911	67,370	1,534	----------	32,856	24,756	7,580	520	----------	1,004	----------	4,058
1910	63,293	1,155	----------	35,141	----------	----------	----------	----------	636	----------	3,719
1909	64,408	1,234	----------	36,561	----------	----------	----------	----------	679	----------	3,812
1908	60,142	1,131	----------	32,735	----------	----------	----------	----------	755	----------	3,338
1907	57,679	896	----------	35,859	----------	----------	----------	----------	589	----------	3,866
1906	55,471	806	----------	31,170	24,750	6,040	380	----------	620	----------	3,471
1905	54,034	781	----------	29,775	----------	----------	----------	----------	486	----------	3,292
1904	51,168	818	----------	30,258	----------	----------	----------	----------	553	----------	3,285
1903	49,289	770	----------	31,029	----------	----------	----------	----------	536	----------	3,763
1902	48,320	1,170	----------	27,119	----------	----------	----------	----------	639	----------	3,499
1901	43,973	2,361	----------	25,546	20,896	4,370	280	----------	1,729	----------	3,402
1900	39,673	2,225	----------	24,644	----------	----------	----------	----------	1,754	----------	3,483
1899	38,937	2,400	----------	23,278	----------	----------	----------	----------	2,137	----------	2,311
1898	33,915	1,843	----------	20,377	----------	----------	----------	----------	1,799	----------	2,752
1897	45,661	2,150	----------	22,067	----------	----------	----------	----------	1,620	----------	2,221
1896	42,077	1,828	----------	21,822	----------	----------	----------	----------	1,441	----------	2,027
1895	39,145	1,463	----------	20,856	----------	----------	----------	----------	1,108	----------	2,049
1894	36,987	1,357	----------	19,855	----------	----------	----------	----------	927	----------	2,166
1893	37,293	1,060	----------	22,750	----------	----------	----------	----------	899	----------	2,473
1892	29,514	1,130	----------	22,647	----------	----------	----------	----------	816	----------	2,051
1891	39,418	1,025	----------	22,312	----------	----------	----------	----------	835	----------	1,928
1890	39,884	1,046	----------	25,313	----------	----------	----------	----------	886	----------	2,105
1889	39,607	857	----------	23,324	----------	----------	----------	----------	723	----------	2,003
1888	34,713	971	----------	19,551	----------	----------	----------	----------	832	----------	1,536
1887	34,420	1,041	----------	20,403	----------	----------	----------	----------	948	----------	1,466
1886	35,161	645	----------	21,767	----------	----------	----------	----------	594	----------	1,489
1885	34,697	862	----------	23,285	----------	----------	----------	----------	769	----------	1,549
1884	34,192	1,230	----------	19,118	----------	----------	----------	----------	1,150	----------	1,284
1883	33,073	1,238	----------	21,162	----------	----------	----------	----------	1,017	----------	1,259
1882	30,270	948	----------	18,091	----------	----------	----------	----------	858	----------	1,135
1881	24,878	678	----------	15,500	----------	----------	----------	----------	565	----------	995
1880	21,761	634	----------	12,903	----------	----------	----------	----------	514	----------	786

See footnotes at end of table.

Series W 96–106. Patent Applications Filed and Patents Issued, by Type and by Patentee: 1790 to 1970—Con.

Year	Inventions, patent applications filed [3]	Patents issued: Inventions	Designs	To residents of foreign countries	Year	Inventions, patent applications filed [3]	Patents issued: Inventions	Designs	To residents of foreign countries
	96	99	104	106		96	99	104	106
1879	20,059	12,125	591	648	1857	4,771	2,674	113	45
1878	20,260	12,345	590	581	1856	4,960	2,302	107	31
1877	20,308	12,920	699	590	1855	4,435	1,881	70	41
1876	21,425	14,169	802	787	1854	3,328	1,755	57	35
1875	21,638	13,291	915	563	1853	2,673	844	86	26
1874	21,602	12,230	886	547	1852	2,639	885	109	20
1873	20,414	11,616	747	493	1851	2,258	752	90	17
1872	18,246	12,180	884	581	1850	2,193	883	83	20
1871	19,472	11,659	903	522	1849	1,955	984	49	17
1870	19,171	12,137	737	644	1848	1,628	583	46	14
1869	19,271	12,931	506	377	1847	1,531	495	60	21
1868	20,420	12,526	445	337	1846	1,272	566	59	19
1867	21,276	12,277	325	275	1845	1,246	473	17	12
1866	15,269	8,863	294	244	1844	1,045	478	12	20
1865	10,664	6,088	221	181	1843	819	493	14	8
1864	6,932	4,630	139	181	1842	761	488	1	11
1863	6,014	3,773	176	125	1841	847	490	---	21
1862	5,038	3,214	195	80	1840	765	458	---	19
1861	4,643	3,020	142	83	1839	[4]800	404	---	10
1860	7,653	4,357	183	49	1838	[4]900	514	---	17
1859	6,225	4,160	107	47	1837	[4]650	426	---	7
1858	5,364	3,455	102	28	1836	[4][5]400	[5]103	---	8

Year	Inventions, patents issued (99)	Year	Inventions, patents issued (99)	Year	Inventions, patents issued (99)	Year	Inventions, patents issued (99)	Year	Inventions, patents issued (99)
1836	[6]599	1826	323	1816	206	1807	99	1798	28
1835	752	1825	304	1815	173	1806	63	1797	51
1834	630	1824	228	1814	210	1805	57	1796	44
1833	586	1823	173	1813	181	1804	84	1795	12
1832	474	1822	200	1812	238	1803	97	1794	22
1831	573	1821	168	1811	215	1802	65	1793	20
1830	544	1820	155	1810	223	1801	44	1792	11
1829	447	1819	156	1809	203	1800	41	1791	33
1828	368	1818	222	1808	158	1799	44	1790	3
1827	331	1817	174						

[1] Since 1942, includes patents issued to Alien Property Custodian, not shown separately.
[2] Excludes patents issued to Alien Property Custodian.
[3] Applications for reissue included with inventions, 1836–1876; design applications included with inventions, 1836–1879.
[4] Estimate.　[5] From July 4 to end of year.　[6] To July 4.

Series W 107–108. Trademarks Registered and Renewed: 1870 to 1970

Year	Registered 107	Renewed 108	Year	Registered 107	Renewed 108	Year	Registered 107	Renewed 108	Year	Registered 107	Year	Registered 107
1970	21,745	6,076	1950	16,817	3,564	1930	13,246	1,661	1910	4,239	1890	1,415
1969	20,613	6,176	1949	15,968	3,788	1929	14,514	1,750	1909	4,184	1889	1,229
1968	21,528	4,646	1948	11,472	5,056	1928	14,133	2,049	1908	5,191	1888	1,059
1967	20,036	3,801	1947	8,976	6,139	1927	14,579	3,063	1907	7,878	1887	1,133
1966	20,259	3,585	1946	8,106	5,725	1926	14,955	4,273	1906	10,568	1886	1,029
1965	18,501	3,165	1945	7,490	4,210	1925	13,815	2,278	1905	4,490	1885	1,067
1964	20,087	2,702	1944	6,025	4,052	1924	15,727	227	1904	2,158	1884	1,021
1963	19,740	2,655	1943	5,595	3,835	1923	14,834	251	1903	2,186	1883	902
1962	17,023	2,809	1942	6,795	2,894	1922	12,793	254	1902	2,006	1882	947
1961	16,595	3,358	1941	8,530	2,765	1921	11,636	117	1901	1,928	1881	834
1960	18,434	3,933	1940	9,974	2,547	1920	10,268	73	1900	1,721	1880	349
1959	18,709	3,272	1939	10,521	1,398	1919	4,208	64	1899	1,649	1879	872
1958	15,351	3,070	1938	10,204	1,051	1918	4,061	38	1898	1,238	1878	1,455
1957	17,480	3,488	1937	11,242	1,524	1917	5,339	52	1897	1,671	1877	1,216
1956	20,753	3,756	1936	10,722	1,888	1916	6,791	55	1896	1,813	1876	959
1955	18,207	4,268	1935	10,886	1,874	1915	6,262	57	1895	1,829	1875	1,138
1954	15,946	3,491	1934	11,362	2,445	1914	6,817	48	1894	1,806	1874	559
1953	15,610	3,103	1933	9,130	1,671	1913	5,065	---	1893	1,677	1873	492
1952	16,172	3,419	1932	9,603	1,587	1912	5,020	---	1892	1,737	1872	491
1951	17,376	3,350	1931	11,400	1,643	1911	4,205	---	1891	1,762	1871	486
											1870	121

Chapter W

Research and Development (Series W 109-180)

W 109–180. General note.

Historical statistics on research and development expenditures and employment by various groups in the major sectors of the economy are of comparatively recent origin. Public interest in representing the input of research and development activity in terms of some widely used measure, such as funds expended or personnel employed, has been largely incidental to concern with major national issues. During the depression years of the 1930's this interest stemmed from the role that research played in the recovery of the economy. Groups such as the National Research Project of the Work Projects Administration (formerly the Works Progress Administration) and the National Resources Planning Board engaged in studies of the interrelationships among trends in research and development, technological change, unemployment, education, and other major economic and social factors. Their interest in measuring research and development was generally subsidiary to a larger preoccupation with such broad national issues as economic recovery, re-employment, and national planning. The research and development estimates which they published were intended to serve primarily as illustrative background materials.

The period of World War II and its aftermath dramatized the critical place of research and development in the Nation's military security program. Groups concerned with measuring research and development during this period included the Committee on Science and Public Welfare (Bowman Committee), the President's Scientific Research Board, and the Research and Development Board of the Department of Defense. Like the earlier groups, these organizations supplemented fragmentary data already on hand with special inquiries and analyses in order to develop background estimates on research and development trends.

The National Science Foundation, a Federal agency established in 1950, undertook as one of its functions the development of such factual data and related analyses on research and development. As a first step, the Foundation initiated an annual survey of Federal funds for research and development, starting with data on funds for scientific research and development at nonprofit institutions for fiscal 1951 and 1952 and moving thereafter to annual surveys of the funds comprising the "Federal Research and Development Budget."

In 1954, the National Science Foundation undertook the first effort to measure the volume of research and development activity, in terms of funds and personnel, through surveys of all major types of organizations in the several sectors of the economy which were known to be performing or financing this activity. Out of this effort grew a continuing Foundation program of surveys designed to facilitate preparation of annual estimates on funds and personnel employed in research and development by the major sectors of the economy. Before the National Science Foundation undertook its first surveys, there was no general agreement on such fundamental matters as the definition of research and development; the distinction between the conduct of research and development and such related activities as academic instruction or industrial production; the distinction between basic and applied research and development; and the major characteristics distinguishing various types of research organizations.

National estimates. National estimates of funds spent on the performance of research and development by the four major sectors of the economy have been made by the National Science Foundation for 1953–70. National estimates of funds received from various sources for the performance of research and development have also been made for 1953–70. These series appear in table B-1 of the National Science Foundation publication, *National Patterns of R&D Resources, 1953–72*, Funds and Manpower in the United States, (NSF 72–300). An analysis of intersectoral flows of transfers of funds for research and development for 1970 appears in table I, below. This table is based on information obtained in the National Science Foundation surveys of funds for research and development in 1970 as presented in table B-1.

The limitations described below indicate that table I should be considered a general approximation rather than an exact statement of the extent to which the different sectors are participating in the financing and performance of research and development.

Detailed information on the scope and limitations of the various surveys appears in the National Science Foundation publications listed below. Generally speaking, the National Science Foundation surveys seek full enumeration of the various segments. The exceptions are industrial firms and the smaller nonprofit institutions for which sampling procedures are employed.

The data in table I are derived basically from survey responses by *performers* of research and development as to how much they spent

Table I. Intersectoral Transfers of Funds Used for Performance of Research and Development: 1970

[In millions of dollars, except as indicated. Based on reports by performers]

Sources of funds, by sector	Research and development performers					Total	
	Federal Government agencies	Industry [1]	Universities and colleges [2]		Other nonprofit institutions [1]	Amount	Percent
			Total	Associated FFRDC's [3]			
Federal Government agencies	3,855	7,779	1,648	737	745	14,764	56.7
Industry		[4] 10,283	61		90	10,434	40.1
Universities and colleges			[4] 461			461	1.8
Other nonprofit institutions			165		[4] 223	388	1.5
Total	3,855	18,062	2,335	737	1,058	26,047	100.0
Percent	14.8	69.3	9.0	2.8	4.1		100.0

[1] Expenditures for Federally Funded Research and Development Centers (FFRDC's) administered by both industry and by nonprofit institutions are included in the totals of their respective sectors. FFRDC's are organizations exclusively or substantially financed by the Federal Government to meet a particular requirement or to provide major facilities for research and training purposes.

[2] Includes agricultural experiment stations.

[3] Federally Funded Research and Development Centers (FFRDC's) administered by individual universities and colleges and by university-consortia.

[4] Includes State and local government funds.

on this activity and where their funds originated. The estimates represent final through-transfers from source organizations financing research and development to performing organizations which ultimately used the funds. Every effort was made to net out intermediate transfers.

Research and development in these series consist of basic and applied research in the sciences (including medical sciences) and in engineering and activities in development, all defined below. In terms of fields, the natural sciences—life, physical, and engineering—as well as the social and psychological sciences are covered in the Federal, universities, and other nonprofit sectors. Industry coverage is limited, at present, to the natural sciences. Research and development excludes routine product testing, quality control, mapping surveys, collection of general-purpose statistics, experimental production, and activities concerned primarily with the dissemination of scientific information and the training of scientific manpower.

Research, which is made up of basic and applied, is systematic, intensive study directed toward fuller scientific knowledge of the subject studied.

Basic research. For three of the sectors—Federal Government, universities and colleges, and other nonprofit institutions—the definition of basic research stresses that it is directed toward increases of knowledge in science with ". . . the primary aim of the investigator being a fuller knowledge or understanding of the subject under study, rather than a practical application thereof." To take account of an individual industrial company's commercial goals, the definition for the industry sector is modified to indicate that basic research projects represent "original investigations for the advancement of scientific knowledge . . . which do not have specific commercial objectives, although they may be in fields of present or potential interest to the reporting company."

Applied research. The core definition in the NSF questionnaire sent to the universities and colleges is: "*Applied research is directed toward practical application of knowledge.*" Here again, the definition for the industry survey takes account of the characteristics of industrial organizations—it covers ". . . research projects which represent investigations directed to discovery of new scientific knowledge and which have specific commercial objectives with respect to either projects or processes." By this definition, applied research in industry differs from basic research chiefly in terms of objectives of the reporting company.

Development. The NSF survey concept of development may be summarized as ". . . the systematic use of scientific knowledge directed toward the production of useful materials, devices, systems or methods, including design and development of prototypes and processes."

Funds used for research and development refer to current operating costs, consisting of both direct and indirect costs including depreciation, insofar as this information is available to respondents. Capital expenditures are excluded by definition in both the industry and the other nonprofit sectors. Under the accounting practices of some Federal agencies, particularly the Department of Defense, data on the Federal R&D funds, which are available in detail only in terms of obligations rather than expenditures, do not include an allowance for depreciation but do include some obligations for capital items. A small amount of capital outlays is also included in the universities and colleges sector.

The National Science Foundation surveys include data on research and development by Federally Funded Research and Development Centers (FFRDC's). These are laboratories or similar research undertakings supported wholly or predominantly by the Federal Government but operated under contract by an industrial, university, or independent organization. Data relating to the performance of research and development at these centers are included within the appropriate sector in the estimates for 1956 and later years.

Several groups of organizations comprise the industry sector as represented in table I. Private industrial firms account for over 95 percent of the total funds for performance of research and development

in this sector. (Data for firms appear in series W 144–160.) The remaining groups are FFRDC's operated by industrial concerns, independent commercial laboratories, and engineering service firms.

The colleges and universities sector consists of institutions of higher education with substantial research programs and of the FFRDC's operated under contract by educational institutions. Included in institutions of higher education are their affiliated research organizations, agricultural research centers, graduate and professional schools, and affiliated hospitals.

Other nonprofit institutions include privately endowed philanthropic foundations, nonprofit research institutes, voluntary health agencies, academies of science, professional societies, museums, zoological gardens, and arboretums, as well as several FFRDC's operated by independent organizations.

The data on transfers of funds were based on estimates from many institutions having somewhat different understandings of costs and expenditures. The estimates for Federal agencies, moreover, were based on obligations rather than expenditures, since information on transfers to the other sectors was available only for obligations. (Additional details appear in series W 126–143.)

For detailed information and trend data on R&D funds and scientific personnel, see the following publications: *National Patterns of R&D Resources, Funds and Manpower in the United States* (annual); *Federal Funds for Research, Development, and Other Scientific Activities* (annual); *Research and Development in Industry* (annual); *Scientific Activities at Universities and Colleges* (biennial); *Scientific Activities of Nonprofit Institutions* (periodic); *American Science Manpower* (biennial); *Scientific, Technical, and Health Personnel in the Federal Government* (annual); and *Employment of Scientists and Engineers in the United States, 1950–66.*

Early major efforts to estimate the volume of research and development. The methodology, scope, and limitations of the various series are often summarized in the publications cited below, and any use of these estimates in descriptive or analytical work should be preceded by a careful review of their limitations. Differences in concepts and scope of these earlier series make comparisons with the later NSF data not generally possible.

George Perazich and Philip M. Field, *Industrial Research and Changing Technology*, Work Projects Administration, National Research Project, Philadelphia, 1940, pp. 5–17 and 52–79. This report presents data on research personnel in industrial laboratories for 1920, 1921, 1927, 1931, 1933, and 1938. The data are based on the six directory listings on industrial research laboratories in the United States published by the National Research Council between 1920 and 1938.

National Resources Committee (later, National Resources Planning Board), *Research, A National Resource*, vol. 1, *Relation of the Federal Government to Research*, Report of the National Resources Planning Board Science Committee, 1938. Section 3, pp. 61–112, of this report presents estimates of Federal expenditures for research in 1937 and 1938. Table D, p. 91, summarizes from other sources a number of earlier estimates of Federal expenditures going back as far as 1901. Section 6, pp. 167–193, contains a discussion of research in American universities and colleges. It also provides a general estimate of the dollar volume of expenditures for research and development for 1935–1936.

National Resources Planning Board, *Research, A National Resource*, vol. II, *Industrial Research*, a report of the National Research Council to the National Resources Planning Board, 1941. Section IV, pp. 173–187 of this report, presents estimates of research personnel in industrial laboratories for 1940; and section II, part 7, pp. 120–123, shows research personnel and expenditures in 31 firms for 1937.

U.S. Senate, Committee on Military Affairs, Subcommittee on War Mobilization (Harley M. Kilgore, Chairman), *Report on the Government's Wartime Research and Development, 1940–44*, 1945. Part I of this report presents detail, and part II summarizes data on funds for research and development for each of 45 Federal agencies and bureaus, with detail on the fiscal sources of funds and the major categories of recipients for fiscal years 1940 through 1944.

Vannevar Bush, *Science, The Endless Frontier, A Report to the President,* July 1945, appendix 3, "Report of the Committee on Science and Public Welfare" (Isaiah Bowman, Chairman). The Bowman Committee's report to Dr. Bush presents the first known national estimates of trends in scientific research and development expenditures in table I, p. 80. It also contains series on scientific research expenditures (based largely on performance of research) for the following major groups: (*a*) Industry—annual expenditures estimates for 1920–1940; (*b*) nonprofit industrial research institutes—annual expenditures estimates for 1930–1942; (*c*) Government (Federal and State)—annual estimates for 1923–1932, 1934–1938, and 1940–1944; (*d*) colleges and universities—biennial estimates, 1930, 1932, 1934, 1936, 1938, 1940, and 1942; (*e*) research institutes (not connected with any industry nor an integral part of any university)—annual estimates for 1930–1940; and (*f*) total scientific research expenditures—total of the foregoing five series for 1930, 1932, 1934, 1936, 1938, and 1940.

The President's Scientific Research Board (John R. Steelman, Chairman), *Science and Public Policy, A Report to the President,* vols. I, II, and IV, 1947. Based on data in Vannevar Bush, *Science, The Endless Frontier* (cited above, vol. I, *A Program for the Nation,* presents for the even years of 1930–1940 estimated expenditures by the Federal Government, industry, universities, and others. Estimates are also made of the average annual expenditures by major groups for 1941–1945 and of expenditures for 1947. Vol. II, *The Federal Research Program,* presents estimates of Federal "expenditures for research and development in the physical and biological sciences" in fiscal year 1947 based on project reports from the individual agencies. Vol. IV, *Manpower for Research,* presents annual estimates and forecasts of scientists and engineers in industrial research laboratories for 1929–1956.

Helen Wood, Robert Cain, and Joseph H. Schuster, *Scientific Research and Development in American Industry, A Study of Manpower and Costs,* Bulletin No. 1148, U.S. Bureau of Labor Statistics, prepared in cooperation with the Department of Defense, 1953. Data in this publication are based on the first survey specifically designed to obtain research and development performance costs and personnel for private firms. The report presents estimates of expenditures for research and development performed in 1951 by firms reporting. Personnel data cover research and development scientists and engineers employed by these firms in January 1951 and 1952.

Office of the Secretary of Defense, *The Growth of Scientific Research and Development,* 1953. This publication presents annual estimates on sources of research and development funds and on performance of research and development for 1941–1952 for the Federal Government, industry, and nonprofit institutions including colleges and universities. Estimates of the number of scientists and engineers employed in research and development by these broad sectors are also shown for the same years. No methodological notes accompany the estimates. They are known to be based on materials in Wood, Cain, and Schuster (cited above); U.S. Senate Committee on Military Affairs, Subcommittee on War Mobilization (cited above); and other published and unpublished sources.

Office of Education, *Statistics of Higher Education; Receipts, Expenditures, and Property, 1953–54,* 1957. This report presents biennial estimates on expenditures for performance of "Organized research" by institutions of higher education, 1930–1954. See series H 732 in this volume. This is the oldest known current series on research expenditures.

More recently, beginning with Bureau of the Budget, *The Budget of the United States Government, 1955,* the Federal budget documents have carried a special analysis of "Federal Research and Development Programs" summarizing expenditures and/or obligations for research and development and R&D plant on an agency basis. In *The Budget, 1972,* this was Special Analysis R and covered fiscal years 1970, 1971, and 1972.

W 109–125. Funds expended for performance of research and development and basic research, by sector, and major function, 1953–1970.

Source: U.S. National Science Foundation, *National Patterns of R&D Resources, 1953–72,* Funds and Manpower in the United States (NSF 72–300).

The four-sector division followed by the National Science Foundation attempts to take account of both the legal nature and major functions of organizations active in financing and performing basic research, applied research, and development. However, grouping diverse types of organizations into discrete sectors requires certain arbitrary judgments because of the mixed nature of many organizations, particularly those in the university and other nonprofit sectors.

The *Federal sector* is made up of the agencies of the Federal Government.

The *industry sector* consists of both manufacturing and nonmanufacturing companies. Manufacturing is surveyed in major industry groupings; and nonmanufacturing, which includes organizations such as those in selected service industries, is treated as a unit. Federally Funded Research and Development Centers (FFRDC's) administered by industrial firms are also included.

The *universities and colleges sector* is composed of all institutions of higher education, both public and private. The term "universities and colleges" is used to refer to the academic institutions as a group without the associated FFRDC's administered by the schools for various Federal agencies. The universities and colleges comprise the following:

Colleges of liberal arts; schools of arts and sciences; professional schools, such as engineering and medical schools, including affiliated hospitals; associated research institutions, and similar organizations, which are integral parts of the universities and colleges; agricultural experiment stations and associated schools of agriculture.

Funds used at the universities and attributed to the universities sector as a source consist of: (a) State and local government funds separately budgeted for research and development, (b) the direct or indirect costs of R&D performance sponsored by outside organizations that were defrayed in part by universities and colleges in accordance with cost sharing or other arrangements, and (c) unrestricted or general funds which the institutions themselves have been free to allocate for research either through their instructional or departmental budget or through their own separately budgeted research. Funds from the Federal Government, industry, or other nonprofit institutions, which are supplied in the form of grants or contracts for research or development at a university, are credited to the appropriate source in the performance of research and development by universities and colleges. Thus, research contracts from industry are treated as university performance funded by industry as the source, whereas funds given to the institution by industry for general educational purposes and used by the school, at its discretion, for research, are treated as university performance financed with the university's own funds.

Institutions in the *other nonprofit sector* fall into two general groups: (1) Organizations that are primarily granting in nature, namely private philanthropic foundations and voluntary health agencies, and (2) public and private organizations that are primarily involved in performing research and development, comprising separately incorporated nonprofit research institutes, professional societies, academies of science, museums, zoological gardens, botanical gardens, arboretums, nonprofit hospitals, and FFRDC's administered by nonprofit organizations.

In these series, both the university and the other nonprofit sectors contain private and public institutions—the latter either closely associated with or considered a part of State or local government. A number of organizations in both sectors, as well as in industry, also receive State and local government funds.

In the Foundation's surveys, respondents in all four sectors indicate the amounts they spend on research and development in their own sector and the sources of these funds. The National Science Foundation bases all national totals on data as reported by performers because institutions doing research and development are in the best position to: (a) indicate how much they spent in the actual conduct of research and development in a given year, (b) classify their work as basic, applied, etc. and (c) identify the sector of the economy in which their financing originated. The use of performer reporting throughout also reduces the possibility of double counting. Because the national time series on Federal funds spent in research and development are based on expenditures reported by organizations which have actually performed the research and development, they differ from the series in *Federal Funds for Research, Development, and Other Scientific Activities* on agency obligations for research and development to be performed in the non-Federal sectors. Federal agency obligations are used in the series only for intramural performance in agency laboratories where they are treated as the equivalent of expenditures. Expenses of Federal personnel engaged in planning and administering intramural and extramural R&D programs are also included in the intramural performance total.

W 126–143. Federal funds for research and development, by agency, 1947–1970.

Source: 1947–1951, U.S. Bureau of the Budget (now the Office of Management and Budget), unpublished data; 1952–1970, U.S. National Science Foundation, *Federal Funds for Research, Development, and Other Scientific Activities*, Vol. XXI.

Obligations represent orders placed, contracts awarded, services received, and similar transactions during a given period, regardless of when the funds were appropriated and when future payment of money is required. One of the limitations of these data is that they are two series compiled at different times and on somewhat different bases. The first series, FY 1947–51, was compiled by the Bureau of the Budget. The second series, FY 1952–70, is based on agency submissions to the National Science Foundation for its annual survey on *Federal Funds for Research, Development, and Other Scientific Activities*. Since Government accounting does not use research and development as a uniform bookkeeping category for all agencies, the data represent estimates by informed persons.

Expenditures represent checks issued and cash payments made during a given period, regardless of when the funds were appropriated.

For agencies operating on a cost-type budget, accrued expenditures and costs are reported instead of obligations. Accrued expenditures represent all costs accrued during the reporting period except those subject to reimbursement from other agencies.

The obligations and expenditures reported cover all transactions from all funds available from direct appropriations, trust funds or special account receipts, corporate income, or other sources, including funds appropriated to the President that an agency received or expects to receive. The amounts reported for each year reflect obligations and expenditures for that year regardless of when the funds were originally authorized or received and regardless of whether they were appropriated, received, or identified specifically for research, development, or R&D plant.

Funds reported for research and development reflect full costs. In addition to costs of specific R&D projects, the applicable overhead costs are also included. The amounts reported include the costs of planning and administering R&D programs, laboratory overhead, pay of military personnel, and departmental administration.

R&D plant (or R&D facilities and fixed equipment, such as reactors, wind tunnels, and radio telescopes) includes acquisition of, construction of, major repairs to, or alterations in structures, works, equipment, facilities, or land, for use in R&D activities at Federal or non-Federal installations. Excluded from the R&D plant category are expendable equipment and office furniture and equipment. Obli-

gations for foreign R&D plant are limited to Federal funds for facilities located abroad and used in support of foreign research and development.

W 144–160. Funds for industrial research and development, by industry, 1956–1970.

Source: U.S. National Science Foundation, *Research and Development in Industry*, annual reports.

The report covering R&D expenditures for 1956 and 1957 follows the general format used in subsequent annual reports. The National Science Foundation also sponsored two industry surveys covering the 1953–56 period, which were conducted by the U.S. Bureau of Labor Statistics (BLS): *Science and Engineering in American Industry, Final Report on a 1953–54 Survey* (NSF 56–16) and *Science and Engineering in American Industry, 1956* (NSF 59–50). Data obtained in the BLS surveys are not directly comparable with U.S. Bureau of the Census figures for 1957–70 because of methodological and other differences in the surveys conducted by the two agencies and have, therefore, been excluded. In addition, the Census surveys, beginning in 1957, have collected data on the R&D activities of Federally Funded Research and Development Centers (FFRDC's) operated by business firms, whereas the earlier BLS surveys did not. To account for the R&D performance of these research centers in 1956, Census adjusted data for that year (collected in the 1957 survey) to provide comparable trend data from 1956 forward.

The surveys in this series have made use of the "shuttle" type questionnaire, permitting respondents to report information for the current year and at the same time make revisions as necessary in figures for the preceding year, which were preentered by the Bureau of the Census.

Research and development as defined in these series, includes basic and applied research in the physical and life sciences (including medicine) and in engineering, and design and development of prototypes and processes. This definition excludes quality control, routine product testing, market exploration, research in the social sciences or psychology, or other nontechnological activities or technical services.

Expenditures, as defined in these series, include salaries of research and development scientists and engineers and their supporting personnel, other direct costs, service and supporting costs, plus attributable overhead expenses incurred in such items as administration, depreciation, and rent. Expenditures also include Federal funds for private industry performance of research and development ranging from about 40 percent of total expenditures in 1953 to about 50 percent in 1970. The totals exclude capital expenditures and patent expenses.

The industry surveys conducted by the Bureau of the Census for the National Science Foundation use the company as the reporting unit. The company is defined as a corporate entity that includes all establishments under common ownership or control. Each company is classified in a single industry on the basis of its primary business activity, although many companies engage in research and development and productive activities outside the industry in which they are classified. Since many firms are active in several diverse product fields, data collected in this survey are not comparable with figures reported elsewhere on an establishment basis.

For the period 1963–70, companies in the survey have been assigned an industry classification based on the 1963 economic censuses conducted by the Bureau of the Census. Similarly, figures for 1958 and earlier years are based on the company classifications resulting from the 1958 economic censuses. To provide a continuous time series, individual industry data for 1959–1962 (previously classified on the 1958 basis) have been adjusted to account for the differences in absolute level resulting from the two classifications. A detailed explanation of the adjustment technique is contained in the Technical Notes section of the industry reports.

W 161–167. Funds for industrial research and development, by character of work, and cost per scientist or engineer, 1953–1970.

Source: U.S. National Science Foundation, series **W 161–165** and **W 167**, *Research and Development in Industry, 1970* (NSF 72–309) pp. 68 and 83; series **W 166**, unpublished data.

For series W 161–165, see the general note for series W 109–180.

W 166, R&D scientists and engineers. Those engaged full time in research and development and the full-time equivalent (FTE) of those working part time. Scientists and engineers are defined as persons engaged in scientific or engineering work at a level which requires a knowledge of physical, life, engineering, or mathematical sciences equivalent at least to that acquired through completion of a 4-year college course with a major in one of those fields.

W 167, cost per R&D scientist or engineer. The number of R&D scientists and engineers used to estimate the cost per R&D scientist or engineer for 1967–70 is the number of man-years; between 1957 and 1966, the arithmetic means of the numbers of R&D scientists and engineers reported in each industry for January in two consecutive years was used.

W 168–180. Employment of natural scientists and engineers, 1950–1970.

Source: U.S. Bureau of Labor Statistics, unpublished data.

Scientists and engineers in these data include those who "work as" *natural* scientists or engineers. This concept, therefore, includes persons without college degrees in science and engineering who were working in engineering and science jobs. It does not include individuals with college degrees in science and engineering who are not working in these fields. Also excluded are social scientists and high school teachers of science subjects, as well as medical scientists who spend the greatest portion of their time providing care to patients.

The basic definitions used in these series are those used in the periodic surveys of scientific and technical personnel in private industry and in State and local governments, conducted by the Bureau of Labor Statistics (BLS). These surveys cover about four-fifths of all scientists and engineers. Following are definitions used in these surveys: (1) Scientists and engineers are workers who perform at a level requiring education or training equivalent to that acquired through completion of a 4-year college course with a major in a natural scientific or engineering field; (2) R&D scientists and engineers are defined as those who spend the greater portion of their time in basic and applied research in the natural sciences (including medical science) and engineering, and in design and development of prototypes and processes; (3) Employment data include all workers employed as scientists and engineers whether full or part time.

Annual estimates refer to January or "early-in-year" employment. Adjustments were necessary to survey data on Federal Government and local governments, as October was generally the date of the surveys in these sectors.

Historically, surveys of science and engineering employment have been made separately for six major sectors of the economy—private industry, Federal Government, State governments, local governments, universities and colleges, and nonprofit organizations. In private industry, surveys of scientific and technical personnel were conducted by BLS for the years 1952, 1954, annually 1959 through 1964, 1966, 1968, and 1969. Data on State government employment, also collected by BLS, are available only for the years 1959, 1962, and 1964. Other nonrecurring BLS surveys in this field include a survey of science and engineering employment in local governments for the year 1963 and a pilot survey covering such employment in six States in 1960. Surveys of science and engineering employment in universities and colleges were conducted by the National Science Foundation in 1954, 1958, 1961, 1965, 1967, and 1969. Scientists and engineers employed by nonprofit organizations were surveyed by BLS in 1958 and the NSF in 1965 and 1967. An NSF survey in 1960 of such employment was limited in scope.

Other sources of information used included BLS establishment data on total wage and salary worker employment and production worker employment; information from the Decennial Census of Population, 1950 and 1960; Bureau of the Census, Current Population Surveys; information on R&D expenditures from the NSF and Department of Defense; information from the NSF's National Register of Scientific and Technical Personnel on scientists, by field, type of employer, and function; and data on full time equivalent R&D employment of scientists and engineers in private industry from NSF reports.

★ ★ ★ ★ ★ ★ ★ ★ ★   **More Recent Data for *Historical Statistics* Series**   ★ ★ ★ ★ ★ ★ ★ ★ ★

Statistics for more recent years in continuation of many of the still-active series shown here appear in annual issues of the *Statistical Abstract of the United States*, beginning with the 1975 edition. For direct linkage of the historical series to the tables in the *Abstract*, see Appendix I in the *Abstract*.

Series **W 109–125**. Funds Expended for Performance of Research and Development and Basic Research, by Sector and Major Function: 1953 to 1970

[Amounts in millions of dollars]

Year	Total funds	Percent Federal as source	Federal Government	Industry Federal funds	Industry Industry funds	Universities and colleges Federal funds	Universities and colleges Industry funds	Universities and colleges funds [1]	Other nonprofit institutions funds [1]	FFRDC's [2]	Other nonprofit institutions Federal funds	Other nonprofit institutions Industry funds	Other nonprofit institutions Other funds [3]	Defense [4]	Space [4]	Other Non-Federal	Other Federal
	109	110	111	112	113	114	115	116	117	118	119	120	121	122	123	124	125
RESEARCH AND DEVELOPMENT [5]																	
1970	26,545	55.6	3,853	7,779	10,283	1,648	61	961	166	737	748	90	220	8,388	2,840	11,786	3,531
1969	26,169	57.0	3,501	8,451	9,867	1,595	60	895	145	725	640	81	209	8,767	2,905	11,253	3,244
1968	25,119	59.5	3,493	8,560	8,869	1,572	55	841	131	719	608	73	198	8,515	3,291	10,173	3,140
1967	23,613	61.1	3,396	8,365	8,020	1,409	48	753	119	673	577	66	187	8,005	3,377	9,209	3,022
1966	22,264	62.8	3,220	8,332	7,216	1,262	42	673	108	630	546	59	176	7,124	4,230	8,260	2,649
1965	20,439	63.8	3,093	7,740	6,445	1,073	41	615	93	629	498	53	159	6,602	4,170	7,397	2,269
1964	19,214	65.3	2,838	7,720	5,792	916	41	555	83	629	450	47	143	6,936	3,555	6,667	2,056
1963	17,371	64.6	2,279	7,270	5,360	760	41	485	73	530	380	48	145	7,053	2,380	6,149	1,789
1962	15,665	63.4	2,098	6,435	5,029	613	40	424	66	470	310	45	135	7,363	1,050	5,749	1,504
1961	14,552	63.7	1,874	6,240	4,668	500	40	371	58	410	240	41	110	7,160	800	5,282	1,310
1960	13,730	63.7	1,726	6,081	4,428	405	40	328	52	360	180	40	90	7,085	426	4,984	1,235
1959	12,540	64.3	1,640	5,635	3,983	306	39	290	47	338	140	35	87	6,684	314	4,477	1,066
1958	10,870	62.5	1,374	4,759	3,630	254	39	257	42	293	111	31	80	5,652	109	4,076	1,033
1957	9,912	61.7	1,220	4,335	3,396	229	34	230	38	240	95	30	65	5,174	99	3,796	843
1956	8,483	57.3	1,040	3,328	3,277	213	29	204	34	194	84	30	50	4,123	76	3,622	662
1955	6,279	55.9	905	2,180	2,460	169	25	185	30	180	75	28	42	2,976	63	2,769	471
1954	5,738	54.7	1,020	1,750	2,320	160	22	167	28	141	67	25	38	2,766	52	2,599	321
1953 [6]	5,207	53.0	1,010	1,430	2,200	138	19	151	26	121	60	20	32	2,473	42	2,447	245
BASIC RESEARCH																	
1970	3,943	62.6	646	158	471	1,296	40	748	110	269	100	25	80				
1969	3,758	63.5	565	160	458	1,275	39	678	95	275	111	22	80				
1968	3,648	64.3	502	180	462	1,268	36	621	86	276	118	20	79				
1967	3,357	64.7	472	202	427	1,124	31	551	79	250	125	19	77				
1966	3,123	63.6	445	173	451	1,009	27	494	71	227	132	18	76				
1965	2,853	63.7	424	186	406	879	26	445	69	208	120	16	74				
1964	2,559	62.3	364	165	384	767	25	402	67	191	108	15	71				
1963	2,196	59.7	299	147	375	610	25	343	58	159	95	14	71				
1962	1,886	57.8	251	143	345	481	25	293	51	136	80	12	69				
1961	1,543	54.5	206	81	314	382	25	250	44	115	57	11	58				
1960	1,326	52.3	160	79	297	299	24	215	38	97	58	10	49				
1959	1,155	52.7	173	72	248	226	24	185	33	92	46	8	48				
1958	973	47.3	126	43	252	178	24	159	29	78	35	6	43				
1957	857	47.6	122	41	230	155	21	136	25	65	25	5	32				
1956	747	46.2	104	37	216	130	18	116	22	51	23	5	25				
1955	608	47.0	90	27	162	103	16	99	19	49	17	5	21				
1954	548	48.4	102	23	143	90	14	85	17	39	11	4	20				
1953 [6]	489	47.9	101	19	132	73	12	73	15	33	8	4	19				

[1] Includes State and local government funds received by these institutions and used for research and development.

[2] Federally Funded Research and Development Centers administered by individual universities and colleges and by university consortia.

[3] Includes estimates for independent nonprofit hospitals and voluntary health agencies.

[4] Defense expenditures consist of all R&D spending by the Department of Defense (DOD) and a portion of Atomic Energy Commission funds. Space R&D expenditures are those of the National Aeronautics and Space Administration. The space activities of DOD are included as spending on defense. The space activities of other Federal agencies are not included; they are estimated to account for less than 5 percent of all space R&D spending.

[5] Basic research, applied research, and development.

[6] Calendar year data for industry and nonprofit institutions combined with Federal and university data for fiscal year 1953 (July 1952–June 1953).

Series W 126–143. Federal Funds for Research and Development, by Agency: 1947 to 1970

[In millions of dollars. For years ending June 30]

Year		Obligations [1]															Expenditures	
	Total	Departments of—									Interior	Atomic Energy Commission	National Aeronautics and Space Administration [5]	National Science Foundation	Veterans Administration	All other [2]	Research and development	R & D plant
		Agriculture	Commerce [2]	Defense					Health, Education, and Welfare [4]									
				Total	Army [3]	Navy [3]	Air Force [3]	Other	Total	National Institutes of Health								
	126	127	128	129	130	131	132	133	134	135	136	137	138	139	140	141	142	143
1970	15,340.3	281.2	121.6	7,360.4	1,659.8	2,257.9	2,990.0	452.7	1,221.0	873.3	157.9	1,346.0	3,799.9	289.0	58.6	704.7	15,157.0	578.9
1969	15,641.1	260.1	72.1	7,696.3	1,643.8	2,124.2	3,498.5	429.6	1,297.4	892.9	207.6	1,405.9	3,963.3	273.8	50.2	414.4	15,695.4	652.2
1968	15,921.4	253.5	83.9	7,709.3	1,563.4	2,024.8	3,621.7	499.3	1,251.8	864.0	190.6	1,369.0	4,429.4	283.5	44.7	305.7	16,333.0	715.9
1967	16,529.3	252.6	74.8	8,049.2	1,661.3	2,108.9	3,794.3	484.6	1,146.6	802.8	170.4	1,257.3	4,867.0	262.4	40.9	408.0	16,073.0	786.1
1966	15,320.4	234.9	55.2	7,023.6	1,585.4	1,601.7	3,342.3	494.2	1,014.4	701.0	143.2	1,212.4	5,050.0	243.7	40.1	303.0	14,970.2	1,047.8
1965	14,614.3	224.6	61.3	6,796.5	1,459.5	1,449.5	3,351.0	536.5	869.4	715.1	113.2	1,240.7	4,951.5	187.2	37.4	132.7	13,811.4	1,077.4
1964	14,225.4	189.0	53.8	7,261.9	1,376.9	1,621.2	3,784.0	479.7	776.9	651.0	106.4	1,236.0	4,286.6	170.2	33.7	110.8	13,758.9	948.1
1963	12,494.7	168.0	52.2	7,285.7	1,297.4	1,597.3	3,944.7	446.3	656.2	566.0	92.1	1,077.9	2,857.4	154.1	29.9	121.1	11,338.5	673.6
1962	10,289.9	157.2	40.1	6,722.9	1,203.5	1,539.1	3,569.8	410.6	576.9	495.1	85.6	1,029.2	1,439.2	113.9	27.5	97.4	9,831.6	555.2
1961	9,058.6	143.4	32.3	6,574.0	1,117.9	1,539.0	3,588.9	328.3	428.5	375.4	73.3	850.2	776.9	84.0	22.0	73.9	8,747.9	539.1
1960	7,551.7	125.8	31.4	5,711.5	1,117.0	1,535.5	2,815.5	243.6	319.8	274.3	64.0	761.7	369.3	74.7	15.1	78.5	7,300.4	443.8
1959	6,693.5	120.7	25.6	5,161.6	1,174.2	1,349.5	2,440.0	197.9	242.8	211.7	60.6	699.8	261.7	60.4	12.8	47.5	5,459.3	347.1
1958	4,569.7	110.2	18.3	3,403.3	603.3	867.9	1,858.6	73.5	184.9	157.4	51.1	644.0	77.1	33.6	10.1	37.3	4,664.4	342.2
1957	3,932.0	99.8	17.7	2,985.6	500.6	804.2	1,643.9	36.9	144.2	124.7	45.2	528.0	55.3	30.6	7.7	17.9	4,118.9	342.9
1956	2,988.2	83.0	18.2	2,268.6	408.0	673.3	1,142.8	44.5	86.0	(NA)	36.1	410.7	49.5	16.0	6.5	13.6	3,231.9	214.1
1955	2,532.8	72.2	15.0	1,945.1	419.3	564.8	939.3	21.7	68.0	(NA)	32.4	327.3	43.0	9.7	5.6	14.5	3,100.1	208.2
1954	2,875.0	59.3	7.8	2,320.0	763.3	615.3	941.4		58.2	48.4	37.7	323.4	47.3	4.6	5.3	11.3	2,884.6	263.3
1953	3,106.0	56.0	10.9	2,577.2	899.6	660.7	1,016.9		49.9	38.0	32.1	309.9	48.4	2.3	5.1	14.1	2,825.6	275.4
1952	1,887.3	55.3	10.3	1,508.5	458.8	551.1	498.6		43.6	33.0	30.7	168.9	50.5	.9	3.9	14.7	1,548.2	268.0
1951	1,481.9	55.1	11.0	1,125.9	307.1	450.2	368.6		37.9		30.4	157.9	45.4	.1	5.1	13.0		
1950	972.6	56.9	22.4	599.7	119.0	257.6	223.1		34.2		28.7	172.2	42.8		3.8	11.8		
1949	937.7	53.2	10.9	626.1	114.7	298.0	213.5		25.2		30.2	140.0	38.3		4.3	9.6		
1948	776.5	45.7	8.9	485.8	97.7	247.3	140.8		24.3		20.3	145.4	33.0		3.1	10.0		
1947	619.5	40.0	5.7	469.3	104.3	252.3	112.7		10.6		16.9	39.9	26.7		1.4	8.9		

NA Not available.
[1] Excludes R & D plant.
[2] Beginning 1966, the Bureau of Public Roads and the Office of Transportation Research and Development, formerly in the Department of Commerce, are included in "All other."

[3] Includes pay and allowances of military R & D personnel beginning in fiscal year 1953, and support from procurement appropriations for development, test, and evaluation, starting with fiscal year 1954.
[4] Federal Security Agency prior to fiscal year 1952.
[5] National Advisory Committee for Aeronautics prior to fiscal year 1958.

Series W 144–160. Funds for Industrial Research and Development, by Industry: 1956 to 1970

[In millions of dollars]

Year	Total	Food and kindred products	Textiles and apparel	Lumber, wood products and furniture	Paper and allied products	Chemicals and allied products	Petroleum refining and extraction	Rubber products	Stone, clay, and glass products	Primary metals	Fabricated metal products	Machinery	Electrical equipment and communications	Motor vehicles and other transportation equipment	Aircraft and missiles	Professional and scientific instruments	All other industries
	144	145	146	147	148	149	150	151	152	153	154	155	156	157	158	159	160
1970	18,062	235	58	48	178	1,766	515	220	157	275	200	1,649	4,352	1,582	5,245	745	837
1969	18,318	205	70	15	188	1,659	467	217	159	257	182	1,536	4,401	1,558	5,909	734	762
1968	17,429	187	58	19	144	1,588	437	205	142	251	183	1,477	4,105	1,491	5,776	660	705
1967	16,385	183	57	12	128	1,507	371	182	136	242	163	1,326	3,867	1,354	5,669	542	649
1966	15,548	164	51	12	117	1,407	371	168	117	232	154	1,217	3,626	1,344	5,526	468	574
1965	14,185	157	38	11	94	1,356	397	162	112	213	145	1,065	3,200	1,230	5,148	403	455
1964	13,512	144	32	12	77	1,284	393	158	109	195	148	1,015	2,972	1,182	5,078	331	384
1963	12,630	130	30	11	69	1,239	317	156	100	183	153	958	2,866	1,090	4,712	284	330
1962	11,464	121	28	10	65	1,175	310	141	96	171	146	914	2,639	999	4,042	309	299
1961	10,908	125	30	10	59	1,101	299	138	88	177	136	901	2,483	936	3,829	297	299
1960	10,509	104	38	10	56	980	296	121	88	177	145	949	2,532	889	3,514	329	287
1959	9,618	91	30	12	49	891	278	115	81	152	138	930	2,329	866	3,090	309	257
1958	8,389	83	26	12	42	792	246	89	75	131	162	781	1,969	856	2,609	294	222
1957	7,731	74	15	14	35	705	211	107	69	108	135	669	1,804	707	2,574	249	(1)
1956	6,605	64	(1)	(1)	36	641	182	(1)	60	90	116	543	1,516	688	2,138	200	(1)

[1] Not available separately; included in total.

Series **W 161–167.** Funds for Industrial Research and Development, by Character of Work, and Cost Per Scientist or Engineer: 1953 to 1970

Year	Research and development (mil. dol.)					R & D scientists and engineers [1]	Cost per R & D scientist or engineer	Year	Research and development (mil. dol.)					R & D scientists and engineers [1]	Cost per R & D scientist or engineer
	Total	Research			Develop-ment				Total	Research			Develop-ment		
		Total	Basic	Applied						Total	Basic	Applied			
	161	162	163	164	165	166	167		161	162	163	164	165	166	167
1970	18,062	4,028	629	3,399	14,034	375,450	$48,100	1960	10,509	2,405	376	2,029	8,104	302,050	$34,800
1969	18,318	3,905	618	3,287	14,413	385,600	47,500	1959	9,618	2,311	320	1,991	7,307	280,200	34,300
1968	17,429	3,766	642	3,124	13,663	381,900	45,600	1958	8,389	2,206	295	1,911	6,183	256,100	32,800
1967	16,385	3,544	629	2,915	12,841	371,950	44,100	1957	7,731	1,941	271	1,670	5,790	236,600	32,700
1966	15,548	3,467	624	2,843	12,081	360,200	43,200	1956	6,605	1,521	253	1,268	5,084	---------	---------
1965	14,185	3,250	592	2,658	10,935	348,400	40,700	1955	4,640	1,117	189	928	3,523	---------	---------
1964	13,512	3,149	549	2,600	10,363	341,900	39,500	1954	4,070	980	166	814	3,090	---------	---------
1963	12,630	2,979	522	2,457	9,651	333,750	37,800	1953	3,630	877	151	726	2,753	---------	---------
1962	11,464	2,937	488	2,449	8,527	319,650	35,900								
1961	10,908	2,372	395	1,977	8,536	312,050	35,000								

[1] For 1957–69, the number of R & D scientists and engineers was derived by using the arithmetic mean of the full-time-equivalent number of R & D scientists and engineers employed in January of two consecutive years; for 1970, man-years were used.

Series **W 168–180.** Employment of Natural Scientists and Engineers: 1950 to 1970

[In thousands]

Year	Total, scientists and engineers	Scientists, by field of employment									Employed in research and development		
		Total	Chemists	Mathe-maticians	Physicists	Geologists, etc.	Other physical	Agricul-tural	Biological	Medical	Total	Engineers	Scientists
	168	169	170	171	172	173	174	175	176	177	178	179	180
1970	1,595	496	133	74	49	31	36	49	71	53	535	342	194
1969	1,568	483	131	73	48	29	35	48	68	51	549	357	192
1968	1,525	462	127	67	46	29	34	47	66	46	553	359	194
1967	1,477	439	123	62	44	28	30	47	63	42	554	358	196
1966	1,418	418	120	54	42	26	29	47	57	43	526	339	186
1965	1,367	397	117	50	40	26	27	44	56	37	513	331	183
1964	1,327	381	115	47	39	23	26	42	54	35	498	322	176
1963	1,281	359	110	44	36	23	25	39	51	31	476	311	165
1962	1,210	337	107	40	34	21	24	35	49	27	442	284	157
1961	1,152	319	103	36	32	21	24	32	47	24	410	263	146
1960	1,104	303	100	34	30	20	22	30	45	22	386	249	138
1959	1,058	291	95	32	29	21	21	30	43	20	362	233	129
1958	1,001	272	91	29	26	20	21	27	39	19	330	210	120
1957	959	251	85	26	24	20	21	26	35	16	309	198	111
1956	874	228	79	23	21	18	19	24	30	14	271	171	100
1955	813	210	74	21	20	17	17	22	27	12	249	156	93
1954	784	204	72	20	19	16	17	22	26	12	244	153	91
1953	749	194	68	18	18	16	17	22	24	11	228	143	85
1952	686	178	63	16	17	14	15	20	23	10	205	126	79
1951	612	161	57	15	15	13	12	18	21	10	175	106	70
1950	557	149	52	14	14	13	10	17	20	9	158	94	64

Chapter X

Financial Markets and Institutions

Flow of Funds (Series X 1-392)

X 1–392. General note.

These data present an integrated picture of financial claims outstanding in the U.S. economy. They summarize the types of claims, who owes them as liabilities, who holds them as assets, and, for some major groups in the economy, how lending and borrowing are related to income and expenditure flows. The data are based on a wide range of information from public and private statistical sources. Directly or indirectly they reflect banking statistics, Treasury accounts, Census data, tax return compilations, balance of payments statements, security market data, and balance sheet tabulations for several kinds of nonbank financial institutions. Data from these diverse sources have been adjusted in many ways to make them consistent with one another in coverage and in definition of types of claim. The process of adjusting them into consistency produces a total system of financial accounts for the economy that includes separate statements of financial position and of transactions for each major institutional group in the system. As a whole, this financial accounting structure constitutes the flow-of-funds system of accounts published by the Federal Reserve System.

Broadly grouped, this section has three parts: (1) a summary of total debt and the structure of assets that finances that debt; (2) statements for households, business, and State and local governments on their saving and investment and financial positions; and (3) summaries for major financial markets of lending and borrowing positions.

Some of the tables include data on both amounts of claims outstanding at year-ends and net flows during years. For most financial claims, the net flows are the changes over years in outstandings and represent the excess of new claims created or acquired during the year over repayments or other disposition. There are exceptions, however, notably in equities in corporate and noncorporate business. Capital supplied to business through corporate stock issues or through proprietors' equity investment appears in the flows as external sources of funds to business and as uses of funds by investors; as equity positions such funds are not included in business liabilities in the tables on outstandings. Corporate equity assets are shown at market value based on prices on stock exchanges, while noncorporate equities are omitted for lack of information on values. Changes in market prices cause the aggregate market value of corporate equities to fluctuate far more from year to year than would be accounted for by net purchases, and the difference is capital gains and losses, mainly unrealized, that are not included in the tables on net flows. For equity markets, therefore, the tables on outstandings and on flows reflect separate aspects of developments.

Tables on flows for households, business, and governments are broader than the tables on outstandings in that they are full statements of saving and investment for the groups covered, including income, spending, and physical asset purchases as well as lending and borrowing. The data on saving and tangible investment for these groups are taken directly from national income accounts, which are summarized in chapter F. The relation between the amounts shown here and national income data are described in the November 1965 *Federal Reserve Bulletin*, pages 1534–1538. For each of these groups, saving and investment are defined to be equal although measured differently, with saving the excess of current receipts over current outlays and investment the sum of outlays for tangibles and financial assets less net borrowing. Because saving and investment are calculated from separate bodies of data, there are inevitable discrepancies between the two that are also shown in the tables.

The tables of net flows for these three groups relate in outstandings to complete balance sheets that include physical assets and net worth as well as the financial assets and liabilities that are included in the tables on outstandings. Changes in net worth in such balance sheets would equal saving (as shown in the flow tables), plus capital gains, while changes in assets less liabilities would equal net investment flows plus the same capital gains.

Complete balance sheets consistent with saving and investment flows are being developed on an economy-wide basis but (as of July 1975) are not in a form that can be included here. These balance sheets require estimates of tangible asset holdings on a uniform valuation basis, with totals for all groups in the economy that are consistent with tangible asset totals of the kind shown in chapter F. Until these estimates are completed only partial balance sheets can be shown, covering financial assets, liabilities, and a net difference that is the financial net worth of each group. When tangible asset holdings can be added to these financial net worth figures, it will be possible to cumulate wealth estimates for individual groups into national wealth totals that are consistent with those shown in chapter F. Most of the financial claims included are both held and owed within the national economy and are canceled out in national wealth cumulations, but they are major elements in the distribution of wealth ownership. At the same time their net sum—the excess of U.S. claims on foreigners over foreign claims on the U.S.—represents the financial component of total national wealth.

The primary interest in these tables on financial claims, however, lies not in their relation to national wealth estimates but rather in the picture of financial structure that they give, the indications of debt burden, liquidity positions, structure of intermediation, and surplus-deficit positions that can be derived from them. While most of the debt is not part of national wealth, the structure of debt—long term or short term—and who owes it—government, business, or households—have important bearings on private spending decisions. The forms of private financial assets—deposits, long-term securities, and so forth—have influences on credit availability as well as on spending. The tables on outstandings are intended to indicate these aspects of financial structure, while the tables on flows give the relation of financial market transactions to nonfinancial activity that generates both the saving from which credit is supplied and the spending for which credit is demanded.

As a group the tables are selective in several ways, since there is not space to include a total statement of all financial activity. Thus, the three summary tables (series X 1–113) encompass all sectors of the economy but are limited primarily to their credit market activities. The tables on individual sectors (series X 114–262) cover all transactions and financial positions of the groups that have been included but represent only the private nonfinancial economy. The principal omissions are banks and other financial institutions, the Federal Government, and foreign transactors. These are covered in somewhat different form in other sections of this volume. The tables on individual financial markets (series X 263–392) are also selective in that they cover all flows into and out of major markets covered but do not include all financial markets. In this area the most important omission is bank loans, which again is covered elsewhere.

Other omissions consist of security credit, commercial paper, and a variety of other credit forms that are relatively small.

X 1–113. General note.

These series are a summary of total credit in the economy and its sources. The forms of credit included are indicated in series X 1–23. Other kinds of financial obligation that are not directly part of credit markets are omitted. Most of these other obligations are represented in series X 114–262.

X 1–23. Debt of nonfinancial borrowers, 1945–1970.

Source: Board of Governors of the Federal Reserve System, *Flow of Funds Accounts: Financial Assets and Liabilities Outstanding, 1945–1971*, and unpublished data.

This set of financial claims, owed by governments, households, nonfinancial business, and foreigners, is an approximation to a base amount of total credit that is used to finance nonfinancial activity in the economy, such as public deficits, business capital formation and inventories, home building, and consumer durables purchases. Government debt omits most public intermediation in financial markets, such as in federally sponsored credit agencies, and the private borrowing omits security credit, book trade accounts, direct foreign investment, other more informal types of financial relationship, and all liabilities of financial intermediaries. For private borrowers the flow of credit included is related closely in total to the volume of capital expenditures, with variations in the relationship and in forms of debt that reflect changing credit conditions.

U.S. Government debt shown is essentially the total for net public borrowing in unified budget presentations. It excludes intragovernment holdings that are part of the larger total of public debt subject to statutory limitation. The unified budget has been published by the Treasury only from the beginning of 1969, but the figures for earlier years have been adjusted to that basis for consistency over time. The figures include Treasury securities, issues by other budget agencies, loan participation certificates, mortgage debt, and Commodity Credit Corporation (CCC) certificates of interest.

State and local government debt is derived from the census of governments.

Corporate and foreign securities are based on Securities and Exchange Commission data on net change in outstandings; the totals for outstandings are Federal Reserve estimates. The figures exclude all issues by financial institutions, and exclude liability for corporate equities outstanding.

Mortgage totals are as published by the Federal Reserve except that they exclude loans in process of disbursement and Federal Government debt in mortgage form.

Bank loans are from banking statistics and are essentially total business loans, farm loans, and loans to individuals after removing credit in the form of open-market paper, CCC-guaranteed loans, consumer credit, and security credit. Loans to financial business are omitted. Consumer credit is as published by the Federal Reserve. Open-market paper consists of dealer-placed commercial paper issued by nonfinancial corporations and bankers' acceptances. Other loans consist mainly of business credit from finance companies and loans by the U.S. Government and federally sponsored credit agencies to business, households, and foreigners. They include foreign loans in aid programs and Export-Import Bank credit.

X 24–63. Funds raised in credit markets by nonfinancial sectors, 1946–1970.

Source: Board of Governors of the Federal Reserve System, *Flow of Funds Accounts: Annual Flows, 1946–1971*, and unpublished data.

See text for series X 1–23.

X 64–113. Sources of credit market funds, 1945–1970.

Source: See source for series X 1–23.

These series distribute, as assets in the economy, the credit totals that appear in series X 1–23 as liabilities, indicating at the same time the position of financial intermediaries and governmental credit agencies in the structure of supply. The series are divided into three sections—credit from public agencies and foreign investors, assets and liabilities of private intermediaries, and assets of private domestic nonfinancial groups. Public agency credit includes—in addition to direct lending by Federal Government agencies—Federal Reserve credit related to money supply and bank reserves, loans by federally sponsored credit agencies, and foreign holdings of credit market instruments. The sponsored credit agencies (series X 71) are a group of institutions that at some time before 1970 had been part of or partly owned by the Federal Government or other sponsored agencies: Federal National Mortgage Association, Federal Home Loan Mortgage Corporation, Federal home loan banks, Federal intermediate credit banks, banks for cooperatives, and Federal land banks. The sponsored agency figures also include mortgage pools backing securities guaranteed by the Government National Mortgage Association. Lending by the sponsored agencies is financed mainly by issues of their own securities to private investors, and in series X 74 these agency issues are brought into total credit holdings of private domestic lenders, shown in series X 75, and private holdings of Government securities, in series X 76. Some of these agency issues finance loans to financial intermediaries (series X 68) that are not part of the debt of nonfinancial sectors (series X 64) and such loans (series X 81) are excluded from net private holdings (series X 75). Foreign holdings (series X 73) are mainly official, such as at central banks, in recent years.

Private domestic holdings of credit instruments are partly in the portfolios of intermediaries (series X 82), and the volume of intermediation is a strong influence on the forms of credit supply. Intermediaries held far more, proportionately, in direct loans to business and housing than nonfinancial investors, whose portfolios of direct credit instruments consist mainly of securities issued in public markets. Hence a period of large credit flows through intermediaries is typically also a period when loan volume is large compared with net new security issues. Intermediary credit supply is heavily dependent on domestic deposit flows to banks and savings institutions, although these institutions also borrow directly in credit markets or from foreign sources to some extent. The relative importance of sources of intermediary funds is indicated in series X 87–93.

Direct lending in credit markets from nonfinancial groups in the private economy (series X 94) exhausts the total of credit outstanding, where, at this level, the total includes borrowing by public credit agencies (series X 74) and private intermediaries (series X 88) as well as nonfinancial sectors (series X 64). For these nonfinancial investors, credit instruments are part of a portfolio that includes deposits at intermediaries that appear earlier as sources of intermediary lending (series X 87). As private assets the deposits are shown beyond credit instrument holdings, together with currency claims on the Federal Reserve. A total portfolio of securities and deposits (series X 105) for private domestic nonfinancial investors appears at the end of this set of assets.

Corporate equity markets (series X 109–113) are excluded entirely from the preceding series on credit market instruments. Holding of equities are stated at year-end market values, and movements in holdings reflect to a large extent capital gains and losses, whether realized or unrealized, that result from market price movements.

X 114–262. General note.

These series present full financial statements for three major groups in the economy—households, business, and State and local governments. They include a variety of obligations that are not directly in the credit markets summarized in the preceding series, such as insurance claims and taxes payable.

FINANCIAL MARKETS AND INSTITUTIONS

X 114–191. General note.

These series consolidate trusts and nonprofit organizations with households mainly because data for a separation of the three groups have been lacking until recent years. From available information, trusts and nonprofit groups appear to hold less than 10 percent of the assets shown in series X 114–147, and their debts are mainly in nonresidential mortgages (series X 140). Apart from these institutional investors, the financial positions shown by series X 114–147 are aggregates for individuals as personal investors and borrowers.

These series omit assets and liabilities connected with noncorporate business, such as trade receivables, commercial and farm mortgages, and business loans from banks; noncorporate business finances are included in series X 192–228. In this respect, the household series shown here differ in coverage from those on individual savings (series F 566–594), which include noncorporate business.

The data for household saving and investment (series X 148–191) include as one item a net flow of equity funds from noncorporate proprietors as households into the business sector, but the assets and liabilities data (series X 114–147) exclude such equities because information is lacking on the value of physical assets of noncorporate business.

Apart from noncorporate equities, the assets and liabilities data give the financial asset and debt positions of households resulting from the investment flows shown by the saving and investment series.

X 114–147. Financial assets and liabilities of households, personal trusts, and nonprofit organizations, 1945–1970.

Source: See source for series X 1–23.

The total shown here for deposits and credit market instruments (series X 115) represents the household component of financial assets (series X 105) in the preceding sources of credit table. Other financial assets consist mainly of corporate equities and claims on life insurance and pension funds.

The credit market instruments liability (series X 138), comprising mainly home mortgages and consumer credit, represents the household component of debt (series X 19) shown in the summary credit table. Other liabilities are related mainly to borrowing for purchasing or carrying securities.

X 148–191. Saving and investment of households, personal trusts, and nonprofit organizations, 1946–1970.

Source: See source for series X 24–63.

Lending less borrowing in series X 114–147 is a measure of the net credit flow from households to other sectors through credit markets. Households are characteristically large net lenders to business and governments, either directly or through intermediaries (series X 165). This net lending is combined with purchases of houses, consumer durables, and nonprofit plant and equipment to give a total investment flow (series X 159) that is, by definition, equal to household saving out of current income (series X 158). Saving and investment are measured from different data sources, however, and a statistical discrepancy exists between them that is shown in series X 191. Series X 148–158 show the relation between personal saving in the national income accounts and gross saving as defined in these tables. The principal adjustments serve to capitalize outlays on consumer durables and growth of claims on government life insurance and employee retirement funds.

X 192–228. General note.

These series cover both corporate and noncorporate business, including farming. Financial sources of funds include net new share issues by corporations as well as net increases in debt claims outstanding. As equities, the share issues are excluded from the liabilities items (series X 199–206).

X 192–206. Financial assets and liabilities of nonfinancial business, 1945–1970.

Source: See source for series X 1–23.

Business financial assets (series X 192–197) are mainly liquidity balances—deposits and credit market instruments—and trade credit. Series X 193–195 are the business element of sources of funds to credit markets in series X 105. Trade credit (series X 196) is almost entirely held by and owed by business and is excluded from the credit market totals in data for debt of nonfinancial borrowers (series X 1–23) and for sources of credit market funds (series X 64–113). The largest component of miscellaneous assets (series X 197) is the direct investment position of corporations in foreign subsidiaries and branches.

Credit market debt (series X 199) is identical to series X 20. As mentioned above, most business trade debt is owed within the group to other firms. "Other" liabilities (series X 206) consist mainly of current accruals such as profit taxes accrued but not yet due.

X 207–228. Saving and investment of nonfinancial business, 1946–1970.

Source: See source for series X 24–63.

Total income before taxes (series X 207) is taken directly from the national income accounts (NIA) and consists of corporate profits and inventory valuation adjustment, proprietors' income from noncorporate business, and part of rental income of persons. Series X 207 excludes rental income that is imputed in national income accounts to owner-occupied houses. That income and all other flows associated with owner-occupied houses are included in the data for households (series X 114–191).

Business gross saving (series X 208) is mainly depreciation charges and other capital consumption allowances that are not cash outlays, but it also includes corporate retained profits after profit taxes and dividends. Noncorporate income is treated as though paid over entirely to proprietors in the household group, and no element of noncorporate retained income is included in the gross savings total. Capital expenditures (series X 211–215) are also from national income accounts (NIA) although not published in the NIA for exactly this group. Expenditures exclude purchases of houses by households, and plant and equipment outlays by nonprofit organizations and by financial business.

In almost all of the years since World War II business capital outlays have been somewhat larger than business gross saving (internal cash flow), and funds raised externally (series X 218) have been correspondingly higher than financial uses of funds (series X 217).

Series X 228 is a statistical discrepancy, the excess of gross saving over an independently measured gross investment total. An important source of this discrepancy is net land purchases, for which estimates are not yet available. These purchases are probably mainly from households and are offset by an equal and opposite element of the household discrepancy, series X 191 (see above).

X 229–262. General note.

Gross saving of State and local governments in series X 247 is the net surplus published in national income accounts less a retirement credit to households that removes employee retirement funds from this group. The retirement funds are viewed here as a form of financial institution parallel to private pension funds, and the data for State and local governments exclude their assets and activities. The basic source of information for these series is the annual surveys of governmental finances published by the Bureau of the Census. Census data are converted from a presumed mid-year fiscal basis to calendar-year estimates on the basis of quarterly data from other sources. Certain adjustments are included which integrate the financial data with national income definitions of the group and its nonfinancial transactions.

Credit market supply of funds by State and local governments included in series X 105 consists of data shown in series X 230–232. Credit market debt (series X 239) is identical with series X 18.

X 229–244. Financial assets and liabilities of State and local governments, 1945–1970.

Source: See source for series X 1–23.

See general note for series X 229–262.

X 245–262. Saving and investment of State and local governments, 1946–1970.

Source: See source for series X 24–63.

See general note for series X 229–262.

X 263–392. General note.

These financial market data series cut across a different dimension of the economy's financial structure from the preceding series. The former are statements for selected institutional groups of transactions and balance sheet positions that relate to the nonfinancial activities of these groups. The market data series, on the other hand, beginning with series X 263–275, for example, indicate for selected types of financial instruments the institutional groups that acquired the claims as assets and that issued them as liabilities. Certain items, however, from the preceding series are repeated here. Corporate bonds held by households, for example, shown in series X 128 as a form of household asset, is shown in series X 345 as one of a set of group holdings of corporate bonds that together account for all of the bonds outstanding. Except in corporate equities, the financial market series present only assets and liabilities outstanding, and net flows to or from the markets can be closely deduced from yearly changes in outstandings. Corporate equities are a special case where changes in market values cause movements in values of holdings that are very different from net transactions. Both value of holdings and net flows are shown for equities.

X 263–275. Money supply, 1945–1970.

Source: See source for series X 1–23.

Demand deposits and currency are the principal means of payment in the U.S., and the amounts held outside banks and the U.S. Government constitute the narrowly defined money supply. These data show the ownership distribution of the money supply and the banking system liability for money and Government cash balances. The figures conform to the definition of money stock as published weekly by the Federal Reserve System, but they are for a single day of the year, December 31, rather than period averages. Series X 265–267, holdings by households, business, and State and local governments are repeated here for series X 116, X 193, and X 230, respectively. Money stock is also held by nonbank financial institutions and by foreigners. These holdings are presented as they appear on the balance sheets of the holder groups. A further element of money supply, shown here as "mail float" (series X 270), is not in the balance sheets of any holders. This float is made up of checks that have been deducted from the books of the check writers but are not yet included in the books of receivers. This is a float in addition to cash items in process of collection and Federal Reserve float, both of which have been deducted already in calculating total money supply. In addition to the money supply, the series presented also include U.S. Government cash balances (series X 271), which are mainly Treasury deposits, and include, in addition, cash and currency held by other agencies.

Liability for cash balances lies partly with the Federal Reserve and certain Treasury accounts, grouped together as "monetary authorities" (series X 272) and partly with commercial banks. The monetary authorities component is mainly currency outside banks but also includes Treasury and foreign official deposits at Federal Reserve Banks and Treasury holdings of currency. The commercial bank liability consists of demand deposits held by nonbanks, after deducting cash items in process of collection and Federal Reserve float.

X 276–292. Time deposits and savings accounts, 1945–1970.

Source: See source for series X 1–23.

Commercial banking liability includes passbook savings deposits and several types of deposit with specific maturity dates. These are shown here as negotiable certificates of deposit (CD's) of $100,000 denomination or more and all others (series X 278 and X 279). The series cover ownership distributions on total time deposits, but not on negotiable CD's separately. Sources for time deposit ownership—mainly bank financial reports and corporate business statements—are inadequate for a separate allocation of CD holdings.

Deposits at nonbank savings institutions are held predominantly by households. In recent years these institutions have also started issuing certificates with stated maturities.

X 293–327. U.S. Government securities, 1945–1970.

Source: See source for series X 1–23.

The ownership estimates shown here cover all of the U.S. Government debt that appears in series X 2 except mortgages. In addition, they include the securities of federally sponsored credit agencies shown in series X 71. The sponsored-agency issues are financial intermediation that is excluded from the debt totals shown in series X 1–23, but they are part of the market for public and agency securities presented here. The sponsored credit agencies are listed in the text for series X 64–113. Almost all of the issues included here, other than sponsored agency securities, are part of public debt subject to statutory limitation, but the totals shown exclude securities held within the Government, such as by social security and civil service retirement funds, and are therefore substantially less than the total debt under ceiling, which includes these intragovernment holdings. Short-term Treasury issues (series X 296) include all marketable securities due within one year of the date shown plus a sliding proportion of those due within two years, as calculated by the Federal Reserve. "Other" Treasury issues (series X 297) are all longer-term marketable securities plus nonmarketable securities other than savings bonds. Budget agency issues and loan participation certificates (series X 299 and X 300) are borrowings by agencies other than the Treasury that became part of net borrowing from the public when the unified form of budget was introduced in 1969. Agency issues are mainly Tennessee Valley Authority and Export-Import Bank securities, and loan participations are obligations of Export-Import Bank, Government National Mortgage Association (GNMA), and a number of other agencies. They include Commodity Credit Corporation certificates up to 1970. For 1970 they also include insured notes sold by Farmers Home Administration, a form of claim that is not included in public borrowing in budget documents. Included in the totals for sponsored-agency debt outstanding are mortgage-backed securities guaranteed by GNMA.

All of the securities are shown at par values, both as liabilities and as assets. The estimates are based primarily on the Treasury Ownership Surveys that are published monthly in the *Treasury Bulletin*. Although definitions of the Government and forms of budget reporting changed substantially from 1945 to 1970 the figures shown here are all on a single definitional basis consistent with budget coverage in 1971. Sponsored-agency debt, for example, includes for all years debt of institutions that were in the group in 1971, even though some or all of the agencies were in the budget in earlier years.

While intragovernmental holdings of debt are excluded, asset holdings include Government investment in sponsored-agency issues, sponsored-agency investment in Government issues, and Federal Reserve holdings of both Treasury and agency securities (series X 302–304). Foreign holdings (series X 305) have in recent years been mainly in the hands of official institutions such as central banks.

The remaining asset holdings (series X 306) comprise the public debt held by private domestic investors and approximate the amount that must compete against other forms of credit for funds in the domestic market. Roughly one-quarter of this total is household savings bonds, Series E and H, shown on the debt side in series X 295.

Savings bonds were the major form of household Government securities for most of the period covered. For other domestic groups, holdings were predominantly marketable Treasury issues, although agency securities increased rapidly toward the end of the period. Household, business, and State and local government holdings (series X 310–312) are duplicated here for series X 121, X 195, and X 233, and in total for series X 95.

X 328–378. Bonds and mortgages, 1945–1970.

Source: See source for series X 1–23.

These data present ownership of the principal forms of private long-term credit instruments, including State and local government securities. Holdings for all groups except households are based on balance sheet tabulations by Government agencies, trade associations, or private research organizations. Household assets are in each case calculated residually by subtracting holdings reported for other groups from the totals outstanding. This procedure puts a questionable valuation on household security assets. While most of the liability totals are stated at par values, the institutional holdings subtracted are book values which represent a mixture of par, cost, and amortized cost values. The resulting distortions in household asset values are probably not large but should be borne in mind.

The totals for debt outstanding come from a variety of sources. For State and local government securities they are taken from the annual surveys of governmental finances published by the Bureau of the Census, with adjustments to shift fiscal-year totals to a December 31 basis. Borrowings by State and local governments from the Federal Government (series X 338) are removed from the total as a separate form of debt. Totals for corporate bonds outstanding are essentially cumulations of net new issues published by the Securities and Exchange Commission, starting from a base total of bonds outstanding in 1944. Foreign bonds held in the U.S. are from balance of payments statistics and are at market value. Mortgage totals are derived mainly from tabulated reports of institutional lenders, with an allowance included for lender groups not covered by the tabulations. The totals are assembled jointly by the Commerce Department, the Federal Home Loan Bank Board, and the Federal Reserve.

Mortgage debt shown for savings and loan associations consists of loans still in process of disbursement. Such loans are included in the associations' assets at their full committed amount. U.S. Govern-

ment mortage debt is on residential properties acquired by the Defense Department and Coast Guard. These mortgages appear in the Treasury Ownership Survey in the *Treasury Bulletin* as "nonsurveyed Government agency securities." They are included in the U.S. Government debt total (series X 2) but not in total Government securities outstanding (series X 293).

Household mortgage debt is entirely on owner-occupied residences. Nonfarm business mortgages are mainly on multi-family rental residential structures and commercial properties. They include small amounts of single-family debt that represent construction loans to builders.

X 379–392. Summary of corporate equities market, 1945–1970.

Source: Board of Governors of the Federal Reserve System, *Flow of Funds Accounts: Financial Assets and Liabilities Outstanding, 1945–1971; Flow of Funds Accounts: Annual Flows, 1946–1971;* and unpublished data.

Holdings of corporate shares are shown here at current market values, based mainly on Securities and Exchange Commission (SEC) tabulations for shares listed on stock exchanges. Movements in these values have been much larger relative to net cash transactions than for debt securities shown in preceding series, and for this market the net transactions are shown separately here. Total market values are as calculated at the Federal Reserve for all shares except open-end investment companies ("mutual funds"). The investment company total is for members of the Investment Company Institute (ICI). The totals include preferred as well as common shares. Purchases of domestic shares represent net new issues and are from the SEC and ICI. U.S. purchases of foreign shares in series X 392 represent net foreign issues, both new and existing, as shown in balance of payments publications.

For financial institutions most of the market values of holdings and net transactions are regularly reported either to trade associations or to the SEC. As in preceding series, household assets and net transactions are calculated residually. The figures indicate that in the later years shown, net purchases by life insurance companies and pension funds were larger than total new issues, while households received more from sales out of their equity portfolios than they paid for new share purchases. These net sales are shown here as negative net purchases and represent household funds transferred out of equities into other uses.

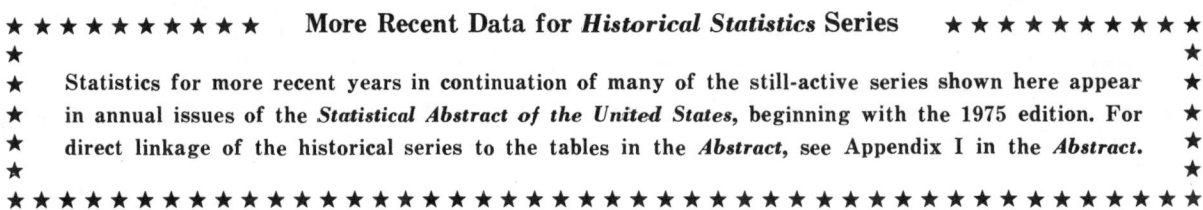

★ ★ ★ ★ ★ ★ ★ ★ ★   **More Recent Data for *Historical Statistics* Series**   ★ ★ ★ ★ ★ ★ ★ ★ ★
★   ★
★   Statistics for more recent years in continuation of many of the still-active series shown here appear   ★
★   in annual issues of the *Statistical Abstract of the United States,* beginning with the 1975 edition. For   ★
★   direct linkage of the historical series to the tables in the *Abstract,* see Appendix I in the *Abstract.*   ★
★   ★
★ ★

Series X 1-23. Debt of Nonfinancial Borrowers: 1945 to 1970

[In billions of dollars. As of December 31]

Year		Total debt	U. S. Government	Other nonfinancial sectors								
				Total	By type of claim							
					Debt capital instruments							
					Total	State and local government securities	Corporate and foreign bonds	Mortgages				
								Total	Home mortgages	Other residential	Commercial	Farm
		1	2	3	4	5	6	7	8	9	10	11
1970		1,459.5	301.4	1,158.2	774.5	146.2	181.1	447.2	275.6	58.0	82.3	31.2
1969		1,364.4	288.6	1,075.9	713.1	132.4	159.4	421.3	262.8	52.2	76.9	29.5
1968		1,278.4	292.2	986.2	665.1	124.4	147.3	393.4	247.1	47.3	71.4	27.5
1967		1,179.7	278.8	900.9	614.1	114.4	133.5	366.3	232.1	43.9	64.8	25.5
1966		1,099.9	265.8	834.1	569.0	106.0	118.6	344.4	220.6	40.3	60.1	23.3
1965		1,033.8	262.2	771.7	530.0	100.3	108.0	321.7	208.9	37.2	54.5	21.2
1964		963.3	260.4	702.9	490.7	93.0	101.6	296.1	193.5	33.6	50.0	18.9
1963		896.6	254.1	642.4	453.8	87.3	96.6	269.9	177.9	29.0	46.2	16.8
1962		838.5	250.2	588.3	417.9	81.4	91.7	244.9	162.7	25.8	41.1	15.2
1961		785.2	243.1	542.0	385.4	76.1	86.1	223.2	150.0	23.0	36.4	13.9
1960		741.0	235.9	505.1	356.2	70.8	80.9	204.4	138.8	20.3	32.4	12.8
1959		705.4	238.0	467.4	331.0	65.6	76.7	188.7	128.7	18.7	29.2	12.1
1958		656.2	230.9	425.3	303.0	59.5	73.4	170.1	116.0	16.8	26.1	11.1
1957		617.2	221.6	395.6	276.5	54.0	66.9	155.6	106.7	15.3	23.2	10.4
1956		589.0	223.8	365.2	253.3	49.6	60.2	143.6	98.1	14.9	20.7	9.8
1955		561.6	229.6	332.0	231.1	45.8	56.3	129.0	87.3	14.3	18.3	9.0
1954		525.7	230.4	295.3	207.2	40.6	53.7	112.9	74.9	13.5	16.3	8.2
1953		500.1	228.0	272.1	185.4	34.6	50.1	100.7	65.6	12.9	14.5	7.7
1952		470.7	220.9	249.7	167.9	30.2	46.8	90.9	58.0	12.3	13.4	7.2
1951		442.0	216.1	225.9	151.6	27.4	42.3	81.9	51.4	11.5	12.5	6.7
1950		418.1	216.5	201.6	135.2	25.2	37.4	72.5	44.9	10.1	11.5	6.1
1949		395.7	217.7	178.0	121.7	21.9	37.4	62.4	37.3	8.6	10.8	5.6
1948		379.3	215.1	164.2	109.6	19.3	34.3	56.0	33.0	7.5	10.2	5.3
1947		366.2	220.8	145.4	96.0	17.2	30.2	48.7	28.0	6.6	9.1	5.1
1946		350.3	228.0	122.3	84.7	15.7	27.3	41.7	22.9	6.1	7.7	4.9
1945		356.3	251.5	104.8	77.6	15.7	26.4	35.5	18.6	5.7	6.4	4.8

Year	Other nonfinancial sectors—Con.											
	By type of claim—Con.					By borrowing sector						
	Other private credit					Foreign	State and local governments	Households	Nonfinancial business			
	Total	Bank loans [1]	Consumer credit	Open-market paper	Other				Total	Corporate	Nonfarm non-corporate	Farm
	12	13	14	15	16	17	18	19	20	21	22	23
1970	383.7	149.8	126.8	16.1	91.0	51.1	151.1	463.2	492.8	368.1	76.4	48.3
1969	362.8	145.0	122.5	12.3	83.1	47.6	137.1	440.6	450.5	335.3	70.1	45.1
1968	321.1	128.0	113.2	9.0	70.9	45.8	128.4	407.9	404.0	299.4	62.7	41.9
1967	286.8	114.1	102.1	7.4	63.2	43.1	117.9	375.8	364.1	268.6	56.2	39.2
1966	265.1	104.3	97.5	5.2	58.1	40.2	109.5	356.2	328.3	241.3	51.2	35.8
1965	241.7	93.9	90.3	4.2	53.3	39.4	103.1	333.8	295.4	217.3	45.8	32.3
1964	212.2	79.8	80.3	4.5	47.7	36.6	95.5	305.1	265.7	196.7	40.0	29.0
1963	188.6	70.4	71.7	3.9	42.6	30.9	89.5	277.2	244.9	183.8	34.7	26.4
1962	170.4	64.0	63.8	3.8	38.7	27.7	83.4	252.4	224.8	170.8	30.2	23.9
1961	156.7	59.5	58.0	3.8	35.4	25.4	77.5	231.6	207.5	159.0	26.9	21.6
1960	148.9	56.6	56.1	2.8	33.4	23.2	72.1	216.3	193.5	149.0	24.6	20.0
1959	136.4	53.4	51.5	1.5	30.0	21.2	66.6	198.6	181.0	139.1	22.9	18.9
1958	122.3	47.3	45.1	1.8	28.1	20.5	60.4	177.2	167.2	129.6	20.6	17.0
1957	119.1	45.7	45.0	1.7	26.7	18.7	54.7	166.1	156.1	121.5	19.0	15.6
1956	111.9	43.6	42.3	1.3	24.7	17.3	50.1	153.2	144.6	111.9	18.0	14.6
1955	100.9	37.2	38.8	.9	24.0	16.5	46.3	137.1	132.1	101.5	16.9	13.7
1954	88.1	31.5	32.5	1.3	22.8	16.4	41.1	117.4	120.5	93.1	15.1	12.3
1953	86.6	31.2	31.4	.9	23.2	16.0	35.4	106.3	114.4	88.6	14.2	11.5
1952	81.9	32.1	27.5	.8	21.4	14.9	31.3	93.8	109.8	84.4	13.7	11.6
1951	74.3	29.9	22.7	.8	21.0	14.6	28.2	82.7	100.4	77.0	12.5	10.8
1950	66.5	24.8	21.5	.6	19.6	12.7	25.8	73.0	90.1	69.0	11.6	9.5
1949	56.4	19.9	17.4	.4	18.7	14.2	22.4	59.7	81.8	63.3	10.0	8.5
1948	54.7	22.0	14.4	.4	17.8	13.6	19.9	51.8	79.0	61.6	9.3	8.1
1947	49.4	21.3	11.6	.4	16.0	12.5	17.7	43.1	72.2	56.0	8.7	7.4
1946	37.6	17.2	8.4	.4	11.6	8.0	16.2	35.2	62.9	48.6	7.3	7.0
1945	27.2	12.3	5.7	.2	9.0	5.1	16.2	28.1	55.5	42.9	6.0	6.6

[1] Not elsewhere classified.

FINANCIAL MARKETS AND INSTITUTIONS

Series X 24–63. Funds Raised in Credit Markets by Nonfinancial Sectors: 1946 to 1970

[In billions of dollars]

Year	Total debt	U. S. Government	Other nonfinancial sectors	By type of claim							
							Debt capital instruments				
			Total	Total	State and local government securities	Corporate and foreign bonds		Mortgages			
							Total	Home mortgages	Other residential	Commercial	Farm
	24	25	26	27	28	29	30	31	32	33	34
1970	94.7	12.8	81.9	60.8	13.8	21.1	25.8	12.8	5.9	5.4	1.8
1969	86.9	−3.6	90.6	49.0	7.9	13.1	27.9	15.7	4.8	5.5	1.9
1968	98.5	13.4	85.1	51.3	10.1	14.0	27.3	15.2	3.5	6.6	2.1
1967	81.0	13.0	68.0	46.2	8.3	15.9	22.0	11.6	3.6	4.7	2.1
1966	67.7	3.6	64.1	39.0	5.7	11.0	22.3	11.4	3.1	5.7	2.1
1965	70.1	1.8	68.3	38.8	7.3	5.9	25.6	15.4	3.6	4.4	2.2
1964	66.2	6.3	59.9	36.3	5.7	4.5	26.1	15.6	4.5	3.8	2.1
1963	58.2	4.0	54.2	35.9	5.9	4.9	25.1	15.1	3.2	5.1	1.6
1962	52.8	7.0	45.8	32.6	5.3	5.5	21.7	12.8	2.8	4.8	1.3
1961	44.1	7.2	36.9	29.1	5.2	5.1	18.8	11.1	2.6	4.0	1.1
1960	35.4	−2.1	37.4	25.0	5.2	4.0	15.7	10.1	1.7	3.2	.7
1959	49.5	7.1	42.4	28.1	6.1	3.4	18.6	12.7	1.8	3.1	1.0
1958	39.1	9.3	29.8	26.6	5.5	6.6	14.5	9.3	1.5	2.9	.7
1957	28.1	−2.2	30.4	23.2	4.4	6.8	12.0	8.6	.5	2.4	.6
1956	27.5	−5.8	33.3	22.3	3.8	3.9	14.6	10.8	.6	2.4	.8
1955	36.0	−.8	36.8	23.9	5.2	2.6	16.1	12.4	.8	2.0	.8
1954	25.5	2.4	23.1	21.6	6.0	3.4	12.1	9.3	.5	1.7	.5
1953	28.0	7.0	20.9	17.5	4.4	3.2	9.9	7.5	.6	1.2	.5
1952	28.9	4.9	24.0	16.4	2.7	4.7	9.0	6.7	.8	.9	.6
1951	22.6	−.4	23.0	15.2	2.2	3.6	9.4	6.5	1.3	1.0	.6
1950	24.3	−1.2	25.4	15.3	3.3	1.9	10.1	7.5	1.5	.6	.5
1949	16.1	2.6	13.6	11.9	2.6	2.9	6.4	4.3	1.2	.7	.3
1948	13.0	−5.7	18.7	13.8	2.2	4.4	7.2	5.0	.9	1.1	.2
1947	15.8	−7.2	23.0	11.3	1.4	2.8	7.1	5.1	.5	1.3	.2
1946	−5.4	−23.4	18.0	7.1	.1	.9	6.1	4.3	.3	1.3	.1

Year	Other nonfinancial sectors—Con.												Net new corporate share issues
	By type of claim—Con.					By borrowing sector							
	Other private credit						State and local governments	Households	Nonfinancial business				
	Total	Bank loans[1]	Consumer credit	Open-market paper	Other	Foreign			Total	Corporate	Nonfarm non-corporate	Farm	
	35	36	37	38	39	40	41	42	43	44	45	46	47
1970	21.1	5.0	4.3	3.8	8.0	3.0	13.9	22.4	42.7	33.0	6.4	3.2	6.8
1969	41.6	16.8	9.3	3.3	12.2	2.9	8.7	32.4	46.6	36.0	7.5	3.2	4.8
1968	33.8	13.8	11.1	1.6	7.3	2.9	10.4	31.9	40.0	31.6	5.7	2.7	−.7
1967	21.8	9.9	4.6	2.1	5.2	4.0	8.5	19.7	35.8	27.4	5.0	3.5	2.4
1966	25.1	10.4	7.2	1.0	6.4	1.6	6.4	23.2	33.0	24.0	5.5	3.5	.9
1965	29.5	14.1	10.0	−.3	5.7	2.2	7.6	28.8	29.6	20.6	5.7	3.3	.3
1964	23.7	9.4	8.5	.7	5.1	4.9	6.0	27.9	21.2	13.2	5.3	2.6	1.6
1963	18.4	6.4	7.9	(Z)	4.1	3.6	6.1	24.8	19.7	12.6	4.5	2.6	−.2
1962	13.3	4.5	5.8	.1	2.8	1.8	5.8	20.8	17.4	11.8	3.3	2.3	.6
1961	7.8	2.9	1.8	1.0	2.0	2.2	5.5	15.3	13.9	10.0	2.3	1.6	2.8
1960	12.4	3.2	4.6	1.3	3.3	1.8	5.4	17.7	12.5	9.8	1.7	1.0	1.7
1959	14.3	6.4	6.4	−.4	1.9	.7	6.3	21.5	14.0	9.6	2.4	1.9	2.4
1958	3.2	1.5	.2	.1	1.4	2.0	5.7	11.0	11.1	8.2	1.6	1.4	2.4
1957	7.2	2.1	2.6	.4	2.1	1.3	4.6	12.9	11.6	9.5	1.0	1.1	2.5
1956	11.0	6.5	3.5	.3	.7	.9	3.9	16.1	12.5	10.5	1.2	.9	2.4
1955	12.9	5.6	6.4	−.4	1.3	.2	5.2	19.7	11.7	8.5	1.8	1.4	2.1
1954	1.5	.4	1.1	.4	−.4	.2	5.7	11.1	6.1	4.5	.9	.8	1.8
1953	3.4	−1.0	3.9	.1	.4	.1	4.1	12.5	4.3	3.9	.5	−.1	1.8
1952	7.5	2.2	4.8	.1	.4	.4	3.1	12.2	8.3	6.4	1.1	.8	2.4
1951	7.9	5.1	1.2	.2	1.4	.5	2.4	9.7	10.3	8.1	.9	1.3	2.0
1950	10.1	4.9	4.1	.2	1.0	.2	3.4	13.3	8.5	5.8	1.7	1.1	1.4
1949	1.7	−2.1	2.9	(Z)	.8	.3	2.5	7.9	2.9	1.8	.7	.4	1.3
1948	4.9	.3	2.8	(Z)	1.8	1.3	2.2	8.7	6.4	5.3	.5	.7	1.1
1947	11.7	4.0	3.2	.1	4.4	4.4	1.4	7.8	9.4	7.5	1.4	.5	1.2
1946	11.0	5.0	2.7	.1	3.2	3.4	(Z)	7.1	7.5	5.8	1.4	.4	1.1

See footnotes at end of table.

Series **X 24–63.** Funds Raised in Credit Markets by Nonfinancial Sectors: 1946 to 1970—Con.
[In billions of dollars]

Year	Private domestic net investment and borrowing in credit markets															
	Households and business					Business						Households				
	Capital outlays²			Net funds raised	Excess net investment⁴	Capital outlays²			Net debt funds raised	Corporate equity issued	Excess net investment⁴	Capital outlays²			Net funds raised	Excess net investment⁴
	Total	Capital consumption³	Net physical investment			Total	Capital consumption³	Net physical investment				Total	Capital consumption³	Net physical investment		
	48	49	50	51	52	53	54	55	56	57	58	59	60	61	62	63
1970	225.5	164.9	60.6	71.8	−11.2	110.1	73.6	36.6	42.7	6.8	−12.9	115.3	91.3	24.0	22.4	1.6
1969	227.1	154.4	72.7	83.3	−10.6	109.3	69.5	39.7	46.6	4.3	−11.2	117.8	84.8	33.0	32.4	.6
1968	208.7	140.4	68.3	71.0	−2.7	99.0	63.2	35.8	40.0	−.8	−3.3	109.7	77.2	32.5	31.9	.6
1967	188.7	128.4	60.3	57.9	2.4	94.0	58.5	35.6	35.8	2.3	−2.5	94.6	69.9	24.7	19.7	5.0
1966	191.2	118.5	72.7	57.3	15.4	97.0	54.2	42.8	33.0	1.2	8.7	94.2	64.3	29.9	23.2	6.7
1965	173.6	110.3	63.3	58.5	4.9	84.1	50.5	33.6	29.6	(Z)	4.0	89.6	59.9	29.7	28.8	.9
1964	152.4	103.2	49.2	50.4	−1.2	70.2	47.3	22.9	21.2	1.4	.3	82.2	55.9	26.3	27.9	−1.6
1963	140.1	96.8	43.3	44.1	−.9	63.8	44.4	19.4	19.7	−.3	(Z)	76.3	52.4	23.9	24.8	−.9
1962	131.9	92.1	39.8	38.7	1.1	60.4	42.3	18.1	17.4	.6	.2	71.5	49.8	21.7	20.8	.9
1961	115.2	85.9	29.3	31.7	−2.5	50.4	38.1	12.3	13.9	2.5	−4.1	64.7	47.8	16.9	15.3	1.6
1960	119.6	83.0	36.6	31.8	4.8	51.8	36.7	15.1	12.5	1.6	1.0	67.8	46.3	21.5	17.7	3.8
1959	118.9	79.6	39.2	37.7	1.5	50.6	35.2	15.4	14.0	2.2	−.8	68.3	44.5	23.8	21.5	2.3
1958	98.2	75.8	22.4	24.2	−1.8	40.5	33.1	7.4	11.1	2.1	−5.8	57.7	42.6	15.0	11.0	4.0
1957	108.0	72.5	35.5	26.9	8.6	46.8	31.8	15.0	11.6	2.4	1.0	61.2	40.8	20.5	12.9	7.6
1956	108.4	66.7	41.7	30.9	10.8	47.2	29.3	17.9	12.5	2.3	3.1	61.2	37.4	23.8	16.1	7.7
1955	106.4	60.9	45.6	33.4	12.2	43.8	27.1	16.7	11.7	1.9	3.1	62.6	33.8	28.9	19.7	9.1
1954	84.1	55.9	28.1	18.8	9.4	32.6	24.4	8.2	6.1	1.6	.5	51.5	31.5	19.9	11.1	8.9
1953	85.5	52.3	33.3	18.6	14.7	34.6	22.2	12.4	4.3	1.8	6.3	50.9	30.0	20.9	12.5	8.4
1952	80.8	48.7	32.1	22.8	9.3	34.8	20.1	14.7	8.3	2.3	4.1	46.0	28.6	17.4	12.2	5.2
1951	88.7	45.1	43.5	21.9	21.6	41.7	18.4	23.3	10.3	1.9	11.1	46.9	26.8	20.2	9.7	10.5
1950	84.3	38.5	45.8	23.2	22.6	36.7	15.9	20.8	8.5	1.4	10.9	47.5	22.5	25.0	13.3	11.7
1949	60.0	34.0	26.0	12.1	14.0	23.4	14.4	9.0	2.9	1.3	4.8	36.6	19.6	17.0	7.9	9.1
1948	68.4	29.9	38.5	16.2	22.3	32.6	12.5	20.1	6.4	1.0	12.6	35.8	17.4	18.4	8.7	9.7
1947	54.2	25.0	29.2	18.4	10.8	24.8	10.4	14.4	9.4	1.2	3.8	29.4	14.6	14.8	7.8	7.0
1946	46.5	19.8	26.7	15.6	11.1	24.7	8.3	16.4	7.5	1.1	7.9	21.8	11.5	10.2	7.1	3.1

Z Less than $50 million, or less than −$50 million. ¹ Not elsewhere classified. ³ Capital consumption includes amounts for consumer durables and excludes financial business capital consumption.
² Capital outlays are totals for residential and nonresidential fixed capital, net change in inventories, and consumer durables, except outlays by financial business. ⁴ Excess of net investment over net funds raised.

Series **X 64–113.** Sources of Credit Market Funds: 1945 to 1970
[In billions of dollars. As of December 31]

Year	Credit market debt claims against nonfinancial sectors																	
	Total	Holdings by public agencies and foreign holdings										Private domestic holdings					
		Total	U.S. Government securities	Residential mortgages	FHLB advances to savings and loan	Other loans and securities	By agency				Agency debt (excluded from total)	Total	U.S. Government securities	Municipal securities	Corporate and foreign bonds	Residential mortgages	Other mortgages—loans	
							U.S. Government	Sponsored credit agencies	Federal Reserve	Foreign							Total	Less FHLB advances
	64	65	66	67	68	69	70	71	72	73	74	75	76	77	78	79	80	81
1970	1,459.5	190.1	86.1	25.5	10.6	67.9	56.7	45.4	62.2	25.7	39.3	1,308.8	253.1	146.2	179.4	309.7	431.0	10.6
1969	1,364.4	161.6	70.4	19.7	9.3	62.2	54.0	35.6	57.2	14.9	30.6	1,233.5	247.3	132.4	159.0	296.8	407.3	9.3
1968	1,278.4	146.8	69.5	15.1	5.3	56.9	51.1	26.5	53.0	16.1	21.9	1,153.5	242.6	124.4	146.4	281.0	364.2	5.3
1967	1,179.7	134.4	66.1	12.3	4.4	51.6	45.7	23.3	49.3	16.1	18.4	1,063.7	229.3	114.4	132.5	265.4	326.5	4.4
1966	1,099.9	123.4	59.3	10.2	6.9	46.9	41.2	23.4	44.5	14.3	19.0	995.5	223.6	106.0	117.3	252.5	303.0	6.9
1965	1,033.8	112.0	55.9	7.4	6.0	42.6	36.9	18.3	41.0	15.9	14.2	936.0	218.2	100.3	107.3	240.5	275.7	6.0
1964	963.3	103.3	52.2	7.1	5.3	38.7	34.1	16.0	37.2	15.9	12.1	872.1	218.3	93.0	100.7	221.9	243.6	5.3
1963	896.6	95.5	48.7	7.2	4.8	34.8	31.4	15.3	33.8	15.0	11.5	812.6	215.1	87.3	95.9	201.5	217.6	4.8
1962	838.5	89.0	44.9	8.5	3.5	32.1	30.0	13.7	30.9	14.4	10.1	759.5	213.5	81.4	91.0	181.8	195.3	3.5
1961	785.2	81.6	41.3	8.4	2.7	29.2	27.5	12.1	28.9	13.0	8.6	712.2	208.8	76.1	85.5	166.0	178.5	2.7
1960	741.0	77.0	39.4	8.2	2.0	27.4	27.5	11.1	27.5	12.5	7.9	671.9	203.1	70.8	80.3	152.3	167.4	2.0
1959	705.4	72.8	38.0	7.2	2.1	25.5	24.9	9.9	26.7	11.3	7.3	639.9	206.3	65.6	76.2	141.1	152.9	2.1
1958	656.2	65.4	34.6	5.3	1.3	24.3	23.1	7.7	26.4	8.3	5.0	595.7	200.7	59.5	73.0	128.1	135.7	1.3
1957	617.2	61.5	32.3	5.2	1.3	22.8	21.7	7.4	24.3	8.2	4.9	560.7	194.1	54.0	66.5	116.9	130.4	1.3
1956	589.0	59.7	32.8	4.0	1.2	21.6	20.9	6.1	25.0	7.7	3.8	533.1	194.4	49.6	59.9	109.0	121.5	1.2
1955	561.6	56.7	31.6	3.4	1.4	20.2	20.3	5.0	24.8	6.5	3.1	508.0	201.0	45.8	56.1	98.2	108.3	1.4
1954	525.7	54.3	30.6	3.0	.9	19.8	19.6	4.0	25.1	5.6	2.1	473.5	201.9	40.6	53.5	85.3	93.0	.9
1953	500.1	54.8	31.0	3.0	1.0	19.8	19.9	3.7	25.9	5.2	2.1	447.4	199.0	34.6	49.8	75.5	89.4	1.0
1952	470.7	50.9	29.2	2.6	.9	18.2	18.0	3.6	24.7	4.6	2.1	421.9	193.8	30.2	46.6	67.7	84.5	.9
1951	442.0	47.3	27.2	2.1	.9	17.0	16.5	3.5	23.8	3.5	2.1	396.8	190.9	27.4	42.1	60.7	76.6	.9
1950	418.1	42.5	24.2	1.5	.8	16.0	16.0	3.1	20.8	3.4	1.8	377.4	194.1	25.2	37.2	53.5	68.2	.8
1949	395.7	38.3	21.2	1.2	.4	15.4	14.5	2.6	19.0	2.2	1.4	358.9	197.9	21.9	37.2	44.8	57.5	.4
1948	379.3	41.2	25.4	.7	.5	14.6	11.3	2.7	23.5	1.9	1.6	339.7	191.3	19.3	34.2	39.8	55.7	.5
1947	366.2	38.1	24.0	.6	.4	13.0	11.8	2.3	22.6	1.4	1.3	329.3	198.0	17.2	30.0	34.0	50.6	.4
1946	350.3	35.3	25.6	.7	.3	8.7	7.5	2.1	23.5	2.1	1.2	316.3	203.6	15.7	27.1	28.3	41.8	.3
1945	356.3	34.7	27.2	.9	.2	6.4	5.2	2.0	24.3	3.1	.9	322.5	225.2	15.7	25.9	23.4	32.5	.2

Series X 64–113.　Sources of Credit Market Funds: 1945 to 1970—Con.

[In billions of dollars.　As of December 31]

Year	Private financial intermediation												Private domestic nonfinancial investors					
	Credit market claims held by private financial institutions					Sources of funds							Credit market claims					
	Total	Commercial banks	Savings institutions	Insurance and pension funds	Other finance	Domestic deposits	Credit market debt	Other					Total	U.S. Government securities	Municipal securities	Corporate and foreign bonds	Commercial paper	Other
								Total	Foreign funds	Treasury balances	Insurance and pension reserves	Other, net						
	82	83	84	85	86	87	88	89	90	91	92	93	94	95	96	97	98	99
1970	1,054.9	444.4	252.2	289.5	68.7	614.3	74.7	365.9	24.5	7.9	242.1	91.3	328.7	135.2	51.8	44.7	21.9	75.0
1969	984.8	412.9	235.7	271.9	64.2	553.9	72.9	357.9	32.9	5.1	228.3	91.7	321.6	142.8	50.4	34.3	23.1	70.9
1968	929.7	393.4	221.6	259.7	55.1	551.5	55.7	322.6	23.6	5.0	216.7	77.3	279.4	126.8	44.1	26.8	14.4	67.3
1967	854.9	354.4	206.1	245.8	48.5	505.3	48.8	300.8	21.0	5.2	206.4	68.2	257.7	119.1	43.8	21.7	10.0	63.0
1966	792.1	318.4	191.3	233.3	49.0	456.1	49.3	286.7	18.7	5.0	195.3	67.7	252.8	120.5	45.8	17.2	8.5	60.7
1965	748.2	302.5	183.0	218.3	44.4	435.9	46.4	265.9	15.0	5.5	181.4	64.0	234.2	111.7	43.2	15.1	6.5	57.7
1964	685.7	273.4	168.7	204.7	38.9	397.4	39.6	248.7	14.3	6.5	170.4	57.6	226.0	109.5	40.6	13.1	6.0	56.8
1963	628.7	250.0	152.5	192.3	34.0	363.3	34.7	230.7	11.8	6.5	159.7	52.7	218.5	108.5	38.8	11.9	4.4	54.9
1962	579.1	232.6	135.1	180.7	30.7	331.3	28.5	219.2	10.3	7.2	150.2	51.5	208.9	104.3	36.4	11.5	3.5	53.1
1961	531.0	213.5	121.1	169.4	27.0	301.6	24.7	204.6	9.8	5.9	140.9	48.0	205.9	102.9	37.4	11.7	3.0	50.9
1960	493.1	198.6	109.3	159.4	25.9	278.4	22.7	192.0	9.5	5.9	133.4	44.2	201.5	103.8	36.0	11.2	2.4	48.2
1959	461.3	189.8	99.8	149.7	22.0	264.2	20.1	177.0	7.3	5.1	125.2	39.4	198.7	108.9	32.8	10.3	1.1	45.6
1958	432.7	184.5	89.4	139.7	19.1	253.4	16.3	163.0	8.0	4.3	116.5	34.3	179.3	96.3	29.0	10.4	1.2	42.5
1957	400.7	169.6	80.4	130.8	19.9	232.9	16.6	151.2	7.0	3.9	109.5	30.8	176.6	98.9	27.6	9.1	1.4	39.6
1956	377.7	164.3	73.2	121.8	18.3	221.9	15.4	140.3	7.0	3.7	101.6	28.0	170.9	99.0	25.5	8.0	1.3	37.0
1955	355.4	158.3	65.9	113.4	17.8	211.0	15.0	129.4	6.5	3.7	93.9	25.2	167.6	101.6	23.0	7.3	1.2	34.6
1954	330.5	153.8	57.7	105.0	14.0	200.3	10.4	119.8	6.7	4.2	87.1	21.8	153.5	94.3	19.4	6.3	1.0	32.4
1953	305.7	144.3	51.3	96.5	13.5	186.5	9.9	109.3	5.9	4.1	80.8	18.5	151.6	96.8	16.8	6.3	1.0	30.8
1952	285.6	140.4	45.5	88.0	11.7	177.0	8.2	100.3	5.8	4.9	74.1	15.5	144.5	93.8	14.4	6.3	.7	29.3
1951	262.4	131.2	40.5	80.5	10.2	165.8	6.8	89.8	5.3	3.4	68.1	13.1	141.2	93.6	13.3	6.5	.5	27.3
1950	246.5	124.2	37.5	74.8	10.0	155.1	6.3	85.1	5.4	2.8	63.1	13.7	137.2	93.4	12.7	5.1	.4	25.5
1949	229.5	117.9	34.2	68.8	8.6	147.6	4.5	77.4	4.8	3.1	58.2	11.3	133.8	90.3	11.7	7.8	.5	23.5
1948	214.9	112.1	31.7	63.5	7.6	144.7	3.6	66.7	4.5	2.3	54.2	5.6	128.4	87.4	10.7	7.9	.3	22.0
1947	207.8	114.3	29.5	58.0	6.0	144.1	2.4	61.3	3.8	1.3	50.0	6.1	124.0	86.1	9.6	8.2	.2	19.9
1946	197.5	111.1	26.9	53.4	6.1	136.7	1.6	59.1	4.2	3.0	46.3	5.6	120.4	84.8	9.1	8.9	.1	17.6
1945	196.9	117.6	24.0	48.8	6.5	123.1	.8	73.0	4.8	24.5	42.9	.8	126.4	92.0	9.4	9.8	(Z)	15.1

Year	Private domestic nonfinancial investors—Con.						Public support rate (percent)	Private financial intermediation (percent)	Total foreign funds	Corporate equities				
	Deposits and currency					Total instruments, deposits and currency				Market value			Held by financial institutions	Other holdings
	Total	Time and savings accounts	Money							Total	Mutual fund shares	Other equities		
			Total	Demand deposits	Currency									
	100	101	102	103	104	105	106	107	108	109	110	111	112	113
1970	664.3	459.2	205.2	155.1	50.0	993.0	13.0	80.6	50.2	928.8	47.6	881.2	147.0	781.8
1969	600.5	402.8	197.7	151.1	46.6	922.1	11.8	79.8	47.8	931.9	48.3	883.6	138.3	793.7
1968	595.2	405.1	190.1	146.4	43.7	874.6	11.5	80.6	39.7	1,035.8	52.7	983.2	141.9	894.0
1967	546.6	371.2	175.4	134.1	41.3	804.2	11.4	80.4	37.0	889.6	44.7	844.9	119.5	770.1
1966	495.2	332.0	163.2	124.0	39.2	748.0	11.2	79.6	33.0	700.7	34.8	665.9	92.6	608.1
1965	473.1	312.8	160.3	123.1	37.2	707.3	10.8	79.9	30.9	778.0	35.2	742.8	96.5	681.6
1964	432.5	280.1	152.4	117.3	35.1	658.5	10.7	78.6	30.2	684.1	29.1	655.0	81.6	602.5
1963	396.0	251.0	145.0	112.3	32.7	614.5	10.7	77.4	26.8	597.0	25.2	571.8	69.7	527.4
1962	362.3	222.3	140.0	109.0	31.0	571.3	10.6	76.2	24.7	505.7	21.3	484.4	57.5	448.2
1961	331.8	194.2	137.7	107.4	30.2	537.8	10.4	74.6	22.8	574.0	22.9	551.1	60.6	513.4
1960	307.9	173.7	134.2	104.7	29.5	509.5	10.4	73.4	21.0	451.0	17.0	434.0	45.6	405.4
1959	293.8	158.5	135.3	105.7	29.6	492.5	10.3	72.1	18.6	454.0	15.8	438.2	41.9	412.1
1958	282.4	147.6	134.8	105.9	28.9	461.7	10.0	72.6	16.2	418.0	13.2	404.7	35.7	382.3
1957	261.4	131.8	129.6	101.1	28.5	437.9	10.0	71.5	15.2	299.0	8.7	290.3	25.2	273.8
1956	250.4	119.3	131.1	102.6	28.5	421.4	10.1	70.8	14.6	338.0	9.0	328.9	25.6	312.4
1955	239.5	109.7	129.8	101.4	28.5	407.1	10.1	70.0	13.1	317.0	7.8	309.2	23.7	293.3
1954	228.3	101.1	127.3	99.2	28.0	381.8	10.3	69.8	12.3	258.0	6.1	251.9	17.7	240.3
1953	214.7	91.1	123.6	95.3	28.3	366.3	11.0	68.3	11.1	179.0	4.1	174.9	12.9	166.1
1952	204.7	82.5	122.2	94.5	27.7	349.2	10.8	67.7	10.4	186.0	3.9	182.1	11.8	174.2
1951	192.3	74.6	117.7	91.2	26.5	333.5	10.7	66.1	8.7	170.0	3.5	166.5	10.2	159.8
1950	180.8	69.6	111.1	85.5	25.6	317.9	10.2	65.3	8.9	146.0	3.3	142.7	9.3	136.7
1949	173.2	67.0	106.2	80.7	25.6	307.0	9.7	64.0	7.0	120.0	3.1	116.9	8.0	112.0
1948	170.9	64.2	106.8	80.5	26.2	299.3	10.9	63.3	6.4	108.0	1.5	106.5	5.5	102.5
1947	170.7	61.6	109.1	82.4	26.7	294.7	10.4	63.1	5.2	109.0	1.4	107.6	5.2	103.8
1946	163.6	58.0	105.6	78.7	26.9	284.0	10.1	62.4	6.4	111.0	1.3	109.7	4.9	106.1
1945	149.8	51.5	98.2	71.6	26.6	276.2	9.7	61.1	7.9	119.0	1.3	117.7	4.7	114.3

Z　Less than $50 million.

Series X 114–147. Financial Assets and Liabilities of Households, Personal Trusts, and Nonprofit Organizations: 1945 to 1970

[In billions of dollars. As of December 31]

Year	Financial assets											
	Total	Deposits and credit market instruments										
		Total	Demand deposits and currency	Savings accounts			Credit market instruments					
				Total	Commercial banks	Savings institutions	Total	U.S. Government securities				
								Total	Short-term	Other direct	Agency issues	Savings bonds
	114	115	116	117	118	119	120	121	122	123	124	125
1970	1,944.3	785.0	126.5	422.4	189.0	233.4	236.1	100.4	16.4	15.2	17.4	51.4
1969	1,867.6	723.9	120.4	377.8	161.5	216.4	225.7	104.8	27.0	11.9	14.8	51.1
1968	1,907.1	681.4	116.7	371.8	163.4	208.4	192.9	92.7	17.5	13.2	10.5	51.5
1967	1,703.4	625.6	104.1	341.5	146.0	195.5	180.0	88.2	12.4	15.6	9.0	51.1
1966	1,468.7	579.6	92.9	306.8	127.9	178.9	179.9	89.0	14.9	16.0	7.9	50.2
1965	1,485.8	540.6	90.3	287.5	115.9	171.6	162.8	80.7	12.9	14.2	4.0	49.6
1964	1,344.7	500.7	82.5	259.5	101.1	158.4	158.7	79.0	9.4	16.7	3.8	49.0
1963	1,214.4	464.1	77.9	232.1	89.4	142.7	154.0	77.0	10.6	15.0	3.3	48.0
1962	1,085.3	430.1	74.1	207.5	79.9	127.6	148.5	73.0	8.0	15.2	2.9	46.9
1961	1,112.1	403.3	72.5	181.8	67.3	114.5	149.0	72.7	7.8	15.9	2.6	46.4
1960	967.9	381.5	70.2	165.3	62.0	103.3	146.0	73.5	8.8	16.3	2.7	45.6
1959	944.6	364.0	69.9	153.8	60.2	93.7	140.3	73.3	11.3	13.1	3.0	45.9
1958	878.4	340.0	68.0	142.1	56.6	85.5	130.0	67.8	7.7	10.9	1.5	47.7
1957	740.9	322.2	65.6	128.0	51.3	76.7	128.6	70.7	9.8	10.8	1.9	48.2
1956	753.6	306.3	66.9	115.9	46.1	69.8	123.5	70.4	7.7	11.4	1.2	50.1
1955	707.8	289.2	65.3	106.3	43.8	62.5	117.6	69.2	6.1	12.0	.9	50.2
1954	627.4	271.5	64.5	97.5	42.1	55.4	109.4	66.6	5.7	10.7	.3	50.0
1953	533.8	259.0	62.9	88.3	39.5	48.8	107.8	68.6	8.1	10.7	.4	49.4
1952	520.6	246.4	61.8	80.0	37.0	43.0	104.6	68.3	6.1	12.8	.3	49.2
1951	486.4	234.6	59.7	72.2	34.2	38.0	102.7	68.1	---------	---------	.2	49.1
1950	447.5	225.1	56.5	67.3	32.4	34.9	101.3	69.1	---------	---------	.2	49.6
1949	413.1	222.4	54.3	64.8	32.4	32.4	103.3	69.6	---------	---------	.1	49.3
1948	394.7	219.4	56.2	62.1	32.2	29.9	101.0	68.6	---------	---------	.2	47.8
1947	388.6	217.8	58.9	59.9	31.9	27.9	99.1	68.2	---------	---------	.1	46.2
1946	380.5	213.4	60.3	56.4	30.8	25.7	96.7	67.1	---------	---------	(Z)	44.2
1945	372.8	203.7	56.4	50.1	27.2	23.0	97.2	68.3	---------	---------	−.1	42.9

Year	Financial assets—Con.										
	Deposits and credit market instruments—Con.				Corporate equities			Life insurance reserves	Pension fund reserves	Security credit	Miscellaneous
	Credit market instruments—Con.										
	State and local obligations	Commercial paper	Corporate and foreign bonds	Mortgages	Total	Investment company shares	Other corporate shares				
	126	127	128	129	130	131	132	133	134	135	136
1970	47.4	6.1	39.8	42.5	763.1	47.6	715.4	130.3	237.4	2.2	26.3
1969	45.4	7.9	27.4	40.2	775.5	48.3	727.2	125.0	216.8	2.6	23.8
1968	38.2	1.9	21.7	38.4	874.4	52.7	821.7	120.0	206.2	3.5	21.6
1967	38.4	(Z)	16.8	36.6	754.6	44.7	709.9	115.4	185.2	2.7	19.8
1966	40.1	2.3	12.8	35.7	595.5	34.8	560.7	110.6	163.2	1.6	18.2
1965	36.4	.1	11.3	34.3	667.0	35.2	631.8	105.9	153.7	1.7	17.0
1964	34.7	(Z)	10.0	35.1	588.7	29.1	559.6	101.1	137.3	1.2	15.7
1963	32.7	.1	9.5	34.8	514.9	25.2	489.7	96.6	122.8	1.2	14.8
1962	31.2	.1	9.7	34.5	437.8	21.3	416.6	92.4	109.5	1.2	14.3
1961	32.2	.2	10.3	33.5	501.6	22.9	478.7	88.6	103.5	1.2	13.8
1960	30.8	.1	9.8	31.8	396.1	17.0	379.0	85.2	90.7	1.1	13.3
1959	27.3	.3	9.4	29.9	402.7	15.8	386.9	82.0	82.1	1.0	12.8
1958	24.3	.3	9.5	28.1	374.0	13.2	360.7	78.5	72.4	1.2	12.3
1957	23.5	.1	8.5	25.8	267.7	8.7	259.0	75.5	62.6	.9	12.0
1956	21.7	.1	7.4	23.9	305.4	9.0	296.4	72.7	56.6	.9	11.7
1955	19.3	.1	6.6	22.4	286.7	.7.8	278.9	69.3	50.4	.9	11.4
1954	16.0	.1	5.5	21.2	235.0	6.1	228.9	66.3	42.6	1.0	10.9
1953	13.5	.1	5.6	20.0	162.4	4.1	158.3	63.6	37.4	.7	10.6
1952	11.5	(Z)	5.7	19.0	170.4	3.9	166.5	60.7	32.4	.7	10.0
1951	10.4	.1	6.0	18.3	156.4	3.5	152.9	57.8	27.5	.8	9.3
1950	10.0	(Z)	4.9	17.4	133.7	3.3	130.4	55.0	24.0	.9	8.7
1949	9.5	(Z)	7.5	16.7	109.5	3.1	106.4	52.1	20.1	.6	8.4
1948	8.8	(Z)	7.7	15.9	100.2	1.5	98.7	49.4	17.2	.6	8.0
1947	7.8	.1	8.1	14.8	101.3	1.4	99.9	46.5	14.8	.6	7.6
1946	7.4	.1	8.7	13.5	103.5	1.3	102.2	43.4	12.5	.7	7.1
1945	7.3	(Z)	9.6	12.0	111.6	1.3	110.4	39.6	11.0	.6	6.3

Z   Less than $50 million, or less than −$50 million.

Series X 114–147. Financial Assets and Liabilities of Households, Personal Trusts, and Nonprofit Organizations: 1945 to 1970—Con.

[In billions of dollars. As of December 31]

Year	Total	Liabilities								Security credit	Trade credit	Deferred and unpaid life insurance premiums
		Credit market instruments										
		Total	Home mortgages	Other mortgages	Installment consumer credit	Other consumer credit	Bank loans	Other loans				
	137	138	139	140	141	142	143	144	145	146	147
1970	483.6	463.2	273.1	20.5	101.2	25.6	21.9	20.9	10.0	5.3	5.1
1969	461.9	440.6	260.4	19.1	98.2	24.3	20.4	18.3	11.9	4.7	4.7
1968	430.8	407.9	244.1	17.8	89.9	23.3	17.5	15.3	14.4	4.2	4.3
1967	395.8	375.8	229.4	16.7	80.9	21.2	14.4	13.3	12.3	3.7	3.9
1966	372.2	356.2	219.0	15.5	77.5	20.0	12.2	11.9	9.0	3.3	3.7
1965	349.4	333.8	206.4	14.2	71.3	19.0	11.9	11.0	9.2	3.0	3.3
1964	319.3	305.1	191.1	13.1	62.7	17.6	10.5	10.1	8.4	2.8	3.0
1963	291.2	277.2	175.1	12.0	55.5	16.3	9.1	9.2	8.6	2.5	2.9
1962	264.1	252.4	160.4	11.0	48.7	15.1	8.6	8.5	6.6	2.4	2.7
1961	243.1	231.6	147.7	10.1	43.9	14.1	8.1	7.7	6.7	2.2	2.5
1960	226.2	216.3	136.8	9.2	43.0	13.2	7.2	7.0	5.4	2.1	2.4
1959	208.4	198.6	126.0	8.3	39.2	12.3	6.7	6.1	5.5	2.1	2.2
1958	186.4	177.2	113.4	7.5	33.6	11.5	5.7	5.4	5.5	1.8	2.0
1957	174.0	166.1	104.6	6.7	33.9	11.1	5.0	5.0	4.4	1.6	1.8
1956	161.2	153.2	95.8	5.9	31.7	10.6	4.8	4.4	4.8	1.5	1.7
1955	144.8	137.1	84.6	5.2	28.9	9.9	4.4	4.1	4.8	1.4	1.5
1954	124.1	117.4	72.4	4.6	23.6	8.9	4.1	3.8	4.1	1.3	1.3
1953	111.8	106.3	63.8	3.9	23.0	8.4	3.7	3.5	3.0	1.2	1.3
1952	98.7	93.8	56.1	3.4	19.4	8.1	3.5	3.3	2.6	1.1	1.2
1951	87.1	82.7	49.7	2.9	15.3	7.4	4.3	3.2	2.4	.9	1.1
1950	77.4	73.0	42.6	2.4	14.7	6.8	3.8	2.9	2.5	.9	1.0
1949	63.2	59.7	35.2	1.8	11.6	5.8	2.7	2.6	1.8	.8	.9
1948	54.9	51.8	31.1	1.3	9.0	5.5	2.5	2.4	1.5	.7	.8
1947	46.3	43.1	26.1	.9	6.7	4.9	2.3	2.2	1.8	.7	.8
1946	38.7	35.2	21.8	.7	4.2	4.2	2.3	2.1	2.2	.6	.7
1945	34.1	28.1	18.0	.5	2.5	3.2	1.8	2.1	4.9	.5	.6

Series X 148–191. Saving and Investment of Households, Personal Trusts, and Nonprofit Organizations: 1946 to 1970

[In billions of dollars]

Year	Personal income	Less: personal taxes and nontaxes	Equals: disposable personal income	Less: personal outlays	Equals: personal savings NIA [1] basis	Credits from government insurance	Capital gains dividends	Net durables in consumption	Net saving	Capital consumption	Gross saving	Gross investment		
												Total	Capital expenditures [2]	
													Total	Residential construction
	148	149	150	151	152	153	154	155	156	157	158	159	160	161
1970	806.3	116.7	689.5	634.7	54.8	9.2	0.9	9.9	74.9	91.3	166.2	174.4	115.3	19.6
1969	750.9	116.5	634.4	596.2	38.2	6.6	2.5	16.2	63.6	84.8	148.4	144.6	117.8	22.0
1968	688.9	97.9	591.0	551.2	39.8	6.0	2.5	16.7	64.9	77.2	142.0	143.5	109.7	21.1
1967	629.3	83.0	546.3	506.0	40.4	5.4	1.7	12.4	59.8	69.9	129.8	131.9	94.6	17.0
1966	587.2	75.4	511.9	479.3	32.5	5.2	1.3	15.2	54.2	64.3	118.5	126.7	94.2	18.9
1965	538.9	65.7	473.2	444.8	28.4	4.8	.9	14.8	49.0	59.9	108.8	113.6	89.5	19.1
1964	497.5	59.4	438.1	411.9	26.2	4.2	.6	11.2	42.1	55.9	98.0	103.0	82.2	19.3
1963	465.5	60.9	404.6	384.7	19.9	3.7	.5	8.9	33.0	52.4	85.4	92.5	76.3	19.0
1962	442.6	57.4	385.3	363.7	21.6	3.6	.5	6.7	32.4	49.8	82.2	85.8	71.5	18.7
1961	416.8	52.4	364.4	343.3	21.2	3.5	.5	2.9	28.0	47.8	75.8	80.9	64.7	17.6
1960	401.0	50.9	350.0	333.0	17.0	3.3	.4	5.1	25.8	46.3	72.1	75.9	67.8	19.7
1959	383.5	46.2	337.3	318.3	19.1	3.0	.4	5.5	28.0	44.5	72.5	78.2	68.3	21.4
1958	361.2	42.3	318.8	296.6	22.3	2.5	.3	.6	25.6	42.6	68.3	75.7	57.7	17.3
1957	351.1	42.6	308.5	287.8	20.7	2.2	.3	4.9	28.1	40.8	68.8	74.5	61.2	18.1
1956	333.0	39.8	293.2	272.6	20.6	2.6	.3	5.9	29.3	37.4	66.7	73.2	61.2	20.2
1955	310.9	35.5	275.3	259.5	15.8	1.8	.2	9.9	27.8	33.8	61.5	67.7	62.6	21.1
1954	290.1	32.7	257.4	241.0	16.4	1.6	.1	4.9	23.0	31.5	54.5	59.1	51.5	16.8
1953	288.2	35.6	252.6	234.3	18.3	1.9	.1	6.4	26.7	30.0	56.7	60.4	50.9	16.2
1952	272.5	34.1	238.3	220.2	18.2	2.0	.1	3.6	23.8	28.6	52.4	55.3	46.0	15.3
1951	255.6	29.0	226.6	209.3	17.3	1.6	.1	5.5	24.5	26.8	51.2	56.2	46.9	15.8
1950	227.6	20.7	206.9	193.9	13.1	1.8	.1	10.2	25.1	22.5	47.7	49.4	47.5	15.6
1949	207.2	18.6	188.6	179.2	9.4	1.7	(Z)	7.0	18.1	19.6	37.7	38.3	36.6	10.7
1948	210.2	21.1	189.1	175.8	13.4	1.5	(Z)	7.1	22.0	17.4	39.4	40.5	35.8	12.1
1947	191.3	21.4	169.8	162.5	7.3	1.8	(Z)	7.5	16.7	14.6	31.2	35.4	29.4	8.3
1946	178.7	18.7	160.0	144.8	15.2	1.8	.1	5.8	22.9	11.5	34.4	37.5	21.8	5.5

See footnotes at end of table.

Series X 148–191. Saving and Investment of Households, Personal Trusts, and Nonprofit Organizations: 1946 to 1970—Con.

[In billions of dollars]

Year	Capital expenditures [2]—Con. Consumer durable goods	Nonprofit plant and equipment	Net financial investment	Net acquisition of financial assets Total	Deposits and credit market instruments [3] Total	Demand deposits and currency	Savings accounts Total	Commercial banks	Savings institutions	Credit market instruments Total	U.S. Government securities	State and local obligations	Commercial paper	Corporate and foreign bonds	Mortgages
	162	163	164	165	166	167	168	169	170	171	172	173	174	175	176
1970	90.5	5.3	59.1	80.5	61.1	6.1	44.5	27.6	17.0	10.4	-4.4	2.0	-1.8	12.4	2.2
1969	90.8	5.1	26.7	57.6	42.9	3.5	6.1	-1.9	8.0	33.3	12.1	7.6	5.9	5.7	2.0
1968	84.0	4.5	33.8	68.6	55.8	12.6	30.4	17.4	13.0	12.9	4.5	-.2	2.0	4.8	1.8
1967	73.1	4.5	37.3	61.0	46.8	11.1	34.8	18.1	16.7	.9	-.8	-1.7	-2.3	4.8	.9
1966	70.8	4.5	32.5	56.1	40.5	2.6	20.5	13.2	7.3	17.5	8.4	3.7	2.2	1.9	1.3
1965	66.3	4.1	24.1	54.3	39.3	7.9	28.0	14.9	13.2	3.4	1.7	1.7	(Z)	.7	-.8
1964	59.2	3.7	20.8	48.9	36.1	4.5	27.4	11.6	15.8	4.2	2.0	2.0	(Z)	-.1	.3
1963	53.9	3.4	16.2	43.3	33.8	3.6	24.6	9.5	15.1	5.5	3.9	1.5	(Z)	-.3	.3
1962	49.5	3.2	14.3	35.3	26.1	.9	25.7	12.6	13.1	-.6	.3	-1.0	-.2	-.6	1.0
1961	44.2	3.0	16.2	33.1	22.8	2.6	16.5	5.4	11.2	3.7	-.5	1.4	.8	.3	1.7
1960	45.3	2.8	8.1	25.9	17.3	.4	11.4	1.8	9.6	5.5	.1	3.5	-.2	.2	2.0
1959	44.3	2.6	9.9	31.9	24.1	2.2	11.3	2.8	8.5	10.5	5.5	3.0	-.1	.3	1.8
1958	37.9	2.5	18.0	30.5	17.9	2.4	14.1	5.3	8.7	1.5	-2.9	.8	.1	1.1	2.3
1957	40.8	2.4	13.3	26.1	15.9	-1.3	12.1	5.2	6.9	5.0	.3	1.8	(Z)	1.0	1.9
1956	38.9	2.1	12.0	28.4	17.2	1.6	9.6	2.3	7.3	6.0	1.2	2.4	(Z)	.9	1.5
1955	39.6	1.9	5.1	25.7	17.7	.8	8.8	1.6	7.1	8.2	2.5	3.4	(Z)	1.1	1.2
1954	32.8	1.9	7.7	20.0	12.2	1.6	9.3	2.6	6.7	1.3	-1.9	2.5	(Z)	-.4	1.2
1953	33.2	1.5	9.4	22.5	12.7	1.1	8.3	2.5	5.8	3.3	.2	2.0	.1	(Z)	1.0
1952	29.3	1.4	9.4	22.0	11.9	2.1	7.8	2.8	5.0	2.0	.3	1.1	(Z)	-.1	.8
1951	29.6	1.5	9.2	18.9	8.1	3.2	4.9	1.8	3.1	.1	-1.0	.3	.1	-.2	.9
1950	30.5	1.4	1.8	16.1	4.7	2.3	2.5	.1	2.4	-.2	-.6	.5	(Z)	-.8	.7
1949	24.6	1.3	1.7	10.0	2.8	-1.9	2.7	.1	2.5	2.1	1.0	.7	(Z)	-.4	.7
1948	22.7	1.0	4.6	13.2	1.8	-2.7	2.3	.3	2.0	2.2	.3	1.0	-.1	-.2	1.2
1947	20.4	.7	6.0	13.6	4.3	-1.4	3.4	1.2	2.3	2.2	1.1	.4	(Z)	-.2	1.3
1946	15.8	.5	15.7	20.3	9.6	3.8	6.3	3.6	2.7	-.5	-1.2	(Z)	(Z)	-.9	1.5

Gross investment—Con.

Year	Net acquisition of financial assets—Con. Investment company shares	Other corporation shares	Life insurance reserves	Pension fund reserves	Other	Net increase in liabilities Total	Credit market instruments Total	Home mortgages	Other mortgages	Installment consumer credit	Other consumer credit	Bank loans [4]	Other loans	Other	Discrepancy
	177	178	179	180	181	182	183	184	185	186	187	188	189	190	191
1970	2.6	-5.2	5.2	19.5	-2.7	21.5	22.4	12.5	1.4	3.0	1.3	1.5	2.6	-0.9	-8.2
1969	5.5	-9.6	4.9	15.8	-2.0	30.8	32.4	16.1	1.3	8.3	1.0	2.8	3.0	-1.6	3.9
1968	4.7	-12.3	4.5	15.4	.5	34.8	31.9	14.9	1.1	9.0	2.1	3.1	1.7	3.0	-1.4
1967	2.6	-6.8	5.0	14.4	-1.0	23.7	19.7	10.5	1.2	3.4	1.2	2.1	1.3	4.0	-2.1
1966	3.7	-4.7	4.6	14.4	-2.3	23.6	23.2	12.3	1.3	6.2	1.0	.4	2.0	.5	-8.2
1965	3.1	-5.1	4.8	12.3	-.1	30.2	28.8	15.2	1.2	8.6	1.4	1.4	.9	1.3	-4.8
1964	1.9	-1.9	4.3	10.9	-2.4	28.1	27.9	16.0	1.0	7.2	1.3	1.4	.9	.3	-5.0
1963	1.2	-4.0	4.1	9.7	-1.6	27.1	24.8	14.8	1.0	6.8	1.2	.4	.7	2.4	-7.1
1962	1.8	-3.9	3.7	9.1	-1.6	21.0	20.8	12.7	1.0	4.8	1.0	.5	.8	.3	-3.6
1961	1.9	-1.5	3.4	8.8	-2.3	16.9	15.3	10.9	.9	.9	.9	.9	.8	1.5	-5.1
1960	1.5	-1.9	3.2	8.4	-2.7	17.8	17.7	10.8	.9	3.7	.9	.6	.9	.1	-3.8
1959	1.7	-1.1	2.9	8.5	-4.3	22.0	21.5	12.6	.8	5.6	.8	1.0	.7	.5	-5.7
1958	1.4	.1	2.9	7.1	1.1	12.5	11.0	8.8	.8	-.2	.4	.7	.5	1.5	-7.4
1957	1.2	.3	2.7	6.7	-.8	12.8	12.9	8.8	.8	2.1	.5	.2	.5	-.1	-5.7
1956	1.1	.9	3.4	6.2	-.4	16.4	16.1	11.2	.7	2.8	.7	.4	.3	.3	-6.4
1955	.9	.2	2.8	5.6	-1.4	20.6	19.7	12.2	.6	5.3	1.0	.3	.3	.9	-6.2
1954	.5	.2	2.7	5.2	-.8	12.3	11.1	8.6	.7	.6	.5	.4	.3	1.3	-4.6
1953	.4	.5	3.0	5.0	1.0	13.1	12.5	7.7	.5	3.6	.3	.2	.3	.7	-3.7
1952	.5	1.0	2.8	4.9	.8	12.6	12.2	6.4	.5	4.1	.7	.3	.1	.5	-2.9
1951	.3	1.3	2.6	3.5	3.0	9.7	9.7	7.1	.6	.6	.7	.5	.3	-.1	-4.9
1950	.2	.5	2.9	3.9	3.8	14.2	13.3	7.4	.5	3.1	1.0	1.1	.3	.9	-1.7
1949	.3	.4	2.7	2.8	.9	8.3	7.9	4.1	.5	2.6	.3	.2	.2	.4	-.6
1948	.1	.9	2.8	2.5	5.2	8.6	8.7	5.0	.4	2.3	.5	.3	.2	-.1	-1.1
1947	.2	.9	3.1	2.2	2.9	7.6	7.8	4.3	.3	2.5	.7	(Z)	.1	-.2	-4.2
1946	.3	.8	3.8	1.5	4.2	4.6	7.1	3.8	.2	1.7	1.0	.5	(Z)	-2.5	-3.1

Z Less than $50 million, or less than −$50 million.
[1] NIA = National income accounts.
[2] Net of sales.

[3] Excludes corporate equities.
[4] Not elsewhere classified.

Series X 192–206. Financial Assets and Liabilities of Nonfinancial Business: 1945 to 1970

[In billions of dollars. As of December 31]

Year	Financial assets						Liabilities									
	Total	Demand deposits and currency	Time deposits	Credit market instruments	Trade credit	Miscel-laneous	Total	Credit market instruments						Net trade debt	Other
								Total	Corpor-ate bonds	Home mort-gages	Other mort-gages	Bank loans [1]	Other loans		
	192	193	194	195	196	197	198	199	200	201	202	203	204	205	206
1970	394.3	52.7	13.5	55.7	176.5	95.9	694.9	492.8	167.9	2.5	151.1	121.7	49.6	131.0	71.0
1969	379.0	52.2	11.8	56.8	170.3	87.9	642.6	450.5	147.6	2.4	139.4	118.4	42.7	122.3	69.8
1968	353.4	50.8	14.2	54.6	153.0	80.8	576.4	404.0	135.6	3.0	128.4	103.7	33.3	104.3	68.1
1967	326.0	49.5	13.8	48.3	139.0	75.3	519.2	364.1	122.7	2.7	117.5	92.7	28.4	94.6	60.5
1966	306.3	48.0	11.7	45.8	131.3	69.4	476.6	328.3	108.0	1.6	108.3	84.7	25.6	88.5	59.8
1965	290.9	47.7	13.1	46.6	120.0	63.5	430.1	295.4	97.8	2.5	98.6	74.3	22.1	78.5	56.2
1964	268.1	47.3	10.8	45.0	107.0	58.0	386.4	265.7	92.4	2.4	89.5	62.0	19.5	69.8	50.8
1963	252.3	46.8	10.8	42.8	98.8	53.2	360.3	244.9	88.4	2.7	80.1	56.8	16.8	67.5	48.0
1962	236.2	46.6	8.4	39.5	92.6	49.1	332.0	224.8	84.5	2.4	71.1	51.5	15.3	63.4	43.8
1961	223.5	46.2	6.9	37.2	88.0	45.2	307.0	207.5	80.0	2.3	63.2	47.7	14.4	60.4	39.1
1960	211.1	45.8	3.9	36.6	82.3	42.5	297.2	193.5	75.3	2.1	56.4	46.3	13.5	57.9	45.7
1959	207.4	48.4	1.5	40.6	78.2	38.7	282.4	181.0	71.9	2.7	51.6	43.8	11.0	55.1	46.2
1958	193.2	50.9	1.9	32.8	72.2	35.3	259.5	167.2	68.9	2.6	46.6	39.0	10.2	51.8	40.5
1957	180.0	48.2	1.0	31.9	66.2	32.6	246.1	156.1	63.2	2.1	42.2	38.7	9.9	48.8	41.2
1956	174.0	47.5	1.0	31.9	64.9	28.7	234.4	144.6	56.9	2.3	39.6	37.1	8.7	48.7	41.6
1955	168.5	47.6	1.0	35.3	59.3	25.2	218.7	132.1	53.3	2.7	36.4	31.4	8.3	45.7	40.9
1954	150.4	46.4	1.1	30.1	49.6	23.1	193.8	120.5	50.4	2.5	33.4	26.3	7.8	37.7	35.6
1953	144.1	44.2	.9	31.4	46.2	21.4	187.2	114.4	47.0	1.8	31.3	26.8	7.6	35.4	37.5
1952	140.8	44.4	.9	29.0	47.0	19.5	179.4	109.8	43.6	1.9	29.5	27.8	7.0	35.1	34.5
1951	135.1	44.1	.9	28.7	44.0	17.4	171.8	100.4	38.9	1.7	27.7	24.8	7.3	36.3	35.2
1950	125.3	41.3	.9	26.9	40.5	15.7	151.2	90.1	35.7	2.3	25.3	20.3	6.5	32.0	29.1
1949	107.6	39.7	.9	22.3	30.3	14.4	125.8	81.8	34.2	2.2	23.2	16.3	5.9	23.6	20.5
1948	103.3	38.8	.9	19.6	31.1	13.0	125.5	79.0	31.4	1.9	21.6	18.3	5.7	24.6	22.0
1947	97.3	38.5	.9	17.8	28.8	11.3	113.8	72.2	27.2	1.9	19.8	18.0	5.3	21.5	20.2
1946	86.5	35.1	.9	17.2	23.7	9.7	97.6	62.9	24.4	1.1	18.0	14.2	5.0	18.1	16.6
1945	85.9	32.8	.9	22.0	21.0	9.2	86.6	55.5	23.5	.6	16.4	9.9	5.0	12.5	18.6

[1] Not elsewhere classified.

Series X 207–228. Saving and Investment of Nonfinancial Business: 1946 to 1970

[In billions of dollars]

Year	Income before taxes	Gross saving	Gross investment	Capital expenditures					Change in inventories
				Total	Fixed investment				
					Total	Business plant and equipment	1-4 family residential construction	Other residential	
	207	208	209	210	211	212	213	214	215
1970	127.5	79.8	72.9	110.1	105.2	93.6	0.8	10.8	4.9
1969	139.5	80.4	68.0	109.3	101.4	90.8	.1	10.6	7.8
1968	142.4	79.8	69.6	99.0	92.0	83.0	.9	8.1	7.1
1967	136.2	78.4	68.5	94.0	85.8	77.8	2.0	6.1	8.2
1966	139.1	77.1	66.6	97.0	82.2	76.1	−.7	6.8	14.8
1965	129.5	71.8	60.4	84.1	74.4	66.3	.7	7.4	9.6
1964	115.3	65.0	56.0	70.2	64.3	56.5	.1	7.7	5.8
1963	106.9	57.3	49.5	63.8	57.9	49.9	1.0	7.0	5.9
1962	102.4	55.0	47.5	60.4	54.4	47.8	.7	5.9	6.0
1961	95.7	48.2	42.3	50.4	48.4	43.3	.9	4.2	2.0
1960	93.4	46.9	40.3	51.8	48.2	45.1	−.2	3.3	3.6
1959	96.2	47.2	41.1	50.6	45.8	41.7	.8	3.2	4.8
1958	87.1	41.2	32.6	40.5	42.0	38.5	1.2	2.3	−1.5
1957	89.3	42.0	41.5	46.8	45.4	43.3	.4	1.7	1.3
1956	88.5	39.7	33.2	47.2	42.5	41.1	.2	1.3	4.7
1955	88.3	39.3	33.8	43.8	37.9	35.7	.9	1.2	6.0
1954	78.0	33.1	29.9	32.6	34.1	31.2	1.6	1.3	−1.5
1953	80.6	30.5	28.1	34.6	34.2	32.4	.6	1.2	.4
1952	82.9	30.0	29.7	34.8	31.7	29.8	1.0	.9	3.1
1951	85.6	28.3	27.8	41.7	31.4	30.0	(Z)	1.4	10.3
1950	76.3	25.3	24.0	36.7	29.9	26.2	.9	2.8	6.8
1949	67.1	25.7	24.2	23.4	26.5	23.5	1.1	1.8	−3.1
1948	74.9	24.4	20.7	32.6	27.9	25.5	.9	1.5	4.7
1947	63.2	17.4	14.8	24.8	25.3	22.5	1.7	1.1	−.5
1946	57.5	11.6	9.8	24.7	18.3	16.6	1.2	.5	6.4

See footnotes at end of table.

Series X 207–228. Saving and Investment of Nonfinancial Business: 1946 to 1970—Con.

[In billions of dollars]

Year	Total	Net financial uses of funds	Net financial investment											Discrepancy
			Net financial sources of funds											
			Total	Corporate share issues	Credit market instruments							Trade debt	Other liabilities	
					Total	Corporate bonds	Home mortgages	Other mortgages	Bank loans¹	Other loans				
	216	217	218	219	220	221	222	223	224	225	226	227	228
1970	−37.3	12.6	49.9	6.8	42.7	20.3	0.3	11.7	3.5	7.0	4.5	−4.0	6.9
1969	−41.3	22.9	64.2	4.3	46.6	12.1	−.4	11.0	14.6	9.3	15.1	−1.9	12.5
1968	−29.5	25.1	54.6	−.8	40.0	12.9	.3	11.0	11.0	4.8	10.5	5.0	10.3
1967	−25.5	18.0	43.6	2.3	35.8	14.7	1.1	9.2	8.0	2.8	9.0	−3.5	9.9
1966	−30.4	13.7	44.1	1.2	33.0	10.2	−1.0	9.7	10.4	3.6	10.1	−.1	10.6
1965	−23.6	21.2	44.8	(Z)	29.6	5.4	.1	9.1	12.3	2.6	12.1	3.1	11.4
1964	−14.2	14.4	28.6	1.4	21.2	4.0	−.3	9.4	5.5	2.6	6.8	−.8	9.0
1963	−14.2	14.7	28.9	−.3	19.7	3.9	.4	9.0	4.9	1.5	7.7	1.8	7.8
1962	−13.0	11.8	24.7	.6	17.4	4.6	.1	8.0	3.9	.9	4.3	2.5	7.5
1961	−8.2	13.0	21.2	2.5	13.9	4.6	.2	6.8	1.4	.9	5.9	−1.1	5.9
1960	−11.5	2.3	13.8	1.6	12.5	3.5	−.6	4.7	2.5	2.5	3.6	−3.9	6.6
1959	−9.5	13.1	22.6	2.2	14.0	3.0	.2	5.1	5.1	.7	5.4	.9	6.1
1958	−7.9	12.4	20.3	2.1	11.1	5.7	.5	4.4	.3	.3	7.6	−.4	8.6
1957	−5.3	5.3	10.6	2.4	11.6	6.3	−.2	2.7	1.6	1.2	−1.8	−1.7	.5
1956	−14.0	4.6	18.6	2.3	12.5	3.6	−.4	3.1	5.7	.5	4.0	−.1	6.6
1955	−10.0	17.2	27.2	1.9	11.7	2.8	.3	3.0	5.0	.6	10.2	3.3	5.4
1954	−2.6	5.6	8.3	1.6	6.1	3.5	.7	2.1	−.4	.2	4.1	−3.6	3.2
1953	−6.6	2.5	9.1	1.8	4.3	3.4	−.1	1.8	−1.0	.3	−.2	3.2	2.4
1952	−5.1	4.9	10.0	2.3	8.3	4.7	.2	1.8	1.9	−.3	−.2	−.5	.3
1951	−13.9	9.1	22.9	1.9	10.3	3.3	−.6	2.4	4.5	.8	2.3	8.4	.4
1950	−12.7	17.2	29.9	1.4	8.5	1.6	.1	2.1	4.0	.7	8.6	11.4	1.3
1949	.7	3.8	3.1	1.3	2.9	2.9	.2	1.7	−2.1	.2	(Z)	−1.1	1.6
1948	−11.9	5.5	17.4	1.0	6.4	4.3	(Z)	1.8	−.1	.4	3.4	6.5	3.7
1947	−10.0	10.4	20.3	1.2	9.4	2.8	.8	1.7	3.8	.2	3.8	6.0	2.5
1946	−14.9	1.0	15.9	1.1	7.5	1.0	.6	1.6	4.3	.1	6.0	1.4	1.8

Z Less than $50 million, or less than −$50 million.   ¹ Not elsewhere classified.

Series X 229–244. Financial Assets and Liabilities of State and Local Governments: 1945 to 1970

[In billions of dollars. As of December 31]

Year	Total	Demand deposits and currency	Time deposits	Financial assets						Liabilities						
				Credit market instruments					Taxes receivable	Total	Credit market instruments					Trade debt
				Total	U.S. Government securities	State and local obligations	Corporate bonds	Home mortgages			Total	State and local obligations			Other loans (U.S. Govt.)	
												Total	Short-term	Other		
	229	230	231	232	233	234	235	236	237	238	239	240	241	242	243	244
1970	71.7	10.0	23.2	36.8	27.4	2.3	4.9	2.2	1.7	157.4	151.1	146.2	14.6	131.7	4.8	6.3
1969	64.9	10.0	13.2	39.1	27.7	2.2	7.0	2.2	2.5	143.0	137.1	132.4	10.7	121.7	4.7	5.9
1968	62.2	8.0	19.1	32.0	22.5	2.2	5.1	2.2	3.2	133.9	128.4	124.4	8.1	116.3	4.0	5.4
1967	55.2	7.4	15.9	29.4	20.2	2.1	4.9	2.2	2.5	122.8	117.9	114.4	8.0	106.4	3.6	4.8
1966	51.2	8.4	13.5	27.1	18.4	2.1	4.4	2.1	2.3	113.6	109.5	106.0	6.2	99.9	3.4	4.2
1965	48.2	9.2	12.2	24.8	16.6	2.2	3.8	2.1	2.1	106.8	103.1	100.3	5.5	94.8	2.8	3.7
1964	43.5	9.6	9.8	22.2	14.7	2.2	3.1	2.2	1.9	98.8	95.5	93.0	4.9	88.1	2.5	3.3
1963	39.2	8.2	8.1	21.7	14.8	2.3	2.4	2.2	1.3	92.5	89.5	87.3	4.3	83.0	2.2	3.0
1962	35.4	7.0	6.5	20.9	14.5	2.6	1.8	2.1	1.1	86.2	83.4	81.4	3.9	77.5	2.0	2.8
1961	32.3	6.1	5.5	19.8	13.7	2.8	1.3	2.0	1.0	80.2	77.5	76.1	3.6	72.4	1.5	2.7
1960	30.8	6.4	4.6	18.9	13.4	2.7	1.5	1.3	.9	74.5	72.1	70.8	3.4	67.4	1.2	2.5
1959	28.8	7.0	3.2	17.7	12.8	2.7	.9	1.4	.9	69.0	66.6	65.6	3.2	62.4	1.0	2.4
1958	27.7	6.9	3.6	16.5	11.7	2.7	.9	1.1	.8	62.6	60.4	59.5	2.8	56.7	.9	2.3
1957	26.6	6.9	2.8	16.1	11.8	2.6	.6	1.0	.9	56.8	54.7	54.0	2.3	51.7	.7	2.1
1956	25.7	6.9	2.4	15.5	11.5	2.5	.6	.9	1.0	52.0	50.1	49.6	2.2	47.4	.5	1.9
1955	25.3	7.3	2.4	14.7	10.8	2.5	.7	.7	1.0	48.0	46.3	45.8	2.1	43.7	.5	1.8
1954	24.6	7.5	2.4	13.9	10.2	2.5	.7	.6	.8	42.7	41.1	40.6	2.0	38.6	.4	1.6
1953	22.9	7.8	2.0	12.3	9.0	2.3	.6	.5	.9	36.9	35.4	34.6	1.9	32.7	.8	1.5
1952	20.9	7.4	1.6	11.0	7.8	2.1	.6	.4	.9	32.7	31.3	30.2	1.8	28.4	1.1	1.4
1951	19.2	7.0	1.5	9.8	6.9	2.1	.5	.3	.9	29.5	28.2	27.4	1.6	25.8	.8	1.3
1950	17.9	6.7	1.4	9.0	6.5	2.0	.3	.2	.8	27.1	25.8	25.2	1.3	24.0	.6	1.3
1949	16.4	6.3	1.3	8.2	6.0	1.7	.2	.2	.6	23.6	22.4	21.9	.9	21.0	.5	1.2
1948	15.7	6.1	1.1	7.7	6.0	1.4	.2	.1	.7	21.0	19.9	19.3	.7	18.6	.6	1.1
1947	14.3	5.7	.9	7.1	5.5	1.4	.1	.1	.6	18.6	17.7	17.2	.5	16.6	.5	.9
1946	12.7	5.1	.7	6.5	4.9	1.5	.1	(Z)	.5	17.0	16.2	15.7	.3	15.4	.5	.8
1945	12.5	4.4	.5	7.1	5.2	1.8	.2	−	.5	16.8	16.2	15.7	.3	15.4	.5	.6

− Represents zero.   Z Less than $50 million.

Series X 245–262. Saving and Investment of State and Local Governments: 1946 to 1970

[In billions of dollars]

Year	Net surplus NIA [1] basis	Less— retirement credit to households	Equals— gross saving	Net financial investment	Net acquisition of financial assets			Credit market instruments	
					Total	Currency and demand deposits	Time deposits	Total	U.S. Government securities
	245	246	247	248	249	250	251	252	253
1970	2.8	6.8	-3.9	-7.5	6.8	-0.1	10.0	-2.3	-0.2
1969	.7	5.0	-4.4	-6.5	2.6	2.1	-5.9	7.1	5.2
1968	-.3	4.7	-5.0	-4.0	7.0	.6	3.2	2.6	2.2
1967	-1.6	4.0	-5.5	-5.1	4.0	-1.0	2.4	2.4	1.8
1966	1.3	3.8	-2.6	-3.8	3.0	-.8	1.3	2.3	1.8
1965	1.0	3.3	-2.4	-3.4	4.6	-.4	2.4	2.5	1.9
1964	1.7	2.8	-1.1	-2.6	3.7	1.2	1.7	.5	-.1
1963	1.2	2.4	-1.2	-2.6	3.8	1.2	1.6	.8	.3
1962	.9	2.5	-1.6	-2.8	3.1	.9	1.0	1.2	.8
1961	-.5	2.5	-3.0	-4.2	1.5	-.3	.9	.8	.2
1960	.2	2.3	-2.1	-3.6	2.0	-.6	1.4	1.2	.6
1959	-.8	2.0	-2.8	-5.3	1.1	.1	-.4	1.3	1.1
1958	-2.3	1.5	-3.8	-4.8	1.1	-.1	.8	.4	-.1
1957	-1.4	1.6	-3.0	-3.8	1.0	.1	.4	.6	.3
1956	-.9	1.4	-2.3	-3.6	.4	-.4	(Z)	.7	.7
1955	-1.3	1.3	-2.6	-4.6	.7	-.2	-.1	.8	.7
1954	-1.1	1.5	-2.6	-4.2	1.7	-.3	.5	1.6	1.2
1953	.1	1.3	-1.1	-2.1	2.1	.4	.3	1.4	1.1
1952	(Z)	1.0	-1.1	-1.5	1.6	.4	.1	1.2	1.0
1951	-.4	.7	-1.2	-1.1	1.3	.3	.2	.7	.4
1950	-1.2	.7	-1.9	-2.0	1.5	.4	.1	.9	.5
1949	-.7	.5	-1.3	-1.9	.7	.2	.2	.5	.1
1948	.1	.4	-.3	-1.0	1.3	.4	.3	.6	.4
1947	1.0	.3	.7	-	1.6	.6	.2	.7	.7
1946	1.9	.3	1.6	(Z)	.2	.7	.2	-.7	-.4

Year	Net acquisition of financial assets—Con.			Net increase in liabilities					Discrepancy
	Credit market instruments—Con.		Tax receivables	Total	Credit market borrowing			Trade debt	
	State and local securities	Other			Total	State and local obligations	U.S. Government loans		
	254	255	256	257	258	259	260	261	262
1970	(Z)	-2.0	-0.9	14.4	13.9	13.8	0.1	0.4	3.6
1969	.1	1.8	-.6	9.1	8.7	7.9	.7	.4	2.1
1968	(Z)	.3	.7	11.0	10.4	10.1	.3	.6	-1.1
1967	-	.6	.3	9.1	8.5	8.3	.2	.6	-.5
1966	(Z)	.5	.2	6.9	6.4	5.7	.6	.5	1.3
1965	-.1	.7	.1	8.0	7.6	7.3	.3	.4	1.0
1964	-.1	.7	.2	6.2	6.0	5.7	.3	.3	1.5
1963	-.2	.7	.2	6.4	6.1	5.9	.2	.2	1.4
1962	-.2	.6	.1	6.0	5.8	5.3	.5	.1	1.2
1961	(Z)	.6	(Z)	5.7	5.5	5.2	.2	.2	1.2
1960	(Z)	.5	(Z)	5.5	5.4	5.2	.2	.1	1.5
1959	(Z)	.2	.1	6.4	6.3	6.1	.2	.1	2.5
1958	.1	.3	-.1	5.9	5.7	5.5	.2	.2	.9
1957	.1	.2	-.1	4.8	4.6	4.4	.2	.2	.8
1956	(Z)	.1	(Z)	4.0	3.9	3.8	.1	.1	1.3
1955	(Z)	.1	.2	5.3	5.2	5.2	(Z)	.2	2.0
1954	.2	.2	-.1	5.9	5.7	6.0	-.3	.2	1.6
1953	.2	.1	(Z)	4.2	4.1	4.4	-.4	.1	1.0
1952	.1	.2	-.1	3.2	3.1	2.7	.3	.1	.5
1951	(Z)	.3	.1	2.4	2.4	2.2	.3	-	(Z)
1950	.3	.1	.2	3.5	3.4	3.3	.1	.1	.1
1949	.3	.1	-.1	2.6	2.5	2.6	-.1	.1	.6
1948	(Z)	.1	.1	2.4	2.2	2.2	.1	.1	.7
1947	(Z)	(Z)	.2	1.6	1.4	1.4	(Z)	.2	.7
1946	-.3	(Z)	(Z)	.2	(Z)	.1	(Z)	.1	1.6

-   Represents zero.
Z   Less than $50 million, or less than −$50 million.

[1] NIA = National income accounts.

Series X 263–275. Money Supply: 1945 to 1970

[In billions of dollars. As of December 31]

Year	Total	Demand deposits and currency: Assets									Net banking system liability			
		Money supply							U.S. Government cash balances	Monetary authorities	Commercial banking			
		Total	House-holds	Non-financial business	State and local govern-ments	Financial sectors	Rest of the world	Mail float			Total	U.S. Government	Other
	263	264	265	266	267	268	269	270	271	272	273	274	275
1970	236.7	227.2	126.5	52.7	10.0	15.6	6.2	16.3	9.5	52.0	184.7	7.9	176.8
1969	224.9	217.9	120.4	52.2	10.0	14.1	6.0	15.2	7.0	48.9	176.0	5.1	171.0
1968	216.4	209.9	116.7	50.8	8.0	14.0	5.7	14.7	6.5	45.7	170.7	5.0	165.7
1967	201.4	193.7	104.1	49.5	7.4	13.0	5.1	14.5	7.7	44.2	157.3	5.2	152.0
1966	187.0	180.4	92.9	48.0	8.4	12.2	4.8	14.1	6.6	41.2	145.8	5.0	140.8
1965	184.3	177.3	90.3	47.7	9.2	12.3	4.4	13.4	7.0	38.8	145.4	5.5	139.9
1964	176.8	168.8	82.5	47.3	9.6	11.9	4.2	13.3	7.9	36.8	140.0	6.5	133.5
1963	168.2	160.4	77.9	46.8	8.2	11.6	3.5	12.4	7.8	34.2	134.0	6.5	127.4
1962	163.1	155.0	74.1	46.6	7.0	11.5	3.2	12.5	8.1	32.3	130.9	7.2	123.7
1961	158.5	151.6	72.5	46.2	6.1	10.6	3.1	13.1	6.8	31.4	127.1	5.9	121.1
1960	152.9	146.1	70.2	45.8	6.4	9.5	2.1	12.1	6.8	30.6	122.3	5.9	116.4
1959	152.7	146.8	69.9	48.4	7.0	9.1	2.1	10.4	5.9	30.8	121.9	5.1	116.8
1958	151.3	146.0	68.0	50.9	6.9	8.9	2.0	9.4	5.3	30.3	121.0	4.3	116.8
1957	145.3	140.2	65.6	48.2	6.9	8.2	2.1	9.1	5.1	30.1	115.2	3.9	111.3
1956	146.0	141.1	66.9	47.5	6.9	7.9	1.8	10.2	4.9	30.1	115.9	3.7	112.2
1955	144.2	139.4	65.3	47.6	7.3	7.8	1.5	9.9	4.9	30.0	114.2	3.7	110.5
1954	142.0	136.4	64.5	46.4	7.5	7.3	1.7	9.1	5.5	29.9	112.1	4.2	107.9
1953	137.5	132.2	62.9	44.2	7.8	6.9	1.5	8.9	5.3	29.8	107.6	4.1	103.5
1952	137.4	130.8	61.8	44.4	7.4	6.6	2.0	8.7	6.6	29.9	107.5	4.9	102.6
1951	130.9	126.0	59.7	44.1	7.0	6.4	1.7	7.0	4.9	28.6	102.3	3.4	98.9
1950	123.9	119.1	56.5	41.3	6.7	5.9	2.0	6.7	4.8	28.2	95.7	2.8	92.9
1949	118.7	113.5	54.3	39.7	6.3	5.2	2.0	6.1	5.2	28.5	90.2	3.1	87.1
1948	118.7	113.9	56.2	38.8	6.1	4.9	2.2	5.7	4.8	29.4	89.4	2.3	87.0
1947	119.2	115.7	58.9	38.5	5.7	4.8	1.7	6.0	3.5	29.3	89.9	1.3	88.6
1946	118.1	112.4	60.3	35.1	5.1	4.5	2.3	5.2	5.7	30.4	87.7	3.0	84.7
1945	132.6	104.8	56.4	32.8	4.4	3.8	2.7	4.7	27.8	31.1	101.4	24.5	76.9

Series X 276–292. Time Deposits and Savings Accounts: 1945 to 1970

[In billions of dollars. As of December 31]

Year	Total held	Commercial banking liability										Savings institutions					Households, total time deposits and savings accounts
		Total	Large negoti-able certif-icates of deposit [1]	Other	Held by							Total	Liabilities			Assets		
					House-holds	Corpo-rate business	State and local govern-ment	U.S. Govern-ment	Mutual savings banks	Foreign		Savings and loan associa-tions	Mutual savings banks	Credit unions	House-holds	Credit unions [2]	
	276	277	278	279	280	281	282	283	284	285	286	287	288	289	290	291	292
1970	466.5	233.1	26.1	207.0	189.0	13.5	23.2	0.4	0.3	6.7	233.4	146.4	71.6	15.4	233.4	(Z)	422.4
1969	411.5	195.1	10.9	184.2	161.5	11.8	13.2	.2	.1	8.4	216.4	135.5	67.1	13.7	216.4	(Z)	377.8
1968	412.9	204.5	23.5	181.0	163.4	14.2	19.1	.4	.2	7.3	208.4	131.6	64.5	12.3	208.4	.1	371.8
1967	379.6	183.7	20.3	163.4	146.0	13.8	15.9	.3	.2	7.6	195.8	124.5	60.1	11.2	195.5	.3	341.5
1966	338.8	159.8	15.7	144.2	127.9	11.7	13.5	.2	.2	6.3	179.0	114.0	55.0	10.0	178.9	.1	306.8
1965	319.7	147.7	16.3	131.4	115.9	13.1	12.2	.3	.2	6.0	172.0	110.4	52.4	9.2	171.6	.4	287.5
1964	286.5	127.6	12.6	115.0	101.1	10.8	9.8	.3	.2	5.4	159.0	101.9	48.8	8.2	158.4	.5	259.5
1963	256.1	113.0	9.9	103.1	89.4	10.8	8.1	.3	.1	4.3	143.1	91.3	44.6	7.2	142.7	.4	232.1
1962	226.5	98.6	6.2	92.4	79.9	8.4	6.5	.3	.2	3.4	127.9	80.2	41.3	6.3	127.6	.4	207.5
1961	197.8	83.0	3.2	79.8	67.3	6.9	5.5	.3	.2	2.9	114.8	70.9	38.3	5.6	114.5	.3	181.8
1960	177.1	73.6	1.1	72.5	62.0	3.9	4.6	.3	.1	2.9	103.5	62.1	36.3	5.0	103.3	.1	165.3
1959	161.8	67.8	___	67.8	60.2	1.5	3.2	.3	.1	2.6	94.0	54.6	35.0	4.4	93.7	.3	153.8
1958	151.9	66.0	___	66.0	56.6	1.9	3.6	.3	.2	3.4	85.9	48.0	34.0	3.9	85.5	.4	142.1
1957	135.0	58.0	___	58.0	51.3	1.0	2.8	.3	.1	2.5	77.0	41.9	31.7	3.4	76.7	.2	128.0
1956	122.7	52.6	___	52.6	46.1	1.0	2.4	.3	.2	2.7	70.1	37.1	30.0	2.9	69.8	.3	115.9
1955	113.3	50.5	___	50.5	43.8	1.0	2.4	.4	.2	2.8	62.8	32.1	28.2	2.4	62.5	.2	106.3
1954	104.8	49.2	___	49.2	42.1	1.1	2.4	.4	.3	2.9	55.6	27.3	26.4	2.0	55.4	.2	97.5
1953	94.3	45.3	___	45.3	39.5	.9	2.0	.3	.2	2.4	48.9	22.8	24.4	1.7	48.8	.1	88.3
1952	85.0	41.9	___	41.9	37.0	.9	1.6	.4	.2	1.8	43.2	19.2	22.6	1.4	43.0	.1	80.0
1951	76.8	38.8	___	38.8	34.2	.9	1.5	.3	.2	1.7	38.1	16.1	20.9	1.1	38.0	.1	72.2
1950	71.9	37.0	___	37.0	32.4	.9	1.4	.2	.2	2.0	34.9	14.0	20.0	.9	34.9	–	67.3
1949	69.2	36.7	___	36.7	32.4	.9	1.3	.2	.2	1.7	32.5	12.5	19.3	.7	32.4	(Z)	64.8
1948	66.2	36.2	___	36.2	32.2	.9	1.1	.1	.2	1.6	30.0	11.0	18.4	.6	29.9	.1	62.1
1947	63.6	35.6	___	35.6	31.9	.9	.9	.1	.2	1.6	28.0	9.8	17.8	.5	27.9	.1	59.9
1946	60.0	34.2	___	34.2	30.8	.9	.7	.1	.2	1.6	25.8	8.6	16.8	.4	25.7	.1	56.4
1945	53.5	30.4	___	30.4	27.2	.9	.5	.1	.1	1.6	23.1	7.4	15.3	.4	23.0	.1	50.1

– Represents zero.
Z Less than $50 million.

[1] $100,000 denomination or larger.
[2] Credit union deposits at savings and loan associations.

Series X 293–327. U.S. Government Securities: 1945 to 1970

[In billions of dollars. As of December 31]

Year	Total out-standing	Treasury direct issues — Total	House-hold savings bonds	Short-term market-able	Other direct	Other — Total	Budget agency issues	Loan partici-pation certifi-cates [1]	Sponsored agency issues [2]	U.S. Government (agency secu-rities)	Sponsored credit agen-cies	Federal Reserve System	Foreign	Private domestic — Total	Private domestic nonfinancial — Total	Direct issues (incl. savings bonds)	Agency issues [1]
	293	294	295	296	297	298	299	300	301	302	303	304	305	306	307	308	309
1970	339.2	290.8	51.4	133.8	105.6	48.4	1.9	7.1	39.3	(Z)	4.2	62.1	19.7	253.1	135.2	111.4	23.8
1969	317.6	278.0	51.1	128.4	98.4	39.7	1.6	7.5	30.6	.1	2.5	57.2	10.6	247.3	142.8	121.2	21.6
1968	312.1	279.2	51.5	119.4	108.3	32.9	1.9	9.4	21.6	1.4	2.7	52.9	12.4	242.6	126.8	111.8	15.1
1967	295.4	268.9	51.1	118.9	98.9	26.5	.5	7.7	18.4	1.3	2.9	49.1	12.9	229.3	119.1	107.3	11.9
1966	282.9	260.0	50.2	110.2	99.5	22.9	.3	3.7	18.9	1.4	2.9	44.3	10.8	223.6	120.5	108.9	11.5
1965	274.2	257.7	49.6	108.8	99.3	16.5	.2	2.4	13.8	(Z)	1.9	40.8	13.2	218.2	111.7	104.6	7.1
1964	270.5	256.4	49.0	105.8	101.6	14.2	.2	2.0	11.9	(Z)	1.8	37.0	13.4	218.3	109.5	103.4	6.1
1963	263.9	251.0	48.0	101.1	101.9	12.9	.2	1.2	11.5	(Z)	2.2	33.6	12.9	215.1	108.5	102.8	5.7
1962	258.4	246.9	46.9	99.8	100.2	11.5	.1	1.4	10.0	−	1.8	30.8	12.3	213.5	104.3	99.3	4.9
1961	250.1	240.7	46.4	98.9	95.3	9.5	.1	.9	8.5	(Z)	1.4	28.9	11.0	208.8	102.9	98.3	4.6
1960	242.5	234.0	45.6	88.2	100.1	8.5	.1	.6	7.9	(Z)	1.5	27.4	10.6	203.1	103.8	99.3	4.5
1959	244.3	236.2	45.9	84.7	105.5	8.1	.8	.2	7.1	−	1.4	26.6	10.0	206.3	108.9	104.2	4.7
1958	235.3	228.8	47.7	79.4	101.7	6.5	.8	.8	4.9	(Z)	1.3	26.3	7.0	200.7	96.3	93.8	2.4
1957	226.3	219.8	48.2	82.2	89.3	6.5	1.4	.3	4.8	(Z)	1.2	24.2	6.9	194.1	98.9	95.9	3.0
1956	227.3	222.5	50.1	75.4	97.0	4.8	.6	.8	3.4	(Z)	1.2	24.9	6.7	194.4	99.0	97.2	1.8
1955	232.6	228.0	50.2	69.0	108.8	4.6	.6	1.0	3.0	(Z)	1.0	24.8	5.8	201.0	101.6	100.3	1.4
1954	232.5	228.1	50.0	65.1	113.0	4.4	--------	2.3	2.1	(Z)	.8	24.9	4.8	201.9	94.3	93.8	.5
1953	230.1	225.7	49.4	79.8	96.6	4.4	--------	2.3	2.1	−	.6	25.9	4.5	199.0	96.8	96.2	.5
1952	223.0	220.3	49.2	63.9	107.3	2.7	--------	.6	2.1	(Z)	.5	24.7	4.1	193.8	93.8	93.4	.5
1951	218.1	215.8	49.1	51.3	115.5	2.3	--------	.2	2.1	(Z)	.4	23.8	3.0	190.9	93.6	93.2	.4
1950	218.3	216.1	49.6	166.6		2.2	--------	.4	1.8	--------	.4	20.8	3.1	194.1	93.4	93.1	.4
1949	219.1	216.7	49.3	167.4		2.5	--------	1.0	1.4	--------	.5	18.9	1.9	197.9	90.3	90.0	.3
1948	216.7	214.2	47.8	166.3		2.5	--------	.9	1.6	--------	.5	23.3	1.6	191.3	87.4	87.0	.4
1947	222.1	220.7	46.2	174.5		1.4	--------	.1	1.3	--------	.3	22.6	1.2	198.0	86.1	85.8	.3
1946	229.2	227.9	44.2	183.8		1.3	--------	.1	1.2	--------	.4	23.4	1.9	203.6	84.8	84.6	.2
1945	252.4	251.2	42.9	208.2		1.2	--------	.3	.9	--------	.4	24.3	2.6	225.2	92.0	92.0	.1

Private domestic holdings—Con.

Year	Private domestic nonfinancial—Con.: House-holds	Cor-porate nonfi-nancial busi-ness	State-local gov-ern-ments	Commercial banking — Total	Treas-ury direct issues	Agency issues	Private nonbank finance — Total	Treas-ury direct issues	Agency issues	Sav-ings and loan asso-ciations	Mutual savings banks	Credit unions	Life insur-ance	Non-life insur-ance	Private pension funds	State-local gov-ern-ment retire-ment funds	Invest-ment com-panies (direct)	Secu-rities brokers and dealers
	310	311	312	313	314	315	316	317	318	319	320	321	322	323	324	325	326	327
1970	100.4	7.4	27.4	76.9	63.2	13.6	41.0	30.1	10.9	12.3	4.9	1.3	4.2	4.3	3.0	6.9	0.9	3.4
1969	104.8	10.4	27.7	67.5	57.4	10.1	36.9	29.1	7.9	11.1	4.7	.8	4.1	4.2	2.8	6.9	.7	1.7
1968	92.7	11.6	22.5	76.9	66.6	10.3	38.9	32.8	6.1	10.9	5.2	.7	4.4	4.7	2.9	7.2	1.1	1.8
1967	88.2	10.7	20.2	73.4	64.3	9.1	36.7	32.4	4.4	10.1	5.4	.5	4.5	4.9	2.5	6.9	.9	1.0
1966	89.0	13.0	18.4	64.0	57.9	6.1	39.2	35.2	3.9	8.6	5.7	.5	4.7	5.6	3.1	7.9	1.4	1.7
1965	80.7	14.4	16.6	67.4	61.4	6.0	39.1	35.8	3.3	8.2	6.2	.3	5.1	6.0	3.6	7.8	.8	1.1
1964	79.0	15.8	14.7	69.8	64.4	5.3	39.1	36.3	2.8	7.6	6.5	.3	5.6	6.0	3.6	7.4	.8	1.4
1963	77.0	16.7	14.8	69.4	64.7	4.7	37.3	34.8	2.4	7.0	6.5	.3	5.9	5.9	3.4	6.9	.7	.7
1962	73.0	16.8	14.5	72.1	67.7	4.4	37.1	34.9	2.2	6.0	6.7	.2	6.2	5.7	3.1	6.5	.7	2.0
1961	72.7	16.5	13.7	70.7	67.7	3.0	35.2	33.3	1.9	5.7	6.6	.2	6.1	5.6	2.8	6.1	.7	1.3
1960	73.5	16.9	13.4	64.9	62.6	2.3	34.5	32.7	1.8	5.2	6.7	.2	6.5	5.6	2.7	5.9	.6	1.0
1959	73.3	22.8	12.8	62.7	60.8	1.9	34.6	33.2	1.5	4.9	7.3	.2	7.0	5.8	2.8	5.6	.6	.4
1958	67.8	16.7	11.7	71.0	68.0	3.0	33.5	32.4	1.1	4.2	7.6	.2	7.3	5.5	2.6	5.1	.4	.6
1957	70.7	16.4	11.8	62.4	60.0	2.4	32.8	31.7	1.1	3.6	7.9	.2	7.1	5.6	2.5	5.2	.3	.4
1956	70.4	17.1	11.5	62.5	60.0	2.4	32.9	32.3	.6	2.9	8.2	.2	7.6	5.7	2.7	5.0	.3	.2
1955	69.2	21.6	10.8	65.3	62.5	2.9	34.1	33.7	.4	2.5	8.6	.1	8.6	6.1	2.9	4.7	.3	.3
1954	66.6	17.5	10.2	69.7	65.9	3.7	34.2	34.0	.2	2.0	8.8	.1	9.1	6.2	2.6	4.4	.2	.7
1953	68.6	19.2	9.0	67.7	64.1	3.6	34.5	34.3	.2	1.9	9.3	.1	9.9	6.1	2.5	3.9	.1	.6
1952	68.3	17.6	7.8	66.0	63.9	2.1	34.0	33.8	.2	1.8	9.5	.1	10.3	5.8	2.3	3.4	.1	.7
1951	68.1	18.7	6.9	63.8	62.0	1.8	33.5	33.4	.1	1.6	9.8	.1	11.0	5.5	2.1	2.9	.1	.3
1950	69.1	17.9	6.5	64.3	62.4	1.8	36.4	36.4	(Z)	1.5	10.9	.1	13.5	5.3	2.0	2.5	.1	.6
1949	69.6	14.7	6.0	69.5	67.4	2.1	38.1	38.1	(Z)	1.5	11.5	.1	15.3	4.8	1.9	2.3	.1	.7
1948	68.6	12.9	6.0	65.0	63.0	2.0	38.9	38.8	.1	1.5	11.6	.1	16.8	4.4	1.7	2.1	.1	.8
1947	68.2	12.3	5.5	70.7	69.6	1.1	41.3	41.3	(Z)	1.7	12.0	.1	20.0	3.9	1.4	1.9	(Z)	.3
1946	67.1	12.8	4.9	76.3	75.3	1.1	42.5	42.5	(Z)	2.0	11.8	.1	21.6	3.3	1.2	1.7	(Z)	.9
1945	68.3	18.5	5.2	92.3	91.2	1.1	40.8	40.8	(Z)	2.4	10.7	.1	20.6	2.7	.9	1.5	(Z)	1.9

− Represents zero.
Z Less than $50 million.
[1] Where not shown separately, loan participations are included with agency issues.

[2] These issues are outside the budget and outside the U.S. Government sector in flow-of-funds accounts. They are included in credit market debt of financial institutions.

Series X 328–378. Bonds and Mortgages: 1945 to 1970

[In billions of dollars. As of December 31]

State and local government securities

| Year | Holdings | | | | | | | | | | Loans from U.S. Government | Total credit market debt |
| | Total | Households | Corporate business | State-local government general funds | Commercial banks | Mutual savings banks | Life insurance companies | Other insurance companies | State-local government retirement funds | Brokers and dealers | | |
	328	329	330	331	332	333	334	335	336	337	338	339
1970	146.2	47.4	2.2	2.3	70.2	0.2	3.3	17.8	2.0	0.9	4.8	151.1
1969	132.4	45.4	2.8	2.2	59.5	.2	3.2	16.3	2.3	.4	4.7	137.1
1968	124.4	38.2	3.8	2.2	58.9	.2	3.2	15.1	2.4	.5	4.0	128.4
1967	114.4	38.4	3.3	2.1	50.3	.2	3.0	14.1	2.4	.5	3.6	117.9
1966	106.0	40.1	3.6	2.1	41.2	.3	3.1	12.6	2.5	.5	3.4	109.5
1965	100.3	36.4	4.6	2.2	38.9	.3	3.5	11.3	2.6	.5	2.8	103.1
1964	93.0	34.7	3.7	2.2	33.7	.4	3.8	11.0	2.9	.7	2.5	95.5
1963	87.3	32.7	3.8	2.3	29.7	.4	3.9	10.6	3.3	.5	2.2	89.5
1962	81.4	31.2	2.7	2.6	26.2	.5	3.9	9.9	3.8	.5	2.0	83.4
1961	76.1	32.2	2.4	2.8	20.5	.7	3.9	9.1	4.3	.3	1.5	77.5
1960	70.8	30.8	2.4	2.7	17.7	.7	3.6	8.1	4.4	.4	1.2	72.1
1959	65.6	27.3	2.7	2.7	17.1	.7	3.2	7.2	4.3	.3	1.0	66.6
1958	59.5	24.3	2.0	2.7	16.7	.7	2.7	6.2	4.0	.2	.9	60.4
1957	54.0	23.5	1.5	2.6	14.1	.7	2.4	5.6	3.5	.2	.7	54.7
1956	49.6	21.7	1.3	2.5	13.1	.7	2.2	4.9	3.1	.1	.5	50.1
1955	45.8	19.3	1.2	2.5	12.9	.6	2.0	4.2	2.7	.3	.5	46.3
1954	40.6	16.0	1.0	2.5	12.7	.6	1.8	3.4	2.4	.3	.4	41.1
1953	34.6	13.5	1.0	2.3	11.0	.4	1.3	2.6	2.1	.4	.8	35.4
1952	30.2	11.5	.8	2.1	10.3	.3	1.1	1.9	1.9	.4	.8	31.3
1951	27.4	10.4	.8	2.1	9.3	.1	1.1	1.4	1.7	.2	1.1	28.2
1950	25.2	10.0	.7	2.0	8.2	.1	1.2	1.1	1.5	.4	.8	25.8
1949	21.9	9.5	.5	1.7	6.6	.1	1.1	.8	1.3	.4	.6	22.4
1948	19.3	8.8	.5	1.4	5.7	.1	.9	.5	1.3	.3	.5	19.9
1947	17.2	7.8	.4	1.4	5.3	.1	.6	.3	1.2	.3	.6	17.7
1946	15.7	7.4	.3	1.5	4.4	.1	.6	.2	.9	.3	.5	16.2
1945	15.7	7.3	.3	1.8	4.0	.1	.7	.2	.8	.3	.5	16.2

Corporate and foreign bonds

| Year | Total, liabilities or assets | Liabilities | | | | Assets of— | | | | | | | | | | |
| | | Corporate business | Finance companies | Commercial banks | Rest of the world | Households | State and local government | Commercial banks | Mutual savings banks | Life insurance companies | Private pension funds | State-local government retirement funds | Other insurance companies | Brokers and dealers | Investment companies | Rest of the world |
	340	341	342	343	344	345	346	347	348	349	350	351	352	353	354	355
1970	206.3	167.9	22.9	2.4	13.2	39.8	4.9	2.7	8.3	74.1	29.7	31.8	8.6	0.5	4.3	1.7
1969	182.0	147.6	20.3	2.3	11.7	27.4	7.0	1.9	6.9	72.7	27.6	27.9	6.3	.4	3.6	.4
1968	168.3	135.6	18.8	2.2	11.7	21.7	5.1	2.0	6.6	71.2	27.0	24.8	5.5	.2	3.4	.9
1967	153.4	122.7	17.9	2.0	10.8	16.8	4.9	1.7	5.3	67.3	26.4	22.3	4.3	.2	3.4	.9
1966	137.2	108.0	16.9	1.7	10.5	12.8	4.4	.9	3.2	63.5	25.2	18.9	3.6	.6	3.0	.9
1965	125.7	97.8	16.1	1.6	10.2	11.3	3.8	.8	2.9	61.1	22.7	16.3	3.0	.6	2.9	1.3
1964	116.6	92.4	14.3	.8	9.2	10.0	3.1	.9	3.1	58.3	21.2	14.2	3.0	.5	2.6	.7
1963	109.0	88.4	12.2	.2	8.2	9.5	2.4	.8	3.2	56.0	19.6	12.3	2.4	.5	2.1	.7
1962	102.4	84.5	10.7	--------	7.2	9.7	1.8	.8	3.5	53.2	18.1	10.4	2.0	.6	1.8	.9
1961	96.5	80.0	10.4	--------	6.2	10.3	1.3	.9	3.6	50.7	16.9	8.5	2.1	.4	1.6	.7
1960	90.8	75.3	9.9	--------	5.6	9.8	1.5	1.1	3.8	48.2	15.7	6.7	1.7	.3	1.6	.7
1959	85.1	71.9	8.3	--------	4.9	9.4	.9	1.3	3.6	46.5	14.1	5.5	1.7	.5	1.2	.6
1958	80.7	68.9	7.2	--------	4.5	9.5	.9	1.4	3.8	44.3	12.8	4.6	1.6	.5	1.1	.6
1957	74.0	63.2	7.1	--------	3.7	8.5	.6	1.4	3.2	41.8	11.3	3.8	1.5	.5	.9	.5
1956	66.5	56.9	6.3	--------	3.3	7.4	.6	1.3	2.7	39.2	9.5	3.0	1.4	.7	.8	.4
1955	61.7	53.3	5.4	--------	3.0	6.6	.7	1.7	2.6	37.0	7.9	2.5	1.2	.7	.7	.3
1954	57.7	50.4	4.0	--------	3.3	5.5	.7	1.9	2.9	35.3	6.9	1.9	1.2	.9	.5	.3
1953	53.8	47.0	3.7	--------	3.1	5.6	.6	2.1	2.8	33.3	5.6	1.4	1.1	.7	.4	.2
1952	49.1	43.6	2.3	--------	3.2	5.7	.6	2.1	2.5	30.6	4.5	.9	1.1	.6	.3	.2
1951	44.3	38.9	2.0	--------	3.4	6.0	.5	2.2	2.2	27.5	3.5	.7	1.0	.6	.3	.3
1950	39.2	35.7	1.7	--------	1.7	4.9	.3	2.2	2.1	24.8	2.8	.6	.8	.5	.3	.2
1949	38.7	34.2	1.4	--------	3.2	7.5	.2	2.1	2.1	22.9	1.9	.6	.7	.6	.2	.2
1948	35.3	31.4	1.0	--------	2.9	7.7	.2	1.9	1.9	20.4	1.5	.3	.7	.6	.2	.2
1947	30.7	27.2	.5	--------	2.9	8.1	.1	2.2	1.5	16.1	1.2	.2	.7	.4	.2	.1
1946	27.7	24.4	.4	--------	2.9	8.7	.1	2.2	1.1	13.1	.9	.2	.6	.4	.1	.2
1945	26.6	23.5	.2	--------	2.9	9.6	.2	2.2	.9	11.3	.7	.1	.5	.5	.1	.5

Series X 328–378. Bonds and Mortgages: 1945 to 1970—Con.

[In billions of dollars. As of December 31]

Year	Total mortgage credit	Liabilities of—								Assets of—			
		Savings and loan associations	U. S. Government	Private nonfinancial sectors						Households	State and local governments, general funds	U. S. Government	FNMA [1] and land banks
				Total	Households	Nonprofit institutions	Business						
							Farm	Nonfarm noncorporate	Corporate				
	356	**357**	**358**	**359**	**360**	**361**	**362**	**363**	**364**	**365**	**366**	**367**	**368**
1970	451.7	3.1	1.5	447.2	273.1	20.5	31.2	45.1	77.3	42.5	2.2	9.5	23.6
1969	425.3	2.5	1.6	421.3	260.4	19.1	29.5	40.3	72.1	40.2	2.2	9.1	17.8
1968	397.5	2.4	1.7	393.4	244.1	17.8	27.5	36.6	67.3	38.4	2.2	8.4	13.3
1967	370.2	2.3	1.7	366.3	229.4	16.7	25.5	33.2	61.6	36.6	2.2	7.3	11.1
1966	347.4	1.3	1.8	344.4	219.0	15.5	23.3	29.5	57.1	35.7	2.1	6.4	9.4
1965	325.8	2.2	1.8	321.7	206.4	14.2	21.2	27.1	52.8	34.3	2.1	5.6	6.8
1964	300.1	2.2	1.8	296.1	191.1	13.1	18.9	24.0	49.0	35.1	2.2	5.7	5.7
1963	274.3	2.5	1.8	269.9	175.1	12.0	16.8	20.6	45.4	34.8	2.2	5.8	5.4
1962	248.6	2.0	1.7	244.9	160.4	11.0	15.2	17.8	40.5	34.5	2.1	6.3	5.9
1961	226.2	1.6	1.5	223.2	147.7	10.1	13.9	15.6	36.0	33.5	2.0	6.1	5.7
1960	206.8	1.2	1.3	204.4	136.8	9.2	12.8	13.6	32.0	31.8	1.3	5.8	5.5
1959	190.8	1.3	.8	188.7	126.0	8.3	12.1	12.8	29.5	29.9	1.4	5.6	4.4
1958	171.8	1.2	.5	170.1	113.4	7.5	11.1	11.6	26.5	28.1	1.1	4.3	3.5
1957	156.5	.9	.1	155.6	104.6	6.7	10.4	10.4	23.6	25.8	1.0	3.9	3.6
1956	144.5	.9	--------	143.6	95.8	5.9	9.8	10.1	21.9	23.9	.9	3.6	2.4
1955	129.9	.9	--------	129.0	84.6	5.2	9.0	9.8	20.3	22.4	.7	3.6	1.6
1954	113.7	.8	--------	112.9	72.4	4.6	8.2	9.1	18.5	21.2	.6	3.3	1.3
1953	101.3	.6	--------	100.7	63.8	3.9	7.7	8.4	16.9	20.0	.5	3.3	1.2
1952	91.4	.5	--------	90.9	56.1	3.4	7.2	8.1	16.1	19.0	.4	2.9	1.1
1951	82.3	.4	--------	81.9	49.7	2.9	6.7	7.5	15.2	18.3	.3	2.4	1.0
1950	72.8	.3	--------	72.5	42.6	2.4	6.1	7.1	14.4	17.4	.2	1.8	1.0
1949	62.7	.3	--------	62.4	35.2	1.8	5.6	6.3	13.5	16.7	.2	1.5	.9
1948	56.2	.2	--------	56.0	31.1	1.3	5.3	5.6	12.7	15.9	.1	1.0	.9
1947	48.9	.2	--------	48.7	26.1	.9	5.1	5.1	11.6	14.8	.1	.9	1.0
1946	41.8	.1	--------	41.7	21.8	.7	4.9	4.3	10.0	13.5	(Z)	1.0	1.0
1945	35.5	(Z)	--------	35.5	18.0	.5	4.8	3.7	8.5	12.0	–	1.4	1.0

Year	Assets of total mortgages—Con.									
	Private financial institutions									
	Total	Commercial banks	Savings institutions			Insurance				Finance companies
			Savings and loan associations	Mutual savings banks	Credit unions	Life insurance companies	Private pension funds	State and local government retirement funds	Other insurance	
	369	**370**	**371**	**372**	**373**	**374**	**375**	**376**	**377**	**378**
1970	374.0	73.3	150.3	57.9	0.8	74.4	4.3	6.8	0.2	5.9
1969	356.0	70.7	140.2	56.1	.7	72.0	4.2	6.0	.2	5.7
1968	335.2	65.7	130.8	53.5	.7	70.0	4.1	5.4	.2	4.9
1967	313.1	59.0	121.8	50.5	.7	67.5	4.1	5.0	.2	4.3
1966	293.9	54.4	114.4	47.3	.6	64.6	3.9	4.5	.1	3.9
1965	276.9	49.7	110.3	44.6	.6	60.0	3.3	3.7	.1	4.5
1964	251.4	44.0	101.3	40.6	.5	55.2	2.7	3.1	.1	3.9
1963	226.1	39.4	90.9	36.2	.5	50.5	2.2	2.6	.1	3.5
1962	199.9	34.5	78.8	32.3	.5	46.9	1.9	2.2	.1	2.7
1961	178.9	30.4	68.8	29.1	.4	44.2	1.6	1.9	.2	2.2
1960	162.5	28.8	60.1	26.9	.4	41.8	1.3	1.5	.1	1.6
1959	149.6	28.1	53.1	25.0	.3	39.2	1.0	1.0	.1	1.6
1958	134.8	25.5	45.6	23.3	.3	37.1	.7	.7	.2	1.4
1957	122.2	23.3	40.0	21.2	.3	35.2	.6	.5	.2	.9
1956	113.7	22.7	35.7	19.7	.2	33.0	.4	.4	.2	1.3
1955	101.7	21.0	31.4	17.5	.2	29.4	.3	.3	.2	1.4
1954	87.3	18.6	26.1	15.0	.1	26.0	.2	.2	.1	.8
1953	76.4	16.9	22.0	12.9	.1	23.3	.2	.2	.1	.6
1952	68.0	15.9	18.4	11.4	.1	21.3	.1	.1	.1	.6
1951	60.3	14.7	15.6	9.9	.1	19.3	.1	.1	.1	.4
1950	52.5	13.7	13.7	8.3	.1	16.1	.1	.1	.1	.5
1949	43.5	11.6	11.6	6.7	.1	12.9	.1	.1	.1	.3
1948	38.3	10.9	10.3	5.8	(Z)	10.8	.1	(Z)	.1	.2
1947	32.2	9.4	8.9	4.9	(Z)	8.7	(Z)	(Z)	.1	.2
1946	26.3	7.2	7.1	4.4	(Z)	7.2	(Z)	(Z)	.1	.2
1945	21.2	4.8	5.4	4.2	(Z)	6.6	–	(Z)	.1	.1

– Represents zero.
Z Less than $50 million.

[1] Federal National Mortgage Association.

Series X 379–392. Summary of Corporate Equities Market: 1945 to 1970

[In billions of dollars. As of December 31]

Year	Type of issue			Investor group										
	Total	Open-end investment companies	Other	Total	Households	Mutual savings banks	Commercial banking	Life insurance companies	Private pension funds	Other insurance companies	State and local government retirement funds	Open-end investment companies	Brokers and dealers	Rest of the world
	379	380	381	382	383	384	385	386	387	388	389	390	391	392
HOLDINGS AT MARKET VALUE (as of December 31)														
1970	928.8	47.6	881.2	928.8	763.1	2.5	0.5	15.4	67.2	13.2	8.0	39.7	0.5	18.7
1969	931.9	48.3	883.6	931.9	775.5	2.2	.4	13.7	61.6	13.3	5.9	40.9	.4	18.1
1968	1,035.8	52.7	983.2	1,035.8	874.4	1.9	.4	13.2	61.4	14.6	4.1	46.1	.2	19.6
1967	889.6	44.7	844.9	889.6	754.6	1.7	.3	10.9	51.1	13.0	2.8	39.2	.6	15.5
1966	700.7	34.8	665.9	700.7	595.5	1.5	.2	8.8	39.5	11.0	2.1	28.9	.6	12.6
1965	778.0	35.2	742.8	778.0	667.0	1.4	.2	9.1	40.7	12.0	1.6	30.9	.5	14.6
1964	684.1	29.1	655.0	684.1	588.7	1.3	.1	7.9	33.5	11.4	1.3	25.6	.5	13.8
1963	597.0	25.2	571.8	597.0	514.9	1.2	.1	7.1	27.7	10.0	1.0	22.1	.6	12.5
1962	505.7	21.3	484.4	505.7	437.8	1.0	.1	6.3	21.9	8.6	.8	18.3	.4	10.3
1961	574.0	22.9	551.1	574.0	501.6	.9	.1	6.3	22.9	9.3	.6	20.3	.3	11.8
1960	451.0	17.0	434.0	451.0	396.1	.8	.1	5.0	16.5	7.5	.4	14.8	.5	9.3
1959	454.0	15.8	438.2	454.0	402.7	.8	.1	4.6	14.5	7.2	.3	13.9	.5	9.4
1958	418.0	13.2	404.7	418.0	374.0	.9	.1	4.1	11.6	6.7	.3	11.7	.5	8.3
1957	299.0	8.7	290.3	299.0	267.7	.8	.1	3.4	7.5	5.2	.2	7.4	.7	6.1
1956	338.0	9.0	328.9	338.0	305.4	.7	(Z)	3.5	7.1	5.6	.2	7.9	.7	7.0
1955	317.0	7.8	309.2	317.0	286.7	.7	(Z)	3.6	6.1	5.4	.1	6.9	.9	6.6
1954	258.0	6.1	251.9	258.0	235.0	.6	(Z)	3.3	3.2	4.5	.1	5.4	.7	5.3
1953	179.0	4.1	174.9	179.0	162.4	.4	(Z)	2.6	2.4	3.3	.1	3.5	.6	3.7
1952	186.0	3.9	182.1	186.0	170.4	.3	(Z)	2.4	1.8	3.2	.1	3.3	.6	3.7
1951	170.0	3.5	166.5	170.0	156.4	.2	(Z)	2.2	1.4	2.9	(Z)	2.9	.5	3.5
1950	146.0	3.3	142.7	146.0	133.7	.2	(Z)	2.1	1.1	2.6	(Z)	2.9	.4	2.9
1949	120.0	3.1	116.9	120.0	109.5	.2	(Z)	1.7	.6	2.2	(Z)	2.7	.6	2.5
1948	108.0	1.5	106.5	108.0	100.2	.2	(Z)	1.4	.5	1.8	(Z)	1.2	.4	2.3
1947	109.0	1.4	107.6	109.0	101.3	.1	(Z)	1.4	.4	1.7	(Z)	1.2	.4	2.5
1946	111.0	1.3	109.7	111.0	103.5	.2	(Z)	1.2	.3	1.7	(Z)	1.0	.4	2.7
1945	119.0	1.3	117.7	119.0	111.6	.2	(Z)	1.0	.2	1.8	(Z)	1.0	.5	2.7
NET PURCHASES AT TRANSACTION VALUE														
1970	9.5	2.6	6.9	9.5	−2.6	0.3	0.1	2.0	4.6	1.0	2.1	1.1	0.2	0.7
1969	10.3	5.5	4.7	10.3	−4.1	.2	(Z)	1.7	5.4	1.0	1.8	2.5	.2	1.6
1968	4.0	4.7	−.7	4.0	−7.6	.3	.1	1.4	4.7	.8	1.3	1.5	−.5	2.1
1967	4.9	2.6	2.3	4.9	−4.2	.2	.1	1.0	4.6	.3	.7	1.5	.1	.7
1966	4.6	3.7	.9	4.6	−1.0	(Z)	.1	.3	3.7	.4	.5	1.0	(Z)	−.3
1965	3.4	3.1	.3	3.4	−1.9	.2	.1	.7	3.1	.1	.4	1.2	.1	−.4
1964	3.5	1.9	1.6	3.5	−.1	.1	(Z)	.5	2.2	.1	.3	.7	−.1	−.3
1963	1.1	1.2	−.1	1.1	−2.7	.1	(Z)	.2	2.2	.2	.2	.6	.1	.2
1962	2.5	1.8	.7	2.5	−2.0	.1	(Z)	.4	2.2	.2	.2	1.1	.1	.2
1961	4.9	1.9	3.0	4.9	.4	.1	(Z)	.5	2.3	.3	.2	1.0	(Z)	.1
1960	3.3	1.5	1.8	3.3	−.4	(Z)	(Z)	.4	1.9	.3	.1	.8	(Z)	.2
1959	4.3	1.7	2.6	4.3	.6	(Z)	(Z)	.2	1.7	.3	.1	.8	(Z)	.2
1958	3.9	1.4	2.5	3.9	.6	.1	(Z)	.1	1.4	.1	.1	1.0	.1	.4
1957	3.9	1.2	2.7	3.9	1.5	.1	(Z)	(Z)	1.1	.1	.1	1.0	−.3	−.1
1956	3.8	1.1	2.7	3.8	1.9	.1	(Z)	(Z)	.9	.1	(Z)	.8	.1	.3
1955	2.9	.9	2.1	2.9	1.1	.1	(Z)	.1	.7	.2	(Z)	.5	.2	.1
1954	2.6	.5	2.1	2.6	.7	.1	(Z)	.3	.7	.2	(Z)	.3	.1	.1
1953	2.3	.4	1.9	2.3	.9	.1	(Z)	.1	.5	.2	(Z)	.4	(Z)	.1
1952	3.0	.5	2.5	3.0	1.6	.1	(Z)	.2	.5	.2	(Z)	.4	(Z)	.1
1951	2.4	.3	2.1	2.4	1.6	(Z)	(Z)	.1	.3	.1	(Z)	.2	(Z)	.1
1950	1.7	.2	1.5	1.7	.7	(Z)	(Z)	.3	.5	.1	(Z)	.1	−.1	(Z)
1949	1.6	.3	1.3	1.6	.8	−	(Z)	.2	.2	.1	(Z)	.2	.2	(Z)
1948	1.2	.1	1.1	1.2	1.0	(Z)	−	(Z)	.1	.1	(Z)	.2	.2	(Z)
1947	1.4	.2	1.2	1.4	1.1	(Z)	(Z)	.2	.1	(Z)	(Z)	.1	(Z)	−.1
1946	1.4	.3	1.1	1.4	1.1	(Z)	−	.3	.1	(Z)	(Z)	.1	−.1	−.1

− Represents zero.

Z Less than $50 million, or less than −$50 million.

Chapter X

Net Public and Private Debt (Series X 393-409)

X 393–409. Net public and private debt, by major sectors, 1916–1970.

Source: U.S. Bureau of Economic Analysis (formerly Office of Business Economics), *Survey of Current Business*, May 1969, p. 11; May 1970, p. 14; and May 1973, p. 13.

The source publications include details for the sectors shown here as well as data on gross debt.

Net debt for the public sectors of the economy represents total outstanding indebtedness minus intrasector holdings of such debt, e.g., total Federal debt minus such portions of that debt as are held by the Treasury and by Federal agencies. State and local debt includes State loans to local units. Net corporate debt represents total corporate debt minus intercompany debts of affiliated companies. Figures for the noncorporate private debt are gross, with no adjustment for intrasector holdings.

All sectors of both gross and net debt exclude (a) deposit liability of banks and banknotes in circulation, (b) value of outstanding policies and annuities of life insurance carriers, (c) short-term debt of individuals and unincorporated nonfinancial business concerns held by other individuals and unincorporated businesses, and (d) nominal corporate debt, such as bonds authorized but not issued, and issued but reacquired.

Series X 395 includes debt of Federal agencies included within the Budget. The debt of Federal agencies not included in the Budget is shown in series X 396. Series X 403 represents agricultural loans to farmers and farmers' cooperatives by institutional lenders. Series X 408 and X 409 include debt owed by farmers for financial and consumer purposes.

★ ★ ★ ★ ★ ★ ★ ★ ★ ★   **More Recent Data for *Historical Statistics* Series**   ★ ★ ★ ★ ★ ★ ★ ★ ★
★   ★
★   Statistics for more recent years in continuation of many of the still-active series shown here appear   ★
★   in annual issues of the *Statistical Abstract of the United States*, beginning with the 1975 edition. For   ★
★   direct linkage of the historical series to the tables in the *Abstract*, see Appendix I in the *Abstract*.   ★
★   ★
★ ★

Series X 393–409. Net Public and Private Debt, by Major Sectors: 1916 to 1970

[In billions of dollars. As of end of year]

Year	Total	Public: Total	Federal [1]	Federal financial agencies [2]	State and local	Private: Total	Corporate: Total	Long [3] term	Short [3] term	Individual and noncorporate: Total	Farm [4]: Production	Farm [4]: Mortgage	Nonfarm mortgage: 1- to 4-family	Nonfarm mortgage: Multifamily residential and commercial	Other nonfarm: Commercial	Other nonfarm: Financial [5]	Other nonfarm: Consumer
	393	394	395	396	397	398	399	400	401	402	403	404	405	406	407	408	409
1970	1,854.1	484.7	301.1	38.8	144.8	1,369.4	793.5	360.2	433.4	575.9	27.5	31.2	274.6	46.3	35.8	33.3	127.2
1969	1,735.0	452.4	289.3	30.6	132.6	1,282.6	734.2	323.5	410.7	548.4	26.0	29.5	261.5	42.4	35.6	32.3	121.1
1968	1,582.5	437.1	291.9	21.4	123.9	1,145.4	631.5	283.6	347.9	513.9	24.3	27.5	246.5	38.4	33.4	33.0	110.8
1967	1,438.7	408.8	286.5	9.0	113.4	1,029.9	553.7	255.6	298.1	476.2	22.8	25.5	232.0	34.9	31.1	29.1	100.8
1966	1,338.7	387.9	271.8	11.2	104.8	950.8	506.6	231.3	275.3	444.2	19.1	23.3	219.6	32.0	29.4	24.5	96.2
1965	1,234.6	373.7	266.4	8.9	98.3	870.0	454.3	209.4	244.9	415.7	18.1	21.2	208.7	28.1	27.0	22.7	89.9
1964	1,151.6	361.9	264.0	7.5	90.4	789.7	409.6	192.5	217.1	380.1	17.1	18.9	193.3	25.6	23.5	21.5	80.3
1963	1,070.9	348.6	257.5	7.2	83.9	722.3	376.4	174.8	201.7	345.8	16.4	16.8	177.1	21.5	21.5	20.8	71.7
1962	996.0	335.9	253.6	5.3	77.0	660.1	348.2	161.2	187.0	311.9	15.0	15.2	161.9	18.4	19.3	18.3	63.8
1961	930.3	321.2	246.7	4.0	70.5	609.1	324.3	149.3	174.9	284.8	13.6	13.9	148.9	15.6	17.9	16.9	58.0
1960	874.2	308.1	239.8	3.5	64.9	566.1	302.8	139.1	163.7	263.3	12.3	12.8	137.4	13.9	16.6	14.2	56.1
1959	833.0	304.7	241.4	3.7	59.6	528.3	283.3	129.3	154.0	245.0	11.7	12.1	127.3	13.7	15.3	13.4	51.5
1958	769.6	287.2	231.0	2.5	53.7	482.4	259.5	121.2	138.4	222.9	12.1	11.1	114.5	13.6	13.7	12.8	45.1
1957	728.3	274.0	223.0	2.4	48.6	454.3	246.7	112.1	134.6	207.6	9.8	10.4	105.2	12.9	13.2	11.1	45.0
1956	698.4	271.2	224.3	2.4	44.5	427.2	231.7	100.1	131.7	195.5	9.6	9.8	96.8	12.6	13.3	11.1	42.3
1955	665.8	273.6	229.6	2.9	41.1	392.2	212.1	90.0	122.2	180.1	9.7	9.0	86.3	12.4	12.4	11.6	38.8
1954	605.9	265.9	229.1	1.3	35.5	340.0	182.8	82.9	100.0	157.2	9.3	8.2	74.1	12.3	10.4	10.4	32.5
1953	581.6	258.9	226.8	1.4	30.7	322.7	179.5	78.3	101.2	143.2	9.1	7.7	64.7	12.0	9.9	8.5	31.4
1952	550.2	249.8	221.5	1.3	27.0	300.4	171.0	73.3	97.7	129.4	8.0	7.2	57.1	11.8	10.3	7.5	27.5
1951	519.2	242.4	216.9	1.3	24.2	276.8	162.5	66.6	95.9	114.3	7.0	6.7	50.4	11.3	9.5	6.7	22.7
1950	486.2	239.8	217.4	.7	21.7	246.4	142.1	60.1	81.9	104.3	6.2	6.1	43.9	10.9	8.9	6.9	21.5
1949	445.8	237.4	217.6	.7	19.1	208.4	118.0	56.5	61.4	90.4	6.4	5.6	36.4	10.7	7.9	6.0	17.4
1948	431.3	232.9	215.3	.6	17.0	198.4	117.8	52.5	65.3	80.6	5.5	5.3	32.0	10.4	7.8	5.1	14.4
1947	415.7	237.4	221.7	.7	15.0	178.3	108.9	46.1	62.8	69.4	3.5	5.1	27.1	10.1	7.1	4.8	11.6
1946	396.6	243.2	229.5	--------	13.7	153.4	93.5	41.3	52.2	59.9	2.7	4.9	22.1	9.7	6.2	5.9	8.4
1945	405.9	265.9	252.5	--------	13.4	140.0	85.3	38.3	47.0	54.7	2.5	4.8	17.7	9.3	4.4	10.3	5.7
1944	370.6	225.8	211.9	--------	13.9	144.8	94.1	39.8	54.3	50.7	2.8	4.9	17.0	9.0	3.7	8.1	5.1
1943	313.2	168.9	154.4	--------	14.5	144.3	95.5	41.0	54.5	48.8	2.8	5.4	16.9	9.2	3.8	5.7	4.9
1942	258.6	117.1	101.7	--------	15.4	141.5	91.6	42.7	49.0	49.9	3.0	6.0	17.3	9.5	4.1	4.0	6.0
1941	211.4	72.4	56.3	--------	16.1	139.0	83.4	43.6	39.8	55.6	2.9	6.4	17.4	9.7	5.0	5.0	9.2
1940	189.8	61.2	44.8	--------	16.4	128.6	75.6	43.7	31.9	53.0	2.6	6.5	16.5	9.6	4.3	5.2	8.3
1939	183.3	59.0	42.6	--------	16.4	124.3	73.5	44.4	29.2	50.8	2.2	6.6	15.5	9.5	3.8	6.0	7.2
1938	179.9	56.6	40.5	--------	16.1	123.3	73.3	44.8	28.5	50.0	2.2	6.8	15.0	9.5	10.1		6.4
1937	182.2	55.3	39.2	--------	16.1	126.9	75.8	43.5	32.3	51.1	1.6	7.0	14.7	9.6	11.3		6.9
1936	180.6	53.9	37.7	--------	16.2	126.7	76.1	42.5	33.5	50.6	1.4	7.2	14.6	9.8	11.2		6.4
1935	175.0	50.5	34.4	--------	16.1	124.5	74.8	43.6	31.2	49.7	1.5	7.4	14.7	10.1	10.8		5.2
1934	171.6	46.3	30.4	--------	15.9	125.3	75.5	44.6	30.9	49.8	1.3	7.6	14.8	10.7	11.2		4.2
1933	168.5	40.6	24.3	--------	16.3	127.9	76.9	47.9	29.0	51.0	1.4	7.7	14.6	11.7	11.7		3.9
1932	175.0	37.9	21.3	--------	16.6	137.1	80.0	49.2	30.8	57.1	1.6	8.5	15.8	13.2	14.0		4.0
1931	182.9	34.5	18.5	--------	16.0	148.4	83.5	50.3	33.2	64.9	2.0	9.1	17.2	13.7	17.6		5.3
1930	192.3	31.2	16.5	--------	14.7	161.1	89.3	51.1	38.2	71.8	2.4	9.4	17.9	14.1	21.6		6.4
1929	191.9	30.1	16.5	--------	13.6	161.8	88.9	47.3	41.6	72.9	2.6	9.6	18.0	13.2	22.4		7.1
1928	186.3	30.2	17.5	--------	12.7	156.1	86.1	--------	--------	70.0	2.7	9.8	29.6		21.6		6.3
1927	177.9	30.3	18.2	--------	12.1	147.6	81.2	--------	--------	66.4	2.6	9.8	26.9		21.8		5.3
1926	169.2	30.3	19.2	--------	11.1	138.9	76.2	--------	--------	62.7	2.6	9.7	24.0		21.2		5.2
1925	162.9	30.6	20.3	--------	10.3	132.3	72.7	--------	--------	59.6	2.8	9.7	21.3		21.1		4.7
1924	153.4	30.4	21.0	--------	9.4	123.0	67.2	--------	--------	55.8	2.7	9.9	18.6		20.6		4.0
1923	146.7	30.4	21.8	--------	8.6	116.3	62.6	--------	--------	53.7	3.0	10.7	16.3		20.0		3.7
1922	140.2	30.7	22.8	--------	7.9	109.5	58.6	--------	--------	50.9	3.1	10.8	14.1		19.7		3.2
1921	136.3	30.1	23.1	--------	7.0	106.2	57.0	--------	--------	49.2	3.3	10.7	12.8		19.4		3.0
1920	135.7	29.9	23.7	--------	6.2	105.8	57.7	--------	--------	48.1	3.9	10.2	11.7		19.3		3.0
1919	128.3	31.1	25.6	--------	5.5	97.2	53.3	--------	--------	43.9	3.5	8.4	10.1		19.3		2.6
1918	117.5	26.0	20.9	--------	5.1	91.5	47.0	--------	--------	44.5	2.7	7.1	9.6			25.1	
1917	94.5	12.1	7.3	--------	4.8	82.4	43.7	--------	--------	38.7	2.5	6.5	9.3			20.4	
1916	82.2	5.7	1.2	--------	4.5	76.5	40.2	--------	--------	36.3	2.0	5.8	8.4			20.1	

[1] Net Federal debt (public and agency) is the outstanding debt held by the public as shown in *The Budget of the United States Government, Fiscal Year 1974*.

[2] Comprises the debt of federally sponsored agencies, in which there is no longer any Federal proprietary interest. Includes obligations of the Federal Land Banks, beginning 1947; debt of the Federal Home Loan Banks, beginning 1951; and debts of the Federal National Mortgage Association, Federal Intermediate Credit Banks, and Banks for Cooperatives, beginning 1968.

[3] Long-term debt has a maturity of 1 year or more; short-term debt, less than 1 year.

[4] Farm production loans and farm mortgages. Farmers' financial and consumer debt is included in the nonfarm categories.

[5] Financial debt is owed to banks for purchasing or carrying securities, customers' debt to brokers, and debt owed to life insurance companies by policyholders.

Chapter X

Money Supply and Gold (Series X 410-443)

X 410–443. General note.

The supply of money, in the sense of a means of payment, is defined broadly to include bank deposits and currency. A more restricted definition of the active money supply includes demand deposits and currency held by the public. Time deposits, including funds deposited in the Postal Savings System, have occasionally been included in the definition of the money supply. Prior to 1934, gold was also a part of the means of payment but in January of that year it was withdrawn from circulation, and, until August 1971, gold served as a means of settlement of international accounts only and, until March 1968, as a purely reserve money domestically.

As used here, the term "currency" includes coin and paper money issued by the Government and by banks. All currency is now issued by the Federal Reserve banks and the U.S. Treasury. In the series in this section three types of currency figures are shown: (a) Total currency stock (series X 420); (b) currency in circulation (series X 423–437), defined as coin and paper money outside the Treasury and Federal Reserve banks; and (c) currency outside banks, that is, currency in circulation less cash in the vaults of banks (series X 410).

Figures on currency in circulation have been compiled by the Treasury Department since 1800. They exclude currency held in the Treasury and Federal Reserve banks, gold and silver coin known to have been exported and, beginning January 31, 1934, all gold coin. They include currency held by the public within the United States, cash in the vaults of banks, currency lost or destroyed, and currency carried abroad and not appearing in the official gold and silver export figures.

At one time gold was the basic form into which all other types of currency could generally be converted. At present (1973–1974), however, the gold stock in most countries is held largely or entirely by central banks and Government treasuries. All gold belonging to the United States is held by the Treasury Department. Private gold holdings are forbidden except in limited amounts for licensed purposes. U.S. residents may purchase, hold, and sell domestic and foreign gold coins situated in the United States and minted before April 5, 1933. Gold coins minted after this date may be held if they have been determined to be of recognized special value to collectors. Gold may be held by Federal Reserve banks for account of foreign central banks or governments. Such earmarked gold, however, is not a part of the monetary gold stock of this country.

Prior to 1934, when gold coin and gold certificates were a part of the means of payment, they are included in series X 421, "currency held in Treasury"; series X 422, "currency in Federal Reserve banks"; and series X 423, "currency in circulation"; as well as in series X 424 and X 425, "gold coin" and "gold certificates" in circulation.

X 410–419. Money stock—currency, deposits, bank vault cash, and gold, 1867–1970.

Source: National Bureau of Economic Research, unpublished data.

See also text for series X 263–275.

Series X 410–419 are annual averages of estimates by Milton Friedman and Anna Jacobson Schwartz.

Series X 411–413 represent total deposits adjusted, i.e., total deposits less U.S. Government deposits, interbank deposits, and cash items in process of collection. A distribution showing demand and time deposits is not available prior to 1915. Figures for bank vault cash are deducted from currency in circulation to arrive at currency outside banks.

M_1 money supply, series X 414, includes currency outside the Treasury and bank vaults, demand deposits at all commercial banks, and foreign demand balances at Federal Reserve Banks. M_2 money supply, series X 415, includes all of the above plus time deposits at commercial banks. Deposits at nonbank thrift institutions are thus excluded from both M_1 money supply and M_2 money supply.

For additional descriptive detail, see Milton Friedman and Anna Jacobson Schwartz, *Monetary Statistics of the United States*, National Bureau of Economic Research (NBER), 1970.

The sources from which the estimates were derived are as follows:

X 410–416: 1867–1906 averages based on quarterly estimates from *Monetary Statistics of the United States*, tables 2 and 21; 1907–1946 averages, on end-of-month estimates from table 1 (*ibid.*), except that series X 416 is from Friedman and Schwartz, *A Monetary History of the United States, 1867–1960*, NBER, 1960, table A-2.

X 410–415: 1947–1963 averages based on monthly averages of daily figures from U.S. Board of Governors of the Federal Reserve System, *Federal Reserve Bulletin*, December 1970, except that series X 411 and X 415 are from *Monetary Statistics . . .*, pp. 48–50; 1964–1970 averages based on daily figures from the *Federal Reserve Bulletin*, November 1971.

X 416: 1947–1970 averages were derived from unpublished monthly averages of the Federal Reserve Board's daily estimates.

X 417: 1869–1878 averages based on end-of-June figures from the *Annual Report of the Secretary of the Treasury, 1928*, p. 552, minus gold presumed lost (see *Annual Report*, Director of the Mint, 1907, pp. 87, 92). 1878–1913 averages based on end-of-month figures from the *Annual Report of the Secretary of the Treasury*, 1898, pp. 59 and 109; 1903, pp. 173 and 205; 1909, p. 190 (corrected for the amount of gold presumed lost); and 1915, p. 319. 1914–1946 averages derived from U.S. Board of Governors of the Federal Reserve System, *Banking and Monetary Statistics*, 1943, pp. 536–538 and *Supplement*, section 14, p. 14 (for 1914–1933, plus $287 million to correct for gold presumed lost). 1947–1970 averages based on daily figures from *Banking and Monetary Statistics, Supplement 10*, pp. 16–19, and *Federal Reserve Bulletin*, monthly issues.

X 418: 1867–1906 averages based on annual or semiannual estimates in *Monetary Statistics . . .*, table 1; 1907–1946 averages derived from end-of-month estimates in table 1; 1947–1970 averages based on 12-month Federal Reserve Board estimates for the last Wednesday of the month from *Monetary Statistics . . .*, table 1, and *Federal Reserve Bulletin*, monthly issues.

X 419: 1897–1954 averages based on annual or quarterly estimates from *Monetary Statistics . . .*, table 1; 1955–1970 averages based on 12-month estimates from *Monetary Statistics . . .*, pp. 42–52, and Federal Home Loan Bank Board, *Selected Balance Sheet Data, All Operating Savings and Loan Associations*.

X 420–423. Currency stock and currency in circulation, 1800–1970.

Source: 1800–1859, U.S. Comptroller of the Currency, *Annual Report, 1896*, vol. I, p. 544; 1860–1970, U.S. Department of the Treasury, *Annual Report of the Secretary of the Treasury*, various issues.

See general note for series X 410–443.

Currency stock (series X 420) and the total of its components (series X 421–423) involve a duplication to the extent that U.S. notes, Federal Reserve notes, Federal Reserve banknotes, and national banknotes, all included in full, are in part secured by gold, also included in full. The duplication of gold certificates, silver certificates, and Treasury notes of 1890 resulting from the equal amounts of gold or silver held as security therefore has been eliminated. For a statement on this point, see footnotes to series X 420 and X 421. A description of security and reserves by type of currency is included in the text for series X 424–437, below. The text for series X 424–437 also describes more refined estimates of gold coin in circulation, 1873–1907 and 1913–1933, which, if incorporated into series X 420–423, would require similar adjustments in "total currency in the United States" and "currency in circulation."

The *Annual Report of the Secretary of the Treasury* for 1922 and subsequent years includes the following information concerning changes in the compilation of series X 420–423. The figures for 1860–1889 have been revised from the best data available in annual reports of the Secretary of the Treasury. The records are not complete and the figures for gold and silver in those years are only estimates. Beginning with 1890, the compilation is based on revised figures for June 30 of each year and therefore differs slightly from the monthly circulation statements issued by the Treasury. The compilation reflects revisions to take account of other changes in the circulation statement, chiefly in 1922 and 1927. These revisions are explained in the *Annual Report of the Secretary of the Treasury* as follows: *1922*, p. 433; *1928*, pp. 70–71 and 551.

X 424–437. Currency in circulation, by kind, 1800–1970.

Source: U.S. Department of the Treasury. *Annual Report of the Secretary of the Treasury, 1947*, p. 543; *1961*, p. 636; *1964*, p. 598; *1967*, p. 656; and *1970*, p. 240; except series X 437, 1800–1859, *Annual Report of the Comptroller of the Currency, 1916*, vol. II, p. 45.

See general note for series X 410–443 and text for series X 420–423.

More detailed annual data on currency stock and circulation, by kind, are shown in the annual reports of the Secretary of the Treasury and the Comptroller of the Currency.

The security and reserve provisions for the different types of currency are described in the *Annual Report of the Secretary of the Treasury*, 1972, p. 245.

X 425, gold certificates. Following the enactment of the Old Series Currency Adjustment Act in 1961, gold certificates (issues prior to series of 1934) are redeemable from the general fund of the Treasury and upon redemption will be retired. Prior to 1961, gold certificates were fully secured by gold in the Treasury.

X 427, silver certificates. Originally secured by silver bullion at monetary value ($1.29⁺ per fine troy ounce) and standard silver dollars held in the Treasury. Since enactment of the Old Series Currency Adjustment Act in 1961, silver certificates issued before July 1, 1929, have been payable from the general fund; certificates issued on or after July 1, 1929, became redeemable from the general fund on June 24, 1968.

X 428, Treasury notes of 1890. In process of retirement since March 1900 upon receipt by the Treasury. Until 1961, secured by silver and by gold reserve; thereafter, redeemable from general fund.

X 431, Federal Reserve notes. Federal Reserve banks secure Federal Reserve notes by depositing like amounts of collateral with Federal Reserve agents. The Federal Reserve Act, as amended, authorizes the use of the following assets for this purpose: (*a*) gold certificates or gold certificate credits; (*b*) certain discounted or purchased commercial paper; (*c*) securities issued by the United States; and (*d*) Special Drawing Rights certificates issued by the Exchange Stabilization Fund. Federal Reserve notes are obligations of the United States and are a first lien on all assets of the issuing Federal Reserve Bank. Following the enactment of the Old Series Currency Adjustment Act of 1961, funds were deposited by the Federal Reserve

banks with the Treasurer of the United States for the redemption of all Series of Federal Reserve notes issued before the series of 1928.

X 432, Federal Reserve banknotes. Secured at issuance by direct obligations of the United States or by commercial paper. Since termination of their issuance on June 12, 1945, the notes have been in process of retirement, and lawful money has been deposited with the Treasurer of the United States for their redemption.

X 433 U.S. notes. Secured by a gold reserve until this requirement was repealed. The Act of May 31, 1879 required that the amount of U.S. notes then outstanding, $346,681,016, be kept in circulation. The Old Series Currency Adjustment Act provided that this amount should be reduced by such amounts of notes as the Secretary of the Treasury might determine to have been destroyed or irretrievably lost. To 1970, the Secretary has made such determinations with respect to $24,142,000 of the U.S. notes issued prior to July 1, 1929.

X 434, national bank notes. Secured at issuance by direct obligations of the United States. From December 23, 1915 these notes have been in process of retirement, and lawful money has been deposited with the Treasurer of the United States for their redemption.

The monetary value of gold was changed from $20.67 per fine ounce to $35.00 per fine ounce on January 31, 1934. The weight of the gold dollar was reduced from 25.8 to 15-5/21 grains of gold, 0.9 fine.

More refined estimates of the amount of gold coin in circulation, 1873–1907, are contained in Bureau of the Mint, *Annual Report of the Director of the Mint, 1907*, p. 87; a discussion of the errors for which adjustments were made is given on pp. 66–95. For 1914–1933, the Board of Governors of the Federal Reserve System published revised estimates of gold coin in circulation (see *Banking and Monetary Statistics*, p. 409), which exclude $287 million of gold coin reported in January 1934 as still in circulation because this amount is believed to have been largely lost or melted down, or otherwise to have disappeared from circulation over the years. The Federal Reserve series has been adjusted in this way for 1914–1933; no similar adjustment has been made in the data included in this volume for gold coin in circulation, total currency in circulation, or total currency stock.

X 438–443. Changes in gold stock, 1914–1970.

Source: Board of Governors of the Federal Reserve System, 1914–1941, *Banking and Monetary Statistics*, p. 536; 1942–1957 (except series X 438 beginning 1953, X 441 beginning 1956, and X 443), *Federal Reserve Bulletin*, June 1949, p. 745, and April 1958, p. 503; **series X 439** and **X 442,** 1958–1970, unpublished data. **Series X 438,** 1953–1970, **X 440,** 1958–1970, and **X 443,** 1942–1970, *Federal Reserve Bulletin*, January issues. **Series X 441,** 1956–1970, U.S. Bureau of the Census, Report FT 2402, annual issues.

For a discussion of the items shown here, see *Banking and Monetary Statistics*, pp. 522–523. See also general note for series X 410–443.

Also available in *Banking and Monetary Statistics* and various issues of the *Federal Reserve Bulletin* are annual data on gold inflow into the United States and contributing factors, net gold imports to the United States by country, and gold production by country.

The data for domestic gold production (series X 440) are those reported by the Director of the Mint, adjusted through 1945 to exclude Philippine production received in the United States. The data for net gold imports or exports (series X 441) are those compiled by the Department of Commerce. The figures for gold under earmark (series X 442–443) represent gold held by the Federal Reserve banks for foreign and international accounts; in the calculation of the changes in gold under earmark, however, consideration has also been given to gold held under earmark abroad for the account of the Federal Reserve banks in 1917–1933.

Series X 410–419. Money Stock—Currency, Deposits, Bank Vault Cash, and Gold: 1867 to 1970

[In billions of dollars.   Annual averages]

Year	Currency held by the public	Deposits adjusted, commercial banks			M₁ Money supply (currency plus demand deposits)	M₂ Money supply (M₁ plus time deposits)	Bank vault cash	Monetary gold stock	Deposits at nonbank thrift institutions	
		Total	Demand	Time					Mutual savings banks	Savings and loan associations
	410	411	412	413	414	415	416	417	418	419
1970	47.69	353.61	162.30	191.31	209.98	401.29	6.48	11.28	68.87	138.62
1969	44.82	340.34	156.94	183.40	201.77	385.17	6.05	10.37	66.03	113.60
1968	41.97	319.66	148.47	171.19	190.41	361.60	5.75	10.71	62.42	127.16
1967	39.37	292.39	138.38	154.01	177.77	331.78	5.38	13.02	57.74	118.95
1966	37.48	270.55	133.58	136.97	171.05	308.02	5.02	13.46	53.62	111.46
1965	35.26	250.64	128.54	122.10	163.79	285.89	4.62	14.26	50.72	105.46
1964	33.49	231.25	123.74	107.51	157.22	264.73	4.24	15.46	46.74	96.08
1963	31.55	217.60	119.74	97.87	151.28	249.15	3.95	15.74	43.02	85.59
1962	30.09	203.83	116.91	86.92	147.00	233.92	3.67	16.36	39.78	74.93
1961	29.10	192.14	114.82	77.31	143.93	221.24	3.40	17.38	37.32	66.06
1960	28.99	181.68	112.62	69.08	141.59	210.67	3.07	19.01	35.42	57.90
1959	28.90	181.19	114.38	66.82	143.27	210.09	2.90	19.95	34.39	51.00
1958	28.37	172.75	109.98	62.77	138.35	201.12	2.77	21.57	32.81	44.66
1957	28.26	163.56	108.48	55.07	136.75	191.82	2.71	22.49	30.75	39.29
1956	27.98	158.89	108.05	50.85	136.02	186.87	2.68	21.81	29.02	34.51
1955	27.63	156.06	106.79	49.25	134.44	183.69	2.59	21.69	27.22	29.62
1954	27.52	149.64	102.75	46.89	130.27	177.16	2.49	21.89	25.32	24.98
1953	27.78	143.41	100.64	42.85	128.34	171.19	2.43	22.42	23.52	20.98
1952	26.70	138.22	98.52	39.70	125.22	164.92	2.34	23.25	21.73	17.57
1951	25.53	130.92	93.67	37.22	119.23	156.45	2.25	22.03	20.35	14.89
1950	25.05	125.76	89.08	36.67	114.14	150.81	2.10	23.91	19.75	13.25
1949	25.50	121.96	85.67	36.30	111.16	147.46	2.02	24.43	18.87	11.72
1948	26.07	122.04	86.24	35.80	112.31	148.11	1.98	23.51	18.12	10.36
1947	26.58	119.42	85.22	34.21	111.79	146.00	1.84	21.38	17.38	9.15
1946	26.48	112.25	79.98	32.27	106.46	138.73	1.90	20.29	16.14	7.96
1945	25.33	101.30	73.90	27.40	99.23	126.63	1.71	20.25	14.36	6.84
1944	21.22	85.60	64.12	21.48	85.34	106.82	1.62	21.21	12.45	5.90
1943	16.35	73.56	55.89	17.67	72.24	89.91	1.54	22.37	11.12	5.22
1942	11.54	59.62	43.82	15.80	55.36	71.16	1.40	22.73	10.40	4.81
1941	8.40	54.11	38.12	15.99	46.52	62.51	1.37	22.54	10.58	4.50
1940	6.76	48.44	32.89	15.55	39.65	55.20	1.24	19.85	10.58	4.22
1939	6.04	43.23	28.11	15.12	34.15	49.27	1.10	16.08	10.39	4.10
1938	5.55	39.96	24.97	14.99	30.52	45.51	1.02	13.25	10.19	4.08
1937	5.59	40.09	25.32	14.77	30.91	45.68	.94	12.15	10.11	4.14
1936	5.23	38.25	24.32	13.93	29.55	43.48	.95	10.58	9.93	4.22
1935	4.80	34.27	21.08	13.19	25.88	39.07	.84	9.06	9.78	4.36
1934	4.63	29.73	17.23	12.50	21.86	34.36	.78	7.74	9.63	4.60
1933	5.09	27.13	14.82	12.31	19.91	32.22	.73	4.35	9.65	5.04
1932	4.92	31.13	16.19	14.94	21.11	36.05	.75	4.24	9.89	5.62
1931	4.16	38.53	19.98	18.55	24.14	42.69	.83	4.70	9.81	6.11
1930	3.73	42.00	22.03	19.97	25.76	45.73	.85	4.47	9.09	6.27
1929	3.90	42.70	22.74	19.96	26.64	46.60	.90	4.28	8.83	6.00
1928	3.89	42.53	22.49	20.04	26.38	46.42	.91	4.21	8.53	5.39
1927	3.98	40.75	22.12	18.63	26.10	44.73	.93	4.56	7.97	4.70
1926	4.00	39.68	22.18	17.50	26.18	43.68	.95	4.45	7.44	4.09
1925	3.96	38.09	21.70	16.39	25.66	42.05	.93	4.38	7.02	3.48
1924	3.96	34.62	19.71	14.91	23.67	38.58	.92	4.44	6.59	2.89
1923	3.96	32.64	18.97	13.67	22.93	36.60	.90	4.06	6.18	2.42
1922	3.69	30.03	17.98	12.05	21.67	33.72	.87	3.80	5.72	2.09
1921	4.04	28.81	17.47	11.34	21.51	32.85	.90	3.29	5.48	1.85
1920	4.48	30.32	19.25	11.07	23.73	34.80	1.02	2.88	5.15	1.60
1919	4.02	26.99	17.77	9.22	21.79	31.01	1.01	3.13	4.71	1.39
1918	2.76	23.97	16.20	7.77	18.96	26.73	1.01	3.16	4.39	1.27
1917	2.17	22.20	14.91	7.29	17.08	24.37	1.40	3.11	4.33	1.16
1916	2.17	18.68	12.53	6.15	14.70	20.85	1.55	2.48	4.13	1.06
1915	1.93	15.66	10.55	5.11	12.48	17.59	1.46	2.00	3.91	.98
1914	1.91	14.48				16.39	1.62	1.88	3.84	.89
1913	1.89	13.84				15.73	1.55	1.88	3.73	.82
1912	1.82	13.31				15.13	1.53	1.82	3.58	.74
1911	1.76	12.36				14.12	1.45	1.76	3.43	.67
1910	1.74	11.60				13.34	1.43	1.66	3.30	.61
1909	1.71	10.97				12.68	1.35	1.65	3.14	.56
1908	1.76	9.68				11.44	1.15	1.64	3.02	.53
1907	1.72	9.88				11.60	1.14	1.49	3.02	.49
1906	1.63	9.45				11.08	1.04	1.35	2.91	.45
1905	1.50	8.74				10.24	1.01	1.24	2.74	.43
1904	1.44	7.80				9.24	1.00	1.21	2.60	.42
1903	1.42	7.26				8.68	.87	1.14	2.50	.41
1902	1.34	6.83				8.17	.85	1.07	2.39	.40
1901	1.27	6.21				7.48	.84	1.02	2.26	.40
1900	1.21	5.39				6.60	.77	.93	2.13	.40
1899	1.10	4.99				6.09	.73	.87	2.00	.41
1898	1.00	4.26				5.26	.70	.74	1.87	.42
1897	.92	3.72				4.64	.65	.60	1.78	.42
1896	.89	3.46				4.35	.58	.53	1.69	
1895	.91	3.52				4.43	.61	.53	1.65	
1894	.93	3.35				4.28	.67	.56	1.57	
1893	1.00	3.26				4.26	.58	.56	1.55	
1892	.96	3.47				4.43	.58	.60	1.52	
1891	.96	3.12				4.08	.52	.62	1.43	
1890	.93	2.99				3.92	.48	.64	1.37	
1889	.87	2.73				3.60	.49	.64	1.30	

Series X 410–419. Money Stock—Currency, Deposits, Bank Vault Cash, and Gold: 1867 to 1970—Con.

[In billions of dollars. Annual averages]

Year	Currency held by the public	Deposits adjusted, commercial banks	M₂ Money supply (M₁ plus time deposits)	Bank vault cash	Monetary gold stock	Deposits at mutual savings banks	Year	Currency held by the public	Deposits adjusted, commercial banks	M₂ Money supply (M₁ plus time deposits)	Bank vault cash	Monetary gold stock	Deposits at mutual savings banks
	410	411	415	416	417	418		410	411	415	416	417	418
1888	0.85	2.55	3.40	0.48	0.65	1.24	1877	0.54	1.11	1.65	0.24	0.13	0.83
1887	.83	2.48	3.31	.46	.61	1.18	1876	.53	1.15	1.68	.24	.10	.84
1886	.78	2.32	3.10	.44	.56	1.12	1875	.54	1.18	1.72	.25	.09	.82
1885	.80	2.07	2.87	.45	.54	1.07	1874	.54	1.11	1.65	.27	.12	.76
1884	.84	1.96	2.80	.37	.51	1.03	1873	.56	1.06	1.62	.24	.11	.70
1883	.87	1.93	2.80	.32	.50	1.00	1872	.55	1.06	1.61	.24	.12	.64
1882	.84	1.79	2.63	.32	.47	.95	1871	.54	.96	1.50	.25	.14	.56
1881	.78	1.66	2.44	.31	.44	.92	1870	.54	.81	1.35	.23	.16	.47
1880	.67	1.36	2.03	.29	.33	.81	1869	.55	.73	1.28	.22	.15	.40
1879	.58	1.08	1.66	.24	.23	.75	1868	.54	.73	1.27	.24	---------	.34
1878	.54	1.04	1.58	.24	.18	.78	1867	.58	.70	1.28	.25	---------	.30

Series X 420–423. Currency Stock and Currency in Circulation: 1800 to 1970

[In thousands of dollars. As of June 30]

Year	Total currency in U.S.[1]	Currency held in Treasury[2]	Currency outside Treasury: In Federal Reserve banks	Currency outside Treasury: In circulation	Year	Total currency in U.S.[1]	Currency held in Treasury[2]	Currency outside Treasury: In Federal Reserve banks	Currency outside Treasury: In circulation	Year[4]	Total currency in U.S.[1]	Currency held in Treasury[2]	Currency outside Treasury in circulation
	420	421	422	423		420	421	422	423		420	421	423
1970	57,416,085	117,164	2,947,949	54,350,972	1922	8,276,070	2,515,005	1,297,893	4,463,172	1874	950,116	86,510	863,606
1969	54,019,573	292,960	2,790,588	50,936,024	1921	8,174,528	2,001,446	1,262,089	4,910,992	1873	903,316	65,065	838,252
1968	51,138,815	496,863	3,001,489	47,640,463						1872	900,571	71,361	829,209
1967	48,126,693	799,071	2,615,178	44,712,443	1920	8,158,496	1,675,026	1,015,881	5,467,589	1871	894,376	100,220	794,156
1966	46,641,417	320,797	3,766,598	42,554,022	1919	7,688,413	2,001,139	810,636	4,876,638				
					1918	6,906,237	1,568,557	855,984	4,481,697	1870	899,876	124,909	774,966
1965	[3]56,689,683	14,411,477	2,554,020	39,719,801	1917	5,678,774	796,005	816,365	4,066,404	1869	873,759	133,118	740,641
1964	55,450,634	12,760,173	4,956,767	37,733,694	1916	4,541,730	299,127	593,345	3,649,258	1868	888,413	116,529	771,884
1963	53,334,680	13,010,106	4,854,775	35,469,798						1867	1,020,927	161,567	859,360
1962	52,194,980	13,720,548	4,704,904	33,769,527	1915	4,050,783	348,236	382,965	3,319,582	1866	1,068,066	128,388	939,678
1961	51,947,136	14,818,780	4,723,662	32,404,694	1914	3,797,825	338,391		3,459,434				
					1913	3,777,021	358,329		3,418,692	1865	1,180,197	96,657	1,083,541
1960	53,070,922	16,608,562	4,397,741	32,064,619	1912	3,701,965	366,744		3,335,220	1864	1,062,841	55,226	1,007,615
1959	53,260,402	16,994,973	4,351,256	31,914,173	1911	3,606,989	343,935		3,263,053	1863	1,010,747	79,473	[5]931,274
1958	54,058,080	18,642,860	4,243,480	31,171,739						1862	629,452	23,754	[5]605,698
1957	55,363,063	19,887,518	4,393,632	31,081,913	1910	3,466,856	318,172		3,148,684	1861	488,006	3,600	[5]484,406
1956	54,008,743	19,060,827	4,232,727	30,715,189	1909	3,451,521	302,695		3,148,826				
					1908	3,423,068	343,913		3,079,155	1860	442,102	6,695	[5]435,407
1955	53,308,618	18,989,892	4,089,403	30,229,323	1907	3,158,111	344,248		2,813,863	1859	443,307	4,339	438,968
1954	53,429,405	19,234,197	4,273,259	29,921,949	1906	3,109,380	334,690		2,774,690	1858	415,208	6,398	408,810
1953	54,015,340	19,729,629	4,160,765	30,124,952						1857	474,779	17,710	457,069
1952	53,853,745	20,610,303	4,217,518	29,025,925	1905	2,919,494	296,154		2,623,340	1856	445,748	19,901	425,847
1951	50,985,939	18,979,646	4,197,063	27,809,230	1904	2,838,023	285,117		2,552,906				
					1903	2,717,646	317,914		2,399,732	1855	436,952	18,932	418,020
1950	52,440,353	21,464,308	3,819,755	27,156,290	1902	2,593,910	314,796		2,279,114	1854	445,689	20,138	425,551
1949	53,103,980	21,736,254	3,874,816	27,492,910	1901	2,511,472	308,275		2,203,198	1853	424,181	21,943	402,238
1948	52,601,129	20,769,375	3,928,896	27,902,859						1852	375,673	14,632	361,041
1947	50,599,352	18,538,131	3,763,994	28,297,227	1900	2,366,220	284,989		2,081,231	1851	341,165	10,912	330,254
1946	49,648,011	17,539,072	3,863,941	28,244,997	1899	2,190,094	286,022		1,904,072				
					1898	2,073,574	235,714		1,837,860	1850	285,367	6,605	278,762
1945	48,009,400	17,517,449	3,745,512	26,746,438	1897	1,906,770	265,787		1,640,983	1849	234,743	2,185	232,558
1944	44,805,301	18,489,163	3,811,797	22,504,342	1896	1,799,975	293,540		1,506,435	1848	240,506	8,101	232,405
1943	40,868,266	19,676,674	3,770,331	17,421,260						1847	225,520	1,701	223,819
1942	35,840,908	19,937,577	3,520,465	12,382,866	1895	1,819,360	217,392		1,601,968	1846	202,552	9,126	193,426
1941	32,774,611	19,781,266	3,380,914	9,612,432	1894	1,805,079	144,270		1,660,809				
					1893	1,738,808	142,107		1,596,701	1845	185,609	7,658	177,950
1940	28,457,960	17,124,764	3,485,695	7,847,501	1892	1,752,219	150,872		1,601,347	1844	175,168	7,857	167,310
1939	23,754,736	13,271,527	3,436,467	7,046,743	1891	1,677,794	180,353		1,497,441	1843	148,564	1,449	147,114
1938	20,096,865	10,132,397	3,503,576	6,460,891						1842	163,734	230	163,504
1937	19,376,690	9,475,429	3,454,205	6,447,056	1890	1,685,123	255,872		1,429,251	1841	187,290	987	186,303
1936	17,402,493	7,800,438	3,360,854	6,241,200	1889	1,658,672	278,311		1,380,362				
					1888	1,691,441	319,270		1,372,171	1840	189,969	3,663	186,305
1935	15,113,035	8,398,521	1,147,422	5,567,093	1887	1,633,413	315,874		1,317,539	1839	222,171	2,467	219,704
1934	[3]13,634,381	6,953,734	1,305,985	5,373,470	1886	1,561,408	308,707		1,252,701	1838	203,639	[6]5,000	198,639
1933	10,078,417	2,085,971	2,271,682	5,720,764						1837	222,186	[6]5,000	217,186
1932	9,004,505	1,513,985	1,795,349	5,695,171	1885	1,537,434	244,865		1,292,569	1836	205,301	[6]5,000	200,301
1931	9,079,624	2,031,632	2,226,059	4,821,933	1884	1,487,250	243,324		1,243,926				
					1883	1,472,494	242,189		1,230,306	1835	154,692	8,893	145,800
1930	8,306,564	2,043,489	1,741,087	4,521,988	1882	1,409,398	235,108		1,174,290	1834	135,840	11,703	124,137
1929	8,538,796	1,935,513	1,856,986	4,746,297	1881	1,349,592	235,355		1,114,238	1833	122,150	2,012	120,138
1928	8,118,091	1,738,889	1,582,576	4,796,626						1832	121,900	4,503	117,397
1927	8,667,282	2,062,851	1,753,110	4,851,321	1880	1,185,550	212,169		973,382	1831	[3]109,100	6,015	93,085
1926	8,428,971	2,070,588	1,473,118	4,885,266	1879	1,033,641	215,009		818,632				
					1878	984,225	164,221		820,004	1830	93,100	5,756	87,344
1925	8,299,382	2,116,582	1,267,591	4,815,208	1877	916,548	102,458		814,090	1820	69,100	[6]2,000	67,100
1924	8,846,542	2,620,299	1,376,935	4,849,307	1876	905,238	98,114		807,124	1810	58,000	[6]3,000	55,000
1923	8,702,788	2,671,678	1,207,836	4,823,275	1875	925,702	91,912		833,789	1800	28,000	[6]1,500	26,500

[1] Excludes gold certificates, silver certificates, and Treasury notes of 1890, since the gold and silver held as security against them are included.
[2] Prior to 1860 consists of specie only; thereafter includes coin, bullion, and paper money. Includes the following categories of currency held in Treasury as published in the circulation statement: Reserves held against U.S. notes and Treasury notes of 1890, held for Federal Reserve banks and agents, and all other money. Excludes amount held as security against gold and silver certificates and Treasury notes of 1890 since the certificates and notes are included elsewhere; for 1860–1933 they are included as currency outside the Treasury, and beginning 1934 they are included either as currency outside the Treasury or as amounts held in the Treasury for Federal Reserve banks and agents, payable in gold certificates.
[3] Agrees with source; however, figures for components do not add to total shown.
[4] Prior to 1860 the exact date of the figures is not known.
[5] Includes total stock of silver dollars and subsidiary silver, 1860–1863; and of gold coin and bullion, 1862–1863. It is not practical to present the amounts in circulation separately for the years mentioned.
[6] Estimated.

Series X 424–437. Currency in Circulation, by Kind: 1800 to 1970

[In thousands of dollars. As of June 30]

Year	Gold coin [1]	Gold certificates [2]	Silver dollars	Silver certificates [2]	Treasury notes of 1890 [2]	Subsidiary silver	Minor coin	Federal Reserve notes [2]	Federal Reserve banknotes [2]	U.S. notes [2]	National banknotes [2]
	424	425	426	427	428	429	430	431	432	433	434
1970	---	3,731	481,675	220,061	11	4,519,799	1,126,617	47,626,751	55,272	296,784	20,271
1969	---	3,804	481,688	222,828	11	4,260,860	1,047,364	44,547,642	56,885	294,478	20,467
1968	---	3,868	481,689	225,266	11	3,877,813	949,604	41,723,506	58,854	299,188	20,664
1967	---	3,973	481,691	394,656	11	3,238,822	920,815	39,290,336	61,057	300,178	20,906
1966	---	4,107	481,694	581,715	11	2,907,355	874,769	37,315,989	64,301	302,781	21,300
1965	---	13,209	481,698	829,177	42	2,355,380	824,585	34,823,233	68,333	301,978	22,167
1964	---	19,379	481,721	1,722,995	142	1,987,138	736,049	32,355,954	73,276	320,721	36,320
1963	---	19,858	411,489	1,846,537	142	1,789,924	676,291	30,291,625	78,247	318,537	37,148
1962	---	29,270	359,590	2,009,073	142	1,663,485	629,423	28,622,224	84,835	318,420	53,066
1961	---	29,803	328,680	2,094,379	1,142	1,548,135	585,234	27,352,908	91,811	318,338	54,262
1960	---	30,394	305,083	2,126,833	1,142	1,484,033	549,367	27,093,693	99,987	318,436	55,652
1959	---	31,046	285,491	2,154,916	1,142	1,415,483	513,876	27,028,617	110,051	316,166	57,385
1958	---	31,797	267,927	2,199,532	1,142	1,346,429	486,571	26,341,854	120,225	316,851	59,411
1957	---	32,541	252,607	2,161,589	1,142	1,315,325	473,904	26,329,345	132,566	321,148	61,745
1956	---	33,483	236,837	2,148,369	1,142	1,258,555	453,044	26,055,247	146,629	317,643	64,239
1955	---	34,466	223,047	2,169,726	1,142	1,202,209	432,512	25,617,775	162,573	319,064	66,810
1954	---	35,481	211,533	2,135,016	1,142	1,164,912	418,754	25,384,606	180,277	320,224	70,005
1953	---	36,596	202,424	2,121,511	1,143	1,150,499	412,952	25,608,669	200,054	317,702	73,403
1952	---	37,855	191,306	2,087,811	1,145	1,092,891	393,482	24,605,158	220,584	318,330	77,364
1951	---	39,070	180,013	2,092,174	1,145	1,019,824	378,350	23,456,018	243,261	318,173	81,202
1950	---	40,772	170,185	2,177,251	1,145	964,709	360,886	22,760,285	273,788	320,781	86,488
1949	---	42,665	163,894	2,060,852	1,145	939,568	355,316	23,209,437	308,821	318,688	92,524
1948	---	45,158	156,340	2,060,869	1,146	918,691	346,112	23,600,323	353,499	321,485	99,235
1947	---	47,794	148,452	2,060,728	1,147	875,971	331,039	23,999,004	406,260	320,403	106,429
1946	---	50,223	140,319	2,025,178	1,149	843,122	316,994	23,973,006	464,315	316,743	113,948
1945	---	52,084	125,178	1,650,689	1,150	788,283	291,996	22,867,459	527,001	322,587	120,012
1944	---	53,964	103,325	1,587,691	1,154	700,022	262,775	18,750,201	597,030	322,293	125,887
1943	---	56,909	83,701	1,648,571	1,155	610,005	235,672	13,746,612	584,162	322,343	132,130
1942	---	59,399	66,093	1,754,255	1,158	503,947	213,144	9,310,135	18,717	316,886	139,131
1941	---	62,872	52,992	1,713,508	1,161	433,485	193,963	6,684,209	20,268	299,514	150,460
1940	---	66,793	46,020	1,581,662	1,163	384,187	168,977	5,163,284	22,373	247,887	165,155
1939	---	71,930	42,407	1,453,573	1,166	361,209	154,869	4,483,552	25,593	265,962	186,480
1938	---	78,500	39,446	1,230,156	1,169	341,942	145,625	4,114,338	30,118	262,155	217,441
1937	---	88,116	38,046	1,078,071	1,172	340,827	144,107	4,168,780	37,616	281,459	268,862
1936	---	100,771	35,029	954,592	1,177	316,476	134,691	4,002,216	51,954	278,190	366,105
1935	---	117,167	32,308	701,474	1,182	295,773	125,125	3,222,913	81,470	285,417	704,263
1934	---	149,740	30,013	401,456	1,189	280,400	119,142	3,068,404	141,645	279,608	901,872
1933	320,939	265,487	27,995	360,699	1,186	256,865	112,532	3,060,793	125,845	268,809	919,614
1932	452,763	715,683	30,115	352,605	1,222	256,220	113,619	2,780,229	2,746	289,076	700,894
1931	363,020	996,510	34,326	377,149	1,240	273,147	117,393	1,708,429	2,929	299,427	648,363
1930	357,236	994,841	38,629	386,915	1,260	281,231	117,436	1,402,066	3,206	288,389	650,779
1929	368,488	934,994	43,684	387,073	1,283	284,226	115,210	1,692,721	3,616	262,188	652,812
1928	377,028	1,019,149	46,222	384,577	1,304	278,175	111,061	1,626,433	4,029	298,438	650,212
1927	384,957	1,007,075	48,717	375,798	1,327	275,605	108,132	1,702,843	4,606	292,205	650,057
1926	391,703	1,057,371	51,577	377,741	1,356	270,072	104,194	1,679,407	5,453	294,916	651,477
1925	402,297	1,004,823	54,289	382,780	1,387	262,009	100,307	1,636,108	6,921	282,578	681,709
1924	393,330	801,381	54,015	364,414	1,423	252,995	96,952	1,843,106	10,066	297,790	733,835
1923	404,181	386,456	57,262	364,258	1,460	247,307	93,897	2,234,660	19,969	302,749	711,076
1922	415,937	173,342	57,973	265,335	1,510	229,310	89,157	2,138,715	71,868	292,343	727,681
1921	447,272	200,582	65,883	158,843	1,576	235,295	91,409	2,599,598	129,942	259,170	721,421
1920	474,822	259,007	76,749	97,606	1,656	248,863	90,958	3,064,742	185,431	278,144	689,608
1919	474,875	327,552	79,041	163,445	1,745	229,316	81,780	2,450,278	155,014	274,119	639,472
1918	537,230	511,190	77,201	370,349	1,851	216,492	74,958	1,698,190	10,970	291,859	691,407
1917	666,545	1,082,926	71,754	468,365	1,970	193,745	68,411	506,756	3,702	311,595	690,635
1916	624,939	1,050,266	66,234	476,279	2,098	171,178	62,998	149,152	1,683	328,227	716,204
1915	587,537	821,869	64,499	463,147	2,245	159,043	58,516	70,810	---	309,796	782,120
1914	611,545	1,026,149	70,300	478,602	2,428	159,966	57,419	---	---	337,846	715,180
1913	608,401	1,003,998	72,127	469,129	2,657	154,458	54,954	---	---	337,215	715,754
1912	610,724	943,436	70,340	469,224	2,916	145,034	50,707	---	---	337,697	705,142
1911	589,296	930,368	72,446	453,544	3,237	138,422	49,049	---	---	338,989	687,701
1910	590,878	802,754	72,433	478,597	3,663	135,584	46,328	---	---	334,788	683,660
1909	599,338	815,005	71,988	477,717	4,203	132,332	42,585	---	---	340,118	665,539
1908	613,245	782,977	76,329	465,279	4,964	124,178	41,139	---	---	339,396	631,634
1907	561,697	600,072	81,710	470,211	5,976	121,777	40,907	---	---	342,270	589,242
1906	668,655	516,562	77,001	471,520	7,337	111,630	38,043	---	---	335,940	548,001
1905	651,064	485,211	73,584	454,865	9,272	101,438	35,458	---	---	332,421	480,029
1904	645,818	465,655	71,314	461,139	12,902	95,528	33,763	---	---	333,759	433,028
1903	617,261	377,259	72,391	454,733	19,077	92,727	32,040	---	---	334,249	399,997
1902	632,394	306,399	68,747	446,558	29,803	85,721	29,724	---	---	334,292	345,477
1901	629,791	247,036	66,921	429,644	47,525	79,235	27,890	---	---	330,045	345,111
1900	610,806	200,733	65,889	408,466	75,304	76,161	26,080	---	---	317,677	300,115
1899	679,738	32,656	61,481	402,137	92,562	69,066	---	---	---	328,627	237,805
1898	657,950	35,812	58,483	390,127	98,306	64,057	---	---	---	310,134	222,991
1897	517,590	37,285	51,940	357,849	83,470	59,616	---	---	---	306,915	226,318
1896	454,905	42,198	52,117	330,657	95,045	60,204	---	---	---	256,140	215,168
1895	479,638	48,381	51,986	319,623	115,943	60,350	---	---	---	319,094	206,953
1894	495,977	66,340	52,565	326,991	134,681	58,511	---	---	---	325,525	200,220
1893	408,536	92,642	56,930	326,824	140,856	65,470	---	---	---	330,774	174,670
1892	408,569	141,094	56,817	326,693	98,259	63,294	---	---	---	339,400	167,222
1891	407,611	120,063	58,826	307,236	40,349	58,219	---	---	---	343,207	162,221
1890	374,259	130,831	56,279	297,556	---	54,033	---	---	---	334,689	181,605
1889	376,482	117,130	54,457	257,156	---	51,477	---	---	---	316,439	207,221
1888	391,114	121,095	55,527	200,760	---	50,362	---	---	---	308,000	245,313
1887	376,541	91,225	55,549	142,118	---	48,584	---	---	---	326,667	276,855
1886	358,220	76,044	52,669	88,116	---	46,174	---	---	---	323,813	307,665
1885	341,668	126,730	39,087	101,531	---	43,703	---	---	---	331,219	308,631
1884	340,624	71,147	40,690	96,427	---	45,661	---	---	---	318,687	330,690
1883	344,653	59,807	35,651	72,621	---	46,474	---	---	---	323,242	347,856
1882	358,251	5,029	32,404	54,506	---	46,380	---	---	---	325,255	352,465
1881	315,313	5,760	29,342	39,111	---	46,839	---	---	---	328,127	349,746

See footnotes at end of table.

Series X 424–437. Currency in Circulation, by Kind: 1800 to 1970—Con.

[In thousands of dollars]

Year	Gold coin [1]	Gold certificates [2]	Silver dollars	Silver certificates [2]	Subsidiary silver	U.S. notes [2]	National bank notes [2]	Fractional currency	Other U.S. currency	State bank notes	Year	State bank notes	Year	State bank notes
	424	425	426	427	429	433	434	435	436	437		437		437
1880	225,696	7,964	20,111	5,790	48,512	327,895	337,415	------	------	------	1859	193,307	1842	83,734
1879	110,505	15,280	8,036	414	61,347	301,644	321,405	------	------	------	1858	155,208	1841	107,290
1878	84,740	24,898	1,209	7	58,918	320,906	311,724	16,368	428	806	1857	214,779	1840	106,969
1877	78,111	32,298	------	------	42,885	337,899	301,289	20,242	456	909	1856	195,748	1839	135,171
1876	74,839	24,175	------	------	26,055	331,447	316,121	32,939	500	1,047				
											1855	186,952	1838	116,139
1875	64,446	17,549	------	------	22,141	349,686	340,547	37,905	551	964	1854	204,689	1837	149,186
1874	78,948	18,015	------	------	14,940	371,421	340,266	38,234	620	1,162	1853	188,181	1836	140,301
1873	62,718	34,251	------	------	13,679	348,464	338,962	38,076	701	1,399	1852	171,673	1835	103,692
1872	76,575	26,412	------	------	12,064	346,169	329,037	36,403	849	1,701	1851	155,165	1834	94,840
1871	72,391	17,790	------	------	12,022	343,069	311,406	34,446	1,064	1,968				
											1850	131,367	1833	91,500
1870	81,183	32,085	------	------	8,978	324,963	288,648	34,379	2,507	2,223	1849	114,743	1832	91,500
1869	62,129	29,956	------	------	5,695	314,767	291,750	30,442	3,343	2,559	1848	128,506	1831	77,000
1868	63,758	17,643	------	------	6,520	328,572	294,369	28,999	28,859	3,164	1847	105,520	1830	61,000
1867	72,882	18,678	------	------	7,082	319,438	286,764	26,306	123,727	4,484	1846	105,552	1820	44,800
1866	109,705	10,505	------	------	8,241	327,792	276,013	24,687	162,739	19,996				
											1845	89,609	1810	28,000
1865	148,557	------	------	------	8,713	378,917	146,138	21,729	236,567	142,920	1844	75,168	1800	10,500
1864	184,346	------	------	------	9,375	415,116	31,235	19,133	169,252	179,158	1843	58,564		
1863	[3] 260,000	------	------	------	[3] 11,000	312,481	------	15,884	93,230	238,677				
1862	[3] 283,000	------	------	------	[3] 13,000	72,866	------	------	53,040	183,792				
1861	266,400	------	------	------	[3] 16,000	------	------	------	------	202,006				
1860	207,305	------	------	------	[3] 21,000	------	------	------	------	207,102				

[1] More refined estimates are available for gold coin in circulation, 1873–1907 and 1914–1933; see text.

[2] For description of reserves held against various kinds of money, see text.
[3] Total stock; circulation figures not available.

Series X 438–443. Changes in Gold Stock: 1914 to 1970

[In millions of dollars; gold valued at $20.67 per fine ounce through January 1934; at $35 thereafter]

Year	Gold stock (end of period) [1]	Increase in gold stock	Domestic gold production [2]	Net gold import (+) or export (−)	Earmarked gold, decrease (+) or increase (−)	Gold under earmark (end of period)	Year	Gold stock (end of period) [1]	Increase in gold stock	Domestic gold production [2]	Net gold import (+) or export (−)	Earmarked gold, decrease (+) or increase (−)	Gold under earmark (end of period)
	438	439	440	441	442	443		438	439	440	441	442	443
1970	11,072	[3] −787	63.5	+196.7	−615	12,926	1941	22,762	719.8	169.1	+982.4	−407.7	2,215.4
1969	11,859	967	60.1	+224.6	+755	12,311	1940	22,042	4,242.2	170.2	+4,744.5	−644.7	1,807.7
1968	10,892	−1,173	53.9	−612.9	+187	13,066	1939	17,800	3,208.0	161.7	+3,574.2	−534.4	1,163.0
1967	12,065	−1,170	53.4	−972.7	−307	13,253	1938	14,592	1,801.5	148.6	+1,973.6	−333.5	628.6
1966	13,235	−571	63.1	−415.3	−50	12,946	1937	12,790	1,367.5	143.9	+1,585.5	−200.4	295.1
1965	[4] 13,806	[3] −1,665	58.6	−1,183.4	−198	12,896	1936	11,423	1,296.5	131.6	+1,116.6	−85.9	94.7
1964	15,471	−125	51.4	−381.9	+256	12,698							
1963	15,596	−461	51.4	−159.4	−254	12,954	1935	10,125	1,867.2	110.7	+1,739.0	+0.2	8.8
1962	16,057	−889.9	54.5	−230.0	−795.3	12,700.4	1934	8,258	4,222.5	92.9	+1,133.9	+82.6	9.0
1961	16,947	−857.2	54.8	−718.8	−62.6	11,905.2	1933	4,036	−190.4	47.1	−173.5	[6] −58.0	59.1
							1932	4,226	52.9	45.9	−446.2	[6] +457.5	73.7
1960	17,804	−1,702.3	58.8	+333.4	−1,981.4	11,842.6	1931	4,173	−133.4	45.8	+145.3	−320.8	458.5
1959	19,507	[3] −1,075.2	57.2	+302.4	−1,323.6	9,861.2							
1958	20,582	−2,275.1	61.6	+259.6	−2,515.0	8,537.6	1930	4,306	309.6	43.4	+280.1	−2.4	137.7
1957	22,857	798.8	63.6	+104.3	+600.1	6,022.7	1929	3,997	142.5	42.5	+175.1	−55.4	135.3
1956	22,058	305.9	65.3	+106.1	+318.5	6,622.8	1928	3,854	−237.9	44.3	−391.9	+119.5	79.9
							1927	4,092	−112.8	43.8	+6.1	−160.2	199.4
1955	21,753	−40.9	65.7	+97.6	−132.4	6,941.3	1926	4,205	92.6	46.3	+97.8	−26.3	39.3
1954	21,793	−297.2	65.1	+16.6	−325.2	6,808.9							
1953	22,091	−1,161.9	69.0	+2.0	−1,170.8	6,483.8	1925	4,112	−100.1	48.0	−134.4	+32.2	13.0
1952	23,252	379.8	67.4	+684.3	−304.8	5,313.0	1924	4,212	255.6	50.6	+258.1	−42.2	45.2
1951	22,873	52.7	66.3	−549.0	+617.6	5,008.2	1923	3,957	315.1	50.2	+294.1	+0.7	3.0
							1922	3,642	268.5	47.3	+238.3	−3.7	3.7
1950	22,820	−1,743.3	80.1	−371.3	−1,352.4	5,625.7	1921	3,373	734.6	48.8	+667.4	[6] +18.7	(NA)
1949	24,563	164.6	67.3	+686.5	−495.7	4,273.3							
1948	24,399	1,530.4	70.9	+1,680.4	−159.2	3,777.7	1920	2,639	−68.4	49.9	+95.0	[6] −145.0	22.0
1947	22,868	[5] 2,162.1	75.8	+1,866.3	+210.0	3,618.4	1919	2,707	−165.8	59.5	−291.7	[6] +127.4	5.0
1946	20,706	623.1	51.2	+311.5	+465.4	3,828.4	1918	2,873	4.9	67.4	+21.0	[6] −46.7	6.9
							1917	2,868	312.2	82.3	+180.6	[6] +51.7	6.9
1945	20,083	−547.8	32.0	−106.3	−356.7	4,293.8	1916	2,556	530.7	91.1	+530.2	−6.1	6.1
1944	20,631	−1,349.8	35.8	−845.4	−459.8	3,937.2							
1943	21,981	−757.9	48.3	+68.9	−803.6	3,477.4	1915	2,025	499.1	99.7	+420.5	------	------
1942	22,739	−23.0	125.4	+315.7	−458.4	2,673.8	1914	1,526	−100.2	93.4	−165.2	------	------

NA Not available.
[1] Beginning 1934, when Exchange Stabilization Fund was established, gold stock includes Treasury gold stock plus gold in Exchange Stabilization Fund; prior to that time represents Treasury gold stock only.
[2] Estimates of the U.S. Bureau of the Mint.
[3] Includes payment of increases in U.S. gold subscription to International Monetary Fund as follows: 1959, $344 million; 1965, $259 million; and 1970, $385 million.

[4] Excludes $259 million gold subscription to the International Monetary Fund in June 1965 for a U.S. quota increase which became effective on Feb. 23, 1966.
[5] Net after payment of $687.5 million in gold as United States gold subscription to the International Monetary Fund.
[6] Adjusted for changes in gold held under earmark abroad by the Federal Reserve banks.

Chapter X

Interest Rates and Security Markets (Series X 444-560)

X 444–560. General note.

Available statistics on interest rates and security prices indicate the cost of credit to borrowers—mainly business concerns and the Federal Government; and the income received by those who lend and invest—primarily individuals, trusts, endowments, banks, and other financial institutions. This section presents a variety of money rate and security market statistics, including principal short-term open-market rates in New York City, the discount rate of the Federal Reserve Bank of New York, commercial paper and bankers' acceptances outstanding, bank rates on short-term loans to business, bond and stock yields and prices, security issues, mutual funds, margin requirements, stock market credit, and the volume of stock exchange trading.

X 444–455. Money market rates, 1890–1970.

Source: Board of Governors of the Federal Reserve System. 1890–1941, *Banking and Monetary Statistics*, pp. 439–442, 448, 460; 1941–1963, *Supplement to Banking & Monetary Statistics*, section 12, "Money Rates and Securities Markets," pp. 37, 48, and 50; 1964–1970, *Federal Reserve Bulletin*, monthly issues.

The rates shown here cover the most important short-term open market instruments in New York City, which is the chief money market of the country. The New York money market is composed of a number of specialized markets for certain types of borrowing and there are usually differences in rates corresponding to differences in the supply of funds relative to the demand for particular types of short-term funds in which the market deals. These markets are called "open" markets since transactions in them are usually made on an impersonal basis with the borrower and lender dealing through agents, as distinct from a "customer" market where the borrower and lender deal directly with each other and where transactions are often made on a personal basis. As a result, lenders may sell paper held, call loans, or refrain from renewing credits upon maturity more freely in the case of open-market paper than in the case of customer loans. Monthly and weekly figures for most of the series shown here are given in the source.

Rates on stock exchange loans are no longer published by the Board of Governors of the Federal Reserve System but data for these series for 1942–1962 were supplied by that agency. For stock exchange call loans (series X 447–448), a single rate only is available beginning in 1957.

Beginning 1929, a new measure of short-term rates became available with the issuance by the Treasury of a new type of security—the Treasury bill, which differs from other types of Treasury marketable securities in that it is sold on a discount basis instead of being offered in the market with a fixed coupon rate. Maturities of Treasury bills have varied up to 9 months, but usually have been 3 months. Two continuous series (X 450–451) are available beginning 1931.

The Federal Reserve Bank of New York discount rates shown (series X 454–455) are the lowest and highest rates during the year on discounts for and advances to member banks under sections 13 and 13a of the Federal Reserve Act. For the period prior to 1921, when a multiplicity of rates prevailed, discount rates on paper of a single class and maturity—usually the type of paper and maturity for which the rate was lowest—are shown. Specifically, from November 16, 1914, the day the Reserve Banks opened, through August 1916, the rate applies to discounts of commercial, agricultural, and livestock paper with maturities of from 31 to 60 days; and from September 1916 to December 1920, to discounts of, and advances secured by, commercial, agricultural, and livestock paper with maturities of 15 days or less. Rates also apply to advances secured by obligations of Federal intermediate credit banks maturing in 6 months. For 1942–1945, the low rate shown is the preferential rate for advances secured by Government securities maturing or callable in one year or less. In this period the rate of 1 percent was continued for discounts of eligible paper and advances secured by such paper or by U.S. Government obligations with maturities beyond 1 year. The discount rates at all Federal Reserve banks and a description of the series through 1941 is contained in *Banking and Monetary Statistics*, pp. 422–424, 439–442, and thereafter in the *Federal Reserve Bulletin*.

X 456–465. Commercial and finance company paper and bankers' acceptances outstanding, 1918–1970.

Source: Board of Governors of the Federal Reserve System. 1918–1941, *Banking and Monetary Statistics*, pp. 465–467; 1942–1952, *Federal Reserve Bulletin*, February 1944, p. 170; January 1946, p. 59; February 1953, p. 146; and 1953–1970, *Federal Reserve Bulletin*, May issues.

Prior to 1948, figures for commercial paper represent the amount of paper outstanding as reported by the principal commercial paper dealers in the country. Some finance company paper sold in the open market is included. Beginning 1948, figures are for commercial paper and finance company paper combined, shown by method of placement. These data represent paper with an original maturity of 9 months or less (including some finance company paper sold in open markets) as reported by a varying number of dealers. Finance company paper placed directly with investors represents the amount reported by a varying number of finance companies. Prior to 1958, a small amount of finance company paper with an original maturity of more than 270 days was included; thereafter, all paper in this maturing group is included.

Figures for bankers' acceptances are amounts outstanding as reported by makers of bankers' acceptances, including banks and bankers in the United States and agencies of foreign banks in this country.

X 466–473. Bank rates on short-term business loans, 1919–1966.

Source: Board of Governors of the Federal Reserve System. 1919–1938, *Banking and Monetary Statistics*, pp. 463–464; 1939–1963, *Supplement to Banking & Monetary Statistics*, section 12, "Money Rates and Securities Markets," p. 61; 1964–1966, *Federal Reserve Bulletin*, March issues.

Data by months through 1938 and by quarters thereafter are available in the source publications. These data are compiled by the Board of Governors from reports submitted by member banks in leading cities throughout the country.

The reporting cities are representative financial centers having large loan markets. Interest rates charged by banks in these cities are more responsive to changes in general monetary conditions than are rates in other places. Because of the financial importance of the cities, their influence would predominate in any compilation designed to show movements of interest rates in large cities.

Figures for series X 470–473 represent averages of prevailing rates reported monthly by banks in a varying number of leading cities on commercial loans and time and demand security loans. These figures are not strictly comparable with those in series X 466–469 but they are believed to represent bank rates on business loans. For series X 466–469, the figures for 1928–1938 are averages of prevailing rates reported monthly by banks in 19 principal cities on business loans only; beginning in 1939, the figures are averages of interest rates charged by banks in the 19 cities on short-term business loans made during the first half of March, June, September, and December. For a description of the figures prior to 1939, see *Banking and Monetary Statistics*, pp. 426–427; beginning 1939, see *Supplement to Banking & Monetary Statistics*, pp. 9–11. Beginning 1948, the source publication includes data on average interest rates by size of loan.

In 1967, these series were revised for expanded coverage. The new series cover new loans and loan renewals made during the first half of the middle month of each calendar quarter. The number of financial centers covered by the survey has been raised from 19 to 35 and the number of respondent banks from 66 to 126. For further details, see *Federal Reserve Bulletin*, May 1967.

X 474–486. General note.

In addition to the sources cited for each individual series, these data (except series X 476 and X 479–482) appear also in U.S. Bureau of Economic Analysis (formerly Office of Business Economics), *Survey of Current Business*. Beginning with the January 1962 issue, the annual figures for the two most current years appear in every issue. Annual data back to 1947 appear in the 1971 edition of *Business Statistics*, a supplement to the *Survey*.

X 474. Yields on U.S. Government bonds, 1919–1970.

Source: Board of Governors of the Federal Reserve System. 1919–1941, *Federal Reserve Bulletin*, May 1945, p. 483; 1941–1963, *Supplement to Banking & Monetary Statistics*, section 12, "Money Rates and Securities Markets," p. 68; 1964–1970, *Federal Reserve Bulletin*, January issues.

Figures are unweighted averages of yields. For 1919–1925, yields cover all outstanding partially tax-exempt Government bonds due or callable after 8 years; for 1926–1934, all such bonds due or callable after 12 years; for 1935–1941, all such bonds due or callable after 15 years. For further description of the series, see *Banking and Monetary Statistics*, p. 429, and *Federal Reserve Bulletin*, May 1945, pp. 483 and 490. Beginning 1942, the series is for fully taxable bonds. Yields cover 1942–March 31, 1952, the bonds due or callable after 15 years; April 1, 1952–March 31, 1953, due or callable after 12 years; April 1, 1953–1970, due or callable in 10 years or more.

X 475. Municipal high-grade bond yields, 1900–1970.

Source: Standard and Poor's Corporation, Trade and Securities Statistics, *Security Price Index Record*, New York, 1971 edition (copyright).

Prior to 1929, this series is an arithmetic average of the yield to maturity of 15 high-grade municipal bonds, based on the mean of monthly high-low prices. Beginning 1929, the series is an average of the 4 or 5 weekly indexes for the month. Annual figures are averages of monthly data. Monthly and weekly data are available in the source.

X 476. Unadjusted index number of yields of American railroad bonds, 1857–1936.

Source: Frederick R. Macauley, *Some Theoretical Problems Suggested by the Movements of Interest Rates, Bond Yields and Stock Prices in the United States Since 1856*, National Bureau of Economic Research, 1938, pp. A 142–161 (copyright).

The railroad industry was selected as the basis for a longtime study of bond yields because no other industry had securities of comparable importance as early as 1857, and for many years no other industry had as high a credit rating. The series is available before and after adjustment to eliminate economic drift due to secular changes in the quality of the bonds included. The unadjusted series is more comparable with currently available series. The series is a chain index number based on the arithmetic average of yields on long-term

high-grade railroad bonds. Yields for individual bonds are based on arithmetic averages of monthly high and low sale prices. With a few exceptions the index includes no bonds with maturities under 10 years, and since 1909 the minimum has been 14 years. The number of bonds on which the index is based was 13 in 1857 and increased gradually to 37 in 1900; it varied between 36 and 45 until 1930 and declined to about 28 in 1935. Annual figures are averages of monthly data.

X 477. Corporate Aaa bond yields, 1919–1970.

Source: Moody's Investors Service, *Moody's Industrial Manual*, New York, 1971 edition, p. a18 (copyright).

This series is an unweighted arithmetic average of the yields for individual bonds, based on closing prices. Prior to 1928, yields are based on the average of the month's high and low sale price for each bond; for 1928 and 1929, on biweekly closing quotations; for 1930 through October 1931, on weekly quotations; beginning November 1931, on daily closing quotations. Annual figures are averages of monthly data.

X 478. Yields on preferred stocks, 1910–1970.

Source: See source for series X 475.

For January 1910–January 1928, this index is computed from the average of the monthly high and low prices of 20 high-grade issues. All prices are converted to a price equivalent to $100 par and a $7 annual dividend before averaging. The yield index is computed from the average price. Beginning February 1928, the index is based on an average of the weekly yields, which are based on Wednesday's closing quotations for 15 (14 from April 1948–September 1965 and 10 thereafter) high-grade noncallable issues. The yield is determined for each issue and the average of the 9, 8, and 4 median yields, respectively, represents the group yield. Annual figures are averages of monthly data.

X 479–482. Yields on common stocks (Cowles Commission), 1871–1937.

Source: Alfred Cowles and Associates, *Common Stock Indexes, 1871–1937*, Principia Press Inc., Bloomington, Ind., 1939, pp. 372–373.

Yields are total actual dividends paid in each calendar year divided by total stock values as represented by an average of the monthly values for the year. The data employed in the construction of this index include, for 1871–1917, all industrial and public utility common stocks, and about 93 percent in market value of the railroad stocks traded on the New York Stock Exchange. The stocks and the periods of their inclusion are given in appendix II of the source volume. Subsequent to 1917 (in some cases 1926 or later) the stocks included in the Standard Statistics weekly indexes are used, which represent 90 percent of all common shares listed on the New York Stock Exchange. For further description of the indexes, see the source volume, pp. 1–50.

X 483–486. Yields on common stocks (Moody's), 1929–1970.

Source: Moody's Investors Service, *Moody's Industrial Manual*, New York, 1971 edition, p. a28 (copyright).

Annual figures are averages of monthly data which are dividends at annual rates based on latest company declarations divided by end-of-month prices.

X 487–491. Basic yields of corporate bonds, by term to maturity, 1900–1970.

Source: 1900–1942, David Durand, *Basic Yields of Corporate Bonds, 1900–1942*, New York, 1942 (copyright); 1943–1955, National Bureau of Economic Research, unpublished data; 1956–1970, Scudder, Stevens, and Clark, New York, unpublished data. Series published monthly in U.S. Bureau of Economic Analysis, *Survey of Current Business*.

Greater detail than is shown here as to yield by years to maturity appears in Durand's volume.

Through 1950, the basic yield series represent the yields estimated as prevailing in the first quarter of each year on the highest grade corporate issues, classified by term to maturity; thereafter, the yields estimated in February only. These series are based on monthly high and low quotations of practically all the actively traded high-grade corporate issues outstanding since 1900.

X 492. U.S. Government bond prices, 1919–1970.

Source: Board of Governors of the Federal Reserve System. 1919–1940, *Federal Reserve Bulletin*, May 1945, p. 483; 1941–1963, *Supplement to Money and Banking Statistics*, section 12, "Money Rates and Securities Markets," p. 98; 1964–1970, *Federal Reserve Bulletin*, January issues.

Prior to 1942, the prices are derived from average yields of partially tax-exempt bonds shown in series X 474 on the basis of a 4 percent 16-year bond through December 1930 and on the basis of a 2¾ percent 16-year bond for 1931–1941. For further description of the series, see *Banking and Monetary Statistics*, p. 429.

For 1942–March 31, 1952, figures for fully taxable issues are average prices of bonds due or first callable after 15 years; for April 1, 1952–March 31, 1953, average prices of fully taxable marketable 2½ percent bonds first callable after 12 years; beginning April 1, 1953, prices are derived from average yields on the basis of an assumed 3 percent 20-year bond. The yield averages used are those on bonds maturing or callable in 10 years or more.

X 493–494. State and local government and corporate Aaa bond prices, 1900–1970.

Source: See source for series X 475, pp. 203 and 224.

The prices are a conversion of the yield indexes, assuming a 4-percent coupon with 20 years to maturity. For a description of the yield series for high-grade State and local government bonds, see text for series X 475. The corporate Aaa bond series is based upon the following: For 1900–1928, the monthly high-low price of 45 high-grade corporate bonds; for 1929–March 1937, a varying group of A1+ bonds, one price monthly (first of month); beginning April 1937, the average of the weekly A1+ indexes. Annual data are averages of weekly figures.

X 495–498. Index of common stock prices, 1871–1970.

Source: See source for series X 475.

These indexes, which are based on the aggregate market value of the common stocks of all the companies in the sample, 500 stocks for all years (425 industrial, 25 railroad, and 50 public utility), express the observed market value as a percentage of the average market value during the base period. From January 1908 to date, these indexes are based on monthly averages of the Standard and Poor's stock price indexes. The indexes for earlier years have been converted to the 1941–43 base from the Cowles Commission stock price indexes, which are an extension of the Standard and Poor's indexes. The same method of construction was used for both, and, as far as possible the same companies. The formula used for this index is generally defined as a "base-weighted aggregative" expressed in relatives with the average value for the base period (1941–43) equal to 10 and with adjustments for arbitrary price changes caused by the issuance of rights, stock dividends, splitups, etc.

X 499–509. Security issues and net change in outstanding corporate securities, 1934–1970.

Source: U.S. Securities and Exchange Commission, *Annual Report*, *1952*, pp. 210–221, and *1958*, pp. 208–216; and *Statistical Bulletin*, May 1958, pp. 9–11, and subsequent issues; except series X 507–509, prior to 1960, unpublished data.

The data for series X 499–506 cover substantially all new issues of securities offered for cash sale in the United States in amounts over $100,000 and with terms to maturity of more than one year. Figures include issues privately placed and publicly offered, whether unregistered or registered with the Securities and Exchange Commission.

The figures for privately placed issues include securities actually issued but exclude securities which institutions had contracted to purchase but had not actually taken during the period covered by the statistics. Also excluded are intercorporate transactions; U.S. Government "Special Series" issues, and other sales directly to Federal agencies and trust accounts; notes issued exclusively to commercial banks; and corporate issues sold through continuous offering, such as issues of open-end investment companies. Issues sold by competitive bidding directly to ultimate investors are classified as publicly offered issues. The figures for new capital include all issues other than those whose proceeds are intended to be used for retirement of securities already outstanding.

The figures for series X 507–509 on net change in outstanding corporate securities are derived by deducting from estimated gross proceeds received by corporations through the sale of securities the amount of estimated gross payments by corporations to investors for securities retired. Included in the latter figures are payments for issues retired with internal funds as well as with proceeds from new issues sold for refunding purposes. These series are based primarily on cash transactions but include conversions and exchanges of one type of security for another, e.g., bonds for stocks.

X 510–515. Corporate security issues, 1910–1934.

Source: 1910–1918, U.S. Bureau of Foreign and Domestic Commerce, *Statistical Abstract of the United States, 1932*, p. 292; 1919–1934, Board of Governors of the Federal Reserve System, *Banking and Monetary Statistics*, p. 487.

The *Commercial and Financial Chronicle* data used for these series, for 1919–1934, include all security issues publicly offered for sale by companies incorporated in the United States. Securities sold privately were included when the compilers were aware of the sale. Issues of foreign companies sold in the United States are excluded. Data are based on the offering price for preferred stock of no par value and for common stock, and on par amounts for bonds, notes, and preferred stock with stated par value. The data prior to 1919 include offerings of foreign corporations.

These series differ from those compiled by the Securities and Exchange Commission (series X 499–506) in a number of respects. The latter include issues on the basis of gross and/or net proceeds, whereas the *Chronicle* series include issues on the basis noted above. The *Chronicle* series include issues for exchange purposes, while the SEC figures include only that portion of such an offering that is sold for cash. The SEC series also include foreign corporate security issues sold in the United States, while the *Chronicle* series exclude them except for the period noted. The basis for inclusion of privately sold securities also differs.

X 516. New State and local government security issues, 1919–1970.

Source: Board of Governors of the Federal Reserve System, 1919–1933, *Banking and Monetary Statistics*, p. 487. U.S. Securities and Exchange Commission, 1934–1945, *Annual Report, 1952*, part 3, p. 211. Board of Governors of the Federal Reserve System, 1946–1963, *Supplement to Banking & Monetary Statistics*, section 12, "Money Rates and Securities Markets," p. 166; 1964–1970, *Federal Reserve Bulletin*, January issues.

Data represent principal amounts of securities offered publicly for sale in the United States by all political subdivisions either for new money or for refunding, retiring, or otherwise acquiring existing securities. They include loans from the U.S. Government. For 1919–1933, figures are as compiled and published by the *Commercial and Financial Chronicle*; for 1934–1956, they are from totals published by the *Chronicle* and the *Bond Buyer*; beginning 1957, the figures are compilations of the Investment Bankers Association of America.

X 517–530.   Market value and volume of sales of stocks and bonds on registered securities exchanges, 1935–1970.

Source: U.S. Securities and Exchange Commission, *Statistical Bulletin*, annual data in various issues (February, March, or April).

The data presented in these series are of two types depending upon the method of aggregation used by each exchange. Reports of some exchanges cover transactions cleared during the calendar month; clearances occur for the most part within five days of the execution of a trade. Reports for other exchanges cover transactions effected on trade dates falling within the report month. The variance introduced by these two different methods of aggregating the data is not considered to be significant and accordingly all registered exchanges are aggregated and reported in monthly summaries.

Stock data include voting trust certificates, certificates of deposit for stocks, and American Depository Receipts for stocks. Bond data have excluded transactions covering United States Government issues since March 1944. Warrants data include trading in rights for all periods.

X 531–535.   Volume of sales on New York Stock Exchange, 1900–1970.

Source: 1900–1909, Board of Governors of the Federal Reserve System, *Banking and Monetary Statistics*, p. 485; 1910–1970, *Commercial and Financial Chronicle*, New York.

Data on stocks (series X 531) show the volume of share trading in round lots on the New York Stock Exchange, as reported by the Exchange ticker; this series excludes odd lots, stopped sales, private sales, split openings, crossed transactions, and errors of omission. Data on bonds are exclusive of stopped sales and, beginning in July 1947, include bonds of the International Bank for Reconstruction and Development.

X 536–539.   Net assets, sales, and redemptions of mutual funds, 1940–1970.

Source: Investment Company Institute, Washington, D.C., *Mutual Fund Fact Book, 1970*, and *Statistical Work Book*, No. 19.

A mutual fund may be defined as a company which combines the funds of many investors whose investment goals are similar, and in turn invests those funds in a wide variety of securities. The selection, purchase, and sale of individual securities by the mutual fund are conducted under the supervision of professional managers. Different mutual funds have a variety of investment objectives, management policies, and degrees of risk. Some funds place strong emphasis on capital growth; others stress current income or a balance between growth and income; some are highly speculative.

Most mutual funds are technically known as open-end investment companies because they stand ready at any time to redeem outstanding shares upon request by the investor. As open-end companies, the number of their shares is not fixed, with the outstanding total varying as new shares are sold to investors and shares are redeemed by investors upon presentation to the company. Shares are generally available from investment dealers or fund sales representatives. In most cases, the offering price includes a sales charge of $7\frac{1}{2}$ to $8\frac{1}{2}$ percent, with lower rates applying on larger purchases. The redemption price is generally the net asset value prevailing at the time the shares to be redeemed are received by the company. The net asset value per share is determined by most companies at least once a day, and is computed by dividing the current market value of the company's total net assets by the number of its shares outstanding.

The origin of investment companies and the concept of diversification date well back into the 19th century. However, most of the growth in mutual funds in the United States, in both the number of companies and total assets, has occurred since World War II, and particularly in the 1950's and 1960's. Growth in net assets over the years has been due not only to excess of share purchases over redemptions, but also to the long-term uptrend in market value of securities in which the mutual funds invest.

Mutual funds are regulated by both Federal and State governments. The major Federal statutes regulating investment companies are the Securities Act of 1933, the Securities Exchange Act of 1934, and the Investment Company Act of 1940. The latter regulates the creation and structure and many of the operations of investment companies. The Federal Acts are administered by the Securities and Exchange Commission.

X 540–542.   Federal Reserve Board margin requirements, 1934–1970.

Source: Board of Governors of the Federal Reserve System, 1934–1963, *Supplement to Banking & Monetary Statistics*, section 12, "Money Rates and Securities Markets," p. 141; 1964–1970, *Federal Reserve Bulletin*, January issues.

Regulations T and U, administered by the Federal Reserve Board, limit the amount of credit that may be extended on a security by prescribing a maximum loan value, which is a specified percentage of its market value at the time of extension; the "margin requirements" shown are the differences between the market value (100 percent) and the maximum loan value.

X 543–546.   Stock market credit, 1931–1970.

Source: Board of Governors of the Federal Reserve System. 1931–1937, *Banking and Monetary Statistics*, p. 501; 1938–1963, *Supplement to Banking & Monetary Statistics*, section 12, "Money Rates and Securities Markets," pp. 142–146; 1964–1970, *Federal Reserve Bulletin*, January issues.

Series X 543–545 relate to credit extended by stock brokers on the basis of reports made by a group of firms estimated to account for at least 90 percent of total credit extended by security brokers and dealers in the United States. Data for 1931–1934 are estimates based on data collected by the New York Stock Exchange, and for 1935–1970 are based on reports collected by the Federal Reserve Board. Customers' debit balances represent credit extended by brokers to their customers, and money borrowed represents most of the credit obtained by these brokers, including money borrowed against customer collateral as well as that for their own activities. Customers' free credit balances represent customers' funds held by brokers pending investment or pending remittances to customers.

Customer credit in the stock market (series X 546) is defined as the sum of customers' net debit balances of the reporting firms, exclusive of those secured by U.S. Government obligations, and bank loans to others than brokers and dealers for purchasing and carrying securities exclusive of U.S. Government securities. As a result of changes in reporting, this series is not entirely comparable. Prior to 1955, customers' net debit balances include balances secured by U.S. Government obligations. Bank loans to others for purchasing and carrying securities are figures of weekly reporting member banks for the last Wednesday of the year, a series beginning in 1938. At the end of 1970 these banks accounted for about seven-tenths of all loans for this purpose. Loans for purchasing and carrying U.S. Government securities are excluded for all reporting banks for 1944–1952, and for reporting banks in New York City and Chicago for 1953–1970. For further details concerning the series, see *Banking and Monetary Statistics*, pp. 435 and 437–438, and *Supplement to Banking & Monetary Statistics*, pp. 18–20.

X 547–550.   Brokers' loans, by groups of lenders, 1918–1938.

Source: Board of Governors of the Federal Reserve System, *Banking and Monetary Statistics*, p. 494.

These data were assembled from various sources and, where gaps occurred, estimates were made. The figures represent loans to brokers by principal groups of lenders—New York City banks, outside banks, and others. Other lenders comprise foreign banking agencies, corporations, other brokers, and individuals. The figures cover primarily loans to brokers and dealers in New York City, most of whom are members of the New York Stock Exchange, but they include also loans to certain investment banking houses that do not have Stock Exchange seats and to brokers and dealers belonging to other stock exchanges. Comparable data are not available after 1938. For a more detailed description of the series, see *Banking and Monetary Statistics*, pp. 434–435.

X 551–560. Short- and intermediate-term consumer credit, by major types, 1919–1970.

Source: Board of Governors of the Federal Reserve System, 1919–1955, *Supplement to Banking & Monetary Statistics*, section 16 (new), "Consumer Credit," p. 33; 1956–1970, *Federal Reserve Bulletin*, monthly issues.

Short- and intermediate-term consumer credit includes credit used to finance the purchase of commodities and services for personal consumption or to refinance debt originally incurred for such purposes. It also includes credit extended to individuals for the purchase of consumer goods that may be used in part for business.

Installment credit, series X 552–556, represents all consumer credit that is scheduled to be repaid in two or more payments. Revolving credit, budget, and coupon accounts are treated as installment credit rather than as charge accounts because they provide for scheduled repayment on a periodic basis. Published estimates of the amount of installment credit outstanding generally include the financing charges on such credit and the cost of insurance or other fees included in the credit contract.

Automobile paper, series X 553, represents credit extended for the purchase of new or used automobiles, whether or not the credit is specifically secured by the automobile purchased. Similarly, "other consumer goods paper," series X 554, represents credit extended for the purchase of such nonautomotive consumer goods as home appliances and furniture, jewelry, mobile homes, and boats.

Automobile credit and other consumer goods credit often are extended to the consumer by a retailer; sometimes the retailer will hold the paper for his own account, but in many instances he will sell it to a sales finance company, a commercial bank, or some other financial institution. In other instances installment paper represents loans made directly by lending institutions to consumers for the purchase of goods and services.

Repair and modernization loans, series X 555, include both Federal Housing Administration-insured credit and noninsured credit extended to consumers to finance the maintenance and improvement of their homes. Such credit may be used for the purchase and installation of equipment, such as heating and air-conditioning systems, hot water heaters, storm windows, and kitchen equipment, as well as for major alterations and additions.

Personal loans, series X 556, include all installment loans not covered in the previous categories that are made by financial institutions to individuals for consumer purposes. Many of these loans are obtained for the consolidation of consumer debts, for the payment of medical, educational, or travel expenses, and for the payment of taxes or insurance premiums. Some loans used for the purchase of automobiles or other consumer goods may be classified as personal loans because the lender cannot identify them with purchases of specific goods.

Noninstallment credit, series X 557–560, consists of those forms of consumer credit that are scheduled to be repaid in a lump sum.

Single-payment loans, series X 558, are noninstallment loans made directly to individuals for consumer purposes. Some credit of this type is used for the purchase of goods, but most is for meeting short-term needs such as for the payment of personal taxes or life insurance premiums.

Charge accounts, series X 559, represent noninstallment balances owed to retail outlets for purchases made by consumers. These are open accounts ordinarily payable in full within 30 days of billing. The charge-account segment also includes the amounts consumers owe on accounts at gasoline service stations or on miscellaneous credit-card accounts and on home-heating-oil accounts. Such indebtedness differs from other charge-account credit in that it does not take the form of outstanding balances on the books of retail outlets.

Service credit, series X 560, consists of the amounts owed by consumers to professional practitioners and service establishments. The largest element in service credit is the amount owed to doctors, hospitals, and other suppliers of medical services. Amounts owed to public utilities, less deposits and prepayments, are also substantial. The remainder of service credit represents amounts owed for a wide variety of services, including education, recreation, and such personal services as laundry, cleaning, and dyeing.

Estimates are described in the *Federal Reserve Bulletin* for December 1968 and October 1972. They are based for the most part on sample reports submitted monthly and are adjusted periodically to more comprehensive data. Figures prior to 1940 are based largely on estimates of the Department of Commerce.

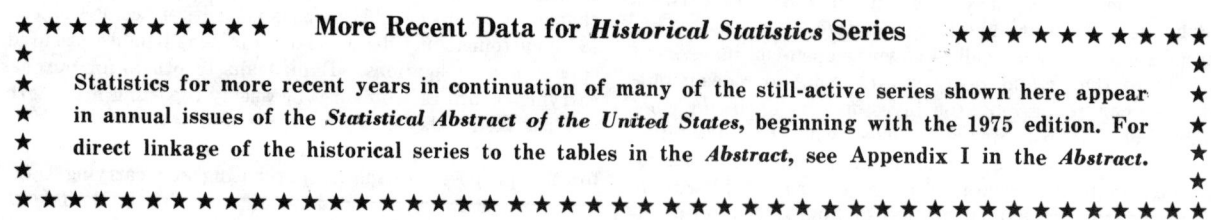

★ ★ ★ ★ ★ ★ ★ ★ ★   **More Recent Data for *Historical Statistics* Series**   ★ ★ ★ ★ ★ ★ ★ ★ ★

★

★ Statistics for more recent years in continuation of many of the still-active series shown here appear ★
★ in annual issues of the *Statistical Abstract of the United States*, beginning with the 1975 edition. For ★
★ direct linkage of the historical series to the tables in the *Abstract*, see Appendix I in the *Abstract*. ★

★   ★

Series X 444–455. Money Market Rates: 1890 to 1970

[**Percent per annum.** Open market rates in New York City]

Year	Stock exchange time loans, 90 days [1]	Prime commercial paper, 4 to 6 months [1]	Finance company paper, placed directly, 3- to 6- months [2]	Stock exchange call loans [3] New	Stock exchange call loans [3] Renewals	Prime bankers' acceptances, 90 days [1]	U.S. Government securities [4] 3-month bills [5] Rate on new issues	U.S. Government securities [4] 3-month bills [5] Market yield	U.S. Government securities [4] Certificates and selected note and bond issues, 9- to 12- months	U.S. Government securities [4] Selected note and bond issues, 3- to 5- years	Federal Reserve Bank of New York discount rate Low	Federal Reserve Bank of New York discount rate High
	444	445	446	447	448	449	450	451	452	453	454	455
1970	----------	7.72	7.23	7.92		7.31	6.458	6.39	6.90	7.37	5.50	6.00
1969	----------	7.83	7.16	7.96		7.61	6.677	6.67	7.06	6.85	5.50	6.00
1968	----------	5.90	5.69	6.31		5.75	5.339	5.34	5.62	5.59	4.50	5.50
1967	----------	5.10	4.89	5.67		4.75	4.321	4.29	4.84	5.07	4.00	4.50
1966	----------	5.55	5.42	5.78		5.36	4.881	[6] 4.86	5.17	5.16	4.50	4.50
1965	----------	4.38	4.27	4.69		4.22	3.954	3.95	4.09	4.22	4.00	4.50
1964	----------	3.97	3.83	4.50		3.77	3.549	3.54	3.76	4.06	3.50	4.00
1963	----------	3.55	3.40	4.50		3.36	3.157	3.16	3.28	3.72	3.00	3.50
1962	4.50	3.26	3.07	4.50		3.01	2.778	2.77	3.02	3.57	3.00	3.00
1961	4.50	2.97	2.68	4.50		2.81	2.378	2.36	2.91	3.60	3.00	3.00
1960	4.99	3.85	3.54	4.99		3.51	2.928	2.87	3.55	3.99	3.00	4.00
1959	4.22	3.97	3.82	4.22		3.49	3.405	3.37	4.11	4.33	2.50	4.00
1958	3.62	2.46	2.12	3.72		2.04	1.839	1.78	2.09	2.90	1.75	3.00
1957	4.35	3.81	3.55	4.50		3.45	3.267	3.23	3.53	3.62	3.00	3.50
1956	3.89	3.31	3.06	4.08	4.03	2.64	2.658	2.62	2.83	3.12	2.50	3.00
1955	3.01	2.18	1.97	3.20	3.20	1.71	1.753	1.73	1.89	2.50	1.50	2.50
1954	2.80	1.58	1.42	3.05	3.05	1.35	.953	.94	.92	1.82	1.50	2.00
1953	2.85	2.52	2.33	3.06	3.06	1.87	1.931	1.90	2.07	2.56	1.75	2.00
1952	2.42	2.33	2.16	2.48	2.48	1.75	1.766	1.72	1.81	2.13	1.75	1.75
1951	2.15	2.16	1.87	2.17	2.17	1.60	1.552	1.52	1.73	1.93	1.75	1.75
1950	1.59	1.45	1.41	1.63	1.63	1.15	1.218	1.20	1.26	1.50	1.50	1.75
1949	1.50	1.49	1.46	1.63	1.63	1.13	1.102	1.11	1.14	1.43	1.50	1.50
1948	1.50	1.44	1.34	1.55	1.55	1.11	1.040	1.05	1.14	1.62	1.00	1.50
1947	1.50	1.03	.94	1.38	1.38	.87	.594	.61	.88	1.32	1.00	1.00
1946	1.35	.81	----------	1.16	1.16	.61	.375	.38	.82	1.16	[7] .50	1.00
1945	1.25	.75	----------	1.00	1.00	.44	.375	.38	.81	1.18	[7] .50	1.00
1944	1.25	.73	----------	1.00	1.00	.44	.375	.38	.79	1.33	[7] .50	1.00
1943	1.25	.69	----------	1.00	1.00	.44	.373	.38	.75	1.34	[7] .50	1.00
1942	1.25	.66	----------	1.00	1.00	.44	.326	.34	----------	1.46	[7] .50	1.00
1941	1.25	.53	----------	1.00	1.00	.44	.103	.13	----------	.73	1.00	1.00
1940	1.25	.56	----------	1.00	1.00	.44	.014	.01	----------	----------	1.00	1.00
1939	1.25	.59	----------	1.00	1.00	.44	.023	.02	----------	----------	1.00	1.00
1938	1.25	.81	----------	1.00	1.00	.44	.053	.05	----------	----------	1.00	1.50
1937	1.25	.94	----------	1.00	1.00	.43	.447	.45	----------	----------	1.00	1.50
1936	1.16	.75	----------	.91	.91	.15	.143	.14	----------	----------	1.50	1.50
1935	.55	.75	----------	.56	.55	.13	.137	.14	----------	----------	1.50	1.50
1934	.90	1.02	----------	1.00	1.00	.25	.256	.26	----------	----------	1.50	2.00
1933	1.11	1.73	----------	1.14	1.16	.63	.515	.52	----------	----------	2.00	3.50
1932	1.87	2.73	----------	2.05	2.05	1.28	.879	.88	----------	----------	2.50	3.50
1931	2.15	2.64	----------	1.74	1.74	1.57	1.402	1.40	----------	----------	1.50	3.50
1930	3.26	3.59	----------	2.87	2.94	2.48	----------	----------	----------	----------	2.00	4.50
1929	7.75	5.85	----------	7.74	7.61	5.03	----------	----------	----------	----------	4.50	6.00
1928	5.86	4.85	----------	6.10	6.04	4.09	----------	----------	----------	----------	3.50	5.00
1927	4.35	4.11	----------	4.05	4.06	3.45	----------	----------	----------	----------	3.50	4.00
1926	4.60	4.34	----------	4.52	4.50	3.59	----------	----------	----------	----------	3.50	4.00
1925	4.23	4.02	----------	4.20	4.18	3.29	----------	----------	----------	----------	3.00	3.50
1924	3.64	3.98	----------	3.10	3.08	2.98	----------	----------	----------	----------	3.00	4.50
1923	5.14	5.07	----------	4.87	4.86	4.09	----------	----------	----------	----------	4.00	4.50
1922	4.53	4.52	----------	4.36	4.29	3.51	----------	----------	----------	----------	4.00	4.50
1921	6.15	6.62	----------	5.97	5.97	5.28	----------	----------	----------	----------	4.50	7.00
1920	8.06	7.50	----------	8.07	7.74	6.06	----------	----------	----------	----------	4.75	7.00
1919	5.83	5.37	----------	6.70	6.32	4.37	----------	----------	----------	----------	4.00	4.75
1918	5.90	6.02	----------	----------	5.28	4.19	----------	----------	----------	----------	3.50	4.00
1917	4.62	5.07	----------	----------	3.43		----------	----------	----------	----------	3.00	3.50
1916	3.25	3.84	----------	----------	2.62		----------	----------	----------	----------	3.00	4.00
1915	2.85	4.01	----------	----------	1.92		----------	----------	----------	----------	4.00	5.00
1914	4.37	5.47	----------	----------	3.43		----------	----------	----------	----------	5.00	6.00

Year	Stock exchange time loans, 90 days [1] 444	Prime commercial paper, 4 to 6 months [1] 445	Stock exchange call loans, renewals [3] 448	Year	Stock exchange time loans, 90 days [1] 444	Prime commercial paper, 4 to 6 months [1] 445	Stock exchange call loans, renewals [3] 448	Year	Stock exchange time loans, 90 days [1] 444	Prime commercial paper, 4 to 6 months [1] 445	Stock exchange call loans, renewals [3] 448
1913	4.64	6.20	3.22	1905	3.82	5.18	4.44	1897	2.68	4.72	1.75
1912	4.16	5.41	3.52	1904	3.10	5.14	1.78	1896	4.83	7.02	4.28
1911	3.22	4.75	2.57	1903	4.84	6.16	3.71	1895	2.82	5.80	1.88
1910	4.03	5.72	2.98	1902	5.05	5.81	5.15	1894	2.30	5.22	1.07
1909	3.26	[8] 4.67	2.71	1901	4.24	5.40	4.00	1893	5.08	7.64	4.57
1908	3.24	[8] 5.00	1.92	1900	3.94	5.71	2.94	1892	3.80	5.40	3.08
1907	6.49	[8] 6.66	7.01	1899	4.19	5.50	5.08	1891	4.83	6.48	3.42
1906	5.71	6.25	6.54	1898	3.31	5.34	2.18	1890	5.31	6.91	5.84

[1] Averages of weekly prevailing rates through 1934; averages of the most representative daily offering rates quoted by dealers thereafter.
[2] Averages of the most representative daily offering rates published by finance companies, for varying maturities in the 90–179 day range.
[3] Seven-day average for week ending Wednesday.
[4] Yields are averages computed from daily closing bid prices.
[5] Bills quoted on bank discount rate basis.
[6] Data for prior years not comparable; series includes the new bill issue the day following the auction, as trading begins on a when-issued basis.
[7] Preferential rate on advances secured by Government securities; see text.
[8] Includes 1 or more interpolated items.

Series X 456–465.　Commercial and Finance Company Paper and Bankers' Acceptances Outstanding: 1918 to 1970

[In millions of dollars. As of end of year]

Year	Commercial and finance company paper [1]			Bankers' acceptances							Year	Commercial and finance company paper [1]
	Total	Placed through dealers	Placed directly	Total	Held by—			Based on—				Total
					Accepting banks	Federal Reserve banks	Others	Imports into U.S.	Exports from U.S.	Other		
	456	457	458	459	460	461	462	463	464	465		456
1970	[2] 31,765	12,262	17,154	7,058	2,694	307	4,057	2,601	1,561	2,895	1923	763
1969	[2] 31,709	10,601	16,814	5,451	1,567	210	3,674	1,889	1,153	2,408	1922	722
1968	20,497	7,201	13,296	4,428	1,544	167	2,717	1,423	952	2,053	1921	663
1967	16,535	4,901	11,634	4,317	1,906	320	2,090	1,086	989	2,241		
1966	13,279	3,089	10,190	3,603	1,198	384	2,022	997	829	1,778	1920	948
1965	9,058	1,903	7,155	3,392	1,223	331	1,837	792	974	1,626	1919	1,186
1964	8,361	2,223	6,138	3,385	1,671	216	1,498	667	999	1,719	1918	881
1963	6,747	1,928	4,819	2,890	1,291	254	1,345	567	908	1,414		
1962	6,000	2,088	3,912	2,650	1,153	196	1,301	541	778	1,331		
1961	4,686	1,711	2,975	2,683	1,272	177	1,234	485	969	1,229		
1960	4,497	1,358	3,139	2,027	662	304	1,060	403	669	954		
1959	3,202	677	2,525	1,151	319	157	675	357	309	485		
1958	2,751	840	1,911	1,194	302	117	775	254	349	590		
1957	2,672	551	2,121	1,307	287	142	878	278	456	574		
1956	2,183	506	1,677	967	227	119	621	261	329	377		
1955	2,035	510	1,525	642	175	61	405	252	210	180		
1954	1,933	733	1,200	873	289	19	565	285	182	406		
1953	1,973	564	1,409	574	172	24	378	274	154	147		
1952	1,749	552	1,197	492	183	20	289	232	125	135		
1951	1,333	449	884	490	197	21	272	235	133	122		
1950	921	345	576	394	192	21	180	245	87	62		
1949	838	270	568	272	128	11	133	184	49	39		
1948	674	277	397	259	146	3	109	164	57	38		
1947	287			261	197	2	62	159	63	39		
1946	228			227	169	7	52	162	29	36		
1945	159			154	112	–	42	103	18	33		
1944	166			129	93	–	35	86	14	28		
1943	202			117	90	–	27	66	11	39		
1942	230			118	93	––	25	57	9	52		
1941	375			194	146	––	49	116	15	63		
1940	218			209	167	–	42	109	18	81		
1939	210			233	175	–	57	103	39	92		
1938	187			270	212	–	58	95	60	116		
1937	279			343	278	2	63	117	87	139		
1936	215			373	315	–	57	126	86	161		
1935	171			397	368	–	29	107	94	196		
1934	166			543	497	1	46	89	140	314		
1933	109			764	442	131	190	94	207	463		
1932	81			710	604	44	62	79	164	468		
1931	120			974	262	556	156	159	222	594		
1930	358			1,556	371	767	417	221	415	919		
1929	334			1,732	191	939	602	383	524	825		
1928	383			1,284	76	813	395	316	497	472		
1927	555			1,081	105	619	357	313	391	377		
1926	526			755	77	437	242	284	261	211		
1925	621			774	93	442	239	311	297	165		
1924	798			821		430		292	305	223		

– Represents zero.
[1] Prior to 1948, total for commercial paper only represents paper maturing within 7 months as reported by principal paper dealers; thereafter, figures for commercial paper and finance company paper combined by method of placement represent paper with an original maturity of 9 months or less as reported by varying number of dealers. [2] Includes paper placed through banks, not shown separately.

Series X 466–473.　Bank Rates on Short-Term Business Loans: 1919 to 1966

[Percent per annum]

Year	Business loan rates				Year	Business loan rates				Year	Customer loan rates			
	Total 19 cities	New York City	7 northern and eastern cities	11 southern and western cities		Total 19 cities	New York City	7 northern and eastern cities	11 southern and western cities		Total leading cities	New York City	Northern and eastern cities	Southern and western cities
	466	467	468	469		466	467	468	469		470	471	472	473
1966	6.0	5.8	6.1	6.2	1946	2.1	1.8	2.1	2.5	1929	6.0	5.9	6.0	6.1
1965	5.1	5.0	5.1	5.3	1945	2.2	2.0	2.5	2.5	1928	5.4	5.2	5.3	5.7
1964	5.0	4.8	5.0	5.3	1944	2.4	2.1	2.7	2.8	1927	5.0	4.5	4.9	5.6
1963	5.0	4.8	5.0	5.3	1943	2.6	2.2	2.9	2.8	1926	5.1	4.7	5.1	5.6
1962	5.0	4.8	5.0	5.3	1942	2.2	2.0	2.3	2.6					
1961	5.0	4.8	5.0	5.3	1941	2.0	1.8	1.9	2.5	1925	5.0	4.5	5.0	5.6
										1924	5.1	4.6	5.1	5.7
1960	5.2	5.0	5.2	5.5	1940	2.1	1.8	2.0	2.5	1923	5.5	5.2	5.5	5.9
1959	5.0	4.8	5.0	5.2	1939	2.1	1.8	2.0	2.5	1922	5.5	5.1	5.5	6.1
1958	4.3	4.1	4.3	4.7	1938	2.5	1.7	2.8	3.3	1921	6.7	6.3	6.8	7.0
1957	4.6	4.5	4.6	4.8	1937	2.6	1.7	2.9	3.3					
1956	4.2	4.0	4.2	4.4	1936	2.7	1.7	3.0	3.4	1920	6.6	6.3	6.7	6.8
										1919	5.7	5.5	5.7	6.0
1955	3.7	3.5	3.7	4.0	1935	2.9	1.8	3.4	3.8					
1954	3.6	3.4	3.6	4.0	1934	3.5	2.5	3.7	4.3					
1953	3.7	3.5	3.7	4.0	1933	4.3	3.4	4.5	5.0					
1952	3.5	3.3	3.5	3.8	1932	4.7	4.2	4.8	5.2					
1951	3.1	2.8	3.1	3.5	1931	4.3	3.8	4.3	4.9					
1950	2.7	2.4	2.7	3.2	1930	4.9	4.4	4.8	5.4					
1949	2.7	2.4	2.7	3.1	1929	5.8	5.8	5.8	5.9					
1948	2.5	2.2	2.6	2.9	1928	5.2	5.0	5.2	5.4					
1947	2.1	1.8	2.2	2.6										

Series X 474–486. Bond and Stock Yields: 1857 to 1970

[Percent per annum]

Year	Bonds U.S. Government 474	Bonds Municipal high grade 475	Bonds Corporate Unadjusted index of yields of American railroads 476	Bonds Corporate Aaa (Moody's) 477	Preferred stocks 478	Common stocks Cowles Commission Total 479	Industrial 480	Railroad 481	Utilities 482	Common stocks Moody's Composite 483	Industrial 484	Railroad 485	Utilities 486
1970	6.59	6.51	----------	8.04	7.22	----------	----------	----------	----------	3.97	3.60	5.97	5.94
1969	6.10	5.81	----------	7.03	6.41					3.42	3.14	4.90	4.88
1968	5.25	4.51	----------	6.18	5.78					3.22	2.93	4.50	4.57
1967	4.85	3.98	----------	5.51	5.34					3.35	3.11	4.82	4.26
1966	4.66	3.82	----------	5.13	4.97					3.57	3.44	4.80	3.99
1965	4.21	3.27	----------	4.49	4.33					3.06	2.98	4.30	3.30
1964	4.15	3.22	----------	4.40	4.32					3.00	2.98	4.05	3.15
1963	4.00	3.23	----------	4.26	4.30					3.17	3.20	4.46	3.12
1962	3.95	3.18	----------	4.33	4.50					3.37	3.37	5.30	3.25
1961	3.90	3.46	----------	4.35	4.66					3.07	3.04	4.94	3.10
1960	4.01	3.73	----------	4.41	4.75					3.60	3.48	5.65	3.84
1959	4.07	3.95	----------	4.38	4.69					3.31	3.12	4.61	3.93
1958	3.43	3.56	----------	3.79	4.45					4.01	3.84	5.60	4.31
1957	3.47	3.60	----------	3.89	4.63					4.33	4.11	6.77	4.92
1956	3.08	2.93	----------	3.36	4.25					4.07	3.89	5.51	4.68
1955	2.84	2.53	----------	3.06	4.01					4.05	3.93	4.89	4.49
1954	2.55	2.37	----------	2.90	4.02					4.75	4.66	6.16	4.81
1953	2.94	2.72	----------	3.20	4.27					5.49	5.51	6.44	5.32
1952	2.68	2.19	----------	2.96	4.13					5.49	5.55	5.88	5.38
1951	2.57	2.00	----------	2.86	4.11					6.11	6.28	6.29	5.78
1950	2.32	1.98	----------	2.62	3.85					6.28	6.52	6.49	5.64
1949	2.31	2.21	----------	2.66	3.97					6.62	6.80	8.44	5.85
1948	2.44	2.40	----------	2.82	4.15					5.77	5.85	6.02	5.85
1947	2.25	2.01	----------	2.61	3.79					5.12	5.05	6.15	5.28
1946	2.19	1.64	----------	2.53	3.53					3.93	3.71	5.28	4.22
1945	2.37	1.67	----------	2.62	3.70					4.17	3.98	5.48	4.90
1944	2.48	1.86	----------	2.72	3.99					4.83	4.57	6.74	6.24
1943	2.47	2.06	----------	2.73	4.06					4.89	4.53	6.87	6.78
1942	2.46	2.36	----------	2.83	4.31					6.64	6.38	7.74	9.75
1941	2.05	2.10	----------	2.77	4.08					6.23	6.31	6.43	7.93
1940	2.26	2.50	----------	2.84	4.14					5.26	5.26	5.36	6.01
1939	2.41	2.76	----------	3.01	4.19					4.14	3.84	3.64	5.28
1938	2.61	2.91	----------	3.19	4.34	----------				4.30	3.77	5.07	6.18
1937	2.74	3.10	----------	3.26	4.45	4.87	4.91	3.76	5.12	4.63	4.61	4.04	5.26
1936	2.69	3.07	3.88	3.24	4.33	4.35	4.27	5.32	4.31	3.50	3.37	2.74	3.67
1935	2.79	3.40	4.24	3.60	4.63	3.88	3.51	2.94	5.97	4.01	3.49	3.93	4.85
1934	3.12	4.03	4.53	4.00	5.29	3.92	3.45	3.09	6.56	4.07	3.40	2.93	5.75
1933	3.31	4.71	5.35	4.49	5.75	4.05	3.56	2.50	6.27	4.22	3.41	2.52	5.67
1932	3.68	4.65	5.73	5.01	6.13	6.69	6.58	5.30	7.36	7.13	7.06	5.63	7.23
1931	3.34	4.01	4.66	4.58	5.04	5.58	5.82	6.89	4.43	5.93	6.14	7.43	4.97
1930	3.29	4.07	4.41	4.55	4.95	4.26	4.45	5.27	3.19	4.45	4.83	5.43	3.30
1929	3.60	4.27	4.60	4.73	5.12	3.48	3.65	4.29	2.29	3.36	3.77	5.36	2.03
1928	3.33	4.05	4.35	4.55	5.12	3.98	3.82	4.76	4.09	----------	----------	----------	----------
1927	3.34	3.98	4.34	4.57	5.51	4.77	4.72	4.89	4.96	----------			
1926	3.68	4.08	4.47	4.73	5.78	5.32	5.24	5.52	5.57				
1925	3.86	4.09	4.73	4.88	5.90	5.19	4.75	5.66	6.13				
1924	4.06	4.20	4.84	5.00	6.08	5.87	5.25	6.44	7.35				
1923	4.36	4.25	4.98	5.12	6.12	5.94	5.40	6.29	7.59				
1922	4.30	4.23	4.85	5.10	6.14	5.80	5.37	5.95	7.62				
1921	5.09	5.09	5.57	5.97	6.80	6.49	5.84	7.08	8.29				
1920	5.32	4.98	5.81	6.12	6.79	6.13	5.54	6.81	8.06	----------			
1919	4.73	4.46	5.29	5.49	6.31	5.75	5.18	6.26	7.37	----------			

Year	Municipal high grade bonds 475	Unadjusted index of yields of American railroad bonds 476	Preferred stocks 478	Common stocks, Cowles Commission Total 479	Industrial 480	Railroad 481	Utilities 482
1918	4.50	5.23	6.70	7.24	7.71	6.32	7.57
1917	4.20	4.79	6.42	7.82	9.79	6.12	6.75
1916	3.94	4.49	6.19	5.62	6.16	5.13	5.72
1915	4.16	4.62	6.48	4.98	4.19	5.21	6.01
1914	4.12	4.44	6.49	5.01	5.32	4.64	6.06
1913	4.22	4.44	6.57	5.37	5.71	5.16	5.66
1912	4.02	4.23	6.27	4.85	4.98	4.73	5.11
1911	3.98	4.19	6.28	4.92	5.36	4.68	5.28
1910	3.97	4.18	6.30	4.84	5.33	4.63	5.04
1909	3.78	4.07	--------	4.31	3.64	4.47	4.57
1908	3.93	4.22	--------	4.93	4.81	4.97	4.93
1907	3.86	4.27	--------	5.38	6.16	5.21	4.78
1906	3.57	4.00	--------	3.96	4.17	3.58	4.67
1905	3.40	3.89	--------	3.53	3.76	3.20	4.77
1904	3.45	3.98	--------	4.18	4.83	3.85	4.64
1903	3.38	4.03	--------	4.65	6.77	3.90	4.60
1902	3.20	3.84	--------	3.71	4.83	3.21	4.03
1901	3.13	3.83	--------	3.85	5.25	3.25	3.84
1900	3.12	3.89	--------	4.50	5.74	3.93	5.30
1899	--------	3.85	--------	3.21	3.62	3.03	3.47
1898	--------	4.03	--------	3.72	5.04	3.38	3.91
1897	--------	4.11	--------	3.90	5.32	3.47	4.73
1896	--------	4.34	--------	4.15	5.56	3.77	4.76
1895	--------	4.27	--------	3.97	5.46	3.50	4.99

Year	Unadjusted index of yields of American railroad bonds 476	Common stocks, Cowles Commission Total 479	Industrial 480	Railroad 481	Utilities 482
1894	4.41	4.62	6.03	4.17	5.94
1893	4.65	5.03	8.12	4.35	5.45
1892	4.53	4.16	5.51	3.77	5.05
1891	4.71	4.28	5.96	3.83	5.44
1890	4.55	4.01	5.07	3.54	6.03
1889	4.43	3.88	4.41	3.35	5.26
1888	4.59	4.18	4.29	3.84	6.11
1887	4.65	4.24	5.13	4.09	4.88
1886	4.55	3.85	5.46	3.75	3.75
1885	4.89	5.09	6.02	4.71	8.14
1884	5.15	6.31	6.25	6.13	8.03
1883	5.23	5.69	6.26	5.47	7.34
1882	5.24	5.18	5.23	5.07	6.18
1881	5.19	4.84	5.06	4.84	4.64
1880	5.60	4.78	6.85	4.64	4.08
1879	5.98	4.70	4.76	4.64	5.25
1878	6.45	5.12	5.34	5.15	4.61
1877	6.62	5.78	5.11	5.94	5.01
1876	6.68	7.02	6.99	7.02	6.98
1875	7.06	6.51	6.06	6.41	7.90
1874	7.53	6.89	6.72	6.80	7.92
1873	7.76	6.54	6.49	6.98	2.81
1872	7.60	5.70	5.10	6.18	2.12
1871	7.78	5.26	4.80	5.48	2.98

Year	Unadjusted index of yields of American railroad bonds 476
1870	7.92
1869	8.13
1868	7.80
1867	7.87
1866	7.95
1865	7.62
1864	6.27
1863	6.34
1862	7.56
1861	8.88
1860	8.59
1859	8.91
1858	9.34
1857	10.25

Series X 487–491. Basic Yields of Corporate Bonds, by Term to Maturity: 1900 to 1970

[Percent per annum]

Year	1 year (487)	5 years (488)	10 years (489)	20 years (490)	30 years (491)
1970	8.15	8.10	8.00	7.60	7.60
1969	7.05	7.05	7.05	6.77	6.54
1968	6.24	6.24	6.20	6.00	5.93
1967	5.29	5.28	5.23	5.00	4.95
1966	5.00	4.97	4.91	4.80	4.75
1965	4.15	4.29	4.33	4.35	4.35
1964	4.00	4.15	4.25	4.33	4.33
1963	3.25	3.77	3.98	4.10	4.16
1962	3.50	3.97	4.28	4.40	4.42
1961	3.10	3.75	4.00	4.12	4.22
1960	4.95	4.73	4.60	4.55	4.55
1959	3.67	3.80	4.03	4.10	4.10
1958	[1]3.21	[1]3.25	3.33	3.47	3.61
1957	[1]3.50	[1]3.50	3.50	[1]3.50	3.68
1956	2.70	2.78	2.86	2.99	3.09
1955	(NA)	[1]2.70	2.80	2.95	3.04
1954	2.40	2.52	2.66	2.88	3.00
1953	[1]2.62	[1]2.75	2.88	3.05	3.15
1952	[1]2.73	[1]2.73	2.73	2.88	3.00
1951	[1]2.05	[1]2.22	2.39	2.59	2.67
1950	[1]1.42	[1]1.90	2.30	2.48	2.58
1949	1.60	1.92	2.32	2.62	2.74
1948	1.60	2.03	2.53	2.73	2.80
1947	[1]1.05	1.65	[1]2.08	2.40	2.50
1946	[1].86	1.32	[1]1.88	2.35	2.43
1945	1.02	1.53	2.14	2.55	2.55
1944	[1]1.08	1.58	2.20	2.60	2.60
1943	1.17	1.71	2.16	2.61	2.65
1942	.81	1.50	2.16	2.61	2.65
1941	.41	1.21	1.88	2.50	2.65
1940	.41	1.28	1.95	2.55	2.70
1939	.57	1.55	2.18	2.65	2.75
1938	.85	1.97	2.60	2.91	3.00
1937	.69	1.68	2.38	2.90	3.08
1936	.61	1.86	2.64	3.04	3.20
1935	1.05	2.37	3.00	3.37	3.50
1934	[1]2.62	3.48	3.70	3.91	3.99
1933	[1]2.60	3.68	4.00	4.11	4.15
1932	[2]3.99	[2]4.58	4.70	4.70	4.70
1931	3.05	3.90	4.03	4.10	4.10
1930	4.40	4.40	4.40	4.40	4.40
1929	5.27	4.72	4.57	4.45	4.42
1928	4.05	4.05	4.05	4.05	4.05
1927	4.30	4.30	4.30	4.30	4.30
1926	4.40	4.40	4.40	4.40	4.40
1925	3.85	4.46	4.50	4.50	4.50
1924	5.02	4.90	4.80	4.69	4.66
1923	5.01	4.90	4.80	4.68	4.61
1922	5.31	5.19	5.06	4.85	4.71
1921	[1]6.94	6.21	5.73	5.31	5.17
1920	6.11	5.72	5.43	5.17	5.10
1919	5.58	5.16	4.97	4.81	4.75
1918	5.48	5.25	5.05	4.82	4.75
1917	4.05	4.05	4.05	4.05	4.05
1916	3.48	4.03	4.05	4.05	4.05
1915	4.47	4.39	4.31	4.20	4.15
1914	4.64	4.45	4.32	4.16	4.10
1913	4.74	4.31	4.12	4.02	4.00
1912	4.04	4.00	3.96	3.91	3.90
1911	4.09	4.05	4.01	3.94	3.90
1910	4.25	4.10	3.99	3.87	3.80
1909	4.03	3.97	3.91	3.82	3.77
1908	[2]5.10	[2]4.30	[2]4.02	3.95	3.95
1907	[2]4.87	[2]3.87	3.80	3.80	3.80
1906	[2]4.75	[2]3.67	3.55	3.55	3.55
1905	3.50	3.50	3.50	3.50	3.50
1904	3.60	3.60	3.60	3.60	3.60
1903	3.45	3.45	3.45	3.45	3.45
1902 [1]	3.30	3.30	3.30	3.30	3.30
1901	3.25	3.25	3.25	3.25	3.25
1900	[2]3.97	[2]3.36	3.30	3.30	3.30

NA Not available.
[1] More than usually liable to error.
[2] One alternative value; the other is equal to the longest term yield shown.

Series X 492–498. Bond and Stock Prices: 1871 to 1970

Year	U.S. Government (492)	State and local government (493)	Corporate Aaa (494)	Total (495)	Industrial (496)	Railroad (497)	Utilities (498)
	Bonds (price per $100 bond)			Standard and Poor's index of common stocks (1941–43 = 10)			
1970	$60.5	$72.3	$61.6	83.22	91.29	32.13	54.48
1969	64.5	79.0	68.5	97.84	107.13	45.95	62.64
1968	72.3	93.5	76.4	98.70	107.49	48.84	66.42
1967	76.6	100.5	81.8	91.93	99.18	46.72	68.10
1966	78.6	102.6	86.1	85.26	91.09	46.34	68.21
1965	83.8	110.6	93.9	88.17	93.48	46.78	76.08
1964	84.5	111.5	95.1	81.37	86.19	45.46	69.91
1963	86.3	111.3	96.8	69.87	73.39	37.58	64.99
1962	86.9	112.0	96.2	62.38	65.54	30.56	59.16
1961	87.6	107.8	95.2	66.27	69.99	32.83	60.20
1960	86.2	103.9	94.7	55.85	59.43	30.31	46.86
1959	85.5	100.7	95.0	57.38	61.45	35.09	44.15
1958	94.0	106.4	102.9	46.24	49.36	27.05	37.22
1957	93.2	105.8	101.3	44.38	47.63	28.11	32.19
1956	98.9	116.3	109.1	46.62	49.80	33.65	32.25
1955	102.4	123.1	114.4	40.49	42.40	32.94	31.37
1954	107.0	125.8	117.2	29.69	30.25	23.96	27.57
1953	99.1	119.7	112.1	24.73	24.84	22.60	24.03
1952	97.3	129.3	115.8	24.50	24.78	22.49	22.86
1951	98.4	133.0	117.7	22.34	22.68	19.91	20.59
1950	102.5	133.4	121.9	18.40	18.33	15.53	19.96
1949	102.7	128.9	121.0	15.23	15.00	12.83	17.87
1948	100.8	125.3	118.2	15.53	15.34	15.27	16.77
1947	103.8	132.8	122.1	15.17	15.17	14.85	18.01
1946	104.8	140.1	123.4	17.08	16.48	19.09	20.76
1945	102.0	139.6	121.6	15.16	14.72	18.21	16.84
1944	100.2	135.7	118.7	12.47	12.34	13.47	12.81
1943	100.5	131.8	118.3	11.50	11.49	11.81	11.34
1942	100.7	126.2	117.4	8.67	8.78	8.81	7.74
1941	109.5	130.9	117.7	9.82	9.72	9.39	10.93
1940	106.6	123.6	116.3	11.02	10.69	9.41	15.05
1939	104.5	119.0	114.7	12.06	11.77	9.82	16.34
1938	101.8	116.6	111.7	11.49	11.39	9.15	14.17
1937	100.1	113.3	110.2	15.41	14.97	16.86	19.07
1936	100.8	113.8	109.6	15.47	14.69	17.71	22.47
1935	$99.5	$108.6	$105.5	10.60	10.13	11.78	15.15
1934	95.4	99.7	98.2	9.84	9.00	14.05	15.79
1933	93.1	91.0	91.2	8.96	7.61	12.75	19.72
1932	88.9	91.7	84.4	6.93	5.37	8.75	20.65
1931	92.8	100.0	92.8	13.66	10.51	23.72	37.18
1930	108.8	99.0	90.9	21.03	16.42	39.82	53.24
1929	104.8	96.5	89.1	26.02	21.35	46.15	59.33
1928	108.3	99.3	91.8	19.95	16.92	40.40	36.86
1927	108.1	100.3	91.6	15.34	12.53	38.17	27.63
1926	103.8	99.0	90.1	12.59	10.04	32.72	24.11
1925	101.7	98.8	88.3	11.15	8.69	29.21	23.28
1924	99.3	97.4	86.6	9.05	6.83	25.02	19.34
1923	95.9	96.7	85.0	8.57	6.54	23.45	18.11
1922	96.6	96.9	85.5	8.41	6.35	23.71	17.39
1921	88.2	86.5	76.6	6.86	5.07	20.15	14.18
1920	85.9	87.7	75.2	7.98	6.50	20.86	13.36
1919	91.9	93.9	81.9	8.78	7.13	22.94	14.79
1918	----------	93.5	82.3	7.54	5.57	22.40	14.70
1917	----------	97.3	87.6	8.50	6.15	24.89	18.24
1916	----------	100.9	90.7	9.47	6.62	28.35	20.26
1915	----------	97.8	89.5	8.31	5.22	26.38	18.65
1914	----------	98.4	90.4	8.08	4.50	27.39	18.14
1913	----------	97.0	90.0	8.51	4.56	29.48	18.92
1912	----------	99.7	92.2	9.53	5.18	32.83	20.92
1911	----------	100.2	92.5	9.24	4.82	32.43	20.00
1910	----------	100.4	92.3	9.35	5.02	32.90	19.08
1909	----------	103.1	93.3	9.71	4.99	34.79	19.39
1908	----------	100.9	90.3	7.78	3.74	28.18	16.11
1907	----------	102.0	90.8	7.84	3.84	28.09	17.36
1906	----------	106.2	95.0	9.64	4.82	34.06	23.25
1905	----------	108.7	96.2	8.99	4.11	31.85	25.59
1904	----------	108.0	93.6	7.05	2.92	24.61	24.19
1903	----------	108.9	93.2	7.21	3.20	24.71	24.48
1902	----------	111.8	95.5	8.42	3.92	28.37	28.25
1901	----------	112.8	94.9	7.84	4.00	25.01	27.82
1900	----------	113.1	93.6	6.15	3.38	18.62	24.22

Series X 492–498. Bond and Stock Prices 1871 to 1970—Con.

Year	Standard and Poor's index of common stocks (1941–43 = 10)				Year	Standard and Poor's index of common stocks (1941–43 = 10)				Year	Standard and Poor's index of common stocks (1941–43 = 10)			
	Total	Industrial	Railroad	Utilities		Total	Industrial	Railroad	Utilities		Total	Industrial	Railroad	Utilities
	495	496	497	498		495	496	497	498		495	496	497	498
1899	6.29	3.67	18.21	27.76	1890	5.27	2.99	15.80	18.14	1880	5.21	2.10	16.08	17.36
1898	5.05	2.74	14.71	23.44	1889	5.32	3.24	15.70	18.59	1879	4.12	1.90	12.44	14.83
1897	4.45	2.32	13.06	20.55	1888	5.20	2.70	15.78	16.96	1878	3.38	1.78	10.00	12.54
1896	4.23	2.22	12.48	18.84	1887	5.53	2.60	17.11	16.93	1877	3.14	1.80	9.22	10.94
					1886	5.36	2.48	16.57	16.80	1876	4.06	2.27	12.00	13.92
1895	4.53	2.50	13.29	19.25										
1894	4.39	2.41	12.95	18.09	1885	4.60	2.19	14.14	14.81	1875	4.45	2.27	13.16	16.43
1893	4.78	2.66	14.15	18.47	1884	4.74	2.06	14.68	15.16	1874	4.57	2.40	13.53	16.44
1892	5.55	3.19	16.58	19.10	1883	5.63	2.25	17.44	19.14	1873	4.80	2.37	14.34	17.06
1891	5.03	2.88	15.22	16.16	1882	5.90	2.41	18.18	20.31	1872	5.03	2.38	15.02	18.79
					1881	6.25	2.45	19.38	21.09	1871	4.69	2.00	14.26	15.91

Series X 499–509. Security Issues and Net Change in Outstanding Corporate Securities: 1934 to 1970

[In millions of dollars]

Year	Total security issues				Classes of corporate securities [1]				Net change in outstanding corporate securities		
	Non-corporate	Corporate			Bonds and notes		Stocks		Total	Bonds and notes	Stocks
		Total gross proceeds	Use of proceeds		Publicly offered	Privately placed	Preferred	Common			
			Retirement of securities	Other							
	499	500	501	502	503	504	505	506	507	508	509
1970	49,721	38,944	----------	----------	25,385	4,880	1,388	7,292	29,628	22,825	6,801
1969	26,003	26,744	----------	----------	12,735	5,613	682	7,714	18,027	13,755	4,272
1968	43,596	21,966	----------	----------	10,731	6,651	637	3,946	13,062	13,962	−900
1967	43,716	24,798	----------	----------	14,990	6,964	885	1,959	18,229	15,960	2,267
1966	26,941	18,074	----------	----------	8,018	7,542	574	1,939	12,258	11,088	1,169
1965	24,116	15,992	----------	----------	5,570	8,150	725	1,547	8,061	8,098	−37
1964	23,165	13,957	----------	----------	3,623	7,243	412	2,679	8,068	6,637	1,431
1963	22,989	12,211	1,528	10,553	4,713	6,143	343	1,011	5,328	5,577	−249
1962	19,251	10,705	754	9,747	4,440	4,529	422	1,314	5,552	4,864	688
1961	22,363	13,165	868	12,017	4,700	4,720	450	3,294	7,819	5,170	2,650
1960	17,387	10,154	271	9,653	4,806	3,275	409	1,664	6,690	4,994	1,696
1959	21,326	9,748	135	9,392	3,557	3,632	531	2,027	6,448	4,073	2,376
1958	22,885	11,558	549	10,823	6,332	3,320	571	1,334	7,977	5,850	2,127
1957	17,687	12,884	214	12,447	6,118	3,839	411	2,516	9,739	7,026	2,713
1956	11,467	10,939	364	10,384	4,225	3,777	636	2,301	7,158	4,611	2,548
1955	16,532	10,240	1,227	8,821	4,119	3,301	635	2,185	6,081	4,188	1,893
1954	20,249	9,516	1,875	7,490	4,003	3,484	816	1,213	5,602	3,799	1,802
1953	19,926	8,898	260	8,495	3,856	3,228	489	1,326	6,688	4,757	1,932
1952	17,675	9,534	664	8,716	3,645	3,957	564	1,369	7,383	4,942	2,441
1951	13,523	7,741	486	7,120	2,364	3,326	838	1,212	5,886	3,583	2,303
1950	13,532	6,361	1,271	4,990	2,360	2,560	631	811	3,469	2,004	1,465
1949	15,059	6,052	401	5,558	2,437	2,453	425	736	4,592	3,285	1,307
1948	13,172	7,078	307	6,652	2,965	3,008	492	614	5,818	4,725	1,093
1947	13,364	6,577	1,352	5,114	2,889	2,147	762	779	4,191	3,005	1,186
1946	11,786	6,900	2,868	3,889	3,019	1,863	1,127	891	2,226	1,114	1,111
1945	48,701	6,011	4,555	1,347	3,851	1,004	758	397	−573	−1,038	464
1944	53,108	3,202	2,389	753	1,892	778	369	163	−516	−653	136
1943	43,348	1,170	739	408	621	369	124	56	−800	−767	−33
1942	34,376	1,062	396	646	506	411	112	34	−336	−389	53
1941	12,490	2,667	1,583	1,041	1,578	811	167	110	−24	−125	101
1940	3,887	2,677	1,854	761	1,628	758	183	108	−273	−342	69
1939	3,523	2,164	1,695	420	1,276	703	98	87	−559	−621	62
1938	3,771	2,155	1,206	904	1,353	691	86	25	549	578	−29
1937	3,018	2,310	1,100	1,138	1,291	327	406	285	−48	−452	404
1936	5,411	4,572	3,368	1,062	3,660	369	271	272	626	575	51
1935	4,352	2,332	1,865	401	1,840	385	86	22	−343	−200	−143
1934	4,512	397	231	152	280	92	6	19	−260	−250	−10

[1] Estimated gross proceeds, which represent the amount paid for the securities by investors.

FINANCIAL MARKETS AND INSTITUTIONS

Series X 510–515. Corporate Security Issues: 1910 to 1934

[In millions of dollars]

Year	Corporate securities — Total (510)	New capital (511)	Retirement of securities (512)	Bonds and notes (513)	Stocks — Preferred (514)	Stocks — Common (515)	Year	Corporate securities — Total (510)	New capital (511)	Retirement of securities (512)	Bonds and notes (513)	Stocks — Preferred (514)	Stocks — Common (515)
1934	490	178	312	456	3	31	1921	2,270	1,702	568	1,994	75	200
1933	380	161	219	227	15	137	1920	2,788	2,563	225	1,750	483	555
1932	644	325	319	620	10	13	1919	2,668	2,246	422	1,122	793	753
1931	2,372	1,551	821	2,028	148	195	1918				1,047	298	
1930	4,957	4,483	474	3,431	421	1,105	1917				1,076	455	
1929	9,376	8,002	1,374	2,620	1,695	5,062	1916				1,405	782	
1928	6,930	5,346	1,584	3,439	1,397	2,094							
1927	6,507	4,657	1,850	4,769	1,054	684	1915				1,111	325	
1926	4,574	3,754	820	3,354	543	677	1914				1,175	262	
1925	4,223	3,605	618	2,975	637	610	1913				1,194	452	
1924	3,521	3,029	492	2,655	346	519	1912				1,350	904	
1923	3,165	2,635	530	2,430	407	329	1911				1,387	352	
1922	2,949	2,215	734	2,329	333	288	1910				1,113	405	

Series X 516. New State and Local Government Security Issues: 1919 to 1970

[In millions of dollars]

Year	Amount (516)	Year	Amount (516)	Year	Amount (516)	Year	Amount (516)	Year	Amount (516)	Year	Amount (516)	Year	Amount (516)
1970	18,164	1962	8,845	1954	6,969	1946	1,204	1939	1,126	1932	849	1925	1,400
1969	11,897	1961	8,566	1953	5,558	1945	795	1938	1,108	1931	1,256	1924	1,399
1968	16,600	1960	7,292	1952	4,401	1944	661	1937	908	1930	1,487	1923	1,063
1967	14,766	1959	7,697	1951	3,278	1943	435	1936	1,121	1929	1,431	1922	1,101
1966	11,405	1958	7,526	1950	3,694	1942	524	1935	1,232	1928	1,415	1921	1,207
1965	11,329	1957	6,926	1949	2,996	1941	956	1934	939	1927	1,510	1920	683
1964	10,847	1956	5,446	1948	3,004	1940	1,238	1933	520	1926	1,366	1919	691
1963	10,538	1955	5,977	1947	2,354								

Series X 517–530. Market Value and Volume of Sales of Stocks and Bonds on Registered Securities Exchanges: 1935 to 1970

[In millions]

Year	All exchanges — Market value, all sales (517)	Stocks — Market value (518)	Stocks — Shares (519)	Bonds — Market value (520)	Bonds — Par value (521)	Rights and warrants — Market value (522)	Rights and warrants — Number of units (523)	New York Stock Exchange — Market value, all sales (524)	Stocks — Market value (525)	Stocks — Shares (526)	Bonds — Market value (527)	Bonds — Par value (528)	Rights and warrants — Market value (529)	Rights and warrants — Number of units (530)
1970	$136,465	$131,126	4,539	$4,763	$6,300	$576	294	$107,649	$103,063	3,213	$4,328	$5,555	$257	233
1969	180,877	175,297	4,963	4,501	5,124	1,079	171	133,173	129,603	3,174	3,550	4,123	19	70
1968	202,772	196,358	5,312	5,670	5,459	744	96	149,395	144,978	3,299	4,402	4,448	14	54
1967	168,258	161,746	4,504	6,087	5,394	424	141	130,791	125,329	2,886	5,428	4,862	34	107
1966	127,914	123,034	3,188	4,261	3,740	619	123	102,754	98,565	2,205	4,101	3,590	88	93
1965	93,325	89,225	2,587	3,794	3,289	305	82	76,878	73,200	1,809	3,643	3,150	34	58
1964	75,328	72,147	2,045	2,882	2,641	298	81	63,284	60,424	1,482	2,783	2,542	77	60
1963	66,157	64,314	1,838	1,740	1,654	103	41	56,564	54,887	1,351	1,667	1,586	11	21
1962	56,564	54,732	1,664	1,730	1,786	102	47	49,019	47,341	1,187	1,666	1,719	13	34
1961	66,068	63,802	2,010	2,023	1,954	243	131	54,785	52,699	1,292	1,964	1,909	122	100
1960	46,901	45,219	1,389	1,607	1,614	75	51	39,552	37,960	958	1,580	1,587	13	29
1959	53,877	51,864	1,605	1,892	1,816	122	94	45,368	43,476	1,039	1,864	1,783	28	76
1958	39,962	38,408	1,400	1,554	1,583	144	93	34,351	32,818	999	1,533	1,561	64	77
1957	33,360	32,206	1,292	1,154	1,253	147	222	28,686	27,547	914	1,140	1,235	96	200
1956	36,360	35,133	1,182	1,227	1,253	114	98	31,064	29,855	784	1,209	1,229	68	85
1955	39,261	37,868	1,212	1,231	1,261	161	108	34,038	32,745	820	1,207	1,226	85	89
1954	29,156	28,130	1,053	1,026	1,121	55	59	25,267	24,264	749	1,003	1,089	15	46
1953	17,488	16,708	716	781	909	47	82	15,010	14,250	520	760	875	32	71
1952	18,179	17,388	732	791	899	59	105	15,531	14,761	522	769	868	42	90
1951	22,127	21,302	863	825	955	45	77	19,013	18,215	643	797	915	27	63

Series X 517–530. Market Value and Volume of Sales of Stocks and Bonds on Registered Securities Exchanges: 1935 to 1970—Con.

[In millions]

Year	All exchanges							New York Stock Exchange						
	Market value, all sales	Stocks		Bonds		Rights and warrants		Market value, all sales	Stocks		Bonds		Rights and warrants	
		Market value	Shares	Market value	Par value	Market value	Number of units		Market value	Shares	Market value	Par value	Market value	Number of units
	517	518	519	520	521	522	523	524	525	526	527	528	529	530
1950___	22,840	21,777	857	1,038	1,278	25	35	19,735	18,725	655	1,000	1,228	10	27
1949___	11,443	10,740	516	703	933	25	38	9,674	9,012	380	662	880	14	26
1948___	13,749	12,904	570	846	1,172	21	30	11,731	10,932	413	798	1,110	10	21
1947___	12,541	11,587	512	954	1,274	59	39	10,617	9,742	358	875	1,176	36	22
1946___	20,001	18,814	802	1,187	1,572	97	46	16,675	15,562	531	1,113	1,489	42	29
1945___	18,112	16,226	744	1,842	2,691	45	22	15,190	13,462	496	1,716	2,509	12	11
1944___	11,780	9,799	464	1,981	3,122	10	6	10,089	8,255	342	1,834	2,925	3	3
1943___	10,986	9,024	485	1,962	3,839	5	6	9,457	7,672	362	1,785	3,593	1	2
1942___	5,570	4,309	220	1,261	2,666	(Z)	2	4,796	3,674	169	1,122	2,478	(Z)	1
1941___	7,603	6,240	310	1,363	2,530	6	7	6,408	5,257	230	1,151	2,269	4	4
1940___	9,726	8,404	372	1,314	2,081	8	5	8,223	7,166	283	1,053	1,760	4	2
1939___	13,347	11,426	467	1,921	2,590	5	5	11,488	9,970	366	1,518	2,121	2	3
1938___	13,927	12,338	542	1,589	2,310	8	11	12,306	11,016	424	1,290	1,932	3	6
1937___	23,709	21,010	837	2,699	3,429	42	35	20,769	18,468	614	2,301	2,967	--------	--------
1936___	27,283	23,621	956	3,661	4,652	25	23	23,323	20,387	702	2,937	3,791	--------	--------
1935 1__	19,115	15,376	662	3,739	4,723	--------	--------	16,138	13,338	499	2,800	3,505	--------	--------

Z Less than $500,000.

1 Stock and bond sales for New York Stock Exchange and New York Curb Exchange, January to March, exclude stopped sales; stock sales for these exchanges also exclude odd-lot sales.

Series X 531–535. Volume of Sales on New York Stock Exchange: 1900 to 1970

[Money figures in millions of dollars]

Year	Stocks (1,000,000 shares)	Bonds, par value				Year	Stocks (1,000,000 shares)	Bonds, par value			
		Total	Corporate	U.S. Government	State, municipal, foreign			Total	Corporate	U.S. Government	State, municipal, foreign
	531	532	533	534	535		531	532	533	534	535
1970_____	2,937	4,495	4,473	(Z)	22	1935_____	382	3,339	2,287	674	378
1969_____	2,851	3,646	3,614	(Z)	32	1934_____	324	3,726	2,239	885	602
1968_____	2,932	3,814	3,767	(Z)	48	1933_____	655	3,369	2,099	501	769
1967_____	2,530	3,956	3,901	(Z)	54	1932_____	425	2,967	1,642	570	755
1966_____	1,899	3,093	3,035	(Z)	58	1931_____	577	3,051	1,846	296	908
1965_____	1,556	2,975	2,912	(Z)	63	1930_____	810	2,764	1,927	116	721
1964_____	1,237	2,524	2,459	(Z)	65	1929_____	1,125	2,982	2,182	142	658
1963_____	1,146	1,483	1,375	(Z)	108	1928_____	920	2,903	1,967	188	749
1962_____	962	1,455	1,361	(Z)	93	1927_____	577	3,269	2,142	290	837
1961_____	1,021	1,636	1,566	(Z)	70	1926_____	451	2,987	2,004	262	721
1960_____	767	1,346	1,271	(Z)	76	1925_____	454	3,384	2,332	391	661
1959_____	820	1,586	1,517	(Z)	69	1924_____	282	3,804	2,345	877	582
1958_____	747	1,382	1,314	(Z)	68	1923_____	236	2,790	1,568	796	425
1957_____	560	1,082	1,031	(Z)	50	1922_____	259	4,370	1,905	1,873	592
1956_____	556	1,069	1,013	(Z)	56	1921_____	173	3,324	1,043	1,957	324
1955_____	650	1,046	962	(Z)	84	1920_____	227	3,977	827	2,861	289
1954_____	573	980	856	(Z)	124	1919_____	317	3,809	622	2,901	286
1953_____	355	776	683	(Z)	93	1918_____	144	2,063	356	1,436	271
1952_____	338	773	693	(Z)	80	1917_____	186	1,057	471	286	300
1951_____	444	824	730	2	92	1916_____	233	1,150	845	1	304
1950_____	525	1,112	1,008	2	103	1915_____	173	961	907	3	51
1949_____	271	818	725	(Z)	93	1914_____	48	462	427	1	34
1948_____	295	1,014	925	1	87	1913_____	83	502	471	2	29
1947_____	254	1,076	970	3	102	1912_____	131	675	648	1	26
1946_____	364	1,364	1,265	19	81	1911_____	127	890	795	3	92
1945_____	378	2,262	2,148	8	106	1910_____	164	635	592	(Z)	43
1944_____	263	2,695	2,585	6	104	1909_____	212	--------	--------	--------	--------
1943_____	279	3,255	3,130	4	120	1908_____	195	--------	--------	--------	--------
1942_____	126	2,311	2,181	7	124	1907_____	195	--------	--------	--------	--------
1941_____	171	2,112	1,929	20	163	1906_____	282	--------	--------	--------	--------
1940_____	208	1,669	1,414	39	216	1905_____	261	--------	--------	--------	--------
1939_____	262	2,046	1,480	311	255	1904_____	187	--------	--------	--------	--------
1938_____	297	1,860	1,484	127	249	1903_____	159	--------	--------	--------	--------
1937_____	409	2,793	2,097	349	347	1902_____	187	--------	--------	--------	--------
1936_____	496	3,576	2,899	319	359	1901_____	265	--------	--------	--------	--------
						1900_____	139	--------	--------	--------	--------

Z Less than $500,000.

Series X 536–539.   Net Assets, Sales, and Redemptions of Mutual Funds: 1940 to 1970

[In thousands of dollars]

Year	Number of funds	Net assets	Sales	Redemptions	Year	Number of funds	Net assets	Sales	Redemptions
	536	537	538	539		536	537	538	539
1970	356	47,618,100	1,230,408	765,375	1954	115	6,109,390	270,594	98,709
1969	269	48,290,733	1,503,002	846,722	1953	110	4,146,061	160,368	56,835
1968	240	52,677,188	1,994,117	1,027,517	1952	110	3,931,407	214,401	49,255
1967	204	44,701,302	1,377,668	743,027	1951	103	3,129,629	194,039	62,150
1966	182	34,829,353	924,435	426,847	1950	98	2,530,563	135,372	82,766
1965	170	35,220,243	1,228,170	512,187	1949	91	1,973,547	125,850	40,650
1964	160	29,116,254	958,489	411,053	1948	87	1,505,762	75,284	34,384
1963	165	25,214,436	648,609	387,643	1947	80	1,409,165	67,276	28,295
1962	169	21,270,735	510,870	285,579	1946	74	1,311,108	82,929	31,958
1961	170	22,788,812	813,127	263,335	1945	73	1,284,185	92,671	29,692
1960	161	17,025,684	481,318	192,556	1944	68	882,191	52,957	16,919
1959	155	15,817,962	541,087	171,650	1943	68	653,653	116,062	51,221
1958	151	13,242,388	482,429	174,773	1942	68	486,850	73,140	25,440
1957	143	8,714,143	331,580	95,759	1941	68	401,611	53,312	45,024
1956	135	9,046,431	342,606	90,661	1940		447,959		
1955	125	7,837,524	290,417	92,501					

Series X 540–542.   Federal Reserve Board Margin Requirements: 1934 to 1970

[Percent of market value.   Prescribed by Board of Governors of Federal Reserve System in accordance with Securities Exchange Act of 1934]

Period	Regulation T — For extensions of credit by brokers and dealers on listed securities	Regulation T — For short sales	Regulation U, for loans by banks on stocks	Period	Regulation T — For extensions of credit by brokers and dealers on listed securities	Regulation T — For short sales	Regulation U, for loans by banks on stocks
	540	541	542		540	541	542
In effect—May 6, 1970	65	65	65	1955, Jan. 4–1953, Feb. 20	50	50	50
1970, May 5–1968, June 8	80	80	80	1953, Feb. 20–1951, Jan. 17	75	75	75
1968, June 7–1968, Mar. 11	70	70	70	1951, Jan. 16–1949, Mar. 30	50	50	50
1968, Mar. 10–1963, Nov. 6	70	70	70	1949, Mar. 29–1947, Feb. 1	75	75	75
1963, Nov. 5–1962, July 10	50	50	50	1947, Jan. 31–1946, Jan. 20	100	100	100
1962, July 9–1960, July 28	70	70	70	1946, Jan. 19–1945, July 5	75	75	75
1960, July 27–1958, Oct. 16	90	90	90	1945, July 4–1945, Feb. 5	50	50	50
1958, Oct. 15–1958, Aug. 5	70	70	70	1945, Feb. 4–1937, Nov. 1	40	50	40
1958, Aug. 4–1958, Jan. 16	50	50	50	1937, Oct. 31–1936, Apr. 1	[2] 55	[3]	55
1958, Jan. 15–1955, Apr. 23 [1]	70	70	70	1936, Mar. 31–1936, Feb. 1	[4] 25–55	[3]	
1955, Apr. 22–1955, Jan. 4 [1]	60	60	60	1936, Jan. 31–1934, Oct. 1	[4] 25–45	[3]	

[1] Effective after close of business.   [2] Effective May 1, 1936.
[3] Requirement prior to Nov. 1, 1937, was margin "customarily required" by broker.

[4] Exact requirement on each security determined by relation of its current price to its lowest price since July 1, 1933.

Series X 543–546.   Stock Market Credit: 1931 to 1970

[In millions of dollars.   As of end of year]

Year	Ledger balances of member firms of New York Stock Exchange carrying margin accounts — Customers' net debit balances [1]	Money borrowed [2]	Customers' net free credit balances	Customer credit in stock market [3]	Year	Customers' net debit balances [1]	Money borrowed [2]	Customers' net free credit balances	Customer credit in stock market [3]	Year	Customers' net debit balances [1]	Money borrowed [2]	Customers' net free credit balances	Customer credit in stock market [3]
	543	544	545	546		543	544	545	546		543	544	545	546
1970	(4)		[5] 2,286	(4)	1957	2,482	1,706	896	3,576	1943	789	567	354	1,367
1969	7,273		2,803	9,852	1956	2,823	2,132	880	3,984	1942	543	380	270	925
1968	9,705		3,717	12,415						1941	600	363	289	1,022
1967	7,883		2,763	10,347	1955	2,791	2,246	894	4,030					
1966	5,329	3,472	1,637	7,443	1954	2,388	1,529	1,019	3,436	1940	677	427	281	1,142
					1953	1,665	1,074	713	2,445	1939	906	637	266	1,412
1965	5,521	3,576	1,666	7,705	1952	1,332	877	727	1,980	1938	991	754	247	1,551
1964	5,079	3,910	1,169	7,053	1951	1,253	659	822	1,826	1937	985	688	278	
1963	5,515	4,449	1,210	7,242						1936	1,395	1,048	342	
1962	4,125	2,785	1,216	5,494	1950	1,237	617	890	1,798					
1961	4,259	2,954	1,219	5,602	1949	821	454	636	1,249	1935	1,258	930	286	
					1948	499	210	586	968	1934	1,170		170	
1960	3,222	2,133	1,135	4,415	1947	517	199	612	1,032	1933	1,270		220	
1959	3,280	2,362	996	4,461	1946	473	163	704	976	1932	800		230	
1958	3,285	2,071	1,159	4,537						1931	1,300		260	
					1945	942	517	652	1,374					
					1944	1,041	768	472	1,394					

[1] Excludes balances with reporting firms of other member firms of major security exchanges and balances of the reporting firms and of general partners of the reporting firms. Figures for November 1931 to August 1935, inclusive, are estimates based on data made available through the courtesy of New York Stock Exchange; such estimates are available only for "Customers' debit balances" and for "Customers' free credit balances."

[2] Includes money borrowed from banks and trust companies in New York City and elsewhere in U.S. and also money borrowed from other lenders (not including members of national securities exchanges). Prior to September 1935, figures reported on a different basis.

[3] For an explanation of this series, see text.   [4] Series discontinued June 1970.
[5] Data not comparable with prior years because of change in series.

Series X 547–550. Brokers' Loans, by Groups of Lenders: 1918 to 1938

[In millions of dollars. As of end of year]

Year	Total	Loans by— New York City banks	Loans by— Outside banks	Loans by— Others	Year	Total	Loans by— New York City banks	Loans by— Outside banks	Loans by— Others	Year	Total	Loans by— New York City banks	Loans by— Outside banks	Loans by— Others
	547	548	549	550		547	548	549	550		547	548	549	550
1938	770	715	15	40	1931	715	540	35	140	1924	2,230	1,150	530	550
1937	770	705	35	30						1923	1,580	720	410	450
1936	1,185	1,095	50	40	1930	2,105	1,280	215	610	1922	1,860	945	410	505
					1929	4,110	1,200	460	2,450	1921	1,190	545	265	380
1935	1,080	1,020	30	30	1928	6,440	1,640	915	3,885					
1934	905	660	180	65	1927	4,430	1,550	1,050	1,830	1920	1,080	390	285	405
1933	915	705	135	75	1926	3,290	1,160	830	1,300	1919	1,610	715	420	475
1932	430	335	20	75	1925	3,550	1,450	1,050	1,050	1918	1,000	575	145	280

Series X 551–560. Short- and Intermediate-Term Consumer Credit, by Major Types: 1919 to 1970

[In millions of dollars. Estimated credit outstanding as of end of year]

Year	Total credit outstanding	Installment credit outstanding Total	Automobile paper	Other consumer goods paper	Repair and modernization loans	Personal loans	Noninstallment credit outstanding Total	Single-payment loans	Charge accounts	Service credit
	551	552	553	554	555	556	557	558	559	560
1970	126,802	101,161	35,490	29,949	4,110	31,612	25,641	9,484	8,850	7,307
1969	122,469	98,169	36,602	27,609	4,040	29,918	24,300	9,096	8,234	6,970
1968	113,191	89,890	34,130	24,899	3,925	26,936	23,301	9,138	7,755	6,408
1967	102,132	80,926	30,724	22,395	3,789	24,018	21,206	8,428	6,968	5,810
1966	97,543	77,539	30,556	20,978	3,818	22,187	20,004	7,972	6,686	5,346
1965	90,314	71,324	28,619	18,565	3,728	20,412	18,990	7,671	6,430	4,889
1964	80,268	62,692	24,934	16,333	3,577	17,848	17,576	6,874	6,195	4,507
1963	71,739	55,486	22,254	14,177	3,437	15,618	16,253	6,101	5,903	4,249
1962	63,821	48,720	19,381	12,627	3,298	13,414	15,101	5,456	5,684	3,961
1961	57,982	43,891	17,135	11,862	3,221	11,673	14,091	5,136	5,324	3,631
1960	56,141	42,968	17,658	11,545	3,148	10,617	13,173	4,507	5,329	3,337
1959	51,544	39,247	16,420	10,631	2,809	9,386	12,297	4,129	5,104	3,064
1958	45,129	33,642	14,152	9,028	2,346	8,116	11,487	3,627	5,060	2,800
1957	44,971	33,868	15,340	8,844	2,101	7,582	11,103	3,364	5,146	2,593
1956	42,334	31,720	14,420	8,606	1,905	6,789	10,614	3,253	4,995	2,366
1955	38,830	28,906	13,460	7,641	1,693	6,112	9,924	3,002	4,795	2,127
1954	32,464	23,568	9,809	6,751	1,616	5,392	8,896	2,408	4,485	2,003
1953	31,393	23,005	9,835	6,779	1,610	4,781	8,388	2,187	4,274	1,927
1952	27,520	19,403	7,733	6,174	1,385	4,111	8,117	2,120	4,130	1,867
1951	22,712	15,294	5,972	4,880	1,085	3,357	7,418	1,934	3,700	1,784
1950	21,471	14,703	6,074	4,799	1,016	2,814	6,768	1,821	3,367	1,580
1949	17,364	11,590	4,555	3,706	898	2,431	5,774	1,532	2,854	1,388
1948	14,447	8,996	3,018	2,901	853	2,224	5,451	1,445	2,722	1,284
1947	11,598	6,695	1,924	2,143	718	1,910	4,903	1,356	2,381	1,166
1946	8,384	4,172	981	1,290	405	1,496	4,212	1,122	2,076	1,014
1945	5,665	2,462	455	816	182	1,009	3,203	746	1,612	845
1944	5,111	2,176	397	791	119	869	2,935	624	1,517	794
1943	4,901	2,136	355	819	130	832	2,765	613	1,440	712
1942	5,983	3,166	742	1,195	255	974	2,817	713	1,444	660
1941	9,172	6,085	2,458	1,929	376	1,322	3,087	845	1,645	597
1940	8,338	5,514	2,071	1,827	371	1,245	2,824	800	1,471	553
1939	7,222	4,503	1,497	1,620	298	1,088	2,719	787	1,414	518
1938	6,370	3,686	1,099	1,442	218	927	2,684	773	1,403	508
1937	6,948	4,118	1,494	1,505	219	900	2,830	792	1,504	534
1936	6,375	3,747	1,372	1,290	364	721	2,628	698	1,428	502
1935	5,190	2,817	992	1,000	253	572	2,373	561	1,354	458
1934	4,218	1,999	614	889	37	459	2,219	473	1,306	440
1933	3,885	1,723	493	799	15	416	2,162	418	1,286	458
1932	4,026	1,672	356	834	18	464	2,354	505	1,374	475
1931	5,315	2,463	684	1,214	22	543	2,852	712	1,635	505
1930	6,351	3,022	986	1,432	25	579	3,329	955	1,833	541
1929	7,116	3,524	1,384	1,544	27	569	3,592	1,040	1,996	556
1928	6,258	2,935	1,134	1,331	28	442	3,323	928	1,901	494
1927	5,344	2,319	765	1,183	26	345	3,025	812	1,765	448
1926	5,227	2,363	977	1,083	24	279	2,864	745	1,701	418
1925	4,715	2,115	914	951	22	228	2,600	671	1,549	380
1924	4,025	1,646	670	779	16	181	2,379	561	1,482	336
1923	3,652	1,368	526	684	12	146	2,284	512	1,456	316
1922	3,166	1,047	295	619	10	123	2,119	430	1,391	298
1921	2,966	919	317	484	9	109	2,047	404	1,358	285
1920	2,964	969	376	490	7	96	1,995	354	1,379	262
1919	2,642	800	304	409	5	82	1,842	306	1,298	238

Chapter X

Banking (Series X 561-820)

X 561–820. General note.

For general statistical purposes it may be said that a bank is a financial institution which accepts money from the general public for deposit in a common fund, subject to withdrawal or transfer by check on demand or on short notice, and makes loans to the general public. The historical series on assets and liabilities of banks reflect these activities and are the basic series on banking. Series X 561–619 and X 634–688 on principal assets and liabilities of banks and on number and total assets by class of bank cover all banks and all commercial banks. Series X 620–633 and X 689–697 provide information on selected aspects of banking: Insured banks, branch banking, suspension of banks, earnings and expenses, bank debits and clearings, savings deposits, and Federal Reserve banks.

Collection and publication of banking and monetary statistics in the United States have been conditioned by the development of the banking and monetary system. Banks in this country have been in part under the jurisdiction of State governments and in part under the Federal Government. At the same time some banks operated before 1933 outside the jurisdiction of both governments, while other banks operated within the jurisdiction of both.

Supervision and regulation of banks have been a primary responsibility of the chartering authority. National banks, organized under Federal law enacted in 1863, are supervised by the Comptroller of the Currency, and State banks, by officials of the respective States.

Two other Federal entities with additional supervisory authority have been superimposed upon the existing banking structure: The Federal Reserve System, established in 1914 to exercise central banking functions, and the Federal Deposit Insurance Corporation, created in 1933 to insure bank deposits. The Federal Reserve System includes all national banks and such State banks as voluntarily join the System. Insurance of bank deposits was made obligatory for banks belonging to the Federal Reserve System and optional for others.

All the supervisory agencies have published some statistics for the banks under their jurisdiction, but there was no centralized collection of statistics for all classes of banks on a uniform basis until 1947. Prior to the National Banking Act of 1863, the only official collection of banking figures for the entire country was made by the Treasury Department under authority of a resolution of the House of Representatives passed in 1832. For 1833–1863, reporting by banks to the Secretary of the Treasury was voluntary. With the exception of some years, the Secretary of the Treasury included in his reports to Congress information regarding the number of State banks which reported to him. For 1863–1873, statistics of national banks only were published in the *Annual Report of the Comptroller of the Currency*.

The need for complete reporting was recognized in the act of 1873, which authorized the Comptroller to obtain balance-sheet data for nonnational banks from State banking authorities, Territorial authorities, or individual incorporated banks. Although coverage was improved, the data obtained were neither uniform nor complete because the various State and Territorial authorities did not request the same information from banks and some States had no department to collect the information. Moreover, in some States many so-called private or unincorporated banks operated outside the jurisdiction of State authority. The Comptroller annually requested that these banks report directly to him, but this procedure met with only limited success.

In spite of the difficulties of collecting statistics for all banks, the coverage and uniformity of the data became progressively better. This improvement came about principally because of greater uniformity in classification of balance-sheet information requested of banks, and because of the creation of banking departments in States that formerly had none, as well as more adequate collection and tabulation of data.

Efforts to promote uniformity in bank statistics culminated in 1938 when representatives of all Federal supervisory agencies worked out a standardized balance-sheet report form. This form was approved by the National Association of State Bank Supervisors and was adopted by the three Federal banking agencies and by many of the State banking departments. Nearly all States now use a form that is substantially consistent with the standard one.

In 1947, the Comptroller of the Currency, the Board of Governors of the Federal Reserve System, and the Federal Deposit Insurance Corporation, which compiled somewhat different balance-sheet data for all banks, worked out an arrangement for the Federal Deposit Insurance Corporation to compile semiannually a uniform series of statistics for all banking institutions.

To provide more adequate historical banking statistics comparable to those available beginning in 1947, the Board of Governors of the Federal Reserve System—with the cooperation of the Comptroller of the Currency, the Federal Deposit Insurance Corporation, and the State bank supervisory authorities—compiled a revised series for all banks in conterminous United States as of June 30 of each year, 1896–1955. These data were published in 1959 in Board of Governors of the Federal Reserve System, *All-Bank Statistics, United States, 1896–1955*. The series cover number of banks and principal assets and liabilities for major classes of banks. The publication also includes similar data for individual States, and for the U.S. outlying areas, which are not included in U.S. totals. Revisions in the earlier data affect primarily the nonnational components, and are largest for figures before 1920.

Compilation of the revised series for national banks presented no major problems. Since 1864, the Comptroller of the Currency has collected condition reports from 3 to 6 times annually from national banks, and has tabulated and published summaries of these reports showing principal assets and liabilities. National bank balance-sheet data were published in detail in *Abstract of Reports of Condition of National Banks* (usually 3 or 4 times a year) through 1962. Assets and liabilities and income and expense data are published in summary form in the *Annual Report*.

Compilation of revised statistics for nonnational banks beginning in 1896 required extensive research into all types of available banking statistics. The main sources of information, other than the records of several large private banks, were the annual reports and statistical publications and records of the Comptroller of the Currency, the Bureau of Internal Revenue, the Board of Governors of the Federal Reserve System, the Federal Deposit Insurance Corporation, and State banking departments, as well as compilations published in bankers' directories. Unofficial compilations of figures for banks in several States were also used.

Under the arrangements made for all-bank data beginning with 1947, the 1947–1955 data in Board of Governors of the Federal Reserve System, *All-Bank Statistics, United States, 1896–1955*, were based on compilations of the Federal Deposit Insurance Corporation, except that data for "other areas," that is, the U.S. outlying areas, were included in U.S. totals.

A financial institution is considered a bank in the revised all-bank series if it accepts deposits from the general public or if it conducts principally a fiduciary business. This is the definition used by the Comptroller of the Currency, the Federal Deposit Insurance Corporation, and the Board of Governors of the Federal Reserve System in the all-bank statistics published beginning with 1947. For complete description of the types of institutions included and of those excluded, see Federal Deposit Insurance Corporation, *Annual Report, 1956*, pp. 88–89.

In 1969, the format and contents of the uniform quarterly Report of Condition and the annual Report of Income, adopted in 1947 by Federal bank supervisory agencies and used by banks in the United States, were substantially revised to provide a better measure of bank performance for the supervisory authorities and the public. Changes in these two reports were effected following extensive discussions among representatives of the Federal and State bank supervisory authorities and the banking industry. For a description of these changes, see the *Federal Reserve Bulletin*, August 1969, pages 642 ff. (Report of Condition) and the July 1970 issue of the *Bulletin*, pages 571–2 (Report of Income).

Beginning June 30, 1969, the three Federal bank supervisory agencies have issued jointly—as of the end of June and December of each year—aggregate data showing the major call report items for all banks in the United States grouped by class, size, and geographic location. This combined report entitled *Assets and Liabilities—Commercial and Mutual Savings Banks* replaces the summary reports of condition formerly issued separately by each of the Federal bank supervisory agencies. The Federal Deposit Insurance Corporation has compiled, beginning in 1969, comprehensive income and end-of-year balance-sheet information for all insured commercial banks grouped by class, size, and geographic location in a report entitled *Bank Operating Statistics*.

X 561–688. General note.

Assets and liabilities are defined here in their usual accounting meaning. Assets are the resources of banks, such as loans, investments, reserves, cash, and balances with other banks; liabilities are the obligations of banks, such as demand and time deposits and capital accounts. The data presented in series X 580–619, X 634–677, and X 683–688, prior to 1956, are for conterminous United States; thereafter, they include Alaska, Hawaii, and U.S. outlying areas.

X 561–565. State banks—number of banks and assets and liabilities, 1811–1830.

Source: *Writings of Albert Gallatin*, edited by Henry Adams, J. B. Lippincott and Company, Philadelphia, 1879, vol. III, pp. 286, 291, and 296.

These are believed to be the most consistent series for the period before 1834. The figures are reprinted in Comptroller of the Currency, *Annual Report, 1876*, p. xl, which also contains estimates derived from an unofficial source of the number of banks, specie holdings, banknote circulation, and capital of banks in the United States for selected years, 1774–1804, and some discussion of early banking statistics. Figures in the Comptroller's report for 1876, together with some additional banking data for the period prior to 1834, are included in Comptroller of the Currency, *Annual Report, 1920*, vol. 2, p. 846.

X 566–579. Second Bank of the United States—resources, liabilities, and profits, 1817–1840.

Source: **Series X 566–577**, U.S. Comptroller of the Currency, *Annual Report, 1876*, app. p. lxxxiii (except series X 577 for 1818–1837, *Annual Report, 1916*, p. 912); **series X 578–579**, Ralph C. H. Catterall, *The Second Bank of the United States*, University of Chicago Press, Chicago, 1903, p. 504.

The Second Bank was chartered by Congress in 1816 for 20 years. Renewal of the charter was denied and reorganization of the bank was effected by the Legislature of the State of Pennsylvania. The bank failed in 1841 and was finally liquidated in 1856. See headnote, table 94, p. 912, Comptroller of the Currency, *Annual Report, 1916*, vol. II; that page also shows assets and liabilities of the First Bank

of the United States in 1809 and 1811, the only two years for which data appear to be available.

X 580–587. All banks—number of banks and principal assets and liabilities, 1834–1970.

Source: 1834–1896, U.S. Comptroller of the Currency, *Annual Report, 1931*, pp. 1018–1025; 1896–1955, Board of Governors of the Federal Reserve System, *All-Bank Statistics, United States, 1896–1955*, pt. I, pp. 30–33; 1956–1970, U.S. Federal Deposit Insurance Corporation, *Annual Report*, various issues.

These series represent a combination of data on two different bases: For 1896–1970, on the revised all-bank series basis and for 1834–1896, on the basis published in annual reports of the Comptroller of the Currency, which is known to provide incomplete coverage, especially of nonnational banks.

The historical tables in the 1931 *Annual Report of the Comptroller of the Currency* provide summary statistics by single years beginning in 1834 for (a) all reporting banks, (b) national banks (beginning in 1863), and (c) all reporting State and private banks (that is, nonnational banks). For nonnational bank data prior to 1873 the sources are as follows: For 1834–1840, Executive Document No. 111, 26th Congress, 2d session; for 1841–1850, Executive Document No. 68, 31st Congress, 1st session. For 1851–1863 (except 1852–1853), figures are from the report on the condition of banks for 1863. Those for 1853 are from Executive Document No. 66, 32d Congress, 2d session, and are incomplete. For 1852, the figures are estimates based on number of banks in 5 years, 1847–1851, and on assets and liabilities in 10 years, 1854–1863. For 1864–1872, all figures except number of banks and capital accounts are estimates based on data for the previous 10 years, 1854–1863.

Prior to 1896, figures shown here include all national banks and all State banks that voluntarily reported to State banking departments in the United States including mutual and stock savings banks, loan and trust companies, and private banks. A few banks in U.S. outlying areas are included. Data for nonnational banks for the earlier years are reported for dates other than June 30 and are known to be incomplete; many of the items have been estimated, as noted above. Where more reliable estimates prior to 1896 are available, they are included in alternate series X 678–682.

Beginning in 1896, more comprehensive data for nonnational banks than those included in the Comptroller's annual reports are available in *All-Bank Statistics, 1896–1955*, cited above. More detailed data than are shown here, by States and by class of banks, are available in this source, together with a description of the composition of the balance-sheet items, the methods by which the figures were compiled, and the classification of banks used.

Beginning in 1896, the figures include national banks and chartered or incorporated State banks, loan and trust companies, stock savings banks, and mutual savings banks. In conformity with the definition of a bank adopted in 1947, they also include unincorporated financial institutions which meet the definition of "bank"; cooperative exchanges in Arkansas which receive deposits; cash depositories in South Carolina; and Morris Plan and industrial banks (unless engaged merely in making loans and investments). In 1933 and 1934 only licensed banks, that is, those operating on an unrestricted basis, are included.

X 583, investments. For the national bank component, 1863–1865, total investments exclude securities other than those of the U.S. Government, which are included in "other assets" in the source. Total investments include all direct U.S. Government obligations and, since 1933, those fully guaranteed as to interest and principal by the U.S. Government; obligations of States and political subdivisions such as securities issued by States, counties, and municipalities, by school, irrigation, drainage, and reclamation districts, and by local housing authorities; and other securities, which comprise primarily obligations of domestic corporations, those of Government agencies not guaranteed by the United States, and foreign securities.

X 585, deposits. Total deposits for national banks for 1863–1865 include State banknotes in circulation and for 1866–1868, bills payable and rediscounts. Beginning 1942, deposit figures exclude reciprocal balances.

X 586, banknotes. Prior to 1864, figures represent State banknotes only; beginning 1896, national banknotes only. In 1865, a prohibitive tax was imposed on State banknotes and as a result only a few such notes were in circulation thereafter. Data for 1870–1910 exclude comparatively small amounts of State banknotes outstanding for which national banks, converted from State banks or merged with State banks, assumed liability.

X 587, capital accounts. Capital accounts include capital, surplus, net undivided profits, reserves for contingencies, and certain other reserve accounts. Capital is here used to designate primarily the original contribution of bank owners to the bank and is ordinarily evidenced by bank stock certificates. Surplus is ordinarily the amount of bank earnings specifically set aside as capital funds. Net undivided profits are earnings not yet set aside for dividends or allocated to surplus. In addition to reserves for contingencies, capital accounts include reserves for undeclared dividends and for accrued interest on capital notes and debentures as well as reserves for retirement of preferred stock or capital notes and debentures. Valuation reserves set up in connection with prospective but undetermined losses on loans, securities, and other assets *are not included* but are deducted from these assets. Prior to 1873, figures for nonnational banks include capital only; beginning 1933, the figures include preferred stock and capital notes and debentures.

X 588–619.   General note.

The following quotation concerning the role of commercial banks in the economy is taken from Board of Governors of the Federal Reserve System, *Banking Studies,* 1941, p. 169:

> Commercial banks are part of the economic organization of the nation. They operate as business concerns and earn a living by rendering services to the public. By lending and investing money, they assist productive processes; by providing checking account services they facilitate and expedite the settlement of financial obligations. There are numerous other banking services, but most of them are related to the primary banking functions of making loans and investments and handling deposits. All these services and operations have to do with money, which may be viewed as the stock in trade of banks.

For further comment on commercial banks and the reason for their separate classification, see text for series X 683–688. See also text for series X 580–587 and general note for series X 561–820. The data presented in series X 588–619, prior to 1956, are for conterminous United States; thereafter, they include Alaska, Hawaii, and U.S. outlying areas.

X 588–609.   All commercial banks—number of banks and principal assets and liabilities, 1896–1970.

Source: 1896–1955, see source for series X 580–587, pt. I, pp. 34–37; 1956–1970, see source for series X 580–587.

X 610–619.   All commercial banks—number of banks and total assets, by Federal Reserve membership and class, 1896–1970.

Source: **Series X 610–611, X 612–615,** (1969–1970), and **X 616–617,** see source for series X 580–587; **series X 612–615,** (1956–1968), U.S. Federal Deposit Insurance Corporation, *Assets and Liabilities—Commercial and Mutual Savings Banks,* semiannual issues; **series X 612–613,** prior to 1956, Board of Governors of the Federal Reserve System, *Member Bank Call Report,* various issues (with adjustments to bring these data into conformity with the revised all-bank series); **series X 614–615,** prior to 1956, derived by deducting from the totals for all commercial banks (series X 588–589) the figures

for all member banks (series X 610–613); **series X 618–619,** are all commercial banks (series X 588–589) less national banks (series X 634–635).

State member commercial banks are those banks chartered by the various States which have voluntarily requested membership in the Federal Reserve System and met the necessary requirements. Nonmember commercial banks are all other State-chartered banks (other than mutual savings banks). See general note for series X 561–820 and text for series X 580–587 and series X 683–688.

X 620–633.   All banks—number of banks and total assets, by deposit insurance status and class, 1934–1970.

Source: 1934–1955, Board of Governors of the Federal Reserve System, unpublished data (compiled in connection with *All-Bank Statistics, United States, 1896–1955*); 1956–1970, U.S. Federal Deposit Insurance Corporation, *Annual Reports* and *Report of Call: Assets, Liabilities, and Capital Accounts—Commercial and Mutual Savings Banks,* June issues, and unpublished data.

See general note for series X 561–820 and text for series X 580–587.

The Federal Deposit Insurance Corporation was created in June 1933 to pay depositors of failed banks the amount of their insured deposits. All national banks and all other member banks of the Federal Reserve System are required by law to be members of the Federal Deposit Insurance Corporation. Banks that are not members of the Federal Reserve System may be admitted to Federal deposit insurance upon meeting certain prescribed conditions.

Detailed statistics on assets and liabilities and earnings, expenses, and dividends of insured banks by class are available in Federal Deposit Insurance Corporation, *Annual Report.*

X 634–655.   National banks—number of banks and principal assets and liabilities, 1863–1970.

Source: See source for series X 580–587.

See also general note for series X 561–820.

National banks are those chartered by the Federal Government and are under the general supervision of the Comptroller of the Currency.

X 656–677.   Nonnational banks—number of banks and principal assets and liabilities, 1863–1970 .

Source: See source for series X 580–587.

Nonnational banks comprised all banks prior to 1863 (see general note for series X 561–820). These banks include State commercial banks, mutual and stock savings banks, private banks, loan and trust companies, and other institutions enumerated in the text for series X 580–587. For comment on incompleteness of nonnational bank data prior to 1896, see text for series X 580–587.

X 678–682.   Nonnational banks—number of banks and selected assets and liabilities, alternate series, 1865–1896.

Source: **Series X 678–679,** David I. Fand, *Banks in the Post-Civil War Period in the United States, 1875–1896,* unpublished doctoral dissertation on file at .University of Chicago. **Series X 680–682,** 1875–1882, U.S. Comptroller of the Currency, *Annual Report, 1885,* pp. clxix–clxxiii (discussion of figures, p. lxviii). **Series X 682,** 1865–1866, U.S. Federal Deposit Insurance Corporation, *Annual Report, 1934,* pp. 103, 112–113; 1867–1876, James K. Kindahl, *Estimates of Nonnational Bank Deposits for the United States, 1867–1875,* unpublished doctoral dissertation on file at University of Chicago, 1954, and Federal Deposit Insurance Corporation, *Annual Report, 1934,* pp. 112–113.

Data for all nonnational banks were compiled from tax returns submitted by banks during this period.

X 678–679, adjusted deposits and vault cash. Adjusted deposits as used here are total deposits (with original source figures adjusted for nonreporting banks and for underreporting by banks) less cash items in process of collection. Data are as of August, 1875–1881, and June, 1882–1896. In the source volume, figures for nonnational commercial banks are shown separately from mutual savings banks.

Figures for capital accounts and total deposits (series X 681–682) are based on information included on semiannual tax returns and are monthly averages for 6 months ending May 31, 1876–1882, and for 6 months ending November 30, 1875.

The figures shown for total deposits (series X 682) for 1865–1876 are the sum of separate estimates for deposits of nonnational commercial banks and mutual savings banks. The methods of estimation are described in the sources cited above. The original source figures for commercial banks were adjusted for nonreporting banks but not for underreporting by banks.

X 683–688. Nonnational banks—number of banks and total assets, by class, 1875–1970.

Source: 1875–1896, U.S. Comptroller of the Currency, *Annual Report*, various issues; 1896–1955, see source for series X 580–587, pts. I and II; 1956–1970, see source for series X 580–587.

These series are a breakdown of number and total assets of nonnational banks shown in series X 656–657.

See also sources and text for series X 580–587.

State commercial banks are all banks other than national and mutual savings banks. The classification of banks as "commercial" is based on function or type of deposit business. Commercial banks include the holding of checking accounts and other deposits subject to withdrawal on demand, and the making of short-term self-liquidating loans to commerce, agriculture, and industry. Mutual savings banks, on the other hand, carry only savings and other time deposits (with some unimportant exceptions) and they invest their funds mostly in mortgage loans and securities. While the distinction between mutual savings and commercial banks is not strictly functional, since the great majority of commercial banks also carry varying proportions of savings and time deposits, it serves to segregate from banks holding demand deposits the group of banks that hold a large amount of deposits which represent principally savings. See series X 588–609 for balance-sheet data for all commercial banks, that is, national and State commercial banks combined.

Private banks are unincorporated institutions that operate ordinarily without a charter from either State or Federal Government. The number and relative importance of these banks has declined over the past half century.

The differences for 1896 in the data compiled by the Federal Reserve Board and by the Comptroller of the Currency indicate the incompleteness of early compilations of banking data, particularly in the case of private banks. Balance-sheet data are available in the Comptroller's annual reports for those banks submitting information to that agency. For separate figures for number and deposits of mutual savings banks, 1865–1896, see Federal Deposit Insurance Corporation, *Annual Report, 1934*, pp. 112–113.

In the source volume for 1896–1955, principal assets and liabilities are available separately for State commercial and mutual savings banks, by States, and for private banks in 18 States; in the remaining States, private banks were not segregated from other banks.

X 689–697. Savings and other time deposits, by type of institution, 1820–1970.

Source: **Series X 689**, sum of series X 690–694. **Series X 690–691**, National Bureau of Economic Research, unpublished data; see text for series X 418–419. **Series X 692**, U.S. National Credit Union Administration, *1970 Annual Report of the Administrator* and *1970 State-Chartered Credit Union Annual Report*. **Series X 693**, U.S. Post Office Department, *Annual Report of the Postmaster General, 1957* and *1969*. **Series X 694**, Board of Governors of the Federal Reserve System, 1892–1941, *Banking and Monetary Statistics*, pp. 34–35; 1942–1947, *Federal Reserve Bulletin*, January 1949, p. 41;

1948–1970, *Federal Reserve Bulletin*, September issues. **Series X 695–696**, U.S. Bureau of the Census, *Statistical Abstract of the United States, 1946*, p. 404. Data furnished by the American Bankers Association. **Series X 697**, U.S. Comptroller of the Currency, 1820–1896, *Annual Report, 1896*, vol. I, p. 720; 1897–1910, *Annual Report, 1920*, vol. I, p. 241.

See general note for series X 561–820.

X 690, mutual savings bank deposits. For definition of mutual savings banks, see text for series X 683–688. See also text for series X 821–833.

X 691, savings and loan association deposits. For definition of savings and loan associations, see text for series X 834–844. Mutually-owned associations accept deposits in the form of share capital; these are legally considered shares in the association and holders of shares are owners rather than creditors, as are depositors in banks. Other types of associations are those having some form of permanent stock ownership.

X 692, credit union deposits. A credit union is a cooperative non-profit organization of individuals with a common bond of occupation, association, or residence. Its objectives are to promote thrift among its members and to provide them with a source of credit at reasonable rates of interest. Credit unions may be incorporated under Federal law or, currently (1970), under any of 44 State laws. Deposits include the purchase of shares, share certificates, or share deposit accounts in the credit union.

X 693, postal savings system deposits. The figures represent the balance to credit of depositors, including items shown on the balance sheets as unclaimed. They include both amounts redeposited in banks and amounts not so redeposited; they exclude amounts in banks in U.S. outlying areas. The Postal Savings System was discontinued as of April 27, 1966, and the accounts were eliminated after June 30, 1967.

X 694, commercial bank deposits. For definition of commercial banks, see general note for series X 561–820 and especially text for series X 588–609 and X 683–688. Deposit figures have been adjusted to exclude interbank deposits, which do not represent money available to the public, and items in process of collection, inclusion of which would represent a double counting of deposits. They exclude U.S. Treasurer's time deposits, open account, beginning 1939, and postal savings redeposited in banks. Beginning 1941, they exclude 3 member mutual savings banks.

X 695–696, national bank and State bank deposits. These data were originally furnished by the American Bankers Association, which discontinued this series after 1942. Savings and other time deposits include deposits evidenced by savings passbooks, time certificates of deposit payable in 30 days or over, time deposits (open account), postal savings redeposited in banks, and for some States, Christmas savings and similar accounts.

Series X 696 includes commercial, stock savings, and private banks and trust companies. Data shown for some of the years for these banks are incomplete for some States or have been estimated for others. Figures exclude 6 States in 1926 and 1927, 4 in 1928–1930, 3 in 1931, 2 in 1932 and 1933, and 1 in 1934–1937.

X 697, savings bank deposits. Data cover mutual and stock savings banks only.

X 698–715. General note.

Deposits in commercial banks are the major portion of the current means of payment. The extent to which such deposits are used is measured by statistics of bank debits. In conjunction with deposit figures, debits figures are a means of determining the rate of turnover of deposits in commercial banks. While these two measurements throw light upon current economic developments, the data must be used with care to measure changes in business conditions. Since factors not related to business activity may affect debits and deposits, these data reflect changes in general business conditions only in a broad way.

X 698–705.   Bank debits and deposit turnover, 1943–1970.

Source: Board of Governors of the Federal Reserve System. 1943–1964, *Supplement to Banking and Monetary Statistics*, Section 5, "Bank Debits"; 1964 (revised)–1970, *Federal Reserve Bulletin*, (monthly data; annual averages from Federal Reserve Board).

Beginning with March 1953, the Board of Governors of the Federal Reserve System has published revised monthly bank debits series comprising only debits to demand deposit accounts of individuals, partnerships, and corporations, and of States and political subdivisions. Series X 698–701, which classify reporting centers into 3 groups—New York City, 6 other leading centers, and 338 other centers—provide a better measure of the activity of checking accounts than the discontinued series presented in X 706–709, which include debits to deposit accounts of the U.S. Government and to time deposits.

The turnover of demand deposits, series X 702–705, computed by dividing debits during a period (and converted to an annual rate) by average deposits against which the debits are made, indicates the number of times a deposit dollar is used during the period.

Monthly data on debits and annual turnover for the period beginning in 1943 are available in the *Federal Reserve Bulletin*, including a seasonally adjusted series for turnover.

X 706–709.   Bank debits to deposit accounts, except interbank accounts, at reporting centers, 1919–1952.

Source: Board of Governors of the Federal Reserve System, 1919–1941, *Banking and Monetary Statistics*, pp. 234–237; 1942–1952, *Federal Reserve Bulletin*, June 1946, p. 630; June 1951, p. 665; and June 1953, p. 612.

Data for individual reporting centers, by months, for 1919–1941, are available in *Banking and Monetary Statistics*; for 1942–1952, they are available upon request from the Board of Governors of the Federal Reserve System.

Figures represent debits or charges on books of reporting member and nonmember commercial banks to deposit accounts of individuals, partnerships, and corporations, the U.S. Government, and State, county, and municipal governments, including debits to time and savings accounts, payments from trust funds on deposit in the banking department, and payments of certificates of deposit. Debits to accounts of other banks or in settlement of clearinghouse balances, payment of certified and officers' checks, charges to expense and miscellaneous accounts, corrections, and similar charges are not included. For a more detailed description of the data, see *Banking and Monetary Statistics*, pp. 230–233, and George Garvy, *Development of Bank Debits and Clearings and Their Use in Economic Analysis*, published in 1952 by the Board of Governors of the Federal Reserve System, especially chap. III, pp. 27–48.

Satisfactory figures are available for New York City and 140 other reporting centers, but the number of other reporting centers, and consequently the total number of all reporting centers, increased substantially for 1919–1952. (For details, see *Banking and Monetary Statistics*, p. 231, and *Federal Reserve Bulletin*, May 1952, p. 514.)

For revised data back to 1943, see series X 698–705.

X 710–715.   Bank debits and deposit turnover, all commercial banks, 1919–1941.

Source: See first source cited for series X 706–709, p. 254.

For definition of debits, see text for series X 706–709; for definition of deposit turnover, see text for series X 698–705. Figures shown here are in part estimated; for a description of these series, see source, p. 232.

X 716–724.   Number of banking offices, by deposit insurance status, 1900–1970.

Source: 1900–1941, Board of Governors of the Federal Reserve System, *Monetary Policy and the Management of the Public Debt*, Joint

Committee on the Economic Report, 82d Congress, 2d session, pt. I, p. 553; 1942–1970, U.S. Federal Deposit Insurance Corporation, *Annual Report*, various issues.

Additional statistics on the number of banking offices are included in Board of Governors of the Federal Reserve System, *Federal Reserve Bulletin* and *Annual Report*, and in Federal Deposit Insurance Corporation, *Annual Report*. The figures for 1900–1932 comprise national and all State-chartered banks except (a) mutual savings banks (data for which are not available until 1933) and (b) unincorporated or private banks not reporting to State banking authorities, other than certain large private banks which began to report to State banking authorities in 1934 and for which data are extended back to 1928. Separate data for State member banks are not available until 1933 (see text for series X 731–740). Beginning in 1942, the figures include banking facilities at military and other Government establishments; see series X 740. See also text for series X 580–587, X 620–633, and X 731–740.

X 725–730.   Bank deposits insured by the Federal Deposit Insurance Corporation and the Deposit Insurance Fund, 1934–1970.

Source: U.S. Federal Deposit Insurance Corporation, *1970 Annual Report*, table 14.

See text for series X 620–633.

The Federal Deposit Insurance Corporation insured deposits in each account up to a maximum of $5,000 from 1934 to September 1950; to $10,000 from September 1950 to October 1966; to $15,000 from October 1966 to December 1969; and to $20,000 since then through 1970.

X 731–740.   Branch banking, 1900–1970.

Source: Board of Governors of the Federal Reserve System. Number of banks and loans and investments or deposits, 1900–1941, *Banking and Monetary Statistics*, pp. 297, 311 (for data on private and mutual savings banks, see also annual tables in the *Federal Reserve Bulletin*); number of branches, 1900–1951, *Monetary Policy and the Management of the Public Debt*, Joint Committee on the Economic Report, 82d Congress, 2d session, pt. I, p. 555; all series for all other years, *Federal Reserve Bulletin*, April, May, June, or July issues.

The figures for number of branches represent some revisions of data previously published in *Banking and Monetary Statistics*. Detailed statistics on branch banking by States, by class of bank, and by location of branches relative to the head office, for selected years since 1900, are available in the sources indicated.

Branch banking is defined as a type of multiple-office banking under which a bank as a single legal entity operates more than one banking office. If a bank operates a single branch office, irrespective of size or functions, other than a "facility" as defined below, it is included here.

The statistics on branches include all branches or additional offices in conterminous U.S. prior to 1959, and include Alaska and Hawaii thereafter, within the meaning of section 5155, United States Revised Statutes, which defines a branch as "any branch bank, branch office, branch agency, additional office, or any branch place of business . . . at which deposits are received, or checks paid, or money lent." Branch figures, however, do not include banking facilities at military and other Government establishments, which began in 1942 through arrangements made by the Treasury Department with banks designated as depositaries and financial agents of the Government. The number of such facilities is shown separately in series X 740.

Branch banking is not to be confused with group and chain banking. Group and chain banking refers to types of multiple-office banking which differ from branch banking principally in legal form and type of control. For data on group and chain banking, see sources cited above.

For mutual savings banks, data are not available for banks operating branches and number of branches until 1933; deposits are available only for the years indicated. Branches of unincorporated (private) banks not reporting to State banking authorities are not included prior to 1934. Separate data for State member and nonmember banks of the Federal Reserve System are available only for the years shown.

Wherever available, figures on loans and investments or deposits of banks operating branches are shown. These figures include the combined deposits or loans and investments of banks and their branches. For 1900–1936, the figures present loans and investments; for 1937–1941 and 1949, they are deposits, except as noted.

X 741–755. Bank suspensions—number and deposits of suspended banks, 1864–1970.

Source: **Series X 741**, sum of series X 742–745; **series X 748**, sum of series X 749–752. **Series X 742–754** (except X 745 and X 752 for 1864–1920), 1864–1891, U.S. Comptroller of the Currency, *Annual Report, 1931*, p. 1040; 1892–1933, Board of Governors of the Federal Reserve System, *Banking and Monetary Statistics*, pp. 283 and 292. **Series X 745** and **X 752**, 1864–1920, U.S. Federal Deposit Insurance Corporation, *Annual Report, 1934*, pp. 112–113; **series X 755**, 1921–1923, *Annual Report, 1940*, p. 66; **series X 742–747** and **X 749–755**, 1934–1970, unpublished data; **series X 741** and **X 748**, 1934–1970, *Annual Report, 1970.*

More detailed statistics for 1921–1941 are available in *Banking and Monetary Statistics*, including the number and deposits of suspended banks, by States and by class of bank, and in the *Federal Reserve Bulletin* for September 1937, pp. 866–910, and December 1937, pp. 1204–1224. The annual reports of the Comptroller of the Currency contain considerable material relating to national banks placed in receivership and losses sustained by depositors and stockholders of national banks.

Comprehensive and dependable statistics on bank suspensions are available only for comparatively recent years, that is, beginning with 1921. Prior to 1921, the figures are useful principally in showing the periods of abnormal banking mortality. Statistics for State banks prior to 1892 are fragmentary and incomplete. While figures for 1892–1920 are believed to be somewhat more reliable than for earlier years, they are not strictly comparable with the figures shown for 1921–1970.

Beginning with 1921, detailed data on the number and deposits of suspended banks were compiled from original reports on bank suspensions. The term "bank suspension" has been defined to comprise all banks closed to the public, either temporarily or permanently, by supervisory authorities or by the banks' boards of directors on account of financial difficulties, whether on a so-called moratorium basis or otherwise, unless the closing was under a special banking holiday declared by civil authorities. In the latter case, if the bank remained closed only during such holiday, it was not counted as a suspension. Banks which, without actually closing, merged with other banks or obtained agreements with depositors to waive or to defer withdrawal of a portion of their deposits likewise were not counted as suspended.

The figures for number of suspended banks for 1933 are not wholly comparable with those for other years. It was difficult in that year to determine the status of some banks because of the changes brought about by the State and national banking holidays and the subsequent reorganization of the banking system. The 1933 figures comprise banks suspended before the banking holiday, licensed banks suspended or placed on a restricted basis following the banking holiday, unlicensed banks placed in liquidation or receivership, and all other unlicensed banks which were not granted licenses to reopen by June 30, 1933. This date was selected because by that time supervisory authorities had completed their examination of practically all the banks not granted licenses immediately following the banking holiday, and had authorized the reopening of banks that could qualify for licenses. Since 1933, suspensions of insured banks have been handled by the Federal Deposit Insurance Corporation.

Deposits for suspended banks are as of the date of suspension for member banks of the Federal Reserve System and for nonmember banks, as of the date of suspension or latest available call date prior thereto, with the exception of unlicensed banks included for 1933. Deposits of unlicensed banks included in suspensions for 1933 are (*a*) for national banks, as of the date of conservatorship; (*b*) for State member banks, as of June 30, 1933, or the nearest call date prior to liquidation or receivership; and (*c*) for nonmember banks, the latest figures available at the time the banks were reported as having been placed in liquidation or receivership, or (for those which later reopened) as of the date license was granted to reopen.

Methods used in deriving the figures for losses borne by depositors (series X 755) for the periods 1865–1880, 1881–1909, and 1901–1920, are described in Federal Deposit Insurance Corporation, *Annual Report, 1940*, pp. 61–73.

There were no bank suspensions in Alaska and Hawaii.

X 756–767. Banks closed because of financial difficulties, 1934–1970.

Source: U.S. Federal Deposit Insurance Corporation, *Annual Report, 1970*, and unpublished data.

The Federal Deposit Insurance Corporation has used two procedures in fulfilling its responsibility to protect bank depositors from loss. It has paid depositors of insured banks placed in receivership up to the maximum limit prescribed by law and it has made loans to, or purchased assets of, financially distressed banks, thereby facilitating assumption of their deposits by another insured bank. The assumption of deposits by another bank enables business to continue with little or no deviation from normal routine, whereas a receivership may disrupt the economic life of the community.

Deposit figures at date of closing are adjusted to reflect subsequent corrections. In the case of banks placed in receivership, deposits at date of closing may be changed to include deposits discovered or reclassified after that date.

Data for losses to depositors in noninsured banks are not available. There were no bank failures in Alaska and Hawaii.

X 768–791. General note.

The earliest available bank earnings data on a nationwide basis are those for national banks beginning in 1869. National banks were required to make earnings reports for the years 1869–1871 whenever dividends were declared; for 1872–1916, at least semiannually whether dividends were declared or not declared; for 1917–1961, for the periods ending in June and December; and for 1962 to the present (1970), annual reports for the calendar year. At first the report form included only cash dividends declared, net profits, and a few related items, but it became progressively more detailed and more comprehensive. Beginning with 1917, a breakdown as to the sources and disposition of earnings has been required.

X 768–775. National banks—earnings and expenses, 1869–1970.

Source: 1869–1941, Board of Governors of the Federal Reserve System, *Banking and Monetary Statistics*, pp. 260–261; 1942–1970, U.S. Comptroller of the Currency, *Annual Report*, various issues.

Data are available for 1919–1941 for all Federal Reserve member banks (national and State member banks combined) in *Banking and Monetary Statistics*, pp. 262–265, and thereafter in various issues of the *Federal Reserve Bulletin*. For example, earnings and expenses are available by type; recoveries and profits, losses and charge-offs, and transfers to and from valuation reserves (beginning in 1948) are shown by character of asset. Data are also available for banks grouped by Federal Reserve District, State, class of bank, and size of bank. Various earnings ratios are available for part of the period.

The figures for gross and net current earnings before 1927 include profits on securities sold; such profits during the second half of 1926, when first reported separately, were $17,388,000. The figures for gross and net earnings up to and including the fiscal year ending June 1919 also include recoveries on charged-off assets; such recoveries in the fiscal year ending June 30, 1919, were $21,066,000. Beginning in 1927 and 1919, respectively, these items are included in series X 772, which is the excess of total losses, charge-offs (including depreciation), and transfers to reserve accounts over total recoveries, profits, and transfers from reserve accounts, or vice versa.

Beginning 1969, data are not fully comparable with those for prior years: (1) net current earnings are reduced by a provision for loan losses; (2) X 770, expenses, includes only those income taxes applicable to current earnings; (3) the effect of taxes on other earnings is reflected in X 772; (4) X 772 is computed by summing securities gains or losses, extraordinary charges or credits, and the excess of transfers from reserves over transfers to reserves, all adjusted for tax effects.

X 776–791. Insured commercial banks—earnings and expenses, 1934–1970.

Source: U.S. Federal Deposit Insurance Corporation, 1934–1941, *Annual Report, 1941*, pp. 158–159 (except ratio of net profits to capital accounts which are from unpublished data); 1942–1970, *Annual Report*, various issues.

For a definition of commercial banks, see general note for series X 561–820 and especially text for series X 588–609 and X 683–688.

More detailed data than are shown here are available in the source. See description of additional data available for national and other Federal Reserve member banks in the text for series X 768–775.

Prior to 1969, reports of income and dividends were submitted to the Federal supervisory agencies on either a cash or an accrual basis. In 1969, banks with assets of $50 million or more, and beginning in 1970, $25 million or more, were required to report consolidated income accounts on an accrual basis. Smaller banks continue to have the option of submitting their reports on a cash or an accrual basis, except that unearned discount on installment loans, and income taxes, must be reported on an accrual basis. For national banks and for State banks in the District of Columbia, not members of the Federal Reserve System, the data are collected by the Comptroller of the Currency; for State bank members of the Federal Reserve System, by the Board of Governors of the Federal Reserve System; for other insured banks, by the Federal Deposit Insurance Corporation.

Earnings data are included for all insured banks operating at the end of the respective years, unless indicated otherwise. Beginning 1958, appropriate adjustments have been made for banks in operation during part of the year but not at the end of the year.

Series X 787 is the excess of total losses, charge-offs, and transfers to reserve accounts over total recoveries, profits, and transfers from reserve accounts, or vice versa. Beginning 1969, series X 787 represents the combination of "extraordinary changes or credits" and "net securities gains or losses."

X 792–795. Bank clearings at principal cities, 1854–1970.

Source: U.S. Comptroller of the Currency, 1854–1881, *Annual Report, 1920*, vol. 2, p. 849; 1882–1919, *Annual Report*, various issues. 1920–1962, *Commercial and Financial Chronicle*, New York, N.Y.; 1963–1970, Dun & Bradstreet, Inc., *Monthly Bank Clearings Report*, p. 2.

The first source cited above gives for New York the number of banks, capital, clearings, balances, average daily clearings, and average daily balances, for years ending September 30, 1854–1920.

For 1882–1919, figures are for all cities reporting to New York Clearing House Association and cover years ending September 30. Beginning 1920, all figures are for calendar years. For 1920–1935, series X 795 is for 146 identical cities. Beginning 1963, series X 793 is for 25 cities outside of New York City. The comparability of figures over the years is affected by (a) changes in the number of cities reporting and (b) the tendency toward consolidation of banks, eliminating former clearings between two or more banks. The source volume suggests that bank debits, series X 698–701 and X 706–709, are a better measure of volume of payment.

X 796–820. General note.

For purposes of administering the Federal Reserve System, the country is divided into 12 districts. There is a Federal Reserve bank in each district and most have one or more branches. Federal Reserve banks are organized as Federal corporations with capital stock subscribed by member banks in the respective districts. Member banks include all national banks and those State banks which have voluntarily requested membership and have met the requirements for joining the System. The number and total assets of national and State member banks are shown separately in series X 610–613 and for the two groups combined in series X 624–625.

The Federal Reserve banks are the principal medium through which the credit policies and general supervisory powers of the Federal Reserve authorities are carried out; they hold the legal reserves of member banks and perform for member banks many services related to those that commercial banks perform for the public, such as furnishing currency for circulation, facilitating the collection and clearance of checks, and providing discount facilities. The Reserve banks also act as fiscal agents, depositaries, and custodians for the U.S. Treasury and other Government units and perform numerous other important functions. The Federal Reserve banks are coordinated and supervised by the Board of Governors of the Federal Reserve System.

X 796–805. Federal Reserve banks—principal assets and liabilities, 1914–1970.

Source: Board of Governors of the Federal Reserve System. 1914–1941, *Banking and Monetary Statistics*, pp. 330–332; 1942–1959, *Annual Report*, various issues; 1960–1970, *Federal Reserve Bulletin*, January issues.

Complete and detailed balance sheets for all Federal Reserve banks combined and for each bank are included in the sources.

Since 1934, the reserves of the Federal Reserve banks have consisted principally of the gold certificate account, which is backed dollar for dollar by gold in the Treasury. The supply of these reserves is dependent primarily upon the size of the monetary gold stock, or more precisely upon that part of the gold stock against which the Treasury has issued gold certificates or gold certificate credits. For a discussion of changes in the items affecting the reserves of Federal Reserve banks, 1914–1934, see *Banking and Monetary Statistics*, p. 325.

Deposits of Federal Reserve banks consist mainly of reserves of member banks, shown in series X 803. They also include the checking account of the U.S. Treasurer, deposits of foreign banks and governments, and other accounts, such as accounts of certain nonmember banks maintained for use in clearing and collecting checks and checking accounts of Government agencies. For further description of the items included in this table, see *Banking and Monetary Statistics*, pp. 324–329, and *Federal Reserve System—Purposes and Functions*, chap. XIII, pp. 173–190.

For statistical series presenting Federal Reserve balance-sheet items and monetary data related to member bank reserves, see *Banking and Monetary Statistics*, pp. 360–401; *Federal Reserve System—Purposes and Functions*, chap. VIII, pp. 107–119; and the opening pages of the tabular section of *Federal Reserve Bulletin*, for example, March 1973, pp. A4–A8.

X 806–812. Federal Reserve banks—earnings and expenses, 1914–1970.

Source: Board of Governors of the Federal Reserve System. 1914–1962, *Annual Report*, various issues; 1963–1970, *Federal Reserve Bulletin*, February issues.

Federal Reserve banks are not operated for profit but they are self-supporting. The nature and the amount of Reserve bank earnings depend largely upon the demand for Reserve bank credit on the part of the member banks and upon Federal Reserve policy as to open-market operations.   Most of the expenses of the Reserve banks are incurred in collecting checks, supplying currency, and performing other services from which no earnings are derived.

Until 1933, the law required that the net earnings of the Federal Reserve banks, after deduction of the annual 6 percent cumulative dividend on paid-in capital stock, be allocated to surplus and to a franchise tax paid to the U.S. Government.   In 1933, Congress abolished the franchise tax at a time when Reserve bank earnings were small and after Congress had directed the Reserve banks to contribute half of their surplus to the capital of the Federal Deposit Insurance Corporation.   From 1947 to 1958, the Reserve banks paid to the Treasury nine-tenths of their net earnings after dividends and after adjustments to maintain their surplus accounts at the level of subscribed capital; in 1959, they began paying all of such earnings to the Treasury.   Since 1964, surplus has been maintained at the level of paid-in capital (which is one-half subscribed capital).

X 813–820.   Federal Reserve banks—member bank reserve requirements, 1917–1970.

Source: Board of Governors of the Federal Reserve System, *Annual Report* and *Federal Reserve Bulletin,* various issues.

Legal limits: These data represent reserve requirements authorized by law (the Federal Reserve Act, as amended).   Since the September 21, 1966, amendment, requirements have been established by the Board of Governors of the Federal Reserve System between specific minimums and maximums set by the law.   On December 31, 1970, these legal limits for ratios of demand deposits were 10 percent and 22 percent for member banks in reserve cities, 7 percent and 14 percent for member banks not in reserve cities.   Ratios of time deposits were 3 percent and 10 percent for all banks.

The Federal Reserve Act as approved December 23, 1913, provided for temporary reserve requirements for member banks to be effective for a period of approximately three years.   Amendment to the Act on June 21, 1917, established percentages below which reserve requirements might not be set, but fixed no upper limits.   Maximum limits at twice the legal minimums were provided by the Act of August 23, 1935.   From August 16, 1948, through June 30, 1949, maximum limits were increased to permit changes in reserve requirements for the purpose of preventing injurious credit expansion.   After June 1949 the limits returned to their former levels.   A 1959 Act changed the maximum reserve requirement on demand deposits of banks in central reserve cities and in reserve cities from twice the legal minimum to 22 percent.   Another provision of that Act discontinued the

central reserve city designation effective July 28, 1962, three years after passage of the Act.   Maximums based on legal minimums for banks outside of reserve cities and for other classes of deposits at all banks were replaced temporarily in September 1966, and permanently in September 1968, by specific maximums and minimums.

Composition of reserves: The temporary reserve requirements in effect until 1917 authorized member banks to hold a part of their reserves as cash in their own vaults and a part on deposit with other banks.   For a fuller discussion of these requirements and the 1917 amendment of the Federal Reserve Act, see *Federal Reserve Bulletin,* November 1938.   Only balances with Federal Reserve banks could be counted as legal reserves from June 21, 1917, until late 1959. Since that time, member banks have also been allowed to count some portion of their vault cash as reserves.   Effective December 1, 1959, vault cash in excess of 4 percent of net demand deposits could be counted by country banks.   The percentage was decreased to $2\frac{1}{2}$ on August 25, 1960.   Central reserve city and reserve city banks were allowed to count vault cash in excess of 2 percent of net demand deposits effective December 3, 1959, and amounts above 1 percent beginning September 1, 1960.   All member banks were allowed to count all vault cash as reserves effective November 24, 1960.

Net demand deposits are demand deposits subject to reserve requirements.   In general, prior to 1917, net demand deposits were made up of (*a*) the gross amount of all demand deposits except those due to other banks, and (*b*) the net excess (if any) of demand deposits due to other banks over demand balances due from other banks and cash items in process of collection.   From 1917 to August 23, 1935, the definition was substantially the same, except that U.S. Government deposits were exempt by law from all reserve requirements and were therefore excluded from net demand deposits.   Beginning August 23, 1935, net demand deposits have been total demand deposits minus cash items in process of collection and demand balances due from domestic banks (also minus war loan and Series E bond accounts during the period April 13, 1943–June 30, 1947).

Reserve cities: Changes in the list of cities classified as "central reserve" and "reserve" for 1914–1960 are shown in the Supplement (1962) to Section 10 of *Banking and Monetary Statistics.*   The central reserve city designation was terminated July 28, 1962.   In 1962–1965, the reserve city designation was discontinued for five cities. Reserve cities on December 31, 1970, included the 36 cities where a Federal Reserve bank or branch is located plus the following: Columbus, Ohio; Des Moines, Iowa; Fort Worth, Texas; Indianapolis, Indiana; Miami, Florida; Milwaukee, Wisconsin; National Stock Yards, Illinois; St. Paul, Minnesota; Tulsa, Oklahoma; and Washington, D.C.

★ ★ ★ ★ ★ ★ ★ ★ ★   **More Recent Data for *Historical Statistics* Series**   ★ ★ ★ ★ ★ ★ ★ ★ ★

★   ★
★   Statistics for more recent years in continuation of many of the still-active series shown here appear   ★
★   in annual issues of the *Statistical Abstract of the United States,* beginning with the 1975 edition. For   ★
★   direct linkage of the historical series to the tables in the *Abstract,* see Appendix I in the *Abstract.*   ★
★   ★

★ ★

Series X 561–565.   State Banks—Number of Banks and Assets and Liabilities: 1811 to 1830

[Money figures in millions of dollars.   As of January 1]

Year	Number of banks	Capital	Circulation	Deposits	Specie
	561	562	563	564	565
1830	329	110.2	48.3	40.8	14.9
1820	307	102.1	40.6	31.2	16.7
1816	246	89.8	68.0	----------	19.0
1815	208	82.3	45.5	----------	17.0
1811	88	42.6	22.7	----------	9.6

Series X 566–579.   Second Bank of the United States—Resources, Liabilities, and Profits: 1817 to 1840

[In thousands of dollars.   Resources and liabilities as of January 1]

Year	Resources							Liabilities					Profits			
													Six months ending January		Six months ending July	
	Loans and dis-counts	Stocks	Real estate	Banking houses	Due from State and foreign banks	Notes of State banks	Specie	Capital	Circu-lation	Deposits	Due to State and foreign banks, etc.[1]	Other liabili-ties	Amount	Divi-dend rate (percent)	Amount	Divi-dend rate (percent)
	566	567	568	569	570	571	572	573	574	575	576	577	578	579	578	579
1840	36,840	16,316	1,229	611	7,469	1,384	1,470	35,000	6,696	3,339	9,127	8,119	--------	--------	--------	--------
1839	41,619	17,957	1,055	424	5,833	1,792	4,154	35,000	5,983	6,779	15,832	9,260	--------	--------	--------	--------
1838	45,257	14,862	1,062	443	3,657	867	3,771	35,000	6,768	2,617	17,449	7,987	--------	--------	--------	--------
1837	57,394	(NA)	817	420	2,285	1,207	2,638	35,000	11,448	2,332	9,211	6,800	--------	--------	--------	--------
1836	59,232	(NA)	1,487	967	4,161	1,736	8,418	35,000	23,075	5,061	2,661	10,100	--------	--------	--------	--------
1835	51,809	(NA)	1,761	1,219	6,532	1,506	15,708	35,000	17,340	11,757	3,119	11,300	--------	--------	--------	--------
1834	54,911	(NA)	1,741	1,189	4,861	1,983	10,039	35,000	19,208	10,839	1,522	8,200	1,430	3.50	1,498	3.50
1833	61,696	(NA)	1,855	1,181	6,795	2,293	8,952	35,000	17,518	20,348	2,092	8,000	1,594	3.50	1,602	3.50
1832	66,294	2	2,137	1,160	4,037	2,172	7,038	35,000	21,356	22,761	1,951	1,600	1,716	3.50	1,861	3.50
1831	44,032	8,675	2,629	1,345	2,383	1,495	10,808	35,000	16,251	17,297	735	2,000	1,345	3.50	1,590	3.50
1830	40,664	11,610	2,886	1,445	2,730	1,465	7,608	35,000	12,924	16,046	(NA)	4,500	1,392	3.50	1,414	3.50
1829	39,220	16,099	2,346	1,557	2,206	1,294	6,098	35,000	11,902	17,062	1,448	3,400	1,325	3.50	1,381	3.50
1828	33,683	17,625	2,295	1,634	357	1,447	6,170	35,000	9,856	14,497	3,165	600	1,203	3.00	1,349	3.50
1827	30,938	17,764	2,039	1,678	2,144	1,068	6,457	35,000	8,549	14,320	280	4,100	1,148	3.00	1,274	3.00
1826	33,425	18,304	1,848	1,793	1,169	1,115	3,960	35,000	9,475	11,215	251	5,500	1,162	2.75	1,218	3.00
1825	31,813	18,422	1,495	1,853	2,154	1,056	6,747	35,000	6,068	12,033	2,407	8,000	1,031	2.50	1,155	2.75
1824	33,432	10,874	1,303	1,872	2,722	705	5,814	35,000	4,647	13,702	1,020	2,400	929	2.50	977	2.50
1823	30,736	11,019	627	1,957	1,432	766	4,425	35,000	4,361	7,622	1,293	2,600	884	2.50	932	2.50
1822	28,061	13,319	563	1,856	2,825	918	4,761	35,000	5,579	8,075	2,040	1,700	719	2.00	1,010	2.25
1821	30,905	9,156	--------	1,887	1,262	677	7,643	35,000	4,567	7,895	2,053	2,000	734	(2)	750	1.50
1820	31,401	7,193	--------	1,297	2,989	1,443	3,393	35,000	3,589	6,569	2,054	500	785	(2)	719	(2)
1819	35,786	7,392	--------	434	3,246	1,878	2,667	35,000	6,564	5,793	1,434	2,600	899	2.50	983	(2)
1818	41,182	9,476	--------	175	2,238	1,837	2,516	35,000	8,339	12,279	1,358	400	1,382	4.00	1,266	3.50
1817	[3]13,485	4,829	--------	--------	8,848	587	1,724	35,000	1,911	11,233	--------	--------	--------	--------	1,022	2.60

NA   Not available.
[1] Comptroller of the Currency, *Annual Report, 1916*, pp. 912–913, shows somewhat different figures as follows (in millions of dollars): Series X 576–1840, 17.3; 1839, 25.1; 1838, 25.5.   Series X 517–1840, 3.0; 1839, no entry; 1838, 0.2.
[2] Carried to contingent fund.

[3] Comptroller of the Currency, *Annual Report, 1916*, p. 912, shows $32.2 million; *American State Papers, Finance*, vol. 3, p. 353, shows $32.4 million as of "last of October."

Series X 580–587. All Banks—Number of Banks and Principal Assets and Liabilities: 1834 to 1970

[In millions of dollars, except number of banks. As of June 30 or nearest available date]

Year	Number of banks	Total assets or liabilities	Assets — Total loans [1]	Assets — Total investments	Assets — Total cash	Liabilities — Total deposits	Liabilities — Bank-notes [2]	Capital accounts
	580	581	582	583	584	585	586	587
1970	14,187	[3] 611,305	[3] 358,433	[3] 142,722	86,817	505,939	----------	47,525
1969	14,194	[3] 594,542	[3] 343,407	[3] 141,609	89,363	496,034	----------	44,408
1968	14,245	529,606	300,381	137,166	76,521	460,146	----------	41,034
1967	14,267	479,590	276,536	123,094	66,397	420,748	----------	38,351
1966	14,328	447,788	261,014	113,320	61,152	394,326	----------	36,197
1965	14,310	412,493	232,784	110,634	58,241	363,892	----------	34,124
1964	14,189	375,349	203,992	107,499	54,247	333,073	----------	31,130
1963	14,006	349,083	180,398	107,892	52,199	310,455	----------	28,691
1962	13,947	321,629	160,709	103,584	49,728	286,037	----------	27,107
1961	13,989	296,445	146,673	96,183	46,541	263,316	----------	25,471
1960	14,019	282,872	141,836	87,191	47,956	249,760	----------	23,857
1959	14,011	273,309	128,143	96,078	43,816	243,016	----------	22,507
1958	14,095	265,861	118,480	97,759	44,628	238,369	----------	21,473
1957	14,184	243,856	112,122	86,314	41,014	218,025	----------	19,983
1956 [4] *	14,247	239,267	106,086	85,888	43,540	216,483	----------	18,911
1955	14,308	229,626	91,353	92,897	42,013	208,845	----------	17,663
1954	14,464	218,896	81,225	92,115	42,555	199,505	----------	16,664
1953	14,533	207,760	77,117	85,965	42,024	189,176	----------	15,791
1952	14,598	201,795	69,742	87,786	41,668	184,147	----------	15,038
1951	14,636	188,338	63,841	83,901	38,236	171,879	----------	14,235
1950	14,676	179,165	52,001	90,962	34,101	163,789	----------	13,577
1949	14,681	170,810	47,078	86,794	34,967	156,488	----------	12,846
1948	14,721	170,052	45,100	87,982	35,000	156,373	----------	12,239
1947	14,715	166,336	38,365	92,729	33,544	153,375	----------	11,719
1946	14,685	171,529	31,506	105,163	33,163	159,293	----------	11,104
1945	14,660	162,169	27,996	101,724	30,740	151,128	----------	10,126
1944	14,674	138,842	25,435	83,329	28,195	128,684	----------	9,333
1943	14,734	116,729	22,248	65,674	26,696	107,297	----------	8,765
1942	14,891	91,930	25,063	38,954	25,595	82,765	----------	8,500
1941	14,975	87,324	25,273	32,667	26,785	78,212	----------	8,441
1940	15,076	79,729	22,311	29,040	25,603	70,854	----------	8,252
1939	15,210	73,193	21,300	28,339	20,550	64,303	----------	8,236
1938	15,419	67,730	21,033	26,267	17,374	59,000	----------	8,107
1937	15,646	68,402	22,435	27,212	15,520	59,485	----------	8,123
1936	15,884	66,854	20,640	27,857	15,038	58,068	----------	8,016
1935	16,047	59,951	20,240	24,176	12,318	51,270	222	7,815
1934	15,913	55,915	21,309	21,262	10,158	46,480	695	7,865
1933	14,771	51,359	22,337	18,125	7,793	41,684	727	7,388
1932	19,317	57,295	28,071	18,406	7,407	45,569	649	8,525
1931	22,242	70,070	35,416	19,973	10,405	57,187	636	9,872
1930	24,273	74,290	40,990	18,090	11,201	60,365	649	10,372
1929	25,568	72,315	41,944	17,305	9,222	58,269	649	9,750
1928	26,401	71,121	39,946	18,146	9,454	58,138	649	8,954
1927	27,255	67,893	37,949	16,649	10,156	56,700	650	8,301
1926	28,350	65,079	36,658	15,562	9,806	54,416	651	7,841
1925	29,052	62,232	34,378	15,056	9,903	52,301	648	7,384
1924	29,601	57,420	32,030	13,843	9,034	47,961	729	7,073
1923	30,444	54,144	30,734	13,474	7,595	44,376	720	6,818
1922	30,736	50,368	28,000	12,328	7,830	41,227	725	6,599
1921	31,076	49,633	29,236	11,169	6,980	38,934	704	6,385
1920	30,909	53,094	31,189	11,043	8,489	41,838	688	6,019
1919	29,767	47,603	25,132	12,024	8,286	37,982	677	5,409
1918	29,480	41,097	22,863	9,609	6,837	33,061	681	5,113
1917	28,919	37,540	20,902	7,925	7,250	30,855	660	4,988
1916	28,362	32,697	18,263	6,833	6,385	26,738	676	4,718
1915	28,017	28,363	15,976	5,982	5,300	22,504	722	4,643
1914	27,864	27,349	15,502	5,701	5,125	21,665	722	4,503
1913	27,285	26,103	14,821	5,400	4,853	20,523	722	4,443
1912	26,472	25,372	14,124	5,440	4,925	20,013	708	4,269
1911	25,815	24,026	13,228	5,136	4,842	18,860	681	4,133
1910	25,151	22,922	12,766	4,839	4,543	17,950	675	3,984
1909	23,734	21,489	11,548	4,746	4,499	16,883	636	3,750
1908	23,161	19,946	10,763	4,4 6	4,043	15,440	613	3,627
1907	21,986	20,114	11,319	4,284	3,848	15,759	548	3,492
1906	20,407	18,740	10,442	4,080	3,635	14,703	510	3,285
1905	18,767	17,511	9,540	3,974	3,455	13,772	445	3,066
1904	17,659	15,848	8,545	3,595	3,202	12,341	399	2,935
1903	16,433	14,901	8,257	3,341	2,828	11,612	359	2,760
1902	15,112	14,026	7,664	3,098	2,855	11,103	309	2,473
1901	14,054	13,037	6,914	2,891	2,866	10,374	319	2,200
1900	13,053	11,388	6,093	2,544	2,395	8,922	265	2,075
1899	12,459	10,679	5,689	2,254	2,382	8,472	199	1,907
1898	12,163	9,218	4,976	1,970	1,914	7,044	190	1,878
1897	12,079	8,432	4,596	1,802	1,703	6,270	197	1,877
1896 [5]	12,112	8,048	4,615	1,689	1,421	5,859	199	1,893

See footnotes at end of table.

Series X 580–587.　All Banks—Number of Banks and Principal Assets and Liabilities: 1834 to 1970—Con.

[In millions of dollars, except number of banks]

Year	Number of banks	Total assets or liabilities	Assets			Liabilities		
			Total loans [1]	Total investments	Total cash [6]	Total deposits [6]	Bank notes [2]	Capital accounts [6]
	580	**581**	**582**	**583**	**584**	**585**	**586**	**587**
1896 [7]	9,469	7,554	4,251	1,675	1,266	5,486	199	1,746
1895	9,818	7,610	4,269	1,565	1,442	5,539	179	1,780
1894	9,508	7,291	4,085	1,445	1,473	5,268	172	1,753
1893	9,492	7,192	4,369	1,366	1,190	5,065	155	1,781
1892	9,336	7,245	4,337	1,284	1,378	5,298	141	1,721
1891	8,641	6,562	4,031	1,179	1,125	4,683	124	1,649
1890	8,201	6,358	3,854	1,173	1,123	4,576	126	1,558
1889	7,244	5,945	3,478	1,129	1,144	4,311	129	1,428
1888	6,647	5,471	3,161	1,131	989	3,891	156	1,348
1887	6,170	5,193	2,943	1,011	999	3,719	167	1,259
1886	4,338	4,542	2,434	1,052	773	3,186	245	1,076
1885	4,350	4,427	2,272	1,042	876	3,078	269	1,040
1884	4,113	4,221	2,261	1,041	678	2,849	295	1,036
1883	3,835	4,208	2,234	1,028	712	2,884	312	973
1882	3,572	4,031	2,051	1,055	755	2,777	309	901
1881	3,427	3,869	1,902	985	782	2,649	313	864
1880	3,355	3,399	1,662	904	655	2,222	318	826
1879	3,335	3,313	1,507	1,139	505	2,149	308	827
1878	3,229	3,081	1,561	875	493	1,921	300	826
1877	3,384	3,204	1,721	852	483	2,006	290	875
1876	3,448	3,183	1,727	818	503	1,993	295	864
1875	[8] 3,336	3,205	1,748	802	527	2,009	318	847
1874	[8] 3,552	2,891	1,564	732	510	1,740	339	789
1873	[8] 3,298	2,731	1,440	721	487	1,625	339	749
1872 [9]	2,419	2,145	1,123	480	490	927	405	748
1871 [9]	2,175	2,003	990	479	485	888	370	706
1870 [9]	1,937	1,781	864	470	406	775	336	648
1869 [9]	1,878	1,736	801	480	418	772	329	616
1868 [9]	1,887	1,736	766	520	418	798	329	596
1867 [9]	1,908	1,674	709	536	398	744	329	578
1866 [9]	1,931	1,673	682	483	480	759	309	560
1865 [9]	1,643	1,357	518	412	392	689	180	452
1864 [9]	1,556	973	555	150	236	380	176	391
1863	1,532	1,209	654	186	307	504	239	412
1862	1,492	1,012	647	99	221	357	184	418
1861	1,601	1,016	697	74	198	319	202	430
1860	1,562	1,000	692	70	196	310	207	422
1859	1,476	983	657	64	229	328	193	402
1858	1,422	849	583	60	170	237	155	395
1857	1,416	953	684	59	177	288	215	371
1856	1,398	880	634	49	167	265	196	344
1855	1,307	817	576	53	155	236	187	332
1854	1,208	795	557	44	163	239	205	301
1853 [10]	750	577	409	22	127	195	146	208
1852 [11]	913	620	430	23	137	182	161	237
1851	879	597	414	22	132	175	155	228
1850	824	532	364	21	115	146	131	217
1849	782	479	332	24	97	121	115	207
1848	751	512	345	27	112	143	129	205
1847	715	458	310	20	94	120	106	203
1846	707	456	312	22	95	125	106	197
1845	707	434	289	20	93	114	90	206
1844	696	427	265	23	104	117	75	211
1843	691	393	255	28	74	78	59	229
1842	692	472	324	25	82	88	84	260
1841	784	608	387	65	112	108	107	314
1840	901	658	463	42	99	120	107	358
1839	840	702	492	36	129	143	135	327
1838	829	682	486	34	119	146	116	318
1837	788	707	525	12	140	190	149	291
1836	713	622	458	12	129	166	140	252
1835	704	498	365	9	108	122	104	231
1834	506	419	324	6	76	102	95	200

* Denotes first year for which figures include Alaska and Hawaii.

[1] Total loans shown as net prior to 1969.　See footnote 3.

[2] Includes circulating notes of both State and national banks.　For State banknotes in circulation, chiefly for 1863–1872, see series X 675; for more complete figures for this series, 1860–1878, see series X 437.　For national banknotes in circulation, 1864–1935, see series X 653.

[3] In 1969 and 1970, loans and securities are stated on a gross basis in total assets of commercial banks.　Total reserves on loans and securities of commercial banks are included in total liabilities.

[4] Excludes one national bank in Alaska.

[5] Comparable with later data.

[6] See series X 679–682 for supplementary figures for nonnational banks: Vault cash, 1875–1896; deposits, 1865–1896; capital accounts, 1875–1882.

[7] Comparable with earlier data.　See series X 656 for number of nonnational banks, 1875–1882.

[8] Number of nonnational banks estimated.

[9] For nonnational banks, all figures except number of banks and capital accounts are estimated; see series X 656–677.

[10] Incomplete.

[11] Estimates based on previous 5 years for number of banks and on 10 years, 1854–1863, for assets and liabilities.

Series X 588-609. All Commercial Banks—Number of Banks and Principal Assets and Liabilities: 1896 to 1970

[In millions of dollars, except number of banks. As of June 30 or nearest available date]

Year	Number of banks	Total assets or liabilities	Loans [1]			Investments				Cash	
			Total	Real estate	Other	Total	U.S. Government obligations	Obligations of States and political subdivisions	Other	Total	Cash items in process of collection
	588	589	590	591	592	593	594	595	596	597	598
1970	13,690	[2] 534,932	[2] 299,356	71,291	228,065	127,701	51,860	63,153	12,687	[2] 85,910	38,516
1969	13,694	[2] 521,242	[2] 286,911	69,079	217,833	126,910	54,242	60,261	12,407	[2] 88,530	44,384
1968	13,743	460,575	247,283	61,967	190,156	123,408	58,805	52,794	11,809	75,562	33,637
1967	13,762	415,437	226,516	55,731	175,198	111,214	54,387	46,994	9,833	65,244	26,470
1966	13,821	388,373	214,386	52,306	166,165	102,500	53,619	40,702	8,180	60,187	22,949
1965	13,805	356,110	189,688	46,548	146,776	99,315	56,986	36,614	5,715	57,221	20,968
1964	13,682	323,349	165,336	41,648	126,946	95,928	59,456	31,477	4,995	53,342	18,867
1963	13,494	301,063	145,733	36,939	111,813	96,160	63,676	27,863	4,621	51,309	18,380
1962	13,434	277,211	129,779	32,194	100,254	91,643	64,550	23,206	3,887	48,844	16,782
1961	13,474	254,627	118,462	29,383	91,503	84,050	61,921	18,766	3,362	45,679	14,912
1960	13,503	243,274	115,767	28,439	89,554	74,961	54,987	16,827	3,147	47,192	14,875
1959	13,492	234,782	103,994	26,857	79,151	83,005	62,208	17,043	3,754	43,035	11,258
1958	13,574	229,182	96,244	23,927	74,159	84,722	64,463	15,789	4,471	43,711	10,952
1957	[3] 13,658	[3] 209,601	91,635	22,736	70,543	73,851	56,895	13,388	3,568	40,175	8,957
1956 *	[3] 13,719	[3] 206,846	87,447	21,990	66,810	73,461	56,869	12,988	3,603	42,623	11,105
1955	[3] 13,780	[3] 199,244	75,181	19,779	56,527	80,080	63,270	12,785	4,025	41,024	9,762
1954	13,936	190,581	67,335	17,226	51,099	79,046	63,508	11,930	3,608	41,568	8,880
1953	14,005	181,427	65,025	16,230	49,734	72,932	58,645	10,533	3,754	41,157	8,826
1952	14,069	177,417	59,233	15,019	45,067	75,204	61,178	9,844	4,182	40,703	8,619
1951	14,107	165,503	54,821	14,144	41,392	71,224	58,521	8,514	4,189	37,385	7,409
1950	14,146	156,914	44,798	12,411	32,978	76,973	65,753	7,392	3,828	33,270	6,813
1949	14,151	149,705	41,028	11,023	30,459	72,750	63,221	5,929	3,600	34,167	6,102
1948	14,189	149,799	39,866	10,233	29,963	73,990	64,798	5,588	3,604	34,168	6,038
1947	14,182	146,974	33,679	8,310	25,369	79,076	70,533	4,965	3,578	32,705	5,831
1946	14,152	153,507	27,159	5,845	21,314	92,417	84,549	4,082	3,786	32,418	5,253
1945	14,126	146,245	23,697	4,501	19,196	90,917	84,136	3,778	3,003	30,157	3,402
1944	14,138	125,031	21,029	4,447	16,582	74,784	68,480	3,472	2,832	27,662	4,126
1943	14,197	104,322	17,673	4,633	13,040	59,020	52,495	3,517	3,008	25,976	3,550
1942	14,353	80,276	20,249	4,875	15,374	33,431	26,439	3,564	3,428	24,844	2,691
1941	14,434	75,356	20,324	4,742	15,582	27,319	20,139	3,670	3,510	25,819	2,517
1940	14,534	67,804	17,393	4,392	13,001	23,793	16,597	3,610	3,586	24,626	1,598
1939	14,667	61,422	16,411	4,099	12,312	23,004	15,740	3,286	3,978	19,852	2,249
1938	14,867	56,185	16,128	3,863	12,265	21,109	14,081	2,779	4,249	16,798	1,953
1937	15,094	56,907	17,471	3,727	13,744	22,138	14,583	2,799	4,756	14,993	2,257
1936	15,329	55,572	15,600	3,530	12,070	23,077	15,344	2,873	4,860	14,497	2,204
1935	15,438	48,905	14,950	3,494	11,456	19,735	12,778	2,689	4,268	11,799	1,226
1934	15,348	44,978	15,719	3,661	12,058	17,072	10,324	2,360	4,388	9,648	1,097
1933	14,207	40,511	16,457	4,202	12,255	14,078	7,496	2,267	4,315	7,368	1,506
1932	18,734	46,304	22,001	4,955	17,046	14,277	6,250	2,299	5,728	6,970	1,372
1931	21,654	59,017	29,307	5,757	23,550	15,686	6,011	2,434	7,241	10,017	2,526
1930	23,679	64,125	35,043	6,146	28,897	14,392	4,874	2,111	7,407	10,910	3,659
1929	24,970	62,442	36,114	6,313	29,801	13,683	4,872	1,955	6,856	9,004	2,394
1928	25,798	61,563	34,488	6,193	28,295	14,466	4,933	1,999	7,534	9,215	2,409
1927	26,650	58,973	32,932	5,992	26,940	13,165	4,494	1,912	6,759	9,901	2,890
1926	27,742	56,781	32,084	5,781	26,303	12,224	4,414	1,723	6,087	9,568	2,683
1925	28,442	54,401	30,222	5,273	24,949	11,755	4,454	1,527	5,774	9,663	2,755
1924	28,988	50,136	28,278	4,710	23,568	10,679	4,260	1,382	5,037	8,787	2,504
1923	29,829	47,332	27,397	4,243	23,154	10,325	4,604	1,182	4,539	7,377	1,677
1922	30,120	44,106	25,040	3,671	21,369	9,359	3,846	1,146	4,367	7,602	1,988
1921	30,456	43,669	26,386	3,354	23,032	8,360	3,262	1,043	4,055	6,771	1,665
1920	30,291	47,509	28,562	3,225	25,337	8,398	3,638	944	3,816	8,264	2,007
1919	29,147	42,462	22,814	2,609	20,205	9,521	4,864	947	3,710	8,061	1,737
1918	28,856	36,352	20,571	2,484	18,087	7,478	3,043	924	3,511	6,613	869
1917	28,298	32,802	18,581	2,395	16,186	5,837	1,300	863	3,674	7,010	768
1916	27,739	28,217	16,067	2,122	13,945	4,870	740	786	3,344	6,148	775
1915	27,390	24,106	13,834	1,960	11,874	4,156	767	663	2,726	5,092	434
1914	27,236	23,155	13,416	1,812	11,604	3,861	782	565	2,514	4,930	587
1913	26,664	22,056	12,820	1,809	11,011	3,697	770	536	2,391	4,681	490
1912	25,844	21,495	12,239	1,677	10,562	3,676	774	530	2,372	4,758	495
1911	25,183	20,320	11,455	1,513	9,942	3,431	742	466	2,223	4,672	519
1910	24,514	19,324	11,072	1,392	9,680	3,156	737	408	2,011	4,387	757
1909	23,098	18,145	10,015	1,199	8,816	3,153	733	412	2,008	4,340	565
1908	22,531	16,664	9,243	1,104	8,139	2,912	706	335	1,871	3,885	431
1907	21,361	16,862	9,810	1,111	8,699	2,744	616	316	1,812	3,706	487
1906	19,786	15,601	9,013	1,026	7,987	2,563	598	279	1,686	3,502	519
1905	18,152	14,542	8,220	870	7,350	2,523	571	236	1,666	3,321	445
1904	17,037	13,035	7,299	756	6,543	2,226	562	259	1,405	3,066	291
1903	15,814	12,190	7,052	698	6,354	2,016	542	223	1,251	2,706	345
1902	14,488	11,427	6,521	617	5,904	1,821	517	199	1,105	2,731	377
1901	13,424	10,572	5,835	545	5,290	1,676	525	190	961	2,740	521
1900	12,427	9,059	5,065	484	4,581	1,410	506	169	735	2,274	276
1899	11,835	8,489	4,718	446	4,272	1,207	435	157	615	2,264	339
1898	11,530	7,170	4,060	420	3,640	1,002	386	128	488	1,800	151
1897	11,438	6,475	3,701	417	3,284	886	358	113	415	1,604	153
1896	11,474	6,167	3,741	436	3,305	818	348	102	368	1,330	136

See footnotes at end of table.

Series X 588–609. All Commercial Banks—Number of Banks and Principal Assets and Liabilities: 1896 to 1970—Con.

[In millions of dollars]

Year	Assets—Con. Cash—Con. Currency and coin	Assets—Con. Cash—Con. Bankers' balances [4]	Other [5]	Liabilities Deposits Total	Liabilities Deposits Interbank [6]	Liabilities Deposits U.S. Government	Liabilities Deposits Other demand	Liabilities Deposits Other time	National banknotes	Capital accounts	Other
	599	600	601	602	603	604	605	606	607	608	609
1970	7,142	40,252	21,966	²436,650	24,515	8,309	196,477	207,349		41,905	²56,377
1969	6,302	37,845	18,892	²429,277	23,647	6,021	196,840	202,769		39,002	²52,963
1968	5,220	36,705	14,322	397,275	19,521	5,324	180,541	191,889		35,923	27,377
1967	4,879	33,896	12,462	362,486	17,603	5,467	163,325	176,090		33,419	19,532
1966	5,267	31,970	11,300	340,598	16,337	11,275	155,941	157,044		31,435	16,339
1965	5,012	31,241	9,887	312,912	15,477	12,100	147,248	138,086		29,588	13,610
1964	4,571	29,903	8,742	286,133	14,468	10,544	140,968	120,153		26,861	10,355
1963	3,506	29,423	7,861	267,207	14,214	11,336	135,362	106,295		24,660	9,195
1962	3,204	28,858	6,945	246,149	13,583	9,870	130,379	92,317		23,254	7,808
1961	2,922	27,846	6,436	225,765	12,929	6,667	126,591	79,577		21,812	7,050
1960	3,277	29,039	5,354	214,425	12,719	6,684	126,615	68,408		20,392	8,456
1959	3,156	28,622	4,747	208,513	12,204	3,117	125,560	67,631		19,192	7,078
1958	3,076	29,684	4,505	205,500	12,514	9,561	119,296	64,129		18,293	5,390
1957	2,791	28,427	3,941	187,348	11,494	3,713	116,766	55,375		16,941	5,313
1956 *	2,321	29,196	3,315	187,299	12,368	5,632	117,854	51,446		16,027	3,520
1955	2,681	28,581	2,959	181,512	15,242	5,414	112,981	47,875		14,906	2,826
1954	2,659	30,029	2,632	174,065	15,497	5,892	106,995	45,681		14,038	2,478
1953	2,590	29,741	2,313	165,548	13,598	3,940	105,735	42,275		13,276	2,603
1952	2,396	29,688	2,277	162,365	13,512	6,118	103,402	39,333		12,599	2,453
1951	1,873	28,103	2,073	151,475	11,946	6,329	96,399	36,801		11,950	2,078
1950	1,829	24,628	1,873	143,845	11,435	3,799	91,882	36,729		11,389	1,630
1949	2,072	25,993	1,760	137,538	10,938	2,302	87,999	36,299		10,781	1,386
1948	2,103	26,027	1,775	138,162	11,435	2,178	88,754	35,795		10,284	1,353
1947	1,851	25,023	1,514	135,933	11,681	1,365	88,030	34,857		9,877	1,164
1946	1,510	25,655	1,513	143,042	12,309	13,413	84,824	32,496		9,392	1,073
1945	1,509	25,246	1,474	136,727	12,586	24,384	72,526	27,231		8,652	866
1944	1,503	22,033	1,556	116,235	11,201	19,511	64,254	21,269		8,011	785
1943	1,485	20,941	1,653	96,175	10,888	8,026	59,661	17,600		7,521	626
1942	1,334	20,819	1,752	72,394	10,278	1,837	44,611	15,668		7,254	628
1941	1,290	22,012	1,894	67,588	10,929	748	39,915	15,996		7,131	637
1940	1,037	21,991	1,992	60,246	10,168	824	33,646	15,608		6,960	598
1939	950	16,653	2,155	53,894	8,220	788	29,691	15,195		6,896	632
1938	936	13,909	2,150	48,814	6,838	596	26,387	14,993		6,770	601
1937	875	11,861	2,305	49,345	6,336	669	27,578	14,762		6,786	776
1936	945	11,348	2,398	48,118	6,903	1,144	26,096	13,975		6,703	751
1935	729	9,844	2,421	41,462	5,644	820	21,731	13,267	222	6,601	620
1934	642	7,909	2,539	36,810	4,581	1,735	17,796	12,698	695	6,625	848
1933	582	5,280	2,608	32,078	3,467	858	16,019	11,734	727	6,190	1,516
1932	715	4,883	3,056	35,658	3,323	433	17,111	14,791	649	7,484	2,513
1931	816	6,675	4,007	47,277	5,150	447	22,569	19,111	636	8,746	2,358
1930	799	6,452	3,780	51,267	5,129	298	25,648	20,192	649	9,318	2,891
1929	740	5,870	3,641	49,385	3,975	375	25,160	19,875	649	8,780	3,628
1928	768	6,038	3,394	49,582	4,282	274	24,857	20,169	649	7,968	3,364
1927	893	6,118	2,975	48,704	4,527	232	25,257	18,688	650	7,392	2,227
1926	911	5,974	2,905	46,952	4,289	235	24,993	17,435	651	7,021	2,157
1925	892	6,016	2,761	45,230	4,330	182	24,325	16,393	648	6,636	1,887
1924	855	5,428	2,392	41,343	4,247	185	22,069	14,842	729	6,420	1,644
1923	743	4,957	2,233	38,175	3,417	305	20,829	13,624	719	6,220	2,218
1922	776	4,838	2,105	35,532	3,353	158	20,106	11,915	725	6,044	1,805
1921	856	4,250	2,152	33,432	2,904	405	18,926	11,197	703	5,936	3,598
1920	1,012	5,245	2,285	36,682	3,729	261	21,571	11,121	688	5,599	4,540
1919	941	5,383	2,066	33,254	3,948	914	19,282	9,110	677	5,014	3,517
1918	865	4,879	1,690	28,708	3,718	1,541	15,747	7,702	681	4,742	2,221
1917	1,464	4,778	1,374	26,501	4,015	146	15,085	7,255	660	4,612	1,029
1916	1,463	3,910	1,132	22,613	3,510	39	12,917	6,147	676	4,367	561
1915	1,452	3,206	1,024	18,612	2,811	48	10,703	5,050	722	4,286	486
1914	1,615	2,728	948	17,806	2,720	66	10,306	4,714	722	4,169	458
1913	1,548	2,643	858	16,808	2,585	49	9,249	4,925	722	4,116	410
1912	1,559	2,704	822	16,455	2,636	58	9,217	4,544	709	3,955	376
1911	1,559	2,594	762	15,452	2,633	48	8,625	4,146	681	3,843	344
1910	1,421	2,209	709	14,644	2,304	54	8,566	3,720	675	3,694	311
1909	1,453	2,322	637	13,789	2,492	70	8,115	3,112	636	3,501	219
1908	1,351	2,103	624	12,425	2,213	130	7,381	2,701	613	3,364	262
1907	1,120	2,099	602	12,727	2,094	180	7,708	2,745	547	3,274	314
1906	1,036	1,947	523	11,791	1,908	89	7,403	2,391	511	3,060	239
1905	1,001	1,875	478	11,028	1,909	75	6,898	2,146	445	2,844	225
1904	1,014	1,761	444	9,739	1,756	110	6,057	1,816	399	2,727	170
1903	865	1,496	416	9,107	1,479	147	5,771	1,710	359	2,555	169
1902	862	1,492	354	8,713	1,498	124	5,541	1,550	309	2,266	139
1901	831	1,388	321	8,114	1,437	99	5,279	1,299	319	1,996	143
1900	756	1,242	310	6,792	1,261	99	4,345	1,087	265	1,878	124
1899	732	1,193	300	6,472	1,126	76	4,295	975	199	1,720	98
1898	701	948	308	5,175	872	53	3,431	819	190	1,701	104
1897	638	813	284	4,486	726	16	2,999	745	197	1,705	87
1896	550	644	278	4,142	571	15	2,844	712	199	1,730	96

* Denotes first year for which figures include Alaska and Hawaii.
[1] Beginning 1948, figures for loan items are shown gross (i.e. before deduction of valuation reserves); they do not add to the totals in 1948–1968 and are not entirely comparable with prior figures. Total loans were shown as net prior to 1969.
[2] In 1969 and 1970, loans and securities are stated on a gross basis in "total assets" of commercial banks. Total reserves on loans and securities of commercial banks are included in "other liabilities."

[3] Figures for member commercial banks exclude, and figures for noninsured nonmember commercial banks include, 1 member nondeposit trust company which is not insured by the Federal Deposit Insurance Corporation.
[4] Includes reserves.
[5] Beginning 1966, excludes corporate stocks, other than Federal Reserve bank stock, of national banks; reported with "other assets." [6] Beginning 1966, includes domestic interbank deposits only. For 1961–1965, includes domestic interbank and postal savings deposits. Prior to 1966, includes deposits of foreign banks.

Series X 610-619. All Commercial Banks—Number of Banks and Total Assets, by Federal Reserve Membership and Class: 1896 to 1970

[As of June 30 or nearest available date]

Year	Member banks of the Federal Reserve System				Nonmember banks		Year	Member banks of the Federal Reserve System				Nonmember banks	
	National banks		State member banks [1]					National banks		State member banks [1]			
	Number	Assets (mil. dol.)	Number	Assets (mil. dol.)	Number	Assets (mil. dol.)		Number	Assets (mil. dol.)	Number	Assets (mil. dol.)	Number	Assets (mil. dol.)
	610	611	612	613	614	615		610	611	612	613	614	615
1970	4,638	[2]314,334	1,166	[2]117,209	7,683	[2]98,368	1942	5,101	44,584	1,543	25,353	7,709	10,340
1969	4,701	[2]307,019	1,236	[2]119,358	7,536	[2]90,202	1941	5,130	41,228	1,423	23,620	7,881	10,508
1968	4,742	266,259	1,296	112,340	7,481	77,705	1940	5,164	36,816	1,234	21,030	8,136	9,958
1967	4,780	242,685	1,327	100,220	7,426	69,011	1939	5,203	33,119	1,127	18,789	8,337	9,514
1966	4,811	226,050	1,382	95,767	7,366	63,091	1938	5,242	30,317	1,096	16,826	8,529	9,042
							1937	5,293	30,272	1,064	17,181	8,737	9,454
1965	4,803	193,748	1,431	102,289	7,301	56,758	1936	5,368	29,643	1,032	16,881	8,929	9,048
1964	4,702	175,250	1,477	94,174	7,222	51,659							
1963	4,537	162,748	1,519	88,453	7,140	47,607	1935	5,425	26,009	985	14,710	9,078	8,186
1962	4,500	149,559	1,568	82,784	7,043	42,787	1934	5,417	23,854	958	13,529	8,973	7,595
1961	4,524	137,299	1,615	76,405	6,997	38,928	1933	4,897	20,813	709	12,226	8,601	7,472
							1932	6,145	22,318	835	13,538	11,754	10,448
1960	4,542	131,433	1,672	72,713	6,933	37,183	1931	6,800	27,430	982	17,406	13,872	14,181
1959	4,559	126,255	1,717	70,980	6,821	35,252							
1958	4,599	122,100	1,754	71,874	6,791	32,650	1930	7,247	28,828	1,068	18,521	15,364	16,776
1957	4,647	112,460	1,794	64,019	6,770	30,703	1929	7,530	27,260	1,177	18,194	16,263	16,988
1956 *	4,667	110,703	1,828	64,090	6,734	29,460	1928	7,685	28,265	1,244	16,390	16,869	16,908
							1927	7,790	26,455	1,309	16,144	17,551	16,374
1955	4,743	107,736	1,864	61,919	7,173	29,589	1926	7,972	25,202	1,403	15,436	18,367	16,143
1954	4,834	108,607	1,883	53,568	7,219	28,406							
1953	4,874	103,418	1,888	50,817	7,243	27,192	1925	8,066	24,252	1,472	14,694	18,904	15,455
1952	4,925	101,253	1,887	50,266	7,257	25,898	1924	8,080	22,525	1,570	13,192	19,338	14,419
1951	4,946	94,394	1,910	47,199	7,251	23,910	1923	8,236	21,454	1,620	12,212	19,973	13,666
							1922	8,244	20,633	1,648	10,960	20,228	12,513
1950	4,971	89,691	1,911	44,033	7,264	23,190	1921	8,150	20,475	1,595	10,375	20,711	12,820
1949	4,987	84,853	1,913	42,388	7,251	22,464							
1948	4,998	85,081	1,924	42,199	7,267	22,519	1920	8,024	23,267	1,374	10,351	20,893	13,891
1947	5,012	83,149	1,913	41,630	7,257	22,195	1919	7,779	21,105	1,042	8,629	20,326	12,727
1946	5,012	85,698	1,872	45,686	7,268	22,123	1918	7,699	18,262	513	6,104	20,644	11,987
1945	5,015	81,491	1,822	44,930	7,289	19,824	1917	7,599	16,231	53	756	20,646	15,815
1944	5,036	70,143	1,734	38,528	7,368	16,360	1916	7,571	13,920	34	307	20,134	13,990
1943	5,060	58,783	1,640	32,028	7,497	13,511	1915	7,597	11,790	17	97	19,776	12,219

Year	National banks		State banks		Year	National banks		State banks	
	Number	Assets (mil. dol.)	Number	Assets (mil. dol.)		Number	Assets (mil. dol.)	Number	Assets (mil. dol.)
	616	617	618	619		616	617	618	619
1914	7,518	11,477	19,718	11,679	1905	5,664	7,325	12,488	7,217
1913	7,467	11,032	19,197	11,024	1904	5,330	6,653	11,707	6,382
1912	7,366	10,857	18,478	10,638	1903	4,935	6,285	10,879	5,905
1911	7,270	10,378	17,913	9,941	1902	4,532	6,007	9,956	5,420
					1901	4,163	5,674	9,261	4,897
1910	7,138	9,892	17,376	9,432	1900	3,731	4,944	8,696	4,115
1909	6,886	9,365	16,212	8,780	1899	3,582	4,709	8,253	3,780
1908	6,817	8,710	15,714	7,954	1898	3,581	3,978	7,949	3,193
1907	6,422	8,472	14,939	8,390	1897	3,610	3,563	7,828	2,912
1906	6,047	7,781	13,739	7,820	1896	3,689	3,354	7,785	2,813

* Denotes first year for which figures include Alaska and Hawaii.
[1] For the period June 1941 through June 1962, member banks include mutual savings banks as follows: 3 before Jan. 1960, 2 through Dec. 1960, and 1 through June 1962; and in 1955–1970, they include 1 nondeposit trust company which is not insured by the Federal Deposit Insurance Corporation. [2] In 1969 and 1970, loans and securities are stated on a gross basis in "total assets" of commercial banks.

Series X 620-633. All Banks—Number of Banks and Total Assets, by Deposit Insurance Status and Class: 1934 to 1970

[As of June 30 or nearest available date. Includes data for U.S. outlying areas]

Year	All banks				Commercial banks [1]						Mutual savings banks [1][2]			
	Insured		Noninsured		Insured				Noninsured nonmember		Insured		Noninsured	
					Member banks [2]		Nonmember banks							
	Number	Assets (mil. dol.)	Number	Assets (mil. dol.)	Number	Assets (mil. dol.)	Number	Assets (mil. dol.)	Number	Assets (mil. dol.)	Number	Assets (mil. dol.)	Number	Assets (mil. dol.)
	620	621	622	623	624	625	626	627	628	629	630	631	632	633
1970	13,818	[3]596,027	369	15,278	5,804	431,543	7,683	98,368	203	5,021	331	66,116	166	10,257
1969	13,806	[3]580,323	388	14,219	5,937	426,377	7,536	90,202	221	4,664	333	63,745	167	9,555
1968	13,851	516,434	394	13,172	6,038	378,599	7,481	77,705	224	4,271	332	60,130	170	8,901
1967	13,867	467,727	400	11,863	6,107	342,905	7,426	69,011	229	3,520	334	55,810	171	8,343
1966	13,891	436,359	437	11,429	6,193	321,817	7,366	63,091	262	3,465	332	51,452	175	7,964
1965	13,862	401,601	448	10,891	6,234	296,037	7,301	56,758	270	3,315	327	48,806	178	7,577
1964	13,728	366,106	461	9,243	6,179	269,425	7,222	51,659	281	2,266	327	45,022	180	6,978
1963	13,527	340,389	479	8,694	6,056	251,201	7,140	47,607	298	2,254	331	41,580	181	6,441

See footnotes at end of table.

Series **X 620–633.**　All Banks—Number of Banks and Total Assets, by Deposit Insurance Status and Class: 1934 to 1970—Con.

Year	All banks				Commercial banks [1]						Mutual savings banks [1][2]			
	Insured		Noninsured		Insured				Noninsured nonmember		Insured		Noninsured	
					Member banks [2]		Nonmember banks							
	Number	Assets (mil. dol.)	Number	Assets (mil. dol.)	Number	Assets (mil. dol.)	Number	Assets (mil. dol.)	Number	Assets (mil. dol.)	Number	Assets (mil. dol.)	Number	Assets (mil. dol.)
	620	621	622	623	624	625	626	627	628	629	630	631	632	633
1962___	13,442	313,496	505	8,134	6,068	232,343	7,043	42,787	323	2,081	331	38,366	182	6,052
1961___	13,461	288,706	528	7,740	6,139	213,704	6,997	38,928	338	1,995	325	36,074	190	5,744
1960___	13,415	273,540	604	9,331	6,214	204,146	6,933	37,183	356	1,944	268	32,211	248	7,387
1959___	13,348	263,714	663	9,594	6,276	197,234	6,821	35,252	395	2,295	251	31,228	268	7,299
1958___	13,383	255,645	712	10,216	6,353	193,974	6,791	32,650	430	2,558	239	29,021	282	7,657
1957___	13,445	233,423	739	10,432	[4]6,441	[4]176,479	6,770	30,703	[4]447	[4]2,419	234	26,241	292	8,013
1956___	13,449	228,524	798	10,743	[4]6,495	[4]174,793	6,734	29,460	[4]490	[4]2,593	220	24,271	308	8,150
1955___	13,505	220,327	845	10,359	[4]6,607	[4]169,660	6,680	27,906	[4]534	[4]2,738	218	22,761	311	7,621
1954___	13,619	209,880	888	10,038	6,718	162,179	6,682	26,464	578	2,960	219	21,237	310	7,078
1953___	13,648	199,176	926	9,579	6,762	154,235	6,673	25,351	610	2,836	213	19,590	316	6,743
1952___	13,655	193,222	983	9,547	6,812	151,519	6,638	23,820	658	3,052	205	17,883	325	6,495
1951___	13,652	179,946	1,026	9,309	6,856	141,592	6,595	21,759	697	3,069	201	16,595	329	6,240
1950___	13,641	170,364	1,077	9,679	6,882	133,724	6,567	20,977	738	3,090	192	15,663	339	6,589
1949___	13,614	161,888	1,109	9,788	6,900	127,241	6,523	19,975	769	3,355	191	14,672	340	6,433
1948___	13,613	161,177	1,154	9,805	6,922	127,280	6,498	19,964	814	3,485	193	13,933	340	6,320
1947___	13,582	157,542	1,179	9,747	6,925	124,779	6,466	19,594	836	3,554	191	13,169	343	6,193
1946___	13,526	162,881	1,203	9,646	6,884	131,384	6,451	19,359	860	3,763	191	12,138	343	5,883
1945___	13,474	154,115	1,228	9,010	6,837	126,421	6,445	17,036	885	3,744	192	10,658	343	5,266
1944___	13,461	131,766	1,254	7,894	6,770	108,671	5,499	13,976	909	3,203	192	9,119	345	4,691
1943___	13,363	105,414	1,411	11,927	6,700	90,811	6,602	11,594	934	2,529	61	3,009	477	9,398
1942___	13,456	80,765	1,474	11,582	6,644	69,937	6,759	8,772	983	1,983	53	2,056	486	9,599
1941___	13,479	74,976	1,540	12,679	6,553	64,848	6,873	8,149	1,051	2,689	53	1,979	489	9,990
1940___	13,534	67,187	1,585	12,825	6,398	57,846	7,085	7,756	1,093	2,485	51	1,585	492	10,340
1939___	13,621	60,832	1,630	12,604	6,330	51,908	7,242	7,531	1,135	2,226	49	1,393	495	10,378
1938___	13,783	55,520	1,676	12,449	6,338	47,144	7,389	7,239	1,179	2,041	56	1,137	497	10,408
1937___	13,943	56,047	1,744	12,585	6,357	47,452	7,530	7,456	1,247	2,228	56	1,139	497	10,357
1936___	14,121	54,718	1,807	12,343	6,400	46,524	7,665	7,072	1,307	2,182	56	1,122	500	10,161
1935___	14,242	48,468	1,849	11,672	6,410	40,719	7,769	6,554	1,352	1,821	63	1,195	497	9,851
1934___	14,150	50,946	1,807	5,149	6,375	37,383	7,540	6,066	1,476	1,708	235	7,497	331	3,441

[1] Comparability of figures for classes of banks is affected somewhat by changes in Federal Reserve System membership, deposit insurance status, and reserve classifications of cities and individual banks, and by mergers, etc.
[2] Member commercial banks exclude, and mutual savings banks include, mutual savings banks which are members of the Federal Reserve System as follows: 3 from 1941 through 1959, 2 in 1960, and 1 in 1961–1970.

[3] In 1969 and 1970, loans and securities are stated on a gross basis in "total assets" of commercial banks. Total loans were shown as net prior to 1969.
[4] Figures for member commercial banks exclude, and figures for noninsured nonmember commercial banks include, 1 member nondeposit trust company which is not insured by the Federal Deposit Insurance Corporation.

Series **X 634–655.**　National Banks—Number of Banks and Principal Assets and Liabilities: 1863 to 1970

[In millions of dollars, except number of banks. As of June 30 or nearest available date]

Year	Number of banks	Total assets or liabilities	Assets								
			Loans [1]			Investments				Cash	
			Total	Real estate	Other	Total [2]	U.S. Government obligations	Obligations of States and political subdivisions	Other [3]	Total	Cash items in process of collection
	634	635	636	637	638	639	640	641	642	643	644
1970_____	4,638	[4]314,334	[4]177,211	40,846	136,364	[4]71,526	28,212	37,064	6,250	52,001	22,872
1969_____	4,701	[4]307,019	[4]171,505	39,930	131,574	[4]71,441	29,489	35,651	6,301	52,344	25,741
1968_____	4,742	266,259	144,272	34,565	112,587	68,558	31,627	30,646	6,286	44,830	20,055
1967_____	4,780	242,685	133,161	31,343	104,475	62,614	29,544	27,660	5,409	39,490	16,450
1966_____	4,811	226,050	125,212	29,407	98,265	57,212	28,891	23,975	4,346	36,794	13,967
1965_____	4,803	193,748	103,377	25,407	80,024	53,612	30,230	20,403	2,979	31,595	11,565
1964_____	4,702	175,250	89,469	22,806	68,437	51,729	31,560	17,527	2,642	29,511	10,354
1963_____	4,537	162,748	78,383	20,064	59,996	51,763	34,011	15,174	2,577	28,641	10,206
1962_____	4,500	149,559	69,771	17,542	53,697	49,470	34,508	12,809	2,153	26,860	8,902
1961_____	4,524	137,299	63,440	15,838	48,950	45,403	33,522	10,124	1,757	25,274	8,063
1960_____	4,542	131,433	62,398	15,278	48,346	39,912	29,298	8,984	1,630	26,380	8,267
1959_____	4,559	126,255	55,816	14,505	42,448	44,166	33,152	9,072	1,942	23,835	6,331
1958_____	4,599	122,100	50,744	12,685	39,054	45,154	34,498	8,347	2,309	23,964	5,918
1957_____	4,647	112,460	48,415	12,022	37,276	39,495	30,345	7,243	1,907	22,525	5,187
1956 [5] *_____	4,667	110,703	45,860	11,552	35,038	39,595	30,555	7,079	1,961	23,545	6,175
1955_____	4,743	107,736	39,422	10,366	29,646	43,890	34,671	7,011	2,208	22,890	5,405
1954_____	4,834	108,607	37,671	9,109	29,136	44,808	35,757	6,941	2,110	24,635	5,489
1953_____	4,874	103,418	36,420	8,443	28,517	41,429	32,958	6,209	2,262	24,279	5,547
1952_____	4,925	101,253	33,054	7,785	25,763	42,982	34,604	5,800	2,578	23,927	5,271
1951_____	4,946	94,394	30,479	7,224	23,664	40,535	32,965	4,959	2,611	22,198	4,616

See footnotes at end of table.

Series X 634–655. National Banks—Number of Banks and Principal Assets and Liabilities: 1863 to 1970—Con.

[In millions of dollars, except number of banks]

Year	Number of banks	Total assets or liabilities	Loans [1]			Investments				Cash	
			Total	Real estate	Other	Total [2]	U.S. Government obligations	Obligations of States and political subdivisions	Other	Total	Cash items in process of collection
	634	635	636	637	638	639	640	641	642	643	644
1950	4,971	89,691	24,591	6,335	18,593	44,132	37,548	4,288	2,296	19,914	4,334
1949	4,987	84,853	22,505	5,677	17,089	41,012	35,487	3,406	2,119	20,324	3,692
1948	4,998	85,081	22,243	5,250	17,192	41,395	36,092	3,204	2,099	20,415	3,829
1947	5,012	83,149	18,764	4,215	15,449	44,218	39,271	2,898	2,049	19,341	3,558
1946	5,012	85,698	14,469	2,740	11,729	51,809	47,271	2,451	2,087	18,607	3,004
1945	5,015	81,491	12,369	2,077	10,292	50,808	47,051	2,196	1,561	17,544	2,184
1944	5,036	70,143	11,213	2,032	9,181	42,130	38,640	2,029	1,461	15,998	2,509
1943	5,060	58,783	9,173	2,129	7,044	33,632	30,102	2,022	1,508	15,154	2,258
1942	5,101	44,584	10,880	2,237	8,643	18,584	14,878	1,956	1,750	14,274	1,671
1941	5,130	41,228	10,897	2,712	8,725	14,922	11,111	2,016	1,795	14,496	1,512
1940	5,164	36,816	9,156	1,993	7,163	12,882	9,094	1,926	1,862	13,857	980
1939	5,203	33,119	8,553	1,821	6,732	12,528	8,753	1,691	2,084	11,061	1,257
1938	5,242	30,317	8,316	1,621	6,695	11,618	7,973	1,424	2,221	9,438	1,107
1937	5,293	30,272	8,797	1,503	7,294	12,097	8,206	1,462	2,429	8,365	1,284
1936	5,368	29,643	7,749	1,367	6,382	12,459	8,435	1,535	2,489	8,368	1,236
1935	5,425	26,009	7,353	1,293	6,060	10,698	7,164	1,396	2,138	6,857	689
1934	5,417	23,854	7,681	1,326	6,355	9,331	5,847	1,225	2,259	5,688	633
1933	4,897	20,813	8,102	1,322	6,780	7,358	4,026	1,158	2,174	4,110	764
1932	6,145	22,318	10,265	1,612	8,653	7,183	3,347	1,114	2,722	3,480	692
1931	6,800	27,430	13,162	1,580	11,582	7,662	3,251	1,107	3,304	4,988	1,262
1930	7,247	28,828	14,874	1,468	13,406	6,875	2,748	893	3,234	5,408	1,808
1929	7,530	27,260	14,805	1,412	13,393	6,651	2,801	838	3,012	4,279	1,228
1928	7,685	28,265	14,921	1,285	13,636	7,141	2,888	839	3,414	4,738	1,412
1927	7,790	26,455	13,849	1,062	12,787	6,388	2,593	743	3,052	4,978	1,635
1926	7,972	25,202	13,322	725	12,597	5,837	2,466	647	2,724	4,788	1,568
1925	8,066	24,252	12,592	636	11,956	5,701	2,512	594	2,595	4,789	1,605
1924	8,080	22,525	11,955	535	11,420	5,103	2,446	505	2,152	4,455	1,468
1923	8,236	21,454	11,778	463	11,315	5,027	2,655	401	1,971	3,660	1,023
1922	8,244	20,633	11,191	371	10,820	4,514	2,240	414	1,860	3,969	1,251
1921	8,150	20,475	11,976	280	11,696	3,919	1,917	393	1,609	3,535	1,106
1920	8,024	23,267	13,499	230	13,269	4,048	2,137	338	1,573	4,493	1,406
1919	7,779	21,105	10,903	184	10,719	4,809	2,941	322	1,546	4,395	1,183
1918	7,699	18,262	10,077	185	9,892	3,836	2,025	320	1,491	3,570	598
1917	7,599	16,231	8,936	185	8,751	2,961	1,043	315	1,603	3,739	530
1916	7,571	13,920	7,767	161	7,606	2,319	703	278	1,338	3,352	522
1915	7,597	11,790	6,663	151	6,512	2,025	749	245	1,031	2,695	250
1914	7,518	11,477	6,443	114	6,329	1,870	764	176	930	2,770	358
1913	7,467	11,032	6,160	77	6,083	1,845	752	175	918	2,659	295
1912	7,366	10,857	5,972	75	5,897	1,822	745	179	898	2,714	295
1911	7,270	10,378	5,632	65	5,567	1,724	717	164	843	2,691	317
1910	7,138	9,892	5,454	65	5,389	1,575	712	149	714	2,549	483
1909	6,886	9,365	4,986	57	4,929	1,594	705	157	732	2,496	338
1908	6,817	8,710	4,639	52	4,587	1,518	679	105	734	2,264	271
1907	6,422	8,472	4,662	52	4,610	1,361	587	93	681	2,157	306
1906	6,047	7,781	4,236	47	4,189	1,240	562	78	600	2,071	345
1905	5,664	7,325	3,928	41	3,887	1,204	527	76	601	1,982	296
1904	5,330	6,653	3,625	38	3,587	1,091	514	67	510	1,740	172
1903	4,935	6,285	3,441	37	3,404	1,025	486	63	476	1,633	250
1902	4,532	6,007	3,246	35	3,211	945	460	57	428	1,685	269
1901	4,163	5,674	2,980	31	2,949	885	450	51	384	1,681	326
1900	3,731	4,944	2,644	26	2,618	775	418	41	316	1,400	180
1899	3,582	4,709	2,508	24	2,484	652	346	36	270	1,428	229
1898	3,581	3,978	2,164	20	2,144	555	304	29	222	1,129	112
1897	3,610	3,563	1,978	18	1,960	484	279	24	181	982	101
1896 [6]	3,689	3,354	1,972	18	1,954	464	274	22	168	801	89

See footnotes at end of table.

Series X 634–655. National Banks—Number of Banks and Principal Assets and Liabilities: 1863 to 1970—Con.

[In millions of dollars, except number of banks]

	Assets—Con.			Liabilities							
	Cash—Con.		Other [3]	Deposits					National banknotes	Capital accounts	Other
Year	Currency and coin	Bankers' balances (including reserves)		Total	Interbank [7]	U.S. Government	Other demand	Other time			
	645	646	647	648	649	650	651	652	653	654	655
1970	4,151	24,978	13,597	255,819	14,106	5,207	114,841	121,666	----------	24,113	[4] 34,402
1969	3,638	22,966	11,728	252,680	13,595	3,734	114,540	120,811	----------	22,635	[4] 31,704
1968	2,967	21,807	8,599	229,772	11,831	3,021	103,335	111,585	----------	20,503	15,984
1967	2,766	20,275	7,419	211,731	11,143	3,381	94,091	103,117	----------	19,098	11,856
1966	2,986	19,841	6,832	198,314	10,246	6,954	89,559	91,556	----------	18,021	9,715
1965	2,723	17,307	5,164	171,528	8,838	6,903	79,494	76,293	----------	15,853	6,367
1964	2,466	16,691	4,541	155,978	8,154	5,989	75,823	66,013	----------	14,262	5,010
1963	1,867	16,568	3,962	145,513	8,183	6,203	72,800	58,327	----------	13,008	4,226
1962	1,687	16,271	3,458	133,728	7,823	5,630	69,661	50,613	----------	12,243	3,588
1961	1,491	15,720	3,182	122,485	7,463	3,749	67,952	43,322	----------	11,439	3,375
1960	1,670	16,443	2,744	116,178	7,490	3,770	67,765	37,154	----------	10,686	4,569
1959	1,603	15,901	2,438	112,659	7,344	1,755	66,975	36,584	----------	10,041	3,555
1958	1,545	16,501	2,238	110,065	7,383	4,941	63,417	34,324	----------	9,451	2,584
1957	1,388	15,950	2,026	100,989	6,854	2,014	62,305	29,815	----------	8,722	2,750
1956 [5] *	1,162	16,208	1,703	100,826	7,364	3,167	62,655	27,640	----------	8,232	1,645
1955	1,364	16,121	1,534	98,631	8,314	3,099	60,917	26,301	----------	7,714	1,391
1954	1,369	17,777	1,493	99,358	9,750	3,576	60,826	25,206	----------	7,686	1,563
1953	1,336	17,396	1,290	94,475	8,594	2,434	60,186	23,261	----------	7,220	1,723
1952	1,239	17,417	1,290	92,719	8,584	3,629	58,862	21,644	----------	6,879	1,655
1951	968	16,614	1,182	86,589	7,625	3,870	55,014	20,080	----------	6,504	1,301
1950	946	14,634	1,054	82,430	7,362	2,363	52,748	19,957	----------	6,180	1,081
1949	1,077	15,555	1,012	78,219	6,945	1,417	50,130	19,727	----------	5,815	819
1948	1,105	15,481	1,028	78,753	7,305	1,327	50,680	19,441	----------	5,533	795
1947	966	14,817	826	77,146	7,432	843	49,932	18,939	----------	5,296	707
1946	788	14,815	813	80,212	7,816	7,648	47,356	17,392	----------	4,862	624
1945	801	14,559	770	76,534	8,251	13,138	40,638	14,507	----------	4,461	496
1944	803	12,686	802	65,585	7,402	10,746	36,214	11,223	----------	4,101	457
1943	793	12,103	824	54,590	7,156	4,542	33,715	9,177	----------	3,816	377
1942	715	11,888	846	40,533	6,497	1,146	24,737	8,153	----------	3,671	380
1941	703	12,281	913	37,273	6,589	516	21,812	8,356	----------	3,590	365
1940	575	12,302	921	33,014	6,083	537	18,189	8,205	----------	3,468	334
1939	527	9,277	977	29,416	4,881	500	15,999	8,036	----------	3,382	321
1938	525	7,806	945	26,763	4,210	392	14,210	7,951	----------	3,266	288
1937	441	6,640	1,013	26,716	3,790	377	14,785	7,764	----------	3,205	351
1936	528	6,604	1,067	26,153	4,167	690	13,786	7,510	----------	3,160	330
1935	402	5,766	1,101	22,477	3,410	435	11,517	7,115	222	3,080	230
1934	350	4,705	1,154	19,896	2,767	887	9,469	6,773	695	2,995	268
1933	286	3,060	1,243	16,742	2,000	448	8,141	6,153	727	2,850	494
1932	336	2,452	1,390	17,428	1,814	212	8,196	7,206	649	3,274	967
1931	367	3,359	1,618	22,164	2,862	234	10,653	8,415	636	3,749	881
1930	340	3,260	1,671	23,235	2,850	170	11,682	8,533	649	3,969	975
1929	297	2,754	1,525	21,586	2,219	226	10,908	8,233	649	3,672	1,353
1928	314	3,012	1,465	22,645	2,701	184	11,466	8,294	649	3,569	1,402
1927	363	2,980	1,240	21,778	2,820	138	11,507	7,313	650	3,237	790
1926	359	2,861	1,255	20,644	2,864	143	11,325	6,312	651	3,088	819
1925	359	2,825	1,170	19,912	2,855	106	11,028	5,923	648	2,969	723
1924	345	2,642	1,012	18,349	2,794	121	10,175	5,259	729	2,915	532
1923	290	2,347	989	16,899	2,384	191	9,570	4,754	719	2,874	962
1922	325	2,393	959	16,323	2,482	102	9,628	4,111	725	2,847	738
1921	373	2,056	1,045	15,142	2,132	247	9,068	3,695	704	2,795	1,834
1920	449	2,638	1,227	17,159	2,824	174	10,676	3,485	688	2,621	2,799
1919	424	2,788	998	15,935	2,974	565	9,612	2,784	677	2,362	2,131
1918	382	2,590	779	14,015	2,796	1,036	7,840	2,343	681	2,249	1,317
1917	752	2,457	595	12,767	3,025	133	7,430	2,179	660	2,197	607
1916	818	2,012	482	10,872	2,713	39	6,391	1,729	675	2,102	271

See footnotes at end of table.

Series X 634–655. National Banks—Number of Banks and Principal Assest and Liabilities: 1863 to 1970—Con.

[In millions of dollars, except number of banks]

Year	Assets—Con. Cash—Con. Currency and coin	Bankers' balances (including reserves)	Other	Liabilities Deposits Total	Interbank [7]	U.S. Government	Other demand	Other time	National banknotes	Capital accounts	Other
	645	646	647	648	649	650	651	652	653	654	655
1915	857	1,588	407	8,817	2,208	48	5,235	1,326	722	2,105	146
1914	1,022	1,390	394	8,560	2,186	66	5,107	1,201	722	2,049	146
1913	968	1,396	368	8,140	2,120	49	4,603	1,368	722	2,045	125
1912	996	1,423	349	8,061	2,178	58	4,611	1,214	708	1,983	105
1911	998	1,376	331	7,673	2,147	48	4,394	1,084	681	1,932	92
1910	865	1,201	314	7,254	1,900	54	4,286	1,014	675	1,850	113
1909	926	1,232	289	6,932	2,037	70	4,082	743	636	1,728	69
1908	889	1,104	289	6,328	1,823	130	3,850	525	613	1,667	102
1907	721	1,130	292	6,188	1,686	180	3,890	432	547	1,603	134
1906	681	1,045	234	5,691	1,545	90	3,766	290	511	1,490	89
1905	679	1,007	211	5,406	1,547	75	3,538	246	445	1,406	68
1904	689	879	197	4,834	1,412	110	3,113	199	399	1,349	71
1903	581	802	186	4,561	1,212	147	3,026	176	359	1,285	80
1902	597	819	131	4,467	1,243	124	2,945	155	309	1,184	47
1901	567	788	128	4,249	1,207	99	2,811	132	319	1,062	44
1900	529	691	125	3,621	1,063	99	2,361	98	265	1,014	44
1899	512	687	121	3,539	933	76	2,443	87	199	947	24
1898	493	524	130	2,799	720	53	1,943	83	190	955	34
1897	435	446	119	2,386	597	16	1,700	73	196	962	19
1896 [6]	363	349	117	2,141	454	16	1,603	68	199	983	31

Year	Number of banks	Total assets or liabilities	Assets Total loans [1]	Total investments [2]	Total cash
	634	635	636	639	643
1896 [8]	3,689	3,536	1,972	464	801
1895	3,715	3,471	2,017	447	894
1894	3,770	3,422	1,944	435	935
1893	3,807	3,213	2,021	357	733
1892	3,759	3,494	2,128	347	919
1891	3,652	3,113	1,964	309	747
1890	3,484	3,062	1,934	311	730
1889	3,239	2,938	1,779	323	757
1888	3,120	2,731	1,628	356	671
1887	3,014	2,637	1,560	329	677
1886	2,809	2,475	1,399	407	593

Year	Number of banks	Total assets or liabilities	Assets Total loans [1]	Total investments [2]	Total cash
	634	635	636	639	643
1885	2,689	2,422	1,258	432	663
1884	2,625	2,283	1,270	449	488
1883	2,417	2,365	1,286	465	541
1882	2,239	2,344	1,209	471	598
1881	2,115	2,326	1,145	484	627
1880	2,076	2,036	995	452	518
1879	2,048	2,020	836	715	398
1878	2,056	1,751	835	460	388
1877	2,078	1,774	902	431	371
1876	2,091	1,826	934	427	400
1875	2,076	1,913	973	443	432

Year	Number of banks	Total assets or liabilities	Assets Total loans [1]	Total investments [2]	Total cash
	634	635	636	639	643
1874	1,983	1,852	926	451	430
1873	1,968	1,851	926	445	439
1872	1,853	1,771	872	450	412
1871	1,723	1,703	789	456	422
1870	1,612	1,566	719	453	361
1869	1,619	1,564	686	466	382
1868	1,640	1,572	656	507	384
1867	1,636	1,494	589	522	361
1866	1,634	1,476	550	468	439
1865	1,294	1,127	362	[9] 394	344
1864	467	252	71	[9] 93	86
1863	66	17	6	[9] 6	5

Year	Liabilities Total deposits	National banknotes	Capital accounts
	648	653	654
1896 [8]	2,141	199	983
1895	2,279	179	987
1894	2,228	172	1,001
1893	1,939	155	1,029
1892	2,327	141	1,011
1891	1,974	124	988
1890	1,979	126	935
1889	1,920	129	875
1888	1,716	155	842
1887	1,650	167	806
1886	1,459	245	760

Year	Liabilities Total deposits	National banknotes	Capital accounts
	648	653	654
1885	1,420	269	725
1884	1,233	295	739
1883	1,337	312	707
1882	1,365	309	660
1881	1,364	312	642
1880	1,085	318	625
1879	1,090	307	615
1878	814	300	629
1877	818	290	656
1876	842	294	679
1875	897	318	687
1874	828	339	676

Year	Liabilities Total deposits	National banknotes	Capital accounts
	648	653	654
1873	836	339	662
1872	805	327	626
1871	791	308	594
1870	706	291	562
1869	716	293	549
1868	745	295	530
1867	685	292	512
1866	695	268	494
1865	614	[10] 132	380
1864	147	[10] 26	79
1863	10	----------	7

* Denotes first year for which figures include Alaska and Hawaii.
[1] Beginning in 1948, figures for loan items are shown gross (i.e. before deduction of valuation reserves); they do not add to the total in 1948–1968 and are not entirely comparable with prior figures. Total loans were shown as net prior to 1969.
[2] Before 1903, includes securities borrowed.
[3] Beginning 1966, other investments exclude corporate stocks, other than Federal Reserve bank stock, of national banks; reported with "other assets."
[4] In 1969 and 1970, loans and securities are stated on a gross basis in "total assets" of commercial banks. Total reserves on loans and securities of commercial banks are included in "other liabilities."
[5] Excludes one national bank in Alaska.
[6] Comparable with later data.
[7] Beginning 1966, includes domestic interbank deposits only; for 1961–1965, includes domestic interbank and postal savings deposits. Prior to 1966, includes deposits of foreign banks.
[8] Comparable with earlier data.
[9] U.S. Government securities only.
[10] Includes State banknotes outstanding.

Series X 656–677. Nonnational Banks—Number of Banks and Principal Assets and Liabilities: 1863 to 1970

[In millions of dollars, except number of banks. As of June 30 or nearest available date]

Year	Number of banks	Total assets or liabilities	Loans [1]			Investments				Cash	
			Total	Real estate	Other	Total	U.S. Government obligations	Obligations of States and political subdivisions	Other [2]	Total	Cash items in process of collection
	656	657	658	659	660	661	662	663	664	665	666
1970	9,549	[3] 296,971	[3] 181,222	87,325	94,030	[3] 71,196	27,453	27,359	16,383	34,816	15,726
1969	9,493	[3] 287,523	[3] 171,902	83,992	88,042	[3] 70,168	28,985	26,115	15,068	37,019	18,734
1968	9,503	263,347	156,109	79,195	79,007	68,608	31,383	22,352	14,872	31,691	13,674
1967	9,487	236,905	143,375	73,281	71,996	60,480	29,147	19,576	11,758	26,907	10,110
1966	9,517	221,738	135,802	68,783	68,871	56,108	29,850	17,011	9,247	24,358	9,044
1965	9,507	218,745	129,407	63,608	67,606	57,022	32,509	16,572	7,940	26,646	9,455
1964	9,487	200,099	114,523	57,041	59,194	55,770	33,912	14,364	7,494	24,736	8,563
1963	9,469	186,335	102,015	51,183	52,408	56,129	35,831	13,149	7,150	23,558	8,233
1962	9,447	172,070	90,938	45,290	47,079	54,114	36,320	10,980	6,814	22,868	7,942
1961	9,465	159,146	83,233	41,560	42,973	50,780	34,680	9,330	6,769	21,267	6,908
1960	9,477	151,439	79,438	38,943	41,722	47,279	32,316	8,540	6,423	21,576	6,638
1959	9,452	147,054	72,327	36,353	37,114	51,912	36,405	8,707	6,800	19,981	4,957
1958	9,496	143,761	67,736	33,344	35,464	52,605	37,381	8,160	7,064	20,664	5,069
1957 *	9,537	131,396	63,707	31,096	33,595	46,819	34,456	6,824	5,538	18,489	3,803
1956 *	9,580	128,564	60,226	29,047	32,023	46,293	34,611	6,577	5,104	19,995	4,973
1955	9,565	121,890	51,931	25,585	27,085	49,007	37,275	6,429	5,303	19,123	4,394
1954	9,630	110,289	43,554	21,999	22,157	47,307	36,767	5,522	5,018	17,920	3,422
1953	9,659	104,342	40,697	19,900	21,373	44,536	35,151	4,702	4,683	17,745	3,307
1952	9,673	100,542	36,688	17,788	19,438	44,804	36,180	4,278	4,346	17,741	3,384
1951	9,690	93,944	33,362	16,057	17,857	43,366	35,761	3,636	3,969	16,038	2,823
1950	9,705	89,474	27,410	13,405	14,505	46,830	39,774	3,189	3,867	14,187	2,509
1949	9,694	85,957	24,573	11,520	13,476	45,782	39,392	2,599	3,791	14,643	2,429
1948	9,723	84,971	22,857	10,340	12,870	46,587	40,682	2,464	3,441	14,585	2,225
1947	9,703	83,187	19,601	8,696	10,905	48,511	43,402	2,131	2,978	14,203	2,290
1946	9,673	85,831	17,037	7,386	9,651	53,354	48,698	1,722	2,934	14,556	2,264
1945	9,645	80,678	15,627	6,663	8,964	50,916	46,657	1,684	2,575	13,196	1,228
1944	9,638	68,699	14,222	6,765	7,457	41,199	37,135	1,599	2,465	12,197	1,627
1943	9,674	57,946	13,075	7,026	6,049	32,042	27,672	1,729	2,641	11,542	1,302
1942	9,790	47,346	14,183	7,380	6,803	20,370	15,442	1,996	2,932	11,321	1,030
1941	9,845	46,096	14,376	7,427	6,949	17,745	12,448	2,190	3,107	12,289	1,015
1940	9,912	42,913	13,155	7,234	5,921	16,158	10,611	2,235	3,312	11,746	627
1939	10,007	40,074	12,747	7,090	5,657	15,811	10,026	2,241	3,544	9,489	999
1938	10,177	37,413	12,717	7,068	5,649	14,649	8,788	2,059	3,802	7,936	851
1937	10,353	38,130	13,638	7,107	6,531	15,115	8,727	2,130	4,258	7,155	978
1936	10,516	37,211	12,891	7,120	5,771	15,398	8,957	2,111	4,330	6,670	972
1935	10,622	33,942	12,887	7,398	5,489	13,478	7,152	2,159	4,167	5,461	541
1934	10,496	32,061	13,628	7,815	5,813	11,931	5,461	2,031	4,439	4,470	469
1933	9,874	30,546	14,235	8,632	5,603	10,767	4,203	2,020	4,544	3,683	746
1932	13,172	34,977	17,806	9,245	8,561	11,223	3,590	2,142	5,491	3,927	684
1931	15,442	42,640	22,254	10,046	12,208	12,311	3,350	2,365	6,596	5,417	1,269
1930	17,026	45,462	26,116	10,312	15,804	11,215	2,625	2,138	6,452	5,793	1,855
1929	18,038	45,055	27,139	10,384	16,755	10,654	2,676	2,022	5,956	4,943	1,169
1928	18,716	42,856	25,025	10,079	14,946	11,005	2,783	2,059	6,163	4,716	1,001
1927	19,465	41,438	24,100	9,690	14,410	10,261	2,752	1,997	5,512	5,178	1,259
1926	20,378	39,877	23,336	9,380	13,956	9,725	2,918	1,834	4,973	5,018	1,119
1925	20,986	37,980	21,786	8,560	13,226	9,355	3,017	1,641	4,697	5,114	1,153
1924	21,521	34,895	20,075	7,704	12,371	8,740	2,935	1,555	4,250	4,579	1,040
1923	22,208	32,690	18,956	6,866	12,090	8,447	3,060	1,451	3,936	3,935	657
1922	22,492	29,735	16,809	6,015	10,794	7,814	2,578	1,429	3,807	3,861	740
1921	22,926	29,158	17,260	5,577	11,683	7,250	2,284	1,330	3,636	3,445	563
1920	22,885	29,827	17,690	5,286	12,404	6,995	2,283	1,256	3,456	3,996	604
1919	21,988	26,498	14,229	4,525	9,704	7,215	2,484	1,373	3,358	3,891	557
1918	21,781	22,835	12,786	4,393	8,393	5,773	1,218	1,388	3,167	3,267	274
1917	21,320	21,309	11,966	4,319	7,647	4,964	306	1,412	3,246	3,511	241
1916	20,791	18,777	10,496	3,947	6,549	4,514	50	1,360	3,104	3,033	256
1915	20,420	16,573	9,313	3,724	5,589	3,957	29	1,232	2,696	2,605	185
1914	20,346	15,872	9,059	3,564	5,495	3,831	29	1,231	2,571	2,355	232
1913	19,818	15,071	8,661	3,513	5,148	3,655	31	1,165	2,459	2,194	196
1912	19,106	14,515	8,152	3,279	4,873	3,618	42	1,101	2,475	2,211	201
1911	18,545	13,648	7,596	3,019	4,577	3,412	38	1,060	2,314	2,151	203
1910	18,013	13,030	7,312	2,827	4,485	3,264	38	1,024	2,202	1,994	275
1909	16,848	12,124	6,562	2,491	4,071	3,152	42	974	2,136	2,003	228
1908	16,344	11,236	6,124	2,378	3,746	2,938	43	912	1,983	1,779	161
1907	15,564	11,642	6,657	2,341	4,316	2,923	49	908	1,966	1,691	182
1906	14,360	10,959	6,206	2,181	4,025	2,840	58	895	1,887	1,564	175
1905	13,103	10,186	5,612	1,950	3,662	2,770	73	883	1,814	1,473	150
1904	12,329	9,195	4,920	1,767	3,153	2,504	86	849	1,569	1,462	120
1903	11,498	8,616	4,816	1,660	3,156	2,316	102	812	1,402	1,195	97
1902	10,580	8,019	4,418	1,529	2,889	2,153	119	766	1,268	1,170	109
1901	9,891	7,363	3,934	1,414	2,520	2,006	153	734	1,119	1,185	196
1900	9,322	6,444	3,449	1,316	2,133	1,769	193	695	881	995	97
1899	8,877	5,970	3,181	1,237	1,944	1,602	228	682	692	954	111
1898	8,582	5,240	2,812	1,177	1,635	1,415	229	644	542	785	40
1897	8,469	4,869	2,618	1,151	1,467	1,318	235	597	486	721	53
1896 [4]	8,423	4,694	2,643	1,146	1,497	1,225	232	562	431	620	47

See footnotes at end of table.

Series X 656–677. Nonnational Banks—Number of Banks and Principal Assets and Liabilities: 1863 to 1970—Con.

[In millions of dollars]

| Year | Assets—Con. Cash—Con. | | | Liabilities | | | | | | | |
	Currency and coin	Bankers' balances (including reserves)	Other	Deposits Total	Interbank[5]	U.S. Government	Other demand	Other time	State banknotes	Capital accounts	Other
	667	668	669	670	671	672	673	674	675	676	677
1970	3,167	15,923	9,736	250,120	10,411	3,110	82,281	154,317	----------	23,412	[3]23,439
1969	2,820	15,464	8,436	243,354	10,055	2,294	82,892	148,113	----------	21,773	[3]22,396
1968	2,412	15,606	6,938	230,374	7,691	2,310	77,739	142,634	----------	20,531	12,442
1967	2,266	14,530	6,144	209,017	6,462	2,093	69,715	130,746	----------	19,253	8,635
1966	2,440	12,875	5,470	196,012	6,093	4,329	66,827	118,763	----------	18,176	7,550
1965	2,440	14,750	5,670	192,364	6,640	5,204	68,148	112,371	----------	18,271	8,110
1964	2,248	13,924	5,071	177,095	6,316	4,562	65,492	100,725	----------	16,868	6,136
1963	1,771	13,555	4,632	164,942	6,032	5,141	62,883	90,885	----------	15,683	5,710
1962	1,649	13,276	4,150	152,309	5,761	4,246	61,008	81,295	----------	14,864	4,897
1961	1,553	12,806	3,866	140,831	5,467	2,923	58,897	73,542	----------	14,032	4,283
1960	1,722	13,216	3,144	133,582	5,231	2,917	58,878	66,555	----------	13,171	4,685
1959	1,665	13,358	2,834	130,357	4,863	1,364	58,613	65,518	----------	12,466	4,232
1958	1,639	13,957	2,755	128,304	5,133	4,623	55,906	62,643	----------	12,022	3,434
1957 *	1,510	13,176	2,380	117,036	4,642	1,702	54,487	56,207	----------	11,261	3,098
1956 *	1,269	13,753	2,050	115,657	5,006	2,468	55,225	52,958	----------	10,679	2,228
1955	1,436	13,293	1,829	110,214	6,931	2,318	52,115	48,850	----------	9,949	1,727
1954	1,408	13,090	1,508	100,147	5,750	2,319	46,216	45,862	----------	8,978	1,164
1953	1,363	13,075	1,364	94,701	5,007	1,508	45,583	42,603	----------	8,571	1,070
1952	1,258	13,099	1,309	91,428	4,929	2,492	44,564	39,443	----------	8,159	955
1951	1,004	12,211	1,178	85,290	4,322	2,462	41,403	37,103	----------	7,731	923
1950	973	10,705	1,047	81,359	4,074	1,438	39,152	36,695	----------	7,397	718
1949	1,092	11,122	959	78,269	3,993	887	37,885	35,504	----------	7,031	657
1948	1,090	11,270	942	77,620	4,131	853	38,089	34,547	----------	6,706	645
1947	968	10,945	872	76,229	4,250	524	38,112	33,343	----------	6,423	535
1946	806	11,486	884	79,081	4,493	5,767	37,482	31,339	----------	6,242	508
1945	785	11,183	939	74,594	4,336	11,247	31,897	27,114	----------	5,665	419
1944	773	9,797	1,081	63,099	3,799	8,766	28,048	22,486	----------	5,232	368
1943	770	9,470	1,287	52,707	3,732	3,485	25,952	19,538	----------	4,949	290
1942	698	9,593	1,472	42,232	3,781	691	19,877	17,883	----------	4,829	285
1941	663	10,611	1,686	40,939	4,340	232	18,107	18,260	----------	4,851	306
1940	536	10,583	1,854	37,840	4,085	287	15,460	18,008	----------	4,784	289
1939	487	8,003	2,027	34,887	3,339	288	13,695	17,565	----------	4,854	333
1938	468	6,617	2,111	32,237	2,628	204	12,188	17,217	----------	4,841	335
1937	483	5,694	2,222	32,769	2,547	292	12,797	17,133	----------	4,918	443
1936	466	5,232	2,252	31,915	2,736	454	12,314	16,411	----------	4,856	440
1935	370	4,550	2,116	28,793	2,234	385	10,216	15,958	----------	4,735	414
1934	341	3,660	2,032	26,584	1,815	848	8,329	15,592	----------	4,870	607
1933	355	2,582	1,861	24,942	1,467	410	7,881	15,184	----------	4,538	1,066
1932	431	2,812	2,021	28,141	1,509	221	8,918	17,493	----------	5,251	1,585
1931	484	3,664	2,658	35,023	2,288	213	11,920	20,602	----------	6,123	1,494
1930	491	3,447	2,338	37,130	2,279	128	13,976	20,747	----------	6,403	1,929
1929	473	3,301	2,319	36,683	1,756	149	14,261	20,517	----------	6,078	2,294
1928	483	3,232	2,110	35,493	1,582	90	13,398	20,423	----------	5,385	1,978
1927	558	3,361	1,899	34,922	1,708	94	13,758	19,362	----------	5,064	1,452
1926	578	3,321	1,798	33,772	1,425	92	13,685	18,570	----------	4,753	1,352
1925	561	3,400	1,725	32,389	1,475	76	13,304	17,534	----------	4,415	1,176
1924	537	3,002	1,501	29,612	1,452	64	11,901	16,195	----------	4,158	1,125
1923	480	2,798	1,352	27,477	1,033	114	11,265	15,065	1	3,944	1,268
1922	482	2,639	1,251	24,904	871	56	10,484	13,493	–	3,752	1,079
1921	506	2,376	1,203	23,792	772	158	9,866	12,996	–	3,590	1,776
1920	589	2,803	1,146	24,679	904	87	10,903	12,785	–	3,398	1,750
1919	541	2,793	1,163	22,047	975	349	9,673	11,050	–	3,047	1,404
1918	506	2,487	1,009	19,046	922	506	7,911	9,707	–	2,864	925
1917	737	2,533	868	18,088	989	13	7,658	9,428	–	2,791	430
1916	668	2,109	734	15,866	798	–	6,530	8,538	1	2,616	294
1915	620	1,800	698	13,687	603	–	5,471	7,613	–	2,538	348
1914	614	1,509	627	13,105	534	–	5,202	7,369	–	2,454	313
1913	596	1,402	561	12,383	465	–	4,649	7,269	–	2,398	290
1912	579	1,431	534	11,952	458	–	4,609	6,885	–	2,286	277
1911	576	1,372	489	11,187	486	–	4,235	6,466	–	2,201	260
1910	576	1,143	460	10,696	404	–	4,281	6,011	–	2,134	200
1909	546	1,229	407	9,951	455	–	4,037	5,459	–	2,022	151
1908	484	1,134	395	9,112	390	–	3,532	5,190	–	1,960	164
1907	420	1,089	371	9,571	408	–	3,820	5,343	1	1,889	181
1906	371	1,018	349	9,012	363	–	3,638	5,011	1	1,795	153
1905	339	984	331	8,366	362	–	3,361	4,643	–	1,660	160
1904	342	1,000	309	7,507	344	–	2,945	4,218	–	1,586	102
1903	300	798	289	7,051	267	–	2,746	4,038	–	1,475	90
1902	281	780	278	6,636	255	–	2,596	3,785	–	1,289	94
1901	281	708	238	6,125	230	–	2,468	3,427	–	1,138	100
1900	245	653	231	5,301	198	–	1,985	3,118	–	1,061	82
1899	237	606	233	4,933	193	–	1,852	2,888	–	960	77
1898	224	521	228	4,245	152	–	1,488	2,605	–	923	72
1897	220	448	212	3,884	129	–	1,299	2,456	1	915	69
1896 [4]	205	368	206	3,718	117	1	1,241	2,361	–	910	66

See footnotes at end of table.

Series X 656–677.　Nonnational Banks—Number of Banks and Principal Assets and Liabilities: 1863 to 1970—Con.

[In millions of dollars, except number of banks]

Year	Number of banks [6]	Total assets or liabilities	Total loans [1]	Total investments	Total cash [6]
	656	657	658	661	665
1896 [7]	5,780	4,200	2,280	1,211	465
1895	6,103	4,139	2,252	1,118	549
1894	5,738	3,869	2,141	1,010	538
1893	5,685	3,979	2,348	1,010	456
1892	5,577	3,752	2,209	936	459
1891	4,989	3,449	2,067	870	378
1890 [8]	4,717	3,296	1,920	863	393
1889 [8]	4,005	3,007	1,699	806	387
1888	3,527	2,739	1,533	775	318
1887	3,156	2,556	1,383	682	322
1886	1,529	2,068	1,035	644	180
1885	1,661	2,005	1,015	610	213
1884	1,488	1,939	991	592	190
1883	1,418	1,843	948	563	171
1882	1,333	1,687	842	584	157
1881	1,312	1,543	757	501	154
1880	1,279	1,364	668	453	138
1879	1,287	1,293	671	424	107
1878	1,173	1,330	726	414	105
1877	1,306	1,430	819	421	112
1876	1,357	1,357	793	391	103
1875	1,260	1,291	775	359	95
1874	[9] 1,569	1,039	638	281	80
1873	[9] 1,330	880	514	276	48
1872 [10]	566	375	252	30	78
1871 [10]	452	299	201	24	62
1870 [10]	325	215	144	17	45
1869 [10]	259	171	115	14	36
1868 [10]	247	164	110	13	34
1867 [10]	272	180	121	14	38
1866 [10]	297	197	132	16	41
1865 [10]	349	231	155	18	48
1864 [10]	1,089	721	484	57	150
1863	1,466	1,192	649	181	303

Liabilities

Year	Total deposits [6]	State banknotes [11]	Capital accounts [6]
	670	675	676
1896 [7]	3,345	----	763
1895	3,260	----	793
1894	3,039	(Z)	751
1893	3,126	(Z)	752
1892	2,970	(Z)	710
1891	2,709	(Z)	661
1890	2,598	(Z)	624
1889	2,391	(Z)	552
1888	2,175	(Z)	506
1887	2,069	(Z)	453
1886	1,727	(Z)	316
1885	1,659	(Z)	315
1884	1,616	(Z)	297
1883	1,547	(Z)	266
1882	1,412	(Z)	240
1881	1,285	(Z)	223
1880	1,137	(Z)	201
1879	1,059	(Z)	211
1878	1,107	(Z)	196
1877	1,188	(Z)	219
1876	1,151	(Z)	185
1875	1,111	(Z)	160
1874	912	(Z)	114
1873	789	(Z)	86
1872	121	78	122
1871	97	62	111
1870	70	45	87
1869	56	36	67
1868	53	34	66
1867	58	38	65
1866	64	41	67
1865	75	48	71
1864	233	150	312
1863	494	239	405

− Represents zero.
* Denotes first year for which figures include Alaska and Hawaii.
Z Less than $500,000.
[1] Beginning in 1948, figures for loan items are shown gross (i.e. before deduction of valuation reserves); they do not add to the totals in 1948–1968 and are not entirely comparable with prior figures. Total loans were shown as net prior to 1969.
[2] Beginning 1966, excludes corporate stocks, other than Federal Reserve bank stock, of national banks; reported with "other assets."
[3] In 1969 and 1970, loans and securities are stated on a gross basis in "total assets" of commercial banks. Total reserves on loans and securities of commercial banks are included in "other liabilities."
[4] Comparable with later data.
[5] Beginning 1966, includes domestic interbank deposits only; for 1961–1965, includes domestic interbank and postal savings deposits. Prior to 1966, includes deposits of foreign banks.
[6] See series X 678–682 for supplementary figures: Number of banks, 1875–1882; capital accounts, 1875–1882; vault cash, 1875–1896; deposits, 1865–1896.
[7] Comparable with earlier data.
[8] Revised from source publication.
[9] Estimated.
[10] All figures except number of banks and capital accounts are estimated, using as a basis the previous 10 years, 1854–1863, inclusive.
[11] For more complete estimates of State banknotes in circulation, 1800–1878, see series X 437.

Series X 678–682.　Nonnational Banks—Number of Banks and Selected Assets and Liabilities, Alternate Series 1865 to 1896

[In millions of dollars, except number of banks]

Year	Adjusted deposits 678	Vault cash 679	Number of banks 680	Capital accounts 681	Total deposits [1] 682	Total deposits [2] 682
1896	3,545	207				
1895	3,604	229				
1894	3,311	226				
1893	3,312	221				
1892	3,409	218				
1891	3,082	187				
1890	2,971	181				
1889	2,694	186				
1888	2,569	191				
1887	2,528	186				
1886	2,395	177				
1885	2,141	161				
1884	2,057	131				
1883	2,016	106				
1882	1,844	109	5,063	235	1,719	
1881	1,823	109	4,681	211	1,527	
1880	1,495	112	4,456	194	1,319	
1879	1,272	84	4,312	201	1,180	
1878	1,275	86	4,400	205	1,243	
1877	1,383	84	4,501	224	1,352	
1876	1,453	85	4,520	219	1,362	1,408
1875	1,450	90	4,488	214	1,372	1,399
1874						1,307
1873						1,276
1872						1,255
1871						1,045
1870						868
1869						751
1868						665
1867						597
1866						443
1865						635

[1] Data for 1875–1882 from Comptroller of the Currency and compiled from tax returns; see text.
[2] Data for 1865–1876 from Federal Deposit Insurance Corporation and are sums of separate estimates; see text.

Series X 683–688. Nonnational Banks—Number of Banks and Total Assets, by Class: 1875 to 1970

[As of June 30 or nearest available date. Figures prior to 1896 are known to be incomplete; for explanation, see text for series X 580–587]

Year	State commercial banks (including private) Number	State commercial banks Assets [1] (mil. dol.)	Private banks [2] Number	Private banks Assets (mil. dol.)	Mutual savings banks [3] Number	Mutual savings banks Assets (mil. dol.)
	683	684	685	686	687	688
1970	9,052	220,598	17	446	497	76,373
1969	8,993	214,223	19	449	500	73,300
1968	9,001	194,316	21	474	502	69,031
1967	8,982	172,752	30	453	505	64,153
1966	9,010	162,322	60	439	507	59,416
1965	9,002	162,362	70	430	505	56,383
1964	8,980	148,099	71	424	507	52,000
1963	8,957	138,314	73	425	512	48,021
1962	8,934	127,652	57	383	513	44,418
1961	8,950	117,328	63	370	515	41,818
1960	8,961	111,841	82	354	516	39,598
1959	8,933	108,527	80	355	519	38,527
1958	8,975	107,083	84	360	521	36,678
1957	9,011	97,142	89	341	526	34,254
1956 *	9,052	96,143	92	352	528	32,421
1955	9,037	91,508	92	355	528	30,382
1954	9,102	81,974	92	374	528	28,315
1953	9,131	78,009	95	357	528	26,333
1952	9,144	76,164	105	362	529	24,378
1951	9,161	71,109	115	382	529	22,835
1950	9,175	67,223	118	372	530	22,252
1949	9,164	64,852	122	378	530	21,105
1948	9,191	64,718	131	374	532	20,252
1947	9,170	63,825	134	394	533	19,362
1946	9,140	67,810	136	362	533	18,021
1945	9,111	64,754	137	317	534	15,924
1944	9,102	54,889	149	276	536	13,810
1943	9,137	45,539	152	261	537	12,407
1942	9,252	35,691	160	237	538	11,655
1941	9,304	34,128	167	228	541	11,969
1940	9,370	30,988	174	223	542	11,925
1939	9,464	28,303	183	812	543	11,771
1938	9,625	25,868	191	665	552	11,545
1937	9,801	26,635	202	837	552	11,496
1936	9,961	25,929	213	761	555	11,283
1935	10,063	22,896	223	623	559	11,046
1934	9,931	21,124	235	508	565	10,938
1933	9,310	19,698	294	486	564	10,848
1932	12,589	23,985	391	512	583	10,991
1931	14,854	31,587	481	760	588	11,052
1930	16,432	35,297	591	963	594	10,164
1929	17,440	35,181	654	874	598	9,873
1928	18,113	33,298	696	901	603	9,557
1927	18,860	32,518	766	915	605	8,920
1926	19,770	31,579	823	809	608	8,298
1925	20,376	30,150	879	736	610	7,831
1924	20,908	27,612	944	820	613	7,284
1923	21,593	25,878	1,024	647	615	6,812
1922	21,876	23,473	1,108	546	616	6,262
1921	22,306	23,194	1,160	588	620	5,964
1920	22,267	24,242	1,691	741	618	5,586
1919	21,368	21,351	1,808	804	620	5,141
1918	21,157	18,090	1,926	953	624	4,745
1917	20,699	16,571	1,974	863	621	4,739
1916	20,168	14,297	2,057	766	623	4,480
1915	19,793	12,316	2,101	857	627	4,257
1914	19,718	11,679	2,201	610	628	4,194
1913	19,197	11,024	2,305	583	621	4,047
1912	18,478	10,638	2,319	595	628	3,877
1911	17,913	9,941	2,374	576	632	3,706
1910	17,376	9,432	2,442	590	637	3,598
1909	16,212	8,780	2,467	625	636	3,344
1908	15,714	7,954	2,525	557	630	3,281
1907	14,939	8,390	2,784	565	625	3,252
1906	13,739	7,820	2,726	575	621	3,139
1905	12,488	7,217	2,777	572	615	2,969
1904	11,707	6,382	2,914	604	622	2,814
1903	10,879	5,905	3,017	584	619	2,711
1902	9,956	5,420	2,896	633	624	2,599
1901	9,261	4,897	2,855	610	630	2,466
1900	8,696	4,115	2,825	507	626	2,328
1899	8,253	3,780	2,761	461	624	2,190
1898	7,949	3,193	2,698	453	633	2,048
1897	7,828	2,912	2,637	441	641	1,957
1896 [4]	7,785	2,813	2,597	457	638	1,881
1896 [5]	4,792	2,057	824	94	988	2,143
1895	5,086	2,085	1,070	131	1,017	2,054
1894	4,714	1,888	904	105	1,025	1,981
1893	4,655	1,965	848	108	1,030	2,014
1892	4,520	1,788	1,161	147	1,059	1,964
1891	3,978	1,595	1,235	152	1,011	1,855
1890 [6]	3,594	1,539	1,344	164	921	1,743
1889 [6]	3,115	1,380	1,324	143	849	1,623
1888	2,726	1,219	1,203	164	801	1,520
1887	2,472	1,179	1,001	175	684	1,378
1886	891	807	----------	----------	638	1,261
1885	1,015	802	----------	----------	646	1,203
1884	852	761	----------	----------	636	1,178
1883	788	724	----------	----------	630	1,119
1882	704	634	----------	----------	629	1,053
1881	683	576	----------	----------	629	968
1880	650	482	----------	----------	629	882
1879	648	428	----------	----------	639	865
1878	510	389	----------	----------	663	941
1877	631	507	----------	----------	675	923
1876 [7]	671	406	----------	----------	686	951
1875 [7]	586	395	----------	----------	674	896

* Denotes first year for which figures include Alaska and Hawaii.

[1] In 1969 and 1970, loans and securities are stated on a gross basis in "total assets" of commercial banks. Total loans were shown as net prior to 1969.

[2] Figures for 1896–1946 are for private banks in 18 States only; private banks were not segregated from other banks in the remaining States in this period. Figures may not be completely accurate; private banks not insured by FDIC are not required to report to any Federal bank supervisory agency.

[3] Includes mutual and stock savings banks, 1875–1896; thereafter, mutual savings banks only. See footnote 2 for series X 630–633.

[4] Comparable with later years.

[5] Comparable with earlier years.

[6] The total of series X 683 and X 687 and the total of series X 684 and X 688 differ from series X 656 and X 657, respectively. The latter are revised data published in the *Annual Report* of the Comptroller of the Currency, 1931, without breakdown by class of bank.

[7] Revised data for number of mutual savings banks, 781 in 1876 and 771 in 1875, are included in *Annual Report* of the Comptroller of the Currency, 1920, vol. 1, p. 241, but total assets for these banks are not available.

Series X 689–697. Savings and Other Time Deposits, by Type of Institution: 1820 to 1970

[In millions of dollars. As of June 30 except as noted]

Year	Total savings and other time deposits	By institution					Year	Total savings and other time deposits	By institution			
		Mutual savings banks	Savings and loan associations	Credit unions [1]	Postal savings system	Commercial banks [2]			Mutual savings banks	Savings and loan associations	Postal savings system	Commercial banks [2]
	689	690	691	692	693	694		689	690	691	693	694
1970	426,929	68,870	138,620	15,523	----------	203,916	1920	17,416	5,150	1,600	157	10,509
1969	412,886	66,030	133,600	13,740	----------	199,516	1919	14,789	4,710	1,390	167	8,522
1968	391,036	62,420	127,160	12,312	53	189,144	1918	13,015	4,390	1,270	148	7,207
1967	361,412	57,740	118,950	11,103	----------	173,566	1917	12,660	4,330	1,160	132	7,038
1966	330,141	53,620	111,460	10,071	192	154,798	1916	11,363	4,130	1,060	85	6,088
1965	302,830	50,720	105,460	9,220	342	137,088	1915	10,220	3,910	980	66	5,264
1964	270,790	46,740	96,080	8,225	415	119,330	1914	9,214	3,840	890	43	4,441
1963	241,915	43,020	85,590	7,164	493	105,648	1913	9,190	3,730	820	34	4,606
1962	213,356	39,780	74,930	6,331	581	91,734	1912	8,653	3,580	740	20	4,313
1961	188,813	37,320	66,060	5,639	702	79,092	1911	8,029	3,430	670	1	3,928
1960	166,056	35,420	57,900	4,981	849	66,906	1910	7,546	3,300	610	----------	3,636
1959	156,363	34,390	51,000	4,441	1,058	65,474	1909	6,870	3,140	560	----------	3,170
1958	144,026	32,810	44,660	3,869	1,214	61,473	1908	5,977	3,020	530	----------	2,427
1957	128,489	30,750	39,290	3,381	1,463	53,605	1907	5,805	3,020	490	----------	2,295
1956	117,907	29,020	34,510	2,914	1,765	49,698	1906	5,220	2,910	450	----------	1,860
1955	109,140	27,220	29,620	2,447	2,007	47,846	1905	4,897	2,740	430	----------	1,727
1954	100,244	25,320	24,980	2,040	2,251	45,653	1904	4,463	2,600	420	----------	1,443
1953	90,895	23,520	20,980	1,691	2,459	42,245	1903	4,198	2,500	410	----------	1,288
1952	82,576	21,730	17,570	1,355	2,619	39,302	1902	3,975	2,390	400	----------	1,185
1951	75,885	20,350	14,890	1,079	2,785	36,781	1901	3,715	2,260	400	----------	1,055
1950	73,700	19,750	13,250	884	3,097	36,719	1900	3,411	2,130	400	----------	881
1949	70,871	18,870	11,720	730	3,259	36,292	1899	3,066	2,000	410	----------	656
1948	68,276	18,120	10,360	630	3,378	35,788	1898	2,862	1,870	420	----------	572
1947	65,290	17,380	9,150	533	3,392	34,835	1897	2,768	1,780	420	----------	568
1946	60,099	16,140	7,960	451	3,119	32,429	1896	2,222	1,690	----------	----------	532
1945	51,411	14,360	6,840	384	2,657	27,170	1895	2,141	1,650	----------	----------	491
1944	41,954	12,450	5,900	355	2,032	21,217	1894	2,026	1,570	----------	----------	456
1943	35,782	11,120	5,220	323	1,576	17,543	1893	2,006	1,550	----------	----------	456
1942	32,438	10,400	4,810	303	1,315	15,610	1892	1,990	1,520	----------	----------	470
1941	32,598	10,580	4,500	287	1,303	15,928	1891	1,430	1,430	----------	----------	----------
1940	31,855	10,580	4,220	223	1,292	15,540	1890	1,370	1,370	----------	----------	----------
1939	31,017	10,390	4,100	169	1,261	15,097	1889	1,300	1,300	----------	----------	----------
1938	30,424	10,190	4,080	127	1,251	14,776	1888	1,240	1,240	----------	----------	----------
1937	30,128	10,110	4,140	98	1,267	14,513	1887	1,180	1,180	----------	----------	----------
1936	29,155	9,930	4,220	68	1,231	13,706	1886	1,120	1,120	----------	----------	----------
1935	28,202	9,780	4,360	38	1,204	12,820	1885	1,070	1,070	----------	----------	----------
1934	27,442	9,630	4,600	28	1,196	11,988	1884	1,030	1,030	----------	----------	----------
1933	26,748	9,650	5,040	23	1,186	10,849	1883	1,000	1,000	----------	----------	----------
1932	30,361	9,890	5,620	22	780	14,049	1882	950	950	----------	----------	----------
1931	34,953	9,810	6,110	----------	342	18,691	1881	920	920	----------	----------	----------
1930	35,235	9,090	6,270	----------	170	19,705	1880	810	810	----------	----------	----------
1929	34,536	8,830	6,000	----------	149	19,557	1879	750	750	----------	----------	----------
1928	33,870	8,530	5,390	----------	148	19,802	1878	780	780	----------	----------	----------
1927	31,119	7,970	4,700	----------	143	18,306	1877	830	830	----------	----------	----------
1926	28,788	7,440	4,090	----------	133	17,125	1876	840	840	----------	----------	----------
1925	26,605	7,020	3,480	----------	131	15,974	1875	820	820	----------	----------	----------
1924	24,104	6,590	2,890	----------	132	14,492	1874	760	760	----------	----------	----------
1923	22,105	6,180	2,420	----------	131	13,374	1873	700	700	----------	----------	----------
1922	19,538	5,720	2,090	----------	136	11,592	1872	640	640	----------	----------	----------
1921	18,395	5,480	1,850	----------	148	10,917	1871	560	560	----------	----------	----------
							1870	470	470	----------	----------	----------
							1869	400	400	----------	----------	----------
							1868	340	340	----------	----------	----------
							1867	300	300	----------	----------	----------

[1] As of December.

[2] Includes certificates of deposit.

Series X 689–697. Savings and Other Time Deposits, by Type of Institution: 1820 to 1970—Con.

[In millions of dollars]

Year	National banks 695	State banks 696	Year	Savings deposits in savings banks 697	Year	Savings deposits in savings banks 697	Year	Savings deposits in savings banks 697
1942	7,842	7,294	1910	4,071	1880	819	1850	43
1941	8,053	7,494	1909	3,713	1879	803	1849	36
			1908	3,661	1878	880	1848	33
1940	7,894	7,272	1907	3,690	1877	866	1847	32
1939	7,693	7,003	1906	3,482	1876	941	1846	27
1938	7,599	6,876						
1937	7,534	6,794	1905	3,261	1875	924	1845	25
1936	7,188	6,265	1904	3,060	1874	865	1840	14
			1903	2,935	1873	802	1835	11
1935	6,869	5,873	1902	2,750	1872	735	1830	7
1934	6,498	5,452	1901	2,597	1871	651	1825	3
1933	5,912	5,453						
1932	6,958	7,283	1900	2,450	1870	550	1820	1
1931	8,045	10,141	1899	2,230	1869	458		
			1898	2,066	1868	393		
1930	8,097	11,176	1897	1,939	1867	337		
1929	7,889	11,426	1896	1,907	1866	283		
1928	8,050	11,695						
1927	7,088	10,963	1895	1,811	1865	243		
1926	6,178	10,993	1894	1,748	1864	236		
			1893	1,785	1863	206		
1925	5,810	10,172	1892	1,713	1862	169		
1924	5,158	9,337	1891	1,623	1861	147		
1923	4,686	8,767						
1922	4,074	7,687	1890	1,525	1860	149		
1921	3,677	7,255	1889	1,425	1859	129		
			1888	1,364	1858	108		
1920	3,463	6,668	1887	1,235	1857	99		
1919	2,776	5,532	1886	1,142	1856	96		
1918	2,336	4,817						
1917	2,173	4,364	1885	1,095	1855	84		
1916	1,716	3,641	1884	1,073	1854	78		
			1883	1,025	1853	72		
1915	1,321	3,541	1882	967	1852	60		
1914	1,454	3,348	1881	892	1851	51		
1913	1,369	3,368						
1912	1,536	3,260						
1911	1,480	3,024						
1910	1,014	----------						

Series X 698–705. Bank Debits and Deposit Turnover: 1943 to 1970

Year	Debits to demand deposit accounts (bil. dol.)				Annual rate of turnover			
	All reporting centers	Leading centers		Other centers	All reporting centers	Leading centers		Other centers
		New York	6 others [1]			New York	6 others [1]	
	698	699	700	701	702	703	704	705
1970	10,237	4,518	2,404	3,315	72.9	154.4	77.6	41.9
1969	9,223	4,069	2,124	3,031	68.0	143.6	68.1	39.8
1968	8,010	3,635	1,756	2,619	62.0	135.5	59.2	36.0
1967	6,662	2,921	1,472	2,269	56.7	120.8	53.4	34.5
1966	5,923	2,502	1,328	2,093	52.8	109.4	50.1	33.3
1965	5,162	2,138	1,141	1,883	48.1	98.8	44.7	31.2
1964 [2]	4,631	1,925	1,031	1,675	44.8	90.2	41.6	29.2
1964 [3]	4,141	1,736	842	1,563	47.7	93.8	47.8	30.8
1963	3,755	1,556	776	1,423	44.3	84.8	44.6	29.0
1962	3,436	1,416	702	1,319	41.5	77.8	41.2	27.7
1961	3,111	1,279	623	1,210	38.2	70.0	36.9	26.2
1960	2,839	1,103	578	1,158	35.5	60.0	34.8	25.7
1959	2,679	1,024	545	1,110	33.4	56.4	32.5	24.5
1958	2,440	959	487	994	31.5	53.6	30.0	22.9
1957	2,357	888	489	979	30.8	49.5	30.4	23.0
1956	2,201	816	463	922	28.9	45.8	28.8	21.8
1955	2,044	767	432	845	27.1	42.7	27.3	20.4
1954	1,887	739	390	758	26.2	42.3	25.8	19.2
1953	1,759	633	386	740	24.6	36.7	25.6	18.9
1952	1,643	598	350	695	23.5	34.4	24.1	18.4
1951	1,543	544	337	661	23.0	31.9	24.0	18.4
1950	1,380	509	299	572	21.9	31.1	22.6	17.2
1949	1,206	446	261	499	20.2	27.9	20.9	15.9
1948	1,227	443	271	513	20.4	26.9	21.6	16.6
1947	1,104	398	247	459	18.7	23.8	19.7	15.5
1946	1,017	407	218	392	18.2	25.1	18.3	14.1
1945	924	383	200	342	17.6	24.1	17.5	13.5
1944	849	327	195	326	17.8	22.3	18.3	14.6
1943	757	281	175	301	17.5	20.4	18.0	15.3

[1] Boston, Philadelphia, Chicago, Detroit, San Francisco-Oakland, and Los Angeles-Long Beach.
[2] Comparable with later years.
[3] Comparable with earlier years.

Series X 706–715. Bank Debits and Deposit Turnover: 1919 to 1952

[In millions of dollars, except rates]

Year	Bank debits to deposit accounts, except interbank accounts, at reporting centers [1]				Bank debits and deposit turnover, all commercial banks [3]					
					Total demand and time deposits			Demand deposits		
	All reporting centers [2]	New York City	140 other centers	Other reporting centers [2]	Debits	Deposits	Annual turnover rate	Debits	Deposits	Annual turnover rate
	706	707	708	709	710	711	712	713	714	715
1952	1,692,136	615,670	895,906	180,560						
1951	1,577,857	551,889	854,050	171,917						
1950	1,403,752	513,970	742,458	147,324						
1949	1,231,053	452,897	648,976	129,179						
1948	1,249,630	449,002	667,934	132,695						
1947	1,125,074	405,929	599,639	119,506						
1946	1,050,021	417,475	527,336	105,210						
1945	974,102	404,543	479,760	89,799						
1944	891,910	345,585	462,354	83,970						
1943	792,935	296,368	419,413	77,153						
1942	[4] 641,778	[4] 226,865	[4] 347,837	[4] 67,074						
1941	537,343	197,724	293,925	45,694	756,000	54,110	14.0	740,000	38,220	19.4
1940	445,863	171,582	236,952	37,329	627,000	48,610	12.9	611,000	33,040	18.5
1939	423,933	171,382	218,295	34,256	592,000	43,670	13.6	577,000	28,550	20.2
1938	405,930	168,778	204,744	32,408	566,000	40,410	14.0	551,000	25,520	21.6
1937	469,462	197,836	235,207	36,419	650,000	40,290	16.1	635,000	25,710	24.7
1936	461,889	208,936	219,669	33,284	628,000	38,660	16.2	614,000	24,810	24.7
1935	402,718	184,006	190,167	28,545	547,000	34,610	15.8	534,000	21,480	24.9
1934	356,613	165,948	165,555	25,110	491,000	30,640	16.0	479,000	18,220	26.3
1933	303,216	[5] 148,449	[5] 134,259	[5] 20,508	437,000	28,500	15.3	424,000	15,850	26.8
1932	347,264	167,964	154,401	24,899	471,000	31,720	14.8	456,000	16,720	27.3
1931	515,294	263,834	217,523	33,937	685,000	37,830	18.1	658,000	19,810	33.2
1930	702,959	384,639	277,317	41,003	931,000	41,550	22.4	892,000	22,090	40.4
1929	982,531	603,088	331,942	47,501	1,276,000	42,720	29.9	1,237,000	23,080	53.6
1928	850,521	500,211	306,194	44,116	1,114,000	42,570	26.2	1,075,000	22,950	46.8
1927	714,328	391,558	282,303	40,467	952,000	40,670	23.4	915,000	22,340	41.0
1926	646,587	339,055	268,902	38,630	872,000	39,340	22.2	838,000	22,210	37.7
1925	605,843	313,373	256,689	35,781	820,000	37,720	21.7	788,000	21,720	36.3
1924	522,627	263,530	228,161	30,936	716,000	34,590	20.7	687,000	19,990	34.4
1923	494,412	238,396	225,331	30,685	685,000	32,920	20.8	658,000	19,280	34.1
1922	451,513	239,855	199,510	12,148	643,000	29,750	21.6	620,000	18,150	34.2
1921	409,338	207,096	191,942	10,300	591,000	28,400	20.8	569,000	17,470	32.6
1920	490,468	241,431	241,595	7,442	721,000	30,350	23.8	700,000	19,800	35.4
1919	460,249	244,119	211,175	4,955	663,000	27,060	24.5	646,000	18,480	35.0

[1] Beginning in May 1942, 60 new reporting centers (affecting series X 706 and X 709) and a number of banks in previously included reporting centers (affecting all series) were added to those centers and banks included for the years prior to 1942. The figures for the period 1942–1952 are therefore not strictly comparable with those for the earlier years. The extent of the change in coverage is reflected for 1942 by comparing the figures shown above with those derived on the old basis, as follows: Series X 706—607,071; series X 707—210,961; series X 708—342,430; series X 709—53,679. (See *Federal Reserve Bulletin*, Aug. 1943, p. 717.)
[2] The number of centers in this group varied considerably; see text.
[3] Excludes interbank deposits and collection items.
[4] Partly estimated for first 4 months.
[5] 11 months only; data for Mar. 1933 not available because of bank holiday.

Series X 716–724. Number of Banking Offices, by Deposit Insurance Status: 1900 to 1970

Year [1]	All banking offices	Commercial bank offices [2]					Mutual savings bank offices [2][4]		
		Total	Member banks [2][3]		Nonmember banks		Total	Insured [5]	Non-insured
			National	State [4][5]	Insured	Non-insured			
	716	717	718	719	720	721	722	723	724
1970	36,910	35,330	17,142	4,798	13,159	231	1,580	1,222	358
1969	35,340	33,858	16,384	4,683	12,546	245	1,482	1,137	345
1968	34,100	32,691	15,700	4,827	11,919	245	1,409	1,072	337
1967	32,983	31,652	14,940	4,983	11,470	259	1,331	1,001	330
1966	31,934	30,673	14,404	4,867	11,103	299	1,261	944	317
1965	30,776	29,556	13,776	4,738	10,723	319	1,220	911	309
1964	29,549	28,370	12,937	4,751	10,356	326	1,179	876	303
1963	28,197	27,064	12,032	4,684	10,012	336	1,133	832	301
1962	26,865	25,768	11,140	4,549	9,718	361	1,097	797	300
1961	25,839	24,782	10,554	4,453	9,407	368	1,057	757	300
1960	24,954	23,954	10,036	4,265	9,253	400	1,000	706	294
1959	* 24,094	* 23,130	* 9,514	4,206	* 9,001	* 409	964	586	378
1958	23,305	22,361	9,109	4,120	8,693	439	944	546	398
1957	22,699	21,772	8,795	3,969	8,545	463	927	535	392
1956	22,123	21,230	8,459	3,884	8,405	482	893	480	413
1955	21,494	20,638	8,055	3,785	8,263	535	856	454	402
1954	20,982	20,147	7,844	3,598	8,132	573	835	439	396
1953	20,608	19,810	7,602	3,536	8,062	610	798	411	387
1952	20,288	19,513	7,465	3,436	7,947	665	775	383	392
1951	20,003	19,244	7,309	3,365	7,879	691	759	367	392

See footnotes at end of table.

Series X 716–724. Number of Banking Offices, by Deposit Insurance Status: 1900 to 1970—Con.

Year [1]	All banking offices	Commercial bank offices [2]					Mutual savings bank offices [2][4]			Year [1]	Commercial bank offices		
		Total	Member banks [2][3]		Nonmember banks		Total	Insured [5]	Non-insured		Total	National banks	State banks [7]
			National	State [4][5]	Insured	Non-insured							
	716	717	718	719	720	721	722	723	724		717	718	719–721
1950	19,708	18,966	7,188	3,271	7,766	741	742	346	396	1932	20,997	7,231	13,766
1949	19,465	18,735	7,060	3,216	7,679	780	730	333	397	1931	22,842	7,478	15,364
1948	19,234	18,520	6,956	3,156	7,582	826	714	325	389				
1947 [6]	19,046	18,342	6,875	3,096	7,521	850	704	318	386	1930	25,694	8,075	17,619
1946	18,863	18,165	6,794	3,022	7,464	885	698	306	392	1929	27,379	8,398	18,981
										1928	28,106	8,563	19,543
1945	18,781	18,096	6,831	2,963	7,397	905	685	293	392	1927	28,714	8,482	20,232
1944	18,741	18,058	6,840	2,866	7,430	922	683	291	392	1926	29,454	8,327	21,127
1943	18,646	17,965	6,782	2,744	7,487	952	681	279	402				
1942	18,562	17,878	6,675	2,619	7,602	982	683	91	592	1925	30,163	8,366	21,797
1941	18,524	17,841	6,682	2,514	7,742	903	683	84	599	1924	30,482	8,299	22,183
										1923	30,931	8,383	22,548
1940	18,561	17,875	6,683	2,344	7,892	956	686	84	602	1922	31,259	8,384	22,875
1939	18,663	17,980	6,705	2,177	8,099	999	683	75	608	1921	31,243	8,222	23,021
1938	18,774	18,084	6,723	2,106	8,226	1,029	690	64	626				
1937	18,927	18,236	6,745	2,075	8,342	1,074	691	67	624	1920	30,368	8,088	22,280
1936	19,066	18,373	6,723	2,032	8,440	1,178	693	67	626	1915	26,660	7,624	19,036
										1910	22,034	7,150	14,884
1935	19,153	18,455	6,715	1,953	8,562	1,225	698	67	631	1905	15,032	5,669	9,363
1934	19,196	18,491	6,705	1,961	[7] 9,825		705	(7)	(7)				
1933	17,940	17,236	6,275	1,817	[7] 9,144		704	(7)	(7)	1900	8,857	3,736	5,121

* Denotes first year for which figures include Alaska and Hawaii.

[1] For 1925, 1926, and 1932–1970, figures are as of December; for earlier years they are as of different dates for banks and branches: For banks, 1927–1931 and 1923–1924, as of December; for 1915–1922, as of June; for branches, 1924 and 1927–1931, as of June; prior to 1924, not for any uniform month. Figures in this table prior to 1947 have not been revised to bring them into conformity with the revised all-bank data referred to in the general note for series X 561–820.

[2] Comparability of figures for classes of banks is affected somewhat by changes in Federal Reserve membership, deposit insurance status, and reserve classifications of cities and individual banks, and by mergers, etc.

[3] Federal deposit insurance is compulsory for member banks of the Federal Reserve System.

[4] None in Alaska and Hawaii.

[5] Member commercial banks exclude, and mutual savings banks include, mutual savings banks which are members of the Federal Reserve System as follows: 3, 1941–1959, 2 in 1960, and 1 in 1961–1970.

[6] In 1947, the series was revised. See footnote 6 to series X 731–740.

[7] Federal insurance of bank deposits did not become effective until Jan. 1, 1934, and the number of nonmember banking offices by insurance status is not available prior to 1935.

Series X 725–730. Bank Deposits Insured by the Federal Deposit Insurance Corporation and the Deposit Insurance Fund: 1934 to 1970

[As of December 31, except as noted. Includes Alaska, Hawaii, and outlying areas]

Year	Deposits in insured banks		Percent of deposits insured	Deposit insurance fund (mil. dol.)	Ratio of deposit insurance fund to—		Year	Deposits in insured banks		Percent of deposits insured	Deposit insurance fund (mil. dol.)	Ratio of deposit insurance fund to—	
	Total (mil. dol.)	Insured [1] (mil. dol.)			Total deposits	Insured deposits		Total (mil. dol.)	Insured [1] (mil. dol.)			Total deposits	Insured deposits
	725	726	727	728	729	730		725	726	727	728	729	730
1970	545,198	349,581	64.1	4,379.6	0.80	1.25	1950	167,818	91,359	54.4	1,243.9	0.74	1.36
1969	495,858	313,085	63.1	4,051.1	.82	1.29	1949	156,786	76,589	48.8	1,203.9	.77	1.57
1968	491,513	296,701	60.2	3,749.2	.76	1.26	1948	153,454	75,320	49.1	1,065.9	.69	1.42
1967	448,709	261,149	58.2	3,485.5	.78	1.33	1947	154,096	76,254	49.5	1,006.1	.65	1.32
1966	401,096	234,150	58.4	3,252.0	.81	1.39	1946	148,458	73,759	49.7	1,058.5	.71	1.44
1965	377,400	209,690	55.6	3,036.3	.80	1.45	1945	157,174	67,021	42.4	929.2	.59	1.39
1964	348,981	191,787	55.0	2,844.7	.82	1.48	1944	134,662	56,398	41.9	804.3	.60	1.43
1963	[2] 313,304	177,381	56.6	2,667.9	.85	1.50	1943	111,650	48,440	43.4	703.1	.63	1.45
1962	[3] 297,548	170,210	57.2	2,502.0	.84	1.47	1942	89,869	32,837	36.5	616.9	.69	1.88
1961	281,304	160,309	57.0	2,353.8	.84	1.47	1941	71,209	28,249	39.7	553.5	.78	1.96
1960	260,495	149,684	57.5	2,222.2	.85	1.48	1940	65,288	26,638	40.8	496.0	.76	1.86
1959	247,589	142,131	57.4	2,089.8	.84	1.47	1939	57,485	24,650	42.9	452.7	.79	1.84
1958	242,445	137,698	56.8	1,965.4	.81	1.43	1938	50,791	23,121	45.5	420.5	.83	1.82
1957	225,507	127,055	56.3	1,850.5	.82	1.46	1937	48,228	22,557	46.8	383.1	.79	1.70
1956	219,393	121,008	55.2	1,742.1	.79	1.44	1936	50,281	22,330	44.4	343.4	.68	1.54
1955	212,226	116,380	54.8	1,639.6	.77	1.41	1935	45,125	20,158	44.7	306.0	.68	1.52
1954	203,195	110,973	54.6	1,542.7	.76	1.39	1934	40,060	18,075	45.1	333.0	.83	1.84
1953	193,466	105,610	54.6	1,450.7	.75	1.37							
1952	188,142	101,842	54.1	1,363.5	.72	1.34							
1951	178,540	96,713	54.2	1,282.2	.72	1.33							

[1] Figures estimated by applying to the deposits in the various types of accounts at the regular call dates the percentages insured as determined from special reports secured from insured banks.

[2] December 20, 1963.

[3] December 28, 1962.

Series X 731–740. Branch Banking: 1900 to 1970

Year [1]	Total	Commercial banks [2]						Mutual savings banks			Number of banking facilities [5]
		Total	Member banks [3]		Nonmember banks [4]			Total	Insured	Noninsured	
			National	State [4]	Insured	Noninsured					
	731	732	733	734	735	736		737	738	739	740

NUMBER OF BANKS OPERATING BRANCHES

Year	731	732	733	734	735	736	737	738	739	740
1970	4,294	3,994	1,684	450	1,840	20	300	213	87	
1969	4,084	3,794	1,591	446	1,738	19	290	206	84	
1968	3,946	3,665	1,550	462	1,633	20	281	199	82	
1967	3,756	3,487	1,477	459	1,530	21	269	190	79	
1966	3,573	3,313	1,406	454	1,435	18	260	183	77	
1965	3,386	3,140	1,331	452	1,336	21	246	176	70	
1964	3,204	2,966	1,233	445	1,269	19	238	172	66	
1963	3,016	2,791	1,133	6 439	1,200	19	225	160	65	
1962	2,840	2,619	1,036	425	1,139	19	221	154	67	
1961	2,696	2,484	986	418	1,062	18	212	146	66	
1960	2,523	2,329	905	404	1,001	19	194	131	63	
1959	* 2,351	* 2,164	* 805	383	* 956	* 20	187	113	74	
1958	2,187	2,010	739	352	899	20	177	107	70	
1957	2,066	1,893	677	340	856	20	173	106	67	
1956	1,962	1,790	627	327	815	21	172	100	72	
1955	1,814	1,659	543	304	790	22	155	94	61	
1954	1,720	1,571	502	276	769	24	149	92	57	
1953	1,609	1,474	444	258	745	27	135	85	50	
1952	1,483	1,359	385	237	708	29	124	78	46	
1951	1,422	1,299	352	226	692	29	123	75	48	
1950	1,354	1,241	324	218	669	30	113	67	46	
1949	1,301	1,191	298	214	648	31	110	65	45	
1948	1,242	1,140	276	202	626	36	102	62	40	
1947 [7]	1,188	1,089	253	194	604	38	99	60	39	
1946	1,143	1,053	235	193	591	34	90	56	34	
1945	1,101	1,016	222	190	570	34	85	52	33	
1944	1,082	999	216	188	563	32	83	51	32	
1943	1,069	989	214	181	563	31	80	49	31	
1942	1,065	985	212	177	565	31	80			
1941	1,054	973	205	174	563	31	81			
1940	1,040	959	200	170	560	29	81			
1939	1,019	939	195	165	549	30	80			
1938	1,001	921	194	161	566		80			
1937	981	903	194	159	527	23	78			
1936	938	859	188		671		79			
1935	901	822	181		641		79			
1934	807	729	176		553		78			
1933	660	584	146		438		76			
1932		681	157		524					
1931		723	164		559					
1930		751	166		585					
1929		764	167		597					
1928		775	171		604					
1927		740	153		587					
1926		744	148		596					
1925		720	130		590					
1924		706	112		594					
1923		671	91		580					
1922		610	55		555					
1921		547	23		524					
1920		530	21		509					
1915		397	12		385					
1910		292	9		283					
1905		196	5		191					
1900		87	5		82					

NUMBER OF BRANCHES

Year	731	732	733	734	735	736	737	738	739	740
1970	22,508	21,424	12,363	3,642	5,371	48	1,084	891	193	219
1969	20,973	19,985	11,550	3,465	4,923	47	988	810	178	223
1968	19,675	18,777	10,797	3,555	4,379	46	898	729	169	236
1967	18,519	17,690	9,991	3,658	3,995	46	829	669	160	238
1966	17,405	16,648	9,407	3,493	3,686	62	757	614	143	260
1965	16,201	15,486	8,754	3,309	3,369	54	715	583	132	270
1964	14,995	14,321	7,940	3,056	3,275	50	674	549	125	280
1963	13,844	13,220	7,204	3,166	2,800	50	624	502	122	278
1962	12,655	12,068	6,423	2,981	2,614	50	587	466	121	277
1961	11,620	11,077	5,827	2,826	2,380	44	543	427	116	276
1960	10,702	10,216	5,298	2,597	2,274	47	486	381	105	267
1959 *	9,835	9,388	4,769	2,490	2,087	42	447	318	129	264
1958	9,038	8,613	4,341	2,360	1,873	39	425	305	120	248
1957	8,373	7,968	3,993	2,173	1,765	37	405	296	109	236
1956	7,728	7,362	3,629	2,053	1,643	37	366	257	109	227

See footnotes at end of table.

Series X 731–740. Branch Banking: 1900 to 1970—Con.

Year [1]	Total	Commercial banks [2]					Mutual savings banks			Number of banking facilities [5]
		Total	Member banks [3]		Nonmember banks [4]		Total	Insured	Noninsured	
			National	State [4]	Insured	Noninsured				
	731	732	733	734	735	736	737	738	739	740

NUMBER OF BRANCHES—Con.

Year [1]	731	732	733	734	735	736	737	738	739	740
1955	7,040	6,710	3,196	1,916	1,563	35	330	234	96	213
1954	6,416	6,108	2,900	1,710	1,462	36	308	221	87	198
1953	5,897	5,627	2,590	1,631	1,365	41	270	192	78	199
1952	5,520	5,274	2,403	1,530	1,300	41	246	177	69	191
1951	5,224	4,994	2,244	1,449	1,260	41	230	165	65	159
1950	4,934	4,721	2,136	1,343	1,190	52	213	152	61	122
1949	4,684	4,485	2,012	1,288	1,132	53	199	141	58	94
1948	4,461	4,279	1,913	1,219	1,079	68	182	132	50	70
1947	4,261	4,090	1,817	1,168	1,038	67	171	124	47	71
1946	4,059	3,902	1,721	1,118	1,001	62	157	115	42	79
1945	3,866	3,723	1,641	1,061	964	57	143	101	42	224
1944	3,772	3,632	1,589	1,035	954	54	140	99	41	292
1943	3,716	3,580	1,573	1,020	935	52	136	95	41	217
1942	3,712	3,575	1,571	1,020	932	52	137	35	102	27
1941	3,699	3,564	1,565	1,015	932	52	135	32	103	-------
1940	3,666	3,531	1,539	1,002	940	50	135	31	104	
1939	3,629	3,497	1,518	1,002	927	50	132	24	108	
1938	3,580	3,445	1,499	992	908	46	135	16	119	
1937	3,540	3,412	1,485	994	891	42	128	11	117	
1936	3,399	3,271	1,398	981	848	44	128	11	117	
1935	3,284	3,156	1,329	952	828	47	128	11	117	
1934	3,133	3,007	1,243	981		783	126	-------	-------	
1933	2,911	2,786	1,121	960		705	125	-------	-------	
1932		3,195	1,220		1,975		-------	-------	-------	
1931		3,467	1,110		2,357		-------	-------	-------	
1930		3,522	1,042		2,480		-------	-------	-------	
1929		3,353	995		2,358		-------	-------	-------	
1928		3,138	934		2,204		-------	-------	-------	
1927		2,914	723		2,191		-------	-------	-------	
1926		2,703	421		2,282		-------	-------	-------	
1925		2,525	318		2,207		-------	-------	-------	
1924		2,297	256		2,041		-------	-------	-------	
1923		2,054	204		1,850		-------	-------	-------	
1922		1,801	140		1,661		-------	-------	-------	
1921		1,455	72		1,383		-------	-------	-------	
1920		1,281	63		1,218		-------	-------	-------	
1915		785	26		759		-------	-------	-------	
1910		548	12		536		-------	-------	-------	
1905		350	5		345		-------	-------	-------	
1900		119	5		114		-------	-------	-------	

Year [1]	Total (mil. dol.)	Commercial bank branches (mil. dol.)						Mutual savings bank branches, total (mil. dol.)
		Total	Member banks [3]		Nonmember banks [4]			
			National	State [4]	Insured	Noninsured		
	731	732	733	734	735	736		737

LOANS AND INVESTMENTS OR DEPOSITS [8]

Year [1]	731	732	733	734	735	736	737
1949	83,260	71,833	39,339	26,703	5,103	688	11,427
1941	43,449	38,496	19,094		19,402		4,953
1939	35,733	30,813	14,924		15,889		4,920
1938		26,587	12,828		13,759		--------
1937		24,989	12,054		12,935		--------
1936		20,706	9,713		10,993		--------
1935		18,744	8,602		10,142		4,457
1933		15,528	6,963		8,565		--------
1932		17,279	7,339		9,940		--------
1931		20,680	8,529		12,151		--------
1930		22,491	9,169		13,322		--------
1929		21,420	8,016		13,404		--------
1928		20,068	7,840		12,228		--------

Year [1]	Commercial bank branches (mil. dol.)		
	Total	Member banks [3]	
		National	State [4]
	732	733	734–736

LOANS AND INVESTMENTS OR DEPOSITS [8]—Con.

Year [1]	732	733	734–736
1927	17,591	6,294	11,297
1926	16,511	5,243	11,268
1925	14,763	4,447	10,316
1924	12,480	3,606	8,874
1923	10,922	2,841	8,081
1922	9,110	2,330	6,780
1921	8,354	1,581	6,773
1920	6,897	689	6,208
1915	2,187	98	2,089
1910	1,272	44	1,228
1905	637	6	631
1900	119	5	114

* Denotes first year for which figures include Alaska and Hawaii.

[1] For years prior to 1924, figures are not for any uniform month. For 1925, 1926, 1932–1970, as of December; for 1924 and 1927–1931, as of June.

[2] Includes 1 national bank in the Virgin Islands, with 2 branches, which became a member of the Federal Reserve System in 1957.

[3] Federal deposit insurance is compulsory for member banks of the Federal Reserve System.

[4] Figures for 1900–1932 comprise State–chartered commercial banks operating branches and their branches and those unincorporated (private) banks operating branches and their branches reporting to State banking authorities. Beginning in 1934, the proportion of private banks reporting was larger than in prior years.

[5] Banking facilities are provided at military and other Government establishments through arrangements made by the Treasury Department with banks. Some of these facilities are operated by banks that have no other type of branch or additional office.

[6] State member bank figures include 1 noninsured trust company without deposits.

[7] In 1947, the series was revised to conform (except that it excludes U.S. outlying areas) to the number of banks in the uniform all-bank series inaugurated in 1947 by the Federal bank supervisory authorities. The revision resulted in a net addition of 115 banks and 9 branches.

[8] Loans and investments, 1900–1936, and deposits, 1937–1941 and 1949, of banks operating branches, except for mutual savings banks for 1935 which are deposits. For other years data are not available. Prior to 1949 commercial bank figures exclude a small amount of deposits of private banks, data for which are available for selected years only as follows: 1935, $46 million; 1939, $102 million; and 1941, $138 million.

Series X 741–755.　Bank Suspensions—Number and Deposits of Suspended Banks: 1864 to 1970

	Number of suspensions							Deposits of suspended banks [2] (mil. dol.)							
			State commercial			Federal Reserve System				State commercial [3]			Federal Reserve System		Losses borne by depositors [3][4]
Year [1]	Total	National	Incorporated	Private (unincorporated)	Mutual savings	Member	Non-member	Total	National	Incorporated	Private (unincorporated)	Mutual savings	Member	Non-member	
	741	742	743	744	745	746	747	748	749	750	751	752	753	754	755
1970	7	1	6	–	–	1	6	53	16	36	–	–	16	36	--------
1969	9	3	6	–	–	5	4	40	12	29	–	–	15	25	--------
1968	3	1	2	–	–	1	2	23	12	11	–	–	12	11	--------
1967	4	1	3	–	–	2	2	11	4	7	–	–	8	3	--------
1966	8	2	6	–	–	2	6	106	4	102	–	–	4	102	--------
1965	9	2	3	4	–	2	7	45	42	1	1	–	42	3	--------
1964	8	1	7	–	–	1	7	24	3	20	–	–	3	20	--------
1963	2	–	2	–	–	–	2	23	–	23	–	–	–	23	--------
1962	3	1	1	1	–	1	2	4	3	1	–	–	3	1	–
1961	9	2	4	3	–	3	6	10	5	4	1	–	7	4	450
1960	2	–	2	–	–	–	2	8	–	8	–	–	–	8	257
1959	3	–	3	–	–	–	3	3	–	3	–	–	–	3	15
1956–1960	20	3	13	4	–	4	16	45	18	25	2	–	19	26	601
1951–1955	23	3	17	3	–	4	19	70	8	59	3	–	27	42	880
1947–1950	23	8	11	4	–	10	13	33	16	15	2	–	24	9	69
1941–1946	49	20	29	–	–	24	25	[5] 59	36	23	–	–	42	17	68
1934–1940	[6] 448	45	383	19	2	61	388	[7] 477	59	412	–	4	232	245	9,173
1933 [8]	4,004	1,101	2,790	109	4	1,275	2,729	3,601	1,611	1,975	13	[9] 2	2,394	1,207	540
1932	1,456	276	1,140	37	3	331	1,125	725	214	494	8	9	269	456	168
1931	2,294	409	1,804	80	1	516	1,778	1,691	439	1,230	21	(Z)	733	958	391
1930	1,352	161	1,131	58	2	188	1,164	869	170	668	15	16	373	496	237
1929	659	64	564	31	–	81	578	231	42	181	8	–	58	173	77
1928	499	57	422	19	1	73	426	143	36	103	3	(Z)	47	96	44
1927	669	91	545	33	–	122	547	199	46	149	4	–	63	136	61
1926	976	123	801	52	–	158	818	260	44	207	9	–	67	193	83
1925	618	118	461	39	–	146	472	168	56	104	8	–	65	102	61
1924	775	122	616	37	–	160	615	210	65	138	8	–	79	132	79
1923	646	90	533	23	–	122	524	150	34	114	2	–	47	103	62
1922	367	49	294	23	1	62	305	93	20	69	2	2	27	66	38
1921	505	52	409	44	–	71	434	172	21	143	9	–	38	134	60

Number of suspensions						Number of suspensions						Number of suspensions				
			State commercial						State commercial [10]							
Year [1]	Total	National	Incorporated	Private (unincorporated)	Mutual savings	Year [1]	Total	National	Incorporated	Private (unincorporated)	Mutual savings	Year [1]	Total	National	State commercial [10]	Mutual savings
	741	742	743	744	745		741	742	743	744	745		741	742	743–744	745
1920	168	7	136	24	1	1901	69	9	15	41	4	1883	33	1	27	5
1919	63	2	59	1	1							1882	22	3	19	–
1918	47	2	35	10	–	1900	36	5	14	16	1	1881	11	–	9	2
1917	49	5	29	15	–	1899	36	10	8	14	4					
1916	52	8	32	12	–	1898	67	11	19	33	4	1880	18	5	10	3
						1897	145	28	64	47	6	1879	37	7	20	10
1915	152	20	93	39	–	1896	155	34	66	41	14	1878	140	10	70	60
1914	151	15	107	27	2							1877	93	8	63	28
1913	105	13	75	15	2	1895	124	34	51	25	14	1876	59	8	37	14
1912	80	6	51	21	2	1894	89	23	39	21	6					
1911	87	5	58	22	2	1893	496	69	228	194	5	1875	28	3	14	11
						1892	83	12	32	36	3	1874	57	10	40	7
1910	63	6	40	12	5	1891	62	16	44		2	1873	41	4	33	4
1909	79	8	37	33	1							1872	19	6	10	3
1908	155	19	83	51	2	1890	37	6	30		1	1871	10	–	7	3
1907	91	12	58	20	1	1889	18	3	15		–					
1906	53	6	34	13	–	1888	33	12	17		4	1870	3	1	1	1
						1887	25	5	19		1	1869	7	1	6	–
1905	80	20	25	35	–	1886	20	6	13		1	1868	14	6	7	1
1904	128	22	53	50	3							1867	8	4	3	1
1903	52	13	22	17	–	1885	46	9	32		5	1866	7	2	5	–
1902	54	4	30	20	–	1884	63	6	54		3					
												1865	6	1	5	–
												1864	2	–	2	–

–　Represents zero.　　Z　Less than $500,000.

[1] For 1864–1891, all series except mutual savings banks are for year ending June 30; for mutual savings banks the date is not specified in the source. For 1892–1920, for all banks other than private, figures are for calendar year; for private banks, figures vary in ending date of reporting year as follows: 1892, June 30; 1893 (14 months), Aug. 31; 1894–1899, Aug. 31; 1900–1919, June 30; and 1920 (18 months), Dec. 31. For 1921–1970, all series are for calendar years. Series X 741 is composite as to reporting period since it comprises the summation of series X 742–745.

[2] Excludes deposits for 7 noninsured banks, for which data were unavailable.

[3] Beginning 1934, based on estimates.

[4] In commercial banks only. Estimated losses to depositors in mutual savings banks were as follows: 1922, $213,000; 1928, $31,000; 1930, $6,530,000; 1931, $157,000; 1932, $4,738,000; 1933, $7,085,000. (See *Annual Report* of the Federal Deposit Insurance Corporation, 1934, p. 113.)

[5] Excludes deposits for 1 foreign-owned bank closed in 1941 by order of the Federal Government, requiring disbursements by the Corporation.

[6] Excludes 1 noninsured bank placed in receivership in 1934 with no deposits at time of closing.

[7] Excludes deposits for two cases requiring disbursements by the Corporation: 1 bank in voluntary liquidation in 1937, 1 noninsured bank in 1938 with insured deposits at date of suspension, its insurance status having been terminated prior to suspension.

[8] Figures not wholly comparable with earlier years; see text.

[9] Figures not comparable with losses to depositors shown in footnote 4 because source data differ for these series.

[10] Prior to 1892, the figures shown include all State commercial banks; separate figures for private bank suspensions are not available.

Series X 756–767. Banks Closed Because of Financial Difficulties: 1934 to 1970

Year	Number of banks					Deposits ($1,000)					Losses in banks insured by Federal Deposit Insurance Corporation ($1,000)	
	Total	Insured by Federal Deposit Insurance Corporation			Not insured by FDIC [4]	Total	In banks insured by Federal Deposit Insurance Corporation			In banks not insured by FDIC [4]	By FDIC [5]	By depositors [6]
		Total insured [1]	With disbursements by FDIC				Total insured [1]	With disbursements by FDIC				
			Deposit payoff cases [2]	Deposit assumption cases [3]				Deposit payoff cases [2]	Deposit assumption cases [3]			
	756	757	758	759	760	761	762	763	764	765	766	767
1970	7	7	4	3	1	52,763	52,340	31,008	21,332	423	11,973	----
1969	9	9	4	5	–	40,120	40,120	8,998	31,122	–	446	----
1968	3	3	–	3	–	22,524	22,524	–	22,524	–	2,371	----
1967	4	4	4	–	–	10,878	10,878	10,878	–	–	5,018	----
1966	8	7	1	6	1	106,171	103,523	774	102,749	2,648	5,576	----
1965	9	5	3	2	4	45,232	43,837	42,865	972	1,395	5,318	----
1964	8	7	7	–	1	23,751	23,322	23,322	–	429	4,951	----
1963	2	2	2	–	–	23,429	23,429	23,439	–	–	1,586	–
1962	3	1	–	1	2	4,220	3,000	–	3,000	1,220	(767)	----
1961	9	5	5	–	4	10,611	8,936	8,936	–	1,675	1,576	450
1960	2	1	1	–	1	7,965	6,930	6,930	–	1,035	–	–
1959	3	3	3	–	–	2,593	2,593	2,593	–	–	105	15
1958	9	4	3	1	5	10,413	8,240	4,156	4,084	2,173	42	8
1957	3	2	1	–	1	12,502	11,247	1,163	–	1,255	–	–
1956	3	2	1	1	1	11,689	11,329	4,702	6,628	360	265	58
1955	5	5	4	1	–	11,953	11,953	6,503	5,450	–	232	8
1954	4	2	–	2	2	2,948	998	–	998	1,950	263	----
1953	5	4	–	2	1	45,101	44,711	–	18,262	390	792	----
1952	4	3	–	3	1	3,313	3,170	–	3,170	143	----	
1951	5	2	–	2	3	6,464	3,408	–	3,408	3,056	3	----
1950	5	4	–	4	1	5,555	5,513	–	5,513	42	1,385	----
1949	9	5	–	4	4	9,217	6,665	–	5,475	2,552	369	----
1948	3	3	–	3	–	10,674	10,674	–	10,674	–	641	----
1947	6	5	–	5	1	7,207	7,040	–	7,040	167	79	----
1946	2	1	–	1	1	494	347	–	347	147	----	
1945	1	1	–	1	–	5,695	5,695	–	5,695	–	----	
1944	2	2	1	1	–	1,915	1,915	456	1,459	–	40	3
1943	5	5	4	1	–	12,525	12,525	6,637	5,888	–	123	12
1942	23	20	6	14	3	19,541	19,186	1,816	17,369	355	688	5
1941	16	14	7	7	2	[7]18,805	18,726	3,739	14,987	79	591	33
1940	48	43	19	24	5	142,787	142,429	5,657	136,773	358	3,783	31
1939	72	60	32	28	12	160,211	157,772	32,738	125,034	2,439	7,153	936
1938	80	73	49	24	7	60,444	59,406	10,018	49,388	1,038	2,425	40
1937	83	76	49	25	7	34,141	33,613	14,896	18,389	528	3,550	110
1936	72	69	42	27	3	28,100	27,508	11,241	16,267	592	2,455	171
1935	32	26	24	1	6	13,987	13,404	9,091	4,229	583	2,707	416
1934	61	9	9	–	52	37,332	1,968	1,968	–	35,364	207	20

– Represents zero.

[1] Includes the following banks not shown separately which reopened or had their deposits assumed by another insured bank without financial aid of the Federal Deposit Insurance Corporation: 1935, 1 bank with deposits of $85 thousand; 1937, 2 banks with deposits of $328 thousand; 1949, 1 bank with deposits of $1,190 thousand; 1953, 2 banks with deposits of $26,449 thousand; 1957, 1 bank with deposits of $10,084 thousand; and 1962, 1 bank with deposits of $3,011 thousand. (See *Annual Report* of Federal Deposit Insurance Corporation, *1941*, pp. 99 and 101; *1949*, p. 191; *1953*, p. 80; *1957*, p. 8; *1962*, p. 4).

[2] Banks placed in receivership with deposits paid, to insurance maximum, by Federal Deposit Insurance Corporation, adjusted to exclude: 1937, 1 bank in voluntary liquidation; 1938, 1 noninsured bank with insured deposits at date of suspension (insured status having been terminated prior to suspension); 1941, 1 foreign-owned bank closed by order of the Federal Government.

[3] Banks in financial difficulties with deposits assumed by other insured banks, with financial aid of Federal Deposit Insurance Corporation.

[4] Previously published data adjusted to add 4 cases in 1934; 1 in 1937; 1 in 1938; 2 in 1939; 1 in 1940; 1 in 1941; and to exclude 1 case in 1935; and 1 case in 1938. Deposits not available for 1 bank in 1938; 2 in 1939; 1 in 1940; 1 in 1941; and 1 in 1954. Excludes 1 bank placed in receivership in 1934, with no deposits at time of closing. Deposits are not available for 7 banks.

[5] Includes loss in the 1938 case mentioned in footnote 2 and estimated loss in cases not yet closed. Beginning 1962, data are changes in amount of the cumulative losses during the year. Figure in parentheses represents net recoveries. Total losses (including estimated losses in active cases) at end of 1970 were $67,703.

[6] Tabulated by Federal Deposit Insurance Corporation from receivership records. Includes loss in the 1938 case mentioned in footnote 2 and estimated loss in cases not yet closed.

[7] Excludes deposits for 1 foreign-owned bank closed in 1941 by order of the Federal Government, requiring disbursements by FDIC.

Series X 768–775. National Banks—Earnings and Expenses: 1869 to 1970

[In millions of dollars, except number of banks. Includes Alaska, Hawaii, and outlying areas]

Year [1]	Number of banks	Gross earnings	Expenses [2]	Net current earnings [2]	Net losses including depreciation (−) or net recoveries (+)	Net profits	Cash dividends declared	Net profits as percent of total capital accounts
	768	769	770	771	772	773	774	775
1970	4,621	20,434	17,542	2,892	−593	2,299	1,278	9.5
1969	4,669	18,221	15,565	2,656	−634	2,022	1,068	9.0
1968	4,716	14,998	12,218	2,779	−848	1,932	897	9.4
1967	4,758	12,651	10,375	2,276	−518	1,757	796	9.2
1966	4,799	11,305	9,099	2,207	−624	1,583	738	8.8
1965	4,815	9,705	7,836	1,870	−482	1,387	683	8.6
1964	4,773	8,148	6,536	1,612	−388	1,213	593	8.5
1963	4,615	7,302	5,917	1,386	−180	1,206	548	9.2
1962	4,503	6,596	5,304	1,292	−223	1,069	518	8.7
1961	4,513	5,955	4,751	1,203	−161	1,042	486	9.1
1960	4,530	5,756	4,450	1,305	−259	1,046	451	9.8
1959	4,542	5,183	3,845	1,338	−538	800	423	8.0
1958	4,585	4,539	3,660	878	+11	889	393	9.4
1957	4,627	4,284	3,252	1,031	−301	730	364	8.3
1956	4,659	3,833	2,768	1,065	−418	647	330	7.9
1955	4,700	3,437	2,551	885	−242	643	310	8.1
1954	4,796	3,226	2,528	699	+42	741	300	9.6
1953	4,864	3,068	2,310	758	−185	573	275	7.9
1952	4,916	2,751	2,067	684	−122	561	259	8.2
1951	4,946	2,454	1,812	642	−135	507	248	7.8
1950	4,965	2,193	1,593	600	−63	538	230	8.7
1949	4,981	2,005	1,442	563	−88	475	205	8.2
1948	4,997	1,900	1,361	540	−116	424	194	7.6
1947	5,011	1,725	1,263	461	−8	453	184	8.6
1946	4,013	1,574	1,138	436	+59	495	170	10.1
1945	5,023	1,349	987	362	+128	490	156	11.0
1944	5,031	1,206	846	360	+52	412	144	10.0
1943	5,046	1,062	746	315	+35	350	132	9.1
1942	5,087	963	695	268	−24	243	128	6.6
1941	5,123	926	642	284	−15	269	133	7.5
1940	5,150	865	599	265	−24	241	133	7.0
1939	5,193	848	581	267	−16	252	131	7.4
1938	5,230	838	577	261	−62	199	123	6.1
1937	5,266	859	586	273	−45	228	122	7.1
1936	5,331	825	565	260	+54	314	120	10.0
1935	5,392	794	549	245	−87	158	113	5.1
1934 [3]	5,467	809	558	251	−405	−153	91	−5.2
1933 [3]	5,159	802	565	236	−523	−286	72	−9.6
1932	6,016	1,000	750	250	−415	−165	135	−5.0
1931	6,373	1,153	850	303	−358	−55	193	−1.5
1930	7,038	1,325	990	336	−177	158	211	4.0
1929	7,408	1,407	988	418	−126	292	227	7.8
1928	7,635	1,351	988	363	−72	291	195	8.2
1927	7,765	1,227	919	308	−50	258	184	7.9
1926	7,912	1,212	857	354	−109	245	169	8.0
1925	8,054	1,160	823	338	−93	244	163	8.2
1924	8,049	1,094	776	318	−104	214	155	7.4
1923	8,184	1,065	758	307	−112	195	152	6.7
1922	8,225	1,043	717	326	−115	211	161	7.4
1921	8,169	1,121	775	347	−166	181	153	6.5
1920	8,130	1,211	817	393	−132	261	162	9.9
1919	7,890	993	671	322	−73	249	135	10.2
1918	7,705	814	510	304	−91	212	130	9.4
1917	7,604	667	411	257	−62	194	126	8.8
1916	7,579	591	371	220	−62	157	115	7.5
1915	7,605	528	322	206	−78	127	114	6.0
1914	7,525	516	301	214	−65	149	121	7.3
1913	7,473	499	285	215	−54	161	120	7.9
1912	7,372	450	259	191	−42	149	120	7.5
1911	7,277	429	232	197	−40	157	115	8.1
1910	7,145	403	210	193	−39	154	106	8.3
1909	6,926	349	177	172	−40	131	93	7.5
1908	6,824	332	151	182	−51	131	97	7.9
1907 [4]	6,429	315	132	183	−31	152	100	[5] 11.4
1906	6,053	279	120	159	−31	128	89	8.6
1905	5,668	249	112	136	−30	106	73	7.5
1904	5,331	249	103	146	−33	113	76	8.4
1903	4,939	235	93	141	−32	110	64	8.6
1902	4,535	221	85	136	−29	107	68	9.0
1901	4,165	188	78	111	−29	82	52	7.7
1900	3,732	194	73	121	−34	87	48	8.6
1899	3,583	157	68	88	−34	54	47	5.7
1898	3,582	143	62	81	−31	50	44	5.2
1897	3,610	138	61	77	−32	44	42	4.6
1896	3,689	142	61	81	−32	50	46	5.1
1895	3,715	135	60	75	−29	47	46	4.8
1894	3,770	140	60	80	−38	42	45	4.2
1893	3,807	152	61	91	−22	69	50	6.7
1892	3,759	149	59	90	−23	67	50	6.6
1891	3,652	151	55	96	−21	76	51	7.7
1890	3,484	145	51	93	−21	72	51	7.7
1889	3,239	135	50	86	−16	70	47	8.0
1888	3,120	129	45	84	−18	65	47	7.8

Year [1]	Number of banks	Net profits	Cash dividends declared	Net profits as percent of total capital accounts
	768	773	774	775
1887	3,014	65	44	8.0
1886	2,809	55	42	7.3
1885	2,689	44	41	6.0
1884	2,625	52	41	7.1
1883	2,417	54	41	7.6
1882	2,239	53	41	8.1
1881	2,115	54	38	8.4
1880	2,076	45	36	7.2
1879	2,048	32	35	5.1
1878	2,056	31	37	4.9
1877	2,078	35	44	5.3
1876	2,091	44	47	6.4
1875	2,076	58	49	8.4
1874	1,983	60	48	8.8
1873	1,968	65	50	9.8
1872	1,853	58	47	9.3
1871	1,723	55	44	9.2
1870	1,612	56	43	9.9
1869 [6]	1,619	29	22	10.7

[1] All data except number of banks are for calendar year, 1919–1970; year ending June 30, 1907–1918; and year ending Aug. 31, 1869–1906. Number of banks are as of end of period.

[2] Income taxes have been treated as an expense throughout. Beginning in 1943, these figures differ from those shown in the source volume, because income taxes in the source volume are shown separately from other expenses and as a deduction from net current earnings.

[3] Licensed banks, i.e., those operating on an unrestricted basis.
[4] 10 months only.
[5] Annual basis.
[6] 6 months only.

Series X 776–791. Insured Commercial Banks—Earnings and Expenses: 1934 to 1970

[In millions of dollars, except number of banks. Includes Alaska, Hawaii, and outlying areas]

Year	Number of banks	Earnings Total	On loans	On securities	Service charges, deposit accounts	Other [1]	Expenses Total	Salaries and wages [2]	Interest on time deposits	Other [1][2][3]	Net current earnings [4]	Net losses (−) or net recoveries (+)	Taxes on net income [3]	Net profits (after income taxes)	Cash dividends	Net profits as percent of capital accounts
	776	777	778	779	780	781	782	783	784	785	786	787	788	789	790	791
1970	13,511	34,716	[5] 23,973	6,539	1,178	3,025	27,789	6,657	10,484	10,648	7,128	[6] −117	[7] 2,174	4,837	2,040	11.76
1969	13,473	30,807	[5] 21,539	5,747	1,120	2,401	24,077	5,879	9,790	8,408	6,730	[6] −231	[7] 2,164	4,335	1,769	11.34
1968	13,488	25,478	16,723	5,381	1,056	2,318	19,354	5,102	8,682	5,571	6,124	−1,431	1,267	3,426	1,589	9.70
1967	13,517	21,782	14,351	4,507	987	1,936	16,554	4,538	7,380	4,636	5,228	−909	1,177	3,142	1,426	9.56
1966	13,541	19,508	13,043	3,849	915	1,701	14,562	4,096	6,2.9	4,207	4,947	−1,232	1,030	2,684	1,307	8.70
1965	13,547	16,817	11,000	3,510	843	1,465	12,486	3,762	5,071	3,653	4,331	−787	1,029	2,515	1,202	8.73
1964	13,493	15,024	9,612	3,326	781	1,305	10,897	3,519	4,088	3,290	4,127	−695	1,148	2,284	1,088	8.65
1963	13,291	13,510	8,517	3,098	729	1,167	9,715	3,284	3,464	2,966	3,795	−415	1,227	2,153	993	8.86
1962	13,124	12,219	7,578	2,852	681	1,107	8,589	3,074	2,845	2,670	3,630	−370	1,256	2,004	941	8.83
1961	13,115	11,070	6,891	2,531	630	1,017	7,440	2,899	2,107	2,435	3,629	−227	1,406	1,996	895	9.37
1960	13,126	10,724	6,699	2,369	590	1,066	6,933	2,854	1,785	2,293	3,791	−404	1,384	2,003	832	10.03
1959	13,114	9,669	5,857	2,278	532	1,002	6,264	2,629	1,580	2,055	3,405	−1,033	884	1,488	776	7.94
1958	13,124	8,501	5,047	2,046	487	922	5,613	2,449	1,381	1,783	2,888	+85	1,271	1,702	726	9.60
1957	13,165	8,050	4,880	1,855	441	875	5,119	2,313	1,142	1,665	2,931	−559	998	1,374	678	8.30
1956	13,218	7,232	4,340	1,713	386	793	4,457	2,136	806	1,516	2,775	−743	815	1,217	617	7.82
1955	13,237	6,378	3,626	1,685	340	727	3,960	1,935	678	1,346	2,418	−468	794	1,156	566	7.90
1954	13,323	5,774	3,206	1,598	312	659	3,638	1,799	618	1,221	2,136	+79	908	1,307	517	9.50
1953	13,432	5,484	3,108	1,505	271	600	3,376	1,687	534	1,154	2,108	−296	786	1,026	474	7.93
1952	13,439	4,932	2,742	1,376	245	569	3,029	1,526	458	1,044	1,903	−218	695	990	442	8.07
1951	13,455	4,395	2,390	1,233	231	542	2,701	1,378	385	938	1,694	−226	559	908	419	7.82
1950	13,446	3,931	1,976	1,241	212	501	2,445	1,226	343	875	1,486	−121	428	937	391	8.51
1949	13,436	3,607	1,734	1,215	194	464	2,284	1,133	328	822	1,323	−167	325	831	354	7.98
1948	13,419	3,404	1,578	1,198	174	454	2,164	1,065	317	782	1,240	−219	275	745	332	7.49
1947	13,403	3,098	1,264	1,259	148	427	1,982	966	298	717	1,116	−32	302	781	315	8.20
1946	13,359	2,863	937	1,395	125	406	1,763	848	269	646	1,100	+125	323	902	299	10.01
1945	13,302	2,482	708	1,300	110	365	1,523	706	233	584	960	+245	299	906	274	10.87
1944	13,268	2,215	681	1,090	107	337	1,357	640	187	530	858	+96	203	751	253	9.73
1943	13,274	1,959	692	861	95	310	1,256	594	164	498	703	+62	128	638	233	8.82
1942	13,347	1,791	805	610	84	291	1,222	564	175	483	569	−48	80	441	228	6.34
1941	13,427	1,730	848	509		373	1,266	527	190	549	464	−10	--------	455	253	6.72
1940	13,438	1,631	769	500		363	1,193	498	201	495	438	−37	--------	401	237	6.01
1939	13,534	1,606	727	522		357	1,160	484	215	461	446	−57	--------	389	232	5.96
1938	13,657	1,584	705	532		347	1,159	474	230	455	425	−125	--------	300	222	4.67
1937	13,795	1,634	710	572		352	1,167	463	235	468	467	−86	--------	381	226	5.94
1936	13,969	1,567	663	574		330	1,126	437	237	451	441	+83	--------	524	223	8.28
1935	14,123	1,486	643	548		295	1,083	411	262	410	403	−196	--------	207	208	3.34
1934	14,137	1,518	691	550	35	243	1,117	402	303	413	401	−741	--------	−340	188	−5.49

[1] Beginning 1961, rentals from bank premises are excluded from "other" earnings and are netted against "other" expenses. [2] Beginning 1961, "other" expenses includes fees paid to directors and committees, formerly included with "salaries and wages." [3] Prior to 1942, taxes on net income have been included with other expenses. Taxes on net income for insured nonmember commercial banks for 1936–1941 are available separately in *Annual Reports* of the Federal Deposit Insurance Corporation.

[4] Prior to 1942, represents net current earnings after deduction of income taxes; thereafter, net current earnings before deduction of income taxes, and beginning 1969, net current earnings before deduction of income taxes and securities gains or losses. See footnote 3. [5] Includes income on Federal funds sold. [6] Net amounts after applicable taxes. [7] Estimated taxes applicable to operating earnings.

Series X 792–795. Bank Clearings at Principal Cities: 1854 to 1970

[In millions of dollars]

Year	New York City (792)	36 cities outside New York City [1][2] (793)
1970	3,745,829	1,359,988
1969	3,299,192	1,287,987
1968	2,427,539	1,149,108
1967	1,831,058	1,064,203
1966	1,507,370	1,010,183
1965	1,280,406	933,673
1964	1,091,636	840,326
1963	970,985	753,781
1962	883,586	734,208
1961	813,738	692,032
1960	738,604	665,194
1959	668,461	649,098
1958	623,611	591,603
1957	581,450	599,274
1956	559,157	569,265
1955	530,883	547,675
1954	532,029	500,884
1953	470,289	492,594
1952	461,724	470,403
1951	431,775	455,621
1950	399,309	403,905
1949	358,845	356,111
1948	371,554	374,727
1947	361,238	338,537
1946	366,065	298,129

Year	Total, United States (794)	New York City (792)	Outside New York City (795)	36 cities outside New York City [1] (793)
1945	----------	334,433	----------	260,331
1944	----------	286,349	----------	249,685
1943	----------	248,560	----------	234,757
1942	----------	192,939	----------	201,060
1941	----------	183,263	----------	172,272
1940	----------	160,878	----------	135,789
1939	----------	165,914	----------	124,286
1938	----------	165,156	----------	114,054
1937	----------	186,740	----------	130,340
1936	----------	193,549	----------	120,054
1935	300,913	181,551	119,362	103,948
1934	264,268	161,507	102,761	89,940
1933	243,891	157,414	86,477	75,301
1932	258,523	160,138	98,385	85,625
1931	411,754	263,270	148,484	129,855
1930	544,542	347,110	197,433	173,045
1929	715,692	477,242	238,450	208,914
1928	623,366	391,727	231,638	201,727
1927	544,414	321,234	223,180	195,124
1926	512,567	290,355	222,212	194,271
1925	500,354	283,619	216,734	190,358
1924	445,747	249,868	195,878	171,736
1923	404,512	213,996	190,515	166,092
1922	384,977	217,900	167,076	145,730
1921	349,757	194,331	155,426	135,699
1920	439,792	243,135	196,657	177,044

Year	Total, United States (794)	New York City (792)	Outside New York City (795)
1919	387,854	214,703	173,151
1918	320,989	174,524	146,464
1917	305,062	181,534	123,528
1916	242,236	147,181	95,055
1915	163,189	90,843	72,347
1914	163,850	89,760	74,089
1913	173,193	98,122	75,071
1912	168,686	96,672	72,014
1911	159,540	92,420	67,119
1910	168,987	102,554	66,433
1909	158,877	99,258	59,620
1908	126,239	73,631	52,608
1907	154,477	95,315	59,161
1906	157,681	103,754	53,927
1905	140,502	91,879	48,623
1904	102,356	59,673	42,684
1903	113,963	70,834	43,130
1902	115,892	74,753	41,139
1901	114,820	77,021	37,799
1900	84,582	51,965	32,618
1899	88,829	57,368	31,461
1898	65,925	39,853	26,072
1897	54,180	31,338	22,842
1896	51,936	29,351	22,585

See footnotes at end of table.

Series X 792–795. Bank Clearings at Principal Cities: 1854 to 1970—Con.

[In millions of dollars]

Year	Total, United States [794]	New York City [792]	Outside New York City [795]	Year	Total, United States [794]	New York City [792]	Outside New York City [795]	Year	New York City [792]	Year	New York City [792]	Year	New York City [792]	Year	New York City [792]
1895	50,975	28,264	22,711	1887	52,127	34,873	17,254	1880	37,182	1872	33,844	1865	26,032	1859	6,448
1894	45,028	24,230	20,798	1886	48,212	33,375	14,837	1879	25,179	1871	29,301	1864	24,097	1858	4,757
1893	58,881	34,421	24,460	1885	37,770	25,251	12,519	1878	22,508	1870	27,805	1863	14,868	1857	8,333
1892	60,884	36,280	24,604	1884	47,387	34,092	13,295	1877	23,289	1869	37,407			1862	6,871	1856	6,906
1891	57,181	34,054	23,127	1883	53,536	40,293	13,243	1876	21,597	1868	28,484	1861	5,916	1855	5,363
1890	59,882	37,661	22,221	1882	61,054	46,553	14,501	1875	25,061	1867	28,675	1860	7,231	1854	5,750
1889	53,501	34,796	18,705	1881	--------	48,566	--------	1874	22,856	1866	28,717				
1888	48,751	30,864	17,887					1873	35,461						

[1] Excludes Los Angeles.   [2] Beginning 1963, figures are for New York City and 25 other cities.

Series X 796–805. Federal Reserve Banks—Principal Assets and Liabilities: 1914 to 1970

[In millions of dollars. As of December 31]

Year	Reserves, total [796]	Total loans and securities [1] [797]	Discounts and advances [798]	Bills bought [799]	U.S. Government securities [800]	Total assets or liabilities and capital accounts [801]	Deposits, Total [802]	Member bank reserve account [803]	Federal Reserve notes in actual circulation [2] [804]	Capital accounts [805]
1970	10,457	62,534	335	57	62,142	85,913	26,687	24,150	50,323	1,404
1969	10,036	57,401	183	64	[3] 57,154	80,854	24,338	22,085	47,473	1,338
1968	10,026	53,183	188	58	52,937	75,885	23,484	21,818	44,726	1,260
1967	11,481	49,455	141	164	49,150	72,026	22,920	20,999	41,642	1,196
1966	12,674	44,682	173	193	44,316	67,043	20,957	19,779	39,339	1,140
1965	13,436	41,092	137	187	40,768	62,652	19,620	18,447	37,074	1,102
1964	15,075	37,324	186	94	37,044	60,389	19,456	18,086	34,659	1,048
1963	15,237	33,818	63	162	33,593	56,176	18,391	17,049	32,381	1,487
1962	15,696	30,968	38	110	30,820	53,931	18,722	17,454	30,151	1,401
1961	16,615	29,062	130	51	28,881	52,470	18,451	17,387	28,802	1,333
1960	17,479	27,491	33	74	27,384	50,859	18,316	17,081	27,924	1,226
1959	19,164	27,181	458	75	26,648	54,028	19,716	18,174	28,262	1,174
1958	19,951	26,460	64	49	26,347	53,095	19,526	18,504	27,872	1,341
1957	22,085	24,360	55	66	24,238	53,028	20,117	19,034	27,535	1,291
1956	21,269	25,034	50	69	24,915	52,910	20,249	19,059	27,476	1,209
1955	21,009	24,921	108	28	24,785	52,340	20,355	19,005	26,921	1,132
1954	21,033	25,076	143	--------	24,932	50,872	20,371	18,876	26,253	1,084
1953	21,354	25,945	28	--------	25,916	52,315	21,422	20,160	26,558	1,025
1952	21,986	24,857	156	--------	24,697	51,852	21,344	19,950	26,250	972
1951	21,468	23,825	19	--------	23,801	49,900	21,192	20,056	25,064	909
1950	21,458	20,848	67	--------	20,778	47,172	19,810	17,681	23,587	869
1949	23,176	18,965	78	--------	18,885	45,643	18,906	16,568	23,483	832
1948	22,966	23,556	223	--------	23,333	50,043	22,791	20,479	24,161	761
1947	21,497	22,646	85	--------	22,559	47,712	19,731	17,899	24,820	696
1946	18,381	23,513	163	--------	23,350	45,006	17,353	16,139	24,945	678
1945	17,863	24,513	249	--------	[4] 24,262	45,063	18,200	15,915	24,649	587
1944	18,687	18,930	80	--------	[4] 18,846	40,269	16,411	14,373	21,731	486
1943	20,096	11,558	5	--------	[4] 11,543	33,955	15,181	12,886	16,906	429
1942	20,908	6,208	6	--------	[4] 6,189	29,019	15,194	13,117	12,193	381
1941	20,764	2,267	3	--------	[4] 2,254	24,353	14,678	12,450	8,192	373
1940	20,036	2,195	3	--------	[4] 2,184	23,262	16,127	14,026	5,931	369
1939	15,524	2,502	7	--------	[4] 2,484	19,027	12,941	11,653	4,959	349
1938	12,166	2,584	4	1	2,564	15,581	10,088	8,724	4,452	344
1937	9,481	2,592	10	1	2,564	12,880	7,577	7,027	4,284	341
1936	9,121	2,461	3	3	2,430	12,525	7,109	6,606	4,284	341
1935	7,835	2,473	5	5	2,431	11,026	6,386	5,587	3,709	335
1934	5,401	2,457	7	6	2,430	8,442	4,405	4,096	3,221	331
1933	3,794	2,670	98	133	2,437	7,041	2,865	2,729	3,080	445
1932	3,331	2,128	235	33	1,855	6,115	2,561	2,509	2,739	430
1931	3,158	1,825	638	339	817	5,672	2,125	1,961	2,624	420
1930	3,082	1,352	251	364	729	5,201	2,517	2,471	1,664	444
1929	3,011	1,548	632	392	511	5,458	2,414	2,355	1,910	448
1928	2,709	1,783	1,056	489	228	5,352	2,440	2,389	1,838	401
1927	2,867	1,591	582	392	617	5,346	2,531	2,487	1,790	366
1926	2,948	1,335	637	381	315	5,150	2,276	2,194	1,851	354
1925	2,824	1,395	643	374	375	5,109	2,257	2,212	1,838	338
1924	3,047	1,249	320	387	540	5,096	2,311	2,220	1,862	330
1923	3,169	1,211	723	355	134	5,066	1,960	1,898	2,247	331
1922	3,166	1,326	618	272	436	5,252	1,974	1,934	2,396	326
1921	3,010	1,524	1,144	145	234	5,151	1,876	1,753	2,409	319
1920	2,250	3,235	2,687	260	287	6,254	1,861	1,781	3,336	302
1919	1,990	3,090	2,215	574	300	6,324	2,022	1,890	3,009	208
1918	2,146	2,291	1,766	287	239	5,250	1,808	1,636	2,659	104
1917	1,672	1,060	660	273	122	3,164	1,583	1,447	1,247	71
1916	757	222	29	129	55	1,211	[5] 879	[5] 722	275	56
1915	555	84	32	24	16	697	[5] 452	[5] 401	189	55
1914	268	11	10	--------	--------	330	[5] 301	[5] 265	11	18

[1] 1914–1959, includes industrial advances not shown separately.
[2] Includes Federal Reserve notes held by the U.S. Treasury or by a Federal Reserve bank other than the issuing bank.
[3] Includes securities loaned—fully secured by U.S. Government securities pledged with Federal Reserve banks.
[4] Includes guaranteed obligations which were not issued until late in 1933. Reserve banks were first authorized to purchase them in 1934. The only holdings of such securities prior to 1939 were $181,000 at the end of 1935, which were included in "other securities."
[5] Figures not comparable with later years in part because prior to June 21, 1917, member banks were not required to keep all of their legal reserves with the Reserve banks; also, for 1914–1916, deferred availability accounts, subsequently shown separately in the source, are included in total deposits.

Series X 806–812. Federal Reserve Banks—Earnings and Expenses: 1914 to 1970

[In thousands of dollars]

Year	Current earnings	Current expenses	Net earnings before payments to U.S. Treasury [1]	Disposition of net earnings				Year	Current earnings	Current expenses	Net earnings before payments to U.S. Treasury [1]	Disposition of net earnings			
				Divi-dends paid	Franchise tax paid to U.S. Treasury [2]	Paid to U.S. Treasury [3]	Trans-ferred to surplus					Divi-dends paid	Franchise tax paid to U.S. Treasury [2]	Paid to U.S. Treasury [3]	Trans-ferred to surplus
	806	807	808	809	810	811	812		806	807	808	809	810	811	812
1970	3,877,218	321,373	3,567,287	41,137	3,493,571		32,580	1940	43,538	29,165	25,860	8,215		82	17,563
1969	3,373,361	274,973	3,097,830	39,237	3,019,161		39,432	1939	38,501	28,647	12,243	8,110		25	4,108
1968	2,764,446	242,350	2,530,616	36,959	2,463,629		30,027	1938	36,261	28,912	9,582	8,019		120	1,443
1967	2,190,404	220,121	1,972,377	35,027	1,907,498		29,851	1937	41,233	28,801	10,801	7,941		177	2,684
1966	1,908,500	207,401	1,702,095	33,696	1,649,455		18,944	1936	37,901	29,874	8,512	7,830		227	455
1965	1,559,484	204,290	1,356,215	32,352	1,296,810		27,054	1935	42,752	31,577	9,438	8,505			635
1964	1,343,747	197,396	1,147,077	30,782	1,582,119		−465,823	1934	48,903	29,241	15,231	8,782			6,450
1963	1,151,120	187,273	964,462	28,912	879,685		55,864	1933	49,487	29,223	7,957	8,874			−917
1962	1,048,508	176,136	872,316	27,412	799,366		45,588	1932	50,019	26,291	22,314	9,282	2,011		11,021
1961	941,648	161,275	783,855	25,570	687,393		70,892	1931	29,701	27,041	2,972	10,030			−7,058
1960	1,103,385	153,882	963,378	23,948	896,816		42,613	1930	36,424	28,343	7,988	10,269	17		−2,298
1959	886,226	144,750	839,771	22,722	910,650		−93,601	1929	70,955	29,691	36,403	9,584	4,283		22,536
1958	742,068	137,722	604,471	21,197	524,059		59,215	1928	64,053	26,905	32,122	8,458	2,585		21,079
1957	763,348	131,814	624,393	20,081	542,708		61,603	1927	43,024	27,518	13,048	7,755	250		5,044
1956	595,649	121,182	474,443	18,905	401,556		53,983	1926	47,600	27,350	16,612	7,329	818		8,464
1955	412,488	110,060	302,162	17,712	251,741		32,710	1925	41,801	27,528	9,449	6,916	59		2,474
1954	438,486	109,733	328,619	16,442	276,289		35,888	1924	38,340	28,431	3,718	6,682	114		−3,078
1953	513,037	113,515	398,463	15,558	342,568		40,337	1923	50,709	29,764	12,711	6,553	3,613		2,546
1952	456,060	104,694	352,950	14,682	291,935		46,334	1922	50,499	29,559	16,498	6,307	10,851		−660
1951	394,656	95,469	297,059	13,865	254,874		28,321	1921	122,866	34,464	82,087	6,120	59,974		15,993
1950	275,839	80,572	231,561	13,083	196,629		21,849	1920	181,297	28,258	149,295	5,654	60,725		82,916
1949	316,537	77,478	226,937	12,329	193,146		21,462	1919	102,381	19,340	78,368	5,012	2,704		70,652
1948	304,161	72,710	197,133	11,920	166,690		18,523	1918	67,584	10,960	52,716	5,541			48,334
1947	158,656	65,393	95,236	11,523	75,224	36	8,453	1917	16,128	5,160	9,582	6,804	1,134		1,134
1946	150,385	57,235	92,524	10,962		67	81,495	1916	5,218	2,274	2,751	1,743			
1945	142,210	48,717	92,662	10,183		248	82,232	1915 }	2,173	2,321	−141	217			
1944	104,392	49,176	58,438	9,500		327	48,611	1914 }							
1943	69,306	43,546	49,528	8,911		245	40,372								
1942	52,663	38,624	12,470	8,669		198	3,604								
1941	41,380	32,963	9,138	8,430		141	566								

[1] Current earnings less current expenses plus other additions and less other deductions.
[2] The Banking Act of 1933 eliminated the provision in the Federal Reserve Act requiring payments of a franchise tax. Beginning in 1947, payments represent interest on Federal Reserve notes; see text.
[3] Payments made pursuant to section 13b of the Federal Reserve Act, relating to loans and discounts for industrial purposes provided for by act of June 19, 1934.

Series X 813–820. Federal Reserve Banks—Member Bank Reserve Requirements: 1917 to 1970

[Percent of deposits. Heavy rules indicate break in series]

Effective date of change [1]	Net demand deposits [2][3]					Time deposits [3][4] (all member banks)			Effective date of change [1]	Net demand deposits [2][3]			Time depo-sits [3][4]
	Central reserve city banks	Reserve city banks		Country banks		Savings deposits	Other time deposits			Central reserve city banks	Reserve city banks	Country banks	
		Under $5 million	Over $5 million	Under $5 million	Over $5 million		Under $5 million	Over $5 million					
	813	814	815	816	817	818	819	820		813	814–815	816–817	818–820
In effect Dec. 31, 1970		17	17½	12½	13	3	3	5	1949—Sept. 1	22	18		
1970—Oct. 1								5	Aug. 25	22½	18½		
1969—Apr. 17		17	17½	12½	13				Aug. 18	23	19		
1968—Jan. 11, 18		16½	17	12	12½				Aug. 11, 16	23½	19½	12	5
									Aug. 1			13	
									June 30, July 1		20	14	6
1967—Mar. 16 Mar. 2						3	3		May 5, 1	24	21	15	7
1966—Sept. 8, 15						3½	3½	6	1948—Sept. 24, 16	26	22	16	7½
July 14, 21								5	June 11	24			
									Feb. 27	22			
1962—Oct. 25, Nov. 1								4	1942—Oct. 3	20			
									Sept. 14	22			
July 28	(5)								Aug. 20	24			
1960—Dec. 1	16½												
Nov. 24				12					1941—Nov. 1	26	20	14	6
Sept. 1	17½								1938—Apr. 16	22¾	17½	12	5
									1937—May 1	26	20	14	6
1958—Apr. 24	18	16½							Mar. 1	22¾	17½	12¼	5¼
1954—July 29, Aug. 1	20	18		12									
June 24, 16	21							5	1936—Aug. 16	19½	15	10½	4½
									1917—June 21	13	10	7	3
1953—July 9, 1	22	19		13									
1951—Jan. 25, Feb. 1	24	20		14									
Jan. 11, 16	23	19		13				6					

[1] When two dates are shown, the first applies to the change at central reserve or reserve city banks and the second to the change at country banks.
[2] For definition of net demand deposits, see text.
[3] Beginning October 16, 1969, member banks were required to maintain reserves at 10 percent against balances above a specified base due from domestic offices to their foreign branches.
[4] Effective January 5, 1967, time deposits such as Christmas and vacation club accounts became subject to same requirements as savings deposits.
[5] Authority of the Board of Governors to classify or reclassify cities as central reserve cities was terminated effective July 28, 1962.

Nonbank Financial Institutions (Series X 821-878)

X 821–878. General note.

Financial institutions other than commercial banks perform a role in credit and capital markets by mobilizing the savings of individuals and channeling these funds among various types of investments. As a result, the flow of savings to these institutions and the allocation of these funds to various investments are important determinants of interest rates and prices of securities.

X 821–833. Assets and liabilities of mutual savings banks, 1896–1970.

Source: Board of Governors of the Federal Reserve System. 1896–1944, *All-Bank Statistics*, 1959, table A-4; 1945–1962, *Supplement to Banking & Monetary Statistics*, section 12, "Money Rates and Securities Markets," table 26; 1963–1970, *Federal Reserve Bulletin*, March 1973, p. A39.

Mutual savings banks are mutual thrift institutions chartered by individual States, primarily those in the northeastern part of the United States. They have no capital stock or stockholders. Incorporators provide initial guaranty and expense funds, and under stated conditions these funds may be returned to them out of subsequent earnings. Most deposits in mutual savings banks take the form of passbook savings. After expenses of operations are paid, all earnings are either distributed as interest to depositors or added to reserves (surplus).

Data for 1930 and earlier years are from the Board of Governors of the Federal Reserve System. For 1931–1945, figures were obtained by the National Association of Mutual Savings Banks from State banking departments and directly from some individual savings banks. Reporting procedures for State banking departments were not completely uniform in this period and differed in some respects from those prescribed by the Federal Deposit Insurance Corporation. Beginning 1946, the data were collected by the National Association directly from individual savings banks and generally conform to FDIC reporting procedures.

X 834–844. Selected assets and liabilities of savings and loan associations, 1900–1970.

Source: U.S. Savings and Loan League, *Savings and Loan Fact Book, 1967*, p. 70; *1971*, p. 79; and *1972*, pp. 95 and 97.

Savings and loan associations—also known as cooperative banks, building and loan associations, and savings associations—are thrift associations chartered by individual States or by the U.S. Government.

Figures were compiled from the following sources: 1900–1933, U.S. Savings and Loan League, Chicago, Ill.; for insured associations, 1934–1949, annual supervisory reports; 1950–1970, monthly supervisory reports; and for uninsured associations, 1932–1970, annual supervisory reports. Resources of associations in liquidation are not included.

X 845–849. Postal Savings System, 1911–1967.

Source: U.S. Post Office Department, *Annual Report of the Postmaster General, 1957* and *1969*, and unpublished data.

The Postal Savings System was discontinued April 27, 1966, and the accounts were eliminated after June 30, 1967.

X 850–863. Outstanding loans and loan insurance or guarantees of Federal and federally sponsored agencies, by economic sector served, 1917–1953.

Source: R. J. Saulnier, Harold G. Halcrow, and Neil H. Jacoby, *Federal Lending and Loan Insurance*, Princeton University Press, 1958, appendix A, pp. 365–380 (copyright).

These series are combinations of data shown separately in the source volume for Federal and federally sponsored agencies. That volume shows amount extended during the year as well as amount outstanding. The economic sectors shown here are the major sectors shown in the source volume and an "other" group which combines minor governmental units and miscellaneous sectors. The coverage and classification are described in the source, chapter I, pp. 3–27, the footnote on pp. 28–29, and footnotes of tables Al to A8. The following paragraphs are adapted from that text.

Federally sponsored agencies include all those having a special financial or administrative connection with the Federal Government, whether or not Federal funds were currently invested in them. Thus, they include agencies that were in some respects private or cooperative in ownership and organization but that operated in part with Federal funds; and agencies that, although no longer using Treasury funds, were specially connected with some Federal agency through the latter's power to appoint policymaking officers and in some cases to review policy decisions.

The Federal agencies represented under the various categories of loans, insurance or guarantees, and stock purchases are summarized in the source in footnotes to the economic sector tables (pp. 365–380) and are shown in greater detail in the source tables covering individual agencies (pp. 381–418). For example, among agencies making direct loans to the business sector were the Export-Import Bank of Washington, the Departments of Army and Navy, the Public Works Administration, the War Finance Corporation, the Reconstruction Finance Corporation, and the Smaller War Plants Corporation. Federal Reserve bank loans and participations in loans of private financing institutions to business under section 13b of the Federal Reserve Act were also included. Guarantees of loans to the business sector included guarantees by the Veterans Administration and by Federal agencies under Regulation V of the Board of Governors of the Federal Reserve System, as well as deferred participation commitments of the Reconstruction Finance Corporation.

Credit programs not covered by the tabulation shown here include loans to foreign governments (except the Export-Import Bank), direct and guaranteed loans by the Commodity Credit Corporation, and loans to State governments. Loans of the Export-Import Bank of Washington which could not be fully separated from lending to foreign concerns and to domestic concerns engaged in foreign trade were included in the business sector.

Outstanding amounts relate to three basic categories of Federal credit activities.

X 850–855, direct loans. These include (*a*) the full amounts of loans extended by specified Federal and federally sponsored agencies; (*b*) the amounts disbursed to private lenders by Federal agencies in purchasing outstanding loans made under Federal insurance or guarantee; and (*c*) the amounts disbursed on loans made in participation with private lenders.

Loans exclude credit extended incident to some other activity, as when the U.S. Commercial Company gave open book credit during

World War II in connection with its sales of commodities, and also grant-in-aid programs. Loans made indirectly—as when the Federal intermediate credit banks discount paper for production credit associations, enabling the latter to make loans to farmers—are included, as well as loans going directly to the ultimate borrower; but there is no double counting that would result from interagency loans.

X 856–860, loan insurance or guarantees. Loan insurance covers the full amounts of loans extended by private lenders and insured by Federal agencies. Loan guarantees cover (a) the amounts federally guaranteed, ranging from 100 percent to seldom lower than 50 percent of a privately made loan; and (b) the amounts of the Federal shares authorized under deferred participations, where the Government was ready to take up an agreed percentage of a privately made loan. Thus, credit actually extended under participation agreements with private lenders is included under direct loans; but during the time when there was merely a commitment outstanding to take up all or some part of a loan at the option of the private lender, the amount of the obligation is included as a loan guarantee.

X 861–863, stock purchases. Such purchases are included if identifiable as primarily credit aid, and they covered the amount of Federal funds invested. Stock purchases represent purchases of, and loans on, preferred stocks of banks and insurance companies, and purchases of capital notes and debentures of banks, by the Reconstruction Finance Corporation; purchases of shares of savings and loan associations by the Home Owners' Loan Corporation and the Treasury Department; purchases of stock of agricultural cooperative

associations by the Tennessee Valley Associated Cooperatives, Inc.; and purchases of Class A stock of production credit associations by the production credit corporations.

X 864–878. Federal and State-chartered credit unions—number, members, savings, loans, and total assets, 1925–1970.

Source: U.S. National Credit Union Administration, *1970 Annual Report of the National Credit Union Administration*, and the *1970 State-Chartered Credit Union Annual Report*.

Early data on operations of credit unions are available in U.S. Bureau of Labor Statistics, *Monthly Labor Review*, 1936–1953 (usually in the latter part of the year), and in BLS Bulletin Nos. 797, 850, 894, and 922.

Data for Federal credit unions, which were authorized by legislation enacted in 1934, represent all operating unions. Data on State-chartered credit unions have been furnished annually by State officials charged with the supervision of such credit unions, to the National Credit Union Administration (formerly Bureau of Federal Credit Unions) since 1951, and to the Bureau of Labor Statistics prior to 1951. Figures for State credit unions represent reporting unions which, in recent years, have included more than 99 percent of all active unions; prior to 1939, the proportion reporting was about 80 percent.

Loans of credit unions (series X 873–875) are principally short-term consumer loans, but they include some real estate mortgage loans and a small amount of business loans.

★ ★ ★ ★ ★ ★ ★ ★ ★ **More Recent Data for *Historical Statistics* Series** ★ ★ ★ ★ ★ ★ ★ ★ ★

Statistics for more recent years in continuation of many of the still-active series shown here appear in annual issues of the *Statistical Abstract of the United States*, beginning with the 1975 edition. For direct linkage of the historical series to the tables in the *Abstract*, see Appendix I in the *Abstract*.

Series X 821–833. Assets and Liabilities of Mutual Savings Banks: 1896 to 1970

[In millions of dollars. 1896–1944, as of June 30 or nearest available date; thereafter, as of end of year]

Year	Total assets or liabilities	Loans			Securities				Cash	Other	Deposits	Other	General reserve accounts
		Total	Mortgage	Other	Total	U.S. Government	State and local government	Corporate and other					
	821	822	823	824	825	826	827	828	829	830	831	832	833
1970	78,995	60,030	57,775	2,255	16,224	3,151	197	12,876	1,270	1,471	71,580	1,690	5,726
1969	74,144	57,605	55,781	1,824	14,320	3,296	200	10,824	912	1,307	67,026	1,588	5,530
1968	71,152	54,693	53,286	1,407	14,208	3,834	194	10,180	996	1,256	64,507	1,372	5,273
1967	66,365	51,514	50,311	1,203	12,721	4,319	219	8,183	993	1,138	60,121	1,260	4,984
1966	60,982	48,271	47,193	1,078	10,734	4,764	251	5,719	953	1,024	55,006	1,114	4,863
1965	58,232	45,295	44,433	862	10,975	5,485	320	5,170	1,017	944	52,443	1,124	4,665
1964	54,238	41,067	40,328	739	11,281	5,791	391	5,099	1,004	886	48,849	989	4,400
1963	49,702	36,614	36,007	607	11,377	5,863	440	5,074	912	799	44,606	943	4,153
1962	46,121	32,658	32,056	602	11,811	6,107	527	5,177	956	695	41,336	828	3,957
1961	42,829	29,377	28,902	475	11,877	6,160	677	5,040	937	640	38,277	781	3,771
1960	40,571	27,118	26,702	416	11,991	6,243	672	5,076	874	589	36,343	678	3,550
1959	38,945	25,127	24,769	358	12,437	6,871	721	4,845	829	552	34,977	606	3,362
1958	37,784	23,358	23,038	320	12,970	7,270	729	4,971	921	535	34,031	526	3,227
1957	35,215	21,224	20,971	253	12,612	7,583	685	4,344	889	490	31,684	427	3,105
1956	33,381	19,807	19,559	248	12,206	7,982	676	3,548	920	448	30,026	369	2,986
1955	31,346	17,490	17,279	211	12,473	8,463	646	3,364	966	416	28,182	310	2,854
1954	29,350	15,033	14,845	188	12,911	8,755	608	3,548	1,026	380	26,351	261	2,738
1953	27,199	12,957	12,792	165	12,930	9,191	428	3,311	983	330	24,388	203	2,608
1952	25,301	11,375	11,231	144	12,703	9,443	335	2,925	917	304	22,610	164	2,527
1951	23,504	9,876	9,747	129	12,457	9,827	140	2,490	883	288	20,900	153	2,450
1950	22,446	8,166	8,039	127	13,233	10,877	2,356		792	255	20,025	137	2,283
1949	21,503	6,585	6,479	106	13,812	11,444	2,368		872	233	19,287	94	2,121
1948	20,482	5,689	5,583	106	13,692	11,509	2,183		877	223	18,400	80	2,002
1947	19,724	4,950	4,856	94	13,680	11,984	1,696		881	213	17,759	71	1,894
1946	18,662	4,526	4,451	75	13,118	11,745	1,373		815	203	16,813	61	1,788
1945	16,962	4,264	4,202	62	11,849	10,650	1,199		606	243	15,332	48	1,582
1944	13,810	4,405	4,351	54	8,545	7,294	156	1,095	533	327	12,449	39	1,322
1943	12,407	4,575	4,522	53	6,654	5,279	234	1,141	720	458	11,122	41	1,244
1942	11,655	4,815	4,743	72	5,522	3,880	388	1,254	751	567	10,372	37	1,246
1941	11,969	4,949	4,858	91	5,348	3,420	536	1,392	966	706	10,624	35	1,310
1940	11,925	4,917	4,835	82	5,247	3,108	551	1,588	977	784	10,608	25	1,292
1939	11,771	4,889	4,812	77	5,336	3,040	647	1,649	697	849	10,409	22	1,340
1938	11,545	4,905	4,826	79	5,158	2,680	704	1,774	575	907	10,186	22	1,337
1937	11,496	4,965	4,884	81	5,074	2,350	793	1,931	527	930	10,141	18	1,337
1936	11,283	5,040	4,956	84	4,780	2,049	773	1,958	541	922	9,950	20	1,313
1935	11,046	5,289	5,196	93	4,441	1,538	866	2,037	520	796	9,809	24	1,213
1934	10,938	5,590	5,480	110	4,190	984	896	2,310	511	647	9,670	27	1,241
1933	10,848	5,880	5,752	128	4,047	733	911	2,403	425	496	9,606	44	1,198
1932	10,991	6,071	5,903	168	4,129	687	957	2,485	437	354	9,911	39	1,041
1931	11,052	6,108	5,869	239	4,287	590	1,038	2,659	388	269	9,910	17	1,125
1930	10,164	5,947	5,635	312	3,697	499	920	2,278	291	229	9,099	12	1,053
1929	9,873	5,830	5,483	347	3,621	604	905	2,112	219	203	8,884	18	971
1928	9,557	5,458	5,171	287	3,681	738	900	2,043	238	180	8,555	16	986
1927	8,920	5,017	4,760	257	3,484	852	827	1,805	255	164	7,996	15	909
1926	8,298	4,574	4,325	249	3,337	970	758	1,609	238	149	7,465	13	820
1925	7,831	4,155	3,923	232	3,302	1,076	709	1,517	240	134	7,071	12	748
1924	7,284	3,753	3,529	224	3,164	1,122	677	1,365	247	120	6,618	13	653
1923	6,812	3,337	3,086	251	3,150	1,112	670	1,368	218	107	6,202	12	598
1922	6,262	2,961	2,715	246	2,968	971	697	1,300	228	105	5,695	12	555
1921	5,964	2,850	2,502	348	2,809	939	680	1,190	209	96	5,503	12	449
1920	5,586	2,627	2,291	336	2,646	783	650	1,213	225	88	5,157	9	420
1919	5,141	2,318	2,100	218	2,503	561	748	1,194	225	95	4,728	18	395
1918	4,745	2,292	2,094	198	2,131	200	783	1,148	224	98	4,353	21	371
1917	4,739	2,321	2,109	212	2,089	50	864	1,175	240	89	4,355	8	376
1916	4,480	2,196	1,986	210	1,963	14	851	1,098	237	84	4,124	5	351
1915	4,257	2,143	1,916	227	1,825	11	813	1,001	208	81	3,893	8	356
1914	4,194	2,085	1,866	219	1,840	12	842	986	196	73	3,859	2	333
1913	4,047	2,001	1,780	221	1,803	12	804	987	172	71	3,715	5	327
1912	3,877	1,885	1,677	208	1,764	13	750	1,001	167	61	3,558	4	315
1911	3,706	1,773	1,570	203	1,705	12	759	934	170	58	3,407	8	291
1910	3,598	1,694	1,500	194	1,684	13	765	906	156	64	3,306	2	290
1909	3,344	1,533	1,349	184	1,593	14	719	860	159	59	3,094	1	249
1908	3,281	1,519	1,326	193	1,544	16	682	846	158	60	3,016	2	263
1907	3,252	1,509	1,282	227	1,540	20	684	836	142	61	3,032	2	218
1906	3,139	1,429	1,202	227	1,517	22	694	801	133	60	2,911	3	225
1905	2,969	1,320	1,121	199	1,452	30	673	749	134	63	2,744	3	222
1904	2,814	1,246	1,049	197	1,370	38	657	675	135	63	2,602	3	209
1903	2,711	1,205	999	206	1,325	46	652	627	122	59	2,505	1	205
1902	2,599	1,143	948	195	1,277	62	624	591	124	55	2,390	2	207
1901	2,466	1,080	901	179	1,215	78	595	542	125	46	2,261	2	203
1900	2,328	1,027	858	169	1,134	105	567	462	121	46	2,129	2	197
1899	2,190	971	815	156	1,047	139	561	347	117	55	2,000	2	188
1898	2,048	915	777	138	968	147	544	277	115	50	1,870	1	177
1897	1,957	895	752	143	916	156	508	252	99	47	1,785	1	171
1896	1,881	874	728	146	870	158	482	230	91	46	1,717	1	163

Series X 834–844. Selected Assets and Liabilities of Savings and Loan Associations: 1900 to 1970

[Includes Alaska, Guam, Hawaii, Puerto Rico, and Virgin Islands]

Year	Number of associations	Total[1]	Mortgage loans[2]				Investment securities[3]	Cash	Savings capital	General reserves and undivided profits	Federal Home Loan Bank advances and other borrowed money
			Total	FHA	VA	Conventional					
	834	835	836	837	838	839	840	841	842	843	844
1970	5,669	176,183	150,331	10,178	8,494	131,659	13,020	3,520	146,404	11,991	10,942
1969	5,835	162,149	140,232	7,909	7,643	124,680	10,873	2,439	135,538	11,228	9,728
1968	5,947	152,890	130,802	6,658	7,012	117,132	11,116	2,962	131,618	10,315	5,705
1967	6,036	143,534	121,805	5,791	6,351	109,663	9,180	3,442	124,493	9,546	4,775
1966	6,112	133,933	114,427	5,269	6,157	103,001	7,762	3,366	113,969	9,096	7,462
1965	6,185	129,580	110,306	5,145	6,398	98,763	7,414	3,900	110,385	8,704	6,444
1964	6,222	119,355	101,333	4,894	6,683	89,756	6,966	4,015	101,887	7,899	5,601
1963	6,248	107,559	90,944	4,696	6,960	79,288	6,445	3,979	91,308	7,209	5,015
1962	6,289	93,605	78,770	4,476	7,010	67,284	5,563	3,926	80,236	6,520	3,629
1961	6,246	82,135	68,834	4,167	7,152	57,515	5,211	3,315	70,885	5,708	2,856
1960	6,320	71,476	60,070	3,524	7,222	49,324	4,595	2,680	62,142	4,983	2,197
1959	6,223	63,530	53,141	2,995	7,186	42,960	4,477	2,183	54,583	4,393	2,387
1958	6,207	55,139	45,627	2,206	7,077	36,344	3,819	2,585	47,976	3,845	1,444
1957	6,169	48,138	40,007	1,643	7,011	31,353	3,173	2,146	41,912	3,363	1,379
1956	6,136	42,875	35,729	1,486	6,643	27,600	2,782	2,119	37,148	2,950	1,347
1955	6,071	37,656	31,408	1,404	5,883	24,121	2,338	2,063	32,142	2,557	1,546
1954	6,037	31,633	26,108	1,170	4,709	20,229	2,013	1,971	27,252	2,187	950
1953	6,012	26,733	21,962	1,048	3,979	16,935	1,920	1,479	22,846	1,901	1,027
1952	6,004	22,660	18,396	904	3,394	14,098	1,787	1,289	19,195	1,658	944
1951	5,995	19,222	15,564	866	3,133	11,565	1,603	1,066	16,107	1,453	894
1950	5,992	16,893	13,657	848	2,973	9,836	1,487	924	13,992	1,280	900
1949	5,983	14,622	11,616	717	2,586	8,313	1,462	880	12,471	1,106	499
1948	6,011	13,028	10,305	563	2,397	7,345	1,455	663	10,964	969	590
1947	6,045	11,687	8,856	--------	--------	--------	1,740	560	9,753	855	542
1946	6,093	10,202	7,141	--------	--------	--------	2,009	536	8,548	751	402
1945	6,149	8,747	5,376	--------	--------	--------	2,420	450	7,365	644	336
1944	6,279	7,458	4,800	--------	--------	--------	1,671	413	6,305	572	199
1943	6,498	6,604	4,584	--------	--------	--------	853	465	5,494	533	135
1942	6,941	6,150	4,583	--------	--------	--------	318	410	4,941	502	153
1941	7,211	6,049	4,578	--------	--------	--------	107	344	4,682	475	256
1940	7,521	5,733	4,125	--------	--------	--------	71	307	4,322	464	233
1939	8,006	5,597	3,806	--------	--------	--------	73	274	4,118	478	227
1938	8,762	5,632	3,614	--------	--------	--------	75	223	4,077	496	244
1937	9,225	5,682	3,464	--------	--------	--------	81	206	4,080	485	247
1936	10,042	5,772	3,286	--------	--------	--------	99	218	4,194	490	194
1935	10,266	5,875	3,292	--------	--------	--------	--------	--------	4,254	--------	--------
1934	10,744	6,406	3,710	--------	--------	--------	--------	--------	4,458	--------	--------
1933	10,596	7,018	4,437	--------	--------	--------	--------	--------	4,750	--------	--------
1932	10,915	7,737	5,148	--------	--------	--------	--------	--------	5,326	--------	--------
1931	11,442	8,417	5,890	--------	--------	--------	--------	--------	5,916	--------	--------
1930	11,777	8,829	6,402	--------	--------	--------	--------	--------	6,296	--------	--------
1929	12,342	8,695	6,507	--------	--------	--------	--------	--------	6,237	--------	--------

Year	Number of associations	Total assets (mil. dol.)
	834	835
1928	12,666	8,016
1927	12,804	7,179
1926	12,626	6,334
1925	12,403	5,509
1924	11,844	4,766
1923	10,744	3,943
1922	10,009	3,343
1921	9,255	2,891
1920	8,633	2,520
1919	7,788	2,127
1918	7,484	1,898
1917	7,269	1,769
1916	7,072	1,599
1915	6,806	1,484
1914	6,616	1,358
1913	6,429	1,248
1912	6,273	1,138
1911	6,099	1,031
1910	5,869	932
1909	5,713	856
1908	5,599	784
1907	5,424	732
1906	5,316	673
1905	5,264	629
1904	5,265	600
1903	5,308	580
1902	5,299	577
1901	5,302	565
1900	5,356	571

[1] Includes assets not shown separately.
[2] Net, after mortgage pledged shares, through 1957. Beginning 1958, includes shares pledged against mortgage loans.
[3] U.S. Government securities only through 1967. Beginning 1968 the total reflects liquid assets and other investment securities. Included are U.S. Government obligations, Federal agency securities, State and local government securities, time deposits at banks, and miscellaneous securities.

FINANCIAL MARKETS AND INSTITUTIONS

Series X 845–849.   Postal Savings System: 1911 to 1967

[As of June 30, except as noted.   Includes Alaska, Hawaii, Puerto Rico, and Virgin Islands]

Year	Offices in operation	Number of depositors [1]	Deposits ($1,000)	Withdrawals ($1,000)	Balance to credit of depositors [2] ($1,000)	Year	Offices in operation	Number of depositors [1]	Deposits ($1,000)	Withdrawals ($1,000)	Balance to credit of depositors [2] ($1,000)
	845	846	847	848	849		845	846	847	848	849
1967	2,658	607,304	–	–	52,950	1938	8,050	2,741,569	929,480	945,355	1,251,799
1966 (June 17)	2,791	803,130	32,750	176,688	200,296	1937	8,068	2,791,371	972,743	936,743	1,267,674
						1936	8,103	2,705,152	933,071	906,261	1,231,673
1965 (June 18)	3,130	997,029	50,428	122,159	344,234						
1964 (June 19)	3,466	1,076,225	63,155	131,945	415,965	1935	8,111	2,598,391	944,960	938,017	1,204,863
1963 (June 21)	4,250	1,164,634	76,442	174,752	484,756	1934	8,059	2,562,082	966,651	955,917	1,197,920
1962 (June 22)	5,205	1,271,858	193,675	212,303	583,067	1933	7,888	2,342,133	1,166,327	763,961	1,187,186
1961 (June 23)	5,484	1,397,538	114,884	251,248	701,696	1932	7,549	1,545,190	860,196	422,792	784,821
						1931	7,459	770,859	366,901	194,756	347,417
1960 (June 24)	5,923	1,550,930	145,082	350,475	838,060						
1959 (June 26)	6,324	1,740,052	192,887	363,042	1,043,453	1930	6,795	466,401	159,959	138,332	175,272
1958 (June 27)	6,871	1,925,852	241,239	489,900	1,213,608	1929	6,770	416,584	112,446	110,945	153,645
1957 [3] (June 28)	7,369	2,200,508	353,628	656,830	1,462,268	1928	6,683	412,250	96,386	91,602	152,143
1956	7,622	2,482,026	606,100	848,627	1,765,470	1927	6,672	411,394	103,607	90,426	147,359
						1926	6,623	399,305	90,751	88,746	134,179
1955	7,750	2,711,110	1,140,503	1,383,926	2,007,996						
1954	7,872	2,934,795	1,197,325	1,403,454	2,251,419	1925	6,655	402,325	89,708	90,349	132,173
1953	8,247	3,162,176	1,342,675	1,502,691	2,457,548	1924	6,758	412,584	94,933	93,790	132,814
1952	8,261	3,339,378	1,460,415	1,631,050	2,617,564	1923	6,802	417,902	88,008	94,073	131,671
1951	8,247	3,529,527	1,603,327	1,912,444	2,788,199	1922	6,774	420,242	96,508	111,161	137,736
						1921	6,300	466,109	133,575	138,461	152,390
1950	8,235	3,779,784	1,827,913	2,007,999	3,097,316						
1949	8,195	3,964,509	1,947,238	2,048,965	3,277,402	1920	6,314	508,508	139,209	149,256	157,276
1948	8,183	4,111,373	2,055,651	2,069,295	3,379,130	1919	6,439	565,509	136,690	117,838	167,323
1947	8,141	4,196,517	2,163,619	1,890,502	3,392,773	1918	6,656	612,188	116,893	100,376	148,471
1946	8,089	4,135,565	2,127,038	1,666,956	3,119,656	1917	7,161	674,728	132,112	86,177	131,955
						1916	8,421	602,937	76,776	56,441	86,020
1945	8,050	3,921,937	1,739,341	1,113,902	2,659,575						
1944	8,057	3,493,079	1,363,028	906,417	2,034,137	1915	9,546	525,414	70,315	48,074	65,685
1943	8,060	3,064,054	1,033,550	771,548	1,577,526	1914	10,347	388,511	47,815	38,190	43,444
1942	8,063	2,812,806	895,080	883,710	1,315,523	1913	12,820	331,006	41,701	28,120	33,819
1941	8,038	2,882,886	923,660	912,916	1,304,153	1912	10,170	243,801	30,732	11,172	20,237
						1911	400	11,918	778	101	677
1940	7,980	2,816,408	923,266	892,149	1,293,409						
1939	7,964	2,767,417	897,339	886,846	1,262,292						

– Represents zero.
[1] Includes depositors whose accounts are reflected on balance sheet as unclaimed.
[2] Includes items shown on balance sheet as unclaimed.

[3] Beginning 1957, data reported on basis of postal fiscal year, 13 4-week accounting periods ending on dates shown.

Series X 850–863.   Outstanding Loans and Loan Insurance or Guarantees of Federal and Federally Sponsored Agencies, by Economic Sector Served: 1917 to 1953

[In millions of dollars.   As of end of year]

Year	Direct loans						Loan insurance or guarantees [4]					Stock purchases [6]		
	Total	Agri- culture [1]	Business [2]	Financial insti- tutions	Housing	Other [3]	Total	Agri- culture [1]	Business	Housing	Other [5]	Total	Agri- culture	Financial insti- tutions
	850	851	852	853	854	855	856	857	858	859	860	861	862	863
1953	13,615	4,939	3,757	952	3,003	965	29,327	124	765	26,504	1,933	46	5	42
1952	13,026	4,748	3,481	864	2,638	1,294	25,737	123	929	23,618	1,067	54	8	47
1951	11,648	4,405	3,329	806	2,161	948	22,876	119	733	21,219	806	96	11	84
1950	10,217	3,972	3,201	816	1,543	684	18,601	109	191	17,886	414	119	16	103
1949	9,103	3,576	3,244	433	1,244	604	14,318	92	246	13,760	221	139	22	116
1948	8,306	3,241	3,112	515	746	691	11,166	81	290	10,576	219	164	29	135
1947	7,264	2,944	2,583	436	651	650	8,239	65	381	7,567	226	195	35	160
1946	6,170	2,736	1,796	315	694	629	6,097	31	395	5,438	234	253	46	207
1945	5,464	2,749	918	220	932	645	5,518	------	537	4,751	229	363	56	308
1944	6,308	3,037	1,147	160	1,279	685	6,333	------	1,564	4,542	226	438	64	374
1943	7,088	3,445	1,170	190	1,549	733	6,335	------	1,715	4,394	225	536	76	460
1942	7,842	3,717	1,096	240	1,917	872	5,082	------	727	4,096	259	674	82	592
1941	8,063	3,825	912	337	2,090	899	3,744	------	38	3,503	203	727	82	645
1940	7,882	3,718	852	374	2,227	712	3,079	------	35	2,796	248	788	61	726
1939	7,750	3,702	768	353	2,254	673	2,234	------	47	2,136	51	848	75	773
1938	7,761	3,670	727	407	2,314	642	1,545	------	34	1,511	--------	909	76	833
1937	8,159	3,650	638	450	2,474	946	1,023	------	4	1,020	--------	924	76	848
1936	8,453	3,642	642	468	2,807	895	705	------	4	701	--------	943	75	868
1935	8,645	3,537	771	622	2,903	812	310	------	3	308	--------	1,063	77	986
1934	7,815	3,126	703	928	2,366	691	32	------	1	30	--------	984	90	893
1933	4,303	2,015	533	1,121	142	493	--------	------	------	------	--------	271	2	269
1932	3,324	1,835	450	832	--------	207	--------	------	------	------	--------	--------	--------	--------
1931	2,031	1,800	140	--------	--------	90	--------	------	------	------	--------	--------	--------	--------

See footnotes at end of table.

Series X 850–863. Outstanding Loans and Loan Insurance or Guarantees of Federal and Federally Sponsored Agencies, by Economic Sector Served: 1917 to 1953—Con.

[In millions of dollars]

Year	Total	Agriculture [1]	Business [2]	Financial institutions	Other [3]	Year	Total	Agriculture [1]	Business [2]	Financial institutions	Other [3]	Year	Total	Agriculture [1]	Business [2]	Financial institutions	Other [3]
	850	851	852	853	855		850	851	852	853	855		850	851	852	853	855
1930	1,779	1,582	125	-------	72	1925	1,476	1,106	353	-------	16	1920	1,034	355	680	-------	(Z)
1929	1,486	1,313	120	-------	53	1924	1,487	1,034	442	-------	11	1919	395	299	94	2	-------
1928	1,438	1,288	113	-------	37	1923	1,431	915	508	-------	8	1918	190	159	30	2	-------
1927	1,474	1,241	204	-------	29	1922	1,303	791	506	-------	5	1917	39	39	-------	-------	-------
1926	1,527	1,184	321	-------	22	1921	1,260	519	740	-------	1						

Z Less than $500,000.
[1] Classification by real-estate and non-real-estate loans available in source tables. Excludes loans and loan guarantees of Commodity Credit Corporation; see text.
[2] Includes loans of Export-Import Bank; see text.
[3] Includes minor governmental units and miscellaneous purposes.
[4] Federal agencies only.   [5] Minor governmental units.
[6] For details on types of stock purchased, see text.

Series X 864–878. Federal and State-Chartered Credit Unions—Number, Members, Savings, Loans, and Total Assets: 1925 to 1970

[As of end of year]

Year	Operating credit unions			Number of members (1,000)			Members' savings (mil. dol.)			Outstanding loans (mil. dol.)			Total assets (mil. dol.)		
	Total	Federal	State [1]	Total	Federal	State	Total	Federal [2]	State [3]	Total	Federal [2]	State	Total	Federal [2]	State
	864	865	866	867	868	869	870	871	872	873	874	875	876	877	878
1970	23,656	12,977	10,679	22,819	11,966	10,853	15,523	7,629	7,894	14,106	6,969	7,137	17,950	8,861	9,089
1969	23,759	12,921	10,838	21,628	11,302	10,326	13,740	6,713	7,027	12,959	6,329	6,630	15,918	7,794	8,124
1968	23,378	12,584	10,794	20,229	10,509	9,720	12,312	5,986	6,326	11,293	5,398	5,895	14,212	6,902	7,310
1967	22,997	12,210	10,787	19,063	9,874	9,189	11,103	5,421	5,682	9,881	4,677	5,204	12,776	6,208	6,568
1966	22,585	11,941	10,644	17,923	9,272	8,651	10,071	4,944	5,127	9,093	4,324	4,769	11,607	5,669	5,938
1965	22,064	11,543	10,521	16,756	8,641	8,115	9,220	4,538	4,682	8,098	3,865	4,233	10,551	5,166	5,385
1964	21,730	11,278	10,452	15,622	8,092	7,530	8,225	4,017	4,208	7,048	3,349	3,699	9,359	4,559	4,800
1963	21,301	10,955	10,346	14,580	7,500	7,080	7,164	3,453	3,711	6,171	2,911	3,260	8,130	3,917	4,213
1962	20,969	10,632	10,337	13,753	7,008	6,745	6,331	3,020	3,311	5,478	2,561	2,917	7,188	3,430	3,758
1961	20,567	10,271	10,296	12,879	6,543	6,336	5,639	2,673	2,966	4,852	2,245	2,607	6,382	3,028	3,354
1960	20,056	9,905	10,151	12,058	6,087	5,971	4,981	2,344	2,637	4,402	2,021	2,381	5,659	2,670	2,989
1959	19,408	9,447	9,961	11,320	5,643	5,677	4,441	2,075	2,366	3,718	1,667	2,051	5,029	2,353	2,676
1958	18,770	9,030	9,740	10,539	5,210	5,329	3,869	1,812	2,057	3,078	1,380	1,698	4,347	2,035	2,312
1957	18,049	8,735	9,314	9,862	4,898	4,964	3,381	1,589	1,792	2,778	1,257	1,521	3,810	1,789	2,021
1956	17,113	8,350	8,763	9,051	4,502	4,549	2,914	1,366	1,548	2,326	1,049	1,277	3,271	1,529	1,742
1955	16,064	7,806	8,258	8,153	4,032	4,121	2.447	1,135	1,312	1,934	863	1,071	2,743	1,267	1,476
1954	14,940	7,227	7,713	7,356	3,599	3,757	2,040	931	1,109	1,552	682	870	2,270	1,033	1,237
1953	13,564	6,578	6,986	6,635	3,255	3,380	1,691	768	923	1,308	574	734	1,895	854	1,041
1952	12,249	5,925	6,324	5,888	2,853	3,035	1,355	597	758	985	415	570	1,516	662	854
1951	11,284	5,398	5,886	5,196	2,464	2,732	1,079	457	622	747	300	447	1,199	505	694
1950	10,571	4,984	5,587	4,610	2,127	2,483	884	362	522	680	264	416	1,006	406	600
1949	9,897	4,495	5,402	4,091	1,820	2,271	730	285	445	515	186	329	827	316	511
1948	9,329	4,058	5,271	3,749	1,628	2,121	630	235	395	399	138	261	701	258	443
1947	8,942	3,845	5,097	3,340	1,446	1,894	533	192	341	280	91	189	591	210	381
1946	8,715	3,761	4,954	3,020	1,302	1,718	451	160	291	188	57	131	495	173	322
1945	8,615	3,757	4,858	2,843	1,217	1,626	384	141	243	126	35	91	435	153	282
1944	8,722	3,815	4,907	2,936	1,306	1,630	355	134	221	121	34	87	398	144	254
1943	9,062	3,938	5,124	3,033	1,312	1,721	323	117	206	122	35	87	355	127	228
1942	9,545	4,145	5,400	3,154	1,357	1,797	303	110	193	149	43	106	341	120	221
1941	9,734	4,228	5,506	3,317	1,409	1,908	287	97	190	220	69	151	323	106	217
1940	8,931	3,756	5,175	2,828	1,128	1,700	223	66	157	191	56	135	254	73	181
1939	7,859	3,182	4,677	2,310	851	1,459	169	43	126	149	38	111	194	48	146
1938	6,737	2,760	3,977	1,869	632	1,237	127	27	100	108	24	84	148	30	118
1937	5,441	2,313	3,128	1,540	484	1,056	98	18	80	78	16	62	116	19	97
1936	4,485	1,751	2,734	1,164	310	854	68	9	59	59	7	52	83	9	74
1935	2,894	772	2,122	642	119	523	38	2	36	36	2	34	50	2	48
1934	2,067	39	2,028	430	3	427	28	(Z)	28	28	(Z)	28	40	(Z)	40
1933	1,772	-------	1,772	360	-------	360	23	-------	23	26	-------	26	35	-------	35
1932	1,472	-------	1,472	301	-------	301	22	-------	22	25	-------	25	31	-------	31
1931	1,244	-------	1,244	286	-------	286	-------	-------	-------	-------	-------	-------	34	-------	34
1929	868	-------	868	265	-------	265	-------	-------	-------	-------	-------	-------	-------	-------	-------
1925	176	-------	176	108	-------	108	-------	-------	-------	-------	-------	-------	-------	-------	-------

Z Less than $500,000.
[1] Reports not received from all operating credit unions; see text.
[2] Data for 1935–1944, partly estimated.
[3] Includes members' deposits.

Chapter X

Insurance (Series X 879-962)

X 879-917. General note.

There are three general sources of primary data about life insurance as a whole: The various State insurance departments through their reports of the life insurance companies operating within their jurisdictions; commercial publishers of life insurance company data; and the trade and other associations of the life insurance companies.

Probably the most widely used of the State insurance department reports are those published annually by the New York Insurance Department. For the approximate period 1860–1880 these reports, which give data on the companies domiciled in the State and the companies of other States authorized to transact business in the State, are most frequently made use of to exhibit the progress of life insurance. The data presented in these reports for this period represent a very high percentage of the total life insurance business. Other State reports often consulted by researchers are those of Massachusetts and Connecticut.

Of the commercial publications, the most frequently used to study the progress of life insurance as a whole is the *Spectator Insurance Year Book*, published annually since 1873 by the Spectator Company, Philadelphia. (For 1873–1937, the publication was known as *The Insurance Year Book*. There were separate "Life" volumes from 1923–1963 and "Property, casualty" volumes through 1960.)

A number of the trade and other associations in the life insurance business prepare industrywide statistics on different aspects of life insurance. The Institute of Life Insurance, New York, a public relations organization formed by the life insurance companies, compiles a number of such statistics and publishes these, as well as data from other associations and from commercial publishers, annually in the *Life Insurance Fact Book*. Two major sources of insurance statistics included in the Institute compilations are the American Life Insurance Association and the Life Insurance Agency Management Association.

To obtain a series of figures over a long period it is not necessary to consult each annual edition of the publications mentioned above. Many of the *New York Insurance Reports* (known also as the *Annual Report of the Superintendent of Insurance*) contain a chronology which gives some of the salient statistics over a long period (sometimes only for selected years). Prior to 1963, the annual *Spectator Insurance Year Book* often gave the aggregates for all available companies for the preceding 10 years and, for the early years of this publication, a summary of data was presented for the companies operating in New York State. Thereafter, the monthly *Spectator Magazine* presents data on life, property, accident, and health companies.

The most recent *Life Insurance Fact Book* will generally give most of the preceding statistics compiled, as well as historical statistics from other sources, as far back as 1890 for some series.

In addition to the *Life Insurance Fact Book*, there are two compilations of historical statistics which are often consulted: J. Owens Stalson, *Marketing Life Insurance, Its History in America*, Harvard University Press, Cambridge, 1942 (the appendixes give data on the number of companies, life insurance sales, life insurance in force, and income as well as many other items from earliest available figures to 1937); and Frederick L. Hoffman, "Fifty Years of American Life Insurance Progress," *Quarterly Publications of the American Statistical Association*, New Series, No. 95, vol. XII, Boston, 1911 (tables of salient statistics, 1860–1910). The statistics presented in these publications do not always agree with the figures given here because in some cases different sources have been used, and in some cases adjustments and corrections of the source material have been made by the Institute of Life Insurance.

Because it represents the exception rather than the rule, it may be of interest to note two instances in which data on life insurance were collected in the decennial census of the United States. *Statistics of the United States in 1860*, 1866, pp. 293–294, contains some statistics on the number of life insurance companies, the amount of life insurance, the number of persons insured, and the annual premium income for 1860. Data on the life insurance business are also shown in the *Report on Insurance Business in the United States at the Eleventh Census: 1890, Part 2, Life Insurance, 1895*. This report contains statistics on life insurance for the decade 1880–1890 for the companies in operation as of December 31, 1889. It does not, however, reflect the business in this decade of companies which ceased to do business before December 31, 1889.

The basic reporting form utilized by all three types of primary sources in preparing their statistics is the annual statement convention blank. This is the prescribed accounting statement which each company must submit to the insurance department of each State in which it is licensed to transact business, setting forth the company's balance sheet, income and disbursement accounts, policy exhibit, and many supporting schedules. The collecting agencies supplement the data from the annual statement form from time to time through mail questionnaires, mostly among the life insurance companies.

An understanding of the historical statistics of life insurance requires some knowledge of the annual statement convention blank—the accounting methods used in preparing the form and changes in the form and methods over the years—and some knowledge of the history of life insurance.

Uniformity in the annual statement convention blank required by the States has been achieved through the efforts of the National Association of Insurance Commissioners. This association is a national organization composed of the officials of the various States who have supervision of insurance affairs within their respective States. It was formed in 1871 (under the name of the National Convention of Insurance Commissioners) and adopted its first convention blank in 1874. This organization has also achieved a degree of uniformity in insurance legislation and departmental rulings among the different States.

The convention blank has undergone revisions from time to time. The most recent significant revision in the annual statement convention blank took place in the form used for reporting the operations for 1951. Where these changes have affected the statistics shown, they are discussed below in the text for the specific series. For a complete discussion of the annual statement form now in use, and a comparison with the superseded form, see E. C. Wightman, *Life Insurance Statements and Accounts*, Life Office Management Association, New York, 1952 and J. C. Noback, *Life Insurance Accounting*, Irwin, Homewood, Ill., 1969. For a detailed discussion of two of the earlier forms, see *Life Insurance Accounts*, 1935 and 1941, by Wightman.

There are many nonstatistical histories of life insurance. A few that may be consulted are: Charles K. Knight, *The History of Life Insurance in the United States to 1870*, unpublished thesis, University of Pennsylvania, 1920; *Marketing Life Insurance, Its History in America* (cited above); and *The Bible of Life Insurance*, George W. Wadsworth, 1932.

The data presented here cover only life insurance as it relates to the insurance companies which are usually referred to as the legal reserve life insurance companies. These are life insurance companies operating under insurance laws specifying the minimum basis for the reserves a company must maintain on its policies. Other types of life insurance include fraternal life insurance which is provided by societies, lodges, and similar fellowship organizations; life insurance with assessment associations, mutual aid groups, and burial societies; life insurance available through savings banks in three States; and veterans life insurance (consisting of U.S. Government Life Insurance and National Service Life Insurance) issued by the Federal Government to members of the Armed Forces and veterans of World Wars I and II.

Though in very recent years the greatest part of all life insurance in force in the United States has been provided by the legal reserve life insurance companies, veterans insurance at its peaks during or immediately after the World Wars exceeded or nearly equaled the totals achieved by the life insurance companies. Fraternal and assessment life insurance combined for the period 1879–1928 was a significant proportion of the life insurance company total (actually exceeding it for a year or two in the 1890's and never amounting to less than 10 percent of the life insurance company total for the period stated).

For historical statistics of veterans, fraternal, and assessment life insurance, see Stalson, *Marketing Life Insurance*, cited above, pp. 806–808 and 816–819.

The data for legal reserve life insurance companies which are presented here are subject to three types of limitations: (a) Changes in the annual statement convention blank on which the companies report their operations; (b) incompleteness of the data in terms of the number of companies for which information is available; and (c) lack of uniformity among the companies in the allocation of certain items to the categories of the convention blank, changes in allocation, and changes made by the publishers of life insurance data in their reporting methods.

Changes in the annual statement blank over the years have been discussed previously. With regard to the completeness of the statistics available, it is extremely difficult to obtain data for any given period on the operations of *all* the life insurance companies operating in the United States. Theoretically, one should be able to compile complete statistics by consulting the insurance reports of each State and the District of Columbia, but in practice this is not feasible. State insurance reports began in the 1850's, but it was not until 1919 that all States (and the District of Columbia) were issuing reports. (A list of the first reports on insurance companies by State departments of insurance is given in Stalson, *Marketing Life Insurance*, cited above, pp. 775–776.) Therefore, until 1919, there is no way of obtaining data from State reports for companies which operated in only those States for which reports were not available. Subsequent to 1919, the difficulties in compiling complete statistics arise from the lack of uniformity in the various reports with regard to the selection of items to be presented and the basis of reporting, and from the failure of some States to issue reports on a regular annual basis.

The life insurance companies omitted from the sources utilized are very small in size relative to those for which data are available. Therefore, even when a fairly large number of these very small companies are omitted, they account for a very small percentage of the total business. For example, in 1970, according to the Institute of Life Insurance, the 1,390 companies for which life insurance in force data were available accounted for 99.96 percent of the total which would have been obtained from the 1,792 companies in existence at the end of 1970. This percentage is doubtlessly lower for the earlier years and for some of the other categories, but it is highly probable that even the oldest figures presented here represent 90 percent or more of the total for all companies. This is true both with regard to the figures taken from sources, such as the *Spectator Insurance Year Book*, which collect data from all available companies, and for the figures for about 1860–1880 which are taken from the reports of the New York Insurance Department. (For a discussion of the percentage of total business accounted for by the New York Insurance Department reports, see Hoffman, "Fifty Years of American Life Insurance Progress," cited above, pp. 11–13.)

The third limitation with regard to the data of legal reserve life insurance companies pertains to the lack of uniformity in allocation of certain items to the categories of the convention blank and changes in allocation. There are many instances where neither the categories of the annual statement convention blank nor the instructions for filing the blank are detailed enough to specify clearly how a certain transaction is to be allocated, so that the treatment becomes a matter of the company's judgment. Thus, for example, of two companies writing monthly debit insurance (a form of life insurance with some of the features of both ordinary and industrial insurance), one may classify it as ordinary and one as industrial. Moreover, a company may decide to change the classification of an item; for the example just cited, a company may transfer at some point its monthly debit business from the industrial to the ordinary classification. Such problems can arise in all the series presented. Even when an accounting procedure tends to become widespread, it is often adopted by different companies at different times.

A further problem arises from the fact that the sources which compile industrywide statistics must often combine the many categories of the annual statement convention blank into broader classifications. From time to time, the manner of combining the categories may be altered or the manner of treating special categories, which are sometimes found in a few companies' convention blank, may be changed.

Related to the problems of changes in the annual statement convention blank and variations in the allocation of items is the problem of changes in method of valuation of policy reserves and assets. The amount of policy reserves reported in a company's convention blank is determined by the types of policies issued, the length of time they have been in force, and the age at issue. The policy reserves are also affected by the mortality table used, the interest assumption, and the reserve basis specified by the various States as the minimum basis for valuation. The assets of a company, and hence its surplus, are also affected by the method of valuation of assets. The problems of changes in valuation of assets and reserves do not appear to be factors of major significance, however, with regard to long-term historical trends of these series.

The general procedure used in preparing these statistics was to examine the various sources and compare the series available as to bases of reporting, completeness of coverage, etc. In those cases where alternative series were available, the selection was determined by completeness of coverage in terms of the number of companies for which data were obtainable, and the basis of reporting most consistent with current practice, on two conditions: (a) That the series be available for a sufficiently long period to preserve the trend, and (b) that component items could be obtained on the same basis or level of coverage as the totals. An illustration might make this clear. For 1879–1887, total assets can be obtained for all the companies operating in New York State. For the same period, totals for a larger group of companies can be obtained from the 1888 *Spectator Insurance Year Book*. The distribution of assets, by type, however, is available only for the companies operating in New York State. Rather than estimate a distribution for the larger asset totals or report a distribution which would not add to the total shown, the New York State figures were used for the total and for the distribution by type. For the period under discussion, the assets of companies operating in New York State represented from 92 to 97 percent of the assets given by the *Spectator Insurance Year Book* for all available companies.

In most cases, the various sources were identical with regard to bases of reporting and completeness of coverage. In these cases, the procedure was to compare the various sources presenting the same data for the same period. Thus for the early period, comparisons were made among the individual *New York Insurance Reports* and the summaries of these reports given in various issues of the *Spectator Insurance Year Book*, *Marketing Life Insurance*, and "Fifty Years of American Life Insurance Progress." For later years, comparisons were made among the various issues of the *Spectator Insurance Year Book* which covered the same period (mainly the 10-year aggregates as compared with the aggregates given in each *Year Book*), *Marketing Life Insurance*, and the *Life Insurance Fact Book* (which utilizes a great deal of material from the *Spectator Insurance Year Book*).

Where the figures in the various sources were in agreement, the data presented were accepted unless some limitations were uncovered while making the comparisons. Where the sources were not in agreement, the reasons for the differences were investigated and the figures considered to be most accurate and complete were accepted.

Some of the figures presented here are original in the sense that they represent adjustments by the Institute of Life Insurance of existing figures for errors in addition, for omissions, or for changes in definition. Wherever possible, published material has been utilized.

X 879. Number of life insurance companies, 1759–1970.

Source: J. Owen Stalson, 1759–1936, *Marketing Life Insurance, Its History in America*, Harvard University Press, Cambridge, 1942, pp. 748–753. Institute of Life Insurance, 1937–1939, estimates; 1940–1970, *Life Insurance Fact Book*, *1974*, p. 87, and unpublished data.

The figures comprise the total number of companies in operation at the end of the year and domiciled in the United States. This number is larger than the number of companies for which life insurance in force data are available (see general note for series X 879–917). For 1941–1949, figures do not include companies which started and then ceased operations within this period. For data on the number of companies formed, discontinued, and in operation, classified by stock and mutual for 1759–1937, see Stalson, cited above, pp. 748–753.

X 880–889. General note.

For 1854–1894, the series were derived by deducting from the insurance in force figures of U.S. life insurance companies the amount of their Canadian and other foreign business, and adding thereto the U.S. business of Canadian and other foreign companies. Data for 1895–1948 were derived from the totals of individual State estimates given in the "Life Insurance in Force by States" section of each *Spectator Insurance Year Book*.

For ordinary life insurance, the figures for 1815–1850 are for all available companies; for 1854–1877, the figures are for life insurance companies reporting to the New York Insurance Department. Beginning with 1878, the data are for all available companies. All the data for group, industrial, and credit life insurance are for all available companies.

Life insurance in force is the sum total of the face amounts (plus additions purchased with dividends) of the life insurance outstanding at a given time. The additional amount of life insurance payable under accidental death provisions (providing for payment of an additional death benefit in case of death as a result of accidental means, often called double indemnity) is not included.

Life insurance in force figures have been adjusted to represent insurance in force on the lives of residents of the United States whether issued by U.S. or foreign companies. For statistics of life insurance in force with U.S. life insurance companies, whether the policyholders are residents of the United States or of some other country, and for the number of policies outstanding, for 1900–1970, see *Life Insurance Fact Book*, *1974*, pp. 25, 27, 30, 33, 35. Estimates by States are available from the "Life Insurance in Force by States" section of the annual *Spectator Insurance Year Book* and the *Life Insurance Fact Book*. For information on life insurance in force by plan of insurance, 1950, 1954, 1957, 1962, 1966, and 1970, see *The Tally of Life Insurance Statistics*, January 1959, pp. 1 and 2, March 1968, pp. 1 and 2, and November 1971, pp. 1 and 2.

For an alternative series of life insurance in force in the United States, for selected years, 1815–1937, see *Marketing Life Insurance*, cited above, pp. 816–817. The alternative series includes fraternal, assessment, and other types of life insurance, and is derived from aggregate figures of U.S., Canadian, and foreign companies, rather than as totals of State figures.

X 880. Number of life insurance policies in force in the United States, 1895–1970.

Source: Institute of Life Insurance, *Life Insurance Fact Book*, various issues.

Data represent all life insurance in force with U.S. life companies, including both direct business and reinsurance acquired. Data include group certificates and credit life insurance.

X 881. Coverage per family of life insurance in force in the United States, 1930–1970.

Source: See source for series X 880.

Families include the units defined by the Bureau of the Census as families, subfamilies, and unrelated individuals.

X 882. Total life insurance in force in the United States, 1815–1970.

Source: 1815–1850, see Stalson, cited above for series X 879, p. 787 (1850 estimate corrected for addition error); 1854–1899, a summation of series X 883 and X 885. 1900–1970, Institute of Life Insurance, *Life Insurance Fact Book*, *1974*, p. 23, and unpublished data.

X 883. Ordinary life insurance in force in the United States, 1815–1970.

Source: 1815–1850, see Stalson, cited above for series X 879, p. 787. Institute of Life Insurance, 1854–1894, unpublished data; 1895–1970, *Life Insurance Fact Book*, *1958*, p. 25, and *1974*, p. 23.

The 1854–1894 figures were compiled from the following sources, using the method described in the general note for series X 880–889: Ordinary insurance in force of U.S. companies: 1854–1858, Spectator Company, *Spectator Insurance Year Book*, 1878, p. 71; 1859–1877, Stalson, cited above for series X 879, p. 820; 1878–1894, *Spectator Insurance Year Book*, various issues (for certain years, adjustments were made). Ordinary business of U.S. companies in Canada: 1869–1894, Stalson, cited above for series X 879, pp. 833–834 (1873 figure adjusted; 1885–1894, industrial business in Canada of U.S. companies subtracted to get ordinary business in Canada). Ordinary business of U.S. companies in foreign countries other than Canada: 1868–1885, Stalson, cited above for series X 879, p. 824; 1886–1888, Hoffman, "Fifty Years of American Life Insurance Progress," cited above in general note for series X 879–962, p. 86; 1889–1894, *Spectator Insurance Year Book*, 1899, p. 466. Ordinary business of Canadian companies in the U.S.: 1889–1894, Stalson, cited above for series X 879, p. 839. Ordinary business of other foreign companies in the U.S.: 1854–1870, series for U.S. branches of British companies estimated by the Institute of Life Insurance; 1871–1881, 1885–1886, State of New York Insurance Department, *New York Insurance Report*, various issues; 1882–1884, data not available, but probably insignificant.

Ordinary life insurance refers to life insurance usually issued in amounts of $1,000 or more, with premiums payable on an annual, semiannual, quarterly, or monthly basis.

X 884. Group life insurance in force in the United States, 1911–1970.

Source: Institute of Life Insurance, *Life Insurance Fact Book*, *1958*, p. 27, and *1974*, p. 23.

Group life insurance is life insurance issued, usually without medical examination, on a group of persons under a master policy. It is usually issued to an employer for the benefit of employees. The individual members of the group hold certificates as evidence of their insurance.

X 885. Industrial life insurance in force in the United States, 1876–1970.

Source: 1876–1894, Institute of Life Insurance, unpublished data; 1895–1970, see source for series X 884, *1958*, p. 31 and *1974*, p. 23.

The 1876–1894 figures were compiled from the following sources, using the method described in the general note for series X 880–889: Industrial insurance in force of U.S. companies: 1876–1894, Spectator Company, *Spectator Insurance Year Book*, various issues (for certain years, adjustments were made). Industrial business of U.S. companies in Canada: 1885–1894, *Spectator Insurance Year Book*, various issues. Canadian and other foreign companies have never written industrial life insurance in the United States, according to available information.

Industrial life insurance is life insurance issued in small amounts, usually not over $500. Premiums are payable on a weekly or monthly basis and are generally collected at the home by an agent of the company.

X 886. Credit life insurance in force in the United States, 1917–1970.

Source: See source for series X 884, *1958*, p. 33 and *1974*, p. 23.

Credit life insurance is term life insurance sold through a lender or lending agency to cover payment of a loan, installment purchase, or other obligation, in case of death. Lending agencies are defined to include agencies that sell merchandise on time and mortgage departments of life insurance companies, as well as banks, finance companies, and other institutions or agencies to or through which financial obligations are incurred. The data refer to insurance on loans of 10 years or less duration.

X 887–889. Average size policy in force in the United States, 1895–1970.

Source: Institute of Life Insurance, *Life Insurance Fact Book*, various issues, and unpublished data.

X 890–893. General note.

Figures represent U.S. life insurance companies' sales (including reinsurance acquired) in the United States and in other countries. Credit life insurance is excluded.

Life insurance sales represent the sum total of the face amount of life insurance sold in a given period (in this case, one year). The additional amount of life insurance payable under accidental death provisions is not included. For definitions of ordinary, group, and industrial, see text for series X 883–885.

X 890. Total sales of life insurance by U.S. life insurance companies, 1854–1970.

Source: 1854–1920, a summation of series X 891–893; 1921–1970, see source for series X 884, *1958*, p. 23 and *1974*, p. 16.

Total life insurance sales in the United States, representing all sales to residents of the United States, whether issued by U.S. or foreign companies, are available, beginning with 1940, from the source, p. 20. These series give number of policies and amount of insurance, by type.

X 891. Sales of ordinary life insurance by U.S. life insurance companies, 1854–1970.

Source: 1854–1910, Spectator Company, *Spectator Insurance Year Book*, various issues (for certain years, adjustments were made by the Institute of Life Insurance); 1911–1920, Institute of Life Insurance, unpublished data (based on data from summary table of Spectator Company, *Spectator Compendium of Official Life Insurance Reports* for each year); 1921–1970, see source for series X 884, *1958*, p. 23 and *1974*, p. 16.

The estimates for 1854–1877 are for life insurance companies reporting to the New York Insurance Department. Thereafter, the data are for all available companies. Beginning 1888, the data are on a paid-for basis; beginning 1893, they exclude revivals, increases, and dividend additions.

Monthly sales and annual sales by States since 1923 are available in Life Insurance Agency Management Association, *Monthly Sales Survey*, various issues. See also *Life Insurance Fact Book*, 1947–1972 editions. For regional data, from 1929–1956, see U.S. Office of Business Economics, *Business Statistics*, *1957 Biennial Edition*.

X 892. Sales of group life insurance by U.S. life insurance companies, 1911–1970.

Source: 1911–1920, Institute of Life Insurance, unpublished data (1911–1918, estimated from a survey of companies writing group life insurance at that time; 1919–1920, compiled from Group Life Exhibit in Spectator Company, *Spectator Compendium of Official Life Insurance Reports*, various issues); 1921–1970, see source for series X 884, *1958*, p. 23 and *1972*, p. 21.

The group life insurance figures are on a paid-for basis. Figures for 1912–1918 may reflect increases in existing contracts to some extent. Beginning 1919, figures exclude revivals, increases, and dividend additions.

X 893. Sales of industrial life insurance by U.S. life insurance companies, 1873–1970.

Source: 1873–1910, Spectator Company, *Spectator Insurance Year Book*, various issues; 1911–1920, *Spectator Compendium of Official Life Insurance Reports*, various issues; 1921–1970, see source for series X 884, *1958*, p. 23 and *1972*, p. 21.

Beginning 1893, figures exclude revivals, increases, and dividend additions.

X 894–907. General note.

The data for 1854–1887 are for life insurance companies reporting to the New York Insurance Department. Thereafter, the data are for all available companies.

In general, before 1951, income and disbursement items were reported on a cash basis (in the accounting use of the term). Beginning 1951, income and disbursement items are reported on an accrual basis (reflecting earned income and incurred claims and expenses).

Before 1951, gross investment income (without deduction of investment expenses) was reported as income, and investment expenses were reported as disbursements (included with "Commissions, expenses, taxes, and other disbursements"). Beginning 1951, investment expenses are deducted from gross investment income and the resulting net figure is reported as income.

X 894–897. Income of U.S. life insurance companies, 1854–1970.

Source: 1854–1910, see first source for series X 893; 1911–1970, see source for series X 884, *1958*, p. 53, *1970*, p. 57, and *1971*, p. 58.

X 895, life insurance premiums. For 1911–1970, this series was obtained by subtracting from premium income as reported in the source, the annuity premium series (series X 896) described below. Since 1947, accident and health premiums have also been subtracted from premium income.

This series includes premiums for ordinary, group, and industrial life insurance, including disability and accidental death provisions. A premium is defined as the payment, or one of the regular periodical payments, a policyholder is required to make for an insurance policy.

X 896, annuity premiums. For 1911–1931, data were obtained by subtracting from the "consideration for annuities" figures given in the aggregates of the *Spectator Compendium* each year, the amount of supplementary contracts involving life contingencies. The series on supplementary contracts involving life contingencies was compiled by the Institute of Life Insurance from data in the *New York Insurance Reports* and the annual editions of Alfred M. Best Co., *Best's Life Insurance Reports*, New York. For 1932–1951, data were obtained directly by summing annuity income items from *Spectator Compendium* aggregates each year. For 1952–1955, data were obtained by summing group and individual annuity data given in Institute of Life Insurance, *The Tally of Life Insurance Statistics*,

August 1956, p. 1; for 1956, Institute of Life Insurance, unpublished data; for 1957, *Life Insurance Fact Book, 1958*, p. 54; for 1958–1964, *1965*, p. 57; for 1965–1970, *1971*, p. 58.

This category includes considerations for group and individual annuities. Before 1911, figures include considerations for supplementary contracts with life contingencies. An annuity is defined as a contract that provides an income for a specified period of time, such as a number of years or for life. A supplementary contract is an agreement by the company to retain the lump sum payable under an insurance policy and to make payments in accordance with the settlement option chosen.

X 897, investment and other income. For 1911–1970, figures include considerations for supplementary contracts both with and without life contingencies. Before 1911, figures include considerations for supplementary contracts without life contingencies.

X 898–907. Disbursements of U.S. life insurance companies, 1854–1970.

Source: 1854–1918, Spectator Company, *Spectator Insurance Year Book*, various issues (for certain years, adjustments were made by the Institute of Life Insurance); 1919–1951, *Spectator Compendium of Official Life Insurance Reports* for each year; 1952–1970, Institute of Life Insurance, unpublished data.

Annual additions to policy reserves are not included. These constitute the greatest portion of the difference between income and disbursements. For data on policy reserves, see series X 916.

Figures for life insurance benefit payments paid to residents of the United States, either by U.S. or foreign companies, may be obtained, for 1940–1957, from the *Life Insurance Fact Book, 1958*, p. 39 and for 1958–1970, from the *1971* edition, p. 43. Death benefit payments in the United States by type of insurance, number of policies, and by State may also be obtained from the annual editions of the *Life Insurance Fact Book*. Monthly benefit figures and quarterly death benefits by States may be obtained from the *Tally of Life Insurance Statistics* through December 1971; the monthly benefit survey was discontinued thereafter. A summary of monthly data for several years may be obtained from U.S. Bureau of Economic Analysis, *Business Statistics*, biennial editions.

X 901, matured endowment payments. This series is defined as the proceeds paid under a policy which provides that a definite sum of money be paid to the policyholder after a specified number of years if he is then living. If the policyholder dies during the endowment period, payment is made to a beneficiary (such proceeds are included as death benefits).

X 903, policy dividends. A policy dividend is defined as a refund of part of the premium on a participating life insurance policy. It is a share of the surplus earnings apportioned for distribution and reflects the difference between the premium charged and actual experience.

X 904, surrender values. A surrender value payment is the amount paid to policyholders upon surrender, for cash, of a policy before it becomes payable by death or maturity.

X 905, disability and accidental death benefits. Disability benefits are payments under a feature added to a life insurance policy, providing for waiver of premium and sometimes payment of monthly income if the insured becomes totally and permanently disabled. For definition of accidental death benefits, see general note for series X 880–889.

Disability provisions became general around 1910 and benefits under these were usually included with annuity payments until 1920. Accidental death benefit provisions became general around 1917 and benefits under these were usually included with death benefits until 1920.

X 906, commissions, expenses, taxes, and other disbursements. This series includes payments on supplementary contracts, with and without life contingencies, and payments of dividends which have been left on deposit.

X 907, dividends to stockholders. Dividends to stockholders were shown as a disbursement in the annual statement convention blank before 1951. For 1951–1970, dividends to stockholders have been shown as a deduction from surplus in the surplus account.

X 908–913. Assets of U.S. life insurance companies, 1854–1970.

Source: 1854–1889, see first source for series X 893; 1890–1970, see source for series X 884, *1958*, pp. 64–91 and *1971*, p. 68.

The data for 1854–1887 are for life insurance companies reporting to the New York Insurance Department. Thereafter, the data are for all available companies.

Assets are on an admitted asset value basis, which is the aggregate value of all the assets used for determination of a company's balance sheet in accord with principles adopted by the insurance departments of the various States. Until about 1909, stocks and bonds were reported at market value. Until 1906, this value was determined by each individual company and, since 1907, by the insurance commissioners. In 1909, New York State required amortization of amply secured bonds, and this soon became the general practice. Stocks and nonamortizable bonds are generally reported at market value. Assets include the assets, distributed by type, of the accident and health departments of life insurance companies.

Shares of Federal savings and loan associations are included with series X 910. Series X 912 includes real estate sold on contract but does not include real estate owned subject to redemption. Foreclosed liens subject to redemption are included in "mortgages" and not transferred to "real estate" until the redemption period is past.

X 914. Net rate of interest earned on assets of U.S. life insurance companies, 1872–1970.

Source: 1872–1909, see first source for series X 893; 1910–1914, Institute of Life Insurance, unpublished data; 1915–1970, see source for series X 884, *1958*, p. 59; *1970*, p. 64; and *1971*, p. 63.

The net rate of interest earned is the ratio of the investment income for the year to the mean assets decreased by one-half the investment income. For 1872–1909, the investment income is gross investment income—i.e., there was no deduction of investment expenses. For 1910–1939, the investment income is net of investment expenses (including direct investment taxes) and the Federal income taxes treated as investment expenses. Beginning 1940, the investment income is net of investment expenses (including direct investment taxes) and all Federal income taxes. For 1872–1950, the assets used in the formula are ledger assets; beginning 1951, the assets are invested assets (including cash) and interest due and accrued.

For a discussion of the level of interest earnings before 1872, see Lester W. Zartman, *The Investments of Life Insurance Companies*, Henry Holt Company, 1906.

X 915. Total liabilities of U.S. life insurance companies, 1859–1970.

Source: 1859–1917, see first source for series X 893; 1918–1951, see second source for series X 893; 1952–1970, Institute of Life Insurance, *Life Insurance Fact Book, 1953–1958*, and *1971* editions.

Data include operations of accident and health departments of life insurance companies. The 1918–1931 figures were compiled by subtracting from total liabilities as given, the amount shown as "amounts set apart." The 1932–1942 figures were compiled by subtracting from total liabilities as given, the amounts shown as "special, voluntary contingency, etc., reserves." The 1943–1951 figures are those shown as total liabilities. The 1952–1970 figures were compiled by adding all the reserve and obligation items shown, excluding only special surplus funds, unassigned surplus, and capital.

X 916. Policy reserves of U.S. life insurance companies, 1860–1970.

Source: 1860–1864, State of New York Insurance Department, *New York Insurance Report*, 1865, pp. clxxv–clxxix; 1865–1889, see first source for series X 893 (for certain years, adjustments were made by Institute of Life Insurance); 1890–1970, see source for series X 884, *1958*, p. 61, *1970*, p. 57, and *1971*, p. 65.

This series includes life, annuity, supplementary contract, disability, and accidental death reserves and, beginning 1947, business of accident and health departments of life insurance companies.

Policy reserves are defined as the funds that an insurance company holds specifically for the fulfillment of its policy obligations. Reserves are so calculated that, together with future premiums and interest earnings, they will enable the company to pay all future claims.

X 917. Capital and surplus of U.S. life insurance companies, 1859–1970.

Source: 1859–1917 (except 1868, 1869, 1870, 1879, and 1881 which are from various *New York Insurance Reports*), see first source for series X 893; 1918–1951, see second source for series X 893; 1952–1970, Institute of Life Insurance, *Life Insurance Fact Book, 1953–1958*, and *1971* editions.

The 1919–1931 figures were compiled by adding to the "unassigned funds and capital" as given, the amounts shown as "amounts set apart." The 1932–1950 figures were compiled by adding to the "unassigned funds and capital" as given, the amounts shown as "special, voluntary, contingency, etc., reserves" (for 1932–1942, "special, voluntary, contingency, etc., reserves" are shown as "liabilities"; for 1943–1950, this item is shown separately). The 1951–1970 figures were compiled by adding the items "special surplus funds," "unassigned surplus," and "capital."

This series includes operations of accident and health departments of life insurance companies.

X 918–932. Assets, policyholders' surplus, and premiums written of the property–liability insurance business, 1931–1970.

Source: A.M. Best Company, Inc., Morristown, N.J., *Best's Aggregates and Averages*, 1959, p. 1, and *1971*, p. 1. (Copyright.)

The aggregates in these series represent the totals of the property-liability insurance business except that the mutual company aggregates do not include a very large number of small companies operated on the township or county plans or on the assessment basis. Life insurance companies writing accident and health business are excluded unless they maintained completely segregated departments and statistics so that the separate department figures could be developed.

Aggregates through 1944 are based on the reported statutory underwriting results, with some companies including Federal income taxes as an expense of operation and others excluding them. For 1942 and 1943, the statutory profit before Federal income was estimated at $115,000,000 for each year and at about $70,000,000 and $65,000,000, respectively, after Federal income taxes. For 1944, the corresponding figures were $100,000,000 and $60,000,000. Beginning 1945, underwriting experience is recorded before Federal income taxes and underwriting results are on a cash basis for reserves.

Prior to 1951, figures included only business written by casualty companies. Figures for all years include Credit, Livestock, and Miscellaneous Unsegregated and Reinsurance Unsegregated Lines.

X 923–927, policyholders' surplus. Represents the sum of paid-in capital, if any, and net reported surplus.

X 928–932, net premiums written. Represents retained premium income, direct or through reinsurance, less payments made for reinsurance ceded.

X 933–946. Underwriting experience for stock and mutual companies, by type of insurance, 1925–1970.

Source: See source for series X 918–932, *1955* issue, pp. 122–125 and 182–185; *1963* issue, pp. 141–144 and 209–212; and *1971* issue, pp. 139–142 and 208–211.

See text for series X 918–932.

X 934, premiums earned. Represents the adjustment of the net premiums written with the increase or decrease during the year in the liability for unearned premiums.

X 935, unearned premiums. Represents the estimated aggregate net amount, after deduction of reinsurance credits, which an insurance company would be obliged to tender to its policyholders as return premiums for the unexpired terms, should it wish to cancel every policy in force.

X 936 and **937**, ratios. As to losses, the ratio of losses and claim expenses incurred to premiums earned is used, but expenses incurred are ratioed to premiums written. When premium volume is increasing or decreasing, the combined loss and expense ratio thus calculated is a more accurate gauge of underwriting than the statutory figure.

X 938 and **939**, underwriting profit or loss. This item is the statutory figure taken from the annual statements of insurance companies and represents a comparison of losses and expenses incurred with premiums earned, adjusted with minor profit and loss items. This statutory figure does not include any adjustment for the estimated gain or loss in the equity in unearned premium liability.

X 947–956. Stock company resources and operating results, 1910–1970.

Source: See source for series X 918–932, *1959*, pp. 20 and 22, and *1971*, pp. 30 and 32.

See text for series X 918–932 and X 933–946.

X 954, investment profit or loss. This item is the statutory figure taken from the annual statements of insurance companies. From 1931 to 1934, arbitrary average values were used in valuing stocks owned by insurance companies; since 1934, market prices have been used for stocks but all bonds not in default have been listed at amortized values. This item, therefore, does not reflect actual market prices for all securities since December 31, 1931, although in most recent years the market prices of high-grade bonds have usually exceeded the amortized values at which they are carried in the statements.

X 957–962. Subscription or premium income and benefit expenditures of private health insurance organizations, 1948–1970.

Source: U.S. Social Security Administration, 1948, 1950, 1955, and 1960–1970, *Social Security Bulletin*, February 1973, tables 17 and 20; all other years, unpublished data.

Blue Cross and Blue Shield data were supplied by the Blue Cross Association and the National Association of Blue Shield plans from data reported to them by the individual plans. The data for insurance companies were compiled by the Health Insurance Association of America from its annual survey of the number of persons covered by insurance companies under group and individual policies. The data for independent health insurance plans are estimates of the Office of Research and Statistics, Social Security Administration, based on its annual survey of these plans.

Series X 879–889.   Life Insurance Companies and Life Insurance in Force in the United States, by Type: 1759 to 1970

[As of December 31]

Year	Number of companies	Policies (mil.)	Coverage per family (dol.)	Life insurance in force — Value (mil. dol.)					Average size policy in force (dol.)		
				Total	Ordinary	Group [1]	Industrial [2]	Credit [3]	Ordinary	Group	Industrial
	879	880	881	882	883	884	885	886	887	888	889
1970	1,802	355	20,900	1,402,123	734,730	551,357	38,644	77,392	6,105	6,905	500
1969	1,790	351	19,500	1,284,529	682,453	488,864	38,614	74,598	5,773	6,473	490
1968	1,776	346	18,400	1,183,354	633,392	442,778	38,827	68,357	5,453	6,074	480
1967	1,723	336	17,200	1,079,821	584,570	394,501	39,215	61,535	5,150	5,733	470
1966	1,711	331	15,900	984,689	541,022	345,945	39,663	58,059	4,938	5,356	450
1965	1,634	320	14,700	900,554	499,638	308,078	39,818	53,020	4,662	5,056	450
1964	1,551	308	13,300	797,808	457,868	253,620	39,833	46,487	4,382	4,637	430
1963	1,490	299	12,200	730,623	420,808	229,477	39,672	40,666	4,136	4,494	420
1962	1,469	290	11,400	675,977	391,048	209,950	39,638	35,341	3,932	4,323	420
1961	1,449	286	10,800	629,493	366,141	192,794	39,451	31,107	3,766	4,167	400
1960*	1,441	282	10,200	586,448	341,881	175,903	39,563	29,101	3,597	4,034	390
1959	1,425	275	9,500	542,128	317,158	160,163	39,809	24,998	3,424	3,875	390
1958	1,365	267	8,800	493,561	288,607	144,772	39,646	20,536	3,227	3,736	380
1957	1,273	266	8,300	458,359	264,949	133,905	40,139	19,366	3,041	3,580	370
1956	1,191	261	7,500	412,630	238,348	117,399	40,109	16,774	2,853	3,361	360
1955	1,107	251	6,900	372,332	216,812	101,345	39,682	14,493	2,721	3,202	350
1954	917	237	6,300	333,719	198,599	86,410	38,664	10,046	2,619	3,018	350
1953	832	229	5,800	304,259	185,007	72,913	37,781	8,558	2,530	2,755	340
1952	730	219	5,300	276,591	170,875	62,913	36,448	6,355	2,452	2,667	330
1951	679	210	4,900	253,140	159,109	54,398	34,870	4,763	2,378	2,535	320
1950	649	202	4,600	234,168	149,116	47,793	33,415	3,844	2,319	2,478	310
1949	612	194	4,300	213,672	138,862	40,207	32,087	2,516	2,264	2,330	300
1948	584	187	4,200	201,208	131,158	37,068	31,253	1,729	2,240	2,280	290
1947	539	182	3,800	186,035	122,393	32,026	30,406	1,210	2,200	2,050	290
1946	514	173	3,600	170,066	112,818	27,206	29,313	729	2,150	2,060	280
1945	473	163	3,200	151,762	101,550	22,172	27,675	365	2,100	1,930	270
1944	451	159	3,100	145,771	95,085	23,922	26,474	290	2,080	1,860	270
1943	437	151	3,000	137,158	89,596	22,413	24,874	275	2,080	1,760	270
1942	435	144	2,800	127,721	85,139	19,316	22,911	355	2,090	1,740	250
1941	438	140	2,800	122,178	82,525	17,359	21,825	469	2,100	1,710	250
1940	444	134	2,700	115,530	79,346	14,938	20,866	380	2,130	1,700	240
1939	446	131	2,600	111,569	77,121	13,641	20,500	307	2,130	1,790	240
1938	435	129	2,600	108,927	75,772	12,503	20,396	256	2,150	1,890	240
1937	436	128	2,600	107,794	74,836	12,638	20,104	216	2,180	1,710	240
1936	372	124	2,500	102,653	72,361	11,291	18,863	138	2,160	1,670	230
1935	373	121	2,400	98,464	70,684	10,208	17,471	101	2,160	1,590	220
1934	371	117	2,400	96,677	70,094	9,472	17,036	75	2,210	1,710	220
1933	375	115	2,400	96,246	70,872	8,681	16,630	63	2,260	1,780	210
1932	392	116	2,600	101,559	75,898	8,923	16,669	69	2,380	1,860	210
1931	413	124	2,800	106,970	79,514	9,736	17,635	85	2,420	1,730	210
1930	438	124	2,800	106,413	78,576	9,801	17,963	73	2,460	1,700	210
1929	438	123		102,086	75,686	8,994	17,349	57	2,470	1,590	190
1928	433	116		92,590	68,430	7,889	16,231	40	2,410	1,580	200
1927	407	110		84,775	63,334	6,333	15,078	30	2,400	1,450	190
1926	396	104		77,642	58,453	5,362	13,803	24	2,350	1,400	180
1925	379	97		69,475	52,892	4,247	12,318	18	2,270	1,340	170
1924	369	90		61,327	47,283	3,127	10,905	12	2,200	1,280	170
1923	358	83		55,097	43,077	2,393	9,618	9	2,160	1,180	160
1922	347	76		48,342	38,053	1,795	8,486	8	2,090	1,150	150
1921	339	70		43,944	34,777	1,527	7,633	7	2,040	1,070	150
1920	335	65		40,540	32,018	1,570	6,948	4	1,990	960	150
1919	314	60		32,971	25,783	1,092	6,092	4	1,860	920	130
1918	295	53		27,924	21,818	630	5,474	2	1,840	840	140
1917	295	49		25,243	19,868	349	5,026	(3)	1,830	780	130
1916	293	45		22,853	18,081	155	4,617		1,800	780	130
1915	295	41		21,029	16,650	100	4,279		1,800	830	130
1914	307	39		19,737	15,661	65	4,011		1,810	970	130
1913	302	37		18,683	14,827	31	3,825		1,810	910	130
1912	305	34		17,301	13,709	13	3,579		1,800	1,080	140
1911	304	31		16,125	12,772	(Z)	3,353		1,790		140
1910	284	29		14,908	11,783		3,125		1,830		140
1909	254	27		13,878	10,960		2,918		1,830		140
1908	211	25		13,085	10,450		2,635		1,850		140
1907	190	24		12,639	10,103		2,536		1,860		140
1906	163	23		12,285	9,871		2,414		1,870		140
1905	126	22		11,863	9,585		2,278		1,880		140
1904	106	20		11,165	9,059		2,106		1,930		140
1903	101	19		10,217	8,264		1,953		1,970		140
1902	95	17		9,369	7,594		1,775		2,020		130
1901	86	16		8,369	6,766		1,603		2,040		130
1900	84	14		7,573	6,124		1,449		2,160		130
1899	82	12		6,822	5,547		1,275		2,210		130
1898	73	11		6,053	4,952		1,101		2,310		130
1897	69	10		5,555	4,563		992		2,340		120
1896	67	9		5,207	4,323		884		2,420		120
1895	67	9		4,988	4,170		818		2,440		120
1894	66			4,847	4,048		799				
1893	66			4,609	3,948		661				
1892	66			4,267	3,685		582				
1891	63			3,868	3,388		481				

See footnotes at end of table.

Series X 879–889. Life Insurance Companies and Life Insurance in Force in the United States, by Type: 1759 to 1970—Con.

[As of December 31]

Year	Number of companies (879)	Total (882)	Ordinary (883)	Industrial [2] (885)
1890	60	3,522.2	3,094.7	427.5
1889	60	3,122.6	2,758.1	364.5
1888	60	2,742.0	2,437.8	304.2
1887	60	2,456.3	2,201.8	254.5
1886	59	2,096.9	1,899.1	197.8
1885	56	2,007.1	1,861.3	145.8
1884	56	1,995.9	1,884.8	111.1
1883	56	1,872.1	1,784.9	87.2
1882	55	1,720.8	1,664.6	56.2
1881	58	1,606.5	1,573.0	33.5
1880	59	1,522.7	1,502.2	20.5
1879	61	1,474.9	1,469.5	5.4
1878	65	1,519.7	1,517.7	2.0
1877	69	1,512.1	1,511.1	1.0
1876	76	1,690.6	1,690.2	.4
1875	86	1,873.9	1,873.9	---------
1874	96	1,947.6	1,947.6	---------
1873	96	2,040.8	2,040.8	---------
1872	108	2,079.2	2,079.2	---------
1871	123	2,083.0	2,083.0	---------
1870	129	2,006.1	2,006.1	---------
1869	127	1,824.8	1,824.8	---------
1868	113	1,534.6	1,534.6	---------
1867	100	1,168.0	1,168.0	---------
1866	79	874.2	874.2	---------
1865	61	589.9	589.9	---------
1864	53	404.3	404.3	---------
1863	50	276.1	276.1	---------
1862	48	191.8	191.8	---------
1861	44	173.3	173.3	---------
1860	43	173.3	173.3	---------
1859	38	151.7	151.7	---------
1858	36	130.5	130.5	---------
1857	37	120.6	120.6	---------
1856	38	106.5	106.5	---------

Year	Number of companies (879)	Total (882)	Ordinary (883)
1855	42	106.0	106.0
1854	43	94.0	94.0
1853	41	(NA)	(NA)
1852	45	(NA)	(NA)
1851	50	(NA)	(NA)
1850	48	97.1	97.1
1849	38	(NA)	(NA)
1848	30	(NA)	(NA)
1847	25	(NA)	(NA)
1846	20	(NA)	(NA)
1845	18	14.5	14.5
1844	16	(NA)	(NA)
1843	15	(NA)	(NA)
1842	15	(NA)	(NA)
1841	14	(NA)	(NA)
1840	15	4.7	4.7
1839	17	(NA)	(NA)
1838	18	(NA)	(NA)
1837	18	(NA)	(NA)
1836	17	(NA)	(NA)
1835	15	2.8	2.8
1834	13	(NA)	(NA)
1833	12	(NA)	(NA)
1832	10	(NA)	(NA)
1831	9	(NA)	(NA)
1830	9	.6	.6
1829	7	(NA)	(NA)
1828	7	(NA)	(NA)
1827	7	(NA)	(NA)
1826	7	(NA)	(NA)
1825	7	.2	.2
1824	7	(NA)	(NA)
1823	7	(NA)	(NA)
1822	7	(NA)	(NA)
1821	6	(NA)	(NA)

Year	Number of companies (879)	Total (882)	Ordinary (883)
1820	6	0.1	0.1
1819	5	(NA)	(NA)
1818	5	(NA)	(NA)
1817	4	(NA)	(NA)
1816	4	(NA)	(NA)
1815	4	(Z)	(Z)
1814	4	---------	---------
1813	3	---------	---------
1812	4	---------	---------
1811	2	---------	---------
1810	2	---------	---------
1809	2		
1808	2		
1807	2		
1806	2		
1805	2		
1804	2		
1803	2		
1802	2		
1801	4		
1800	4		
1799	4		
1798	4		
1797	4		
1796	4		
1795	4		
1794	4		
1793	2		
1792	2		
1791	2		
1790	3		
1789	3		
1788	3		
1787	3		
1786	2		

Year	Number of companies (879)
1785	2
1784	2
1783	2
1782	2
1781	2
1780	2
1779	2
1778	2
1777	2
1776	2
1775	2
1774	2
1773	2
1772	2
1771	2
1770	2
1769	2
1768	1
1767	1
1766	1
1765	1
1764	1
1763	1
1762	1
1761	1
1760	1
1759	1

* Denotes first year for which figures include Alaska and Hawaii.
NA Not available.   Z Less than $50,000 or less than $500,000.
[1] Initial year 1911.
[2] First weekly premium policy issued 1873; industrial agency system introduced 1875.
[3] Initial year 1917.

Series X 890–893. Sales of Life Insurance, by U.S. Life Insurance Companies, by Type: 1854 to 1970

[In millions of dollars]

Year	Total (890)	Ordinary (891)	Group (892)	Industrial [1] (893)
1970	[2] 213,907	138,356	[2] 68,939	6,612
1969	172,811	124,124	42,192	6,495
1968	[3] 162,091	112,820	[3] 42,596	6,675
1967	[3] 154,070	103,823	[3] 43,195	7,052
1966	130,659	95,987	27,589	7,083
1965	[2] 149,812	89,643	[2] 52,867	7,302
1964	111,899	79,430	25,149	7,320
1963	95,882	68,862	19,854	7,166
1962	84,624	61,259	16,260	7,105
1961	85,317	58,888	19,181	7,248
1960	78,417	56,183	15,328	6,906
1959*	75,107	55,138	13,077	6,892
1958	72,918	50,839	15,061	7,018
1957	71,748	48,937	16,016	6,795
1956	60,037	38,941	14,518	6,578
1955	[3] 50,243	32,207	[3] 11,637	6,399
1954	[3] 47,453	26,824	[3] 13,669	6,960
1953	38,134	24,908	6,609	6,617
1952	32,954	21,579	5,285	6,090
1951	28,857	19,000	4,261	5,596
1950	29,989	18,260	6,237	5,492
1949	24,215	15,848	2,911	5,456
1948	23,380	15,787	2,998	4,595
1947	23,637	16,131	2,768	4,738
1946	22,805	16,244	2,152	4,409
1945	15,391	10,577	1,302	3,512
1944	14,124	9,184	1,621	3,319
1943	13,281	8,022	1,924	3,335
1942	11,888	7,041	1,657	3,190
1941	12,564	7,935	1,197	3,432
1940	11,087	7,022	747	3,318
1939	10,935	6,886	844	3,205
1938	11,045	6,745	507	3,793
1937	12,572	7,593	800	4,179
1936	12,165	7,314	626	4,225
1935	12,298	7,550	715	4,033
1934	11,928	7,363	534	4,031
1933	10,846	6,786	427	3,633
1932	12,305	7,896	720	3,689
1931	15,066	10,161	927	3,978
1930	17,265	11,905	1,381	3,979
1929	17,755	12,305	1,379	4,071
1928	16,942	11,654	1,508	3,780
1927	15,582	10,777	1,008	3,797
1926	15,217	10,508	1,174	3,535
1925	14,278	10,060	1,075	3,143
1924	12,039	8,764	649	2,626
1923	11,061	8,273	549	2,239
1922	8,885	6,720	298	1,867
1921	7,957	6,248	128	1,581
1920	9,415	7,634	441	1,340
1919	7,882	6,369	433	1,080
1918	4,731	3,520	268	943
1917	4,553	3,500	184	869
1916	3,893	2,986	90	817
1915	3,285	2,437	48	800
1914	3,098	2,305	41	752
1913	3,175	2,414	22	739
1912	2,886	2,125	13	748
1911	2,688	2,008	(Z)	680
1910	2,371	1,742	---------	629
1909	2,232	1,574	---------	658
1908	1,884	1,379	---------	505
1907	1,782	1,272	---------	510
1906	1,963	1,377	---------	586
1905	2,283	1,666	---------	617
1904	2,316	1,729	---------	587
1903	2,217	1,660	---------	557
1902	2,064	1,488	---------	576
1901	1,895	1,326	---------	569
1900	1,755	1,221	---------	534
1899	1,609	1,118	---------	491
1898	1,286	883	---------	403
1897	1,196	803	---------	393
1896	1,034	687	---------	347

See footnotes at end of table.

Series X 890–893.　Sales of Life Insurance, by U.S. Life Insurance Companies, by Type: 1854 to 1970—Con.

[In millions of dollars]

Year	Total	Ordinary	Industrial [1]	Year	Total	Ordinary	Industrial [1]	Year	Total	Ordinary
	890	**891**	**893**		**890**	**891**	**893**		**890**	**891**
1895	1,113	744	369	1880	228	193	35	1865	245	245
1894	1,274	712	562	1879	178	173	5	1864	156	156
1893	1,131	797	334	1878	168	166	2	1863	90	90
1892	1,096	819	277	1877	179	178	1	1862	44	44
1891	1,006	779	227	1876	233	233	1	1861	25	25
1890	984	742	242	1875	299	299	(1)	1860	36	36
1889	871	669	202	1874	352	352	(1)	1859	30	30
1888	723	545	178	1873	466	466	(1)	1858	23	23
1887	697	538	159	1872	490	490		1857	21	21
1886	609	477	133	1871	489	489		1856	20	20
1885	432	339	94	1870	588	588		1855	17	17
1884	418	329	89	1869	615	615		1854	15	15
1883	394	317	77	1868	580	580				
1882	321	269	52	1867	472	472				
1881	268	231	37	1866	405	405				

* Denotes first year for which figures include Alaska and Hawaii.
Z　Less than $500,000.　[1] First weekly premium policy issued in 1873; industrial agency system introduced 1875.　Yearly sales, 1873–1875, probably less than $500,000.

[2] Includes servicemen's group life insurance of $27.4 billion in 1965 and $16.8 billion in 1970.　[3] Includes Federal employees group life insurance of $6,756 million in 1954, $1,928 million in 1955, $8.2 billion in 1967, and $3.4 billion in 1968.

Series X 894–907.　Income and Disbursements of U.S. Life Insurance Companies: 1854 to 1970

[In millions of dollars]

Year	Income				Disbursements									
						Payments to policyholders							Commissions, expenses, taxes, and other disbursements	Dividends to stockholders
	Total income [1]	Life insurance premiums	Annuity premiums	Investment and other income [2]	Total disbursements	Total [1]	Death benefits [3]	Matured endowments	Annuity payments	Policy dividends [4]	Surrender values	Disability and accidental death benefits [3]		
	894	**895**	**896**	**897**	**898**	**899**	**900**	**901**	**902**	**903**	**904**	**905**	**906**	**907**
1970	49,054	21,679	3,721	12,287	39,032.4	25,599.9	7,162.3	1,004.8	1,724.5	3,758.8	2,930.6	241.3	12,944.7	487.8
1969	45,628	20,491	3,762	11,632	36,085.9	23,369.2	6,841.1	975.5	1,520.7	3,597.7	2,785.4	222.4	12,201.3	515.4
1968	41,863	19,364	2,993	10,776	32,710.7	21,320.5	6,371.2	985.4	1,353.0	3,426.0	2,502.0	192.1	11,012.2	378.0
1967	38,635	18,094	2,671	9,983	29,914.9	19,502.4	5,775.6	1,041.6	1,233.0	3,248.0	2,274.1	200.4	10,149.6	262.9
1966	36,134	17,160	2,416	9,314	27,936.7	18,252.3	5,408.3	1,012.3	1,115.0	3,039.2	2,152.4	190.8	9,418.1	266.3
1965	33,167	16,083	2,260	8,563	25,214.9	16,543.0	4,923.2	955.6	1,006.6	2,794.8	1,981.8	179.6	8,434.8	237.1
1964	30,674	15,128	1,912	8,021	23,485.6	15,245.3	4,587.1	905.3	923.3	2,589.3	1,863.8	172.4	7,995.4	244.9
1963	28,584	14,266	1,742	7,471	22,036.7	14,210.8	4,277.7	823.5	874.9	2,439.8	1,826.1	159.9	7,640.9	185.0
1962	26,000	13,215	1,484	6,627	19,759.1	13,106.1	3,936.1	725.5	790.1	2,253.2	1,808.1	153.5	6,481.2	171.8
1961	24,397	12,546	1,385	6,139	18,609.1	12,288.3	3,624.8	719.3	736.5	2,080.9	1,820.3	145.7	6,134.5	186.3
1960	23,007	11,998	1,341	5,642	17,498.5	11,425.0	3,442.7	678.5	690.2	1,889.3	1,650.4	139.6	5,914.0	159.5
1959*	21,790	11,487	1,494	5,168	16,139.1	10,388.8	3,171.4	625.2	629.3	1,664.4	1,520.1	126.5	5,570.7	179.6
1958	20,249	10,753	1,424	4,778	15,126.7	9,891.2	2,971.7	759.8	578.0	1,566.3	1,457.3	133.4	5,082.2	153.3
1957	19,333	10,241	1,408	4,558	14,197.3	9,222.7	2,785.7	733.4	529.4	1,473.7	1,290.5	127.9	4,837.3	137.3
1956	17,865	9,592	1,293	4,281	12,492.4	8,055.6	2,495.3	655.5	502.7	1,358.2	1,024.4	117.8	4,302.1	134.7
1955	16,544	8,903	1,288	3,998	11,263.9	7,267.5	2,289.6	615.0	453.2	1,270.9	922.5	118.2	3,891.5	104.9
1954	15,280	8,239	1,209	3,717	10,246.8	6,570.1	2,111.6	543.1	417.3	1,117.6	868.6	118.9	3,585.6	91.1
1953	14,271	7,778	1,190	3,424	9,416.5	5,976.5	2,023.7	475.5	411.7	985.2	714.3	118.2	3,347.7	92.3
1952	13,076	7,228	1,094	3,193	8,467.4	5,371.4	1,881.4	440.7	369.0	868.4	644.0	112.8	3,037.0	59.0
1951	12,012	6,785	961	2,972	7,838.6	4,983.4	1,749.2	504.0	345.7	796.9	618.6	101.7	2,803.2	52.0
1950	11,337	6,249	939	3,148	7,189.7	4,402.7	1,593.3	493.8	257.2	679.3	666.3	132.7	2,696.6	90.4
1949	10,376	5,926	768	2,865	6,475.6	3,997.4	1,483.7	469.7	239.7	634.5	588.7	128.5	2,416.1	62.1
1948	9,751	5,679	799	2,594	5,955.5	3,670.7	1,443.3	436.2	229.9	600.5	472.9	124.9	2,240.2	44.6
1947	9,114	5,370	718	2,461	5,469.4	3,338.3	1,335.7	415.6	214.4	567.0	389.9	122.0	2,092.6	38.5
1946	8,068	4,982	644	2,442	4,611.1	2,848.3	1,274.5	404.6	199.0	507.2	327.3	135.7	1,728.9	33.9
1945	7,674	4,589	570	2,515	4,218.6	2,718.8	1,282.2	413.7	184.8	472.4	240.7	125.0	1,469.3	30.5
1944	7,011	4,265	528	2,218	3,972.1	2,527.9	1,203.1	360.6	173.7	437.7	235.4	117.4	1,420.1	24.1
1943	6,442	3,942	415	2,085	3,781.2	2,407.5	1,092.5	324.6	165.2	410.1	295.0	120.1	1,335.5	38.2
1942	6,029	3,753	368	1,908	3,739.6	2,443.2	993.0	268.1	159.3	434.5	453.8	134.5	1,282.2	14.2
1941	5,855	3,607	413	1,835	3,827.4	2,550.2	989.7	264.3	152.0	429.7	573.1	141.4	1,258.7	18.5
1940	5,658	3,501	386	1,771	3,914.0	2,680.7	976.9	275.1	142.3	456.1	688.5	141.8	1,215.2	18.1
1939	5,453	3,431	345	1,677	3,826.9	2,641.5	943.2	241.6	133.6	456.5	731.6	135.0	1,165.9	19.5
1938	5,357	3,368	393	1,596	3,744.4	2,578.1	934.0	175.9	123.2	446.9	771.2	126.9	1,152.7	13.6
1937	5,257	3,354	376	1,527	3,610.3	2,437.0	937.3	154.7	109.9	435.4	669.3	130.4	1,155.1	18.2
1936	5,180	3,216	440	1,524	3,518.0	2,429.2	919.2	154.2	94.8	418.3	712.7	130.0	1,076.1	12.7
1935	5,072	3,182	491	1,399	3,593.0	2,535.1	877.4	145.0	76.1	424.2	882.5	129.9	1,047.5	10.4
1934	4,786	3,107	400	1,279	3,661.7	2,704.9	875.4	129.4	58.2	437.7	1,077.8	126.4	945.2	11.6
1933	4,622	3,057	254	1,311	3,917.4	3,016.4	877.1	121.0	42.2	499.4	1,356.6	120.1	891.9	9.1
1932	4,653	3,314	181	1,158	3,997.7	3,087.0	905.3	122.6	36.5	562.7	1,346.1	113.8	896.7	14.0
1931	4,850	3,477	176	1,197	3,537.8	2,606.6	915.2	117.0	29.0	584.6	861.0	99.8	914.2	17.0
1930	4,594	3,416	101	1,077	3,198.5	2,246.8	855.8	112.0	23.3	553.7	614.2	87.8	929.8	21.9
1929	4,337	3,251	92	994	2,882.3	1,961.5	807.8	108.8	21.2	513.2	448.0	62.5	898.5	22.3
1928	4,088	3,037	98	953	2,547.9	1,698.7	705.9	89.9	16.8	465.8	369.2	51.1	828.1	21.1
1927	3,673	2,814	52	807	2,295.2	1,499.9	613.5	89.2	13.0	417.9	324.5	41.8	777.0	18.3
1926	3,330	2,577	39	714	2,123.8	1,373.2	569.1	98.7	11.3	376.9	282.9	34.3	737.4	13.2

See footnotes at end of table.

Series X 894–907. Income and Disbursements of U.S. Life Insurance Companies: 1854 to 1970—Con.

[In millions of dollars]

Year	Income				Disbursements									
						Payments to policyholders							Commissions, expenses, taxes, and other disburse-ments	Divi-dends to stock-holders
	Total income [1]	Life insur-ance pre-miums	Annuity pre-miums	Invest-ment and other income	Total disburse-ments	Total [1]	Death bene-fits	Matured endow-ments	Annuity pay-ments	Policy divi-dends [4]	Sur-render values	Dis-ability and accidental death benefits		
	894	895	896	897	898	899	900	901	902	903	904	905	906	907
1925	3,018	2,340	38	640	1,936.5	1,246.2	493.4	114.5	10.0	351.1	248.6	28.6	675.8	14.5
1924	2,703	2,096	20	587	1,813.2	1,205.1	449.7	138.6	10.1	351.1	235.7	19.9	596.4	11.7
1923	2,427	1,881	13	533	1,680.4	1,089.1	420.8	142.9	10.0	274.7	225.3	15.4	579.0	12.3
1922	2,149	1,671	11	467	1,493.9	1,005.7	370.1	138.3	9.5	259.8	218.4	9.6	477.5	10.7
1921	1,951	1,523	11	417	1,289.0	840.0	338.9	121.9	10.7	192.0	167.2	9.3	443.0	6.0
1920	1,764	1,374	7	383	1,198.3	744.6	350.0	101.2	9.4	157.5	119.0	7.5	448.4	5.3
1919	1,560	1,187	17	356	1,105.7	739.9	354.1	103.7	10.9	159.5	111.7	_____	361.6	4.2
1918	1,325	980	11	334	998.9	710.2	372.9	80.0	11.1	145.2	101.0	_____	283.6	5.0
1917	1,249	916	10	323	845.8	590.2	264.6	74.6	10.0	136.7	104.3	_____	251.8	3.8
1916	1,118	835	10	273	792.4	566.4	256.4	63.5	9.1	125.3	112.0	_____	220.9	5.2
1915	1,043.1	776.4	5.7	261.0	768.5	544.7	237.4	63.4	8.9	111.3	123.8	_____	220.5	3.3
1914	985.0	738.8	5.4	240.8	704.7	509.5	222.1	60.7	8.1	107.9	110.6	_____	192.0	3.3
1913	945.6	708.5	4.6	232.5	660.6	469.6	209.6	56.0	8.4	101.2	94.4	_____	186.9	4.1
1912	893.4	666.3	4.9	222.2	629.2	448.8	205.2	55.7	7.8	92.8	87.4	_____	178.2	2.1
1911	836.1	625.9	4.2	206.0	579.9	414.3	194.1	48.5	7.4	83.1	81.2	_____	163.6	2.0
1910	781.0	587.7	5.7	187.6	540.3	387.3	180.7	46.4	7.4	75.4	77.5	_____	150.9	2.1
1909	748.0	560.2	5.0	182.8	505.4	360.7	172.3	41.2	7.4	63.0	76.8	_____	143.2	1.4
1908	703.9	542.0	3.9	158.0	467.7	335.8	164.7	34.9	7.2	54.5	74.5	_____	130.2	1.7
1907	678.7	528.4	4.7	145.6	438.8	309.7	164.2	33.0	7.3	46.3	58.9	_____	128.0	1.1
1906	667.2	521.5	5.1	140.6	426.9	287.3	153.0	29.3	7.1	40.3	57.7	_____	138.6	1.0
1905	642.1	507.7	8.3	126.1	411.9	265.0	149.7	28.0	6.8	36.1	44.4	_____	145.9	1.0
1904	599.1	477.2	11.1	110.8	391.8	247.1	144.5	25.3	6.3	33.6	37.4	_____	143.9	.9
1903	553.6	438.7	8.8	106.1	360.5	225.8	131.7	24.6	5.6	31.4	32.6	_____	133.8	.9
1902	504.5	396.5	10.4	97.6	322.0	199.9	118.4	22.4	4.9	26.9	27.3	_____	121.2	.9
1901	458.0	357.6	8.7	91.7	302.8	192.4	117.9	21.3	4.4	24.3	24.6	_____	109.6	.8
1900	400.6	318.4	6.3	75.9	267.6	168.7	100.7	18.3	4.1	22.9	22.7	_____	97.9	1.0
1899	365.4	285.6	6.2	73.6	250.3	160.0	96.2	15.4	3.7	21.4	23.4	_____	89.5	.8
1898	325.5	252.6	5.1	67.8	222.5	146.8	82.7	14.0	3.4	20.0	26.8	_____	74.9	.9
1897	304.9	237.3	6.0	61.6	209.0	139.4	78.6	12.4	3.0	18.5	27.0	_____	68.8	.8
1896	283.7	222.9	5.0	55.8	202.6	136.2	77.3	12.3	2.6	17.2	26.7	_____	65.5	.9
1895	271.9	216.1	3.6	52.2	189.8	125.1	73.1	10.9	2.4	15.4	23.4	_____	63.8	.8
1894	262.0	207.1	2.6	52.3	182.3	118.4	69.3	8.3	2.3	14.8	23.6	_____	63.1	.8
1893	241.7	195.0	2.0	44.7	170.4	112.7	66.6	8.5	2.3	15.1	20.2	_____	56.9	.8
1892	227.6	181.9	2.6	43.1	156.4	104.5	63.9	8.0	2.1	14.7	15.9	_____	51.2	.7
1891	213.4	170.0	2.9	40.5	144.6	97.0	55.8	8.5	2.0	14.2	16.5	_____	46.9	.6
1890	195.6	153.6	3.2	38.8	134.2	90.0	50.9	8.9	1.8	14.5	14.0	_____	43.7	.5
1889	176.2	137.2	2.9	36.1	120.8	82.1	44.9	9.1	1.5	14.1	12.4	_____	38.3	.5
1888	153.9	117.9	2.4	33.6	108.7	76.5	41.1	8.1	1.4	14.5	11.5	_____	31.7	.5
1887	133.7	101.6	1.9	30.2	96.0	68.9	35.9	6.5	1.2	14.9	10.4	_____	26.6	.4
1886	119.1	89.1	1.7	28.3	84.1	61.5	30.8	6.9	1.1	13.2	9.4	_____	22.3	.3
1885	107.0	78.8	1.2	27.0	82.8	61.6	30.3	7.6	1.1	13.0	9.6	_____	20.8	.4
1884	98.1	71.8	1.3	25.0	78.6	59.5	27.1	8.8	1.0	13.0	9.5	_____	18.8	.4
1883	93.4	66.0	2.2	25.2	72.5	56.4	25.4	7.9	.8	13.4	8.8	_____	15.8	.3
1882	85.7	59.4	1.7	24.6	66.7	52.8	23.0	6.4	.6	13.6	9.3	_____	13.6	.3
1881	80.2	54.9	1.9	23.4	66.3	52.7	22.8	7.9	.5	12.6	8.9	_____	13.3	.3
1880	77.7	53.0	1.2	23.5	67.5	53.2	21.9	7.9	.3	13.2	9.9	_____	13.9	.3
1879	77.8	53.1	.7	24.0	69.0	57.4	22.6	8.8	.3	13.5	12.2	_____	11.3	.3
1878	80.5	56.8	.5	23.2	72.1	60.9	19.7	9.2	.3	14.6	17.1	_____	11.0	.2
1877	86.2	62.7	.3	23.2	74.3	60.7	21.0	4.9	.2	15.4	19.2	_____	13.3	.4
1876	96.4	71.8	.3	24.3	76.6	63.1	22.3	3.0	.2	16.2	21.4	_____	13.2	.3
1875	108.6	83.4	.4	24.8	80.0	65.5	25.0	2.0	.2	17.9	20.4	_____	14.1	.4
1874	115.7	89.2	.2	26.3	81.2	64.9	[5] 25.7	(5)	.1	16.6	22.5	_____	16.0	.4
1873	118.4	95.8	.2	22.4	84.5	66.8	[5] 27.1	(5)	.1	22.9	16.7	_____	17.2	.5
1872	117.3	96.5	.1	20.7	78.2	59.7	[5] 25.6	(5)	.1	20.1	13.9	_____	18.0	.5
1871	113.5	96.6	.1	16.8	77.5	56.7	[5] 28.7	(5)	.1	14.6	13.3	_____	20.2	.6
1870	105.0	90.2	.1	14.7	63.9	44.9	[5] 19.5	(5)	.1	15.8	9.6	_____	18.3	.6
1869	98.5	86.0	.1	12.4	54.5	36.6	[5] 15.6	(5)	.1	15.7	5.1	_____	17.3	.6
1868	77.4	67.8	.1	9.5	41.0	26.5	10.1	.9	.1	11.7	3.8	_____	13.8	.6
1867	56.5	50.4	(Z)	6.1	26.3	16.5	7.6	.6	(Z)	6.2	2.1	_____	9.5	.3
1866	40.4	35.8	(Z)	4.6	17.2	10.2	6.1	.3	(Z)	2.5	1.2	_____	6.8	.2
1865	24.9	[6] 21.6	(6)	3.3	10.6	6.3	[7] 4.1	(7)	(7)	1.5	.7	_____	4.0	.3
1864	16.1	[6] 13.1	(6)	3.0	7.0	4.6	[7] 3.1	(7)	(7)	1.0	.4	_____	2.3	.1
1863	10.6	[6] 8.5	(6)	2.1	5.8	3.7	[7] 2.3	(7)	(7)	1.0	.4	_____	1.9	.1
1862	7.4	[6] 5.7	(6)	1.7	3.8	2.8	[7] 1.7	(7)	(7)	.6	.5	_____	.9	.1
1861	6.3	[6] 4.9	(6)	1.4	3.6	2.8	[7] 1.5	(7)	(7)	.6	.7	_____	.8	.1
1860	6.0	[6] 4.8	(6)	1.2	2.9	2.1	[7] 1.4	(7)	(7)	.5	.2	_____	.7	.1
1859	5.2	[6] 4.0	(6)	1.2	2.6	1.9	[7] 1.3	(7)	(7)	.4	.1	_____	.8	(Z)
1858	4.5	[6] 3.6	(6)	.9	2.4	_____	1.2	_____	_____	_____	_____	_____	_____	_____
1857	4.0	[6] 3.2	(6)	.8	2.1	_____	1.2	_____	_____	_____	_____	_____	_____	_____
1856	3.8	[6] 3.0	(6)	.8	2.0	_____	1.0	_____	_____	_____	_____	_____	_____	_____
1855	3.5	[6] 3.0	(6)	.5	2.0	_____	1.2	_____	_____	_____	_____	_____	_____	_____
1854	3.2	[6] 2.6	(6)	.6	2.0	_____	1.0	_____	_____	_____	_____	_____	_____	_____

* Denotes first year for which figures include Alaska and Hawaii.
Z Less than $50,000.
[1] Beginning 1947, includes data on operations of accident and health departments of U.S. life insurance companies, not shown separately; therefore components will not add to totals.
[2] Beginning 1951, investment income is net of investment expenses.
[3] Beginning 1951, accidental death benefits included with death benefits; figures for series X 456 are for disability benefits only. Accidental death benefits approximately $30 million in 1951.
[4] Beginning 1947, includes policy dividends paid by accident and health departments of U.S. life insurance companies.
[5] Matured endowments included with death benefits.
[6] Annuity premiums included with life insurance premiums.
[7] Matured endowments and annuity payments included with death benefits.

Series X 908–917. Assets, Earning Rate, Liabilities, and Capital and Surplus of U.S. Life Insurance Companies: 1854 to 1970

Year (As of Dec. 31)	Assets (mil. dol.) Total	Bonds	Stocks	Mortgages	Real estate	Other [1]	Net rate of interest earned on assets	Liabilities (mil. dol.) Total	Policy reserves	Capital and surplus (mil. dol.)
	908	909	910	911	912	913	914	915	916	917
1970	207,254	84,166	15,420	74,375	6,320	26,973	5.30	189,931	167,556	17,323
1969	197,208	81,773	13,707	72,027	5,912	23,789	5.12	180,154	158,550	17,054
1968	188,636	79,406	13,230	69,973	5,571	20,456	4.95	171,804	150,308	16,832
1967	177,832	75,766	10,877	67,516	5,187	18,486	4.82	162,084	142,418	15,748
1966	167,455	72,215	8,832	64,609	4,885	16,914	4.73	152,539	134,711	14,916
1965	158,884	70,152	9,126	60,013	4,681	14,912	4.61	145,048	127,620	13,836
1964	149,470	67,963	7,938	55,152	4,528	13,889	4.53	136,589	120,698	12,881
1963	141,121	66,083	7,135	50,544	4,319	13,040	4.45	129,088	114,301	12,033
1962	133,291	63,722	6,302	46,902	4,107	12,258	4.34	122,035	108,384	11,256
1961	126,816	60,932	6,258	44,203	4,007	11,416	4.22	116,240	103,285	10,576
1960	119,576	58,555	4,981	41,771	3,765	10,504	4.11	109,902	98,473	9,674
1959 *	113,650	56,686	4,561	39,197	3,651	9,555	3.96	104,533	93,975	9,117
1958	107,580	54,233	4,109	37,062	3,364	8,812	3.85	98,773	88,604	8,807
1957	101,309	51,356	3,391	35,236	3,119	8,207	3.75	93,085	84,075	8,224
1956	96,011	49,107	3,503	32,989	2,817	7,595	3.63	88,321	79,738	7,690
1955	90,432	47,741	3,633	29,445	2,581	7,032	3.51	83,424	75,359	7,008
1954	84,486	46,294	3,268	25,976	2,298	6,650	3.46	78,103	70,903	6,383
1953	78,533	44,402	2,573	23,322	2,020	6,216	3.36	72,819	66,683	5,714
1952	73,375	41,974	2,446	21,251	1,903	5,801	3.28	68,119	62,579	5,256
1951	68,278	39,650	2,221	19,314	1,631	5,462	3.18	63,428	58,547	4,850
1950	64,020	39,366	2,103	16,102	1,445	5,004	3.13	59,381	54,946	4,639
1949	59,630	39,274	1,718	12,906	1,247	4,485	3.06	55,472	51,498	4,158
1948	55,512	37,979	1,428	10,833	1,055	4,217	2.96	51,803	48,158	3,709
1947	51,743	36,757	1,390	8,675	860	4,061	2.88	48,307	44,882	3,436
1946	48,191	35,350	1,249	7,155	735	3,702	2.93	44,885	41,702	3,306
1945	44,797	32,605	999	6,636	857	3,700	3.11	41,556	38,667	3,241
1944	41,054	28,711	756	6,686	1,063	3,838	3.23	38,318	35,577	2,736
1943	37,766	24,836	652	6,714	1,352	4,212	3.33	35,343	33,049	2,423
1942	34,931	21,558	608	6,726	1,663	4,376	3.44	32,775	30,797	2,156
1941	32,731	19,051	601	6,442	1,878	4,759	3.42	30,769	28,945	1,962
1940	30,802	17,092	605	5,972	2,065	5,068	3.45	28,964	27,238	1,838
1939	29,243	15,734	587	5,683	2,139	5,100	3.54	27,512	25,827	1,731
1938	27,755	14,473	586	5,445	2,179	5,072	3.59	26,122	24,495	1,633
1937	26,249	13,272	558	5,230	2,192	4,997	3.69	24,706	23,202	1,543
1936	24,874	11,869	615	5,128	2,149	5,113	3.71	23,274	21,800	1,600
1935	23,216	10,041	583	5,357	1,990	5,245	3.70	21,826	20,404	1,390
1934	21,844	8,533	482	5,875	1,693	5,261	3.92	20,417	19,030	1,427
1933	20,896	7,189	487	6,701	1,267	5,252	4.25	19,475	18,077	1,421
1932	20,754	6,843	574	7,336	935	5,066	4.65	19,308	17,839	1,446
1931	20,160	6,806	567	7,673	684	4,430	4.93	18,750	17,384	1,410
1930	18,880	6,431	519	7,598	548	3,784	5.05	17,524	16,231	1,356
1929	17,482	6,001	416	7,316	464	3,285	5.05	16,159	14,948	1,323
1928	15,961	5,655	285	6,778	403	2,840	5.05	14,711	13,596	1,250
1927	14,392	5,146	145	6,200	351	2,550	5.05	13,238	12,279	1,154
1926	12,940	4,653	125	5,580	303	2,279	5.09	11,919	11,061	1,021
1925	11,538	4,333	81	4,808	266	2,050	5.11	10,623	9,927	915
1924	10,394	4,034	64	4,175	239	1,882	5.17	9,551	8,939	843
1923	9,455	3,783	57	3,662	243	1,710	5.18	8,657	8,130	798
1922	8,652	3,656	56	3,122	197	1,621	5.12	7,943	7,449	709
1921	7,936	3,390	69	2,792	186	1,499	5.02	7,332	6,903	604
1920	7,320	3,298	75	2,442	172	1,333	4.83	6,752	6,338	568
1919	6,791	3,241	76	2,094	168	1,212	4.66	6,209	5,830	582
1918	6,475	3,012	82	2,075	179	1,127	4.72	5,903	5,407	572
1917	5,941	2,537	83	2,021	179	1,121	4.81	5,336	5,033	605
1916	5,537	2,309	83	1,893	174	1,078	4.80	4,967	4,696	570
1915	5,190	2,095	81	1,779	173	1,062	4.77	4,648	4,399	542
1914	4,935	1,982	83	1,706	171	993	4.69	4,364	4,166	571
1913	4,659	1,909	86	1,618	166	880	4.67	4,137	3,934	522
1912	4,409	1,859	96	1,485	176	793	4.59	3,880	3,695	529
1911	4,164	1,787	100	1,358	171	748	4.59	3,646	3,473	518
1910	3,876	1,660	130	1,227	173	686	4.55	3,386	3,226	490
1909	3,644	1,616	146	1,084	167	631	4.79	3,171	3,029	473
1908	3,380	1,473	147	987	167	606	4.77	2,939	2,829	441
1907	3,053	1,281	133	921	170	548	4.80	2,736	2,651	317
1906	2,924	1,299	160	826	170	469	4.68	2,557	2,473	367
1905	2,706	1,211	173	724	171	427	4.68	2,372	2,295	334
1904	2,499	1,066	173	672	181	407	4.63	2,168	2,101	331
1903	2,265	897	165	624	178	401	4.61	1,979	1,916	286
1902	2,092	872	132	573	170	345	4.58	1,798	1,738	294
1901	1,911	792	103	532	166	318	4.61	1,640	1,584	271
1900	1,742	707	95	501	158	281	4.67	1,493	1,443	249
1899	1,595	654	83	468	154	236	4.81	1,366	1,322	229
1898	1,463	581	72	455	145	210	4.87	1,246	1,203	217
1897	1,345	503	56	452	138	196	4.86	1,141	1,119	204
1896	1,244	445	54	442	135	168	4.91	1,067	1,048	177
1895	1,160	423	53	412	125	147	5.00	998	980	162
1894	1,073	369	50	394	117	143	4.93	931	915	142
1893	988	323	47	374	105	139	4.95	869	853	119
1892	919	306	39	351	97	126	5.08	802	789	117
1891	841	270	31	334	86	120	5.36	740	727	101
1890	771	241	30	310	81	109	5.10	679	670	92
1889	714.5	251.7		283.3	75.7	103.8	5.27	624.3	616.3	90.2
1888	657.1	231.6		262.5	68.6	94.4	5.43	574.6	566.8	82.5
1887	597.6	207.8		244.9	63.4	81.5	5.47	524.7	518.4	72.9
1886	561.6	197.7		227.5	59.9	76.5	5.39	459.8	452.8	101.8
1885	524.7	182.6		212.9	58.0	71.2	5.42	431.5	425.0	93.2
1884	492.2	152.1		205.7	54.6	79.8	5.48	410.1	403.3	82.1

See footnotes at end of table.

Series X 908–917. Assets, Earning Rate, Liabilities, and Capital and Surplus of U.S. Life Insurance Companies: 1854 to 1970—Con.

Year (As of Dec. 31)	Assets (mil. dol.) Total	Bonds	Stocks	Mortgages	Real estate	Other [1]	Net rate of interest earned on assets	Liabilities (mil. dol.) Total	Policy reserves	Capital and surplus (mil. dol.)
	908	909	910	911	912	913	914	915	916	917
1883	472.4	137.6		187.6	51.7	95.5	5.54	391.9	385.2	80.5
1882	450.0	124.0		172.7	51.4	101.9	5.55	373.1	366.4	76.9
1881	429.6	129.2		160.2	51.1	89.1	5.51	357.1	349.9	72.5
1880	418.1	124.8		164.8	51.6	76.9	5.48	346.5	338.8	71.6
1879	401.7	116.2		173.8	49.2	62.5	5.83	336.3	328.3	65.4
1878	404.1	112.8		189.1	42.8	59.4	5.94	339.6	329.5	64.5
1877	396.4	100.8		201.1	31.6	62.9	6.37	334.8	326.3	61.6
1876	407.4	85.7		217.9	29.2	74.6	6.55	346.3	337.5	61.1
1875	403.1	73.9		219.7	22.6	86.9	6.79	342.3	334.1	60.8
1874	387.3	65.3		210.1	18.3	93.6	6.89	328.4	320.3	58.9
1873	360.1	56.6		189.8	15.0	98.7	6.93	311.5	300.2	48.6
1872	335.2	54.7		164.3	12.5	103.7	6.90	288.3	277.4	46.9
1871	302.6	52.4		134.9	10.8	104.5	----------	254.6	243.3	48.0
1870	269.5	48.1		108.0	9.0	104.4	----------	221.0	209.3	48.5
1869	229.1	45.1		83.6	7.0	93.4	----------	180.3	170.9	48.8
1868	176.8	40.9		58.0	4.8	73.1	----------	135.8	126.0	41.0
1867	125.6	33.2		37.0	3.6	51.8	----------	88.6	81.2	37.0
1866	91.6	28.3		23.7	2.3	37.3	----------	65.6	59.8	26.0
1865	64.2	22.4		16.5	1.7	23.6	----------	49.3	42.8	14.9
1864	49.0							34.7	31.0	14.3
1863	37.8							28.6	24.0	9.2
1862	30.1							23.8	17.5	6.3
1861	26.7							18.3	15.3	8.4
1860	24.1							17.1	14.4	7.0
1859	20.5							15.4	----------	5.1
1858	15.9									
1857	14.0									
1856	15.0									
1855	12.7									
1854	11.4									

* Denotes first year for which figures include Alaska and Hawaii.

[1] Includes cash, policy loans, collateral loans, due and deferred premiums, and all other assets.

Series X 918–932. Assets, Policyholders' Surplus, and Premiums Written of the Property-Liability Insurance Business: 1931 to 1970

[In millions of dollars]

Year	Assets Total	Stock companies	Mutual companies	Recip-rocals	Lloyds	Policyholders' surplus Total	Stock companies	Mutual companies	Recip-rocals	Lloyds	Premiums written Total	Stock companies	Mutual companies	Recip-rocals	Lloyds
	918	919	920	921	922	923	924	925	926	927	928	929	930	931	932
1970	58,594	42,568	14,140	1,831	55	18,521	14,014	4,046	443	18	32,867	22,430	8,980	1,433	25
1969	52,369	37,992	12,746	1,574	56	16,719	12,699	3,606	395	19	29,225	19,970	8,023	1,206	25
1968	51,226	37,691	12,032	1,442	60	19,107	14,887	3,775	423	22	26,026	17,833	7,111	1,054	29
1967	46,562	34,183	11,020	1,296	62	17,501	13,580	3,512	382	26	23,829	16,343	6,509	948	28
1966	42,288	31,035	10,046	1,150	57	15,556	12,007	3,189	338	22	22,090	15,197	6,017	849	27
1965	41,843	31,299	9,437	1,051	56	17,112	13,660	3,106	326	20	20,063	13,855	5,413	769	26
1964	39,865	30,077	8,788	950	50	16,990	13,691	2,970	315	15	18,317	12,648	4,973	673	24
1963	37,076	27,9 9	8,164	876	46	15,747	12,642	2,788	306	11	17,175	11,881	4,656	616	22
1962	34,217	25,780	7,588	802	47	14,144	11,146	2,697	288	12	16,034	11,207	4,239	566	22
1961	33,690	25,585	7,270	787	48	14,594	11,719	2,565	299	11	15,474	10,783	4,134	531	25
1960	30,132	22,777	6,581	727	48	11,930	9,495	2,163	263	9	14,973	10,527	3,900	523	23
1959	28,602	21,801	6,080	669	52	11,633	9,381	1,993	247	12	14,084	9,931	3,646	481	27
1958	26,309	20,115	5,539	608	46	10,679	8,619	1,825	224	10	12,828	9,077	3,282	445	24
1957	23,449	17,889	4,981	535	43	8,859	7,073	1,575	202	9	12,096	8,640	3,035	399	22
1956	23,106	17,811	4,727	529	39	9,607	7,800	1,587	212	8	11,130	7,991	2,759	358	22
1955	22,305	17,275	4,481	513	35	9,461	7,694	1,553	208	7	10,539	7,662	2,510	347	20
1954	20,416	15,789	4,115	475	37	8,392	6,697	1,494	191	10	9,908	7,144	2,412	331	22
1953	17,872	13,772	3,641	420	40	6,573	5,192	1,211	162	9	9,673	7,000	2,325	321	26
1952	16,397	12,779	3,211	368	39	6,246	4,964	1,136	138	8	8,770	6,411	2,058	277	24
1951	14,756	11,535	2,861	320	40	5,739	4,543	1,062	125	10	7,775	5,759	1,761	229	25
1950	13,476	10,603	2,552	287	35	5,331	4,217	990	114	9	6,866	5,138	1,506	199	23
1949	12,100	9,520	2,295	252	34	4,720	3,708	902	101	10	6,356	4,760	1,393	180	23
1948	10,530	8,288	2,003	212	27	3,897	3,066	743	80	8	5,877	4,403	1,299	159	17
1947	9,408	7,465	1,745	176	21	3,636	2,905	658	65	7	5,113	3,862	1,104	133	13
1946	8,315	6,630	1,525	142	18	3,546	2,879	607	54	6	4,052	3,063	879	100	9
1945	7,851	6,309	1,398	128	16	3,806	3,151	595	53	7	3,230	2,425	720	78	7
1944	7,010	5,617	1,259	119	15	3,335	2,729	547	53	6	2,985	2,258	650	70	8
1943	6,408	5,141	1,144	109	14	3,050	2,494	501	49	5	2,774	2,091	610	66	7
1942	5,798	4,661	1,023	100	14	2,721	2,222	448	45	6	2,841	2,165	602	67	7
1941	5,435	4,432	903	88	12	2,606	2,164	397	41	5	2,583	1,989	529	59	6
1940	5,145	4,229	822	82	12	2,633	2,209	378	41	5	2,230	1,730	444	51	6
1939	4,921	4,063	768	79	10	2,563	2,179	342	38	4	2,022	1,571	397	49	5
1938	4,781	3,976	720	75	9	2,354	1,972	342	37	3	1,929	1,508	370	46	5
1937	4,549	3,800	669	72	9	2,184	1,828	319	33	3	2,029	1,579	394	49	8
1936	4,690	3,987	629	66	9	2,416	2,079	296	36	6	1,827	1,445	332	43	7
1935	4,160	3,528	564	62	6	2,095	1,784	272	36	3	1,668	1,332	295	37	3
1934	3,689	3,128	499	58	4	1,749	1,472	241	33	3	1,580	1,282	264	32	2
1933	3,627	3,111	456	54	6	1,528	1,288	205	32	3	1,437	1,182	226	27	2
1932	4,142	3,571	507	58	6	1,478	1,243	197	34	4	1,547	1,288	226	31	2
1931	4,440	3,830	537	64	8	1,728	1,466	219	37	6	1,833	1,532	261	38	2

Series X 933-946.   Underwriting Experience for Stock and Mutual Companies, by Type of Insurance: 1925 to 1970

Year	Stock companies							Mutual companies						
	Net premiums (mil. dol.)			Ratios		Underwriting profit or loss		Net premiums (mil. dol.)			Ratios		Underwriting profit or loss	
	Written	Earned	Unearned	Losses incurred to premiums earned	Expenses incurred to premiums written	Total (mil. dol.)	Ratio to premiums earned	Written	Earned	Unearned	Losses incurred to premiums earned	Expenses incurred to premiums written	Total (mil. dol.)	Ratio to premiums earned
	933	934	935	936	937	938	939	940	941	942	943	944	945	946
TOTAL														
1970	22,430	21,448	11,386	69.7	29.6	-146	-0.7	8,713	8,383	3,304	73.3	23.4	202	2.4
1969	19,970	19,108	10,426	70.3	30.3	-384	-2.0	7,773	7,463	2,969	76.5	24.1	-123	-1.6
1968	17,833	17,236	9,589	68.8	31.2	-187	-1.1	6,887	6,659	2,664	74.4	24.6	13	.2
1967	16,343	15,853	8,994	67.2	31.7	28	.2	6,278	6,121	2,447	72.7	24.5	129	2.1
1966	15,197	14,655	8,522	66.1	31.9	110	.8	5,788	5,617	2,290	70.9	24.2	234	4.2
1965	13,855	13,379	8,025	69.2	32.7	-419	-3.1	5,196	5,036	2,126	73.1	25.0	56	1.1
1964	12,648	12,347	7,578	68.0	33.9	-341	-2.8	4,767	4,651	1,970	73.4	25.9	3	.1
1963	11,881	11,595	7,285	66.3	34.7	-210	-1.8	4,447	4,240	1,855	71.4	26.5	35	.8
1962	11,599	11,285	7,061	64.5	34.5	9	.1	4,038	4,047	1,649	66.7	25.7	307	7.6
1961	10,783	10,707	6,744	64.4	35.0	36	.3	3,945	3,883	1,657	63.6	25.6	404	10.4
1960	10,527	10,264	6,672	63.6	34.8	70	.7	3,723	3,650	1,594	64.2	25.6	352	9.6
1959	9,931	9,526	6,407	62.5	35.3	74	.8	3,475	3,357	1,518	64.7	25.3	306	9.1
1958	9,077	8,841	6,003	63.7	36.3	-87	-1.0	3,120	3,022	1,403	64.9	25.6	263	8.7
1957	8,640	8,325	5,771	66.2	36.7	-359	-4.3	2,890	2,791	1,306	65.5	25.8	215	7.7
1956	7,991	7,744	5,455	63.4	37.1	-134	-1.7	2,609	2,527	1,206	65.0	26.3	201	7.9
1955	7,662	7,342	5,232	58.2	36.7	259	3.5	2,385	2,331	1,112	61.3	26.0	285	12.2
1954	7,144	6,992	4,921	56.9	36.7	387	5.5	2,278	2,223	1,055	59.3	25.3	329	14.8
1953	7,000	6,658	4,756	57.2	35.9	336	5.0	2,186	2,080	1,005	60.3	24.4	292	14.1
1952	6,411	5,994	4,422	58.4	36.0	186	3.1	1,884	1,770	886	60.5	24.7	233	13.2
1951	5,759	5,377	4,007	60.2	36.9	13	.2	1,659	1,551	777	60.3	24.8	204	13.1
1950	2,933	2,821	1,239	60.0	35.7	84	3.0	1,327	1,289	346	65.6	22.2	150	11.6
1949	2,664	2,562	1,130	55.7	36.1	173	6.7	1,171	1,139	306	61.0	23.1	174	15.3
1948	2,442	2,284	1,019	56.6	35.6	121	5.3	1,059	1,017	273	58.7	23.7	169	16.6
1947	2,075	1,913	863	58.1	36.3	48	2.5	887	844	230	61.5	23.8	114	13.4
1946	1,614	1,482	701	61.2	37.7	-33	-2.2	688	648	192	64.6	24.3	62	9.6
1945	1,325	1,251	568	58.0	36.1	47	3.8	540	517	146	64.0	23.9	57	11.0
1944	1,223	1,183	497	53.8	37.0	94	8.0	485	474	123	61.4	23.9	67	14.2
1943	1,130	1,126	449	53.3	39.0	83	7.4	440	435	111	59.4	23.8	72	16.5
1942	1,110	1,084	446	51.1	40.1	81	7.4	427	416	105	57.0	23.2	79	19.0
1941	997	951	421	52.7	39.1	58	6.0	364	350	94	60.3	23.7	52	14.9
1940	870	849	374	51.9	40.6	54	6.3	294	287	78	59.9	23.9	45	15.6
1939	821	813	354	50.8	41.0	62	7.7	257	253	70	57.7	23.5	46	18.2
1938	812	800	349	51.6	40.5	55	6.9	231	226	64	58.8	22.0	42	18.7
1937	824	800	336	52.9	39.2	52	6.6	235	228	60	60.2	21.1	41	18.2
1936	746	726	313	55.1	38.1	34	4.7	200	192	53	61.4	21.2	30	15.7
1935	673	659	281	58.5	38.3	11	1.6	168	162	46	61.1	21.4	26	15.8
1934	645	636	269	61.2	38.7	-5	-.7	141	135	40	63.7	21.4	18	13.2
1933	591	598	260	62.7	40.3	-17	-2.8	110	108	34	61.4	23.7	15	14.1
1932	636	673	281	66.3	41.9	-31	-4.6	108	110	33	60.4	24.5	17	15.2
1931	769	777	332	65.7	41.2	-51	-6.6	122	123	36	62.1	23.4	17	14.0
1930	838	840	359	63.4	40.9	-39	-4.7	132	131	36	62.9	22.6	18	14.0
1929	866	841	366	60.0	39.7	-22	-2.5	135	130	36	65.1	21.6	15	11.9
1928	805	779	345	58.0	39.5	4	.5	121	116	33	61.8	20.1	18	15.9
1927	763	740	316	58.7	39.2	-8	-1.1	105	100	27	61.3	20.6	16	15.9
1926	710	682	296	59.5	39.4	-8	-1.2	88	84	24	58.3	20.7	14	16.2
1925	633	599	270	57.7	39.3	-11	-1.8	70	67	19	63.0	19.0	11	15.9
HOMEOWNERS MULTIPLE-PERIL INSURANCE														
1970	1,960	1,860	1,593	69.2	33.6	-86	-4.6	604	564	406	66.9	34.7	-23	-4.1
1969	1,785	1,667	1,493	69.6	33.8	-96	-5.8	535	490	366	65.8	35.4	-22	-4.5
1968	1,606	1,499	1,374	69.0	34.9	-96	-6.4	471	441	323	67.3	35.5	-23	-5.3
1967	1,419	1,344	1,267	69.2	35.5	-90	-6.7	420	395	295	65.8	35.6	-14	-3.6
1966	1,324	1,205	1,192	64.2	35.7	-41	-3.4	378	354	270	60.5	35.4	6	1.6
1965	1,183	1,086	1,081	71.0	36.2	-114	-10.5	340	313	245	68.8	35.8	-24	-7.6
1964	1,036	964	987	74.0	38.1	-144	-14.9	297	270	218	70.1	36.8	-29	-10.6
1963	967	853	917	69.3	38.7	-113	-13.2	263	230	191	64.2	37.7	-17	-7.2
1962	825	725	803	65.7	39.5	-77	-10.6	214	195	158	59.1	36.5	2	1.0
1961	701	593	703	64.6	39.8	-69	-11.7	183	156	139	54.2	36.9	4	2.5
1960	617	443	592	58.5	39.8	-62	-14.0	147	113	114	54.0	36.8	-2	-1.8
1959	421	297	418	51.4	39.9	-23	-7.9	102	75	80	43.9	35.4	6	8.1
1958	281	208	292	56.3	41.1	-24	-11.7	64	50	53	45.4	36.0	4	8.1
1957	195	131	211	57.8	41.9	-29	-20.2	46	31	38	47.1	37.4	-1	-2.7
1956	149	67	147	56.8	42.3	-34	-50.7	30	14	23	43.3	37.2	-3	-22.9
1955	59	18	48	58.5	38.4	-15	-83.1	9	3	7	41.4	32.9	-1	-45.4

Series X 933–946. Underwriting Experience for Stock and Mutual Companies, by Type of Insurance: 1925 to 1970—Con.

Year	Stock companies							Mutual companies						
	Net premiums (mil. dol.)			Ratios		Underwriting profit or loss		Net premiums (mil dol.)			Ratios		Underwriting profit or loss	
	Written	Earned	Unearned	Losses incurred to premiums earned	Expenses incurred to premiums written	Total (mil. dol.)	Ratio to premiums earned	Written	Earned	Unearned	Losses incurred to premiums earned	Expenses incurred to premiums written	Total (mil. dol.)	Ratio to premiums earned
	933	934	935	936	937	938	939	940	941	942	943	944	945	946
COMMERCIAL MULTIPLE-PERIL INSURANCE														
1970	1,119	1,034	747	56.1	34.7	65	6.3	212	194	121	49.5	35.1	23	12.1
1969	941	863	662	58.8	35.5	22	2.5	173	155	103	53.0	34.9	13	8.3
1968	794	719	584	60.8	36.3	−6	−.8	139	121	86	57.4	35.0	3	2.1
1967	677	597	510	56.1	37.2	10	1.6	101	91	67	57.0	35.3	4	3.9
1966	566	479	430	56.7	36.5	1	.2	83	72	57	51.4	35.1	6	7.8
1965	444	362	344	60.4	37.0	−21	−5.8	65	54	45	55.8	36.2	(Z)	.4
1964	325	248	263	57.3	37.4	−15	−6.2	47	35	33	56.3	35.7	−2	−4.6
1963	234	154	185	58.9	36.2	−21	−13.9	29	19	20	54.2	33.1	−1	−5.4
1962	143	89	106	55.9	36.8	−13	−15.2	15	10	10	45.5	31.9	(Z)	4.8
1961	75	55	53	55.5	37.1	−3	−6.2	7	5	4	45.9	35.5	(Z)	7.5
1960	51	40	33	65.8	37.4	−5	−13.5	5	4	2	57.2	36.3	(Z)	.8
1959	34	32	22	65.9	37.9	−2	−6.6	4	3	2	64.9	32.3	(Z)	−4.6
1958	27	25	19	78.5	37.8	−5	−20.0	2	2	1	54.9	41.0	(Z)	4.9
1957	26	18	16	86.2	37.6	−7	−39.8	2	2	1	67.2	40.0	(Z)	−17.6
1956	16	11	7	76.4	34.7	−3	−26.9	2	1	1	54.3	35.1	(Z)	−4.0
WORKMEN'S COMPENSATION-INSURANCE														
1970	2,489	2,411	704	71.6	20.7	170	7.0	1,003	996	205	70.8	15.8	132	13.2
1969	2,233	2,174	626	71.0	21.2	158	7.3	967	954	197	69.5	16.4	132	13.8
1968	2,006	1,954	571	70.2	21.5	151	7.7	855	879	185	68.5	16.6	130	14.7
1967	1,791	1,729	519	71.5	22.2	95	5.5	810	796	178	72.6	16.6	84	10.6
1966	1,614	1,568	456	73.0	22.5	60	3.9	734	722	164	69.7	16.7	96	13.3
1965	1,405	1,365	411	72.2	23.5	50	3.6	638	625	153	70.1	17.4	76	12.2
1964	1,274	1,248	372	71.9	24.0	44	3.6	595	588	140	71.8	17.7	60	10.3
1963	1,164	1,134	347	72.7	24.6	23	2.0	561	552	133	73.4	17.9	46	8.4
1962	1,072	1,044	317	72.5	24.8	21	2.0	532	528	124	69.8	17.2	68	12.9
1961	987	968	290	74.9	25.0	−4	−.4	497	488	121	71.2	17.1	56	11.5
1960	943	918	271	73.5	25.1	7	.7	477	469	112	70.8	17.0	56	11.9
1959	861	844	246	74.1	25.3	1	.1	436	434	105	71.7	17.6	46	10.5
1958	803	798	229	71.5	25.8	20	2.5	406	404	103	70.2	18.0	47	11.7
1957	789	777	224	70.2	25.9	27	3.5	411	404	101	65.0	17.4	70	17.3
1956	726	712	212	68.0	25.8	40	5.7	385	382	94	66.3	17.0	63	16.5
1955	670	656	198	66.9	25.9	44	6.7	365	361	91	64.9	17.2	64	17.8
1954	646	632	183	64.4	25.7	59	9.3	371	366	87	62.9	16.4	75	20.5
1953	642	618	170	69.2	24.9	31	5.0	389	378	83	67.6	15.3	63	16.7
1952	568	555	146	72.5	25.8	6	1.1	350	342	71	70.0	15.6	48	14.0
1951	506	497	134	76.8	26.5	−19	−3.8	312	306	63	70.2	16.2	41	13.4
1950	439	437	124	70.9	27.8	5	1.1	258	257	56	69.8	16.7	34	13.4
1949	457	449	122	61.6	27.7	46	10.2	262	258	55	63.6	16.9	50	19.3
1948	469	452	114	60.9	27.5	48	10.7	263	255	52	58.9	16.5	61	24.1
1947	415	402	97	62.2	27.8	37	9.1	228	244	44	60.4	16.3	51	23.0
1946	325	322	84	65.4	29.2	17	5.1	173	174	40	66.4	16.4	30	17.2
1945	308	304	81	66.7	26.7	19	6.3	169	165	40	64.7	16.3	31	18.6
AUTOMOBILE LIABILITY, BODILY INJURY														
1970	4,093	3,895	1,643	77.8	26.6	−226	−5.8	2,116	2,049	648	76.0	21.5	38	1.9
1969	3,597	3,486	1,451	76.2	27.3	−154	−4.4	1,897	1,841	581	76.8	22.3	3	.2
1968	3,291	3,204	1,344	75.9	28.0	−149	−4.7	1,693	1,642	526	78.5	22.5	−29	−1.8
1967	3,087	2,996	1,255	74.9	28.1	−115	−3.8	1,535	1,496	476	79.7	22.6	−44	−2.9
1966	2,872	2,773	1,168	75.4	28.3	−133	−4.8	1,408	1,366	437	80.2	22.4	−45	−3.3
1965	2,624	2,519	1,073	75.8	29.0	−152	−6.0	1,247	1,209	397	79.5	23.3	−43	−3.5
1964	2,365	2,298	973	75.4	30.1	−145	−6.3	1,149	1,120	363	81.3	24.3	−69	−6.2
1963	2,194	2,144	906	72.5	30.5	−81	−3.8	1,056	1,006	333	79.3	25.1	−57	−5.6
1962	2,079	2,018	860	71.4	30.9	−65	−3.2	941	948	285	72.8	24.5	28	2.9
1961	1,940	1,914	799	72.3	31.0	−73	−3.8	910	901	291	71.7	24.8	29	3.2
1960	1,873	1,847	774	72.1	30.7	−60	−3.3	852	839	281	72.4	24.6	22	2.6
1959	1,769	1,701	748	74.6	30.9	−115	−6.8	795	761	269	78.3	24.0	−26	−3.4
1958	1,602	1,542	679	78.5	31.9	−180	−11.6	695	667	234	80.2	24.3	−37	−5.5
1957	1,461	1,390	621	81.6	33.0	−226	−16.3	610	583	206	79.6	24.8	−32	−5.6
1956	1,289	1,243	550	76.0	33.1	−128	−10.3	525	506	180	77.2	25.4	−18	−3.5
1955	1,189	1,158	509	69.3	32.8	−35	−3.0	467	459	159	74.4	25.5	−1	−.3
1954	1,114	1,090	480	64.2	32.6	27	2.5	442	433	151	69.0	24.9	24	5.5
1953	1,068	1,019	455	64.8	32.2	15	1.5	413	392	142	70.0	24.4	17	4.3
1952	938	866	406	70.2	32.6	−48	−5.5	339	315	121	71.5	25.2	4	1.3
1951	770	720	335	72.3	33.6	−59	−8.2	275	257	97	67.5	25.4	14	5.4
1950	652	628	280	65.4	34.1	−5	−.8	217	210	76	66.1	24.6	18	8.5
1949	606	580	255	59.2	34.1	30	5.2	196	189	69	60.6	24.8	26	13.7
1948	553	519	229	62.4	34.7	3	.6	175	167	61	58.5	26.2	23	14.0
1947	470	424	194	65.5	35.4	−20	−4.7	151	140	53	61.9	25.7	14	10.3
1946	357	317	148	74.0	35.9	−46	−14.4	121	109	42	67.8	26.0	4	3.3
1945	257	241	108	65.8	36.8	−12	−4.9	87	82	30	59.4	26.9	10	11.9

Z Less than $500,000.

Series X 933–946. Underwriting Experience for Stock and Mutual Companies, by Type of Insurance: 1925 to 1970—Con.

	Stock companies							Mutual companies						
	Net premiums (mil dol.)			Ratios		Underwriting profit or loss		Net premiums (mil dol.)			Ratios		Underwriting profit or loss	
Year	Written	Earned	Unearned	Losses incurred to premiums earned	Expenses incurred to premiums written	Total (mil. dol.)	Ratio to premiums earned	Written	Earned	Unearned	Losses incurred to premiums earned	Expenses incurred to premiums written	Total (mil. dol.)	Ratio to premiums earned
	933	934	935	936	937	938	939	940	941	942	943	944	945	946
AUTOMOBILE LIABILITY, PROPERTY DAMAGE														
1970	1,792	1,689	726	80.0	27.0	−146	−8.6	957	919	300	84.7	21.8	−68	−7.3
1969	1,540	1,484	626	81.8	28.1	−163	−11.0	832	798	263	90.2	22.5	−109	−13.6
1968	1,396	1,356	570	76.7	28.7	−84	−6.2	727	702	230	83.5	22.9	−51	−7.2
1967	1,294	1,241	530	73.3	29.0	−43	−3.5	650	630	205	78.5	23.3	−16	−2.5
1966	1,177	1,122	479	74.0	29.0	−50	−4.4	589	568	185	78.8	22.9	−14	−2.5
1965	1,040	985	425	77.1	29.6	−82	−8.3	514	496	166	80.2	23.8	−24	−4.9
1964	911	886	373	78.2	30.9	−89	−10.0	461	447	148	81.8	24.9	−33	−7.5
1963	853	846	349	73.0	31.5	−41	−4.8	424	406	134	78.1	25.4	−19	−4.7
1962	831	810	342	69.9	32.0	−22	−2.7	388	394	116	72.1	24.9	13	3.4
1961	790	791	322	66.0	32.2	14	1.8	383	383	122	68.6	25.6	22	5.9
1960	784	780	323	65.6	31.6	21	2.7	374	371	122	69.2	25.3	20	5.3
1959	762	740	320	65.6	32.1	10	1.4	356	344	119	70.6	24.7	14	3.9
1958	701	676	298	67.9	33.4	−17	−2.5	319	307	107	71.2	25.2	8	2.7
1957	647	634	274	70.5	34.6	−37	−5.8	285	277	97	71.9	25.9	4	1.4
1956	615	608	262	65.7	34.9	−5	−.9	255	251	88	72.4	26.5	1	.6
1955	602	593	257	58.2	34.2	42	7.1	238	237	82	65.0	26.7	19	8.1
1954	578	566	250	54.2	34.0	62	11.0	231	227	80	61.7	26.0	27	11.8
1953	557	521	237	59.6	33.6	24	4.5	220	207	76	64.8	25.1	18	8.6
1952	465	433	201	69.2	34.3	−27	−6.1	176	164	63	75.8	25.9	−6	−3.7
1951	386	363	168	75.4	35.3	−47	−12.9	142	134	51	81.0	26.6	−12	−9.1
1950	328	315	142	64.6	36.2	−7	−2.2	114	110	40	70.1	25.6	4	3.3
1949	299	284	129	61.3	35.9	2	.8	102	98	36	65.7	26.5	6	6.6
1948	262	239	114	67.9	36.0	−18	−7.4	89	83	32	68.1	27.4	2	2.4
1947	207	176	90	78.5	36.6	−38	−21.4	70	62	26	75.5	27.1	−4	−6.1
1946	137	117	60	93.4	37.3	−43	−36.9	49	43	18	87.5	27.6	−8	−18.8
1945	94	89	40	86.0	38.0	−23	−26.4	33	32	12	81.5	28.1	−4	−11.3
AUTOMOBILE PHYSICAL DAMAGE (FIRE, THEFT, COLLISION, AND COMPREHENSIVE)														
1970	3,275	3,143	1,647	(1)	(1)	−2	(1)	1,548	1,486	486	(1)	(1)	15	(1)
1969	2,883	2,768	1,518			−126		1,314	1,262	424			−117	
1968	2,620	2,537	1,406			−1		1,146	1,109	373			−2	
1967	2,426	2,373	1,321			145		1,032	1,008	337			96	
1966	2,314	2,191	1,269			151		944	914	313			112	
1965	2,031	1,905	1,148			−17		829	794	283			41	
1964	1,782	1,712	1,029			−47		727	704	248			15	
1963	1,650	1,595	960			12		662	628	227			27	
1962	1,543	1,481	905			26		591	597	193			57	
1961	1,397	1,440	843			100		567	567	200			76	
1960	1,440	1,438	782			93		554	551	199			74	
1959	1,424	1,377	886			87		532	519	196			76	
1958	1,283	1,316	839			54		490	475	183			67	
1957	1,302	1,271	873			−38		447	430	169			32	
1956	1,210	1,245	841			24		404	398	152			45	
1955	1,343	1,251	880			124		385	380	143			75	
1954	1,202	1,234	790			208		371	369	139			89	
1953	1,291	1,192	812			124		362	343	138			61	
1952	1,205	1,076	724			65		308	291	118			49	
1951	998	982	595			83		267	255	102			43	
1950	196	174	101			24		173	163	61			41	
1949	162	151	81			29		144	137	52			38	
1948	132	114	66			15		127	119	45			28	
1947	101	85	48			3		105	96	36			13	
1946	73	59	32			−12		77	66	27			−6	
1945	36	30	18			−7		46	41	16			−8	
FIRE INSURANCE														
1970	1,836	1,788	1,374	59.1	36.0	70	3.9	364	360	218	54.3	33.7	42	11.7
1969	1,677	1,625	1,327	60.7	37.6	8	.5	341	332	210	53.7	34.4	36	10.9
1968	1,507	1,478	1,275	61.6	38.9	−19	−1.3	320	314	202	54.5	35.1	30	9.7
1967	1,380	1,405	1,248	60.3	39.7	10	.7	302	303	196	54.2	34.3	35	11.7
1966	1,321	1,352	1,273	59.6	40.8	9	.6	284	287	197	51.7	34.5	41	14.2
1965	1,272	1,329	1,311	60.0	42.1	−5	−.3	276	277	200	52.2	35.2	36	12.8
1964	1,259	1,341	1,371	59.9	43.6	−11	−.8	275	281	202	53.6	35.4	33	11.8
1963	1,288	1,377	1,454	65.4	44.3	−95	−6.9	284	277	208	57.7	36.2	15	5.3
1962	1,356	1,400	1,544	58.5	44.5	−24	−1.7	267	290	201	49.3	34.0	57	19.5
1961	1,337	1,411	1,587	55.8	45.0	23	1.6	282	293	225	47.4	34.9	56	19.0
1960	1,387	1,422	1,661	55.2	44.7	17	1.2	280	288	236	46.8	35.2	55	19.0
1959	1,434	1,390	1,694	54.3	44.6	−4	−.3	276	280	244	49.2	35.3	45	16.0
1958	1,363	1,348	1,654	55.3	45.4	−17	−1.3	263	265	247	46.6	35.8	47	17.8
1957	1,336	1,327	1,642	55.2	45.8	−19	−1.4	258	257	247	45.8	35.4	48	18.6
1956	1,332	1,313	1,633	55.2	45.5	−17	−1.3	250	248	246	45.0	35.8	47	18.9
1955	1,317	1,314	1,618	49.3	45.0	74	5.6	244	239	243	42.1	35.4	52	21.9
1954	1,308	1,308	1,621	47.1	44.4	111	8.5	238	231	238	41.2	34.4	54	23.3
1953	1,306	1,285	1,618	48.5	43.9	88	6.8	228	219	230	38.2	33.5	58	26.6
1952	1,289	1,236	1,594	46.7	43.2	101	8.2	218	200	218	37.9	33.5	51	25.6
1951	1,301	1,164	1,541	47.0	42.1	69	5.9	203	178	200	37.6	33.8	43	24.0

[1] 1945–1970, sufficient data not available to compute ratios.

Series X 947-956. Stock Company Resources and Operating Results: 1910 to 1970

[In millions of dollars, except percent]

Year	Resources					Operating results				
	Assets	Liabilities	Capital	Surplus	Policy-holders' surplus [1]	Investment income		Investment profit or loss [2]	Underwriting profit or loss [3]	
						Total	Percent of mean assets		Total	Percent of premiums earned
	947	948	949	950	951	952	953	954	955	956
1970	42,568	28,553	1,878	9,326	14,014	1,439	3.57	1,250	−154	−0.72
1969	37,992	24,293	1,578	8,690	12,699	1,238	3.27	−492	−396	−2.07
1968	37,691	22,804	1,500	10,136	14,887	1,101	3.06	2,279	−201	−1.17
1967	34,183	20,603	1,367	9,324	13,580	987	3.03	2,302	10	.07
1966	31,035	19,028	1,320	8,388	12,007	896	2.87	−552	103	.70
1965	31,297	17,639	1,316	9,391	13,660	852	2.78	1,466	−425	−3.19
1964	30,077	16,386	1,350	9,576	13,691	782	2.69	1,821	−348	−2.81
1963	27,989	15,347	1,290	8,868	12,642	721	2.69	2,017	−219	−1.89
1962	25,780	14,633	1,251	7,843	11,146	673	2.62	−230	3	.02
1961	25,585	13,865	1,175	8,126	11,719	621	2.57	2,516	30	.28
1960	22,777	13,282	1,112	6,745	9,495	592	2.66	655	66	.64
1959	21,801	12,419	1,030	6,502	9,381	534	2.55	1,021	71	.74
1958	20,115	11,496	951	5,995	8,619	489	2.57	2,074	−93	−1.05
1957	17,889	10,816	957	5,009	7,073	461	2.58	−166	−361	−4.33
1956	17,811	10,011	934	5,536	7,800	430	2.45	580	−136	−1.75
1955	17,275	9,581	911	5,532	7,694	394	2.38	1,147	255	3.49
1954	15,789	9,091	832	4,858	6,697	363	2.46	1,583	385	5.50
1953	13,772	8,580	797	3,793	5,192	326	2.37	267	333	5.00
1952	12,779	7,815	759	3,598	4,964	294	2.30	549	185	3.08
1951	11,535	6,992	739	3,264	4,543	273	2.47	545	13	.24
1950	10,603	6,386	736	3,034	4,217	253	2.52	600	191	4.00
1949	9,520	5,812	671	2,656	3,708	215	2.42	528	421	9.51
1948	8,288	5,222	620	2,187	3,066	188	2.39	152	200	4.99
1947	7,465	4,560	615	2,050	2,905	172	2.44	109	−49	−1.44
1946	6,630	3,751	594	1,960	2,879	154	2.38	−12	−152	−5.78
1945	6,309	3,158	579	2,199	3,151	147	2.47	517	33	1.47
1944	5,617	2,888	530	1,946	2,729	141	2.62	331	72	3.37
1943	5,141	2,646	513	1,781	2,494	133	2.72	332	153	7.42
1942	4,661	2,440	493	1,575	2,222	123	2.71	84	74	3.43
1941	4,432	2,268	491	1,520	2,164	128	2.95	39	55	2.96
1940	4,229	2,020	484	1,573	2,209	122	2.93	58	70	4.28
1939	4,063	1,884	473	1,561	2,179	116	2.88	138	89	5.78
1938	3,976	2,004	461	1,511	1,972	115	2.97	233	97	6.40
1937	3,800	1,972	448	1,389	1,828	126	3.24	−286	85	5.64
1936	3,987	1,908	444	1,635	2,079	120	3.21	359	69	4.98
1935	3,528	1,744	429	1,355	1,784	108	3.23	332	83	6.35
1934	3,128	1,655	419	1,053	1,472	112	3.58	25	59	4.62
1933	3,111	1,824	418	869	1,288	106	3.17	107	64	5.10
1932	3,571	2,328	449	794	1,243	125	3.38	−9	−3	−.24
1931	3,830	2,364	604	862	1,466	154	3.92	60	−11	−.69
1930	4,021	2,197	650	1,174	1,824	164	3.92	−148	−23	−1.30
1929	4,322	2,285	639	1,398	2,037	152	3.65	84	31	1.74
1928	4,009	2,186	552	1,270	1,822	140	3.76	242	62	3.65
1927	3,463	2,039	443	981	1,424	124	3.80	285	26	1.59
1926	3,058	1,897	397	764	1,161	112	3.83	158	−49	−3.17
1925	2,809	1,742	372	695	1,067	116	4.31	163	−57	−4.01
1924	2,557	1,584	341	631	973	113	4.59	190	−48	−3.57
1923	2,348	1,479	323	546	869	115	5.02	71	−12	−.94
1922	2,225	1,365	296	563	859	113	5.25	151	7	.58
1921	2,080	1,335	246	498	745	109	5.32	114	−23	−1.90
1920	2,004	1,336	236	432	668	105	5.61	53	−29	−2.47
1919	1,739	1,106	205	428	633	86	5.38	42	51	5.18
1918	1,447	917	184	346	529	63	4.64	37	20	2.34
1917	1,271	776	173	323	496	61	5.05	15	5	.77
1916	1,142	652	169	321	491	64	5.89	49	3	.56
1915	1,039	582	158	300	457	56	5.58	41	15	2.71
1914	984	561	152	271	423	54	5.61	11	−17	−3.26
1913	935	515	150	269	419	45	4.84	9	5	1.01
1912	917	495	138	284	422	49	5.48	28	9	2.02
1911	860	460	128	271	399	41	4.90	31	6	1.49
1910	799	432	122	246	367	38	4.78	20	23	5.70

[1] Includes voluntary reserves.
[2] Includes investment income.
[3] Beginning 1942, before Federal income taxes.

Series X 957-962. Subscription or Premium Income and Benefit Expenditures of Private Health Insurance Organizations: 1948 to 1970

[In millions of dollars, except percent]

TOTAL

Year	Subscription or premium income	Benefit expenditures Total Amount	Total Percent of premium income	Hospital care	Physicians' services	Other types of care
	957	958	959	960	961	962
1970	17,185	15,744	91.6	10,007.8	4,908.2	118.1
1969	14,658	13,069	89.2	8,356.2	4,028.9	528.6
1968	12,861	11,310	87.9	7,328.7	3,476.2	424.6
1967	11,105	9,545	85.9	6,133.4	2,964.3	447.1
1966	10,564	9,142	86.5	5,993.1	2,831.1	317.6
1965	10,001	8,729	87.3	5,789.8	2,679.8	259.3
1964	8,984	7,832	87.2	5,187.4	2,427.2	217.5
1963	8,054	6,980	86.7	4,641.5	2,153.0	184.8
1962	7,411	6,344	85.6	4,196.9	1,991.7	155.2
1961	6,673	5,965	89.4	3,766.3	1,796.1	133.0
1960	5,841	4,996	85.3	3,304.5	1,592.6	99.2
1959	5,139	4,399	85.6	2,944.5	1,454.3	(1)
1958	4,498	3,877	86.2	2,591.4	1,285.9	(1)
1957	4,144	3,474	83.8	2,304.5	1,169.5	(1)
1956	3,624	3,015	83.2	2,021.8	992.9	(1)
1955	3,150	2,536	80.5	1,678.4	857.3	(1)
1954	2,756	2,179	79.1	1,442.4	736.5	(1)
1953	2,405	1,919	79.8	1,287.0	632.2	(1)
1952	1,993	1,604	80.5	1,073.8	530.1	(1)
1951	1,660	1,353	81.5	896.8	455.8	(1)
1950	1,292	992	76.8	680.0	311.9	(1)
1949	1,015	767	75.6	538.9	227.9	(1)
1948	862	606	70.3	455.0	151.0	(1)

INSURANCE COMPANIES

Year	Subscription or premium income	Benefit expenditures Total Amount	Total Percent of premium income	Hospital care	Physicians' services	Other types of care
	957	958	959	960	961	962
1970	8,746	7,656	87.5	4,645.1	2,488.8	46.7
1969	7,569	6,306	83.3	3,845.0	2,072.0	306.0
1968	6,933	5,791	83.5	3,573.5	1,890.8	267.7
1967	5,858	4,837	82.6	3,036.0	1,545.0	256.0
1966	5,595	4,585	81.9	2,911.0	1,462.0	212.0
1965	5,224	4,265	81.6	2,729.0	1,359.0	177.0
1964	4,652	3,763	80.9	2,404.0	1,210.0	149.0
1963	4,136	3,332	80.6	2,127.0	1,078.0	127.0
1962	3,810	3,012	79.0	1,928.0	979.0	105.0
1961	3,427	2,706	79.0	1,735.0	885.0	86.0
1960	3,027	2,389	78.9	1,541.0	784.0	64.0
1959	2,639	2,080	78.8	1,371.0	709.0	(1)
1958	2,314	1,809	78.2	1,186.0	623.0	(1)
1957	2,175	1,655	76.1	1,080.0	575.0	(1)
1956	1,839	1,411	76.7	927.0	483.6	(1)
1955	1,627	1,179	72.5	738.8	440.2	(1)
1954	1,390	983	70.8	609.0	374.0	(1)
1953	1,181	855	72.4	544.7	310.0	(1)
1952	958	699	73.0	437.8	260.9	(1)
1951	798	588	73.7	367.3	220.2	(1)
1950	605	400	66.1	254.0	146.0	(1)
1949	461	295	63.8	192.0	103.0	(1)
1948	461	228	54.2	---	---	---

BLUE CROSS-BLUE SHIELD

Year	Subscription or premium income	Benefit expenditures Total Amount	Total Percent of premium income	Hospital care	Physicians' services	Other types of care
	957	958	959	960	961	962
1970	7,371	7,060	95.8	4,933.7	1,969.8	57.7
1969	6,156	5,903	95.9	4,155.4	1,565.4	179.9
1968	5,187	4,840	93.3	3,462.8	1,242.3	129.4
1967	4,555	4,083	89.6	2,853.9	1,102.8	126.1
1966	4,328	3,975	91.9	2,844.0	1,076.4	55.0
1965	4,169	3,913	93.9	2,824.3	1,048.6	40.0
1964	3,785	3,574	94.4	2,570.3	973.1	31.0
1963	3,399	3,180	93.6	2,302.5	856.0	21.0
1962	3,119	2,894	92.8	2,080.9	797.7	15.0
1961	2,805	2,585	92.2	1,857.3	715.1	13.0
1960	2,482	2,287	92.1	1,634.5	642.6	10.0
1959	2,157	1,995	92.5	1,423.7	571.1	(1)
1958	1,867	1,768	94.7	1,263.9	504.1	(1)
1957	1,668	1,543	92.5	1,099.9	447.1	(1)
1956	1,493	1,353	90.6	965.8	387.9	(1)
1955	1,292	1,147	88.8	831.6	315.1	(1)
1954	1,133	985	86.9	718.0	266.6	(1)
1953	989	851	86.0	623.7	227.8	(1)
1952	881	736	86.5	549.6	186.9	(1)
1951	685	605	88.3	451.7	153.3	(1)
1950	574	491	85.5	382.9	107.7	(1)
1949	455	383	84.2	307.4	75.4	(1)
1948	365	308	84.4	---	---	---

INDEPENDENT PLANS

Year	Subscription or premium income	Benefit expenditures Total Amount	Total Percent of premium income	Hospital care	Physicians' services	Other types of care
	957	958	959	960	961	962
1970	1,068	1,027	96.2	429.0	449.6	13.7
1969	933	859	92.1	355.8	391.5	42.7
1968	740	678	91.6	292.4	343.1	1.4
1967	692	625	90.3	243.5	316.5	65.0
1966	641	581	90.7	238.1	292.7	50.6
1965	608	551	90.6	236.5	272.2	42.3
1964	547	495	92.4	213.1	244.1	.7
1963	518	468	90.3	212.0	219.0	36.8
1962	482	438	90.9	188.0	215.0	35.2
1961	441	404	91.6	174.0	196.0	7.0
1960	332	320	96.4	129.0	166.0	25.2
1959	343	324	94.5	149.8	174.2	(1)
1958	317	300	94.6	141.5	158.8	(1)
1957	301	272	90.4	124.6	147.4	(1)
1956	292	250	85.6	129.0	121.4	(1)
1955	230	210	91.3	108.0	102.0	(1)
1954	233	211	90.6	115.4	95.9	(1)
1953	635	213	90.6	118.6	94.4	(1)
1952	184	169	91.8	86.4	82.3	(1)
1951	177	160	90.4	77.8	82.3	(1)
1950	113	101	89.4	43.1	58.2	(1)
1949	99	89	89.9	39.5	49.5	(1)
1948	76	70	92.1	---	---	---

[1] Included in "Hospital care" and "Physicians' services."

Government

Elections and Politics (Series Y 1-271)

Y 1–26. Methods of electing presidential electors, 1788–1836.

Source: Charles O. Paullin, *Atlas of the Historical Geography of the United States*, Carnegie Institution of Washington and American Geographical Society of New York, 1932, p. 89 (courtesy of the Carnegie Institution).

The presidential electors of each State, now chosen by popular vote in all States, are selected, according to the Constitution, "in such manner as the legislature thereof may direct."   The development of political party direction of the electoral college was not anticipated in the Constitution and, during the early years of the Republic, electors were chosen in the several States by a number of different devices. The principal methods were election by the State legislature itself, by State electors popularly chosen to elect presidential electors, and by direct popular vote for the electors. With few exceptions, presidential electors have been elected by popular vote since 1828. The Legislature of South Carolina, however, continued to elect presidential electors until 1860. Since the Civil War, legislatures have chosen electors only twice—in Florida in 1868 and in Colorado in 1876.

Y 27–78. Voter participation in presidential elections, by State, 1824–1968.

Source: Walter Dean Burnham, Dept. of Political Science, Massachusetts Institute of Technology, unpublished data. The explanatory notes which follow were prepared by Professor Burnham.

The United States, unlike some other countries, has never developed an automatic, governmentally-operated system for enrolling potential voters. The uniform practice since the earliest times has been that each of the States is the sole judge of the electoral procedures which it prescribes within its jurisdiction, subject only to constitutional amendments, congressional legislation enacted pursuant to such amendments or other portions of the Constitution, and Federal judicial decisions. All of these may limit or abolish the States' discretion in specified areas of legal procedure pertaining to elections; otherwise, the general rule stated here has continuously applied to the conduct of elections in the United States.[1]

[1] *Only the most salient* of such interventions are mentioned here, specifically as they apply to the composition of the potentially eligible electorate. They are:
The Reconstruction Act of March 2, 1867, which (with the Supplemental Act of March 23, 1867) required that the ten ex-Confederate States still without Federal representation eliminate all racial barriers to the suffrage as a precondition for readmission.
The Fifteenth Amendment to the Constitution (1870), which forbade either the States or the Federal Government to deny the right of citizens to vote "on account of race, color, or previous condition of servitude," and subsequent implementing legislation of 1870, 1871, and 1875. (See also *Guinn v. United States*, 238 U.S. 347 (1915), in which the Supreme Court struck down the "grandfather clause" as a patent attempt to evade the command of this Amendment.)
The Nineteenth Amendment to the Constitution (1920), which enfranchised women on the same constitutional terms as men.
The Supreme Court's invalidation of the white primary, and of the doctrine that political parties, being private associations, could exclude Negroes or any others they chose to exclude from their nominating processes. (*Smith v. Allwright*, 321 U.S. 649, (1944).)
The Twenty-third Amendment to the Constitution (1961), extending presidential suffrage to the District of Columbia.
The Twenty-fourth Amendment to the Constitution (1964), prohibiting the levying of a poll tax or any other tax as a prerequisite to voting in Federal elections. (See also the Supreme Court's extension of this prohibition to State and local elections as well, *Harper v. Virginia State Board of Elections*, 383 U.S. 663 (1966).)
The Civil Rights Act of 1965 suspending all literacy tests in Alabama, Alaska, Georgia, Louisiana, Mississippi, South Carolina, Virginia, 40 counties in North Carolina, and one county in Arizona, and establishing Federal registrars in the affected areas.
The Civil Rights Act of 1970, which continued suspension for another five years; extended it to all literacy tests; lowered the minimum voting age from 21 to 18 in all Federal and State elections; and lowered the minimum residence requirement for voting in presidential elections to a uniform 30 days.
The Twenty-sixth Amendment to the Constitution (1971) which formally reaffirmed the lowering of the voting age minimum from 21 to 18 years.

As a result of this heterogeneity, it is not possible to achieve precise *statements* of the eligible electorate. The data in series Y 27–78 are *estimates,* and should be read throughout with that point in mind.

Every estimate of voting participation is, in effect, a ratio between a numerator and a denominator. Errors in estimates may occur because of errors in the numerator, the denominator, or both. Problems with the numerator include the following: (1) The reported vote cast may have been heavily inflated by fraudulent ballot-box stuffing, as for example in Plaquemines Parish, Louisiana, in 1844, or in Kansas City, Missouri, between 1934 and 1938; (2) the stated vote may be only a fraction of the real vote cast, either because of fradulent suppression of returns, other forms of pressure on the electorate, or failure of subdivisions to report within the legal time limit (the latter very frequently occurring in Texas); (3) more or less major compiling or reporting errors, without fraudulent intent, may exist, and clearly did in a number of cases in the nineteenth century; and (4) available returns may be significantly fragmentary because the original records were lost.

Problems with the denominator, i.e. the population base, relate primarily to its derivation. Information which has been compiled into the denominator falls into the following classifications: (1) Age cohorts; (2) sex by age for and following every point at which women were enfranchised by State law or by the Nineteenth Amendment; (3) race, which substantially means adding the Negro adult male population to the denominator base in 1868 (ten Southern States) or 1870; (4) citizenship status, reported separately as "male citizens" in 1870, and in more detail beginning with the 1900 census.

The following possible elements of a denominator have *not* been compiled, though they have entered into State legislation regulating eligibility to vote: (1) Literacy of the adult male/adult population; (2) taxpaying components of the adult male/adult population; (3) other components (for example, the total number registered) which define those legally entitled to vote at any given time. There are two reasons for such exclusions: Many of such devices were deliberately employed, particularly between 1890 and shortly after 1960, to violate the letter and the spirit of the Fifteenth Amendment; and they are extremely heterogeneous—for example, some States have registration reporting covering all jurisdictions, some do not, and the times for which such information is available are extremely diverse.

The four major components of the denominator, the estimated eligible population, alone can be developed more or less accurately for all States and time periods but even these have very significant problems. In general, the denominator estimates are much more precise from 1900 on than they are for years prior to that date. The reason for this lies in the changing nature of census reporting of critical components which enter the calculation.

Age cohorts. From 1870, the adult male/adult population is specifically enumerated so that the whole number of those 21 years old and over can be stated. This was not the practice earlier. Procedures followed here were to sum all white male age cohorts entirely above 21, and to add to that sum a fraction of any age cohort which bracketed that age, *i.e.,* which included both males above and below 21 years. The fraction was derived by a simple division of the relevant bracketed age grouping, and addition of the quotient to the sum already derived. For example: The 1820 census yields free white male age classifications of 16–25, 26–44, and 45 and over. For Maine in that year, the total number of free white males 26 and over was

46,920. The total number falling in the 16–25 age classification was 28,530. There being ten years in that classification, symmetrically divided five (16–20) and five (21–25), figure of 28,530 was divided by two, yielding 14,265; this was, in turn, added to the sum of free white males 26 and over (46,920) to produce a total estimated electorate of 61,185. (The figure of 61,185 is too precise but serves to provide the basis from which such estimates could best be derived; the procedure for dividing bracketed age classifications in the census arbitrarily presupposes a linear or uniform age distribution among all the years in the grouping. State-by-State actuarial estimates for this period could easily permit a different procedure. The effect of the procedure used is, unquestionably, to inflate the denominator from its "true" value and thus to generate a lower turnout figure than was actually achieved in these years.)

The following table indicates the bracketed age cohorts and the criteria for division and compilation:

Age Cohorts in the United States Census, 1790–1860 [a]

| Census | Bracketed age classification | Distribution of years | | Divisor |
		Below 21	21 and over	
1790 [b]	16 and over			(b)
1800	16–25	16–20	21–25	2
1810	16–25	16–20	21–25	2
1820	16–25	16–20	21–25	2
1830	20–29	20	21–29	10
1840	20–29	20	21–29	10
1850	20–29	20	21–29	10
1860	20–29	20	21–29	10

[a] *Throughout*, the basis is that of free white males. This excludes a small fraction of free Negroes who were at least nominally entitled to vote in several States. No estimate of citizenship exists except for 1860.

[b] The procedure for estimation in 1790 is a simple transfer from 1800 data: The proportion in each State of the *total* free white male population of age 16 and over which is estimated to be of age 21 and over.

Sex components. Women were universally enfranchised in 1920, but a number of States gave women suffrage earlier. In order of enfranchisement, the States which extended suffrage to women *before* 1920 were: Wyoming, as territory, 1869; Colorado, 1893; Utah, 1896; Idaho, 1897; Washington, 1911; California, 1911; Oregon, 1913; Arizona, 1913; Kansas, 1913; Montana, 1914; Nevada, 1914; Illinois, 1916, presidential only; Michigan, 1918; and New York, 1918. In all cases, appropriate sex-related adjustments were made in the denominator effective with the first election to which they applied.

Racial components. Negroes were enfranchised in ten Southern States effective with the 1868 election and nationally by the Fifteenth Amendment (1870). Prior to 1868, the proportion of free Negroes allowed to vote at all was extremely small; and the States in which they were allowed to vote had very small Negro populations. No effort, therefore, has been made to include a component for other than white races in the denominator prior to 1868/70. In Vermont, Maine, Massachusetts, and New York this means a tiny *deflation* of the denominator from its probable true value, and an equally small overestimation of the participation rates prior to 1870.

Citizenship components. This element represents the most difficult of the four major denominator components to estimate for the period prior to 1890–1900, for the following reasons: First, the 1928 election was the first presidential election in which American citizenship was a *universal* prerequisite for voting. In particular, the period from about 1840 through about 1910 was one in which a considerable number of States permitted aliens (those who had filed first papers, as a rule) to vote in elections. Every effort has been made here to identify by State and at what times these were legally qualified to vote. The denominator is thus grounded in part upon a legal definition which is heterogeneous across space and, for the States in which aliens were once allowed to vote, across time as well.

Second, the population census during most of the nineteenth century is not helpful in decomposing the foreign-born population, when reported, by citizenship status. Prior to 1870, no basis for estimation exists at all from the census materials. In 1870, males of 21 and over are reported in two columns, one of which specifies male *citizens*. Combining this with analysis of the size of the foreign-born component of the voting-age male population, certain probable inferences can be made about the proportion of foreign-born males of legal age who had been naturalized, and about these compared with later censuses for which specific proportions are reported. No help is given on this question in the 1880 census. The 1890 census (Population, part II, p. lxvi) gives a percentage breakdown by State of the foreign-born population by status: Naturalized, first papers, aliens, unknowns. From 1900 onward, census figures are provided for these categories in absolute numbers.

A period of particular difficulty in estimation lies between 1860 and 1890. Prior to 1860 no effort is made to decompose the denominator (population base) estimate by citizenship. For 1860 and the years interpolated to 1870, the same *proportion* of citizens over 21 to all males over 21 which the 1870 census employs is used to derive the estimated potential electorate of 1860. Where proportions exist for 1890 and 1870 and the State requires citizenship status of its voters through this period, the mean of the two proportions is used for estimating the 1880 proportion and thus the denominator. Where States permitted alien voting, an effort was made to estimate the proportion of naturalized and first-paper foreign–born to all foreign-born for 1870, based upon the mean of 1890 and 1900 proportions. No such refinements were made for 1860.

There is some reason to believe that these proportions were relatively stable, particularly in States where the frontier stage of settlement had passed. With the raw figures of the 1870 census and the percentage decomposition of foreign-born males of voting age in 1890, the general outlines of this stability can be seen in the example of Ohio. In 1870, citizen males constituted 92.4 percent of the total male population of voting age; in 1890, 93.7 percent; in 1900, 94.4 percent.[2] From this an interpolated estimate of 93.1 percent was derived for 1880, and the 1870 figure, 92.4 percent, was used to calculate the estimated eligible electorate of the 1860 voting-age male population.

Distribution of Ohio Male Population of Voting Age, 1890–1910

| Year | Citizens | | | Aliens | Total males 21 and over |
	Native white	Naturalized	Negro		
1890	76.0	15.1	2.6	6.3	1,016,464
1900	78.8	13.0	2.6	5.6	1,212,233
1910	76.5	9.6	2.7	11.2	1,484,265

States which permitted alien suffrage and subsequently abolished it are presented below, with the effective year of abolition so far as is known.

Alien-Suffrage States

State	Effective year of abolition	State	Effective year of abolition
Arkansas	1925	Nebraska	1910
Colorado	1902	North Dakota	1898–1902
Illinois	1870	Ohio	1851
Indiana	1921	Oregon	1914
Iowa	1857	South Dakota	1918
Michigan	1894	Wisconsin	1908
Minnesota	1896		

The problems of estimation are clearly more acute in the citizenship area than in any other. *The figures presented here are to be considered provisional and subject to revision*; no claim is made that the denominators and the participation estimates derived from them are the best

----
[2] In 1910, as the consequence of the influx of the "new immigration" after 1900, this figure falls to 88.8 percent, corresponding to a percentage decline of naturalized to all foreign-born from 70.3 percent in 1890, to 69.6 percent in 1900, and to only 46.2 percent in 1910.

possible estimates. Limited explorations suggest that the probable margin of error in turnout estimates—at least for States requiring citizenship qualifications—is well under 1 percent for the 1870–1900 period.

One final remark about method involves the ratio between numerator and denominator. In the absence of any better estimation, the biennial figures are compiled throughout on the basis of *linear interpolation* between one decennial census year and the next. Obviously, patterns of population growth and decline are never perfectly linear and may deviate widely from that assumption. This is particularly visible as a problem in the "mining-camp" States of the West, especially in Nevada before World War I. A metal lode was discovered at a point in time following a census. Voting-age males poured into the State until the lode was exhausted; and then they left. All of this produced extreme deviations of empirical population realities from any linear model, with resultant wild fluctuations in turnout. Fortunately, the linear model does not appear sharply inconsistent with reality in well-settled States. In any event, no known alternative to it appears to exist throughout most of American political and demographic history except in those few States which published adequate censuses falling between Federal census years.

Y 79-186. General note.

The election of the President of the United States is provided for in the Constitution, article II, section 1, through the establishment of an electoral college in each State, for each presidential election. The method of casting the electoral vote was modified in 1804 by the adoption of the 12th amendment to the Constitution. The number of electors, and therefore of electoral votes, is "equal to the whole number of Senators and Representatives to which the State may be entitled in Congress." Because of the varied practices in choosing electors in earlier years, the record of popular votes is inadequate to explain the elections until after 1824.

In four elections the entire electoral vote of certain States remained uncast: (a) 1789—no electoral vote was cast in New York because the legislature failed to agree on electors; (b) 1864—no vote in Confederate States (Alabama, Arkansas, Florida, Georgia, Louisiana, Mississippi, North and South Carolina, Tennessee, Texas, and Virginia); (c) 1868—no vote in Mississippi, Texas, and Virginia because these States had not yet been "readmitted" to the Union; (d) 1872—the vote of Arkansas was rejected, the count of the popular vote in Louisiana was disputed, and the votes of both sets of electors were rejected by Congress.

In addition to the sources cited below, the following references were used in compiling the data for series Y 79–186: U.S. Congress, Clerk of the House of Representatives, *Platforms of the Two Great Political Parties, 1932 to 1944*, pp. 437–447, and *Statistics of the Presidential and Congressional Elections*, various issues; Julius F. Prufer and Stanley J. Folmesbee, *American Political Parties and Presidential Elections*, McKinley Publishing Company, Philadelphia, 1928; Charles O. Paullin, cited above for series Y 1–26, pp. 88–104; Bureau of the Census, *Vote Cast in Presidential and Congressional Elections, 1928–1944*.

Y 79-83. Electoral and popular vote cast for President, by political party, 1789-1968.

Source: 1789–1832, Edward Stanwood, *A History of the Presidency*, two volumes, Houghton Mifflin Company, Boston, 1928, various pages (copyright); 1836–1892, W. Dean Burnham, *Presidential Ballots, 1836–1892*, Johns Hopkins Press, Baltimore, 1955, pp. 246–257 and 887–889 (copyright); 1896–1932, Edgar Eugene Robinson, *The Presidential Vote*, Stanford University Press, Stanford, 1934, pp. 46

and 402 (copyright); 1936–1944, Edgar Eugene Robinson, *They Voted for Roosevelt*, Stanford University Press, Stanford, 1947, p. 183 (copyright); 1948–1960, Governmental Affairs Institute, Washington, D.C., *American at the Polls*, 1965, pp. 15–22 (copyright); 1964–1968, Governmental Affairs Institute, *America Votes 7*, 1968, pp. 1 and 2, and *America Votes 8*, 1970, pp. 1 and 2 (copyright).

Y 84-134. Electoral vote cast for President, by State and political party, 1804-1968.

Source: For complete citation of the following, see sources cited for series Y 79–83: 1804–1832, Stanwood, various pages; 1836–1892, Burnham, pp. 887–889; 1896–1932, Robinson, *The Presidential Vote*, p. 402 (copyright); 1936–1944, Robinson, *They Voted for Roosevelt*, pp. 56–57 (copyright); 1948–1960, Governmental Affairs Institute, Washington, D.C., *America at the Polls*, 1965, pp. 15–22 (copyright); 1964–1968, Governmental Affairs Institute, *America Votes 7*, 1968, pp. 1 and 2, and *America Votes 8*, 1970, pp. 1 and 2 (copyright).

Y 135-186. Popular vote cast for President, by State and political party, 1836-1968.

Source: For complete citation of the following, see sources cited for series Y 79–83: 1836–1892, Burnham, pp. 246–257; 1896–1932, Robinson, *The Presidential Vote*, pp. 46–53 (copyright); 1936–1944, Robinson, *They Voted for Roosevelt*, pp. 59–182 (copyright); 1948–1960, Governmental Affairs Institute, Washington, D.C., *America at the Polls*, 1965, pp. 15–22 (copyright); 1964–1968, Governmental Affairs Institute, *Amercia Votes 7*, 1968, pp. 1 and 2, and *America Votes 8*, 1970, pp. 1 and 2 (copyright).

Variations in figures reported for some States account for small differences between the sum of State data and the total shown for the United States.

Y 187-188. Costs of presidential general elections, 1860-1968.

Source: 1860–1900, *Congressional Record*, vol. 45, 61st Congress, 2d Session, 1910, p. 4931, except for series 187, 1892–1924, from Louise Overacker, *Money in Elections*, Macmillan Company, New York, 1932, p. 73; 1928–1944, Louise Overacker, *Presidential Campaign Funds*, Boston University Press, 1946, p. 32; 1948, William Goodman, *The Two Party System in the United States*, D. Van Nostrand Company, Inc., New York, 1956, p. 517 (copyright); 1952–1968, Citizens' Research Foundation, Princeton. Data presented in *History of American Presidential Elections, 1789–1968*, vol. IV, Arthur M. Schlesinger, Jr., Editor, McGraw-Hill Book Co., New York, 1971 (copyright).

Figures represent spending by all national level committees, but not by the candidates themselves. Figures for Republicans, 1912, and Republicans and Democrats, 1916–1944, include amounts transferred to the States as well. National-level committees proliferated after 1940, when the Hatch Act limitation of $3 million on the expenditures of a single committee and the $5,000 limitation on individual contributions went into effect.

For campaigns from 1860 to 1912, figures are estimates at best. For 1912 and later campaigns, figures are relatively reliable. Although the value of the dollar shrank and the voting population expanded more than fourfold from 1912 to 1952, the cost per vote was 19 cents in both of those campaigns. Between 1912 and 1952, however, the cost per vote fluctuated widely. By 1968, the cost per vote had increased to 60 cents.

Y 189-198. Congressional bills, acts, and resolutions, 1789-1970.

Source: U.S. Congress, *Calendars of the U.S. House of Representatives and History of Legislation*; Library of Congress, Legislative Reference Service, unpublished tabulations; U.S. Congress, *Congressional Record*, various issues.

---

[3] These include such States as Iowa, Michigan, Massachusetts, and above all, New York between 1845 and 1875. There is a mass of potentially useful and still unrecovered or unsused State material which should be employed for the nineteenth century. Such material includes lists of taxables triennially compiled from 1814 through 1828 in Pennsylvania (available in *Hazard's Register* (1825(1835)), and the Missouri State census of 1844, available only as an appendix to the *Missouri Senate Journal* (1845).

Some measure of the activities of the U.S. Congress can be gained from the number of bills and resolutions which have been introduced in Congress and from the number of public and private laws which have been passed. The abrupt reduction in the number of private bills enacted into law beginning with the 60th Congress was the result of combining many private bills, particularly pension bills, into omnibus enactments.

Y 199–203. Congressional bills vetoed, 1789–1970.

Source: U.S. Congress. Senate Library, *Presidential Vetoes*, U.S. Government Printing Office, 1969, p. v, and *Calendars of the U.S. House of Representatives and History of Legislation*, annual issues.

The term "veto," which does not appear in the Constitution, indicates the action of the President when he disapproves a bill and returns it with his objections to the House of Congress which originated the measure. These regular vetoes differ from pocket vetoes, which result when a bill fails to become law because the President has not signed it within 10 days but cannot return it with objections because the Congress has adjourned during the same period. For a bill to pass over a veto, both Houses of Congress must vote to override the veto.

Y 204–210. Political party affiliations in Congress and the Presidency, 1789–1970.

Source: 1st to 74th Congress, Library of Congress, Legislative Reference Service, "Political Trends—Both Houses of Congress—1789–1944" (typewritten tabulation based on *Encyclopedia Americana*, 1936 edition, vol. 7, pp. 516–518, 1st to 69th Congresses; and on Harold R. Bruce, *American Parties and Politics*, 3d edition, Henry Holt and Co., New York, 1936, pp. 174–179, 70th to 74th Congresses); 75th to 91st Congresses, U.S. Congress, *Congressional Directory*, annual volumes.

It is generally recognized today that popular government operates only through the agency of organized political parties. During the early development of the United States, party alignments and the function of political parties were neither fully appreciated nor provided for. Party alignments developed during the formative period, but designations for the different groups were not firmly fixed.

In the classification by party, the titles of parties during early years have been so designated as to be recognizable in the records of the periods concerned, and also to show the thread of continuity which tends to run from early alignments into the present 2-party system. Inasmuch as the party of Thomas Jefferson (generally known at the time as the Republican party) has with a considerable measure of continuity survived to the present time as the Democratic party, the name later accepted by the Jeffersonian Republicans of "Democratic-Republican" is used in the tables to avoid any confusion of the early Jeffersonian Republican with the present-day Republican party. Opposed to the early Republican party was the Federalist party, which was dominant in the first national administration and which, with interruptions, can be traced tenuously by elements of popular support through the National Republican, the Whig, and the Free Soil parties to the Republican party of today.

Y 211–214. Vote cast for Representatives, by political party, 1896–1970.

Source: 1896–1950, Governmental Affairs Institute, Washington, D.C., unpublished data. (Figures adapted by Richard M. Scammon from Cortez A. M. Ewing, *Congressional Elections, 1896–1944*, University of Oklahoma Press, Norman, 1947, and from unpublished work sheets used in its preparation and the biennial reports of the Clerk of the House of Representatives giving statistics of Congressional voting.) 1952–1962, U.S. Bureau of the Census, *Congressional District Data Book (Districts of the 88th Congress)*; 1964–1968, Governmental Affairs Institute, Washington, D.C., *America Votes 8*, 1970

(copyright); 1970, U.S. Congress, Clerk of the House, *Statistics of the Congressional Election.*

Y 215–271. General note.

The number of members in the House of Representatives is fixed by the Congress at the time of each apportionment. The population figures used for apportionment purposes are those determined for the States by each decennial census. No reapportionment was made following the 1920 census, and no change in total House membership has been made since 1912. However, the legislation granting statehood to Alaska and Hawaii allotted one Representative to each of those States and, during 1960 to 1962, increased the total of members to 437. The total reverted to 435 after reapportionment following the 1960 census. The original assignment of Representatives for each State, to be in effect until after the first enumeration of the population, and the requirement that each State have at least one Representative are stated in the Constitution.

Prior to the passage of the 14th amendment, Representatives were apportioned among the States "according to their respective numbers, which shall be determined by adding to the whole number of free persons, including those bound to service for a term of years, and excluding Indians not taxed, three-fifths of all other persons." (Art. I. sec. 2.) In effect, censuses between 1790 and 1860 included three-fifths of slaves in the apportionment population. Since the passage of the 14th amendment in 1868, Representatives have been apportioned "among the several States according to their respective numbers, counting the whole number of persons in each State, excluding Indians not taxed." At the time of the 1940 apportionment, it was determined that there were no longer any Indians who would be classed as "not taxed" under apportionment law.

In 1970, for the first time, the following classes of persons abroad were allocated to their home States for inclusion in the apportionment population: (1) members of the Armed Forces; (2) civilian employees of any Federal department or agency who were citizens of the United States or who had a home State; (3) spouses and children who were living abroad with persons classified in groups 1 and 2 above; and (4) other relatives living abroad in groups 1 and 2 who were citizens of the United States or who had a home State.

For detailed information about apportionment methods, see House Report 91–1314: *The Decennial Population Census and Congressional Apportionment*, 1970.

Y 215–219. Apportionment of Representatives among the States, 1790–1970.

Source: U.S. Bureau of the Census, *U.S. Census of Population: 1970*, vol. I, p. VIII.

See general note for series Y 215–271 for information about the apportionment population.

Y 220–271. Apportionment of membership in House of Representatives, by State, from adoption of Constitution to 1970.

Source: U.S. Bureau of the Census, *U.S. Census of Population: 1970*, vol. I, p. 53.

Membership is shown as of the date of the fixing of the new House apportionment plus members added for new States admitted during the subsequent decade. Major boundary changes affecting State representation in the House occurred in 1820, when Maine separated from Massachusetts, and in 1863, when West Virginia separated from Virginia.

Prior to 1850, apportionment ratios were chosen arbitrarily; from 1850 to 1900, ratios were the apportionment population of the United States divided by a predetermined number of Representatives; from 1910 on, apportionment ratios were computed by dividing a fixed number (435) of Representatives into the apportionment population. For additional information, see general note for series Y 215–271.

Series Y 1–26. Methods of Electing Presidential Electors: 1788 to 1836

[L—by legislature; G T—by people, on general ticket; D—by people, in districts; A—by people, in the State at large; E—by electors. The number in parentheses following the symbol "D" is the number of districts into which the State was divided. As a rule, each district elected 1 elector. The number in parentheses following the symbol "A" is the number of electors elected at large]

Series No.	State	1836	1832	1828	1824	1820	1816	1812	1808	1804	1800	1796	1792	1788–1789
1	New Hampshire	G T	G T	G T	G T	G T	G T	G T	G T	G T	L	G T and L [1]	G T [2]	G T and L [1]
2	Massachusetts	G T	G T	G T	G T	D (13) and A (2)	L	D (6) [3]	L	D (17) and A (2)	L	D (14) and L [4]	D (4) and L [5]	D (8) and L [6]
3	Rhode Island	G T	G T	G T	G T	G T	G T	G T	G T	G T	G T	L	L	---
4	Connecticut	G T	G T	G T	G T	G T	L	L	L	L	L	L	L	L
5	New York	G T	G T	D (30) and E [7]	L	L	L	L	L	L	L	L	L	---
6	New Jersey	G T	G T	G T	G T	G T	G T	L	G T	G T	L	L	L	L
7	Pennsylvania	G T	G T	G T	G T	G T	G T	G T	G T	G T	L	G T	G T	G T
8	Delaware	G T	G T	L	L	L	L	L	L	L	L	L	G T	D (3) [8]
9	Maryland	G T	D (4) [9]	D (9) [10]	D (9) [10]	D (9) [10]	D (9) [10]	D (9) [10]	D (9) [10]	D (9) [10]	D (10)	D (10)	G T	G T
10	Virginia	G T	G T	G T	G T	G T	G T	G T	G T	G T	G T	D (21)	D (21)	D (12)
11	North Carolina	G T	G T	G T	G T	G T	G T	L	D (14)	D (14)	D (12)	D (12)	L [11]	---
12	South Carolina	L	L	L	L	L	L	L	L	L	L	L	L	L
13	Georgia	G T	G T	G T	L	L	L	L	L	L	L	L	G T	L
14	Vermont	G T	G T	G T	G T	G T	G T	G T	G T	G T				
15	Kentucky	G T	G T	G T	D (3) [12]	D (3) [13]	D (3) [13]	D (3) [13]	D (2) [13]	D (2) [13]	D (4)	D (4)	D (4)	
16	Tennessee	G T	G T	D (11)	D (11)	D (8)	D (8)	D (8)	D (5)	D (5)	E [14]	E [14]		
17	Ohio	G T	G T	G T	G T	G T	G T	G T	G T	G T				
18	Louisiana	G T	G T	G T	L	L	L	L						
19	Indiana	G T	G T	G T	G T	L								
20	Mississippi	G T	G T	G T	G T	G T								
21	Illinois	G T	G T	G T	D (3)	D (3)								
22	Alabama	G T	G T	G T	G T	L								
23	Maine	G T	G T	D (7) and A (2)	D (7) and A (2)	D (7) and A (2)								
24	Missouri	G T	G T	G T	D (3)									
25	Arkansas	G T												
26	Michigan	G T												

[1] A majority of the popular vote was necessary for a choice. In case of a failure to elect, the legislature supplied the deficiency.

[2] A majority of votes was necessary for a choice. In case of a failure to elect 1 or more electors a second election was held by the people, at which choice was made from the candidates in the first election who had the most votes. The number of candidates in the second election was limited to twice the number of electors wanted.

[3] 1 district chose 6 electors; 1, 5 electors; 1, 4 electors; 2, 3 electors each; and 1, 1 elector.

[4] A majority of votes was necessary for a popular choice. Deficiencies were filled by the General Court, as in 1792. It also chose 2 electors at large. In 1796 it chose 9 electors, and the people, 7.

[5] 2 of the districts voted for 5 members each, and 2 for 3 members each. A majority of votes was necessary for a choice. In case of a failure to elect by popular vote the General Court supplied the deficiency. In the election of 1792, the people chose 5 electors and the General Court, 11.

[6] Each of the 8 districts chose 2 electors, from which the General Court (i.e., the legislature) selected 1. It also elected 2 electors at large.

[7] 1 district elected 3 electors; 2, 2 electors each; and 27, 1 elector each. The 34 electors thus elected chose 2 presidential electors.

[8] Each qualified voter voted for 1 elector. The 3 electors who received most votes in the State were elected.

[9] 1 district chose 4 electors; 1, 3 electors; 1, 2 electors; 1, 1 elector.

[10] During the years 1804–1828, Maryland chose 11 electors in 9 districts, 2 of the districts elected 2 members each.

[11] The State was divided into 4 districts, and the members of the legislature residing in each district chose 3 electors.

[12] 2 districts chose 5 electors each, and 1 chose 4 electors.

[13] Each district chose 4 electors.

[14] In 1796 and 1800, Tennessee chose 3 presidential electors—1 each for the districts of Washington, Hamilton, and Mero. 3 "electors" for each county in the State were appointed by the legislature, and the "electors" residing in each of the 3 districts chose 1 of the 3 presidential electors.

Series Y 27–78. Voter Participation in Presidential Elections, by State: 1824 to 1968

[In percent]

Series No.	State	1968	1964	1960	1956	1952	1948	1944	1940	1936	1932	1928	1924	1920	1916	1912	1908	1904	1900	1896
27	**United States**	60.6	61.7	64.0	60.6	63.3	53.0	55.9	62.5	61.0	56.9	56.9	48.9	49.2	61.6	58.8	65.4	65.2	73.2	79.3
28	Alabama	52.8	36.1	31.2	27.6	24.2	12.6	15.0	18.9	18.8	17.5	19.1	13.5	20.6	24.3	22.6	21.5	24.2	38.9	51.9
29	Alaska	53.0	48.0	59.2																
30	Arizona	50.6	56.8	53.8	47.8	53.9	45.4	42.2	57.0	52.0	55.1	47.9	44.4	46.8	48.7	38.6				
31	Arkansas	54.1	51.2	41.1	38.0	36.9	21.9	19.3	18.2	17.3	22.1	21.4	15.3	20.9	40.0	30.7	40.2	33.8	40.8	48.2
32	California	62.0	66.1	67.9	64.0	69.4	63.2	65.1	73.4	66.0	64.0	59.0	50.8	47.2	58.0	46.9	60.2	61.7	69.9	75.0
33	Colorado	64.0	67.6	71.7	69.2	76.2	64.5	67.9	79.7	75.5	75.3	68.4	62.5	56.0	60.5	59.1	65.4	71.0	71.2	65.2
34	Connecticut	68.8	71.3	77.1	75.8	80.9	71.2	77.2	74.6	70.8	72.6	57.9	58.7	73.8	71.5	76.3	80.5	79.7	83.3	
35	Delaware	68.7	69.5	74.5	72.7	78.4	68.5	66.9	79.4	79.8	76.3	75.3	68.1	75.1	86.1	84.1	86.2	82.0	81.9	64.6
36	District of Columbia	34.7	39.4																	
37	Florida	53.8	51.9	50.0	43.6	47.6	34.1	33.5	40.9	31.3	30.5	33.0	17.0	30.3	33.8	24.2	26.2	24.4	29.9	40.0
38	Georgia	44.7	45.3	32.9	31.3	31.9	21.4	17.6	17.7	17.7	16.5	15.7	11.5	10.5	23.7	18.9	22.0	23.8	24.4	34.3
39	Hawaii	53.3	52.4	58.9																	
40	Idaho	71.9	75.2	80.6	75.2	78.2	63.1	64.5	77.0	71.8	74.4	66.0	65.2	61.1	67.4	59.8	65.8	65.3	77.8	76.1
41	Illinois	69.3	72.6	76.5	72.4	76.0	70.3	74.8	82.2	81.6	74.6	73.4	64.1	60.5	66.8	74.7	81.6	80.5	89.9	95.7
42	Indiana	69.5	71.7	76.9	73.7	75.7	67.2	71.7	81.1	78.7	78.9	74.9	70.7	71.0	81.9	77.8	89.9	89.7	92.1	95.1
43	Iowa	67.9	70.0	76.8	74.0	75.8	62.4	64.3	75.5	73.5	69.1	68.9	68.4	64.5	75.0	74.2	77.6	79.7	91.0	96.1
44	Kansas	63.4	63.6	71.8	67.4	71.7	65.0	62.2	75.1	76.6	64.1	68.0	65.8	76.3	82.5	78.1	91.2	85.5	89.2	
45	Kentucky	51.3	54.8	60.5	60.5	57.0	47.9	51.9	59.5	59.9	67.4	67.7	61.0	71.8	82.8	74.6	84.0	77.7	87.0	89.2
46	Louisiana	54.9	47.1	45.1	36.0	40.2	27.5	25.1	29.4	27.3	23.4	20.1	12.4	14.1	21.6	19.3	19.8	15.6	21.7	35.8
47	Maine	66.4	65.0	74.0	61.8	63.1	49.0	57.3	65.0	64.4	66.3	60.2	44.9	46.9	65.1	63.4	53.2	49.5	56.0	63.0

Series Y 27–78. Voter Participation in Presidential Elections, by State: 1824 to 1968—Con.

[In percent]

Series No.	State	1968	1964	1960	1956	1952	1948	1944	1940	1936	1932	1928	1924	1920	1916	1912	1908	1904	1900	1896
48	Maryland	55.2	54.7	58.3	54.6	57.5	41.7	46.7	57.2	58.1	51.2	56.8	41.0	52.3	68.1	64.8	70.9	69.6	85.9	87.3
49	Massachusetts	66.4	68.4	76.9	72.0	75.0	71.5	71.0	78.7	75.9	69.5	74.0	56.6	53.3	62.8	63.4	65.1	67.6	67.4	70.6
50	Michigan	64.9	66.2	72.7	71.1	68.5	55.6	63.7	66.6	62.1	62.0	56.3	53.7	55.1	72.9	69.8	75.9	78.9	89.0	95.3
51	Minnesota	71.7	73.7	77.1	68.7	72.6	65.7	63.0	72.3	69.7	66.2	68.5	62.0	59.5	65.0	61.2	66.1	64.3	76.7	75.2
52	Mississippi	53.3	34.1	25.7	21.0	23.8	16.0	15.0	14.7	14.4	13.8	15.2	12.0	9.4	20.0	15.1	16.5	15.6	16.9	22.1
53	Missouri	64.9	65.2	72.6	68.8	71.8	61.0	62.2	74.4	77.3	70.9	69.1	63.3	67.6	81.5	74.9	79.7	74.9	83.1	88.5
54	Montana	68.4	70.6	71.7	71.6	71.8	62.3	59.0	72.2	70.8	70.3	63.5	59.2	61.4	68.0	63.3	61.9	65.8	75.3	73.8
55	Nebraska	60.0	66.6	72.1	67.6	71.9	58.2	67.9	75.4	75.6	72.1	71.5	63.8	55.7	84.5	77.1	77.8	70.1	80.2	74.1
56	Nevada	55.9	60.0	61.0	65.9	69.7	64.0	64.8	75.7	69.1	73.2	63.0	56.1	61.0	73.6	68.1	92.1	59.2	71.4	69.2
57	New Hampshire	68.5	71.4	80.2	74.4	79.2	70.3	73.5	79.6	77.8	77.5	77.8	67.4	67.5	77.3	78.2	80.8	81.6	83.9	78.1
58	New Jersey	65.8	69.2	71.8	68.9	72.3	63.0	69.1	76.1	75.0	72.0	75.6	60.7	59.1	70.7	69.1	82.4	83.6	85.9	88.4
59	New Mexico	60.0	62.8	64.5	56.8	60.5	53.4	48.8	66.6	68.7	69.7	60.3	61.8	62.3	77.8	59.6				
60	New York	59.7	64.4	66.9	67.9	71.2	65.0	70.9	75.7	72.6	66.1	68.3	56.3	51.6	71.6	72.1	79.7	83.3	84.6	84.3
61	North Carolina	54.1	51.9	54.1	47.4	51.3	35.4	38.0	42.7	47.4	44.0	43.1	35.9	44.6	49.8	46.1	52.0	46.1	70.2	85.3
62	North Dakota	70.0	72.9	79.1	71.3	75.5	61.6	61.5	78.4	78.0	74.5	72.4	63.8	67.4	77.7	60.8	73.2	61.4	65.2	63.1
63	Ohio	62.7	65.3	71.3	66.4	69.7	58.4	66.9	75.4	71.8	65.5	66.9	57.8	62.6	76.5	74.8	87.5	83.1	91.5	95.5
64	Oklahoma	60.0	62.4	64.3	61.4	68.6	52.5	52.8	60.5	56.4	54.4	50.5	47.4	48.6	60.4	57.4	71.5			
65	Oregon	64.6	67.2	72.4	71.1	69.6	56.5	58.4	67.1	62.5	60.7	57.7	55.3	52.3	54.2	51.8	47.3	47.6	58.3	69.9
66	Pennsylvania	64.3	66.0	70.7	65.5	66.5	56.0	59.8	67.6	72.5	53.1	62.7	45.8	42.8	63.4	64.4	71.8	74.3	75.0	81.8
67	Rhode Island	65.6	69.3	77.3	73.2	79.8	66.0	65.0	75.6	78.0	71.7	68.9	66.3	57.9	65.8	62.7	62.4	63.4	56.2	59.2
68	South Carolina	46.0	38.7	31.4	24.7	29.1	12.8	9.8	10.1	12.5	12.3	8.5	6.4	8.6	17.5	14.6	20.6	18.4	18.0	25.2
69	South Dakota	72.8	75.4	78.8	74.7	74.4	63.3	59.3	79.5	77.5	76.5	72.0	59.4	56.6	60.9	61.9	69.5	73.0	85.4	78.0
70	Tennessee	53.2	51.5	50.4	45.9	44.7	28.7	28.2	30.6	30.0	26.5	25.7	23.3	35.4	46.6	45.1	48.1	47.7	56.6	70.8
71	Texas	48.2	44.1	42.4	37.9	43.5	26.0	28.2	30.1	24.8	27.2	24.8	25.8	21.7	35.0	30.8	33.6	29.6	61.4	88.3
72	Utah	75.2	78.0	78.9	77.2	82.9	76.0	75.0	83.1	77.9	80.0	73.4	69.7	69.6	79.5	66.4	73.0	78.4	84.5	79.4
73	Vermont	62.9	67.0	72.9	66.5	66.8	54.5	56.9	66.8	68.5	66.6	66.8	51.3	45.3	58.2	56.8	48.9	50.7	57.9	67.5
74	Virginia	50.5	41.6	34.4	31.8	29.9	21.6	22.3	22.1	23.0	22.1	24.0	18.1	19.4	27.1	25.7	27.4	27.7	59.6	71.0
75	Washington	64.3	67.2	74.1	70.4	72.6	63.2	67.0	70.6	66.5	64.2	56.6	54.7	50.8	59.0	60.9	64.9	64.9	63.1	
76	West Virginia	69.3	73.0	77.9	74.6	76.3	65.8	65.5	83.0	84.9	81.9	76.4	75.2	71.7	83.6	81.9	86.9	89.2	91.3	93.6
77	Wisconsin	65.6	68.6	73.5	67.8	72.5	59.8	65.7	72.4	68.9	65.1	65.9	57.3	52.3	70.2	68.7	68.7	72.0	77.5	84.9
78	Wyoming	65.3	74.1	73.9	67.4	72.5	59.6	63.3	74.8	74.0	74.9	68.7	71.0	52.3	54.9	50.3	49.2	50.8	51.1	50.7

Series No.	State	1892	1888	1884	1880	1876	1872 [1]	1868	1864	1860	1856	1852	1848	1844	1840	1836	1832	1828	1824
27	**United States**	74.7	79.3	77.5	79.4	81.8	71.3	78.1	73.8	81.2	78.9	69.6	72.7	78.9	80.2	57.8	55.4	57.6	26.9
28	Alabama	68.5	56.6	54.2	58.8	72.8	79.6	77.9	(2)	78.7	71.0	45.3	69.7	80.3	89.7	64.9	31.5	54.6	49.1
31	Arkansas	55.0	68.9	59.1	59.5	64.7	67.6	49.0	(2)	79.5	60.2	48.6	55.9	63.5	67.6	28.9	------	------	------
32	California	73.8	76.5	68.8	67.1	75.9	57.9	72.3	64.6	71.2	81.6	75.7							
33	Colorado	54.6	57.4	52.4	57.4	(3)													
34	Connecticut	85.4	85.5	79.9	81.4	82.0	71.3	80.1	76.3	73.3	81.8	72.3	72.3	80.0	75.7	52.3	46.0	27.2	14.9
35	Delaware	80.4	68.8	76.0	81.9	73.4	73.3	84.3	79.8	79.5	78.5	75.0	80.4	85.8	82.8	69.5	67.1		
37	Florida	35.3	85.0	83.1	85.9	93.5	77.0	(3)	(2)	79.5	77.6	56.9	64.0						
38	Georgia	53.1	37.6	41.0	49.4	63.5	55.2	73.2	(2)	85.1	82.8	54.8	86.0	92.6	88.8	61.8	29.0	31.8	
40	Idaho	63.1																	
41	Illinois	86.0	82.9	84.4	89.9	87.5	75.0	76.7	69.2	80.5	72.4	64.7	70.5	76.0	86.0	43.5	46.0	52.4	24.3
42	Indiana	89.0	93.3	92.2	94.4	94.6	85.3	92.5	82.9	89.4	88.3	80.3	78.5	84.7	84.4	69.2	71.9	68.7	37.1
43	Iowa	88.5	87.9	90.0	93.7	99.1	79.0	97.1	95.4	94.2	87.0	80.2	90.7						
44	Kansas	80.7	88.2	85.1	80.8	65.7	77.8	51.3	31.8										
45	Kentucky	73.8	81.1	70.8	75.5	80.9	66.2	69.9	44.0	74.1	76.7	64.2	73.9	80.7	74.3	61.1	74.0	70.7	25.4
46	Louisiana	45.1	50.0	49.8	50.3	77.9	76.4	75.9	(2)	58.6	53.6	48.7	51.1	47.1	39.4	19.2	22.3	36.2	
47	Maine	63.5	71.7	75.0	85.0	71.5	57.9	74.4	73.2	68.9	78.1	61.2	68.4	71.3	83.7	37.7	66.2	42.7	19.1
48	Maryland	79.9	84.8	79.9	79.8	82.7	75.0	72.6	57.7	81.1	80.0	72.8	76.0	81.4	84.5	67.6	55.7	70.3	53.7
49	Massachusetts	74.6	71.7	69.3	71.2	72.3	62.0	66.9	63.8	65.8	69.8	57.8	64.6	65.8	66.7	43.4	39.4	25.7	29.0
50	Michigan	73.2	80.9	76.0	75.5	78.0	64.0	77.4	66.2	80.0	81.1	71.3	74.5	79.8	84.9	35.0			
51	Minnesota	66.6	76.3	68.2	68.9	71.3	67.5	71.1	57.5	74.9									
52	Mississippi	18.8	43.8	49.2	50.1	79.7	71.1	(1)	(2)	89.5	78.3	61.7	80.7	86.1	88.2	64.4	28.0	56.6	41.3
53	Missouri	77.4	81.8	77.0	78.0	76.6	66.6	43.0	36.3	69.1	54.7	46.3	62.5	77.8	75.1	36.1	41.0	54.0	19.8
54	Montana	74.2																	
55	Nebraska	66.2	75.9	67.8	67.7	53.0	43.7	46.1											
56	Nevada	70.1	71.4	61.6	76.5	90.0	74.4	73.7	157.5										
57	New Hampshire	85.8	90.2	87.4	93.3	92.0	80.9	82.3	84.3	80.7	87.9	65.7	67.4	68.9	86.3	38.2	70.1	74.3	18.0
58	New Jersey	90.3	91.9	88.6	95.4	94.8	81.4	89.5	81.0	89.4	83.1	79.8	82.7	87.2	80.4	69.2	68.8	71.0	35.6
60	New York	86.3	92.3	87.5	89.3	89.6	80.9	91.7	89.3	95.5	89.9	84.7	79.6	92.1	91.9	70.5	84.2	80.2	
61	North Carolina	78.0	85.2	86.3	83.0	90.1	71.9	81.2	(2)	70.9	66.7	65.8	71.4	78.8	82.4	53.0	31.3	56.9	41.8
62	North Dakota	56.7																	
63	Ohio	86.2	91.9	93.4	94.4	94.4	84.4	90.4	87.6	88.3	82.3	80.6	77.5	83.6	84.5	75.5	73.9	75.9	34.8
65	Oregon	58.4	53.5	63.0	79.1	70.4	60.5	85.8	91.8	97.8									
66	Pennsylvania	75.7	83.0	82.3	88.8	83.5	68.6	88.3	85.0	78.4	80.8	72.6	76.3	77.3	77.5	53.1	52.3	56.5	18.8
67	Rhode Island	63.0	53.4	48.1	48.7	49.4	40.2	46.6	58.8	59.4	62.9	57.8	41.1	45.1	33.2	23.8	26.3	17.1	12.0
68	South Carolina	29.1	35.0	43.0	83.9	101.0	60.4	79.6	(2)	(4)	(4)	(4)	(4)	(4)	(4)	(4)	(4)		
69	South Dakota	70.7																	
70	Tennessee	64.0	77.6	73.1	75.1	74.6	66.2	39.7	(2)	80.9	82.9	72.9	83.4	89.8	89.7	57.3	31.3	55.0	28.3
71	Texas	79.4	78.3	80.2	68.8	54.6	56.3	(1)	(2)	67.4	58.1	42.6	69.6						
73	Vermont	60.4	71.4	70.5	81.6	83.3	69.1	75.9	77.0	63.0	72.5	63.5	70.5	70.8	73.8	52.5	50.0	54.5	
74	Virginia	75.3	83.2	81.7	64.1	77.6	66.2	(1)	(2)	71.5	67.8	63.3	47.3	54.2	54.7	35.2	31.1	27.7	11.6
75	Washington	67.3																	
76	West Virginia	90.3	94.5	86.7	82.6	83.6	61.2	58.0	51.6										
77	Wisconsin	76.8	81.1	82.2	82.4	83.9	70.6	79.8	66.8	79.0	80.8	59.6	58.3						
78	Wyoming	47.7																	

[1] Mississippi, Texas, and Virginia did not participate in the election.
[2] Confederate States did not participate in the election.
[3] Florida (in 1868) and Colorado (in 1876) cast 3 Republican electoral votes through its legislature rather than by popular vote.
[4] South Carolina chose its electors through its legislature.

Series Y 79–83. Electoral and Popular Vote Cast for President, by Political Party: 1789 to 1968

[Excludes unpledged tickets and minor candidates polling under 10,000 votes. Various party labels may have been used by a candidate in different States; the more important of these are listed below]

Year	Number of States	Presidential candidate	Political party	Electoral	Popular	Year	Number of States	Presidential candidate	Political party	Electoral	Popular
	79	80	81	82	83		79	80	81	82	83
1968____	50	Richard M. Nixon	Republican	301	31,785,480	1920___	48	Warren G. Harding	Republican	404	16,143,407
		Hubert H. Humphrey	Democratic	191	31,275,166			James M. Cox	Democratic	127	9,130,328
		George C. Wallace	American Independent	46	9,906,473			Eugene V. Debs	Socialist	–	919,799
		Henning A. Blomen	Socialist Labor	–	52,588			P. P. Christensen	Farmer-Labor	–	265,411
		Dick Gregory	(1)	–	47,133			Aaron S. Watkins	Prohibition	–	189,408
		Fred Halstead	Socialist Workers	–	41,388			James E. Ferguson	American	–	48,000
		Eldridge Cleaver	Peace and Freedom		36,563			W. W. Cox	Socialist Labor	–	31,715
		Eugene J. McCarthy	(2)	–	25,552	1916___	48	Woodrow Wilson	Democratic	277	9,127,695
		E. Harold Munn	Prohibition	–	15,123			Charles E. Hughes	Republican	254	8,533,507
								A. L. Benson	Socialist	–	585,113
1964____	50	Lyndon B. Johnson	Democratic	486	43,129,566			J. Frank Hanly	Prohibition	–	220,506
		Barry M. Goldwater	Republican	52	27,178,188			Arthur E. Reimer	Socialist Labor	–	13,403
		Eric Hass	Socialist Labor	–	45,219	1912___	48	Woodrow Wilson	Democratic	435	6,296,547
		Clifton DeBerry	Socialist Workers	–	32,720			Theodore Roosevelt	Progressive	88	4,118,571
		E. Harold Munn	Prohibition	–	23,267			William H. Taft	Republican	8	3,486,720
								Eugene V. Debs	Socialist	–	900,672
1960____	50	John F. Kennedy	Democratic	³303	34,226,731			Eugene W. Chafin	Prohibition	–	206,275
		Richard M. Nixon	Republican	219	34,108,157			Arthur E. Reimer	Socialist Labor	–	28,750
		Eric Hass	Socialist Labor	–	47,522	1908___	46	William H. Taft	Republican	321	7,675,320
		Rutherford L. Decker	Prohibition	–	46,203			William J. Bryan	Democratic	162	6,412,294
		Orval E. Faubus	National States Rights	–	44,977			Eugene V. Debs	Socialist	–	420,793
		Farrell Dobbs	Socialist Workers	–	40,165			Eugene W. Chafin	Prohibition	–	253,840
		Charles L. Sullivan	Constitution	–	18,162			Thomas L. Hisgen	Independence	–	82,872
								Thomas E. Watson	People's	–	29,100
1956____	48	Dwight D. Eisenhower	Republican	457	35,590,472			August Gillhaus	Socialist Labor	–	14,021
		Adlai E. Stevenson	Democratic	⁴73	26,022,752	1904___	45	Theodore Roosevelt	Republican	336	7,628,461
		T. Coleman Andrews	States' Rights	–	111,178			Alton B. Parker	Democratic	140	5,084,223
		Eric Hass	Socialist Labor	–	44,450			Eugene V. Debs	Socialist	–	402,283
		Enoch A. Holtwick	Prohibition	–	41,937			Silas C. Swallow	Prohibition	–	258,536
1952____	48	Dwight D. Eisenhower	Republican	442	33,936,234			Thomas E. Watson	People's	–	117,183
		Adlai E. Stevenson	Democratic	89	27,314,992			Charles H. Corregan	Socialist Labor	–	31,249
		Vincent Hallinan	Progressive	–	140,023	1900___	45	William McKinley	Republican	292	7,218,491
		Stuart Hamblen	Prohibition	–	72,949			William J. Bryan	Democratic ⁵	155	6,356,734
		Eric Hass	Socialist Labor	–	30,267			John C. Wooley	Prohibition	–	208,914
		Darlington Hoopes	Socialist	–	20,203			Eugene V. Debs	Socialist	–	87,814
		Douglas A. MacArthur	Constitution	–	17,205			Wharton Barker	People's	–	50,373
		Farrell Dobbs	Socialist Workers	–	10,312			Jos. F. Malloney	Socialist Labor	–	39,739
1948____	48	Harry S. Truman	Democratic	303	24,179,345	1896___	45	William McKinley	Republican	271	7,102,246
		Thomas E. Dewey	Republican	189	21,991,291			William J. Bryan	Democratic ⁵	176	6,492,559
		Strom Thurmond	States' Rights	39	1,176,125			John M. Palmer	National Democratic	–	133,148
		Henry Wallace	Progressive	–	1,157,326			Joshua Levering	Prohibition	–	132,007
		Norman Thomas	Socialist	–	139,572			Charles H. Matchett	Socialist Labor	–	36,274
		Claude A. Watson	Prohibition	–	103,900			Charles E. Bentley	Nationalist	–	13,969
		Edward A. Teichert	Socialist Labor	–	29,241	1892___	44	Grover Cleveland	Democratic	277	5,555,426
		Farrell Dobbs	Socialist Workers	–	13,614			Benjamin Harrison	Republican	145	5,182,690
1944____	48	Franklin D. Roosevelt	Democratic	432	25,606,585			James B. Weaver	People's	22	1,029,846
		Thomas E. Dewey	Republican	99	22,014,745			John Bidwell	Prohibition	–	264,133
		Norman Thomas	Socialist	–	80,518			Simon Wing	Socialist Labor	–	21,164
		Claude A. Watson	Prohibition	–	74,758	1888___	38	Benjamin Harrison	Republican	233	5,447,129
		Edward A. Teichert	Socialist Labor	–	45,336			Grover Cleveland	Democratic	168	5,537,857
1940____	48	Franklin D. Roosevelt	Democratic	449	27,307,819			Clinton B. Fisk	Prohibition	–	249,506
		Wendell L. Willkie	Republican	82	22,321,018			Anson J. Streeter	Union Labor	–	146,935
		Norman Thomas	Socialist	–	99,557	1884___	38	Grover Cleveland	Democratic	219	4,879,507
		Roger Q. Babson	Prohibition	–	57,812			James G. Blaine	Republican	182	4,850,293
		Earl Browder	Communist	–	46,251			Benjamin F. Butler	Greenback-Labor	–	175,370
		John W. Aiken	Socialist Labor	–	14,892			John P. St. John	Prohibition	–	150,369
1936____	48	Franklin D. Roosevelt	Democratic	523	27,752,869	1880___	38	James A. Garfield	Republican	214	4,453,295
		Alfred M. Landon	Republican	8	16,674,665			Winfield S. Hancock	Democratic	155	4,414,082
		William Lemke	Union	–	882,479			James B. Weaver	Greenback-Labor	–	308,578
		Norman Thomas	Socialist	–	187,720			Neal Dow	Prohibition	–	10,305
		Earl Browder	Communist	–	80,159	1876___	38	Rutherford B. Hayes	Republican	185	4,036,572
		D. Leigh Colvin	Prohibition	–	37,847			Samuel J. Tilden	Democratic	184	4,284,020
		John W. Aiken	Socialist Labor	–	12,777			Peter Cooper	Greenback	–	81,737
1932____	48	Franklin D. Roosevelt	Democratic	472	22,809,638	1872___	37	Ulysses S. Grant	Republican	286	3,596,745
		Herbert C. Hoover	Republican	59	15,758,901			Horace Greeley	Democratic	(⁶)	2,843,446
		Norman Thomas	Socialist	–	881,951			Charles O'Connor	Straight Democratic		29,489
		William Z. Foster	Communist	–	102,785			Thomas A. Hendricks	Independent-Democratic	42	------------
		William D. Upshaw	Prohibition	–	81,869			B. Gratz Brown	Democratic	18	------------
		Verne L. Reynolds	Socialist Labor	–	33,276			Charles J. Jenkins	Democratic	2	------------
		William H. Harvey	Liberty	–	53,425			David Davis	Democratic	1	------------
1928____	48	Herbert C. Hoover	Republican	444	21,391,993			(Not voted)		17	------------
		Alfred E. Smith	Democratic	87	15,016,169	1868___	37	Ulysses S. Grant	Republican	214	3,013,421
		Norman Thomas	Socialist	–	267,835			Horatio Seymour	Democratic	80	2,706,829
		Verne L. Reynolds	Socialist Labor	–	21,603			(Not voted)		23	------------
		William Z. Foster	Workers	–	21,181						
		William F. Varney	Prohibition	–	20,106						
1924____	48	Calvin Coolidge	Republican	382	15,718,211						
		John W. Davis	Democratic	136	8,385,283						
		Robert M. LaFollette	Progressive	13	4,831,289						
		Herman P. Faris	Prohibition	–	57,520						
		Frank T. Johns	Socialist Labor	–	36,428						
		William Z. Foster	Workers	–	36,386						
		Gilbert O. Nations	American	–	23,967						

See footnotes at end of table.

Series Y 79–83. Electoral and Popular Vote Cast for President, by Political Party: 1789 to 1968—Con.

Year	Number of States	Presidential candidate	Political party	Electoral	Popular	Year	Number of States	Presidential candidate	Political party	Vote cast, electoral
	79	80	81	82	83		79	80	81	82
1864	36	Abraham Lincoln	Republican	212	2,206,938	1812	18	James Madison	Democratic-Republican	128
		George B. McClellan	Democratic	21	1,803,787			De Witt Clinton	Fusion	89
		(Not voted)	---------	81				(Not voted)		1
1860	33	Abraham Lincoln	Republican	180	1,865,593	1808	17	James Madison	Democratic-Republican	122
		J. C. Breckinridge	Democratic (S)	72	848,356			C. C. Pinckney	Federalist	47
		Stephen A. Douglas	Democratic	12	1,382,713			George Clinton	Independent-Republican	6
		John Bell	Constitutional Union	39	592,906			(Not voted)		1
1856	31	James Buchanan	Democratic	174	1,832,955	1804	17	Thomas Jefferson	Democratic-Republican	162
		John C. Fremont	Republican	114	1,339,932			C. C. Pinckney	Federalist	14
		Millard Fillmore	American	8	871,731					
1852	31	Franklin Pierce	Democratic	254	1,601,117	1800 [9]	16	Thomas Jefferson	Democratic-Republican	73
		Winfield Scott	Whig	42	1,385,453			Aaron Burr	Democratic-Republican	73
		John P. Hale	Free Soil	–	155,825			John Adams	Federalist	65
1848	30	Zachary Taylor	Whig	163	1,360,967			C. C. Pinckney	Federalist	64
		Lewis Cass	Democratic	127	1,222,342			John Jay	Federalist	1
		Martin Van Buren	Free Soil	–	291,263	1796 [9]	16	John Adams	Federalist	71
1844	26	James K. Polk	Democratic	170	1,338,464			Thomas Jefferson	Democratic-Republican	68
		Henry Clay	Whig	105	1,300,097			Thomas Pinckney	Federalist	59
		James G. Birney	Liberty	–	62,300			Aaron Burr	Anti-Federalist	30
1840	26	William H. Harrison	Whig	234	1,274,624			Samuel Adams	Democratic-Republican	15
		Martin Van Buren	Democratic	60	1,127,781			Oliver Ellsworth	Federalist	11
1836	26	Martin Van Buren	Democratic	170	765,483			George Clinton	Democratic-Republican	7
		William H. Harrison	Whig	73				John Jay	Independent-Federalist	5
		Hugh L. White	Whig	26	} [7] 739,795			James Iredell	Federalist	3
		Daniel Webster	Whig	14				George Washington	Federalist	2
		W. P. Mangum	Anti-Jackson	11				John Henry	Independent	2
1832	24	Andrew Jackson	Democratic	219	687,502			S. Johnston	Independent-Federalist	2
		Henry Clay	National Republican	49	530,189			C. C. Pinckney	Independent-Federalist	1
		William Wirt	Anti-Masonic	7		1792 [9]	15	George Washington	Federalist	132
		John Floyd	Nullifiers	11				John Adams	Federalist	77
		(Not voted)		2				George Clinton	Democratic-Republican	50
1828	24	Andrew Jackson	Democratic	178	647,286			Thomas Jefferson	---------	4
		John Q. Adams	National Republican	83	508,064			Aaron Burr		1
1824	24	John Q. Adams		[8] 84	108,740	1789 [9]	10	George Washington		69
		Andrew Jackson	No distinct party designations	[8] 99	153,544			John Adams		34
		Henry Clay		37	47,136			John Jay		9
		W. H. Crawford		41	46,618			R. H. Harrison		6
1820	24	James Monroe	Republican	231				John Rutledge		6
		John Q. Adams	Independent-Republican	1				John Hancock		4
		(Not voted)		3				George Clinton		3
1816	19	James Monroe	Republican	183				Samuel Huntington		2
		Rufus King	Federalist	34				John Milton		2
		(Not voted)		4				James Armstrong		1
								Benjamin Lincoln		1
								Edward Telfair		1
								(Not voted)		12

– Represents zero.

[1] Total vote for Gregory includes write-in votes as well as votes for the Freedom and Peace Party, the Peace Freedom Alternative, the Peace and Freedom Party, and the New Party.

[2] Total vote for McCarthy includes write-in votes as well as votes for the Alternative in November Party, and the New Party.

[3] 6 Democratic electors in Alabama, all 8 unpledged Democratic electors in Mississippi, and 1 Republican elector in Oklahoma voted for Senator Harry F. Byrd.

[4] 1 Democratic elector in Alabama voted for Walter Jones.

[5] Includes a variety of joint tickets with People's Party electors committed to Bryan.

[6] Greeley died shortly after the election and presidential electors supporting him cast their votes as indicated, including 3 for Greeley, which were not counted.

[7] Whig tickets were pledged to various candidates in various States.

[8] No candidate having a majority in the electoral college, the election was decided in the House of Representatives.

[9] Prior to the election of 1804, each elector voted for 2 candidates for President; the one receiving the highest number of votes, if a majority, was declared elected President, the next highest, Vice President. This provision was modified by adoption of the 12th amendment, which was declared ratified by the legislatures of three-fourths of the States in a proclamation of the Secretary of State, Sept. 25, 1804.

Series Y 84-134.   Electoral Vote Cast for President, by State and Political Party: 1804 to 1968

[Electoral votes are given for the period following the revision of the method of election in 1804, using these letter symbols for the various political parties: A—American; AJ—Anti-Jackson; AM—Anti-Masonic; C—Coalition; CU—Constitutional Union; D—Democratic; DR—Democratic-Republican; F—Federalist; N—Nullification; NR—National Republican; PP—People's Party; PR—Progressive; R—Republican; SD—Southern Democratic; SR—States' Rights; W—Whig.   In the 1824 election, party lines were so indistinct that names of the individual candidates have been used]

Series No.	State	1968	1964	1960	1956	1952	1948	1944	1940	1936	1932	1928	1924	1920	1916	1912	1908
84	Alabama	10A	10R	[1]5D	[2]10D	11D	11SR	11D	11D	11D	11D	12D	12D	12D	12D	12D	11D
85	Alaska	3R	3D	3R													
86	Arizona	5R	5R	4R	4R	4R	4D	4D	3D	3D	3D	3R	3R	3R	3D	3D	
87	Arkansas	6A	6D	8D	8D	8D	9D	9D	9D	9D	9D	9D	9D	9D	9D	9D	9D
88	California	40R	40D	32R	32R	32R	25D	25D	22D	22D	22D	13R	13R	13R	13D	2D, 11PR	10R
89	Colorado	6R	6D	6R	6R	6R	6D	6R	6R	6D	6D	6R	6R	6R	6D	6D	5D
90	Connecticut	8D	8D	8D	8R	8R	8R	8D	8D	8D	8R	7R	7R	7R	7R	7D	7R
91	Delaware	3R	3D	3D	3R	3R	3R	3R	3D	3D	3R	3R	3R	3R	3R	3D	3R
92	District of Columbia	3D	3D														
93	Florida	14R	14D	10R	10R	10R	8D	8D	7D	7D	7D	6R	6D	6D	6D	6D	5D
94	Georgia	12A	12R	12D	12D	12D	12D	12D	12D	12D	12D	14D	14D	14D	14D	14D	13D
95	Hawaii	4D	4D	3D													
96	Idaho	4R	4D	4R	4R	4R	4D	4D	4D	4D	4D	4R	4R	4R	4D	4D	3R
97	Illinois	26R	26D	27D	27R	27R	28D	28D	29D	29D	29D	29R	29R	29R	29R	29D	27R
98	Indiana	13R	13D	13R	13R	13R	13R	13R	14R	14D	14D	15R	15R	15R	15R	15D	15R
99	Iowa	9R	9D	10R	10R	10R	10D	10R	11R	11D	11D	13R	13R	13R	13R	13D	13R
100	Kansas	7R	7D	8R	8R	8R	8R	8R	9R	9D	9D	10R	10R	10R	10R	10D	10R
101	Kentucky	9R	9D	10R	10R	10D	11D	11D	11D	11D	11D	13R	13R	13D	13D	13D	13D
102	Louisiana	10A	10R	10D	10D	10D	10SR	10D	10D	10D	10D	10D	10D	10D	10D	10D	9D
103	Maine	4D	4D	5R	5R	5R	5R	5R	5R	5R	5R	6R	6R	6R	6R	6D	6R
104	Maryland	10D	10D	9D	9R	9R	8R	8D	8D	8D	8D	8R	8R	8R	8D	8D	2R, 6D
105	Massachusetts	14D	14D	16D	16R	16R	16D	16D	17D	17D	17D	18D	18R	18R	18R	18D	16R
106	Michigan	21D	21D	20D	20R	20R	19R	19D	19R	19D	19D	19R	15R	15R	15R	15PR	14R
107	Minnesota	10D	10D	11D	11R	11R	11D	11D	11D	11D	11D	12R	12R	12R	12R	12PR	11R
108	Mississippi	7A	7R	(3)	8D	8D	9SR	9D	9D	9D	9D	10D	10D	10D	10D	10D	10D
109	Missouri	12R	12D	13D	13D	13R	15D	15D	15D	15D	15D	18R	18R	18R	18D	18D	18R
110	Montana	4R	4D	4R	4R	4R	4D	4D	4D	4D	4D	4R	4R	4R	4D	4D	3R
111	Nebraska	5R	5D	6R	6R	6R	6R	6R	7R	7D	7D	8R	8R	8R	8D	8D	8D
112	Nevada	3R	3D	3D	3R	3R	3D	3D	3D	3D	3D	3R	3R	3R	3D	3D	3D
113	New Hampshire	4R	4D	4R	4R	4R	4R	4D	4D	4D	4R	4R	4R	4R	4D	4D	4R
114	New Jersey	17R	17D	16D	16R	16R	16R	16D	16D	16D	16D	14R	14R	14R	14R	14D	12R
115	New Mexico	4R	4D	4R	4R	4R	4R	4D	4D	3D	3D	3R	3R	3R	3D	3D	
116	New York	43D	43D	45D	45R	45R	47R	47D	47D	47D	47R	45R	45R	45R	45R	45D	39R
117	North Carolina	12R, 1A	13D	14D	14D	14D	14D	14D	13D	13D	13D	12R	12D	12D	12D	12D	12D
118	North Dakota	4R	4D	4R	4R	4R	4R	4R	4D	4D	4D	5R	5R	5R	5D	5D	4R
119	Ohio	26R	26D	25R	25R	25R	25D	25R	26D	26D	26D	24R	24R	24R	24D	24D	23R
120	Oklahoma	8R	8D	[4]7R	8R	8R	10D	10D	11D	11D	11D	10R	10D	10D	10D	10D	7D
121	Oregon	6R	6D	6R	6R	6R	6R	6D	5D	5D	5D	5R	5R	5R	5R	5D	4R
122	Pennsylvania	29D	29D	32D	32R	32R	35R	35D	36D	36D	36R	38R	38R	38R	38R	38PR	34R
123	Rhode Island	4D	4D	4D	4R	4R	4D	4D	4D	4D	4D	5R	5R	5R	5D	5D	4R
124	South Carolina	8R	8R	8D	8D	8D	8SR	8D	8D	8D	8D	9D	9D	9D	9D	9D	9D
125	South Dakota	4R	4D	4R	4R	4R	4R	4R	4R	4D	4D	5R	5R	5R	5R	5PR	4R
126	Tennessee	11R	11D	11R	11R	11R	11D, 1SR	12D	11D	11D	11D	12R	12D	12D	12D	12D	12D
127	Texas	25D	25D	24D	24R	24R	23D	23D	23D	23D	23D	20R	20D	20D	20D	20D	18D
128	Utah	4R	4D	4R	4R	4R	4D	4D	4D	4D	4D	4R	4R	4R	4D	4R	3R
129	Vermont	3R	3D	3R	3R	3R	3R	3R	3R	3R	3R	4R	4R	4R	4R	4R	4R
130	Virginia	12R	12D	12R	12R	12R	11D	11D	11D	11D	11D	12R	12D	12D	12D	12D	12D
131	Washington	9D	9D	9R	9R	9R	8D	8D	8D	8D	8D	7R	7R	7R	7D	7PR	5R
132	West Virginia	7D	7D	8D	8R	8D	8D	8D	8D	8D	8D	8R	8R	8R	7R, 1D	8D	7R
133	Wisconsin	12R	12D	12R	12R	12R	12D	12R	12D	12D	12D	13R	13PR	13R	13R	13R	13R
134	Wyoming	3R	3D	3R	3R	3R	3D	3R	3D	3D	3D	3R	3R	3R	3D	3D	3R

Series No.	State	1904	1900	1896[5]	1892	1888	1884	1880	1876	1872[6]	1868	1864	1860	1856
84	Alabama	11D	11D	11D	11D	10D	10D	10D	10D	10R	8R	(8)	9SD	9D
87	Arkansas	9D	8D	8D	8D	7D	7D	6D	6D		5R	(8)	4SD	4D
88	California	10R	9R	8R, 1D	1R, 8D	8R	8R	1R, 5D	6R	6R	5R	5R	4R	4D
89	Colorado	5R	4D	4D	4PP	3R	3R	3R	3R					
90	Connecticut	7R	6R	6R	6D	6D	6D	6R	6D	6R	6R	6R	6R	6R
91	Delaware	3R	3R	3R	3D	3D	3D	3D	3R	3D	3D	3D	3SD	3D
93	Florida	5D	4D	4D	4D	4D	4D	4D	4R	4R	3R	(8)	3SD	3D
94	Georgia	13D	13D	13D	13D	12D	12D	11D	11D	[9]8D	9D	(8)	10SD	10D
96	Idaho	3R	3D	3D	3PP									
97	Illinois	27R	24R	24R	24D	22R	22R	21R	21R	21R	16R	16R	11R	11D
98	Indiana	15R	15R	15R	15D	15R	15R	15R	15D	15R	13R	13R	13R	13D
99	Iowa	13R	13R	13R	13R	13R	13R	11R	11R	11R	8R	8R	4R	4D
100	Kansas	10R	10R	10D	10PP	9R	9R	5R	5R	5R	3R	3R		
101	Kentucky	13D	13D	12R, 1D	13D	13D	13D	12D	12D	12D	11D	11R	12CU	12D
102	Louisiana	9D	8D	8D	8D	8D	8D	8D	8R		7D	(8)	6SD	6D
103	Maine	6R	6R	6R	6R	6R	6R	7R	7R	7R	7R	7R	8R	8R
104	Maryland	1R, 7D	8R	8R	8D	8D	8D	8D	8D	8D	7D	7R	8SD	8A
105	Massachusetts	16R	15R	15R	15R	14R	14R	13R	13R	13R	12R	12R	13R	13R
106	Michigan	14R	14R	14R	9R, 5D	13R	13R	11R	11R	11R	8R	8R	6R	6R
107	Minnesota	11R	9R	9R	9R	7R	7R	5R	5R	5R	4R	4R		
108	Mississippi	10D	9D	9D	9D	9D	9D	8D	8D	8R	(7)	(8)	7SD	7D
109	Missouri	18R	17D	17D	17D	16D	16D	15D	15D	15D	11R	11R	9D	9D
110	Montana	3R	3D	3D	3R									
111	Nebraska	8R	8R	8D	8R	5R	5R	3R	3R	3R	3R			
112	Nevada	3R	3D	3D	3PP	3R	3R	3D	3R	3R	3R	2R		

See footnotes at end of table.

Series Y 84–134. Electoral Vote Cast for President, by State and Political Party: 1804 to 1968—Con.

[Electoral votes are given for the period following the revision of the method of election in 1804, using these letter symbols for the various political parties: A—American; AJ—Anti-Jackson; AM—Anti-Masonic; C—Coalition; CU—Constitutional Union; D—Democratic; DR—Democratic-Republican; F—Federalist; N—Nullification; NR—National Republican; PP—People's Party; PR—Progressive; R—Republican; SD—Southern Democratic; SR—States' Rights; W—Whig. In the 1824 election, party lines were so indistinct that names of the individual candidates have been used]

Series No.	State	1904	1900	1896 [5]	1892	1888	1884	1880	1876	1872 [6]	1868	1864	1860	1856
113	New Hampshire	4R	4R	4R	4R	4R	4R	5R	5R	5R	5R	5R	5R	5R
114	New Jersey	12R	10R	10R	10D	9D	9D	9D	9D	9R	7D	7D	4R, 3D	7D
116	New York	39R	36R	36R	36D	36R	36D	35R	35R	35R	33D	33R	35R	35R
117	North Carolina	12D	11D	11D	11D	11D	11D	10D	10D	10R	9R	(8)	10SD	10D
118	North Dakota	4R	3R	3R	(10)	--------	--------	--------	--------	--------	--------	--------	--------	--------
119	Ohio	23R	23R	23R	22R, 1D	23R	23R	22R	22R	22R	21R	21R	23R	23R
121	Oregon	4R	4R	4R	3R, 1PP	3R	3R	3R	3R	3R	3D	3R	3R	
122	Pennsylvania	34R	32R	32R	32R	30R	30R	29R	29R	29R	26R	26R	27R	27D
123	Rhode Island	4R	4R	4R	4R	4R	4R	4R	4R	4R	4R	4R	4R	4R
124	South Carolina	9D	9D	9D	9D	9D	9D	7D	7R	7R	6R	(8)	8SD	8D
125	South Dakota	4R	4R	4D	4R	--------	--------	--------	--------	--------	--------	--------	--------	--------
126	Tennessee	12D	12D	12D	12D	12D	12D	12D	12D	12D	10R	(8)	12CU	12D
127	Texas	18D	15D	15D	15D	13D	13D	8D	8D	8D	(7)	(8)	4SD	4D
128	Utah	3R	3R	3D	--------	--------	--------	--------	--------	--------	--------	--------	--------	--------
129	Vermont	4R	4R	4R	4R	4R	4R	5R	5R	5R	5R	5R	5R	5R
130	Virginia	12D	12D	12D	12D	12D	12D	11D	11D	11R	(7)	(8)	15CU	15D
131	Washington	5R	4R	4D	4R	--------	--------	--------	--------	--------	--------	--------	--------	--------
132	West Virginia	7R	6R	6R	6D	6D	6D	5D	5D	5R	5R	5R	5R	
133	Wisconsin	13R	12R	12R	12D	11R	11R	10R	10R	10R	8R	8R	5R	5R
134	Wyoming	3R	3R	3D	3R	--------	--------	--------	--------	--------	--------	--------	--------	--------

Series No.	State	1852	1848	1844	1840	1836 [11]	1832	1828	1824	1820	1816	1812	1808	1804
84	Alabama	9D	9D	9D	7D	7D	7D	5D	5 Jackson	3DR	--------	--------	--------	--------
87	Arkansas	4D	3D	3D	3D	3D								
88	California	4D												
90	Connecticut	6D	6W	6W	8W	8D	8NR	8NR	8 Adams	9DR	9F	9C	9F	9F
91	Delaware	3D	3W	3W	3W	3W	3NR	3NR	(12)	4DR	13 3F	4C	3F	3F
93	Florida	3D	3W											
94	Georgia	10D	10W	10D	11W	11W	11D	9D	9 Crawford	8DR	8DR	8DR	6DR	6DR
97	Illinois	11D	9D	9D	5D	5D	5D	3D	(14)	3DR				
98	Indiana	13D	12D	12D	9W	9W	9D	5D	5 Jackson	3DR	3DR			
99	Iowa	4D	4D											
101	Kentucky	12W	12W	12W	15W	15W	15NR	14D	14 Clay	12DR	12DR	12DR	13 7DR	8DR
102	Louisiana	6D	6W	6D	5W	5D	5D	5D	(15)	3DR	3DR	3DR		
103	Maine	8D	9D	9D	10W	10D	10D	8NR, 1D	9 Adams	9DR				
104	Maryland	8D	8W	8W	10W	10W	16 5NR, 3D	6NR, 5D	(17)	11DR	18 8DR	5C, 6DR	2F, 9DR	2F, 9DR
105	Massachusetts	13W	12W	12W	14W	14W	14NR	15NR	15 Adams	15DR	22F	22C	19F	19DR
106	Michigan	6D	5D	5D	3W	3D	--------	--------	--------	--------	--------	--------	--------	--------
108	Mississippi	7D	6D	6D	4W	4D	4D	3D	3 Jackson	12 2DR	--------	--------	--------	--------
109	Missouri	9D	7D	7D	4D	4D	4D	3D	3 Clay	19 3DR	--------	--------	--------	--------
113	New Hampshire	5D	6D	6D	7D	7D	7D	8NR	8 Adams	7DR	8DR	8C	7F	7DR
114	New Jersey	7D	7W	7W	8W	8W	8D	8NR	8 Jackson	8DR	8DR	8C	8DR	8DR
116	New York	35D	36W	36D	42W	42D	42D	16NR, 20D	(20)	29DR	29DR	29C	21 13DR	19DR
117	North Carolina	10D	11W	11W	15W	15D	15D	15D	15 Jackson	15DR	15DR	15DR	3F, 11DR	14DR
119	Ohio	23D	23D	23W	21W	21W	21D	16D	16 Clay	8DR	8DR	13 7DR	3DR	3DR
122	Pennsylvania	27D	26W	26D	30W	30D	30D	28D	28 Jackson	13 24DR	25DR	25DR	20DR	20DR
123	Rhode Island	4D	4W	4W	4W	4D	4NR	4NR	4 Adams	4DR	4DR	4C	4F	4DR
124	South Carolina	8D	9D	9D	11D	11AJ	11N	11D	11 Jackson	11DR	11DR	11DR	10DR	10DR
126	Tennessee	12W	13W	13W	15W	15W	15D	11D	11 Jackson	13 7DR	8DR	8DR	5DR	5DR
127	Texas	4D	4D	--------	--------	--------	--------	--------	--------	--------	--------	--------	--------	--------
129	Vermont	5W	6W	6W	7W	7W	7AM	7NR	7 Adams	8DR	8DR	8DR	6DR	6DR
130	Virginia	15D	17D	17D	23D	23D	23D	24D	24 Crawford	25DR	25DR	25DR	24DR	24DR
133	Wisconsin	5D	4D	--------	--------	--------	--------	--------	--------	--------	--------	--------	--------	--------

[1] 6 electors voted for Harry F. Byrd.
[2] 1 elector voted for Walter Jones.
[3] 8 electors voted for Harry F. Byrd.
[4] 1 elector voted for Harry F. Byrd.
[5] Electors classed here as Democratic were elected in many States on joint Democratic and People's Party fusion tickets.
[6] Electoral votes from Arkansas and Louisiana were not counted. Due to the death of Greeley, Democratic electors divided their votes among Hendricks (42), Brown (18), Jenkins (2), and Davis (1).
[7] Mississippi, Texas, and Virginia did not participate in the election.
[8] Confederate States did not participate in the election.
[9] Excludes 3 votes for Greeley, which were not counted.
[10] 1 each for Republican, Democratic, and People's Party.

[11] Whig electors divided their votes among Harrison (73), White (26), and Webster (14).
[12] Vote was as follows: 2 for Crawford, 1 for Adams.
[13] 1 elector did not vote.
[14] Vote was as follows: 2 for Jackson, 1 for Adams.
[15] Vote was as follows: 3 for Jackson, 2 for Adams.
[16] 2 electors did not vote.
[17] Vote was as follows: 7 for Jackson, 3 for Adams, 1 for Crawford.
[18] 3 electors did not vote.
[19] 1 elector voted for John Quincy Adams.
[20] Vote was as follows: 26 for Adams, 5 for Crawford, 4 for Clay, 1 for Jackson.
[21] 6 electors voted for George Clinton.

Series Y 135–186. Popular Vote Cast for President, by State and Political Party: 1836 to 1968

[In thousands. Rep.—Republican; Dem.—Democratic; A.I.—American Independent.   Vote listed is normally that of the highest candidate for presidential elector for each party]

Series No.	State	1968				1964			1960			1956			1952		
		Total	Rep.	Dem.	A. I.	Total	Rep.	Dem.	Total	Rep.	Dem.	Total	Rep.	Dem.	Total	Rep.	Dem.
135	United States	73,212	31,785	31,275	9,906	70,645	27,178	43,130	68,838	34,108	34,227	62,034	35,590	26,023	61,551	33,936	27,315
136	Alabama	1,050	147	197	691	690	479	----	570	238	324	497	196	281	426	149	275
137	Alaska	83	38	35	10	67	23	44	61	31	30	----	----	----			
138	Arizona	487	267	171	47	481	243	238	398	221	177	290	177	113	261	152	109
139	Arkansas	620	191	188	241	560	243	314	429	185	215	407	186	213	405	177	226
140	California	7,252	3,468	3,244	487	7,058	2,879	4,172	6,507	3,260	3,224	5,466	3,028	2,420	5,142	2,897	2,198
141	Colorado	811	409	335	61	777	297	476	736	402	331	657	394	258	630	380	246
142	Connecticut	1,256	557	622	77	1,219	391	826	1,223	566	657	1,117	712	405	1,097	611	482
143	Delaware	214	97	89	28	201	78	123	197	96	100	178	98	79	174	90	83
144	District of Columbia	171	31	140	–	199	29	170	----	----	----						
145	Florida	2,188	887	677	624	1,854	906	949	1,544	795	749	1,126	644	480	989	544	445
146	Georgia	1,250	380	334	536	1,139	617	523	733	274	459	670	223	445	656	199	457
147	Hawaii	236	91	141	3	207	44	163	185	92	92	----	----	----			
148	Idaho	291	165	89	37	292	144	149	300	162	139	273	167	106	276	181	95
149	Illinois	4,620	2,175	2,040	391	4,703	1,906	2,797	4,757	2,369	2,378	4,407	2,623	1,776	4,481	2,457	2,014
150	Indiana	2,124	1,068	807	243	2,092	911	1,171	2,135	1,175	952	1,975	1,183	784	1,955	1,136	802
151	Iowa	1,168	619	477	66	1,185	449	733	1,274	722	551	1,235	729	502	1,269	809	452
152	Kansas	873	479	303	89	858	387	464	929	561	363	866	567	296	896	616	273
153	Kentucky	1,056	462	398	193	1,046	373	670	1,124	603	522	1,054	572	476	993	495	496
154	Louisiana	1,097	258	310	530	896	509	387	808	231	407	618	329	244	652	307	345
155	Maine	393	169	217	6	381	119	262	422	241	181	352	249	102	352	232	119
156	Maryland	1,235	518	538	179	1,116	385	731	1,055	490	566	933	560	373	902	499	395
157	Massachusetts	2,332	767	1,469	87	2,345	550	1,786	2,469	977	1,487	2,349	1,393	948	2,383	1,292	1,084
158	Michigan	3,306	1,371	1,593	332	3,203	1,060	2,137	3,318	1,620	1,687	3,080	1,714	1,360	2,799	1,552	1,231
159	Minnesota	1,589	659	858	69	1,554	560	991	1,542	758	780	1,340	719	618	1,379	763	608
160	Mississippi	655	89	151	415	409	357	53	298	74	108	248	61	144	286	113	173
161	Missouri	1,810	812	791	206	1,818	654	1,164	1,934	962	972	1,833	914	918	1,892	959	930
162	Montana	274	139	114	20	279	113	164	278	142	135	271	155	116	265	157	106
163	Nebraska	537	321	171	45	584	277	307	613	381	233	577	378	199	610	422	188
164	Nevada	154	73	61	20	135	56	79	107	52	55	97	56	41	82	51	32
165	New Hampshire	297	155	131	11	288	104	184	296	158	138	267	177	90	273	166	107
166	New Jersey	2,875	1,325	1,264	262	2,848	964	1,868	2,773	1,363	1,385	2,484	1,607	850	2,419	1,374	1,016
167	New Mexico	327	170	130	26	329	133	194	311	154	156	254	147	106	239	132	106
168	New York	6,792	3,008	3,378	359	7,166	2,244	4,913	7,291	3,446	3,830	7,096	4,346	2,748	7,128	3,953	3,105
169	North Carolina	1,587	627	464	496	1,425	625	800	1,369	655	713	1,166	575	591	1,211	558	653
170	North Dakota	248	139	95	14	258	108	150	278	154	124	254	157	97	270	192	77
171	Ohio	3,960	1,791	1,701	467	3,969	1,471	2,498	4,162	2,218	1,944	3,702	2,263	1,440	3,701	2,100	1,600
172	Oklahoma	943	450	302	192	932	413	520	903	533	370	859	474	386	949	518	431
173	Oregon	820	408	359	50	786	283	501	776	408	367	736	406	329	695	421	271
174	Pennsylvania	4,748	2,090	2,259	379	4,823	1,674	3,131	5,007	2,440	2,556	4,577	2,585	1,982	4,581	2,416	2,146
175	Rhode Island	385	122	247	16	390	75	315	406	148	258	388	226	162	414	211	203
176	South Carolina	667	254	197	215	525	309	216	387	189	198	301	76	136	341	168	173
177	South Dakota	281	150	118	13	293	130	163	306	178	128	294	172	122	294	204	90
178	Tennessee	1,249	473	351	425	1,144	509	635	1,052	557	481	939	462	457	893	446	444
179	Texas	3,079	1,228	1,267	584	2,627	959	1,663	2,311	1,121	1,168	1,955	1,081	860	2,076	1,103	969
180	Utah	423	239	157	27	401	182	220	375	205	169	334	216	118	330	194	135
181	Vermont	161	85	70	5	163	55	108	167	98	69	153	110	43	154	110	43
182	Virginia	1,361	590	442	322	1,042	481	558	771	405	362	698	386	268	620	349	269
183	Washington	1,304	589	616	97	1,259	470	780	1,242	629	599	1,151	620	523	1,103	599	493
184	West Virginia	754	308	374	73	792	254	538	838	396	442	831	449	382	874	420	454
185	Wisconsin	1,692	810	749	128	1,692	638	1,050	1,729	895	831	1,551	955	587	1,607	980	622
186	Wyoming	127	71	45	11	143	62	81	141	77	63	124	75	50	129	81	48

Series No.	State	1948				1944			1940			1936			1932		
		Total	Rep.	Dem.	States' Rights	Total	Rep.	Dem.	Total	Rep.	Dem.	Total	Rep.	Dem.	Total	Rep.	Dem.
135	United States	48,794	21,991	24,179	1,176	47,969	22,015	25,607	49,891	22,321	27,308	45,643	16,675	27,753	39,732	15,759	22,810
136	Alabama	215	41	–	171	245	45	199	294	42	251	276	35	238	242	35	205
138	Arizona	177	78	95	–	138	56	81	150	54	95	124	33	87	118	36	79
139	Arkansas	242	51	150	40	213	64	149	200	42	157	179	32	147	219	27	190
140	California	4,022	1,895	1,913	1	3,521	1,513	1,989	3,269	1,351	1,878	2,638	836	1,767	2,266	848	1,324
141	Colorado	515	240	267	–	505	269	234	549	280	266	489	181	295	457	190	251
142	Connecticut	884	438	423	–	832	391	435	782	361	418	691	279	382	594	288	282
143	Delaware	139	70	68	–	125	57	68	136	61	75	128	54	70	113	57	54
145	Florida	578	194	282	90	483	143	339	485	126	359	327	78	249	275	69	206
146	Georgia	419	77	255	85	328	57	268	313	24	265	293	37	255	256	20	234
148	Idaho	215	102	107	–	208	100	107	235	107	128	200	66	126	187	71	109
149	Illinois	3,984	1,961	1,995	–	4,036	1,939	2,079	4,218	2,047	2,150	3,957	1,570	2,283	3,408	1,433	1,882
150	Indiana	1,656	821	808	–	1,672	876	781	1,783	899	874	1,651	692	935	1,575	677	862
151	Iowa	1,038	494	522	–	1,053	547	500	1,215	632	579	1,143	488	622	1,037	414	598
152	Kansas	789	423	352	–	734	442	287	860	489	365	859	394	462	790	348	423
153	Kentucky	823	341	467	10	868	392	473	968	410	557	923	370	539	983	395	581
154	Louisiana	416	73	136	204	349	68	282	372	52	320	330	37	293	269	19	249
155	Maine	265	150	112	–	296	155	141	321	164	156	304	169	126	298	167	129
156	Maryland	597	295	287	2	608	293	315	660	270	385	625	231	390	511	184	314
157	Massachusetts	2,107	909	1,152	–	1,961	921	1,035	2,027	940	1,077	1,840	769	943	1,580	737	800
158	Michigan	2,110	1,039	1,003	–	2,205	1,084	1,107	2,086	1,040	1,033	1,805	700	1,017	1,665	740	872
159	Minnesota	1,212	484	693	–	1,126	527	590	1,251	596	644	1,130	350	699	1,003	364	601
160	Mississippi	192	5	19	168	180	12	169	176	7	168	162	4	157	146	5	140
161	Missouri	1,579	655	917	–	1,572	761	807	1,834	871	958	1,829	698	1,111	1,610	565	1,025
162	Montana	224	97	119	–	207	93	113	248	100	146	231	64	160	216	78	127
163	Nebraska	489	265	224	–	563	330	233	616	352	264	608	248	347	570	201	359

– Represents zero.   Z Less than 500.

Series Y 135–186.　Popular Vote Cast for President, by State and Political Party: 1836 to 1968—Con.

[In thousands.　Rep.—Republican; Dem.—Democratic.　Vote listed is normally that of the highest candidate for presidential elector for each party]

Series No.	State	1948				1944			1940			1936			1932		
		Total	Rep.	Dem.	States' Rights	Total	Rep.	Dem.	Total	Rep.	Dem.	Total	Rep.	Dem.	Total	Rep.	Dem.
164	Nevada	62	29	31	–	54	25	30	53	21	32	44	12	32	41	13	29
165	New Hampshire	231	121	108	(Z)	230	110	120	218	110	125	218	105	108	206	104	101
166	New Jersey	1,950	981	895	–	1,964	961	988	1,974	945	1,016	1,819	719	1,084	1,630	775	806
167	New Mexico	187	80	105	–	152	71	81	183	79	104	169	62	106	151	54	95
168	New York	6,177	2,841	2,780	–	6,317	2,988	3,304	6,302	3,027	3,252	5,596	2,181	3,293	4,689	1,938	2,535
169	North Carolina	791	259	459	70	791	263	527	823	214	609	839	223	616	712	208	498
170	North Dakota	221	115	96	(Z)	220	119	100	281	155	124	274	73	163	256	72	178
171	Ohio	2,936	1,446	1,453	(Z)	3,153	1,582	1,571	3,320	1,587	1,733	3,012	1,128	1,747	2,610	1,228	1,302
172	Oklahoma	722	269	453	–	722	319	401	826	349	474	750	245	501	705	188	516
173	Oregon	524	261	243	–	480	225	249	481	220	258	414	123	267	369	136	214
174	Pennsylvania	3,735	1,902	1,752	–	3,795	1,835	1,940	4,078	1,890	2,171	4,138	1,690	2,354	2,859	1,454	1,296
175	Rhode Island	328	136	189	–	299	123	175	321	139	182	310	125	164	266	115	147
176	South Carolina	143	5	34	103	103	5	91	100	2	95	115	2	114	104	2	102
177	South Dakota	250	130	118	–	232	135	97	308	177	131	296	126	160	288	99	184
178	Tennessee	550	203	270	74	511	200	309	523	169	352	477	147	328	390	127	259
179	Texas	1,250	303	824	114	1,144	192	816	1,117	212	905	850	103	742	856	98	753
180	Utah	276	124	149	–	248	98	150	248	93	154	217	65	150	207	85	117
181	Vermont	123	76	46	–	125	72	54	143	78	64	144	81	62	137	79	56
182	Virginia	419	172	201	43	388	145	242	347	109	236	335	98	235	298	90	204
183	Washington	905	386	476	–	856	362	487	794	322	462	692	207	460	615	209	353
184	West Virginia	749	316	429	–	716	323	393	868	372	496	830	325	503	744	331	405
185	Wisconsin	1,277	591	647	–	1,339	675	650	1,406	679	705	1,259	381	803	1,115	348	707
186	Wyoming	101	48	52	–	101	52	49	112	53	59	103	39	63	97	40	54

Series No.	State	1928			1924				1920			1916			1912			
		Total	Rep.	Dem.	Total	Rep.	Dem.	Progressive	Total	Rep.	Dem.	Total	Rep.	Dem.	Total	Rep.	Dem.	Progressive
135	United States	36,812	21,392	15,016	29,086	15,718	8,385	4,831	26,748	16,143	9,130	18,531	8,534	9,128	15,037	3,487	6,297	4,119
136	Alabama	249	121	128	165	43	113	8	234	75	156	131	29	99	118	10	82	23
138	Arizona	91	53	39	74	31	26	17	67	37	30	58	21	33	23	3	10	7
139	Arkansas	202	78	123	139	41	85	13	183	72	106	168	47	112	124	24	69	22
140	California	1,797	1,162	614	1,282	733	106	425	943	625	229	1,000	463	466	678	4	283	284
141	Colorado	392	254	133	342	195	75	70	292	173	105	294	102	179	266	58	114	72
142	Connecticut	553	297	252	400	246	110	42	366	229	121	214	107	100	190	68	75	34
143	Delaware	105	69	35	90	52	33	5	95	53	40	52	26	25	49	16	23	9
145	Florida	254	144	102	109	31	62	9	145	45	91	81	15	56	52	4	36	5
146	Georgia	231	65	130	166	30	123	13	149	43	106	160	11	128	121	6	94	21
148	Idaho	154	100	53	148	70	24	54	136	89	47	135	55	70	106	33	34	26
149	Illinois	3,107	1,769	1,313	2,470	1,453	577	432	2,095	1,420	534	2,193	1,153	950	1,146	254	405	386
150	Indiana	1,421	848	563	1,272	703	492	72	1,263	696	511	719	341	334	654	151	282	162
151	Iowa	1,010	624	379	972	537	160	274	895	635	228	515	279	221	492	120	185	162
152	Kansas	713	514	193	662	408	156	98	570	369	185	628	276	314	365	75	144	120
153	Kentucky	941	558	381	814	397	376	38	919	452	456	520	242	270	453	116	219	102
154	Louisiana	216	51	165	122	25	93	4	126	39	88	93	6	80	79	4	60	9
155	Maine	262	180	81	192	138	42	11	198	136	59	136	70	64	130	27	51	48
156	Maryland	528	301	224	359	162	148	47	428	236	181	262	117	138	232	55	113	58
157	Massachusetts	1,578	776	793	1,130	703	281	141	994	681	277	532	269	248	489	156	174	142
158	Michigan	1,372	965	397	1,160	875	152	122	1,038	756	231	647	338	284	548	151	150	213
159	Minnesota	971	561	396	822	421	56	339	736	519	143	387	180	179	334	64	106	126
160	Mississippi	152	26	125	112	8	100	3	82	12	69	86	4	80	64	2	57	4
161	Missouri	1,501	834	663	1,310	648	575	84	1,332	727	575	787	369	398	699	208	331	124
162	Montana	194	113	79	174	74	34	66	179	109	57	178	67	101	80	19	28	22
163	Nebraska	547	346	198	464	219	137	106	383	248	120	287	118	159	249	54	109	73
164	Nevada	32	18	14	27	11	6	10	27	15	10	33	12	18	20	3	8	6
165	New Hampshire	197	115	81	165	99	57	9	159	95	63	89	44	44	88	33	35	18
166	New Jersey	1,548	925	616	1,086	675	298	109	904	611	257	494	269	211	434	89	179	146
167	New Mexico	118	70	48	114	55	49	10	106	58	47	67	31	34	49	18	20	8
168	New York	4,406	2,193	2,090	3,264	1,820	951	475	2,899	1,871	781	1,706	869	759	1,588	455	656	390
169	North Carolina	635	349	286	482	191	284	7	538	233	305	290	121	168	244	29	144	69
170	North Dakota	240	131	107	199	95	14	90	204	160	37	115	53	55	86	23	30	26
171	Ohio	2,508	1,628	864	2,016	1,176	478	358	2,021	1,182	780	1,164	514	604	1,037	278	425	230
172	Oklahoma	618	394	219	528	226	256	41	489	248	218	292	97	148	253	91	119	–
173	Oregon	320	205	109	279	143	68	68	239	144	80	262	127	120	137	35	47	38
174	Pennsylvania	3,160	2,055	1,077	2,145	1,401	409	308	1,853	1,218	504	1,297	704	522	1,218	273	396	445
175	Rhode Island	237	118	119	210	125	77	8	168	107	55	88	45	40	78	28	30	17
176	South Carolina	69	3	63	51	1	49	1	67	2	64	64	2	62	50	1	48	1
177	South Dakota	262	158	103	204	101	27	75	182	111	36	129	64	59	117	–	49	59
178	Tennessee	353	195	157	301	131	159	11	428	219	207	273	117	153	253	60	133	55
179	Texas	708	367	340	656	130	483	43	486	115	288	373	65	287	302	29	220	27
180	Utah	177	95	81	157	77	47	33	146	82	57	143	54	84	112	42	37	24
181	Vermont	135	90	44	103	80	16	6	90	68	21	64	40	23	63	23	15	22
182	Virginia	305	165	140	224	73	140	10	231	87	142	154	49	103	137	23	90	22
183	Washington	501	336	157	422	220	43	151	399	223	84	381	167	183	322	70	87	114
184	West Virginia	643	376	264	584	289	257	37	510	282	221	290	143	140	264	57	113	79
185	Wisconsin	1,017	544	450	841	312	68	454	701	499	113	447	221	192	400	131	164	62
186	Wyoming	83	53	29	80	42	13	25	55	35	17	52	22	28	42	15	15	9

– Represents zero.　Z Less than 500.

Series Y 135–186. Popular Vote Cast for President, by State and Political Party: 1836 to 1968—Con.

[In thousands. Rep.—Republican; Dem.—Democratic. Vote listed is normally that of the highest candidate for presidential elector for each party. Democratic vote in 1896 and 1900 includes a variety of joint elector tickets with the People's Party, and party totals generally include votes cast for the presidential candidate under other designations than that of the party itself]

Series No.	State	1908			1904			1900			1896			1892			
		Total	Rep.	Dem.	Total	Rep.	Dem.	Total	Rep.	Dem.	Total	Rep.	Dem.	Total	Rep.	Dem.	People's
135	United States	14,884	7,675	6,412	13,521	7,628	5,084	13,968	7,218	6,357	13,907	7,102	6,493	12,061	5,183	5,555	1,030
136	Alabama	105	26	74	109	22	80	160	56	97	195	56	130	233	9	138	85
139	Arkansas	152	57	88	117	48	64	128	45	81	140	38	101	148	47	88	12
140	California	387	214	127	332	205	89	303	165	125	299	147	123	270	118	118	25
141	Colorado	264	124	127	244	135	100	221	93	123	187	26	159	96	39	-	54
142	Connecticut	190	113	68	191	111	73	180	103	74	174	110	57	165	77	82	4
143	Delaware	48	25	22	44	24	19	42	23	19	32	17	13	37	18	19	
145	Florida	49	11	31	39	8	27	40	7	28	46	11	31	35		30	5
146	Georgia	132	41	72	130	24	84	121	34	81	156	59	93	221	48	129	42
148	Idaho	98	53	36	73	48	18	58	27	29	30	6	23	19	9		11
149	Illinois	1,155	630	451	1,076	633	328	1,132	598	503	1,088	607	465	874	399	426	22
150	Indiana	721	349	338	682	369	274	663	335	310	637	324	306	552	254	263	22
151	Iowa	495	275	201	486	308	149	530	308	209	521	289	224	443	220	196	21
152	Kansas	376	197	161	329	213	86	352	186	161	336	159	172	325	157		163
153	Kentucky	490	235	244	436	205	217	468	227	235	446	218	218	341	136	175	24
154	Louisiana	76	9	64	54	5	48	68	14	54	101	22	77	114	26	88	
155	Maine	106	67	35	97	65	28	108	66	38	118	80	35	116	63	48	2
156	Maryland	239	117	116	224	109	109	264	136	122	251	137	105	213	93	114	1
157	Massachusetts	457	266	156	445	258	166	415	239	157	402	279	106	391	203	177	3
158	Michigan	538	333	175	520	362	134	544	316	211	546	293	237	467	223	202	20
159	Minnesota	330	196	109	293	217	55	316	190	113	342	194	140	268	123	101	30
160	Mississippi	67	4	60	59	3	53	58	6	51	70	5	63	53	1	41	10
161	Missouri	716	347	347	644	321	296	684	314	352	674	305	364	542	228	268	41
162	Montana	69	32	29	64	35	22	64	25	37	53	10	42	44	19	18	7
163	Nebraska	267	127	131	226	139	53	241	122	114	223	103	115	200	87	24	83
164	Nevada	25	11	11	12	7	4	10	4	6	10	2	8	11	3	1	7
165	New Hampshire	90	53	34	90	54	34	92	55	35	84	57	21	89	46	42	
166	New Jersey	467	265	183	432	245	165	401	222	165	371	221	134	336	156	171	1
168	New York	1,638	870	667	1,618	860	684	1,548	822	678	1,424	820	551	1,337	609	655	16
169	North Carolina	252	115	137	208	82	124	292	133	158	330	154	175	278	101	133	45
170	North Dakota	95	58	33	70	53	14	58	36	21	47	26	21	36	18		18
171	Ohio	1,122	572	503	1,004	600	345	1,040	544	475	1,014	526	477	851	405	405	15
172	Oklahoma	256	107	127													
173	Oregon	111	63	38	90	60	17	84	47	33	97	49	45	78	35	14	27
174	Pennsylvania	1,265	746	447	1,237	841	338	1,173	713	424	1,194	728	427	1,003	516	452	9
175	Rhode Island	72	44	25	69	42	25	57	34	20	55	37	14	53	27	24	
176	South Carolina	66	4	62	56	3	53	51	4	47	66	7	59	71	13	55	2
177	South Dakota	115	68	40	101	72	22	96	55	40	83	41	41	71	35	9	27
178	Tennessee	257	118	136	243	105	132	274	123	145	318	149	164	266	101	136	24
179	Texas	298	69	218	233	51	167	422	131	268	539	163	369	423	75	240	101
180	Utah	109	61	43	102	62	33	93	47	45	78	13	65				
181	Vermont	53	40	11	52	40	10	56	43	13	64	51	10	56	38	16	
182	Virginia	137	53	83	131	48	81	264	116	146	295	135	155	292	113	164	12
183	Washington	184	106	58	145	102	28	108	57	45	94	39	52	88	37	30	19
184	West Virginia	258	138	111	240	133	101	221	120	99	202	105	94	171	80	84	4
185	Wisconsin	454	248	167	443	280	124	442	266	159	447	268	166	371	171	177	10
186	Wyoming	36	21	15	31	20	9	25	14	10	21	10	10	17	8		8

Series No.	State	1888			1884			1880			1876			1872		
		Total	Rep.	Dem.	Total	Rep.	Dem.	Total	Rep.	Dem.	Total	Rep.	Dem.	Total	Rep.	Dem.
135	United States	11,383	5,447	5,538	10,053	4,850	4,880	9,217	4,453	4,414	8,422	4,037	4,284	6,460	3,597	2,843
136	Alabama	175	57	117	154	59	93	152	56	91	172	69	103	170	90	79
139	Arkansas	157	60	86	126	51	73	109	42	61	97	39	58	79	41	38
140	California	250	125	118	197	102	89	164	80	80	156	79	76	96	54	41
141	Colorado	91	50	37	64	36	28	54	28	25						
142	Connecticut	154	75	75	137	66	67	133	67	64	122	59	62	96	50	46
143	Delaware	30	13	16	30	13	17	29	14	15	24	11	13	22	11	10
145	Florida	67	27	40	60	28	32	52	24	28	48	24	24	33	18	15
146	Georgia	142	40	100	143	48	94	157	54	103	181	51	130	143	63	76
149	Illinois	748	370	348	673	337	312	622	318	277	553	277	259	430	242	185
150	Indiana	537	263	261	495	239	245	471	232	226	430	207	214	350	186	164
151	Iowa	404	212	180	377	197	178	323	184	106	295	174	112	205	132	71
152	Kansas	331	183	103	266	154	90	201	122	60	124	78	38	100	67	33
153	Kentucky	344	155	184	276	118	153	267	106	149	260	97	160	189	89	100
154	Louisiana	116	31	85	109	46	63	103	38	65	146	75	71	129	72	57
155	Maine	128	74	50	130	72	52	144	74	65	116	66	50	91	61	29
156	Maryland	211	100	106	186	86	97	173	79	94	164	72	92	135	67	68
157	Massachusetts	345	184	152	303	147	122	283	165	112	259	150	109	199	133	65
158	Michigan	475	236	213	403	193	150	353	185	132	317	167	141	222	139	79
159	Minnesota	262	143	104	190	112	70	151	94	53	124	73	49	91	56	35
160	Mississippi	115	29	85	121	44	78	116	34	76	165	53	112	129	82	47
161	Missouri	521	236	262	441	203	236	397	154	209	351	145	202	271	119	151
163	Nebraska	203	108	80	134	77	54	87	55	29	58	32	17	25	17	8
164	Nevada	12	7	5	13	7	6	18	9	10	20	10	9	15	8	6
165	New Hampshire	91	46	43	84	43	39	86	45	41	80	42	39	69	37	31
166	New Jersey	304	144	152	261	123	128	246	121	123	220	104	116	168	92	77
168	New York	1,320	650	636	1,167	562	563	1,104	556	535	1,016	490	522	830	441	387
169	North Carolina	286	135	148	268	125	143	241	116	125	234	108	125	165	95	70
171	Ohio	839	416	395	785	400	368	725	375	341	659	331	323	529	282	244
173	Oregon	62	33	27	53	27	25	41	21	20	30	15	14	20	12	8
174	Pennsylvania	998	526	447	900	473	395	875	445	407	755	385	362	562	349	213
175	Rhode Island	41	22	18	33	19	12	29	18	11	26	16	11	19	14	5
176	South Carolina	80	14	66	93	22	70	171	58	112	183	92	91	95	72	23
178	Tennessee	304	139	159	259	124	134	243	108	130	223	90	133	181	86	95
179	Texas	364	94	236	326	93	226	241	57	156	151	45	106	116	48	68
181	Vermont	63	45	17	59	40	17	65	46	18	65	44	20	52	41	11
182	Virginia	304	150	152	285	139	145	212	84	97	237	96	141	185	93	92
184	West Virginia	159	78	79	132	63	67	113	46	57	100	42	57	62	32	30
185	Wisconsin	355	177	155	320	161	146	266	144	114	257	130	124	192	105	86

- Represents zero.

Series Y 135–186.   Popular Vote Cast for President, by State and Political Party, by States: 1836 to 1956—Con.

[In thousands.   Rep.—Republican; Dem.—Democratic.   Vote listed is normally that of the highest candidate for presidential elector for each party]

Series No.	State	1868			1864			1860					1856			
		Total	Rep.	Dem.	Total	Rep.	Dem.	Total	Rep.	Dem.	Southern Dem.	Constitutional Union	Total	Rep.	Dem.	American
135	**United States**	**5,720**	**3,013**	**2,707**	**4,011**	**2,207**	**1,804**	**4,690**	**1,866**	**1,383**	**848**	**593**	**4,045**	**1,340**	**1,833**	**872**
136	Alabama	149	76	72				90		14	49	28	75		47	29
139	Arkansas	41	22	19				54		5	29	20	33		22	11
140	California	109	55	54	106	62	44	120	39	38	34	9	110	21	53	36
142	Connecticut	99	51	48	87	45	42	80	43	17	16	3	81	43	35	3
143	Delaware	19	8	11	17	8	9	16	4	1	7	4	14		8	6
145	Florida							13			8	5	11		6	5
146	Georgia	160	57	103				107		12	52	43	99		57	42
149	Illinois	448	250	198	348	190	159	337	171	158	2	5	239	96	106	38
150	Indiana	344	177	167	280	150	130	272	139	116	12	5	235	94	119	22
151	Iowa	194	120	74	135	86	48	128	70	55	1	2	90	44	36	9
152	Kansas	44	30	14	21	17	4									
153	Kentucky	155	39	116	90	27	63	146	1	26	53	66	133		70	63
154	Louisiana	114	33	80				51		8	23	20	43		22	21
155	Maine	113	70	42	109	64	45	101	63	30	6	2	110	67	39	3
156	Maryland	93	30	62	70	37	32	93	2	6	42	42	87		39	47
157	Massachusetts	196	136	59	175	127	49	169	107	34	6	22	167	108	39	20
158	Michigan	226	129	97	160	89	72	155	88	65	1		126	72	52	2
159	Minnesota	72	44	28	42	25	17	35	22	12	1					
160	Mississippi							69		4	40	25	59		34	24
161	Missouri	152	87	66	104	73	31	165	17	59	31	58	106		58	49
163	Nebraska	15	10	6												
164	Nevada	12	6	5	16	10	7									
165	New Hampshire	68	38	31	69	36	33	66	38	26	2		70	37	32	24
166	New Jersey	163	80	83	129	61	68	121	58	63			100	28	47	24
168	New York	850	420	430	731	369	362	677	363	314			597	276	196	125
169	North Carolina	181	97	85				96		3	49	45	85		48	37
171	Ohio	519	280	239	471	266	206	443	232	187	11	12	386	187	171	28
173	Oregon	22	11	11	18	10	8	14	5	3	5					
174	Pennsylvania	656	342	314	574	296	277	476	268	17	179	13	460	148	231	82
175	Rhode Island	20	13	6	23	14	9	20	12	8			20	11	7	2
176	South Carolina	108	62	45												
178	Tennessee	82	57	25				144		11	64	69	140		74	66
179	Texas							63			48	15	48		32	16
181	Vermont	56	44	12	56	42	13	45	34	9		2	51	40	11	1
182	Virginia							167	2	16	74	74	150		90	60
184	West Virginia	49	29	20	34	23	10									
185	Wisconsin	194	109	85	145	80	63	152	86	65	1		120	66	53	1

Series No.	State	1852			1848			1844			1840			1836		
		Total	Whig	Dem.	Total	Whig	Dem.	Total	Whig	Dem.	Total	Whig	Dem.	Total	Whig	Dem.
135	**United States**	**3,162**	**1,385**	**1,601**	**2,879**	**1,361**	**1,222**	**2,701**	**1,300**	**1,338**	**2,412**	**1,275**	**1,128**	**1,505**	**740**	**765**
136	Alabama	44	15	27	62	30	31	63	26	37	63	29	34	37	17	21
139	Arkansas	20	7	12	17	8	9	15	6	10	12	5	7	4	1	2
140	California	77	36	41												
142	Connecticut	67	30	33	62	30	27	65	33	30	57	32	25	38	19	19
143	Delaware	13	6	6	12	6	6	12	6	6	11	6	5	9	5	4
145	Florida	7	3	4	7	4	3									
146	Georgia	62	17	35	92	48	45	86	42	44	72	40	32	47	24	23
149	Illinois	155	65	80	125	53	56	108	46	59	93	46	47	33	15	18
150	Indiana	184	81	95	153	70	75	140	68	70	117	65	52	74	41	32
151	Iowa	35	16	18	22	10	11									
153	Kentucky	111	57	54	115	67	49	113	61	52	91	59	33	69	37	33
154	Louisiana	36	17	19	34	18	15	27	13	14	19	11	8	7	4	4
155	Maine	82	33	42	87	35	40	85	34	46	93	47	46	38	15	23
156	Maryland	75	35	40	72	28	34	69	36	33	62	34	29	48	26	22
157	Massachusetts	125	53	45	134	61	35	130	68	52	126	73	52	78	42	35
158	Michigan	83	34	42	65	24	31	56	24	28	44	23	21	12	6	7
160	Mississippi	45	18	27	52	26	27	46	20	26	37	20	17	20	10	10
161	Missouri	69	30	39	73	33	40	73	31	41	53	23	30	18	7	11
165	New Hampshire	51	15	29	50	15	28	49	18	27	59	26	33	25	6	19
166	New Jersey	84	39	44	78	40	37	76	38	37	64	33	31	52	26	26
168	New York	525	235	263	456	219	114	486	232	238	442	226	213	306	139	167
169	North Carolina	79	39	40	80	44	36	82	43	39	79	46	34	50	24	27
171	Ohio	353	153	169	329	139	155	312	155	149	273	148	124	203	106	97
174	Pennsylvania	386	179	199	369	185	173	331	160	167	288	144	144	179	87	91
175	Rhode Island	17	8	9	11	7	4	12	7	5	9	5	3	6	3	3
178	Tennessee	115	59	57	122	64	58	120	60	60	108	60	48	62	36	26
179	Texas	20	5	15	17	5	12									
181	Vermont	44	22	13	48	23	11	49	27	18	51	32	18	35	21	14
182	Virginia	133	59	74	92	45	47	96	45	51	86	43	44	54	23	30
185	Wisconsin	62	21	32	39	14	15									

Series Y 187–188. Costs of Presidential General Elections: 1860 to 1968

Year	Republicans 187	Democrats 188	Year	Republicans 187	Democrats 188
1968 [1]	$25,402,000	$11,594,000	1912 [4]	$1,071,549	$1,134,848
1964	16,026,000	8,757,000	1908	1,655,518	629,341
1960	10,128,000	9,797,000	1904	2,096,000	700,000
1956	7,778,702	5,106,651	1900	3,000,000	425,000
1952	6,608,623	5,032,926	1896	3,350,000	675,000
1948 [2]	2,127,296	2,736,334	1892	1,700,000	2,350,000
1944	2,828,652	2,169,077	1888	1,350,000	855,000
1940	3,451,310	2,783,654	1884	1,300,000	1,400,000
1936	8,892,972	5,194,741	1880	1,100,000	355,000
1932	2,900,052	2,245,975	1876	950,000	900,000
1928	6,256,111	5,342,350	1872	250,000	50,000
1924 [3]	4,020,478	1,108,836	1868	150,000	75,000
1920	5,417,501	1,470,371	1864	125,000	50,000
1916	2,441,565	2,284,590	1860	100,000	50,000

[1] American Independent Party, with George Wallace as candidate, spent $7,223,000.
[2] Progressive Party, with Henry Wallace as candidate, spent $1,133,863; States' Rights, with Strom Thurmond as candidate, spent $163,442.
[3] Progressive Party, with R. M. LaFollette as candidate, spent $236,963.
[4] Progressive Party, with T. Roosevelt as candidate, spent $665,420.

Series Y 189–198. Congressional Bills, Acts, and Resolutions: 1789 to 1970

[Excludes simple and concurrent resolutions]

Period of session	Congress	Measures introduced			Measures passed						
		Total	Bills	Joint resolutions	Total	Public			Private		
						Total	Acts	Resolutions [1]	Total	Acts	Resolutions [1]
		189	190	191	192	193	194	195	196	197	198
Jan. 1969–Jan. 1971	91st	26,303	24,631	1,672	941	695	695	----------	246	246	----------
Jan. 1967–Oct. 1968	90th	26,460	24,786	1,674	1,002	640	640	----------	362	362	----------
Jan. 1965–Oct. 1966	89th	24,003	22,483	1,520	1,283	810	810	----------	473	473	----------
Jan. 1963–Oct. 1964	88th	17,480	16,079	1,401	1,026	666	666	----------	360	360	----------
Jan. 1961–Oct. 1962	87th	18,376	17,230	1,146	1,569	885	885	----------	684	684	----------
Jan. 1959–Sept. 1960	86th	18,261	17,230	1,031	1,292	800	800	----------	492	492	----------
Jan. 1957–Aug. 1958	85th	19,112	18,205	907	1,720	936	936	----------	784	784	----------
Jan. 1955–July 1956	84th	17,687	16,782	905	1,921	1,028	1,028	----------	893	893	----------
Jan. 1953–Dec. 1954	83d	14,952	14,181	771	1,783	781	781	----------	1,002	1,002	----------
Jan. 1951–July 1952	82d	12,730	12,062	668	1,617	594	594	----------	1,023	1,023	----------
Jan. 1949–Jan. 1951	81st	14,988	14,219	769	2,024	921	921	----------	1,103	1,103	----------
Jan. 1947–Dec. 1948	80th	10,797	10,108	689	1,363	906	906	----------	457	457	----------
Jan. 1945–Aug. 1946	79th	10,330	9,748	582	1,625	733	733	----------	892	892	----------
Jan. 1943–Dec. 1944	78th	8,334	7,845	489	1,157	568	568	----------	589	589	----------
Jan. 1941–Dec. 1942	77th	11,334	10,793	541	1,485	850	850	----------	635	635	----------
Jan. 1939–Jan. 1941	76th	16,105	15,174	931	1,662	1,005	894	111	657	651	6
Jan. 1937–June 1938	75th	16,156	15,120	1,036	1,759	919	788	131	840	835	5
Jan. 1935–June 1936	74th	18,754	17,819	935	1,724	987	851	136	737	730	7
Mar. 1933–June 1934	73d	14,370	13,774	596	975	539	486	53	436	434	2
Dec. 1931–Mar. 1933	72d	21,382	20,501	881	843	516	442	74	327	326	1
Apr. 1929–Mar. 1931	71st	24,453	23,652	801	1,522	1,009	869	140	513	512	1
Dec. 1927–Mar. 1929	70th	23,897	23,238	659	1,722	1,145	1,037	108	577	568	9
Dec. 1925–Mar. 1927	69th	23,799	23,250	549	1,423	879	808	71	544	537	7
Dec. 1923–Mar. 1925	68th	17,462	16,884	578	996	707	632	75	289	286	3
Apr. 1921–Mar. 1923	67th	19,889	19,133	756	930	654	549	105	276	275	1
May 1919–Mar. 1921	66th	21,967	21,222	745	594	470	401	69	124	120	4
May 1917–Dec. 1919	65th	22,594	21,919	675	453	405	349	56	48	48	----------
Dec. 1915–Mar. 1917	64th	30,052	29,438	614	684	458	400	58	226	221	5
Mar. 1913–Mar. 1915	63d	30,053	29,367	686	700	417	342	75	283	271	12
Apr. 1911–Mar. 1913	62d	38,032	37,459	573	716	530	457	73	186	180	6
Mar. 1909–Mar. 1911	61st	44,363	43,921	442	884	595	526	69	289	286	3
Dec. 1907–Mar. 1909	60th	38,388	37,981	407	646	411	350	61	235	234	1
Mar. 1905–Mar. 1907	59th	34,879	34,524	355	7,024	775	692	83	6,249	6,248	1
Mar. 1903–Mar. 1905	58th	26,851	26,504	347	4,041	575	502	73	3,466	3,465	1
Mar. 1901–Mar. 1903	57th	25,460	25,007	453	2,790	480	423	57	2,310	2,309	1
Dec. 1899–Mar. 1901	56th	20,893	20,409	484	1,942	443	383	60	1,499	1,498	1
Mar. 1897–Mar. 1899	55th	18,463	17,817	646	1,437	552	449	103	885	880	5
Dec. 1895–Mar. 1897	54th	14,585	14,114	471	948	434	356	78	514	504	10
Mar. 1893–Mar. 1895	53d	12,226	11,796	430	711	463	374	89	248	235	13
Dec. 1891–Mar. 1893	52d	14,893	14,518	375	722	398	347	51	324	318	6
Mar. 1889–Mar. 1891	51st	19,630	19,163	467	2,251	611	531	80	1,640	1,633	7
Dec. 1887–Mar. 1889	50th	17,078	16,664	414	1,824	570	508	62	1,254	1,246	8
Mar. 1885–Mar. 1887	49th	15,002	14,618	384	1,452	424	367	57	1,028	1,025	3
Dec. 1883–Mar. 1885	48th	11,443	10,961	482	969	284	219	65	685	678	7
Mar. 1881–Mar. 1883	47th	10,704	10,194	510	761	419	330	89	342	317	25
Mar. 1879–Mar. 1881	46th	10,067	9,481	586	650	372	288	84	278	250	28
Mar. 1877–Mar. 1879	45th	8,735	8,413	322	746	303	255	48	443	430	13
Mar. 1875–Mar. 1877	44th	6,230	6,001	229	580	278	251	27	302	292	10
Mar. 1873–Mar. 1875	43d	6,434	6,252	182	859	415	392	23	444	441	3
Mar. 1871–Mar. 1873	42d	5,943	5,725	218	1,012	531	515	16	481	479	2

See footnote at end of table.

Series Y 189–198.   Congressional Bills, Acts, and Resolutions: 1789 to 1970—Con.

Period of session	Congress	Measures introduced			Measures passed						
						Public			Private		
		Total	Bills	Joint resolutions	Total	Total	Acts	Resolutions [1]	Total	Acts	Resolutions [1]
		189	190	191	192	193	194	195	196	197	198
Mar. 1869–Mar. 1871	41st	5,314	4,466	848	769	470	313	157	299	235	64
Apr. 1867–Mar. 1869	40th	3,723	3,003	720	765	354	226	128	411	380	31
Mar. 1865–Mar. 1867	39th	2,348	1,864	484	714	427	306	121	287	228	59
Mar. 1863–Mar. 1865	38th	1,708	1,402	306	515	411	318	93	104	79	25
Mar. 1861–Mar. 1863	37th	1,661	1,370	291	521	428	335	93	93	66	27
Mar. 1859–Mar. 1861	36th	1,746	1,595	151	370	157	131	26	213	192	21
Mar. 1857–Mar. 1859	35th	1,686	1,544	142	312	129	100	29	183	174	9
Dec. 1855–Mar. 1857	34th	1,608	1,515	93	433	157	127	30	276	265	11
Mar. 1853–Mar. 1855	33d	1,660	1,552	108	540	188	161	27	352	329	23
Mar. 1851–Mar. 1853	32d	1,167	1,011	156	306	137	113	24	169	156	13
Mar. 1849–Mar. 1851	31st	1,080	978	102	167	109	88	21	58	51	7
Dec. 1847–Mar. 1849	30th	1,433	1,305	128	446	176	142	34	270	254	16
Mar. 1845–Mar. 1847	29th	1,051	956	95	303	142	117	25	161	146	15
Dec. 1843–Mar. 1845	28th	1,085	979	106	279	142	115	27	137	131	6
Mar. 1841–Mar. 1843	27th	1,210	1,146	64	524	201	178	23	323	317	6
Dec. 1839–Mar. 1841	26th	1,122	1,081	41	147	55	50	5	92	90	2
Mar. 1837–Mar. 1839	25th	1,631	1,566	65	532	150	138	12	382	376	6
Dec. 1835–Mar. 1837	24th	1,107	1,055	52	459	144	130	14	315	314	1
Dec. 1833–Mar. 1835	23d	993	946	47	390	128	121	7	262	262	--------
Dec. 1831–Mar. 1833	22d	1,000	976	24	462	191	175	16	271	270	1
Mar. 1829–Mar. 1831	21st	856	842	14	369	152	143	9	217	217	--------
Dec. 1827–Mar. 1829	20th	632	612	20	235	134	126	8	101	100	1
Mar. 1825–Mar. 1827	19th	622	609	13	266	153	147	6	113	113	--------
Dec. 1823–Mar. 1825	18th	498	481	17	335	141	137	4	194	194	--------
Dec. 1821–Mar. 1823	17th	492	492	--------	238	136	130	6	102	102	--------
Dec. 1819–Mar. 1821	16th	480	480	--------	208	117	109	8	91	91	--------
Mar. 1817–Mar. 1819	15th	507	507	--------	257	156	136	20	101	101	--------
Dec. 1815–Mar. 1817	14th	465	465	--------	298	173	163	10	125	124	1
Mar. 1813–Mar. 1815	13th	400	400	--------	273	185	167	18	88	88	--------
Mar. 1811–Mar. 1813	12th	406	406	--------	209	170	163	7	39	39	--------
Mar. 1809–Mar. 1811	11th	348	348	--------	119	94	91	3	25	25	--------
Oct. 1807–Mar. 1809	10th	266	266	--------	105	88	87	1	17	17	--------
Mar. 1805–Mar. 1807	9th	219	219	--------	106	90	88	2	16	16	--------
Oct. 1803–Mar. 1805	8th	217	217	--------	111	93	90	3	18	18	--------
Mar. 1801–Mar. 1803	7th	161	161	--------	95	80	78	2	15	15	--------
Dec. 1799–Mar. 1801	6th	157	157	--------	112	100	94	6	12	12	--------
Mar. 1797–Mar. 1799	5th	234	234	--------	155	137	135	2	18	18	--------
June 1795–Mar. 1797	4th	132	132	--------	85	75	72	3	10	10	--------
Mar. 1793–Mar. 1795	3d	122	122	--------	127	103	94	9	24	24	--------
Mar. 1791–Mar. 1793	2d	105	105	--------	77	65	64	1	12	12	--------
Mar. 1789–Mar. 1791	1st	144	144	--------	118	108	94	14	10	8	2

[1] Public and private resolutions are carried only as public and private laws beginning with the 77th Congress.

Series Y 199–203.   Congressional Bills Vetoed: 1789 to 1970

Period	President	Vetoed bills			Vetoes sustained	Bills passed over veto	Period	President	Vetoed bills			Vetoes sustained	Bills passed over veto
		Total	Regular	Pocket					Total	Regular	Pocket		
		199	200	201	202	203			199	200	201	202	203
1969–1970	Nixon	11	7	4	9	2	1869–1877	Grant	93	45	48	89	4
1963–1969	L. Johnson	30	16	14	30	--------	1865–1869	A. Johnson	29	21	8	14	15
1961–1963	Kennedy	21	12	9	21	--------	1861–1865	Lincoln	6	2	4	6	--------
1953–1961	Eisenhower	181	73	108	179	2	1857–1861	Buchanan	7	4	3	7	--------
1945–1953	Truman	250	180	70	238	12	1853–1857	Pierce	9	9	--------	4	5
1933–1945	F. Roosevelt	635	372	263	626	9	1850–1853	Fillmore	--------	--------	--------	--------	--------
1929–1933	Hoover	37	21	16	34	3	1849–1850	Taylor	--------	--------	--------	--------	--------
1923–1929	Coolidge	50	20	30	46	4	1845–1849	Polk	3	2	1	3	--------
1921–1923	Harding	6	5	1	6	--------	1841–1845	Tyler	10	6	4	9	1
1913–1921	Wilson	44	33	11	38	6	1841	W. H. Harrison	--------	--------	--------	--------	--------
1909–1913	Taft	39	30	9	38	1	1837–1841	Van Buren	1	--------	1	1	--------
1901–1909	T. Roosevelt	82	42	40	81	1	1829–1837	Jackson	12	5	7	12	--------
1897–1901	McKinley	42	6	36	42	--------	1825–1829	John Q. Adams	--------	--------	--------	--------	--------
1893–1897	G. Cleveland	170	42	128	165	5	1817–1825	Monroe	1	1	--------	1	--------
1889–1893	B. Harrison	44	19	25	43	1	1809–1817	Madison	7	5	2	7	--------
1885–1889	G. Cleveland	414	304	110	412	2	1801–1809	Jefferson	--------	--------	--------	--------	--------
1881–1885	Arthur	12	4	8	11	1	1797–1801	John Adams	--------	--------	--------	--------	--------
1881	Garfield	--------	--------	--------	--------	--------	1789–1797	Washington	2	2	--------	2	--------
1877–1881	Hayes	13	12	1	12	1							

Series Y 204–210. Political Party Affiliations in Congress and the Presidency: 1789 to 1970

[Letter symbols for political parties: Ad—"Administration"; AM—Anti-Masonic; C—Coalition; D—Democratic; DR Democratic-Republican; F—Federalist; J.—Jacksonian; NR—National Republican; Op—"Opposition"; R—Republican; U—Unionist; W—Whig. Figures are for the beginning of the first session of each Congress]

Year	Congress	House			Senate			President
		Majority party	Principal minority party	Other (except vacancies)	Majority party	Principal minority party	Other (except vacancies)	
		204	205	206	207	208	209	210
1969–1970	91st	D–245	R–189	----------	D–57	R–43	----------	R (Nixon)
1967–1968	90th	D–246	R–187	----------	D–64	R–36	----------	D (L. Johnson)
1965–1966	89th	D–295	R–140	----------	D–68	R–32	----------	D (L. Johnson)
1963–1964	88th	D–258	R–177	----------	D–67	R–33	----------	D (L. Johnson)
1961–1962	87th	D–263	R–174		D–65	R–35	----------	D (Kennedy) D (Kennedy)
1959–1960[1]	86th	D–283	R–153		D–64	R–34		R (Eisenhower)
1957–1958	85th	D–233	R–200		D–49	R–47		R (Eisenhower)
1955–1956	84th	D–232	R–203	----------	D–48	R–47	1	R (Eisenhower)
1953–1954	83d	R–221	D–211	1	R–48	D–47	1	R (Eisenhower)
1951–1952	82d	D–234	R–199	1	D–49	R–47	----------	D (Truman)
1949–1950	81st	D–263	R–171	1	D–54	R–42		D (Truman)
1947–1948	80th	R–245	D–188	1	R–51	D–45		D (Truman)
1945–1946	79th	D–242	R–190	2	D–56	R–38	1	D (Truman)
1943–1944	78th	D–218	R–208	4	D–58	R–37	1	D (F. Roosevelt)
1941–1942	77th	D–268	R–162	5	D–66	R–28	2	D (F. Roosevelt)
1939–1940	76th	D–261	R–164	4	D–69	R–23	4	D (F. Roosevelt)
1937–1938	75th	D–331	R–89	13	D–76	R–16	4	D (F. Roosevelt)
1935–1936	74th	D–319	R–103	10	D–69	R–25	2	D (F. Roosevelt)
1933–1934	73d	D–310	R–117	5	D–60	R–35	1	D (F. Roosevelt)
1931–1933	72d	D–220	R–214	1	R–48	D–47	1	R (Hoover)
1929–1931	71st	R–267	D–167	1	R–56	D–39	1	R (Hoover)
1927–1929	70th	R–237	D–195	3	R–49	D–46	1	R (Coolidge)
1925–1927	69th	R–247	D–183	4	R–56	D–39	1	R (Coolidge)
1923–1925	68th	R–225	D–205	5	R–51	D–43	2	R (Coolidge)
1921–1923	67th	R–301	D–131	1	R–59	D–37	----------	R (Harding)
1919–1921	66th	R–240	D–190	3	R–49	D–47	----------	D (Wilson)
1917–1919	65th	D–216	R–210	6	D–53	R–42	----------	D (Wilson)
1915–1917	64th	D–230	R–196	9	D–56	R–40	----------	D (Wilson)
1913–1915	63d	D–291	R–127	17	D–51	R–44	1	D (Wilson)
1911–1913	62d	D–228	R–161	1	R–51	D–41	----------	R (Taft)
1909–1911	61st	R–219	D–172	----------	R–61	D–32	----------	R (Taft)
1907–1909	60th	R–222	D–164	----------	R–61	D–31	----------	R (T. Roosevelt)
1905–1907	59th	R–250	D–136	----------	R–57	D–33	----------	R (T. Roosevelt)
1903–1905	58th	R–208	D–178	----------	R–57	D–33	----------	R (T. Roosevelt)
1901–1903	57th	R–197	D–151	9	R–55	D–31	4	R (T. Roosevelt) R (McKinley)
1899–1901	56th	R–185	D–163	9	R–53	D–26	8	R (McKinley)
1897–1899	55th	R–204	D–113	40	R–47	D–34	7	R (McKinley)
1895–1897	54th	R–244	D–105	7	R–43	D–39	6	D (Cleveland)
1893–1895	53d	D–218	R–127	11	D–44	R–38	3	D (Cleveland)
1891–1893	52d	D–235	R–88	9	R–47	D–39	2	R (B. Harrison)
1889–1891	51st	R–166	D–159	----------	R–39	D–37	----------	R (B. Harrison)
1887–1889	50th	D–169	R–152	4	R–39	D–37	----------	D (Cleveland)
1885–1887	49th	D–183	R–140	2	R–43	D–34	----------	D (Cleveland)
1883–1885	48th	D–197	R–118	10	R–38	D–36	2	R (Arthur)
1881–1883	47th	R–147	D–135	11	R–37	D–37	1	R (Arthur) R (Garfield)
1879–1881	46th	D–149	R–130	14	D–42	R–33	----------	R (Hayes)
1877–1879	45th	D–153	R–140	----------	D–39	R–36	1	R (Hayes)
1875–1877	44th	D–169	R–109	14	R–45	D–29	2	R (Grant)
1873–1875	43d	R–194	D–92	14	R–49	D–19	5	R (Grant)
1871–1873	42d	R–134	D–104	5	R–52	D–17	5	R (Grant)
1869–1871	41st	R–149	D–63	----------	R–56	D–11	----------	R (Grant)
1867–1869	40th	R–143	D–49	----------	R–42	D–11	----------	R (A. Johnson)
1865–1867	39th	U–149	D–42	----------	U–42	D–10	----------	R (A. Johnson) R (Lincoln)
1863–1865	38th	R–102	D–75	9	R–36	D–9	5	R (Lincoln)
1861–1863	37th	R–105	D–43	30	R–31	D–10	8	R (Lincoln)
1859–1861	36th	R–114	D–92	31	D–36	R–26	4	D (Buchanan)
1857–1859	35th	R–118	D–92	26	D–36	R–20	8	D (Buchanan)
1855–1857	34th	R–108	D–83	43	D–40	R–15	5	D (Pierce)
1853–1855	33d	D–159	W–71	4	D–38	W–22	2	D (Pierce)
1851–1853	32d	D–140	W–88	5	D–35	W–24	3	W (Fillmore)
1849–1851	31st	D–112	W–109	9	D–35	W–25	2	W (Fillmore) W (Taylor)
1847–1849	30th	W–115	D–108	4	D–36	W–21	1	D (Polk)
1845–1847	29th	D–143	W–77	6	D–31	W–25	----------	D (Polk)
1843–1845	28th	D–142	W–79	1	W–28	D–25	----------	W (Tyler)
1841–1843	27th	W–133	D–102	6	W–28	D–22	2	W (Tyler) W (W. Harrison)
1839–1841	26th	D–124	W–118	----------	D–28	W–22	----------	D (Van Buren)
1837–1839	25th	D–108	W–107	24	D–30	W–18	4	D (Van Buren)
1835–1837	24th	D–145	W–98	----------	D–27	W–25	----------	D (Jackson)
1833–1835	23d	D–147	AM–53	60	D–20	NR–20	8	D (Jackson)
1831–1833	22d	D–141	NR–58	14	D–25	NR–21	2	D (Jackson)
1829–1831	21st	D–139	NR–74	----------	D–26	NR–22	----------	D (Jackson)
1827–1829	20th	J–119	Ad–94	----------	J–28	Ad–20	----------	C (John Q. Adams)
1825–1827	19th	Ad–105	J–97	----------	Ad–26	J–20	----------	C (John Q. Adams)
1823–1825	18th	DR–187	F–26	----------	DR–44	F–4	----------	DR (Monroe)
1821–1823	17th	DR–158	F–25	----------	DR–44	F–4	----------	DR (Monroe)

See footnote at end of table.

Series **Y 204–210.**　Political Party Affiliations in Congress and the Presidency: 1789 to 1970—Con.

[Letter symbols for political parties: Ad—"Administration"; AM—Anti-Masonic; C—Coalition; D—Democratic; DR—Democratic-Republican; F—Federalist; J—Jacksonian; NR—National Republican; Op—"Opposition"; R—Republican; U—Unionist; W—Whig]

		House		Senate		President
Year	Congress	Major party	Principal minority party	Major party	Principal minority party	
		204	**205**	**207**	**208**	**210**
1819–1821	16th	DR–156	F–27	DR–35	F–7	DR (Monroe)
1817–1819	15th	DR–141	F–42	DR–34	F–10	DR (Monroe)
1815–1817	14th	DR–117	F–65	DR–25	F–11	DR (Madison)
1813–1815	13th	DR–112	F–68	DR–27	F–9	DR (Madison)
1811–1813	12th	DR–108	F–36	DR–30	F–6	DR (Madison)
1809–1811	11th	DR–94	F–48	DR–28	F–6	DR (Madison)
1807–1809	10th	DR–118	F–24	DR–28	F–6	DR (Jefferson)
1805–1807	9th	DR–116	F–25	DR–27	F–7	DR (Jefferson)
1803–1805	8th	DR–102	F–39	DR–25	F–9	DR (Jefferson)
1801–1803	7th	DR–69	F–36	DR–18	F–13	DR (Jefferson)
1799–1801	6th	F–64	DR–42	F–19	DR–13	F (John Adams)
1797–1799	5th	F–58	DR–48	F–20	DR–12	F (John Adams)
1795–1797	4th	F–54	DR–52	F–19	DR–13	F (Washington)
1793–1795	3d	DR–57	F–48	F–17	DR–13	F (Washington)
1791–1793	2d	F–37	DR–33	F–16	DR–13	F (Washington)
1789–1791	1st	Ad–38	Op–26	Ad–17	Op–9	F (Washington)

[1] Excludes Hawaii; 2 Senators (1–R, 1–D) and 1 Representative (D) seated August 1959.

Series **Y 211–214.**　Vote Cast for Representatives, by Political Party: 1896 to 1970

[In thousands]

Year	Total	Republican	Democratic	Other	Year	Total	Republican	Democratic	Other
	211	**212**	**213**	**214**		**211**	**212**	**213**	**214**
1970	54,173	24,415	28,923	835	1932	37,657	15,575	20,540	1,542
1968	66,285	32,142	33,244	900	1930	24,777	13,032	11,044	701
1966	53,143	25,635	27,044	463	1928	33,906	19,163	14,361	382
1964	67,154	28,288	38,549	317	1926	20,435	11,643	8,284	508
1962	50,634	24,021	26,467	146	1924	26,884	14,932	10,854	1,098
1960	63,110	28,625	34,222	263	1922	20,409	10,548	9,131	730
1958	44,984	19,565	25,306	112	1920	25,214	14,773	9,038	1,403
1956	58,610	28,533	29,951	126	1918	12,579	6,600	5,421	558
1954	42,749	20,095	22,453	200	1916	16,140	7,810	7,468	862
1952	57,723	28,470	28,715	538	1914	13,275	5,650	5,727	1,898
1950	40,342	19,750	19,785	807	1912	13,517	4,602	6,128	2,787
1948	45,933	20,920	23,820	1,193	1910	11,669	5,427	5,536	706
1946	34,398	18,400	15,221	777	1908	14,021	6,975	6,466	580
1944	45,103	21,303	22,808	992	1906	10,552	5,350	4,659	543
1942	28,074	14,203	12,934	937	1904	12,697	6,837	5,298	562
1940	46,951	21,393	24,092	1,466	1902	10,654	5,250	4,980	424
1938	36,236	17,047	17,612	1,577	1900	13,626	6,973	6,086	567
1936	42,886	17,003	23,944	1,939	1898	11,513	5,258	5,373	882
1934	32,256	13,558	17,385	1,313	1896	14,652	6,845	6,339	1,468

Series **Y 215–219.**　Apportionment of Representatives Among the States: 1790 to 1970

Year	Congress	Population base [1] (1,000)	Apportionment act			Apportionment population per Representative	Year	Congress	Population base [1] (1,000)	Apportionment act			Apportionment population per Representative
			Number of States	Number of Representatives [2]	Date of act					Number of States	Number of Representatives [2]	Date of act	
		215	**216**	**217**	**218**	**219**			**215**	**216**	**217**	**218**	**219**
1970	93d	[3]204,053	50	435	Nov. 15, 1941	469,088	1870	43d–47th	38,116	37	292	Feb. 2, 1872 [5]	130,533
1960	88th–92d	178,559	50	435	Nov. 15, 1941	410,481	1860	38th–42d	29,550	34	241	May 23, 1850 [6]	122,614
1950	83d–87th	149,895	48	435	Nov. 15, 1941	334,587	1850	33d–37th	21,767	31	234	May 23, 1850 [7]	93,020
1940	78th–82d	131,006	48	435	Nov. 15, 1941	301,164	1840	28th–32d	15,908	26	223	June 25, 1842	71,338
1930	73d–77th	122,093	48	435	June 18, 1929	280,675	1830	23d–27th	11,931	24	240	May 22, 1832	49,712
1920	(4)	(4)	(4)	435	(4)	(4)	1820	18th–22d	8,972	24	213	Mar. 7, 1822	42,124
1910	63d–72d	91,604	48	435	Aug. 8, 1911	210,583	1810	13th–17th	6,584	17	181	Dec. 21, 1811	36,377
1900	58th–62d	74,563	45	386	Jan. 16, 1901	193,167	1800	8th–12th	4,880	16	141	Jan. 14, 1802	34,609
1890	53d–57th	61,909	44	356	Feb. 7, 1891	173,901	1790	{ 3d–7th	3,616	15	105	Apr. 14, 1792	34,436
1880	48th–52d	49,371	38	325	Feb. 25, 1882	151,912		{ 1st–2d	————	13	65	Constitution 1789	[8]30,000

[1] Excludes the population of the District of Columbia, the population of outlying areas, the number of Indians not taxed, and (prior to 1870) two-fifths of the slave population.　[2] Actual number apportioned at the beginning of the decade.
[3] Includes 1,575,000 persons in population abroad; see text.
[4] No apportionment was made after the census of 1920.

[5] Amended by the act of May 30, 1872.
[6] Amended by the act of March 4, 1862
[7] Amended by the act of July 30, 1852.
[8] The minimum ratio of population to Representatives stated in the Constitution (art. I, sec. 2).

Series Y 220-271. Apportionment of Membership in House of Representatives, by States, From Adoption of Constitution to 1970

[Population figures used for apportionment purposes are those determined for States by each decennial census.　No reapportionment based on 1920 population census]

Series No.	Item	1970	1960	1950	1940	1930	1910	1900	1890	1880	1870	1860	1850	1840	1830	1820	1810	1800	1790	Constitution
220	Apportionment ratio 1,000	469	410	345	301	281	211	194	174	152	131	127	93	71	48	40	35	33	33	[1] 30
221	**STATE** Total number of Representatives	435	435	[2] 437	435	435	435	391	357	332	[3] 293	[4] 243	[5] 237	232	242	213	186	142	106	65
222	Alabama	7	8	9	9	9	10	9	9	8	8	6	7	7	5	3	[6] 1			
223	Alaska	1	1	[6] 1																
224	Arizona	4	3	2	2	1	[7] 1													
225	Arkansas	4	4	6	7	7	7	7	6	5	4	3	2	1	[6] 1					
226	California	43	38	30	23	20	11	8	7	6	4	3	2	[6] 2						
227	Colorado	5	4	4	4	4	4	3	2	1	[6] 1									
228	Connecticut	6	6	6	6	6	5	5	4	4	4	4	4	4	6	6	7	7	7	5
229	Delaware	1	1	1	1	1	1	1	1	1	1	1	1	1	[6] 1	1	2	1	1	1
230	Florida	15	12	8	6	5	4	3	2	2	2	2	1	[6] 1						
231	Georgia	10	10	10	10	10	12	11	11	10	9	7	8	8	9	7	6	4	2	3
232	Hawaii	2	2	[6] 1																
233	Idaho	2	2	2	2	2	2	1	1	[6] 1										
234	Illinois	24	24	25	26	27	27	25	22	20	19	14	9	7	3	1	[6] 1			
235	Indiana	11	11	11	11	12	13	13	13	13	13	11	11	10	7	3	[6] 1			
236	Iowa	6	7	8	8	9	11	11	11	11	9	6	2	[6] 2						
237	Kansas	5	5	6	6	7	8	8	8	7	3	1								
238	Kentucky	7	7	8	9	9	11	11	11	11	10	9	10	10	13	12	10	6	2	
239	Louisiana	8	8	8	8	8	8	7	6	6	6	5	4	4	3	3	[6] 1			
240	Maine	2	2	3	3	3	4	4	4	4	5	5	6	7	8	7	[8] 7			
241	Maryland	8	8	7	6	6	6	6	6	6	6	5	6	6	8	9	9	9	8	6
242	Massachusetts	12	12	14	14	15	16	14	13	12	11	10	11	10	12	13	13	17	14	8
243	Michigan	19	19	18	17	17	13	12	12	11	9	6	4	3	[6] 1					
244	Minnesota	8	8	9	9	9	10	9	7	5	3	2	[6] 2							
245	Mississippi	5	5	6	7	7	8	8	7	7	6	5	5	4	2	1	[6] 1			
246	Missouri	10	10	11	13	13	16	16	15	14	13	9	7	5	2	1				
247	Montana	2	2	2	2	2	2	1	1	[6] 1										
248	Nebraska	3	3	4	4	5	6	6	6	3	1	[6] 1								
249	Nevada	1	1	1	1	1	1	1	1	1	1	[6] 1								
250	New Hampshire	2	2	2	2	2	2	2	2	2	3	3	3	4	5	6	6	5	4	3
251	New Jersey	15	15	14	14	14	12	10	8	7	7	5	5	5	6	6	6	6	5	4
252	New Mexico	2	2	2	2	1	[6] 1													
253	New York	39	41	43	45	45	43	37	34	34	33	31	33	34	40	34	27	17	10	6
254	North Carolina	11	11	12	12	11	10	10	9	9	8	7	8	9	13	13	13	12	10	5
255	North Dakota	1	2	2	2	2	3	2	1	[6] 1										
256	Ohio	23	24	23	23	24	22	21	21	21	20	19	21	21	19	14	6	[6] 1		
257	Oklahoma	6	6	6	8	9	8	[6] 5												
258	Oregon	4	4	4	4	3	3	2	2	1	1	1	[6] 1							
259	Pennsylvania	25	27	30	33	34	36	32	30	28	27	24	25	24	28	26	23	18	13	8
260	Rhode Island	2	2	2	2	2	3	2	2	2	2	2	2	2	2	2	2	2	2	1
261	South Carolina	6	6	6	6	6	7	7	7	7	5	4	6	7	9	9	9	8	6	5
262	South Dakota	2	2	2	2	2	3	2	2	[6] 2										
263	Tennessee	8	9	9	10	9	10	10	10	10	10	8	10	11	13	9	6	[6] 1		
264	Texas	24	23	22	21	21	18	16	13	11	6	4	2	[6] 2						
265	Utah	2	2	2	2	2	2	1	[6] 1											
266	Vermont	1	1	1	1	1	2	2	2	2	3	3	3	4	5	5	6	4	2	
267	Virginia	10	10	10	9	9	10	10	10	10	9	11	13	15	21	22	23	22	19	10
268	Washington	7	7	7	6	6	5	3	2	[6] 1										
269	West Virginia	4	5	6	6	6	6	5	4	4	3									
270	Wisconsin	9	10	10	10	10	11	11	10	9	8	6	3	[6] 2						
271	Wyoming	1	1	1	1	1	1	1	1	[6] 1										

[1] The minimum ratio of population to Representatives stated in the Constitution (art. 1, sec. 2).

[2] Membership temporarily increased to 437 after legislation granting statehood to Alaska and Hawaii in 1959.　See footnote 6.

[3] Membership originally fixed at 283 but increased to 292 by act of May 30, 1872 (17 Stat. L. 192).　See footnote 6.

[4] Membership increased from 233 to 241 by act of Mar. 4, 1862 (12 Stat. L. 353). See footnote 6.

[5] Membership increased from 233 to 234 by act of July 30, 1852 (10 Stat. L. 25). See footnote 6.

[6] Assigned after apportionment.

[7] Included in apportionment act in anticipation of statehood.

[8] Included in the 20 members originally assigned to Massachusetts but credited to Maine after its admission as a State, Mar. 15, 1820 (3 Stat. L. 555).

Government Employment and Finances (Series Y 272-848)

Y 272–848. General note.

Governmental services in the United States are provided through a complex organizational structure made up of numerous public bodies and agencies. In addition to the widely recognized pattern of Federal, State, county, municipal, and township governments, there exist many offshoots in the form of single-function and multiple-function districts, authorities, commissions, boards, and other entities that have varying degrees of autonomy. The basic pattern differs widely from State to State. Within a particular State, the various classes of local units may also differ in their characteristics.

Identification and enumeration of governmental units is, of course, a prerequisite to comprehensive reports on their activities. Thus, the U.S. Bureau of the Census report, *Census of Governments, 1967*, vol. I, *Governmental Organization*, provides information on numbers of governmental units by type, size, and location.

The summary historical table from the 1967 Census of Governments, reproduced below, presents the numbers of different types of governmental units for 1942, 1952, 1957, 1962, and 1967.

Table I. Governmental Units, by Type: 1942 to 1967

Type of government	Number of units				
	1967	1962	1957	1952	1942
Total_____	81,299	91,237	102,328	116,743	155,116
U.S. Government_____	1	1	1	1	1
States_____	50	50	48	48	48
Counties_____	3,049	3,043	3,047	3,049	3,050
Municipalities_____	18,048	18,000	17,183	16,778	16,220
Townships and towns____	17,105	17,142	17,198	17,202	18,919
School districts_____	21,782	34,678	50,446	67,346	108,579
Special districts_____	21,264	18,323	14,405	12,319	8,299

Comparable data for the number of governments are not available for earlier years, principally because definition of the concept of "a governmental unit" and enumeration of the units in existence are beset with many difficulties. Professor William Anderson of the University of Minnesota has done extensive work in this field, and the enumerations by the Bureau of the Census in 1942 and later reflect his contributions.

Anderson's monograph, *The Units of Government in the United States: An Enumeration and Analysis*, first published in 1934 and revised in 1936, was extensively revised in 1942 and finally republished in 1945 with an appendix comparing the author's enumeration of governments with that of the 1942 Census of Governments. (Public Administration Service, Chicago, 1945.) Anderson reported 175,418 governments in the United States in 1930–33 and 165,049 in 1941. The 1942 Census of Governments adopted a more selective definition, eliminating 9,729 school districts and 204 other units from enumeration as separate entities. Anderson reported that he had "good reason to believe that the Bureau's figures represent a more accurate enumeration." (Source cited above, p. 48.)

The comparative totals reported by Anderson, on the basis of his definitions and procedures, are summarized in table II.

A governmental unit as defined in the 1967 Census of Governments (*Governmental Organization*, cited above, p. 13) is as follows:

A government is an organized entity which, in addition to having governmental character, has sufficient discretion in the management of its own affairs to distinguish it as separate from the administrative structure of any other governmental unit. To be counted as a government, any entity must possess all three of the attributes reflected in the foregoing definition: Existence as an organized entity, governmental character, and substantial autonomy.

Characteristics taken as evidence of the "essential attributes" of a separately existing governmental unit include organization, active operation, and the possession of specific corporate powers; the popular election or appointment of officers; the power to levy taxes or to issue debt that bears interest exempt from Federal taxation; responsibility for performing a function commonly regarded as governmental; public accountability; and considerable administrative and fiscal independence.

Despite the variety and apparent simplicity of these criteria, the proper classification of some local governmental entities remains doubtful and, in such cases, account has been taken of (*a*) local attitudes as to whether the type of unit involved is independent, and (*b*) the effect of the classification upon the collection and presentation of statistics of governmental finances and employment.

Table II. Governmental Units, by Type: 1930–33 and 1941

Type of government	1941	1930–33	Change in number
Total_____	165,049	175,418	−10,369
U.S. Government_____	1	1	–
States_____	48	48	–
Counties_____	3,050	3,053	−3
Incorporated places (cities, villages, etc., and D.C.)_____	16,262	16,366	−104
Towns (as in New England) and organized townships (in a total of 23 States)_____	18,998	20,262	−1,264
School districts_____	118,308	127,108	−8,800
Other units_____	8,382	8,580	−198

– Represents zero.

Two broad categories of governmental units may be distinguished —special-purpose organizations, such as school, park, and sanitary districts; and general-purpose governments, each with a broad spectrum of powers and duties, ranging in size from small village and town governments to the large metropolitan city, State, and Federal governments.

These diverse units can be represented by at least two kinds of measures that are universally applicable: (*a*) the number of persons serving in each governmental unit and their compensation, and (*b*) the broad financial aspects of the operations, as represented by revenues, expenditures, and indebtedness. The collection and reporting of such data are complicated by the large numbers and frequent changes of the governmental units to be covered, by changes (often unrecorded) in their internal structures and external relationships, and by the great diversity that exists in organizational forms, employment relationships, financial procedures, the adequacy and availability of records, and the categories and terminologies used in those records and in public reporting. For the most part, data for the Federal Government are derived from regular personnel and fiscal reports, published annually or oftener. Those for the States and large cities are compiled from annual public reports or other official records of each unit and its component organizational subdivisions; and those of other local governments are derived from surveys based on similar reports and records of carefully selected samples of each type of government.

Complete censuses of governments, covering governmental structure, personnel, expenditures, revenues, debt, and other selected aspects of all governments in the United States, were conducted for 1932, 1942, 1957, 1962, and 1967. Earlier periodic censuses (for decennial years for 1850–1890 and for 1902, 1912, and 1922) were narrower in scope, particularly with reference to expenditures and personnel.

The various censuses of governments and also the annual reports on personnel and finances, differ not only in completeness, but also in some of the basic concepts and classifications. Consequently, the preparation of historically comparable data covering all governmental units is extremely difficult. As is evident in the historical series for the Federal Government, events and changing concepts greatly affect the comparability, over long periods, of data for a single government. The problem of continuity in concepts and classifications is greatly multiplied in summaries for all governmental entities.

For such reasons, the consolidated historical series now available are for selected years beginning with 1902. The data available for earlier years are either inadequate for classifications now used or require more extensive reworking than could be achieved with available resources.

State and local government data in this chapter include Alaska and Hawaii for years after admission as States; they omit outlying areas of the United States. The District of Columbia is classified as a local government.

For references to publications containing the original data and statistics for individual State and local governments, see text for series Y 652–848.

For still another approach to the role of Government operations in the economy, see series F 66–70, reporting Government purchases of goods and services, in which the Federal Government totals for 1938–1970 are subdivided between national defense and other purposes. For national income originating in "Government" as an industry, see series F 141; and for estimates of "Government product" in the national income accounts, see series F 129.

Y 272–334. General note.

Statistics on government employment and payrolls in the United States appear in *The Trend of Government Activity in the United States Since 1900*, by Solomon Fabricant, assisted by Robert E. Lipsey, National Bureau of Economic Research, New York, 1952, pp. 161–203. Fabricant and Lipsey relate their figures to the government employment data for 1929–1949 and earlier periods published by the Office of Business Economics and predecessor agencies. The latter figures differ from the former chiefly in omitting, for national income accounts, all Federal Government employees abroad. Also differentiated are earlier estimates prepared for the National Bureau of Economic Research by Simon Kuznets in *National Income and Its Composition, 1919–1938*, New York, 1941, vol. II, pp. 811–826. This study did not have data from the Work Projects Administration-Bureau of Labor Statistics compilations noted below. For reference to other studies for earlier years, see text for series Y 332–334.

The WPA-BLS figures, mentioned above, cover 1929–1939. They were obtained as part of a larger survey of State and local governments conducted in 1938–1943 by the Bureau of Labor Statistics and financed and staffed by the Work Projects Administration. Annual estimates of employment and payrolls of State and local governments and the underlying detailed estimates of States, by classes of governments and major fields of employment, were published by the Bureau of Labor Statistics in *Employment and Pay Rolls of State and Local Governments*, January 1946.

Sample surveys by the Bureau of the Census began in 1940 on a quarterly basis, giving reports of January, April, July, and October data. School data prior to 1946 were from the Office of Education and reported only for State and local aggregates, so that pre-1946 detail by level and type of government relates only to the non-school data.

State-by-State estimates were issued by the Bureau of the Census at least once a year from the early 1940's, except for 1951. Summary data were provided on the school (education) component, but other functional detail was supplied only for State and municipal governments until 1952. Development of separate payroll figures on full-time employees was begun in 1951, and derivation of employment figures on a full-time equivalent basis was initiated in 1952. Beginning with 1953, national and State-by-State data have been reported by function, on the full-time equivalent number of employees of State and local governments for the month of October (except 1957 data, which were for April).

Beginning with 1955, the Bureau of Labor Statistics assumed responsibility for providing monthly statistics on government employment and payrolls.

Both series Y 272–289 and Y 332–334 cover all types of special-purpose districts as well as general-purpose local governments and all branches of the State governments; and both include the employees of government utilities as well as of general government services and agencies. Education employment includes noninstructional staff and the educational employees of State as well as local governments. Both tabulations omit military personnel and persons on work relief.

Federal Government employment and payrolls for 1952–70, series Y 273 and Y 291, respectively, are derived from Civil Service Commission data. Prior to 1952, these figures (Y 273 and 291) are basically the Bureau of Labor Statistics figures and, therefore, differ in coverage and date from the Civil Service Commission's historical tabulations for the Federal Government alone (series Y 308–317).

Differences from labor force data.—Data collected from the governmental employers, such as the Bureau of the Census and Bureau of Labor Statistics compilations on public employment referred to above, necessarily differ from government employment statistics derived from broad surveys of the labor force (see, for example, series Y 332–334).

Data on the labor force, and therefore on government workers, are collected by the Bureau of the Census in monthly surveys and published in its *Current Population Reports*. These surveys involve direct personal interviews with selected samples of households throughout the Nation. Governments are listed as an industry group, and members of the labor force who report that they are government workers are so classified.

Y 272–307. Public employees and government monthly payrolls, by type of government, 1940–1970.

Source: 1940–1967, U.S. Bureau of the Census, *U.S. Census of Governments: 1967*, vol. 6, No. 5, *Historical Statistics on Governmental Finance and Employment*; 1968–1970, *Public Employment*, annual issues.

Data on Federal employment and payrolls were obtained from the Bureau of Labor Statistics (BLS) prior to 1952 and the Civil Service Commission since that time. BLS figures were based on Civil Service data. Substantially all basic data for State and local governments were collected by mail surveys of the Bureau of the Census. However, prior to 1946, data on school employment were derived from the U.S. Office of Education publication, *Biennial Survey of Education in the United States*.

The reports on public employment outline the development of the Bureau of the Census reporting of statistics on public employees and payrolls, record data for the years back to 1940, and provide information on the concepts and definitions used. Additional data on Federal, State, and local governments are contained in the *U.S. Census of Governments: 1957*, vol. 2, *Governmental Employment*; the *U.S. Census of Governments: 1962*, vol. 3, *Compendium on Public Employment*; and the *U.S. Census of Governments: 1967*, vol. 3, *Public Employment*.

Public employees, as defined for the purpose of the Bureau of the Census survey of government employment, include all paid officials and civilian employees of Federal, State, and local governmental units. Employees of contractors, persons working on a contract basis, and persons on work relief are not considered public employees. The term, however, does include fee officials, paid volunteer firemen, student help, and other persons employed on a part-time basis even though they may receive only nominal compensation for their services. Military personnel and their pay are omitted.

Figures for full-time equivalent employees, series Y 273–289, represent the number of persons that could have been employed, for the payroll amounts reported, if all personnel were engaged on a full-time basis at the average monthly rates applying to full-time workers for the particular functions and levels of government involved. Full-time employees are those persons employed during the pay period for the number of hours per week prescribed for full-time work in the jurisdiction concerned. The term includes temporary and emergency employees working on a full-time basis during the pay period.

Payrolls, series Y 290–307, include salaries, wages, fees, and other compensation earned in the calendar month by officials and other employees. Amounts reported are gross pay before deductions for withholding taxes, retirement contributions, social security, and other purposes. Full-time payrolls, series Y 292–307, are amounts paid to full-time employees as defined above.

Figures for State governments include, in addition to data for the regular departments and agencies, data for boards, commissions, authorities, institutions of higher education, and other semiautonomous agencies of State government. State employees include all persons paid by the State government.

Figures for municipalities (series Y 283–284 and Y 301–302) are for city, borough, village, and—except in New England, New York, and Wisconsin—town governments. They include boards, commissions, and semiautonomous districts and authorities controlled by such governments, as well as the regular municipal departments and agencies. In a number of States, some or all of the public schools serving city areas are operated by city governments, and city figures include their employees.

Figures for counties (series Y 285–286 and Y 303–304) include data for semiautonomous county agencies and for public schools or school facilities operated by county governments in a few of the States.

Data on school districts are restricted to independent districts operating public schools. They do not include data for school systems operated by State, city, county, or township governments. Between 76 and 81 percent of all local government education employees in October of each year, 1946–1970, were employees of independent school districts.

In addition to townships of the Midwestern States, which have limited governmental functions and play a minor role, township data include figures for New England, New York, and Wisconsin towns, and Pennsylvania and New Jersey townships, where town and township governments are important in the local government structure. The New England town figures include school information for four States (all except New Hampshire and Vermont) in which town governments administer public schools. Data on special districts are for special-purpose units of local government set up to perform a specific service or services in a local area, but which are administratively and fiscally independent of the broader types of local government having jurisdiction in the area. These units range in size from drainage districts and other agricultural-resources districts having only intermittent activity or employment up to such entities as the Chicago Transit Authority, the Port of New York Authority, and other large-scale governmental employers.

Y 308–317. Paid civilian employment of the Federal Government, 1816–1970.

Source: U.S. Civil Service Commission, unpublished data.

The data for 1816–1891 were compiled by the Civil Service Commission from *Official Register of the United States;* for 1901–1911, from the *Annual Report* of the Civil Service Commission and *Official Register;* for 1908–1970, from the Civil Service Commission, *Annual Report* and *Federal Civilian Manpower Statistics,* formerly titled *Monthly Report of Federal Employment,* and supplemented throughout by Civil Service Commission records.

Prior to 1938, the data are for employees on the rolls, with or without pay; for 1938–1942, the number on the payroll with pay; and for 1943–1970, the number in active duty status.

Employees and officials of the legislative, judicial, and executive branches are included. Employees of the District of Columbia are not included; they are considered employees of a local government.

The figures exclude military personnel but include civilian employees of the military departments. However, mechanics and other workmen at army arsenals and navy yards are not included prior to 1881.

The data for the Post Office, series Y 314, exclude contractors but include substitutes, partly estimated.

Series Y 311 represents personnel employed under the act of January 16, 1883, establishing the Civil Service Commission and the competitive (classified) service. This service includes all civilian positions in the executive branch of the Federal Government that are not specifically exempted by or pursuant to statute, or by the Civil Service Commission. It also includes all positions in the legislative and judicial branches which are specifically made subject to the civil service laws by statute. Figures represent positions, including vacancies, prior to 1947; since 1948, they represent employees serving under competitive appointment, primarily in the executive branch.

Y 318–331. Paid civilian employment in full-time positions in the Federal Government, 1948–1970.

Source: U.S. Civil Service Commission, *Pay Structure of the Federal Civil Service,* table 2, annual issues.

Over the years, the data in this table reflect increased coverage of paid Federal civilian employees. The data for 1948–1951 include only those employees in the conterminous United States; all later data are worldwide figures. Prior to 1954, only executive branch employees are shown; later data include all legislative branch employees except employees of Congress. Employees of the District of Columbia are not included as they are considered employees of a local government. The figures exclude military personnel but include civilian employees of the military departments.

Changes have also taken place over the years in the various employee pay systems. Data on the crafts, protective, and custodial schedule are shown for 1948–1951; some data on a different basis are also available in the annual issues cited above for 1952–1955. After 1955, this schedule was discontinued. The data for the Postal Pay Act do not include postal substitutes as full-time employees until 1953. Postal seasonal Christmas assistants are not included. The data for "other" employees include foreign nationals employed overseas after 1951.

Y 332–334. State and local government employment, 1929–1970.

Source: U.S. Bureau of Labor Statistics, *Employment and Earnings, United States, 1909–71,* BLS Bulletin 1312–8, p. 576.

Data for 1929–1939 are derived from a WPA-BLS survey (see general note for series Y 272–334). Figures for 1940–1954 are from Bureau of the Census reports on public employment and for 1955–1970, from Bureau of Labor Statistics compilations.

These series include regular full-time teachers for the summer vacation period, whether or not they were specifically paid in those months; elected officials of small local units and paid volunteer firemen are omitted as nominal employees.

Series Y 332–334 differ from series Y 274–276 because the former measure average monthly employment, whereas the latter are for October 31 of each year (except for 1957).

For a discussion of studies conducted by Federal agencies, see general note for series Y 272–334. Estimates of employment and payrolls for the years 1909–1927 appear in Wilford I. King, *The National Income and Its Purchasing Power,* National Bureau of

Economic Research, 1930, pp. 360–365; and for 1926, a study by William E. Mosher and Sophie Polah based on approximately 500 reports from State and local governments, published in "Public Employment in the United States," supplement to *National Municipal Review*, vol. XXI, No. 1, January 1932.

Relying heavily on the Mosher-Polah article and public employment data issued by the Bureau of Foreign and Domestic Commerce in connection with certain of its national income studies, Simon Kuznets, in *National Income and Its Composition, 1919–1938*, National Bureau of Economic Research, 1941, vol. II, pp. 811–826, published revised estimates of government employees and payrolls for 1919–1938.

Y 335–338. Summary of Federal Government finances—administrative budget, 1789–1939.

Source: U.S. Department of the Treasury, *Statistical Appendix to Annual Report of the Secretary of the Treasury, 1970*, pp. 8–13 and 60–61.

Receipts and expenditures for 1789–1915 are based on warrants issued; for 1916–1939, on daily Treasury statements. Total gross public debt is on the basis of public debt accounts for 1791–1915, and on the basis of daily Treasury statements for 1916 to date. For description of the *Daily* and *Monthly Statements of the Treasury*, explanation of "warrants issued," "public debt accounts," and other pertinent items, see the source, pp. 1 and 2.

The receipts and expenditures data exclude amounts received in trust and expended from trust accounts. They also exclude amounts borrowed through the sale of Government securities and amounts paid to retire public debt. Receipts include the proceeds of sales of some types of Government-owned assets, including land. For recent years, however, proceeds from the disposition of some categories of Government property (including sales of commodities and securities purchased and repayments received on account of loans made by the Government) are reported as deductions from expenditures, rather than as receipts. Postal receipts and expenditures are included net for each year throughout the series; that is, a postal surplus is included in receipts and a postal deficit in expenditures.

Subject to the foregoing qualifications, figures for Federal Government receipts (series Y 335) represent "total receipts" through 1912 and "net receipts" thereafter. In determining net receipts, the following items are deducted from total receipts:

Refunds of receipts, principally for the overpayment of taxes, 1913–1939, are deducted from total receipts. (For earlier years, such refunds are included in expenditures.)

Certain interfund transactions are excluded from receipts and expenditures starting in 1932; for prior years, the amounts of such transactions are insignificant. Refunds of receipts are excluded from receipts and expenditures starting in 1913; comparable data are not available for prior years.

Transfers of tax receipts to the Federal old-age and survivors insurance trust fund from 1937; to the railroad retirement account from 1938.

Capital transfers, consisting of payments to the Treasury principally by wholly owned Government corporations for retirement of capital stock and for disposition of earnings. (Although the exclusion applies to all fiscal years for 1931–1939, the only transfer of this kind identified for that period was an item of $250 thousand in 1937.)

Figures for expenditures for 1931–1939 likewise are net of refunds paid and of capital transfers, but include any such payments in earlier years.

The surplus or deficit (series Y 337) is the difference between receipts and expenditures in any fiscal year. The change in public debt during any year is usually determined in large part by the surplus or deficit; it is, however, affected also by the increase or decrease in the Treasury cash balance and by various other financial operations. Consequently, there is only an approximate relationship between

series Y 337 and the year-to-year differences in the debt reported in series Y 338.

For comments on the total gross public debt (series Y 338) and other aspects of the public debt, see text for series Y 493–504.

In a statement on "Some Historical Aspects of Federal Fiscal Policy, 1790–1956" (in *Federal Expenditure Policy for Economic Growth and Stability*, papers submitted by panelists appearing before the Subcommittee on Fiscal Policy, Joint Economic Committee, 85th Congress, 1st sess., Nov. 5, 1957, Joint Committee Print, pp. 60–83), the official historical series on Federal receipts and expenditures—such as series Y 335 and Y 336—were characterized by Professor Paul B. Trescott as subject to "certain deficiencies for the economist" stemming in part from "capricious patterns of inclusion and exclusion." Important before 1870, according to Trescott, was lack of conformity between the accounts of the Treasury, which the official data summarize, and the accounts of the collecting and disbursing officers who actually dealt with the public. He reported that the payment of $28 million of surplus revenue to the States in 1837 was omitted from Treasury accounts; that more than $100 million reported in Treasury figures of expenditures in the Civil War years was accumulated in disbursing officers' balances; and that various other adjustments were desirable. In compiling alternative totals of receipts and expenditures on the basis of various official records additional to Treasury accounts, Trescott has adopted special concepts, so that the resulting totals are designed primarily to measure money-flows. To some extent, his work incorporates a revised expenditure series compiled by M. Slade Kendrick in *A Century and a Half of Federal Expenditures*, National Bureau of Economic Research, New York, Occasional Paper 48, revised, 1955. Kendrick's data are as nearly as possible on a cash-payment basis for 1917–1952 (see Appendix B, especially p. 67).

The adoption of the unified budget concept reflected in series Y 339–342 was in part designed to eliminate these problems of comparability, but the data have not been worked back prior to 1954. From 1940 to 1953 the consolidated cash data shown in series Y 339–342 are closer to the concept currently in use than the administrative budget, while the only official data available for years prior to 1940 are the administrative budget figures.

The differences between the administrative budget and consolidated cash statement were slight prior to the mid-1930's when the Social Security trust funds began. From 1934 to 1939, cash receipts totaled $30.3 billion and administrative budget receipts totaled $26.2 billion; cash payments totaled $45.4 billion while administrative budget expenditures were $44.9 billion; the cash deficit totaled $15.0 billion and the administrative budget deficit totaled $18.7 billion.

Y 339–342. Summary of Federal Government finances, 1929–1970.

Source: U.S. Office of Management and Budget. For all series, 1929–1939, unpublished data. Series Y 339–341, 1940–1970, *The Budget of the United States Government, 1973*, p. 553. Series Y 342, 1940–1962, *Federal Government Finances* (unbound mimeographed tables); 1963–1970, *The Budget of the United States Government, 1973*, p. 543.

The unified Federal budget concept was first introduced in 1968 to incorporate reforms recommended by the President's Commission on Budget Concepts, whose report was published in 1967. Among the principal recommendations of the Commission incorporated into the new unified budget concept are the following:

(1). The Federal budget should include all federally controlled funds—whether labeled "Federal funds" or "trust funds"—so that it provides a picture of the total impact of the government on the economy.

(2). Any privately-owned activities—even if federally chartered —are not to be included in the Federal budget.

(3). Federal receipts shall consist of all income which arises out of the Government's sovereign capacity to govern (that is, taxes and compulsory payments plus unfettered gifts to the Government). All income derived from business-type activities (such as the sale of public lands) are recorded as negative outlays.

The objective was to provide a consistent, comprehensive overview of total Federal finances regardless of the legal technicalities over who "owns" the money the Federal Government controls.

In order to provide comparable data over a period of years, the Bureau of the Budget (now Office of Management and Budget) and the Department of the Treasury jointly produced a set of data back to 1954. It was felt that the differences from the consolidated cash statement were too minor to warrant the additional work required to produce completely comparable data for earlier years. For most purposes there is no serious discontinuity in using the consolidated cash data for the 1940–1953 period and unified budget data for subsequent years. For example, over the period from fiscal year 1954 to 1958 the consolidated cash receipts averaged only 3 percent higher ($1.9 billion annually) than the unified budget receipts; cash payments averaged $2\frac{1}{2}$ percent higher ($1.6 billion annually) than unified budget outlays; and the cash statement averaged a $.03 billion surplus while the unified budget averaged a $.3 billion deficit.

The consolidated cash statement was the broadest budgetary measure of Federal finances prior to the adoption of the unified budget. It differs from the unified budget primarily for the following reasons:

(1). The cash statement has a much more inconsistent treatment of income from business types of transactions. It treats large amounts of such income as offsets to outlays (called payments in the cash series) whereas other large amounts of such income are included in receipts.

(2). The cash statement includes transactions of wholly privately-owned enterprises (such as the Federal Home Loan Banks).

(3). The cash statement records interest when the cash is paid; the unified budget records interest when it is earned (accrued).

Consolidated cash data for current periods are no longer being produced since the existence of alternative budget concepts creates inordinate confusion.

At the same time that the budget concepts were reformed the debt concepts were also reformed; for many years there were two principal debt concepts: Public debt and debt subject to the debt limit. The public debt is that debt which originates from the Treasury Department. For most of our history this was the total debt, but in the past few decades the Congress has authorized other agencies (such as the Tennessee Valley Authority and the Federal Housing Administration) to borrow money without going through the Treasury Department. As a result, the public debt series does not include several billion dollars worth of Federal debt. The debt subject to limit includes almost all public debt but only part of the agency debt. Hence, a new comprehensive debt series was developed which includes both public and agency debt. This debt series is called "Gross Federal debt" (series Y 342 and Y 488) and data on a comparable basis have been compiled back to 1939. The differences between the gross Federal debt and the public debt (series Y 338 and Y 493) are quite large in the 1939–1944 period because of the large volume of agency borrowing which occurred in the 1930's, particularly in 1934.

Y 343–351. Federal Government receipts, by source, 1940–1970.

Source: U.S. Office of Management and Budget, *Federal Government Finances* (unbound mimeographed tables), October 31, 1972.

For 1940–1953, data are consolidated cash totals; for 1954–1970, data are based on the unified budget concept. The cash data are comparable to the unified budget data except for the "other miscellaneous receipts and "total" columns, where the cash receipts include certain transactions that are offset against outlays in the unified budget. In general, these differences have no effect on the surplus or deficit. For further details, see text for Y 339–342.

Y 352–357. Federal Government receipts—administrative budget, 1789–1939.

Source: U.S. Department of the Treasury, *Statistical Appendix to the Annual Report of the Secretary of the Treasury, 1971*, pp. 8–12, except series Y 356, *Annual Report of the Secretary of the Treasury, 1946*, pp. 422–423.

See text for series Y 335–338, for a discussion of receipts according to the administrative budget concept.

Y 358–373. Internal revenue collections, 1863–1970.

Source: U.S. Department of the Treasury, *Annual Report of the Secretary of the Treasury, 1929*, pp. 419–424; *1946*, pp. 406–409; and *Statistical Appendix to Annual Report of the Treasury, 1970*, pp. 46–51.

The three *Annual Reports* overlap as to years covered. To the extent that they differ in the grouping of items in any given year, the tabulation shown here generally follows the latest compilation; however, some exceptions are indicated below.

In *Historical Statistics of the United States, 1789–1945*, series P 109–119, the corresponding figures exclude trust fund receipts for 1935–1945. The data shown here for series Y 358–373 follow later Treasury practice by including, among internal revenue collections, all taxes collected by the Internal Revenue Service, whether assigned to general revenue or to trust funds.

These data, from Internal Revenue Service reports of collections, differ from figures shown in other series. The variations reflect differences in the time or stage of operations when the receipts are recorded. Taxes are included in budget receipts when reported in the account of the Treasurer of the United States. Internal Revenue Service reports of collections through 1954 include taxes for which returns (and payments) were received in internal revenue offices. Under arrangements begun in 1950 for withheld individual income tax and old-age and survivors insurance taxes, and later extended to railroad retirement taxes and many excises, these taxes are paid directly into Treasury depositaries. The depositary receipts, issued as evidence of such payment, are attached to quarterly returns submitted to the Internal Revenue Service by employers and taxpayers. Under this procedure, the amounts are included in budget receipts in the month and year when the depositary receipts are issued. Effective July 1, 1954, this accounting practice was extended to Internal Revenue Service reports of collections, so that the reported collections after fiscal 1954 likewise include depositary receipts in the month when the depositary receipts are issued.

Excise taxes paid into depositaries cannot be fully classified in terms of specific taxes until the supporting returns are received. Consequently, the collections shown for designated excise taxes in fiscal years after 1954 are subject to an undistributed adjustment. (For the amounts involved, see *Statistical Appendix to Annual Report of the Secretary of the Treasury, 1970*, p. 50.)

The principal taxes included in totals but not shown separately are as follows:

1863–1915. Income and profits, largely 1863–1874 and 1914–1915 (see comments below for series Y 359); corporation excise, 1910–1914; occupational (special) taxes, 1863–1871, 1898–1902, and 1915.

1916–1957. Occupational (special) taxes, 1916–1928; insurance, 1918–1922; soft drinks, 1918–1924; and agricultural adjustment taxes, 1934–1936.

Y 358, total collections. For items included in this series but not shown separately in series Y 359–373, see source publications.

Y 359, individual income taxes. Although not shown separately for 1863–1915, this was an important tax source under revenue legislation enacted during the Civil War. The first collections in 1863 and for other years are shown below as tabulated in the *Annual Report of the Secretary of the Treasury, 1929*, p. 419.

The income tax legislation of the Civil War period expired in 1871 (see text for series Y 393–411). The collections in 1895 were under an act of 1894 that was declared unconstitutional. This type of tax was not imposed in other years during 1872–1913. The amounts shown in table III for 1873, 1874, 1876, 1881, and 1884 were late collections.

Table III. Individual Income Tax Collections: 1863 to 1895
[In thousands of dollars. For years ending June 30]

Year	Amount	Year	Amount	Year	Amount	Year	Amout
1895	77	1874	139	1870	37,776	1866	72,982
1884	56	1873	5,062	1869	34,792	1865	60,979
1881	3	1872	14,437	1868	41,456	1864	20,295
1876	1	1871	19,163	1867	66,014	1863	2,742

Separate figures for the individual income tax collections are not available for 1914, 1915, and 1918–1924.

Since 1951, withheld income taxes and old-age and survivors insurance taxes on employees and employers, and since 1957, disability insurance taxes on employees and employers have been paid into the Treasury in combined amounts without separation as to type of tax. Since June 1965, hospital insurance taxes have been deposited in the same way. Similarly, since 1951 and 1957, respectively, the old-age and survivors insurance and the disability insurance taxes on self-employment incomes have been paid in combination with income tax other than that withheld. The distribution of these collections by type of tax is based on estimates made in accordance with section 201(a) of the Social Security Act (42 U.S.C. 401(a)). Included in income taxes withheld by employers for 1951–1956 are amounts subsequently transferred to the Government of Guam under an act approved August 1, 1950 (48 U.S.C. 1421h). Since 1956 these amounts are excluded.

The relative importance of withholding by employers as a method of income tax collection is shown in table IV for the period since withholding was instituted.

Table IV. Individual Income Tax Collections, by Method of Collection: 1943 to 1970
[In millions of dollars. For years ending June 30]

Year	Total	Withheld by employers	Other collections	Year	Total	Withheld by employers	Other collections
1970	103,652	77,416	26,236	1956	35,338	24,016	11,322
1969	97,440	70,182	27,258	1955	31,650	21,254	10,396
1968	78,252	57,301	20,951	1954	32,814	22,077	10,737
1967	69,371	50,521	18,850	1953	32,536	21,132	11,404
1966	61,298	42,811	18,486	1952	29,274	17,929	11,345
1965	53,661	36,840	16,820	1951	22,997	13,090	9,908
1964	54,590	39,259	15,331	1950	17,153	9,889	7,264
1963	52,988	38,719	14,269	1949	18,052	10,056	7,996
1962	50,650	36,246	14,403	1948	20,998	11,534	9,464
1961	46,153	32,978	13,175	1947	19,343	9,842	9,501
1960	44,946	31,675	13,271	1946	18,705	9,858	8,847
1959	40,735	29,001	11,733	1945	19,034	10,264	8,770
1958	38,569	27,041	11,528	1944	18,261	7,823	10,438
1957	39,030	26,728	12,302	1943	6,630	686	5,944

Y 360, corporation income taxes. Includes excess profits tax, 1917 and 1934–1946; unjust enrichment tax, 1937–1946; and undistributed profits tax, 1937–1939.

The corporation income tax law, effective March 1, 1913, was preceded by a corporate excise tax enacted in 1909, under which collections were as shown in table V (see Treasury Department, *Annual Report of the Secretary of the Treasury, 1929,* p. 420).

For 1914, 1915, and 1918–1924, the Treasury reports do not separate corporate income tax from individual income tax collections.

Collections shown for 1952–1970 include taxes on business income of exempt corporations. Also included is the income tax on the

Alaska Railroad, which was repealed for taxable years after June 30, 1952.

Table V. Collections Under the Corporate Excise Tax Act of 1909: 1910 to 1914
[In thousands of dollars. For years ending June 30]

Year	Amount	Year	Amount
1914	10,671	1911	33,512
1913	35,006	1910	20,960
1912	28,583		

Y 361, employment taxes. Includes the employer, employee, and self-employed taxes for the Federal old-age, survivors, and disability insurance system; the Federal unemployment insurance tax on employers; and the railroad retirement tax on employers and employees. Collections are received in combination with individual income taxes and the distribution by type of tax is based on estimates, as noted above in text for series Y 359.

Omitted from this series are railroad unemployment insurance contributions, collected by the Railroad Retirement Board under the Railroad Unemployment Insurance Act of 1938, as amended (45 U.S.C. 360). Although based on payrolls, this levy is not considered an internal revenue tax.

State unemployment insurance taxes also are not internal revenue collections, although the proceeds are deposited in the unemployment trust fund in the Federal Treasury.

Y 362, estate and gift taxes. Comprises, for 1863–1871 and 1899–1907, taxes on legacies, successions, and inheritances. The estate and gift taxes are shown separately for 1917 and later in the Treasury reports cited above. The figures for 1917–1924 and 1927–1932, inclusive, are for estate tax only. As indicated below for series Y 440–449, estate tax rate increases under the Revenue Act of June 2, 1924, were repealed retroactively February 26, 1926. Gift tax rates levied in 1924 were also reduced retroactively by the act of 1926. Estate and gift tax collections reported for 1925 and 1926 may include amounts collected at the higher rates and subsequently refunded; the refunds were reported as expenditures rather than as deductions from revenue. (See Bureau of Internal Revenue, *Statistics of Income, 1946,* part 1, pp. 430–431; *Annual Report of the Secretary of the Treasury, 1926,* pp. 291 and 350; *1927,* pp. 965–966.)

Y 363–371 and **Y 373,** excise taxes. Series Y 363, excise taxes total, and series Y 366, manufacturers' excise tax subtotal, are shown for years in which these totals appear in the Treasury annual reports cited above. Taxes of these types were collected also in other years.

For the years for which they are shown, these totals include various taxes not specified in the table. The "manufacturers' excise taxes" include special taxes relating to manufacture and sale. For 1863–1868, the manufacturers' excise subtotal includes a tax on raw cotton. For 1916–1970, the series includes taxes on sales under the act of October 22, 1914; manufacturers', consumers', and dealers' excise taxes under war revenue and subsequent acts; and for 1932 and later, manufacturers' excises under the act of 1932, as amended. Excise taxes on soft drinks are in the total for series Y 363 but not in series Y 366.

Y 364, alcohol. Comprises taxes on distilled spirits, beer, wines, and other products and includes occupational taxes. Includes amounts collected by the customs service on imports of distilled spirits and beer. Beginning in 1954, the reported amounts include taxes collected in Puerto Rico on alcohol products of Puerto Rican manufacture coming into the United States.

Y 365, tobacco. Comprises taxes on cigarettes, cigars, and other tobacco products. Beginning in 1954, the reported amounts include taxes collected in Puerto Rico on Puerto Rican tobacco products coming into the United States.

Y 367, automobiles and accessories. Includes tax collected for "passenger automobiles and motorcycles," "automobile trucks and buses," and "parts and accessories for automobiles." Tax on motorcycles repealed effective September 1, 1955; tax on parts and accessories for automobiles (except truck parts) repealed effective January 1, 1966.

Y 370, admissions. Comprises "general admissions" and "cabarets," as shown separately in the *Annual Report of the Secretary of the Treasury, 1970*, for 1936–1970. Tax repealed effective December 31, 1965.

Y 371, telephone, telegraph, radio, and cable facilities. Includes in all years the taxes on "telephone, telegraph, radio, and cable facilities," and also, for 1942 and later, the tax on "local telephone services." General and toll telephone and typewriter service reduced to 3 percent effective January 1, 1966; retroactively restored to 10 percent rate on June 28, 1968. Private communications service, telegraph service, and wire equipment service repealed effective January 1, 1966.

Y 372, capital stock tax. This tax was not levied for years ending in the period July 1, 1926, through June 30, 1932, and for years ending after June 30, 1945. Collections after the fiscal year 1950 are included in excises, series Y 363.

Y 374–380. Fiduciary income tax returns, 1937–1970.

Source: U.S. Internal Revenue Service, 1937–1965, *Statistics of Income, Fiduciary Income Tax Returns*; 1970, unpublished data.

These series were tabulated from returns (Form 1041) before official audit. All returns were used for 1937–1939, but only taxable returns were used for 1940–1951. Data for years after 1951 are based on a sample of returns filed. Prior to 1937, data for fiduciary income tax returns were shown combined with individual income tax returns.

Fiduciary returns show annual income from estates in process of settlement or any other trust for which the fiduciary acts as administrator. Only certain small trusts are excused from filing. For the period covered, returns were required if income equaled or exceeded the amounts specified for the following years:

Income of an estate—for 1937–1939, gross income of $5,000 or net income taxable to the fiduciary of $1,000; 1940, gross income of $800; 1941, gross income of $750; 1942–1947, gross income of $500; 1948–1970, gross income of $600.

Income of a trust—for 1937, gross income of $5,000 or net income taxable to the fiduciary of $1,000; 1938 and 1939, gross income of $5,000 or net income of $100; 1940, gross income of $800 or net income of $100; 1941, gross income of $750 or net income of $100; 1942–1947, gross income of $500 or net income of $100; 1948–1953, gross income of $600 or net income of $100; 1954–1970, gross income of $600 or any taxable income of the fiduciary.

For any tax year, a return was required if any beneficiary of the estate or trust was a nonresident alien.

Total income (series Y 375) is gross income reported in accordance with the law for each tax year. For 1937–1952, this is after business and rental expenses and allowable loss from sales of capital assets and other property, and it includes capital gains as required under the various acts. For 1954 and later years, it includes gross profit from business, gross rents, and the entire capital gain without adjustment.

Net income or taxable income (series Y 376) as shown for 1954 and later years is less inclusive than the amounts shown for earlier years. For 1937–1952, this series represents total income less allowable nonbusiness deductions and the amount distributable to beneficiaries. For these years, it is not the amount taxed, since the exemption allowed to trusts and estates has not been deducted from the net income taxable to the fiduciary. For 1954 and later years, the series shows income taxable to the fiduciary. This is total income after deduction of the exemption as well as all business and rental expenses, the authorized nonbusiness deductions, distributions to beneficiaries, and the fiduciary's share of dividend exclusions and of long-term capital gain.

Y 381–392. Corporation income tax returns, 1909–1970.

Source: U.S. Internal Revenue Service (formerly Bureau of Internal Revenue), 1909–1915, *Annual Report of the Commissioner of Internal Revenue*, various issues; 1916–1970, *Statistics of Income, Corporation Income Tax Returns*, annual issues.

Income tax returns are required annually of all corporations except those specifically exempt, such as fraternal, civic, and charitable organizations not operating for profit.

Data for 1909–1915 are from returns received during the fiscal year beginning July 1 of the year specified. The data for 1915 include information from approximately 32,000 returns received during the preceding fiscal year.

Data for 1916–1970 are for returns with accounting periods that ended between July 1 of the year specified and June 30 of the following year (for example, figures for 1916 are for accounting periods ending July 1, 1916, to June 30, 1917). A large proportion of the corporations' accounting periods coincide with the calendar year, and the calendar year is therefore used to identify the "income year." For the "income year" 1967, for example, 44.6 percent of the returns were for accounting periods that ended in December 1967; 22.5 percent for periods that ended during July–November 1967; 32.9 percent for periods that ended in the first half of 1968.

Data are based on returns as filed, prior to audit adjustments, carrybacks, renegotiation of war contracts, or other changes made after the returns were filed. For 1951–1970, data are based on a probability sample described in the annual *Statistics of Income*. Only the most important changes in law affecting historical comparability of the data can be noted here; others are specified in the annual *Statistics of Income*—for example, the varying provisions regarding life insurance company taxation.

Because of consolidated returns for affiliated corporations, the number of returns (series Y 381, Y 382, Y 386, and Y 392) is not the same as the number of corporations.

Total receipts of the corporations (series Y 383 and Y 387) include gross sales and receipts from operations, interest less amortizable bond premium, rents, royalties, net gain from capital assets (as defined by law) and other property, dividends, and other taxable income—all before "total deductions." These series also include nontaxable dividends from domestic corporations for 1918–1935 and nontaxable interest, but exclude all other nontaxable income. The data for 1916–1922 represent gross income. This was smaller than the total receipts by the amounts of wholly tax-exempt interest received on certain government obligations and, for 1918–1921, of nontaxable dividends.

Total deductions include the cost of goods sold and (beginning in 1932) the cost of operations, as well as other negative amounts reported under sources of income.

Net income (less deficit) (series Y 384 and Y 388) is gross taxable income less allowable current-year deductions, except statutory deductions. This category excludes tax-exempt interest on government obligations and, for 1918–1935, dividends from domestic corporations; these are included in total receipts. Beginning in 1936, contributions or gifts were deductible in determining net income. A deduction for amortization of emergency facilities was first allowable in 1940; the deduction was later extended to grain facilities and other items. Beginning with 1963, net income (less deficit) includes constructive taxable income from related foreign corporations.

Income tax (series Y 389), as shown for 1909–1915, represents tax collections. For 1909–1912, these amounts correspond to the corporate excise tax collections noted for the fiscal years 1910–1913 in the text for series Y 360, above. For the income year 1913, the amount represents income tax and excise tax. Beginning with 1916, "income tax" is the tax liability on the returns, but before deduction of credit for taxes paid to foreign countries or U.S. possessions. For 1936–1938, the amounts include surtax on undistributed profits, as well as normal tax. For 1940 and 1941, the series includes the income defense tax; for 1941–1970, normal tax and surtax; for 1942–1970, alternative tax; for 1963–1970, tax from recomputing prior year investment credit; for 1967–1970, the surcharge; for 1969–1970, the additional tax for tax preferences.

Excess profits tax (series Y 390) for 1917–1922 comprises war profits tax and excess profits tax, and for 1933–1945, a declared-value excess profits tax effective for tax years that ended before July 1, 1946. Data for 1940 include the declared-value excess profits defense tax, and for 1940–1946, the excess profits tax under the Second Revenue Act of 1940. Amounts for 1942–1944 are for tax liability on the excess profits tax returns less a credit for debt retirement and the net postwar refund. Deferments under section 710(a)(5) of the 1939 Internal Revenue Code (relating to abnormalities under section 722) are reflected in the data for 1942 but not for 1943–1946. Amounts for 1943–1946 are after adjustments under various other relief provisions. The data for 1950–1954 are for the excess profits tax effective with respect to tax years from July 1, 1950, to December 31, 1953. For all years, the tax shown is before credit for foreign taxes paid.

Dividends paid (series Y 385 and Y 391) exclude liquidating dividends. They include all other dividends. In including dividends paid in the corporation's own stock, this series differs from similar series published elsewhere (e.g., U.S. Bureau of the Census, *Statistical Abstract of the United States, 1973*, table 640). For selected years, the amounts paid in stock, as included in the historical table, are as shown in table VI.

Table VI. Stock Dividends Paid: 1935 to 1970

[In thousands of dollars]

Income year	Included in series Y 385	Included in series Y 391	Income year	Included in series Y 385	Included in series Y 391
1970	1,922,810	1,679,308	1960	1,965,587	1,865,572
1969	2,715,063	2,570,607	1959	2,173,518	2,091,226
1968	3,303,905	3,194,340	1958	1,603,895	1,507,144
1967	3,233,481	3,095,337	1957	1,777,670	1,696,463
1966	2,677,450	2,583,276	1956	2,725,210	2,676,783
1965	2,239,629	2,154,005	1955	1,996,477	1,965,391
1964	3,092,238	3,029,011	1954	1,350,041	1,316,460
1963	2,118,090	2,048,090	1953	1,110,260	1,089,355
1962	2,148,904	2,026,498			
1961	2,176,709	2,092,000	1950	1,292,460	1,278,908
			1940	139,989	130,578
			1935	135,851	112,162

Inactive corporation returns (series Y 392) are those which show no items of income or deductions.

Y 393–411. Individual income tax returns, 1913–1970.

Source: U.S. Internal Revenue Service, *Statistics of Income, Individual Income Tax Returns*, annual issues.

The data represent returns of residents and citizens, including those with addresses outside Alaska, Hawaii, and conterminous United States. Detailed tabulations for each year, 1961–1970, with data by levels of gross income and by States, appear in *Statistics of Income, 1970, Individual Income Tax Returns*, 1970, pp. 307–322.

As noted above in the text for internal revenue collections (series Y 359), the individual income tax has been a continuing element of the revenue system since 1913, but was included in Federal revenue legislation in two earlier periods.

During the Civil War decade, this tax was included in the first revenue act of the war, in 1861, at a flat rate of 3 percent on incomes above $800. Before the initial rate took effect, it was superseded in 1862 by rates of 3 percent on up to $10,000, 5 percent above that amount of net income, and an individual exemption of $600. Rates were raised further in 1864. The highest rates, levied for a single year, were 10 percent on net income of $600 to $5,000, 12.5 percent on $5,000 to $10,000, and 15 percent above $15,000. In 1867, the rate became a flat 5 percent on income of more than $1,000; for 1870 and 1871, the rate was 2.5 percent and the exemption $2,000. The law expired at the end of 1871.

An individual income tax law adopted in 1894 was patterned generally after the law of 1867. It provided a 2 percent tax rate on individual and corporate net income, with a $4,000 exemption for individuals. Personal property received by gift or inheritance was to be included in net income. The act was declared unconstitutional in 1895 in a Supreme Court decision (Pollock v. Farmers' Loan and Trust Co., 157 U.S. 429, 158 U.S. 601). The personal income tax was not again levied until after adoption in 1913 of the Sixteenth Amendment to the Constitution. For data showing individual income tax collections covering the period 1863–1895, see text for series Y 359.

The data for 1913–1970 relate to returns filed under the income tax laws of 1913 and subsequent years. A return is required of every citizen or resident with gross or net income above a specified minimum. The requirements for filing have changed from time to time and are summarized below.

Table VII. Requirements for Filing Individual Income Tax Returns: 1913 to 1970

Year	Return required if net or gross income equaled or exceeded amount specified	
	Single, or married and not living with spouse	Married couple, joint return [1]
1970	Gross, $1,700 [2]	Gross, $2,300 [3]
1954–1969	Gross, $600 [4]	Gross, $600 each spouse [4]
1948–1953	Gross, $600	Gross, $600 each spouse
1944–1947	Gross, $500	Gross, $500 each spouse
1942–1943	Gross, $500 [5]	Gross, $1,200 [6]
1941	Gross, $750	Gross, $1,500
1940	Gross, $800	Gross, $2,000
1932–1939	Net, $1,000 or gross, $5,000	Net, $2,500 or gross, $5,000
1925–1931	Net, $1,500 or gross, $5,000	Net, $3,500 or gross, $5,000
1924	Net, $1,000 or gross, $5,000	Net, $2,500 or gross, $5,000
1921–1923	Net, $1,000 or gross, $5,000	Net, $2,000 or gross, $5,000
1917–1920	Net, $1,000	Net, $2,000
1913–1916	Net, $3,000	Net, $3,000

[1] Through 1943, amount shown is combined net or combined gross income.
[2] Gross income of $2,300 if age 65 or over.
[3] Gross income of $2,900, if one spouse age 65 or over; $3,500 if both age 65 or over.
[4] Gross income of $1,200 for each person age 65 or older.
[5] Also, for 1943, required to file if liable for 1942 tax, regardless of 1943 gross income.
[6] Also, for 1943, required to file if gross income of either spouse exceeded $624 or if either was liable for 1942 tax, regardless of 1943 gross income.

A joint return could be filed by husband and wife if income of both was included or if one spouse had no income.

For 1951–1970, a return was required of any individual whose net earnings for self-employment tax were $400 or more, regardless of the gross income requirement for filing.

In addition, under the current tax payment system instituted in 1943, returns were filed to claim refunds of taxes overpaid, even though the individual was not otherwise required to file.

Fiduciary income of an estate or trust for 1913–1936 was reported on an individual return form when there remained in the hands of the fiduciary net income which was taxable to him and not distributed to beneficiaries. Such a return for net income taxable to the fiduciary was required under the same conditions as those stated above for single persons during this period.

Data for 1913–1915 were derived from annual reports of the Commissioner of Internal Revenue, net income being determined on the basis of number of returns filed and the average net income in each class. Subsequent data were taken from returns, unaudited except to insure proper execution. Data for 1916 were tabulated from each return, but for later years were compiled by sampling techniques to represent the universe of returns, Form 1040 and 1040A (replaced by W–2 for 1944–1947). Tabulated data cover individual and fiduciary returns with net income of $3,000 or more, 1913–1916; returns with net income of $1,000 or more, 1917–1920; returns with net income, 1921–1927; all individual and fiduciary returns with net income, but only individual returns with no net income, 1928–1936; individual returns with net income or no net income, 1937–1943; and individual returns with adjusted gross income or no adjusted gross income, 1944–1970, except that returns with no information were excluded for 1953–1956.

In the great majority of cases, the returns are for the calendar year, although some returns are for accounting periods ended during the calendar year. Also, some returns cover income attributable to several tax years. Prior to 1957, the tabulations of adjusted gross income (series Y 397) included only income attributed to the current tax year. For 1957 and later years adjusted gross income includes the whole amount received by the taxpayer within his tax year even if it was reported as income earned over a period of time that included prior tax years.

Adjusted gross income for 1944–1970 is total income reported for tax purposes less deductions for certain expenses generally related to the acquisition of income. These deductions include business and rental expenses, certain travel and transportation expenses of employees, depreciation allowed life tenants of property held in trust, allowable loss from the sale of capital assets and other property, adjustments for long-term capital gain, net operating loss deductions, and for 1954–1970, excludable sick pay, the limited exclusion of dividends, and expenses of salesmen. For 1964–1970, deductions of expenses of employees moving to a new job and deductions of pension plan contributions of self-employed persons were allowed.

Under the Internal Revenue Code of 1954, taxable income (series Y 398) for 1954–1970 is the base on which the tax is computed. It consists of adjusted gross income less nonbusiness deductions, standard or itemized. Itemized deductions are for taxes, contributions, interest, and other specified purposes, and also include all personal exemptions. The figures for taxable income embrace all returns, including those showing the so-called "optional tax," i.e., a tax determined by reference to a simplified tax table involving standard deductions rather than itemized nonbusiness deductions.

During 1948–1969, personal exemptions were $600 a year for each person—the taxpayer, his spouse, and dependents. A taxpayer aged 65 or older was allowed an additional $600 exemption for himself and, if a joint return was filed, for his wife if she was 65 or older. Likewise, an additional $600 exemption was allowed a blind taxpayer or a blind spouse. For 1970 the exemption amount was raised to $625.

Total income (series Y 405 and Y 409) for 1913–1943 is the gross income reported for income tax purposes under the act in effect for the income year. It is the total income after deduction of business and rental expenses and allowable loss on sales of capital assets and other property. Capital gain is included to the extent provided under successive acts.

Net income (series Y 406) for 1913–1943 is total income less authorized deductions. However, in the *Statistics of Income* for 1922–1931 the allowable prior-year loss was not deducted, and for 1924–1933 a capital loss that gave rise to a tax credit was not deducted. In the case of fiduciary net income, distribution to the beneficiary was an authorized deduction for 1913–1936. Net income in all years is measured before deduction of personal exemptions; it is not the tax base. The series is not available after 1943.

The small amounts of tax reported for 1938–1941 for returns with no net income (series Y 411) are an alternative tax on a small number of returns which showed a long-term capital loss and, for 1940 and 1941, a defense tax. For 1943, a victory tax was due on 17,438 returns with no net income.

Y 412–439. Individual income tax liability and effective rates, for selected income groups, 1913–1970.

Source: U.S. Department of the Treasury, unpublished data.

Maximum earned net income is assumed where it affects the amount of tax liability. In the case of the married couple (four exemptions), the computations assume prior to 1948 that only one spouse had income. Beginning with the income year 1948, all married couples have been permitted to combine their incomes in a joint return and to split the taxable income equally for purposes of the tax computation; a joint return on the split-income basis is therefore assumed for the married couple for the income years 1948–1970.

For the same years, persons of age 65 or older and blind persons were allowed additional exemptions; consequently, the illustrative data for 1948–1970 apply equally to any married couple claiming 4 exemptions, whether the additional exemptions were for dependents, age, or blindness.

The effective tax rate is the tax liability as a percentage of the amount of net income. The liability is the amount for income tax only, including the defense and victory taxes of 1940 and 1943; it does not include the self-employment tax for social security, applicable for 1951–1970.

Net income, as used here, is gross income (after 1943, adjusted gross income) minus nonbusiness deductions for contributions, interest, taxes, medical and dental expenses, and other allowable expenses, but before deduction of personal exemptions. Also excluded from net income (and from adjusted gross income) is tax-exempt interest on government obligations, excludable sick pay under the Revenue Act of 1954, certain expenses related to the acquisition of income, and other nontaxable income.

Statutory changes have been made from time to time in the allowable nonbusiness deductions. For example, the deduction for medical expenses was amended several times during 1944–1970. Another type of nonbusiness deduction, the amount allowed for contributions, was limited to 20 percent of adjusted gross income prior to 1954; for 1954–1970, taxpayers were allowed to deduct more than 20 percent to the extent that the excess (limited to 10 percent of adjusted gross income through 1969; 30 percent in 1970) was for contributions to hospitals, churches, or educational institutions.

In consequence of these and other changes, a given amount of net income could be associated with somewhat different amounts of gross income in different years. Even in any one year, a given amount of net income could be associated with different amounts of gross income for different taxpayers in accordance with their varying allowable deductions.

Beginning with the income year 1941, taxpayers with gross income of not more than $3,000 from specified sources were allowed to use a simplified return, Form 1040A, with the tax determined by a table that allowed a standard percentage of earned income credit and deductions from income. Taxpayers who did not use the short form were required to itemize deductions. In either case, the 1943 victory tax had to be computed separately. Legislation simplifying the filing of tax returns made available (beginning in 1944) the option of a standard deduction of 10 percent of adjusted gross income, limited to $500 for 1944–1947. For 1948–1970, the limit was raised to $1,000 for single persons and for married persons filing joint returns. In general, this implies that, for 1944–1947, net incomes of $4,500 or less and, for 1948–1970, net incomes of $9,000 or less, as shown in the table, would represent adjusted gross incomes at least ten-ninths as large. (That is, $800 net represents at least $889 of adjusted gross income; $1,000 net, at least $1,111 gross; $4,500 net, at least $5,000 gross; etc.)

For some types of analysis, effective rates based on gross rather then net income might be more pertinent. Such rates can be computed by making uniform assumptions about the deductions associated with the several specified levels of net income. For example, if it is assumed that the standard deductions made up the whole difference between adjusted gross and net income in cases in which the standard deduction was available, the effective percentage rate of tax on adjusted gross income in these cases would be nine-tenths of the effective rates shown in series Y 412–439. For another type of computation of effective tax rates, see Internal Revenue Service, *Statistics of Income, 1970, Individual Income Tax Returns*, p. 149.

The history since 1913 of the personal exemptions (including credits for dependents) and of the range of tax rates applicable to taxable individual incomes is summarized below in table VIII, from the following publications: 1913–1950, Treasury Department, *Annual Report of the Secretary of the Treasury, 1940*, pp. 466–467, and *1950*, p. 251; 1951–1957, Joint Economic Committee, *The Federal Revenue*

System: Facts and Problems, 1959, 86th Congress, 1st session, p. 189; and 1958–1970, unpublished Treasury Department data.

Table VIII. Federal Individual Income Tax Exemptions, and First and Top Bracket Rates: 1913 to 1970

Income year	Single	Married				Tax rates			
		None	Dependents			First bracket		Top bracket	
			1	2	3	Rate (percent)	Income	Rate (percent)	Income over—
1970 [1][2]	$625	$1,250	$1,875	$2,500	$3,125	14	$500	71.75	$100,000
1969 [2][3]	600	1,200	1,800	2,400	3,000	14	500	77	100,000
1968 [2][4]	600	1,200	1,800	2,400	3,000	14	500	75.25	100,000
1965–1967 [2]	600	1,200	1,800	2,400	3,000	14	500	70	100,000
1964 [2]	600	1,200	1,800	2,400	3,000	16	500	77	200,000
1954–1963 [2]	600	1,200	1,800	2,400	3,000	20	2,000	[5]91	200,000
1952–1953 [2]	600	1,200	1,800	2,400	3,000	22.2	2,000	[5]92	200,000
1951 [2]	600	1,200	1,800	2,400	3,000	20.4	2,000	[5]91	200,000
1950 [2]	600	1,200	1,800	2,400	3,000	17.4	2,000	[5]84.36	200,000
1948–1949 [2]	600	1,200	1,800	2,400	3,000	16.6	2,000	[5]82.13	200,000
1946–1947	500	1,000	1,500	2,000	2,500	19	2,000	[5]86.45	200,000
1944–1945	500	1,000	1,500	2,000	2,500	23	2,000	[5]94	200,000
1942–1943 [6]	500	1,200	1,550	1,900	2,250	[7]19	2,000	88	200,000
1941	750	1,500	1,900	2,300	2,700	[7]10	2,000	81	5,000,000
1940	800	2,000	2,400	2,800	3,200	[7]4.4	4,000	81.1	5,000,000
1936–1939	1,000	2,500	2,900	3,300	3,700	[7]4	4,000	79	5,000,000
1934–1935	1,000	2,500	2,900	3,300	3,700	[7]4	4,000	63	1,000,000
1932–1933	1,000	2,500	2,900	3,300	3,700	4	4,000	63	1,000,000
1930–1931	1,500	3,500	3,900	4,300	4,700	[8]1⅛	4,000	25	100,000
1929	1,500	3,500	3,900	4,300	4,700	[8]⅜	4,000	24	100,000
1925–1928	1,500	3,500	3,900	4,300	4,700	[8]1⅛	4,000	25	100,000
1924	1,000	2,500	2,900	3,300	3,700	[8]1½	4,000	46	500,000
1923	1,000	[9]2,500	2,900	3,300	3,700	3	4,000	56	200,000
1922	1,000	[9]2,500	2,900	3,300	3,700	4	4,000	56	200,000
1921	1,000	[9]2,500	2,900	3,300	3,700	4	4,000	73	1,000,000
1919–1920	1,000	2,000	2,200	2,400	2,600	4	4,000	73	1,000,000
1918	1,000	2,000	2,200	2,400	2,600	6	4,000	77	1,000,000
1917	1,000	2,000	2,200	2,400	2,600	2	2,000	67	2,000,000
1916	3,000	4,000	4,000	4,000	4,000	2	20,000	15	2,000,000
1913–1915	3,000	4,000	4,000	4,000	4,000	1	20,000	7	500,000

[1] Includes 2.5 percent surcharge, but lowest bracket unaffected; maximum effective rate on earned income is 60 percent.
[2] Additional exemptions of $600 ($625 in 1970) are allowed to taxpayers and their spouses on account of blindness and/or age 65 or older.
[3] Includes 10 percent surcharge, but lowest bracket unaffected.
[4] Includes 7.5 percent surcharge, but lowest bracket unaffected.
[5] Subject to maximum effective rate limitation: 90 percent for 1944–45, 85.5 percent for 1946–47, 77 percent for 1948–49, 80 percent for 1950, 87.2 percent for 1951, 88 percent for 1952–53, and 87 percent for 1954–59.
[6] Exclusive of victory tax.
[7] Before earned income credit allowed as a deduction equal to 10 percent of earned net income.
[8] After earned income credit equal to 25 percent of tax on earned income.
[9] If net income exceeds $5,000, married person's exemption is $2,000.

Y 440–449. Federal estate tax returns, 1916–1970.

Source: U.S. Internal Revenue Service, *Statistics of Income, Estate Tax Returns.*

These data are from returns filed, before audit. Data for returns filed in 1966 and 1970 are based on a sample.

The Federal estate tax is a levy upon the transfer of property by a decedent. It differs from inheritance taxes, in which, generally, the tax is on the privilege of receiving property by inheritance and is levied upon the heirs.

The base of the tax is the value of the gross estate transferred, adjusted for exclusions, deductions, and exemptions. The tax is imposed at graduated rates, and certain credits are allowed against the tax so computed.

The estate tax in its present form became a permanent part of the Federal tax system in 1916, but four times earlier death taxes had been imposed by the Federal Government. During 1797–1802, a stamp tax applied to succession to personal property by inheritance. The Civil War Revenue Act of 1862 included an inheritance tax which was substantially increased in 1864; this tax was repealed in 1870. The income tax act of 1894 included an inheritance tax that was abandoned when the income tax was declared unconstitutional. The Revenue Act of 1898, for financing the Spanish-American War,

included a short-lived tax applicable to all estates of over $10,000, except those inherited by spouses.

Table IX summarizes the history of Federal estate tax rates and exemptions for 1916–1970. An estate tax return was required if the value of the gross estate at the date of death exceeded the allowable specific exemption as shown in the table and footnote 1.

The estate of an individual who died in the period June 6, 1932, through August 16, 1954, was subject to two estate taxes—basic and additional. Basic tax was at the rates provided in the 1926 act; additional tax was the excess of a tentative tax at rates provided by the act in force at date of death, over the basic tax. Under the 1954 Code, these two taxes were combined and a single tax rate applied to the net taxable estate.

Table IX. Estate Tax Rates, Specific Exemption, and Insurance Exclusion: 1916 to 1970

Date of death	Tax rates, range (percent)	Minimum rate applies to first—	Maximum rate applies above—	Specific exemption [1]	Insurance exclusion
Oct. 22, 1942–1970	3.0–77	$5,000	$10,000,000	$60,000	---------
Sept. 21, 1941–Oct. 21, 1942	3.0–77	5,000	10,000,000	40,000	$40,000
Aug. 31, 1935–Sept. 20, 1941	[2]2.0–70	10,000	50,000,000	40,000	40,000
May 11, 1934–Aug. 30, 1935	1.0–60	10,000	10,000,000	50,000	40,000
June 6, 1932–May 10, 1934	1.0–45	10,000	10,000,000	50,000	40,000
Feb. 26, 1926–June 6, 1932	1.0–20	50,000	10,000,000	100,000	40,000
Feb. 24, 1919–Feb. 26, 1926	[3]1.0–25	50,000	10,000,000	50,000	40,000
Oct. 4, 1917–Feb. 24, 1919	2.0–25	50,000	10,000,000	50,000	---------
Mar. 3–Oct. 3, 1917	1.5–15	50,000	5,000,000	50,000	---------
Sept. 9, 1916–Mar. 2, 1917	1.0–10	50,000	5,000,000	50,000	---------

[1] For estate of resident citizen or alien. The same specific exemption was granted for estates of nonresident citizens dying after May 10, 1934. Exemptions were not granted to estates of nonresident aliens until Oct. 22, 1942, when a $2,000 exemption became available.
[2] For deaths from June 26, 1940, to Sept. 20, 1941, a defense tax was added equal to 10 percent of the net estate tax (computed at the rates of 2 to 70 percent) after deduction of credits for gift taxes and State death taxes.
[3] Higher rates, ranging from 1 percent to a top-bracket rate of 40 percent on the excess over $10,000,000 were provided in the Revenue Act of June 2, 1924, but the rates of the 1921 act were restored retroactively Feb. 26, 1926. Refunds were authorized for overpayments made at the higher rates. The net tax (series Y 445 and Y 449) was computed at the lower rates (*Statistics of Income, 1925*, pp. 70–71, 82).
Source: Adapted from Internal Revenue Service, *Statistics of Income*, various issues; U.S. Department of the Treasury, *Annual Report of the Secretary of the Treasury, 1940*, pp. 478–479, and *1950*, p. 258.

A marital deduction for bequests to the surviving spouse applied to the estates of persons who died after 1947. The deduction is limited to the smaller of either one-half the value of the adjusted gross estate or the value of the qualifying property interests which pass to the surviving spouse. The impact of this provision is reflected in the statistics.

Gross estate (series Y 442 and Y 447) includes all property possessed to the extent of the decedent's interest therein at death, including certain transfers made during life without full consideration, joint estates, tenancies by the entirety, dower and courtesy of surviving spouse, and life insurance on the life of the decedent if the estate was administered under the 1942 or subsequent acts. The value of the gross estate may be either the value at date of death or as of the date one year after death, whichever the executor elected in case death occurred on or after August 31, 1935.

Net taxable estate (series Y 443 and Y 448) is gross estate less the deductions and specific exemptions allowed under the act in effect at date of death. These have varied somewhat among the different acts.

Y 450–456. Federal gift tax returns, 1924–1966.

Source: U.S. Internal Revenue Service, *Statistics of Income, Gift Tax Returns.*

These data are from returns filed, before audit. Data for returns filed in 1961, 1963, and 1966 are based on a sample. Data have not been tabulated in years for which no figures are shown.

The Federal gift tax, like the estate tax, is a levy upon transfers of property by gift. The tax is a liability of the person making the gift and is based upon the value of the transferred property.

The gift tax was first levied for 1924 and 1925. For these years, a return was required for gifts of property located in the United States, made by individuals, corporations, associations, partnerships, trusts, or estates, if total gifts exceeded the sum of authorized deductions for exemption, charitable gifts, and previously taxed property, and if the aggregate exceeded $500 to any one donee.

The present gift tax was introduced in 1932 in connection with substantial revisions in the estate tax. The rates were three-fourths of those in the estate tax, and this relationship was maintained through subsequent revisions (subject, however, to differences in the effective dates of rate and exemption changes). A return was required during 1932–1970 if aggregate gifts in the year to any donee exceeded the allowable annual exclusion per donee and for gifts of future interests regardless of value. Tax rates, specific exemptions, and annual exclusions are summarized in table X.

Table X. Gift Tax Rates, Exemptions, and Exclusions: 1924 to 1970

Calendar year of gift	Tax rates, range (percent)	Minimum rate applies to first—	Maximum rate applies above—	Specific exemption [1]	Annual exclusion per donee
1943–1970	2.25–57.75	$5,000	$10,000,000	$30,000	$3,000
1942	2.25–57.75	5,000	10,000,000	40,000	4,000
1939–1941	[2] 1.5–52.5	10,000	50,000,000	40,000	4,000
1936–1938	1.5–52.5	10,000	50,000,000	40,000	5,000
1935	75–45	10,000	10,000,000	50,000	5,000
1932 [3]–1934	75–33.5	10,000	10,000,000	50,000	5,000
1924 [4]–1925	1–25	50,000	10,000,000	50,000	500

[1] During 1924–1925, allowed in each calendar year; in later years, allowed only once.
[2] From June 26, 1940, through 1941, subject to additional defense tax equal to 10 percent of basic tax liability.
[3] In effect for gifts June 7, 1932, and later.
[4] In effect June 24, 1924.
Source: Adapted from Internal Revenue Service, *Statistics of Income*, various issues; U.S. Department of the Treasury, *Annual Report of the Secretary of the Treasury, 1940*, pp. 478–579, and *1950*, p. 258.

Since 1932 the tax has applied to individuals only (citizens, residents, or nonresident aliens) for transfer of property situated in the United States.

Gift tax rates are progressive in application; that is, current graduated rates are applied to (a) the aggregate net taxable gifts made after June 6, 1932, and to (b) the aggregate net gifts exclusive of those made in the current year—the excess of tax in (a) over (b) being the current tax liability.

As indicated in table X, the donor is allowed to exclude gifts of less than a specified amount to each recipient in each year. This annual exclusion was $3,000 for each donee for the years 1943–1970. In addition, a specific exemption ($30,000 during 1943–1970) is allowed each citizen or resident and may be taken, at his option, entirely in a single year or spread over a number of years. After April 2, 1948, a marital deduction of one-half of the value of gifts made between a husband and wife was allowed citizens and residents.

Total gifts (series Y 452 and Y 456) is the value of property (real property or tangible or intangible personal property) transferred without full consideration in money or money's worth, whether transferred in trust or otherwise, whether direct or indirect, or of future interests. Generally, gifts of less than the allowable annual exclusion for each donee are not reported, except that gifts of future interests must be included regardless of value (and, for 1939–1942, gifts in trust).

Net taxable gift (series Y 453) is the tax base. It is the value of total gifts minus the exclusion for each donee, deductions, and specific exemptions.

Y 457–465. Outlays of the Federal Government, 1789–1970.

Source: All series except Y 463, U.S. Department of the Treasury, *Statistical Appendix to Annual Report of the Secretary of the Treasury, 1970*, pp. 8–16. **Series Y 463**, 1789–1946, Department of the Treasury, *Annual Report, 1946*, pp. 422–423; 1947–1970, U.S. Office of Management and Budget (formerly Bureau of the Budget), *Budget of the United States Government*, annual issues, 1949–1970.

Data for 1954–1970 are unified budget outlays. For earlier years data are for the administrative budget, so they exclude expenditures from trust funds. Series Y 466–471 show consolidated cash data for the years 1940 through 1953. The consolidated cash data are more comparable to the unified budget data than are the administrative budget data, but data on cash payments by agency are not available.

In the case of public enterprise funds (including the postal service) and various intra-governmental funds, expenditures included in the total are on a *net* basis—that is, their collections are deducted from gross expenditures and the results are the net expenditures included in Federal Government expenditure accounts. In the case of the postal service, the net postal expenditure is included in the total and "other" (series Y 457 and Y 462) expenditures in the years in which there was a postal deficit. For a historical series showing gross postal expenditures in relation to postal receipts, see references in text for series Y 352–357.

Expenditures for 1789–1915 are based on warrants issued; for 1916–1952, on the *Daily Statement of the United States Treasury*; for 1953–1970, on the Treasury's *Monthly Statement of Receipts and Expenditures of the United States Government*.

In the *Monthly Statement*, expenditures are reported on the basis of checks issued by disbursing officers, except for interest on the public debt and payments made in cash. Where payment is made by the issuance of bonds or by an increase in their redemption value, instead of by the issuance of checks, such an issuance or increase is an expenditure. Interest on the public debt is reported on an accrual basis. For years prior to those reported in the *Monthly Statement*, interest on the public debt is reported on the same basis as other expenditures.

The figures for 1916–1952 were compiled from daily reports received by the Treasurer of the United States from Government depositaries and Treasury offices holding Government funds. On this basis, the expenditures include payments on checks outstanding at the beginning of the fiscal year and do not include checks unpaid at the end of the year. Beginning with the fiscal year 1947, expenditures of several departments and establishments were reported on the basis of checks issued, so that the detail in the daily statement was partly based on checks issued, partly on checks paid. The change to the monthly statement basis eliminated the necessity for showing an item of "adjustment to daily Treasury statement basis" in tabulations presenting components of the expenditure total.

Y 466–471. Outlays of the Federal Government, by major function, 1900–1939.

Source: U.S. Bureau of the Budget, unpublished data.

Basic data are from the following:

1900–1914. Adapted from Bureau of the Budget compilation for 1900–1948 in U.S. Congress, *Congressional Record*, 80th Congress, 2d session, vol. 94, pt. 2, March 11, 1948, pp. 2576–2577. Series Y 469, veterans services and benefits, supplied from the Treasury compilation in series Y 463 (see below). Tax refunds of $10 million a year deducted from 1913 and 1914 to conform to the *1959 Federal Budget Mid-Year Review* (September 1958), p. 42, where budget receipt and expenditure totals are shown for each year, 1900–1939, with refunds excluded starting in 1913.

1915–1920. *Congressional Record*, cited above, but with tax refunds deducted.

1921–1938. Unpublished Bureau of the Budget table for 1920–1939, September 17, 1958; but with series Y 468, International affairs and finance, supplied from *Congressional Record*, cited above.

1939. Unpublished Bureau of the Budget table for 1939–1950, February 1959.

As Federal Government operations expanded in volume and variety, the limited classification of expenditures exemplified in series Y 457–465 (even when supplemented with additional items and subdivided to give more specific categories) was inadequate to delineate the scope of Government programs and to focus attention on significant shifts in the purpose of expenditures. The text for series Y 472–487 explains the development to and definitions of the current Government expenditures.

Series Y 469, veterans services and benefits, may be slightly understated for 1900–1914, as it comprises only the payments for veterans compensation and pensions, the same as series Y 463. Any such understatement in series Y 469 apparently would not exceed $12 million a year and is balanced by an equal overstatement in the residual series, Y 471, for "All other."

Refunds are excluded from series Y 466–471 since 1912. Consequently, total expenditures, series Y 466, for 1913–1930 deviate from those shown in series Y 336 and Y 457 by the amount of refunds.

Y 472–487.   Outlays of the Federal Government, by major function, 1940–1970.

Source: U.S. Office of Management and Budget, *Federal Government Finances* (mimeographed tables), October 31, 1972.

A systematic classification of expenditures by major functional categories and more specific subfunctions was introduced in the budget for the fiscal year 1948. Although each succeeding annual budget modified some of the categories or shifted particular items from one classification to another, continuity of the series was maintained by adjusting the data for prior years so that the data for each function is as consistent as feasible. Details concerning the composition of the classifications shown here (including the subfunctional groupings) may be found in the 1973 budget document.

In 1967 the President's Commission on Budget Concepts recommended substantial changes in the budget concept. These changes were first reflected in the 1969 Budget but the data were carried back on a comparable basis through 1954. While historical data on the current budget basis are not available prior to 1954, the consolidated cash statements are a reasonable approximation for earlier years. The principal differences between the cash and unified budget data are: (1) many proprietary receipts are included in the consolidated cash statement as income but are offsets to outlays under the unified budget, (2) the cash statement has certain timing adjustments not made in the unified budget, and (3) certain activities—such as two privately-owned but federally-chartered banking institutions—are included in the cash totals but excluded from the unified budget totals. In all cases, the functional data for the consolidated cash statement have been made as comparable as feasible; the discontinuities are concentrated in the unallocable column. For a more complete discussion see text for series Y 339–342.

For years prior to 1940, the figures in series Y 457–465 are a rough approximation of certain functional categories. The sum of expenditures for the Department of the Army and the Department of the Navy are roughly equivalent to the national defense function; interest on the public debt is roughly equivalent to the interest function, and veterans compensation and pensions (series Y 463) is roughly equivalent to veterans benefits and services (series Y 469).

Y 488–492.   Gross Federal debt outstanding, 1939–1970.

Source: U.S. Office of Management and Budget, *Federal Government Finances* (mimeographed tables), October 31, 1972.

Gross Federal debt is the broadest generally used measure of the Federal debt. It is composed primarily of the public debt (direct borrowing by the Treasury) but also includes agency debt (such as borrowing by the Tennessee Valley Authority or the Postal Service). About three-fourths of the gross debt is held by the public, and about

one-fourth is held by Government accounts. The Government-held debt results from the fact that the surpluses of trust funds are normally invested in public debt securities. The interest payments on this Government-held debt are made from one account within the budget to another account within the budget and do not, therefore, affect the budget deficit or surplus. Only the debt owed to the public gives rise to net budget expenditures for interest.

The Federal Reserve System is an independent, federally-chartered, central banking system. As the System is not included in the Federal budget, debt held by the System is included in "debt held by the public." Interest paid on Federal debt held by the System is not, therefore, an intrabudgetary transaction. However, since 1947 the Federal Reserve System has made annual payments to the Treasury from its surplus, which, in turn, arises primarily as a result of interest payments made by the Treasury to the Federal Reserve. In 1970, these payments amounted to $3.3 billion, equal to the bulk of interest payments to the Federal Reserve System. Thus, interest payments to the Federal Reserve System have very little net effect on the budget deficit or surplus.

This series differs from series Y 493–504, which excludes Federal agency debt issuances. See also text for series Y 493–504.

Y 493–504.   Public debt of the Federal Government, 1791–1970.

Source: **Series Y 493–497**, U.S. Department of the Treasury, *Statistical Appendix to Annual Report of the Secretary of the Treasury, 1970*, pp. 60–61. **Series Y 498–499**, 1855 and 1892–1915, U.S. Bureau of Foreign and Domestic Commerce, *Statistical Abstract of the United States, 1921*, p. 829; 1856–1891 and 1916–1970, U.S. Department of the Treasury, *Annual Report, 1891*, p. XCIV, *1946*, p. 546, and *Statistical Appendix, 1970*, pp. 220–221. **Series Y 500–504**, 1880–1915, U.S. Department of the Treasury, unpublished data; 1916–1970, *Annual Report, 1946*, p. 459, *1958*, pp. 472–473, *1967*, p. 506, and *Statistical Appendix, 1970*, p. 66.

The total public debt (series Y 493) as reported at the end of each fiscal period is essentially the formal funded debt of the Federal Government, both long-term and short-term. It includes savings bonds at current redemption value. It differs from gross Federal debt (series Y 488) in that public debt represents borrowing by the Department of the Treasury; gross Federal debt also includes borrowing by Federal agencies. (The Federal agency debt outstanding at the end of fiscal 1970 was $12.5 billion.)

Studies by Paul B. Trescott and others have suggested that the debt totals (series Y 493) as compiled by the Treasury Department for the early years of the Republic—1791 into the early 1800's—may omit obligations incurred otherwise than by the issuance of Treasury obligations and may include some contingent liabilities that would be excluded by the definitions adopted in later years. (Trescott, unpublished memoranda; see also Paul Studenski and Herman E. Krooss, *Financial History of the United States*, McGraw-Hill, New York, 1952, p. 3, footnote 1.) See also text for series Y 335–338.

Although nearly all the public debt is interest-bearing, the total includes some obligations that bear no interest and matured debt on which interest has ceased. In recent years, a substantial part of the public debt has been held in the trust funds and other Treasury investment accounts. (For the ownership of Federal public debt securities at several dates for 1960–1970, see the *Annual Report of the Secretary of the Treasury, 1970*, p. 14, and *Statistical Appendix* (ibid.), p. 230.) Certain unfunded obligations of the Government are not counted in the public debt—for example, a potential obligation of the Government for unpaid employer contributions to the civil service retirement and disability fund.

The formal concept of "the public debt," as used in Federal fiscal reports, appears to have emerged following initial enactment of a statutory ceiling on the debt of the Federal Government. Such a ceiling was first provided in the Second Liberty Bond Act of 1917; prior to May 26, 1938, the limitation applied to particular segments of the debt, not to the total. The debt ceiling has been modified from time to time in subsequent legislation. For a tabular summary of the debt limit legislation, 1917–1970, see *Statistical Appendix to Annual Report of the Secretary of the Treasury, 1970*, p. 108. See also Marshall A. Robinson, *The National Debt Ceiling, An Experiment in Fiscal Policy*, The Brookings Institute, Washington, D.C., 1959.

Despite the close relationship of "the public debt" (series Y 493) to the debt limitation, series Y 493 includes a relatively small amount of obligations not subject to statutory limitations. Robinson, cited above, points out (p. 8) that "the Federal debt is part of a larger structure of Federal Government obligations.... The legally defined gross Federal debt ... is the debt that falls under the debt limitation, and it is what general usage calls the national debt." For a rough estimate of some additional obligations not included in "total gross debt," see a compilation by the Comptroller General of the United States, in *Investigation of the Financial Condition of the United States: Hearings Before the Senate Committee on Finance*, 85th Congress, 1st session, vol. 1, June 26, 1957, pp. 81–82, 269.

Various writers have contended that the most meaningful measure of the national debt in economic terms is "debt owed to the public." "Debt held by the public," series Y 490, closely corresponds to this concept, which includes Federal agency as well as Treasury (public) debt issues.

The computed annual interest charge, series Y 498, represents the amount of interest that would be paid if each interest-bearing issue outstanding at the end of the year should remain outstanding for a year at the applicable annual rate of interest. The charge is computed for each issue by applying the appropriate annual interest rate to the amount outstanding on that date. The aggregate charge is the total of the computed amounts for all interest-bearing issues. The average annual rate is computed by dividing the computed annual interest charge for the total of outstanding issues by the corresponding principal amount. Beginning December 31, 1958, the computed average rate is based upon the rate of effective yield for issues sold at premiums or discounts. Before that date the computed average rate was based upon the coupon rates of the securities.

Y 505–848. General note.

The concepts and terms used in these series were originally developed for the Bureau of the Census reporting on finances of State and local governments. These concepts have also been applied to Federal Government data to provide comparable comprehensive aggregates covering all levels of government.

For a full discussion of basic concepts and terminology and of the classifications of revenue and expenditure, see the source for years 1902–1967 for series Y 505–566, pp. 1–12. A few of the more important items are discussed here.

General revenue and general expenditure, as used in these series, refer to all sources or purposes other than certain specifically defined utility, liquor store, and insurance trust operations.

Intergovernmental revenue and intergovernmental expenditure refer to transactions between the Federal, State, and local governments. To avoid double counting, such transactions are netted out of aggregates comprising the groups of governments concerned. Transactions with governments of other countries are not defined as intergovernmental. The value of intergovernmental aid "in kind" (for example, commodities or other property given by the Federal Government to State or local government agencies) is not included in either intergovernmental or other revenue of the receiving government; the expenditures involved in granting such aid are included in direct expenditure of the granting government.

Besides intergovernmental aid "in kind," the following types of transactions between governments have not been isolated for special treatment as intergovernmental revenue or expenditure:

a. Contributions by local governments to State-administered retirement systems that cover their employees. These are included without distinction as part of the "current operation" expenditure of the local governments, and the receipts are included with State insurance trust revenue.

b. Interest paid or received on obligations of one government held by another government.

c. Transactions in which governments deal as ordinary suppliers and customers—e.g., in purchasing property, utility services, or supplies from one another.

Direct expenditure comprises all expenditure other than intergovernmental expenditure.

Since the data utilized for each individual government represent a consolidation of amounts from its various funds, payments between funds are eliminated for census reporting. Thus, a government employer contribution to a retirement fund it administers is not counted as expenditure, nor is the receipt of this contribution by the retirement fund considered revenue; only the payment out of the fund for retirement benefits is classified in the census tabulations as a governmental expenditure (in this particular illustration, an insurance trust expenditure).

The substantial amount of interest paid by the U.S. Treasury to the Federal insurance trust funds, which have all their reserves invested in Federal securities, is excluded from Federal interest expenditure and insurance trust revenue to avoid double counting in Federal financial aggregates. However, the principle of eliminating interfund transactions is not followed in the case of interest paid by a State or local government on any of its own securities held as an investment by insurance funds it administers—mainly because of the difficulty of identifying such transactions.

Y 505–566. Federal, State, and local government finances, 1902–1970.

Source: U.S. Bureau of the Census, 1902–1967, *Census of Governments, 1967*, vol. 6, No. 5, *Historical Statistics on Governmental Finances and Employment*; 1968–1970, *Governmental Finances in 1970–71*.

These data are a consolidation of data for the Federal Government in series Y 567–637 and for State and local governments in series Y 652–709. The amounts in these series are net of intergovernmental transactions between the Federal, State, and local governments.

Y 567–637. Federal Government finances, 1902–1970.

Source: See source for series Y 505–566.

The Bureau of the Census classification of Federal fiscal data was used in annual reports on *Governmental Finances* for the fiscal years 1952 through 1970. Derivation of the Federal Government data for earlier years is described on pp. 8–9 of *Historical Summary of Governmental Finances in the United States* (*Census of Governments: 1967*, vol. IV, No. 3).

The classification used by the Bureau of the Census for reporting State and local government finance statistics differs from the classification used in the U.S. Budget. Accordingly, it was necessary to recast U.S. Budget data. This involved not only (1) grouping of individual Federal receipt items and "budget expenditure" amounts for various agencies and appropriation items in accordance with the functional framework used for reporting of State and local government finances, but also (2) applying certain adjustments to Federal "budget receipts" and "budget expenditures" data in order to arrive at "revenue" and "expenditure" amounts, as reported here. These adjustments took account of the following major differences between these series:

(1) The financial transactions of government enterprises are included in Federal budget figures only to the extent of their net effect (plus or minus) upon budget expenditures; Census figures include gross revenue and expenditure of government enterprises (other than loan and investment transactions).

(2) Receipts from various enterprises or market-oriented Federal activities, from interest on loans the government has made, from sales of property or products, and from certain other reimbursements from non-Federal sources, as well as receipts from charges

for quarters and subsistence furnished to employees are treated in the Federal budget as offsets against expenditures and result in reducing Federal expenditure totals of related activities. For census purposes, these amounts are counted as revenue and added back to expenditure.

(3) Federal budget receipts and expenditures now include various financial transactions of trust funds which were excluded before fiscal 1967. Such transactions are included in census reporting of Federal revenue and expenditure, except for trust funds handled on an agency basis for State and local governments (e.g., the State accounts in the unemployment compensation fund, and District of Columbia funds).

(4) Although interfund and intragovernmental transactions are netted out of Federal budget totals, such transfer amounts are included in Federal figures for various receipts and expenditure categories. Census figures exclude such transfers.

(5) Federal budget expenditures include interest accrued but not paid during the fiscal year; census data on interest are on a disbursement basis.

(6) The net excess of loan disbursements or loan repayments of Federal loan accounts is added to expenditures or to receipts in developing budget totals. Such loan transactions are excluded from census reporting of Federal data.

In the 1967 Census of Governments reports, the introductory text includes detail for 1942–1967 for the census category, "National defense and international relations," showing how related items in Federal budget reports are regrouped in the Census of Governments classifications; and for 1902–1967, showing the census treatment of items grouped in Federal budget reports under "Veterans services and benefits." Other functional categories also differ from those shown for the Federal Government in series Y 335–471.

Federal Government indebtedness and the change in debt outstanding (series Y 601–604) correspond with "public debt" as reported by the U.S. Treasury. Consequently, series Y 601 is the same as series Y 493.

Y 638–651.   Federal grants to State and local governments, 1930–1970.

Source: U.S. Social Security Administration, *Social Security Bulletin*, September 1971, p. 16. These series were compiled from the following Department of the Treasury sources: *Annual Report of the Secretary of the Treasury*, 1939–1940 and 1946–1970, supplemented by Federal agency published and unpublished reports; 1941–1945, *Annual Report of the Secretary of the Treasury, Combined Statement of Receipts, Expenditures, and Balances of the United States Government* and agency reports.

The definition of Federal grants used in compiling these series differs from that used by the Treasury Department. These data are confined to grants for cooperative Federal-State or Federal-local programs administered at the State and/or local level and to those programs in which the bulk of the funds is channeled through agencies of State and local governments. Emergency grants and the value of grants-in-kind, such as surplus foods distributed domestically or Braille materials for the blind, are included when they conform to these criteria. Shared revenues and payments in lieu of taxes are excluded from series Y 638–651 although included in the Treasury series, as are programs in which the States or localities act solely as agents of the Federal Government. Loans are excluded by definition.

The categories of grants (health, education, etc.) follow the organization of programs in the Social Security Administration's social welfare expenditures series, with the addition of the "Highways" and "All other" groups. "All other" grants are often presented with further breakdown of "Urban affairs," "Agriculture and natural resources," and "Miscellaneous" grants. A detailed list of the grants programs in each group can be found in the source annual as well as

in the Federal grants article in the *Social Security Bulletin*, usually in the June issue.

Y 652–848.   State and local government finances, 1902–1970.

Source: See source for series Y 505–566.

Periodic surveys of State and local government finance began in 1850; for that year and 1860 the data were published in conjunction with reports of the population census. For 1870–1922, the State and local government data were reported at approximately decennial intervals under the title, *Wealth, Debt, and Taxation*; for 1932, as *Financial Statistics of State and Local Governments*; and for 1942, 1957, 1962, and 1967, as the *Census of Governments*.

Census Bureau statistics on governmental finances, as initially published, have been broadly comparable within the three periods: Pre-1937, 1937 to 1950, and 1951 and subsequent years, but are less directly comparable from one period to another. The financial statistics shown here for 1950 and earlier years are substantially taken from several earlier studies, by which the statistics for particular years, as originally published, were recast and supplemented to derive comprehensive data in terms of the basic classification pattern which has applied since 1951.

For a summary discussion of the periodic censuses and annual Census Bureau reporting on governmental finances, see Census of Governments, 1967, vol. 6, No. 5: *Historical Statistics on Governmental Finances and Employment*, pp. 6–12. That report, and the similar "Historical" reports from the 1962 and 1957 censuses on governments present comparable nationwide data, by level of government, for selected years back to 1902, outline data classification changes, discuss the development of historically consistent data, and cite key source documents. They also provide combined State-local figures, by State, for selected years back to 1942.

For financial statistics of the individual State and local governments in 1967, see the detailed reports of the *Census of Governments, 1967*, especially vol. 4, presenting a separate bulletin for each State area.

For financial statistics in detail for the individual State governments, see the annual compilation by the Bureau of the Census, *State Government Finances*, issued for 1942–1957, as *Compendium of State Government Finances*; and for 1915–1941, as *Financial Statistics of States*. There were no volumes for 1920 and for 1932–1936; partial data were published for 1921; and data for 1932 were collected for 41 States but were not compiled fully or published.

Reports for earlier years used systems different from those applied since 1951. Figures for individual States on the later reporting basis are available in Bureau of the Census, *Revised Summary of State Government Finances, 1942–1950*, (State and Local Government Special Studies No. 32, 1953).

For detail for individual large city governments, and in many years for every city with population above 25,000 or 30,000, see the annual compilations published by the Department of Labor for 1898–1901 and by the Bureau of the Census for 1902–1941 (with gaps for the years 1914 and 1920), as *Financial Statistics of Cities* (with early variations in title), for 1942–1957, as *Compendium of City Government Finances*, and since 1957, as *City Government Finances*. Prior to 1932, the city statistics covered cities of 30,000 inhabitants or more in the preceding decennial census. For 1932–1941, coverage was limited to cities of 100,000 or more; for 1942–1959, the population minimum was 25,000; and beginning 1960, a 50,000 minimum has been applied. Since 1956, nationwide aggregates have been published annually, including sample-based estimates for the smaller municipalities.

A series on county governments also was published for 1943–1946, following the inclusion of all county governments in the Census of Governments for 1942. The county series yielded nationwide aggregates of county transactions and individual statistics for large counties.

Series Y 272–289.　Public Employees, by Type of Government: 1940 to 1970

[In thousands.　As of October 31 except as noted]

Year	All governments	Federal [1] (civilian)	State and local — Total	State and local — Education	State and local — Other than education	State — Total	State — Education	State — Other than education	Local [2] — All local — Total	Local — All local — Education	Local — All local — Other than education	Local — Municipalities — Total	Local — Municipalities — Other than education	Local — Counties — Total	Local — Counties — Other than education	Local — School districts	Local — Townships and special districts — Total	Local — Townships and special districts — Other than education
	272	273	274	275	276	277	278	279	280	281	282	283	284	285	286	287	288	289
ALL EMPLOYEES																		
1970	13,028	2,881	10,147	5,297	4,850	2,755	1,182	1,573	7,392	4,115	3,277	2,244	1,815	1,229	949	3,316	604	513
1969	12,685	2,969	9,716	5,061	4,655	2,614	1,112	1,501	7,102	3,949	3,154	2,165	1,747	1,163	902	3,176	599	504
1968	12,342	2,984	9,358	4,829	4,530	2,495	1,037	1,458	6,864	3,792	3,072	2,112	1,714	1,151	881	3,028	573	477
1967	11,867	2,993	8,874	4,550	4,324	2,335	940	1,395	6,539	3,610	2,929	1,993	1,633	1,077	832	2,919	549	463
1966	11,388	2,861	8,527	4,313	4,214	2,211	866	1,344	6,316	3,447	2,869	1,971	1,613	1,043	805	2,850	543	452
1965	10,589	2,588	8,001	3,960	4,041	2,028	739	1,289	5,973	3,221	2,752	1,884	1,560	979	767	2,598	510	425
1964	10,064	2,528	7,536	3,674	3,862	1,873	656	1,217	5,663	3,018	2,645	1,817	1,514	936	737	2,436	474	395
1963	9,736	2,548	7,188	3,437	3,751	1,775	602	1,173	5,413	2,835	2,578	1,782	1,498	875	698	2,300	456	380
1962	9,388	2,539	6,849	3,224	3,625	1,680	555	1,126	5,169	2,670	2,499	1,696	1,434	862	686	2,161	449	379
1961	9,100	2,484	6,616	3,050	3,566	1,625	518	1,106	4,992	2,532	2,460	1,734	1,448	821	654	2,049	427	358
1960	8,808	2,421	6,387	2,918	3,469	1,527	474	1,053	4,860	2,444	2,416	1,692	1,439	788	571	1,921	581	494
1959 *	8,487	2,399	6,088	2,745	3,343	1,454	443	1,011	4,634	2,302	2,332	1,636	1,399	767	568	1,820	599	451
1958	8,297	2,405	5,892	2,589	3,303	1,408	406	1,002	4,484	2,183	2,302	1,594	1,369	738	564	1,752	549	406
1957 [3]	8,047	2,439	5,608	2,461	3,147	1,300	375	925	4,307	2,086	2,221	1,539	1,319	726	562	1,651	394	341
1956	7,685	2,410	5,275	2,283	2,992	1,268	353	915	4,007	1,930	2,077	1,485	1,277	674	530	1,533	318	270
1955	7,432	2,378	5,054	2,169	2,886	1,199	333	866	3,855	1,835	2,020	1,436	1,238	648	512	1,455	315	269
1954	7,232	2,373	4,859	2,050	2,809	1,149	310	839	3,710	1,740	1,970	1,420	1,220	628	497	1,365	297	254
1953	7,048	2,385	4,663	1,949	2,714	1,082	294	788	3,580	1,654	1,926	1,382	1,187	597	473	1,293	308	267
1952	7,105	2,583	4,522	1,872	2,649	1,060	293	768	3,461	1,580	1,881	1,341	1,154	573	454	1,234	312	273
1951	6,802	2,515	4,287	1,759	2,528	1,070	316	754	3,218	1,443	1,774	1,297	1,102	505	435	1,136	280	238
1950	6,402	2,117	4,285	1,723	2,562	1,057	312	745	3,228	1,411	1,817	1,311	1,106	500	429	1,102	317	282
1949	6,203	2,047	4,156	1,658	2,497	1,037	306	731	3,119	1,352	1,767	1,281	1,082	476	410	1,056	307	275
1948	6,042	2,076	3,966	1,581	2,385	963	286	677	3,002	1,295	1,707	1,249	1,039	469	406	986	298	263
1947	5,791	2,002	3,789	1,529	2,260	909	271	638	2,880	1,258	1,622	1,202	996	434	375	962	282	251
1946	6,001	2,434	3,567	1,457	2,110	804	233	572	2,762	1,224	1,539	1,155	955	417	361	934	257	223
1945	6,556	3,375	3,181	1,267	1,914			473			1,441		879		316			246
1944	6,537	3,365	3,172	1,311	1,861			456			1,405		855		329			221
1943	6,358	3,166	3,192	1,320	1,872			464			1,408		858		322			228
1942	5,915	2,664	3,251	1,320	1,931			503			1,428		872		333			223
1941	4,970	1,598	3,372	1,320	2,052			547			1,505		901		335			268
1940	4,474	1,128	3,346	1,320	2,026			551			1,475		887		345			242
FULL-TIME EQUIVALENT EMPLOYEES																		
1970	11,338	2,810	8,528	4,258	4,271	2,302	803	1,499	6,226	3,455	2,772	1,922		1,098		2,786	420	
1969	11,053	2,893	8,160	4,063	4,097	2,179	746	1,433	5,981	3,316	2,664	1,858		1,053		2,656	412	
1968	10,780	2,901	7,879	3,898	3,982	2,085	694	1,391	5,795	3,204	2,590	1,813		1,034		2,555	392	
1967	10,364	2,908	7,455	3,658	3,797	1,946	620	1,326	5,509	3,039	2,470	1,715	1,410	973	765	2,449	371	99
1966	10,030	2,767	7,263	3,543	3,720	1,864	575	1,289	5,399	(NA)	(NA)	1,701	(NA)	948	(NA)	2,369	381	(NA)
1965	9,489	2,552	6,937	3,337	3,600	1,751	508	1,243	5,186	2,829	2,357	1,638	(NA)	893	(NA)	2,287	368	(NA)
1964	(NA)	(NA)	6,586	3,132	3,454	1,639	460	1,179	4,947	2,671	2,275	1,584	(NA)	859	(NA)	2,164	341	(NA)
1963	(NA)	(NA)	6,282	2,948	3,334	1,558	422	1,136	4,724	2,526	2,198	1,549	(NA)	804	(NA)	2,056	315	(NA)
1962	8,428	2,470	5,958	2,730	3,228	1,478	390	1,088	4,480	2,340	2,140	1,486	1,259	784	634	1,901	309	246
1961	(NA)	(NA)	5,845	2,652	3,193	1,435	(NA)	(NA)	4,410	(NA)	(NA)	1,491	(NA)	760	(NA)	1,836	300	(NA)
1960	(NA)	(NA)	5,570	2,525	3,045	1,353	(NA)	(NA)	4,217	(NA)	(NA)	1,447	(NA)	728	(NA)	1,729	302	(NA)
1959	(NA)	(NA)	5,342	2,396	2,946	1,302	(NA)	(NA)	4,039	(NA)	(NA)	1,406	(NA)	703	(NA)	1,635	288	(NA)
1958	(NA)	(NA)	5,171	2,270	2,901	1,259	(NA)	(NA)	3,912	(NA)	(NA)	1,372	(NA)	678	(NA)	1,572	289	(NA)
1957 [3]	7,133	2,340	4,793	2,093	2,700	1,154	258	896	3,638	1,834	1,805	1,297	1,105	647	504	1,452	242	194
1956			4,687	2,032	2,655	1,136			3,551			1,292		632		1,415	213	
1955			4,487	1,935	2,552	1,081			3,406			1,252		604		1,341	209	
1954			4,309	1,826	2,483	1,024			3,284			1,234		587		1,264	199	
1953			4,126	1,737	2,389	966			3,160			1,200		561		1,197	203	
1952			4,012	1,678	2,334	958			3,054			1,175		538		1,146	196	
1951			3,815	1,577	2,238	973			2,843			1,145		458		1,060	179	
FULL-TIME EMPLOYEES ONLY																		
1951			3,643			903			2,740	1,298	1,442	1,112	942	442	375	1,024	161	125
1950			3,472			841			2,630	1,258	1,372	1,066	889	418	351	985	162	
1949			3,376			822			2,554	1,216	1,338	1,043	871	400	337	953	157	
1948			3,192			756			2,437	1,161	1,276	1,018	837	375	314	889	156	
1947			3,044			708			2,336	1,134	1,202	973	796	353	297	873	137	
1946			2,825			623			2,202	1,091	1,111	920	754	328	274	842	112	
1945											1,026		685		251			
1944											1,019		673		254			
1943											1,013		669		252			
1942											1,023		679		253			
1941											1,060		699		264			
1940											1,043		687		260			

* Denotes first year for which figures include Alaska and Hawaii.
NA Not available.
[1] Includes Federal civilian employees outside continental United States.　Prior to 1953, figures are as of September 30.

[2] Local government data, except for 1967, 1962, and 1957, are subject to sampling variation.
[3] As of April 30.

Series Y 290-307.　Government Monthly Payrolls, by Type of Government: 1940 to 1970

[In millions of dollars.　For October except as noted]

Year	All govern- ments	Fed- eral [1] (civi- lian)	State and local			State			Local [2]									
									All local			Municipalities		Counties		School districts	Townships and special districts	
			Total	Educa- tion	Other than educa- tion	Total	Educa- tion	Other than educa- tion	Total	Educa- tion	Other than educa- tion	Total	Other than educa- tion	Total	Other than educa- tion		Total	Other than educa- tion
	290	291	292	293	294	295	296	297	298	299	300	301	302	303	304	305	306	307
ALL EMPLOYEES																		
1970	8,334.2	2,427.9	5,906.4	3,169.7	2,736.1	1,612.1	630.2	981.8	4,294.2	2,539.4	1,754.8	1,360.7	1,061.7	639.5	490.4	2,031.7	262.3	202.5
1969	7,587.6	2,335.3	5,252.3	2,830.6	2,421.7	1,430.5	554.4	876.0	3,821.7	2,276.1	1,545.6	1,195.6	930.7	571.6	433.7	1,816.3	238.2	181.3
1968	6,889.2	2,137.3	4,751.9	2,544.8	2,207.1	1,256.6	477.0	779.6	3,495.2	2,067.7	1,427.5	1,097.1	868.3	531.8	394.0	1,644.0	222.4	173.4
1967	6,055.5	1,842.3	4,213.2	2,244.0	1,969.2	1,105.5	406.3	699.3	3,107.7	1,837.8	1,270.0	971.5	768.9	465.4	352.2	1,475.0	195.8	148.7
1966	5,463.0	1,664.8	3,798.2	2,020.2	1,777.9	975.2	353.0	622.2	²2,823.0	1,677.1	1,155.7	891.7	703.3	414.4	313.1	1,332.9	184.0	139.3
1965	4,884.0	1,483.7	3,400.3	1,777.7	1,622.5	849.2	290.1	559.1	2,551.1	1,487.7	1,063.4	818.2	648.6	377.3	288.1	1,188.6	167.0	126.6
1964	4,572.4	1,475.2	3,097.2	1,607.9	1,489.3	761.1	257.5	503.6	2,336.1	1,350.4	985.7	760.5	606.7	345.5	264.8	1,079.9	150.3	114.1
1963	4,263.5	1,423.2	2,840.3	1,463.8	1,376.6	696.4	230.1	466.3	2,143.9	1,233.6	910.3	707.9	569.5	311.2	240.8	992.3	132.6	99.9
1962	3,966.2	1,346.9	2,619.3	1,325.1	1,294.2	634.6	201.8	432.8	1,984.7	1,123.3	861.4	662.3	534.0	295.4	229.0	899.3	127.7	98.5
1961	3,633.5	1,213.6	2,419.9	1,204.6	1,215.3	586.2	177.0	409.2	1,833.7	1,027.6	806.1	630.4	501.7	272.2	211.6	811.6	120.0	92.8
1960 *	3,332.8	1,117.8	2,215.0	1,095.0	1,120.0	524.1	151.2	372.9	1,690.9	943.9	747.0	583.4	470.5	249.4	197.9	735.4	117.9	(NA)
1959 *	3,114.4	1,072.7	2,041.7	999.3	1,042.4	485.4	139.2	346.2	1,556.3	860.0	696.3	547.9	446.0	229.1	(NA)	669.5	108.9	(NA)
1958	2,977.2	1,091.4	1,885.8	905.7	980.1	446.5	121.5	325.0	1,439.3	784.1	655.2	511.2	417.8	212.8	(NA)	618.2	104.6	(NA)
1957 ⁴	2,533.1	918.6	1,614.5	757.8	856.7	372.5	95.2	277.3	1,242.0	662.5	579.5	461.0	375.9	184.3	142.4	520.1	76.6	61.2
1956	2,509.4	943.7	1,565.7	734.3	831.4	366.5	93.1	273.4	1,199.2	641.2	558.0	450.0	365.4	176.4	138.4	503.7	69.0	54.2
1955	2,264.5	845.7	1,418.8	661.7	757.1	325.9	83.0	242.9	1,092.9	578.7	514.2	413.8	336.8	161.8	126.2	453.3	64.0	51.0
1954	2,103.1	784.8	1,318.3	600.0	718.2	300.7	73.4	227.3	1,017.5	526.7	490.8	396.2	324.4	151.7	118.9	409.9	59.7	47.6
1953	2,013.6	793.1	1,220.5	552.0	668.5	278.6	68.6	210.0	941.9	483.3	458.6	367.6	301.1	140.6	110.5	376.0	57.8	46.9
1952	1,979.6	855.9	1,123.7	502.9	620.8	260.3	65.0	195.3	863.4	437.8	425.6	345.0	282.7	123.9	97.0	338.9	55.7	45.8
1951	1,865.4	857.4	1,008.0	452.5	555.5	245.8	68.1	177.7	762.3	384.5	377.8	314.9	253.9	101.3	86.1	298.6	47.5	37.8
1950	1,527.9	613.4	914.6	409.4	505.2	218.4	61.0	157.4	696.2	348.4	347.8	290.0	230.2	92.5	78.7	267.1	46.7	39.0
1949	1,406.0	539.2	866.7	384.8	481.9	209.8	58.5	151.3	656.9	326.3	330.6	277.2	219.7	86.4	73.6	249.2	44.3	37.3
1948	1,329.0	533.9	795.1	353.0	442.0	184.9	50.9	134.0	610.1	302.1	308.0	266.0	206.2	78.1	66.6	223.4	42.6	35.2
1947	1,183.7	481.4	702.3	318.5	383.7	160.8	44.8	116.0	541.5	273.7	267.7	236.3	181.2	68.4	58.1	202.0	34.8	28.4
1946	1,155.5	571.5	584.0	260.1	323.9	128.0	34.6	93.5	456.0	225.6	230.4	205.8	160.0	58.4	50.7	166.4	25.4	19.8
1945	1,109.9	642.3	467.6	200.0	267.6			72.9			194.7		133.2		42.6			19.0
1944	1,103.0	684.8	418.2	172.2	246.0			64.2			181.8		125.0		39.4			17.4
1943	1,084.4	672.7	411.7	175.7	236.0			64.0			172.0		119.3		36.9			15.7
1942	880.2	486.1	394.1	175.4	218.7			59.5			159.2		109.7		34.5			14.9
1941	649.4	254.1	395.3	175.4	219.9			62.1			157.8		108.4		34.5			14.8
1940	565.8	177.0	388.8	175.3	213.5			58.8			154.7		104.9		34.3			15.5
FULL-TIME EMPLOYEES ONLY [5]																		
1970			5.597,6	2,933.6	2,664.0	1,508.5			4,089.1			1,312.4		617.7		1,912.6	246.4	
1969			4,977.5	2,624.6	2,352.9	1,339.9			3,637.6			1,154.8		550.5		1,709.8	122.6	
1968			4,504.9	2,366.7	2,138.2	1,177.6			3,327.4			1,059.3		510.7		1,549.6	207.8	
1967			4,007.0	2,097.8	1,909.1	1,035.9	354.2	681.8	2,971.0	1,743.6	1,227.4	942.3	749.1	449.3	341.3	1,396.8	182.5	41.9
1966			3,622.5	1,908.4	1,713.7	909.6	(NA)	(NA)	2,712.8	(NA)	(NA)	858.6	(NA)	400.5	(NA)	1,284.1	169.6	(NA)
1965			3,250.5	1,682.7	1,567.8	803.2	(NA)	(NA)	2,447.3	(NA)	(NA)	787.6	(NA)	364.4	(NA)	1,140.7	154.6	(NA)
1962 *			2,506.1	1,253.5	1,252.7	602.5	179.9	422.6	1,903.7	1,073.6	830.1	641.1	518.4	284.9	221.7	859.6	118.1	90.0
1957 ⁴			1,543.8	717.3	826.5	369.9	98.4	271.5	1,173.9	619.0	554.9	445.2	365.0	160.8	134.9	498.2	69.7	54.9
1956			1,514.0	707.8	806.2	366.1	99.0	267.2	1,147.9	608.9	539.0	437.8	355.8	157.1	134.1	489.5	63.5	49.1
1955			1,371.5	638.0	733.5	326.4	89.6	236.9	1,045.0	548.5	496.6	402.7	328.0	143.7	122.6	439.9	58.6	46.0
1954			1,268.0	575.6	692.4	296.1	77.7	218.5	971.8	497.9	473.9	385.8	316.3	134.0	114.9	397.7	54.3	42.7
1953			1,172.6	529.3	643.2	274.2	73.3	200.9	898.3	456.0	442.3	357.0	293.1	123.8	106.8	364.5	52.9	42.4
1952			1,078.5	482.2	596.3	254.0	67.5	186.4	824.5	414.6	409.9	335.5	275.4	109.4	93.1	328.8	50.8	41.4
1951			962.7	433.8	528.9	228.1	60.8	167.4	734.6	373.1	361.5	305.9	245.4	97.7	82.6	288.4	42.7	33.5

* Denotes first year for which figures include Alaska and Hawaii.
NA　Not available.
¹ Federal payroll figures represent pay for the number of working days in month specified.　Thus, changes in amount of payroll reflect in part differences in number of working days covered.　Prior to 1953, data are for the month of September.

² Local government data, except for 1967, 1962, and 1957, are subject to sampling variation.
³ Revised total figure; revised figures for detail not available.
⁴ Data are for the month of April.
⁵ Data are not available for any of the series for 1958–1961 and 1962–1963.

Series Y 308–317. Paid Civilian Employment of the Federal Government: 1816 to 1970

[As of June 30 except as noted]

Year	Employees			Competitive civil service employees (classified)	Executive branch				Legislative branch	Judicial branch [4]
	Total [1]	Washington, D.C. [2]	All other areas		Total	Defense [3]	Post Office	Other		
	308	309	310	311	312	313	314	315	316	317
1970	2,981,574	327,369	2,654,205	2,453,292	2,943,818	1,219,125	741,216	983,477	30,869	6,887
1969	3,076,414	328,077	2,748,337	2,549,506	3,040,129	1,341,587	739,002	959,540	29,577	6,708
1968	3,055,212	329,879	2,725,333	2,569,752	3,019,976	1,316,977	730,977	972,022	28,675	6,561
1967	3,002,461	318,609	2,683,852	2,485,863	2,967,964	1,302,605	716,603	948,756	28,178	6,319
1966	2,759,019	299,429	2,459,590	2,367,100	2,726,144	1,138,126	675,423	912,595	26,908	5,967
1965	2,527,915	279,997	2,247,918	2,154,992	2,496,064	1,033,775	595,512	866,777	25,947	5,904
1964	2,500,503	269,993	2,230,510	2,153,658	2,469,645	1,029,756	585,313	854,576	25,048	5,810
1963	2,527,960	266,737	2,261,223	2,164,163	2,497,699	1,050,007	587,161	860,531	24,523	5,738
1962	2,514,197	257,350	2,256,847	2,159,050	2,484,655	1,069,543	588,477	826,635	23,974	5,568
1961	2,435,804	246,266	2,189,538	2,096,635	2,407,025	1,042,407	582,447	782,171	23,621	5,158
1960	2,398,704	239,873	2,158,831	2,050,938	2,370,826	1,047,120	562,868	760,838	22,886	4,992
1959	2,382,807	234,358	2,148,449	2,042,034	2,355,054	1,078,178	549,951	726,925	22,853	4,900
1958	2,382,491	230,271	2,152,220	2,032,944	2,355,292	1,097,095	538,416	719,781	22,347	4,852
1957	2,417,565	236,330	2,181,235	2,067,285	2,390,561	1,160,915	521,198	708,448	22,340	4,664
1956	2,398,736	232,707	2,166,029	2,042,007	2,372,266	1,179,836	508,587	683,843	22,115	4,355
1955	2,397,309	231,873	2,165,436	2,004,853	2,371,462	1,186,580	511,613	673,269	21,711	4,136
1954	2,407,676	228,501	2,179,175	1,992,057	2,381,659	1,208,892	507,135	665,632	21,972	4,045
1953	2,558,416	242,678	2,315,738	2,138,899	2,532,150	1,332,068	506,555	693,527	22,312	3,954
1952	2,600,612	261,569	2,339,043	2,247,692	2,574,132	1,337,095	507,779	729,258	22,517	3,963
1951	2,482,666	265,980	2,216,686	2,144,882	2,455,901	1,235,498	482,281	738,122	22,835	3,930
1950	1,960,708	223,312	1,737,396	1,656,803	1,934,040	753,149	484,679	696,212	22,896	3,772
1949	2,102,109	225,901	1,876,208	1,771,927	2,075,148	879,875	501,743	693,530	23,382	3,579
1948	2,071,009	214,544	1,856,465	1,707,220	2,043,981	870,962	474,911	698,108	23,551	3,477
1947	2,111,001	213,515	1,897,486	1,692,065	2,082,258	859,142	445,683	777,433	25,669	3,074
1946	2,696,529	242,263	2,454,266	------------	2,665,520	1,416,225	453,953	795,342	27,946	3,063
1945	3,816,310	264,770	3,551,540	------------	3,786,645	2,634,575	416,314	735,756	26,959	2,706
1944	3,332,356	276,758	3,055,598	------------	3,304,379	2,246,454	374,758	683,167	25,314	2,663
1943	3,299,414	284,665	3,014,749	------------	3,273,887	2,200,064	339,005	734,818	22,903	2,624
1942	2,296,384	276,352	2,020,032	------------	2,272,082	1,291,093	338,090	642,899	21,657	2,645
1941	1,437,682	190,588	1,247,094	990,233	1,416,444	556,073	335,008	525,363	18,712	2,526
1940	1,042,420	139,770	902,650	726,895	1,022,853	256,025	323,481	443,347	17,099	2,468
1939	953,891	129,314	824,577	662,832	935,797	195,997	314,478	425,322	15,802	2,292
1938	882,226	120,744	761,482	562,909	864,534	163,457	311,440	389,637	15,609	2,083
1937	895,993	117,020	778,973	532,073	878,214	160,737	304,852	412,625	15,609	2,170
1936	867,432	122,937	744,495	498,725	850,395	148,369	281,314	420,712	14,976	2,061
1935	780,582	108,673	671,909	455,229	765,712	147,188	275,483	343,041	12,970	1,900
1934	698,649	94,244	604,405	450,592	685,108	133,092	281,770	270,246	11,667	1,874
1933	603,587	70,261	533,326	456,096	590,984	101,228	286,935	202,821	10,847	1,756
1932	605,496	73,455	532,041	467,161	592,560	100,420	296,136	196,004	11,159	1,777
1931	609,746	76,303	533,443	468,050	596,745	107,980	297,159	191,606	11,192	1,809
1930	601,319	73,032	528,287	462,083	588,951	103,462	297,895	187,594	10,620	1,748
1929	579,559	68,266	511,293	445,957	567,721	103,098	295,695	168,928	10,240	1,598
1928	560,772	65,506	495,266	431,763	549,238	94,005	293,023	162,210	9,894	1,640
1927	547,127	63,814	483,313	422,998	535,599	85,717	291,249	158,633	9,848	1,680
1926	548,713	64,722	483,991	422,300	537,251	92,208	288,573	156,470	9,742	1,720
1925	553,045	67,563	485,482	423,538	541,792	94,772	284,550	162,470	9,493	1,760
1924	543,484	68,000	475,484	415,593	532,048	92,331	279,679	160,038	9,636	1,800
1923	536,900	70,062	466,838	411,398	525,746	94,001	268,951	162,794	9,314	1,840
1922	543,507	73,645	469,862	420,688	532,210	107,126	260,100	164,984	9,417	1,880
1921 [5]	561,142	82,416	478,726	448,112	550,020	138,293	251,300	160,427	9,202	1,920
1920 [5]	655,265	94,110	561,155	497,603	645,408	237,212	242,400	165,796	7,897	1,960
1919 [6]	794,271	106,073	688,198	592,961	784,180	(NA)	(NA)	(NA)	8,091	2,000
1918	854,500	120,835	733,665	642,432	844,480	(NA)	(NA)	(NA)	7,980	2,040
1917	438,500	48,313	390,187	326,899	429,727	91,982	215,883	121,862	6,693	2,080
1916	399,381	41,804	357,577	296,926	391,133	63,395	212,215	115,523	6,128	2,120
1915	395,429	41,281	354,148	292,291	387,294	58,286	212,012	116,996	5,975	2,160
1914	401,887	40,016	361,871	292,460	393,555	57,989	212,973	122,593	6,132	2,200
1913	396,494	38,975	257,519	282,597	388,217	55,476	213,103	119,638	6,037	2,240
1912	400,150	38,555	361,595	217,392	391,918	60,015	214,770	117,133	5,942	2,290
1911	395,905	39,782	356,123	227,657	387,673	60,283	211,546	115,844	5,902	2,330
1910	388,708	38,911	349,797	222,278	380,428	58,320	209,005	113,103	5,910	2,370
1909	372,379	35,936	336,443	234,940	364,078	54,425	205,360	104,293	5,891	2,410
1908	356,754	34,647	322,107	206,637	348,479	50,665	199,904	97,910	5,825	2,450
1907	------------	------------	------------	194,323	------------	------------	------------	------------	------------	------------
1906				184,178						
1905				171,807	------------	------------	------------	------------	------------	------------
1904				154,093						
1903				135,453						
1902				107,990						
1901	239,476	28,044	211,432	106,205	231,056	44,524	136,192	50,340	5,690	2,730

See footnotes at end of table.

Series Y 308–317. Paid Civilian Employment of the Federal Government: 1816 to 1970—Con.

[As of June 30 except as noted]

Year	Employees			Competitive civil service employees (classified)	Executive branch				Legislative branch	Judicial branch [4]
	Total [1]	Washington, D.C. [2]	All other areas		Total	Defense [3]	Post Office	Other		
	308	309	310	311	312	313	314	315	316	317
1900				94,893						
1899				93,144						
1898				89,306						
1897				85,886						
1896				87,044						
1895				54,222						
1894				45,821						
1893				43,915						
1892				37,523						
1891	157,442	20,834	136,608	33,873	150,844	20,561	95,449	34,834	3,867	2,731
1890				30,626						
1889				29,650						
1888				22,577						
1887 [7]				19,345						
1886 [8]				17,273						
1885 [9]				15,590						
1884 [10]				13,780						
1881	100,020	13,124	86,896		94,679	16,297	56,421	21,961	2,579	2,762
1871	51,020	6,222	44,798		50,155	1,183	36,696	12,276	618	247
1861	36,672	2,199	34,473		36,106	946	30,269	4,891	393	173
1851	26,274	1,533	24,741		25,713	403	21,391	3,919	384	177
1841	18,038	1,014	17,024		17,550	598	14,290	2,662	332	156
1831	11,491	666	10,825		11,067	377	8,764	1,926	289	135
1821	6,914	603	6,311		6,526	161	4,766	1,599	252	136
1816	4,837	535	4,302		4,479	190	3,341	938	243	115

NA Not available.
[1] Excludes employees of the Central Intelligence Agency and the National Security Agency.
[2] Data prior to June 1941 relate to District of Columbia only. Beginning July 1941, Alexandria city, Arlington County, and part of Fairfax County, Va. were added; parts of Montgomery and Prince Georges Counties, Md. were also added. Beginning 1950, all of Fairfax County, Va. and all of Montgomery and Prince Georges Counties, Md. are included. Beginning 1952, Falls Church city, Va. is included. Beginning 1965, Fairfax city, Va. is included. Beginning 1968, Loudoun and Prince William Counties, Va. are included.

[3] Prior to 1947, War and Navy Departments; beginning 1881, includes mechanics and other workmen at army arsenals and navy yards.
[4] Estimated for 1908–1928.
[5] As of July 31.
[6] As of Nov. 11.
[7] Jan. 16, 1886–June 30, 1887.
[8] Jan. 16, 1885–Jan. 15, 1886.
[9] Jan. 16, 1884–Jan. 15, 1885.
[10] July 16, 1883–Jan. 15, 1884.

Series Y 318–331. Paid Civilian Employment in Full-Time Positions in the Federal Government: 1948 to 1970

[As of June 30 except as noted. Excludes employees of Congress and Federal courts, maritime seamen of Department of Commerce, and small number for whom rates were not reported]

Year	Employees (thousands)							Average pay (dollars) [2]						
	Total	Classification Act of 1949			Wage system [1]	Postal Pay Act	Other	Total	Classification Act of 1949			Wage system	Postal Pay Act	Other
		Total	General schedule [1]	Crafts, protective, and custodial schedule [1]					Total	General schedule	Crafts, protective, and custodial schedule			
	318	319	320	321	322	323	324	325	326	327	328	329	330	331
1970	2,806	1,287		674		673	172	9,234	11,065		6,976		8,120	8,741
1969	2,879	1,299		746		657	178	7,980	9,367		6,249		7,343	7,461
1968	2,867	1,302		737		639	190	7,426	8,654		5,835		6,932	6,857
1967	2,784	1,252		757		605	170	7,014	8,148		5,538		6,574	6,805
1966	2,574	1,189		681		570	135	6,920	7,904		5,508		6,437	7,426
1965	2,398	1,112		621		534	131	6,868	7,707		5,887		6,219	7,032
1964	2,370	1,090		627		524	130	6,479	7,293		5,530		5,889	6,618
1963	2,387	1,084		658		521	125	6,149	6,808		5,358		5,744	6,298
1962	2,372	1,058		676		517	120	5,739	6,286		5,202		5,283	5,907
1961	2,291	1,007		663		503	118	5,664	6,216		5,086		5,292	5,775
1960	2,237	973		667		483	114	5,273	5,705		4,935		4,854	5,344
1959	2,239	970		688		474	107	5,165	5,611		4,742		4,837	5,292
1958	2,231	962		700		461	108	5,031	5,510		4,531		4,808	4,945
1957	2,272	971		747		447	108	4,540	4,848		4,275		4,326	4,490
1956	2,264	950		768		441	106	4,398	4,749		4,012		4,330	4,331
1955	2,255	993		731		434	97	4,250	4,602		3,790		4,196	4,356
1954	2,214	975		711		434	95	4,047	4,225		3,862		3,955	4,022
1953	2,344	1,014		803		431	97	3,937	4,144		3,685		3,916	3,942
1952	2,379	1,076		851		352	100	3,775	4,043		3,350		4,002	3,718
1951	2,121	1,005	886	119	719	348	49	3,481	3,596	3,700	2,814	3,245	3,523	4,302
1950	1,628	801	702	99	430	362	35	3,504	3,667	3,788	2,807	3,133	3,488	4,502
1949 [3]	1,702	817	711	106	490	349	43	3,283	3,407	3,524	2,624	3,025	3,257	4,149
1948	1,639	794	691	103	473	328	40	2,928	3,027	3,140	2,267	2,757	2,839	3,843

[1] Beginning 1956, under amended Classification Act of 1949, approximately ⅓ of CPC employees were classified under General Schedule, and ⅔ were classified under Wage Boards.

[2] Arithmetic means based on annual rates and other rates converted to annual equivalents.
[3] Data as of July 1.

Series Y 332–334. State and Local Government Employment: 1929 to 1970

[In thousands. Excludes nominal employees. Estimated monthly average]

Year	Total 332	School 333	Other functions 334	Year	Total 332	School 333	Other functions 334	Year	Total 332	School 333	Other functions 334
1970	9,830	5,108	4,722	1955	4,727	2,101	2,626	1940	3,206	1,327	1,879
1969	¹9,444	4,917	¹4,528	1954	4,563	2,005	2,558	1939	3,090	1,293	1,797
1968	9,109	4,693	4,416	1953	4,340	1,893	2,447	1938	3,054	1,265	1,789
1967	8,679	4,445	4,234	1952	4,188	1,787	2,402	1937	2,923	1,231	1,692
1966	8,227	4,150	4,077	1951	4,087	1,712	2,375	1936	2,842	1,198	1,644
1965	7,696	3,782	3,914	1950	4,098	1,680	2,418	1935	2,728	1,174	1,554
1964	7,248	3,515	3,733	1949	3,948	1,620	2,328	1934	2,647	1,145	1,502
1963	6,868	3,295	3,573	1948	3,787	1,550	2,237	1933	2,601	1,144	1,457
1962	6,550	3,092	3,458	1947	3,582	1,499	2,083	1932	2,666	1.171	1,495
1961	6,315	2,942	3,373	1946	3,341	1,415	1,926	1931	2,704	1,184	1,520
1960	6,083	2,816	3,267	1945	3,137	1,380	1,757	1930	2,622	1,173	1,449
1959 *	5,850	2,670	3,180	1944	3,116	1,378	1,738	1929	2,532	1,143	1,389
1958	5,648	2,554	3,094	1943	3,174	1,388	1,786				
1957	5,399	2,436	2,963	1942	3,270	1,411	1,859				
1956	5,069	2,262	2,806	1941	3,320	1,392	1,928				

* Denotes first year for which figures include Alaska and Hawaii.

¹ Beginning 1969, approximately 39,000 civilian technicians of the National Guard were transferred from State to Federal status in accordance with Public Law 90–486.

Series Y 335–338. Summary of Federal Government Finances—Administrative Budget: 1789 to 1939

[In thousands of dollars. For 1789–1842, years ending December 31; 1844–1939, June 30; 1843 figures are for January 1–June 30]

Year	Budget receipts¹ 335	Budget expenditures² 336	Surplus or deficit³ (−) 337	Total public debt⁴ 338	Year	Budget receipts¹ 335	Budget expenditures² 336	Surplus or deficit³ (−) 337	Total public debt⁴ 338	Year or period	Budget receipts¹ 335	Budget expenditures² 336	Surplus or deficit³ (−) 337	Total public debt⁴ 338
1939	4,979,066	8,841,224	−3,862,158	40,439,532	1890	403,081	318,041	85,040	1,122,397	1840	19,480	24,318	−4,837	5,251
1938	5,588,012	6,764,628	−1,176,617	37,164,740	1889	387,050	299,289	87,761	1,249,471	1839	31,483	26,899	4,584	3,573
1937	4,955,613	7,733,033	−2,777,421	36,424,614	1888	379,266	267,925	111,341	1,384,632	1838	26,303	33,865	−7,562	10,434
1936	3,997,059	8,421,608	−4,424,549	33,778,543	1887	371,403	267,932	103,471	1,465,485	1837	24,954	37,243	−12,289	3,308
					1886	336,440	242,483	93,957	1,555,660	1836	50,827	30,868	19,959	337
1935	3,705,956	6,497,008	−2,791,052	28,700,893	1885	323,691	260,227	63,464	1,578,551	1835	35,430	17,573	17,857	38
1934	3,014,970	6,644,602	−3,629,632	27,053,141	1884	348,520	244,126	104,394	1,625,307	1834	21,792	18,628	3,164	38
1933	1,996,844	4,598,496	−2,601,652	22,538,673	1883	398,288	265,408	132,879	1,721,959	1833	33,948	23,018	10,931	4,760
1932	1,923,892	4,659,182	−2,735,290	19,487,002	1882	403,525	257,981	145,544	1,856,916	1832	31,866	17,289	14,577	7,012
1931	3,115,557	3,577,434	−461,877	16,801,281	1881	360,782	260,713	100,069	2,019,286	1831	28,527	15,248	13,279	24,322
1930	4,057,884	3,320,211	737,673	16,185,310	1880	333,527	267,643	65,884	2,090,909	1830	24,844	15,143	9,701	39,123
1929	3,861,589	3,127,199	734,391	16,931,088	1879	273,827	266,948	6,879	2,298,913	1829	24,828	15,203	9,624	48,565
1928	3,900,329	2,961,245	939,083	17,604,293	1878	257,764	236,964	20,800	2,159,418	1828	24,764	16,395	8,369	58,421
1927	4,012,794	2,857,429	1,155,365	18,511,907	1877	281,406	241,334	40,072	2,107,760	1827	22,966	16,139	6,827	67,475
1926	3,795,108	2,929,964	865,144	19,643,216	1876	294,096	265,101	28,995	2,130,846	1826	25,260	17,036	8,225	73,987
1925	3,640,805	2,923,762	717,043	20,516,194	1875	288,000	274,623	13,377	2,156,277	1825	21,841	15,857	5,984	81,054
1924	3,871,214	2,907,847	963,367	21,250,813	1874	304,979	302,634	2,345	2,159,933	1824	19,381	20,327	−945	83,788
1923	3,852,795	3,140,287	712,508	22,349,707	1873	333,738	290,345	43,393	2,151,210	1823	20,541	14,707	5,834	90,270
1922	4,025,901	3,289,404	736,496	22,963,382	1872	374,107	277,518	96,589	2,209,991	1822	20,232	15,000	5,232	90,876
1921	5,570,790	5,061,785	509,005	23,977,451	1871	383,324	292,177	91,147	2,322,052	1821	14,573	15,811	−1,237	93,547
1920	6,648,898	6,357,677	291,222	24,299,321	1870	411,255	309,654	101,602	2,436,453	1820	17,881	18,261	−380	89,987
1919	5,130,042	18,492,665	−13,362,623	25,484,506	1869	370,944	322,865	48,078	2,545,111	1819	24,603	21,464	3,140	91,016
1918	3,645,240	12,677,359	−9,032,120	12,455,225	1868	405,638	377,340	28,298	2,583,446	1818	21,585	19,825	1,760	95,530
1917	1,100,500	1,953,857	−853,357	2,975,619	1867	490,634	357,543	133,091	2,650,168	1817	33,099	21,844	11,255	103,467
1916	761,445	712,967	48,478	1,225,146	1866	558,033	520,809	37,223	2,755,764	1816	47,678	30,587	17,091	123,492
1915	683,417	746,093	−62,676	1,191,264	1865	333,715	1,297,555	−963,841	2,677,929	1815	15,729	32,708	−16,979	127,335
1914	725,117	725,525	−408	1,188,235	1864	264,627	865,323	−600,696	1,815,831	1814	11,182	34,721	−23,539	99,834
1913	714,463	714,864	−401	1,193,048	1863	112,697	714,741	−602,043	1,119,774	1813	14,340	31,682	−17,341	81,488
1912	692,609	689,881	2,728	1,193,839	1862	51,987	474,762	−422,774	524,178	1812	9,801	20,281	−10,480	55,963
1911	701,833	691,202	10,631	1,153,985	1861	41,510	66,547	−25,037	90,582	1811	14,424	8,058	6,365	45,210
1910	675,512	693,617	−18,105	1,146,940	1860	56,065	63,131	−7,066	64,844	1810	9,384	8,157	1,228	48,006
1909	604,320	693,744	−89,423	1,148,315	1859	53,486	69,071	−15,585	58,498	1809	7,773	10,281	−2,507	53,173
1908	601,862	659,196	−57,334	1,177,690	1858	46,655	74,185	−27,530	44,913	1808	17,061	9,932	7,128	57,023
1907	665,860	579,129	86,732	1,147,178	1857	68,965	67,796	1,170	28,701	1807	16,398	8,354	8,044	65,196
1906	594,984	570,202	24,782	1,142,523	1856	74,057	69,571	4,486	31,974	1806	15,560	9,804	5,756	69,218
1905	544,275	567,279	−23,004	1,132,357	1855	65,351	59,743	5,608	35,588	1805	13,561	10,506	3,054	75,723
1904	541,087	583,660	−42,573	1,136,259	1854	73,800	58,045	15,755	42,244	1804	11,826	8,719	3,107	82,312
1903	561,881	517,006	44,875	1,159,406	1853	61,587	48,184	13,403	59,805	1803	11,064	7,852	3,212	86,427
1902	562,478	485,234	77,244	1,178,031	1852	49,847	44,195	5,652	66,199	1802	14,996	7,862	7,134	77,055
1901	587,685	524,617	63,068	1,221,572	1851	52,559	47,709	4,850	68,305	1801	12,935	9,395	3,541	80,713
1900	567,241	520,861	46,380	1,263,417	1850	43,603	39,543	4,060	63,453	1800	10,849	10,786	63	83,038
1899	515,961	605,072	−89,112	1,436,701	1849	31,208	45,052	−13,844	63,062	1799	7,547	9,666	−2,120	82,976
1898	405,321	443,369	−38,047	1,232,743	1848	35,736	45,377	−9,641	47,045	1798	7,900	7,677	224	78,409
1897	347,722	365,774	−18,052	1,226,794	1847	26,496	57,281	−30,786	38,827	1797	8,689	6,134	2,555	79,229
1896	338,142	352,179	−14,037	1,222,729	1846	29,700	27,767	1,933	15,550	1796	8,378	5,727	2,651	82,064
1895	324,729	356,195	−31,466	1,096,913	1845	29,970	22,937	7,033	15,925	1795	6,115	7,540	−1,425	83,762
1894	306,355	367,525	−61,170	1,016,898	1844	29,321	22,338	6,984	23,462	1794	5,432	6,991	−1,559	80,748
1893	385,820	383,478	2,342	961,432	1843	8,303	11,858	−3,555	32,743	1793	4,653	4,482	171	78,427
1892	354,938	345,023	9,914	968,219	1842	19,976	25,206	−5,230	20,201	1792	3,670	5,080	−1,410	80,359
1891	392,612	365,774	26,839	1,005,807	1841	16,860	26,566	−9,706	13,594	1789–1791	4,419	4,269	150	77,228

¹ Excludes receipts from borrowing. Prior to 1913, total receipts; thereafter, net receipts (see text).

² Excludes debt repayment. Prior to 1913, total expenditures; thereafter, net expenditures (see text).

³ Receipts compared with expenditures.

⁴ As of end of period.

Series Y 339–342. Summary of Federal Government Finances: 1929 to 1970

[In billions of dollars. For years ending June 30. Data for 1929–1953 are consolidated cash statement figures; for 1954–1970, unified budget figures]

Year	Receipts	Outlays	Surplus or deficit (−)	Total gross Federal debt	Year	Receipts	Outlays	Surplus or deficit (−)	Total gross Federal debt	Year	Receipts	Outlays	Surplus or deficit (−)	Total gross Federal debt
	339	340	341	342		339	340	341	342		339	340	341	342
1970	193.7	196.6	−2.8	382.6	1955	65.5	68.5	−3.0	274.4	1940	6.9	9.6	−2.7	50.7
1969	187.8	184.5	3.2	367.1	1954	69.7	70.9	−1.2	270.8	1939	6.6	9.4	−2.9	48.2
1968	153.7	178.8	−25.2	369.8	1953	71.5	76.8	−5.3	266.0	1938	7.0	7.2	−.1	-------
1967	149.6	158.3	−8.7	341.3	1952	68.0	68.0	(Z)	259.1	1937	5.6	8.4	−2.8	-------
1966	130.9	134.7	−3.8	329.5	1951	53.4	45.8	7.6	255.3	1936	4.2	7.6	−3.5	-------
1965	116.8	118.4	−1.6	323.2	1950	40.9	43.1	−2.2	256.9	1935	3.8	6.3	−2.4	-------
1964	112.7	118.6	−5.9	316.8	1949	41.6	40.6	1.0	252.6	1934	3.1	6.5	−3.3	-------
1963	106.6	111.3	−4.8	310.8	1948	45.4	36.5	8.9	252.0	1933	2.1	4.7	−2.6	-------
1962	99.7	106.8	−7.1	303.3	1947	43.5	36.9	6.6	257.1	1932	2.0	4.8	−2.7	-------
1961	94.4	97.8	−3.4	292.9	1946	43.5	61.7	−18.2	271.0	1931	3.2	4.1	−1.0	-------
1960	92.5	92.2	.3	290.9	1945	50.2	95.2	−45.0	260.1	1930	4.0	3.1	.9	-------
1959	79.2	92.1	−12.9	287.8	1944	47.8	94.0	−46.1	204.1	1929	3.8	2.9	.9	-------
1958	79.6	82.6	−2.9	279.7	1943	25.1	78.9	−53.8	142.6					
1957	80.0	76.7	3.2	272.4	1942	15.1	34.5	−19.4	79.2					
1956	74.5	70.5	4.1	272.8	1941	9.2	14.0	−4.8	57.5					

Z Less than $50 million.

Series Y 343–351. Federal Government Receipts, by Source: 1940 to 1970

[In millions of dollars. As of June 30. Data for 1940–1953 are consolidated cash statement figures; for 1954–1970, unified budget data]

Years	Total	Customs	Individual income taxes	Corporation income taxes	Social insurance taxes and contributions	Excise taxes	Estate and gift taxes	Deposit of earnings of the Federal Reserve System	Other
	343	344	345	346	347	348	349	350	351
1970	193,743	2,430	90,412	32,829	45,298	15,705	3,644	3,266	158
1969	187,784	2,319	87,249	36,678	39,918	15,222	3,491	2,662	247
1968	153,671	2,038	68,726	28,665	34,622	14,079	3,051	2,091	400
1967	149,552	1,901	61,526	33,971	33,349	13,719	2,978	1,805	303
1966	130,856	1,767	55,446	30,073	25,567	13,062	3,066	1,713	162
1965	116,833	1,442	48,792	25,461	22,258	14,570	2,716	1,372	222
1964	112,662	1,252	48,697	23,493	22,012	13,731	2,394	947	138
1963	106,560	1,205	47,588	21,579	19,804	13,194	2,167	828	194
1962	99,676	1,142	45,571	20,523	17,046	12,534	2,016	718	125
1961	94,389	982	41,338	20,954	16,438	11,860	1,896	788	131
1960	92,492	1,105	40,741	21,494	14,684	11,676	1,606	1,093	94
1959	79,249	925	36,776	17,309	11,722	10,578	1,333	491	114
1958	79,636	782	34,724	20,074	11,239	10,638	1,393	664	122
1957	79,990	735	35,620	21,167	9,997	10,534	1,365	434	138
1956	74,547	682	32,188	20,880	9,323	9,929	1,161	287	97
1955	65,469	585	28,747	17,861	7,866	9,131	924	251	104
1954	69,719	542	29,542	21,101	7,210	9,945	934	341	104
1953	71,495	596	29,780	21,238	6,821	9,878	881	298	2,003
1952	68,011	533	27,918	21,226	6,496	8,852	818	278	1,890
1951	53,390	609	21,604	14,101	5,714	8,648	708	189	1,817
1950	40,940	407	15,747	10,449	4,386	7,550	698	192	1,511
1949	41,576	367	15,544	11,192	3,809	7,502	780	187	2,195
1948	45,357	403	19,310	9,678	3,966	7,356	890	100	3,654
1947	43,531	477	17,930	8,614	3,333	7,182	771	15	5,209
1946	43,537	424	16,132	12,235	3,078	6,646	668	----------	4,354
1945	50,162	341	18,396	16,360	3,438	5,893	637	----------	5,097
1944	47,818	417	20,179	15,255	3,428	4,379	507	----------	3,653
1943	25,097	308	6,473	9,587	3,013	3,769	441	----------	1,506
1942	15,104	369	3,238	4,740	2,429	3,121	420	----------	787
1941	9,202	365	1,589	1,849	2,004	2,386	403	----------	606
1940	6,879	331	1,110	978	1,715	1,844	353	----------	548

Series Y 352–357. Federal Government Receipts—Administrative Budget: 1789 to 1939

[In thousands of dollars. For 1789–1842, years ending December 31; 1844–1939, June 30; 1843 figures are for January 1–June 30]

Year or period	Total [1] (352)	Customs (353)	Internal revenue (354)	Other receipts: Total, excluding sales of public lands (355)	Other receipts: Sales of public lands (356)	Refunds, transfers, interfund transactions (357)
1939	4,979,066	318,837	5,161,221	187,765	248	−688,758
1938	5,588,012	359,187	5,674,318	208,156	96	−653,649
1937	4,955,613	486,357	4,597,140	210,094	71	−337,978
1936	3,997,059	386,812	3,512,852	216,293	74	−118,898
1935	3,705,956	343,353	3,277,690	179,424	87	−94,512
1934	3,014,970	313,434	2,640,604	161,516	99	−100,584
1933	1,996,844	250,750	1,604,424	224,523	103	−82,853
1932	1,923,892	327,755	1,561,006	116,964	170	−81,834
1931	3,115,557	378,354	2,429,781	381,504	230	−74,082
1930	4,057,884	587,001	3,039,295	551,646	396	−120,058
1929	3,861,589	602,263	2,938,019	492,968	315	−171,661
1928	3,900,329	568,986	2,794,971	678,391	385	−142,019
1927	4,012,794	605,500	2,869,414	654,480	621	−116,601
1926	3,795,108	579,430	2,837,639	545,686	754	−167,648
1925	3,640,805	547,561	2,589,176	643,412	624	−139,343
1924	3,871,214	545,638	2,795,157	671,250	522	−140,831
1923	3,852,795	561,929	2,624,473	820,734	657	−154,341
1922	4,025,901	356,443	3,213,253	539,408	895	−83,203
1921	5,570,790	308,564	4,596,426	719,943	1,530	−54,143
1920	6,648,898	322,903	5,405,032	966,631	1,910	−45,667
1919	5,130,042	184,458	4,315,285	652,514	1,405	−22,215
1918	3,645,240	179,998	3,186,034	298,550	1,969	−19,343
1917	1,100,500	225,962	809,366	88,996	1,893	−23,825
1916	761,445	213,186	512,702	56,647	1,888	−21,089
1915	683,417	209,787	415,670	72,455	2,167	−14,494
1914	725,117	292,320	380,041	62,312	2,572	−9,556
1913	714,463	318,891	344,417	60,803	2,910	−9,648
1912	692,609	311,322	321,612	59,675	5,393	
1911	701,833	314,497	322,529	64,807	5,732	
1910	675,512	333,683	289,934	51,895	6,356	
1909	604,320	300,712	246,213	57,396	7,701	
1908	601,862	286,113	251,711	64,038	9,732	
1907	665,860	332,233	269,667	63,960	7,879	
1906	594,984	300,252	249,150	45,582	4,880	
1905	544,275	261,799	234,096	48,380	4,859	
1904	541,087	261,275	232,904	46,908	7,453	
1903	561,881	284,480	230,810	46,591	8,926	
1902	562,478	254,445	271,880	36,153	4,144	
1901	587,685	238,585	307,181	41,919	2,965	
1900	567,241	233,165	295,328	38,748	2,837	
1899	515,961	206,128	273,437	36,395	1,678	
1898	405,321	149,575	170,901	84,846	1,243	
1897	347,722	176,554	146,689	24,479	865	
1896	338,142	160,022	146,763	31,358	1,006	
1895	324,729	152,159	143,422	29,149	1,103	
1894	306,355	131,819	147,111	27,426	1,674	
1893	385,820	203,355	161,028	21,437	3,182	
1892	354,938	177,453	153,971	23,514	3,262	
1891	392,612	219,522	145,686	27,404	4,030	
1890	403,081	229,669	142,607	30,806	6,358	
1889	387,050	223,833	130,882	32,336	8,039	
1888	379,266	219,091	124,297	35,878	11,202	
1887	371,403	217,287	118,823	35,293	9,254	
1886	336,440	192,905	116,806	26,729	5,631	
1885	323,691	181,472	112,499	29,720	5,706	
1884	348,520	195,067	121,586	31,866	9,811	
1883	398,288	214,706	144,720	38,861	7,956	
1882	403,525	220,411	146,498	36,617	4,753	
1881	360,782	198,160	135,264	27,358	2,202	
1880	333,527	186,522	124,009	22,995	1,017	
1879	273,827	137,250	113,562	23,016	925	
1878	257,764	130,171	110,582	17,012	1,080	
1877	281,406	130,956	118,630	31,820	976	
1876	294,096	148,072	116,701	29,323	1,129	
1875	288,000	157,168	110,007	20,825	1,414	
1874	304,979	163,104	102,410	39,465	1,852	
1873	333,738	188,090	113,729	31,919	2,882	
1872	374,107	216,370	130,642	27,094	2,576	
1871	383,324	206,270	143,098	33,955	2,389	
1870	411,255	194,538	184,900	31,817	3,350	
1869	370,944	180,048	158,356	32,539	4,020	
1868	405,638	164,465	191,088	50,086	1,349	
1867	490,634	176,418	266,028	48,189	1,164	
1866	558,033	179,047	309,227	69,759	665	
1865	333,715	84,928	209,464	39,322	997	
1864	264,627	102,316	109,741	52,569	588	
1863	112,697	69,060	37,641	5,997	168	
1862	51,987	49,056	−	2,931	152	
1861	41,510	39,582		1,928	871	
1860	56,065	53,188	−	2,877	1,779	
1859	53,486	49,566	−	3,921	1,757	
1858	46,655	41,790	−	4,866	3,514	
1857	68,965	63,876	−	5,089	3,829	
1856	74,057	64,023	−	10,034	8,918	
1855	65,351	53,026	−	12,325	11,497	
1854	73,800	64,224	−	9,576	8,471	
1853	61,587	58,932	−	2,655	1,667	
1852	49,847	47,339	−	2,507	2,043	
1851	52,559	49,018	−	3,542	2,352	
1850	43,603	39,669	−	3,935	1,860	
1849	31,208	28,347	−	2,861	1,689	
1848	35,736	31,757	(Z)	3,978	3,329	
1847	26,496	23,748	(Z)	2,748	2,498	
1846	29,700	26,713	3	2,984	2,694	
1845	29,970	27,528	4	2,438	2,077	
1844	29,321	26,184	2	3,136	2,060	
1843	8,303	7,047	(Z)	1,256	898	
1842	19,976	18,188	(Z)	1,788	1,336	
1841	16,860	14,487	3	2,370	1,366	
1840	19,480	13,500	2	5,979	3,293	
1839	31,483	23,138	3	8,342	7,076	
1838	26,303	16,159	2	10,141	3,082	
1837	24,954	11,169	5	13,779	6,776	
1836	50,827	23,410	(Z)	27,416	24,877	
1835	35,430	19,391	10	16,028	14,758	
1834	21,792	16,215	4	5,573	4,858	
1833	33,948	29,033	3	4,913	3,968	
1832	31,866	28,465	12	3,389	2,623	
1831	28,527	24,224	7	4,295	3,211	
1830	24,844	21,922	12	2,910	2,329	
1829	24,828	22,682	15	2,131	1,517	
1828	24,764	23,206	17	1,541	1,018	
1827	22,966	19,712	20	3,234	1,496	
1826	25,260	23,341	22	1,898	1,394	
1825	21,841	20,099	26	1,716	1,216	
1824	19,381	17,878	35	1,468	984	
1823	20,541	19,088	34	1,418	917	
1822	20,232	17,590	68	2,575	1,804	
1821	14,573	13,004	69	1,500	1,213	
1820	17,881	15,006	106	2,769	1,636	
1819	24,603	20,284	230	4,090	3,274	
1818	21,585	17,176	955	3,454	2,607	
1817	33,099	26,283	2,678	4,138	1,991	
1816	47,678	36,307	5,125	6,246	1,718	
1815	15,729	7,283	4,678	3,768	1,288	
1814	11,182	5,999	1,663	3,520	1,136	
1813	14,340	13,225	5	1,111	836	
1812	9,801	8,959	5	837	710	
1811	14,424	13,313	2	1,108	1,040	
1810	9,384	8,583	7	793	697	
1809	7,773	7,296	4	473	442	
1808	17,061	16,364	8	689	648	
1807	16,398	15,846	13	539	466	
1806	15,560	14,668	20	872	765	
1805	13,561	12,936	22	602	540	
1804	11,826	11,099	51	677	488	
1803	11,064	10,479	215	370	166	
1802	14,996	12,438	622	1,936	189	
1801	12,935	10,751	1,048	1,137	168	
1800	10,849	9,081	809	958	(Z)	
1799	7,547	6,610	779	157	−	
1798	7,900	7,106	644	150	12	
1797	8,689	7,550	575	564	84	
1796	8,378	6,568	475	1,334	5	
1795	6,115	5,588	338	188	----------	
1794	5,432	4,801	274	357	----------	
1793	4,653	4,255	338	60	----------	
1792	3,670	3,443	209	18	----------	
1789–1791	4,419	4,399	----------	19	----------	

− Represents zero.
Z Less than $500.

[1] Refunds of receipts are excluded starting in 1913; comparable data are not available for prior years. Certain interfund transactions are also excluded starting in 1932; for prior years, the amounts of such transactions are insignificant.

Series Y 358–373. Internal Revenue Collections: 1863 to 1970

[In thousands of dollars. For years ending June 30. Total columns include components not shown separately]

Year	Total collections	Individual income taxes	Corporation income taxes	Employment taxes	Estate and gift taxes [1]	Excise taxes — Total [2]	Alcohol	Tobacco	Manufacturers' — Total	Manufacturers' — Automobiles and accessories	Manufacturers' — Tires, tubes, and tread rubber	Manufacturers' — Gasoline, lubricating oils	Admissions [3]	Telephone, telegraph, radio, and cable facilities	Capital stock tax [2]
	358	359	360	361	362	363	364	365	366	367	368	369	370	371	372
1970	195,722,096	103,651,585	35,036,983	37,449,188	3,680,076	15,904,264	4,746,382	2,094,212	6,683,061	2,497,382	614,795	3,517,586	−71	1,469,562	
1969	187,919,560	97,440,406	38,337,646	33,068,657	3,530,064	15,542,787	4,555,560	2,137,585	6,501,146	2,534,647	631,527	3,283,715	11	1,316,378	
1968	153,636,838	78,252,045	29,896,520	28,085,898	3,081,979	14,320,396	4,287,237	2,122,277	5,713,973	2,054,746	489,139	3,123,103	1,150	1,105,478	
1967	148,374,815	69,370,595	34,917,825	26,958,241	3,014,406	14,113,748	4,075,723	2,079,869	5,478,347	1,917,383	503,753	3,025,467	3,399	1,101,853	
1966	128,879,961	61,297,552	30,834,243	20,256,133	3,093,922	13,398,112	3,814,378	2,073,956	5,613,869	2,148,840	481,803	2,914,965	81,404	907,917	
1965	114,434,634	53,660,683	26,131,334	17,104,306	2,745,533	14,792,779	3,772,634	2,148,594	6,418,145	2,565,926	440,467	2,763,230	95,591	1,078,937	
1964	112,260,257	54,590,354	24,300,863	17,002,504	2,416,304	13,950,232	3,577,499	2,052,545	6,020,543	2,325,676	411,483	2,694,686	88,079	910,196	
1963	105,925,395	52,987,581	22,336,134	15,004,486	2,187,457	13,409,737	3,441,656	2,079,237	5,610,309	2,087,161	398,860	2,571,726	82,583	880,605	
1962	99,440,839	50,649,594	21,295,711	12,708,171	2,035,187	12,752,176	3,341,282	2,025,736	5,132,949	1,755,717	361,562	2,485,726	74,775	843,478	
1961	94,401,086	46,153,001	21,764,940	12,502,451	1,916,392	12,064,302	3,212,801	1,991,117	4,896,802	1,654,107	279,572	2,444,599	70,282	827,302	
1960*	91,774,803	44,945,711	22,179,414	11,158,589	1,626,348	11,864,741	3,193,714	1,931,504	4,735,129	1,792,706	304,466	2,097,542	84,099	738,297	
1959 [4]	79,797,973	40,734,744	18,091,509	8,853,744	1,352,983	10,764,993	3,002,096	1,806,816	3,958,789	1,420,785	278,911	1,773,938	95,094	690,435	
1958	79,978,476	38,568,559	20,533,316	8,644,386	1,410,925	10,821,292	2,946,461	1,734,021	3,974,135	1,542,827	259,820	1,706,625	97,602	650,185	
1957	80,171,971	39,029,772	21,530,653	7,580,522	1,377,999	10,653,026	2,973,195	1,674,050	3,761,925	1,500,822	251,454	1,531,818	119,088	613,210	
1956	75,112,649	35,337,642	21,298,522	7,295,784	1,171,237	10,009,464	2,920,574	1,613,497	3,456,013	1,711,603	177,872	1,104,981	146,273	557,233	
1955	66,288,692	31,650,106	18,264,720	6,219,665	936,267	9,217,934	2,742,840	1,571,213	2,885,016	1,319,327	164,316	1,024,496	145,357	520,449	
1954	69,919,991	32,813,691	21,546,322	5,107,623	935,122	9,517,233	2,783,012	1,580,229	2,689,133	1,152,155	152,567	904,922	310,264	771,981	
1953	69,686,535	32,536,217	21,594,515	4,718,403	891,284	9,946,116	2,780,925	1,654,911	2,862,788	1,173,672	180,047	964,000	359,522	775,873	
1952	65,009,586	29,274,107	21,466,910	4,464,264	833,147	8,971,158	2,549,120	1,565,162	2,348,943	889,729	161,328	808,461	389,138	705,771	
1951	50,445,686	22,997,308	14,387,569	3,627,480	729,730	8,703,599	2,546,808	1,380,396	2,383,677	894,123	198,383	666,286	376,305	644,980	
1950	38,957,132	17,153,308	10,854,351	2,644,575	706,226	7,598,405	2,219,202	1,328,464	1,836,053	664,429	151,795	604,342	412,697	559,620	
1949	40,463,125	18,051,822	11,553,669	2,476,113	796,538	7,578,846	2,210,607	1,321,875	1,771,533	589,747	150,899	585,407	434,701	535,911	266
1948	41,864,542	20,997,781	10,174,410	2,381,342	899,345	7,409,941	2,255,327	1,300,280	1,649,234	485,872	159,284	559,525	438,628	468,776	6,138
1947	39,108,386	19,343,297	9,676,459	2,024,365	779,291	7,283,376	2,474,762	1,237,768	1,425,395	366,711	174,927	515,691	456,223	417,690	1,723
1946	40,672,097	18,704,536	12,553,602	1,700,828	676,833	6,684,178	2,526,165	1,165,519	922,671	131,908	118,092	480,297	415,268	380,082	352,121
1945	43,800,388	19,034,313	16,027,213	1,779,177	643,055	5,944,630	2,309,866	932,145	782,511	72,845	75,257	498,428	357,466	341,587	371,999
1944	40,121,760	18,261,005	14,766,796	1,738,372	511,211	4,463,674	1,618,775	988,483	503,462	36,020	40,334	323,690	205,289	231,474	380,702
1943	22,371,386	6,629,932	9,668,956	1,498,705	447,496	3,797,503	1,423,646	923,857	504,746	26,132	18,345	332,104	154,451	158,161	328,795
1942	13,047,869	3,262,800	4,744,083	1,185,362	432,540	3,141,183	1,048,517	780,982	771,898	123,621	64,811	416,019	115,033	75,022	281,900
1941	7,370,108	1,417,655	2,053,469	925,856	407,058	2,399,417	820,056	698,077	617,373	105,234	51,054	381,242	70,963	27,331	166,653
1940	5,340,452	982,017	1,147,592	833,521	360,071	1,884,512	624,253	608,518	447,152	77,847	41,555	257,420	21,888	26,368	132,739
1939	5,181,574	1,028,834	1,156,281	740,429	360,716	1,768,113	587,800	580,159	396,975	56,666	34,819	237,516	19,471	24,094	127,203
1938	5,658,765	1,286,312	1,342,718	742,660	416,874	1,730,853	567,979	568,182	417,152	56,666	31,567	235,213	20,801	23,977	139,349
1937	4,653,195	1,091,741	1,088,101	265,745	305,548	1,764,561	594,245	552,254	450,581	84,382	40,819	227,996	19,740	24,570	137,499
1936	3,520,208	674,416	753,032	48	378,840	1,547,293	505,464	501,166	382,716	62,311	32,208	204,443	17,112	21,098	94,943
1935	3,299,436	527,113	578,678		212,112	1,363,802	411,022	459,179	342,145	50,617	26,638	189,332	15,380	19,741	91,508
1934	2,672,239	419,509	400,146		113,138	1,287,854	258,911	425,169	385,291	43,271	27,630	227,830	14,614	19,251	80,168
1933	1,619,893	352,574	394,218		34,310	838,738	43,174	402,739	243,600	17,825	14,980	141,162	15,521	14,565	
1932	1,557,729	427,191	629,566		47,422	453,550	8,704	398,579	87				1,859		
1931	2,428,229	833,648	1,026,393		48,078	520,110	10,432	444,277	138				2,779		
1930	3,040,146	1,146,845	1,263,414		64,770	565,070	11,695	450,339	2,665				4,231		47
1929	2,939,054	1,095,541	1,235,733		61,897	539,927	12,777	434,445	5,712				6,083		5,956
1928	2,790,536	882,727	1,291,846		60,087		15,308	396,450	51,952				17,725		8,689
1927	2,865,683	911,940	1,308,013		100,340		21,196	376,170	66,850				17,941		8,970
1926	2,836,000	879,124	1,094,980		119,216		26,452	370,666	150,220				23,981		97,386
1925	2,584,140	845,426	916,233		108,940		25,905	345,247	140,877				30,908		90,003
1924	2,796,179	(NA)	(NA)		102,967		27,586	325,639	200,922				77,713	34,662	87,472
1923	2,621,745	(NA)	(NA)		126,705		30,358	309,015	185,117				70,175	30,381	81,568
1922	3,197,451	(NA)	(NA)		139,419		45,609	270,759	174,361				73,385	29,272	80,612
1921	4,595,357	(NA)	(NA)		154,043		82,623	255,219	229,398				89,731	28,442	81,526
1920	5,407,580	(NA)	(NA)		103,636		139,871	295,809	267,969				76,721	27,677	93,020
1919	3,850,150	(NA)	(NA)		82,030		483,051	206,003	79,400				50,920	17,902	28,776
1918	3,698,956	(NA)	(NA)		47,453		443,840	156,189	36,637				26,357	6,299	24,996
1917	809,394	180,108	207,274		6,077		284,009	103,202	775						
1916	512,723	67,944	56,994				247,454	88,064	4,219						10,472

See footnotes at end of table.

Series Y 358–373. Internal Revenue Collections: 1863 to 1970—Con.

[In thousands of dollars. For years ending June 30. Total columns include components not shown separately]

Year	Total collections	Estate and gift taxes [1]	Excise taxes Alcohol	Tobacco	Total manufacturers' [5]	Stamp taxes (including playing cards)	Year	Total collections	Estate and gift taxes [1]	Excise taxes Alcohol	Tobacco	Total manufacturers' [5]	Stamp taxes (including playing cards)
	358	362	364	365	366	373		358	362	364	365	366	373
1915	415,681	----	223,949	79,957	----	24,130	1888	124,326	----	92,630	30,662	10	(Z)
1914	380,009	----	226,180	79,987	----	714	1887	118,837	----	87,752	30,108	22	8
1913	344,424	----	230,146	76,789	----	655	1886	116,903	----	88,769	27,907	24	8
1912	321,616	----	219,660	70,590	----	616							
1911	322,526	----	219,648	67,006	----	582	1885	112,421	----	85,742	26,407	23	2
							1884	121,590	----	94,990	26,062	24	166
1910	289,957	----	208,602	58,118	----	566	1883	144,553	----	91,269	42,104	72	7,053
1909	246,213	----	192,324	51,887	----	502	1882	146,523	----	86,027	47,392	82	7,569
1908	251,666	----	199,966	49,863	----	460	1881	135,230	----	80,854	42,855	149	7,375
1907	269,664	50	215,905	51,811	----	573							
1906	249,103	142	199,036	48,423	----	489	1880	123,982	----	74,015	38,870	228	7,134
							1879	113,450	----	63,300	40,135	299	6,238
1905	234,188	774	186,319	45,660	----	427	1878	110,654	----	60,358	40,092	430	5,937
1904	232,904	2,072	184,893	44,656	----	376	1877	118,549	----	66,950	41,107	238	6,004
1903	230,741	5,357	179,501	43,515	----	423	1876	116,768	----	65,998	39,795	509	6,049
1902	271,868	4,843	193,127	51,938	----	13,807							
1901	306,872	5,212	191,698	62,482	1	39,558	1875	110,072	----	61,226	37,303	864	6,084
							1874	102,191	----	58,749	33,243	625	5,683
1900	295,316	2,884	183,420	59,355	3	41,295	1873	113,504	----	61,424	34,386	1,267	7,131
1899	273,485	1,235	167,928	52,493	5	44,109	1872	130,890	----	57,734	33,736	4,616	15,296
1898	170,867	----	132,062	36,231	1	1,055	1871	143,198	2,505	53,671	33,759	3,632	14,530
1897	146,620	----	114,481	30,710	9	251							
1896	146,831	----	114,454	30,712	1	260	1870	184,303	3,092	61,925	31,351	3,017	15,611
							1869	159,124	2,435	51,171	23,431	3,345	15,505
1895	143,246	----	111,503	29,705	(Z)	382	1868	190,375	2,823	24,612	18,730	61,650	14,047
1894	147,168	----	116,674	28,618	2	----	1867	265,065	1,865	39,600	19,765	91,531	15,239
1893	161,005	----	127,269	31,890	7	1	1866	310,120	1,171	38,489	16,531	127,231	14,258
1892	153,858	----	121,347	31,000	2	(Z)							
1891	146,035	----	111,901	32,796	4	(Z)	1865	210,856	547	22,466	11,401	73,318	10,889
							1864	116,966	311	32,619	8,592	36,223	5,715
1890	142,595	----	107,696	33,959	9	8	1863	41,003	57	6,805	3,098	16,525	4,140
1889	130,894	----	98,036	31,867	6	(Z)							

* Denotes first year for which figures include Alaska and Hawaii.
NA Not available.   Z Less than $500.
[1] Prior to 1916, series entitled "legacies, successions, inheritances" taxes.
[2] Beginning 1951, capital stock tax included in excise taxes; see text.
[3] Repealed, effective noon Dec. 31, 1965.
[4] Includes Alaska.
[5] Prior to 1916, series entitled "manufactures and products" taxes.

Series Y 374–380. Fiduciary Income Tax Returns: 1937 to 1970

[In thousands of dollars, except number of returns]

Income year	Taxable returns Number of returns	Total income	Net income or taxable income [1]	Income tax (after credits) [2]	Nontaxable returns Number of returns [3]	Total income [4]	Deficit (reduced by net income)
	374	375	376	377	378	379	380
1970	379,899	4,985,751	1,851,047	611,056	647,384	5,137,876	511,692
1965	343,596	5,310,590	1,947,684	658,885	453,905	3,201,180	149,414
1962	259,934	3,296,959	1,222,574	429,987	338,226	2,640,139	179,941
1960	226,382	2,810,714	1,045,676	361,665	353,278	2,456,308	221,972
1958	188,805	2,445,266	888,993	308,599	369,552	2,609,791	215,150
1956	172,185	2,543,617	901,626	326,945	318,511	2,340,802	192,716
1954	127,779	1,868,922	696,999	263,893	297,136	1,993,002	149,568
1952	132,927	1,307,721	626,760	234,933	289,736	1,480,439	56,808
1951	116,210	1,202,376	590,847	210,765	(NA)	(NA)	(NA)
1950	115,252	1,233,957	615,614	208,756	(NA)	(NA)	(NA)
1949	99,577	926,824	462,775	144,030	(NA)	(NA)	(NA)
1948	101,283	986,806	530,360	176,309	(NA)	(NA)	(NA)
1947	109,997	973,583	509,244	173,071	(NA)	(NA)	(NA)
1946	121,725	1,065,765	594,924	205,457	(NA)	(NA)	(NA)
1945	113,560	856,594	478,495	175,605	(NA)	(NA)	(NA)
1944	92,369	655,623	357,017	131,078	(NA)	(NA)	(NA)
1943	97,156	695,395	375,766	139,933	(NA)	(NA)	(NA)
1942	81,483	572,753	299,633	103,670	(NA)	(NA)	(NA)
1941	84,884	700,790	340,808	90,210	(NA)	(NA)	(NA)
1940	67,388	583,926	278,827	54,963	(NA)	(NA)	(NA)
1939	62,879	574,502	252,953	37,460	150,461	817,334	58,763
1938	52,881	506,172	236,444	39,098	147,945	785,316	60,816
1937	44,531	556,811	294,990	48,406	138,442	976,511	26,862

NA Not available.
[1] Prior to 1954, net income taxable to fiduciary before exemptions; thereafter, taxable income after exemptions.
[2] For 1937–1942 and 1944, income tax before credits. Tax for 1940–1941 includes defense tax, and for 1943, victory tax.
[3] For 1954–1970, excludes returns with no information.
[4] For 1952–1970, represents total income less deficit in total income.

Series Y 381–392. Corporation Income Tax Returns: 1909 to 1970

[In thousands of dollars, except number of returns. Includes data for Alaska and Hawaii]

Income year	Number of corporation returns	Active corporation returns										Number of inactive corporation returns [4]
		All returns				Returns with net income						
		Number	Total receipts [1]	Net income (less deficit)	Dividends paid [2]	Number	Total receipts [1]	Net income	Income tax [3]	Excess profits tax	Dividends paid [2]	
	381	382	383	384	385	386	387	388	389	390	391	392
1970	1,747,629	1,665,477	1,750,728,260	64,050,106	33,935,487	1,008,337	1,453,122,279	83,710,924	33,251,216	----------	31,843,899	82,152
1969	1,737,877	1,658,820	1,680,432,985	80,218,685	35,666,040	1,045,520	1,461,061,949	93,432,590	39,360,025	----------	34,397,194	79,057
1968	1,614,768	1,541,670	1,507,785,705	85,961,988	34,866,834	999,328	1,349,977,425	95,102,002	39,694,253	----------	33,789,727	73,098
1967	1,609,900	1,534,360	1,374,598,532	78,181,729	31,472,498	988,906	1,221,446,354	86,653,746	33,301,013	----------	30,536,187	75,540
1966	1,537,857	1,468,725	1,306,517,897	80,527,706	29,710,630	939,846	1,180,714,247	87,740,224	34,449,174	----------	29,181,075	69,132
1965	1,490,103	1,423,980	1,194,600,662	73,889,821	28,237,082	915,311	1,079,661,387	80,796,801	31,661,573	----------	27,629,664	66,123
1964	1,437,209	1,373,517	1,086,739,483	61,575,194	26,397,101	858,515	968,052,709	68,734,651	27,856,983	----------	25,792,604	63,692
1963	1,381,677	1,323,187	1,008,742,704	54,284,740	23,223,371	808,045	887,327,015	61,315,228	26,298,372	----------	22,583,943	58,490
1962	1,318,757	1,268,042	949,305,342	49,606,038	21,713,684	783,195	825,254,516	56,248,301	23,930,297	----------	20,828,623	50,715
1961	1,240,759	1,190,286	873,177,644	45,893,900	20,214,489	715,589	750,598,885	52,401,331	22,188,057	----------	19,445,730	50,473
1960	1,187,642	1,140,574	849,131,939	43,505,174	19,158,788	670,239	724,451,248	50,382,345	21,866,299	----------	18,472,558	47,068
1959	1,119,835	1,074,120	816,799,884	46,797,267	18,415,099	670,581	719,416,050	51,651,374	22,524,687	----------	17,887,911	45,715
1958	1,032,632	990,381	735,338,092	38,522,869	16,555,619	611,131	632,342,814	43,489,773	18,814,304	----------	16,005,167	42,251
1957	984,516	940,147	720,413,567	44,476,464	16,691,403	572,936	625,621,466	48,664,002	20,581,934	----------	16,099,259	44,369
1956	924,961	885,747	679,868,168	46,884,912	17,223,610	559,710	614,857,002	50,184,217	21,364,290	----------	16,870,178	39,214
1955	842,125	807,303	642,248,036	47,478,271	15,588,909	513,270	584,975,387	50,328,887	21,740,890	----------	15,366,051	34,822
1954	754,019	722,805	554,822,450	36,328,435	13,263,471	441,177	484,727,486	39,572,830	16,823,241	37,711	12,907,270	31,214
1953	730,974	697,975	558,242,262	39,484,687	12,711,017	441,767	506,450,081	41,819,445	18,255,625	1,613,424	12,511,979	32,999
1952	705,497	672,071	531,307,298	38,456,179	12,626,377	442,577	486,441,344	40,431,697	17,596,969	1,550,725	12,475,019	33,426
1951	687,310	652,376	517,039,183	43,545,590	12,728,622	439,047	479,243,451	45,333,173	19,623,441	2,458,676	12,576,500	34,934
1950	665,992	629,314	458,130,069	42,613,304	12,845,423	426,283	430,687,780	44,140,741	15,929,488	1,387,444	12,733,663	36,678
1949	649,957	614,842	393,449,692	28,194,837	10,253,335	384,772	350,168,722	30,576,517	9,817,308	----------	10,068,108	35,115
1948	630,670	594,243	410,965,648	34,425,024	10,411,182	395,860	379,309,471	36,273,250	11,920,260	----------	10,287,867	36,427
1947	587,683	551,807	367,745,578	31,422,728	9,065,813	382,531	343,273,851	33,381,291	10,981,482	----------	8,914,555	35,876
1946	526,363	491,152	288,954,237	25,192,886	8,024,178	359,310	265,597,448	27,184,592	8,606,695	268,145	7,762,034	35,211
1945	454,460	421,125	255,447,753	21,138,957	6,415,201	303,019	239,045,611	22,165,206	4,182,705	6,612,045	6,246,856	33,335
1944	446,796	412,467	262,200,531	26,304,481	6,304,239	288,904	252,962,944	27,123,741	4,353,620	10,530,430	6,210,584	34,329
1943	455,894	420,521	249,682,493	27,819,245	5,952,524	283,735	240,766,898	28,717,966	4,479,166	11,446,417	5,851,265	35,373
1942	479,677	442,665	217,680,512	23,051,611	5,679,802	269,942	206,160,215	24,052,358	4,337,728	7,918,668	5,559,812	37,012
1941	509,066	468,906	190,432,017	16,332,542	6,879,727	264,628	175,181,820	18,111,095	3,744,568	3,423,334	6,676,037	40,160
1940	516,783	473,042	148,236,787	8,919,429	6,228,770	220,977	125,180,472	11,203,224	2,144,292	404,254	6,018,903	43,741
1939	515,960	469,617	132,878,224	6,734,565	5,836,617	199,479	105,658,383	8,826,713	1,216,450	15,806	5,649,475	46,343
1938	520,501	471,032	120,453,946	3,672,882	5,098,013	169,884	80,267,477	6,525,979	853,578	5,988	4,856,345	49,469
1937	529,097	477,838	142,443,379	7,353,991	7,702,687	192,028	109,202,739	9,634,837	1,232,837	43,335	7,479,719	51,259
1936	530,779	478,857	132,722,602	7,326,218	7,724,305	203,161	105,011,693	9,478,241	1,169,765	21,613	7,514,539	51,922
1935	533,631	477,113	114,649,717	1,695,950	6,076,471	164,231	77,638,952	5,164,723	710,156	[5] 24,969	4,763,164	56,518
1934	528,898	469,804	101,489,954	[6] 94,170	5,074,142	145,101	63,118,536	4,275,197	588,375	[5] 7,673	3,996,018	59,094
1933	504,080	446,842	84,234,006	[6] 2,547,367	3,229,502	109,786	46,906,664	2,985,972	416,093	6,976	2,466,339	57,238
1932	508,636	451,884	81,637,988	[6] 5,643,574	4,028,677	82,646	31,855,431	2,153,113	285,576	----------	2,410,341	56,752
1931	516,404	459,704	108,056,952	[6] 3,287,545	6,314,613	175,898	52,267,013	3,683,368	398,994	----------	3,949,767	56,700
1930	518,736	463,036	136,588,320	1,551,218	8,598,422	221,420	89,910,937	6,428,813	711,704	----------	7,073,549	55,700
1929	509,436	456,021	161,158,206	8,739,758	9,808,454	269,430	130,064,831	11,653,886	1,193,436	----------	9,199,848	53,415
1928	495,892	443,611	153,304,973	8,226,617	7,632,852	268,783	127,787,507	10,617,741	1,184,142	----------	7,104,022	52,281
1927	475,031	425,675	144,899,177	6,510,145	7,125,677	259,849	115,732,970	8,981,884	1,130,674	----------	6,427,654	49,356
1926	455,320	455,320	142,629,445	7,504,693	6,702,942	258,134	118,420,378	9,673,403	1,229,797	----------	6,246,430	----------
1925	430,072	430,072	134,779,997	7,621,056	5,733,906	252,334	114,086,725	9,583,684	1,170,331	----------	5,319,791	----------
1924	417,421	417,421	119,746,703	5,362,726	4,849,349	236,389	97,560,316	7,586,652	881,550	----------	4,461,811	----------
1923	398,933	398,933	119,019,865	6,307,974	5,060,403	233,339	97,793,737	8,321,529	937,106	----------	4,607,787	----------
1922	382,883	382,883	[7] 100,920,515	4,770,035	6,784,765	212,535	[7] 80,331,680	6,963,811	775,310	8,466	6,349,786	----------
1921	356,397	356,397	[7] 91,249,274	457,829	[8]	171,239	[7] 60,051,123	4,336,048	366,444	335,132	[8]	----------
1920	345,595	345,595	[7] 118,205,562	5,873,231	[8]	203,233	[7] 93,824,225	7,902,655	636,508	988,726	[8]	----------
1919	320,198	320,198	[7] 99,918,749	8,415,872	[8]	209,634	[7] 88,261,006	9,411,418	743,536	1,431,806	[3]	----------
1918	317,579	317,579	[7] 86,464,281	7,671,739	[8]	202,061	[7] 79,706,659	8,361,511	653,198	2,505,566	[8]	----------
1917	351,426	351,426	[7] 84,693,239	10,100,753	[8]	232,079	[7] 79,540,005	10,730,360	503,698	1,638,748	[8]	----------
1916	341,253	341,253	[7] 35,327,631	8,109,005	[8]	206,984	[7] 32,531,097	8,765,909	171,805	----------	[8]	----------
1915	366,443	366,443	[8]	[9]	[8]	190,911	[8]	5,310,000	56,994	----------	[8]	----------
1914	299,445	299,445	[8]	[9]	[8]	174,205	[8]	3,940,000	39,145	----------	[8]	----------
1913	316,909	316,909	[8]	[9]	[8]	188,866	[8]	4,714,000	43,128	----------	[8]	----------
1912	305,336	305,336	[8]	[9]	[8]	61,116	[8]	4,151,000	35,006	----------	[8]	----------
1911	288,352	288,352	[8]	[9]	[8]	55,129	[8]	3,503,000	28,583	----------	[8]	----------
1910	270,202	270,202	[8]	[9]	[8]	54,040	[8]	3,761,000	33,512	----------	[8]	----------
1909	262,490	262,490	[8]	[9]	[8]	52,498	[8]	3,590,000	20,960	----------	[8]	----------

[1] In 1918–1924, railroads and other public utility corporations frequently reported only net income, resulting in understatements estimated at $5 billion in 1918 and 1919 and nearly twice that amount in 1920 and 1921; not estimated for 1922–1924.
[2] Excludes liquidating dividends.
[3] For 1941–1943, includes a small amount of surtax from returns with no net income but with partially tax-exempt interest from Government obligations. For 1941–1970, includes a small amount of tax from returns with no net income because of special provisions for insurance companies; for 1963–1970 includes tax from recomputing prior year investment credit; for 1967–1970, includes the surcharge; and for 1969–1970, includes the additional tax for tax preferences.

[4] Prior to 1927, included among those reporting no net income.
[5] The declared-value excess profits tax includes a small amount of tax from returns with no net income because the excess profits tax applied to interest on Government obligations exempt from income tax.
[6] Deficit.
[7] Gross income. "Total receipts" is not available separately for returns with net income and returns with no net income.
[8] Not tabulated.
[9] Amount of deficit for returns with no net income is not available.

Series Y 393–401. Individual Income Tax Returns: 1944 to 1970

[In thousands of dollars, except number of returns]

Income year	Number of returns			Returns with adjusted gross income				Returns with no adjusted gross income	
	Total	Taxable	Non-taxable [1]	Number	Adjusted gross income	Taxable income	Income tax (after credits)	Number [1]	Adjusted gross deficit
	393	394	395	396	397	398	399	400	401
1970	74,279,831	59,317,371	14,962,460	73,862,448	631,692,540	400,859,064	83,909,314	417,383	2,451,726
1969	75,834,388	63,721,394	12,112,994	75,375,731	605,578,947	388,153,971	86,568,215	458,657	2,032,867
1968	73,728,708	61,288,708	12,440,000	73,347,156	556,304,955	352,799,662	76,637,902	381,552	1,884,469
1967	71,651,909	58,672,938	12,978,971	71,282,525	506,641,751	315,108,212	62,919,958	369,384	1,832,272
1966	70,160,425	56,709,076	13,451,349	69,786,185	470,271,721	286,296,994	56,087,084	374,240	1,821,142
1965	67,596,300	53,700,794	13,895,506	67,198,928	430,663,208	255,082,124	49,529,695	397,372	1,461,969
1964	65,375,601	51,306,338	14,069,263	64,943,284	398,212,083	229,875,078	47,152,855	432,317	1,552,252
1963	63,943,236	51,323,221	12,620,015	63,511,244	370,270,618	209,090,323	48,203,580	431,992	1,492,546
1962	62,712,386	50,092,363	12,620,023	92,290,595	349,860,992	195,320,479	44,902,840	421,791	1,159,526
1961	61,499,420	48,582,765	12,916,655	61,061,589	330,935,737	181,779,732	42,225,498	431,831	1,074,453
1960	61,027,931	48,060,985	12,966,946	60,592,712	316,557,566	171,627,771	39,464,156	435,219	1,091,184
1959	60,271,297	47,496,913	12,774,384	59,838,162	306,616,924	166,540,616	38,645,299	433,135	1,521,945
1958	59,085,182	45,652,134	13,433,048	58,700,924	282,166,418	149,337,414	34,335,652	384,258	1,012,326
1957	59,825,121	46,865,315	12,959,806	59,407,673	281,308,431	149,363,077	34,393,639	417,448	987,865
1956	59,197,004	46,258,646	12,938,358	58,798,843	268,583,814	141,532,061	32,732,132	398,161	859,546
1955	58,250,188	44,689,065	13,561,123	57,818,164	249,429,182	128,020,111	29,613,722	432,024	898,865
1954	56,747,008	42,633,060	14,113,948	56,306,704	230,235,855	115,331,301	26,665,753	440,304	1,014,480
1953	57,838,184	45,223,151	12,615,033	57,415,885	229,863,409	----------	29,430,659	422,299	1,155,153
1952	56,528,817	43,876,273	12,652,544	56,107,089	216,087,449	----------	27,802,831	421,728	797,541
1951	55,447,009	42,648,610	12,798,399	55,042,597	203,097,033	----------	24,227,780	404,412	760,548
1950	53,060,098	38,186,682	14,873,416	52,655,564	179,874,478	----------	18,374,922	404,534	726,202
1949	51,814,124	35,628,295	16,185,829	51,301,910	161,373,205	----------	14,538,141	512,214	799,280
1948	52,072,006	36,411,248	15,660,758	51,745,649	164,173,861	----------	15,441,529	326,309	657,847
1947	55,099,008	41,578,524	13,520,484	54,799,936	150,295,275	----------	18,076,281	299,072	559,193
1946	52,816,547	37,915,696	14,900,851	52,600,470	134,330,006	----------	16,075,913	216,077	247,206
1945	49,932,783	42,650,502	7,282,281	49,750,991	120,301,131	----------	17,050,378	181,792	292,472
1944	47,111,495	42,354,468	4,757,027	46,919,590	116,714,736	----------	16,216,401	191,905	249,771

[1] Includes returns with no information, 1944–1952 and 1957.

Series Y 402–411. Individual Income Tax Returns: 1913 to 1943

[In thousands of dollars, except number of returns]

Income year	Returns with net income [1]						Returns with no net income			
	Number of returns			Total income	Net income [2]	Income tax [3]	Number	Total income	Net deficit	Tax
	Total	Taxable	Nontaxable							
	402	403	404	405	406	407	408	409	410	411
1943	43,506,553	40,222,699	3,283,854	106,614,214	99,209,862	14,449,441	215,485	170,866	225,683	643
1942	36,456,110	27,637,051	8,819,059	85,876,118	78,589,729	8,823,041	163,136	181,486	198,598	(NA)
1941	25,770,089	17,502,587	8,267,502	63,841,047	58,527,217	3,815,415	99,828	264,032	292,023	2,326
1940	14,598,074	7,437,261	7,160,813	40,277,645	36,309,719	1,440,967	112,697	239,583	311,385	473
1939	7,570,320	3,896,418	3,673,902	25,816,147	22,938,918	890,934	82,461	228,690	284,327	300
1938	6,150,776	2,995,664	3,155,112	21,549,277	18,660,929	726,120	100,233	318,769	354,156	615
1937	6,301,833	3,326,912	2,974,921	23,891,481	20,941,302	1,093,163	83,904	250,394	308,518	----------
1936	5,413,499	2,861,108	2,552,391	21,888,373	19,240,110	1,214,017	73,272	248,530	286,632	----------
1935	4,575,012	2,110,890	2,464,122	17,316,505	14,909,812	657,439	94,609	288,653	381,353	----------
1934	4,094,420	1,795,920	2,298,500	15,092,960	12,796,802	511,400	104,170	344,055	412,859	----------
1933	3,723,558	1,747,740	1,975,818	13,393,825	11,008,638	374,120	168,449	725,817	1,141,331	----------
1932	3,877,430	1,936,095	1,941,335	14,392,080	11,655,909	329,962	206,293	831,592	1,480,922	----------
1931	3,225,924	1,525,546	1,700,378	17,268,451	13,604,996	246,127	184,583	1,299,750	1,936,878	----------
1930	3,707,509	2,037,645	1,669,864	22,319,446	18,118,635	476,715	144,867	1,204,383	1,539,452	----------
1929	4,044,327	2,458,049	1,586,278	29,844,758	24,800,736	1,001,938	92,545	902,251	1,025,130	----------
1928	4,070,851	2,523,063	1,547,788	28,987,634	25,226,327	1,164,254	72,829	420,649	499,213	----------
1927	4,101,547	2,440,941	1,660,606	26,208,561	22,545,091	830,639				----------
1926	4,138,092	2,470,990	1,667,102	25,447,436	21,958,506	732,471				----------
1925	4,171,051	2,501,166	1,669,885	25,272,035	21,894,576	734,555				----------
1924	7,369,788	4,489,698	2,880,090	29,578,997	25,656,153	704,265				----------
1923	7,698,321	4,270,121	3,428,200	29,247,593	24,777,466	661,666				----------
1922	6,787,481	3,681,249	3,106,232	24,871,908	21,336,213	861,057				----------
1921	6,662,176	3,589,985	3,072,191	23,328,782	19,577,213	719,387				----------
1920	7,259,944	5,518,310	1,741,634	26,690,270	23,735,629	1,075,054				----------
1919	5,332,760	4,231,181	1,101,579	22,437,686	19,859,491	1,269,630				----------
1918	4,425,114	3,392,863	1,032,251	17,745,761	15,924,639	1,127,722				----------
1917	3,472,890	2,707,234	765,656	[4] 14,538,146	13,407,303	691,493				----------
1916	437,036	362,970	74,066	8,349,902	6,298,578	173,387				----------
1915	336,652	----------	----------	----------	4,600,000	67,944				----------
1914	357,515	----------	----------	----------	4,000,000	41,046				----------
1913 [5]	357,598	----------	----------	----------	3,900,000	28,254				----------

NA Not available.
[1] Includes fiduciary returns with net income filed on Form 1040, 1913–1936.
[2] For 1941–1943, total income on Form 1040A was also used as net income.
[3] Tax for 1924–1931, after earned income credit and capital loss credit; 1932–1933, after capital loss credit only; 1943, after foreign tax credit and tax paid at source. Tax for 1940–1941 includes defense tax and for 1943, victory tax.
[4] Somewhat understated because net income was used also as total income on returns with income of $1,000 to $2,000. [5] Data pertain to last 10 months of year.

Series Y 412–439. Individual Income Tax Liability and Effective Rates, for Selected Income Groups: 1913 to 1970

Group and revenue act	Income year or period	$600	$1,000	$2,000	$3,000	$5,000	$6,000	$8,000	$10,000	$15,000	$20,000	$25,000	$50,000	$100,000	$1,000,000
		412	413	414	415	416	417	418	419	420	421	422	423	424	425
		SINGLE EXEMPTION—LIABILITY [1] (Dollars)													
1969	1970[2]		53	208	391	792	1,018	1,511	2,065	3,788	5,934	8,423	22,770	56,435	702,179
1964[3]	1969[2]		56	222	425	856	1,098	1,628	2,224	4,077	6,380	9,053	24,453	60,584	753,577
	1968[2]		56	219	415	836	1,073	1,591	2,174	3,984	6,235	8,847	23,897	59,207	736,450
	1965–1967		56	209	386	778	998	1,480	2,022	3,706	5,800	8,230	22,230	55,076	685,070
	1964		64	233	420	834	1,069	1,588	2,177	3,954	6,165	8,744	23,559	58,890	751,378
1954[4]	1954–1963[5]		80	280	488	944	1,204	1,780	2,436	4,448	6,942	9,796	26,388	66,798	[6]869,478
1951	1952–1953[5]		89	311	542	1,052	1,342	1,992	2,728	4,968	7,762	10,940	28,466	69,688	[6]880,000
	1951[5]		82	286	498	964	1,234	1,816	2,486	4,528	7,072	9,976	26,578	67,274	[6]872,000
1950	1950		70	244	428	843	1,080	1,604	2,201	4,032	6,301	8,898	23,997	60,770	[6]800,000
1948	1948–1949		66	232	409	811	1,040	1,546	2,124	3,894	6,089	8,600	23,201	58,762	[6]770,000
1945	1946–1947	19	95	285	485	922	1,169	1,720	2,347	4,270	6,645	9,362	25,137	63,541	[6]840,147
1944[7]	1944–1945	23	115	345	585	1,105	1,395	2,035	2,755	4,930	7,580	10,590	27,945	69,870	[6]900,000
1942	1943[8][9]	17	107	333	574	1,105	1,401	2,052	2,783	4,968	7,626	10,644	28,058	69,665	[6]899,500
	1942[8]	15	89	273	472	920	1,174	1,742	2,390	4,366	6,816	9,626	25,811	64,641	854,616
1941	1941		21	117	221	483	649	1,031	1,493	2,994	4,929	7,224	20,882	53,214	733,139
1940	1940[10]		4	44	84	172	255	449	686	1,476	2,666	4,253	14,709	44,268	718,404
1936, 1938[11]	1936–1939			32	68	140	216	378	560	1,104	1,834	2,804	9,334	33,354	680,184
1934	1934–1935			32	68	140	216	378	560	1,104	1,834	2,804	9,334	31,404	572,324
1932	1932–1933			40	80	160	240	420	600	1,140	1,800	2,640	8,720	30,220	571,220
1928	1929[12]			2	6	13	22	52	90	285	555	922	4,250	14,930	230,930
	1928, 1930–1931			6	17	40	56	101	154	386	694	1,099	4,664	15,844	240,844
1926	1925–1927[13]			6	17	40	56	101	154	386	694	1,234	4,954	16,134	241,134
1924	1924			15	30	60	90	150	225	585	1,045	1,635	6,165	22,645	429,645
1921	1923			30	60	120	180	315	450	855	1,350	1,980	6,540	22,665	413,040
	1922			40	80	160	240	420	600	1,140	1,800	2,640	8,720	30,220	550,720
	1921			40	80	160	250	450	670	1,310	2,070	2,960	9,270	31,220	663,270
1918	1919–1920			40	80	160	250	450	670	1,310	2,070	2,960	9,270	31,270	663,270
	1918			60	120	240	370	650	950	1,790	2,750	3,840	11,150	35,150	703,150
1917	1917			20	40	120	170	275	395	770	1,220	1,820	5,220	16,220	475,220
1916	1916					40	60	100	140	240	340	490	1,340	3,940	102,940
1913	1913–1915[14]					20	30	50	70	120	170	270	770	2,520	60,020
		SINGLE EXEMPTION—EFFECTIVE RATE [15] (Percent)													
1969	1970[2]		5.3	10.4	13.0	15.8	17.0	18.9	20.6	25.3	29.7	33.7	45.5	56.4	70.2
1964[3]	1969[2]		5.6	11.1	14.2	17.1	18.3	20.4	22.2	27.2	31.9	36.2	48.9	60.6	75.4
	1968[2]		5.6	11.0	13.8	16.7	17.9	19.9	21.7	26.6	31.2	35.4	47.8	59.2	73.6
	1965–1967		5.6	10.4	12.9	15.6	16.6	18.5	20.2	24.7	29.0	32.9	44.5	55.1	68.5
	1964		6.4	11.6	14.0	16.7	17.8	19.8	21.8	26.4	30.8	35.0	47.1	58.9	75.1
1954[4]	1954–1963[5]		8.0	14.0	16.3	18.9	20.1	22.2	24.4	29.7	34.7	39.2	52.8	66.8	[6]86.9
1951	1952–1953[5]		8.9	15.5	18.1	21.0	22.4	24.9	27.2	33.1	38.8	43.8	56.9	69.7	[6]88.0
	1951[5]		8.2	14.3	16.6	19.3	20.6	22.7	24.9	30.2	35.4	39.9	53.5	67.3	[6]87.2
1950	1950		7.0	12.2	14.3	16.9	18.0	20.0	22.0	26.9	31.5	35.6	48.0	60.8	[6]80.0
1948	1948–1949		6.6	11.6	13.6	16.2	17.3	19.3	21.2	26.0	30.4	34.4	46.4	58.8	[6]77.0
1945	1946–1947	3.2	9.5	14.3	16.2	18.4	19.5	21.5	23.5	28.5	33.2	37.5	50.3	63.5	[6]84.0
1944[7]	1944–1945	3.8	11.5	17.3	19.5	22.1	23.3	25.4	27.6	32.9	37.9	42.4	55.9	69.9	[6]90.0
1942	1943[8][9]	2.8	10.7	16.7	19.1	22.1	23.4	25.7	27.8	33.1	38.1	42.6	56.1	69.7	[6]90.0
	1942[8]	2.5	8.9	13.7	15.7	18.4	19.6	21.8	23.9	29.1	34.1	38.5	51.6	64.6	85.5
1941	1941		2.1	5.9	7.4	9.7	10.8	12.9	14.9	20.0	24.6	28.9	41.8	53.2	73.3
1940	1940[10]		.4	2.2	2.8	3.4	4.3	5.6	6.9	9.8	13.3	17.0	29.4	44.3	71.8
1936, 1938[11]	1936–1939			1.6	2.3	2.8	3.6	4.7	5.6	7.4	9.2	11.2	18.7	33.4	68.0
1934	1934–1935			1.6	2.3	2.8	3.6	4.7	5.6	7.4	9.2	11.2	18.7	31.4	57.2
1932	1932–1933			2.0	2.7	3.2	4.0	5.3	6.0	7.6	9.0	10.6	17.4	30.2	57.1
1928	1929[12]			.1	.2	.3	.4	.7	.9	1.9	2.8	3.7	8.5	14.9	23.1
	1928, 1930–1931			.3	.6	.8	.9	1.3	1.5	2.6	3.5	4.4	9.3	15.8	24.1
1926	1925–1927[13]			.3	.6	.8	.9	1.3	1.5	2.6	3.5	4.9	9.9	16.1	24.1
1924	1924			.8	1.0	1.2	1.5	1.9	2.3	3.9	5.2	6.5	12.3	22.7	43.0
1921	1923			1.5	2.0	2.4	3.0	3.9	4.5	5.7	6.8	7.9	13.1	22.7	41.3
	1922			2.0	2.7	3.2	4.0	5.3	6.0	7.6	9.0	10.6	17.4	30.2	55.1
	1921			2.0	2.7	3.2	4.2	5.6	6.7	8.7	10.4	11.8	18.5	31.3	66.3
1918	1919–1920			2.0	2.7	3.2	4.2	5.6	6.7	8.7	10.4	11.8	18.5	31.3	66.3
	1918			3.0	4.0	4.8	6.2	8.1	9.5	11.9	13.8	15.4	22.3	35.2	70.3
1917	1917			1.0	1.3	2.4	2.8	3.4	4.0	5.1	6.1	7.3	10.4	16.2	47.5
1916	1916					.8	1.0	1.3	1.4	1.6	1.7	2.0	2.7	3.9	10.0
1913	1913–1915[14]					.4	.5	.6	.7	.8	.9	1.1	1.5	2.5	6.0

See footnotes at end of table.

Series Y 412–439. Individual Income Tax Liability and Effective Rates, for Selected Income Groups: 1913 to 1970—Con.

FOUR EXEMPTIONS—LIABILITY [1] (Dollars)

Group and revenue act	Income year or period	$600	$1,000	$2,000	$3,000	$5,000	$6,000	$8,000	$10,000	$15,000	$20,000	$25,000	$50,000	$100,000	$1,000,000
		426	427	428	429	430	431	432	433	434	435	436	437	438	439
1969	1970 [2]				70	374	547	928	1,317	2,445	3,772	5,310	16,205	44,772	685,961
1964 [3]	1969 [2]				84	405	604	1,016	1,434	2,651	4,079	5,733	17,446	48,114	736,230
	1968 [2]				84	400	591	993	1,402	2,591	3,986	5,603	17,050	47,021	719,498
	1965–1967				84	386	552	924	1,304	2,410	3,708	5,212	15,860	43,740	669,300
	1964				96	430	608	1,000	1,400	2,582	3,988	5,604	16,846	46,356	731,832
1954 [4]	1954–1963 [5] [16]				120	520	720	1,152	1,592	2,900	4,464	6,268	18,884	51,912	[6] 854,576
1951	1952–1953 [5] [16]				133	577	799	1,282	1,774	3,236	5,000	7,004	21,088	56,032	[6] 871,224
	1951 [5] [16]				122	530	734	1,174	1,622	2,972	4,552	6,406	19,232	52,640	[6] 858,408
1950	1950 [16]				104	452	626	1,016	1,417	2,607	4,030	5,672	17,152	47,208	[6] 791,430
1948	1948–1949 [16]				100	432	598	974	1,361	2,512	3,888	5,476	16,578	45,643	[6] 769,314
1945	1946–1947				190	589	798	1,292	1,862	3,639	5,890	8,522	24,111	62,301	[6] 838,850
1944 [7]	1944–1945	3	15	45	275	755	1,005	1,585	2,245	4,265	6,785	9,705	26,865	68,565	[6] 900,000
1942	1943 [8] [9]	1	14	58	267	730	979	1,553	2,208	4,207	6,693	9,574	26,392	67,803	[6] 898,800
	1942 [8]			13	191	592	810	1,322	1,914	3,758	6,088	8,814	24,845	63,479	853,384
1941	1941				58	271	397	717	1,117	2,475	4,287	6,480	19,967	52,160	731,930
1940	1940 [10]					75	114	246	440	1,118	2,143	3,571	13,741	42,948	717,036
1936, 1938 [11]	1936–1939					48	84	184	343	831	1,469	2,327	8,621	31,997	678,436
1934	1934–1935					48	84	184	343	831	1,469	2,327	8,621	30,162	570,898
1932	1932–1933					68	108	236	416	956	1,616	2,456	8,536	30,036	571,036
1928	1929 [12]					3	6	14	40	201	471	838	4,166	14,846	230,846
	1928, 1930–1931					8	19	42	83	281	589	994	4,559	15,739	240,739
1926	1925–1927 [13]					8	19	42	83	281	589	1,129	4,849	16,029	241,039
1924	1924					26	41	81	141	475	935	1,525	6,055	22,535	429,535
1921	1923					51	96	207	342	747	1,242	1,872	6,432	22,557	412,932
	1922					68	128	276	456	996	1,656	2,496	8,576	30,076	550,576
	1921					68	138	306	526	1,166	1,886	2,816	9,126	31,126	663,126
1918	1919–1920				24	104	154	338	558	1,198	1,958	2,848	9,158	31,158	663,158
	1918				36	156	226	482	782	1,622	2,582	3,672	10,982	34,982	702,982
1917	1917				12	64	114	219	339	714	1,164	1,764	5,164	16,164	475,164
1916	1916					20	40	80	120	220	320	470	1,320	3,920	102,920
1913	1913–1915 [14]					10	20	40	60	110	160	260	760	2,510	60,010

FOUR EXEMPTIONS—EFFECTIVE RATE [15] (Percent)

Group and revenue act	Income year or period	$600	$1,000	$2,000	$3,000	$5,000	$6,000	$8,000	$10,000	$15,000	$20,000	$25,000	$50,000	$100,000	$1,000,000
1969	1970 [2]				2.3	7.5	9.1	11.6	13.2	16.3	18.9	21.2	32.4	44.8	68.6
1964 [3]	1969 [2]				2.8	8.1	10.1	12.7	14.3	17.7	20.4	22.9	34.9	48.1	73.6
	1968 [2]				2.8	8.0	9.8	12.4	14.0	17.3	19.9	22.4	34.1	47.2	71.9
	1965–1967				2.8	7.7	9.2	11.6	13.0	16.1	18.5	20.8	31.7	43.7	66.9
	1964				3.2	8.6	10.1	12.5	14.0	17.2	19.9	22.4	33.7	46.4	73.2
1954 [4]	1954–1963 [5] [16]				4.0	10.4	12.0	14.4	15.9	19.3	22.3	25.1	37.8	51.9	85.5
1951	1952–1953 [5] [16]				4.4	11.5	13.3	16.0	17.7	21.6	25.0	28.0	42.2	56.0	87.1
	1951 [5] [16]				4.1	10.6	12.2	14.7	16.2	19.8	22.8	25.6	38.5	52.6	85.8
1950	1950 [16]				3.5	9.0	10.4	12.7	14.2	17.4	20.2	22.7	34.3	47.2	79.1
1948	1948–1949 [16]				3.3	8.6	10.0	12.2	13.6	16.7	19.4	21.9	33.2	45.6	76.9
1945	1946–1947				6.3	11.8	13.3	16.2	18.6	24.3	29.5	34.1	48.2	62.3	83.9
1944 [7]	1944–1945	.5	1.5	2.3	9.2	15.1	16.8	19.8	22.5	28.4	33.9	38.8	53.7	68.6	[8] 90.0
1942	1943 [8] [9]	.2	1.4	2.9	8.9	14.6	16.3	19.4	22.1	28.0	33.5	38.3	52.8	67.8	[8] 89.9
	1942 [8]			.7	6.4	11.8	13.5	16.5	19.1	25.1	30.4	35.3	49.7	63.5	85.3
1941	1941				1.9	5.4	6.6	9.0	11.2	16.5	21.4	25.9	39.9	52.2	73.2
1940	1940 [10]					1.5	1.9	3.1	4.4	7.5	10.7	14.3	27.5	42.9	71.7
1936, 1938 [11]	1936–1939					1.0	1.4	2.3	3.4	5.5	7.3	9.3	17.2	32.0	67.8
1934	1934–1935					1.0	1.4	2.3	3.4	5.5	7.3	9.3	17.2	30.2	57.1
1932	1932–1933					1.4	1.8	3.0	4.2	6.4	8.1	9.8	17.1	30.0	57.1
1928	1929 [12]					.1	.1	.2	.4	1.3	2.4	3.4	8.3	14.8	23.1
	1928, 1930–1931					.2	.3	.5	.8	1.9	2.9	4.0	9.1	15.7	24.1
1926	1925–1927 [13]					.2	.3	.5	.8	1.9	2.9	4.5	9.7	16.0	24.1
1924	1924					.5	.7	1.0	1.4	3.2	4.7	6.1	12.1	22.5	43.0
1921	1923					1.0	1.6	2.6	3.4	5.0	6.2	7.5	12.9	22.6	41.3
	1922					1.4	2.1	3.5	4.6	6.6	8.3	10.0	17.2	30.1	55.1
	1921					1.4	2.3	3.8	5.3	7.8	9.6	11.3	18.3	31.1	66.3
1918	1919–1920				.8	2.1	2.6	4.2	5.6	8.0	9.8	11.4	18.3	31.2	66.3
	1918				1.2	3.1	3.8	6.0	7.8	10.8	12.9	14.7	22.0	35.0	70.3
1917	1917				.4	1.3	1.9	2.7	3.4	4.8	5.8	7.1	10.3	16.2	47.5
1916	1916					.4	.7	1.0	1.2	1.5	1.6	1.9	2.6	3.9	10.3
1913	1913–1915 [14]					.2	.3	.5	.6	.7	.8	1.0	1.5	2.5	6.0

[1] Actual tax liability on selected net incomes and necessary assumptions.
[2] Includes income tax surcharge, generally 7.5 percent in 1968, 10 percent in 1969, and 2.5 percent in 1970, except in low tax brackets.
[3] Revenue Act of 1964.
[4] Internal Revenue Code of 1954.
[5] Excludes self-employment tax.
[6] Taking into account the following maximum effective rate limitations: For 1944–1945, 90 percent; 1946–1947, 85.5 percent; 1948–1949, 77 percent; 1950, 80 percent; 1951, 87.2 percent; 1952–1953, 88 percent; 1954–1957, 87 percent.
[7] Individual Income Tax Act of 1944.
[8] Tax liabilities unadjusted for transition to current payment basis.
[9] Includes net victory tax. Computed by assuming that deductions are 10 percent of victory tax net income; i.e., that victory tax net income is ten-ninths of selected net income.
[10] Includes defense tax.
[11] Rates and exemptions for 1936 and 1938 acts were identical and resulted in the same tax liabilities.
[12] Normal tax rates of 1928 act were reduced for 1929 only by Joint Resolution of Congress.
[13] Provisions of 1926 act were retroactive to 1925.
[14] Mar. 1, 1913–Dec. 31, 1915.
[15] Tax liability divided by stated net income.
[16] Split income basis.

Series Y 440–449. Federal Estate Tax Returns: 1916 to 1970

[In thousands of dollars, except number of returns]

Filing year	Total number of returns	Citizens and resident aliens [1]					Nonresident aliens [4]			
		Number of returns (taxable and nontaxable)	Gross estate	Net taxable estate [2]	Credit for State inheritance taxes paid	Net estate tax [3] (after credits)	Number of returns (taxable and nontaxable)	Gross estate	Net taxable estate [2]	Net estate tax [3] (after credits)
	440	441	442	443	444	445	446	447	448	449
1970		133,944	29,670,558	8,036,640	332,656	2,999,965				
1966	98,905	97,339	21,936,168	9,159,917	280,423	2,414,310	1,566			
1963	79,743	78,393	17,007,239	7,070,827	207,620	1,840,972	1,350			
1961	65,789	64,538	14,622,073	6,014,498	195,581	1,618,548	1,251	43,733	23,336	4,142
1957	47,381	46,473	10,293,669	4,342,072	146,769	1,176,710	908	28,884	20,987	4,589
1955	37,565	36,595	7,467,443	2,990,810	86,249	778,342	970	22,803	15,948	2,913
1954	37,672	36,699	7,411,754	2,969,174	85,842	778,504	973	23,383	16,206	3,096
1951	29,002	27,958	5,504,961	2,188,878	64,535	577,401	1,044	20,666	16,052	3,081
1950	27,144	25,858	4,918,094	1,916,645	48,940	483,520	1,286	24,157	18,192	3,229
1949	25,904	24,552	4,933,215	2,106,827	65,831	567,421	1,352	24,511	19,356	3,407
1948	24,381	23,356	4,774,783	2,584,595	82,725	714,707	1,025	16,266	12,602	1,825
1947	22,007	20,899	4,224,210	2,319,310	69,850	621,966	1,108	27,198	21,872	4,389
1945	16,550	15,898	3,436,901	1,900,159	64,517	531,052	652	13,524	10,997	1,876
1944	14,857	14,303	2,907,620	1,508,953	46,285	404,635	554	8,712	7,272	1,146
1943	16,033	15,187	2,627,367	1,396,697	35,966	362,164	846	10,471	8,703	1,212
1942	17,396	16,215	2,724,513	1,524,881	45,626	308,342	1,181	12,620	11,455	1,349
1941	17,122	15,977	2,777,657	1,561,215	53,636	291,758	1,145	15,783	14,553	1,641
1940	16,876	15,435	2,632,659	1,479,268	45,337	250,360	1,441	15,540	13,916	1,196
1939	16,926	15,221	2,746,143	1,537,975	53,111	276,707	1,705	21,745	20,347	2,231
1938	17,642	15,932	3,046,977	1,724,589	59,842	314,620	1,710	22,648	20,670	2,182
1937	17,032	15,037	2,767,739	1,622,618	58,252	305,784	1,995	26,019	23,995	2,665
1936	13,321	11,605	2,296,257	1,245,395	44,218	195,301	1,716	16,163	14,627	1,069
1935	12,724	11,110	2,435,282	1,316,838	43,864	153,763	1,614	24,609	22,888	1,703
1934	11,853	10,353	2,244,107	1,150,533	33,922	95,228	1,500	23,178	20,033	988
1933	10,275	8,727	2,026,931	970,868	28,295	59,429	1,548	34,025	30,056	1,986
1932	8,507	7,113	2,795,818	1,391,569	61,642	22,364	1,394	34,570	31,868	1,310
1931	9,889	8,333	4,042,381	2,327,319	137,663	44,540	1,556	33,195	29,013	660
1930	10,382	8,798	4,108,517	2,376,973	113,388	39,003	1,584	57,106	50,481	2,614
1929	10,343	8,582	3,843,514	2,268,323	122,110	43,303	1,761	49,732	45,653	1,085
1928	10,236	8,079	3,503,239	1,943,429	94,452	40,561	2,157	51,032	49,075	1,398
1927	10,700	9,353	3,146,290	1,735,840	59,600	40,931	1,347	26,945	25,777	755
1926	14,567	13,142	3,386,267	1,951,969	36,732	101,324	1,425	21,656	20,567	481
1925	16,019	14,013	2,958,364	1,621,008	10,707	86,223	2,006	42,725	37,861	1,099
1924	14,513	13,011	2,540,922	1,372,421		71,451	1,502	25,600	23,395	488
1923	15,119	13,963	2,774,741	1,504,621		88,384	1,156	29,587	27,440	726
1922 (Jan. 15–Dec. 31)	13,876	12,563	2,955,959	1,652,832		117,624	1,313	58,113	52,142	2,938
1916–1922 [5]	45,126	42,230	8,785,642	5,407,674		351,138	2,896	107,597	101,849	5,378

[1] Includes returns for nonresident citizens who died on or after May 11, 1934.
[2] Net taxable estate includes net estate for returns filed under 1926 and prior acts, net estate for additional tax for returns filed under 1932 through 1953 acts, and net taxable estate for returns filed under 1954 Code.
[3] Net estate tax is the combined basic tax and additional tax whenever applicable, and includes defense tax for returns filed under 1940 act.
[4] Includes returns for nonresident citizens who died prior to May 11, 1934.
[5] Sept. 9, 1916–Jan. 15, 1922.

Series Y 450–456. Federal Gift Tax Returns: 1924 to 1966

[In thousands of dollars, except number of returns]

Filing year [1]	Total number of returns	Taxable returns				Nontaxable returns	
		Number of returns	Total gifts	Net taxable gift	Gift tax	Number of returns	Total gifts
	450	451	452	453	454	455	456
1966	112,796	29,547	2,372,850	1,454,998	412,962	83,249	1,589,099
1963	85,689	20,598	1,401,552	790,314	183,290	65,091	1,248,430
1961	78,232	17,936	1,219,482	657,024	157,687	60,296	1,096,581
1959	77,920	15,793	928,130	478,289	104,838	62,127	941,932
1956	49,189	14,736	923,470	517,583	113,005	34,453	434,009
1953	44,695	8,464	474,767	258,478	55,528	36,231	537,287
1951	41,703	8,360	501,377	304,131	67,426	33,343	498,141
1950	39,056	8,366	578,431	337,719	77,605	30,690	485,769
1949	31,547	6,114	325,682	178,035	36,087	25,433	382,699
1948	26,200	6,559	377,889	209,148	45,338	19,641	363,034
1947	24,857	6,822	438,681	256,594	64,402	18,035	338,932
1946	24,826	6,808	425,640	265,246	62,336	18,018	329,964
1945	20,095	5,540	288,739	169,625	36,633	14,555	246,820
1944	18,397	4,979	276,121	148,420	37,781	13,418	222,891
1943	16,987	4,656	208,738	123,936	29,637	12,331	203,916
1942	16,906	4,380	222,296	120,653	24,665	12,526	257,927
1941	25,788	8,940	714,400	484,319	69,819	16,848	367,082
1940	15,623	4,930	346,679	225,972	34,445	10,693	223,363
1939	12,226	3,929	219,594	131,577	18,701	8,297	152,010
1938	11,042	3,515	230,763	138,801	17,839	7,527	169,010
1937	13,695	4,128	317,787	180,939	22,758	9,567	250,322
1936	13,420	3,770	258,000	134,979	15,664	9,650	224,783
1935	22,563	8,718	1,710,061	1,196,001	162,798	13,845	420,453
1934	9,270	2,528	692,428	537,083	68,383	6,742	196,325
1933	3,683	878	155,859	101,793	8,943	2,805	85,149
1932 (June 7–Dec. 31)	1,747	245	36,025	17,879	1,111	1,502	45,363
1925	848	768	[2] 187,275	91,289	2,715	80	15,789
1924	1,528	1,411	328,803	170,182	7,242	117	18,289

[1] Prior to 1959, year of gift.
[2] Exclusive of total gifts on 4 returns of nonresident donors.

Series Y 457–465. Outlays of the Federal Government: 1789 to 1970

[In thousands of dollars. For 1789–1842, years ending December 31; 1844–1970, June 30; 1843 figures are for January 1–June 30. Data for 1789–1953 are administrative budget figures; for 1954–1970, unified budget figures]

Year	Total¹	Department of Defense	Interest on the public debt	Other Total²³	Other Veterans compensation and pensions⁴	Other Department of Health, Education, and Welfare⁵	Other Department of Agriculture
	457	458–460	461	462	463	464	465
1970	196,587,786	78,360,168	19,303,670	98,923,948	5,307,901	52,337,602	8,306,563
1969	184,556,043	79,144,789	16,588,237	88,823,017	4,879,320	46,599,029	8,330,318
1968	178,832,655	78,672,894	14,573,008	85,586,754	4,605,253	40,576,498	7,306,961
1967	158,254,257	68,762,932	13,391,068	76,100,256	4,301,855	34,607,693	5,841,151
1966	134,651,927	55,445,394	12,013,863	67,192,670	4,214,289	27,959,129	5,513,411
1965	118,429,745	47,179,329	11,346,455	59,903,961	4,109,144	22,732,251	6,795,400
1964	118,583,708	50,702,893	10,665,858	57,214,957	3,961,206	21,695,149	7,458,178
1963	111,311,144	49,242,562	9,895,304	52,173,279	3,871,438	20,248,874	7,332,799
1962	106,812,594	⁶49,283,445	9,119,760	48,409,389	3,704,671	4,210,376	6,294,074
1961	97,794,579	⁶45,688,376	8,957,242	43,148,961	3,621,506	3,680,977	5,383,802
1960	92,223,354	⁶43,968,848	9,179,589	39,074,917	3,368,224	3,400,075	4,842,599
1959	92,104,459	44,602,920	7,592,769	39,908,769	3,274,568	3,089,040	6,529,383
1958	82,575,093	39,916,689	7,606,774	35,051,629	3,104,494	2,636,400	4,368,422
1957	76,740,583	38,719,035	7,244,193	30,777,355	2,869,989	2,292,686	4,560,472
1956	70,460,329	35,692,897	6,786,599	27,980,833	2,797,509	2,067,375	4,760,671
1955	68,509,184	35,629,779	6,370,362	26,509,044	2,680,834	1,989,947	4,275,011
1954	70,889,744	40,625,674	6,382,486	23,881,584	2,481,514	1,977,284	2,613,484

Year	Total¹	Department of the Army (formerly War Department)	Department of the Navy	Department of the Air Force	Interest on the public debt	Other Total²³	Other Veterans compensation and pensions⁴
	457	458	459	460	461	462	463
1953	74,119,798	17,054,333	11,874,830	15,085,228	6,503,580	23,601,826	2,420,140
1952	65,303,201	17,452,710	10,231,265	12,851,619	5,859,263	18,908,343	2,177,893
1951	43,970,284	8,635,939	5,862,549	6,358,604	5,612,655	17,500,538	2,171,475
1950	39,544,037	5,789,468	4,129,546	3,520,633	5,749,913	20,354,478	2,222,926
1949	39,474,413	7,862,397	4,434,706	1,690,461	5,339,396	20,147,453	2,153,828
1948	32,955,232	7,698,556	4,284,619	----------	5,211,102	15,760,955	2,080,130
1947	38,923,379	9,172,139	5,597,203	----------	4,957,922	19,196,115	1,929,226
1946	60,326,042	27,986,769	15,164,412	----------	4,721,958	12,452,902	1,261,415
1945	98,302,937	50,490,102	30,047,152	----------	3,616,686	14,148,997	772,190
1944	94,986,002	⁶49,438,330	26,537,634	----------	2,608,980	16,401,058	494,959
1943	79,367,714	⁶42,525,563	20,888,349	----------	1,808,160	14,145,642	442,394
1942	34,036,861	14,325,508	8,579,589	----------	1,260,085	9,871,679	431,294
1941	13,254,948	3,938,943	2,313,058	----------	1,110,693	5,892,255	433,148
1940	9,055,269	907,160	891,485	----------	1,040,936	6,215,689	429,178
1939	8,841,224	695,256	672,722	----------	940,540	6,532,705	416,721
1938	6,764,628	644,264	596,180	----------	926,281	4,597,954	402,779
1937	7,733,033	628,104	556,674	----------	866,384	5,681,871	396,047
1936	8,421,608	618,587	528,882	----------	749,397	6,524,742	399,066

Year	Total¹	Department of the Army (formerly War Department)	Department of the Navy	Interest on the public debt	Other Total²³	Other Veterans compensation and pensions⁴
	457	458	459	461	462	463
1935	6,497,008	487,995	436,266	820,926	4,751,821	373,805
1934	6,644,602	408,587	296,927	756,617	5,182,470	319,322
1933	4,598,496	434,621	349,373	689,365	3,125,137	234,990
1932	4,659,182	476,305	357,518	599,277	3,226,082	232,521
1931	3,577,434	486,142	353,768	611,560	2,125,964	234,402
1930	3,320,211	464,854	374,164	659,348	1,821,846	220,609
1929	3,127,199	425,946	364,562	678,330	1,658,361	229,781
1928	2,961,245	400,990	331,335	731,764	1,497,156	229,401
1927	2,857,429	369,114	318,909	787,020	1,382,386	230,556
1926	2,929,964	364,090	312,743	831,938	1,421,193	207,190
1925	2,923,762	370,981	346,137	881,807	1,324,837	218,321
1924	2,907,847	357,017	332,249	940,603	1,277,978	228,262
1923	3,140,287	397,051	333,201	1,055,924	1,354,111	264,148
1922	3,289,404	457,756	476,775	991,001	1,363,872	252,577
1921	5,061,785	1,118,076	650,374	999,145	2,294,190	260,611
1920	6,357,677	1,621,953	736,021	1,020,252	2,979,451	213,344
1919	18,492,665	9,009,076	2,002,311	619,216	6,862,063	221,615
1918	12,677,359	4,869,955	1,278,840	189,743	6,338,820	181,138
1917	1,953,857	377,941	239,633	24,743	1,311,541	160,318
1916	712,967	183,176	153,854	22,901	353,036	159,302
1915	746,093	202,060	141,836	22,903	379,295	164,388
1914	725,525	208,349	139,682	22,864	354,630	173,440
1913	714,864	202,129	133,263	22,899	356,573	175,085
1912	689,881	184,123	135,592	22,616	347,550	153,591
1911	691,202	197,199	119,938	21,311	352,753	157,981
1910	693,617	189,823	123,174	21,343	359,277	160,696
1909	693,744	192,487	115,546	21,804	363,907	161,710
1908	659,196	175,840	118,037	21,426	343,893	153,892
1907	579,129	149,775	97,128	24,481	307,744	139,310
1906	570,202	137,326	110,474	24,309	298,093	141,035
1905	567,279	126,094	117,550	24,591	299,044	141,774
1904	583,660	165,200	102,956	24,646	290,857	142,559
1903	517,006	118,630	82,618	28,556	287,202	138,426
1902	485,234	112,272	67,803	29,108	276,051	138,489
1901	524,617	144,616	60,507	32,343	287,151	139,324
1900	520,861	134,775	55,953	40,160	289,973	140,877
1899	605,072	229,841	63,942	39,897	271,392	139,395
1898	443,369	91,992	58,824	37,585	254,968	147,452
1897	365,774	48,950	34,562	37,791	244,471	141,053
1896	352,179	50,831	27,148	35,385	238,816	139,434
1895	356,195	51,805	28,798	30,978	244,615	141,395
1894	367,525	54,568	31,701	27,841	253,415	141,177
1893	383,478	49,642	30,136	27,264	276,436	159,358
1892	345,023	46,895	29,174	23,378	245,576	134,583
1891	365,774	48,720	26,114	37,547	253,393	124,416

Year	Total¹	Department of the Army (formerly War Department)	Department of the Navy	Interest on the public debt	Other Total²	Other Veterans compensation and pensions⁴
	457	458	459	461	462	463
1890	318,041	44,583	22,006	36,099	215,352	106,937
1889	299,289	44,435	21,379	41,001	192,473	87,625
1888	267,925	38,522	16,926	44,715	167,761	80,289
1887	267,932	38,561	15,141	47,742	166,488	75,029
1886	242,483	34,324	13,908	50,580	143,671	63,405
1885	260,227	42,671	16,021	51,386	150,149	56,102
1884	244,126	39,430	17,293	54,578	132,826	55,429
1883	265,408	48,911	15,283	59,160	142,053	66,013
1882	257,981	43,570	15,032	71,077	128,302	61,345
1881	260,713	40,466	15,687	82,509	122,051	50,059
1880	267,643	38,117	13,537	95,758	120,231	56,777
1879	266,948	40,426	15,125	105,328	106,069	35,121
1878	236,964	32,154	17,365	102,501	84,944	27,137
1877	241,334	37,083	14,960	97,125	92,167	27,964
1876	265,101	38,071	18,963	100,243	107,824	28,257
1875	274,623	41,121	21,498	103,094	108,912	29,456
1874	302,634	42,314	30,933	107,120	122,268	29,038
1873	290,345	46,323	23,526	104,751	115,745	29,359
1872	277,518	35,372	21,250	117,358	103,538	28,553
1871	292,177	35,800	19,431	125,577	111,370	34,444
1870	309,654	57,656	21,780	129,235	100,982	28,340
1869	322,865	78,502	20,001	130,694	93,668	28,477
1868	377,340	123,247	25,776	140,424	87,894	23,782
1867	357,543	95,224	31,034	143,782	87,503	20,937
1866	520,809	284,450	43,324	133,068	59,968	15,605
1865	1,297,555	1,031,323	122,613	77,398	66,221	16,339
1864	865,323	690,792	85,726	53,685	35,119	4,984
1863	714,741	599,299	63,222	24,730	27,490	1,079
1862	474,762	394,368	42,668	13,190	24,535	853
1861	66,547	22,981	12,421	4,000	27,144	1,036
1860	63,131	16,410	11,515	3,177	32,029	1,103
1859	69,071	23,244	14,643	2,638	28,546	1,220
1858	74,185	25,485	13,985	1,567	33,148	1,217
1857	67,796	19,262	12,748	1,678	34,108	1,312
1856	69,571	16,948	14,092	1,954	36,577	1,298
1855	59,743	14,774	13,312	2,314	29,342	1,450
1854	58,045	11,734	10,799	3,071	32,442	1,238
1853	48,184	9,947	10,919	3,666	23,652	1,778
1852	44,195	8,225	8,953	4,000	23,017	2,404
1851	47,709	11,812	9,006	3,697	23,195	2,290
1850	39,543	9,400	7,905	3,782	18,456	1,870
1849	45,052	14,853	9,787	3,566	16,846	1,330
1848	45,377	25,502	9,408	2,391	8,076	1,211
1847	57,281	38,306	7,901	1,119	9,956	1,748
1846	27,767	10,793	6,455	843	9,676	1,810

See footnotes at end of table.

Series Y 457–465. Outlays of the Federal Government: 1789 to 1970—Con.

[In thousands of dollars]

Year	Total	Department of the Army (formerly War Department)	Department of the Navy	Interest on the public debt	Other Total [2]	Other Veterans compensation and pensions [4]	Year	Total	Department of the Army (formerly War Department)	Department of the Navy	Interest on the public debt	Other Total [2]	Other Veterans compensation and pensions [4]
	457	458	459	461	462	463		457	458	459	461	462	463
1845___	22,937	5,753	6,297	1,040	9,847	2,397	1818___	19,825	5,623	2,954	6,016	5,232	891
1844___	22,338	5,179	6,498	1,834	8,826	2,031	1817___	21,844	8,004	3,315	6,389	4,136	297
1843___	11,858	2,957	3,728	524	4,649	843	1816___	30,587	16,012	3,908	7,213	3,453	189
1842___	25,206	6,612	8,397	774	9,423	1,379							
1841___	26,566	8,806	6,001	285	11,474	2,388	1815___	32,708	14,794	8,660	5,755	3,499	70
							1814___	34,721	20,351	7,311	4,593	2,466	90
1840___	24,318	7,097	6,114	175	10,932	2,604	1813___	31,682	19,652	6,447	3,599	1,984	87
1839___	26,899	8,917	6,182	400	11,400	3,143	1812___	20,281	11,818	3,959	2,451	2,052	91
1838___	33,865	12,897	6,132	15	14,821	2,156	1811___	8,058	2,033	1,966	2,466	1,594	75
1837___	37,243	13,683	6,647	(NA)	16,914	2,672							
1836___	30,868	12,169	5,808	(NA)	12,891	2,883	1810___	8,157	2,294	1,654	2,845	1,363	84
							1809___	10,281	3,346	2,428	2,866	1,641	88
1835___	17,573	5,759	3,865	58	7,891	1,955	1808___	9,932	2,901	1,884	3,428	1,719	83
1834___	18,628	5,696	3,956	202	8,773	3,364	1807___	8,354	1,289	1,722	3,370	1,974	71
1833___	23,018	6,704	3,901	304	12,108	4,589	1806___	9,804	1,224	1,650	3,723	3,206	82
1832___	17,289	5,446	3,956	773	7,114	1,184							
1831___	15,248	4,842	3,856	1,384	5,166	1,171	1805___	10,506	713	1,598	4,149	4,047	82
							1804___	8,719	875	1,190	4,267	2,388	80
1830___	15,143	4,767	3,239	1,914	5,223	1,363	1803___	7,852	822	1,215	3,849	1,966	63
1829___	15,203	4,724	3,309	2,543	4,627	950	1802___	7,862	1,179	916	4,125	1,642	85
1828___	16,395	4,146	3,919	3,099	5,232	851	1801___	9,395	1,673	2,111	4,413	1,197	74
1827___	16,139	3,939	4,264	3,486	4,450	976							
1826___	17,036	3,943	4,219	3,973	4,900	1,557	1800___	10,786	2,561	3,449	3,375	1,402	64
							1799___	9,666	2,467	2,858	3,186	1,155	95
1825___	15,857	3,660	3,049	4,367	4,781	1,309	1798___	7,677	2,010	1,381	3,053	1,232	105
1824___	20,327	3,341	2,905	4,997	9,085	1,499	1797___	6,134	1,039	383	3,300	1,412	92
1823___	14,707	3,097	2,504	4,923	4,183	1,781	1796___	5,727	1,260	275	3,195	997	101
1822___	15,000	3,112	2,224	5,173	4,491	1,948							
1821___	15,811	4,461	3,319	5,087	2,943	243	1795___	7,540	2,481	411	3,189	1,459	69
							1794___	6,991	2,639	61	3,490	800	81
1820___	18,261	2,630	4,388	5,126	6,116	3,208	1793___	4,482	1,130	(NA)	2,772	580	80
1819___	21,464	6,506	3,848	5,164	5,946	2,416	1792___	5,080	1,101	(Z)	3,202	777	109
							1789– 1791__	4,269	633	1	2,349	1,286	176

NA Not available.
Z Less than $500.
[1] Effective Jan. 3, 1949, amounts refunded by the Government, principally for overpayment of taxes, are reported as deductions from total receipts rather than as outlays. Also, effective July 1, 1948, payments to the Treasury, principally by wholly owned Government corporations for retirement of capital stock and for disposition of earnings, are excluded in reporting both budget receipts and outlays. Neither change affects the budget surplus or deficit. Figures beginning with fiscal 1913 have been adjusted accordingly for comparability.

[2] Includes interest payments by Government corporations and other business-type activities on securities issued to the Treasury.
[3] Beginning 1954, undistributed intrabudgetary transactions are deducted from total. Beginning 1932, interfund transactions are deducted from total.
[4] Excludes education and training.
[5] Social Security trust fund outlays are reflected under the Department of the Treasury through fiscal 1962, and under the Department of Health, Education, and Welfare, thereafter.
[6] Includes military assistance.

Series Y 466–471. Outlays of the Federal Government, by Major Function: 1900 to 1939

[In millions of dollars. For years ending June 30]

Year	Total	Major national security	International affairs and finance	Veterans services and benefits	Interest	All other	Year	Total	Major national security	International affairs and finance	Veterans services and benefits	Interest	All other
	466	467	468	469	470	471		466	467	468	469	470	471
1939_____	8,858	1,075	20	560	950	6,254	1920_____	6,357	3,997	435	332	1,024	569
1938_____	6,792	1,030	19	581	933	4,229	1919_____	18,448	13,548	3,500	324	616	460
1937_____	7,756	937	18	1,137	872	4,792	1918_____	12,662	7,110	4,748	235	198	371
1936_____	8,494	914	18	2,350	756	4,456	1917_____	1,954	602	891	171	25	265
							1916_____	713	305	6	171	23	208
1935_____	6,521	711	19	607	826	4,358							
1934_____	6,694	540	12	557	770	4,815	1915_____	746	297	5	176	23	245
1933_____	4,623	648	16	863	701	2,395	1914_____	725	298	5	173	23	226
1932_____	4,659	703	19	985	619	2,333	1913_____	715	293	5	175	23	219
1931_____	3,578	733	16	1,040	628	1,161	1912_____	690	284	5	154	23	224
							1911_____	691	283	(1)	158	21	[1] 229
1930_____	3,320	734	14	821	697	1,054							
1929_____	3,127	696	14	812	719	886	1910_____	694	284	(1)	161	21	[1] 228
1928_____	2,933	656	12	806	731	728	1909_____	694	308	(1)	162	22	[1] 202
1927_____	2,837	578	17	786	787	669	1908_____	659	294	(1)	154	21	[1] 190
1926_____	2,888	586	17	772	832	681	1907_____	579	247	(1)	139	24	[1] 169
							1906_____	570	247	(1)	141	24	[1] 158
1925_____	2,881	591	15	741	882	652							
1924_____	2,890	647	15	676	941	611	1905_____	567	244	(1)	142	25	[1] 156
1923_____	3,137	680	14	747	1,056	640	1904_____	584	268	(1)	143	25	[1] 148
1922_____	3,285	929	10	686	991	669	1903_____	517	202	(1)	138	29	[1] 148
1921_____	5,058	2,581	83	646	999	749	1902_____	485	180	(1)	138	29	[1] 138
							1901_____	525	206	(1)	139	32	[1] 148
							1900_____	521	191	(1)	141	40	[1] 149

[1] Figures for "International affairs and finance" included with "All other."

Series Y 472–487.   Outlays of the Federal Government, by Major Function: 1940 to 1970

[In millions of dollars.   For years ending June 30.   Data for 1940–1953 are consolidated cash statement figures; for 1954–1970, unified budget figures]

Year	Total outlays	National defense	International affairs and finance	Space research and technology	Veterans benefits and services	Health	Income security	Education and manpower	Agriculture and rural development	Natural resources and environment	Commerce and transportation	Community development and housing	General government	Interest	Undistributed intragovernmental transactions [1]	Unallocable [2]
	472	473	474	475	476	477	478	479	480	481	482	483	484	485	486	487
1970	196,588	80,295	3,570	3,749	8,677	12,907	43,790	7,289	6,201	2,568	9,310	2,965	3,336	18,312	−6,380	....
1969	184,548	81,232	3,785	4,247	7,640	11,611	37,699	6,525	6,218	2,169	7,921	1,961	2,866	15,791	−5,117	....
1968	178,833	80,517	4,619	4,721	6,882	9,608	34,108	6,739	5,940	1,722	8,094	4,076	2,561	13,744	−4,499	....
1967	158,254	70,081	4,547	5,423	6,897	6,667	31,164	5,853	4,373	2,036	7,594	2,616	2,510	12,588	−3,936	....
1966	134,652	56,785	4,490	5,933	5,920	2,509	29,016	4,258	3,676	2,036	7,171	2,644	2,292	11,285	−3,364	....
1965	118,430	49,578	4,340	5,091	5,722	1,704	25,702	2,284	4,805	2,056	7,399	288	2,210	10,357	−3,109	....
1964	118,584	53,591	4,117	4,170	5,681	1,716	25,110	1,751	5,184	1,966	6,511	−185	2,040	9,810	−2,877	....
1963	111,311	52,257	4,115	2,552	5,520	1,379	24,084	1,502	5,138	1,498	5,765	−880	1,810	9,215	−2,644	....
1962	106,813	51,097	4,492	1,257	5,625	1,130	22,530	1,406	4,122	1,675	5,430	589	1,650	8,321	−2,513	....
1961	97,795	47,381	3,357	744	5,688	873	21,227	1,227	3,340	1,554	5,062	191	1,491	8,108	−2,449	....
1960	92,223	45,908	3,054	401	5,426	756	18,203	1,060	3,322	1,002	4,790	971	1,327	8,299	−2,296	....
1959	92,104	46,617	3,267	145	5,428	654	17,247	870	5,365	1,193	4,467	851	1,168	7,070	−2,238	....
1958	82,575	44,371	3,063	89	5,184	540	15,016	820	3,224	870	3,033	109	1,243	6,944	−1,931	....
1957	76,741	42,760	3,074	76	4,870	461	11,522	672	3,082	752	2,171	832	1,643	6,679	−1,853	....
1956	70,460	40,305	2,181	71	4,810	342	9,789	674	3,991	251	1,791	80	1,331	6,292	−1,448	....
1955	68,509	40,245	2,038	74	4,522	271	9,122	573	4,023	493	1,128	12	1,187	6,030	−1,209	....
1954	70,890	46,645	1,503	90	4,341	288	7,760	437	2,373	941	1,118	−639	1,247	6,012	−1,226	....
1953	76,769	50,413	2,268	79	4,522	318	6,128	425	2,965	1,517	1,826	397	1,497	6,450	−1,422	−614
1952	67,962	44,015	2,954	67	5,350	330	5,206	322	1,086	1,409	1,807	589	1,463	5,834	−1,302	−1,168
1951	45,797	22,544	3,822	62	5,530	307	4,442	221	691	1,311	1,482	501	1,312	5,628	−1,204	−852
1950	43,147	13,119	4,775	54	8,837	252	4,707	219	2,818	1,246	1,618	250	1,174	5,744	−1,189	−477
1949	40,570	13,097	6,121	49	6,601	183	3,580	165	2,547	1,089	1,482	295	1,060	5,414	−1,074	−39
1948	36,493	13,015	4,651	38	6,445	150	2,782	171	604	770	1,063	100	1,294	5,135	−998	1,273
1947	36,931	13,059	4,552	35	6,907	146	2,762	97	1,274	554	664	260	1,224	4,903	−904	1,398
1946	61,738	44,731	2,739	32	3,364	173	2,509	110	478	322	849	−579	885	4,694	−813	2,244
1945	95,184	81,585	3,312	38	1,132	186	1,173	234	1,623	329	4,147	−191	758	3,549	−624	−2,067
1944	93,956	76,874	3,642	30	709	152	1,080	197	1,228	412	7,740	307	886	2,544	−503	−1,342
1943	78,909	63,212	3,320	23	613	73	1,136	198	785	510	7,515	297	791	1,786	−366	−984
1942	34,500	23,970	1,841	12	603	61	1,454	188	1,833	541	3,549	207	480	1,263	−308	−1,194
1941	13,980	6,062	146	8	629	53	1,628	142	1,530	459	2,152	122	384	1,116	−258	−193
1940	9,589	1,504	52	3	628	48	1,460	73	1,580	481	2,643	28	354	1,049	−224	−90

[1] Represents employer share of employee retirement and interest received by trust funds.

[2] Allowance for differences between the unified budget and the consolidated cash statement.

Series Y 488–492.   Gross Federal Debt Outstanding: 1939 to 1970

[In millions of dollars.   As of June 30]

Year	Gross Federal debt	Held by Federal Government accounts	Held by the public			Year	Gross Federal debt	Held by Federal Government accounts	Held by the public		
			Total	The Federal Reserve System	Other				Total	The Federal Reserve System	Other
	488	489	490	491	492		488	489	490	491	492
1970	382,603	97,723	284,880	57,714	227,166	1955	274,366	47,751	226,616	23,607	203,009
1969	367,144	87,661	279,483	54,095	225,388	1954	270,812	46,313	224,499	25,037	199,462
1968	369,769	79,140	290,629	52,230	238,399	1953	265,963	47,580	218,383	24,746	193,637
1967	341,348	73,819	267,529	46,719	220,810	1952	259,097	44,339	214,758	22,906	191,852
1966	329,474	64,784	264,690	42,169	222,521	1951	255,288	40,962	214,326	22,982	191,344
1965	323,154	61,540	261,614	39,100	222,514	1950	256,853	37,830	219,023	18,331	200,692
1964	316,763	59,210	257,553	34,794	222,759	1949	252,610	38,288	214,322	19,343	194,979
1963	310,807	56,345	254,461	32,027	222,434	1948	252,031	35,761	216,270	21,366	194,904
1962	303,291	54,918	248,373	29,663	218,710	1947	257,149	32,810	224,339	21,872	202,467
1961	292,895	54,291	238,604	27,253	211,351	1946	270,991	29,130	241,861	23,783	218,078
1960	290,862	53,686	237,177	26,523	210,654	1945	260,123	24,941	235,182	21,792	213,390
1959	287,767	52,764	235,003	26,044	208,959	1944	204,079	19,283	184,796	14,899	169,897
1958	279,693	53,329	226,363	25,438	200,925	1943	142,648	14,882	127,766	7,149	120,617
1957	272,353	52,931	219,421	23,035	196,386	1942	79,200	11,447	67,753	2,640	65,113
1956	272,763	50,537	222,226	23,758	198,468	1941	57,531	9,308	48,223	2,180	46,043
						1940	50,696	7,924	42,772	2,458	40,314
						1939	48,156	6,735	41,421	2,551	38,870

Series Y 493–504. Public Debt of the Federal Government: 1791 to 1970
[For 1791–1842, as of January 1; thereafter, as of June 30]

Year	Principal of public debt outstanding					Computed annual interest charge	Computed rate of interest	Composition of interest-bearing debt				
	Total debt		Matured	Non-interest-bearing[3]	Interest-bearing[4]			Bonds		Treasury bills[6]	Notes[7]	Special issues[8]
	Amount[1]	Per capita[2]						U.S. savings bonds	Other bonds[5]			
	493	494	495	496	497	498	499	500	501	502	503	504
	1,000 dollars	Dollars	1,000 dollars	1,000 dollars	1,000 dollars	1,000 dollars	Percent	Million dollars	Million dollars	Million dollars	Million dollars	Million dollars
1970	370,918,707	1,811.12	365,990	1,527,194	369,025,522	20,338,884	5.557	51,281	65,551	78,050	97,821	76,323
1969	353,720,254	1,740.64	460,746	1,530,062	351,729,445	17,086,631	4.891	51,711	81,430	69,039	82,761	66,790
1968	347,578,406	1,727.94	253,982	2,923,917	344,400,507	15,403,812	4.499	51,712	93,789	65,580	73,793	59,526
1967	326,220,938	1,638.36	284,263	3,650,723	322,285,952	12,952,924	4.039	51,213	100,243	64,899	49,774	56,155
1966	319,907,088	1,624.66	307,674	4,168,359	315,431,055	12,516,398	3.988	50,537	105,439	57,348	50,987	51,120
1965	317,273,899	1,630.46	292,260	3,868,822	313,112,817	11,466,618	3.678	50,043	107,183	54,537	52,699	48,650
1964	311,712,899	1,622.49	295,293	4,061,045	307,356,562	10,900,361	3.560	49,299	92,962	51,028	67,436	46,627
1963	305,859,633	1,614.74	310,416	3,595,487	301,953,731	10,119,295	3.360	48,314	86,619	69,891	52,328	44,801
1962	298,200,823	1,597.60	437,628	3,321,194	294,442,001	9,518,857	3.239	47,607	79,915	56,518	65,464	44,939
1961	288,970,939	1,572.58	349,355	2,949,975	285,671,609	8,761,496	3.072	47,514	86,796	50,062	56,257	45,043
1960	286,330,761	1,584.70	444,609	2,644,969	283,241,183	9,316,067	3.297	47,544	88,250	51,065	51,483	44,899
1959	284,705,907	1,606.11	476,455	2,396,090	281,833,362	8,065,917	2.867	50,503	93,401	65,860	27,314	44,756
1958	276,343,218	1,586.89	597,325	1,048,333	274,697,560	7,245,155	2.638	51,984	100,725	55,326	20,416	46,246
1957	270,527,172	1,579.30	529,242	1,512,368	268,485,563	7,325,147	2.730	54,622	92,170	43,893	30,973	46,827
1956	272,750,814	1,621.38	666,052	2,201,694	269,883,068	6,949,700	2.576	57,497	94,210	37,111	35,952	45,114
1955	274,374,223	1,660.11	588,601	2,044,354	271,741,268	6,387,226	2.351	58,365	94,133	33,350	42,642	43,250
1954	271,259,599	1,670.41	437,185	1,912,648	268,909,767	6,298,069	2.342	58,061	93,660	37,920	37,039	42,229
1953	266,071,062	1,667.48	298,421	1,826,623	263,946,018	6,430,991	2.438	57,886	95,084	35,561	34,878	40,538
1952	259,105,179	1,650.84	418,692	1,823,625	256,862,861	5,981,357	2.329	57,685	90,221	45,642	25,575	37,739
1951	255,221,977	1,654.20	512,047	1,858,165	252,851,765	5,739,616	2.270	57,572	93,881	23,123	43,624	34,653
1950	257,357,352	1,696.67	264,771	1,883,228	255,209,353	5,612,677	2.200	57,536	104,490	31,951	28,876	32,356
1949	252,770,360	1,694.75	244,757	1,763,966	250,761,637	5,605,930	2.236	56,260	112,306	40,964	8,456	32,776
1948	252,292,247	1,720.71	279,752	1,949,146	250,063,348	5,455,476	2.182	53,274	114,464	36,345	15,769	30,211
1947	258,286,383	1,792.05	230,914	2,942,058	255,113,412	5,374,409	2.107	51,367	121,607	41,071	13,702	27,366
1946	269,422,099	1,905.42	376,407	934,820	268,110,872	5,350,772	1.996	49,035	119,929	51,843	24,972	22,332
1945	258,682,187	1,848.60	268,667	2,056,904	256,356,616	4,963,730	1.936	45,586	107,149	51,177	33,633	18,812
1944	201,003,387	1,452.44	200,851	1,259,181	199,543,355	3,849,255	1.929	34,606	80,132	43,557	26,962	14,287
1943	136,696,090	999.83	140,500	1,175,284	135,380,306	2,678,779	1.979	21,256	58,164	28,425	16,663	10,871
1942	72,422,445	537.13	98,300	355,727	71,968,418	1,644,476	2.285	10,188	38,588	5,604	9,703	7,885
1941	48,961,444	367.09	205,000	369,044	48,387,400	1,218,239	2.518	4,314	30,652	1,603	5,698	6,120
1940	42,967,531	325.23	204,591	386,444	42,376,496	1,094,620	2.583	2,905	27,012	1,302	6,383	4,775
1939	40,439,532	308.98	142,283	411,280	39,885,970	1,036,937	2.600	1,868	25,698	1,308	7,243	3,770
1938	37,164,740	286.27	141,362	447,452	36,575,926	947,084	2.589	1,238	22,361	1,154	9,147	2,676
1937	36,424,614	282.75	118,530	505,974	35,800,109	924,347	2.582	800	20,522	2,303	10,617	1,558
1936	33,778,543	263.79	169,363	620,390	32,988,790	838,002	2.559	316	18,312	2,354	11,381	626
1935	28,700,893	225.55	230,662	824,989	27,645,241	750,678	2.716	62	14,874	2,053	10,023	633
1934	27,053,141	214.07	54,267	518,387	26,480,488	842,301	3.181	----------	16,510	2,921	6,653	396
1933	22,538,673	179.48	65,911	315,118	22,157,643	742,176	3.350	----------	14,223	3,063	4,548	323
1932	19,487,002	156.10	60,079	265,650	19,161,274	671,605	3.505	----------	14,250	3,341	1,261	309
1931	16,801,281	135.45	51,819	229,874	16,519,589	588,987	3.566	----------	13,531	2,246	452	291
1930	16,185,310	131.51	31,717	231,701	15,921,892	606,032	3.807	----------	12,111	1,420	1,626	764
1929	16,931,088	139.04	50,749	241,398	16,638,941	656,654	3.946	----------	12,125	1,640	2,267	607
1928	17,604,293	146.09	45,335	241,264	17,317,694	671,353	3.877	----------	13,021	1,252	2,582	462
1927	18,511,907	155.51	14,719	244,524	18,252,665	722,676	3.960	----------	15,222	686	1,986	359
1926	19,643,216	167.32	13,360	246,086	19,383,771	793,424	4.093	----------	16,928	453	1,799	204
1925	20,516,194	177.12	30,259	275,028	20,210,907	829,680	4.105	----------	16,842	533	2,740	95
1924	21,250,813	186.23	30,278	239,293	20,981,242	876,961	4.180	----------	16,025	808	4,148	----------
1923	22,349,707	199.64	98,739	243,925	22,007,044	927,331	4.214	----------	16,535	1,031	4,441	----------
1922	22,963,382	208.65	25,251	227,793	22,710,338	962,897	4.240	----------	15,965	1,829	4,916	----------
1921	23,977,451	220.91	10,688	227,862	23,738,900	1,029,918	4.339	----------	16,119	2,700	4,920	----------
1920	24,299,321	228.23	6,745	230,076	24,062,500	1,016,592	4.225	----------	16,218	2,769	5,075	----------
1919	25,484,506	242.56	11,176	236,383	25,236,947	1,054,205	4.178	----------	17,188	3,625	4,422	----------
1918	12,455,225	119.13	20,243	237,475	12,197,508	468,619	3.910	----------	9,911	1,706	369	----------
1917	2,975,619	28.77	14,232	248,837	2,712,549	83,625	3.120	----------	2,412	273	27	----------
1916	1,225,146	12.02	1,473	252,110	971,563	23,085	2.376	----------	967	----------	4	----------

See footnotes at end of table.

Series Y 493–504. Public Debt of the Federal Government: 1791 to 1970—Con.

Year	Principal of public debt outstanding					Computed annual interest charge	Composition of interest-bearing debt		Year	Debt [1]
	Total debt		Matured	Non-interest-bearing [3]	Interest-bearing [4]		Other bonds [5]	Treasury bills [6]		
	Amount [1]	Per capita [2]								
	493	494	495	496	497	498	501	502		493
	1,000 dollars	*Dollars*	*1,000 dollars*	*1,000 dollars*	*1,000 dollars*	*1,000 dollars*	*Million dollars*	*Million dollars*		*1,000 dollars*
1915	1,191,264	11.85	1,507	219,998	969,759	22,937	970	----------	1850	63,453
1914	1,188,235	11.99	1,553	218,730	967,953	22,891	968		1849	63,062
1913	1,193,048	12.27	1,660	225,682	965,707	22,835	966		1848	47,045
1912	1,193,839	12.52	1,760	228,301	963,777	22,787	964		1847	38,827
1911	1,153,985	12.29	1,880	236,752	915,353	21,337	915		1846	15,550
1910	1,146,940	12.41	2,125	231,498	913,317	21,276	913		1845	15,925
1909	1,148,315	12.69	2,884	232,114	913,317	21,276	913	----------	1844	23,462
1908	1,177,690	13.28	4,130	276,056	897,504	21,101	883	14	1843	32,743
1907	1,147,178	13.19	1,087	251,257	894,834	21,629	895	(Z)	1842	13,594
1906	1,142,523	13.37	1,128	246,236	895,159	23,248	895	(Z)	1841	5,251
1905	1,132,357	13.51	1,370	235,829	895,158	24,177	895	(Z)	1840	3,573
1904	1,136,259	13.83	1,971	239,131	895,157	24,177	895	(Z)	1839	10,434
1903	1,159,406	14.38	1,205	243,659	914,541	25,542	915	(Z)	1838	3,308
1902	1,178,031	14.88	1,281	245,680	931,070	27,543	913	(Z)	1837	337
1901	1,221,572	15.74	1,416	233,016	987,141	29,789	987	(Z)	1836	38
1900	1,263,417	16.60	1,176	238,762	1,023,479	33,541	1,023	(Z)	1835	38
1899	1,436,701	19.21	1,218	389,434	1,046,049	40,848	1,046	(Z)	1834	4,760
1898	1,232,743	16.77	1,263	384,113	847,367	34,387	847	(Z)	1833	7,012
1897	1,226,794	16.99	1,347	378,082	847,365	34,387	847	(Z)	1832	24,322
1896	1,222,729	17.25	1,637	373,729	847,364	34,387	847	(Z)	1831	39,123
1895	1,096,913	15.76	1,722	378,989	716,202	29,141	716	(Z)	1830	48,565
1894	1,016,898	14.89	1,851	380,005	635,042	25,394	635	(Z)	1829	58,421
1893	961,432	14.36	2,094	374,301	585,037	22,894	585	(Z)	1828	67,475
1892	968,219	14.74	2,786	380,404	585,029	22,894	585	(Z)	1827	73,987
1891	1,005,807	15.63	1,615	393,663	610,529	23,616	610	(Z)	1826	81,054
1890	1,122,397	17.80	1,816	409,268	711,313	29,418	711	(Z)	1825	83,788
1889	1,249,471	20.23	1,911	431,705	815,854	33,752	816	(Z)	1824	90,270
1888	1,384,632	22.89	2,496	445,613	936,523	38,992	936	(Z)	1823	90,876
1887	1,465,485	24.75	6,115	451,678	1,007,692	41,781	1,008	(Z)	1822	93,547
1886	1,555,660	26.85	9,704	413,941	1,132,014	45,510	1,132	(Z)	1821	89,987
1885	1,578,551	27.86	4,101	392,299	1,182,151	47,014	1,182	(Z)	1820	91,016
1884	1,625,307	29.35	19,656	393,088	1,212,564	47,926	1,212	(Z)	1819	95,530
1883	1,721,959	31.83	7,831	389,899	1,324,229	51,437	1,324	(Z)	1818	103,467
1882	1,856,916	35.16	16,261	390,845	1,449,810	57,365	1,449	(Z)	1817	123,492
1881	2,019,286	39.18	6,724	386,994	1,625,568	75,019	1,625	1	1816	127,335
1880	2,090,909	41.60	7,621	373,295	1,709,993	79,634	1,709	1	1815	99,834
1879	2,298,913	46.72	37,015	374,181	1,887,716	83,774	----------		1814	81,488
1878	2,159,418	44.82	5,594	373,089	1,780,736	94,654			1813	55,963
1877	2,107,760	44.71	16,649	393,223	1,697,889	93,161			1812	45,210
1876	2,130,846	46.22	3,902	430,258	1,696,685	96,104			1811	48,006
1875	2,156,277	47.84	11,426	436,175	1,708,676	96,856			1810	53,173
1874	2,159,933	49.05	3,216	431,786	1,724,931	98,796			1809	57,023
1873	2,151,210	50.02	51,929	402,797	1,696,484	98,050			1808	65,196
1872	2,209,991	52.65	7,927	401,270	1,800,794	103,988			1807	69,218
1871	2,322,052	56.72	1,949	399,406	1,920,697	111,949			1806	75,723
1870	2,436,453	61.06	3,570	397,003	2,035,881	118,785			1805	82,312
1869	2,545,111	65.17	5,112	388,503	2,151,495	125,524			1804	86,427
1868	2,583,446	67.61	1,246	390,874	2,191,326	128,460			1803	77,055
1867	2,650,168	70.91	1,739	409,474	2,238,955	138,892			1802	80,713
1866	2,755,764	75.42	4,436	429,212	2,322,116	146,068			1801	83,038
1865	2,677,929	75.01	2,129	458,090	2,217,709	137,743			1800	82,976
1864	1,815,831	52.08	367	455,437	1,360,027	78,853			1799	78,409
1863	1,119,774	32.91	172	411,767	707,834	41,854			1798	79,229
1862	524,178	15.79	231	158,591	365,356	22,049			1797	82,064
1861	90,582	2.80	159	----------	90,423	5,093			1796	83,762
1860	64,844	2.06	161	----------	64,683	3,444			1795	80,748
1859	58,498	1.91	165	----------	58,333	3,126			1794	78,427
1858	44,913	1.59	170	----------	44,743	2,447			1793	80,359
1857	28,701	.93	198	----------	28,503	1,673			1792	77,228
1856	31,974	1.30	169	----------	31,805	1,869			1791	75,463
1855	35,588	1.30	170	----------	35,418	2,314				
1854	42,244	1.59	199	----------	42,045					
1853	59,805	2.32	162	----------	59,642					
1852	66,199	2.67	----------	----------						
1851	68,305	2.85	----------	----------						

Z Less than $500,000.
[1] Figures for 1791 through 1852 are not entirely comparable with later figures.
[2] Based on Bureau of the Census estimated population. Beginning 1959, estimates include Alaska and, 1960, Hawaii.
[3] Includes old demand notes; U.S. notes (gold reserve deducted since 1900); postal currency and fractional currency less the amounts officially estimated to have been destroyed; and also the deposits held by the Treasury for the retirement of Federal Reserve banknotes, and for national banknotes of national banks failed, in liquidation, and reducing circulation, which, prior to 1890, were not included in the published debt statements. Does not include gold, silver, or currency certificates, or Treasury notes of 1890 for redemption of which an exact equivalent of the respective kinds of money or bullion was held in the Treasury.

[4] Exclusive of bonds issued to Pacific Railways (provision was made by law to secure the Treasury against both principal and interest) and the Navy pension fund (which was not a debt, the principal being the property of the United States). The Statement of the Public Debt included the railroad bonds from issuance and the Navy fund from Sept. 1, 1896, until the Statement of June 30, 1890.
[5] Includes Treasury, Panama Canal, Depositary, and U.S. retirement plan bonds.
[6] Includes certificates of indebtedness. Also includes refunding certificates of deposit, 1880–1907, inclusive.
[7] Includes old Treasury (War) savings securities from 1918 through 1929.
[8] Comprises special issues to Government agencies and trust funds.

Series Y 505–521. Federal, State, and Local Government Revenue, by Source: 1902 to 1970

[In millions of dollars]

Year	Total revenue [1]	General revenue										Insurance trust revenue						
		Total	Taxes							Charges and miscellaneous	Utility and liquor stores revenue	Total [2]	Employee retirement	Unemployment insurance			Old-age and survivors insurance	Other
			Total	Individual income	Corporation income	Sales, gross receipts, and customs	Property	Other taxes, including licenses					Total	Contributions	Interest (credited by U.S. Government)		
	505	506	507	508	509	510	511	512	513	514	515	516	517	518	519	520	521
1970___	333,810	272,480	232,877	101,224	36,567	48,619	34,054	12,413	39,603	8,614	52,716	8,206	3,224	2,654	569	38,485	2,802
1969___	312,638	258,242	222,708	96,157	39,858	44,345	30,673	11,675	35,534	7,840	46,557	7,133	3,174	2,683	491	33,649	2,600
1968___	265,639	217,323	185,126	76,034	31,183	39,186	27,747	10,976	32,197	7,502	40,814	6,240	3,103	2,685	418	29,029	2,441
1967___	252,563	206,696	176,121	67,352	36,198	36,336	26,047	10,188	30,575	6,911	38,956	5,492	3,422	3,057	365	27,663	2,380
1966___	225,547	188,368	160,742	60,206	32,111	33,726	24,670	10,029	27,626	6,619	30,558	4,870	3,476	3,188	288	20,023	2,189
1965___	202,585	169,691	144,953	52,882	27,390	32,904	22,583	9,191	24,739	6,355	26,539	4,494	3,387	3,145	241	16,742	1,916
1964___	192,412	160,740	138,292	52,488	25,188	30,538	21,241	8,838	22,448	5,975	25,697	4,078	3,404	3,198	205	16,386	1,828
1963___	180,302	151,751	130,811	50,855	23,084	28,661	19,833	8,378	20,940	5,532	23,019	3,729	3,331	3,150	181	14,195	1,765
1962___	168,062	142,397	123,816	48,608	21,831	26,922	19,054	7,402	18,581	5,308	20,357	3,438	2,967	2,802	164	12,289	1,663
1961___	158,741	133,969	116,331	43,951	22,220	25,112	18,002	7,047	17,637	5,116	19,657	3,190	2,669	2,473	196	12,131	1,667
1960 *__	153,102	130,618	113,120	43,178	22,674	24,452	16,405	6,411	17,499	4,877	17,608	2,868	2,476	2,295	183	10,656	1,606
1959 [3]__	133,055	114,178	99,636	38,713	18,310	21,769	14,983	5,862	14,542	4,536	14,341	2,641	1,935	1,754	181	8,294	1,472
1958___	130,403	112,466	98,387	36,483	21,092	21,102	14,047	5,661	14,079	4,211	13,726	2,365	1,807	1,587	220	8,044	1,508
1957___	129,151	112,723	98,632	37,374	22,151	20,594	12,864	5,650	14,091	4,127	12,301	2,130	1,799	1,588	210	6,857	1,515
1956___	119,651	104,494	91,593	33,725	21,770	19,160	11,749	5,190	12,900	3,854	11,303	1,872	1,536	1,349	187	6,442	1,453
1955___	106,404	93,264	81,072	29,984	18,604	17,221	10,735	4,527	12,192	3,688	9,452	1,622	1,345	1,157	188	5,087	1,398
1954___	108,255	95,844	84,476	30,669	21,879	17,643	9,967	4,317	11,369	3,496	8,914	1,502	1,488	1,284	204	4,554	1,370
1953___	104,781	93,124	83,704	30,881	22,055	17,279	9,375	4,112	9,420	3,324	8,333	1,332	1,571	1,389	182	4,060	1,369
1952___	100,245	89,230	79,066	28,919	22,072	15,689	8,652	3,735	10,163	3,108	7,907	1,253	1,612	1,452	160	3,547	1,495
1950___	66,680	58,486	51,100	16,533	11,081	12,997	7,349	3,140	7,386	2,712	5,482	965	1,190	1,042	148	2,107	1,219
1948___	67,005	59,666	51,218	19,848	12,092	12,092	6,126	2,881	8,448	2,511	4,828	672	1,337	1,193	144	1,616	1,203
1946___	61,532	55,130	46,380	16,579	12,280	9,950	4,986	2,586	8,750	2,033	4,369	571	1,282	1,154	128	1,201	1,316
1944___	64,778	58,617	49,095	20,043	15,188	7,012	4,604	2,249	9,522	1,633	4,528	498	1,518	1,432	86	1,260	1,251
1942___	28,352	24,347	20,793	3,481	4,999	5,776	4,537	2,000	3,554	1,277	2,728	285	1,218	1,159	59	869	356
1940___	17,804	14,858	12,688	1,183	1,279	4,109	4,430	1,687	2,170	998	1,948	214	931	896	35	538	265
1938___	17,484	15,023	12,949	1,495	1,498	3,815	4,440	1,701	2,074	877	1,584	182	731	706	25	387	284
1936___	13,588	12,533	10,583	819	858	3,389	4,093	1,424	1,950	747	308	158	23	23	_____	_____	127
1934___	11,300	10,463	8,854	485	435	2,885	4,076	973	1,609	590	247	136	_____	_____	_____	_____	111
1932___	10,289	9,578	7,977	479	677	1,485	4,487	849	1,601	463	248	126	_____	_____	_____	_____	122
1927___	12,191	11,551	9,451	949	1,351	1,558	4,730	862	2,100	403	237	92	_____	_____	_____	_____	145
1922___	9,322	8,894	7,387	2,040		1,306	3,321	721	1,507	266	162	59	_____	_____	_____	_____	103
1913___	2,980	2,862	2,271	_____	35	670	1,332	234	591	116	2	2	_____	_____	_____	_____	_____
1902___	1,694	1,632	1,373	_____	_____	515	706	152	259	62	_____						

* Denotes first year for which figures include Alaska and Hawaii.
[1] To avoid duplication, transactions between governments are excluded; see text.
[2] Excludes interest on Federal securities held by Federal agencies and funds; see text. [3] Includes Alaska.

Series Y 522–532. Federal, State, and Local Government Expenditure and Governmental Debt: 1902 to 1970

[In millions of dollars. For 1962 and earlier years, figures relate to governmental fiscal years ending within the particular calendar year. Since 1962, figures for local governments are grouped in terms of fiscal years which closed within the 12 months ending June 30]

Year	Expenditure								Expenditures for personal services	Indebtedness	
	Total [1]	Capital outlay			Current operation	Assistance and subsidies	Interest on debt [2]	Insurance benefits and repayments		Debt outstanding at end of fiscal year	Increase or decrease (−) in debt during year
		Total	Construction	Other							
	522	523	524	525	526	527	528	529	530	531	532
1970_____	332,985	47,519	28,402	19,118	197,020	20,764	19,160	48,521	110,499	514,489	27,221
1969_____	308,344	47,246	26,836	20,410	181,547	18,288	17,663	43,600	99,068	487,268	18,532
1968_____	282,645	47,057	24,772	22,285	165,515	16,450	15,496	38,127	89,375	468,736	28,856
1967_____	257,800	42,101	23,832	18,269	153,458	14,694	13,985	33,561	81,270	439,880	13,669
1966_____	224,813	39,981	22,411	17,569	130,488	13,363	12,857	28,126	72,963	426,958	10,172
1965_____	205,550	33,744	20,885	12,860	122,481	11,952	12,493	24,880	65,724	416,786	12,851
1964_____	196,431	36,905	19,420	17,485	111,496	11,119	12,750	24,161	61,361	403,935	13,019
1963_____	184,996	36,272	18,005	18,269	103,471	10,277	11,716	23,259	56,976	390,916	(NA)
1962_____	176,240	35,220	17,298	17,922	98,146	9,586	11,660	21,628	54,153	379,479	14,767
1961_____	164,875	32,320	16,987	15,333	91,723	9,710	10,931	20,191	50,215	363,994	7,708
1960 *_____	151,288	31,946	15,832	16,113	81,654	9,690	10,402	17,596	47,136	356,286	7,470
1959 [3]_____	145,748	32,228	16,385	15,842	78,950	7,283	10,658	16,631	44,994	348,816	14,286
1958_____	134,931	30,838	14,922	15,916	71,637	7,653	10,278	14,524	41,857	334,530	10,964
1957_____	125,463	28,866	13,782	15,084	68,966	6,873	9,488	11,269	39,486	323,566	1,947
1956_____	115,796	26,363	12,771	13,592	64,110	6,531	9,215	9,576	37,573	321,619	2,978
1955_____	110,717	28,736	12,612	16,125	58,133	5,904	8,942	9,002	34,916	318,641	8,450
1954_____	111,332	27,369	11,739	15,631	62,494	5,713	8,271	7,484	33,538	310,190	10,338
1953_____	110,054	26,403	10,498	15,904	63,051	5,660	8,933	6,006	33,070	299,852	10,648
1952_____	99,847	24,873	9,723	15,151	56,112	4,986	8,387	5,489	29,766	289,205	5,867

See footnotes at end of table.

Series Y 522–532. Federal, State, and Local Government Expenditure and Governmental Debt: 1902 to 1970—Con.

[In millions of dollars]

Year	Total [1]	Capital outlay			Current operation	Assistance and subsidies	Interest on debt [2]	Insurance benefits and re-payments	Expenditures for personal services	Debt outstanding at end of fiscal year	Increase or decrease (−) in debt during year
		Total	Construction	Other							
	522	523	524	525	526	527	528	529	530	531	532
1950	70,334	----------	6,840		51,584		5,017	6,894	20,530	281,472	7,703
1948	55,081	----------	4,376		43,226		4,866	2,614	17,345	270,948	−4,153
1946	79,707	----------	2,536		70,356		4,422	2,392	28,413	285,339	9,986
1944	109,947	----------	5,117		101,201		2,786	842	26,760	218,482	63,013
1942	45,576	----------	8,232		34,625		1,732	986	10,966	91,759	22,891
1940	20,417	----------	3,139		14,624		1,686	968	7,649	63,251	2,748
1938	17,675	----------	2,662		12,835		1,624	554	7,047	56,601	714
1936	16,758	----------	2,427		12,551		1,558	222	6,353	53,253	5,305
1934	12,807	----------	2,155		8,888		1,571	193	5,338	45,982	3,855
1932	12,437	----------	1,876		8,968		1,422	171	4,729	38,692	2,918
1927	11,220	----------	2,095		7,560		1,426	139	4,255	33,393	−57
1922	9,297	----------	1,397		6,398		1,418	84	3,303	33,072	432
1913	3,215	----------	561		2,451		196	7	1,427	5,607	----------
1902	1,660	----------	202		1,350		108	----------	970	3,285	----------

* Denotes first year for which figures include Alaska and Hawaii.
NA Not available.
[1] To avoid duplication, transactions between governments are excluded; see text.
[2] Includes interest on debt of utilities operated by local governments.
[3] Includes Alaska.

Series Y 533–566. Federal, State, and Local Government Expenditure, by Function: 1902 to 1970

[In millions of dollars]

Year	Total expenditure [1]	General expenditure															
		Total	National defense and international relations		Postal service	Education				Highways	Public welfare				Hospitals	Health	Police
			Total	Military services only		Total	State institutions of higher education	Local schools	Other education		Total	Categorical public assistance	Other public assistance	Other public welfare			
	533	534	535	536	537	538	539	540	541	542	543	544	545	546	547	548	549
1970	332,985	275,017	84,253	76,550	7,722	55,771	12,924	37,461	5,386	16,746	17,517	6,917	554	10,046	9,693	3,895	4,903
1969	308,344	255,924	84,496	77,179	6,993	50,377	11,551	33,752	5,074	15,738	14,730	5,737	515	8,479	8,593	3,337	4,242
1968	282,645	236,348	83,874	76,747	6,485	43,614	10,214	29,305	4,095	14,654	11,245	4,849	420	5,975	7,801	2,778	3,700
1967	257,800	216,888	74,638	66,782	6,227	40,214	8,932	27,590	3,692	14,033	9,592	4,388	295	4,909	6,951	2,506	3,331
1966	224,813	189,406	60,832	53,770	5,706	34,837	7,207	25,091	2,539	12,895	6,965	3,829	266	2,872	6,297	2,065	3,033
1965	205,550	173,613	55,810	48,385	5,261	29,613	5,863	21,966	1,785	12,348	6,420	3,697	256	2,467	5,865	1,805	2,792
1964	196,431	166,088	57,326	49,341	4,775	27,342	5,278	20,399	1,665	11,828	5,880	3,491	258	2,131	5,461	1,618	2,586
1963	184,996	156,002	56,386	47,973	4,402	24,480	4,466	18,759	1,255	11,315	5,538	3,327	250	1,961	5,106	1,540	2,446
1962	176,240	149,159	55,172	46,950	4,101	22,814	4,042	17,739	1,032	10,508	5,147	3,266	259	1,623	4,791	1,344	2,326
1961	164,875	139,161	51,210	43,068	4,025	21,214	3,570	16,608	1,036	9,995	4,779	3,084	335	1,362	4,549	1,132	2,210
1960 *	151,288	128,600	48,922	41,340	3,730	19,404	3,202	15,166	1,036	9,565	4,462	3,006	310	1,145	4,213	1,031	2,030
1959 [2]	145,748	124,217	49,688	41,230	3,499	18,119	2,920	14,034	1,165	9,726	4,193	2,897	301	995	4,074	993	1,880
1958	134,931	115,714	47,626	38,998	3,327	16,836	2,582	13,032	1,222	8,702	3,866	2,700	275	890	3,805	761	1,769
1957	125,463	109,765	47,500	39,073	3,034	15,098	2,206	11,657	1,235	7,931	3,534	2,538	195	801	3,416	735	1,623
1956	115,796	102,156	43,388	35,553	2,899	14,160	1,814	11,165	1,182	7,035	3,184	2,319	244	621	3,068	671	1,486
1955	110,717	97,828	43,472	35,782	2,726	12,710	1,570	10,129	1,012	6,520	3,210	2,278	329	603	2,721	707	1,358
1954	111,332	100,365	49,265	40,519	2,669	11,196	1,418	8,947	831	5,586	3,103	2,234	308	561	2,676	692	1,254
1953	110,054	100,733	53,583	43,847	2,686	10,117	1,361	7,822	934	5,053	2,956	2,167	272	516	2,548	698	1,160
1952	99,847	91,291	48,187	38,962	2,612	9,598	1,267	6,862	1,469	4,714	2,830	2,033	303	493	2,460	739	1,080
1950	70,334	60,701	18,355	12,118	2,270	9,647	1,107	5,906	2,634	3,872	2,964	2,010	538	416	2,050	661	864
1948	55,081	50,088	16,075	10,642	1,715	7,721	895	4,363	2,463	3,071	2,144	1,473	357	314	1,398	536	724
1946	79,707	75,582	50,461	42,677	1,381	3,711	397	2,886	428	1,680	1,435	1,014	216	205	762	380	549
1944	109,947	107,823	85,503	74,670	1,085	2,805	380	2,344	81	1,215	1,150	842	166	142	568	289	497
1942	45,576	43,483	26,555	22,633	878	2,696	296	2,225	175	1,765	1,285	761	345	179	517	197	444
1940	20,417	18,125	1,590	1,567	808	2,827	290	2,292	245	2,177	1,314	611	438	265	537	195	386
1938	17,675	16,273	1,041	1,021	776	2,653	268	2,172	213	2,150	1,233	483	485	265	496	182	378
1936	16,758	15,835	932	916	751	2,365	231	1,904	230	1,945	997	731		266	461	131	331
1934	12,807	12,086	553	541	651	2,005	177	1,623	205	1,829	979	796		183	416	119	306
1932	12,437	11,748	721	702	794	2,325	234	2,050	41	1,766	445	366		79	462	121	349
1927	11,220	10,590	616	599	711	2,243	196	2,017	30	1,819	161	79		82	347	84	290
1922	9,297	8,854	875	864	553	1,713	143	1,541	29	1,296	128	57		71	287	65	204
1913	3,215	3,022	250	245	270	582	49	522	11	419	57	17		40	80	33	92
1902	1,660	1,578	165	162	126	258	13	238	7	175	41	11		30	45	18	50

See footnotes at end of table.

Series Y 533–566. Federal, State, and Local Government Expenditure, By Function: 1902 to 1970—Con.

[In millions of dollars]

	General expenditure—Con.											Insurance trust expenditure					
Year	Local fire protection	Local sanitation	Natural resources		Local parks and recreation	Housing and urban renewal	Veterans services, not elsewhere classified	Financial administration and general control	Interest on general debt [3]	Air and water transport and terminals [4]	Other and unallocable [4]	Utility and liquor stores expenditure	Total	Employee retirement	Unemployment compensation	Old-age and survivors insurance	Other
			Total	Stabilization of farm prices and income													
	550	551	552	553	554	555	556	557	558	559	560	561	562	563	564	565	566
1970	2,024	3,413	11,469	4,261	1,888	3,189	5,455	6,370	18,411	3,969	18,329	9,447	48,521	6,399	2,816	35,828	3,478
1969	1,793	2,969	10,024	2,933	1,645	2,505	5,097	5,563	16,992	3,623	17,207	8,820	43,600	5,641	2,089	32,474	3,396
1968	1,623	2,707	9,200	2,598	1,412	2,841	4,773	4,966	14,873	3,343	16,459	8,170	38,127	4,979	2,126	27,951	3,071
1967	1,499	2,523	10,145	3,496	1,291	2,413	4,448	4,537	13,406	3,212	15,924	7,350	33,561	4,584	2,012	23,919	3,045
1966	1,376	2,571	10,301	4,206	1,187	2,415	4,531	4,105	12,278	2,899	15,113	7,282	28,126	3,915	1,981	19,793	2,437
1965	1,306	2,360	10,990	5,803	1,104	2,198	4,210	3,842	11,430	2,727	13,533	7,058	24,880	3,455	2,413	16,618	2,393
1964	1,222	2,267	10,042	4,989	1,022	2,037	4,208	3,583	10,649	2,513	11,729	6,184	24,161	3,170	2,772	15,830	2,388
1963	1,161	1,996	9,511	4,993	902	1,688	3,961	3,362	9,846	2,481	9,879	5,736	23,260	2,848	2,927	15,015	2,470
1962	1,124	1,958	10,468	5,963	886	1,701	4,224	3,187	9,173	2,470	7,764	5,453	21,628	2,642	3,019	13,669	2,298
1961	1,087	1,774	9,756	5,508	857	1,320	4,049	3,025	9,309	2,338	6,530	5,523	20,191	2,339	3,715	11,889	2,248
1960 *	995	1,727	7,087	3,404	770	1,142	3,801	2,859	9,332	1,984	5,546	5,088	17,596	2,161	2,639	10,798	1,997
1959 [2]	914	1,609	7,966	4,559	729	838	3,706	2,750	6,959	1,755	4,821	4,901	16,631	1,936	3,523	9,388	1,784
1958	873	1,505	6,160	2,890	685	801	3,576	2,536	7,360	1,409	4,117	4,693	14,524	1,773	2,979	8,043	1,728
1957	810	1,443	6,137	3,283	608	624	3,224	2,405	6,603	1,370	3,669	4,429	11,269	1,534	1,633	6,515	1,589
1956	737	1,326	6,630	4,118	541	562	3,185	2,235	6,297	1,358	3,394	4,065	9,576	1,332	1,383	5,361	1,500
1955	694	1,142	6,338	3,892	509	611	3,058	2,060	5,684	1,066	3,242	3,886	9,002	1,152	1,990	4,333	1,527
1954	653	1,058	6,377	3,863	424	742	2,913	1,997	5,515	1,137	3,105	3,482	7,484	1,090	1,648	3,276	1,471
1953	598	908	4,816	2,271	374	768	2,823	1,866	5,477	1,305	2,998	3,316	6,006	948	1,008	2,728	1,321
1952	586	992	3,252	638	324	875	2,570	1,801	4,814	1,070	2,784	3,067	5,489	831	1,022	1,983	1,653
1950	488	834	5,005	2,712	304	573	3,258	1,555	4,862	624	2,515	2,739	6,894	629	1,980	726	3,559
1948	406	670	2,223	592	243	245	3,926	1,325	4,722	550	2,394	2,379	2,614	541	821	512	740
1946	294	370	3,111	2,012	179	221	2,588	1,163	4,286	1,190	1,821	1,733	2,392	503	985	321	584
1944	251	245	2,731	1,532	123	574	530	1,087	2,650	4,741	1,779	1,281	842	298	70	185	289
1942	236	229	2,468	929	128	622	481	828	1,591	890	1,672	1,106	986	247	386	110	243
1940	235	207	2,730	694	162	267	501	739	1,552	374	1,524	1,324	968	209	509	16	234
1938	231	226	2,089	326	130	109	590	725	1,513	266	1,485	848	554	193	202	5	154
1936	205	204	2,158	602	104	71	1,699	662	1,455	269	1,095	701	222	157	--------	--------	65
1934	189	177	1,241	382	126	3	508	533	1,473	213	765	528	193	135	--------	--------	58
1932	210	223	326	--------	147	–	928	601	1,323	198	809	518	171	103	--------	--------	68
1927	203	312	206	--------	153	1	579	526	1,348	254	737	491	139	64	--------	--------	75
1922	158	189	140	--------	85	1	505	439	1,370	302	544	359	84	36	--------	--------	48
1913	76	97	44	--------	57	--------	177	256	170	90	272	186	7	7	--------	--------	--------
1902	40	51	17	--------	29	--------	141	175	97	22	128	82	--------	--------	--------	--------	--------

* Denotes first year for which figures include Alaska and Hawaii.
– Represents zero.
[1] To avoid duplication, transactions between governments are excluded; see text.
[2] Includes Alaska.

[3] Excludes interest on Federal securities held by Federal agencies and funds.
[4] Any State and local amounts for "Air and water transport and terminals" prior to 1951 are included under "Other and unallocable."

Series Y 567–589. Federal Government Revenue, by Source: 1902 to 1970

[In millions of dollars]

		General revenue											
	Total revenue	Total	Taxes										
Year			Total taxes	Individual income	Corporation income	Sales, gross receipts, and customs						Death and gift	Other taxes
						Total	Customs duties	Motor fuel	Alcoholic beverages	Tobacco products	Other		
	567	568	569	570	571	572	573	574	575	576	577	578	579
1970	205,562	163,582	146,082	90,412	32,829	18,297	2,430	3,776	4,726	2,094	5,271	3,644	900
1969	199,637	162,845	145,996	87,249	36,678	17,826	2,319	3,508	4,534	2,138	5,326	3,491	753
1968	165,239	133,240	117,554	68,726	28,665	16,275	2,038	3,325	4,269	2,122	4,520	3,051	838
1967	161,351	130,869	115,121	61,526	33,971	15,806	1,901	3,178	3,958	2,077	4,692	2,978	840
1966	141,142	118,547	104,095	55,446	30,073	14,641	1,767	2,955	3,698	2,066	4,155	3,066	869
1965	125,837	106,720	93,710	48,792	25,461	15,786	1,442	2,792	3,667	2,142	5,743	2,716	954
1964	120,959	102,300	90,507	48,697	23,493	14,776	1,252	2,696	3,478	2,048	5,301	2,394	1,148
1963	114,557	98,145	86,797	47,588	21,579	14,215	1,205	2,558	3,345	2,075	5,032	2,167	1,248
1962	106,441	92,016	82,262	45,571	20,523	13,428	1,142	2,451	3,248	2,022	4,565	2,016	724
1961	101,341	87,062	77,470	41,338	20,954	12,649	982	2,333	3,124	1,986	4,224	1,896	633
1960	99,800	87,088	77,003	40,715	21,494	12,603	1,105	1,984	3,106	1,927	4,481	1,606	585
1959	85,459	75,249	67,257	36,719	17,309	11,332	925	1,656	2,915	1,798	4,038	1,333	563
1958	86,006	76,112	68,007	34,724	20,074	11,273	782	1,592	2,860	1,728	4,311	1,393	543
1957	87,066	78,403	69,815	35,620	21,167	11,127	735	1,498	2,893	1,669	4,333	1,365	537
1956	81,294	73,162	65,226	32,188	20,880	10,469	682	1,055	2,846	1,607	4,279	1,161	528

Series Y 567–589. Federal Government Revenue, by Source: 1902 to 1970—Con.

[In millions of dollars]

Year	Total revenue	General revenue											
		Total	Taxes									Death and gift	Other taxes
			Total taxes	Individual income	Corporation income	Sales, gross receipts, and customs							
						Total	Customs duties	Motor fuel	Alcoholic beverages	Tobacco products	Other		
	567	568	569	570	571	572	573	574	575	576	577	578	579
1955	71,915	65,322	57,589	28,747	17,861	9,578	585	972	2,694	1,571	3,757	924	478
1954	75,835	69,798	62,409	29,542	21,101	10,367	542	845	2,716	1,580	4,684	934	465
1953	74,239	68,687	62,796	29,816	21,238	10,352	596	906	2,781	1,655	4,414	881	508
1952	71,798	66,615	59,744	27,921	21,226	9,332	532	720	2,549	1,565	3,966	818	446
1951	56,731	52,125	46,032	21,643	14,106	9,143	609	589	2,494	1,378	4,073	708	432
1950	43,527	40,061	35,186	15,745	10,488	7,843	407	534	2,165	1,325	3,412	698	412
1948	47,254	44,277	37,876	19,305	9,678	7,650	403	479	2,203	1,297	3,268	890	353
1946	46,405	43,629	36,286	16,157	11,833	6,964	424	406	2,479	1,156	2,499	669	[1] 663
1944	51,399	48,663	40,321	19,701	14,737	4,723	417	271	1,592	986	1,457	507	[1] 653
1942	16,062	14,788	12,265	3,205	4,727	3,425	369	370	1,037	779	870	421	[1] 487
1940	7,000	6,194	4,878	959	1,123	2,127	331	226	613	607	350	357	[1] 312
1938	7,226	6,595	5,344	1,277	1,333	2,021	343	204	556	567	351	413	[1] 300
1936	5,176	5,086	3,882	666	745	1,905	372	177	493	499	[2] 364	377	[1] 189
1934	3,886	3,801	2,942	405	386	1,877	299	203	248	424	[2] 703	110	[1] 164
1932	2,634	2,542	1,813	405	598	733	311	----------	8	398	16	41	36
1927	4,469	4,396	3,364	879	1,259	1,088	585	----------	20	376	107	90	47
1922	4,261	4,221	3,371	1,939		1,152	318	----------	44	270	520	139	[1] 142
1913	962	962	662	----------	35	612	310	----------	223	77	2	–	15
1902	653	653	513	----------	----------	487	243	----------	187	49	8	5	21

Year	General revenue—Con.				Insurance trust revenue					
	Charges and miscellaneous general revenue									
	Total	Postal receipts	Sales of agricultural products [3]	Other	Total [4]	Employee retirement	Unemployment compensation	Old-age and survivors insurance	Veterans life insurance	Railroad retirement
	580	581	582	583	584	585	586	587	588	589
1970	17,500	6,181	880	10,439	41,980	1,713	123	38,485	679	980
1969	16,848	5,986	492	10,370	36,793	1,479	126	33,649	600	939
1968	15,686	5,408	1,096	9,182	31,999	1,375	131	29,029	606	858
1967	15,748	4,866	2,216	8,666	30,482	1,220	137	27,663	668	795
1966	14,452	4,584	2,074	7,794	22,595	1,126	139	20,023	623	683
1965	13,010	4,339	1,890	6,781	19,117	1,071	143	16,742	525	636
1964	11,793	4,120	1,975	5,698	18,659	1,006	144	16,386	529	593
1963	11,347	3,727	2,026	5,595	16,412	946	150	14,195	563	559
1962	9,754	3,420	1,362	4,972	14,425	877	147	12,289	548	564
1961	9,592	3,300	1,799	4,493	14,279	866	150	12,131	561	571
1960	10,085	3,260	1,748	5,077	12,712	769	153	10,656	527	607
1959	7,992	3,054	772	4,166	10,210	770	102	8,294	519	525
1958	8,105	2,566	1,475	4,064	9,894	677	90	8,044	507	575
1957	8,588	2,512	2,092	3,984	8,663	644	74	6,857	472	616
1956	7,936	2,435	1,324	4,177	8,132	577	31	6,442	441	641
1955	7,733	2,363	1,187	4,183	6,594	442	16	5,087	450	599
1954	7,390	2,269	1,134	3,987	6,037	432	18	4,554	430	603
1953	5,891	2,093	544	3,254	5,552	423	15	4,060	428	625
1952	6,871	1,967	800	4,104	5,183	418	10	3,547	473	735
1951	6,093	1,777	1,772	2,544	4,606	377	15	3,119	520	575
1950	4,875	1,677	933	2,265	3,466	359	10	2,107	440	550
1948	6,401	1,411	414	4,576	2,977	239	131	1,616	434	557
1946	7,343	1,221	700	5,422	2,776	282	117	1,201	893	283
1944	8,342	1,113	343	6,886	2,736	270	109	1,260	834	263
1942	2,523	860	385	1,278	1,274	90	76	869	98	141
1940	1,316	767	----------	549	806	45	46	538	56	121
1938	1,251	729	----------	522	631	39	----------	387	59	146
1936	1,204	665	----------	539	90	33	----------	----------	57	----------
1934	859	587	----------	272	85	29	----------	----------	56	----------
1932	730	588	----------	142	91	33	----------	----------	58	----------
1927	1,032	683	----------	349	73	25	----------	----------	48	----------
1922	850	485	----------	365	40	14	----------	----------	26	----------
1913	300	267	----------	33	----------	----------	----------	----------	----------	----------
1902	140	122	----------	18	----------	----------	----------	----------	----------	----------

– Represents zero.
[1] Includes capital stock tax.
[2] Includes agricultural adjustment taxes.

[3] In connection with price support program; excludes sales to Federal Government agencies.
[4] Excludes interest on Federal securities held by Federal agencies and funds.

Series Y 590–604. Federal Government Expenditure, by Character and Object, and Federal Government Debt: 1902 to 1970

[In millions of dollars]

Year	Total	Inter-governmental expenditure to State and local governments	Direct expenditure — Total	Capital outlay — Total	Con-struction	Other [1]	Current operation [1]	Assistance and subsidies [1]	Interest on debt	Insurance benefits and repayments	Expenditure for personal services	Debt Outstanding Total	Held by Federal Government	Other	Increase or decrease (−) during year
	590	591	592	593	594	595	596	597	598	599	600	601	602	603	604
1970	208,190	23,257	184,933	17,869	4,150	13,719	99,105	12,674	14,037	41,248	47,501	370,919	95,170	275,749	17,199
1969	196,165	19,421	176,744	19,006	3,932	15,074	95,369	11,562	13,260	37,547	43,373	353,720	84,815	268,905	6,142
1968	184,464	18,053	166,411	21,326	3,972	17,354	90,204	10,801	11,607	32,474	40,379	347,578	74,136	273,442	21,357
1967	166,849	15,027	151,821	17,868	4,470	13,398	85,618	9,679	10,373	28,283	36,819	326,221	75,705	250,515	6,314
1966	143,022	13,115	129,907	17,652	4,610	13,041	70,276	9,048	9,589	23,342	32,904	319,907	66,618	253,289	2,633
1965	130,059	11,062	118,996	13,209	4,472	8,737	68,552	8,366	8,940	19,930	29,629	317,274	63,236	254,038	5,561
1964	125,949	10,097	115,852	17,818	4,031	13,787	61,809	8,865	8,293	19,067	28,051	311,713	60,964	250,749	5,853
1963	118,805	8,507	110,298	18,635	3,752	14,884	57,728	7,979	7,682	18,273	26,237	305,860	58,206	247,654	7,659
1962	113,428	7,735	105,693	18,429	3,673	14,756	55,410	7,952	7,162	16,740	25,424	298,201	56,296	241,905	9,230
1961	104,863	7,011	97,852	16,229	3,773	12,456	51,923	7,323	7,485	14,892	23,754	288,971	56,002	232,969	2,640
1960	97,284	6,994	90,289	16,842	3,480	13,361	45,336	6,884	7,662	13,565	22,691	286,331	55,259	231,072	1,625
1959	93,531	6,355	87,177	16,877	3,662	13,215	45,581	7,329	5,543	11,847	22,466	284,706	54,554	230,152	8,363
1958	86,054	4,835	81,219	16,852	3,218	13,634	40,775	7,119	6,116	10,356	21,071	276,343	55,842	220,501	5,816
1957	81,783	3,873	77,910	16,250	3,396	12,854	40,983	6,660	5,497	8,520	20,779	270,527	55,501	215,026	−2,224
1956	75,991	3,347	72,644	14,956	3,416	11,540	38,582	6,595	5,311	7,200	20,454	272,751	53,470	219,281	−1,623
1955	73,441	3,099	70,342	18,030	3,564	14,467	34,947	6,282	4,845	6,238	19,377	274,374	50,536	223,838	3,114
1954	77,692	2,967	74,725	18,244	4,001	14,244	40,986	5,637	4,796	5,061	19,195	271,260	49,340	221,920	5,189
1953	79,990	2,873	77,117	18,498	3,735	14,763	43,086	6,376	4,863	4,294	19,970	266,071	47,560	218,511	6,966
1952	71,568	2,585	68,984	17,437	3,337	14,100	37,579	5,916	4,262	3,790	17,721	259,105	44,335	214,770	3,883
1951	48,935	2,383	46,552	....	2,218		37,312		4,221	2,801	13,564	255,222	40,958	214,264	−2,135
1950	44,800	2,371	42,429	....	1,671		31,839		4,404	4,515	10,487	257,357	37,830	219,527	4,587
1948	35,592	1,771	33,821	....	1,291		26,790		4,323	1,417	8,915	252,292	35,761	216,531	−5,994
1946	66,534	894	65,640	....	1,566		59,123		3,865	1,086	22,468	269,422	29,121	240,301	10,740
1944	100,520	1,072	99,448	....	4,555		92,254		2,151	488	21,772	201,003	18,920	182,083	64,307
1942	35,549	887	34,662	....	6,991		26,276		1,026	369	6,451	72,422	10,340	62,082	23,461
1940	10,061	884	9,177	....	1,311		6,686		899	281	3,347	42,968	6,803	36,165	2,528
1938	8,449	762	7,687	....	1,124		5,552		840	171	3,023	37,165	4,466	32,699	740
1936	9,165	908	8,257	....	1,162		6,312		717	66	2,797	33,779	1,959	31,820	5,008
1934	5,941	976	4,965	....	985		3,186		734	60	2,144	27,053	1,332	25,721	4,514
1932	4,266	232	4,034	....	318		3,083		582	51	1,188	19,487	607	18,880	2,686
1927	3,533	123	3,410	....	174		2,442		764	30	1,110	18,512	759	17,753	−1,131
1922	3,763	118	3,645	....	161		2,487		988	9	919	22,963	432	22,531	−1,014
1913	970	12	958	....	119		816		23	....	401	1,193	(Z)	1,193	−1
1902	572	7	565	....	38		498		29	....	160	1,178	....	1,178	−44

Z Less than $500,000.

[1] Prior to 1952, amounts for "Other capital outlay" and "Assistance and subsidies" are included under "Current operation."

Series Y 605–637. Federal Government Expenditure, by Function: 1902 to 1970

[In millions of dollars]

Year	Total expenditure	Total general expenditure (direct and inter-governmental)	Intergovernmental expenditure Total	Education	Highways	Public welfare	Employment security administration	Other and unallocable	Total direct	General expenditure Total general	National defense and international relations Total	Military services only	Postal service	Education [1]	Highways	Public welfare
	605	606	607	608	609	610	611	612	613	614	615	616	617	618	619	620
1970	208,190	166,942	23,257	5,844	4,608	7,574	664	4,567	184,933	143,685	84,253	76,550	7,722	3,053	319	2,837
1969	196,165	158,618	19,421	4,775	4,352	6,358	616	3,320	176,744	139,197	84,496	77,179	6,993	3,139	321	2,620
1968	184,464	151,990	18,053	4,727	4,291	5,407	592	3,036	166,411	133,937	83,874	76,747	6,485	2,456	173	1,388
1967	166,849	138,565	15,027	3,920	4,059	4,234	564	2,250	151,821	123,538	74,638	66,782	6,227	2,295	100	1,374
1966	143,022	119,679	13,115	3,014	3,953	3,579	486	2,083	129,907	106,564	60,832	53,770	5,706	1,550	125	208
1965	130,059	110,129	11,062	1,677	3,997	3,098	413	1,877	118,996	99,067	55,810	48,385	5,261	1,050	127	105
1964	125,949	106,882	10,097	1,371	3,628	2,973	415	1,710	115,852	96,786	57,326	49,341	4,775	1,056	164	114
1963	118,805	100,532	8,507	1,115	2,981	2,752	342	1,317	110,298	92,025	56,386	47,973	4,402	751	165	118
1962	113,428	96,689	7,735	1,169	2,748	2,448	461	909	105,693	88,953	55,172	46,950	4,101	598	151	63
1961	104,863	89,971	7,011	1,030	2,586	2,178	370	847	97,852	82,960	51,210	43,068	4,025	640	151	59
1960	97,284	83,719	6,994	950	2,905	2,070	325	745	90,289	76,724	48,922	41,340	3,730	685	137	58
1959	93,531	81,685	6,355	826	2,575	1,973	298	682	87,177	75,330	49,688	41,230	3,499	836	134	57
1958	86,054	75,698	4,835	653	1,478	1,799	288	617	81,219	70,863	47,626	38,998	3,327	917	135	48
1957	81,783	73,263	3,873	604	944	1,557	245	523	77,910	69,390	47,500	39,073	3,034	964	115	49
1956	75,991	68,792	3,347	535	732	1,458	224	397	72,645	65,445	43,388	35,553	2,899	940	82	45

See footnotes at end of table.

Series Y 605–637. Federal Government Expenditure, by Function: 1902 to 1970—Con.

[In millions of dollars]

Year	Total expenditure	Total general expenditure (direct and intergovernmental)	Intergovernmental expenditure						Direct expenditure							
			Total	Education	Highways	Public welfare	Employment security administration	Other and unallocable	Total direct	General expenditure						
										Total general	National defense and international relations		Postal service	Education [1]	Highways	Public welfare
											Total	Military services only				
	605	606	607	608	609	610	611	612	613	614	615	616	617	618	619	620
1955	73,441	67,203	3,099	521	589	1,429	187	373	70,342	64,104	43,472	35,782	2,726	802	68	42
1954	77,692	72,631	2,967	475	530	1,439	198	325	74,725	69,664	49,265	40,519	2,669	639	60	43
1953	79,990	75,696	2,873	508	510	1,332	196	327	77,117	72,823	53,583	43,847	2,686	727	66	42
1952	71,568	67,778	2,585	436	415	1,181	182	369	68,984	65,193	48,187	38,962	1,280	64	42	
1951	48,935	46,134	2,383	311	400	1,194	176	302	46,552	43,751	25,953	19,136	2,403	1,885	56	25
1950	44,800	40,285	2,371	369	429	1,131	215	227	42,429	37,914	18,355	12,118	2,270	2,470	69	24
1948	35,592	34,175	1,771	418	318	724	158	153	33,821	32,404	16,075	10,642	1,715	2,342	35	45
1946	66,534	65,448	894	149	79	424	75	167	65,640	64,554	50,461	42,677	1,381	355	8	26
1944	100,520	100,032	1,072	193	147	420	36	276	99,448	98,960	85,503	74,670	1,085	12	15	17
1942	35,549	35,180	887	76	164	383	72	192	34,662	34,293	26,555	22,633	878	110	275	60
1940	10,061	9,780	884	154	195	278	62	195	9,177	8,896	1,590	1,567	808	189	604	158
1938	8,449	8,278	762	112	264	218	46	122	7,687	7,516	1,041	1,021	776	162	500	164
1936	9,165	9,099	908	147	285	290	3	183	8,257	8,191	932	916	751	188	520	170
1934	5,941	5,881	976	61	279	495	1	140	4,965	4,905	553	541	651	174	320	90
1932	4,266	4,215	232	12	191	1	--------	28	4,034	3,983	721	702	794	14	25	1
1927	3,533	3,503	123	10	83	1	--------	29	3,410	3,380	616	599	711	8	10	10
1922	3,763	3,754	118	7	92	1	--------	18	3,645	3,636	875	864	553	8	2	9
1913	970	970	12	3	--------	2	--------	7	958	958	250	245	270	5	--------	5
1902	572	572	7	1	--------	1	--------	5	565	565	165	162	126	3	--------	4

Year	Direct expenditure—Con.																
	General expenditure—Con.											Insurance trust expenditure					
	Hospitals	Health	Police	Natural resources		Housing and urban renewal	Veterans services, not elsewhere classified	Financial administration and general control	Interest on general debt [3]	Air and water transportation and terminals	Other and unallocable	Total	Employee retirement	Unemployment compensation	Old-age and survivors insurance	Veterans life insurance	Railroad retirement
				Total [2]	Stabilization of farm prices and income												
	621	622	623	624	625	626	627	628	629	630	631	632	633	634	635	636	637
1970	1,830	2,089	409	8,737	4,261	1,051	5,388	1,688	14,037	2,556	7,716	41,248	2,770	93	35,828	971	1,586
1969	1,582	1,828	341	7,472	2,933	603	5,046	1,458	13,260	2,439	7,599	37,547	2,420	97	32,474	1,023	1,533
1968	1,519	1,514	290	6,729	2,598	1,209	4,740	1,319	11,607	2,420	8,214	32,474	2,150	76	27,951	909	1,388
1967	1,392	1,425	282	7,801	3,496	944	4,425	1,224	10,373	2,427	8,611	28,283	1,976	71	23,919	1,060	1,257
1966	1,328	1,124	257	8,262	4,203	1,009	4,510	1,131	9,589	2,157	8,776	23,342	1,696	88	19,793	572	1,194
1965	1,340	969	243	9,260	5,803	948	4,190	1,069	8,940	2,036	7,716	19,930	1,447	115	16,618	633	1,116
1964	1,290	879	220	8,207	4,989	895	4,189	1,016	8,293	1,863	6,497	19,067	1,326	134	15,830	684	1,092
1963	1,178	830	209	8,014	4,993	509	3,941	923	7,682	1,833	5,082	18,273	1,183	167	15,015	844	1,064
1962	1,118	675	196	9,097	5,963	548	4,129	850	7,162	1,805	3,288	16,740	1,064	211	13,669	772	1,024
1961	1,053	542	193	8,429	5,508	377	3,965	788	7,485	1,623	2,420	14,892	956	252	11,889	814	982
1960	978	472	173	5,898	3,404	284	3,689	746	7,662	1,405	1,885	13,565	896	275	10,798	679	916
1959	932	411	170	6,890	4,559	223	3,645	747	5,543	1,206	1,350	11,847	792	248	9,388	651	768
1958	844	260	159	5,161	2,890	200	3,455	693	6,116	936	986	10,356	699	222	8,043	672	719
1957	797	235	155	5,205	3,283	119	3,186	680	5,497	951	903	8,520	591	133	6,515	612	670
1956	752	215	156	5,724	4,118	125	3,097	675	5,311	852	1,184	7,200	507	106	5,361	628	599
1955	667	238	129	5,545	3,892	112	2,997	607	4,845	798	1,055	6,238	430	206	4,333	698	570
1954	714	245	124	5,615	3,863	131	2,811	622	4,796	829	1,101	5,061	411	140	3,276	749	485
1953	685	271	122	4,111	2,271	138	2,710	602	4,863	1,050	1,167	4,294	363	98	2,728	645	460
1952	715	299	141	2,476	638	106	2,428	608	4,262	862	1,111	3,790	300	49	1,983	1,073	384
1951	668	299	104	3,027	1,360	124	2,601	547	4,221	670	1,168	2,801	270	51	1,498	665	317
1950	666	297	88	4,335	2,712	121	2,796	514	4,404	624	881	4,515	268	131	726	3,088	302
1948	461	244	80	1,727	592	69	3,293	445	4,323	550	1,000	1,417	244	62	512	377	222
1946	195	129	70	2,809	2,012	107	2,534	460	3,865	1,190	964	1,086	266	17	321	330	152
1944	100	101	83	2,499	1,532	528	529	488	2,151	4,741	1,109	488	103	1	185	65	134
1942	85	38	50	2,254	929	386	480	250	1,026	890	955	369	78	9	110	46	126
1940	87	36	21	2,512	694	37	501	178	899	374	902	281	69	15	16	68	113
1938	96	31	19	1,867	326	106	590	183	840	266	875	171	64	--------	5	22	80
1936	110	15	17	1,965	602	71	1,699	162	717	269	605	66	44	--------	--------	22	--------
1934	107	10	15	1,082	382	3	508	101	734	213	344	60	39	--------	--------	21	--------
1932	113	14	31	161	--------	–	928	131	582	198	270	51	28	--------	--------	23	--------
1927	68	8	20	112	--------	1	579	114	764	254	105	30	14	--------	--------	16	--------
1922	87	7	14	79	--------	1	425	126	988	302	160	9	6	--------	--------	3	--------
1913	1	4	3	30	--------	--------	177	45	23	90	55	--------	--------	--------	--------	--------	--------
1902	2	1	--------	8	--------	--------	141	34	29	22	30	--------	--------	--------	--------	--------	--------

– Represents zero.

[1] Service academies are included under "National defense and international relations."

[2] Includes amounts not shown separately.

[3] Excludes interest on Federal securities held by Federal agencies and funds.

Series Y 638–651. Federal Grants to State and Local Governments, by Purpose: 1930 to 1970

[Amounts in millions of dollars. Includes Puerto Rico, Guam, and Virgin Islands. On basis of checks issued for years ending June 30]

Year	All grants [1]	Social welfare										Highway		All other
		Total		Public assistance		Health		Education		Miscellaneous social welfare				
		Amount	Percent of all grants	Amount	Percent of all grants	Amount	Percent of all grants	Amount	Percent of all grants	Amount	Percent of all grants	Amount	Percent of all grants	
	638	639	640	641	642	643	644	645	646	647	648	649	650	651
1970	23,585	16,546	70.2	7,445	31.6	1,043	4.4	3,017	12.8	5,041	21.4	4,392	18.6	2,648
1969	19,767	13,863	70.1	6,280	31.8	866	4.4	2,726	13.8	3,990	20.2	4,162	21.0	1,747
1968	18,173	12,511	68.8	5,319	29.3	823	4.6	2,781	15.4	3,588	19.5	4,197	23.1	1,464
1967	14,820	9,845	66.4	4,175	28.2	436	2.9	2,370	16.0	2,864	19.3	4,022	27.1	953
1966	12,519	7,634	61.0	3,528	28.2	365	2.9	1,595	12.7	2,147	17.2	3,975	31.8	909
1965	10,630	5,672	53.4	3,059	28.8	346	3.3	705	6.6	1,560	14.7	4,018	37.8	941
1964	9,774	5,352	54.8	2,944	30.1	322	3.3	579	5.9	1,507	15.4	3,644	37.3	778
1963	8,324	4,825	58.0	2,730	32.8	292	3.5	558	6.7	1,246	15.0	3,023	36.3	477
1962	7,703	4,535	58.9	2,432	31.6	263	3.4	491	6.4	1,348	17.5	2,783	36.1	385
1961	6,921	3,950	57.1	2,167	31.3	240	3.5	460	6.6	1,083	15.6	2,623	37.9	349
1960	6,838	3,610	52.8	2,059	30.1	214	3.1	441	6.5	896	13.1	2,942	43.0	286
1959	6,316	3,450	54.6	1,966	31.1	211	3.3	376	6.0	897	14.2	2,614	41.4	251
1958	4,794	3,095	64.6	1,795	37.4	176	3.7	308	6.4	816	17.0	1,519	31.7	181
1957	3,936	2,848	72.4	1,556	39.6	162	4.1	280	7.1	848	21.6	955	24.3	133
1956	3,441	2,615	76.0	1,455	42.3	133	3.9	276	8.0	751	21.8	740	21.5	85
1955	3,096	2,403	77.6	1,427	46.1	119	3.8	296	9.6	561	18.1	597	19.3	97
1954	2,958	2,346	79.3	1,438	48.6	140	4.7	248	8.4	519	17.6	538	18.2	74
1953	2,759	2,162	78.4	1,330	48.2	173	6.3	259	9.4	400	14.5	517	18.8	80
1952	2,329	1,854	79.6	1,178	50.6	187	8.0	156	6.7	333	14.3	420	18.0	56
1951	2,253	1,802	80.0	1,186	52.6	174	7.7	93	4.1	350	15.5	400	17.8	50
1950	2,212	1,731	78.2	1,123	50.8	123	5.6	82	3.7	402	18.2	429	19.4	53
1949	1,840	1,366	74.2	928	50.4	67	3.6	76	4.2	295	16.0	410	22.3	64
1948	1,581	1,229	77.8	718	45.4	55	3.5	120	7.6	335	21.2	318	20.2	33
1947	1,549	1,302	84.1	614	39.6	63	4.1	65	4.2	560	36.2	199	12.8	48
1946	844	701	83.1	439	52.0	71	8.4	58	6.8	133	15.7	75	8.8	68
1945	917	700	76.3	410	44.7	79	8.6	103	11.3	108	11.7	87	9.5	130
1944	983	700	71.3	405	41.2	60	6.1	136	13.8	99	10.1	144	14.7	138
1943	991	691	69.7	396	39.9	30	3.1	171	17.2	94	9.5	174	17.6	126
1942	926	694	74.9	375	40.4	29	3.1	151	16.3	139	15.0	158	17.1	74
1941	915	624	68.2	330	36.0	26	2.8	113	12.3	156	17.0	171	18.7	120
1940	967	531	54.9	271	28.0	22	2.3	51	5.2	187	19.4	165	17.0	272
1939	1,031	446	43.2	247	24.0	15	1.4	50	4.8	134	13.0	192	18.6	393
1938	790	365	46.2	216	27.3	15	1.9	48	6.1	86	10.8	247	31.2	178
1937	818	230	28.1	144	17.6	13	1.6	38	4.6	36	4.4	341	41.6	247
1936	1,015	107	10.5	28	2.8	4	.4	37	3.7	37	3.7	224	22.1	684
1935	2,197	28	1.3	–	–	–	–	26	1.2	3	.1	275	12.5	1,893
1934	1,803	24	1.4	–	–	–	–	22	1.2	2	.1	222	12.3	1,557
1933	190	25	13.2	–	–	–	–	23	12.3	2	.9	163	86.0	2
1932	214	26	12.1	–	–	–	–	24	11.3	2	.8	186	87.1	2
1931	180	25	13.9	–	–	–	–	24	13.1	1	.8	154	85.2	2
1930	100	23	23.2	–	–	(Z)	–	22	21.8	1	1.3	76	75.5	1

– Represents zero.
Z Less than $500,000.

[1] Excludes shared revenues, payments in lieu of taxes, and grants for programs administered by the States as agents of the Federal Government.

Series Y 652–670. State and Local Government Revenue, by Source: 1902 to 1970

[In millions of dollars]

Year	Revenue from all sources		Intergovernmental revenue (from Federal Government)	Revenue from State and local sources								
				Total [1]	General revenue							Charges and miscellaneous
	Total	General revenue (direct and intergovernmental)			Total	Taxes						
						Total	Individual income	Corporation income	Sales and gross receipts	Property	Other taxes	
	652	653	654	655	656	657	658	659	660	661	662	663
1970	150,106	130,756	21,857	128,248	108,898	86,795	10,812	3,738	30,322	34,054	7,868	22,103
1969	132,153	114,550	19,153	113,001	95,397	76,712	8,908	3,180	26,519	30,673	7,432	18,686
1968	117,581	101,264	17,181	100,400	84,083	67,572	7,308	2,518	22,911	27,747	7,087	16,511
1967	106,581	91,197	15,370	91,211	75,827	61,000	5,826	2,227	20,530	26,047	6,370	14,827
1966	97,619	83,036	13,214	84,405	69,822	56,647	4,760	2,038	19,085	24,670	6,094	13,175
1965	87,777	74,000	11,029	76,748	62,971	51,243	4,090	1,929	17,118	22,583	5,521	11,729
1964	81,455	68,443	10,002	71,453	58,440	47,785	3,791	1,695	15,762	21,241	5,296	10,655
1963	74,408	62,269	8,663	65,745	53,606	44,014	3,267	1,505	14,446	19,833	4,963	9,593
1962	69,492	58,252	7,871	61,621	50,381	41,554	3,037	1,308	13,494	19,054	4,662	8,827
1961	64,531	54,037	7,131	57,400	46,907	38,861	2,613	1,266	12,463	18,002	4,518	8,045
1960 *	60,277	50,505	6,974	53,302	43,530	36,117	2,463	1,180	11,849	16,405	4,220	7,414
1959 ²	53,972	45,306	6,377	47,596	38,929	32,379	1,994	1,001	10,437	14,983	3,966	6,550
1958	49,262	41,219	4,865	44,397	36,354	30,380	1,759	1,018	9,829	14,047	3,725	5,974
1957	45,929	38,164	3,843	42,085	34,320	28,817	1,754	984	9,467	12,864	3,748	5,503
1956	41,692	34,667	3,335	38,357	31,332	26,368	1,538	890	8,691	11,749	3,501	4,964

See footnotes at end of table.

Series Y 652–670. State and Local Government Revenue, by Source: 1902 to 1970—Con.

[In millions of dollars]

Year	Revenue from all sources		Intergovernmental revenue (from Federal Government)	Revenue from State and local sources								
						General revenue						
							Taxes					
	Total	General revenue (direct and intergovernmental)		Total [1]	Total	Total	Individual income	Corporation income	Sales and gross receipts	Property	Other taxes	Charges and miscellaneous
	652	653	654	655	656	657	658	659	660	661	662	663
1955	37,619	31,073	3,131	34,489	27,942	23,483	1,237	744	7,643	10,735	3,125	4,459
1954	35,386	29,012	2,966	32,420	26,046	22,067	1,127	778	7,276	9,967	2,918	3,979
1953	33,411	27,307	2,870	30,541	24,437	20,908	1,065	817	6,927	9,375	2,723	3,529
1952	31,013	25,181	2,566	28,447	22,615	19,323	998	846	6,357	8,652	2,471	3,292
1950	25,639	20,911	2,486	23,153	18,425	15,914	788	593	5,154	7,349	2,030	2,511
1948	21,613	17,250	1,861	19,752	15,389	13,342	543	592	4,442	6,126	1,638	2,047
1946	15,983	12,356	855	15,128	11,501	10,094	422	447	2,986	4,986	1,254	1,407
1944	14,333	10,908	954	13,379	9,954	8,774	342	451	2,289	4,604	1,089	1,180
1942	13,148	10,418	858	12,290	9,560	8,528	276	272	2,351	4,537	1,092	1,031
1940	11,749	9,609	945	10,804	8,664	7,810	224	156	1,982	4,430	1,018	854
1938	11,058	9,228	800	10,258	8,428	7,605	218	165	1,794	4,440	988	823
1936	9,360	8,395	948	8,412	7,447	6,701	153	113	1,484	4,093	858	746
1934	8,430	7,678	1,016	7,414	6,662	5,912	80	49	1,008	4,076	699	750
1932	7,887	7,267	232	7,655	7,035	6,164	74	79	752	4,487	772	871
1927	7,838	7,271	116	7,722	7,155	6,087	70	92	470	4,730	725	1,068
1922	5,169	4,781	108	5,061	4,673	4,016	43	58	154	3,321	440	657
1913	2,030	1,912	12	2,018	1,900	1,609	---------	---------	58	1,332	219	291
1902	1,048	986	7	1,041	979	860	---------	---------	28	706	126	119

Year	Revenue from State and local sources—Con.						
	Utility and liquor stores revenue	Insurance trust revenue					
				Unemployment compensation			Other
		Total	Employee retirement	Total	Contributions	Interest (credited by U.S. Govt.)	
	664	665	666	667	668	669	670
1970	8,614	10,736	6,493	3,101	2,531	569	1,143
1969	7,840	9,764	5,654	3,049	2,557	491	1,061
1968	7,502	8,815	4,865	2,972	2,554	418	977
1967	6,911	8,474	4,272	3,285	2,920	365	917
1966	6,619	7,964	3,744	3,337	3,049	288	883
1965	6,355	7,422	3,423	3,244	3,002	241	755
1964	5,975	7,038	3,072	3,260	3,054	205	706
1963	5,532	6,607	2,783	3,181	3,000	181	643
1962	5,308	5,932	2,561	2,820	2,655	164	550
1961	5,116	5,378	2,324	2,519	2,323	196	535
1960 *	4,877	4,896	2,099	2,323	2,142	183	472
1959 [2]	4,536	4,131	1,871	1,833	1,652	181	428
1958	4,211	3,832	1,688	1,717	1,497	220	426
1957	4,127	3,638	1,486	1,725	1,514	210	427
1956	3,854	3,171	1,295	1,505	1,318	187	371
1955	3,688	2,858	1,180	1,329	1,141	188	349
1954	3,496	2,877	1,070	1,470	1,266	204	337
1953	3,324	2,781	909	1,556	1,374	182	316
1952	3,108	2,724	835	1,602	1,442	160	287
1950	2,712	2,016	606	1,180	1,032	148	229
1948	2,511	1,851	433	1,206	1,062	144	212
1946	2,033	1,593	289	1,165	1,037	128	140
1944	1,633	1,792	228	1,409	1,323	86	154
1942	1,277	1,454	195	1,142	1,083	59	117
1940	998	1,142	169	885	850	35	88
1938	877	953	143	731	706	25	79
1936	747	218	125	23	23	---------	70
1934	590	162	107	---------	---------	---------	55
1932	463	157	93	---------	---------	---------	64
1927	403	164	67	---------	---------	---------	97
1922	266	122	45	---------	---------	---------	77
1913	116	2	2	---------	---------	---------	---------
1902	62	---------	---------	---------	---------	---------	---------

* Denotes first year for which figures include Alaska and Hawaii.
[1] To avoid duplication, transactions between State and local governments are excluded; see text.

[2] Includes Alaska.

Series Y 671–681.　State and Local Government Expenditure, by Character and Object, and State and Local Government Debt: 1902 to 1970

[In millions of dollars]

Year	Expenditure									Debt	
	Total [1]	Current operation	Capital outlay			Assistance and subsidies	Interest on debt [2]	Insurance benefits and repayments	Expenditure for personal services	Out-standing at end of fiscal year	Increase or decrease (−) during year
			Total	Construction	Other						
	671	672	673	674	675	676	677	678	679	680	681
1970	148,052	97,915	29,650	24,252	5,399	8,090	5,123	7,273	62,998	143,570	10,022
1969	131,600	86,178	28,240	22,904	5,336	6,726	4,403	6,053	55,695	133,548	12,390
1968	116,234	75,311	25,731	20,800	4,931	5,649	3,889	5,653	48,996	121,158	7,499
1967	105,978	67,840	24,233	19,362	4,871	5,015	3,612	5,278	44,451	113,659	7,355
1966	94,906	60,212	22,330	17,801	4,528	4,315	3,268	4,782	40,059	107,051	7,539
1965	86,686	54,062	20,535	16,413	4,123	4,127	3,012	4,950	36,095	99,512	7,290
1964	80,579	49,687	19,087	15,389	3,698	3,885	2,826	5,094	33,310	92,222	7,166
1963	74,698	45,743	17,637	14,253	3,385	3,737	2,595	4,986	30,739	85,056	(NA)
1962	70,547	42,736	16,791	13,625	3,166	3,708	2,424	4,888	28,729	80,802	5,526
1961	67,023	39,800	16,091	13,214	2,877	3,608	2,225	5,299	26,461	75,023	5,068
1960 *	60,999	36,318	15,104	12,352	2,752	3,518	2,028	4,031	24,445	69,955	5,845
1959 [3]	58,572	33,369	15,351	12,723	2,628	3,329	1,740	4,784	22,528	64,110	5,923
1958	53,712	30,862	13,986	11,704	2,282	3,159	1,537	4,168	20,786	58,187	5,148
1957	47,553	27,983	12,616	10,387	2,230	2,828	1,376	2,749	18,707	53,039	4,171
1956	43,152	25,528	11,407	9,354	2,053	2,620	1,220	2,376	17,118	48,868	4,601
1955	40,375	23,186	10,706	9,048	1,658	2,660	1,059	2,764	15,539	44,267	5,336
1954	36,607	21,508	9,125	7,738	1,386	2,634	916	2,423	14,343	38,931	5,149
1953	32,937	19,965	7,905	6,763	1,142	2,558	797	1,711	13,100	33,782	3,682
1952	30,863	18,533	7,436	6,386	1,051	2,472	724	1,698	12,045	30,100	1,984
1950	27,905	15,948	6,047	5,169	879	2,918	613	2,379	10,043	24,115	3,116
1948	21,260	13,415	3,725	3,085	640	2,381	543	1,197	8,430	18,656	1,841
1946	14,067	9,690	1,305	970	334	1,209	557	1,306	5,945	15,917	−754
1944	10,499	7,848	709	562	147	952	635	354	4,988	17,479	−1,294
1942	10,914	7,057	1,477	1,241	236	1,056	706	617	4,515	19,337	−570
1940	11,240	6,176	2,515	1,828	687	1,075	787	687	4,302	20,283	220
1938	9,988	5,969	1,858	1,538	320	994	784	383	4,024	19,436	−26
1936	8,501	5,228	1,524	1,265	259	752	841	156	3,556	19,474	297
1934	7,842	4,650	1,407	1,170	237	815	837	133	3,194	18,929	−659
1932	8,403	5,179	1,876	1,558	318	388	840	120	3,541	19,205	232
1927	7,810	4,590	2,356	1,921	435	93	662	109	3,145	14,881	1,074
1922	5,652	3,477	1,518	1,236	282	152	430	75	2,384	10,109	1,446
1913	2,257	1,505	548	442	106	24	173	7	1,026	4,414	-------
1902	1,095	796	205	164	41	15	79	-------	540	2,107	-------

* Denotes first year for which figures include Alaska and Hawaii.
NA　Not available.

[1] To avoid duplication, transactions between State and local governments are excluded.
[2] Includes interest on debt of utilities operated by local governments.
[3] Includes Alaska.

Series Y 682–709.　State and Local Government Expenditure, by Function: 1902 to 1970

[In millions of dollars]

Year	Total [1]	General expenditure												
		Total general	Education				High-ways	Public welfare				Hos-pitals	Health	Police
			Total	State institutions of higher education	Local schools	Other education		Total	Cate-gorical public assist-ance	Other public assist-ance	Other public welfare			
	682	683	684	685	686	687	688	689	690	691	692	693	694	695
1970	148,052	131,332	52,718	12,924	37,461	2,332	16,427	14,679	6,902	480	7,298	7,863	1,806	4,494
1969	131,600	116,728	47,238	11,551	33,752	1,935	15,417	12,110	5,691	446	5,974	7,011	1,509	3,901
1968	116,234	102,411	41,158	10,214	29,305	1,637	14,481	9,857	4,817	349	4,690	6,282	1,264	3,410
1967	105,978	93,350	37,919	8,932	27,590	1,397	13,932	8,218	4,381	266	3,571	5,559	1,081	3,049
1966	94,906	82,843	33,287	7,207	25,091	989	12,770	6,757	3,822	236	2,701	4,969	941	2,776
1965	86,686	74,678	28,563	5,863	21,966	735	12,221	6,315	3,690	234	2,391	4,525	836	2,549
1964	80,579	69,302	26,286	5,278	20,399	609	11,664	5,766	3,478	226	2,062	4,171	739	2,366
1963	74,698	63,977	23,729	4,466	18,759	504	11,150	5,420	3,290	238	1,892	3,928	710	2,237
1962	70,547	60,206	22,216	4,043	17,739	434	10,357	5,084	3,257	258	1,570	3,673	669	2,130
1961	67,023	56,201	20,574	3,570	16,608	396	9,844	4,720	3,075	335	1,312	3,496	590	2,017
1960 *	60,999	51,876	18,719	3,202	15,166	351	9,428	4,404	2,997	310	1,096	3,235	559	1,857
1959 [2]	58,572	48,887	17,283	2,920	14,034	329	9,592	4,136	2,886	301	949	3,142	582	1,710
1958	53,712	44,851	15,919	2,582	13,032	305	8,567	3,818	2,689	275	853	2,961	501	1,610
1957	47,553	40,375	14,134	2,206	11,657	272	7,816	3,485	2,525	195	765	2,619	500	1,468
1956	43,152	36,711	13,220	1,814	11,165	241	6,953	3,139	2,310	244	585	2,316	456	1,330

See footnotes at end of table.

Series Y 682–709. State and Local Government Expenditure, by Function: 1902 to 1970—Con.

[In millions of dollars]

General expenditure

Year	Total¹ (682)	Total general (683)	Education: Total (684)	State institutions of higher education (685)	Local schools (686)	Other education (687)	Highways (688)	Public welfare: Total (689)	Categorical public assistance (690)	Other public assistance (691)	Other public welfare (692)	Hospitals (693)	Health (694)	Police (695)
1955	40,375	33,724	11,907	1,570	10,129	210	6,452	3,168	2,269	382	517	2,053	471	1,229
1954	36,607	30,701	10,557	1,418	8,947	192	5,527	3,060	2,224	308	527	1,962	447	1,130
1953	32,937	27,910	9,390	1,361	7,822	207	4,987	2,914	2,159	301	454	1,863	427	1,038
1952	30,863	26,098	8,318	1,267	6,862	189	4,650	2,788	2,023	303	461	1,745	440	939
1950	27,905	22,787	7,177	1,107	5,906	164	3,803	2,940	2,010	538	392	1,384	364	776
1948	21,260	17,684	5,379	895	4,363	121	3,036	2,099	1,473	357	269	937	292	644
1946	14,067	11,028	3,356	397	2,886	73	1,672	1,409	1,014	216	179	567	251	479
1944	10,499	8,863	2,793	380	2,344	69	1,200	1,133	842	166	125	468	188	414
1942	10,914	9,190	2,586	296	2,225	65	1,490	1,225	761	345	119	432	159	394
1940	11,240	9,229	2,638	290	2,292	56	1,573	1,156	611	438	107	450	159	365
1938	9,988	8,757	2,491	268	2,172	51	1,650	1,069	483	485	101	400	151	359
1936	8,501	7,644	2,177	231	1,904	42	1,425	827	731		96	351	116	314
1934	7,842	7,181	1,831	177	1,623	31	1,509	889	796		93	309	109	291
1932	8,403	7,765	2,311	234	2,050	27	1,741	444	366		78	349	107	318
1927	7,810	7,210	2,235	196	2,017	22	1,809	151	79		72	279	76	270
1922	5,652	5,218	1,705	143	1,541	21	1,294	119	57		62	200	58	190
1913	2,257	2,064	577	49	522	6	419	52	17		35	79	29	89
1902	1,095	1,013	255	13	238	4	175	37	11		26	43	17	50

General expenditure—Con. / Insurance trust expenditure

Year	Local fire protection (696)	Local sanitation (697)	Natural resources (698)	Local parks and recreation (699)	Housing and urban renewal (700)	Financial administration and general control (701)	Interest on general debt (702)	Air and water transport and terminals (703)	Other and unallocable (704)	Utility and liquor stores expenditure (705)	Insurance trust: Total (706)	Employee retirement (707)	Unemployment compensation (708)	Other (709)
1970	2,024	3,413	2,732	1,888	2,138	4,682	4,374	1,413	10,681	9,447	7,273	3,629	2,723	921
1969	1,793	2,969	2,552	1,645	1,902	4,105	3,732	1,184	9,660	8,820	6,053	3,221	1,992	840
1968	1,623	2,707	2,471	1,412	1,632	3,647	3,266	923	8,278	8,170	5,653	2,829	2,050	774
1967	1,499	2,523	2,344	1,291	1,469	3,313	3,032	785	7,336	7,350	5,278	2,608	1,941	728
1966	1,376	2,571	2,039	1,187	1,406	2,974	2,690	742	6,358	7,282	4,782	2,219	1,893	671
1965	1,306	2,360	1,861	1,104	1,250	2,773	2,490	691	5,833	7,058	4,950	2,298	2,008	644
1964	1,222	2,267	1,835	1,022	1,142	2,567	2,356	650	5,249	6,184	5,094	1,844	2,638	612
1963	1,161	1,996	1,497	902	1,179	2,439	2,164	648	4,817	5,736	4,987	1,665	2,760	562
1962	1,124	1,958	1,371	886	1,153	2,338	2,011	665	4,571	5,453	4,888	1,578	2,808	502
1961	1,087	1,774	1,327	857	943	2,237	1,824	715	4,194	5,523	5,299	1,383	3,463	453
1960 *	995	1,727	1,189	770	858	2,113	1,670	579	3,772	5,088	4,031	1,265	2,364	402
1959 ²	914	1,609	1,076	729	615	2,003	1,416	549	3,532	4,901	4,784	1,144	3,275	365
1958	873	1,505	999	685	601	1,843	1,244	473	3,252	4,693	4,168	1,074	2,757	337
1957	810	1,443	932	608	505	1,725	1,106	419	2,804	4,429	2,749	943	1,500	307
1956	737	1,326	906	541	437	1,560	986	506	2,298	4,065	2,376	825	1,277	274
1955	694	1,142	793	509	499	1,452	838	268	2,249	3,886	2,764	722	1,784	258
1954	653	1,058	762	424	611	1,375	718	308	2,109	3,482	2,423	679	1,507	237
1953	598	908	705	374	631	1,263	614	255	1,942	3,316	1,711	585	910	216
1952	586	992	776	324	769	1,193	552	208	1,815	3,067	1,698	530	973	195
1950	488	834	670	304	452	1,041	458		2,096	2,739	2,379	361	1,849	169
1948	406	670	496	243	176	880	399		2,027	2,379	1,197	297	759	141
1946	294	370	302	179	114	703	421		911	1,733	1,306	237	968	102
1944	251	245	232	123	46	599	499		670	1,281	354	195	69	90
1942	236	229	214	128	236	578	565		718	1,106	617	169	377	71
1940	235	207	218	162	230	561	653		622	1,324	687	140	494	53
1938	231	226	222	130	3	542	673		610	848	383	129	202	52
1936	205	204	193	104	---	500	738		490	701	156	113	---	43
1934	189	177	159	126	---	432	739		421	528	133	96	---	37
1932	210	223	165	147	---	470	741		539	518	120	75	---	45
1927	203	312	94	153	---	412	584		632	491	109	50	---	59
1922	158	189	61	85	---	313	382		464	359	75	50	---	45
1913	76	97	14	57	---	211	147		217	186	7	7	---	---
1902	40	51	9	29	---	141	68		98	82	---	---	---	---

* Denotes first year for which figures include Alaska and Hawaii.
¹ To avoid duplication, transactions between State and local governments are excluded; see text.
² Includes Alaska.

Series Y 710–735. State Government Revenue, by Source: 1902 to 1970

[In millions of dollars]

Year	Revenue from all sources		Intergovernmental revenue		Revenue from State sources										
	Total	General revenue (direct and intergovernmental)	From Federal Government	From local governments	Total	General revenue								
						Total	Taxes			Sales and gross receipts					
							Total	Individual income	Corporation income	Total	General	Motor fuel	Alcoholic beverages	Tobacco products	Other
	710	711	712	713	714	715	716	717	718	719	720	721	722	723	724
1970	88,939	77,755	19,252	995	68,691	57,507	47,962	9,183	3,738	27,254	14,177	6,283	1,420	2,308	3,065
1969	77,584	67,312	16,907	868	59,809	49,537	41,931	7,527	3,180	24,050	12,443	5,644	1,246	2,056	2,660
1968	68,460	59,132	15,228	707	52,525	43,197	36,400	6,231	2,518	20,979	10,441	5,178	1,138	1,886	2,335
1967	61,082	52,071	13,616	673	46,793	37,782	31,926	4,909	2,227	18,575	8,923	4,837	1,041	1,615	2,159
1966	55,246	46,757	11,743	503	43,000	34,511	29,380	4,288	2,038	17,044	7,873	4,627	985	1,541	2,019
1965	48,827	40,930	9,874	447	38,507	30,610	26,126	3,657	1,929	15,059	6,711	4,300	917	1,284	1,847
1964	45,167	37,648	9,046	417	35,703	28,184	24,243	3,415	1,695	13,957	6,084	4,059	864	1,196	1,755
1963	40,993	33,882	7,832	411	32,750	25,639	22,117	2,956	1,505	12,873	5,539	3,851	793	1,124	1,565
1962	37,595	31,157	7,108	373	30,115	23,677	20,561	2,728	1,308	12,038	5,111	3,665	740	1,075	1,448
1961	34,603	28,693	6,412	370	27,821	21,911	19,057	2,355	1,266	11,031	4,510	3,431	688	1,001	1,401
1960 *	32,838	27,363	6,382	363	26,094	20,618	18,036	2,209	1,180	10,510	4,302	3,335	650	923	1,300
1959 [1]	29,164	24,448	5,888	364	22,912	18,196	15,848	1,764	1,001	9,287	3,697	3,058	599	675	1,257
1958	26,191	21,772	4,461	302	21,427	17,008	14,919	1,544	1,018	8,750	3,507	2,919	566	616	1,142
1957	24,656	20,382	3,500	427	20,728	16,454	14,531	1,563	984	8,436	3,373	2,828	569	556	1,109
1956	22,199	18,389	3,027	269	18,903	15,093	13,375	1,374	890	7,801	3,036	2,687	546	515	1,017
1955	19,667	16,194	2,762	226	16,678	13,205	11,597	1,094	737	6,864	2,637	2,353	471	459	944
1954	18,834	15,299	2,668	215	15,951	12,417	11,089	1,004	772	6,573	2,540	2,218	463	464	889
1953	17,979	14,511	2,570	191	15,218	11,750	10,552	969	810	6,209	2,433	2,019	465	469	823
1952	16,815	13,429	2,329	156	14,330	10,944	9,857	913	838	5,730	2,229	1,870	442	449	740
1950	13,903	11,262	2,275	148	11,480	8,839	7,930	724	586	4,670	1,670	1,544	420	414	621
1948	11,826	9,257	1,643	97	10,086	7,517	6,743	499	585	4,042	1,478	1,259	425	337	542
1946	8,576	6,284	802	63	7,712	5,419	4,937	389	442	2,803	899	886	402	198	419
1944	7,695	5,465	926	55	6,714	4,484	4,071	316	446	2,153	720	684	267	159	323
1942	6,870	5,132	802	56	6,012	4,274	3,903	249	269	2,218	632	940	257	130	258
1940	5,737	4,382	667	58	5,012	3,657	3,313	206	155	1,852	499	839	193	97	224
1938	5,293	4,141	633	48	4,612	3,460	3,132	218	165	1,674	447	777	176	55	219
1936	4,023	3,672	719	39	3,265	2,914	2,618	153	113	1,394	364	687	126	44	173
1934	3,421	3,212	933	36	2,452	2,243	1,979	80	49	978	173	565	62	25	153
1932	2,541	2,423	222	45	2,274	2,156	1,890	74	79	726	7	527	–	19	173
1927	2,152	2,015	107	51	1,994	1,857	1,608	70	92	445	--------	259	–	--------	186
1922	1,360	1,254	99	27	1,234	1,128	947	43	58	134	--------	13	–	--------	121
1913	376	376	6	10	360	360	301	--------	--------	55	--------	--------	2	--------	53
1902	192	190	3	6	183	181	156	--------	--------	28	--------	--------	--------	--------	28

Year	Revenue from State sources—Con.										
	General revenue—Con.				Liquor stores revenue	Insurance trust revenue					
	Taxes—Con.			Charges and miscellaneous		Total	Employee retirement	Unemployment compensation			Other
	Property	Motor vehicle and operators' licenses	Other					Total	Contributions	Interest (credited by U.S. Govt.)	
	725	726	727	728	729	730	731	732	733	734	735
1970	1,092	2,955	3,741	9,545	1,748	9,437	5,205	3,090	2,524	566	1,143
1969	981	2,685	3,509	7,606	1,663	8,609	4,509	3,039	2,550	488	1,061
1968	912	2,485	3,275	6,797	1,557	7,771	3,831	2,963	2,547	416	977
1967	862	2,311	3,042	5,856	1,470	7,541	3,351	3,273	2,910	363	917
1966	834	2,236	2,940	5,131	1,361	7,128	2,918	3,326	3,040	286	884
1965	766	2,021	2,691	4,483	1,270	6,627	2,638	3,234	2,994	239	755
1964	722	1,917	2,536	3,942	1,195	6,324	2,369	3,250	3,046	203	706
1963	688	1,780	2,316	3,523	1,161	5,950	2,136	3,171	2,992	179	642
1962	640	1,667	2,180	3,116	1,134	5,304	1,942	2,812	2,649	162	550
1961	631	1,641	2,133	2,854	1,119	4,791	1,745	2,511	2,317	194	535
1960 *	607	1,573	1,957	2,583	1,128	4,347	1,558	2,316	2,136	181	472
1959 [1]	566	1,492	1,740	2,348	1,085	3,631	1,376	1,827	1,647	179	428
1958	533	1,415	1,658	2,089	1,058	3,361	1,224	1,711	1,493	218	426
1957	479	1,368	1,701	1,923	1,065	3,209	1,063	1,719	1,510	209	427
1956	467	1,295	1,548	1,718	1,019	2,791	919	1,500	1,315	185	371
1955	412	1,184	1,306	1,608	962	2,511	837	1,325	1,138	187	350
1954	391	1,098	1,251	1,328	974	2,560	757	1,466	1,263	203	337
1953	365	949	1,250	1,198	967	2,501	634	1,551	1,370	181	316
1952	370	924	1,082	1,087	924	2,462	579	1,597	1,438	159	287

* Denotes first year for which figures include Alaska and Hawaii. [1] Includes Alaska.
– Represents zero.

Series Y 710–735.　State Government Revenue, by Source: 1902 to 1970—Con.

[In millions of dollars]

Year	Property	Motor vehicle and operators' licenses	Other	Charges and miscellaneous	Liquor stores revenue	Total	Employee retirement	Unemployment compensation			Other
								Total	Contributions	Interest (credited by U.S. Govt.)	
	725	726	727	728	729	730	731	732	733	734	735
1950	307	755	888	909	810	1,831	425	1,176	1,028	148	229
1948	276	593	747	774	857	1,711	296	1,203	1,059	144	212
1946	249	439	616	482	798	1,494	193	1,162	1,034	128	140
1944	243	394	520	413	528	1,702	142	1,405	1,319	86	154
1942	264	431	472	370	373	1,366	115	1,134	1,076	58	117
1940	260	387	453	344	281	1,074	108	878	844	34	88
1938	244	359	472	328	262	890	85	726	702	24	79
1936	228	360	370	296	183	168	75	23	23	--------	70
1934	273	305	294	264	90	119	64	--------	--------	--------	55
1932	328	335	348	266	-	118	54	--------	--------	--------	64
1927	370	301	330	249	-	137	40	--------	--------	--------	97
1922	348	152	212	181	-	106	29	--------	--------	--------	77
1913	140	5	101	59	-	--------	--------	--------	--------	--------	--------
1902	82	--------	46	25	2	--------	--------	--------	--------	--------	--------

- Represents zero.

Series Y 736–782.　State Government Expenditure, by Character and Object, by Function, and State Government Debt: 1902 to 1970

[In millions of dollars]

Year	Total	Intergovernmental expenditure	Total	Current operation	Capital outlay			Assistance and subsidies	Interest on debt	Insurance benefits and repayments	Expenditure for personal services	Outstanding at end of fiscal year	Increase or decrease (−) during year
					Total	Construction	Other						
	736	737	738	739	740	741	742	743	744	745	746	747	748
1970	85,055	28,892	56,163	30,971	13,295	11,185	2,110	4,387	1,499	6,010	17,786	42,008	2,455
1969	74,227	24,779	49,448	27,052	12,701	10,610	2,091	3,509	1,275	4,911	15,592	39,553	3,887
1968	66,254	21,950	44,304	23,379	12,210	10,053	2,158	2,960	1,128	4,626	13,799	35,666	3,194
1967	58,760	19,056	39,704	20,201	11,544	9,550	1,994	2,665	1,026	4,268	12,011	32,472	2,908
1966	51,123	16,928	34,195	16,855	10,193	8,287	1,906	2,301	894	3,952	10,561	29,564	2,530
1965	45,639	14,174	31,465	14,930	9,307	7,600	1,707	2,236	822	4,170	9,257	27,034	1,993
1964	42,583	12,968	29,616	13,492	8,820	7,263	1,558	2,175	765	4,364	8,408	25,041	1,865
1963	39,583	11,885	27,698	12,449	8,110	6,717	1,393	2,112	721	4,306	7,722	23,176	1,153
1962	36,402	10,906	25,495	11,290	7,214	5,960	1,254	2,118	635	4,238	7,051	22,023	2,004
1961	34,693	10,114	24,578	10,384	6,865	5,699	1,166	2,044	584	4,701	6,524	19,993	1,450
1960 *	31,596	9,443	22,152	9,534	6,607	5,509	1,098	2,015	536	3,461	5,914	18,543	1,613
1959 [1]	31,125	8,689	22,436	8,775	7,059	5,937	1,122	1,891	453	4,259	5,474	16,930	1,536
1958	28,080	8,089	19,991	8,161	5,946	5,022	924	1,813	396	3,675	5,063	15,394	1,656
1957	24,235	7,440	16,796	7,330	5,163	4,318	845	1,639	351	2,313	4,473	13,738	848
1956	21,686	6,538	15,148	6,758	4,564	3,872	692	1,531	311	1,984	4,132	12,890	1,692
1955	20,357	5,986	14,371	6,234	3,992	3,404	589	1,482	251	2,411	3,795	11,198	1,598
1954	18,686	5,679	13,008	5,886	3,347	2,831	515	1,486	193	2,096	3,491	9,600	1,776
1953	16,850	5,384	11,466	5,540	2,847	2,472	375	1,501	162	1,416	3,232	7,824	950
1952	15,834	5,044	10,790	5,173	2,658	2,323	336	1,402	144	1,413	2,956	6,874	652
1950	15,082	4,217	10,864	4,450	2,237	1,966	272	1,891	109	2,177	2,450	5,285	1,137
1948	11,181	3,283	7,897	3,837	1,456	1,268	188	1,499	86	1,020	1,960	3,676	708
1946	7,066	2,092	4,974	2,701	368	292	75	663	84	1,158	1,240	2,353	−154
1944	5,161	1,842	3,319	2,134	330	288	42	527	101	226	1,061	2,776	−214
1942	5,343	1,780	3,563	1,827	642	560	82	466	122	505	961	3,257	−233
1940	5,209	1,654	3,555	1,570	737	643	94	517	130	601	902	3,590	58
1938	4,598	1,516	3,082	1,503	701	612	89	448	128	302	848	3,343	−32
1936	3,862	1,417	2,445	1,192	634	553	81	416	124	79	685	3,413	−9
1934	3,461	1,318	2,143	985	619	540	79	356	119	64	576	3,248	167
1932	2,829	801	2,028	982	786	686	100	83	114	63	616	2,832	223
1927	2,047	596	1,451	762	492	430	62	43	83	71	465	1,971	145
1922	1,397	312	1,085	562	302	263	39	122	45	54	343	1,131	230
1913	388	91	297	218	48	42	6	17	14	---------	125	379	47
1902	188	52	136	114	2	2	---------	10	10	---------	65	230	11

See footnotes at end of table.

Series **Y 736–782.** State Government Expenditure, by Character and Object, by Function, and State Government Debt: 1902 to 1970—Con.

[In millions of dollars]

Year	Total expenditure	Total general expenditure (direct and intergovernmental)	Intergovernmental expenditure, by function						Direct expenditure, by function								
										General expenditure							
											Education					Public welfare	
			Total	Education	Highways	Public welfare	Other specified purposes	General local government support	Total	Total	Total	State institutions of higher education	Local schools	Other education	Highways	Total	Categorical cash assistance
	749	750	751	752	753	754	755	756	757	758	759	760	761	762	763	764	765
1970	85,055	77,642	28,892	17,085	2,439	5,003	1,408	2,958	56,163	48,749	13,780	11,011	437	2,332	11,044	8,203	3,534
1969	74,227	68,023	24,779	14,858	2,109	4,402	1,275	2,135	49,448	43,244	12,304	10,004	365	1,935	10,414	6,464	2,827
1968	66,254	60,395	21,950	13,321	2,029	3,527	1,079	1,993	44,304	38,446	10,957	8,982	339	1,637	9,819	5,122	2,421
1967	58,760	53,305	19,056	11,845	1,861	2,897	868	1,585	39,704	34,249	9,384	7,728	300	1,357	9,423	4,291	2,243
1966	51,123	46,090	16,928	10,177	1,725	2,882	783	1,361	34,195	29,162	7,572	6,353	231	989	8,624	3,138	1,986
1965	45,639	40,446	14,174	8,351	1,630	2,436	655	1,102	31,465	26,273	6,181	5,258	189	735	8,214	2,998	1,970
1964	42,583	37,242	12,968	7,664	1,524	2,108	619	1,053	29,616	24,275	5,465	4,649	207	609	7,850	2,796	1,935
1963	39,583	34,377	11,885	6,993	1,416	1,919	545	1,012	27,698	22,491	4,718	3,992	222	504	7,425	2,712	1,909
1962	36,402	31,281	10,906	6,474	1,327	1,777	490	839	25,495	20,375	4,270	3,634	202	434	6,635	2,509	1,863
1961	34,693	29,118	10,114	5,963	1,266	1,602	462	821	24,578	19,004	3,792	3,170	226	396	6,230	2,311	1,767
1960 *	31,596	27,228	9,443	5,461	1,247	1,483	447	806	22,152	17,784	3,396	2,856	189	351	6,070	2,221	1,728
1959 [1]	31,125	26,006	8,689	4,957	1,207	1,409	391	725	22,436	17,318	3,093	2,614	150	329	6,414	2,124	1,683
1958	28,080	23,537	8,089	4,598	1,167	1,247	390	687	19,991	15,449	2,728	2,305	117	305	5,507	1,944	1,563
1957	24,235	21,087	7,440	4,212	1,082	1,136	341	668	16,796	13,647	2,342	1,958	112	272	4,875	1,826	1,481
1956	21,686	18,857	6,538	3,541	984	1,069	313	631	15,148	12,319	2,138	1,678	219	241	4,367	1,603	1,364
1955	20,357	17,176	5,986	3,150	911	1,046	288	591	14,371	11,190	1,905	1,468	227	210	3,899	1,600	1,321
1954	18,686	15,788	5,679	2,930	871	1,004	274	600	13,008	10,109	1,715	1,324	199	192	3,254	1,548	1,298
1953	16,850	14,678	5,384	2,737	803	981	271	592	11,466	9,294	1,634	1,277	150	207	2,781	1,534	1,307
1952	15,834	13,697	5,044	2,523	728	976	268	549	10,790	8,653	1,494	1,180	125	189	2,556	1,410	1,192
1950	15,082	12,250	4,217	2,054	610	792	279	482	10,864	8,033	1,358	1,107	87	164	2,058	1,566	1,337
1948	11,181	9,469	3,283	1,554	507	648	146	428	7,897	6,186	1,081	895	65	121	1,510	962	820
1946	7,066	5,245	2,092	953	339	376	67	357	4,974	3,153	518	397	48	73	613	680	589
1944	5,161	4,508	1,842	861	298	368	41	274	3,319	2,666	489	380	40	69	540	577	506
1942	5,343	4,549	1,780	790	344	390	32	224	3,563	2,769	391	296	30	65	790	523	414
1940	5,209	4,384	1,654	700	332	420	21	181	3,555	2,730	375	290	29	56	793	527	321
1938	4,598	4,092	1,516	656	317	346	17	180	3,082	2,576	347	268	28	51	815	453	257
1936	3,862	3,640	1,417	573	285	245	151	163	2,445	2,223	297	231	24	42	754	422	[2]395
1934	3,461	3,327	1,318	434	247	211	281	145	2,143	2,009	228	177	20	31	738	363	[2]337
1932	2,829	2,766	801	398	229	28	6	140	2,028	1,965	278	234	17	27	843	74	[2]61
1927	2,047	1,976	596	292	197	6	3	98	1,451	1,380	218	196	------	22	514	40	[2]29
1922	1,397	1,343	312	202	70	4	1	35	1,085	1,031	164	143	------	21	303	38	[2]27
1913	388	388	91	82	4	------	------	5	297	297	55	49	------	6	26	16	[2]10
1902	188	186	52	45	2	------	------	5	136	134	17	13	------	4	4	10	[2]6

Direct expenditure, by function—Con.

Year	Public welfare—Con.		Hospitals	Health	Police	Natural resources	Veterans services, not elsewhere classified	Financial administration and general control	Interest on general debt	Social insurance administration	Correction	Other and unallocable	Liquor stores expenditure	Insurance trust expenditure			
	Other cash assistance	Other public welfare												Total	Employee retirement	Unemployment compensation	Other
	766	767	768	769	770	771	772	773	774	775	776	777	778	779	780	781	782
1970	145	4,524	4,002	786	688	2,158	65	1,720	1,499	767	1,051	2,985	1,404	6,010	2,376	2,713	921
1969	91	3,545	3,582	676	585	2,035	49	1,496	1,275	665	914	2,786	1,293	4,911	2,088	1,984	840
1968	57	2,643	3,233	599	516	1,954	31	1,310	1,128	606	838	2,332	1,233	4,626	1,810	2,042	774
1967	54	1,994	2,857	501	441	1,801	23	1,175	1,026	545	747	2,036	1,187	4,268	1,606	1,934	728
1966	57	1,096	2,533	433	385	1,532	21	1,024	894	500	664	1,842	1,081	3,952	1,398	1,884	671
1965	62	965	2,317	384	348	1,343	20	948	822	457	632	1,609	1,022	4,170	1,238	2,288	644
1964	59	801	2,127	337	315	1,185	19	871	765	426	586	1,534	977	4,364	1,125	2,627	612
1963	60	743	2,006	324	297	1,097	20	830	721	411	536	1,393	900	4,306	995	2,750	562
1962	61	585	1,878	283	276	973	95	763	635	399	508	1,152	882	4,238	933	2,802	502
1961	78	466	1,799	260	261	906	84	726	584	351	479	1,223	873	4,701	791	3,456	453
1960 *	76	417	1,664	232	245	842	112	654	536	313	425	1,073	907	3,461	700	2,359	402
1959 [1]	66	375	1,627	223	228	813	61	619	453	303	413	948	860	4,259	626	3,268	365
1958	55	326	1,549	211	214	753	121	569	396	270	370	818	869	3,675	587	2,751	337
1957	49	296	1,373	198	179	688	38	531	351	234	328	685	836	2,313	511	1,495	307
1956	37	203	1,268	202	159	670	88	477	311	215	295	526	845	1,984	437	1,273	274
1955	44	234	1,145	193	139	597	61	447	251	207	268	478	770	2,411	373	1,780	258
1954	32	218	1,089	187	130	563	102	419	193	190	250	469	803	2,096	355	1,504	237
1953	37	188	1,014	170	119	531	113	399	162	187	238	411	757	1,416	292	908	216
1952	37	182	968	164	106	539	142	361	144	177	223	369	723	1,413	247	971	195
1950	92	137	788	159	85	468	462	317	109	172	198	293	654	2,177	163	1,845	169
1948	58	84	533	130	65	344	633	266	86	150	153	273	691	1,020	123	756	141

See footnotes at end of table.

Series **Y 736–782.** State Government Expenditure, by Character and Object, by Function, and State Government Debt: 1902 to 1970—Con.

[In millions of dollars]

Year	Public welfare—Con. Other cash assistance	Other public welfare	Hospitals	Health	Police	Natural resources	Veterans services, not elsewhere classified	Financial administration and general control	Interest on general debt	Social insurance administration	Correction	Other and unallocable	Liquor stores expenditure	Insurance trust expenditure Total	Employee retirement	Unemployment compensation	Other
	766	767	768	769	770	771	772	773	774	775	776	777	778	779	780	781	782
1946	35	56	308	116	45	207	54	192	84	60	97	179	663	1,158	92	965	102
1944	32	39	253	78	41	164	1	162	101	35	83	142	426	226	71	65	90
1942	72	37	235	64	40	159	1	164	122	59	80	141	288	505	65	369	71
1940	170	36	236	64	34	144	--------	151	130	64	86	126	224	601	56	492	53
1938	165	31	209	59	30	128	--------	146	128	48	85	128	204	302	48	202	52
1936	(2)	27	180	41	19	93	--------	130	124	3	73	87	143	79	36	--------	43
1934	(2)	26	167	36	15	85	--------	108	119	1	70	79	70	64	27	--------	37
1932	(2)	13	181	34	15	119	--------	114	114	--------	87	106		63	18	--------	45
1927	(2)	11	146	24	7	94	--------	96	83	--------	64	94		71	12	--------	59
1922	(2)	11	105	20	4	61	--------	69	45	--------	64	158		54	9	--------	45
1913	(2)	6	47	6	1	14	--------	38	14	--------	28	52		--------	--------	--------	--------
1902	(2)	4	28	4	--------	9	--------	23	10	--------	14	15	2	--------	--------	--------	--------

* Denotes first year for which figures include Alaska and Hawaii.
¹ Includes Alaska.

² Other cash assistance included with categorical public assistance.

Series **Y 783–795.** Local Government Expenditure, by Character and Object, and Local Government Debt: 1902 to 1970

[In millions of dollars]

Year	Expenditure Total	Intergovernmental expenditure (to States)	Direct expenditure Total	Current operation	Capital outlay Total	Construction	Other	Assistance and subsidies	Interest on debt ¹	Insurance benefits and repayments	Expenditure for personal services	Debt Outstanding at end of fiscal year	Increase or decrease (−) during year
	783	784	785	786	787	788	789	790	791	792	793	794	795
1970	92,522	633	91,889	66,943	16,355	13,067	3,289	3,703	3,624	1,263	45,212	101,563	7,568
1969	82,698	546	82,152	59,126	15,539	12,294	3,245	3,217	3,128	1,141	40,103	93,995	8,503
1968	72,357	427	71,930	51,932	13,521	10,747	2,773	2,689	2,761	1,027	35,197	85,492	4,307
1967	66,648	374	66,274	47,639	12,689	9,811	2,877	2,349	2,587	1,008	32,439	81,185	4,463
1966	60,994	283	60,711	43,357	12,137	9,514	2,622	2,014	2,374	830	29,498	77,487	5,009
1965	55,482	262	55,221	38,999	11,360	8,905	2,456	1,891	2,191	780	26,838	72,478	5,297
1964	51,199	235	50,964	36,197	10,267	8,127	2,140	1,709	2,061	730	24,902	67,181	5,300
1963	47,237	235	47,002	33,294	9,528	7,536	1,992	1,625	1,875	680	23,017	61,881	2,942
1962	45,279	226	45,053	31,446	9,577	7,665	1,912	1,590	1,789	651	21,678	58,779	3,521
1961	42,641	196	42,445	29,416	9,226	7,515	1,711	1,564	1,641	598	19,937	55,030	3,618
1960 *	39,056	209	38,847	26,785	8,497	6,843	1,654	1,503	1,492	570	18,531	51,412	4,232
1959 ²	36,341	205	36,136	24,594	8,292	6,786	1,506	1,438	1,287	525	17,055	47,180	4,387
1958	34,023	302	33,721	22,701	8,040	6,682	1,358	1,346	1,141	493	15,723	42,793	3,492
1957	31,057	300	30,757	20,653	7,454	6,069	1,385	1,189	1,025	436	14,234	39,301	3,323
1956	28,273	269	28,004	18,771	6,843	5,482	1,361	1,089	910	392	12,986	35,978	2,909
1955	26,230	226	26,004	16,951	6,713	5,644	1,069	1,179	807	353	11,744	33,069	3,738
1954	23,814	215	23,599	15,622	5,778	4,907	871	1,148	723	327	10,851	29,331	3,374
1953	21,662	191	21,471	14,425	5,058	4,291	767	1,057	635	296	9,868	25,957	2,731
1952	20,229	156	20,073	13,360	4,778	4,063	715	1,070	580	285	9,089	23,226	1,332
1950	17,041	(3)	³17,041	11,498	3,810	3,203	607	1,027	504	202	7,593	18,830	1,979
1948	13,363	(3)	³13,363	9,578	2,269	1,817	452	882	457	177	6,470	14,980	1,133
1946	9,093	(3)	³9,093	6,989	937	678	259	546	473	148	4,705	13,664	−600
1944	7,180	(3)	³7,180	5,714	379	274	105	425	534	128	3,927	14,703	−1,080
1942	7,351	(3)	³7,351	5,230	835	681	154	590	584	112	3,554	16,080	−337
1940	7,685	(3)	³7,685	4,606	1,778	1,185	593	558	657	86	3,400	16,693	162
1938	6,906	(3)	³6,906	4,466	1,157	926	231	546	656	81	3,176	16,093	6
1936	6,056	(3)	³6,056	4,036	890	712	178	336	717	77	2,871	16,061	306
1934	5,699	(3)	³5,699	3,665	788	630	158	459	718	69	2,618	15,681	−826
1932	6,375	(3)	³6,375	4,197	1,090	872	218	305	726	57	2,925	16,373	9
1927	6,359	(3)	³6,359	3,828	1,864	1,491	373	50	579	38	2,680	12,910	929
1922	4,567	(3)	³4,567	2,915	1,216	973	243	30	385	21	2,041	8,978	1,216
1913	1,960	(3)	³1,960	1,287	500	400	100	7	159	8	901	4,035	----------
1902	959	(3)	³959	682	203	162	41	5	69	----------	475	1,877	----------

* Denotes first year for which figures include Alaska and Hawaii.
¹ Includes interest on debt of utilities operated by local governments.

² Includes Alaska.
³ Minor amounts of intergovernmental expenditure to States not segregable from "Direct expenditure."

Series Y 796–816. Local Government Revenue, by Source: 1902 to 1970

[In millions of dollars]

Year	Revenue from all sources		Intergovernmental revenue		Revenue from local sources							
					Total	General revenue						
	Total [1]	General revenue (direct [1] and intergovernmental)	From Federal Government	From State governments		Total	Taxes					Charges and miscellaneous
							Total	Individual income [2]	Sales and gross receipts	Property	Other taxes [3]	
	796	797	798	799	800	801	802	803	804	805	806	807
1970	89,082	80,916	2,605	26,920	59,557	51,392	38,833	1,630	3,068	32,963	1,173	12,558
1969	79,274	71,943	2,245	23,837	53,192	45,861	34,781	1,381	2,470	29,692	1,239	11,080
1968	70,171	63,181	1,954	20,342	47,875	40,886	31,171	1,077	1,932	26,835	1,327	9,714
1967	64,608	58,235	1,753	18,434	44,419	38,045	29,074	916	1,956	25,186	1,016	8,971
1966	59,268	53,172	1,378	16,391	41,499	35,404	27,361	472	2,041	23,836	1,012	8,044
1965	53,408	47,528	1,155	14,010	38,242	32,362	25,116	433	2,059	21,817	807	7,245
1964	49,578	44,084	956	12,873	35,749	30,256	23,542	376	1,806	20,519	841	6,714
1963	45,586	40,558	831	11,760	32,995	27,967	21,897	311	1,574	19,145	867	6,070
1962	43,147	38,346	763	10,879	31,506	26,705	20,993	309	1,456	18,414	815	5,711
1961	40,483	35,899	719	10,185	29,579	24,995	19,804	258	1,432	17,370	744	5,192
1960 *	37,324	33,027	592	9,522	27,209	22,912	18,081	254	1,339	15,798	692	4,831
1959 [4]	33,572	29,621	489	8,399	24,684	20,733	16,531	230	1,150	14,417	734	4,202
1958	31,348	27,723	404	7,974	22,970	19,345	15,461	215	1,079	13,514	652	3,885
1957	29,021	25,531	343	7,321	21,357	17,866	14,286	191	1,031	12,385	679	3,580
1956	26,352	23,137	309	6,590	19,453	16,238	12,992	164	889	11,282	657	3,246
1955	24,166	21,092	368	5,987	17,811	14,737	11,886	143	779	10,323	641	2,851
1954	22,402	19,562	298	5,635	16,468	13,629	10,978	122	703	9,577	576	2,651
1953	21,007	18,371	300	5,384	15,323	12,687	10,356	96	718	9,010	530	2,331
1952	19,398	16,952	237	5,044	14,117	11,671	9,466	85	627	8,282	473	2,205
1950	16,101	14,014	211	4,217	11,673	9,586	7,984	64	484	7,042	394	1,602
1948	13,167	11,373	218	3,283	9,666	7,872	6,599	44	400	5,850	305	1,273
1946	9,561	8,227	53	2,092	7,416	6,082	5,157	33	183	4,737	204	925
1944	8,535	7,340	28	1,842	6,665	5,470	4,703	26	136	4,361	180	767
1942	8,114	7,122	56	1,780	6,278	5,286	4,625	27	133	4,273	192	661
1940	7,724	6,939	278	1,654	5,792	5,007	4,497	18	130	4,170	179	510
1938	7,329	6,651	167	1,516	5,646	4,968	4,473	----------	120	4,196	157	495
1936	6,793	6,179	229	1,417	5,147	4,533	4,083	----------	90	3,865	128	450
1934	6,363	5,820	83	1,318	4,962	4,419	3,933	----------	30	3,803	100	486
1932	6,192	5,690	10	801	5,381	4,879	4,274	----------	26	4,159	89	605
1927	6,333	5,903	9	596	5,728	5,298	4,479	----------	25	4,360	94	819
1922	4,148	3,866	9	312	3,827	3,545	3,069	----------	20	2,973	76	476
1913	1,755	1,637	6	91	1,658	1,540	1,308	----------	3	1,192	113	232
1902	914	854	4	52	858	798	704	----------	----------	624	80	94

Year	Revenue from local sources—Con.								
	Utilities revenue					Liquor stores revenue	Insurance trust revenue		
	Total	Water supply system	Electric power system	Transit system	Gas supply system		Total	Employee retirement	Unemployment compensation [5]
	808	809	810	811	812	813	814	815	816
1970	6,608	2,687	2,385	1,135	401	258	1,299	1,288	11
1969	5,931	2,464	2,166	934	366	245	1,155	1,145	10
1968	5,683	2,313	2,119	919	332	262	1,044	1,035	10
1967	5,246	2,187	1,881	860	319	195	933	921	12
1966	5,069	2,115	1,911	743	300	189	837	826	11
1965	4,908	2,004	1,833	776	295	177	795	785	10
1964	4,616	1,917	1,718	715	266	164	713	703	10
1963	4,216	1,804	1,488	675	249	155	657	647	10
1962	4,026	1,725	1,422	643	236	148	627	619	8
1961	3,856	1,621	1,450	588	197	141	587	579	8
1960 *	3,613	1,529	1,307	581	196	136	549	541	7
1959 [4]	3,320	1,388	1,178	565	190	131	500	495	6
1958	3,041	1,256	1,096	516	173	112	471	464	6
1957	2,944	1,235	1,011	541	157	118	429	423	6
1956	2,718	1,162	887	542	127	117	380	376	5
1955	2,609	1,092	870	544	104	117	347	343	4
1954	2,403	971	787	554	90	119	317	313	4
1953	2,237	939	713	500	85	120	280	275	5
1952	2,071	839	683	479	70	113	262	256	5
1950	1,808	705	574	468	61	94	185	181	4
1948	1,565	640	474	399	52	89	140	137	3
1946	1,169	556	348	227	38	66	99	96	3
1944	1,066	521	305	208	32	39	90	86	4
1942	887	439	251	170	27	17	88	80	8
1940	704	401	220	58	25	13	68	61	7
1938	605	371	169	47	18	10	63	58	5
1936	558	369	131	41	17	6	50	50	----------
1934	499	342	115	32	10	1	43	43	----------
1932	463	317	111	25	10	----------	39	39	----------
1927	403	247	111	35	10	----------	27	27	----------
1922	266	175	72	----------	13	6	16	16	----------
1913	116	99	16	----------	1	----------	2	2	----------
1902	60	56	3	----------	1	----------	----------	----------	----------

* Denotes first year for which figures include Alaska and Hawaii.
[1] Duplicative transactions between levels of government are excluded.
[2] Includes minor amounts of corporation income tax.
[3] Includes licenses.   [4] Includes Alaska.   [5] Washington, D.C., only.

Series Y 817–848. Local Government Expenditure, by Function: 1902 to 1970

[In millions of dollars]

Year	Total	Intergovernmental expenditure (to States)	Direct expenditure — Total	General expenditure — Total general	Education Total	Local schools	Institutions of higher education	Highways	Public welfare Total	Categorical cash assistance	Other cash assistance	Other public welfare	Hospitals	Health	Police	Fire protection
	817	818	819	820	821	822	823	824	825	826	827	828	829	830	831	832
1970	92,522	633	91,889	82,582	38,938	37,024	1,914	5,383	6,477	3,368	335	2,774	3,861	1,019	3,806	2,024
1969	82,698	546	82,152	73,483	34,934	33,387	1,547	5,003	5,646	2,863	354	2,429	3,429	833	3,316	1,793
1968	72,357	427	71,930	63,966	30,200	28,966	1,233	4,663	4,735	2,396	292	2,047	3,049	666	2,894	1,623
1967	66,648	374	66,274	59,101	[1]28,534	27,290	1,204	4,510	3,927	2,138	212	1,577	2,703	580	2,609	1,499
1966	60,994	283	60,711	53,680	25,715	24,860	855	4,146	3,620	1,836	179	1,605	2,436	508	2,391	1,376
1965	55,482	262	55,221	48,405	22,382	21,777	605	4,007	3,317	1,719	171	1,426	2,208	452	2,201	1,306
1964	51,199	235	50,964	45,027	20,822	20,192	630	3,814	2,970	1,543	167	1,260	2,044	402	2,051	1,222
1963	47,237	235	47,002	41,486	19,011	18,537	474	3,725	2,708	1,465	206	1,037	1,921	386	1,934	1,161
1962	45,279	226	45,053	39,831	17,946	17,538	408	3,722	2,575	1,394	197	985	1,795	386	1,854	1,124
1961	42,641	196	42,445	37,197	16,782	16,382	400	3,614	2,409	1,308	257	845	1,697	330	1,756	1,087
1960 *	39,056	209	38,847	34,092	15,323	14,977	346	3,358	2,183	1,269	234	680	1,571	327	1,612	995
1959 [2]	36,341	205	36,136	31,570	14,190	13,884	306	3,178	2,012	1,203	235	574	1,515	359	1,482	914
1958	34,023	302	33,721	29,403	13,192	12,915	277	3,060	1,874	1,126	220	528	1,412	292	1,396	873
1957	31,057	300	30,757	26,729	11,793	11,545	248	2,941	1,659	1,043	146	470	1,246	303	1,290	810
1956	28,273	269	28,004	24,392	11,082	10,946	136	2,586	1,536	946	207	382	1,048	254	1,172	737
1955	26,230	226	26,004	22,534	10,003	9,902	102	2,553	1,568	947	285	336	908	277	1,091	694
1954	23,814	215	23,599	20,593	8,842	8,748	94	2,272	1,512	927	276	309	873	260	1,000	653
1953	21,662	191	21,471	18,616	7,756	7,672	84	2,207	1,380	853	236	292	849	258	919	598
1952	20,229	156	20,073	17,444	6,824	6,737	87	2,094	1,378	831	266	280	777	276	833	586
1950	17,041	(3)	[3]17,041	14,754	5,819	5,819		1,745	1,374	673	446	255	596	205	691	488
1948	13,363	(3)	[3]13,363	11,498	4,298	4,298		1,526	1,137	653	299	185	404	162	579	406
1946	9,093	(3)	[3]9,093	7,875	2,838	2,838		1,059	729	425	181	123	259	135	434	294
1944	7,180	(3)	[3]7,180	6,197	2,304	2,304		660	556	336	134	86	215	110	373	251
1942	7,351	(3)	[3]7,351	6,421	2,195	2,195		700	702	347	273	82	197	95	354	236
1940	7,685	(3)	[3]7,685	6,499	2,263	2,263		780	629	290	268	71	214	95	331	235
1938	6,906	(3)	[3]6,906	6,181	2,144	2,144		835	616	226	320	70	191	92	329	231
1936	6,056	(3)	[3]6,056	5,421	1,880	1,880		671	405		336	69	171	75	295	205
1934	5,699	(3)	[3]5,699	5,172	1,603	1,603		771	526		459	67	142	73	276	189
1932	6,375	(3)	[3]6,375	5,800	2,033	2,033		898	370		305	65	168	73	303	210
1927	6,359	(3)	[3]6,359	5,830	2,017	2,017		1,295	111		50	61	133	52	263	203
1922	4,567	(3)	[3]4,567	4,187	1,541	1,541		991	81		30	51	95	38	186	158
1913	1,960	(3)	[3]1,960	1,767	522	522		393	36		7	29	32	23	88	76
1902	959	(3)	[3]959	879	238	238		171	27		5	22	15	13	50	40

Direct expenditure — Con.

Year	Sanitation	Natural resources	Parks and recreation	Housing and urban renewal	Financial administration and general control	Interest on general debt	Other and unallocable	Utilities Total	Water supply system	Electric power system	Transit system	Gas supply system	Liquor stores expenditure	Insurance trust Total	Employee retirement	Unemployment compensation [4]
	833	834	835	836	837	838	839	840	841	842	843	844	845	846	847	848
1970	3,413	574	1,888	2,115	2,961	2,875	7,248	7,820	3,211	2,486	1,753	370	223	1,263	1,253	10
1969	2,969	517	1,645	1,887	2,609	2,457	6,444	7,316	3,019	2,216	1,750	332	212	1,141	1,133	8
1968	2,707	517	1,412	1,613	2,337	2,138	5,411	6,721	2,740	2,123	1,559	299	216	1,027	1,019	8
1967	2,523	542	1,291	1,441	2,139	2,007	4,797	6,006	2,587	1,847	1,285	287	157	1,009	1,002	7
1966	2,571	507	1,187	1,382	1,950	1,796	4,097	6,042	2,716	1,949	1,114	263	159	830	822	8
1965	2,360	518	1,104	1,227	1,825	1,668	3,829	5,886	2,505	1,983	1,127	272	150	780	770	10
1964	2,267	650	1,022	1,125	1,697	1,590	3,350	5,067	2,255	1,614	948	251	140	730	719	11
1963	1,996	400	902	1,167	1,608	1,444	3,123	4,704	2,197	1,458	814	235	132	680	670	10
1962	1,958	398	886	1,145	1,574	1,376	3,091	4,445	2,077	1,378	771	219	126	651	645	6
1961	1,774	421	857	936	1,512	1,240	2,782	4,532	2,106	1,461	755	210	119	599	592	7
1960 *	1,727	347	770	850	1,459	1,134	2,436	4,066	1,881	1,244	750	191	115	570	565	5
1959 [2]	1,609	263	729	612	1,384	963	2,360	3,923	1,764	1,273	711	174	118	525	518	7
1958	1,505	246	685	599	1,274	848	2,147	3,720	1,624	1,260	686	150	104	492	487	6
1957	1,443	244	608	503	1,195	755	1,939	3,494	1,584	1,102	652	156	98	436	432	4
1956	1,326	236	541	435	1,083	675	1,681	3,119	1,461	895	636	128	101	392	388	4
1955	1,142	196	509	497	1,005	587	1,504	3,023	1,479	819	600	125	93	353	348	5
1954	1,058	199	424	609	956	525	1,410	2,577	1,150	751	586	90	102	327	323	4
1953	908	173	374	628	864	452	1,250	2,457	1,084	723	582	68	102	296	294	2
1952	992	237	324	766	832	408	1,117	2,246	973	631	581	61	98	285	283	2
1950	834	202	304	452	724	349	971	2,005	849	534	570	52	80	202	198	4
1948	670	152	243	176	614	313	818	1,612	628	438	499	47	76	177	174	3
1946	370	95	179	114	511	337	521	1,014	426	305	247	36	56	148	145	3
1944	245	68	123	46	437	398	411	822	355	227	215	25	33	128	124	4
1942	229	55	128	236	414	443	437	804	368	216	201	19	14	112	104	8
1940	207	74	162	230	410	523	346	1,090	404	257	411	18	10	86	84	2
1938	226	94	130	3	396	545	349	636	385	156	82	13	8	81	81	
1936	204	100	104	--------	370	614	327	553	344	117	81	11	5	77	77	--------
1934	177	74	126	--------	324	620	271	457	292	102	57	6	1	69	69	--------
1932	223	46	147	--------	356	627	346	518	320	92	99	7		57	57	--------
1927	312	--------	153		316	501	474	491	349	94	38	10	--------	38	38	--------
1922	189	--------	85		244	337	242	359	255	75	25	4	--------	21	21	--------
1913	97	--------	57		173	133	137	186	159	25	1	1	--------	21	21	--------
1902	51	--------	29		118	58	69	80	71	8	1	1	--------	7	7	--------

[1] Includes minor amounts of expenditure by municipalities on behalf of school districts, not shown separately. [2] Includes Alaska. [3] Minor amounts of intergovernmental expenditure to States not segregable from "Direct expenditure." [4] Washington, D.C., only.

Chapter Y

Armed Forces and Veterans (Series Y 849-1031)

Y 849-855. Estimates of total cost of U.S. wars.

Source: U.S. Congress, Joint Economic Committee, *The Military Budget and National Economic Priorities*, part I, pp. 149 and 150, 91st Congress, 1st session (statement of James L. Clayton, University of Utah, at Hearings before the Subcommittee on Economy in Government); and for **series Y 853**, U.S. Veterans Administration, *Annual Report of Administrator of Veterans Affairs*.

Details concerning individual estimates and the sources used by Professor Clayton are given in the source document.

An earlier study, *Cost of U.S. Wars* (typewritten form), was made by Raymond E. Manning, Senior Specialist in Taxation and Fiscal Policy, Legislative Reference Service, The Library of Congress, October 1956. This report gives details as to the period covered, the costs which are included and those excluded, and the assumptions and statistical method used for the computations for each war from the American Revolution through the Korean conflict.

Y 856-903. Selected characteristics of the Armed Forces, by war.

Source: The President's Commission on Veterans Pensions, *Veterans' Benefits in the United States*, vol. I; Staff Report No. IV, "Veterans in our Society," House Committee Print 261, 84th Cong., 2d session; and revised estimates prepared by the Department of Defense.

The time coverage for a particular war may vary from series to series. See source for exact coverage.

The number of personnel serving in the Revolutionary War is not known, but estimates range from 184,000 to 250,000. In the War of 1812, it is estimated that 286,730 served and in the Mexican War, 78,718. In the Civil War, estimates for Confederate forces range from 600,000 to 1,500,000.

Y 904-916. Military personnel on active duty, 1789-1970.

Source: U.S. Department of Defense, reports and unpublished data.

Primary sources of Army data are as follows: 1789, 1794, and 1795, *American State Papers, Military Affairs*, vol. 1 (except for officers, 1789, Thomas H. S. Hamersly, *Complete Regular Army Register of the United States for One Hundred Years (1779-1879)*, Washington, D.C., 1880); 1801-1821, *American State Papers, Military Affairs*, vol. 2; 1822-1939, *War Department Annual Reports* (except as follows: Regular Army, 1847 and 1866, Francis B. Heitman, *Historical Register and Dictionary of the United States Army*, vol. 2, Washington, D.C., 1903; Army Nurse Corps, 1920, Army field clerks, 1917, and Quartermaster Corps field clerks, 1917 and 1918, *Special Report 196*, Revised, Statistics Branch, War Department, General Staff, 1927; 1919 and 1920, Quartermaster Corps field clerks, *Regular Report 189*, Statistics Branch, War Department, General Staff, 1922; 1940-1957, Office of The Adjutant General, *Strength of the Army*, monthly reports. For data on U.S. Military Academy cadets, 1802-1821, *American State Papers, Military Affairs*, vol. 2; 1822-1920, *Official Register of the Officers and Cadets at the United States Military Academy* (except as follows: 1871, 1910, 1913, 1915, 1917, and 1918, *War Department Annual Reports*); 1921-1941, *War Department Annual Reports*; 1942-1970, *Strength of the Army*, monthly reports.

Some of the figures for the Navy and Marine Corps appear in the following sources: Gordon R. Young (ed.), *Army Almanac*, Stackpole Company, Harrisburg, Pennsylvania, 1959; Bureau of Navy Personnel, *Navy and Marine Corps, Military Personnel Statistics*, June and December 1956; Navy Department, Bureau of Personnel, *Progress Report*, March 1948.

Officers include warrant officers, flight officers, nurses, medical specialists, and field clerks. Enlisted personnel include U.S. Military Academy cadets, U.S. Naval Academy midshipmen, U.S. Air Force Academy cadets, and other officer candidates.

Army data (series Y 905-907) begin with 1789, the year in which the Department of War (now Department of the Army) was established. Although a "regular" Army has existed continuously from that time, the total strengths cannot be documented from available records, nor can reliable estimates be made for 1790-1793 and 1796-1800. Beginning 1861, the data include all military personnel on extended active duty with the Army (Regulars, volunteers, militia, inductees, Reserves, National Guardsmen, and reactivated retired Regular personnel) and U.S. Military Academy cadets. Data prior to 1861 are for Regular Army and cadets only, except for 1836-1840 (Seminole Indian War) and 1846-1848 (Mexican War). Source documents for other years do not contain adequate strength statistics on nonregular personnel called out during the War of 1812 or for short periods of service during the numerous Indian disturbances. For most years prior to 1878, data were compiled from the latest returns received; some of the reports used, especially those from the frontier garrisons, were weeks or months in transit.

The Army figures include the Army Nurse Corps beginning 1898; Army field clerks and field clerks in the Quartermaster Corps for 1917-1925; warrant officers beginning 1919; flight officers for 1943-1947; and the Women's Army Corps (formerly the Women's Army Auxiliary Corps) and the Women's Medical Specialist Corps (later redesignated the Army Medical Specialist Corps), beginning 1943. All data for these categories are as of June 30, except the 1898 figure for the Army Nurse Corps which is as of September 15.

The Army Nurse Corps became a part of the permanent Army military establishment in 1901. It traces its origin, however, to 1898, when authority was received to employ by contract as many nurses as needed during the war with Spain. For this reason, data on nurses have been included for 1898-1900.

The positions of Army field clerks and field clerks in the Quartermaster Corps were created by Act of Congress, August 29, 1916. Field clerks of both classes were subject to the rules and articles of war, and had the status of officers, although not commissioned officers. By Act of Congress, April 27, 1926, the Secretary of War was authorized and directed to appoint as warrant officers all field clerks then in active service.

The Army figures for 1908-1947 include strength of the Army Air Force and predecessor agencies. Those beginning with 1948 consist of military personnel under the command of the Army only, resulting from the establishment of the Department of the Air Force as an executive department by the National Security Act of 1947. Data for 1948 and 1949 include a small number of Department of the Air Force military personnel assigned for duty with Army commands, and data for 1948-1955 exclude a larger number of Department of the Army military personnel assigned for duty with Air Force commands.

Navy data for 1794, 1795, and 1798 are an approximation of the "on board" personnel authorized by Congress in conjunction with the construction of six frigates to reconstitute a Navy which had existed for 1775-1785 under the Continental Congress. A separate Navy Department was authorized and organized in 1798. Since the crews usually were obligated, during the early years of the Navy, for only a specific sailing or mission, rather than a continuous tour of duty, the strengths shown are more in the nature of averages and are therefore noted as estimated. Data exclude an unknown number of Naval Militia, supplied by the States, who served during the War of

1812, the Mexican War, and the Spanish-American War. Since 1916, naval reservist and retired personnel on extended active duty have been included.

The Marine Corps was founded in 1775 by the Continental Congress and served during the Revolutionary War, but ceased to exist in 1783. It was reactivated in 1794 when Congress authorized the building of the six frigates and a small number of marines were used as guards. The data in series Y 914–916 begin with 1798, since reliable estimates are not available for prior years. Since 1917, reservist and retired personnel on active duty have been included.

Y 917–926.   Classification of selective service registrants, 1940–1970.

Source: U.S. Selective Service System. **Series 917**, 1940, *Selective Service in Peacetime*, Appendix 20. **Series 917–925**, 1941–1947, *Summary Reports of Classification, Continental United States, March 31, 1941–April 1, 1947*, vol. 1, parts 1–3; 1948–1950, *Statistics and Special Reports Digests, September 1948–September 1951*, U.S. Summary, vol. 1, part E; 1951–1952, *Statistics—Periodic Reports of Classifications, U.S. and State Summaries, October 1951–February 1956*, vol. II, part B, section 1, Regular Registrants; 1953–1970, compiled from Selective Service System Form 116. **Series 926**, 1940–1945, *Quotas, Calls, and Inductions*, Special Monograph No. 12, vol. II, Appendices F–H; 1946–1947, unpublished data; 1948–1970, compiled from Selective Service Form 262.

The Selective Service System is responsible for the registration, examination, classification, selection, and delivery for induction into the Armed Forces of all men required by law to register, or, in lieu of induction, for ordering them to perform civilian work. The law also provides exemptions or deferments from service for many persons for reasons of previous service, essential occupation, family dependency, etc.

The Selective Training and Service Act of 1940, which became law on September 16, 1940, was the first peacetime conscription law in U.S. history. The classification system under that Act provided for classification of registrants into four main groups in the order of their being called into the Armed Forces: Class I, persons available for training and service after the physical examination; Class II, persons available for training and service but temporarily deferred as necessary in defense industries for varying periods up to six months; Class III, persons who had dependents requiring their support; and Class IV, persons who were exempted from training and service by statute, or were nondeclarant aliens, or had completed military service (up to Pearl Harbor), or conscientious objectors against both combatant and noncombatant service, or who were physically, mentally, or morally unfit for service. Within these main classes there were certain subdivisions which indicated more specifically the status of the registrants.

For details concerning changes over time in legislation, classification, registration regulations, etc., see the annual and semiannual reports of the Director of the Selective Service System and the System's series of special monographs. A list of monographs covering the early years appears on the inside front cover of *Quotas, Calls, and Inductions*, cited in the source note.

Y 927–942.   Disposition of defendants charged with violation of selective service acts, 1945–1970.

Source: U.S. Administrative Office of the U.S. Courts, *Federal Offenders in the United States District Courts, 1970*, table H10.

Statistics reflect defendants charged with violations of the Selective Training and Service Act of 1940 and the Universal Military Training and Service Act of 1948.

These data exclude District of Columbia, Canal Zone, Guam, and Virgin Islands.

Y 943–956.   Estimated number of veterans in civil life, by age, 1865–1970.

Source: U.S. Veterans Administration, reports and unpublished data.

Age distribution for veterans of World War I, Spanish-American War, Civil War, Mexican War, and War of 1812 were obtained by procedures used in estimating the number of living veterans in civil life, as described in the text for series Y 957–970. The ages for veterans of Indian wars and Regular Establishment (peacetime service) were obtained from records of the Veterans Administration and predecessor agencies. Age distribution for Regular Establishment veterans is not included after 1965.

The ages of World War II veterans included in the total for 1945 were based on the ages of those veterans on the Veterans Administration disability compensation rolls on June 30, 1945. The estimated number of veterans by age, for 1950 and thereafter, were derived by the application of appropriate survival rates to the male and female components of the potential World War II veteran population as of July 25, 1947. In this particular case, the potential World War II veteran population is defined as: (a) The estimated number of men and women who had served in World War II and who had returned to civil life prior to July 25, 1947, and (b) those still in the service as of July 25, 1947. The age distribution of this population was derived from the Veterans Administration's sample of approximately 1 percent of the records of the men and women separated from the Armed Forces between September 16, 1940, and July 25, 1947, and from estimates provided by the Armed Forces for World War II participants who were still in service on the latter date.

The ages of Korean conflict veterans included for 1955 and thereafter were derived from the Veterans Administration's sample of approximately 1 percent of Department of Defense records for persons returning to civil life between June 27, 1950, and June 30, 1970.

The ages of veterans who served between the end of the Korean conflict and the inception of the Vietnam era included in 1966 and thereafter were derived from the Veterans Administration's sample of approximately 1 percent of Department of Defense records for persons returning to civil life in the period February 1, 1955, through August 4, 1964.

The ages of veterans who served in the Vietnam era included in 1966 and thereafter were derived from the Veterans Administration's sample of approximately 1 percent of Department of Defense records for persons returning to civil life between August 4, 1964, and June 30, 1970.

Y 957–970.   Estimated number of veterans in civil life, by period of service, 1865–1970.

Source: U.S. Veterans Administration, reports and unpublished data.

The estimates for the War of 1812 were derived by a backward chain computation involving the application of appropriate survival rates to the age distribution of the 165 living veterans of this war on the pension rolls in 1892. It was assumed that all living veterans of the War of 1812 were on the pension rolls after 1873.

Estimates for the Mexican War were computed by applying appropriate survival rates to the age distribution of the 2,195 living Mexican War veterans on the pension rolls in 1907. For 1890 and later years, the estimates were based on the assumption that 90 percent of the living Mexican War veterans were on the pension rolls. Estimates for years prior to 1890 were based on a backward chain computation.

Estimates for the Indian wars include only veterans on pension rolls of the Veterans Administration or predecessor agencies.

The Civil War estimate for 1865 was based on Armed Forces data. Estimates for years after 1865 were computed from actuarial projections, based on the American Experience Mortality Table, 1868, applied to the age distribution of one million Civil War participants included in Surgeon General, *The Medical Department of the U.S. Army in the World War*, vol. XV, *Statistics*, part I, 1921. The totals so obtained were modified by the assumptions that 75 percent of the living Civil War veterans were on the pension rolls in 1900–1915 and that practically all living Civil War veterans were on the rolls in 1920 and later years. The estimates pertain to Union forces only.

For the Spanish-American War, estimates for 1905 and later years were computed by application of appropriate survival rates to the 1902 age distribution of Spanish-American War participants (not shown here). For 1900, the estimate is based on total participants, inservice deaths, and discharges to civil life.

Estimates for World War I were computed by applying appropriate survival rates to the 1918 distribution of World War I participants by year of age based on records of 3.7 million War Risk Insurance applications (*The Medical Department of the U.S. Army . . .*, cited above).

For World War II, the Korean conflict, the Vietnam era, and service between the Korean conflict and Vietnam era, the estimates were derived from Armed Forces data on the number of persons returned to civil life less Veterans Administration estimates of deaths and less the number who reenlisted from civil life.

Data on the Regular Establishment include only former members of the peacetime forces receiving disability compensation or pension from the Veterans Administration or predecessor agencies.

The following periods are covered by the specified wars for determining veterans status:

War of 1812—June 18, 1812, through February 17, 1815
Mexican War—April 25, 1846, through May 30, 1848
Civil War—April 12, 1861, through April 13, 1865
Indian wars—1817 through 1898 (approximately)
Spanish-American War—April 21, 1898, through July 4, 1902 (includes the war with Spain, Boxer Rebellion, and Philippine Insurrection. For persons serving in the Moro Province, hostilities ended July 15, 1903)
World War I—April 6, 1917, through November 11, 1918 (for persons serving in Russia, the war ended April 1, 1920)
World War II—September 16, 1940, through July 25, 1947
Korean conflict—June 27, 1950, through January 31, 1955
Service between Korean conflict and Vietnam era—February 1, 1955, through August 4, 1964
Vietnam era—service after August 4, 1964

Y 971–983. Expenditures of Veterans Administration and predecessor agencies from appropriated funds, by period of service, 1790–1970.

Source: U.S. Veterans Administration. Original data are taken from annual reports of the Administrator of Veterans Affairs, Veterans Bureau, Bureau of Pensions, National Home for Disabled Volunteer Soldiers, and records of the Veterans Administration.

The data pertain to expenditures from appropriated funds (see text for series Y 984–997) for veterans and their dependents through June 30, 1970. Thus, they include expenditures for pensions since 1790 and for care in the National Homes (now Veterans Administration domiciliaries) since 1867. Grants-in-aid for the care of veterans in State homes were first made in 1889 and are included thereafter.

Expenditures on behalf of World War I veterans, made originally as allowances for the dependents of enlisted men in the Armed Forces, compensation for death and disability, medical care and treatment, vocational rehabilitation and training, and insurance against death or permanent disability, are included since October 1917. Subsequent adjustments of benefits for World War I veterans and for veterans of the earlier wars (e.g., extension of hospital benefits) are reflected in the ensuing years. Expenditures for World War II veterans began in 1941, and for veterans of the Korean conflict in 1951.

Trust and working fund expenditures (e.g., the U.S. Government Life and National Service Life Insurance Trust Funds, the Adjusted Service Certificate Trust Fund, and the General Post Fund) are excluded; transfers from appropriations to the insurance trust funds, however, are included. Also excluded are expenditures made by

other Federal and State agencies (e.g., unemployment compensation paid to Korean conflict veterans by the Department of Labor, expenditures for retirement pay by the Department of Defense, and bonus payments made by State governments).

Of the $174.8 billion in total expenditures through 1970, $139.0 billion (79 percent) was directly allocated by war. The distribution of the remaining expenditures was estimated. Therefore, the figures are subject to a varying and unknown degree of error. For example, variations in average hospital costs between wars, or unusual administrative workloads are not reflected in the distribution factors used.

Y 984–997. Expenditures for veterans benefits and services by Veterans Administration and predecessor agencies, 1790–1970.

Source: U.S. Veterans Administration, *Annual Report of the Administrator of Veterans Affairs*, various issues, and unpublished data.

Data are based on checks paid through December 31, 1947, and on vouchers approved for payment thereafter. The data are gross, since they include expenditures made from amounts earned (in the form of reimbursements) by the various accounts. Expenditures from revolving funds are also gross, i.e., receipts have not been netted out of these funds except in minor instances noted elsewhere. Accordingly, these data do not agree with those reported in the statements of the Treasury Department and the Bureau of the Budget.

Y 984, total expenditures. This series measures the gross cost of benefits and services (including capital expenditures and administrative costs) provided veterans and their beneficiaries, irrespective of the source of funds. Included are expenditures from general and special funds appropriated by the Congress, revolving and management funds authorized to finance a continuing cycle of operations using receipts derived from these operations, and trust funds held by the Government for the benefit of veterans and their beneficiaries. Transfers from appropriations to insurance trust funds, from which the actual expenditures are made, are not included in the total, in order to avoid duplication. Expenditures from the Veterans Administration Revolving Supply Fund, established July 1, 1954, also are excluded from the total, since these amounts generally duplicate expenditures made by Veterans Administration administrative appropriations for supplies, equipment, and certain services procured through the fund.

Y 985, compensation and pensions. Data represent total expenditures less refund of overpayments.

Y 986, insurance and servicemen's indemnities. Data include direct payments to beneficiaries from insurance appropriations, servicemen's indemnities, and benefits and dividends paid from insurance trust funds. Some noncash transactions (e.g., interest credited to dividends left on deposit) also are included as expenditures from the trust funds. Transfers from appropriations to the insurance trust funds, from which the benefit payments are made, are not included in these amounts. Beginning fiscal year 1949, the reporting of expenditures from the U.S. Government Life Insurance and National Service Life Insurance trust funds was changed from a net to a gross basis. This resulted in an understatement in varying amounts for prior years. The cumulative differences for the prior years between the net figures and what the figures would have been on a gross basis have been added in a lump sum to the 1948 figures. This adjustment amounted to $295,651,000.

Y 987, education and training. This series includes subsistence allowances, tuition, supplies, and equipment of veterans training under Public Law 346, education and training allowances to veterans training under Public Law 550, veterans and servicemen training under Public Law 89–358, and educational assistance for dependents and survivors of totally disabled or deceased veterans under Public Laws 634, 88–361, and 90–631.

Y 988, vocational rehabilitation. Data include subsistence allowances, tuition, supplies, and equipment of veterans training under Public Laws 16, 894, and 87–815, and vocational rehabilitation allowances for World War I veterans.

Y 989, unemployment and self-employment allowances. Includes allowances to World War II veterans to assist in their readjustment to civilian employment. Similar allowances paid to Korean conflict and Vietnam veterans by the Department of Labor are excluded.

Y 990, loan guaranty. Includes payments on defaulted loans, and the cost of property and securities acquired. The amounts are gross and do not reflect the cost of the loan guaranty program to the Government. Refunds and recoveries on claims paid returned to the general fund and deposits to the loan guaranty revolving fund amounted to $2.9 billion through June 30, 1970. Other losses of the program are subject to further recovery from the liquidation of securities and repayments by borrowers.

Y 991, direct loans. Includes direct mortgage loans and advances to veterans, interest expenses on capital borrowed from the U.S. Treasury, and other expenses (excluding Veterans Administration administrative expenses) of the direct loan program. Expenditures are gross and do not reflect the cost of this program to the Government. Through June 30, 1970, receipts paid into the direct loan fund amounted to $3.1 billion, bringing net expenditures to $108 million. This will be further reduced, as the program matures, by payments of interest and principal by borrowers.

Y 992, miscellaneous benefit payments. Includes statutory burial allowances; expenditures not classified as to purpose from the compensation and pensions appropriation; automobiles and other conveyances for disabled veterans; specially adapted homes for paraplegic veterans; payments to participants in the yellow fever experiments; military and naval family allowances of World War I veterans; marine and seamen's insurance in World War I; adjusted service compensation (World War I bonus); General Post Fund expenditures; withdrawals of the personal funds of patients held by the Veterans Administration as banker and funds due incompetent beneficiaries; soldiers' and sailors' civil relief; and the vocational rehabilitation revolving fund. These expenditures are gross with the exceptions of soldiers' and sailors' civil relief and the vocational rehabilitation revolving fund, which are on a net basis.

Y 993, medical, hospital, and domiciliary services. Figures include expenditures for hospital nursing bed care, and domiciliary care, out-patient medical and dental treatment, medical research, and related costs; appropriations to the Canteen Service Revolving Fund; and grants to the Republic of the Philippines for medical care and treatment of veterans. Beginning 1921, the data are estimated. Prior to July 1, 1879, the fiscal year of the National Home for Disabled Volunteer Soldiers ended on various dates. For this period, the data have been proportionately adjusted by the Veterans Administration to reflect expenditures for years ending June 30.

Y 994, hospital and domiciliary facilities. These data include expenditures for the construction and equipping of hospitals and domiciliary facilities, and major alterations, improvements, and repairs thereof; grants to the Republic of the Philippines for the construction and equipping of a hospital; grants for construction of State extended care facilities; expenditures from funds allotted under the National Recovery Act of 1933 and Public Works Administration Act of 1938; and $436,623,692 transferred to the Department of the Army, Corps of Engineers, for the construction of hospitals.

Y 995, administration and other benefits. Includes expenses for vocational counseling of veterans, beneficiary travel for certain programs, reporting allowances paid schools for certifying the attendance of veteran trainees, private laws for relief, and all administrative salaries and expenses.

Y 996–997, expenditures from general and special fund appropriations. Series Y 996 represents expenditures from appropriations made by the Congress to finance the general and ordinary operations of the Veterans Administration and predecessor agencies. The figures differ from amounts shown under total expenditures (series

Y 984) after 1917 in that they do not include expenditures from trust funds, working funds, and deposit funds. Transfers from appropriations to insurance trust funds (series Y 997) are included in the figures for series Y 996.

Y 998–1009. Veterans pensions and compensation—number of veterans and expenditure, by type, 1866–1970.

Source: U.S. Veterans Administration, records. Data were compiled from various annual reports of the Administrator of Veterans Affairs, and of the Commissioner of Pensions.

The basic distinction between pension and compensation is that pension is a benefit payable for total and permanent disability or death which is not attributable to the veteran's military service. Compensation is payable for the disability or death resulting from injury or disease incurred in, or aggravated by, military service. In the series relating to death benefits, the number of veterans refers to the number of deceased veterans whose dependents are receiving benefits, rather than to the number of dependents in receipt of such benefits; the data on expenditures refer to the amount received by these dependents. In the disability cases, the data refer to the number of veterans, and the amount of money paid to these veterans in the form of retirement pay administered by the Veterans Administration or its predecessor agencies.

For 1866–1890, separate data are not available for the death and disability series. Likewise, information is not available which would permit a separation of the data on the pensions and compensation earned for military service prior to 1904. As a result, all data on veterans of the Spanish-American and earlier wars have been arbitrarily included in the pension series.

The compensation data refer (with the qualifications as noted above for the series on deaths) to the number of, or expenditures paid to, veterans of the Regular Establishment, World War I, World War II, the Korean conflict, and Vietnam. Data on these veterans were first included in 1904, 1918, 1942, 1951, and 1965, respectively.

Y 1010–1027. Patients receiving hospital or domiciliary care authorized by Veterans Administration, 1921–1970.

Source: U.S. Veterans Administration, *Annual Report of the Administrator of Veterans Affairs*, various issues, and unpublished data.

These data do not in all cases agree with information previously published in some of the earlier annual reports of the Veterans Administration. Revisions were made to adjust some of the data for earlier years for comparability with current data.

The data for admissions is by type of patient; through 1960 neurological patients were included with neuropsychiatric, thereafter with general. Tuberculosis patients are included with general.

The data for all veterans receiving hospital care (series Y 1014) and veterans with service-connected disabilities (series Y 1019) are identical prior to 1925. The act which made Veterans Administration hospital care available to veterans with nonservice-connected disability was passed in 1924, and it was not until 1925 that such patients were admitted to Veterans Administration hospitals.

Data for veterans receiving hospital care for service-connected disabilities (series Y 1019–1022) exclude those veterans with service-connected disabilities who are being treated for nonservice-connected ailments.

Series Y 1018 shows the number of nonveteran patients in Veterans Administration hospitals. This group of patients is made up for the most part of persons still in the military service who have not yet attained veteran status, and cases admitted to Veterans Administration hospitals for humanitarian reasons.

Domiciliary care was provided by the National Homes for Disabled Volunteer Soldiers through July 30, 1930; later, it was provided by other agencies. The number of veterans in State homes receiving domiciliary care (series Y 1025) is shown because the Veterans Administration contributes to the support of veterans cared for in approved State homes who would be eligible for admission to Veterans Administration domiciliaries.

Y 1028–1031. Government life insurance administered by Veterans Administration—number of policies, income received, and benefits paid, 1921–1970.

Source: U.S. Veterans Administration, *Annual Report of the Administrator of Veterans Affairs*, various issues, and unpublished data.

The U.S. Government, through the Veterans Administration, operates two life insurance programs for veterans and servicemen. The insurance program which had its origin in World War I is known as U.S. Government Life Insurance (USGLI); and the program which had its inception in 1940 is called National Service Life Insurance (NSLI). The administrative expenses of these programs are borne by the U.S. Government. All USGLI is participating (that is, entitled to dividends from any earnings). This program was closed to new issues effective April 25, 1951. All NSLI issued prior to April 25, 1951, with some minor exceptions, is participating and entitled to dividends. This type of insurance also was closed to new issues in 1951. Veterans separated from military service without a service-connected disability on or after April 25, 1951, and before January 1, 1957, could apply for nonparticipating NSLI on the 5-year non-convertible term plan only. Conversion to permanent plans was made available in 1959. This insurance is known as Veterans Special Life Insurance.

Veterans separated with a service-connected disability on or after April 25, 1951, are eligible to apply, within one year after service-connection is established, for permanent plan or term policies. This insurance is known as service-disabled veterans insurance.

In 1964 Congress enacted legislation which provided for a limited reopening of NSLI for a period of one year beginning May 1, 1965, to qualifying disabled veterans. To qualify they must have been eligible to buy National Service Life Insurance between October 8, 1940, and January 1, 1957, and have had either (1) a service-connected disability or (2) a nonservice disability, or a combination of service and nonservice disabilities so serious that they could not obtain commercial insurance at the highest rates. This insurance is known as Veterans Reopened Insurance.

The maximum amount of all Government insurance for veterans is $10,000 on one life. Excluded from these series are data on the Servicemen's Indemnity program, which was in effect from June 27, 1950, to January 1, 1957. This program provided free life insurance in the amount of $10,000 (less any USGLI or NSLI in force) while in military service and for 120 days thereafter.

Income received (series Y 1030) includes: (1) Premiums received from policy holders for insurance and disability income benefits, including premiums waived because of disability, (2) advances from Congressional appropriations to the service-disabled veterans insurance fund, (3) interest on investments in U.S. Treasury Certificates of Indebtedness and in U.S. Treasury notes, (4) interest on policy loans and on premiums paid in arrears, (5) dividends credited to insureds or deposited to accumulate at interest, and (6) reimbursements from the U.S. Government as the Government's contribution for death and disability claims due to the extra hazards of military or naval service, for gratuitous insurance, and for other obligations.

Benefits paid (series Y 1031) include: (1) The actual cash payments to beneficiaries of deceased insureds, (2) cash payments to insureds under the total and permanent disability provisions of USGLI policies, (3) monthly income payments under total disability income provisions of USGLI and NSLI policies issued before April 25, 1951, (4) premiums waived for total disability, (5) cash surrender values paid on contracts surrendered, (6) payments on matured endowment policies, (7) dividends paid and dividends previously credited or left on deposit and later withdrawn, (8) interest added on dividend credits and deposits, (9) adjustments in policy liens, receivables, and overpayments waived, (10) transfers to U.S. Government in the Veterans Special Life Insurance program, and (11) administrative costs in the Veterans Reopened Insurance program.

★ ★ ★ ★ ★ ★ ★ ★ ★ **More Recent Data for *Historical Statistics* Series** ★ ★ ★ ★ ★ ★ ★ ★ ★ ★

★ Statistics for more recent years in continuation of many of the still-active series shown here appear in annual issues of the *Statistical Abstract of the United States*, beginning with the 1975 edition. For direct linkage of the historical series to the tables in the *Abstract*, see Appendix I in the *Abstract*.

Series Y 849–855. Estimates of Total Cost of U.S. Wars

[In millions of dollars, except percent]

War	Estimated total war costs	Original war costs [1]	Veterans' benefits			Estimated interest payments on war loans	
			Total costs under present laws [2]	Percent of original war costs	Total costs to 1970	Total	Percent of original war costs
	849	850	851	852	853	854	855
Vietnam conflict [3]	352,000	110,000	[4] 220,000	[4] 200	2,461	[5] 22,000	[5] 20
Korean conflict	164,000	54,000	99,000	184	15,016	11,000	20
World War II	664,000	288,000	290,000	100	87,445	86,000	30
World War I	112,000	26,000	75,000	290	45,585	11,000	42
Spanish-American War	6,460	400	6,000	1,505	5,436	60	15
Civil War (Union only)	12,952	3,200	8,580	260	8,570	1,172	37
Mexican War	147	73	64	88	64	10	14
War of 1812	158	93	49	53	49	16	17
American Revolution	190	100	70	70	70	20	20

[1] Based on expenditures of Departments of the Army and Navy to World War I and major national security expenditures thereafter. Usually the figures begin with the year the war began but in all cases they extend one year beyond the end of the actual conflict.

[2] To World War I, estimates are based on Veterans Administration data. For World War I, World War II, and Korean conflict, estimates are those of the 1956 report of the President's Commission on Veterans' Pensions plus 25 percent (the increase in the average value of benefits since the Commission made its report).

[3] Estimates based on assumption that war would end by June 30, 1970 (except for veterans' benefit costs to 1970). Occupation costs not included. Background data:

		Bil. dol.
Original cost:		
a. Major national security expenditures for Vietnam conflict, 1965–70 fiscal years		108.5
b. Cost of supporting American personnel in South Vietnam, 1954–64, at $25,000 per man per year		1.5
Total		110.0

Veterans' benefits:	
Medium estimate, 200 percent of original cost	220.0
Interest on war debt:	
Medium estimate, 20 percent of original cost	22.0
Total, medium estimate	352.0

[4] Medium-level estimate of 200 percent (high, 300; low, 100) based on figures expressing relationship of veterans' benefits payments to original costs of other major U.S. wars.

[5] Medium-level estimate of 20 percent (high, 30; low, 10) based on figures showing interest payments on war loans as percentage of original costs of other major U.S. wars.

Series Y 856–903. Selected Characteristics of the Armed Forces, by War

Series No.	Characteristic	Civil War (Union forces only)	Spanish-American War	World War I	World War II	Korean conflict	Series No.	Characteristic	Civil War (Union forces only)	Spanish-American War	World War I	World War II	Korean conflict
856	Military personnel___1,000__	2,213	307	4,744	16,354	5,764		Annual rate per 1,000 average strength:					
857	Army___1,000__	2,129	281	4,057	11,260	2,834							
858	Air Force___1,000__					1,285	883	Total deaths	104.4	36.6	35.5	11.6	5.5
859	Navy___1,000__	} 84 {	23	599	4,183	1,177	884	Battle deaths	40.1	(NA)	17.1	8.6	3.4
860	Marines___1,000__		3	79	669	424	885	Other deaths	64.3	(NA)	18.4	3.0	2.1
861	Coast Guard___1,000__			9	241	44							
								Medical care:					
	Draftees:							Army:					
862	Classified___1,000__	777		24,234	36,677	9,123		Admissions for care, all causes:					
863	Examined___1,000__	522		3,764	17,955	3,685	886	Number___1,000__	6,455	317	4,039	17,919	2,717
864	Rejected___1,000__	160		803	6,420	1,189	887	Annual rate per 1,000 average strength	2,478	2,146	978	704	511
865	Inducted___1,000__	46		2,820	10,022	1,560		Noneffectiveness, total:					
866	Average duration of service____months__	20	8	12	33	19	888	Man-days lost_1,000__	(NA)	4,355	86,947	413,393	49,810
867	Officers____months__	(NA)	8	14	39	24	889	Daily rate per 1,000 average strength	(NA)	80.7	57.7	44.5	25.7
868	Enlisted____months__	(NA)	8	12	33	18	890	Wounded who died subsequently___percent__	13.3	6.3	8.1	4.5	2.6
	Overseas service:						891	Annual nonbattle death rate per 1,000 average strength	68.7	25.9	15.4	3.0	2.0
869	Percent of total who served overseas	(NA)	29	53	73	56							
870	Average months served overseas [1]	(NA)	1.5	5.5	16.2	13.4		Navy and Marine Corps: Admissions for care, all causes:					
871	Occupation of enlisted personnel____percent__	[2] 100.0	[2] 100.0	[2] 100.0	100.0	100.0	892	Number___1,000__	(NA)	25	1,073	5,514	1,200
872	Technical and scientific____percent__	0.2	0.5	3.7	10.4	12.7	893	Annual rate per 1,000 average strength	(NA)	1,038	1,024	553	337
873	Administrative and clerical____percent__	0.7	3.1	8.0	12.6	18.1		Noneffectiveness, total:					
874	Mechanics and repairmen____percent__	0.1	1.0	8.5	16.6	15.3	894	Man-days lost_1,000__	(NA)	248	12,705	115,700	23,998
875	Craftsmen____percent__	0.5	.1	13.0	5.9	4.7	895	Daily rate per 1,000 average strength	(NA)	28.3	33.2	31.8	18.5
876	Service workers__percent__	2.4	6.5	12.5	9.6	12.4	896	Wounded who died subsequently___percent__	(NA)	5.9	9.0	3.2	2.2
877	Operators and laborers____percent__	2.9	2.2	20.2	6.1	6.5	897	Annual nonbattle death rate per 1,000 average strength	(NA)	17.6	11.6	2.8	1.9
878	Military-type occupations, not elsewhere classified____percent__	93.2	86.6	34.1	38.8	30.3		Military pay (current dol.): Basic pay (annual rate):					
	Casualties, number:						898	All personnel___dollars__	231	282	510	1,017	1,776
879	Total deaths	364,511	2,446	116,516	405,399	54,246	899	Officers____dollars__	717	2,101	2,141	2,442	4,453
880	Battle deaths	140,414	385	53,402	291,557	33,629	900	Enlisted____dollars__	202	205	417	856	1,473
881	Other deaths	224,097	2,061	63,114	113,842	20,617		Pay and allowances (annual rate):					
882	Wounds not mortal	281,881	1,662	204,002	670,846	103,284	901	All personnel___dollars__	510	528	968	1,811	2,940
							902	Officers____dollars__	1,912	2,489	2,698	3,777	6,234
							903	Enlisted____dollars__	427	444	870	1,587	2,584

NA Not available. [1] During hostilities only. [2] Army personnel only.

Series Y 904–916. Military Personnel on Active Duty: 1789 to 1970

[As of June 30, beginning 1878 for Army, 1900 for Navy, and 1798 for Marine Corps. For prior years, the month for which most complete records were available was used]

Year	Grand total [1]	Army Total	Army Officers	Army Enlisted	Air Force [2] Total	Air Force [2] Officers	Air Force [2] Enlisted	Navy Total	Navy Officers	Navy Enlisted	Marine Corps Total	Marine Corps Officers	Marine Corps Enlisted
	904	905	906	907	908	909	910	911	912	913	914	915	916
1970 [3]	3,066,294	1,322,548	166,721	1,155,827	791,349	129,803	661,546	692,660	80,761	611,899	259,737	24,941	234,796
1969	3,460,162	1,512,169	172,590	1,339,579	862,353	135,476	726,877	775,869	85,199	690,670	309,771	25,698	284,073
1968	3,547,902	1,570,343	166,173	1,404,170	904,850	139,691	765,159	765,457	85,425	680,032	307,252	24,555	282,697
1967	3,376,880	1,442,498	143,517	1,298,981	897,494	135,485	762,009	751,619	81,902	669,717	285,269	23,592	261,677
1966	3,094,058	1,199,784	117,786	1,081,998	887,353	130,724	756,629	745,205	79,805	665,400	261,716	20,512	241,204
1965	2,655,389	969,066	112,120	856,946	824,662	131,578	693,084	671,448	77,866	593,582	190,213	17,258	172,955
1964	2,687,409	973,238	110,870	862,368	856,798	133,389	723,409	667,596	76,400	591,196	189,777	16,843	172,934
1963	2,699,677	975,916	108,302	867,614	869,431	133,763	735,668	664,647	75,549	589,098	189,683	16,737	172,946
1962	2,807,819	1,066,404	116,050	950,354	884,025	134,908	749,117	666,428	75,302	591,126	190,962	16,861	174,101
1961	2,483,771	858,622	99,921	758,701	821,151	128,793	692,358	627,089	69,981	557,108	176,909	16,132	160,777
1960	2,476,435	873,078	101,236	771,842	814,752	129,689	685,063	617,984	69,559	548,425	170,621	16,203	154,418
1959	2,504,310	861,964	101,690	760,274	840,435	131,602	708,833	626,340	69,795	556,545	175,571	16,065	159,506
1958	2,600,581	898,925	104,716	794,209	871,156	132,939	738,217	641,005	71,560	569,445	189,495	16,741	172,754
1957	2,795,798	997,994	111,187	886,807	919,835	140,563	779,272	677,108	73,703	603,405	200,861	17,434	183,427
1956	2,806,441	1,025,778	118,364	907,414	909,958	142,093	767,865	669,925	71,770	598,155	200,780	17,809	182,971
1955	2,935,107	1,109,296	121,947	987,349	959,946	137,149	822,797	660,695	74,527	586,168	205,170	18,417	186,753
1954	3,302,104	1,404,598	128,208	1,276,390	947,918	129,752	818,166	725,720	77,280	648,440	223,868	18,593	205,275
1953	3,555,067	1,533,815	145,633	1,388,182	977,593	130,769	846,824	794,440	81,731	712,709	249,219	18,731	230,488
1952	3,635,912	1,596,419	148,427	1,447,992	983,261	128,742	854,519	824,265	82,247	742,018	231,967	16,413	215,554
1951	3,249,455	1,531,774	[4] 130,540	1,401,234	788,381	107,099	681,282	736,680	70,513	666,167	192,620	15,150	177,470
1950	1,460,261	593,167	72,566	520,601	411,277	57,006	354,271	381,538	44,641	336,897	74,279	7,254	67,025
1949	1,615,360	660,473	77,272	583,201	419,347	57,851	361,496	449,575	47,975	401,600	85,965	7,250	78,715
1948	1,445,910	554,030	68,178	485,852	387,730	48,957	338,773	419,162	45,416	373,746	84,988	6,907	78,081
1947	1,582,999	991,285	132,504	858,781	---------	---------	---------	498,661	52,434	446,227	93,053	7,506	85,547
1946	3,030,088	1,891,011	267,144	1,623,867	---------	---------	---------	983,398	141,161	842,237	155,679	14,208	141,471

Year	Grand total [1]	Army Total	Army Officers	Army Enlisted	Navy Total	Navy Officers	Navy Enlisted	Marine Corps Total	Marine Corps Officers	Marine Corps Enlisted
	904	905	906	907	911	912	913	914	915	916
1945	12,123,455	8,267,958	891,663	7,376,295	3,380,817	331,379	3,049,438	474,680	37,067	437,613
1944	11,451,719	7,994,750	776,980	7,217,770	2,981,365	276,153	2,705,212	475,604	32,788	442,816
1943	9,044,745	6,994,472	579,576	6,414,896	1,741,750	179,676	1,562,074	308,523	21,384	287,139
1942	3,858,791	3,075,608	206,422	2,869,186	640,570	69,564	571,006	142,613	7,138	135,475
1941	1,801,101	1,462,315	99,536	1,362,779	284,427	29,092	255,335	54,359	3,339	51,020
1940	458,365	269,023	18,326	250,697	160,997	13,604	147,393	28,345	1,800	26,545
1939	334,473	189,839	14,486	175,353	125,202	12,023	113,179	19,432	1,380	18,052
1938	322,932	185,488	13,975	171,513	119,088	10,739	108,349	18,356	1,359	16,997
1937	311,808	179,968	13,740	166,228	113,617	10,367	103,250	18,223	1,312	16,911
1936	291,356	167,816	13,512	154,304	106,292	10,247	96,045	17,248	1,208	16,040
1935	251,799	139,486	13,471	126,015	95,053	10,115	84,938	17,260	1,163	16,097
1934	247,137	138,464	13,761	124,703	92,312	9,972	82,340	16,361	1,187	15,174
1933	243,845	136,547	13,896	122,651	91,230	9,947	81,283	16,068	1,192	14,876
1932	244,902	134,957	14,111	120,846	93,384	9,967	83,417	16,561	1,196	15,365
1931	252,605	140,516	14,159	126,357	93,307	9,849	83,458	18,782	1,196	17,586
1930	255,648	139,378	14,151	125,227	96,890	9,540	87,350	19,380	1,208	18,172
1929	255,031	139,118	14,047	125,071	97,117	9,434	87,683	18,796	1,181	17,615
1928	250,907	136,084	14,019	122,065	95,803	9,401	86,402	19,020	1,198	17,822
1927	248,943	134,829	14,020	120,809	94,916	9,440	85,476	19,198	1,198	18,000
1926	247,396	134,938	14,143	120,795	93,304	9,091	84,213	19,154	1,178	17,976
1925	251,756	137,048	14,594	122,454	95,230	8,918	86,312	19,478	1,168	18,310
1924	261,189	142,673	13,784	128,889	98,184	8,651	89,533	20,332	1,157	19,175
1923	247,011	133,243	14,021	119,222	94,094	8,410	85,684	19,674	1,141	18,533
1922	270,207	148,763	15,667	133,096	100,211	8,334	91,877	21,233	1,135	20,098
1921	386,542	230,725	16,501	214,224	132,827	9,979	122,848	22,990	1,087	21,903
1920	343,302	204,292	18,999	185,293	121,845	10,642	111,203	17,165	1,104	16,061
1919	1,172,602	851,624	91,975	759,649	272,144	19,357	252,787	48,834	2,270	46,564
1918	2,897,167	2,395,742	130,485	2,265,257	448,606	23,631	424,975	52,819	1,503	51,316
1917	643,833	421,467	34,224	387,243	194,617	8,383	186,234	27,749	776	26,973
1916	179,376	108,399	5,175	103,224	60,376	4,022	56,354	10,601	348	10,253
1915	174,112	106,754	4,948	101,806	57,072	3,593	53,479	10,286	338	9,948
1914	165,919	98,544	5,033	93,511	56,989	3,406	53,583	10,386	336	10,050
1913	154,914	92,756	4,970	87,786	52,202	3,273	48,929	9,956	331	9,625
1912	153,174	92,121	4,775	87,346	51,357	3,074	48,283	9,696	337	9,359
1911	144,846	84,006	4,585	79,421	51,230	2,886	48,344	9,610	328	9,282
1910	139,344	81,251	4,535	76,716	48,533	2,699	45,834	9,560	328	9,232
1909	142,200	84,971	4,299	80,672	47,533	2,630	44,903	9,696	328	9,368
1908	128,500	76,942	4,047	72,895	42,322	2,463	39,859	9,236	283	8,953
1907	108,375	64,170	3,896	60,274	36,119	2,238	33,881	8,086	279	7,807
1906	112,216	68,945	3,989	64,956	35,053	2,133	32,920	8,218	278	7,940
1905	108,301	67,526	4,034	63,492	33,764	2,079	31,685	7,011	270	6,741
1904	110,129	70,387	3,971	66,416	32,158	2,014	30,144	7,584	255	7,329
1903	106,043	69,595	3,927	65,668	29,790	1,893	27,897	6,658	213	6,445
1902	111,145	81,275	4,049	77,226	23,648	1,822	21,826	6,222	191	6,031
1901	112,322	85,557	3,468	82,089	20,900	1,742	19,158	5,865	171	5,694
1900	125,923	101,713	4,227	97,486	18,796	1,683	17,113	5,414	174	5,240
1899	100,166	80,670	3,581	77,089	16,354	1,588	14,766	3,142	76	3,066
1898	235,785	209,714	10,516	199,198	22,492	1,432	21,060	3,579	98	3,481
1897	43,656	27,865	2,179	25,686	11,985	1,399	10,586	3,806	71	3,735
1896	41,680	27,375	2,169	25,206	12,088	1,425	10,663	2,217	72	2,145

See footnotes at end of table.

Series Y 904–916.   Military Personnel on Active Duty: 1789 to 1970—Con.

Year	Grand total [1]	Army			Navy			Marine Corps		
		Total	Officers	Enlisted	Total	Officers	Enlisted	Total	Officers	Enlisted
	904	905	906	907	911	912	913	914	915	916
1895	42,226	27,495	2,154	25,341	11,846	1,412	10,434	2,885	71	2,814
1894	42,101	28,265	2,146	26,119	11,460	1,405	10,055	2,376	67	2,309
1893	39,492	27,830	2,158	25,672	9,529	1,486	8,043	2,133	63	2,070
1892	38,677	27,190	2,140	25,050	9,448	1,468	7,980	2,039	66	1,973
1891	37,868	26,463	2,052	24,411	9,247	1,510	7,737	2,158	66	2,092
1890	38,666	27,373	2,168	25,205	9,246	1,489	7,757	2,047	61	1,986
1889	39,452	27,759	2,177	25,582	9,921	1,530	8,391	1,772	54	1,718
1888	39,035	27,019	2,189	24,830	10,115	1,528	8,587	1,901	72	1,829
1887	38,763	26,719	2,200	24,519	10,113	1,542	8,571	1,931	61	1,870
1886	38,636	26,727	2,102	24,625	9,909	1,549	8,360	2,000	66	1,934
1885	39,098	27,157	2,154	25,003	10,057	1,611	8,446	1,884	65	1,819
1884	39,400	26,666	2,147	24,519	10,846	1,660	9,186	1,888	66	1,822
1883	37,278	25,652	2,143	23,509	9,842	1,819	8,023	1,784	60	1,724
1882	37,850	25,811	2,162	23,649	10,170	1,911	8,259	1,869	63	1,806
1881	37,845	25,842	2,181	23,661	10,101	1,866	8,235	1,902	70	1,832
1880	37,894	26,594	2,152	24,442	9,361	1,713	7,648	1,939	69	1,870
1879	38,022	26,601	2,127	24,474	9,453	1,695	7,758	1,968	62	1,906
1878	36,444	26,023	2,153	23,870	8,087	1,582	6,505	2,334	77	2,257
1877	34,094	24,140	2,177	21,963	8,057	1,591	6,466	1,897	73	1,824
1876	40,591	28,565	2,151	26,414	10,046	1,646	8,400	1,980	76	1,904
1875	38,105	25,513	2,068	23,445	10,479	1,571	8,908	2,113	76	2,037
1874	43,609	28,640	2,081	26,559	12,700	1,595	11,105	2,269	85	2,184
1873	43,228	28,812	2,076	26,736	11,654	1,655	9,999	2,762	87	2,675
1872	42,205	28,322	2,104	26,218	11,680	1,699	9,981	2,203	77	2,126
1871	42,238	29,115	2,105	27,010	10,610	1,702	8,908	2,513	74	2,439
1870	50,348	37,240	2,541	34,699	10,562	1,551	9,011	2,546	77	2,469
1869	51,632	36,953	2,700	34,253	12,295	1,649	10,646	2,384	70	2,314
1868	66,412	51,066	2,835	48,231	[2] 12,268	1,976	10,292	3,078	81	2,997
1867	74,786	57,194	3,056	54,138	14,081	1,801	12,280	3,511	73	3,438
1866	76,749	57,072	(NA)	(NA)	16,340	2,297	14,043	3,337	79	3,258
1865	1,062,848	1,000,692	(NA)	(NA)	58,296	6,759	51,537	3,860	87	3,773
1864	1,031,724	970,905	(NA)	(NA)	57,680	5,679	52,001	3,139	64	3,075
1863	960,061	918,354	(NA)	(NA)	38,707	4,209	34,498	3,000	69	2,931
1862	673,124	637,264	(NA)	(NA)	[2] 33,454	3,224	30,230	2,406	51	2,355
1861	217,112	186,845	(NA)	(NA)	27,881	1,114	26,767	2,386	48	2,338
1860	27,958	16,215	1,080	15,135	9,942	1,150	8,792	1,801	46	1,755
1859	28,978	17,243	1,070	16,173	9,884	1,117	8,767	1,851	47	1,804
1858	29,014	17,678	1,099	16,579	9,729	1,068	8,661	1,607	52	1,555
1857	27,345	15,918	1,097	14,821	9,676	1,031	8,645	1,751	57	1,694
1856	25,867	15,715	1,072	14,643	8,681	1,027	7,654	1,471	57	1,414
1855	26,402	15,911	1,042	14,869	8,887	1,236	7,651	1,604	52	1,552
1854	21,134	10,894	956	9,938	8,879	1,254	7,625	1,361	49	1,312
1853	20,667	10,572	961	9,611	8,841	1,250	7,591	1,254	49	1,205
1852	21,349	11,376	957	10,419	8,805	1,232	7,573	1,168	47	1,121
1851	20,699	10,714	944	9,770	8,792	1,246	7,546	1,193	43	1,150
1850	20,824	10,929	948	9,981	8,794	1,273	7,521	1,101	46	1,055
1849	23,165	10,744	945	9,799	11,345	1,282	10,063	1,076	46	1,030
1848	60,308	47,319	2,865	44,454	11,238	1,141	10,097	1,751	42	1,709
1847	57,761	44,736	[2] 2,863	[2] 41,873	11,193	1,126	10,067	1,832	75	1,757
1846	39,165	27,867	[2] 2,003	[2] 25,864	10,131	1,053	9,078	1,167	41	1,126
1845	20,726	8,509	826	7,683	11,189	1,095	10,094	1,028	42	986
1844	20,919	8,730	813	7,917	11,103	1,063	10,040	1,086	40	1,046
1843	20,741	9,102	805	8,297	[2] 10,555	1,055	9,500	1,084	43	1,041
1842	22,851	10,780	781	9,999	10,782	998	9,784	1,289	46	1,243
1841	20,793	11,319	754	10,565	8,274	940	7,334	1,200	44	1,156
1840	21,616	12,330	789	11,541	8,017	932	7,085	1,269	46	1,223
1839	19,317	10,691	749	9,942	7,676	922	6,754	950	34	916
1838	17,948	9,197	717	8,480	7,656	847	6,809	1,095	28	1,067
1837	22,462	12,449	873	11,576	8,452	801	7,651	1,561	37	1,524
1836	16,874	9,945	[3] 857	[3] 9,088	5,588	787	4,801	1,341	43	1,298
1835	14,311	7,337	680	6,657	5,557	756	4,801	1,417	68	1,349
1834	13,396	7,030	669	6,361	5,451	695	4,756	915	46	869
1833	12,895	6,579	666	5,913	5,420	664	4,756	896	43	853
1832	12,478	6,268	659	5,609	5,312	642	4,670	898	38	860
1831	11,173	6,055	613	5,442	4,303	612	3,691	815	35	780
1830	11,942	6,122	627	5,495	4,929	615	4,314	891	37	854
1829	12,096	6,332	608	5,724	4,869	555	4,314	895	43	852
1828	11,431	5,702	540	5,162	4,797	506	4,291	932	40	892
1827	11,627	5,885	546	5,339	4,796	505	4,291	946	43	903
1826	11,586	5,989	540	5,449	4,762	471	4,291	835	39	796
1825	11,089	5,903	562	5,341	4,405	505	3,900	781	35	746
1824	11,008	5,973	532	5,441	4,095	531	3,564	940	50	890
1823	10,871	6,117	525	5,592	[2] 4,053	553	3,500	701	20	681
1822	9,863	5,358	512	4,846	3,774	534	3,240	731	23	708
1821	10,587	5,773	547	5,226	3,935	484	3,451	879	35	844
1820	15,113	10,554	696	9,858	3,988	537	3,451	571	19	552
1819	13,259	8,506	705	7,801	[2] 4,068	568	3,500	685	21	664
1818	14,260	8,155	697	7,458	[2] 5,545	545	5,000	560	24	536
1817	14,606	8,446	647	7,799	[2] 5,494	494	5,000	666	14	652
1816	16,743	10,231	735	9,496	[2] 6,040	500	5,540	472	21	451
1815	40,885	33,424	2,272	31,152	6,773	531	6,242	688	8	680
1814	46,858	38,186	2,271	35,915	[2] 8,024	524	7,500	648	11	637
1813	25,152	19,036	1,476	17,560	[2] 5,525	525	5,000	591	12	579
1812	12,631	6,686	299	6,387	5,452	442	5,010	493	10	483
1811	11,528	5,608	396	5,212	5,364	454	4,910	556	14	542

See footnotes at end of table.

Series Y 904–916. Military Personnel on Active Duty: 1789 to 1970—Con.

Year	Grand total [1]	Army			Navy			Marine Corps		
		Total	Officers	Enlisted	Total	Officers	Enlisted	Total	Officers	Enlisted
	904	905	906	907	911	912	913	914	915	916
1810	11,554	5,956	441	5,515	[2] 5,149	450	4,699	449	9	440
1809	12,375	6,977	533	6,444	[2] 4,875	450	4,425	523	10	513
1808	8,200	5,712	327	5,385	1,616	191	1,425	872	11	861
1807	5,323	2,775	146	2,629	[2] 2,145	191	1,954	403	11	392
1806	4,076	2,653	142	2,511	1,105	191	914	318	11	307
1805	6,498	2,729	159	2,570	[2] 3,191	191	3,000	578	22	556
1804	5,323	2,734	216	2,518	[2] 2,200	200	2,000	389	25	364
1803	4,528	2,486	174	2,312	[2] 1,700	200	1,500	342	25	317
1802	5,432	2,873	175	2,698	[2] 2,200	200	2,000	359	29	330
1801	7,108	4,051	248	3,803	[2] 2,700	200	2,500	357	38	319
1800	(NA)	(NA)	(NA)	(NA)	[2] 5,400	400	5,000	525	38	487
1799	(NA)	(NA)	(NA)	(NA)	[2] 2,200	200	2,000	368	25	343
1798	(NA)	(NA)	(NA)	(NA)	[2] 1,856	150	1,706	83	25	58
1795	5,296	3,440	212	3,228	[2] 1,856	150	1,706			
1794	5,669	3,813	[2] 235	3,578	[2] 1,856	150	1,706			
1789	718	718	46	672						

NA Not available.
[1] Excludes Coast Guard.
[2] Included with Army prior to 1948. Includes Army personnel assigned to Air Force Command. See text.

[3] Estimated.
[4] Includes 178 Navy medical officers on duty with the Army.

Series Y 917–926. Classification of Selective Service Registrants: 1940 to 1970

[In thousands. Data for 1940–1947 are for varying dates and age groups, as noted, and refer to conterminous United States; totals include classes not shown separately. Data for 1948–1970 are as of December 31 and include Puerto Rico and outlying areas]

Year	Classification status of registrants, 18½ to 26 years old									Inducted
	Total	Class I: Available for military service	Class IV: Conscientious objectors	Class I: Fulfilling military obligation	Class IV: Completed military obligation	Class II and III: Deferred	Class IV: Exempted	Class IV: Disqualified for military service	Unclassified	
	917	918	919	920	921	922	923	924	925	926
1970	22,705	2,596	28	3,504	3,801	6,151	130	5,959	537	163
1969	21,785	1,469	16	3,885	3,308	6,971	130	5,583	425	284
1968	20,829	1,446	13	3,887	2,946	6,798	126	5,189	424	296
1967	19,901	1,412	11	3,802	2,672	6,578	121	4,909	396	228
1966	18,971	1,165	9	3,733	2,521	6,091	115	4,988	350	382
1965	17,968	1,485	10	3,167	2,399	5,830	103	4,640	334	231
1964	16,835	2,006	11	2,856	2,304	4,899	95	4,149	514	112
1963	16,027	1,743	8	2,645	2,243	3,613	82	3,593	2,101	119
1962	15,410	2,298	10	2,543	2,175	2,534	79	3,598	2,174	82
1961	14,868	2,329	10	2,448	2,132	2,302	76	3,421	2,152	119
1960	14,057	2,287	9	2,180	2,191	2,014	70	3,315	1,992	87
1959	13,179	2,295	9	2,069	2,211	1,804	68	3,145	1,578	96
1958	12,376	2,132	8	2,037	2,231	1,607	67	2,936	1,359	142
1957	11,674	2,105	7	1,969	2,275	1,372	64	2,574	1,309	139
1956	11,087	1,904	6	1,903	2,281	1,361	63	2,293	1,275	152
1955	10,609	1,736	5	4,221	113	1,419	67	2,122	926	153
1954	10,157	1,564	5	4,219	255	1,439	70	1,992	612	253
1953	9,727	1,116	3	4,052	578	1,529	72	1,818	559	472
1952	8,993	1,117	5	3,364	1,253	1,483	75	1,532	164	438
1951	8,638	1,154	8	2,375	1,995	1,288	67	1,283	468	552
1950	9,239	1,402	12	870	2,699	1,236	50	907	2,063	220
1949	8,924	1,233	9	271	2,719	882	34	523	3,253	10
1948	8,946	501	5	47	213	212	17	234	7,718	20
1947 [1]	3,690	268	8	(NA)	(NA)	278	(NA)	2,217	(NA)	(NA)
1946 [2]	3,459	268	9	(NA)	(NA)	305	(NA)	2,261	(NA)	184
1945 [3]	8,817	444	(NA)	6,228	(NA)	809	(NA)	1,288	(NA)	946
1944 [3]	8,654	480	(NA)	5,803	117	841	(NA)	1,364	(NA)	1,592
1943 [4]	22,138	1,090	(NA)	8,970	(NA)	8,560	(NA)	3,353	(NA)	3,324
1942 [5]	28,477	1,572	11	5,778	(NA)	15,690	190	2,418	2,820	3,033
1941 [6]	14,690	982	6	974	99	10,760	213	1,098	558	924
1940 [7]	16,317									19

NA Not available.
[1] As of Apr. 1, ages 18–29. Excludes classes I–C (already in Armed Forces) and III–A (registrants having dependents).
[2] As of Dec. 2. See also footnote 1.
[3] As of Dec. 1, ages 18–25.

[4] As of Dec. 1, ages 18–37.
[5] As of Dec. 31, ages 18–37.
[6] As of Sept. 30, ages 21–35.
[7] As of Oct. 20, ages 21–35.

Series Y 927–942. Disposition of Defendants Charged with Violation of Selective Service Acts: 1945 to 1970

Year	Total defend-ants	Not convicted		Acquitted by		Convicted and sentenced	Plea of guilty or nolo con-tendere	Convicted by		Type of sentence — Imprisonment [1]					Pro-bation, fine, and other	Average sentence of im-prison-ment (in mo.)
		Total	Dis-missed	Court	Jury	Total		Court	Jury	Total	1 year and 1 day and under [2]	Over 1 year 1 day to 3 years	3–5 years	5 years and over		
	927	928	929	930	931	932	933	934	935	936	937	938	939	940	941	942
1970	2,833	1,806	1,570	222	14	1,027	570	321	136	450	53	144	208	45	577	33
1969	1,744	844	747	88	9	900	511	252	137	544	40	155	261	88	356	36
1968	1,192	408	353	49	6	784	520	196	68	580	44	131	301	104	204	37
1967	996	248	224	22	2	748	538	141	69	666	47	270	291	58	82	32
1966	516	145	132	11	2	371	265	74	32	301	61	128	95	17	70	26
1965	341	99	88	8	3	242	197	28	17	189	64	90	30	5	53	21
1964	276	70	63	6	1	206	161	32	13	146	46	77	22	1	60	21
1963	338	73	66	7	–	265	212	46	7	189	79	65	36	9	76	22
1962	274	49	46	2	1	225	182	31	12	164	58	75	28	3	61	22
1961	244	45	37	8	–	199	160	33	6	141	45	59	35	2	58	23
1960	239	73	65	7	1	166	131	31	4	126	47	48	28	3	40	22
1959	258	56	44	11	1	202	159	39	4	152	46	63	39	4	50	23
1958	325	96	66	26	4	229	154	66	9	190	66	81	42	1	39	22
1957	357	95	75	17	3	262	183	70	9	194	60	85	41	8	68	24
1956	371	185	167	16	2	186	109	67	10	123	35	50	35	3	63	24
1955	719	430	367	57	6	289	157	106	26	217	54	105	47	11	72	25
1954	822	398	278	116	4	424	194	185	45	356	78	137	126	15	68	26
1953	630	285	236	39	10	345	185	129	31	280	61	101	84	34	65	29
1952	561	248	222	16	10	313	160	97	56	272	58	77	97	40	41	31
1951	368	212	202	6	4	156	105	24	27	123	35	37	29	22	33	30
1950	449	274	272	1	1	175	156	6	13	109	78	24	6	1	66	13
1949	506	214	202	3	9	292	263	20	9	213	134	62	17	–	79	15
1948	833	529	511	7	11	304	264	11	29	212	133	69	9	1	92	14
1947	2,074	937	908	18	11	1,137	898	178	61	775	394	317	61	3	362	14
1946	2,651	999	953	26	20	1,652	1,130	222	300	1,339	547	501	244	47	313	21
1945	4,287	1,449	1,399	25	25	2,838	1,823	319	696	2,368	438	775	744	411	470	32

– Represents zero.
[1] Includes sentences of more than 6 months which are to be followed by a term of probation (mixed sentences).
[2] Includes split sentences where a defendant receives a sentence on a one-count indictment of 6 months or less in a jail type institution, followed by a term of probation. Included in these figures are mixed sentences involving confinement for 6 months or less on one count, to be followed by a term of probation on one or more other counts.

Series Y 943–956. Estimated Number of Veterans in Civil Life, by Age: 1865 to 1970

[In thousands. As of June 30. Includes all veterans of the Vietnam era, service between Korean conflict and the Vietnam era, Korean conflict, World War II, World War I, Spanish-American War, Civil War, Mexican War, and War of 1812, as well as those veterans of the Indian wars and former members of the Regular Establishment (peacetime) who were on the benefit rolls of Veterans Administration or predecessor agencies. Veterans who served in 2 or more wars prior to the Korean conflict are included 2 or more times; veterans who served in both World War II and the Korean conflict, and in the Vietnam era, Korean conflict, and World War II are included only once]

Year	Total, all ages	Under 20 years	20 to 24 years	25 to 29 years	30 to 34 years	35 to 39 years	40 to 44 years	45 to 49 years	50 to 54 years	55 to 59 years	60 to 64 years	65 to 69 years	70 years and over	Unknown
	943	944	945	946	947	948	949	950	951	952	953	954	955	956
1970	27,647	24	1,693	2,628	2,321	3,039	4,017	5,066	3,895	1,934	1,034	326	1,670	–
1969	26,925	18	1,527	2,361	2,318	3,291	4,243	5,071	3,469	1,709	894	315	1,709	–
1968	26,273	24	1,282	2,193	2,382	3,482	4,511	4,958	3,082	1,514	752	376	1,717	–
1967	25,805	31	1,095	2,149	2,541	3,580	4,791	4,785	2,680	1,374	610	466	1,703	–
1966	25,534	39	1,100	2,078	2,799	3,759	4,977	4,451	2,360	1,253	476	646	1,596	–
1965	21,834	(Z)	13	314	2,458	3,967	5,137	4,036	2,059	1,152	387	958	1,353	–
1964	22,013	–	13	580	2,930	4,222	5,148	3,596	1,823	996	378	1,200	1,127	–
1963	22,166	(Z)	13	906	3,316	4,508	5,025	3,189	1,614	835	451	1,365	944	–
1962	22,275	(Z)	20	1,426	3,502	4,773	4,839	2,765	1,461	676	555	1,478	780	–
1961	22,403	(Z)	98	1,976	3,715	4,955	4,494	2,429	1,333	530	772	1,461	640	–
1960	22,534	(Z)	281	2,425	3,962	5,127	4,060	2,115	1,219	426	1,138	1,260	521	–
1959	22,666	(Z)	521	2,890	4,222	5,139	3,624	1,873	1,054	418	1,423	1,091	411	–
1958	22,727	(Z)	857	3,195	4,498	5,023	3,227	1,665	889	503	1,617	944	309	–
1957	22,634	4	989	3,535	4,810	4,854	2,803	1,513	720	624	1,743	816	223	–
1956	22,372	17	1,446	3,526	5,008	4,528	2,469	1,380	563	866	1,720	691	158	–
1955	21,861	26	1,398	3,866	5,143	4,095	2,155	1,265	445	1,288	1,482	555	143	–
1950	19,077	1	2,196	5,023	4,064	2,154	1,280	458	1,390	1,653	650	72	136	–
1945	6,498	28	637	740	497	380	130	1,295	1,764	718	77	111	77	44
1940	4,286	–	–	–	–	16	1,287	1,848	773	86	131	72	35	38
1935	4,494	–	–	–	16	1,323	1,917	815	93	149	86	31	28	36
1930	4,680	–	–	17	1,356	1,974	849	98	162	97	37	13	56	21
1925	4,894	–	17	1,386	2,026	877	103	172	105	41	15	6	130	16
1920	5,146	17	1,416	2,075	903	107	180	112	44	18	7	3	245	19
1915	773	–	–	(Z)	19	145	100	40	16	8	3	8	417	17
1910	977	–	(Z)	20	150	105	42	17	8	4	11	380	238	2
1905	1,192	(Z)	21	156	109	44	18	9	4	13	458	208	150	2
1900	1,224	12	91	64	26	11	5	3	14	521	251	121	104	1
1895	1,187	–	–	–	–	–	–	13	578	289	148	85	71	3
1890	1,341	–	–	–	–	–	14	628	321	171	105	67	35	–
1885	1,475	–	–	–	–	15	670	347	189	121	82	44	7	–
1880	1,593	–	–	–	16	710	370	216	142	133	93	53	5	10
1875	1,698	–	–	17	748	390	216	142	103	59	7	(Z)	16	–
1870	1,802	–	17	784	411	228	152	109	65	8	(Z)	(Z)	28	–
1865	1,908	18	820	430	239	159	116	70	9	1	(Z)	(Z)	37	–

– Represents zero.   Z Less than 500.

Series Y 957–970. Estimated Number of Veterans in Civil Life, by Period of Service: 1865 to 1970

[In thousands. As of June 30]

Year	Total veterans	War of 1812	Mexican War	Civil War	Indian wars [1]	Spanish-American War	World War I	World War II [2]	Korean conflict Total [2]	Korean conflict Without World War II service	Service between Korean conflict and Vietnam [3][4]	Vietnam [3][5] Total [6]	Vietnam [3][5] Without Korean conflict service	Regular Establishment [7]
	957	958	959	960	961	962	963	964	965	966	967	968	969	970
1970	27,647				(Z)	5	1,536	14,458	5,867	4,605	3,125	4,173	3,918	185
1969	26,925				(Z)	6	1,647	14,592	5,847	4,590	3,134	3,169	2,956	183
1968	26,273				(Z)	8	1,766	14,718	5,814	4,567	3,139	2,234	2,070	180
1967	25,805				(Z)	10	1,888	14,832	5,797	4,563	3,142	1,493	1,370	195
1966	25,534				(Z)	12	2,007	14,916	5,770	4,568	3,147	962	884	175
1965	21,834				(Z)	15	2,121	14,969	5,718	4,568	3,152	456	434	161
1964	22,013				(Z)	18	2,226	15,048	5,708	4,574	3,119			147
1963	22,166				(Z)	22	2,343	15,100	5,663	4,567	2,617			134
1962	22,275				(Z)	26	2,455	15,126	5,586	4,546	2,156			122
1961	22,403				(Z)	31	2,565	15,156	5,531	4,538	1,760			113
1960	22,534				(Z)	36	2,673	15,202	5,482	4,520	1,380			103
1959	22,666			(Z)	(Z)	43	2,778	15,243	5,448	4,507	967			95
1958	22,727			(Z)	(Z)	48	2,876	15,288	5,353	4,431	569			84
1957	22,634			(Z)	(Z)	55	2,971	15,332	5,105	4,202	186			74
1956	22,372			(Z)	(Z)	63	3,061	15,370	4,686	3,812	30			66
1955	21,861			(Z)	(Z)	72	3,150	15,405	3,999	3,171	4			63
1954	20,951			(Z)	(Z)	80	3,230	15,425	2,912	2,153				63
1953	20,196			(Z)	(Z)	89	3,308	15,440	1,955	1,297				62
1952	19,338			(Z)	(Z)	99	3,382	15,369	867	428				60
1951	18,919			(Z)	(Z)	108	3,452	15,200	211	100				59
1950	19,077			(Z)	1	118	3,518	15,386	(Z)	(Z)				54
1949	18,945			(Z)	1	127	3,587	15,182						48
1948	18,745			(Z)	1	136	3,651	14,914						43
1947	18,262			(Z)	1	146	3,711	14,361						43
1946	16,655			(Z)	1	155	3,768	12,687						44
1945	6,498			(Z)	1	164	3,821	2,469						43
1944	5,689			(Z)	1	173	3,871	1,601						43
1943	5,002		1	1	1	182	3,917	858						43
1942	4,485		1	2	2	190	3,961	289						42
1941	4,337		2	2	2	198	4,002	95						38
1940	4,286			2	2	206	4,040							36
1935	4,494			13	4	244	4,201							32
1930	4,680			49	5	274	4,336							16
1925	4,894		(Z)	127	4	298	4,453							12
1920	5,146		(Z)	244	4	317	4,566							15
1915	773		1	424	1	332								15
1910	977		2	624	2	349								
1905	1,192		5	821	2	364								
1900	1,224	(Z)	9	1,000	1	214								
1895	1,187	(Z)	14	1,170	3									
1890	1,341	(Z)	19	1,322										
1885	1,475	3	23	1,449										
1880	1,593	10	26	1,557										
1875	1,698	16	28	1,654										
1870	1,802	28	30	1,744										
1865	1,908	46	32	1,830										

Z Less than 500.   [1] Includes only veterans on the benefit rolls of the Veterans Administration or predecessor agencies.

[2] Includes veterans who served in both World War II and the Korean conflict.

[3] Public Law 89-358, March 3, 1966, conferred veteran status on all persons serving on active duty in the Armed Forces after January 31, 1955. Veterans with service between the Korean conflict and Vietnam era (February 1, 1955–August 4, 1964) and Vietnam era veterans (service after August 4, 1964) included in the total veteran count beginning June 1966.

[4] Veterans whose only service was on active duty between January 31, 1955, and August 5, 1964. Excludes men who served on active duty for training only.

[5] Service after August 4, 1964.

[6] Includes veterans who served in both the Vietnam era and the Korean conflict or World War II.

[7] Former members of Regular Establishment (peacetime) receiving disability compensation from the Veterans Administration or predecessor agencies. Beginning June 1966, Regular Establishment veterans are excluded from total veterans since they are for the most part included as veterans with service between the Korean conflict and Vietnam era or as veterans of a war period.

Series Y 971–983. Expenditures of Veterans Administration and Predecessor Agencies From Appropriated Funds, by Period of Service: 1790 to 1970

[In thousands of dollars. For years ending June 30]

Year	Total, all wars	War of 1812	Mexican War	Civil War	Indian wars	Spanish-American War	World War I	World War II	Korean conflict	Between Korean conflict and Vietnam	Vietnam era	Regular Establishment	Undistributed and other
	971	972	973	974	975	976	977	978	979	980	981	982	983
Total	[1]174,760,880	[2]48,747	[3]64,284	[4]8,569,583	123,225	5,430,693	48,970,260	87,450,145	15,190,502	2,049,917	2,617,062	4,159,608	[5]16,809
1970	8,905,065			1,014	167	54,475	1,943,366	3,880,834	898,251	480,794	1,327,690	318,474	
1969	7,907,776			945	190	60,948	1,910,450	3,521,688	675,500	844,240	624,258	269,557	
1968	7,290,882			1,090	206	58,999	1,901,226	3,295,979	755,536	535,088	464,537	278,221	
1967	6,913,666			1,132	205	65,413	1,891,630	3,483,144	794,651	189,796	200,576	287,119	
1966	6,410,840			1,309	243	70,390	1,980,136	3,323,174	707,581			328,007	
1965	6,150,021			1,522	297	78,947	1,962,712	3,108,782	720,802			276,959	
1964	6,008,129			1,774	362	89,899	1,946,465	3,058,185	664,094			247,350	
1963	5,866,233			1	2,052	400	96,909	1,947,434	2,856,483	746,745			216,209	(Z)
1962	5,636,630			2	2,533	468	103,872	1,907,004	2,661,322	767,487			193,940	2
1961	5,567,531			1	2,740	547	113,160	1,870,473	2,447,984	956,369			176,253	4

See footnotes at end of table.

Series Y 971–983. Expenditures of Veterans Administration and Predecessor Agencies From Appropriated Funds, by Period of Service: 1790 to 1970—Con.

[In thousands of dollars.   For years ending June 30]

Year	Total, all wars	War of 1812	Mexican War	Civil War	Indian wars	Spanish-American War	World War I	World War II	Korean conflict	Regular Establishment	Undistributed and other
	971	972	973	974	975	976	977	978	979	982	983
1960	5,389,378	----------	2	3,130	632	123,733	1,693,360	2,398,350	1,008,037	162,129	5
1959	5,343,711	----------	3	3,428	712	130,155	1,564,592	2,354,010	1,151,933	138,873	5
1958	5,205,941	----------	3	2,458	724	129,569	1,445,443	2,270,189	1,234,720	122,831	4
1957	4,884,506	----------	3	2,839	863	137,279	1,349,830	2,059,223	1,231,723	102,742	4
1956	4,801,885	----------	4	3,257	983	145,738	1,284,202	2,135,904	1,140,840	90,955	2
1955	4,483,137	----------	5	3,697	1,101	152,663	1,188,768	2,137,246	914,123	85,532	2
1954	4,282,592	----------	5	4,112	1,192	164,889	1,067,701	2,416,000	548,801	79,891	1
1953	4,354,220	----------	8	4,739	1,326	163,000	1,019,190	2,869,785	216,054	80,116	2
1952	4,944,187	----------	11	5,168	1,348	160,434	903,432	3,747,014	53,706	73,070	4
1951	5,356,639	----------	13	6,974	1,532	164,525	851,288	4,255,015	4,003	73,284	5
1950	6,627,657		14	6,864	1,719	168,449	793,337	5,593,899	----------	63,369	6
1949	6,660,350		17	7,938	1,920	174,787	717,947	5,705,569	----------	52,166	6
1948	6,497,681		23	9,081	1,971	175,716	647,393	5,624,766	----------	38,725	6
1947	7,470,600		26	9,104	2,008	153,191	573,034	6,696,915	----------	36,316	6
1946	4,425,001	(Z)	27	10,513	2,169	145,783	444,965	3,794,869	----------	26,667	8
1945	2,084,668	(Z)	31	12,007	2,348	148,109	400,440	1,494,977	----------	26,747	9
1944	743,596	(Z)	39	14,070	2,324	132,116	355,691	213,346	----------	25,999	11
1943	605,693	(Z)	50	16,776	2,517	130,189	375,435	54,327	----------	26,385	14
1942	556,198	(Z)	55	19,791	2,782	132,593	370,162	7,851	----------	22,949	15
1941	553,013	(Z)	66	23,504	3,025	133,744	366,260	5,244	----------	21,155	15
1940	557,690	(Z)	85	28,255	3,313	134,166	372,522	----------	----------	19,334	15
1939	555,175	(Z)	103	33,615	3,554	131,774	371,627	----------	----------	14,487	15
1938	581,923	1	117	39,791	3,671	125,160	398,895	----------	----------	14,273	15
1937	579,352	1	133	47,292	3,664	121,591	392,619	----------	----------	14,036	16
1936	580,249	1	155	56,340	3,911	116,189	391,916	----------	----------	11,720	17
1935	556,857	3	181	64,400	4,013	83,413	393,314	----------	----------	11,515	18
1934	496,215	3	199	70,797	3,887	61,415	350,201	----------	----------	9,695	18
1933	780,758	4	286	99,204	5,039	131,328	537,434	----------	----------	7,437	26
1932	789,251	4	327	109,315	4,865	122,829	544,910	----------	----------	6,977	24
1931	714,022	5	347	123,400	4,797	110,375	468,926	----------	----------	6,172	----------
1930	639,213	6	397	127,458	4,786	91,700	409,307	----------	----------	5,559	
1929	631,248	7	475	145,301	4,646	84,230	391,305	----------	----------	5,284	
1928	625,144	9	547	151,718	4,123	77,476	386,452	----------	----------	4,819	
1927	618,791	10	572	169,124	2,141	63,338	379,084	----------	----------	4,522	
1926	628,271	7	438	174,645	1,951	35,806	411,088	----------	----------	4,336	

Year	Total, all wars [6]	War of 1812	Mexican War	Civil War	Indian wars	Spanish-American War	World War I	Regular Establishment	Undistributed and other	Year or period	Total, all wars [6]	War of 1812	Mexican War	Civil War	Indian wars
	971	972	973	974	975	976	977	982	983		971	972	973	974	975
1925	607,246	9	511	190,003	2,011	29,929	380,780	4,003	----------	1895	147,606	561	2,340	143,821	820
1924	647,283	13	585	207,148	1,970	25,197	408,400	3,970	----------	1894	147,408	668	2,291	143,366	871
1923	737,000	18	724	243,965	1,964	21,071	465,051	4,207	----------	1893	165,315	758	2,257	161,783	251
1922	736,731	20	781	241,662	1,844	13,933	474,415	4,076	----------	1892	147,784	876	2,254	144,295	----------
1921	652,157	24	894	252,792	1,614	8,046	384,582	4,205	----------	1891	125,351	1,115	2,499	121,284	----------
1920	494,183	21	683	207,948	1,784	5,748	273,806	4,193	----------	1890	112,647	1,359	2,598	----------	----------
1919	499,311	18	765	217,640	1,594	4,813	270,236	4,245	----------	1889	95,066	1,521	2,672	----------	----------
1918	260,898	21	892	176,653	971	5,379	72,622	4,360	----------	1888	84,512	1,755	2,624	----------	----------
1917	169,264	19	852	159,237	428	4,948	----------	3,780	----------	1887	79,451	1,984	142	----------	----------
1916	167,393	19	815	157,447	488	4,887	----------	3,737	----------	1886	68,931	1,727	----------	----------	----------
1915	173,729	23	939	163,778	526	4,821	----------	3,642	----------	1885	70,196	1,911	----------	----------	----------
1914	180,866	28	1,077	170,928	575	4,663	----------	3,586	9	1884	62,184	2,157	----------	----------	----------
1913	183,138	33	1,207	173,038	545	4,735	----------	3,569	11	1883	64,361	2,448	----------	----------	----------
1912	162,125	38	1,191	152,355	538	4,585	----------	3,418	----------	1882	56,882	2,656	----------	----------	----------
1911	166,448	45	1,348	156,651	592	4,508	----------	3,302	2	1881	52,771	3,135	----------	----------	----------
1910	169,492	52	1,492	159,861	640	4,343	----------	3,102	----------	1880	58,585	3,573	----------	----------	----------
1909	171,458	64	1,647	161,747	659	4,279	----------	2,972	----------	1879	35,526	3,317	----------	----------	----------
1908	162,398	70	1,512	153,267	553	4,009	----------	2,853	----------	1878	28,764	1,128	----------	----------	----------
1907	147,482	86	1,381	138,808	587	3,770	----------	2,727	----------	1877	30,145	1,373	----------	----------	----------
1906	148,421	103	1,423	139,767	650	3,726	----------	2,614	----------	1876	29,887	1,622	----------	----------	----------
1905	150,851	117	1,572	142,191	686	3,667	----------	2,512	----------	1875	31,106	1,981	----------	----------	----------
1904	150,716	144	1,739	142,248	778	3,318	----------	2,376	----------	1874	31,908	2,305	----------	----------	----------
1903	147,079	165	1,687	142,295	447	2,369	----------	3	----------	1873	28,681	2,875	----------	----------	----------
1902	146,575	188	1,729	142,253	435	1,865	----------	2	----------	1872	31,454	2,411	----------	----------	----------
1901	147,275	216	1,788	143,409	488	1,247	----------	(Z)	----------	1871	30,081	----------	----------	----------	----------
1900	146,887	255	1,893	143,726	545	344	----------	----------	----------	1870	30,543				
1899	146,822	301	2,014	143,775	601	31	----------	----------	----------	1869	29,658				
1898	152,814	357	2,150	149,559	644	----------	----------	----------	----------	1868	24,164				
1897	147,903	400	2,190	144,455	707	----------	----------	----------	----------	1867	21,276				
1896	145,789	471	2,277	142,093	777	----------	----------	----------	----------	1866	15,858				
										1790–1865	96,445				

Z   Less than $500.
[1] Includes $70,045,000 for the Revolutionary War spent prior to 1911.
[2] Includes $132,000 spent prior to 1872, not shown by year.
[3] Includes $78,000 spent prior to 1887, not shown by year.
[4] Includes $1,168,119,000 spent prior to 1891, not shown by year.
[5] Includes $16,487,000 spent prior to 1911, not shown by year.
[6] Amounts in footnotes 1 to 5, which affect years prior to 1911, are not shown annually by war but are distributed by years in this column.

Series Y 984–997. Expenditures for Veterans Benefits and Services by Veterans Administration and Predecessor Agencies: 1790 to 1970

[In thousands of dollars. For years ending June 30]

Year	Total expenditures	Compensation and pensions	Insurance and servicemen's indemnities[1]	Readjustment benefits					Miscellaneous benefit payments	Medical, hospital, and domiciliary services	Hospital and domiciliary facilities	Administration and other benefits	Expenditures from general and special fund appropriations	
				Education and training	Vocational rehabilitation	Unemployment and self-employment allowances	Loan guaranty	Direct loans					Total	Transfers to insurance trust funds
	984	985	986	987	988	989	990	991	992	993	994	995	996	997
Total[2]	194,364,921	94,415,801	25,349,218	21,599,199	2,599,252	3,804,876	4,005,094	3,508,283	6,639,876	24,255,295	1,862,119	6,326,846	174,760,880	7,626,965
1970[2][3]	10,122,477	5,253,840	1,169,451	991,443	41,643	----------	248,961	180,403	153,926	1,748,432	74,605	262,605	8,905,065	11,381
1969	9,025,846	4,848,852	1,068,437	661,095	29,965	----------	282,955	208,546	139,825	1,515,851	47,872	222,448	7,907,776	9,790
1968	8,425,437	4,519,304	1,083,335	446,490	22,755	----------	328,090	208,382	144,238	1,418,953	49,883	204,007	7,290,882	6,968
1967	8,003,404	4,392,834	1,039,099	286,597	19,186	----------	368,873	161,660	155,364	1,325,705	60,035	194,051	6,913,666	9,066
1966	7,325,325	4,305,368	867,999	30,988	17,426	----------	378,028	92,432	141,686	1,229,254	83,464	178,689	6,410,840	8,256
1965	[2]6,967,530	4,042,144	783,139	37,443	14,533	(Z)	363,926	171,394	118,376	1,181,512	76,996	178,125	6,150,021	8,910
1964	6,866,474	3,900,203	827,763	58,566	11,757	(Z)	355,314	237,280	113,536	1,119,811	68,576	173,666	6,008,129	8,527
1963	[2]6,816,023	3,814,749	930,873	88,209	9,243	(Z)	309,520	246,332	104,737	1,071,790	66,170	174,640	5,866,233	8,053
1962	[2]6,529,104	3,652,598	882,269	142,557	10,336	(Z)	234,993	252,827	102,998	1,022,323	53,008	175,330	5,636,630	8,351
1961	[2]6,636,402	3,568,396	1,068,544	237,264	11,837	(Z)	159,885	286,271	96,241	978,048	51,428	178,917	5,567,531	9,829
1960	[2]6,215,378	3,314,761	831,760	382,861	17,910	(Z)	121,829	312,777	89,088	912,967	56,854	174,768	5,389,378	11,120
1959	[2]6,129,139	3,225,527	796,315	574,029	22,307	1	120,933	203,971	81,232	880,787	45,145	178,838	5,343,711	12,426
1958	[2]5,948,131	3,062,211	761,075	698,415	26,095	2	80,039	228,868	63,189	823,963	32,904	171,627	5,205,941	15,570
1957	[2]5,553,871	2,828,516	696,646	776,277	30,598	5	60,125	130,219	58,915	768,076	36,342	168,799	4,884,506	19,993
1956	[2]5,402,035	2,748,989	686,013	766,900	38,134	[4]2	40,062	103,118	55,726	760,409	26,882	176,944	4,801,885	79,041
1955	5,170,768	2,634,293	724,069	664,514	40,770	[4]200	28,831	125,126	51,000	696,750	32,510	173,105	4,483,137	31,160
1954	5,075,185	2,450,518	869,579	544,119	41,294	[4]245	44,640	117,709	51,537	712,828	51,043	192,163	4,282,592	73,477
1953	5,013,733	2,376,307	737,575	667,802	57,768	[4]516	65,843	92,760	63,809	662,858	88,183	201,344	4,354,220	84,725
1952	5,869,841	2,105,973	1,110,193	1,325,403	97,902	76	78,355	87,276	63,267	662,683	113,011	235,702	4,944,187	204,644
1951	5,953,879	2,035,988	607,104	1,943,341	176,875	8,378	90,108	60,932	62,530	594,084	103,878	270,661	5,356,639	44,555
1950	9,278,335	2,009,462	3,108,957	2,595,728	272,292	138,191	58,671	----------	41,222	592,082	151,532	310,198	6,627,657	474,648
1949	6,987,596	1,891,283	401,454	2,703,862	335,200	509,592	40,038	----------	40,700	574,178	124,025	367,264	6,660,350	89,154
1948	7,040,503	1,820,685	[5]676,932	2,498,884	333,313	677,256	64,354	----------	39,780	519,722	16,980	392,597	6,497,681	144,458
1947	6,972,077	1,731,973	328,211	2,122,292	221,147	1,447,916	75,493	----------	44,409	415,813	153,880	430,943	7,470,600	833,278
1946	3,382,777	1,215,688	340,594	350,561	45,087	1,000,909	5,229	----------	18,007	213,816	34,313	158,573	4,425,001	1,389,296
1945	1,140,829	732,535	175,935	8,693	8,348	23,512	----------	----------	21,744	101,611	15,801	52,650	2,084,668	1,130,490
1944	723,445	494,364	86,392	----------	659	----------	----------	----------	10,077	98,041	4,851	29,061	743,596	104,947
1943	619,764	442,360	55,508	----------	[4]3	----------	----------	----------	8,063	86,623	2,720	24,493	605,693	36,492
1942	642,917	431,284	56,516	----------	[4]4	----------	----------	----------	49,974	81,973	4,046	19,128	556,198	4,813
1941	612,721	433,114	69,588	----------	[4]4	----------	----------	----------	9,626	78,458	4,541	17,398	553,013	1,636
1940	637,611	429,138	87,899	----------	[4]3	----------	----------	----------	15,690	74,497	13,638	16,752	557,690	1,516
1939	597,461	416,704	70,965	----------	[4]2	----------	----------	----------	14,045	69,651	10,958	15,140	555,175	2,760
1938	627,399	402,769	111,727	----------	[4]1	----------	----------	----------	20,757	66,626	9,347	16,174	581,923	2,431
1937	891,426	396,030	114,880	----------	[4]9	----------	----------	----------	289,957	64,154	8,964	17,450	579,352	2,568
1936	[6]3,835,661	398,992	118,862	----------	[4]6	----------	----------	----------	[6]3,234,247	62,481	2,938	18,147	580,249	3,459
1935	605,686	374,407	123,297	----------	[4]9	----------	----------	----------	29,802	57,047	2,903	18,239	556,857	4,230
1934	540,991	321,377	124,494	----------	[4]7	----------	----------	----------	28,065	45,962	3,170	17,930	496,215	4,847
1933	827,825	550,559	145,426	----------	[4]16	----------	----------	----------	27,034	65,435	13,517	25,870	780,758	5,674
1932	835,357	545,777	146,397	----------	[4]17	----------	----------	----------	25,958	75,020	12,876	29,346	789,251	6,080
1931	752,816	488,389	137,325	----------	[4]22	----------	----------	----------	21,862	68,591	9,040	27,631	714,022	6,551
1930	675,788	418,433	139,212	----------	[4]20	----------	----------	----------	23,263	60,426	8,241	26,233	639,213	8,235
1929	665,342	418,821	135,704	----------	[4]3	----------	----------	----------	26,191	54,682	4,044	25,903	631,248	7,946
1928	652,712	410,765	131,277	----------	234	----------	----------	----------	27,189	53,121	5,222	24,904	625,144	7,158
1927	640,549	403,630	128,415	----------	2,206	----------	----------	----------	24,180	53,235	4,599	24,284	618,791	4,413
1926	649,143	372,281	142,507	----------	25,840	----------	----------	----------	20,927	53,113	4,511	29,964	628,271	4,350
1925	617,486	346,748	109,762	----------	60,486	----------	----------	----------	7,657	55,024	3,895	33,914	607,246	3,336
1924	652,101	345,490	106,036	----------	106,962	----------	----------	----------	17	48,422	9,215	35,959	647,283	2,685
1923	740,783	388,607	103,334	----------	149,433	----------	----------	----------	[4]264	59,262	2,644	37,767	737,000	2,785
1922	740,624	377,158	104,801	----------	166,051	----------	----------	----------	5,231	77,062	917	9,404	736,731	4,273
1921	664,538	380,026	96,961	----------	99,065	----------	----------	----------	23,831	53,128	----------	11,527	652,157	----------
1920	514,980	316,418	85,974	----------	34,652	----------	----------	----------	54,084	5,829	----------	18,023	494,183	----------
1919	701,131	233,461	43,798	----------	67	----------	----------	----------	400,589	5,512	----------	17,704	499,311	----------
1918	327,100	180,177	840	----------	----------	----------	----------	----------	134,806	6,920	----------	4,357	260,898	----------

See footnotes at end of table.

Series Y 984–997. Expenditures for Veterans Benefits and Services by Veterans Administration and Predecessor Agencies: 1790 to 1970—Con.

[In thousands of dollars. For years ending June 30]

Year	Total expenditure 984	Compensation and pensions 985	Medical, hospital, and domiciliary services 993	Administration and other benefits 995	Expenditures from general and special fund appropriations 996	Year or period	Total expenditure 984	Compensation and pensions 985	Medical, hospital, and domiciliary services 993	Administration and other benefits 995	Expenditures from general and special fund appropriations 996
1917	169,264	160,895	6,806	1,563	169,264	1890	112,647	106,094	3,027	3,526	112,647
1916	167,393	159,155	6,581	1,657	167,393	1889	95,066	88,843	2,756	3,467	95,066
1915	173,729	165,518	6,431	1,780	173,729	1888	84,512	78,951	2,046	3,515	84,512
1914	180,866	172,418	6,382	2,066	180,866	1887	79,451	73,753	1,945	3,753	79,451
1913	183,138	174,172	6,423	2,543	183,138	1886	68,931	64,091	1,595	3,245	68,931
1912	162,125	152,986	6,690	2,449	162,125						
1911	166,448	157,325	6,606	2,517	166,448	1885	70,196	65,172	1,631	3,393	70,196
						1884	62,184	57,912	1,437	2,835	62,184
1910	169,492	159,974	6,860	2,658	169,492	1883	64,361	60,428	1,341	2,592	64,361
1909	171,458	161,974	6,632	2,852	171,458	1882	56,882	54,313	1,103	1,466	56,882
1908	162,398	153,093	6,504	2,801	162,398	1881	52,771	50,583	1,116	1,072	52,771
1907	147,482	138,155	6,018	3,309	147,482						
1906	148,421	139,000	5,897	3,524	148,421	1880	58,585	56,689	961	935	58,585
						1879	35,526	33,664	1,024	838	35,526
1905	150,851	141,143	5,986	3,722	150,851	1878	28,764	26,786	945	1,033	28,764
1904	150,716	141,094	5,773	3,849	150,716	1877	30,145	28,183	928	1,034	30,145
1903	147,079	137,760	5,326	3,993	147,079	1876	29,887	27,936	936	1,015	29,887
1902	146,575	137,504	5,240	3,831	146,575						
1901	147,275	138,531	4,875	3,869	147,275	1875	31,106	29,270	853	983	31,106
						1874	31,908	30,207	734	967	31,908
1900	146,887	138,462	4,583	3,842	146,887	1873	28,681	26,982	695	1,004	28,681
1899	146,822	138,355	4,320	4,147	146,822	1872	31,454	29,753	750	951	31,454
1898	152,814	144,652	4,048	4,114	152,814	1871	30,081	28,519	699	863	30,081
1897	147,903	139,950	3,965	3,988	147,903						
1896	145,789	138,221	3,577	3,991	145,789	1870	30,543	29,351	591	601	30,543
						1869	29,658	28,513	580	565	29,658
1895	147,606	139,812	3,456	4,338	147,606	1868	24,164	23,102	509	553	24,164
1894	147,408	139,987	3,457	3,964	147,408	1867	21,276	20,785	_____	491	21,276
1893	165,315	156,907	3,540	4,868	165,315	1866	15,858	15,451	_____	407	15,858
1892	147,784	139,394	3,491	4,899	147,784						
1891	125,351	117,313	3,338	4,700	125,351	1790–1865	96,445	96,445	_____	_____	96,445

Z Less than $500.
[1] Largely includes payments from trust accounts.
[2] Detail does not add to total because of adjustments for overpayments collected and items written off as uncollectible under the readjustment benefits program.

[3] Data for 1970 are on an accrued expenditures basis. Prior year data based on nonaccrual basis.
[4] Credit.
[5] Includes adjustments for prior years; see text.
[6] Includes total payments to veterans and beneficiaries on adjusted service certificates.

Series Y 998–1009. Veterans Pensions and Compensation—Number of Veterans and Expenditure, by Type: 1866 to 1970

[For years ending June 30]

Year	Number of veterans[1] (1,000)						Expenditure (mil. dol.)					
	Total		Pensions		Compensation		Total		Pensions		Compensation	
	Death 998	Disability 999	Death 1000	Disability 1001	Death 1002	Disability 1003	Death 1004	Disability 1005	Death 1006	Disability 1007	Death 1008	Disability 1009
1970	1,541	3,181	1,169	1,089	372	2,092	1,502	3,752	907	1,357	595	2,395
1969	1,497	3,160	1,125	1,120	372	2,040	1,385	3,466	849	1,318	536	2,148
1968	1,443	3,164	1,075	1,152	368	2,012	1,296	3,228	779	1,272	517	1,956
1967	1,388	3,182	1,025	1,182	363	2,000	1,210	3,183	713	1,263	497	1,920
1966	1,339	3,201	974	1,207	365	1,994	1,172	3,133	689	1,300	483	1,833
1965	1,294	3,217	929	1,224	365	1,993	1,111	2,931	640	1,224	471	1,707
1964	1,239	3,197	872	1,203	367	1,994	1,047	2,853	585	1,155	462	1,698
1963	1,183	3,181	810	1,191	373	1,990	995	2,820	547	1,151	448	1,669
1962	1,122	3,150	745	1,162	377	1,988	965	2,688	510	1,124	455	1,564
1961	1,067	3,107	683	1,106	384	2,001	926	2,642	461	1,072	465	1,570
1960	951	3,009	559	981	392	2,028	824	2,491	354	911	470	1,580
1959	916	2,934	528	880	388	2,054	811	2,414	339	815	472	1,599
1958	884	2,850	497	785	387	2,065	776	2,286	309	729	467	1,557
1957	863	2,797	478	720	385	2,076	729	2,100	295	657	434	1,443
1956	837	2,739	454	654	383	2,085	694	2,055	281	604	413	1,451
1955	808	2,669	426	832	382	1,837	664	1,970	265	538	400	1,432
1954	778	2,590	403	533	375	2,057	612	1,838	243	475	369	1,364
1953	748	2,506	379	485	369	2,021	608	1,768	231	431	377	1,337
1952	707	2,418	353	437	353	1,981	538	1,568	195	364	343	1,204
1951	683	2,374	339	394	343	1,980	501	1,535	190	330	311	1,205

See footnotes at end of table.

Series Y 998–1009. Veterans Pensions and Compensation—Number of Veterans and Expenditure, by Type: 1866 to 1970—Con.

[For years ending June 30]

Year	Number of veterans [1] (1,000)						Expenditure (mil. dol.)					
	Total		Pensions		Compensation		Total		Pensions		Compensation	
	Death	Disability	Death	Disability	Death	Disability	Death	Disability	Death	Disability	Death	Disability
	998	999	1000	1001	1002	1003	1004	1005	1006	1007	1008	1009
1950	658	2,368	322	345	336	2,023	485	1,524	181	295	304	1,229
1949	636	2,314	302	290	334	2,024	457	1,434	171	253	286	1,181
1948	603	2,315	279	249	324	2,066	385	1,436	152	234	233	1,201
1947	566	2,354	253	233	314	2,121	367	1,365	138	194	229	1,171
1946	502	2,130	227	219	275	1,911	305	910	108	167	198	744
1945	369	1,144	177	220	193	924	185	547	69	166	116	381
1944	253	813	124	221	129	593	126	368	50	80	76	288
1943	239	622	127	227	112	395	113	330	52	139	61	190
1942	236	624	129	231	107	392	111	320	53	132	58	188
1941	238	619	130	229	108	390	113	320	54	132	59	188
1940	239	610	130	224	110	386	115	314	55	130	60	184
1939	240	603	130	225	109	378	109	308	55	129	54	179
1938	236	601	132	225	104	375	101	301	56	126	45	176
1937	243	599	136	227	107	371	96	300	60	121	37	179
1936	251	601	144	230	107	371	100	299	63	119	37	180
1935	253	586	146	215	107	371	96	278	61	96	35	182
1934	258	581	153	218	105	363	94	228	59	80	34	148
1933	273	998	169	636	103	362	122	428	85	228	37	200
1932	284	994	182	641	102	354	124	421	87	215	38	206
1931	289	791	192	468	97	323	124	365	91	168	32	197
1930	298	543	203	241	95	301	128	290	94	120	34	170
1929	306	526	215	245	91	281	132	287	100	126	32	162
1928	318	517	229	245	89	271	124	287	92	132	32	154
1927	327	490	240	233	86	257	126	278	96	131	30	147
1926	334	473	252	233	83	240	125	247	93	111	32	136
1925	334	457	264	232	70	224	124	223	97	117	26	107
1924	335	427	274	236	62	191	122	223	102	125	20	99
1923	341	437	282	241	59	196	133	256	113	146	20	110
1922	341	431	286	244	55	187	124	253	106	144	17	109
1921	346	423	294	254	52	169	127	253	108	147	19	106
1920	350	420	302	271	47	149	115	201	93	117	22	85
1919	336	338	307	299	29	40	101	133	95	124	6	9
1918	308	342	302	325	6	16	81	99	80	97	1	3
1917	303	370	298	354	5	16	55	106	54	103	1	3
1916	306	403	302	388	5	16	46	113	45	110	1	3
1915	310	438	306	422	4	15	47	119	46	116	1	3
1914	315	471	310	456	4	15	47	125	46	123	1	3
1913	317	504	312	489	4	15	47	127	46	124	1	3
1912	322	538	318	524	4	14	48	105	47	103	1	2
1911	322	570	317	557	4	14	48	109	47	107	1	2
1910	318	603	314	589	4	13	48	112	47	110	1	2
1909	314	633	310	620	4	12	47	115	46	113	1	2
1908	293	659	289	647	4	12	35	118	34	116	1	2
1907	287	680	283	669	4	11	35	104	34	102	1	2
1906	284	701	281	691	4	11	35	104	34	103	1	2
1905	281	718	277	708	3	10	35	106	34	104	1	2
1904	274	721	271	711	3	10	35	106	34	104	1	2

Year	Number of veterans [1] (1,000)		Expenditure (mil. dol.)		Year	Number of veterans [1] (1,000)	Expenditure (mil. dol.)	Year	Number of veterans [1] (1,000)	Expenditure (mil. dol.)
	Death	Disability	Death	Disability						
	998	999	1004	1005		998–999	1004–1005		998–999	1004–1005
1903	267	729	34	104	1890	538	106	1877	232	28
1902	260	739	33	104	1889	490	89	1876	232	28
1901	249	749	32	106	1888	453	79			
					1887	406	74	1875	235	29
1900	241	753	31	107	1886	366	64	1874	236	30
1899	237	754	32	107				1873	238	27
1898	235	759	35	110	1885	345	65	1872	232	30
1897	229	747	34	106	1884	323	58	1871	207	29
1896	222	749	32	106	1883	304	60			
					1882	286	54	1870	199	29
1895	219	751	32	108	1881	269	51	1869	188	29
1894	215	754	33	107				1868	170	23
1893	206	760	37	120	1880	251	57	1867	155	21
1892	173	703	31	109	1879	243	34	1866	127	15
1891	139	537	31	86	1878	224	27			

[1] Series Y 998, Y 1000, and Y 1002 represent the number of deceased veterans whose dependents were receiving pension or compensation. Series Y 999, Y 1001, and Y 1003 represent the number of living veterans who were receiving pension, compensation, disability allowance, or retirement pay.

Series Y 1010–1027. Patients Receiving Hospital or Domiciliary Care Authorized by Veterans Administration: 1921 to 1970

[Includes beneficiaries admitted and cared for in Army, Navy, other Federal, State, and civil (contract) hospitals. Patients receiving hospital care: 1921–54 as of June 30; 1955–62 as of May 31; 1963–70 as of census date]

Year	Patients admitted to hospitals			Patients receiving hospital care [1]					
					Veterans				Non-veterans
	Total	Neuro-psychiatric	General	Total	Total	Tuber-culosis	Neuro-psychiatric	General	
	1010	1011	1012	1013	1014	1015	1016	1017	1018
1970	711,289	102,919	608,370	88,870	88,174	2,433	50,735	35,006	696
1969	689,459	92,809	596,650	92,185	91,720	2,800	56,565	32,355	465
1968	670,600	86,316	584,284	99,970	99,325	3,420	62,840	33,065	645
1967	654,474	79,724	574,750	106,930	106,535	3,915	67,490	35,130	395
1966	641,469	71,288	570,181	109,338	109,178	4,340	68,020	36,818	160
1965	627,993	63,506	564,487	112,345	112,040	5,075	67,780	39,185	305
1964	634,308	61,152	563,156	112,715	112,275	5,950	67,760	38,565	440
1963	610,887	56,336	554,551	112,500	111,975	5,970	68,115	37,890	525
1962	589,975	54,246	535,729	111,302	110,941	7,180	61,742	42,019	361
1961	565,654	50,513	515,141	112,749	112,448	8,052	62,247	42,149	301
1960	539,243	64,927	474,316	113,246	112,919	8,665	62,325	41,929	327
1959	521,428	61,370	460,058	111,380	111,052	9,871	61,953	39,228	328
1958	512,754	59,283	453,471	110,721	110,278	10,678	61,638	37,962	443
1957	510,855	58,815	452,040	110,715	110,247	12,224	61,550	36,473	468
1956	517,455	60,186	457,269	112,660	112,131	13,595	61,703	36,833	529
1955	498,187	54,235	443,952	110,257	109,649	14,836	59,349	35,464	608
1954	477,915	(NA)	(NA)	108,357	107,509	[4] 15,636	[4] 54,916	[4] 36,957	848
1953	468,349	60,776	407,573	102,323	101,470	[4] 15,292	[4] 52,559	[4] 33,619	853
1952	495,056	47,116	447,940	103,774	102,974	15,362	53,053	34,042	800
1951	509,720	44,389	465,331	100,517	99,800	14,825	52,987	31,988	717
1950	577,715	48,200	529,515	102,303	101,862	14,361	54,419	33,082	441
1949	554,863	50,708	504,155	107,073	106,685	14,810	55,150	36,725	388
1948	534,723	55,869	478,854	103,576	103,263	13,045	54,790	35,428	313
1947	532,881	61,924	470,957	104,443	104,176	12,436	53,913	37,827	267
1946	349,092	53,136	295,956	87,257	86,998	8,475	48,687	29,836	259
1945	243,994	45,654	198,340	70,246	69,965	6,864	44,078	19,023	281
1944	197,858	34,464	163,394	63,890	63,581	6,314	40,076	17,191	309
1943	167,428	22,845	144,583	56,850	56,597	5,149	36,345	15,103	253
1942	182,158	24,480	157,678	56,103	55,847	5,090	34,596	16,161	256
1941	191,745	24,040	167,705	58,241	57,988	4,758	34,257	18,973	253
1940	182,136	24,315	157,821	56,450	56,216	4,848	32,882	18,486	234
1939	168,237	22,694	145,543	53,745	53,472	5,041	31,080	17,351	273
1938	154,361	23,471	130,890	50,640	50,385	5,062	29,299	16,024	255
1937	144,861	22,292	122,569	46,235	45,935	4,987	26,246	14,702	300
1936	125,224	19,063	106,161	41,251	40,899	4,553	24,025	12,321	352
1935	114,160	17,429	96,731	41,728	41,316	5,283	22,781	13,252	412
1934	63,900	12,536	51,364	38,733	38,026	5,283	21,475	11,268	707
1933	137,910	20,408	117,502	33,844	33,518	5,804	19,791	7,923	326
1932	148,662	21,556	127,106	43,469	43,334	6,985	19,528	16,821	135
1931	109,649	16,665	92,984	35,145	35,055	6,560	16,936	11,559	90
1930	92,115	13,523	78,592	30,556	30,447	6,733	15,035	8,679	109
1929	83,188	12,796	70,392	27,897	27,784	6,547	13,781	7,456	113
1928	73,270	11,454	61,816	26,257	26,139	6,542	13,057	6,540	118
1927	71,967	11,499	60,468	25,440	25,318	6,956	12,748	5,614	122
1926	69,441	12,489	56,952	25,965	25,858	7,863	12,902	5,093	107
1925	76,812	15,216	61,596	27,218	27,071	9,792	12,224	5,055	147
1924	64,053	12,119	51,934	22,978	22,726	8,831	9,875	4,020	252
1923	82,814	14,095	68,719	23,805	23,604	9,886	9,403	4,315	201
1922	134,354	----------	----------	27,240	26,869	10,849	9,231	6,789	371
1921	91,440	----------	----------	26,237	26,237	10,337	7,499	8,401	----------

Year	Veterans with service-connected disabilities receiving hospital care [1]				Veterans receiving domiciliary care [2]			Operating expenses of VA hospitals (mil. dol.)	Per diem cost in VA hospitals (dol.)
	Total	Tuber-culosis	Neuro-psychiatric	General	Total	Veterans Administration	State homes [3]		
	1019	1020	1021	1022	1023	1024	1025	1026	1027
1970	22,215	262	17,353	4,600	18,680	11,998	6,682	1,278.8	38.42
1969	23,240	345	19,715	3,180	19,552	12,412	7,140	1,145.4	34.16
1968	25,865	385	22,510	2,970	20,058	12,592	7,466	1,088.6	30.53
1967	28,455	530	24,885	3,040	20,382	12,694	7,688	1,034.4	27.41
1966	31,131	541	26,930	3,660	21,319	13,091	8,228	976.1	24.90
1965	32,130	635	27,775	3,720	23,526	14,380	9,146	946.4	23.75
1964	32,965	810	28,455	3,700	24,575	15,229	9,346	904.5	22.43
1963	34,635	865	30,075	3,695	25,173	16,012	9,161	873.3	21.56
1962	33,756	1,155	29,040	3,561	25,435	16,373	9,062	858.3	20.87
1961	34,998	1,357	30,108	3,533	26,197	16,812	9,385	822.5	19.93
1960	36,149	1,610	30,910	3,629	26,274	16,856	9,418	763.0	18.44
1959	37,136	2,013	31,182	3,941	26,518	16,840	9,678	732.6	17.82
1958	37,727	2,405	31,774	3,548	25,991	16,673	9,318	676.2	16.81
1957	39,063	3,138	32,083	3,842	25,846	16,908	8,938	617.7	15.45
1956	40,195	3,769	32,536	3,890	25,786	17,047	8,739	602.9	15.22

See footnotes at end of table.

Series Y 1010–1027. Patients Receiving Hospital or Domiciliary Care Authorized by Veterans Administration: 1921 to 1970—Con.

[Includes beneficiaries admitted and cared for in Army, Navy, other Federal, State, and civil (contract) hospitals. Patients receiving hospital care: 1921–54 as of June 30; 1955–62 as of May 31: 1963–70 as of census date]

Year	Veterans with service-connected disabilities receiving hospital care [1]				Veterans receiving domiciliary care [2]			Operating expenses of VA hospitals (mil. dol.)	Per diem cost in VA hospitals (dol.)
	Total	Tuber-culosis	Neuro-psychi-atric	General	Total	Veterans Adminis-tration	State homes [3]		
	1019	1020	1021	1022	1023	1024	1025	1026	1027
1955	41,078	4,576	32,312	4,190	25,774	16,972	8,802	542.2	13.93
1954	40,711	[4] 5,150	[4] 30,106	[4] 5,455	25,291	16,945	8,346	530.6	14.05
1953	39,092	[4] 5,638	[4] 28,502	[4] 4,952	25,035	16,919	8,116	486.2	13.61
1952	36,182	5,917	26,564	3,701	24,792	16,892	7,900	474.9	13.24
1951	35,597	6,253	25,397	3,947	24,564	16,790	7,774	409.8	11.66
1950	34,596	5,323	25,347	3,926	24,307	16,870	7,437	384.6	10.90
1949	35,919	6,242	24,755	4,922	22,000	15,288	6,712	353.4	10.24
1948	34,872	6,158	23,478	5,236	20,552	14,402	6,150	307.7	9.05
1947	35,525	6,408	22,854	6,263	18,637	13,113	5,524	271.1	8.67
1946	28,806	3,921	20,282	4,603	15,190	10,547	4,643	136.2	5.22
1945	23,375	3,219	18,072	2,084	13,161	9,002	4,159	80.3	3.42
1944	18,476	2,398	14,608	1,470	13,852	9,447	4,405	72.1	3.38
1943	14,580	1,491	12,312	777	15,328	10,430	4,898	65.7	3.37
1942	13,324	1,185	11,393	746	20,101	14,371	5,730	59.1	2.96
1941	12,825	849	11,098	878	22,662	16,696	5,966	55.4	2.78
1940	12,670	873	10,826	971	22,926	16,708	6,218	49.9	2.60
1939	12,534	1,013	10,383	1,138	21,687	15,709	5,978	48.0	2.68
1938	12,394	1,045	10,209	1,140	19,136	13,514	5,622	44.2	2.65
1937	12,182	1,133	9,956	1,093	15,296	10,364	4,932	43.3	2.81
1936	11,906	1,123	9,818	965	16,741	12,008	4,733	42.4	2.82
1935	12,168	1,340	9,669	1,159	14,566	10,406	4,160	39.9	2.78
1934	11,451	1,145	9,241	1,065				32.6	2.51
1933	13,925	1,574	11,056	1,295				33.4	2.99
1932	15,199	1,991	11,414	1,794				32.0	3.44
1931	15,773	2,616	11,342	1,815				30.4	3.72
1930	16,418	3,278	11,170	1,970				28.5	3.86
1929	16,024	3,399	10,777	1,848				28.2	4.01
1928	16,597	3,802	10,809	1,986				26.1	4.00
1927	18,087	4,818	10,988	2,281				25.3	4.00
1926	20,811	6,576	11,438	2,797				25.3	4.19
1925	23,266	8,848	11,038	3,380				23.4	4.04
1924	22,726	8,831	9,875	4,020				19.2	4.55
1923	23,604	9,886	9,403	4,315				21.7	4.99
1922	26,869	10,849	9,231	6,789				23.5	4.74
1921	26,237	10,337	7,499	8,401					

NA Not available.
[1] From 1962–1970, type of care based on 20-percent sample of annual patient census.
[2] Average daily member load.
[3] Average daily number for fiscal year.
[4] Estimated.

Series Y 1028–1031. Government Life Insurance Administered by Veterans Administration—Number of Policies, Income Received, and Benefits Paid: 1921 to 1970

[As of June 30]

Year	Policies in force		Income received	Benefits paid	Year	Policies in force		Income received	Benefits paid
	Number	Face value				Number	Face value		
	1028	1029	1030	1031		1028	1029	1030	1031
		1,000 dol.	1,000 dol.	1,000 dol.			1,000 dol.	1,000 dol.	1,000 dol.
1970	5,540,553	37,743,432	1,046,184	930,053	1945	16,512,099	126,034,439	2,412,815	287,219
1969	5,623,206	38,201,658	1,033,429	870,809	1944	15,068,150	110,707,707	1,263,124	124,864
1968	5,713,489	38,716,495	993,151	850,941	1943	9,394,598	63,304,655	693,624	76,414
1967	5,817,697	39,314,131	1,030,385	885,118	1942	3,217,499	16,986,809	263,188	66,176
1966	5,879,886	39,574,793	956,582	783,573	1941	972,860	3,847,972	121,498	71,816
1965	5,823,981	39,102,968	932,567	767,035	1940	609,094	2,565,327	116,159	91,989
1964	5,885,857	39,469,983	930,156	809,444	1939	606,071	2,562,354	130,808	97,397
1963	5,935,798	39,655,027	967,993	903,286	1938	602,963	2,569,893	159,772	99,481
1962	5,999,125	40,051,309	907,923	853,299	1937	596,982	2,578,339	185,251	120,396
1961	6,214,879	41,659,027	954,856	1,032,072	1936	593,213	2,590,922	193,146	123,785
1960	6,319,847	42,382,403	896,437	791,640	1935	590,865	2,605,400	193,617	130,670
1959	6,401,240	42,973,665	881,990	759,440	1934	598,266	2,666,733	196,844	141,810
1958	6,485,256	43,624,978	810,392	720,567	1933	616,069	2,782,709	208,826	149,112
1957	6,565,985	44,202,158	776,705	656,207	1932	641,247	2,977,330	216,342	158,712
1956	6,442,956	42,890,932	758,047	649,903	1931	646,055	3,024,445	210,865	148,982
1955	6,449,437	42,623,425	810,683	662,750	1930	648,248	3,042,743	208,080	142,870
1954	6,530,816	42,802,077	784,615	755,058	1929	650,066	3,059,919	206,157	141,523
1953	7,003,942	46,706,290	797,789	804,819	1928	660,374	3,113,649	204,143	136,978
1952	7,538,729	50,837,910	838,360	822,818	1927	587,980	2,893,045	196,352	130,536
1951	7,625,694	51,559,594	896,129	1,026,661	1926	553,660	2,781,587	185,682	136,784
1950	6,113,308	37,972,928	814,455	3,144,507	1925	552,340	2,865,029	167,735	127,005
1949	6,038,865	37,952,323	1,128,508	450,525	1924	562,000	2,984,573	142,936	109,103
1948	6,291,263	38,065,025	783,577	376,281	1923	560,065	3,070,210	137,521	105,218
1947	6,380,103	37,535,634	1,347,322	383,374	1922	581,778	3,348,400	131,865	104,363
1946	9,814,873	67,514,994	2,280,700	369,715	1921	651,054	3,849,376	115,109	101,410

Colonial and Pre-Federal Statistics

Z 1–615.   General note.

It would have been possible to distribute these series for the colonial and pre-Federal period among the chapters covering each of the appropriate subject fields.   It was felt, however, that a separate chapter especially organized to cover this period would be more valuable in itself and would also provide a more suitable, less-exacting context for the statistics, many of which are relatively roughhewn.

In the past, statistics for the colonial and pre-Federal period were largely dependent on compilations made during the 17th and 18th centuries by historians such as Whitworth and Macpherson.   Present-day scholars, however, no longer rely solely upon such compilations.   They are ferreting out statistical information from original records hitherto left unused in archives and reconstructing statistical series of their own from other sources.   Several of the series presented here are appearing in print for the first time.   Compilers of the new series are identified in the source citations.

The Public Records Office in London (sometimes hereafter abbreviated PRO) contains many collections of records which throw light on commerce between England and the colonies and to some extent on the development of agriculture and manufacturing in the colonies, particularly when considered with reference to the mercantilist laws passed by the mother country, as has been done here.   The laws in question are cited at various points in the text below by reference to their regnal year and chapter numbers—for example, 5 Geo. II c 22 (the fifth year of the reign of King George II, chapter 22).

The collections in the Public Records Office in London, which are the original sources for many of the data presented here, are identified there by title and call numbers.   For example, one collection is titled "American Inspector General's Ledgers" and is further identified as "PRO Customs 16/1."   The most important of these collections or ledgers of imports and exports are the following: The English Inspector General's Ledgers (PRO Customs 3); the Scottish Inspector General's Ledgers (PRO Customs 14); the American Inspector General's Ledgers (PRO Customs 16/1); and the colonial naval office lists (usually found in C. O. 5).

The English, Scottish, and American Inspector Generals' Ledgers are conveniently arranged for statistical purposes, but are so voluminous that it is far more convenient to utilize contemporary tabulations drawn from them when such secondary sources are available.   The lists kept by the naval officers of that period (for the purpose of helping to enforce the navigation laws) merely provide chronological data concerning the ships which entered and cleared port, together with their cargoes and destinations.

The task of using the naval office lists has in some instances been lightened by colonial newspapers, such as the *South Carolina Gazette*, which published data taken from customhouse records.   Also of general assistance in the preparation of many series presented in this chapter are the compilations from naval office lists prepared by a Works Progress Administration project conducted at the University of California, entitled "Trade and Commerce of the English Colonies in America," and referred to below as WPA compilations.

Z 1–19.   Estimated population of American Colonies, 1610–1780.

Source: Compiled by Stella H. Sutherland, Due West, South Carolina, chiefly from the following sources: B. J. Brawley, *A Short History of the American Negro*, MacMillan, 1913; Elizabeth Donnan (editor), *Documents Illustrative of the History of the Slave Trade to America*, 4 vols., Carnegie Institution of Washington, D.C., 1930–35; Evarts B.

Greene and Virginia D. Harrington, *American Population Before the Federal Census of 1790*, Columbia University Press, New York, 1932; Stella H. Sutherland, *Population Distribution in Colonial America*, AMS Press, Inc., New York, 1966; E. R. Turner, "The Negro in Pennsylvania," *Prize Essays of the American Historical Association*, Washington, D.C., 1911; Bureau of the Census, *A Century of Population Growth*, 1909; Thomas J. Wertenbaker, *The Planters of Colonial Virginia*, Princeton, 1922; and George W. Williams, *The History of the Negro Race in America From 1619 to 1880*, 2 vols., New York, 1883.   (Also, a wide variety of source material was consulted for general information.)

The original data were obtained from the reports of the colonial officials to the Lords Commissioners of Trade and Plantations.   Not infrequently a census supplied sworn evidence of the number of inhabitants; for other reports, the militia or the tax lists or both were used, commonly accompanied by an estimate of the whole population as indicated by the rolls or lists.   Estimates made by colonial officials and by other informed contemporaries who did not disclose the figures upon which their conclusions were based have occasionally been included in these series.   However, such estimates were selected in accordance with the general pattern of population growth.

The ratio of the militia to the whole population was generally 1 to 5⅓, but there were many exceptions.   In Massachusetts, it was 1 to 6 in 1751 and 1 to 4 in 1763; in Connecticut, 1 to 6 in 1722 and 1756 and 1 to 7 in 1749, 1761, and 1774; it was 1 to 6 in Virginia and 1 to 7 in South Carolina at various times.   No generalization can safely be made as to the ratio borne by the northern polls and ratables and by the southern taxables and tithables to the whole population of the Colonies.   In every Province the figure was different.   In the North, it ranged from 1 to 4 to 1 to 5½; in Pennsylvania, it was 1 to 7 in the 1750's, but 1 to 5.8 was the more common figure; in Maryland and Virginia, where both male and female slaves appeared on the tax lists, the ratio was 1 to 3 or 3.5 in the 17th century and 1 to 2.4 or 2.6 in the 18th century.   The North Carolina white taxables were multiplied by 4 and the Negro taxables by 2.

The figures for Negroes for the 17th century, which are doubtlessly too low, are largely estimates based upon references to purchase and sale, to laws governing slavery, and occasionally to reports of more or less exact numbers.

Z 20–23.   Percent distribution of the white population, by nationality, 1790.

Source: American Council of Learned Societies, "Report of Committee on Linguistic and National Stocks in the Population of the United States" (based on studies by Howard F. Barker and Marcus L. Hansen), *Annual Report of the American Historical Association, 1931*, vol. I, Washington, D.C., 1932, p. 124.

Distribution was made primarily on the basis of family names.   For explanation of methods used, see source.

Z 24–132.   Population censuses taken in the colonies and States during the colonial and pre-Federal period, 1624-25 to 1786.

Source: Compiled by Robert C. Klove, U.S. Bureau of the Census, with the counsel of Stella Sutherland, chiefly from the following sources: Evarts B. Greene and Virginia D. Harrington, *American Population Before the Federal Census of 1790*, Columbia University Press, New York, 1932 (reprinted by Peter Smith, Gloucester, Mass., 1966) and W. S. Rossiter, *A Century of Population Growth, From the*

First Census of the United States to the Twelfth: 1790–1900, U.S. Bureau of the Census, 1909.

The original data were obtained as follows:

Z 24–37, Connecticut.

1756 *Connecticut Colony Public Records*, XIV, p. 492. Rossiter has made corrections, p. 164. Greene and Harrington give the same figures as Rossiter, pp. 58–61.

1774 *Ibid.*, pp. 485–491. From Rossiter, pp. 166–169. Rossiter has made some corrections in addition from the original records. Greene and Harrington use the same source and give approximately the same figures but do not give as much detail, pp. 58–61.

1782 Jedidiah Morse, *American Geography*, Boston, 1792, pp. 217–218. From Greene and Harrington, p. 61.

Delaware.

	Total	White	Negro
1782	44,095	41,195	2,900

From unpublished manuscripts in the State House in Dover, Delaware, examined by Stella Sutherland. Only the census totals for Kent County (9,782) and Sussex County (12,660) are available. Newcastle County is missing, but Sutherland has estimated a total for Newcastle (21,153) which is included in the State total. She also made separate estimates for white and Negro.

Z 38–49, Maine.

1764–65 Josiah H. Benton, Jr., *Early Census Making in Massachusetts, 1643 to 1765*, Boston, 1905. With addition corrections by Rossiter, p. 162. Benton used the Crane MS (manuscript) for Massachusetts and Maine which was discovered about 1900. Greene and Harrington also preferred the Crane MS as published by Benton (see footnote a, pp. 21–22). Rossiter's figures are used in this table because they give more detail. The earlier Dana MS was published in Joseph B. Felt, "Statistics of the Population in Massachusetts" (in *American Statistical Association Collections*, I, 121–216), Boston, 1897. Felt does not include Negro and other persons and the total population is slightly less.

William D. Williamson, in *The History of the State of Maine, 1602–1820*, Hallowell, 1839, gives population for the three counties in Maine on p. 373 and also estimates for the plantations which were omitted in the enumeration. His source is the *Columbian Centinel* published in 1822 which, according to Greene and Harrington, was based on the Dana MS. His total is considerably larger and does indicate that the Dana MS included Negroes.

Z 50–62, Maryland.

1704 *Maryland Archives*, XXV, p. 256. From Greene and Harrington, p. 129.

1710 *Ibid.*, pp. 258–259. From Greene and Harrington, p. 129.

1712 *Ibid.*, p. 259. From Greene and Harrington, p. 129.

1755 *Gentleman's Magazine*, vol. XXXIV, p. 261. With corrections by Rossiter, p. 185. Rossiter gives more detail than Greene and Harrington, pp. 125–126, but the latter have some figures that vary considerably from those given by Rossiter. The total population is only 60 more. Greene and Harrington take their figures from a different source, *Maryland Records Miscellaneous*, 1755–75, 11 in Force, Transcripts (copied from Ezra Stiles' MS) in Library of Congress Transcripts.

1782 Jedidiah Morse, *American Geography*, Boston, 1792, p. 350. Also in Greene and Harrington, p. 127. Morse gives a partial breakdown of the totals and indicates that this census was taken by several assessors in March 1782.

Z 63–77, Massachusetts.

1764–65 See source for Maine, 1764–65. (Addition corrections by Rossiter, p. 161.)

1776 Jesse Chickering, *Statistical View of the Population of Massachusetts, 1765–1840*, Boston, 1846, p. 9. From Greene and Harrington, p. 17.

1784 Jedidiah Morse, *American Geography*, Boston, 1792, p. 172. From Greene and Harrington, p. 46.

Z 78–90, New Hampshire.

1767 *Provincial Papers of New Hampshire*, vol. VII, pp. 168–170. With corrections by Rossiter, pp. 149–150.

1773 *Ibid.*, vol. X, pp. 625–636. With corrections by Rossiter, p. 150.

1775 *New Hampshire Historical Society Collections*, vol. I, pp. 231–235. From Rossiter, pp. 152–154. Rossiter did not total the figures, which are given by towns. He indicated that the census was incomplete, with data for several towns not reported. The town figures in Greene and Harrington (pp. 74–79), which are town totals only, differ in a few instances from those given by Rossiter.

1786 *Provincial Papers of New Hampshire*, vol. X, pp. 637–689. With correction by Rossiter, p. 156, and Greene and Harrington, p. 74. Many towns did not distinguish whites, Negroes, and others.

Z 91–97, New Jersey.

1726 *New Jersey Archives*, 1st Series, V, p. 164. With corrections by Rossiter, p. 184, and Greene and Harrington, p. 109.

1738 *New Jersey Archives*, 1st Series, VI, pp. 242–243. With corrections by Rossiter, p. 184, and Greene and Harrington, p. 110. Both report Negroes as "Negroes and Other and Slaves."

1745 *New Jersey Archives*, 1st Series, VI, pp. 242–243. With corrections by Rossiter, p. 184, and Greene and Harrington, p. 111. Both report Negroes as "Slaves."

1772 *New Jersey Archives*, 1st Series, X, pp. 452–453. From Stella H. Sutherland, *Population Distribution in Colonial America*, Columbia University Press, New York, 1936; reprinted AMS Press, Inc., New York, 1966, pp. 98–99. Separate figures for whites and Negroes available for only 8 counties.

1784 New Jersey Department of State: *Compendium of Censuses, 1726–1905*, Trenton, 1906, p. 41; and Jedidiah Morse, *American Geography*, Boston, 1792, p. 284.

Z 98–104, New York.

1698 F. B. Hough, *Census of the State of New York, 1855*, iv.; also *Calendar of State Papers, Colonial Series: America and West Indies, 1697–98*, 532, 978, vi. From Rossiter, p. 170, and Greene and Harrington, p. 92.

1703 *Ibid.*, iv. From Rossiter, p. 170, and Greene and Harrington, p. 95.

1712–14 *New York Colonial MS*, vol. LVII, Secretary's office. From Rossiter, p. 181.

1723 *New York Documentary History* (ed. E. B. O'Callaghan), Albany, 1849–51, vol. I, p. 693. From Rossiter, p. 181, and Greene and Harrington, p. 96.

1731 *Ibid.*, vol. I, p. 694. With corrections, Rossiter, p. 181, and Greene and Harrington, p. 97.

1737 *Ibid.*, vol. I, p. 694. With corrections by Rossiter, p. 182, and Greene and Harrington, p. 98.

1746 *Ibid.*, vol. I, p. 695, not including Albany County. From Rossiter, p. 182, and Greene and Harrington, p. 99.

1749 *Ibid.*, vol. I, p. 695. With corrections by Greene and Harrington, p. 100.

1756 *Ibid.*, vol. I, p. 696. With corrections by Greene and Harrington, p. 101.

1771 *Ibid.*, vol. I, p. 697. With corrections by Rossiter, p. 183, and Greene and Harrington, p. 102.

1786 F. B. Hough, *Census of the State of New York, 1855*, viii. From Rossiter, p. 183, and Greene and Harrington, p. 104.

Z 105–113, Rhode Island.

1708 *Rhode Island Colonial Records*, vol. IV, p. 59. With correction from Rossiter, p. 162, and Greene and Harrington, p. 65.

1730 Census in "R. I. State Papers" in *Massachusetts Historical Society Collections*, 2d Series, VII, p. 113. From Greene and Harrington, p. 66.

1748 See source for 1730. From Greene and Harrington, p. 63.

1755 "Acct. of the People in the Colony of R. I." with Governor Hopkin's letter, Dec. 24, 1755, *Proprieties V:* 159 (iv), in *Historical Society of Pennsylvania Transcripts.* From Greene and Harrington, p. 67.

1774 John R. Bartlett, *Census of Rhode Island for 1774*, Providence, 1858, p. 239. With corrections from Rossiter, p. 162.

1783 *Rhode Island Colonial Records*, VII, p. 299. With corrections from Greene and Harrington, pp. 69–70.

Z 114–120, Vermont.

1771 *London Documents*, xliv, p. 144; *New York Documentary History* (ed. E. B. O'Callaghan), Albany, 1849–51, p. 474; F. B. Hough, *Census of the State of New York*, 1955, vii. From Rossiter, p. 183, and Greene and Harrington, p. 102.

Z 121–132, Virginia.

1624–25 *Virginia Magazine of History and Biography* (Virginia Historical Society), VII, pp. 364–367; Alexander Brown, *First Republic in America*, Boston and New York, 1898, pp. 617–627. From Greene and Harrington, p. 144. Irene W. D. Hecht in "The Virginia Muster of 1624/5 as a source for Demographic History," *William and Mary Quarterly*, Third Series, vol. XXX, No. 1, January 1973, gives the total population as 1,218 and other details.

1634 *Virginia Colonial Records*, p. 91. "After this list was brought in there arrived a Ship of Holland with 145 persons from Bermudas; and since that 60 more in an English ship from Bermudas also." George Chalmers, *Coll. Va.*, I, p. 18, New York Public Library. From Greene and Harrington, p. 145.

1699 *Colonial Office Papers*, 5:1312, No. 19, XI in Library of Congress Transcripts; *Calendar of State Papers, Colonial Series: America and West Indies*, 1701, 635, No. 1040, XI. From Greene and Harrington, p. 137.

1701 *Colonial Office Papers* 5:1312, No. 19, X. From Greene and Harrington, p. 147–148.

Z 133–168. General note.

The two basic sources for the study of the colonial Negro are population statistics (see series Z 1–19 and Z 21–132) and commercial statistics concerning slave importations. Although direct knowledge of the colonial Negro's natural increase is scarce, available evidence indicates that this increase must have been considerable. It is reported in 1708 that about half of Boston's 400 Negro servants were born there, and Governor James Glen of South Carolina stated in 1749 that the number of Negroes in his colony increased rather than diminished during the nine years when prohibitive taxes and war "prevented any from being imported" (Elizabeth Donnan, ed., *Documents Illustrative of the History of the Slave Trade to America*, Carnegie Institution of Washington, D.C., 1935, vols. III and IV, pp. 24 and 303, respectively). Otherwise, discrepancies between import and population figures (especially in later years) would call for the existence of an illegal trade in Negroes of an extent to which other evidence gives little support.

Donnan's *Documents . . .*, cited above, provides the greatest single source on the subject of the slave trade. She supplies references to many of the varied sources which provide such knowledge as we have of the 17th century, most helpful of which are the statistical reports prepared to help settle disputes between the Royal African Company and the separate traders.

After the first quarter of the 18th century, data on the slave trade usually rest upon the colonial naval office lists (PRO C. O. 5). Colonial newspapers sometimes reported the tallies which had been made in the customhouse; Donnan, *Documents . . .*, cited above, reproduces the individual entries for most of the lists which have survived, and the WPA compilations (see general note for series Z 1–615) give annual totals. In preparing the series on slaves, photographic copies of the naval office lists (PRO C. O. 5) were used when the Donnan entries and the WPA compilations did not agree. It is important to note, however, that the naval office lists report importations by sea rather than overland movements of slaves. Also, it is not always known how many of the Negroes survived after their entry was recorded. The Virginia statistics for 1710–1718 (Donnan, cited above, vol. IV, pp. 175–181) show that of 4,415 Negro slaves entered, 231 died within the time allowed to recover the duty and 103 were drawn back for exportation—7.5 percent of the total importations.

In the case of the Southern Colonies, the statistics for Virginia and South Carolina are reasonably complete; those for Maryland and Georgia are spotty; and those for North Carolina are virtually nonexistent.

In New England, the Negro population appears to have been due to natural increase rather than extensive importations. Governor Dudley of Massachusetts reported in 1708 that about one-half of Boston's Negro servants were born there (Donnan, cited above, vol. III, p. 24), and a comparison of the 1768–1773 trade figures, series Z 133–145, with the population figures, series Z 1–19, suggests that natural increase had become even more important than importations by the revolutionary era.

In the Middle Colonies the first Negroes were probably brought to New York from Spanish or Dutch prizes in 1625 or 1626. Dutch records are meager but show a consignment of 5 in 1660 and another of 300 in 1664. After the English conquest, New York for a time had an indeterminate trade in slaves with the pirates of Madagascar (Donnan, cited above, vol. III, pp. 405–406, 420, and 423). In Pennsylvania, the number of slaves was always small and their entry often discouraged by high taxes. Donnan (cited above, vol. III, pp. 408–409) believes that data about the slave trade there must be sought in merchant's account books, newspaper advertisements, and items of ship news, some of which appear in Edward R. Turner, "The Negro in Pennsylvania," *Prize Essays of American Historical Association*, Washington, D.C., 1911. In New Jersey, the slave trade centered in the eastern part of the colony, but here too the number of slaves imported was relatively small.

Z 133–145. Slave trade, by origin and destination, 1768–1772.

Source: Compiled by Lawrence A. Harper, University of California, from the American Inspector General's Ledgers of Imports and Exports, Public Records Office, London, Customs 16/1.

Z 146–149. Slave trade in Virginia, 1619–1767.

Source: 1619–1699, Elizabeth Donnan, ed., *Documents Illustrative of the History of the Slave Trade to America*, Carnegie Institution of Washington, D.C., 1935, vol. IV, pp. 4–6, 49–65 (copyright), and Philip A. Bruce, *Economic History of Virginia in the Seventeenth Century*, vol. II, Macmillan, New York, 1895, pp. 66–85; 1700–1726, Donnan, *Documents Illustrative . . .*, vol. IV, pp. 173–187; 1727–1767, Donnan, vol. IV, pp. 187–234, and WPA compilations of colonial naval office lists (see general note for series Z 1–615).

The title of these series refers to "slaves" because that was the status of most Negroes listed, but it should be remembered that until the middle of the 17th century Negroes came as servants, not as slaves. Unless otherwise noted, these figures show the total trade at all Virginia ports. When one or more quarters of a port's naval office lists are missing, the total for the full year has been estimated, the calculations resting upon a chronological or geographic extension—whichever involved the least element of conjecture. The totals depend upon such estimates in all years after 1726 except 1737–1740, 1743–1745, 1750, 1758, 1761–1762, and 1764, when full records exist for all the ports except Accomack, which can be disregarded because of its lack of direct participation in the slave trade. No figure is given in which the total includes more than 20 percent estimate.

In the case of slaves exported, the highly variable nature of this trade did not warrant estimative totals. Of the slaves exported, 1,055 went to Maryland, 12 to North Carolina, 9 to Rhode Island, 8 and a shipment (number unspecified) to Barbados, 3 to Madeira, 2 to Great Britain, 2 to Georgia, and 1 to Boston.

Z 150–154. Slave trade in New York, 1701–1764.

Source: 1701–1718, E. B. O'Callaghan, ed., *Documents Relative to the Colonial History of the State of New York*, vol. V, Weed, Parsons & Co., Albany, 1855, p. 814; 1719–1764, Donnan, cited above for series Z 146–149, vol. III, pp. 462–509, and WPA compilations of colonial naval office lists (see general note for series Z 1–615).

Figures for New York for 1731 were partially estimated, for missing quarters, by Lawrence A. Harper, University of California. The estimates were derived by obtaining the ratio of the number of slaves imported for each quarter to the number annually imported. This ratio was based on figures covering a period of eight years in which quarterly data were available.

Figures for exports, 1701 to 1718, are not available.

Z 155–164. Slaves imported into Charleston, S.C., by origin, 1706–1775.

Source: Compiled by W. Robert Higgins, Murray State University, Murray, Kentucky.

The number of slaves from each source was obtained, unless otherwise designated, from the "Shipping Returns," and "Duty Books 'A,' 'B,' and 'C.'" The figures for 1717 to 1734 include all Negroes brought to South Carolina through the port of Charleston; for 1735 to 1775, the recorded number was of Negroes imported for sale. The number of cargoes was determined from information given in the same sources. The total number of slaves imported came from the same sources except for 1706 through 1724, which came from a report in 1737 by a committee of the South Carolina assembly containing a record of slave importations published in London. The number of cargoes for this period are from Elizabeth Donnan, ed., *Documents Illustrative of the History of the Slave Trade to America*, vol. IV, p. 255.

The ports or locations from which the slaves were exported to Charleston are listed below:

From African ports—Anamaboe, Angola, Bance Island, Bonny, Calabar, Cape Coast, Cape Mount, Gambia, Gold Coast, Senegal, Sierra Leone, and Widah (Ouidah). By far the most frequent designation in the books was simply "Africa."

From Caribbean ports—Anguilla, Antigua, Bahamas (Providence), Barbados, Bermuda, Cuba (Havana, Oporto, Portola, Santa Cruz), Curacao, Dominica, Grenada and the Grenadines, Gaudeloupe, Haiti (including Cap Nicholas), Jamaica (including Spanish Town), Montserrat, Nevis, St. Christopher, St. Croix, St. Eustatius, St. Vincent, and Tobago.

From North American ports—Connecticut (New London), East Florida (St. Augustine), Georgia (Savannah), Massachusetts (Boston, Plymouth, and Salem), New Hampshire (Portsmouth), New York (New York city), North Carolina (Cape Fear), Pennsylvania (Philadelphia), Rhode Island, Virginia, and West Florida (Pensacola).

For further information see W. Robert Higgins, "The Geographical Origins of Negro Slaves in Colonial South Carolina," *The South Atlantic Quarterly*, vol. LXX, No. 1, Winter, 1971, or W. Robert Higgins, *The Slave Trade of Colonial South Carolina*, University of South Carolina Press, Columbia, South Carolina (forthcoming).

Z 165–168. British-American and West African slave prices, 1638–42 to 1773–75.

Source: Compiled by Richard N. Bean, University of Houston, from Richard N. Bean, *The British Transatlantic Slave Trade, 1650–1775*, unpublished Ph.D. dissertation, University of Washington, 1971, and Richard N. Bean, *Additional Slave Prices*, University of Houston, Department of Economics, Working Paper Series 741, No. 4, 1974.

Because of the scarcity of data, Bean included in his series almost every available observation on slave prices in order to get a continuous series. The numbers presented here were gleaned from such sources as commercial correspondence, government archives, published document collections, monographs, and occasionally undocumented citations in secondary sources. Some prices are for actual large scale transactions while others are simply estimates by informed contemporaries. Bean found no reasonable method to weight the observations according to their quality. Instead, he relied on the central limits theorem, operating through five-year averaging, to lessen the effect of the measurement errors. Since many of the price observations are averages for unspecified numbers of slaves, no attempt was made to weight the transaction prices by the number of slaves involved. British-American slave prices are adjusted to eliminate the effect of differential transport costs from Africa to places other than Jamaica.

Bean has suggested that anyone wishing to review his sources and methods of deriving these prices borrow copies of his unpublished Ph.D. dissertation and the working paper through inter-library loans from the universities cited.

Z 169–191. Components of private wealth per free capita for the Thirteen Colonies, by region, 1774.

Source: Calculated by Alice Hanson Jones. See Jones' "Wealth Estimates for the American Middle Colonies, 1774," *Economic Development and Cultural Change*, vol. 18, no. 4, pt. 2, July 1970; "La fortune privée en Pennsylvanie, New Jersey, Delaware, 1774," *Annales: Économies, Sociétes, Civilisties*, vol. 24, no. 2, Paris, France, Armand Colin, Mars-Avril, 1969, pp. 235–249; "Wealth Estimates for the New England Colonies about 1770," *Journal of Economic History*, vol. 32, no. 1, March 1972, pp. 98–127; *Wealth of the Colonies on the Eve of the American Revolution*, Columbia University Press, New York (forthcoming) and *American Colonial Wealth: Documents and Methods*, Arno Press, Inc., New York (forthcoming). Jerome Cornfield gave guidance in drawing the sample in the pilot study for the Middle Colonies. Stephen E. Fienberg and F. Kinley Larntz, Jr., gave guidance in sample drawing for the other regions. Mr. Larntz guided the final execution of the sampling and development of the weighting procedures.

Wealth is estimated on the basis of a sample drawn from all estates probated in the Thirteen Colonies in 1774. To select the sample, every county then in existence was given a chance to be drawn proportionate to its total wealthholding population in 1774. Each county, or cluster of counties, drawn into the sample represents an equal stratum of living wealthholders. Wealthholders are defined to include all free adult males aged 21 and over, white and Negro, and 10 percent of all free adult females, chiefly widows, except no Negro females in the South. Slaves and indentured servants are not counted as wealthholders. Because of the sample design and weighting procedures followed, the combination of data from sample countries within a region yields an unbiased regional estimate of wealth of probated estates, and the regional estimates combined, except for the weakness of the New York data, yield an unbiased estimate for all Thirteen Colonies. The data for probated decedents are adjusted, through the weighting procedure, to the age structure of the living and to include an allowance for wealth of persons not probated, and hence to represent the larger statistical population of living wealthholders.

The counties included in the sample and numbers of probate cases for each are:

New England: Total 381. Connecticut: Litchfield 31, New Haven 37; Massachusetts: Essex 102, Hampshire 27, Plymouth 35, Suffolk 100, Worcester 49. *Middle Colonies:* Total 217. Pennsylvania: Northampton 21, Westmoreland 7, Philadelphia 135; New Jersey: Burlington 25; Delaware: Kent 29. *South:* Total 298. Maryland: Queen Anne 38, Anne Arundel 27; Virginia: Charlotte-Halifax 25, Southampton-Brunswick-Mecklenburg 23, Charlotte-Spotsylvania-Fairfax 30; North Carolina: Halifax 39, Orange 32; South Carolina: Charles Town District 87. In addition, 23 probate inventories from nine counties in New York, together with regional data for New England and Middle Colonies, serve to form an estimate for New York which is part of the Thirteen Colonies total but is not shown separately.

All the inventories probated in 1774 within the sampled counties or county-clusters are included, with a few exceptions. In Essex County, Massachusetts, there was a cut-off at 102 cases, taking all surnames alphabetically from A to part way through the P's. In several counties or county-clusters some cases randomly drawn from 1773 or 1775 were added to provide an adequate number of cases. In the then frontier county of Westmoreland, Pennsylvania, three cases for 1774, two for 1773, and two for 1775 are all that exist for those dates. For New York, the 23 cases used represent all the cases located that were probated in any year from 1772 through 1775 not only in the two sample counties of Suffolk and Albany but in any county in the province.

Data from each county or county-cluster received equal weight in its regional average, inasmuch as each represents an equal stratum of living wealthholders. The procedure means that the counties with larger numbers of cases do not dominate or bias their respective regional averages, yet that full use could be made of all the available cases. For the New York estimate, the 23 cases received 10 percent weight, the New England average 30 percent, and the Middle Colonies average 60 percent. The assumption here is that if more cases for New York had survived, they would have shown wealth resembling that found in the adjoining New England and Middle Colonies, somewhat more like the latter than the former. The Thirteen Colonies total gives each component regional average, including the estimate for New York, an importance in proportion to its 1774 living wealthholder population.

For all regions, data on portable physical wealth and on financial assets came from the probate inventories with occasional adjustments for data found in estate accounts. For New England, the inventories

are also the source of data on land. In the other regions, land was usually not shown in the inventories. For the Middle Colonies, original data on land come from tax lists and, for the South, from deeds and land grants. Data on financial liabilities for New England come from documents filed with probate inventories or from accounts of estate administrators or executors; in the other regions they came from the estate accounts.

Average wealth of the nonprobate-type living (persons who, upon death, would probably not have their estates probated) is assumed to equal one-fourth the average wealth of age-adjusted probated (i.e., probate-type living) in New York, the Middle Colonies, and the South, but one-half in New England. The larger figure is used for New England because a higher proportion of the wealthholders there were not probated. The numbers of living wealthholders (of either probate-type or nonprobate-type) is estimated as follows: Thirteen Colonies total 434,835; New England 137,934; New York 45,128; Middle Colonies 98,448; South 153,325. The proportions of these wealthholders estimated to be of nonprobate-type are: New England 66 percent, New York 40, Middle Colonies 36, South 27.

The numbers of free capita used to construct this table, i.e., the total free population in 1774, men, women, and children, white and Negro, are estimated as follows: Thirteen Colonies total 1,820,019; New England 582,285; New York 180,116; Middle Colonies 405,033; South 652,585. These numbers are estimated to form the following proportions of the total population, free and nonfree: Thirteen Colonies total 77.3 percent; New England 95.8; New York 88.8; Middle Colonies 92.5; South 59.0. The total population figures were interpolated to 1774 on the basis of compound annual rates of population growth, separately for whites and for Negroes, from series Z 1–17 of the previous edition of this volume (U.S. Bureau of the Census, *Historical Statistics of the United States: Colonial Times to 1957*). The proportions of indentured whites and of free Negroes which underlie the figures on free population are estimated from secondary sources listed more fully in the first and last bibliography titles cited above. The underlying age structure of the living population, used for age adjustment from decedent to 1774 living wealthholders, is based on proportions of free whites in the 1800 census, modified slightly in the proportions of children. Complete population tables for 1774 will appear in *Wealth of the Colonies*, Columbia University Press, forthcoming.

Wealth figures in original documents were always stated in local pounds, shillings, and pence of the particular province, which were of varying values in relation to each other and to the English pound sterling. All local pounds have been reduced to equivalent pounds sterling, using as exchange rates the following numbers of local pounds and decimal equivalents thereof as equal to one pound sterling: Massachusetts and Connecticut 1.33; New York 1.79; Pennsylvania, New Jersey, and Delaware 1.70; Maryland common money 1.67, Maryland current money 1.33; Virginia 1.32; North Carolina 1.77; South Carolina 7.00.

Z 192–194. Agriculture censuses in Maine, Massachusetts, and New Jersey, 1784.

Source: Jedidiah Morse, *American Geography*, Boston, 1792, pp. 172 and 284.

It may be assumed that the limited information on agriculture presented in this table for Maine, Massachusetts, and New Jersey for 1784 was collected at the same time that the population was enumerated. Maine was a part of Massachusetts until it became a State in 1820. Other agricultural statistics of this type, except for a few estimates for parts of colonies, do not appear to exist for the colonial and pre-Federal period.

Z 195–212. Basic weekly diets in Britain and America, 1622–1790.

Source: Compiled by Austin White (graduate student, University of California) based on the following: **Series Z 195**, M. S. Rose, *A Laboratory Handbook for Dietetics*, Macmillan, New York, 1937. **Series Z 196–212**, 1622, see source for series Z 253–265, vol. II, p. 318; 1632,

E. M. Leonard, *The Early History of English Poor Relief*, Cambridge University Press, Cambridge, 1900, pp. 198–199; 1638, John Josselyn, "An Account of Two Voyages to New England Made During the Years 1638–1663," *Massachusetts Historical Society Collections*, Third Series, III, 1833, pp. 220–221; 1676, Philip A. Bruce, *Institutional History of Virginia in the Seventeenth Century . . .*, vol. II, Putnam, New York, 1910, p. 87; first half of 18th century, William Douglass, *A Summary, Historical and Political, of the First Planting, Progressive Improvement, and Present State of the British Settlements in North America*, vol. I, R & J Dodsley, London, 1760, p. 536; 1735, Abbot Smith, *Colonists in Bondage*, University of North Carolina Press, Chapel Hill, 1947, p. 212; 1744–1746, Howard Chapin, *The Tartar, the Armed Sloop of the Colony of Rhode Island in King George's War*, Providence, 1922, p. 17; 1747, Isabel M. Calder, *Colonial Captivities, Marches and Journeys*, Macmillan, New York, 1935, p. 40; 1755, Basil Sollers, "The Acadians (French Neutrals) Transported to Maryland," *Maryland Historical Magazine*, vol. III, March 1908, pp. 8–10; 1757, John Fitzpatrick, ed., *The Writings of George Washington*, vol. II, U.S. Government Printing Office, Washington, D.C., 1931, p. 72; 1761, "Brigade Order Books, Montreal, September 29, 1761," *Journals of the Hon. William Hervey, from 1755 to 1814*, Paul and Mathew, Bury St. Edmunds, England, 1906, p. 154; about 1770, Walter Besant, *London in the Eighteenth Century*, A & C Black, London, 1903, p. 556; 1775, Fitzpatrick, cited above, vol. III, p. 409; 1776, "Journal of the Committees of Observation of the Middle District of Frederick County, Maryland," *Maryland Historical Magazine*, vol. XI, December 1916, p. 310; 1780 (Continental Army), John W. Wright, "Some Notes on the Continental Army," *William and Mary Quarterly*, vol. XI, 1931, p. 105; 1780 (French prisoners), Rupert C. Jarvis, ed., *Customs Letter-Book of the Port of Liverpool*, Manchester, 1954, p. 106; about 1790, Fitzpatrick, cited above, vol. XXXI, pp. 186–187; before 1861 (majority of slaves), Kenneth Stampp, *The Peculiar Institution*, Alfred A. Knopf, New York, 1956, p. 282.

Data for calories per day, series Z 195, have been recalculated from those shown in *Historical Statistics . . . Colonial Times to 1957* and rounded to the nearest 100. Exact precision cannot be expected in reducing colonial data to modern caloric terms. Also, the totals might have been reduced before actual consumption by spoilage, human carelessness, and dishonesty, or increased by fish, game, and produce in season. Researchers interested in the subject should write to Professor Lawrence A. Harper, Department of History, University of California, Berkeley.

Z 213–226.   Value of exports to and imports from England by American Colonies and States, 1697–1791.

Source: 1697–1773, Charles Whitworth, *State of the Trade of Great Britain in Its Imports and Exports Progressively from the Year 1697*, G. Robinson, London, 1776; 1774–1776, David Macpherson, *Annals of Commerce, Manufactures, Fisheries and Navigation*, vol. III, Mundell & Son, Edinburgh, 1805, pp. 564, 585, and 599; 1777–1791, compiled by Jacob M. Price, University of Michigan, from Public Record Office, London, B.T. 6/185 ff.106v–117v.

The English Inspector General's Ledgers (Public Records Office, London, Customs 2 and 3) provide the original source for these figures. Unfortunately, Whitworth's erroneous title has caused many to believe the figures relate to Britain rather than to England but otherwise his volume has much value. The source tables cover all countries and appear in two formats: One gives England's trade with any one country, annually; the other shows all the countries with which England traded each year. Those interested in studying broader trends will find value in the decennial averages in John, Lord Sheffield, *Observations on the Commerce of the American States*, 6th edition, London, 1784. G. N. Clark's *Guide to English Commercial Statistics, 1696–1782* (Royal Historical Society Guides and Handbooks, No. 1, London, 1938) provides a valuable history and analysis of the basic statistics and a useful appendix which has a chronological list of statistical material for 1663–1783 and specifies where the data may be found.

Users of this material should note the basis on which the values rest. Smuggling does not constitute a material factor during the years under consideration. However, other difficulties arise with respect to the question of the volume of exports and the value of all the trade. The repeal of the export duties on woolen manufactures in 1701 (11 W. III c 20) and of the remaining export duties in 1721 (Geo. II c 15) removed the penalty for false entries on exports, and some merchants overstated their quantity for reasons of real or fancied prestige—a practice which may have injected an element of error of about 4 percent (Clark, cited above, pp. 16, 27, and 35).

Another problem arose in determining the value of the merchandise imported as well as exported. The authorities of the early 18th century were greatly interested in the balance of trade and at first tried to ascertain the real commercial value of merchandise. However, the difficulties of doing so, and the increasing recognition that there were intangible elements which the records could not disclose, led to the abandonment of attempts to keep the values current by the end of the second decade of the 18th century.

The so-called "official values" became stereotyped between 1705 and 1721 (Clark, cited above, pp. 17–23), a fact which diminished their value for use in striking a balance of trade but increased their usefulness as a rough-and-ready index of the relative increase or decrease of the volume of trade.

This table has been revised from that published in the *Historical Statistics . . ., Colonial Times to 1957* volume to include figures for the years 1777–1791. Also, several figures have been corrected, as indicated by footnote 1. The source for these corrections is: John J. McCusker, "The Current Value of English Exports, 1697 to 1800," *William and Mary Quarterly*, Third Series, vol. XXVIII, No. 4, October 1971, p. 612, footnote 8.

See also general note for series Z 1–615.

Z 227–244.   Value of exports to and imports from Scotland by American Colonies and States, 1740–1791.

Source: Compiled by Jacob M. Price, University of Michigan, from records as follows: 1740–1773, House of Lords Record Office, London, 20 Nov. 1775; 1774–1791, Public Record Office, London, B.T., 6/185 ff.188v–204.

Z 245–252.   Value of exports to and imports from England by New York, 1751–1775.

Source: Virginia D. Harrington, *The New York Merchant on the Eve of the Revolution*, Columbia University Press, New York, 1935, p. 354 (copyright).

Z 253–265.   Tonnage capacity of ships, 1769 and 1770, and value of exports and imports of American Colonies, 1769, by destination and origin.

Source: David Macpherson, cited above in source for series Z 213–226, vol. III, pp. 571–572.

The tonnage figures shown are those used commercially—not those computed when the Royal Navy was purchasing vessels (see text for series Z 266–285). The statistics given by Macpherson are substantially the same as those given in Public Records Office, London, Customs 16/1, except that Macpherson put the 1769 inward-bound tonnage data for Southern Europe in the West Indies column (and vice versa)—an error which has been corrected here.

The value figures for 1769 provide only a rough-and-ready index of the relationship among the different trades. Totals include figures for the Islands of Newfoundland, Bahama, and Bermuda (a factor which statistically makes only a minor difference). These data are based on the official valuations used in the customhouse which, according to Macpherson, considerably understate the true amount. This defect, however serious for some purposes, does not destroy the value of the figures for comparative purposes. Also, it must be remembered that the value figures exclude the intercolonial coastwise trade which the tonnage figures show to have been as large as any other.

See also series Z 213–226, which provide a broader and more representative base for studying the relative relationship of the Thirteen Colonies trade with England.

It should be noted that the use of these figures on volume of the traffic for the various trades for estimating the amount of shipping given full-time employment must allow for repeated voyages of the same vessel.

Z 266–285. Number and tonnage capacity of ships outward and inward bound, to and from 5 cities, by destination and origin, 1714–1772.

Source: Compiled by Lawrence A. Harper, University of California, from photographic copies of the naval office lists in the British Public Records Office (C. O. 5), except for: 1714–1717, Boston, and 1715–18, New York City, E. B. O'Callaghen, ed., *Documents Relative to the Colonial History of the State of New York*, vol. V, Weed, Parsons, and Company, Albany, 1855, p. 618; 1733 and 1734, Philadelphia, *Pennsylvania Gazette* for those years; 1752, Port Hampton, Francis C. Huntley, "The Seaborne Trade of Virginia in Mid-Eighteenth Century: Port Hampton," *Virginia Magazine of History and Biography*, vol. LIX, No. 3, July 1951, pp. 302–303; 1763 and 1764, New York, and 1765 and 1766, New York, Boston, and Philadelphia, see source for series Z 245–252, pp. 356–358; and 1768–1772, all ports, American Inspector General's Ledgers, Public Records Office, London, Customs 16/1.

Where the classification in *Documents Relative to the Colonial History* . . . did not correspond to that used here, the necessary adjustments were made by reference to the Colonial Naval Office lists (PRO C. O. 5).

The colonial naval officers appointed to enforce the English navigation laws as well as the collectors appointed by the English Commissioners of Customs under the act of 1673 (25 Car. II c 7) were charged with reporting the entry and clearance of ships as well as their cargoes. Many of the copies of the naval office lists have survived from the 18th century. When they have not, records of the names and destinations of the ships (but not their tonnages) may be obtained from the shipping news in the colonial newspapers. Such data of entries and clearances provide the best rough-and-ready index of the course of trade and its relative volume.

Although the figures concerning the entry of goods such as molasses might be distorted by illicit trade, the severity of the penalty (forfeiture) for failure to enter one's ship and the difficulty of concealing the offense help to warrant the accuracy of ship entry figures. Tonnage figures, however, present a special problem. Ralph Davis in "Organization and Finance of the English Shipping Industry in the Late Seventeenth Century" (doctoral thesis, University of London, 1955) states (pp. 476–479) that *the tonnage* as calculated when the English Navy was contracting *for the purchase* of a vessel was 25 to 33 percent greater than the *conventional "tons burden"* recorded in the customhouse books. Since the "tons burden" figures for the same ship remain constant in the passbooks and customs entries during the span of time here involved (although not necessarily for all periods), the difference between this purchase tonnage and the conventional tonnage will ordinarily not affect use of the data shown here.

See also general note for series Z 1–615.

Z 286–290. Value of commodity exports and imports, earnings, and value of slaves imported into British North American Colonies, 1768–1772.

Source: James F. Shepherd and Gary M. Walton, *Shipping, Maritime Trade, and the Economic Development of Colonial North America*, Cambridge University Press, London, 1972, table 1 (copyright).

The regions used are defined as follows: *Northern Colonies*—Newfoundland, Quebec, and Nova Scotia; *New England*—New Hampshire, Massachusetts, Rhode Island, and Connecticut; *Middle Colonies*—New York, New Jersey, Pennsylvania, and Delaware; *Upper South*—Maryland and Virginia; and *Lower South*—North Carolina, South

Carolina, and Georgia. Florida includes East and West Florida, and has been grouped with the Bahama and the Bermuda Islands principally because the overseas trade from these colonies was small relative to the other regions. The Northern Colonies are not listed under Africa because there was no trade between them.

The source for the commodity export and import data was the American Inspector-General's Ledgers (Great Britain, Public Records Office, Customs 16/1) except that imports from Great Britain were taken from the English and Scottish customs records for these years (Great Britain, Public Records Office, Customs 3 and Customs 14, respectively). Price data were taken from various sources. Commodity exports are estimated f.o.b. values and commodity imports are estimated c.i.f. values. Shipping earnings include earnings from exports on colonial-owned ships plus earnings of colonial-owned ships carrying imports since the imports are valued c.i.f. Shipping earnings of colonial-owned ships carrying goods between foreign ports were estimated to have averaged 13,000 pounds sterling annually during 1768–1772. This estimate is included in the totals of shipping earnings, but not in the earnings estimated for the various routes between overseas areas and the colonies. These earnings are allocated to the total shipping earnings of each region as follows in pounds sterling: New England, 6,000; Middle Colonies, 3,000; and the Southern Colonies, 3,000. (1,000 pounds sterling were lost in rounding.) Other invisible earnings include interest, insurance, and mercantile profits earned by colonial residents in their trade with overseas areas. Because of the likely small amounts involved, no estimates were made for Africa. The source contains a discussion of the problems and procedures of estimation and the validity of the estimates.

Other items which affected the colonial balance of payments but which are not reflected in the estimates are the sale of ships to overseas residents, the immigration of indentured servants, and expenditures by the British government for civil government and defense in the colonies. The source also presents a discussion of the probable magnitudes of these items.

Z 291–293. Average annual coastal exports, imports, and balances of trade, by region, 1768–1772.

Source: James F. Shepherd and Samuel H. Williamson, "The Coastal Trade of the British North American Colonies, 1768–1772," *The Journal of Economic History*, XXXII, 4, December 1972, p. 798 (copyright).

The estimates of values for coastal exports from, and imports into, each colonial port district are based upon quantity data taken from the American Inspector-General's Ledgers (Great Britain, Public Records Office, Customs 16/1), and price data taken from various sources. The computed values were then aggregated according to the regional definitions specified in the text for series Z 286–290. It is important to note that these are *not* net exports from, or net imports into, each region. Exports and imports that took place between ports within each region, as well as those to or from other regions, are included in each regional total. Total export and import values should be approximately the same; the discrepancy is due principally to discrepancies in quantities recorded in the customs records.

See source for a discussion of the procedures of estimation and the validity of the estimates.

Z 294. Value and quantity of articles exported from British Continental Colonies, by destination, 1770.

Source: David Macpherson, cited above in source for series Z 213–226, vol. III, pp. 572–573, supplemented by American Inspector General's Ledgers, Public Records Office, London, Customs 16/1.

Data do not include coastwise shipments as do the figures in the American Inspector General's Ledgers (PRO Customs 16/1). Macpherson (see source for series Z 213–226) states that he omitted fractional parts of the quantities but their value is retained in the value column. Because of this and an error which Macpherson saw but had no means of correcting, the value column may not be entirely comparable with the quantity columns. The value figures are not the market values (which Macpherson believes to have been higher) but are the official customhouse values at the ports of exportation. Customs 16/1 presents the quantities in all cases for a longer time span, 1768–1772, but the data there are not so conveniently totaled as in Macpherson.

See also general note for series Z 1–615.

Z 295–304. Coal exported from James River ports in Virginia, by destination, 1758–1765.

Source: Howard N. Eavenson, *The First Century and a Quarter of American Coal Industry*, Waverly Press, Inc., Baltimore, 1942, pp. 32–34, and WPA compilations (see general note for series Z 1–615) of naval office lists at the University of California.

These figures were compiled from the colonial naval office lists by Eavenson. They represent only the years for which records are complete in the case of both the Upper and Lower James. Comparison with the colonial exports for 1768–1772 (compiled by Eavenson, p. 36, from PRO Customs 16/1) shows that the James River shipments constituted the great bulk of the exports from the Thirteen Colonies. Out of a total of 2,798 net tons recorded, 1,220 net tons were shipped from the Upper James, 180 from the Lower James, 1,100 from Nova Scotia, 117 from New Hampshire, and only minor quantities from other ports (which may have been used as ballast and originally may have come from Great Britain).

Chaldrons were not converted into tons at the Newcastle rate of 5,936 pounds equal to 2.97 net tons but on the measure used after the Revolutionary War, a chaldron equaling 36 bushels or 1.44 net tons.

Z 305–325. Coal imported, by American ports, 1768–1772.

Source: American Inspector General's Ledgers, Public Records Office, London, Customs 16/1.

Chaldrons and bushels were converted to net tons as described in text for series Z 295–304.

The WPA compilations (see general note for series Z 1–615) from the naval office lists show earlier entries of coal in the several ports, from time to time. The great bulk came from Britain, the remainder (except in the case of exports from James River ports) apparently were transshipments, but it is not until 1768 that records give a good cross section of the traffic.

Z 326–417. General note.

Iron was listed in colonial commerce as "pig iron" which derived its name from the shape assumed by the molten iron when poured from the furnace, after being separated from the ore, and "bar iron" which consisted of malleable iron produced in bloomeries or at the forge. Iron manufactures not specifically described by name, such as anchors, axes, pots, nails, scythes, etc., were listed as "cast iron" if poured into forms and "wrought iron" if forged from malleable iron, except in the English Inspector General's records (PRO Customs 3) where the term "wrought iron" seems to have included both cast and malleable iron products.

The statistical picture of iron in the colonies can be reconstructed in part from data concerning iron works in the colonies and in part from the records of colonial trade. The beginning of this industry came early in the various American colonies: Virginia 1622, Massachusetts 1645, Connecticut 1657, New Jersey 1680, Maryland 1715, Pennsylvania 1716, and New York shortly before 1750. By 1775, the colonies had at least 82 charcoal furnaces which produced about 300 tons each, or a total of 24,600 tons, of pig iron and more than 175 iron forges, some being bloomeries which made bar iron directly from the ore. Most of them, however, were refinery forges which used pig iron. Each of the 175 forges produced an average of 150 tons of bar iron a year, or 26,250 tons in all. In addition, there were slitting mills and other iron works.

Arthur C. Bining, in *British Regulation of the Colonial Iron Industry*,

cited below for series Z 326–330, p. 134, provides a table comparing American production with the world total (see text table I). These estimates include pig iron, cast iron wares made at blast furnaces, and bar iron produced at bloomeries directly from the ore.

Table I. Iron Production of American Colonies and the World
[In tons]

Year	American Colonies	World
1800	45,000	400,000
1790	38,000	325,000
1775	30,000	210,000
1750	10,000	150,000
1700	1,500	100,000

The figures shown in series Z 326–417 for the movement of the various types of iron in commerce throw light on England's efforts to encourage Americans to produce pig and bar iron by freeing those products from import duties in England, and to limit further manufacture by prohibiting the erection of any new slitting or rolling mills, tilt hammer forges, or steel furnaces (23 Geo. II c 29; 30 Geo. II c 16). Iron was not added to the list of enumerated products which could be shipped only to Britain (or another colony) until 1764 (4 Geo. III c 15), and even then the law only forbade shipments to Europe.

Comparisons of colonial production with export figures will help provide estimates of the home market, which can be reduced to an approximate *per capita* base by reference to series Z 1–19.

See also general note for series Z 1–615.

Z 326–330. Pig iron exported to England, by colony, 1723–1776.

Source: 1723–1755, and **series Z 326** only, 1761–1776, Arthur Cecil Bining, *British Regulation of the Colonial Iron Industry*, University of Pennsylvania Press, Philadelphia, 1933, pp. 126–133 (copyright); 1756–1760, and **series Z 327–330**, 1761–1776, English Inspector General's Ledgers, Public Records Office, London, Customs 3.

Basically, all the figures come from the Inspector General's accounts although Bining obtained his from House of Lords manuscript, No. 185, and Harry Scrivenor, *Comprehensive History of the Iron Trade*, Longman, Brown, Green, and Longmans, London, 1841.

J. L. Bishop, *A History of American Manufactures . . .*, cited below for series Z 348–353, p. 625, gives an earlier figure when he states that the first iron sent to England from America was from Nevis and St. Christopher, followed in 1718 by 3⅛ tons from Virginia and Maryland. Series Z 326 is that of Bining and, where possible, footnotes explain the reasons for differences between his totals and those of the extended figures. The customs records were stated in terms of tons, hundredweights, quarters, and pounds, but they have here been rounded to tons.

Z 331–337. Pig iron exported from American Colonies, by destination and colony, 1768–1772.

Source: American Inspector General's Ledgers, Public Records Office, London, Customs 16/1.

The difference in total exports given in series Z 331 for Great Britain and that in series Z 326 for England should reflect trade with Scotland except for the variation in terminal dates and the lapse of time required to cross the Atlantic. The trade, however, seems to have been minor. J. L. Bishop, *A History of American Manufactures . . .*, cited below for series Z 348–353, p. 628, gives figures showing that the pig iron exported to Scotland totaled only 264 tons in the 10 years from 1739 to 1749 and 229 tons in the 6 years from 1750 to 1756.

No figures are available for pig iron imported from England by the colonies. Such imports were probably negligible.

Z 338–347. Pig iron imported by American Colonies from other Continental Colonies, 1768–1772.

Source: See source for series Z 331–337.

In addition to the colonies shown, these series also cover New

Hampshire, New Jersey, Georgia, and Florida. However, these colonies imported no pig iron for 1768–1772.

Z 348–353. Bar iron imported from England by American Colonies, 1710–1750.

Source: 1710–1735, J. L. Bishop, *A History of American Manufactures From 1608 to 1860*, vol. I, Edward Young & Co., Philadelphia, 1861, p. 629; 1750, English Inspector General's Ledgers, Public Records Office, London, Customs 3.

Shipments of bar iron from England to the Colonies declined sharply in the last quarter century before the Revolution. Figures are not available for 1736–1749 to determine when the decline first became evident.

Imports were relatively few after 1750. The English and American Inspector Generals' Ledgers show that New England imported 6 tons in 1764, and again in 1769, and 1,053 bars in 1773. South Carolina imported 19 bars in 1770 and 3 hundredweight in 1773.

Z 354–359. Bar iron exported to England, by colony, 1718–1776.

Source: 1718–1755, and **series Z 354**, 1761–1776, Bining, cited above for series Z 326–330, pp. 128–133; 1756–1760, and **series Z 355–359**, 1761–1776, English Inspector General's Ledgers, Public Records Office, London, Customs 3.

The original sources show data in tons, hundredweights, quarters, and pounds, but they have here been rounded by Lawrence A. Harper (University of California) to the nearest ton.

The source indicates that no bar iron was exported during 1710–1717 and for years which have been omitted in these series.

Z 360–373. Bar iron imported by American Colonies from other Continental Colonies, 1768–1772.

Source: See source for series Z 331–337.

Z 374–383. Bar iron exported by American Colonies, by destination and colony, 1768–1772.

Source: See source for series Z 331–337.

The difference in total exports given in series Z 374 for Great Britain and those in series Z 354 for England should reflect exports to Scotland, except for the variation in terminal dates and the lapse of time required to cross the Atlantic. According to J. L. Bishop, these exports were minor—only 11 tons from 1739 to 1749 (see text for series Z 331–337).

Z 384–397. Cast iron imported and exported by American Colonies, by origin and destination, 1768–1772.

Source: See source for series Z 331–337.

Additional information may be obtained concerning imports from England in the English Inspector General's Ledgers (PRO Customs 3) and in the WPA compilations (see general note for series Z 1–615) of the colonial naval office lists. English exports to the Colonies list, in addition to the generic heading "cast iron," such items as ordnance, iron pots, melting pots, and Flemish iron pots. The WPA compilations show an active coastal trade in pots as well as a surprisingly large quantity of sugar pots and sugar molds going to Kingston, Jamaica, especially from Philadelphia.

The figures for 1769–1771 may include some shipments from Scotland but the amounts probably are negligible.

The source also indicates additional minor quantities of cast iron exported to Southern Europe, Wine Islands, and West Indies.

Z 398–405. Wrought iron imported from England by American Colonies, 1710–1773.

Source: 1710–1735, Bishop, cited above for series Z 348–353, p. 629; 1750–1764, and 1773, English Inspector General's Ledgers,

Public Records Office, London, Customs 3; 1769–1771, see source for series Z 331–337.

The figures for 1769–1771 may include some shipments from Scotland but the amounts probably are negligible.

The American Inspector General's figures for 1768–1772 (PRO Customs 16/1) disclose no exports of wrought iron from the Colonies to England, but the figures do show some shipments to the West Indies.

Z 406–417. Selected iron products imported and exported by American Colonies, 1768–1772.

Source: See source for series Z 331–337.

Figures are probably underestimated since the items included may have been listed under more general designations. The colonists were not necessarily dependent upon importation but may have manufactured their own nails and other articles from bar iron which was either home-produced or imported.

Since colonial imports of axes and scythes came so predominantly from the other colonies, and steel and nails from Great Britain, no note has been taken of the negligible importations of these items from other sources.

Z 418–431. Value of furs exported to England by British Continental Colonies, 1700–1775.

Source: Murray G. Lawson, "Fur—A Study in English Mercantilism, 1700–1775," *University of Toronto Studies*, History and Economics Series, vol. IX, University of Toronto Press, Toronto, 1943, pp. 108–109 (copyright).

As pointed out in the source, the fur trade is inextricably interwoven with the manufacture of beaver hats. Thus, the Hat Act of 1732 (5 Geo. II c 22) forbidding the exportation of hats by any colony, combined with the enumeration of beaver skins and furs in 1722 (8 Geo. I c 15), sought to protect the English hat manufacturers. These series show the importance to the English of their colonial supply of fur. Comparison of these figures with those shown in series Z 213–226 will demonstrate the relative unimportance of fur in the colonial balance of trade.

The source also specifies the different kinds and quantity of fur England imported from the colonies and elsewhere, as well as the quantity and value of the different markets of the world—data given in even greater detail in the original tables which Lawson has left with the WPA compilations at the University of California in Berkeley.

See also general note for series Z 1–615.

Z 432–435. Indigo and silk exported from South Carolina and Georgia, 1747–1788.

Source: **Series Z 432–434**, 1747–1775, Lewis C. Gray, *History of Agriculture in the Southern United States to 1860*, vol. II, Carnegie Institution of Washington, D.C., 1933, p. 1024 (copyright), (except 1766, WPA compilations of colonial naval office lists, Public Records Office, London, C. O. 5; and 1768–1772, photographic copies of the American Inspector General's Ledgers, Public Records Office, London, Customs 16/1); 1783–1788, compiled by Jacob M. Price, University of Michigan, from records of the Public Record Office, London B.T. 6/21 ff.311–312. **Series Z 435**, Lewis C. Gray, cited above, vol. I, p. 187.

See also general note for series Z 1–615.

The data on indigo are reasonably complete. Although South Carolina contemplated the production of indigo as early as 1672, little came of it, presumably because of the competition from the British West Indies. When the British Islands began to emphasize sugar rather than indigo, England had to depend upon the French West Indies for her supplies of indigo until South Carolina (thanks to the enterprise of Eliza Lucas) again entered the field. The first successful crop in 1744 was largely devoted to seed but South Carolina was soon exporting in quantity. In due course, Georgia became a competitor but British Florida did not enter the picture until late. Even during the last 5 years of the colonial period, British Florida's production ranged only between 20,000 and 60,000 pounds (Gray, cited above, vol. I, pp. 54 and 291–295).

The great bulk of indigo went to Britain (which wanted it as a source of blue dye), not only because of its enumeration in the act of 1660 (12 Charles II c 18), but also because of the bounty England paid of 6 pence per pound (21 Charles II c 30). However, Customs 16/1 and the WPA compilations (see general note for series Z 1–615) show that minor quantities went to other Continental Colonies. Gray's Carolina figures, which were taken by him from an English source, apparently do not include coastwise shipments. This omission is relatively unimportant since the coastwise figures for 1768–1773 (as shown in Customs 16/1) represented only 1.6 percent of the total exports. The figures for Georgia (compiled by an American customs official) include shipments coastwise as well as to England—a matter of statistical significance as they constituted 5.1 percent of Georgia's total for 1768–1773.

Comparison of Gray's figures for 1747–1765 with those for 1768–1773 in Customs 16/1 suggests that Gray's figures are not for Charleston and Savannah alone, as shown by his headings, but for South Carolina and Georgia. In the case of South Carolina, the two series agree exactly in 1768, the one year when we have figures from both sources. Since Gray's source (British Museum, Kings Manuscripts, 206, f. 29) is the same for the earlier years, 1747–1765, it seems probable that the figures for these years also refer to South Carolina as a whole.

Customs 16/1 does not conclusively answer the problem in the case of Savannah. It shows for 1768–1772 that Savannah was the only Georgia port exporting indigo except in 1772. For this year, Gray's figures differ slightly from those shown in Customs 16/1 for Savannah alone and also those for Georgia as a whole. The decision to change the heading from Savannah to Georgia rests upon the fact that Bernard Romans (*A Concise Natural History of East and West Florida*, vol. I, New York, 1775, p. 104) specifies Georgia rather than Savannah.

Whether or not the figures are for Savannah or Georgia seems statistically insignificant. In South Carolina, however, ports other than Charleston provided 7.8 percent of that colony's exports to England for 1768–1773. Whatever may be true of Gray's figures, those given for 1768–1773 from Customs 16/1 do include all South Carolina ports and all of Georgia, but the only figure available for South Carolina for 1766 (from the WPA compilations) is for Charleston alone.

The figures on silk are from records compiled by the Georgia Comptroller of Customs (Gray, cited above, vol. I, p. 187). See also text for series Z 436–440.

Z 436–440. Silk exported and imported by North and South Carolina, 1731–1755.

Source: Chapman J. Milling, ed., *Colonial South Carolina*, University of South Carolina Press, Columbia, 1951, p. 104 (copyright).

Despite vigorous efforts to encourage colonial silk production by both British and colonial governments, more silk moved west than east across the Atlantic. Early figures gathered by Gray (cited above for series Z 432–435, vol. I, pp. 184–187) show that in 1654 Virginia reported the production of only 8 pounds; in 1656, 10 pounds (wound silk); in 1668, 300 pounds (sent to Charles II, type specified); in 1730, 300 pounds (raw), and that the Carolinas sent "several bales" to London in 1710 and again in 1716. Georgia's first efforts succeeded in sending only 20 pounds of silk to England in 1739. In 1741, she produced 600 pounds of cocoons (of which 16 pounds made 1 pound of silk) as against 37 pounds of wound silk in all the previous years of the colony. In 1749, the Salzburgers (a religious colony of industrious peasants and artisans) alone produced 762 pounds of cocoons and 50 pounds, 13 ounces, of spun silk. In 1764, the Colonies'

total product amounted to 15,212 pounds of cocoons. See also text for series Z 432–435.

The figures for the Carolinas (1731–1755) were taken from British records and appear in Governor James Glen's *Description of South Carolina* (Milling, cited above, p. 104).

Z 441–472. General note.

Colonial statistics concerning production and consumption of tobacco have not been developed yet, and perhaps they can never advance beyond the rough estimate stage. For the present, only general deductions from export statistics and other evidence can be made.

Figures for trans-Atlantic shipments of tobacco in the 17th century leave much to be desired (see text for series Z 457–459) but those for the 18th century are reasonably satisfactory. The 18th century statistics of English imports rest upon contemporary compilations from customhouse entries. The figures for Scotland are less exact and in the early years they do not rise above mere estimates. However, Scotland's tobacco imports were relatively minor in those years. Fortunately, as their relative importance grew, the Scottish statistics became more reliable.

British imports represented virtually all the colonial exports. The figures given in series Z 441–448 and Z 449–456 give the landed weight in Britain. Due to the tobacco's loss of moisture while crossing the Atlantic, the landed weight in Britain is about 5 percent less than the shipping weight in America (Arthur P. Middleton, *Tobacco Coast*, the Mariners' Museum, Newport News, Va., 1953, p. 104; Rupert C. Jarvis, *Customs Letter-Books of the Port of Liverpool, 1711–1813*, the Chetham Society, Manchester, 1954).

Unfortunately, the English Inspector General's Ledgers of Imports and Exports (PRO Customs 3) do not differentiate between shipments from Virginia and Maryland as do the Scottish (PRO Customs 14) and the American (PRO Customs 16/1).

The validity of British statistics as a reflection of the American tobacco trade depends, of course, upon colonial obedience to the regulations requiring shipment (with minor exceptions) of colonial tobacco to England (Britain after 1707)—at first by royal order and after 1660 by the Navigation Act of 12 Car. II, c 18.

Until the English drove the Dutch from New Netherland (first in 1664 and finally in 1674) great opportunities existed for illicit trade in America. The rules also appear not to have been consistently enforced in Europe (see text for series Z 457–459). In the 1680's there was a flareup of illegal shipments to Ireland but it reflected a sudden change in the law. The offending vessels were apprehended and the great bulk of the Irish trade thereafter seems to have followed legal channels. There were lurid accounts of smuggling to Scotland at the turn of the century but the quantity of tobacco involved should be viewed in proportion to the trade as a whole. One cannot reasonably expect the illegal shipments at that time to exceed the shipments made a decade later with full sanction of the law. In fact, the illegal shipments presumably were much less because Scotland as a whole at the end of the 17th century had only one-fourth of the shipping it had within 5 years after direct trade was permitted. The Clyde ports, which were most concerned with the American trade, had only one-tenth of their later shipping (L. A. Harper, *The English Navigation Laws*, Columbia University Press, New York, 1939, pp. 260–261). In view of this difference in the shipping available, the volume of illegal trade would seem not to have been more than 250,000 pounds, and a comparison with series Z 441–448 shows that it represented at most 1 percent of the tobacco crossing the Atlantic lawfully.

During the 18th century there was undoubtedly some smuggling of tobacco but it does not seem likely to impair the validity of the colonial import statistics. The illicit trader's greatest profit did not lie in evading the provisions of the Navigation Act but in escaping the high taxes laid on tobacco in England. The most effective technique consisted in importing the tobacco and reexporting it legally to a nearby port (such as the Isle of Man) whence small craft could "run" it ashore again duty-free (for details, see Jacob M. Price, *The Tobacco Trade and the Treasury, 1685–1733: British Mercantilism in its Fiscal Aspects*, unpublished doctoral dissertation, Harvard University, 1954).

American historians have pointed to the small amount of the "plantation duties" collected on intercolonial trade as evidence of the breakdown of the laws. If the American colonists consumed the 5 pounds per capita of the Bermudians in the early 18th century, the 2 pounds of the English at the beginning of the 18th century, or even their 1 pound per capita at the end of the 18th century (Alfred Rive, "The Consumption of Tobacco Since 1600," *Economic Journal Supplement, Economic History Series*, vol. I, Jan. 1926, p. 63; H. C. Wilkinson, *Bermuda in the Old Empire*, Oxford University Press, London, 1950, p. 14), the colonies would have provided a sizable market of 2,000,000 to 10,000,000 pounds at the time of the Revolution. But that is a figure which can and must be greatly discounted. In the first place, it should be cut in half because the Southern Colonies had about half the population and provided their own source of supply. Similarly, allowance must be made for tobacco produced in the Northern colonies. Pennsylvania, Delaware, New York, Rhode Island, Connecticut, and Massachusetts all at one time or another grew tobacco (George L. Beer, *The Origins of the British Colonial System, 1578–1660*, Macmillan, New York, 1908, p. 88; J. B. Killebrew, *Report on the Culture and Curing of Tobacco in the United States*, Department of the Interior, Census Office, Washington, D.C., 1884, pp. 147 and 237; Vertrees J. Wyckoff, *Tobacco Regulation in Colonial Maryland*, Johns Hopkins University Studies in Historical and Political Science, Extra Volumes, New Series, No. 22, Baltimore, 1936, pp. 37, 38, and 65). Philadelphia, Lewes, and New Castle appear in the WPA compilations (see general note for series Z 1–615) as suppliers to other ports like New York and Boston. New York itself exported tobacco (and even more snuff) coastwise as well as to England, and the exports from New England continued large even into the 1750's. In the 1760's, Rhode Island tobacco crops provided surpluses sufficient to warrant shipping 200,000 pounds to Surinam, a colony in South America (James B. Hedges, *The Browns of Providence Plantations*, Harvard University Press, Cambridge, 1952, pp. 30–40).

It need not be assumed that the colonists were averse to violating the law. It may be that violations on a significant scale were not good business. The fact that the 200,000 pounds of Rhode Island tobacco sent to Surinam went there illegally means little. It was a type of tobacco not in general demand and constituted less than one-third of one percent of the annual legal trade.

Z 441–448.   Tobacco imported by England, by origin, 1697–1775.

Source: Compiled by Jacob M. Price, University of Michigan.

The basic sources used by Price are the same as those used by him for his doctoral dissertation (see below).

The English Inspector General's Ledgers (PRO Customs 3), which are the original source of the data, distinguish between entries in London and in the rest of the Kingdom (the outports) but Price has combined them in the interest of saving space.

Z 449–456.   American tobacco imported and reexported by Great Britain, 1697–1791.

Source: 1697–1775, Jacob M. Price, *The Tobacco Trade and the Treasury, 1685–1733: British Mercantilism in its Fiscal Aspects*, unpublished doctoral dissertation, Harvard University, 1954; 1783–1791, compiled by Jacob M. Price, University of Michigan.

The basic sources of the data for England in Price's doctoral dissertation were the Inspector General's Ledgers of Imports and Exports (PRO Customs 2 and 3) except as follows (see general note for series Z 1–615 for an explanation of the call numbers which follow): 1703–1722, from PRO CO 390/5/47; 1717–1722, confirmed in PRO T. 1/281/18, BM Add. MS. 33,038 fol. 159; 1722 (London import only), from PRO T 64/276B/327; 1763–1769 (import only), from PRO T. 64/276B/328; 1770–1773 (import only), from PRO T. 64/276B/

332; 1770–1771 (export), from PRO T. 64/276/330; 1772, 1774–1775 (import and export), from PRO T. 17/1,3,4; 1773–1775 (export), from Adam Anderson, *An Historical and Chronological Deduction of the Origin of Commerce*, vol. IV, J. Walter, London, 1707–1709, p. 447; 1783–1791, PRO Customs 17/8–14.

For Scotland, Price's data came from the Scottish Ledgers of Imports and Exports (PRO Customs 14), except as follows: 1707–1711 (import and export), from PRO T. 1/39/29; 1715–1717 (import and export), from PRO CO 390/5/13; 1721–1724 (import and export), from PRO T. 1/282/23; 1725–1731, 1752–1754, 1763, 1769 (import and export), from PRO T. 36/13; 1738–1747 (import and export), from PRO T. 1/329 fol. 125.

Total imports and reexports for 1708–1731 and 1752–1754 were obtained by adding figures not strictly comparable with each other. Scottish imports and reexports for 1708–1717 are averages of estimates for several years.

Z 457–459.   American tobacco imported by England, 1616–1695.

Source: 1616–1621, Vertrees J. Wyckoff, *Tobacco Regulation in Colonial Maryland*, Johns Hopkins University Studies in Historical and Political Science, Extra Volumes, New Series, No. 22, Baltimore, 1936, pp. 20–36 (copyright); 1622–1631, Neville Williams, "England's Tobacco Trade in the Reign of Charles I," *The Virginia Magazine of History and Biography*, October 1957, pp. 403–449, Virginia Historical Society, Richmond (copyright); 1637–1640, Stanley Gray and V. J. Wyckoff, "The International Tobacco Trade in the Seventeenth Century," *Southern Economic Journal*, VII, July 1940, pp. 18–25, University of North Carolina, Chapel Hill (copyright); 1663–1695, compiled by J. M. Price from PRO CO 388/2 ff.7,13 (1663, 1669), outports for 1669 from Lonsdale MS, B. M. Sloane MS.1815 ff.34–7 (1683–1689), PRO T. 1/36/9 fo.50 (1689–1693), and Gray and Wyckoff, cited above (1672–1682); 1693–1695, House of Lords Record Office, parchment collection.

The figures here are not as satisfactory as those given in series Z 441–448 and Z 449–456. The total imports for 1686 and 1688 were obtained by adding figures not strictly comparable with each other. Imports of the outports (English ports other than London) for 1682–1688 are averages of estimates for several years. In a few instances the figures from Gray and Wyckoff include minor quantities of Spanish and Brazilian tobacco.

As indicated in the general note for series Z 441–472, the figures shown prior to the time when the Dutch were driven from New Netherland should not be relied upon too greatly. Rive (cited in source above, pp. 57–75) suggests that the doubling of the London import figures between 1637 and 1638 may have been due to better patrolling of the Channel. There is much evidence to show that the laws restricting tobacco importations to London and excluding Spanish tobacco were disregarded at least in part (Beer, cited above in general note for series Z 441–472, pp. 197 ff.; Williams, cited in source above, pp. 419–420; Wyckoff, cited in source above, pp. 32–34).

An alternate approach to studying the import figures is to consider the estimates of tobacco which might be produced or purchased. English proposals for limitations on tobacco importation included the following: 55,000 pounds in 1620; 200,000 pounds in 1625 and 1626; 250,000 pounds in 1627; 600,000 pounds in 1635; and 1,600,000 pounds in 1638 (Beer, cited above in general note for series Z 441–472, pp. 120, 138, 154, and 158). Virginia meantime wanted the King in 1628 to take at least 500,000 pounds annually and by 1639 sought to reduce the tobacco crop to 1,500,000 that year and 1,300,000 pounds for each of the next two years (Killebrew, cited above in general note for series Z 441–472, pp. 215–216).

Another weakness of the figures for these series lies in their failure to show which colonies supplied the tobacco; however, other data provide some opportunities to estimate the quantity which the various colonies contributed. Virginia and Bermuda ran neck and neck in 1620 at 50,000 to 55,000 pounds each. In 1628, Virginia's shipments were twice those of Bermuda, and thereafter Virginia drew far ahead (Beer, cited above in general note for series Z 441–472, p. 120; and

Williams, cited in source above, pp. 421–449). Her production had risen from 20,000 pounds in 1619 and went on to 18,150,000 in 1688 and 18,295,000 pounds in 1704 (R. A. Brock, "A Succinct Account of Tobacco in Virginia, 1607–1790," in J. B. Killebrew, cited above in general note for series Z 441–472, p. 224). Bermuda's production increased to 500,000 pounds at the most in the 1680's (George L. Beer, *The Old Colonial System, 1660–1754*, vol. II, Macmillan, New York, 1912, p. 91). At the end of the century, Bermuda's exports to England became negligible, and by the first quarter of the 18th century Bermuda was importing from Virginia some of the 20,000 pounds consumed by her population, which was estimated at 3,600 whites and 5,000 slaves in the 1680's (H. C. Wilkinson, *Bermuda in the Old Empire*, Oxford University Press, London, 1950, p. 14).

The West Indies were said to have begun growing tobacco as early as 1625; by 1628, reports show the shipment of about 100,000 pounds, but by the middle of the century sugar began to take over as the predominant crop (Beer, *The Origins . . .*, cited above in general note for series Z 441–472, pp. 89–90).

Meanwhile Maryland, which probably had produced no more than 100,000 pounds annually by 1639 (Wyckoff, cited in source above, p. 49), so increased her output that she contributed about 36 percent of the combined Virginia-Maryland total in 1688—a percentage she approximated at the turn of the 17th century (Margaret Shove Morriss, *Colonial Trade of Maryland, 1689–1715*, Johns Hopkins University Studies in Historical and Political Science, Series XXXII, No. 3, Baltimore, 1914, pp. 31–36) and during the period 1768 to 1773 (see series Z 467–468).

In the Colonies further south, North Carolina was said to be growing about 2,000 hogsheads, or 1,000,000 pounds, of tobacco in the 1670's—an estimate which seems more generous than the subsequent pattern of exports justifies (Beer, *The Old Colonial System, 1660–1754*, cited above, vol. II, p. 195).

Z 460–472. American tobacco exported and imported, by origin and destination, 1768–1772.

Source: Compiled by Lawrence A. Harper, University of California, from American Inspector General's Ledger of Imports and Exports, Public Records Office, London, Customs 16/1.

Although they cover only a few years, these series provide the only known comprehensive data which permit a complete analysis of the pre-Revolutionary colonial tobacco trade.

In the source, some export figures for 1768 and 1770 for Virginia, North Carolina, and South Carolina were shown in hogsheads or barrels. When the weights of these units were not indicated, they were converted to pounds by Harper, by using the average weights of these units as reflected in the shipments to Great Britain from the respective colonies for 1768–1772.

Also, the source shows the South Carolina export to Great Britain for 1771 as 433 hogsheads totaling 40,333 pounds. This obviously is an erroneous ratio. Since the hogshead figure is more comparable to other data shown here than the pounds figure, the former is assumed to be correct. It has been converted to pounds in the same manner as the 1770 export figures mentioned above.

Z 473–480. Tea imported from England by American Colonies, 1761–1775.

Source: Compiled by Lawrence A. Harper, University of California, from the English Inspector General's Ledgers, Public Records Office, London, Customs 3.

Figures for tea imports shown in the American Inspector General's Ledgers (PRO Customs 16/1) for 1768–1772 closely approximate those shown here for the corresponding years (O. M. Dickerson, *The Navigation Acts and the American Revolution*, University of Pennsylvania Press, Philadelphia, 1951, pp. 99–100).

Z 481–499. General note.

Information on rice in the colonial period is limited primarily to the material on the clean rice which entered commercial trading. Presumably, the weight of this rice bore approximately the same ratio to the rough rice of the plantation at that time as it does now, that is, 100/162. There are no known satisfactory statistics on rice production and only scattered data concerning domestic consumption. Lord Carteret told the Board of Trade in 1715 that South Carolina "spent in the country" one-third of the 3,000 tons of rice she was producing at that time. By the pre-Revolutionary period, comparison of total exports with net imports for 1769–1772 indicates that only 3 percent of total exports was consumed in the nonrice-producing colonies.

The basic sources of statistics on clean rice in commerce are the records of importations in the British Public Records Office kept by the English Inspector General of Imports and Exports (Customs 2 and 3, since 1696), by the Scottish Inspector General (Customs 14, since 1755), by the American Inspector General (Customs 16/1, 1768–1772), and the records kept by the colonial naval officers (supplemented by those kept by the deputies of the London Commissioners of Customs for the comparatively few instances when these records have survived).

Data from these basic sources appear in: Gray, *History of Agriculture . . .*, cited above for series Z 432–435, pp. 1020–1023; Francis Yonge, *A View of the Trade of South Carolina*, London, 1722; C. J. Gayle, "The Nature and Volume of Exports From Charleston, 1724–1774," *The Proceedings of the South Carolina Historical Association*, Columbia, 1937, pp. 30–31; G. K. Holmes, *Rice Crop of the United States, 1712–1911* (Circular 34, Department of Agriculture, Bureau of Statistics, 1912); Francis Yonge, *Narratives of the Proceedings of the People of South Carolina*, in B. R. Carroll, *Historical Collections of South Carolina*, vol. II, Harper & Bros., New York, 1836, p. 156; *The Case of the Province of South Carolina* (Carroll, vol. II, p. 265); Gov. James Glen, *Description of South Carolina* (Carroll, vol. II, p. 26); "An Account of Sundry Goods Imported and . . . Exported . . . From the First of November 1738 to the First of November 1739" (printed as a broadside by P. Timothy, Charleston, 1739), Bernard Romans, *Natural History of East and West Florida*, New York, 1775; and WPA compilations from the Charleston Naval Office lists (see general note for series Z 1–615).

Fortunately, the British records measure the quantities imported in hundredweights, but the American statistics usually give only the number of barrels and other containers exported. Where half-barrels were reported, the number was divided by two and the result included in the barrel totals.

Miscellaneous units in the American figures have been converted to barrels. The term "cask" has been considered synonymous with "barrel," following the usage of the American Inspector General's Accounts for 1768, but the remaining figures are rough approximations suggested by the weights of other commodities as given in M. Postlethwayt, *The Universal Dictionary of Trade and Commerce*, W. Strahan, London, 1774; J. H. Alexander, *Universal Dictionary of Weights and Measures*, D. Van Nostrand, New York, 1867, and the *Oxford English Dictionary*. A tierce has been considered to equal $1\frac{1}{3}$ barrels; a hogshead, 2 barrels; a puncheon, $2\frac{2}{3}$ barrels; a butt, 4 barrels; small barrels and small casks, $\frac{1}{2}$ of a barrel; seroons, boxes, and bags, $\frac{2}{5}$ of a barrel; kegs, $\frac{1}{5}$; and bushels, $\frac{1}{8}$. Colonial containers varied so greatly that these estimates seldom, if ever, represented the exact relationship. When discussing weights and measures for other uses, additional information should be obtained and corrections, as may be necessary, should be made in the formulas employed here. For present purposes, these maverick units constitute such a negligible part of the whole that errors in estimating their weight seem unlikely to exceed those involved in rounding.

The significant problem lies in determining the weight of the barrel, the principal unit. Holmes (cited above, p. 4) stated that it weighed 350 pounds in 1717; 400 pounds, 1718–1729; and 500 pounds, 1730–1788, but as Gray (cited above, vol. II, p. 1020) points out, these figures conflict with those given by others. Although Governor Johnson of South Carolina stated in 1719 that the average barrel contained about 350 pounds, Francis Yonge, the collector at Charleston, gave the figure of 400 pounds for 1719–1721; a Savannah Rice Association study declared it to be 325 pounds for 1720–1729; a contemporary report in 1731 and Governor Glen of South Carolina in 1749 said the barrel contained 500 pounds, but other documents say that it was 500–600 pounds in 1763; "something over 600 pounds in 1768–1769"; 550 pounds for 1764–1772; and 540 pounds net in 1772. O. M. Dickerson, *The Navigation Acts and the American Revolution* (cited above in text for series Z 473–480, p. 59) states that the formula used by the customs service for converting barrels to hundredweight had each barrel containing $4\frac{1}{2}$ hundredweight, or 504 pounds (but the records do not disclose when the formula was calculated nor how often it was revised).

Fortunately, an examination of the surviving official statistics enables one to obtain averages calculated on broad bases. The decennial totals for 1720–1729 and 1730–1739 (Gov. James Glen, cited above) give both the number of barrels and the total weight shipped, showing the average barrel to weigh 373 pounds during the first decade and 448 pounds during the second. Similarly, the naval office lists for 1756–1767, which record both the number of barrels and pound weights shipped to Southern Europe and the West Indies, give a weighted average of about 525 pounds each for some 20,000 barrels.

Comparisons of the number of barrels shipped to Britain from America with the weight recorded for the rice arriving there provide another means of estimating the average weight of the rice barrel. For present purposes, it can be assumed to have been 350 pounds until 1720, and then to have risen 10 pounds a year until 1730, when it remained at a plateau of 450 pounds until after 1740; then it began to ascend at the rate of 5 pounds a year until it reached its pre-Revolutionary peak of 525 pounds in 1755. It must be remembered, however, that the weight of the barrels might vary radically. New York's Naval Office list for 1764 shows one shipment averaging $183\frac{1}{2}$ pounds a barrel and another 698 pounds.

Z 481–485. Rice exported from producing areas, 1698–1789.

Source: 1698–1774, compiled by Lawrence A. Harper, University of California, from references discussed below; 1783–1789, compiled by Jacob M. Price, University of Michigan.

These series attempt to provide a comprehensive statistical summary comparable to those available for the postcolonial period. Barrels have been converted to pounds on the bases described in the general note for series Z 481–499.

There was the problem of totaling the exports from the three South Carolina ports (Charleston, Beaufort-Port Royal, and Georgetown-Wynyaw) and those of Georgia. Shipments from other colonies can be considered as having originated in South Carolina and Georgia, except possibly those of North Carolina, and even in this case most of the exports probably went through South Carolina. In any event, North Carolina's exports are grouped with South Carolina's shipments in the English import figures, under the generic heading, "Carolinas." Shipments to Scotland seem to have been infrequent and insignificant until the French and Indian War (1754–1763).

The Charleston figures, with the exceptions noted below, are those compiled by Gayle (cited above in general note for series Z 481–499) from the *South Carolina Gazette*, although his figures for less than 12 months have been extended to full year bases for 1750, 1756, 1757, 1763, and 1767. For 1698–1724, the figures have been calculated on the assumption that all American rice imports recorded in the English Inspector General's Ledgers were equal to $\frac{7}{8}$ of Charleston's total exports, as suggested in 1719 by Francis Yonge, the customs collector at Charleston, a conclusion corroborated by a comparison of the WPA compilations of Charleston exports with the English imports for 1717, 1718, 1719, and 1724, and by Edward Randolph's remark in 1700 that $\frac{1}{10}$ of Charleston's exports went to the West Indies alone (Carroll, cited above in general note for series Z 481–499). For 1731, the figures come from the WPA compilations of the Charleston Naval Office list (see general note for series Z 1–615), and

for 1734 and 1758, directly from the *South Carolina Gazette;* for 1765, from the *Charleston Year Book* (1880) as copied by Holmes (cited above in general note for series Z 481–499); for 1766, from photographic copies of the Charleston Naval Office list (PRO C. O. 5); for 1768–1772, from the American Inspector General's Ledgers (PRO Customs 16/1); for 1773 and 1774, from Gray (cited above for series Z 432–435, p. 1022), although his partial figure for 1773 has been extended to complete the year. The years terminate October 31 except 1698 (September 28); 1699–1724, 1731 (December 24); and 1768–1773 (January 4 of the following year).

Neither Beaufort-Port Royal nor Georgetown-Wynyaw (South Carolina) seem to have had much importance until 1732. Although the former had its first collector in 1729, there was a lapse of $2\frac{1}{2}$ years before his successor took over (PRO AO 1/804/1038, AO 1/805/1039); and the latter appears to have had its first collector in June 1732 (*South Carolina Gazette*, June 24, 1732). Scattered naval office records show Georgetown exporting 385 barrels for the year 1734 and 509 for the first quarter in 1735; and Beaufort, 342 during the first half of 1736. In 1739, Georgetown exported 2,202 barrels and Beaufort, 2,165 barrels (broadside, cited above, general note for series Z 481–499), an approximate equality which also existed in the period 1768–1772 (PRO Customs 16/1). For lack of a better basis, their exports will be considered for present purposes to have been equal from 1733 to 1768, when exact figures are available and used. In 1739, the exports of the two together equalled $6\frac{1}{2}$ percent of South Carolina's exports—a percentage which dropped by 1769–1772 to 4.4 percent. Thus, from 1739 to 1768, the Beaufort and Georgetown contributions have been assumed to be 5 percent of the total South Carolina exports. A different formula was used for the years prior to 1739, when their percentage was growing from the $2\frac{1}{2}$ percent which they enjoyed in 1734 (calculated by doubling the Georgetown figures which have survived for that year). On the necessarily arbitrary assumption that the rate of increase was uniform, the two ports each year from 1734 to 1739 added 0.7 percent to their share of South Carolina's exports. Extending the same formula backwards, their share of the Carolina total was 1.8 percent in 1733 and 1.1 percent in 1732.

Romans, cited above, general note for series Z 481–499, provides figures for Georgia for 1756–1767. A comparison of his figures for Georgia's total exports with those of receipts from Georgia in England (see series Z 493–499) for the decade 1756–1765 shows a ratio of one barrel exported for every 2.07 hundredweight received; and for 1740, 1742, 1750, and 1753–1755, the barrels shipped from Georgia have been computed in accordance with that formula, on the basis of English receipts (series Z 493–499). Figures for 1768–1772 come from PRO Customs 16/1. In 1773 and 1774, Georgia is assumed to have contributed 13.9 percent of the total exports, as it did from 1768 to 1772. Years end January 4 of the year following, except for the years for which figures are calculated, as noted above. For those years, no exact date can be assigned and the data are therefore not strictly comparable.

The figures for 1768–1772 provide the best basis for the later period, but for present purposes the 1768 list was not included in the basic calculations described above because it lacks data for coastwise exports; however, it provides the best base for estimating the imports for that year. All that need be assumed is that the ratio of the coastwise exports to the other exports was the same in 1768 as the average of the other four years.

The coastwise entries for 1769–1773 show both inward and outward entries. Thus, to avoid duplications in the Carolina and Georgia entries, only the net exports coastwise have been included. This adjustment cannot be made prior to 1769, but samples from the WPA compilations (see general note for series Z 1–615) indicate that it is very minor.

The data for the various colonies are shown here, not because the individual details are necessarily accurate, but in order that scholars possessing more complete information may adjust the figures wherever possible.

The object of presenting these series is to provide the best possible pattern of the over-all development. The errors in detail are as likely as not to offset one another. Except for 1713–1731, when the estimates of the size of the barrels varied radically, the totals shown here should be within 5 percent of the true figure.

Data for 1783–1789 were compiled from records of Public Record Office, London Board of Trade, 6/21 ff.311–312. Shipping seasons for the crops of these years were: 1789 (crop of 1788), no limiting dates given; 1788 (crop of 1787), November 30, 1787–November 22, 1788; 1787 (crop of 1786), November 23, 1786–November 30, 1787; 1786 (crop of 1785), November 19, 1785–November 23, 1786; 1785 (crop of 1784), December 3, 1784–November 19, 1785; 1784 (crop of 1783), November 12, 1783–December 3, 1784; and 1783 (crop of 1782), January 17, 1783–November 12, 1783.

Z 486–492. Rice exported from Charleston, S.C., by destination, 1717–1766.

Source: Compiled by J. R. House from the WPA compilations of naval office lists at the University of California, Berkeley (see general note for series Z 1–615).

The differences in totals here and in series Z 481–485 may result in part from the differences in year-ending dates, as shown in the tabular headnotes.

Z 493–499. Rice exported to England, by origin, 1698–1776.

Source: Compiled by Lawrence A. Harper, University of California, from English Inspector General's Ledgers of Imports and Exports, Public Records Office, London, Customs 3 (except 1727, from PRO T.64/276B/323).

A large proportion of the exported rice was reexported by England, not only to Northern but also to Southern Europe.

Z 500–503. Pitch, tar, and turpentine exported from Charleston, S.C., 1725–1774.

Source: 1725–1755, 1760–1764, 1767–1771, Charles J. Gayle, "The Nature and Volume of Exports from Charleston, 1724–1774," *The Proceedings of the South Carolina Historical Association*, Columbia, 1937, p. 31; 1756–1759, 1765, 1772–1774, *South Carolina Gazette*, Charleston, S.C., various issues.

The basic source for these series has been the *South Carolina Gazette*, which obtained the figures from the customhouse books and ran them as cumulative totals from November 1st of most years. The editorial policy of the *Gazette* was not consistent, however; it did not always list the same commodities each year, and sometimes it discontinued the cumulative totals before October 31st.

The WPA compilations (see general note for series Z 1–615) from the English copies of these same records (PRO C. O. 5) provide an alternate source for some years. They also distinguish in detail the destination of the various shipments.

Z 504–509. Timber and timber products exported from Charleston, S.C., and Savannah, Ga., 1754–1774.

Source: Series Z 504–506, 1754–1755, 1760–1764, 1767–1771, Gayle, cited above for series Z 500–503, p. 31; 1756–1759, 1765, 1772–1774, *South Carolina Gazette*, Charleston, S.C., various issues. Series Z 507–509, Oliver M. Dickerson, *The Navigation Acts and the American Revolution*, University of Pennsylvania Press, Philadelphia, 1951, pp. 26–27 (copyright).

The original figures for Savannah were compiled by the Comptroller at that port. For discussion of Charleston figures, see text for series Z 500–503.

Z 510–515. Number and tonnage of vessels built, by type, 1768–1773.

Source: Compiled by Jacob M. Price, University of Michigan, from George Chalmers, *Opinions On Interesting Subjects . . . Arising From American Independence*, London, 1784, p. 105.

Z 516–529. Vessels built in Thirteen Colonies and West Florida, 1769–1771.

Source: Compiled by Jacob M. Price, University of Michigan, from John, Lord Sheffield, *Observations On the Commerce of the American States*, 6th edition, London 1784, p. 96.

Z 530–533. Number of vessels engaged in whaling, and quantity and value of oil acquired, Nantucket, Mass., 1715–1789.

Source: 1715–1785, Obed Macy, *The History of Nantucket*, Hilliard, Gray & Co., Boston, 1835, pp. 54–55 and 232–233; 1787–1789, U.S. Congress, *American State Papers*, Class 4, "Commerce and Navigation" (two volumes), vol. I, Gales and Seaton, Washington, D.C., 1832, p. 16.

The figures shown on pp. 232–233 of the source are stated to be from the Massachusetts Historical Society's Collections. Those on pp. 54–55 cite no authority; however, the Macy family descended from the first settlers and Obed Macy's data, which are generally consistent with information from other sources, provide the best figures now available.

The development of whaling in Nantucket followed the process typical of all the colonies [Walter S. Tower, *A History of the American Whale Fishery* (publications of the University of Pennsylvania, series in Political Economy and Public Law, No. 20), Philadelphia, 1907]. The early settlers first processed drift whales, then they engaged in the offshore fisheries which probably reached their height at Nantucket in 1726 when 86 whales were taken (Alexander Starbuck, *The History of Nantucket*, C. E. Goodspeed & Co., Boston, 1924, p. 356). The first deep-sea venture occurred about 1712 when a strong wind blew an offshore vessel to sea where it caught a spermaceti whale (Macy, cited above, p. 36). By 1746, Nantucket whalers were making their way to Davis Straits and by 1774 they were sailing as far away as the coast of Brazil (Macy, cited above, p. 54).

The figures for Nantucket may be viewed in better perspective by noting that in 1730 the New England whaling fleet totaled 1,300 tons, and in 1763 that of Massachusetts consisted of 180 sailing vessels. (Raymond McFarland, *A History of the New England Fisheries*, D. Appleton and Company, New York, 1911, p. 86.) At the time of the Revolution, New England had 304 whalers totaling 27,840 tons out of an estimated American fleet of 360 vessels (Tower, cited above, p. 45; Starbuck, cited above, p. 176).

Z 534–538. State of the cod fishery of Massachusetts, 1765–1775.

Source: Stella H. Sutherland, *Population Distribution in Colonial America*, AMS Press, Inc., New York, 1966 (copyright). (The original source of the data is Timothy Pitkin, *A Statistical View of the Commerce of the United States*, p. 84.)

Dr. John J. McCusker, University of Maryland, in "Weights and Measures in the Colonial Sugar Trade: The Gallon and the Pound and Their International Equivalents," *William and Mary Quarterly*, Third Series, vol. XXX, No. 4, October 1973, pp. 605 and 606, has supplied the following information on the definition of "quintal":

"The usual multiple of the pound was the *hundred*, called frequently the *quintal* and more fully the *hundredweight* (abbreviated cwt. or Ct. in eighteenth-century accounts). The hundredweight usually but not always equalled one hundred times the basic unit.

"By the middle of the seventeenth century, the *great hundred* of 112 pounds had become established for the English sugar trade as the standard hundredweight in the mother country but not consistently in the colonies. The English colonists on the North American continent bought and sold sugar by the great or long hundredweight, yet used the short hundredweight of 100 pounds for tobacco and codfish, commodities for which the mother country employed the long hundredweight."

Z 539–550. Daily wages of selected types of workmen, by area, 1621–1781.

Source: 1621–1670 and 1776–1781, Richard B. Morris, *Government and Labor in Early America*, Octagon Books, New York, 1975 (copyright 1946, and new foreword copyright © 1975, by Richard B. Morris); 1710, Richard Walsh, *The Charleston Sons of Liberty*, University of South Carolina Press, Columbia, 1959 (copyright).

The figures do not represent actual payments, which may have been higher, but they represent what the lawmakers believed was the proper maximum wage rate. Figures are payments to master craftsmen; journeymen received less (for example, 20 pence instead of 2 shillings in 1641).

For New Haven there were two wage rates—one for the summer, which is shown in these series, and one for the winter. For each occupation the winter rate was 6 shillings less in 1640 and 4 shillings less in 1641. Apparently the lower rate for the winter was paid because of the shorter workday.

The legislative rates also throw light on other labor facts. When New Haven set the rate for mowers in 1640, correlation of the daily wage (2 s. 6 d.) with the rate for mowing an acre of fresh marsh shows that they considered it a day's work, although they believed that mowing a salt marsh would take longer and be worth 3 shillings. The next year they confessed the ratio was inadequate when they lowered the daily wages without board to 20 d. and raised the rate for mowing to 3 s. per acre for fresh marsh and 3 s. 6 d. for salt marsh (Morris, cited above, pp. 79–80).

For discussion of the working day, see text for series Z 551–556.

Z 551–556. Daily and monthly wages of agricultural laborers in Maryland, 1638–1676.

Source: Manfred Jonas, "Wages in Early Colonial Maryland," *Maryland Historical Magazine*, vol. LI, March 1956, pp. 27–38.

The source also gives additional information on the cost of living. Its basic data came from scattered items in the *Archives of Maryland* (a series of annual volumes published by the Maryland Historical Society, Baltimore).

In Maryland, during the first half of the 17th century, the working month seems to have extended from 23 to 25 days and the working day from 10 to 12 hours. The 3 winter months were generally not included within the terms of labor contracts. Persons hired by the day worked the same hours and did not get lodging, but received at least 2 meals at the job (Jonas, cited above, pp. 30 and 34–35). In the other colonies the working day was probably much the same. New Haven, for example, specified in 1640 that a day's work was from 10 to 12 hours in summer and 8 hours in winter (Morris, *Government and Labor ...*, cited above for series Z 539–550, pp. 59, 79, and 84).

Z 557. Index of wholesale prices estimated for colonial and pre-Federal years, 1720–1789.

Source: U.S. Congress, *Hearings Before the Joint Economic Committee*, 86th Congress, 1st session, Part II, *Historical and Comparative Rates of Production, Productivity, and Prices* (statement presented by Ethel D. Hoover, U.S. Bureau of Labor Statistics).

This index (which extends to 1958 in the source) was obtained by combining and splicing index numbers constructed by various investigators for different markets, to approximate a continuous series. The annual indexes were calculated by working forward and backward from the selected base period, 1850–59. No adjustments were made to the original series for differences in coverage or in methods of calculation. However, when wholesale prices in two or more markets were combined, the necessary conversions to a common base period were made, and occasional estimates, as noted in other parts of the source, were used.

For this series, weighted combinations were made of the available index series for three major markets (Philadelphia, New York, and Charleston), except for the years prior to 1732 and the Revolutionary War years. For these years, the estimates were based on Philadelphia prices only. The weights used to combine markets were rough approximations, based chiefly on estimates of the population and trade for each area and on the representative character and adequacy of the available indexes.

Z 558–577. Average annual wholesale prices of selected commodities in Philadelphia, 1720–1775.

Source: Anne Bezanson, Robert D. Gray, and Miriam Hussey, *Prices in Colonial Pennsylvania*, University of Pennsylvania Press, Philadelphia, 1935, pp. 422–424 (copyright).

The primary source of the original data was the list of "prices current" which first appeared in 1719 in the *American Mercury* and which was continued in that and other newspapers. Gaps were usually filled by reference to merchants' account books and letterbooks (as discussed and listed in the source cited, pp. 3–5, 351–354, and 434–438). The annual averages were computed "by taking the arithmetic mean of the 12 average monthly prices in each year. When any monthly price was missing the available data were averaged quarterly and the annual figure derived from the quarterly averages. ... In some cases it was necessary to estimate a quarterly price by averaging the last monthly quotation in the previous quarter with the first monthly quotation in the following quarter. No annual price was estimated completely. ..."

The source volume was sponsored by the International Scientific Committee in Price History, as were a number of other studies of colonial prices drawn together in A. H. Cole, *Wholesale Commodity Prices in the United States: 1700–1861*, Harvard University Press, Cambridge, 1938. In addition to discussion and analyses of prices, this publication offers a statistical supplement of monthly prices for the principal commercial centers. The tables in it, however, rest primarily upon the Philadelphia prices until the 1750's. Prior to 1750, Boston has only two series, wheat and molasses, which begin in 1720. Although there are gaps in the data, Charleston has series for bread, corn, rice, rum, wine, molasses, and staves beginning 1732; sugar beginning 1744; beef, pork, and indigo in 1747; and coffee, leather, and lumber in 1749. New York has series for flour, bread, rice, sugar, salt, rum, and molasses beginning 1748; and for wheat, beef, and pork beginning 1749.

Price series for the following Philadelphia commodities are shown in the source (not included here because of space limitations): Brown bread, white bread, London loaf sugar, Pennsylvania loaf sugar, indigo, bar iron, pig iron, hogshead staves, pipe staves, turpentine, and gunpowder. In addition to the annual averages, the source contains average monthly prices and monthly and annual indexes (both arithmetic and geometric) of 20 commodities in Philadelphia.

The unit of measure of Madeira wine (pipe) consists of 110 gallons. Barrels, in the case of beef and pork, consist of 31.5 gallons and hundredweights equal 112 pounds, except for tobacco where it equals 100 pounds.

Z 578–582. Prices of Maryland tobacco, 1711–1775.

Source: Carville V. Earle, *The Evolution of a Tidewater Settlement System: All Hallow's Parish, Maryland, 1650–1783*, Ph.D. dissertation, University of Chicago, 1973.

The prices of tobacco are from the probate records, inventories and accounts of Anne Arundel and Prince Georges counties between 1711 and 1775. The year runs from January 1 to December 31. Each year contains at least eight prices; the mean annual average is presented here. The prices are in British sterling. Accompanying the price series is a list of exchange rates for converting Maryland current money to sterling. In the probate records, where the tobacco prices appear, the monies of account are varied Maryland currencies which are overvalued in relation to sterling. Exchange rates between one of these currencies, Maryland current money, and sterling are frequent, and these administered rates provide the data for the exchange rate series. For each year, the modal exchange rate is entered.

So long as tobacco prices are in current money, they may be converted to sterling with this series. One problem concerns the years 1772 and 1773 when current money exchanged at 33⅓ and 66⅔; accordingly, for these years, two exchange rates and two tobacco prices are shown. A second problem occurs in 1757 when no one exchange rate is predominant; therefore, the mean exchange rate is used in preference to the mode.

Z 583. Farm prices of Maryland tobacco, 1659–1710.

Source: Russell R. Menard, "Farm Prices of Maryland Tobacco, 1659 to 1710," *Maryland Historical Magazine*, LXVIII, 1973, pp. 80–85.

The series presents yearly means based on crop appraisals and other data found in all Maryland probate inventories filed between 1659 and 1710. Full documentation and a description of procedure is provided in the source.

Z 584. Farm prices of Chesapeake tobacco, 1618–1658.

Source: Russell R. Menard, "A Note on Chesapeake Tobacco Prices, 1618 to 1660," (forthcoming) *Virginia Magazine of History and Biography* (copyright).

The series presents yearly means of price quotations found in correspondence, accounts of sales, promotional literature, court records, official proclamations, and legislative acts. Price quotations for Chesapeake tobacco in Europe and prices that appear to be deliberate exaggeration or understatements of the actual price were excluded from the mean. The means are based on few observations: in no one year did the number exceed ten; in most only two or three prices were found.

See source for further documentation and description of procedures.

Z 585. Annual rate of exchange on London for Pennsylvania currency, 1720–1775.

Source: See source for series Z 558–577, p. 432.

This series is derived from data in papers of Pennsylvania merchants and the Minutes of the Provincial Council (1739), supplemented in some years by Victor S. Clark, *History of Manufactures in the United States, 1893–1928*, vol. III, Carnegie Institution of Washington, D.C., 1916–1949, pp. 361–362. Bezanson et al., in *Prices . . .*, cited above, p. 431, also give monthly rates of exchanges during the same period.

Z 586. Annual price of an ounce of silver at Boston, Mass., 1700–1749.

Source: A. H. Cole, *Wholesale Commodity Prices in the United States: 1700–1861*, Harvard University Press, Cambridge, 1938, p. 119 (copyright).

The original shilling prices were taken from the Suffolk files by A. M. Davis, *Currency and Banking in the Province of Massachusetts Bay*, vol. I, Macmillan, New York, 1901, pp. 368 and 370. Where more than one price was given for a year, the high and low figures were averaged to determine the price for that year.

Z 587–598. Partial list of bills of credit and Treasury notes issued by American Colonies, 1703–1775.

Source: B. U. Ratchford, *American State Debts*, Duke University Press, Durham, 1941, pp. 26–27 (copyright).

These series attempt to show the issues of bills of credit and treasury notes emitted by the Colonies between 1703 and 1775. The £82,000 in bills issued by Massachusetts between 1690 and 1702 are not included, nor are the issues of Georgia, which never had a large debt. Under the trustees, the principal circulating medium in Georgia was the "sola" bills, issued only in the original by the trustees. A total of £135,000 of these bills of exchange were issued but only £1,149 remained unredeemed in 1752. Thereafter, Georgia emitted at least two issues of bills: One of £3,000 in 1756 and one of £7,410 in 1761 (Ratchford, cited above, p. 19).

Ratchford concedes that the list may be incomplete and that many of the issues listed were not made at the time nor in the exact amount stated. Sometimes the law authorizing the issue constitutes the only evidence, and nothing indicates "how, when, or to what extent the issue was actually made."

The original source for 1737–1748 for Massachusetts is A. M. Davis, cited above in text for series Z 586. Davis expressed all issues in the terms of old tenor (the form of bills which existed in February 1737). Ratchford did not follow this procedure because he did not feel sufficiently acquainted with the circumstances in each case to make the conversion with assurance. For all other years, the data rest upon a variety of sources cited in the footnotes of Ratchford's first chapter, which provide a helpful bibliography for further reference.

The footnotes to these series indicate the principal purposes for which the larger issues were made. For years when several issues appeared for different purposes, the footnotes indicate the purpose for issuing the majority of the bills.

Z 599–610. Paper money outstanding in American Colonies, 1705–1775.

Source: See source for series Z 587–598, p. 28.

The original sources of the data are various monographs cited in Ratchford's first chapter. Unfortunately, the authors of these monographs did not always attempt to find or to make estimates themselves. Some of the estimates are those of legislative committees or public officials and, less frequently, of contemporary writers. Many of the estimates for 1739 and 1748 come from William Douglass whose work is discussed in Charles Bullock, Introduction, *Economic Studies of the American Economic Association*, vol. II, No. 1. Georgia did not warrant a separate series, the only estimate being one for £5,500 for 1761.

For approximately a fifth of the figures, the actual year of issuance differs from that indicated in this table by one or two years; for exact year of issuance, see source.

Z 611–615. Tax collections in America under the different revenue laws, 1765–1774.

Source: Oliver M. Dickerson, *The Navigation Acts and the American Revolution*, University of Pennsylvania Press, Philadelphia, 1951, p. 201 (copyright).

Tax records have long been an untapped source of economic data. Dickerson has gathered figures from the English Treasury Papers for both the revenues collected under the Navigation Act of 1673 (25 Car. II c 7) and the new revenue measures which followed the French and Indian War (1763). He estimates (p. 202) that seizures (often highly technical) under the new revenue program cost the Americans not less than £60,956 "exclusive of fees, direct plunder, and costs of defending suits in the admiralty courts."

Series Z 1–19. Estimated Population of American Colonies: 1610 to 1780

Series No.	Colony	1780	1770	1760	1750	1740	1730	1720	1710	1700	1690	1680	1670	1660	1650	1640	1630
	WHITE AND NEGRO																
1	Total	2,780,369	2,148,076	1,593,625	1,170,760	905,563	629,445	466,185	331,711	250,888	210,372	151,507	111,935	75,058	50,368	26,634	4,646
2	Maine [1]	49,133	31,257	20,000											1,000	900	400
3	New Hampshire [2]	87,802	62,396	39,093	27,505	23,256	10,755	9,375	5,681	4,958	4,164	2,047	1,805	1,555	1,305	1,055	500
4	Vermont [3]	47,620	10,000														
5	Plymouth [4]										7,424	6,400	5,333	1,980		1,020	390
6	Massachusetts [1][2][4]	268,627	235,308	202,600	188,000	151,613	114,116	91,008	62,390	55,941	49,504	39,752	30,000	20,082	14,037	8,932	506
7	Rhode Island [2]	52,946	58,196	45,471	33,226	25,255	16,950	11,680	7,573	5,894	4,224	3,017	2,155	1,539	785	300	
8	Connecticut [2]	206,701	183,881	142,470	111,280	89,580	75,530	58,830	39,450	25,970	21,645	17,246	12,603	7,980	4,139	1,472	
9	New York [2]	210,541	162,920	117,138	76,696	63,665	48,594	36,919	21,625	19,107	13,909	9,830	5,754	4,936	4,116	1,930	350
10	New Jersey [2]	139,627	117,431	93,813	71,393	51,373	37,510	29,818	19,872	14,010	8,000	3,400	1,000				
11	Pennsylvania [2]	327,305	240,057	183,703	119,666	85,637	51,707	30,962	24,450	17,950	11,450	680					
12	Delaware [2]	45,385	35,496	33,250	28,704	19,870	9,170	5,385	3,645	2,470	1,482	1,005	700	540	185		
13	Maryland [2]	245,474	202,599	162,267	141,073	116,093	91,113	66,133	42,741	29,604	24,024	17,904	13,226	8,426	4,504	583	
14	Virginia [2]	538,004	447,016	339,726	231,033	180,440	114,000	87,757	78,281	58,560	53,046	43,596	35,309	27,020	18,731	10,442	2,500
15	North Carolina [2]	270,133	197,200	110,442	72,984	51,760	30,000	21,270	15,120	10,720	7,600	5,430	3,850	1,000			
16	South Carolina [2]	180,000	124,244	94,074	64,000	45,000	30,000	17,048	10,883	5,704	3,900	1,200	200				
17	Georgia [2]	56,071	23,375	9,578	5,200	2,021											
18	Kentucky [5]	45,000	15,700														
19	Tennessee [6]	10,000	1,000														
	NEGRO																
1	Total	575,420	459,822	325,806	236,420	150,024	91,021	68,839	44,866	27,817	16,729	6,971	4,535	2,920	1,600	597	60
2	Maine [1]	458	475	300													
3	New Hampshire [2]	541	654	600	550	500	200	170	150	130	100	75	65	50	40	30	
4	Vermont [3]	50	25														
6	Massachusetts [1][2]	4,822	4,754	4,566	4,075	3,035	2,780	2,150	1,310	800	400	170	160	422	295	150	
7	Rhode Island [2]	[7]2,671	3,761	3,468	3,347	2,408	1,648	543	375	300	250	175	115	65	25		
8	Connecticut [2]	[7]5,885	5,698	3,783	3,010	2,598	1,490	1,093	750	450	200	50	35	25	20	15	
9	New York [2]	21,054	19,112	16,340	11,014	8,996	6,956	5,740	2,811	2,256	1,670	1,200	690	600	500	232	10
10	New Jersey [2]	10,460	8,220	6,567	5,354	4,366	3,008	2,385	1,332	840	450	200	60				
11	Pennsylvania [2]	7,855	5,761	4,409	2,872	2,055	1,241	2,000	1,575	430	270	25					
12	Delaware [2]	2,996	1,836	1,733	1,496	1,035	478	700	500	135	82	55	40	30	15		
13	Maryland [2]	80,515	63,818	49,004	43,450	24,031	17,220	12,499	7,945	3,227	2,162	1,611	1,190	758	300	20	
14	Virginia [2]	220,582	187,605	140,570	101,452	60,000	30,000	26,559	23,118	16,390	9,345	3,000	2,000	950	405	150	50
15	North Carolina [2]	91,000	69,600	33,554	19,800	11,000	6,000	3,000	900	415	300	210	150	20			
16	South Carolina [2]	97,000	75,178	57,334	39,000	30,000	20,000	12,000	4,100	2,444	1,500	200	30				
17	Georgia [2]	20,831	10,625	3,578	1,000												
18	Kentucky [5]	7,200	2,500														
19	Tennessee [6]	1,500	200														

Series No.	Colony	1620	1610
	WHITE AND NEGRO		
5	Plymouth	102	
14	Virginia	[8]2,200	350

[1] For 1660–1750, Maine counties included with Massachusetts. Maine was a part of Massachusetts until it became a separate State in 1820.
[2] One of the original 13 States.
[3] Admitted to statehood in 1791.
[4] Plymouth became a part of the Province of Massachusetts in 1691.
[5] Admitted to statehood in 1792.
[6] Admitted to statehood in 1796.
[7] Includes some Indians.
[8] Includes 20 Negroes.

Series Z 20–23. Percent Distribution of the White Population, by Nationality: 1790

Series No.	Area	Total	English	Scotch	Irish		German	Dutch	French	Swedish	Spanish	Unassigned
					Ulster	Free State						
20	Total States	100.0	60.9	8.3	6.0	3.7	8.7	3.4	1.7	0.7		6.6
	Maine [1]	100.0	60.0	4.5	8.0	3.7	1.3	.1	1.3			21.1
	New Hampshire	100.0	61.0	6.2	4.6	2.9	.4	.1	.7			24.1
	Vermont	100.0	76.0	5.1	3.2	1.9	.2	.6	.4			12.6
	Massachusetts [1]	100.0	82.0	4.4	2.6	1.3	.3	.2	.8			8.4
	Rhode Island	100.0	71.0	5.8	2.0	.8	.5	.4	.8	.1		18.6
	Connecticut	100.0	67.0	2.2	1.8	1.1	.3	.3	.9			26.4
	New York	100.0	52.0	7.0	5.1	3.0	8.2	17.5	3.8	.5		2.9
	New Jersey	100.0	47.0	7.7	6.3	3.2	9.2	16.6	2.4	3.9		3.7
	Pennsylvania	100.0	35.3	8.6	11.0	3.5	33.3	1.8	1.8	.8		3.9
	Delaware	100.0	60.0	8.0	6.3	5.4	1.1	4.3	1.6	8.9		[2]4.4
	Maryland (incl. Dist. of Col.)	100.0	64.5	7.6	5.8	6.5	11.7	.5	1.2	.5		1.7
	Virginia (incl. West Virginia)	100.0	68.5	10.2	6.2	5.5	6.3	.3	1.5	.6		.9
	North Carolina	100.0	66.0	14.8	5.7	5.4	4.7	.3	1.7	.2		1.2
	South Carolina	100.0	60.2	15.1	9.4	4.4	5.0	.4	3.9	.2		1.4
	Georgia	100.0	57.4	15.5	11.5	3.8	7.6	.2	2.3	.6		1.1
	Kentucky and Tennessee	100.0	57.9	10.0	7.0	5.2	14.0	1.3	2.2	.5		1.9
	OTHER AREAS											
21	Northwest Territory	100.0	29.8	4.1	2.9	1.8	4.3		57.1			
22	Spanish, United States	100.0	2.5	.3	.2	.1	.4				96.5	
23	French, United States	100.0	11.2	1.6	1.1	.7	8.7		64.2		12.5	

[1] Maine was a part of Massachusetts until it became a State in 1820.   [2] Corrected figure; does not agree with source.

Series **Z 24-132.** Population Censuses Taken in the Colonies and States During the Colonial and Pre-Federal Period: 1624-25 to 1786

Year and age	Total popula-tion	CONNECTICUT								Negro			Indian		
		White								Total	Male	Female	Total	Male	Female
		Total	Male			Female									
			Total	Married	Single	Total	Married	Single							
	24	25	26	27	28	29	30	31	32	33	34	35	36	37
1782	209,177	[1] 202,904							[2] 6,273					
1774	197,842	[3] 191,378	96,182	30,524	65,658	94,296	30,636	63,660	5,101	2,883	2,218	1,363	635	728
Under 10 years		61,164	31,114	–	31,114	30,050	–	30,050	2,471	1,306	1,165	746	391	355
10-20 years		46,828	24,271	222	24,049	22,557	697	21,860						
20-70 years		78,310	38,807	28,866	9,941	39,503	29,017	10,486	2,630	1,577	1,053	617	244	373
Over 70 years		4,176	1,990	1,436	554	2,186	922	1,264						
1756	130,612	126,976							3,019			617		

Year and age	Houses	Families	Total popula-tion	MAINE								
				White			Negro and mulatto			French neutral		
				Total	Male	Female	Total	Male	Female	Total	Male	Female
	38	39	40	41	42	43	44	45	46	47	48	49
1784			50,493									
1776			47,767	47,279			488					
1764-65	2,486	3,481	[4] 21,857	21,451	10,870	10,581	344	192	152	62	27	35
Under 16 years				10,709	5,532	5,177				36	16	20
16 years and over				10,742	5,338	5,404				26	11	15

Year, age, and sex	Total population	MARYLAND								
		White			Mulatto			Negro		
		Total	Free	Servant	Total	Free	Slave	Total	Free	Slave
	50	51	52	53	54	55	56	57	58	59
1782	254,050	[5] 170,688						[6] 83,362		
1755	[7] 153,505	108,193	99,352	8,841	3,608	1,460	2,148	41,704	357	41,347
Under 16 years (not taxable)	77,444	53,321	51,773	1,548	2,026	811	1,215	22,097	111	21,986
Male	39,802	27,752	26,637	[8] 1,115	996	419	577	11,054	71	10,983
Female	37,642	25,569	[9] 25,136	[10] 433	1,030	392	638	11,043	40	11,003
16 years and over (taxable)	48,811	28,469	23,386	5,083	1,388	554	834	18,954	188	18,766
Male	40,165	28,469	23,386	[11] 5,083	749	307	442	10,947	119	10,828
Female	8,646	–	–	–	639	247	392	[12] 8,007	69	7,938
16 years and over (not taxable)	27,250	26,403	24,193	2,210	194	95	99	653	[13] 58	[13] 595
Male		672	[14] 672	–						
Female		25,731	23,521	[15] 2,210						
1712	46,151	37,743						8,408		
1710	42,741	34,796						7,945		
1704	34,912	30,437						[16] 4,475		

Year	MARYLAND—Con.			
	White			
	Total	Masters and taxable men	Women	Children
	51	60	61	62
1712	37,743	11,029	9,081	17,633
1710	34,796	11,091	8,294	15,411
1704	30,437	[17] 11,026	[18] 7,163	12,248

See footnotes at end of table.

Series Z 24–132. Population Censuses Taken in the Colonies and States During the Colonial and Pre-Federal Period: 1624–25 to 1786—Con.

MASSACHUSETTS

Year and age	Houses	Families	Total population	White Total	White Male	White Female	Negro and mulatto Total	Negro Male	Negro Female	Indian Total	Indian Male	Indian Female	French neutral Total	French Male	French Female
	63	64	65	66	67	68	69	70	71	72	73	74	75	76	77
1784			307,018												
1776			290,900	286,139			4,761								
1764–65	31,707	43,483	223,841	216,700	106,611	110,089	4,891	2,824	2,067	1,681	728	953	569	274	295
Under 16 years				103,447	52,859	50,588							261	133	128
16 years and over				113,253	53,752	59,501							308	141	167

NEW HAMPSHIRE

Year and age	Total population	Free white Total	Free white Male Total	Male Single	Male Married	Free white Female Total	Female Single	Female Married	Female Widowed	Slave Total	Slave Male	Slave Female	Other
	78	79	80	81	82	83	84	85	86	87	88	89	90
1786	95,849	95,452								46			351
1775	81,300	80,644	41,016			39,628				[19] 656			
Under 16 years			20,863										
16–50 years			14,231										
Over 50 years			3,436										
In Army			2,486										
1773	73,097	72,423	36,739			35,684	22,228	11,887	1,569	674	379	295	
Under 16 years			18,334	18,334	—								
16–60 years			16,867	6,263	10,604								
60 years and over			1,538										
1767	52,720	52,087	26,264			25,823	15,992	8,467	1,364	633	384	249	
Under 16 years			12,924	12,924	—								
16–60 years			12,180	4,510	7,670								
60 years and over			1,160										

NEW JERSEY

Year and age	Total population	White Total	White Male	White Female	Negro Total	Negro Male	Negro Female
	91	92	93	94	95	96	97
1784	149,435	138,934			[20] 10,501		
1772	122,003						
1745	61,403	[21] 56,797	29,339	27,458	4,606	2,588	2,018
Under 16 years		28,007	14,253	13,754			
16 years and over		28,790	15,086	13,704			

NEW JERSEY—Con.

Year and age	Total population	White Total	White Male	White Female	Negro Total	Negro Male	Negro Female
	91	92	93	94	95	96	97
1738	46,676	42,695	22,270	20,425	3,981	2,208	1,773
Under 16 years	21,963	20,339	10,639	9,700	1,624	849	775
16 years and over	24,713	22,356	11,631	10,725	2,357	1,359	998
1726	32,442	29,861	15,737	14,124	2,581	1,435	1,146
Under 16 years	15,585	14,506	7,558	6,948	1,079	563	516
16 years and over	16,857	15,355	8,179	7,176	1,502	872	630

NEW YORK

Year and age	Total population	White Total	White Male	White Female	Negro Total	Negro Male	Negro Female
	98	99	100	101	102	103	104
1786	[22] 238,897	219,996	112,465	107,531	18,889	9,521	9,368
Under 16 years		106,573	54,807	51,766			
16–60 years		} 113,423	52,927	} 55,765			
Over 60 years			4,731				
1771	163,348	143,474	73,990	69,484	19,874	10,623	9,251
Under 16 years	74,456	65,986	33,628	32,358	8,470	4,414	4,056
16–60 years	} 88,892	} 77,488	36,115	} 37,126	11,404	5,362	} 5,195
Over 60 years			4,247			847	
1756	96,790	83,242	43,261	39,981	13,548	7,570	5,978
Under 16 years	45,713	39,653	20,669	18,984	6,060	3,280	2,780
16–60 years	} 51,077	} 43,589	19,825	} 20,997	7,488	3,797	} 3,198
Over 60 years			2,767			493	

NEW YORK—Con.

Year and age	Total population	White Total	White Male	White Female	Negro Total	Negro Male	Negro Female
	98	99	100	101	102	103	104
1749	73,348	62,756	32,355	30,401	10,592	5,696	4,896
Under 16 years	34,688	30,069	15,457	14,612	4,619	2,379	2,240
16–60 years	} 38,660	} 32,687	15,332	} 15,789	5,973	2,950	} 2,656
Over 60 years			1,566			367	
1746	61,589	52,482	26,860	25,622	9,107	4,857	4,250
Under 16 years	29,924	25,744	12,938	12,806	4,180	1,964	2,216
16–60 years	} 31,665	} 26,738	12,522	} 12,816	4,927	2,529	} 2,034
Over 60 years			1,400			364	
1737	60,437	51,496	25,740	25,756	8,941	4,948	3,993
Under 10 years	19,261	16,585	8,347	8,238	2,676	1,397	1,279
10 years and over	41,176	34,911	17,393	17,518	6,265	3,551	2,714

See footnotes at end of table.

Series Z 24–132. Population Censuses Taken in the Colonies and States During the Colonial and Pre-Federal Period: 1624–25 to 1786—Con.

NEW YORK—Con.

Year and age	Total population	White Total	White Male	White Female	Negro Total	Negro Male	Negro Female
	98	99	100	101	102	103	104
1731	50,286	43,055	24,853	18,202	7,231	4,334	2,897
Under 10 years	19,362	16,916	10,243	6,673	2,446	1,402	1,044
10 years and over	30,924	26,139	14,610	11,529	4,785	2,932	1,853
1723	40,564	34,393	17,583	16,810	6,171	3,364	2,807
Adults	21,842	17,846	9,083	8,763	3,996	2,186	1,810
Children	18,722	16,547	8,500	8,047	2,175	1,178	997
1712–1714	[23] 22,608	16,979	8,601	8,378	2,425	1,334	1,091
Under 16 years	9,294	8,450	4,389	4,061	844	434	410
16–60 years	10,110 {	7,853	3,850	4,003	} 1,581	900	681
Over 60 years		676	362	314			

NEW YORK—Con.

Year and age	Total population	White Total	White Male	White Female	Negro Total	Negro Male	Negro Female
	98	99	100	101	102	103	104
1703	20,665	18,282	9,197	9,085	2,258	1,174	1,084
Under 16 years	10,483	9,634	4,710	4,924	849	467	382
16 years and over	[24] 10,182	8,648	4,487	4,161	1,409	707	702
1698	18,067	15,897			2,170		
Adults		9,743	5,066	4,677			
Children		6,154					

RHODE ISLAND

Year and age	Families	Total population	White Total	White Male	White Female	Negro Total	Negro Male	Negro Female	Indian
	105	106	107	108	109	110	111	112	113
1783		51,887	48,556			[25] 2,806			525
1774	9,450	59,607	54,460	26,763	27,697	3,668			1,479
Under 16 years			25,079	12,731	12,348				
16 years and over			29,381	14,032	15,349				
1755		40,536	35,839	17,860	17,979	4,697	2,387	2,310	
Adults			18,121	9,177	8,944	2,542	1,277	1,265	
Children			17,718	8,683	9,035	2,155	1,110	1,045	
1748		34,128	29,755			3,101			1,272
1730		17,935	15,302			1,648			985
1708		7,181	[26] 2,432			426			

VERMONT [27]

Year and age	Total population	White Total	White Male	White Female	Negro Total	Negro Male	Negro Female
	114	115	116	117	118	119	120
1771	4,669	4,650	2,503	2,147	19	13	6
Under 16 years	2,389	2,383	1,249	1,134	6	2	4
16–60 years	2,280 }	2,267 {	1,187	1,013	13 {	10	2
Over 60 years			67			1	

VIRGINIA

Year	Total population	White Total	White Free Male	White Free Female	White Servants Male	White Servants Female	White Children	Negro Total	Negro Male	Negro Female	Negro Children	Indians
	121	122	123	124	125	126	127	128	129	130	131	132
1701	[28] 57,596											
1699	[29] 58,040											
1634	4,909											
1624–25	1,227	1,202	432	176	441	46	107	23	11	10	2	2

– Represents zero.

[1] Corrected total from Greene and Harrington, p. 61. Morse gives total of 202,877 including 39,388 males between the ages of 16 and 50 and 103,735 females.
[2] Includes Indians. [3] Includes 900 not distributed by sex.
[4] 24,020 total per Williamson with 23,685 whites and 332 Negroes. Also, 2,789 houses and 3,572 families, not including estimates for the plantations.
[5] Including 35,268 free males above 18 years of age.
[6] Including 27,626 under 8 years of age; 13,399 males and females 8 to 14 years of age; 16,246 males from 14 to 45 years of age; 13,832 females from 14 to 36 years of age; and 12,259 males above 45 years of age and females above 36 years of age.
[7] 153,565 per Greene and Harrington, p. 126.
[8] Including 1,048 hired or indented and 67 convicts.
[9] 24,141 per Greene and Harrington, p. 126.
[10] Including 412 hired or indented and 21 convicts.
[11] Including 3,576 hired or indented and 1,507 convicts.
[12] 9,007 per Greene and Harrington, p. 126.

[13] Past labor or cripples. [14] Including 35 clergy and 637 poor men.
[15] Including 1,824 hired or indented and 386 convicts. [16] Slaves.
[17] Masters, freemen, and servants. [18] Freewomen and servants.
[19] Reported as Negroes and slaves.
[20] 1,959 were slaves.
[21] Includes 9,736 Quakers and reported Quakers who are whites and distributed by sex and age. [22] Total includes 12 Indians who paid taxes.
[23] Includes 3,204 persons in Kings and Richmond counties not returned in detail. An "imperfect" census according to Rossiter.
[24] Total includes 125 over 60 years of age not distributed by sex or race.
[25] Including 464 mulattoes.
[26] Including 1,015 freemen, 1,362 militia, and 55 white servants.
[27] These figures cover Cumberland and Gloucester counties which were superseded after Vermont became a State. Vermont was enumerated in the New York Census of 1771. [28] Includes 21,712 tithables and 35,884 untithables.
[29] Includes 21,606 tithables and 36,434 untithables.

Series Z 133–145.   Slave Trade, by Origin and Destination: 1768 to 1772

[For years ending January 4 of following year]

Year and origin or destination	Total	New Hampshire	Massachusetts	Rhode Island	Connecticut	New York	Pennsylvania	Maryland	Virginia	North Carolina	South Carolina	Georgia	Florida
	133	134	135	136	137	138	139	140	141	142	143	144	145
1772													
Imports	10,165	4	4	2		23		175	2,104	155	7,201	328	169
Africa	6,638					19		86	1,271		5,145	117	
West Indies	3,146	4		2		4		82	794	145	2,027	69	19
Continental Colonies	381		4					7	39	10	29	142	150
Exports	495	4				2	20				5	463	1
West Indies	3					2							1
Continental Colonies	492	4					20				5	463	
1771													
Imports	4,970			12		9		227	762	82	3,100	758	20
Africa	2,754							194	13	7	2,051	489	
West Indies	2,020			7		8		27	744	68	998	148	20
Continental Colonies	196			5		1		6	5	7	51	121	
Exports	341		1	6	1		1	2			297	5	28
West Indies	3							2			1		
Continental Colonies	338		1	6	1		1				296	5	28
1770													
Imports	3,069					69		532	905	115	123	1,144	181
Africa	2,266					67		517	631			875	176
West Indies	600					2		14	274	103	81	126	
Continental Colonies	203							1		12	42	143	5
Exports	144		1	13				1		19	88	22	
West Indies	27							1		14	5	7	
Continental Colonies	117		1	13						5	83	15	
1769													
Imports	6,736	4		6			10	203	493	169	4,888	687	276
Africa	5,161			6				180	234	36	4,138	448	119
West Indies	1,222	4					10	23	258	79	675	91	82
Continental Colonies	353								1	54	75	148	75
Exports	336				4				1		5	298	28
West Indies	9								1		5	3	
Continental Colonies	327				4							295	28
1768													
Imports	2,496	12		70	14	19		301	354	198	249	1,001	278
West Indies [1]	2,204	12		59	14	19		288	354	170	187	971	130
Continental Colonies	292			11				13		28	62	30	148
Exports	282	1		34				14		14	39	61	119
West Indies	107			8				1		1		5	92
Continental Colonies	175	1		26				13		13	39	56	27

[1] Includes Africa.

Series Z 146–149.   Slave Trade in Virginia: 1619 to 1767

[For years ending December 24, except 1619–1699, unknown. *Italic* figures do not purport to be complete]

Year	Imported Total	Imported Africa	Imported Elsewhere	Exported
	146	147	148	149
1767	61	([1])	61	([1])
1766	112	108	4	4
1765	66	([1])	66	([1])
1764	967	922	45	10
1763	1,195	1,080	115	3
1762	1,810	1,787	23	92
1761	1,581	1,470	111	28
1760 [2]	1,158	1,152	6	52
1758 [2]	43	—	43	—
1757	4	([1])	4	([1])
1756	1	([1])	1	2
1755 [2]	565	456	109	2
1754 [2]	399	249	150	([1])
1753	21	([1])	21	9
1752	[2] 3,515	[2] 3,515	([1])	11
1751 [2]	1,194	982	212	([1])
1750	1,010	849	161	—
1749 [2]	2,338	1,826	512	([1])
1747	28	([1])	28	([1])
1746	1,647	1,299	348	10
1745	654	512	142	—
1744	672	486	186	—
1743	1,428	1,320	108	—
1742	1,529	1,095	434	63
1741	947	687	260	36
1740	1,646	934	712	6
1739	1,710	1,623	87	7
1738	1,101	839	262	—

Year	Imported Total	Imported Africa	Imported Elsewhere	Exported
	146	147	148	149
1737	2,174	2,044	130	263
1736 [2]	3,222	3,166	56	52
1735	2,104	1,798	306	([1])
1734	1,587	1,231	356	47
1733 [2]	1,720	1,245	475	21
1732	1,291	1,223	68	149
1731	184	130	54	([1])
1730 [2]	[2] 276	[2] 276	([1])	([1])
1729	4	([1])	4	4
1728	26	24	2	4
1727	735	—	735	24
1726	2,149			55
1725	781			142
1724	464			
1723	694			
1722	239			
1721	1,960			
1720	1,368			
1719	1,842			
1710–1718 [3]	552	233	319	
1709	326			
1708	593			
1707	713			
1706	1,013			
1705	1,639			
1704	987			
1703	156			
1702	481			

Year	Imported Total	Imported Africa	Imported Elsewhere
	146	147	148
1701		796	
1700		229	
1699 [4]	349		
1687		120	
1685	191	[5] 190	1
1684		34	
1679		245	
1678		120	
1677		[5] 150	
1674		[5] 650	
1665 [4]	59		
1662 [4]	80		
1656 [4]	30		
1652 [4]	7		
1649 [4]	17		
1643 [4]	18		
1642 [4]	7		
1639 [4]	46		
1638 [4]	30		
1637 [4]	28		
1636 [4]	7		
1635 [4]	26		
1628		100	
1623	1		
1622	1		
1621	1		
1619	21	—	21

— Represents zero.

[1] Information lacking or too incomplete to calculate.

[2] Figures have been extended on basis of partial data.

[3] Annual average. Source also shows 72 Indian slaves imported; 231 slaves died and 103 drawn back for exportation during the 9 years.

[4] Number of headrights granted.

[5] Number of Negroes shipped, not those actually arrived.

Series Z 150–154. Slave Trade in New York: 1701 to 1764

[For years ending December 24, except 1701–1718, unknown; 1754–1764, January 4 of following year]

Year	Imported				Exported
	Total	Africa	Continental Colonies	Elsewhere	
	150	151	152	153	154
1764	35	----	----	35	1
1763	205	196	----	----	9
1754	65	65	----	----	41
1748	¹10	----	----	10	¹0
1743	7	----	----	7	¹0
1742	14	----	2	12	----
1741	55	----	7	48	----
1740	56	----	4	52	5
1739	100	----	11	89	----
1738	118	3	51	64	----
1737	99	----	3	96	¹0
1736	¹13	----	----	13	¹0
1735	121	----	2	119	----
1734	52	----	1	51	7
1733	257	100	1	156	5
1732	¹139	¹0	1	138	3
1731	²309	²130	²2	²177	¹0
1730	165	----	7	158	¹4
1729	211	----	11	200	8
1728	130	----	4	126	14
1727	221	----	3	218	1

Year	Imported				Exported
	Total	Africa	Continental Colonies	Elsewhere	
	150	151	152	153	154
1726	176	----	32	144	6
1725	211	59	6	146	6
1724	64	----	8	56	5
1723	101	----	1	100	3
1722	96	----	----	96	----
1721	205	117	2	86	4
1720	77	----	11	66	4
1719	104	----	----	104	¹8
1718	517	70	----	447	----
1717	334	266	----	68	----
1716	62	43	----	19	----
1715	55	38	----	17	----
1714	53	----	----	53	----
1712	77	77	----	----	----
1711	55	55	----	----	----
1710	53	53	----	----	----
1705	24	24	----	----	----
1704	8	----	----	8	----
1703	16	----	----	16	----
1702	165	----	----	165	----
1701	36	----	----	36	----

¹ Partial year.

² Figures have been extended on basis of partial data.

Series Z 155–164. Slaves Imported Into Charleston, S.C., by Origin: 1706 to 1775

[Data for number of slaves for 1740–1745, 1749–1767, and 1770–1771 for some ports are projections based upon a division of the average duty per slave over time into the total annual duty paid]

Year	Total importations		From African ports		From Caribbean ports		From North American ports		From other locations	
	Slaves	Cargoes	Slaves	Cargoes	Slaves	Cargoes	Slaves	Cargoes	Slaves	Cargoes
	155	156	157	158	159	160	161	162	163	164
Total	¹83,825	1,261	67,269	453	11,220	666	464	133	18	9
1775	3	1	–	–	–	–	3	1	–	–
1774	4,592	87	4,261	49	213	28	115	9	3	1
1773	7,845	97	7,246	47	553	29	40	19	6	2
1772	4,740	90	3,072	18	1,611	53	57	19	–	–
1771	2,035	77	1,293	8	698	51	44	18	–	–
1770	1,596	19	1,557	9	23	7	²16	3	–	–
1769	4,652	67	4,053	25	589	38	10	4	–	–
1768 ³	6	3	–	–	4	1	1	1	1	1
1767 ³	4	1	–	–	–	–	4	1	–	–
1765	6,520	106	4,415	37	2,032	65	73	4	–	–
1764	2,604	65	2,068	13	²529	46	5	4	2	2
1763	1,341	29	1,137	8	201	18	3	3	–	–
1762	470	14	441	2	23	6	6	6	–	–
1761	1,497	13	1,483	9	9	3	5	1	–	–
1760	3,716	22	3,669	17	46	4	1	1	–	–
1759	1,839	20	1,665	11	173	8	1	1	–	–
1758	3,204	29	3,048	14	155	14	1	1	–	–
1757	1,251	18	906	5	344	12	1	1	–	–
1756	1,612	20	1,568	12	37	4	7	4	–	–
1755	1,594	50	1,156	10	422	30	16	10	–	–
1754	2,040	33	1,616	12	414	17	10	4	–	–
1753	1,356	27	1,016	7	339	19	1	1	–	–
1752	1,619	30	1,051	5	567	24	1	1	–	–
1751	608	22	340	2	267	19	1	1	–	–
1750	739	14	658	6	81	8	–	–	–	–
1749	13	2	–	–	13	2	–	–	–	–
1748	424	9	409	5	15	4	–	–	–	–
1747	6	1	–	–	6	1	–	–	–	–

See footnotes at end of table.

Series Z 155–164.　Slaves Imported Into Charleston, S.C., by Origin: 1706 to 1775—Con.

Year	Total importations		From African ports		From Caribbean ports		From North American ports		From other locations	
	Slaves	Cargoes	Slaves	Cargoes	Slaves	Cargoes	Slaves	Cargoes	Slaves	Cargoes
	155	156	157	158	159	160	161	162	163	164
1745	7	3	–	–	7	3	–	–	–	–
1744 [4]	291	6	289	5	2	1	–	–	–	–
1742 [4]	81	2	–	–	81	2	–	–	–	–
1741 [4]	1	1	–	–	–	–	1	1	–	–
1740	740	12	714	6	26	6	–	–	–	–
1739	2,017	16	1,975	12	42	4	–	–	–	–
1738	2,508	20	2,495	18	13	2	–	–	–	–
1737	1,063	13	1,055	8	1	1	1	1	6	3
1736	3,526	24	3,500	19	25	4	1	1	–	–
1735	2,723	28	2,641	11	80	15	2	2	–	–
1734	1,805	39	1,319	7	480	29	6	3	–	–
1733	179	3	[2] 160	1	19	2	–	–	–	–
1732	996	18	810	4	168	12	18	2	–	–
1731	1,766	25	1,611	9	144	13	11	3	–	–
1727	652	9	[2] 610	3	[2] 42	6				
1726	[5] 1,751									
1725	[5] 433	1			[2] 4	[2] 1				
1724	[6] 800	12	763	5	35	5	2	2		
1723	436	4	[2] 192	1	38	3				
1722 [4]	323	4			[2] 38	4				
1721 [4]	165									
1720 [4]	601									
1719 [4]	541	19	[2] 221	3	[2] 212	16				
1718	[6] 566	17	392	4	174	13				
1717	[6] 619	19	394	6	225	13	–	–	–	–
1716	67									
1715	81									
1714	419									
1713	159									
1712	76									
1711	170									
1710	131									
1709	107									
1708	53									
1707	22									
1706	24									

– Represents zero.
[1] Total number of slaves imported is greater than sum of source of importation; detailed figures are incomplete for early years.
[2] Incomplete; records missing.
[3] A three year prohibition of external slave trade was in effect during 1766 to 1768.
[4] A prohibitively high duty on slave importation was in effect during 1719 to 1722 and 1741 to 1744.

[5] Totals for 1725 and 1726 were obtained from BPRO Transcripts, C.O. 5, p. 387, and Elizabeth Donnan, ed., *Documents Illustrative of the History of the Slave Trade to America*, vol. IV, p. 267.　Detailed figures for the source of importation for these years and earlier are missing.
[6] Data from the "Shipping Records" of the Naval Officer of Charleston.

Series Z 165–168.　British-American and West African Slave Prices: 1638–42 to 1773–75

[Averages]

Period	British-American slave prices		West African slave prices		Period	British-American slave prices		West African slave prices	
	Number of observations	Price in pounds sterling	Number of observations	Price in pounds sterling		Number of observations	Price in pounds sterling	Number of observations	Price in pounds sterling
	165	166	167	168		165	166	167	168
1773–75	19	44.08	11	17.04	1698–1702	26	23.68	24	5.21
1768–72	28	38.39	17	17.72	1693–97	9	26.02	5	4.19
1763–67	21	34.74	18	15.91	1688–92	5	23.85	4	3.37
1758–62	11	35.61	11	13.71	1683–87	10	19.95	13	3.92
1753–57	27	33.10	22	13.66	1678–82	29	19.32	20	3.28
1748–52	7	27.12	28	14.01	1673–77	19	21.92	5	2.04
1743–47	9	31.04	8	11.21	1668–72	20	21.14	4	3.03
1738–42	11	26.64	6	17.43	1663–67	15	21.14	2	5.41
1733–37	5	18.50	13	15.37	1658–62	3	21.12	1	3.01
1728–32	14	24.91	13	12.86	1653–57	2	24.09	1	11.38
1723–27	18	23.92	18	11.87	1648–52	3	27.70	1	6.72
1718–22	13	24.11	21	11.13	1643–47	3	20.20	3	1.87
1713–17	9	25.67	23	9.88	1638–42	3	16.50	2	3.91
1708–12	24	24.37	14	8.75					
1703–07	26	26.37	13	8.87					

Series Z 169–191. Components of Private Wealth Per Free Capita for the Thirteen Colonies, by Region: 1774

[In pounds sterling. One pound sterling in 1774 = $37.86 in 1973. Figures are averages per capita excluding slaves and indentured servants]

Series No.	Kind of wealth	Thirteen Colonies	New England	Middle Colonies	South
169	Net worth	74.1	32.7	51.3	131.9
170	Physical wealth	76.0	38.2	46.0	136.8
171	Land	37.7	27.3	27.8	55.4
172	Portable physical wealth	38.3	10.9	18.2	81.3
173	Servants and slaves	21.3	.2	1.9	57.7
174	Producers' durables	8.0	4.5	7.1	12.2
175	Livestock	5.8	2.9	5.2	9.0
176	Farm tools, other equipment of household	1.9	1.3	1.4	2.8
177	Equipment of clearly separable nonfarm business	.3	.4	.3	.1
178	Materials	.1	(Z)	.1	.3
179	Producers' perishables	2.4	.6	2.5	4.0
180	Crops	2.2	.2	2.4	3.9
181	Other	.2	.4	.1	.1
	Physical wealth—Con.				
	Portable physical wealth—Con.				
182	Consumers' durables	4.9	4.3	3.9	6.3
183	Apparel	.9	.9	1.2	.8
184	Other	4.0	3.4	2.7	5.6
185	Consumers' perishables	.4	.2	.3	.7
186	Separable nonfarm business inventories	.9	1.0	1.7	.3
186a	Nonseparable items [1]	.3	.2	.7	–
187	Financial assets	12.3	6.8	16.0	14.0
188	Cash	1.5	.4	2.0	1.9
189	Other "good"	10.3	6.3	13.9	10.7
190	"Doubtful," "bad," "desperate"	.6	(Z)	.1	1.3
191	Financial liabilities	14.2	12.2	10.6	18.8

– Represents zero. Z Less than 0.05 pound.

[1] Occasional adjustments from supplementary information in estate accounts were appropriately added to or subtracted from affected wealth subcategory when information was sufficiently specific. Where no breakdown of such an adjustment as "what the goods sold for more than appraised," in the Middle Colonies, it appears here. Also includes, for New England, several cases where no subdivision of "Personal estate" was shown on the probate inventory.

Series Z 192–194. Agriculture Censuses in Maine, Massachusetts, and New Jersey: 1784

State	Acres of improved land	Number of horses	Number of horned cattle
	192	193	194
Maine	165,810	5,448	49,006
Massachusetts	921,563	43,969	237,993
New Jersey	2,032,587	52,488	102,221

Series Z 195–212. Basic Weekly Diets in Britain and America: 1622 to 1790

[In pounds or gallons unless otherwise specified]

Year	Calories per day	Biscuits	Bread	Flour	Oatmeal	Peas	Rice	Cornmeal	Fish	Beef	Pork	Bacon	Cheese	Butter	Beer	Molasses	Rum	Other
	195	196	197	198	199	200	201	202	203	204	205	206	207	208	209	210	211	212
Before 1861, majority of slaves in U.S.	3,400–4,100							1 peck			3½ or 3½							
About 1790, slaves on Washington's plantation	2,800							11.3	2.4									[1] 0.42
1780, French prisoners returned to France and English repatriates	3,100		7							7					3½			
1780, Continental Army ration	2,600–4,000		7 or 7					1¾		7 or 6⅛								
1776, Tory prisoners in Maryland	3,600–4,200		7 or 7			3 pts		1 qt		7 or 5¼						7 gills		[2] 7 gills
1775, Continental Army ration	3,000–5,400		7 or 7			[3] 3 pts		[4] 1 pt		7 or 7 or 5¼					1¾ or 63/100			[5] ⅞
About 1770, convicts sent to Va., Md., and Carolinas from England	2,000		4⅔		1⅔	1				⅔	½		⅔			1¼ lb		[6] ⅓ gill
1761, British Army in Canada	3,300–3,800			7		3 pts	½			7 or 4				⅜				
1757, Va. Militia in the field	2,900			7														[1] 7
1755, Acadians sent to Md	1,400			5							1							
1747, English prisoners of French, at Quebec	1,800–2,300		7			[7] 1¾pts				1 5/16 or 3½ or 1¾					1 4/5			(8)
1744–1746, R. I. Armed Sloop	4,000		7			[3] 2 qts				4	2			1			7/16	
1735, Ga. trustees, diet for passengers	3,600		6⅛	2		1 pt			½	3 1/5	2			1/10	21 pts			[9] 2/5
First half of 18th century, Mass. Militia:																		
Post allowance	3,100		7			3½ pts					4⅔					1/6		
Marching allowance	2,700		7								7						7 gills	
First half of 18th century, Mass. privateers	4,600		7			1 qt		1 pt		3	4				7			
1676, Va. Militia	4,400	7								3½		3½	3½					
1638, Josslyn voyage to New England, immigrants	4,900		7		7/50 gal	1⅛ pts			1½	4⅞			¾	¼	7			(10)
1632, children's hospital at Norwich, England	2,700		6 9/16							1⅛			1⅜	14½oz	2 3/16			[11] 3 pts
1622, British naval vessels [12]	5,300–6,200	7							1½	8			¾	⅜	7			
		7				2 pts			1½	4	2		¾	⅜	7			
		7				2 pts			1½	4		2	¾	⅜	7			

[1] Meat.
[2] Vinegar.
[3] Peas or beans.
[4] ½ pint of rice or 1 pint of cornmeal.
[5] Milk.
[6] Gin.
[7] With pork ration only.
[8] 10½ spoonfuls of oil, and 21 spoonfuls of vinegar, with fish only.
[9] Suet or plums.
[10] Vinegar and mustard; quantity unknown.
[11] Pottage.
[12] Sailors received 1 of the 3 different diets.

Series Z 213–226. Value of Exports To and Imports From England by American Colonies and States: 1697 to 1791

[In pounds sterling. For years ending December 24, except as noted]

Year	Total Exports (213)	Total Imports (214)	New England Exports (215)	New England Imports (216)	New York Exports (217)	New York Imports (218)	Pennsylvania Exports (219)	Pennsylvania Imports (220)	Virginia and Maryland Exports (221)	Virginia and Maryland Imports (222)	Carolina Exports (223)	Carolina Imports (224)	Georgia Exports (225)	Georgia Imports (226)
1791	1,011,313	4,014,416	75,750	580,737	151,605	772,187	54,141	697,132	447,358	1,440,194	230,879	431,880	51,580	92,286
1790	1,043,389	3,258,238	98,383	338,784	97,607	497,699	50,540	728,439	483,962	1,292,207	253,022	359,592	59,875	41,517
1789	893,296	2,306,529	88,488	347,624	80,769	400,693	36,050	349,691	446,543	803,043	215,890	359,214	25,556	46,264
1788	883,618	1,709,928	66,306	232,744	97,607	301,932	30,489	203,394	406,422	656,678	258,029	291,429	24,765	23,751
1787	780,444	1,794,214	67,399	200,693	80,731	339,444	34,796	206,213	344,217	744,143	229,086	281,647	24,215	22,074
1786	743,644	1,431,255	45,303	125,128	69,397	204,285	22,834	203,870	376,027	701,834	198,454	181,410	31,629	14,728
1785	775,892	2,078,744	56,648	162,939	56,844	390,965	55,984	344,986	350,122	857,069	212,229	278,389	44,065	44,396
1784	701,190	3,418,407	49,831	521,743	43,360	653,508	68,828	653,678	352,742	1,099,782	163,540	442,465	22,889	47,231
1783	314,058	1,435,229	26,350	199,558	83,413	547,132	30,053	239,462	93,888	199,657	74,589	226,737	5,765	22,683
1782	28,676	256,325			7,690	186,242					14,182	69,743	6,804	340
1781	99,847	847,883	2,068		2,905	502,977					94,368	330,847	506	14,059
1780	18,560	825,431	32		15,532	496,602	37				708	236,941	2,251	91,888
1779	20,579	349,797	808		14,862	349,712	570				3,732		607	85
1778	17,694	33,986	372		16,192	26,449	56	7,537		58		1,074		
1777	12,619	57,295	1,880		8,430	57,295	17					2,234		
1776	103,964	55,415	762	55,050	2,318		1,421	365	73,226		13,668		12,569	
1775	1,920,950	196,162	116,588	71,625	187,018	1,228	175,962	1,366	758,356	1,921	579,549	6,245	103,477	113,777
1774	1,373,846	2,590,437	112,248	562,476	80,008	437,937	69,611	625,652	612,030	528,738	432,302	378,116	67,647	57,518
1773	1,369,229	2,079,412	124,624	527,055	76,246	289,214	36,652	426,448	589,803	[1]428,904	456,513	344,859	85,391	62,932
1772	1,258,515	3,012,635	126,265	824,830	82,707	343,970	29,133	507,909	528,404	793,910	425,923	449,610	66,083	92,406
1771	1,339,840	4,202,472	150,381	1,420,119	95,875	653,621	31,615	728,744	577,848	920,326	420,311	409,169	63,810	70,493
1770	1,015,535	1,925,571	148,011	394,451	69,882	475,991	28,109	134,881	435,094	717,782	278,907	146,273	55,532	56,193
1769	1,060,206	1,336,122	129,353	207,993	73,466	74,918	26,111	199,909	361,892	488,362	387,114	306,600	82,270	58,340
1768	1,251,454	2,157,218	148,375	419,797	87,115	482,930	59,406	432,107	406,048	475,954	508,108	289,868	42,402	56,562
1767	1,096,079	1,900,923	128,207	406,081	61,422	417,957	37,641	371,830	437,926	437,028	395,027	244,093	35,856	23,334
1766	1,043,958	1,804,333	141,733	409,642	67,020	330,829	26,851	327,314	461,693	372,548	293,587	296,732	53,074	67,268
1765	1,151,698	1,944,114	145,819	451,299	54,959	382,349	25,148	363,368	505,671	383,224	385,918	334,709	34,183	29,165
1764	1,110,572	2,249,710	88,157	459,765	53,697	515,416	36,258	435,191	559,408	515,192	341,727	305,808	31,325	18,338
1763	[1]1,106,161	1,631,997	74,815	258,854	[1]53,989	238,560	38,228	284,152	642,294	555,391	282,366	250,132	14,469	44,908
1762	742,632	1,377,160	41,733	247,385	58,882	288,046	38,091	206,199	415,709	417,599	181,695	194,170	6,522	23,761
1761	847,892	1,652,078	46,225	334,225	48,648	289,570	39,170	204,067	455,083	545,350	253,002	254,587	5,764	24,279
1760	761,099	2,611,764	37,802	599,647	21,125	480,106	22,754	707,998	504,451	605,882	162,769	218,131	12,198	
1759	639,909	2,345,453	25,985	527,067	21,684	630,785	22,404	498,161	357,228	459,007	206,534	215,255	6,074	15,178
1758	670,720	1,712,887	30,204	465,694	14,260	356,555	21,383	260,953	454,362	438,471	150,511	181,002		10,212
1757	610,684	1,628,348	27,556	363,404	19,168	353,311	14,190	268,426	418,881	426,287	130,889	213,949		2,571
1756	659,356	1,352,178	47,359	384,371	24,073	250,425	20,095	200,169	337,759	334,897	222,915	181,780	7,155	536
1755	939,553	1,112,997	59,533	341,796	28,054	151,071	32,336	144,456	489,668	285,157	325,525	187,887	4,437	2,630
1754	1,007,759	1,176,279	66,538	329,433	26,663	127,497	30,649	244,647	573,435	323,513	307,238	149,215	3,236	1,974
1753	972,740	1,452,944	83,395	345,523	50,553	277,864	38,527	245,644	632,574	356,776	164,634	213,009	3,057	14,128
1752	1,004,182	1,148,127	74,313	273,340	40,648	194,030	29,978	201,666	569,453	325,151	288,264	150,777	1,526	3,163
1751	835,651	1,233,168	63,287	305,974	42,363	248,941	23,870	190,917	460,085	347,027	245,491	138,244	555	2,065
1750	814,768	1,313,083	48,455	343,659	35,634	267,130	28,191	217,713	508,939	349,419	191,607	133,037	1,942	2,125
1749	663,524	1,230,386	39,999	238,286	23,413	265,773	14,944	238,637	434,618	323,600	150,499	164,085	51	5
1748	716,626	830,433	29,748	197,682	12,358	143,311	12,363	75,330	494,852	252,624	167,305	160,172		1,314
1747	660,715	726,669	41,771	210,640	14,992	137,984	3,832	82,404	492,619	200,088	107,500	95,529		24
1746	559,500	755,926	38,612	209,177	8,841	86,712	15,779	73,699	419,371	282,545	76,897	102,809		984
1745	554,431	535,253	38,948	140,463	14,038	54,957	10,130	54,280	399,423	197,799	91,847	86,815		939
1744	667,524	640,881	50,248	143,982	14,527	119,920	7,446	62,214	402,709	234,855	192,594	79,141		769
1743	880,807	829,273	63,185	172,461	15,067	135,487	9,596	79,340	557,821	328,195	235,136	111,499	2	2,291
1742	659,227	800,052	53,166	148,899	13,536	167,591	8,527	75,295	427,769	264,186	154,607	127,063	1,622	17,018
1741	912,291	885,492	60,052	198,147	21,142	140,430	17,158	91,010	577,109	248,582	236,830	204,770		2,553
1740	718,416	813,382	72,389	171,081	21,498	118,777	15,048	56,751	341,997	281,428	266,560	181,821	924	3,524
1739	754,276	695,869	46,604	220,378	18,459	106,070	8,134	54,452	444,654	217,200	236,192	94,445	233	3,324
1738	620,212	751,270	59,116	203,233	16,228	133,438	11,918	61,450	391,814	258,860	141,119	87,793	17	6,496
1737	775,382	682,434	63,347	223,923	16,833	125,833	15,198	56,690	492,246	211,301	187,758	58,986		5,701
1736	699,764	677,624	66,788	222,158	17,944	86,000	20,786	61,513	380,163	204,794	214,083	101,147		2,012
1735	652,326	668,664	72,899	189,125	14,155	80,405	21,919	48,804	394,995	220,381	145,348	117,837	3,010	12,112
1734	611,350	556,275	82,252	146,460	15,307	81,758	20,217	54,392	373,090	172,086	120,466	99,658	18	1,921
1733	669,633	548,890	61,958	184,570	11,626	65,417	14,776	40,565	403,198	186,177	177,845	70,466	203	1,695
1732	519,036	531,253	64,095	216,600	9,411	65,540	8,524	41,698	310,799	148,289	126,207	58,298		828
1731	650,863	536,266	49,048	183,467	20,756	66,116	12,786	44,260	408,502	171,278	159,771	71,145		
1730	572,585	536,860	54,701	208,196	8,740	64,356	10,582	48,592	346,823	150,931	151,739	64,785		
1729	575,282	422,958	52,512	161,102	15,833	64,760	7,434	29,799	386,174	108,931	113,329	58,366		
1728	605,324	517,861	64,689	194,590	21,141	81,634	15,230	37,478	413,089	171,092	91,175	33,067		
1727	637,135	502,927	75,052	187,277	31,617	67,452	12,823	31,979	421,588	192,965	96,055	23,254		
1726	526,303	553,297	63,816	200,882	38,307	84,866	5,960	37,634	324,767	185,981	93,453	43,934		
1725	415,650	549,693	72,021	201,768	24,976	70,650	11,981	42,209	214,730	195,884	91,942	39,182		
1724	462,681	461,584	69,585	168,507	21,191	63,020	4,057	30,324	277,344	161,894	90,504	37,839		
1723	461,761	411,590	59,337	176,486	27,992	53,013	8,332	15,952	287,997	123,853	78,103	42,246		
1722	437,696	424,725	47,955	133,722	20,118	57,478	6,882	26,397	283,091	172,754	79,650	34,374		
1721	493,871	331,905	50,483	114,524	15,681	50,754	8,037	21,548	357,812	127,376	61,858	17,703		
1720	468,188	319,702	49,206	128,767	16,836	37,397	7,928	24,531	331,482	110,717	62,736	18,290		
1719	463,054	393,000	54,452	125,317	19,596	56,355	6,564	27,068	332,069	164,630	50,373	19,630		
1718	[2]457,471	[2]425,333	61,591	131,885	27,331	62,966	5,588	22,716	316,576	191,925	46,385	15,841		
1717	[2]426,090	[2]439,666	58,898	132,001	24,534	44,140	4,499	22,505	296,884	215,962	41,275	25,058		
1716	[2]424,389	[2]402,042	69,595	121,156	21,971	52,173	5,193	21,842	281,343	179,599	46,287	27,272		

See footnotes at end of table.

Series Z 213–226. Value of Exports To and Imports From England by American Colonies and States: 1697 to 1791—Con.

[In pounds sterling]

Year	Total		New England		New York		Pennsylvania		Virginia and Maryland		Carolina	
	Exports	Imports	Exports	Imports	Exports	Imports	Exports	Imports	Exports	Imports	Exports	Imports
	213	214	215	216	217	218	219	220	221	222	223	224
1715	[2] 297,246	[1] 451,366	66,555	164,650	21,316	54,629	5,461	[1] 16,182	174,756	199,274	29,158	16,631
1714	[2] 395,774	[2] 333,443	51,541	121,288	29,810	44,643	2,663	14,927	280,470	128,873	31,290	23,712
1713	[2] 303,222	[2] 284,556	49,904	120,778	14,428	46,470	178	17,037	206,263	76,304	32,449	23,967
1712	[2] 365,971	[2] 309,691	24,699	128,105	12,466	18,524	1,471	8,464	297,941	134,583	29,394	20,015
1711	[2] 324,698	[2] 297,626	26,415	137,421	12,193	28,856	38	19,408	273,181	91,535	12,871	20,406
1710	[2] 249,814	[2] 293,659	31,112	106,338	8,203	31,475	1,277	8,594	188,429	127,639	20,793	19,613
1709	[2] 324,534	[2] 269,596	29,559	120,349	12,259	34,577	617	5,881	261,668	80,268	20,431	28,521
1708	286,435	240,183	49,635	115,505	10,847	26,899	2,120	6,722	213,493	79,061	10,340	11,996
1707	284,798	413,244	38,793	120,631	14,283	29,855	786	14,365	207,625	237,901	23,311	10,492
1706	187,073	161,691	22,210	57,050	2,849	31,588	4,210	11,037	149,152	58,015	8,652	4,001
1705	150,961	291,722	22,793	62,504	7,393	27,902	1,309	7,206	116,768	174,322	2,698	19,788
1704	321,972	176,088	30,823	74,896	10,540	22,294	2,430	11,819	264,112	60,458	14,067	6,621
1703	204,295	296,210	33,539	59,608	7,471	17,562	5,160	9,899	144,928	196,713	13,197	12,428
1702	335,788	186,809	37,026	64,625	7,965	29,991	4,145	9,342	274,782	72,391	11,870	10,460
1701	309,134	343,826	32,656	86,322	18,547	31,910	5,220	12,003	235,738	199,683	16,973	13,908
1700	395,021	344,341	41,486	91,918	17,567	49,410	4,608	18,529	317,302	173,481	14,058	11,003
1699	255,397	403,614	26,660	127,279	16,818	42,792	1,477	17,064	198,115	205,078	12,327	11,401
1698 [3]	226,055	458,097	31,254	93,517	8,763	25,279	2,720	10,704	174,053	310,135	9,265	18,462
1697 [3]	279,852	140,129	26,282	68,468	10,093	4,579	3,347	2,997	227,756	58,796	12,374	5,289

[1] Corrected figures, wrong in 1957 volume; see text.
[2] Corrected figures. Figures shown in source for 1709–1718 incorrectly presented as totals of components.
[3] For years ending Sept. 28.

Series Z 227–244. Value of Exports To and Imports From Scotland by American Colonies and States: 1740 to 1791

[In pounds sterling]

Year	Total		New England		New York		Pennsylvania		Maryland	
	Exports	Imports	Exports	Imports	Exports	Imports	Exports	Imports	Exports	Imports
	227	228	229	230	231	232	233	234	235	236
1791	209,033	182,866	8,002	3,464	51,979	12,901	7,602	–	22,182	20,070
1790	173,542	147,682	1,189	2,481	34,428	22,364	3,383	1,191	11,302	12,532
1789	188,893	156,894	2,494	1,904	29,252	19,030	5,021	–	13,588	293
1788	176,224	140,171	946	840	28,743	14,241	9,109	2,318	30,241	2,258
1787	219,898	113,191	682	297	21,585	6,429	3,484	–	26,142	2,976
1786	172,211	99,476	1,705	89	22,008	5,896	7,722	–	7,919	96
1785	229,282	117,705	410	–	14,798	4,828	24,230	1,722	4,387	5,362
1784	319,604	48,140	4,818	1,248	56,040	3,943	35,813	1,435	11,521	4,789
1783	108,636	34,670	2,998	176	56,020	19,366	5,796	801	2,458	–
1782	44,324	106,827	–	–	44,324	106,827	–	–	–	–
1781	147,568	44,310	–	–	101,219	32,866	–	–	–	–
1780	171,317	79,687	–	2,200	73,705	52,308	–	8,662	–	–
1779	62,626	33,815	–	–	62,505	33,599	–	216	–	–
1778	35,210	24,834	–	–	28,693	21,303	6,517	–	–	1,177
1777	35,553	3,991	–	–	35,553	3,161	–	–	–	–
1776	905	81,852	905	–	–	–	–	–	–	13,606
1775	24,193	536,112	13,489	11,587	241	9,204	–	758	–	140,644
1774	253,032	473,070	14,175	11,550	21,701	3,472	19,973	–	24,454	84,235
1773	233,053	517,954	16,110	7,454	6,739	2,304	9,492	–	15,887	91,232
1772	298,088	541,896	19,592	12,775	5,494	–	18,032	70	50,747	122,517
1771	374,472	606,464	15,718	12,542	1,529	19	18,725	20,042	52,999	125,424
1770	335,964	482,206	22,243	9,432	4,229	29,115	4,753	2,956	54,458	97,667
1769	268,849	471,307	15,701	13,422	1,013	39,916	5,070	2,001	51,512	98,353
1768	233,101	405,128	11,010	9,429	7,743	4,694	9,722	2,265	40,774	97,242
1767	267,187	376,810	10,105	19,309	6,022	3,072	11,291	5,022	30,538	94,908
1766	177,666	383,542	9,773	15,809	2,088	315	6,854	1,292	37,790	78,859
1765	175,811	421,944	17,404	29,754	4,996	4,932	5,653	3,963	27,012	84,543
1764	224,949	337,962	28,792	9,104	8,894	8,197	3,096	6,440	18,234	56,625
1763	260,943	353,811	20,405	4,282	17,698	–	11,913	250	20,923	71,846
1762	169,961	326,347	14,258	9,403	22,563	2,981	–	616	19,579	59,535
1761	144,520	312,713	4,245	5,627	3,774	811	–	1,038	45,664	92,270
1760	186,014	389,394	12,132	2,006	10,959	13,241	1,597	92	43,044	84,288
1759	160,544	209,858	22,715	755	13,789	6,224	4,626	1,584	15,858	45,883
1758	135,235	315,970	11,723	71	7,360	286	1,984	–	19,147	68,485
1757	123,794	209,431	7,841	4,513	10,174	303	641	1,176	16,615	35,523
1756	111,665	162,151	9,957	14,418	8,063	1,630	106	2,390	14,097	40,239

– Represents zero.

Series Z 227–244. Value of Exports To and Imports From Scotland by American Colonies and States: 1740 to 1791—Con.

[In pounds sterling]

Year	Total Exports	Total Imports	New England Exports	New England Imports	New York Exports	New York Imports	Pennsylvania Exports	Pennsylvania Imports	Maryland Exports	Maryland Imports
	227	228	229	230	231	232	233	234	235	236
1755	110,086	185,480	6,218	6,243	1,024	1,121	2,001	4,852	8,493	23,853
1754	121,313	167,481	7,976	7,055	666	1,357	1,079	1,395	9,877	25,414
1753	157,542	215,217	12,386	6,319	3,767	936	2,547	—	6,046	27,003
1752	155,090	187,011	13,754	5,975	1,555	2,019	1,309	1,217	7,609	20,928
1751	164,205	199,521	21,242	6,402	1,417	—	2,214	5	17,550	27,123
1750	127,196	160,797	14,385	3,205	1,944	—	500	896	14,341	26,246
1749	114,819	178,582	11,370	4,629	1,466	—	1,521	—	9,109	31,387
1748	191,634	162,677	25,961	2,703	—	—	61	—	19,231	18,105
1747	190,560	117,192	18,259	5,545	2,787	—	5,157	1,148	16,211	6,234
1746	174,954	99,981	22,827	2,477	—	—	407	—	6,000	10,924
1745	97,207	124,140	5,601	979	—	—	1,658	1,269	4,640	17,734
1744	89,656	103,494	7,112	2,419	—	—	2,800	—	555	16,186
1743	130,460	119,799	7,003	1,615	—	—	—	—	8,237	22,947
1742	108,654	101,725	13,022	1,988	—	—	2,634	564	11,272	15,611
1741	78,951	86,118	4,380	3,978	—	—	735	778	2,449	19,029
1740	82,090	52,146	5,714	2,301	—	—	936	595	528	9,910

Year	Virginia Exports	Virginia Imports	North Carolina Exports	North Carolina Imports	South Carolina Exports	South Carolina Imports	Georgia Exports	Georgia Imports
	237	238	239	240	241	242	243	244
1791	85,844	104,846	11,758	19,606	21,666	18,362	—	3,617
1790	85,748	70,280	15,665	14,952	21,009	18,358	818	5,524
1789	95,837	92,519	19,643	19,984	22,025	23,087	1,033	77
1788	79,363	95,992	9,668	15,505	17,560	8,725	594	292
1787	135,479	76,142	13,350	7,200	17,570	17,186	1,606	2,961
1786	115,068	75,548	6,643	10,024	11,146	7,811	—	12
1785	153,647	88,097	12,444	7,283	19,366	8,559	—	1,854
1784	161,043	32,720	30,611	2,210	19,758	1,795	—	—
1783	17,719	11,175	7,656	991	15,989	2,161	—	—
1782	—	—	—	—	—	—	—	—
1781	—	—	—	—	46,349	11,057	—	387
1780	—	15,296	—	—	69,519	1,221	28,093	—
1779	—	—	—	—	—	—	121	—
1778	—	—	—	—	—	2,354	—	—
1777	—	830	—	—	—	—	—	—
1776	—	68,172	—	74	—	—	—	—
1775	—	348,041	395	25,878	140	—	9,928	—
1774	136,874	341,407	28,491	32,380	5,859	—	1,505	26
1773	144,636	374,243	19,653	24,586	16,366	3,563	4,170	14,572
1772	170,913	385,556	18,562	16,716	11,481	4,262	3,267	—
1771	250,401	423,105	14,033	16,458	19,765	8,874	1,302	—
1770	224,917	315,236	17,968	16,911	4,259	10,366	3,137	526
1769	175,069	299,715	11,847	11,312	8,637	6,588	—	—
1768	152,795	273,364	6,330	8,708	4,727	9,426	—	—
1767	184,506	237,156	14,884	12,247	9,694	5,096	147	—
1766	109,391	255,481	7,063	12,467	4,707	19,319	—	—
1765	108,642	288,860	7,408	4,342	4,696	4,954	—	596
1764	155,266	244,723	4,437	6,849	6,230	6,024	—	—
1763	175,112	272,251	4,843	1,822	10,049	3,360	—	—
1762	104,976	242,057	2,557	1,086	6,028	10,669	—	—
1761	86,514	196,992	400	3,382	3,923	11,268	—	1,325
1760	112,021	270,299	3,141	1,938	3,120	17,530	—	—
1759	96,381	124,179	460	7,253	6,715	21,512	—	2,468
1758	89,296	221,320	305	4,343	5,420	20,449	—	1,016
1757	85,676	156,956	1,484	812	1,363	10,148	—	—
1756	74,399	95,006	—	—	5,043	8,468	—	—
1755	91,002	145,659	431	1,716	917	2,036	—	—
1754	96,288	130,237	1,046	1,473	4,381	550	—	—
1753	120,901	177,324	173	—	11,722	3,635	—	—
1752	124,991	154,814	2,070	281	3,802	1,777	—	—
1751	113,449	163,488	2,713	430	5,620	2,073	—	—
1750	94,529	128,804	—	349	1,497	1,297	—	—
1749	85,144	137,895	576	365	5,633	4,306	—	—
1748	146,381	128,049	—	—	—	13,820	—	—
1747	146,337	91,285	—	—	1,809	12,980	—	—
1746	142,361	75,734	—	—	3,359	10,846	—	—
1745	82,033	103,563	—	595	3,275	—	—	—
1744	77,905	77,392	—	789	1,284	6,708	—	—
1743	112,550	93,253	460	1,694	2,210	290	—	—
1742	81,726	79,575	—	1,710	—	2,277	—	—
1741	70,204	62,330	838	—	345	3	—	—
1740	74,724	38,125	—	1,215	188	—	—	—

— Represents zero.

Series Z 245–252. Value of Exports To and Imports From England by New York: 1751 to 1775

[In pounds sterling. For years ending December 24. Foreign manufactures "In time" are those which could receive a drawback (refund) of duties; "Out of time" are those which could not. Outports are all ports in England other than London]

	Between New York and London				Between New York and outports			
	Exports to London	Imports from London			Exports to outports	Imports from outports		
Year		English manufactures	Manufactures of other nations			English manufactures	Manufactures of other nations	
			In time	Out of time			In time	Out of time
	245	246	247	248	249	250	251	252
1775	95,106	1,140	55	----------	91,912	----------	33	----------
1774	49,381	250,728	61,908	10,612	30,627	108,271	5,673	746
1773	54,476	127,433	69,942	4,205	21,771	71,470	16,166	----------
1772	58,743	183,663	30,809	10,246	23,964	111,175	7,688	390
1771	72,895	393,345	66,842	23,031	22,981	158,764	11,588	52
1770	55,192	284,973	45,494	15,248	14,691	119,451	10,555	272
1769	38,585	48,991	3,900	2,325	34,881	16,327	3,230	146
1768	50,510	299,481	96,381	8,111	36,606	72,484	6,180	293
1767	35,502	258,012	57,586	17,705	25,921	75,249	9,067	339
1766	45,683	184,866	18,940	47,374	21,338	58,024	18,285	3,341
1765	38,233	217,488	20,288	81,312	16,727	42,285	19,909	1,068
1764	28,922	336,352	37,486	99,032	24,776	34,250	7,837	459
1763	29,978	133,444	30,094	34,140	24,011	38,024	2,828	30
1762	17,730	216,165	23,357	28,091	41,152	19,962	472	----------
1761	16,721	89,631	25,851	7,103	31,927	18,449	3,927	232
1760	6,328	387,839	42,124	18,065	14,797	28,628	2,995	455
1759	10,012	483,952	59,804	58,826	11,673	23,903	4,300	----------
1758	3,442	263,290	30,136	43,946	10,819	16,154	2,772	256
1757	9,828	228,378	43,149	37,522	9,340	34,780	8,864	620
1756	13,136	169,234	31,753	9,478	10,937	31,311	8,253	396
1755	17,987	114,451	17,097	4,191	10,067	14,756	525	51
1754	21,289	87,499	13,501	7,845	5,374	13,600	5,052	----------
1753	45,866	199,578	25,769	24,951	4,687	16,825	10,418	325
1752	38,485	124,329	21,846	28,916	2,164	13,113	5,213	613
1751	36,997	124,190	25,530	48,177	5,367	33,191	17,072	780

Series Z 253–265. Tonnage Capacity of Ships, 1769 and 1770, and Value of Exports and Imports of American Colonies, 1769, by Destination and Origin

[For years ending January 4 of following year]

Year and destination or origin	Total	New Hampshire	Massachusetts	Rhode Island	Connecticut	New York	New Jersey	Pennsylvania	Maryland	Virginia	North Carolina	South Carolina	Georgia
	253	254	255	256	257	258	259	260	261	262	263	264	265
1770 TONNAGE													
Outward bound	351,664	20,192	70,282	20,661	20,263	26,653	1,181	49,654	33,474	45,179	21,490	32,031	10,604
Great Britain and Ireland	[1] 98,825	1,910	13,778	955	426	7,357	----------	7,999	17,967	25,123	7,393	12,457	3,460
Southern Europe and Africa	37,237	185	5,419	755	180	3,018	----------	11,395	5,337	3,682	655	6,291	320
British and foreign West Indies	[1] 108,050	12,419	20,957	6,779	9,923	7,005	648	14,839	5,118	10,096	6,893	8,194	5,179
America, Bermuda, and Bahamas	107,552	5,678	30,128	12,172	9,734	9,273	533	15,421	5,052	6,278	6,549	5,089	1,645
Inward bound	331,942	15,362	65,271	18,667	19,223	25,539	1,018	50,901	30,477	44,803	20,963	29,804	9,914
Great Britain and Ireland	82,934	1,200	13,916	400	210	5,722	----------	7,917	13,693	21,236	6,202	10,163	2,275
Southern Europe and Africa	37,717	----------	6,213	101	----------	3,354	140	15,010	5,005	4,403	440	2,256	· 795
British and foreign West Indies	106,713	10,300	19,917	7,121	8,656	8,695	365	15,883	5,093	9,547	5,930	10,588	4,618
America, Bermuda, and Bahamas	104,578	3,862	25,225	11,045	10,357	7,768	513	12,091	6,686	9,617	8,391	6,797	2,226
1769 TONNAGE													
Outward bound	339,302	19,744	63,666	17,775	17,966	26,859	1,093	42,986	30,996	52,008	23,113	33,855	9,241
Great Britain and Ireland	99,121	2,822	14,044	540	580	6,470	----------	7,219	16,116	24,594	7,805	15,902	3,029
Southern Europe and Africa	42,601	170	5,102	863	200	3,483	----------	12,070	6,224	7,486	1,030	5,773	200
British and foreign West Indies	96,382	12,878	17,532	6,060	9,201	5,466	555	11,959	3,358	11,397	6,945	6,377	4,654
America, Bermuda, and Bahamas	101,198	3,874	26,988	10,312	7,985	11,440	538	11,738	5,298	8,531	7,333	5,803	1,358
Inward bound	332,146	16,446	66,451	16,836	18,016	26,632	936	45,028	30,688	47,237	23,076	31,107	9,693
Great Britain and Ireland	90,710	915	14,340	415	150	5,224	----------	9,309	15,486	20,652	6,415	15,281	2,523
Southern Europe and Africa	34,151	480	6,595	226	105	2,730	25	10,745	4,095	4,600	700	3,325	525
British and foreign West Indies	94,916	9,500	17,898	5,958	7,790	6,964	257	12,521	4,533	11,612	6,702	6,893	4,288
America, Bermuda, and Bahamas	112,369	5,551	27,618	10,237	9,971	11,714	654	12,453	6,574	10,373	9,259	5,608	2,357
1769 VALUE													
Exports____ pounds sterling	2,852,441		550,090			231,906	2,532	410,757		991,402		569,585	96,170
Great Britain	1,531,516		142,776			113,382	----------	28,112		759,961		405,015	82,270
Southern Europe and Africa	573,015	561	86,503	9,255	2,567	52,199	----------	204,313	66,556	73,635	3,310	73,501	614
West Indies	747,910	40,431	123,394	65,207	79,395	66,325	2,532	178,331	22,303	68,946	27,944	59,815	13,286
Imports_____pounds sterling	2,623,412		564,034			188,976	1,991	399,821		851,140		535,714	81,736
Great Britain	1,604,976		223,696			75,931	----------	204,980		714,944		327,084	58,341
Southern Europe and Africa	228,682	652	21,908	2,761	267	15,625	327	14,249	10,083	16,462	2,013	130,347	13,987
West Indies	789,754	48,529	155,387	56,840	53,994	97,420	1,664	180,592	32,198	77,454	10,604	65,666	9,408

[1] Figures disagree with source used here (Macpherson); corrected to agree with sum of components and with original source (PRO Customs 16/1).

Series Z 266–285. Number and Tonnage Capacity of Ships Outward and Inward Bound, To and From 5 Cities, by Destination and Origin: 1714 to 1772

[Prior to 1768, for years ending December 24, except as noted; 1768–1772, January 4 of following year. In some years, detail will not add to total since ships were sometimes counted twice; see text]

Series No.	Destination or origin	1772 Number	1772 Tonnage	1771 Number	1771 Tonnage	1770 Number	1770 Tonnage	1769 Number	1769 Tonnage	1768 Number	1768 Tonnage	1765–66, tonnage[1]	1755 Number	1755 Tonnage	1754 Number	1754 Tonnage	1714–17[2] Number	1714–17[2] Tonnage
	BOSTON																	
266	**Outward bound**	845	42,506	794	38,995	800	36,965	828	37,045	612	33,695	30,444	406	21,295	447	26,669	416	20,927
267	Great Britain	57	6,178	55	5,750	56	5,819	66	6,707	67	6,428	5,286	35	2,975	26	2,510	48	3,985
268	Ireland	1	170					1	60	2	170	436	2	100	3	165		
269	Europe	11	555	22	1,113	15	813	20	1,081	22	1,333	1,075	29	1,853	31	2,465	19	1,185
270	Africa	5	420	4	267	6	415	4	495			275			1	75		
271	Bahama Islands	8	215	12	320	5	100	6	175	1	20	50	1	50	5	260	4	124
272	Bermuda Islands	1	70	1	40			1	20				3	80			5	124
273	Caribbean	178	10,703	136	9,171	131	8,248	143	8,995	147	10,095	7,806	133	7,945	149	10,521	191	10,897
274	Thirteen Colonies	443	17,528	439	16,764	464	16,638	457	16,132	281	11,451	11,926	122	4,854	156	7,052	117	3,583
275	Other American Colonies	141	6,667	125	5,570	123	4,932	130	3,380	93	4,218	3,590	81	3,438	76	3,621	28	891
276	**Inward bound**	852	43,633	821	39,420	819	38,360	879	40,483	549	31,983	33,786	287	14,585	303	17,575	(NA)	(NA)
277	Great Britain	93	9,325	72	7,502	74	6,830	75	7,333	69	6,946	7,163	32	3,040	43	4,448		
278	Ireland							1	100	1	220	80	2	85	2	110		
279	Europe	20	1,343	17	1,055	23	1,640	31	2,129	22	1,871	2,018	27	1,963	37	2,763		
280	Africa																	
281	Bahama Islands	11	340	9	215	4	110	5	160			163			7	345		
282	Bermuda Islands	1	70	2	85	1	45	1				80	2	60				
283	Caribbean	204	12,469	196	12,155	188	11,088	172	10,495	160	10,811	6,295	48	2,391	71	4,432		
284	Thirteen Colonies	427	14,713	382	12,827	422	14,118	430	14,200	204	8,266	14,375	149	5,651	139	5,347		
285	Other American Colonies	96	5,373	143	5,581	107	4,529	164	6,046	91	3,869	3,612	28	1,475	11	445		

Series No.	Destination or origin	1772 Number	1772 Tonnage	1771 Number	1771 Tonnage	1770 Number	1770 Tonnage	1769 Number	1769 Tonnage	1768 Number	1768 Tonnage	1765–66, tonnage[1]	1764, tonnage[3]	1763, tonnage[3]
	NEW YORK CITY													
266	**Outward bound**	700	28,574	524	25,433	612	26,653	787	26,859	480	23,566	19,862	16,982	15,741
267	Great Britain	39	4,280	45	4,830	46	4,665	47	3,955	56	5,130	2,872	2,952	2,079
268	Ireland	19	1,610	27	2,476	29	2,692	30	2,515	30	2,522	2,035	1,882	1,460
269	Europe	48	2,449	40	2,029	58	2,920	78	3,278	45	2,360	3,190	1,087	1,000
270	Africa	9	260	4	115	2	98	5	205	2	35	290	140	70
271	Bahama Islands	5	88	7	135	8	144	2	35	4	67	50	93	35
272	Bermuda Islands	3	85	6	153	4	95	8	127	7	172	190	230	115
273	Caribbean	199	8,076	194	7,708	189	7,005	125	5,466	156	6,981	8,385	7,898	7,507
274	Thirteen Colonies	324	8,859	134	4,968	188	5,655	430	9,068	125	3,754	1,129	1,495	2,450
275	Other American Colonies	54	2,867	67	3,019	88	3,379	62	2,210	55	2,545	1,721	1,205	1,025
276	**Inward bound**	710	28,861	557	25,042	600	25,539	725	26,650	462	21,847	18,214	16,750	11,129
277	Great Britain	61	6,117	63	6,850	39	4,055	41	3,785	79	7,158	4,842	4,040	3,980
278	Ireland	11	915	13	1,411	19	1,667	18	1,435	15	1,387	880	1,647	550
279	Europe	38	2,480	27	1,344	44	3,124	39	2,700	31	1,500	710	2,385	1,390
280	Africa					4	230	1	30	2	130	295		65
281	Bahama Islands	11	268	9	210	11	284	4	42	9	204	75	103	205
282	Bermuda Islands	5	215	4	105	1	30	2	90	3	115	45	370	200
283	Caribbean	208	8,170	220	8,191	226	8,695	179	6,964	158	6,301	8,265	7,430	4,124
284	Thirteen Colonies	352	9,247	184	5,416	217	5,941	394	9,884	139	3,952	2,450	645	615
285	Other American Colonies	24	1,449	37	1,515	39	1,513	47	1,720	26	1,100	652	130	

Series No.	Destination or origin	1754 Number	1754 Tonnage	1739 Number	1739 Tonnage	1735 Number	1735 Tonnage	1734 Number	1734 Tonnage	1733 Number	1733 Tonnage	1727 Number	1727 Tonnage	1726 Number	1726 Tonnage	1715–18[2] Number	1715–18[2] Tonnage
	NEW YORK CITY—Con.																
266	**Outward bound**	322	13,322	269	10,012	207	7,358	184	6,374	223	7,704	214	8,052	211	7,855	215	7,464
267	Great Britain	31	2,085	9	795	12	838	8	645	9	690	11	1,030	12	988	21	1,461
268	Ireland	23	1,615	16	820	3	200	2	160	5	160						
269	Europe	19	725	21	1,040	17	904	9	475	6	275	6	465	8	515	10	630
270	Africa	4	130					1	60							1	40
271	Bahama Islands	3	60	1	20	3	60	1	20	4	145					3	75
272	Bermuda Islands	3	75	3	78	1	45	4	90	6	168	5	160	3	90	5	107
273	Caribbean	180	6,351	113	4,333	95	2,836	87	2,771	103	3,624	104	4,149	95	3,378	104	3,608
274	Thirteen Colonies	51	2,076	97	2,451	73	2,321	70	1,959	85	2,349	86	2,138	90	2,761	68	1,406
275	Other American Colonies	12	440	10	505	5	250	5	278	6	305	2	110	5	155	3	137
276	**Inward bound**	266	10,921	261	9,738	196	6,759	213	7,442	217	7,433	215	7,672	202	7,716	(NA)	(NA)
277	Great Britain	28	2,475	27	2,224	26	1,648	18	1,350	24	1,823	17	1,473	31	2,470		
278	Ireland	10	650	4	360	3	240	4	215	3	100			1	80		
279	Europe	25	1,055	22	1,320	25	1,436	24	1,571	12	640	7	420	10	615		
280	Africa	5	205							1	120			1	25		
281	Bahama Islands	6	120	1	20	2	40	6	145	3	65	2	40				
282	Bermuda Islands	3	80	14	426	13	365	19	525	15	426	11	305	9	275		
283	Caribbean	177	6,020	105	3,643	83	2,509	78	2,707	97	3,271	95	3,775	85	3,072		
284	Thirteen Colonies	23	931	93	2,069	47	882	71	1,366	78	1,629	87	1,753	69	1,452		
285	Other American Colonies	7	280	11	321	5	124	5	241	6	204	3	135	5	149		

NA Not available.
[1] Ending date of year unknown. For Boston, figures given in source for trade with the remainder of Massachusetts do not follow pattern of other entries and are, therefore, not a component of total. Totals were not taken from source but represent sum of detail as shown in source.

[2] Annual averages for years ending June 23. For Boston, the sum of the detail does not equal the total shown since the total includes entries for unknown ports.
[3] For year ending January 4 of following year.

Series **Z 266–285.** Number and Tonnage Capacity of Ships Outward and Inward Bound, To and From 5 Cities, by Destination and Origin: 1714 to 1772—Con.

Series No.	Destination or origin	1772 Number	1772 Tonnage	1771 Number	1771 Tonnage	1770 Number	1770 Tonnage	1769 Number	1769 Tonnage	1768 Number	1768 Tonnage	1765–66, tonnage [1]	1734, number	1733, number
	PHILADELPHIA													
266	**Outward bound**	759	44,822	741	43,029	769	47,292	678	40,871	641	36,944	39,262	191	185
267	Great Britain	23	3,123	27	3,222	25	3,208	37	4,049	40	4,134	1,830	21	12
268	Ireland	24	2,491	25	3,470	49	4,791	32	3,170	38	3,482	4,830	16	17
269	Europe	88	8,415	79	7,110	125	10,940	136	12,040	88	7,255	4,455	22	20
270	Africa	1	20	3	90	---	---	1	30	---	---	300	---	---
271	Bahama Islands	11	282	13	253	10	126	---	---	---	---	317	---	---
272	Bermuda Islands	4	125	3	55	2	75	---	---	3	100	242	6	2
273	Caribbean	268	15,674	230	13,449	243	13,842	202	11,114	206	12,019	13,494	74	87
274	Thirteen Colonies	307	12,872	332	13,655	283	12,370	246	9,085	229	8,116	10,834	50	45
275	Other American Colonies	33	1,820	29	1,725	32	1,940	24	1,383	37	1,838	2,960	2	2
276	**Inward bound**	730	42,300	719	41,740	750	47,489	698	42,333	528	34,970	36,872	210	190
277	Great Britain	63	7,757	71	8,157	42	4,705	46	5,504	60	6,924	4,455	24	26
278	Ireland	12	1,125	16	1,545	26	2,267	32	2,995	15	1,470	4,100	11	8
279	Europe	88	8,120	69	6,345	154	13,620	108	9,685	63	5,001	4,230	17	16
280	Africa	---	---	---	---	---	---	---	---	---	---	40	---	---
281	Bahama Islands	10	247	12	208	11	156	---	---	---	---	405	---	---
282	Bermuda Islands	2	70	6	155	1	10	---	---	3	110	425	12	10
283	Caribbean	247	12,947	232	13,397	221	14,946	214	11,726	139	11,677	11,724	79	77
284	Thirteen Colonies	287	11,024	294	11,058	274	10,670	243	9,160	218	7,978	9,688	68	58
285	Other American Colonies	21	1,010	19	875	21	1,115	55	3,263	30	1,810	1,805	---	---

Series No.	Destination or origin	1772 Number	1772 Tonnage	1771 Number	1771 Tonnage	1770 Number	1770 Tonnage	1769 Number	1769 Tonnage	1768 Number	1768 Tonnage	1752 Number	1752 Tonnage	1739 Number	1739 Tonnage	1733 Number	1733 Tonnage	1731 Number	1731 Tonnage	1727 Number	1727 Tonnage
	HAMPTON, VA.																				
266	**Outward bound**	356	22,293	301	18,593	244	13,851	266	17,046	246	15,776	156	8,008	98	3,966	82	3,769	101	4,501	104	4,577
267	Great Britain	36	5,454	34	4,530	27	3,184	29	4,110	33	5,252	20	2,285	6	745	11	1,110	16	1,633	22	2,046
268	Ireland			3	360	2	270	1	100	1	200										
269	Europe	14	1,155	20	1,790	15	1,405	20	2,096	14	1,209	14	1,195	7	410	6	440	5	300	2	60
270	Africa											1	25								
271	Bahama Islands	3	60	3	55	3	30	6	65	5	115	1	15								
272	Bermuda Islands	10	235	5	123	12	306	3	68	7	205	8	220	8	240	5	140	13	332	19	483
273	Caribbean	205	11,930	180	9,450	141	7,410	146	8,136	148	7,376	81	3,462	44	1,607	50	1,664	53	1,795	41	1,366
274	Thirteen Colonies	88	3,459	56	2,285	42	1,156	59	2,396	37	1,369	31	806	33	964	10	415	14	441	20	622
275	Other American Colonies					2	90	2	75	1	50										
276	**Inward bound**	332	23,966	317	21,857	282	18,915	281	19,843	254	19,673	169	10,557	102	5,746	87	4,816	88	5,009	94	4,023
277	Great Britain	62	9,623	62	8,216	56	8,320	59	8,532	55	8,411	37	4,912	21	2,535	19	2,285	21	2,525	18	1,785
278	Ireland	1	170	1	130	2	195	1	105												
279	Europe	10	1,050	10	878	13	1,080	15	1,595	9	1,065	10	1,015	5	330	4	440	1	40	2	130
280	Africa	1	150			1	103					2	140			1	25				
281	Bahama Islands	3	80	5	105	5	55	7	80	3	35	1	15			2	60			1	120
282	Bermuda Islands	7	185	6	150	8	198	9	236	3	75	4	120	9	330	5	131	5	127	16	421
283	Caribbean	158	8,598	156	8,532	132	6,298	134	7,575	134	8,152	78	3,580	40	1,579	50	1,769	46	1,760	37	1,273
284	Thirteen Colonies	88	4,025	77	3,846	64	2,656	50	1,425	50	1,935	37	775	29	1,122	10	351	15	557	20	294
285	Other American Colonies	2	85			1	10	6	295												

Series No.	Destination or origin	1772 Number	1772 Tonnage	1771 Number	1771 Tonnage	1770 Number	1770 Tonnage	1769 Number	1769 Tonnage	1768 Number	1768 Tonnage	1735 Number	1735 Tonnage	1734 Number	1734 Tonnage	1732 Number	1732 Tonnage	1731 Number	1731 Tonnage
	CHARLESTON, S. C.																		
266	**Outward bound**	485	31,548	487	31,031	451	29,976	433	31,147	429	31,551	247	14,530	219	12,841	183	10,322	198	12,366
267	Great Britain	115	15,610	119	15,792	81	11,727	109	14,681	121	15,873	88	7,919	81	7,330	73	6,234	94	8,424
268	Ireland																		
269	Europe	16	1,774	26	2,882	53	6,291	56	5,773	48	5,515	30	2,685	22	1,830	20	1,665	15	1,185
270	Africa	2	290	1	30														
271	Bahama Islands	25	452	25	497	21	690	16	333	22	345	41	582	28	385	22	249	23	404
272	Bermuda Islands	11	323	12	398	11	343	8	205	9	293			1	40	2	40	1	20
273	Caribbean	129	5,749	163	6,131	163	7,374	113	5,807	113	5,808	22	670	28	1,359	33	1,134	34	1,280
274	Thirteen Colonies	166	6,724	124	4,875	98	3,012	106	3,698	83	2,852	65	2,644	59	1,897	33	1,000	31	1,059
275	Other American Colonies	21	626	17	426	24	539	25	650	33	865	1	30					1	14
276	**Inward bound**	452	29,933	489	31,592	455	27,554	433	29,096	448	34,449	232	13,220	226	13,278	174	9,504	191	12,101
277	Great Britain	79	10,932	79	11,878	61	9,153	115	14,551	139	18,125	57	4,896	53	5,122	43	3,650	55	5,375
278	Ireland	11	1,110	3	310	5	440			11	1,010	4	320	7	700	3	204	1	74
279	Europe	24	2,565	21	2,361	20	2,256	13	1,310	18	2,023	38	3,130	17	1,500	12	980	10	870
280	Africa	25	2,171	11	993			21	2,215			9	885	7	645	5	495	9	755
281	Bahama Islands	22	585	29	517	22	466	20	245	21	355	27	453	30	445	21	293	18	264
282	Bermuda Islands	14	386	20	606	15	395	10	395	9	273	1	70	4	115	7	230	9	198
283	Caribbean	120	6,121	163	8,208	184	9,563	114	6,123	129	8,238	42	2,039	60	3,665	46	2,225	55	3,501
284	Thirteen Colonies	138	5,538	132	5,788	115	4,223	104	3,071	88	3,410	57	2,743	64	2,825	42	1,843	42	2,030
285	Other American Colonies	19	525	31	931	33	1,058	36	1,186	33	1,015	15	254	4	56	2	74	3	74

[1] Ending date of year unknown.

Series Z 286–290. Value of Commodity Exports and Imports, Earnings, and Value of Slaves Imported into British North American Colonies: 1768 to 1772

[In thousands of pounds sterling. See text for definition of colonial regions]

1772

Overseas area of trade and major colonial region	Exports (286)	Imports (287)	Shipping earnings (288)	Other invisible earnings (289)	Value of slaves imported (290)
All areas	3,487	5,128	643	261	392
Northern Colonies	229	417	12	4	–
New England	509	1,335	354	113	(Z)
Middle Colonies	688	1,332	181	92	1
Upper South	1,219	1,244	} 95	} 51	89
Lower South	800	727			300
Florida, Bahama and Bermuda Islands	42	73	1	1	1
Great Britain and Ireland	1,902	4,080	145	38	---------
Northern Colonies	40	394	2	–	---------
New England	78	912	60	17	---------
Middle Colonies	105	979	55	8	---------
Upper South	1,003	1,100	} 28	} 13	---------
Lower South	637	635			---------
Florida, Bahama and Bermuda Islands	39	60	–	–	---------
Southern Europe and Wine Islands	592	84	116	54	---------
Northern Colonies	168	12	8	3	---------
New England	59	20	48	16	---------
Middle Colonies	237	32	40	24	---------
Upper South	96	10	} 20	} 11	---------
Lower South	32	9			---------
Florida, Bahama and Bermuda Islands	–	1			---------
West Indies	964	964	365	169	126
Northern Colonies	21	11	2	1	–
New England	347	403	235	80	(Z)
Middle Colonies	344	321	83	60	(Z)
Upper South	120	134	} 44	} 27	35
Lower South	129	83			90
Florida, Bahama and Bermuda Islands	3	12	1	1	1
Africa	29	–	5	---------	266
New England	25	–	5	---------	–
Middle Colonies	2	–	–	---------	1
Upper South	–	–	–	---------	54
Lower South	2	–	–	---------	210
Florida, Bahama and Bermuda Islands	–		–	---------	–

1771

Overseas area of trade and major colonial region	Exports (286)	Imports (287)	Shipping earnings (288)	Other invisible earnings (289)	Value of slaves imported (290)
All areas	3,252	6,104	626	223	182
Northern Colonies	332	375	14	6	–
New England	500	1,783	348	109	(Z)
Middle Colonies	527	1,758	174	65	(Z)
Upper South	1,256	1,464	} 89	} 42	37
Lower South	593	632			141
Florida, Bahama and Bermuda Islands	44	92	1	1	4
Great Britain and Ireland	1,866	5,346	158	39	---------
Northern Colonies	83	353	2	1	---------
New England	88	1,446	60	18	---------
Middle Colonies	127	1,551	66	9	---------
Upper South	1,081	1,339	} 30	} 11	---------
Lower South	446	572			---------
Florida, Bahama and Bermuda Islands	41	85	–	–	---------
Southern Europe and Wine Islands	557	67	117	47	---------
Northern Colonies	236	12	10	4	---------
New England	78	15	55	21	---------
Middle Colonies	146	22	36	15	---------
Upper South	65	10	} 16	} 7	---------
Lower South	32	7			---------
Florida, Bahama and Bermuda Islands	–	1	–	–	---------
West Indies	813	691	337	137	79
Northern Colonies	13	10	2	1	–
New England	319	322	225	70	(Z)
Middle Colonies	253	185	69	41	(Z)
Upper South	110	115	} 40	} 24	29
Lower South	115	53			46
Florida, Bahama and Bermuda Islands	3	6	1	1	4
Africa	16	–	2	---------	103
New England	15	–	2	---------	–
Middle Colonies	1	–	–	---------	–
Upper South	–	–	–	---------	8
Lower South	(Z)	–	–	---------	96
Florida, Bahama and Bermuda Islands	–	–	–	---------	–

1770

Overseas area of trade and major colonial region	Exports (286)	Imports (287)	Shipping earnings (288)	Other invisible earnings (289)	Value of slaves imported (290)
All areas	2,983	3,991	615	230	108
Northern Colonies	155	439	8	3	–
New England	496	821	323	100	–
Middle Colonies	609	1,067	188	84	3
Upper South	1,169	1,234	} 95	} 42	53
Lower South	534	362			45
Florida, Bahama and Bermuda Islands	20	68	1	1	7
Great Britain and Ireland	1,582	3,038	151	35	---------
Northern Colonies	39	423	1	–	---------
New England	96	457	66	16	---------
Middle Colonies	139	717	59	10	---------
Upper South	951	1,117	} 25	} 9	---------
Lower South	340	261			---------
Florida, Bahama and Bermuda Islands	17	63	–	–	---------
Southern Europe and Wine Islands	565	76	126	50	---------
Northern Colonies	106	6	5	2	---------
New England	62	14	42	13	---------
Middle Colonies	214	43	51	23	---------
Upper South	116	5	} 28	} 12	---------
Lower South	67	7			---------
Florida, Bahama and Bermuda Islands	–	1	–	–	---------
West Indies	815	877	322	145	23
Northern Colonies	10	10	2	1	–
New England	318	350	205	71	(Z)
Middle Colonies	255	307	75	51	(Z)
Upper South	102	112	} 39	} 21	10
Lower South	127	94			12
Florida, Bahama and Bermuda Islands	3	4	1	1	(Z)
Africa	21	–	4	---------	85
New England	20	–	4	---------	–
Middle Colonies	1	–	–	---------	3
Upper South	–	–	–	---------	43
Lower South	–	–	–	---------	33
Florida, Bahama and Bermuda Islands	–		–	---------	7

1769

Overseas area of trade and major colonial region	Exports (286)	Imports (287)	Shipping earnings (288)	Other invisible earnings (289)	Value of slaves imported (290)
All areas	2,947	3,014	607	224	240
Northern Colonies	122	296	7	3	–
New England	464	616	313	97	(Z)
Middle Colonies	553	645	176	76	(Z)
Upper South	1,238	892	} 110	} 47	26
Lower South	551	498			205
Florida, Bahama and Bermuda Islands	19	67	1	1	8
Great Britain and Ireland	1,620	2,099	147	35	---------
Northern Colonies	26	288	1	–	---------
New England	90	228	62	16	---------
Middle Colonies	120	325	57	9	---------
Upper South	990	774	} 27	} 10	---------
Lower South	379	429			---------
Florida, Bahama and Bermuda Islands	15	55	–	–	---------
Southern Europe and Wine Islands	604	81	145	56	---------
Northern Colonies	87	4	4	2	---------
New England	70	26	46	14	---------
Middle Colonies	225	30	52	23	---------
Upper South	153	14	} 43	} 17	---------
Lower South	69	5			---------
Florida, Bahama and Bermuda Islands	–	2	–	–	---------
West Indies	699	834	299	133	46
Northern Colonies	9	4	2	1	–
New England	281	362	195	67	(Z)
Middle Colonies	207	290	64	44	(Z)
Upper South	95	104	} 37	} 20	11
Lower South	103	64			32
Florida, Bahama and Bermuda Islands	4	10	1	1	3
Africa	24	–	4	---------	194
New England	23	–	4	---------	(Z)
Middle Colonies	1	–	–	---------	–
Upper South	–	–	–	---------	16
Lower South	(Z)	–	–	---------	173
Florida, Bahama and Bermuda Islands	–	–	–	---------	4

See footnotes at end of table.

Series Z 286–290. Value of Commodity Exports and Imports, Earnings, and Value of Slaves Imported into British North American Colonies: 1768 to 1772—Con.

[In thousands of pounds sterling]

Overseas area of trade and major colonial region	Exports 286	Imports 287	Shipping earnings 288	Other invisible earnings 289	Value of slaves imported 290	Overseas area of trade and major colonial region	Exports 286	Imports 287	Shipping earnings 288	Other invisible earnings 289	Value of slaves imported 290
1768						**1768—Con.**					
All areas	2,403	3,489	561	171	83	All areas—Con.					
Northern Colonies	96	224	5	2	–	West Indies	583	574	293	103	(1)
New England	416	714	296	82	3	Northern Colonies	8	10	1	1	(1)
Middle Colonies	420	1,209	165	53	1	New England	252	258	193	55	(1)
Upper South	929	825	}94	}33{	24	Middle Colonies	162	169	62	30	(1)
Lower South	538	452			50	Upper South	73	82	}36	}16{	(1)
Florida, Bahama and Bermuda Islands	4	65	1	1	5	Lower South	85	47			(1)
						Florida, Bahama and Bermuda Islands	3	8	1	1	(1)
Great Britain and Ireland	1,429	2,837	144	35	(1)						
Northern Colonies	20	208	1	–	(1)	Africa	13	–	3	----	(1)
New England	89	441	55	15	(1)	New England	13	–	3	----	(1)
Middle Colonies	155	1,005	61	11	(1)	Middle Colonies	(Z)	–	–	----	(1)
Upper South	784	728	}27	}9{	(1)	Upper South	–	–	–	----	(1)
Lower South	380	399			(1)	Lower South	–	–	–	----	(1)
Florida, Bahama and Bermuda Islands	1	56	–	–	(1)	Florida, Bahama and Bermuda Islands	–	–	–	----	(1)
Southern Europe and Wine Islands	378	78	109	33	(1)						
Northern Colonies	68	6	3	1	(1)						
New England	62	15	39	12	(1)						
Middle Colonies	103	35	39	12	(1)						
Upper South	72	15	}28	}8{	(1)						
Lower South	73	6			(1)						
Florida, Bahama and Bermuda Islands	–	1	–	–	(1)						

– Represents zero. Z Less than 500 pounds sterling.

[1] Imports of slaves in 1768 were not given in the source by place of origin.

Series Z 291–293. Average Annual Coastal Exports, Imports, and Balances of Trade, by Region: 1768 to 1772

[In thousands of pounds sterling. See text for series Z 286–290 for definitions of colonial regions]

Region	Exports 291	Imports 292	Balance 293	Region	Exports 291	Imports 292	Balance 293
Total	767	743	+24	Upper South	88	73	+15
				Lower South	103	76	+27
Northern Colonies	35	87	−52	Florida, Bahama and Bermuda Islands	17	40	−23
New England	304	289	+15				
Middle Colonies	220	178	+42				

Series Z 294. Value and Quantity of Articles Exported From British Continental Colonies, by Destination: 1770

[Value in pounds sterling, quantities in units as indicated. For year ending January 4 of following year. Includes Newfoundland, Bahamas, and Bermuda]

Article	Value, total	Total[1]	Great Britain	Ireland	Southern Europe	West Indies	Africa	Article	Value, total	Total[1]	Great Britain	Ireland	Southern Europe	West Indies	Africa
			VALUE								QUANTITY SHIPPED[4]				
Total	3,437,715	(2)	1,752,515	118,777	691,912	848,934	21,678	Potash_____tons_	35,192	1,173	1,173	-------	-------	-------	-------
								Pearlash_____tons_	29,469	737	737	-------	-------	-------	-------
Foreign merchandise (mostly from West Indies)	[3]81,555	(2)	65,860	4,698	5,992	4,755	297	Spermaceti candles_lb_	23,688	379,012	4,865	450	14,167	351,625	7,905
								Tallow candles_____lb_	1,238	59,420	-------	-------	1,630	57,550	240
Articles shipped as American produce	3,356,160	(2)	1,686,654	114,079	685,920	844,179	21,382	Coal_____chaldrons__	25	20	20	-------	-------	20	-------
								Castorium_____lb_	1,680	7,465	7,465	-------	-------	-------	-------
								Fish, dried__quintals__	375,394	660,003	22,086	450	431,386	206,081	-------

See footnotes at end of table.

Series Z 294. Value and Quantity of Articles Exported From British Continental Colonies, by Destination: 1770—Con.

[Value in pounds sterling, quantities in units as indicated]

Article	Value, total	Total [1]	Great Britain	Ireland	Southern Europe	West Indies	Africa	Article	Value, total	Total [1]	Great Britain	Ireland	Southern Europe	West Indies	Africa
		QUANTITY SHIPPED [4]—Con.								QUANTITY SHIPPED [4]—Con.					
Fish, pickled____bbl_	22,551	30,068	123	25	307	29,582	31	Shoes_____pairs_	394	3,149				3,149	
Flaxseed_____bu_	35,169	312,612	6,780	305,083	749			Ship stuff_____bbl_	9,959	7,964			7,327	640	
Indian corn_____bu_	43,376	578,349		150	175,221	402,958	20	Onions_____value_	6,495	(2)			117	6,379	
Oats_____bu_	1,243	24,859			3,421	21,438		Pitch_____bbl_	3,200	9,144	8,265			822	57
Wheat_____bu_	131,467	[5]751,240	11,739	149,985	588,561	955		Tar, common_____bbl_	24,427	81,422	78,115			3,173	134
								Tar, green_____bbl_	261	653	653				
Peas and beans____bu_	10,077	50,383			1,046	49,337		Turpentine_____bbl_	6,806	17,014	15,125			1,807	82
Ginseng_____lb_	1,243	74,604	74,604												
Hemp_____cwt_	130	86	86					Rosin_____bbl_	279	223	195			28	
Iron, pig_____tons_	30,089	6,017	5,747	267				Oil of turpentine__bbl_	103	41	11			30	
Iron, bar_____tons_	36,961	[4]2,470	2,102	85	[4]10	[4]273		Masts, yards, etc._no_	16,630	3,045	3,043			2	
								Walnut wood____value_	115	(2)	106	9			
Iron, cast_____tons_	33	2				2		Pine, oak, cedar							
Iron, wrought____tons_	167	8				8		boards_____ft_	58,618	42,756,306	6,013,519	329,741	486,078	35,922,168	4,800
Indigo_____lb_	131,552	584,672	584,593			83									
Whale oil_____tons_	85,013	5,667	5,202	22	175	268		Pine timber_____tons_	4,405	11,011	10,582	50	64	315	
Whale fins_____lb_	19,121	112,971	112,971					Oak timber_____tons_	3,487	3,874	3,710	10	10	144	
								Houses framed____no_	3,260	163				163	
Linseed oil_____tons_	488	168	161			7		Staves and heading_no_	61,619	20,546,326	4,921,020	2,828,762	1,680,403	11,116,141	
Copper ore_____tons_	854	41	41					Hoops_____no_	8,668	3,852,383	18,912		7,072	3,817,899	8,500
Lead ore_____tons_	83	6	6												
Bread and flour___tons_	504,553	45,868	263	3,583	18,501	23,449	72	Shook hogsheads__no_	7,835	62,678			549	62,099	30
Meal_____bu_	443	4,430				4,430		Cattle_____no_	14,328	3,184				3,184	
								Horses_____no_	60,228	6,692				6,692	
Potatoes_____bu_	127	3,382				3,382		Sheep and hogs___no_	4,479	12,797				12,797	
Beef and pork____bbl_	66,035	(2)			244	[6]2,870	439	Poultry_____doz_	1,177	2,615				2,615	
Butter_____lb_	3,492	167,613				167,313	300								
Cheese_____lb_	933	55,997				55,997		Furs_____value_	91,486	(2)	91,486				
New England rum__gal_	21,836	[5]349,381	600	7,931	45,310	2,574	292,966	Deer skins_____lb_	57,750	799,807	799,622	185			
								Tobacco_____value_	906,638	(2)	904,982			1,569	87
Rice_____bbl_	340,693	[5]151,418	74,073		36,296	[5]40,932	117	Tallow and lard____lb_	3,857	185,143	800			183,893	450
Rough rice_____bu_	615	8,200				8,200		Beeswax_____lb_	6,426	128,523	62,794	10,980	50,529	1,820	2,400
American loaf sugar_lb_	333	10,648			600	8,548	1,500								
Raw silk_____lb_	542	541	541												
Soap_____lb_	2,165	86,585			550	85,035	1,000								

[1] Fractional quantities have been dropped; therefore, total may not equal sum of components.
[2] Information needed to provide totals is not available.
[3] Figure as given in source; components add to 81,602.
[4] Except for a few items where value is shown.
[5] Figures disagree with source used here (Macpherson); corrected to agree with sum of components and with original source (PRO Customs 16/1).
[6] Quantity in tons of beef and pork.

Series Z 295–304. Coal Exported From James River Ports in Virginia, by Destination: 1758 to 1765

[In net tons of 2,000 pounds. For years ending January 4 of following year]

Series No.	Destination	1765	1763	1762	1761	1760	1758	Series No.	Destination	1765	1763	1762	1761	1760	1758
295	Salem_____	161	112					300	Piscataway_____	214	168				
296	Boston_____	60	232	288				301	Philadelphia_____	21	102	47	60		
297	Nantucket_____		34					302	New Castle_____		24				
298	Rhode Island_____	256	136	156				303	Lower James_____						8
299	New York_____		247	40	136	182	24	304	West Indies and Bermuda_____		21		15	12	

Series Z 305–325. Coal Imported, by American Ports: 1768 to 1772

[In net tons of 2,000 pounds. For years ending January 4 of following year]

Series No.	Port	Imports from Continental Colonies				Imports from Great Britain			Series No.	Port	Imports from Continental Colonies, 1771	Imports from Great Britain		
		1772	1771	1770	1768	1771	1770	1769				1771	1770	1769
305	New Hampshire_____		50		130	89	158	293	316	Rappahannock_____		96		150
306	Falmouth_____					3		12	317	James River—lower____		384	432	815
307	Salem and Marblehead__	83	183	23	101		162	30	318	James River—upper____				56
308	Boston_____	204	174		153	527	989	1,894	319	York River_____		181		
309	Rhode Island_____		13	76		206	208	159	320	Roanoke_____		19		
310	New Haven_____						69	37	321	Brunswick_____		46		3
311	New London_____		37						322	Charleston_____	244	774	901	1,819
312	New York_____		226			2,248	337	1,537	323	Savannah_____	4	93	69	74
313	Philadelphia_____		122	69	86	1,119	1,507		324	Sunbury_____			15	
314	Patuxent_____			40		239	65	107	325	St. Augustine_____	3	23		
315	North Potomac____					316		65						

Series Z 326–330. Pig Iron Exported to England, by Colony: 1723 to 1776

[In tons of 2,240 pounds. For years ending December 24]

Year	Total	Virginia and Maryland	New York	Pennsylvania	Other [1]
	326	327	328	329	330
1776	[2]316	208	43	----	60
1775	2,996	1,467	1,015	385	130
1774	[2]3,452	1,458	1,533	323	131
1773	2,938	1,581	984	209	163
1772	[2]3,725	1,879	756	706	364
1771	[2]5,303	2,624	778	1,553	379
1770	4,233	1,572	1,031	1,381	248
1769	3,402	1,616	864	634	288
1768	2,953	1,718	520	665	50
1767	3,313	2,070	357	785	101
1766	[2]2,887	1,741	548	299	----
1765	[2]3,264	2,071	564	301	29
1764	2,554	1,837	371	307	40
1763	2,566	2,325	108	132	----
1762	[2]1,767	1,733	19	7	23
1761	2,766	2,512	76	149	29
1760	[3]3,265	3,123	51	61	30
1759	[2][3]1,596	1,429	103	128	12

Year	Total	Virginia and Maryland	New York	Pennsylvania	Other [1]
	326	327	328	329	330
1758	[3]3,717	3,448	49	195	25
1757	[3]2,699	2,462	157	80	
1756	[3]3,011	2,468	201	234	[3]108
1755	3,441	2,133	457	836	15
1754	3,245	2,591	116	513	25
1753	2,738	2,347	97	243	51
1752	2,979	2,762	41	156	20
1751	3,210	2,950	33	200	27
1750	2,924	2,509	76	318	21
1749	1,759	1,575	17	167	----
1748	2,156	2,018	22	115	1
1747	2,157	2,119	13	25	----
1746	1,861	1,729	29	103	----
1745	2,274	2,131	19	97	27
1744	1,862	1,748	6	88	20
1743	3,005	2,816	81	63	45
1742	2,075	1,926	----	144	5
1741	3,457	3,261	----	153	43

Year	Total	Virginia and Maryland	Pennsylvania	Other [1]
	326	327	329	330
1740	2,275	2,020	159	96
1739	2,418	2,242	170	6
1738	2,359	2,113	228	18
1737	2,316	2,120	169	27
1736	2,729	2,458	271	----
1735	2,561	2,362	196	3
1734	2,196	2,042	147	7
1733	2,405	2,310	95	----
1732	2,333	2,226	107	----
1731	2,250	2,081	169	----
1730	1,717	1,527	189	1
1729	1,132	853	274	5
1728	886	643	243	----
1727	484	407	77	----
1726	296	263	33	----
1725	137	137	----	----
1724	202	202	----	----
1723	15	15	----	----

[1] Includes pig iron exported from New England, Carolina, Barbados, Canada, Newfoundland, and Jamaica.
[2] Reason for discrepancy in total and sum of components is unknown.
[3] American Colonies only.

Series Z 331–337. Pig Iron Exported From American Colonies, by Destination and Colony: 1768 to 1772

[In hundredweights. For years ending January 4 of following year]

Year and destination	Total	Massachusetts	Rhode Island	New York	Pennsylvania	Maryland	Virginia
	331	332	333	334	335	336	337
1772							
Total	98,098	1,521	6,325	26,755	9,408	33,405	20,684
Great Britain	74,320	1,301	1,075	15,585	8,840	27,215	20,304
Ireland	610				160	150	300
Continental Colonies	22,688	220	5,250	11,170	8	6,040	
West Indies	480				400		80
1771							
Total	[1]128,306	810	7,820	15,770	30,886	45,245	27,455
Great Britain	101,316	810	2,760	10,300	29,986	30,005	27,455
Ireland	1,280			700		580	
Continental Colonies	[1]25,680		5,060	4,740	900	14,660	
West Indies	30			30			
1770							
Total	133,079	1,020	6,957	26,490	31,947	35,150	31,515
Great Britain	114,944	1,020	3,697	21,515	31,387	25,810	31,515
Ireland	5,350			1,250	560	3,540	
Continental Colonies	12,725		3,260	3,725		5,740	
West Indies	60					60	
1769							
Total	112,186	2,365	5,980	23,795	21,896	24,830	33,320
Great Britain	93,866	1,360	2,310	14,960	21,676	20,240	33,320
Ireland	930	370		40	220	300	
Continental Colonies	17,390	635	3,670	8,795		4,290	
1768							
Total	[2]71,194	1,077	2,220	31,119	12,102	6,422	17,494
Great Britain	[2]62,356	1,077	1,820	29,819	10,006	1,780	17,094
Continental Colonies	8,838		400	1,300	2,096	4,642	400

[1] Includes 320 hundredweights exported by Connecticut.
[2] Includes 760 hundredweights exported by New Jersey.

Series Z 338–347. Pig Iron Imported by American Colonies From Other Continental Colonies: 1768 to 1772

[In hundredweights. For years ending January 4 of following year]

Year	Total	Massachusetts	Rhode Island	Connecticut	New York	Pennsylvania	Maryland	Virginia	North Carolina	South Carolina
	338	339	340	341	342	343	344	345	346	347
1772	25,768	5,680	9,620	620	4,770	160	----	4,918	----	----
1771	27,625	3,640	3,875	1,420	1,980	5,590	1,060	10,040	20	----
1770	14,127	2,710	3,405	1,640	740	2,872	----	2,700	----	60
1769	15,535	4,555	3,020	1,340	3,280	20	----	3,320	----	----
1768	12,447	1,654	----	360	1,920	4,523	430	3,560	----	----

Series Z 348–353. Bar Iron Imported From England by American Colonies: 1710 to 1750

[In tons of 2,240 pounds. For years ending December 24]

Year	Total	New England	New York	Pennsylvania	Virginia and Maryland	Carolina	Year	Total	New England	New York	Pennsylvania	Virginia and Maryland	Carolina
	348	349	350	351	352	353		348	349	350	351	352	353
1750	5	1	-------	-------	3	1	1718	190	154	3	4	27	2
1735	218	101	108	-------	3	6	1717	207	141	43	9	10	4
1734	363	263	90	-------	2	8	1716	539	373	147	10	9	-------
1733	465	371	55	2	12	25	1715	511	373	111	8	17	2
1732	488	413	58	3	5	9	1714	419	279	98	25	8	9
1731	365	243	102	5	4	11	1713	302	211	49	7	8	27
1730	250	150	92	-------	2	6	1712	326	282	32	2	5	5
1729	405	338	58	4	1	4	1710	226	201	10	13	2	-------

Series Z 354–359. Bar Iron Exported to England, by Colony: 1718 to 1776

[In tons of 2,240 pounds. For years ending December 24]

Year	Total	New England	New York	Pennsylvania	Virginia and Maryland	Other [1]	Year	Total	New England	New York	Pennsylvania	Virginia and Maryland	Other [1]	Year	Total	Virginia and Maryland	Other [1]
	354	355	356	357	358	359		354	355	356	357	358	359		354	358	359
1776	28	-------	-------	-------	28	-------	1761	39	-------	-------	3	36	-------	1744	57	57	-------
1775	916	5	361	88	462	-------	1760	127	-------	-------	29	98	-------	1741	5	5	-------
1774	[2]639	-------	284	114	244	-------	1759	273	-------	-------	199	74	-------	1740	5	5	-------
1773	[2]838	5	498	137	289	-------	1758	355	-------	-------	10	341	[3]4	1736	5	-------	[4]5
1772	[2]966	-------	561	-------	382	18	1757	73	-------	19	19	35	-------	1735	55	44	[4]11
1771	2,222	1	1,493	18	709	-------	1756	181	-------	2	31	148	-------	1733	1	-------	[5]1
1770	1,716	9	984	93	598	32	1755	390	-------	12	79	299	-------	1730	9	-------	9
1769	1,780	46	861	208	659	5	1754	271	-------	7	110	154	-------	1727	3	3	-------
1768	1,990	7	909	357	712	3	1753	248	2	-------	148	98	-------	1726	1	-------	[6]1
1767	1,326	13	401	342	569	-------	1752	82	-------	-------	65	17	-------	1724	7	7	-------
1766	1,258	9	400	88	744	15	1751	5	-------	2	-------	3	-------	1721	15	15	-------
1765	1,079	-------	194	85	639	160	1750	6	-------	-------	-------	6	-------	1720	4	4	-------
1764	[2]1,059	-------	241	272	247	1	1748	4	-------	-------	-------	4	-------	1719	1	1	-------
1763	[2]310	-------	39	21	234	3	1747	83	-------	-------	-------	83	-------	1718	3	3	-------
1762	[2]110	-------	-------	3	107	3	1746	196	-------	-------	3	193	-------				
							1745	4	-------	-------	-------	4	-------				

[1] Includes bar iron exported from Antigua, Canada, Jamaica, Barbados, and others as noted.
[2] Reason for discrepancy between total and sum of components is unknown.
[3] From Carolina.
[4] From Pennsylvania.
[5] From New York.
[6] From New England.

Series Z 360–373. Bar Iron Imported by American Colonies From Other Continental Colonies: 1768 to 1772

[In hundredweights. For years ending January 4 of following year]

Year	Total	New Hampshire	Massachusetts	Rhode Island	Connecticut	New York	New Jersey	Pennsylvania	Maryland	Virginia	North Carolina	South Carolina	Georgia	Florida
	360	361	362	363	364	365	366	367	368	369	370	371	372	373
1772	33,156	4,169	14,367	2,304	1,588	220	6	940	16	4,540	1,749	2,778	352	127
1771	28,084	3,079	10,869	2,240	2,351	880	--------	494	47	2,420	2,604	2,590	419	91
1770	28,338	3,717	[1]13,052	1,240	2,295	120	--------	166	--------	2,105	1,186	3,961	324	172
1769	21,860	2,390	8,648	1,175	1,734	710	--------	530	97	1,546	1,352	3,127	525	28
1768	16,905	1,500	7,977	2,322	271	236	145	684	45	71	1,401	1,775	317	161

[1] Plus 154 bars.

Series Z 374–383. Bar Iron Exported by American Colonies, by Destination and Colony: 1768 to 1772

[In hundredweights. For years ending January 4 of following year]

Year and destination	Total	Massa-chusetts	Rhode Island	Connect-icut	New York	New Jersey	Pennsyl-vania	Mary-land	Virginia	Other [1]
	374	375	376	377	378	379	380	381	382	383
1772										
Total	60,916	1,110	354	538	17,245	140	22,008	17,272	2,091	158
Great Britain	19,708				9,930		900	7,797	1,081	
Continental Colonies	35,848	1,110	314	504	4,805	100	[2]19,253	8,875	729	158
West Indies	4,620		40	34	2,370	40	[2]1,595	260	281	
Other	740				140		260	340		
1771										
Total	76,513	985	500	85	28,892	94	21,942	20,080	3,713	222
Great Britain	42,300	2	20		23,650		200	15,531	2,897	
Continental Colonies	29,310	983	320	65	3,607	14	19,413	4,207	489	212
West Indies	3,980		120	20	935	80	2,196	302	327	
Other	923		40		700		133	40		10
1770										
Total	78,228	1,029	686	180	33,629	108	22,967	14,823	4,453	353
Great Britain	42,047	100	40		25,985		1,577	10,530	3,815	
Continental Colonies	28,949	929	[3]606		4,674	108	18,776	3,200	484	172
West Indies	5,457		40	180	1,635		[4]2,594	673	154	181
Other	1,775				1,335		20	420		
1769										
Total	75,869	1,009	641	556	24,358	230	21,805	17,965	9,184	121
Great Britain	43,105	124	98		17,090		4,415	12,925	8,453	
Continental Colonies	26,378	885	543	446	5,223	230	14,628	3,789	514	120
West Indies	4,826			110	1,385		2,652	461	217	1
Other	1,560				660		110	790		
1768										
Total	77,857	1,127	3,199	223	4,422	140	20,969	35,114	12,307	356
Great Britain	50,271	[5]	739	38			[6]6,189	[7]31,265	[8]11,704	336
Continental Colonies	24,403	1,107	2,400	171	3,874	140	12,621	3,714	356	20
West Indies	3,123	20		14	548		[9]2,159	135	247	
Other	60		60				[10]			

[1] Includes N.H., N.C., S.C., Ga., and Fla.
[2] Includes 40 cwt. exported through New Castle, Del.
[3] Plus 150 bars.
[4] Includes 134 cwt. exported through New Castle, Del.
[5] 42 bars.
[6] Plus 10,627 bars exported to Great Britain and 166 bars to Ireland.

[7] Plus 730 bars.
[8] Plus 11,664 bars.
[9] Includes 45 cwt. exported through New Castle, Del. In addition to the 2,159 cwt., there were 2,125 bars exported.
[10] Source states that 735 bars were exported to Southern Europe.

Series Z 384–397. Cast Iron Imported and Exported by American Colonies, by Origin and Destination: 1768 to 1772

[In hundredweights. For years ending January 4 of following year]

| Series No. | Colony | Imports | | | | | | | | Exports | | | | | | | |
| | | From other Continental Colonies | | | | | From Great Britain | | | To other Continental Colonies | | | | | To West Indies | | |
		1772	1771	1770	1769	1768	1771	1770	1769	1772	1771	1770	1769	1768	1771	1770	1769
384	Total	4,936	4,884	4,039	3,824	4,733	968	969	2,621	5,231	5,503	6,309	3,926	2,025	97	42	165
385	New Hampshire	217	402	[1]72	40				[1]	5	11	18	29	18			
386	Massachusetts	128	138	[1]121	44	43	8	[1]		2,070	1,714	[2]2,029	1,972	860		25	10
387	Rhode Island	72	97		194	7				2,538	2,795	[2]1,206	1,422	711	21		65
388	Connecticut	964	2,364	[1]1,150	1,581	256				77	315	[2]37	129	41		7	
389	New York	1,773	422	[1]150	318	785			[1]	180	206	[2]61	142	20	20	6	
390	New Jersey		10	24	116						2						
391	Pennsylvania [3]	58	45	[1]1,357	155	359		106	[1]231	311	290	356	137	188	3		70
392	Maryland	280	266	236	285	1,496	[1]	[1]30	[1]1,426	4	39	2,513	95	51	53		
393	Virginia	138	290	347	391	65	733	626	528	8	82			99			
394	North Carolina	1,131	532	297	633	1,066	[1]178	78	6	8	12			2			20
395	South Carolina	142	313	192	67	363		60	359	30	37	89		35			
396	Georgia	3	5	3		270	[1]49	69	[1]71							4	
397	Florida	30		90		23	[1]		[1]								

[1] In addition, the following number of pots were imported: From other Continental Colonies, 1770, N.H.—4, Mass.—20, Conn.—103, N.Y.—52, Pa.—130; from Great Britain, 1771, Md.—2,432, N.C.—169, Ga.—150, Fla.—4; 1770, N.H.—187, Mass.—12 pots and 250 pounds, Md.—107; 1769, N.Y.—100, Pa.—231, Md.—34, Ga.—71, Fla.—2.

[2] In addition, the following number of pots were exported: Mass.—510, R.I.—116, Conn.—20, N.Y.—104, and 35 potash kettles from Mass.
[3] Includes figures for New Castle, Del., as follows: Imports from other Continental Colonies, 1770, 1 cwt.; 1771, 40 cwt. Exports to other Continental Colonies, 1771, 3 cwt.

Series Z 398–405. Wrought Iron Imported From England by American Colonies: 1710 to 1773

[In hundredweights. For years ending December 24 except 1769–1771, January 4 of following year]

Year	Total	New England	New York	Pennsylvania	Virginia and Maryland	Carolina	Georgia	Florida	Year or period	Total	New England	New York	Pennsylvania	Virginia and Maryland	Carolina
	398	399	400	401	402	403	404	405		398	399	400	401	402	403
1773	56,988	2,634	5,972	19,652	12,554	12,155	1,855	2,166	1731	26,753	9,727	2,628	2,946	9,682	1,770
1771	59,186	4,209	11,497	----	38,546	[1]3,212	1,068	[2]654	1730	20,604	7,330	2,775	2,629	6,390	1,480
1770	19,756	2,250	3,860	176	7,664	4,393	1,402	11	1729	16,357	7,394	1,904	851	4,866	1,342
1769	33,685	[3]2,907	620	[4]1,565	21,734	[5]5,773	[6]878	[7]208	1718	13,097	3,110	1,396	887	6,735	969
1764	29,720	6,290	4,883	5,303	4,866	7,993	385	----	1717	15,705	3,819	1,145	1,147	8,728	866
1758	35,549	3,455	6,280	8,687	10,128	6,849	150	----	1716	15,571	5,398	1,094	963	7,446	670
1750	29,508	7,884	4,384	4,765	8,684	3,733	58	----	1715	17,802	5,796	1,380	988	8,947	691
1735	23,845	6,544	2,137	2,102	9,709	3,353	----	----	1714	14,343	4,633	1,137	924	6,598	1,051
1734	23,155	6,192	2,291	3,150	8,641	2,881	----	----	1713	11,176	4,883	986	1,040	2,860	1,407
1733	22,643	7,105	1,610	2,420	8,815	2,693	----	----	1712	13,729	5,345	639	540	5,654	1,551
1732	22,800	8,598	2,380	2,208	7,446	2,168	----	----	1710–11	10,309	4,597	567	988	3,014	1,143

[1] Plus 5 casks and 4 cases.
[2] Plus 15 casks and 1 case.
[3] Plus 41 casks and 13 packs.
[4] Plus 1 cask.
[5] Plus 49 packs.
[6] Plus 11 packs.
[7] Plus 7 packs.

Series Z 406–417. Selected Iron Products Imported and Exported by American Colonies: 1768 to 1772

[For years ending January 4 of the following year. Data are for imports from or exports to other colonies unless otherwise noted]

Year	Imports						Exports					
	Wrought iron	Anchors	Scythes	Nails[1]	Steel[1]	Axes	Wrought iron — Other colonies	Wrought iron — West Indies	Anchors	Scythes	Axes — Other colonies	Axes — West Indies
	406	407	408	409	410	411	412	413	414	415	416	417
	Cwt.	Number	Dozens	Cwt.	Cwt.	Number	Cwt.	Cwt.	Number	Dozens	Number	Number
1772	351	68	494	([2])	([2])	5,603	301	47	[3]80	454	6,800	2,673
1771	513	[4]109	[5]340	5,668	1,599	7,144	391	153	70	[6]540	7,574	2,385
1770	[7]256	[7]126	297	[8]22,283	[9]1,578	6,063	[10]103	167	[11]156	377	7,483	1,961
1769	[11]1,289	[11]12	[5]102	[8]3,161	[9]2,126	6,665	[12]1,101	----	([13])	400	5,606	4,059
1768	([2])	([2])	([2])	([2])	([2])	5,568	[12]162	279	([14])	([2])	2,688	([2])

[1] Imported from Great Britain.
[2] No listing.
[3] Plus 36 to West Indies.
[4] Plus, from Great Britain, 15 in 1771.
[5] Plus, from Great Britain, 129 bundles in 1771 and 46 bundles and 1 dozen in 1769.
[6] 30 dozen to West Indies.
[7] Wrought iron entry coastwise in source includes 43 cwt. of anchors which may not have been included in number of anchors. Also, 27 anchors were imported from Great Britain.
[8] Plus 1,993 casks in 1770 and 84 casks in 1769 from Great Britain and 102 barrels in 1770 from other colonies.
[9] Plus 4,030 bars, 12.5 faggots, and 36 long steel in 1770, and 1 bundle and 41 faggots in 1769.
[10] Includes 110 cwt. of anchors which also have been included in the number of anchors.
[11] Wrought iron entry coastwise included 363 cwt. of anchors which may not have been included in the number of anchors.
[12] Anchors only.
[13] 15 anchors to Africa. All the wrought iron entries this year consisted of anchors.
[14] In addition to coastwise exports listed under wrought iron, 1 anchor went to the West Indies.

Series Z 418–431. Value of Furs Exported to England by British Continental Colonies: 1700 to 1775

[In pounds sterling. For years ending December 24]

Series No.	Colony	1775	1770	1765	1760	1750	1739[1]	1730	1725	1720	1710	1700
418	Total	53,709	47,758	49,293	19,985	22,817	25,196	22,348	23,541	19,377	7,840	16,284
419	Continental Colonies	51,058	44,394	45,925	14,637	17,491	22,536	19,804	21,903	19,128	5,165	13,712
420	Canada	34,486	28,433	24,512	1,930	----	----	----	----	----	----	----
421	Carolina	128	26	491	20	12	9	57	46	4	27	576
422	Florida	108	68	----	----	----	----	----	----	----	----	----
423	Georgia	63	9	53	----	3	----	----	----	----	----	----
424	Hudson's Bay	5,640	9,213	9,770	8,321	8,143	13,452	12,335	11,180	9,839	----	2,360
425	New England	1,642	2,453	2,811	946	1,015	2,481	2,010	1,862	2,119	1,595	2,435
426	Newfoundland	1,913	403	648	470	420	551	500	452	457	553	223
427	New York	3,939	2,340	5,565	1,023	5,710	5,073	2,611	6,952	5,393	2,148	4,962
428	Nova Scotia	210	132	78	24	----	----	----	156	----	----	----
429	Pennsylvania	2,866	1,148	1,927	1,879	1,909	329	1,642	923	849	88	723
430	Virginia and Maryland	63	169	70	21	282	641	493	488	467	754	2,433
431	All other colonies	2,651	3,364	3,368	5,348	5,326	2,660	2,544	1,638	249	2,675	2,572

[1] Since the English customs records for 1740 are not complete, the records for 1739 were used.

Series Z 432–435. Indigo and Silk Exported From South Carolina and Georgia: 1747 to 1788

[For years ending January 4 of following year, except as noted]

Year	Indigo (1,000 pounds) Total (432)	South Carolina (433)	Georgia (434)	Silk [1] (pounds) (435)
1788		[2]833.5		
1787		[2]974.1		
1786		[2]757.1		
1785		[2]626.2		
1784		[2]713.9		
1783		[2][3]289.5		
1775[4]		1,122.2		
1774[5]		747.2		
1773[6]		720.6		
1772	[7]759.8	[7]746.7	13.1	485
1771	454.1	434.2	19.9	438
1770	573.1	550.8	22.3	290
1769	416.6	402.7	13.9	332

Year	Indigo (1,000 pounds) Total (432)	South Carolina (433)	Georgia (434)	Silk [1] (pounds) (435)
1768	[8][9]517.7	[8]498.0	[9]19.7	541
1767	(NA)	([10])	12.9	671
1766	[2]506.2	491.8	14.4	1,084
1765	351.9	335.8	16.0	711
1764	543.2	529.1	14.2	898
1763	447.7	438.9	8.7	953
1762	264.4	255.3	9.1	380
1761	385.6	384.1	1.6	332
1760	519.3	507.6	11.7	558
1759	696.2	695.7	.6	734
1758	572.6	563.0	9.6	358
1757	894.5	876.4	18.2	358
1756	232.1	222.8	9.3	268
1755	308.0	303.5	4.5	438

Year	Indigo, South Carolina (1,000 pounds) (433)
1754	129.6
1753	28.5
1752[11]	3.8
1751[12]	19.9
1750[12]	63.1
1749[12]	138.3
1748[12]	62.2
1747[12]	138.3

NA Not available.
[1] Savannah, Ga., only.
[2] For Charleston, the only South Carolina port for which data are available; other South Carolina ports averaged 7.8 percent of the colony's totals for 1768–1773.
[3] 827 casks at 350 lb. each.
[4] For 6½ months ending Feb. 24.
[5] For 11 months ending Oct. 6.
[6] For year ending Nov. 11.
[7] Plus 302 casks and 5 boxes.
[8] Plus 196 casks.
[9] Plus 357 casks.
[10] From Oct. 31, 1767, to Sept. 8, 1768, Charleston exported 530,092 pounds of indigo.
[11] For 9½ months ending Jan. 5 of following year.
[12] For year ending Mar. 24 of following year.

Series Z 436–440. Silk Exported and Imported by North and South Carolina: 1731 to 1755

[In pounds. For years ending December 24]

Year	Exports of raw silk (436)	Imports: Silk, wrought (437)	Silk with worsted (438)	Silk with inkle (439)	Silk with grosgrain (440)
1755	5.5	3,416	2,634	337	
1754		2,682	2,300	374	150
1753	11	3,027	2,236	190	
1752		3,365	2,860	218	7
1751		2,404	1,933	291	
1750	118	1,519	1,258	223	50
1749	46	1,772	1,065	74	
1748	52	1,772	1,658	155	34
1747		1,313	2,050	386	

Year	Exports of raw silk (436)	Imports: Silk, wrought (437)	Silk with worsted (438)	Silk with inkle (439)	Silk with grosgrain (440)
1746		929	590	330	3
1745		544	615	184	40
1744		1,035	1,296	181	
1743		1,427	1,262	122	
1742	18.5	1,576	1,350	144	
1741		2,798	2,452	440	7
1740		1,454	1,492		
1739		1,273	877		
1738		1,111	1,177		

Year	Silk, wrought (437)	Silk with worsted (438)
1737	691	790
1736	1,223	516
1735	1,487	864
1734	943	937
1733	1,015	1,341
1732	774	892
1731	970	537

Series Z 441–448. Tobacco Imported by England, by Origin: 1697 to 1775

[In thousands of pounds. For years ending December 24, except as noted]

Year	Total (441)	Virginia and Maryland (442)	Carolina (443)	Georgia (444)	Pennsylvania (445)	New England (446)	Other [1] (448)
1775	55,968	54,458	834	109		57	510
1774	56,057	54,785	1,191	71			10
1773	55,929	54,915	964	50			(Z)
1772	51,501	50,667	684	135			15
1771	58,093	56,888	1,136	35			34
1770	39,188	38,986	190	8			4
1769	33,797	33,552	203	1			41
1768	35,555	35,457	88				9
1767	39,145	39,096	44				4
1766	43,318	43,193	114				12
1765	48,320	47,600	704			3	13
1764	54,433	53,662	765		4		2
1763	65,179	64,500	647		6		27
1762	44,111	41,862	2,226		10		13
1761	47,075	45,818	796		450		11

Year	Total (441)	Virginia and Maryland (442)	Carolina (443)	Pennsylvania (445)	New England (446)	Other [1] (448)
1760	52,347	51,283	989	10	7	59
1759	34,782	34,652	120	4		6
1758	43,969	43,623	273			73
1757	42,232	41,542	369			321
1756	33,291	32,943	289	1	(Z)	58
1755	49,084	48,610	241	14	2	217
1754	58,867	57,977	836	46		8
1753	62,686	61,913	451	35	285	2
1752	57,250	56,591	83	68	505	3
1751	45,979	45,745	162	67	4	(Z)
1750	51,339	50,785	12	34	447	61
1749	44,648	44,190	321	122		15
1748	50,695	49,646	393	66	319	271
1747	51,289	50,765	287	107	124	6
1746	39,990	39,567	81	228		114

See footnotes at end of table.

Series Z 441–448. Tobacco Imported by England, by Origin: 1697 to 1775—Con.

[In thousands of pounds]

Year	Total 441	Virginia and Maryland 442	Carolina 443	Pennsylvania 445	New England 446	New York 447	Other[1] 448
1745	41,073	40,897	----	166	----	----	10
1744	41,434	41,119	35	159	3	----	118
1743	56,767	55,666	515	18	----	----	568
1742	43,467	42,838	558	30	(Z)	----	41
1741	59,449	59,007	70	221	7	----	144
1740	36,002	35,372	49	427	48	----	106
1739	46,724	45,866	552	305	----	----	1
1738	40,120	39,868	----	226	----	----	26
1737	50,208	49,946	86	154	----	----	22
1736	37,904	37,682	108	100	(Z)	----	14
1735	40,069	39,818	----	250	----	----	1
1734	35,563	35,216	----	338	1	----	8
1733	40,085	39,854	----	169	----	----	62
1732	30,891	30,847	----	21	14	----	9
1731	41,595	41,194	2	90	----	----	309
1730	35,080	34,860	16	73	----	----	131
1729	39,951	39,785	----	161	(Z)	----	5
1728	42,588	42,328	1	155	1	----	103
1727	43,275	43,026	----	225	----	----	24
1726	32,311	32,159	----	142	1	----	9
1725	21,046	20,968	----	66	----	2	12
1724	26,634	26,612	(Z)	13	----	1	9
1723	29,297	29,259	6	23	(Z)	2	7
1722	28,543	28,383	8	140	----	1	10
1721	37,292	36,949	47	254	41	----	1
1720	34,526	34,138	8	365	4	1	10
1719	33,684	33,503	1	177	2	(Z)	1
1718	31,840	31,740	4	94	1	----	(Z)
1717	29,600	29,450	(Z)	102	47	(Z)	1
1716	28,316	28,305	(Z)	3	(Z)	----	8
1715	17,810	17,783	----	18	(Z)	----	9
1714	29,264	29,248	----	----	1	9	6
1713	21,598	21,573	(Z)	----	12	2	11
1712	30,523	30,502	----	7	4	4	6
1711	28,122	28,100	----	----	1	6	15
1710	23,498	23,351	2	117	2	(Z)	26
1709	34,547	34,467	1	65	----	2	12
1708	28,975	28,716	7	184	57	1	10
1707	28,088	27,684	6	83	192	46	77
1706	19,780	19,379	5	94	17	5	280
1705	15,661	15,573	----	47	9	----	32
1704	34,864	34,665	7	86	9	2	95
1703	20,075	19,451	2	313	113	3	193
1702	37,209	36,749	3	304	67	----	86
1701	32,189	31,754	----	270	44	1	120
1700	37,840	37,166	8	398	23	12	233
1699	31,253	30,641	3	65	16	32	496
1698[2]	8,478	8,359	(Z)	67	(Z)	9	43
1698[3]	23,052	22,738	(Z)	22	2	7	283
1697[3]	35,632	35,329	1	118	1	27	156

Z Less than 500 pounds.
[1] Includes Portugal and Madeira Islands, rest of Europe, Turkey, Africa, East Indies, Antigua, Barbados, Bermuda, Jamaica, St. Kitts, and others and prize.
[2] For Sept. 29–Dec. 24.
[3] For years ending Sept. 28.

Series Z 449–456. American Tobacco Imported and Reexported by Great Britain: 1697 to 1791

[In millions of pounds. For years ending December 24 unless otherwise noted. Outports are English ports other than London]

Year	Imports Total 449	England Total 450	England London 451	England Outports 452	Scotland[1] 453	Reexports Total 454	Reexports England 455	Reexports Scotland[1] 456
1791	53	38	----	----	14	54	44	10
1790	58	47	----	----	11	37	28	9
1789	59	48	----	----	12	38	29	8
1788	49	39	----	----	10	16	7	9
1787	40	32	----	----	8	34	27	8
1786	45	38	----	----	8	27	21	6
1785	43	34	----	----	9	35	26	9
1784	44	40	----	----	4	31	28	3
1783	18	16	----	----	2	8	6	2
1775	102	56	----	----	46	74	44	30
1774	97	56	----	----	41	79	45	34
1773	100	56	38	18	45	97	50	46
1772	97	51	36	15	45	94	50	44
1771	105	58	43	15	47	87	41	46
1770	78	39	27	12	39	73	33	40
1769	70	34	24	9	36	59	24	35
1768	69	36	23	12	33	67	31	36
1767	68	39	26	14	29	63	36	26
1766	73	43	27	16	29	63	33	30
1765	81	48	29	20	33	68	39	29
1764	81	54	37	17	26	85	54	31
1763	98	65	47	18	33	65	41	24
1762	71	44	22	22	27	62	36	25
1761	73	47	27	20	26	66	37	29
1760	85	52	28	24	32	64	40	25
1759	50	35	18	16	15	50	32	19
1758	70	44	24	20	26	43	26	17
1757	60	42	22	20	18	46	28	18
1756	46	33	19	14	12	38	26	12
1755	64	49	27	22	15	45	34	10
1754	79	59	33	26	20	73	53	20
1753	87	63	37	25	24	74	50	23
1752	78	57	33	24	21	69	49	20
1751	----	46	26	20	----	----	39	----
1750	----	51	26	26	----	----	33	----
1749	----	45	21	23	----	----	44	----
1748	----	51	28	23	----	----	43	----
1747	64	51	29	23	13	52	39	13
1746	52	40	19	21	12	49	32	16
1745	55	41	22	19	14	43	33	10
1744	52	41	24	17	11	51	42	10
1743	67	57	33	24	11	58	47	11
1742	53	43	24	19	10	52	44	8
1741	68	59	41	19	9	54	46	8
1740	41	36	19	17	5	42	35	7
1739	53	47	31	16	7	43	38	5
1738	45	40	25	15	5	37	33	4
1737	----	50	32	19	----	----	41	----
1736	----	38	25	13	----	----	32	----
1735	----	40	26	14	----	----	33	----
1734	----	36	24	12	----	----	27	----
1733	----	40	27	13	----	----	26	----
1732	----	31	20	11	----	----	31	----
1731	46	42	29	13	4	34	29	5
1730	41	35	24	11	6	33	27	5
1729	47	40	27	13	7	38	31	7
1728	50	43	29	14	7	35	29	6
1727	50	43	28	16	7	32	26	5
1726	36	32	20	12	4	31	28	3
1725	25	21	14	7	4	16	13	3
1724	32	27	18	8	6	28	18	11
1723	34	29	21	9	5	24	22	1
1722	35	29	19	9	7	25	21	4
1721	41	37	----	----	4	30	26	4
1720	----	35	----	----	----	----	23	----
1719	----	34	----	----	----	----	20	----
1718	----	32	----	----	----	----	19	----
1717	32	30	----	----	2	21	19	2
1716	31	28	----	----	2	19	17	2
1715	20	18	----	----	2	15	13	2
1714	----	29	----	----	----	----	20	----
1713	----	22	----	----	----	----	17	----
1712	----	31	----	----	----	----	19	----
1711	30	28	----	----	1	16	15	1
1710	25	23	----	----	1	16	15	1
1709	36	35	----	----	1	22	21	1
1708	30	29	----	----	1	18	17	1
1707	----	28	15	13	----	----	21	----
1706	----	20	12	8	----	----	11	----
1705	----	16	----	----	----	----	11	----
1704	----	35	25	10	----	----	20	----
1703	----	20	----	11	----	----	17	----
1702	----	37	25	12	----	----	14	----
1701	----	32	21	11	----	----	21	----
1700	----	38	25	12	----	----	25	----
1699	----	31	18	13	----	----	22	----
1698[2]	----	23	10	13	----	----	18	----
1697[2]	----	36	26	10	----	----	18	----

[1] For 1721–1731 and 1752–1754, for years ending Sept. 28; 1755–1775, years ending Jan. 4 of following year.
[2] For years ending Sept. 28.

Series Z 457–459. American Tobacco Imported by England: 1616 to 1695

[In thousands of pounds. For years ending September 28 except 1637–1640, unknown; 1672–1682, 1693–1695, December 24; 1690–1692, November. Leaders denote no satisfactory data available. Outports are English ports other than London]

Year	Total	London	Outports	Year	Total	London	Outports	Year	Total	London	Outports
	457	458	459		457	458	459		457	458	459
1695		19,937.4		1680		11,943.0		1629	178.7	89.0	89.7
1694	27,836.7	17,280.7	10,556.0	1679		12,983.0		1628	552.9	420.1	132.8
1693	27,464.1	19,866.0	7,598.1	1678		14,455.0		1627	376.9	335.3	41.6
1692		13,423.5		1677		11,735.0		1626	333.1	213.3	119.8
1691		14,830.5		1676		11,127.0		1625	131.8	111.1	20.7
				1672	17,559.0	10,539.0	7,020.0	1624	203.0	187.3	15.6
1690		12,638.0						1623	134.6	119.4	15.2
1689		14,392.6		1669	15,039.6	9,037.3	6,002.3	1622	61.6	59.4	2.2
1688	28,385.5	14,890.5	13,495.0	1663		7,371.1		1621	73.8	73.8	
1687	27,567.0	14,072.0	13,495.0	1640		1,257.0					
1686	28,036.5	14,541.5	13,495.0	1639		1,345.0		1620	119.0	118.0	1.0
				1638		3,134.0		1619	45.8	45.8	
1684			13,495.0					1618	49.7	49.5	.2
1683			13,495.0	1637		1,537.0		1617	18.8	18.8	
1682	21,399.0	12,592.0	8,807.0	1631	272.3	209.7	62.5	1616	2.5	2.3	.2
1681		14,472.0		1630	458.2	360.6	97.5				

Series Z 460–472. American Tobacco Exported and Imported, by Origin and Destination: 1768 to 1772

[In thousands of pounds. For years ending January 4 of following year]

Year and destination	Total	New Hampshire	Massachusetts	Rhode Island	Connecticut	New York	Pennsylvania	Maryland	Virginia	North Carolina	South Carolina	Georgia	Florida
	460	461	462	463	464	465	466	467	468	469	470	471	472
1772													
Exports	106,979.4	2.0	23.7	14.0	1.7	58.6	26.4	33,909.2	70,632.3	1,604.8	527.6	179.1	
Great Britain	106,574.0							33,902.0	70,449.4	1,573.4	479.0	170.2	
West Indies	178.0		.5	1.8	.3	6.7	[1]22.3	2.5	147.0	11.8	7.4		
Coastwise	194.4	2.0	23.2	4.1	1.4	36.6		4.7	35.9	19.6	35.7	8.9	
Southern Europe and Africa	33.0			8.1		15.3	4.1				5.5		
Imports, coastwise	[2]87.4		13.7	16.6	.6	25.1	30.8			.1	[3]	.5	
1771													
Exports	112,921.2	4.4	58.0	11.4	5.0	48.2	4.4	38,963.0	71,468.7	1,886.6	436.6	34.9	
Great Britain	112,508.6							38,931.4	71,268.7	1,872.2	401.4	34.9	
West Indies	181.7		55.6	9.9		2.9	1.0	15.3	160.5	2.0			
Coastwise	197.5	4.4	55.6	9.9	2.1	29.1	1.1	16.3	39.5	12.4	27.1		
Southern Europe and Africa	33.4		2.4	1.5		19.1	2.3				8.1		
Imports, coastwise	141.5	12.2	39.3	7.2	1.0	66.7	14.8	.1					.2
1770													
Exports	89,744.3	3.7	20.9	.4	13.5	34.6	6.5	27,272.0	61,048.5	1,097.3	233.2	13.4	.3
Great Britain	89,321.4							27,266.8	60,811.1	1,084.7	145.5	13.3	
West Indies	165.4				10.8	3.4		3.1	145.6	2.4		.1	
Coastwise	248.2	3.7	20.9	.4	2.7	21.9	6.5	2.1	91.8	10.2	87.7		.3
Southern Europe and Africa	9.3					9.3							
Imports, coastwise	158.7	5.9	39.0	5.4		72.6	32.4					.5	2.9
1769													
Exports	84,207.3		46.7	11.2	29.3	12.6	1.2	25,790.8	57,445.2	554.7	310.4	5.2	
Great Britain	83,945.2		.3		13.9	1.3		25,781.8	57,337.8	549.6	275.4	.6	
West Indies	102.3			2.3	13.9	1.3		1.2	78.2	3.4	.1	1.6	
Coastwise	155.2		45.5	6.6	15.4	10.6	1.2	7.8	29.2	1.0	34.9	3.0	
Southern Europe and Africa	4.6		.9	2.3		.7			.7				
Imports, coastwise	95.2	10.6	38.1		1.2	34.4	[1]4.7			1.0	.2		5.0
1768													
Exports	69,683.1		11.8	3.1	23.2	5.0		24,382.3	44,876.9	380.8			
Great Britain	69,519.1							24,382.3	44,769.7	367.1			
West Indies	139.2			1.4	23.2	1.0			107.2	6.4			
Coastwise	20.5		11.8	1.4						7.3			
Southern Europe and Africa	4.3			.3		4.0							
Imports, coastwise	22.1		3.7			10.0	5.5				.8	.7	1.4

[1] Coastwise exports for 1772 include 14,589 lb. exported by Delaware; coastwise imports for 1769 include 224 lb. imported by the Jerseys.

[2] Plus 5 pigtails.

[3] 5 pigtails.

Series Z 473–480. Tea Imported From England by American Colonies: 1761 to 1775

[In pounds. For years ending December 24]

Year	Total 473	New England 474	New York 475	Pennsylvania 476	Virginia and Maryland 477	Carolina 478	Georgia 479	Florida 480
1775	22,198	8,005	----	----	8,825	----	----	5,368
1774	73,274	30,161	1,304	----	31,273	4,332	3,661	2,543
1773	739,221	206,312	208,385	208,191	26,491	83,959	5,070	813
1772	264,882	151,184	530	128	78,117	22,916	10,265	1,742
1771	362,257	282,857	1,035	495	32,961	36,385	5,420	3,104
1770	110,386	85,935	269	----	18,270	1,175	2,980	1,757
1769	229,439	86,004	4,282	81,729	37,355	12,982	4,426	2,661
1768	873,744	291,899	320,214	174,883	41,944	34,639	5,212	4,953
1767	480,376	152,435	177,111	87,741	36,088	24,261	2,325	415
1766	361,001	118,982	124,464	60,796	29,177	20,112	6,798	672
1765	518,424	175,389	226,232	54,538	23,280	36,067	2,918	----
1764	489,252	143,234	265,385	41,949	18,249	18,374	1,989	72
1763	188,785	37,525	83,870	18,281	23,481	22,860	2,768	----
1762	161,588	51,618	70,460	7,884	12,773	17,850	1,003	----
1761	56,110	6,992	3,837	144	22,244	22,893	----	----

Series Z 481–485. Rice Exported From Producing Areas: 1698 to 1789

[In barrels, except as indicated. Data are for various terminal dates, primarily December 24, January 4 (of the succeeding year), and October 31; see text]

Year	Total Pounds 481	Total Barrels[1] 482	Charleston, S.C. 483	Beaufort and Georgetown, S.C. 484	Georgia 485
1789	----	----	100,000	----	----
1788	----	----	82,400	----	----
1787	----	----	65,195	----	----
1786	----	----	66,557	----	----
1785	----	----	63,732	----	----
1784	----	----	61,974	----	----
1783	----	----	24,255	----	----
1774	76,265,700	145,268	118,482	6,594	20,192
1773	81,476,325	155,193	126,940	6,681	21,572
1772	69,218,625	131,845	104,821	4,076	22,948
1771	81,755,100	155,724	125,151	5,209	25,364
1770	83,708,625	159,445	131,805	5,568	22,072
1769	73,078,950	139,198	115,582	6,900	16,716
1768	77,284,050	147,208	125,538	7,045	14,625
1767	63,465,150	120,886	104,125	5,480	11,281
1766	48,396,600	92,184	74,031	3,896	14,257
1765	65,710,575	125,163	107,292	5,647	12,224
1764	55,907,250	106,490	91,960	4,840	9,690
1763	61,959,450	118,018	104,800	5,516	7,702
1762	47,435,325	90,353	79,652	4,192	6,509
1761	58,430,275	111,391	101,389	5,336	4,666
1760	35,327,250	67,290	60,807	3,200	3,283
1759	30,472,575	58,043	51,718	2,722	3,603
1758	38,527,650	73,386	67,464	3,551	2,371
1757	33,976,950	64,718	58,634	3,086	2,998
1756	45,344,250	86,370	79,203	4,170	2,997
1755	59,057,775	112,491	104,682	5,510	2,299
1754	49,179,520	94,576	88,570	4,662	1,344
1753	19,747,675	38,345	35,523	1,870	952
1752	42,245,850	82,835	78,208	4,116	511
1751	32,751,270	64,854	61,611	3,243	----
1750	27,372,500	54,745	51,190	2,694	861
1749	21,381,030	43,194	41,034	2,160	----
1748	28,368,550	57,895	55,000	2,895	----
1747	27,643,060	56,996	54,146	2,850	----
1746	27,335,040	56,948	54,101	2,847	----
1745	29,813,375	62,765	59,627	3,138	----
1744	39,963,630	85,029	80,778	4,251	----
1743	35,935,200	77,280	73,416	3,864	----
1742	22,706,060	49,361	46,196	2,431	734
1741	38,720,955	85,101	80,846	4,255	----
1740	43,326,000	96,280	91,110	4,785	385

Year	Total Pounds 481	Total Barrels[1] 482	Charleston, S.C. 483	Beaufort and Georgetown, S.C. 484
1739	32,167,800	71,484	67,117	4,367
1738	16,327,350	36,283	34,324	1,959
1737	20,201,400	44,892	42,827	2,065
1736	24,804,000	55,120	52,971	2,149
1735	21,259,800	47,244	45,732	1,512
1734	13,991,850	31,093	30,323	770
1733	23,245,200	51,656	50,726	930
1732	16,866,000	37,480	37,068	412
1731	21,753,450	48,341	48,341	----
1730	18,774,900	41,722	41,722	----
1729	14,248,960	32,384	32,384	----
1728	12,884,950	29,965	29,965	----
1727	11,291,280	26,884	26,884	----
1726	9,442,710	23,031	23,031	----
1725	7,093,600	17,734	17,734	----

Year	Total, pounds 481	Year	Total, pounds 481
1724	8,654,447	1710	1,600,983
1723	8,797,304	1709	1,510,679
1722	9,732,377	1708	675,327
1721	7,963,615	1707	561,185
1720	6,485,662	1706	267,309
1719	4,001,210	1704	759,536
1718	2,956,727	1703	694,493
1717	2,881,335	1702	612,646
1716	4,584,927	1701	194,618
1715	2,367,605	1700	394,130
1714	3,139,361	1699	131,207
1713	3,850,533	1698[2]	10,407
1711	1,181,430		

[1] Number of pounds per barrel varied from year to year; see text.

[2] Year ending Sept. 28; exports from Sept. 29 to Dec. 24, 1698, were 1,597 pounds.

Series Z 486–492. Rice Exported From Charleston, S.C., by Destination: 1717 to 1766

[In barrels. For 1717–1738, for years ending December 24; for 1758–1766, ending January 4 of following year]

Year	Total	England	Scotland	Continental Colonies	British West Indies	Foreign West Indies	Countries south of Cape Finisterre	Year	Total	England	Scotland	Continental Colonies	British West Indies	Countries south of Cape Finisterre
	486	487	488	489	490	491	492		486	487	488	489	490	492
1766	85,862	39,468	2,862	3,297	11,730	3,369	25,136	1735	44,418	28,345	---	667	713	14,693
1763	103,451	51,335	3,703	16,117	16,466	1,490	14,340	1734	37,303	24,849	---	605	1,061	10,788
1762	82,159	33,217	4,573	10,921	20,239	1,970	11,239	1732	38,942	26,766	---	1,417	1,504	9,255
1759	51,037	18,517	9,359	4,546	5,962	490	12,163	1731	48,337	38,331	---	1,737	1,872	6,397
1758	61,501	30,687	7,214	4,611	6,432	---	12,557	1724	19,908	16,452	---	2,199	1,257	---
1738	32,372	27,331	---	596	643	---	3,802	1719	13,357	8,423	31	3,210	1,693	---
1737	37,896	32,322	---	511	594	---	4,469	1718	8,421	6,187	---	1,005	1,229	---
1736	53,376	38,158	---	798	1,164	---	13,256	1717	10,380	7,257	---	1,980	1,143	---

Series Z 493–499. Rice Exported to England, by Origin: 1698 to 1776

[In hundredweights. For years ending December 24, except as noted]

Year	Total	Carolina	Georgia	New England	New York	Pennsylvania	Virginia and Maryland	Year	Total	Carolina	Georgia	New England	New York	Pennsylvania	Virginia and Maryland
	493	494	495	496	497	498	499		493	494	495	496	497	498	499
1776	6,342	3,507	2,835	---	---	---	---	1737	154,318	154,010	(NA)	128	---	180	---
1775	576,916	452,822	110,020	4,232	7,312	2,530	---	1736	151,234	150,797	(NA)	---	---	437	---
1774	425,988	339,911	69,387	870	5,696	9,980	144								
1773	457,073	378,291	72,469	---	2,455	3,858	---	1735	118,295	116,441	1,444	---	309	97	4
1772	[1]479,226	405,121	64,078	---	360	6,321	2,146	1734	80,263	79,448	---	286	222	300	7
1771	[1]452,664	375,727	59,417	349	7,666	9,399	52	1733	147,272	147,021	---	124	---	83	44
								1732	101,838	101,387	---	401	---	50	---
1770	280,847	222,556	48,846	8,183	66	1,196	---	1731	164,515	161,246	---	1,784	37	1,448	---
1769	434,444	362,063	71,484	92	305	500	---								
1768	431,891	380,720	41,398	6,457	565	2,719	32	1730	139,384	136,578	---	1,365	507	922	12
1767	288,537	257,936	27,530	193	1,650	1,072	156	1729	119,202	117,550	---	1,120	232	300	---
1766	[1]238,680	193,915	44,387	88	24	175	---	1728	100,466	95,973	---	1,986	1,918	589	---
								1727	89,942	89,942	---	(NA)	(NA)	(NA)	(NA)
1765	357,099	319,164	28,495	554	6,916	1,501	469	1726	69,092	67,041	---	499	1,465	87	---
1764	320,734	291,546	20,377	1,631	4,574	2,277	329								
1763	271,505	251,476	9,494	1,537	5,354	3,644	---	1725	53,670	52,268	---	754	585	63	---
1762	148,754	138,777	7,786	750	408	1,033	---	1724	63,383	59,385	---	3,115	556	327	---
1761	238,750	224,964	7,220	164	4,562	1,840	---	1723	67,613	60,952	---	5,746	488	425	2
								1722	76,034	72,238	---	2,457	366	940	33
1760	108,673	95,773	11,628	---	309	958	5	1721	62,215	54,873	---	5,574	620	1,058	90
1759	109,596	102,001	6,358	481	523	233	---								
1758	102,794	95,741	(NA)	305	4,819	1,929	---	1720	50,669	44,915	---	5,444	175	118	17
1757	74,741	72,785	(NA)	1,375	67	514	---	1719	31,259	26,233	---	4,035	147	813	31
1756	167,261	156,279	5,931	1,359	3,621	71	---	1718	23,097	19,530	---	2,303	1,130	129	5
								1717	22,509	17,484	---	3,822	641	439	123
1755	312,845	306,720	3,945	342	1,837	1	---	1716	35,820	27,555	---	5,709	871	1,424	261
1754	276,935	273,862	2,782	62	204	25	---								
1753	123,682	120,221	1,970	---	225	---	1,266	1715	18,497	14,405	---	2,013	1,272	807	---
1752	267,210	261,387	1,047	1,815	1,387	174	1,400	1714	24,527	22,264	---	1,620	210	433	---
1751	202,943	196,863	---	4,363	923	794	---	1713	30,083	28,517	---	1,393	165	---	8
								1711	9,231	8,678	---	174	379	---	---
1750	166,672	164,378	1,783	505	---	6	---	1710	12,508	12,265	---	128	105	---	10
1749	122,401	121,614	---	748	---	39	---	1709	11,802	11,274	---	289	232	---	7
1748	144,068	143,515	(NA)	---	209	344	---	1708	5,276	5,220	---	49	---	---	7
1747	86,018	85,939	(NA)	79	---	---	---	1707	4,385	4,120	---	173	83	---	9
1746	51,736	50,202	(NA)	1,094	431	---	9	1706	2,089	2,058	---	---	3	21	7
1745	75,153	73,792	(NA)	38	317	1,006	---								
1744	196,968	195,249	(NA)	1,323	156	240	---	1704	5,933	5,550	---	217	79	28	59
1743	243,091	241,820	---	244	60	888	79	1703	5,426	5,320	---	17	62	---	27
1742	136,117	134,368	1,518	52	---	179	---	1702	4,786	4,568	---	---	218	---	---
1741	263,093	261,110	(NA)	360	1,006	613	4	1701	1,521	1,457	---	---	64	---	---
1740	313,571	308,178	798	1,597	1,374	1,624	---	1700	3,079	3,037	---	26	4	---	12
1739	254,879	253,380	---	1,350	105	---	44	1699	1,025	1,018	---	---	---	7	---
1738	128,337	128,187	---	149	---	---	1	1698 [2]	81	81	---	---	---	---	---

NA Not available.
[1] Includes exports from Florida in 1766, 91 cwt.; 1771, 54 cwt.; 1772, 1,200 cwt.

[2] Year ending Sept. 28. Data for Sept. 29 to Dec. 24, 1698, were 11 cwt. for Carolina and 2 cwt. for Virginia and Maryland.

Series Z 500–503. Pitch, Tar, and Turpentine Exported from Charleston, S.C.: 1725 to 1774

[In barrels. For years ending October 31. Leaders denote no data available]

Year	Pitch 500	Tar 501	Turpentine 502	Tar (green) 503	Year	Pitch 500	Tar 501	Turpentine 502	Tar (green) 503	Year	Pitch 500	Tar 501	Turpentine 502
1774[1]	870	1,176	1,394	---	1757[3]	4,962	2,103	337	397	1740	11,377	2,436	577
1773[2]	821	1,236	1,043	396	1756[5]	3,058	2,711	1,195	1,070	1739	7,890	2,722	33
1772[3]	4,125	2,728	864	2,995	1755	5,869	2,596	2,171	547	1738	16,088	5,417	845
1771	7,429	2,259	1,353	1,142	1754	11,025	2,295	5,375	369	1737	11,987	8,501	4,411
					1753	15,220	6,008	6,496	---	1736	11,736	1,491	5,193
1770	4,133	827	1,335	2,111	1752	20,483	2,651	6,271					
1769	5,256	1,278	3,201	3,849	1751	11,441	5,070	1,401		1735	24,036	5,636	8,061
1768[3]	6,948	1,454	5,761	822	1750[4]	11,157	3,858	812		1734	28,874	7,336	4,552
1767[3]	12,339	2,232	3,787	---	1749	7,796	3,765	1,582		1733	18,165	6,604	2,212
					1748	5,521	3,075	2,397		1732	32,593	4,575	2,466
1765[2]	8,751	2,183	653	392	1747	13,737	4,422	5,162		1731	9,385	1,725	1,560
1764	7,459	3,093	1,643	65	1746	18,016	1,519	4,262					
1763[4]	6,087	1,265	3,042	411						1730	10,825	2,014	1,073
1762	6,315	1,244	1,438	289						1729	8,377	3,441	1,913
1761[4]	6,626	1,438	4,874	---	1745	8,823	1,286	988		1728	3,186	2,269	1,232
					1744	7,678	17,552	1,245		1727	13,654	10,950	1,252
1760	5,754	886	2,420	97	1743	9,755	2,206	2,012		1726	29,776	8,322	715
1759	7,813	2,236	1,333	405	1742	15,808	3,115	1,986		1725	57,422	2,333	133
1758	2,521	1,720	937	328	1741	11,831	1,811	1,691					

[1] Data for 4 months.
[2] Data for 7 months.
[3] Data for 10 months.
[4] Data for 11 months.
[5] Data for 9 months.

Series Z 504–509. Timber and Timber Products Exported From Charleston, S.C., and Savannah, Ga.: 1754 to 1774

[Charleston, for years ending October 31; Savannah, unknown]

Year	Charleston, S.C. Lumber (feet) 504	Shingles 505	Staves 506	Savannah, Ga. Timber (feet) 507	Shingles 508	Staves 509	Year	Charleston, S.C. Lumber (feet) 504	Shingles 505	Staves 506	Savannah, Ga. Timber (feet) 507	Shingles 508	Staves 509
1774[1]	119,923	858,100	27,400	---	---	---	1763[4]	647,112	1,225,160	362,065	917,384	1,470,120	594,356
1773[2]	528,637	1,313,500	79,875	---	---	---	1762	414,754	896,500	163,990	417,449	685,265	325,477
1772[2]	647,047	1,392,075	207,280	2,163,582	3,525,930	988,471	1761	610,952	1,354,500	236,327	307,690	606,650	50,969
1771	675,000	709,000	101,228	2,159,072	2,224,598	403,253							
							1760	545,333	1,354,500	135,992	---	---	---
1770	697,393	1,305,625	117,860	1,805,992	2,896,991	466,276	1759	1,018,490	1,204,890	146,172	---	---	---
1769	592,026	2,072,947	282,180	1,634,331	3,474,588	747,903	1758	639,012	724,000	145,529	---	---	---
1768[3]	760,125	2,131,000	182,940	1,787,258	3,669,477	806,609	1757[3]	234,303	664,100	83,617	---	---	---
1767[3]	450,118	1,717,800	240,813	1,767,199	2,570,725	748,166	1756[5]	202,316	522,420	109,890	---	---	---
1766	---	---	---	1,101,466	2,036,947	737,898							
							1755	780,776	952,880	168,121	---	---	---
1765[2]	697,648	---	186,375	1,879,454	3,722,050	661,416	1754	764,607	822,120	102,290	---	---	---
1764	948,121	1,553,365	228,015	1,043,535	2,061,151	423,251							

[1] Charleston data for 4 months.
[2] Charleston data for 7 months.
[3] Charleston data for 10 months.
[4] Charleston data for 11 months.
[5] Charleston data for 9 months.

Series Z 510–515. Number and Tonnage of Vessels Built, by Type: 1768 to 1773

[Vessels built and registered in British North America, Bahamas, and Bermuda]

Year registered	Total Number 510	Tonnage 511	Topsails Number 512	Tonnage 513	Sloops and schooners Number 514	Tonnage 515	Year registered	Total Number 510	Tonnage 511	Topsails Number 512	Tonnage 513	Sloops and schooners Number 514	Tonnage 515
Total	3,124	170,837	928	100,610	2,196	70,227							
1773	638	38,029	212	24,500	426	13,529							
1772	557	32,423	184	19,854	373	12,569	1770	515	24,198	130	11,216	385	12,982
1771	478	25,275	131	14,695	347	10,580	1769	450	21,460	114	11,247	336	10,213
							1768	486	29,452	157	19,098	329	10,354

Series Z 516–529.   Vessels Built in Thirteen Colonies and West Florida: 1769 to 1771

Year and type of vessel	Total	New Hampshire	Massachusetts	Rhode Island	Connecticut	New York	New Jersey	Pennsylvania	Maryland	Virginia	North Carolina	South Carolina	Georgia	West Florida
	516	517	518	519	520	521	522	523	524	525	526	527	528	529
1771														
Topsails_____	128	15	42	15	7	9	–	15	10	10	–	3	2	–
Sloops and schooners___	293	40	83	60	39	28	2	6	8	9	8	4	4	2
Tons_____	24,092	4,991	7,704	2,148	1,483	1,698	70	1,307	1,645	1,678	241	560	543	24
1770														
Topsails_____	118	27	31	16	5	8	–	18	7	6	–	–	3	–
Sloops and schooners___	283	20	118	49	41	10	–	8	10	15	5	3	3	1
Tons_____	20,620	3,581	7,274	2,035	1,522	960	–	2,354	1,545	1,105	125	52	57	10
1769														
Topsails_____	114	16	40	8	7	5	1	14	9	6	3	4	–	1
Sloops and schooners___	276	29	97	31	43	14	3	8	11	21	9	8	2	–
Tons_____	20,081	2,452	8,013	1,428	1,542	955	83	1,469	1,344	1,269	607	789	50	80

– Represents zero.

Series Z 530–533.   Number of Vessels Engaged in Whaling, and Quantity and Value of Oil Acquired, Nantucket, Mass.: 1715 to 1789

[Year ending date unknown]

Year or period	Number of vessels	Tons burden, each vessel	Oil Barrels	Oil Value (£) [1]	Year	Number of vessels	Tons burden, each vessel	Oil Barrels	Oil Value (£) [1]	Year	Number of vessels	Tons burden, each vessel	Oil Barrels	Oil Value (£) [1]
	530	531	532	533		530	531	532	533		530	531	532	533
1787–1789____	36	113	_____	12,060	1770_____	[3] 125	75–110	[3] 14,331	_____	1763_____	60	_____	9,238	_____
1785_____	15	_____	(2)	(2)	1769_____	119	_____	19,140	_____	1762_____	78	_____	9,440	_____
1784_____	28	_____	5,400	14,500	1768_____	[3] 125	75	[3] 15,439	_____	1756_____	80	75	12,000	27,600
1783_____	19	_____	2,260	16,280	1767_____	108	_____	16,561	_____	1748_____	60	50–75	11,250	19,648
1772–1775____	150	90–180	30,000	167,000	1766_____	118	_____	11,969	_____	1730_____	25	38–50	3,700	3,200
1772_____	98	_____	7,825	_____	1765_____	101	_____	11,512	_____	1715_____	6	38	600	[4] 1,100
1771_____	115	_____	12,754	_____	1764_____	72	_____	11,983	_____					

[1] £, pound sterling.   See source for value per ton.
[2] Ships still at sea at time of reporting.

[3] Different figures are quoted by the source (p. 233) from the Massachusetts Historical Society Collection.
[4] Includes the value of 11,000 pounds of whale bone.

Series Z 534–538.   State of the Cod Fishery of Massachusetts: 1765 to 1775

Port	Vessels, annually	Tonnage	Seamen	Quintals to Europe	Quintals to the West Indies	Port	Vessels, annually	Tonnage	Seamen	Quintals to Europe	Quintals to the West Indies
	534	535	536	537	538		534	535	536	537	538
Total_____	**665**	**25,630**	**4,405**	**178,800**	**172,500**	Scituate_____	10	400	70	1,000	3,000
						Duxborough_____	4	160	28	400	1,200
Marblehead_____	150	7,500	1,200	80,000	40,000	Kingston_____	6	240	42	800	1,600
Gloucester_____	146	5,530	888	35,000	42,500	Yarmouth_____	30	900	180	3,000	6,000
Manchester_____	25	1,500	200	10,000	10,000	Wellfleet_____	3	90	21	300	600
Beverly_____	15	750	120	6,000	6,000	Truro_____	10	400	80	1,000	3,000
Salem_____	30	1,500	240	12,000	12,000	Provincetown_____	4	160	32	500	1,100
Newburyport_____	10	400	60	2,000	2,000	Chatham_____	30	900	240	4,000	8,000
Ipswich_____	50	900	190	8,000	5,500	Nantucket_____	8	320	64	1,000	2,200
Plymouth_____	60	2,400	420	8,000	16,000	Maine_____	60	1,000	230	4,000	8,000
Cohasset_____	6	240	42	800	1,600	Weymouth_____	2	100	16	200	600
Hingham_____	6	240	42	800	1,600						

Series Z 539–550. Daily Wages of Selected Types of Workmen, by Area: 1621 to 1781

[£, pound sterling; s, shilling; d, pence. Pay in local currency; not comparable from colony to colony]

Area and year	With board furnished						Without board furnished					
	Carpenters	Masons and bricklayers	Joiners and riggers	Coopers	Tailors	Laborers	Carpenters	Masons and bricklayers	Joiners and riggers	Coopers	Tailors	Laborers
	539	540	541	542	543	544	545	546	547	548	549	550
	s. d.	s. d.	s. d.	s. d.	s. d.	s. d.	s. d.	s. d.	s. d.	s. d.	£ s. d.	s. d.
Virginia, 1781							5–0	5–0		5–0	5–0	2–0
Providence, 1779							72–0	73–0	72–0		[1]17–0–0	48–0
Rhode Island, 1776					[1]3–0		5–0	6–6	5–0	5–0		3–0
South Carolina, 1710							3 to 5–0	6–0	3 to 5–0	4–0	5–0	([2])
Massachusetts, 1670						2–0	2–0	2–0		[3]2–8	1–8	1–3
New Haven, 1641							2–0	2–0	2–0	2–0		18
New Haven, 1640							2–6	2–6	2–6	2–6		2–0
Massachusetts, 1633	14	14	14		12	8	2–0	2–0	2–0			18
Virginia, 1621	3–0	3–0	4–0	3–0	2–0	2–0	4–0	4–0	5–0	4–0	3–0	3–0

[1] Per suit.
[2] 1s. 3d. to 2s.
[3] For 32-gal. barrel.

Series Z 551–556. Daily and Monthly Wages of Agricultural Laborers in Maryland: 1638 to 1676

[s, shilling; d, pence]

Year	Daily wages — In tobacco			Monthly wages — In tobacco		
	Pounds of tobacco	Price per pound	Sterling	Pounds of tobacco	Price per pound	Sterling
	551	552	553	554	555	556
		s.	s. d.		s.	s. d.
1676				300	[1]1.0	25–0
1670				175	[1]1.5	21–10
1669 [2]	20	1.5	2–6	320	1.5	40–0
1669 [2]				125	1.5	15–8
1669 [2]				150	1.5	18–9
1667				600	.5	25–0
1662				266	1.2	26–8
1660 [2]				200	1.0	16–8
1660 [2]				250	1.0	20–10
1656	15	[1]2.0	2–6			
1655 [2]	25	2.0	4–2			
1655 [2]	20	2.0	3–4			
1654				600	[1]2.0	100–0
1652				600	[1]2.0	100–0
1649	10	3.0	2–6			
1648	15	[1]2.0	2–6	250	[1]2.0	41–8
1647	20	1.5	2–6	170	1.5	21–3
				170	1.5	21–3
1645				187	[1]1.2	23–4
1644 [2]	10	[1]1.5	1–3	167	[1]1.2	20–10
1644 [2]				133	[1]1.2	16–8
1644 [2]				100	.6	5–0
1642	15	.6	9			
1641	20	[1]1.2	2–0			
1638						8–4

[1] Estimate.
[2] Source does not explain why 2 (or 3) sets of figures are given.

Series Z 557. Index of Wholesale Prices Estimated for Colonial and Pre-Federal Years: 1720 to 1789

[1850–59 = 100]

Year	Index	Year	Index	Year	Index	Year	Index	Year	Index	Year	Index	Year	Index
1789	94.0	1779	2,969.1	1769	81.2	1759	85.8	1749	76.1	1739	59.6	1729	62.9
1788	97.4	1778	598.1	1768	80.7	1758	73.9	1748	74.3	1738	69.4	1728	63.1
1787	103.9	1777	329.6	1767	81.7	1757	69.6	1747	65.6	1737	69.3	1727	66.3
1786	105.1	1776	108.0	1766	81.7	1756	69.5	1746	55.0	1736	62.6	1726	68.7
1785	105.0	1775	78.0	1765	76.7	1755	71.2	1745	53.7	1735	66.3	1725	65.7
1784	112.7	1774	84.3	1764	77.2	1754	71.4	1744	57.1	1734	67.0	1724	60.4
1783	119.1	1773	90.9	1763	83.5	1753	78.2	1743	59.7	1733	59.7	1723	57.3
1782	139.6	1772	98.2	1762	83.4	1752	75.6	1742	69.7	1732	58.0	1722	55.5
1781	5,085.8	1771	84.9	1761	77.5	1751	72.0	1741	73.6	1731	59.2	1721	53.4
1780	10,544.1	1770	80.0	1760	81.5	1750	73.9	1740	59.6	1730	66.6	1720	58.6

Series Z 558–577. Average Annual Wholesale Prices of Selected Commodities in Philadelphia: 1720 to 1775

[In Pennsylvania currency; in shillings per unit of quantity indicated, except series Z 573 in pounds]

Year	Corn	Wheat	Tobacco	Rice	Bread Middling	Bread Ship	Flour	Beef	Pork	Salt Coarse	Salt Fine	Molasses	Sugar, muscovado	Rum New England	Rum West Indies	Madeira wine	Barrel staves	Pitch	Tar	Cotton
	558	559	560	561	562	563	564	565	566	567	568	569	570	571	572	573	574	575	576	577
	Bu.	Bu.	Cwt.¹	Cwt.	Cwt.	Cwt.	Cwt.	Bbl.	Bbl.	Bu.	Bu.	Gal.	Cwt.	Gal.	Gal.	Pipe	Mil.	Bbl.	Bbl.	Lb.
1775	2.90	5.68		17.38			15.36	57.00	64.88	2.13	3.71	1.75	52.96	2.17	3.05	64.06	72.54	15.13	13.81	1.48
1774	2.83	6.93		16.92	31.08	14.57	18.12	54.31	69.50	1.38	2.05	1.79	55.56		3.03	55.17	63.49	14.70	13.79	1.44
1773	3.14	7.42		18.34	30.93	17.30	18.92	54.58	83.97	1.69	2.22	1.74	50.02	2.20	3.25	56.75		14.70	14.32	1.27
1772	3.69	7.74	32.29	23.39	31.23	19.95	20.26	57.05	93.46	1.85	1.85	1.75	49.18	2.19	3.44	54.03	71.85	14.54	14.32	1.27
1771	3.50	6.78	32.50	16.86	28.93	15.68	17.50	51.48	80.31	1.65	1.55	1.77	50.86	2.18	3.35	50.00	75.15	12.19	12.41	1.24
1770	3.60	5.92	28.73	16.29	28.53	14.11	15.71	51.39	77.04	1.63	1.89	1.86	51.80	2.19	3.01	49.58	68.68	11.54	11.33	1.32
1769	2.80	5.48	25.12	17.71	25.45	13.65	15.04	55.21	80.29	1.43	1.81	1.78	52.74	2.16	3.29	48.02	61.32	11.93	10.17	1.37
1768	2.57	6.31	21.83	17.74	26.38	15.91	16.89	52.41	73.43	1.61	1.53	1.81	46.42	2.23		47.73	65.47	14.34	11.01	1.71
1767	2.93	6.25	21.89	17.54	27.47	16.80	17.16	55.35	71.76	1.64	1.76	1.74	49.43	2.08	3.00	50.97	79.60	16.16	11.69	1.93
1766	3.29	5.73	20.42	16.69	24.54	15.44	14.81	55.21	76.88	1.70		1.92	55.74	2.23	3.02	48.92	67.71	17.25	11.90	
1765	3.01	4.70	18.13	14.34	24.92	13.88	13.50	58.75	74.36	1.70		1.76	52.94	2.04	3.02	47.29	70.63	17.33	12.40	
1764	2.74	4.60	17.71	14.52	23.84	12.95	12.81	60.00	98.26	1.92		1.63	48.73	2.05	3.26	50.56	64.90	15.28	12.36	1.36
1763	3.75	6.06	19.48	15.50	30.18	17.82	16.94	60.29	86.95	2.21		1.99	49.79	2.59	3.72	49.34	66.04	14.93	12.30	1.87
1762	3.48	5.66	21.42	13.90	28.88	17.49	16.82	58.04	85.63	2.86		2.29	52.15	2.79	3.94	50.79	90.85	13.47	14.06	2.04
1761	2.42	5.03	21.52	16.58	25.18	12.67	14.82	54.91	73.92	1.98	2.86	2.42	49.14	3.04	3.93	48.83	86.91	14.06	11.25	1.45
1760	2.96	5.11	20.43	19.00	24.36	13.40	14.96	53.72	69.30	2.14	2.97	2.70	47.85	3.54	4.73	50.31	68.82	14.47	10.82	1.32
1759	2.99	4.96	20.42		22.14	14.33	14.59	48.66	69.19	2.13	2.40	2.87	45.18	3.94	4.99	45.26	60.69	16.07	10.68	1.51
1758	1.94	3.89	18.33		21.84	13.98	12.27	48.18	59.49	2.36	2.41	2.51	47.70	3.12	3.72	39.46	60.73	15.11	9.75	1.40
1757	1.72	3.79	17.74	14.84	21.24	14.16	11.31	46.43	60.94	2.83	2.56	2.45	47.99	2.74	3.17		50.82	15.19	9.85	1.52
1756	2.50	4.34	15.88	14.50	21.21	13.65	12.76	48.96	61.42	2.15	2.39	2.04	48.83	2.35	2.73	32.78	41.63	13.93	11.42	1.49
1755	2.16	4.49	15.08	16.50	21.42	14.50	13.76	47.85	65.94	1.49	1.54	1.89	48.39	2.27	2.84	29.56	51.54	14.92	11.54	1.40
1754	2.34	4.46	17.77	17.06	21.64	15.89	14.11	45.13	61.19	1.47	1.63	2.00	50.85	2.44	3.22	28.96	55.94	15.71	10.67	1.58
1753	2.91	4.48	19.47	20.97	21.52	13.87	12.80	45.70	63.20	1.43	1.85	2.03	51.70	2.47	3.08	30.70	56.87	16.05	9.76	1.65
1752	2.56	4.38	19.90	16.32	21.94	13.17	13.13	48.44	72.35	1.26	1.53	1.94	47.04	2.39	3.22	30.10	53.28	20.06	11.07	1.90
1751	2.79	4.28	20.19	17.29	22.37	14.20	12.34	48.44	69.97	1.16	1.30	1.86	47.04	2.51	3.49	30.07	51.50	21.56	11.07	2.18
1750	2.56	4.51	19.98	20.63	23.82	15.23	13.10	38.17	63.99	1.41	1.69	1.69	51.98	2.53	3.46	29.74	68.36	18.91	12.89	1.89
1749	2.63	5.66	17.10	18.98	26.30	17.60	16.59	40.16	60.16	2.18	2.51	2.08	46.83	2.72	3.77	28.77	68.79	15.41	10.49	1.65
1748	2.28	5.04	18.00	15.83	19.67	13.89	15.41	44.29	61.04	3.17	3.07	2.82	51.63	3.60	4.63	25.60	61.06	14.76	11.06	1.77
1747	1.92	3.29	16.38	11.40	16.48	11.53	10.01	40.55	57.66	3.58	3.84	2.63	55.01	3.62	4.46	24.42	56.03	13.19	10.30	1.94
1746	1.82	2.87	13.93	6.99	14.95	10.15	9.07	41.13	53.79	3.76	3.75	2.50	47.15	2.69	3.03	22.90	40.63	11.42	9.11	1.83
1745	1.69	2.60	13.05	10.00	13.06	8.81	8.01	36.88	53.02	2.63	2.56	2.34	43.02	2.65	3.25	27.50	39.79	13.50	10.38	1.33
1744	1.53	2.49	12.65	11.03	13.32	8.47	7.68	41.94	60.49	2.05	2.23	1.80	49.97	2.52	3.20	27.85	40.00	13.90	10.92	1.19
1743	2.14	2.84	16.25	11.96	14.31	9.06	8.69	44.75	68.52	1.94	2.20	1.87	38.94	2.36	3.16	27.38	40.85	14.25	10.40	.99
1742	2.69	3.58	17.65	16.17	15.96	11.77	10.98	36.63	54.17	2.90	2.67	2.28	40.94	2.84	3.64	24.35	47.81	16.21	12.75	1.01
1741	2.74	4.47	14.83	16.58	19.58	15.83	13.66	40.63	49.83	2.47	2.19	1.82	36.40	2.46	2.96	21.83	49.17	17.54	14.08	1.16
1740	1.50	3.25	13.92	12.75	13.56	10.31	8.72	35.63	46.04	1.67	2.20	1.65	37.88	1.81	2.53	20.17	39.42	14.29	10.88	1.29
1739	1.41	2.82	15.63	17.08	13.01	9.60	8.03	35.75	54.88	1.24	2.16	1.59	38.08		2.33	21.58	44.58	11.42	9.42	1.33
1738	2.10	3.48	17.00	20.67	16.75	12.58	11.16	36.67	59.58	1.35	2.19	1.60	38.98		2.29	22.00	47.56	11.33	8.63	1.22
1737	2.08	3.88	17.41	17.44	16.71	11.78	11.71	36.06	54.44	1.22	2.24	1.68	35.64		2.65	20.88	45.36	10.85	8.56	1.17
1736	1.89	3.24	15.08	17.15	12.77	10.94	9.61	33.50	41.72	1.36	1.92	1.68	32.81		2.24	21.58	35.21	12.25	8.98	1.09
1735	1.58	3.85	15.65	18.50	14.58	12.33	11.47	30.61	37.59	1.56	2.08	1.65	35.64		2.36	21.47	36.37	12.83	9.63	1.07
1734	2.02	3.55			13.75	10.90	10.51	30.56	43.58		2.04	1.50	29.20		2.63			12.92	10.14	1.01
1733	2.10	3.06			12.85	10.39	8.84		47.54		2.36	1.39	28.94		2.30			17.17	12.25	1.08
1732	1.81	2.70	15.53		11.91		8.17		49.41	1.95	2.40	1.37	33.35		2.50			13.75	10.10	.97
1731	1.65	2.47	13.45	15.04	11.72		8.02	36.31	55.97	1.88	3.14	1.36	33.21		2.64			14.31	11.10	1.13
1730	1.93	3.68			14.88		11.56		59.24		3.09	1.54	32.13		2.51			15.00	11.04	
1729	2.15	3.70	15.08	18.74	14.00		10.65		51.65		2.15	1.53	35.00		2.60			12.08	11.00	
1728	2.26	3.39	16.06		13.72		10.02	36.72	59.17		1.85	1.51	35.17		2.61			13.11	11.92	
1727	2.02	3.27	17.87		13.46		11.46		47.79		2.07	1.43	32.63		2.87			18.40		
1726	2.13	3.82	17.22		14.08		12.51		48.58		1.85	1.45	36.35		3.19			19.19		
1725	2.13	3.87	33.46	19.98	12.79		12.12	30.17	39.29	2.51	2.83	1.46	33.44		2.85			18.42		
1724	2.12	3.36		14.56	11.92		10.95	30.65	36.00	2.23	3.14	1.49	29.42		2.35			15.50	10.67	
1723	1.86	2.73	14.13		11.67		8.80	30.58	40.48	2.05	2.81	1.30	36.88		2.57		22.50	12.63	11.38	
1722	1.73	2.97	10.25	13.92	12.54		8.93	30.67	45.00	1.19	1.65	1.24	31.88		2.94	20.50	22.50	13.50	10.25	
1721	1.76	3.05	10.04	15.44	13.00		8.83	30.00	45.00	1.46	1.85	1.16	33.13		2.31	19.08	22.50	12.00	8.33	
1720	1.73	3.08	13.79	16.92	13.31		9.26	30.00	46.46	2.31	2.31	1.34	35.52		2.68	17.99	22.50	14.17	9.83	

¹ Cwt. of tobacco was an exception to the rule that cwt. equaled 112 lb.; it equaled only 100 lb.

Series Z 578–582.   Prices of Maryland Tobacco: 1711 to 1775

[In pence sterling per pound]

Year	Number of observations	Prices			Exchange rate	Year	Number of observations	Prices			Exchange rate
		Mean	High	Low				Mean	High	Low	
	578	579	580	581	582		578	579	580	581	582
1775	14	1.67	2.43	1.20	33⅓	1743	36	0.67	1.20	0.19	100
1774	12	1.41	2.52	.90	33⅓	1742	50	.67	1.00	.30	100
1773 [1]	10	1.33	2.34	.86	66⅔	1741	23	.62	1.05	.24	100
1773 [1]	10	1.64	2.93	1.13	33⅓						
1772 [1]	19	1.44	1.92	.86	66⅔	1740	29	.80	1.20	.30	100
1772 [1]	19	1.64	2.40	1.08	33⅓	1739	8	1.01	1.50	.45	33⅓
1771	18	1.90	2.70	.90	33⅓	1738	18	1.02	1.80	.45	33⅓
						1737	10	.93	1.50	.45	33⅓
1770	26	2.06	2.52	1.13	33⅓	1736	14	1.02	2.25	.36	33⅓
1769	14	2.23	3.00	1.35	33⅓						
1768	14	1.81	3.00	1.13	33⅓	1735	16	.93	1.50	.45	33⅓
1767	22	1.63	2.16	.72	33⅓	1734	28	.97	1.26	.54	33⅓
1766	10	1.45	1.80	1.17	33⅓	1733	13	.84	1.13	.54	33⅓
						1732	9	.74	.90	.36	33⅓
1765	12	1.33	1.62	.90	33⅓	1731	10	.65	.90	.23	33⅓
1764	10	1.26	1.50	1.04	33⅓						
1763	20	1.10	1.44	.88	50	1730	15	.67	1.13	.27	33⅓
1762	30	1.39	3.00	---------	50	1729	9	.70	.99	.38	33⅓
1761	12	1.54	2.00	1.00	50	1728	14	.67	.75	.26	33⅓
						1727	14	.82	1.13	.75	33⅓
1760	15	1.60	2.72	.80	50	1726	11	.91	1.13	.26	33⅓
1759	13	2.05	3.00	1.28	50						
1758	14	1.29	2.73	.73	65	1725	11	1.05	1.80	.54	33⅓
1757	17	1.16	1.90	.63	57.78	1724	10	.90	1.08	.72	33⅓
1756	11	1.07	1.21	.91	65	1723	12	1.07	1.13	.75	33⅓
						1722	14	.86	1.13	.75	33⅓
1755	16	.85	1.60	.40	50	1721	11	.97	1.50	.45	33⅓
1754	16	1.04	1.33	.60	50						
1753	24	1.16	1.60	.60	50	1720	12	1.19	1.50	.75	33⅓
1752	11	1.48	1.60	.80	50	1719	20	1.04	1.50	.75	33⅓
1751	15	1.16	1.54	.31	75	1718	16	.89	1.35	.75	33⅓
						1717	12	.79	1.13	.75	33⅓
1750	16	1.16	1.89	.60	100	1716	18	.80	1.44	.63	33⅓
1749	26	.76	1.50	---------	100						
1748	16	.67	1.00	.24	100	1715	10	.72	.75	.45	33⅓
1747	30	.45	1.00	---------	100	1714	19	.71	.75	.29	33⅓
1746	11	.61	1.00	.30	100	1713	17	1.00	1.00	.95	Par
						1712	16	1.00	1.00	1.00	Par
1745	26	.56	1.20	.15	100	1711	12	.97	1.00	.60	Par
1744	41	.63	1.00	.15	100						

[1] Two exchange rates provided during 1772 and 1773, so prices are given for each rate; see text.

Series Z 583–584.   Farm Prices of Maryland Tobacco, 1659 to 1710, and Chesapeake Tobacco, 1618 to 1658

[In pence sterling per pound.   All figures rounded to the nearest twentieth of a pence]

Year	Maryland tobacco price	Year	Maryland tobacco price	Year	Maryland tobacco price	Year	Maryland tobacco price	Year	Chesapeake tobacco price	Year	Chesapeake tobacco price	Year	Chesapeake tobacco price
	583		583		583		583		584		584		584
1710	0.85	1697	0.90	1684	0.80	1671	1.05	1658	2.10	1645	1.50	1633	5.00
1709	.90	1696	.85	1683	.80			1657	2.00	1644	2.55	1632	3.40
1708	.90			1682	.80	1670	1.15	1656	2.25	1643	1.80	1631	4.00
1707	.90	1695	.75	1681	.90	1669	1.15			1642	4.20		
1706	.80	1694	.75			1668	1.25	1655	2.00			1624	13.00
		1693	.75	1680	1.00	1667	1.10	1654	2.80	1640	2.50	1623	16.00
1705	.80	1692	.80	1679	1.05	1666	.90	1653	2.60	1639	3.00	1622	18.00
1704	.90	1691	.80	1678	1.15					1638	3.00	1621	20.00
1703	.85			1677	1.15	1665	1.10	1649	3.00	1637	3.00		
1702	1.00	1690	.80	1676	1.05	1664	1.35	1648	1.50	1636	5.35	1620	12.00
1701	.95	1689	.70			1663	1.55	1647	2.00			1619	27.00
		1688	.75	1675	1.00	1662	1.60	1646	2.20	1635	5.00	1618	27.00
1700	1.00	1687	.85	1674	1.00	1661	1.50						
1699	1.05	1686	1.00	1673	1.00	1660	1.50						
1698	1.00	1685	1.00	1672	1.00	1659	1.65						

Series Z 585.   Annual Rate of Exchange on London for Pennsylvania Currency: 1720 to 1775

[Pennsylvania currency for 100 £ sterling]

Year	Rate	Year	Rate	Year	Rate	Year	Rate	Year	Rate	Year	Rate
1775	166.04	1766	165.35	1757	165.95	1748	174.33	1740	164.06	1731	153.13
1774	169.74	1765	171.58	1756	172.52	1747	184.56	1739	170.00	1730	151.69
1773	165.80	1764	172.38	1755	168.88	1746	179.25	1738	167.50	1729	150.00
1772	161.21	1763	173.13	1754	168.15	1745	175.70	1737	167.50	1728	150.00
1771	165.57	1762	175.84	1753	167.96	1744	167.35	1736	165.13	1727	150.00
1770	153.99	1761	174.12	1752	166.66	1743	160.31	1735	162.50	1722	133.33
1769	158.31	1760	160.30	1751	170.63	1742	159.69	1733	165.00	1721	133.33
1768	166.36	1759	154.71	1750	171.10	1741	145.18	1732	161.10	1720	133.33
1767	166.20	1758	159.21	1749	172.36						

Series Z 586. Annual Price of an Ounce of Silver at Boston, Mass.: 1700 to 1749

[In paper shillings. Base 1700]

Year	Price	Year	Price	Year	Price	Year	Price	Year	Price	Year	Price	Year	Price
1749	60.00	1737	26.75	1729	20.50	1721	13.00	1713	8.50	1705	8.00		
1747	55.00	1736	26.75	1728	17.25	1720	12.33	1712	8.50	1704	7.00		
1746	38.50	1735	27.50	1727	16.00	1719	12.00	1711	8.33	1703	7.00		
1745	36.00	1734	25.50	1726	16.00	1718	11.00	1710	8.00	1702	7.00		
1744	30.00	1733	22.00	1725	15.50	1717	10.00	1709	8.00	1701	7.00		
1741	28.00	1732	20.00	1724	16.25	1716	10.00	1708	8.00	1700	7.00		
1739	28.50	1731	18.75	1723	15.00	1715	9.00	1707	8.00				
1738	27.00	1730	20.00	1722	14.25	1714	9.00	1706	8.00				

Series Z 587–598. Partial List of Bills of Credit and Treasury Notes Issued by American Colonies: 1703 to 1775

[In thousands of colonial pounds except for Maryland in 1769 and 1773, which are in thousands of dollars]

Year	Massa-chusetts 587	Connect-icut 588	New Hampshire 589	Rhode Island 590	New York 591	Pennsyl-vania 592	New Jersey 593	Maryland 594	Delaware 595	Virginia 596	North Carolina 597	South Carolina 598
1775				60		6						
1773						162		[1] 480		[2] 36		
1772						25						
1771			2		[1] 120	15				30	[3] 66	
1770												70
1769						30		[1] 318		10		[2] 107
1768				2		20					20	
1767				1				65				
1766						55	[3] 25					
1764		[3] 7					[3] 10					
1763		[3] 10					[3] 30	1		20		
1762	[3] 60	[3] 65	20	[3] 13			[3] 25				[3] 20	
1761	[3] 70	[3] 45	[3] 20									
1760		[3] 70	[3] 15	[3] 27	[3] 60	[3] 100	[3] 45		[3] 4	52	[3] 12	[3] 392
1759		[3] 70	[3 4] 13	[3] 20	[3] 100	[3] 100	[3] 50		[3] 27	62		
1758		[3] 30	[3] 21	21	[3] 100	[3] 100	[3] 60		[3] 12	89	[3] 11	
1757			[3] 20			[3] 100	[3] 40			180	[3] 15	[3] 229
1756			[3] 36	[3 4] 14	[3] 62	[3] 85	[3] 18	[3] 40	[3] 2	[3] 35	[3] 4	
1755		[4] 62	[3] 40	[3] 240	[3] 63	[2] 15	[3] 40			[3] 60		33
1754	10							[2] 4	[2] 3		[3] 40	
1753												[2] 20
1752												
1751				[1 4] 25								
1748	[3] 400			30							[2 4] 21	[2] 107
1747	[3] 348			[3] 15	[3] 28							
1746	[3] 662	[3] 23	[3] 60	[3] 11	[3] 53	5	[3] 16	[2] 6	20			[1] 210
1745	[3] 1,040	[3] 40	[1] 27	[3] 9								
1744	[3] 344	[3] 19	1	[1 4] 50		[2] 10		[2] 1	[1] 6			
1743	85											
1742	117		[4] 30					[2] 1				
1741	120			16								
1740	80	[3 4] 49	[3] 2	[1 4] 30		[2] 10	[2] 80	[2] 8	[2] 6			
1739					[2] 10							
1738	26			[1] 110								
1737	81		10	30	[1] 48			[2] 1				
1736	48										[2] 53	[1] 210
1735	39				12				[1] 12			
1734	30			2								
1733	79	[1] 30		[1] 104			[1] 40	90				
1731	24			[1] 60								[2] 107
1730	13		1		[2] 3		[1] 20					
1729	20	6	[2] 2			[1] 30			[1] 12		[1] 40	
1728	36	4		[1] 48								
1727	88	4	2		[2] 3		[2] 25					[2] 20
1726	25		3	[2] 50		7						
1725	70		[3] 2									63
1724	55	4	[3] 2									
1723	40			2	2	[1] 45	[1] 40		[1] 11			
1722	45	4	[2] 10								[2] 12	
1721	17			[1] 100								
1720	[1] 65											34
1719	15	4										
1718	11											
1717	9		[1] 15		17							
1716	[1] 111		2				5					[3] 15
1715	44		1	[1] 40	28						[2] 24	[3] 35
1714	[1] 50		1									
1713	14	[2] 22									[3] 8	
1712	25		[2] 2								[3] 4	[1] 52
1711	[1] 95	10	4	6	[3] 10		[3] 5					[3] 7
1710	44	5	3	[3] 7								
1709	46	[3] 19	[3] 3		13		[3] 3					

Year	Massa-chusetts 587	South Carolina 598
1708	32	8
1707	32	8
1706	44	
1705	18	
1704	32	
1703	32	[3] 6

[1] Loans.
[2] Reissues or exchanges.
[3] War costs.

[4] Indicates years in which there were issues of different tenor on a different basis from previous issues.

Series Z 599–610. Paper Money Outstanding in American Colonies: 1705 to 1775

[In thousands of colonial pounds]

Year	Massachusetts	Connecticut	New Hampshire	Rhode Island	New York	Pennsylvania	New Jersey	Delaware	Maryland	Virginia	North Carolina	South Carolina
	599	600	601	602	603	604	605	606	607	608	609	610
1775		27			120	422			295		80	
1770						344	190			88	79	
1765					260	432	248			303	75	498
1760			212			486	155				50	
1752		340	114			84			60			
1748	2,135	281	114	550		85	38		60		21	133
1744	305		30			85		14	90			
1739	243	60	23	340	80	80	60	17	90		53	250
1735	309		22			69	23	20	90		53	
1730	311		27	320		69	18				40	107
1725	351		27			39	37	11				116
1720	230		22								12	
1715	170	27	8	51	36		5				24	
1710	89	20		7	7							74
1705	28											

Series Z 611–615. Tax Collections in America Under the Different Revenue Laws: 1765 to 1774

[In pounds sterling]

Year	New revenue measures			Navigation act (1673)
	Total	Sugar act (1764, 1766)	Townshend revenue act (1767)	
	611	612	614	615
1774	27,995	27,074	921	672
1773	42,103	39,531	2,572	2,517
1772	45,870	42,570	3,300	1,490
1771	31,761	27,086	4,675	1,446
1770	33,637	30,910	2,727	1,828

Year	New revenue measures				Navigation act (1673)
	Total	Sugar act (1764, 1766)	Stamp act (1765)	Townshend revenue act (1767)	
	611	612	613	614	615
1769	45,499	39,938		5,561	1,294
1768	37,861	24,659		13,202	1,160
1767	34,041	33,844		197	3,905
1766	26,696	26,696			7,373
1765	17,383	14,091	3,292		2,954

Appendix:

Contributors to This Edition of Historical Statistics

[Listed below, by chapter and subject, are the names of persons other than those listed on pp. viii–x, who contributed new or revised data or text additions and revisions to this edition, to the extent they could be identified. In some cases, manuscript was provided for the book without specific identification of the persons engaged in its compilation, preparation, or review]

Subject	Contributor	Subject	Contributor
Chapter N		**Chapter Q—Con.**	
General review	Robert E. Lipsey, National Bureau of Economic Research, Inc.	State highway finances	Helen C. Millson, Federal Highway Administration
Value of public and private construction	Dollie Finn, Bureau of the Census	Road and highway funds	David Sacks, Federal Highway Administration
Construction contracts awarded	Jonah Otelsberg, F. W. Dodge Corp.	Motor vehicle factory sales	Jacques J. Evers, Automobile Manufacturers Association, Inc.
Construction bidding volume	Linda Marcotte, Engineering News-Record	Motor vehicle registrations and fuel	Alexander French and Laurence L. Liston, Federal Highway Administration
Railroad construction cost indexes	Edward P. Johnson, Interstate Commerce Commission	Travel mileage of motor vehicles	W. J. Page, Federal Highway Administration
Wholesale price indexes, construction materials	David Slack, Bureau of Labor Statistics	Motor vehicle deaths and death rates	Barbara Carraro, National Safety Council
Housing units, major Federal programs	H. G. Ries, Department of Housing and Urban Development	Public transit	Robert C. Stark, American Transit Association
Low-rent public housing units	Robert E. Ryan, Department of Housing and Urban Development	Railroad mileage, equipment, traffic, finances	William F. Betts, Association of American Railroads
Nonfarm residential mortgage debt	David F. Seiders, Board of Governors of the Federal Reserve System	Railroad passenger and freight operations	William G. Norris, Interstate Commerce Commission
Nonfarm mortgages and real estate foreclosures	Nellie C. Hartke, Federal Home Loan Bank Board	New passenger train cars	John L. Dale, Association of American Railroads
Federal housing finance programs	Fordyce A. Voss, Department of Housing and Urban Development	Railroad employment and wages	Joseph A. Edwards and Charles N. Graham, Interstate Commerce Commission
FNMA purchases and sales	F. X. McGrath, Federal National Mortgage Association	Employment and wage scale, merchant vessels	Lester E. Bartholow and Esther M. Love, Maritime Administration
Chapter P		Documented vessels	Robert O. McDonald, Coast Guard
Corporate sales and profits	William Levin, Federal Trade Commission	Documented vessels on Western rivers	Erik F. Haites, University of Western Ontario, and Gary M. Walton, Indiana University
Capital in manufacturing industries	Gerald F. Donahoe and John C. Musgrave, Bureau of Economic Analysis	Waterborne cargo tonnage	W. A. C. Connelly, Corps of Engineers
Concentration in manufacturing	Willis K. Jordan, Bureau of the Census	Great Lakes traffic	Oliver T. Burnham, Lake Carriers' Association
Alcohol and tobacco products	Rex D. Davis, Internal Revenue Service	Panama Canal traffic	F. R. Johnson, Panama Canal Co.
Rayon, acetate, and noncellulosic yarns	Stanley B. Hunt, Textile Economics Bureau, Inc.	Aircraft production	Gene P. King, Federal Aviation Administration
Refined petroleum products	William G. Carrico and Charles Hennig, Bureau of Mines		
Steel	Kenneth C. Allen and Robert Platt, American Iron and Steel Institute	**Chapter R**	
		Telephone and telegraph	T. F. Finn, American Telephone and Telegraph Co.; Courtney S. Snyder, U.S. Independent Telephone Association; and Robert E. Stromberg, Federal Communications Commission
Chapter Q			
Road mileage and Federal-aid highway system	Robert Sherrer, Federal Highway Administration	Radio and TV stations, finances, employment	Larry D. Eads, Federal Communications Commission

Appendix: Contributors to This Edition—Con.

Subject	Contributor	Subject	Contributor
Chapter R—Con.		**Chapter U—Con.**	
Radio and TV sets produced	Horace L. Johnson, Electronic Industries Association	Foreign trade related to production	Herbert H. Glantz, Bureau of International Commerce
Families with radio and TV sets	Richard Ravich, National Broadcasting Co., Inc.	Value of exports, imports, and duties	Jeremiah N. King and Lala B. Pipkin, Bureau of the Census
Radio and TV advertising	Patrick J. Kelly, Decker Communications, Inc.	Indexes of exports and imports	Seymour Etkin, Bureau of International Commerce
Safety and special radio stations	Bertie E. Hislop, Federal Communications Commission	**Chapter V**	
Postal service	Arthur H. Klotz, Jr., and J. R. Runyon, U.S. Postal Service	Business concerns and failures	Rowena Wyant, Dun & Bradstreet, Inc.
Books published	Frederico Fico and Isabel Pang, R. R. Bowker Co.	Business formations index	Betty F. Tunstall, Bureau of Economic Analysis
Newsprint and newspapers	Albert Weis, Editor and Publisher	Mergers in manufacturing and mining	Mary Ann Comps, Federal Trade Commission
		Corporate finances	Hazel Beatty, Internal Revenue Service
Chapter S		Nonfinancial corporations, gross product and unit costs	John A. Gorman, Bureau of Economic Analysis
General review	Milton F. Searl, Resources for the Future, Inc.	Finances of utility industries	Joseph P. Kucharski, Federal Power Commission
Horsepower of all prime movers	John A. Waring, Takoma Park, Maryland		
Electric energy and generating plants	Paul Hayes and Annetta R. McMillin, Federal Power Commission	**Chapter W**	
Electric energy use	C. W. Lines, Federal Power Commission	National productivity indexes and real gross private product	Shelby A. Herman, Bureau of Economic Analysis
Rural electrification program	Marvin T. Hearst, Rural Electrification Administration	Indexes of output per manhour	Ed Henneberger and Arthur S. Herman, Bureau of Labor Statistics
Waterpower	T. A. Phillips, Federal Power Commission	Copyright registrations	Donald S. Reines, Copyright Office
		Patents	Ethan A. Hurd, Patent Office
Chapter T		Research and development	Robert O. Santos, National Science Foundation
Department store sales and stocks indexes	Jerrie Ledson, Board of Governors of the Federal Reserve System		
Retail trade margins	D. Anne Fisher, Bureau of Economic Analysis	**Chapter X**	
Service establishments and receipts	John R. Wikoff, Bureau of the Census	Changes in gold stock	Margaret Garber, Board of Governors of the Federal Reserve System
Advertising indexes	Robert J. Coen, McCann-Erickson, Inc.	Money market rates	Elizabeth Sette, Board of Governors of the Federal Reserve System
Newspaper advertising linage	Bernice Bowman, Bureau of Economic Analysis	Bond and stock yields	Leo V. Barry, Jr., Bureau of Economic Analysis
		Corporate securities	Robert H. Menke, Securities and Exchange Commission
Chapter U		New York Stock Exchange sales	George S. Morrissey and George Troester, Commercial and Financial Chronicle
Balance of payments	Evelyn M. Parrish, Bureau of Economic Analysis	Commercial and non-national banks, assets and liabilities	Benjamin Christopher, Federal Deposit Insurance Corporation
U.S. international investment position	Nancy R. Keith, Bureau of Economic Analysis		
Investment in foreign countries	Julius N. Friedlen, Bureau of Economic Analysis	Commercial banks	Loree D. Bernard, Betty Jean Johnson, and Bessie McCrea, Board of Governors of the Federal Reserve System
U.S. foreign grants and credits	E. Seymour Kerber, Bureau of Economic Analysis		

APPENDIX

Appendix: Contributors to This Edition—Con.

Subject	Contributor	Subject	Contributor
Chapter X—Con.		**Chapter Y—Con.**	
National banks, earnings and expenses	David C. Motter and Irving Ward, Comptroller of the Currency	Individual income tax liability	Gabriel G. Rudney, Department of the Treasury
Federal Reserve Banks, assets and liabilities	Adrian P. Francoeur, Board of Governors of the Federal Reserve System	Outlays of the Federal Government	Matthew J. Conroy, Office of Management and Budget
Federal Reserve member bank reserves	Dorothy Werner, Board of Governors of the Federal Reserve System	Federal grants	Alfred M. Skolnik, Social Security Administration
Credit unions	Herman Nickerson, Jr., and Vincent J. Olive, National Credit Union Administration	Armed Forces characteristics	John L. Donnelly, Department of Defense
Life insurance in force	Ilene Freidus and Rosemarie Shomstein, Institute of Life Insurance	Selective service registrants	Phyllis G. Knowles, Selective Service System
Property and liability insurance	Robert J. Schrader and William Steurer, Alfred M. Best Co.	Defendants charged with Selective Service Act violations	Sam G. Moy, Administrative Office of the United States Courts
Health insurance	Marjorie S. Mueller, Social Security Administration	Veterans population	Millard Klein, Veterans Administration
		VA expenditures for veterans benefits	Paul Kamenick, Veterans Administration
Chapter Y		**Chapter Z**	
Vote cast for Representatives	W. Pat Jennings, Office of the Clerk, House of Representatives	Slave imports	W. Robert Higgins, Murray State University
Campaign expenditures	Herbert Alexander, Citizens Research Foundation	Slave prices	Richard N. Bean, University of Houston
Federal civilian employment	Christine Steele, Civil Service Commission	Components of private wealth	Alice Hanson Jones, Washington University
State and local government employment	Gerald Storch, Bureau of Labor Statistics	Trade between England and Colonies	John J. McCusker, University of Maryland
Corporate income, estate, and gift taxes	Lloyd K. Gilmour, Internal Revenue Service	Export-import values	James F. Shepherd, Whitman College, and Gary M. Walton, Indiana University
Individual income tax returns	Floyd Reeves, Internal Revenue Service	Tobacco prices	Carville Earle, University of Maryland, and Russell R. Menard, Annapolis, Maryland

[Entries are series numbers. Each statistical series has been allocated to the time period for which the earliest figure in the series appears. For most series, an entry for a given time period means that the figures are presented for that and all later time periods]

Chapter	Before 1800	1800–1819	1820–1839	1840–1859	1860–1879	1880–1889	1890–1899
A. Population	A 1–2, 5, 7, 43, 49–52, 57, 63–66, 69, 92, 99, 119–134, 172–179, 184–189, 195–200, 202–210, 217–218, 221, 228, 230–232, 240–241, 243–244, 249–251, 253, 256–257, 263, 288, 291, 335–349	A 3–4, 48, 62, 146–148, 219, 224–225, 229, 233, 235, 244, 246	A 47, 61, 91, 93, 98, 100, 143–145, 149–151, 211, 214, 220, 236, 262	A 45–46, 59–60, 106–107, 113–114, 135, 139, 190–194, 215, 226, 234, 242, 248, 254–255, 260	A 94–97, 101–105, 108–112, 115–118, 152–157, 201, 213, 216, 223, 227, 237–239, 258–259, 261	A 9–10, 12–13, 44, 58, 73–81	A 54–56, 70–72, 136–138, 140–142, 158–171, 245, 247, 252, 320–334
B. Vital Statistics and Health and Medical Care		B 6, 9, 67, 69–81, 83–92, 278, 281–282	B 5, 82	B 68, 93, 96, 126–135, 148, 275–276, 283, 285	B 193–213	B 279–280, 288–290	
C. Migration			C 89–96, 98–102, 104–105, 109–115, 119–120, 130–136, 138–142	C 1–7, 10–24, 228–240, 242–245, 248, 251–255, 258–260, 262–264, 268, 273, 278–289, 293–294	C 8–9, 25–60, 62–73, 97, 103, 106, 116–118, 137, 241, 246, 249, 265, 267, 274–275, 290–292, 295	C 61	C 121–129, 159, 161, 181, 188–194
D. Labor	D 715–717	D 167–172, 174–176, 178, 180–181, 705–711	D 75–77, 152–153, 156–157, 166, 718–721	D 154–155, 158–165, 173, 177, 179, 712, 714	D 11–13, 16–17, 19, 26–28, 78–84, 683–686, 688, 728–738, 921–926	D 713, 845, 977–980, 982–985	D 14, 24–25, 29–41, 49–51, 53–55, 57–60, 62, 85–86, 687, 765–783, 786–801, 814, 846–876, 940–945, 952–969
E. Prices and Price Indexes	E 52–60, 62–63, 90–111, 115–117	E 112–114, 118–129, 131–133, 135	E 183	E 61, 130, 134, 174–182, 184	E 214		E 23, 40, 42–51, 87–89, 185–187, 189, 191–195, 197, 202
F. National Income and Wealth			F 238–249	F 287–294, 423, 425–429, 431–436, 438, 445, 447, 449–453, 455–460, 462, 469	F 1–5, 10–16, 71–83, 85, 88–91, 93, 96–110, 112, 115–118, 120, 123–129, 210–225, 250–260	F 295–296, 424, 430, 448, 454, 535–539	F 6–9, 540–551, 638–652, 656–659, 661–667
G. Consumer Income and Expenditures				G 889, 907	G 573–581, 911	G 564–572, 582–587	G 881–884, 887–888, 906
H. Social Statistics	H 803		H 801	H 433–441, 789, 792, 805–807, 809–810	H 420, 422, 424, 492–493, 496, 502–503, 520–522, 524, 526–528, 598–601, 664–665, 668, 689, 694–698, 706–707, 751–754, 757, 760–762, 764, 791, 894–898	H 418–419, 426, 494, 498–499, 504, 666–667, 756, 763, 1168–1170	H 1–3, 16–17, 21, 28, 32, 40, 427, 429–430, 432, 487, 489–490, 545, 548–549, 552, 554, 557–558, 560–561, 708–709, 717, 747–748, 758–759, 788, 790, 793, 800, 815–816, 862–863

[Entries are series numbers. Each statistical series has been allocated to the time period for which the earliest figure in the series appears. For most series, an entry for a given time period means that the figures are presented for that and all later time periods]

Chapter	1900–1909	1910–1919	1920–1929	1930–1939	1940–1949	1950–1970
A. Population	A 11, 14–18, 23–42, 180–183, 350	A 19, 22, 309–312, 351–352	A 20	A 6, 8	A 289–290, 292–308, 313–319, 359–371	A 21, 53, 67–68, 82–90, 212, 222, 264–287, 353–358
B. Vital Statistics and Health and Medical Care	B 1, 8, 36–41, 107–125, 149–152, 154–163, 165–192, 277, 319–320, 329, 345–350, 423–424, 444, 446–452	B 7, 42–66, 94–95, 97–98, 139–147, 164, 286–287, 292–293, 295–296, 299, 301–304	B 3–4, 10, 136–138, 214–217, 221–228, 230–233, 235–250, 252–254, 256–259, 261, 284, 294, 300, 321–328, 330, 351–358, 371, 373, 375, 377, 379, 425–427, 445	B 2, 99–105, 262–274, 291, 298, 372, 374, 376, 378, 380–388, 401–402, 407–408, 429–437	B 11–35, 106, 153, 220, 229, 234, 251, 255, 260, 305–318, 331–334, 337–338, 341–344, 359–370, 389–400, 403–406, 409–422, 428, 438–443, 453–456	B 218–219, 297, 335–336, 339–340, 457–459
C. Migration	C 162, 168–169, 180, 182–183, 195–202, 205–208, 210–211, 213–215, 218, 223–224, 227, 256, 296–301	C 158, 166–167, 203–204, 216–217, 219–221, 225–226, 257, 269–272	C 76–80, 143–154, 157, 160, 170–179, 184–187, 247, 250, 261, 266	C 108, 209, 212, 222, 302–311, 313–326, 328–331	C 81–88, 107, 163–165	C 74–75, 155–156, 276–277, 312, 327
D. Labor	D 1–10, 127–130, 133–134, 137–139, 145, 182–240, 242–264, 266–271, 273–278, 280–281, 285–295, 297–308, 310, 312–331, 334–340, 342–344, 346–377, 379–391, 393–406, 408–412, 414–430, 432–446, 448–449, 451–460, 463–466, 468–472, 474–481, 483, 485–486, 488–491, 495, 497–545, 547–563, 565–577, 579–607, 609–661, 663–679, 681–682, 723–727, 739–764, 784–785, 802–804, 811–813, 818–823, 826–829	D 265, 272, 279, 296, 309, 311, 332–333, 341, 345, 378, 392, 407, 413, 431, 450, 461, 467, 473, 482, 484, 487, 492–494, 496, 564, 578, 608, 680, 824–825, 830–844, 1022, 1024–1028	D 140–141, 241, 282–284, 462, 722, 807, 810, 893–907, 909–916, 918–920, 970–973, 975–976, 981, 1029, 1034, 1036	D 15, 18, 131–132, 135–136, 146–147, 546, 662, 805–806, 808–809, 815–817, 877–888, 892, 908, 917, 927–931, 934–937, 939, 946–951, 974, 986–989, 994–996, 998–1000, 1002–1008, 1010–1012, 1014–1016, 1030–1033, 1035	D 20–23, 42, 52, 56, 61, 63–74, 87–115, 142–144, 148–151, 447, 689–704, 889–891, 990–993, 997, 1001, 1009, 1013, 1017–1021	D 43–48, 116–126, 932–933, 938, 1023
E. Prices and Price Indexes		E 24–25, 41, 73–74, 78, 84, 137, 150, 155–156, 188, 190, 196, 198–201, 203, 212–213	E 1–22, 28–29, 31–32, 34, 36–38, 204	E 30, 35, 138–146, 149, 152–153, 157–173, 205–211	E 26–27, 33, 39, 64–72, 75–77, 79–83, 85–86, 147	E 136, 148, 151, 154
F. National Income and Wealth	F 31, 186–191, 377–380, 383–384, 386–396, 400–410, 412–422, 437, 439–444, 446, 461, 463–468	F 84, 86–87, 92, 94–95, 111, 113–114, 119, 121–122, 653–654, 660	F 17–30, 32–67, 70, 144–185, 192–209, 226–237, 261–275, 278–286, 297–298, 300–308, 310–348, 385, 411, 470–534, 552–560, 562–565, 595–619, 621–637, 655	F 68–69, 276–277, 620	F 130–143, 309, 381–382, 397–399, 566–594, 668–723	F 299, 349–376, 561
G. Consumer Income and Expenditure	G 470–494, 554–563, 850–856, 885, 890–893, 895, 897–898, 900, 903–905, 908–910, 912–914	G 337–352, 534–553, 588–601, 849, 894, 899, 902, 915	G 269–313, 319–331, 333–336, 416–421, 423–469, 772–797, 843–848, 896	G 314–318, 332, 353–415, 422, 515–533, 679–696, 754–771, 828–842, 857–865, 886, 901	G 1–138, 179–181, 184–206, 208–268, 643–678, 735–753, 813–827, 866–880	G 139–178, 182–183, 207, 495–514, 602–642, 697–734, 798–812
H. Social Statistics	H 431, 550–551, 555, 559, 562, 755, 804, 808, 811–813, 868–870, 878–882, 884–885, 887–892, 899, 971–974, 979–986, 1013, 1017, 1021, 1023, 1025	H 5, 417, 423, 425, 486, 488, 495, 497, 500, 505–507, 547, 556, 563–564, 567–568, 570–573, 575–576, 578–582, 584–585, 690–693, 716, 814, 851–852, 856–857, 860–861, 877, 921, 924–931, 939–945, 948–951, 975–976, 978	H 4, 8, 13–15, 18–20, 22–23, 25–26, 29–30, 33, 35–37, 39, 41–43, 45, 47, 260–266, 393–404, 421, 478–479, 483, 491, 501, 523, 525, 529–530, 535–537, 540–542, 546, 553, 565–566, 569, 587–597, 699, 718–721, 723, 725–726, 739, 741, 743, 765–787, 802, 833–835, 850, 853–855, 858–859, 864, 873–875, 883, 886, 893, 932–938, 1135–1146, 1148–1151, 1153–1154	H 6–7, 9–10, 27, 31, 34, 38, 44, 48–55, 57–64, 66–68, 174–181, 183–185, 238–240, 242–244, 267–274, 276–278, 280–283, 285–287, 290, 293, 296, 299, 302, 333–343, 346–351, 353–377, 380, 382–389, 392, 405–416, 428, 477, 480–482, 485, 513–519, 531–534, 538–539, 543–544, 574, 583, 656–661, 722, 724, 727–738, 745–746, 749–750, 817–819, 821–823, 832, 839–842, 849, 876, 962–970, 999–1011, 1147, 1152, 1155–1167	H 11–12, 24, 56, 69, 115–132, 134–156, 158–173, 186–189, 191–195, 197–202, 204–211, 213–219, 221–225, 227–237, 241, 245–246, 249–250, 252–257, 305–332, 344–345, 378–379, 381, 390–391, 442–448, 453–476, 508–512, 602–617, 641–653, 684–688, 700–705, 710–715, 740, 742, 820, 836–837, 843–848, 865, 867, 871–872, 900–914, 917–920, 946–947, 977, 987, 990–998, 1020, 1022, 1029–1037, 1040–1046, 1049–1050, 1054–1058, 1062–1068, 1070–1110, 1112–1124	H 46, 65, 70–114, 133, 157, 182, 190, 196, 203, 212, 220, 226, 247–248, 251, 258–259, 275, 279, 284, 288–289, 291–292, 294–295, 297–298, 300–301, 303–304, 352, 449–462, 484, 577, 586, 618–640, 654–655, 662–663, 669–683, 744, 794–799, 824–831, 838, 866, 915–916, 922–923, 952–961, 988–989, 1012, 1014–1016, 1018–1019, 1024, 1026–1028, 1038–1039, 1047–1048, 1051–1053, 1059–1061, 1069, 1111, 1125–1134

[Entries are series numbers.   Each statistical series has been allocated to the time period for which the earliest figure in the series appears.   For most series, an entry for a given time period means that the figures are presented for that and all later time periods]

Chapter	Before 1800	1800–1819	1820–1839	1840–1859	1860–1879	1880–1889	1890–1899
J. Land, Water, and Climate	J 1–2, 4–7, 26, 32, 248, 254	J 3, 9, 20, 250–251, 253, 255	J 21, 23–25, 249, 252, 256–259, 264–267	J 22, 50–52, 56, 61, 260–263	J 10, 13, 15	J 14, 16, 18, 27–28, 55, 59–60, 62–65, 164–166, 201, 206–208, 239–241, 276–277	J 86–87, 89, 91, 179–184, 191–193, 197–200, 202, 215–220, 233–235, 242–244
K. Agriculture	K 554	K 240–250, 445–459	K 407–409, 503, 507, 512, 515, 527, 530, 551, 608	K 4–7, 10–12, 14–15, 17–40, 45–63, 65–67, 72, 74, 76, 78–79, 193, 518, 533, 536, 595, 598–599, 601–602	K 13, 41–44, 68–71, 73, 75, 77, 178–181, 414, 502, 504, 506, 508, 511, 513–514, 516, 526, 528–529, 531–532, 534–535, 537, 550, 552–553, 555, 557, 559–573, 596, 600, 607	K 1–2, 8, 82, 85–86, 89, 109–113, 124–128, 162–173, 517, 597	K 64, 93–98, 373–374, 519, 538–540, 558, 584–585, 587, 590–591, 593
L. Forestry and Fisheries	L 98–99, 211	L 100, 172			L 113–127, 129–135, 137, 166, 169, 268	L 224, 229, 236–241, 243, 245–250, 252, 263–267, 270–273, 275–278, 280–282, 286, 290–291	L 101, 104, 107, 110, 128, 136, 167–168, 170–171, 174, 178–187, 242, 251, 274, 283–285
M. Minerals	M 218, 268	M 76–78, 93, 123, 188, 217, 243, 248	M 269	M 1, 3–5, 8, 83–85, 92, 138–139, 235, 241, 247, 250, 255, 270	M 2, 9–10, 12, 79, 86–87, 100–101, 127–128, 130, 141, 189, 196, 205, 210, 222, 246, 253–254, 271, 276	M 6, 13–18, 20–21, 24, 26–36, 54–67, 80, 88, 96, 122, 126, 134, 190–192, 195, 198–200, 203, 208, 214–215, 221, 223–224, 256, 258	M 23, 72–75, 82, 90–91, 103, 105, 107, 111–112, 142, 209, 211, 257, 262, 275
N. Construction and Housing			N 114		N 70–71, 111–113, 115–117, 138	N 62–65, 72–77, 139, 156, 162–164, 167, 196–199	N 192–195, 232–245, 259–260, 262–269, 272, 302–307
P. Manufactures				P 1, 5, 9–10	P 17, 69, 73, 107–112, 123, 126–146, 149–172, 174, 176, 227–228, 231–232, 235–236, 239–241, 253, 262–268, 270, 294–295, 318–332, 334–336, 339–344, 347, 349–353, 355–360, 362, 364–374	P 4, 7–8, 70, 124–125, 173, 230, 233–234, 293, 302, 307, 348	P 16, 40–41, 45, 47, 49, 51–58, 60–62, 64–65, 67–68, 71–72, 214–215, 224, 247–249, 251–252, 260–261, 286, 290, 296–301, 333, 337, 345
Q. Transportation	Q 418, 425, 429–434, 436, 506–508, 518–523	Q 419, 435, 464–466, 481–483, 485–486, 559–563	Q 321, 329, 512–514, 556–558, 564	Q 347–349, 351–352, 459–463, 484, 509–511, 515–517, 548–551	Q 274, 278, 283, 322–328, 346, 350, 353–355, 417, 426, 437, 552	Q 47–49, 275–277, 279–282, 427–428	Q 96, 264–273, 284, 287–291, 295, 301, 304, 306–307, 311–312, 314, 317–318, 330, 339–341, 343–345, 356, 358–363, 367–371, 373–377, 398–407, 473–480
R. Communications	R 163–165, 190			R 71–72, 166–167, 246–247	R 1–2, 6, 46–55, 73–74, 89, 168, 188–189	R 9–10, 17, 19–20, 23, 25–29, 92, 169, 192	R 7–8, 11–12, 91, 193–194

[Entries are series numbers. Each statistical series has been allocated to the time period for which the earliest figure in the series appears. For most series, an entry for a given time period means that the figures are presented for that and all later time periods]

Chapter	1900–1909	1910–1919	1920–1929	1930–1939	1940–1949	1950–1970
J. Land, Water, and Climate	J 8, 17, 33–34, 57–58, 92–109, 173–178, 188–190, 194–196, 209–214, 221–223, 225, 227–232, 278	J 53–54, 167–172, 185–187, 203–205, 224, 226, 245–247, 268–273	J 11–12, 30, 45–49, 66–84, 274–275	J 19, 35–38, 88, 236–237	J 29, 39–44, 85, 90, 110–163, 238	J 31
K. Agriculture	K 80–81, 83–84, 87–88, 100, 114–123, 130–134, 136–140, 142–146, 148–152, 192, 251–252, 254–255, 392–403, 520–522, 541–549, 556, 575, 578–580, 583, 586, 588–589, 592, 594, 603–604, 606, 609–611, 617–618	K 16, 101–104, 174–177, 182–187, 189, 194–203, 259–260, 264–267, 269–302, 344–365, 367–372, 376, 410–413, 415–429, 460–463, 466–468, 471–477, 481–482, 485–501, 523–524, 576–577, 581–582, 605, 619	K 3, 9, 129, 135, 141, 147, 153, 188, 220–229, 231–239, 375, 377, 379, 381–388, 390–391, 404–406, 478–480, 505, 509–510, 525, 574, 612–613, 620–623	K 105–108, 154–161, 230, 256–258, 261–263, 268, 303–334, 339–341, 366, 378, 380, 430–444, 483–484, 614–616	K 90–92, 99, 190–191, 204–219, 253, 335–338, 342–343, 389, 464–465, 469–470	
L. Forestry and Fisheries	L 10–11, 15–18, 22–29, 56–78, 80–84, 87–97, 173, 175–177, 206, 262, 292, 294–295, 298, 304	L 12–14, 19, 30, 44–46, 102, 105–106, 108–109, 199–203, 205, 279, 287, 289, 319–320, 369–370	L 20–21, 47–49, 52–55, 79, 103, 111–112, 188–190, 208–210, 225–228, 230–235, 244, 253, 288, 296–297, 299–303, 305–310, 313, 315–318, 338–351, 354–360, 362–365, 367–368	L 37–43, 50–51, 191–198, 204, 254–261, 269, 311–312, 314, 321–327, 333, 361, 366	L 31–36, 85–86, 207, 293, 328–332, 352–353	L 1–9, 138–165, 212–223, 334–337
M. Minerals	M 25, 38–53, 81, 104, 135, 147, 152–155, 193, 197, 202, 204, 212–213, 225, 236, 242, 244, 249, 251, 261, 273	M 19, 37, 68, 89, 94–95, 97–98, 102, 108–110, 113–121, 124–125, 129, 131–133, 136, 140, 143–144, 156–157, 161–165, 167–171, 194, 201, 206–207, 216, 226–227, 229–230, 232–234, 237–240, 259, 263, 266, 277–282, 285–288, 290–291, 293, 297–298, 303	M 69–70, 99, 106, 137, 148–151, 166, 172–174, 176–187, 219–220, 267	M 7, 22, 158, 160, 175, 245, 252, 260, 272, 274, 283–284, 300–301	M 71, 145–146, 228, 264–265, 289, 294–295, 299, 304–305	M 11, 159, 231, 292, 296, 302, 306
N. Construction and Housing	N 78, 159–161	N 1–8, 11–21, 25–29, 32–35, 37, 40–47, 49, 55–61, 66–69, 79–81, 83–93, 96–101, 108, 118–132, 135–137, 261	N 9–10, 23–24, 30–31, 36, 38–39, 48, 50, 52–54, 82, 94–95, 140, 143, 148–149, 151–152, 155, 200–202, 205–206, 208–210, 213–214, 216–218, 221–222, 224–226, 229–230, 273, 276, 278–282, 284, 301	N 22, 51, 102–107, 109–110, 133–134, 157–158, 165–166, 168–169, 180, 182–184, 203–204, 211–212, 219–220, 227–228, 270–271, 274, 277, 283, 285–296, 300	N 141–142, 144–147, 150, 153–154, 170–172, 174–176, 178–179, 181, 185–191, 207, 215, 223, 231, 246–248, 275, 297	N 173, 177, 249–258, 298–299
P. Manufactures	P 3, 15, 197, 212–213, 216–220, 250, 269, 279, 303, 310–311, 314, 317, 346, 361	P 13, 50, 147–148, 175, 229, 244, 254–259, 281–282, 308–309, 316, 338, 354, 363	P 14, 46, 113–121, 221, 237–238, 242–243, 271, 277, 283–285, 288–289, 304–306, 312, 315	P 12, 42–44, 48, 205, 208, 210, 222–223, 225–226, 236a, 246, 291–292	P 6, 11, 18–21, 23–39, 63, 66, 74–106, 122, 177–196, 198–199, 201, 203, 206–207, 209, 211, 245, 272–276, 278, 280, 287, 313	P 2, 22, 59, 200, 202, 204
Q. Transportation	Q 56, 148–153, 155, 300, 305, 313, 316, 372, 542–545	Q 65–68, 82–95, 156–158, 208–219, 222–223, 225, 242, 293–294, 296–297, 331–338, 357, 391–392, 411, 438–448, 546, 553–555, 565–567, 573–576	Q 50–52, 54–55, 57–58, 60–64, 97–128, 154, 199–201, 226–232, 241, 243–244, 251, 257–263, 285–286, 298–299, 308, 319–320, 342, 364–366, 378–379, 384–389, 393–397, 408–410, 412, 414, 420–424, 524–540, 577–578, 580–584, 586, 588, 604, 606–607, 609–610, 614, 619, 624–627, 634–636	Q 12–35, 53, 59, 69–81, 159–162, 202–207, 224, 233–240, 245–250, 252–253, 256, 292, 309–310, 315, 380–383, 390, 413, 487–505, 579, 585, 587, 589, 591–603, 605, 608, 615–618, 628–633, 637	Q 36–46, 129–147, 163–196, 220–221, 254–255, 302–303, 449–458, 467–472, 547, 568–569, 590, 611–613, 620–623	Q 1–11, 197–198, 415–416, 541, 570–572
R. Communications	R 13–14, 18, 21–22, 30, 75–77, 79, 81, 83–84, 86–88, 90, 244–245, 248–251, 256–257	R 15–16, 24, 31–38, 40–45, 56–63, 65–68, 80, 82, 140, 145–146, 191, 252, 254	R 3–5, 39, 64, 78, 85, 93, 102, 104, 141, 170, 172–187, 224–226, 228, 230–231, 253, 255	R 69–70, 106–122, 143, 147, 171, 232–243	R 94–96, 103, 105, 123–138, 144, 148–150, 153–161, 218–223, 227, 229	R 97–101, 139, 142, 151–152, 162, 195–217

[Entries are series numbers. Each statistical series has been allocated to the time period for which the earliest figure in the series appears. For most series, an entry for a given time period means that the figures are presented for that and all later time periods]

Chapter	Before 1800	1800–1819	1820–1839	1840–1859	1860–1879	1880–1889	1890–1899
S. Energy				S 1, 3–10, 12	S 11	S 13	S 2
T. Distribution and Services					T 1–2, 15–16, 220–221, 225, 228, 231, 233–234, 236, 239–241, 243–244, 384–385, 388–390, 444	T 222, 227, 229–230	T 223–224, 232
U. International Transactions and Foreign Commerce	U 1–3, 8–10, 13–15, 17–23, 40, 190–193, 196, 275, 277–280, 296, 298, 300, 317, 324–328, 335	U 274, 276, 281, 287, 294	U 4, 11, 16, 187–189, 194–195, 197–200, 207–224, 282, 286, 289, 295, 297, 299, 301, 307–308, 310, 318–323, 329–330, 333–334, 336–348, 351–352	U 26, 33, 285, 303, 306, 331–332, 349–350	U 7, 24, 27, 34, 37, 201–202, 206, 225–248, 264–273, 305	U 283–284, 288, 290–293, 309, 311–315	U 28–30, 302, 304
V. Business Enterprise				V 20, 23–24, 27, 30	V 271–274, 279–280, 283–284	V 275–278	V 39–40
W. Productivity and Technological Development	W 99		W 96, 106	W 104	W 58, 60–61, 82, 85, 87-88, 92, 107	W 1–8, 13, 55–56, 97	W 12, 89
X. Financial Markets and Institutions	X 879	X 420–421, 423, 437, 561–563, 565–567, 569–579, 882–883	X 564, 568, 580–587, 697	X 476, 792, 890–891, 894–895, 897–900, 903–904, 906–908, 915, 917	X 410–411, 415–418, 424–427, 429, 433–436, 479–482, 495–498, 634–636, 639, 643, 648, 653–654, 656–658, 661, 665, 670, 675–676, 678–684, 687–690, 741–745, 768, 773–775, 885, 893, 896, 901–902, 909–914, 916	X 685–686, 769–772, 794–795	X 419, 428, 444–445, 448, 588–609, 616–619, 637–638, 640–642, 644–647, 649–652, 655, 659–660, 662–664, 666–669, 671–674, 677, 691, 694, 821–833, 880, 887, 889
Y. Government	Y 1–16, 79–82, 189–190, 192–200, 202, 204–205, 207–208, 210, 215–221, 228–229, 231, 238, 241–242, 250–251, 253–254, 259–261, 263, 266–267, 335–338, 352–356, 457–459, 461–463, 493, 849–855, 904–907, 911–916, 971, 984–985, 996	Y 17–19, 90–91, 94, 98, 101–102, 104–105, 113–114, 116–117, 119, 122–124, 126, 129–130, 201, 222, 234–235, 239–240, 245, 256, 308–310, 312–317	Y 20–28, 31, 34–35, 38, 41–42, 45–50, 52–53, 57–58, 60–61, 63, 66–67, 70, 73–74, 83–84, 87, 97, 103, 106, 108–109, 135–136, 139, 142–143, 146, 149–150, 153–158, 160–161, 165–166, 168–169, 171, 174–175, 178, 181–182, 191, 206, 209, 225, 243, 246	Y 32, 37, 43, 71, 77, 88, 93, 99, 127, 133, 140, 145, 151, 179, 185, 203, 226, 230, 236, 244, 258, 264, 270, 494–495, 497–498	Y 44, 51, 55–56, 65, 68, 76, 89, 100, 107, 111–112, 121, 132, 152, 159, 163–164, 173, 176, 184, 187–188, 227, 237, 248–249, 269, 358, 362, 364–366, 373, 496, 856–857, 859–860, 862–866, 871–887, 890–891, 898–903, 943–955, 957–960, 972, 993, 995, 998–999, 1004–1005	Y 33, 141, 233, 247, 255, 262, 268, 271, 311, 501–502, 973	Y 40, 54, 62, 69, 72, 75, 78, 96, 110, 118, 125, 128, 131, 134, 148, 162, 170, 177, 180, 183, 186, 211–214, 265, 867–870, 888–889, 892–897, 956, 961, 974–976
Z. Colonial and Pre-Federal Statistics	Z 1–615						

[Entries are series numbers. Each statistical series has been allocated to the time period for which the earliest figure in the series appears. For most series, an entry for a given time period means that the figures are presented for that and all later time periods]

Chapter	1900–1909	1910–1919	1920–1929	1930–1939	1940–1949	1950–1970
S. Energy	S 15–24, 32–36, 40, 44–46, 48–49, 52–53, 57, 74–88, 90–91, 94, 109, 112–114, 116, 119–120	S 37–39, 41–43, 108, 118, 121–124, 126–132	S 14, 50–51, 54–56, 58–59, 66, 71, 92–93, 95, 100–107, 110–111, 160–167, 176–189	S 115, 117, 133–151, 190–218	S 25–31, 47, 60–63, 67–70, 72–73, 89, 125, 152–157, 168–175	S 64–65, 96–99, 158–159
T. Distribution and Services	T 226, 235, 237–238, 242, 386–387	T 272–273	T 3–5, 7–14, 17–19, 21–33, 35–42, 70–71, 75, 79–81, 84, 87–112, 116–172, 176–219, 245–270, 274–286, 288–290, 292–293, 300–302, 304–306, 308–310, 312–314, 316–318, 320–322, 324–326, 328–330, 332–334, 336–338, 340–342, 344–346, 348–350, 352–353, 360–362, 364–366, 368–369, 438–439, 485–491	T 43–45, 47–50, 52–55, 57–69, 72–74, 76–78, 82–83, 85, 113–115, 173–175, 271, 287, 291, 294–299, 303, 307, 311, 315, 319, 323, 327, 331, 335, 339, 343, 347, 351, 354–359, 363, 367, 370–374, 391, 393, 398, 400–415, 418–437, 440–443, 445–454, 459–479, 482–484	T 6, 20, 34, 46, 51, 56, 375–383, 394–397, 399, 416–417, 455–458, 480–481	T 86, 392
U. International Transactions and Foreign Commerce	U 5, 25, 316	U 6, 12, 31–32, 35–36, 38, 203–205	U 41–44, 46, 249–263	U 47–51, 55, 59, 63, 67, 74	U 39, 75–96, 102–186	U 45, 52–54, 56–58, 60–62, 64–66, 68–73, 97–101
V. Business Enterprise	V 216, 225–231, 234–246, 249–270	V 38, 41–65, 213–215, 219–224, 232–233, 247–248, 281–282, 285–305	V 13–19, 25–26, 28–29, 66–77, 108–119, 123–128, 167–177, 217–218	V 1–12, 120–122, 129–140, 178–212	V 21–22, 31–37, 78–107, 141–166, 306–332	
W. Productivity and Technological Development	W 30, 83, 100–102	W 31, 36–38, 40, 43, 47, 50–54, 57, 64, 67–81, 84, 90–91, 93–95, 108	W 59, 86	W 14–21, 32, 34–35, 39, 41, 44–45, 48, 65, 98, 103, 105	W 9–11, 22–29, 32a–33, 42, 46, 49, 62–63, 66, 126–132, 134, 136–138, 140–141	W 109–125, 133, 135, 139, 142–180
X. Financial Markets and Institutions	X 430, 475, 487–491, 493–494, 531, 717–721, 732–736, 834–835	X 393–395, 397–399, 402–409, 412–414, 422, 431–432, 438–443, 447, 449, 454–456, 470–474, 477–478, 492, 510–516, 532–535, 547–560, 610–615, 693, 695–696, 706–715, 796–810, 812–820, 845–853, 884, 886, 888, 892, 947–956	X 400–401, 459–469, 483–486, 746–755, 793, 836, 842, 855, 864, 866–867, 869, 905, 933–946	X 450–451, 499–509, 517–530, 540–546, 620–633, 692, 716, 722–731, 737–739, 756–767, 776–787, 789–791, 811, 840–841, 843–844, 854, 856, 858–863, 865, 868, 870–878, 881, 918–932	X 1–121, 124–277, 279–298, 300–301, 303–342, 344–357, 359–392, 396, 446, 452–453, 457–458, 536–539, 698–705, 740, 788, 837–839, 857, 957–961	X 122–123, 278, 299, 302, 343, 358, 962
Y. Government	Y 64, 120, 172, 257, 381–382, 386, 388–389, 466–467, 469–471, 505–507, 510–514, 522, 524–528, 530–531, 533–552, 554, 556–561, 567–569, 572–573, 575–581, 583, 590–592, 594–598, 600–601, 603–608, 610, 612–618, 620–622, 624, 627–631, 652–657, 660–664, 671–677, 679–680, 682–699, 701–705, 710–716, 719, 724–725, 727–729, 736–741, 743–744, 746–753, 756–760, 762–765, 767–769, 771, 773–774, 776–778, 783, 785–791, 793–794, 796–802, 805–810, 812, 817, 819–833, 835, 837–842, 844, 962, 982, 1000–1003, 1006–1009	Y 30, 59, 86, 115, 138, 167, 224, 252, 357, 359–360, 370–372, 383–384, 387, 390, 402–407, 414–425, 429–443, 445–449, 468, 499, 503, 509, 515–516, 529, 562–563, 571, 602, 623, 665–666, 678, 706–707, 722, 726, 742, 770, 792, 804, 814–815, 843, 846–847, 861, 970, 977, 983, 986, 988, 992	Y 332–334, 339–341, 363, 385, 391–392, 408–410, 444, 450–456, 504, 508, 521, 532, 555, 566, 570, 584–585, 588, 599, 609, 619, 626, 632–633, 636, 658–659, 670, 681, 709, 717–718, 721, 730–731, 735, 745, 754–755, 779–780, 782, 795, 811, 963, 994, 997, 1010–1022, 1026–1031	Y 342, 361, 367–369, 374–380, 411, 488–492, 500, 517–520, 553, 564–565, 574, 587, 589, 611, 625, 635, 637–651, 667–669, 700, 708, 720, 723, 732–734, 761, 766, 775, 781, 813, 816, 834, 836, 845, 1023–1025	Y 272–307, 318–331, 343–351, 393–397, 399–401, 412–413, 426–428, 460, 472–487, 582, 586, 634, 772, 803, 848, 908–910, 917–942, 964, 978, 987, 989–990	Y 29, 36, 39, 85, 92, 95, 137, 144, 147, 223, 232, 398, 464–465, 523, 593, 784, 818, 858, 965–969, 979–981, 991
Z. Colonial and Pre-Federal Statistics						

Subject Index

[Numbers in *italics* refer to text pages]

[Numbers in *italics* refer to text pages]

[Numbers in *italics* refer to text pages]

[Numbers in *italics* refer to text pages]

[Numbers in *italics* refer to text pages]

[Numbers in *italics* refer to text pages]

[Numbers in *italics* refer to text pages]

[Numbers in *italics* refer to text pages]

Library of Congress Cataloging in Publication Data

United States. Bureau of the Census.
   **Historical statistics of the United States,
colonial times to 1970.**

Includes bibliographical references and indexes.

   1. United States—Statistics.   I. Title.
HA202.B87 1976   317.3   75-38832

☆ U.S. GOVERNMENT PRINTING OFFICE : 1976 O—499-508